W9-CHS-892

THREATENED BIRDS OF THE AMERICAS:
THE ICBP/IUCN RED DATA BOOK

Threatened Birds of the Americas

The ICBP/IUCN Red Data Book

Third edition, part 2

N. J. COLLAR, L. P. GONZAGA, N. KRABBE,
A. MADROÑO NIETO, L. G. NARANJO, T. A. PARKER III
and D. C. WEGE

SMITHSONIAN INSTITUTION PRESS
WASHINGTON AND LONDON
in cooperation with
INTERNATIONAL COUNCIL FOR BIRD PRESERVATION
CAMBRIDGE, U.K.

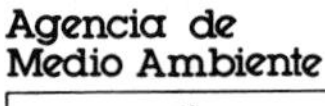

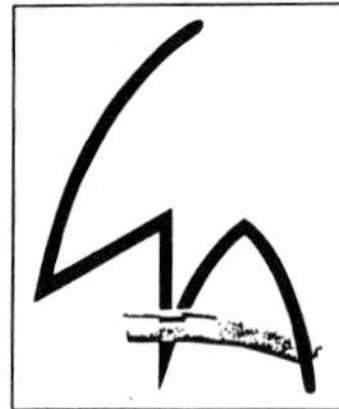

ISBN 1-56098-267-5

Printed by Page Bros (Norwich) Ltd. U.K

Cover illustration:
Marvellous Spatuletail *Loddigesia mirabilis* by Norman Arlott

Cover design:
CBA, Cambridge, U.K.

Contents

Foreword

This kind of book can only be produced by an organization like ICBP which enjoys the goodwill and support of a large global network of people deeply committed to conservation. As with the preceding volume *Threatened birds of Africa* the information in this Red Data Book has been provided by hundreds of ornithologists and conservation experts from all over the world, motivated by a great love for that uniquely rich fauna and flora of the Neotropics and by a profound concern about the precarious status of so many of the region's species and habitats they depend on. I am truly delighted about the international cooperation on many levels that made this volume possible and I am particularly grateful for the generous support from a number of Spanish government and regional sources during the past two years that has allowed us to complete this important conservation report.

On re-reading my opening remarks in the African volume I am struck by how some things have remained unchanged since 1984, while others are profoundly different. No difference, alas, can be reported in the number of species that are globally threatened; no slowing down even of the rate at which that number is growing, as evidenced for example in the list of near-threatened species reported in this book (Appendix D), which is as long again as the list of threatened species itself.

No change either *why* these species are threatened: although the Caribbean, Central and South America are less densely populated than the African continent, there is in the Americas likewise a never-ending quest for more land, for more natural resources to be used, in order to provide a livelihood for more people. All this is usually happening at the expense of the wildlife and their habitats, in particular the tropical forests which are largely responsible for the enormous biological richness of the region.

What is now markedly different, however, is a vastly increased public concern about the status of and the threats to the world's biological diversity – the variety of species and ecosystems that make up our biosphere. *Biodiversity*, a word hardly known outside conservation science circles in the mid-eighties, has now become a term commonly used by politicians and the media alongside other global environmental issues, such as global warming and the depletion of the ozone layer. Through the adoption of the Biodiversity Convention at the Earth Summit in Rio in June 1992 the conservation of threatened species, habitats and ecosystems has been firmly put on the global conservation agenda.

In this context, a Red Data Book like this volume, which contains an in-depth analysis of the problems affecting the most threatened and vulnerable members of the biosphere, is of renewed significance. While conservation programmes today hardly address single-species issues any more but follow more integrated approaches to cover specific sites and habitats, a focus on individual species, which are the building blocks of ecosystems, and a focus in particular on indicator and flagship species (such as many birds), is still an indispensable tool for identifying priority areas and sites and for drawing up management recommendations. How information on status and distribution of individual species, such as presented in this book, can be used for the identifying regional priorities for biodiversity conservation has been demonstrated in ICBP's recent publication *Putting biodiversity on the map*, which is an important companion volume to this Red Data Book.

The information and recommendations contained in this book need wide dissemination. First and foremost, they must be available to politicians and government officials who have a mandate from their people to look after their countries' natural heritage and wealth. I am therefore delighted that, for the first time in the history of Red Data Books, we are able to publish it in two languages (with a Spanish edition being sponsored by Quinto Centenario) and thus overcome part of language barrier all too often associated with this kind of text.

Like all Red Data Books *Threatened birds of the Americas* is a call for action, to be taken, jointly or independently, by different countries, international agencies, national institutions, individuals, the world community. Many of the threatened species in this book occur in only *one* country, giving that government the challenge of *ultimate* responsibility for the survival of a species. But they do not have *sole* responsibility: for those governments who are willing to take action, help and assistance should be, and often are, available from an ever-increasing number of national and international, governmental and non-governmental conservation organizations. The purpose of this book also is to motivate further such international assistance.

Finally I would like to thank all those who, over the years, have made a wide range of contributions to this book. Above all, my deep appreciation goes to the team of authors who, under Nigel Collar's leadership and uncompromising devotion to scientific accuracy, have yet again produced such a superb volume.

Christoph Imboden
Director-General ICBP

August 1992

Introduction

Nadie puede escribir un libro. Para
Que un libro sea verdaderamente,
Se requieren la aurora y el poniente,
Siglos, armas y mar que une y separa.

– Jorge Luis Borges, "Ariosto y los árabes"

Books like this get abandoned, not completed. The expectation that any assessment of threatened species can be definitive, or that the compilation of data in it can be exhaustive, is illusory. The best that can happen is to aim for the closest approximation to these things, for certainly if species are to be saved it is in the first place through information. The guiding principle behind this book has been to search out, analyse and include any and all material relevant to the conservation of the species it judges threatened. I and my co-authors have followed this through to an agreed deadline, and at a certain point, still (inevitably) fretting whether species X ought to have been added and species Y not, we have had to stop. Within days it will be out of date; by the time it is actually published, someone will have given us conclusive evidence for another species to be included or for another to be judged safe (probably species Y). Nevertheless, here it is: I hope it will stand between many birds and extinction. That is its purpose.

Throughout the 1950s ICBP and IUCN worked semi-informally on the identification of threatened species (it is interesting to note the Phelps' successful petition to IUCN to list the Red Siskin *Spinus cucullatus* as threatened as long ago as 1952); ICBP's first efforts can be found in the pages of its *Bulletins* of the period. Red Data Books began in the mid-1960s as a formalization of this process (which already had the stimulus provided by Greenway 1958), the work being published in loose-leaf ring-bound form, so that each species could be updated with a fresh sheet as new information came in. However, there is an inevitable cycle to such work, and with different authors came different editions: the birds were addressed first by Vincent (1966-1971), now unobtainable, and then by King (1978-1979), this latter being issued in paperback, still in print, in 1981 (King 1981).

1981 was also the year in which ICBP, having the previous year established its headquarters in Cambridge alongside IUCN's newly founded Red Data Book unit (now the World Conservation Monitoring Centre), began a new and much more protracted cycle of analysis of threatened bird species. This volume is, technically, the second of a projected four-part third edition of the ICBP Red Data Book, following on from *Threatened birds of Africa and related islands* (Collar and Stuart 1985), and to be finished with volumes on Europe and Asia, and Australasia and the Pacific. Although on present evidence it might take another 11 years to complete the cycle, proper funding would see the project through well before the year 2000.

Work on *Threatened birds of the Americas* began in late 1985, and a major candidate list of species was circulated for comments in February 1986. At that time, the scope of the book was to have been the New World in its entirety. However, a two-year hiatus in the period 1988-1990, when funds and thus work almost completely dried up, was followed by the sudden commitment of new money from Spanish sources in mid-1990, on condition that publication coincided with the 500th anniversary of Columbus's voyage of discovery. The Americas being rich in both birds (including – though not disproportionately – threatened ones: 327 against Africa's 172) and information on them, the task had somehow to be rendered attainable, and by the end of 1991 it was apparent that (the 25) threatened birds in North America and on the "Neotropical Pacific" islands belonging to American countries would need to be reallocated to the projected final volume. This is by no means satisfactory, but considerations of time have demanded it; and it can at least be said that all United States species will thus be treated in a single volume, and that the characteristics of threats to oceanic island species are such that the grouping of the Revillagigedos, Galápagos, Desventuradas, Juan Fernández and other islands in one volume will also bestow a certain uniformity. The species in question are, at least, profiled in Appendix A.

Considerations of time also lie behind the decision not to furnish an account of the Atitlán Grebe *Podilymbus gigas* which, although extant when King (1978-1979) documented its plight, now seems certain not to survive (Hunter 1988, LaBastille 1990). So recently extinct a species would normally still have received full treatment, if only as a case history or valediction; but our schedule has been unsparing.

The problem of categories of threat

The original idea behind Red Data Books was not just to flag which species are at risk but to indicate some sort of priority according to the perceived degree of threat they face. IUCN developed a system of categories that, with modifications, served as the international standard for 20 years or so, and has been widely used in threatened species analyses at the regional and national levels as well.

Paradoxically, however, while IUCN's Red Data Book programme tailed off in the mid-1980s, the system of categories devised for it took on new significance, since in place of a single "compiler" (who was charged with deciding categories) the responsibility for classification passed to the chairs and activists of the Species Survival Commission's specialist groups, so that the problem of retaining consistency, taxing enough for one person, became hydra-headed. Difficulties and dissatisfactions with the IUCN categories, exacerbated by the multiplication of people seeking to apply them, led to an abortive debate in the form of an SSC symposium in Madrid in 1984 (Fitter and Fitter 1987), with some specialist groups simply abandoning their use in action plans drawn up in the late 1980s. Most recently an attempt has been made to introduce quantification into the process of categorization through the thoughtful analysis of Mace and Lande (1991).

The system these authors proposed as a replacement for the old IUCN categories – involving the estimation of probabilities of extinction within given periods of time – is gaining wide currency, partly because it offers concrete advantages in some contexts and partly because it has a particular constituency within IUCN's widest-ranging and most influential species-oriented agency, the Captive Breeding Specialist Group. However, by its creators' own admission, the system is still being tested, and remains open to modification and even rejection. It is certainly my own view that the application of their criteria to many of the birds in this book is of as little or as much use as the application of the old IUCN categories, the result being that there is no easy choice to be made here about how to indicate priority.

Various constraints, not least time, have ruled out an attempt at applying the Mace–Lande criteria (this can and may well be done in due course, if only to test them on creatures other than amenable mammals). Although I have stayed with the IUCN system, I have also sought to impose a parallel arrangement on the species (grouping them by numbers from 1 to 12) which allows a somewhat sharper focus on their status and needs. This arrangement has been found roughly to fit with the IUCN system, but should not be construed as an attempt to replace it or to offer an alternative to Mace–Lande. The results of the exercise are given in Appendix B, where the categories invoked are explained along with the more familiar ones of IUCN. At the top right of each species account the IUCN category is given as a letter or combination of letters, with the numerical grouping adjacent in superscript.

However, I remain convinced that the plain fact of inclusion in this book is more significant for a species than the category it occupies. The individual species accounts are – or at least should be – self-justifying entities. Readers can decide for themselves what level of urgency exists, either by giving different weight to the evidence presented or by taking into consideration evidence that we have missed. Publishing literally means placing in the public domain, and it is vital that the many judgements and decisions made in this book can be scrutinized and understood, and hence supported and acted upon. On the other hand, there is an unwritten part of this book, forming its shadow, composed of the many species that crowd on the fringes of eligibility and have been found wanting: these birds are termed "near-threatened". Collar and Stuart (1985) had time and space to give each a paragraph outlining its circumstances and hence justifying its status, but the sheer number in the Americas (325 against Africa's 93) has prevented a similar exercise here, and the best we can offer is their names in Appendix D, with the hope that at some stage it may be possible to publish annotations that will explain and justify their listing. This would be particularly important where the decisive information remains otherwise unobtainable, and where readers may thus be left unapprized of what can have caused us (a) to include a bird on the list, (b) to exclude it from consideration altogether (which might be a taxonomic matter as much as one of conservation status), or (c) to downgrade it from King (1978-1979) or from Collar and Andrew (1988).

Taxonomy, subspecies, proper names

The preparation of this book has straddled a period of shifting confidence and allegiance in systematic analysis. In the mid-1970s CITES adopted Morony *et al.* (1975) as its taxonomic authority, and King (1978-1979) largely did likewise. Collar and Stuart (1985) also took it as the basic guide, but spent most of a page indicating points of divergence. Work on the Americas again began by building on Morony *et al.* (1975) but, with the publication of so many new species and the revision and splitting of many others (as, e.g., in AOU 1983), the book cannot be said to depend on any one source of authority. The importance of remaining flexible and receptive to new opinion and information must be obvious, since the existence of species is at stake; that such opinion and information should be very sound is, however, equally relevant, since the costs of intervention on behalf of these species, in terms of time, manpower, money and indeed credibility, are high.

On the whole, ICBP has always inclined towards the splitting rather than the lumping of species. This is partly to compensate for the abandonment of documenting threatened subspecies, which are simply too numerous and often too ill-defined to be accessible to detailed review and analysis, and which would inevitably distract activity from the primary task of treating full species. Thus if a good case exists for the elevation of a race to species level, it tends to be accepted; in this book, the optional Remarks section explains these and other matters that bear on a form's taxonomic status. Because of the number of cases where a new species or split exists, the decision has been taken to list and treat species alphabetically within genera.

The English names of birds very largely follow Sibley and Monroe (1990). The vernacular and scientific names of other life-forms mentioned generally follow the individual sources that cite them, although some effort has been made at least to standardize plant genera by recourse to Mabberley (1987). The scientific name is usually given once, thereafter only the English or vernacular name; bird names have initial letters capitalized, those of other animals and plants being in lower case throughout. We often include local names of plants, since these may be valuable to fieldworkers. The names of places are generally spelt in accordance with *The Times atlas of the world* (= TAW 1986) or, where too small to be featured there, with some other identified authority (this is discussed further in the following section under Distribution).

Textual organization

Every species judged as threatened within the scope of this book is treated in a standard manner. There is a brief summary in italics, followed by sections on Distribution, Population, Ecology, Threats, Measures Taken and Measures Proposed, with an optional Remarks. In previous Red Data Books, each species account had its own reference list, so that essentially the text was self-contained. Here, however, considerations of space have compelled us to create a single reference list at the end.

Metric measurement is used throughout, except in quotation, and our conversions of miles, feet, etc., have generally been adjusted to reflect the approximations in the original figures ("roughly 15 miles" would become "c.25 km"; "around 5,000 feet" "c.1,500 m").

Direct quotation is used on occasions when it is felt likely to be helpful, commonly in the Population section for phrasing used on abundance, but also when indicating a source of ambiguity, imprecision, error or contradiction. This includes direct quotation in translation; very occasionally, the original in whatever language is offered, most notably in the case of the Glaucous Macaw *Anodorhynchus glaucus*, since the sources of what is known of this species are extremely inaccessible and they deserve as little mediation as possible. Errors in original sources are generally indicated when noted and if significant. In cases of conflicting evidence or viewpoint we have endeavoured to represent the situation fairly and in such a manner that the issue is not prejudiced.

The problem of the validity of sight records is always likely to be controversial. The rule generally applies here to include all records provided by correspondents or uncovered by research, with an indication if there are grounds for doubt or surprise. Very rarely does a record – particularly if published – get omitted entirely, as for example the Plain Pigeon *Columba inornata* in Central Park, New York (*Auklet* 1990: 6-7), despite the photographic evidence. Always accepting that false records may weaken the sense of urgency with which a species must be addressed, from the conservation standpoint it is marginally better that records be published than not: published claims can be subject to scrutiny and in many cases direct checking, while unpublished ones cannot.

Distribution is commonly the longest section, given that most information relevant to a species's conservation often concerns its range. The text is usually organized in an explicit geographical sequence, most often with localities and their states, provinces or departments arranged from north to south, although there are variations appropriate to context. Longer texts are usually broken down into paragraphs by some national subdivision, with distinct sections for countries (headed by the name in bold) and other subsections for lesser political (or sometimes geographical and even taxonomic) entities (headed by the name in italics); separate paragraphs are almost always used for Brazilian states. As noted above, place-names are generally spelt as they are in TAW (1986), and otherwise in accordance with another (usually indicated) authority. We use lower case initial for río and rio when these refer to rivers rather than settlements; for reasons of conformity this practice extends to other words for watercourses (e.g. riacho, ribeirão). Accents in both Spanish and Portuguese have been added where known or where obviously needed, but many small place-names, often originally listed on specimen labels or in catalogues, defy the process; even some fairly major sites (for example, some of the volcanoes listed under Distribution: Guatemala for the Horned Guan *Oreophasis derbianus*) seem to have lost accents that ought to be there, and in such cases it has been policy to leave them as found.

Localities that appear in TAW (1986) and, in the case of Brazil, either TAW (1986) or GQR (1991), are not traced further (although it is inevitable that sometimes an oversight will have occurred); localities not in TAW (or GQR) are, where possible, given coordinates by reference to (a) the ornithological gazetteers published through MCZ, (b) general gazetteers published by the U.S. Department of the Interior, (c) various identified maps, and (d) other stated sources. Untraced localities are mostly acknowledged as such, but we attempt to place them where the evidence suggests they most likely belong; in cases where a locality (such as a farm) cannot be expected to appear on a map we have indicated an adjacent locality that does.

This system has been applied as fully as possible. We recognize that a gazetteer at the end of the book might have served better, but for a long period the texts were prepared in the expectation that each would be almost entirely internally coherent, with its own reference list (as in Collar and Stuart 1985), so that individual species accounts could easily be copied and used.

By the time the decision to create a single reference list was taken it was too late to rework all the texts so as to create a gazetteer.

Ideally, maps should exist for all the species documented here; but time and space once more militated against this. However, we have provided a selection of maps for some of the more interesting distributions. On these maps, the numbers against each distribution point correspond to the superscript numbers in the text.

Population This is often a short and sometimes rather unsatisfactory section, assembling all kinds of material referring to a species's status, abundance and trends, ranging from the blandest generalizations through varying levels of subjective assessment to the most precise counts and estimates. Generally the sequence begins with vague historical comments that allow some impression of former abundance, then focuses down as sharper and more quantified evaluations emerge towards the present. Direct quotation helps obviate the risks of a kind of "Chinese whispers" in which an original meaning distorts under the successive repetitions of authors who rely on each other rather than the source itself.

Ecology Factors concerning a species's habitat, food and breeding are arranged in that order, commonly with a paragraph for each, although where the text is short a single paragraph is used. Information on movements or other matters may appear as a fourth paragraph or be appended to one of the others, as appropriate.

Threats Longer texts are broken down into paragraphs, each generally treating a separate issue. The listing of a species as threatened usually has to be justified by the identification of a particular threat, but there are just a few species included here where the risk is potential rather than actual, and nothing is listed.

Measures Taken Because of the recent issuance of a major threatened species list (Bernardes *et al.* 1990) – the birds of which are in fact largely based on ICBP's early evaluations for this book in 1986 – species officially recognized under Brazilian law as threatened are indicated in this section. However, it is otherwise recognized that the listing of a species in law is largely irrelevant to its conservation, and there has been no systematic attempt to indicate other legal status in this section except with regard to CITES. If a species has been found in a particular protected area, this is automatically indicated here, even though of course the protected area will never simply have been created for the sake of the species and in a strict sense no measure has been taken. Actions taken and those proposed get different weightings: under Measures Proposed we commonly advocate surveys to determine status and needs, but those that have already taken place (sometimes in direct response to our drafts being circulated) do not necessarily get listed in the Measures Taken section, which would then start to get needlessly overcrowded.

However, we have done what we can to indicate worthy and relevant activities, and where possible and appropriate we have added the source of support for the work. So much of such work is customarily assisted by WWF, WCI, CI, TNC, RARE, ICBP Pan American Section and other leaders in conservation that some offence might unwittingly be given by our failure to identify the organizations in question. This has not been intentional.

Measures Proposed This is commonly the section with the highest level of direct authorial input, since it is often the case that no steps are being planned, leaving judgement of what best needs to be done to the compiler of the account. Given that seven people worked on the book, some variation in emphasis and opinion must be detectable between recommendations made for species, although each text has been read and adjusted by me and almost always one other author. Much greater variation comes when faithfully repeating the recommendations made by others, so that some species may have lengthy proposals on very specific matters or on issues at one remove from the subject itself (as for example increasing the staffing of a protected area in which a threatened bird occurs), whereas others receive no such consideration. We have always tried to give a fair representation of proposals made by others, but of course our judgement may have been influenced by developments since those proposals were made, or simply by a fuller understanding than that of the proposers themselves.

We have in this section or else in Remarks, as appropriate, attempted to cross-refer to other threatened species with which the bird in question is sympatric. This exercise seeks to turn attention from threatened species to key sites, and in so doing to point out the major opportunities that exist for securing as many (threatened) birds as possible for particular units of investment.

Remarks What will not fit in the rest of the text tends to go under Remarks. It is a section for registering conflicts of evidence, problems in textual analysis, additional testimony and, most usually, any matters bearing on the taxonomic distinctiveness of the species under review.

Referencing

Everything written in *Threatened birds of the Americas* ought to be traceable to source. Even if this principle results in rather heavy reading, particularly in the Distribution sections, the reasoning behind it can hardly need rehearsing. The point is that the referencing of every fact gives the future researcher and conservationist a clear basis of confidence in the information he or she is using, as well as a specific line of pursuit in cases where his or her findings challenge what was known or believed until then. Moreover, unpublished data must be credited to its provider, both to honour the trust involved and to engender such trust in any prospective contributors. The fate of species may ultimately depend on such good faith.

We have therefore endeavoured to ensure that every statement of fact in this book is fully and consistently attributed. Any sentence ending without accreditation either represents a summary whose sources are explicit (given in advance or clearly to follow) or else carries a judgement or deduction that is the responsibility of the authors, and ultimately therefore of the senior author. Opinions expressed do not represent official policy of ICBP (there is a single case where initials – mine – have been added to an opinion in order to reinforce this last point). Information (as opposed to opinion or deduction) provided by authors is accompanied by his respective initials. Throughout the book semi-colons are used as a way of increasing the distance between full stops and hence reducing the number of times a source needs to be given; in the Distribution section, however, semi-colons usually separate individual facts, each of which is attributed to source, but (as will usually be obvious) in rare cases where no source appears before a semi-colon this is because it is the next in sequence.

Personal communications are cited as either *in litt.* or verbally (with the year involved), to distinguish whether or not a written record of the information in question is retained. There are unavoidable complications where an informant is not the original source (or, worse, not the only such source) of a piece of information, and of course sometimes an informant – in all innocence – may have omitted to indicate that source and will appear to be credited for it. Where the first source is cited, we have had to take on trust the accuracy of the report as well as the original observer's willingness to have it published through an intermediary; in such cases original observers are indicated by use of "*per*" after their name(s). There are a few cases where letters on file have been addressed to people associated with ICBP such as the late P. Barclay-Smith, W. Belton, W. B. King and R. Wirth, and these are indicated accordingly.

In Collar and Stuart (1985) a source for information from a skin in a museum (mostly the authors themselves) was indicated. The much greater use of museum material in this American study has made the practice of crediting personal sources far too cumbersome, but since the museum itself remains identified as the institutional source there has been little loss in accountability. While a high proportion of museum material was again examined and documented by the authors themselves, it is still the case that the blanket anonymity in noting specimens masks the contributions made by certain colleagues, and readers are referred to Acknowledgements for a guide to this matter. It is important to note that museum specimens are indicated only when they supply or supplement (e.g. with a date) a record; if the relevant data are already published, museum material is not mentioned.

For the sake of brevity and clarity, initials have been used in certain references (e.g. OG, IGN) but these are all expanded in the reference list. In citing book titles, we have often inserted appropriate punctuation where for reasons of presentation this does not appear on the title page. Journal titles are abbreviated generally in accordance with common practice; we use "Nat." for "Natural" and its compounds, "Natn." for "National".

This is perhaps the point where as senior author I should indicate that responsibility for the many decisions made and systems used in this book, ranging from which species to include to how to cite a reference, rests entirely with me.

Initials and glossary

Institutions, museums and conservation bodies referred to in the text by their abbreviations are as follows: AFA, American Federation of Aviculture; AMNH, American Museum of Natural History; ANSP, Academy of Natural Sciences of Philadelphia; APECO, Asociación Peruana para la Conservación de la Naturaleza; BMNH, British Museum (Natural History), recently and lamentably renamed the "Natural History Museum"; CAS, California Academy of Sciences; CBSG, Captive Breeding Specialist Group of IUCN; CCACS, Coleção C. A. C. Seabra (Rio de Janeiro); CI, Conservation International; CIAL, Coleção Instituto Adolfo Lutz (São Paulo); CIDA, Canadian International Development Agency; CITES, (Washington) Convention on International Trade in Endangered Species of Fauna and Flora; CM, Carnegie Museum of Natural History (Pittsburgh); CMN, Canadian Museum of Nature (Ottawa); CNPq, Conselho Nacional de Pesquisas (Brazil); CONAF = Corporación Nacional Forestal (Chile); COP, Colección Ornitológica Phelps (Caracas); CPNI, Coleção Parque Nacional do Itatiaia (Rio de Janeiro state); CVC, Corporación Autónoma Regional del Valle del Cauca, Colombia; DMNH, Delaware Museum of Natural History; DZMG, Departamento de Zoologia, Universidade Federal de Minas Gerais (Belo Horizonte); EBD, Estación Biológica de Doñana (Seville); FBCN, Fundação Brasileira para a Conservação da Natureza; FMNH, Field Museum of Natural History (Chicago); FUNDAECO, Fundación para el Ecodesarrollo y la Conservación (Guatemala); IBAMA, Instituto Brasileiro do Meio Ambiente e dos Recursos Naturais Renováveis; IBGE, Instituto Brasileiro de Geografia e Estatística; IBUNAM, Instituto de Biología, Universidad Nacional Autónoma de México; ICN, Instituto de Ciencias Naturales, Universidad Nacional de Colombia (Bogotá); IML, Instituto Miguel Lillo (San Miguel de Tucumán); IND, Unidad Investigativa Federico Medem, INDERENA (Bogotá); INDERENA, Instituto Nacional de los Recursos Naturales Renovables y del Medio Ambiente (Colombia); IRSNB, Institut Royal des Sciences Naturelles (Brussels); IUCN, International Union for Conservation of Nature and Natural Resources (World Conservation Union); IWRB-TWRG, International Waterfowl and Wetlands Research Bureau's Threatened Waterfowl Research Group; JWPT, Jersey Wildlife Preservation Trust; LACM, Los Angeles County Museum of Natural History; LSUMZ, Louisiana State University Museum of Zoology; MACN, Museo Argentino de Ciencias Naturales "Bernardino Rivadavia" (Buenos Aires); MCML, Merseyside County Museums, Liverpool; MCN, Museu de Ciências Naturais (Rio Grande do Sul); MCNAS, Museo de Ciencias Naturales "Augusto Schulz" (Argentina); MCZ, Museum of Comparative Zoology (Cambridge, U.S.A.); MECN, Museo Ecuatoriano de Ciencias Naturales (Quito); MFASF, Museo Florentino Ameghino de Santa Fe, Argentina; MHNCI, Museu de Historia Natural Capão da Imbuia (Curitiba); MHNJP, Museo de Historia Natural "Javier Prado" (Lima); MHNG, Muséum d'Histoire Naturelle, Geneva; MHNUC, Museo de Historia Natural, Universidad del Cauca (Popayán); MLZ, Moore Laboratory of Zoology, Occidental College (Los Angeles); MNHN, Muséum National d'Histoire Naturelle (Paris); MNHNM, Museo Nacional de Historia Natural (Montevideo); MNHNS, Museo Nacional de Historia Natural (Santiago); MNHUK, Museum of Natural History, University of Kansas; MNRJ, Museu Nacional de Rio de Janeiro; MSC, Museu do Seminário do Colégio Coração de Jesus (Corupá, Santa Catarina); MVZ, Museum of Vertebrate Zoology, University of California; MZFC, Museo de Zoología de la Facultad de Ciencias (UNAM); MZUCR, Museo de Zoología, Universidad de Costa Rica;

MZUFV, Museu de Zoologia, Universidade Federal de Viçosa, Minas Gerais; NHMW, Naturhistorisches Museum (Vienna); NRM, Naturhistoriska Riksmuseet (Stockholm); NYZS, New York Zoological Society; PUC-RS, Pontifícia Universidade Católica de Rio Grande do Sul; RARE, formerly Rare Animal Relief Effort, now RARE Center for Tropical Conservation; RMNH, Rijksmuseum van Natuurlijke Historie (Leiden); ROM, Royal Ontario Museum; SBMNH, Santa Barbara Museum of Natural History; SDMNH, San Diego Museum of Natural History; SWC, Southwestern College (Kansas); TNC, The Nature Conservancy; UCLA, University of California at Los Angeles; UFPE, Universidade Federal de Pernambuco; UMMZ, University of Michigan Museum of Zoology; UMZC, University Museum of Zoology (Cambridge, U.K.); UNAM, Universidad Nacional Autónoma de México; UNP, Universidad Nacional de la Plata; USNM, (United States) National Museum of Natural History (Washington); UV, Universidad del Valle (Cali); WCI, Wildlife Conservation International; WFVZ, Western Foundation of Vertebrate Zoology (Los Angeles); WPTI, Wildlife Preservation Trust International; WWF, World Wildlife Fund or World Wide Fund for Nature; YPM, Peabody Museum, Yale University (New Haven); ZFMK, Zoologisches Forschungsinstitut und Museum Alexander Koenig (Bonn); ZGAP, Zoologische Gesellschaft für Arten- und Populationsschutz; WHSRN, Western Hemisphere Shorebird Reserve Network; ZMB, Zoologisches Museum (Berlin); ZMUC, Zoological Museum, University of Copenhagen.

Foreign terms used without translation (and not italicized) in the text include: *caatinga*, xerophytic scrubland; *campesino*, landless farmer, peasant; *campo limpo*, open grassland; *campo sujo*, bushy grassland; *capoeira*, second growth; *cerrado*, open canopy (grassy) woodland; *igapó*, permanently flooded forest; *terra firme*, dryland (forest); *várzea*, seasonally flooded forest. The term "Atlantic Forest" is used in a broad sense to embrace the southern subdivision sometimes referred to as "Paranense Forest".

Acknowledgements

This book has been funded by many different sources. In Spain, the Instituto Nacional para la Conservación de la Naturaleza (ICONA) and the Agencia de Medio Ambiente (AMA) of Madrid provided the support needed for the major effort to finish the work, channelled through the Sociedad Estatal Quinto Centenario. In Brazil, the Companhia Vale do Rio Doce (CVRD) provided part-time support for LPG over two years, 1986–1988. In the U.S.A., the Bleitz Wildlife Foundation (administered through the Western Foundation of Vertebrate Zoology) made a major contribution to work (particular thanks go to J. F. Clements, E. N. Harrison, J. Kiff and L. F. Kiff), Conservation International covered the expenses of TAP's participation in the project (and here we should especially thank R. A. Mittermeier, B. Bailey and T. Werner), the Frank M. Chapman Fund supported NJC's work gathering label data at the American Museum of Natural History, and the Pan American Section of ICBP paid for NJC's participation in the 1988 Neotropical Ornithological Congress; Mrs Elizabeth Jones, Mr and Mrs John D. Mitchell, and Carl Zeiss Optical, Inc., also made significant contributions. IUCN funded NJC for the first years of the project. Much valued financial support also came from Ing. A. M. Sada in Mexico, the Bromley Trust in the U.K., the late Mr W. H. Phelps, Jr, in Venezuela, and the Canadian Nature Federation on behalf of ICBP-Canada. ICBP itself made good a considerable shortfall, so that all members and supporters of the organization can claim to have contributed to the book's production. To all these ICBP extends the warmest thanks for their generosity.

It will be obvious that a great deal of information in this book derives from museum collections. Most of this was gathered by the authors, but inevitably late decisions to consider a species meant that curators and managers had to be asked to provide further data. Longest-suffering victims of this process were M. LeCroy (AMNH), M. B. Robbins (ANSP) and D. E. Willard (FMNH), to whom we extend our special thanks for many kindnesses and much patience. However, the magnanimity and welcome shown by all staff at the museums we visited was extraordinary, and we particularly thank R. Aveledo Hostos (COP), E. Bauernfeind (NHMW),

M. R. Browning (USNM), J. Cabot (EBD), H. F. de A. Camargo (MZUSP), N. Carnevalli (DZMG), J. W. Fitzpatrick and S. M. Lanyon (FMNH), F. B. Gill (ANSP), G. K. Hess (DMNH), R. D. James (ROM), J. L. Pontes (MZUFV), K. C. Parkes and J. M. Loughlin (CM), R. A. Paynter (MCZ), J. V. Remsen (LSUMZ), F. Sibley (YPM), D. M. Teixeira and J. B. Nacinovic (MNRJ), C. Voisin (MNHN) and C. Weber (MHNG) for their memorable courtesy and assistance. Thanks also go to long-standing friends on the staff of BMNH, in particular P. R. Colston and M. P. Walters, for hosting many visits in the past six years. In addition, K. L. Garrett and M. C. Wimer (LACM), L. F. Kiff (WFVZ), J. R. Navas (MACN) and J. C. Torres-Mura (MNHNS) sent much data on many specimens in their care (other contributors of museum data are named in the main list below). This is also the place to mention again M. LeCroy and AMNH for the donation to ICBP of a large number of museum publications used in this work, and M. A. Traylor and FMNH for the donation to ICBP of the critically important *Catalogue of birds of the Americas* (1918–1949).

Much research was undertaken in libraries, and we particularly wish to express our warmest thanks to L. Birch at the Alexander Library in the Edward Grey Institute, Oxford, A. Vale and F. E. Warr at the British Museum, Tring, A. Datta and her staff at the Natural History Museum General Library, London, and I. Dawson at the Royal Society for the Protection of Birds, Sandy, all of whom showed the greatest understanding and support. We also thank J. Winterburn (Zoology Library, Cambridge), R. Fairclough and his staff (Map Room, University Library, Cambridge), and M. White and K. Grose (IUCN Library, Gland) for their unfailing assistance.

It is a delight to contemplate the number of people who have contributed their unpublished information or in other ways helped in our inquiries. If this book has any stature or authority, it is because it represents the breadth and judgement of ornithologists and conservationists throughout the Americas who are concerned to see the species they know survive. It is, in a real sense, a book by the people, for the people. Here they are:

E. I. Abadie, J. Abramson, C. I. Acevedo, F. Achaval, G. Alayón García, M. Alberico, M. Albornoz, A. B. Altman, E. Alvarez, H. Alvarez-López, V. S. Alves, D. W. Anderson, K. S. Anderson, A. V. Andors, G. I. Andrade, M. A. Andrade, R. F. Andrle, J. P. Angle, L. de Anjos, P. T. Z. Antas, D. Anthony, R. Antonelli Filho, G. Arango, S. Arango, B. Araya Mödinger, P. Arctander, W. J. Arendt, S. Arías, T. Arndt, S. D. Arruda, P. Atkinson, M. Babarskas, S. F. Bailey, T. Bakker, C. S. Balchin, M. R. Ballantyne, R. C. Banks, L. F. Baptista, M. Barker, L. A. R. Bege, D. J. Bell, W. Belton, J. W. Beltrán, G. A. Bencke, P. Bertagnolio, C. Bertonatti, B. J. Best, the late R. C. Best, R. O. Bierregaard, L. C. Binford, D. Blanco, R. Bleiweiss, H. Bloch, D. E. Blockstein, N. A. Bó, B. A. de Boer, D. Bohlen, W. C. A. Bokermann, the late J. Bond, M. R. Bornschein, C. Bosque, J. E. Botero, W. R. P. Bourne, M. Boussekey, P. E. Bradley, J. Brandbyge, the late A. Brandt, M. A. Brazil, A. Bräutigam, S. R. Broad, K. M. Brock, H. P. Brokaw, M. de L. Brooke, M. R. Browning, D. F. Bruning, P. J. Bubb, D. W. Buden, W. Burke, P. J. Butler, J. Cabot, H. F. de A. Camargo, W. Campbell, P. Canevari, M. Carbonell, J. M. Carrión, C. E. Carvalho, G. D. A. Castiglioni, I. Castro, S. M. Caziani, G. Ceballos, S. Charity, N. Chávez C., M. B. Christiansen, M. I. Christie, C. T. Clarke, R. O. S. Clarke, J. F. Clements, J. Clinton-Eitniear, the late S. Coats, A. G. M. Coelho, A. Colman, J. A. Colón, J. R. Contreras, S. G. D. Cook, P. Coopmans, R. Corado, G. Cox, J. P. Croxall, J. Cuddy, J. P. Cuello, H. Currie, M. A. Da-Ré, C. Dauphiné, T. J. Davis, F. Delgado, E. Derlindati, B. Dewynter, M. V. Dias, J. A. Dick, R. W. Dickerman, J. M. Dietz, P. K. Donahue, H. Dos Santos, A. F. G. Douse, S. R. Drennan, D. C. Duffy, the late J.-L. Dujardin, H. (Mrs J. S.) Dunning, E. P. Edwards, J. W. Eley, V. Emanuel, L. H. Emmons, G. Engblom, E. Enkerlin, P. Escalante, R. Escalante, J. Escobar, L. A. Espinosa G., D. Espinosa G., P. G. H. Evans, W. T. Everett, J. A. Faaborg, C. A. Faanes, P. W. Fairbairn, L. Fazio, P. Feinsinger, A. Fernández Badillo, D. Fisher, J. W. Fitzpatrick, R. ffrench, J. Fletcher, E. Flores, P. S. M. da Fonseca, B. C. Forrester, D. M. R. Fortaleza, M. S. Foster, R. Foster, R. M. Fraga, I. Franke, P. W. Freeman, J. de Freitas, M. L. D. de Freitas, O. Frimer, P. G. Gadd, M. Galetti, D. Gallegos-Luque, E. R. García, D. S. Gardner, N. J. Gardner, K. L. Garrett, O. H. Garrido, M. R. Gaskin, A. R. M. Gepp, F. B. Gill, J. A. Giraldo, A. Giraudo,

R. Gnam, J. Goerck, E. Godínez, M. A. Gómez Garza, H. González Alonso, F. González García, G. M. González R., M. J. González, P. González, A. J. Goodwin, M. L. Goodwin, S. Gorzula, T. Granizo Tamayo, P. R. Grant, G. R. Graves, A. Green, G. Green, P. Greenfield, P. Gregory, A. Gretton, J. Guarnaccia, C. G. Guerra, P. Gutiérrez, B. Haase, J. Haffer, S. M. Haig, R. van Halewyn, M. Hancock, G. Harris, P. V. Hayman, A. M. Haynes-Sutton, M. Heath, M. Held, J. I. Hernández Camacho, E. Hernández-Prieto, N. Hilgert de Benavides, S. L. Hilty, P. Hocking, T. R. Howell, J. del Hoyo, P. Hubbell, the late R. A. Hughes, P. S. Humphrey, L. A. Hunter, S. H. Hurlbert, M. B. Hutt, J. Ingels, T. P. Inskipp, M. Isler, P. Isler, F. M. Jaksic, C. James, J. F. de la Jara, D. F. Jeggo, J. R. Jehl, J. M. Jiménez López, A. D. Johns, Andrés Johnson, Arlyne Johnson, P. A. Johnsgard, P. J. Jones, G. M. Jonkel, P. Kaestner, H. W. Kale, J. R. Karr, G. Kattan, K. Kaufman, A. R. Keith, M. G. Kelsey, M. Kessler, L. F. Kiff, J. R. King, W. B. King, G. Kirwan, Z. Kock, S. Krapovickas, J. A. Kushlan, O. Læssøe, F. R. Lambert, J. M. Lammertink, D. V. Lanning, A. Laurie, C. Levey, M. Levy, M. van Liefde, A. Lieberman, A. Long, M. V. López, N. López Kochalka, B. M. López Lanús, A. López Ornat, R. Low, S. C. Luçolli, C. S. Luthin, N. C. Maciel, S. A. J. Malone, F. Man Ging, L. O. Marcondes-Machado, L. C. Marigo, M. Marin A., T. Marlow, J. T. Marshall, J. C. Martínez-Sánchez, P. Martuscelli, J. C. Mathéus P., S. Matola, G. T. de Mattos, N. G. McCartney, M. A. McDonald, P. McGill-Harelstad, C. McIntosh, J. W. McNeely, M. K. McNicholl, L. B. McQueen, G. Medina-Cuervo, G. F. Mees, A. de Meijer, J. M. Meyers, J. Meza, D. Michael, S. J. Midence, B. W. Miller, C. M. Miller, S. Miller, A. Mitchell, M. L. Mondragón, I. Mora, R. Morales, E. S. Morton, S. G. Mosa, C. A. Munn, E. Murgueitio R., J. B. Nacinovic, E. Nadachowski, T. Narosky, A. G. Navarro, J. R. Navas, R. Naveen, A. J. Negret, J. Nicholls, G. Nilsson, I. C. T. Nisbet, F. C. Novaes, L. G. Olarte, S. Oldfield, B. Ølgård, W. L. R. Oliver, S. L. Olson, J. P. O'Neill, J. R. van Oosten, J. E. Orejuela, D. C. Oren, R. I. Orenstein, E. G. Ortiz, F. Ortiz Crespo, R. Otoch, J. A. Ottenwalder, H. Ouellet, S. G. Paccagnella, N. Pacheco V., C. L. Paiva, K. C. Parkes, R. F. Pasquier, P. E. Paryski, R. A. Paynter, D. Paz, M. R. de la Peña, C. A. Peres, N. Pérez, R. A. Pérez-Rivera, A. T. Peterson, R. W. Peterson, the late W. H. Phelps, A. R. Phillips, C. Pickup, J. E. Pierson, R. B. Pineschi, F. A. Pitelka, E. Pitter, M. A. Pizo, M. A. Plenge, F. B. Pontual, F. S. Porto, W. Post, M. K. Poulsen, T. G. Prins, R. P. Prŷs-Jones, V. M. Pulido, H. A. Raffaele, C. Rahbek, R. B. Ramírez P., C. Ramo, M. A. Ramos, D. Ramsaroop, R. Ranft, J. H. Rappole, J. F. Rasmussen, K. H. Redford, P. Regalado Ruíz, J. V. Remsen, L. M. Renjifo, A. Repizzo, C. Restrepo, G. B. Reynard, J. C. Riveros Salcedo, C. S. Robbins, M. B. Robbins, P. J. Roberts, P. Robertson, S. Robinson, P. Rockstroh, O. Rocha O., D. Rodríguez Batista, J. P. Rodríguez, A. Romero, D. Rootes, L. Rosselli, P. Roth, P. Y. Roumain, J. C. Rowlett, R. A. Rowlett, M. Rumboll, the late A. Ruschi, M. K. Rylander, A. M. Sada, M. Sallaberry, J. Sánchez, M. Sander, F. Sarmiento, P. A. Scharf, N. Schechaj, G. Scheres, P. Scherer Neto, N. Schischakin, R. P. Schlatter, C. Schouten, K.-L. Schuchmann, T. S. Schulenberg, S. E. Senner, the late M. A. Serna, C. Sharpe, J. N. Shepherd, L. L. Short, the late H. Sick, F. Silva, J. M. C. da Silva, T. Silva, K. M. Silvius, I. Simão, F. Simon, C. Sims, D. Sirí Núñez, R. A. Sloss, N. G. Smith, D. W. Snow, N. F. R. Snyder, V. Solar Manzano, A. L. Spaans, G. J. Speight, F. Spivy-Weber, K. T. Standring, B. R. Stein, M. Steinitz-Kannan, A. Stockton de Dod, R. W. Storer, D. F. Stotz, S. D. Strahl, R. J. Straneck, C. Strang, I. J. Strange, F. C. Straube, S. N. Stuart, A. Studer, O. Suárez Morales, A. M. Sugden, M. Sulley, S. Sulley, R. Summers, R. Sutton, J. Swallow, B. Swift, A. Taber, E. Tabilo Valdivieso, N. (Mrs J. T.) Tanner, A. Tarak, D. M. Teixeira, J. W. Terborgh, J.-M. Thiollay, B. T. Thomas, M. C. Thompson, J. B. Thomsen, S. Thorn, W. A. Thurber, R. E. Tomlinson, F. Toral, the late C. Torres de Assumpção, J. C. Torres-Mura, O. Tostain, E. P. Toyne, P. W. Trail, M. A. Traylor, D. B. Trent, P. L. Tubaro, A. Tye, S. J. Tyler, M. P. Valle, J. P. Vannini, N. Varty, R. Vasile, R. Vaz-Ferreira, E. Velarde, E. Velasco Abad, C. Venegas C., J. L. Venero González, J. Ventosilla, V. Velloso, R. Vides Almonacid, J. Vielliard, F. J. Vilella, Y. A. Vilina, J. A. Villa L., C. G. Violani, W. A. Voss, K. H. Voous, F. Vuilleumier, W. Wake, B. P. Walker, H. Walter, F. E. Warr, S. L. Warter, J. Wattel, D. R. Waugh, S. Webb, T. Webber, D. S. Weber, D. Weyer, S. Whitehouse, A. Whittaker, M. Whittingham, D. A. Wiedenfeld, S. R. Wilbur, D. S. Wilcove,

J. W. Wiley, R. Williams, D. Willis, E. O. Willis, M. H. Wilson, R. G. Wilson, D. B. Wingate, K. Winker, R. Wirth, D. S. Wood, W. Woodrow, B. Woods E., C. A. Woods, R. Woods, C. Wotzkow, J. M. Wunderle, C. Yamashita, P. Yorio, H. G. Young, K. Young and E. Zerda-Ordóñez. We offer our apologies to anyone who feels unjustly omitted from this list.

Most of the names above will be found in the species accounts, but some will not: it is important to recognize that many species were excluded on the basis of information provided, but such contributions of data are of course no less valuable to the project. At the other end of the scale are people whose names figure repeatedly, and whose reward must largely lie simply in that repetition. Nevertheless, certain among them deserve very particular acknowledgement: R. S. Ridgely, for days of help and advice at the start of the project and a continuous stream of data right through to its last hours; D. A. Scott, who took upon himself to think through a first candidate list in 1985 and adduced a mass of supporting evidence; J. Fjeldså, who provided extensive advice and judgement on many species and was a committed supporter of the project throughout; B. M. Whitney, who read over many texts and contributed large quantities of new data; and M. Pearman, who made available all his records from several years' travel in South America. At the national and regional level, we must particularly thank J. C. Chebez, M. Nores and D. Yzurieta for their indefatigable efforts to improve the texts for Argentina and adjacent areas, F. E. Hayes for the provision of his comprehensive list of records and references concerning Paraguay, J. F. Pacheco for collating his (many) and other records from Brazil, F. G. Stiles for commenting carefully on all Colombian and Costa Rican texts, and S. N. G. Howell for extensive up-to-date information from Mexico and adjacent countries.

Certain ICBP staff have played a major part in this book, no-one more so than A. J. Stattersfield, who took charge of the complicated and necessarily very painstaking business of storing and cross-referring information received in letters, and overhauled and for long maintained the system of hard-copy retrieval that made it possible to write this book – her contribution has been inestimable; and much support has come from the other members of ICBP's Research Department, notably G. Walton in the library. R. Pfaff typed and processed large parts of the book, and undertook myriad minor tasks in its final standardization; L. Delgado Rodríguez and M. Risebrow liaised with the Spanish funders and coordinated production; A. Long oversaw the compilation of the maps and helped check Appendix D; and I. Hughes, M. Hines and N. Parker undertook various tasks. Programme staff A. T. Juniper, M. G. Kelsey, R. Phillips, M. R. W. Rands, G. Shillinger and R. Wirth assisted in the provision of information. Ch. Imboden and C. J. Bibby commented on the first draft of this Introduction, and both were instrumental in persuading me to undertake the priority grouping review in Appendix B. I warmly thank them all.

In Spain we owe very special thanks to J. del Hoyo, E. de Juana, L. Maestre and J. Varela for their strong support in various ways. The Sociedad Española de Ornitología kindly assisted over funding arrangements.

We are greatly obliged to J. Fjeldså and M. Hoppe Wolf for contributing their sketches of some of the species treated in this book, and to N. Arlott for his dust-jacket drawing of the Marvellous Spatuletail *Loddigesia mirabilis*.

Permission to quote the first stanza of "Ariosto y los árabes" by Jorge Luis Borges (from *El hacedor*, 1960) was very kindly given by María Kodama and Emecé Editores S.A.

Finally, on behalf of ICBP I must acknowledge with gratitude the support of the institutions of my co-authors, i.e. Universidade Federal de Rio de Janeiro (LPG), Zoologisk Museum, Copenhagen (NK), Universidad del Valle (LGN), and Conservation International and the Museum of Zoology, Louisiana State University (TAP); and I personally must thank all my co-authors for their dedication, enthusiasm, understanding and good fellowship in bringing this work to a conclusion – or perhaps I should say, to the point where it could conscionably be abandoned.

N. J. Collar *August 1992*

BLACK TINAMOU *Tinamus osgoodi* K[12]

This uncommon gamebird is known from two small areas of humid forest separated by almost 2,000 km, the northern subspecies hershkovitzi *in the East Andes of Colombia chiefly at 1,400-1,500 m (status unknown), the nominate form only on the eastern Andean slope in Cuzco department, south-east Peru, at 600-1,400 m (where a sizeable population may be safe within Manu National Park).*

DISTRIBUTION The Black Tinamou is represented by two subspecies confined to two widely disjunct areas (2,000 km apart), on the western slope of the East Andes at the head of the Magdalena valley, Huila department, Colombia, and at five localities along a 100 km stretch of the eastern Andean slope of Cuzco department, Peru. The few known sites (coordinates from Paynter and Traylor 1981, Stephens and Traylor 1983) are as follows:

Colombia (race *hershkovitzi*) near San Adolfo (1°37'N 75°59'W) on the río Aguas Claras (a tributary of the río Suaza), where three specimens (in FMNH) were taken at 1,400 and 1,500 m in June 1951 (also Blake 1953); and nearby in Cueva de los Guácharos National Park (c.1°35'N 76°00'W), where one was seen at 2,100 m in 1976 (Hilty and Brown 1986);

Peru (nominate *osgoodi*) Cordillera del Pantiacolla (c.12°35'S 71°15'W), where birds were recorded at 900-1,350 m in August, September and November 1985 (D. F. Stotz *in litt.* 1989); Tono (c.13°03'S 71°10'W), where one was heard in December 1985 (D. F. Stotz *in litt.* 1989); Consuelo (c.13°08'S 71°15'W), where birds were recorded almost daily in October and November 1981 between 1,100 and 1,400 m (D. F. Stotz *in litt.* 1989; also specimen in FMNH taken in November 1981); c.15 km east of Quincemil (13°16'S 70°38'W), an area of low ridges at 800-900 m in the Marcapata valley, where a bird was seen in December 1974 (TAP); and Cadena (formerly Hacienda Cadena at 13°24'S 70°43'W), in the Marcapata valley, where specimens (in AMNH, FMNH, LSUMZ, USNM and YPM) were collected between 600 and 1,200 m from 1949 to 1951 and in 1958 (also Conover 1949, Traylor 1952).

This species undoubtedly occurs in Manu National Park, as all three first-mentioned localities lie within 5 km of its boundary (D. F. Stotz *in litt.* 1989), on ridges that extend into the park (TAP). Undiscovered populations may exist locally in poorly known parts of the eastern Andean slope.

POPULATION Near San Adolfo, Colombia, this tinamou was perhaps not rare in June 1951 (T. S. Schulenberg *in litt.* 1989), although there is no available information on the present state of its habitat there. With only one recent record from Colombia, the species was considered "very rare" by Hilty and Brown (1986). In Peru, the bird was common at Cadena at least until 1958 (Traylor 1952: also seven specimens in LSUMZ and YPM, all collected in 1958), and at Consuelo near Manu National Park it was fairly common (recorded more or less daily) in 1981; however, it was found to be uncommon in the Cordillera del Pantiacolla in 1985 (D. F. Stotz *in litt.* 1989). Most habitat destruction in the species's Peruvian range occurs below 900 m, thus giving little reason to suggest that the population has declined (D. F. Stotz *in litt.* 1989).

ECOLOGY The Black Tinamou inhabits humid forest in the foothill tropical and upper tropical zones at 600 to 1,500 m, possibly higher in Colombia, from where there is a sight record at 2,100 m (Blake 1953, Parker *et al.* 1982, Hilty and Brown 1986; see also Distribution). At Consuelo, Peru, one was taken near a mossy ridge-top at 1,390 m; it responded to playback of its own voice, and had its stomach and crop full of nuts (FMNH label data). On a steep-sided ridge east of Quincemil, an individual was flushed from the ground in epiphyte-laden forest confined to the upper slopes and ravines of a semi-isolated, low mountain (TAP). Nothing further is known of its habits, although birds with active gonads have been taken in Peru in March, June and

November (three specimens in FMNH and YPM), with a quarter-grown chick in February (specimen in FMNH). No date is given for the "clutch" of two eggs reported by Traylor (1952).

THREATS The species is almost certainly threatened by habitat destruction in Colombia, where most foothill forest on the western slope of the East Andes has been logged for agriculture (see Threats under Moustached Antpitta *Grallaria alleni* and Red-bellied Grackle *Hypopyrrhus pyrohypogaster*). In Peru there is some habitat destruction in the part of its range outside Manu National Park, particularly below 900 m and along roads, but most of the forest is still intact (D. F. Stotz *in litt.* 1989), and there is extensive, undisturbed habitat to the north and south (TAP). The species is apparently hunted for food (Traylor 1952).

MEASURES TAKEN Although the Black Tinamou apparently occurs in Cueva de los Guácharos National Park in Huila, Colombia (9,000 ha, from 1,700 m up) (Hilty and Brown 1986, Hernández Camacho *et al.* undated), there is no evidence that it holds a viable population (for other threatened species known to occur in this park, see equivalent section under Moustached Antpitta). In Peru, such a population undoubtedly occurs in the large Manu National Park (1,530,000 ha) (D. F. Stotz *in litt.* 1989, IUCN 1992), and the species may well occur to the south in the recently established Tambopata-Condamo Reserve (1,480,000 ha: IUCN 1992).

MEASURES PROPOSED Satellite images of the foothill tropical and upper tropical zones along the entire Amazonian slope of the Andes should be analysed to assess the present extent of suitable natural habitat before any effective initiatives to protect this and the 100 (and more) other species of bird restricted to these zones can be proposed. A special effort to investigate the state of the habitat at the type-locality of the Colombian race should be undertaken, and protection of suitable remaining habitat must be encouraged (see also equivalent section for Moustached Antpitta). Increased protection for existing reserves in south-eastern Peru is essential, as is establishment of additional protected areas to the north and south. The recently proposed Alto Madidi National Park in northern La Paz, Bolivia (TAP), would encompass extensive areas of lower montane forest on outlying Andean ridges, the habitat of this and many additional species with very narrow elevational ranges (TAP). In addition to the biological importance of these forests, their value as watershed catchments is inestimable.

CHOCO TINAMOU *Crypturellus kerriae* I[7]

This poorly known tinamou is endemic to forested foothills in the border region in Darién province, Panama, and Chocó department, Colombia, where it has been recorded on just a small number of occasions. Although the species may be safe within the Darién National Park, Panama, suitable forest in Colombia is disappearing.

DISTRIBUTION The Chocó Tinamou is known from just two areas, one in easternmost Darién on the border of Panama and Colombia, the other in central Chocó department, north-west Colombia.

Panama Records of this species are restricted to the slopes of Cerros de Quía (7°35'N 77°27'W), which form the central part of the border between Colombia and Panama, at the southern end of Cerro Pirre (Haffer 1975, Wetmore *et al.* 1984). Two specimens (male and female) were collected in February and March 1970 on Cerros de Quía near a trail leading down to the río Mono: the bird was also found more generally on the steep slopes of the higher ridges in this area (Wetmore *et al.* 1984). More recently, the species was believed heard on the slopes of Cerro Pirre, above Cana, although this has not been confirmed with specimens or sightings (Ridgely and Gwynne 1989).

Colombia The type and one other specimen were taken during June–July 1912 at Baudó: Baudó (= Pizarro, 4°48'N 77°22'W) is at sea level, and the specimens were taken at 450 m, apparently on the río Baudó in the Serranía de Baudó (c.6°00'N 77°05'W) (Chapman 1917a, Paynter and Traylor 1981, Hilty and Brown 1986; coordinates from Paynter and Traylor 1981). There have apparently been no further records from Colombia.

POPULATION Nothing is known about the population of the Chocó Tinamou in Colombia: however, in Cerros de Quía, Panama, Wetmore *et al.* (1984) found it fairly common on the steep slopes of the higher ridges, noting that birds were heard regularly but seen only occasionally (usually as they rose in rapid flight). Ridgely and Gwynne (1989) suggested that the species is "apparently uncommon to rare".

ECOLOGY This tinamou is apparently one of humid primary forest (in the tropical zone) on foothill slopes, records coming from 300 to 760 m (Wetmore *et al.* 1984, Blake 1977). Wetmore *et al.* (1984) heard birds regularly during February and March, and the type-specimen (a female), collected in June–July, is apparently an immature, both facts suggesting that like many species in this region breeding occurs between March and June (Haffer 1975).

THREATS The forest in Darién, on the border of Panama and Colombia (including Cerros Pirre and de Quía) is seemingly mostly unaffected by agricultural or logging activities (CNPPA 1982), and in the Serranía de Baudó there are still large expanses of forest (A. J. Negret *in litt.* 1987). However, both the Colombian side of the border and the Serranía de Baudó (especially around Ensenada Utría) have been identified as the having the highest conservation priority (within the Colombian Chocó) owing to the incursion of roads encouraging settlement, and by timber companies causing further deforestation (IUCN TFP 1988a).

MEASURES TAKEN In Panama, the Darién National Park (597,000 ha), covers about 80% of the border area with Colombia and includes the Cerro Tacarcuna massif (CNPPA 1982, Ridgely and Gwynne 1989). In Colombia, Los Katíos National Park (72,000 ha) covers areas along the border (CNPPA 1982), although the bird has not been recorded there; and Ensenada Utría National Park (c.50,000 ha) protects some areas of the Serranía de Baudó (IUCN TFP 1988a), although again it is unknown whether the Chocó Tinamou occurs in the immediate area (for further details see equivalent section under Speckled Antshrike *Xenornis setifrons*).

MEASURES PROPOSED Where possible, efforts on behalf of this species should seek to address the needs of the other threatened birds in this area, namely Speckled Antshrike and Baudó Oropendola *Psarocolius cassini* (details concerning the conservation of the threatened and endemic birds in this area are in the equivalent section under Speckled Antshrike).

MAGDALENA TINAMOU *Crypturellus saltuarius* E/Ex[4]

This gamebird (still of some taxonomic uncertainty) is known only from the type-specimen taken during 1943 in the río Magdalena valley, Colombia, where it is apparently at risk from human disturbance of the dry deciduous forest that grows (or grew) in the area.

DISTRIBUTION The Magdalena Tinamou (see Remarks) is only known from the type-specimen (in USNM) taken at Ayacucho (8°36'N 73°35'W, c.150 m), on the lower middle río Magdalena, Cesar department, north-central Colombia (Wetmore 1950, Paynter and Traylor 1981).

POPULATION This species is known from just a single male taken on 9 June 1943 (in USNM), and has seemingly not been recorded since that date.

ECOLOGY Nothing is known, although the type-locality is (or was) covered by low, dry, deciduous forest and savannas (Paynter and Traylor 1981, LGN). An unattributed remark (on USNM printout) suggests that the type-specimen is an immature bird.

THREATS Clearance of the dry forests for cattle-ranching and farming in this area is a serious threat to the Magdalena Tinamou, and hunting by locals (of tinamous in general) is to be expected (A. J. Negret *in litt.* 1987, LGN).

MEASURES TAKEN There are no protected areas in the vicinity of the type-locality of this species, most of the land being privately owned and used for cattle-ranching (CNPPA 1982, LGN).

MEASURES PROPOSED A thorough search for this tinamou in suitable (remaining) habitat close to the type-locality is urgently needed, to assess both the conservation status of the bird and its taxonomic position (see Remarks).

REMARKS Several authors (e.g. Carriker 1955b, Blake 1977, Hilty and Brown 1986), based on comparison of specimens and interspecific mallophagan ectoparasites, have suggested that the Magdalena Tinamou is in fact a subspecies of the widespread Red-legged Tinamou *Crypturellus erythropus*, from northern Colombia, northern Venezuela, the Guianas and northern Brazil (Hilty and Brown 1986).

KALINOWSKI'S TINAMOU *Nothoprocta kalinowskii* E/Ex[4]

This tinamou is known from two old specimens collected in either grassland or scrub at two high Andean localities over 900 km apart in Peru.

DISTRIBUTION Kalinowski's Tinamou is known from only two specimens taken at widely disjunct localities (over 900 km apart) in Peru. The type-specimen was collected in Cuzco department in May 1894, apparently at 4,575 m in the "Cordillera de Licamachay" (von Berlepsch and Stolzmann 1901, 1906). Licamachay was not located by Vaurie (1972), but according to Blake (1977) and Stephens and Traylor (1983) it is south of and near to Cuzco town. The only other known specimen (in AMNH) was collected in western La Libertad department in May 1900, at Hacienda Tulpo (c.8°08'S 78°01'W: Stephens and Traylor 1983), apparently at c.3,000 m on the Pacific slope c.19 km east of Santiago de Chuco, and south-east of Huamachuco (Ménégaux 1910).

POPULATION This tinamou is known from just two specimens, the last of which was taken in 1900. Although it cannot be common within its range, the species may survive locally in small numbers.

ECOLOGY At Hacienda Tulpo in La Libertad (at 3,000 m) there were pastures, potato and barley fields (Ménégaux 1910). If the Cuzco specimen was really taken at 4,575 m it must have come from an area of grassland (NK; Blake 1977), or possibly *Polylepis* woodland (NK). If, however, it was taken lower, Parker *et al.* (1982) may be correct in describing its habitat as montane scrub, the habitat to be expected at 3,000 m on the Pacific slope of La Libertad department (NK).

THREATS None is known apart from the general hunting of all species of tinamou. The presence of man in the high Andes for thousands of years may have seriously altered its habitat.

MEASURES TAKEN None is known.

MEASURES PROPOSED The rediscovery of the species must be the first target (for which visits to and enquiries at the two known localities represent a starting point), after which fieldwork should concentrate on its habitat requirements and distribution. A full taxonomic evaluation of the species, involving careful examination of the two known skins, would be helpful (see below).

REMARKS Hellmayr and Conover (1942), who only knew of the Cuzco specimen, suggested that *kalinowskii* was probably a subspecies of Ornate Tinamou *N. ornata*. This possibility was also mentioned by Blake (1977), although he was aware of the specimen from La Libertad, and that the intervening region is inhabited by *N. ornata branickii*. However, he formally maintained *kalinowskii* as a species, and later (Mayr and Cottrell 1979) made no reference to the issue, thus apparently rejecting the possible conspecificity of *kalinowskii* and *ornata*.

TACZANOWSKI'S TINAMOU *Nothoprocta taczanowskii* V[9]

This poorly known tinamou inhabits semi-humid montane scrub near the treeline in southern Peru. It is uncommon and perhaps local, and is affected by frequent burning of grassland, and by the cutting of high-elevation copses and shrubby patches for use as firewood.

DISTRIBUTION Taczanowski's Tinamou has been recorded from Junín, Apurímac, Cuzco and Puno departments, southern Peru, where it is known from sixteen specimens and a number of recent observations, at the following localities (coordinates from Stephens and Traylor 1983):

Junín vicinity of Maraynioc (11°22'S 75°24'W), near the source of the río Aynamayo (= río Vítoc), where specimens (in AMNH, FMNH, MCZ and Warsaw) have been taken between 3,300 and 3,650 m, most recently in 1939 (also Taczanowski 1874, 1884-1886, Sclater and Salvin 1874, von Berlepsch and Stolzmann 1902, Peters and Griswold 1943);

Apurímac Pomayaco (untraced, but in the río Pampas valley, c.1.5 hours ride from Ahuayro at c.13°22'S 73°52'W), where a specimen (in BMNH) was taken in 1939 (also Morrison 1948); Bosque de Chincheros (c.13°30'S 73°45'W), where a specimen (in FMNH) was collected at 2,900 m in 1970 (also Blake 1977, Mayr and Cottrell 1979); Bosque Ampay (c.13°38'S 72°57'W), where there have been several recent sightings at elevations ranging from 2,700 to 4,000 m (J. Fjeldså *in litt.* 1990); Bosque de Naupallagta, probably east of Caraybamba (c.14°23'S 73°09'W) on the road to Antabamba (14°19'S 72°55'W), where a specimen (in MHNJP) was taken at 3,650 m in 1977 (also Fjeldså and Krabbe 1990);

Cuzco Canchaillo (13°08'S 72°19'W), where the species has recently been seen at c.3,500 m (TAP); Cachupata (c.13°17'S 71°22'W), 32 km east of Paucartambo, on the east slope of the Andes in the Madre de Díos drainage, where specimens (in BMNH) were taken at 3,500 m (also Sclater and Salvin 1874, Taczanowski 1884-1886, Salvadori 1895a, Peters 1931, Hellmayr and Conover 1942, Blake 1977, Mayr and Cottrell 1979; see Remarks);

Puno Valcón (c.14°26'S 69°24'W), on the eastern slope of the Andes, where two specimens (in LSUMZ) were taken at c.3,000 m in 1980 (also Fjeldså and Krabbe 1990).

POPULATION This tinamou was described as being fairly common at Maraynioc in 1939, but was so wary that it was difficult to shoot (Peters and Griswold 1943), and thus scarcity of museum specimens may not reflect its true rarity. The species was uncommon at Bosque Ampay in November 1989 (J. Fjeldså *in litt.* 1990). The status of "rare" given by Parker *et al.* (1982) was intended for Kalinowski's Tinamou *Nothoprocta kalinowskii* adjacent to it in the book, while the status for that species, "uncommon", was meant for the present species (TAP).

ECOLOGY Taczanowski's Tinamou inhabits humid and semi-humid montane scrub at the edge of fields and puna grassland, at elevations ranging from 2,700 to 4,000 m (Peters and Griswold 1943, Morrison 1948, J. Fjeldså *in litt.* 1990). At Canchaillo, Cuzco, it was found in near-pristine grassland with scattered *Lupinus* bushes and small thickets of *Gynoxys* shrubbery, just above treeline forest (TAP). At Pomayaco, Apurímac, a specimen was collected on the fringe of humid temperate woods, which lie as a belt above the arid río Pampas valley, and which change abruptly above to the lower level of the puna zone (Morrison 1948). At Maraynioc, Junín, the species occurred in small copses and on the grassy slopes, and was most frequently encountered around small potato fields scattered through the area (Peters and Griswold 1943). Judging from the photographs in Peters and Griswold (1943) these copses were composed, at least partly, of *Buddleia*, *Gynoxys* and *Polylepis* (NK). At Bosque Ampay, Apurímac, the species was also found in a mosaic habitat: small tuber fields and strongly grazed patches interspersed with copses, small woods and scrub (*Podocarpus*, *Escallonia myrtilloides*, *Vallea stipularis*, *Barnadesia*, *Hesperomeles* and others) (J. Fjeldså *in litt.* 1990). Birds may run rapidly whenever there is much cover, but if surprised in the open will usually freeze until almost stepped on (Peters and Griswold 1943).

At Bosque Ampay the species was noted to feed in the open (mainly on tuber crops) only early in the morning, and would hide at the edge of shrubbery and woods the rest of the day (J. Fjeldså *in litt.* 1990). At Maraynioc it was found to be fond of potatoes, which it dug out of the ground, often returning to the same fields (Peters and Griswold 1943); also at this locality, females with eggs in the oviduct, a chick, and a male with active gonads were taken in April and May (Peters and Griswold 1943; specimens in FMNH and MCZ). At Valcón, Puno, a chick was collected in October (Fjeldså and Krabbe 1990; specimen in LSUMZ). The Pomayaco bird from October had inactive gonads and was moulting (specimen in BMNH), and an immature bird was collected in September in Cuzco (Taczanowski 1874, Sclater and Salvin 1874).

THREATS The isolated temperate woodlands and adjacent shrubby grasslands in the high Andes have been diminishing for hundreds of years owing to the activities of man (Fjeldså 1987), including frequent burning of grassland, and the cutting of high-elevation copses and shrubby patches for use as firewood (NK, TAP). The species is being hunted for food (NK).

MEASURES TAKEN None is known.

MEASURES PROPOSED Taczanowski's Tinamou should be studied to clarify its ecological requirements and distributional limits. The upper elevations (above 3,500 m) of existing protected areas should be extended to incorporate (at least a few) large areas of treeline habitat from which domestic livestock should be excluded (and annual burning prohibited). These habitats occur in or near Manu National Park, above the Machupicchu "sanctuary", above the Tambopata-Condamo Reserve (all in Peru), and along the western edge of the recently proposed Alto Madidi National Park in Bolivia (Parker *et al.* 1990). An additional high-elevation biological reserve or national park should be established somewhere between the río Huallaga canyon (in Huánuco) and the río Apurímac canyon (in Ayacucho), while in densely settled areas farmers should be encouraged to leave plenty of shrubbery and open, park-like woodland bordering their fields in order to stop wind- and soil-erosion: all this would benefit a large number of plant and animal species confined to small areas in the high Andes of central and southern Peru (TAP).

REMARKS One of the two specimens taken by H. Whitely in Cuzco was described as a distinct species and named *Nothoprocta godmani* by Taczanowski (1884-1886). However, Sclater and Salvin (1873) had considered this specimen an immature, arguing that while the type of *taczanowskii* agrees in general coloration with the larger of the two Cuzco specimens, it corresponds in dimensions with the smaller, which was later designated the type of *godmani*. Taczanowski (1884-1886) nevertheless gave the measurements of *godmani* as all being smaller than those of the type of *taczanowskii*, except for the middle toe, which he gave as longer; he made no reference to the other Cuzco bird, under either *tacznowskii* or *godmani*. Hellmayr and Conover (1942) believed that Taczanowski had referred both Cuzco specimens to *godmani*, and they left the question of the status of *godmani* open, but referred to the type of *godmani* as an immature bird. Subsequent authors have uncritically included the Cuzco specimens under *taczanowskii* (e.g. Blake 1977, Mayr and Cottrell 1979).

LESSER NOTHURA *Nothura minor* I[7]

Rapid and extensive conversion of its grassland and cerrado habitat to agriculture in central and south-east Brazil appears to be threatening this poorly known small tinamou, for which there are almost no recent records.

DISTRIBUTION The Lesser Nothura is endemic to central-southern Brazil from central Mato Grosso and Goiás south to central São Paulo. The species's occurrence in Bahia (von Ihering and von Ihering 1907) is unsubstantiated (Hellmayr and Conover 1942). In the following account, records are arranged from north to south within states, as follows:

Federal District Brasília in May 1963 (specimen in MPEG) and December 1965 (specimen in MNRJ), and in Brasília National Park in November 1983 (specimen in MNRJ) and 1987-1990 (TAP), prefiguring the disclosure of the species's occurrence alongside the Dwarf Tinamou *Taoniscus nanus* in the IBGE Roncador Biological Reserve south of Brasília (Teixeira and Negret 1984);

Goiás Luziânia, September 1979 (specimen in MNRJ); Goiânia, January 1968 (two specimens in LSUMZ); Emas National Park, 1985 and 1987 (A. Negret verbally 1987, R. S. Ridgely verbally 1988, TAP);

Minas Gerais (see Remarks 1) rio Preto near Paracatu, January 1967 (specimen in MNRJ); Tejuco (= Diamantina, type-locality) (von Spix 1824, Hellmayr and Conover 1942); Agua Suja (= Romaria in Paynter and Traylor 1991) (Laubmann 1934); Lagoa Santa (Reinhardt 1870); Serra do Cipó at Alto da Palácio, July 1977 (Willis and Oniki in press);

Mato Grosso Chapada (= Chapada dos Guimarães: Paynter and Traylor 1991), September 1882 and June 1885 (Allen 1891-1893; specimens in AMNH, plus one undated in BMNH); Serra da Chapada (untraced but perhaps the same as the preceding), 700-900 m, September 1902 (specimen in BMNH);

Mato Grosso do Sul Fazendas Corralinho and Carrapatos (near Campo Grande) on successive dates, 31 August and 1 September 1938 (Pinto 1964, specimens in MZUSP); Fazenda Capão Bonita, Vacaria, c.110 km south of Campo Grande, September 1937 (specimen in FMNH); and Fazenda Barra Mansa, somewhere on the rio Brilhante, also south of Campo Grande, June 1954 (Pinto 1964, specimen in MZUSP);

São Paulo São José do Rio Pardo, 1927 (Pinto 1938); Lagoa Branca (specifically at Casa Branca), April 1957 (specimen in LACM); Ribeirão Bonito, September 1929 (Pinto 1938, 1964, specimen in MZUSP); "Irisanga" (= Orissanga, 22°12'S 46°57'W in Paynter and Traylor 1991), December 1822 (von Pelzeln 1868-1871); Itirapina, recently (E. O. Willis *in litt.* 1986, TAP; see Remarks 2); Botucatu airfield, February 1947 (Pinto 1964, specimen in MZUSP); Fazenda da Florida, Bofete, April 1938 (Pinto 1964, specimen in MZUSP); Itatinga, September 1902 (Hellmayr and Conover 1942, specimen in AMNH); Sorocaba, specifically Salto, May 1937 (Pinto 1964, specimen in MZUSP); Itapetininga, March and June 1927, July 1928 (Pinto 1938, 1964, specimens in MCZ, FMNH, MZUSP); Fazenda Cambará, Aracaçu, October 1938 (Pinto 1964, specimen in MZUSP); Fazenda do Rio Verde (just north of Itararé), August 1820 (von Pelzeln 1868-1871); Itararé, September 1820, "February, March" (von Pelzeln 1868-1871; see Remarks 3).

POPULATION This bird may be overlooked (D. M. Teixeira *in litt.* 1987), and even common locally (J. Vielliard *in litt.* 1986), yet recent specimens and documented sight records are paltry in number, suggesting a steep decline: E. O. Willis (*in litt.* 1986) mentioned having one recent locality (a small grassland area near Itirapina: TAP) in São Paulo, source of most records historically, and the other recent records are from Brasília and Emas National Parks and the IBGE reserve in Distrito Federal (see Distribution). Lesser Nothuras apparently occur in low densities in these few known modern localities: in Brasília National Park, up to three individuals were heard singing in an area of c.20 ha of campo sujo, but none was found in much larger but seemingly suitable areas of the same habitat (TAP); and in Emas National Park a few individuals could be flushed during long walks through lush campo limpo, and others were occasionally seen along roadsides through the same habitat, but the species was seemingly greatly outnumbered by the Spotted Nothura *Nothura maculata* (TAP, R. S. Ridgely *in litt.* 1992).

ECOLOGY The Lesser Nothura inhabits cerrado, sometimes in the same areas as Spotted Nothura, though in scrubbier grassland ("campo mais sujo") (Sick 1985), primarily in undisturbed areas of campo limpo and campo sujo habitat (TAP), being unable to adapt to man-modified habitats, unlike the Spotted Nothura (de Magalhães 1978); it is also notable that this species has been recorded at many of the same localities (Lagoa Santa, Orissanga, Itararé, Itapetininga, Brasília) as the Dwarf Tinamou (see relevant account). J. Natterer (von Pelzeln 1868-1871) recorded solitary individuals of this species from high grass on the plains, noting that they run fast and that, when hunted with dogs, often hide in armadillo holes and can usually then be caught by hand (this reluctance to fly, even when almost stepped on, also being noted in recent fieldwork: TAP). At Emas these inconspicuous birds are usually encountered singly in open expanses of grassland (campo limpo) with scattered bushes and small trees, often in areas where large termite mounds are numerous; they apparently prefer areas with a continuous cover of tall grasses and sedges, and are almost impossible to see in such areas (in contrast to Spotted Nothura) (TAP). One small area of campo sujo in Brasília National Park supported a small population over a period of at least four years, during which the site remained unburnt; no individuals were seen or heard in nearby, similar-looking habitat that was burnt at least twice during that period (TAP). In preferred habitat at both Brasília and Emas, Lesser Nothuras were found in close proximity to four other bird species that are similarly threatened in central Brazil (near-threatened at the global level): Ocellated Crake *Micropygia schomburgkii*, Cock-tailed Tyrant *Alectrurus tricolor*, Sharp-tailed Tyrant *Culicivora caudacuta* and Black-masked Finch *Coryphaspiza melanotis* (TAP). There is no information on diet. The male collected in Mato Grosso do Sul in September had testes enlarged (FMNH label data), and juveniles have been captured in January (Reinhardt 1870), March (Pinto 1938) and June (Allen 1891-1893); this suggests that breeding normally takes place during the rainy season, October–February. The species has been noted to fall prey to Burrowing Owls *Speotyto cunicularia* (Teixeira and Negret 1984).

THREATS The near-total destruction of open grasslands both in south-east Brazil (São Paulo) and in the vast central planalto (Mato Grosso, Goiás and Minas Gerais) must be regarded as one of the great ecological catastrophes in South America, all the more regrettable because so utterly neglected as an international conservation issue. The speed and extent of the conversion of the Brazilian grassland ecosystems to large-scale agriculture is astonishing, most largely disappearing only since 1960: new farming techniques, such as liming to cure aluminium toxicity and acid soils, has allowed agrobusiness to develop throughout the region, with large-scale development involving eucalyptus, pines, sugarcane and soybeans (de Magalhães 1978, E. O. Willis *in litt.* 1986), and more than 95% of potential arable or stock-raising land has probably already been appropriated or otherwise thoroughly degraded (TAP; also E. O. Willis *in litt.* 1990). Relatively pristine tracts of upland grassland south of 15°S are now confined to portions of five national parks and a small number of other types of reserve: most natural grassland vegetation elsewhere in Brazil seems likely to disappear altogether by the end of the century (TAP).

As a result of this development, nearly all the species endemic or near-endemic to the open vegetation of central Brazil have suffered drastic declines (Teixeira and Negret 1984, Cavalcanti 1988, Willis and Oniki 1988b), and a few may even be extinct through large parts of their former range, these being the Lesser Nothura and the threatened Dwarf Tinamou, Blue-eyed Ground-dove *Columbina cyanopis*, White-winged Nightjar *Caprimulgus candicans*, Rufous-sided Pygmy-tyrant *Euscarthmus rufomarginatus*, Ochre-breasted Pipit *Anthus nattereri*, Black-and-tawny Seedeater *Sporophila nigrorufa*, Cinereous Warbling-finch *Poospiza cinerea* and possibly also the mysterious

Cone-billed Tanager *Conothraupis mesoleuca* (see relevant accounts). Most of the remaining campo and cerrado habitat specialists of the region (e.g. the near-threatened Cock-tailed Tyrant, Sharp-tailed Tyrant and Black-masked Finch) would also be considered threatened but for the fact that they retain reasonably healthy populations in the grasslands of north-central Bolivia (see Parker *et al.* 1991); these latter stand also to gain from the preservation of natural grasslands advocated for Corrientes province, Argentina (see Measures Proposed under Strange-tailed Tyrant *Yetapa risora*). The Bearded Tachuri *Polystictus pectoralis* is another species whose populations in this region (nominate *pectoralis*) have been virtually exterminated (see Remarks 4 under White-winged Nightjar; also Remarks 2 below).

Lush campo sujo habitat in Emas National Park is not currently secure (see Threats under White-winged Nightjar).

MEASURES TAKEN The Lesser Nothura is protected under Brazilian law (Bernardes *et al.* 1990). The species occurs in the IBGE Roncador Biological Reserve, where it shares its habitat with the threatened Dwarf Tinamou (Teixeira and Negret 1984), and in Brasília and Emas National Parks (28,000 ha and 132,000 ha respectively: IBAMA 1989; see Distribution).

MEASURES PROPOSED Detailed studies of this and the other grassland and cerrado tinamous of central Brazil (Red-winged Tinamou *Rhynchotus rufescens*, Spotted Nothura and Dwarf Tinamou) are most desirable, with particular emphasis on the ecology of Lesser Nothura and Dwarf Tinamou. This and other species listed in Threats should be prime targets of a major scheme of terrestrial reconnaisance and biological survey throughout the remaining patches of appropriate habitat within their ranges, notably in the three protected areas from which it is known (Emas and Brasília National Parks and the IBGE reserve), but also the other major parks and reserves of the region: Serra das Araras Ecological Reserve (28,000 ha) in Mato Grosso, which is proving to be rich in endemic Brazilian Shield fauna and flora (E. O. Willis *in litt.* 1991); Chapada dos Guimarães National Park (33,000 ha), also in Mato Grosso, although much of the region's best campo sujo habitat appears to lie to the north of the park boundary, to which therefore an extension might be made (TAP); Chapada dos Veadeiros National Park (60,000 ha) in Goiás; Grande Sertão Veredas National Park (84,000 ha) and Serra da Canastra National Park (71,500 ha), both in Minas Gerais (areas from IBAMA 1989). The northern and western ranges of the Brazilian Shield, such as Serra do Cachimbo, Serra dos Apiacás and Serra do Roncador, support poorly known campo and cerrado plant and animal communities (TAP) that deserve investigation for this group of birds and which can hopefully be protected against modification by man.

Improved fire management techniques should be employed in all national parks and biological reserves to ensure that all stages of campo vegetation (campo limpo, campo sujo, campo cerrado) are present at all times. Much research is needed on the effects of fire and grazing on the structure and floristic composition of central Brazilian grasslands, and on the ecological role of fire in the distribution and abundance of campo birds. Work to illuminate these matters might also be directed at determining the possibility of reclaiming and restoring certain degraded areas.

REMARKS (1) There is a specimen in USNM labelled "Conceição do Lerro, Brazil" and also from Belo Horizonte Zoo, dated August 1933 and with the information that its habitat is "campo" and its abundance is great. Conceição do Lerro cannot be traced, but the locality in question was presumably near to Belo Horizonte and at least within Minas Gerais; a Conceição da Barra, now Cassiterita, is at 21°07'S 44°28'W (in OG 1963b). (2) The near-threatened Bearded Tachuri retains a small population in the same remnant patch of grassland at Itirapina (E. O. Willis *in litt.* 1991), which considerably adds to the importance of the site (see Remarks 4 under White-winged Nightjar *Caprimulgus candicans*). (3) According to the itinerary in von Pelzeln (1868-1871), J. Natterer, the collector involved, was not at Itararé except in August/September 1820 and possibly January 1821, although there is some confusion about his activities and whereabouts at the start of 1821 (see, e.g., Remarks 4 under Red-tailed Amazon *Amazona brasiliensis*). These skins from February and March presumably represent purchased items.

DWARF TINAMOU *Taoniscus nanus* I[7]

Rapid and extensive conversion of its grassland and cerrado habitat to agriculture appears to be threatening this poorly known small ground-dwelling bird from central and south-east Brazil (once recorded also in Argentina).

DISTRIBUTION The Dwarf Tinamou is known with certainty from a relatively small area of central Brazil, where it was only discovered in the 1960s, some scattered localities in south-east Brazil, almost all now from long ago, some vague records from Minas Gerais, and two skins from Argentina. The original description was based on one in de Azara (1802-1805) naming "Misiones" as the (presumed) provenance (de Azara said it was very scarce there, not necessarily implying that this was his source of birds), apparently assumed to indicate the province in Argentina (Hellmayr and Conover 1942, Pinto 1964, 1978) although presumably it might equally well have implied the department in Paraguay. Neither seems to have been widely accepted in the literature (see Remarks 1); however, the neglected records of the species from the Argentine "chaco" (see below) tend to heighten the possibility of de Azara's reports stemming from near-adjacent southern Paraguay. It is notable that several authorities mention Paraguay (e.g. Burmeister 1856, Pinto 1938), presumably believing that de Azara had been referring to that country and not Argentina; Podtiaguin (1941-1945) even listed, without supporting evidence, the departments of Misiones and Alto Paraná (and the records below from Mato Grosso do Sul show how close the species is known to approach the country).

Brazil On the assumption that the range of the Dwarf Tinamou in Brazil is continuous or nearly so, its area of occurrence has been judged very large (da Silveira 1967, Teixeira and Negret 1984). However, the map in da Silveira (1967) is a gross exaggeration and generalization of the known range (extending it hundreds of kilometres to the south of any record), and on current evidence the species has practically disappeared from the south-east of its range while its status in central Brazil remains to be clarified.

Federal District Records are from: near Brasília, in the IBGE Roncador Biological Reserve, 15°55'S 47°52'W, early 1980s (Teixeira and Negret 1984; see Remarks 2); and the vicinity of the city, mid-1960s (da Silveira 1967, 1968).

Goiás Records are from: Cristalina, 1965, and presumably at the same or adjacent (but unspecified) localities, 1966 (da Silveira 1967, 1968).

Minas Gerais Hellmayr and Conover (1942) explained why the listing of this state (e.g. by Pinto 1938) was based on a nineteenth-century error. Nevertheless, M. A. de Andrade (*in litt.* 1988) referred to old records of the species around Sete Lagoas and Lagoa Santa (the latter mentioned in Warming 1908), while in the late 1980s a local hunter at Poços de Caldas in the far south-west (relatively close to Orissanga, below) described the species convincingly and indicated that it occurred there locally (F. C. Straube verbally 1988), and in April 1973 a bird was seen at Lagoa Chapadão do Ferro, Serra Negra, near Patrocínio (G. T. de Mattos verbally 1987).

Mato Grosso do Sul There are two records: from Rio Brilhante (not clear if the river or the town), undated (Pinto 1978), and Bonito, August 1991 (J. F. Pacheco verbally 1992).

São Paulo Records (north to south) are from: Franca, before 1822 (Schlegel 1880); Sarandy (= Sarandi), the only one in São Paulo listed in OG (1963b) now being called Jurucê, at 21°04'S 47°45'W, May 1938 (specimen in MCZ); "Irisanga" (= Orissanga, 22°12'S 46°57'W in Paynter and Traylor 1991), January 1823 (von Pelzeln 1868-1871; see Remarks 3); Bartira, 22°15'S 51°02'W, in the west of the state, July 1922 (Pinto 1938; see Remarks 4); Itapetininga, July 1927, June and July 1928, May, June and July 1930 (Hellmayr and Conover 1942; nine specimens in AMNH, ANSP, BMNH, FMNH, MCZ); Buri, 1929 (Pinto 1964); Itararé, on the border with Paraná, January, February and March 1821 (von Pelzeln 1868-1871; see Remarks 5). E. O. Willis (*in litt.* 1986) mentioned having one recent locality for the species.

Paraná The only record appears to be from "Jaguaraiba" (= Jaguariaíva), in the north (not far from Itararé), September 1820 (von Pelzeln 1868-1871; see Remarks 6).

Argentina Two specimens (in BMNH) are from "chaco austral, Argentina", one from the "coast of river Bermejo", the other also from "River Bermejo", i.e. in either Formosa or Chaco provinces; neither is dated but they were received in 1900 and 1901. Although first published in Collar and Andrew (1988), these records did not appear in Sibley and Monroe (1990) or Canevari *et al.* (1992).

POPULATION Already 50 and over 100 years ago the Dwarf Tinamou was being called "one of the rarest neotropical birds" (Hellmayr and Conover 1942) and the rarest of species (Schlegel 1880), although this was at a time when its range was believed to extend only through São Paulo, Paraná and Misiones in Argentina. In fact de Azara (1802-1805) had already made the point that its great scarcity (in Misiones) was probably more perceived than actual, given that it hides in the grass and only flies when about to be stepped on. Old reports spoke of it being common around Sete Lagoas and Lagoa Santa, Minas Gerais, but with no further records it is assumed to have become rare in the state (M. A. de Andrade *in litt.* 1988), as it was also in São Paulo (Pinto 1964); the local hunter at Poços de Caldas who apparently knew the species reported it uncommon in the area but common in Goiás (F. C. Straube verbally 1988), and indeed Teixeira and Negret (1984) reiterated the view that the species might be not so much rare as difficult to locate. However, the massive agricultural conversion of its habitat is such that confidence over its present situation cannot be high (Teixeira and Negret 1984), and the species seems likely to be in very steep decline.

ECOLOGY The species has been claimed to occur in "gallery forest, savannah country and the cerrados... in small flocks" (da Silveira 1967, 1968; see Remarks 7); de Azara (1802-1805) reported it from dense scrub and grassland ("campos muy cerrados de broza y pasto alto y espeso"). Teixeira and Negret (1984) never found other than singles and pairs, however, and mentioned cerrado and campo sujo as habitat, the latter being defined as scattered bushes less than 2 m in height on dense grassland composed mainly of Gramineae (*Axonopus*, *Echinolaena*, *Paspalum*, *Panicum* and *Schizachyrium*), the birds most often being seen (not as a habitat preference but because of relative ease of observation) in open, burnt-over vegetation and along trails; they seemed to be more active in the early morning or afternoon, especially after or during drizzle. In general it would seem likely to be a campo sujo specialist (TAP). A specimen originally in MNRJ from the IBGE reserve, Brasília, November 1982, was in campo limpo at 1,000 m; an observation in Minas Gerais was when a bird crossed a road in partially cleared, weed-invaded cerrado (G. T. de Mattos verbally 1987).

At the Fazenda Carneiro (see Remarks 6) the species was recorded from grassland; a bird was so unwilling to fly that it was caught by hand, and its stomach and crop were found to contain seeds (von Pelzeln 1868-1871). Elsewhere the species has been reported to spend most of its time searching through the vegetation for small arthropods (pecking at nests of termites *Proconitermes araujoi* to catch the emerging insects) and grass seeds (Teixeira and Negret 1984). It is notable that two of five specimens from the mid-1960s were caught alive, apparently by hand, while a third was killed by a dog (da Silveira 1968); Teixeira and Negret (1984) attributed their being able to capture specimens by hand to the dizzying effects of smoke on the birds (see Threats), but it is clear from the above that they react to approaching danger by freezing, whether dizzy or not. De Azara (1802-1805) kept a bird briefly which would eat only spiders.

Both birds from the Argentine "chaco" (the habitat in question may rather have been remnant campo areas, not dry forest or monte scrub), neither dated, were "full of eggs" on dissection (BMNH label data). A non-moulting male from September (a time when songs were very common) was very fat, with testes starting to develop; an adult with two tiny chicks was seen in October (Teixeira and Negret 1984). Males from Itararé, January and March, were "young" (von

Pelzeln 1868-1871), and indeed that from January is juvenile (specimen in NHMW: C. G. Violani *in litt.* 1987; also Teixeira and Nacinovic 1990).

THREATS Grasslands both in south-east Brazil (São Paulo and Paraná) and in the country's vast central planalto are under enormous pressure from agriculture (see Threats under Lesser Nothura *Nothura minor*). Moreover, these birds are directly harmed by extensive grass fires, and may also suffer predation by raptors when fleeing them (Teixeira and Negret 1984).

MEASURES TAKEN The Dwarf Tinamou is protected under Brazilian law (Bernardes *et al.* 1990). The species occurs in the IBGE Roncador Biological Reserve, where it shares its habitat with the Lesser Nothura (Teixeira and Negret 1984; see relevant account).

MEASURES PROPOSED Teixeira and Negret (1984) indicated that the voice of this species is now known, and that much singing, albeit difficult to distinguish from crickets, can be heard in the breeding season. This will aid the needed surveys for this species, which should, however, be integrated into a major scheme of terrestrial reconnaissance and biological survey as adumbrated in the equivalent section under Lesser Nothura.

REMARKS (1) Sibley and Monroe (1990) referred to reports from north-east Argentina (Misiones) as needing confirmation, citing Teixeira and Negret (1984); Teixeira and Negret (1984) referred to "recent observations" from the same area as needing confirmation, citing Olrog (1979); Olrog (1979) contains nothing on this matter. It may be that all this refers to the original citation based on de Azara (1802-1805). (2) In addition to the material considered by Teixeira and Negret (1984), the IBGE collection in Brasília contains a male and female from the Roncador reserve, dated August 1984 (C. Yamashita *in litt.* 1987). (3) The skin in NHMW is actually dated 25 February 1823 (C. G. Violani *in litt.* 1987). (4) Paynter and Traylor (1991) quoted Pinto (1964) as saying that Bartira is in "the campos of Capivari" (this is in fact based on the label in MZUSP, which says "Bartyra, campos de Capivary"), and pointed out that the only Bartira they could trace (coordinates as given) was nowhere near Capivari, and assumed therefore it was incorrect; however, GQR (1991) shows a ribeirão Capivara extending close to the coordinates for Bartira, and it is assumed here that the grasslands in its headwaters were what was intended. (5) These specimens were, of course, all collected by J. Natterer; an undated, uncredited skin in AMNH from Itararé very likely also proceeds from Natterer at this time. (6) It is possible to assume from both von Pelzeln (1868-1871) and Hellmayr and Conover (1942) that a second locality, "Fazenda do S. Coronel Luciano Carneiro", existed in the state (the latter authors qualified it as being equivalent to or near "Boa Vista" and gave the "other" locality as "Rio Jaguaraiba"); but the absence of a specimen labelled from the fazenda or of its mention in von Pelzeln's account of J. Natterer's itinerary suggests that it was the particular site at which Natterer stayed when at Jaguariaíva; Paynter and Traylor (1991) omitted the locality, perhaps having reached a similar conclusion. (7) The published text in da Silveira (1968) reads "secondary forest", but the author amended this in providing a copy to H. Sick (LPG).

COLOMBIAN GREBE *Podiceps andinus* E/Ex[4]

Probably now extinct, this waterbird was originally restricted to a few lakes throughout the Bogotá–Ubaté plateaus, Colombia, and was apparently last seen in 1977. The reasons for its decline cannot be determined with confidence, but habitat alteration, hunting and the introduction of exotic fish probably played significant roles.

DISTRIBUTION The Colombian Grebe (see Remarks) is known to have bred exclusively at a number of lakes between 2,500 and 3,100 m on the Bogotá–Ubaté plateaus, Cundinamarca and Boyacá departments, Colombia (Meyer de Schauensee 1966, Hilty and Brown 1986). Most records (specimens in AMNH, ANSP, FMNH, USNM) are from Laguna de Tota on the eastern side of the East Andes (5°33'N 72°55'W; 3,015 m): however, on the Ubaté plateau records come from Laguna de Fúquene (5°28'N 73°45'W; 2,580 m) and Laguna de Cucunubá (5°17'N 73°48'W); and on the Bogotá plateau, birds have been noted at La Caro (c.4°52'N 74°02'W; c.2,550 m), Laguna de la Florida (c.4°43'N 74°09'W; c.2,600 m), Laguna de la Herrera (4°42'N 74°18'W; 2,600 m), and Embalse del Muña (c.4°32'N 74°18'W, 2,555 m) (Olivares 1969, Fjeldså and Krabbe 1990, Fjeldså in press; coordinates from Paynter and Traylor 1981).

POPULATION This bird was recorded on the Ubaté plateau (specifically Laguna de Fúquene) during the 1940s, with a few birds still present in the 1950s, and unconfirmed reports of flocks at Laguna de Cucunubá during the early 1970s (Fjeldså in press): on the Bogotá plateau, its disappearance was seemingly complete by the end of the 1940s (Fjeldså 1984). At Laguna de Tota, the Colombian Grebe was recorded as abundant in 1945, usually in groups of 10-30 individuals (Borrero 1947, Fjeldså in press). Even during the 1960s the bird was considered relatively common at this locality (Nicéforo and Olivares 1964), with 300 individuals reported there in 1968 (King 1978-1979; also Fjeldså in press). However, since that date the species is only known from a report of a single bird in 1972 (Fjeldså in press), and two (possibly three) on 13 and 15 February 1977 (King 1978-1979, Fjeldså in press). Despite a number of searches (at all known localities, and practically all other potential sites) looking specifically for this species (e.g. by G. I. Andrade, G. Arango and LGN in the period 1975–1980, J. Fjeldså in 1981, and N. Varty and co-workers in 1982), the Colombian Grebe has not been recorded unequivocally since the 1970s and is almost certainly extinct (Fjeldså 1984 and in press, Varty *et al.* 1986: see Measures Proposed).

ECOLOGY All the lakes formerly inhabited by the Colombian Grebe have in common their high altitude, cold oligotrophic waters, and shorelines with a dense growth of reeds: however, they range widely in size and depth (LGN). Fjeldså and Krabbe (1990) described the habitat as "marshes and lakes with tall marginal reeds and extensive shallows full of submergent water-weeds". At Laguna de Tota in the 1960s, the main submergent in the lake was *Potamogeton illinoiensis* (Borrero 1963), although this is now no longer the case (Fjeldså in press). The *Potamogeton* habitat was probably important for the Colombian Grebe's various prey items (Fjeldså in press). The only published information on the breeding habits of the species are from Borrero (1947), who reported several females ready to lay in August, while J. I. Hernández Camacho (verbally 1980) mentioned that this grebe apparently depended on cattails and other reeds to build and anchor its floating nests.

THREATS In 1981, Fjeldså (in press) noted the following about the various localities and areas where the Colombian Grebe had previously been recorded: (1) the wetlands at the northern end of the Bogotá plateau, near La Caro, were almost totally drained, and the few remaining *Scirpus* marshes, partly overgrown oxbows and waterdams were all unsuitable for the species; (2) wetlands associated with the río Bogotá at Laguna de la Florida were also drained, and badly polluted; (3)

Laguna de la Herrera was almost drained, and comprised 350 ha of marsh habitat (*Scirpus*), *Azolla*-covered mud, and scarcely any open water; (4) Lagunas de Fúquene (45 km^2) and de Cucunubá (3.5 km^2) had complex marginal vegetation zones but the water quality was totally unsuitable – the soil erosion from surrounding deforested hills had reduced water transparency to 10-30 cm and almost totally eliminated the submergent vegetation (again *Potamogeton illinoiensis*), the situation presumably being exacerbated by the large populations of carp *Cyprinus* sp. At Laguna de Tota, the main submergent community comprised *Potamogeton illinoiensis* in the 1960s (see Ecology), but in 1981, Fjeldså (in press) found that this had primarily been replaced with a dense monoculture of *Elodea canadense* which locally filled the water up to the surface.

Various other factors have helped cause the apparent extinction of the Colombian Grebe at Laguna de Tota: (1) intensive onion cultivation around the lake during the early 1960s, leading to a lowering of the water-level and to increased usage of fertilizers and pesticides; (2) introduction of rainbow trout *Salmo gairdneri* in 1944, possibly resulting in the predation of chicks, but more likely affecting the availability of suitable food items; and (3) hunting pressure in the breeding colonies (Varty *et al.* 1986; also Fjeldså 1984). It seems likely that the major decline at Laguna de Tota occurred in the 1950s and early 1960s through habitat loss caused by falling water-levels and changes in the aquatic plant community – *Elodea canadense* seemingly being unsuitable for this bird to dive for food in (Fjeldså 1984 and in press, Varty *et al.* 1986).

MEASURES TAKEN None is known.

MEASURES PROPOSED Although it now seems unlikely that a population of this species still exists, Fjeldså (in press) has suggested that groups of birds may have been straying around (see records of flocks on Laguna de Cucunubá in the 1970s in Population), and that they may still exist on a suitable lake elsewhere in the Andes (see Fjeldså in press for elaboration of this hypothesis).

REMARKS Historically there has been continuous debate as to the taxonomic status of the Colombian Grebe, i.e. whether it is a full species (e.g. Simmons 1962) or a subspecies of the widespread Eared (Black-necked) Grebe *Podiceps nigricollis* (e.g. Meyer de Schauensee 1952, 1959, 1966, Blake 1977, Mayr and Cottrell 1979). Currently, the bird is regarded as a full species, and it will presumably need comparative allozyme analyses to put the argument finally to rest (Fjeldså in press).

JUNIN GREBE *Podiceps taczanowskii* E[1]

This flightless waterbird is confined to Lago de Junín in the highlands of west-central Peru, where it is seriously threatened by pollution from mining activities, by regulation of the water level for a hydroelectric plant supplying the mines, and by plans to divert water down the Pacific slope to supply Lima.

DISTRIBUTION The Junín (Flightless) Grebe (see Remarks 1) is restricted to Laguna Chinchaycocha de Junín (appearing on most maps as Lago de Junín or Laguna de Junín), a 14,320 ha lake (with an additional 11,900 ha of temporarily flooded meadows surrounding it), situated at 4,080 m in Junín department, western Peru (at 10°51'-11°06'S 76°17-33'W) (Fjeldså 1981b). The species is now absent from the heavily polluted north-western end of the lake.

POPULATION Although several thousand birds may formerly have occurred on the lake, the total population now appears to be only between 200 and 300 individuals.

Morrison (1939b), who was at the lake without intermission from 18 January to 11 May 1938, found the species to be extremely abundant. In mid-November 1961, several hundred birds were seen at the southern end of the lake (Storer 1967, F. B. Gill verbally 1985, J. Fjeldså *in litt.* 1985), suggesting that well over 1,000 inhabited the lake at this time.

Along 9.5 km of the southern coast, 70 birds were counted in October 1977, with 75 counted there (along 12 km) in January 1978 (when some birds may have been brooding); during both counts no grebe was present far offshore, and extrapolation to the shores of the entire lake gave estimates of 390 and 330 birds, respectively (Fjeldså 1981b). Considering the absence of this species from the heavily polluted northern end, and information from locals suggesting that it is most numerous between Ondores and Pari, becoming gradually sparser north of Pari and towards the south-east of the lake but occurring inside a reed-barrier which separates small lakes outside Huayre and Carhuamayo, the population was estimated to be 300 birds including immatures: the number of birds observed taking part in displays or seen in pairs suggested that not many more than 100 pairs were present (Fjeldså 1981b). What was believed to be the entire population, 250-300 including young, was counted in May 1979, in the central part of the lake, with none near the reed-borders (Fjeldså 1981b; see also Harris 1981). For comparison with these numbers 45-55 Silvery Grebes *Podiceps occipitalis* and 3,500-4,000 White-tufted Grebe *Rollandia rolland* were estimated to inhabit the lake in 1977/1978 (Fjeldså 1981b).

Fifty-seven Junín Grebes were counted along 8 km of the southern coast in October 1981, thus suggesting a small decline in the total population to some 250 birds, although some could still have been present in the central part of the lake as no breeding behaviour was observed (J. Fjeldså *in litt.* 1987). Brief observations outside Ondores in November 1983 were inconclusive: some grebes were well offshore, as was the case in February 1985, when only 20 were seen between Ondores and Pari (J. Fjeldså *in litt.* 1987). Locals explained that although it had rained heavily in December–February 1983/1984 the rain had stopped early, so the water level in the dry season of 1984 was even lower than the exceptionally low level of 1983, forcing White-tufted Grebes (a food competitor) out of the reeds (into Junín Grebe habitat), with a resultant high mortality of the former (and possibly the latter) (J. Fjeldså *in litt.* 1987).

Little rain fell in the rainy season of 1984/1985, so in February 1985 the water level was already approaching that of October 1977 (J. Fjeldså *in litt.* 1987). From brief observations along the southern coast in 1983 and 1985, the population was estimated to be as small or smaller than in 1981 (J. Fjeldså *in litt.* 1987).

In July and August 1986 147 individuals were censused, all but one being observed over 1 km from the outer reed-border: censuses were carried out from a boat along two transects, one almost the full length of the lake, and one across the southern end at Ondores; a general decrease in the north-westerly direction along the length of the lake was noted (Balharry 1989). The long transect

(6 km long, 0.4 km wide) had on average 25 birds on two trips, the 3.5 km transect 21 birds on six trips; extrapolation from these two transects gave 260 and 375 birds respectively (Balharry 1989). Considering the decrease of birds in the north-westerly direction, the population may have actually been c.250 birds, i.e. much the same as in 1981. A brief visit during May 1992 (relying on information from F. Tueros) suggested that the population may be only c.100 individuals, and that the birds had not been able to breed that season (T. Valqui and J. Barrio *in litt.* 1992; see Threats).

ECOLOGY The detailed studies of the Junín Grebe in the rainy season of 1977/1978 (Fjeldså 1981a,b) are, except when otherwise noted, the source used in the following account.

Lago de Junín is situated 4,080 m above sea level, but remains permanently ice-free, despite air temperatures well below freezing at night in the dry season (May–September). It is a shallow, weakly alkaline, gypsotrophic lake, averaging 4 m deep (with a maximum depth of 10 m), with 143 km^2 of open water (of which c.25 km^2 are more than 1 km from the reed-border: Balharry 1989), surrounded by 156 km^2 of reedbeds of 0.5-2 m tall rush *Juncus andecolus* and, in the more fertile and permanently flooded parts, the 2-4 m tall tule *Scirpus californicus*. Thirty percent of the reedbeds are unbroken, the rest being shallow water with *Chara* (submergent) vegetation interrupted only by scattered patches and floating islands of *Juncus*. In some areas intricate mosaics of channels and small lakes are formed, while in others there are large open "lakes" within the reedbeds: most such areas dry up during the dry season. The grebe breeds in patches of tall *Scirpus* in deep water, and during the breeding season forages along the coast in open water, usually 8-75 m from the reed-border (although a few occur in the larger "lakes" in the reedbeds), only exceptionally venturing closer than 5 m or as far as 500 m from the reed-border. Considerable parts of the open lake are shallow with dense *Chara*-cover over the marl bottom, this lying close beneath the surface in the dry season, but 1.5-2.5 m deep in the rainy season, when it is the grebe's favourite habitat. In the dry season the grebes move into the deeper central parts of the lake (at depths of 5.5-9.0 m: Balharry 1989), where the bottom, besides *Chara*, may have taller weeds such as *Myriophyllum elatinoides*, *Potamogeton ferrugineum* and *P. strictus*, *Ranunculus trichophyllus* and *Zannichellia*, but usually has scanty growth and large bare areas. Nothing is known about the grebe's diet at this season, but in the rainy season fish of the genus *Orestias* form the majority of the biomass ingested. In the dry season numerous small *Orestias* survive in the reed and mud swamps, but when they disperse in the rainy season their population densities decrease.

Stomachs of the Junín Grebe (11 adults and two downy young taken in October and January) held chironomid midges, adults and nymphs of the corixid bug *Trichorixa reticulata*, *Orestias* fish, the amphipod *Hyalella simplex*, and maggots and pupae of ephydriid flies: 62% of the fish were less than 25 mm long and made up c.49% of the diet, bigger fish c.41.5%, corixids 6.2% and midges 2%. Considering the differential rate of digestion, some 93-95% of the effective diet is fish. In October there were on average 40 fish per stomach, in January (when most fish had moved into the tules) only 11 per stomach. The relation of diets to available food (as seen in plankton-net samples from the respective feeding areas), as well as the proportions of different types of prey in the stomachs, suggest that bugs act as a buffer food when the supply of fish fails; conversely, feeding on midges appears to be an opportunistic habit. Like its close relative the Silvery Grebe, which it also resembles in habitat selection, the Junín Grebe is a highly sociable species, spending most of the year in small close flocks, rarely as many as 12 together, but usually in twos followed by one or two singles (and sometimes a Silvery Grebe); when foraging they move in a line and dive synchronously, waiting for each other to catch up.

Egg-laying occurs from late November to March, nests being placed in colonies on semi-floating *Scirpus* beds, with 8-20 nests each 1-4 m apart, the clutch-size 1-3 but usually two. After hatching, the young are carried by the male (which is then nearly prevented from diving and thus poorly nourished) and fed by the (well-nourished) female. Pairs with young are solitary. Breeding success appears to be low. Of the pairs with known number of young seen in May

1979, 17 had one young, seven had two, one had three, and 63.4% of all apparently adult birds had no young.

THREATS Lago de Junín has deteriorated greatly due to pollution over an ever-increasing area of the bottom (so far mainly in the northern end and in the deepest, central part, the latter being the wintering grounds of the Junín Grebe), with flocculated iron oxides from the mines that release waste into the río San Juan, and regulation of the water level since 1955 for a hydroelectric power plant supplying the mines (Fjeldså 1986b). The fluctuations in the water level have increased in recent years (Fjeldså 1986b), and abrupt changes of a metre or more, leaving bird nests and fish spawning grounds out of the water, have been noted (B. A. Luscombe *in litt.* 1988). In 1992, it was noted that the lake was experiencing one of the driest periods for decades, and that open water was only left in the centre: the resultant lack of suitable nesting habitat (and failure to observe any young) suggested that (as of the end of May) the birds had not been able to breed (T. Valqui and J. Barrio *in litt.* 1992: see Ecology). Presumably owing to lake bottom contamination, numerous dead fish (*Orestias* sp. of all sizes) were found along the northern shores in 1989, and during the first five months of 1992 up to 10 dead grebes were reported each month (three dead Junín Grebes were found along 2 km of shoreline during three days in May 1992) around the entire lake (T. Valqui and J. Barrio *in litt.* 1992).

In 1977 and 1978 plans were announced to make the lake a water reservoir for Lima: annual fluctuations in water level of up to 5 m were anticipated, which would alter the conditions in the lake completely and, although the pollution would be stopped, the great fluctuations in water level, combined with increasing possibilities for cattle-grazing (see Remarks 2) in the marsh areas during the dry season, would certainly destroy all tall marsh vegetation (Fjeldså 1981b). Junín Grebes could possibly nest on floating weeds (as can Silvery Grebes when necessary), but the complete seasonal dessication of the marshes might seriously alter food availability, partly because of much larger numbers of White-tufted Grebes entering Junín Grebe habitat, and partly because stable production of relevant foods would be impaired by the destruction of submergent vegetation (owing to seasonal drought and turbid water: Fjeldså 1981b). There might be short periods with great production of some invertebrates, which, however, would favour Silvery Grebes rather than Junín Grebes, and it is unlikely that the Junín Grebe would survive such changes (Fjeldså 1981b). Fortunately, worries on behalf of nature and local cattle-raising interests have, together with economic factors, caused postponement and division of the plan into several alternatives (Fjeldså 1984). Contamination with lead, mentioned as a possible danger by Vincent (1966-1971), does not seem to have reached alarming levels (Fjeldså 1981b). However, for unknown reasons, this species is heavily infested with stomach nematodes: although the direct impact of these parasites may be slight, this infestation was heavier than in other grebes (averaging at least 10 times more than other species analysed at the same time) and may indicate poor health (Fjeldså 1981b).

During October, when the grebes approach the reed-borders to breed, and the reedbeds are still too dry for the White-tufted Grebe to enter, the Junín Grebe may suffer severe competition for food from the much more numerous White-tufted Grebe (which, however, on average takes larger fish: overlap in exploitation during this period has, on the basis of diet studies, been calculated at 60-65% (Fjeldså 1981b). Although the Silvery Grebe is seemingly unaggressive, other grebes avoid feeding in places with many of them, probably because their scudding to and fro disturbs hunting by other species; with the present small population of Silvery Grebe in Lago de Junín (c.50 individuals) there seems to be no great competition for space from that species, but it is very common in the numerous small lakes of the region, and an influx to Lago de Junín from lakes that dry up might occur (Fjeldså 1981b, J. Fjeldså verbally 1990).

MEASURES TAKEN Lago de Junín is a national reserve (Dourojeanni *et al.* 1968, IUCN 1992). A thorough study of the grebe and its requirements during the breeding season was undertaken in 1978/1979 (Fjeldså 1981a,b).

Translocation In November 1983 a search for a lake suitable for a transfer of some of the grebes was undertaken in view of their dwindling population and the general deterioration of Lago de Junín: Lake Chacacancha was chosen, as it was found to meet the requirements of the grebe, and locals claimed that there were no trout in the lake (J. Fjeldså verbally 1983). In February 1985 four adult birds (a pair, a male and a female) were transferred (Goriup 1985, J. Fjeldså *in litt.* 1986); in August 1986 one or more birds still survived (Balharry 1989), but by January 1987 all had disappeared (Fjeldså 1987). It turned out that there were trout in the lake after all (Fjeldså 1987, Balharry 1989), and local fishermen suggested that the grebes had got caught in the nets used for catching them (J.Fjeldså verbally 1987). Further plans for transfers were frozen until a more suitable lake could be found: however, most larger lakes in the region are considered unsuited to the grebe (J. Fjeldså *in litt.* 1990).

Monitoring and management of the lake Drill cores from various places in Lago de Junín were taken in 1986 (Balharry 1989), and they could possibly serve as a standard for measuring changes in pollution of the lake (J. Fjeldså verbally 1990). This may also be possible through a continuation of the monitoring of water quality, started by the company "Binnie and Partners", hired to help with the water reservoir plans (Proyecto Transvase Mantaro), but halted in February 1987 (B. A. Luscombe *in litt.* 1987). Future conservation of the lake and its endemic life is now in the hands of Asociación de Ecología y Conservación (ECCO) which has tried to obtain the cooperation of the national mining company (CENTROMEN) in order to stop abrupt changes in the water level and, if possible, to keep water levels high when the grebe commences breeding (B. A. Luscombe *in litt.* 1987). ECCO, with some financial aid from the Peruvian Consejo Nacional de Ciencias y Tecnología (CONCYTEC), acquired the ecological (including water-quality monitoring) results from the work of "Binnie and Partners", and launched four studies in 1988 and 1989 in Lago de Junín, despite lack of funds and no boat: one on zooplankton, one on fish, one on the giant toad *Batrachophrynus macrostomus* and one on birds, the latter two not yet published (B. A. Luscombe *in litt.* 1989). Work is now dangerous owing to guerilla activity in the Lago de Junín area (B. A. Luscombe *in litt.* 1989, T. Valqui *per* J. Fjeldså verbally 1990), which has led to an almost complete closure of the mines in this region: the advance of the pollution may have stopped temporarily (J. Fjeldså verbally 1990). A brief survey of the lake (on behalf of ICBP) was undertaken in May 1992, as a preliminary stage to more extensive work planned for July and August 1992 (T. Valqui and J. Barrio *in litt.* 1992).

MEASURES PROPOSED In October 1986 a proposal for research and conservation management relating to Lago de Junín and the Junín Grebe was submitted to the ICBP by

J. Fjeldså, suggesting: grebe counts covering the whole lake and studies of seasonal movements; sampling of potential grebe food in the various habitats used throughout the year, so as to reach a better understanding of the extent to which the apparent decline is caused by seasonal or occasional food shortage, or by competition and habitat degradation, as previous studies suggest; collection of data on nest-sites, time of breeding, clutch-size and breeding success; counts by local people (for Proyecto Transvase Mantaro) on other waterbirds in the lake and detailed studies of habitat use by all waterbirds during an annual cycle (preferably in the same areas as studied 1977/1978) to determine how the fluctuation in water level affects the birds of the lake; studies of whether seasonal variation in the lakes of the surrounding mountains causes a periodic influx of birds from these other areas, and to what extent this influx affects the local birds; monitoring of changes in some other nearby lakes for reference; investigation of Laguna Yanacocha, c.15 km west of Ondores, as a possible transfer site for the grebe; and research on other endemic and rare animals of Lago de Junín (see Remarks 3). As a result of the preliminary work during May 1992, an ICBP-funded survey has been scheduled to go ahead during July and August 1992, aimed at realizing some of the proposals outlined above (T. Valqui and J. Barrio *in litt.* 1992).

REMARKS (1) The Junín Grebe is closely related to the Silvery Grebe, and was probably derived from that species by isolation in Lago de Junín during the last glaciation (Fjeldså 1981a). (2) The meadows surrounding Lago de Junín are grazed by almost 200,000 cattle (Fjeldså 1986a). (3) Lago de Junín is a biologically important area: besides endemic forms such as the toad *Batrachophrynus macrostomus*, the Junín Grebe, and Junín Rail *Laterallus tuerosi* (see relevant account), and possibly the virtually unknown Peruvian Rail *Rallus peruvianus* (see Remarks under Bogotá Rail *Rallus semiplumbeus*), it holds a full complement and larger concentrations of waterbirds than most other Andean lakes (Dourojeanni *et al.* 1968, Harris 1981, Fjeldså 1983b).

CAHOW or BERMUDA PETREL *Pterodroma cahow* (E)[5]

Once an abundant nesting seabird throughout Bermuda, this petrel was thought extinct for three centuries before 18 pairs were rediscovered breeding on tiny suboptimal islets in Castle Harbour between 1951 and 1961, since when intensive management (including the elimination of nest-site competition) has wrought a slow but steady increase to over 40 breeding pairs in the 1990s.

DISTRIBUTION The Cahow (see Remarks 1) or Bermuda Petrel is endemic to the island of Bermuda, Atlantic Ocean, where at the time of the early settlers' arrival in the sixteenth century it was widespread throughout the main island and its adjacent satellites, although it is now confined to four of the smallest islets (1 ha in total area) in Castle Harbour, east Bermuda (Bent 1922, Beebe 1935, Murphy and Mowbray 1951, Wingate 1985). Virtually nothing is known of its range at sea, but it probably wanders to the offshore waters of the southern Atlantic states (Clapp *et al.* 1982), with a possible sight record off the coast of North Carolina at 35°18'N 74°45'W on 18 April 1983 (Lee 1984). The only tangible evidence of the species away from its breeding grounds is that of fossil bones of at least one individual on Crooked Island, Bahamas (see Olson and Hilgartner 1982).

POPULATION At the time of Bermuda's discovery by European explorers in the early sixteenth century, the island had no indigenous human inhabitants or other mammals and there were large nesting colonies of seabirds, notably the endemic petrel (Wingate 1985). Evidence from first travellers, early settlers (see, e.g., Verrill 1902, Bent 1922, Beebe 1935, Bradlee *et al.* 1931) and fossil bones shows that the species must have been extremely abundant throughout the island (Shufeldt 1916, Wingate 1960, 1978), but excessive human exploitation for food and introduced mammal predators (see Threats) quickly relegated it to a few offshore islands, notably Cooper's, so that as early as 1621 it was believed extinct (Verrill 1902, Nichols and Mowbray 1916, Shufeldt 1916, Bent 1922, Murphy and Mowbray 1951, Wingate 1960, 1985), a view that persisted for three centuries until its haltingly slow rediscovery from 1906 to 1951 (Beebe 1935, Murphy and Mowbray 1951; see Remarks 2). By 1951 when the first breeding sites were discovered the species was in fact very close to extinction, with only 18 pairs remaining (Wingate 1978). It was estimated that since nest-site competition with White-tailed Tropicbirds *Phaethon lepturus* started, the decline of the Cahow must have been in the order of 50% every 30 years, and thus in 1906, when the first specimen was collected on Castle Island (a site where cahows no longer breed), the population may have numbered around 70 nesting pairs (Wingate 1978). As a result of continuous management efforts (see Measures Taken), the species's total population in Castle Harbour has steadily increased since 1962 from 18 pairs (eight young fledged) to 43 established pairs (23 young fledged) and five establishing pairs in 1992 (45 being the maximum in 1989, as of 1992 with 28 young fledged) (D. B. Wingate *in litt.* 1991, 1992). The total population is estimated at approximately 150 birds (D. B. Wingate *in litt.* 1992). Following management of Nonsuch Island (see Measures Taken), which could easily accommodate a population in excess of 1,000 pairs (many more with the use of artificial burrows), eventual recolonization by the species is expected (Wingate 1985).

ECOLOGY Cahows are believed to range widely on the open ocean, returning to land only to breed, where they are strictly nocturnal in habits (Wingate 1973). Their food consists primarily of cephalopods (small squid) and lesser amounts of shrimp and probably small fish (Wingate 1972). The stomach of a bird collected in June 1935 contained 17 beaks of cephalopods and several crystalline lenses of the same organism (Murphy and Mowbray 1951). The breeding season runs from late October to mid-June (Wingate 1973). Eggs are laid in January, hatch in late February and early March, and young birds fledge in late May and early June (Murphy and Mowbray 1951, Wingate 1978). The Cahows originally burrowed their nests into the soft soils of Bermuda, but predation by introduced mammals exterminated them everywhere except on the smallest offshore islets where soil cover was too sparse to permit burrowing, the birds being obliged to occupy natural erosion crevices in the cliffs and cliff talus instead (a breeding habitat already heavily used by the tropicbirds) (Wingate 1978; see Threats). Like other species of the genus, Cahow adults often cease tending their chicks long before they are able to fly, since the fat accumulated by the fledglings can provide enough energy to reach fledging condition: 15 days from abandonment to the chick's departure was not unusual; however, chicks that grow fast are tended up to fledging, while those that grow slowly are more likely to be abandoned (Wingate 1972; see Warham 1990).

THREATS The Cahow has suffered the typical fate of oceanic island birds in being exposed to a multiplicity of threats, many interlinked, and all assuming an exaggerated significance in inverse relation to population size.

Early impact of man: habitat loss, exploitation, predation Pigs were introduced late in the sixteenth century by early voyagers and, by the time of the first human settlements in 1612, they had already decimated the seabirds on the main island; other man-introduced animals (e.g. rats, domestic cats and dogs) appeared with the early settlements and the impact of these new predators, combined with extensive burning, deforestation and human capture of birds and eggs for food, greatly reduced the seabird population, bringing the Cahows to the verge of extinction (Verrill 1902, Bent 1922, Murphy and Mowbray 1951, Wingate 1960).

Nest-site competition Even the smallest Castle Harbour islets were marginal breeding habitat because they were accessible to rats and were so eroded that they lacked sufficient soil to enable the birds to excavate nesting burrows; as a consequence, the Cahows were forced to nest in the few deep natural holes and crevices in the cliffs (optimum breeding habitat of the White-tailed Tropicbird) with the resultant nest-site competition invariably favouring the tropicbirds and leading to the deaths of more than 60% of Cahow chicks at the time the population was first rediscovered (Wingate 1978, 1985).

Pesticide contamination Detection of high levels of pesticides such as DDT and other chlorinated hydrocarbon compounds in unhatched Cahow eggs and dead chicks (one egg contained more than 11 ppm) was presumably a cause for the observed decline in reproductive success during the first decades after the species's rediscovery (Wurster and Wingate 1968), but the use of DDT rapidly declined in North America in the late 1960s and in the early 1970s reproductive success of the Cahows climbed back towards its earlier 60% fledging rate (Zimmerman 1975, King 1978-1979, D. B. Wingate *in litt.* 1992).

Airbase and military development and disturbance In 1941, after an agreement between the U.S.A. and the U.K., an airbase was established on the former breeding site of Cooper's Island, which was connected to the larger St David's Island through dredging and filling (Murphy and Mowbray 1951). By 1950 this airbase had grown considerably, airlines were using it to bring thousands of visitors in a prosperous post-war tourist boom, and the island population was increasing rapidly (Wingate 1960; see Measures Proposed). Furthermore, bright lights on a nearby NASA installation were believed to have contributed to the abandonment of one islet (D. B. Wingate *in litt.* 1992); but in 1987 the U.S. Naval Air Station installed an array of extremely bright security lights near Cooper's Island within half a mile of the breeding islets; appeals to rectify the problem resulted in all of the offending lights being turned off by early November 1990 and a surge of pre-breeding activity immediately followed (D. B. Wingate *in litt.* 1991).

Natural disasters In January–March 1987 a vagrant Snowy Owl *Nyctea scandiaca* targeted the species, resulting in the loss of at least five pre-breeding birds from two of the four breeding islets (D. B. Wingate *in litt.* 1991; also Amos 1991). In 1989, Hurricane Hugo may have been implicated in an unusually high (doubled) mortality rate in the population; this and the above events are believed to have resulted in drastically lower breeding success and a small reduction in the number of established breeding pairs in 1990 (D. B. Wingate *in litt.* 1991).

Global warming A longer-term concern, given the small size of the breeding islets, is the threat of sea-level rise and increased storm activity owing to anticipated global warming; after 25 years with no significant flooding problems, there have been four major burrow flooding events in recent years, two of them occurring during the 1991 breeding season and causing failure for at least two pairs (D. B. Wingate *in litt.* 1991).

MEASURES TAKEN The Cahow has been the subject of an intensive conservation and research programme since the rediscovery of its breeding grounds in 1951 (see, e.g., Wingate 1972, 1985, Zimmerman 1975). This resulted in the establishment of the 10 ha Castle Harbour Islands National Park, consisting of nine small islands (Wingate 1985). Nonsuch Island (6 ha, the largest of the Castle Harbour islands) was selected in 1962 for restoration as a living museum, and after 1966 received full government recognition and support as a project of the Conservation Division; restoration has involved the elimination and/or exclusion of exotic species, reforestation with indigenous flora and the artificial creation of additional habitats, the island's small size and isolation making it possible to eliminate or exclude most exotic species including rats (Wingate 1985). In 1954 artificial entrances for the Cahow nesting crevices were devised in order to avoid competition from White-tailed Tropicbirds, and since 1961 this system has completely prevented mortality from tropicbirds, effectively trebling the Cahow's reproductive success (Wingate 1978, 1985). Another manipulative technique has been the construction of artificial burrows on the level tops of the Cahow breeding islets in an effort to re-establish the original separation in breeding niches between the soil-burrowing petrel and the cliff-nesting tropicbird (Wingate 1985). The Cahow population has responded with a gradual but accelerating increase (see Population). Ultimately, this increasing population is expected to spill over onto the larger neighbouring soil-covered islands such as Nonsuch, where soil-burrowing will once again become possible (Wingate 1985). The problem of burrow flooding (see Threats) has been overcome by the construction (in autumn 1991) of a protective sea-wall in order to shelter low-lying nest-sites on the most vulnerable islet; this action proved to be effective when Hurricane Grace sent waves over that islet in late October 1991 which would probably otherwise have killed at least two nesting pairs (D. B. Wingate *in litt.* 1992). Consideration is now being given to accelerating long-term plans to attract Cahows to breed on Nonsuch Island, using techniques developed by Podolsky and Kress (1992) for Dark-rumped Petrels *Pterodroma phaeopygia* on the Galápagos (D. B. Wingate *in litt.* 1992).

The steady nurturing of the Cahow back from the brink of extinction has been the personal mission of D. B. Wingate for over 30 years; there are few cases in bird conservation where one figure has been so closely associated with and dedicated to a particular species, and the world is forever in his debt for his singular and continuing achievements.

MEASURES PROPOSED A proposal to restore Cooper's Island (where, according to the early histories, the bird widely nested: see, e.g., Bent 1922, Beebe 1935, Wingate 1960) as a wilderness area for the preservation of all Bermuda's endangered species of flora and fauna, much as is being done on Nonsuch Island today, represents a very important but very long-term investment in Cahow conservation: it would involve the dismantling of present installations and the re-opening of the natural channel (which formerly kept ground predators from spreading from St David's Island), and would thus also benefit Nonsuch Island in terms of reduced disturbance and risk of predator invasion (D. B. Wingate *in litt.* 1991). Unfortunately, there is little likelihood of this proposal being realized before the end of the 99-year lease agreement signed in 1941 unless circumstances change radically (D. B. Wingate *in litt.* 1992).

REMARKS (1) This is an onomatopoeic name (*cahow*, *cahowe* or *cowhaw*) given by early settlers of the island (Jobling 1991). (2) The species's rediscovery is generally regarded as having occurred in 1951 (with the discovery of breeding pairs), but the first bird taken alive in modern times was collected on Castle Island on 22 February 1906, although it was erroneously attributed to "*Aestrelata gularis*" or Peale's Petrel *Pterodroma inexpectata* (see Bradlee 1906, Hellmayr and

Conover 1948), and not until 1916 was it named as "*Aestrelata cahow*" (Nichols and Mowbray 1916). In June 1935 a dead bird found at St David's Island lighthouse became the second known specimen of this mystery species (Beebe 1935). In June 1941 a third specimen was found dead, having flown into a telephone cable on St George's Island, and in March 1945 a dead adult apparently killed in a fight with a tropicbird was washed up on Cooper's Island (D. B. Wingate *in litt.* 1992). A summary of nineteenth century references to the species is provided by Bent (1922), from which it is clear that great confusion existed with other Procellariidae, notably Audubon's Shearwater *Puffinus lherminieri* (see also Murphy and Mowbray 1951, Wingate 1964c).

JAMAICA PETREL *Pterodroma caribbaea* E/Ex[4]

Predation by introduced mongooses and human exploitation for food caused the extinction or near-extinction of this very poorly known seabird of the forested mountains of eastern Jamaica, which recent evidence suggests is (or was) a good species.

DISTRIBUTION The Jamaica Petrel (see Remarks 1) formerly nested in the Blue Mountains of Jamaica, where specimens were taken at the summit in 1829 (Bancroft 1835) and in Cinchona Plantation on the south flank at about 1,600 m in November and December 1879 (Bond 1956b, Benson 1972, Imber 1991). Carte (1866) was aware of the species in the north-eastern end of Jamaica, and the John Crow Mountains, adjacent to the Blue Mountains, were known to harbour birds at the end of the nineteenth century (see Scott 1891-1893); Bourne (1965) reported that "birds are still said to call at night" in the John Crow Mountains. It is conceivable that the species also nested in the mountains of Guadeloupe and Dominica, since there is evidence of nesting black petrels in Guadeloupe (see Bent 1922, Murphy 1936, Imber 1991, Remarks 2 under Black-capped Petrel *Pterodroma hasitata*), and Verrill (1905) reported that the Jamaica Petrel nested in Dominica (see Remarks 2) in La Birne, Pointe Guignarde, Lance Bateaux, Morne Rouge and Scott's Head. Virtually nothing is known about the species's range at sea other than Bond's (1936) report of a possible sighting west of the Bimini Group, Bahama Islands.

POPULATION When first reported in the literature in 1789 it was considered plentiful (see Godman 1907-1910). Gosse (1847) was aware of the existence of the "Blue-Mountain Duck" in the Blue Mountains, although he could not provide further information. In 1866 two additional specimens were taken in the same region (Carte 1866), and between November and December 1879 at least 22 specimens were collected at Cinchona (see Imber 1991). The investigation conducted by Scott (1891-1893) in 1891 led him to consider the species to be "nearly if not quite exterminated": for this assessment he investigated and gathered information from local people, discovering that a man living several miles away from Mooretown (south of the John Crow Mountains) knew of the species and indicated that at one time it had been exploited for food and that not long before he himself had taken a pair from one of the burrows; furthermore, when Scott's assistant was conducted to the area (late February or early March 1891) where these birds had previously been taken, they dug out some twenty-five burrows, but were unable to find a single bird, though in many of the holes excavated they found mongooses. Furthermore, the information given by Scott (1891-1893) revealed that while the species was considered extirpated from the Blue Mountains it was still "abundant" in the John Crow Mountains (perhaps the last area occupied by the species in the island). Godman (1907-1910) indicated that the petrels were believed to be "nearly extinct", for despite careful searches and the offer of a reward no birds were found. Hellmayr and Conover (1948) listed the species as extinct, and Smith (1968) referred to it as "probably extinct", with the last specimen collected at Cinchona around 1880, although he entertained the possibility of birds still being present on high, inaccessible cliffs in the mountains, obviously unaware of Bourne's (1965) recent rumours of petrels in the John Crow Mountains. Most modern assessments have considered the species extinct or possibly so (e.g. Lack 1976, Bond 1978, Mayr and Cottrell 1979, Haynes 1987, Haynes *et al.* 1989, Downer and Sutton 1990) and several searches in the 1970s and early 1980s in the John Crow Mountains were unproductive (van Halewyn and Norton 1984), yet Wingate (1964a,b) and Imber (1991) have suggested it may still be alive as gadfly petrels are known to persist for decades or centuries in imperceptible numbers, e.g. the Cahow *Pterodroma cahow* (see relevant account), the Magenta Petrel *P. magentae* (see King 1978-1979) or Madeira Petrel (or Freira) *P. madeira* (see Collar and Stuart 1985).

That the species nested on Guadeloupe is not entirely clear (see Remarks 2 under Black-capped Petrel). On the assumption that "black" petrels nested on the Soufrière, these (either the

Jamaica Petrel or a dark morph of the Black-capped Petrel) must have been abundant, as J. B. Labat's narrative of a hunting expedition conducted on 14 and 15 March 1696 described how a party of six men captured more than 200 birds hauled from their burrows.

ECOLOGY Very little is known. Carte (1866) was already aware of the Jamaica Petrel's nocturnal habits and of its excavating burrows (1.8 to 3 m long) for nesting, feeding on "fishes", and returning to the burrows "before dawn". Godman (1907-1910) compiled earlier reports that burrows were only found "in the crevices of almost inaccessible mountains" or in holes under trees "in the unfrequented woods" at elevations of 1,800 and 2,100 m. The "black" petrels referred to by J. B. Labat in the mountains of Guadeloupe dug their nests in the soil, and the breeding season would have begun early in October (see Bent 1922); eggs were probably laid during January since the young were hatched by March, and by the end of May the fledglings made their way to sea (Murphy 1936).

THREATS The petrel's colonies in Jamaica were known to have been invaded by mongooses by the end of nineteenth century (Scott 1891-1893, Godman 1907-1910; see Population), although Imber (1991) appears to have overlooked this information, arguing that there is no evidence to support the Jamaica Petrel's being affected by these predators. Apart from the mongoose, man appears to have continuously exploited the petrels for food (Scott 1891-1893). If the species ever occurred in Guadeloupe and Dominica it obviously suffered a similar fate to the Black-capped Petrel (see relevant account).

MEASURES TAKEN The Blue and John Crow Mountains are currently being eastablished as a national park (Varty 1991, N. Varty verbally 1992).

MEASURES PROPOSED Searches for the species should be conducted in Jamaica (the Blue and John Crow Mountains), in Dominica and Guadeloupe, timed to coincide with the courtship, mating and prelaying periods (i.e. October to December) (Imber 1991; also Wingate 1964b). Further taxonomic studies are urgently required in order to clarify the relationship of the Jamaica and Black-capped Petrels. Specimens in MCZ may help, as there are skins of Black-capped Petrel from Guadeloupe showing substantial differences in size and coloration which originally marked them out as a different species (see Remarks 2 under Black-capped Petrel). For an overview of the importance of the endemic forests birds (not including the Jamaica Petrel) in the Blue and John Crow Mountains, see Varty (1991).

REMARKS (1) The taxonomic position of this petrel has been a source of much controversy: it was first described by Carte (1866) under the name of "*Pterodroma caribbaea*". Murphy (1936) treated it as a dark morph of the Black-capped Petrel and hence presumably did other authors (e.g., Bond 1956b, Smith 1968, Mayr and Cottrell 1979, AOU 1983, Harrison 1983, van Halewyn and Norton 1984, 1987, Haynes 1987, Haynes *et al.* 1989, Downer and Sutton 1990, Sibley and Monroe 1990). However, Hellmayr and Conover (1948), Bourne (1965) and Benson (1972) still maintained its taxonomic distinctiveness, Bourne (1965) indicating that it "appears to be a small dark race" of the Black-capped Petrel. Recently Imber (1991) has suggested that the Jamaican Petrel should be treated as a distinct species mainly based on biometric comparisons between the two species which showed the Jamaican form to be somewhat smaller and presumably more closely related to the Gon-gon or Cape Verde Petrel *Pterodroma feae* (for which see Collar and Stuart 1985). It is however important to note the apparent variation that Black-capped Petrels can show (Noble 1916, Murphy 1936), and further comparisons are perhaps in order to clarify the taxonomy position. That the Black-capped Petrel has two colour morphs (as with other *Pterodroma* species: e.g. Harris 1983, Warham 1990) would appear rather attractive as an explanation of the mystery of "black" birds nesting on Soufrière, Guadeloupe, in 1696 (see Remarks 2 under Black-capped Petrel); only a quarter of a century before, in the same locality, birds were described as having "white and black" plumage, this being explained by Murphy (1936) as a possible alternation of prevailing plumage-types, as one genetic factor or another gains ascendancy in the breeding population. However, Imber (1991) pointed out that Murphy's assertion that polymorphic species and subspecies retain the same underwing pattern does not hold true in this case, and added that there is no evidence for Black-capped Petrels breeding on Jamaica as would be expected if *caribbaea* merely represented a morph. Until further investigation on this problem is made, we are inclined to follow Imber (1991) in giving specific status to the Jamaica Petrel.

(2) Verrill (1905) referred to the Black-capped Petrel and Jamaica Petrel as both being present in the island. He claimed to have obtained specimens of the two species (two of the Jamaica Petrel), but the current location of this material is apparently unknown. Prior to Verrill (1905), F. A. Ober (in Lawrence 1878a) said of the Diablotin of Dominica that "it may be identical with the Jamaica Petrel", although he had not seen the bird and was apparently basing himself on "Prof. Baird".

BLACK-CAPPED PETREL *Pterodroma hasitata* I[7]

Human exploitation for food, predation by introduced mammals and in one case an earthquake have been blamed for the decline and local extinction of this seabird, which survives in small colonies in cliffs and montane forest on Haiti, Dominican Republic, Cuba and probably Dominica (in that order of known importance). Records at sea both in the Caribbean and off the North American Atlantic seaboard indicate a greater numerical strength than that reflected at the known or suspected sites.

DISTRIBUTION The Black-capped Petrel occurs in tropical and subtropical water masses in the western North Atlantic Ocean between 10° and 40°N (Haney 1987). It is currently known to breed in some of the Hispaniolan forested mountain ranges (Massif de la Selle and Massif de la Hotte in Haiti and Sierra de Baoruco in the Dominican Republic) and in Cuba (Sierra Maestra) and formerly in Dominica (possibly still; see Population), Guadeloupe and Martinique (see Remarks 1). Black-capped Petrels at sea appear to be closely associated with the western edge of the Gulf Stream in the North American South Atlantic Bight (Cape Cañaveral, Florida, to North Carolina) (Lee 1977, 1984, Lee and Booth 1979, Clapp *et al.* 1982, Haney 1983, 1987). Records in the Caribbean Sea south of the Greater Antilles to near the coasts of Venezuela suggest that the species is also found there at least during the winter and spring months (Mörzer Bruyns 1967a). Unless otherwise stated coordinates in the following account are taken from DMATC (1972, 1973), OG (1955b, 1963a), except for coordinates at sea which are provided by the original source of each record.

Cuba Although not yet proven, it is believed that the species nests in the south-eastern coastal slopes of Sierra Maestra, on "La Bruja" (= Loma la Bruja, 19°59'N 76°48'W) mountain, near Ocujal, where a presumed colony was discovered in December 1977 (Bond 1978, Garrido 1985). Furthermore, Garrido (1985) indicated the possibility of another colony in Sancti Spíritus, near Playa Yaguanabo, Trinidad (Yaguanabo is at 21°54'N 80°12'N).

Haiti

Massif de la Hotte A nesting colony was discovered in 1984 on the south-facing cliffs of Pic Macaya (18°23'N 74'02'W), and a possible second colony was believed to exist on the north-west face of Pic Formon (c.18°22'N 74'02'W, read from the map in Woods and Ottenwalder 1986) (Woods 1987).

Massif de la Selle In confirmation of a prediction in Wetmore (1939), Wingate (1964a) reported 11 nesting colonies in 1963, nine of them within the present boundaries of La Visite National Park (eight on the La Selle escarpment between Morne La Visite, 18°24'N 72°51'W, and Morne Kadeneau, 18°21'N 72°12'W, a ridge including Morne Cabaio and Tête Opaque, and one on the south-west boundary of the park) (see Wingate's 1964a map) and two more on the northern side of Morne La Selle (18°22'N 71°59'W) and at Dubois (c.18°24'N 71°56'W, read from the map in Wingate 1964a).

Dominican Republic There are records of three birds near the north coast of the country in April 1900 (Wetmore and Swales 1931), and four birds were taken at Moca (19°24'N 70°31'W) in May 1928 (Hobley 1932, Wetmore 1932a). In July 1977 a small group of these petrels was observed off the north-east point of Isla Beata and in October 1978 three birds were observed flying north-east near Alto Velo Island (Wiley and Ottenwalder 1990). In July 1977 fishermen reported petrels nesting in the Cabo Falso cliffs (17°47'N 71°41'W) on the Península de Barahona, although this was not proved (Wiley and Ottenwalder 1990). A moribund bird was found at Laguna del Rincón (18°17'N 71°14'W), Barahona, in June 1979 (see Ottenwalder and Vargas M. 1979). A relatively small breeding colony (the only known in the country to date) was discovered in February 1981 near the border with Haiti, at Loma de Toro (this being above Zapotén, 18°19'N 71°41'W), Sierra de Baoruco (Bond 1982, Woods and Ottenwalder 1983, D. B. Wingate *in litt.* 1981, A. Stockton de Dod *in litt.* 1986).

Guadeloupe The nesting of the species in former times is well documented: it was known to have nested on Soufrière mountain, Basse Terre, during the nineteenth century (Lawrence 1891; see Remarks 2 and Remarks 2 under the Jamaica Petrel *Pterodroma caribbaea*). Nesting occurred up until 1847 (see Threats) on the north-east slopes of the Nez Cassé (= Soufrière) (Noble 1916). However, there is a record of a bird collected a few years before 1891 "even as low" as Camp Jacob (Lawrence 1891).

Dominica The species was known to breed on the island on Morne Diablotin and Morne au Diable (15°37'N 61°26'W) since late in the eighteenth century (Verrill 1892, Feilden 1894, Godman 1907-1910). Verrill (1905) referred to the species as "rare near the coast" but did not mention inland localities, and also referred to "large petrels" (which he tentatively attributed to this species) "not infrequently seen" at night, near the end of the pier at Roseau. At this same locality a bird was picked up alive in May 1932 (Hobley 1932, Wetmore 1932b) and so was an immature in August 1988 (P. G. H. Evans *in litt.* 1992). In June 1984 seven birds were observed on the sea 5.6 km off the south-east coast of the island and in November 1984 two were seen and heard flying at Petit Coulibri in the direction of Morne Vert in southern Dominica (P. G. H. Evans *in litt.* 1992).

Martinique The Black-capped Petrel was considered a possible former breeder (Bond 1956b, Grenway 1967). It was recorded on the island between 1827 and 1844 (see Lawrence 1878d), but no further information was given. There are bones (presumably of the species) found on the island which probably represent pre-Columbian remains (Wetmore 1952; also Olson and Hilgartner 1982).

Range at sea Black-capped Petrels are associated with the waters of the Caribbean and notably along south-eastern United States Atlantic coasts in the Gulf Stream near the shelf edge, principally off Virginia, Maryland, North and South Carolina, Georgia and Florida (Mörzer Bruyns 1967b, Lee 1977, 1984, Lee and Booth 1979, Haney 1983, 1987, Harrison 1983; see also the map in Haney 1987 and Population). There are occasional records east of the Gulf Stream in the western Sargasso Sea (a bird observed in January 1965 at 25°02'N 71°58'W) (Nieboer 1966) but this appears to be unusual inasmuch as none was observed during two weeks of daily observations in August 1984 (see Haney 1987). There are no pelagic observations from the Gulf of Mexico (Clapp *et al.* 1982, Haney 1987). It is possible that Black-capped Petrels occur regularly farther north than present records suggest, especially where the Gulf Stream meanders and warm core rings occur near the shelf edge (Haney 1987). There are a few records of birds in the waters of the Bahamas: one was observed off Savannah Sound, Eleuthera, at 31°48'N 75°58'W, in January 1913 (Nichols 1913), and five birds were seen off the east coast of Great Abaco, at 26°02'N 76°03'W, on 19 August 1988 (Bourne 1989), while there is a bone (presumably of this species) from Crooked Island, which is the first indication for the Bahamas (Olson and Hilgartner 1982, Buden 1987a). Black-capped Petrels have been observed mainly in winter and spring in Caribbean waters near some of the Greater and Lesser Antilles (Cuba, Hispaniola, Puerto Rico, Virgin Islands, Guadeloupe, Dominica and Martinique), this probably representing birds near nesting colonies (Verrill 1905, Godman 1907-1910, Wetmore and Swales 1931, Bond 1956b, Mörzer Bruyns 1967a, Garrido 1985, Norton 1983, 1984, Haney 1987, Cheshire 1990, Wiley and Ottenwalder 1990), but the species has also been recorded in summer (e.g. Bourne and Dixon 1973). Records in the southern Caribbean Sea off the coast of Venezuela between 12°36'N

71°41'W and 12°00'N 73°12'W on 1 May 1962 (c.40 birds observed singly) suggest that the bird can also be commonly found in this region. There is a record from Brazil (Mathews 1934, Hellmayr and Conover 1948), although they give no further details.

North American stragglers Stray Black-capped Petrels have been regularly reported both inland and along the Atlantic coasts of North America (Ontario, Maine, Vermont, New Hampshire, New York, Connecticut, Ohio, Kentucky, Virginia, Florida) since at least 1846, as a result of oceanic storms and hurricanes (the hurricane of 27 August 1893 and Hurricane Hugo of September 1989 are responsible for several specimens collected well inland in different localities of the United States and Canada) (Allen 1904, Bent 1922, Murphy 1936, Sutton 1940, Holman 1952, Bond 1968, Woolfenden 1974, Clapp *et al.* 1982; AOU 1983, D. B. Wingate *in litt.* 1991; also AMNH, CM and ROM label data).

United Kingdom stragglers There is a single specimen record from Norfolk in 1852 (Cramp and Simmons 1977) and a recent sight record from the Rockall Bank (Dannenberg 1982, Bourne 1983).

POPULATION The Black-capped Petrel appears to have suffered a steep decline, having been almost entirely extirpated from its former breeding colonies in Guadeloupe, Dominica and Martinique, where it was reported very common up to the nineteenth century (see, e.g., Bent 1922), after which the location of the diminishing breeding colonies was lost to science and the species was considered to be "perhaps on the verge of extinction" (Bent 1922). Nesting colonies remained unknown during the first half of the twentieth century until discovered in the Massif de la Selle, Haiti in 1963; further breeding areas were subsequently found in Sierra Maestra, Cuba (1977), in the Massif de la Hotte, Haiti (1984), and Sierra de Baoruco, Dominican Republic (1981) (see Distribution). During the twentieth century there were numerous records at sea (Bond 1956b; see below), and the recent pelagic surveys off the Atlantic coast of the USA have shown that the species is far from rare and must still be fairly numerous as a breeding bird in the Caribbean (Halewyn and Norton 1984, Lee 1984, Haney 1987).

Cuba The status of the species on the island is unknown.

Haiti Wingate (1964a), relying on the volume of the chorus heard (see Remarks 3), estimated that each of the 11 colonies contained at least 50 pairs and probably many more. Their inaccessible location, in contrast to historical accounts, suggests an obvious decline, but the population trend was unclear and local people where not aware of any change in petrel abundance during their lifetime (Wingate 1964a). In February 1980, the colonies in the Massif de la Selle were visited again and, although peasants had recently invaded some areas above the breeding cliffs (see Threats), still no evidence of decline in the population on the western end of the ridge (Tête Opaque, Cabaio and La Visite) was noted (D. B. Wingate *in litt.* 1981). In the winter of 1984, some of the colonies within the La Visite National Park were surveyed again and this time it was believed that there were fewer colonies within the same area (one colony still existed on Morne La Visite and two in the Tête Opaque area) (Woods 1987). Following Wingate's (1964a) estimate of 50 birds per colony, Woods (1987) suggested a possible total of 300 birds in the park (a 40% reduction in 20 years: see Remarks 4). Another previously unreported nesting colony was discovered in the Massif de la Hotte in 1984 (see Distribution, Remarks 5).

Dominican Republic The possibility of the species nesting on the island was indicated by Wetmore (1932a) and supported by Bond (1956b), but only proven in February 1981, when the number of nests on Loma del Toro was estimated at 40-50 pairs (see Bond 1982, Woods and Ottenwalder 1983). Further fieldwork might result in additional colonies being found in the poorly explored mountains ranges (e.g. Sierra de Neiba, Cordillera Central and Cordillera Septentrional) (Woods and Ottenwalder 1983, van Halewyn and Norton 1984), although searches conducted in Pico Duarte (see Woods and Ottenwalder 1983) failed to detect any, so Wingate's (1964a) estimate of 4,000 possible birds in the whole of Hispaniola (by extrapolating his findings in Haiti and the apparent suitable habitat in the Dominican Republic) remains to be confirmed.

Guadeloupe The species appears to have nested in great numbers according to the information provided by Bent (1922), and although it was believed to be extinct after 1847 (see also Threats) Verrill (1905) still referred to it as "not uncommon in Martinique and Guadeloupe channel" (see Population under Jamaica Petrel).

Dominica According to the evidence provided by Bent (1922) and Lawrence (1878a) the species must have been "abundant" during the second half of the nineteenth century, and there is evidence of it nesting in the mountains of the island at least since the late eighteenth century (Godman 1907-1910). The last nineteenth-century breeding record appears to have been in 1882 on Morne au Diable (Feilden 1894); searches conducted late in the same century on the slopes of both Morne au Diable and Morne Diablotin were unsuccessful (Ober 1880, Feilden 1894, Godman 1907-1910, Murphy 1936; see Remarks 6). No further nesting has been recorded on the island but there were early twentieth-century reports (Verrill 1905, Hobley 1932). A local guide assured Porter (1930c) that the "Diablotin" was still present in "very small numbers" in the mountains, and described it and its habitats with great accuracy. Two years later a bird was found in Roseau (see Distribution), and this led to the protection of the species in the country (see Measures Taken). Searches by Wingate (1964a) in October and November 1961 on Morne Diablotin were unsuccessful, but he recognized that it was only possible to check a small proportion of potential breeding sites given the steep terrain and impenetrable nature of the rainforest. In 1977 there were unverified records of the species on Morne Diablotin (Halewyn and Norton 1984), while at present it is believed that a small population "almost certainly exists", although breeding has yet to be proven (Evans 1989), the recent evidence being: the observation of birds relatively near the southern coast in June 1984; the observation of two birds flying at Petit Coulibri in the direction of Morne Vert; and an immature picked up exhausted on the beach in Roseau in August 1988 (P. G. H. Evans *in litt.* 1992). Although a small colony may exist on the slopes of one of the coastal mountains in south-eastern Dominica, breeding has yet to be proven (P. G. H. Evans *in litt.* 1992). Recent searches for the species on Morne Diablotin and in the coastal mountains in the south-eastern parts of the island (a fairly inaccessible area where a small colony can easily be overlooked) have been conducted, as have transects on the sea off the west coast between February and May, without result (P. G. H. Evans *in litt.* 1992).

Martinique Nothing is known of former numbers; its use for food by Carib Indians might suggest abundance, while its supposed extinction in the pre-Columbian era suggests the opposite (both facts in van Halewyn and Norton 1984). Verrill (1905) reported it as "not uncommon in the Martinique and Guadeloupe channels".

Population at sea *(Virginia and Maryland)* Single birds and small groups have been seen off the coast (Harrison 1983); (*North Carolina*) Lee and Rowlett (1979) reported having observed 70-100 birds since the first sighting for the state in 1972, and LeGrand (1984) observed 10 birds on 3 March 1984 and four on 11 May 1984. Furthermore, Lee (1984) reported seeing the species on many occasions at sea off the coasts of North Carolina, with more than 1,000 birds observed in nine years (1975-1984). (*South Carolina and Georgia*) Mörzer Bruyns (1967b) reported at least 12 birds in the Gulf Stream in September 1966; one bird was observed off South Carolina in August 1967 (Bourne and Dixon 1973) and Haney (1983) observed a total of six off the coast of Georgia on the outer continental shelf (40-200 m depth) in February 1983, while during cruises to outer continental shelf and Gulf Stream waters conducted in May through October 1983 the species was observed monthly with the highest numbers in May (100+), June (80+), and October

(40+) (Clapp *et al.* 1982, Haney 1983). Further records in South Carolina's offshore waters (out to a distance of 162 km) between October 1983 and May 1985 yielded a total of 158 birds with a maximum of 50 counted on 13 June 1984 (Haney 1986), and 65 birds were counted on 13 April 1984 off Georgia (see LeGrand 1984) and 16 birds singly and in groups were observed on 24 May 1989 far off the South Carolina coast at 33°05'N 76°02'W (Cheshire 1990); (*Florida*) there are records off the coast including as many as 13 and 38 birds observed in one day (see Clapp *et al.* 1982), a recent record being of one observed at 29°08'N 78°04'W on 25 May 1988 (Cheshire 1990).

ECOLOGY Black-capped Petrels use warm oceanic waters, generally off the continental shelf, such as the waters of the Gulf Stream off the south-eastern United States, which apparently constitute a major foraging area during the non-breeding season, although birds are observed there throughout the year; it is not clear if birds present in these waters during the breeding season are non-breeders (perhaps sub-adults), although it is conceivable that breeding birds could range approximate 1,200 km from Haiti between incubation shifts (Clapp *et al.* 1982, Lee 1984, Haney 1987). Lee (1984) found that 85-95% of his sightings occurred in deep-water areas (900-1,800 m) with very few over water less than 180 m deep, and Haney (1987) indicated that Gulf Stream meanders and deflections affected petrel distribution at meso-scales (100-1,000 km) between Florida and North Carolina; locally (10-100 km), petrel distribution was influenced by the presence of upwelling associated with eddies and the mesas, ridges and hills on the Blake Plateau. Primary marine habitat off North Carolina lies seaward of the continental shelf break (200 m isobath) (an area including but not limited to the Gulf Stream), petrels occurring almost exclusively within the cross-shelf interval of Gulf Stream frontal meandering in the South Atlantic Bight; thus the species appears to be linked to the current boundary and where current-generated turbulence at seamounts on the Blake Plateau creates upwelling (Haney 1987). Petrel affinities for the Gulf Stream current boundary result in changes in the species's distribution with respect to depth and distance offshore: off Florida, it occurred over shallower depths and closer to land than further north off Georgia and South Carolina; broader cross-shelf distributions at higher latitudes also corresponded to this increase in the cross-shelf range of frontal meandering (see figures 2 and 3 in Haney 1987).

Little is known about the feeding requirements of the species: the stomach of one specimen taken contained remains of cephalopod beaks and lenses, larger in size than those found for the Cahow (Wingate 1964a). It probably feeds (like other gadfly petrels) on squid and fish in areas of turbulence and upwellings created by sea ridges and the continental shelf break (Haney 1987; also Warham 1990).

Black-capped Petrels nest in burrows excavated in the soil of steep forested cliffs in the mountains (e.g. Noble 1916, Bent 1922, Murphy 1936, Wingate 1964a). In Haiti, colonies were located on forested cliffs 500 m or more in height and above 1,300 m altitude, most being located between 1,500 and 2,000 m above sea level, either where a sufficient soil cover existed for excavating their 1-3 m deep burrows, or where rock crevices on the face of cliffs could be used (Wingate 1964a, Woods 1987). The breeding season runs from early November to mid-May (Wingate 1964a; see also Bent 1922), although birds in Haiti arrive at colonies late in September (Woods 1987); peak breeding occurs in late December, January and February; eggs (one) are laid during January and February, the young fledge in the spring and vocalizations are no longer heard after April; from May until late September the birds are away from their breeding grounds (Wingate 1964a, Woods 1987). A similar regime (September–March) was described in the nineteenth century from Guadeloupe (see Godman 1907-1910). A bird taken on 30 June 1938 in Port-au-Prince was considered a juvenile "not long out of the nest" (Wetmore 1939).

THREATS Human predation and introduced mammals (in one case also an earthquake) are believed to be the major causes of decline, although a combination of these is presumably responsible for the extinction and decline of some of the known or formerly known colonies.

Cuba None is known.

Haiti The mongoose is thought to have reached La Selle Ridge about 1941, although the effect of this introduced predator on nesting colonies is not known (Wingate 1964a, Woods 1987); while mongooses have been blamed for the presumed extinction of the Jamaica Petrel (see relevant account), they cannot be for the virtual extinction of the population on Dominica, since they have never been introduced there (Wingate 1964a). Human predation does not appear to have been a major problem in Haiti, where the colonies are inaccessible to humans, but Wingate (1964a) described the only way known to local people for securing birds for food (see Remarks 7). Rats *Rattus norvegicus* and *R. rattus* have been trapped in the area, the former being caught only near dwellings and the latter, although present even on the steep cliffs, not believed to be a significant predator (Wingate 1964a). Further threats (perhaps the most important) derive from the difficult economic situation in the country which has resulted in peasant colonization of the forested slopes of mountain ridges, resulting in further deforestation, burning, etc.: a visit to the breeding areas in the Massif de la Selle in February 1980 confirmed that peasants had recently invaded the pine- and cloud-forest areas above the breeding cliffs and were even cutting and burning forest on parts of the cliff itself; although no decline of the petrel population was noted, there is no doubt that the long-term effect of this invasion is going to be disastrous for the species (D. B. Wingate *in litt.* 1981). Woods (1987) noted that dogs, cats and mongooses are becoming more abundant in the nesting areas and that suitable habitat is being cleared in both the Massif de la Selle and Massif de la Hotte; dogs having been observed digging petrels from burrows (Woods 1987).

Dominican Republic The nests in the colony in the Sierra de Baoruco were almost certainly accessible to man (see Bond 1982). There has been recent concern over the possible effects that the installation of a communication antenna could have on the population.

Dominica Intensive and continuous exploitation for food has been well documented since the seventeeth century: this is perhaps the major cause for the almost total extinction of the species in Dominica (where the mongoose is absent), although the introduction of the common opossum *Didelphis marsupialis*, which may have arrived in Dominica in the 1830s (Feilden 1894) has also been blamed (Feilden 1894, Nicoll 1904, Godman 1907-1910, Hobley 1932).

Guadeloupe Petrel hunting is known to have occurred since at least the mid-seventeenth century (see also Threats under Jamaica Petrel), which must have resulted in the almost total extermination of the population; however, local informants who had taken part in hunting parties in the mountains of the island asserted that extinction resulted from a powerful earthquake in 1847 (Bent 1922; see Remarks 8).

Martinique The species is thought to have become extinct in the pre-Columbian era, and is known to have been collected for food by Carib Indians (see van Halewyn and Norton 1984).

MEASURES TAKEN On paper the presence of colonies in four protected areas in three countries is encouraging, but in practice this is only a partial gain.

Cuba The Sierra Maestra National Park embraces the chief presumed nesting area on the island, and according to Garrido (1985) the presumed breeding site is inaccessible.

Haiti At least nine of the 11 colonies found by Wingate (1964a) were within the current boundaries of the La Visite National Park, and the only known colony in the Massif de la Hotte (see Distribution) is within the Pic Macaya National Park (Wood 1987); but see Threats.

Dominican Republic The only currently known nesting site is protected within the Sierra de Baoruco National Park (DVS 1990).

Dominica The species has been protected since 1932 (Hobley 1932), but searches to find it during the second half of the twentieth century have been unsuccessful (see Population).

MEASURES PROPOSED This is an uncomfortably problematic bird to work on, requiring substantial effort for little certain reward. In most cases what is first needed is simply the location of colonies, which could be highly exacting in itself; but the subsequent study and management of these colonies would probably also need to be on a scale virtually unknown for a nocturnal seabird nesting in tropical forest. The problem is compounded rather than ameliorated by the fact that as many as five nations may host breeding populations (particularly if the suspicion that a major undiscovered site exists): each of the countries involved can claim to have higher individual priorities.

Cuba Further investigation is required; colonies may well exist elsewhere in the many mountain ranges of the island.

Haiti No fires should be allowed on the peaks of the mountains during the winter months, and no peasants should be allowed to capture petrels (Woods 1987). Wingate (1964a) recommended the gathering of additional information on the status and life history of the Black-capped Petrel, which might be feasible with the services of a professional rock-climber; Woods (1987) suggested that all dogs and cats in the national parks be killed, no gardens or trails be allowed anywhere near the steep cliffs within the boundaries of the parks, and no fires be allowed in a buffer zone that extends down to an elevation of at least 1,400 m below the cliffs within each park; this buffer zone should extend all the way to the base of the mountains and the flat areas below. Woods (1987) did not recommend the control of rats in La Visite National Park until a way can be found to guarantee the security of the populations of the endemic hutia *Plagiodontia aedium* that occur in close proximity to the colonies of the petrels all along the La Visite ridge; but goats and sheep also occur widely and should be removed from both national parks since they are capable of destroying valuable forest cover and disturbing nesting petrels.

Dominican Republic More searches are required in order to locate possible unknown colonies; these should be conducted in the Sierra de Neiba, Cordillera Central and Cordillera Septentrional (Ottenwalder and Vargas M. 1979, Woods and Ottenwalder 1983). DVS (1990) recommended managing the nesting area in the Sierra de Baoruco so as to minimize possible threats (e.g. fires).

Dominica Further searches for the species might result in additional colonies being found in the inland or southern coastal mountains (see van Halewyn and Norton 1984, P. G. H. Evans *in litt.* 1992).

REMARKS (1) The species is generally listed as breeding (or formerly breeding) in the mountains of Jamaica as a melanistic morph or subspecies *caribbaea*. However, following Imber (1991), here this form is given full specific status (see Jamaica Petrel *Pterodroma caribbaea* account for further discussion of taxonomic problems).

(2) J. B. Labat's account of hunting petrels ("Diablotin") on Soufrière in 1696 has aroused debate, as his plate and text both referred to a bird of uniformly dark plumage. This was tentatively attributed to (a morph of) the Black-capped Petrel by Bent (1922) and Murphy (1936),

although they both suggested it might refer to the Jamaica Petrel (Bent 1922; see Distribution under Jamaica Petrel). It remains a mystery whether the "black" petrels reported by Labat were (a) the Jamaica Petrels nesting sympatrically with the Black-capped Petrel, (b) a dark morph of the latter (see below) or (c) simply a mistake in description. However, before Labat's visit there was an account written in 1654 which clearly referred to the "devil" having a "white and black plumage" (see Bent 1922). Furthermore, Lawrence (1891) provided clear evidence of Black-capped Petrels being hunted in the mid-nineteenth century "amongst the rocks and mountains surrounding the Soufrière", these being described as "not pure black", and there is a record from Camp Jacob (see Distribution) of a petrel "black above and white below"; he also noted Labat's description of the black "Diablotin", and questioned whether this description was erroneous or whether there were two birds bearing the name "Diablotin". A further taxonomic complication is introduced by information given by Lafresnaye (1844) and Noble (1916), namely that two different sorts of closely related white-breasted (specimens in MCZ: Noble 1916, R. A. Paynter *in litt.* 1992) petrels formerly bred in Guadeloupe, the respective birds coming to nest at different seasons, and choosing quite different altitudes on the island for the sites of their colonies; although such a distinction ("*Aestrelata diabolica*" and "*A. haesitata*" [*sic*]) has not been recognized (Murphy 1936, Hellmayr and Conover 1946), it is possible that Lafresnaye's (1844) reference to different-sized white-breasted petrels with different nesting altitude preferences and breeding season may be the result of confusion between Black-capped Petrels and Audubon's Shearwaters *Puffinus lherminieri* (which are also known to breed on the island, e.g. Mayr and Cottrell 1979).

(3) This estimate was possible as a result of the experience gained in work on the closely related Cahow *Pterodroma cahow* of Bermuda (see relevant account).

(4) This estimated number would hold true if the number of pairs per colony had remained the same in the 20-year period since their discovery, but it is likely that the number of pairs per colony had diminished in parallel with an overall decline in the number of colonies (Woods 1987). The average number of vocalizations was recorded for use in future assessments and comparisons of population trends (see table 2 in Woods 1987).

(5) As with colonies reported from the Massif de la Selle, Woods (1987) could not estimate the number of pairs but an average number of vocalizations was again recorded (see Woods 1987).

(6) The statement by Hobley (1932) that F. A. Ober captured a bird in 1871 is clearly in error as Ober (1880) himself stated that he failed to find the species.

(7) The "sen sel" consisted in lighting moderate fires on the cliff top above a colony on winter foggy and moonless nights where disoriented birds crash into and around the fires; D. B. Wingate himself had the opportunity to catch four birds in one night after several attempts, and in the same area reported 15 petrels being caught and eaten in a nearby logging camp (Wingate 1964a).

(8) This extraordinary event may indeed have caused the extinction of the population on the island after severe and persistent over-exploitation by man: the whole side of Nez Cassé, on which the petrels were known to breed, collapsed and fell into the valley (see Bent 1922).

PERUVIAN DIVING-PETREL *Pelecanoides garnotii* V[9]

Destruction of breeding habitat by guano harvesting, exploitation for food, overfishing and introduced predators have all contributed to the steep decline of this once abundant seabird of the coasts and offshore islands of Peru and Chile.

DISTRIBUTION The Peruvian Diving-petrel is endemic to the Humboldt Current occurring along the west coast of South America from Isla Lobos de Tierra (06°27'S) in Peru to as far south as Isla Chiloé (42°30'S) in Chile (Mayr and Cottrell 1979, Hays 1989).

Peru Insular colonies (from north to south) were previously known from Lobos de Tierra, Lobos de Afuera, Macabi, Guanape, Mazorca, Pescadores, Chincha Norte, Ballestas, San Gallán and La Vieja (see map in Hays 1989); this author appears to omit two islands where the species was believed to nest according to Murphy (1936), namely Isla San Lorenzo (12°05'S 77°15'W, in Stephens and Traylor 1983) and Isla Frontón (12°07'S 77°11'W, in Stephens and Traylor 1983) (see Remarks 1). According to Hays (1989), the bulk of the surviving colonies today may be restricted to San Gallán and La Vieja (see Population). Other localities where specimens have been either collected or observed and are not mentioned above are: Pacasmayo, November 1964 (specimen in USNM); Salaverry, undated (Murphy 1936); Ancón, a large series taken in April and May 1913 (specimens in AMNH and ANSP; see Remarks 2); Callao and Callao Bay, several dates (specimens in AMNH, ANSP and BMNH; also Godman 1907-1910); near Pucusana (12°29'S 76°48'W, in Stephens and Traylor 1983) in July 1987 (B. Haase verbally 1987); Chilca, and Pisco Bay, undated (Murphy 1936); Independencia Bay, July 1907 and January 1935 (specimens in LACM and USNM); c.65 km north of Mollendo and c.8 km offshore, September 1924 (specimen in USNM); near Islay, during austral summer, 1914-1918 (Pässler 1922).

Chile Most of the records refer to birds collected along the coast, the only recorded nesting places being Pan de Azúcar, Pájaros, Chañaral, Choros, and Mocha islands (see below), although the species was believed to nest on Isla Santa María in the Arauco Bay (Pässler 1922; also Murphy 1936). Localities where the species has been observed and/or collected are: Arica, undated (specimens in MNHNS), 1913 (Murphy 1936) and February 1990 (P. Roberts *in litt.* 1990); off Pisagua, where two birds were observed in June 1984 (B. Araya Mödinger *in litt.* 1991); Iquique, undated (Darwin 1841), August 1893 (Schalow 1898), 1913 (Murphy 1936) and July 1931 (Philippi 1941); off Iquique, where 16 birds were observed in May 1981 (after 175 minutes sailing northwards), and one bird in June 1984 (after 186 minutes sailing northwards) (B. Araya Mödinger *in litt.* 1991); off Antofagasta, where a bird was observed in June 1984 (after 63 minutes sailing northwards) (B. Araya Mödinger *in litt.* 1991); Taltal, 1913 (Murphy 1936), 1914-1918 (Pässler 1922); off Taltal, were a bird was observed in June 1984 (after 40 minutes sailing southwards) (B. Araya Mödinger *in litt.* 1991); close inshore at Pan de Azúcar National Park, where c.15 birds were observed close inshore on 27 January 1991 (M. Pearman *in litt.* 1991); Isla Pan de Azúcar (26°09'S 70°42'W, in Paynter 1988), currently breeding (Vilina in press); Caldera, March 1956 (specimen in MNHNS); near Isla Grande (27°14'S 71°00'W), where five birds where counted in September 1982 and 20 in June 1984 (after 92 and 128 minutes sailing from mainland to the island) (data and coordinates from B. Araya Mödinger *in litt.* 1991); Isla Chañaral, where two eggs (one fresh, one hard-set) were collected in December 1938 and December 1943 (see Remarks 3), and birds were observed near the island during periodic censuses conducted in 1989 and 1990 (Vilina in press; see Population); Isla Choros, where 51 nests (at least one containing an egg) were found in October 1982 and 18 birds were counted (after 25 minutes sailing from mainland to the island) in November 1984 (B. Araya Mödinger *in litt.* 1991), and 31 and 160 birds were counted respectively between the island and mainland in April and December 1991 (Y. A. Vilina *in litt.* 1991); Isla de los Pájaros, where four eggs were collected in October 1893 (Schalow 1898; see Remarks 4), and three and five birds were counted in November 1984 and June 1988 respectively (after 92 minutes sailing from mainland to the island on the former date and 12 minutes on the latter) (B. Araya Mödinger *in litt.* 1991); Coquimbo, where birds were observed and two collected in November 1881 (Salvin 1883, Godman 1907-1910); Zapallar, undated, where considerable groups have been reported (Goodall *et al.* 1951); Quintero, April 1940 (specimen in YPM); Valparaiso, 1893 (Schalow 1898), February 1903 (specimens in BMNH), July 1924 (specimen in USNM); Coronel, where a bird was collected on 26 March 1918 (Pässler 1922; also Stresemann 1922); Talcahuano, undated (specimen in MNHNS); San Vicente de Talcahuano (= Bahía de San Vicente, at 36°44'S 73°09'W), where considerable groups have been reported (Goodall *et al.* 1951); Isla Santa María, where the species was believed to nest, as many birds were observed in summer in the vicinity of the island (Pässler 1922; also Stresemann 1922); Lebu, where considerable groups have been reported (Goodall *et al.* 1951); Isla Mocha, which according to Mayr and Cottrell (1979) would be the southernmost breeding station; Corral (Valdivia harbour), the southernmost known locality for the species as stated by Hays (1989) (see Remarks 5).

POPULATION The evidence is that the Peruvian Diving-petrel has suffered a massive decline throughout its range.

Peru Formerly quite numerous, the species is now in serious decline (Hays 1989; also Lesson 1828, Godman 1907-1910, Murphy and Harper 1921, Murphy 1936). Most of the surviving populations in Peru are now restricted to Isla San Gallán and Isla La Vieja, and although formerly they nested abundantly on Lobos de Tierra, Macabi, Gaunape, Pescadores and Ballestas they have drastically decreased and apparently now no longer breed there (Hays 1989; also Murphy 1936; see Remarks 6). On Isla San Gallán, recent studies found about 100 colonies with c.1,200 nests, of which 30% were active, and the number of nests per colony was generally less than 10 (Jahncke Aparicio and Riveros-Salcedo 1991). Hays (1989) estimated that the species's Peruvian population could consist of c.4,000 individuals, but more recently it was estimated at only 1,500 individuals (Vilina in press), the previous number of 10,000 given by Duffy *et al.* (1984) being considered an overestimate. Records of sightings at sea have also decreased, e.g. large concentrations were sighted in Independencia Bay during the 1960s, but on a recent trip (in November 1985) in the same area only two individuals were seen (Hays 1989), although the species still appears to be common at Paracas (Gardner 1986, P. K. Donahue *in litt.* 1987) and it was "abundant" near Pucusana in July 1987 (B. Haase verbally 1987).

Chile The same pattern of decline may have occurred although not as well documented as in Peru (Murphy 1936; also Goodall *et al.* 1951). The species was reported to be common early this century near Valparaiso (Nicoll 1904), and in July 1938 a large flock was noted at the entrance to Iquique harbour (Philippi 1941). Goodall *et al.* (1951) observed "considerable flocks" at various localities between 37° and 38°S (see Distribution). It nested in great numbers on Isla Chañaral, and one observer in 1938 reported that the island was a "swarming mass" of the birds, and the number of burrows that he found suggested that the colony "must have been enormous"; six years later (1944), after the introduction of a pair of foxes (in 1941), the same observer found "well over" 200,000 skeletons (Araya and Duffy 1987). Jehl (1973) reported scattered Peruvian Diving-petrels along the Chilean coast, but in the Golfo de Arauco and Isla Chañaral it was abundant with hundreds seen in June-July 1970; however, it is now very scarce at Isla Chañaral, no burrows were found in 1982 and no skeletons were seen during a visit to the island in November 1985 (Araya and Duffy 1987); subsequent visits between September 1989 and October

1990 failed to detect breeding signs on the island (see Remarks 7), and a maximum of 100 birds were counted near the island during periodic censuses conducted in 1989 and 1990 (dates and numbers of birds recorded are given by Vilina in press). The species is still being seen in Chilean waters (P. Roberts *in litt.* 1990, B. Araya Mödinger *in litt.* 1991, M. Pearman *in litt.* 1991), although relatively small numbers were counted during censuses conducted offshore in different areas (see Distribution) during the 1980s (B. Araya Mödinger *in litt.* 1991). The only known breeding populations are currently found on Isla Pan de Azúcar and Isla Choros; in October 1982 B. Araya Mödinger (*in litt.* 1991) found 51 nests on the latter, with at least one nest with an egg, and recently 300 active nests have been reported (Vilina and Capella 1991), while on Isla Pan de Azúcar B. Araya Mödinger (*in litt.* 1991) found 80 to 100 burrows on the north-east side of the hill in October 1990, and Vilina and Capella (1991) have recently found 220 active nests. The nesting pairs involved show a very small population when compared to previous numbers of breeding pairs reported for Isla Chañaral (see above).

ECOLOGY The Peruvian Diving-petrel occurs on the sea coasts of Peru and Chile, where it is mainly encountered in offshore waters near its breeding grounds and is closely associated with the relatively close inshore upwelling waters of the Humboldt Current (Murphy 1936, Hays 1989). It is only known to nest on offshore islands, although in Peru it has been reported nesting on the mainland (Duffy *et al.* 1984, Hays 1989; see Remarks 8).

Feeding is very much dependent on the rich stocks of the Humboldt Current; anchovies *Engraulis* and silversides *Odontesthes* constitute the main staple of the birds, which also congregate in areas of water discoloured by clouds of *Munida* and other crustaceans on which they may feed directly, e.g. the majority of twelve stomachs examined containing only traces of gravel and varying amounts of small crustaceans, identified merely as the megalops stage of a crab, of which more than 120 were in one stomach (Murphy 1936, Duffy *et al.* 1984, Hays 1989). Prey is captured during short, shallow dives from the surface using wing-propulsion (Murphy 1936). The diving-petrels moult their wing feathers simultaneously and thus lose the ability to fly, so for a time each year become exclusively aquatic; apparently this does not affect their ability to forage, since flightless petrels proved to be as full of crustaceans or small fish as flighted individuals (Murphy 1936). The birds often concentrate with other oceanic birds near shoals of fish, but are generally encountered in small groups flying just above the water and diving from time to time (Murphy 1936; also Lesson 1828). Their movements are mainly sporadic, although Murphy (1936) noticed that during the southern summer birds are commoner in the Peruvian and Chilean bays than in winter, when many of them were recorded as far as 20 km offshore.

The species nests on islands with a thick guano layer in which it excavates deep burrows, but it also digs in sandy soils or uses natural crevices in the salty substrate, or beneath rocks especially when guano extraction has been too intense (Coker 1920, Murphy 1936, Hays 1989). Jahncke Aparicio and Riveros-Salcedo (1991) found that on Isla San Gallán c.60% of current nests are placed in crevices. Nests are preferably situated windward (i.e. southerly), as this provides lift from their burrows, and gentle slopes (less than 30%) are preferred (Murphy 1936, Jahncke Aparicio and Riveros-Salcedo 1991). Recent studies on Isla San Gallán showed that colony size can vary from isolated nests to more than 30, but nowadays mosts colonies found (80%) comprised less than 10 nests (Jahncke Aparicio and Riveros-Salcedo 1991; also Murphy 1936). Breeding has been reported as occurring from January to March and from September to December (Hays 1989) but evidence from museum specimens and from the literature shows that breeding is also known from May to July, and even within the same colony breeding is frequently asynchronous (Coker 1920, Murphy and Harper 1921, Murphy 1936); whether there is year-round breeding or perhaps two peaks per year is not clear from present levels of information. The clutch-size is always one (Jahncke and Riveros 1989).

THREATS Guano extraction, direct exploitation and commercial fisheries can be mentioned as three of the major threats affecting the Peruvian Diving-petrel (Duffy *et al.* 1984, Hays 1989, Jahncke and Riveros 1989). Guano extraction has been one of the main reasons for its disappearance from some of the Chilean and Peruvian islands (Schlatter 1984; see Distribution), mainly through the removal of ancient layers which appear to be essential for nesting purposes (see Ecology); however, in the course of such activities, the capture of adults for sale as food by both harvesters as well as fishermen was once on a large scale and remains a serious problem (Coker 1920, Murphy 1936, Hays 1989, Vilina and Capella 1991). Commercial fisheries for many decades overexploited the rich anchovy shoals of the Peruvian and Chilean coasts, resulting in the collapse of the fish stocks in the early 1970s (e.g. Idyll 1973). Incidental catch in fishing nets is a further problem derived from fishing activities (Duffy *et al.* 1984, Hays 1989). Anchovies have never recovered from the 1972 collapse, yet overfishing of the surviving stocks has continued (Duffy *et al.* 1984). In El Niño years the anchovies become unavailable, causing massive mortality of seabirds (Barber and Chávez 1983), but although the seabirds endemic to the Humboldt Current have evolved to adapt to such unpredictable changes, various additional influences of man (Hays 1984) mean that the impact of El Niño events is greatly magnified. During the 1982-1983 El Niño, diving-petrels were found dead in considerable numbers on beaches throughout their range in Peru (Hays 1989).

Exploitation for food still occurs on the two last major breeding islands (San Gallán and La Vieja), where local fishermen use lanterns to attract the birds at night and during the guano harvest dig them out from their burrows (Hays 1989). Similar problems appear to occur as well at the Chilean seabird colonies (e.g. Isla Choros) (Vilina and Capella 1991; also Schlatter 1984), although nothing is known about the numbers affected by this practice. The impact of natural predators such as Peregrines *Falco peregrinus*, Kelp Gulls *Larus dominicanus* and Turkey Vultures *Cathartes aura* may now be substantially greater, given the species's overall population trend (Hays 1989). Introduced animals such as dogs on San Gallán (Murphy 1936) and rats on certain islands in Chile (Schlatter 1984) are further sources of concern. Introduced foxes have been blamed for the massive depletion of the once huge colonies at Isla Chañaral (Araya Mödinger and Duffy 1987). Despite certain initiatives in Peru (see Measures Taken), enforcement has generally not been strict enough: fishing boats operate close to the islands, making them accessible for egging and trafficking in birds; airplanes, especially military craft, fly over them; and what is left of the fishing industry still sets its nets where birds are feeding (Duffy *et al.* 1984). Jahncke Aparicio and Riveros-Salcedo (1991) remarked that increasing tourism on Isla San Gallán threatens the species's preferred nesting habitat. In Chile, the formal protection of Isla Choros (see Measures Taken) has not proved effective (Y. A. Vilina *in litt.* 1991).

MEASURES TAKEN Measures taken so far have clearly been insufficient in maintaining a stable overall population.

Peru The government recognizes that this species is in danger of extinction (Pulido 1991). The two major Peruvian breeding sites, San Gallán and La Vieja islands, are both within the boundaries of the Paracas National Reserve, but the activities of fishermen on San Gallán are currently not controlled (Hays 1989).

Since 1909, the islands from which the Peruvian Diving-petrel has been recorded have been protected by the state-owned guano company, which has been responsible for the conservation of seabirds in Peru, with guards provided, headlands fenced off with predator-proof walls, and avian predators such as rats removed from the islands; laws prohibit all boats from approaching within two miles of the guano islands, fishing boats from operating within three to five miles, purse-seining at shoals of fish where birds were already present, and overflights of colonies by aircraft lower than 500 m (Duffy *et al.* 1984). In 1978 the company improved its administration of the guano islands, and radios were provided, cats and domestic fowl prohibited and dogs reduced; the few guards suspected of dealing in eggs and nestlings were moved (Duffy *et al.* 1984).

Chile The Peruvian Diving-Petrel is not included in any conservation plan (Vilina in press), but the two extant reproductive colonies are within protected areas (i.e. Pan de Azúcar National Park, which protects the Isla Pan de Azúcar, and Pingüino de Humboldt National Reserve, which includes the Isla Choros – but for the latter see Threats) (Y. A. Vilina *in litt.* 1991).

MEASURES PROPOSED The following proposals are mostly a slightly modified repetition of those in Duffy *et al.* (1984) and Hays (1989): (1) a life history study of the Peruvian Diving-petrel should urgently be carried out, with particular emphasis on determining the timing and frequency of breeding; (2) it is crucial to investigate and monitor the species throughout its range; (3) any remaining island or coastal breeding colonies should be located in both countries (see Remarks 8) and afforded effective protection, while those already under protection (e.g. San Gallán in Peru and Choros in Chile) should have their existing regulations enforced and, as noted by Jahncke Aparicio and Riveros-Salcedo (1991), tourism should be carefully controlled; (4) during the guano harvest at any of the islands where the species nests, labourers should be prevented from killing petrels, something that in Peru could be enforced by PESCA-PERU, the entity responsible for the protection and exploitation of the guano islands (when the timing of breeding is accurately determined, recommendations should be made to PESCA-PERU and the corresponding body in Chile to conduct the guano harvest outside the species's breeding season); (5) the guano harvest in those areas where the species has breeding colonies must be stopped, but in the absence of this a study to find the least harmful harvesting procedure would be valuable (see also Coker 1908); (6) better-trained guards are needed on the islands and training courses at regular intervals would improve their efficiency; (7) prevention of overfishing is urgent, existing laws in both countries should be effectively enforced, and catch levels should be sufficiently low for fish stocks to survive a year of recruitment failure; (8) a commission should investigate how the guano islands could be made greater tourist attractions without damaging them; (9) introduced predators such as foxes, dogs, rats, etc., should be eliminated from the islands.

REMARKS (1) Murphy (1936) gave these two islands together with San Gallán and La Vieja as possibly the only ones with Peruvian Diving-petrel colonies as they have considerable sand and soil deposits in contrast to those from which large amounts of guano have been removed, and which have thus been rendered unsuitable for breeding purposes (see also Population). (2) Forty-three specimens collected by R. H. Beck are labelled simply as Ancón, Peru, but as some of these birds were nesting (see Ecology) it is most likely that the collecting locality was in the Islas Pescadores which are just offshore of Ancón. (3) The identity of the species for these records is not in question as birds were seen at the colony for the 1938 record and a brooding bird was photographed in the nest for the 1943 record (information on labels in WFVZ). (4) This is the only known nesting evidence for the species on Isla de los Pájaros. (5) Records from Calbuco and Ancud (i.e. adjacent to northern Isla Chiloé) (Schalow 1898) appear to have been accepted by Mayr and Cottrell (1979), who include Isla Chiloé as the southernmost locality for the species, despite the fact that both Pässler (1922) and Hellmayr and Conover (1948) attributed these observations to the similar Magellanic Diving-petrel *Pelecanoides magellanicus*, which is known to occur in that area (Hellmayr and Conover 1948, Mayr and Cottrell 1979). (6) The species's nocturnal habits and extended breeding season (see Ecology) make it very difficult not only to make accurate censuses but also simply to ascertain whether colonies on certain islands have been abandoned or not. (7) The results obtained in this survey do not mean that the species does not breed on the island, since the inaccessibility of some sectors did not allow proper investigation; nevertheless, any nests would be few and scattered (Vilina in press). (8) The most likely mainland areas in Peru are in Paracas National Reserve (Hays 1989).

WEST INDIAN WHISTLING-DUCK *Dendrocygna arborea* V[9]

Despite its large range through the Bahamas, Turks and Caicos, Cuba, Caymans, Jamaica, Haiti, Dominican Republic, Puerto Rico, U.K. Virgin Islands, St Croix, St Kitts-Nevis and Antigua and Barbuda, this fresh- and saltwater marsh-dwelling duck has suffered everywhere from relentless hunting pressure and wetland drainage, so that today its status is precarious. Much more attention needs to be given to wetland conservation within its range, and authorities have to find ways of reducing levels of (now almost universally) illegal hunting on their territories. Cuba and the Bahamas in particular deserve fuller survey.

DISTRIBUTION The West Indian Whistling-duck is widely scattered throughout most of the Caribbean from the Bahamas, Greater Antilles and adjacent islands and in a great number of the smaller archipelagos east to the Lesser Antilles (Leeward Islands only; see Remarks 1). Unless otherwise stated coordinates in the following account are taken from OG (1955b, 1958, 1963a), DMATC (1972, 1973) and Scott and Carbonell (1986), with records roughly from west to east; significant numbers of birds observed or collected (when data were available in the original source) are generally discussed under Population. The species was recorded accidentally in Bermuda in November 1907 (see Bond 1956b) and in Texas, U.S.A. (see Remarks 2). A small feral population may exist in Florida (see Owre 1973).

Bahamas Records (north to south) on individual islands are: (*Abaco*) May 1973 (J. Patterson *in litt.* 1973 to W. B. King); (*Andros*) January 1879 (specimen in FMNH), May 1884 (specimen in ROM), January 1902 (Bonhote 1903), March 1922 (five specimens in AMNH); western Andros, April 1890 (Northrop 1891) and currently, where it probably breeds (Scott and Carbonell 1986); on the ponds situated a few miles from the mouth of Fresh Creek (c.24°43'N 77°47'W, read from ACB 1976), undated (Cory 1880); (*New Providence*) unspecified (Bond 1971); artificial pond at Nassau, December 1984 (C. A. Faanes *in litt.* 1986); (*Cat*) c.3 km east of Smith Bay (24°21'N 75°28'W), near New Bight (c.24°18'N 75°26'W) and 1.5 km east of McQueens (c.24°11'N 75°28'W), June 1986 (Buden 1987c; coordinates read from the map in Buden 1987c); (*San Salvador*) unspecified (Brudenell-Bruce 1975, King 1978-1979); (*Rum Cay*) c.2.5 km north of Cotton Field Point (23°39'N 74°52'W) and Yard Pond (23°39'N 74°57'W), June 1987 (Buden 1990; coordinates from ACB 1976); (*Long*) unspecified (King 1978-1979); (*Hog Cay*) (23°24'N 75°28'W), currently (P. D. Graham *in litt.* 1991); (*Ragged*) Little Ragged (22°10'N 75°43'W), April 1907 (see Buden 1987b); (*Crooked*) where a downy young was taken in March 1934 (Buden 1987a); (*Acklins*) in the early 1970s (see Buden 1987a); (*Inagua*) "Inagua", February and April 1888 (four specimens in FMNH and MCZ) and still present in 1973 (see Population); Great Inagua, Horse Pond, near Mathewtown, where a nest was found in February 1909 (Todd and Worthington 1911), September 1966 (H. F. Mayfield *per* J. T. Emlen *in litt.* to W. B. King) and undated (Campbell 1978); Inagua National Park and Lake Rosa (21°05'N 73°30'W), currently (Scott and Carbonell 1986).

Turks and Caicos Records are: (*Caicos*) Ft George Cay (c.21°54'N 72°05'W, read from the map in Buden 1987a), where a flock in flight tentatively identified as this species was observed in July 1930 (see Buden 1987a); Stubbs Cay (a small cay next to Ft George Cay), July 1930 (see Buden 1987a); North Caicos, Sawgrass and Bellfield Landing ponds (untraced), July and September 1987 (Norton and Clarke 1987); (*Turks*) Grand Turk, where a few birds were under domestication by local salt merchants in July 1930 (see Buden 1987a).

Cuba Records include:

Mainland (*Pinar del Río*) Laguna La Deseada (untraced), San Cristóbal (22°43'N 83°03'W), July 1932 (five specimens in FMNH); 1 km from the coast south of San Cristóbal, October 1955 (three specimens in YPM; also Ripley and Watson 1956); (*La Habana*) Laguna de Ariguanabo (22°56'N 82°33'W), February 1920 (six specimens in AMNH); "Guariguanabo" (presumably Ariguanabo), where the species was still present in 1943 (Barbour 1943); (*Matanzas*) "Ciénaga de Zapata", March 1913 (two specimens in MCZ); "Zanja La Cocodrila" (22°34'N 81°39'W), where a female with three ducklings were observed in May 1968 (Garrido 1980); Península de Zapata, near Bahía Cochinos, December 1991 (J. M. Jiménez López *in litt.* 1992); Guamá (on the south-eastern corner of Laguna del Tesoro, 22°21'N 81°07'W), undated (Garrido 1980) and June 1978 (Clements 1979; also J. F. Clements *in litt.* 1991); (*Sancti Spíritus*) sanctuary at Soledad (apparently botanical gardens, now evidently Pepito Tey, 28°08'N 80°20'W: see Figure 1 in Rutten 1934), where the species bred regularly (Barbour 1923, 1943); Soledad (presumably same as previous locality), March 1941 (specimen in CM); Jibaro wetlands (21°00'N 79°10'-80°00'W), currently (Scott and Carbonell 1986); (*Ciego de Avila*) Cayo Coco, October 1973 (Garrido 1976); (*Camagüey*) Cayo Romano, before 1981 (Acosta and Berovides 1984); (*Granma*) Laguna el Leonero (Leonero, 20°41'N 77°04'W), Ciénaga de Birama (at the mouth of the río Cauto), April 1971 (Bond 1972); "Fca de la Punta", c.6.5 km west of Guamo (on the río Cauto), January 1949 (six specimens in USNM); (*Guantánamo*) San Carlos de Río Seco (possibly San Carlos, 20°09'N 75°09'W), July 1909 (specimen in AMNH); "La Laguña" (untraced), Los Caños (20°03'N 75°09'W), January 1919 (specimen in USNM); mangroves along the bay between Manatí (20°05'N 75°06'W) and Los Caños, January 1913 (three specimens in USNM); Manatí, March 1912 (specimen in AMNH);

Adjacent islands and archipelagos (*Isle of Pines* or *Isla de la Juventud*) (records north to south) "Rincon Lagoon" (north-east coast: see the map in Todd 1916), 1904 (Todd 1916); McKinley (21°53'N 82°55'W), Santa Bárbara and río de las Nuevas (21°56'N 82°56'W), sometime before 1911 (see Todd 1916); "Santa Fé", 1904 (Bangs and Zappey 1905); Los Indios (21°42'N 83°00'W), 1904 (Todd 1916); western end of the Ciénaga de Lanier, near Siguanea (21°38'N 82°58'W), September 1912 (specimen in FMNH), November 1912 and April 1913 (Todd 1916); Ciénaga de Lanier (21°35'N 82°48'W), May 1904 (Bangs and Zappey 1905; five specimens in MCZ) down to the present (Scott and Carbonell 1986); La Vega (possibly San Francisco de la Vega: see the map in Todd 1916), October 1925 (specimen in YPM); Pasadita (Ciénaga de Lanier: see the map in Todd 1916), 1904 (Todd 1916); (*Archipiélago de los Canarreos*) Cayo Matías (21°34'N 82°26'W), resident around 1985 (Acosta *et al.* 1988); Cayo Cantiles (21°36'N 82°02'W), where large numbers have been recorded (see Garrido and Schwartz 1968).

Cayman Islands The species is a breeding resident on Grand Cayman (Westerly Freshwater Wetlands, 19°16'N 81°18'W; Central Mangrove Swamp and Booby Cay, 19°20'N 81°16'W; Meagre Bay Pond and Pease Bay Pond, 19°17'N 81°13'W; Conocarpus Swamps and Frank Sound Wetland, 19°19'N 81°10'W; Malportas Pond, Rock Pond and Point Pond, 19°21'N 81°12'W) and Little Cayman (Tarpon Lake and Wearis Bay Wetlands, 19°41'N 80°02'W; Charles Bight Wetland and Sesuvium Swamp, 19°42'N 79°59'W), feeding areas in the latter also including Booby Pond and nearby Heronry, 19°40'N 80°04'W, and North Mangrove Swamp, 19°42'N 80°03'W (Scott and Carbonell 1986). The species is not considered to be resident on Cayman Brac but it is occasionally observed there (Bond 1972, Bradley 1985, van Liefde 1992).

Jamaica Records are from: Negril Aerodrome, May 1989 (Levy 1989); Negril Morass (18°19'N 78°20'W), currently (Scott and Carbonell 1986); morasses of Westmoreland (Westmoreland parish, at 18°14'N 78°09'W), where the species was a numerous breeder (Gosse 1847); Mount Edgecumbe (*sic*) Swamp (Mount Edgecombe at 18°08'N 78°01'W), currently (A. Sutton *in litt.* 1990 to IWRB-TWRG); Font Hill (St Elizabeth) (18°04'N 77°56'W), currently (A. Sutton *in litt.* 1990 to IWRB-

TWRG); Parottee (presumably Parottee Salt Pond, 17°58'N 77°50'W), December 1976 (see Kear 1979); Parottee Salt Pond, and Black River Lower Morass (18°03'N 77°48'W), currently (Scott and Carbonell 1986, Downer and Sutton 1990); Falmouth Swamps (18°30'N 77°40'W), currently (Downer and Sutton 1990); Long Bay (17°51'N 77°01'W), near Spanish Town, December 1861 (specimen in USNM); Salt Island Lagoon (17°53'N 76°59'W), currently (Downer and Sutton 1990); Caymanas Dam (Caymanas at 18°01'N 76°54'W), currently (Downer and Sutton 1990); Great Salt Pond (17°58'N 76°52'W), October 1862 (specimen in USNM); Passage Fort (17°59'N 76°52'W), October 1863, October 1864 and November 1865 (three specimens in AMNH, MCZ); Grant's Pen (18°02'N 76°47'W), currently (Downer and Sutton 1990).

Haiti Records are from: Ile-à-Vache, May 1930 (Wetmore 1932c); Les Basses (18°35'N 73°42'W), January 1918 (Wetmore and Swales 1931); Étang Miragoane (18°24'N 73°03'W), 1927 and February 1928 (Bond 1928a, Danforth 1929); near Gonaïves (19°27'N 72°41'W), 1927 (Danforth 1929); Artibonite Sloughs beyond St Marc, where a few birds were observed in 1927 (Danforth 1929); Rivière Estère (Rivière L'Estère, at 19°54'N 72°38'W; see Remarks 3) reportedly common sometime before 1809 (see Wetmore and Swales 1931); Source Matelas (18°43'N 72°22'W), undated (see Wetmore and Swales 1931); "Lac Assuei" (= Étang Saumâtre), June 1938 (specimen in FMNH); Étang Saumâtre, April 1917 (Wetmore and Swales 1931) and March 1918 (Wetmore and Swales 1931) down to the present (see Scott and Carbonell 1986); Trou Caïman (18°40'N 72°09'W), April 1917 (Wetmore and Swales 1931); Fort Liberté, reported to Bond (1928a); Les Salines (untraced), 1927 (Danforth 1929).

Dominican Republic Records are from: "Santo Domingo", April 1895 (specimen in FMNH); Lago Enriquillo, October 1919 (see Wetmore and Swales 1931) and at least until 1981 (Stockton de Dod 1981); Laguna del Salodillo (= Laguna de Saladilla, 19°39'N 71°43'W), near Copey (19°41'N 71°41'W), June 1927 (Danforth 1929), March 1985 (C. A. Faanes *in litt.* 1986) down to the present (see Scott and Carbonell 1986); Montecristi (= Monte Cristi or Fernando de Montecristi, 19°52'N 71°39'W), currently (A. Stockton de Dod *in litt.* 1986); Laguna Salada (17°41'N 71°28'W), February 1977 and May 1978 (see Vargas Mora and González Castillo 1983); Bucán de Base (17°38'N 71°26'W), July 1977 (Wiley and Ottenwalder 1990); Laguna de Oviedo (17°46'N 71°21'W), Laguna de Cabral (Cabral at 18°15'N 71°13'W), mangroves near Gaspar Hernández (19°37'N 70°17'W), Rincón de San Francisco de Macorís (San Francisco de Macorís at 19°18'N 70°15'W), Bayaguana (18°45'N 69°38'W) and Pilancón (18°54'N 69°36'W), where the species was present at least until 1981 (all six preceding localities from Stockton de Dod 1981); several localities in the Bahía de Samaná ("Samaná Bay", "Samaná Bay, San Lorenzo", "San Lorenzo Bay", "Sanchez" (*sic*), "La Cañita" ["swamp at mouth of Yuna River"]), April 1883 (four specimens in FMNH), July 1883 (two specimens in ANSP), July and September 1916 and February 1919 (12 specimens in AMNH and in USNM), May 1927 (Wetmore and Swales 1931); (*Isla Beata*), "regularly" reported by 1977 (see Wiley and Ottenwalder 1990). Untraced localities are: Almezein, late eighteenth century (Fisher 1981), Jicomé and Esperanza (which are common names of settlements), where the species was present up to 1981 (Stockton de Dod 1981).

Puerto Rico Records are from: *(Mona Island)*, where the species was observed before 1974 (Bond 1974) and before 1977 (King 1978-1979); (*Mainland*) Aguada (18°23'N 67°11'W), where it was regularly observed in 1982-1983 (J. A. Colón *in litt.* 1986); Boquerón (18°01'N 67°10'W), regularly (J. A. Colón *in litt.* 1986); near Mayagüez (18°12'N 67°09'W), 1875 (Gundlach 1878b); Cartagena Lagoon (18°01'N 67°06'W), currently (Scott and Carbonell 1986); Laguna de Guánica (18°00'N 66°56'W), 1876 (Gundlach 1878b) and regularly observed in 1982-1983 (J. A. Colón *in litt.* 1986); Tiburones Swamp (18°28'N 66°41'W), currently (Scott and Carbonell 1986); Tortuguero Lagoon and Cabo Caribe Swamp (18°27'N 66°27'W), probably breeding (see Scott and Carbonell 1986); Torrecillas (18°20'N 66°26'W), shortly before 1973 (H. A. Raffaele *in litt.* 1973 to W. B.

King); Cibuco Swamp (18°28'N 66°23'W), where the species is considered to be resident (see Scott and Carbonell 1986); Anegado Lagoon (posibly Anegado Shoal, at 18°27'N 66°07'W), December 1921 and a nest found in December 1922 (see Wetmore 1927b); Torrecilla Alta (18°25'N 65°54'W), currently (see Scott and Carbonell 1986); Canóvanas (Barrio Canóvanas, at 18°23'N 65°53'W) and Río Grande (18°23'N 65°50'W), regularly (J. A. Colón *in litt.* 1986); Humacao Swamp (18°11'N 65°46'W), where a flock of c.80 birds was observed shortly before 1973 (H. A. Raffaele *in litt.* 1973 to W. B. King) down to the present (Scott and Carbonell 1986, J. A. Colón *in litt.* 1986, Raffaele 1989); mangrove swamps near Mameyes (18°22'N 65°46'W), reported to Wetmore (1927b); Roosevelt Roads Naval Reservation, 18°14'N 65°37'W, currently (Scott and Carbonell 1986); (*Vieques Island*) on the "larger lagoons", where it was reported to occur at times (Wetmore 1916); wetlands on the southern shore of the island, notably at Laguna Kiani (18°07'N 65°34'W), currently (Scott and Carbonell 1986).

Virgin Islands (U.K.) The species has been recorded from Virgin Gorda, where two adults and three downy young were collected in December 1889 (specimens in BMNH and FMNH), and recently before 1976 (Bond 1976).

St Croix (U.S.A.) The species was collected in July and September 1858 (Newton 1859), December 1939, November and December 1940 and January and February 1941 (seven specimens in FMNH).

Antigua and Barbuda The species has been listed as breeding in Antigua (see Bond 1980), and in Barbuda it was recorded in November 1903 (specimen in USNM) and January 1976 (Bond 1977), and it is currently present (Faaborg and Arendt 1985) in the coastal mangroves in the north-west (see Lewis and Renton 1989) and in the Bull Hole and inland mangroves (17°35'N 61°46'W) (Scott and Carbonell 1986).

St Kitts-Nevis There is an undated specimen in MCZ from St Kitts.

POPULATION The West Indian Whistling-duck has clearly suffered an alarming decline throughout its range, but the scant information available does not allow a precise evaluation of its current status.

Bahamas Cory (1880) referred to the species as "not uncommon" on some of the larger islands; this assessment is supported by other authors visiting some of the larger islands during the nineteenth and early twentieth centuries (see below), but the species now seems to be rare or very rare almost everywhere.

(*Abaco*) According to J. Patterson (*in litt.* 1973 to W. B. King), the species was formerly found in "much greater numbers", but "rare" with only few records in recent years.

(*Andros*) It was considered "quite abundant" on the ponds situated a few miles from the mouth of Fresh Creek (Cory 1880), and Bonhote (1903) referred to it as "often seen" along the west coast, although "generally in small parties". There appears to be no more recent assessment.

(*New Providence*) The status of the species in the past in unknown. There was a sighting of seven or eight birds at Nassau in December 1984 (C. A. Faanes *in litt.* 1986).

(*Cat*) Buden (1987c) reported it an "uncommon to fairly common" resident, although breeding is undocumented. During May-July 1986, birds were seen and heard in the southern half of the island; villagers throughout the island considered it a permanent resident and an agricultural pest (Buden 1987c).

(*San Salvador*) The status of the species remains unclear (see Scott and Carbonell 1986).

(*Rum Cay*) It was reported for the first time in June 1989, and is probably resident although breeding is undocumented; a flock of 10-15 birds was observed at Yara Pond and 43 were counted at a small freshwater pond c.2.5 km north of Cotton Field Point (Buden 1990).

(*Hog Cay*) This small 100 ha cay supports a resident population which during the "past 15 years" reached a maximum of approximately 380 birds (P. D. Graham *in litt.* 1991).

(*Ragged*) The only known observation, on Little Ragged, 1907, concerned six birds (Buden 1987b).

(*Crooked*) The species is known to have bred in March 1934 (Buden 1987a).

(*Acklins*) The species's status is uncertain. There is a record of c.20 in two flocks in the early 1970s (see Buden 1987a).

(*Inagua*) Todd and Worthington (1911) found the species "not uncommon" but "exceedingly shy" on Great Inagua; reproduction was confirmed as a nest was found in February 1909. A small but "apparently secure population" was reported in 1973 (see King 1978-1979), but Campbell (1978) considered it a rarity. The species is currently present in "tens of birds" in Inagua National Park (see Scott and Carbonell 1986), but C. A. Faanes (*in litt.* 1986) failed to detect it there after several searches in suitable habitat during April 1985.

Turks and Caicos A few domesticated birds in 1930 in Turks (see Buden 1987a) suggest a breeding population, but there are no recent records, and C. A. Faanes (*in litt.* 1986) failed to find the species in the mid-1980s. On Caicos there are records from 1930 (see Distribution) and two flocks of 11 and 15 (probably family groups) were observed in July and September 1987 (Norton and Clarke 1987).

Cuba (*Mainland*) Gundlach (1876) referred to the species as "very common" in appropriate habitat (see Ecology) but Barbour (1923, 1943) noted that the species had been "greatly reduced" in numbers as a consequence of lowland deforestation, having disappeared "from many localities where but a few years ago they were very abundant"; he referred to "one small band" being left at Ariguanabo, and it was still to be found "about the Ciénaga" (presumably Ciénaga de Zapata) and was "still abundant" in remote (less densely populated) coastal regions. He also reported it breeding "regularly" in the sanctuary at Soledad, where sightings of "twenty or more" resting during the day were not uncommon. Ripley and Watson (1956) also noted its increasing rarity, calling it "formerly common". In 1974 numbers declined drastically at the Jibaro wetlands, after a pest control programme in the rice paddies (see Scott and Carbonell 1986). On Cayo Cantiles, Archipiélago de los Canarreos, the species was known to occur in large flocks (see Garrido and Schwartz 1969). Garrido and García Montaña (1975) still considered it common, and although Garrido (1984) referred to a "notably decrease of its populations", and then expressing the belief that it still was "locally common in swamps, along coasts, and even on keys, in good numbers" and reporting that it was actually recovering as a result of its protection against hunting (Garrido 1985; but see Threats). In the Ciénaga de Zapata Gundlach (1893) had found it "very common" but nowadays the species is considered rare there: in six years it was only observed twice, 12 being the largest number recorded (L. Fazio *in litt.* 1992). There are still occasional sightings in this area (e.g. a group of five in December 1991 near Bahía Cochinos: J. M. Jiménez López *in litt.* 1992). In Camagüey, Pinar del Río and some of the cays (e.g. Cayo Coco), the species is considered "not uncommon" (A. Kirkconnell and O. H. Garrido *per* L. Fazio *in litt.* 1992).

(*Isle of Pines*) Bangs and Zappey (1905) found the species in "considerable" numbers in 1904 (with birds collected in the Ciénaga de Lanier), while Todd (1916) recorded it several times in the northern part of the island along the río de las Nuevas, and considered it "quite common" in the western extreme of the Ciénaga de Lanier. Later, Ripley and Watson (1956) noted a decline in the Ciénaga de Lanier, where it had become "rare".

Cayman Islands Johnston *et al.* (1971) considered it an "uncommon breeding resident" on Grand Cayman and Little Cayman, although D. W. Johnston in 1973 judged it "reasonably common", "less so" on Cayman Brac (see King 1978-1979) and Bradley (1985) considered it a "rare breeding resident". The overall population was estimated at over 400 birds (for numbers observed in each of the wetlands mentioned under Distribution see Scott and Carbonell 1986), but very few individuals have been seen or heard during organized evening watches on the edges of mangrove forests in the centre of Grand Cayman (van Liefde 1992). The species appears to be fairly secure in Little Cayman, where the human population is very small and the wetlands still intact; rough counts there yielded numbers up to 125 birds (van Liefde 1992). According to local hunters, the species was formerly numerous on Grand Cayman, where it was "easy to find" and "easy to hunt", but now is "almost impossible to find" (van Liefde 1992).

Jamaica Gosse (1847) found the West Indian Whistling-duck "numerous", breeding in the morasses of Westmoreland, and Sclater and Salvin (1876) described it as a breeding resident in "numerous and compact flocks". By the 1920s Bangs and Kennard (1920) reported it a "rather common resident" although they had already noted a decline as a result of the introduction of the mongoose *Herpestes*; however, they speculated that it might have changed its breeding habits, "probably" keeping its young in places too wet for the mongoose and apparently "regaining its former abundance". Bond (1956b) called it "common" on the island. At present, the species "regularly" occurs in Negril Morass and the Black River Lower Morass, this being considered the last stronghold of the species on the island (Scott and Carbonell 1986). Downer and Sutton (1990) still thought it "locally common" but extremely shy and difficult to see.

Haiti The evidence assembled by Wetmore and Swales (1931) shows that the species must have been very common late in the eighteenth, nineteenth and early twentieth centuries. By 1918 it was reported to be the "most common duck" in the country (see Wetmore and Swales 1931), and Danforth (1929) found it "very abundant" at Les Salines and near Gonaïves in 1927 with birds seen near Grand Goave, Lake Miragoane and the Artibonite Sloughs. The species occurs regularly at Etang Saumâtre (see Scott and Carbonell 1986) and although currently considered "extraordinarily rare" (C. A. Woods verbally 1992), P. Y. Roumain (*in litt.* 1991) indicated that it can still be found in small numbers at night in isolated swamps and in rice-growing areas.

Dominican Republic Cory (1885) called the West Indian Whistling-duck "probably resident, but not abundant". It seems to have been locally common in the early decades of the twentieth century, judging from the comments in Wetmore and Swales (1931), who considered it "fairly common" in the lowlands, notably in the Bahía de Samaná (18 specimens in AMNH and USNM were collected in 1916), Laguna de Saladilla and Lago Enriquillo, a site where Danforth (1929) reported it "very abundant" in June 1927 (12 birds shot). Later observations include a group of seven birds in Laguna Salada in February 1977 (see Vargas Mora and González Castillo 1983), and in this same year marines on Beata Island reported it "regularly" in mangroves, and "many" were observed at Bucán de Base (Wiley and Ottenwalder 1990). Stockton de Dod (1981) considered the species to be on the way to extinction. By 1986, "some colonies" were reported from Montecristi, although it was "very rare" elsewhere on the northern coast (A. Stockton de Dod *in litt.* 1986). DVS (1990) counted it amongst the country's threatened species.

Puerto Rico The species has suffered a great decline, having once been recorded at "many localities" and locally in numbers (Gundlach 1878b). Wetmore (1927b) described it as "formerly common" but "now locally fairly common", at a time when this was its status at Laguna Cartagena, where according to local informants it was observed at times in flocks of up to one hundred (Wetmore 1927b). Danforth (1936) also referred to its former abundance, but reported "now they are scarce" because of hunting. Further assessments in the second half of this century are from Bond (1956b), who judged it "rare", and King (1978-1979), who, quoting other sources, indicated that the species was "very rare" despite a record of c.80 birds near Humacao in the early 1970s. This large flock and the "limited comeback" of the species in the area resulted presumably from the re-flooding of some former marshlands (H. A. Raffaele *in litt.* 1986, J. W. Wiley *in litt.*

1986). Despite this, H. A. Raffaele (*in litt.* 1986) achieved only a single sighting of a group of five birds despite active fieldwork during the early 1970s. By 1984, the species's population was estimated only at about 150-250 individuals (J. A. Colón *in litt.* 1986), and although regularly reported from several localities in 1986 (see Distribution), at present it is only known to occur regularly in the Humacao area, being very rare elsewhere (Raffaele 1989). The species was known to occur on the "larger lagoons" of Vieques Island (Wetmore 1916); at present it is known from Laguna Kiani (Scott and Carbonell 1986). On Mona Island it is occasional (see Distribution).

Virgin Islands The species was presumably resident in Virgin Gorda, where there is a record of a pair with downy young in 1889; other records on this island are from the early 1970s (see Distribution), the species today being considered very rare (Raffaele 1990). Scott and Carbonell (1986) did not mention the species for any of the British or U.S. islands and according to S. Oldfield (*in litt.* 1988) it no longer occurs on Anegada.

St Croix Newton (1859) reported the species "pretty common on the mangrove lagoons" in 1857 and 1858, although its breeding status could not be proved. Beatty (1930) considered it a "very rare" resident, adding that 15 years ago it used to breed and was "very common". There are seven specimens (in FMNH) collected in December 1939, November and December 1940 and January and February 1941.

Antigua and Barbuda The species appears to be resident with certainty only on Barbuda, where a "large population" was reported in a suitable area during 1983-1984 (Faaborg and Arendt 1985), but no estimation of its population exists (Lewis and Renton 1989).

ECOLOGY The West Indian Whistling-duck inhabits both fresh and saline waterbodies such as lagoons, swamps, mangroves, ricefields and palm savannas (Gundlach 1876, Cory 1880, Todd 1916, Wetmore and Swales 1931, Garrido and García Montaña 1975, Raffaele 1989, DVS 1990). It is known to spend the daylight hours hidden in the vegetation, e.g. mangroves (Bradley 1985, Garrido 1984), "maciales" *Typha* (Cuba) (Barbour 1943), woodlands (Stockton de Dod 1978, Garrido 1984, N. Varty verbally 1992) or even in the hills (Puerto Rico) (Raffaele 1989).

The species feeds mostly at night, birds generally being seen at dusk when flying in flocks to the feeding haunts in search of the highly appreciated fruit of the royal palm trees *Roystonea* sp. (e.g. Cuba, Jamaica, Dominican Republic, Puerto Rico), fruits, seeds and grasses or crops, notably rice and corn (Gundlach 1893, Bangs and Zappey 1905, Wetmore 1927b, Wetmore and Swales 1931, Barbour 1943, Stockton de Dod 1978, Garrido 1984, Bradley 1985, Buden 1987c, Downer and Sutton 1990). Stomach contents of birds taken on the Isle of Pines were "grass" (Todd 1916) and in the Dominican Republic "small seeds" but mostly grasses (Danforth 1929).

The breeding season is ill-defined and variable from one island to another and even within one particular island: in Cuba the commonest breeding months are from June to October (Gundlach 1876, Davis 1941, Ripley and Watson 1956, Balát and González 1982), but there are records from December and January (Gundlach 1893, Bond 1977, Balát and González 1982); in Jamaica breeding was believed to occur from October to December (Biaggi 1970) but Downer and Sutton (1990) judged it to occur from May to October; in Grand Cayman nesting runs from May to June, but it has also been reported in November/December for two consecutive years (van Liefde 1992), and in Little Cayman from February to May (Bradley 1985); in Haiti laying has been reported in January (Wetmore and Swales 1931) and birds collected in November in the Dominican Republic had fully enlarged gonads (specimens in AMNH); in Puerto Rico the breeding season is considered variable (Raffaele 1989). Nests have been reported in tree holes, on horizontal branches, in clumps of bromeliads, in reeds near the ground or on the ground among roots of fallen trees in bushy cover, but normally not far from water; clutches generally contain 10-16 eggs

(Gundlach 1876, Barbour 1943, Biaggi 1970, Stockton de Dod 1978, Bradley 1985, Downer and Sutton 1990). Very little is known about the species's movements from island – or groups of islands – to island, but displacements appear to occur: Stockton de Dod (1978) indicated that (in the Dominican Republic) the species "disappears" from time to time but "usually only for short periods in January, February or March.

THREATS The West Indian Whistling-duck is suffering from destruction of wetlands in most of its wide range, primarily as a result of human activities and development projects (see Scott and Carbonell 1986 for threats affecting the most important wetlands within the species's range). The good quality of its flesh has resulted in indiscriminate hunting (see Remarks 4), which, combined with the loss of suitable habitat, has resulted in the alarming decline that the species has suffered throughout its range (see, e.g., Gundlach 1878a, 1893, Cory 1892, Danforth 1936, Barbour 1943, Campbell 1978, Scott and Carbonell 1986). The use of pesticides in agriculture (the rapid adaptation of the species to feeding on crops, notably rice and corn, has been well documented: see Ecology) is another factor that has provoked massive mortality (e.g. in Cuba: Garrido 1985). Egg-collecting and keeping captive birds as pets have been widespread influences (see, e.g., Gundlach 1893, Todd 1916, Wetmore and Swales 1931, Barbour 1943, Bond 1961, Stockton de Dod 1981 amongst others).

Bahamas Although the species is protected it is still prized by hunters (Campbell 1978).

Cuba Hunting, egg-collecting and pesticide usage have been the major causes of decline (see above).

Cayman The Development Plan of 1977 for Grand Cayman adopted in 1981 called for the incorporation of 97% of Grand Cayman's wetlands into urban (e.g. tourist complexes) and agricultural schemes: the implementation of this plan is in progress, and the ultimate removal of 97% of the island's wetland habitat would result in a dramatic decline in wildfowl populations and represent an important loss of one of the best refuges within the species's range (see Scott and Carbonell 1986). Furthermore, some of the ponds used for feeding at night on Grand Cayman are currently being encroached upon by housing, with much resulting disturbance; some have been ploughed, levelled for more pasture or filled in by developers; and man-associated animals (e.g. dogs, cats) are said to be proliferating (van Liefde 1992). In addition the species is being negatively affected by hunting (Scott and Carbonell 1986, van Liefde 1992).

Jamaica The species's strong decline in the island has been in part attributed to the introduction of the Indian mongoose *Herpestes* (Bangs and Kennard 1920, Kear and Williams 1978). Despite recognition of wetlands as areas of special conservation value (see Measures Taken), they remain under threat, particularly from drainage for agriculture, housing and industrial development (details in Scott and Carbonell 1986).

Haiti Despite the extreme degradation of terrestrial environments owing in part to the density and poverty of the human population (see Threats under White-winged Warbler *Xenoligea montana*), the wetlands in the country have suffered comparatively less, but continuing conversion of freshwater marshes to rice-growing areas, drainage for other forms of cultivation, cutting of mangroves for charcoal, and local pollution from domestic sewage have been identified as the major threats; pesticides are not widely used and there is relatively little disturbance from hunting and fishing activities (Scott and Carbonell 1986; see Remarks 5).

Dominican Republic Habitat loss, hunting and the use of pesticides are the major problems (Stockton de Dod 1978, J. W. Wiley *in litt.* 1986, DVS 1990).

Puerto Rico The species is suffering from illegal hunting (J. A. Colón *in litt.* 1986, J. W. Wiley *in litt.* 1986), intensive industrial development and the expansion of agriculture and "sanitary" land-fills, causing a deterioration of the wetlands (excessive drainage, diversion of watercourses, infilling for construction, excessive use of fertilizers, insecticides and herbicides: see Scott and Carbonell 1986).

Virgin Islands Wetlands in both the British and U.S. Virgin Islands have suffered much deterioration as a result of development projects and tourism (Scott and Carbonell 1986, Norton *et al.* 1986).

Antigua and Barbuda In Antigua vast areas of mangroves and wetlands have been destroyed by coastal developments (see CCA 1991a), and in Barbuda, although the original habitats on the island are still in reasonable condition, new development projects threaten the salt-pond and mangrove swamp (see CCA 1991a).

MEASURES TAKEN

Bahamas The species is (only nominally) protected (Campbell 1978; see Threats). It is known to occur in the Inagua National Park (Scott and Carbonell 1986), and on Hog Cay (a privately owned approximate 100 ha cay) it has increased in numbers considerably in recent years as a consequence of regular feeding by the owner (see Population).

Turks and Caicos On Caicos, the Sawgrass Pond (where a family group was observed in July 1977) has been protected as a Ramsar site (Norton and Clarke 1987).

Cuba Hunting of the species is forbidden (Garrido 1985); but see Threats. The protected areas where the species is known to occur or have occurred are: Península de Zapata and Ciénaga de Lanier National Parks, within Archipiélago de Camagüey (Cayo Coco and Cayo Romano Natural Reserves) and Cayo Cantiles Faunal Refuge (see Wright 1988).

Cayman The species is protected against hunting (Scott and Carbonell 1986); but see Threats. The following wetlands where the species is known to be present are protected (as listed in Scott and Carbonell 1986): Central Mangrove Swamp and Booby Cay (only the 150 m wide fringe of mangroves around North Sound and Booby Cay); Meagre Bay Pond, Malportas Pond, Rock Pond and Point Pond, Westerly Ponds, Salt Water Pond and Booby Pond (only the mangrove fringe). The Cayman Island Bird Club is trying to assess the species by determining the sites where it occurs regularly (van Liefde 1992).

Jamaica Hunting of the species is prohibited (King 1978-1979); but see Threats. Wetlands are considered by the National Physical Plan and Parish Development Orders as areas of special conservation value (see Scott and Carbonell 1986); but again see Threats. Some of the important wetlands for the species (Negril Morass, Black River Lower Morass, Canoe Valley and Portland Bight Swamp) have been proposed for different degrees of protection under the National Physical Plan (see Scott and Carbonell 1986; also JCEP 1987).

Haiti None is known.

Dominican Republic The species is protected (DVS 1990). Los Haitises, Isla Cabreros, Jaragua and Monte Cristi National Parks are of great importance for the species (see Distribution).

Puerto Rico Shooting is prohibited (King 1978-1979); but see Threats. The wetlands of Torrecilla Alta and Roosevelt Roads Naval Reservation (see Remarks 6) have received some degree of protection (see Scott and Carbonell 1986).

Virgin Islands Hunting of the species has been outlawed since 1976 (J. A. Colón *in litt.* 1986).

MEASURES PROPOSED This endangered and poorly known species deserves more attention and close monitoring throughout is huge range in order to clarify its current status. Protection of any of the important wetlands (as listed in Scott and Carbonell 1986) within this range is obviously a priority. Educational campaigns to show the importance of wetlands for the conservation of wildlife and particularly the critical situation of the West Indian Whistling-duck should also be conducted.

Bahamas Very little ornithological exploration has been conducted in most of the larger islands with potential habitat for the species (see Scott and Carbonell 1986); moreover, there is almost no information on the hundreds of small islands and cays where the species may possibly nest or roost. Clearly, therefore, some survey work is needed to furnish a solid database on which conservation initiatives can be built. The remarkable population increase on Hog Cay (see Measures Taken) shows that relatively small management efforts on small islands can help support the species; this particular achievement deserves fuller study, for example through a long-term programme of monitoring the population and marking individual birds.

Cuba Further field investigation is needed to clarify the current status of the species in some of the most important wetlands listed in Scott and Carbonell (1986).

Cayman Islands The implementation of the Development Plan for Grand Cayman should be urgently reviewed and important wetland areas (see Scott and Carbonell 1986) excluded from any development project. The importance of these wetlands for wildlife in general has already been stressed by Bradley (1985) and Scott and Carbonell (1986), and their particular value for the West Indian Whistling-duck (one of the most important areas within its overall range) should be emphasized as an indication of the islands' international obligations to conservation.

Jamaica The following areas should be afforded protection: Negril Morass, Black River Lower Morass, Parottee Salt Pond and Great Salt Pond. The species would also benefit from the conservation of other wetlands in the country where suitable habitat is present.

Haiti Protection of the wetlands is urgently required: none of the 11 important sites has yet been gazetted (Scott and Carbonell 1986). As priorities, the Caracol area and Baie de Fort Liberté, the floodplain and delta of the Artibonite river, Étang Saumâtre, Étang Miragoane and eastern Ile-à-Vache deserve attention. There are, however, other important wetlands listed in Scott and Carbonell (1986) (e.g. Cayemite Islands and Baie des Bararderes, Baie d'Aquin, the wetlands on Gonave Island) where, from their habitat descriptions, the West Indian Whistling-duck may well be present.

Dominican Republic The proposed extensions to the Los Haitises and Isla Cabritos National Parks (see DVS 1990) are of great importance for the conservation of the species; this would also benefit the threatened Ridgway's Hawk *Buteo ridgwayi* (see Measures Proposed under this species).

Puerto Rico A minimum step should be to gazette the currently unprotected wetlands in which the species has been reported (see Distribution).

Antigua The remaining mangrove areas (in the north-eastern part of the island) should be protected, with restriction of access (see figure 3.1.3 in CCA 1991a).

Barbuda Codrington Lagoon's extensive mangrove forest and seven-mile barrier beach should be considered for nomination as a Ramsar site as suggested in CCA (1991a). The creation of the following proposed protected areas would also be valuable: Codrington Lagoon Bird Sanctuary, Codrington Lagoon and Goat Island and the Flashes (CCA 1991a). Furthermore, the Bull Hole and inland mangroves (see Distribution) are important for the species and thus some action to ensure and protect the population found there is needed.

REMARKS (1) Hellmayr and Conover (1948) included Guadeloupe, Martinique and Barbados within the species's range, but there is no evidence to support its occurrence there other than as a casual vagrant (see Bond 1956b). (2) A ROM printout credits J. H. Fleming for the remark "original label lost, came with other *Dendrocygna* from Brownsville, Texas, that were taken from 1891-1894; this is an Armstrong skin and is no doubt a Texas record". The occurrence of stragglers in the Gulf of Mexico is certainly likely during severe Caribbean storms and hurricanes. (3) OG (1955) also lists "Rivière de l'Estère" at 19°24'N 72°42'W. (4) Hunting is a reason for concern despite having been protected in most of its range (see Measures Taken). Sympatric occurrence in some areas with the commoner Fulvous Whistling-duck *Dendrocygna bicolor* makes it easy to confuse and thus it is difficult to protect it effectively against hunting, especially in rice plantations (Garrido 1984, O. H. Garrido *in litt.* 1992). (5) The difficult economic situation in the country is also responsible for the general lack of guns, which presumably has prevented much shooting of this and other species (C. A. Woods verbally 1992). (6) The Roosevelt Roads Naval Reservation (the extent to which this is different from the Naval Station of the same name listed under Yellow-shouldered Blackbird *Agelaius xanthomus* is not clear) has no legal habitat protection, but intrusion is prevented by the naval authorities (Scott and Carbonell 1986).

BRAZILIAN MERGANSER *Mergus octosetaceus* E[1]

Perturbation and pollution (largely as direct and indirect consequences of deforestation) of the shallow, fast-flowing rivers that are this duck's habitat in south-central Brazil, eastern Paraguay and northern Argentina have led to its exceptional rarity and the isolation of very small numbers in distant reserves.

DISTRIBUTION The Brazilian Merganser is restricted to south-central Brazil (Goiás, Minas Gerais, Mato Grosso do Sul, São Paulo, Paraná and Santa Catarina) and the neighbouring regions of Paraguay and Argentina (Misiones), in the basins of the upper Paraná, Tocantins and São Francisco rivers and on a single tributary (arroyo Soberbio) of the río Uruguay (see Remarks 1), with two old records from the rio Itajaí, Santa Catarina. Records generally refer to single birds observed or collected (exceptions are indicated), and coordinates are taken from OG (1968), Paynter (1985) and Paynter and Traylor (1991).

Argentina Misiones is the only province from where the Brazilian Merganser has ever been reported. Unreferenced records below are based on single collected specimens listed in Partridge (1956) and Johnson and Chebez (1985), localities (north to south; see Remarks 2) being: arroyo Yacuy (25°34'S 54°11'W), October 1947 (see Remarks 3); Saltos del río Iguazú, before 1914; close above the Iguazú falls, April 1956 (Delacour 1959); Garganta del Diablo (the largest waterfall on the río Iguazú), where a pair with young was observed sometime between 1942 and 1950 and another pair was seen in 1977 (Johnson and Chebez 1985); Destacamento Apepú, Iguazú National Park, 1978 (Johnson and Chebez 1985); arroyo Urugua-í (25°54'S 54°36'W; see Remarks 4), in the years 1947-1954 (26 specimens in AMNH, BMNH, FMNH, MACN, MNRJ, UNP, USNM, YPM; see Remarks 5), July 1960 (specimen in LACM), June 1984 (three birds observed; exact localities in Johnson and Chebez 1985), August 1985 (Forcelli 1987) and July 1988 (Luthin 1988); arroyo Uruzú (25°55'S 54°39'W), sometime between August and September 1986 (P. Canevari *in litt.* 1992) and January 1989 (A. Johnson, A. Giraudo and J. C. Chebez *in litt.* 1992); arroyo Aguaray-guazú (26°08'S 54°39'W), May 1948; arroyo Piray-miní (untraced but in Eldorado department, at 26°15'S 54°25'W), where a bird was collected in the 1970s (J. C. Chebez *in litt.* 1992); arroyo Piray-guazú (26°27'S 54°42'W; see Remarks 6), May and September 1951 and August 1952; arroyo Tigre (a tributary of the arroyo Piray-guazú; see, e.g., the map in Johnson and Chebez 1985), 1977 (Johnson and Chebez 1985); arroyo Paranay-guazú (26°41'S 54°48'W), where a pair was reported in 1984 (M. Nores *in litt.* 1984 to W. Belton); arroyo Garuhapé (26°47'S 54°56'W), September 1882; arroyo Mandarinas (a tributary of the arroyo Soberbio, 27°15'S 54°12'W, the only tributary of the río Uruguay on which the species has ever been recorded), where several birds were observed in November 1953 (Johnson and Chebez 1985); arroyo Victoria (26°52'S 54°39'W; another tributary of the arroyo Soberbio), November 1969 (Johnson and Chebez 1985); Bonpland (= Bonplano, 27°29'S 55°29'W), April 1912 (see Remarks 7).

Brazil Records of the species from the states of Bahia and Rio de Janeiro are not accepted here (see Remarks 8). Localities (north to south) are:

Goiás rio das Pedras (a tributary of the rio Paranã), Nova Roma (13°51'S 46°57'W), June 1950 (Sick 1958); upper rio Tocantins, 1953, 1960 and 1972 (Sick 1985); rio Preto (14°05'S 47°42'W), headwaters of the rio Tocantins, Chapada dos Veadeiros National Park, where pairs were observed on five different occasions between October 1986 and January 1987 (coordinates and data from Yamashita and Valle 1990); Veadeiros, rio São Miguel, March and April 1940 (specimens in FMNH); Guardamor (= Guarda Mor, c.16°00'S 50°40'W), where five birds were collected in

October 1823 (von Pelzeln 1868-1871); Emas National Park, where a pair was observed in August 1990 (A. Whittaker *in litt.* 1992);

Minas Gerais (see Remarks 9) ribeirão do Salitre, affluent of rio Quebra-Anzol, in the Serra Negra (c.19°17'S 46°55'W) at 900-950 m, near Salitre de Minas (= Salitre, 19°05'S 46°48'W), where two birds were seen sometime between June and August 1973 (G. T. de Mattos *in litt.* 1988 to H. Sick, G. T. de Mattos *in litt.* 1992); "Minas", probably on the rio das Velhas (a tributary of rio São Francisco, early in 1819 (Stresemann 1954; also Partridge 1956); rio São João (untraced but on the northern boundary of Serra da Canastra National Park), sometime between 1978 and 1980 (J. M. Dietz *in litt.* 1986); wetlands of the Serra da Canastra National Park, down to the present (Scott and Carbonell 1986, Bartmann 1988, M. Pearman *in litt.* 1990; see Population); Fazenda Boquerão (on the rio São Francisco, below Serra da Canastra National Park), currently (M. Pearman *in litt.* 1990, Gardner and Gardner 1990b; see Population);

Mato Grosso do Sul headwaters of the rio Sucuriú, mid 1940s (P. T. Z. Antas *per* D. A. Scott *in litt.* 1992; specimen in MZUSP);

São Paulo unspecified, 1819 (Stresemann 1954; also Burmeister 1856); Salto Grande, rio Paranapanema, May 1903 (Pinto 1938); Itararé (24°07'S 49°20'W), where a pair was observed (specimen in BMNH) in August 1820 (von Pelzeln 1868-1871);

Paraná Salto da Ariranha (c.24°22'S 51°27'W), on the rio Ivaí, November 1922 (Sztolcman 1926);

Santa Catarina unspecified (Burmeister 1856), including specimens taken in the state before 1871 (Stresemann 1935, 1954) and 1887 (in AMNH); Blumenau (von Berlepsch 1873-1874) and Taió (both localities on the rio Itajaí), 1827 (Stresemann 1948, Sick *et al.* 1981); Laguna, before 1877 (Mertens and Steinbacher 1955; see Remarks 10).

Paraguay According to Bertoni (1901) the Brazilian Merganser inhabited small streams along the Paraguayan side of the Paraná drainage in the department of Alto Paraná (see Remarks 11); his observations were from 1891. The only precisely known locality in the country is the río Carapá near Catueté (c.24°08'S 54°35'W, read from DSGM 1988), Canindeyú department, where a bird was observed in February 1984 (Scott and Carbonell 1986, N. López Kochalka verbally 1990).

POPULATION The Brazilian Merganser's overall population would appear to be extremely small, given that it is present only at a few scattered sites throughout its large range. There may in fact be only three small and isolated populations; one in Argentina (Misiones) and two in Brazil (Goiás and Minas Gerais). A total of around 250 birds (in Ellis-Joseph *et al.* 1992) represents a vaguely informed guess, and may indeed approximate to the truth, although on the evidence provided here the number could equally well be much less than 250.

Argentina Between 1942 and 1978 records of the species in Iguazú National Park included a group of up to three or four individuals and a pair with youngsters, the observer remarking that it was not a usual bird and never abundant (Johnson and Chebez 1985).

At least 30 specimens (26 from río Urugua-í; see Threats, Remarks 12) were collected on the eastern rivers and streams that flow from the highlands in the interior of the province into the upper Paraná between 1947 and 1954, a time when the species was considered "not rare" although found in low densities (Partridge 1956; see also Distribution). In August 1951 two pairs had their feeding grounds in rapids on the río Urugua-í near "km 10", the first occasion when more than two birds were observed together in Argentina (Partridge 1956). Subsequent records from the river occurred in 1960 (see Remarks 13) and 1984, when three birds were seen (Johnson and Chebez 1985), August 1985 (Forcelli 1987) and July 1988 (Luthin 1988), indicating that a small population is extant along its course. In the arroyo Paranay-guazú, the species has only been recorded once (a pair in 1984) despite the habitat there (up to 1984) still being in fairly good condition (M. Nores *in litt.* 1984 to W. Belton). The Brazilian Merganser is nowadays considered to be very rare and one of the most threatened species in Argentina (Canevari *et al.* 1991).

Brazil Stresemann (1954) believed that the species was apparently not rare around 1820 in the states of Rio de Janeiro, Minas Gerais and São Paulo (but see Remarks 8). The judgement a century later that the bird was "maybe vanishing" (Phillips 1929) was doubtless based on the chronic paucity of specimens. Sick and Teixeira (1979) considered it rare in Brazil, although they indicated that its status was little known. Its population certainly appears to be highly fragmented, the only two known remaining populations being in Serra da Canastra and Chapada dos Veadeiros National Parks (the recent record from Emas cannot yet be judged to reflect a resident population) in the states of Minas Gerais and Goiás, most of the other records listed under Distribution referring to old specimens or to sites where the species is likely to have been extirpated. In 1980, the population in the Serra da Canastra National Park and surrounding areas was estimated at about 50 pairs (Scott and Carbonell 1986), but between 1981 and 1985 Bartmann (1988) could only find two pairs within the park (on the upper rio São Francisco), with a third pair c.50 km downstream, and concluded that the estimate of 50 pairs was too high; he reported 23 sightings (mostly of pairs, once of three birds together) in 68 hours of observation. In the same general area (Fazenda Boquerão), the species is known to have been present during 1987, when five young were reared, and in July 1989, when a pair with ducklings was observed (M. Pearman *in litt.* 1990). In the upper rio Tocantins drainage area, birds were been reported in 1950, 1953, 1960, 1972, 1986 and 1987 (see Distribution), overall numbers probably being very small; a pair was observed on five occasions in 1986 and 1987 (Yamashita and Valle 1990).

Paraguay Despite Bertoni's (1901) view that it was very rare, Partridge (1956) believed that a thorough search along the many tributaries on the western side of the Paraná drainage in Paraguay would probably reveal that the merganser's status there was similar to that in Misiones (i.e., "not rare"). This may have been true at the time, but extensive searches in canoe and on foot during July–September 1989 failed to detect the species along 105 km of the río Carapá, 22 km of the río Itambey, and 71 km of the río Ñacunday, and along accessible points of arroyo Pozuelo, río Yacuy Guazú and río Tambey (Granizo Tamayo and Hayes in prep., Hayes and Granizo Tamayo in press). The species's future in Paraguay is uncertain and recent ecological changes (see Threats) may have left too little habitat to permit a viable population (Granizo Tamayo and Hayes in prep.).

ECOLOGY The Brazilian Merganser is a shy inhabitant of silent streams and rivers flowing through remote, undisturbed forest, and prefers upper river tributaries interspersed with rapids and waterfalls from low elevations up to c.1,000 m where steep escarpments and deep valleys with gallery forests are present (Bertoni 1901, Partridge 1956, Johnson and Chebez 1985, Scott and Carbonell 1986, Bartmann 1988; see Remarks 14). On the rio Preto, Chapada dos Veadeiros, the habitat is cerrado, and the major requirement of the species is probably the presence of rapids and clear waters (Yamashita and Valle 1990), as suggested elsewhere (e.g. Partridge 1956, Johnson and Chebez 1985, Bartmann 1988, Granizo Tamayo and Hayes in prep.) rather than the type of vegetation bordering the rivers.

Brazilian Mergansers are good swimmers and dive with great agility in pursuit of fish; they feed actively during the day, especially in the morning and evening; feeding occurs mostly in shallow, fast-flowing waters (Partridge 1956, Bartmann 1988). Examination of 11 stomachs and gullets in Misiones revealed that the species feeds primarily on fish and occasionally on aquatic insects and snails; however, in one case 80% of the contents of the stomach and gullet consisted of remains of the larvae of a large dobson fly (*Corydalis*) and also a few (0.8%) snail shells

(Partridge 1956). Fish size found in the gullet varied from 6 to 19 cm long, and these included mojarra (Characinidae), catfish (Pimelodidae), "virolito" *Parodon* (Hemiodontidae) (Partridge 1956). In the Serra da Canastra, Bartmann (1988) believed that the staple of adults was the "lambari" *Astyanax fasciatus* with sizes up to 15 cm, while ducklings fed on insects on the water surface or in the shallows with their heads submerged, probably consuming aquatic invertebrates (Trichoptera, Plecoptera, Diptera). Fish seemed to replace invertebrate food in the growing ducklings. The stomach of a female taken in November in Santa Catarina contained vegetable matter (Sztolcman 1926). "Fish" fauna in the rio Preto, Chapada dos Veadeiros seemed very poor, merely consisting of "lambaris" and small "cascudos" (C. Yamashita *in litt.* 1987)

The mergansers rest perched on stones, branches or fallen trees projecting from the water; they fly close to the surface following the river's course, increasing altitude to as much as 15 to 30 m when potential risks are present (Giai 1950, Partridge 1956). Rivers and streams in Misiones, Argentina, were believed to be inhabited by isolated, sedentary populations; pairs probably never leave their territory (Partridge 1956, Johnson and Chebez 1985, Bartmann 1988), and may spend their entire lives along one river or stream (Partridge 1956). Bartmann (1988) found that one pair with a duckling at the Serra da Canastra occupied a stretch of river estimated to be c.7 km in length. The breeding season runs from June, when birds in Argentina have been seen displaying (Giai 1950), with incubation in July and August (Partridge 1958). However, records of display in August (Partridge 1958) possibly indicate slight variation in seasonality (or, e.g., preparation for a replacement clutch). A nest discovered on 24 August 1954 was in a tree-cavity (*Peltophorum dubium*) c.25 m above water level (Partridge 1956). Flightless young have been reported throughout August, including the only known nest from which chicks left on 30 August 1954 (Giai 1950, Partridge 1956, Bartman 1988, M. Pearman *in litt.* 1990; see Remarks 15).

THREATS The Brazilian Merganser has been suffering from steady habitat loss as a result of human activities, the main cause of the species's decline probably being the increasing turbidity of rivers and streams throughout its range as a result of watershed degradation and erosion (Partridge 1956, Johnson and Chebez 1985, Scott and Carbonell 1986).

Among natural predators are the near-threatened Black-and-white Hawk-Eagle *Spizastur melanoleucus* (Giai 1951, Partridge 1956), otters (Bartmann 1988) and fish (Partridge 1956).

Argentina The riverine habitat of the Brazilian Merganser has suffered from staggering deforestation, especially since the 1950s, and from the construction of a dam on the arroyo Urugua-í which flooded large areas where the species had previously been reported by Partridge (1956), Johnson and Chebez (1985) and Forcelli (1987) including the area in which the only known nest was found (Chebez 1984, 1990, Johnson and Chebez 1985). In addition, the lower Urugua-í basin has been greatly transformed by reforestation with pines *Pinus elliotii* and *Araucaria angustifolia*; this has involved increasing human activity in the area with obvious negative consequences for the species (Johnson and Chebez 1985). Hunters searching for mammals on the riversides must have disturbed the mergansers and would occasionally have shot them (Johnson and Chebez 1985). From 1942 to 1978 the water quality of the río Iguazú deteriorated seriously, owing to deforestation in the upper basin of the river in Brazil; similar habitat degradation has also been noted in other streams in Misiones, namely Aguary-guazú, Garuhapé and Yabebirí (Johnson and Chebez 1985). The species's increasing rarity has resulted in transactions with local people of as much as US$6,000 for a single stuffed specimen (Johnson and Chebez 1985), a problem already flagged in the 1940s by Giai (1976), although who was or is buying such material is not clear; Johnson and Chebez (1985) implied that museums might be involved. The collection of 26 specimens in the period 1947–1954 (see Population) cannot have helped the species.

Brazil Agricultural development, watershed degradation and soil erosion have occurred everywhere outside national parks and nature reserves within the species's range (Bartmann 1988). According to C. Yamashita (*in litt.* 1992), many small dams have extirpated considerable amounts of potential habitat. Extensive diamond mining occurs near the Fazenda Boquerão (M. Pearman *in litt.* 1990).

Paraguay The Alto Paraná region has suffered great changes in the last 15 years, including the construction of the Itaipú and Acaray dams, which flooded large areas of prime merganser habitat; deforestation has also caused land erosion and hence an increased amount of siltation in the watersheds (Granizo Tamayo and Hayes in prep.). Economic development of the area accompanied the construction of the dams, resulting in a large influx of people with inevitable new pressures on the environment (e.g. the use of pesticides in agriculture, which have already caused mass fish deaths: Granizo Tamayo and Hayes in prep). Furthermore, Itapúa department has now been greatly deforested (F. E. Hayes *in litt.* 1991).

MEASURES TAKEN Very little has been done over the years to promote the long-term security of this interesting but problematic animal.

Argentina Some 55,500 ha of Atlantic forest are protected within the Iguazú National Park, but the scant records from the area show that this does not guarantee the species's survival in the country (Johnson and Chebez 1985). In 1988 the provincial government of Misiones – with considerable financial assistance from ICBP (using a donation from the late J. S. Dunning) and Fundación Vida Silvestre Argentina – established two natural provincial reserves of great importance for the species, namely the Urugua-í (84,000 ha, incorporating the Islas Malvinas Provincial Park) and the Yacuy; this has resulted in the protection of the upper reaches of arroyos Urugua-í, Uruzú and Yacuy and, because these reserves are contiguous with the Iguazú National Park, a huge continuous protected area is now effectively in place (Chebez and Rolón 1989, J. C. Chebez *in litt.* 1992). Educational proposals emphasizing the importance of wildlife in general and the Brazilian Merganser in particular have been put to the government of Misiones by the Fundación Vida Silvestre Argentina and Asociación Ornitológica del Plata (see Johnson and Chebez 1985).

Brazil The species is protected under Brazilian law (King 1978-1979, Bernardes *et al.* 1990), and seemingly very small numbers are protected by the Serra da Canastra, Chapada dos Veadeiros and Emas National Parks (see Distribution). In the first of these, protection was regarded as excellent (Scott and Carbonell 1986).

Paraguay None is known apart from the unsuccessful searches conducted in 1989 (Hayes and Granizo Tamayo in press).

MEASURES PROPOSED The Brazilian Merganser has been proposed for inclusion on Appendix I of CITES (Johnson and Chebez 1985, Granizo Tamayo and Hayes in prep.; see Remarks 17). However, the overriding requirements are for more survey work throughout its range, monitoring of known populations, and further biological studies to clarify the ecological factors affecting such parameters as territory size and breeding success.

Argentina Proposals by Johnson and Chebez (1985) to protect and manage the upper reaches of the Urugua-í and to protect the entire Yacuy have been accepted and implemented (see Measures Taken), but there remain several further points to be addressed: (1) a thorough search of remaining populations using rowing boats, at least in the breeding season, should be conducted on the rivers and streams of northern and central Misiones, in the following order: upper Urugua-í and Yacuy basin, arroyo Piray-guazú and its tributary arroyo Tigre, arroyo Garuhapé, Aguaray-guazú, Yabebirí, upper río Iguazú, the arroyo Soberbio, San Antonio, San Francisco, Piray-miní and Paraíso; (2) regulations against hunting should be established and fully enforced; (3) an educational campaign should be launched to highlight the enormous importance of the wildlife of the province of Misiones with particular emphasis on the Brazilian Merganser (see Measures Taken).

On the evidence given by Bertoni (1901) and Partridge (1956), Johnson and Chebez (1985) did not recommend captive breeding.

Brazil It is very important to regulate the increasing amount of tourism in the Serra da Canastra National Park (Bartmann 1988), and those pairs breeding outside the park (e.g. Fazenda Boquerão and rio São João; see Distribution) should be afforded protection. A comprehensive study and survey of the birds both here and in the Chapada dos Veadeiros National Park are needed, and a broader investigation of possible sites in appropriate habitat throughout its potential range from Goiás south to the Argentina border is long overdue. Furthermore, the similar habitat requirements of the Brazilian Merganser and the Fasciated Tiger-heron *Tigrisoma fasciatum* (see Yamashita and Valle 1990) suggest that searches where the latter species was recorded in northern Goiás on the rio Piratinga, Formoso municipality (where habitat has great similarities with that in the Chapada dos Veadeiros National Park), would perhaps result in further localities for the mergansers (G. T. de Mattos *in litt.* 1992).

Paraguay Although most of the rivers considered likely to hold populations were visited in 1989, searches are still needed along the following ríos and arroyos: Piraty, Alto Acaray, Pozuelo and Guarapey; the relatively recent sighting of the species on the río Carapá (see Distribution) indicates the need for continued monitoring (it was surveyed without success in 1989) in order to ascertain whether the species may yet survive there (Granizo Tamayo and Hayes in prep). The only chance for the species in the country lies in protecting what little habitat remains, especially along the río Carapá (F. E. Hayes *in litt.* 1991).

REMARKS (1) Meyer de Schauensee (1966, 1982) and thus presumably Blake (1977), Mayr and Cottrell (1979), Sick and Teixeira (1979) and Johnson and Chebez (1985) included the río Paraguay as part of the Brazilian Merganser's range. However, this is not supported by precise localities and was not indicated by earlier reviewers (e.g. Hellmayr and Conover 1948, Partridge 1956) or in recent extensive waterbird surveys (F. E. Hayes *in litt.* 1992). (2) Further details (e.g. exact collecting dates, collectors, age and sex of the specimens plus a map showing collecting localities) can be found in Partridge (1956) and Johnson and Chebez (1985). (3) Two additional specimens, taken at the same locality, were probably collected in 1949 (see Johnson and Chebez 1985). (4) Most specimen labels simply read "arroyo Urugua-í", but exact localities where birds have been reported feeding and nesting are "km 10" and "km 30" eastward from the río Paraná (Partridge 1956). (5) Birds collected from 1947 to 1954 were secured in every month from March to September; also in December. (6) The labels of two specimens in AMNH read: "Puerto Piray, 15 km" and "18 km" respectively; the reverse of the latter explains this as 18 km east of the río Paraná. Date or collector of two additional specimens from the same arroyo is not indicated (Johnson and Chebez 1985). (7) According to Partridge (1956) and Johnson and Chebez (1985), the specimen in question was probably procured on the río Yabebirí (north of Bonpland). (8) A specimen from "Bahia" taken before 1859 (Fisher 1981) was presumably a trade skin originating elsewhere in Brazil. The occurrence of the species in Rio de Janeiro was indicated by Stresemann (1954), but apparently as a guess. (9) De Mattos *et al.* (1985) claimed to have the first observations of the species in the state, but this is mistaken (G. T. de Mattos *in litt.* 1992). (1O) This locality was regarded as uncertain (Mertens and Steinbacher 1955). (11) Bertoni (1901, 1914) referred to "Alto Paraná", presumably meaning the province, although in the former publication he indicated a latitude of 27°S, which corresponds to Itapúa department (where the species was most likely to be found). (12) Data are from the list of specimens provided by Johnson and Chebez (1985) plus specimens in BMNH, FMNH, UNP and YPM. (13) Johnson and Chebez (1985) referred to a lapse of 30 years during which the species was not recorded on the arroyo Urugua-í, evidently unaware of the specimen collected in July 1960 (see Distribution). (14) Von Ihering (1898) thought that the species might occur along the coast, but this has never been shown. It has been suggested that the species's apparent absence from the río Paraná is due to the dorado *Salminus maxillosus*, a serious threat to ducklings but absent from the smaller rivers whose cataracts bar the progress of migratory fish (Giai 1950, Partridge 1956). (15) Extensive information on the species's natural history (including nesting behaviour of adults) can be found in Partridge (1956) and Giai (1950, 1951 and 1976). (16) Argentina could unilaterally place the species on Appendix III, which would automatically prohibit trade out of the country.

GUNDLACH'S HAWK *Accipiter gundlachi* V/R[10]

This secretive raptor, once widespread on Cuba and still found throughout, has become ever rarer with the loss and disturbance of wooded habitats and particularly in response to human persecution (it specializes on birds and is known to take poultry). Five main population centres are known to remain, three for the nominate race in west and central Cuba, two for the race in the east of the island.

DISTRIBUTION Gundlach's Hawk is endemic to Cuba, where it occurs as two distinct subspecies, the nominate in western and central Cuba and *wileyi* in the east (Wotzkow 1991). The following records are organized by and within provinces from west to east (see Remarks 1), and unless otherwise stated coordinates are taken from OG (1963a):

Pinar del Río Mil Cumbres (22°45'N 83°24'W), currently (Wotzkow 1985); Sierra del Rosario, where it was observed in the 1970s (Reynard *et al.* 1987); Los Palacios (22°35'N 83°15'W; see Remarks 2), May and November 1934 (two specimens in AMNH); Cabañas los Pinos, within La Güira National Park, this being a few km north-west of San Diego de los Baños (22°39'N 83°22'W), where a bird was observed in November 1987 (A. Mitchell *in litt.* 1991); San Cristóbal (22°43'S 83°03'W), February 1944 (Wotzkow 1991); Villa Soroa, north-west of Candelaria (22°44'N 82°58'W), where a bird was observed in February 1989 and another in February 1991 (A. Mitchell *in litt.* 1991);

Habana Cayajabos (22°52'N 82°51'W), undated (Wotzkow 1991); Artemisia, May 1934, January, February and April 1935, 1942, March 1944, December 1949 and February 1950 (specimens in AMNH, ANSP and MCZ; also Wotzkow 1991); Hanábana (*sic*) (Habana), from where the type was described in 1860 (AOU 1983); Cojimar (23°10'N 82°18'W), undated (Barbour 1923); near Tapaste (23°02'N 82°08'W), where a single bird was found during 1985 and 1986 (Wotzkow 1991); Santa Bárbara (c.23°04'N 82°07'W, read from ICGC 1978), March 1985 (Wotzkow 1991);

Matanzas (all from the Península de Zapata) "Ciénaga de Zapata", around 1860, nesting (Gundlach 1893); Santo Tomás (22°24'N 81°25'W), undated (O. H. Garrido *in litt.* 1991); Cárdenas (23°02'N 81°12'W), July 1841 (Lembeye 1850); Soplillar (22°17'N 81°09'W), where six nests were reported between 1981 and 1984 (Wotzkow 1986), and April 1985, when two juveniles were examined (Wotzkow 1991); Laguna del Tesoro (22°21'N 81°07'W), currently (Wotzkow 1985); "Boca de Guamá" (untraced, but about half-way between the resort of Guamá, at the south-eastern corner of Laguna del Tesoro and the Bay of Pigs), where a bird was observed in June 1978 (Clements 1979; also J. F. Clements *in litt.* 1991); "Zapata Swamp", where a nest containing young was found in May 1871 (Wotzkow 1986); La Majagua (22°15'N 81°06'W in García *et al.* 1987), between October 1983 and August 1984 (García *et al.* 1987); Los Sábalos (22°15'N 81°05'W in González *et al.* 1990), January 1988 (González *et al.* 1990); Playa Girón (22°04'N 81°02'W), currently (Wotzkow 1985); Los Avalos (untraced but within the Zapata Swamp), where a nest found in April 1985 contained two chicks (Wotzkow 1986);

Cienfuegos Soledad (22°28'N 80°28'W), undated (Bond 1956b); near Cienfuegos, undated (Bond 1963); Laguna de Guanaroca (22°04'N 80°24'W), in 1962 (García undated) and January 1963 (Wotzkow 1991); between Trinidad (21°48'N 79°59'W) and Casilda (see below), January 1963 (Bond 1963);

Sancti Spíritus Casilda, January 1963 (Wotzkow 1991) and currently (Garrido 1985);

Villa Clara Sierra del Escambray (22°14'N 79°54'W), undated (Reynard *et al.* 1987);

Camagüey Cayo Romano, undated (see Wotzkow Alvarez 1988); Cayo Coco (22°30'N 78°25'W), undated (Regalado Ruíz 1981) and October 1973 (Garrido 1973); near Camagüey (the city), recently (Wotzkow 1991); Loma Hato (21°50'N 77°30'W), Cayo Guajaba, in 1984 (Garrido *et al.* 1986); Nuevitas (21°33'S 77°16'W), August 1987 (Wotzkow 1991);

Granma Bartolomé Masó municipality (20°10'N 76°57'W), sometime between 1980 and 1987 (Torres Leyva *et al.* 1988); Pico Verde, Buey Arriba (20°09'N 76°45'W), where a nest containing three chicks was found in February 1985 (Wotzkow 1986), April 1985 and September 1985 (Wotzkow 1991; also Torres Leyva *et al.* 1988); El Quemado (possibly in the area of Pinar Quemado, c.20°07'N 76°43'W, read from ICGC 1978), between 1980 and 1987 (Torres Leyva *et al.* 1988); Nuevo Yao (c.20°11'N 76°43'W, read from ICGC 1978), between 1980 and 1987 (Torres Leyva *et al.* 1988);

Holguín Yaguabo (20°37'N 76°25'W), río Cauto, March 1972 (Wotzkow 1991); Cacocum municipality (20°44'N 76°23'W), sometime between 1980 and 1987 (Torres Leyva *et al.* 1988); Cupecillo (21°06'N 76°11'W) and Floro Pérez (c.21°01'N 76°14'W read from ICGC 1978), sometime between 1980 and 1987 (Torres Leyva *et al.* 1988); near Gibara (21°07'N 76°08'W), where two specimens were secured, one from Finca Santa María in 1962, and at río Gibara in 1963 (Bond 1964; also García undated, Wotzkow 1985 and Reynard *et al.* 1987); Gibara (two undated specimens) (Wotzkow 1991); río Corojal (untraced but near Gibara), where a nest was found in June 1987 (Torres Leyva *et al.* 1988); Rafael Freire municipality (21°02'N 76°00'W), sometime between 1980 and 1987 (Torres Leyva *et al.* 1988); Altos del Puio Mayari (*sic*), untraced (but probably near Mayarí); Cayo Saetía (20°47'N 75°45'W), December 1985 (Llanes Sosa *et al.* 1987; also Wotzkow Alvarez 1988) and sometime between 1980 and 1987 (Torres Leyva *et al.* 1988); La Zoilita, El Culebro and El Palenque, currently (these three localities are on the northern slopes of the Sierra del Cristal, 20°33'N 75°31'W) (Abreu *et al.* 1989); La Zoilita, sometime between between 1980 and 1987 (Torres Leyva *et al.* 1988), March 1988 (Wotzkow 1991); "Buena Vista" Ranch (untraced), May 1987 (two birds collected) (Wotzkow 1991);

Santiago de Cuba Pico Turquino (19°59'N 76°50'W), Sierra Maestra, currently (O. H. Garrido *in litt.* 1991), this presumably being the same as the less precise site given by Reynard *et al.* (1987); "Santiago de Cuba", undated (Wotzkow 1991);

Guantánamo "Guantánamo", February 1889, June 1889 (Wotzkow 1991); Cupeyal (20°35'N 75°11'W), January 1968 (see Wotzkow Alvarez 1988) and from February to March 1985 when a nesting pair was observed (Alayón García 1987); Sierra del Guaso (20°16'N 75°11'W), currently (O. H. Garrido *in litt.* 1991); Las Municiones (La Munición in ICGC 1978, c.7 km north-east of El Manguito, 20°21'N 75°08'W), where a nest containing four eggs was found in February 1985 (Wotzkow 1986, Torres Leyva *et al.* 1988); 3 km south of La Munición, March 1985 (Reynard *et al.* 1987); Sierra de Moa, between 1985 and 1987 (Alayón García et al. 1987); Cuchillas del Toa Biosphere Reserve (20°27'N 74°58'W), e.g. Ojito de Agua, Calentura, Farallones de Moa, April 1986 (Alayón García *et al.* 1987, Reynard *et al.* 1987, Wotzkow 1991, O. H. Garrido *in litt.* 1991); near Baracoa (20°21'N 74°30'W), currently (Reynard *et al.* 1987);

An untraced locality in Cuba is Júcaro, where several undated observations were made (Lembeye 1850). A record from Cayo Cantiles in the Archipiélago de los Canarreos is now attributed to Cooper's Hawk *Accipiter cooperii*; the fact that the species has not even been recorded on the neighbouring Isle of Pines is another reason for doubting this record (Garrido and Schwartz 1969, Buden and Olson 1989).

POPULATION The evidence is conflicting: Gundlach (1861) reported the species to be "rather rare" but "not very rare in the mountains" (Gundlach 1893) and García (undated) wrote that it was fairly common during the nineteenth century; Phillips (1929) considered to be "well on the road to extinction" and Barbour (1943) regarded it as "one of the rarest hawks in the world"; Brown and Amadon (1968) considered the species to have been "always rare" and perhaps "nearly or quite extinct"; Garrido (1967) judged it to be the rarest of Cuban hawks, yet neither he (Garrido

1985) nor Bond (1968) regarded it as to be in danger of extinction. However, it is now accepted that the species was once much more widely distributed and has disappeared from many places where it was perhaps still present 30 years ago (e.g. Habana province, where it could still be found in the vicinity of Artemisia in the 1930s and 1940s) (Wotzkow 1991, O. H. Garrido *in litt.* 1991). L. Fazio *in litt.* (1992) considered it to be "very rare" in Pinar del Río and Oriente provinces. From the information given by Wotzkow (1985), Torres *et al.* (1988), Abreu *et al.* (1989) and in Distribution, the current population is restricted to the following five areas (the first three holding nominate *gundlachi*, the last two the race *wileyi)*: (1) area of Mil Cumbres, Pinar del Río, where three pairs have been estimated; (2) Zapata Swamp, where about 20 pairs are estimated around Playa Girón and Laguna del Tesoro; (3) Sierra del Escambray, Villa Clara (no estimation made); (4) Gibara, south of Holguín (e.g. Cacocum, Yaguabos), Mayarí and Sierra del Cristal (all in Holguín province) and nearby areas in the Sierra del Guasó, Sierra de Moa and Sierra de Toa and Baracoa (Guantánamo province); (5) Granma province, on the northern slopes of Sierra Maestra in the area between Bartolomé Masó, Buey Arriba and El Quemado.

ECOLOGY The secretive Gundlach's Hawk is not considered specialized in its habitat requirements, as it can be found in forest, open woodland, forest borders, swamps, mangroves and mountains below 800 m (Gundlach 1876, Garrido and Schwartz 1969, Garrido 1985, Wiley 1986, Torres Leyva *et al.* 1988, Wotzkow 1991).

It appears to feed exclusively on birds, and among the species known to have fallen its victims are: Northern Bobwhite *Colinus virginianus*, White-crowned Pigeon *Columba leucocephala*, a nighthawk *Chordeiles* sp., doves *Zenaida* spp., Cuban Parrot *Amazona leucocephala*, Red-legged Thrush *Turdus plumbeus* and Cuban Crow *Corvus nasicus*; females (the larger sex) prefer parrots and pigeons, which are mainly hunted in open areas, while males tend to capture the more abundant and mobile doves and thrushes in forest undergrowth (Wotzkow 1986; also Gundlach 1871-1875, Reynard *et al.* 1987). Gundlach's Hawk has also been observed hunting and chasing domestic hens and pigeons on poultry farms, even entering the installations on foot (Wotzkow 1985; also Gundlach 1876).

Breeding occurs from February to June, but chicks have been found in February (Wotzkow 1986, Torres Leyva *et al.* 1988), suggesting that the breeding season could start as early as January. The nest is built in high trees, including júcaro *Bucida buceras*, pine *Pinus* spp., jubilla *Dipholis jubilla*, soplillo *Lysiloma bahamensis*, ocuje *Calophyllum antillarum* and yaba *Andira jamaicensis*, 7-20 m from the ground and situated close to the main trunk below the canopy (Wotzkow 1986, Torres Leyva *et al.* 1988); however, one has been found in a mangrove (Wotzkow 1991). Clutch-size varies from two to four (Wotzkow 1986).

THREATS Gundlach's Hawk has been reported to be a major predator of poultry (Barbour 1923, Abreu *et al.* 1989; see also Ecology), which, although not well documented, may explain the considerable human persecution it suffers (Wiley 1985a, Reynard *et al.* 1987); in the Cupeyal area, farmers reported shooting three birds late in 1967 (Bond 1968). Habitat loss and human disturbance are also affecting the species's population, as it appears to be very sensitive to environmental changes, which in turn can affect the availability of prey (Wotzkow 1986, 1991). The present lack of fuels in Cuba is causing more woodland to be cut (L. Fazio *in litt.* 1992). Wiley (1986) reported that young birds are being taken for captivity or for the international raptor trade.

MEASURES TAKEN Little is known about the security of the species within protected areas in Cuba. The information under distribution, plus a few comments found in the literature, reveal that some of the protected areas (as listed in Wright 1988) may be of value, namely: Sierra

Maestra, Ciénaga de Zapata and Sierra del Cristal National Parks; Cupeyal del Norte and El Sábalo Nature Reserves; Cayo Coco and Cayo Saetía Faunal Refuges, and Baconao, Sierra del Rosario and Cuchillas del Toa Biosphere Reserves.

MEASURES PROPOSED Sierra de Mil Cumbres has been proposed for some form of protection (Wright 1988), which would be likely to benefit the small known population in Pinar del Río. However, the other four main areas for the species, listed at the end of Population, also require careful evaluation, study and management, none of them currently falling within an established protected area. Surveys to identify viable populations in other areas of Cuba are needed, bearing in mind the newly discovered distinctness of birds in eastern Cuba, and detailed studies of the ecology and population dynamics of birds of both races in different habitats would be welcome as a means of increasing confidence in the appropriate measures for the management of the species as a whole; in particular, some illumination of the reasons it is so sensitive to environmental changes when it is so catholic in its choice of habitat would be very valuable. Shooting and trade should be properly penalized (see Wiley 1986).

REMARKS (1) Some localities which were given under old province boundaries have now been included within the present political division of provinces (see ICGC 1978). (2) A. Mitchell *(in litt.* 1992) has pointed out that these specimens may have been collected in the wooded hills of the río Los Palacios nearby San Diego de Los Baños, rather that at Los Palacios (the town), which is surrounded by flat agricultural land and probably was even in 1934.

WHITE-NECKED HAWK *Leucopternis lacernulata* V/R[10]

This raptor occupies primary patches of lowland Atlantic Forest in eastern Brazil, and must be considered threatened owing to its low density and to the highly fragmented and restricted nature of the remaining habitat.

DISTRIBUTION The White-necked Hawk (see Remarks 1) is endemic to the Atlantic Forest region of Brazil, with records from Alagoas and southern Bahia south through eastern Minas Gerais, Espírito Santo, Rio de Janeiro, São Paulo and Paraná to Santa Catarina. In the following account, records are given within states from north to south with coordinates from Paynter and Traylor (1991) unless otherwise stated.

Alagoas An adult female was collected at Usina Sinimbu, 9°55'S 36°08'W, February 1957 (Pinto and de Camargo 1961), and the species was recently observed in the Pedra Talhada forest near Quebrangulo (A. Studer verbally 1992).

Bahia In 1816 the species was recorded on the rio Peruípe, 17°43'S 39°16'W, and specifically at Viçoza, now evidently Nova Viçosa (Wied 1831-1833, Hellmayr and Conover 1949). Four birds were collected at Ilhéus in March, May and September 1944 (specimens in MZUSP). A pair was displaying in June 1990 in Monte Pascoal National Park (Gardner and Gardner 1990b).

Minas Gerais Records are from: the rio Jequitinhonha valley in the far north-east, recently (M. A. Andrade *in litt.* 1988); Serra do Cipó National Park, 1980 (A. Brandt *in litt.* 1987); rio Piracicaba, close to its confluence with the rio Doce, September 1940 (Pinto 1952, Pinto and de Camargo 1961; specimen in MZUSP); rio Doce, September 1906 (Pinto 1938); Rio Doce State Park, recently (M. A. Andrade *in litt.* 1988); Matas do Tororo, 25 km north of Raul Soares, September 1957 (specimen in LACM); and rio Cágado, 22°02'S 43°09'W (in OG 1963b), an affluent of the upper rio da Pomba (Burmeister 1856; see Remarks 2). An untraced locality is Piedade de Ponte Nova, where two birds were seen in 1979 (A. Brandt *in litt.* 1987).

Espírito Santo The species was probably seen at Fazenda São Joaquim (formerly Klabin), now the Córrego Grande Biological Reserve, October 1986 (Gonzaga *et al.* 1987). Certain records are from: Sooretama Biological Reserve, in recent years (Scott and Brooke 1985, J. F. Pacheco *in litt.* 1986, B. M. Whitney *in litt.* 1991, TAP) and adjacent CVRD Linhares Reserve, also in recent years (Scott 1985, B. M. Whitney *in litt.* 1987, 1991, D. F. Stotz *in litt.* 1988); Lagoa Juparanã, November 1929 (specimen in AMNH); Pau Gigante (now Ibiraçu), undated (von Ihering and von Ihering 1907) and October 1940 (specimen in MZUSP); Santa Teresa, January 1941 (specimen in MNRJ); Augusto Ruschi (Nova Lombardia) Biological Reserve, since 1986, ranging up to 900 m (Gonzaga *et al.* 1987, C. E. Carvalho *in litt.* 1987, B. M. Whitney *in litt.* 1991); Chaves, near Santa Leopoldina, September 1942 (specimen in MZUSP); and the rio Jucu estuary, December 1815 (Wied 1831-1833).

Rio de Janeiro Records are from: Fazenda União, near Rocha Leão, August 1989, July, September and November 1990 (J. F. Pacheco *in litt.* 1992); foothills of the Serra de Madureira, Gericinó massif, 1980 (J. F. Pacheco *in litt.* 1986); Desengano State Park and adjacent areas (rio Mocotó, near Campos; Agulha, near Santa Maria Madalena; Morumbeca do Imbé), recently (C. E. Carvalho *in litt.* 1987, J. F. Pacheco *in litt.* 1987); Cantagalo, last century (von Ihering 1900a); Poço das Antas Biological Reserve, late 1981 (Scott and Brooke 1985); Serra dos Órgãos National Park and foothills in the area, recently (J. F. Pacheco *in litt.* 1986, C. E. Carvalho *in litt.* 1987); Santo Aleixo, undated (Gonzaga 1986); Xerém, several times recently (J. F. Pacheco *in litt.* 1986, C. E. Carvalho *in litt.* 1987); sporadic ones in or around Rio de Janeiro city, i.e. Serra do Tinguá near Nova Iguaçu, 1981 (J. F. Pacheco *in litt.* 1986), Jacarepaguá, August 1956 (specimen in LACM), Parque da Cidade, undated (Mitchell 1957), Estrada das Paineiras, September 1959 (Sick and Pabst 1968), Horta Florestal next to Tijuca National Park, recently (J. F. Pacheco *in litt.* 1986, C. E. Carvalho *in litt.* 1987) and Gávea, August 1967 (Aguirre and Aldrighi 1983); Saí ("Registo do Sai"), 22°56'S 44°00'W, April 1818 (von Pelzeln 1868-1871); Fazenda Patrimônio, Mangaratiba, 1986 (J. F. Pacheco *in litt.* 1986); Angra dos Reis (at Fazenda Japuhyba), October 1945 (specimen in MNRJ); and Parati, 100 m, October 1990 (B. M. Whitney *in litt.* 1991).

São Paulo Records (see Remarks 3) are from: Ubatuba, 50 m, October 1991 (J. L. Rowlett and B. M. Whitney *in litt.* 1991); Boracéia Biological Station, 23°39'S 45°54'W, 800 m, recently (D. F. Stotz *in litt.* 1988); suburbs and outskirts of São Paulo, in the Serra da Cantareira, Horto Florestal, July 1952 (specimen in MZUSP), at Ipiranga, March 1935 (Pinto 1938) and at Vila Ema, March 1947 (specimen in MZUSP); Icapara, 24°41'S 47°25'W, July 1970 (two specimens in MNHN); Iguape, April 1900 (von Ihering and von Ihering 1907, Pinto 1938); rio Ribeira estuary, July 1964 (specimen in MZUSP); Ilha do Cardoso State Park, recently (D. F. Stotz *in litt.* 1988, P. Martuscelli *in litt.* 1991).

Paraná The only records appear to be from: Santa Cruz Forest Reserve, 25°35'S 48°35'W, July 1946; and Represa de Guaricana, 25°43'S 48°50'W, March 1985 (Straube 1991, whence coordinates; Bornschein and Straube 1991).

Santa Catarina There are specimen and sight records from around Joinville: Hellmayr and Conover (1949) mentioned two skins, a bird was seen at Salto do Piraí, 8 km north-north-west of Vila Nova, near Joinville, July 1991 (M. Pearman *in litt.* 1991: see Measures Proposed), and another was over the rio Mississipi (*sic*) near Joinville, December 1989 (Bornschein and Straube 1991). The only other record is from Blumenau (von Berlepsch 1873-1874).

POPULATION Although once described as "common in many areas" (Wied 1831-1833), "not really rare" (Burmeister 1856), and not listed as threatened by Sick (1969, 1972) or Sick and Teixeira (1979; see Remarks 4), the relative paucity of records for this bird of prey suggest a species now in low numbers scattered between isolated forest patches, well deserving to be considered "evidently rare and local" (Brown and Amadon 1968). Survey work at Poço das Antas and Sooretama reserves concluded that it was uncommon and rare respectively (Scott and Brooke 1985), although separate work at the latter site led to its classification as uncommon (TAP). A very conjectural assessment based on one and a pair of soaring birds in the right weather and season at CVRD's Forest Reserve was that less than 30 pairs could be expected to be present (B. M. Whitney *in litt.* 1987).

ECOLOGY The White-necked Hawk seems largely confined to lowland forest (see records under Distribution), with the Mantled Hawk *Leucopternis polionota* tending to replace it at higher altitudes and further inland within the Atlantic Forest region (see Remarks 4); however, some overlap certainly occurs (Sick 1985) and indeed the latter species penetrates to sea-level (Straube and Bornschein 1991), possibly on a seasonal basis, and the ecological separation between the two species remains entirely obscure; the two have been recorded together at Serra dos Órgãos, Morumbeca, Agulha, Xerém and Tinguá in Rio de Janeiro (J. F. Pacheco *in litt.* 1987) and Guaricana in Paraná (F. C. Straube *in litt.* 1987). Habitat is the mid-storey of primary forest (D. F. Stotz *in litt.* 1989), although birds will perch atop dead trees for long periods (Wied 1831-1833, Burmeister 1856). In Ilha do Cardoso State Park they are restricted to the sand-plain forest, making occasional movements to the mainland (P. Martuscelli *in litt.* 1991). Food has been given as reptiles, mammals, birds and insects (Mitchell 1957), large spiders, Orthoptera, beetles and ants (Brown and Amadon 1968), and beetles, spiders and small snakes, taken on the ground (Sick 1985). That the species might tend to take invertebrates as a staple is suggested by the contents of three stomachs of specimens in MZUSP, respectively: several spiders and insects; insects; a large quantity of diverse insects. Moreover, Martuscelli (1991) observed a bird follow an army ant swarm and take a large nocturnal gastropod *Megalobulimus paranaguensis* flushed by the ants. There are no breeding data.

THREATS Destruction of forest within this species's range has been extremely serious, such that only small fragments of the original biome remain (for a full discussion see Sick and Teixeira 1979). Habitat loss is the threat in Minas Gerais (M. A. Andrade *in litt.* 1988). In São Paulo in areas of forest clearance it is further persecuted as a chicken stealer (P. Martuscelli *in litt.* 1991).

MEASURES TAKEN The White-necked Hawk is protected under Brazilian law (Bernardes *et al.* 1990). It has been recorded from Pedra Talhada Biological Reserve in Alagoas, Monte Pascoal National Park in Bahia, Sooretama Biological Reserve and the adjacent CVRD Linhares Reserve, Augusto Ruschi (Nova Lombardia) Biological Reserve, all in Espírito Santo, Rio Doce State Park in Minas Gerais, Desengano State Park, Poço das Antas Biological Reserve and on the fringes of Serra dos Órgãos, Tijuca and Bocaina National Parks in Rio de Janeiro, Boracéia Biological Reserve and Ilha do Cardoso State Park in São Paulo and Santa Cruz Forest Reserve in Paraná. Despite this array of apparent havens, the species probably lives at such low densities and the areas in question are so far apart that they offer no guarantee of long-term security.

MEASURES PROPOSED Fuller surveys for this and other threatened species of bird need to be undertaken in, for example, the Jequitinhonha valley in Minas Gerais and the Serra do Mar in São Paulo, Paraná and, perhaps especially, Santa Catarina, an ornithologically much neglected state which may yet prove to harbour important populations of many Atlantic Forest species. Biological studies of the species are likely to prove very difficult, given its evidently retiring nature, but ornithologists should be on the alert for any nests, so that chance discoveries can be followed up immediately by intensive investigation. The tower in the CVRD Forest Reserve (see, e.g., Collar 1986) offers an opportunity to study forest raptor display and dispersion (see Population), and the White-necked Hawk would be the key focus of such a study. Consideration of a reserve at Salto do Piraí in Santa Catarina has been suggested as this is the only locality in the world for Kaempfer's Tody-tyrant *Hemitriccus kaempferi* (see Measures Proposed in relevant account).

REMARKS (1) This is apparently a poor name, since the bird is no more white-necked than the sympatric Mantled Hawk; "Band-tailed Mantled Hawk" has been claimed as far more diagnostic (Mitchell 1957). (2) Paynter and Traylor (1991) listed rio Cágado as untraced, although it is given in OG (1963b); Hellmayr and Conover (1949) place rio Cágado and rio da Pomba together, as if two localities were involved. (3) E. O. Willis *in litt.* (1986) mentioned this species from two unspecified localities in the state. (4) It is curious that Sick (1969, 1972) and Sick and Teixeira (1972) listed the Mantled Hawk as threatened when this bird has a much more extensive range (into Paraguay and Argentina: King 1978-1979) and, by virtue of its occupation of more upland areas, enjoys considerably more habitat security; thus for example in São Paulo it had been found in 12 forest areas as against the White-neck's two (E. O. Willis *in litt.* 1986) and in Paraná it has been found to be fairly abundant and capable of using plantations (Straube and Bornschein 1991).

GREY-BACKED HAWK *Leucopternis occidentalis* E[2]

This rare hawk inhabits deciduous and evergreen forests in western Ecuador and immediately adjacent north-west Peru, where it is threatened by rampant habitat destruction; it retains large populations at only a few sites, notably Machalilla National Park in Ecuador and Tumbes National Forest in Peru.

DISTRIBUTION The Grey-backed Hawk (see Remarks 1) is restricted to western Ecuador and immediately adjacent north-west Peru: in western Ecuador it has been found on the coastal hill range in Esmeraldas, Manabí and Guayas provinces, in the western lowlands in Pichincha and Los Ríos provinces, and on the Andean slopes in the south-west in Azuay, El Oro and Loja provinces; in north-west Peru, the only confirmed records come from Tumbes department. Unless otherwise stated coordinates in the following account are from Paynter and Traylor (1977), Stephens and Traylor (1983), Best and Clarke (1991), Williams and Tobias (1991), or read from IGM (1989).

Ecuador Records in the coastal range are from: (*Esmeraldas*) Cerro Mutiles (Reserva Jardín Tropical "Luis Vargas Torres"), not located but on a ridge south-east of Esmeraldas, east of río Esmeraldas (sighting in January 1991: TAP); Cabeceras de Bilsa, c.100-300 m, east of Bilsa and north-east of Muisne, i.e. at c.0°42'N 79°52'W (sightings in January 1991: TAP); (*Manabí*) Filo de Monos, 47 (road) km north-west of El Carmen, i.e. at c.0°05'S 79°51'W (specimen in WFVZ collected in July 1988); Mongoya, 200 m, presumably near the river of the same name at c.0°10'S 79°50'W (two specimens in BMNH collected in July 1942; see Remarks 2); Cordillera de Balzar, at c.0°55'S 79°55'W (specimen in BMNH collected before March 1880; see Remarks 3); Cerro Achi, 600 m, at 1°23'S 80°39'W (sighting in January 1991: TAP); Machalilla National Park, on the coast near the Guayas border, at c.1°35'S 80°46'W (recent sightings: King 1978-1979; also sightings of at least two pairs on Cerro San Sebastián in 1991: TAP, R. S. Ridgely *in litt.* 1991); (*Guayas*) Quebrada Canoa, Cerro Blanco reserve, Cordillera de Chongón, at c.2°09'S 80°03'W, c.14 km west of Guayaquil (a possibly nesting pair sighted in January 1991: TAP).

Records in the western lowlands are from: (*Pichincha*–see Remarks 4) Santo Domingo de los Colorados, 490 m, at 0°15'S 79°09'W (given as 0°13'S 79°06'W on label of specimen in AMNH collected in July 1914); Río Palenque reserve (200 m), near the border with Manabí and Los Ríos, at c.0°30'S 79°30'W (King 1978-1979, coordinates and altitude from Leck 1979; species apparently no longer present: see Population); (*Los Ríos*) Valencia, 100 m, (c.15 km north-east of) Quevedo, at 0°56'S 79°21'W (specimen in ANSP collected in October 1950); Quevedo, 100 m, at 1°02'S 79°29'W (specimen in BMNH collected before 1884); Jauneche reserve, at 1°10'S 79°30'W, recently (TAP).

On the Andean slopes in the south-west there are records from: (*Azuay*) Manta Real, at c.2°30'S 79°17'W (singles sighted in July and August 1991: TAP, R. S. Ridgely *in litt.* 1991); above Naranjal, at c.2°35-45'S 79°30-35'W (King 1978-1979); (*El Oro*) Uzhcurumi, 3°19'S 79°36'W (several noted in February 1991: Best 1992); 9.5 km by road west of Piñas (near Buenaventura), 900-950 m, at 3°40'S 79°42'W (Robbins and Ridgely 1990: two specimens in ANSP and MECN collected in June and July 1985, and several subsequent sightings, for which see Population); San Pablo, east of Zaruma, 3°41'S 79°33'W, at 1,200 m (birds seen during September 1991: Williams and Tobias 1991); "Las Piñas, 1,100 m, Alamor range, Loja" (Chapman 1926; specimen in AMNH collected in September 1921), not located by Paynter and Traylor (1977) but judged here to be the Piñas in El Oro, at 3°40'S 79°42'W; Salvias, 1,050 m, at 3°47'S 79°21'W (Chapman 1926; specimen in AMNH collected in August 1920); (*Loja*) Quebrada Cebollal, 945 m, at 3°55'S 80°03'W (Chapman 1926; specimen in USNM collected in September 1921); east of Vicentino, 1,400 m, at c.3°56'S 79°55'W (at least one pair sighted in

February 1991: Best 1992); between Vicentino and Alamor, 1,200-1,400 m (at least two pairs sighted in February 1991: Best 1992); El Tigre (untraced), on the Arenillas–Alamor road, 600 m (one bird in September 1991: Williams and Tobias 1991); near Quebrada Las Vegas (near Alamor), 3°59'S 79°57'W (birds seen calling, including three together in August 1991: Williams and Tobias 1991); Alamor, 1,385 m, at 4°02'S 80°02'W (Chapman 1926; specimen in AMNH collected in October 1920); Tierra Colorada, 1,400-1,850 m, at 4°02'S 79°57'W (one pair sighted in February 1991: Best 1992); Guainche (between Alamor and Celica), 975 m (Chapman 1926; specimen in AMNH collected in August 1921; also sighting of a pair in March 1989 at 4°05'S 79°58'W: Rahbek *et al.* 1989; and sighting of at least one pair at 1,600-1,800 m in February 1991: Best 1992); on the Alamor–Celica road, at 4°09'S 79°50'W, 1,900 m (pair seen in March 1989: Bloch *et al.* 1991); Celica, 2,100 m, at 4°07'S 79°59'W (Chapman 1926; specimen in AMNH collected in September 1920; also daily sightings of several at 1,900-2,100 m west of Celica in August 1989: R. S. Ridgely *in litt.* 1989); Puyango, 300 m, at c.3°52'S 80°05'W (Chapman 1926; specimen in AMNH collected in October 1921).

Peru Records come from June and early July 1979, late February and early March 1986, and late July 1988 at El Caucho and Campo Verde, Tumbes department, at 3°49'S 80°17'W and 3°51'S 80°11'W respectively, in the hills between these localities, and at Pampa de Hospital 24 km to the north-west (Wiedenfeld *et al.* 1985, M. Kessler *in litt.* 1988, Parker *et al.* 1989). A record of the species from above San José de Lourdes in the extreme southern part of Cordillera del Condor (Robbins *et al.* 1987) is the only report of the species east of the Andes, and is now doubted by M. B. Robbins and R. S. Ridgely (R. S. Ridgely *per* B. J. Best *in litt.* 1992).

POPULATION As 90% or more of lowland Ecuador where the species formerly occurred is now deforested, a great decline must have taken place, and the species is now confined to only a few areas (R. S. Ridgely *in litt.* 1989), and similar levels of deforestation have doubtless affected the species's range in Peru. In the following account, evidence is presented from north to south.

Ecuador This hawk was found to be uncommon at Cabeceras de Bilsa, Esmeraldas, in January 1991 (TAP). In the Machalilla National Park, Manabí, some 8-9 birds were seen during four days in 1978 (R. S. Ridgely *in litt.* 1989), and in January 1991 the species was again found to be fairly common (TAP), with at least two pairs on Cerro San Sebastián during the year (TAP, R. S. Ridgely *in litt.* 1991). The species was formerly "not rare" at the Río Palenque reserve, Pichincha (M. Marin *per* M. B. Robbins *in litt.* 1988); however, it has not been seen there recently (P. Greenfield *in litt.* 1989), and there may in fact be no reliable records since 1977 (R. S. Ridgely *in litt.* 1989). There are no recent records from Los Ríos (see Distribution), and only single birds were recorded in Azuay during July and August 1991 (see Distribution). In El Oro, several birds were noted at Uzhcurumi in February 1991 (Best 1991); on the slope 8-10 km west of Piñas (near Buenaventura), numbers seem to be largely unchanged since 1985, despite further habitat destruction (R. S. Ridgely *in litt.* 1989), with five or more (including two pairs and a presumed immature bird) seen in June and July 1985 (Robbins and Ridgely 1990), 3-4 seen there in August 1988 and April 1989 (P. Greenfield *in litt.* 1989), two presumed pairs of adults present in March 1990 (B. M. Whitney *in litt.* 1991), two presumed pairs in February–March 1991 (Best 1992), several pairs present in September 1991 (Williams and Tobias 1991), with one, one and four birds being noted there on consecutive days in January 1992 (G. Kirwan and T. Marlow *in litt.* 1992); slightly further east at San Pablo, a pair was seen daily during September 1991 (Williams and Tobias 1991). In Loja almost all recent records come from the Vicentino–Alamor–Celica area: one pair east of Vicentino in February 1991 (Best 1992), two pairs between Vicentino and Alamor (including one in Quebrada Las Vegas) in February 1991 (Best 1992), one pair at Quebrada Las Vegas in August 1991 (Williams and Tobias 1991), a pair at Tierra Colorado in February 1991

(Best 1992), one pair between Alamor and Celica in March 1989 (Bloch *et al.* 1991), with a pair in March 1989 and at least one pair in February 1991 at Guainche (Rahbek *et al.* 1989, Best 1992), daily sightings of several in August 1989 west of Celica (R. S. Ridgely *in litt.* 1989), and a pair displaying 5 km north-west of Celica in February 1991 (Best 1992).

In its small Peruvian range the species is "uncommon" (Parker *et al.* 1982) or rare (Wiedenfeld *et al.* 1985), M. Kessler (*in litt.* 1988) recording only two singles and a pair during a six-day survey in Tumbes National Forest during late February and early March 1986, and Parker *et al.* (1989) reported finding two pairs and a subadult, 15 and 5 km south-west and 5 km north-east of El Caucho in late July 1988.

ECOLOGY The Grey-backed Hawk inhabits deciduous and evergreen forests, mainly at 100-1,400 m, but locally (as around Celica) as high as 2,100 m (Brown and Amadon 1968, Meyer de Schauensee 1970, Blake 1977, R. S. Ridgely *in litt.* 1989). The preferred habitat was probably moist evergreen forest (as described by Dodson *et al.* 1985, and Dodson and Gentry 1991), a forest type now restricted to a few small patches in the río Guayas basin and north on the slopes of the coastal mountains to the east of Esmeraldas. The species avoids drier areas such as Tambo Negro (Best 1991), and appears to rely on more humid areas than many other Tumbesian endemics (Williams and Tobias 1991). In Peru it has been recorded in both low-elevation (500 m) deciduous forest (dominated by *Ceiba trichistandra*), as well as in semi-deciduous *Cavanillesia platanifolia* dominated forest at 750 m (Parker *et al.* 1989), but in Ecuador most recent sightings are from evergreen moist forest and wet forest on the lower slopes of the Andes (Piñas) (P. Greenfield *in litt.* 1989). Between Alamor and Celica it survives in very scattered, fragmented and disturbed forest patches (R. S. Ridgely *in litt.* 1989, Best 1992), this area being described as having 30-40% forest cover, 50% of which is probably secondary in nature (Bloch *et al.* 1991). Birds occur singly, in pairs or small groups of 3-4, singles or loose pairs, often perched quietly in the mid-upper levels of large open trees (both within forest and in cleared agricultural areas with scattered tall trees) as is typical of other members of the genus, but unlike those species (and like White Hawk *Leucopternis albicollis*) it often soars, sometimes to considerable heights (Wiedenfeld *et al.* 1985, M. Kessler *in litt.* 1988, P. Greenfield *in litt.* 1989, R. S Ridgely *in litt.* 1989, Robbins and Ridgely 1990, Best 1992).

In the Alamor–Celica area, birds were seen occasionally to sally short distances within and above the canopy, although none was seen actively hunting (Best 1991). One bird in Peru was seen carrying a 14 cm long teiid lizard (Parker *et al.* 1989), and another a snake (R. S. Ridgely *in litt.* 1989). A bird near Quebrada Las Vegas was carrying a 30-40 cm snake, and another took an Ecuadorian Thrush *Turdus maculirostris* in the bottom shelf of a mist-net (Williams and Tobias 1991). A recently collected female (specimen in ANSP) had crab, beetle (Scarabidae) and *Conocephalus* katydid (Tettigoniidae) remains in the stomach (Robbins and Ridgely 1990), and a male (in MECN) collected at the same site a few days later had eaten two small rodents and a freshwater crab *Pseudotelphusa* sp. (J. C. Mathéus *in litt.* 1989). The latter specimen was collected in a small remnant of humid forest at 900 m, where it sat in the sun near the road in an open area: others seen at this site were observed fishing crabs in a brook, or soaring high above the forest (J. C. Mathéus *in litt.* 1989, Robbins and Ridgely 1990). One or two individuals that regularly perched on low branches overhanging forest streams in steep ravines (on Cerro San Sebastián and Cerro Blanco) were apparently attracted to large numbers of small frogs *Colostethus* sp. and *Leptodactylus* sp. concentrated around small pools (TAP).

As with many species endemic to this region, breeding apparently takes place during the rainy season from December to April: a pair circling noisily just above the canopy at El Caucho, in March 1986, was possibly nesting (M. Kessler *in litt.* 1988), as was a pair in the Cordillera de Chongón in January 1991 (TAP). One of two birds between Alamor and Vicentino was seen carrying nest-material in February 1991 (Best 1992, NK). Nearby, at Celica, also in February 1991, a pair was seen involved in aerial display (Best 1991), but by August and September of that year (in the Celica–Alamor area) display activity was virtually absent, although two birds were seen calling during aerial play (Williams and Tobias 1991). A presumed immature was seen near Piñas in June 1985, and a female taken there at the same time was sexually inactive (Robbins and Ridgely 1990).

THREATS The dry and moist forest habitats of this and numerous additional endemic bird species in western Ecuador and adjacent north-west Peru are among the most threatened of Neotropical habitats, facing near-total destruction (Dodson and Gentry 1991). Only a few small and widely scattered patches of (mostly degraded) tall forest survive, one of the largest surviving below 500 m being the Jauneche reserve of only 130 ha (TAP). A few dry and moist forest endemics also range into adjacent wet forests on the lower Andean slopes and north as far as Esmeraldas, but that forest type is also threatened within Ecuador. Throughout western Ecuador moist lowland forest covered about 32,000 km^2 (40%) in 1958, but only 1,500 km^2 (4%) in 1988: dry forest covered about 28,000 km^2 (35%) in 1958, but a mere 200 km^2 (less than 1%) in 1988 (Dodson and Gentry 1991). Between Alamor and Celica the area has been described as comprising highly disturbed, scattered and disturbed forest patches, with just 30-40% forest cover, 50% of which is apparently secondary in nature (R. S. Ridgely *in litt.* 1989, Bloch *et al.* 1991, Best 1992), and habitat destruction is continuing rapidly (NK).

A few larger islands of moist forest persist in the coastal cordillera of Manabí, as at 500-700 m in Machililla National Park (which is, however, ineffectively protected, and only part of which holds suitable habitat: see below), and even as far north as Cerro Mutiles near Esmeraldas city, but all remnants of this habitat are being eroded away or otherwise degraded (TAP, A. Gentry verbally 1991). The Machalilla National Park suffers from the activities of numerous families living within its boundaries (TAP, R. S. Ridgely *in litt.* 1991), and there is little other than its remoteness to protect the Tumbes National Forest in Peru (M. Kessler verbally 1991). Floristically similar forests to those in south-west Ecuador can be found on the lower Andean slopes in Piura and Lambeyeque, Peru: these are important for a number of the other threatened endemics to this region, and are also gravely threatened (see Threats under Grey-breasted Flycatcher *Lathrotriccus griseipectus*).

In addition to rampant deforestation throughout this densely settled region (south-west Ecuador and north-west Peru), further habitat degradation is caused by considerable trampling of the undergrowth by livestock and clearance of bamboo (by local people) for pack-animal food: this especially affects undergrowth inhabitants such as the threatened Blackish-headed Spinetail *Synallaxis tithys*, Henna-hooded Foliage-gleaner *Hylocryptus erythrocephalus*, Rufous-necked Foliage-gleaner *Syndactyla ruficollis*, and Grey-headed Antbird *Myrmeciza griseiceps* (Parker *et al.* 1985, Best and Clarke 1991), but also leads to the general deterioration of the remnant forest patches and thus presumably influences all threatened species.

MEASURES TAKEN Small but perhaps significant populations of the Grey-backed Hawk occur in only two relatively large protected areas, the Machalilla National Park and the Tumbes National Forest (and possibly also in the adjacent Cerros de Amotape National Park). The species has been reported from several very small reserves such as Río Palenque, Jauneche, and Cerro Blanco, none of which is large enough to support more than a few pairs: it also occurs in the small "Luis Vargas Torres" reserve in Esmeraldas (see Distribution).

The coverage of protected areas in western Ecuador and north-west Peru is far from adequate (as is the degree to which they are protected), considering the large number of endemic (including 17 threatened) bird species reliant on the region's specialized forest types. The following (from north to south) is a list of the formally protected areas that harbour many of the threatened species endemic to the region (see Measures Proposed for a list of the threatened species recorded at each site): none (except perhaps the Jauneche reserve) appears to receive adequate protection (Dodson and Gentry 1991):

Ecuador (1) Reserva Jardín Tropical Luis Vargas Torres (Cerro Mutiles), east of Esmeraldas city; (2) Machalilla National Park (55,000 ha: IUCN 1992; 0-800 m), which remains ineffectively established, suffering throughout from the activities of numerous families living (indeed owning the land) within its boundaries (Ridgely 1981a, R. S. Ridgely *in litt.* 1991, TAP); (3) Centro Científico Río Palenque, a 167 ha reserve of which only 87 ha is mature forest (NK); (4) Cerro Blanco Protected Forest, in the Cordillera de Chongón (2,000 ha; from 0-500 m), the land being donated by the Cemento Nacional company (sometimes referred to as the "Reserva Cemento Nacional", and run with the involvement of Fundación Natura (C. Strang *in litt.* 1991); (5) Jauneche reserve, El Oro (130 ha), which is apparently well protected (Dodson and Gentry 1991: see above), and owned and operated by the University of Guayaquil as a biological research station (Best 1992); (6) Arenillas Military Reserve, a large tract of forest controlled by the army between Arenillas and Huaquillas (R. S. Ridgely *in litt.* 1992);

Peru (7) Tumbes National Forest, recently renamed Reserva de la Biosfera del Noroeste Peruano (75,100 ha: IUCN 1992); and (8) Cerros de Amotape National Park (91,300 ha; 200-1,600 m) (IUCN 1992): these latter two adjacent protected areas encompass the largest remaining tracts of deciduous and moist forest west of the Andes, but they receive only meagre protection; both are far from secure, and are ultimately threatened with habitat destruction (M. Kessler verbally 1991, TAP).

MEASURES PROPOSED Western Ecuador and adjacent north-west Peru (the Tumbesian centre of endemism) is a critically important region for conservation, with an exceptionally high rate of floristic endemism (Dodson and Gentry 1991); no fewer than 48 species of bird are restricted to it (ICBP 1992, Crosby *et al.* in prep.), 13 of which appear in the following list of 17 considered to be threatened: Grey-backed Hawk, White-winged Guan *Penelope albipennis*, Bearded Guan *P. barbata*, Ochre-bellied Dove *Leptotila ochraceiventris*, El Oro Parakeet *Pyrrhura orcesi*, Esmeraldas Woodstar *Acestura berlepschi*, Little Woodstar *A. bombus*, Blackish-headed Spinetail *Synallaxis tithys*, Rufous-necked Foliage-gleaner *Syndactyla ruficollis*, Henna-hooded Foliage-gleaner *Hylocryptus erythrocephalus*, Grey-headed Antbird *Myrmeciza griseiceps*, Grey-breasted Flycatcher *Lathrotriccus griseipectus*, Pacific Royal Flycatcher *Onychorhynchus occidentalis*, Ochraceous Attila *Attila torridus*, Slaty Becard *Pachyramphus spodiurus*, Pale-headed Brush-finch *Atlapetes pallidiceps* and Saffron Siskin *Carduelis siemiradskii* (the attila and becard are in fact essentially endemic to this region, but were for various reasons omitted from the analysis in ICBP 1992).

A suggestion presented by Dodson and Gentry (1991) for the conservation of the endemic flora in this region also holds true for the avifauna: there is a desperate need for the identification and survey of all forest remnants be accomplished as soon as possible, using satellite imagery and overflights for "ground-truthing" (it is parenthetically to be noted, as a measure already taken, that several important surveys – the projects led by B. J. Best and R. Williams – directly resulted from measures proposed in earlier drafts of species accounts in this book). Further information on the distributional limits, potential seasonal movements and behavioural ecology (including the extent to which species can tolerate habitat degradation and disturbance) for each of the species mentioned above is also requisite. However, despite these exigencies, it is already clear that various areas are vitally important for the conservation of these threatened (and endemic) species: some are already formally (or privately) protected (see Measures Taken), but others have recently been identified as having concentrations of the threatened species, and their protection must therefore be of the highest priority. Further initiatives, specific to each of these areas, are given below (where applicable), along with the threatened species known to occur there (the requirements of individual species are discussed under the relevant accounts); all of these areas require further work, and those already designated as reserves need more adequate protection, and preferably some expansion in size to incorporate any remaining forest that exists adjacent to their boundaries.

Río Palenque holds: Little Woodstar, Grey-breasted Flycatcher, Ochraceous Attila, Slaty Becard.

Machililla National Park holds: Grey-backed Hawk, Ochre-bellied Dove, Esmeraldas Woodstar, Little Woodstar, Blackish-headed Spinetail, Henna-hooded Foliage-gleaner, Grey-breasted Flycatcher, Pacific Royal Flycatcher, Ochraceous Attila, Saffron Siskin. This park is possibly (with perhaps the exception the Tumbes National Forest) the single most important site for the threatened species mentioned above, and deserves far more careful protection from the Ecuadorian authorities than is currently being given (R. S. Ridgely *in litt.* 1991). Effective protection of Machalilla National Park, the only protected area where the Esmeraldas Woodstar is known to occur, should be ensured. Ideally, a research station should be set up as a centre for studies and activities within the park, but there also a need for more wardens with powers to stop illegal settling, hunting and deforestation (B. J. Best *in litt.* 1991). Maintaining the integrity of the small areas of moist forest near the coast just south of this park should also be a priority, and the more extensive tracts of forest on the higher ridges inside the park (e.g. Cerro San Sebastián) should receive immediate attention. People with rights to part of the land in Machalilla National Park should be compensated for ceding these rights and either moved elsewhere or employed in the management of the park; as an immediate measure, they should be restrained from clearing additional areas of forest and from allowing their livestock to roam freely through the forest, especially that of Cerro San Sebastián.

Cerro Blanco Protected Forest and Cordillera de Chongón holds: Grey-backed Hawk, Ochre-bellied Dove, Blackish-headed Spinetail, Grey-breasted Flycatcher, Saffron Siskin. There is a proposal from Fundación Natura to create a 2,000 ha buffer-zone around the Cerro Blanco reserve, involving other landowners and reforestation schemes (C. Strang *in litt.* 1991); with its close proximity to Guayaquil (c.15 km), it would also be an ideal area for an educational and interpretive centre. Additional tracts of dry and moist forest should be identified, surveyed and protected in some way (e.g. as carefully managed extractive reserves, as well as watershed management areas).

Jauneche reserve holds: Grey-backed Hawk, Grey-breasted Flycatcher, Pacific Royal Flycatcher, Ochraceous Attila.

Manta Real on the Pacific slope of Azuay (near the border with Cañar) at 300-1,000 m, is currently in the process of being protected (P. Greenfield *in litt.* 1990) and holds: Grey-backed Hawk, El Oro Parakeet, Grey-breasted Flycatcher, Pacific Royal Flycatcher, Ochraceous Attila, Slaty Becard. Fairly large but diminishing blocks of forest remain along the lower slopes of the Andes in the Cordillera de Molletura, south of Manta Real in Azuay (TAP); these are in urgent need of survey and some form of protection.

Arenillas Military Reserve holds: Blackish-headed Spinetail and probably Slaty Becard, but should be searched for the presence of White-winged Guan and other species.

Cordillera de Chilla (incorporating the west slope from Uzhcurumi 30 km south to Piñas, the important forest areas west of Piñas and also the wooded ravines to the east of Piñas) holds: Grey-backed Hawk, Bearded Guan, Ochre-bellied Dove, El Oro Parakeet, Rufous-necked Foliage-gleaner, Grey-breasted Flycatcher, Pacific Royal Flycatcher, Ochraceous Attila. In the late 1980s, just west of Piñas, an extensive tract of relatively untouched forest stretched out to the north, although in all other directions the forest was either in small isolated patches or absent: forest to the south and towards Piñas had long since been denuded, but downslope deforestation appeared to have occurred more recently (Robbins and Ridgely 1990). The Cordillera de Chilla has apparently only 10 patches of habitat (totalling 400 ha) suitable for the Bearded Guan (see relevant account), and quite clearly all of these must be targeted for immediate protection.

Sabanilla (10 km below the town, and 20 km by road north of Zapotillo) holds: Little Woodstar, Blackish-headed Spinetail, Henna-hooded Foliage-gleaner, Grey-breasted Flycatcher, Saffron Siskin, and other rare endemics listed in the equivalent section under Saffron Siskin; the site seems ideal for the as-yet unrecorded Ochre-bellied Dove (M. B. Robbins *in litt.* 1992). This area still holds some relatively good deciduous forest, and is apparently a stronghold for the Henna-hooded Foliage-gleaner and Saffron Siskin (M. B. Robbins *in litt.* 1992). As neither the spinetail, foliage-gleaner nor siskin was recorded in the area in 1991, it is essential that a survey is undertaken during a non-El Niño year (Best 1992, B. J. Best *in litt.* 1992).

Cordillera de Alamor–Cordillera de Celica (300-2,000 m) holds: Grey-backed Hawk, Ochre-bellied Dove, Little Woodstar, Blackish-headed Spinetail, Rufous-necked Foliage-gleaner, Henna-hooded Foliage-gleaner, Grey-headed Antbird, Grey-breasted Flycatcher, Pacific Royal Flycatcher, Ochraceous Attila, Slaty Becard. Protection of forest patches in this area is critically important due to the large number of threatened species present, and identification of suitable areas must be of the highest priority.

Sozoranga–Tambo Negro holds: Ochre-bellied Dove, Blackish-headed Spinetail, Rufous-necked Foliage-gleaner, Henna-hooded Foliage-gleaner, Grey-headed Antbird, Grey-breasted Flycatcher. Sozoranga (1,300-1,800 m) comprises small patches of semi-deciduous forest, and Tambo Negro (550-1,100 m; between Macará and Sabiango) is mainly deciduous forest (Best 1991), and represents the largest intact forest block (c.15 km^2, with an intact understorey) in western Loja and El Oro provinces, extending into northern Peru (Best 1992). Although the forest at Sozoranga and Tambo Negro is not linked, it is close enough to allow species to move seasonally into their preferred habitat types (Best 1992), making this forest block critically important for protection.

Angashcola and Amaluza hold: Bearded Guan and Rufous-necked Foliage-gleaner.

Tumbes National Forest (and probably the adjacent Cerros de Amotape National Park) holds: Grey-backed Hawk, Ochre-bellied Dove, Blackish-headed Spinetail, Rufous-necked Foliage-gleaner, Henna-hooded Foliage-gleaner (for which it is a major stronghold), Grey-headed Antbird (mostly too low for this species), Grey-breasted Flycatcher, Pacific Royal Flycatcher, Ochraceous Attila, Slaty Becard, Saffron Siskin. Tumbes National Forest (and Cerros de Amotape National Park) should be secured against possible invasion by colonists (M. Kessler *in litt.* 1991), and adequate protection initiated as an absolute priority. As with Machalilla National Park, it would be ideal for a research station to be set up as a centre for studies and activities within the park, but there also need to be more wardens with powers to stop illegal settling, hunting and deforestation (B. J. Best *in litt.* 1991). A detailed ornithological survey of Cerros de Amotape National Park is urgently needed, during which the White-winged Guan should be searched for.

Middle and upper Marañón drainage holds: Henna-hooded Foliage-gleaner, Grey-breasted Flycatcher and Slaty Becard, but is a centre of avian endemism in its own right, holding (amongst the threatened species) at various altitudes: Peruvian Pigeon *Columba oenops*, Yellow-faced Parrotlet *Forpus xanthops*, Marvellous Spatuletail *Loddigesia mirabilis*, Grey-winged Inca-finch *Incaspiza ortizi* (see equivalent section under Peruvian Pigeon).

Cruz Blanca–Palambla–Canchaque holds: Bearded Guan, Ochre-bellied Dove, Rufous-necked Foliage-gleaner, Henna-hooded Foliage-gleaner, Grey-headed Antbird, Grey-breasted Flycatcher, Slaty Becard. The immediate vicinity of Palambla is devoid of forest, but there is still some unexplored forest away from the road, and White-winged Guan has been found in eight valleys (with forest) between Palambla and Abra de Porculla (50 km to the south) (see Distribution under

Henna-hooded Foliage-gleaner). Conservation initiatives in this area should consider the montane threatened species: several large areas of upper montane forest still exist on the west slope of the Andes in Piura between Ayabaca and Cruz Blanca (see Measures Proposed under Bearded Guan).

The largest remaining moist/wet forest in western Ecuador south of the río Esmeraldas/Guaillabamba lies to the north-east of Muisne in an area (of c.200 km^2) drained by the ríos Bilsa and Vince (TAP); this forest will survive for only a few years if the present rate of clearance continues (TAP), and should be surveyed urgently for the presence of threatened species, and protected accordingly.

Further studies (on the status of the forest, the species, and their ecological requirements) are required in each of these areas (as outlined above), and their findings should be used to produce management plans for the protected areas and strategy documents for the others (B. J. Best *in litt.* 1991). The watershed importance (to the banana industry, for example) of forests on the lower slopes of the Andes, especially those at 500-1,000 m from near Manta Real to near Piñas, has apparently been overlooked or ignored by government officials, and this should be stressed at all levels when areas are proposed for protection.

An environmental education campaign initiated in reserves and settlements, using interpretive facilities and guided walks within the reserves, should be combined with a parallel programme of education in sustainable agricultural techniques (perhaps using model farms as demonstrations), both aiming at a more sustainable usage of the remaining forest fragments (B. J. Best *in litt.* 1991). The conservation of the White-winged Guan and Pale-headed Brush-finch generally falls outside of this sort of integrated approach, and both species require individual action plans (see relevant accounts).

REMARKS (1) The Grey-backed Hawk is closely related to the White Hawk and has been judged conspecific with it, but is now maintained as a distinct species (Blake 1977); it is perhaps also closely related to the near-threatened Mantled Hawk *Leucopternis polionota* (Meyer de Schauensee 1966). (2) Concerning Mongoya, Paynter and Traylor (1977) listed "Mangaya", with no province noted, although the BMNH label, which is interpretable as both Mangaya and Mongoya, specifies Manabí; OG (1957b) gave the río Mongoya as at 0°10'S 79°38'W and this fits fairly well with the river as marked in IGM (1989). (3) Comments concerning the Cordillera de Balzar are in Remarks under Saffron Siskin. (4) A specimen in AMNH collected on 20 October 1914 labelled "near the crater of Pichincha, 3,660 m" (i.e. Pichincha province, at 1°10'S 78°33'W) (Chapman 1926) is undoubtedly mislabelled, as all other known records are at considerably lower elevations.

CROWNED EAGLE *Harpyhaliaetus coronatus* V[9]

This open-country raptor has been recorded over a large area of central and southern South America, but at such low densities that concrete evidence on its population status is lacking, as are good data on ecology and threats; it requires much study.

DISTRIBUTION The Crowned Eagle occurs in the lowlands of south-central South America: Bolivia, Brazil, Paraguay, Argentina and Uruguay (Alvarez 1933, Hellmayr and Conover 1949, Barattini and Escalante 1958, Meyer de Schauensee 1982, Sibley and Monroe 1990; see Remarks 1). Unless otherwise stated, coordinates are taken from Paynter (1985, 1989) and Paynter and Traylor (1975, 1991), and records at individual localities are of single birds or pairs collected or observed.

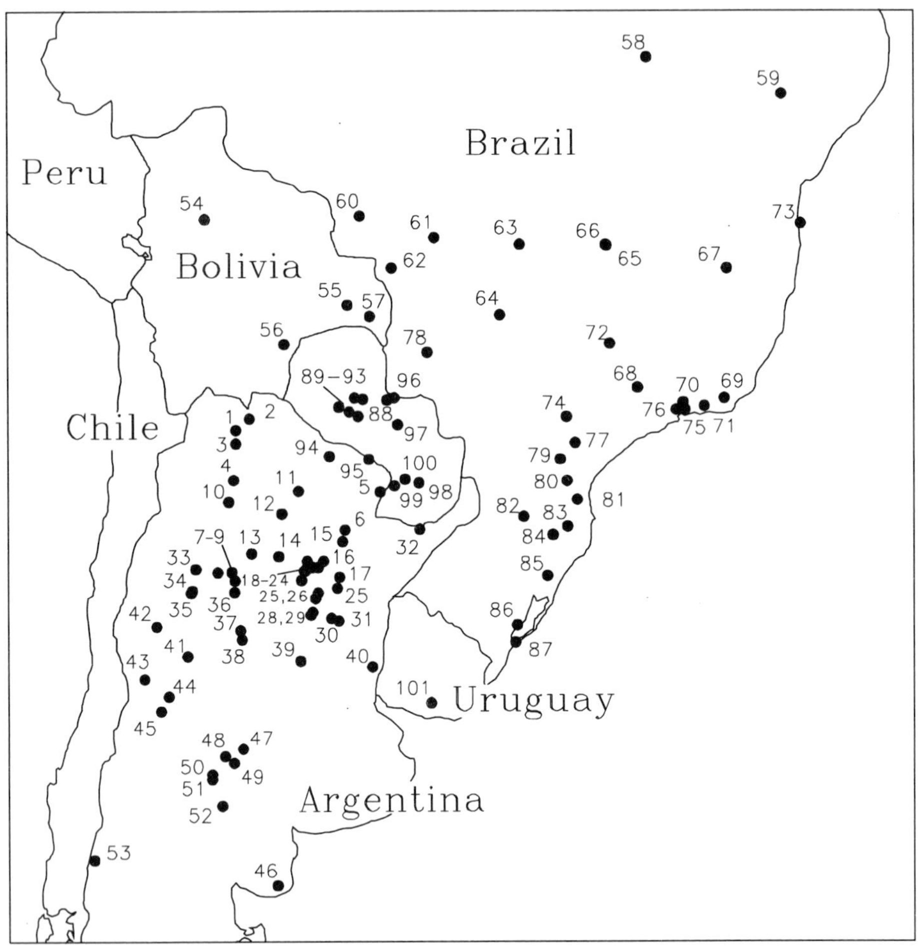

Argentina Records by province (north to south) are: (*Jujuy*) "west of Jujuy" (no further details given) (Olrog 1959); Calilegua National Park[1] (23°35'S 64°54'W), undated (C. Bertonatti and A. Serret *per* J. C. Chebez *in litt.* 1992); (*Salta*) Orán[2], 1970 (G. Hoy *per* J. C. Chebez *in litt.* 1992);

Rivadavia[3], July 1929 (Esteban 1953); Yatasto[4], June 1985 (B. M. López Lanús *in litt.* 1991); (*Formosa*) north of Formosa city[5], December 1987 (B. M. Whitney *in litt.* 1988); (*Chaco*) "Chaco", undated (Fontana 1881); Charadai[6], July 1986 (T. Narosky *in litt.* 1992); "Estina" (*sic*) (untraced), August 1890 (specimen in ROM); (*Misiones*) unspecified (Pereyra 1950); (*Catamarca*) unspecified (Olrog 1963); Recreo[7], August 1982 (T. Narosky *in litt.* 1992); 30 km south-east of Recreo[8], August 1982 (M. Nores *in litt.* 1992); El Médano[9] (29°19'S 65°44'W), undated (R. Miatello *per* M. Nores *in litt.* 1992); (*Tucumán*) río Vipos[10] (26°31'S 65°14'W), undated (Lillo 1902); Tucumán province (no further details given) (Freiberg 1943, Olrog 1963, Lucero 1983); (*Santiago del Estero*) in the eastern part of the province, 1934 (Giai 1952); Reserva Provincial Copo[11] (26°05'S 62°00'W in Nores *et al.* 1991), undated (S. M. Caziani *in litt.* 1992), February 1989 (D. A. Gómez *per* S. Krapovickas *in litt.* 1992) and recently (J. C. Chebez *in litt.* 1992); Tintina[12], undated (specimen in MFASF); Monte Redondo[13] (28°34'S 64°10'W), where three birds were observed in October 1980 (Nores *et al.* 1991); 15 km south of Icaño[14] (28°41'S 62°54'W), August 1902 (Ménégaux 1925); (*Santa Fe*) Los Amores[15] (28°06'S 59°59'W), July 1976 (T. Narosky *in litt.* 1992); west of Los Amores, November 1989; Ruta 13[16] (c.28°52'S 60°52'W); Vera department[17], October 1989; Pozo Borrado[18] (c.28°52'S 61°37'W), Nueve de Julio department, July 1987 (approximate coordinates and data from M. R. de la Peña *in litt.* 1991, also for the following 14 localities); Tostado[19], February 1945 (specimen in MACN; also Giai 1950); 10 km east of Tostado[20], November 1989; Antonio Pini[21] (c.29°07'S 61°37'W), July 1987; c.10 km south of Antonio Pini, September 1988; Ruta 75[22] (c.29°07'S 61°22'W), Nueve de Julio department, October 1989; Fortín los Pozos[23] (c.29°07'S 61°07'W), Nueve de Julio department, where two adults (2 km apart) were observed on 11 February 1988; north-east of Monteriore[24], Ruta 75 (c.29°37'S 61°52'W), November 1989; Calchaquí[25], undated (specimen in MACN); Santurce[26] (c.30°07'S 61°07'W), San Cristóbal department, January 1988; San Cristóbal[27], November 1974 and August 1978; Constanza[28] (c.30°52'S 61°22'W), San Cristóbal department, nesting in October 1979 and December 1982; Virginia (c.30°52'S 61°22'W), Castellanos department, August 1989; Ataliva[29] (30°59'S 61°27'W), July 1988; Cayastacito[30] (31°06'S 60°30'W), September 1974; 25 km west of Cayastá[31] (31°12'S 60°10'W), May 1989 (all, including approximate coordinates, from M. R. de la Peña *in litt.* 1991); Los Molles (untraced: Paynter 1985), September 1932 (Freiberg 1943); (*Corrientes*) "Corrientes province" (no further details given) (d'Orbigny 1835-1844); "Corrientes province", where three birds were observed, 1986-1988 (Contreras 1989); near Puerto Valle[32] (27°37'S 56°26'W), 1973 (Chebez 1989); (*La Rioja*) El Cantadero[33] (29°11'S 66°44'W), July 1986 (coordinates and data from M. Nores *in litt.* 1992); Patquía[34], undated (Anon. 1931); Guayapa[35] (30°07'S 66°57'W), September 1956 (Hayward 1967); (*Córdoba*) Monte de las Barrancas[36] (30°05'S 64°58'W), three undated observations (Nores *et al.* 1983); Copina[37] (31°34'W 64°42'W), undated (Nores *et al.* 1983); Valle de Calamuchita[38] (31°55'S 64°38'W), undated (Nores *et al.* 1983); General Roca department[39] (General Roca, at 32°44'S 61°55'W), September 1916 (specimen in MACN); (*San Juan*) Sierra de Villicum[40], Albardón, June 1984 (de Lucca 1992); (*Entre Ríos*) unspecified (specimen in MACN); banks of the Gato[41] (probably arroyo la Punta del Gata at 32°57'S 58°36'W), north-west of Gualeguaychú (33°01'S 58°31'W), between July 1871 and February 1872 (Lee 1873); (*San Luis*) (locality not given), where a bird was captured in 1973 (D. Ochoa de Masramón *per* J. C. Chebez *in litt.* 1992), and a bird in Buenos Aires Zoo was captured in this province in 1986 (J. C. Chebez *in litt.* 1992); Sierra de las Quijadas[42] (32°33'S 67°07'W), September 1990 (Haene and Gil undated; also R. Clark *per* J. C. Chebez *in litt.* 1992); (*Mendoza*) Tupungato[43], undated (one bird collected) (Reed 1916); Ñacuñán Ecological Reserve[44] (34°03'N 67°58'W) (from evidence provided in de Lucca 1992); San Rafael[45], undated (Reed 1916); (*Buenos Aires*) near Carmen de Patagones[46], where d'Orbigny (1835-1844) reported it during his visit to the area (7 January to 1 September 1829); (*Buenos Aires/Río Negro*) banks of the río Negro (d'Orbigny 1835-1844; see Remarks 2). (*La Pampa*) five sites in the area between Conhelo and

El Odre[47-51], marked on a map provided by J. R. Contreras (*in litt.* 1992); Parque Nacional Lihuel-Calel[52] (38°02'S 65°33'W), where three birds (an immature and two adults) were observed in October 1988 (M. Babarskas *in litt.* 1992); (*Río Negro*) "río Negro" (Sclater and Hudson 1888-1889), undated (see Remarks 3); (*Neuquén*) Lanín National Park[53] (39°55'S 71°25'W), accidental (J. C. Chebez *in litt.* 1992). A bird in BMNH is labelled as "River Negro, Patagonia". Temminck (1838) reported the species on the banks of the río de la Plata, but this cannot be attributed to any particular province

Bolivia The species's occurrence in the country is poorly documented, most sources failing to be more specific than "eastern Bolivia" (e.g. Hellmayr and Conover 1949, Brown and Amadon 1968, Blake 1977, Mayr and Cottrell 1979, Meyer de Schauensee 1982, Remsen and Traylor 1989, Sibley and Monroe 1990), and a bird in BMNH collected before 1888 is simply labelled "Bolivia".

Beni The only known record appears to be from Beni Biological Station[54] (14°38'S 66°18'W), presumably in 1989 (see Rocha O. 1990c).

Santa Cruz The species was listed for the province by West (1979) but the only records appear to be one from the northern chaco (somewhere along the Corumbá–Santa Cruz railway[55]) (Reichholf 1974), one in a remnant chaco grassland (surrounded by chaco woodland) at Perforación[56], 20°03'S 62°38'W, June 1990 (TAP), and one in grassland at the edge of dry forest at Guayacanes[57], 18°49'S 58°42'W, June 1991 (TAP, including coordinates for both the preceding).

Brazil Records (see Remarks 4) within states (roughly from north to south) are from:

Maranhão east of Balsas[58], near Buritirana in the Serra do Itapicurú, where a pair together with an immature bird were observed sometime between 22 June and 24 July 1985 (Roth 1985);

Bahia "north-western Bahia", where a pair was observed in April-June 1986 (Roth 1986); riacho da Melância[59] (09°08'S 39°54'W), Fazenda Concórdia, July 1990 (F. B. Pontual *in litt.* 1992);

Mato Grosso near Uirapuru[60], July 1987 (C. Yamashita *in litt.* 1987); Chapada[61] (= Chapada dos Guimarães), October 1883 (Allen 1891-1893; specimen in AMNH), with a pair in grassy cerrado there in September 1991 (TAP); reportedly Descalvados[62] (= Descalvado; 16°45'S 57°42'W) (Stone and Roberts 1934); reportedly on the rio Xingu, where it was well known among the Indians (Stone and Roberts 1934; also Hellmayr and Conover 1949); rio das Mortes or rio Xingu, where the species was recorded once (February to November 1970: Reichholf 1974); "Mato Grosso" (locality not given), April 1962 (Aguirre and Aldrighi 1983);

Goiás Araguay[63] (= Registro do Araguaia), October 1823 (von Pelzeln 1868-1871; also Paynter and Traylor 1991); Emas National Park[64], July 1981 (F. B. Pontual *in litt.* 1992) and August 1991 (J. F. Pacheco verbally 1991);

Distrito Federal Brasília National Park[65], November 1978, January 1987 (pair observed twice: C. Yamashita *in litt.* 1987), and November 1991 (P. G. Gadd *in litt.* 1991); Brasília[66], April 1963 (specimen in MNRJ);

Minas Gerais Chapada de São Domingos[67], Carbonita, July 1988 (G. T. de Mattos *in litt.* 1991); Caldas[68], 1855 (Gyldenstolpe 1927);

Rio de Janeiro unspecified (specimen in MNRJ); Nova Friburgo[69], July 1987, when three birds were seen (Luigi 1988), one evidently being collected (specimen in MNRJ); Várzea[70], Resende, April 1988 (J. F. Pacheco verbally 1988); Serra do Tinguá[71] (22°36'S 43°27'W in Scott and Brooke 1985), where an adult and an immature (apparently on migration) were observed on 29 November 1980 (Scott and Brooke 1985);

São Paulo Paraná[72] (= Porto do rio Paraná; c.19°59'S 47°46'W), April 1823 (von Pelzeln 1868-1871; also Paynter and Traylor 1991); Pontal[73], June 1991 (J. F. Pacheco verbally 1991); Chavantes[74], 1927 (Pinto 1938); Fazenda Albion[75], Bananal municipality, December 1989 (F. B. Pontual *in litt.* 1992); Serra da Bocaina[76] (22°45'S 44°45'W), where a bird (apparently of this species) was shot by a farmer in 1987 and another was observed in June 1988 (F. B. Pontual *in litt.* 1992); Ytararé[77] (= Itararé), August 1820 (von Pelzeln 1868-1871);

Mato Grosso do Sul by the road between Aquidauana and Miranda[78], February 1987 (C. Yamashita *in litt.* 1987); in cerrado north of Campo Grande, 1988, where a pair was reportedly nesting (*per* TAP);

Paraná Castro[79], June 1907 (Pinto 1938); Fazenda do Pitangui[80] (= Pitangui, untraced but between Curitiba and Castro), December 1820 (von Pelzeln 1868-1871; also Paynter and Traylor 1991);

Santa Catarina Corupá[81], undated (specimen in MSC: L. A. R. Bege *in litt.* 1991); Videira municipality, August 1984 (Albuquerque 1986; P. Scherer Neto *in litt.* 1992); Limoeiro (untraced), Agua Doce municipality[82], 1985 (Bornschein and Straube 1991); Lontras[83], undated (Sick *et al.* 1981, L. A. R. Bege *in litt.* 1991); Lages[84], 1990 (Bornschein and Straube 1991);

Rio Grande do Sul unspecified (specimen in MNRJ); alongside the road 5 km north of São Francisco de Paula[85], March 1978 (Belton 1984-1985); São Lourenço do Sul[86], undated (von Ihering 1898); São José do Norte[87], some time between June and August 1914 (Gliesch 1930).

Paraguay The following records fall to the west (Chaco) and east (Región Oriental) of the río Paraguay:

Chaco 200 km west of Puerto Casado[88], this being at 22°20'S 57°55'W, Alto Paraguay department, September 1939 (specimen in FMNH); 190 km west of Puerto Casado[89], June 1940 (two specimens in FMNH); General Díaz[90] (see Remarks 5), June 1945 (specimen in FMNH); Lichtenau[91] (c.22°50'S 59°40'W), Presidente Hayes, April 1963 (Steinbacher 1968); Colonia Neuland[92] (c.22°38'S 60°09'W, read from DSGM 1988), Boquerón, in 1988 or 1989 (Neris and Colman 1991); Ruta Trans-Chaco (km 187)[93], Presidente Hayes, September 1989 (J. Escobar *in litt.* 1991); near Estancia San José[94] near río Confuso, c.15 km south-west of km 75 on the Ruta Trans-Chaco), July 1989 (AMN); "Gran Chaco", sometime between February and November 1970 (Reichholf 1974); Fortín Page[95] (c.24°47'S 58°45'W), Presidente Hayes, 12 July 1890 (Kerr 1892: see Remarks 6);

Región Oriental Near Estancia Centurión[96] (= Centurión, c.22°15'S 57°35'W), Concepción[97], May 1989 (F. E. Hayes *in litt.* 1991); Villa Rica[98] (= Villarrica, Guairá, February 1907 (specimen in BMNH); Cerro Acahay[99] (25°52'S 57°35'W), Paraguarí, undated (Acevedo *et al.* 1990, whence also coordinates); "Alto Paraná"[100] region, undated (Bertoni 1914).

Uruguay Kothe (1912) reported two specimens from Montevideo, but this obscure record was called in question by Hellmayr and Conover (1949); hence presumably the scepticism of Cuello and Gerzenstein (1962) and Gore and Gepp (1978) over the occurrence of the species in the country. The listing of the species for Uruguay by Steullet and Deautier (1935-1946) appears to have been guesswork based on the proximity of localities in neighbouring countries (R. Escalante *in litt.* 1991), and presumably Pinto (1938) and Freiberg (1943) simply followed suit. However, Barattini and Escalante (1958) postulated the occurrence of the species in Uruguay based on a drawing by D. A. Larrañaga, who died in 1848. Moreover, an apparently overlooked record for the country is that of Alvarez (1933), who reported a bird shot somewhere by the río Santa Lucía Grande[101] on an ungiven date, and who added various notes about its status and habits (i.e. implying that it occurred more widely; see Population).

POPULATION Although the Crowned Eagle's range is relatively large, it appears generally to be rare and very difficult to find throughout (see Remarks 7); TAP has spent dozens of hours in campo and cerrado habitat in Brazil and Bolivia, yet has found the species on very few occasions. While it is true that this is a naturally low-density raptor, and on the basis of the information assembled here there is little clear evidence of a decline, trends are always very difficult to detect in low-density populations and it seems very likely that a loss of numbers has occurred.

Argentina The species has been considered "uncommon to rare" in eastern Formosa (B. M. Whitney *in litt.* 1988), "scarce" in Tucumán, where it "probably nests" (Lucero 1983), "rare" (Giacomelli 1923) and "scarce" (Hayward 1967) in La Rioja, "scarce" in Córdoba (Nores *et al.* 1983) and in Santa Fe (de la Peña 1977a), and the data presented by Chebez (1989) and Contreras (1989) suggest that it is rare in Corrientes, whence there are only four records. Narosky and Yzurieta (1987) included the species in the category "scarce or difficult to see".

Bolivia Apart from the few records in Distribution, the species's status is practically unknown.

Brazil The judgement that the Crowned Eagle is rare (Albuquerque 1986) is fully justified by the notable paucity of records from its extensive range in the country, most of them referring to old specimens (see Distribution).

Paraguay De Azara (1802-1805) commented that there are "some" in Paraguay, and Kerr (1892) reported the species to be rare in the lower Pilcomayo area. J. Escobar *in litt.* (1991) considered it "occasional" in the chaco, and AMN only observed it once in the humid chaco, despite having spent several months in both dry and humid chaco in 1989 and 1990.

Uruguay The only information about the species's status in the country is that given by Alvarez (1933), who reported it to be fairly scarce. The species has not certainly been recorded for at least the last 60 years, and R. Escalante (*in litt.* 1991) regarded it as possibly extinct in the country.

ECOLOGY The Crowned Eagle is more often found in the lowlands in semi-open seasonal dry country (palm savanna, thin woodland, steppes with bushes), chaco and cerrado in the lowlands east of the Andes, although it sometimes occurs in moderate altitude hill ranges of western Argentina and south-eastern Brazil (von Pelzeln 1868-1871, Olrog 1959, Hayward 1967, Brown and Amadon 1968, Reichholf 1974, Blake 1977, Nores *et al.* 1983, Narosky and Yzurieta 1987, Chebez 1989; also Distribution). Birds observed in the lowland humid chaco in Argentina and Paraguay were in open, periodically flooded grassland areas with scattered palms *Copernicia alba* (Kerr 1892, B. M. Whitney *in litt.* 1988, AMN): however, an immature bird observed in Bahia was found in caatinga (F. B. Pontual *in litt.* 1992).

Food has been reported to consist of birds (e.g. tinamous), mammals (including skunks *Conepatus* sp., armadillos, weasels, rodents), reptiles and carrion (sheep, armadillos) (de Azara 1802-1805, Temminck 1838, Lee 1873, Sclater and Hudson 1888-1889, Ménégaux 1925, Alvarez 1933, Giai 1950, Brown and Amadon 1968, de la Peña 1977a, Sick 1985, Canevari *et al.* 1991, F. E. Hayes *in litt.* 1991). Alvarez (1933) examined the stomach of a shot bird which contained a chick, and he also mentioned lambs and poultry among its prey items.

A nest placed on the communal nest of Monk Parakeets *Myiopsitta monachus* at 15 m in a large eucalyptus tree held one egg on 28 October 1979 and a chick on 5 December 1982 (de la Peña 1977a, M. R. de la Peña *in litt.* 1991). The nest is placed on trees or in ravines and generally consists of a large platform in which a single egg is laid (de la Peña 1985, Canevari *et al* 1991).

The Crowned Eagle has been described as partially crepuscular (Olrog 1959, Brown and Amadon 1968, Sick 1985) and tame, reluctant to fly off when approached (Brown and Amadon 1968). Its movements are poorly known: it is considered sedentary in Argentina (Dabbene 1910, Narosky and Yzurieta 1987), but the map in Narosky and Yzurieta (1987) shows an area of "low density" towards its southern range (i.e. Río Negro and southern Buenos Aires, where nineteenth-century records exist; see Distribution), and Scott and Brooke (1985) reported two birds (apparently on migration) outside its previously known range on 29 November 1980 in eastern Brazil (see Distribution).

THREATS The causes of the Crowned Eagle's apparent rarity in Bolivia remain unknown. In Brazil, the species suffers from hunting pressure (C. Yamashita *in litt.* 1987) and probably also from the effects of habitat clearance both in central and southern Brazil, cerrado being replaced by soy crops in the former (C. Yamashita *in litt.* 1986) and natural grasslands being developed for agriculture and afforestation (with exotic trees) in the latter (Albuquerque 1986); see particularly Threats under Lesser Nothura *Nothura minor*. In Paraguay, although appropriate habitat in the chaco is still in fairly good condition, increasing colonization (farming, cattle-raising) is rapidly destroying wooded areas and natural grasslands, and hunting, although prohibited in Paraguay, is a common practice, with large raptors and storks being especially targeted (AMN). On the rio Xingu, Mato Grosso, Brazil, in the 1930s the species was often found to be kept alive by natives for whom it had a religious significance (Stone and Roberts 1934).

MEASURES TAKEN The species is protected in Argentina (MAG 1954), and in both Brazil and Paraguay it has been included on the national lists of threatened fauna (Acevedo *et al.* 1990, Bernardes *et al.* 1990). Records from protected areas are few; those from Emas and Brasília National Parks and Beni Biosphere Reserve appear to be the most encouraging.

MEASURES PROPOSED This species presents a major challenge to conservation, owing to its very low density or at least very patchy distribution. The first requirement must be to identify one or more general areas in which some reasonable population exists; these will then need close study to determine ecological constraints, breeding success, migratory patterns and other factors relevant to the development and implementation of a long-term conservation strategy (which may well need to be international in scope). It may be appropriate to integrate the first task, that of identifying key areas for the species, with a wider programme of survey that targets other, if smaller, bird species also in difficulty in the same general region and habitat.

REMARKS (1) Other countries or regions have been erroneously included within the range of the species, doubtless because it was considered conspecific with the Solitary Eagle *Harpyhaliaetus solitarius* (see, e.g., Hellmayr 1932, Hellmayr and Conover 1949). (2) From d'Orbigny (1835-1844, 1843) it is not clear if he observed the species on both sides of the river (Buenos Aires and Río Negro provinces). (3) Hudson (1872), when referring to the species, commented: "... my observations have been confined to the valley of the río Negro and to the adjacent high grounds..." (also Paynter 1985). (4) Untraced localities are: 12 km south of "Geomõ" (*sic*), where a female was taken on 27 August 1902 and 15 km south of the same locality, where a male was collected on 25 August 1902 (sepcimens in MNHN). (5) It is not clear whether the collector was at Fortín General Díaz (22°07'S 58°40'W) or at Laguna General Díaz (22°18'S 59°01'W), the former in Alto Paraguay and the latter in Presidente Hayes department (but relatively close to each other) (see Paynter 1989). (6) Evidence in Kerr (1892) suggests that a female specimen in BMNH labelled "Pilcomayo" and simply dated 12 June may well be the same bird. (7) The species's habitat preferences and its easily detected presence (see Ecology) suggest that it is indeed rare even though large areas of its distribution still remain well preserved (e.g. the Argentinian, Paraguayan and Bolivian chaco).

HISPANIOLAN HAWK *Buteo ridgwayi* I[7]

Habitat loss on a major scale, combined with persecution, have caused this forest raptor to decline severely throughout its range in Haiti and the Dominican Republic, and its stronghold now appears to be a poorly protected national park (Los Haitises) in the north-east of Hispaniola.

DISTRIBUTION The Hispaniolan Hawk is endemic to Hispaniola (Dominican Republic and Haiti) and the surrounding small islands, Beata and Alto Velo (Dominican Republic), Gonave, Grande Cayemite, Petite Cayemite and Ile-à-Vache (Haiti) (Wiley and Wiley 1981, Wiley 1986). Wiley (1985a) referred to the species having been widespread on the island but now with its range much reduced. Previously published localities for the species with many new sites have been mapped by Wiley and Wiley (1981; see Remarks 1).

Dominican Republic From Wiley and Wiley (1981), it is apparent that the great majority of mainland (Hispaniolan) records (24 of 27 mapped), current and historical, stem from the eastern two-thirds of the country, with the greatest concentration in the north-east within a 75 km radius of the río Yuna estuary, largely focused on Los Haitises mountain range; they appear to omit two localities, namely Casavito, which is "Casabito" (19°02'N 70°31'W, in DMATC 1972) (Stockton de Dod 1978), and Santo Domingo, "east of Santo Domingo city", where individuals were seen on 4 and 8 July 1927 (Danforth 1929); they also misspell Neiba as "Nieba". Its stronghold now appears to be an area in north-east Dominican Republic called Los Haitises.

Haiti On the mainland there appears to be but one record away from the Massif du Nord.

POPULATION At the end of the last century, one observer saw the species frequently in the Dominican Republic (Cherrie 1896; see Remarks 2). In the first half of the present century, however, observers and reviewers thought it to be rare in some degree on the mainland (Peters 1917, Wetmore and Swales 1931, Wetmore 1932a, Friedmann 1950). However, studies in the mid-1970s by Wiley and Wiley (1981) support the judgement of Bond (1956b) and Stockton de Dod (1978) that the Hispaniolan Hawk is common at least in one area, inasmuch as its overall population in Los Haitises, from the territory size data under Ecology below, is likely to be fairly healthy (seen "often" as against being "encountered infrequently" in other habitats searched on the island: Wiley and Wiley 1981). However, it has obviously also suffered local decline and extinction, being (e.g.) only occasionally seen in the largest tracts of degraded forest above Miches on the north coast and, also on the north coast, now entirely gone from the Samana peninsula (which includes the type-locality), where forest clearance has been very extensive (Wiley and Wiley 1981). In both Haiti and the Dominican Republic forests are still being destroyed (see Threats) and the species must therefore still be in steady decline.

Earlier this century it was common on both Cayemites (Haiti) and in 1962 it was common on Ile-à-Vache (Wiley and Wiley 1981) where perhaps together with a few of the less disturbed satellite Haitian islands it may still exist in good numbers (Wiley 1985a), but there is no more recent information on its numerical status on any of Hispaniola's offshore islands other than that it was not found during a field study in July 1977 and a single bird was recorded twice in the north-west of Alto Velo Island on a one-day visit in October 1978 (Wiley and Ottenwalder 1990); none was seen on Gonave Island during fieldwork in February 1985 (M. A. McDonald *in litt.* 1991), and after aerial surveys of the islands of Haiti J. A. Ottenwalder (*in litt.* 1992) found that with the exception of Grande Cayemite and Tortue (although the species has not been reported from the latter) most of the other islands are heavily disturbed (e.g. Ile-à-Vache) and/or densely populated (e.g. Gonave).

ECOLOGY The Hispaniolan Hawk has been recorded from a wide variety of habitats, as catalogued by Wiley and Wiley (1981): (1) subtropical dry forest; (2) subtropical moist forest, comprising (a) pine forest, (b) lowland scrub (as, e.g., on the Cayemites, according to Wetmore and Swales 1931), (c) lowland/littoral woodland, (d) lower montane hardwood forest, (e) lower montane pasture and agricultural land, (f) lower montane cut-over pine/hardwood, and (g) lowland riparian woods/marsh; and (3) subtropical wet forests, comprising (a) lower montane limestone karst forest (as at Los Haitises) and (b) rainforest. Although the species apparently has a wide tolerance of habitat types, it is commoner in virgin forest than in degraded areas (Wiley 1986), but forest edge and open habitats are also used for hunting purposes (for hunting methods see Wiley and Wiley 1981). The elevational distribution of the species is accordingly broad, from sea level to about 2,000 m (Wiley and Wiley 1981, Wiley 1985a), although from the evidence in Distribution it appears to be much commoner at lower than at higher elevations. The forest vegetation in the Los Haitises range is typefied by cupey *Clusia rosea*, granadillo *Buchenavia capitata*, mahogany *Swietenia mahogani*, silk-cotton tree *Ceiba pentandra*, masa *Tetragastris balsamifera*, muskwood *Guarea trichilioides* and corcho bobo *Pisonia albida*, and the area in general consists of virgin forest mixed with active and abandoned small farms (Wiley and Wiley 1981).

A survey of the literature and museum specimen labels indicated that food of the Hispaniolan Hawk includes rats *Rattus*, mice *Mus*, Common Ground-doves *Columbina passerina*, Red-legged Thrushes *Turdus plumbeus*, and lizards *Leiocephalus melanochlorus*, *Anolis* and *Amaevia taeniura* (Wiley and Wiley 1981). Breeding birds in 1976 brought to the nest lizards (28%), snakes (28%), mammals (rats and bats) (19.5%) and birds (8.5%), but only one frog despite an abundance of frogs in the forest; by biomass, mammals formed 48.1%, lizards 20.7% and snakes 17.6% (Wiley and Wiley 1981). Of 70 identified prey brought to two nests, the most numerous species were the snake *Uromacer oxyrhynchus* (13), the lizard *Anolis baleatus* (12) and the rat *Rattus rattus* (11) (for a complete list, plus items found in the nests, see Wiley and Wiley 1981).

The adjacent home ranges/territories of three pairs in Los Haitises, 1976, were calculated as 53.7, 47.4 and 72.2 (mean 57.8) ha (see Remarks 3) and the distances between their nests was 300, 880 and 1,000 m (average 727 m), two nests overlooking cultivated valleys, the third being in virgin forest, two being in dead trees, one in a living, at 6.1, 23.3 and 36.6 m from the ground, all three being more prominent than those around them (Wiley and Wiley 1981). Of four further nests reported, at least one (15 m up in the crown) was in a tree taller than its neighbours, and was under construction on 15 February (Stockton de Dod 1978); another, on Ile-à-Vache, 10 m up in the crown of a royal palm *Roystonea regia*, was under construction on 28 April (Wetmore and Lincoln 1933), while the two others, in the Massif du Nord in Haiti, 8 and 12 m up in pines, each held downy young on 2 May (Bond 1928a). In Los Haitises, nest-building was in February–March and egg-laying (clutch-size two) in March, with a minimum incubation period of 28-29 days; at the only nest where success was proved, two young took 12 weeks to fledge, were still being fed by their parents in week 13, and were still at least present in the territory in week 16 (Wiley and Wiley 1981).

The species has been noted for its tameness on the offshore islands (Wetmore and Swales 1931, Wiley and Wiley 1981).

THREATS Forest destruction and disturbance including shooting, appear to be the major threats to the Hispaniolan Hawk, and there is particular concern for wet forest: even in Los Haitises, a recently created national park (see Measures Taken), "clear-cutting and burning for farming continue at an alarming rate", and the rate and extent of forest destruction in Haiti (one of the most environmentally degraded countries in the world: see, e.g., Threats under White-winged

Warbler *Xenoligea montana*) leaves little hope for the future of the hawk there (Wiley and Wiley 1981, Wiley 1985a).

MEASURES TAKEN The Hispaniolan Hawk is protected by law in the Dominican Republic, although this does not prevent the species being shot (Wiley 1985a); on paper, Los Haitises National Park gives protection to what is evidently one of the most important remaining populations of the species (but see Threats).

MEASURES PROPOSED Wiley (1985a) urged that agricultural activities should be excluded from Los Haitises National Park, and additional populations should be identified and habitats preserved. The offshore islands where the species has been recorded need to be checked for surviving populations. A long-term study of the population ecology of the species would yield important information on the viability of birds in the various habitats from which they have been recorded. The proposed extention of the Los Haitises National Park (see DVS 1990) would also be of great value for the conservation of the Hispaniolan Hawk as its density there is higher than elsewhere in the island; Los Haitises National Park is also one of the few areas where the threatened Plain Pigeon *Columba inornata* (see relevant account) can be found in the Dominican Republic (see map II.15 in DVS 1990).

REMARKS (1) Although the named islands on the map in Wiley and Wiley (1981) are intended to indicate the occurrence on them of the Hispaniolan Hawk (see Wiley 1986), it is not immediately clear whether the same is true of the named mountain ranges; there is, for example, no published record from the Sierra de Baoruco, and published data for the Massif du Nord and Sierra de Neiba (Bond 1928a, Stockton de Dod 1978) refer only to the single localities pinpointed on the Wiley and Wiley (1981) map. (2) Wiley and Wiley (1981) mistakenly attributed to Christy (1897) the view that the Hispaniolan Hawk was "common in some areas" in the last century. (3) Calculations were based on flat projection, the actual surface areas being larger through altitudinal variations in the terrain.

LESSER COLLARED FOREST-FALCON *Micrastur buckleyi* K[12]

A virtually unknown small raptor of western Amazonian forest interior, this species has only been recorded from eastern Ecuador, north-east and south-central Peru, and in one area of western Brazil, although it seems likely to prove to be relatively widespread and secure.

DISTRIBUTION The Lesser Collared Forest-falcon is known from a few localities in Amazonian Ecuador, Peru and Brazil. It probably also occurs in south-east Amazonas, Colombia (Sibley and Monroe 1990). In the following account, records are given from north to south and unless otherwise stated coordinates and elevations are taken from Paynter and Traylor (1977) and Stephens and Traylor (1983).

Ecuador Records are based on specimens, all obtained before 1940, from: San José Nuevo ("San José de Sumaco"), 500-1,000 m, 0°26'S 77°20'W, in Napo, March 1923 (Traylor 1948; specimen in AMNH; see Remarks 1); río Suno, c.500 m, 0°42'S 77°08'W, in Napo (Traylor 1948); and Sarayacu (the type-locality), 700 m, 1°44'S 77°29'W, in Pastaza, February 1880 (Swann 1920, Traylor 1948); Cordillera de Cutucú, 1,800 m, November 1938 (two specimens in BMNH whose existence and identity were first indicated in Robbins *et al.* 1987; identity confirmed by P. R. Colston verbally 1992).

Peru Records are from: Orosa, 3°26'S 72°08'S, c.100 m on the río Amazonas in Loreto department, November 1936 (Amadon 1964; specimen in AMNH); near Kusú, 4°27'S 78°18'W, hilly lowlands on the río Comaina, Amazonas department, August 1978 (specimen in LSUMZ; see Remarks 2); near Huampami, unlocated, on the río Cenepa (4°35'S 78°12'W), c.210 m, Amazonas department, August 1977 (specimen in LSUMZ); Perico, 5°15'S 78°45'W, c.200 m on the río Chinchipe in Cajamarca department, July 1923 (Amadon 1964; specimen in AMNH); Yarinacocha, 8°15'S 74°43'S, c.100 m on the río Ucayali, Ucayali (but formerly in Loreto) department, July 1946 (Traylor 1948, 1958, O'Neill and Pearson 1974; specimen in FMNH); Boca Manu, untraced but c.11°50'S 71°20'W, 360 m, the airstrip at the confluence of ríos Manu and Alto Madre de Dios, Madre de Dios department, 21-22 July 1989 (B. M. Whitney *in litt.* 1991, whence coordinates); Hacienda Villacarmen, 12°50'S 71°15'W, 600 m in south-eastern Cuzco department, July 1958 (Blake 1977; specimen in FMNH).

Brazil The species was discovered in March 1992 near Porongaba upriver on the rio Juruá from Mário Lobão (Porto Wálter) in Acre, two specimens being collected and a sight-record being made (C. A. Peres and A. Whittaker *in litt.* 1992).

POPULATION There is no information on numbers. Although the species has been described as "rare" (Amadon 1964, Blake 1977), birds of the genus *Micrastur* are very inconspicuous (Thiollay 1984) and this particular form is extremely similar to the Collared Forest-falcon *M. semitorquatus*, with which it is sympatric (Traylor 1948), so that lack of records need not be entirely attributable to rarity.

ECOLOGY The species's habitat is described as "lowland forest" (Blake 1977) but in the tropical and subtropical zones (Meyer de Schauensee 1966); the records from 1,800 m in Cordillera Cutucú are somewhat anomalous in this regard. At Yarinacocha the bird was described as irregular in the middle stratum of inundated primary forest on the east side of the lake there (O'Neill and Pearson 1974), but this may possibly have referred to the single record from this locality. The birds found on the rio Juruá were in both várzea and terra firme forest (C. A. Peres and A. Whittaker *in litt.* 1992). The bird located at Boca Manu in July 1989 was juvenile, and perched c.4 m above ground at the edge of the airstrip in 15-20 m tall *Cecropia*-dominated second growth, giving food-begging calls about once per minute; it had probably been out of the nest for less than a week (B. M. Whitney *in litt.* 1991). The August 1978 specimen from Amazonas, Peru, had testes somewhat enlarged; that from August 1977 did not, though its skull was ossified, and its stomach contained one *Mesomys* (LSUMZ specimen label data). The shorter tarsus and smaller feet of this species (Traylor 1948) suggest an ecological adaptation for foraging in trees rather than for capturing or even pursuing prey on the ground (as recorded for the genus *Micrastur* by Willis *et al.* 1983).

THREATS The habitat in at least part of this bird's range is being cleared (J. P. O'Neill *in litt.* 1986); problems of deforestation in the Cordillera de Cutucú are outlined in Threats under White-necked Parakeet *Pyrrhura albipectus*.

MEASURES TAKEN None is known.

MEASURES PROPOSED The first requirement is to determine the species's true distribution, status and ecology, following which its management can be planned. However, on the basis of recent records it would seem fairly likely that this is not a serious candidate for attention, and that it can be conserved in many areas being managed or established for more obviously pressing cases.

REMARKS (1) San José Nuevo has apparently disappeared (Paynter and Traylor 1977). (2) The coordinates are as given on the label; in Stephens and Traylor (1983) they are 4°27'S 78°16'W.

PLUMBEOUS FOREST-FALCON *Micrastur plumbeus* V[9]

This poorly known small raptor of foothill forest interior is restricted to the Pacific slope of the Andes in south-western Colombia and north-western Ecuador.

DISTRIBUTION The Plumbeous Forest-falcon (see Remarks 1) is known from a few localities on the Pacific slope in south-west Colombia and north-west Ecuador (coordinates below are taken from Paynter and Traylor 1977, 1981).

Colombia Records of this species come from: (*Chocó*) La Vieja (c.5°24'N 76°23'W), where a specimen (in AMNH) was taken at 300 m in October 1912; (*Cauca*) río Munchique, El Tambo (c.2°35'N 77°15'W), where a female (in ANSP) was taken at 915 m in October 1938 (also Bond and Meyer de Schauensee 1940); "La Costa", El Tambo (c.2°25'N 76°49'W, 1,000 m, below Cerro Munchique) (Hellmayr and Conover 1949); Cerro Munchique (c.2°32'N 76°57'W, 40 km west of Popayán) (Hellmayr and Conover 1949); and (*Nariño*) La Guayacana (1°26'N 78°27'W: mistakenly called Guayana in Hellmayr and Conover 1949), where a male and juvenile were taken at 250 m in April 1944, with a female (in LACM) collected there at 225 m in August 1959 (von Sneidern 1954: see Remarks 2).

Ecuador Localities are restricted to Esmeraldas province and are as follows: Carondelet on the río Bogotá (1°06'N 78°42'W, 18 m), this being the type-locality (Sclater 1918); Pulún (1°05'N 78°40'W, 50 m) where a male (in BMNH) was collected in the early 1900s (also Hellmayr and Conover 1949); El Placer, c.15 km west of Lita (c.0°51'N 78°34'W, 670 m), where two specimens (in ANSP, MECN) were collected at 670 m in August 1987; and río Zapallo Grande (0°44'N 78°56'W, c.100 m) (Hellmayr and Conover 1949).

POPULATION There is no information on numbers. Although the species is described as "rare" (Meyer de Schauensee 1948-1952, Hilty and Brown 1986), birds in the genus *Micrastur* are very inconspicuous (Thiollay 1984) and this particular form is extremely similar to the Barred Forest-falcon *M. ruficollis*, with which it is sympatric (Brown and Amadon 1968): for this reason, lack of records need not be wholly attributable to rarity.

ECOLOGY Records of this species appear to come from between c.20 and 1,000 m (see Distribution), and as such it inhabits lowland and foothill tropical forest, although Brown and Amadon (1968), and hence Blake (1977), speculated that the bird reaches the subtropical zone. The stomach contents of birds taken recently (in ANSP, MECN) at El Placer, Esmeraldas, were found to contain a crab and lizard. One of the specimens taken at La Guayacana, Nariño, in April 1944 was a "juvenile" (von Sneidern 1954), while the female (in ANSP) taken at El Placer in August 1987 was deemed not to be in breeding condition.

THREATS Although considerable areas of primary tropical forest still remain within the range of this species (LGN), Gentry (1989) mentioned that in Nariño rapid deforestation is currently occurring, with many areas totally cleared. In Esmeraldas, human population pressure is similarly causing problems (Gentry 1989), and many areas have been cleared or degraded (Evans 1988b: see Measures Taken).

MEASURES TAKEN In Colombia, sites where this species has been recorded around río and Cerro Munchique are located within the Munchique National Park (44,000 ha) (CNPPA 1982); there is a second protected area nearby (Los Tambitos Natural Reserve: A. J. Negret verbally 1991) which is potentially important for it. Further areas are currently being surveyed with the aim of establishing new reserves (J. W. Beltrán verbally 1992). There appear to be no protected areas covering localities where this species has been recorded in Ecuador, although the Cotacachi–Cayapas Ecological Reserve (204,400 ha: IUCN 1992) is very close to El Placer and the río Zapollo Grande (CNPPA 1982) and undoubtedly holds the species, but despite its status as a reserve the tropical forest there is being opened up for logging (NK).

MEASURES PROPOSED The true distribution of the Plumbeous Forest-falcon, its population density and basic ecological requirements all need to be determined. Its range overlaps with the ranges of a number of other threatened species, namely Banded Ground-cuckoo *Neomorphus radiolosus* (both occurring in Munchique National Park: also see equivalent section under Multicoloured Tanager *Chlorochrysa nitidissima*) and Scarlet-breasted Dacnis *Dacnis berlepschi* (see relevant accounts and also equivalent section under Hoary Puffleg *Haplophaedia lugens*), and any conservation initiatives should where possible (and where sympatry occurs) consider the requirements of all these species.

REMARKS (1) Meyer de Schauensee (1966) thought this species a possible race of Lined Forest-falcon *M. gilvicollis*, and noted that Plumbeous would be considered a distinct species if Lined were merged with Barred Forest-falcon *M. ruficollis*, as suggested by Amadon (1964). However, Lined and Barred have been found to be valid species (Schwartz 1972), so Plumbeous may yet prove to be an isolated race of Lined. (2) Meyer de Schauensee (1948-1952) suggested that the three birds from La Guayacana were taken between 600 and 700 m.

WHITE-WINGED GUAN *Penelope albipennis* E[1]

Discovered in dry north-westernmost Peru in 1876 and generally presumed extinct for a century thereafter, this guan is now known from a small number of dry wooded valleys in the Andean foothills of Peru (chiefly in Lambayeque), where it numbers possibly less than a hundred individuals and is seriously endangered by forest clearance.

DISTRIBUTION The White-winged Guan is restricted to a small area of north-west Peru, although the exact extent of its distribution there remains to be clarified; that it might or does occur in adjacent Ecuador is dealt with in the last paragraph in this section.

The species was originally described from a specimen collected in December 1876 on Condesa island, 3°31'S 80°29'W, in the Santa Lucia swamps of the Tumbes river delta, Tumbes, and a second specimen was obtained a month later, January 1877, at the Hacienda Pabur, 5°15'S 80°20'W, 200 km to the south and 130 km inland, in Piura, while a third specimen from the same locality is believed to be the live-caught offspring of the second (Taczanowski 1877, 1884-1886, Vaurie 1966b, de Macedo 1978, 1979). At the time of its first discovery, the species was reported at second-hand to inhabit mangroves at the mouth of the Zarumilla ("Zurumilla") on the border with Ecuador, and to be found in all the larger river valleys of western Peru as far south as the Chicama in La Libertad (but there was no sight record from there, *contra* Meyer de Schauensee 1966), in particular those at Lambayeque and "Nancho (Rio de Saña)" in adjacent Cajamarca (Taczanowski 1884-1886).

A century later, in September 1977, the general veracity of these reports was established with the rediscovery and collection of one specimen of the species in Quebrada San Isidro, 5°35'S 79°48'W, on the Hacienda Querpón, Querpón, some 40 km south of Hacienda Pabur (de Macedo 1978, 1979), and the subsequent rapid discovery of c.25 other localities, of which 17 or more were suspected to hold breeding pairs (Ortiz 1980). All these recently discovered sites lie within Lambayeque department (although some were erroneously referred to Piura by de Macedo 1978 and Dejonghe and Mallet 1978) from 5°31'S, near the border of Piura department, to 6°22'S, east of Chiclayo, localities being: near Hacienda Chiernique, 5°34'S 79°55'W, at Jaguay Grande (only visiting birds July–December), Chacra de Paulino (vagrants) and Quebrada de Vacas (2-3 pairs); Quebrada de Querpón, 5°37'S 79°49'W, at Olla Serrana (one pair), San Isidro (three pairs), El Guabo (vagrants) and El Chirimoyo (vagrant); Hacienda Boca Chica, 5°42'S 79°48'W, at Quebrada de Pavas (3-4 pairs) and Quebrada Mugo Mugo (vagrants, perhaps 1-2 pairs); El Tocto, 5°47'S 79°41-42'W, at Quebrada La Pachinga (2-3 pairs), Quebrada Paltorán (vagrants, perhaps 1-2 pairs: this valley in conjunction with the former is where the guan occurs highest, at times up to 1,200 m), Quebrada Cachaco–Quebrada Rosas (one pair), Quebrada Caballito (one pair; but see Population), Quebrada Granada (one pair), Quebrada Peña Blanca (one pair), a second Quebrada Paltorán (two pairs, possibly the same as those in Quebrada Granada and Quebrada Pomapara) and Quebrada Pomapara (one pair); Hacienda Recalí, 5°51-52'S 79°41'W, at Quebrada El Algodonal–Oberito (one pair), Quebrada Oberito (3-4 pairs), Quebrada Las Torcazas (perhaps one pair) and Quebrada El Barranco (vagrants) (Ortiz 1980); río Olmos, 5°54'S 79°35-36'W, at Quebrada Oberal, Quebrada Naranja and Quebrada Agua Blanca (E. G. Ortiz *in litt.* 1988); Lajas, 6°21'S 79°29'W, at Quebrada Negrohuasi (1-2 or more pairs) and El Reloj (one pair) (Ortiz 1980); and near Chongoyape, east of Chiclayo, at 6°39'S 79°24'W (Eley 1982). Details of most of these localities are given by Ortiz (1980).

Dozens of valleys in this area were found not to hold guans (Ortiz 1980), and although Ortiz (1980) claimed that more could possibly be found, it seems unlikely that there would be many in view of the areas covered (NK, E. G. Ortiz *in litt.* 1988). A nest was found 27 May 1978 in the vicinity of El Cabuyo in Quebrada de Pavas, at 5°40'S 79°45'30"W (Ortiz 1980, Williams 1980). More birds can probably be found both within and outside the currently known range (Ortiz 1980). The Andean foothills to the north of Hacienda Pabur – notably the Cerros de Amotape National

Park in Piura – may also hold the species (Delacour and Amadon 1973, King 1978-1979), and the islands of the Tumbes delta certainly appear to hold vegetation similar to that in which the species now occurs (de Macedo 1978, 1979). In 1988 soldiers and cattle herders in Bosque Nacional de Tumbes reported the presence of a large black guan in evergreen forest along the Ecuadorian border; several informants were certain that the birds had white flight-feathers as in the present species, but their memory might have been influenced by a poster of it on display at the military post, leaving a chance that the species was actually Crested Guan *Penelope purpurascens*, which is known from west Ecuador within 25 km of the Peruvian border (Parker *et al.* 1989).

That the species might be found in the large, little disturbed swampy region of coastal Ecuador anywhere south of Guayaquil (Delacour and Amadon 1973) was almost borne out in August 1980 when White-tailed Jays *Cyanocorax mystacalis* were heard giving imitations of guan alarm calls in a fairly undisturbed *Ceiba*-dominated forest east of Arenillas in coastal El Oro; although the birds being imitated might have been Crested Guans, which occur as close as El Chiral, the latter (in Ecuador at least) normally occupy humid forest, and the suspicion remains that the White-winged Guan was (or had recently been) present (R. S. Ridgely *in litt.* 1992; see Remarks 1).

POPULATION By report the species was common and found close to the town of Tumbes up to around 1850, but by the late 1870s it had become "everywhere rare" (Taczanowski 1884-1886). The report that it was "close to complete extermination", with a guessed-at 15 pairs remaining on Condesa, the last remaining site for the species in Tumbes (Taczanowski 1884-1886), was clearly responsible for the uncritical assumption of extinction that followed (Vaurie 1966b, 1968, Blake 1977). On being rediscovered, the total population was estimated to be a few hundred birds at most (de Macedo 1978). E. G. Ortiz (1980, *in litt.* 1987) showed the existence of 54-68 or more birds in Lambayeque in 1978 (these are detailed by site in Distribution), and stated that more birds could probably be found within this region, but he and J. P. O'Neill speculated the total population to number fewer than 100 birds (Eley 1982), and according to local residents the population has declined in recent years, notably after the land reforms of 1968, which gave public access to much land previously belonging to large haciendas (Ortiz 1980). At an unspecified date presumably in the late 1980s further surveys resulted in observations of under 200 birds and an estimate of only a few hundred in total (Díaz Montes 1991).

Populations at individual sites presumably vary, depending on patterns of local movement and breeding success; thus for example Ortiz (1980) reported one pair resident in Quebrada Caballito, M. Kessler (*in litt.* 1988) reported two groups (one of three birds) in February 1986, five were there in June 1987 (M. Pearman *in litt.* 1989), and an estimated 12 (six seen together) in August 1989 (B. M. Whitney *in litt.* 1991); see Remarks 2.

ECOLOGY The White-winged Guan inhabits dry wooded slopes and ravines in the deep valleys of the western Andean foothills from about 300 to 900 m, rarely up to 1,200 m, but may well also have occurred in coastal gallery forests (Ortiz 1980, Eley 1982; also de Macedo 1979). That its long tarsus implies adaptation to stream-side and mangrove habitats (Vaurie 1968) is, however, an error of tarsus-length assessment (Delacour and Amadon 1973). On Condesa, an island densely fringed with mangrove, the habitat consists of trees characteristic of dry north Peruvian forests, notably mesquite *Prosopis chilensis*, wattle *Acacia macracantha* and the groundsels *Baccharis lanceolata* and *B. salicifolia*; the guans would pass the day in impenetrable thickets and only leave at dawn and dusk to forage amongst the mesquite, whose pods appeared to supplement a staple early-year diet of buckthorn *Scutia spicata* berries (Taczanowski 1884-1886, de Macedo 1978, 1979). In Lambayeque it typically inhabits forested slopes in valleys with small permanent streams (valleys without constant presence of water being frequented only temporarily) and dry deciduous forest with safe (70%) cover, food plants and little human disturbance (Ortiz 1980). Characteristic plants (in order of predominance) are: in the valley bottoms the trees *Ficus* sp. (in the humid parts near the streams), "chamelico" (unidentified), *Ceiba trichistandra*, *Acacia macracantha*, *Pithecellobium multiflorum* and "cerezo" (unidentified), the bushes *Encelia* sp.,

Cestrum sp. and "santa maría" (unidentified), and in muddy places with abundant water also the grass *Gynerium sagittatum*; on the slopes the trees *C. trichistandra*, *Loxopterygium huasango*, *Cordia rotundifolia*, *Erythrina* sp., *Bursera graveolens* and *Genipa americana*, and the bushes *Encelia* sp., *Grabowskia boerhaaviaefolia*, *Oenothera verrucosa*, "solumpe" (unidentified) and *Croton* sp.; and for the upper reaches of the valley the trees *L. huasango*, *C. trichistandra*, *Erythrina* sp., *B. graveolens* and *G. americana*, the bushes "solumpe", *Croton* sp. and *G. boerhaaviaefolia*, also many cacti *Cereus* sp., and in the rocky parts an abundance of *Puya* sp. (Ortiz 1980). A list of 105 species of plants from its habitat is presented by Ortiz (1980). It is usually found in pairs or small family groups, but during the non-breeding season as many as 10 may be seen together (Ortiz 1980). It is territorial, especially during the breeding season, and is most active early in the morning and late in the day (Ortiz 1980). Activity starts at 05h45 when it leaves its perch, typically a well-hidden branch c.3 m above the ground, and performs short, vertical, ascending flights with noisy, powerful wingbeats, a behaviour typical of many species of guans (Ortiz 1980). Following the morning display, it descends to the valley bottom to drink and eat until 07h30-08h00 (sometimes to as late as 10h00), and then finds a cool, shady place where it will eat and rest without much movement till 16h30 or 17h00, when it again becomes active till 18h45, whereafter it finds a place to roost, often different from that used the previous night (Ortiz 1980). During the dry season some guans, mainly younger birds, travel to other valleys in search of food, water and breeding sites (Ortiz 1980). Within the valleys the guans are mainly found in the most humid parts, especially during the dry season, when these areas are confined to the higher parts of the valleys, but if undisturbed they will descend in the morning to places with greater abundance of water at lower elevations (Ortiz 1980). Flights in the open are avoided if possible, but occasionally as much as 200 m may be covered in a single glide (Ortiz 1980). B. M. Whitney (*in litt.* 1991) noted that birds in August kept to moist ravines through the heat of the day, but moved around in trees devoid of leaves on dry slopes early and late in the day, and when flying across a quebrada made no noise whatsoever.

The diet consists of fruits, flowers, leaves, buds and seeds, and possibly a few insects, though the latter needs confirmation (Ortiz 1980). Fig trees *Ficus* sp., whose fruits are among the most favoured, grow in humid places at low elevations and are frequented when the fruits are ripe (March–July and October–December) (Ortiz 1980). Other fruits include the fleshy berries of *Celtis iguanea* (May–July and October) and the unidentified "naranjillo" (June), the drupes of *Geoffroea striata* (July–September), and the fairly dry pods of *Pithecellobium multiflorum* (May–October), *Prosopis* sp. (February–April), *Acacia macracantha* (February–March, June–July and September) and *Caesalpinia corymbosa* (April, June–July and September); of flowers only the petals are devoured in the case of *Erythrina* sp. (February–April and August–November), while the whole flower is eaten from the unidentified "cerezo" (March–May and July–August); flowers of *Encelia* sp., abundant on the slopes March–May, are much sought after by the guans, who also eat the thin leaves and buds; buds are also taken from *Alternanthera* sp. (March–April), and in January fruits, leaves and buds may be taken from the unidentified "hoja tiesa"; seeds are principally extracted from the fruits of "*Bombax discolor*" (= *Ceiba trichistandra*) (June–August) and the unidentified leguminacean "chaquiro" (throughout the year); occasionally guans will visit fields in April, where they may eat shoots of maize, sweet potatoes and beans; only in Quebrada Cachaco or Quebrada Paltorán (which of the two was unspecified) in the El Tocto area are they known to eat coffee fruits (June–July) (Ortiz 1980, where details of 43 different food plants are given).

During the breeding season the loud calls, which are most often given between 06h00 and 06h45 and which can be heard over 1 km away, can be used to establish the presence or absence of guans in an area (Ortiz 1980). The only confirmed nest of the species was found in late May 1978, 2.5 m up in a small, heavily leaning vine-covered tree in dense forest at 470 m on steep slopes near a stream; it held three infertile eggs (Williams 1980). However, breeding is also confirmed at sea level in December–January, since the female collected in January 1877 had charge of two two-day-old chicks (Taczanowski 1884-1886), although the nearby thick untidy nest of dry branches 3 m off the ground could have been of another species, e.g. a heron (Williams 1980).

THREATS Hunting was identified as the sole cause of the species's disappearance from around Tumbes, c.1850-1877, and birds were then described as very timid (Taczanowski 1884-1886); indeed their current restriction (apparently) to the Andean foothills is probably attributable to hunting pressure along the coast (Eley 1982). However, in these foothills it is in serious danger of extinction owing to habitat destruction, with trees being felled for charcoal or wood to use in fruit-boxes and parquet (de Macedo 1978, 1979). Hunting of the guan continues in these foothills, mainly in Quebrada Mugo Mugo where many people have firearms, but in most of the remainder of the guan's range firearms are scarce and ammunition too expensive for the residents to use on an animal of only 1.5 kg (Ortiz 1980). Slings are sometimes used, and in Quebrada Negrohuasi four guans were killed with slings in early 1978 (Ortiz 1980). Hunting pressure increased after land reform in 1968, before which time the areas were privately owned and had little public access (Ortiz 1980). Nevertheless, habitat destruction is by far the greatest threat, as there is an ever-increasing pressure by man looking for wood, water and new areas to cultivate (Ortiz 1980). Recent studies have indicated that "chronic extreme drought, the unstable nature of the north-east dry forests and other factors such as infertility still limit the population size" (Díaz Montes 1991).

Natural predators Local people reported that the Black-chested Buzzard-eagle *Geranoaetus melanoleucus* is the principal predator of the guan in some areas, and they knew of at least two cases where guans had been killed by this hawk (Ortiz 1980). A guan of which the several-months-old, eaten remains were found in Quebrada San Isidro may also have died this way (Ortiz 1980). A Solitary Eagle *Harpyhaliaetus solitarius* was seen making an unsuccessful pass at a guan in Quebrada San Isidro on 13 June 1978 (Schulenberg and Parker 1983). Also Bay-winged Hawk *Parabuteo unicinctus*, known to have killed guans in other areas (Brown and Amadon 1968), occurs within the range of the White-winged Guan (Ortiz 1980). The mustelid *Eira barbara*, also occurring here, can take guans, though this is not common (Ortiz 1980). A number of predators probably take eggs or chicks of the guan, but there is no specific information on this (Ortiz 1980).

MEASURES TAKEN Within two months of the species's rediscovery in September 1977 the then Rare Animal Relief Effort (now RARE) gave US$3,000 to provide interim protection for the species at Quebrada San Isidro, organized by G. del Solar (unattributed paper on ICBP's files). RARE and WCI have continued to fund research and conservation of the species (Díaz Montes 1991). The species and its habitat is now completely protected by law (it is also covered by the U.S. Endangered Species Act: Nowak 1990), and a reserve at Quebrada Negrohuasi has been established; this protection, however, only exists on paper and has had little real effect (Ortiz 1988). The Cerro de Amotape National Park (91,300 ha: IUCN 1992) in Piura may hold the species (King 1978-1979).

Captive breeding A breeding programme of captive birds is being carried out on G. de Solar's fruit farm near Olmos (Ortiz 1988). In August 1989 around 24 birds were held at the establishment (B. M. Whitney *in litt.* 1991). In November 1990 APECO and Stichting Crax formally agreed to start a breeding centre with the support of G. de Solar, using the 23 captive birds (four reproductive pairs) and with the long-term aim of reintroduction into natural habitats (Díaz Montes 1991).

MEASURES PROPOSED A "national sanctuary" for the White-winged Guan has been proposed (Díaz Montes 1991), although whether as a general concept or as a decided area is unclear; certainly, however, such a reserve is highly desirable, and would also benefit at least two other threatened species, namely Grey-headed Antbird *Myrmeciza griseiceps* and Henna-hooded Foliage-gleaner *Hylocryptus erythrocephalus*, as well as a very large number of Tumbesian dry forest and scrub endemics (see ICBP 1992, Crosby *et al.* in prep.; also Cracraft 1985 for partial list).

Meanwhile, a concerted, systematic effort to discover more sites holding the White-winged Guan is required: this should involve the identification (by aerial photographs or satellite imagery) and investigation of all suitable dry forest areas in Tumbes, Piura, Lambayeque and even La Libertad; surveys of any habitat at the mouth of the Zarumilla on the Ecuador border; and a re-survey of Condesa and other islands in the Tumbes delta. In Ecuador the species merits searching for in any dry forests associated with coastal mangrove habitat bordering the Golfo de Guayaquil (see also Remarks 1). Additional data on the conservation of dry/moist forest birds in western Ecuador and north-west Peru are in the equivalent section under Grey-backed Hawk *Leucopternis occidentalis*.

REMARKS (1) R. S. Ridgely (*in litt.* 1992) added that there have been no subsequent records of guans from the region, including the large tract of forest controlled by the military between Arenillas and Huaquillas; these are surely worth investigation. (2) The fact that a high count was achieved at the height of the dry season, when birds were concentrated in evergreen thickets (B. M. Whitney *in litt.* 1992), may indicate that other seasons produce inaccurately low census figures owing to the lower detectability of the species.

BEARDED GUAN *Penelope barbata* **V/R[10]**

This guan occupies a fairly restricted range in humid montane forest in southern Ecuador and northern Peru, and is probably declining owing to habitat destruction and hunting; an important reserve for it is Podocarpus National Park, Ecuador, but several others in Peru, notably on Cerro Chinguela, are needed.

DISTRIBUTION The Bearded Guan is confined to the southern quarter of Ecuador and adjacent north-western Peru (see Remarks 1). The record from Tamiapampa, Amazonas (Taczanowski 1882, 1884-1886, Hellmayr and Conover 1942), is undoubtedly erroneous (see Remarks 2). Localities for the species (north to south within provinces and departments respectively, with coordinates, unless otherwise stated, from Paynter and Traylor 1977, Stephens and Traylor 1983 or read from IGM 1989), are:

Ecuador (*Azuay*) río Mazan, above 3,050 m, at c.2°52'S 79°10-11'W (M. Pearman *in litt.* 1991; guans here were reported to be Andean Guan *Penelope montagnii* by Robinson 1988, so corroboration is desirable); Guasipamba, Ingapucará, Santa Isabel, at c.3°10'S 79°30'W (sightings in September 1990: F. Toral verbally 1990, who also reported a sighting of Andean Guan just north-east of Pucará; again corroboration is desirable); río Rircay (3°24'S 79°21'W in OG 1957b) where a tail-feather of this species (not *montagnii*) was found in 1991 (R. Williams *in litt.* 1992); (*El Oro*) Taraguacocha (the type-locality), Cordillera de Chilla, at 3°40'S 79°40'W (Chapman 1921, 1926; specimen in AMNH); (*Loja*) Huaico, 2,800 m, untraced, although there is an Angu Huiacu just south-west of Ona (just inside Loja), i.e. at c.3°30'S 79°10'W (read from IGM 1969b) (Hellmayr and Conover 1942; specimen in FMNH collected August 1939); between Selva Alegre and Manu, 2,850-3,000 m, Cordillera de Chilla, at 3°31'S 79°22'W (observed mid-May 1989: Rahbek *et al.* 1989; see Population); Acanama near San Lucas, c.3,000 m, at 3°42'S 79°13'W (observed mid-June 1989: Rahbek *et al.* 1989; coordinates from Bloch *et al.* 1991); San Lucas (2,500-2,750 m), at 3°45'S 79°15'W (apparently misquoted as San José by Vaurie 1966) (Ogilvie-Grant 1893, Chapman 1926; two specimens in BMNH); Finca de D. Espinosa, north side of Loja–Zamora road, 2,550 m, at 3°58'S 79°09'W (D. Espinosa and F. R. Lambert verbally 1991); every surveyed locality along the west slope of Podocarpus National Park from the Cajanuma area south to Quebrada Honda, 2,700 m (occasionally to 2,900 m), at c.4°05-10'S 79°10'W (evidently year-round: Rahbek *et al.* 1989, C. Rahbek *in litt.* 1992; see Threats, Measures Proposed); Malacatos, 1,600 and 1,900 m, at 4°14'S 79°15'W (Hellmayr and Conover 1942; four specimens in FMNH collected August 1939); Loma Angashcola, 2,550-3,100 m, at 4°34'S 79°22'W, and Cofradia, 2,600-2,740 m, at 4°34'30"S 79°22'W (large population found in July–August 1990: R. Williams *in litt.* 1991);

Peru (*Piura*) Cerro Chacas, 2,625 m, Ayabaca province, at 4°36'S 79°44'W (pair observed and several birds heard 23-24 September 1989: Best and Clarke 1991); slope of Cerro Mayordano, 2,950 m, c.44 km by road east-south-east of Ayabaca, Ayabaca being at 4°38'S 79°43'W (three specimens in MHNJP collected in late September 1987); both slopes of Cerro Chinguela, 2,400-2,900 m, Piura and Cajamarca departments, at c.5°07'S 79°23'W (Parker *et al.* 1985; two specimens in LSUMZ collected August 1975 and June 1980); Huancabamba, 2,600 m, at 5°14'S 79°28'W (Vaurie 1966; specimen in FMNH collected May 1954; see Remarks 3); below Cruz Blanca, 1,800-3,000 m, at c.5°20'S 79°32'W (sightings: Parker *et al.* 1985); Palambla, 1,220 m, at 5°23'S 79°37'W (Carriker 1934; two specimens in ANSP collected June 1933); Abra de Porculla, 1,830 m, Piura, near border of Lambayeque department, at 5°51'S 79°31'W (Carriker 1934; two specimens in ANSP collected May 1933); (*Lambayeque*) upper reaches of Quebrada Paltorán, mainly above 1,500 m, but regularly down to 1,200 m, at 5°44'S 79°40'W (Ortiz 1980; coordinates read from IGM 1966); Bosque de Chiñama, 2,200-2,500 m, Ferreñafe province, at 6°02'S 79°27'W (sightings by I. Franke and others in August 1988: T. S. Schulenberg *in litt.* 1989;

coordinates read from IGM 1967); (*Cajamarca*) Tambillo, east slope of West Andes, at 6°10'S 78°45'W (Taczanowski 1879, Hellmayr and Conover 1942; two specimens in MHNJP: Koepcke 1961); Llama (2,100 m), at 6°31'S 79°08'W (Koepcke 1961; two specimens in MHNJP collected April 1951); 7 km north and 3 km east of Chota, 2,635 m, Chota at 6°33'S 78°39'W (two specimens in LSUMZ collected September 1977); Hacienda Udima, c.1,800 m, near Taulis, at 6°49'S 79°06'W (Koepcke 1961; specimen in MHNJP collected December 1952); trail to Monte Seco, 1,800 m, río Saña drainage, possibly the same as Hacienda Montesco at c.6°52'S 79°05'W (skeleton in FMNH collected May 1987); and Hacienda Taulis, 1,700, 2,400, c.2,500 and 2,700 m, at 6°54'S 79°03'W (Koepcke 1961; five specimens, two in AMNH collected June and July 1926, three in MHNJP collected February and August 1952 and April 1954).

POPULATION The species was described in the last century as "common" in northern Peru (Taczanowski 1884-1886), and it is probably true that this was its status in both countries until habitat loss became so widespread (C. Rahbek *in litt.* 1992). It was regarded as uncommon in Peru by Parker *et al.* (1982), and on Cerro Chinguela it was found to be uncommon and probably decreasing (Parker *et al.* 1985). It may, however, still be fairly common in unexplored areas within its range, and there are no recent reports of its status in the vicinity of Hacienda Taulis (T. S. Schulenberg *in litt.* 1988), where seven of the known 29 specimens were collected. The Ecuadorian population in 1989 was estimated to be between 500 and 3,000 pairs, probably about 1,500 pairs; the Cordillera de Chilla apparently has the greatest density, but only some 10 patches of habitat (e.g. 4 km^2 in extent), each holding 5-10 pairs (Rahbek *et al.* 1989, C. Rahbek *in litt.* 1992); about 400 km^2 of habitat in Cordillera Cordoncillo and Páramos de Matanga (the latter now virtually devoid of forest: NK) might hold the species (although it has yet only been found in the southern end of this region); and about 1,000 km^2 of habitat exists from Podocarpus National Park to the Peruvian border, possibly more, especially if much forest remains below 2,500 m on the east slope; for the two last areas a density of one pair per km^2 was estimated (M. K. Poulsen, C. Rahbek, J. F. Rasmussen and H. Bloch *in litt.* 1990).

ECOLOGY This species inhabits humid montane forest and cloud-forest (Delacour and Amadon 1974, Parker *et al.* 1985, Rahbek *et al.* 1989,, B. J. Best and C. T. Clarke *in litt.* 1989), usually between 1,500 and 3,000 m, but regularly down to 1,200 m in Lambayeque (see Distribution). Recent observations were mostly of pairs or small groups of 3-4 (Parker *et al.* 1985, Rahbek *et al.* 1989, B. J. Best and C. T. Clarke *in litt.* 1989). At Chota they were found to be remarkably tame (T. S. Schulenberg *in litt.* 1988), and a similar behaviour was seen in three localities in Ecuador (Rahbek *et al.* 1989).

There are few reliable data on food, save that a pair was seen eating yellowish green fruits (slightly larger than cherries) of an unidentifiable (probably undescribed) tree on several occasions in Podocarpus National Park (Rahbek *et al.* 1989). Although not proven, the large amount of undigested seeds in its droppings makes it seem likely that the guan is an important disperser of seeds (NK).

A report in Delacour and Amadon (1973) that the nesting season coincides with that of the Wattled Guan *Aburria aburri*, with chicks being met with from December to February, precisely echoes one in Taczanowski (1884-1886), and is supported by an observation of two adults with a two-thirds grown chick in Podocarpus National Park, March 1990 (B. M. Whitney *in litt.* 1991); however, at Acanama a pair with chicks was observed on 17 June (Bloch *et al.* 1991), on Cerro Chinguela a female with two small young was found on 29 July (Parker *et al.* 1985), at Cofradia a very recently fledged juvenile was in the company of its parents (including roosting on what was believed its former nest) in late July 1990 (R. Williams *in litt.* 1992), and a female from Taulis collected on 24 July had slightly enlarged ovaries (specimen in AMNH).

THREATS Ninety-nine per cent of Podocarpus National Park is out to mining concession (deposits of gold exist within its area), and although up to 1991 only a small part was being mined the situation remains very unsatisfactory, particularly with the development of new plans involving a Norwegian company (ECUNOR) and concomitant considerations of reducing the park's legal extent to one-third of its present size (C. Rahbek *in litt.* 1992, also Toyne and Jeffcote 1992, Sheean 1992; see Measures Proposed). Moreover, a cadre of illegal independent goldminers is already present in the park, and is capable of inflicting as much damage on it in the long term as the Norwegian company (E. P. Toyne *per* C. Rahbek verbally 1992). Pressure from settlers in the region is relatively high, and will greatly increase in future; at Quebrada Honda, for example, some dwellings have already been established inside the park boundary and small-scale logging is occurring (C. Rahbek *in litt.* 1992), and colonists are clearing forest at río Bombuscara and do not accept the park as a legally established entity (Toyne and Jeffcote 1992).

Hunting and habitat destruction are blamed for the probable decline of the Bearded Guan in northern Peru (Parker *et al.* 1985); forest at Abra de Porculla and Palambla is now mostly destroyed within 10 km of thc highways in both areas, although good habitat still exists to the north and south of Palambla (T. S. Schulenberg *in litt.* 1989, TAP). The confiding nature of the species renders it especially vulnerable to hunting (Rahbek *et al.* 1989). In 1977 the species was noted to be hunted at Chota by the few people in this area who then had guns (T. S. Schulenberg *in litt.* 1988). In the río Rircay it is hunted, according to locals (R. Williams *in litt.* 1992). Increased mining in Podocarpus National Park will inevitably increase the hunting pressure on the species, as the workforce will remain poor and in need of supplementary protein (C. Rahbek *in litt.* 1992).

MEASURES TAKEN The species occurs in Podocarpus National Park, Ecuador, established in 1982 and covering 146,000 ha (Rahbek *et al.* 1989, Toyne and Jeffcote 1992), but see Threats. It may also occur at Río Mazan, now apparently effectively protected (see equivalent section under Violet-throated Metaltail *Metallura baroni*).

MEASURES PROPOSED Only one large protected area, Podocarpus National Park, contains viable populations of this and other upper montane forest and páramo endemics of southern Ecuador and adjacent northern Peru; it harbours a further six threatened species, namely Golden-plumed Parakeet *Leptosittaca branickii*, White-breasted Parakeet *Pyrrhura albipectus*, Red-faced Parrot *Hapalopsittaca pyrrhops*, Neblina Metaltail *Metallura odomae*, Coppery-chested Jacamar *Galbula pastazae*, and Masked Mountain-tanager *Buthraupis wetmorei* (see relevant accounts; also Bloch *et al.* 1991). This park is in urgent need of better protection and management (Bloch *et al.* 1991), not only because of new plans to mine a very large portion of it (see Threats) but also because a large part of the Bearded Guan population in the region occurs just outside the park boundaries; with relatively minor extensions the park could become the world stronghold of the species (C. Rahbek *in litt.* 1992).

Additional montane forest reserves in southern Ecuador and adjacent northern Peru are badly needed. The remaining tracts of forest in the Cordillera de Chilla (El Oro, Ecuador) not only support large populations of the present species, but may also be a stronghold for other threatened species such as the Red-faced Parrot (see relevant account). Forests on the eastern slopes of Cerro Chinguela (Piura, Peru) support these and a variety of additional little-known species, including the near-endemic Neblina Metaltail, and the only Peruvian populations of more than 20 additional cloud-forest species (Parker *et al.* 1985). Several large areas of upper montane forest (at 2,000-3,300 m) still exist on the western slope of the Andes in Piura between Ayabaca and Cruz Blanca (I. Franke verbally 1991), and a reserve in this region would protect a great diversity of montane plant and animal species confined to a small area on the western slopes of the Andes (TAP). Large patches of similar forest also survive to the south, in the upper río Sana and río Chanchay valleys in central Cajamarca (including known collecting sites for the Bearded Guan such as Chugur, Taulis, Seques, and Paucal) (I. Franke verbally 1991).

REMARKS (1) North of Cordillera de Chilla or western Azuay (see Distribution), the Bearded Guan is replaced by the Andean Guan *Penelope montagnii*, which occurs in west Ecuador south possibly to Azuay, and in east Ecuador south at least to Cordillera Zapote-Najda, east-south-east of Cuenca, in west Morona-Santiago province near the border of Azuay (NK; specimens in ZMUC). It is yet to be established where on both the west and the east slope the two replace one another. Although not found there during a recent survey (Krabbe 1991), a high elevation species of *Penelope* may occur in Cordillera del Condor along the Peruvian border in south-east Ecuador, but it remains to be established whether it is *montagnii* or *barbata*. South and east of río Marañón *montagnii* reappears from Cordillera de Colán, Amazonas, southwards (Parker *et al.* 1985), raising the suspicion that the Bearded Guan is but a sub- or semispecies of the Andean Guan (NK). Peruvian specimens have been separated as the race *inexpectata* (Carriker 1934, Koepcke 1961), but Carriker was apparently unaware of the existence of *barbata* when he applied the name (Hellmayr and Conover 1942), while Koepcke seems to have compared the Peruvian birds with only a single Ecuadorian specimen. Traits of the distinguishing characters of *inexpectata* (general coloration and somewhat vermiculated belly) were reported to occur in some Ecuadorian specimens by Fjeldså and Krabbe (1990), who suspected they were only signs of immaturity, so the validity of *inexpectata* seems doubtful, and it was not recognized by Delacour and Amadon (1973). (2) Birds collected in the last century at Tambillo and Tamiapampa, Peru, were originally ascribed to "*Penelope sclateri*" (Taczanowski 1884-1886), but were later identified as belonging to the *Penelope argyrotis* (Band-tailed Guan) group (of which *barbata* has been judged a race) by Hellmayr and Conover (1942, also 1932), who added: "but whether they are the same as *P. a. barbata* or a separate form with more denuded throat can only be determined by actual comparison". Actual comparison seems not to have occurred, as Vaurie (1966b, 1968), and Delacour and Amadon (1973) made no reference to this issue yet failed to mention Amazonas (for Tamiapampa) in the distribution of *barbata*, nor did either locality earn mention under their treatments of the Andean Guan *P. montagnii*, to which the form *sclateri* belongs. As *montagnii* has been collected in Amazonas (see Distribution), it seems likely that Taczanowski's description refers to the Tambillo specimens only (T. S. Schulenberg *in litt.* 1988). (3) This specimen is presumably from above Huancabamba to the east or west, for the town lies in a semi-arid valley devoid of forest (TAP).

CHESTNUT-BELLIED GUAN *Penelope ochrogaster* V/R[10]

This seemingly very rare guan occupies a broad but poorly defined area of central Brazil, inhabiting patches and galleries of semi-deciduous forest in drier areas. It could prove to have a low population, and has been recorded from only one protected area.

DISTRIBUTION The Chestnut-bellied Guan is known from some scattered localities in central Brazil, from Goiás to western Minas Gerais and southern Mato Grosso. It possibly occurs also in adjacent Bolivia, where appropriate habitat is extensive (C. Yamashita *in litt.* 1987). In the following account localities are arranged from north to south, with coordinates taken from Paynter and Traylor (1991).

Tocantins There is a record from Macaúba, Ilha do Bananal, May 1962 (specimen in MNRJ), this being within the confines of the Araguaia National Park, according to TAW (1986); and there are sight records of small numbers in the park from the late 1970s and early 1980s (R. S. Ridgely verbally 1986).

Goiás There are two localities: the middle rio Paranã, near Monte Alegre de Goiás (mouth of the rio São Domingos), 1932/1933 (Pinto 1938, 1964; two specimens in MCZ), and Leopoldina (now Aruanã), rio Araguaia, July 1906 (Hellmayr 1908).

Mato Grosso Records are from São Domingos, 13°30'S 51°23'W, September 1949 (Pinto and de Camargo 1952); Pindaíba, August 1949 (Pinto and de Camargo 1952); "Engenho do Pari" near Cuiabá, June 1825 (von Pelzeln 1868-1871); Flechas, 16°02'S 57°15'W, July 1825 (von Pelzeln 1868-1871); near Cáceres, 1909 (specimen in MNRJ); Poconé, on the northern border of the Pantanal, currently (C. Yamashita *in litt.* 1987, A. Whittaker *in litt.* 1991); near Descalvados, 1825 and 1916 (von Pelzeln 1868-1871, Naumburg 1930); around (but not within) the Pantanal National Park at the confluence of the rios Paraguai and Cuiabá at four localities, namely Fazenda Sara (17°42'S 57°04'W), Fazenda Belice (17°46'S 57°14'W), Rita Velha (17°49'S 57°14'W) and Morro Campo (17°54'S 57°22'W), early 1992 (R. B. Pineschi *in litt.* 1992, whence coordinates); and at Porto Jofre across the river from Mato Grosso do Sul, August 1991 (TAP).

Mato Grosso do Sul There is a single record from the northernmost part of the state along the rio Piquiri, 1909 (specimen in MNRJ); but the record from Porto Jofre above suggests it must occur in adjacent areas south of the rio Cuiabá.

Minas Gerais A series collected at Pirapora, right bank of the rio São Francisco, in 1912 and 1913 (Pinto 1938, 1952), represents the only known record of this species in Minas Gerais, and a report of its recent occurrence in this area (de Mattos *et al.* 1984) is in error (G. T. de Mattos verbally 1987).

POPULATION Numbers are not known. The Chestnut-bellied Guan has been considered "a rare species, at least in collections" (Delacour and Amadon 1973) and "certainly rare" (C. Yamashita *in litt.* 1986), although another view is that it is "uncommon, but not particularly threatened" (J. Vielliard *in litt.* 1986). The extraordinary paucity of records, both specimen and sight, suggests that the bird is at least either highly localized or highly secretive. The commonest source of records is Poconé, and there at least it appears to be moderately common and enjoys relatively light hunting pressure (A. Whittaker *in litt.* 1991).

ECOLOGY Virtually nothing has been reported of the habits of this guan, which is said probably to occur in the better-timbered areas along rivers or in swamps (Delacour and Amadon 1973) and to inhabit forest interspersed with campo (Sick 1985). On both occasions J. Natterer encountered the species it was by the side of a stream, in one case the birds (a pair) being perched in trees (von Pelzeln 1868-1871). Its preferred habitat at Poconé has been given as "cordilheiras" of semi-deciduous gallery forest (C. Yamashita *in litt.* 1987), which grow on higher terrain that is rarely flooded (Alho and Rondon 1987), with, e.g., guatambu *Aspidosperma* sp., goncaleiro

Astronium urundeuva, louro *Ocotea* sp., laranjeira *Sebastiana* sp., tarumarana *Vitex* sp. and paratudo *Tabebuia* sp.; in the dry season, July–October, the ground under this vegetation is full of fallen leaves (C. Yamashita *in litt.* 1987). This was also the habitat of birds found in the same area in early 1992 (R. B. Pineschi *in litt.* 1992). At Porto Jofre two were in seasonal swamp forest with numerous fruiting figs *Ficus* and other 15-20 m high trees, notably *Vochysia divergens*, *Inga* sp., *Triplaris* sp. and *Pithecellobium multiflorum* (TAP).

The species has been observed feeding on flowers of a tree *Tabebuia* together with Bare-faced Curassow *Crax fasciolata*, Blue-throated Piping-guan *Pipile cumanensis* and Chaco Chachalaca *Ortalis canicollis*; it is sympatric at Poconé also with Rusty-margined Guan *Penelope superciliaris*, and is the rarest of the cracids in the semi-deciduous forest in the Pantanal (C. Yamashita *in litt.* 1986, 1987). There are no breeding data; three birds collected in June and July were not in moult (von Pelzeln 1868-1871).

THREATS None is known, but the species is presumably hunted for food like most large cracids in South America. It is difficult to pronounce on the extent or even existence of habitat loss, given the general uncertainty over the species's preferences, but it is to be noted that much agricultural development is occurring within its range (see, e.g., Threats under Blue-eyed Ground-dove *Columbina cyanopis* and Hyacinth Macaw *Anodorhynchus hyacinthinus*).

MEASURES TAKEN The species is protected under Brazilian law (Bernardes *et al.* 1990). It has been recorded at least around the periphery of the Pantanal National Park (R. B. Pineschi *in litt.* 1992); however, the record from a site within the present Araguaia National Park is the only certain evidence of its occurrence within a protected area.

MEASURES PROPOSED Surveys are needed to delimit the Chestnut-bellied Guan's current range and assess its status more accurately. Pantanal and Araguaia National Parks merit particular attention. Work at Poconé, the only site at which the species can be found with relative ease (C. Yamashita *in litt.* 1987), should be undertaken to determine its ecology there, with a view to applying the insights in a general evaluation of its likely distribution and situation.

REMARKS The Chestnut-bellied Guan forms a superspecies with two near-threatened cracids, the White-browed Guan *Penelope jacucaca* and White-crested Guan *P. pileata* (e.g. Vaurie 1968, Delacour and Amadon 1973, Sick 1985). It is locally known in Poconé as "jacucaca" (C. Yamashita *in litt.* 1987).

CAUCA GUAN *Penelope perspicax* **R**[11]

This guan has suffered from the almost total loss of its humid forest habitat in the middle and upper Cauca valley, Colombia, to which it is almost wholly confined; however, it survives in three protected areas, although poaching is prevalent in two of them.

DISTRIBUTION The Cauca Guan (see Remarks 1) is endemic to the upper tropical and subtropical zones of western Colombia (being principally confined to the middle Cauca valley), with records from both slopes of the West Andes and the western slopes of the Central Andes (Vaurie 1968, Blake 1977).

Localities for the species, as given in Hellmayr and Conover (1932, 1942), Meyer de Schauensee (1948-1952), Vaurie (1966a) or else as indicated, with elevations and coordinates from Paynter and Traylor (1981), are (north to south): (*Risaralda*) Ucumarí Regional Park, Pereira municipality, 1,850 m, on the western slope of the Central Andes, from 1989 to the present (E. Nadachowski *in litt.* 1992, E. Velasco *in litt.* 1992, LGN); (*Quindío*) Salento, 1,895 m, 4°38'N 75°34'W; (*Valle del Cauca*) Bosque de Yotoco Reserve (on the ridge and east slope of the West Andes, not above Buga, *contra* King 1978-1979), 3°52'N 76°24'W, and again in the period 1988–1989 (E. Velasco *in litt.* 1992); Pavas, 1,350 m, 3°41'N 76°35'W; heights of Caldas (apparently the same as Dagua), 816 m, 3°40'N 76°41'W; San Luis (type-locality), 1,350 m, 3°40'N 76°40'W; Lomitas, 1,400 m, 3°38'N 76°38'W; Bitaco valley, 1,350 m, 3°36'N 76°36'W (see Remarks 2); Miraflores, 2,050 m, 3°35'N 76°10'W; San Antonio, 1,750 m, 3°30'N 76°38'W; río Lima, near San Antonio, untraced; Primavera, also near San Antonio, untraced (see Remarks 3); Palmira, 1,066 m, 3°32'N 76°16'W; (*Cauca*) Santa Helena, 3°10'N 76°14'W, on the western slopes of the Central Andes, 1989 (E. Velasco *in litt.* 1992, including coordinates); río Mechengue, 2°40'N 77°12'W; Charguayaco, 2,200 m, 2°40'N 76°57'W; Munchique, 2°32'N 76°57'W; a remnant woodlot on the eastern flank of the western cordillera belonging to Cartón de Colombia (but given in a paper concerning records from Munchique National Park), September 1987 but not subsequently, despite searches (Negret 1991); Valle de Patía, 900 m, c.2°27'N 76°36'W, recently (A. Negret *in litt.* 1992, including coordinates and altitude); Patía, 1950s (specimen in MHNUC).

Two other sites are Clementina, named in Hellmayr and Conover (1942) as in the Western Andes but not traced by Paynter and Traylor (1981) (specimen in AMNH collected on 5 April 1898; see Remarks 4); and La Palma, south-west of San Agustín, at the head of the Cauca valley, 1°47'N 76°22'W, identified as the source of an egg by Delacour and Amadon (1973) but treated with some scepticism by Hilty and Brown (1986), evidently for being so far out of range. Hilty and Brown (1986) also commented that the species is unlikely to be found extensively on the Pacific slope (i.e. west slope of the West Andes), most records there being from low passes.

POPULATION At the beginning of this century the species was regarded as "not uncommon" (Chapman 1917a). Since then, however, habitat loss has obviously made it much scarcer, with almost no further specimens being collected: of 16 skins in AMNH, ANSP, CM and MCZ, 15 were obtained between 1898 and 1918, the exception being a female from Charguayaco in ANSP, collected 10 July 1955; the only other post-1918 specimen is a bird (in MHNUC) from Patía taken in the 1950s (LGN). The dearth of recent records before the mid-1980s and the destruction of forest in the Cauca valley caused real concern that the species was approaching extinction (Delacour and Amadon 1973, King 1978-1979, Hilty and Brown 1986); however, new observations in Ucumarí and Yotoco (see Distribution), plus live specimens (held captive in Cali) from Santa Helena (taken as a young bird) and Yotoco (egg removed from nest and incubated) (E. Velasco *in litt.* 1992), indicate that, at least in these areas, small but stable populations still remain; indeed, the density of that in Ucumarí appears fairly high, with (e.g.) 16 birds counted over 10/11 November 1990 (C. I. Acevedo and L. M. Renjifo *in litt.* 1992). The species is rare in Munchique National Park, despite extensive forest cover (C. I. Acevedo and L. M. Renjifo *in litt.* 1992).

ECOLOGY The Cauca Guan is an inhabitant of humid forest at 1,300-2,100 m (Hellmayr and Conover 1932, Hilty and Brown 1986). It is known to occur both in primary forest and second growth, including groves near dirt roads (LGN). Birds forage and apparently roost in flocks up to 16 individuals, from low trees and shrubs (c.3 m) almost to the canopy at up to 20 m (LGN). Food has been studied by E. Nadachowski (*in litt.* 1992). Concerning breeding, there is the somewhat unsatisfactory egg dating from 3 May (see Distribution), a one-third-grown juvenile collected near Pavas on 29 March 1908 (specimen in MCZ), a nest with two eggs (presumably one taken for captive rearing: see Population) from Yotoco (date unknown) (E. Velasco *in litt.* 1992) and a nest with two eggs at Ucumarí (date unknown) (E. Nadachowski *in litt.* 1992).

THREATS The deforestation of the middle Cauca valley has been almost total (Delacour and Amadon 1973, King 1978-1979, Hilty and Brown 1986), and it is more than likely that hunting has compounded the problem: poaching is prevalent in Ucumarí and the species is also persecuted in Munchique National Park (L. M. Renjifo *in litt.* 1992). However, the squatters who moved into the Bosque de Yotoco in 1977 (King 1978-1979) were prevented from taking up residence there (see below).

MEASURES TAKEN In the 1970s the Bosque de Yotoco was being given token protection by a local college (King 1978-1979), but squatters have now been effectively excluded and hunting and logging prohibited (LGN). The species also occurs in the Ucumarí Regional Park and Munchique National Park (see Distribution). All three sites have guards and human disturbance is prohibited by law. Recent surveys and studies have been conducted by E. Velasco and E. Nadachowski, gathering data on habitat, food preferences, population density, etc. (LGN).

MEASURES PROPOSED The three protected areas where the Cauca Guan is known to survive at present merit intensive conservation efforts, and ongoing studies in them should be fully supported; in two of them, Munchique and Ucumarí, poaching clearly has to be eliminated. Moreover, the apparently disjunct population around Cerro Munchique appears largely to have been ignored in calculations of the chances of the species's survival, and it is to be noted first that the (apparently) most recent specimen comes from this area, and that at río Mechengue there was "dense rainforest" in the lower reaches in 1970 (Paynter and Traylor 1981), possibly therefore also higher up, this being a locality also worth investigating for the near-threatened Baudó Guan *Penelope ortoni*. Any sites not investigated in recent years, such as Salento (see equivalent section under Moustached Antpitta *Grallaria alleni*), Patía and, possibly, La Palma, merit investigation. Obviously, any conservation initiatives focused on this species should consider the needs of the threatened species known to be sympatric with it, which for Munchique National Park, Bosque de Yotoco Reserve and Ucumarí Regional Park are listed in the equivalent section under Multicoloured Tanager *Chlorochrysa nitidissima*.

REMARKS (1) This bird has long existed as a subspecies of either Crested Guan *P. purpurascens* (Peters 1934) or Spix's Guan *P. jacquacu* (Meyer de Schauensee 1966, Vaurie 1968, Blake 1977); it is better considered a full member of a superspecies that includes these and others, including *ortoni* (LGN). (2) Paynter and Traylor (1981) synonymize "Bitaco valley" with Bitaco at the coordinates given for the former, but San Luis, the type-locality, is identified as in the Bitaco valley (see, e.g., Hellmayr and Conover 1942), and it may in fact be that specimens labelled as from the "Bitaco valley" were taken at San Luis, and hence that one locality exists, not two; Bitaco and San Luis certainly exist as separate localities within the valley, however (LGN). (3) Primavera might be a small village in the municipality of Darién, Valle del Cauca, on the west slope of the West Andes at c.3°56'S 76°31'W (LGN). (4) Clementina is likely to be

Rancho Clemtino, as Paynter and Traylor (1981) noted an MCZ specimen (not of this species) from this locality on the same date; however, they could not trace it beyond guessing it to be in Valle del Cauca.

BLACK-FRONTED PIPING-GUAN *Pipile jacutinga* V/R[10]

This largely arboreal frugivore of the Atlantic Forest formations of eastern Brazil, eastern Paraguay and north-eastern Argentina used to be abundant, but the combination of enormous hunting pressure and the destruction of its habitat, in particular the forest palms on which it chiefly depends, has rendered it now very rare except for a few protected areas in southern Brazil and in Argentina.

DISTRIBUTION The Black-fronted Piping-guan (see Remarks 1) once occurred in south-eastern Brazil from southern Bahia to Rio Grande do Sul, and in adjacent areas of south-eastern Paraguay and north-eastern Argentina in Misiones and Corrientes (Delacour and Amadon 1973, King 1978-1979), but it has disappeared from most places where it was once common, being currently very local (Sick 1985).

Brazil Records from western Paraná and both northern and north-eastern Paraguay (in Amambay) suggest that the species might occur in Mato Grosso do Sul, but there are no records. In the following account, localities are listed from north to south with coordinates from Paynter and Traylor (1991). *Bahia* Records are from Barracão de Cima on the rio Gongogi, October 1915 (specimen in USNM); ribeirão Issara, c.15°05'S 39°45'W, and ribeirão Quiricos, c.14°48'S 39°16'W, both affluents of the rio Ilhéus, December/January 1816/1817 (Wied 1820-1821, Pinto 1964; see Bokermann 1957); the rio Jucurucu, where it was seen several times around Cachoeira Grande and one specimen was secured, April 1933 (Pinto 1935); and the Monte Pascoal National Park, where it was found in 1977 (King 1978-1979, Sick and Teixeira 1979, Sick 1985).

Espírito Santo There is no strong evidence to suggest the species survives in the state. Records are from Fazenda Klabin in 1973 (King 1978-1979, Sick and Teixeira 1979) although only a fraction of this site, now the Córrego Grande Biological Reserve, remains (see Threats) and the species appears to be absent (Gonzaga *et al.* 1987); Fazenda Boa Lembrança, rio Itaúnas, near Conceição da Barra, October 1950 (Aguirre and Aldrighi 1983); Sooretama Biological Reserve and its former forested environs (including córrego Braço do Sul, rio São José, August 1937: Aguirre and Aldrighi 1983), 1977 (King 1978-1979, Sick and Teixeira 1979), although reported to have disappeared around 1953 (Sick 1969, 1972; also Gochfeld and Keith 1977, Scott and Brooke 1985); the mountains of Limoeiro-Jatiboca (900-1,000 m, near Itarana), regular in 1939 and 1942 (Sick 1969, 1972); Forno Grande, near Castelo, late 1960s (Sick 1969, 1972).

Minas Gerais The species was formerly common in the valley of the rio Jequitinhonha, and in the Serra do Brigadeiro (20°30'–21°S 42°20–40'W), but is now restricted to one locality in each, respectively: the Rio Doce State Park near Dionísio, where five birds were seen at two sites in 1981 and where today its numbers may even be increasing, and the Serra do Boné, 1,850 m, where a few individuals survive in a *Euterpe*-rich area of forest (G. T. de Mattos *in litt.* 1987, 1992). However, it may also occur in the state's portion of Itatiaia National Park (see Rio de Janeiro below).

Rio de Janeiro Records are from the valley of the rio Paraíba do Sul at São Fidélis and Cantagalo (Wied 1820-1821, von Ihering 1900a, Pinto 1964), where it still occurred in the late 1960s (Sick 1969, 1972); Teresópolis (Sick 1972, 1985), where it is believed still present locally (presumably within the Serra dos Órgãos National Park, but in very reduced numbers (Sick 1985 *contra* Scott and Brooke 1985); Itatiaia National Park, in or around November 1903, September 1950, 1978 (Pinto 1951, 1954a, 1964, Sick and Teixeira 1979, Sick 1985); Angra dos Reis, January 1924 (specimen in MNHN); the coastal slopes of the Serra do Mar at Mambucaba (Sick 1969) and Parati (Sick and Teixeira 1979), both these localities being adjacent to the Serra da Bocaina National Park. It is almost certain that the species occurred originally in and around Rio de Janeiro (Sick and Pabst 1968).

São Paulo It used to occur in every forest along big rivers in the interior of the state (see below), but has long since disappeared (Sick 1972, 1985, Sick and Teixeira 1979, D. F. Stotz *in litt.* 1988). Records within a strip roughly 200 km from the coast are from: Fazenda Barreiro Rico, c.22°45'S 48°09'W, near Anhembi, last shot in 1926 (Willis 1979, whence coordinates); Serra da Bocaina, still present in 1977 (Sick and Teixeira 1979); Ipanema, April 1819 or 1820 (von Pelzeln 1868-1871); Boracéia Biological Station, April 1988 (D. F. Stotz *in litt.* 1988); São Sebastião, May 1903 (four specimens in AMNH); Ilhabela State Park (i.e. Ilha de São Sebastião), on the coast, currently (several pairs being seen in 1978 along the road which crosses the island), and seasonally frequent on the eastern side of the island according to local reports (W. C. A. Bokermann *in litt.* 1987); Carlos Botelho State Park, 24°04'S 47°58'W, monthly between January 1985 and September 1986 (A. C. Dias *per* S. G. Paccagnella *in litt.* 1987; see Measures Taken), November 1988 (C. Yamashita *in litt.* 1988), January 1990 (Pacheco and da Fonseca 1990) and in October 1991, when 3-4 were seen, two of them displaying (B. M. Whitney *in litt.* 1991); Itararé, August 1820, March 1821 (von Pelzeln 1868-1871; see Remarks 2); Rocha (untraced but in the rio Juquiá valley: D. F. Stotz *in litt.* 1988, Paynter and Traylor 1991), August and September 1961 (two specimens in MZUSP); Iporanga (untraced but c.25 km north-north-west of Juquiá: Paynter and Traylor 1991), October 1961 (specimen in MZUSP); mountains north of Sete Barras, August 1929 (specimen in MCZ); "Port. V. Travessão" on the rio Ipiranga, March 1957 (two specimens in YPM); Iguape, undated (von Ihering and von Ihering 1907, Pinto 1964); Ilha do Cardoso State Park, currently (P. Martuscelli *in litt.* 1990). An untraced locality is Taquaral, April 1930 (specimen in MCZ: see Paynter and Traylor 1991). In the far west of the state there are records from Itapura, August 1904 (von Ihering and von Ihering 1907, Pinto 1938, 1964); the rio Paranapanema on Ilha da Serra do Diabo, 22°37'S 52°21'W (Pinto 1964); and the rio Paraná (Pinto 1964). The species was reported to exist also at Jacupiranga (now Jacupiranga State Park) and Sete Barras (now incorporated into Carlos Botelho State Park), although this remained to be confirmed (Willis and Oniki 1981a).

Paraná Straube (1990) referred to the species being known from a little fewer than 20 localities in the state (many more than are traced here). Records include: Londrina, formerly (Sick 1985); Porto Camargo, undated (Pinto 1964); rio das Cinzas, July 1927 (Pinto 1938, 1964; see Remarks 3); Salto Ubá, 24°30'S 51°28'W, on the rio Ivaí, November 1922 (Sztolcman 1926); Barreiros (untraced), Sertão, c.21°35'S 52°40'W, and Cruzeiro do Oeste, all also in the rio Ivaí valley, along with other unspecified sites there, August and September 1945, July 1951 and November 1956 (Straube and Bornschein 1989); rio Piquiri, undated (Straube and Bornschein 1989); Iguaçú National Park in 1977 and 1979 (Sick 1985), and throughout the 1980s (TAP); the rio Paraná valley, July 1951 (Straube and Bornschein 1989); Antonina and Guaraqueçaba, in the early 1970s (Cominese Filho *et al.* 1986); Cubatão, 25°50'S 48°48'W, February 1989 (Straube 1990); the flooding areas of the Salto Segredo hydroelectric dam at Fazenda Iguaçu, 25°55'S 52°10'W, May 1987 (Straube 1988; also F. C. Straube *in litt.* 1987). It probably still occurs also in the region of Morretes, on the coastal slopes of the Serra do Mar (F. C. Straube *in litt.* 1987). It has disappeared from interior Paraná (Sick 1972, 1985, Sick and Teixeira 1979).

Santa Catarina Records are from: Joinville, 1904 (Pinto 1938); Jaraguá (do Sul), undated (Hellmayr and Conover 1942); Blumenau, undated (von Berlepsch 1873-1874); rio Itajaí, 1860s, in large numbers (Sick 1985; see Population); Morro do Funil near Pouso Redondo, 1,050 m, where one was seen in November 1979 (Sick *et al.* 1981); Serra do Tabuleiro State Park, near São Bonifácio, where several birds were observed on privately owned land within the park in May 1986 (B. T. Pauli *per* C. Yamashita verbally 1987).

Rio Grande do Sul Records are from: Turvo Forest Park, 27°15'S 53°57'W, near Yucumã Falls, rio Uruguay, where five were seen in April 1979 (de Oliveira 1982; also Albuquerque 1981); Nonoai Forest Reserve, 27°21'S 52°57'W, where one was seen in July 1971 (Belton 1984-1985; also source of coordinates); Bom Jesus (i.e. Aparados da Serra, 66 km from Vacaria), where one was collected in July 1961 (de Oliveira 1982); probably in Santiago municipality, April 1849 (de Oliveira 1982); between Canela and São Francisco de Paula, where one was seen in around

1970 (Belton 1984-1985); Barra do Ouro, near Rolante, where five were seen in August 1971, with two or more on subsequent unspecified dates (de Oliveira 1982); Taquara, undated (von Ihering 1899a, Gliesch 1930; see Remarks 4); Arroio Grande, seasonally (von Berlepsch and von Ihering 1885; see Remarks 5); presumably near Porto Alegre, since a specimen was found in the market there during the 1920s (Gliesch 1930); and by report south of Porto Alegre as far as rio Camaquã, 31°17'S 51°47'W (von Ihering 1899a). Records along the río Uruguay in Corrientes, Argentina (see Distribution), just across from still forested areas in the state, offer hope that the species still occurs in these latter localities (Belton 1984-1985).

Paraguay In eastern Paraguay the species occurs north as far as the southern part of Amambay where it overlaps with the Blue-throated Piping-guan *Pipile cumanensis* (Vaurie 1968). Records (roughly north to south, by department, with coordinates from Paynter 1989) are from: (*Amambay*) Capitán Bado in the Cordillera ("Cerro") de Amambay, undated (Hellmayr and Conover 1942); (*Canindeyú*) Mbaracayú Reserve (Sierra de Maracaju), February 1988 (F. E. Hayes *in litt.* 1991); (*Alto Paraná*) río Acaray, río Monday, 25°33'S 54°41'W, and other rivers between 23° and 26°S, at the turn of the century (Bertoni 1901); Reserva Limoy, near the Itaipú Dam, currently (N. Pérez *in litt.* 1988); (*Caaguazú*) Caaguazú, between the end of June and mid-August 1893 (Salvadori 1895b); río Yuquerí, 25°15'S 55°39'W, 240 m, February 1932 (three-quarters grown specimen in MCZ); río Yguazú, 25°20'S 55°00'W, 220 m, March 1932 (four-fifths grown specimen in MCZ); (*Paraguarí*) Caballero ("General Caballero, near Villarica": Hellmayr and Conover 1942), 25°41'S 56°50'W, between the end of June and mid-August 1893 (Salvadori 1895b); (*Itapúa*) Capitán Meza, 1912, 1938 and 1939 (specimens in MACN).

Argentina Records are all from Misiones and adjacent north-east Corrientes, and chiefly from the northern half of Misiones (Nores and Yzurieta 1988a), as follows (coordinates being from OG 1968 or Paynter 1985): (*Misiones*) Iguazú National Park, currently (Chebez 1985b, M. Nores and D. Yzurieta *in litt.* 1986); Brazo del Yacuy (presumably part of arroyo Yacuy at 25°34'S 54°11'W), 1947 (specimen in MACN; see Remarks 6); arroyo Urugua-í, at kms 10, 20 and 30, 25°54'S 54°36'W, 1950s (Chebez 1990); arroyo Uruzú, 25°55'S 54°17'W, December 1983 (P. Canevari *in litt.* 1987); Piñalitos, 25°59'S 53°54'W, undated but in 1950s (Chebez 1990; see Remarks 7); Puerto Segundo, 25°59'S 54°38'W, 1917 (specimen in IML); Colonia General J. J. Lanusse, by local report (P. Canevari *per* S. M. Caziani *in litt.* 1988); Piray Miní, untraced but in Eldorado department (Paynter 1985), where a good population currently exists (J. C. Chebez *in litt.* 1992); arroyo Aguaray-Guazú, undated (Giai 1950; see Remarks 7); Tobuna, 26°28'S 53°54'W, 1950s (Chebez 1990); Puerto Leoni, 26°59'S 55°10'W, río Parana, where one seen in January 1987 (F. Moschione *per* S. M. Caziani *in litt.* 1988); Puerto Gisela, 27°01'S 55°27'W, 1926 (Nores and Yzurieta 1988a); Piñal Seco (río Pepirí Guazú, 27°10'S 53°50'W), currently (Nores and Yzurieta 1988a); El Soberbio, 27°18'S 54°13'W, 1871 or 1971 (specimen in a museum in Santa Fe: S. Caziani *in litt.* 1988); Santa Ana, 27°22'S 55°34'W, undated (Dabbene 1913); near Posadas, currently (Chebez 1985b); (*Corrientes*) along the río Uruguay at the Estancia Rincón de las Mercedes, 6 km south-west of Colonia Garabí, September 1967 (Short 1971; see Remarks 8); in forest along the río Paraná 14 km north of Ituzaingó, probably in October 1967 (Short 1971) and certainly post-1980 (Canevari and Caziani 1988).

POPULATION The species has suffered a steep decline throughout its range, resulting in its virtual extinction in the northern portion of its range and its restriction to certain areas in the south where it used to be very much commoner and indeed seasonally abundant.

Brazil In Espírito Santo in the 1940s it was found as rare as or rarer than the Red-billed Curassow *Crax blumenbachii* (see relevant account) (Delacour and Amadon 1973) and very few have been seen at Sooretama in recent years and indeed the bird has reportedly already vanished there (Gochfeld and Keith 1977); any extant population must be on the verge of extinction (Scott and Brooke 1985). Its current status in Minas Gerais is unknown (M. A. de Andrade *in litt.*

1988). In the state of Rio de Janeiro as early as the late nineteenth century it was reported to be increasingly rare at Cantagalo (Euler 1900), but individuals still appeared on the southern slopes of the Serra dos Órgãos (Goeldi 1894), where the species disappeared before the 1920s (Sick 1972), having been considered common at Teresópolis around 1916 (Sick 1985); small numbers are still, however, believed to survive in the area (see Distribution), although it is now almost certainly absent from the coastal ranges of eastern Rio de Janeiro (Scott and Brooke 1985). In the Carlos Botelho State Park, southern São Paulo, isolated individuals or groups of two to eight (isolated birds and groups of up to three being found more frequently) were observed 117 times between January 1985 and September 1986 (A. C. Dias *per* S. G. Paccagnella *in litt.* 1987); this is probably the best population in protected areas (M. T. J. Pádua *per* H. Sick verbally 1987), the species being frequent at least during the fruiting of palms *Euterpe edulis* (see Ecology), which are abundant there but have been extirpated outside the reserve (W. C. A. Bokermann *in litt.* 1986). This bird was once common to the point of being sold in markets in Rio Grande do Sul and Paraná in the 1940s (Sick and Teixeira 1979) and was shot in considerable numbers (a photograph shows "a pyramid" of dead birds) in the 1930s at Londrina, Paraná, while on the lower rio Itajaí, Santa Catarina, no fewer than around 50,000 birds were killed in just a few weeks during the cold winter of 1866 (Sick 1985). Numbers in Iguaçu National Park in the 1980s were always very low, and birds may even have been crossing from Argentina and were thus being double-counted (TAP).

Paraguay The species was evidently once abundant in much of eastern Paraguay, since Bertoni (1901) referred to its remaining so along certain rivers (specifically Monday and Acaray) despite having been exterminated wherever high levels of human settlement had occurred. It is probably now an uncommon resident of such large tracts of forest as remain in eastern Paraguay (F. E. Hayes *in litt.* 1981).

Argentina In the early 1950s it was repeatedly found to be abundant along arroyo Urugua-í (Chebez 1990), but it soon afterwards showed signs of alarming decline (Canevari and Caziani 1988, Canevari *et al.* 1991) and is now very rare throughout the country (Chebez 1990); it is commonest at Piñal Seco, Misiones, on the río Pepirí Guazú, where four individuals were seen in June 1985 and the local people know it well (M. Nores and D. Yzurieta *in litt.* 1986), and in 1986 it was found to be very common along the arroyo Uruzú in what is now the Urugua-í Provincial Park (J. C. Chebez *in litt.* 1992). In Iguazú National Park a small increase in the species's population has been noted (J. C. Chebez *in litt.* 1986).

ECOLOGY Wied (1831-1833) considered the Black-fronted Piping-guan a bird of the interior of tall, closed primary forests, but never found it close to sea coasts. It has been found in the Serra do Mar region "at any elevation" in rough, rocky places covered by thick high forest rich in palms *Euterpe edulis* (Sick 1985). In Espírito Santo it was found in luxuriant lowland forest to the north of the rio Doce alongside the Red-billed Curassow (Sick 1972, 1985). In Corrientes birds were seen in gallery forests (Short 1971), which are outliers of the formerly continuous forests of Misiones and adjacent Paraguay and Brazil (Delacour and Amadon 1973). In Misiones the species is very much tied to riverine strips of forest (M. Rumboll *in litt.* 1986), a point confirmed by studies in the 1950s along the arroyo Urugua-í, where all birds seen and collected were close to the stream, (almost) never in the interior forest (Chebez 1990), by observations in the 1980s (P. Canevari *in litt.* 1987), and by work at Piñal Seco along the río Pepirí Guazú (M. Nores *in litt.* 1992); observations in Iguaçu National Park in Brazil indicate the same, with birds mainly confined to forest within 100 m of the river, as is the case with many populations of Blue-throated Piping-guan in Amazonia (TAP). It inhabits higher strata of the vegetation, but sometimes descends to the ground to feed on fallen fruits of, e.g., bicuiba *Virola* (Aguirre and Aldrighi 1983). In Bahia, 1933, two or more birds were almost always seen perched on the branches of high trees in virgin forest: in the mornings they used to visit big araçazeiros *Psidium* full of ripe fruit, or rested in the highest branches of some nearby tree (Pinto 1935).

Fruits, seeds, grains and buds are listed as food by Canevari *et al.* (1991). Fruits of *Euterpe* are its favourite food (Aguirre and Aldrighi 1983, Sick 1985). Nuts of these trees are regurgitated in numbers and litter the forest floor, thereby attracting the attention of hunters (Sick 1985). Food in Carlos Botelho State Park consists mainly of *Cecropia* and *Euterpe* fruits but also includes figs, wild guava and other fruit (A. C. Dias *per* S. G. Paccagnella *in litt.* 1987). Other fruits recorded as food are *Psidium* (Pinto 1935, Aguirre 1947), *Hymaenea* and *Myrcia* (Aguirre 1947). In the one case where a bird was found away from water, it was eating alecrín *Holocalyx balansae* and cocú *Allophyllus edulis* (J. C. Chebez *in litt.* 1992). Wied (1831-1833) recorded the remains of both fruit and insects in the stomachs, and W. H. Partridge once found birds eating molluscs among stones at the side of arroyo Urugua-í, and on another occasion found them on mud where they were possibly taking salt (Chebez 1990). Birds formerly migrated vertically in the Serra do Mar in São Paulo in response to the availability of *Euterpe* fruit, which ripen earlier at lower elevations (Sick 1985). Vertical movements are still noted on Ilha do Cardoso, where the species ranges between 100 and 900 m (P. Martuscelli *in litt.* 1991). Regular displacements of the species in Santa Catarina occurred during the fruiting of pindaúba *Xylopia* in March and April, when flocks of 10 to 15 were seen; it used to appear in numbers in Santa Catarina during cold winters (see Population) and was periodically present also in south-central Rio Grande do Sul (Sick 1985), e.g. at Arroio Grande, where it arrived in May and June in flocks of 4-16 and left in December after nesting (von Berlepsch and von Ihering 1885; von Ihering 1900b gave the same information but for the north of the state).

Nests at Arroio Grande were commonly placed in a thick tree in the hollow of a fork formed by three or four branches, without any lining, both parents apparently incubating the 2-3 eggs and tending the young, which hatched at the end of November (von Berlepsch and von Ihering 1885, von Ihering 1900b). In Misiones, Argentina, females were forming eggs in August, a female and her two agile young were collected high in trees over arroyo Urugua-í on 28 October 1949, and an adult with two already fully feathered young were taken on 8 November 1952 (Chebez 1990). A pair from rio Paraná, São Paulo, were in breeding condition in late October (specimens in MZUSP) and a three-quarters grown male and a four-fifths grown female from Paraguay were collected on 26 February and 3 March respectively (see Distribution). Young have been observed in Carlos Botelho State Park in January (A. C. Dias per S. G. Paccagnella *in litt.* 1987). A male collected in November 1940 in Espírito Santo reportedly had considerably enlarged gonads (Delacour and Amadon 1973), but these were much smaller than those of another specimen collected in August 1941, while a female from the state in January 1941 had undeveloped ovaries (specimens in MNRJ). However, both Wied (1831-1833) and Euler (1900) referred to a nest with 2-3 eggs in February, and Bertoni (1901) reported a clutch-size of up to four.

THREATS The Black-fronted Piping-guan is threatened by both habitat loss and incessant poaching (Sick and Teixeira 1979, Cominese Filho *et al.* 1986, Chebez 1990, Straube 1990). Although the former has been seen as the more important cause of its decline (King 1978-1979) and has certainly eliminated it from most of its range (Delacour and Amadon 1973), the impact of hunting over the centuries cannot easily be understated (see below).

Habitat destruction Monte Pascoal National Park is under severe pressure (Redford 1989). The species's (chiefly riverine) habitat is especially susceptible to deforestation and hydroelectric developments (J. C. Chebez *in litt.* 1986), both known sites for it in Corrientes (see Remarks 8) facing loss through the construction of the Yacireta–Apipe dam on the río Paraná and the Garabí dam on the río Uruguay (Chebez 1985b, 1990). The species is sensitive to disturbance, disappearing as soon as clearings are made in the forest (Aguirre and Aldrighi 1983). Destruction of palms within forested areas may have been a particular factor in the steep decline of the species (Nores and Yzurieta 1988a); in Paraguay such exploitation has been massive (J. Escobar *in litt.* 1991). In this regard it is worth noting the similar impact such activity appears to have had on the largely sympatric Blue-bellied Parrot *Triclaria malachitacea* (see Threats in relevant account).

Hunting This bird has evidently long been persecuted both for its meat and, by Indians, for its feathers, evidence of the former being (e.g.) in the form of many feathers of this and the Red-billed Curassow strewn around a site near ribeirão Issara in 1817 (see Wied 1831-1833). It is avidly pursued by both predators and hunters in its remaining forests (Coimbra-Filho and Magnanini 1968). Its disappearance from Sooretama in Espírito Santo was caused by hunting (Gochfeld and Keith 1977). In the Carlos Botelho State Park, apparently one of the few places where a good population survives, one poacher shot eight birds by the roadside (C. Yamashita *in litt.* 1986). In Ilha do Cardoso State Park hunting is the major cause of decline (P. Martuscelli *in litt.* 1991). In Paraná the species declined during the expansion of coffee plantations in the north of the state, being shot in numbers in the 1930s at Londrina (Sick 1985; see Population), and hunting persisted until the 1970s, as attested by bird remains in the camps of settlers around Antonina and Guaraqueçaba (Cominese Filho *et al.* 1986). Appearing only periodically in the regions colonized by Europeans in Santa Catarina the birds developed no fear of firearms: in Itajaí, half a dozen were killed consecutively in the same tree and nearly 100 were shot in another tree, and the record of 50,000 killed in a few weeks in 1866 (see Population) evokes the history of the loss of the Eskimo Curlew *Numenius borealis* (see Appendix A) and Passenger Pigeon *Ectopistes migratorius* (see, e.g., Greenway 1958); but in the states of Rio de Janeiro and Minas Gerais they were very wild, possibly as a result of centuries-long persecution by man (see Sick 1985). Already at the turn of the century Bertoni (1901) reported that hunting had "totally exterminated" the species from populated areas of Paraguay, and this factor has certainly continued down to the present (J. Escobar *in litt.* 1991). Relatively frequent in Misiones until a few years ago, it has been pursued relentlessly this century for its much-prized meat (Chebez 1985b). Its decline along the arroyo Urugua-í may have been linked to its persistent use for food during a major expedition there in the late 1940s and early 1950s (Canevari and Caziani 1988), though given the size of the area at the time this seems unlikely (J. C. Chebez *in litt.* 1992). The record of the species from arroyo Uruzú in 1983 consisted of remains of a bird that had been hunted there (P. Canevari *in litt.* 1987). It was reported as occasionally taken by hunters at Estancia Rincón de las Mercedes in Corrientes (Short 1971), but may be extinct there now (J. C. Chebez *in litt.* 1992).

MEASURES TAKEN The species is listed on Appendix I of CITES, and protected under Brazilian law (Bernardes *et al.* 1990). Its hunting has been prohibited by law in Brazil since 1951 (Sick 1969, 1972). In Brazil the importance needs stressing of Monte Pascoal National Park in Bahia, Rio Doce State Park in Minas Gerais, Itatiaia and (possibly) Serra da Bocaina National Parks in Rio de Janeiro, Boracéia Biological Station, Ilhabela State Park (where neither poaching nor deforestation has been known to occur: W. C. A. Bokermann *in litt.* 1987), Carlos Botelho State Park and Ilha do Cardoso State Park in São Paulo, Iguaçu National Park in Paraná, Serra do Tabuleiro State Park in Santa Catarina (which covers 900 km^2, 80% being montane: L. A. R. Bege *in litt.* 1991), Turvo Forest Park (possibly important for Helmeted Woodpecker *Dryocopus galeatus*: see relevant account) and Nonoai Forest Reserve (apparently important for Vinaceous Amazon *Amazona vinacea*: see relevant account) in Rio Grande do Sul. A study of the species's population and ecological requirements began at Carlos Botelho State Park in 1989 (S. G. Paccagnella verbally 1989) but details remain unknown. An attempt to reintroduce the species to Sooretama Biological Reserve is reported to have been made, but failed (Gochfeld and Keith 1977); there seems to be no documentation of this initiative. Creation of a forest reserve on the Atlantic slopes of the Serra do Mar between Mangaratiba and Parati, Rio de Janeiro, was suggested (Sick 1969), apparently in ignorance of the existence, since 1961, of the Serra da Bocaina National Park in part of this very region. The 1988 record of the species from the Mbaracayú Reserve, a proposed national park, is important further evidence of the value of this site in Paraguay (see Measures Taken and Proposed under Vinaceous Amazon). In Misiones, Argentina, strict control in Iguazú National Park is believed to have led to some recovery of the species in the first five years of the 1980s (M. Rumboll *in litt.* 1986), and this park remains critically important to the survival of the species, although other parks, such as the Islas Malvinas Provincial Reserve and the newly created Alto Urugua-í Reserve, may also prove of great value (Canevari and Caziani 1988, Nores and Yzurieta 1988a), the former having now been integrated into the Urugua-í Provincial Park (J. C. Chebez *in litt.* 1992; see Chebez and Rolón 1989).

Captive breeding has been achieved several times in Brazil (Junqueira 1938, Sick 1969, Cominese Filho *et al.* 1986) as well as in Italy (Taibel 1968). However, there appears to have been extensive deliberate hybridization of birds with other members of the genus *Pipile* (R. Wirth *per* D. F. Jeggo *in litt.* 1986), and this cannot be regarded as a conservation measure of any merit.

MEASURES PROPOSED Survey of the Serra da Bocaina National Park in Rio de Janeiro and the Jacupiranga State Park in São Paulo would be valuable to confirm the species's presence. The Brazilian parks and reserves where birds are known still to occur (listed under Measures Taken) merit full maintenance. The establishment of Mbaracayú Reserve as a national park in Paraguay is clearly very important; the record of the species there consisted of a bird that had been shot (F. E. Hayes *in litt.* 1991), which indicates a problem of wardening and education that will have to be confronted at this site (and clearly many others). It has been suggested that other nature reserves like the existing Moconá Provincial Park in San Pedro and the Alto Urugua-í reserve in General Belgrano departments should be created in Misiones (Chebez 1985b), and Piñal Seco, with its important population, particularly deserves this treatment (Nores and Yzurieta 1988a). Moconá should be extended to include the Yabotí basin and to the north, and the area around Piray Miní and that of the Sierra Morena (in Iguazú department) should be established as reserves (J. C. Chebez *in litt.* 1992). Basic research into the ecology and movements of this bird is clearly important, and this might be allied with a study of *Euterpe* palms and their significance for two other threatened bird species, the Blue-bellied Parrot and the Cinnamon-vented Piha *Lipaugus lanioides* (see relevant accounts).

Captive breeding could aid further reintroduction of the species in parks and reserves, especially the Serra dos Órgãos, Itatiaia and Tijuca National Parks (Coimbra-Filho and Magnanini 1968); however, it seems that the enhancement of protection of the remaining populations and forests is more a priority (see Threats); Serra dos Órgãos and Itatiaia possibly continue to hold a population (see Distribution), and one attempted reintroduction has already failed (see Measures Taken).

REMARKS (1) The proposed inclusion of *Pipile* in *Aburria* (Delacour and Amadon 1973) has been rejected, but all the species of *Pipile* might be merged into one (Sick 1985). The Red-throated Piping-guan *P. cujubi* has been treated as a race of *P. jacutinga* (Pinto 1964, 1978), but this has not generally been accepted (e.g. Vaurie 1968, Delacour and Amadon 1973, Sick 1985). (2) The itinerary in von Pelzeln (1868-1871) indicates that J. Natterer was never in Itararé in March, the closest date being April. (3) There are other specimens from Rio das Cinzas, all with the name barely legible: one in MCZ dated 16 May 1903, one in AMNH dated 15 May 1903 collected by A. Hempel, and one in YPM dated 16 March 1909. However, the MCZ specimen label has "S. Sebastião, E. de S. Paulo" crossed out, yet AMNH has four other specimens collected by Hempel from São Sebastião, three of them on 18 May 1903. From this it appears that an error perhaps in dating has crept in. FMNH appears to have two skins, listed in Hellmayr and Conover (1942) as "Rio das Linga" (dated in the database 15 March 1903) but which Paynter and Traylor (1991) indicate as a misreading of Rio das Cinzas; this also applies to "Rio das Linyas", May 1903, on two specimen labels in MHNG. (4) The listing of Taquara (Mundo Novo) possibly simply referred to the nearby locality of Arroio Grande, as von Berlepsch and von Ihering (1885) indicated that the species had not been found at Taquara. (5) The siting of Arroio Grande in the southern littoral of Rio Grande do Sul on the map in de Oliveira (1982) is mistaken. (6) MACN data on this species were sent by S. M. Caziani (*in litt.* 1988), who gave the locality as reproduced; however, Nores and Yzurieta (1988a) referred to this site as Barra del Yacuy, while J. C. Chebez (*in litt.* 1992) has corrected this to "bajo del Yacuy". (7) Nores and Yzurieta

(1988a) pointed out that Refugio Piñalitos is on arroyo Aguaray-Guazú, but this is not the same as the Piñalitos in General Belgrano department (J. C. Chebez *in litt.* 1992). (8) Chebez (1985b) referred to three localities in Corrientes, apparently counting estancia Rincón de las Mercedes and Colonia Garabí as two.

TRINIDAD PIPING-GUAN *Pipile pipile* E[2]

Hunting and habitat destruction have reduced Trinidad's only endemic bird species to two small populations in the primary forests of the Northern and Southern Ranges; key site conservation and more public awareness are both urgently needed.

DISTRIBUTION The Trinidad Piping-guan (see Remarks 1) is endemic to the island of Trinidad, Trinidad and Tobago. According to hunters interviewed in the 1980s, the species was widely distributed through the island 30-40 years ago (James and Hislop 1988), although by the 1930s it was believed to occur only in the north and south (Belcher and Smooker 1934-1937), a situation also judged true in the 1950s (Junge and Mees 1958). Certainly today the known population centres exist only in the Northern Range at Madamas, Aripo, Cumaca/Platanal, Hollis Dam, Salibia/Matura and Grand Riviere, and in the Southern Range in the Trinity Hills (some other former localities are under Threats); probably the main centre for the species is the eastern half of the Northern Range (James and Hislop 1988; also R. P. ffrench *in litt.* 1981).

POPULATION Two small, well separated populations now survive. The species was evidently once abundant, since in the last century birds were easily tamed and often kept like poultry (Léotaud 1866), but Chapman (1894) noted that hunting was rendering it "a rare bird", and Belcher and Smooker (1934-1937) referred to its "extreme rarity". Howbeit, according to hunters interviewed in the 1980s, large numbers existed 30-40 years ago on the island (James and Hislop 1988), but the bird was already thought of as rare by the 1950s (Junge and Mees 1958). Although historically reported to be gregarious, moving about in flocks of 12-15 (in one doubted report, 50: ffrench 1992), there were no such records in the 1980s, the highest number together being five, although nine were recorded on one day at a particular locality (James and Hislop 1988). Some 250 km^2 of habitat still existed in the early 1970s (see King 1978-1979), but around 1980 one rough estimate was of only 100 birds remaining (L. Calderon *per* R. Sutton verbally 1981).

ECOLOGY The Trinidad Piping-guan inhabits remote primary forests (typically vine- and epiphyte-rich closed-canopy tracts with sparse ground cover) where there is minimal human disturbance; areas preferred are hilly (400-900 m) with steep ridges, deep valleys and abundant watercourses, the vegetation being lower montane rainforest in the north and semi-evergreen seasonal forest in the south (Léotaud 1866, Beard 1946, James and Hislop 1988). Principal tree associations in the north are serette–debasse *Byrsonima spicata–Licania biglandulosa*, crappo–guatecare *Carapa guianensis–Eschweilera subglandulosa* and pois-doux–redwood *Inga macrophylla–Guarea guarea*, while in the south the habitat is characterized by acurel–moussara *Trichilia smithii–Brosimum alicastrum* (James and Hislop 1988). Birds are arboreal, moving in small parties through trees 20-40 m up, although in the recent past in (presumably now cleared) lowland forest areas the species could be found on the forest floor or in the lower branches of trees; over much of the day the birds stay hidden and seemingly inactive in dense tangles high in the trees, and records during the rainy season (May–December) are relatively few, for reasons unknown (James and Hislop 1988). The distribution of the species appears to be closely linked to the distribution and availability of certain preferred food-trees, birds moving over large areas in the Northern Range in search of fruit; there have been records from coffee plantations adjacent to primary forest (James and Hislop 1988).

Feeding tends to occur most often in the evening, 16h00-20h00, i.e. extending for an hour or two after dark (verified by continued dropping fruit, which abruptly ceases), although it is occasionally noted in the morning; birds chiefly take fruit and seeds of forest trees, including *Ocotea*, *Pouteria*, *Bursera*, *Didymopanax*, *Erythroxylum* and, in second growth, *Lantana*, occasionally also cultivated crops (ffrench 1992, James and Hislop 1988). Léotaud (1866) also mentioned young leaves. Hunters reported that when birds were observed on the ground they were scratching the forest floor in search of insects; others have reported drinking from streams and forest epiphytes (James and Hislop 1988).

The sparse breeding information suggests a protracted season: mating was reported in March and apparent mating behaviour in April; developing eggs were in a bird found dead in January; two chicks were seen in March, and small (juvenile) birds in November, January, February and May (James and Hislop 1988). Reports indicated that the nest is stick platform "placed quite near the ground within a tangle of vegetation" (Belcher and Smooker 1934-1937), that the clutch-size is two and that nests may be predated by snakes (James and Hislop 1988). Not only does feeding persist into darkness but birds also become active (with noisy flights) as early as 03h00, apparently as a form of display, since flight in the daytime is relatively silent (James and Hislop 1988).

THREATS Principal causes of the great decline in the species appear to be habitat destruction and illegal hunting, the latter perhaps more critical in recent years.

Habitat destruction Heavy timber extraction or the total conversion of forests to commercial timber plantations has taken place in many areas of the Southern Range (e.g. at Casthill, Moruga and Guyaguare) (James and Hislop 1988). Similar disturbance and loss has occurred in the Northern Range, particularly in the foothills, at such sites as Valencia, Matura, Rampanalgas, Cumana and Toco, where hunters' reports indicated a former abundance of the piping-guan, and significant threats to forest remain at Aripo, Cumaca/Platanal, Madamas, Matura/Salibia and Grand Riviere (James and Hislop 1988). Access roads for agriculture and tourism (and always accompanied by squatters) are likely to result in further declines in the species: one such road is being built into Cumaca, close to a known area, while another is planned to run from Blanchisseuse to Matelot and could affect populations at Madamas and Grande Riviere (James and Hislop 1988).

Hunting Because its flesh is "tender and tasty" (Léotaud 1866) and "deservedly esteemed" (Chapman 1894), persecution has long affected the species adversely, although Belcher and Smooker (1934-1937), while accepting its rarity, wrote of "its one-time popularity as a table bird" as if this was no longer so. However, evidence gathered in the 1980s suggests that up to 20 years ago the species was shot often simply for sport, although since then hunting has been for subsistence (James and Hislop 1988). The pressure appears to have been high, with up to 10 birds reported shot "in one sitting", chiefly in the Southern Range from Casthill to Guyaguare (James and Hislop 1988). As with the Ring-tailed Pigeon *Columba caribaea* (see relevant account), hunters reported birds being attracted to columns of smoke at camps in the forest, and that shooting of one bird did not disturb the flock so that others could then be picked off (James and Hislop 1988). Hunting continues and, even though the meat is not prized (despite the nineteenth-century accolades), the species is used by bushmeat poachers whilst hunting the more profitable mammals of remote forests (James and Hislop 1988). Lack of reports in recent years from some of the more easily accessible areas of the Northern Range, where ecological conditions for the species appear ideal, suggests that hunting pressure there is too high for populations to replace themselves (James and Hislop 1988).

MEASURES TAKEN The Trinidad Piping-guan has never been listed as a gamebird, and the present Conservation of Wildlife Act, in force since 1963, has listed it as a protected species (James and Hislop 1988). Its preferred habitat falls mainly within forest reserves or state forests (some of which are surrounded by extensive tracts of private land, largely abandoned cocoa, coffee and citrus estates), but these provide no special protection to wildlife since forestry practices predominate, entry is unrestricted, and both illegal logging and squatting are commonplace (James and Hislop 1988).

Conservation education The government's Wildlife Section mounted public awareness campaigns about the species throughout the 1980s, involving the publication of popular articles, the distribution of posters to schools, lectures to school children and hunters' groups (with field trips for the former), and a free television "advertisement" for a few months in 1985, this last proving to be the single most effective instrument of popular enlightenment (James and Hislop 1988). The Point-à-Pierre Wildfowl Trust contributed to this work by producing calendars with and postcards of the species (James and Hislop 1988).

MEASURES PROPOSED Proposals for a system of national parks and other protected areas have been in place since 1980 without implementation, but in any case (from the standpoint of piping-guan conservation) now need modification (on a phased-in basis as more is learnt of the species), although some known key areas in both the Northern and Southern Ranges should receive immediate attention (James and Hislop 1988; see Remarks 2). Further research (lasting at least one year) on the ecology of the species is needed, and this can only be done with the support and participation of an international conservation group (James and Hislop 1988). Similar outside support is needed to assist the Wildlife Section in its awareness campaigns targeting rural communities, hunters, land-use managers and politicians, and in its efforts to enforce existing laws concerning hunting, squatting and logging (James and Hislop 1988).

Elevation to specific status (see Remarks 1) renders the Trinidad Piping-guan the only bird species endemic to the country, and as such it might be adopted as the national bird (with the White-tailed Sabrewing *Campylopterus ensipennis* – see relevant account – as Tobago's emblem).

REMARKS (1) Reinstatement of this bird as a full species (as was formerly judged by Chapman 1894 and Hellmayr 1906a) has only been recent, and remains somewhat tentative, the new arrangement proposing specific status for the Blue-throated Piping-guan *Pipile cumanensis* and for the Red-throated Piping-guan *P. cujubi* (Sibley and Monroe 1990). It is clear, however, that *P. pipile* and *P. cumanensis* are very closely related (see, e.g., Vaurie 1967a). (2) Efforts to establish protected areas in the Northern Range should, as far as possible, attempt to address the little-known threatened endemic race *aripoensis* of the Scaled Antpitta *Grallaria guatimalensis* (see King 1978-1979, ffrench 1992).

HORNED GUAN *Oreophasis derbianus* V/R[10]

A highly distinctive, little-known bird of high cloud-forest in southernmost Mexico and adjacent western Guatemala, this guan is at risk from habitat destruction and hunting within its limited range, and requires an intensive survey to assess its current status and needs, and the creation of several further protected areas.

DISTRIBUTION The Horned Guan (see Remarks 1) is restricted to the Sierra Madre del Sur in southern Oaxaca (reportedly) and Chiapas, extreme southern Mexico, and the region of high ranges and volcanoes in adjacent south-west Guatemala, with one record from eastern Guatemala and a probable record from Honduras (see Remarks 2). Patchiness of distribution is discussed under Threats.

Mexico Localities for the species, as given by Andrle (1967) and Vaurie (1967c) or as otherwise stated (with coordinates derived from OG 1956a or as otherwise stated), are (west to east): (*Oaxaca*) by local report, the Sierra Madre in the extreme east of the state, probably on Picacho Prieto (Binford 1989) although Cerro Baúl is mentioned by Vannini and Rockstroh (1988), with a claimed confirmation from the state in 1988 (*Cracid Newsletter* 1,1 [1991]: 4); (*Chiapas*) by local report, in the mountains west of Cintalapa, 16°44'N 93°43'W; by local report, the Sierra Madre above Tonalá; Cerro Venado, 1987 (González-García 1988a); by local report, "the trail over the Sierra from San Juan Custepeques", 15°41'N 93°00'W (coordinates from A. Long *in litt.* 1992); El Triunfo, 15°37'N 92°48'W (coordinates from A. Long *in litt.* 1992); near Santa Ana de la Laguna, 15°43'N 92°32'W; Cerro Toquián Grande, 1987 (González-García 1988a); Pinabete, c.15°13'N 92°13'W (read from DCM 1958); Volcán Tacaná (Mexican side: see Remarks 3), 15°07'N 92°06'W (Taylor 1975b; also probably in 1984: see Measures Proposed: Captive breeding); "Frailesca" (untraced) on Cerro Pico de Loro, 15°35'N 92°01'W (see Remarks 4). Of these sites, the most important are El Triunfo and the unprotected Volcán Tacaná (González-García 1988a).

Seemingly good potential sites for the species include Cerro Tres Picos (16°11'N 93°37'W: A. Long *in litt.* 1992) (although this seems likely to be the same area as that indicated by "above Tonalá"), Cerro La Angostura and Cerro Cebú (both in core areas of El Triunfo Biosphere Reserve), although these and three others (all north-west of El Triunfo), Cerro Semental, Cerro Tecoluma and Cerro Tomate, were searched unsuccessfully in March–June 1987; nevertheless, local hunters on Cerro Cebú and Cerro La Angostura reported them easy to shoot on account of their tameness, two being taken on the former in 1985 (González-García 1988a).

Guatemala Localities for the species, as given by Andrle (1967) and Vaurie (1967c) or as otherwise stated (with coordinates from OG 1965), are (northern sector, west to east, followed by southern sector, west to east): Jucup and Tzununcap in the region of San Sebastián Coatan, 15°44'N 91°34'W; north-west of San Pedro Soloma, 15°43'N 91°27'W; above Huehuetenango; San Miguel Uspantan, 15°23'N 19°50'W; Chicaman, 15°24'N 90°46'W (though the site specified was the left bank of the río Negro, i.e. well south of Chicaman itself and over a range of hills); Cobán, 15°29'N 90°19'W; Volcán Tacaná (Guatemala side: see Remarks 3), 15°08'N 92°06'W; Volcán Tajumulco, 15°02'N 91°55'W; Volcán Santa María, 14°45'N 91°33'W (where, however, no records were obtained in one year's fieldwork in the mid-1980s: Vannini and Rockstroh 1988); Zunil Ridge (Volcán Zunil), 14°44'N 91°27'W (where additionally in 1970 a feather was found at 3,300 m and birds were reported by locals: R. F. Andrle *in litt.* 1988), this evidently including the modern birding site for the species, Fuentes Georgina, at c.14°46'N 91°26'W, where (e.g.) five were observed in July 1990 (Wall 1992; coordinates from J. del Hoyo *in litt.* 1992); Volcán San Pedro, 14°39'N 91°16'W; Volcán Toliman (Volcán San Lucas), 14°37'N 91°11'W; Volcán Atitlán, 14°35'N 91°11'W; Chiul (presumably "Chibul"), El Quiche, 15°24'N 91°05'W; Chichoy, 14°48'N 91°03'W (see Remarks 5), although searches of the Tecpán ridge near Chichoy in 1970 were negative (R. F. Andrle *in litt.* 1988); (Finca) Santa Elena, 14°48'N 91°01'W; Cerro Tecpan, 14°47'N 91°01'W; (Finca) Chichavac, 14°48'N 90°59'W; Volcán de Fuego, 14°29'S 90°53'W; and, 110 km north-north-east (as predicted by Vannini and Rockstroh 1988), the Sierra de las Minas at c.2,500 m, about 20 km north-west of Río Hondo (Howell and Webb 1992).

In addition to these sites, the following were identified by Andrle (1967) as likely to hold populations of the species: Cerro Tumbador, 14°52'N 91°56'W (coordinates are for "El Tumbador"); Volcán Lacandon, 14°49'N 91°42'W; Cerro Tecun Uman, 14°50'N 91°30'W; Cerro Santa Clara, 14°39'N 91°17'W; Volcán Acatenango, 14°30'N 90°53'W. Of these, the Tecun Uman ridge was searched in 1970 with negative results (R. F. Andrle *in litt.* 1988). Volcán de Agua, considered a possible site by Vannini and Rockstroh (1988), was ascended in 1970, but not suffiently high to encounter the species (R. F. Andrle *in litt.* 1988). It is clear that there may be many other sites within the scope of this range where the species still occurs or occurred until recently; Vannini and Rockstroh (1988) mentioned the Sierra de Chuacús as an area in which residual populations may occur, and the Volcán Siete Orejas as the purported source of a captive bird near Quetzaltenango.

POPULATION Numbers have clearly decreased very seriously over the past century, as there is nowhere today where the species is considered any better than uncommon. In Guatemala a hundred years ago, however, it was "fairly abundant" above Chicaman (Salvin and Godman 1888-1904) and in the 1930s it was reported to have been fairly common at Chichoy (Carriker and Meyer de Schauensee 1935); it was still abundant in the 1960s on the Pacific slope of Volcán Tajumulco, but both there and at Chichoy the situation has deteriorated, and although Tajumulco may have continued to hold one of the largest of the remaining populations (Andrle 1967), in recent years political and military activities in the area may have led to a substantial decline (P. Rockstroh *per* M. J. González *in litt.* 1988). Elsewhere in Guatemala even by the 1930s a great decline was recognized since birds had not been found for years in places where they were formerly common (Griscom 1932); however, according to a local hunter, the species remains common in the newly discovered locality, the Sierra de las Minas (Howell and Webb 1992), and there are other parts of the species's range where the inaccessibility of the terrain will render it relatively secure for some years (P. Rockstroh *per* M. J. González *in litt.* 1988). Andrle (1969) considered that the largest populations occur along the Pacific slopes from Volcán Tacaná on the Mexico border south-east to Volcán de Fuego, and that this may have been the evolutionary centre of the species's abundance; but it is within this area that much habitat has been lost (see Threats). In 1970 aerial surveys showed substantial habitat remaining on Volcanes Toliman, Atitlán and Zunil, and some on San Pedro (R. F. Andrle *in litt.* 1988). In Mexico also a decline at El Triunfo was apparent in the mid-1960s (Andrle 1967). At the end of the 1970s an estimate was made that less than 1,000 birds survived (King 1978-1979; a figure evidently accepted by González-García 1988b), and comment that the species is amongst the rarest of the cracids (e.g. Estudillo López 1986) is common.

ECOLOGY The habitat of the Horned Guan is humid, evergreen, montane broadleaf forest ("cloud-forest") composed of many different tree and shrub species, sometimes mixed with cypress or pine, with ground and tree-ferns, epiphytes, mosses and lianas generally abundant; "here are moldering ranks of fallen trees and a luxuriant undergrowth, everything saturated with moisture because the sun is prevented from penetrating by the closed canopy" (Andrle 1967). Details of variation in composition of broadleaf habitats between localities are provided by Andrle (1967). On Volcán de Fuego the species was chiefly to be found in belts of the "hand plant *Chirostemen platanoides*" (Salvin 1860, Salvin and Godman 1888-1904), but this tree, now identified as *Chiranthodendron pentadactylon*, is seemingly absent from other mountains in its range (Andrle 1967). Details of the *Quercus–Matudea–Hedyosmum–Dendropanax* community that is the habitat of the species at El Triunfo (A. Long *in litt.* 1992) appear in Long and Heath (1991: 139-141) and Williams Linera (1991). A territorial polygynous male at El Triunfo repeatedly visited several "palo colorado" trees *Symplococarpus flavifolium* which provided food but also appeared to serve as look-outs or as advertising posts (González-García and Bubb 1989). The bird occasionally penetrates stands of pine and cypress (Andrle 1967), and has been described as occupying cloud-forest in the transition zone between deciduous and coniferous forests at 1,500-3,200 m (Estudillo López 1986). The altitudinal range in Mexico is from around 1,600 to 2,700 m, in Guatemala from around 2,130 up to 3,350 m, although there are very few sites with suitable habitat above 3,300 m; in Guatemala the greatest abundance appears to occur between 2,400 and 3,100 m (Andrle 1967). Wagner (1953) claimed that in the breeding season the species occupies areas above the limits of cloud-forest on the windswept, bushy mountain peaks, and hence was much more terrestrial than other cracids, while outside the breeding season it enters the forest and then was often to be found feeding in rides cut by coffee-planters; however, while it is the case that certain other workers have reported it to be terrestrial for much of the time (Salvin 1860, Salvin and Godman 1888-1904, Blake 1953), the accumulated evidence – including a very short tarsus – is against the species being any more ground-haunting than other cracids (Andrle 1967, Vaurie 1968), nor does it imply a breeding season exodus to higher levels (see Andrle 1967). That it is "primarily terrestrial" (Land 1970) is clearly unlikely; but it has been observed walking and never flying upslope (P. J. Bubb *in litt.* 1991).

Studies at El Triunfo in the 1980s revealed that the species eats the fruit of at least 35 plants (notably in the Lauraceae, Araliaceae and Liliaceae), the leaves of five others, and both of one, as follows (this list extending and superseding information in Andrle 1967, González-García 1984): *Ilex tolucana*, *Anthurium* sp. (leaves), *Dendropanax pallidus*, *D. populifolius*, *Oreopanax capitatus*, *Epiphyllum crenatum* var. *crenatum*, *Hedyosmum mexicanum*, *Eupatorium chiapense* (leaves), *Schistocarpha bicolor* (leaves), *Licaria alata*, *Nectandra sinuata*, *Nectandra* sp., *Ocotea chiapensis*, *O. matudae*, *O. uxpanapana*, *Persea* sp., *P. liebmanii*, *Phoebe bourgeviana*, *P. siltepecana*, *Smilax jalapensis*, *S. lanceolata*, *S. mollis*, *S. purpusii*, *S. subpubescens*, *Conostegia volcanalis*, *Morus* sp., *Trema micrantha*, *Zunillia cucullata*, *Cobaea scandens* (leaves), *Rhamnus capraefolia* var. *grandiflora*, *Cestrum* aff. *guatemalense*, *Solanum* sp. (fruit and leaves), *Symplococarpum flavifolium*, *Urera alcifolia*, *U. caracasana*, *Citharexylum mocinnii*, "cola de caballo" (Scrophulariaceae) (leaves), "coxoc" (Ulmaceae), "cafecillo" and "cacho de carnero" (families unknown) (F. González-García *in litt.* 1992). The *Prunus* mentioned by Salvin (1860) remains of uncertain identity. Other authors also mention buds, shoots and invertebrates (Wagner 1953, Andrle 1967, González-García 1984), the last being regarded as readily taken, notably soft-bodied insects such as Orthoptera and larvae, with the young largely dependent on insects (Alvarez del Toro 1976); however, on the basis of the most recent fieldwork, this is the only cracid so far studied that is strictly vegetarian (F. González-García *in litt.* 1992), with even the young being fed bill-to-bill by the mother on regurgitated fruit and fragments of green leaves (*Cestrum*) (González-García and Bubb 1989, González-García 1991). Contrary to the expectations of Andrle (1969), food competition with Highland Guans *Penelopina nigra* has been observed at El Triunfo, a male Horned Guan chasing away a pair of the latter from a fruiting tree seven times on four dates in March/April 1989, but although capable of winning encounters on the basis of its greater size the Horned Guan may suffer overall, being far less numerous than the Highland Guan and less able to reach fruits on slender twigs; the two species appeared to be entirely dependent on the same locally concentrated food resources (P. J. Bubb *in litt.* 1991).

The breeding season appears to be earlier than in other cracids of the region (Mexico), falling in the low rainfall months of February and March (or even January or earlier, as on Volcán Tacaná in 1987: González-García 1988a), so that by May when the rains return the young are already half-grown (Wagner 1953; also Alvarez del Toro 1976): this appears largely confirmed by the territorial calling of males in Guatemala, which starts in January and ends in April, and by the collection there of a month-old bird on 26 March (Andrle 1967), less positively by fortnight-old young on 21 April at El Triunfo (Parker *et al.* 1976). Apparent variation in breeding season, judged from females with young, may well result from serial polygyny (González-García 1988a), although the following evidence of polygyny appears at least partly simultaneous: in the territory of one male which had copulated with a female on 2 April (1989, in El Triunfo) a different female was observed with a week-old chick on 4 April and a third female with two two-week-old chicks on 9 April; the first female was expected to lay eggs a few days after copulation, with hatching in early May (P. J. Bubb *in litt.* 1991). One male was found to have occupied an area of only c.8(-20) ha throughout the breeding season (González-García and Bubb 1989). The report of a nest placed on the ground fuelled the belief that this was normal (Wagner 1953), and while subsequent reports also ascribed nesting to cliffs and the tops of rocks, others referred to low trees (Andrle 1967). In the 1980s the first nests known to science were found high in isolated, epiphyte-rich trees with few branches, close to a ravine with a stream (González-García 1984, 1988a; Wagner 1953 reported that territories needed flowing water, and González-García 1988b repeated this); another nest (or possibly one of those from which the foregoing was generalized), at 3,330 m, was high above the ground, hollowed out of plants growing on and around the trunk (Taylor 1975b); a nest in 1990 was 16.5 m up in the first branches of a rather isolated "trompillo" *Ternstroemia lineata* on a 45° slope at 2,325 m (González-García 1991). The clutch-size is two; incubation is by the female alone (which at one nest left the eggs three times per day – morning, midday, and afternoon – and at another four times a day, less towards hatching, partly perhaps owing to much rain at that time), and lasts 34-35 days (González-García 1984, 1988a, 1991). The female at the 1990 nest confined herself to an area of 9(-15) ha during the incubation period (González-García 1991). Hatching at this nest was virtually simultaneous (one or two hours' difference); these chicks received their first feed after some 40 hours, although this might have been delayed by poor weather, and left the nest after 67 hours, although in 1988 chicks stayed six days in their nest, probably owing to rain (González-García 1991); the manner of their reaching the ground has not been described. Care of the young is entirely by the female (González-García and Bubb 1989). Experience from captive birds suggests that males take up to four years to mature, while females do so perhaps in only one (F. González-García *in litt.* 1992). Except when breeding, the species is moderately gregarious (Blake 1953), but this may only be family groups that remain together throughout the non-breeding period (Wagner 1953).

THREATS The combination of extensive and intensifying deforestation with relentless hunting pressure has caused grave concern for this species's future: in the 1960s both these factors were prevalent in key areas, including Tajumulco, the Tecpán Ridge, the Sierra de los Cuchumatanes, and throughout Chiapas (Andrle 1967). In the Sierra Madre in southern Chiapas there are many farming communities, especially adjacent to the road connecting Huixtla over the ridge to Motozantla, with coffee being grown as high as 1,800-1,900 m (A. Long *in litt.* 1992). In western Guatemala, the potential area for the species was some 6,000 km^2, but habitat loss has reduced this by half; moreover, while many montane areas have escaped deforestation above the 1,600 m "coffee limit", this has not been the fate of Volcanes Tajumulco and Tacaná, nor even the Sierra de los Cuchumatanes, where it extends above 2,000 m (Vannini and Rockstroh 1988) or even to 3,000 m (Veblen 1976). Volcanes Santa María, de Fuego and Acatenango have suffered considerable loss owing to volcanic activity (Vannini and Rockstroh 1988). In eastern Guatemala, any populations will be severely threatened by marble-mining, which involves clearance of the cloud-forests covering the mountain ridges (P. Rockstroh *in litt.* 1988).

Whilst deforestation causes more permanent loss, and is thus ultimately the most serious threat, hunting (mostly subsistence, by coffee-plantation workers) is a very serious threat too, notably in areas with concentrations of villages such as at Volcán Tacaná (Alvarez del Toro 1981, González-García 1988a). Hunting was judged to be the cause of the species's local extermination below 2,700 m on the Tecpán Ridge, Guatemala, by the mid-1930s (Andrle 1967). Compounding this, livestock-grazing in the undergrowth of forest seriously alters and degrades its character (Andrle 1969, Parker *et al.* 1976). Military operations in the Atitlán complex (Volcanes Toliman, Atitlán and San Pedro) have compounded farming and hunting in reducing numbers in the region, and the same possibly holds true for any population on Volcán de Agua (Vannini and Rockstroh 1988). Captive breeding (see below) cannot perhaps be described as a threat to this species (although it is to be noted that the eggs from the first two nests ever recorded in science were taken for rearing in a private collection: Estudillo López 1986), but it does not appear to be relevant to its conservation and could possibly distract authorities from the more serious undertaking of habitat conservation.

The patchiness of this species's occurrence has been mentioned by Alvarez del Toro (1976), who noted that it is absent from seemingly suitable areas; the explanation for this might obviously be hunting, but it might also have to do with interspecific competition (see second paragraph under Ecology) or with undetected characteristics of the habitat. However, A. Long (*in litt.* 1992) has judged that mostly the species has been overlooked in many localities.

MEASURES TAKEN The species is legally protected from hunting or capture in both Mexico and Guatemala, but the laws are unenforced; it is listed on Appendix I of CITES (King 1978-1979).

Following the recognition that since 1960 El Triunfo was being destroyed by settlers, (Alvarez del Toro 1976), the Instituto de Historia Natural in Chiapas, Mexico, intervened and a 10,000 ha reserve was established there in May 1972 (King 1978-1979, González-García 1988a); this has recently been expanded and established as a biosphere reserve under federal law by presidential decree, consisting of 119,000 ha in five nuclei and a buffer zone (González-García 1991, A. Long *in litt.* 1992). Apart from this, valuable studies of the species continued throughout the 1980s, supported by various conservation bodies including WCI and the Brehm Fund (e.g. González-García 1984, 1988a,b, 1991). Other reserves in the Sierra Madre de Chiapas include the 73,800 ha La Sepultura Ecological Reserve (proposed), the 60,450 ha La Frailescana Forestry Reserve (decreed in January 1978), the 15,000 ha Pico el Loro–Paxtal Cloud-forest Reserve (proposed) and the less than 10,000 ha Volcán Tacaná region (proposed) (see Heath and Long 1991: 242).

Several volcanoes which support Horned Guan populations in Guatemala are considered national parks, and in the 1960s Guatemalan wildlife officials were trying to establish specific reserves for the species (Andrle 1969); one such, aimed also (and chiefly) at conserving the Resplendent Quetzal *Pharomachrus mocinno*, was established in 1972 on the southern slopes of Volcán Atitlán at 1,700-2,450 m, but only then covered 400 ha and was not known to hold any Horned Guans (LaBastille 1973). In any case, reserves in Guatemala that hold the species remain virtually unmanaged owing to political and military exigencies (P. Rockstroh *per* M. J. González *in litt.* 1988); however, one that does is Lago de Atitlán National Park, while three private reserves, Finca Mocca (Suchitepequez), Finca El Faro (Quetzaltenango) and Finca Pueblo Viejo (Alta Verapaz), possibly hold populations (Vannini and Rockstroh 1988).

MEASURES PROPOSED The importance of El Triunfo as a refuge for the Horned Guan and, at a lower altitude, the Azure-rumped Tanager *Tangara cabanisi* (see relevant account), as well as for the near-threatened Resplendent Quetzal, which migrates altitudinally between the habitat of the guan and the tanager (A. Long verbally 1992), cannot easily be exaggerated, and such further support as the area needs should be always accorded high priority. However, many further sites deserve conservation, such as those enumerated in the section above, and even these appear to be insufficient in quantity. What is needed is an entirely new analysis of the crisis over deforestation in the range of the Horned Guan: the areas surveyed and flown over in the 1960s (see Andrle 1967) need to be checked by the same methods again, with real thoroughness and care, so that a definitive understanding can be reached and clear position occupied by the conservation community (see Remarks 6). Major tracts of remaining forest require active conservation in both Mexico and Guatemala, this to involve the exclusion of cattle (Andrle 1967, Parker *et al.* 1976): such initiatives must (and in the case of El Triunfo, do) aim at the real integration of local community interests with the broader goal of permanent species conservation, and hence require a major educational component (González-García 1988a, A. Long *in litt.* 1992).

Volcán Tacaná merits special attention as an area in which a bi-national park could be established for the species (González-García 1991).

The whole question of what forms the northern and southern limits of the species's range, and why, deserves investigation. In this regard, the species merits being looked for on the higher slopes of Picacho Prieto, Oaxaca (Binford 1989), while the higher parts of the Sierra de las Minas in Guatemala, which had already been proposed as a national park before the discovery of the species there (S. N. G. Howell *in litt.* 1991), clearly need careful exploration, as does the Cerro Volcán Pacayita in Honduras (see Remarks 2).

Captive breeding A programme has been established "to avoid the extinction of this remarkable bird" (Estudillo López 1986), supported by the Brehm Fund (*Flying Free* 7,1-2 [1987]: 5-6), yet the general evidence is that the restocking of areas with shot-out populations is not a pressing need. Nevertheless, the Miguel Alvarez del Toro Zoo (Tuxtla Gutiérrez) received five one-year-old birds from Tapachula (therefore probably captured on Volcán Tacaná) in 1989 (P. J. Bubb *in litt.* 1991). Some 15 young have been bred from the stock held by J. Estudillo López (F. González-García *in litt.* 1992).

REMARKS (1) The Horned Guan occupies its own genus, and is arguably not only the most distinctive of its family but also one of the most striking members of the entire Central American fauna. (2) Local inhabitants have reported large birds with single red horns in the Cerro Volcán Pacayita Biological Reserve (S. J. Midence verbally 1988), which rises to 2,516 m and covers 97 km^2 between Lempira and Ocotepeque departments, Honduras (Cruz 1986). (3) It will be noted that Volcán Tacaná is listed for both Mexico and Guatemala. (4) Andrle (1967) appeared confused about the position of Pico de Loro, reporting it as 50 km "northwest" of Escuintla when evidently north-east was intended, but even so his positioning of it east of Santa Ana de la Laguna appears largely at odds with it being 50 km north-east of Escuintla. (5) OG (1965) gives two sets of coordinates for Chichoy, the other being 14°41'N 91°04'W. (6) As implied in Andrle (1969) and Delacour and Amadon (1973), in the late 1960s and early 1970s R. F. Andrle continued surveying actual and potential sites identified in his earlier (1967) study; however, the work had to be abandoned and the results were never published, except now under Distribution above in the form of notes supplied *in litt.* in 1988.

ALAGOAS CURASSOW *Mitu mitu* E[1]

This large ground-dwelling frugivore, only known in recent decades from a few forest patches in Alagoas, north-east Brazil, is now probably extinct in the wild owing to habitat loss and hunting, and its only chance of survival lies in a private captive population that numbered 11 in 1984.

DISTRIBUTION The Alagoas Curassow, here separated from the Razor-billed Curassow *Mitu tuberosa* (see Remarks 1), is known only from the north-eastern Brazilian coast, having first been encountered in the early seventeenth century in Pernambuco (Marcgrave 1648) and rediscovered in October 1951 in São Miguel dos Campos, Alagoas, when an adult female was collected (Pinto 1952, 1954a, Sick 1985). A report of its occurrence in northern Bahia (Burmeister 1856) has been much repeated (Pinto 1952, 1964, 1978, Vaurie 1968, Delacour and Amadon 1973) but is unreliable (Coimbra-Filho 1970). In recent decades, at any rate, the species has almost certainly been restricted to Alagoas (Pinto 1952), where by December 1970 the largest relict forests (then 8,500 ha) were to be found in São Miguel dos Campos (Coimbra-Filho 1971), and it still survived there more recently (Sick 1985), being restricted to the few forests in São Miguel dos Campos, Roteiro, Barra de São Miguel, Pilar and Marechal Deodoro (Teixeira 1986). At present, however, this bird is extinct or virtually so in the wild (D. M. Teixeira *in litt.* 1987: see Population); there is an unconfirmed report of one being shot at São Miguel dos Campos around 1988, apparently in an area of 800 ha of lowland forest which is all that now remains of such habitat in the state (D. Willis verbally 1992; see Threats, Measures Proposed).

POPULATION The plight of this curassow and its near extinction have been widely recognized ever since its rediscovery in 1951 for, despite then having been fairly easily found in the region (a hunter reported killing many), a rapid recent decline to a situation of "extreme rarity" was evident (Pinto 1952, 1954a). In the following decade it was presumed to have become extinct (Vaurie 1968), the date for this being fixed at around 1960 (Coimbra-Filho 1970), but evidence gathered during fieldwork in Alagoas showed that it was "still extant, though extremely reduced", that "no more than about 20 were left in São Miguel dos Campos forests", and that it "may be extinct before long, perhaps 2-3 years" (Coimbra-Filho 1971). It was again regarded as "possibly extinct" in following years (Delacour and Amadon 1973, King 1978-1979) but was acknowledged to be still found in Alagoas in the late 1970s (see next paragraph), albeit in "very reduced numbers"(Sick and Teixeira 1979, LPG). In the 1980s it remained "imminently threatened with extinction" (Sick 1985), its situation being "especially desperate" and the population calculated to be "probably less than 60 individuals" (Teixeira 1986), which certainly appears to represent an overestimate, even if the captive population was included (see below). Efforts made between 1983 and 1985 to capture birds for an official captive-breeding programme were unsuccessful, but an "old, hard-fleshed" individual was hunted in 1984 near São Miguel dos Campos (A. G. M. Coelho *in litt.* 1986). One bird said to have been sighted in early 1987 (R. A. Mittermeier *per* R. Wirth *in litt.* 1987) was killed shortly afterwards in a disastrous attempt to capture it for the bird trade (D. M. Teixeira verbally 1987); this may be a version of the 1988 report mentioned in the last sentence under Distribution.

A captive population has been kept since 1977 by a private bird-fancier (P. Nardelli) in Rio de Janeiro, who obtained the original stock in the late 1970s both from a local bird-keeper and from the wild in Alagoas (Sick 1980, LPG). In June 1979 four birds, tentatively sexed as one male and three females, were kept in this aviary (Sick 1980), and in early 1984 at least 10 adult-sized birds and a chick were apparently living there (Sick 1986). These are the only birds known on earth.

ECOLOGY The Alagoas Curassow is or was confined to lowland forest (Teixeira 1986) and the specimen collected at the time of the species's rediscovery was on a trail inside primary forest near the mouth of the rio São Miguel; the ground at the collecting site was covered with fruits of a big tree known regionally as "castelo" (*Phyllanthus*: Pinto 1954a), which were reportedly sought as food by a variety of mammals and birds such as deer, pacas, agoutis, curassows, tinamous, doves and toucans; the specimen's stomach and oesophagus were full of such fruits (Pinto 1952). The bird was also reported to be fond of "mangabeira" fruits (Coimbra-Filho 1971).

THREATS The extinction of this curassow was forecast as long ago as its rediscovery, owing to hunting and the imminent cutting of its last forest refuges (Pinto 1952). Destruction of habitat duly proceeded and the bird was ceaselessly hunted, although already extremely scarce and difficult to find in 1970 (Coimbra-Filho 1971) but, despite claims, no intervention was known to have been made (Coimbra-Filho 1974, King 1978-1979) other than some legal gestures (see Measures Taken), so that it became "extremely threatened" both by the expansion of sugarcane plantations and by poaching (Sick and Teixeira 1979). The sugarcane problem intensified in the late 1970s through a government programme (Proalcool) designed to supply the country's need for fuel alcohol (LPG). Despite the warning that "extinction will soon occur if the last survivors are not preserved in a forest reserve" (Sick 1972, 1983), the situation was allowed to deteriorate to the point where "there does not seem to be a single relict of lowland forest whose quality and size justify a reserve" (Teixeira 1986), particularly after demand for sugarcane forced up land prices there, one hectare of forest costing US$500 in the middle 1980s (Sick 1985). Ironically, however, there appears to have been a reasonably extensive area of lowland forest at São Miguel dos Campos that survived into the late 1980s, but which was cleared over a very short period (six months), leaving a mere 800 ha (D. Willis verbally 1992). Populations of the species may have been affected also by pesticides drifting from nearby cane fields into the birds' last forest refuges (Teixeira 1986).

MEASURES TAKEN This bird (as *Mitu mitu mitu*) is listed on Appendix I of CITES and protected under Brazilian law (Bernardes *et al.* 1990). Attempts were made to establish a captive breeding programme involving IBDF (now IBAMA) and UFPE, but these failed (A. G. M. Coelho *in litt.* 1986). Some birds have been reared in captivity since 1977 (see Population), but it is not at all clear how successful this private programme has been.

MEASURES PROPOSED Although it has been suggested that a detailed population survey of this curassow should be undertaken (Coimbra-Filho 1971) and that areas in Alagoas must be selected that can be protected as reserves for the reintroduction in the wild of captive-bred birds (Sick 1972, 1980, 1983) it has become apparent that almost no sites exist (see Threats) and that the "reconstruction of an acceptable area through the unification of a number of existing [forest] fragments [in] a slow process of reforestation... will run into many obstacles" (Teixeira 1986). Nevertheless, the area of some 800 ha at São Miguel dos Campos may possibly hold a few birds (D. Willis verbally 1992; see Remarks 2), and is in any case important for certain other threatened species (see Remarks 3); it therefore merits urgent investigation and protection.

Captive breeding It thus seems that the species will survive, at least in the short term, only by captive breeding (Sick 1985), which may not be difficult (*contra* Sick 1983) to judge from the good reproductive potential of its close relative, the Razor-billed Curassow, in captivity (Coimbra-Filho 1971). However, adequate management of the existing captive stock is an urgent need (and this would include public accountability through the involvement of the appropriate government and international institutions, and a full recovery plan drawn up under the aegis of CBSG). It is an extraordinary circumstance that the entire population of a species protected under national law should be held by a private bird-fancier, and even more remarkable that the agencies responsible for implementing that law have apparently developed no formal agreement for the birds' management and propagation.

REMARKS (1) The case for regarding the Alagoas Curassow as specifically distinct from the Razor-billed Curassow *Mitu tuberosa* (Pinto 1952, 1954a, *contra* Pinto and de Camargo 1957, Coimbra-Filho 1970, Sick 1980) is accepted here. The lumping of the genus *Mitu* with *Crax* has been proposed (Delacour and Amadon 1973, see also King 1978-1979) but this "lacks a reasonable basis, for both live side side by side, while as a rule congeneric species of this family replace each other geographically" (Sick 1985). At the time of the rediscovery of this bird in Alagoas, there still supposedly survived there a species of *Crax*, which was the "*Mitu poranga*" (Pinto 1952), almost certainly a subspecies of the Bare-faced Curassow *Crax fasciolata* (Pinto 1952, Sick 1969), described from the same area (Marcgrave 1648). (2) D. Willis (*in litt.* 1992) has pointed out that the Amazonian relative Razor-billed Curassow lives at a density of four pairs per hundred hectares, so that a forest of 800 ha could conceivably be managed so as to hold 32 pairs. (3) The same forests in Alagoas held also the threatened Pernambuco Solitary Tinamou *Tinamus solitarius pernambucensis*, Marcgrave's Bearded Bellbird *Procnias averano averano* (Coimbra-Filho 1971, Teixeira 1986), Red-browed Amazon *Amazona rhodocorytha* and endemic subspecies of the White-shouldered Antshrike *Thamnophilus aethiops* and Dusky Antbird *Cercomacra tyrannina* (Teixeira 1986).

NORTHERN HELMETED CURASSOW *Pauxi pauxi* E[2]

The nominate race of this curassow was formerly common in the northern mountains of central Venezuela, but deforestation and hunting have much reduced it there, although its status in the Andes of Merida and the adjacent departments of Colombia is unknown; the race gilliardi *from the Sierra de Perijá on the Colombia/Venezuela border is also believed to be under great pressure.*

DISTRIBUTION The Northern Helmeted Curassow exists in two forms, nominate *pauxi* ranging through the northern coastal mountains of central Venezuela from Miranda west into the Cordillera de Mérida across the border into Colombia in extreme south-west Norte de Santander and northernmost Boyacá; and race *gilliardi* in the Sierra de Perijá (Serranía de los Motilones) on both sides of the border in north-east Colombia and western Venezuela. The population of *gilliardi* is judged very probably to extend further south (Wetmore and Phelps 1943) and possibly even to make contact with nominate *pauxi* at the junction of the Colombian and Venezuelan Andes (Vaurie 1967c, 1968); nevertheless, while accepting the possible bias created by the distribution of fieldwork, the current concentration of records suggests that the species's two main centres are the Sierra de Perijá and the 250 km stretch of mountains west of Caracas. Localities, as given in Hellmayr and Conover (1942), Wetmore and Phelps (1943), Phelps and Phelps (1958, 1962), Vaurie (1967c) or as otherwise stated, with coordinates from Paynter and Traylor (1981) and Paynter (1982), are:

Venezuela (nominate *pauxi*, east to west): Cerro Negro 10°03'N 66°18'W (these coordinates placing it within the Guatopo National Park [see CNPPA 1982], whence there are apparently more recent records: S. D. Strahl verbally 1988); near Caracas, c. 10°30'N 66°55'W; Maracay, 10°15'N 67°36'W, and Rancho Grande, 10°22'N 67°41'W (Schäfer and Phelps 1954), both these being part of the Henri Pittier National Park (see CNPPA 1982); Cumbre de Valencia (type-locality: Blake 1977), 10°20'N 68°00'W; San Esteban, 10°26'N 68°01'W; Montalbán, 10°13'N 68°20'W; near Tucacas, 10°48'N 68°19'W; Nirgua, 10°09'N 68°34'W; Lagunita de Aroa, 10°26'N 68°54'W; mountains inland from Aroa, 10°15'N 68°55'W; Cubiro, 9°47'N 69°35'W, this evidently close to or in the Yacambú National Park (see CNPPA 1982), whence there are apparently more recent records (S. D. Strahl verbally 1988) including one in April 1992 (F. Rojas *per* C. Sharpe verbally 1992); "Montaña del Capas" (presumably Quebrada La Capaz), 8°43'N 71°24'W; Montañas de Limones, Mérida (untraced); La Azulita, 8°43'N 71°27'W; Burgua, 7°26'N 72°00'W;

(race *gilliardi*, north to south) Fila Macoíta–Apón (the ridges between the rivers Apón and Macoíta), 10°24'N 72°33'W; Campamento Avispa, 10°10'N 72°48'W; Cerro Yin-taina (also Manastara; Cerro Jurustaco; and "Sierra de Perijá west of Machiques"), all at or around 10°05'N 72°55'W; upper río Negro, 10°02'N 72°56'W (judged from TAW 1986); La Sabana (also Cerro Ayapa and Kunana: specimens in COP), all at or around 10°00'N 72°50'W; (upper) río Tucuco, 9°55'N 72°50'W (judged from TAW 1986);

Colombia (nominate *pauxi*, east to west) in the extreme south-east Norte de Santander and extreme north Boyacá, with plausible hunters' reports from adjacent westernmost Arauca in the río Crave Norte (Vaurie 1968, evidently based on Nicéforo 1955), specific localities (certain and reported) being (1) on the río Valegrá (Chucarima; El Porvenir, south of Labateca), (2) río Margua (La Dominga in the río Saravita canyon; San Alberto, between Quebrada Talco [Falco in Nicéforo and Olivares 1965] and the headwaters of the río San Lorenzo), (3) Quebrada La China on the río Cubugón (Alto de Herrera north of Santa Librada; headwaters of La China; Santa Librada and to the south; west slopes of Cerro de San Agustín; Palo Negro; El Porvenir; Quebrada Güíjica), (4) upper río Cobaría (río Tecauca) (in the San Francisco de Cobaría region, 2,800 m), and (5) the valley of the Cravo Norte above Tame (Nicéforo 1955; see Remarks);

(race *gilliardi*, north to south) El Bosque, above Carraipia, 11°09'N 72°20'W; Monte Elias, Sierra Negra, 10°51'N 72°43'W; Tierra Nueva, Sierra Negra (type-locality), 10°35'N 72°45'W; Hiroca ("Eroca"), 9°42'N 73°05'W.

POPULATION In the last century this species was common in the mountains of northern Venezuela (Summerhayes 1874, Funck 1875), and even in the 1950s was thought to be fairly abundant (Ginés and Aveledo 1958), although by then it was considered scarce at Rancho Grande, with a population of some 25-50 birds (Schäfer and Phelps 1954), and virtually exterminated in settled areas (Schäfer 1953). It has recently been described as occurring at a naturally low level of abundance, with less than one pair per 20-40 ha or 5-10 birds per km^2, but nevertheless in drastic decline (Strahl and Silva 1987). The nominate subspecies was described as already very rare in Colombia over 25 years ago (Nicéforo and Olivares 1965), and there appears to be no subsequent evidence of its status there or indeed of the race *gilliardi* in either Colombia or Venezuela.

ECOLOGY The species occupies very dense, wet, cool, mountain forest ("cloud-forest") on steep slopes in the subtropical and adjacent upper tropical and temperate zones, 500-2,000 m but usually and preferably 1,000-1,500 m in dense subtropical cloud-forest (Schäfer and Phelps 1954, Delacour and Amadon 1973, Meyer de Schauensee and Phelps 1978): it avoids forest edge and particularly selects humid gorges with a thick undergrowth of dwarf palms and terrestrial aroids, requiring the presence of associations of *Heliconia*, *Cyclanthus*, *Calathea*, *Anthurium* and *Dieffenbachia* (Schäfer 1953, Hilty and Brown 1986). However, females tend to select somewhat drier places when nesting (Schäfer 1953). Birds are highly site-faithful, and roost, nest, sing and seek safety in lower branches, rarely moving up into the middle storey (Schäfer 1953, Schäfer and Phelps 1954, Hilty and Brown 1986).

The species is largely terrestrial, foraging on the ground for fallen fruit and seeds but also taking grasses, buds and leaves (Schäfer 1953).

Territorial singing begins in December (or when the dry season ends), territories apparently being only 10 ha or less (300 x 300 m); pair formation (one case of apparent male bigamy, with the two nests 130 m apart inside one territory) takes place in February, nest-building (by the female) at the end of March, hatching of young (two eggs are laid, and only the female incubates, the male never associating with her from nest-building until hatching) in mid-May, but although nesting is entirely over by July, care of the young by both adults continues into October, when the moult is complete (Schäfer 1953). These breeding data are matched in the Sierra de Perijá, source of a laying female, 7 April, a breeding-condition male, 21 June, and a juvenile, 11 August (Hilty and Brown 1986). The nest is placed in forks or on horizontal branches some 4-6 m from the ground (Schäfer 1953). Incubation in captivity lasted 30 days in one instance (Taylor 1975a). The species is usually found in pairs or family parties throughout the year, and young remain with their mothers until October or November (Funck 1875, Schäfer 1953); this and other evidence above suggests some divergence of mating system from that observed in the closely related Southern Helmeted Curassow *Pauxi unicornis* (see relevant account), and indeed Schäfer (1953) considered the bird monogamous.

Daily (foraging) activity is restricted to the first hours of the day and the last of the afternoon; territorial singing often occurs at night in the early breeding season, but usually also over the midday hours from April to June (Schäfer 1953).

THREATS Deforestation and indiscriminate hunting both in Venezuela and Colombia are to blame for the substantial decline in this species (Schäfer 1953, Negret 1987). The low density of the species renders it vulnerable to human disturbance, and it is hunted even in national parks (Strahl and Silva 1987). In Henri Pittier National Park there is also heavy disturbance from the Maracay–Ocumare and Maracay–Choroni roads (M. Pearman *in litt.* 1991). It is also hunted by Indians who use the helmet in necklaces (Wetmore and Phelps 1943). In Colombia the race *pauxi* is (or was) hunted zealously by both colonists and Indians, again (in the case of the latter) not only for its meat but also for its helmet (Nicéforo and Olivares 1965).

MEASURES TAKEN The species occurs (but is hunted) in Rancho Grande (Henri Pittier) National Park, Venezuela (Schäfer and Phelps 1954, S. D. Strahl verbally 1988), and also in Guatopo and Yacambú National Parks (S. D. Strahl verbally 1988). In Colombia it is present on the eastern slope of both El Cocuy and Tamá National Parks (J. I. Hernández Camacho verbally 1988). A major educational campaign to generate interest in saving the species in both Venezuela and Colombia is now being mounted (Strahl and Silva 1987); ProVita Animalium is currently running such a campaign in the Yacambú National Park, Venezuela (C. Sharpe verbally 1992).

MEASURES PROPOSED A thorough analysis of the current status of the species and the threats it faces throughout its range would provide the best basis for determining an appropriate course of action; to a large extent this ought, in Venezuela, to be a component of a general survey to assess the needs of the threatened and endemic avifauna of the northern mountains and the Andes of Mérida, and the decisions taken should represent the interests of all such species. One measure already suggested, for the curassow at least, is the establishment of a "binational" park in the Sierra de Perijá/Serranía de los Motilones (Negret 1987).

REMARKS J. I. Hernández Camacho (verbally 1988) has pointed out that the first records of the species in Colombia date from 1761 when nine captive birds were noted recorded as having come from "La Salina de Chita", Boyacá.

SOUTHERN HELMETED CURASSOW *Pauxi unicornis* V/R[10]

An exceptionally poorly known species, this curassow has been found in lower montane forest at three localities in Bolivia and two in Peru, and appears to be genuinely localized and vulnerable to hunting.

DISTRIBUTION The Southern Helmeted Curassow is known from three localities, fairly close together, in Bolivia (nominate *unicornis*) and two in Peru (race *koepckeae*).

Peru On 17 July 1969 two specimens, identified as a new race, *koepckeae*, were procured at 1,200 m on the south-west slopes of the Cerros del Sira in the rio Llulla Pichis watershed, 9°26'S 74°45'W in Huánuco department. The consideration existed that these birds represent a relict population isolated on the Sira, which does not form part of the true Andean chain (Weske and Terborgh 1971), but in their original description of the species, Bond and Meyer de Schauensee (1939) referred to vague nineteenth-century reports from north-east Peru and the mountains of northern Peru, and in late May 1992 a bird (race undetermined) was encountered in the Cerros de Távara at precisely 13°30'S 69°41'W, near the confluence of the ríos Távara and Tambopata in the southern department of Puno at 800 m (TAP; see also Population).

Bolivia The species was first discovered in July 1937 in the hills above Bolívar, near Palmar, 17°06'S 65°29'W, at 760 m in the Yungas de Cochabamba, when a pair was secured (Bond and Meyer de Schauensee 1939, Vaurie 1967c; coordinates from Paynter *et al.* 1975). Searches in the late 1960s and early 1970s produced two more skins from near "Guanay, Arepucho, apparently also located in the Cochabamba area" (Weske and Terborgh 1971; see Remarks), these presumably the specimens also reported as from "rio Catacapes, upper rio Beni" (Meyer de Schauensee 1982): there is a rio Catacajes (also spelt Cotacajes) at roughly 17°S 68°W in TAW (1986), although an account of these searches suggests that El Guanay and, in particular, Carmen-Pampa (where the species was found) are in the "Yungas of Totora" (Cordier 1971), Totora being at some distance south-east of the Catacajes (see TAW 1986; but also see Remarks). Another vague account mentions the río Sagta at the base of the yungas, as if this related to the locality at which three live birds were collected, the dates not being given (Estudillo López 1986). More recently the species has been located and studied at 700 m on the upper río Saguayo within the boundaries of the Amboró National Park, whose southern border lies at 17°51'S between the ríos Surutú and Yapacani (Cox and Clarke 1988).

POPULATION The species is evidently rare in Bolivia (see Cordier 1971) and is likely also to be so in Peru (Weske and Terborgh 1971); nevertheless, the discovery of a bird in southern Peru in May 1992 fulfilled an expectation that the species would be present on ridges and outliers from the Cerros del Sira southwards into the Bolivian yungas (TAP).

ECOLOGY In Bolivia the species inhabits densely forested regions of heavy rainfall, preferably at 450-1,100 m, in extremely rugged terrain drained by white-water streams (Cordier 1971). In Amboró National Park, birds were found in semi-open tropical forest on steep slopes; the presence of cliffs, banks and steep ridge-tops may be important to allow birds to escape predators by downhill gliding (Cox and Clarke 1988). In the Cerros del Sira, Peru, which is a range of rugged hills covered (at least in the early 1970s) in undisturbed humid forest, the two specimens were collected together in a lushly vegetated ravine near the lower elevational limit of cloud-forest (Weske and Terborgh 1971).

A major food is the seeds of a tree named almendrillo, renowned for its exceptionally hard wood (Cordier 1971). Locals have reported three types of "laurel" (*Nectandra*) and "negrillo" (Lauraceae) as food, and birds have been flushed from below fruit-bearing trees; they are generally active between dawn and 08h30 and 16h00 and dark, but may feed on moonlit nights, having been noted to be far more active on days following moonless nights (Cox and Clarke 1988).

In Amboró National Park at the start of the rains in early September, the scattered local population coalesces into small groups and then gathers at a deep forest site where males call ("boom") in a dispersed lek; a quantitative analysis of data on birds calling in October 1988 gave an estimated mean of 40 birds in a 1 km^2 plot (presumably the "deep forest site") in the main study area (Cox 1990). After mating, females move away to nest alone; the only nest found to date was a substantial structure that held only one egg (considered laid on 24 October 1989), and was placed 5 m up in the fork of an isolated tree in a rocky stream bed at its confluence with the río Saguayo, at 600 m (G. Cox *in litt.* 1989, Cox 1990).

THREATS Professional hunters have caused a decline in Bolivia, where in addition local people in the "Yungas of Totora" fashion cigarette-lighters from the species's "horn" (Cordier 1971); in and around Amboró the bird is much eaten and its skewered head claimed to be used in folk dances (Hardy 1984: see also Threats under Bolivian Recurvebill *Simoxenops striatus*).

MEASURES TAKEN Efforts to secure the integrity of the Amboró National Park (see Hardy 1984) must have contributed to the long-term security of this species (see equivalent section under Bolivian Recurvebill). A study of the species in the park, the "1987 Horned Curassow Expedition", by R. O. Clarke and G. G. Cox, is a major step towards determining its status and needs there, as well as obtaining some basic biological data which will have wider applicability.

MEASURES PROPOSED International support is required for the maintenance of Amboró National Park (see equivalent section under Bolivian Recurvebill). The other localities known for the species in Bolivia need further investigation, with a view to assessing the potential threats of hunting and deforestation. In Peru consideration might be given to establishing protected area status for the Cerros del Sira, only home of the Sira Tanager *Tangara phillipsi* (see relevant account). Equally, however, further work is likely to reveal new populations in the low Andean foothills and outlying ridges in the region of the Peru/Bolivia border, and care must be taken to align initiatives to protect areas for this species with other conservation interests in this area.

REMARKS Cordier's (1971) account of his searches is confusing, and the other information about his localities gained elsewhere (see Distribution) fails to clarify matters. However, Arepucho is at 17°15'S 65°14'W (in OG 1955a). Meanwhile, AGSNY (1940) shows a Carmenpampa just south (upriver) of Espiritu Santo on the river of the same name, at c.17°09'S 65°34'W, not far from a locality called Palmar (c.17°06'S 65°24'W), although no "El Guanay" is marked and the locality is well north-west of Arepucho (Espiritu Santo is in TAW 1986, at 17°05'S 65°39'W). Camacho Lara (1947) complicated the issue further by showing a "Pampa El Carmen" north of Arepucho (though this is a region rather than a settlement) and still further (1958) by indicating the Yungas de Totora well to the south-west of Arepucho.

BLUE-BILLED CURASSOW *Crax alberti* E[3]

Occupying a restricted range in northern Colombia in humid forest of the lowlands and foothills, this large gamebird has suffered serious decline and widespread local extinction owing to deforestation and hunting, such that the location of any surviving populations is unknown and surveys and associated conservation efforts are now exigent.

DISTRIBUTION The Blue-billed Curassow is endemic to northern Colombia in the foothills of the Sierra Nevada de Santa Marta, the north-west lowlands, the northern Andean foothills west of the río Magdalena, and the western slopes of the middle Magdalena valley. In their otherwise very accurate map of the species's (former) range, Hilty and Brown (1986) showed a continuous distribution around the base of the Santa Marta massif, but there appear to be no records from the west or south. In fact its entire range may now have contracted to only a few remnant forest patches (Negret 1987). In the following list dates have been largely omitted, since so few are given in the original sources, but from a comparison of these records with many of the museum skins on which they are based it appears that almost all of them were made before 1950 (those known to be later are indicated).

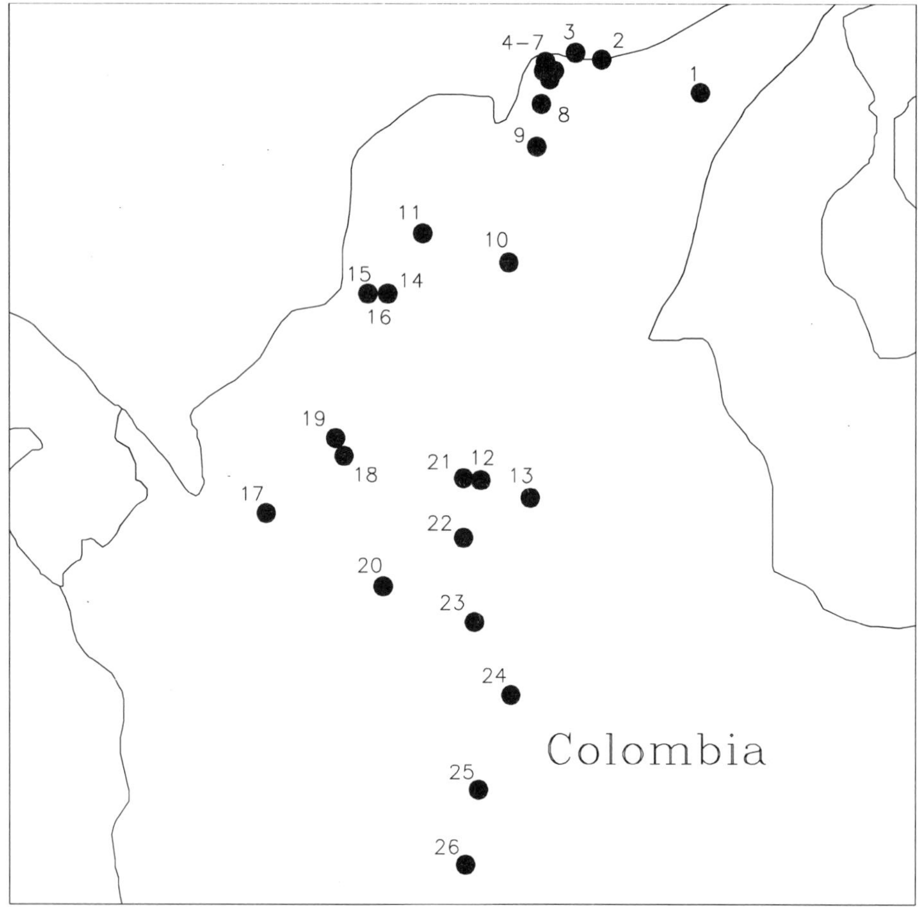

Localities (see Remarks 1) for the species, with coordinates from Paynter and Traylor (1981), are here arranged by department, north-east to south-west as far as 9°N, then north-west to south-east: (*La Guajira*) La Cueva[1] (see Remarks 2), 11°01'N 72°56'W (Vaurie 1967b; female in USNM labelled *Crax annulata*, collected on "old trail, Fonseca-Ríohacha", 560 m, 13 April 1945); (*Magdalena*) Don Diego[2], 11°15'N 73°42'W (Todd and Carriker 1922); Los Naranjos[3] ("Naranjo"), 11°18'N 73°54'W (Allen 1900); San Lorenzo[4], Cuchilla, 11°10'N 74°04'W (Todd and Carriker 1922); Cincinati[5], 11°06'N 74°06'W (Vaurie 1967b); Bonda[6], 11°14'N 74°08'W (Allen 1900); La Tigrera[7], 11°10'N 74°09'W (Vaurie 1967b); along the río Frío[8] and on the Quebrada Mateo near Río Frío, 10°55'N 74°10'W (Darlington 1931); Aracataca[9], 10°36'N 74°12'W (Darlington 1931); Costarrica[10] ("Camp Costa Rica"), 9°44'N 74°25'W (Vaurie 1967b; two females in USNM identified further as from "Petróleos Ariguaní, 76 km north-east of Plato", 75 m, collected on 1 February 1947); (*Bolívar*) San Juan Nepomuceno[11], 9°57'N 75°05'W, in the Serranía de San Jacinto, 1960 or 1961 (Haffer 1975); Regeneración[12], 8°06'N 74°38'W (male in USNM from "Q. San Marcos–Lower Rio Cauca", 30 m, 9 February 1948); Volador[13], 7°58'N 74°15'W (Vaurie 1967b; male in USNM labelled as from "25 miles west of Simití" ["El Tigre"], 730 m, 27 May 1947); (*Sucre*) Colosó[14], Serranía de San Jacinto, 9°30'N 75°21'W (Blake 1955, Haffer 1975; specimen in FMNH labelled as from "Las Campanas"[15], 9°30'N 75°30'W, 18 May 1949); (*Córdoba*) Alto de Quimarí[16], 8°07'N 76°23'W (Meyer de Schauensee 1950, Vaurie 1967b); Socorré[17] (see Remarks 3), 7°51'N 76°17'W (Blake 1955, Haffer 1967, Vaurie 1967b; female in FMNH labelled also "upper río Sinú", 27 March 1949; male in USNM labelled from "1½ miles below the mouth of río Verde", 115 m, collected on 22 April 1949); Catival[18] (see Remarks 3), 8°17'N 75°41'W (Blake 1955, Haffer 1967, Vaurie 1967b; female in FMNH labelled from the upper río San Jorge[19], 8°25'N 75°45'W, 21 July 1949); (*Antioquia*) Puerto Valdivia[20], 7°18'N 75°23'W (Hellmayr and Conover 1942); Nechí[21], 8°07'N 74°46'W (Vaurie 1967b); El Real[22], río Nechí, 7°40'N 74°46'W (Vaurie 1967b); Remedios[23] (El Amparo), 7°02'N 74°41'W, December 1974 (Serna 1980); Puerto Berrío[24], 6°29'N 74°24'W, July 1978 (Serna 1980); río La Miel[25] (captive birds), 5°46'N 74°39'W (Meyer de Schauensee 1948-1952); (*Tolima*) west of Honda[26], 5°12'N 74°45'W (Chapman 1917a).

POPULATION The species was not common anywhere in the Santa Marta region at the beginning of the century, though perhaps most numerous in the humid lowlands of the north coast (Todd and Carriker 1922), along which a road now runs (TAW 1986). In the Serranía de San Jacinto by the 1970s it was "becoming very rare" (Haffer 1975; see Remarks 4), and this status is expected wherever its habitat has been settled (Hilty and Brown 1986). By the 1980s it had "disappeared from most places" in which it was found, albeit uncommon, 30 years before (Estudillo López 1986). Indeed the species is now believed extinct throughout most of its range, with only a few small isolated populations surviving away from the Santa Marta region (Negret 1987). There appear to be no recent observations and the only certain evidence that the species survives at all may be the record of four in trade in 1987 (see Threats).

ECOLOGY This curassow inhabits forested regions in the tropical zone, i.e. humid lowlands, foothills and lower mountain forests up to 1,200 m (but less commonly above 600 m), feeding chiefly on the ground (Todd and Carriker 1922, Darlington 1931, Blake 1977, Hilty and Brown 1986). Young birds have been recorded in July (Allen 1900, Todd and Carriker 1922), and a three-quarters grown juvenile (from Nechí, in FMNH) is also from this month; however, the male from Regeneración and two females from Costarrica, all taken in February, had enlarged gonads (greatly so in one female), as did the female from La Cueva in April (see Distribution).

THREATS Destruction of lowland forest in northern Colombia is taking place at such a rate as to cause serious concern (King 1978-1979). Haffer (1967) referred to rapid deforestation associated with agriculture east of the Golfo de Urabá, in the secondary contact zone with Great Curassow *Crax rubra*, and to the survival of forest remnants in the Serranía de San Jacinto only "along some of the deeply incised valleys" (Haffer 1975); similarly, Paynter and Traylor (1981) noted that by 1960 forest at Puerto Valdivia was confined to ridges. At Río Frío, Santa Marta, the species was much hunted 50 years ago (Darlington 1931), and this was and is doubtless true of the bird throughout its range. There is also evidence that the species is sometimes traded, with four birds being imported illegally into Japan in July 1987 (Tokunaga 1987).

MEASURES TAKEN None is known.

MEASURES PROPOSED Surveys are needed of any major remaining regions of forest to identify the current status and distribution of this species (this is now being planned: Strahl 1991), and several protected areas should be established to conserve this and other endemic and/or threatened and near-threatened species of northern Colombia (threatened species known to have occurred sympatrically with this curassow in the vicinity of Puerto Valdivia are listed in the equivalent section under Antioquia Bristle-tyrant *Phylloscartes lanyoni*). Although (at least formerly) present in the upper Sinú valley (Quimarí, Socorré), the species has not been recorded from the Paramillo National Park there (Negret 1987), and further survey of this protected area to check for its presence is important (this should be extended to the Recurve-billed Bushbird *Clytoctantes alixii* and Red-bellied Grackle *Hypopyrrhus pyrohypogaster*, both of which at one time occurred in this area: see relevant accounts). The conservation of any Blue-billed Curassows remaining in the coastal lowlands of the Santa Marta region, where they possibly reached their maximum abundance, requires consideration as one of the highest priorities in Colombia.

Captive breeding Very few specimens are in captivity, a breeding pair with three offspring being at Houston Zoo in 1987 (W. T. Todd *per* R. Wirth *in litt.* 1987). Given that the species in the wild could now be virtually extinct, the development of a full-scale recovery plan utilizing as many captive individuals as possible is urgently needed, under the auspices of the CBSG. However, this does not mean that the export of more wild-caught specimens from Colombia should be countenanced.

REMARKS (1) Hellmayr and Conover (1942) accepted the record of a live pair from Cartagena, Bolívar department (Sclater 1876), as indicating occurrence there, but the birds presumably originated in the interior; Vaurie (1967b) implied Bogotá as a site, but the specimen in question was undoubtedly a trade skin. A record of *Crax annulata*, a synonym of *C. alberti*, from Isla de Charo, Arauca department, on the Venezuelan frontier (Nicéforo María 1947), refers to Yellow-knobbed Curassow *C. daubentoni* (Vaurie 1967b, J. I. Hernández Camacho verbally 1988). (2) Vaurie (1967b) listed La Cueva for Magdalena. (3) Vaurie (1967b) listed Alto de Quimarí, Socorré and Catival for Bolívar. (4) Hilty and Brown (1986) somewhat misrepresented Haffer (1975) in saying that the bird is "now quite scarce" in the Serranía de San Jacinto.

RED-BILLED CURASSOW *Crax blumenbachii* R[11]

Formerly fairly widespread in lowland Atlantic Forest in south-east Brazil from Bahia south to Rio de Janeiro, this species is now restricted to five protected forest patches – Una and Monte Pascoal (Bahia, although several unprotected sites have recently been found in the state), Rio Doce (Minas Gerais), Sooretama and Linhares (Espírito Santo) – several of which are under threat. The total population must be very small, although birds have bred well in captivity.

DISTRIBUTION The Red-billed Curassow (see Remarks 1) is endemic to eastern Brazil where it is currently restricted to five forest reserves. However, to judge from occurrence of place-names in which the word *mutum* appears, it was once fairly widespread in southern Bahia, eastern Minas Gerais, Espírito Santo and north-east Rio de Janeiro (Sick 1969, 1970, 1972, 1985). The record of the species from Bolivia (Gyldenstolpe 1945), repeated by Meyer de Schauensee (1966), is in error (Vaurie 1968, Gochfeld and Keith 1977). Records in the following account are arranged from north to south, with coordinates from Paynter and Traylor (1991).

Bahia The species is known from forest patches around Camamu, currently at least by local report (da Silva and Nacinovic 1991); Ilhéus, where it was recorded on the rio Salgado, 14°54'S 39°26'W, January 1817, with many remains of hunted birds at ribeirão Issara, c.15°05'S 39°45'W, at the same time (Wied 1820-1821; see Bokermann 1957), and one specimen was collected in 1944 (Stresemann 1954, Pinto 1964); Una Biological Reserve, in the recent past (Coimbra-Filho 1970, S. Lindbergh *per* C. Yamashita *in litt.* 1987); rio Jequitinhonha (as rio Belmonte), specifically on Ilha do Chave, c.15°57'S 39°33'W, September 1816 (Wied 1820-1821, 1831-1833; see Bokermann 1957); Monte Pascoal National Park, where it was recorded in 1977 (King 1978-1979, Sick and Teixeira 1979, Sick 1985) and in October 1986 (Gonzaga *et al.* 1987); rio Itanhém (as rio Alcobaça), formerly (Wied 1831-1833), although accordingly to local reports recently traded individuals came from near Teixeira de Freitas (da Silva and Nacinovic 1991), which stands on the Itanhém; rio Mucuri, at Morro da Arara, formerly (Wied 1820-1821, 1831-1833; see Bokermann 1957). Reports from near Prado and Marajú (Teixeira and Antas 1982) cannot be confirmed as the areas in question are now cleared (LPG), while records from rio Salgado and rio Jucurucu (Pinto 1964) could not be traced to source and may be in error. Despite a claim of its occurrence there, the species is almost certainly absent from the CVRD Porto Seguro Reserve (Gonzaga *et al.* 1987).

Minas Gerais The few records in this state are from "Villa do Fanado" at "Alto dos Bois", near Minas Novas, early in the last century (de Sainte-Hilaire 1830); Mairinque (Mayrink), December 1908 (Pinto 1938, 1952); near the rio Xopotó, 20°45'S 43°05'W, a probable record in 1850 (Burmeister 1853); the Rio Doce State Park (36,000 ha) near Dionísio, currently (M. A. de Andrade *in litt.* 1986, G. T. de Mattos verbally 1987, *in litt.* 1992); and below São Caetano on the Rio Pomba, 21°38'S 42°04'W, undated (Burmeister 1853, 1856). The species has been introduced to two reserves in the state which are not known formerly to have held it (see Measures Taken), though it is not known if stocks have survived.

Espírito Santo Localities include Fazenda São Joaquim on the northern state border and the rio Itabapoana, which forms the southern state border, suggesting that the species originally extended throughout the state. Records are from forest at Fazenda São Joaquim (Fazenda Klabin), now much reduced and converted to the Córrego Grande Biological Reserve (King 1978-1979, Sick and Teixeira 1979), although it was not found there in October 1986 and is almost certainly extinct (Gonzaga *et al.* 1987); córrego do Engano, near Conceição da Barra, where four birds were collected at 245-285 m, three of them in October 1944 (specimens in AMNH, FMNH); Sooretama Biological Reserve (including córrego Cupido and rio São José, whence specimens in MNRJ and AMNH from 1939 and 1941 respectively and one from 1942; also Pinto 1945, Stresemann 1954, Sick 1970), currently (King 1978-1979, Sick 1969, 1983, Scott and Brooke 1985, C. E. Carvalho *in litt.* 1987, Aleixo *et al.* 1991) and, more recently recognized, the contiguous CVRD Linhares

Reserve, currently (Collar 1986, Collar *et al.* 1987, Collar and Gonzaga 1988; see Population); Lagoa Juparanã, where it was formerly common on the banks (de Sainte-Hilaire 1833, specimen in MNRJ); rio Doce, rio Itapemirim and rio Itabapuana (Itabapoana), formerly (Wied 1831-1833).

Rio de Janeiro The species was first described from forests in the state (von Spix 1824), one sixteenth-century report from around the city of Rio de Janeiro possibly referring to birds traded by Indians from other areas (Sick and Pabst 1968). The only specific sites for the species are the valley of the rio Paraíba do Sul, where it reputedly occurred until 1963 near São Fidélis, and Cantagalo (Sick 1969, 1972), where it was known only through old hunters' reports (Euler 1868, von Ihering 1900a). Reports from Desengano State Park and Santa Maria Madalena required verification (Teixeira and Antas 1982).

POPULATION In the early nineteenth century the Red-billed Curassow must have been a relatively common bird in Atlantic Forest in Espírito Santo and Bahia, Wied (1831-1833) referring to it being "not rare", "frequent" on the rios Doce, Mucuri, Alcobaça and Belmonte, and "everywhere a very favourite game bird", with de Sainte-Hilaire (1833) clearly implying that it was common on the shores of Lagoa Juparanã. However, Burmeister (1856) noted that it was already rather scarce in well settled areas, and since then the species has continued to decline not only as its habitat disappeared but also with the extensive penetration of all remaining habitat by hunters, so that since the mid-twentieth century (despite the mistaken optimism that "with such a wide range, in many places little disturbed" the species seemed unlikely to be in great danger: Greenway 1958), it was recognized to be "on the road to extinction" (Stresemann 1954) and "one of the most threatened Brazilian birds" (Sick 1972; also Delacour and Amadon 1973, King 1978-1979). In the late 1970s it was still decreasing owing to illegal hunting and continuing deforestation in southern Bahia, having vanished from some biological reserves in Espírito Santo where, in small numbers, it could be found some years before; by this time, although no population estimates were known, only "a few hundred individuals" were guessed to exist (Teixeira and Antas 1982). By the 1980s only five localities could be shown to hold the species, although very recent research has disclosed one or two more, by local report (see Distribution).

Two of the certain localities, Sooretama Biological Reserve and the adjacent CVRD Linhares Reserve, form the chief stronghold. As long ago as August 1939 local people reported it "not rare" in this area (Sick 1970), and, despite the anomalous and presumably mistaken impression that it was "very rare" there in September 1942 (Pinto 1945), in 1954 and 1961 up to 25 birds were observed together being fed at Sooretama (Sick 1970) and up to six were seen together at the same site, plus two others, over six days in September 1973 (Gochfeld and Keith 1977), when "perhaps fifty at the most" were thought to survive in the reserve (Delacour and Amadon 1973). In 1977 "perhaps 60 or more" were reported there (King 1978-1979) and a minimum of 26 birds (nine males, 11 females and four indeterminate, plus two chicks) was seen over three weeks, December 1980 to January 1981, suggesting that the total population was considerably more than 60 (Scott and Brooke 1985). Another equally important population was subsequently found in the CVRD Linhares Reserve where 25 birds (19 males, five females and one indeterminate) were recorded at 16 sites during a two-week survey of the species, 4-17 October 1985 (Collar 1986, Collar *et al.* 1987, Collar and Gonzaga 1988); just over a year later managers at the reserve were expressing confidence that over 100 birds existed there (B. M. Whitney *in litt.* 1987).

Numbers in Monte Pascoal National Park were believed to be much less than at Sooretama in 1978 (King 1978-1979) and are likely to be even more reduced now (Gonzaga *et al.* 1987: see Threats). No population estimates are known from the Rio Doce State Park and Una Biological Reserve, but numbers are likely to be very small at least in the latter (LPG), where it was said to be rare (Coimbra-Filho 1970), seven birds being seen there on 24-25 November 1986 (S. Lindbergh *per* C. Yamashita *in litt.* 1987) and wardens seeing the species very rarely (LPG). In the mid-1970s there were "possibly as few as 10" in what was then Fazenda Klabin (King 1978-1979), where the species is now almost certainly extinct (Gonzaga *et al.* 1987).

ECOLOGY The Red-billed Curassow inhabits high primary forest in hot, humid regions (Sick 1985; see Remarks 2). The statement that it occurs in both "lowland and highland forests" (Teixeira and Antas 1982) is surely in error, as none of the localities from which it has been recorded lies above (or much above) 500 m. Although recorded "in secluded parts of forests" (Wied 1831-1833), the possibility cannot be discounted that the species prefers habitat that includes forest edge, as all records in the CVRD Linhares Reserve were made from forest tracks that caused a break in the canopy (Collar *et al.* 1987, Collar and Gonzaga 1988; see also Scott and Brooke 1985) and at the rio São José the birds were noted to visit "small areas with lower vegetation as on the banks of the larger rivers, small floodplains, and steep banks, all, however, covered by woods", and were notably to be found at treefalls (Sick 1970). One male was heard calling 8 m up in dense cover in cut-over second-growth forest at Sooretama (Gochfeld and Keith 1977). In the CVRD Linhares Reserve the curassows have been found chiefly in the low-lying eastern half, below the 50 m contour, which could reflect a need for damp substrates and/or proximity to water (Collar *et al.* 1987, Collar and Gonzaga 1988), although further study of the situation there suggested that disturbance and poaching might have contributed to its absence or scarcity in the western half (Gonzaga unpublished). On the Jequitinhonha Wied (1820-1821) found that they were most frequently to be found when the river was in flood. The birds in Sooretama are quite habituated to man, feeding with chickens round the forestry camp in the mornings and evenings (Sick 1970, Gochfeld and Keith 1977, Scott and Brooke 1985) and being seen along a busy dirt road in the reserve (Scott and Brooke 1985). Birds come out onto tracks after rain to dry and preen (Collar and Gonzaga 1988) and like to drink, taking water as it drips from the leaves after heavy rain or walking to the nearest watering places (Sick 1970) such as fresh puddles on tracks (Gonzaga unpublished). The species lives much on the ground (Wied 1831-1833), being less arboreal than guans *Penelope* and piping-guans *Pipile* (Sick 1970).

Food consists of fruits, buds, seeds and insects (Wied 1831-1833, Sick 1970, Teixeira and Antas 1982, Teixeira and Snow 1982), and is taken on the ground in high forest with rich undergrowth and deep shadow, but is also picked off bushes and trees (Burmeister 1856, Sick 1970, Teixeira and Snow 1982). Grit is always found in their stomachs (Sick 1970), although not by Wied (1831-1833), who anticipated it. Fruits included in the diet are, e.g., sapucaia *Lecythis pisonis*, bicuiba *Virola bicuhyba*, aricanga palm *Geonoma* (Aguirre 1947, Sick 1970), murici *Byrsonima* (Aguirre 1947, Teixeira and Antas 1982), *Byrbicuiba* (Sick 1970, Teixeira and Antas 1982), *Eugenia*, *Ferdinandusa*, *Eschweilera* (Teixeira and Snow 1982) and *Pithecellobium* (Teixeira and Antas 1982). "Hard fruits and nuts", some impossible to split with a hammer, have been found in birds (Wied 1831-1833). Centipedes and venomous spiders *Lycosa* are not rejected as prey (Sick 1985). The statement that "a characteristic sign of [the species's] foraging is bushes with leaves half-eaten" (Teixeira and Snow 1982) seems of little practical scope, since such damage must result from the activities of many other animals in the same habitat. Several other birds and mammals including the Rusty-margined Guan *Penelope superciliaris* and the threatened Black-fronted Piping-guan *Pipile jacutinga* like the same fruits (Aguirre 1947, Sick 1970) and one male curassow was seen feeding on the ground in the company of three Rusty-margined Guans (Gochfeld and Keith 1977).

The main period for the low, booming song seems to be from the middle of September to October, being rarely heard in December and January (Sick 1970); however, booming was heard at Linhares in December 1986 and was heard rather little there in late September (B. M. Whitney *in litt.* 1991), implying variation that presumably reflects seasonal conditions. An apparent variation in the laying date between years is probably due to an extended breeding season within each year (Collar and Gonzaga 1988): thus young have been said to hatch in October (Sick 1970); pairing time was reported as especially from September to November in Espírito Santo (Teixeira and Antas 1982); or from November to January (Wied 1831-1833); a female with two chicks was reported in January (Scott and Brooke 1985); another with one half-grown female was seen on 19 February (Gonzaga unpublished) and a nest was found with two eggs on 15 November at a time when other birds were claimed to have well-grown young around 100 days old (Teixeira and Snow 1982). The nest is placed in lower trees (Teixeira and Antas 1982), a report that it may also be made on the ground (Burmeister 1856) being doubted (Ogilvie-Grant 1897). One nest was 6 m up in a obliquely leaning tree, one of a group growing from the water at the edge of a lagoon; it was solidly based on an arboreal termite nest, well shaded, and well concealed by the surrounding foliage (Teixeira and Snow 1982). Another, probably an old curassow nest, was on a dense viny thicket which covered some fallen trees, at a height of scarcely 2 m (Sick 1970); Wied (1831-1833) reported that the nest was made of twigs and sticks and placed in a tree 8-10 feet (2.5-3 m) from the ground. Clutch-size is commonly two (Sick 1970, Teixeira and Antas 1982, Teixeira and Snow 1982), sometimes one (Sick 1970); Wied (1831-1833) was told it was four. Incubation takes 28 days (Teixeira and Antas 1982) and the young remain with the mother several (up to at least four) months, following her the whole day (Sick 1970, 1985). In one study the female was recorded incubating alone (Teixeira and Snow 1982). The females are capable of breeding at two or three years, being fertile for at least 11 years (Teixeira and Antas 1982). Siblings are always of opposite sexes (Sick 1985). The species is claimed to be polygamous (Delacour and Amadon 1973) and the observation on the "far-reaching" call of the male "calling the hens around him" (Wied 1831-1833) seems to imply that, but the sex ratio may be affected by hunting (Delacour and Amadon 1973).

Birds have been reported as usually found in pairs throughout the year (Wied 1831-1833); groups seen during the winter seldom comprise more than four birds and are surely family units (Sick 1970) but an observation of four males together at the beginning of the breeding season in October could refer to birds that had failed to establish a territory (Collar and Gonzaga 1988).

THREATS This species has declined mainly as a result of chronic habitat destruction and hunting pressure (Coimbra-Filho and Magnanini 1968, Sick and Teixeira 1979, Teixeira and Snow 1982) and is clearly extremely vulnerable, although perhaps not in imminent danger (Scott and Brooke 1985). Nevertheless, the very protection afforded to the population in Sooretama also brings a threat, since predators are attracted into the reserve by the relative abundance of prey to be found there (Coimbra-Filho and Magnanini 1968). Trade is also an enduring threat (see below).

Habitat destruction It was reported that in 1973 almost all the forest in north-east Espírito Santo, where the species formerly occurred, had been cleared, much of it within the year, and that the rate of forest destruction, mainly for charcoal, markedly accelerated in the preceding decade (Gochfeld and Keith 1977). The rate of forest destruction in eastern Brazil is so severe that in the past decade it has become evident that virtually no areas of lowland forest survive in the belt north of Rio de Janeiro that are not under active protection (Collar *et al.* 1987); the surrounding areas may be completely cultivated, like the São José region in the vicinity of Sooretama (Sick 1970) or largely abandoned after timber exploitation followed by cattle-grazing for a few years (LPG). Two decades ago Sooretama was considered "nearly abandoned" and lacked permanent policing (Sick 1969), and it was reported that a state governor once contracted a firm to log out and replace Sooretama with eucalyptus and pines, which was only prevented by federal intervention (Gochfeld and Keith 1977). Concerns about the future of Monte Pascoal as a protected area have been expressed as the forest there faces a major problem from its Indian population (Padua 1983, Gonzaga *et al.* 1987, Redford 1989). In the middle of the last century it was land clearance and settlement that caused the species's retreat northwards to the Paraíba do Sul valley (Euler 1868) and its extinction at São Fidelis, the last site in Rio de Janeiro, was due to clearance of forest there in 1963 (Sick 1969, 1972). The almost certain extinction at Fazenda São Joaquim (Fazenda Klabin) must unquestionably be related to the clearance of three-quarters of the forest there since the 1970s, less than 1,500 ha remaining in October 1986 (Gonzaga *et al.* 1987).

Hunting This bird is valued as food because of its size, although the flesh is quite dry (Sick 1970). In the early nineteenth century it was "everywhere a very favourite game bird... often caught in snares and eagerly hunted... especially in the period when they give their loud, deep calls" (Wied 1831-1833); it was much hunted (e.g.) near the ribeirão Issara alongside the Black-fronted Piping-guan (Wied 1831-1833), and at Lago Juparanã by the people of Linhares (de Saint-Hilaire 1833), while it was well-known in the rios Mucuri and Doce, where it was one of the most prized gamebirds (Goeldi 1894). Three specimens obtained in 1939 in Espírito Santo were killed by local hunters whose traps consisted of a heavy log hung above the ground over maize and manioc (Sick 1970).

Trade At the Caxias bird-market, Rio de Janeiro (see Carvalho 1985), the species had not been available for nearly 20 years (C. Torres *in litt.* 1985). Nevertheless, the species is highly prized by illegal marketeers (Teixeira and Antas 1982). It is to be noted that about fifty percent of the birds succumb to stress soon after capture: a "specialist" reported that most Red-billed Curassows, when removed from the nets, are already dead (Teixeira and Antas 1982). The apparent ease with which the species could still be obtained from the wild in the mid-1980s was a source of both surprise and concern (Collar and Gonzaga 1988) with reports of capture even in biological reserves and national parks (Teixeira and Antas 1982); in August 1984 a dealer with a pair from Sooretama claimed that certain wardens were working for him (C. Torres *in litt.* 1985).

MEASURES TAKEN All areas where the species currently occurs are forest reserves (see Distribution). Sooretama has been considered "a well protected nature reserve" (King 1978-1979) and in 1981 Red-billed Curassows at Sooretama seemed "to be doing well" and were considered "under very good protection" (Scott and Brooke 1985); however, although it is patrolled and permits are needed to enter it, no complacency is permissible (Gochfeld and Keith 1977; see Threats, Measures Proposed). Protection of CVRD's privately owned Linhares Reserve has been judged excellent (Collar 1986, Collar *et al.* 1987), with poaching not perceived as a problem there (Collar and Gonzaga 1988). This bird is listed on Appendix I of CITES and protected under Brazilian law (Bernardes *et al.* 1990). Its hunting has been prohibited in Espírito Santo since 1947 (Sick 1969).

Captive breeding and (re)introduction The view that this bird can only be saved in future by captive breeding (Sick 1985) is not wholly supported by the evidence above, since proper conservation and management (including anti-poaching controls) of the remaining sites must be the primary requisite (Collar and Gonzaga 1988). Nevertheless, it is clear that "reserve" stocks of this bird in captivity are important in themselves and as sources of birds for reintroductions (Teixeira and Antas 1982), following the guidelines laid down in Black (1991). The species has already been successfully bred in captivity, in Brazil (see, e.g., Euler 1868, 1900, who records egg-laying, King 1978-1979, da Silveira and Pais 1986, Collar and Gonzaga 1988) and is known to be held in zoos outside the country as well (Olney 1977, Geerlings 1992). In 1985, at least 67 adult birds were known to be held in zoos and private aviaries in Brazil (see da Silveira and Pais 1986, Collar and Gonzaga 1988). Nearly half of these were kept by R. M. A. Azeredo of Fundação Crax (with support from Stichting Crax) in Minas Gerais and, fulfilling the need perceived by da Silveira and Pais (1986) to expand the captive population urgently, his stock grew from 34 birds in October 1985 up to 75 in May 1987 (Collar and Gonzaga 1988) and had reached 258 (45 breeding pairs) by July 1991 (G. Scheres *in litt.* 1991). In December 1990 15 pairs from this stock were released ("reintroduced", although there is no evidence of former occurrence at the site) into the Caratinga Reserve (Fazenda Montes Claros) in eastern Minas Gerais (*Atualidades Ornitológicas* no.39 [1991]: 1). In the middle of 1991 20 further pairs from this stock were introduced into the CENIBRA Reserve at Ipatinga, Minas Gerais, although this area is regarded as seriously deficient in appropriate habitat (G. T. de Mattos *in litt.* 1992).

MEASURES PROPOSED It has become a matter of permanent concern that the protection of Sooretama Biological Reserve should be enhanced and maintained, with the introduction of stronger measures against poaching and trapping (Sick 1969, Gochfeld and Keith 1977, Teixeira and Antas 1982, Scott and Brooke 1985) and possibly even the control of predators (Coimbra-

Filho and Magnanini 1968). CVRD deserves congratulation and encouragement for its high-standard protection of the adjacent Linhares Reserve. However, a conservation education project was to be implemented by CVRD around the Linhares Reserve, adopting this species as the campaign's symbol (V. Velloso verbally 1987), but has apparently been shelved; it needs revival. Searches of other remaining forest tracts within the species's range for unknown populations has been urged (Gochfeld and Keith 1977) and partially achieved more recently (Gonzaga *et al.* 1987, Collar and Gonzaga 1988, da Silva and Nacinovic 1991); the discovery that unprotected relict populations may survive in 3,000–5,000 ha forest patches around Camamu must be followed up with thorough investigations and, if results are positive, strong action to maintain and manage the sites. Meanwhile, surveys are still needed, especially at Rio Doce State Park, Monte Pascoal National Park and Una Biological Reserve to assess the species's status more accurately in these areas. Ecological research on the species at Linhares to start permanent monitoring has also been suggested (Collar *et al.* 1987, Collar and Gonzaga 1988).

Captive breeding and (re)introduction The fate of the stock introduced to the Caratinga and CENIBRA Reserves needs to be monitored and reported. Certain other areas exist where attempts might be made to introduce captive-bred birds, e.g. Fazenda São Joaquim and the nearby Córrego do Veado Biological Reserve (see IBAMA 1989, Oliver and Santos 1991), but only if sufficient wardening could be provided to prevent all stock being poached out. Oliver and Santos (1991) provided an inventory of other smaller reserves within the species's range. G. T. de Mattos (*in litt.* 1992) has suggested that bolstering the population in Rio Doce State Park would be welcome; however, this would need to be done only after careful evaluation of the health of the birds to be reintroduced (see Black 1991 for general guidelines).

REMARKS (1) Detailed comparisons of skins of the Red-billed Curassow and Wattled Curassow *Crax globulosa* (see relevant account) reveals that "the males are sometimes indistinguishable and the females very similar" (Teixeira and Sick 1981). The two forms cannot, however, be considered conspecific, as the Wattled Curassow does not possess the low, booming song of the Red-billed (Delacour and Amadon 1973). (2) Calling the habitat "Amazonian primary forest" (King 1978-1979) is misleading, although the habitat certainly resembles Amazonian forests in its components (Rizzini 1979).

WATTLED CURASSOW *Crax globulosa* I[7]

Although seemingly very widespread in the Amazon basin of Brazil, Colombia, Ecuador, Peru and Bolivia, this species appears to be almost wholly unknown, and it may be suffering seriously as a consequence of loss of riverine habitat.

DISTRIBUTION The Wattled Curassow occupies the Amazon basin on rivers chiefly in Brazil and Peru, but also in Bolivia, Colombia and Ecuador. The records show a curious distribution in the middle and upper Amazon and in the middle and upper Madeira, and it is a seemingly anomalous record like that from the río Caquetá in Colombia that suggests that the species's range is very incompletely known: Gyldenstolpe (1951) believed it would be found on the rio Purus in Brazil, and indeed it might be expected on the Juruá (now proven) and all or any of the other rivers in the massive dendritic system of the Amazon basin (and, considering the number of apparently unexplored and undisturbed rivers such as the Coari, Tefé, Jutaí, Jandiatuba and Branquinho, this seems likely); on the other hand, to generalize and hence to assume its distribution, such as in the map in Delacour and Amadon (1973) or when Meyer de Schauensee (1964) converted the two known records from Colombia into "forests east of the Andes from Caquetá southward to the Amazon", is an unaffordable risk.

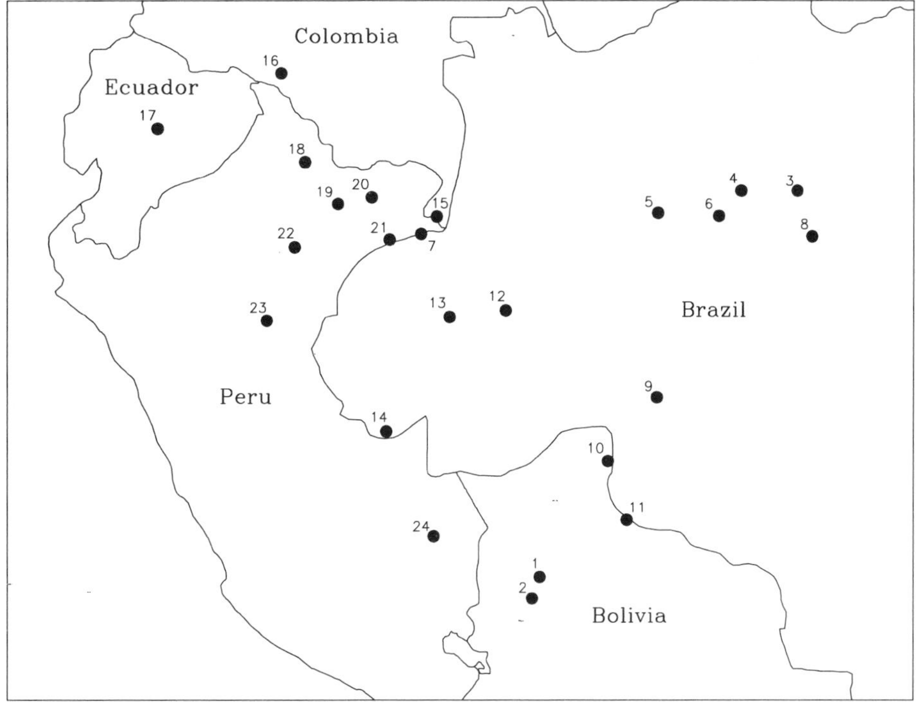

Bolivia There are three records from the lower río Beni, one without further data, one from El Desierto[1], 13°45'S 67°20'W, and one from Puerto Salinas[2], 14°20'S 67°33'W (Allen 1889, Hellmayr and Conover 1942, Gyldenstolpe 1945; coordinates from Paynter *et al.* 1975).

Brazil The species has been found along the Amazon west of the junction with the rio Madeira, and along the rio Madeira itself, extending south-west to the Bolivian border, and there are reports from the middle and upper rio Juruá.

Records on or associated with the Amazon (as the Solimões), and all from Amazonas state, are from the Paraná do Manhana (untraced, but an affluent of rio Japurá), September 1927 (specimen in MNRJ); Manaus[3] (i.e. Barra do Rio Negro), June and July 1834 (von Pelzeln 1868-1871, still the only record: Novaes 1978b); rio Manacapuru[4] ("rio Manacapuri"), October 1925 (specimens in CM); Catuá island near Ega[5] (now Tefé), c.3°45'S 64°00'W (on AGSNY 1940), c.1850 (Bates 1863); and Ilha do Comprido[6], now Ilhas Codajás, just west of the mouth of the rio Purus, July 1935 to January 1936 (Pinto 1938, Hellmayr and Conover 1942, Vaurie 1967b, Paynter and Traylor 1991; specimens in FMNH), plus at the mouth of the rio Javari[7] apparently at c.4°12'S 70°42'W, July 1977 (Hilty and Brown 1986, Paynter and Traylor 1991).

Records from the rio Madeira and its tributaries, all made by J. Natterer in 1829-1830 (von Pelzeln 1868-1871), are from Borba[8] (Amazonas), January 1830, and in Rondônia at: Salto do Teotônio[9], c.8°51'S 64°02'W (on AGSNY 1940 and in Paynter and Traylor 1991), October 1829; Piori, untraced but close to (upriver from) the preceding, October 1829; Cachoeira do Bananeira[10], c.10°36'S 65°25'W on the Mamoré (on ASGNY 1940 and in Paynter and Traylor 1991), September 1829; and Volta do Gentio[11], 12°12'S 64°53'W, on the rio Guaporé along the Bolivian border, August 1829.

Records from the rio Juruá are based on (entirely reliable: birds well described) reports from hunters along the middle section of the river, e.g. at rubber-tapping sites around and downriver of Itamarati[12] (C. A. Peres and A. Whittaker *in litt.* 1992); older inhabitants remember it from their youth around Eirunepé[13], but it is extinct there now (C. A. Peres and A. Whittaker *in litt.* 1992). Indians just inside Peru have reported the presence of the species in the headwaters of the rio Envira[14] (Embira), a tributary of the rio Juruá in south-west Acre (Ortiz 1988).

Colombia There are two records, one from Isla Loreto[15] ("Isla de Mocagua") on the Amazon, 3°51'S 70°15'W, and one from Tres Troncos[16], La Tagua, 0°08'N 74°41'W, on the río Caquetá, a tributary of the Solimões (Meyer de Schauensee 1948-1952, Blake 1955; coordinates from Paynter and Traylor 1981). However, S. Defler is believed to have found the species recently in the south-east (M. G. Kelsey verbally 1992).

Ecuador The species is known from the río Napo and the río Negro[17] (presumably that at 1°24'S 78°13'W: see Paynter and Traylor 1977) (Chapman 1926, Hellmayr and Conover 1942, Vaurie 1967b), with several being recorded along Quebrada Papaya, a small blackwater north-bank tributary of the Napo, in June 1982 (TAP); there are also records from the mouth of the río Curaray (see Remarks 1), including statements by Huitotos Indians in 1982 that the species (locally called *piurí*) still occurs up the Napo towards the Curaray confluence, while from the lower Napo only the oldest man spoken to remembered the bird (TAP).

Peru Records (arranged here from north to south, with coordinates from Stephens and Traylor 1983) are chiefly from the Amazon and its major tributaries in the department of Loreto in the north-east: from the mouth of the río Curaray[18] (see Remarks 1); in the basin of the río Napo, according to LSUMZ field studies (Ortiz 1988, TAP), with specimen records from there (Sclater and Salvin 1870) and nearby río Mazán and Iquitos[19] (Hellmayr and Conover 1942, Vaurie 1967b); north of the río Amazonas at Pebas and Apayacu[20], 3°19'S 72°06'W (Sclater and Salvin 1870, Taczanowski 1884-1886, Vaurie 1967b); along the río Yavarí[21] on the Brazilian frontier (Ortiz 1988, TAP); the lower río Marañón (Sclater and Salvin 1873, Ortiz 1988, TAP), whence also a specimen so labelled and another from Samiria[22], 4°42'S 74°18'W (Hellmayr and Conover 1942, Vaurie 1967b); the lower río Ucayali (Sclater and Salvin 1873, Ortiz 1988), whence also a specimen from Sarayacu[23], 6°44'S 75°06'W (Taczanowksi 1886, Hellmayr and Conover 1942, Vaurie 1967b); and far to the south, in Madre de Dios, at the mouth of the río Colorado[25], 12°39'S 70°20'W, a tributary of the rio Madeira (Hellmayr and Conover 1942, Vaurie 1967b). Because of his reports of birds just inside the Brazilian border (see above), Ortiz (1988) drew attention to the possibility of the species occurring inside Peru south-west of the headwaters of the Envira, i.e. just south-west of 10°S 72°W.

POPULATION In Bolivia on the lower río Beni a century ago the species was, with the Razor-billed Curassow *Mitu tuberosa*, considered abundant and found both singly and in flocks of 5-15 (Allen 1889), although this report cannot be considered reliable (see Remarks 2). In Peru in the 1960s it was reported less common and more local than the Razor-billed Curassow (Koepcke and Koepcke 1963) and it is now regarded as extremely rare there and the highest cracid conservation priority after White-winged Guan *Penelope albipennis* (Ortiz 1988); local people within its range refer to it as having disappeared almost totally in the past 30 years (TAP). There have been no reports from eastern Ecuador for at least 10 years, despite much work in the region on cracids (A. Johnson verbally 1991). In Colombia it appears to be extinct along the río Caquetá (J. V. Rodríguez *per* S. Defler verbally 1988), and the species was not recorded during several years' fieldwork to the north of, in and near the Amacayacu National Park, near Leticia, in the late 1980s (S. Defler verbally 1988, M. G. Kelsey verbally 1992). Recent surveys by R. Garcés in various parts of lower Amazonia suggest that the species has indeed disappeared from Ecuador, Colombia and Peru (Strahl 1991), and that other than at the Javari estuary south of Leticia (see Distribution) there appear to be no recent records; several ornithologists now express serious concern over the fate of the species throughout its range (J. V. Remsen *in litt.* 1986, S. D. Strahl verbally 1988, TAP). Nevertheless, although Koepcke and Koepcke (1963) thought it rare in zoos, Delacour and Amadon (1973) called it "one of the commoner curassows in captivity", and the recent evidence of traders is that the bird was still common in the mid-1980s in remote regions of Bolivia (J. Estudillo López verbally 1988) and in southern Colombia, western Brazil and north-east Peru, where local people offer it for sale at small airstrips (F. O. Lehmann verbally 1988). The testimony of hunters on the rio Juruá in Brazil is certainly that the bird is far rarer than the Razor-billed Curassow, but nevertheless still routinely found (C. A. Peres and A. Whittaker *in litt.* 1992).

ECOLOGY The habitat is humid lowland (to 300 m) tropical-zone forest (Hilty and Brown 1986). In one report the drier areas within such habitat are favoured and swampy areas shunned (Koepcke and Koepcke 1963), while in five others an association with water is apparent: in one, várzea was occupied (Hilty and Brown 1986); in another, the species was twice found near the edge of a lake or pond (Bates 1863: 282, 292); in the third, birds are specifically stated to inhabit riverine island forests, várzeas locally, near streams and black-water rivers (Ortiz 1988); in the fourth, birds were flushed from dry levees into vine tangles in 14-18 m high várzea along a small blackwater stream (TAP); in the fifth, hunters reported the species as primarily occupying várzea at least for most of the year, contrasting this with the Razor-billed Curassow, which uses both várzea and terra firme forest (C. A. Peres and A. Whittaker *in litt.* 1992). If the species is indeed an ecological counterpart of the east Brazilian Red-billed Curassow *Crax blumenbachii* (see relevant account), as suggested by Teixeira and Sick (1981), then an association with water would certainly be likely. It may be more arboreal than other curassows, keeping mostly to the trees (Koepcke and Koepcke 1963; hence presumably Hilty and Brown 1986), and indeed Bates (1863: 282) reported a "flock" (from which a bird was collected) some 30 m up in the canopy. There are no published data on food or breeding in the wild; however, six of nine specimens collected in 1935-1936 on Ilhas Codajás, Solimões, had gonad condition noted: two males had small testes in July 1935, two had them enlarged in July and August 1935; and two females had small ovaries in July 1935 and January 1936 (specimens in FMNH). The extent to which birds move in pairs is unknown, but if this happens only when breeding it is worth noting that a pair was shot on 19 or 20 August 1829 on the Guapore, Brazil (von Pelzeln 1868-1871).

THREATS A century ago the species was much exploited for food in northern Bolivia (Allen 1889); in Peru it was regarded as suffering great hunting pressure in the early 1960s (Koepcke and Koepcke 1963) and this continues (Ortiz 1988). In eastern Ecuador the increased traffic in shotguns since 1970, owing to the opening up of the region to oil exploration and extraction, render this bird all the more vulnerable, if indeed it still occurs (A. Johnson verbally 1991). Destruction and development of várzea along the Brazilian Amazon is a major conservation concern (TAP). Despite all this, the reasons why this species should have vanished so comprehensively from ornithological knowledge in the twentieth century remain puzzling; and there are still vast areas of várzea on the upper Solimões, Juruá and Purus (D. F. Stotz *in litt.* 1988).

MEASURES TAKEN None is known in the wild, and despite its rarity and status as a gamebird the species is not protected under Brazilian law. In captivity, efforts are being made to breed the species at the Cracids Breeding and Conservation Center "Lanaken", Belgium, where 16 birds are held (Geerlings 1992).

MEASURES PROPOSED Given the large (and potentially enormous) range of this species, a useful first step would be to identify any protected areas in the five countries concerned within which the Wattled Curassow might be expected, and to survey them. Second, particular areas where the species has previously been recorded should be resurveyed: such areas should be selected after consultations over their current condition (in Peru the best hope for a good population may be the upper río Napo: Ortiz 1988). Third, areas where the species may be anticipated, such as in the vast areas of várzea along the Solimões, Purus and the Juruá, require exploration (D. F. Stotz *in litt.* 1988; but see Remarks 3); in particular, the Ilhas Codajás, source of at least 16 specimens (Vaurie 1967b), merits new investigation. There appear to be a number of captive specimens and it would be of great value to trace their origin.

REMARKS (1) Paynter and Traylor (1977, 1983) doubtless correctly favoured Peru over Ecuador for the location of the mouth of the río Curaray, but it is worth noting that of four specimens from this locality, all collected between 25 January and 14 February 1926 by the Olallas, two (in ANSP and MCZ; the others in AMNH) explicitly state "Ecuador" on the labels; it is also worth noting that the Curaray forms two confluences, one well inside Peru with the Napo, the other virtually at the border with the Cononaco, and if this latter is the site in question the collecting could have occurred within Ecuadorian territory. (2) Allen (1889) simply repeated the remarks of the collector, who supposed that the Wattled and Razor-billed Curassows "were only individuals of different age and the same species", which means that his comments on abundance may chiefly refer to the latter. (3) Some of these seemingly remote areas have been explored without evidence of the species, however; see, e.g., von Ihering (1905b) and Snethlage (1908).

BEARDED WOOD-PARTRIDGE *Dendrortyx barbatus* E[2]

Confined to the dwindling and highly fragmented cloud-forests of eastern Mexico, this rare game-bird has become locally extinct and is severely threatened elsewhere, largely as a result of habitat destruction on a major scale, although hunting may have played a part.

DISTRIBUTION The Bearded Wood-partridge is endemic to the mountains of the Sierra Madre Oriental in southern San Luis Potosí (and possibly Querétaro: see Remarks 1) and northern Hidalgo, southwards along the escarpment to central Veracruz and Puebla, Mexico. In the following account coordinates are taken from OG (1956a).

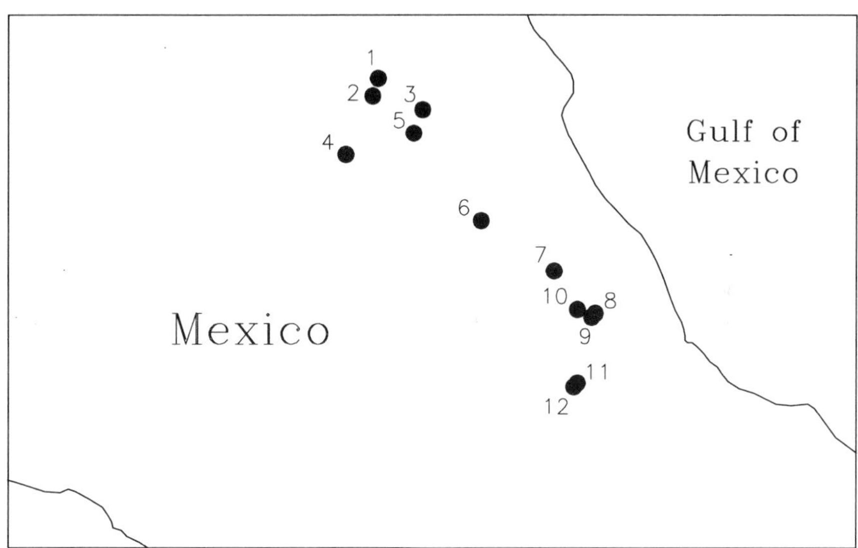

San Luis Potosí This species has been recorded from the south-east near the borders with Querétaro, Hidalgo and Veracruz, almost exclusively in the vicinity of Xilitla. It was first collected in the state in 1947 when a female and three downy young were taken on 12 June and a male on 2 September at 1,220-1,310 m on Cerro Miramar (one of several peaks west of Xilitla: A. G. Navarro and A. T. Peterson *in litt.* 1991). From Cerro San Antonio[1] (just west of Xilitla), specimens were collected in July 1950 (a male) and November 1951 (a male and female; all in LSUMZ: Lowery and Newman 1951). West of Cerro San Antonio, the species was recorded between 1,525-2,135 m at Cerro Conejo, in December 1951 (Davis 1952). Specimens were taken c.10 km west of Ahuacatlán[2] (21°19'N 99°03'W; c.8 km south-west of Xilitla) at 1,830 m, in June 1951 (a half-grown juvenile) and in August 1951 (two males and a female; all in LSUMZ), with further observations also being made "west of Ahuacatlán" during November and December 1951 at 1,525 m (Davis 1952; see Remarks 1).

Hidalgo There are apparently just three specimens (all in LSUMZ) from Hidalgo: a male taken 15 November 1958, 35 km south of Tamazunchale[3]; and two hatchlings taken at Apetsco[4] (= Apesco, at 20°49'N 99°18'W) in April 1948. Birds have been recorded at Puerto El Rayo[5], north-east of Tlanchinol, where live birds were obtained from cloud-forest, and locals reported the species in remnant forest blocks at less than 915 m (Johnsgard 1988, P. A. Johnsgard *in litt.* 1991: see Remarks 2); and nearby at c.8 km north of Tlanchinol, where S. N. G. Howell (*in litt.* 1987, 1991) saw one at c.1,525 m in December 1986. These sites are all in north-central Hidalgo *contra* Johnsgard (1973, 1988) and AOU (1983).

Puebla In the north of the state, the Bearded Wood-partridge has been collected at Scapa[6], 5 km north-east of Huachinango (two males taken at 1,220 m on 14 December 1947, in MLZ), with a pair found near Teziutlán[7] (19°49'N 97°21'W) in February 1977 (D. A. Scott *in litt.* 1985). Further south, Johnsgard (1973) reported the species from Orizaba, Puebla (details given under Veracruz).

Veracruz Most records of the Bearded Wood-partridge come from the Cofre de Perote area of the state, nine specimens coming from "Jalapa" (two taken in 1872 and 1881, the remainder with no data but apparently collected at the end of the nineteenth century; in ANSP, BMNH, MCZ). Jalapa has been doubted as an actual collecting locality (Chapman 1898, Loetscher 1941), a better description probably being the "vicinity of" or the "environs of" Jalapa, both terms used by Sclater (1857a, 1859a), although at the time these specimens were collected Jalapa was situated within cloud-forest and was presumably a suitable locality (A. G. Navarro and A. T. Peterson *in litt.* 1991). A female (in LSUMZ) was collected in 1968 near Coatepec[8] (19°27'N 96°58'W), and in June/July 1893 11 specimens (in USNM) were taken at "Jico"[9] (Xico at 19°25'N 97°00'W), both localities just south and west of Jalapa and east of Cofre de Perote. Cofre de Perote[10] (19°29'N 97°08'W) was mentioned as a locality by Leopold (1959) and Johnsgard (1973), the latter describing the species as occurring sympatrically there with Long-tailed Wood-partridge *Dendrortyx macroura*. Whether "Cofre de Perote" actually refers to the Jalapa, Coatepec and Xico records is unknown, although these records invariably come from the lower slopes of the mountain. Further south in Veracruz, records come from the vicinity of Pico de Orizaba: two specimens were taken at "Orizaba"[11] during the nineteenth century (in MCZ) and a male was collected at Nogales[12] (18°49'N 97°10'W), south-west of Orizaba, in July 1891 (in MNHN). Leopold (1959) mentioned Pico de Orizaba as a locality although again it is unknown if this is a generalization stemming from the Orizaba and Nogales records, Sumichrast (1881) listing the species from the "alpine region of Orizaba". Johnsgard (1973), as mentioned earlier, recorded it from Orizaba, Puebla: Pico de Orizaba straddles the Veracruz–Puebla border and he may well have been referring to a record from the Puebla side of the mountain. The Bearded Wood-partridge has also been collected at Dos Caminos, km 354 (untraced, but on the road from Teziutlán to Nautla and km 354 from Mexico City: M. A. Traylor *in litt.* 1991), where a male and female were taken at 1,370 m in August 1948 (specimens in FMNH).

POPULATION Little specific information exists. At the end of the nineteenth century, Salvin and Godman (1888-1904) wrote that in the highland forests of Veracruz it is a rarer bird than the Long-tailed Wood-partridge. At around this time, 10 specimens (seven males, two females and a juvenile, in USNM) were taken at Xico, 4-15 July 1893, suggesting that on the lower slopes of Cofre de Perote the species was not uncommon. It was not recorded again until the late 1940s (see Lowery and Newman 1951), Loetscher (1941) concluding that it was locally rare or very rare and suggesting that there was a remote possibility of its extinction.

When the species was "rediscovered" in 1947 around Xilitla, San Luis Potosí (see Distribution), Lowery and Newman (1951), who collected a female and three young on Cerro San Antonio (12 June 1947), considered it a not uncommon resident in the area. Most "recent" specimens come from the Xilitla area (in LSUMZ), and observations include 17 seen in five days during November and December 1951 (Davis 1952); these latter break down as six seen in one day between 1,220-1,525 m, two seen in a day west of Ahuacatlán, and three in a day at Cerro Conejo, all of which suggests that a sizeable population existed in this part of San Luis Potosí, although its present status is very doubtful owing to the almost total removal of forest (see Threats).

In Hidalgo the species is apparently rare near Tlanchinol, where one was seen in December 1986, although locals said that the bird could be heard fairly frequently (S. N. G. Howell *in litt.* 1991). In 1990, no birds were observed near this site and the locals this time claimed that the species no longer occurred in the immediate vicinity, although with fairly extensive areas of forest left in the area it could still be present (S. N. G. Howell *in litt.* 1991).

In Veracruz, the present status of the population is unknown, although a female collected in 1968 near Coatepec (in LSUMZ) suggests an extant population in the Cofre de Perote area; however, recent investigations by ornithologists from MZFC (around Xico, Cofre de Perote and Jalapa) revealed no evidence of the bird, most of the forest in central Veracruz having been destroyed (A. G. Navarro and A. T. Peterson *in litt.* 1991). There have been no specimens taken in the Orizaba area since the late nineteenth century, although Leopold's (1959) comment that the species is sympatric with Long-tailed Wood-partridge on Pico de Orizaba, and Johnsgard's (1973) similar comment, imply that there may be more recent records. A population may survive near Teziutlán, Puebla (see Distribution).

ECOLOGY The endemic Bearded Wood-partridge is resident in humid montane forests of the subtropical and possibly the lower temperate zones (Loetscher 1941, AOU 1983). Most records of this bird come from between 1,220 and 2,135 m (see Distribution), although Johnsgard (1988) was told by locals in Hidalgo that the species occurred in primary forest remnants at elevations of less than 915 m (see Remarks 2). The species is mostly associated with montane cloud-forests (Lowery and Newman 1951, Johnsgard 1988), and more specifically in the Xilitla region it has been found in the oak–sweetgum–treefern association at 1,220-1,525 m; west of Ahuacatlán it was seen in an area of mixed pine and oak where the ground was covered with scattered shrubs and grass (epiphytes and vines being relatively scarce), at 1,525 m on the dry side of the mountain; on the wet slope of Cerro Conejo between 1,525-2,135 m in woods of mostly pine, with some oak lower down (Davis 1952); and near Tlanchinol, in humid evergreen montane forest (with oaks and treeferns) (S. N. G. Howell *in litt.* 1991), P. A. Johnsgard (*in litt.* 1991) describing this area as a patchwork of cloud-forest with small plantings of maize and beans.

In Hidalgo, the species reportedly visits planted fields in forest openings when the black beans are ripening (Johnsgard 1988). A male taken at Orizaba in July 1891 (in MNHN) was found to contain fruit and seed. Captive birds were noted to relish soft fruit and fairly large seeds such as soaked black beans and maize kernels (Johnsgard 1988).

In the Xilitla region, downy young have been noted on 28 April, 2 May, 6 June, with three on 12 June (all in LSUMZ; see also Lowery and Newman 1951) and at Xico, Veracruz, one was collected on 9 July 1893 (in USNM). Clutch-size is unknown although Johnsgard (1988) kept five birds apparently all from the same brood, suggesting that the clutch would normally be slightly greater than five. The incubation period in captivity was noted at 28-30 days (Johnsgard 1988). Adult Bearded Wood-partridges are extremely difficult to secure (Lowery and Newman 1951), probably only flushing to nearby trees on the approach of hunting dogs (Leopold 1959). The species is thought to be sympatric with Long-tailed Wood-partridge in a few areas such as Pico de Orizaba and Cofre de Perote (Salvin and Godman 1888-1904, Leopold 1959, Johnsgard 1988), although S. N. G. Howell (*in litt.* 1991) has suggested that a habitat difference exists between the two species, Bearded Wood-partridge preferring humid evergreen montane forest and Long-tailed Wood-partridge usually found at higher elevations in pine evergreen forest.

THREATS The Bearded Wood-partridge is reliant upon a limited area of humid montane forest, and as a result is vulnerable to deforestation: rampant destruction of the primary forest within its range (S. N. G. Howell *in litt.* 1987) has resulted in little hope for the species's long-term survival (Johnsgard 1988). Most of the cloud-forest in central Veracruz has been destroyed (A. G. Navarro and A. T. Peterson *in litt.* 1991), and the forests near Xilitla (San Luis Potosí) and around Teziutlán (Puebla), which in the past supported sizeable populations of this species (see Population), have also been extensively cut and cleared (S. N. G. Howell *in litt.* 1991). Cloud-forest in Querétaro (in which the bird presumably occurred: see Remarks 1) is located in a very narrow area on the border with San Luis Potosí and Hidalgo (very close to or once continuous with forest near Xilitla), and (as of July 1991) is almost completely destroyed (A. G. Navarro and A. T. Peterson *in litt.* 1991).

Local residents in Hidalgo report the species from primary forest remnants lower than 915 m (c.300 m below its usual altitudinal range: see Ecology), which (if correct: see Remarks 2) suggests that it can tolerate a certain degree of deforestation and habitat fragmentation (although probably not in combination with hunting), but it is unknown whether these reports refer to the same birds that visit fields of ripening black beans (see Ecology) and which in fact still rely upon pristine forest higher up once this seasonal food source has gone. The Tlanchinol area of Hildalgo has been cleared rapidly during the last two years, although it still contains some large patches of good habitat (A. G. Navarro and A. T. Peterson *in litt.* 1991).

Adult birds are very difficult to secure (Lowery and Newman 1951), *Dendrortyx* species in general being hunted little in Mexico; only when dogs are used, flushing the birds into nearby trees, can they be shot (Leopold 1959). Nevertheless, S. N. G. Howell (*in litt.* 1987) has suggested that subsistence hunting is a threat and, speaking to locals in an area of forest where the species still occurs, found that dogs and traps were used to secure the birds. Also, three downy young were purchased from locals in the Xilitla region (specimens in LSUMZ) and Johnsgard (1988) obtained live specimens (presumably the five from one brood mentioned in Ecology) that had been captured in cloud-forest in Hidalgo, all of which suggests that young are caught and raised (for food) at least on an opportunistic level.

MEASURES TAKEN There are three national parks within the immediate range of the species, all in Veracruz. The Cofre de Perote National Park covers areas where the species has been recorded (see Distribution), although agricultural practices are carried out in at least part of the park and may well still threaten the bird there (Vargas Márquez 1984). Further south in Veracruz are the Cañon del Río Blanco National Park (55,690 ha), situated along route 150 from Orizaba to the Puebla border, and Pico de Orizaba National Park (19,750 ha, straddling the Puebla–Veracruz border: Anon. 1989), both of which include areas where the species is known to have occurred, although its current status there is unknown (see Population).

MEASURES PROPOSED The priority for the Bearded Wood-partridge is obviously to locate any existing viable populations and to protect the habitat in these areas. Such protection should be augmented with a total hunting ban, and more realistically an education programme to persuade locals not to hunt this species. An aerial survey would perhaps speed up the process of identifying suitable patches of remaining habitat which could then be targeted for fieldwork and protection.

The Tlanchinol area of Hidalgo appears to be the immediate priority for protection, with possibly more surviving habitat and birds than most other areas (but see Threats), although the area around Tenango de Daria still holds good forest (A. G. Navarro and A. T. Peterson *in litt.* 1991) and also warrants investigation. Any suitable remaining forest in the Xilitla (San Luis Potosí) and Teziutlán (Puebla) (see Population) regions needs protection, with surveys to determine the viability of each area for this species.

The status of any populations and suitable habitat (if in fact any still exists) within the present Veracruz national parks needs to be assessed (the Dwarf Jay *Cyanolyca nana* – see relevant account – was originally known from the same parks, although it has not been recorded there in recent years). The precise ecological requirements of the partridge are still unknown, and a detailed study is needed to help with the identification of other suitable (potential) areas.

REMARKS (1) The San Luis Potosí–Querétaro border lies just c.5-8 km west of Ahuacatlán, obviously further by road, but suggesting that records from up to 10 km west of Ahuacatlán may possibly be from Querétaro state and not San Luis Potosí. (2) The altitude of 915 m seems particularly low and its origin is unknown. The village of Puerto El Rayo is apparently at c.1,675 m, and nearby Tlanchinol at c.1,525 m; however, it is possible that suitable habitat exists (or existed) as low as 915 m close to these villages.

GORGETED WOOD-QUAIL *Odontophorus strophium* V/R[10]

This rare wood-quail is endemic to the severely threatened subtropical and temperate zone forests encompassing a small area of the western slope of the East Andes, Colombia. Until 1923 only known from Cundinamarca, recent records have come from one of the only remaining areas of suitable habitat, around Virolín in Santander department.

DISTRIBUTION The Gorgeted Wood-quail is restricted to two areas on the western slope of the East Andes in Santander and Cundinamarca departments, Colombia, encompassing a maximum longitudinal range of some 280 km (Romero-Zambrano 1983). The few precise records and localities, with coordinates (unless otherwise stated) from Paynter and Traylor (1981), are as follows:

Santander Cuchilla del Ramo, on the río Zapatoca (6°48'N 73°26'W; near Betulia: coordinates from Romero-Zambrano 1983), a male and chicks taken in May 1970 (Romero-Zambrano 1983, Brooke 1988b); and Virolín (6°05'N 73°12'W), in the vicinity of which three specimens were collected at Finca La Argentina in November 1979, Finca La Lanosa in December 1979, and Caño Luisito in March 1981 (Romero-Zambrano 1983), and within a 3 km radius of which (i.e. Virolín) birds were shot (by a hunter) and groups heard during March 1988, all between 1,800 and 2,050 m (Brooke 1988b);

Cundinamarca San Juan de Ríoseco (4°51'N 74°38'W), a male (in AMNH) taken in November 1923 (also Apolinar-María 1946); Subia (4°34'N 74°27'W), a male (in AMNH) taken in July 1913 (also Chapman 1917a); río Beura (untraced, but in the vicinity of Bogotá), a specimen (in MCZ) taken in August 1912; and (label data only partially legible, but apparently) "Finca de Nonnardo, Agualarga" (untraced, but also in the vicinity of Bogotá), a female (in AMNH) taken in May 1920.

POPULATION Until recently, this species was known from very few records (four specimens with information other than "Bogotá" or "Colombia" on their labels), all originating in Cundinamarca during or prior to 1923 (see above). There have been no subsequent records from Cundinamarca, but in 1970 it was found to the north in Santander when breeding was proven near Betulia, and three specimens were collected between 1979 and 1981 in the vicinity of Virolín, where a good population was deemed to exist (Romero-Zambrano 1983). Despite this, the species was considered very rare and endangered (King 1978-1979, Hilty and Brown 1986, Johnsgard 1988) until March 1988, when at least seven groups of birds were heard (with three birds shot, and at least three others seen), also in the vicinity of Virolín (Brooke 1988b).

It has been concluded that the oak forest in the Virolín area may be especially favoured by the species and may possibly harbour high densities of birds, although its status in this whole forest block (north-east of Virolín) remains unknown (Brooke 1988b). The large-scale destruction and fragmentation of forest on the western slope of the East Andes, especially in Cundinamarca (see Threats), suggest that the Gorgeted Wood-quail has suffered a serious long-term population decline, and may now exist in relatively small numbers in just a few remaining forest blocks, the largest of which appears to be near Virolín (see Hilty and Brown 1986, Brooke 1988b).

ECOLOGY The Gorgeted Wood-quail inhabits the floor of humid subtropical and lower temperate zone forests (Hilty and Brown 1986, Johnsgard 1988, Fjeldså and Krabbe 1990), at altitudes known to range from 1,750 to 2,050 m (Romero-Zambrano 1983, Brooke 1988b). However, Hilty and Brown (1986) suggested a range of 1,500-1,800 m, and Brooke (1988b) could see no reason (with reference to the forest structure) for birds at Virolín not to range as high as 2,500 m. The bird apparently favours primary forest dominated by oaks (*Quercus humboldtii* and *Trigonobalanus* sp.) and laurels (e.g. *Nectandra* sp. and *Persea* sp.) (Romero-Zambrano 1983). However, in the Virolín area (described as primary oak forest with areas of pasture and secondary forest), Brooke (1988b) noted birds calling from forest that was regenerating after logging, although it seems likely that the species relies on primary forest during at least part of its life-cycle. Just prior to breeding, it occurs in small groups, with three birds seen together, and seven groups (of unknown size) recorded from a relatively small area around Virolín during March 1988 (Brooke 1988b).

The forest around Virolín is characterized by a number of plant species, all but the last three of which are suspected of featuring in the wood-quail's diet: *Quercus humboldtii*, *Trigonobalanus* sp., *Cavendishia guatapensis*, *C.* cf. *nitida*, *Macleania rupestris*, *Miconia theaezans*, *Myrica pubescens*, *Rapanea ferruginea*, *Nectandra laurel*, *Ficus boyacensis*, *Norantea mixta*, *Thibaudia floribunda*, *Tibouchina lepidota*, and *Persea mutisii* (Romero-Zambrano 1983). The stomach contents of recent specimens indicate a diet of arthropods and fruits, and there is some evidence suggesting that the fruits and seeds preferred by the species are those of the plants mentioned above (Romero-Zambrano 1983).

The breeding season (in Santander) appears to coincide with the two periods of peak annual rainfall, i.e. March–May and September–November (see Fundación Natura 1990), with a breeding condition bird taken in March 1981 (and groups of birds calling in March 1988), juveniles in May 1970, another in breeding condition in November 1979, and an immature in December 1979 (Romero-Zambrano 1983, Brooke 1988b).

THREATS The humid subtropical and temperate zone forests of the western slope of the East Andes have been largely cleared, and at least in Cundinamarca there is now almost no forest left (Hilty and Brown 1986, J. Fjeldså *in litt.* 1986, Brooke 1988b), although King (1978-1979) mentioned that small patches of forest remained near Subia, but were probably too small and disturbed to harbour this species.

The only remaining forest block of significant size within the range of this rare wood-quail is in the vicinity of Virolín: this forest block is an extensive area (c.10,000 ha) of primary humid forest extending for c.50 km north-east from Virolín in a band c.25 km wide ranging up to 3,000 m (Brooke 1988b, J. Hernández Camacho and G. I. Andrade *in litt.* undated). The valley bottom near Virolín is at c.1,800 m, and has been mostly cleared for grazing, with forest (which may have experienced some selective felling but is essentially primary) starting at c.1,950 m (Brooke 1988b). Tree-felling and hunting are largely confined to the peripheral kilometre (at least around Virolín), but although the area is rugged it is not so precipitous as to preclude felling in the future (Brooke 1988b). The presence of at least seven groups of birds in an area of active hunting suggested that this species may be able to withstand some hunting pressure (Brooke 1988b), but this is presumably only true if there are adjacent tracts of undisturbed forest with a substantial population of birds in the area, i.e. hunting remains a major threat to relict populations in remnant forest patches (also G. I. Andrade verbally 1991).

MEASURES TAKEN Based on recommendations from ICBP (which reflected the importance of area as recognized by INDERENA and Romero-Zambrano 1983), M. de L. Brooke (supported by ICBP and Fundación Natura) undertook an ornithological survey of the oak-dominated forest in the Virolín area (concentrating on the Gorgeted Wood-quail) in March 1988 (Brooke 1988b). As a result of this work, and the known biological importance of the area, Fundación Natura (with assistance from ICBP, Financiera Eléctrica Nacional and The Nature Conservancy) set out to design a protected area encompassing the most important forest areas around Virolín: a final proposal for the Cachalú Wildlife Sanctuary (previously named Virolín) was submitted to INDERENA for formal designation in 1990 (G. I. Andrade *in litt.* 1988, 1990, Fundación Natura 1990).

MEASURES PROPOSED The obvious priority for the Gorgeted Wood-quail is to ensure the effective preservation of the remaining forest around Virolín, which should be facilitated by the protected area outlined above. Further suitable areas in Santander and any remaining forest patches in Cundinamarca need to be identified, their importance assessed and protection ensured if more than one isolated population (however large it may be) of the species is to survive. Surveys and research are needed to determine the population status of this species in Cachalú Wildlife Sanctuary, and also the effects of hunting and the extent to which the birds use secondary habitats. These forests on the western slope of the East Andes (including those in the vicinity of Virolín) are also important for the Black Inca *Coeligena prunellei*, the requirements of which should be integrated into any future conservation initiatives or management (see relevant account).

AUSTRAL RAIL *Rallus antarcticus* E/Ex[4]

Known from a fair number of records from southern Argentina and southern Chile, this marshbird has not been recorded since 1959, and may already be extinct or nearly so, owing presumably to the destruction of wet grasslands by grazing sheep and man's activities.

DISTRIBUTION The Austral Rail has been recorded from Buenos Aires province, Argentina, and Valparaiso province, Chile, south to Tierra del Fuego, but the only definite austral summer (i.e. breeding season) records are from "central Chile" plus Llanquihué and Magallanes provinces, Chile, and Río Negro, Chubut and north-eastern Tierra del Fuego provinces, Argentina. On the following evidence the species may possibly breed or have bred throughout its Chilean range, while it still needs to be established whether Argentine records from Buenos Aires are of migrants only.

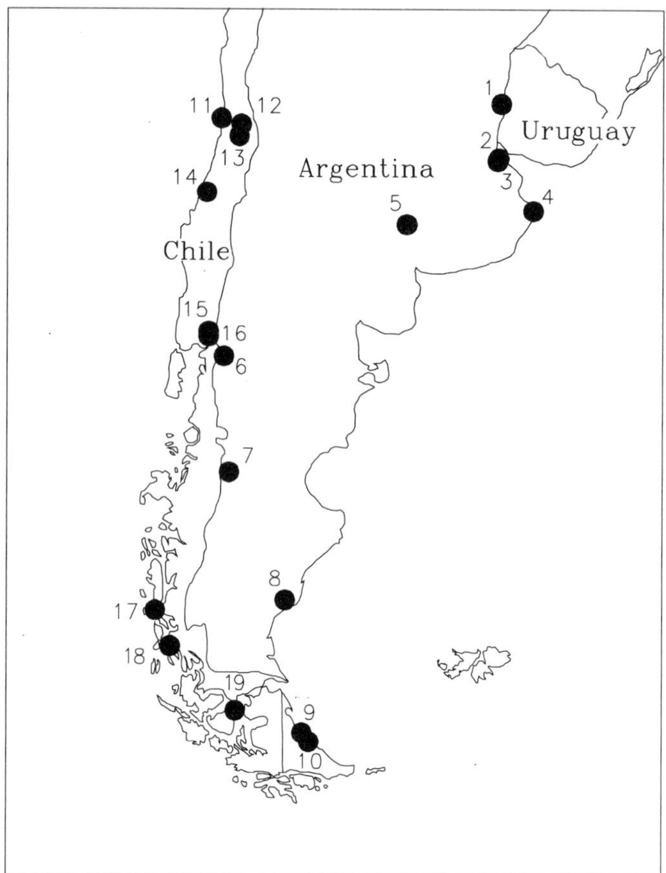

Argentina Records (north to south, coordinates from Paynter 1985) are: (*Entre Ríos*) near Concepción del Uruguay[1], where there were possible nineteenth-century sightings (Barrows 1884); (*Buenos Aires*) possibly Barracas al Sud[2] (adjacent to Avellaneda, 34°39'S 58°22'W), where two nests with eggs were found in early November 1900 (Hartert and Venturi 1909) but no parent birds were procured, so that the record remains doubtful (Hellmayr and Conover 1942); Partido de Lomas de Zamora[3] (34°45'S 58°25'W), where a specimen (in BMNH) was killed by dogs in the swamp in June 1884 (Withington and Sclater 1888, Sharpe 1894); Cabo San Antonio[4], where a bird was collected in July 1899 (Gibson 1920); Carhué[5], April 1881 (Barrows 1884; specimen in MCZ); (*Río Negro*) El Bolsón[6] (41°58'S 71°31'W), where a bird was collected in October 1959 (Navas 1962); (*Chubut*) Valle del Lago Blanco[7] (c.45°54°S 71°15'W), November 1901 (specimen in BMNH; also Hellmayr and Conover 1942); (*Santa Cruz*) lower río Chico[8], March 1897 (Scott and Sharpe 1904; specimen in FMNH); (*Tierra del Fuego*) río Grande Norte[9] (53°47'S 67°42'W, exact locality and date obtained unknown; specimen labelled "Río Grande Norte" donated to AMNH by the museum at Punta Arenas: Humphrey *et al.* 1970; see also Chapman 1933); Viamonte[10], February 1931 (Humphrey *et al.* 1970; specimen in BMNH).

Chile SOMA (1935-1942) listed Talca and Linares provinces for the species, but in the absence of supporting evidence they are not considered further here. Records (north to south, coordinates from OG 1967) are: "Central Chile", where eight eggs were collected in October of an unspecified year (Oates 1901); (*Valparaiso*) "Valparaiso"[11] (old record determined by J. Fjeldså *in litt.* 1988); (*Santiago*) Fundo (*sic*), San Ignacio[12] (33°20'S 70°42'W), where a nest with six eggs found in November 1940 was attributed to this species, although identity was considered uncertain (six eggs in WFVZ); Viluco[13] (33°47'S 70°48'W), undated (Philippi 1858); (*Colchagua*) Cauquenes[14], undated (Reed 1877); (*Llanquihué*) Puntiagudo[15] (41°05'S 72°16'W), Peulla and Cayutué[16] (41°16'S 72°16'W) (all three at Lago Todos los Santos), undated (Goodall *et al.* 1951, Johnson 1965); (*Magallanes*) Bahía Tom[17] (50°12'S 74°47'W), north-eastern Isla Madre de Dios, where a bird was collected in April 1879 (Sharpe 1881); Puerto Mayne[18] (51°19'S 74°05'W), Isla Evans, where a bird was collected in March 1880 (Sharpe 1881); Punta Arenas[19], January 1876 (specimens in BMNH; Sclater and Salvin 1878a) and February 1883 (Oustalet 1891). There are additional records without specific data from "Chile", "Central Chile", "Santiago province" and "Straits of Magellan", this last being the type-locality (Hellmayr 1932).

POPULATION The Austral Rail has evidently become extremely rare and the absence of records in the past 30 years from a region where ornithological activity has not been insignificant gives serious cause for alarm. Only two specimens have been collected since 1901, one in 1931 and one in 1959 (see Distribution). Withington (1888) found the species to be rather common at Carhué in Buenos Aires in early April 1881. Rails are generally difficult to detect, but the paucity of specimens and sightings of this species suggests that it was already genuinely rare at the turn of the century. J. Koslowsky only secured a single specimen during intensive collecting from 1899 to 1901 in Chubut, Argentina (Hellmayr and Conover 1942), and a similarly experienced collector, A. Kovács, also only ever recorded a single individual in Patagonia (Navas 1962). In Llanquihué, Chile, a Dr Wolffhügel (in Johnson 1965) saw a few every winter, and stated that the species bred in the reedbeds in Lago Todos los Santos, both at Peulla and Puntiagudo, as well as in the extensive reedbeds at the mouth of río Cayutué; no data concerning these records were given. Recent searches in the area produced no records, and the species is not even known by the guards of the present-day park (D. Willis *in litt.* 1991; see Measures Taken).

ECOLOGY Johnson (1965) considered the species "possibly the least known Chilean bird". It inhabits marshy fields, lake shores with rushy areas, and reedbeds (Johnson 1965, Meyer de Schauensee 1970, Fjeldså and Krabbe 1990), although a few birds were known to spend the winter months in the garden of a house garden at Cayutué, where they appeared to be very tame (Johnson 1965).

Little is known about feeding; one stomach contained a mass of partially digested Trichoptera *Limnophilus meridionalis* (Humphrey *et al.* 1970), and during winter at Cayutué very tame birds were observed feeding on grubs found underneath decomposing leaves, and even eating the leftovers of a dog's dinner (Johnson 1965). Its diet is probably not very different from that of the similar Virginia Rail *Rallus limicola*, which Ripley (1977) stated consists of slugs, snails, small fish, insect larvae and earthworms.

Nesting probably occurs throughout its range (Navas 1962), but the only nest which can be safely attributed to this species was found in October in central Chile and contained eight eggs (Oates 1901). The nest found near San Ignacio, Santiago (possibly belonging to this species), on 1 November 1940 contained six fresh eggs, and was placed on the ground under a thick bramble *Rubus* bordering an irrigation canal; the eggs were in a depression with a scanty lining of grass bents and rushes (information from WFVZ card index). Two more nests attributed to this species were found in a lagoon, early November 1900, each 20 cm above the water in a grass tussock, and each containing four eggs (Hartert and Venturi 1909).

Northwards post-breeding migration seems to occur or to have occurred, at least in the most southerly populations; this would take place at the end of March and early in April (Navas 1962).

THREATS The reasons for the species's scarcity are not clear; Fjeldså (1988) has identified the overgrazing and disappearance of practically all tall-grass habitat in Patagonia as a possible cause. Scott and Carbonell (1986) reported the proposed development of Lago Todos los Santos despite its protected area status (see below).

MEASURES TAKEN None is known other than that Lago Todos los Santos is protected within the contiguous Puyehue and Vicente Pérez National Parks (Scott and Carbonell 1986; but see above).

MEASURES PROPOSED It is difficult to suggest a conservation strategy for such an unknown and wide-ranging species, but clearly the first priority is simply to locate remaining populations. Localities where the species was previously found and where preferred habitats still exist should be surveyed; other suitable areas within its range should be visited as well in case any overlooked populations survive. Surveys would be most useful at the beginning of the breeding season (i.e. October for northern populations and later, perhaps November and December, for the more southerly ones), when an effort should be made to record its voice, which could then greatly facilitate the further location of birds.

BOGOTA RAIL *Rallus semiplumbeus* V/R[10]

Restricted to the savanna and páramo marshes of Cundinamarca and Boyacá departments in the East Andes of Colombia, the Bogotá Rail has healthy populations in just a few remaining marsh areas, all of which are threatened by drainage, habitat loss and the effects of agrochemicals.

DISTRIBUTION The Bogotá Rail is restricted to the marshes and lakes of the Bogotá–Ubaté savannas and some surrounding higher altitude areas, in the East Andes in Boyacá and Cundinamarca departments, Colombia (see Remarks). Although the current distribution is primarily restricted to relatively few lake or marsh areas, specific localities (coordinates from Paynter and Traylor 1981) for this species area as follows:

(*Boyacá*) Laguna de Tota (5°33'N 72°55'W; at 3,015 m), where probably the largest population exists (Blake 1959, Varty *et al.* 1986, Fjeldså and Krabbe 1990, J. Fjeldså *in litt.* 1992); (*Cundinamarca*) Laguna de Fúquene (5°28'N 73°45'W; at 2,580 m on the Cundinamarca–Boyacá border), where birds were seen in October 1991 (J. Fjeldså *in litt.* 1992); Laguna de Cucunubá (5°17'N 73°48'W; at 2,500 m, Valle de Ubaté), where a bird was seen in October 1991 (J. Fjeldså *in litt.* 1992); Subachoque (4°56'N 74°11'W; at 2,685 m near the north-western limit of the Bogotá savanna), from which there is an undated specimen (in ICN); Torca (c.4°53'N 74°05'W; at 2,600 m, 26 km north of Bogotá), where two males (in ICN) were taken in September 1950; Cota (4°49'N 74°06'W; at 2,605 m, 25 km north of Bogotá: Olivares 1969); Laguna de Pedropalo (c.4°45'N 74°24'W), where the species was recorded at 2,100 m in January 1991 (F. G. Stiles *in litt.* 1992); "Suba Marshes" and Laguna de Juan Amarillo (= Tibabuyes), c.3 km west of Suba (4°45'N 74°05'W; at 2,560 m), where four specimens (in LACM) were collected in March 1960, with one heard in January 1992 (L. M. Renjifo *in litt.* 1992); El Prado (4°43'N 74°02'W; at c.2,600 m, 5 km north of Bogotá), where three males (in ANSP, ICN) were collected in March 1960; near Funza (4°43'N 74°13'W), where birds were recorded on a small marsh in November 1991 (F. G. Stiles *in litt.* 1992); Laguna de la Florida (c.4°43'N 74°09'W; at c.2,600 m, west of Bogotá near Aeropuerto Internacional Eldorado), whence come the majority of recent records (Hilty and Brown 1986, F. R. Lambert *in litt.* 1989, M. Pearman *in litt.* 1990, J. Fjeldså *in litt.* 1992, P. Kaestner *in litt.* 1992); near La Florida on a small roadside pool, where one was seen in January 1987 (M. Pearman *in litt.* 1990: see also Population); La Holanda (4°42'N 74°15'W; c.25 km west of Bogotá), where a male (in AMNH) was collected at 2,650 m in May 1913; Usaquén (4°42'N 74°02'W; at 2,590 m, a north-eastern suburb of Bogotá), where a female (in ICN) was taken during November 1952; La Herrera (4°42'N 74°18'W; at c.2,600 m, 20 km north-west of Bogotá), where many birds have been seen during recent years (Varty *et al.* 1986, J. Fjeldså *in litt.* 1992, LGN); 15 km east-north-east of Bogotá (4°36'N 74°05'W) in a small marsh beside the road to Guatavita lake, where the species has recently been recorded (P. Kaestner *in litt.* 1992); Techo (c.4°36'N 74°08'W; at 2,570 m, 8 km west of Bogotá), where a male (in ICN) was taken during September 1952; Embalse del Muña (c.4°32'N 74°18'W; at 2,550 m), where a female (in ICN) was taken in June 1943; south of "Laguna Chingaza" (Páramo de Chingaza is at 4°31'N 73°45'W; 35 km east of Bogotá), where a bird and an empty nest were found at 3,300 m in October 1991 (J. Fjeldså *in litt.* 1992); also the adjacent Carpanta Biological Reserve, where the bird was recorded in October 1989 (F. G. Stiles *in litt.* 1992); and Laguna Chisacá (4°17'N 74°13'W; at 4,000 m, 45 km south-west of Bogotá), where a female (in ICN) was taken between 3,900 and 4,000 m in April 1960.

POPULATION The Bogotá Rail is uncommon to locally fairly common (Chapman 1917a, Hilty and Brown 1986), and despite the destruction of its habitat (see Threats), there are indications that the bird may occur in numerous localities where suitable habitat (albeit in small patches) remains (J. Fjeldså *in litt.* 1986, P. Kaestner *in litt.* 1992). Laguna de Tota supports the largest population of the species, with Varty *et al.* (1986) estimating the 1982 population to be between 30 and 50 pairs, although they recognized that this was probably an underestimate as most records were just of calling birds (33 counted). Two breeding territories observed at Laguna de Tota during 1982 were between 0.2 and 0.45 ha in area (Varty *et al.* 1986). In 1991, J. Fjeldså (*in litt.* 1992) judged the number to be closer 400 individuals. At La Herrera, 11 birds were counted along a 250 m transect in August 1982 (Varty *et al.* 1986), and in 1991 the population was estimated at 50 territories, thus representing the second largest known concentration (J. Fjeldså *in litt.* 1992). Elsewhere, at (Parque) La Florida, 4-8 birds have consistently been recorded (since 1989), with up to 12 individuals noted along one edge of the main marsh: a more precise population estimate at this locality (in 33 ha) is being made by I. E. Lozano, and currently (May 1992) stands at c.20 pairs (F. G. Stiles *in litt.* 1992: see Measures Taken). Outside of the park, another sizeable area of marsh also supports a small population, and a c.6 ha marsh near Funza supported at least five birds in November 1991 (F. G. Stiles *in litt.* 1992). Despite several birds being seen at Laguna de Fúquene, the unsuitability of the vegetation suggests that the population density there is not high (J. Fjeldså *in litt.* 1992).

ECOLOGY The Bogotá Rail has been recorded in the temperate zone marshes from 2,500 m up to 4,000 m on the páramo, occurring at least occasionally down to 2,100 m at Laguna de Pedropalo (see Distribution). Birds inhabit rushy fields, reedbeds (often with open, regenerating burnt areas), reed-filled ditches (including *Juncus* sp.), fens fringed with dwarf bamboo *Swallenochloa* sp., and often feed along the water's edge, in flooded pasture, wet fen, or within patches of dead waterlogged vegetation nearby (Varty *et al.* 1986, Fjeldså and Krabbe 1990). The characteristic wetland where these birds occur is fringed with tall, dense reeds (comprising *Scirpus californicus*, *Typha latifolia*, with less *Cortadera* sp.) and some *Alnus acuminata* swamp, with the shallows full of *Elodea*, *Myriophyllum brasiliense*, *Potamogeton* etc. (Varty *et al.* 1986, Fjeldså and Krabbe 1990). Few of these marshes remain, owing to the strong influence of pollution and siltation: in these circumstances, the submergent vegetation disappears and carpets of *Azolla* sp., *Ludwigia peploides*, and *Limnobium stoloniferum* spread over the surface (Fjeldså and Krabbe 1990), although even this can be utilized by the species (J. I. Hernández Camacho verbally 1991).

This rail primarily feeds on aquatic invertebrates and insect larvae, although birds have been observed taking worms, dead fish and molluscs, and may also take small frogs, tadpoles and plant material (Varty *et al.* 1986, L. M. Renjifo *in litt.* 1992). Although they are closely associated with *Typha* reedbeds, food availability in this vegetation is low, and they seem to prefer wet fen and marsh shoreline areas for foraging (Varty *et al.* 1986): at Laguna La Florida, birds forage mainly in areas with a thin carpet of floating plants, such as *Azolla* sp. and *Limnobium* sp., but avoiding the introduced *Eichhornia crassies* (I. E. Lozano *per* L. M. Renjifo *in litt.* 1992). Bogotá Rails are active from dawn to dusk and, although generally skulking, they visit more open areas (including reed edge) early in the morning (Hilty and Brown 1986, Varty *et al.* 1986).

Nesting territories (0.2-0.45 ha) of two pairs studied at Laguna de Tota comprised a combination of vegetation types, but the (three) nests found were all in *Typha* sp. beds (one of these areas was mixed with *Scirpus* sp.) (Varty *et al.* 1986). Pairs with between two and four juveniles were recorded at the end of July and the beginning of August, and there was some indication that one pair was starting a second brood, suggesting a breeding season at Laguna de Tota from July to late September (Varty *et al.* 1986): two specimens (in ROM) taken at this locality in February 1950 are labelled "juvenile" and "immature".

THREATS Only a few lakes with high plant productivity exist in the Andes of Colombia, but until recent disturbance by man the Ubaté and Bogotá plateaus had enormous marshes and swamps (Fjeldså and Krabbe 1990). These savanna wetlands are strongly influenced by pollution and siltation, with the submergent plants disappearing to be replaced by floating mats of vegetation: such habitat destruction has caused the once outstanding diversity of waterbirds to vanish (Fjeldså and Krabbe 1990). All of the major savanna wetland localities are threatened with final destruction, mainly from drainage (Varty *et al.* 1986, J. Fjeldså *in litt.* 1986). At Laguna de Tota, there remain less than 175 ha of "wetland" vegetation, some of which is unsuitable for rails and all of which is threatened by numerous factors: (1) tourism, although this is probably not a major threat during the main breeding season, except through the disturbance caused by the increasing use of motorboats; (2) hunting of all waterbird species; (3) burning of vegetation; (4) harvesting of reeds (possibly not a significant threat); (5) onion cultivation, which is now the major source of revenue, about 90% of the flat lakeside agricultural land being used for this crop; (6) insecticide usage, possibly reducing food availability and poisoning birds; (7) eutrophication from untreated sewage effluent and agrochemicals; and (8) fluctuations and general decreases in water level, caused by drainage and increasing water demand, which have a detrimental effect on the shallow water plant community and allow agricultural encroachment into the reedbeds (Varty *et al.* 1986). Laguna de la Herrera has greatly decreased in size during recent years, although there remain c.250-350 ha of marsh (reed-marsh with extensive open mudflats covered in *Azolla* sp. and *Hydrocotyle* sp. but hardly any water): however, even this is threatened by the development of limestone quarries (which has had a dramatic effect on the western side of the marsh), and by cattle trampling the reedbeds (causing further drying of the marsh) (Varty *et al.* 1986, J. Fjeldså *in litt.* 1992): this lake, one of the largest in the Bogotá savanna, has been without water from August 1991 until at least June 1992 owing to irrigation projects run by the Corporación Autónoma Regional de las Cuencas de los Ríos Bogotá, Ubaté and Suárez (CAR) (L. M. Renjifo *in litt.* 1992). Laguna de Fúquene, although not ideal for the rail (owing to the wide fringe of tall reeds: J. Fjeldså *in litt.* 1992), suffers from agricultural activities within the watershed, soil erosion causing a high content of suspended material, and severe hunting pressure (Varty *et al.* 1986), and is also affected by the work of CAR (L. M. Renjifo *in litt.* 1992: see above). Parque La Florida is a popular recreational area bisected by a road, to the south of which is a highly disturbed boating area with little suitable vegetation, and to the north a fenced-off area of c.2 ha with reeds (Varty *et al.* 1986): the vegetation around this lake is in places apparently cleared or cut, and in 1989 a new dyke was under construction, the potential effect of which was unknown (F. R. Lambert *in litt.* 1989): water flowing into this marsh is polluted with sewage and agrochemicals from surrounding farms and greenhouses (I. E. Lozano *per* L. M. Renjifo *in litt.* 1992).

MEASURES TAKEN Páramo populations of the Bogotá Rail are to be found within Chingaza National Park (50,370 ha), the adjacent Carpanta Biological Reserve, and possibly in Sumapaz National Park (154,000 ha) (Hernández Camacho *et al.* undated): however, the savanna wetlands enjoy no legal protection, although CAR is charged with the task of providing water for drinking and industrial use, and as such is concerned with conservation initiatives and management plans for the many wetlands within its jurisdiction in Cundinamarca, plus Laguna de Tota, Boyacá (Varty *et al.* 1986). A detailed study of the species at Parque La Florida is currently being undertaken (supported by an ICBP-PACS small grant) in order to discover the population size and further aspects of the species's ecology (I. E. Lozano *in litt.* 1991, M. G. Kelsey *in litt.* 1992: see Population and Ecology for some of the preliminary findings): the protected status of this site is unknown.

MEASURES PROPOSED The ecological requirements of the Bogotá Rail are already sufficiently well known to allow the design of an effective conservation plan, and the priority must be to secure the long-term future of the larger remaining wetlands, although any such initiatives need to consider the region's other threatened species, for which see the equivalent section under Apolinar's Wren *Cistothorus apolinari*, but also Rusty-faced Parrot *Hapalopsittaca amazonina* and Black Inca *Coeligena prunellei*, with which (amongst other threatened species) this rail is sympatric in some paramó areas.

Any searches for the species should perhaps concentrate in the páramo areas which have apparently enjoyed a less disturbed history than the savanna wetlands: the species may well be found to occur widely and in significant populations within these areas. However, an assessment of the population within the savanna wetlands, especially that portion of it that exists within small remnant marshes away from the main lake areas, is also a priority for this bird, the status of which is unclear outside of the few main localities. The effective protection of Laguna de la Florida (including the control of incoming water quality), where there appears to be a significant population (see Population), should be an early measure to help conserve this species.

REMARKS Fjeldså and Krabbe (1990) reported an unconfirmed record of this species from Ecuador, and noted that the Peruvian Rail *Rallus peruvianus* (known from just one old specimen of uncertain origin though believed to be in Peru) may in fact represent a subspecies of Bogotá Rail.

PLAIN-FLANKED RAIL *Rallus wetmorei* E[2]

This extremely rare and poorly known rail is restricted to brackish lagoons along a small stretch of the north Venezuelan coast, from where there are very few recent records. It is severely threatened by the loss and deterioration of its wetland habitat.

DISTRIBUTION The Plain-flanked Rail is restricted to the coast of northern Venezuela in eastern Falcón, northern Carabobo and Aragua states. The few records of this species are as follows (coordinates from Paynter 1982):

Falcón near Chichiriviche, where A. B. Altman (*in litt.* 1988) heard of an unconfirmed sighting, but did not see it there himself in two visits; Cuare Wildlife Refuge (10°55'N 68°20'W), where the bird has apparently been recorded (Scott and Carbonell 1986: see Remarks); and Tucacas (10°48'N 68°19'W), where a female (in COP) was taken in January 1950, with five males, four females, and two others (in ANSP, BMNH, COP) taken there during May 1951;

Carabobo Puerto Cabello (10°28'N 68°01'W), where four males, three females and two others (in COP, FMNH, USNM) were collected in September 1945; Borburata (10°26'N 67°58'W, 5 km south-east of Puerto Cabello), where a female (in COP) was collected (at sea level) in November 1944; and Patanemo (10°28'N 67°55'W, 10 km east of Puerto Cabello), where a bird (in AMNH) was taken in September 1945;

Aragua La Ciénaga (c.10°28'N 67°49'W, between Ocumare de la Costa and Turiamo), where the type-specimen (in COP) was taken on the west shore of the bay in April 1943 (Zimmer and Phelps 1944); and beside a lagoon near Playa de Cata (c.10°30'N 67°44'W), 15 km east of La Ciénaga, where a pair of birds was seen in April 1991 (A. F. Badillo *in litt.* 1992).

POPULATION The status of the Plain-flanked Rail is unknown (Ripley 1977), but the fact that 11 birds were collected at Tucacas during May 1951 (see above), and nine were taken at Puerto Cabello in September 1945 (see above) suggests that the species was at least locally common. Despite many subsequent collecting trips to the type-locality, this species was not found there again (Zimmer and Phelps 1944), and although a pair was found nearby (15 km east) in the Cata valley in 1991, this was the first record after a decade of periodic ornithological observations within the area (A. F. Badillo *in litt.* 1992). Records of this rail come from between 1943 (when it was discovered) and 1951, after which time the only reports are from Chichiriviche (unconfirmed), Cuare Wildlife Refuge, and east of La Ciénaga; this seems to indicate that the species's population has declined (especially as the localities are easily accessible to ornithologists).

ECOLOGY Very little is known of the Plain-flanked Rail, but it is apparently sedentary (Ripley 1977; see Distribution), and occurs in coastal mangroves at Tucacas, Puerto Cabello and Patanemo (specimens in AMNH, ANSP, BMNH, FMNH, USNM); Meyer de Schauensee and Phelps (1978) added "shallow saltwater lagoons" to the habitat description. At La Ciénaga, the species was taken (see above) in a "mangrove swamp" of c.150 ha on the west shore of the (sea) bay (Zimmer and Phelps 1944, Ripley 1977); east of this locality, the lagoon near Playa de Cata is apparently covered in emergent vegetation (A. F. Badillo *in litt.* 1992). The habitat at Cuare Wildlife Refuge was described in Scott and Carbonell (1986) as a shallow sea bay bordered in most parts by mangrove swamps, and a large area of seasonally flooded brackish lagoons and marshes (with halophytic vegetation dominated by saltwort *Batis maritima*); the area is surrounded by dry thorn and cactus scrub. The type-specimen, collected in April, was apparently in breeding condition (Zimmer and Phelps 1944); a male (in BMNH) taken in May had enlarged testes; and a bird (in AMNH) taken in September is an apparent juvenile, all of which suggests a breeding season starting in April or May.

THREATS Ripley (1977) wrote that this species was generally subject to pressure from development along the north coast both from weekend houses (with consequent destruction of the mangrove habitat), and expanding oil exploration. More specifically, threats to the Cuare Wildlife Refuge include: (1) the expansion of the town of Chichiriviche; (2) invasion of the area by illegal squatters; (3) construction of large tourist hotels nearby, and on an area currently occupied by squatters; (4) numerous roads within the refuge, leading to excessive tourist pressure; (5) the dangers of pollution from domestic sewage, pesticides, and mercury; (6) a proposal to reduce the area of the refuge by 150 ha, to exclude the area occupied by squatters and an area on which a golf course is to be built (involving a 35 ha landfill); (7) plans to move the squatters to the centre of the refuge; and (8) the construction of a road along the northern edge of the refuge (already under way) without any provision to allow the flow of water to and from the sea (Scott and Carbonell 1986, J. L. Mateo *in litt.* 1991). The lagoon near Playa de Cata, where a pair of birds was seen in 1991, has been modified by the construction of a dike that has closed the lagoon's connection with the sea, seriously threatening the existence of the presumably small, localized population of this rail (A. F. Badillo *in litt.* 1992). The Playa de Cata is one of the most popular beaches along this central part of the Venezuelan coast, and the dike has been constructed to facilitate development for tourism (A. F. Badillo *in litt.* 1992).

MEASURES TAKEN The Cuare Wildlife Refuge (11,825 ha) "protects" a large area of suitable habitat for this species, but is under serious threat (see above), being poorly wardened, with no game guards and no notices (Scott and Carbonell 1986: see Threats); yet this refuge is Venezuela's only RAMSAR site (IUCN 1992). The Laguna de Turiamo (1,600 ha) at the north-western end of Henri Pittier National Park (Scott and Carbonell 1986), is close to La Ciénaga and may well support a population of this species, as may the Morrocoy National Park (32,000 ha), north-east of Tucacas (Scott and Carbonell 1986, B. Swift *in litt* 1988).

MEASURES PROPOSED Clearly, the integrity of the Cuare Wildlife Refuge needs to be ensured, as this area is apparently one of the most important coastal wetlands in Venezuela (Scott and Carbonell 1986), and is currently one of the only places where the Plain-flanked Rail is known to occur. Adequate wardening of the reserve, combined with an awareness campaign, prevention of illegal hunting and careful control of the tourist usage of the area with environmental impact assessments (on all planned developments) are all needed to safeguard the site (see Threats). Official protection of the threatened coastal mangrove habitat would also represent an important step towards the effective conservation of this and other species. Surveys need to be undertaken in the other protected areas (see above) to determine whether or not this rail is present, and an ecological study of the bird would help in the identification of other suitable localities. The tourist developments near Playa de Cata (see Threats) should also be investigated to determine if any remedial action could reduce the long-term environmental impact on the lagoon.

REMARKS It is very possible that the unconfirmed record from "near Chichiriviche" may in fact be the one reported by Scott and Carbonell (1986).

ZAPATA RAIL *Cyanolimnas cerverai* I[7]

This apparently flightless marsh-dwelling rail remains known from only two sites within the Zapata Swamp, Cuba, where it is assumed to have suffered particularly from dry-season burning of habitat and perhaps also from introduced predators.

DISTRIBUTION The Zapata Rail is endemic to Cuba, and for many years since it was first described in 1927 it was believed to occur only in a very restricted area about 1.5 km north of Santo Tomás (22°24'N 81°25'W in OG 1963a), Matanzas province (Barbour and Peters 1927, Garrido and García Montaña 1975). However, Barbour's (1928) surmise that the species would be found elsewhere in the Zapata area was borne out in June 1978 when a bird was observed in one of the channels leading to Guamá village (in the south-eastern corner of Laguna del Tesoro (22°21'N 81°07'W in OG 1963a) and a young bird was photographed at Guamá, Laguna del Tesoro, on 12 June 1978 (Clements 1979, Garrido 1985, J. F. Clements *in litt.* 1991), this new locality being about 65 km from Santo Tomás (Bond 1985). Fossil bones from cave deposits in Pinar del Río province and on the Isle of Pines (Isla de la Juventud) have been attributed to this species (Olson 1974), suggesting a wider former distribution (Garrido 1985). Few specimens have been taken; those in ANSP and MCZ are labelled "Santo Tomás, Península de Zapata, Cuba", one in AMNH "Ciénaga de Zapata, Cuba".

POPULATION At least four birds were collected in 1927 (specimens in MCZ) and Bond (1971) had no difficulty in finding the species in 1931, when two birds were collected and others seen and heard. However, thereafter it was not seen for several decades (Regalado Ruíz 1981). Garrido (1980) failed to find the species in more than five expeditions to the Santo Tomás area, therefore considering it to be "very scarce" and obviously "much less common than 50 years before". The voice was recorded in the mid-1970s, and more birds were observed in 1979 and 1980 (Morton 1979, Garrido 1985). These records together with the new locality for the species at Laguna del Tesoro led Garrido (1985) to comment that the species "may be more widespread in the swamp than previously thought" and that "if no disastrous fires or droughts occur, the rail should not be in any danger". Bond (1971) pointed out the secretive habits of rails and that there are "vast stretches of virtually impenetrable swamp land in the vicinity of Santo Tomás". However, the burnings (see Threats) that occur in the swamp could be a major reason for the scarcity of the species, as it is apparently almost flightless (Regalado Ruíz 1981, Olson 1974). Sulley and Sulley (1992) considered the species to be rare although "regularly heard in the Santo Tomás area".

ECOLOGY The Zapata Rail inhabits dense bush-covered swampland near higher ground at Santo Tomás (Bond 1979) where sawgrass *Cladium jamaicense* and "arraigán" *Myrica cerifera* are common (King 1978-1979, Regalado Ruíz 1981); the habitat where it was found in the Laguna del Tesoro region has not been described. Other aspects of its life history are poorly known (Ripley 1977). Bond (1973) noted that the two specimens collected in January 1931 had "somewhat enlarged testes", and the first nest ever reported was found near Santo Tomás on 7 September 1982; it was situated c.60 cm above water level in a hummock of sawgrass and contained three eggs (Bond 1984).

THREATS Some areas of the Zapata Swamp have been drained, but these are not extensive and should have caused no great harm to the rail's habitat (King 1978-1979). Extensive grass-cutting formerly occurred for roof-thatch, but probably much more devastating for the species are the common man-started fires during the dry season (Morton 1979, Regalado Ruíz 1981), which still occur today (O. H. Garrido *in litt.* 1991). Barbour (1928) and Garrido (1985) both noted the presence of the introduced mongoose *Herpestes* and rats *Rattus*, which could constitute a very substantial additional threat.

MEASURES TAKEN The Zapata Rail has been afforded protection with an area of 10,000 ha in the Corral de Santo Tomás Faunal Refuge, and Laguna del Tesoro falls within the Guana, Playa Larga, Playa Girón Nature Tourism Area (Wright 1988; see also ICGC 1978), but no information exists concerning the benefit these measures bestow upon the Zapata Rail.

MEASURES PROPOSED A survey of the species is urgently needed, with a special effort to delimit accurately its range, numbers and potential threats (see Remarks). Dry-season burning of the swamp must be investigated and controlled.

REMARKS The Zapata Rail occurs in the same area of the Zapata Swamp as the threatened Zapata Wren *Ferminia cerverai* and the nominate race of the threatened Cuban Sparrow *Torreornis inexpectata*, and clearly any intensive survey work on one of these forms (all of them need it) should be expanded to include the other two.

DOT-WINGED CRAKE *Porzana spiloptera* I[7]

Records of this poorly known wetland bird of southern Uruguay and northern Argentina come chiefly from Buenos Aires province; the evidence links a probable decline to the development of marsh areas and particularly the intrusion of cattle.

DISTRIBUTION The Dot-winged Crake has been recorded from southern Uruguay and Buenos Aires west to La Rioja province, Argentina (Hellmayr and Conover 1942). In most cases, records at individual localities are of single birds being collected or observed.

Argentina Records within provinces below are organized from north to south with coordinates taken from Paynter (1985).

La Rioja The species has only been recorded from Paso del Recreo (untraced, but presumably in the north-central part of the province near La Rioja: Paynter 1985) (Giacomelli 1923; see Remarks 1).

San Juan There is a record from "east of San Juan" (Dabbene 1910); apparently based on this, Hellmayr and Conover (1942) and Olrog (1963) listed the species with no further information (see Remarks 2).

San Luis Olrog (1963, 1978) and Nores *et al.* (1983) listed the species with no further information.

Córdoba Records are from Bañados del río Dulce (30°31'S 62°32'W), where eight to ten birds were observed on 1 November 1973, two on 8 February and one on 16 October 1974 (Nores and Yzurieta 1975). A bird collected in May 1925 is simply labelled "Provincia de Córdoba" (specimen in MACN).

Santa Fe A bird was collected in "Santa Fé" in April 1906. De la Peña (1977b) included the species for the province, but no localities were given.

Buenos Aires Records are from: Isla Ella (untraced), somewhere in the Paraná Delta (J. C. Chebez *in litt.* 1992; also a site for Marsh Seedeater *Sporophila palustris*: see relevant account), February 1917 (specimen in BMNH); Otamendi (near Campana), currently (Narosky and di Giacomo in prep., M. Pearman *in litt.* 1991); a small area (c.4 ha) in the río Luján marshes (34°16'S 58°58'W), where a maximum of two birds was observed in 1989 and 1991 (M. Babarskas, B. M. López Lanús *per* M. Pearman *in litt.* 1991); Zelaya (34°21'S 58°52'W), October 1924 and November 1925 (Pereyra 1927), and June 1934 (specimen in MACN); Belgrano (34°34'S 58°28'W), where the type was caught in a garden by a dog in August 1876 (Durnford 1877); Barracas al Sud (34°39'S 58°22'W), where two birds (male and female) were taken in June 1900 (Hartert and Venturi 1909) and a female in November 1904 (specimen in AMNH); Punta Lara (34°49'S 57°59'W), near Villa Elisa (34°51'W 58°04'S), undated (Narosky and di Giacomo in prep.); Pradere (35°15'S 62°55'W), undated (Serié 1923); Veinticinco de Mayo, September 1982 (B. M. López Lanús *per* M. Pearman *in litt.* 1991); Estación Biológica Punta Rasa (= Punta Norte del Cabo San Antonio, 36°17'S 56°47'W), October 1986 (M. Babarskas *in litt.* 1992), with a juvenile following an adult there sometime in 1987-1988 (reported to M. Pearman), June 1989 (M. Pearman *in litt.* 1990), and November 1990 (B. M. Whitney *per* M. Pearman *in litt.* 1991); neighbourhood of Cabo San Antonio, where two birds were taken in September 1899 (Gibson 1920) and it was recorded around 1986 or 1987 (J. C. Chebez *in litt.* 1992); San Clemente del Tuyú (36°22'S 56°43'W), March 1971 (specimen in MACN) and May 1978 (M. Nores and D. Yzurieta *in litt.* 1986); General Lavalle, October 1933 (specimen in MACN); Azul (36°47'S 59°51'W), undated (Narosky and di Giacomo in prep.); "Albufera Mar Chiquita" (= Laguna Mar Chiquita) (37°37'S 57°24'W), currently (Narosky and di Giacomo in prep.). A female collected in 1868 is simply labelled "Buenos Aires" and another bird was collected in "Provincia de Buenos Aires" in June 1934 (specimens in MACN).

Uruguay The species has been recorded at two localities (coordinates from Rand and Paynter 1981): Barra de Pando (= Arroyo Pando, 34°48'S 55°52'W), Canelones department, sometime prior to 1926 (Dabbene 1926; see Remarks 3), and Arroyo Solís Grande (34°49'S 55°24'W), Maldonado department, February 1973 (Escalante 1980).

POPULATION The status of this poorly known and secretive bird is far from clear. Pereyra (1927, 1938) reported it to be "abundant" in the cord grass *Spartina densiflora* in north-eastern Buenos Aires province, and Durnford (1877) "frequently" flushed a "small crake" (see Remarks 4) from the grass near the river at Belgrano. Narosky and Yzurieta (1987) included the Dot-winged Crake in the category of "rare" or "very difficult to find", while M. Pearman (*in litt.* 1990) reported it to be "scarce" but "regularly seen" at Punta Rasa Biological Reserve, where it was observed by two Asociación Ornitológica del Plata groups during 1986, and where B. M. Whitney *in litt.* (1991) has found it "fairly common". The observations in this reserve and at río Luján (see Distribution) suggest that the species may prove to be far commoner in Buenos Aires province than records suggest, with lack of sightings attributable to lack of observers (M. Pearman *in litt.* 1991); however, T. Narosky (*in litt.* 1992) believes that the population at Punta Rasa is decreasing (see Threats). Giacomelli (1923) considered the species "rare" in La Rioja, and de la Peña (1977b) also referred to it as "rare" and "difficult to see", and while it was common in Bañados del río Dulce (Córdoba) in 1975 its habitat there seems to have been affected (M. Nores *in litt.* 1992; see Threats); the bird's current status in this and other interior provinces of Argentina remains uncertain and more investigation is obviously needed to clarify the situation. In Uruguay, it was considered "rare" and probably a "local resident" (Gore and Gepp 1978); the record of an immature in February (see Distribution) suggested breeding in the area but not necessarily permanent residence (R. Escalante *in litt.* 1991).

ECOLOGY The Dot-winged Crake occurs in fresh and brackish surroundings, temporary and tidal marshes, swamps, wet marshy meadows, grassland, sometimes dry grassland, cord grass, riparian scrub and even on occasion gardens (Durnford 1877, Meyer de Schauensee 1970, Blake 1977, de la Peña 1977b, Ripley 1977, Gore and Gepp 1978, Narosky 1985, Narosky and Yzurieta 1987, M. Pearman *in litt.* 1990). The species's habitat in the río Luján marshes is dominated by *Spartina densiflora* and small areas of *Eryngium*; in this area, all observations have occurred in dense *Spartina* (to a height of 70 cm) with permanent saline (brackish) surface water; a bird at Veinticinco de Mayo was flushed from *Paspalum* (M. Pearman *in litt.* 1991). Feeding habits are little known; Gibson (1920) noted that a bird collected at Cabo de San Antonio was feeding on insects, seeds and marsh weeds. The only recorded nest was found near Buenos Aires, although no other details were given (*Ibis* [5]6 [1888]: 285; also Hellmayr and Conover 1942).

THREATS Reclamation of wetlands for agricultural purposes, overgrazing and burning of grasslands (T. Narosky *in litt.* 1991) are perhaps the most serious current risks. M. Pearman (*in litt.* 1991) noted that both in río Luján and at Punta Rasa (two apparently healthy areas for the species) cattle are absent; however, the latter area is at risk of being altered by a recreational development project, and it is believed that the population there is declining presumably because of an increase in visitors in recent years (T. Narosky *in litt.* 1992). Flooding of Mar Chiquita appears to have affected the habitat adversely in the Bañados del río Dulce (M. Nores *in litt.* 1992), but whether this is a natural or man-made phenomenon is not clear.

MEASURES TAKEN The Dot-winged Crake occurs in the río Dulce marshes, a small part of which has been protected, in the Laguna Mar Chiquita, which has been protected as a provincial reserve (Scott and Carbonell 1986), and in the recently created Otamendi Strict Nature Reserve (T. Narosky *in litt.* 1992), which is also important for the Speckled Crake *Coturnicops notata* (see relevant account).

MEASURES PROPOSED Surveys in appropriate habitat within the known range should be conducted; results would probably be optimal during the austral summer when an effort should be made to record the species's voice, e.g. in Punta Rasa Biological Reserve and by the río Luján, which could then greatly facilitate the further location of birds elsewhere. Moreover, near these localities a study might be made of the species's ability to colonize suitable areas following the better management of cattle; the results could be of importance for future conservation of this and other threatened rallids such as Austral Rail *Rallus antarcticus* (see relevant account).

REMARKS (1) This record however, could well refer to the similar Black Crake *Laterallus jamaicensis* (J. C. Chebez *in litt.* 1992). (2) Despite being listed under Dot-winged Crake by Hellmayr and Conover (1942), this record may also refer to the Black Crake (J. C. Chebez *in litt.* 1992). (3) According to Dabbene (1926) three specimens (date not given) were kept alive in the Zoological Garden in Montevideo, but were not preserved (Escalante 1980). (4) After having been given a bird of this species, Durnford (1877) attributed his previous sightings at Belgrano to the same species, although he could not be absolutely certain.

RUSTY-FLANKED CRAKE *Laterallus levraudi* V[9]

This poorly known rail is confined to the Caribbean slope of north-western Venezuela, where recent records are confined to two areas of man-made habitat. It is likely that the bird has suffered habitat loss owing to the general degradation of wetlands within its range.

DISTRIBUTION The Rusty-flanked Crake is endemic to the Caribbean slope of north-western Venezuela, where it has been recorded infrequently from few localities; a claimed specimen from Paraíba, Brazil (Ripley and Beehler 1985) has been discounted as a misattribution (Teixeira *et al.* 1989). Records of this species are as follows (coordinates, unless otherwise stated, deriving from Paynter 1982):

Lara Yacambu National Park (c.9°40'N 69°32'W; coordinates from DGPOA), where the species apparently frequents a man-made pool (B. Swift *in litt.* 1988);

Yaracuy Nirgua (10°09'N 68°34'W), a locality mentioned by Phelps and Phelps (1958), probably referring to a specimen (in COP) taken at 600 m at Hacienda Panchito (same coordinates as for Nirgua) during December 1939 (see Paynter 1982);

Carabobo Urama (10°27'N 68°19'W; 23 km west of Puerto Cabello), where a specimen (in COP) was taken at 20 m during July 1940; La Cabrera (10°16'N 67°40'W; on the north-eastern shore of Lago de Valencia), where five females (in ANSP, COP) were taken at 400 m during July 1942;

Aragua Lago de Valencia, where specimens (in COP, FMNH) were taken in April 1908, September 1942 and September 1946; Isla (Punto) Chambergo (10°14'N 67°47'W; in Lago de Valencia; coordinates from OG 1961), where a male (in COP) was taken at 460 m during October 1947; Embalse de Taguaiguai (10°08'N 67°27'W; 15 km east of Lago de Valencia, and also known as Bella Vista: A. B. Altman *in litt.* 1988), where birds were seen in January and February 1985 and apparently later that year (A. B. Altman *in litt.* 1988, B. Swift *in litt.* 1988);

Distrito Federal "vicinity of Caracas", whence comes the type-specimen (Sclater and Salvin 1868c);

Miranda San José de Río Chico (10°18'N 65°59'W), where six birds (five males and one female in AMNH, COP, USNM) were collected at 20 m during mid-September 1940.

POPULATION The status of the Rusty-flanked Crake is generally unknown: B. Swift (*in litt.* 1988) considered the species to be "common at least locally", although the only records since the 1940s have been observations of a small population at Yacambu National Park, and of 2-3 individuals seen in January and February 1985 at Embalse de Taguaiguai, with 6-12 individuals there (in an area of c.3-4 ha), presumably later that year (B. Swift *in litt.* 1986, 1988, A. B. Altman *in litt.* 1988). The fact that this species was at least historically locally common is demonstrated by the collection of five females in two days (July 1942) at La Cabrera, and five males and a female taken in three days (September 1940) at San José de Río Chico (see Distribution). With so little known of its current distributional status, it is difficult to assess whether or not the population has experienced any significant decline.

ECOLOGY The Rusty-flanked Crake apparently inhabits lakes, lagoons, swamps, flooded pasture and sometimes dry grassland (Meyer de Schauensee and Phelps 1978), where it is seemingly resident from the coastal plain (c.20 m) up to 600 m (see Distribution). Since the 1940s the only records have been from two man-made habitats (see Population), at one of which (Embalse de Taguaiguai) birds were seen in dense fringing aquatic vegetation (A. B. Altman *in litt.* 1988). Nothing is known of feeding or breeding in this species.

THREATS Lago de Valencia is polluted by industrial waste, and wetlands in irrigated areas are affected by pesticides (Scott and Carbonell 1986). Several of the major lakes within the range of the Rusty-flanked Crake are in conservation districts intended to preserve water levels, although success in achieving this has been mixed (B. Swift *in litt.* 1988). More specifically, the water level in the reservoir at Embalse de Taguaiguai had dropped sufficiently by January 1986 that the "shore" was c.300 m from the area where this species was originally seen: the crakes have not been seen there subsequently (B. Swift *in litt.* 1986, A. B. Altman *in litt.* 1988). A dam is being constructed near Yacambu, although it is unknown what (if any) effects this will have on the species (M. L. Goodwin *in litt.* 1992).

MEASURES TAKEN None is known, although the Rusty-flanked Crake has recently been found at the edge of its known range within the Yacambu National Park (B. Swift *in litt.* 1988). However, the Yacambu National Park does not have any significant wetland areas (Scott and Carbonell 1986), and the crake was found inhabiting a man-made pond (see above).

MEASURES PROPOSED An assessment of the precise year-round ecological requirements of the Rusty-flanked Crake is necessary before a realistic conservation strategy can be developed. However, protection of suitable habitat, perhaps extending to the creation of habitat as a spin-off from the dam construction (see Threats) in Yacambu National Park is an important task, as is the discovery of the current status of the species at Embalse de Taguaiguai (which should also be protected and monitored if the bird is found still to be present there). Surveys in and around (Isla Chambergo) Lago de Valencia are also needed to determine the overall status of the species, and to make a more detailed assessment of the threats facing it.

JUNIN RAIL *Laterallus tuerosi* E[2]

This secretive species inhabits the rushy vegetation of the wide marsh habitats fringing Lago de Junín, central Peru, where it may be fairly common but is at risk from pollution and water-level changes, and would benefit from a package of measures targeting the general welfare of the lake.

DISTRIBUTION The Junín Rail is known only from the shores of Lago de Junín ("Laguna Chinchaycocha de Junín"), 4,080 m in the Andes in Junín department, central Peru; while it is likely that it occurs through large portions of the 15,000 ha of marshland surrounding the lake, the only specific area for it is near Ondores and Pari on the south-west shore of Lago de Junín (Fjeldså 1983, J. Fjeldså *in litt.* 1992).

POPULATION It may be common within the appropriate (*Juncus*-zone) habitat, by report "sometimes appearing in semicolonies of a dozen birds" (Fjeldså 1983).

ECOLOGY It inhabits the "vast marshes" bordering Lago de Junín, but detailed information on habitat selection is lacking: birds were seen "in the inner parts of 4 km wide *Juncus* zones, in areas with mosaics of small beds of 1 m tall *Juncus andecolus* and open areas of waterlogged marl sparsely covered by weeds", these beds having "small openings with a velvety bottom vegetation of mosses and low herbs as e.g. *Castelleja fissifolia*, *Cardamine bonariensis*, *Mimulus glabratus*, *Epilobium denticulatus* and globular algae, *Nostoc*, on flooded parts" (Fjeldså 1983). This description was condensed to "rushy areas with open spaces with partly flooded moss or short matted grass" by Fjeldså and Krabbe (1990), who pointed out that its close relative the Black Rail *Laterallus jamaicensis* is crepuscular and extremely secretive, running mouse-like through vegetation rather than flushing.

Breeding is reported to occur at the end of the dry season, i.e. in September–October (Fjeldså and Krabbe 1990 say "in the rainy season"); only two eggs are laid (Fjeldså 1983). The "semicolonies" referred to under population may be the consequence of patchy distribution of optimal habitat or reflect some unknown feature of the species's behavioural ecology.

THREATS Pollution and man-made changes in water level have been affecting the lake since at least 1955 (for details, see Threats under Junín Grebe *Podiceps taczanowskii*) and may adversely influence the fringing vegetation in which this rail lives (J. Fjeldså verbally 1987).

MEASURES TAKEN The status of the lake and efforts to reduce pollution and water-level changes are described in the corresponding section under Junín Grebe.

MEASURES PROPOSED This bird merits further study as part of an integrated initiative to manage Lago de Junín for its endemic wildlife (see corresponding section under Junín Grebe).

REMARKS The Junín Rail was described as a distinctive race of the Black Rail (Fjeldså 1983) and was subsequently retained as such (Fjeldså and Krabbe 1990), but both these sources admit the bird's possible status as a full species, as already accorded it by Collar and Andrew (1988).

RUFOUS-FACED CRAKE *Laterallus xenopterus* V/R[10]

This evidently highly secretive marsh-dwelling bird has been recorded in two areas of Paraguay and one in central Brazil, and its status and needs remain essentially unknown.

DISTRIBUTION The Rufous-faced Crake is known from just three widely separated areas, two in Paraguay and one, over 1,200 km to the north-east, in Brazil.

Paraguay The type-specimen was collected at Horqueta (see Remarks 1), 40 km east of the río Paraguay in Concepción department, in November 1933 (Conover 1934). Two specimens were collected 6.3 km north-east (by road) of Curuguaty (24°31'S 55°42'W in Paynter 1989), Canindeyú department, in July 1976 and July 1979, and two were collected 13.3 km north-east (by road) of Curuguaty in August 1978 and July 1979 (Myers and Hansen 1980). It has been suggested that the species may also be found in the wetlands of Concepción (J. Escobar *in litt.* 1991; see also Remarks 2).

Brazil A specimen was taken in Brasília National Park, Federal District, in July 1978 (Sick 1979d, Myers and Hansen 1980), and there have been subsequent field observations from this area and the IBGE Ecological Reserve, also adjacent to Brasília (Negret and Teixeira 1984, D. M. Teixeira *in litt.* 1987). One was seen in the Brasília Zoological Garden area in March 1989 (J. F. Pacheco verbally 1992). Presumably the species occurs in wetlands southwards towards Paraguay.

POPULATION Numbers are not known. The species is doubtless commoner than suggested by the number of records, since the areas in question are poorly studied, and *Laterallus* rails are secretive birds (Myers and Hansen 1980, Storer 1981, D. M. Teixeira *in litt.* 1987). In the Federal District the species has been judged "relatively frequent" (Negret and Teixeira 1984).

ECOLOGY The Brazilian specimen was captured in a snap-trap (baited with peanut butter, cracked corn, and banana) set in perennial bunch-grass growing in a marsh, in water 3-4 cm deep; the average height of the grass, which completely covered the ground, was 53 cm; this marsh was being used extensively by small mammals, especially *Oxymycterus roberti*, *Zygodontomys lasiurus* and *Cavia fulgida* (Myers and Hansen 1980), was bordered by gallery forest on one side and cerrado on the other (see below), and in December 1978 was dry (Sick 1979d). Paraguayan specimens entered traps (baited with peanut butter and rolled oats) set near the edge of a marsh in coarse, grass-like vegetation approximately 1.5-2 m in height, the marsh itself being mostly covered by water 2-3 cm deep or else, in moist places without standing water, by dense bunch-grass-like vegetation no more than 30 cm in height, with plants of the genus *Xyris* and several other monocotyledons present; the vegetation formed a dense mat difficult for a large animal to enter, but penetrated by numerous small channels between clumps of grass in which Ash-throated Crake *Porzana albicollis*, Red-and-white Crake *Laterallus leucopyrrhus* and the mammals *Oxymycterus delator*, *Akodon cursor* and *Lutreolina crassicauda* were also captured (Myers and Hansen 1980; see also Storer 1981). Similar marshes (cañadones or wet campos) commonly form in eastern Paraguay and adjacent parts of Brazil; they range from a few to several hundred metres in width and may form a zone on gently sloping valley sides between upland cerrado and riparian forests (Myers and Hansen 1980). The gonads of the Paraguayan specimens taken in July and August were small (Myers and Hansen 1980). The paucity of records of this species indicates that it must be extremely secretive in its behaviour.

THREATS None is known in Paraguay. Wet campos are under threat in central Brazil from drainage and the drying effects of adjacent eucalyptus cultivation, the latter phenomenon being witnessed in one part of Brasília National Park; burning may also affect this vegetation, but its impact is not known (R. B. Cavalcanti *in litt.* 1986), although it is considered a potential threat

(Negret and Teixeira 1984). A fuller review of the destruction of primary grasslands in central Brazil is in Threats under Lesser Nothura *Nothura minor*.

MEASURES TAKEN None is known, except that the species occurs in Brasília National Park and the IBGE Ecological Reserve, where it shares its habitat with the near-threatened Ocellated Crake *Micropygia schomburgkii* (Negret and Teixeira 1984).

MEASURES PROPOSED Work is needed at the two adjacent 1970s sites in Paraguay to relocate the species and record its voice, so that further surveys based on knowledge of calls and the use of taped playback can better define its range and assess its status more accurately. The voice might also be taped in Brasília, and used to determine the range of the species in the Federal District and beyond.

REMARKS (1) What is presumably intended to denote the type-locality on the distribution map in Ripley (1977) actually indicates somewhere in Brazil (Storer 1981). (2) Podtiaguin (1941-1945) listed Lima (San Pedro department) and Pedro Juan Caballero (Amambay) as localities, indicating "C. Schultz" as the collector at the first site and the Paraguay National History Museum as the source of the second; neither of these has received further substantiation.

SPECKLED CRAKE *Coturnicops notata* I[7]

An enigmatic species (mostly found in inundation zones, but twice taken on ships at sea), this tiny marsh-haunting bird has been recorded once or a few times from Colombia, Venezuela, Guyana, Brazil, Paraguay, Uruguay and Argentina, with the most recent information tending to suggest that it may be much more under-recorded than genuinely rare.

DISTRIBUTION The Speckled Crake (see Remarks 1) has been found over a massive range in South America, but extremely sparsely, with only one or a few records per country. There is a possible record from the Falkland Islands/Islas Malvinas (see Remarks 2).

Colombia The only record is of one bird collected east of the Andes on the margins of the río Guayabero, 2°36'N 72°47'W, 400 m, in southern Meta department at the southern base of the Serranía de la Macarena, 18 March 1959 (Olivares 1959, Meyer de Schauensee 1962, Hilty and Brown 1986; coordinates from Paynter and Traylor 1981; see Remarks 3).

Venezuela There are two records: a female from Mérida, June 1914 or 1916 (Phelps and Phelps 1961, Meyer de Schauensee 1962); and two females from Aparición, 9°24'N 69°23'W, Portuguesa state, August "1960" (Meyer de Schauensee 1962; coordinates from Paynter 1982; see Remarks 4).

Guyana The only record is from the Abary River, 6°33'N 57°44'W, September 1907 (Meyer de Schauensee 1962; coordinates from Stephens and Traylor 1985).

Brazil Records are from four localities: (*São Paulo*) in the east of the state, at (north to south) Pindamonhangaba (Pinto 1964, 1978); Taubaté, 500 m, May 1976, August 1982, April 1984 and apparently throughout each year (Teixeira and Puga 1984; specimen in MNRJ); Ipiranga (a suburb of São Paulo city), September 1924 (Pinto 1938, Meyer de Schauensee 1962); (*Rio Grande do Sul*) Hamburgo Velho (now a suburb of Novo Hamburgo), 1928 (Meyer de Schauensee 1962, Belton 1984-1985).

Paraguay There are three records: a male was collected at Laguna General Díaz, 22°18'S 59°01'W, Presidente Hayes department, in June 1945 (Blake 1977; specimen in FMNH; coordinates from Paynter 1989); a female was collected 7 km east of Horqueta, Concepción department, in December 1937 (Brodkorb 1938, Meyer de Schauensee 1962); and Puerto Bertoni, Alto Paraná department, is indicated without further details by Bertoni (1939) and Podtiaguin (1941-1945).

Uruguay There are five records: a specimen was collected at Sarandí, Durazno department, in April 1918 (Tremoleras 1920, Cuello and Gerzenstein 1962; see Remarks 5); a specimen (in MACN) was collected at an unspecified locality in Durazno in June 1915; a brood of three was found (one being captured alive) on a farm near Juan Lacaze, Colonia department, in December 1985 (Arballo 1990); one was seen in Parque Lecoqc (*sic*), Montevideo department, in March 1985 (Arballo 1990); and one flew aboard a ship off Cabo Santa María, Rocha department, in around November or December 1875 (*Proc. Zool. Soc. London* 1876: 255, Meyer de Schauensee 1962; see Remarks 6). The species has also been reported, without supporting evidence, from Bañados del Este (*World Birdwatch* 12,1-2 [1990]: 4).

Argentina There are at least 10 records, here listed from north to south: Esteros de Iberá 5 km west of Santo Tomé, Corrientes, May 1991 (F. R. Lambert verbally 1992); Córdoba province, before 1890 (Stempelmann and Schulz 1890, Meyer de Schauensee 1962), and the Bañados del río Dulce, Córdoba, where a bird was seen in November 1973 (Nores and Yzurieta 1975, Nores *et al.* 1983; hence in Scott and Carbonell 1986), and where it is speculated very probably to breed (Nores and Yzurieta 1980); Otamendi Strict Nature Reserve, río Luján marshes, north-west of the capital, Buenos Aires province, October 1991 (B. M. López Lanús *per* M. Pearman and J. C.

Chebez *in litt.* 1992); "Buenos Aires", September 1904 (Pinto 1938); Isla Paulino, near Berisso, south of Buenos Aires city, 1980s (F. Moschione *per* M. Pearman *in litt.* 1992); Punta Lara (34°49'S 57°59'W in Paynter 1985) in Buenos Aires province, January 1962 (female in IML); San Miguel del Monte in Buenos Aires province, March 1984 (male in MACN; also Navas 1991), this bird being caught by hand by a tractor driver in a ploughed field (J. R. Mata and J. D. Córdoba *per* J. C. Chebez *in litt.* 1992); on board the *Beagle* in the río de la Plata, 1831 (Gould 1841); and "Patagonia", probably near Carmen de Patagones near the río Negro estuary, 1829, in either Río Negro or Buenos Aires province (Hellmayr and Conover 1942, Meyer de Schauensee 1962, Navas 1991). J. C. Chebez (*in litt.* 1986) referred to the species's probable occurrence in La Pampa province.

POPULATION The Speckled Crake has been described as very rare (Cuello and Gerzenstein 1962, Blake 1977, Hilty and Brown 1986, Navas 1991), "excessively rare" (Phelps and Phelps 1961) and even as "one of the rarest Neotropical birds" (Hellmayr and Conover 1942, Ripley 1977; also Canevari *et al.* 1991). However, its discovery at Taubaté in Brazil "indicates that it is not so much scarce as difficult to find" (Teixeira and Puga 1984). It seems likely that this will prove to be the case, but until rather more evidence can be mustered it is prudent to consider the species genuinely rare.

ECOLOGY The habitat has been characterized as rice and alfalfa fields, swamps, and humid woodland edge, 200-1,500 m (Meyer de Schauensee and Phelps 1978), also grassy savanna and dense marshy vegetation (Hilty and Brown 1986; see Remarks 7). Several specimens have been taken at night in open savanna or rice fields using lights (Ripley 1977). At Taubaté in Brazil the species inhabits dense vegetation in flooded rice fields (Teixeira and Puga 1984). In Uruguay the brood of three was found in wheat stubble on a farm, and the single bird near Montevideo was in a flooded meadow (Arballo 1990). In Córdoba, Argentina, it was recorded from the densest part of flooded grasslands (Nores and Yzurieta 1980), while the bird in Corrientes was flushed from the wettest part of a marsh with rushes and floating vegetation (F. R. Lambert verbally 1992) and one on the río Luján marshes was in flooded *Spartina densiflora* (B. M. López Lanús *per* M. Pearman verbally 1992). In Colombia the single record was made only 100 m from where the country's first Ocellated Crake *Micropygia schomburgkii* was found (Olivares 1959).

The stomach of a bird collected in May at Taubaté contained 80% small grass seeds, 15% remains of arthropods, and 5% fine gravel (Teixeira and Puga 1984).

Data on breeding are sparse: the bird above from May had well-developed testes (Teixeira and Puga 1984), while a brood of three was found in Uruguay in December (Arballo 1990); moreover, despite being judged immature (Meyer de Schauensee 1962) the two August birds from Venezuela had enlarged gonads (ANSP label data).

There has been some speculation that the Speckled Crake undertakes migrations between the north and south of the South American continent (Meyer de Schauensee 1962, 1966, Blake 1977, Ripley 1977, Meyer de Schauensee and Phelps 1978, Hilty and Brown 1986, Canevari *et al.* 1991), and this has even been taken as a certainty (Gore and Gepp 1978), but the state of the gonads of the Venezuelan birds from August and the presence of the species in April, May, June and August in Brazil and Paraguay (see Distribution) tend to annul this possibility. The view that either it has a very much fuller distribution than demonstrated so far or its occurrences in Colombia and at sea indicate that birds occasionally erupt large distances in a random pattern from their centre of distribution in the tropical savannas of northern and eastern South America (Ripley 1977: 16) seems appropriate, except that the centre of distribution cannot be assumed to be in tropical savannas. It is worth noting that both birds caught at sea were taken in November or December (see Distribution), this possibly indicating some post-breeding dispersal. In view of the remarkable parallel with the White-winged Flufftail *Sarothrura ayresi* (see Remarks 1), it is also worth noting that the latter species appears to be nomadic in response to rainfall, selecting as habitat the less flooded parts of (seasonal) marshes (see Collar and Stuart 1985).

THREATS None is known.

MEASURES TAKEN It is not clear whether the site at which the Colombian specimen was collected lies within the boundaries of the Macarena National Park (which, however, is itself threatened: Struhsaker 1976). The Bañados del río Dulce in Córdoba, Argentina, are at present a WHSRN reserve (M. Nores *in litt.* 1992). The Otamendi Strict Nature Reserve near Buenos Aires is also important for Dot-winged Crake *Porzana spiloptera* (see relevant account).

MEASURES PROPOSED Using tape-recordings presumably available from the captive bird described by Teixeira and Puga (1984), searches could be made by ornithologists with playback equipment during any lacustrine surveys in any part of lowland South America. Further study of the species at a possibly constant site, such as Taubaté in Brazil, is desirable.

REMARKS (1) The establishment of the race *duncani* for northern populations of this species has been discredited in Meyer de Schauensee (1962) who, however, pointed out the striking similarity in the history of this bird with that of the (also threatened) White-winged Flufftail of Ethiopia and southern Africa (see Collar and Stuart 1985); a further similarity that now emerges is that both were thought possibly to be migratory between the north and the south of their ranges, although this appears increasingly unlikely to be so for both. It is perhaps noteworthy, too, that both possess white secondaries, conspicuous in flight. (2) A specimen was captured alive near Port Stanley in April 1921, but following its death the skin was not kept (Bennett 1926), so the record cannot be verified (Meyer de Schauensee 1962); nevertheless, Bennett (1926) "carefully examined it while still alive", suggesting his identification was likely to have been correct and, since birds have twice been caught on ships along the South Atlantic coast (see Distribution), the likelihood of birds straggling to the Falklands/Malvinas is high. (3) Meyer de Schauensee (1962) referred to both "río Guaviare" and "río Guayabero", the latter being described as a major tributary of the former by Paynter and Traylor (1981). (4) Despite the year 1960 being given, the labels on these skins indicate 1954 (M. B. Robbins *in litt.* 1992). (5) Rand and Paynter (1981) were uncertain which of several localities with the name Sarandí might have been intended, but it seems most likely that it was the relatively large Sarandí del Yí. (6) This bird was kept alive and donated to the London Zoo in January 1876, where it survived until December 1880 (BMNH label data). (7) Hilty and Brown (1986) cited Ripley (1977) as their authority for these habitat types, but this is mistaken.

HORNED COOT *Fulica cornuta* K[12]

This high-altitude Andean waterbird lives at low densities in a scatter of low-saline lakes in Argentina, Bolivia and Chile, where it may be suffering from certain human pressures; fieldwork is needed to clarify its status and needs.

DISTRIBUTION The Horned Coot is known from a few high-altitude Andean lakes of the puna zone in south-western Bolivia, north-western Argentina and northern Chile. Records within provinces below are organized from north to south. Unless otherwise stated coordinates are taken from Paynter (1985, 1988) and OG (1967, 1968).

Argentina

Jujuy Records are from: Laguna de Pozuelos, currently (M. Nores and D. Yzurieta *in litt.* 1986, Fjeldså and Krabbe 1990), with three or four pairs nesting there in January 1987 (M. Nores *in litt.* 1991); a small lake 4 km west of Laguna de Pozuelos, where nesting was reported in November 1984 (M. Rumboll *in litt.* 1986); Laguna Larga (untraced, but near Laguna de Pozuelos, and conceivably the same as the previous site), December 1981 (P. Canevari *in litt.* 1987, 1992); La Lagunilla (untraced, but near Laguna de Pozuelos), where c.80 have been reported (date unknown) (F. N. Contino *per* M. Nores and D. Yzurieta *in litt.* 1986); Laguna Pululos (22°35'S 66°44'W), where "large numbers" were reported before 1941 (Crespo 1941) and where nesting occurred in October 1982 (P. Canevari *in litt.* 1992).

Salta The species was recorded during a survey from 19 November to 6 December 1984 at Laguna Socompa (24°30'S 68°14'W; Vides-Almonacid 1990) (see Remarks 1).

Catamarca The species is only known from Laguna Blanca, December 1918 (three specimens in AMNH and IML; also Esteban 1953).

Tucumán Localities are: the Cumbres Calchaquíes range (centred on 26°27'S 65°43'W), February 1903 (two specimens in AMNH and IML; Hartert and Venturi 1909); also within this mountain range three birds were collected at the Lagunas de Amaichá (untraced, but probably near Amaichá del Valle at 26°36'S 65°55'W; see Remarks 2) in February 1905 (specimens in MNHN); Laguna El Negrito (= Lagunas de Huaca Huasi, 26°40'S 65°44'W: coordinates from R. Vides-Almonacid *in litt.* 1992), November and December 1947 (four specimens in IML), and where it was a typical inhabitant (Olrog 1949); Lagunas de Huaca Huasi and Laguna Escondida (untraced, but within the Cumbres Calchaquíes range), where periodical censuses between 1981 and 1985 recorded the species in very low numbers (including a nesting pair: Vides-Almonacid 1988; see Population); Tafí del Valle (26°52'S 65°41W), March 1948 (Olrog 1949; see Remarks 3); Laguna del Cerro Pelado (untraced, but possibly in the Aconquija range; see Remarks 4), February 1903 (specimen in AMNH; also Baer 1904); Sierra de Aconquija, currently (Fjeldså and Krabbe 1990); Laguna Cerritos, Laguna Los Patos (both in Cerro Muñoz at 26°46'S 65°51'W) and Laguna La Manga (in the base of Morro El Zarzo = Nevado de las Animas, 15 km south-west of Cerro Muñoz), where the species was observed in March and September 1982 and in April and October 1984 (Vides-Almonacid 1988; see Population for numbers observed).

San Juan The species has been recorded breeding at Reserva de San Guillermo (29°08'S 69°30'W), undated (J. C. Pujalte *per* P. Canevari *in litt.* 1987), this being the southernmost known locality for the species.

Bolivia

Oruro A bird was taken at Lago Poopo in June 1903 (Ménégaux 1909).

Potosí Records are from: near Potosí, where the type-specimen was collected in December 1853 (Hellmayr and Conover 1942); small lagoons within the Eduardo Avaroa National Faunal Reserve (21°30'-21°56'S 67°35'-68°05'W in Scott and Carbonell 1986; see the map in Rocha O. 1990b) namely: Laguna Khastor and Laguna Chojllas, where 550 and 782 birds were recorded respectively in October-November 1989 (Rocha O. 1990a; see Population); Laguna Totoral,

November 1982, Laguna Catalcito, where small numbers have been recorded, and Laguna Pelada, one of the most important localities for the species (Cabot and Serrano 1982, Scott and Carbonell 1986; see Population); Laguna Verde, where at least eight birds and three eggs were collected on several dates between 1952 and 1958 (specimens and eggs in ANSP, FMNH, MNHN, MNHNS, WFVZ and YPM) (see Remarks 5).

Chile The Horned Coot occurs from the lakes of the Lauca National Park (18°25'S) south to Lago Valeriano and El Cajón del Encierro (28°46'S) (Johnson 1965, Scott and Carbonell 1986). Behn and Millie (1959) remarked that the species would probably be found in other localities where similar conditions to those at Lago Caritaya and Santa Rosa exist, but some of these remain unknown because the difficulty of access.

Tarapacá The northernmost locality for the species, once thought to be Tranque Caritaya (19°01'S 69°19'W), where 10 birds were observed and four eggs (in WFVZ) were collected in February 1957, now appears to be the lakes of Lauca National Park (18°25'S 69°10'W; coordinates from Scott and Carbonell 1986) (Behn and Millie 1959, Scott and Carbonell 1986).

Antofagasta Localities are: río Loa, "casual" (no further details given) (Goodall *et al.* 1951); Lago Ascotán, February 1884 (Philippi 1888), and a bird collected in 1886 (specimen in MNHNS); near Calama, where a pair (apparently accidentals) were recorded in July 1940 (Olrog 1948; see Remarks 2); Laguna Verde (23°14'S 67°46'W), October 1955 and July 1957 (three specimens in YPM); Lago Loyoques (Salar de Loyoques at 23°15'S 68°18'W), where an egg was taken in December 1952 (held in WFVZ); Laguna Meñique (untraced, but near Salar de Atacama), where a "large group" was recorded on 21 February 1989 (Narosky 1990).

Atacama Localities are: Laguna de Santa Rosa (27°05'S 69°10'W), from at least the 1950s down to the present (see Population); and the headwaters of the río Huasco, where the species has been recorded in several lagoons of the Cajón del Encierro (28°59'S 69°52'W) including (to the end of the paragraph): Lagunita de Encierro, where nest-building was in progress in November 1946 (Ripley 1957a); Laguna Chica (28°48'S 69°52'W), February 1945 (specimen in MCZ) and a nest found in November 1945 (Behn and Millie 1959); Laguna Pachuy (untraced), where five eggs were collected in January 1946 (Behn and Millie 1959); Laguna Grande (28°53'S 70°04'W), where nests were found in 1936, 1945 and 1946 (Ripley 1957a, Behn and Millie 1959), and Laguna Valeriano (29°03'S 69°52'W), undated (Johnson 1965), this being the southernmost extreme of its range, except that of the apparently isolated population in San Juan province of Argentina.

POPULATION The Horned Coot has been considered "rare and extremely local" (Ripley 1977). Large concentrations have been recordered only occasionally (see below), but in general its density appears to be low, and lower than other species of coot (Vides-Almonacid 1988). However, no apparent decline is known to have occurred (King 1978-1979), although local populations are believed to fluctuate greatly between periods of drought and rain (Fjeldså and Krabbe 1990).

Argentina The Horned Coot has not been reported in large numbers except at Laguna Pululos, where large numbers were reported prior to 1941 (Crespo 1941), and c.40 pairs with nests were observed in October 1982 (P. Canevari *in litt.* 1992), although large numbers no longer occur (Vides-Almonacid 1988); Fjeldså and Krabbe (1990) believed that "good numbers" occur around Sierra de Aconquija and at Laguna de Pozuelos, but no numbers are given. Apart from this, modest numbers have been recorded in the Aconquija range at Laguna Cerritos, Laguna Los Patos and Laguna La Manga, where maximum total numbers of 135 (of which 106 were juveniles) and 98 birds respectively were present in March and September 1982, but only 10 and 12 birds in April and October 1984 (numbers for each lagoon are given in Vides-Almonacid 1988), and at La Lagunilla, where c.80 birds have been recorded, undated (F. N. Contino *per* M. Nores and D. Yzurieta *in litt.* 1986). M. Rumboll *in litt.* (1986) found c.28 nests in a small lake 4 km west of Laguna de Pozuelos in November 1984, and the species was found in small numbers at Laguna de Pozuelos, Laguna Larga and Laguna Pululos in the early 1980s (P. Canevari *per* M. Nores and

D. Yzurieta *in litt.* 1986, M. Nores *in litt.* 1991). The species was found "very scarce" at Laguna Socompa and in the lagoons within the Cumbres Calchaquíes range (Laguna de Huaca Huasi and Laguna Escondida), where from December 1981 to February 1985 the maximum population consisted of six individuals (a family group in December 1981 and two pairs with young in February 1985) (Vides-Almonacid 1988, 1990), and in March 1986 three nests and 10 juveniles were found (R. Grau *per* R. Vides-Almonacid *in litt.* 1992).

Bolivia Little has been published about numbers of the Horned Coot. Probably the largest concentration ever recorded within its range was at Laguna Pelada, where 2,800 individuals were counted in November 1982 (Cabot and Serrano 1982). Other large counts include 90 birds at Laguna Totoral in November 1982 (Cabot and Serrano 1982), 550 (18 active nests found) and 782 (11 active nests found) birds in Laguna Khastor and Chojllas respectively in October-November 1989 (Rocha O. 1990a). According to this author, although the species's population is small there is no evidence to support a decline. Besides these records and that of 36 birds observed at Laguna Verde in July 1957 (Peña 1961), other localities given under Distribution simply refer to single or a few specimens collected.

Chile The overall population is estimated to consist of 620 individuals (Glade 1988: 22). Largest numbers have been found at Laguna de Santa Rosa, where counts include: 100 birds (including immatures and juveniles) and c.30 nests (not all of which were in use), between 29 January and 5 February 1958 (Behn and Millie 1959); 252 birds (58 nests in an advanced stage of construction and 30 nests in early stages), October 1986 (Correa and Oyarzo 1987); 107 birds, 17 chicks out of the nest and 27 nests (nine of them containing chicks), January 1988; 77 birds and 32 nests, October 1988 (both from CONAF 1988); 72 adults and 28 active nests, October 1990; 54 adults and 23 active nests, November 1990 (both from Oyarzo and Cisternas 1990); 68 adults, 49 chicks and 31 active nests; 159 birds (37 of which were juveniles), May 1991 (both from Oyarzo and Cisternas 1991). At Laguna Grande 50 birds were reported arriving after dusk in April 1956 and departing the following morning (Behn and Millie 1959, Johnson 1965). Other records, except that at Tranque Caritaya, where 10 birds were observed (see Distribution), refer to single or a few specimens collected and/or observed.

ECOLOGY The Horned Coot inhabits barren Andean highland lakes both fresh and brackish, where it is chiefly found at altitudes varing from 3,000 to 5,200 m (Fjeldså and Krabbe 1990), although records at Calama (2,266 m) in July 1940 and at Tafí del Valle (2,000 m) in March 1948 show that occasional movements to lower altitudes may occur in winter or while harsh weather conditions at higher altitudes are present (Olrog 1948, 1949).

The Horned Coot's diet remains little studied but consists mostly of aquatic plants (*Myriophyllum*, *Potamogeton* and *Ruppia*) which are apparently absent in saltmarshes, which may explain the species's avoidance of highly saline environments commonly found in the puna (Behn and Millie 1959, Johnson 1965, Vides-Almonacid 1988, Fjeldså and Krabbe 1990). Stomach contents of three birds from Laguna Verde (Bolivia) consisted of aquatic grasses and volcanic sand (Peña 1961), and five stomachs from birds collected at Laguna Santa Rosa contained sand, *Ruppia* seeds and stems (Behn and Millie 1959). These latter authors pointed out that where *Myriophyllum* is present, the species prefers it to *Ruppia*. There is evidence that the Horned Coot may fly from one feeding ground to another (see data for Laguna Grande under Population: Chile).

The breeding season is fairly well documented and mainly occurs from October to February, although birds can be paired and building nests as early as September (Ripley 1977, CONAF 1988, Vides-Almonacid 1988, Fjeldså and Krabbe 1990). Nests can be enormous, and usually consist of mounds of stones built up from the bottom of the lake and then covered with soft vegetable matter (*Myriophyllum*, *Ruppia*, etc.), or else entirely made of it; clutches vary from three to five eggs (Behn and Millie 1959, Johnson 1965, Ripley 1977). Little is known about reproductive success, but in Laguna Santa Rosa, Chile, 25% of the chicks did not reach the juvenile stage (Oyarzo and Cisternas 1991).

Little is known about seasonal altitudinal movements or displacements from one feeding locality to another; surveys conducted at Laguna Santa Rosa showed that birds are absent during the winter months when the surface of the lake is frozen and food unavailable (CONAF 1988, Oyarzo and Cisternas 1990). Winter is thus the more likely season to find the species at lower elevations; long displacements may take place to areas where conditions are less severe.

THREATS As previously mentioned (see Population), little is known about population trends. Vides-Almonacid (1988) commented that the reduced population of the Horned Coot in Tucumán perhaps could be related to unpredictable ecological changes in the lagoons (e.g. droughts and floods), although this should not constitute a threat itself as the species has evolved in such extreme ecosystems; but such changes, when occurring together with other threats noted by Vides-Almonacid (1988) and J. C. Torres-Mura *in litt.* (1986), such as hunting, egg-harvesting, exploitation of habitat (piping water to coastal cities and towns or mining centres), may prove fatal. Other potential threats such as predation by the Andean Gull *Larus serranus* has been reported (R. Vides-Almonacid *in litt.* 1992) although it is believed not to occur very often (Behn and Millie 1959). In Tucumán, the trampling of nests by cattle and the contamination of waterbodies with their ordure are also reasons for concern (R. Vides-Almonacid *in litt.* 1992).

MEASURES TAKEN In Chile the Horned Coot has been officially considered threatened in the "vulnerable" category, and CONAF is carrying out periodic censuses and surveillance with the purpose of gaining further knowledge on the species (Glade 1988); a study of the species at Laguna Santa Rosa is being conducted by CONAF, but no information on this is yet available (I. Castro *in litt.* 1989). Some of the lakes where the species occurs have been protected (see Remarks 6) and are listed as follows: (in Argentina) Laguna Pozuelos National Monument, Laguna Blanca Provincial Reserve (Scott and Carbonell 1986) and San Guillermo Provincial Reserve (Vides-Almonacid 1988); (in Bolivia) Eduardo Avaroa National Faunal Reserve (Scott and Carbonell 1986), which includes Laguna Totoral, Laguna Catalcito and Laguna Pelada (one of the most important localities known for the species: see Population).

MEASURES PROPOSED Detailed studies should be conducted in the three countries where the species occurs (see Remarks 7), concentrating on: (1) overall breeding population estimates for each country, including visits to those areas where the species has not been reported but where it is likely to occur; (2) studies on the biology of the species, (i.e.) habitat requirements, feeding and ecology, seasonal movements, etc., all of which should be mainly focused on identifying possible threats; (3) a global strategy for conservation which can guarantee the species's long-term survival, obviously involving the creation of new protected areas within the Andean puna, as well as enforcement of existing laws which already protect them. In Argentina, the establishment of a protected area in the already proposed mountainous areas of Sierra del Aconquija (Tucumán and

Catamarca provinces) and Cumbres Calchaquíes (Tucumán and Salta provinces) comprising more than 300,000 ha (R. Vides-Almonacid *in litt.* 1992) would result in a major step towards protecting prime habitat of the species and thus ensuring its survival in the country. This initiative will also benefit populations of the White-tailed Shrike-tyrant *Agriornis andicola*, Rufous-throated Dipper *Cinclus schulzi* and Tucumán Mountain-finch *Poospiza baeri* (see relevant accounts).

REMARKS (1) This appears to be the only published locality for this province, although Salta has previously been mentioned as one of the provinces where the species is to be found (Blake 1977, Vides-Almonacid 1988). (2) According to R. Vides-Almonacid (*in litt.* 1992) these lagoons could well be Laguna Cerritos and Laguna Los Patos (see Distribution), but it is also possible that the lagoon in question was "Laguna Amaicheña" (= Laguna de los Amaicheños), which is c.5 km north-west of Lagunas de Huaca Huasi. (3) This locality together with that of Calama in Chile are at an unusually low altitude, probably related to bad weather conditions, as pointed out by Olrog (1949; see Ecology). (4) The specimen's label indicates an altitude for the collecting locality of 5,000 m; Paynter (1985) pointed out that Laguna del Cerro Pelado could possibly be in vicinity of Cerro Pelado (26°55'S 65°44'W), although this mountain attains an altitude of only c.2,500 m and altitudes approaching 5,000 m are found no nearer than 25 km to the south-west on the Catamarca border. (5) A bird taken by L. Peña in July 1954 and labelled as "Laguna Verde, Chile/Bolivia" (specimen in ANSP) could have been collected at Laguna Verde, Antofagasta, at 23°14'S 67°42'W, as a visit of L. Peña to Laguna Verde in 1954 has been attributed to the Laguna Verde in Antofagasta, Chile, by Paynter (1988), who has pointed out Peña's confusion of these two localities, although he visited and collected birds in both of them (see Distribution). (6) Although under legal protection, some of these areas still witness illegal hunting, egg-collecting and cattle-grazing, but whether these practices affect the Horned Coot is not known (for details affecting these areas see Scott and Carbonell 1986). (7) The study that CONAF is carrying out at Laguna Santa Rosa, Chile, could serve as a model for further projects elsewhere in Chile or in Bolivia and Argentina, bur details are first needed.

OLROG'S GULL *Larus atlanticus* K[12]

Low overall numbers (less than 1,400 breeding pairs) and the vulnerability of the few known colonies tend to suggest that this largely crab-eating gull of the coast of Argentina (where it breeds) and Uruguay (where some birds winter) merits fuller protection and intensified study and monitoring.

DISTRIBUTION Olrog's Gull (see Remarks 1) is endemic to the Argentinian Atlantic coast, where until recently the only known breeding sites were in Bahía San Blas in the province of Buenos Aires (Olrog 1967, Devillers 1977). However, newly discovered colonies in the province of Chubut considerably extend the known breeding range to the south (see below and Remarks 2). The species disperses north along the coast of Uruguay (Gore and Gepp 1978, Escalante 1984), accidentally in southern Brazil (Vooren and Chiaradia 1990), and south along the Patagonian coasts (Olrog 1967; see Remarks 3). Unless otherwise stated, coordinates in the following account are taken from Rand and Paynter (1981) and Paynter (1985) and records at individual localities are of single birds or small groups collected or observed.

Brazil The only two known records are from Rio Grande do Sul, where a bird was captured in winter 1971 near Rio Grande (Belton 1984-1985) and a juvenile was photographed in June 1989 at Cassino Beach (Vooren and Chiaradia 1991).

Uruguay Records (west to east) are from: (*San José*) Playa Autódromo (= Playa Penino, c.34°45'S 56°25'W), July 1959 (Zorrilla de San Martín 1959); Playa Penino, August 1960 (Vaz-Ferreira and Gerzenstein 1961), November 1960 and August 1964 (Escalante 1966), with 93 adults and 11 immatures being seen on 27 June 1970 (Gore and Gepp 1978) and an unspecified number in December 1978 (Escalante 1980); (*Montevideo*) Bahía de Montevideo, June and July 1959 (Vaz-Ferreira and Gerzenstein 1961); (*Canelones*) Arroyo Pando (34°48'S 55°52'W), June 1961 (Escalante 1970); (*Maldonado*) Playa Brava (34°58'S 54°56'W), Punta del Este, July 1964 (Escalante 1966); Barra del Arroyo Maldonado (= Arroyo Maldonado, at 34°55'S 54°51'W), July 1961, May 1963, July 1964 and July 1965, with 28 juveniles in September 1982 (Escalante 1962, 1966, 1984); Laguna José Ignacio (34°51'S 54°43'W), June 1959 (Vaz-Ferreira and Gerzenstein 1961), and July 1961 (Escalante 1962).

Argentina Records are organized within province from north to south, as follows:

Buenos Aires Isla Martín García (34°11'S 58°15'W), undated (Narosky and di Giacomo in prep.); río de la Plata, outside the Jorge Newbery Airport, January 1989 (H. G. Young *in litt.* 1989); Tigre (34°25'S 58°34'W), June 1978 (Narosky and di Giacomo in prep.); Paraná delta (34°25'S 58°35'W), May 1991 (coordinates and data from M. Babarskas *in litt.* 1991); San Fernando (34°26'S 58°34'W), Buenos Aires, July 1988 (B. M. López Lanús *in litt.* 1991); Buenos Aires harbour, September 1991 (M. Pearman *in litt.* 1991); San Isidro, undated (Narosky and di Giacomo in prep.); Ribera Norte, San Isidro, several observations during the mid- and late 1980s and in 1990 (J. C. Chebez *in litt.* 1992); Costanera Sur Reserve (34°36'S 58°27'W), currently (M. Pearman *in litt.* 1991); Capital Federal (34°38'S 58°28'W), July 1988 and July 1990 (coordinates and data from M. Babarskas *in litt.* 1992); Moreno (= Mariano Moreno, 34°39'S 58°48'W), undated (Narosky and di Giacomo in prep.); Quilmes, December 1917 and October 1918 (specimens in MACN); Punta Lara (34°49'S 57°59'W), "only in the autumn and winter months" (Klimaitis and Moschione 1987); mouth of río Salado, June 1990 (Narosky and di Giacomo in prep); Punta Rasa (36°22'S 56°45'W), various dates from March 1971 to December 1986 (Narosky and di Giacomo in prep.), with 26 birds on 12 July 1987 and a maximum of 182 on 8 May 1988 (coordinates and data from D. Blanco *in litt.* 1991); ría de Ajó (36°20'S 56°54'W), June 1937 (specimens in UNP; also Casares 1939); Dolores, October 1924 (specimen in MACN); San Clemente del Tuyú (36°22'S 56°43'W), Cabo San Antonio and vicinity, during the summer months (November to February) and in November 1962 (Olrog 1967); General Lavalle, September

1937 (Pereyra 1938; see Remarks 4); Santa Teresita (36°32'S 56°41'W), May 1991 (Narosky and di Giacomo in prep.); Mar del Tuyú (c.15 km north of Mar de Ajó; see below) undated (Narosky and di Giacomo in prep.); Mar de Ajó (c.20 km north of Punta Sur del Cabo San Antonio), undated (Narosky and di Giacomo in prep.); Punta Médanos, 5 km north of Punta Sur del Cabo San Antonio, undated (Narosky and di Giacomo in prep.); Cariló, c.5 km south of Pinamar (37°07'S 56°50'W), January 1984 (Narosky and di Giacomo in prep.); Villa Gesell (37°15'S 56°57'W), undated (Narosky and di Giacomo in prep.); Mar Chiquita (= Laguna Mar Chiquita, 37°37'S 57°24'W), "winter visitor" and February 1977 (Narosky and di Giacomo in prep.), with 20 birds in January 1991 (M. Nores *in litt.* 1992) and the species reported common in winter 1991 (J. C. Chebez *in litt.* 1992); Mar del Plata, August 1926 (specimen in MACN), also reportedly abundant on the beaches in September 1956 (Olrog 1958a) and common in July 1982, July 1986 (several adults) and June 1988 (M. Babarskas *in litt.* 1992, B. M. López Lanús *in litt.* 1992); main pier of Mar del Plata, where c.200 birds were observed on 21 June 1989 (M. Pearman *in litt.* 1991); Mar del Sur, May 1960 (specimen in MACN); San Cayetano (38°25'S 59°40'W), undated (Narosky and di Giacomo in prep.); Necochea, where c.20 birds were recorded in June 1989, and 40-100 birds followed a trawler on a pelagic trip from Necochea in June 1989, and on another such trip (to c.25 km offshore) more than 10 birds were observed in June 1991 (M. Pearman *in litt.* 1991); Quequén Harbour (just east of Necochea), where more than 15 birds were observed in June 1991 (M. Pearman *in litt.* 1991); Costa Bonita (c.12 km east of Necochea), January 1969 (T. Narosky *in litt.* 1992), between 1983-1985 (Narosky and Fiameni 1987), January 1986 (M. Nores *in litt.* 1992), December 1986, June 1987 (T. Narosky *in litt.* 1992), with more than 40 birds in June 1991 (M. Pearman *in litt.* 1991); Quequén (38°32'S 58°42'W) and Costa Bonita, where 10 birds were observed in June 1988 (B. M. López Lanús *in litt.* 1991); Orense (38°40'S 59°47'W), undated (Narosky and di Giacomo in prep.); Cuatreros (38°42'S 62°24'W), December 1990 (Narosky and di Giacomo in prep.); General Daniel Cerri (38°44'S 62°24'W), July 1991 (data and coordinates from T. Narosky *in litt.* 1992); Puerto Ingeniero White, December 1938 (Casares 1939); Puerto Belgrano, December 1952 and January 1953 (Olrog 1958b), reportedly common there (12 birds taken) in June 1971 (Jehl and Rumboll 1976) and reportedly very common in dumps in autumn 1981 (J. C. Chebez *in litt.* 1992); Isla Brightman (= Caleta Brightman, 39°24'S 62°10'W in OG 1968), nesting in November 1990 (P. Yorio *in litt.* 1992; see Population); Riacho Azul, Bahía Unión, undated (Narosky and di Giacomo in prep.); Bahía San Blas, nesting on several small islands in the bay (Daguerre 1933, Olrog 1967, Devillers 1977; see Population, Remarks 4), this including breeding colonies in November 1990 at Isla Puestos (c.12 km north-west of Isla de los Riachos), Isla Gama and Isla Jabalí (40°36'S 62°12'W in OG 1968) (P. Yorio *in litt.* 1992; see Population); Faro Segunda Barraca (c.40°46'S 62°16'W), April 1931 (Steullet and Deautier 1935-1946);

Río Negro San Antonio Oeste, January 1973 (Contreras 1978); Canal del Indio, San Antonio Oeste, March to June between 1989 and 1991 (P. González *in litt.* 1991); Balneario Las Grutas (40°48'S 65°05'W; read from map provided by P. González *in litt.* 1991), January 1989 (M. Pearman *in litt.* 1991); Balneario El Cóndor (río Negro mouth), Punta Bermeja and Punta Mejillón, Caleta de los Loros (c.41°00'S 64°00'W), present in small numbers throughout the year (D. Paz *in litt.* 1991); Reserva Provincial "Area Complejo Islote Lobos" (41°26'S 65°28'W), November (year not given) (coordinates and data from D. Paz *in litt.* 1991); El Horno (c.41°56'S 65°03'W), January 1974 (Contreras 1978);

Chubut Puerto Lobos, January 1973 and January 1974 (Contreras 1978); Punta Norte and Puerto Pirámides (Península de Valdés), January 1973 (Contreras 1978); Puerto Pirámides, January 1989 (H. G. Young *in litt.* 1989); 2 km east of Puerto Pirámides, January 1989 (M. Pearman *in litt.* 1990); Islote Galfrascoli (45°02'S 65°52'W in OG 1968) and Islas Vernaci (45°11'S 66°30'W), nesting in November 1990 (P. Yorio *in litt.* 1992; see Population); Comodoro Rivadavia, where c.80 birds were recorded in January 1989 (M. Pearman *in litt.* 1990);

Santa Cruz Puerto Deseado, January 1940 (Olrog 1948);

Tierra del Fuego Río Grande, 24 January 1989, and Ushuaia, 29 January 1989 (M. Pearman *in litt.* 1990).

POPULATION The overall population of Olrog's Gull was believed to be very small (Devillers 1977), and until November 1990 the species was only known to breed in a few small colonies in the Bahía San Blas, Buenos Aires province, where Olrog (1967) found 12 nests in November 1963 and Devillers (1977) located two colonies occupied by some 400 individuals in November 1975. Current studies at breeding colonies (including those in Chubut) conducted in November 1990 have resulted in a estimated total population of 1,239±127 breeding pairs, with numbers at individual localities as follows (brackets indicate the number of estimated pairs): Isla Brightman (315±35); Isla Puestos (363±36); Isla Gama (309±30); Isla Jabalí (163±16); Islote Galfrascoli (19); Islas Vernaci (70±10) (P. Yorio *in litt.* 1992; see Remarks 2). Outside the breeding season Escalante (1984) noted that between 1966 and 1968 the number of individuals in a flock along the coast between San José and Maldonado departments, Uruguay, never exceeded 55 birds, although Gore and Gepp (1978) reported the species as a "fairly common" wintering visitor to the country's coasts, with a maximum of 104 birds recorded at Playa Penino on 27 June 1970. In Argentina, it was reported to be abundant (commoner than Kelp Gulls *Larus dominicanus*) on the beaches of Mar del Plata and at sea, as far as 10 miles from the coast, in September 1956 (Olrog 1958a), and it was "common" in the Mar del Plata harbour on July 1982 (B. M. López Lanús *in litt.* 1991). Jehl and Rumboll (1976) found it common in the vicinity of Puerto Belgrano, where more than 200 birds (no more than four subadults and one juvenile) were present in the area from 25 to 28 June 1971. Narosky and Fiameni (1987) found it "abundant" at Costa Bonita between 1983 and 1985, and D. Blanco (*in litt.* 1991) observed 115 and 182 birds respectively at Punta Rasa on 7 and 8 May 1988, although Klimaitis and Moschione (1987) reported it scarce and only found during autumn and winter. Observations at Comodoro Rivadavia gave numbers of c.80 birds on 22 January 1989 and it was found common on a pelagic trip from Necochea in the same year (see Distribution); c.200 birds were present at Mar del Plata pier on 21 June 1989, and at Costanera Sur several observations during 1990 and 1991 included 18 birds on 3 August 1991, c.30 (a majority of second-year birds) on 7 September 1991 and 20 (including many second-year birds) on 8 September 1991 (M. Pearman *in litt.* 1991). In Río Negro province it appears frequently (Contreras 1978), with small numbers (no more than 17) present throughout the year (D. Paz *in litt.* 1991).

ECOLOGY Olrog's Gull occurs along the coasts on beaches, rocky coasts, harbours (see Remarks 5), coastal and brackish lagoons and, notably, estuaries (Olrog 1958a, Gore and Gepp 1978, Escalante 1984, M. Nores *in litt.* 1992).

Its diet is fairly specialized and consists mainly of crabs *Chasmagnathus granulatus*, *Cyrtograpsus* sp. and *Uca* sp., as well as mussels, the former being obtained from mudbanks at low tide and the latter from rocky coasts (Escalante 1970, 1984, Devillers 1977). The stomach and gullet contents of eight specimens taken on mudflats consisted of: *Chasmagnathus granulatus* (six birds), *Chasmagnathus* sp. and several mussels (one bird) and *Cyrtograpsus* sp. (one bird) (Escalante 1966; also Daguerre 1933). More rarely, Olrog's Gull has been reported feeding on waste from boats (Jehl and Rumboll 1976, Escalante 1984, Klimaitis and Moschione 1987) and scavenging inside a sea-lion colony (H. G. Young *in litt* 1989). Further details of its feeding behaviour are in Escalante (1966).

Nesting starts in September/October, as fairly well-grown chicks have been found in early November (Devillers 1977, also Olrog 1967; see Remarks 6). Nesting colonies are established on flat sandy islands just above water level (they may be partly inundated at high tide), where grasses and halophytic plants (i.e. *Salicornia*, *Suaeda*, etc.) are scarce (Olrog 1967, Devillers 1977, Escalante 1984). The nests may be placed in grass tussocks (Olrog 1967), and Devillers (1977) described them as elevated platforms of twigs, grass stems, pieces of *Salicornia*, or as scrapes lined with the same materials. Colonies were situated 500 m (Olrog 1967) and 100 m (Devillers

1977) from the high-tide line, and were reported to be remarkably compressed, some nest platforms touching each other. Devillers (1977) reported two colonies on two islands, one formed by 70 individuals and the other being divided into two subcolonies located 50 m from each other, with 70 and 160 adults c.60 and 20 m respectively from the nearest Kelp Gull colony; five additional pairs bred elsewhere at the periphery of another Kelp Gull colony (Devillers 1977).

The species's seasonal movements are insufficiently studied, but birds are commonly found along Uruguayan coasts in the autumn, winter and spring months, i.e. April/May to October/November (Gore and Gepp 1978, Escalante 1980), as well as along the Buenos Aires province coast (see Distribution). D. Blanco (*in litt.* 1991) noted that at Punta Rasa birds arrive in May. Records suggest that southward displacements are less frequent, and are more likely to occur during the austral summer, after breeding (five records from southern Chubut, Santa Cruz and Tierra del Fuego are all from January: see Distribution).

THREATS The chief cause of concern in this species is its extreme vulnerability in the breeding season: the number of known breeding sites is very small. At those in Buenos Aires province, egg-collecting for food already occurs regularly (Olrog 1967); moreover, there is a permanent danger from the possible development of tourism, increase in fishing traffic, petroleum exploitation and other activities (Devillers 1977, Escalante 1984). Diseases and man-induced changes in its habitat (e.g. contamination of feeding areas) could cause a shortage of prey items.

MEASURES TAKEN The species occurs in several provincial reserves, namely Ribera Norte, Costanera Sur, Rincón de Ajó, Campos del Teyú, Mar Chiquita (J. C. Chebez *in litt.* 1992). Some islands in Bahía San Blas, Bahía Anegada and Bahía Blanca, and most in Bahía Samborombón, have also been protected as provincial reserves, although in practice these islands are by no means effectively protected (T. Narosky *in litt.* 1992). Further south reserves include: Punta Bermeja, Caleta Los Loros and Islote Lobos in Río Negro, Punta Pirámides in Chubut and ría de Puerto Deseado in Santa Cruz, some of which periodically hold great concentrations of the species, although again protection of the sites is not adequately enforced (J. C. Chebez *in litt.* 1992).

MEASURES PROPOSED Existing colonies should immediately be afforded rigorous protection, involving the exclusion (at least during the breeding season) of both unauthorized persons and potential domestic predators (i.e. dogs, cats, etc.). A study should be conducted to locate the most important resting and feeding areas year-round (Escalante 1984), as well as other possible unreported breeding colonies. Detailed studies of the species's feeding requirements as well as of the conservation status of its main staples should be conducted to detect and prevent possible threats and food shortages (Escalante 1984).

REMARKS (1) Olrog's Gull's taxonomic status has been uncertain owing to its affinities with the Band-tailed Gull *Larus belcheri*, but the view that it represents a good species (see Olrog 1958a, Devillers 1977, Escalante 1970, 1984) is accepted here. (2) Data on these newly found colonies was provided by P. Yorio (*in litt.* 1992) based on Harris and Yorio (in press) (unseen at the time of going to press). (3) A record of this species from the island of South Georgia has now been proved to refer to the Kelp Gull (Escalante 1980). (4) Magno (1971) referred in vague terms to nests found together with those of the Brown-hooded Gull *L. maculipennis* at General Lavalle but surprisingly does not mention the colonies previously reported by Olrog (1967) at Bahía San Blas. (5) Athough it can be found in man-modified environments, the species is apparently less adaptive than other gulls of the region (e.g. Kelp and Brown-hooded), as indicated by Escalante (1966) and by its feeding habits (see further under Ecology). (6) Colonies at Bahía San Blas are apparently regularly egged, thus timing of breeding can vary somewhat from year to year (Devillers 1977).

RING-TAILED PIGEON *Columba caribaea* V[9]

Illegal hunting and extensive habitat loss (compounded by a recent hurricane) have reduced the population and range of this montane forest frugivore, whose main hope of survival rests with the full implementation of national parks within its habitat on Jamaica.

DISTRIBUTION The Ringed-tailed Pigeon is endemic to Jamaica, where it is restricted to the least disturbed forested mountains, notably Cockpit Country, Blue Mountains and John Crow Mountains (Lack 1976, Downer and Sutton 1990). However there are also recent breeding records (parishes in bracketed italics) from: (*St Elizabeth*) Black River gorge, May 1990; (*St Andrew*) Red Hills (untraced), April 1990; Stony Hill (18°05'N 76°48'W), June 1990; and Barbican area (untraced), May 1990 (all records from *Gosse Bird Club Broadsheet* 55 [1990]: 19), while a bird was observed in a private garden in Brown's Town, St Ann (Helwig 1987). Records from other areas, historical and recent, include the following localities (from west to east, coordinates from OG 1955b): (*St James*) Hillcroft near Rocklands, where four birds were observed in late November 1985 (Salmon 1986); (*Trelawney*) undated (see Remarks 1) (two specimens in AMNH and USNM); Windsor (18°22'N 77°37'W), May 1859 (specimen in BMNH) and sometime before 1976 (Lack 1976); Mahogany Hall (untraced), November 1858 (specimen in BMNH); (*St Ann*) unspecified (Ridgway 1916); (*St Catherine*) Moneague, undated (Ridgway 1916); Spanish Town, March 1865 (two specimens in BMNH and MCZ) and undated (specimen in ANSP); (*St Mary*) Highgate mountains, where the species was known to have been abundant (Gosse 1847); "St Mary" where it was known to occur around 1950 (Jeffrey-Smith 1956); (*St Andrew*) unspecified, October 1883 (specimen in FMNH); "St Andrews", October 1908 (specimen in MCZ); junction of Jack's Hill and Sunset Drive, St Andrew hills, where a possible bird was observed in February 1986 (Fletcher 1986); (*Portland*) Rio Grande valley, undated (Spence 1977); Priestman's River, January and February 1891 (six specimens in CM, FMNH and MCZ); St George (St George Cliffs at 17°53'N 76°54'W), May 1882 (specimen in FMNH); (*St Thomas*) Cuna Cuna (18°00'N 76°22'W), July 1905 (specimen in USNM); Mansfield property, near Bath, June 1904 (specimen in USNM); mountains above Bath, March 1906 (specimen in MCZ).

POPULATION The Ring-tailed Pigeon appears to have suffered a steep decline in many parts of the country where it was formerly abundant (Gosse 1847, Scott 1891-1893, Lack 1976; also Distribution). Gosse (1847) found it abundant in the Highgate mountains, an area where the species no longer occurs, and Scott (1891-1893) referred to birds as "so common" in the vicinity of Boston (see Remarks 2) at altitudes between 300 m and 600 m that he "frequently used them as food". Bangs and Kennard (1920) considered the species "rather local" in distribution and "nowhere abundant" except in some of the very wildest mountain regions, while Bond (1940) referred to it as "widely distributed" in the wilder parts of the island, being "locally fairly common"; this opinion was maintained by Bond (1956b) and in Greenway (1958, 1967). Jeffrey-Smith (1956) referred to the species to be "still seen in fairly large numbers" in the mountains of Portland (i.e. Blue Mountains), Cockpit Country and St Mary; this last has not been mentioned in recent accounts (e.g. Lack 1976, Downer and Sutton 1990) and presumably no longer harbours the species. Lack (1976) reported it "common" in the forests of the Cockpit Country, John Crow Mountains and in the eastern part of the Blue Mountains, although he asserted that its range had been reduced by hunting. Sykes and Beach (1983) reported a flock of 15 birds within the Cockpit Country in August 1982. Helwig (1987) believed it to be "in danger of extermination", and although Downer and Sutton (1990) still considered it "fairly common locally" it is generally accepted that the species is still decreasing (Haynes *et al.* 1989). After the passage of Hurricane Gilbert in September 1988, local people in the forest areas in the Cockpit Country, Blue Mountains and John Crow Mountains all agreed to have seen "far fewer" Ring-tailed Pigeons in April–July 1989 compared with the same period the previous year; however, no strong decline was indicated by comparing the 1989 census with previous ones (1976 and 1985), although this may partly be a reflection of increased movements (hence greater detectability) in search of scarcer food rather than their true numbers, and marked declines may occur in the longer term (Varty 1991). Varty (1991) recorded 57, 41 and 39 birds (13.3, 17.3 and 31.4 birds per 10-hour period) during counts in the Blue Mountains, John Crow Mountains and Cockpit Country respectively in April–July 1989.

ECOLOGY The Ringed-tailed Pigeon is restricted to the forested mountain areas and hills (up to almost 2,000 m), descending to lower elevations (down to 300 m and even 150 m) in autumn and winter (March 1863, Scott 1891-1893, Bangs and Kennard 1920, Lack 1976, Goodwin 1983, Downer and Sutton 1990, Varty 1991). The species is known to move between areas of fruiting trees, when it tends to occur in groups of six or eight (March 1863, Varty 1991). It has been considered the most arboreal of all Jamaican columbids (Gosse 1847), feeding only occurring in the canopy on a variety of arboreal fruits and seeds: *Chrysophyllum oliviforme*, *Annona muricata*, *Calyptronoma occidentalis*, mistletoe (Loranthaceae), *Sapium jamaicense*, *Cordia collococca*, *Bumelia* sp., *Eugenia* sp., *Ficus* sp., *Laurus* sp., *Nectandra antillana* (see Davis *et al.* 1985). The Ring-tailed Pigeon is an important disperser of relatively large-seeded fruits, such as *N. antillana* (and other Lauraceae with similar fruits, such as *N. patens* and *Licaria triandra*) and *Xylopia muricata*; it may have a mutualistic relationship with the endemic *N. antillana* (Davis *et al.* 1985).

Nesting occurs in the spring and summer months (March 1863, Varty 1991). The nest consists of a thick mat or platform of sticks bedded with leaves, twigs and bark, constructed near the summit of some lofty tree enveloped in tangled masses of trailing plants (March 1863).

THREATS Illegal year-round hunting and destruction of forests threaten the species's survival, and it is likely that all remaining natural areas will be subject to severe disturbance in the near future (Haynes *et al.* 1989). Gosse (1847) long since remarked that the species was highly appreciated by hunters for its excellent flesh, and despite protection this holds true today: furthermore, regulations against hunting are poorly enforced and even senior politicians and Jamaica's elite overlook these particular laws (Haynes-Sutton 1988, Haynes *et al.* 1989). The seasonal concentrations of Ring-tailed Pigeons at known localities make it especially vulnerable to illegal shooting (Varty 1991). Gosse (1847) reported them being attracted to fires lit beneath fruiting trees in the forest, a hunter's trick also reported for the Maroon Pigeon *Columba*

thomensis of São Tomé (see Collar and Stuart 1985) and the Trinidad Piping-guan *Pipile pipile* (see relevant account); Gosse implied that birds came to the smoke in order to avoid mosquitoes, but this explanation is somewhat fanciful.

Haynes *et al.* (1989) have indicated the existence of illegal trade of some species for pets, including the Ring-tailed Pigeon. The effects of strong hurricanes (e.g. Gilbert in September 1988: see Haynes-Sutton 1988, Varty 1991), which cause great damage to forest vegetation, are believed to affect frugivorous species negatively by damaging food trees, which need many years to regenerate; this, coupled with continuing human destruction and disturbance of the forests, constitutes an important threat to the species (Varty 1991; also Population). Furthermore, Varty (1991) noted extensive recent clearance in the three main forest areas where the species is still present (see Distribution): for instance, clearance in the Blue Mountains was spreading to higher, steeper areas, and fires there were recorded on several occasions in May and June 1989.

MEASURES TAKEN The species is legally protected (see Haynes *et al.* 1989), but see Threats. The Blue and John Crow Mountain National Park is being established, and the majority of the land covered by natural forest there and in Cockpit Country is classified as forest reserve, wherein a wide range of activities, including felling, are prohibited or restricted (Varty 1991, N. Varty verbally 1992); but again see Threats.

MEASURES PROPOSED The forests of Cockpit Country should be declared a national park, and "corridors" linking these forests and lowland areas should be maintained (Varty 1991); an overview of the importance of Cockpit Country and the Blue and John Crow Mountains for other endemic mountain forest birds is in Varty (1991) and under Jamaican Petrel *Pterodroma caribbaea.*

REMARKS (1) The specimen was collected by W. Osborn and thus presumably sometime during the mid-nineteenth century. (2) The specimens collected at Priestman's River (see Distribution) are the same as those referred to by Scott (1891-1893) as from the "vicinity of Boston", the two localities being 5 km apart.

PLAIN PIGEON *Columba inornata* I[7]

Hunting and habitat loss have combined to reduce this once abundant and widespread pigeon of Cuba, Jamaica, Haiti, the Dominican Republic and Puerto Rico to the situation where it is threatened everywhere and gravely at risk in Cuba (highest known population c.100 pairs), Jamaica and Puerto Rico (apparently under 300 birds); a recent decline has occurred in the Dominican Republic, and only in Haiti, where firearms and ammunition are too expensive, are there reports of birds in some numbers. Captive breeding is being used to attempt to reverse trends in Puerto Rico, but protection of habitat there is still needed; elsewhere surveys are imperative to obtain an adequate perspective on the species's conservation.

DISTRIBUTION The Plain Pigeon (see Remarks 1) is endemic to the Greater Antilles, i.e. Cuba (including Isla de la Juventud or Isle of Pines), Jamaica, Hispaniola and Puerto Rico. In the following account, records are arranged from west to east and, unless otherwise indicated, refer either to one individual observed or to an unspecified number of individuals (as in the original source), with coordinates taken from OG (1955b, 1958, 1963a) and DMATC (1972, 1973):

Cuba (*Pinar del Río*) forests of Península de Guanahacabibes, where several pairs were observed in the surroundings of Cabo San Antonio in July 1957 (Vaurie 1957) and down to the present (O. H. Garrido *in litt.* 1991, A. Mitchell *in litt.* 1992); Cayo Real (21°58'N 83°35'W), Cayos de San Felipe, sometime in the 1970s (Garrido and García Montaña 1975, Garrido 1986, O. H. Garrido *in litt.* 1991); (*Habana*) neighbourhood of "Havana", where the type-specimen was collected (Vigors 1827); (*Matanzas*) Ciénaga de Zapata, reported nesting on an ungiven date (Gundlach 1871-1875), and currently (O. H. Garrido *in litt.* 1991); Zanja "La Cocodrila" (in the area of Santo Tomás, 22°24'N 81°25'W), Península de Zapata, where the species has sporadically been observed (Garrido 1980); Santo Tomás, May 1933 and April 1935 (four specimens in FMNH); Soplillar (22°17'N 81°09'W), December 1991 (J. M. Jiménez López *in litt.* 1992); (*Cienfuegos*) San Blas (21°59'N 80°13'W), Trinidad Mountains, where the species was found common between February and July 1933 (Rutten 1934); (*Villa Clara*) "Las Villas (formerly Santa Clara)" (see Remarks 2), apparently in the mid-1950s (Bond 1956b); (*Sancti Spíritus*) along the río Agabama (21°51'N 79°50'W), where the species was common in March and April 1933 (Rutten 1934); (*Camagüey*) "Camagüey" (the province), apparently in the mid-1950s (Bond 1956b); Cayo Romano, undated (Acosta and Berovides 1984); Santa Rosa (21°17'N 78°04'W), February 1923 (eight specimens in AMNH, BMNH, CM and FMNH) and March 1923 (specimen in USNM); La Belén (= Belén, 21°00'N 77°43'W) and other areas near the Sierra de Najasa (21°03'N 77°47'W), currently (O. H. Garrido *in litt.* 1991); (*Granma*) Birama (20°48'N 77°12'W, presumably in the area of Esteros de Birama, 20°38'N 77°13'W), where a population possibly still exists (0. H. Garrido *in litt.* 1991); (*Guantánamo*) Guantánamo Bay, undated (Gundlach 1878b); regions near Guantánamo (Garrido and García Montaña 1975); in the area of Los Caños (20°03'N 75°09'W), where it was not rare early in the twentieth century (O. H. Garrido *in litt.* 1991); Cuchillas del Toa Biosphere Reserve (20°27'N 74°58'W) (Ojito de Agua area), sometime between 1985 and 1987 (Giraldo Alayón *et al.* 1987); (*Isle of Pines*) Santa Bárbara (21°49'N 83°01'W), sometime between 1909 and 1914 (see Todd 1916); Los Indios (21°42'N 83°00'W), August, September and December 1912 (seven specimens in CM and FMNH) and January 1913 (four specimens in AMNH and CM) with a nest on 29 April 1910 which contained eggs on 4 May (Todd 1915b, 1916); Cañada Mountains (= Sierra de la Cañada, 21°45'N 82°57'W), "Nuevas River" (= río de las Nuevas, 21°56'N 82°56'W), McKinley (21°53'N 82°55'W, see Remarks 3) to Nueva Gerona, sometime between 1909 and 1914 (see Todd 1916); San Pedro (21°37'N 82°53'W), March 1902 (specimen in AMNH); "Santa Fé" (21°45'N 82°45'W), around the mid-nineteenth century (see Todd 1916); Palma Alta (21°34'N 82°40'W), March 1902 (specimen in AMNH);

Jamaica Amity (18°15'N 78°06'W), apparently mid-1950s (Jeffery-Smith 1956); St Elizabeth parish, apparently mid-1950s (Bond 1956b); Trelawney, February 1908 (specimen in AMNH); woods of Trelawney, where the species was evidently heard in the mid-1950s (Jeffery-Smith 1956; also Ridgway 1916); Freeman's Hale (untraced, but in Trelawney parish), September 1959 (specimen in USNM); Balaclava (18°10'N 77°39'W), apparently mid-1950s (Jeffery-Smith 1956); Barbecue Bottom (between Clark's Town and Albert Town: see the map in Downer and Sutton 1990), where three birds were observed in April 1979 (see Pérez-Rivera 1990), the species being still present (Downer and Sutton 1990); Grove Valley, near Mandeville, in the 1930s (Bond 1940); Cumberland Valley (= Cumberland, 18°07'N 77°26'W), undated (Ridgway 1916); Clarendon Plains, currently (Downer and Sutton 1990); Old Harbour, where "several" were shot in 1952 (Bond 1956b, Jeffery-Smith 1956); Moneague, undated (Ridgway 1916); Fern Gully (mountains south of Ocho Ríos: see the map in Downer and Sutton 1990), where 15 birds were observed in April 1979 (see Pérez-Rivera 1990), the species being still present (Downer and Sutton 1990); eastern St Mary parish, where a flock of eight birds was observed in the 1970s (Spence 1977); St Catherine, mid-1950s (Bond 1956b); Spanishtown (= Spanish Town), February 1864 (three specimens in AMNH and BMNH; also Salvadori 1893); Port Henderson, where about 30 birds were observed in January 1977 (see Pérez-Rivera 1990); Hardwar Gap (18°05'N 76°43'W), where a possible bird was observed flying in January 1971 (Lack 1973); Yallahs, currently (Downer and Sutton 1990); Salt Ponds, February 1864 (specimen in AMNH) and where c.25 birds were observed in December 1978 (see Pérez-Rivera 1990); Blue Mountains, mid-1950s (Bond 1940), several observations in 1973 (see Pérez-Rivera 1990) and present by 1977 (Spence 1977); Mona Reserve (see the map in Downer and Sutton 1990), 1972 (see Pérez-Rivera 1972);

Haiti Ile de la Tortue ("Tortuga Island") (Bond 1928a, 1940); (*northern peninsula*) Massif du Nord (untraced, but presumably in Nord department) (Bond 1928a); Ennery, March 1928 (specimen in ANSP); Montagnes Noires (19°23'N 72°27'W) (Bond 1928a); 1.6 km north of L'Atalaye (see Remarks 4), where the species was taken in January 1929 (see Wetmore and Swales 1931; also USNM label data); Poste Charbert, near Caracol (19°42'N 72°01'W), where it was common in April 1927 (see Wetmore and Swales 1931); along the road between Maïssade (19°10'N 72°08'W) and Hinche, where several birds were observed in April 1927 and a specimen was then collected in "Ravine Papaye", Hinche, where birds were reportedly common (Wetmore and Swales 1931; two specimens in USNM); Hinche, March 1929 (see Wetmore and Swales 1931); woods near the mouth of the Artibonite river, where five birds were observed in July 1927 (Danforth 1929); c.6 km south-east of Cerca la Source (19°10'N 71°42'W), where the species was "plentiful" in March 1927 (see Wetmore and Swales 1931; also USNM label data); (*southern peninsula*) Trou Caïman (19°16'N 72°39'W; see Remarks 5), December 1928 (specimen in FMNH); La Visite National Park (see the map in Woods and Ottenwalder 1986), where 40-50 individuals were observed on several occasions, apparently around 1984 (M. A. McDonald *in litt.* 1986); Saumatre (= Étang Saumâtre) (Bond 1928a), with two birds flying in the direction of Morne La Selle foothills in 1983 (J. A. Ottenwalder *in litt.* 1986); Forêt des Pins, Marie Claire (18°18'N 71°49'W), February 1959 (specimen in YPM); "Boucan Chat" (presumably Boucan Chatte, 18°19'N 71°45'W), March 1959 (specimen in YPM);

Dominican Republic Sierra de Neiba, currently (D. Sirí Núñez *in litt.* 1992); Lago Enriquillo (Bond 1928a) and in dry areas there around 1978 (Stockton de Dod 1978); Isla Cabritos National Park, Lago Enriquillo, where a total of 67 birds were reported in 1986 (D. Sirí Núñez *in litt.* 1992); Aguacate, a military post above Sapotén (18°19'N 71°41'W), Loma de Toro (a few km to the west of Pueblo Viejo, 18°14'N 71°31'W), around 1978 (Stockton de Dod 1978); Río Limpio (19°15'N 71°31'W) and Loma Nalga de Maco (19°13'N 71°29'W), recently (SEA/DVS 1992); Hoyo de Palempito (18°06'N 71°28'W), around 1978 (Stockton de Dod 1978); a wooded area near the southern extreme of Laguna Salada (17°41'N 71°28'W), where five birds were observed in March 1983 (Vargas Mora and González Castillo 1983); Bucán de Base (17°38'N 71°26'W), near Laguna Salada, where a flock of about 200 birds were observed in 1977 (see Vargas Mora and

González Castillo 1983); "desiertos de Oviedo" (Oviedo at 17°47'N 71°22'N), around 1978 (Stockton de Dod 1978); Bucán de Isidro (untraced but presumably in the Península de Barahona), where it was reported common until 1978 (see Vargas Mora and González Castillo 1983); Jaybón (= Jaibón, 19°37'N 71°09'W), February 1935 (specimen in USNM); Constanza (18°55'N 70°45'W), September and October 1916 (three specimens in CM and USNM), April 1919 (two specimens in USNM), June 1922 (specimen in AMNH); near Constanza, where it was fairly common in May 1927 (Wetmore and Swales 1931), 1976 (Pérez-Rivera 1990) and around 1978 (Stockton de Dod 1978); Loma Tina (18°47'N 70°44'W), January 1917 (ten specimens in AMNH; also Wetmore and Swales 1931); Azua, 1976 (Pérez-Rivera 1990); Reserva Científica Ebano Verde (near Jarabacoa; see the map in DVS 1990), where three birds were observed in May 1992 (D. Sirí Núñez *in litt.* 1992); mouth of río Yuna, May 1927 (Wetmore and Swales 1931); Los Haitises (19°05'N 69°45'W), around 1981 (Stockton de Dod 1981); Samaná Bay, June 1883 (two specimens in ANSP); San Lorenzo, Samaná Bay, July 1916 (specimen in USNM), March 1919 (three specimens in USNM), and probably nesting in March 1919 (see Wetmore and Swales 1931); Sánchez (see Remarks 6), where the species was taken in November 1916 (see Wetmore and Swales 1931; five specimens in AMNH) and February 1919 (see Wetmore and Swales 1931); Maguá (18°59'N 69°14'W; see Remarks 7), where a bird was collected in February 1883 (Cory 1885); Parque Nacional del Este, undated (Hoppe 1989, which maps the site). Untraced localities are: mouth of the arroyo Barrancota, where a few birds were observed in May 1927 (Wetmore and Swales 1931); Canotes, undated (Stockton de Dod 1978); Sánchez Ramírez, 1976 (see Pérez-Rivera 1981; R. A. Pérez-Rivera *in litt.* 1992);

Puerto Rico (*Añasco municipality*) Añasco (18°17'N 67°08'W), where two birds were observed in 1926 (Danforth 1936) and the species was believed to be reproducing around 1977 (Pérez-Rivera 1977b; see Population); (*Lares*) on the road from Lares (18°19'N 66°52'W) to Utuado (18°15'N 66°42'W), where several birds were shot in July 1876 (Gundlach 1878b); (*Utuado*) "Caguana" (= Barrio Caguanas), reported to Gundlach (1878a); Barrio Caguanas (18°18'N 66°45'W), where it was being hunted until 1956 (Pérez-Rivera 1981; also Population) and possibly breeding around 1977 (Pérez-Rivera 1977b, Population); Utuado (18°15'N 66°42'W), April 1912 (specimen in CM) and still present in June 1980 (Pérez-Rivera 1981); caves in Hacienda Jobo (untraced but near Utuado), where bones of the species have been found (Wetmore 1922); (*Yauco*) "Altura de Yauco" (Yauco at 18°02'N 66°51'W), where hunters reported seeing the species on an ungiven date; (*Guayanilla*) Punta Verraco (17°59'N 66°47'W), reported by hunters on an ungiven date; (*Arecibo*) one or more sites where the species is known to have been hunted on an ungiven date; (*Ponce*) Ponce municipality, where Plain Pigeons were hunted and sold as food in 1961; mangroves of "El Tuque" (untraced), June 1980, with hunters reportedly securing the species at "Tuque" (near Peñuelas, 18°03'N 66°43'W) (all five from Pérez-Rivera 1981); "Barrio Canas" (= Barrio Cañas, 18°01'N 66°40'W), where several bones were found in 1934 in a midden (Wetmore 1938); (*Manatí*) around Manatí town (18°25'N 66°30'W), where the species was rediscovered in 1958 and at some stage hunted (Pérez-Rivera 1978, 1981); (*Morovís*) caves in the vicinity of Morovís (18°20'N 66°24'W), where bones of the species have been identified (Wetmore 1927); (*Salinas*) near Campamento de la Guardia Nacional (untraced, but on route no.1 (see USGS 1951) to Cayey, where the species was observed in December 1979 (Pérez-Rivera 1981); (*Aibonito*), 1970–1980 (Pérez-Rivera and Collazo Algarín 1976, Pérez-Rivera 1981); (*Cayey*) near Cayey, from April to June of an unstated year (Pérez-Rivera 1981); Toita de Cayey (= Toita, 18°08'N 66°11'W), nesting around 1980 (Pérez-Rivera 1981); Arenas de Cayey (= Arenas, 18°10'N 66°08'W), around 1977 (Pérez-Rivera 1977b); area of Guavate (18°08'N 66°05'W), where the species is known to have bred (Pérez-Rivera 1984; also Population); (*Cidra*) vicinity of Lake Cidra (18°11'N 66°10'N), currently (see Population); (*Aguas Buenas*) along route 156 (which links Aguas Buenas, 18°15'N 66°06'W, and Caguas, 18°14'N 66°02'W), 1970–1980, mainly in areas with canyons (tributaries of the río Bayamón) (Pérez-Rivera 1981); (*Guayama*) surroundings of Lago Carite (18°04'N 66°06'W), where it has been reported by hunters, and in June 1980 a bird was heard calling in appropriate habitat for breeding (Pérez-Rivera 1981); (*Caguas*) km 3 of "Autopista de las Américas" (linking Cayey and Caguas) towards "las Quebradillas" (= Quebrada de las Quebradillas, 18°12'N 66°03'W), 1970–1980 (Pérez-Rivera 1981); in the bamboo areas of the río Turabo (18°13'N 66°01'W), 1970–1980 (Pérez-Rivera 1981); in the area next to "Peaje de Caguas-Cayey", 1970–1980 (Pérez-Rivera 1981); Borinquén (18°10'N 66°02'W), 1970–1980 (March–August) (Pérez-Rivera 1981); (*Gurabo*) Gurabo municipality, in the 1950s (Pérez-Rivera 1981); bamboos of the río Gurabo (18°17'N 66°06'W), February 1977 (Pérez-Rivera 1981); Estación Experimental Agrícola de Gurabo (Gurabo at 18°16'N 65°58'W), 1974 (Pérez-Rivera 1981); margins of the río Grande de Loíza (near Gurabo: see USGS 1951), where 20 birds were observed in February 1980 (Pérez-Rivera 1981); Florida (18°11'N 65°57'W), May 1977 (Pérez-Rivera 1981); (*Juncos*) c.3 km before Juncos (18°14'N 65°55'W) along the motorway to Caguas from Humacao, October 1980, November 1980 and March 1981 (Pérez-Rivera 1981); (*Las Piedras*) Las Piedras (18°11'N 65°53'W), where the species was hunted sometime before 1976; c.1 km from Barrio Tejas (18°09'N 65°51'W), December 1980 (Pérez-Rivera 1981); (*Naguabo*) Naguabo municipality, undated (Pérez-Rivera 1977b).

POPULATION The Plain Pigeon has declined dramatically throughout its range, being almost wiped out from Puerto Rico, Jamaica and Cuba, where it is considered it in immediate danger of extinction, its status in Hispaniola being "not being much better", i.e. also considered threatened; thus if no urgent, strong measures are taken the species could well become extinct in the next 50 years (Pérez-Rivera 1990). Bangs and Kennard (1920) noted the decline throughout its range, and reported that it had been common "in the early days" but referred to it as "disappearing rapidly".

Cuba The Plain Pigeon appears to have been abundant in former times on both the mainland and the Isle of Pines (Todd 1916, Barbour 1923, Garrido 1986), but according to Todd (1916) by the start of this century its numbers were very much reduced and it was practically extinct in many parts. Bangs and Kennard (1920) believed it to be on the verge of extinction, and Barbour (1923) considered it an "excessively" rare bird. During the second half of the nineteenth century, it appears to have been recorded in the Ciénaga de Zapata and shores of Guantánamo Bay in great numbers, but not in the interior of the island, and even by the start of the twentieth century it was considered nearly extinct in the two localities mentioned (Gundlach 1871-1875, Barbour 1923). However, Rutten (1933) found it "really common" in the Trinidad Mountains near San Blas (February–July 1933) and along the río Agabama (March and April 1933), while the number of specimens collected at Santa Rosa, Camagüey, in February 1923 (eight: see Distribution) suggests that at that time it was still common there, and Bond (1940), presumably drawing in part on this evidence, referred to the species as locally common in the provinces of Santa Clara (presumably what is today Villa Clara) and Camagüey. Later, Bond (1956b) indicated that it was rare in Oriente and in extreme western Pinar del Río (Península de Guanahacabibes), but his contention that the species was well established in parts of Cuba (Bond 1961) has not been confirmed by further field research. Nowadays it is very localized in Guanahacabibes, the Zapata peninsula and in parts of the Sierra de Najasa (where the population is presumed to be no larger that 15 pairs), but a small population may also exist in the Esteros de Birama (see Distribution) (O. H. Garrido *in litt.* 1991). Whether birds are still present in nearby areas in Guantánamo, as indicated by Garrido and García Montaña (1975) and Garrido (1986), is unknown. The relatively recent record of the species in Cayo Real may indicate a small population there (Garrido 1986) and another may exist in the southern parts of Pinar del Río (Garrido 1986). A small recovery of the population in the Península de Guanahacabibes as a result of educational programmes has been noted (Garrido 1986), and at around 100 pairs or less this is the strongest known population in the country (O. H. Garrido *in litt.* 1991). On the Isle of Pines the species was abundant but evidently suffering early in the twentieth century, when "large bags" were "the rule" after hunts conducted by local people (Todd 1916, Garrido 1986; also Distribution); but Barbour (1923) could not find the species from 1915 to 1918 despite many visits to the island at all times of the year, and thus he believed it to have "probably gone", while Bond (1940, 1956b) considered it rare and local. Garrido (1986) noted the lack of recent records, although he believed that small groups might still be confined to some areas, but it is now judged that the species has indeed been exterminated there (O. H. Garrido *in litt.* 1991).

Jamaica The species appears to have been scarce a century ago, and from March (1863) and Scott (1891-1893) it is not readily clear whether it was ever a common species. Scott (1891-1893) referred in vague terms to its former abundance, himself being unable to find the species in the north-east part of the island around Boston, and March (1863) referred to small groups of six or eight passing from the hills to the fields to feed on "guinea corn". During the present century the species has steadily declined, becoming very rare (Lack 1973, Pérez-Rivera 1990). Bangs and Kennard (1920) believed that it was on the verge of extinction, Bond (1940) considered it "apparently rare and local", while Jeffery-Smith (1956) referred to it as "rarely seen but far from extinct". In 1952 several were shot near Old Harbour (Bond 1956b) and Bond (1961) considered it "rare" but "probably in no immediate danger". Spence (1973) indicated that it appears regularly in the foothills of the Blue Mountains when *Ficus* trees are fruiting, and Lack (1976) noted that the last published record was in July and August 1963, although he observed a bird which he believed to be this species in January 1971. Vogel *et al.* (1989) considered the Plain Pigeon "very rare" with no nesting "observed in recent years", and Downer and Sutton (1990) also considered it a very rare and endangered resident. More recent records (see Distribution) could well prove to be of birds from just one or two breeding localities, and the species's current status may well be similar to or even worse than that in Puerto Rico, given the possible damage caused to it by Hurricane Gilbert (Pérez-Rivera 1990).

Haiti Bond (1928a) considered the Plain Pigeon the "most common pigeon" in the north and to be local in the south, not uncommon on Tortuga Island but absent on Gonave. In April 1927, Wetmore and Swales (1931) considered it the "most common" of the large pigeons in the vicinity of Hinche and particularly along the Ravine Papaye, where resting groups of 2-10 were found, and it was also common at Poste Charbert, near Caracol. In March 1927 it was "very plentiful" at Cerca-la-Source (see Wetmore and Swales 1931). M. A. McDonald (*in litt.* 1986) reported seeing 40-50 birds in La Visite National Park on several occasions (see Remarks 8), and C. A. Woods (verbally 1992) judged the species to be locally common, apparently owing to the lack of firearms amongst the poverty-stricken populace (see Remarks 9).

Dominican Republic The Plain Pigeon appears to have been abundant in the mid-nineteenth century (see Pérez-Rivera 1990), and according to Stockton de Dod (1987) it was once very common, flying in "clouds". Wetmore and Swales (1931) found it locally common but only in the wooded interior of the island, e.g. "fairly common" near Constanza in May 1927. Bond (1940) considered it to be locally common, and Bond (1961) and Greenway (1967) referred to it as well established in parts of Hispaniola, but none of them provided further details. Stockton de Dod (1978) believed that the population in the island was "substantial" although it could not be considered common, and later (Stockton de Dod 1981) thought the species relatively common ("población regular") although reduced in numbers. Perhaps the largest concentration recorded in recent times is of a flock of 200 in flight at Bucán de Base in August 1977 (W. Arendt in Vargas Mora and González Castillo 1983). The species was reported to be common near Bucán de Isidro around 1978 (see Vargas Mora and González Castillo 1983) and near Sánchez Ramírez (see Pérez-Rivera 1981). A. Stockton de Dod (*in litt.* 1986) reported that a "substantial" population still existed in the country. In 1986 67 birds were reported from Isla Cabritos, Lago Enriquillo, but the population there is believed to have declined (D. Sirí Núñez *in litt.* 1992). Also in 1986 a search for the species (covering c.3,500 km and conducted in different parts of the Cordillera Central and Los Haitises) resulted in failure to locate any birds, the areas where the species was present 10 years before having been cleared or used for agriculture (Pérez-Rivera 1990). From this survey and information provided by hunters and aviculturists, Pérez-Rivera

(1990) concluded that the species currently has a very restricted distribution with the healthiest populations being in the extreme south-west and in the north-east in the least transformed areas of Los Haitises. D. Sirí Núñez (*in litt.* 1992) has also reported a considerable decline, with a few individuals still present in the Sierra de Neiba; furthermore Pérez-Rivera (1990) indicated that if habitat destruction continues at its current rate the species will be soon in danger of extinction.

Puerto Rico The Plain Pigeon appears to have been abundant and widespread in former times, with reports of "hundreds" in the first half of the nineteenth century (see Pérez-Rivera 1990; also Wiley 1985b), but when the bird was described in 1866 it was already rare, with only one specimen being collected in 1860 (see Pérez-Rivera 1978). In 1878, it was reported from around Lares (Gundlach 1878a,b) but the next specimen was not collected until 1912 near Utuado (see Distribution). Neither Bowdish (1902-1903) nor Wetmore (1927, 1928) observed the species while working in Puerto Rico in the late nineteenth and in the early twentieth centuries. Danforth (1936) observed the species in 1926 in Añasco, after which he considered it to have become extinct around 1936 (hence Bond 1941). Although there was evidence of hunting during the early 1950s in a few widely scattered areas (Pérez Rivera 1981, Wiley 1985b), Bond (1956b) still believed that the species was extinct. It was rediscovered in 1958 near Manatí, and in 1959 a bird was shot near Naguabo (see Pérez-Rivera 1981), but it was not until 1963 that a population was discovered around the Lake of Cidra (see, e.g., Bond 1964, Wiley 1985b, Pérez-Rivera 1990) and only in 1973 was the first nest reported (Pérez-Rivera and Collazo 1976), the first census in the area yielding 63 birds (Wiley 1985b). Nesting pigeons have since been found in neighbouring districts and individuals have been seen far from the Cidra area (Pérez-Rivera 1981, USFWS 1982, Wiley 1985b). In November 1976 a census revealed the existence of about 200 individuals (Pérez-Rivera 1977a), and Pérez-Rivera (1977b) reported finding nests in Toita and Arenas de Cayey (the first record of the pigeons nesting outside the Cidra area, possibly reflecting a population increase or else a retreat to areas where competition with the Scaly-naped Pigeon *Columba squamosa* could be avoided; see Threats). Pérez-Rivera (1981) indicated that the species's range appeared to be larger than was previously believed and located in four areas, namely (1) Añasco, (2) Yauco–Ponce, (3) Lares–Manatí and (4) Salinas and Guayama towards the north in Caguas and to the east as far as Naguabo (see map 2 in Pérez-Rivera 1981). The population is known to have decreased since the first investigations started in 1973, and in July, August and September 1983 censuses resulted in an average of 33 birds, this being the smallest number recorded for 10 years, and only five nests were found between 1982 and 1983 at Cidra (in the fourth area listed above), whereas between March and July 1975 at least 15 active nests had been found in just one of the nesting sites in the Cidra area (Propiedad Cancio) (Pérez-Rivera 1984). A small population at Guavate (within the Cidra–Cayey area) stood at 21 birds in April 1981, only two in August 1982, but 12-14 in January 1983 (Pérez-Rivera 1984). According to Wiley (1985b) the population remained at about 70 birds between late 1976 and 1983 (69 in a November 1983 census around Cidra: Pérez-Rivera 1984), but nesting success had apparently declined, with a substantial reduction in breeding effort: despite extensive searches, only six nests were located in 1984, and all failed (Wiley 1985b). However, periodic censuses conducted in the same area of Cidra between 1984 and 1991 resulted as follows (figures represent the minimum number of birds): November 1984 155, December 1985 129, June 1986 122, August 1986 221, January 1987 118, September 1987 193, April 1988 148, December 1988 70, September 1989 204, October 1990 255, February 1991 196 (Pérez-Rivera and Ruiz-Lebrón 1992). Larger numbers were detected from August to November (when less reproductive activity exists and flocking behaviour is more common; see Ecology), while from December to June (main breeding period) bird are less detectable as they tend to remain in the nesting areas (Pérez-Rivera and Ruiz-Lebrón 1992). Although the above figures appear to suggest an increase in the population (notably from 1988 to 1991), this has been attributed to an improvement of the census method rather than an improvement in what was being censused; moreover, a population decline is predicted as a result of the current destruction of nesting, roosting and feeding areas by development at Cidra and by the recent passage of Hurricane Hugo (Pérez-Rivera and Ruiz-Lebrón 1992; see Threats). The Plain Pigeon's estimated density in the municipality of Cidra between 1985 and 1989 was in the order of 0.4-1.2 birds per km^2 and elsewhere birds were detected only twice in 2,400 point counts conducted at 90 sampling stations (Rivera-Milán 1992).

ECOLOGY The Plain Pigeon is known to occupy very different habitats at all altitudes, including forested lowlands (primary and second growth), desert thorn-scrub, mountain forest (pinewoods or broadleaf rainforest), coastal mangroves, open savannas and cultivated country (e.g. Gosse 1847, Gundlach 1878b, Bond 1928a, 1956b, Vaurie 1957, Wiley 1985b, Garrido 1986). However, its habitat preferences appear to be slightly different in each of the islands within its range, although this presumably is due to habitat alteration and thus different availability of resources. In Cuba the species has been more frequently reported in open country, lowland forests, mangroves and swampy areas (Gundlach 1871-1875, 1878a, Todd 1916, Garrido 1986), although it has also been reported from two mountainous areas (Trinidad Mountains and Sierra de Najasa: see Distribution). In Jamaica the species was formerly widespread at all altitudes (Gosse 1847), but it duly retreated into the mountain rainforest (Gosse 1847), and March (1863) described it as a "highland pigeon", although it still made forays to lowland fruit trees to feed (King 1978-1979), and feeds in coastal mangroves, chiefly in the southern coastal plains (Downer and Sutton 1990). In northern Haiti it was known to occur in the upland pine-forest (Bond 1928a), and in the Dominican Republic it was found in dry coastal deserts, mangroves and in the mountains in both pine and broadleaf woodland (Wetmore and Swales 1931, Stockton de Dod 1978, Vargas Mora and González Castillo 1983). In Puerto Rico it frequented lowland forests (Danforth 1936), but is now mainly restricted to second-growth areas with native and exotic plants and patches of farmland and cattle pastures (USFWS 1982, Wiley 1985b).

The Plain Pigeon feeds on fruits, berries, seeds, buds, leaves and flowers (R. A. Pérez-Rivera *in litt.* 1992; see below). In Cuba it was reported feeding on the berry of the "ateye tree" *Cordia callococca* (see Greenway 1967) and Rutten (1934) reported it eating the fruit of the royal palm *Roystonea regia*. In Jamaica it was known to descend to the plains in search of ripening "guinea corn" in January and February (March 1863), and it has been observed feeding on fruiting fig *Ficus* (Spence 1973). In Puerto Rico the bulk of the diet consists of fruits of the royal palm *Roystonea borinquena*, *Cestrum diurnum*, and *Didymopanax morototoni*, and although the species can obtain its food near or on the ground (including cattle-spilt grain), it shows the characteristics of a highly arboreal pigeon, doing most of its feeding in trees (Pérez-Rivera 1978, 1985, Pérez-Rivera *et al.* 1988, which see for further information on the species's diet in Puerto Rico).

The (typical pigeon) nest is placed in trees (including mangroves, pines, hardwoods, etc.) at moderate heights above the ground on horizontal branches of trees or epiphytic plants, with one (Puerto Rico) or two eggs (March 1863, Wetmore and Swales 1931, Bond 1957, Greenway 1967, Pérez-Rivera and Collazo Algarín 1976, Pérez-Rivera 1978, 1984, Balát and González 1982, Garrido 1986). In Puerto Rico, reproduction has been intensively studied (e.g. Pérez-Rivera and Collazo Algarín 1976, Pérez-Rivera 1978, Wiley 1985b, Pérez-Rivera *et al.* 1988) and birds are known to nest chiefly in bamboo groves and hardwood canyons: the first habitat consists of mature dense stands of bamboo, which occur along the banks of shallow ravines formed by runoff water, or at the edges of a large water-body, while the hardwood associations are in little canyons, mostly formed by second-growth vegetation such as *Cecropia peltata*, *Didymopanax morototoni*, *Spathodea campanulata*, *Eugenia jambos* and *Miconia prasina*. The site selected for nesting is always characterized by the presence of bulky vegetation and proximity to water: of 40 nests studied 75% were found in bamboo vegetation, and of the remaining 25% five were in *Eugenia jambos*, three in *Cydista aequinoctalis*, one in *Bucida buceras* and another in *Spathodea campanulata*; the nests have been found at heights ranging from 6 to 21 m, the average being 14.5 m in bamboo and 9.6 m in hardwood vegetation (Pérez-Rivera 1978). Mean distances between nests in Puerto Rico were found to be 12 m, with (simultaneous and successful) nests observed as close as 6 m, although fighting between males caused the loss of an egg (i.e. nest failure) in a case where two nests were only 4 m apart (Pérez-Rivera and Collazo Algarín 1976). Breeding in Cuba has been reported in April, May and July (Todd 1916, Greenway 1967, Balát and González 1982, Garrido 1986), in Jamaica from April to July (Downer and Sutton 1990) and in Hispaniola in April (nest found: Wetmore and Swales 1931) through to July (egg in specimen collected on 22 June: AMNH label data). In Puerto Rico, the breeding season is not clearly defined, and can occur all year round, although egg-laying peaks are from December to June (Pérez-Rivera and Collazo Algarín 1976, Pérez-Rivera 1978, USFWS 1982, Pérez-Rivera *et al.* 1988). The incubation period in the wild has been reported to be from 13 to 15 days, and squabs fledge at the age of 21 to 23 days (Pérez-Rivera 1978, USFWS 1982, Pérez-Rivera *et al.* 1988). Pérez-Rivera (1978) indicated that reproductive success in Puerto Rico was 44.4% and 50% in 1975 and 1976 respectively, and Wiley (1985b) found that, from a total of 78 pairs studied in 1974 and 1975, 61% failed to fledge young. After the breeding season, notably in autumn, Plain Pigeons have a tendency to occur in flocks and thus become more detectable (Pérez-Rivera and Ruiz-Lebrón 1992).

THREATS Habitat destruction and excessive hunting can be blamed for the species's critical situation throughout its range (Wetmore and Swales 1931, King 1978-1979, Vogel *et al.* 1989, Pérez-Rivera 1990, O. H. Garrido *in litt.* 1991). The Plain Pigeon has a reputation of having no wariness and thus being an easy target for hunters (Greenway 1967); this fact was also stressed by Todd (1916) in referring portentously to the heavy persecution to which it was subjected on the Isle of Pines; in Barbour's (1923) words "such a stupid bird, so good to eat, never could survive". Despite being protected throughout its range, illegal hunting has continued to be a problem (King 1978-1979, Pérez-Rivera 1984, 1990, O. H. Garrido *in litt.* 1991). Natural factors such as hurricanes can also be very damaging to reduced populations of pigeons (e.g. Varty 1991; see below).

In addition to the above threats, in Puerto Rico the main problem in the Cidra area (the last stronghold of the species: see Population) is urban development (see Pérez-Rivera and Ruiz-Lebrón 1992), transformation for cattle-grazing, and large areas being planted with "pangola" *Digitaria decumbens* which restricts the growth of thistles and thus limits the source of food. Further threats are predation of eggs and chicks by rats, Pearly-eyed Thrashers *Margarops fuscatus*, Red-legged Thrushes *Mimocichla plumbea*, and man, who uses chicks for food (Pérez-Rivera and Collazo Algarín 1976, Pérez-Rivera 1978), and parasitism of chicks by larvae of the fly *Philornis pici*, which is known to have affected five chicks collected for captive breeding (Pérez-Rivera and Collazo Algarín 1976, Pérez-Rivera 1985). Wiley (1985b) found that rats destroyed 10% of the nests and Pearly-eyed Thrashers 2% (and he noted that the pigeon tended to be commoner where the thrasher was rarer), but the most important cause of nest failure (56%) was man and man-related activities (e.g. cattle-grazing, cutting of nesting habitat, malicious destruction of nests). Competition with the territorially more vigorous Scaly-naped Pigeon for food and nest-sites may be another problem: Plain Pigeons have been forced to nest in the introduced bamboo, which is less suitable than the hardwood as it is less protected against heavy rains; this competition seems likely to increase since hardwood areas are being altered or eliminated for human development (see below) and Scaly-naped Pigeons seem to be moving into the bamboo to nest (Pérez-Rivera 1977a,b, 1978). Small woodlots often surrounded by housing tracts or industrial complexes are being lost at an alarming rate to continuing urban and industrial growth, and local government is interested in the further development of Cidra (Pérez-Rivera 1984, 1990, Wiley 1985b, Pérez-Rivera and Ruiz-Lebrón 1992; see table 5 in this last reference for examples of destruction of important areas for the Plain Pigeon in the municipality of Cidra from 1988 to 1991), an effect that is presumably responsible for an increase in sightings of Plain Pigeons in nearby municipalities as habitat at Cidra disappears; this dispersion can result in further conservation problems as it would require the identification and protection of additional areas (Pérez-Rivera and Ruiz-Lebrón 1992). Although agents of the commonwealth occasionally patrol Cidra, shooting is still heard around Plain Pigeon habitat (Wiley 1985b, Pérez-Rivera and Ruiz-

Lebrón 1992). The passage of Hurricane Hugo in September 1989 is known to have damaged at least one important area for the Plain Pigeon in the municipality of Cidra (Pérez-Rivera and Ruiz-Lebrón 1992), and no attempt at breeding was detected after the hurricane up to April 1990 (Pérez-Rivera 1990).

MEASURES TAKEN To date the only positive intervention for the Plain Pigeon has been on Puerto Rico.

Cuba The species is protected against hunting, but this is not enforced (see Threats). It benefits to some degree from the following protected areas: Ciénaga de Zapata National Park, Cayo Romano and Cayos de San Felipe National Reserves, Santo Tomás Faunal Refuge, Guanahacabibes Biosphere Reserve; according to O. H. Garrido (*in litt.* 1991), La Belén, Camagüey, is currently a protected area.

Jamaica The species is protected against hunting at all times, but regulations have sometimes been inadequately enforced (King 1978-1979, Vogel *et al.* 1989). The Blue and John Crow Mountains are currently being established as a national park (Varty 1991, N. Varty verbally 1992).

Haiti The species has been reported from La Visite National Park, but its current status there is unknown.

Dominican Republic The species is protected (Stockton de Dod 1981) but illegally hunted (Pérez-Rivera 1990). From the information given under Distribution it occurs or has occurred in the following national parks: Jaragua, Baoruco, Isla Cabritos, the contiguous Armando Bermúdez and José del Carmen Ramírez, Los Haitises and del Este (see Distribution; also the map in Hoppe 1989), and the importance of the proposed extension of the Los Haitises National Park is stressed in Measures Taken under Hispaniolan Hawk *Buteo ridgwayi*.

Puerto Rico The Plain Pigeon is protected by commonwealth law; a recovery team for the species was formed in 1976 and a recovery plan was approved in 1982 (USFWS 1982), but the U.S. Fish and Wildlife Service disbanded the team (Wiley 1985b). In 1989 a new recovery team was named for the Plain Pigeon but it was again disbanded (R. A. Pérez-Rivera *in litt.* 1992). The municipality of Cidra was closed to hunting in 1967 expressly to preserve the Plain Pigeon, and additional areas known to be used by the species were closed to hunting in 1978 (USFWS 1982, Wiley 1985b): the Department of Natural Resources provided surveillance in the Cidra area, but this did not prevent illegal hunting as was shown by the 1982-1983 censuses (USFWS 1982, Pérez-Rivera 1984). Educational campaigns have been conducted in the Cayey area (Pérez-Rivera 1977a). In 1983 the University of Puerto Rico (Humacao Campus) began a research programme on captive propagation for Plain Pigeons; in April 1988 Plain Pigeons bred successfully for the first time in captivity, and as of 1992 there were 116 in captivity (Díaz-Soltero 1988, Pérez-Rivera *et al.* 1988, R. A. Pérez-Rivera *in litt.* 1992). Furthermore, a new aviary has been constructed (under a cooperative agreement between USFWS, the Department of Natural Resources of Puerto Rico and the University of Puerto Rico) to produce at least 60 birds per year in order to enter the release phase of the project (planned to start in August 1992) (R. A. Pérez-Rivera *in litt.* 1992). Although a reintroduction site was selected in the Río Abajo Commonwealth Forest between Utuado and Arecibo (R. A. Pérez-Rivera *in litt.* 1987, Díaz-Soltero 1988) this area has been discarded and instead 10 birds equipped with radio transmitters will be released at Cidra; late in 1993 reintroduction is planned in the Guajataca State Forest (R. A. Pérez-Rivera *in litt.* 1992). In addition a group of professors of the University of Puerto Rico has incorporated a foundation for the conservation of the species (Fundación para la Conservación de la Paloma Sabanera), which is starting an educational campaign in Cidra (in August 1992) and aims to provide funds and logistical support for the captive breeding programme and to acquire critical habitat ($50,000 are already available to buy land to protect the species) (R. A. Pérez-Rivera *in litt.* 1992).

MEASURES PROPOSED Protection of habitat and effective control of widespread illegal hunting throughout the Plain Pigeon's range are the major problems that need to be tackled.

Cuba A survey to clarify and locate the existence of the last populations of the species is long overdue (searches in southern Pinar del Río and in the Esteros de Birama could result in additional populations being discovered: Garrido 1986, O. H. Garrido *in litt.* 1991); the total population size should be ascertained, and further searches in areas where the species was once present (e.g. Guantánamo province) are needed. Current threats to the species must be studied, as must the degree of protection afforded by the existing protected areas; this could be implemented together with work on the Blue-headed Quail-dove *Starnoenas cyanocephala* (at least in areas where both species are present; see relevant account). A captive breeding programme for several columbids (including the Plain Pigeon) is being prepared, this including a cooperative agreement between the Instituto de Sistemática y Ecología (Academia de Ciencias de Cuba) and the University of Puerto Rico (R. A. Pérez-Rivera *in litt.* 1992).

Jamaica Surveys are urgently needed to locate the last important breeding areas for the species and to estimate the total population. An educational campaign for the protection of the species from illegal hunting could be extended to include the Ring-tailed Pigeon *Columba caribaea*, with which there is much overlap in range and habitat requirements (see relevant account).

Haiti Although the species is apparently still locally common (see Population), it is important to conduct fieldwork in order to confirm this and to identify important areas, the population sizes within them, and possible threats; this could well be linked to similar efforts conducted in the Dominican Republic.

Dominican Republic More studies on the species's distribution are needed, and its current status needs clarification, since the most recent reports have suggested a steep decline (see Population). It would be of great value to estimate population sizes within the existing protected areas and to assess whether these are adequately protected.

Puerto Rico The Plain Pigeon would greatly benefit from the implementation of a package of measures: (a) designation of (in legal terms) "Critical habitat" for the species in the municipalities of Cidra and Cayey is long overdue and should urgently be implemented in order to ensure the protection of the habitat while the captive breeding and re-establishment programmes are developed; (b) any development project in the municipalities of Cidra and Cayey should be well vetted in order to avoid damage to the species's critical habitat; (c) illegal shooting of the species should be prevented, for which much more surveillance is needed; (d) more educational campaigns in favour of the species are needed (Wiley 1985b, Pérez-Rivera and Ruiz-Lebrón 1992, P. A. Pérez-Rivera *in litt.* 1992).

REMARKS (1) Although the Plain Pigeon has long been considered a polytypic species (e.g. Peters 1937, Hellmayr and Conover 1942), it is currently not clear whether it should be treated as monotypic (Banks 1986) or polytypic (Pérez-Rivera 1990). (2) There is some confusion of old province names in this record, which appears to fall within that currently called Villa Clara. (3) The species was known to be nesting at McKinley around 1911 (see Todd 1916). (4) There are two adjacent localities bearing the same name at 19°20'N 72°16'W and 19°21'N 72°18'W (DMATC 1973). (5) There are two localities sharing this name, the one chosen here being based on the specimen label data, which specifies 40 miles west of Port-au-Prince. (6) In this same area Christy's (1897) report of the species clearly reflects that it was extremely abundant at the head of Samaná Bay in June, July and August 1895, but Wetmore and Swales (1931) believed that he had confused the Plain Pigeon with the White-headed Pigeon *C. leucocephala*, a species not listed in his account but which they found abundant in that area. (7) Although there are several localities in the Dominican Republic with this name, the specimen (in FMNH) is labelled "Seibo, Magua", so coordinates are those given for the Maguá within the Seibo administration. (8)

Observations of large flocks in Hispaniola (e.g. 40-50 individuals and up to 200 birds: see Distribution) have to be treated with caution, as after the breeding season (i.e. from August to December) Plain Pigeons tend to form large flocks that contain significant proportions of the total population, moving back and forth (see Ecology) over such an area as to create a false impression of their true numerical strength: thus around Cidra, Puerto Rico, hunters are known to have overestimated the population size after sightings of large post-breeding flocks (R. A. Pérez-Rivera *in litt.* 1992). (9) Although the population in Haiti lacks firearms, it is most likely that squabs are taken from nests and adults trapped, since pigeons are an important source of protein; in the Dominican Republic, people have been observed selling doves and pigeons at the roadsides (R. A. Pérez-Rivera *in litt.* 1992).

PERUVIAN PIGEON *Columba oenops* V[9]

The restricted range (chiefly the upper Marañón valley of northern Peru) and restricted habitat (chiefly riparian woodland, under great pressure) conspire to render this already fairly uncommon pigeon vulnerable; it needs to be surveyed and studied.

DISTRIBUTION The Peruvian Pigeon is endemic to a small area of north-central Peru almost entirely within the upper Marañón valley in the departments of Cajamarca and Amazonas, with one record (the first in the following list) from Piura and two (the last) from La Libertad. Records (coordinates from Stephens and Traylor 1983) are from: km 21 on the Olmos–Bagua road, one bird in June 1987 (M. Pearman *in litt.* 1989); San Felipe, 5°46'S 79°19'W, October 1924 (two specimens in AMNH); Perico, near Bellavista, 5°15'S 78°45'W, September 1916 (Bangs and Noble 1918, Hellmayr and Conover 1942) and July/August 1923 (five specimens in AMNH); Bellavista, 5°37'S 78°39'W, 1950s (Dorst 1957a); Hacienda Morerilla, c.5°38'S 78°23'W, April 1955 (Dorst 1957a,b); Bagua, 5°40'S 78°31'W, 1950s (Dorst 1957a); from Abra de Porculla east to 5 km before Jaen on the Olmos–Marañón road, c.5°51'S 79°31'W, 1970s (Krabbe 1979); between Pedro Ruíz and Chachapoyas, 6°10'S 77°54'W, 1970s (Krabbe 1984, from whom coordinates are derived); Hacienda Limón, 6°50'S 78°05'W, October 1933 (Bond 1955; specimen in ANSP); Balsas, 6°50'S 78°01'W, undated (Hellmayr and Conover 1942); Malca, 7°35'S 78°09'W, April 1894 (Salvin 1895, Baron 1897; specimen in AMNH; see Remarks 1); Chagual, 7°50'S 77°38'W, 1,050 m, August 1979 (two specimens in LSUMZ); Viña (= Viñas), Huamachuco, 7°57'S 77°38'W, March 1894 and February/March 1895 (Salvin 1895, Godman 1899).

POPULATION The first judgement of the status of this pigeon was by Bangs and Noble (1918) who, following an expedition within its range in 1916, considered it "apparently rare in northwestern Peru, as only one or two small flocks were seen". Dorst (1957b) judged it uncommon in the "humid forests" of the region. Parker *et al.* (1982) classified it as "fairly common" within its range, but this referred to a relatively small, inaccessible portion of the upper río Marañón around Balsas and in the valley bottom east of Huamachuco (TAP). The species is now quite scarce in the heavily populated northern part of its range, as around Jaen and Bagua (Chica and Grande); at Balsas small groups (3-6) and singles were seen in riparian woods and nearby trees around small ranches in 1975 (TAP).

ECOLOGY The habitat of the Peruvian Pigeon is riparian forest and adjacent (probably seasonally) dry forest on the steep slopes of the upper río Marañón valley (TAP; see Remarks 2). At Balsas, this species was observed primarily in tall trees (especially large willows *Salix humboldtiana* and pepper trees *Schinus molle*) along the riverbanks, the open forest of the slopes above being dominated by a *Ceiba* sp. and a variety of smaller leguminous trees such as *Acacia* and probably *Prosopis* (TAP). Similarly, birds encountered in 1916 "frequented the banks of a deep river valley" (Bangs and Noble 1918). Baron (1897) described Hacienda Malca as having low brushwood and cacti on the hills, and willow and pepperwood in the canyons; presumably, from the two foregoing sentences, the pigeon was found in the trees of the canyon. Elevations for the species include 850 m (at Balsas: Stephens and Traylor 1983), 1,700 m (at Viñas), 1,800 m (at San Felipe), 2,000 m (at Hacienda Limón) and 2,400 m (at Malca) (sources as in Distribution). Little has been recorded about food, save that three of four skins in BMNH are labelled (by O. T. Baron) "Food: coca seeds" (see Remarks 3), or breeding, save that a bird collected in April was juvenile (Dorst 1957b).

THREATS The gradual degradation and loss of riparian and dry forest habitats in the upper Marañón valley must represent a serious threat to a species confined to such a small geographic area (TAP). Whether this species suffers from hunting is not known, but the fact that birds in 1916 were "very shy" (Bangs and Noble 1918) suggests it then did.

MEASURES TAKEN None is known.

MEASURES PROPOSED This species urgently requires a full survey with a careful evaluation of the extent of and threats to its habitat, and any other pressures it may be experiencing, such as hunting. Some of this work could be part of a broader investigation of the status and ecology of the threatened endemic birds of the upper Marañón valley, such as Yellow-faced Parrotlet *Forpus xanthops*, Marvellous Spatuletail *Loddigesia mirabilis* and Grey-winged Inca-finch *Incaspiza ortizi*, the threatened non-endemic Henna-hooded Foliage-gleaner *Hylocryptus erythrocephalus*, Slaty Becard *Pachyramphus spodiurus* and Grey-breasted Flycatcher *Lathrotriccus griseipectus* (see relevant accounts) plus endemics or near-endemics such as Chestnut-backed Thornbird *Phacellodomus dorsalis*, Great Spinetail *Siptornopsis hypochondriacus* (near-threatened), Marañón Spinetail *Synallaxis maranonica*, Marañón Crescent-chest *Melanopareia maranonica*, Marañón Thrush *Turdus maranonicus*, Little Inca-finch *Incaspiza watkinsi*, Buff-bridled Inca-finch *I. laeta* and Buff-bellied Tanager *Thlypopsis inornata* (ICBP 1992, Crosby *et al.* in prep., TAP; see Remarks 4).

REMARKS (1) Salvin (1895) incorrectly wrote Malea for Malca; and while he understood that Baron (1897) intended by "Malca, Cajabamba" to qualify the position of the first by reference to the second, Peters (1937) mistook them for two separate localities for the species. (2) Dorst (1957b) treated the pigeon as a bird of "humid forest", which he characterized as denser, taller and at lower elevations than dry forest in the same region. (3) At Viña, Baron (1897) reported a large pigeon feeding on the ripe seeds of the coca plant, gorging itself to such an extent as to burst its crop when falling from a tree after being shot, but that the crops were always empty in birds shot before 08h00. Given what he recorded on the BMNH labels of the Peruvian Pigeon, it seems likely this was the species intended in this passage. (4) Current insurgency renders the region in question problematic; however, researchers should be poised to conduct biological inventories and investigations as soon as peace is restored.

BLUE-EYED GROUND-DOVE *Columbina cyanopis* E[3]

Although records of this ground-feeding pigeon derive from a very wide area of interior Brazil, it remains extremely rare, possibly as the result of natural factors, although probably (at least now) also owing to massive habitat loss.

DISTRIBUTION The few records of the Blue-eyed Ground-dove come from Goiás, Mato Grosso and São Paulo states in central Brazil. Its listing for Minas Gerais (de Mattos *et al.* 1984) is apparently in error; although the species might conceivably occur in the westernmost parts of that state, it was not found there during an ornithological survey between February and November 1987 (A. Brandt *in litt.* 1987).

Mato Grosso Five specimens were collected (two of them "near the new barracks") at Cuiabá in the period from December 1823 to February 1825 (von Pelzeln 1868-1871). The species was again found near Cuiabá once in the 1980s (D. M. Teixeira *in litt.* 1987). Birds were seen at the Serra das Araras Ecological Station (15°45'S 57°15'W), between Cuiabá and Cáceres, February 1986, although another observer apparently did not find the species there in 1987 (J. M. C. da Silva *in litt.* 1987),

Goiás Two specimens were collected (others were seen) on Fazenda Transvaal "near" Rio Verde (see Remarks) in the valley of the rio Claro, one between March and June 1940 (Pinto 1941, 1945) and the other in October 1941 (Pinto 1945, 1949).

São Paulo A specimen was taken at Itapura, left bank of the rio Paraná, state of São Paulo, in October 1904 (von Ihering and von Ihering 1907, Pinto 1937, 1945).

POPULATION Numbers are not known, though the small number of records and the broad scatter of localities indicate that this bird must be very rare; the total population could prove to be extremely low and restricted. Indeed, it has been considered one of the rarest Brazilian birds (Sick 1965, 1985), perhaps on the road to extinction (Pinto 1937, 1949), having avoided detection by collectors who explored the region of Cuiabá and elsewhere, and who obtained large amounts of zoological material during long stays in the interior (Pinto 1937, 1941, 1949). It has, however, been speculated that the species might often be misidentified, especially under poor conditions (D. M. Teixeira *in litt.* 1987). In the Serra das Araras Ecological Station "a small population" was found during brief observations in 1986 and the possibility of finding the species again in this area was expected to increase with increased survey work (J. M. C. da Silva *in litt.* 1986, 1987).

ECOLOGY The rarity of the Blue-eyed Ground-dove suggests some unknown but presumably natural factor influencing the species in what appears to be (at least until recently) extensive areas of various possible habitats in central Brazil (a similar consideration affects the Cone-billed Tanager *Conothraupis mesoleuca*: see relevant account). It has been recorded from grassland inside cerrado (J. M. C. da Silva *in litt.* 1986), and was once observed also in a rice field after harvest (D. M. Teixeira *in litt.* 1987). The specimens from Goiás were taken in open grassland ("campo descoberto"), and other individuals were seen by the collector, both singly and in pairs, always on the ground like other ground-doves (Pinto 1949). The specimens from Cuiabá were obtained in January, February and December; of these, two males (one from January) were in moult (von Pelzeln 1868-1871).

THREATS None has been positively identified, the reasons for the extraordinary historical scarcity of the species remaining a matter of speculation; however, in the past few decades in particular the grassland habitats of central Brazil have come under unsustainable pressure from agricultural development, which must have seriously compromised the survival of this species (see Threats under Lesser Nothura *Nothura minor*).

MEASURES TAKEN The Blue-eyed Ground-dove is protected under Brazilian law (Bernardes *et al.* 1990). The species has been recorded in the Serra das Araras Ecological Station, which covers 28,000 ha, and might also be expected in Emas National Park (18°45'S 52°45'W in Paynter and Traylor 1991), which covers 132,000 ha (see Redford 1987), the only other protected area within its range.

MEASURES PROPOSED Any general ornithological work in the areas from which the species is known, or where it might be expected (notably Emas National Park, also possibly the Iquê-Juruena Ecological Station: see equivant section under Cone-billed Tanager), should where possible be extended to include searches to locate this species (also the Cone-billed Tanager), to provide information on its ecology, including possible seasonal movements, and to determine its conservation status. Surveys for this species should, however, be integrated into a major scheme of terrestrial reconnaissance and biological survey as adumbrated in the equivalent section under Lesser Nothura. Collection of further specimens should not be countenanced.

REMARKS Fazenda Transvaal (Transwaal) could not be traced by Paynter and Traylor (1991) but was placed in Rio Verde municipality, i.e. near Rio Verde. However, D. F. Stotz (*in litt.* 1988) has pointed out that the farm is c.100 km from the town, and that the municipality should be either Paranaiguara or Cachoeira Alta.

PURPLE-WINGED GROUND-DOVE *Claravis godefrida* E/Ex[4]

Probably a bamboo specialist, this unobtrusive ground-dove has become extremely rare in the forests of south-east Brazil, eastern Paraguay and northern Argentina, and has doubtless suffered from the fragmentation of its habitat and the increasing infrequency of bamboo flowerings. Studies are needed to clarify its needs, if a population can ever be found.

DISTRIBUTION The Purple-winged Ground-dove is endemic to the Atlantic forest region of south-eastern South America, extending from southern Bahia (no records this century) and eastern Minas Gerais south through Espírito Santo to Santa Catarina (no records this century) in Brazil into eastern Paraguay and Misiones, Argentina.

Brazil Records of this species suggest that its centre of distribution lay from eastern Minas Gerais south to São Paulo, but current localities are very few and unpredictable (see Ecology).

Bahia The only records (though at a time when the species was well known to the local people) are from the rio Belmonte (now Jequitinhonha, and including Ilha Cachoeirinha) (whence a specimen in AMNH) and rio Mucuri in the south (Wied 1820-1821, 1833, Pinto 1949), apart from one specimen in BMNH (Salvadori 1893) and one in MNHG from unspecified localities.

Espírito Santo The only records are from Santa Teresa in May 1956 (specimen in MNRJ) and the Augusto Ruschi (Nova Lombardia) Biological Reserve (in Santa Teresa), where a single bird was seen in winter 1986 (C. E. Carvalho *in litt.* 1987).

Minas Gerais Records (north to south) are from Lagoa Santa, where four males were collected in August 1837 (Krabbe undated; also Reinhardt 1870, Pinto 1950a); Fazendinha, Serra do Caparaó, 1,350 m (i.e. adjacent to the present Caparaó National Park), August 1929 (specimen in AMNH); Viçosa, August 1937 (specimen in MZUFV); and São Francisco, 22°36'S 45°18'W, 1,580 m, March 1901 (specimen in AMNH; coordinates from Paynter and Traylor 1991).

Rio de Janeiro Older records are from Cantagalo (Cabanis 1874, von Ihering 1900a); Nova Friburgo (Burmeister, von Ihering 1900a); Luiz d'Almeida, November 1818 (von Pelzeln 1868-1871; see Remarks 1); and rio Macacu (Goeldi 1894). All the twentieth-century records are from two main localities: Teresópolis (see Population), at Socavão, June 1926 (specimen in MNRJ), Fazenda Comari and Boa Fé, February and March 1943 (Davis 1945; also specimen in MZUSP), and Ingá, 1984 (J. B. Nacinovic verbally 1987), all adjacent to the present Serra dos Órgãos National Park, where a bird was seen at 1,400 m in December 1980 and others reported in recent years (Scott and Brooke 1985); and the Itatiaia National Park, 830 m, September 1953, 1,200 m, August 1950, June 1951 (Pinto 1954b), 1978 (Sick and Teixeira 1979), November 1980 at c.1,250 m (TAP, R. S. Ridgely verbally 1987), August 1983 (C. E. Carvalho *in litt.* 1987), and at 2,300 m in January 1989 (R. B. Pineschi verbally 1989; see Ecology). A statement that the species was formerly also in Guanabara (now the municipality of Rio de Janeiro city) (Sick 1985) has not been traced to source.

São Paulo Nineteenth-century records are from Piracicaba (von Ihering 1898), Mato Dentro and Ipanema (von Pelzeln 1868-1871); and Alto da Serra (near Ribeirão Pires: see Pinto 1945), August 1899 (specimen in MZUSP; also Pinto 1964). Other older records are: Victoria (now Botucatu; see Pinto 1945), 570 m, May 1902 (two specimens in AMNH); Serra da Cantareira (north of São Paulo city, now a forest reserve; see Pinto 1945, CONSEMA 1985), October 1937 (specimen in MZUSP; also Pinto 1938, 1964); Vila Carrão, Fazenda Gavião (c.23°32'S 46°37'W in Paynter and Traylor 1991), c.12 km from São Paulo, October 1946 (male in FMNH); and BR2 (now BR116) highway near the divide with Paraná, beyond Registro, April 1959 (specimen in MZUSP). The only recent records are of a pair seen at Boracéia Biological Station in February 1987 (D. F. Stotz *in litt.* 1991) and a single bird near Ubatuba in September 1991 (TAP).

Paraná Apart from secondhand information of its occurrence in the state in 1978 (Sick and Teixeira 1979), the only record seems to be the one from the Guaricana reserve (25°43'S 48°58'W), 500-800 m, where one individual was reportedly seen by P. Scherer Neto in May 1981 (Straube 1990, whence also coordinates). However, the records from Iguazú Falls in Argentina (see below) suggest the likelihood of the species's occurrence across the river in the Brazilian Iguaçu National Park.

Santa Catarina The only record is from Blumenau (von Berlepsch 1873-1874, Pinto 1949, 1964).

Paraguay The species was recorded from the upper rio Paraná twice, at 26°53'S in July 1893 and at 25°43'S on an unstated date (Bertoni 1901).

Argentina Early in this century the species was doubtfully recorded from Misiones (see Navas and Bó 1986), but a specimen was collected there, along arroyo Urugua-í in October 1957 (Navas and Bó 1986), a pair was seen near Wanda in December 1974 and another bird was mist-netted at Iguazu National Park in August 1977 (Olrog 1979, Chebez 1986c).

POPULATION From the evidence of most of the records above, based on the collection or observation of only single or a few individuals at any one time, it would appear that this ground-dove has always been a rare species throughout its range, and that it is now close to extinction. Only Wied (1831-1833) seems to have established evidence of its reasonable abundance in Bahia, since he found local people who knew it well enough to have a name for it and where he himself recorded the basics of its habits (including the fact that outside the breeding season it could be found in small groups and flocks). Goeldi (1894) reported having several times captured the species, which in certain periods seemed to be one of the commonest doves on the hot lowlands around the (Guanabara) bay in Rio de Janeiro. Also from this state comes a secondhand report that the species used to be much commoner in the first decades of this century around Teresópolis, where flocks of 50 to 100 birds occurred in November and December during the flowering of some bamboo species, migrating away at winter's approach; it was claimed that numbers decreased progressively as the town grew and forests became rare, so that the last flocks were reduced to only ten individuals, and the species finally disappeared in the late 1940s (Sick 1972).

Indications of its occurrence in Teresópolis in the mid-1970s (Sick and Teixeira 1979) were interpreted as a reappearance of the species, possibly owing to the bamboo cycle (Sick 1985), but numbers involved in recent records, from Teresópolis and elsewhere, remain very low in all cases. Assumption that such a decline has taken place throughout the species's range led to its inclusion and acceptance in lists of threatened birds (Sick 1972, King 1978-1979, Scott and Brooke 1985), despite suggestions that the species is probably locally common (e.g. D. W. Snow in Scott and Brooke 1985). Although this and other forest ground-doves may be easily overlooked, as stated by Sick (1985), the great scarcity of records tends to indicate genuine rarity. Even during several mass bamboo flowering episodes at Itatiaia during the 1980s the species could not be found (TAP). W. H. Partridge collected only one in the many months and years that he and his co-workers were exploring the arroyo Urugua-í (Navas and Bó 1986). In Iguazú National Park there have been reports in the early 1980s (M. Rumboll *in litt.* 1986), but there may be some confusion involved in such records, since none was seen (or known of by local report) on either side of the river (i.e. also in Iguaçu National Park, Brazil) during visits throughout the period 1977-1990 (TAP), and park guards and other visiting ornithologists appear not to have reported it for at least the past eight years (J. C. Chebez *in litt.* 1992).

ECOLOGY The Purple-winged Ground-dove has been recorded around bamboo in dense forest and forest border (Scott and Brooke 1985, Sick 1985, D. F. Stotz *in litt.* 1988, Straube 1990), or simply in forest edge and adjacent shrubbery (Wied 1831-1833), seemingly preferring hillier, more broken terrain (Chebez 1986c).

From the evidence of these records, bamboo seeds constitute its preferred food, as noticed long ago by local hunters in Rio de Janeiro (Goeldi 1894), and the infrequent and irregular availability of this resource seems to affect the local abundance of the species (King 1978-1979; see Population). It has also been recorded feeding on small seeds on the ground and on papaya and other giant fruits (Wied 1831-1833; hence evidently Burmeister 1856), and on sedge and grass seeds in the campo region of Itatiaia, which had burnt some months before; this after-fire bloom also attracted many Uniform Finches *Haplospiza unicolor*, otherwise a bamboo seed feeder, Grassland Yellow-finch *Sicalis luteola* and the rare (near-threatened) Blackish-blue Seedeater *Amaurospiza moesta*, another bamboo seedeater (R. B. Pineschi verbally 1989; see Remarks 2).

According to Wied (1831-1833), the species occurs in small flocks except during the breeding season, and its nest is placed in a thick, bushy tree. The species arrived in flocks around Teresópolis in November and December to breed, during the fruiting of the bamboos *Guadua angustifolia* and *Chusquea ramosissima* and remained there until the autumn, i.e. presumably March (Chebez 1986c). There are no other breeding data from the wild.

THREATS This and two other bamboo specialists (Temminck's Seedeater *Sporophila falcirostris* and Buffy-throated Seedeater *S. frontalis*: see relevant accounts) seem to be in difficulties even with moderate deforestation, which extends the intervals between major bamboo crops (E. O. Willis *in litt.* 1986). The remaining tracts of lowland and montane forest in south-east Brazil, although extensive enough for many forest species, might now be too fragmented for a specialized feeder such as this, which must be particularly wide-ranging (Scott and Brooke 1985). Although the Purple-winged Ground-dove is now apparently uncommon or infrequent in the cagebird trade and in captivity, and seems always to have been so at least in Brazil (see Remarks 3), the taking of wild birds in any numbers would certainly represent a considerable and possibly unsustainable additional impact.

MEASURES TAKEN The species has been protected by Brazilian law since 1973 (LPG, Bernardes *et al.* 1990), but its occurrence in some parks and reserves along the Serra do Mar in Brazil and at Iguazú National Park in Argentina (probably also in Brazil) is only partially reassuring, since the numbers observed remain so small and the species's needs are so poorly understood.

MEASURES PROPOSED An appeal has been made for a complete ban on the capture of wild birds for the pet trade, as any partial controls would be so open to abuse as to be ineffective (Scott and Brooke 1985). Effective control in already created forest reserves, mainly during periods of bamboo flowering, would almost certainly enhance survival chances of this and other species, but the identification and protection of additional areas where the species occurs seem to be of equal importance. A better understanding of its particular requirements, through further study (mist-netting could prove fruitful), is probably crucial to its long-term conservation; such work might best be started at the most predictable of its current sites, namely Itatiaia National Park in Brazil. Studies could perhaps be combined in a programme on other Atlantic Forest bamboo specialist birds, notably the threatened seedeaters above plus White-bearded Antshrike *Biatas nigropectus* and Fork-tailed Pygmy-tyrant *Hemitriccus furcatus* (see Measures Proposed under the former).

REMARKS (1) This locality, called São Luís de Almeida by Pinto (1964), was untraced by Paynter and Traylor (1991), but must lie in the west of the state near Piraí. (2) Recurrent fires on the high plateaus of Itatiaia seem to be most harmful to adjacent cloud-forest, which is invaded by weeds after burning, while field plants sprout again after some months and the vegetation usually resumes its original facies (R. B. Pineschi verbally 1989). (3) This species used to be frequent in captivity (King 1978-1979), and Naether (1983) reported J. Delacour as saying that 40 years before several hundred were imported into France and other European countries. Goeldi

(1894) mentioned that it appeared commonly at times in Rio de Janeiro market but that it was rarely seen in captivity (possibly most birds were exported from the Rio market at those times).

TOLIMA DOVE *Leptotila conoveri* **V/R**[10]

This pigeon is endemic to the eastern slope of the Central Andes of Colombia, where it has been recorded at only a few localities in one of the most disturbed montane forest areas of this region.

DISTRIBUTION The Tolima Dove is apparently known from just three areas on the eastern slope of the Central Andes in Tolima and Huila departments, Colombia (coordinates are from Paynter and Traylor 1981). (*Tolima*) The bird was originally described from Toche (4°32'N 75°25'W, near Ibagué), on the southern slope of Nevado del Tolima, where specimens (in AMNH, ANSP, FMNH) were taken between 2,075 and 2,255 m during April and May 1942 (also Bond and Meyer de Schauensee 1943), with others (a male and female in IND) between 2,000 and 2,200 m during June 1985. More recently (between 1988 and 1990), birds have been recorded at Juntas (untraced), c.30 km north-north-west of Ibagué; and 7 km east of Tapias at km 27, west of Ibagué (both by P. Kaestner *in litt.* 1992). (*Huila*) Other records of this species come from near the headwaters of the río Magdalena in Huila department, localities being as follows: El Isno (= Isnos, c.1°55'N 76°15'W, 10 km north-east of San Agustín), where three females and a male (in ANSP, FMNH, ICN) were collected at 1,600 m in July 1942; San Agustín (1°53'N 76°16'W), a locality mentioned by Meyer de Schauensee (1948-1952) but which probably refers to birds collected at Isnos; near San Agustín, where two individuals were seen in March 1990 (A. J. Negret *in litt.* 1991); and Belén (1°26'N 76°05'W, 45 km south-west of La Plata), where a male and female (in USNM) were taken at 2,135 m in March and April 1952.

POPULATION Numbers are unknown, but on the evidence above they must be low. Fjeldså and Krabbe (1990) considered the species to be very local, and some searches in the upper Magdalena valley have been unsuccessful in finding the bird (King 1978-1979, also P. Kaestner *in litt.* 1992), although two were recorded near San Agustín in March 1990 (A. J. Negret *in litt.* 1991). Observations by P. Kaestner (*in litt.* 1992) between 1988 and 1990 confirmed that the species survives north and west of Ibagué, Tolima, with birds being seen (flushed from the road) just once near Juntas, and on two (of six) occasions near Tapias.

ECOLOGY Specimens of this bird (see Distribution) come from between 1,600 and 2,255 m, although Hilty and Brown (1986) gave an altitudinal range of between 1,800 and 2,500 m. The Tolima Dove has been recorded from humid forest and bushy forest borders in the subtropical (and possibly the lower limit of the temperate) zone (Hilty and Brown 1986, Fjeldså and Krabbe 1990): at the type-locality, one bird was obtained in forest and the others in second growth. In the vicinity of Ibagué, P. Kaestner (*in litt.* 1992) found the species beside a road at the bottom of a steep valley which was covered in secondary forest and coffee. Birds collected at Belén during March and April were in breeding condition, as were those taken in June at Toche (see Distribution).

THREATS When the type-series was collected, the head of the valley near Toche was heavily forested (Bond and Meyer de Schauensee 1943), but now much of this habitat within the species's known range has been destroyed (Hilty and Brown 1986). However, records from coffee groves and secondary growth suggest that like most members of this genus it may be able to survive in degraded habitat (but see Measures Proposed).

MEASURES TAKEN None of the protected areas along the Central Andes includes localities where the Tolima Dove has been recorded.

MEASURES PROPOSED Surveys need to be undertaken to determine the current range and ecological requirements of this species. In particular, studies are needed on populations that exist in secondary habitats in order to decide whether they are viable, and consequently to assess the true extent and nature of the threats that the species faces. Patches of remaining primary habitat in the foothill areas on the eastern slope of the Central Andes, in both Tolima and Huila, need protected area status to ensure that this and other bird species (see below) are conserved. It may also prove to be of equal importance to focus an education programme on the value of maintaining secondary habitats, to the benefit not only of conservation (of both this species, and perhaps the Yellow-headed Brush-finch *Atlapetes flaviceps*: see below), but also of water quality and erosion control (F. G. Stiles *in litt.* 1992). Obviously, any fieldwork or conservation initiatives should take into account proposals for the Yellow-headed Brush-finch (see relevant account), which is sympatric with the Tolima Dove between Toche and Ibagué, and has also been observed in secondary habitats. Other threatened species known to occur in this area include Yellow-eared Parrot *Ognorhynchus icterotis*, Bicoloured Antpitta *Grallaria rufocinerea* and Red-bellied Grackle *Hypopyrrhus pyrohypogaster* (see relevant accounts). The endemic wax palm *Ceroxylum quindiuense* forests in the vicinity of Toche (between 2,000 and 2,800 m) have recently been the subject of a broad integrated conservation programme developed by Fundación Herencia Verde and ICBP (and supported by CORTOLIMA, the Corporación Autónoma Regional del Tolima), and it is hoped that this will benefit a number of the threatened species mentioned above (M. G. Kelsey and L. M. Renjifo *in litt.* 1991).

OCHRE-BELLIED DOVE *Leptotila ochraceiventris* E[2]

This enigmatic pigeon inhabits deciduous and evergreen moist forests in the tropical and subtropical zones of western Ecuador and north-west Peru, but has occurred in lower montane cloud-forests. All types of forest within its range are threatened with near-total destruction, and the situation is compounded by its poorly understood seasonal displacements.

DISTRIBUTION The Ochre-bellied Dove is known from Manabí, Los Ríos, Guayas, Chimborazo, El Oro and Loja provinces in western Ecuador, and Tumbes and Piura departments in north-west Peru, at elevations ranging from sea level to 1,830 m, but there are additional recent sightings as high as 2,625 m. Eighteen of the existing 19 museum specimens were collected between 1913 and 1931 at 11 localities in six widely scattered areas, although there have recently been a fair number of sight records. Coordinates in the following account are from Stephens and Traylor 1983, Paynter and Traylor 1977, Best 1991, 1992, Williams and Tobias 1991, or read from IGM 1989), with localities arranged north to south as follows:

Ecuador (*Manabí*) Chone, (20 m), 0°41'S 80°06'W (Chapman 1926; specimen in AMNH taken in December 1912); Cerro San Sebastián, 500-700 m, Machalilla National Park, at c.1°35'S 80°40'W (sightings January 1991, and one now in ANSP collected in August 1991: TAP, R. S. Ridgely *in litt.* 1991); (*Los Ríos*) río San Antonio-sur, (100 m), at 1°48'S 79°27'W (Hellmayr and Conover 1942; two specimens in FMNH taken in September 1931); Isla Silva-sur (sea level), near the border with Guayas, at 1°57'S 79°44'W (Hellmayr and Conover 1942; specimen in FMNH); (*Guayas*) Daule, (sea level), at 1°50'S 79°56'W (Chapman 1926; specimen in AMNH taken in April 1913); La Palma, (2-3 m), near the border with Los Ríos, at 1°55'S 79°41'W (Hellmayr and Conover 1942; specimen in FMNH taken in October 1931); Quebrada Canoas, Cerro Blanco reserve, at c.2°09'S 80°03'W (sightings January 1991: TAP); (*Chimborazo*) río Coco, 915 m, at 2°05'S 79°00'W (Chapman 1926); (*El Oro*) Santa Rosa, sea level, at 3°27'S 79°58'W (Chapman 1926; specimen in AMNH taken in July 1921); south of Piñas, 1,100 m, at 3°40'S 79°43'W (two seen in August 1980: Robbins and Ridgely 1990); 9 km by road west of Piñas, 850-900 m, at c.3°40'S 79°45'W (recorded in August 1980 and 1988: P. Greenfield *in litt.* 1989, Robbins and Ridgely 1990); wooded ravine east of Piñas (three birds seen on consecutive days in July 1990: P. K. Donahue *in litt.* 1990); Zaruma, 1,585 and 1,830 m, at 3°41'S 79°37'W (Chapman 1914a, 1926; four specimens in AMNH, one in MCZ, one in BMNH taken in September 1913); (*Loja*) north-east of but near Vicentino, 900 m, at 3°57'S 79°57'W (heard in February 1991: Best 1992); ravines around Quebrada Las Vegas, at c.1,250 m, 3°59'S 79°57'W (several recorded between August and October 1991: Williams and Tobias 1991); along the Vicentino–Alamor road (birds seen drinking on several occasions from August to October 1991: Williams and Tobias 1991); Alamor, 1,385 m, at 4°02'S 80°02'W (Chapman 1926; specimen in AMNH taken in September 1921; also captive bird, said to have been taken just above the town, seen in February 1991: Best 1992); west of Alamor (a small number found in degraded habitat in August and September 1991: Williams and Tobias 1991); Guainche, 975 m, between Alamor and Celica, at 4°07'S 79°59'W (Chapman 1926; specimen in ANSP taken in August 1921); west of Celica, 1,800 m (sighting in August 1989: R. S. Ridgely *in litt.* 1989); small forest patch above Celica (one seen in December 1990: M. Pearman *in litt.* 1991); Catacocha, 1,500-1,700 m, at 4°03'S 79°40'W (heard and seen in March 1991: Best 1992); north of El Empalme, c.4°15'S 79°50'W (one seen between August and October 1991: Williams and Tobias 1991); Quebradas Suquinda and Yaguana, 1,750 m, at 4°18'S 79°49'W and 4°19'S 79°48'W (sightings in September 1989 and July 1990: Best and Clarke 1991, R. Williams *in litt.* 1991); between Utuana and Sozoranga, 1,750-1,800 m, at 4°20'S 79°46'W (heard in February 1991: Krabbe 1991, Best 1992); just above the town of Sozoranga, at 4°20'S 79°47'W (sightings in early 1991: Best 1992); Quebrada Hueco Hondo, 500-1,000 m,

Tambo Negro, at 4°24'S 79°51'W (sightings in September 1989 and heard calling March 1991: Best and Clarke 1991, Best 1992);

Peru (*Tumbes*) Campo Verde, 750 m, at c.3°51'S 80°12'W (sightings in February and March 1986: M. Kessler *in litt.* 1988); Cerro San Carlos, near Campo Verde, c.750 m (small numbers seen in late July 1988: Parker *et al.* ms); (*Piura*) Cerro Chacas, 2,625 m, north of Ayabaca town, at 4°36'S 79°34'W (sighting in late September 1989: Best and Clarke 1991); Palambla, at 5°23'S 79°37'W (Koepcke 1961; two specimens in AMNH collected in September and October 1922, and, like others collected there by H. Watkins, labelled 1,190-1,980 m). A bird seen at Canchaque, c.1,300 m, near Palambla in January 1986 appeared to be this species (M. Kessler *in litt.* 1989, Parker *et al.* ms). This dove now appears to be absent from all lowland areas, mainly owing to habitat destruction (R. S. Ridgely *in litt.* 1989: see Threats).

POPULATION The only place the Ochre-bellied Dove has been reported to be common is at Campo Verde, Peru, where up to 25 were seen in one morning in late February and early March 1986 (M. Kessler *in litt.* 1988). In late July 1988 small numbers (up to six in a morning) were seen at c.750 m on the west slope of Cerro San Carlos, near Campo Verde (Parker *et al.* ms). On Cerro San Sebastián in Machalilla National Park it was seemingly rare in January 1991 (TAP), while a substantial population was found there in August 1991, presumably owing to increased song activity (R. S. Ridgely *in litt.* 1991). At Quebrada Canoas in the Cerro Blanco reserve, at least three males were heard in January 1991 along c.100 m of dense deciduous woodland bordering riparian forest in a deep ravine (TAP). In the Sozoranga region the species was found in deciduous forest perhaps as large as 20 km^2 at Tambo Negro, as well as in smaller patches of subtropical forest in Quebradas Yaguana and Suquinda; it was shy and occurred at low densities, although up to seven individuals were noted at once along a small stream where they gathered to drink at Tambo Negro, and 2-3 birds were found in each of the quebradas at Yaguana and Suquinda, alongside larger numbers of White-tipped Dove *Leptotila verreauxi*, in August and September 1989 (Best and Clarke 1991). Small numbers were recorded at various localities near Alamor in August–October 1991 (Williams and Tobias 1991), one was heard at Vicentino, three at Catacocha, four below Utuana, and three at Tambo Negro, with four seen just above Sozoranga, all in early 1991 (Best 1992). South of Piñas two birds were seen in August 1980, and west of Piñas there have been but two sightings, in August 1988 and April 1989, each of 2-3 individuals (P. Greenfield *in litt.* 1989), but a well-sized population may exist in western Azuay province, where much forest similar to that west of Piñas still remains (see account of El Oro Parakeet *Pyrrhura orcesi*). It was not found at Palambla during a recent thorough survey (Parker *et al.* 1985), but may possibly still be found in less accessible forest nearby (NK), of which some can be seen from the road (T. S. Schulenberg *in litt.* 1988), and the possible recent sighting at Canchaque leaves hope that the species still inhabits that region. Almost all the semi-humid areas in the southern half of lowland western Ecuador are now cultivated (NK), and apart from the recent records in the vicinity of Alamor there are apparently no reports from any of the old localities reported by Chapman (1926), most of which are now totally deforested (Robbins and Ridgely 1990).

ECOLOGY The Ochre-bellied Dove inhabits the undergrowth and floor of both evergreen and deciduous forest, with records from the latter habitat even during the leafless period (June to December: see above), when significant numbers were recorded at Tambo Negro (M. Kessler *in litt.* 1988, Parker *et al.* ms, Robbins and Ridgely 1990, Best and Clarke 1991, Best 1992). Although formerly found down to sea level it now mostly occurs at 500-1,800 m, locally as high as 2,625 m (see below). It may previously have been most numerous in moist forests that once covered large areas in the río Guayas basin and slopes of the coastal cordillera to the north-west, a habitat that has been almost entirely destroyed (Dodson and Gentry 1991; for a description of Ecuadorian moist forest see Dodson *et al.* 1985), but it also occurs in dry deciduous forest, wet lower montane forest, semi-deciduous (subtropical) cloud-forest, and humid cloud-forest (see below). On Cerro San Sebastián, Ecuador, and Cerro San Carlos, Peru, the species was observed in evergreen moist forest with a dense understorey of small trees and woody vines, both important components of this habitat (TAP, Dodson *et al.* 1985). At Campo Verde, Peru, the species occurs in a mixed evergeen forest (Wiedenfeld *et al.* 1985) that may be too humid for the bombaceans *Ceiba trichistandra* and *Cavanillesia platanifolia*, both dominant in the dry forest habitat of adjacent areas where the dove occurs seasonally (M. Kessler *in litt.* 1988, Parker *et al.* ms). In the Sozoranga, Catacocha, Celica and Ayabaca regions the species was found in tall deciduous forest dominated by emergent *C. trichistandra*, as well as more varied, evergreen and semi-deciduous forest patches at higher elevations (TAP); at Tambo Negro, south of Sozoranga, birds were observed in August and September 1989 when the forest was dry and leafless but the understorey still green (Best and Clarke 1991). At Cerro Chacas, Peru, where all forest below 2,000 m has been cleared, it was found in humid cloud-forest at 2,625 m in late September 1989, this representing the only temperate zone record (Best and Clarke 1991, Best 1992). West of Piñas, Robbins and Ridgely (1990) reported it uncommon or rare in wet cloud-forest (1,100 m), with two in August of 1980 and 1988. In late February and early March 1986 at Campo Verde it was not encountered in the nearby drier, lower forest (M. Kessler *in litt.* 1988), while in late July 1988 it was only in the semi-deciduous forest on the west slope of Cerro San Carlos at 750 m (Parker *et al.* ms). Observations outside forest include a group of four feeding in low scrub, adjacent to degraded forest in a ravine just above Sozoranga (Best and Clarke 1991, Best 1992), and in August–September 1991 one bird was seen near El Empalme in *Acacia* scrub adjacent to an area of *C. trichistandra* dominated woodland, and a small number were found in heavily degraded habitat west of Alamor, twice on the edge of maize fields, but otherwise in hedges and small areas of woodland (Williams and Tobias 1991). That the Ochre-bellied Dove may breed in deciduous as well as evergreen forest is suggested by seasonal song activity recorded in both habitats (M. Kessler *in litt.* 1988, Parker *et al.* ms, Robbins and Ridgely 1990, Best and Clarke 1991, Best 1992; see below). The seasonal movements of this enigmatic dove are unclear: at Piñas (very wet evergreen forest), birds have only been found during July and August, despite intensive searching throughout the year (B. J. Best *in litt.* 1992). Seasonal movements are apparent at a number of other sites such as Quebrada Hueco Hondo, Machalilla National Park and the Cerro Blanco reserve, although the species is apparently resident at Quebrada Yaguana, near Sozoranga (C. Clarke *in litt.* 1992). The dove may withdraw from deciduous forest during the driest parts of the dry season (which, however, varies in intensity from year to year) into more humid areas, although they may simply move to the more humid elements within deciduous forest, such as river courses (Best 1992).

The Ochre-bellied Dove is typically wary and difficult to observe, inhabiting the forest floor and undergrowth, often walking quietly on the shaded forest floor beneath low trees and bushes (or scrub) where the leaf-litter is especially thick (TAP, M. Kessler *in litt.* 1988, Parker *et al.* ms, Best and Clarke 1991, Williams and Tobias 1991). On being disturbed, birds typically fly a few metres and perch in the undergrowth (dense tangles of vines or a low branch of a nearby tree), or land back on the ground (TAP, M. Kessler *in litt.* 1988, Best and Clarke 1991, Williams and Tobias 1991). The species is most easily observed during the first half of the day when drinking, which at Tambo Negro during August and September 1989 (the driest part of the dry season) took place at stream beds which still maintained pools or slow trickles of water, and up to seven birds could then be seen together (Best and Clarke 1991). Similarly, in August and September 1991, birds were seen drinking on several occasions in small pools along the sandy Alamor–Vicentino road (Williams and Tobias 1991). At Tambo Negro, in August and September 1989, birds were noted to feed on the marble-sized fruits of a *Trichilia* tree, which they removed with a downward tug (Best and Clarke 1991). Birds apparently call from perches c.2 m above the ground (Robbins and Ridgely 1990, Williams and Tobias 1991).

In the Sozoranga region and Cerro Chacas the Ochre-bellied Dove was never heard in August and September (1989) in sharp contrast to the very vocal White-tipped Dove (B. J. Best and C. Clarke *in litt.* 1989), while it was very vocal in the Sozoranga region in semi-deciduous forest near Utuana in early February and early March (1991), and in deciduous forest at Tambo Negro in early March (1991) after five weeks of rain (Best 1992); however, a bird was heard west of Alamor, Loja, during late August 1991 (Williams and Tobias 1991). Near Piñas, El Oro, the species was heard calling in August, but not in September, February, March or April (P. Greenfield *in litt.* 1989, Robbins and Ridgely 1990, Best 1992, NK), and at Campo Verde it was very vocal in late February and early March (M. Kessler *in litt.* 1988), although none was heard there in July (Parker *et al.* ms). On Cerro San Sebastián there was little singing in the wet season in January, whilst in August 1991, when few other species of bird were breeding, song activity was high and the one specimen collected was in breeding condition (R. S. Ridgely *in litt.* 1991). However, a little further south in the Cerro Blanco reserve, song activity was high in January 1991, and a male was seen displaying before a female (TAP). The specimen from Daule was taken in April and had slightly enlarged gonads (AMNH). The remaining 17 specimens were taken in July–October and in December: three taken in September at Zaruma and one in October from Palambla all had inactive gonads, whilst two September birds from Palambla and Zaruma had them slightly enlarged (specimens in AMNH, ANSP, BMNH, FMNH and MCZ).

THREATS This species is threatened by massive deforestation throughout its small range. Most of its forest habitat below 700 m has disappeared altogether. The landowners of the few small subtropical valleys at Sozoranga, where the species has been noted, have no current desire to cut the trees down, but a change of mind will cause the doves to disappear from the subtropical zone in this region (B. J. Best and C. Clarke *in litt.* 1989). Most places where the dove is found in the Catacocha, Sozoranga and Celica regions, however, will be cleared if conservation action is not taken immediately (NK), and although it occurs in heavily degraded habitat near Alamor, it is unknown if such areas could sustain viable breeding populations (Williams and Tobias 1991). Settlers claiming rights to the land live inside Machalilla National Park, and continue to clear small areas of moist forest for agriculture (TAP). There is little control over human activities within Tumbes National Forest, despite the presence of military authorities who restrict access to the area. The planned re-opening of the main road leading into this forest will no doubt result in increased logging and hunting (TAP).

MEASURES TAKEN The species is known to occur in three protected areas, Machalilla National Park, the Cerro Blanco reserve and Tumbes National Forest (see Grey-backed Hawk *Leucopternis occidentalis* for details).

MEASURES PROPOSED Effective protection of the three reserves where the species is known to occur should be a high priority: aside from Tumbes, Machalilla National Park is perhaps the most important area for this and many other threatened endemics of the region, especially Ochraceous Attila *Attila torridus* (see relevant account). Intensive searches for the species should be undertaken, concentrating on its temporal distribution and assessing its precise ecological requirements. The area 10 km from Sabanilla, Loja, which comprises relatively good deciduous forest, seems ideal for this species and should be checked for its presence (M. B. Robbins *in litt.* 1992; see equivalent sections under Grey-backed Hawk and Saffron Siskin *Carduelis siemiradzkii*). Additional dry/moist forest reserves should be established in south-west Ecuador, especially in the Chilla mountains, El Oro province, the Celica mountains and Tambo Negro, Loja Province, as these areas host a wide range of other threatened bird taxa. All the threatened bird species endemic to lowland south-west Ecuador and north-west Peru should be considered in a conservation action plan for this region, for which see the equivalent section under Grey-backed Hawk.

GRENADA DOVE *Leptotila wellsi* E[1]

This rare dove is confined to Grenada, West Indies, where there is an extremely vulnerable and much reduced population of about 100 individuals that is still threatened by habitat alteration and destruction.

DISTRIBUTION The Grenada Dove, here treated as a full species (following Blockstein and Hardy 1989, and *contra* AOU 1983), is endemic to the island of Grenada, West Indies, where records come from two disjunct areas (see distribution maps and historical records listed in Blockstein 1988, 1991). In the north-east, the species was historically reported from: Green Island (Bond 1956b); near Levera Pond (Blockstein 1988, Johnson 1988); and from "islets just off the coast" (Blockstein 1988), possibly referring to the Levera archipelago. However, most records come from the west coast and the south-west peninsula, the localities involved including: (on the west coast) Halifax Harbour (the lower hillsides, including those along the Salle and Douce rivers: Blockstein 1991); Beausejour estate (Blockstein 1991); Fontenoy (Lawrence 1884); (and on the south-west peninsula) on the golf course between Grand Anse and Saint Georges (Johnson 1988); Mont Tout (Blockstein 1988); Petit Bouc (Blockstein 1988); Mount Hartman estate, whence come the majority of records (Blockstein 1988, 1991: see Remarks); Grand Anse estate (Blockstein 1988); Point Salines (Blockstein 1988); and Glover's Island, where the species was collected in May 1886 (Wells 1886).

POPULATION Until the late 1980s, the status of this species was essentially unknown owing to the paucity of records (e.g. there were no records between 1905 and 1929, and then none again until 1961; see Blockstein 1988). The Grenada Dove has long been considered rare (see Blockstein 1991), although Clark (1905) suggested that it was very numerous on some islets. In 1987, 49 singing males were located in a 500 ha area in the south-east corner of the south-west peninsula (Blockstein 1988). The majority of these birds (80%) were on the hills of the Mount Hartman estate and adjacent government farm, the others being at Petit Bouc, Mont Tout, and Grand Anse estate; the total population was estimated at c.100 individuals (Blockstein 1988). Between December 1989 and January 1990, 25 to 30 singing males were located on the south-west peninsula, with 23 to 28 of them being on the Mount Hartman estate (c.90% were concentrated on 1 km of the main ridge) (Blockstein 1991), and a similar survey in July 1991 finding 24-27 singing males there (B. Rusk *per* D. E. Blockstein *in litt.* 1992). Also during the 1989-1990 survey, 10 males were found at Halifax Harbour, and three at Beausejour estate, giving a total of 38 to 43 singing males and an estimated total population of 75-85 individual birds (Blockstein 1991). The Grenada Dove has not been recorded from the Levera area (including the offshore islands) since the period 1960-1977, and following a thorough search in 1989-1990 it has been suggested that this north-eastern population is now extinct (Blockstein 1991). The overall population of Grenada Doves declined substantially (c.40-50%, allowing for the inclusion of two small groups not located in 1987) between 1987 and 1990, with a loss of individuals at Mount Hartman estate and the virtual disappearance of satellite populations on the south-west peninsula outside Mount Hartman estate (Blockstein 1991). The 10 males at Halifax Harbour constitute an important buffer to the Mount Hartman population (from which they have probably been distinct throughout historical times), although the small (three males in 1989-1990, but just one in 1991) population at Beausejour appears to be doomed (Blockstein 1991, B. Rusk *per* D. E. Blockstein *in litt.* 1992: see Threats).

ECOLOGY The Grenada Dove inhabits lowland (up to c.150 m) dry-scrub woods, including those on abandoned agricultural land (e.g. sugar plantations: Blockstein 1988, 1991). At Mount Hartman estate this secondary vegetation has grown into deciduous thorn-scrub thickets, with a canopy 6-8 m high, and consists mostly of *Acacia* spp., *Bauhinia ungulata*, and *Randia mitis* with occasional emergent trees, especially *Bursera simaruba* (Blockstein 1988), Johnson (1988) adding *Gliricidia* sp., *Pithecellobium* sp., *Tabebuia* sp. and *Tecoma* sp. to a more general list of secondary dry-scrub wood species. Blockstein (1991) noted that areas containing Grenada Doves were characterized by a fairly closed canopy, large areas of bare ground, and a substantial shrub component. The leguminous sapling *Haematoxylum campechianum* was found to be the dominant species in such woods (Blockstein 1991). During surveys in 1987 and 1989-1990, no Grenada Doves were seen outside the forest although some were observed foraging near the edge of clearings (Blockstein 1991). Territorial males sing from branches 1-6 m above the ground, although the species forages exclusively on the ground and is generally a terrestrial bird (Blockstein 1988, 1991). Food is as yet unrecorded, although birds probably take seeds (Blockstein 1991). The breeding season is unclear: males were singing and holding territories during late July 1987 at Mount Hartman estate (Blockstein 1988), and single nests were found there in July 1988 (Blockstein 1991) and July 1991 (B. Rusk *per* D. E. Blockstein *in litt.* 1992). However, during surveys from December 1989 to January 1990, males were found singing and noted to be holding territories: a nest was found (on a palm frond, 4 m above the ground) in January at Halifax Harbour, which by mid-February had a nestling (Blockstein 1991). It is likely that the breeding season is longer on the wetter west coast than in the drier south-west peninsula (the seasonally deciduous south-west shrub woodlands had lost their leaves by mid-January); singing by the doves was very intense throughout December–January on the west coast, but became sporadic in the south-west by late December (Blockstein 1991).

THREATS The Grenada Dove is threatened primarily by habitat destruction, but is probably also affected by a number of other factors. Much of the native vegetation of Grenada has been altered (the vegetation in the dry zone is almost entirely secondary), and of the remaining habitat suitable for the species, over 10% was recently (early 1980s) destroyed for the construction of the Point Salines airport (Blockstein 1988). To add to this, the rest of the south-west peninsula has been fragmented by roads and is rapidly being developed for homes and tourist facilities (Blockstein 1988). Building of luxury homes, especially along ridge-tops, is a serious threat (building on ridge-tops is illegal, but continues unabated), the Grand Anse estate area being a major area of construction (Blockstein 1988).

During much of the past century, areas in the south-west peninsula were cleared for planting or pasture and then abandoned, subsequently growing back into dense thorn-scrub: the government-owned Mount Hartman estate is the prime example, being an abandoned sugarcane plantation that is currently the only large area of undeveloped land (Blockstein 1988). Since the 1970s, land use has become more intensive with more clearing resulting in fewer wooded areas (Blockstein 1988): the lower slopes of the Mount Hartman estate, in July 1987, were being bulldozed for a government-subsidized sugarcane plantation, and by 1989 essentially all of the lowlands at Mount Hartman had been planted in cane (Blockstein 1991). This clearance has had the further effect of pushing subsistence farmers onto lower slopes that had been shrubland in 1987, and of forcing people who cut saplings and brush for charcoal production to cut higher onto the hillside: thus, the habitat quantity and quality have deteriorated (Blockstein 1991). A plan for a new development on Hog Island, which may include a golf course on the adjacent lowlands of Mount Hartman estate, could (if the golf course goes ahead) lead to the dove's extinction (D. E. Blockstein *in litt.* 1992: see Measures Taken).

The virtual disappearance of the satellite populations in the south-west peninsula (outside Mount Hartman) may be due to several factors: some habitat destruction has occurred along Mont Tout, but there appear to have been no major changes since 1987, and it is possible that the decline of this subpopulation is simply due to stochastic events in the population (Blockstein 1991). The small population along the west coast at Halifax Harbour may persist, but the birds at Beausejour appear to be doomed: the three males and two females at Beausejour are in a small patch of habitat (the only piece of second-growth saplings in the area), and clearing for a new housing development was taking place next to this patch in 1990 (Blockstein 1991): only a single bird was located there in 1991 (see Population). Overgrazing and loss of vegetation is apparently responsible for the extinction of this species from the offshore islets (Blockstein 1988). Introduced mongooses *Herpestes auropunctatus* occur in high density on the south-west peninsula, and may at least occasionally prey on Grenada Dove fledglings (Blockstein 1988). It has been suggested (Bond 1956b) that the increasing Violet-eared Dove *Zenaida auriculata* may be outcompeting the Grenada Dove for food, and therefore contributing to its rarity: however, D. E. Blockstein (*in litt.* 1992) found no evidence of sympatry between the two species.

MEASURES TAKEN Initial population and ecological surveys of this species have been undertaken (Blockstein 1988, 1991, D. E. Blockstein *in litt.* 1992), although this needs to be part of a long-term monitoring effort (see below). The Grenada Dove has been given legal protection from hunting and egg collecting, but the threats to the bird from these activities are insignificant (Blockstein 1988). The problem of development is great (see above), and there is currently a moratorium against building on ridge-tops in the south-west peninsula; however, this law is not enforced and as a result building continues unabated (Blockstein 1988, 1991). There are no protected areas within the current distribution of this species (i.e. the west coast and south-west peninsula), although the Levera National Park "protects" the area where doves were present until the 1970s (Blockstein 1991). Although the government has decided to proceed with the development of Hog Island, it has at least temporarily turned down the plan to build the golf course on the Mount Hartman estate, and is apparently "committed to do its best to conserve the bird's habitat" (*Grenadian Voice* 21 December 1991: 3). In October 1991 RARE Center started a one-year educational campaign featuring the Grenada Dove, using the species to highlight concern for all Grenadian wildlife and to increase pride in their one unique (and recently designated national) bird (D. E. Blockstein *in litt.* 1992).

MEASURES PROPOSED Recommendations for the conservation of this species were made by Blockstein (1988) after his initial survey. These proposals had not been implemented by the time he published the results of a second survey (Blockstein 1991), and consequently a restated but refined set of recommendations were made, as follows: (1) designation of the Mount Hartman estate as a national critical conservation area and natural landmark, involving (a) the leasing of wooded ridges to a group such as the Grenada National Trust, (b) prohibition of additional clearing of wooded hillsides and brush at Mount Hartman, (c) authorization of the government forestry department to work in lowland dry forests such as Mount Hartman, including reforestation of trees for charcoal and cattle browse, community forestry and extension work, (d) appointment of a warden to enforce (b); (2) similar designation of the hills around Halifax Harbour as a national critical area; (3) strict enforcement of the moratorium against building on ridge-tops in the south-west peninsula; (4) stationing of a conservation biologist in Grenada to continue research and conduct a public education programme regarding native wildlife, especially endangered species; (5) updating wildlife laws in Grenada; (6) appointment of a government wildlife conservation and management officer; (7) continued census and monitoring of the dove and other bird species; (8) restoration of degraded drylands in and around Levera National Park, with the ultimate aim of restoring populations of Grenada Dove to the area (Blockstein 1991).

REMARKS The records in Bond (1961, 1963) and Schwartz and Klinikowski (1963), from 4 km south of Saint Georges on the road between Grand Anse and Point Salines, presumably refer to birds in the Mount Hartman estate.

BLUE-HEADED QUAIL-DOVE *Starnoenas cyanocephala* I[7]

Once common and widespread on its native Cuba, this ground-haunting pigeon has become extremely rare almost everywhere through the combined effects of hunting and the destruction of its (chiefly lowland) forest habitat.

DISTRIBUTION The Blue-headed Quail-dove (see Remarks 1) is endemic to Cuba including the Isle of Pines (Isla de la Juventud), although it was originally thought to occur in Jamaica and Florida as well (see Remarks 2). Unless otherwise stated, coordinates below are taken from OG (1963a), with records organized by and within provinces from west to east (see Remarks 3), as follows:

Pinar del Río about 20 km before reaching Cabo San Antonio, Península de Guanahacabibes, 1974 (García undated); El Veral, Península de Guanahacabibes, where a pair was observed sometime before 1968 (Garrido and Schwartz 1968); Sierra de los Organos (22°25'N 84°00'W) and Sierra de Güira (22°40'N 83°26'W), currently (Garrido 1986); Pan de Guajaibón (22°48'N 83°22'W) (see Rodríguez and Sánchez 1991); La Güira National Park, north-west to San Diego de los Baños (22°39'N 83°22'W), where a bird was observed in March 1989 (J. F. Clements *in litt.* 1991); Cabaña Los Pinos (inside La Güira National Park), where a bird was observed in November 1987 (A. Mitchell *in litt.* 1991); San Diego de los Baños itself (outside the current park), April 1900 (two specimens in USNM); Palacios (probably Los Palacios, 22°35'N 83°15'W), February 1886, and near Palacios at La Serrana (untraced), February 1933 (six specimens in FMNH); hillside north of Candelaria (22°44'N 82°58'W), October 1955 (specimen in YPM; also Ripley and Watson 1956); Nortey (22°49'N 82°56'W) in the Sierra del Rosario, undated (Garrido 1986), with untraced localities within the province being San Marcos and Sierra Chiquita (see Rodríguez and Sánchez 1991);

Isle of Pines (Isla de la Juventud) Carapachibey (21°27'N 82°56'W) to Guayacanal (21°30'N 82°46'W), around 1965 (Garrido 1986); Caballos Mountains (21°53'N 82°46'W), undated (Bangs and Zappey 1905);

Habana "Havana", February 1886 and March 1892 (four specimens in FMNH); "near Havana", January and March 1929 and April 1936 (three specimens in DMNH, FMNH and YPM); Minas (23°07'N 82°12'W), April 1934 (two specimens in FMNH); Arcos de Canasí (23°07'N 81°47'W), undated (O. H. Garrido *in litt.* 1991); Nueva Paz (22°46'N 81°45'W), undated (O. H. Garrido *in litt.* 1991);

Matanzas Caobí (22°51'N 81°49'W) and El Portugués (22°52'N 81°48'W) (see González and Sánchez 1991); near Bodega, Vieja (untraced, but near Santo Tomás 22°24'N 81°25'W), Península de Zapata, undated (Garrido 1980); near Bemba (now known as Jovellanos, 22°48'N 81°12'W: see, e.g., Mapa de la Isla de Cuba 1900), undated (specimen in AMNH); in the woodlands from Soplillar (22°17'N 81°09'W) south-east to Cayo Ramona (22°09'N 81°02'W), currently (González Alonso *et al.* 1990, Rodríguez and Sánchez 1991, R. García *per* A. Mitchell *in litt.* 1991, Sulley and Sulley 1992), with untraced localities within the province being El Cenote and Nueva Paz (see Rodríguez and Martínez 1991);

Cienfuegos–Sancti Spíritus Pico de San Juan (on the border of the two provinces) by local report (Chapman 1892);

Ciego de Avila Palo Alto (21°36'N 78°59'W), April 1915 and nearby, January 1934 (two specimens in MCZ); Loma de Cunagua (22°06'N 78°27'W), currently (Rodríguez and Sánchez 1991, O. H. Garrido *in litt.* 1991);

Camagüey near Vertientes (21°16'N 78°09'W), March 1926 (four specimens in FMNH, MCZ and USNM); Algarrobo (21°28'N 78°05'W), March and April 1925 (six skins in AMNH, BMNH and MCZ); Sierra de Cubitas (21°41'N 77°55'W), April 1933 (Rutten 1934) and undated (Allen 1962, O. H. Garrido *in litt.* 1991); La Mula (untraced, but near Nuevitas at 21°33'N 77°16'W), April 1925 (two specimens in AMNH and MCZ), with untraced localities including San

Berenito (*sic*), April and March 1924, 1925 and 1934 (specimens in AMNH, BMNH and MCZ), Delisio (*sic*), March 1925 (specimens in MCZ; see Remarks 4), Los Angeles, March 1924 (specimen in MCZ; see Remarks 5);

Granma Cabo Cruz (19°51'N 77°44'W), undated (O. H. Garrido *in litt.* 1991); Las Coloradas (untraced), currently (Rodríguez and Sánchez 1991);

Holguín Holguín, June 1904 (specimen in MCZ), and Santiago (20°53'N 76°09'W), March 1905 (specimen in AMNH);

Santiago de Cuba Pico Turquino (15°59'N 76°50'W), undated (O. H. Garrido *in litt.* 1991); near Paso Estancia (20°24'N 75°58'W), June 1906 (specimen in WFVZ); Baconao (19°54'N 75°28'W), currently (Rodríguez and Sánchez 1991, O. H. Garrido *in litt.* 1991); Pico Cuba (untraced), currently (Rodríguez and Sánchez 1991);

Guantánamo Bayate, 1906 (specimens in AMNH, BMNH, FMNH and MCZ; see Remarks 6); Boca de Jaibo (20°02'N 75°14'W), August 1919 (specimen in USNM); Guantánamo town, 1911, 1912, 1913 and 1926 (specimens in AMNH and USNM); Lajas (20°05'N 75°10'W), June 1916 (specimen in USNM); San Carlos (20°09'N 75°09'W), April 1912; Romilia woods (Romelia = Hector Infante, 20°10'N 75°06'W), January and June 1911, January 1912 and January 1913 (four specimens in AMNH and USNM); Río Seco and nearby (20°12'N 75°04'W), 1908, 1911, 1912 and 1916 (eight specimens in AMNH, CM and USNM).

POPULATION The number of birds collected in the past (at least 105 specimens in the museums listed above), together with comments in the literature (see, e.g., d'Orbigny 1839, Gundlach 1871-1875, Cory 1887, Barbour 1923, Bond 1956b, García undated), testifies to a former abundance and hence a steep decline that was already pointed out by Gundlach (1871-1875; see also Threats). Ripley and Watson (1956) reported finding the Blue-headed Quail-dove rather common on the hillsides north of Candelaria in 1955, and Barbour (1923) found it "very common" in 1915 in the lowlands near Palo Alto, where he shot "a good many", with the "guajiros" having "dozens caged to sell...", adding that in Oriente (see Remarks 7), "the bird is still common where it has not been trapped too hard". Garrido and Schwartz (1968) believed that it was still to be found in numbers in the Península de Guanahacabibes, although they could only observed a pair. It was presumably very rare on the Isle of Pines (Garrido and García Montaña 1975), where the species was first reported by local people to Bangs and Zappey (1905) in the Caballo Mountains (now extirpated: O. H. Garrido *in litt.* 1991) and somewhere on the south coast; a bird was collected in August 1909 (see Todd 1916). In 1965 Garrido (1986) found a few birds in the southern parts of the island, but the species seems now to be extinct there (Rodríguez and Sánchez 1991, O. H. Garrido *in litt.* 1991). At present the Blue-headed Quail-dove is so much rarer and less widespread than formerly that it has for some years been considered in danger of extinction (Allen 1962, Goodwin 1983, Garrido 1986). However, it still appears to occur in reasonable numbers in the forested area between Soplillar and Cayo Ramona (R. García *per* A. Mitchell *in litt.* 1991); in March and April 1987, 13 birds were ringed in the area of Soplillar and Los Sábalos (Rodríguez and Sánchez 1991), and a group of five birds was observed in this same area in January-February 1991 (Sulley and Sulley 1992).

ECOLOGY The Blue-headed Quail-dove mainly inhabits lowland forest undergrowth and occasionally highland forest where suitable open woods are also sometimes to be found; it appears to need thick overhead cover, but with an open and preferably stony forest floor (Gundlach 1871-1875, Barbour 1923, Goodwin 1983, Rodríguez and Sánchez 1991). Generally it is found in pairs (Garrido 1986). It mainly feeds from the ground on seeds, fallen berries and snails; it has also been reported in pea plantations at the time of year when the shells start opening (Goodwin 1983, Rodríguez and Sánchez 1991; also d'Orbigny 1839). It lays one or two eggs in a simple nest low in shrubbery or on bare ground under bushes or among the roots of trees (Bond 1979, García undated, Valdés Miró 1984, Garrido 1986, WFVZ label data), although it has also been said to build its nest with twigs in epiphytic *Tillandsia* (Cabanis 1856, Gundlach 1871-1875). Breeding occurs from April to July (Rodríguez and Sánchez 1991, USNM and WFVZ label data).

THREATS The present scarcity of the Blue-headed Quail-dove is mainly due to human persecution and the destruction of its habitat (Goodwin 1983, Rodríguez and Sánchez 1991). It has been persistently hunted as its flesh was highly appreciated, birds often being trapped alive and sent to markets in both Cuba and Jamaica (Albin 1738, Hayes 1794, d'Orbigny 1839, Gundlach 1871-1875, Cory 1887, Scott 1891-1893, Barbour 1923, Garrido 1986), this still occurring on the Península de Zapata (O. H. Garrido *in litt.* 1991). Such pressure made numbers decline annually, and the price paid for them rose accordingly (Gundlach 1871-1875). Despite Cuba being reported to have the "lowest annual deforestation rate in Latin America" (in Santana 1991), habitat loss, mainly for agricultural land, has forced the Blue-headed Quail-dove to retreat into pockets of habitat (Garrido 1986).

MEASURES TAKEN The species presumably benefits from the following protected areas (as listed in Wright 1988): Península de Guanahacabibes Biosphere Reserve, La Güira, Sierra Maestra and Península de Zapata National Parks, Santo Tomás and Loma de Cunagua Faunal Refuges, and Guaná, Playa Larga, Playa Girón Tourist Natural Areas. The species is protected against hunting although this law is not adequately enforced (see Threats).

MEASURES PROPOSED Intensive studies are needed to clarify the current status of the Blue-headed Quail-dove and to determine whether it occurs in any of the protected areas listed above, a task that should perhaps be combined with similar studies of the Plain Pigeon *Columba inornata* in those areas where the two overlap (see relevant account). Enforcement of existing hunting legislation should be increased, but this would best be done through a campaign of general public education concerning this and other threatened birds endemic to Cuba.

REMARKS (1) The Blue-headed Quail-dove is the sole representative of its genus. (2) The species is now considered to have been introduced unsuccessfully in the Florida Keys, Hawaiian Islands and Jamaica (Long 1981; also AOU 1983). (3) Some localities which were labelled under old province boundaries have now been included within the present political division of provinces (see ICGC 1978). (4) Probably the locality is Delirio, but there are several places with this name in Camagüey (see, e.g., OG 1963a). (5) Los Angeles is a too common a place-name in Camagüey to be traceable. (6) Two localities are called Bayate, one in Santiago de Cuba and the other in Guantánamo. The museum labels do not specify the province, but the larger Bayate (20°20'N 75°22'W) in Guantánamo is almost certainly intended. (7) Oriente was the name of the easternmost province, today split into Granma, Holguín, Santiago de Cuba and Guantánamo (e.g. ICGC 1978).

GLAUCOUS MACAW *Anodorhynchus glaucus* E/Ex[4]

The possibly extinct Glaucous Macaw was formerly fairly widespread but clearly very local in south-central South America in northern Argentina, southern Paraguay, north-eastern Uruguay and Brazil from Paraná state southwards, being mostly found along major rivers where it nested in cliffs; the species is now so rare as to be considered extinct, but claims that the cause of its decline must have been natural are made in ignorance of the impact of human colonization of the river systems where it occurred, since it is clear that gallery forest destruction, disturbance at breeding colonies, direct human exploitation and, perhaps most importantly, agricultural development of palm savannas, were likely to have been major influences.

DISTRIBUTION The Glaucous Macaw (see Remarks 1) appears to be or have been endemic to the middle reaches of the major rivers (Uruguay, Paraná and Paraguay) and adjacent areas and watercourses in south-eastern South America, with most records coming from Corrientes province, Argentina. Considerable difficulty attends the elaboration of records owing to problems in tracing all relevant material, the vagueness of old accounts, the ways they have been mediated by subsequent literature, and some doubts about the identity of the species in question. There have been only two acceptable records this century, one direct (in Uruguay in 1951) and one indirect (based on local reports in Paraná, Brazil, in the early 1960s).

Argentina Firm records are from the north-east of the country in north and central Corrientes province (see Remarks 2), with more circumstantial reports from southern Misiones, eastern Chaco and even possibly Entre Ríos and Santa Fe; there is also a skin in MHNG simply labelled "Frontière du Paraguay, Rep. Argentina". Nores and Yzurieta (1988b) thought the species would also have penetrated eastern Formosa. The evidence that follows is presented roughly from north to south.

Chaco Chebez (1986a) noted that a writer a century before (Fontana 1881) had listed the Glaucous Macaw as a bird of the Chaco, i.e. Chaco province (but also presumably Formosa), without evidence.

Misiones Dabbene (1910) cited a source for the species from the province "on the río Uruguay", and Misiones was subsequently listed as part of the species's range by Pereyra (1943, 1950) and King (1978-1979), regarded as probable by Forshaw (1989), but omitted by Ridgely (1981a); Ridgely (1979) also wrote that "despite its being mentioned as occurring around Iguaçu Falls, there is no present evidence for its doing so, on either the Brazilian or Argentinian side" (the source of such reports is unknown).

Corrientes De Azara (1802-1805) recorded the species personally from between 27 and 29°S, while A. d'Orbigny communicated to Bourjot Saint-Hilaire (1837-1838) that his records were from between 27 and 31°S; however, it would appear (see Remarks 3) that on the Paraná d'Orbigny only found the species as far south as Santa Lucía, which is almost exactly at 29°S. D'Orbigny himself only treated the species incidentally in a general narrative of his travels, the first mention being of a bird collected in July 1827 in the Rincón de San Luís, on the northern arm of the río Batel (d'Orbigny 1835: 168), i.e. in the Batel marshes (28°30'S 58°20'W in OG 1968); this is evidently the source of the record from what Chebez (1986a) called the Rincón Batel or "esteros Batel", and which he considered the southernmost record of the species; the skin may well be the one now preserved in MNHN, labelled simply "Corrientes" (Chebez 1986a; see Remarks 4). Two further specimens from Corrientes collected on 1 August 1854 (in USNM) were evidently taken on the río Riachuelo, just south of Corrientes town (see Remarks 5, 6). Chebez (1986a) indicated that d'Orbigny found the bird near Corrientes town itself, but this was a generalization, not based on a specific record in d'Orbigny (1835) (J. C. Chebez *in litt.* 1992). D'Orbigny (1835: 219-221) himself referred to encountering the species on the westward-flowing stretch of the Paraná, first at Iribucua (see Remarks 7) and immediately afterwards upstream at (and a little upstream from)

Ita-Ibaté ("Itá Ibaté", at 27°26'S 57°20'W, in Paynter 1985), apparently on a south-east-facing cliff on an island in the Paraná (see Remarks 8).

Entre Ríos/Santa Fe The species was reported by local people to de Azara (1802-1805) to extend – apparently on the río Paraná (i.e. the río de la Plata of de Azara's title) – as far south as 33°30'S, which if true would take the range into southern Entre Ríos and, across the river, Santa Fe.

Bolivia Two chicks were reputedly taken from a nest, sometime before 1983 or 1984, between Santa Cruz (Santa Cruz province) and Corumbá (in Brazil on the Bolivian border); for this and other "evidence" concerning Bolivia, see Remarks 9.

Brazil Evidence for the occurrence of the species in Brazil is not primarily based on the authority of skins – except for two very old specimens simply labelled "Brazil" in MCML (Fisher 1982) and MCZ – or of competent ornithologists, but remains highly impressive at least in three instances.

Rio Grande do Sul The naturalist F. Sellow found a blue macaw nesting in holes in rock cliffs at Caçapava do Sul around New Year 1824 (see Stresemann 1948; identity as Glaucous Macaw accepted by Belton 1984-1985, Sick 1985). The species was reported from the east banks of the Uruguay river in the eighteenth century (Sánchez Labrador 1767), and although this might refer equally to present-day Uruguay as to Rio Grande do Sul, it seems most likely to have referred to both.

Santa Catarina Sick *et al.* (1981) concluded that Glaucous Macaw was the subject of a passage in a text by de Saint-Hilaire (1851) in which he reported finding relatively small, blue-green macaws with yellow eye-rings common along part of the coast near Laguna (although not seen in other regions) in 1820: before arriving at Laguna he passed an island actually called Ilha das Araras because it was a resting place for birds of this species. Sick (1985) appeared somewhat more tentative in his view of this record, but the details are at least as convincing as any other early traveller's record (see Remarks 10), even if the locality is somewhat more anomalous.

Paraná A blue-green macaw with yellow at the base of the bill, smaller and rarer than the Green-winged Macaw *Ara chloroptera*, was reported by locals as living on the steep banks of the rio Iguaçu in the south-west of the state at roughly 26°S 52°W, 1961-1964; this equally can only have been Glaucous Macaw (Straube 1988). This evidence gives strength to the unsupported reports from the Iguaçu Falls (see under Argentina). There is in addition the curious testimony of a letter from G. Rossi dalla Riva in southern São Paulo state (Miracatu) in April 1970, who wrote "it seems certain that the [species] nests in a locality not very far from here (a locality that... I prefer not to reveal otherwise local collectionists would immediately send their hunters and trappers)" (Bertagnolio 1981): it is not impossible that the locality in question was in São Paulo state.

Mato Grosso do Sul/Mato Grosso There is a claim for its survival along the Paraguay river north of Corumbá, plus a vague report of captive birds coming from between 15° and 16°30'S 60°W (Silva 1989a; see Remarks 9).

Paraguay Although Paraguay has always figured as part of the range of the Glaucous Macaw, the evidence is surprisingly tenuous, and seemingly based on ten or so skins and two testimonies from the eighteenth century (there is a remote possibility that the birds seen nesting at Ita-Ibaté were on the Paraguayan side of the Paraná: see Remarks 8). Thus Sánchez Labrador (1767) reported the bird rare on the río Paraguay, while de Azara (1802-1805) found the species only as far north as 27°S, i.e. just inside southernmost Paraguay (but mentioned the species from the Paraná and Uruguay rivers, omitting reference to the Paraguay: hence, doubtless, the question mark against the species in the country by von Berlepsch 1887). In addition, there are specimens labelled from Paraguay in MACN (Orfila 1936-1938), apparently two in RMNH (Finsch 1867-1868), two in BMNH, undated but received before 1859 and 1883 respectively, two in ANSP (undated but acquired by the museum in 1846 or soon afterwards: M. B. Robbins *in litt.* 1991), and two in AMNH, both of them London Zoo specimens (1886-1895 and 1898-1912). There is a wholly mysterious reference to "Río Pelotas, Kl.3 (Alto Paraná)" as a locality (Podtiaguin 1941-1945); there is a river of this name indicated (in Beyer 1886) as a small tributary of the upper Paraná (though not in the modern province of Alto Paraná) just south of Salto de Guaíra, i.e. at the easternmost point of the country. Searches in south-east Paraguay in July/August 1977 were fruitless, local people knew nothing of the species, and even dealers in Asunción, who were well aware of the potential value of a specimen, had never been able to obtain one (Ridgely 1981a).

Uruguay Sánchez Labrador (1767), de Azara (1802-1805) and d'Orbigny (in Bourjot Saint-Hilaire 1837-1838) all found the species on the Uruguay river, and although their records could have referred to the present Brazilian section as much as to the Uruguayan, it seems most likely that both were involved; and indeed there is good reason to interpret d'Orbigny's information to mean that he found the species as far south on the Uruguay as 31°S (see Remarks 3), i.e. through Artigas department into Salto. Burmeister (1856), Finsch (1867-1868) and Goeldi (1894) even asserted that its range extended as far south as Montevideo, but without clear evidence (the latter two were doubtless copying the first, whose statements on species distributions are sometimes questionable); Tremoleras (1920) merely listed the species for Uruguay, although he provided more precise localities for species if known. It is wholly improbable that d'Orbigny's longitudinal limit was the cause of the subsequent listing of Artigas as a locality (Steullet and Deautier 1935-1946, SOMA 1935-1942), and the source of this information remains unknown; the species's one-time presence in Artigas has been treated as possible (King 1978-1979), probable (Ridgely 1981a, Forshaw 1989) or certain (Silva 1989a), while Cuello and Gerzenstein (1962) and Gore and Gepp (1978) assumed the bird to be probably (still) a rare or local resident in the north. A sight-record of the species by R. Vaz-Ferreira has come to light only recently (Nores and Yzurieta 1983; hence Chebez 1986a, Silva 1989a), and involved a single bird perched on a fence-post some 10 km south of Bella Unión in north-west Artigas, on the old road to Salto, in March 1951 (not 1950 as in the above references); surveys in this general area, 1952-1955 and 1978-1988, yielded no records, and the precise locality of the 1951 sighting has been altered by eucalyptus plantations (R. Vaz-Ferreira *in litt.* 1991). This record may conceivably have been known to Decoteau (1982), who made the otherwise unsubstantiated claim that "evidence now reveals that this bird could still be around in very small groups in Uruguay". Finally, there was apparently a pair of skins in ZMB from Uruguay (Finsch 1867-1868), a record which seems to have been overlooked (although today only an unlabelled male can be found there: G. Mauersberger *in litt.* 1991).

POPULATION Lack of records of the Glaucous Macaw both in the wild and in captivity for most of this century has led to the near-universal view of its probable extinction, always however accepting a remote chance of its survival (Vielliard 1979, Ridgely 1981a, Sick 1985, Chebez 1986a, Forshaw 1989). Only Silva (1989a) has claimed to have items of evidence that "incontrovertibly prove that it is extant" (see Remarks 9). If it does survive, its numbers must be extremely low (King 1978-1979).

In the second half of the eighteenth century the species was abundant ("muchísimas") on the east bank of the río Uruguay, becoming rare in the woods of the río Paraguay (Sánchez Labrador 1767). That de Azara (1802-1805) found it quite common along the río Paraná (Ridgely 1981a) somewhat exaggerates the record: in fact he merely reported seeing "some pairs" between 27° and 29°S. That d'Orbigny (1835) found it still common along the Paraná near Corrientes in 1827 (as suggested in Sick and Teixeira 1979, Sick 1985, Chebez 1986a) is similarly uncertain – the evidence under Distribution suggests that it grew commoner higher up the Paraná towards Misiones – particularly as it seems highly probable that the Glaucous Macaw was one (and perhaps all) of the "rare birds" obtained in 1854 just south of Corrientes by Page (1859; see Remarks 5), which suggests that its status in the area was then not strong. Indeed, in a much overlooked commentary on the species (reproduced in Remarks 3), d'Orbigny informed Bourjot

Saint-Hilaire (1837-1838) that the birds were not very numerous. De Saint-Hilaire's (1851) record in 1820 from coastal Santa Catarina specified that though the species was common at the one locality it was never seen elsewhere on his (extensive) travels. Overall, the species may have been fairly or at least locally common for perhaps the first third of the nineteenth century, but no museum specimens are known to have been obtained directly from the wild after 1860 (see Remarks 6), and only very small numbers of captive birds apparently came into trade thereafter: three in Amsterdam Zoo, from at least 1862 to at least 1868 (Silva 1989a); several in Hamburg, 1878 (Silva 1989a); "several" in Antwerp Zoo in 1886 (*Proc. Zool. Soc. London* 1886: 320); two in London Zoo (the first stemming from Antwerp Zoo: see *Proc. Zool. Soc. London* 1886: 417) between 1886 and 1912 (these birds originating in Paraguay: see above); one in Berlin Zoo, 1892 (Neunzig 1921, Sick 1985); one in the Jardin d'Acclimatation, Paris, 1895-1905 (Sick and Teixeira 1980, Ridgely 1981a, Forshaw 1989), although Silva (1989a) gave its dates as 1896-1914; somewhere in Denmark, 1900, and the Netherlands, 1928 (Silva 1989a). Tavistock (1926) referred to it as "very seldom imported" (i.e. into Britain), which nevertheless indicates somewhat more than just the two in London Zoo; Smith (1991b) wrote confidently of one in Cambridge, U.K., "more than half a century ago". There was a specimen in Buenos Aires Zoo in 1936 (Orfila 1936-1938), and although it might equally have been a Lear's Macaw *Anodorhynchus leari* (Ridgely 1981a), it was seen by Porter (1938), who said that it had been there for over 20 years and was known to be over 45 years old ("evidently suffering from senile decay"); one was supposedly in the Netherlands in the 1970s (Silva 1989a), one in Sweden then or in the 1980s (J. Cuddy verbally 1992), and another or others in Brazil in the mid-1970s (Silva 1989a), one of these belonging to G. Rossi dalla Riva, apparently from the site he claimed existed near São Paulo, and which died in January 1976 (Bertagnolio 1981), although Low (1986) thought any such specimen could have been *leari*; Low's (1986) own report of a specimen in Australia is regarded with scepticism by Forshaw (1989). Decoteau's (1982) claim of a breeding pair in Europe at the time of his writing is mystifying. Reports of extant birds in a British newspaper (*Mail on Sunday* 2 June 1991 and 29 March 1992) are unsubstantiated.

Because this species became rare before or early in the second half of the last century, its documentation in the literature virtually does not exist. A report in 1895 that the species was very rare in north-east Argentina (see Holmberg 1939) appears to have been repeated in 1959 (Forshaw 1978), with no fresh evidence from the field. Sick and Teixeira (1979) seem to be the first to point out that the species had not been seen anywhere this century (which was an accurate assessment then, only seriously challenged now by the records from Paraná and Uruguay), although Forshaw (1978), in calling it extremely rare, had not then regarded it as extinct except in Brazil. It was evidently the conclusions of Ridgely's (1979, 1981a) field- and deskwork that pushed opinion towards the view that the Glaucous Macaw is probably extinct throughout its range.

ECOLOGY The dependence of the Glaucous Macaw on riverine habitats (including their fringing subtropical forest) is strongly suggested by the consistency with which records (see Distribution) derive from along major rivers. It is possible, of course, that these records reflect true habitat choice less than travellers' dependence on river transport, and certainly it is fair to suggest that the species ranged away from the rivers into the "lightly wooded savannas", like other *Anodorhynchus* species (Ridgely 1981a, Forshaw 1989), a view to which d'Orbigny's (1835) hitherto insufficiently considered record from marshland in the Rincón de San Luís, and de Saint-Hilaire's (1851) from coastal Santa Catarina, lend weight. Nevertheless, d'Orbigny's generalizing notes to Bourjot Saint-Hilaire (1837-1838) referred to the species keeping to the interior of littoral woodland, and Sánchez Labrador (1767) noted its abundance in the forests ("bosques") on the east bank of the Uruguay, so that altogether the fragmented image is one of a species which, like Lear's Macaw (see relevant account), is at least partly constrained by use of traditional nesting and roosting sites in cliffs, and which therefore occurs locally, but then relatively commonly, where such cliffs exist (which, in the region in question, may have meant principally along rivers).

For all this, Olrog (1984; hence presumably also Canevari *et al.* 1991), from undisclosed sources, noted the species as reported from savannas and "bosques de pino de Brasil" (*Araucaria angustifolia* pinewoods), and Chebez (1986a), also from undisclosed sources, as woodland ("parque") or forest or scrub patches surrounded by grassland and marsh or palm-covered zones near steep-banked rivers (in both cases the habitat simply represents the prevalent vegetation types in the region: J. C. Chebez *in litt.* 1992); for "pantanal" as habitat, see Remarks 9. De Saint-Hilaire's (1851) record from Santa Catarina concerned birds gathered on an evidently low island in a river or lagoon close to the sea, with adjacent terrain also low and covered in scrub; it was mid-May, and the island was apparently used for roosting and resting; from context (see Remarks 10) it does not appear that any rock-faces could have been in the vicinity, and the consideration arises that possibly this record refers to wintering immigrants from the interior.

The importance of palms is suggested by Goeldi's (1894) casual and unattributed report that the species feeds on the nuts of tucum and mucujá, which evidently led Sick (1985) to write that it "lived in valleys with palms (tucum, mucujá)" (this is evidently assumption, based on Hyacinth Macaw *Anodorhynchus hyacinthinus*: see Remarks 11). De Azara (1802-1805) merely remarked that its food consisted only of fruits, seeds and dates, while Silva (1989a), in recording that the bird's food is undescribed, said it was believed to be the fruit of *"Atalea"* (i.e. *Scheelea*) *phaletera*. In fact, d'Orbigny informed Bourjot Saint-Hilaire (1837-1838) that its food was the kernel of various types of palm (see Remarks 3). Recent analysis of bill structure and nuts from palms in the region, involving comparisons with Lear's and Hyacinth Macaws, which are both heavily dependent on palm nuts (see relevant accounts), has indicated that, as might be expected, the Glaucous Macaw was adapted to consume palm nuts as its staple, the only palm within its range showing the appropriate size and type of nut being the palmera yatay or chatay *Butia yatay* (C. Yamashita and M. P. Valle *in litt.* 1991), and this perception has provided the clearest explanation for the species's extinction (see Threats). Most interestingly, J. C. Chebez (*in litt.* 1992) has traced a reference (Martin de Moussy 1860) that states that the fruits of the yatay were indeed the basic food of the Glaucous Macaw (see Remarks 12).

The importance of rivers is suggested by records of birds nesting in the river banks: de Azara (1802-1805) noted that they nested in both tree holes and vertical river banks, more frequently in the latter, along both the Paraná and Uruguay; d'Orbigny (1835), on 20 December 1827, observed pairs occupying the "enormous holes that they dug in the cliffs to make their nests", and F. Sellow recorded it nesting (at New Year) in holes in cliffs at Caçapava do Sul (see Stresemann 1948, Belton 1984-1985). That two eggs were laid (Goeldi 1894, Orfila 1936-1938) seems reasonable, but twice a year (Goeldi 1894) does not (see Remarks 11).

THREATS The apparently rapid decline of this species, when there was little habitat destruction or disturbance and when hunting pressure could not have been strong, was regarded as somewhat mysterious by Ridgely (1981a), Sick (1985) and Forshaw (1989), who speculated (or agreed with speculation) that natural phenomena – such as disease or a cold period that reduced its food supply – could have been responsible; Low (1984) even claimed that "man played no part in its extinction". As Ridgely (1981a) pointed out, though little subtropical forest survives in Brazil there is (or was in the late 1970s) much left in south-east Paraguay and north-east Argentina, and even a good deal of gallery forest; moreover, if confinement to gallery forest had made it more vulnerable to hunting, other game species survived in them well enough. However, the fact that in the 1820s the species was still apparently fairly common at least in Argentina (see Distribution, Population) suggests that its decline may have come half a century later than assumed above; moreover, the fact that extensive habitat remains in Paraguay and north-east Argentina, i.e. Misiones, is of no particular significance if, as the evidence mustered under Distribution suggests, the species barely penetrated Paraguay and in Misiones it was only present in the south.

Chebez (1986a) thought that the navigation and settlement of the Paraná and Uruguay rivers probably transformed conditions along them, and this is borne out by (e.g.) various references in d'Orbigny (1835) to the widespread clearance of trees on the shores of the Paraná between

Corrientes town and Misiones, including the cutting of palms (C. Bertonatti *in litt.* 1991). J. C. Chebez (*in litt.* 1992) has added that Corrientes was founded as early as 1588, and has therefore been the focus for man-induced changes in the region for over four centuries. The evidence that the species was dependent on palm nuts (see Ecology) points to the most likely cause of its demise, for, as indicated above, settlement of the major river basins within the species's range was accompanied by the widespread loss of palm groves, either through direct clearance (yatays indicated good soils for agriculture) or through the total suppression of regeneration by the colonists' cattle, which were already an economic mainstay of the region when de Azara was there (C. Yamashita and M. P. Valle *in litt.* 1991, J. C. Chebez *in litt.* 1992).

Chebez (1986a) also thought that the size and appearance of the bird made it a significant target for hunters, and even that the taking of young as pets – a tradition extending back into the eighteenth century – could have been important. Again, d'Orbigny recorded its use as food (see Remarks 3 and 7), and if this was a widespread habit among travellers, merchants and prospective settlers, and if, as indeed seems likely, the Glaucous Macaw was closely associated with riverine cliffs along major navigation routes, it is easy to see how it might have been exploited for food or sport at quite different rates or at least with quite different results from the other game species dwelling in gallery forests; and it would appear consistent with the evidence that the species's major period of decline was only after 1830 and possibly not until 1850.

Obviously any modern trade in eggs, skins or live specimens of the species, if still extant, could be very harmful (Bertagnolio 1981, Silva 1989a). Inquiries made in Argentina over the past 10 years reveal that only one bird-exporter had reliably seen a Glaucous Macaw in captivity, many years before: but even this indicates that the species was indeed in trade at one stage (C. Bertonatti *in litt.* 1991). Rumours of birds in trade in Brazil in 1979 (Sick 1981), presumably refer to the birds Silva (1989a) claimed to be in captivity in the mid-1970s (see Population); Silva (1989a) also reported that four birds were imported into the U.S.A. in the 1980s, and it is very obvious from his account that keen interest in the species exists amongst dealers and aviculturists.

MEASURES TAKEN The Glaucous Macaw is protected under Brazilian law (Bernardes *et al.* 1990) and has been listed on Appendix I of CITES since its inception (King 1978-1979). Silva (1989a) claimed to be keeping secret the exact site of his supposed extant population (see Remarks 9) as an alleged protection against traders and trappers, although he admitted sharing this secret with E. Koopmann and his daughter G. Cáceres, bird dealers from Asunción, Paraguay, at whose home two young Spix's Macaw *Cyanopsitta spixii* were seized in 1987 (see Measures Taken and Remarks 14 in the relevant account).

MEASURES PROPOSED Chebez (1986a) has called for a careful survey of all rivers and gallery forest in Argentina to see if a population cannot be found; this forlorn sentiment may be echoed with respect to northern Uruguay and the remoter regions of southern Brazil from Rio Grande do Sul north through Santa Catarina to Paraná. Remoter marshland areas of northern and western Corrientes where rich stands of palm, particularly the chatay, may still perhaps occur should also be considered for searching. It ought to be possible to revisit some of the old sites for the species, if only to discover if subfossil remains exist (e.g. in the cliffs near Itá Ibaté or at Caçapava do Sul). Meanwhile Silva (1989a) planned to visit the area of Brazil in which he claimed the species survives (see Remarks 9, including the last sentence where a second proposed search is mentioned) to assess numbers there and at a nearby reputed locality, and to set in motion plans for habitat conservation; but whether anything has resulted is not clear. Silva (1989a) has also called for the management of birds said to be in captivity in California so that they begin breeding, although Clubb and Clubb (1991) express scepticism over the existence of any such stock and indeed the value of any such actions.

REMARKS (1) Glaucous and Lear's Macaws are so closely related that they could be treated as races of one species (Forshaw 1989, Smith 1991b), and certainly with Hyacinth Macaw they form a superspecies (Vielliard 1979, Sick and Teixeira 1980). All three – hence the genus *Anodorhynchus* – are now at risk, both Glaucous and Lear's being highly critical.

(2) Faced with the quality of evidence concerning Corrientes (for which see also Remarks 12), it is staggering that Meyer de Schauensee (1966) could blindly follow Olrog (1963, 1979) in asserting that "there is no authentic Argentine record of this bird", and that he could continue to exclude the country from its range (Meyer de Schauensee 1970, 1982).

(3) Bourjot Saint-Hilaire (1837-1838) reported that d'Orbigny "a recontré le Guacamayo bleu depuis le 27° jusqu'au 31° latit. australe, aux bords de l'Uraguay [*sic*], du Parana, et jusqu'à Sainte-Lucie di [*sic*] Corrientes"; since Santa Lucía is on the Paraná, it seems reasonable to deduce that the 31°S refers to the río Uruguay, which conforms well with other evidence presented under the country of the same name. D'Orbigny's neglected notes to Bourjot continue: "Ces individus ne sont pas très-nombreux; ils se tiennent dans l'intérieur des bois du littoral, sont sédentaires, vivent par couples, timides, peu querelleurs; ont le vol lent, droit, prolongé; ne se posent jamais à terre, mais passent de branches en branches; vivent de l'amande du noyau des différents palmiers; nichent dans les falaises des rivières, et ont un cri désagréable... On mange leur chair." Given the great value of this testimony, it is mystifying to find Finsch (1867-1868) describing Bourjot's entire text as "mit grosser Leichtfertigkeit behandelt und gänzlich werthlos" ("put together with great sloppiness and totally worthless"), unless he felt (though he did not say) that it simply referred to the wrong species (see Remarks 8).

(4) A Boucard skin from Corrientes was exhibited in London in 1879 (*Proc. Zool. Soc. London* 1879: 551), which may have been that from MNHN, as both BMNH skins are from Paraguay. The MNHN skin from Corrientes (there is another, from "Buenos Aires") is also labelled "Flamant Corrientes", but it is not clear that a specific locality is thereby intended, and in any case none has been traced on nineteenth century maps of the province (NJC).

(5) The collector of the USNM material was T. J. Page, who provided a general narrative of his explorations at that time in Page (1859): although no dates are attached to his activities between an entry for 4 July and another for September 1854, his account makes it clear that most of this time was occupied with a hunting trip, introduced (p.264) as follows: "Wishing to see the country adjacent to the river during the rainy season, and with the hope of adding something new to our collections, I determined to make a little boat-cruise up the Riachuelo, a small stream that rises in the interior and empties into the Parana nine miles below Corrientes. I was fortunate in obtaining some rare birds..." The species is listed in an appendix of birds as *Anodorhynchus cinereus* (Cassin 1859).

(6) There is a third specimen in USNM, not labelled from Corrientes but, like the other two, tagged as collected during the "Exploration of the Paraná: Capt. T. J. Page"; another hand has pencilled in "March 1860", i.e. six years after the other two, suggesting possibly a different provenance. This is the specimen mentioned by Ridgely (1981a) as the last wild bird collected, and hence the date of 1860 repeatedly crops up as a key date in the species's history, after which it is seen as extremely rare. Regrettably, Page appears to have published nothing on his second exploration of the river. A complete review of Page's material in USNM might allow some reconstruction of his itineraries, though this is doubtful; but it is worth noting that in March 1860 he also collected a specimen of Bearded Tachuri *Polystictus pectoralis* at "Irarana", which seems likely to have been in Chaco or Corrientes (see Remarks 2 under Strange-tailed Tyrant *Yetapa risora*).

(7) Iribucua, though untraced by Paynter (1985), is marked on a map in Parchappe and d'Orbigny (1835) as at approximately 27°20'S 57°50'W, and d'Orbigny (1835: 219) described it as 24 leagues (roughly 120 km) from Corrientes. It is not, however, clear that Glaucous Macaw was collected precisely at this locality. The relevant passage, coming in a section concerning embarcation at Iribucua, reads: "Nous étions réduits à vivre de notre chasse, consistant en canards musqués, en pénélopes et en aras bleus; mais la chair de ces oiseaux est si coriace, que je ne pouvais en manger."

(8) The relevant passage (d'Orbigny 1835: 220) reads: "...nous démarrâmes [from Ita-Ibaté] et fîmes force de rames contre le courant... Une falaise élevée, couverte de bois, était à notre gauche; à droite s'étendait le Parana, qui, lorsque sa rive opposée n'était pas masquée par des côtes, nous offrait presqu'une lieue de largeur; et, au-delà, le territoire du Paraguay. Tout le long de la falaise, on voyait disséminés des couples d'aras d'un bleu glauque, dont les échos des bois répétaient incessamment les cris aigus. Chaque couple se montrait soit sur le bord des énormes trous qu'ils se creusent dans les falaises, afin d'y déposer leur nichée, soit perché sur les branches pendantes des arbres qui couronnent la côte". If the cliff was on the left and they were rowing against the current, the cliff was either on a riverine island or else in Paraguay. It would be barely worth noting that Finsch (1867-1868) considered that these observations referred "without doubt" to Hyacinth Macaws *A. hyacinthinus* (he was, in this, without doubt wrong), were it not for his extraordinary dismissal of everything (including notes by d'Orbigny) written about the Glaucous Macaw by Bourjot (see Remarks 3 above).

(9) Silva (1989a) gave four pieces of evidence that "incontrovertibly" establish the continued existence of the Glaucous Macaw. The first of these, (a), Vaz-Ferreira's 1951 sight-record, can be dismissed merely on the subsequent 40-year time gap (but also on the evidence provided under Distribution for Uruguay concerning subsequent search-efforts in the relevant region). The other three refer to (b) a chick offered for sale, (c) several specimens in trade, and (d) a 1988 sighting by a hired trapper. The chick story (b) derives from an apparent avicultural acquaintance of Silva's who declined the offer of a curiously coloured Hyacinth Macaw chick (taken with its sibling in Bolivia somewhere between Santa Cruz and Corumbá) and then decided it might have been a Glaucous; this is patently unacceptable as hard evidence. The specimens in trade story (c) concerns four Glaucous Macaws supposedly finding their way into California ("vehemently denied, but two knowledgeable sources confirmed that they were indeed *glaucus*"); this, too, is unacceptable until the birds are produced and their identity proven. However, the story's authenticity is assumed to be bolstered by C. Cordier reporting to Silva that, just before this shipment, he had seen Glaucous Macaws in a Bolivian dealer's compound, and that they came from the borderland area of Bolivia and Brazil at 15°-16°30'S 60°W; Silva invoked the authority of J. Delacour to certify Cordier's competence in this matter, although the area indicated by the coordinates is completely different from that where Silva then asserted the species survives, as if this anomaly were of no significance to the overall veracity of his case. The location of the 1988 "sighting" (d) was in the Pantanal on the eastern edge of the Paraguay river, i.e. inside Brazil, and the hired trapper who reported the sighting also reported being told of a cliff site for the species on the western edge of the same river; this trapper was the man who reputedly caught a Glaucous Macaw in the 1970s which went first to Germany and then "reportedly" (the word is Silva's, although later in his account he omitted this qualification) to the Netherlands. All this amounts to is hearsay: the man who saw the chick could have been mistaken; the California shipment could all be an inflated rumour; Cordier's testimony is flimsy; and the trapper's powers of identification might not be quite sufficient.

The story of the sighting (d) differs somewhat from an apparent version of the same in Smith (1991b): while Silva said the trapper had previously caught a specimen in the 1970s, Smith said that up to around April 1988 the trapper had never seen the like of such a bird; and while Silva only agreed to work with the trapper (from the chronology this appears to be shortly before February 1988) so long as none of the birds was caught, Smith reported that the man in question actually caught three in around April that year, although these somehow ended up in the hands of his employer's rival (i.e. cannot be traced). Smith (1991b) also claimed that trappers in Bolivia had encountered the same bird "which was widely scattered"; moreover, Smith (1991b) gave credence to a British newspaper report in June 1991 that the species was being offered for sale in Argentina, and disclosed that a third-hand report by a British peace-worker had identified an area in Bolivia where the species still survives and to which he (Smith) would be travelling in 1991/1992.

(10) De Saint-Hilaire (1851) was travelling from Villa Nova to Laguna, and the relevant passage (p.377) reads: "La première pointe qui se présenta à nous s'appelle Tapiruva... Avant d'y arriver nous passâmes en face d'un îlot inhabité qu'on nomme *Ilha das Araras* (l'île des aras), parce qu'il sert d'asile à une espèce d'aras communs sur cette côte et que je n'avais encore recontrées nulle part. Ces oiseaux, dont le plumage est d'un bleu verdâtre, ont le tour des yeux jaune; le seul que je vis de près me parût plus petit que l'espèce commune. Entre la pointe d'Embituva, que j'avais laissée derrière moi depuis quelques jours, et celle de Tapiruva, le terrain, à une faible distance de la mer, s'élève un peu, et l'on y voit des arbrisseaux d'un vert foncé pressés les uns contre les autres. Après avoir passé derrière la pointe de Tapiruva, nous nous trouvâmes sur une seconde plage... En cet endroit, les sables s'étendent fort loin de la mer, et au délà de cet espace entièrement nu on ne voit qu'une végétation maigre..."

(11) Goeldi's (1894) and Orfila's (1936-1938) stated source for the breeding information is de Azara; but there is nothing confirming these attributions in the relevant pages of de Azara (1802-1805). Goeldi's (1894) source for the dietary information was evidently his own imagination, as he introduced it with the phrase "ao que parece" ("as it seems"): he had presumably read Finsch (1867-1868) on Hyacinth Macaw, who said its chief food was nuts of mucujá *Acrocomia lasiospatha* and tucumá *Astryocaryum tucuma* (this itself being based on Bates 1863: see Remarks 3 under Hyacinth Macaw), and had extrapolated from that; in this regard it is worth noting that Goeldi's rendering of d'Orbigny's experience ("for some time he lived exclusively off the unpalatable meat of this macaw") is completely mistaken (see Remarks 7 above), and thus scarcely enhances the reliability of the dietary information in his account.

(12) After describing macaws that are evidently Green-winged (in Misiones) and Blue-and-yellow *Ara ararauna* (in Paraguay), Martin de Moussy (1860) wrote: "La province de Corrientes possède un autre Ara plus petit, mais à longue queue comme les précédents, qui vit principalement dans les bois de palmiers, où il se nourrit du fruit du Yatai: sa couleur est violette."

HYACINTH MACAW *Anodorhynchus hyacinthinus* V/R[10]

The Hyacinth Macaw has been seriously reduced by massive, illegal trade to an estimated 3,000 birds divided between three main areas of Brazil: the eastern Amazonian region (chiefly Pará), where it lives in várzeas and savannas adjacent to tropical forest; the Gerais of the north-east, where it is a bird of cerrado and palm stands; and the pantanals of Mato Grosso (and marginally western Bolivia and north-eastern Paraguay). In all areas it exploits hard palm fruits and nests in either tree-holes or, in the Gerais, cliffs; strict enforcement of legal bans on trade, and various related action, is needed to save the species in each of its three known main areas, but further surveys should determine whether populations exist elsewhere.

DISTRIBUTION The Hyacinth Macaw is found chiefly in the centre of Brazil, south of the Amazon, but is also recorded from the extreme north-west of Paraguay and eastern Bolivia (see Remarks 1). The report in Niles (1981) of the species being present but "not plentiful" in Guyana is assumed to be an error. A specimen from Argentina is irrelevant (see Remarks 2).

Brazil On the basis of all the evidence available, the species is known from the Tapajós River in Pará east through Maranhão to Piauí and the rio São Francisco in Bahia and Minas Gerais, south through Tocantins and Goiás to Mato Grosso and Mato Grosso do Sul. On the basis of their own and other "recent" evidence, Munn *et al.* (1987, 1989) identified three distinct regions within this range into which the species has now retreated, one in the north focused on the Serra dos Carajás and the Amazon tributaries that drain from and round it, one in the east in the "Gerais" region where four states (Tocantins, Maranhão, Piauí and Bahia) meet, and one in the pantanal region of the south where three countries meet.

Munn *et al.* (1989) thought it "likely that the species originally ranged from just south of the Amazon in Pará to the drainage of the Paraná and Paraguay rivers in Paraguay and southern Brazil", implying full occupation of the intervening lands, as represented on the map in Forshaw (1989), which incorporates almost the entire states of Pará and Mato Grosso in the species's range. In fact, however, the records, both ancient and modern, indicate no occurrence west of the rio Xingu and the rio das Mortes between 4 and 15°S, so that the known range forms a broad arc that only covers the far east and south of Mato Grosso. The barrier that constrains the species in the west is presumably the eastern frontier of continuous Amazonian rainforest (see Ecology), so that in fact many populations, albeit at low density, may yet be found to exist in areas west of the rios Xingu and das Mortes where savannas and other more open formations occur naturally (the record from as far west as Alta Floresta bears this out). Equally, it is possible that the reports of the species from north of the Amazon even into Amazonas state reflect its ability to penetrate along rivers in várzea and into natural patches of savanna.

Amapá In October 1895 the species was common (though reportedly a dry season immigrant) on the rio Cunaní above and below Cunaní town, and at Lago do Tralhoto just to the north of Cunaní, where birds were breeding (Goeldi 1897). These observations (it is not clear if the area has ever been revisited) remain unique for the state (Novaes 1978a), although Vielliard (1979) speculated that the species might be or have been found as far as the frontiers with the Guyanas, and indeed J.-L. Dujardin (verbally 1991) had met hunters from Amapá who report the species there, while Smith (1991c), without indicating his source, casually mentioned his intention to survey a population there that is "less disturbed" than that in the Pantanal.

Amazonas Silva (1989a) referred to "a recent sighting of a group north of Manaus", and J. B. Thomsen (verbally 1991) also has a trapper's report of the species between Manaus and Roraima; until further information these records are best treated as provisional.

Pará Although Meyer de Schauensee (1966, 1982) and Pinto (1978) excluded the north bank of the Amazon from the species's range, a flock of seven near Breves, flying towards Ilha de Marajó on 17 January 1984, and others on 8 January 1984 flying towards north bank of the Amazon somewhere between Almeirim and Prainha, indicate the contrary, at least temporarily (da Silva and Willis 1986). These records give substance to specimen evidence from Monte Alegre on the north bank (Snethlage 1914), although Monte Cussari on the opposite south bank was probably the source of the skin (Novaes 1978a). Silva (1989a) had a dubious report of the species from Ilha de Marajó at the mouth of the Amazon.

Other localities in the state include (west to east, north of 4°S) rio Cuparí (Bates 1863), Tauari (Griscom and Greenway 1941), and Caxiricatuba (i.e. near Belterra: Pinto 1945) (specimen in MZUSP), all on the lower Tapajós; Diamantina, near Santarem, 1880s (Riker and Chapman 1890-1891); Trans-Amazonian Highway, east and west of Altamira (da Silva and Willis 1986), in the east as far as the headwaters of the Curuá-Una (Sick 1985), specifically Prainha on the Curuá-tinga (three specimens in MNRJ); rio Iriri (possibly therefore at Altamira) (specimens in MNRJ and MPEG), and at its confluence with the Xingu, apparently the highest concentration of the species in the state (Silva 1989a), with sight records from 3°39'S 52°22'W in August/September 1986 (Graves and Zusi 1990); Patos (now Nazaré dos Patos just below the Tucuruí Dam), on the Tocantins, and up- but not downriver from there (Wallace 1853a, Bates 1863); the Tucuruí area itself in the mid-1980s (Johns 1986); and along a considerable length (its entire east-north-east course downriver of present-day Pindobal) of the rio Capim (Goeldi 1903); for rio Gurupi see Maranhão. South of 4°S, records (all recent) are from three general areas, the Serra dos Carajás, the Gorotire–Kayapo lands, and an area south of the rio Pau d'Arco near Redenção (Munn *et al.* 1987); the second of these lies on the upper Xingu, an area previously identified, apparently from hearsay, by Wallace (1853a).

Maranhão There is a specimen in ANSP from the rio Gurupi, forming the border with Pará, from 1928. The text and map in Snethlage (1927-1928) indicate records of the species on the Maranhão side of the Parnaíba south of Uruçuí, i.e. roughly from 7°30'S. Reiser (1926) found the species at Barra do Galiota (Galeota) across the Parnaíba from Piauí, somewhat south of 8°S (also a specimen in AMNH). However, Munn *et al.* (1987) mapped in the entire southernmost part of the state, south of Carolina and Balsas, based on recent field reports.

Piauí Reiser (1926) recorded the species regularly in June and July 1903 on the upper Parnaíba, extending from Gilbués north to São Estevão at roughly 8°S (a Lagoa Estevão is at 7°32'S 45°03'W in OG 1963b), an intervening locality being "Xingu, near Santa Maria"; a pair from this river in Piauí are mentioned by Hellmayr (1908) as being in BMNH, but cannot now be found there. Corrente (or Correntes), south of Gilbués, is a further locality (Pinto and de Camargo 1961). Munn *et al.* (1987) mapped the area of extreme south-west Piauí in which all these places lie as the only part of the state from which recent records exist, without reference to that from Picos, on the eastern border of the rio Parnaíba basin, apparently in the 1970s, and evidently the north-easternmost record of all for the species (Vielliard 1979).

Bahia In 1903 Reiser (1926) saw captive birds from the rio Preto in the far north-west; and in 1940 birds were "seen frequently" on the rio Grande, near Barreiras (Aguirre and Aldrighi 1983). Munn *et al.* (1987) included the first area within their "Gerais" centre, and mapped a large area south-west of the second (not therefore covering the rio Grande itself) as one from which the species has now disappeared.

Tocantins Sick (1985) referred to the northern part of Goiás, i.e. what is now Tocantins, in the region of the rio Tocantins, as especially important; yet the evidence seems remarkably tenuous. Stager (1961) observed and collected the species between the Serra Dourada and Peixe, i.e. in the southernmost part of the state, but Munn *et al.* (1987) indicated the population there to be extinct. However, Munn *et al.* (1987) reported the species present in Araguaia National Park, in the northernmost part of Ilha do Bananal (they treated this as the south-easternmost extension of the Amazonian Brazil centre, the only area outside the state of Pará), and they mapped a large area of the north-east of the state, from Filadélfia south through the Chapada das Mangabeiras to Dianópolis (mentioning that the western limits of the species's range in this area include Santa Teresa de Tocantins and Ponte Alta do Tocantins), as part of the "Gerais" centre. However, the centre evidently extends further south into the south-eastern corner of the state, given specimens (in MNRJ) from Taguatinga, rio da Palma and Arraias. It is worth noting that von Spix (1824) recorded the species from "Goyaz province near the community of Santa Maria" ("Provinciae Goyatazes prope pagum St. Mariae"), this presumably being the present-day Santa Maria do Tocantins, lying at the western edge of the "Gerais" centre.

Goiás Older records are from the north-west quarter of the state at Crixás (des Murs 1855, Pinto 1938), Pilar de Goiás (specimen in MZUSP), Uruaçu (Aguirre and Aldrighi 1983) and the lower rio das Almas at Fazenda Formiga (Pinto 1936, 1938); the single area in the state mapped by Munn *et al.* (1987) to indicate modern records covers precisely these four sites, although it is described as "near Mozarlândia". Less specifically the Araguaia at or near Registro do Araguaia was a locality for the species in 1823 (von Pelzeln 1868-1871), with two females collected on the river in June 1906 (Hellmayr 1908), while the Araguaia between Aruanã and Ilha do Bananal was a source of repeated sightings in 1932 (Fleming 1933); indeed, Hellmayr (1908) commented that "the Araguaya seems to be one of the principal hunting-grounds of this beautiful bird".

Mato Grosso The last record under Goiás applies equally to Mato Grosso, since the Araguaia divides the two states; and the species was collected across the river from Dumbá (close to Aruanã), which is on the right (Goiás) bank of the Araguaia (Pinto and de Camargo 1952). In this south-east region of the state there are also records from Garapú, on rio Sete de Setembro (specimen in MPEG); Chavantina (Xavantina) and Pindaíba, both on the rio das Mortes (Pinto and de Camargo 1948, 1952, Sick 1955). All these records were omitted from the map in Munn *et al.* (1987), presumably because none is more recent than 1952, although one from 12°54'S 51°52'W in August–September 1968 (Fry 1970) is also omitted.

A highly significant new record is of a low-density population near Alta Floresta in the central-north of the state, west of the rio Teles Pires, late 1989 (TAP). This extends the range westwards in the state by some 600-700 km, and indicates how lack of ornithological exploration may have seriously biased assessments of the species's status not only in the state but globally. It would appear very likely that populations occur throughout the entire north-western quarter of the state.

In the south of the state, below 15°S, the species evidently occurs patchily across pantanal habitat. Published or specimen localities are extremely scarce, four being Fazenda de Cima and rio (ribeirão) das Flechas (von Pelzeln 1868-1871) (both these being south-west of Cuiabá), Poconé (Forshaw 1989) and Bocaina de Descalvados (or Descalvado) (Naumburg 1930), 8 km and 18 km south, 1931 (Stone and Roberts 1935). Nevertheless, Munn *et al.* (1987) delineated an area encompassing both these sites south-west of Cuiabá in the upper Paraguai basin, and representing 12 sites for recent records. They also mapped as a separate entity the region that straddles the Bolivian border from below San Matías (Bolivia) south to Lagoa Uberaba; and they demarcated the general area of pantanal north-east from Porto Jofre up to and around Rondonópolis as one of unknown possible significance, although one apparently in which no known food-plants grow. However, in July 1988 up to six were present 35 km north of Porto Jofre and seven roosted in palms at Porto Jofre (M. Pearman, S. G. D. Cook *in litt.* 1988).

Mato Grosso do Sul The general area of pantanal delineated for Mato Grosso (see immediately above) by Munn *et al.* (1987) extends south-east from Porto Jofre into the upper Taquari and the rio Coxim – there are 10 specimens from Coxim (in MCZ, MNRJ and MZUSP; also Pinto 1938) despite the reported absence from the central Pantanal of known food-plants. Munn *et al.* (1987) indicated four other semi-discrete areas, (1) astride the Bolivian border north of Corumbá as far as the state border, (2) in the Pantanal do Rio Negro, (3) north of Miranda and (4) in the south-west corner adjacent to Porto Murtinho (whence six specimens in MNRJ and MZUSP taken at Salobra: see Pinto 1945). These account for almost all previous records from the state (including, e.g., Dubs 1983, Ridgely 1983), but there are specimens in FMNH from Piraputanga (OG 1963b gives two adjacent sites, west of Campo Grande), although they were taken in 1926.

Minas Gerais In the nineteenth century the species was reported from Contendas (18°03'S 47°21'W in OG 1963b) (see Pinto 1952), and from the São Francisco basin, notably at the confluence of the rio das Velhas, i.e. near Pirapora (Burmeister 1856). Sick (1985) also mentioned "middle rio São Francisco" but it is assumed this is a repetition of Burmeister. Modern records are from Paracatu, Arinos, Formoso and Buritis in the north-west (M. A. de Andrade *in litt.* 1986), and these seem to have been overlooked by Munn *et al.* (1987).

São Paulo The listing of the species for the extreme western part of the state in the lower rio Tietê, rio Paraná (Pinto 1978), is based on a century-old report in von Ihering (1898) that referred particularly to Itapura (a locality for, among others, Golden-capped Parakeet *Aratinga auricapilla*: see relevant account); however, absence of a specimen led von Ihering (1905a) to reject the species for the state and the record is today regarded as totally unreliable (C. Yamashita *in litt.* 1990).

Bolivia The species occurs in the far east of Santa Cruz, south and south-west of San Matías (Remsen and Ridgely 1980, Ridgely 1981a, 1989), and astride the border with Brazil (Munn *et al.* 1987). A second area bordering Brazil, just north of Corumbá, may hold the species (Munn *et al.* 1987). López (in press) had a second-hand report of up to five birds in Noel Kempff Mercado National Park, which would represent a substantial range extension.

Paraguay Historically, Finsch (1867-1868) referred to the southern limit of the species as being formed by the Paraguayan settlement named Albuquerque, although this has not been traced. The species is apparently now found, at least seasonally, in extreme north-eastern Paraguay, where in August 1977 along the río Apa it was well known to hunters, who said it crosses over at times from adjacent Mato Grosso (Ridgely 1981a). Although in 1987 only one resident pair was reported to be present in the entire country, in the río Apa region (Munn *et al.* 1987), there have been records in the period 1988-1989 from Concepción department (Estancias Centurión, San Luis de la Sierra, Reyes Cué, Mirabeaud and Satí, as far as Loma Porá to the south of San Luis de la Sierra) which suggest a small resident population there (López in press; see Remarks 3). Nores and Yzurieta (1984b) considered it present in Canindeyú department, but the basis for this is not clear. A flock of six birds crossed the río Paraguay into the country at 21°37'S (Puerto María, Alto Paraguay department) on 11 August 1988 (Hayes *et al.* 1990, F. E. Hayes *in litt.* 1991).

POPULATION Munn *et al.* (1989) put a range of between 100,000 and three million for the numbers prior to the advent of Amerindians. However, owing to the species's large but even now patchily known (and perhaps truly patchy) range, an idea of an original population size, say at the beginning of the last century when the Hyacinth Macaw was first described, is unapproachable. A few fragments of qualitative evidence exist, such as that on the Tocantins above Patos it was "very abundant" in 1848 (Wallace 1853a), in one part of Amapá the species was common at the end of the last century (see Distribution), in many parts of Mato Grosso in the 1910s it was abundant (Naumburg 1930), and in the pantanal of the state in 1931 it was frequent, several groups containing from one to eight pairs (Stone and Roberts 1935), while in one area of the Gerais up to 50 were seen apparently feeding on a burnt area in what was considered the richest area for the species in the upper Parnaíba (Reiser 1926), in another (near Gilbués) "hundreds" were startled from a roost in a swamp (Naumburg 1928), and in yet another (Peixe, in central Goiás) in 1956 small flocks of from three to six individuals were seen (Stager 1961). Despite indications of a great decline in numbers and the fragmentation of the species's range wrought by trade since the early 1970s, neither Ridgely (1981a) nor Sick (1985) considered it "truly rare" in the early 1980s. However, in early 1987 the first attempt at a comprehensive review and survey of the species (Munn *et al.* 1987, 1989) estimated the then world population at 3,000 individuals, with a range of 2,500 to 5,000; of the three main known areas for the species, around 750 were judged to survive in Amazonian Brazil (following, amongst other things, a reported 70% decline since 1974 of numbers at Carajás), 1,500 survived in the pantanals (of which some 200 were inside Bolivia and just two inside Paraguay), and 1,000 existed in the Gerais (mostly in Tocantins; only 100 were believed left in Piauí, following the extirpation of the species from around Corrente and Gilbués, where 10-15 years before it was common). There are no figures for Minas Gerais, except that in 1986 26 birds were confiscated that had been trapped in the state (M. A. de

Andrade *in litt.* 1988). Munn *et al.* (1989) argued that each of the three main populations needs to be managed as a separate biological entity whose numbers do not sink below 500. The world's population of captive specimens is now certainly bigger than that in the wild, many thousands being held in zoos and private collections (C. Yamashita *in litt.* 1988).

ECOLOGY As a species of the seasonally drier forests of the eastern Amazon and the drainages south and east of the Amazon basin, but with the ability to exploit different types of food in different parts of its range, the Hyacinth Macaw occurs in habitats with very different topography, vegetation and climate (Munn *et al.* 1989). In the Amazonian part of its range it occupies seasonally moist forest with a broken canopy of brazil-nut trees *Bertholletia excelsa* and an understorey of low trees and bamboo (Munn *et al.* 1987, 1989) and at Tucuruí it was recently found in tall terra firme forest, even foraging within selectively logged areas (Johns 1986), although other evidence is of palm-rich várzea as the preferred habitat there (da Silva and Willis 1986; also Riker and Chapman 1890-1891, Sick 1985). Wallace (1853a), noting its absence from alluvial lowlands, considered that the distribution of the species's food-plants must be influenced by geological factors, and Goeldi (1903) characterized it tentatively as an inhabitant of the upper part of rivers in "Lower Amazonia", particularly in the vicinity of rapids; while it seems always to shun continuous humid forest (Ridgely 1981a), it occurs at its edge and flies over it in search of foraging habitat (Roth 1988c, 1989a). In the south-west pantanals it occupies moist palm groves interspersed with grassy marshes and gallery forests (Munn *et al.* 1987, 1989), and its (virtual) absence west of the río Paraguay is explained by the lack of this combination there (Ridgely 1983). In the Gerais region of north-east Brazil it is a bird of open dry forest in rocky valleys and plateaus (Munn *et al.* 1987, 1989): in the upper reaches of various rivers and their tributaries in this region there are wet areas called "brejos", either with gallery forest or buriti *Mauritia vinifera* palm stands, often in cliff-sided valleys cutting through the plateaus, and the combination of cerrado across the plateaus and in the valleys (where the birds forage), buriti stands (where they loaf and sometimes breed: but see Threats), and cliffs (where they breed), proves ideal (Roth 1988c, 1989a; also Snethlage 1927-1928: 477-478, 510-511, Stager 1961, Sick 1965). In central Goiás in 1934 the species appeared wholly allied to buriti palm stands, the birds coming daily in small groups to tall trunks of burnt specimens to explore and expand cavities in them (Pinto 1936; see also Sick 1955). The roost-site in one instance was buriti palms on a river bank (Reiser 1926), but another study has indicated that the nest-cavity may be used by one of the pair for roosting throughout the year (C. L. Paiva *in litt.* 1989).

Food consists of seeds, nuts, fruits and vegetable matter (Forshaw 1989). Munn *et al.* (1987, 1989) indicated that the Hyacinth Macaw is dependent on about eight species of palm (see Remarks 4, 5), two or three in each of its three known main areas: thus in the Amazonian region it utilizes inajá *Maximiliana regia*, babaçú *Orbignya martiana* and tucuman *Astrocaryum* sp. (reports of its eating brazil nuts being unpersuasive); in the pantanals acuri *Scheelea phalerata* and bocaiúva *Acrocomia* sp. (but also occasionally *Copernicia australis*: Silva 1989a); and in the Gerais piaçava *Attalea funifera* and catolé *Syagrus coronata*, although also occasionally (not as a major food, *contra* Pinto 1936) buriti (also Ribeiro 1920, Aguirre 1958, A. Studer verbally 1987). The endosperm and/or mesocarp of fruits of these species are obtained through the exceptional power of the bill and jaw of this parrot, the largest of its kind in the world (Munn *et al.* 1989). In the Gerais, the two main food-plants have no stem, and birds therefore forage from the ground (Sick 1985, Roth 1989a); they gather on burnt areas, as foraging is then rendered much easier (Reiser 1926, Snethlage 1927-1928, Roth 1989a), and similarly, in the pantanals, flocks come regularly to paddocks and around ranch buildings where cattle congregate, to feed on the palm nuts eaten but not digested by the cattle (Ridgely 1989, Munn *et al.* 1991). There is a report that at Poconé the local population of c.30-40 birds eat oil palm nuts (presumably *Elaeis guineensis*) from the plantations along the roadside (A. Whittaker *in litt.* 1991). Other foods may be taken, though in much smaller proportions: thus while the crop and stomach contents of one specimen collected in Mato Grosso do Sul comprised crushed palm nuts, another taken at the same locality held three fruits (Myrtaceae), possibly *Ficus* sp. (Schubart *et al.* 1965); the species "appreciates coconut palm buds" (Sick 1985); and four birds in flooded terrain were once witnessed eating *Pomacea* snails (Roth 1989a). Birds are presumed to take minerals from exposed clay near rivers (Silva 1989a); and have been seen to take salt from blocks laid out for cattle (C. L. Paiva *in litt.* 1989, Silva 1989a, Clark 1991).

It has been speculated that in the lower Amazon seasonal movements may take place over large distances, possibly related to the phenology of some plants (da Silva and Willis 1986). Certainly in Amapá the species was reported to be a dry season breeding immigrant, absent during certain months (Goeldi 1897). Wallace (1853a) recorded its absence from alluvial lowlands, but in the same account mentioned its presence at "the sea-coast" and "sometimes close up to the banks of the Amazon", which suggests that movements must occur: indeed while Sclater and Salvin (1867), working on Wallace's collection and presumably his notes also, wrote that it is "not found in the Amazons valley proper, and appears to be restricted to the slightly elevated plateau south of the Lower Amazons", Wallace (1853b) himself indicated that the food-plants later identified by Bates (1863; see above) were present throughout the alluvial lowlands. Snethlage (1927-1928) indicated movements into burnt areas of savanna in the Gerais at the end of the dry season, but also only recorded the species after reaching the plateau. Flights between roosting or nesting sites and feeding areas are often over long distances and at great heights (Forshaw 1989). The species is most active in the morning and late afternoon, flying normally in groups of 2-8 to and from its feeding grounds (Roth 1989a); feeding can begin as early as 05h00 (Clark 1991), while high daytime temperatures appear to inhibit foraging activity (da Silva *et al.* 1991).

Throughout its range the Hyacinth Macaw nests in holes in trees, but in the Gerais it also uses holes in cliffs, at one stage in equal proportion to tree holes, although in more recent years, with the destruction of trees to obtain young, almost exclusively in cliffs (Munn *et al.* 1987, 1989, Roth 1989a). The extent to which the cliff holes are excavated by the birds, as claimed by Descourtilz (1854-1856), is unknown. At Carajás the brazil-nut tree provides nest-sites (Munn *et al.* 1987, 1989, Roth 1989a), although elsewhere in Amazonian Brazil the birds' preference for várzea forest is equally for the palms' roosting and nesting sites as for their food (Sick 1985); breeding there appears to occur in the dry season, starting in July (Roth 1989a), while nesting in "miritý [= buriti] palms" was recorded in October, Amapá (Goeldi 1897). In the pantanals the nest-tree is almost always either manduvi *Sterculia striata*, chimbuva *Enterolobium contortisiliquum* or angelim *Torresea cearensis*, the only species that reach sufficient diameter for nesting (Munn *et al.* 1987, 1989, C. L. Paiva *in litt.* 1989). Of 21 nests, 1990-1991, 20 were in *S. striata*, which were commonest in small patches of vegetation dominated by acuri palms, cavity entrances were on average 8 m from the ground, and 67% were in the main trunk (Guedes 1991, Guedes and Harper 1991); of 25 nests at another site in the same period, 23 were in *S. striata*, the other two being in *E. contortisiliquum* and *Andira cuiabensis*, the average distance between active nests was 3.64 km, and density over the 50,000 km^2 ranch was 0.027 nests per km^2 (Munn *et al.* 1991); of six nests at a third site, one was in an isolated tree by the roadside while the others were all inside forest patches (C. L. Paiva *in litt.* 1989). Roth (1989a) reported that buriti palms are also used there, and that breeding is from the end of the dry season in September; C. Yamashita (*in litt.* 1988) found nesting there from late August to January at the beginning of the rainy season (see also Dubs 1983, Clark 1991). In the Gerais large dead or dying buriti palms are or at least were used (Sick 1985, Munn *et al.* 1987, 1989, Roth 1989a); local reports in Piauí of eggs being laid in December (Reiser 1926) are supported by the find of a cliff-nest in that month in 1979, c.100 km from Formosa do Rio Preto (A. Studer verbally 1987), although Roth (1989a) saw a pair acting as if with eggs or young in August, and Snethlage (1927-1928) reported cliff-nests occupied in September–October. In captivity, the incubation period is 27 days (Low 1991d), or 28-30 days, with the fledging period approximately three months (Forshaw 1989). The clutch-size is normally two, sometimes three, and occasionally as many as three fledge from one nest, though usually only one (Roth 1989a). However, possibly only 15-30% of the population, at least in the pantanals, attempt to breed each year: so 50 pairs may produce as few as 10-30 or even 7-25 offspring per year in natural conditions (Munn *et al.* 1987, 1989). Certainly breeding success appears highly variable between years (possibly influenced by success in the preceding year): Smith (1991c) claimed that only one chick per nest is raised (and thought that only three young were likely to fledge from ten nests during an investigation of his own), Munn *et al.* (1991) also considered one young to be the rule (of four nests whose outcome was certain, three failed entirely and one fledged one young, while in three other nests only one young was present), Guedes and Harper (1991) found that of five active nests in early 1991 one fledged two young and the others one each, while Clark (1991) reported obvious success of birds in June 1989, when half the pairs seen had offspring, and of these latter pairs half had one and half had two offspring, whereas in the following year at the same site he saw no evidence of any breeding success at all. Nestling growth may be slowed by the very high temperatures, humidity and insolation that inhibits daytime foraging by parents (da Silva *et al.* 1991). Immatures appear to remain with adults for almost a year (Clark 1991). Sexual maturity is only reached, in captive individuals, at four years (Silva 1989a).

THREATS The Hyacinth Macaw is especially vulnerable to capture, shooting and habitat destruction because it is so noisy, intrinsically fearless, curious, sedentary, predictable, and extremely specialized on only one or two species of palm in each part of its range (Munn *et al.* 1987). Following this generalization, it is important to stress that the cardinal cause of the species's decline is trapping for the cagebird trade, as widely agreed (Ridgely 1981a, Munn *et al.* 1987, 1989, Forshaw 1989, Roth 1989a, Silva 1989a, Smith 1991c).

Trade Quantification of trade figures in the past two decades remains unreliable, owing to the amount of smuggling, routing through non-CITES countries, and internal consumption in South America; nevertheless, Munn *et al.* (1989) noted that while CITES declarations indicate 702 birds imported into the U.S.A. during 1981-1984, quarantine sources show a figure of 1,382, suggesting that CITES declarations may have revealed only a fraction even of the then "legal" trade in the species. At this time each bird was selling for around $2,000 in the U.S.A. (Ridgely 1983), although $5,000-7,000 was the figure given in Inskipp *et al.* (1988) (which see for a breakdown of trade figures in the early 1980s).

To develop some impression of the impact of trapping for trade it is worth taking note of three extraordinary sets of figures provided by aviculturists: first, as an example of the difficulty of keeping young birds alive (a reason why trade in adults, which affects populations much more seriously, prevails), Silva (1989a: 153-154) recorded a Paraguayan dealer receiving 300 unfeathered young in 1972 and losing all but three (a 99% mortality); second, he reported a trapper once working an area for three years, with one assistant, from which he was collecting 200-300 Hyacinth Macaws a month (though clearly only in certain seasons, unless a total catch of 7,200-10,800 is seriously being proposed); third, Smith (1991c) reported a trapper who caught a thousand in one year (1980), who knew of two other teams operating at similar levels, and who suggested a minimum 10,000 were taken from the wild during the 1980s.

Concentration on trapping adult birds, because young survive so poorly (see above), has depleted populations much more rapidly (Munn *et al.* 1987, 1989, Roth 1989a); while in the Gerais young were (nevertheless) taken by felling nest-trees (see above), this could equally have had the effect of removing adults, if no other nest-sites were available in the region. Trapping methods for adults include liming perches at traditional roost-sites and using clap-nets on baited areas, both of which can lead very rapidly to the extermination of a local population, since the species is so extremely site-faithful (Ridgely 1981a, Munn *et al.* 1987, 1989, Roth 1989a, C. Yamashita *in litt.* 1987, 1988).

Transportation and smuggling are obviously well organized, for even birds from the Gerais leave Brazil through Paraguay and Bolivia (P. Roth *in litt.* 1985), chiefly by plane from private airstrips on estates in Mato Grosso do Sul, or via Corumbá, whence either to Santa Cruz in Bolivia (the largest exporting centre in that country) or down the Paraguay River to Asunción or Concepción, and thence abroad (Ridgely 1981a, 1983, J. V. Remsen *in litt.* 1986, Munn *et al.*

1987, 1989): of the 1,113 birds that entered the U.S.A. between 1975 and 1982, 1,089 were exported from Bolivia, 16 from Paraguay and only two from Brazil (Nores and Yzurieta 1984b). Listing on Appendix I of CITES (see Measures Taken) in 1987 appears only to have enhanced the rarity value of the species and fuelled the illegal market, for from August 1987 to November 1988 no fewer than 700 birds are known to have been trapped and traded (Munn *et al.* 1989). The internal market for the species in Brazil and adjacent countries is unknown but probably large; it appears sporadically in the illegal market in Rio de Janeiro in lots of up to four birds (C. E. Carvalho *in litt.* 1987).

Other threats: Amazonian Brazil The increased commercial sale of feather art by the Kayapo Indians of Gorotire (up to 10 Hyacinth Macaws are needed to make a single headdress) is of concern (Munn *et al.* 1987, 1989); meat-hunting by recent settlers also exists, e.g. along the Trans-Amazonian Highway (Munn *et al.* 1987, 1989; also Sick 1985), although Wallace's (1853a) evidence from the Tocantins indicates that this has been a chronic problem ("at almost every house feathers were on the ground, showing that this splendid bird is often shot for food"); habitat loss to hydroelectric power schemes on the rios Tocantins and Xingu has been significant (A. D. Johns *in litt.* 1986); habitat modification through human encroachment embraces the entire length of the rio Capim, according to the map in Wetterburg *et al.* (1981); and perhaps the current conversion of the region to cattle-ranching may yet prove the most irreversibly damaging influence (Munn *et al.* 1989).

Other threats: the pantanals Apart from trapping, the only real threat in this region is lack of nest-sites: although food-trees are left standing (they also provide food for cattle), nest-trees are cleared for the sake of cattle, sometimes because the cavities play host to vampire bats, sometimes because high-ground (i.e. dry) forest is cleared for wet-season pasture (Munn *et al.* 1987, 1989, 1991, da Silva *et al.* 1991); indeed, the most favoured nest-tree, manduvi, is characteristic of fertile soils, and hence many are lost to make way for pastures (Guedes 1991). However, in addition, Sick (1985) reported that the Hyacinth Macaw is killed in the region because eating bocaiúva buds makes the palm, which furnishes good wood for fence posts, die, and because it is accused of scaring away the cattle; and C. L. Paiva *in litt.* (1989) recorded poor regeneration of *Scheelea* food-trees owing to cattle-grazing, and serious competition for nest-cavities from African bees *Apis mellifera* (although some nests seem to enjoy or endure an association with these bees, without harm: Guedes 1990). Loss of eggs or chicks in nests was thought attributable to cold (if rain entered the cavity), predators (possibly coatis) or, most probably, moquitoes (Smith 1991c). Birds have been seen defending nests against Red-and-green Macaws *Ara chloroptera* (Guedes and Harper 1991).

Other threats: the Gerais In 1903 the species was little trapped but hunted for its feathers and meat (Reiser 1926). However, subsequent human movement into the region has led to an intensification of agriculture, as most of the cerrado, its preferred feeding habitat, makes very fertile farmland (Roth 1989a; also P. T. Z. Antas *in litt.* 1986); moreover, meat-hunting continues as the area is so poor that bush-meat of any kind is sought for its protein value (Munn *et al.* 1987, 1989).

MEASURES TAKEN The species is protected under Brazilian law (Bernardes *et al.* 1990), has been listed on Appendix I of CITES since 1987 (but see Threats) and is banned from export in all countries of origin (Inskipp *et al.* 1988, Munn *et al.* 1989). Singapore's accession to CITES is regarded as a major step towards closing down illegal trade in the species (Low 1991d). The Hyacinth Macaw occurs in only a few Brazilian national parks and reserves, e.g. the Cara-Cara Reserve (now the Pantanal National Park) in Mato Grosso and the Araguaia National Park in Goiás, neither of which are entirely secure (Ridgely 1981a); but only a small, low-density population exists in the latter, and only a few individuals if any exist in the extreme north of the former, the nearest area with a reasonable population of the species being 30 km north of its northern limit (C. Yamashita *in litt.* 1986, 1987). The ranch-owners in the pantanals have become sensitized to the problem, and many no longer allow trappers on their properties; similar attitudes are developing in the Gerais (Munn *et al.* 1989). At Poconé the owners of many local fazendas protect the birds despite their use of oil palms (see Ecology) (A. Whittaker *in litt.* 1991).

MEASURES PROPOSED Munn *et al.* (1987) called for a package of six measures of which (1), moving the species to Appendix I of CITES, was almost immediately implemented; the others were (2) to list the species as Endangered under the U.S. Endangered Species Act, for further protection in the U.S.A.; (3) to encourage a "media blitz" in Brazil against keeping the species and buying illegal birds, and in favour of stiffer penalties for law-breakers; (4) to break the network of smugglers in Brazil and adjacent countries through arrest and prosecution of key individuals, and an overall increase in IBAMA's enforcement competence and strength; (5) to create Bolivian and Paraguayan trade management authorities under presidential control (the former located in Santa Cruz); (6) to manage and replant the species's food-trees, erect nest-boxes as an experiment, and consider captive-breeding programmes at one site in the Pantanal and another in the Gerais. In respect of this last, however, the aviculturist Smith (1991c) remarked that "it is highly improbable that such a specialised feeder could ever be re-established as a wild bird from captive stock in which case aviary stock is absolutely irrelevant for the survival of this species". This may be valid, except that it takes no account of captive breeding's potential in supplying the market; the species used to be rare in captivity and very little bred (see Low 1972 for early successes) but it has in the past few years begun to be bred by a number of people (see Low 1991d) and with considerable sophistication (see Abramson 1991), so that a studbook now exists (Clubb and Clubb 1991). Meanwhile, Munn *et al.* (1989) have called for stricter international enforcement of the ban on trade in the species, and strong international pressure on those countries permitting the smuggling out or importation of birds. In the pantanals, the species could survive in good numbers if ranch-owners would leave standing all large actual and potential nest-trees and eliminate all trapping on their properties; and with the erection of nest-boxes, the fencing off of certain saplings and the planting of others, its long-term prospects would be further improved (da Silva *et al.* 1991).

Further important action must be to investigate the status of the species in areas not apparently addressed in the survey by Munn *et al.* (1987, 1989), for example (1) in the precise region of Amapá where it was common in the 1890s, (2) the middle reaches of the rio Capim in Pará, if not too seriously damaged since the 1890s, (3) the area of southern Piauí east of the main Gerais region as far as Picos, where birds were seen in the recent past, (4) north-western Minas Gerais where populations are scattered over a considerable area from the evidence under Distribution, but whose status is poorly known (M. A. de Andrade *in litt.* 1988), (5) the extensive region of south-eastern Mato Grosso from which rather old records derive but which appears to have been neglected ever since. Indeed, the entire question of the species's status and distribution at the vaguely perceived western edge of its range needs to be addressed by a vigorous combination of fieldwork (including plane flights) and the study of existing and currently planned vegetation and forest-cover maps (including those from satellite images). Following from this is the question of whether existing protected areas that hold the species can be supported, or whether they should be extended or even (for example in north-east Tocantins) created. Munn *et al.* (1989) also urged further studies of breeding biology in relation to such factors as nest-site shortage (with the erection of nest-boxes if the results indicate the need), and such studies are now beginning: hence Guedes and Harper (1991), Munn *et al.* (1991), da Silva *et al.* (1991), these last in turn calling for radio-telemetry studies to determine whether food shortages are causing problems. Munn *et al.* (1989) also called for the prevention of meat-hunting in the Gerais by improving local people's diet, and the prohibition of the sale of Indian feather art (although their traditional use of feathers should remain unchallenged).

REMARKS (1) Griscom and Greenway (1941) recognized subspecific difference between birds from Mato Grosso (race *maximiliani*) and the Lower Amazon. (2) A specimen (in MACN) was collected at 1,000 m on the río Caraparí in Orán department, Salta, in July 1930 (J. R. Navas *in* *litt.* 1991); the río Caraparí lies at around 22°08'S 63°43'W, rising in extreme north-central Salta and flowing north-west almost to the Bolivian border, where it meets another branch flowing south from Tarija and thus forms the Quebrada Macueta (Paynter 1985). This astonishing record must represent an escape, a straying bird or most likely a mislabelling. (3) Estancia Centurión is the source of a record of the near-threatened Bearded Tachuri *Polystictus pectoralis*, May 1989 (F. E. Hayes *in litt.* 1991), a piece of evidence that underscores the biological value of the site (see Remarks 4 under White-winged Nightjar *Caprimulgus candicans*). (4) Palm nomenclature in various accounts reflects the unresolved taxonomy of the group: the *Attalea* was identified by Reiser (1926) as *A. compta*; the *Acrocomia* by Aguirre (1958) and C. Yamashita (*in litt.* 1988) as *A. sclerocarpa*, by Bates (1863) and Finsch (1867-1868) as *A. lasiospatha* (local name "mucujá"), by Hohenstein (1987) as *A. totai* and by C. L. Paiva (*in litt.* 1989) as *A. mokayayba*; the *Astrocaryum* by Bates (1863) and Finsch (1867-1868) as "*Astryocaryum*" *tucuma* (local name "tucumá"); and the *Syagrus* by Forshaw (1989) as *S. commosa*; moreover, Munn *et al.* (1987, 1989) referred to *Astrocaryum* as *Astocaryum* and *Atrocaryum* respectively, and various authors spell *Attalea Atalea*. Worse yet, *Scheelea phalerata* is sometimes placed in the genus *Attalea*, and the specific name *phalerata* is sometimes also given to *Orbignya martiana* (latter in Munn *et al.* 1987, former in Munn *et al.* 1989, Silva 1989a); finally, Munn *et al.* (1989) refer to acuri as "bacurí", while buriti is sometimes "miriti". (5) Bates (1863) recorded the species's use of *Astrocaryum* (tucumá) on the Tapajós, and of *Acrocomia* (mucujá) on the Tocantins; in the former case, all six of the specimens he collected had been eating the fruit, and in the latter, he made it clear that this was the most favoured of "several palms". It is curious that no-one else mentions *Acrocomia* as a food-plant in Amazonian Brazil.

LEAR'S MACAW *Anodorhynchus leari* E[1]

By the time the home of this blue macaw was finally traced in 1978 it numbered only some 60 birds in the wild, restricted to two cliff-nesting colonies in the Raso da Catarina in north-eastern Bahia, Brazil, where without considerable intervention it faces extinction in the fairly near term from the destruction and disturbance of its feeding habitat (licuri palm stands) compounded by hunting for food and for trade.

DISTRIBUTION Lear's (or Indigo) Macaw (see Remarks 1) is confined to the middle course of the rio Vaza-Barris south of the Raso da Catarina plateau, north-eastern Bahia, Brazil, in an area of probably no more than 8,000 km^2 (see below). However, for more than a century European and American zoos had occasionally received specimens (see Remarks 2) in consignments of Hyacinth Macaws *Anodorhynchus hyacinthinus* originating from Pará (probably Belém), Bahia (Salvador), Santos and Rio de Janeiro, but the provenance of the rarer, smaller macaws could not be established beyond "probably some part of Brazil" (Salvadori 1891, Astley 1907, Peters 1937). This situation of ignorance prevailed until Pinto (1950c), visiting Santo Antão municipality in Pernambuco, was shown a captive specimen that had come from Juazeiro, a town on the right bank of the rio São Francisco in Bahia (a locality also noted for Spix's Macaw *Cyanopsitta spixii*: see relevant account). However, successive expeditions – to north-western Bahia and southern Piauí in 1958 (Pinto and de Camargo 1961), central Goiás in 1956 (Stager 1961), northern Bahia and Ceará in 1964 (Sick *et al.* 1987), again north-western Bahia in 1974 and 1976 (Sick 1979b,c) and north-western Bahia and southern Piauí and Maranhão in 1977 (Sick *et al.* 1987) – failed to find the species in the wild: no macaws were found around Juazeiro either in 1964 or in 1977 (Sick *et al.* 1979, Sick and Teixeira 1980) and it was evident that the captive specimen had been transported there, possibly along the rio São Francisco (King 1978-1979, Ridgely 1981a; see Remarks 3); thus in the year of its rediscovery the range of the species was given as "north-eastern Brazil, in the region of the lower rio São Francisco" (Pinto 1978).

The home of Lear's Macaw was finally traced in December 1978 to the area given above, although the rio Vaza-Barris flows directly into the Atlantic and is not part of the São Francisco basin (Sick 1979b,c, 1981, Sick *et al.* 1979, 1987, Sick and Teixeira 1980, 1983, also Freud 1980; popular recent account in Seitre 1990). The species is apparently restricted to that area, although formerly it was somewhat wider spread, probably reaching the rio São Francisco to the north near the town of Paulo Afonso (Sick *et al.* 1987); similar canyons north of Raso da Catarina, said by local people to have been used as roosts, were surveyed in 1978/1979 with no positive result (LPG). The species now occurs in two colonies (roosting sites, and probably for both also breeding sites) either side of the Vaza-Barris, one at Toca Velha, the other at Serra Branca; its feeding grounds extend south-west to Monte Santo and Euclides da Cunha (Sick *et al.* 1987). Its present range has been estimated to occupy an area of 15,000 km^2 (Yamashita 1987), but no recent records are known from outside an area of approximately only 8,000 km^2 (LPG), and indeed the evidence of recent work (see Ecology) is that birds forage within an area of only 450 km^2.

It is naturally not impossible that other small populations exist but, given the fairly intensive surveys of the interior of north-east Brazil in the past 10 years for this and two other blue macaws, Spix's and Hyacinth (see relevant accounts), the chances are very small; nevertheless, searches in northern Bahia in 1991 for possible additional populations of Spix's Macaw resulted in convincing reports of Lear's Macaw from several new areas (details withheld) that require follow-up (F. B. Pontual *in litt.* 1992; see also Remarks 4).

POPULATION Lear's Macaw "was common" in north-east Bahia 60-100 years ago, old people in the area remembering "large flocks... flying overhead" (Hart 1991). However, the current total population is not known to be more than 60 individuals living in two colonies (Yamashita 1987), and at best the total population consists of far less than 200 birds (Yamashita 1987); the statement that "there are possibly some hundreds of specimens left, living in several colonies" (Sick *et al.* 1987; also Sick and Teixeira 1983) must therefore now be regarded with caution, and the earlier view that the Raso da Catarina population probably numbers no more than 100 birds, perhaps fewer (Ridgely 1981a), allowed to prevail. Indeed in four consecutive simultaneous counts (May, July, August and November 1989) at the two roost sites, although the numbers at each always varied, the total came to 61 (Machado and Brandt 1990). In July 1990 the total was 66 (D. S. Gardner *in litt.* 1990). On 24 September 1991 a concentration of 46 birds was observed c.45 km east of Canudos, and a local man reported that a second, smaller population lived some 15 km to the west, and that in his view the total number stood between 50 and 100 birds (B. M. Whitney *in litt.* 1991).

ECOLOGY The range of Lear's Macaw is within the "caatinga" (thorn scrub) region of north-east Brazil at altitudes from about 380 to 800 m, with daily temperatures varying between 15 and 45°C (Yamashita 1987); the birds roost in sandstone cliffs or canyons (locally known as "talhados" or "serras": Sick *et al.* 1979, 1987) that vary in height from 30 to 60 m, using fairly small weathered holes which are often within 0.5 m of one another in the top third of the cliff faces; as many as four use a single hole; some birds roost outside the holes, clinging to the cliff or on narrow ledges (Yamashita 1987). Individuals leave their roosting places before dawn for the feeding grounds, arriving at them between 06h00 and 07h00 (in a later study 05h00 and 06h00, although as late as 10h00 or more in August, after ranging more widely for food); they leave for the roosts between 16h00 and 18h00 and arrive back around dusk (Sick and Teixeira 1980, Sick *et al.* 1987, Yamashita 1987, Brandt and Machado 1990, Machado and Brandt 1990).

The view that the chief food of the species is nuts of mucujá *Acrocomia lasiospatha* and tucuma *Astrocaryum tucuma* (Finsch 1867-1868) was a guess based on what was known of the food of Hyacinth Macaw (see Ecology in relevant account and that also of Glaucous Macaw *Anodorhynchus glaucus*). In fact Lear's Macaw feeds principally on the hard nuts of licuri *Syagrus coronata* palm trees found in the caatinga and pastures cleared for cattle-grazing (Yamashita 1987); these palms grow on top of the Raso da Catarina plateau and on crystalline soils in the surrounding lower lands; within the macaw's range they are particularly abundant in the municipality of Euclides da Cunha, being less common on the plateau's sandy soils (Sick *et al.* 1987). Studies in 1988 showed that birds from the Toca Velha roost were feeding in eight discrete areas (between 20 and 32 km distant) scattered over some 140 km^2, these areas ranging from 10 to 440 ha and containing 150-600 licuri palms; birds from the Serra Branca roost were known to use only a single site (12 km distant) of 400 ha containing around 1,000 licuri palms that were so productive as to render foraging elsewhere unnecessary (Brandt and Machado 1990). Studies in 1989 raised the number of feeding areas for the Toca Velha birds to 15, covering 300 km^2, and for the Serra Branca birds to eight (see Remarks 5), covering 150 km^2 and ranging from six to 14 km from the roost site (Machado and Brandt 1990). Feeding activity occurs mainly between 06h00 and 09h00 and between 14h00 and 16h00 (Brandt and Machado 1990). The birds feed in trees in small subgroups of two or three (maximum four) individuals or search for fallen nuts on the ground (also those deposited by cattle), taking turns at keeping watch (Sick and Teixeira 1980, Sick *et al.* 1987, Yamashita 1987, Brandt and Machado 1990, Machado and Brandt 1990). Up to five palms may be visited in a feeding period, birds preferring near-ripe fruits and each consuming around 350 licuri palm nuts per day, a figure which suggests that this food resource is a main factor (direct and indirect) limiting population growth (Brandt and Machado 1990; see Threats, also Remarks 6). Other foods indicated by local people are the fruits of pinhão *Jatropha pohliana*, umbu *Spondias tuberosa* and mucunã *Dioclea* (Sick *et al.* 1987); the first two of these (both unripe) were noted by Brandt and Machado (1990) and Machado and Brandt (1990), who otherwise saw sisal flowers *Agave* sp. (apparently nectar) being used once, braúna *Melanoxylon* sp. seeds being taken from July to September 1989 (licuri then being largely unavailable), and maize *Zea mays* being taken extensively in July 1988. There is a report that birds forage on "*Cocos schizophylla*" nuts (P. Roth in Silva 1989a; see Remarks 7). Adults may return to the same palm trees on consecutive days, a fact exploited by hunters (Sick *et al.* 1987).

The holes in the cliff faces are said by local people to serve also for nesting (Sick and Teixeira 1980), but to date nesting has only been recorded from adjacent cliffs (see below). The breeding season was said to coincide with Lent and with the period of licuri harvest (i.e. maximum production), from February to April (Sick *et al.* 1987), and copulation has been recorded in September (B. M. Whitney *in litt.* 1991) and November (Brandt and Machado 1990), with nesting activity in December (C. Yamashita *in litt.* 1987): thus indeed breeding may be timed so that the period of maximum food availability (January, in 1989: Brandt and Machado 1990) coincides with the period of maximum consumption (Hart 1991 related timing of breeding to the rainy season, starting between December and February and lasting till April/May). The nesting pair observed in 1986 occupied an isolated cliff near the rest of the colony (C. Yamashita *in litt.* 1987). In another account of possibly the same event, communal roosting at a traditional cliff was disrupted by the increasing territorialism of a pair "intending to nest in one of the deep burrows in the traditional roosting cliffs", the non-breeding birds scattering in small groups to roost in other cliffs instead; two or three breeding pairs tolerated each other in the same area, although their burrows were not in sight of each other and trips to and from feeding areas involved noisy challenges from each pair (Hart 1991). In July–October 1988 two young were observed (Brandt and Machado 1990). In May 1989 five young were produced by three pairs (one pair with one, two with two) (Machado and Brandt 1990). Thus there has been clear evidence of breeding, albeit with low productivity, in three out of four years, 1986–1989. Young birds take almost twice as long as adults to open nuts, and their diet is supplemented by relatives throughout their first year of life (Brandt and Machado 1990). Breeding has occurred in captivity but few details have been published; it took 13 weeks (87 days in Hart 1991) from hatching for a young bird to be fully feathered and flying, and another three weeks to be self-sufficient (see Bish 1985, Silva 1989a).

THREATS The distribution of Lear's Macaw certainly appears relictual, and the species could even be declining owing to natural causes. The general disturbance of the area is, however, testimony to the prevalence of human pressures in the region: two heavily travelled roads cross the range of the macaw, the area has been densely populated since the late eighteenth century (or "since 1870": Hart 1991), and there are many foot and donkey trails that provide wide access (Yamashita 1987). Hart (1991) attributed this general level of disturbance to (a) the opening up of the region 25 years ago by Petrobrás, the Brazilian oil company, whose new roads into the region were immediately used by settlers and hunters, and (b) the relocation of many families in the region by government agency; she added that if indeed oil is found in the immediate area the species will soon become extinct.

Trade The species may now be more at risk than ever, simply because its precise whereabouts are now well known: even in the late 1970s it was recognized that the area would need to be rigorously protected from bird trappers (Ridgely 1981a), a situation which still applies: between 1983 and April 1988, three birds are known to have been offered for sale in the markets at Jeremoabo, all apparently young taken from the colony (Toca Velha) just south of the Raso da Catarina, two in 1986 and one in 1988 (C. Yamashita *in litt.* 1988). There was, moreover, the incident reported under Measures Taken.

Hunting Hunting both for food and for sale of wildlife products in regional markets represents a serious problem in the area (Yamashita 1987), but the extent to which it has affected the Lear's Macaw population is unclear; two birds are known to have been shot for food since the species's rediscovery (Sick *et al.* 1987, A. Brandt verbally 1988). The inability of the licuri palm stands to supply the birds' needs throughout the year forces them to forage more widely, notably in July, which renders them more vulnerable to hunters, especially if they take to eating cultivated maize (Brandt and Machado 1990).

Farming and tree use The local economy depends on subsistence agriculture and free-range cattle and goat-farming; cattle consumption of racemes and unripe fruit of licuri palms in the dry season may limit the supply of ripe nuts for macaws; although these birds prefer mature fruit and cattle prefer green fruit, many farmers believe that macaws compete with cattle for food (C. Yamashita *in litt.* 1988). Licuri palms are not regenerating in any areas used by livestock (Brandt and Machado 1990), and many adult plants in traditional feeding sites of the bird are now senescent (C. Yamashita *in litt.* 1988); it is already apparent that the existing areas of palm used by the species are inadequate at seasons of greater scarcity (see Brandt and Machado 1990), so this trend is extremely serious and will prove fatal to Lear's Macaw unless reversed. Burning to renew pastures compounds this problem (Ribeiro 1990b) and poses a further threat (see below). In July 1990 a main feeding area was actually being cleared of licuri palms (D. S. Gardner *in litt.* 1990). Moulted feathers showed fault bars indicating the occurrence of food privation (C. Yamashita *in litt.* 1986). The dependence of the birds on braúna seeds in winter 1989 reveals a further vulnerability, since braúna is prized as a building material, so although the trees are left standing when land is cleared for pasture this is merely so that they can be exploited at a later date (Machado and Brandt 1990). There are projects for reforestation with algarroba *Prosopis* in the area (C. Yamashita *in litt.* 1986), this being promoted in north-east Brazil (principally Pernambuco) as a multiple-use miracle plant (see de Azevedo 1984) although its environmental impact appears to be unknown (LPG).

Disturbance The Toca Velha roosting site is subject to some disturbance owing to the proximity of the town of Canudos and the presence of some families living in the accesses to the canyon (Machado and Brandt 1990). Ribeiro (1990b) mentioned the impending development of a road close to a breeding area, resulting in more traffic and disturbance.

Fire Licuri palms are mostly situated in very dry, grassy pastures, winds are nearly constant in the region, and there is a local penchant for burning to clear areas: one major fire in the region could eradicate a major portion of the species's food-supply in a matter of days (B. M. Whitney *in litt.* 1991).

Natural causes Certain individuals in the two known colonies have been noted to have crossed tail-feathers, which may be evidence of inbreeding in the population (C. Yamashita *in litt.* 1986). The sandstone cliffs that are currently used as roosting sites by the macaws are fractured, and for unknown reasons birds roost in only a few canyons, although many others are seemingly available; high thermal variation from day to night produces slides in the cliffs (Yamashita 1987), as do torrential rainfalls (LPG), and a slide occurring at night or during nesting could have a disastrous effect on the population (Yamashita 1987). Sick and Teixeira (1980) and Sick (1981) refer to birds on cliffs defending themselves against dense swarms of flies, implying these might be problematic (mosquitoes may affect breeding success in Hyacinth Macaws: see Threats in relevant account).

MEASURES TAKEN The species is protected under Brazilian law (Bernardes *et al.* 1990) and is listed on Appendix I of CITES. That the area where Lear's Macaw was rediscovered happened already to be part of an established federal reserve, the Raso da Catarina Ecological Station appeared to be good fortune (Sick *et al.* 1979; see Remarks 8). However, although 99,772 ha in size (Ribeiro 1990b) and having the Serra Branca cliff-site just inside its southern boundary (LPG), the station has no resident group of birds; cattle consume the unripe racemes there, so little food is available and the birds visit only sporadically (Yamashita 1987). Nevertheless, in fulfilment of an obvious need to protect the species from trapping (Ridgely 1981a), two guards were installed at Cocorobó (now Canudos) in 1980, and are still present (LPG). The movements of all strangers in the area are monitored, and their access to sensitive sites is denied (Hart 1991). On one occasion, a man believed to be working for a Rio de Janeiro bird-fancier was arrested while driving in the area with a large birdcage in the back of his truck (LPG). Landowners in the area have proved to be interested in protecting the macaws against the intrusions of hunters and trappers, and there has been much local liaison and education to promote regional interest in the conservation of the species; at one point this involved the publicizing of the shooting of a bird by a poor farmer and the exemplary (i.e. intended to be one-off) clemency shown him by police travelling eight hours to make the arrest (Hart 1991).

In fulfilment of other clear needs, namely a survey for further populations (Ridgely 1981a) and a study of the feeding biology of the birds and food production in the area (LPG and C. Yamashita verbally to WWF-U.S. 1985), fieldwork on both has taken place, funded largely by WWF-U.S. (see Sick *et al.* 1987 for the former, Brandt and Machado 1990, Machado and Brandt 1990 for the latter). Moreover, farmers growing corn have been promised compensation if they resist driving birds from their crops; a plan for the large-scale planting of licuri palm seedlings has been received with enthusiasm; and one landowner has bought up an area and allowed it to return to a natural state, with many young licuri palms now producing much fruit (Hart 1991).

MEASURES PROPOSED Continued research into the general biology of the species (proposed in Machado and Brandt 1990) is clearly of enormous importance for valid management, and must be undertaken. However, the view of Machado and Brandt (1990) that an on-site captive breeding programme could possibly accompany this research seems inappropriate: it would be an extremely expensive and necessarily risky option and at least should not be considered until the recommendations below have been successfully implemented (an increase in the stock of birds without an increase in the carrying capacity of the habitat would be of little value, while an increase in the latter could lead to an increase in the former without the trouble and expense of captive breeding).

The ecological station's enlargement to include more of the species's range was early hoped for (Sick *et al.* 1979, 1987), called for (in an ICBP Parrot Group resolution in April 1980: Ridgely 1981a) and, apparently, worked for (see Sick and Teixeira 1983), yet never implemented (LPG); it is important that roosting and nesting sites remain completely inaccessible to people (Sick and Teixeira 1980). However, nothing has yet been achieved in this regard, except the passing of a law in 1983 to establish the reserve officially (Machado and Brandt 1990), and the development (by Machado and Brandt 1990) of a detailed plan for land acquisition and/or the establishment of reserves, including the ecological station.

Meanwhile, a permanent food supply for the birds needs to be assured by fencing off key areas that hold licuri palms, and by planting seedlings chiefly of licuri palm but also of other native and introduced foodplants (mentioned under Ecology); in the longer term the creation of new feeding areas (identified in accordance with the results of the continuing programme of biological research) will be needed to compensate for intensifying disturbance from development near current feeding sites (Machado and Brandt 1990).

Education programmes will be necessary to achieve the support and sympathy of local communities for the conservation of the species and its habitats; in tandem with this should go a programme of wardening and liaison that extends current arrangements (Machado and Brandt 1990).

An investigation of the Cachoeira do Rio Preto region may be worthwhile in view of local claims of a second type of blue macaw there (see Remarks 4 and accompanying reservations). Sites in northern Bahia from which the species was reported or described during searches for Spix's Macaw by F. B. Pontual and M. A. Da-Ré in 1991 (see Distribution) need urgent investigation; IBAMA has been informed (M. G. Kelsey verbally 1992).

Several individual birds and a few pairs exist in captivity in various places around the world: at the start of the 1980s one report claimed that 11 birds existed in the U.S.A. alone (Decoteau 1982); in 1987 there were at least 13 in total, namely one in Antwerp (this went to N. Kawall in Brazil), one in Mulhouse and one in Basle (these were united as a pair in Mulhouse, then loaned in 1992 to H. Sissen in the U.K.), one in Monaco (now dead), two in Bourton-on-the Water (U.K.) (both now dead, one after going to H. Sissen), one (with N. Kawall, now paired with the Antwerp bird) in São Paulo, one in Los Angeles (now dead), four in Tampa (at least one now dead) and one in Miami (R. Wirth *in litt.* 1987, with 1992 updates in brackets); in addition, there was one in Paris Zoo (this was in fact the same as the first bird held at Mulhouse: R. Wirth verbally 1992) and another in São Paulo Zoo (Silva 1989a), and more recently an assertion of one or more held in San Diego Zoo (incorrect: R. Wirth verbally 1992) and Vogelpark Walsrode (Lantermann and Schuster 1990), one in Yorkshire (U.K.) (this being the bird from Bourton-on-the-Water, now dead) and one male in South Africa (Barnicoat 1982, Sissons [*sic*, = Sissen] 1991), this last now in Yorkshire along with the two (senescent) birds loaned from Mulhouse (NJC). Although informed comment on the situation in the U.S.A., where a total of four birds (two of them captive-bred) existed in 1990, is that "aviculturists in the U.S. cannot do anything to save this species" (Clubb and Clubb 1991), there is clearly a case for seeking to determine the whereabouts of all captive stock, and to maximize its reproductive and genetic potential (and indeed that of the species) through the establishment of a consortium under the impartial aegis of the IUCN Captive Breeding Specialist Group, with the full support and involvement of the Brazilian authorities.

REMARKS (1) A modest suggestion – not, in the journalistic calumny of Ribeiro (1990b), an uncompromising insistence – that Lear's would prove to be a hybrid between Hyacinth and Glaucous Macaw (Voous 1965) was obviously discounted following the discovery of a wild population (King 1978-1979, Vielliard 1979). On the other hand, both Glaucous and Lear's could perhaps be regarded as vicariant forms of a single species, forming a superspecies with Hyacinth Macaw (Vielliard 1979, Forshaw 1989). (2) One such consignment, to Germany in 1893, apparently consisted of a fair number of birds (see Neunzig 1921), and Delacour (1939) possessed no fewer than seven in the late 1930s. (3) Juazeiro is only 150 km by road from the present centre of the species's range, so transportation by river would have been unnecessary. (4) During attempts to locate populations of Spix's Macaw in Bahia, Roth (1989b) reported that several people in a relatively small area of the upper rio Preto (Cachoeira do Rio Preto) distinguished two types of large blue macaw, although only Hyacinth Macaw was encountered. This needs to be treated cautiously, however, as in that region Hyacinth Macaw is known as "arara-preta" (black macaw) and Blue-and-yellow Macaw *Ara ararauna* as "arara-azul" (blue macaw) (LPG; also Reinhardt 1870). (5) Machado and Brandt (1990) referred to seven feeding sites for the Serra Branca birds, but their table of these sites lists seven without including the major site used in their 1988 study (Brandt and Machado 1990), and it is presumed here that the total number of feeding sites is eight. (6) In view of the high rate of food consumption reported here, it is interesting to note that Tavistock (1926) reported the species "quite hardy, and I had a freshly imported one which went without food for two days and two nights on the top of an oak tree in the depth of winter". (7) The scientific name should be *Syagrus schizophylla*, but in any case it appears this was a misidentification of *S. coronata* (LPG). (8) The view that because the species had so long gone undetected at the Raso da Catarina Ecological Station governmental presence there must have been slight (Ridgely 1981a) was mistaken, as the station had only just been established and indeed the first leaflet it issued (just before the species was rediscovered) mentioned the presence nearby of blue macaws (LPG).

SPIX'S MACAW *Cyanopsitta spixii* E[1]

This enigmatic and exquisite macaw, known for over a century and a half from small numbers of traded birds from somewhere in the interior of Brazil, was traced in the 1980s to some remnant caraiba gallery woodland adjoining the rio São Francisco in northern Bahia. However, at that stage only three birds remained and these were all believed captured for illegal trade in 1987 and 1988, although a single bird, now well publicized and guarded, was discovered at the site in July 1990 (still present in June 1992). At this time evidence was assembled to suggest that the species might have been heavily dependent on caraiba woodland for nest-sites, so that its long-term rarity could be attributed to the long-since loss of most such habitat, although its exploitation for the illegal bird trade since around 1970 is certainly responsible for its current proximity to extinction. As this plight became clear in the mid-1980s, efforts were made to identify birds held captive around the world, and the total of publicly acknowledged birds was 27 in June 1992, although at least 14 of these are offspring and the degree of relatedness between all the birds is unknown. A Permanent Committee for the Recovery of Spix's Macaw has been established by the Brazilian government and this includes most holders.

DISTRIBUTION Spix's Macaw is a distinctive parrot (see Remarks 1) endemic to the arid interior of east-central Brazil, and is known with certainty from just one site in northern Bahia, at which a single bird survives. Many other localities have been claimed for the species, such that they constitute an area embracing some 300,000 km^2 in north-west Bahia, southern Pernambuco, southern Piauí, southern Maranhão and eastern Tocantins (as northern Goiás is now known) (Roth 1988b, 1990). In particular, an 80,000 km^2 area called the "Gerais", where the states of Bahia, Piauí, Maranhão and Tocantins meet, has been the source of most unconfirmed reports of this parrot (Roth 1988b, 1990); Silva (1989a) reported a Belém dealer in 1986 giving the Gerais as a source of a few birds in recent years. However, modern evidence of the species's habitat requirements suggests that most if not all unconfirmed sites are false (see Remarks 2). On the basis of the following two paragraphs, the species's original range may now be proposed as a 50 km wide belt of the 150-200 km stretch of the rio São Francisco between Juazeiro (and possibly even Remanso) and Abaré, the south side in Bahia, the north side in Pernambuco (see Remarks 3).

Bahia The only entirely certain records (possibly but not provenly from the same site) are from the banks of the rio São Francisco, near Juazeiro (Joazeiro), where the type was collected in April 1819 (von Spix 1824, Hellmayr 1906c), and from the riacho Melância (Melância Creek), some 20 km south-east of Curaçá, where one bird was found to be present in July 1990 (Roth 1986, 1990, Juniper and Yamashita 1990, 1991, Juniper 1991; see Population) and was still there in early June 1992 (M. A. Da-Ré *per* F. B. Pontual *in litt.* 1992). There is also a strong but second-hand report from the riacho da Vargem, near Abaré, some 100 km east of Curaçá (Juniper and Yamashita 1990, 1991).

The view that the type came from Curaçá, since birds there were reported to appear irregularly on the rio São Francisco (Roth 1985, 1987a, 1990), has been widely repeated (Arndt *et al.* 1986, Strunden *et al.* 1986, Forshaw 1989, Silva 1989a), even to the point of identifying one specific area (Barra Grande) as the type-locality (Juniper and Yamashita 1990; see Remarks 4). All of this is no more than possible; Juazeiro lies 90 km south-west of Curaçá (both being on the right bank of the São Francisco) and it cannot conceivably now be established that the locality where von Spix found his bird in 1819 is identical to that discovered in the 1980s (see Remarks 5, 6). The fact that Juniper and Yamashita (1990) were able to find a new (but recently trapped-out: hence not absolutely certain) locality, riacho da Vargem, on the basis of their identification of the species's habitat constraints, further indicates the inappropriateness of assuming the precise origin of von Spix's bird. Indeed, Roth (1986) himself suggested that the species's distribution, if allied to caraiba trees *Tabebuia caraiba* along creeks, would originally have extended 50 km either side of the São Francisco between Juazeiro in the west and Santa Maria de Boa Vista in the east (indeed the caatinga formation extended as far west as Remanso and east to Orocó) and, now that this association has been affirmed (Juniper 1990, Juniper and Yamashita 1990, 1991), such a proposed original range appears very plausible, although in fact riacho da Vargem extends it much further eastwards, to Abaré; Roth (1985, also 1986, 1987c) referred to local reports of birds from Curaçá wandering as far as Orocó (Pernambuco), but Orocó is well west of Abaré. (It is clear, of course, that birds would once have ranged widely through the general region indicated by the localities mentioned above, and even now would not necessarily be inhibited from travelling between islands of habitat.)

The most widely accepted other area for the species is the Formosa do Rio Preto, Riachão (i.e. rio do Ouro region, in the Gerais), where three and then four individuals were seen flying over a buriti palm grove on 25 December 1974 (Sick and Teixeira 1979, Sick 1981, 1985; incorrect year in King 1978-1979). This record was carefully followed up by Roth (1986, 1988a, 1989b, 1990; also by Juniper and Yamashita 1990), who could find no-one who knew the species among several with great experience of the local avifauna, and the cerrado habitat was fundamentally different from that at Curaçá: the conclusion was that either the species might be found in the denser gallery woodland of the region, or it is more nomadic there (see Ecology, last paragraph), or the record was a misidentification; but in any case that any population there must now be extinct or nearly so. However, it is to be noted that, for reasons unknown, Pinto (1938, 1978) listed both rio Preto and rio São Francisco in Bahia as recorded localities, and indeed was a party to the search for it there in 1958 (Pinto and de Camargo 1961).

Pernambuco The former occurrence of Spix's Macaw in southern Pernambuco, along the stretches of the rio São Francisco adjacent to the known sites in Bahia, is based only on local information given to Roth (1985, 1986, 1987c), but is consistent with his evidence that appropriate habitat (caraiba woodland) existed there in former decades. Indeed, in 1991 a trapper working for the main dealer in the species (Carlinhos: see Threats: Trade) reported that a few decades ago the species was commoner in the state than in Bahia, but that with the loss of the trees the birds moved south across the São Francisco; however, he claimed to have seen a pair along the rio Brígida in 1988 (F. B. Pontual *in litt.* 1992).

Piauí On 18 and 21 June 1903, respectively three and two Spix's Macaws were seen at Lago de Parnaguá, the first observation being of birds coming to drink, the second of a pair flying from south to north (Reiser 1926; also Hellmayr 1929a), and these records form the main basis for the inclusion of southern Piauí in the range of the species (e.g. Forshaw 1978, Ridgely 1981a, Sick 1985). Pinto (1938, 1978), for reasons unknown, also included the upper rio Parnaíba (which divides southern Piauí and Maranhão) in his summary of the species's distribution (see under Maranhão). The Lago de Parnaguá area was investigated in 1958 without success (Pinto and de Camargo 1961), but it is not clear that it was ever visited by P. Roth (see, e.g., Roth 1990). It was, however, investigated in June 1990 without success (Juniper and Yamashita 1991). A confident 1979 report of the species at Fazenda Bom Recreio, near Manoel Emídio, in the Gurgueia valley close to the Uruçui Preto river system, was followed up, but inquiries at the fazenda, and a search of the region extending to the headwaters of the rio Estiva, revealed no evidence to confirm the report; and, again, the habitat was cerrado (Roth 1987d, 1988a, 1989b, 1990). Roth (1985) found a trapper at Gilbués who clearly knew Spix's Macaw, and Silva's (1989a) version of this could be read to imply that the birds had been seen locally, but Roth (1988a) indicated that the man in question had trapped the species at Curaçá (although it was also he who was responsible for identifying the rio Parnaibinha in Maranhão as a locality). A pair of macaws fitting the species's description was seen during an archaeological survey at Serra Branca in Serra da Capivara National Park, March/April 1975, and local people around the park appear to know the species, although it seems now to have disappeared there (Olmos in press); such information, while valuable as a possible pointer, inevitably has to be treated with caution.

Within the Gerais, the region of São Raimundo Nonato, Piauí, claimed for the species by several aviculturists and dealers, has the most similar habitat (in terms of its caatinga composition) to that at Curaçá; moreover Remanso (Bahia), where in 1903 Reiser (1926) saw a captive bird, is not distant; however, searches in April 1986, July 1987 and January 1988 yielded nothing (Roth 1986, 1988a), and it appears that the habitat similarity did not include mature gallery woodland.

The Piauí section of the Chapada das Mangabeiras was also reported in 1989 as a source of recent possible sightings, and was therefore investigated in 1990, along with other reputed areas for the species in southern Piauí not covered in surveys, 1985-1988; results were negative, and misidentifications seemed to be responsible for all these records. Nevertheless, Keller (1992) revived the idea that a small population (at least six birds) might still exist somewhere in the state, and implied that P. Roth had seen and photographed them.

Maranhão Apart from the inclusion of the upper rio Parnaíba in the species's range (see under Piauí above), five specimens in trade, 1976-1977, including two young, were reputedly from southern Maranhão (three of them, seized in 1976, went to São Paulo Zoo) (Sick and Teixeira 1979; hence Ridgely 1981a, Roth 1988a). Local reports at first suggested birds might be found on a 60 km stretch of the rio Parnaibinha from Morro da França and Fazenda Promissão to Fazenda Galiléia, but investigation revealed that all this appeared based on misidentification, and no other evidence – including that of a search around Curupá just west of the Parnaíba, and at Baixa Funda, just across the border from Lizarda in Tocantins – was found to confirm or suggest the species's presence in Maranhão (Roth 1987d, 1988a,b, 1990), although Roth (1985) himself referred to four small unidentified macaws he glimpsed in Serra do Itapecurú, between Buritirana and Balsas (apparently never followed up).

Tocantins In eastern Tocantins (the region adjacent to southernmost Maranhão) the species was reported by hunters to H. Sick and R. S. Ridgely in 1977 (Ridgely 1981a), although Goiás (as Tocantins then was) did not earn mention by Sick and Teixeira (1979) or Sick (1985). The most specialized trapper of Spix's Macaw reported regularly visiting the border region between Tocantins and Maranhão, and some recently captured birds probably originated in the region (Roth 1988a). Keller (1987) reported being offered birds that came from "northern Goiás", and referred to repeated allusions by trappers and traders to Tocantinha and Filadélfia, to which Roth (1988a) added the sites of Pedro Afonso and São Miguel do Araguaia. Inquiries and surveys in 1988 in the "Xalapão" region (untraced), and from Filadélfia through Tocantinha and Lizarda to the rio do Sono and Dianópolis, produced no evidence of the species (Roth 1988a,b, 1989b, 1990).

POPULATION A single bird was all that was known to survive in the wild in July 1990 (Juniper 1990, Juniper and Yamashita 1990), while there were 16 acknowledged birds in captivity in November of that year (see penultimate paragraph, this section). In June 1992 the single bird remained (M. A. Da-Ré *per* F. B. Pontual *in litt.* 1992), while the conclusively proven captive stock stood at 27.

Population in the wild The Curaçá population (i.e. that at the Barra Grande and adjacent riacho Melância) was judged to consist of 30 or more pairs at the start of the century (Roth 1985, 1986, 1990) and on the evidence in Threats: Trade it would appear that a good proportion of this number was still present in the late 1970s. However, by 1985 no more than five (including two pairs) were reported remaining, following 15 years of trapping and no successful breeding (Roth 1985, 1986, 1990). In that year the eggs of a breeding pair were broken by a trapper during a nest inspection (Roth 1985), although in a later account this event was not mentioned, rather that at least one pair attempted to breed, but failed owing to heavy rains; later in the year one bird was shot dead by local trappers trying to cripple it and capture it alive (Roth 1986 *contra* Roth 1990, who said it was shot for food, and Keller 1992, who said it was shot by the proprietor of a local fazenda). In 1986 only three birds remained, including a pair which attempted to breed; trappers damaged the eggs and, when the birds relayed at a site 4-5 km distant (but still along the riacho Melância), trappers sealing the nest entrance caused the eggs again to be broken (Roth 1986). From December 1986 to early March 1987 the birds were not reported as present; they appeared with the first rains (10 March) and seemed not to have bred (Roth 1987b,c), although two young were taken at some locality by trappers that February/March (see below). The three birds were present up to the end of April 1987, but from May only two were observed (Silva 1989a indicated, without giving a source, that the missing bird had been trapped), and in December 1987 one of these two was reported captured, in January 1988 the other (Silva 1988b imparted the information, without indicating a source, that one of these two birds died soon after capture); this was done by a trapper with a group of armed men under instructions from a dealer in Petrolina, after which the species was considered extinct at Curaçá (Roth 1988a,b, 1990, Munn *et al.* 1989). However, in July 1990 a new search of reported and reputed localities finally resulted in the discovery of a single bird, probably male, at riacho Melância (see above; also Remarks 7).

It is widely agreed that any surviving or recent populations of Spix's Macaw must be or must have been small, and that the species must always (i.e. in the past two centuries) have been "rare" (King 1978-1979, Ridgely 1981a, Sick 1981). The degree of rarity might have depended on the extent of its range, but its relative rarity within that range would seem to have been constant (see Remarks 8). It seems never to have been noted that von Spix (1824), in his original description, referred to the species as "very rare" (see Remarks 5), which for so relatively large and conspicuous a bird is clearly good evidence that indeed its population was low and scattered even at the start of the nineteenth century. From its discovery in 1819 to its rediscovery in 1985/1986, the species was recorded in the wild only twice in published sources, in 1903 (Reiser 1926) and 1974 (Sick 1985), but neither of these records can be regarded as unassailable (see Distribution, Remarks 2). Very small numbers of birds have been in trade at least since the 1870s, and the species has always been considered extremely rare in aviculture (Dutton 1897, Low 1972). Museum skins are also very rare, and most are preserved specimens of captive birds, although the labels do not always help in judging this (ANSP has two skins acquired from Paris in 1846 or soon afterwards: M. B. Robbins *in litt.* 1991; MHNG has one labelled "Bahia, Brazil" which it received in 1892). The very low but relatively constant volume of live and dead specimens over the decades is consistent with an interpretation of the ecological evidence that the small numbers of the species lived in a specific and limited habitat close to the rio São Francisco, a main channel of communications from interior Brazil (Juniper and Yamashita 1990; see Ecology, also Remarks 8).

That populations of the species, albeit small and scattered, might exist elsewhere other than at Curaçá had long been indicated not only by records and reports (see Distribution) but also by evidence of birds entering trade, especially in recent years. In March 1987 two young Spix's Macaws were seized by the authorities in Paraguay (see Measures Taken), and although Thomsen and Munn (1988) maintained that they originated from Curaçá, Roth (1987b, 1988a) believed that they were from another (albeit pressurized) population, particularly as he had evidence that two different young birds were being sold illegally in 1987 and knew of offers to obtain young in 1988. Such evidence, coupled with the view (almost certainly mistaken) that the species's habitat was intact, continued to suggest to Sojer (1989) and Sojer and Wirth (1989) that Spix's Macaw occurred somewhere else at low density, and presumably stimulated Roth's further pursuit of hearsay reports at the expense of searches for new areas of the habitat he had already identified for the species. The persistence of a population elsewhere was confirmed and the likely provenance of new birds on the market identified when in July 1990 ICBP-backed researchers, using habitat features as a guide, discovered the gallery woodland at riacho da Vargem, which local people reported to have held a steadily trapped-out population up to as recently as 1989 (Juniper and Yamashita 1990). Moreover, Keller (1992) referred to chicks being exported from Brazil that had been captured after 1988 and not in the Curaçá area.

The problem posed by lack of certainty concerning other populations, particularly when the range is believed vast and the ecological requirements assumed to be unspecialized, is illustrated by the fact that, only 10 years ago, Spix's Macaw was not regarded as the most endangered Neotropical parrot after the probably extinct Glaucous Macaw *Anodorhynchus glaucus*, the distinction going instead to the Red-tailed Amazon *Amazona brasiliensis* (Ridgely 1981a), and indeed the species was not even discussed by Greenway (1958, 1967) or listed as threatened by Vincent (1966-1971).

Population in captivity Trade in Spix's Macaw has always been light, indicating the long-term rarity of the species; but it has still been considered easier to find a captive bird than a wild one. BMNH received a specimen from a dealer in 1859 and a second in 1884, this latter having been held in London Zoo since 1878 (see also *Proc. Zool. Soc. London* 1878: 976); AMNH has a specimen received in London Zoo in 1894 and which died there in 1900 (longevity recorded also in Mitchell 1911). These two London Zoo birds were evidently the only two that Dutton (1897) reported ever having seen (the former being acquired from the Jardin d'Acclimatation, the latter by W. Rothschild from a Mr Jamrach), although he evidently soon saw (and bought) a third specimen (Dutton 1897, 1900) which was six or seven years old and "picking up a good deal of conversation" in 1902 (*Avicult. Mag.* 8 [1902]: 277). At this time Blaauw (1900) noted Spix's Macaw in the collections at Berlin Zoo, de Grahl (1986) and Brack (1987a) indicating that one had been there in 1893, and Neunzig (1921) affirming that it had arrived that year and at least one other had followed it.

From this, Low's (1972) assertion that the first specimens of the species came to Europe in the 1920s can be seen to be mistaken. However, in the 1920s there certainly was a flush of importations into Europe and North America, Tavistock (1929) referring to the species as "formerly extremely rare, but a few have been brought over during recent years" (see Remarks 9), indeed in sufficient quantity that he could add that it "sometimes makes a fair talker". Thus in the U.K. Paignton (Primley) Zoo held one in 1926 and a pair in 1927, although these were not being held together in 1931 (Seth-Smith 1926, Hopkinson 1927, 1931). What were apparently two different birds from the above were exhibited in 1927 and 1930–1932 (Seth-Smith 1927, 1932, Prestwich 1930a, 1931), at least two were in London Zoo in 1930 (Prestwich 1930b) and another was at a private zoo in Liverpool in 1932 (Stokes 1932), suggesting at least seven in the country around 1930, although any resale would mean some double counting: it is impossible, for example, to tell if two that had been kept by Marsden (1927) died or were sold on. In the U.S.A. Plath (1930, 1934, 1937, 1969) reported keeping one from 1928 to 1946, and knew of no authentic records in the country before 1927. However, AMNH possesses the skin of a captive bird (male) which either died or was received in 1926; another was received in 1928, and a third in 1935; USNM has a female from the National Zoo in 1937; and ANSP has two from Philadelphia Zoo, received in August 1931 and January 1947. A Miss Dalton-Burgess (English, according to de Grahl 1986) held a female that laid an egg in 1927 (Brack 1987a); egg-laying had already been recorded without details the previous year (Tavistock 1926). There was at least one in France in 1929 or 1930 (Stokes 1930) and Vienna Zoo held a bird in 1929 (Brack 1987a).

After the importations of the 1920s the trade in the species appears to have waned. Low (1984) remarked that the number of specimens documented in the avicultural literature of the previous 50 years did not exceed single figures outside Brazil. That birds went abroad in this period, especially in the 1970s, is borne out by, e.g., Ridgely's (1981a) encounter in 1977 with Paraguayan dealers who had obtained specimens in the recent past. A captive female received by MNHN in 1953 may have been a long-lived bird from the 1920s. The only record otherwise of captive birds in the 1950s is amongst the conflicting accounts of the first successful captive breeding of the species, by Alvaro Rossman Carvalhães, of Santos, São Paulo: according to Low (1984, 1986, 1990) and Keller (1987), Carvalhães had a pair that produced eight young over several years in the 1950s, one of which went to Naples Zoo, the rest remaining in Brazil, and most dying as non-reproductive adults; the breeding pair is presumably that referred to in King (1978-1979) as dying in the mid- to late 1970s. However, according to Silva (1989a; also 1990a, 1991a), Carvalhães bred over 15 in the 1960s and 1970s, and some of these "reared young for Ulisses Moreira" (this apparently indicating second-generation breeding) three times in the late 1960s (Roth 1987a referred to Ulisses Morães's [*sic*] success as occurring in the 1970s). According to F. Simon, Carvalhães hatched over two dozen birds (documentation provided by J. B. Thomsen *in litt.* 1991); according to Nogueira-Neto (1973), Carvalhães held no fewer than four pairs of this species (by implication these were all caught from the wild), but he had also bred them and a pair had been passed to Moreira. Moreira's success may explain why Sick (1981, also 1969) implied that there had been more than one breeder of the species in Brazil, while Low (1984, 1986) and Roth (1986) insisted that no other breeding had occurred there or elsewhere. A report that several birds came on the market in the late 1970s that had been bred at São Paulo Zoo (Brack 1987a) is patently erroneous (confirmed by F. Simon *in litt.* 1992); Brack (1987a) reported Carvalhães's success ("many chicks") as being in 1970, and successful breeding in Santos in 1983. There were two birds in Rio de Janeiro Zoo in January 1974 (Strunden 1974), and one was found at the home of J. L. do Nascimento in Macururé, Bahia, in July 1979, this bird having been a gift three years before from D. L. de Moraes of Amargosa (also Bahia), who had kept it for 15 years (LPG).

The errors, contradictions, silence and disinformation that afflict the history of Spix's Macaw in captivity were magnified as fieldwork in the 1980s highlit the species's critical plight in the wild and placed the last hope of saving it on captive breeding, engendering a series of initiatives to identify the whereabouts of birds. Initially Ridgely (1981a) had reported "extremely few in captivity even in Brazil, and now almost none abroad", although King (1978-1979) was told there were then 13 in Europe. G. A. Smith (*in litt.* to W. B. King 1978) knew of two six-month-old birds being sent (apparently from the U.K.) to the U.S.A. in early 1977. Decoteau (1982) asserted that at the start of the 1980s there were three "known" pairs in the U.S.A., all breeding ("well-kept secrets, and rightfully so"), and that there were several pairs in Europe, of which one, in Belgium, had been most prolific, producing three good young for six years down to the time of writing, with another pair breeding in Germany; none of these claims gains support from independent testimony, but A. Decoteau (*per* J. R. van Oosten *in litt.* 1991) asserted that the birds in the U.S.A. were in Maine and are all dead, while the whereabouts of those in Belgium is no longer known to him. Low (1984) wrote that no more than 10 were held in Brazil, one of which was in Paraná, although Low (1986) revised the figure up to around 20, adding that N. Kawall had told G. A. Smith that three or four birds, probably from two nesting pairs, came onto the market in Brazil each year. Roth (1985, 1986, 1987a) simultaneously wrote of 40-50 in captivity, half of them in Brazil, thus: at least 12 in São Paulo (including three in the zoo), at least three in Rio de Janeiro, four in Recife, and scattered individuals elsewhere; then 1-2 in Walsrode (Germany), a pair in Naples Zoo (reported to be two females: G. A. Smith *in litt.* to W. B. King 1978), a pair in Portugal, four in Yugoslavia, a pair in Singapore, four with the "Caribbean Wildlife Preservation Trust" (confirmed by W. L. R. Oliver *in litt.* to J. B. Thomsen 1991), two at "Canary Island Parrot Park" (= Loro Parque, Tenerife), and one in California. De Grahl (1986) and Brack (1987a,b), more retrospectively, reported a pair in the Rio de Janeiro Zoo, 1974 (one of these had died by December 1975: Aguirre and Aldrighi 1983), a pair held by G. Rossi dalla Riva, Brazil, one of which died in 1976 (in fact he had two pairs, possibly all dead in 1976: see Bertagnolio 1981), and, outside Brazil, a pair on exhibition in Rotterdam in 1971, one held by G. A. Smith in 1978 (imported from Portugal in 1976: Smith 1975-1977, also Low 1980a; see Remarks 10), four in the Philippines, two in 1975 (then four, but by 1986 one) at Walsrode, two at Loro Parque, and two in 1975 (then one) in Naples Zoo. Arndt *et al.* (1986) and Strunden *et al.* (1986) provided similar lists, adding that at least two were in Switzerland and that others might be in Portugal, U.K., Japan, U.S.A. and Yugoslavia. Yugoslavia was discounted after investigations by Vestner (1987), while Thomsen and Munn (1988) added Singapore and France to the list of possible countries where birds were held, and Hoppe (1988) anticipated a fairly large number of clandestine holders, reporting a colleague being shown a photograph of two birds for sale from a dealer in Thailand. A bird was in the possession of Sir Crawford McCullogh of Lismore in Northern Ireland (U.K.) in 1969, as a recording of it, deposited and catalogued at the British Library of Wildlife Sounds, was made on 4 March that year (R. Ranft *in litt.* 1991). DeDios (*sic*) and Hill (1990) referred to a bird in a Los Angeles "pet home" around 1980 (A. de Dios *per* P. Scherer Neto *in litt.* 1992 has disclaimed responsibility for this information). A pair is reported to have gone to Sweden in recent years (J. Cuddy verbally 1992).

For the Tenerife initiative (see Measures Taken), Keller (1987) could only enumerate 14 (and possibly only 11) in Brazil: possibly three with an unnamed São Paulo holder (Pedro Callado, according to Roth 1988b); one, probably female, with an unnamed Rio de Janeiro holder; a pair with N. Kawall, São Paulo; one, Piauí; two with J. A. Camargo Cardoso, São Paulo (who obtained them from a dealer in Floriano, Keller [1992] claiming that these were taken as chicks from the wild in 1982); and five in São Paulo Zoo. This was duly repeated by Arndt (1987) and Roth (1988b), the former adding that seven of the 14 were illegal and therefore unlikely to become available for a breeding programme, while only 10 birds existed outside Brazil, the latter noting that Kawall now only had one bird and that Camargo Cardoso, having had four, now only possessed one or two; the lost birds were presumably the "at least three" noted by Roth (1987d) to have died in July–August 1987 (with the comment that "not all holders... give their birds optimal conditions and the birds still suffer an unnecessarily high mortality in captivity"). C. Keller (*in litt.* 1991) recorded that Callado's birds either died or were sold, that the Rio bird died, that the Piauí bird went to Europe, and that Camargo Cardoso's birds died. Sojer (1989) and Sojer and Wirth (1989) noted the loss of the Naples bird, and Roth (1989b) the loss of one at São Paulo Zoo (in 1988), all of Camargo Cardoso's by 1988, and one at Walsrode, and the apparent addition of two in the Philippines. Silva (1989a; and 1990a, 1991a) gave two rather differing accounts of these last – in one of which the pair and two young were acquired from Singapore (see Remarks 11), in the other the pair producing all their young in the Philippines – adding that their number in 1990 was seven; DeDios (*sic*) and Hill (1990) give the second version, as does Low (1990), and it is accepted as true by T. Silva (*per* P. Scherer Neto *in litt.* 1992).

At November 1990 the birds publicly acknowledged in captivity numbered 16, with others acknowledged early in 1991 (in Hämmerli 1991), as follows: *São Paulo Zoo* (Brazil) four (three males aged 13, four and four years respectively, one female aged 13 years, all chromosomically sexed); *N. Kawall* (São Paulo, Brazil) two (one female, chromosomically sexed, this bird being taken as an adult from the wild in 1982 [Keller 1992], one male – estimated to be about 20 years old [Patzwahl 1991] received the month before from *W. W. Brehm of Vogelpark Walsrode* in Germany: see Measures Taken: Permanent Committee); *M. G. F. dos Santos* (Recife, Brazil) one (a female, said by the holder in notes to the Permanent Committee to have been taken from the wild as a six-month-old in July 1987, which matches a newspaper report by Cesar [1990], but in another version it was taken as a chick from a nest in riacho da Melância in February 1988: Keller 1992); *A. de Dios of Birds International* (Philippines) seven (three males, three females, one sex unknown, all derived from a pair acquired in November 1979: DeDios [*sic*] and Hill 1990); *W. Kiessling of Loro Parque* (Tenerife, Spain) two (male and female, endoscopically sexed: Silva 1990a, 1991a), these last not being old enough for breeding until 1989, when a single egg was laid (Low 1990; see Remarks 12). In addition, in early 1991 *J. Hämmerli* possessed a pair in Switzerland that he acquired in 1978 and from which he had successfully bred five offspring (Hämmerli 1991). There are also reports of a second pair with an undisclosed number of offspring, again in Switzerland; moreover, in early 1991 the Brazilian government was apparently in negotiations with an unnamed Brazilian aviculturist who had come forward under amnesty claiming to hold a pair and two captive-bred young (J. B. Thomsen *in litt.* 1991).

At November 1991 the birds publicly acknowledged in captivity numbered 25, as follows: *São Paulo Zoo* three (one male transferred to M. G. F. dos Santos); *N. Kawall* a pair, *M. G. F. dos Santos* a pair, *A. de Dios* a pair and eight offspring, of which one was male, five female and two unsexed, *W. Kiessling* a pair, *J. Hämmerli* a pair and four offspring (M. G. Kelsey *in litt.* 1991). In addition there was reportedly a 12-year-old bird in Germany whose owner wanted DM 30,000 for it, a pair also in Germany, a pair in Madrid, two in Argentina, two in Brazil, one in the U.S.A. and possibly one in Japan (T. Silva *per* M. G. Kelsey *in litt.* 1991). By June 1992 the Loro Parque pair had produced two offspring (T. Silva *in litt.* 1992 to M. G. Kelsey).

ECOLOGY Spix's Macaw is now believed, with ample justification, to be associated with gallery woodland in which mature specimens of caraiba, caraibeira or craibeira trees *Tabebuia caraiba* dominate, within the caatinga (i.e. dry scrub) zone of the Brazilian interior (Juniper 1990, Juniper and Yamashita 1990, 1991; see Threats). The importance of gallery woodland and the caraiba tree was first reported by Roth (1985), who was told how Spix's Macaw preferred the more humid areas of caatinga near small rivers ("riachos") where water was available and where the vegetation formed gallery forest. Roth (1986, also 1987c) later himself remarked that the most striking feature of the species's habitat was the high number of (mostly seasonal) creeks characterized by caraiba growth. The caraiba tree was reported to him as important for nesting and roosting, and direct observation in 1986 tended to confirm this, the birds habitually perching on the same branches, typically the most prominent and least leaved, and indeed they would use the same breeding holes (the first site used by the surviving pair in 1986 was one reputedly used continuously by the species for 50 years) and even the same flight-paths; such very traditional behaviour greatly facilitates the endeavours of trappers (Roth 1985, 1990). The one survivor at riacho Melância was flying around 20 km each day in late 1991, and was difficult to follow (M. A. Da-Ré *per* M. G. Kelsey *in litt.* 1991).

Juniper and Yamashita (1991) also determined that Spix's Macaws probably favour caraiba woodland because of nest-site availability, and they thought that this woodland was related to caatinga vegetation, since caraiba trees do not appear to form such formations elsewhere; the requisites for these formations included seasonally inundated watercourses above a certain size (8 m in width) and the presence of fine alluvial deposits. On the basis of discussions, aerial photographs and surveys, only some 30 km^2 of such woodland remain in Bahia, in three patches (Juniper and Yamashita 1990).

The general caatinga habitat of the region is characterized by the predominance of Euphorbiaceae (*Jatropha* and *Cnidoscolus*), along with caatingueira *Caesalpinia*, joazeiro *Zizyphus joazeiro* and several species of cactus, e.g. facheiro *Cereus squamosus* (on the highest tops of which Spix's Macaws were reported sometimes to roost), xique-xique *Pilocereus gounellei*, *Opuntia* spp. (Roth 1986, 1990). Spix's Macaw eats the seeds of favela or faveleira *Cnidoscolus phyllacanthus* and pinhão-brabo *Jatropha pohliana*, and the fruits of *Z. joazeiro* and pau-de-colher *Maytenus rigida* were reported eaten also, as well as (though this Roth doubted) those of the very local licuri palm *Syagrus coronata* (Roth 1985, 1986, 1988b, 1990; see Remarks 13). Food could not then be a limiting factor, as *Cnidoscolus* and *Jatropha* are among the commonest plants in the region and available even during very dry periods (Roth 1986). Mari-mari *Geoffroea spinosa*, a characteristic tree along the creeks, was said by one trapper to be a food source (F. B. Pontual *in litt.* 1992). However, in 1991/1992 the lone survivor was seen to use only one food source, the fruits and/or seeds of braúna *Melanoxylon* sp. (various observers *per* and including F. B. Pontual *in litt.* 1992). An early record of the species favouring passion-fruit may well refer to a taste developed in captivity (see Remarks 3). Reiser (1926) recorded birds coming to drink at a lakeside, "evidently from a great distance", the birds showing considerable wariness although, when finally drinking, doing so deliberately and uninterruptedly. The lone survivor has also shown a clear lack of confidence when drinking (from small pools), moving slowly down from branch to branch, calling nervously, and quickly flying to a high perch as soon as finished (C. R. Moura and M. A. Da-Ré *per* F. B. Pontual *in litt.* 1992).

Stands of buriti palm *Mauritia flexuosa* do not occur in the habitat at Curaçá (Roth 1986, 1990), yet groves of this plant, which grow locally within the caatinga in swampy or seasonally wet areas, have been identified as the key habitat of the species (Meyer de Schauensee 1970, Sick and Teixeira 1979, Ridgely 1981a, Sick 1985). Roth's (1986, 1987c, 1990) clear perception of the importance of caraiba woodland did not lead him to question the veracity of these reports about buriti palm use, since (despite finding evidence from the Gerais unconvincing) he presumably felt the records in question were indisputable; hence searches for the species in such habitat continued (and occupied much time), and resulted in the speculation – possibly influenced by similar comments in Keller (1987) – that Spix's Macaw's structural proximity to Red-bellied Macaw *Ara manilata* might reflect an ecological proximity, since the latter has a close association with buriti palms (Roth 1988a). Indeed, a dependence on buriti palm was speculated to be a cause of Spix's Macaw's unpredictability and even nomadism within a region, since stands would ripen in different areas depending on local conditions; equally, however, the rarity of Spix's Macaw was regarded as puzzling, given the general abundance of such stands in the "Gerais" region (Roth 1988a; see Remarks 14).

The breeding period was reported to be November to March, though variable with rainfall; birds use traditional holes in caraiba trees (also, according to two trappers, holes in braúnas: F. B. Pontual *in litt.* 1992) for nesting (and are very traditional in their habits in general); the number of young is two or three, and because they have a relatively small crop they need to be fed more frequently than other macaws (Roth 1985; also 1987c, 1990). In captivity up to four eggs have been laid in a clutch, with two-day intervals between eggs; the incubation period is 26 days, the fledging period is two months, and the young are fed by their parents for some three months after fledging (Hämmerli 1991). Birds remain normally in pairs (the single bird in July 1990 had formed a bond with a Blue-winged Macaw *Ara maracana*: Juniper 1990, Juniper and Yamashita 1990), though in the past they would occur in flocks up to 15 (Roth 1985); their occurrence in flocks was noted by von Spix (1824; see Remarks 5). They sometimes disappear from an area for several days or even weeks (Roth 1985, 1990). The survivor at riacho Melância was again paired with a Blue-winged Macaw in December 1991 and was then seen investigating a nest-hole (M. G. Kelsey *in litt.* 1991).

If the identification of birds at buriti stands was correct, it is worth considering that caraiba woodland clearance may have resulted in the displacement of populations for which only the availability of nest-sites was a problem; they might thus have become chronically nomadic (being long-lived birds suffering no food shortages) through the inability to locate suitable breeding habitat, and chance observation could have been responsible for the misattribution of habitat preference in the species. It is conceivable (if highly improbable) that the reappearance of the species at riacho Melância in 1990 was a genuine reoccupation, and explicable through tree loss elsewhere (but locals claim that the lone bird was always at the site: F. B. Pontual *in litt.* 1992).

THREATS The rarity of this species has always been puzzling, and could not be attributed to its present most serious threat, trade. However, an explanation is immediately apparent in Juniper and Yamashita's (1990, 1991) new evaluation of its habitat, whose destruction has evidently been proceeding over centuries (see below).

Trade The single most immediate threat to Spix's Macaw in the past 20 years has been, as speculated by Ridgely (1981a), trapping for the cagebird trade (Roth 1985, 1990; Thomsen and Munn 1988). There was evidently a period in the late 1960s and early 1970s when captive-bred birds (evidently Carvalhães's: see below) were available more than wild-caught ones (Sick 1969, King 1978-1979), but before this period wild nestlings were usually targeted (Sick 1969) and after it predominantly wild adults (Roth 1988b *contra* Sick 1985). Ridgely (1981a) thought the species's rarity in aviculture reflected the difficulty in procuring specimens, but in reality it seems to have reflected the species's genuine rarity in nature. Decoteau (1982) reported being offered a pair by an English dealer for US$20,000 in 1979, which indicates the costs likely to have been incurred by bird-fanciers who now hold or recently held specimens.

Despite this, Keller (1992) wrote of some 40 birds in the Curaçá population being reduced by trappers to four. In the years immediately preceding and including 1985, over 25 birds were reportedly taken from the Curaçá population, at first only young birds but later also adults caught on limed sticks (and without much care: on at least one occasion the parents were shot in the process of removing young from the nest) (Roth 1985). In 1984 12 birds (seven adults, five young) were reportedly removed, all but two young (which were hand-reared and sent to São Paulo) by a dealer in Piauí; two adults died soon after capture, some were sold in São Paulo for the equivalent of US$2,000 each (at a time when Hyacinth Macaws *Anodorhynchus hyacinthinus* were traded for $50), and others probably left Brazil through Paraguay (Roth 1985, 1986). Thomsen and Munn (1988) independently found sources to account for 23 birds being removed from the Curaçá population in the period 1977-1987, when trade in the species was controlled by two dealers: from 1977 to 1985, one ("Carlinhos" from Petrolina, Pernambuco) traded 15 birds, of which 13 were adults, the two nestlings being the first to be taken from the breeding area (in

1988 they were held near São Paulo); from 1984 to 1987, the other (Nascimento from Floriano, Piauí) moved eight birds, four of them nestlings taken in 1986 and 1987 from the same nest as the 1985 nestlings (the 1987 nestlings seized in Paraguay – see Measures Taken – being described as from the one remaining nest).

There is thus a conflict with Roth's evidence (see Population) that no breeding occurred in 1986 or 1987, although the discovery of a new site at riacho da Vargem supports Roth's (1988a) contention that another population must then have existed (there is a another less important conflict over the taking of adults and young, one study suggesting adults were the initial target and only later the young, the other *vice versa*). Keller (1987), presumably on the basis of solid inside information, reported no fewer than six young Spix's Macaws being for sale in 1987, all being exported from Brazil: two died during transport (a point noted also by Roth 1987d), two were then captured in Paraguay, and two "got away". More recently, Keller (1992) judged that as many as 25 young were taken in the period 1978-1988, and claimed that in 1982 alone no fewer than 21 birds (19 adults and two young) were caught with lime: of these, 13 adults died of food privation or poor treatment, one died on the way to São Paulo, one adult (female) went to N. Kawall, four could not be traced, and the two chicks went to J. A. Camargo Cardoso (see Remarks 15).

Inbreeding There is as yet no clear evidence that genetic relatedness might be causing problems, but it needs to be recognized that, apart from the fact that half of the known birds in the world are the offspring of the other half, the parents and current non-breeders are themselves very possibly closely related; it is even possible that one or more existing pairs are composed of siblings or of parent and offspring.

Private ownership Private ownership of Spix's Macaws has become a serious obstacle to the conservation of the species (a) because private demand is responsible for fuelling the exploitation of remaining populations, (b) because ownership is a matter of jealousy, prestige and possessiveness that is fundamentally different in psychological origin from the spirit of cooperation and selflessness needed to generate a scientifically based recovery programme (see, e.g., comments in Strunden *et al.* 1986, Brack 1987b, Forshaw 1989, Silva 1989a, Smith 1991a), and (c) because there are questions of legality that at least until very recently have remained intractable both inside and outside Brazil. As long ago as the late 1970s it was observed that "because most captive specimens are in private hands, there has been no comprehensive program to ensure that they are paired and housed under conditions conducive to breeding" (King 1978-1979). A broadsheet entitled "No chance for the Spix's Macaw?" put out by ZGAP, translating Arndt *et al.* (1986) and Strunden *et al.* (1986), concluded (English corrected) that "anybody who opposes an international coordinated breeding project can only be acting out of selfish reasons and would personally be responsible for the extinction of this species. The present owners should consider that they have caused the present situation by the demand and by buying the birds". Evidence that the attitude of most private owners remained intransigent as late as 1988 is given under Measures Taken concerning the Tenerife and Curitiba initiatives.

Hunting Hunting for food was identified as a serious pressure on all edible wildlife in interior Brazil, and one that Spix's Macaw was reported to have experienced in the Curaçá region (Roth 1985, 1990).

African bees When a hybrid African strain of the bee *Apis mellifera* spread through the Curaçá region some years previously (when invading new areas they are supposedly at their most aggressive), they were reported to have attacked incubating Spix's Macaws (which are tight sitters), killing some of them (Roth 1985); this was later modified and recorded as a possible occurrence (Roth 1988b, 1990). Thomsen and Munn (1988) were also told by trappers that recent breeding success had been low owing to hole occupation by African bees. However, Juniper and Yamashita (1990) found that only two out of 40 potential nest-holes obviously held bees in July 1990.

Habitat destruction The assumption that habitat loss has not been a significant factor in the decline of Spix's Macaw has long prevailed (e.g. King 1978-1979, Ridgely 1981a, Sojer 1989,

Sojer and Wirth 1989), and even Roth (1988a) wrote of a puzzling abundance of food and habitat for so rare a species, seemingly thus discounting the report he was given that Spix's Macaw had disappeared from Pernambuco and that caraiba trees had been cleared there (Roth 1986). It appears to have been Silva (1989a) who first expressed the causative link in these two events when he wrote "where craibeiras have been felled, as in the Pernambuco side of the São Francisco River, the species has disappeared"; yet Roth (1990) continued to ask why the bird could be so rare and what special circumstances determined its population size and distribution.

The rio São Francisco forms a major corridor down which settlers of interior Brazil have moved for over 300 years, and local farmers have indicated that caraiba woodland grows in places most favoured for the cultivation of subsistence crops such as maize; they are also the areas where pasture lasts longest into the dry season, and hence most human habitation has been along creeks, posing additional pressure through firewood-gathering (Juniper and Yamashita 1990, 1991). Moreover, very old specimens of caraiba now dominate the remaining woodlands, the result of chronic and excessive grazing pressure by domestic stock that has largely prevented regeneration (there is some – see Measures Proposed: Preservation in the wild): the gallery woodlands are themselves in real danger of disappearance (Juniper and Yamashita 1990, 1991). All this is evidence that habitat destruction over the centuries almost certainly explains the rarity of Spix's Macaw since it first became known to science, and it indicates that even now habitat degeneration remains a threat to the species (Juniper and Yamashita 1990, 1991).

MEASURES TAKEN Spix's Macaw is protected under Brazilian law (Bernardes *et al.* 1990) and is listed on Appendix I of CITES (King 1978-1979).

Preservation in the wild The initial (as well as the most recent) searches for the species in the wild, sponsored in both cases by ICBP and perhaps prompted by Ridgely's (1981a) call for a thorough study of the situation, were responsible for its precise location (Roth 1985, 1986, Juniper and Yamashita 1990, 1991). The first efforts to protect the wild birds, as recommended by Roth (1986), were taken by ZGAP, which provided funds to pay local people to act as guards at Curaçá, apparently from May 1986 to May 1987 (Roth 1987b,c, Sojer 1989, Sojer and Wirth 1989). Later survey work was also funded by IBDF and WWF (Roth 1988b, 1989b). Following the discovery of one bird at Curaçá in 1990, ICBP sought to make funds available for its temporary surveillance until appropriate government protection (through IBAMA, and overseen by M. A. Da-Ré) could be established (in July 1991: see below). Local enthusiasm for the species at Curaçá has led to the opening of an "Ararinha Azul" restaurant and the use of an effigy on a float during Independence Day celebrations, and this sense of community pride has been boosted by the local distribution of 5,000 posters and some tee-shirts (M. G. Kelsey *in litt.* 1991).

Searches for other populations This was naturally a major feature of the work undertaken by Roth (1985, 1986, 1988a, 1989b), and considerable progress was made in evaluating and eliminating areas. Still further progress – almost to the point where possible sites were exhausted (but see Measures Proposed) – resulted from survey work in 1990 (Juniper 1990). In 1991 M. A. Da-Ré and F. B. Pontual made further searches in southern Pernambuco and northern Bahia, but without finding new populations or evidence of them (M. G. Kelsey *in litt.* 1992).

Control of trade The rescue and return (to São Paulo Zoo) of two wild nestlings, smuggled via Petrolina (Keller 1987) to Paraguay (see Remarks 16) in late March 1987 (not 1988 as in Sojer 1989, Sojer and Wirth 1989), and bound for West Germany where a buyer was prepared to pay $40,000 for them (details, with some background inaccuracies, in, e.g., Hardie 1987, Ress 1987, Graham 1988), was a particular credit to TRAFFIC (notably J. S. Villalba-Macías), CITES, IBDF and various conservation personnel from WWF-U.S. and WCI.

Captive breeding Calls for urgent action involving private owners have been made since the critical situation in the wild was first grasped: Arndt *et al.* (1986) proposed an action plan with (a) a species management plan developed by CBSG in collaboration with IBDF, (b) the support of all captive holders, and (c) the retention of any offspring to build the captive stock. On 5 May 1987 TRAFFIC (Sudamérica) issued a memorandum proposing the formal establishment of a recovery committee (J. B. Thomsen *in litt.* 1991). Brack (1987b) and at one stage Silva (1989a) proposed the confiscation of privately held captive birds, at least in Brazil, perhaps unaware of the insurmountable practical and legal difficulties in such a measure. Roth (1987c) called for the urgent cooperation among holders in Brazil to begin a captive breeding programme. Thomsen and Munn (1988) sought a recovery plan which would (a) establish an *in situ* breeding operation in Brazil, as legal and logistical obstacles there appeared less than outside the country, and (b) concentrate studies on the known wild birds rather than on searches elsewhere (but between the drafting and publication of this proposal the last birds then known were trapped). Details of captive management in the Philippines are in Low (1990) and in Switzerland in Hämmerli (1991).

The Tenerife initiative on captive breeding In 1987 an initiative involving ICBP, CBSG, ZGAP and Loro Parque to bring together the holders of captive birds and develop plans for a consortium resulted in a meeting in August at Loro Parque itself. Despite considerable efforts by many interested parties to identify and invite them, no holders of birds attended except the host, W. Kiessling, and the meeting "largely failed" (Silva 1989a); certainly Low's (1988) assertion that the holders outside Brazil agreed to cooperate in pairing and lending birds is wrong. The meeting was, however, a step forward (Arndt 1987; see also Low 1987, Kiessling and Low 1987), as the CBSG proposals and conditions for the practical needs of a captive breeding programme remain valid (see Measures Proposed, last section).

The Curitiba initiative on captive breeding On 16 September 1988 an agreement on the captive breeding of Spix's Macaw, preliminary in nature while the involvement of IBDF was still pending, was signed by A. Mafuz Saliba for São Paulo Zoo and J. S. Villalba-Macías for both the CITES Secretariat and TRAFFIC (documentation provided by J. B. Thomsen *in litt.* 1991). At the ICBP/IUCN Parrot Specialist Group meeting in Curitiba, Brazil, October 1988, this agreement was introduced to the Brazilian private holders (who did not receive it well), and it was forwarded to IBDF for endorsement and participation. Silva (1989a) wrote that "news of this event stimulated several aviculturists into sending their birds to other, more capable collections", which is no more true than Low's (1988) remarks about the outcome of the Tenerife meeting. On 19 December 1988 IBDF issued a formal endorsement of and declaration of participation in the agreement (documentation provided by J. B. Thomsen *in litt.* 1991). (IBDF was replaced by IBAMA by law 7735/89 on 22 February 1989.)

Permanent Committee for the Recovery of Spix's Macaw This committee only formed after a series of meetings with varying degrees of official endorsement, as follows.

On 24 August 1989 the first unofficial meeting of a "committee for the Spix's Macaw" was held in São Paulo Zoo, and on 22 September 1989 IBAMA established a Spix's Macaw Working Group to establish the sexes of birds in Brazil, develop a management plan for the species, investigate its wild status, propose the structure of a permanent committee for its recovery, and identify interested institutions and individuals for their involvement in this committee (N. Schischakin *in litt.* 1990). Four days later a second, but still unofficial, meeting of this group took place to discuss sexing of birds (documentation provided by J. B. Thomsen *in litt.* 1991). In October 1989 the CITES meeting in Lausanne was the forum for a discussion involving W. Kiessling, A. de Dios, TRAFFIC and CITES, evidently concerning the movement of birds between certain facilities (see Silva 1990a, 1991a). The first two official meetings of the Working Group took place at São Paulo Zoo on 23 and 30 October, and resulted in draft statutes of the proposed Permanent Committee being prepared and forwarded to IBAMA (documentation provided by J. B. Thomsen *in litt.* 1991). The sexing of all birds in São Paulo was achieved in early 1990 by N. Schischakin of the Houston Zoo (*in litt.* 1990), and the Permanent Committee and its statutes were established under law (Portarias 330 and 331) on 13 March 1990 and formally published on 20 March (documentation provided by J. B. Thomsen *in litt.* 1991).

The inaugural meeting of the Permanent Committee was held at IBAMA's headquarters in Brasília on 12-13 July 1990, establishing C. S. Schenkel as its president and P. T. Z. Antas as studbook keeper, and binding itself to meet at least once a year and to develop an action plan involving literature surveys, the identification of areas to be investigated, a survey of birds in captivity and a management plan for them (minutes provided by J. S. Villalba-Macías *per* J. B. Thomsen *in litt.* 1991). The only published account of this meeting claimed that it "resulted in the Brazilians accepting all Spix's Macaws as legal – they had considered a great part of them as smuggled native fauna – and in a resolution calling for the governments of the countries where the birds are held to consider the birds as legal, provided their owners join the special committee and agree to work towards saving the species by 15 October of this year" (Silva 1990b); in fact, a formal announcement of this was still pending much later in the year (see Silva 1991b, and below).

An unofficial meeting of the committee took place in September 1990 when it was decided (1) to implant a microchip in and take a DNA record of each bird before the next meeting in March 1991 (Silva 1990b, 1991b), (2) to reject ICBP's proposal (to release a captive bird to form a mate for the last wild individual: see below) on the grounds of there being too few captive specimens and of too great a risk to wild birds from trappers (Silva 1991b), and (3) to build a massive aviary at the Curaçá site into which to induce the wild bird to fly and breed in semi-captivity with a suitable mate (Silva 1991b,c); at this meeting discussions also took place on how to involve currently secret and illegal holders of the species (Silva 1991b). Simultaneously, US$35,000 were raised by the Loro Parque Association for the Preservation of Parrots to support fieldwork on the species, to help construct a giant aviary within its range, and to guard the remaining bird and any mate provided for it (Silva 1990b, 1991c). At this meeting the expectations of the committee were that a male held in São Paulo Zoo would be exchanged with a female in the Philippines (Silva 1990b, 1991b). Soon afterwards, in October 1990, the male at Walsrode was loaned to N. Kawall to pair with the latter's female (Silva 1990b, *Papagaien* 6 [1990]: 169, Patzwahl 1991).

Only on 25 October 1990 did the Brazilian government issue a decree (Portaria 2161) not to confiscate or seek to confiscate specimens of Spix's Macaw if the holders agreed to participate in the Permanent Committee's work to manage the remaining captive population (documentation provided by J. B. Thomsen *in litt.* 1991), and only on 5 February 1991 was this resolution notified to parties by the CITES Secretariat (the whole exercise being an attempt to enlist the cooperation of those holders with sufficient conscience and public-mindedness who otherwise would be driven to conceal their illegal possessions for fear of prosecution under international law) (documentation provided by J. B. Thomsen *in litt.* 1991).

The second meeting of the Permanent Committee took place on 20 April 1991 at São Paulo Zoo, at which one of the holders (M. G. F. dos Santos) donated US$2,000 and CI donated US$8,000 towards the conservation of the species, allowing, among other things, for the appointment of a biologist to guard the single wild bird, and in July 1991 M. A. Da-Ré took up this position (M. G. Kelsey *in litt.* 1991).

The third meeting of the Permanent Committee took place on 28-29 November 1991 in Recife, at which, among many other matters, (1) a population viability analysis conducted by CBSG was commissioned, (2) the exchange of a Swiss-held female with a Philippines-held female, to form two new pairs, was made conditional upon the acceptance by the Swiss authorities of the legality of the stock held by J. Hämmerli, and (3) a working group was established to consider reintroducing birds to the wild, following the offer by A. de Dios of an individual to join the wild bird (M. G. Kelsey *in litt.* 1991).

MEASURES PROPOSED In the following account the "Measures to avert imminent extinction of Spix's Macaw" outlined by ICBP in September 1990 are treated in the first section, although point four refers to captive breeding.

Preservation in the wild Following the discovery of one wild bird at riacho Melância in July 1990, ICBP made the following recommendations (adumbrated in Juniper 1990 and Juniper and Yamashita 1990; also *CBSG News* 2,1 [1991]: 17). (1) An immediate priority must be to continue to safeguard the one remaining bird in the wild, a vital step because (a) it is likely to be much easier to introduce captive-bred birds to the area if a wild one is present (so much traditional knowledge held by that bird could be lost by its capture for any breeding programme), and (b) the conservation of the gallery woodland, very necessary if birds are to be set free there in the future, is much more defensible if a wild bird remains present. (2) A mate for this bird (thought to be male) should be found from among the captive stock for release at the earliest stage, so that wild breeding can commence as soon as possible, and so that other birds can begin to learn from the wild bird, whose experience of the local environment (food resources, roost-sites, predators, etc.) may be absolutely critical to the re-establishment of a wild population. (3) The gallery woodland habitat needs fencing in sections for 5-10 year periods, to allow regeneration beyond the reach of grazing and browsing stock. (4) A breeding facility needs to be established in the immediate area, fully equipped and professionally run, the benefits of which would include (a) a neutral site encouraging cooperation, (b) the optimal climate for the species and the proper setting for the eventual release of birds, (c) a facility from which to monitor and manage wild and captive birds as a single entity, and (d) the generation of local interest and goodwill, which is of ultimate importance to all these efforts.

A project has now been developed by the Permanent Committee to investigate the distribution and conservation of caraiba woodland in Bahia (M. G. Kelsey verbally 1991); further research by the Royal Botanic Gardens in Kew in 1991 indicated that this formation is indeed of enormous botanical interest and that caraiba trees grow extremely slowly, the majority being some 200-300 years old and with little regeneration in at least the past 50 years (C. Stirton *per* M. G. Kelsey verbally 1991). However, at least one farmer already fences off areas (to provide forage when the annual supply reaches its lowest point), and experiments are now being conducted by M. A. Da-Ré to decide management regimes for further regeneration (M. G. Kelsey *in litt.* 1992).

Search for other populations Any further search for other wild birds must not compromise efforts to conserve the single known specimen by implying that such work may prove superfluous. However, now that a specific habitat type has been identified, it is important to visit every other area where such habitat is or may be found, including (a) a more extensive survey of the riacho da Vargem; (b) a detailed survey of the north side of the rio São Francisco between Abaré and Petrolina in case some stands of caraiba trees survive, despite reports; and (c) a survey westwards from Petrolina and Juazeiro as far as Remanso, which Roth (1986) regarded as the westernmost extension of the same caatinga habitat as that at Curaçá, and which might hold some creeks with caraiba gallery woodland. In addition to this, Roth (1986) argued for surveys of more humid valleys with gallery forests in the Gerais (Roth 1987d saw caraiba-lined creeks in the Parnaíba and Parnaibinha headwaters in southern Maranhão; and Roth 1988a also wanted Xique-xique, Bahia, investigated), and, as they seem not to have been done in his subsequent fieldwork, there is a case for undertaking them now. There is also, obviously, a case for mounting a concerted search for mature gallery woodland anywhere else within the 300,000 km^2 area from which reports of the species have emerged, but this should be done in consultation with naturalists and scientists who already know the areas as well as with maximum use of modern aids such as aerial photographs (or indeed aerial surveys). Roth (1988b) also advocated using dealers, by whatever means available, to help identify new sources of birds; but this has obvious drawbacks.

The search for other birds in captivity, to maximize the number of specimens available to help the important captive breeding initiative now under way, must proceed, and avicultural societies should do all they can to urge covert holders of the species to surrender them to their national authorities, if necessary through third parties.

Control of trade Roth (1988b) identified the dealers and trappers specializing in Spix's Macaw and called for their activities to be stopped, which would require full-time work by a Brazilian. IBAMA clearly has an opportunity to bring charges against dealers known to have acted illegally.

Captive breeding Although plans for captive propagation are now the responsibility of IBAMA's Permanent Committee for the Recovery of Spix's Macaw, the provisions of the CBSG's proposed Memorandum of Agreement, drawn up after the Tenerife initiative, are summarized in the following paragraph for information.

The current known captive birds constitute the founder stock for the propagation programme, and are to be registered with any offspring in a studbook, never offered for sale, and managed to a plan developed and directed by a Consortium for Propagation, this plan seeking to achieve optimal age matches and genetic lineages. The consortium, consisting of holders, plus representatives of the Brazilian government, CBSG and ICBP, shall meet once a year at its own expense to review events and discuss recommendations, including the commissioning of scientific or husbandry studies to secure the species's captive breeding. Action shall be taken by consensus if possible, otherwise according to majority vote, and all actions taken to manipulate the husbandry of the species shall be part of a systematic plan, to be properly documented in reports to the consortium. Offspring from the managed captive population, when it is secure, shall be donated to a release programme in due course.

Amongst other recommendations made in pursuit of successful breeding are (a) medical examination and quarantine for any birds being paired for the first time, (b) genetic fingerprinting of all birds to help determine their relatedness and confirm their identification, (c) sexing of all birds by laparoscopy or chromosome analysis, (d) protocols on housing and dietary quality and on veterinary management, and (e) preservation of skins, bodies and tissues of all birds that die (N. Schischakin *in litt.* and verbally 1990).

Comments on the captive breeding of this species, by Smith (1991a), are as follows: "The truth is that captive-breeding attempts so far have been appalling. The few reared do not make up for the numbers of adults that have died, and continue to die". If the most recent results tend to offset these remarks, made by a former holder of the species, their value remains in reminding all parties that time is as critical a factor as any other in the conservation of Spix's Macaw; and in this regard it certainly appears that the minimum of one meeting per year for the Permanent Committee is too few for the optimal management of its complex affairs (NJC).

REMARKS (1) Spix's (or Little Blue) Macaw, an exceptionally beautiful species, much smaller than members of the genus *Anodorhynchus* with which it is associated because of its colour, occupies its own genus and, according to Sick (1981), is "not a real macaw". Low (1984) thought no-one would consider it a parakeet ("conure"), evidently unaware that this is precisely what Dutton (1900) had done.

(2) The uniform doubt accorded in this account to all sight-records except those from Curaçá seems preferable to an exercise that gives more weight to some sightings than others, but, as suggested in the last paragraph under Ecology, the possibility exists that some records could have been genuine, referring to displaced birds. An example of a patently erroneous sight record (readily repeated by Goeldi 1894) is from the río Ucayali in Peru (von Berlepsch 1889).

(3) It is of interest to note that the species appears to have been seen and described ("grösser als ein *Psittacus*, das ganze Gefieder ist graublau") by G. Marcgrave when he worked in Pernambuco in 1638 (Herrmann 1989), although (as with the more certain Golden Parakeet *Guaruba guarouba*: see relevant account) the individual(s) in question may have been in captivity (particularly as Marcgrave remarked its preference for passion-fruit).

(4) Barra Grande and the riacho Melância are adjacent and, seemingly, contiguous, so although treated separately by Juniper and Yamashita (1990), they are here regarded as one area (as evidently they were by Roth 1985, 1986, 1987b).

(5) Von Spix (1824) actually wrote: "habitat gregarius, rarissimus licet, propre Joazeiro in campis ripariis fluminis St. Francisci, voce tenui insignis" ("it lives in flocks, although very rare, near Joazeiro in the region bordering the rio São Francisco, [and is] notable for its thin voice"); the point about its voice is confirmed by Smith (1975-1978).

(6) Juniper and Yamashita (1991; also Juniper 1991) drew attention to a sighting by E. Kaempfer of the species in 1927 "at a railway station at Joazeiro in Bahia" (Naumburg 1928, 1935), which they took, with some reason, to indicate a specific field record. However, copies of Kaempfer's correspondence (held in AMNH and forwarded by M. LeCroy *in litt.* 1990) reveal that the record was of one "alive on the railway station", i.e. in a cage presumably awaiting

transportation. That the species was either so coveted that disinformation about it existed as long ago as the 1920s (which seems improbable) or that it was genuinely rare and little known at that time, at least in the vicinity of Joazeiro, is indicated by the facts that before he made his discovery on the station Kaempfer wrote from the town (twice) that "nobody knew anything about such a parrot", and that when finally found he was informed that it came from the central Bahian mountains (see Naumburg 1928). It is worth noting that Reiser (1926) also met with professed ignorance of the species when he asked after it in Joazeiro in 1903.

(7) Keller's (1992) version is that, after the bird was shot, two others "fled" towards Barro Vermelho (in the Serra da Borracha), and the fourth and last remained under the protection of the same proprietor who had shot its companion.

(8) As a sidelight on how little was known of Spix's Macaw in the last century, Forbes (1881) noted that he found a stuffed specimen in a Recife museum labelled from Angola.

(9) It would appear that the importations occurred in and after 1926, since in that year Tavistock (1926) had baldly reported it "very rarely imported".

(10) Smith (1975-1978) readily conceded that "as my chances of obtaining another are nil I shall try to hybridise it with another species of small macaw".

(11) The magazine *Singapore Aviculture* 3(2), June 1983: 13-16, carried photographs of "Mr. & Mrs. Spix's... and family" which appear to represent an adult pair and two young, although all four are not shown together and it is conceivable that the adults shown are just the two young at a later stage of development. It is these four birds that Silva (1989a) indicated went to the Philippines, by implication in 1983. If it is the case that only a pair went to the Philippines, and in 1979, the question obviously arises of the fate of the birds illustrated in the magazine.

(12) Low's (1990) assertion that the Loro Parque birds were too young to breed until 1989 must be set against their registration (incidentally, as two males) in the *International Zoo Yearbook* 26 (1986) (see Silva 1990a), which indicates that the birds must have been in Loro Parque in 1985 or earlier. Indeed, it is not without exasperation that one reads in an article, clearly based on an interview with the holder himself, that "Wolfgang Kiessling managed to obtain a doddering pair in 1984" (Stern and Stern 1990: 70). Keller (1992) considered them probably the survivors of three birds (one died) he once saw in private hands in São Paulo and which were sold and taken to Tenerife some years ago.

(13) C. Yamashita (*in litt.* 1990) pointed out that faveleiro and pinhão are both colonizers, and that only *Maytenia* would seem to have been in the original vegetation of the region. Licuri palms are the staple of Lear's Macaw *Anodorhynchus leari*, and therefore would seem unlikely to be utilized by the much weaker-billed Spix's.

(14) What is surprising is that Roth's early recognition of the importance of caraiba woodland at Curaçá – he even indirectly equated the loss of Spix's Macaw in Pernambuco with the clearance of these trees – did not promptly lead to a survey of the region for similar habitat, since such action by Juniper and Yamashita (1990) resulted in the immediate discovery of an entirely new site which, from local reports, held birds up to 1989; Roth (1985, 1986) had also had the testimony of certain trappers, confirmed in 1987 by Thomsen and Munn (1988), that the source of all captive birds was the one small area around Curaçá.

(15) Keller (1992) apparently obtained this information in an interview with Carlinhos on 8 November 1991, when F. B. Pontual (*in litt.* 1992) was also present, this latter indicating that on subsequent days (when Keller was no longer present) other versions and figures were offered, so that no confidence can be placed in any one account of the trapping-out of the last population.

(16) The dealers in Asunción who were caught in possession of young birds in 1987 were E. Koopmann and his daughter G. Cáceres (J. B. Thomsen verbally 1991).

BLUE-THROATED MACAW *Ara glaucogularis* E[3]

The Blue-throated Macaw is currently restricted to a small area of savanna and gallery forest in northern Bolivia, where it is exploited for the cage-bird trade although its precise whereabouts have not been discovered by ornithologists. It appears to be rare (possibly less than 1,000 birds in total) within its range and urgently requires fieldwork to determine its status and conservation needs.

DISTRIBUTION The Blue-throated Macaw (see Remarks 1) is known to be distributed in northern Bolivia, in the southern half of Beni department and in north-western Santa Cruz department, but it has never been found in the wild by field ornithologists, so that no precise data exist on its current whereabouts. There have been additional sightings and references from Argentina and Paraguay attributed to this species, at least some of which are attributed to its confusion with Blue-and-yellow Macaw *Ara ararauna* (Ridgely 1981a, Ingels *et al.* 1981).

Bolivia Records are from two departments, Santa Cruz and Beni. Apart from data on three museum skins, all information derives from trappers and dealers in the cagebird trade. Coordinates in the following account are from OG (1955a) and Paynter *et al.* (1975).

Santa Cruz The type was taken at Santa Cruz de la Sierra (480 m), Santa Cruz department, Bolivia, at 17°48'S 63°10'W, in or before 1863 (Dabbene 1920, 1921, Ingels *et al.* 1981), and there are two specimens taken on 26 January 1920, at 400 m, and 4 July 1922, at 500 m, from Buena Vista, Santa Cruz department, Bolivia, at 17°27'S 63°40'W (Ingels *et al.* 1981). A keeper at the zoological garden in Santa Cruz de la Sierra, where at that time (1983) three specimens of the macaw were kept, reported that they had been captured at San Ignacio de Velasco (300 m), at 16°22'S 60°58'W, in central Santa Cruz (Nores and Yzurieta 1986). However, the late N. Kempff Mercado reported that he had never heard of the species inhabiting this locality, that the six specimens at the Santa Cruz Zoo in 1984 had been captured on the ranch of Sr Gasser between Santa Rosa de Yacuma and Trinidad, and that another of their specimens (now dead and not preserved) had been captured near Buena Vista in western Santa Cruz (Nores and Yzurieta 1986, M. Nores *in litt.* 1989). At 10 de Mayo, a town c.75 km west of Buena Vista, Blue-and-yellow Macaws were found to be common, but no Blue-throated Macaws could be found (Nores and Yzurieta 1986). Trappers told Lanning (1982) that though they worked throughout Santa Cruz they had not found it in other than the north-western corner of the department.

Beni Traders reported to Lanning (1982) that they had found the species in the south-west of the department in the area from Santa Rosa (230 m), at 14°10'S 66°53'W, east 150 km to Santa Ana (220 m), at 13°45'S 65°35'W, and San Miguel (220 m), at 13°55'S 65°23'W, and also in the south-east of the department in the area of "Monteverde" near San Nicolas (220 m), at 14°16'S 64°25'W. A Bolivian resident familiar with the trapping and export of macaws reported that the range extends from 40 km south-west of Santa Rosa at Reyes (230 m), 14°19'S 67°23'W, east to San Nicolas, with the highest concentrations near Santa Rosa and San Nicolas (Riviere *et al.* 1986). One dealer reported that specimens exported to European zoos originate in southern Beni, south of Trinidad (240 m), at 14°46'S 64°50'W, along the upper río Mamoré (Ingels *et al.* 1981). Here the Blue-throated Macaw, Blue-and-yellow Macaw and Scarlet Macaw *A. macao* occur sympatrically, the Blue-throated being outnumbered by Blue-and-yellow by 100:1 (Ingels *et al.* 1981). Other dealers (especially R. Romero) likewise report the species from south-eastern Beni, south of Trinidad, in the drainage of the upper río Mamoré, where it occurs regularly, usually in pairs, and always greatly outnumbered by Blue-and-yellow, with which it often mingles (Ridgely 1981a). Traders reported to Lanning (1982) that they collected the species in south-eastern Beni near Caimanes (230 m) (misspelt "Canaima" in Lanning 1982: D. V. Lanning *in litt.* 1989), at 15°26'S 64°05'W, and in adjacent north-western Santa Cruz.

Searches for the macaw in southern Bolivia in southern Santa Cruz, Chuquisaca and Tarija departments in 1981-1982 proved negative, and local inhabitants did not know of any "blue and yellow" macaws in the region (Lanning 1982). However, a "blue and yellow" macaw captured in 1975, on the southern edge of Bolivia in the area of Yacuiba (580 m), Tarija, at 22°02'S 63°45'W, is presumed to be this species (Olrog 1979), although a photograph of the bird leaves the identification equivocal (Ingels *et al.* 1981).

Argentina The species has been reported from Misiones province in northern Argentina (Orfila 1936, Pereyra 1950), although the source of this information has so far not been located (Ingels *et al.* 1981). A sight record of three pairs in 1952 in a deep valley of the río Carapari near Bolivia in Salta province, north-west Argentina, and a previous sighting at Orán somewhat further south in Salta (Hoy 1969), were presumably of this species (Ridgely 1981a, Nores and Yzurieta 1988b), although later searches have not revealed it there and local residents do not know it; possibly the birds in question were only wanderers from further north (Ridgely 1981a). Lynch Arribálzaga (1920) reported the species from the area of río Bermejo in Chaco province, Argentina, and as the río Bermejo also runs in Salta and along the border of Formosa province, Ingels *et al.* (1981) assumed that this record was the basis for Olrog's (1959) inclusion of those provinces in the bird's range; Olrog (1963, 1968, 1979) himself was quick to deny all evidence of the species in the country.

Paraguay The persistent inclusion of this country in the range of the Blue-throated Macaw appears to rest entirely on its mention by de Azara (1802-1805) (Ingels *et al.* 1981); there is, however, an extraordinary discussion of the species by Podtiaguin (1941-1945), treated here under Remarks (2). De Azara (1802-1805) wrote that according to the Guaraní Indians, this macaw now occurs neither south of 24°30'S, nor within 50 leagues (c.275 km) of the capital, where it was previously common. The macaw described by de Azara seems to be referable to Blue-and-yellow Macaw (Ingels *et al.* 1981), Blue-throated Macaw (Ridgely 1981a), or both (Nores and Yzurieta 1986). Although neither of the two species seems to occur in Paraguay today (Ridgely 1981a), at least Blue-and-yellow Macaw did so formerly (Sánchez Labrador 1767, Brabourne 1914, Dabbene 1920), and records of Blue-throated Macaw from Villa Franca, Desmochados and "Guzu-Cua" (possibly Guazú-Cuá), Paraguay (SOMA 1935-1942), may in fact be referable to Blue-and-yellow Macaw (Ingels *et al.* 1981). Nevertheless, as both species occur sympatrically in Bolivia they may well have done so in Paraguay in the past.

POPULATION One exporter estimated a total of about 1,000, another a total of about 500 (Lanning 1982). The estimate of 5,000 to 7,000 by Riviere *et al.* (1986) is based on the proportion of Blue-throated Macaws caught relative to Blue-and-yellows, while in the same paper they admit that the reason none was trapped prior to 1979 was that no trappers had "caller birds" to lure them in. In 1981 about 60 (Lanning 1982) and between 1979 and 1984 approximately 175 were exported (Riviere *et al.* 1986). Nilsson (1985) reported that 111 were imported into the U.S.A. between 1980 and 1983, but that by 1984 the importation had ceased.

ECOLOGY The region inhabited by the species lies at elevations between 200 and 250 m, and is tropical savanna with scattered "islands" of trees and ribbons of gallery forest along the watercourses; the savanna is inundated by rains from October to April, the trees and palms being on slightly higher land and on better-drained soils (Lanning 1982). Traders report that the macaw's preferred food is palm nuts (Lanning 1982). According to the traders the species travels in pairs, rarely small flocks of up to five, and has not been seen to congregate in large flocks as the Blue-and-yellow Macaw sometimes does, although (*contra* N. Kempff Mercado *per* M. Nores *in litt.* 1989) it sometimes mingles with that species (Ridgely 1981a, Lanning 1982). Captive birds are smaller and slimmer than Blue-and-yellow Macaws, and built for flying very fast; they appear notably inquisitive, and their high trilling call is much closer to Red-fronted Macaw *Ara rubrogenys* than to anything made by Blue-and-yellow, all of which lends weight to the possibility that the species is adapted for travelling long distances in search of various unpredictable foods and has little to do with the Blue-and-yellow Macaw (J. Abramson verbally 1992). According to the hunters, the macaw nests in cavities in trees from November to March, and raises one or two young per nest (Lanning 1982). The second egg is laid two days after the first (Riviere *et al.* 1986, Leibfarth 1988), and the incubation period is 28 days for each egg; the young leave the nest 90-94 days after hatching (Leibfarth 1988).

THREATS If the population is only 500-1,000 birds, and 60 birds were exported in one year (Lanning 1982), then trapping must be a serious threat to the species (Low 1984). It is not known to what extent this abuse continues at present, and one of the significant threats to the species is conservationists' fundamental ignorance of its distribution, status, ecological needs, level of exploitation and loss of habitat.

MEASURES TAKEN In 1983 all further international trade of the species became prohibited as it was placed on Appendix I of CITES (WTMU 1988), and it also became formally protected against capture and trade within Bolivia in 1984 (Riviere *et al.* 1986). However, its greatest protection is afforded by the remoteness of its habitat and its elusiveness (Riviere *et al.* 1986). There are at least four reports of successful breeding in captivity (Hayward 1983, Kiessling 1985, Riviere *et al.* 1986, Leibfarth 1988).

MEASURES PROPOSED The first priority with this species is to find it in the wild, then to assess its ecological needs, status and the pressures upon it, and to draw up an effective management plan based on these findings. Fieldwork to discover the chief centres of occurrence within Bolivia should be conducted as soon as possible, on a coordinated basis (e.g. through ICBP), since there are many individual plans and proposals to undertake the work. Meanwhile, thorough inspection of all shipments of "blue and yellow" macaws should be undertaken both at export and import sites (Lanning 1982), and particularly the throat should be investigated, as it is often painted black so as to look like Blue-and-yellow Macaw (B. Woods E. *in litt.* 1986). The captive population needs to be managed carefully to maintain genetic diversity, and a studbook is being established (Clubb and Clubb 1991). This is clearly a species that could benefit from concerted efforts to maximize captive numbers through aviculture, with a view to stemming any illegal pressure on wild birds, and to establishing a good reserve until more is learnt of the wild population.

REMARKS (1) The species has been known for over 100 years as Caninde Macaw or Wagler's Macaw under the scientific name *Ara caninde*, based on a description from Paraguay by de Azara (1802-1805). It is not clear, however, whether de Azara was referring to a single specimen or giving a general description of the birds he observed: if the former it was possibly a hybrid, as he noted that the crown was green (it is blue in Blue-throated Macaw, green in Blue-and-yellow), the face had three horizontal black lines (again as in Blue-and-yellow, Blue-throated having four or five that are blue-green) and the gular area was broadly turquoise blue (as in Blue-throated), not black (as in Blue-and-yellow). It is thus hard to accept Dabbene's (1920) view that the description of the throat was acceptably of Blue-and-yellow Macaw, or the statement by Ingels *et al.* (1981) that de Azara's description is unequivocally of that species. Dabbene (1920) renamed the blue-throated species on the basis of the specimen taken at Santa Cruz de la Sierra, first calling it *A. azarae*, and later (Dabbene 1921) *A. glaucogularis*. However, Dabbene's papers went largely unremarked, and the use of *A. caninde* persisted (e.g. Forshaw 1981). Ingels *et al.* (1981) designated the specimen on which Dabbene (1920) had based his description as the type, and suggested the English name Blue-throated Macaw.

(2) Podtiaguin (1941-1945; specifically 1944: 114-115) referred to two specimens (young birds) being collected at Colonia Esperanza on 18 June 1939, and another at Colonia Nueva Italia in "Dep. Villeta" (Villeta is south of Asunción), adding that in certain years the species travels

widely, that it is not then rare to find it in Paraguay, and that the only reason it is not more often reported is the complete absence of ornithologists in the country. These skins appear to be lost and the entire commentary fails to match the facts as given in the account above.

RED-FRONTED MACAW *Ara rubrogenys* V[9]

Confined to a small area of high, arid valleys in south-central Bolivia, where it numbers only a few thousand individuals (possibly only a thousand), this unusual macaw has suffered from capture for the cagebird industry, from persecution as a pest in peanut and maize fields, and from loss of trees within its habitat. It is the object of several concurrent projects.

DISTRIBUTION The Red-fronted Macaw is confined to south-central Bolivia, where it has been collected and sighted around the headwaters of río Yapacani and along the drainages of the río Mizque and río Grande, in western Santa Cruz, south-eastern Cochabamba and extreme northern Chuquisaca departments. There are sight records from along the río Pilcomayo drainage in Chuquisaca and immediately adjacent western Potosí department. Although only three localities of museum specimens appear to have been published before around 1990 (des Murs 1855, Bond and Meyer de Schauensee 1942-1943, Remsen *et al.* 1986), no fewer than 21 of the (at least) 29 museum specimens in existence are labelled with locality, all but one having been taken in or before 1937 (specimens in AMNH, ANSP, CM, EBD, FMNH, MNHN and UMMZ). The locality identified by des Murs (1855), "Estella", is untraced. In the following account coordinates are from OG (1955a).

Santa Cruz The species has been collected in the upper río Yapacani drainage in Santa Cruz at El Palo, 1,900 m, at 18°06'S 64°12'W (Remsen *et al.* 1986; specimen in CM), and sighted between El Trigal (1,740 m) at 18°17'S 64°09'W (whence a specimen in MNHN) and Valle Grande (2,085 m) at 18°28'S 64°06'W (Romero 1974a, Ridgely 1981a, Lanning 1982, 1991). Records from along the río Mizque drainage in Santa Cruz include (from east to west): 30 km east of Comarapa, 2,000 m, at 18°05'S 64°21'W (sighting: Nores and Yzurieta 1986); Tin-Tin, 2,150 m, at 18°01'S 64°25'W (specimens in FMNH, MNHN); Pulquina (1,690 m), at 18°06'S 64°25'W (sight records: Ridgely 1981a, Lanning 1982, 1991); and Saipina (1,475 m), at 18°06'S 64°34'W (sight records: Ridgely 1981a, Lanning 1982, 1991).

Cochabamba Records include (from east to west): Pérez (1,472 m), at 18°06'S 64°44'W (sight records: Lanning 1982); Ele-Ele, 1,525 m, at 18°06'S 64°45'W (Bond and Meyer de Schauensee 1942-1943, Lanning 1991); Pojo, 2,500 m, at 17°45'S 64°49'W (two specimens in CM); 25 km north of Aiquile, 1,800 m, at 18°00'S 65°07'W (sight records: Lanning 1982); 22 km north of Aiquile, 2,150 m at 18°02'S 65°08'W (sight record: Nores and Yzurieta 1986); Aiquile, 2,150 m, at 18°12'S 65°10'W (specimens in FMNH, UMMZ); and Mizque, 2,290 m, at 17°56'S 65°19'W (four specimens in AMNH).

Chuquisaca One specimen (in AMNH) labelled "Río Grande, 1,100 m" was evidently taken near Bella Vista, at c.18°40'S 64°17'W (see Remarks 1). Lanning (1982) reported 12 sightings along a tributary of río Grande in the north of the department, at 1,600-1,900 m near Chuqui Chuqui, at 18°50'S 65°07'W; C. Cordier (in Alderton 1985) noted the occurrence of these parrots north-west of this area, around río Caine at the headwaters of río Grande (where later they were studied by Boussekey et al. 1991a,b, 1992), and on 1 August 1989 M. Kessler (*in litt.* 1989) during a survey of only four hours found 40-50 macaws just east of Torotoro, 2,100-2,500 m, on the border of Cochabamba and Potosí departments, Torotoro being at c.18°07'S 65°46'W; this is considered the best *Schinopsis* "forest" (see Ecology) in the entire region (M. Kessler *in litt.* 1989). Lanning (1982) reported four sightings along río Pilcomayo at the eastern border of Potosí, near Uyuni, at 19°27'S 64°50'W.

Judging from the extent of habitat, Lanning (1982) estimated the range of the Red-fronted Macaw to be c.18,000 km^2 in south-east Cochabamba and adjacent parts of Santa Cruz and Chuquisaca, and c.2,000 km^2 along the río Pilcomayo in Potosí and Chuquisaca. All of the specimens from museums mentioned above were taken between 29 September and 28 December, except the singles from Trigal, collected 30 June, El Palo, collected 20 July, and Chapare, dated 21 July (but this was captive when it died). Lanning (1982) noted that the macaw is a strong flier and very mobile, and that it could probably be seen throughout its range at any time of the year, although this was doubted by Clarke and Duran Patiño (1991).

POPULATION Ridgely (1981a) estimated a total population of no more than 1,000-3,000 birds, while Lanning (1982), having found the distribution to be somewhat larger, estimated a total of 3,000-5,000 birds. This latter estimate has been recently doubted, because it was based partly on the view that the species moves very little within its home range, whereas modern evidence seems to be that it moves considerably; thus a census of the main area of the ríos Grande and Mizque in 1991 revealed 555-626 birds, with reports suggesting that altogether less than 1,000 persist (Clarke and Duran Patiño 1991). Half those questioned in this more recent work judged that the species was rarer than it was 8-10 years before, and a third considered it scarce or rare, with reported loss of populations at Comarapa and Pererata and a substantial decline around Trigal (Clarke and Duran Patiño 1991). In a study area of 200 ha in the río Caine, average daily sightings of 180 birds suggested a total population there of around 60 individuals (Boussekey *et al.* 1991a,b, 1992).

ECOLOGY The Red-fronted Macaw inhabits mountainous, fairly arid scrubby regions intersected with narrow gorges and wider floodplains, generally at elevations from 1,100 to 2,500 m (Ridgely 1981a, Lanning 1982, Clarke and Duran Patiño 1991; specimens in AMNH, ANSP, CM and FMNH). In western Santa Cruz department it was found in March and April in valleys with desert-like shrubby vegetation, and somewhat taller, though still dry woodland on some upper slopes and ridges, and was never seen in better developed patches of woodland (Ridgely 1981a). Lanning (1982) reported it from a mixture of scrub and semi-arid deciduous woodland. Clarke and Duran Patiño (1991) note that the lower río Grande system has been classified as temperate dry woodland, the lower río Mizque system as subtropical cactus woodland, and the upper ríos Grande and Mizque system as temperate cactus woodland; of these, they felt that the last was the most preferred habitat. Common genera of trees, usually less than 5-7 m tall, and shrubs in these woodlands are *Prosopis*, *Carica*, *Acacia*, *Mimosa*, *Gourleia*, *Schinus*, *Erythrina*, *Salix*, *Alnus* and *Dodonea* as well as balsa trees and large columnar cacti (*Cereus* spp.) (Lanning 1982, Fjeldså 1987). The study area in the río Caine was xerophytic (300-600 mm of rain per year, all between November and April) and dominated by cacti (*Cleistocactus* sp., the endemic *Lobivia caineana*, *Echinopsis* sp., *Opuntia* sp., *Quiabentia pereziensis*) plus bromeliads *Hetchia* or *Dyckia* sp. and *Tillandsia*, spiny bushes (notably *Prosopis kuntzei*) and, rarely, small trees 4-10 m tall, of which the commonest was *Schinus molle* (Boussekey *et al.* 1991a,b, 1992). At Torotoro M. Kessler (*in litt.* 1989) found the Red-fronted Macaw on the edges of irrigated fields near the river bed and very extensive *Schinopsis–Aspidosperma–Prosopis–Jacaranda* forest on the slopes (both the valley bottoms and the ridges above, at 2,500-3,000 m or more, are settled). During the day it travels alone, in pairs or small groups, rarely up to 20 individuals (Romero 1974a, Lanning 1982, Nores and Yzurieta 1986), while flocks of 30-80 birds may be seen in wide-ranging roosting flights (Ridgely 1981a). The birds are reliably reported to roost in sheer, vegetation-free cliffs, preferring those overhanging running water, adjacent to the larger rivers, higher than 40 m, and free of human disturbance (Clarke and Duran Patiño 1991), and E. Pitter and M. Bohn Christiansen (*in litt.* 1991) found two roost-sites in holes in 50 m high cliffs, although they also witnessed overnight roosting in trees near fields; for further data on daily movements, etc., see the last paragraph in this section.

In a recent survey in the río Grande, local residents identified well over twenty food-plants of the species, the four most consistently reported being two legumes (soto *Schinopsis quebracho* and algarroba *Prosopis chilensis*), a cactus (carapari *Cereus* or *Neocardenasia* sp.) and chañara (unidentified) (Clarke and Duran Patiño 1991), confirming reports by Romero (1974a,b), Ridgely (1981a) and S. Arías (verbally 1988); a recent survey in the río Caine produced a rather different list (entirely based on local reports) consisting of *Schinus molle*, *Aspidosperma* sp., *Prosopis kuntzei* and *P. juliflora*, *Cnidoscolus* sp. and two grasses, *Tribulus* sp. and *Cenchrus* sp.

(Boussekey *et al.* 1991a,b, 1992); moreover, Lanning (1991) recorded birds feeding 12 times on the fruits of *Jatropha hieronymii*, a common tree in the valleys where the species occurs, while Silva (1989a) singled out *Erythrina cristigalli* as a food-plant (presumably derived from Romero 1974b). Chewing of *Aspidosperma* leaves occurs during the resting periods, apparently for their juice (E. Pitter and M. Bohn Christiansen *in litt.* 1991). However, cultivated crops also form part of the species's diet, so that it is considered a pest by local farmers (Ridgely 1981a, Lanning 1982, E. Pitter and M. Bohn Christiansen *in litt.* 1991). Local farmers report that at the end of the breeding season (March–April) birds range into maize fields at up to 3,000 m, which are then in the main "milk" stage, and stay in these areas until groundnuts become available around May–June (Clarke and Duran Patiño 1991; also Boussekey *et al.* 1991a,b; see Threats); the same informants denied that the birds actively dig for the nuts, rather glean what have been missed during harvest or else pick over the stacks prior to their storage (Clarke and Duran Patiño 1991), but active digging was reported in Alderton (1985) and by both R. S. Ridgely (*in litt.* 1988) and E. Pitter and M. Bohn Christiansen (*in litt.* 1991), who all noted that this was chiefly for nuts left behind after the harvest and after the fields have been ploughed, much less prior to the harvest. Once a flock of 200 birds was seen feeding in a maize field (Nores and Yzurieta 1984a, 1986), six were once observed sitting on the ground in a bean field, presumably feeding on the beans (M. Kessler *in litt.* 1989), and frequent feeding on a small grass seed (from a common weed, so that on average 14 per minute were consumed) has been noted (E. Pitter and M. Bohn Christiansen *in litt.* 1991). Apricots are occasionally taken (S. Arías verbally 1988). In October–November 1990 in the río Caine a local population of around 60 birds appeared to be feeding exclusively on some 30 ha of cultivated ground, and according to the local farmers they do so at times throughout the year; thus they follow the plough during the October groundnut sowing, seek the green shoots as they begin to appear, forage on the maturing crop in June, and glean the ungathered nuts after harvest (Boussekey *et al.* 1991a,b). In a side valley of the río Grande, 1991/1992, birds foraged mainly on the fruits of *Zizyphus mistol* in November/December, on planted corn in January/February, and fruits of *Jatropha risinifolia* from February to April (E. Pitter and M. Bohn Christiansen *in litt.* 1992). Birds drink in small groups, not going to the main river but to adjacent streams where the water flows slowly; drinking follows feeding in the morning period, lasting some 10 minutes, and occurs during the afternoon feeding session (Boussekey *et al.* 1991a,b).

Ridgely (1981a) was told by local people that the macaws nest semi-colonially on certain cliffs during September–February, and Lanning (1982, *in litt.* 1989) reported it to breed in inaccessible cavities (holes and cracks) in large sandstone cliffs during December–March, although the two closest nests he found were 200 m apart on separate cliffs (see Lanning 1991). Attempted copulation (on the ground) was witnessed twice in late October, and the earliest clutches are presumably laid in November or December; however, birds seen in November that appeared to be 6-8 months old must have hatched in March and thus represented late breeding, with eggs laid in February (Boussekey *et al.* 1991a,b). Fieldwork in 1992 strongly suggested that the breeding season is timed to coincide with maximum fruit production of wild plants, in February–March (M. Boussekey *in litt.* 1992). Romero (1974a) believed the species to be monogamous, as he always observed it in pairs; this was confirmed by Boussekey *et al.* (1991a,b, 1992), who noted that even in feeding groups a pair (sometimes with a juvenile) would always stay closer to each other than they did to the other birds. Nest-sites are in cliffs, and local reports indicate that nests are dispersed and not colonially grouped (Boussekey *et al.* 1991a,b, 1992). In one case incubation in captivity took c.26 days, and nine weeks after hatching the young could feed by themselves (DeLoach 1983); young birds fledge at about 70-73 days (Robiller *et al.* 1988). Of 26 observations (in late 1990) of pairs accompanied by immatures, 24 (92%) involved one young, one involved two and one three (Boussekey *et al.* 1991a,b); at the same site at the equivalent stage of the following year, however, pairs with two or three young were seen just as often as pairs with only one offspring, and counts of larger groups of foraging birds (up to 74) indicated that approximately one-third were first-year birds (E. Pitter and M. Bohn Christiansen *in litt.* 1991).

Immatures in October–November participated little in foraging, often either sitting on the ground next to their foraging parents or remaining perched in a nearby bush (presumably they are still then being fed bill-to-bill) (Boussekey *et al.* 1991a,b).

Daily activity, October–November (1990), took the following pattern: between 05h30 and 07h00 the birds arrived from their (undiscovered) roosting cliffs, flying towards the feeding areas; between 07h30 and 10h00 they returned in the direction of the roosting cliffs, resting quietly in trees in the shade over the long midday period, though occasionally indulging in noisy social activity; between 14h30 and 17h30 they flew back again to feed; and between 17h00 and 18h30 they again returned towards the roosting cliffs (Boussekey *et al.* 1991a,b); in 1991 this pattern was repeated, except that return to forage following the midday rest period was generally delayed until 16h00 (E. Pitter and M. Bohn Christiansen *in litt.* 1991). However, in another study extending from December to March, the periods of activity were 05h30-09h30, 11h30–13h30 and 15h30–19h30 (Lanning 1991).

THREATS The Red-fronted Macaw has suffered capture for the cagebird industry and persecution by local farmers, and is now threatened by habitat destruction.

Trade Both Ridgely (1981a) and Lanning (1982) considered the capture of this species for the pet-trade a serious threat (see Remarks 2). The macaws, including both breeding adults and subadult birds, are caught with mist-nets and cannon-nets after being lured into baited fields (Ridgely 1981a). Imports into the U.S.A. went from 16 in 1977 to 82 in 1978, and 125 in the first eight months of 1979 (Nilsson and Mack 1980). In 1981 alone 300 were estimated to have been exported (see Robiller *et al.* 1988). Local people in the río Caine valley reported in 1991 that trappers from Cochabamba came every year until 1987 to capture birds (E. Pitter and M. Bohn Christiansen *in litt.* 1991); this conforms well with Robiller *et al.* (1988), who referred to "several hundred birds in trade annually in recent years", and reported seeing (in 1986) 20 wild-caught birds in a Singapore dealer's establishment, destined for the Philippines (Robiller *et al.* 1988).

Persecution Local farmers consider it a pest on their crops of maize and peanuts and kill the species by shooting it or baiting it with poisoned maize, so that around 1980 it was judged that the species would be extinct within 10 to 15 years if further hunted (D. Wells in Alderton 1985); Romero (1974b) said the birds were shot both as pests and for their tail-feathers, and also expressed concern for its security. However, neither Ridgely (1981a), Lanning (1982) nor, retrospectively, C. Cordier (in Müller-Bierl and Cordier 1991; see Remarks 2) regarded persecution by local farmers as a serious threat to the macaw, arguing that few of the farmers have firearms, a view largely confirmed in recent studies by Boussekey *et al.* (1991a,b, 1992), E. Pitter and M. Bohn Christiansen (*in litt.* 1991) and Clarke and Duran Patiño (1991), although the last, in noting that five farmers out of 24 admitted to killing birds occasionally, with nobody claiming more than two per year, regarded the overall number lost annually as of some importance if the population is as low as they judge it (see Population).

Habitat destruction Although habitat destruction was not regarded as a serious threat by Ridgely (1981a; also *in litt.* 1989) or Lanning (1982), C. Cordier (in Alderton 1985) argued that the algorroba tree, which he (and also S. Arías verbally 1988) stated to be an important food-source of these macaws (see also Ecology), is being heavily cut to make charcoal for the tin-smelting plant near the town of Oruro, and that the macaws will therefore turn to more frequent use of maize and peanuts as a food-source, this again leading to further persecution. In recent years in the main part of the range (although not in the río Caine: Boussekey *et al.* 1991a,b, 1992) the problem of habitat loss has become more acute, and is held directly to blame for the decline in numbers believed to have occurred through the 1980s: thus (1) the flood-plain valleys have lost 40% of their natural vegetation to agriculture, (2) the use of the macaw's food-plant soto (but also even various preferred cacti) as firewood to produce sugar "cake" (used in local alcohol production) entails a serious loss of food, and (3) outside the flood-plains an intensifying cattle industry is causing erosion and much habitat loss (Clarke and Duran Patiño 1991). In the río

Caine, the only threat has been judged the improvements to roads that lead to the archaeological tourist site of Torotoro, 20 km to the north (Boussekey *et al.* 1991a,b), but another perception is that this area has also suffered seriously from habitat loss, with the few remaining small forested areas along the river (used by the birds in the dry season) being heavily degraded by grazing goats, charcoal extraction and firewood collection (E. Pitter and M. Bohn Christiansen *in litt.* 1991). It may therefore be no coincidence that the only locality where M. A. Carriker found it in the 1930s (Ele-Ele) was the one in which xerophytic vegetation was more abundant than anywhere else he visited (see Bond and Meyer de Schauensee 1942-1943).

Natural enemies appear chiefly to be birds of prey: an unidentified raptor, possibly a Roadside Hawk *Buteo magnirostris*, was reported to have taken a chick from the nest, and panic was witnessed amongst birds when Andean Condors *Vultur gryphus* flew close to their nests on the río Grande (Clarke and Duran Patiño 1991) and when vultures (three species), Black-chested Buzzard-eagles *Geranoaetus melanoleucus* and Crested Caracaras *Polyborus plancus* flew close while they were feeding on the ground in the río Caine valley (Boussekey *et al.* 1991a,b, E. Pitter and M. Bohn Christiansen *in litt.* 1991), while direct attacks by Peregrines *Falco peregrinus* have been witnessed (E. Pitter and M. Bohn Christiansen *in litt.* 1991).

MEASURES TAKEN The Red-fronted Macaw was placed on Appendix I of CITES in 1983 (largely in response to the study by Lanning 1982, funded by ICBP Pan American Section and NYZS), thus receiving protection against all international trade and transport (WTMU 1988), and a 1984 ban on the export of all live animals and birds from Bolivia has now become indefinite (Clarke and Duran Patiño 1991). As an apparent consequence, trapping of birds in crop-fields, the traditional method of capture, seems genuinely to have stopped in the late 1980s (Boussekey *et al.* 1991a,b, Clarke and Duran Patiño 1991), although at Omereque on the upper río Mizque a band of smugglers was reported still to be taking 20-40 birds annually (Clarke and Duran Patiño 1991). Demand for birds in the U.S.A. apparently diminished during the 1980s owing to successful captive breeding (Clubb and Clubb 1991). Only the eight or so breeding birds on the río Zapillar exist within a protected area, namely the Amboró National Park (Clarke and Duran Patiño 1991). The study by Boussekey *et al.* (1991a,b, 1992), reported here (and now leading to a cooperative programme: see below), was undertaken in direct response to the circulation of a draft of this text in 1988. Other fieldwork is being undertaken by E. Pitter and M. Bohn Christiansen, funded by WWF-Denmark, and in early 1992 5,000 posters urging protection of the species and its habitat were made, distributed and apparently well received throughout the region (S. Arías *per* M. Bohn Christiansen *in litt.* 1992).

MEASURES PROPOSED The Red-fronted Macaw would benefit from a package of measures including site protection, elimination of trade, education campaigns, appropriate technological aid, and continuing study and monitoring. Except for the last two paragraphs, the recommendations below are based on Clarke and Duran Patiño (1991), who set out certain points in considerable detail. Some of these points will be addressed in a cooperative programme between Espace ZOOlogique (France) and Santa Cruz University, Natural History Museum and Zoo (M. Boussekey *in litt.* 1992).

Fieldwork A census in the río Grande is needed to confirm assumptions about the macaw's status there and to help plan the proposed wildlife sanctuary (see below); further study of the populations west of the main Sucre highway and in the Pilcomayo drainage is also needed.

Site protection The entire río Mizque valley (south of Saipina as far as its confluence with río Grande) and that part of the río Grande from El Oro to the main Sucre highway should be declared a wildlife sanctuary, and a minor adjustment to the limits of the Amboró National Park is needed to include the small breeding population in the río Chañawaykho.

Elimination of trade The national authorities should formally notify civic authorities and all regional corregidors (over 50 listed) to enforce the prohibition on the persecution and trapping of the macaw, with punitive action in Omereque against the trading ring in that area.

Education A small educational campaign highlighting the local and national endemism of the macaw, involving radio broadcasts, posters and videos, ought to generate considerable popular support for the species.

Appropriate aid The local sugar industry in the species's range, responsible for much tree consumption, would benefit by the introduction of fuel-efficient methods for the production not only of sugar cake but also molasses, whose addition to cattle fodder might reduce grazing pressure in the region.

Habitat conservation In the río Caine valley, a strategy and a campaign to preserve the remaining native vegetation are vital, with replanting of native trees both to provide alternative food sources for the birds and to counter the extensive soil erosion now taking place (E. Pitter and M. Bohn Christiansen *in litt.* 1991).

Captive breeding Silva (1989a) provided an indication of the surprisingly wide representation this species has in captivity, and stated that lack of protection in the wild will throw the onus of conservation onto captive breeding. However, while captive breeding has obviously greatly helped by reducing the demand for wild-caught birds, and while the development of a studbook, already established (Clubb and Clubb 1991), remains important, there is no immediate need to consider captive breeding a major option in efforts to secure the species.

REMARKS (1) The specimen labelled "río Grande, 1,100 m" was taken by on 6 November 1915 (AMNH label data) by collectors who were on the upper río Grande between Pucará and Villa Serrano on that day, and it seems likely that they obtained the specimen on the right bank of the river, in Chuquisaca department, perhaps in the vicinity of Bella Vista, at c.18°40'S 64°17'W, and certainly no more than a two-day mule ride from Pescado (now Villa Serrano), Chuquisaca, at 19°06'S 64°22'W (A. V. Andors *in litt.* 1988).

(2) Alderton (1985) used the testimony of C. Cordier, along with published information by D. Wells (*Avicult. Bull.*, July 1981), to discredit the work of Lanning (1982), which had led to the placing of the species on Appendix I of CITES. Wells had indicated that the species was a crop pest and much persecuted by farmers (something not observed or reported by Lanning), and Alderton (1985), in criticizing Lanning for this failure, expressed frustration that "with a ban on legal trade, the only option available to the farmers is to kill the birds"; he used Cordier's information at other points to indicate apparent inadequacies in Lanning's work. It is therefore worth noting that Cordier has subsequently expressed two opinions in line with Lanning's (whether accurate or not) and made one admission that stands awkwardly against the testimony of Wells, these being that: (a) persecution by farmers did not constitute a problem for the species (Müller-Bierl and Cordier 1991); (b) intensive trapping of the birds represented a very serious threat (Robiller *et al.* 1988); and (c) depredation of crops was greatly overemphasized by dealers in order to justify their exploitation of the species (Robiller *et al.* 1988).

GOLDEN-CAPPED PARAKEET *Aratinga auricapilla* V[9]

Although occupying a wide range in central-eastern Brazil from Bahia and Goiás south to Paraná (one record from adjacent Paraguay), the Golden-capped Parakeet has become extinct in many regions and extremely local in others, owing to the loss of its forest habitat and, perhaps, the impact of national trade levels; much survey and biological work is needed as well as the continued or new protection of key sites, notably in Minas Gerais.

DISTRIBUTION Apart from a single citation for Paraguay, at Puerto Bertoni[1] (Podtiaguin 1941-1945), 25°38'S 54°40'W in Paynter (1989), close to the Paraná border, the Golden-capped Parakeet is endemic to central south-eastern Brazil, from eastern and central-southern Bahia and eastern Goiás through Minas Gerais to Espírito Santo (no records since 1950), Rio de Janeiro (one recent record), São Paulo (two recent records) and northern Paraná (one recent record). Nominate *auricapilla* is confined to northern and central parts of Bahia; birds from southern Bahia tend to be intermediate between this race and *aurifrons* (see Pinto 1935); the race *aurifrons* occupies the rest of the range given (see, e.g., Forshaw 1989; also Remarks).

Ridgely (1981a) cited Santa Catarina as "reportedly" in the species's range, and Forshaw (1989) included it as the southernmost state, but there seems to be no evidence for this; moreover, a dubious nineteenth-century record for Rio Grande do Sul is not acceptable (Belton 1984-1985), and neither state was included in the species's range by Pinto (1978). However, the records from Ilha Solteira, Itapura and Nova Independência on the banks of the rio Paraná in São Paulo (see below) suggest the possibility of its occurrence across the river in Mato Grosso do Sul.

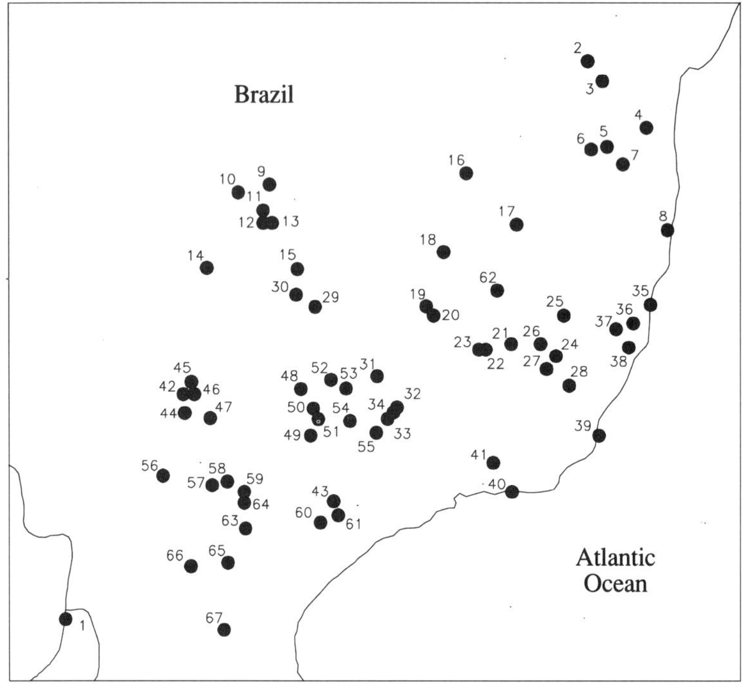

Bahia Localities (from north to south) include: Santo Amaro area[2], late 1970s; Lençóis (400 m), February 1989 (one pair); Macaco Seco, near Andaraí, November 1913; Iracema[3] (mapped in Naumburg 1930; now Iramaia), October 1927; rio Gongogi at Cajazeiras[4], June 1928, and at the confluence with rio Novo, December 1932; Conquista[5] (now Vitória da Conquista) and nearby Porcos[6] (Wied 1831-1833; see Bokermann 1957); Verruga[7], rio Pardo, July 1921; in and around Monte Pascoal National Park[8], late 1970s (specimens in AMNH, FMNH, MCZ, MZUSP; also Hellmayr 1929a, Pinto 1935, Ridgely 1981a, J. F. Pacheco verbally 1991).

Goiás Localities (north to south) include rio das Almas[9], Jaraguá (Fazenda Thomé Pinto), August 1934; Goiás city[10], recently (C. Yamashita *in litt.* 1987); "Fontas", Inhumas[11], November 1962; Trindade[12], March 1967; Goiânia[13] (in one case specifically "Campo-limpo"), November 1962, September 1963, February and April 1966, April, May and November 1967; Rio Verde[14], April 1940; Caldas Novas[15], March 1945 (unless otherwise stated, all records are based on specimens in CMN, MNRJ, MNHN, MZUSP; also Pinto 1936, Ridgely 1981a).

Minas Gerais Localities (north to south, apart from those west of 46°W: see further below) include: Januária[16], rio São Francisco, November 1931; Fazenda Ramaiana[17], Joaima, March 1970; Pirapora[18], January 1937; mouth of rio Indaiá, rio São Francisco, Morada Nova[19], September 1947 (Aguirre and Aldrighi 1983); Barra de Paraopeba[20], May 1930; Dom Joaquim[21], October 1968; Lagoa Santa[22] (Reinhardt 1870) and Pedro Leopoldo[23] and Lagoa Santa, 1971-1973 (A. Brandt *in litt.* 1987); Caratinga Reserve[24] (Fazenda Montes Claros), October 1986 (M. A. Brazil and D. R. Waugh *in litt.* 1986), September and October 1987 (A. Brandt *in litt.* 1987), July 1988 (S. G. D. Cook *in litt.* 1988) and October 1990 (R. S. Ridgely *in litt.* 1991); rio Doce on the lower Piracicaba, right bank, August 1940, and on the lower Suaçuí[25], September 1940; Rio Doce State Park[26], 1977 (Ridgely 1981a), 1981 (A. Brandt *in litt.* 1987); Raul Soares[27], June 1949 and July 1957; Casa Queimada, Serra do Caparaó[28], August 1929 (where no source before semi-colon, records are from specimens in AMNH, FMNH, LACM, MCZ, MNRJ, MZUFV, MZUSP, UFMG). Records west of 46°W are from the rio (= ribeirão) Jordão near Araguari[29], June 1901 (Hellmayr 1906c) and several localities along the rios Araguari and Quebra Anzol[30], February to November 1987 (A. Brandt *in litt.* 1987); between Piumhi and Vargem Bonita, May 1990 (Gardner and Gardner 1990b); Serra da Canastra National Park[31], October 1983 (LPG); Carmo do Rio Claro[32], February 1959 (specimen in MNRJ); Monte Belo[33] (Fazenda Monte Alegre) and Conceição de Aparecida[34] (J. F. Pacheco *in litt.* 1986, C. E. Carvalho *in litt.* 1987). A record for Itatiaia is given under Rio de Janeiro.

Espírito Santo Localities include: rio Itaúnas (in one case specifically Conceição da Barra[35]), September and October 1950; rio São José[36], September 1942; São Domingos[37], August 1940; Lagoa Juparanã[38], December 1929 (specimens in AMNH, MNRJ, MCZ and MZUSP; also Aguirre and Aldrighi 1983).

Rio de Janeiro Wied (1831-1833) found it on the lower reaches of the rio Paraíba[39]; BMNH has two skins labelled "Rio de Janeiro"[40] received in 1895; MCML had five of which at least one was from Rio de Janeiro (Forbes and Robinson 1897); and a flock was seen at Valença[41] in December 1990 (J. F. Pacheco verbally 1991). A turn-of-the-century sight record (in Pinto 1951, 1954) from middle altitude on the forested slopes of the Serra de Itatiaia (part of which is in Minas Gerais) must now (given the area's relatively high observer coverage) be doubted.

São Paulo Localities in the northern half of the state (west to east) are: Itapura[42], October 1938 and January 1957 (and indeed the entire lower Tietê[43] at the end of the nineteenth century); Nova Independência[44], February 1957; Ilha Solteira[45], August 1990 (group of eight); Ilha Seca[46], February 1940; Valparaíso[47], June and July 1931; Avanhandava, November 1903; Fazenda Varjão, Lins, January and February 1941; Barretos[48], no date; Silvania[49], December 1937; Fazenda Tres Barras[50], Pitangueiras, September 1945; Pontal[51] (a small resident population), 1991; Ituverava[52], May and August 1911; Franca[53], no date; Fazenda São Miguel[54], Cajuru, May 1943; Caconde[55], May 1900; localities in the southern half (west to east) are (all but the last three) in the Paranapanema valley at: Porto Marcondes[56], east of Teodoro Sampaio, May 1945 (site now submerged by the Taquaruçu dam: LPG); opposite the rio Tibagi (Tibaji) confluence[57], May 1945; Corredeira das Flores[58], Assis, rio Paranapanema, September 1943; Fazenda Palmira (south of Assis), September 1943; Fazenda Cayoá[59], Salto Grande, rio Paranapanema, August 1903; Itapetininga[60], nineteenth century; Ipanema[61] ("Campo de Guarapiranga"), July 1820; and Tejuco[62], evidently close to present-day Campinas, November 1822 (specimens in AMNH, CM, FMNH,

LACM, MCZ, MZUSP, YPM; also von Pelzeln 1868-1871, von Ihering 1898, Hellmayr 1906c, von Ihering and von Ihering 1907, Pinto 1932, 1938, 1945, Aguirre and Aldrighi 1983, C. Yamashita *in litt.* 1990, J. F. Pacheco verbally 1991).

Paraná Localities (north to south) include: rio das Cinzas[63], May 1903; Jacarezinho[64], March 1901 (von Ihering and von Ihering 1907 used "Ourinho", which is the old name: see Pinto 1945: 273); Fazenda Monte Alegre[65] (i.e. presumably "Castro" in Pinto 1938), August 1907 (Pinto 1932, 1935); rio Baile and Cândido de Abreu[66], November 1929 (same day and collector) (specimens in AMNH, FMNH, MZUSP, USNM; see corresponding section under Vinaceous Amazon *Amazona vinacea*); and the banks of the rio Jordão close to its confluence with the rio Iguaçu[67], c.30 birds, June 1987 (Straube 1988).

POPULATION In general the Golden-capped Parakeet has become rare, although where it can still be found it may sometimes prove common (see below); the area over which it is or was distributed is massive, and it is clearly likely that some populations (possibly major ones) remain to be discovered, but Ridgely's (1981a) conclusion – fully supported by Forshaw (1989), who pleaded for the species's listing "as rare in the *IUCN Red Data Book*" – that a very substantial decline must have occurred in recent decades, cannot be disputed, except inasmuch as the decline may have been in progress for two hundred years. Wied (1831-1833) apparently found it common on the Paraíba in Rio de Janeiro state, since he referred to its being rare further north until he penetrated the hinterland of Bahia around Vitória da Conquista, when it "again" became common, with "many flocks" consisting of 12-20 birds; the Paraíba population has evidently now almost gone, apparently along with all those in Espírito Santo, while there has been no indication of the species's continuing abundance anywhere in Bahia (see Distribution, Ridgely 1981a). In what must now be considered the core of its range, Minas Gerais, it was common in almost all remaining forest fragments surveyed from February to November 1987, but uncommon in secondary growth and pastureland with interspersed trees and palms in the same region; it was always seen in groups of 2-15 individuals (A. Brandt *in litt.* 1987); over 40 birds were seen in the Caratinga Reserve in 1988 (S. G. D. Cook *in litt.* 1988). In Goiás there is no evidence that it occurs in large numbers (C. Yamashita *in litt.* 1987). In two areas of São Paulo state (Itapetininga municipality and the lower rio Tietê) the species was reported to be common in the 1890s (von Ihering 1898), which clearly no longer obtains. The 1987 and 1990 records from Paraná and Rio de Janeiro are encouraging but presumably refer to small, isolated and doubtless diminishing populations.

ECOLOGY The Golden-capped Parakeet is clearly not a typical Atlantic Forest species, yet its distribution shows it to reach or have reached the Atlantic Forest borders, while extending through generally much drier inland regions in semi-deciduous forest. Ridgely (1981a) noted that, unlike the other two members of the Sun Parakeet *A. solstitialis* superspecies, the Golden-capped is a forest-based bird (in fact the Jandaya Parakeet *A. jandaya* is also a woodland bird, but of less humid formations: C. Yamashita verbally 1991); thus while the Golden-capped favours fringes and small clearings, at least a patch of forest must be nearby. In southern Minas Gerais it occurs in the same areas as Peach-fronted Parakeet *A. aurea* and inhabits the canopy of forest patches alongside Maroon-bellied Parakeet *Pyrrhura frontalis* (J. F. Pacheco *in litt.* 1986); in the north of the state it occurs alongside Blue-chested Parakeet *P. cruentata* (de Mattos and de Andrade 1988; see relevant account). Descourtilz's (1854-1856) view that it is rarely found in virgin forests, but frequently seen in extensive secondary growth, may be based on its use of forest edge (even in 1822 at Tejuco in São Paulo it was recorded at the edge of forest in dry trees: von Pelzeln 1868-1871); the evidence under Population concerning its relative abundance in forest and second growth certainly suggests the importance of primary habitat. There seems to be no altitudinal constraint on the species, which was recorded at 2,180 m in the Serra do Caparaó (specimen in AMNH).

Food is fruits and seeds: an undated specimen in UFMG had eaten guiabo (okra) seeds; one in MNRJ from March contained corn and seeds; and one in MZUSP from September held fruits (and had been taken in capoeira). The species likes maize (Wied 1831-1833), and in the last century at least was notorious as a pest in corn plantations, which were visited by large flocks, these birds favouring any soft sweet fruit (Descourtilz 1854-1856).

Breeding is poorly documented; of eight specimens (in AMNH) collected in June (two), August (two), October (one) and December (three) whose gonads were examined, only one from June had them slightly enlarged, the others being dormant; however, an October specimen in UFMG had developed testes, and birds were in pairs, November (von Pelzeln 1868-1871).

THREATS Extensive land clearance in the south-eastern parts of the species's range has clearly had a major impact, and its present distribution is now heavily fragmented; moreover, most of the last forest patches in this region continue to be cut (Ridgely 1981a; also Forshaw 1989). The impact of this fragmentation will depend on the carrying capacity of remaining protectable forests, their distance from each other, and the dispersive ability of the species; it is possible that some populations can stay in contact through the use of riverine forest corridors.

There appear to be no records of human persecution of this species in response to its depredation of crops, but it remains exploited for trade: it is relatively common in illegal markets in Brazil, being offered for sale in lots of up to 15 birds (C. E. Carvalho *in litt.* 1987). The situation at the international level is confused by the similarity in both appearance and scientific name of the Peach-fronted Parakeet (also known, even more confusingly, as the Golden-crowned Parakeet, e.g. in Low 1972), and there are consequently no reliable data on levels of trade in the past decade (see Inskipp *et al.* 1987); however, it is known that *auricapilla* was imported into West Germany "in hundreds" in the early 1980s (R. Wirth verbally 1992).

MEASURES TAKEN The species has been recorded from several protected areas, namely the Monte Pascoal National Park in Bahia and the Rio Doce State Park, Fazenda Montes Claros (Caratinga Reserve), Serra da Canastra National Park and (presumably) Serra do Caparaó National Park in Minas Gerais; it has also been found in or very close to the Chapada Diamantina National Park in Bahia (at Lençóis and Andaraí), but the high observer coverage in recent decades has failed to confirm it in Itatiaia National Park.

MEASURES PROPOSED Despite its extensive range, this species needs to be comprehensively surveyed and studied. A research programme into its population dynamics and dispersive capacity, and a detailed analysis of its habitat and feeding requirements at various sites where it occurs in Goiás, Bahia, Minas Gerais and São Paulo, should partner a general review of its status in these states (making every effort to locate major new populations and define the limits of its range). Certain sites for the species in eastern Minas Gerais deserve particularly urgent investigation since they appear also to hold populations of other threatened birds (including parrots): the Rio Doce State Park and the Caratinga Reserve are two crucial localities. The record of the flock from Valença in Rio de Janeiro is notable as this area also holds a small population of Vinaceous Amazon (see relevant account); further study there is to be encouraged. The species is not protected by Brazilian law, and this should be rectified.

REMARKS The Golden-capped Parakeet has been regarded as a subspecies, *A. solstitialis auricapilla* (Pinto 1978, Sick 1985). However, we follow Ridgely (1981a) in tentatively regarding *A. jandaya*, *A. solstitialis* and *A. auricapilla* as members of a superspecies. There is a zone of contact between *A. auricapilla* and *A. jandaya* in northern Goiás, but hybrids are uncommon, typical *jandaya* being found only 40 km north of Brasília; there is an ecological separation between them in Formosa in that region, *jandaya* occurring in less forested areas on calcareous soil (C. Yamashita *in litt.* 1986).

CUBAN PARAKEET *Aratinga euops* V[9]

The Cuban Parakeet has become a rare bird throughout Cuba owing to excessive trapping and the loss of its semi-deciduous woodland and palm savanna habitat, such that it now appears to survive in only a few more remote regions of the country, notably the Península de Zapata and the Cuchillas del Toa; a full status survey should be undertaken to determine whether and what further management is needed.

DISTRIBUTION The Cuban Parakeet was originally recorded throughout Cuba except for La Habana province (Garrido and García Montaña 1975; also García undated), although currently its range has contracted into seemingly rather few core areas (identified below as those from which there are recent records). Even in the second half of the nineteenth century it had disappeared (or was believed to have disappeared) from most of the island, still occurring in the Ciénaga de Zapata (Zapata Swamp), Bahía de Cochinos (Bay of Pigs) region, Trinidad mountains, the Bayamo region and the Isla de la Juventud (Isle of Pines) (Gundlach 1871-1875, 1876), and by 1915 the population in the Zapata Swamp was thought probably the only one west of Camagüey (Barbour 1923, 1943); in fact, it is clear from the dates attaching to the localities enumerated below that both Gundlach and Barbour were allowing their understandable alarm to inflate the confidence they placed in their distributional information. In the following account, records or reports (excluding Isla de la Juventud: see Population) are given from west to east by province, and all coordinates are derived from OG (1963a) or from a reading of ICGC (1978), as follows:

Pinar del Río Península de Guanahacabibes, apparently a modern stronghold (Silva 1989a) although never previously listed as a site (and denied as a locality by O. H. Garrido *in litt.* 1991); La Mulata, 22°52'N 83°23'W, where a small flock was seen in 1933 (Rutten 1934) although the species is now regarded as extinct there (O. H. Garrido *in litt.* 1991; but see Remarks 3 concerning El Pan de Guajaibón);

Matanzas Península de Zapata, perhaps the single most important (and certainly the best known) site, with many records down to the present, localities within it including Santo Tomás, Soplillar and Caleta Rosario (Gundlach 1871-1875, 1876, Barbour 1923, 1943, Ripley and Watson 1956, Garrido 1980); the northern edge between Buenavista and Australia, January 1991 (M. Sulley and S. Sulley *in litt.* 1991); the Bay of Pigs (Bahía [Ensenada] de Cochinos) region (Gundlach 1871-1875, 1876), including a modern development area called Guamá (see Remarks 2) where the species currently occurs (A. Mitchell verbally 1991) and between which and Playa Girón it has been seen (Dathe and Fischer 1979-1981; M. Sulley and S. Sulley *in litt.* 1991);

Cienfuegos–Villa Clara–Sancti Spíritus near Cienfuegos, 1986 (I. Gabrielli *per* P. Bertagnolio *in litt.* 1991); the Trinidad (San Juan) mountains at the junction of these three provinces (Gundlach 1871-1875, 1876, Barbour 1923, 1943, Rutten 1934, Davis 1941, Silva 1981b), including San Juan and San Pablo villages, 1892 (Chapman 1892, Ridgway 1916) and adjacent areas to the north such as Soledad (apparently botanical) Gardens (this is now evidently Pepito Tey, 22°08'N 80°20'W: see Figure 1 in Rutten 1934), presumably in the late 1930s (Barbour 1943), Mina Carlotta, 22°04'N 80°10'W, April 1941 (specimens in CM), Barajaguá, 22°10'N 80°07'W, undated (Bond 1956b), the Hanabanilla Falls, 22°06'N 80°04'W, 1917 (Barbour 1923, 1943), although these are now dammed (ICGC 1978), and the Sierra de Escambray, 22°14'N 79°54'W, apparently recently (Silva 1989a);

Villa Clara Remedios, February 1864 (specimens in ANSP, USNM; also Ridgway 1916, Barbour 1923, 1943);

Sancti Spíritus Sancti Spíritus, July 1933 (specimen in USNM), although either the town or the province could be intended; near Laguna Taje (21°47'N 79°44'W) at Finca Guasacualo, January 1949 (specimen in USNM); Guasimal, in the 1920s, 21°44'N 79°28'W (Bond 1958); Los Galleguitos, 21°36'N 79°18'W, apparently recently (O. H. Garrido *in litt.* 1991); "Finca Rosamaria", 1930s (see Remarks 1);

Ciego de Avila west and north-west of Júcaro, 1915 (Barbour 1923, 1943);

Camagüey the Granja Agrícola near Camagüey town, 1933 (Rutten 1934); Sierra de Najasa, 21°05'N 77°50'W, 1980s (Berovides Alvarez *et al.* 1982, Acosta Cruz and Mugica Valdés 1988, Alfonso Sánchez *et al.* 1988); "San Michel", 1933 (Rutten 1934), this evidently being San Miguel de Bagá, 21°26'N 77°20'W;

Granma the Bayamo region (Gundlach 1871-1875, 1876), within which there is apparently recent evidence of presence on the río Cauto at the coast (Robiller 1990); the extensive Sierra Maestra, identified as a possible (Silva 1981b) and later a certain site (Silva 1989a), although the only other (but inconclusive) supporting evidence seems to be four skins in USNM from December 1901 simply labelled Guamá (Ridgway 1916; see Remarks 2);

Holguín Mayarí on the Bahía de Nipe, February 1904 (specimen in BMNH); La Zoilita mountains in the Sierra del Cristal, centred on 20°26'N 75°30'W, 1985-1986 (Abreu *et al.* 1989, whence coordinates);

Guantánamo "Río Seco, San Carlos", September 1913 (specimen as labelled in USNM), names which only occur (in OG 1963a) in close geographical combination just east of Guantánamo town (a less precise match occurs in Pinar del Río); Capital Virginia, Yateras, December 1917 (specimen in USNM), evidently at 20°18'N 75°03'W, with the untraced Capital Alcachopa, Yateras, January 1918 (specimen in USNM) somewhere nearby; Reserva Natural de Cupeyal, approximately 20°30'N 75°00'W (straddling the border with Holguín), 1985 (Alayón García 1987); on the río Jaguaní, c.20°28'N 74°56'W (read from ICGC 1978), 1987 (O. H. Garrido *in litt.* 1991: see Population); just north of the Cupeyal reserve by the village of Farallones, and just east in the hills of Ojito de Agua, where groups of up to 20 birds were occasionally seen, early 1991 (J. M. Lammertink *in litt.* 1991); Sierra (Cuchillas) del Toa, mid-1980s (Alayón García *et al.* 1987, Silva 1989a) and in particular La Melba, at 20°28'N 74°44'W, evidently recently (O. H. Garrido *in litt.* 1991). There are in addition three localities that cannot be traced with sufficient confidence to be placed correctly in this list (see Remarks 3).

POPULATION Generalized accounts of abundance indicate that in the early years of the nineteenth century the Cuban Parakeet was a very common bird throughout the country (d'Orbigny 1839), that by mid-century it was "common" or at least "not rare" (Cabanis 1856, Gundlach 1861), that by the 1870s its range had begun to contract, being found only in certain areas although still common within them (Gundlach 1871-1875, 1872), that it was "disappearing fast" in the first half of the twentieth century (Barbour 1923, 1943) and that, although at mid-century it was still considered "not uncommon in the wilder, heavily forested, parts of Cuba" (Bond 1956b), by the 1970s it was a rare species (Garrido and García Montaña 1975), having declined so alarmingly that urgent protection was considered necessary to prevent its total extinction (García undated). Silva (1981b) also predicted that, without protection of habitat or (at a separate point in his narrative) without captive breeding, total extinction would follow.

On the Isla de la Juventud the species was formerly abundant, but by the 1890s it was rather rare and likely to become extinct within a few years (Gundlach 1893; see Threats); at the start of the twentieth century it was nearly if not entirely exterminated, with none seen and its extinction affirmed by locals (Bangs and Zappey 1905), and it was not found during a year of fieldwork there, 1912-1913 (Todd 1916). Two "recent" (i.e. presumably in the early 1970s) records of flocks in the north (Garrido and García Montaña 1975) were "impugned" by Silva (1981b, 1989a), although he accepted another report that birds had survived on the island until the 1950s.

Older records of its local status elsewhere derive from: Chapman (1892), who found the species common (flocks of 10-20 generally seen) at two out of four study sites in the Trinidad region a century ago; Barbour (1923, 1943), who wrote of only small flocks in the Zapata Swamp, a single small flock near the Hanabanilla Falls, "a few" in the Trinidad mountains, diminishing numbers in the Guantánamo basin, and the probable clearance of all the forest near Júcaro where the species had been abundant in 1915 (adding "this will be one of the next birds to become completely extinct in Cuba, as it already is in the Isle of Pines"); Rutten (1934), who found it common in groups of up to 50 in the Trinidad mountains, saw several flocks near San Miguel de Bagá, and one small group daily near Camagüey town, but only once recorded the species in Pinar del Río (a small flock).

Recent records of its local status are from: Garrido (1980), who found the species not very common on the Península de Zapata (a flock of 42 was seen there in early 1992, but overall it is very rare: L. Fazio *in litt.* 1992), with flocks being seen much less often than those of the White-headed Amazon *Amazona leucocephala*, a perception borne out by the presence of the amazon but not the parakeet in certain general reviews of the avifauna of the area (e.g. García *et al.* 1987, González Alonso *et al.* 1990; see also the map in Wiley 1991); Abreu *et al.* (1989), who in La Zoilita mountains again found the species less frequent than the White-headed Amazon, although the flock-sizes were rather larger with up to 15 birds; and Alayón García (1987) and Alayón García *et al.* (1987), who recorded a few individuals in Reserva Natural de Cupeyal and found birds relatively abundant in the Cuchillas del Toa, these observations deriving from the same fieldwork (the search for the Ivory-billed Woodpecker *Campephilus principalis*; see relevant account) that led to the report (in Forshaw 1989) of the species being locally common in suitable habitat, although less plentiful overall than the White-headed Amazon. There is, however, a remarkable record by O. H. Garrido (*in litt.* 1991) of a flock of 600-800 birds flying over the río Jaguaní during 1987 searches for the Ivory-bill.

Two general assessments of the species's recent status are less pessimistic than those of García (undated) and Silva (1981b) cited above: first, Silva (1989a) himself, although treating the Cuban Parakeet in a book on threatened parrots, was informed that "it remains common in the western, central and eastern regions of Cuba" (given the island's shape, however, this is unhelpful); second, Robiller (1990) was informed that it is still locally common, despite its overall rarity. Large flocks, judged to be 200-300 strong, were observed in 1986 near Cienfuegos (I. Gabrielli *per* P. Bertagnolio *in litt.* 1991). Assessments of its frequency at Najasa are given in Berovides Alvarez *et al.* (1982), Acosta Cruz and Mugica Valdés (1988) and Alfonso Sánchez *et al.* (1988).

On the basis of all the foregoing, it seems likely that the Cuban Parakeet persists in moderate numbers in several areas where accessibility is poor, and in general it may be that, having suffered an enormous decline (from being one of the most numerous of Cuban endemic birds), it now possesses a relatively small though stable population.

ECOLOGY The Cuban Parakeet dwells in savannas (notably where rich in palms of the genera *Copernicia* and *Thrinax*), in areas with many trees on cultivated land, and on the edges of woodland, but not inside woodland itself (Gundlach 1871-1875, 1876, 1893); yet Barbour (1923, 1943) characterized the species as essentially one of virgin forest, while others compromised in calling it a bird of both woodland and palm savanna (Garrido and García Montaña 1975; also García undated) and of barely accessible forests in the mountains, though also of coastal regions and occasionally open country (Bond 1956b, Robiller 1990). Birds have been seen flying over semi-deciduous woodland areas (Alayón García 1987) and over open country with eucalyptus groves (Dathe and Fischer 1979-1981), but while it occupies a variety of such habitats plus degraded patches of evergreen forest and small woodlands in palm savanna, fundamentally it seems to survive only in and near larger tracts of original forest (TAP).

Food consists of tree-fruit, berries, seeds, also nuts, blossoms, and leaf-buds (Robiller 1990). More specifically, Gundlach (1871-1875, 1876) listed the seeds of millet and other grasses, but also those of forest trees such as ayúa *Xanthoxylon*, júcaro *Terminalia*, and also smaller fruits of e.g. mamoncillo *Melicoccus*; Chapman (1892) identified a favourite food as the berries of the royal palm (no scientific name given but presumably *Roystonea regia*, mentioned in Silva 1989a); Barbour (1943) noted birds attracted to the ripening fruit of jobo *Spondias luteus*; and Silva (1981b, 1989a), building on some of the above and adding information of his own, listed guava *Psidium guajava*, mangoes *Mangifera indica*, papaya *Carica papaya*, mamoncillo *Melicoccus bijugatus*, palm nuts (e.g. *Roystonea regia*), sweet pods and seeds of *Cordia collococca* and guaba *Inga vera*, and ripening jobo, adding that on the Isla de la Juventud birds fed almost exclusively on palm nuts and the shoots of *Pinus caribbea*. In the first half of the nineteenth century the species was a crop pest, taking the flowers and fruit of oranges, the heads of maize and the berries (but discarding the seeds) of coffee (d'Orbigny 1839; also or hence Gundlach 1872).

Breeding is deferred until late April or early May, so as to coincide with maximum fruit availability (Chapman 1892). Egg-laying is believed to occur in May, based on well incubated eggs taken in June and July and the fact that many young were already then present; but fresh-laid eggs have been found as late as mid-July (Bond 1958, Balát and González 1982); this may be explained by a single report (in Robiller 1990) that refers to two broods per year, in May and August. Although García (undated) gave the clutch-size as three, it reaches at least five (Balát and González 1982); up to five young were in nest-holes examined (Bond 1958). Nests are placed in hollows in dry, sometimes broken palms *Sabal florida*, in one case recorded at a height of 3 m from the ground (Balát and González 1982); Gundlach (1876) was told of nesting in "jatas" and other palms (Gundlach 1871-1875 indicated fan-palms), otherwise in holes in trees; García (undated) referred to nests in dead trunks of miraguano trees, which Silva (1989a) identified as *Coccothrinax miraguama*. A museum label states "in some palms 2 to 3 nests" (Balát and González 1982), which possibly indicates colonial breeding in a single tree, although it probably refers to small concentrations of nests in stands of palms. Barbour (1923, 1943; also Bond 1958, Silva 1989a) recorded nesting in hollow trees, frequently palms ("palmas canas", for which Rutten [1934] gave the name *Sabal parviflora*), the birds favouring old woodpecker borings and in particular those of Cuban Green Woodpecker *Xiphidiopicus percussus*, often those excavated in arboreal termite nests; Silva (1981b) noted that only active termitaria are used as abandoned ones are too brittle, while Silva (1989a) recorded a case in which the parakeets evicted the woodpeckers from an active nest, and themselves laid a fortnight later. The incubation period is 22-23 days in captivity (Silva 1981b gave 26), young fledge at 45-50 days, and independence occurs 2-3 weeks after fledging (Bauer 1989, Robiller 1990; see also Silva 1989a).

Some seasonal movements may occur; Davis (1941) referred to flocks occasionally descending from the Trinidad mountains in September and October. Birds sometimes associate with White-headed Amazons (Ripley and Watson 1956, Silva 1989a, Robiller 1990).

THREATS The Cuban Parakeet has suffered from a combination of habitat loss, persecution as a crop pest, and exploitation as a trade item. The problem of habitat loss has received little attention, but has almost certainly been highly significant; thus while it is difficult to reconcile Barbour's (1923, 1943) judgement (that the species required virgin forest and was unable to adapt to changed conditions) with other testimony (see Ecology) including the very fact that it was persecuted as a crop pest (see below), his anticipation of the clearance of the only forests where he had found the species abundant (near Júcaro: see Population) suggests an incompletely stated awareness of the impact of the steady, chronic loss of primary habitats during this century. It is, at any rate, intensive clearance of forest that is blamed for rendering it rare in recent years (Bauer 1989).

The species was much persecuted in the last century as an agricultural pest, although no less sought after as a cage-bird (d'Orbigny 1839; also Gundlach 1872). Trapped birds could be either killed or traded, and the evidence is that the latter option was increasingly taken in the second half of the century: Gundlach (1893) reported such a degree of persecution on the Isla de la Juventud that he feared for the bird's survival there (hundreds of young birds exported each year, and many others lost in the capturing process); and indeed Bangs and Zappey (1905) could only confirm that the species had been "exterminated in very recent years", i.e. in the late 1890s. Barbour (1923, 1943) referred to the bird as "stupid to a degree" when being hunted; he reported many being caught for pets, their nests becoming ever more the target of trappers the higher the price they fetched. García (undated) ascribed the species's decline in large part to this chronic exploitation, noting that it was the species most preferred by visitors to Cuba, which at one stage added to the demand for it; legal protection did not, apparently, stop (or immediately stop) the trade to eastern European countries (Silva 1981b). Moreover, the market for the species may continue internally:

in 1981 it was noted that palms were commonly being cut near Soplillar in order to obtain young parakeets, and that this had the effect of reducing the number of available nest-sites, and thus of greatly constraining the species, at least in the accessible parts of the Zapata Swamp (de las Pozas and González 1984).

MEASURES TAKEN Exportation of the species was (at some unspecified date) prohibited owing to foreign demand (García undated). Silva (1989a) referred to a breeding programme at the Cuban National Zoo, but involving only four birds and without success at his time of writing. The only protected areas which hold the species appear to be the Cupeyal Nature Reserve (Alayón García 1987) and the Península de Zapata National Park (Wiley 1991), although the status of the species in the latter is not clear. Apart from these, ICGC (1978) marks several protected areas that may be of significance: these include the national park and nature reserve (apparently called El Faro and El Veral respectively) on the Península de Guanahacabibes (but the species does not occur on the peninsula, according to one authority: see Distribution), El Pan de Guajaibón Nature Reserve (if this is the El Pan de Guajaibón referred to by Silva 1981b: see Remarks 3), the faunal reserves (Corral de Santo Tomás and Las Salinas) adjacent to the Península de Zapata National Park, the Pico Potrerillo National Park in the Trinidad mountains, La Plata National Park in the Sierra Maestra, the Sierra del Cristal Nature Reserve, and a curious complex centred on the Cuchillas del Toa in which a "Nature Tourism Area" is bordered by three smaller, unnamed national parks and the Jaguaní Nature Reserve. There is a protected area at Najasa in which the species occurs (Berovides Alvarez *et al.* 1982).

MEASURES PROPOSED Silva (1989a) identified three issues to address: the preservation of the species's habitat; an investigation of its status and biology; and an evaluation of the need and potential for the establishment of groups in aviaries. Of these the second seems most appropriate to undertake first, since the evidence particularly of its status is somewhat feeble and inconsistent; the first requires careful consideration so that all the threatened endemic birds of Cuba can be integrated into and benefit from any new initiatives on protected areas; while the third is certainly an option worth pursuit by aviculture as a safeguard, but always accepting that the results of the first two initiatives may render it superfluous.

REMARKS (1) Silva (1989a) gave "Finca Rosamaria" in "Las Villas", the only locality in OG (1963a) approximating to this being Central Rosa María, now named Central Aracelio Iglesias, a sugar-processing plant at 22°19'N 79°04'W. (2) According to ICGC (1978), Guamá is a south-facing region of the Sierra Maestra centred on 20°02'N 76°20'W (actually in westernmost Santiago de Cuba province), although a river of that name rises on the north slopes and gives its name to a settlement at 20°12'N 76°38'W (in Granma); but OG (1963a) lists at least another 12 localities of this name, presumably all less significant but not necessarily so in 1901; it is assumed at any rate that the Guamá in question is not the modern locality for the species near the Bay of Pigs, but that this latter is the same as the "Boca de Guama" of Clements (1979). (3) Three localities defy confident attribution. (a) A skin in UMMZ is labelled "Santa María, Oriente, Libana" and dated August 1951, but there is no "Libana" in any gazetteer, and too many Santa Marías; OG (1963a) lists several localities named Líbano or Monte Líbano for the former Oriente province, namely at 20°18'N 75°09'W (very close to Virginia but with no Santa María nearby), 20°03'N 76°03'W (a Santa María is some way north-west), and, perhaps most likely, 21°07'N 76°36'W, i.e. south of Puerto Padre, in a region where there are so many Santa Marías that they are numbered (Onze, Doce, etc.). However, O. H. Garrido (*in litt.* 1991) believed the site would be in the Sierra del Guaso; as there is a río Guaso at 20°02'S 75°09'W (in OG 1963a) the site in question is probably the first, i.e. that at 20°18'S 75°09'W. (b) Four skins in USNM are from "Bayate, Linea Central" and dated early 1910: of several Bayates, two lie on or very near the (presumably) central railway line (as it may have been in 1910), but at opposite ends of the island, at 22°44'N 82°57'W and 20°22'N 75°56'W; O. H. Garrido (*in litt.* 1991) considered the site in question to be the latter.

(c) Silva (1981b) referred to El Pan de Guajaibón in "Las Villas" province, but OG (1963a) only lists one such locality, at 22°48'N 83°22'W, which is not in what was formerly Las Villas but is very close to La Mulata and currently a protected area (see Measures Taken).

GOLDEN PARAKEET *Guaruba guarouba* V[9]

This highly distinctive parrot is endemic to the Amazonian basin of Brazil, occurring in northern Maranhão and Pará (with a single recent record from Rondônia) where it suffers from both the destruction of its rainforest habitat and the depredations of trappers and hunters: better protection of the Gurupi Biological Reserve, Amazonia National Park and intervening areas is needed, along with stronger enforcement of existing trade laws.

DISTRIBUTION The Golden Parakeet (see Remarks 1) occurs in northern Brazil from north-western Maranhão west through Pará as far as the Tapajós (Amazonia) National Park and along the Trans-Amazonian Highway, with recent evidence of a population in Rondônia in western Brazil (see below). The discovery of this last undermines previous attempts to judge its range ("probably does not extend south of southern Pará": Ridgely 1981a), and the fact that the Rondônia habitat conforms with that in Pará suggests that further populations await discovery when appropriate areas are investigated. Suggestions that the species occurred perhaps as far east as Ceará (Hellmayr 1929a, Peters 1937), and the assertion that it formerly extended over the whole of north-east Brazil (Pinto 1946, 1978, Ruschi 1979) as far as Pernambuco and Bahia (Burmeister 1856), were at least in part based on its description by Marcgrave (1648), who travelled no further west than western Ceará; however, the specimen he saw was probably a bird traded east by Indians (Oren and Willis 1981, Oren and Novaes 1986a).

Maranhão The map in Oren and Novaes (1986a) indicates five localities for the species in the north-west of the state, surrounded to the north, east and south by a belt (reaching as far as 5°S 45°W) from which the species has (almost) disappeared (a record of birds from the rio Gurupi close to the coast in November 1985 suggests a remnant population: P. Roth verbally 1986). The northernmost of the five mapped localities lies within this belt, and is the state's only specimen record, hence presumably the Serra do Pirocaua (Hellmayr 1912, 1929a). The other four records lie within or close to the Gurupi Biological Reserve, and the easternmost one appears to lie within the drainage of the rio Pindaré, where Ridgely (1981a) also encountered the species.

Pará The map in Oren and Novaes (1986a) indicates twenty-five localities for the species in the northern half of the state (above 5°S), although it has disappeared from the area east of Belém and north of the rio Capim (embracing the rio Guamá drainage) across to the border with Maranhão (the rio Gurupi). Oren and Novaes (1986a) gave their sources as Snethlage (1914), Hellmayr (1929a), Pinto (1938), specimens in MNRJ, MPEG and MZUSP, and recent reliable observations, the most notable of which are in Oren and Willis (1981); these appear to be almost all the sources available, and although Oren and Novaes (1986a) did not name all these localities or provide dates the comprehensiveness of their map is sufficient guide to the species's distribution; however, two localities apparently unrepresented on the map are Villarinho do Monte on the rio Xingu and Recreio (c.1°42'S 52°12'W) on the rio Matari (specimens in AMNH; coordinates from Paynter and Traylor 1991).

Rondônia The species was recently found 500 km south-west of its previously known range in the Jamari National Forest (9°07'S 62°54'W) on the right bank of the rio Madeira, where six birds were seen repeatedly in October/November 1989 (Yamashita and França in press).

POPULATION Although long considered rare (Descourtilz 1854-1856) or becoming so (Pinto 1946), it is possible that early explorers, following watercourses and penetrating little into the higher areas between them, failed to find the species's optimal habitat (see Ecology) and gained a distorted view of its abundance. Ridgely (1981a) acknowledged that it avoids várzea and is thus found away from the Amazon or its tributaries; even so, he only found a flock of six in "over a week in seemingly ideal little disturbed forest in Maranhão (drainage of the rio Pindare)". While observers with longer experience in the region report that where good forest remains (as in parts even of Maranhão) the species may still be seen regularly (P. Roth *in litt.* 1985, A. D. Johns *in litt.* 1986), overall numbers have declined very considerably (Ridgely 1981a, P. Roth *in litt.* 1986).

ECOLOGY The Golden Parakeet frequents tropical rainforest, almost exclusively terra firme forest and mainly in hilly upland areas, ranging primarily in the canopy (Oren and Willis 1981, Ridgely 1981a, Oren and Novaes 1986a). The extent to which the species benefits from partial forest clearance is moot: one report referred to its appearance in an area only after conversion of forest to agriculture (Hellmayr 1912; also Müller 1912); on the Xingu, the species was noted in riverine grasslands, and around Pará in clearings in primary forest (Snethlage 1913). Várzea (seasonally flooded forest) is only known to be used around Tucuruí, the birds regularly wandering from adjacent upland forest along the rio Tocantins (Oren and Novaes 1986a; also, by implication, Snethlage 1913; see last paragraph in this section); Johns (1986) referred to the species being common around Tucuruí in igapó (permanently flooded forest), presumably in error for várzea. Use of tall forest takes place during the dry (non-breeding) season, May–November, but when breeding the birds seek out cleared areas (e.g. new fields with isolated living or dead trees for nesting) adjacent to forest (Oren and Novaes 1986a). Tree hollows are used for roosts in the non-breeding season both inside forest and in cleared areas, and are often changed on successive nights (Oren and Novaes 1986a).

The species feeds on fruits, berries, seeds and nuts, procured in the treetops. Although its preferred food was thought to be sapucaia *Lecythis* (Descourtilz 1854-1856) or *Euterpe* palm nuts (Sick 1985), observations reveal the following species as food: cajuí *Anacardium* cf. *spruceanum*, cashew *A. occidentale*, mango *Mangifera indica*, breu *Protium* spp. and *Tetragastris* spp., maize *Zea mays*, ananí *Symphonia* sp., lacre *Visnia gujanensis*, ingá *Inga* spp., murucí *Byrsonima crassifolia*, andiroba *Carapa guianensis*, cecropia *Cecropia* spp., and bacaba *Oenocarpus bacaba*, in all cases the birds consuming the fruits or pseudofruits except for ananí, of which the buds and flowers were eaten (Oren and Novaes 1986a). Feeding on bacaba palm, as well as on an unidentified lauraceous tree, was also noted by Oren and Willis (1981; see Remarks 2). A collected specimen contained a crushed seed (Schubart *et al.* 1965) and others (taken in várzea) berries (specimens in MNRJ, MPEG; see Remarks 3). The species utilizes some cultivated crops, and Descourtilz's (1854-1856) claim that it spends most of the day in corn plantations is at least partially borne out by recent work indicating that maize crops, which unfortunately ripen just before the young fledge, are attacked (Oren and Novaes 1986a).

The breeding season, as noted above, runs from December to April; however, a completely formed egg was found in the oviduct of a specimen collected on 13 October 1912 (Snethlage 1935), and a female was caught on the nest on the rio Gurupi, 9 October 1926 (specimen in ANSP), suggesting some variation, perhaps in response to weather conditions. Breeding appears to be communal, with several females contributing to a clutch: in a captive group of three males and three females all six cared for the 14 chicks produced, and in the wild hunters reported up to nine birds (often at very different stages of development) in nests with multiple attendants, but only 2-3 in those of single pairs; nevertheless, it is just possible that only one female lays in a nest, adjusting her clutch-size to the number of assistants available (Oren and Novaes 1986a). The nest-site is a cavity in the highest part of an isolated tree 15-30 m tall, in the main trunk or a thick branch; of four nest-trees in one study, one was a living taxí *Sclerolobium* sp. (Leguminosae), while the others were unidentified because dead, and all were within a few hundred metres of intact forest (Oren and Novaes 1986a). The end of January has been indicated as the time when young are regularly taken from nests (Forshaw 1989). In captive birds, incubation lasts around 30 days and sexual maturity is reached in about three years (Oren and Novaes 1986a). Roosting is gregarious, with up to nine birds sharing a tree-hole "dormitory", the birds moving in flocks up to 30 between roost-sites and feeding areas (Oren and Novaes 1986a).

Johns (1986) cited Sick (1985) as asserting that the species breeds exclusively in the heavily disturbed region of south-east Pará and Maranhão states, but migrates outwards during the non-breeding season as far as the rio Tapajós (none of which appears to be in Sick 1985); on the basis of this Johns (1986) considered that the forests of the Tucuruí area might form an important staging post "during the February–April migration". Whether any predictable seasonal movements occur remains to be established, but it certainly appears that birds can wander over huge areas and are not predictably found in one area at any season (TAP).

THREATS The species's prime threat is habitat destruction, its eastern distribution having become fragmented as a result of road construction, subsequent development and settlement, with accompanying widespread forest clearance: the Belém-Brasília Highway, with its 30-40 km wide swath of clearing, now bisects the Golden Parakeet's range from north to south, while the newer Trans-Amazonian Highway cuts across it from east to west, these highways and their ancillary networks spurring the clearance of much newly accessible forest (Ridgely 1981a, P. Roth *in litt.* 1985). The Tucuruí site (see Ecology) is now partly inundated by a hydroelectric project (Oren and Willis 1981) whose notoriety was established in Caufield (1985). Tucuruí is on the Tocantins, and the entire area east of the river to the Maranhão border is undergoing major development involving lumber operations, gold-mining, cattle-ranching and the construction and operation of a massive railroad connecting the Serra dos Carajás to the port of São Luís (Caufield 1985, Oren and Novaes 1986a).

The Golden Parakeet is one of the world's most highly desired aviary birds (Low 1972), commanding extremely high prices (U.S.$10,000-15,000 around 1980); despite the prohibition of commercial export, therefore, very small numbers were still being smuggled out of Brazil around 1980 (Ridgely 1981a), and indeed throughout the 1980s international smuggling has continued (Silva 1989a). The internal pet trade, though also illegal, is much less controlled (Oren and Novaes 1986a) and, since an average worker from Pará can sell a Golden Parakeet for five times his monthly wage (Keller 1987), young are still taken from nests in some quantity (P. Roth *in litt.* 1985, Oren and Novaes 1986a). A century ago the species was much trapped and domesticated by Indians for its feathers (Goeldi 1894), a practice that might be deleterious now in certain areas. When not being pursued for live capture, it is hunted for food, particularly after the larger game species have been shot out of an area, and the birds are also shot both in retaliation for their attacks on maize crops and, in the Tapajós (Amazonia) National Park (at least around 1980), as sport by weekend and holiday hunters (Oren and Willis 1981, Oren and Novaes 1986a).

Natural predators are reportedly White-breasted and Channel-billed Toucans *Ramphastos tucanus* and *R. vitellinus*, which take eggs and nestlings at nests in clearings, with monkeys, tayra *Eira barbara* and snakes taking a toll in the forest (Oren and Novaes 1986a).

MEASURES TAKEN The species is protected under Brazilian law (Bernardes *et al.* 1991) and thus commercial export from Brazil is prohibited (Ridgely 1981a); the species is on Appendix I of CITES (King 1978-1979). However, highlighting the species through laws may actually have added to pressure by identifying the bird to dealers as of special value (Oren and Novaes 1986a). A population is relatively well protected in the Tapajós (Amazonia) National Park, which covers 994,000 ha (IBAMA 1989) in the region of the rio Tapajós, and is the only nature reserve in the species's range in Pará; hunting in the area, both by local subsistence farmers and weekend and holiday intruders, was expected to diminish as IBDF (now IBAMA) training of new guards improved the protection of the site (Oren and Willis 1981).

MEASURES PROPOSED The obvious first candidate for the fulfilment of Ridgely's (1981a) call for the preservation of a large forest tract for the species is the 341,000 ha Gurupi Biological Reserve, created by decree in January 1988 but which must be urgently demarcated and wardened to protect this and several other important species (e.g. the near-threatened Hooded Gnateater *Conopophaga roberti*) in western Maranhão (Oren 1988). The integrity of the Tapajós (Amazonia) National Park at the western end of the species's known range in Pará must equally be maintained, and intervening areas protected and managed so that populations can survive and interbreed. A certain amount of fieldwork, seeking to establish the species's western and southern limits in Pará, to clarify its habitat requirements, and to discover the size and distribution of the population in Rondônia, with the overall aim of understanding where else birds may yet be found, needs to be undertaken. Measures must also be implemented to control the exploitation of the Golden Parakeet in internal trade (Oren and Novaes 1986a). Because it is yellow and green like the national flag, the Golden Parakeet has been proposed as the national bird of Brazil (Sick 1985, 1987); it is time this measure was taken, which would perhaps result in higher vigilance for the species than at present.

REMARKS (1) The species is so distinct from *Aratinga* parakeets that it merits its own genus, *Guaruba* (Sick 1985, 1990). (2) Oren and Willis (1981) referred to a flock perched in a brazil-nut tree *Bertholletia excelsa*, which Forshaw (1989) mistook as a record of birds feeding. (3) Forshaw (1978), who apparently examined the relevant MPEG skin, reported that the berries were cultivated, but this is in error.

GOLDEN-PLUMED PARAKEET *Leptosittaca branickii* V/R[10]

This poorly known parrot is found very locally in temperate Andean forests in Colombia, Ecuador and Peru, in the first two of which it has suffered from much habitat loss; its nomadism, which may be related to a heavy dependence on Podocarpus *cones, renders it highly problematic to conserve.*

DISTRIBUTION The Golden-plumed Parakeet is known from at least 70 specimens, and has been recorded from at least 30 localities scattered through the Andes in Colombia, Ecuador and Peru.

Colombia The species is known from two regions on the west slope of the Central Andes (all coordinates, unless otherwise stated, are from Paynter and Traylor 1981), as follows:

the Nevado del Ruiz–Nevado del Tolima region on the borders of Tolima, Risaralda, Quindío and Caldas departments (in and around Los Nevados National Park), localities being Hacienda Jaramillo, over 3,000 m, at 4°47'N 75°26'W, September 1918 (Carriker 1955a; nine specimens in CM, all labelled "Santa Ignacia"); above Santa Rosa de Cabal, recently (Hilty and Brown 1986); Laguneta, 3,050 m, at 4°35'N 75°30'W, April 1942 (specimen in ANSP); Alto Quindío Acaime Natural Reserve, 4°37'N 75°28'W, and the nearby Cañon del Quindío Natural Reserve, on the west slope of the Central Andes in Quindío, ranging into adjacent forest on the east slope in Tolima, and present throughout the year (E. Murgueitio R. *in litt.* 1987; also Renjifo 1991, L. M. Renjifo *in litt.* 1992, whence coordinates; see Ecology); Rincón Santo, Salento, 2,800 m, December 1989 (J. A. Giraldo *in litt.* 1992); and Ucumarí Regional Park, Risaralda, recently (LGN);

the Volcán Puracé region in Cauca department, localities being: Las Papas valley, río Caquetá, 3°08'N 64°46'W, eight seen in February 1988 (Negret and Acevedo 1990); río Aguas Blancas, at 2°58'N 76°14'W, February 1954 (Carriker 1955a; coordinates from LGN); Cerro Munchique, at c.2°32'N 76°57'W (Lehmann 1957; Negret and Acevedo 1990 place this within the national park); Gabriel López, 2,835 m, at 2°29'N 76°18'W, February 1955 (specimen in USNM); Laguna San Rafael and in canyons or over the largely forested north-west end of Puracé National Park, December 1982 and more recently (Hilty and Brown 1986, M. Pearman *in litt.* 1988, B. M. Whitney *in litt.* 1991), with several flocks of 8-12 birds (a total of 31 on one day in May 1989: Negret and Acevedo 1990) near Laguna San Rafael, c.3,350 m, and near Quebrada Tierra Adentro, c.3,200 m, March 1987, when c.60 were seen (M. Pearman *in litt.* 1989), and February 1989 (F. R. Lambert *in litt.* 1989); Puracé, 2,900 m, at c.2°24'N 76°27'W, February 1954 (five specimens in USNM and YPM); Termales de San Juan, 2°20'N 76°05'W, 12 seen in June 1986 (Negret and Acevedo 1990; coordinates from LGN); Coconuco, 3,050 m, at 2°20'N 76°28'W, June 1939 (seven specimens in ANSP *contra* Carriker 1955a, who believed them all in Sweden), four seen in January 1983 (B. M. Whitney *in litt.* 1991) and six seen in May 1989 (Negret and Acevedo 1990); río Quilcacé, Sotará, c.2°12'N 76°31'W, 23 seen in February 1990 (Negret and Acevedo 1990; coordinates from LGN); río San Francisco canyon, c.1°13'N 77°17'W, where two flocks of 13 and 21 were seen in April 1989 (Negret and Acevedo 1990; coordinates from LGN).

The view that the species may occur in the intervening region (Hilty and Brown 1986) is borne out by a record from Bolo Azul (untraced), Cauca department, in November 1989 (Negret and Acevedo 1990), while to the south of the second main area it has been recorded on the east slope of Nariño at Llorente, 1,800 m, at 0°49'N 77°37'W (Fitzpatrick and Willard 1982), with a flock heard on the east shore of Lago del Guamés (= La Cocha) in Tungurahua Natural Reserve in April 1992 (L. M. Renjifo *in litt.* 1992).

Ecuador The species is known from four or five localities (coordinates, unless otherwise stated, are from Paynter and Traylor 1977): (*Imbabura*) Pimampiro (c.2,000 m) on the west slope, at 0°26'N 77°58'W, September 1931 (two specimens in FMNH); (*Azuay*) recent sightings at 3,100-

3,400 m at Río Mazan, adjacent to Cajas National Recreation Area, west side of the interandean plateau, at 2°52'S 79°08'W (Gretton 1986, J. R. King verbally 1988, M. Hancock *in litt.* 1989; location and coordinates read from LANDSAT 1987 and IGM 1981); (*El Oro*) Taraguacocha, 2,970-3,350 m, in the Chilla mountains, at 3°40'S 79°40'W, August 1920 (two specimens in AMNH and MCZ); (*Morona-Santiago*) sightings and tape-recordings in June 1984 and 1987 at San Vicente, 3,100-3,200 m, Zapote Najda mountains, eastern slope of the Andes near the Azuay border, at c.3°1'S 78°38'W (NK; coordinates read from IGM 1981); (*Loja*) 7 km north-east of San Lucas, 3,100 m, at 3°42'S 79°13'W, September 1990 (one in MECN collected from a flock of 35); Acanama near San Lucas, 3,000 m, at 3°42'S 79°13'W, recently (Bloch *et al.* 1991, whence coordinates); the Vilcabamba area, September 1982 (Lemire 1991); between Yangana and Valladolid, c.3,100 m, at 4°27'S 79°10'W, recently (P. Greenfield *in litt.* 1989, Bloch *et al.* 1991); Podocarpus National Park, at c.4°06'S 79°10'W, February, May and August 1989 (M. Hancock *in litt.* 1989, Bloch *et al.* 1991; coordinates read from IGM 1981).

Peru There are no records from Cerro Chinguela, Piura, northern Peru (Parker *et al.* 1985), but further east and south (coordinates from Stephens and Traylor 1982) there are records from: (*Cajamarca*) locality unspecified (Ridgely 1981a); (*Amazonas*) Cordillera Colán, 1,390-3,125 m, at c.5°34'S 78°17'W, August and September 1978 (specimens in LSUMZ); (*San Martín*) Puerto del Monte, c.3,250 m, c.30 km north-east of Los Alisos, at c.7°32'S 77°29'W, August 1981 (three specimens in LSUMZ); (*La Libertad*) Cumpang, 2,400 m, at 8°12'S 77°10'W, August 1900 (Ménégaux 1910); Mashua, 3,350 m, east of Tayabamba, on Ongón trail, at c.8°12'S 77°14'W, September 1979 (specimen in LSUMZ); (*Huánuco*) Acomayo region (Bosque Shaigua, Bosque Tapra, Mision Punta, Rosapampa, Huailaspampa, Hacienda Huaravilla, Zapatagocha, Carpish Tunnel), 2,400-2,750 m, Carpish Mountains, north-east of Huánuco, at 9°40-46'S 76°02-12'W (many specimens in ANSP, BMNH, FMNH and LSUMZ), with several recent sightings (Parker and O'Neill 1976, Forshaw 1989, NK); (*Pasco*) Rumicruz, 2,950 m, at 10°44'S 75°55'W, February 1922 (specimen in AMNH); (*Junín*) Huacapistana, at 11°14'S 75°29'W, April 1930 (two specimens in ANSP); Maraynioc, "3,050-3,950 m", at 11°22'S 75°25'W (type: von Berlepsch and Stolzmann 1894); (*Cusco*) between Shintuya and Paucartambo, 2,200 m, flock of 25 observed, July 1989 (R. S. Ridgely *in litt.* 1989).

POPULATION The status of this species is difficult even to guess at, owing to its nomadic behaviour and inaccessible haunts (see Ecology), factors which certainly help explain why it has been judged very rare (Ridgely 1981a). Most records are of small flocks of 6-10 individuals (Ridgely 1981a, Forshaw 1989, Hilty and Brown 1986, NK), but larger flocks certainly still occur (see below), and in Alto Quindío the mean flock size was 19 (Renjifo 1991). Nevertheless, numbers in Colombia are indisputably small and vulnerable (Negret and Acevedo 1990). In Ecuador there is no recent information concerning its occurrence in the north-west, but a flock of 18-22 birds was seen almost daily at Río Mazan in 1986 and 1987 (Gretton 1986, J. R. King verbally 1988), and on some days an additional flock would join to form a flock of 41-42 (Gretton 1986) or even 50 birds (J. R. King verbally 1988), and judging from the extent of apparently suitable habitat there (read from LANDSAT 1987: NK) the population at Río Mazan and the adjacent Cajas National Recreation Area may number several hundred (NK; see also King 1989). In the far south up to 100 birds were present near Vilcabamba in September 1982, but this appeared unusual (Lemire 1991). The species is very local and uncommon in Peru (Parker *et al.* 1982, J. W. Terborgh *in litt.* 1986), but if it proves widespread there, as surmised by Ridgely (1981a), total numbers may reach thousands.

ECOLOGY The Golden-plumed Parakeet normally inhabits temperate cloud-forest and elfin woodland at 2,400-3,400 m, mean 2,875 m (Ridgely 1981a, Graves 1985, Hilty and Brown 1986), in Ecuador notably *Podocarpus* forest (Gretton 1986), but occasionally it may be found as low as 1,400 m (see Distribution); in Peru it is a bird of "stunted timberline forests" (O'Neill 1987).

Birds usually perch largely hidden in the canopy and rarely stay more than 5-10 minutes in each tree (A. Gretton verbally 1988, NK). In Puracé National Park birds roost in the páramo zone above 3,000 m and at dawn descend in compact, noisy flocks to the remnant Andean woodlots in the steep canyons (Negret and Acevedo 1990).

Of 25 perches recorded in one day in early August 1986 at Río Mazan, 20 were in *Podocarpus* trees, and all positive records of feeding at Río Mazan in August and September 1986 and 1987 concerned *Podocarpus* cones (Gretton 1986 and verbally 1988, J. R. King verbally 1988, King 1989). Of 19 feeding observations in Alto Quindío Acaime Natural Reserve, Colombia, 11 involved fruit of *Podocarpus oleifolius* and eight those of *Prumnopytis montanus*; visits to fruiting trees by a flock might last an hour and a half, but generally were much shorter and involved much nervous flying between trees (Renjifo 1991). Birds also forage on *Croton* seeds, fruits of *Ficus* and Melastomataceae, and, according to local reports, cultivated maize (Negret and Acevedo 1990, Renjifo 1991). One stomach of a September bird in the eastern Andes of Ecuador held over 500 tiny seeds, one seed 5x3 mm, sand and a little earth (NK). If the birds depend largely on cones, they may suffer the same unpredictability in crops that make both species of *Rhynchopsitta* parrots in Mexico nomadic (see relevant accounts). The species is certainly nomadic, such that it may disappear from a site after being recorded there for many years, only to reappear much later (TAP), and there are records of flocks passing over non-forested regions in Colombia (Hilty and Brown 1986) and Ecuador (Gretton 1986, J. R. King verbally 1988); at Río Mazan it was considered to be seasonal outside the breeding season (King 1989).

The only records of breeding are two laying females and a male with greatly enlarged testes all taken on 26 February at Puracé, Colombia (specimens in USNM, YPM), two birds mating in a flock of eight individuals, early August 1986 at Río Mazan (A. Gretton verbally 1988), and birds apparently nest-prospecting in holes in dead *Ceroxylum quindiuense* palms in Alto Quindío, Colombia, in May 1990 (Renjifo 1991).

THREATS In Colombia and perhaps Ecuador numbers have declined owing to heavy deforestation, while the population in Peru seems to be stable (Ridgely 1981a, Negret and Acevedo 1990). The land in Caldas, Risaralda, Quindío and Tolima in Colombia is now largely deforested, as is the region surrounding Volcán Puracé (Ridgely 1981a), and indeed the intervening area has suffered similarly (R. S. Ridgely *in litt.* 1988). The nomadic or erratic movements of the species suggest that it may be particularly at risk from loss of habitat, and render it highly problematic to conserve simply through protected areas. Selective logging of *Podocarpus* could cause the elimination of local populations (L. M. Renjifo *in litt.* 1992). Hunting is also identified as a problem in Colombia, where the species is sometimes trapped as a "pest" on maize crops (Negret and Acevedo 1990), although the numbers involved must be small. Trade appears to be no problem: birds are virtually unknown in captivity (Ridgely 1981a).

MEASURES TAKEN The species is known to occur (see Distribution) in nine protected areas: (*Colombia*) Alto Quindío Acaime, Cañon del Quindío and Tungurahua Natural Reserves, Ucumarí Regional Park, Munchique, Puracé and Los Nevados National Parks, (*Ecuador*) Río Mazan (now apparently effectively protected: see equivalent section under Violet-throated Metaltail *Metallura baroni*) and Podocarpus National Park, and (*Peru*) Río Abiseo National Park; however, it undoubtedly occurs in Manu National Park, Peru (R. S. Ridgely *in litt.* 1989).

MEASURES PROPOSED More research on this poorly known parrot is needed before measures can be taken (Ridgely 1981a). In particular, the causes of its nomadism urgently require study and, assuming that these are related to a patchy and unpredictable food supply, the forests that appear to provide its needs with greatest frequency (including for breeding) should be catalogued, mapped and, as far as possible, given protection. The recent record based on voice from Tungurahua Natural Reserve, Colombia, should be followed up, particularly as *Podocarpus oleifolius* is abundant there (L. M. Renjifo *in litt.* 1992).

The Golden-plumed Parakeet is sympatric with a large number of other threatened species, whose best interests should also be considered in any initiatives: for lists of these species and details of other proposals see the equivalent sections under Bicoloured Antpitta *Grallaria rufocinerea* (for Alto Quindío Acaime Natural Reserve), Multicoloured Tanager *Chlorochrysa nitidissima* (for Ucumarí Regional Park), Colourful Puffleg *Eriocnemis mirabilis* (for Munchique National Park), Bicoloured Antpitta (for Puracé National Park), Rufous-fronted Parakeet *Bolborhynchus ferrugineifrons* (for Los Nevados National Park), Violet-throated Metaltail (for Río Mazan) and Bearded Guan *Penelope barbata* (for Podocarpus National Park).

REMARKS This bird occupies its own genus, but as its calls are somewhat like those of larger species of *Aratinga* it is probably referable to that genus (R. S. Ridgely *in litt.* 1989 and in Hilty and Brown 1986), although B. M. Whitney (*in litt.* 1991) has pointed out that some calls are distinctive (see also comments in Forshaw 1989), its facial plumes are also distinctive, and it neither overlaps *Aratinga* altitudinally nor is replaced geographically by a member of that genus.

YELLOW-EARED PARROT *Ognorhynchus icterotis* E[3]

Although formerly found at scattered localities in all three ranges of Colombia and in north-west Ecuador, when it was in places common or even abundant, this distinctive parrot is now rare owing to the widespread loss of its wax palm habitat, with recent records from only a few localities in the southern half of the West Andes and at the head of the Magdalena valley in Colombia and in Carchi and Cotopaxi provinces, north-west Ecuador.

DISTRIBUTION The Yellow-eared Parrot (see Remarks) has been recorded from humid montane forest and partially cleared terrain, especially where there are wax palms *Ceroxylon* spp. in all three ranges of Colombia, and in Carchi, Imbabura, Pichincha and Cotopaxi provinces, north-west Ecuador, mainly at 2,000-3,000 m, though occasionally down to 1,200 m and up to 3,400 m (Chapman 1926, Ridgely 1981a, Hilty and Brown 1986, P. Greenfield verbally 1986). On the basis of the evidence below, for which all coordinates unless otherwise stated are from Paynter and Traylor (1977, 1981), the species may currently be confined to the Cerro Munchique region in Cauca department and Alto Quindío, Colombia, and the north-western slope in Ecuador, though a small population may also persist near the head of the Magdalena valley, Huila department, Colombia (Ridgely 1981a, Hilty and Brown 1986).

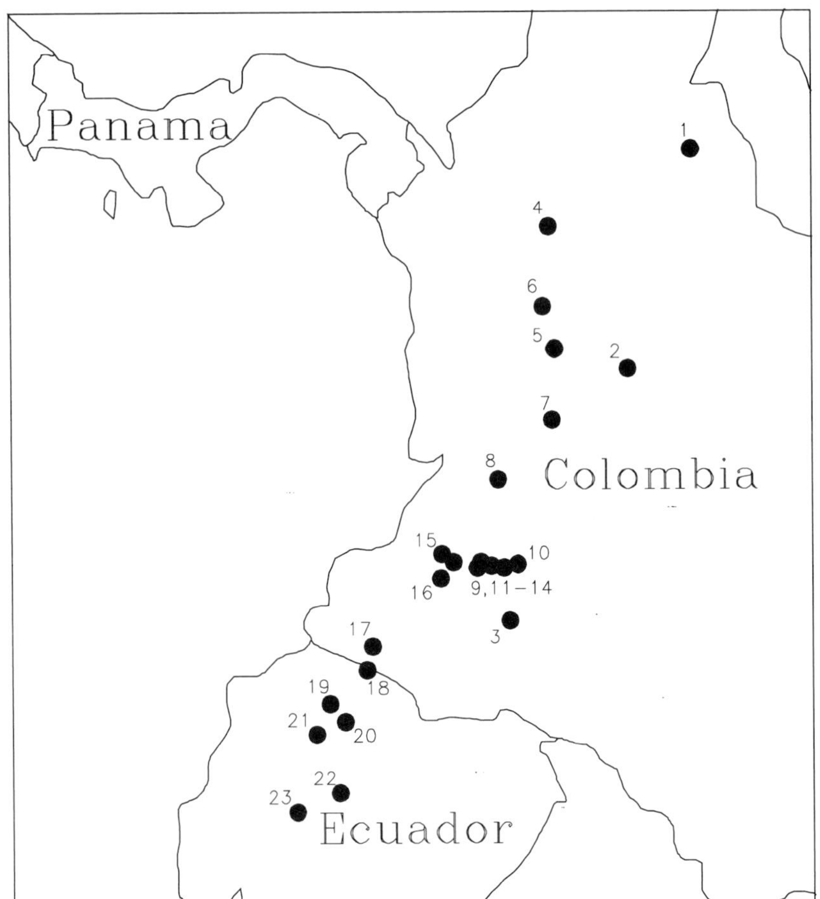

Colombia Records (see Remarks 2) are from:

East Andes Ocaña (1,200 m), on the west slope but on the eastern watershed of Sierra de Ocaña[1], Norte de Santander department, at 8°15'N 73°20'W (Peters 1937); old "Bogotá" specimens (in AMNH, USNM), although these cannot confidently be attributed to the East Andes; Zipaquirá[2], 1,525 m, on the east slope in Cundinamarca department, at 5°02'N 74°00'W, late last century (one specimen in BMNH), although again this record is questionable (J. I. Hernández Camacho verbally 1991); a small group sighted in 1975 in Cueva de los Guácharos National Park[3], Huila department, at 1°35'N 76°00'W (Hilty and Brown 1986);

Central Andes La Frijolera[4], 1,525 m, on the west slope in Antioquia department, December 1914 and January 1915, at c.7°10'N 75°25'W (specimens in AMNH and USNM); San Félix[5], west slope in Caldas department, at 5°26'N 75°20'W (Rodríguez and Hernández Camacho 1988); La Ceja[6], río Toche valley between 2,500 and 2,800 m, where a flock of less than 10 was seen flying over wax palms in May 1991 (J. I. Hernández Camacho verbally 1991); Alto Quindío Acaime Natural Reserve (Renjifo 1991: see Population); río Toché[7], 2,070 m, on the east slope in Tolima department, at 4°26'N 75°22'W, October 1911 (12 specimens in AMNH, FMNH, MCZ and USNM); Miraflores east of Palmira[8], 2,070 m, on the west slope in Valle del Cauca department, at c.3°35'N 76°10'W, April 1911 (specimen in AMNH); Laguna San Rafael páramo[9], c.3,400 m, on the summit in Cauca department, at c.2°25'N 76°25'W, where a pair was sighted in May 1976 (Hilty and Brown 1986); La Plata[10], on the east slope in Huila department, at 2°23'N 75°53'W, March 1939 (specimen in ANSP); Tijeras[11], 2,560 m, on the east slope in Huila, at 2°22'N 76°16'W, March 1952 and February 1958 (specimens in LACM and USNM); Moscopán[12], 2,450 m, on the east slope on the border of Huila and Cauca departments, at c.2°20'N 76°05'W, March 1954 (specimens in YPM); Coconuco[13], 2,750 m, on the west slope in Cauca department, at 2°20'N 76°28'W, December 1939 (specimens in ANSP);

West Andes El Tambo[14] below Cerro Munchique, 2,100 m, on the east slope in Cauca department, at 2°25'N 76°49'W, September 1939 (specimen in ANSP); on the north-east slope of Cerro Munchique[15], at 3,400 m, in Cauca department, where a flock of 25 was seen in July 1978 (Hilty and Brown 1986), and whence presumably come two specimens labelled "coast range west of Popayan, Cauca, 10,340'" (3,150 m) and dated 13 and 17 July 1911 (in AMNH); río Timbío[16], an affluent of upper río Patía, 1,280 m, on the west slope in Cauca, at 2°11'N 77°00'W, January 1939 (specimen in ANSP); Ricaurte[17], 2,000 and 2,500 m, at 1°13'N 77°59'W, on the west slope in Nariño, where four specimens (in FMNH and LACM) were collected in April 1958 (Blake 1959); and adjacent La Planada Nature Reserve, where birds appeared in February 1983, February 1984 and February 1985, almost to the day, although on the last occasion they stayed until mid-May (Orejuela 1985, Rodríguez and Hernández Camacho 1988), with annual records continuing into the late 1980s but then ceasing (J. E. Orejuela verbally 1992).

Ecuador Records are given from north to south. What was presumably this species was heard at c.2,400 m in Carchi, at c.0°53'N 78°04'W[18] (coordinates read from IGM 1981), in January 1982, but during an ANSP expedition in July and August 1988 none was recorded despite intensive searching (R. S. Ridgely *in litt.* 1989). A bird was collected at Intag[19] ("1,200 m") on the west slope in Imbabura province at c.0°24'N 78°36'W in December 1877 (specimen in BMNH), and another at Hacienda Piganta, 2,620 m, on the west side of Mojanda mountains[20], northern part of Pichincha province, at 0°09'N 78°23'W, on 15 June in a year before 1921 (Lönnberg and Rendahl 1922). A few birds were sold on the cagebird market in around 1970, and one of these had supposedly been captured near Mindo[21], Pichincha province, at c.0°02'S 78°48'W (R. Wirth *in litt.* 1989); Mindo, however, remains one of the ornithologically best known parts of Ecuador, so this bird was presumably a straggler (NK). There is a recent specimen (in MECN) labelled "Lita"[22], i.e. on the border of Imbabura and Carchi provinces, at 0°52'S 78°28'W, and a local claimed in 1990 that a small flock can still be seen there between November and February (T. Arndt *in litt.* 1991). Four freshly shot birds, three of which are preserved in Museo de Mundo Jovenil, Quito, were collected recently by J. Aro (a bird trapper in Quito) near El Corazón[23], Cotopaxi, at 1°08′S 79°05′W, supposedly at a place called La Calera (not located) (I. Mora verbally 1991).

POPULATION Although Chapman (1917a) reported the Yellow-eared Parrot "common and in places abundant" in the subtropical zone of the Central Andes of Colombia, these sites are now almost entirely deforested, and are unsuited for the parrot (Ridgely 1981a). There is still considerable forest on the west slope of the West Andes north and south of Cerro Munchique, so it is possible that this region retains an undetected population (Ridgely 1981a). Lehmann (1957) had found birds numerous in the Moscopán region of Huila in the period from December to April up until the early 1950s, but in July 1956 he observed only one. Despite spending considerable time in the same region, Ridgely (1981a) reported seeing only a single pair on one occasion, on the east slope in Puracé National Park (R. S. Ridgely *in litt.* 1989), and the region is now largely deforested (King 1978-1979). The bird does not appear to be regular in the East Andes at the head of Magdalena valley, although considerable forest, some of it at present well protected, exists there (Ridgely 1981a). The only recent records are from La Planada Nature Reserve in Nariño, where over three years birds returned in increasing numbers, perhaps because of the relative lack of disturbance there, with a flock of 21 in 1985 (Orejuela 1985), Alto Quindío, Colombia, where birds were seen in May 1991 (see Distribution) following reports by local people that the species was still present (Renjifo 1991), and an undisclosed area of central western Ecuador, whence a few skins and some traded individuals were reported in the late 1980s (NK). Thus, on present knowledge, the total population could be very small and on the verge of extinction.

ECOLOGY The Yellow-eared Parrot inhabits humid forest and partially cleared terrain, especially where there are wax palms *Ceroxylon* spp., at 2,000-3,000 m, occasionally down to 1,200 m and up to 3,400 m (Ridgely 1981a, Hilty and Brown 1986). The association with wax palms appears to be strong; however, the species is absent from one region in Napo, northern Ecuador, where a wax palm is abundant (Ridgely 1981a, R. S. Ridgely *in litt.* 1989).

The bird feeds on wax palms, probably of all species but certainly *Ceroxylon quindiuense* (J. I. Hernández Camacho verbally 1991). At Reserva de la Planada in Nariño all observations of feeding over a period of three months involved fruits of *Sapium* spp. (Orejuela 1985, Rodríguez and Hernández Camacho 1988). Flocks probably wander seasonally in search of food (Hilty and Brown 1986).

In May 1911 it was found nesting in colonies at río Toché, Tolima department, Colombia, the nest-holes being just under the lowest leaves, more than 25 m up in wax palms, and in places nearly every palm had an occupied nest-hole (Chapman 1917a: 29). On 27 October 1911 12 specimens (in AMNH, FMNH, MCZ and USNM; also Chapman 1917a) were collected at this same locality, one (in USNM) being indicated as having undeveloped gonads. A female laying and a male with large testes were collected in March 1954 at Moscopán (specimens in YPM). A male and a female collected in December 1914 in Antioquia, and a female collected in April 1911 in Valle del Cauca, all had undeveloped gonads (specimens in AMNH). The presence of the parrots at the wax palms in Tolima in both May and October (Chapman 1917a; specimens in MCZ, AMNH, USNM and FMNH) suggests that the palms were attractive as both breeding and feeding sites.

THREATS Extensive deforestation over much of its range is responsible for the serious decline of the Yellow-eared Parrot (Ridgely 1981a). Two wax palm species, *Cerxylon alpinum* and *C. quindiuense*, with which these parrots have been associated, are now considered vulnerable or endangered owing to lack of regeneration (Moore 1977, Ridgely 1981a); the problem is caused less by cattle-grazing than by the species' inability to regenerate in stands of introduced kikuyu grass (J. I. Hernández Camacho verbally 1991). The parrot has always been extremely rare in captivity (Ridgely 1981a). Its colonial habits render it highly vulnerable to hunting, capture and forest clearance, and it may already be very close to extinction.

MEASURES TAKEN In Colombia the species has been recorded in Munchique, Purac茅 and Cueva de los Gu谩charos National Parks, plus La Planada Nature Reserve, although it may not be regular in any of them (Ridgely 1981a, Hilty and Brown 1986). Only in Munchique National Park and La Planada Nature Reserve have there been (relatively) recent sightings of enough birds to suggest that a viable population may exist there or nearby. The parrot may occur in Nevado de Huila National Park (King 1978-1979), also Los Nevados and Las Hermosas National Parks. In Ecuador the recent creation of the Cotocachi-Cayapas Ecological Reserve in Imbabura and Esmeraldas provinces may protect the southernmost part of the species's known range (Ridgely 1981a).

MEASURES PROPOSED Additional study of this parrot is badly needed, as is protection of areas found to harbour any of its populations (Ridgely 1981a). It is obviously now very pressing that searches take place around Cerro Munchique to determine whether a significant population occurs in the forests there; such work could be combined with field studies to clarify the status in this area of many other threatened bird species (see below). The Cotocachi-Cayapas Ecological Reserve in Imbabura and Esmeraldas provinces, north-west Ecuador, needs strengthened management (Ridgely 1981a). The Yellow-eared Parrot is sympatric with a number of other threatened species, and any conservation initiatives should take into account their best interests: details are in the equivalent sections under Moustached Antpitta *Grallaria alleni* (for Cueva de los Gu谩charos National Park), Bicoloured Antpitta *G. rufocinerea* (for Alto Quind铆o Acaime Natural Reserve and Purac茅 National Park), Tolima Dove *Leptotila conoveri* (for the r铆o Toche wax palm area), Colourful Puffleg *Eriocnemis mirabilis* (for Munchique National Park) and Hoary Puffleg *Haplophaedia lugens* (for La Planada Nature Reserve and vicinity).

REMARKS (1) The Yellow-eared Parrot is a highly distinctive bird in its own genus. (2) A record based on three specimens (in AMNH and ROM) collected on 31 January and 1 February 1907 at the untraced "Torne", Valle del Cauca department, may refer to the Central or West Andes.

THICK-BILLED PARROT *Rhynchopsitta pachyrhyncha* V[9]

Now endemic to the pine forests of the Sierra Madre Occidental in Mexico, this parrot formerly ranged into and probably bred in the U.S.A. and has done so recently owing to a major and ingenious reintroduction project. Extensive deforestation has occurred throughout its Mexican range, none of which enjoys protection. Because it is nomadic in response to variations in cone abundance, it requires the preservation of substantial areas of pine in different parts of its range if it is to be secure.

DISTRIBUTION The Thick-billed Parrot ranges through the Sierra Madre Occidental of north-west Mexico principally in the states of Chihuahua and Durango (the only states for which breeding has been proved), with smaller or occasional populations in Sonora, Sinaloa, Jalisco and Michoacán and, formerly, in the the U.S.A. in the states of Arizona and New Mexico; the species is now being reintroduced to Arizona, and has bred there.

Mexico In the following text, records are arranged approximately from north-west to south-east, with coordinates taken from OG (1956a) and indicating the approximate locations of certain sites only otherwise to be found on the map in Lanning and Shiflett (1983).

Sonora Records are all from the mountainous north-east region in: the Sierra de Madera, 30°20'N 108°52'W, an extension of the Sierra de Nácori, present by reliable local report made in 1931 (Scheffler 1931; hence van Rossem 1945); the Sierra Huachinera, 30°16'N 108°45'W, Sierra de Oposura, 29°55'N 109°29'W, and Sierra de Nácori (not listed in OG 1956a), all in the 1950s (Marshall 1957, from whose map the last-named is roughly at 29°50'N 108°45'W).

Chihuahua Records extend throughout the mountainous westerly side of the state, and it is evident that the species ranges widely on both slopes of the Sierra Madre Occidental (as indicated, e.g., by Bergtold 1906, Lanning and Shiflett 1981, 1983), specific localities including: Janos, February 1920 (skin in UMMZ); southward from 60 km west of Casas Grandes (Bergtold 1906), thus immediately embracing the following sites down to Madera; Pacheco (Colonia Pachaco, Pachico, Tachico) and environs, where nesting proved (Salvin and Godman 1888-1904, Allen 1893, Thayer 1906), including río Gavilán, 12 km south-west of Pacheco (specimen in MVZ) and Azules, where breeding proved (Lanning and Shiflett 1983); Colonia García, 29°59'N 108°20'W (see Remarks 1 under Imperial Woodpecker *Campephilus imperialis*), and environs, where nesting proved (Thayer 1906; skins from 1948 in MVZ); "Chuichupa", i.e. Chuhuichupa, 29°38'N 108°22'W, and southward (Bergtold 1906), but also eastward to Ojo Negro, where breeding proved (Lanning and Shiflett 1983); Babicora, June 1902 (specimens in FMNH); Madera, where breeding proved (Lanning and Shiflett 1983); Arroyo Mesteño, 29°26'N 107°04'W, in the Sierra del Nido, August 1961 (specimen in MVZ); Arroyo del Nido, 29°36'N 106°38'W, also in the Sierra del Nido, June 1957, one bird with a brood-patch (specimens in MNHUK, MVZ); Cebadilla, where breeding proved (Lanning and Shiflett 1983, from whose map the site must lie 20 km north-west of the next; see Remarks 2); "Yaguirachic", i.e. Yahuirachic, 28°35'N 108°09'W, July 1957 (specimens in MVZ), and Vallecillo, where breeding proved (Lanning and Shiflett 1983, from whose map the site appears identical to the preceding; see Remarks 3); near the village of Tutuaca, 28°29'N 108°12'W, in the 1970s (V. Emanuel *in litt.* 1992, with coordinates from OG 1956a; this the site of the "sizeable population" on the border with Sonora reported in King 1978-1979); Pinos Altos, June/July 1888 (van Rossem 1934), 28°15'N 108°17'W (the same locality as for Imperial Woodpecker: see relevant account); Bravo, evidently nearby as also July 1888 and recorded by the same collector (van Rossem 1934); Cumbre at the top of the Barranco de Cobre (Cerro Cobre at 27°01'N 108°39'W) on the border with Sonora and Sinaloa, May 1950 (Stager 1954); Jesús María, the only likely site of this name being 26°52'N 107°39'W, undated (van Rossem 1934); mountains west of Parral (Bergtold 1906), i.e. presumably modern-day Hidalgo del Parral; Laguna Juanota, 26°30'N 106°29'W, July 1937 (specimen in MLZ); Guadalupe y Calvo, August and September 1898 (specimens in USNM) and adjacent Cerro Mohinora, 26°06'N

107°04'W, where breeding proved (*Condor* 40 [1938]: 189; also Hubbard and Crossin 1974, Lanning and Shiflett 1983); Los Frailes, 25°39'N 106°55'W, on the state line with Durango, June 1937 (specimens in MLZ). Vagrancy must account for a record from Ciudad Chihuahua (mentioned in Bent 1940).

Durango Records are scattered throughout the west and south of the state in the Sierra Madre Occidental, thus: Cócono, where breeding proved (Lanning and Shiflett 1983, whose map suggests 26°15'N 106°10'W); Vacas, where breeding proved (Lanning and Shiflett 1983, whose map suggests 26°10'N 106°W); Arroyo del Buey, May 1903, and San Andrés, November 1903 (both untraced, but in the north-west, the former being described as in the Sierra del Candella, the latter apparently close to the Sonora border) (Miller 1906); Camellones, where breeding proved (Lanning and Shiflett 1983; see Remarks 4); Nevado, where breeding proved (Lanning and Shiflett 1983, whose map suggests 25°10'N 105°40'W; but see Remarks 4); Laguna del Progreso, untraced but c.80 km west-north-west of Ciudad Durango, June 1950 (specimen in FMNH); Coyotes, September 1904 (specimen in FMNH), the only localities given by OG (1956a) in the state being just north of Ciudad Durango at 24°15'N 104°42'W or south-west (perhaps more probable given the records below) at 23°49'N 105°20'W; (near) Ciudad Durango and to the south-west on the road to Mazatlán (Salvin and Godman 1888-1904); by local report in winter at El Salto (also on this road) and at Rancho Las Margaritas and west of Rancho El Cortijo, 1950s, although not observed in the summers (Fleming and Baker 1963); over the canyon of the río San Juan (untraced but some 30 km south-west of Ciudad Durango), spring 1931 (Bailey and Conover 1935).

Coahuila Scarlet-fronted birds have been seen in flocks of Maroon-fronted Parrots in winter at San Antonio de las Alazanas, and possibly were wanderers from the Sierra Madre Occidental (see Remarks 1 under the latter species).

Sinaloa The species has been recorded from only two areas, both at the border with Durango, 10 km west of Palmito: at Rancho Carrizo, April 1972, and Rancho Liebre, May 1964 (Hubbard and Crossin 1974) and January 1982, at 2,100 m (B. M. Whitney *in litt.* 1991), the only Palmito traceable to near Sinaloa in OG (1956a) being in Durango at 25°11'N 106°59'W; and at 10 km east of Santa Lucía, 23°27'N 105°53'W, May 1959 (specimen in WFVZ).

Jalisco Records are confined to the Nevado (Volcán[es]) de Colima (twin peaks of Volcán de Fuego and Volcán de Nieve) in the south of the state, with skins from April 1892 (in USNM) and February 1904 (in AMNH), and observations in January 1972, birds then suspected of being winter visitors although local breeding was possible (Schnell *et al.* 1974), and February 1981, at 1,880 m (B. M. Whitney *in litt.* 1991).

Michoacán Records are from one main area, around Uruapan: to the west, on the Cerro de Tancítaro ("Tancitario" in TAW 1986), July 1940 and July 1941 (Blake and Hanson 1942); and 7 km to the east, at Rancho La Cofradia, June 1939 (specimen in MLZ). However, there is an old record from Angangueo in the extreme east of the state (van Rossem 1945).

México There is a single record of the species from Popocatépetl on the border with Puebla in the last century (Sumichrast 1881, Salvin and Godman 1888-1904). Given the relative proximity of this mountain to Angangueo in Michoacán, it seems likely that the record refers to Thick-billed and not Maroon-fronted Parrot *Rhynchopsitta terrisi* (see relevant account).

Veracruz Records are from Cofre de Perote (Sumichrast 1881; skins mentioned by van Rossem 1945; see Remarks 5); and Pico de Orizaba (Volcán Citlaltépetl) at the (apparently no longer thus named) village of Moyoapam (Sumichrast 1881) and from around the peak at the border with Puebla, where "during the summer of 1891" Cox (1895) saw a flock of parrots "above the deep pine forest about midway between upper and lower timber lines", these being attributed by Loetscher (1940) to this species. Ridgely (1981a) thought these records might pertain to Maroon-fronted Parrots, as indeed they may; but owing to the stronger evidence of wandering in the Thick-billed Parrot, and given the records above from Michoacán and México states, there remains an equally good chance that records from Veracruz involved Thick-bills. If the specimens referred to could be traced, the matter might be resolved.

U.S.A. The Thick-billed Parrot was at first thought to be an irregular, invasive visitor, irrupting across the Mexican border into south-eastern Arizona (notably the Chiricahua Mountains, which remain the key area for the species) and south-western New Mexico, remaining some months or even over a year or more, but then draining back into Mexico (Vorhies 1934, Wetmore 1935); this view certainly prevailed over comment by Lusk (1900) and Smith (1907) that the species might be resident or at least much more regular than supposed. However, while irruptive behaviour certainly existed (and probably accounts entirely for records from New Mexico, the most recent of which was in autumn 1964 on Animas Peak: Woodard 1980), interviews with old-timers indicated that the species was formerly "an every-year resident" (presumably therefore a year-round resident) in at least one part of southern Arizona (the Chiricahuas), with lack of breeding reports being possibly no more than an observational artefact (Snyder and Wallace 1988, Snyder and Johnson 1989). Thus, apart from evidence that in the immediate pre- and post-Columbus periods the species apparently occurred as far north as Flagstaff (Wetmore 1931, Hargrave 1939; see Remarks 6), recent interviews have revealed its presence at the start of the twentieth century, seasonally at least, in the Catalina, Rincon, Galiuro, Santa Rita, Patagonia and Chiricahua mountain ranges (Johnson and Snyder 1987; other records from this period in Phillips *et al.* 1964). Modern records of introduced birds are dealt with under Measures Taken.

POPULATION The overall status of any parrot species is difficult to assess owing chiefly to its unpredictably wide-ranging behaviour, but this bird is particularly problematic. If indeed it is highly nomadic both within and between years (see Ecology), as much evidence suggests, this has two dangers: first, that it inflates its range in a manner that makes it appear generally (and permanently) more widespread and numerous than it is; and second, it creates the impression of a high numerical representation at certain sites as if this were a permanent condition. Thus Marshall (1957) often saw the species in his study areas in the Sierra Madre Occidental in 1951 and 1952 (including flocks of 50 and 60), but in 1955 saw birds only twice; whereas in the Sierra Huachinera (an outlier of the main massif) he saw none in 1953 and many in 1954. Hubbard and Crossin (1974) considered overall numbers to have declined in the decade or more prior to their own review, citing Fleming and Baker's (1962) failure to find birds in Durango in the summers of 1957-1961, and other anonymous reports; yet birds have subsequently been found breeding widely in Durango (Lanning and Shiflett 1981, 1983). Records from the south of the range, e.g. of the species being "moderately abundant" at Cerro de Tancítaro, Michoacán (Blake and Hanson 1942), and of flocks up to 120 on the Nevado de Colima, Jalisco, in 1972 and 1973 (Schnell *et al.* 1974) and of over 250 there in 1981 (B. M. Whitney *in litt.* 1991), may well refer to temporary populations (even though present for several years), or perhaps temporary augmentations of permanent but small local populations; but it is to be noted that Beebe (1905) found the species "abundant" on the Nevado de Colima in early 1904.

One construction that can be placed on the evidence is that there may be certain core areas, perhaps those with greatest diversity of acceptable food-plants (so that birds there can compensate for temporary loss of one source by exploiting another), which host important populations virtually permanently, but that otherwise many populations (in some years doubtless inflated by one or more years of breeding success) move widely through the Sierra Madre Occidental in search of fruiting stands of pine, breeding opportunistically wherever and for as long as conditions are favourable. Given the longevity and learning ability of parrots in general, and the capacity to traverse large distances rapidly in this species, sometimes merely in response to impending adverse weather (see Measures Taken for evidence of this), the birds probably develop a broad knowledge of massive areas of habitat.

Despite limited ability to judge the overall situation, it must be true that the numbers of this species have declined, given the extent of habitat conversion reported under Threats. Moreover, irruptions into the U.S.A. have not taken place since around 1920, and observers no longer refer to such phenomena as an "immense flock... estimated at from 700 to 1000" (Smith 1907) or mountains being "alive with these parrots" (Bergtold 1906). How serious the decline has been remains obscure, and it is not possible to judge whether Monson's (1965) pessimism over the species's future is justified or not.

ECOLOGY The Thick-billed Parrot inhabits temperate conifer forests, i.e. (with increasing altitude) mature pine–oak, pine, and fir forests, from roughly 1,200 to 3,600 m (but most usually between 2,000 and 3,000 m), where it occurs in locations varying from plateau-like tops of mountains with open pine or pine–oak woodland and parkland, to thick pine and fir stands below high cliffs or rimrock outcrops used for roosting (Sumichrast 1869, Marshall 1957, Monson 1965, Hubbard and Crossin 1974, Schnell *et al.* 1974, Woodard 1980, Lanning and Shiflett 1983); in winter it is a bird of the snow zone (Snyder and Johnson 1989). At one locality, Cerro Tancítaro in Michoacán, in July of successive years birds were found to range from the lowlands (tropical deciduous forest) to the highlands (pines), roosting in the former and feeding in the latter (Blake and Hanson 1942), but this seems anomalous.

Food is principally the seeds of various pines, supplemented at certain times with acorns. In the one detailed study of the species, Arizona pine *Pinus arizonica* and Mexican white pine *P. ayacahuite*, the two common pines of north-west Mexico, were the usual food sources, although birds were also seen to eat the smaller seeds of Aztec pine *P. teocote* on occasion (Lanning and Shiflett 1983). Irrupting birds in Arizona, 1917-1918, fed chiefly on Chihuahua pines *P. leiophylla* until the crop was consumed, then switched to acorns, probably of all four oaks *Quercus* represented in the area, and in very cold weather the birds that remained behind took food from the ground in places where the wind had blown away the snow-layer; in previous invasions they were reported to have eaten pinyon *P. edulis* and/or Mexican pinyon *P. cembroides*, but no-one could substantiate newspaper claims that cultivated crops were attacked (Wetmore 1935, Cottam and Knappen 1939). In 82 feeding observations of released birds in this same region of Arizona, 1986, 34 were on Chihuahua pine, 25 on Mexican pinyon, 15 on Apache pine *P. latifolia*, six on Douglas fir *Pseudotsuga taxifolia* (cones and terminal buds) and one each on ponderosa pine *Pinus ponderosa* and Arizona white oak *Quercus arizonica*, although the ponderosa pine may have been under-recorded as it is a species of high altitudes (to which birds were seen to fly); birds usually started each day on Mexican pinyon, possibly because its large seeds provided a rapid increase in energy reserves (Snyder and Wallace 1988). Elsewhere (Cerro de Tancítaro, Michoacán) birds have been recorded taking "pinyon" seeds but also fruits of a cherry *Prunus capuli* and legume seeds (Blake and Hanson 1942), and (in Barranca de Cobre, Chihuahua) the terminal buds of Chihuahua and Lumholtz pines *P. lumholtzii* (Stager 1954). Feeding can be solitary, but is usually a group activity (mean size eight) (Lanning and Shiflett 1983). Feeding bouts of released birds commonly lasted 1-2 hours and took place irregularly through the day, birds rarely staying in one place for more than two hours (Snyder and Wallace 1988). Released birds sometimes drank before feeding in the morning, and often did so before roosting at night (Snyder and Wallace 1988); Wetmore (1935) reported birds sometimes drinking at a river before roosting, Arizona, and in the north-west Sierra Madre Occidental Marshall (1957) was told of a waterfall to which thousands came to drink.

The breeding season is timed to coincide with peak abundance in pine seeds (Lanning and Shiflett 1983), and this may lead to some variation: in August 1905 nests with fresh eggs and nests with young were found, and in two cases two large young and one fresh egg were found in the same nest (Thayer 1906); much the same schedule was noted by Bergtold (1906), although he found a nest with half-fledged young on 5 October; and Lanning and Shiflett (1981, 1983) noted in 1979 that birds returned to their breeding areas in April and May, egg-laying occurred between mid-June and the end of July, young hatched from mid-July to late August and fledged when about two months old, between mid-September and late October. On the other hand, Smith (1907) and Wetmore (1935) reported birds in juvenile plumage in late August, suggesting egg-laying in late May, and Bent (1940) gave a laying date of 10 May; Lusk (1900) collected a juvenile as early as mid-June. Cliffs within the Sierra Madre Occidental are mostly rhyolitic and contain few holes (Lawson and Lanning 1981), therefore unlike its close relative the Maroon-fronted Parrot the Thick-bill nests in cavities in trees, primarily pines: 42 of 55 nests found, 1979, were in the two species of pine that were also the chief source of food (see above), Arizona and Mexican white; nine were in quaking aspen *Populus tremuloides* and four in Douglas fir; standing dead pines (pine snags) provided cavities in 32 cases (Lanning and Shiflett 1981, 1983); other descriptions, including evidence that the species utilized old holes of the possibly extinct Imperial Woodpecker (see relevant account), are in Bergtold (1906) and Thayer (1906). Nests were found between 2,300 and 3,070 m; 28 (51%) were on north or north-east slopes, where the largest trees were often located; the 10 cavities in live pines were in parts of the tree that had died from lightning strike, disease or age (Lanning and Shiflett 1981, 1983). Cavities in the 1979 study were 8-28 (mean 17) m above ground, and most had probably been excavated by Common Flickers *Colaptes auratus* or other woodpeckers; of 12 re-examined in 1980, one held young, indicating some re-use in successive seasons (Lanning and Shiflett 1981, 1983). Nesting density was variable, apparently dependent on nest-site availability: in 1979 a pine and an aspen each held two simultaneously active nests, although pairs were usually more scattered, and in 14 cases no other nests were found within a kilometre radius (Lanning and Shiflett 1981, 1983). Although Thayer (1906) reported a clutch-size of 1-3, Lanning and Shiflett (1981, 1983) found 2-4 eggs per nest, with three being commonest, and 1-3 young fledging, a fairly high success rate; they summarized captive breeding studies (but see, e.g., Witt 1978), where birds laid up to three eggs at 2-3 day intervals, incubation starting with the first egg and lasting 25-28 days per egg, while Snyder *et al.* (1989b) reported on a pair that laid two eggs on 14 and 19 August that hatched on 10 and 12 September, giving incubation periods of 27 and 24 days respectively.

As typical of parrots, birds remain in pairs, so that flocks are commonly even-numbered, members of pairs flying very close to each other (Bergtold 1906, Leopold 1937). Roosting is gregarious and may take place in cliffs (see above), but reintroduced birds, Arizona, used trees, invariably densely crowned pines or firs providing good protection from nocturnal predators; on one occasion they changed the site after encountering a Goshawk *Accipiter gentilis* en route to roost (Snyder and Wallace 1988). In the 1917-1918 invasion of Arizona, birds flew up the mountains to roost in the summer and autumn, but came as low as 1,500 m in the coldest weather (Wetmore 1935). The problem of this species's movements is discussed under Population, and more information on food and breeding is given under Measures Taken.

THREATS The loss of the Thick-billed Parrot from the United States avifauna (see the last paragraph in this section) has created considerable sensitivity about its fate in Mexico, beginning with Leopold (1937), who feared that an impending programme of road construction would result in the loss of the species, and continuing with Monson (1965), who saw it as unable to outface an expanding human population and its guns, sawmills, cattle and goats. However, Tavistock's (1929) report that the bird was disdained by local people as neither good to keep (a point confirmed by Low 1972) nor good to eat holds true today, with Lanning and Shiflett (1981) discovering that use as a food resource or for pets (locally) is minimal. The explanation of the decline in numbers of this species is therefore chiefly habitat destruction, although international trade has played a part in recent years, and other factors may have been important.

Habitat destruction Marshall (1957) was perhaps first to point out that "almost all" the Sierra Madre Occidental, at least in Chihuahua, was being logged, "but somewhat selectively". Vincent (1966-1971) saw that removal of large trees would be particularly damaging to the species, and his concern was shared by Hubbard and Crossin (1974) and by Schnell *et al.* (1974), who in 1973 discovered a new road through pristine pine forest on Nevado de Colima, Jalisco, with a lumbering facility operating along it. Commercial logging of live pines for lumber and dead pines for pulp began in the early 1900s and has grown steadily: a pulp mill operating in Chihuahua since the mid-1960s, when reported on in 1980, had the capacity to process 1,800-3,600 pine snags every day (this seems inconceivable), and another mill, this time in Durango, was due to open in the early 1980s (Lanning and Shiflett 1981, 1983). All dead pines that can be extracted invariably are; and old residents of the region testified to the disappearance of the parrot with the disappearance of their nest trees, so that in 1979 large areas could be traversed in which no suitable nest-sites existed (Lanning and Shiflett 1981, 1983). In a re-examination of 12 nest-sites from the previous year, one held dead chicks apparently as a result of logging disturbance of the area, and two trees had been lost owing to logging (Lanning and Shiflett 1983), i.e. in one year 25% of nest-sites were affected adversely by man. Under overnment regulations, living pines are selectively cut only when their breast-height diameters exceed 40-50 cm; and only one of the 42 nests in pines in 1979 was in a tree with a diameter under 50 cm (Lanning and Shiflett 1981, 1983).

Trade Although over 100 birds were imported into the U.K. in the early 1970s, trade thereafter dropped sharply both there and in the U.S.A. (Lanning and Shiflett 1981). However, in 1985 and 1986 there was an enormous increase in illegal Thick-bills entering the U.S.A., with numbers estimated varying from several hundred to several thousand (Snyder and Wallace 1988, Snyder and Johnson 1989, N. F. R. Snyder *in litt.* 1992). In summer 1988 U.S. Customs confiscated 37 in Texas (Johnson *et al.* 1989, Snyder *et al.* 1989b).

Other (including natural) factors The absence of the Imperial Woodpecker from Texas was indicated as the reason the Thick-billed Parrot did not nest in the state, since the latter uses the former's old nest-holes (Phillips *et al.* 1964). If such an association were real, the decline and disappearance of the woodpecker (owing, apparently, chiefly to hunting: see relevant account) must have affected the parrot, by reducing the number of nest-sites available; but the parrot's successful use of old flicker holes suggests it did not (N. F. R. Snyder *in litt.* 1992). Widespread failures of pine cone crops have also been blamed (Hubbard and Crossin 1974), although this could only be problematic in combination with other factors. Natural causes of nest failure may include rain in the cavity (Lanning and Shiflett 1983). Hawks are a major threat to wild birds (see Measures Taken) and are much feared (Wetmore 1935).

Causes of disappearance in the U.S.A. Although regarded as poor food in Mexico (see above), mounting evidence from interviews has suggested that in southern Arizona around the turn of the century this and many other species were greatly reduced in numbers through subsistence hunting by woodsmen and miners, and this, combined with considerable logging to provide props and track for the mining industry, may have depleted the (resident) parrot populations to zero (Johnson and Snyder 1987, Johnson *et al.* 1989, Snyder and Johnson 1989, Snyder *et al.* 1989a). It is worth noting here that birds apparently unfamiliar with man showed extraordinary tameness, as witness the photograph in Smith (1907) and the remark by Beebe (1905) that "it is either a very stupid bird or controlled by its curiosity, for the flocks followed us everywhere as we made our way over the slippery ground".

MEASURES TAKEN The Thick-billed Parrot is listed as Endangered under U.S. law and is on Appendix I of CITES (Lanning and Shiflett 1983). However, it is not known whether the species occurs, at least on a regular basis, in a single protected area in Mexico. The survey of the species in 1979, much as urged by Jeggo (1975), were funded by RARE (then the Rare Animal Relief Effort) (Lanning and Shiflett 1981, 1983).

Reintroduction into U.S.A. The only real steps to provide for this bird have come in the form of a reintroduction scheme in south-eastern Arizona under the auspices of the Arizona Fish and Game Department, the U.S. Fish and Wildlife Service, the U.S. Forest Service, and Wildlife Preservation Trust International, with the active cooperation of the Avicultural Breeding and Research Center, the Wild Bird Sanctuary, and many zoos; the following account of this project is conflated from Johnson and Snyder (1987), Koschmann and Price (1987), Snyder and Wallace (1987), Snyder and Johnson (1988, 1989), Johnson *et al.* (1989), Snyder *et al.* (1989a,b) and Johnson *et al.* (1991), with corrections and additions by N. F. R. Snyder (*in litt.* 1992).

Sufficiently large numbers of confiscations had followed the illegal importations of birds in 1985-1986 (see Threats: Trade) for a programme of release into the wild to be developed and initiated during 1986, based in the Chiricahua Mountains, Arizona, not only the major source of U.S. records of the species but also an area largely under the jurisdiction of the U.S. Forest

Service and managed for recreation, wildlife and watershed. The release of 29 confiscated wild-caught birds took place (after considerable preparation, including imping damaged feathers and conditioning birds to improve their flight capacity) in Cave Creek Canyon in September and October 1986, some birds being fitted with radio transmitters to monitor their movements. Seven were quickly lost (probably to hawk predation: a major problem for adjusting birds not yet up to full flying strength during the first week of freedom), and in early November the remaining birds split into two groups of 14 and eight, the latter flying south, apparently into Mexico not to be seen again, the former disappearing for three weeks in December to the Pinaleño Mountains (these movements predicting by a day the arrival of low pressure systems in the area); they spent the winter in Cave Creek Canyon, foraging and roosting from 1,600 to 2,700 m, until the following June, during which time their number fell by one, while in the spring five more birds were released to join them (see Remarks 7), one of these falling victim probably to a Goshawk.

On 14 June 1987 the 17 birds flew north-west to Tonto Creek north-east of Phoenix on the Mogollon Rim, some 320 km from the release site, foraging almost exclusively on ripening Douglas fir cones through July. A bird was found dead in Oak Creek Canyon along the Verde River, 100 km north-west of Tonto Creek, and an imped feather was found in the White Mountains close to the New Mexico border, indicating still wider dispersal of the birds. No breeding was proved. In September five birds returned to the release site (see Remarks 8), and a bird was released to join them; in October another four returned. Throughout October, the 10 birds fed on ponderosa pines at lower elevations (1,600-2,000 m), then moved up the mountains to feed chiefly on Aztec pines, one bird dying in December; four months later they were down again, again feeding on Chihuahua pines, with four strong pairs now evident. Meanwhile, in mid-November two experimental releases of hand-reared captive-bred birds failed owing to their inability to flock, watch for predators, or (despite long conditioning) recognize food sources, although one bird, parent-reared, performed much better and was integrating into the flock when it was taken by a predator.

On 10 April 1988 three wild-caught birds were released to join the flock of nine, but by June one had been lost. In mid-June, only four days off the previous year's date, eight birds flew again to the Mogollon Rim, while in the same month a pair of birds was released to join the three left behind, these five staying in the Chiricahuas over the summer. The eight in the Tonto basin fed on abundant ponderosa and pinyon pine cones, and exhibited much mating activity; but they then disappeared, and were only rediscovered in the basin in late September when first eight and then 12 birds were present, this increase being due to two incomers that had split from the five in the Chiricahuas and, most significantly, two young birds bred by one pair. These two offspring were among nine birds that returned to the Chiricahuas in November and wintered there, feeding on an abundant cone crop.

Early in February 1989 another bird was released and quickly integrated, but one of the wild-bred young disappeared at this time. By late spring there were eight birds present in the flock, and seven of these survived the spring migration to the Tonto basin (three pairs breeding, all in ponderosa snags). At this stage it was recognized that stocks in the wild needed further bolstering as soon as possible, since this species seems particularly dependent on flocking as an anti-predator mechanism. Unfortunately, no birds were available for immediate release, and by late summer the effects of an extremely severe drought were being seen in a near-total loss of pine cones in the region. This food failure was the primary cause of breeding failure in all three active pairs in 1989, and the birds soon adopted erratic movements in an apparent search for food, migrating back to the Chiricahuas in early September, back up to the Tonto basin a few days later, then soon back to the Chiricahuas again, where they were able to subsist on a marginal crop of Douglas fir for several weeks. However, they again soon left the mountains and, with the loss of the last bird with a radio transmitter, became impossible to track. The crop failure continued through 1990; although at least some birds are known to have survived this period, they did not regroup in former areas and their present status is unknown.

Food supplies were somewhat better in 1991, and at the end of November 18 birds (eight believed wild-caught, 10 captive-reared) were released into the Chiricahuas, all at least one year old and all having been subjected to rigorous flight conditioning. Nevertheless, within three days five were killed by Goshawks *Accipiter gentilis*, two died of starvation, one died of unknown causes, one was lost to radio contact and one was recaptured because it failed to join the eight survivors, which soon began flocking cohesively and foraging well. However, after a month these birds were taken back into captivity, partly because of the predation factor and partly because the wild cone crop was proving inadequate to sustain the birds. Further releases will concentrate on integrating parent-reared captive-bred birds with wild-caught birds, once more favourable food conditions return.

MEASURES PROPOSED The preservation of a number of very large tracts of forest where the species occurs in several parts of its range (to allow for periodic local failure of cone crops) has been deemed urgent (Monson 1965, Woodard 1980). Any such initiatives would best be taken only after considerable research into the status of this and two other extremely rare endemics of the same region, the Eared Trogon *Euptilotis neoxenus* and Imperial Woodpecker (see relevant accounts), so that all three (if the last survives at all) can be catered for, along with other significant species such as the near-threatened Spotted Owl *Strix occidentalis*; nevertheless, it is clear that this is indeed a pressing and important undertaking with major ramifications, and one which ought to excite the interest and commitment of conservationists and agencies on both sides of the Mexican border. Lanning and Lawson (1981, 1983) called for the adoption of forest management practices that allow five or more dead pines to be left standing per hectare, with perhaps some small reserves to protect optimal primary forest habitat.

REMARKS (1) The Thick-billed Parrot is here treated as a distinct species from the Maroon-fronted Parrot *Rhynchopsitta terrisi* (see Remarks 1 under that species). Because both members are threatened, so is the genus. (2) OG (1956a) gives a Cerro Cebadilla at 28°49'N 108°17'W. (3) OG (1956a) gives a Cerro el Vallecillo at 28°32'N 107°38'W. (4) Possibly the map in Lanning and Shiflett (1983) transposes the sites of Camellones and Nevado, since OG (1956a) places the only Nevado (Cerro Nevado) in the state at 25°02'N 106°05'W. (5) Sclater's (1859a) record from "Jalapa" is attributed to the virtually adjacent Cofre de Perote by Salvin and Godman (1888-1904) and Loetscher (1941). (6) Hargrave (1939) found remains of four birds at an Indian site occupied between 700 and 1300 AD on the San Francisco Mountain near Flagstaff, but warned these might have been traded; however, Wetmore's (1931) evidence from 1593 suggests they were not. (7) Snyder and Johnson (1989) said three birds augmented the wild flock at this date, but this appears to be a slip for June 1988; indeed, this paper adds a 1989 postscript that entirely omits reference to proof of breeding during 1988. (8) Johnson and Snyder (1987) considered the returning flock of five was a remnant of the eight that flew south into Mexico the year before; but this view is not expressed in any of the other papers.

MAROON-FRONTED PARROT *Rhynchopsitta terrisi* V[9]

With a population not known with certainty to exceed 2,000 and habitat (mature pine forest generally between 2,000 and 3,500 m) covering up to no more than 7,000 km², this colonial cliff-nesting parrot risks gradual decline through forest destruction and needs the benefit of protected areas in both the north and south of its limited range in the Sierra Madre Oriental, Mexico.

DISTRIBUTION The Maroon-fronted Parrot (see Remarks 1) is confined to a small area of north-east Mexico in a narrow section of the Sierra Madre Oriental some 300 km long and averaging 60 km in width, covering south-east Coahuila, west-central and southern Nuevo León, and south-west Tamaulipas; of the approximate 18,000 km² thus delineated, only 20-40% or some 3,500-7,000 km² contains appropriate habitat (Lanning and Lawson 1977), and if indeed the southernmost breeding site is Cerro Potosí (see below) then the entire breeding range of the species is only the northern third of this area. Records from Veracruz do not necessarily pertain to this species (see Remarks 2).

Localities for the species from north to south are as follows (with some distances and orientations derived from Lanning and Lawson 1977): (*Nuevo León*) mountains south-west of Monterrey in the region of San Isidro, Laguna Sánchez and "San José de Bosquillos" (correctly, San José de las Boquillas: N. F. R. Snyder *in litt.* 1992), with four sites (including "Highrise" cliff and "Las Cuevas") 7 km and 31 km north-east, 5 km west and 17 km south of Laguna Sánchez (Lawson and Lanning 1981, Valenzuela *et al.* 1981, Sada 1987, M. A. Gómez Garza *in litt.* 1991; see Remarks 3); (*Coahuila*) at 26 km east of Saltillo (Lanning and Lawson 1977; see Remarks 4); west of Saltillo reportedly in the small range extending to just beyond General Cepeda (D. V. Lanning verbally to W. B. King 1978; also Woodard 1980); Diamante Pass, 8 km south-east of Saltillo (Burleigh and Lowery 1942); Las Vacas, 13 km south-east of Saltillo (Ely 1962), the precise site of one specimen (in DMNH) being 3 km south on the north slope of [Mount] Zapalinamé; an unspecified area in mountains south of Saltillo (Ely 1962); the Sierra Guadalupe south-west of Saltillo (Lawson and Lanning 1981); various sites adjacent to San Antonio de las Alazanas (itself 50 km south-east of Saltillo), namely Los Lirios, 15 km to the north (Lanning and Lawson 1977) and Mesa de las Tablas and Ciruela (16 km and 22 km respectively to the east) (Hardy and Dickerman 1955; also Urban 1959; see Remarks 3); then (again in *Nuevo León*) a cliff 25 km north-east of Cerro Potosí (and 40 km south-east of Laguna Sánchez), the southernmost known breeding site of the species, found in 1991 (D. V. Lanning and N. F. R. Snyder *in litt.* 1992); on Cerro Potosí 15 km north-west of Galeana, and at 10 km south-east of Galeana (Moore 1947); a high mountain area (notably Cerro Viejo) around Zaragoza, north-west of Ciudad Victoria (Lanning 1978), this apparently being north of the border of Tamaulipas; Cerro Peña Nevada, c.100 km south of Cerro Potosí and on the Tamaulipas border (Lanning and Lawson 1977); (*Tamaulipas*) in the Sierra de Guatemala at La Joya de las Salas, 20 km north-west of Gómez Farías (Robins and Heed 1951) and Rancho del Cielo, between La Joya valley and Gómez Farías (Robins and Heed 1951); Lanning and Lawson (1977) mentioned Ocampo along with Gómez Farías as the southernmost point of the range, but without indication of a record.

POPULATION Given the reports of habitat destruction (evidently throughout this century and before) within the range of the Maroon-fronted Parrot, King's (1978-1979) assumption of a decline is entirely justified. Assessment of the modern situation is compromised by the species's seasonal movements and vagrancy, with regular or occasional local abundance being no helpful guide. Indeed, even some assertions about total numbers are based on mistaken assumptions: thus Lawson and Lanning (1981), by reporting a roost of 1,400 in the north of the species's range in September and another of 1,600 in the south in January, prompted Ridgely (1981a) to interpret this as yielding at least 3,000 birds (later summarized as "estimated at only 3,000 plus"), whereas a study of the evidence indicates a possible migration from north to south in November (see

Ecology), so that the two roosts could conceivably – if improbably – have been of the same birds. In fact, the count of 1,400 in September was thought to consist entirely of non-breeding birds, so this was very definitely a minimum figure for the area in question, at or near the Highrise cliff near San Antonio de las Alazanas (Lawson and Lanning 1981). Lanning and Lawson (1977) had earlier counted 800-1,000 birds in early April 1977 east of Saltillo, believed another thousand could exist in the region between San Antonio de las Alazanas and Cerro Potosí, and thus were confident of 2,000 in the northern part of the range, probably to be revised upward with further exploration; nevertheless, given the view that birds do not breed on or south of Cerro Potosí (see Distribution), the figure of 2,000 could serve as a baseline total. Generally, it seems much too small; in fact Lanning (1978) counted 1,600 at the "southern" (Cerro Viejo) roost while estimating 2,000, and it seems improbable that the entire population of the species was concentrated at this one site.

Recent observations at Highrise and adjacent cliffs showed a significant increase in the number of nesting pairs compared with the late 1970s, suggesting both that the number of usable nest-holes was not limiting the population in the 1970s and that food supplies had been adequate in the intervening years (D. V. Lanning and N. F. R. Snyder *in litt.* 1992).

ECOLOGY The prime habitat of the Maroon-fronted Parrot appears to be mixed conifer forests, mostly at higher elevations; birds descend as low as 1,300 m and have been found at 3,700 m on the highest ridge visited, but are most frequently encountered between 2,000 and 3,500 m (Lanning and Lawson 1977, D. V. Lanning *in litt.* 1992). Principal food is pine seeds, including those of Arizona pine *Pinus arizonica*, *P. gregii*, Aztec pine *P. teocote*, *P. montezumae* and Mexican pinyon *P. cembroides*; the birds depend on this broad variety as each species's cone crop varies from year to year (*P. cembroides* generally produces seed only once every five years) and moreover shows local variation in abundance within years (Lawson and Lanning 1981). Other foods taken include seeds of a fir *Abies*, acorns of a *Quercus* and nectar (and also seeds: M. A. Gómez Garza *in litt.* 1991) from *Agave macroculnis* (as many as 30 birds have been seen on a single plant); Acorn Woodpeckers *Melanerpes formicivorus* have been seen trying to drive parrots off a snag where they were evidently breaking into the former's acorn cache, but also off agave blooms (Lanning and Lawson 1977, Lawson and Lanning 1981; also Ely 1962). Birds have not been recorded feeding, despite their availability, on the seeds of Douglas fir *Pseudotsuga menzesii* or Arizona cypress *Cupressus arizonica*, although mass roosting in a stand of the latter was once witnessed (Lanning and Lawson 1977, Lawson and Lanning 1981) and general use of the former is reported (Ely 1962). Birds need water and have been seen queuing and squabbling at a small seep high on a sheer cliff at which no more than two could drink at a time; while at a stream on Cerro Potosí (supposedly the only source of water on the mountain, close to the radar station: Valenzuela *et al.* 1981) birds were seen picking off fragments of ice from beside a waterfall and taking bites of snow from adjacent patches (Lanning and Lawson 1977).

Dependence on pine seed explains three aspects of the species's life history: (1) its non-breeding nomadism; (2) its breeding period, in late summer and fall, coinciding with seed ripening; (3) the location of nest-sites near areas of mixed-conifer forest, which give the highest likelihood of a perennial food supply (Lawson and Lanning 1981). Despite speculation of tree-nesting (see King 1978-1979), nesting occurs exclusively in holes in limestone cliffs, there being few trees of sufficient size to offer nest-holes (see Threats); in places nesting appears to be colonial, such that a favoured locality like "Highrise" held 17 and probably 28 nests in 1979, although this may be a function of hole availability, since some 100 nests were estimated along a 28 km length of cliff that included Highrise, 1979 (Lawson and Lanning 1981). In 1978 most young had fledged at Highrise by mid-November (Lawson and Lanning 1981); in 1981 at evidently the same site there were no birds present on 7 November and local people reported their disappearance four weeks earlier (Valenzuela *et al.* 1981); assuming that the species is similar to the Thick-billed Parrot *Rhynchopsitta pachyrhyncha*, with an incubation period of 26 days and a fledging period of two months (see relevant account), egg-laying would have taken place in mid-

August in 1978 but in early July in 1981. Such variations in timing of breeding are evidently normal and related to variations in timing and abundance of pine crops; thus two males from one locality had enlarged testes on 30 May 1959 (in FMNH), while in the previous year a male from the same region had enlarged testes as late as 21 October (in DMNH). All this evidence points to the fact that the close synchrony of nesting in this species recorded by Snyder *et al.* (1987: 100) is a regular occurrence. In 1979 one to three (possibly four) young were reared per successful nest, with asynchronous fledging over several days; generally all birds desert the area very soon afterwards (Lawson and Lanning 1981; also Valenzuela *et al.* 1981). In six of eight fledgings observed in 1978 the young birds followed the parents; in two they preceded them (Snyder *et al.* 1987: 165).

The nomadism referred to above outside the breeding season remains within a relatively small area, and in fact some pattern of occurrence has emerged: thus in the northernmost part of the species's range, i.e. south-east Coahuila and west-central Nuevo León, birds could not be found in January 1978 and were reportedly absent each year (or largely so: some birds may be present throughout, at least at one site: Sada 1987) from October to March, whereas in the southernmost part of the range, i.e. south-west Tamaulipas, locals reported some birds present throughout the year (no proof of breeding) but with a dry season influx from October to April (Lanning 1978; also Robins and Heed 1951). The record of flocks totalling over 600 flying south very high over Las Vacas (Coahuila) on 16 November (Ely 1962) certainly suggests migration and conforms well with the above evidence. At Cerro Potosí in the middle of the range locals reported the species present throughout the year, whereas the major roost near Zaragoza, to the south but also in the middle of the range, was only occupied from mid-November to February/March (Lanning 1978).

The species is highly sociable and forms communal roosts throughout the year (presumably serving as foraging information centres), although breeding pairs spend the night at the nest and even in roosting flocks pairs remain together (Ely 1962, Lanning and Lawson 1977, Lawson and Lanning 1981). Birds roost in trees and cliffs (D. V. Lanning *in litt.* 1992), leaving at dawn and dispersing widely to feeding areas, often seen travelling over 40 km along one ridge between a feeding and a roosting site (Lanning and Lawson 1977) or very high overhead in pairs or small groups flying from one mountain to another (Ely 1962): there are two peaks of activity with a lull over the middle of the day, with non-breeders at Highrise for example often gathering during this lull in flocks of several hundred on the cliffs and in the adjacent forest to rest and preen (Lawson and Lanning 1981). Nocturnal roosting can involve the use of pre-roost assembly-points in the late afternoon (Ely 1962) or else the steady accretion of birds from three hours before sunset, though with a final urgent rush of birds at sunset itself before they settle for the night (Lanning and Lawson 1977). The varied weather of the mountains influences birds' movements: in the cold of early morning they fly low over slopes and valleys, but in the heat of the day they fly above ridges and cliffs, often soaring; they avoid bad weather, skirting round heavy clouds and thunderheads, and returning early to roosts ahead of afternoon storms (Lanning and Lawson 1977).

THREATS Habitat destruction has been considered the major threat: the species's mixed-conifer forests are being destroyed by fire, logging and clearance for agriculture, with for example fire claiming c.5,000 ha of habitat in two of the best areas, Sierra de la Marta in 1975 and Cerro Potosí in 1978 (as much as 50% of the habitat on the latter was destroyed). Indeed at Cerro Potosí an active logging mill was responsible for extensive lumbering in November 1981, when the birds there appeared to be food-stressed (Lawson and Lanning 1981, Valenzuela *et al.* 1981); however, in 1991 there was considerable regeneration of pines on both Cerro Potosí and Sierra de la Marta, with logging on the former perceived as very selective and the pine cover there still good (D. V. Lanning and N. F. R. Snyder *in litt.* 1992). At Highrise cliff some 200 local people are dependent on the adjacent forest for their firewood, building timber and grazing, and at Las Cuevas, where a colony of up to nine pairs exists, an access road was built for loggers in 1989, resulting in no breeding that year as well as devastation to the area, although three pairs nested in 1990 (M. A. Gómez Garza *in litt.* 1991). Heavy grazing by goats and other livestock prevents pinewood regeneration in some areas (Lanning and Lawson 1977). As long ago as the late 1950s it was observed that "much of the original conifer forest has been destroyed" in the north of the species's range (Ely 1962), although as recently as the late 1970s the forests in the south (Tamaulipas) were still largely intact (Lanning and Lawson 1977); however, if birds are migratory between the two their survival will depend on the preservation of areas of forest in both regions.

Otherwise the species is relatively untroubled: although around Highrise herders sometimes kill birds with slingshots for fun, or let their dogs take grounded fledglings (M. A. Gómez Garza *in litt.* 1991), it is not actively hunted for food because locals believe it bad eating; it is not persecuted because it does not eat corn or apple crops; and it is not trapped for trade because the nests are inaccessible and because it makes a poor talker (Lawson and Lanning 1981). It is certainly almost unknown in captivity, with possibly only a single bird in the U.S.A. in the late 1980s (Silva 1989a). Nevertheless, there is some danger of trade becoming significant, and vigilance will be required. Red-tailed Hawks *Buteo jamaicensis* and Common Ravens *Corvus corax* are capable of eating parrot eggs and young, and Spotted Owls *Strix occidentalis* (see Remarks 5) may also do so (Lawson and Lanning 1981).

MEASURES TAKEN The Maroon-fronted Parrot is listed on Appendix I of CITES and is protected under local law, though this is not enforced (King 1978-1979). A status survey of the species was funded by ICBP PACS in 1978 (Lanning 1978). A large part of the range is covered by the Cumbres de Monterrey National Park, the largest such park (246,500 ha) in Mexico (Anon. 1989), but it appears to be poorly protected (only two guards operated there up to 1982: Vargas Márquez 1984) and damage to habitat through tree clearance within it is such that its value as a protected area appears nugatory (see Anon. 1991a, Low 1991). Plans to reforest the area of Sierra de la Marta burnt in 1975 involved establishing 180 trees per hectare of four different pine species, of which only one was native to the area (Lawson and Lanning 1981); the outcome so far appears to be encouraging (see Threats).

MEASURES PROPOSED The preservation of a number of very large tracts of forest where the species occurs in several parts of its range (to allow for periodic local failure of cone crops) has been deemed urgent (Woodard 1980); one such tract might be around Highrise cliff (see Remarks 5). This is vital for local people, too, as the lower-lying agricultural landscape and two large cities, Monterrey and Saltillo, depend on these forests for moderating climate, stabilizing soils and supplying water (Lawson and Lanning 1981). A research programme in resource management to determine whether sustained-yield logging can continue has been called for (Forshaw 1989). Ridgely (1981a) urged formal protection of the birds' nesting cliffs and feeding areas. Most recently, proposals have been formulated to purchase and warden an area of forest in which the species breeds called "El Condominio", and to initiate a captive breeding project (Anon. 1991a, Low 1991); there may be great merit in the first part of this scheme, but there seems to be no evidence that captive breeding will benefit the species. Perhaps most usefully at this stage an educational campaign, emphasizing the local endemism of the species and generating grass-root interest in its conservation, would help develop a new awareness of the heritage of the region's forests and in particular erect a barrier of popular opposition to any attempts to begin trapping and trading the birds (N. F. R. Snyder *in litt.* 1992).

REMARKS (1) The Maroon-fronted Parrot was originally described as a full species (Moore 1947), then lumped as a race of Thick-billed Parrot (Hardy and Dickerman 1955) and then, based on the view that colour pattern is particularly significant for recognition in parrots, separated again (Hardy 1967). An explanation of some mixed characters of the two forms is that some Thick-bills wander to the Sierra Madre Oriental in winter (scarlet-fronted birds have been reported from San Antonio de las Alazanas, Coahuila, at that time) and then stay and miscegenate (Ely 1962); if this is the case, it dissolves Hardy's (1967) argument. Nevertheless, Ridgely (1981a) and Lawson and Lanning (1981) accepted specific status, and their judgement is acknowledged here before that of (e.g.) King (1978-1979), Forshaw (1989) and Silva (1989a). That the genus *Rhynchopsitta* is very close to the macaws is captured in the idea that the two forms might be called "macawlets" (in Robins and Heed 1951). Because both members are threatened, so is the genus. (2) It has been suggested that records from Veracruz refer to the Maroon-fronted Parrot, not the Thick-billed (Ridgely 1981a); however, the chances seem to favour the latter (see Distribution: Veracruz under Thick-billed Parrot). (3) Laguna de Sánchez is at 25°21'N 100°17'W in OG (1956a) and is marked as such on AGSNY (1954), with San Isidro a few kilometres to the west and "Boquillas" (*sic*) further west still; the ridge to the south where the birds presumably occur is also the state line between Nuevo León and Coahuila, and "San Antonia de las Alzanas" (*sic*) is only 40 km distant west-south-west over the mountains, with Ciruela and "Mesa de Tablas" (*sic*) only c.20 km to the south-west. (4) The cliffs 26 km east of Saltillo may be identical with one of the sites listed as in the mountains south-west of Monterrey. (5) The fact that the near-threatened Spotted Owl is common at Highrise suggests the special value of creating a reserve there.

WHITE-NECKED PARAKEET *Pyrrhura albipectus* K[12]

This poorly known parakeet is confined to upper tropical rainforest in three small areas of south-eastern Ecuador, where its numbers appear to be fairly low and where habitat destruction is beginning to have an effect.

DISTRIBUTION The White-necked Parakeet (see Remarks 1) is known from three general areas – in and around Podocarpus National Park, in the Cordillera de Cutucú, and in the Cordillera del Condor – in south-eastern Ecuador. Altogether 12 specimens (in AMNH, ANSP, MECN, WFVZ and ZMUC) have been collected, and there are recent sightings from all three areas (Ridgely 1981a, Robbins *et al.* 1987, Bloch *et al.* 1991, Krabbe in prep., M. Marin verbally 1991, C. Rahbek verbally 1992).

Podocarpus area The type and two other specimens (one with a lost label, but presumably from the same locality since taken at the same time: Chapman 1926) were collected at "610 m" (see Remarks 2) at Zamora, Zamora-Chinchipe (previously Loja) province, south-east Ecuador, on the eastern slope of the Andes, October 1913 (Chapman 1914a). In February and March 1980, flocks were seen on the slope above Zamora at 1,000-1,600 m (Ridgely 1981a), in February 1988 a few birds were seen there (P. Greenfield *in litt.* 1989), in May 1989 10-50 birds flying upstream were recorded daily at Río Bombuscara Visitors' Center (Podocarpus National Park), c.940 m, on the slope south-west of Zamora (Bloch *et al.* 1991), and birds were studied at this last site in August/September 1990 (Toyne and Jeffcote 1992); in March 1990 at least 18 birds were found in three flocks in the río Jamboe valley (east of the Bombuscara drainage) at 1,120-1,250 m (B. M. Whitney *in litt.* 1991); in late 1991 and early 1992 birds were found at Romerillos, 1,600-1,900 m (untraced but also inside Podocarpus National Park) (C. Rahbek verbally 1992; also Toyne and Jeffcote 1992); in December 1989 a flock of at least 10 was seen along the Loja–Zamora road (C. S. Balchin *in litt.* 1990); in March 1990 a flock of six was seen in the río Zamora (río Sabanilla) valley at c.1,330 m (B. M. Whitney *in litt.* 1991); in December 1990 several small flocks (maximum five) were seen on a 5 km stretch of the road between 1,700 and 1,800 m, in two cases below Sabanilla (M. Pearman *in litt.* 1991), and birds were seen there at c.1,600 m in January 1992 (C. Rahbek verbally 1992). Records around Podocarpus are thus from much of the year; the species's apparent absence in June (NK) and July (Ridgely 1981a) may be illusory, especially if the evidence of local breeding (see Ecology) obtained in September is accepted.

Cordillera de Cutucú Two specimens were collected in this range, Morona-Santiago province, Ecuador, one at 1,200 m (specimen in AMNH), and one at 2,000 m (specimen in ANSP), both in December 1940. In April 1984 a male (now in ZMUC) was collected from a flock of about eight birds on the western slope of the central part of the cordillera at 1,250 m; it was in extremely worn plumage, and the testes had apparently been recently enlarged, suggesting that it had just finished breeding, presumably locally (NK). In June and July 1984 several flocks of 4-10 birds each were encountered on the same slope, at 1,200 to 1,700 m, one bird being collected (Robbins *et al.* 1987; see Remarks 1). Definite records from these mountains are thus from 1,200 to 1,700 m, in the months of December, April, June and July.

Cordillera del Condor In August 1989, at 1,000 m and again in September 1990, at 1,700 m, the species was found in the central part of this cordillera, at c.4°00'S 78°34'W, and three specimens (now in ANSP, MECN and WFVZ) were taken (M. Marin verbally 1991, Krabbe in prep.). Another, previously unpublished specimen in WFVZ was taken in the cordillera in c.1988 (M. Marin verbally 1990). The species has not been recorded in the southern (Peruvian) part of this range (Robbins *et al.* 1987).

POPULATION In Cordillera del Cutucú the White-necked Parakeet is uncommon (Ridgely 1981a, Robbins *et al.* 1987, NK). At a site in Cordillera del Condor where a bird was collected in c.1988, only one flock of c.5 birds was found in an area of about 1 km^2 (M. Marin verbally 1990). Near Chinapinza in the central part of Cordillera del Condor, a flock of five was resident in an area of 2 ha, and two other flocks, one of 12 and one of five, briefly visited the area a few times over 16 days in September 1990 (Krabbe in prep.); the specimen taken nearby at 1,000 m in August 1989 was collected from a flock of 18-20 birds (M. Marin verbally 1991). In Podocarpus National Park in 1990 flocks were usually of 5-8 birds, with 3-13 the extremes in size, except for a possible sighting of 25 (Toyne and Jeffcote 1992). The total population of the species may comprise a few thousand individuals.

ECOLOGY The few definite observations of the species suggest that its ecology is fairly similar to congeners. It travels in small groups of 4-20 individuals, and forages in fruiting trees in primary forest and clearings (Ridgely 1981a, Bloch *et al.* 1991, Krabbe in prep.). Its altitudinal range is c.900 to 2,000 m (see Distribution). The adult male collected in April 1984 kept watch from an open branch while the rest of the flock fed in adjacent trees (NK).

On five occasions in September 1990 in Cordillera del Condor the food plant of the species was identified, always the inflorescences of the slender, woody, composite vine *Piptocarpha* cf. *poeppigiana* (a widespread species in both eastern and western Ecuador: B. Ølgård verbally 1990); two specimens taken there had their stomachs crammed with these flowers, one of them also a small unidentified seed (Krabbe in prep.). *Piptocarpha poeppigiana* climbs young trees, and in some cases the parrots would descend as low as 1-2 m above the ground to feed on its flowers; at this locality the species was very confident, allowing approach as close as 3 to 4 m, and because it was only vocal in flight it could go undetected for long periods while feeding, even when close to humans (Krabbe in prep.). Other studies during the same period in Podocarpus National Park identified four food sources, the seeds of *Mollia gracilis* (much favoured), fruits of *Ficus* aff. *mutisii* and *Miconia* cf. *punctata*, and the flowers of the liana *Mikania leiostachya*, with drinking noted from rainwater in epiphytic plants (Toyne and Jeffcote 1992).

All 22 individuals seen in Cordillera del Condor in September 1990 were adults (NK), and the one taken in Cordillera de Cutucú in April appeared to have just finished breeding (see Distribution). However, in Podocarpus National Park a juvenile was observed being fed by an adult in early September, and breeding was assumed to have occurred in May–July (Toyne and Jeffcote 1992).

THREATS Although the upper tropical zone is being cleared along the east slope of the Andes at an alarming rate (NK; also P. Greenfield verbally 1986), much forest of the subtropical zone is still intact within the parrot's range. However, the Podocarpus National Park is under severe pressure (see Threats under Bearded Guan *Penelope barbata*); in the valley of the Jamboe there is little undisturbed habitat below 1,100 m, and clearance of forest is proceeding upwards (B. M. Whitney *in litt.* 1991). Moreover, Shuar Indians of the Cutucú region, in order to claim their land legally, are forced to clear at least part of it for agriculture, and some clearance of subtropical forest there has already begun (NK). In Cordillera del Condor the subtropical forest is largely intact, being inhabited only by gold prospectors and used for hunting by Shuar Indians; in contrast the upper tropical zone forest has been almost completely felled for timber up to 1,000 to 1,200 m, at least along the central part of the range, and eventually this cutting will expand into the subtropical zone and threaten the species (NK). Thus the main threat is habitat destruction, but two of the birds in MECN, which both died in 1989, had been purchased in the cagebird market in Quito (P. Greenfield *in litt.* 1989), and two other captive individuals were encountered in Ecuador in 1990, suggesting a small but continuing pressure from internal trade (Toyne and Jeffcote 1992).

MEASURES TAKEN The Cordillera de Cutucú is a reserve for the Shuar Indians, who traditionally build no more than two or three houses together, with some 2 km to the next settlement, thus ensuring enough forest as hunting grounds for each family; the Shuars generally hunt and do very little farming, which so far has left the Cutucú mountains one of the least disturbed forested regions in Ecuador (NK); but see Threats. If the White-necked Parakeet breeds at the type-locality, it may be safe on the lower eastern slope of the Podocarpus National Park, Loja, which stretches almost to Zamora; but again see Threats.

MEASURES PROPOSED As the Cordillera de Cutucú apparently represents the breeding grounds for a number of local or otherwise uncommon, scarce or rare species of bird (Robbins *et al.* 1987), including the Spot-winged Parrotlet *Touit stictoptera*, it is of the utmost importance to preserve the forest in its present condition (Ridgely 1981a, NK). The Shuar policy of not letting non-Shuars into the Cutucú region without permission should be encouraged, and laws obliging them to clear forest in order to claim land should be revoked (NK). The Shuars need to know the significance of the White-necked Parakeet, and to report immediately any attempts by trappers to obtain specimens; indeed, monitoring of internal trade in the species must be developed. However, perhaps the major task is to assure the long-term future of Podocarpus National Park (see equivalent section under Bearded Guan).

REMARKS (1) There is some question over the taxonomic status of the White-necked Parakeet. In the Cordillera de Cutucú, some flocks encountered between 1,000 and 1,200 m appeared to be either mixed flocks of *Pyrrhura albipectus* and Maroon-tailed Parakeet *P. melanura berlepschi* (previously considered a distinct species, Berlepsch's Parakeet *P. berlepschi*: see Ridgely and Robbins 1988), or were possibly hybrids between the two, as some individuals had white to yellow breasts which had only faint dark barring or completely lacked it; one specimen was collected, and most closely matches *P. m. berlepschi* (Robbins *et al.* 1987). However, all 22 individuals seen in Cordillera del Condor in September 1990 were adult *albipectus*, showing no sign of hybridization with *melanura* (Krabbe in prep.). (2) The altitude of 610 m recorded for the Zamora specimens is undoubtedly erroneous, as the nearest place at that altitude is 70 km north–east of Zamora (IGM 1981), so presumably these birds were collected above Zamora at the same altitudes (1,000-1,600 m) as those seen there in recent years (NK).

FLAME-WINGED PARAKEET *Pyrrhura calliptera* V/R[10]

The Flame-winged Parakeet occupies upper subtropical and temperate forest in the East Andes of Colombia, where it is confined to the east slope in both Boyacá and Cundinamarca, having at least formerly also occurred in the latter on the west slope. Forest destruction has been extensive within its restricted range and, although still locally numerous, it now survives in highly fragmented populations.

DISTRIBUTION The Flame-winged Parakeet is known from over 50 specimens taken at 17 or more localities in Boyacá and Cundinamarca departments, in the East Andes of Colombia (the record from Macizo de Tamá means that it may possibly occur in Venezuela: J. I. Hernández Camacho verbally 1991). In the following account coordinates are from Paynter and Traylor (1981).

West slope Records are all prior to 1914 (and all from *Cundinamarca*): Villa Gómez, at c.5°17'N 74°12'W, 1872 (specimen in BMNH); Anolaima, at c.4°46'N 74°28'W, 1913 (specimen in AMNH), this being the probable source of many specimens labelled "Bogota" (Chapman 1917a), of which there are over 27 in various museums; Subía, 1,900 m, at 4°34'N 74°27'W, 1913 (Chapman 1917a); La Aguadita, at 4°25'N 74°20'W (Rodríguez and Hernández Camacho 1988); Silvania, at 4°24'N 74°24'W (Rodríguez and Hernández Camacho 1988); El Roble, 2,450 m, at 4°23'N 74°19'W, 1913 (Chapman 1917a); Fusagasugá, 1,850 m, at 4°21'N 74°22'W, 1913 (Chapman 1917a). All west slope specimens thus appear to have been taken in the upper subtropical zone at 1,850-2,450 m, perhaps as low as 1,500-1,600 m (Villa Gómez, Anolaima, Silvania).

East slope Localities are: (*Boyacá*) Macizo de Tamá, at c.7°25'N 72°26'W, i.e. close to the border with Venezuela (see Remarks 1); Boca del Monte, according to Paynter and Traylor (1981) at c.2,250 m, north-west of and near Chinivaque, which is at 6°09'N 72°20'W, 1917 (specimens in CM); upper río Cusiana at 2,000-3,000 m, this river rising on Páramo de Toquilla, which is at c.5°37'N 72°50'W, October 1967 and July 1984 (specimens in ICN and IND; see Remarks 2) and sightings in 1977 (Hilty and Brown 1986); Laguna de Tota, (3,015 m), at 5°33'N 72°55'W, 1963 (Hilty and Brown 1986); Ramiriquí, at c.5°24'N 73°20'W (Hilty and Brown 1986); (*Casanare*) La Salina (untraced), where two birds were taken at Los Arrayanes, Vereda Rodrigoque (specimens in ICN); (*Cundinamarca*) Páramo de Guasca (c.3,000 m), at 4°55'N 73°52'W (Forshaw 1981, Rodríguez and Hernández Camacho 1988; specimen in ICN); Guasca, (2,720 m), at 4°52'N 73°52'W; below Páramo de Choachi, 2,980 m, at 4°33'N 73°58'W; Choachi, (1,966 m), at 4°32'N 73°56'W (all from Rodríguez and Hernández Camacho 1988); Páramo Chingaza, including Chingaza National Park and adjacent areas (see Measures Taken), at 3,100-3,400 m, at c.4°31'N 73°45'W (Hilty and Brown 1986, Rodríguez and Hernández Camacho 1988, L. Rosselli *in litt.* 1991); Fómeque, 2,000 m, at 4°29'N 73°54'W (Rodríguez and Hernández Camacho 1988); the Monterredondo–El Calvario road, close to the former (4°17'N 73°48'W), at 1,800-2,000 m (F. G. Stiles *per* L. Rosselli *in litt.* 1991; see Remarks 3). East slope records thus range from 1,800 to 3,400 m.

There are three specimens in BMNH collected in 1914 at Peños which, however, cannot be located; it may well, however, be El Peñon, at 4°26'N 74°18'W. Rodríguez and Hernández Camacho (1988) suspected that the species occurs as far south as Páramo de Sumapaz, western Meta department (at 3°45'N 74°25'W).

POPULATION Although reported "common" in the subtropical zone on the west slope in Cundinamarca by Chapman (1917a), there seem to be no records after 1913, and the region is now mostly deforested (Ridgely 1981a); a few forest patches, harbouring many other bird species, still exist, but the parakeet could not be found in one of these during intense fieldwork from April 1972 to January 1973 at Finca Rancho Grande, 1,700 m, 4°36'N 74°20'W (Munves 1975). On the east slope the parakeet ranges over 300 km from north-west Boyacá to the Bogotá region in Cundimamarca, and it was reported fairly common in the upper río Cusiana valley in February 1977, with over 40 seen and heard (Hilty and Brown 1986). Nevertheless, there has been a steep decline throughout Cundinamarca (Orejuela 1985). In Chingaza National Park small numbers were seen daily from September to November 1979 (Hilty and Brown 1986), and students from Universidad de los Andes have encountered it in the park on virtually all their field trips (F. R. Lambert *in litt.* 1989). However, the population on the east slope presumably continues to diminish rapidly, as there seems no reason to believe that the deforestation reported by Ridgely (1981a) should have ceased.

ECOLOGY The Flame-winged Parakeet inhabits humid upper subtropical and temperate forest at 1,850-3,000 m, where it sometimes flies over, and even feeds in, adjacent clearings amongst stubble, as well as elfin woodland and regenerating second growth at 3,000-3,400 m (Forshaw 1981, Hilty and Brown 1986, F. R. Lambert *in litt.* 1989). Forshaw (1981) reported it a bird of cold montane moorlands, although Ridgely (1981a) suspected that this is at best only a seasonal phenomenon. Rodríguez and Hernández Camacho (1988) described the habitat as often clouded Andean and subandean forest (including *Weinmannia tormentosa*, *Quercus humboldtii* and other communities), secondary forest, subpáramo and peatbog páramo with bushes. Recent studies in and near Chingaza National Park by L. Rosselli (*in litt.* 1991) have indicated that the species occurs in páramo and subpáramo with scattered small forest patches (with *Clusia* trees common), also in an area of forest in which the dominant trees are *Clusia* spp., *Weinmannia* spp., *Brunellia colombiana* and several Melastomataceae.

Food includes blueberries ("mora") and other fruits, such as those of *Cecropia* (data on skins in ICN, IND). Observational records are of fruit of *Clusia* spp., *Ficus* sp. and *Brunellia colombiana*, and by report blackberries *Rubus*, the seeds of *Espeletia uribeii*, and cultivated maize (L. Rosselli *in litt.* 1991).

Birds collected in March and April on the west slope in Cundinamarca were not in breeding condition (specimens in AMNH). Two from July (río Cusiana) had developing gonads, one of two in August (Casanare) had developed gonads, while four of five from October (río Cusiana) had developed gonads (specimens in ICN, IND), as did five from Laguna de Tota in the same month (Olivares 1971), suggesting breeding in this and adjacent months. This parakeet usually occurs in small fast-flying bands of 6-14 that behave like others of the genus (Hilty and Brown 1986).

THREATS Rapid deforestation poses a threat to the species, although it is in no immediate danger of extinction, being still fairly common locally and with much habitat still remaining in Boyacá (Ridgely 1981a, S. L. Hilty *in litt.* 1986). The Laguna de Tota area is now nearly totally deforested (R. S. Ridgely *in litt.* 1989). A road is to be built through Chingaza National Park, and this will probably affect an important forest area for the parakeets (L. Rosselli *in litt.* 1991). Except as pets locally (L. Rosselli *in litt.* 1991) the parakeet has apparently never been held in captivity, and certainly not outside of Colombia (Ridgely 1981a). Birds are occasionally hunted by local farmers in retaliation for their feeding on maize crops, but this is likely to become a serious problem only after further deforestation (L. Rosselli *in litt.* 1991).

MEASURES TAKEN The Flame-winged Parakeet occurs in Chingaza National Park, but fieldwork there in 1991 suggested that most of the local population remains outside the park boundaries (L. Rosselli *in litt.* 1991). However, a small (roughly 1,000-2,000 ha) forest just outside the western part of the park, called Reserva Florestal del Río Blanco, is probably very important for the species; 400 ha have already been purchased by the Empresa de Acueducto (L. Rosselli *in litt.* 1991). The 1,200 ha private Carpanta Biological Reserve, 4°35'N 73°40'W, also adjacent to Chingaza, harbours a population of the species, mainly in its upper reaches (L. Rosselli *in litt.* 1991; see *Fundación Natura Annual Report* 1989: 5-6; 1990: 4-6; coordinates from L. M.

Renjifo *in litt.* 1992); so does Valle de Jesus Forest, c.4°50'N 73°40'W, this being a communal reserve in need of more formal protection (L. M. Renjifo *in litt.* 1992).

MEASURES PROPOSED It is important that certain areas still with forest be formally and effectively protected while there is still forest left to protect (notably in Boyacá); proper management of the parks already established should also be ensured (Ridgely 1981a, Orejuela 1985). The Río Blanco Reserve requires further support in order to ensure its survival and that of the important population of Flame-winged Parakeets it harbours (L. Rosselli *in litt.* 1991). Pisba National Park north-east of Laguna de Tota and Sierra Nevada de Cocuy National Park on the border of Boyacá and Arauca departments (see Hilty and Brown 1986) are two protected areas that deserve to be investigated for presence of this species. The significance of the Monterredondo area has been greatly enhanced by a recent discovery there that must make this one of the highest priority sites for conservation in the species's range (see Remarks 3). More fieldwork is needed to establish whether it still exists on the west slope in Cundinamarca. Work is also needed to determine the birds' movements and annual requirements, since without such information it is impossible to manage the species in the long term (L. Rosselli *in litt.* 1991).

REMARKS (1) This record is from J. I. Hernández Camacho (verbally 1991), who recalls the species's mention at this locality in a book by a missionary; but the name and author of the book have escaped his memory. (2) The five 1967 specimens in ICN from the río Cusiana are labelled as from Hacienda Comijoque; the two in IND are also from this hacienda, but also labelled "Município Pajarito, Inspección Policia Corinto, 2,000 m". (3) The area at Monterredondo forms the type- and only locality of a new antpitta *Grallaria* (see *Wilson Bull.* 104, 1992), and hence is of extreme importance: steps are clearly needed to secure the region against further degradation (F. G. Stiles *in litt.* 1992).

BLUE-CHESTED PARAKEET *Pyrrhura cruentata* R[11]

The Blue-chested Parakeet survives in scattered Atlantic Forest fragments from southern Bahia south to Rio de Janeiro, Brazil and, although sometimes fairly common where it occurs, faces extinction from the continuing clearance of its lowland habitat: preservation of key sites and possibly a study of its ability to survive in cacao plantations are needed.

DISTRIBUTION The Blue-chested Parakeet is endemic to the Atlantic Forest region of south-eastern Brazil from Bahia south of Salvador and south-eastern Minas Gerais south through Espírito Santo to Rio de Janeiro state.

Bahia Older records are from as far north as Jequié (Serra do Palhão), November 1932; Boa Nova, 790 m, June 1928; rio Gongogi, Cajazeiras, 300 m, June 1928, and at the confluence of the rio Novo, December 1932; and Ilhéus, February and July 1944 and January 1945 (specimens in AMNH, MCZ, MZUSP; also Pinto 1935); moreover, Wied (1831-1833) encountered the species as far north as Ilhéus, reporting it as much rarer in the hinterland of the state, where he obtained it on the rio Catolé and on the Ilha Cachoeirinha in the rio Jequitinhonha (Wied 1820-1821). It is not known if any populations persist in these areas today, but ones currently exist in the small CEPLAC experimental stations either side of the Jequitinhonha at Canavieiras and Barrolândia, where birds were seen in October 1987 (LPG), and in the CVRD Porto Seguro Reserve, where birds were seen in October 1986 (Gonzaga *et al.* 1987), all three sites being north of the anticipated northern limit of the species, Monte Pascoal National Park (Ridgely 1981a). Between this park and the border with Espírito Santo records are from the rio Jucurucú (Cachoeira Grande do Sul), March/April 1933 (Pinto 1935, and in MCZ), and rio Mucuri (Wied 1831-1833).

Minas Gerais Older records (north to south) are from the eastern part of the state at Salto da Divisa, undated; Machacalis, December 1954; Teófilo Otoni, September/October 1908; lower rio Piracicaba at the confluence with rio Doce, August 1940; 35 km to the north of Raúl Soares, July 1957; and Matipó, June 1919 and January and July 1936 (Pinto 1937, 1938, 1952, and specimens in LACM, MZUSP and MZUFV). Of these, the Piracicaba confluence and the Raúl Soares site are close to or in the Rio Doce State Park where the species persists (G. T. de Mattos *in litt.* 1987; also Pinto 1945), although this is not the only site for it in the state (*contra* speculation in Ridgely 1981a), while at rio Matipó an observation was made in 1979 (A. Brandt *in litt.* 1987). Four further localities are the Caratinga Reserve (Fazenda Montes Claros, near Raúl Soares) (Mittermeier *et al.* 1982), where the species was common in October/November 1986 (L. C. Marigo verbally 1986) and in September 1987 (A. Brandt *in litt.* 1987); Fazenda Ramaiana, Joaima (in the north-east, near Machacalis), where a female was collected in March 1970 (in MNRJ); Almenara, Serra da Mombuca (rio Jequitinhonha) also in the north-east, where a female (presumably that labelled as from Fazenda Gangogi, Divisópolis, in CGTM) was collected in October 1975 (G. T. de Mattos *in litt.*, verbally 1987), and Mantena, recently (de Mattos and de Andrade 1988). The locality Pirapora is almost certainly an error (see Remarks 1).

Espírito Santo Older records are (north to south) from the rio Itaúnas, September 1950; rio São José, September 1942; São Domingos, August 1940; rio Doce, December 1905 to April 1906; Baixo Guandu (in one case precisely Fazenda da Serra), October 1925 and December 1929; Linhares (also precisely rio Pequeno and rio Juparanã), October 1939, November 1940 and February 1952; Lagoa Juparanã (in one case precisely Santana), October 1925 and November 1929; (córrego) Cupido, August 1939 (this now within the Sooretama Reserve); Rancho Fundo, Colatina, August 1940; Pau Gigante (now Ibiraçu) (in one case precisely Lauro Muller), August to November 1940; Agua Boa, Santa Cruz, October 1940 (specimens in AMNH, MCZ, MNRJ, MZUSP and USNM; also Pinto 1938). The key site for the species in the state (and indeed anywhere) is Sooretama Biological Reserve (Ridgely 1981a) and the adjacent CVRD Linhares Reserve (see Population), on the rio Barra Seca (whence two specimens, August 1939: Aguirre and Aldrighi 1983). Other recent records (all to the north or north-west of Sooretama) are from

Pedro Canário, four birds collected in February 1973 (in MNRJ), and Córrego do Veado Biological Reserve (Gonzaga *et al.* 1987) (both are close to rio Itaúnas), Córrego Grande (Fazenda Klabin) Biological Reserve (Gonzaga *et al.* 1987) and Córrego das Queixadas, Barra de São Francisco (G. T. de Mattos *in litt.*, verbally 1987).

Rio de Janeiro Nineteenth-century records are from Lagoa de Maricá; Gurapina; Fazenda Tiririca; Serra de Inoa; and the rio Paraíba (Wied 1820-1821, 1831-1833; see Remarks 2); Registo do Sai, April 1818 (von Pelzeln 1868-1871); (Serra das) Araras (i.e. Piraí), November 1818 (von Pelzeln 1868-1871; see Remarks 3); Nova Friburgo (Burmeister 1856); and Cantagalo (Cabanis 1874, von Ihering and von Ihering 1907); records from Rio de Janeiro (von Spix 1824, von Ihering and von Ihering 1907, and seven skins in AMNH, BMNH, MCZ and USNM) cannot be attributed to the city itself but refer to the state. However, in 1969 and 1970 a total of 66 Blue-chested Parakeets were claimed to have been "reintroduced" (in fact this was an introduction) successfully (breeding confirmed through the presence of offspring) into Tijuca National Park above Rio city (Coimbra-Filho and Aldrighi 1971, 1972, Coimbra Filho *et al.* 1973), although no further records are known, despite much observer coverage of the area, other than a report in Silva (1989a) (certainly in error) that the species "remains rather common and is perfectly established there". During 1987 the species was rediscovered in the state near the Desengano State Park (São Julião, 50-110 m; rio Mocotó, near Sossego; Serra da Penação), with small flocks of birds (up to 15; 23 in 1988) being seen (J. F. Pacheco *in litt.* 1987, verbally 1988); and in August 1989 and September and November 1990 the species was recorded at Fazenda União, Rocha Leão, in the municipality of Casimiro de Abreu (J. F. Pacheco verbally 1991).

São Paulo The only records for the state are from Araras in the north-east in November 1818, which is considered here in error (see Remarks 3), and (by report) from the lower rio Tietê in the far west (von Ihering 1898), which is sufficiently anomalous to be probably also in error. Nevertheless, von Ihering (1898) thought the species could occur near Bananal, just inside the São Paulo border from Rio, Ridgely (1981a) identified coastal north-east São Paulo as the most likely place where birds might survive in the southern part of their range, and Silva (1989a) followed Sick (1985) in including the north-east of the state as part of the range; but there seems to be no evidence, fresh or otherwise, for any of this.

POPULATION The Blue-chested Parakeet was common in the states of Bahia and Rio de Janeiro in the 1890s (von Ihering 1898). Over half a century ago it was recognized that while the species's habitat is restricted it nevertheless generally remains common where present (Pinto 1935), and this perception persists in modern assessments (e.g. Ridgely 1981a, Scott and Brooke 1985). At present the species's stronghold is the Sooretama Reserve and the adjacent CVRD Linhares Reserve in northern Espírito Santo, where a large population is found (Ridgely 1981a): thus flocks of up to 20 were seen almost daily in Sooretama from 30 December to 21 January 1980/1981 (Scott and Brooke 1985), while in the CVRD Linhares Reserve in October 1985 flocks of up to 20 were seen (Collar and Gonzaga 1985), with similar values in December 1986 (flocks varying in size from as few as six to as many as about 20, 8-12 seeming commonest), yielding an estimated daily total of at least 40 birds (B. M. Whitney *in litt.* 1987) and in 1988 30 per day (D. F. Stotz *in litt.* 1988). Numbers in the much smaller reserves listed under Distribution cannot be high, but in the comparably large Monte Pascoal National Park the species seems relatively less abundant (Ridgely 1981a) and it was not found there by Gonzaga *et al.* (1987). However, it was common at the CVRD Porto Seguro Reserve, January 1988 (B. M. Whitney *in litt.* 1988).

ECOLOGY The Blue-chested Parakeet inhabits humid primary forest and forest edge and, to a lesser extent, small clearings and thinned forest, remaining hidden in the canopy of the trees (Wied 1831-1833, Ridgely 1981a, Scott and Brooke 1985, Sick 1985); it also persists or at least persisted (see Threats), albeit apparently in smaller numbers, in agricultural regions where many forest trees are retained, e.g. to shade cacao (Ridgely 1981a). It is never seen in either dry forest or cerrado, only in primary moist evergreen forest (G. T. de Mattos *in litt.* 1987). Ridgely's

(1981a) altitudinal limit of around 400 m is too low, given the records from Boa Nova (Bahia) at 790 m and various sites in Minas Gerais up to 960 m, but these make the species's absence from certain areas, such as Augusto Ruschi (Nova Lombardia) Biological Reserve in Espírito Santo or the higher parts of Desengano State Park, difficult to explain unless in terms of its replacement there by Maroon-bellied Parakeet *Pyrrhura frontalis*.

It feeds on fruits of secondary growth trees (e.g. *Trema micrantha*, *Cecropia*) in forest edges along tracks (LPG). Stomach contents of specimens in MNRJ are given as seeds, red berries, fruit. In a study in Minas Gerais, birds ate pitomba *Talisia esculenta* in June/July, folha-do-balo *Alchornea iricurana* in September, plus canudo-de-pito *Mabea fistulifera* and an unidentified Myrtaceae at unspecified times; foraging was done chiefly in the canopy and birds never fed outside the forest, although they cross open areas between forest patches (de Mattos and de Andrade 1988). Twenty-three individuals were once seen perched in an isolated flowering tree in pasture adjacent to forest (J. F. Pacheco verbally 1991), and birds will associate with other parrots in a fruiting tree, e.g. Golden-capped Parakeet *Aratinga auricapilla* at Fazenda Ramaiama (de Mattos and de Andrade 1988). Corn seeds are mentioned as food taken by this species (Moojen *et al.* 1941), but feeding on agricultural crops has not been observed in the wild.

A female collected in Minas Gerais, October, had an egg in the oviduct, and a nest of the species was found 10 m up in a hollow tree in December (G. T. de Mattos *in litt.* 1987). Of the five specimens collected in November and December whose gonad condition was recorded, none was developed, whereas of the five such from June, two were slightly developed (specimens in AMNH); a bird collected in August had testes slightly enlarged; one in September had them fully enlarged (in MNRJ). Two to four eggs are laid in holes in trees, incubation lasting 22-25 days, and the fledging period is 45 days (de Mattos and de Andrade 1988). In captivity, birds became adult at two years and bred at three; 7-8 eggs were laid, incubation lasted 24 days and the fledging period was two months (Spenkelink-van Schaik 1984, Silva 1989a). Independent young appear to form flocks in December and January (de Mattos and de Andrade 1988).

Descourtilz (1854-1856) referred to the species's presence in Minas Gerais and Espírito Santo only between April and September, which is certainly incorrect; there is no evidence for any migration.

THREATS Forest clearance throughout the species's range is clearly culpable for its highly patchy modern distribution (King 1978-1979, Ridgely 1981a, Forshaw 1989). The southern part of this range (Espírito Santo and Rio de Janeiro) has been heavily inhabited for a century or more, and virtually all lowland forest has long since been cut (Ridgely 1981a); yet even now forest at the lower levels in Desengano State Park is being steadily cleared by the private owners of the land (J. F. Pacheco verbally 1991). Although found in the late 1970s in cacao plantations (see Ecology), modern developments provide little hope for the long-term utilization of such habitat: older shade trees are not replaced, new (1980s) shading techniques involve the use of banana and *Erythryna* trees (and hence the clearance of standing forest), and in any case unstable prices have driven many farmers to convert their land to pasture (LPG). Forest at the privately owned Fazenda São Joaquim (Fazenda Klabin), although now an IBAMA-run biological reserve (Córrego Grande), has been reduced over the past two decades from 4,000 ha to only 1,200 ha (Gonzaga *et al.* 1987). Monte Pascoal National Park is under severe pressure (Redford 1989).

In the 1810s, when a common species, it was apparently little persecuted because a poor talker and hard to maintain (Wied 1831-1833). However, recently in Sooretama the species has been under pressure from trapping in numbers for the cagebird trade (R. Wirth *in litt.* 1984), although it remains rare in the illegal markets within Brazil (C. E. Carvalho *in litt.* 1987) and in captivity in general (Ridgely 1981a, Spenkelink-van Schaik 1984); over 70 have been bred by one U.K. collector (Low 1991e).

MEASURES TAKEN The species is protected by Brazilian law (Bernardes *et al.* 1990), placed on Appendix I of CITES, and listed as endangered under the U.S. Endangered Species Act (King

1978-1979). Some of its present remnant populations should persist if the protected areas where they are found continue to be preserved (Ridgely 1981a; also King 1978-1979); but see Threats. On the basis of the evidence under Population, the two critical areas for the species are the CVRD Porto Seguro Reserve in Bahia and the Sooretama Biological Reserve and adjacent CVRD Linhares Reserve in Espírito Santo, although Desengano State Park (possibly: no records yet inside the boundaries) and Fazenda União in Rio de Janeiro and Rio Doce State Park and Fazenda Montes Claros (Caratinga Reserve) in Minas Gerais are clearly important (see Remarks 4). Ridgely's (1981a) urging that the few remaining forest patches should be surveyed in the southern part of the species's range has largely been fulfilled in the past decade.

MEASURES PROPOSED Reservation of such additional forest tracts as still exist in southern Bahia and elsewhere would also be very worthwhile (Ridgely 1981a). The few remaining patches of forest within the northern part of the species's range (southern Bahia, north-eastern Minas Gerais) could still harbour small and so far undetected populations, and merit being identified and searched. Support for existing key sites is clearly imperative, and CVRD must be urged to maintain the full extent of forest cover at its Porto Seguro Reserve. Research is possibly needed to test whether the species anywhere survives and breeds successfully in cacao plantations, as hoped in King (1978-1979) and Ridgely (1981a); but in any case see Threats. A proposal to reforest three million hectares in the valleys of the rios Doce and Jequitinhonha in Minas Gerais, involving CVRD (*Brasil Environment* no.7, August 1991), is an opportunity to integrate the revitalizing of the regional economy with the conservation of various Atlantic Forest bird species such as this and the Red-browed Amazon *Amazona rhodocorytha* (see relevant account).

REMARKS (1) Pinto (1952) gave Pirapora as the source of a specimen, without comment, despite its being so far west, out of the Atlantic Forest region, that some error seems likely; in fact his source, Moojen (1943), simply listed the species as "Matipó Pirapora" (Moojen was the collector of the Matipó specimens in MZUFV), and is of such poor typographic quality that some error here seems certain. (2) Bokermann (1957) provided the localities of Wied's explorations; from this it is worth noting that Wied only went up the Paraíba as far as São Fidelis. (3) The record from Araras (von Pelzeln 1868-1871) was originally (and evidently correctly) attributed by von Ihering (1898) to Rio de Janeiro but, possibly through confusion with Areias in the extreme north-east of São Paulo state, the species was listed for that region by (e.g.) Pinto (1935) and many subsequent authorities. An analysis of J. Natterer's itinerary and collecting dates (as given in von Pelzeln 1868-1871) indicates that in fact the true locality was the Serra das Araras as given in Distribution: Rio de Janeiro (J. F. Pacheco verbally 1991). (4) The nominate form of White-eared Parakeet *P. leucotis leucotis* is very similar in distribution and, apparently, ecological requirements to Blue-chested Parakeet, and is likewise becoming rare and in need of protection (King 1978-1979, Ridgely 1981a); it is listed as threatened under Brazilian law (Bernardes *et al.* 1990).

EL ORO PARAKEET *Pyrrhura orcesi* V/R[10]

This recently described species is restricted to humid forest on the west slope of the Andes in Azuay and El Oro provinces, south-west Ecuador, where it occurs at altitudes between 300 and 1,300 m. It is threatened by habitat destruction, but plans are under way to protect part of its range.

DISTRIBUTION The El Oro Parakeet (see Remarks) seems to be confined to wet forest on the Pacific slope of the Andes in Azuay and El Oro provinces, Ecuador, between the río San Antonio valley at 2°30'S and the Balsas region at 3°45'S, at 300 to 1,300 m elevation, possibly lower. It was discovered in remnant patches of cloud-forest c.9.5 road km west of Piñas, 900 m, in El Oro, at 3°39'S 79°45'W, in August 1980 (Ridgely and Robbins 1988; coordinates – also for the following – read from IGM 1989). Specimens were secured at the same locality in June and early July 1985, and in August 1986 additional specimens were collected east of Naranjal, Azuay, all birds being seen or collected at altitudes ranging from 600 to 1,100 m (Ridgely and Robbins 1988). A further specimen (in BMNH) had been collected in September 1939 at Piedras, 300 m, El Oro, at 3°38'S 79°56'W (Ridgely and Robbins 1988). A flock was heard at an elevation of 1,300 m, above Uzhcurumi, some 30 km north of the type-locality, on the north-western slope of Cordillera de Chilla, El Oro, at 3°23'S 79°32'W in March 1991 (NK). Despite extensive searches, the species was not found north of the Naranjal site (Ridgely and Robbins 1988), i.e. (presumably) north of the río San Antonio valley. There are several recent sightings from the Pacific slope of Azuay, the northernmost being at Manta Real, 600-1,080 m, near río Tigay, 13 road km from Troncal on the road to Shucay, at c.2°30'S 79°17'W, others being along the road under construction from north of Naranjal to Cuenca, near the border of Guayas province, 900-1,200 m, at 2°34'S 79°20'W, and near Escuela San Luis, 600-1,000 m (not located but south-east of Naranjal), along the road that heads east from Hacienda Balao Chica (c.18 road km south of Naranjal) and crosses to the south side of río Jagua, i. e. at c.2°52'S 79°32'W (J. C. Mathéus *in litt.* 1991, NK). It seems possible that the parakeet may range down to the lowest part of the slope where it is forested, i.e. down to 50 m at places in western Azuay such as near río Siete at c.3°05'S (NK). South of the type-locality the bird has never been found despite extensive previous collecting and two recent expeditions (Chapman 1926, Wiedenfeld *et al.* 1985, R. S. Ridgely *in litt.* 1990, B. J. Best *in litt.* 1991).

POPULATION At the El Oro site a highly conservative count gave a total of 55-60 birds, and at the Naranjal site over 20 were encountered (Ridgely and Robbins 1988). On 6 August 1988 over 75 birds (including a flock of 60) were seen at the type-locality, despite significant further loss of habitat (R. S. Ridgely and P. Greenfield *in litt.* 1989), but in April 1989 only small numbers were encountered, so seasonal movements may take place (P. Greenfield *in litt.* 1989) or else a real drop in numbers had occurred. Other counts at the Piñas site are of 40-50 birds at 1,270 m and six at 1,200 m on 13 March 1990 (B. M. Whitney *in litt.* 1991), five flocks of 15, five, four, one and 10 on 25-26 September 1990 (NK), a total of 12 on 15 December 1990 (M. Pearman *in litt.* 1991), two flocks of five and 14 on 1 February 1991 (NK), three flocks of 10, 7-10 and 7-10 on 27 February to 1 March 1991 (B. J. Best *in litt.* 1991) and one flock of seven on 14-16 April 1991 (NK). Along the new Cuenca road five to six flocks, each of 5-6 birds, was seen on 27 September 1990, and a flock of four was seen there on 22 December 1990 (J. C. Mathéus *in litt.* 1991, NK), while at San Luis a flock of four and another of 12 were seen in February 1991 (J. C. Mathéus *in litt.* 1991). The 300-1,300 m zone between Naranjal and Piñas covers c.750 km^2 (read from IGM 1989). As far as can be gathered from satellite photos (LANDSAT 1987) some 50-80% of the forest remains (NK). A probable density of the closely related Maroon-tailed Parakeet *Pyrrhura melanura* would be in the order of 3-30 birds per km^2

(NK), which for *orcesi* would give a total population of c.2,000 birds at worst and 20,000 birds at best.

ECOLOGY The El Oro Parakeet inhabits very humid upper tropical forest (Ridgely and Robbins 1988). At the type-locality, forest canopy height on the more level areas exceeded 20 m, although average canopy height was lower on steeper slopes; trees and the relatively dense understorey were laden with epiphytes; moisture is carried by westerly winds from the Pacific Ocean c.75 km west of the type-locality, and on 4 August 1980, and during investigations in June and July 1985, the forest was usually shrouded by clouds from dawn until about midday (Ridgely and Robbins 1988), and similar or even foggier weather with frequent rain was noted in September and January, while in mid-April clouds hung high above the ridge and no rain fell in three days, and according to a local had not done so for two weeks (NK). The forest at the Naranjal site was very similar to the El Oro site, except that it was even more fragmented by human activity; at both localities the parakeet moved in flocks of 4-12 birds, flocks consisting of adults and young of both sexes (Ridgely and Robbins 1988).

West of Piñas the birds were observed feeding repeatedly at a fig (*Ficus* cf. *macbridei*) and on the fruit of the tiliacean *Heliocarpus popayanensis*, while at the Naranjal site they were observed feeding only on the fruit of a euphorb *Hieronyma sp.* (Ridgely and Robbins 1988). The 40-50 birds at Piñas in March 1990 were feeding on the fruits of several large *Ficus* trees (B. M. Whitney *in litt.* 1992), while in mid-February 1991 small flocks there fed on berries and in *Cecropia* trees (B. J. Best *in litt.* 1991). Three birds were observed drinking from a small bromeliad at the top of a tree in a clearing (M. Pearman *in litt.* 1991).

Given that some fledged young were begging food in late June, the main breeding period was speculated to be from March through to May (Ridgely and Robbins 1988); fledged young were also observed being fed in August 1988 (R. S. Ridgely *in litt.* 1989).

THREATS The natural forest habitat at the type-locality and the Naranjal site has been reduced significantly by human activity; at the El Oro site, between 10 and 15 large trees were being removed daily from a small tract of accessible forest in 1985; typically, once the larger trees are removed, the area is burnt and cattle are brought in (Ridgely and Robbins 1988); this process was still continuing in August 1988 (R. S. Ridgely *in litt.* 1989); another observer judged that 5% of the forest disappeared between visits in April 1986 and May 1987 (M. Pearman *in litt.* 1989), and even in late 1990 there was clear evidence of continuing deforestation (M. Pearman *in litt.* 1991). Although the parakeet was relatively numerous and appears to be thriving in patchy forest now found at the two first known localities, significant further disturbance and fragmentation of the forest may eliminate vital nesting and feeding sites; fortunately there is still extensive, mostly inaccessible forest remaining between the two sites (Ridgely and Robbins 1988).

MEASURES TAKEN None is known, but "Fundación Natura", an Ecuadorian nature conservation organization, has plans to set up a reserve in the northernmost part of the parakeet's range (P. Greenfield *in litt.* 1989).

MEASURES PROPOSED It has been strongly recommended that a sizeable tract of land within the bird's range be preserved, not only to ensure that a large population is protected, but also to protect other forms that have distributions restricted to this region (Ridgely and Robbins 1988), for an enumeration of which see Remarks under Grey-backed Hawk *Leucopternis occidentalis*.

REMARKS The species is evidently a close relative of the Maroon-tailed Parakeet, but regarded as a distinct species mainly on the basis of the extent and colour tone of its red forehead, even in young birds, as well as differences in the pattern of the underparts (Ridgely and Robbins 1988). Also its calls are considerably higher pitched (NK).

RUFOUS-FRONTED PARAKEET *Bolborhynchus ferrugineifrons* V/R[10]

This parakeet is restricted to the Central Andes of Colombia, from Caldas to Cauca departments, where it occurs at 3,200 to 4,000 m in shrubland of the temperate forest/páramo ecotone. The total population has been put at 1,000-2,000 individuals, although habitat degradation is such that the true figure may be lower.

DISTRIBUTION The Rufous-fronted Parakeet (see Remarks), described from a single "Bogotá" specimen (Lawrence 1880b), has been sighted or collected in only two areas of the Central Andes of Colombia (all coordinates are from Paynter and Traylor 1981), (1) the Nevado del Ruiz–Nevado del Tolima volcanic complex lying at the juncture of Caldas, Risaralda, Quindío and Tolima departments, and (2) the slopes of Volcán Puracé, Cauca department, c.280 km south-south-west of Nevado del Tolima; however, it is probably a low-density resident all the way from Nevado del Ruiz to Volcán Puracé (Graves and Giraldo 1987). Records are:

the Nevado del Ruiz–Nevado del Tolima area the páramo de Ruiz, September 1918 (Carriker 1955a); Nevado del Ruiz, c.4,000 m, in 1975, when a few small parrots were presumed to be this species (Ridgely 1981a); the vicinity of Laguna de Otún (3,950 m), 4°47'N 75°26'W, south-west of Nevado de Santa Isabel, Risaralda, where many were seen and two collected in August 1985 (Graves and Giraldo 1987); Alto Quindío Acaime Natural Reserve, 4°37'N 75°28'W, September 1989 and April 1990, and the nearby Cañon del Quindío Natural Reserve on the southern boundary of Los Nevados National Park (Renjifo 1991, L. M. Renjifo *in litt.* 1992, whence coordinates); Hacienda Indostán (3,280 m), Anzoátegui municipality, Tolima, where one specimen was collected (Graves and Giraldo 1987); the Manizales-Ruiz road on the north slope of Nevado del Ruiz at 3,540 m, when a flock of three was observed in January 1986 (Graves and Giraldo 1987); the río Guali–Libani road on the north-west slope of Nevado del Ruiz, when a pair was seen in January 1986 (Graves and Giraldo 1987); the río Guali canyon, 4,000 m, where eight were seen in April 1992 (J. A. Giraldo *in litt.* 1992); and in the páramo zone of Nevado del Tolima, 1985 (J. I. Hernández Camacho verbally 1991);

Volcán Puracé in Cauca department, where a specimen (in USNM) was collected in February 1955 at Gabriel López ("2,835 m"), 2°29′N 76°18′W, and another (in FMNH) nearby in January 1957 at Malvasá, 3,000 m.

An entirely untraced locality is Alto Valle de Lagunillas, where in 1985 the species was found at 3,800-3,900 m in the lower páramo potato plantations and in small patches of highland forest (J. I. Hernández Camacho verbally 1991).

POPULATION Although the Rufous-fronted Parakeet is reported to be fairly common in the vicinity of Laguna de Otún, Risaralda department, with farmers in the area considering it very common, and despite the scarcity of sightings up to the mid-1980s and the low number of museum specimens being attributable to the remoteness of its restricted geographic and elevational range (Graves and Giraldo 1987), this is still a very low-density species: using a conservative estimate of one individual per square kilometre, and assuming it to occur from Nevado del Ruiz to Volcán Puracé, the total population could easily number up to 1,000-2,000 individuals (Graves and Giraldo 1987), although owing to the degradation of the páramo habitat this computation is considered over-optimistic (Renjifo 1991).

ECOLOGY Although recorded as low as 2,835 m (Ridgely 1981a) and in both forest and páramo (J. I. Hernández Camacho verbally 1991), the habitat preference of the Rufous-fronted Parakeet is probably the shrubland and sparsely wooded slopes on the temperate forest/páramo ecotone at 3,200-4,000 m (Ridgely 1981a, Graves and Giraldo 1987). It usually occurs in noisy flocks of 10-15 individuals that are easily approached (Graves and Giraldo 1987).

The species is primarily a ground-feeder, having been observed taking grass-seeds, in one case possibly *Calamagrostis effusa*, seeds of "frailejones", and achenes and flowers of *Espeletia hartwegiana* (Renjifo 1991, J. I. Hernández Camacho verbally 1991).

The male collected in January 1957 at Malvasá, Cauca department, had enlarged testes (specimen in FMNH). The nest has not been described in detail, but the prediction that it would prove to be a burrow in an earthen bank or cliff-face, as in other high-elevation Andean members of the genus (Forshaw 1981), appears to have been fulfilled with a report of nesting in rock crevices in Los Nevados National Park (J. I. Hernández Camacho verbally 1991).

THREATS Despite the severe deforestation below 3,300 m in the Central Andes of Colombia, much habitat above this level is more or less intact, and is exploited mainly by firewood-cutters and for grazing (Graves and Giraldo 1987). Nevertheless, the páramo has suffered considerably through burning and over-grazing, even and especially at the southern end of the Los Nevados National Park, and this seems seriously to have affected the species (Renjifo 1991, L. M. Renjifo *in litt.* 1992); moreover, the conversion of páramo elsewhere to potato-fields, which involves much burning, is suspected of jeopardizing the species (J. I. Hernández Camacho verbally 1991). Rufous-fronted Parakeets are occasionally kept as pets by farmers in the Nevado del Tolima region (Graves and Giraldo 1987), and in 1983 two birds were imported into French Guiana (Arndt 1986). Otherwise there are no reports of the species in captivity (Ridgely 1981a), as information on imports into West Germany in the 1970s was erroneous (Arndt 1986).

MEASURES TAKEN The species is known to occur within the boundaries of Los Nevados National Park, Colombia (Graves and Giraldo 1987), but this is of small comfort (see Threats); it also occurs in the Alto Quindío Acaime Natural Reserve, but at very low densities (Renjifo 1991: see equivalent section under Moustached Antpitta *Grallaria rufocinerea*).

MEASURES PROPOSED This bird needs very careful searching for (Orejuela 1985), monitoring and study to determine its status and requirements at certain key localities where it stands best chance of being conserved; among these are the Laguna de Otún and the Alto Quindío Acaime and Cañon del Quindío Natural Reserves (see Distribution, also equivalent section under Moustached Antpitta). In Los Nevados National Park, this species may also occur with Fuertes's Parrot *Hapalopsittaca fuertesi*, Yellow-eared Parrot *Ognorhynchus icterotis* and Brown-banded Antpitta *Grallaria milleri* (see relevant accounts), all of which should be considered in any conservation initiatives aimed at increasing the protection of the park (see Threats). Extension of the park boundaries to embrace more habitat at lower elevations would benefit Moustached Antpitta (which may occur in the lowest parts of the park) and Red-bellied Grackle *Hypopyrrhus pyrohypogaster* (see relevant accounts), but for the Rufous-fronted Parakeet what is urgently needed in the park is a major reduction in livestock and agriculture (L. M. Renjifo *in litt.* 1992). This goes also for Las Hermosas, Nevado del Huila and Puracé National Parks, where the species might be expected (L. M. Renjifo *in litt.* 1992).

REMARKS The Rufous-fronted Parakeet and Andean Parakeet *Bolborhynchus orbygnesius* appear to form a superspecies in the narrow sense, by being recently derived sister species that occupy similar habitats and have similar behaviour, in addition to having allopatric distributions (Graves and Giraldo 1987).

YELLOW-FACED PARROTLET *Forpus xanthops* V[9]

This small parrot occurs in the arid woodland and scrub of the upper Marañón valley in north-central Peru, where it has recently declined seriously owing to trapping for trade and the apparent deterioration of its habitat.

DISTRIBUTION The Yellow-faced Parrotlet (see Remarks 1) is endemic to the upper Marañón valley in three departments from southern Amazonas and Cajamarca south into extreme eastern La Libertad, north-central Peru. Records (north to south, with coordinates from Stephens and Traylor 1983) are from: (*Cajamarca*) Bellavista, 5°37'S 78°39'W (Dorst 1957a); both banks of the Marañón somewhere between the Vacapampa (= Huacapampa) valley and Leimebamba (Baron 1897), i.e. in this department and the next; (*Amazonas*) Bagua, 5°40'S 78°31'W (Dorst 1957a; see Remarks 2); Corral Quemado, where the Olmos–Marañón highway crosses the Marañón, 5°44'S 78°40'W (Krabbe 1979); Balsas, above and west of Cajamarca, 6°50'S 78°01'W (Krabbe 1984); (*La Libertad*) Chagual, 7°50'S 77°38'W (Bond 1955), also from July and August 1979 (five specimens in LSUMZ); Soquián, 7°51'S 77°41'W (Bond 1955); Viña (= Viñas), Huamachuco, 7°57'S 77°38'W (Salvin 1895).

POPULATION All the evidence is that this species was fairly common within its restricted range: its discoverer judged it "not rare" at the type-locality (Baron 1897), and it was later reported "particularly abundant and in large flocks" (Dorst 1957b), common (O'Neill 1981, 1987, Parker *et al.* 1982) or common in at least part of its range, and with its overall population "almost certainly stable" (Ridgely 1981a). However, in recent years it has suffered a serious decline, becoming notably rare around settlements and near roads (Riveros Salcedo *et al.* 1991).

ECOLOGY The Yellow-faced Parrotlet is a bird of the arid tropical zone of the upper Marañón valley, where it inhabits desert scrub, dry forest and riparian thickets (Parker *et al.* 1982), or in another version "cactus–*Prosopis* desert" (O'Neill 1987), at an elevation of 600 to 1,700 m (Ridgely 1981a). Baron (1897), who noted that the species flies in flocks, recorded the habitat at the localities where he encountered them as brushwood and cacti. Dorst (1957b), who also saw large flocks, noted its use of the tops of low trees and bushes, that it regularly occurred in cactus areas and that it sometimes settled on the ground. Near Balsas in 1975 the species was found in small flocks of several to more than a dozen individuals, in desert terrain with scattered bushes, small *Acacia*-like trees and numerous columnar cacti; one small flock fed on the seeds of a leguminous tree, and others were flushed from the tops of fruiting cacti; the species was also recorded in open, leafless forest dominated by a large species of *Ceiba*, and was noted flying in and out of willows *Salix humboldtiana* and other riverside trees (TAP). Birds feed on the seeds of balsas trees and cacti (Baron 1897). The only breeding data appear to be from captive birds, which have laid clutches of 3-6 eggs, with an incubation period of 21 days, a period of 35 days to fledging, another two weeks after that to independence of the young, and as many as three broods a year (Robiller 1990; see also Mitchell 1991).

THREATS Two factors (trade and habitat destruction) have contributed to the recent decline in this species; of the two it may be trade that is more to blame.

Trade This apparently did not exist as an influence in the late 1970s, Ridgely (1981a) being unaware of the species's presence in captivity, at least outside Peru. O'Neill (1981) ambiguously wrote of the absence of its persecution, presumably referring to trapping rather than to shooting for food or as a pest. However, while Mitchell (1991) considered them scarce in the U.K., Robiller (1990) revealed that in the late 1980s the species was relatively common in captivity, his earliest knowledge of it in trade (outside of Peru) dating from 1975. In 1988 research by Riveros Salcedo *et al.* (1991) showed that it was much valued in the pet trade within Peru and that, despite legal protection granted four years earlier, local commerce continued; the rarity of the bird near roads and villages was attributed to poaching.

Habitat destruction At the time of the species's discovery, cultivation of the Marañón valley was already proceeding apace, to judge from the comments in Baron (1897): the type-locality, Viña, was "a narrow strip of cultivated land, planted with coca and some fruit-trees". However, apart from a comment by O'Neill (1981) that goat damage to the local vegetation might represent a problem, it took until 1988 before the progressive deterioration of habitat was identified as an issue (Riveros Salcedo *et al.* 1991).

MEASURES TAKEN The species was accorded legal protection around 1984 (Riveros Salcedo *et al.* 1991), although to little effect (see Threats). The timely survey of the species undertaken in 1988 was funded by AFA (Riveros Salcedo *et al.* 1991).

MEASURES PROPOSED Control of trade and proper law enforcement are regarded as essential to save the species (Riveros Salcedo *et al.* 1991). However, this would perhaps best be pursued alongside an educational campaign that highlights the biological endemism of the Marañón valley (see equivalent section under Peruvian Pigeon *Columba oenops*); moreover, further study of the parrot's year-round ecological needs appears still to be important, along with some clearer understanding of human land-use practices in the region, in order to determine appropriate management options.

REMARKS (1) This species is closely related to the Pacific Parrotlet *Forpus coelestis*, but was considered distinct in size and pattern (Salvin 1895); even during a period when the two were lumped it was regarded as "a very distinct form that would be regarded as a separate species by some ornithologists" (Bond 1955). (2) Ridgely (1981a) thought the species would be found north of Balsas although he believed no records existed; in fact, Dorst (1957a) had already proved him right.

BROWN-BACKED PARROTLET *Touit melanonota* V/R[10]

This is a very poorly known (but small and inconspicuous) species, recorded this century from Rio de Janeiro state and three sites in São Paulo; it inhabits forest, chiefly in hills, but descends to lower levels (perhaps seasonally), and appears to be a victim of widespread habitat loss and fragmentation, although many recent records are from protected areas.

DISTRIBUTION The Brown-backed Parrotlet is confined to south-eastern Brazil from southern Bahia south to southern São Paulo (Ridgely 1981a, Forshaw 1989). There appear, however, to be no records from Espírito Santo, and those from Bahia are at least a century old. Minas Gerais is not listed below but records from the Itatiaia massif, through which the border with Rio de Janeiro runs, indicate its likely occurrence in that part of the state.

Bahia The only locality for the species in Brazil during extensive travels within its range, 1815-1817, was the rio Peruípe at around 18°S (Wied 1831-1833), the precise site being mapped by Bokermann (1957) as around 17°45'S 39°50'W. Two further specimens exist labelled simply Bahia (acquired in 1875 and 1890 by UMZC and BMNH respectively).

Rio de Janeiro The great majority of records stem from Rio de Janeiro city and its immediate environs, including at least three nineteenth-century specimens (two in BMNH; also Fisher 1981): Descourtilz (1854-1856) found it in the Corcovado mountain forests in Rio de Janeiro city; specimens (in CCACS) from Tijuca National Park date from October 1966 (Sick 1969, LPG), seven were observed there in July 1979 (A. Greensmith *per* D. Willis *in litt.* 1988), three in November 1980 (Ridgely 1981a) and one in July 1988 (J. F. Pacheco verbally 1988); there are records from the Pedra Branca State Park, February 1987 at 200 m, and March 1988; the Parque da Cidade on the fringe of Tijuca National Park, October 1985 (one bird), at 50 m; and Xerém, 120 m, June 1987 (two) (J. F. Pacheco *in litt.* 1987, verbally 1991). Elsewhere in the state the species has been recorded from the Serra de Cantagalo (Descourtilz 1854-1856); the Serra dos Órgãos National Park (Ribeiro 1920, Ridgely 1981a), where one pair was seen in July 1991 at 1,200 m (J. F. Pacheco verbally 1991); Teresópolis (Ribeiro 1920); near Desengano State Park (São Julião, near rio Mocotó), May 1987, seven and four individuals at 20 and 120 m respectively (J. F. Pacheco *in litt.* 1987) and again on September 1988 at 150 m (J. F. Pacheco verbally 1991), with further records from the same region (Serra dos Marreiros, near Renascença, 1,000 m, and rio do Colégio, near São Fidélis, 950 m) in April 1989 (J. F. Pacheco verbally 1991); Itatiaia National Park, two males, one female, October 1961, 800 m (LPG; also Sick 1969, 1985), and two there in September 1989 at 1,400 m (M. Kessler *in litt.* 1989), with recent records on the Itatiaia massif at Visconde de Mauá (Maromba), 1,200 m, and Maringá (near Mirantão), also 1,200 m, March 1991 (J. F. Pacheco verbally 1991); and at other unspecified localities in the Serra do Mar (Sick 1969). An old, undated specimen in AMNH labelled "near Freiburg" presumably comes from Nova Friburgo.

São Paulo Descourtilz (1854-1856) reported it from unspecified forests in the state. Confirmed records (east to west) are from: Bananal, on the Serra da Bocaina, 1,000 m, September 1989 (J. F. Pacheco verbally 1991); Praia do Prumirim, Ubatuba, June 1980 (specimen in MNRJ); Iguape, 1898 (three specimens in MZUSP; also von Ihering and von Ihering 1907, Pinto 1938, 1946); and (in fulfilment of a third-hand report of the species still surviving in the "littoral", probably south-west of São Paulo city, in the 1960s: Bertagnolio 1981), the Ilha do Cardoso State Park (P. Martuscelli *in litt.* 1991). In addition, von Ihering (1898) repeated a report that the species appeared in July and August on the rio Iririaia; it should occur in the Boracéia watershed reserve in north-eastern São Paulo (Ridgely 1981a); and unidentified parrotlets *Touit* were recorded in Ubatuba Reserve in the late 1970s (Willis and Oniki 1981a), Forshaw (1989) inclining to believe that they were *melanonota*, for unstated reasons; the record from Praia do Prumirim notwithstanding, they could have been Golden-tailed Parrotlets *T. surda* or indeed even both species.

POPULATION In the last century the Brown-backed Parrotlet was quite rare in the forests around Rio de Janeiro, though somewhat more abundant in the Serra de Cantagalo and still more so in São Paulo's forests (Descourtilz 1854-1856). Wied's (1831-1833) record from Bahia involved the collecting of 21 with two shots from a larger flock perched in the crown of a tree. Pinto (1946) thought it was perhaps formerly common (not "occasionally common" as in Silva 1989a) in the coastal forests of São Paulo, but regarded it now as very rare. Modern commentators have agreed that it is indeed a rare species, but with the proviso that parrotlets of the genus *Touit* seem generally to occur at very low densities, and their inconspicuous habits unquestionably result in their often being overlooked (Sick 1969, King 1978-1979, Ridgely 1981a, Scott and Brooke 1985); indeed, most recent records for Rio de Janeiro state stem from knowledge of the species's calls, after much fruitless fieldwork in the areas involved (J. F. Pacheco verbally 1991). Ridgely (1981a) predicted it not to prove as rare as the Golden-tailed Parrotlet (see relevant account), because more forest remains in the Serra do Mar than in the adjacent lowlands. There have been a few records of small flocks on the Ilha do Cardoso in recent years (P. Martuscelli *in litt.* 1991).

ECOLOGY The species favours humid forests on lower montane slopes, at about 500-1,000 m (Ridgely 1981a). However, the view that it rarely if ever descends to the coastal lowlands, the habitat of the Golden-tailed Parrotlet (Ridgely 1981a), may oversimplify the truth: several records under Distribution are from lowland areas, namely the rio Peruípe in Bahia, the sites in Rio de Janeiro state where altitudes are given, and Praia do Prumirim and Ilha do Cardoso (where at lower levels it occupies "sand-plain forest", the same habitat as Golden-tailed Parrotlet: see relevant account) in São Paulo; moreover, the Golden-tailed Parrotlet is evidently not in any case an exclusively lowland species, so that ecological separation between the two cannot be attributed simply to altitude.

The species lives in small flocks of 4-10 individuals, keeping constantly hidden in the foliage and feeding on the seeds of large leguminous trees (Descourtilz 1854-1856). The birds remain in or below the forest canopy, creeping along larger branches and not perching in the open (Ridgely 1981a). In the primary forests bordering the Peruípe, the birds had been eating seed kernels and were very fat; at that time of year (June, winter), they wandered more widely and were found both in the interior and at the coast (Wied 1831-1833). In the Itatiaia massif birds have been seen eating the fruits of *Rapanea acuminata* (Pineschi 1990).

There are no breeding data. On the evidence above (and under Distribution: São Paulo), it seems likely that the species undertakes some type of seasonal migration or dispersal, in some areas possibly only over quite short altitudinal distances, but in others perhaps more pronounced (Sick and Teixeira 1979 called it "migratory like other psittacids"). This implies a wider dependence on habitat than might otherwise be apparent, and hence a greater vulnerability (both past and present) to forest loss or modification.

THREATS The fragmentation of the species's range by extensive forest destruction has been and remains the one significant threat (Ridgely 1981a). Habitat destruction is affecting the species on the Ilha do Cardoso (P. Martuscelli *in litt.* 1991).

MEASURES TAKEN The species is protected under Brazilian law (Bernardes *et al.* 1990) and listed on Appendix II of CITES. It occurs in five protected areas in Rio de Janeiro state, namely Tijuca, Serra dos Órgãos and Itatiaia National Parks, and Desengano and Pedra Branca State Parks. In São Paulo state, the Ilha do Cardoso State Park holds this and some 15 other threatened bird species (P. Martuscelli *in litt.* 1991), and is therefore of crucial importance to conservation; and the Ubatuba Reserve is part of Ubatuba Experimental Station (Willis and Oniki 1981a), this being at the foot of the Serra do Mar State Park; for this and other possible protected areas in the state, see below.

MEASURES PROPOSED Silva (1989a), noting that the species is difficult to maintain in captivity and therefore that no trapping should be allowed, called for research into the species's biology and, as "the very greatest priority by the Brazilian government", the "preservation of remaining forests". More specifically, there is a strong case to be made for the conservation of forest at Ubatuba in São Paulo state, Ilha do Cardoso must be spared any further tree loss, Boracéia Biological Station, the Serra da Bocaina National Park and the Serra do Mar State Park (all in São Paulo state) need investigation for the species's presence, and fieldworkers in Bahia and Espírito Santo should be primed to look for it at suitable localities (based on the flimsy evidence under Distribution and Ecology). The proposed augmentation of numbers in Tijuca National Park through introductions (Coimbra-Filho and Aldrighi 1971) was, however, surely supererogatory.

SPOT-WINGED PARROTLET *Touit stictoptera* K[12]

This poorly known parrot has been found in six areas in Colombia, Ecuador and northern Peru. It may be partly overlooked and more widespread, but as an inhabitant of the upper tropical and lower subtropical zone it is threatened by deforestation, at present mostly so in Colombia.

DISTRIBUTION The Spot-winged Parrotlet is known from 11 specimens collected at eight different localities, with sightings at three additional sites, all falling within six general areas in Colombia, Ecuador and Peru. However, it must often be overlooked by anyone not familiar with its calls (Ridgely 1981a, Davis 1986), and may be more or less continuously distributed in the eastern foothills of the Andes from the Macarena mountains, Meta department, Colombia, to northern San Martín department, Peru (Ridgely 1981a, NK).

Colombia The type was described by Sclater (1862) on the basis of a "Bogotá" specimen, which could have been taken anywhere from the head of the Magdalena valley to the llanos east of the East Andes (Chapman 1917a). Later records (three) are from: Fusagasugá, west slope of the East Andes in Cundinamarca department (Dugand 1945a,b reported eight skins; two are in ANSP, collected July and November 1944) at 4°21'N 74°22'W (Paynter and Traylor 1981; see Remarks); ridge south-west of Entrada, 1,070 m, east slope of the northern end of the Macarena mountains, Meta department (Blake 1962; specimen in BMNH, collected in January 1950, during fieldwork described in Philipson *et al.* 1951), located at either c.3°08'N 73°52'W or c.3°00'N 73°45'W (Paynter and Traylor 1981); San Andrés, Cauca department, undated (Hilty and Brown 1986), located at 2°38'N 76°04'W on the east slope of the Central Andes, at 1,600 m (Paynter and Traylor 1981), apparently erroneously referred to the west slope by Forshaw (1978), Ridgely (1981a) and Hilty and Brown (1986). Hilty and Brown (1986) mentioned eastern Nariño as a probable area.

Ecuador Records (unreferenced coordinates read from IGM 1982) are from: (*Napo*) San Rafael, Coca Falls, 1,200 m (flock of six sighted in June 1979: Ridgely 1980) at 0°03'S 77°32'W; a little below Baeza (one collected March 1899 and another seen: Goodfellow 1901-1902; specimen in AMNH), Baeza located at 1,525 m at 0°27'S 77°53'W (Paynter and Traylor 1977); along the new Hollin-Loreto road, upper tropical zone, south or south-east of Cerro Sumaco, at c.0°47'S 77°47'W (flocks of about 10 sighted by R. A. Rowlett and others in the late 1980s and early 1990s: P. Greenfield *in litt.* 1989, M. Pearman *in litt.* 1991); (*Morona-Santiago*) upper río Upano valley at 1,600 m (flock of 12 sighted in August 1979: Ridgely 1980) at c.2°14'S 78°16'W; Yapitia, 1,625 m, west slope of Cordillera de Cutucú (one in ANSP, collected 25 June 1984; also one in MECN taken about the same time; also sighted daily in flocks of less than 10 individuals at the same locality, between 1,500 and 1,800 m from 22 June to 3 July 1984: Robbins *et al.* 1987) at c.2°40-43'S 78°05-06'W (Robbins *et al.* 1987, NK); (*Zamora-Chinchipe*) north of Zumba, 1,200 m (flock of 18-20 sighted in August 1989: R. S. Ridgely *in litt.* 1989).

Peru Records are from: above San José de Lourdes, Cordillera del Condor, Cajamarca department, July 1976 (Davis 1986; specimen in LSUMZ), San José de Lourdes being at 1,180 m at 5°04'S 78°54'W (Stephens and Traylor 1983); Pomará, "335 m", left bank of lower Marañón river in Amazonas department, July 1924 (specimen in AMNH), located at 500 m ("335 m" on the label seems therefore erroneous) at 5°16'S 78°26'W (Stephens and Traylor 1983); c.15 trail km north-east of Jirillo on the Balsapuerto trail, c.2 trail km past the Jesús del Monte settlement, San Martín department, at 6°03'S 76°44'W, where two specimens were collected and flocks of 5-25 seen daily at 1,350-1,450 m from 26 October to 24 November 1983 (Davis 1986).

POPULATION The Spot-winged Parrotlet must generally be rare (Ridgely 1981a), having been recorded "fairly common" only in the Cordillera de Cutucú (Robbins *et al.* 1987) and in San Martín (Davis 1986). In the Magdalena valley, Colombia, it certainly no longer exists at Fusagasugá, where forest destruction has been nearly total (Ridgely 1981a), and is possibly already extirpated from the entire East Andes (J. I. Hernández Camacho verbally 1991), and although it is recorded from the Macarena buffer zone, this East Andean outlier is also very heavily disturbed by settlers (J. I. Hernández Camacho verbally 1991; see also Threats); there is a slight possibility that it still occurs at San Andrés, Cauca department, but considering the close proximity of a road, probably no subtropical forest remains there (NK).

ECOLOGY Almost all specimens and sightings have been recorded from tall humid montane forest (David 1986, Hilty and Brown 1986, NK); one specimen in San Martín was actually collected in savanna-like habitat, and another nearby in stunted forest on a ridge-top (Davis 1986). In San Martín birds preferred tall humid forest, but were not restricted to it (Davis 1986). O'Neill (1987) thought it "restricted to poor-soil forests" in Peru. Most records are from 1,050 to 1,700 m, although it has been recorded as low as 500 m and possibly as high at 2,300 m (see Distribution). It travels in small flocks of 5-12 (Ridgely 1980, Davis 1986, Robbins *et al.* 1987), sometimes as many as 25 together (Davis 1986), usually flying well above the canopy (Davis 1986), less often low over or through the canopy (Ridgely 1981a, Davis 1986).

The crop and stomach of the Cutucú specimen contained fruit, while one specimen from San Martín had green seeds in its stomach (Davis 1986, J. V. Remsen *in litt.* 1989). Local people at Fusagasugá, Colombia, claimed that this parrot frequently raided maize crops when the grain was ripening, and that it occasionally fed in *Ficus* and *Clusia* trees above the town, close to 2,200 or 2,300 m (Dugand 1945a). The stomach of one collected below Fusagasugá contained numerous small fruits of a loranthacean mistletoe (Dugand 1945a).

The only suggestion of breeding is from Baeza, Ecuador, where Goodfellow (1901-1902) reported seeing only two birds in March. Specimens collected in June (Cordillera de Cutucú), July (Cajamarca and Amazonas) and October–November (San Martín) all had undeveloped gonads (Davis 1986; specimens in AMNH and ANSP), with observations of flocks being from June–August in east Ecuador (Ridgely 1980, Robbins *et al.* 1987) and October–November in San Martín, Peru (Davis 1986).

THREATS The Spot-winged Parrotlet may be in no immediate danger, as much habitat remains in eastern Ecuador and north-eastern Peru (Ridgely 1981a, NK), but in this case it has been chronically under-recorded; however, one observer, noting that it appears very local, has reported rapid deforestation along the Loreto road in Ecuador since its opening in 1988 (M. Pearman *in litt.* 1991), forest in the Cordillera de Cutucú is at some risk (see Threats under White-necked Parakeet *Pyrrhura albipectus*), while the species may nearly have been extirpated from Colombia (Ridgely 1981a, Hilty and Brown 1986), where for example the Macarena National Park is imperilled by invading colonists (Struhsaker 1976, Ridgely 1981a).

MEASURES TAKEN This parrotlet is known to occur in two Ecuadorian protected areas: the Cayambe-Coca Ecological Reserve and the Sangay National Park (Ridgely 1981a). It has been collected in what is now Macarena National Park, Colombia (but see Threats).

MEASURES PROPOSED All three protected areas in which the parrot is known to occur require continued vigilance to maintain their ecological integrity, with the situation in Macarena being especially critical at this time (Ridgely 1981a). Action needed for the Cordillera de Cutucú is outlined in the equivalent section under White-necked Parakeet.

REMARKS Although both 1944 specimens from Fusagasugá are labelled "1,750 m", Dugand (1945a) stated that they were collected below the town, at c.1,600 m; he also mentioned the claim by local people that the species is occasionally found above the town, at 2,200-2,300 m, and suggested that its occurrence in the general area may be seasonal, as a thorough search by one of his assistants in April 1945 failed to locate it, as did the AMNH expedition during late March and early April 1913 (Chapman 1917a); however, J. I. Hernández Camacho (verbally 1991) reported that they were temporarily common at the locality up to the late 1940s, and were then collected in coffee groves.

GOLDEN-TAILED PARROTLET *Touit surda* V/R[10]

The rare Golden-tailed Parrotlet has been recorded from four states in north-east Brazil and from Bahia south to São Paulo, all in the Atlantic Forest region of the country; it appears to be migratory in some degree, and has evidently suffered from habitat destruction, although many recent records are from protected areas.

DISTRIBUTION The Golden-tailed Parrotlet is endemic to eastern Brazil in four adjacent north-eastern states (*T. s.* "*ruficauda*": see Remarks 1) and from southern Bahia south to São Paulo (*T. s. surda*). The evidence is that this is a species of Atlantic Forest and, while the record below from Ceará is accepted here, a record from Pará (Wied 1831-1833, Burmeister 1856; see also von Ihering and von Ihering 1907) and one from the rio Claro, Goiás (specimen in BMNH; see also Ribeiro 1920, Pinto 1935), are not admitted (although Goiás was accepted by Meyer de Schauensee 1966 and Sick 1985); nor does there appear to be any evidence of its occurrence in Minas Gerais (*contra* King 1978-1979).

Ceará There is a remarkable record of three perched birds seen in the municipality of Camocim, in the north of the state, in 1984 (R. Otoch *in litt.* 1987).

Paraíba A female was collected at Mamanguape, Uruba, 12 July 1957 (Pinto and de Camargo 1961).

Pernambuco The species was recorded by Swainson (1820-1823) "in the vicinity of Pernambuco", i.e. near present-day Recife. Two birds collected at Dois Irmãos, Recife, 2 December 1944, formed the basis of the subspecies *ruficauda* (Berla 1954), although of course these were not the first records for the state (*contra* Berla 1946). There is an undated skin from the state in MCML (Fisher 1981).

Alagoas A bird was collected at São Miguel dos Campos, 26 September 1951 (Pinto 1954a), and three were taken at Usina Sinimbu, February 1957 (in LACM and MZUSP) (see Threats). Four males (one from a flock of four, another from a flock of about six, and two together) were collected at Pedra Branca ("Serra Branca"), Murici, 500-550 m, 11-12 May 1984 and 22 January 1986 (specimens in MNRJ). A solitary pair was observed briefly at Pedra Talhada Biological Reserve at c.700 m on 22 October 1990 (B. M. Whitney *in litt.* 1991).

Bahia At least nine nineteenth-century skins, in AMNH, BMNH, MCML (Fisher 1981), MCZ and USNM, are merely labelled "Bahia". Wied (1831-1833) collected a pair in March at the Mucuri estuary, i.e. in the very far south of the state. In this century records of the species are (north to south) from Jequié, Serra do Palhão (on the rio de Contas), December 1932 (Pinto 1935); Fazenda Santa Maria, rio Gongogi, December 1932 (Pinto 1935); Itabuna, June and July 1919 (specimens in MZUSP: see Remarks 2); Ilhéus, July 1944 (two in MZUSP); CEPLAC Lemos Maia Experimental Station, Una, October 1987 (minimum of three seen perched: LPG); Monte Pascoal National Park, September 1977 (a pair) (Ridgely 1981a). Ridgely (1981a) considered that if the species has a stronghold it is in southern Bahia.

Espírito Santo Wied (1831-1833) found the species as far as 19°S, i.e. the northern reaches of the state, noting that numbers were caught with lime, notably around São Mateus. All but one twentieth-century records are from further south, the exception being Fazenda Klabin (now Córrego Grande Biological Reserve), three in September 1979 (A. Greensmith *per* D. Willis *in litt.* 1988); then Sooretama Biological Reserve (flock of eight) and adjacent CVRD Linhares Reserve, December 1986, January 1987 and July/August 1988 (Pacheco and Fonseca 1987, C. E. Carvalho *in litt.* 1987, B. M. Whitney *in litt.* 1987, D. F. Stotz *in litt.* 1988); Pau Gigante (now Ibiraçu), September 1940 (specimen each in MZUSP and USNM); Augusto Ruschi (Nova Lombardia) Biological Reserve, small flocks recorded on repeated visits in October/November, 1980-1986 (TAP), at 800 m, January 1987 (flock of eight) (B. M. Whitney *in litt.* 1987), and a flock of 14 on successive days, September/October 1989 (M. Kessler *in litt.* 1989).

Rio de Janeiro A male was collected near Rio de Janeiro before 1848 (Fisher 1981), and a specimen was taken at Nova Friburgo before 1891 (in BMNH; also von Ihering 1900a). Twentieth-century records are from Cabo Frio, sporadically from June to September since 1970 (Sick and Teixeira 1979); Majé, March 1984 (flock of about eight) and probably also 1982 (Gonzaga 1986); Desengano State Park, 830 m, August 1987 (three birds) and at São Julião, rio Mocotó (lowlands near Desengano), July 1988 (J. F. Pacheco *in litt.* 1987, verbally 1988); Tinguá, August 1939 (female in MNRJ); Serrinha, near Itatiaia National Park, 1988 (Pineschi 1990). Specimens with which the type-material of *ruficauda* were compared were from Teresópolis (Berla 1954), a locality mentioned, along with Serra dos Órgãos, by Ribeiro (1920).

São Paulo An old specimen purportedly from the state required confirmation (Pinto 1935), provided by a single perched bird seen at Boracéia Biological Station, 800 m, January 1987 (D. F. Stotz *in litt.* 1988), and by its presence on Ilha do Cardoso State Park (P. Martuscelli *in litt.* 1991). Unidentified parrotlets *Touit* were recorded in Ubatuba Reserve in the late 1970s (Willis and Oniki 1981a), Forshaw (1989) inclining to believe that they were Brown-backed Parrotlets *T. melanonota*, for unstated reasons; in fact they could have been *surda* or indeed even both species. The species was reportedly common on the lower rio Tietê (i.e. in the west of the state) at the end of the nineteenth century (von Ihering 1898).

POPULATION Throughout the last century (apart from the last remark under Distribution) this species was regarded as rare (Swainson 1820-1823, Wied 1831-1833, Burmeister 1856, Finsch 1867-1868), and its continuing evasion of observation has perpetuated this view ("apparently now very rare": Scott and Brooke 1985). Whatever the relative degrees of rarity over the past two hundred years, Ridgely (1981a) is clearly safe in assuming that a great decline in numbers has taken place in that period owing to habitat destruction, but also that the species is often overlooked; indeed, records from Rio de Janeiro and Espírito Santo states made after he lamented their absence (notably in a reserve – Sooretama – that he thought "seemingly suitable") indicate this problem. Several small flocks (of four, five, seven and eight individuals, plus a singleton, i.e. minimum of eight, maximum of 25) were observed from a tower in the CVRD Linhares Reserve (contiguous with Sooretama), 19-20 December 1986; they clearly covered a large area of forest, and these numbers therefore possibly represent a high proportion of the reserve's total population (B. M. Whitney *in litt.* 1987). On Ilha do Cardoso there have been a few recent records of flocks up to 12 (P. Martuscelli *in litt.* 1991). No other data on numbers exist other than the records given under Distribution.

ECOLOGY From the evidence of the records above, this species inhabits lowland and adjacent mountain forest (Sick 1985). However, the view that it is a lowland bird reaching up to c.500 m, after which it is probably replaced by the Brown-backed Parrotlet, and indeed that the two species may never be locally sympatric (Ridgely 1981a), appears to be confounded by records at 800 m or more from Augusto Ruschi, Desengano State Park and Boracéia, especially when combined with evidence that *T. melanonota* itself may be found at lower levels (see relevant account). On the Ilha do Cardoso the Golden-tailed Parrotlet inhabits "sand-plain forest" (P. Martuscelli *in litt.* 1991). That it also inhabits forest edge (Sick 1985) seems mistaken, given the general evidence above, although the flock at Majé was in the canopy at the edge of a small second-growth woodlot almost completely surrounded by open country (Gonzaga 1986).

This flock fed on the unripe fruits of an anacardiaceous tree, *Spondias lutea* (Gonzaga 1986). In the Itatiaia massif birds fed on ripe fruits of *Rapanea schwackeana* (Pineschi 1990). In the forest along the rio Gongogi, Bahia, a fruiting myrtaceous tree was frequently visited by birds in December (Pinto 1935).

There are no data on breeding, except that the gonads of the MZUSP female collected in Alagoas, September, were undeveloped. The species may undertake seasonal movements: in the state of Rio de Janeiro it has been found occasionally in two lowland localities near the foothills of the Serra do Mar, appearing from June to September in one of them, Cabo Frio (Sick and

Teixeira 1979), and during some weeks of March in the other, Majé (Gonzaga 1986). Small flocks, believed of this species, occurred seasonally at fruiting trees in areas that had been mostly deforested (Ridgely 1981a).

THREATS The massive deforestation which has taken place within its range has been regarded as the main cause of its decline (Ridgely 1981a, Forshaw 1989). The population of the species in the north-east must be at most serious risk from this phenomenon, with for example the localities Usina Sinimbu and São Miguel dos Campos now entirely cleared of forest (LPG). The Ilha do Cardoso is suffering from deforestation (P. Martuscelli *in litt.* 1991). Ridgely (1981a) thought it might occur in cacao plantations in southern Bahia, and that if so there should still be some suitable habitat left for its survival; but these plantations offer little security (see Threats under Blue-chested Parakeet *Pyrrhura cruentata*).

The relative tameness of this bird, which allows it to be easily captured (Sick 1985, LPG), may be an additional factor of risk wherever it still occurs. However, trade in the species appears to be extremely light.

MEASURES TAKEN The Golden-tailed Parrotlet is protected under Brazilian law (Bernardes *et al.* 1990). The species's occurrence in various protected areas, e.g. Lemos Maia Experimental Station, Monte Pascoal National Park, Sooretama Biological Reserve and adjacent CVRD Linhares Reserve, Augusto Ruschi Biological Reserve, Desengano State Park, Boracéia Biological Station (which has no legal protection or definition of boundaries: H. F. de A. Camargo verbally 1991) and Ilha do Cardoso State Park, is only partially reassuring, since the numbers observed remain so small and the species's needs (including its possible seasonal displacements) are so poorly understood.

MEASURES PROPOSED Surveys of the species in the field are needed, particularly now that its calls have been identified during recent fieldwork (e.g. by B. M. Whitney *in litt.* 1987, LPG). Better protection for existing reserves such as Ilha do Cardoso is obviously essential. The conservation of the Pedra Branca forests at Murici is a self-evident imperative, this being apparently the largest remaining continuous forest area in extreme north-east Brazil (Teixeira 1987) and holding several other threatened birds (see Remarks under Alagoas Foliage-gleaner *Philydor novaesi*).

REMARKS (1) The subspecies *ruficauda* seems unlikely to be valid; if it is, it must take the name given to the species by Swainson (1820-1823), *chryseura*, which itself was evidently close to preceding *surda*. (2) Pinto's (1935) dates of January and April for these specimens are in error, as confirmed by Pinto (1938, 1945).

RUSTY-FACED PARROT *Hapalopsittaca amazonina* V/R[10]

This parrot occurs in the Andes of Venezuela and Colombia; all three races are confined to humid upper montane forest and scrub at 2,200 to 3,000 m, appear to be very local throughout their ranges, very rare at most localities, and threatened by habitat destruction.

DISTRIBUTION The Rusty-faced Parrot (see Remarks) appears to be patchy in its occurrence throughout its range in the Andes of Venezuela and Colombia.

Venezuela The subspecies *theresae* has been recorded in Mérida and Táchira states as follows: (*Mérida*) Quintero, 2,800 m, August 1941; Valle, 2,500 m; El Escorial páramo, 2,500 m; and La Culata páramo, 3,000 m, all four on the south slope of Sierra del Norte, c.25 km north-east, c.15 km north, c.10 km north-west and 17 km north-east of the town of Mérida, respectively; the Pico Humboldt trail, Sierra Nevada National Park, c.11 km east of the town of Mérida (flock of six seen in December 1983 just above the first refuge: C. S. Balchin *in litt.* 1988); (*Táchira*) Boca de Monte (Pregonero) in the interior Andes at 2,300-2,400 m, c.90 km south-west of the town of Mérida; along the Queniquea road in March 1981 (Phelps and Phelps 1958, Meyer de Schauensee and Phelps 1978, Paynter 1982, R. S. Ridgely *in litt.* 1988; specimens in AMNH, COP, FMNH and UMMZ). The species, including subspecies *amazonina*, is recorded as ranging from 2,300 to 3,000 m in Venezuela (Meyer de Schauensee and Phelps 1978), but the sight record of a pair along the Queniquea road was at 2,200 m (R. S. Ridgely *in litt.* 1988).

The subspecies *amazonina* is recorded from one locality in Venezuela: Páramo de Tamá, 2,500-3,000 m, Táchira department (Phelps and Phelps 1958, Meyer de Schauensee and Phelps 1978; also sightings in January 1983: C. S. Balchin *in litt.* 1988).

Colombia The subspecies *amazonina* is known from seven areas within the East Andes (coordinates unless otherwise stated are from Paynter and Traylor 1981): (*Norte de Santander*) Gramalote, east slope, at c.7°53'N 72°48'W, September 1946 (Carriker 1955a); Ramírez, west slope c.4 km north of Cáchira, at 7°48'N 73°05'W, October 1916 (Carriker 1955a); (*Santander*) La Pica, west slope north-east of Molagavita, at c.6°45'N 72°45'W, February 1917 (Carriker 1955a); (*Cundinamarca*) Valle de Jesus Forest, c.4°50'N 73°40'W, adjacent to the following locality, where 6-8 were seen feeding in secondary forest in July 1991 (A. Repizzo and L. M. Renjifo *in litt.* 1992); Chingaza National Park east of Bogotá (whence a feather), the adjacent La Bolsa area (whence a flock), recently (L. M. Renjifo *per* L. Rosselli *in litt.* 1991) and also the adjacent Carpanta Biological Reserve, 4°35'N 75°28'W, at 2,600 m, 1988 and 1989 (S. Arango *in litt.* 1992, L. M. Renjifo *in litt.* 1992, whence coordinates); Sumapaz Natural Reserve, c.4°N 71°25'W, above Cabrera, where one was seen flying over secondary habitat in August 1991 (L. M. Renjifo *in litt.* 1992); and El Roble, 2,438 m, above Fusagasugá, south-west of Bogotá on the west slope, at c.4°23'N 74°19'W (specimens in AMNH). (*Caldas*) The subspecies *velezi* was discovered in 1986; it is known from four specimens taken in 1969 and 1976 at two localities, both above Manizales on the north-western face of Nevado del Ruiz, in Municipio de Manizales, near the border of Tolima, sites being Cuenca Hidrográfica de "Río Blanco", 2,450 m, and Hacienda La Morena (Bosque del Taira), 2,400 m; several additional sightings of flocks above Manizales between 1969 and 1985 were at elevations between 2,250 and 2,650 m, at least one of these being at a reforestation plot in the Gallinazo watershed (Graves and Uribe Restrepo 1989); two were seen on the río Blanco at 2,400 m in December 1991 (J. A. Giraldo *in litt.* 1992).

There are recent sight records of *Hapalopsittaca* parrots, possibly of this form (at Finca Merenberg considerable red on the face was noted) from the upper Magdalena valley: in 1973 on the east slope of the Central Andes in Puracé National Park, Cauca department; in 1976 on the west slope of the East Andes in Cueva de los Guácharos National Park, Huila department, at 1°35'N 76°00'W; and in 1976 on the east slope of the Central Andes at Finca Merenberg, Huila department, at 2°14'N 76°08'W (Ridgely and Gaulin 1980, Hilty and Brown 1986). These records may indicate that the range of *velezi* extends south along the east slope of the Central Andes to the head of the Magdalena valley (Graves and Uribe Restrepo 1989; see also Distribution under Fuertes's Parrot *Hapalopsittaca fuertesi*).

POPULATION The species is very locally distributed in Venezuela (Phelps and Phelps 1958), and its status in the country is critical (Desenne and Strahl 1991). In Colombia it is rare, with no recent records from the northern part of the East Andes (Hilty and Brown 1986), although some substantial and hitherto remote forest areas still do exist within its range, particularly in Santander and Boyacá (Ridgely 1981a). Although Chapman (1917a) recorded it as "common" at El Roble, a region now completely deforested, no-one has since reported it in any numbers (Ridgely 1981a). There have been several sightings of flocks, presumably of *velezi*, above Manizales between 1969 and 1985, the largest and latest being of 25 individuals (Graves and Uribe Restrepo 1989), but unless its range is found to be considerably larger than currently known, the total population of *velezi* must be small. Other recent records of *Hapalopsittaca* parrots in Venezuela and Colombia are of two to seven individuals (Hilty and Brown 1986, C. S. Balchin verbally 1989), and so few that the total population would seem to be very small. It is possible that the species has invaded the Central Andes of Colombia in the course of this century (Graves and Uribe Restrepo 1989; see also account of Fuertes's Parrot).

ECOLOGY The Rusty-faced Parrot mainly inhabits very wet cloud-forest at 2,500 to 3,000 m, sometimes ranging down to 2,000 m into adjacent subtropical forest (Chapman 1917a, Meyer de Schauensee and Phelps 1978, Ridgely 1981a, Hilty and Brown 1986), although the subspecies *velezi* has as yet been recorded only between 2,250 and 2,650 m, albeit in *Alnus acuminata* reforestation plots as well as in patches of cloud-forest (Graves and Uribe Restrepo 1989). It probably usually flies high above the forest like its close relative the Red-faced Parrot *H. pyrrhops* (see relevant account), in pairs or groups of four to seven (Ridgely 1981a, Hilty and Brown 1986), although as many as 25 *velezi* have been seen together (Graves and Uribe Restrepo 1989); it perches conspicuously in treetops (Hilty and Brown 1985, C. S. Balchin verbally 1989). The type-specimen of *velezi*, taken on 20 July 1976, had seeds and fruit in its stomach, and inactive gonads (Graves and Uribe Restrepo 1989). Birds in Carpanta Biological Reserve have been seen eating *Clusia* fruit and the berries of mistletoes (S. Arango *in litt.* 1992); this conforms with the perception that the genus *Hapalopsittaca* may exploit mistletoes extensively (see Ecology under Red-faced Parrot). There appear to be no breeding data beyond the inactivity of the type of *velezi* in July.

THREATS Up to the end of the 1970s the Rusty-faced Parrot had never been held in captivity, probably not even locally (Ridgely 1981a); even in the 1980s there was little evidence of trade, at least in Venezuela (Desenne and Strahl 1991). All the subspecies have declined seriously owing to widespread forest destruction (Ridgely 1981a); thus for example the one area where the species was ever described as common (El Roble in Colombia) is now entirely cleared (see Population), and the forest within its range in western Venezuela is being rapidly destroyed, such that the two protected areas there, El Tamá and Sierra Nevada National Parks, are among the most threatened in Venezuela (Desenne and Strahl 1991). The inclusion in the El Tamá National Park management plan of a provision for a mining concession covering 10,000 ha (within the park) is especially worrying (M. L. Goodwin *in litt.* 1992).

MEASURES TAKEN In Venezuela the species occurs in Sierra Nevada National Park and presumably El Tamá National Park (see Distribution), but this is of little comfort (see Threats). In Colombia Los Nevados (possibly), Puracé, Cueva de los Guácharos and Chingaza National Parks all hold the species, at least seasonally, as does Finca Merenberg (Hilty and Brown 1986, Graves and Uribe Restrepo 1989), Carpanta Biological Reserve (for which see *Fundación Natura Ann. Rep.* 1989: 5-6; 1990: 4-6) and Sumapaz Natural Reserve.

MEASURES PROPOSED Establishment of additional protected forest areas is obviously very much needed, as is more effective protection of those areas which have already been established (Ridgely 1981a); current efforts to protect forests in the relevant protected areas, namely Chingaza, Carpanta and Sumapaz, deserve greater support, the first needing help with its lower forest, the second two being too small for good populations, while the Valle de Jesus Forest should be legally protected (L. M. Renjifo *in litt.* 1992). Clearly more work must be done on the distribution and ecology of this species in both countries, with particular emphasis on determining management options (Desenne and Strahl 1991). The forests in the Cordillera de Mérida require urgent protection (this especially applies to forests in the Sierra Nevada and El Táma National Parks, Venezuela), not only for this species, but also for the 25 other endemic birds found there (ICBP 1992, Crosby *et al.* in prep.), of which five are threatened, namely: Northern Helmeted Curassow *Pauxi pauxi*, Táchira Emerald *Amazilia distans* (at lower altitudes), Táchira Antpitta *Grallaria chthonia*, Hooded Antpitta *Grallaricula cucullata* and Rufous-browed Hemispingus *Hemispingus goeringi* (see relevant accounts: also Remarks 1 under Flame-winged Parakeet *Pyrrhura calliptera*). A number of other areas are important for Rusty-faced Parrot, and in turn harbour other threatened species: (1) Chingaza National Park and Carpanta Biological Reserve also embrace a population of Bogotá Rail *Rallus semiplumbeus*; (2) the río Blanco watershed appears to be an ideal area for protection, and harbours a population of Bicoloured Antpitta *Grallaria rufocinerea*; (3) Puracé National Park holds populations of five other threatened species which are listed in the equivalent section under Bicoloured Antpitta; and (4) Cueva de los Guácharos National Park (where this species probably occurs) holds four other threatened species which are listed in the equivalent section under Moustached Antpitta *G. alleni*.

REMARKS The Rusty-faced Parrot was considered conspecific with the Red-faced Parrot (see relevant account) by Peters (1937), a treatment not followed here. Fuertes's Parrot (see relevant account), though first described as a full species (Chapman 1912), was later also treated as a race of *amazonina* by Peters (1937), a view adopted by several subsequent authors (e.g. Forshaw 1973, Morony *et al.* 1975), but with the finding that the new form *velezi* was virtually sympatric with *fuertesi* it became evident that the latter must again have full specific status (Graves and Uribe Restrepo 1989).

FUERTES'S PARROT *Hapalopsittaca fuertesi* E[1]

This very rare and local parrot is known only from humid temperate forest on the west slope of the Central Andes of Colombia near the border of Quindío, Risaralda and Tolima departments, where it is threatened by habitat destruction. The only definite records since its discovery in 1911 are at Alto Quindío from 1989 to the present.

DISTRIBUTION Fuertes's Parrot (see Remarks under Rusty-faced Parrot *Hapalopsittaca amazonina*) is endemic to the west slope of the Central Andes of Colombia, where it is known with certainty only from the type-series dating from 1911 and by observations since 1989. The type-series consists of seven specimens collected at two localities some 40 km apart: Laguneta, 3,140 m (Chapman 1912), on the west slope of the Central Andes, Quindío department, 4°35'N 75°30'W (Paynter and Traylor 1981), and Santa Isabel, 3,810 m (Chapman 1912), on the west slope of Nevado de Santa Isabel in the Central Andes, Risaralda department, 4°47'N 75°28'W (Paynter and Traylor 1981), in August and September 1911 (specimens in AMNH). In 1980, *Hapalopsittaca* parrots, either this species or Rusty-faced Parrots (see relevant account), were sighted above Santa Rosa de Cabal at 3,750 m in a small forest remnant near río Campoalegre, on the west slope of the Central Andes, Risaralda, close to the Tolima border (Orejuela and Alberico 1980, Orejuela 1985). From 1989 to 1991 birds were seen in the Alto Quindío Acaime Natural Reserve, 4°37'N 75°28'W, and in the nearby Cañon del Quindío Natural Reserve, Quindío department (Renjifo 1991, L. M. Renjifo *in litt.* 1992). Sightings at the head of the Magdalena valley (Hilty and Brown 1986) may be of *fuertesi* or (more likely) *amazonina* (Ridgely 1980).

POPULATION The fact that *fuertesi* was never observed by A. A. Allen and L. E. Miller during their expedition to the Central Andes in 1911, but only by their field assistant, may indicate that it was then uncommon and that *H. amazonina velezi* (which they did not record) was not yet present (Graves and Uribe Restrepo 1989). The finding of *velezi* in 1969 and later years may indicate that *fuertesi* has been displaced (or possibly genetically swamped: NK) by that form sometime between 1911 and 1969 (Graves and Uribe Restrepo 1989). If the two replace each other altitudinally (see discussion under Ecology), then the 1980 sightings at 3,750 m at Santa Rosa de Cabal (see Distribution) would seem to indicate that *fuertesi* still exists in the region, but the population would be very small. Meanwhile, the only certainly known population survives in the Acaime and Cañon del Quindío reserves in Alto Quindío, where the average flock size in 7.9 and the largest group seen consisted of 25 birds: the population is very small (L. M. Renjifo *in litt.* 1992).

ECOLOGY The habitat at 3,140 m at Laguneta was fairly open (possibly therefore disturbed) forest, with a few small palms and tree ferns; the large trees, of which some were oaks, were rather sparingly branched and thinly leaved, and heavily clad in epiphytes (Chapman 1917a). The altitudinal range of the species at Alto Quindío is from 2,610 to 3,490 m, but 80% of the records have been in the narrow band at 2,900-3,150 m (Renjifo 1991). The known elevational range of *H. amazonina velezi* (2,250-2,650 m) and of *fuertesi* (2,610-3,810 m) suggests that the two replace each other altitudinally; however, already in 1911 forest was mostly cleared below 2,835 m on the trail to Santa Isabel, so the lower elevational limits of *fuertesi* may have been artificially truncated (Graves and Uribe Restrepo 1989). The distance between collecting localities for *fuertesi* and *velezi* is small (less than 25 km) relative to the dispersal abilities of *Hapalopsittaca* (Graves and Uribe Restrepo 1989; see also Ecology under accounts of Red-faced Parrot *H. pyrrhops* and Rusty-faced Parrot). There appear to be no data on food or breeding, but the genus's possible dependence on mistletoes is mentioned in Ecology under Red-faced Parrot.

THREATS Extensive clearance of forest in the region of the type-locality was already advanced in 1911 (Chapman 1917a), and is now widespread and thorough (Ridgely 1981a). Possible competition from the Rusty-faced Parrot is mentioned in Population and Ecology above. There are, however, no immediate threats to the population in Alto Quindío (L. M. Renjifo *in litt.* 1992).

MEASURES TAKEN In 1973, the establishment of Los Nevados National Park, covering 380 km^2 at 2,600-5,400 m in portions of Tolima, Risaralda, Quindío and Caldas departments, resulted in the protection of three snow-covered peaks, Ruiz, Santa Isabel and Tolima (Hilty and Brown 1986); but there is no evidence that the species occurs within its limits. It is known to survive only in the Acaime and Cañon del Quindío Natural Reserves, Alto Quindío (see Distribution).

MEASURES PROPOSED Highest priority needs to be given to support for the Acaime and Cañon del Quindío Natural Reserves, where the ecology of Fuertes's Parrot, especially in respect of feeding and breeding, should be researched, and every step taken to ensure optimum management to maximize the population there (a number of other threatened species occur in the Acaime reserve, and are listed in the equivalent section under Bicoloured Antpitta *Grallaria rufocinerea*); expansion of both reserves, which are probably too small for long-term security, is strongly recommended (L. M. Renjifo *in litt.* 1992) and, given that these two protected areas may hold the world's only population of this beautiful parrot, this has the force of an imperative (being addressed by ICBP and Fundación Herencia Verde: see under Bicoloured Antpitta). The possibility that the species occurs in the Los Nevados National Park (and the adjacent Navarco Nature Reserve: J. I. Hernández Camacho verbally 1991) should be investigated, and appropriate management must follow if it does (other threatened species known to occur in this park, and which should be considered in any conservation initiatives, are listed in the equivalent section under Rufous-fronted Parakeet *Bolborhynchus ferrugineifrons*). The remnant patch of forest in which it may have been sighted in 1980 and adjacent habitat should also be investigated and protected (Ridgely 1981a: see also equivalent section under Moustached Antpitta *G. alleni*).

RED-FACED PARROT *Hapalopsittaca pyrrhops* E[2]

This rare parrot is confined to the upper montane forests on the eastern Andean slopes at 2,500-3,500 m in the southern half of Ecuador and immediately adjacent Peru, and is threatened by habitat destruction.

DISTRIBUTION The Red-faced Parrot (see Remarks 1) is only known from a few records and a few localities in central and southern Ecuador and immediately adjacent Peru (Parker *et al.* 1985).

Ecuador Traceable records (see Remarks 2) in the country (north to south, most coordinates from Paynter and Traylor 1977) are from three provinces, as follows:

(*Morona-Santiago*) 2-4 birds seen on three occasions, October 1976, at Planchas and El Placer (a few kilometres upstream from Planchas) at 2,800-2,900 m in the upper río Palora valley, both on the east slope of the Andes in the new Sangay National Park (Ridgely 1980);

(*Azuay*) two birds in June 1978 near Laguna Llaviuco, Cajas National Recreation Area (Ridgely 1980), and 1-5 birds seen on 10 occasions in August/September 1987 at Río Mazan, adjacent to Cajas National Recreation Area, 2°52'S 79°08'W at 3,150-3,500 m, most at 3,200 m (King 1989; coordinates read from LANDSAT 1987 and IGM 1981); Gima at the headwaters of río Palmar, c.22 km east of Girón, and c.35 km south of Cuenca, 3°12'S 78°57'W, 1877 (in one case March) (two specimens in AMNH, BMNH; also Chapman 1926); four birds in July 1978 at "Pongo", 2,900 m, south-west of Girón (Ridgely 1980);

(*Loja*) small groups feeding on 9 and 10 May, and a flock of 16 roosting 10-11 May 1989 at 2,850-3,000 m between Selva Alegre and Manu, Chilla mountains, at 3°31'S and 79°22'W (Bloch *et al.* 1991), with 18 at Selva Alegre on 14 April 1992 (Toyne *et al.* in prep.); San Lucas, which is at 2,490 m in the pass between the Cordoncillo and Chilla mountains, 3°45'S 79°15'W, 1876 (Salvin 1876; specimen in BMNH); Acanama near San Lucas, Cordillera Cordoncillo, at 3°42'S 79°13'W, where local reports were confirmed when a group of c.20 were seen at 3,200 m in September 1991 (R. Williams verbally 1991; coordinates from Bloch *et al.* 1991); Cajanuma, Podocarpus National Park, at 4°05'S 79°10'W, where a pair was seen in February and the species heard in May 1989, at c.2,850 m (Bloch *et al.* 1991).

Peru Pairs were recorded in October 1977 and June 1978 on Cerro Chinguela at 2,530-2,960 m, Piura department, Peru (Parker *et al.* 1985), 5°07'S 79°23'W (Stephens and Traylor 1983), with a single bird there in August 1989 (B. M. Whitney *in litt.* 1991).

POPULATION In Ecuador the species is very uncommon and local, all but two sightings being of 1-5 birds (see Distribution), while in Peru it is very rare, with only single pairs observed at the one locality known (Parker *et al.* 1985).

ECOLOGY The Red-faced Parrot inhabits very wet upper montane cloud-forest and low, open forest and shrubbier growth near the páramos at 2,500-3,500 m (Ridgely 1980, 1981a, Parker *et al.* 1985, J. R. King verbally 1988, Bloch *et al.* 1991). It typically flies 30-50 m above the forest (J. R. King verbally 1988, Bloch *et al.* 1991) in singles, pairs, or groups of four to five, rarely more (Ridgely 1980, 1981a, Parker *et al.* 1985, J. R. King *in litt.* 1988, Bloch *et al.* 1991).

The Black-winged Parrot *Hapalopsittaca melanotis*, observed in the yungas of Cochabamba, Bolivia, in October 1991, proved to be particularly fond of fruits of cloud-forest mistletoes of the genus *Gaiadendron*, with flocks of up to 50 individuals apparently wandering in search of areas with an abundance of these plants (J. Fjeldså verbally 1991); it may well be that the Red-faced Parrot has a similar preference. At Río Mazan, Ecuador, Red-faced Parrots perched conspicuously atop trees (*Podocarpus* aff. *sprucei*) (J. R. King verbally 1988). In the Chilla mountains in May the species was observed in forest 20-22 m tall, and foraged secretively 12-20 m up within dense canopy, once down to the undergrowth some 6 m up; the trees used for feeding were not identified, but were never *Podocarpus*, which is frequent in the area (Bloch *et al.* 1991). However, a study of birds between March and May 1992 revealed their use of the fruits of a *Miconia* sp., berries of a *Viburnum* sp., shoots, flowers and seeds of two *Weinmannia* spp. trees, the flowers and pods of a *Clethra* sp. (all these being mature trees some 25 m tall), and parts (not specified) of two ericaceous trees, *Cavendishia bracteata* and *Disterigma alaternoides* (Toyne *et al.* in prep.).

At Río Mazan a pair was recorded on three occasions, 28-30 August 1987; over 9-16 September single birds were seen four times, and on 26 September a flock of five birds was seen (what was presumably the same flock was briefly glimpsed or heard on 25 and 27 September); despite intensive fieldwork by observers familiar with the call, no birds were recorded there from 28 September to 9 October (J. R. King *in litt.* 1988). These observations suggest that a pair bred there from August through the first three weeks of September and, after rearing three young, left the valley at the end of September (J. R. King *in litt.* 1988; also King 1989).

THREATS The Red-faced Parrot has declined seriously owing to widespread forest destruction (Ridgely 1981a). In the Chilla Mountains, where it has been found most numerous, forest clearance is severe at the elevations it inhabits, and what may be one of the last suitable forests there, a 4 km^2 patch, will, at the present rate of burning and felling, have disappeared in a few years (Bloch *et al.* 1991). The problems facing Podocarpus National Park are outlined in Threats under Bearded Guan *Penelope barbata*.

MEASURES TAKEN Sangay National Park, Cajas National Recreation Area and Podocarpus National Park, Ecuador, all hold small numbers of the species, at least seasonally (Ridgely 1980, J. R. King *in litt.* 1988, Bloch *et al.* 1991). At least at Cajas, remnant forest patches were constantly being whittled away in 1978 (Ridgely 1981a), but the adjacent Río Mazan area, where this parrot is also found, is now apparently effectively protected (see equivalent section under Violet-throated Metaltail *Metallura baroni*).

MEASURES PROPOSED An effort to protect the forest patch between Selva Alegre and Manu in the Chilla mountains should be made, to protect not only the present species and the Bearded Guan, which also has an especially dense population there (see relevant account), but also an unusually high diversity of other birds (Bloch *et al.* 1991). The need to assure the survival of this area, Podocarpus National Park and Cerro Chinguela is indicated in the equivalent section under Bearded Guan.

REMARKS (1) Although formerly considered to be a full species, *Hapalopsittaca pyrrhops* was treated as a race of the Rusty-faced Parrot *H. amazonina* by Peters (1937). We here restore it as a full species, a treatment advocated by Ridgely (1981a) and Graves and Uribe Restrepo (1989). (2) A young bird from the "upper Napo" (Ménégaux 1908) was considered likely to refer to this form (Chapman 1926); if correct, this record would extend the species's range into north-central Ecuador. The other problematic record concerns the type-locality, Santa Rita (Salvin 1876), which could not be located by Paynter and Traylor (1977); there are two skins, collected by C. Buckley in 1880, in BMNH.

RED-NECKED AMAZON *Amazona arausiaca* R[11]

This amazon is confined to Dominica, where it occurs chiefly in the forests around Morne Diablotin but, having suffered from a combination of habitat loss at lower levels, hunting, trade and hurricanes, in recent years it has benefited from joint government and non-government efforts to protect its habitat and sensitize local citizens to its needs, and its numbers have risen from possibly as few as 150 in 1980 to possibly more than 500 in 1992.

DISTRIBUTION The Red-necked Amazon is endemic to Dominica, West Indies, where its population is centred on the slopes of Morne Diablotin in the north of the island, but with a tiny outlying population in the central east and the possibility of some birds surviving in the far south (see Figure 3 in Evans 1991). Its centre of abundance may always have been Morne Diablotin, where it was "found more commonly than in any other part of the island" by Bond (1941b), although it formerly extended beyond the range of Imperial Amazon *Amazona imperialis* (see relevant account) throughout the mountainous interior of the island (Bond 1928b), including the northern peninsula or Morne aux Diables (where in 1992 it was found once more, apparently resident), and often visited trees along the Indian River near Portsmouth in August–October (Nichols *et al.* 1976), where in fact small numbers continue to be recorded (Evans 1991) and where, in the 1920s, numbers used to be sold cheaply at Portsmouth market (Porter 1930b). From Figure 3 in Evans (1991) it appears that the species has undergone a range contraction since 1950 far more notable than that of the Imperial Amazon; despite sightings throughout the south of the island in 1981, following the devastations of two hurricanes (see Threats), birds have evidently largely disappeared from south of Morne Diablotin, at least for the present (details of its 1978, i.e. pre-hurricane, distribution are in Evans 1991). In the two years to 1990, however, some recovery and expansion of range back into lower-lying areas in the north and north-east of the island were being noted (Evans 1991), and in 1991 and 1992 the species has been seen west of Morne Trois Pitons in the south of the island, near Pont Cassé west towards Cochrane, with sporadic sightings also in the central region around Emerald Pool, above Castle Bruce and the Carib territory: all of which possibly indicates a return to areas occupied before Hurricane David (P. G. H. Evans *in litt.* 1992).

POPULATION In the nineteenth century (or at least in the late 1870s and in March–May 1890) the species was thought rarer ("not abundant") than the Imperial Amazon, although seen in rather larger flocks (Verrill 1892); in 1880 it was reported as "now scarce and... seldom seen away from the deepest woods of the widest part of the island", the offer of a "good reward for a dead specimen" producing no result (Lawrence 1880a). Whether this relative rarity was real or apparent, and whichever explanation of it was true, are matters deserving further consideration. However, at the start of the twentieth century Verrill (1905) reported that, although "in 1890 I found this parrot far rarer and more difficult to procure than the 'Ciceroo' [Imperial Amazon] and confined almost entirely to the windward coast... it is now far more abundant than the [Imperial Amazon]"; Bond (1928b) judged it probably the most numerous of the four Lesser Antillean parrots, and a non-specialist observer in 1929 found it common, seeing it many times daily (17 in one day) on Morne Diablotin and several times on Morne Trois Pitons (Howes 1929); curiously, however, a third observer at around this time insisted it was "much rarer than is generally thought" and believed that, on account of its greater vulnerability to hunting in the lowlands, "twenty years or so will see the end of this very interesting species" (Porter 1930b). In 1971 D. Lack (*in litt.* 1971 to P. Barclay-Smith) reported it "in reasonably large numbers on Diablotin and reasonably safe", but elsewhere in the 1970s it was becoming rare: thus around 1950 one observer recollected "clouds" on Morne Negres Marrons although by the mid-1970s few if any remained there or indeed on Morne Trois Pitons (Nichols *et al.* 1976), and the general consensus was that it was "not seen in the same numbers or in the same places that it was ten years ago" (Swank and Julien 1975).

Fieldwork targeted at or at least encompassing the species has been more or less continuous since the mid-1970s, resulting initially in informed guesses by three observers of 400, 250-300 and 350 birds remaining in 1975 (Nichols *et al.* 1976), the last figure gaining the greatest currency through several repetitions (e.g. in Nichols 1976, 1977b; see Remarks 1). However, the reported sighting in 1977 of a single flock of around 350 on Hampstead Ridge north of Morne Diablotin suggested that the 1975 total estimate of 350 may have been too low (Snyder and Snyder 1979; *ICBP Newsletter* 2[1], 1980). The combined impacts of the two hurricanes in 1979 and 1980 (see Threats) was estimated to have halved the population to 150-225 (Anon. 1981a). Nichols (1981c) put the figure at 200; Evans (1986a) estimated around 300 in 1985 but, owing to fuller data analysis rather than any event, back at around 200 in 1987 (Evans 1988a), although a genuine recovery now seems to be under way with an estimated 300 in May 1990 (Evans 1991; for upper Picard valley, 1978-1990, with the clear effect of the 1979 hurricane, see Figure 6 in Evans 1991). Unanalysed results from fieldwork in April 1992 suggest that the current total population is likely to exceed 500 but to be less than 1,000, probably nearer the former than the latter; it is possible that the 1990 estimate was too low, rather than that there was a very large increase in the period 1990-1992 (P. G. H. Evans *in litt.* 1992).

Nichols (1981c) lamented the fact that the private Dominican bird-keeper D. Green had 15 birds captive in mid-1980 but only five in mid-1981, a significant loss of the then total global population.

ECOLOGY The Red-necked Amazon occupies the canopy of rainforest in the mountainous interior, but concentrating at lower altitudes than the Imperial (300-800 m as opposed to 600-1,300 m) (Evans 1988a, 1991). It ranges as high as Imperial (see Figure 9 in Evans 1991) but tolerates some agricultural activity close by and will return (at least at first) to old feeding areas after their conversion to (fruit-)farms (Nichols *et al.* 1976, Anon. 1981b). Birds formerly moved to at least one lowland (coastal) area in the period August–October (see Distribution), and would then (at least sometimes) be in "open country" (Porter 1930b).

Ecological separation of Red-necked from Imperial Amazon, and a list of plants whose fruits are eaten by both, are given in Ecology under the latter; the Red-neck is known also to take (unless otherwise stated the fruits of) coco poule *Cordia elliptica* and *C. laevigata*, pistolet or pipirie *Pithecellobium jupunba*, mauricif *Byrsonima martinicensis*, the palm *Euterpe dominicana*, wild almond *Anacardium occidentale* (buds), penipice *Pouteria multiflora*, pommier *Dussia martinicensis*, caconier *Ormosia monosperma*, caconier blanc *O. krugii*, zolivier *Buchenavia capitata*, savonette *Lonchocarpus* sp. (fruits and buds), ti citron *Ilex macfadenii*, feuille cigene *Anthurium* sp. and cord sec (a vine) (Evans 1988a; also Anon. 1981b), and while bois cote *Tapura antillana* and kaklin *Clusia venosa* were two of three species listed as (usually) only taken by Imperials (Evans 1988a) both were listed for both parrots in the wake of Hurricane David (Zamore 1980) when the Red-neck was also noted to feed near ground level on young shoots (Gregoire 1981). In the nineteenth century birds were reported to descend valleys to feed on wild guavas (Lawrence 1878), and in the 1920s "their chief food during certain seasons of the year" was reported to be "the seeds of one of the huge forest palms" (Porter 1930b). Butler (1989) reported observations of Red-necked Amazons occasionally feeding in trees beneath the canopy layer and even sometimes settling on the ground. Unfortunately the species also shows a propensity for cultivated citrus, which is likely to establish it as an enemy of farmers within its range (P. G. H. Evans *in litt.* 1992).

The main breeding season for both species of Dominican amazon is February–June (particularly March–May), coinciding with the dry season and perhaps therefore related to greater food abundance during the nestling and fledgling period (Evans 1988a). The first three nests discovered during research in the mid-1970s were all in gommiers *Dacryodes excelsa*, all found in May, and all with one young (two well-feathered, the third not described), but the fourth was in an unidentified tree with two young (Nichols *et al.* 1976, Nichols 1977b); subsequently both gommier and chataignier *Sloanea berteriana*, two dominant rainforest trees, were found to be primarily used for nesting (Evans 1988a), although a bois diable *Licania ternatensis* has also been used (Zamore 1982). The reproductive rate is low, with two eggs being laid perhaps only every second year and pairs seldom raising more than one young per clutch (Gregoire 1981; also Evans 1988a); nevertheless, at one nest-site (presumably) the same pair (reputedly) reared two young in each of three successive years (Amberger 1989a). Age of first breeding and whether nest-sites are limiting remain unknown (Evans 1988a). A fledged young was still clearly smaller than its parents, October 1980 (Anon. 1981b). During November–January birds tend to be more nomadic, owing apparently to a relative scarcity of food, and will fly long distances in pairs or small flocks; about an hour after their arrival in a feeding area, birds tend to form large, loose feeding flocks, e.g. 50-70 in the Syndicate–Picard area, 50 in Woodford Hill heights, and 70-100 in the Bense–Dos d'Ane heights (Anon. 1981b; also Evans 1988a, Butler 1989, P. G. H. Evans *in litt.* 1992). The greater gregariousness of Red-necked than Imperial Amazon has long been noted (e.g. Lawrence 1878, Verrill 1892, Nichols *et al.* 1976, Evans 1988a). Comments on diurnal activity and roosting, given in Ecology under Imperial Amazon, apply almost identically for this species.

THREATS The introductory paragraph in Threats under Imperial Amazon is relevant also for this species.

Habitat destruction Because a lower altitude species than the Imperial, the Red-necked Amazon was considered to be at much greater risk from clearance of forest (Gochfeld 1974, King 1978-1979, Gregoire 1981). This assumption has not been borne out by developments, although the incidents reported below of pairs competing unsuccessfully with Imperial pairs for nest-sites suggest that some displacements caused by deforestation have taken place. Further information about habitat loss is in Threats under Imperial Amazon.

Hunting Hunting was the most serious factor limiting the population through into the 1970s. The species was shot for food, September–February, in the 1870s (Lawrence 1878), and this was doubtless what made it so wild and difficult for Verrill (1892) to procure in 1890; it was still being hunted in the 1920s (Bond 1928b, Porter 1929), with Porter (1930b) being told of such things as (a) "twelve a day being killed by white residents who were fond of eating Parrot-pie", (b) a man shooting 30 dead in the process of winging two that could be sold as pets, and (c) a man in the interior being able to "trace the passage of a small flock... from hill to hill by the reports from the rifles of the native gunners as they followed the birds from one part to another". By the mid-1970s hunting was still the single most serious threat to the species (Nichols *et al.* 1976); indeed, because more accessible altitudinally, it was considered to be in greater danger from hunting than the Imperial Amazon (Gochfeld 1974). Even after the 1979 hurricane and in spite of Forestry Division efforts, there were believed to be "strong hunting pressures" on the species (Snyder and Snyder 1979; *ICBP Newsletter* 2[1], 1980; Zamore 1980, Gregoire 1981), and in November 1981 four Frenchmen from Guadeloupe were apprehended while hunting in the Forest Reserve (Anon. 1981b); nevertheless, throughout the rest of the 1980s there was little evidence of other than occasional shooting (P. G. H. Evans *in litt.* 1992).

Trade Owing at least in part to the inaccessibility of nests from which to take young, hunting for cage-birds involved the highly destructive practice of "wing-shooting", which resulted in the accidental deaths of many birds (as reported, e.g., by Lawrence 1878, Porter 1929). Gregoire (1981) estimated that 40 birds (of each species) were being shot every year (i.e. even in the 1970s) as a consequence of this practice; much of this was apparently from local rather than international interest (Nichols *et al.* 1976). However, the fact that illegally exported birds had been able to remain in foreign hands (Christian 1991) had been noted by other European aviculturists, and this was thought to be likely to contribute to further attempts to capture and smuggle birds abroad (Nichols 1981c); but the situation is now considered under control (see Measures Taken under Imperial Amazon).

Natural causes: hurricanes General background to the two hurricanes of 1979 and 1980 is given in Threats under Imperial Amazon. The first of these is believed to have halved the number of Red-necked Amazons (see Population); but despite the loss of fruit in the second, the observation of a fledged young in October (Anon. 1981b) indicates that its effects may have been more limited.

Natural causes: predators and competitors Possible predators include opossum *Didelphis marsupialis*, rats *Rattus*, boas *Constrictor constrictor* and Broad-winged Hawks *Buteo platypterus*, although only the first, believed introduced in the later nineteenth century, has been thought in any way serious (Nichols *et al.* 1976). Owing to their greater sympatry in lower rainforest, competition for nest-sites from Pearly-eyed Thrashers *Margarops fuscatus* was thought to be more serious for Red-necked than for Imperial Amazons, and interactions were witnessed at the first nest found; nevertheless, they were judged not to have been a major force in the decline of the Red-neck in the 25 years to 1975, being insufficiently common while potential nest-sites remained abundant (Nichols 1976, Nichols *et al.* 1976). The idea that Red-necked Amazons might be in direct competition with Imperials (see, e.g., King 1978-1979) cannot be confirmed, with no interactions when seen feeding together ("feeding and living in harmony": Porter 1929) and with evidence that both were in steep decline together (Nichols *et al.* 1976); however, nest-site competition between the species (won by Imperials) was witnessed twice in 1981 and attributed to Red-necks being forced into higher altitudes by habitat destruction below (Anon. 1981b). Escape of exotic parrot pets might pose a threat in the future, with two African Greys *Psittacus erithacus* reported flying in a flock of Red-necks in the early 1970s (Nichols *et al.* 1976).

MEASURES TAKEN These are discussed in the equivalent section under Imperial Amazon.

MEASURES PROPOSED These are discussed in the equivalent section under Imperial Amazon. It is, however, worth noting that perhaps the earliest proposal to save this species was Porter's (1930b) idea, inspired by the colony of Greater Birds-of-paradise *Paradisaea apoda* that had been established on Little Tobago in 1909 (see ffrench 1992), of translocating a number to "some small uninhabited island" to be maintained "under strict supervision".

REMARKS Anon. (1981a) cited "Nichols and Nichols" as the source of information that there were 300-450 birds present in 1972, something which hence crops up even in Evans (1988a); but there is no evidence in any writing by any Nichols that 1972 was a year used for estimating numbers or that "300-450" were then indicated as population figures. These figures may therefore be forestry personnel assessments (P. G. H. Evans *in litt.* 1992).

YELLOW-SHOULDERED AMAZON *Amazona barbadensis* K[12]

The Yellow-shouldered Amazon is a bird of xerophytic vegetation ranging disjunctly along the north Venezuelan coastal region onto Margarita, La Blanquilla and the Dutch island of Bonaire. Numbers on the mainland seem generally low; those on the islands appear to fluctuate, but have all declined. The species is widely exploited for trade, which at least in Venezuela serves a strong internal pet market. Tourist and associated developments on Margarita are a serious threat. The mainland requires systematic survey.

DISTRIBUTION The Yellow-shouldered Amazon occurs in a few disjunct areas along the northern coastlands of Venezuela and on the Venezuelan islands of Margarita and La Blanquilla, plus Bonaire in the Netherlands Antilles, having become extinct on Aruba and possibly also Curaçao in the Netherlands Antilles (for subspecies see Remarks 1).

Venezuela *mainland* Although the species is generally indicated as from arid regions of the coast (Phelps and Phelps 1958), records relate to two highly disjunct general areas, in the west in the states of Falcón and Lara and in the east in those of Anzoátegui and Sucre, within which populations appear themselves to be local and disjunct; the map (Figure 3) in Desenne and Strahl (1991) is not entirely accurate, given the details below, but offers the postulation that the species might extend across the top of the Lago de Maracaibo onto the Península de Guajira, and hence into Colombia.

Within the western general area, the species can be seen for sale along the roadside anywhere between Maracaibo (in Zulia state) and Puerto Cabello (in Carabobo state) (R. B. Ramírez *in litt.* 1988), although site of sale and site of capture obviously need not be identical. Field surveys indicated that the species occurs in Falcón as follows: in the west from the Zulia border east through Casigua (specimens in COP; at 11°02'N 71°01'W in OG 1961) to around Dabajuro (Phelps and Phelps 1958, Ridgely 1981a); in the central north around Coro (Hartert 1893), 20 km south of Coro on the Barquisimeto road (Arndt 1989), 85 km inland at Agua Clara (Arndt 1989), evidently on the same road since at 11°10'N 69°59'W in OG (1961), and around Las Veritas, 10°55'N 70°12'W, and indeed throughout the Distrito Democracia, chiefly along the ríos Pedregal and Japure (H. Dos Santos *per* C. Bosque *in litt.* 1992, whence coordinates); the Península de Paraguaná (Voous 1957, 1983, Low 1972; see Remarks 2) which, although cited by Ridgely (1981a) as an area from which the species is inexplicably absent, holds small numbers in a private reserve managed by Fundación Bioma at Piedra Honda, 11°57'N 70°00'W, in the Sierra de San Luís (Desenne and Strahl 1991, H. Dos Santos *per* C. Bosque *in litt.* 1992, whence coordinates); in Lara to the west of Barquisimeto, in March 1975 (Low 1981; see Remarks 3); and at Sanare, at the junction of the Chichiriviche road with the highway from Morón to Coro (M. Pearman *in litt.* 1991).

Within the eastern general area, records in Anzoátegui state are all from the north, around Puerto Píritu and between there and Barcelona, 40 km to the east (Phelps and Phelps 1958, Low 1981, Ridgely 1981a), birds repeatedly being found in the area (A. B. Altman *in litt.* 1988), although missed despite intensive searches in July 1988 (Arndt 1989); records in Sucre are from the Península de Araya (= Cariaco) in 1908 (Lowe 1909) and 1979 (G. Medina-Cuervo *in litt.* 1986), with a specific locality being Chacopata (S. Gorzula *in litt.* 1986), at 10°33'N 63°49'W (Office of Geography 1961).

Margarita Records from this large (950 km^2: Andrade 1987) island are from the western third (see Remarks 4) which comprises the Península de Macanao and its isthmus, and prior to recent studies they were notably at Robledar (= Robledal) and Boca de Pozo on the west coast (see Remarks 5), Punta de Tunar (= Punta Tunal) on the north coast (Yépez Tamayo 1964), San Francisco and the Barranco del Maiz in the centre (Yépez Tamayo 1964, Vierheilig and Vierheilig 1988), and Boca del Río and the mangroves of the Laguna de la Restinga which lies behind the long beach connecting Macanao to the main island (Lowe 1907b, Yépez Tamayo 1964, Vierheilig and Vierheilig 1988, Arndt 1989; see DCN 1964). However, recent work has indicated that, while the species is widespread on the peninsula (concentrating at well-wooded quebradas, and with a high proportion of records between sea level and 250 m), it does not breed (and perhaps never occurs; but see Remarks 6) in the Restinga mangroves, this being a misattribution based on Blue-crowned Parakeet *Aratinga acuticaudata* (K. M. Silvius *in litt.* 1992). There are four main roost-sites on Macanao, all at 50-150 m above sea level: Quebrada de la Chica, ríos San Francisco/Guainamal, río Chacaracual or La Montaña, and río Guayacancito (Silvius 1989).

La Blanquilla Lowe (1907a, 1911) found the species in the eastern part of this relatively small (50 km^2: Low 1983) island, most abundantly in January, while Cory's (1909) collector reported it from the west, to which the natives claimed it was confined; but Phelps (1948), too, found it in the east.

Netherlands Antilles *Bonaire* Most recorded localities, clearly forming the core of the species's range, lie in the hilly north-west portion of this medium-sized (280 km^2: Reijns and van der Salm 1981) island, west and north-west of Rincón. Within this area, moving clockwise from the north as read from CSD (1963), localities mentioned in the published literature are: Sabana, La Sana, Dos Pos (Poos), Montaña (= Montagne), Karpata, Lagún (Lake) Goto, Ceru Wecúa (Seroe Wekoewa) or Saliñ'e Tam (Saliña Dam, Tam), Brasiel, Saliña Frans, Boca Slagbaai, (Mount) Brandaris, Put Bronswinkel, Saliña Runchi and Saliña Bartol (Rooth 1968; also Hartert 1893, Rutten 1931, Phelps and Phelps 1951, Voous 1957, Reijns and van der Salm 1981); one further locality, Kernadoe (Low 1981; untraced on CSD 1963), is close to Fontein and about 1 km east of some radio antennae (R. Low *in litt.* 1991). Many more sites are marked without being named on the map in Reijns and van der Salm (1980, 1981), and others are named in the unpublished work of Spaans (1973), Mellink and Molina (1984) and Joordens (1985). Several of these localities in north-west Bonaire fall within the Washington-Slagbaai National Park (see Measures Taken). The two chief sites outside this area are both immediately north-east of Rincón, namely Onima (Low 1981, Voous 1983), marked as a small marsh on CSD (1963), and Fontein, a north-facing escarpment (Hartert 1893, Low 1981, 1983, Reijns and van der Salm 1981, Voous 1983). The map in Reijns and van der Salm (1980, 1981) indicates an otherwise undocumented area in the hilly country south of Rincón along the south-facing coast, extending east beyond Barcadera to the longitude of Fontein; Low's (1981) claim that birds appear south of Rincón only while food is scarce would therefore appear mistaken. However, all other localities mentioned do appear to reflect vagrancy by food-stressed birds, namely Kralendijk and to the south-east at Nikiboko, Wanapa and Lima (Rooth 1968, Low 1981). Voous (1983) also referred to the island of Klein Bonaire opposite Kralendijk as a site for the species, although it is not mentioned by other researchers and from CSD (1963) appears completely flat and covered in rock and scrub. An untraced locality is Terra Cora, where a bird (in ZMA) was collected in April 1978.

Aruba Details of the species's former distribution on this island are given in Voous (1957).

Curaçao Evidence that birds ever occurred on Curaçao is tenuous and ancient (see Voous 1957, 1983), although its position in relation to Bonaire, Aruba and the Península de Paraguaná suggest they ought to have done. In the late 1970s some escaped cagebirds were reported from the hills of Sint Christoffel (Voous 1983).

POPULATION The evidence generally points towards the total population of the Yellow-shouldered Amazon being several thousands, but there are insufficient data for much confidence other than to doubt that the total is merely "in the order of a few hundreds – possibly exceeding one thousand" (Low 1983).

Venezuela *mainland* Although feared rare, a brief survey in March/April 1981 proved the species numerous in both Falcón and Anzoátegui, with no evidence of a recent decline (Ridgely 1981a). Ninety years earlier Hartert (1893) had found it common at Coro and being exported to the country's cities in large numbers; and as recently as July 1988 single birds and groups up to five were observed, with locals claiming it occurred in thousands around Coro and in good numbers further inland, all of which tended to be borne out by the numbers of birds held captive in local households (Arndt 1989). A roost at a village near Las Veritas (name and coordinates supplied) in Falcón held some 700 birds in November 1989, and local people described the bird as abundant in the district (H. Dos Santos *per* C. Bosque *in litt.* 1992). On the Península de Paraguaná only a small population of some 30-40 birds is known (H. Dos Santos *per* C. Bosque *in litt.* 1992). On the Península de Araya recently the species was seen frequently (several times per day) (G. Medina-Cuervo *in litt.* 1986). Other recent reports are of two groups (eight and three respectively) at Lago de Píritu, 10 km west of Puerto Píritu, and of seven birds seen midway from there to Barcelona, June 1991 (J. Swallow *in litt.* 1991), and at least 35 at the intersection of the Chichiriviche road with the Morón–Coro road, August 1990 (M. Pearman *in litt.* 1991). The situation is confused by local reports that the species is "not common" in Venezuela (Low 1981), by Arndt's (1989) failure to find it at all in Anzoátegui, and by the patchy ornithological coverage which has resulted in the records from Lara, Sucre and seemingly even the Península de Paraguaná (see Distribution) being omitted in the major summaries of the species (e.g. Meyer de Schauensee and Phelps 1978, Ridgely 1981a, Forshaw 1989).

Margarita On the Península de Macanao the species was relatively abundant in the early 1960s, with flocks of up to 30 being seen (Yépez Tamayo 1964). Three unrelated surveys of the peninsula in the late 1980s resulted in total estimates of 150-200 birds (Vierheilig and Vierheilig 1988), of not more than several hundred (Arndt 1989), and of between 650 and 800 (Silvius 1989; see Remarks 7).

La Blanquilla The species was "pretty common" on the island ("several fairly large bands") on 5 April 1906 (Lowe 1907a). At around this time another researcher found birds "common in a grove on the westerly end" but "according to the natives... on no other part of the island" (Cory 1909). However, Lowe (1911) indicated that he had found it in a woodland belt along the eastern side of the island, in "numbers which exceeded, out of all proportion, anything which we have ever seen in any of the West Indian or Venezuelan islands", with "as many as forty or more... flying together" and "several hundred" being seen in the course of a single morning; and it was there, too, that numerous flocks were encountered in 1944 (Phelps 1948: see Remarks 8). A census in August 1988 revealed less than 100 birds (Desenne and Strahl 1991), although a figure of 100-200 is given in Rojas (1991).

Netherlands Antilles *Bonaire* Birds were common near Fontein at the end of the last century, when nine were collected during a brief visit (Hartert 1893). In 1951-1952 the population was estimated to be 50-100 pairs (Voous 1957, 1983) or 60-80 pairs (in Rooth 1968), and in 1961 the same observer (K. H. Voous) thought there were fewer birds than 10 years previously (Rooth 1968). Rooth (1968) himself concluded that over 100 pairs were present, 1959-1960, but he saw so few birds on a brief visit in 1966 that in January 1968 he conducted a more detailed survey, resulting in an estimate of nearer 50 than 100 pairs. The general figures of 50-100 pairs were again affirmed in 1972-1973 (Voous 1983): more precisely, Spaans (1973) felt that between 90 and 180 birds were present and, allowing that not all would be pairs, indicated that the total breeding population could be less than 45 pairs and would certainly be less than 90 pairs. Several droughts, 1976-1978, resulted in declines estimated at one-third (Reijns and van der Salm 1981) or one-half or more (from 300 or 400 birds to 200 or even 100 in 1978) (Low 1981, Voous 1983). Nevertheless, in early 1980, two large roosts near Lake Goto and Saliña Tam held 180 and 120 birds respectively with several smaller roosts elsewhere in the north-west of the island, giving a total of at least 375 birds (Reijns and van der Salm 1981; see Remarks 9). In August 1984 216 birds were counted (Mellink and Molina 1984), in October/November 1985 a survey found at least 323 birds (Joordens 1985), and in October/November 1987 a total of 401 birds roosted among eight different sites (van Helmond and Wijsman 1988).

Aruba Hartert (1893) considered the species "not rare in the more wooded and rocky parts of the island", which Voous (1983) interpreted as the south. However, by 1930 birds were scarce, by 1943 rare, and by 1947 probably extinct (Voous 1957). Subsequent records in 1955, 1961, 1965 and 1974 refer either to captive birds that were set free or to stragglers from the Península de Paraguaná (Voous 1983).

ECOLOGY On the Venezuelan mainland the Yellow-shouldered Amazon occurs in xerophytic vegetation consisting of monotonous dry scrublands dominated by cacti and thornbush with scattered small trees on sandy soil (Meyer de Schauensee and Phelps 1978, Ridgely 1981a, Arndt 1989); the Península de Araya, "everywhere of an arid and hilly nature", has (or had) vegetation like the lower parts of Margarita (Lowe 1909). The assertion that the species is restricted to lowlands up to 100 m (Meyer de Schauensee and Phelps 1973) is disproved by observations well inland in Falcón and Lara, although the habitat is evidently the same (Low 1981, Arndt 1989). A partial correlation appears to exist between the species's mainland distribution and the southern limit of the South Caribbean Dry Zone, in which rainfall is less than 1,000 mm per year (see, e.g., map 4 in Sugden 1982). On the Caribbean islands, too, the species ranges beyond 100 m, with birds roosting in cliffs at 150-200 m and foraging at up to 450 m on Margarita (Arndt 1989), and being reported from Mount Brandaris (Hartert 1893) and Kernadoe "at high elevation" (Low 1981) on Bonaire. Nevertheless, on these islands the habitat is similar to the mainland, with (e.g.) one important gorge for the species on Margarita containing cacti, thornbush, scrub, isolated trees and groups of trees (Vierheilig and Vierheilig 1988); mangroves are sometimes used (along with open fields) on Bonaire (Voous 1983). In some places cliffs are used for nesting as well as roosting (Low 1981, Arndt 1989). The overall importance of woodland to the species is unclear: several early accounts (e.g. Lowe 1911) referred to its presence in woodland on La Blanquilla (although this island is predominantly flat and barren, with patches of acacia and cactus: Lowe 1907a, Low 1983) and in "lowland forests" in the Coro district (Hartert 1893); the survival of remnants of such areas could conceivably be decisive in determining its distribution, and hence explain the absence of the species from large expanses of apparently suitable habitat (see Ridgely 1981a). Woodland may simply be important for providing secure nest-sites in areas where cliff-nesting is impossible, in which case the absence of the species from given areas might be a seasonal phenomenon, with breeding birds confined to areas with suitable nest-sites, but at other times ranging much more widely: this might explain why Ridgely (1981a) considered the species absent from around Coro, based on researches in March/April, when Arndt (1989) found it relatively abundant only 20 km to the south in July.

Food consists of various wild and cultivated fruits, seeds and flowers, with virtually all data stemming from Bonaire. Voous (1983) listed the tree fruits shimarucu (West Indian cherry) *Malpighia punicifolia*, watekeli *Bourreria succulenta*, palu di Bonaire *Casearia tremula*, wayacá *Guaiacum officinale*, almond *Terminalia catappa*, hoba *Spondias mombin*, benbom *Moringa oleifera*, apeldam *Zizyphus spina-cristi* and probably palu di lora *Capparis coccolobifolia* as food, plus the seeds from the pods of dividivi *Caesalpinia coriaria*, maraca *Crotalaria incana*, wabi *Acacia tortuosa*, indju or kwi *Prosopis juliflora*, tumba rabu *Leucaena leucocephala* and other Fabaceae and Mimosaceae. Reijns and van der Salm (1980, 1981) mentioned some of these but also fruits of *Bursera bonairensis*, the nectar-rich blossoms of the calabash-tree *Crescentia cujete*, the tops of the cactus (datu) *Lamaireocereus griseus* and the sweet fruits of the organpipe or candle cactus (cadushi) *Cereus repandus*, these last being available throughout the year. Voous (1983) implied that *Cereus* is only taken in times of food shortage but Hartert (1893) noted it in the species's diet on Bonaire along with *Melocactus*, *Morinda* (or possibly *Moringa*) and *Guava*, while on the Península de Araya in Venezuela birds were also seen consuming *Cereus* fruits (G. Medina-Cuervo *in litt.* 1986), and Voous (1957) himself collected three birds whose stomachs were entirely filled with cactus fruit; the juice of cactus fruit makes the face dirty (Hartert 1893) and this is possibly what Low (1981) interpreted as discoloration caused by nest-site preparation. Seeds, flowers, fruits, nectar and/or shoots of five cacti (cardón *Ritterocereus griseus*, yaurero *Subpilocereus repandus*, *Pilocereus lanuginosus*, *Melocactus lobelii* and *M. caesius*), five legumes (*Platymiscium diadelphum*, yaque *Prosopis juliflora*, guíchere *Pithecellobium unguis-cati*,

Piptadenia flavia and *Piscidia piscipula*), and plants from several families (*Bulnesia arborea*, *Guaiacum officinale*, *Bourreira cumanensis*, *Tabebuia chrysantha*, *Capparis odoratissima*, *Casearia tremula*, *Zizyphus mauritania*) provide food for the parrots on Margarita, and the distributions of the four whose common name is given, along with that of palosano (for nesting), are regarded as major reasons for the relative abundance of birds at lower altitudes (Silvius 1989); indeed, subsequent work has shown the cardón to be critically important as a year-round food source (Silvius 1991; see Measures Proposed). In addition, Voous (1983) mentioned reports that the species favours the fruits of mango, sapodillo, kenepa, pomegranate, papaya, avocado and soursop, also the seeds of millet (most or all of this seemingly being derived from Reijns and van der Salm 1980), and hence is sometimes destructive in fruit gardens and fields (its taking of millet was a cause of its destruction in Aruba). Birds certainly feed in disused plantations on Bonaire (Low 1981, 1983), probably take maize when available (Spaans 1973), and with severe aridity venture into villages to forage in gardens, even from tables (Reijns and van der Salm 1981). Around San Francisco de Macanao on Margarita the species causes (or used to cause) damage to maize (Yépez Tamayo 1964). On La Blanquilla Lowe (1911) recorded birds utilizing "the small yellow fruit-like seeds of some guaiacum trees and the fruits of the cactus". On the Venezuelan mainland near Las Veritas plants eaten included cardón de lefaria *Cereus deficiens*, cují *Prosopis juliflora* and unidentified plants called trompillo, curarí and baitoa (H. Dos Santos *per* C. Bosque *in litt.* 1992).

On the Venezuelan mainland near Coro, 1988, the age of young captive birds indicated breeding from as early as March but otherwise April and May, locals reporting nests being made in trees on nearby mountain slopes (Arndt 1989); in another account the trees used in Falcón are *Bulnesia arborea* and *Prosopis juliflora*, and the season extends from the end of March to the end of August, with a clutch-size of 3-4 (H. Dos Santos *per* C. Bosque *in litt.* 1992; also Rojas 1991). This generally accords with various items of evidence from the islands. Locals reported breeding, Bonaire, from March to July (but also in October, which was considered possible, at least occasionally), and behavioural cues indicated breeding in late April with hatching in May and fledging in July (Low 1981, 1983); Spaans's (1973) and Voous's (1983) information for the same island modifies this only slightly, with a reported breeding season from February to June and still begging young as late as October, but with one park guard indicating a July–September breeding season. On Margarita the season is from the end of March (most clutches are laid in April) to the middle of August (most young leave the nest in August) (Arndt 1989, Silvius 1989, Rojas 1991). A female from La Blanquilla (in YPM) had undeveloped ovaries on 23 March 1960. Presumably breeding is a response to local conditions and its timing may therefore vary quite considerably between years. Clutch-size is reportedly 2-3 on Bonaire (Low 1981, 1983) and 4-6 has been claimed, Margarita (Vierheilig and Vierheilig 1988), although in 1990 the proven range was 2-5, average 3.4 (Rojas 1991), with (in the wild) an incubation period of 26 days (22 days in the case of a fifth egg in a clutch) and a fledging period of 59 days, with equivalent figures for captive birds of 24-27 (Noegel 1986) and 77 (Low 1983) respectively. Up to 30% of the population appeared to be breeding in 1989 on Margarita, the palosano *Bulnesia arborea* being much the most favoured for nesting in: of 31 nest-sites examined, 24 were in palosanos, two in mucos *Capparis pachaca*, three in quebrahachos *Caesalpinia mollis* and two in yaureros *Subpilocereus repandus*, although in other parts of the island guayacan *Guaiacum officinale* is known to be used (Silvius 1989). In the following year (providing good evidence that nest-sites are reoccupied in successive years), a study of 34 nests showed that 27 were in quebradas or by rivers, four were on hillsides, two were on flat ground away from quebradas and one was in a cliff, with 27 being in palosano, three in quebrahachos and one each in cotoperí *Talissia oliviformes*, guayacan and yaurero (Rojas 1991). On Bonaire the species uses both tree-holes and limestone cliffs, favoured trees being *Spondias*, *Capparis*, *Bursera* and *Guaiacum*, plus the cactus *Cereus repandus* (Hartert 1893, Rooth 1968, Low 1981, 1983, Voous 1983, Mellink and Molina 1984); on Aruba, hollow trees were reportedly used (Hartert 1893). On Bonaire, up to 90% of broods may be predated by rats, people or others, although nest-site competition (from Brown-throated Parakeets *Aratinga pertinax* and Pearly-eyed Thrashers *Margarops fuscatus*) appears to be slight (Mellink and Molina 1984). On Margarita, predation of newly fledged birds by raptors is thought probably high (Silvius 1989), and nest predation by the snakes *Constrictor constrictor* and *Corallus enydris* has been documented and many other potential nest predators, both reptile and mammal, identified (Rojas 1991). Extrapolating from estimates of breeding population size plus data on clutch-size, hatching success and fledging success, Rojas (1991) proposed that a breeding population of 70-106 pairs lay 238-360 eggs, 65% hatch into 155-234 chicks, and 50% are taken by nest-robbers, leaving 78-117 young to fledge; he thought that in 1990 the breeding population was probably 95 pairs, producing 323 eggs, 210 chicks and 105 recruits into the population.

Generally birds occur in pairs and small groups, but sometimes in larger flocks (60-80 and even over 100) when feeding, and commonly form communal roosts at least outside the breeding season (Meyer de Schauensee and Phelps 1978, Reijns and van der Salm 1981, Voous 1983); even when in flocks, however, birds clearly remain in close-knit pairs (Lowe 1911, Spaans 1973). On Bonaire, apparently in July, Hartert (1893) recorded nocturnal roosting in rocks, with birds leaving to forage at daybreak, returning between 08h00 and 09h00, moving out again in the afternoon and flying in again just before sunset. The two main nocturnal roosts on Bonaire in early 1980 were in fairly narrow, deep valleys in the lee of the hill (Reijns and van der Salm 1981), and Voous (1957, 1983) recorded diurnal resting in the crowns of various trees in secondary seasonal forest and cactus vegetation, with activity confined to the early morning and late afternoon. The steady fall-off in numbers at the 1980 nocturnal roosts through February and March has been interpreted as birds moving elsewhere in response to newly available foods (Silva 1989a) and as dispersal to breed (Forshaw 1989). Years with good rain may result in sufficient fruit for flocking behaviour to diminish (Rooth 1968).

On La Blanquilla Lowe (1911) found birds in large numbers in January but much diminished in the same location in February; believing the birds to be confined to this eastern area (and in this he might have been right, since Cory may have slipped in indicating occurrence on the western side of the island: see Population), he could only explain the difference by postulating occasional movements of birds to Margarita.

THREATS The most prevalent threat to the Yellow-shouldered Amazon is (largely internal) trade, but this is compounded by local threats such as tourism (on Margarita) and by various "natural" developments including drought; there are no published claims that habitat destruction has been highly significant, yet ecological studies in progress have shown it to be important on Margarita (see below), and a rigorous analysis of the historical evidence would probably reveal the same for parts of the mainland (see Measures Proposed). On Aruba the extinction of the species has been attributed by Voous (1983) to shooting and poisoning in response to crop damage, although earlier he (Voous 1957: hence also Low 1981, 1983) blamed it on the usurpation of land by a large oil-refining industry, and Silva (1989a) assumed that drought and the taking of nestlings as pets may have been no less factors than they are on Bonaire. International trade in the species has always been considered minimal (Low 1981, 1983, Silva 1989a), but recent evidence (Venezuelan parrot shipments confiscated in Aruba, and others seen in Curaçao coming from Falcón) indicate that unknown numbers are entering foreign markets (M. L. Goodwin *in litt.* 1992).

Venezuela *mainland* A century ago Hartert (1893) referred to the rarity of museum skins "in spite of the numbers that are kept in confinement", explaining that "large numbers are sent to the bird-shops of the larger towns of Venezuela and to Curaçao" from mainland locations. Although in 1981 Ridgely (1981a) found (a) mainland birds to be unusually fearless, indicating lack of persecution, (b) only small numbers being held locally as pets, and (c) no appreciable trade, Arndt (1989) later encountered a situation (in Falcón) more similar to that recorded by Hartert (although wild birds were still very approachable), with the species much favoured as pets by local people (almost every fourth house having a specimen in one area), and with birds also being sold very cheaply (equivalent of US$3), which suggested how common they then were as traded items. This was confirmed by a contemporaneous but independent assessment which showed that at least eight birds could be found for sale at the roadside between Puerto Cabello and Maracaiba on any date, indicating a heavy threat from trade in Falcón (R. B. Ramírez *in litt.* 1988), and again by research in 1990 which revealed that near Las Veritas the capture of chicks (using a barbed *Bromelia* leaf) is an intensive and widespread activity during May, at the end of which it is easy to find six or more birds in most homes, the birds being sold to dealers for international trade or roadside resale between Coro and Maracaibo (H. Dos Santos *per* C. Bosque *in litt.* 1992). Roadside sale of birds also occurs in Anzoátegui (Desenne and Strahl 1991). "Habitat destruction" was regarded as a major factor (A. B. Altman *in litt.* 1988); on the Península de Araya this takes the form of slow but probably irreversible pressure from overgrazing by goats and firewood-gathering by local people (S. Gorzula *in litt.* 1986); overgrazing was strongly in evidence at the one site in Lara (Low 1981). On the Península de Paraguaná the species was reportedly commoner 30 years ago, but has declined perhaps for natural reasons, e.g. increasingly long dry seasons, absence of water and of nest-sites, there being no evidence of trade, despite the peninsula being much used for the illicit transfer of the species to the Netherlands Antilles from the hill country around Coro (H. Dos Santos *per* C. Bosque *in litt.* 1992).

Margarita Burgeoning tourism and local trade now affect the species, tourism much more problematically. As an indication of the development of Margarita as a resort, Andrade (1987) reported a growth in visitors from 270,868 in 1971 to two million in 1986 and a projected six million by 2010, with a concomitant rise in the resident population from 197,000 in 1981 to 515,000 in 2010. Although it was thought that the Península de Macanao had remained untouched by this growth, and remains sparsely populated and little visited, it was feared that the new identity of the island as a resort would result in ecological disturbances and transformations that could affect the species (Vierheilig and Vierheilig 1988). In fact sand-mining for the construction business had already begun on Macanao in the late 1980s, slowly destroying the birds' primary foraging habitat as well as the four key roosting areas and nesting trees, such that habitat loss in general counted as a greater threat to the species even than the taking of young (Silvius 1989, Desenne and Strahl 1991). Up to 50 birds per year are killed as crop pests (Silvius 1991); nevertheless, it is the local exploitation of the species for pets that most obviously has an impact, with at least 50% of young being taken by traders in 1989 (Silvius 1989); "the vast majority of the fishermen living on Macanao owned one or two *A. barbadensis* as pets" and the species's "increasing scarcity... has caused locals to abstain from felling nest-trees in order to ensure a recapture the following year", a barbed leaf or fishing hook now being used to extract the featherless chicks (Desenne and Strahl 1991). Indeed, the high number of confiscations during 1988 suggested that organized efforts, possibly indicating international trade, were operating (Desenne and Strahl 1991). Periodic drought probably also causes high mortality amongst adults, but it is possible that the most important factor limiting the population on the island is nest-site availability, caused in part by the loss of nest-trees owing to sand-mining and to the (formerly) destructive actions of some trappers when taking the young (Silvius 1989).

La Blanquilla Young are taken by fishermen (Desenne and Strahl 1991), presumably as pets. Silva (1989a) noted that the island was at one stage leased as a goat ranch, the impact of which can hardly have been beneficial to the native vegetation: Lowe (1907a) referred to "large numbers of donkeys, horses, and goats all over the island", and Murphy (1952) said it was "devastated by overpopulation of domestic animals".

Nethelands Antilles *Bonaire* The taking of young for the local pet-trade (bird-catchers know the nest-sites well) is the most serious threat (Voous 1983), this seemingly affecting cliff-nesters more than tree-nesters (Low 1981, 1983); in the late 1970s as many as 100 birds were estimated to be in captivity on the island at a time when the wild population may not have been much more (Low 1981, 1983). Birds so taken may also be sold elsewhere within the Netherlands Antilles for up to US$110 (Rooth 1968, Silva 1989a, J. de Freitas *in litt.* 1991). The species is considered a pest and is sometimes shot by farmers because of the damage done to crops and orchards (Reijns and van der Salm 1981), but this presumably only occurs when drought stresses birds. Drought is in fact a serious second threat, since the reduction in food-supply leads not only to the shooting but also to the starvation or capture of birds as they move into villages in other parts of the island; in 1978 200 were estimated to have died, which may have been 50-75% of the population, as a result of drought from February to June, and in 1982 a similarly caused mortality occurred (Low 1981, Reijns and van der Salm 1981, Voous 1983). Although this pressure is natural, the human occupation of Bonaire and defence of its cultivated resources represents a constraint on the parrots which unnaturally amplifies their vulnerability at such times. Other natural problems for the species involve nest-predation by and possibly nest-site competition from the endemic race (*bonairensis*) of the Pearly-eyed Thrasher, although this, too, suffers in droughts (Voous 1983), nest-predation by rats *Rattus* and nest disturbance by iguanas (R. van Halewyn *in litt.* 1986).

MEASURES TAKEN The Yellow-shouldered Amazon is protected by law in Venezuela, although this is not enforced (G. Medina-Cuervo *in litt.* 1986; also Desenne and Strahl 1991). Similarly the species has been protected by law on Bonaire since 1952, when its capture and export were forbidden (Low 1983), but to no great avail (see Threats), despite intervention by ICBP's Pan American Section in 1962 (not 1963 in Silva 1989a), which resulted in assurances of enforcement. The only part of its mainland range under protection is the private Fundación Bioma reserve on the Península de Paraguaná (see Distribution). The island of Margarita already possesses two national parks, three regional parks and 37 other protected areas (Andrade 1987) but none covers a significant population of Yellow-shouldered Amazons (K. M. Silvius *in litt.* 1992); however, a recent agreement was reached between WCI, Pro Vita Animalium and the Venezuelan Ministry of the Environment to conserve the species's habitat, increase public awareness of its plight, reduce trade and coordinate efforts for captive breeding, law enforcement and local education (*WCI Bulletin* March/April 1990: 7). Calls for ecological studies and precise evaluation of the situation on Margarita (Low 1981, Arndt 1989) have been answered by the initiation of two projects currently in progress, one investigating the species's ecology (e.g. Silvius 1989, 1991, Rojas 1991) and the other representing an educational campaign (Desenne and Strahl 1991); these initiatives have already started to produce important results, such as the fledging of 30 young in both 1990 and 1991 from nests that were traditionally poached (Silvius 1991). On Bonaire the species occurs in the 3,800 ha Washington-Slagbaai National Park, which embraces Goto, Saliña Tam, Slagbaai and Mount Brandaris, and is administered by STINAPA, the Netherlands Antilles National Parks Foundation (Voous 1983). In 1978 STINAPA flew in 2,000 kg of mangoes and sweet gourds to help feed starving birds (Low 1981, 1983).

MEASURES PROPOSED Most published suggestions and exhortations refer to the islands, but it seems likely that the mainland holds far larger populations of the species and must not be neglected. The first requirement is therefore for a comprehensive survey of the mainland areas at various seasons to determine more clearly the distribution and status of the species and to initiate quantitative studies on its ecology, with particular emphasis on food, nesting habitat and the possible importance of woodland (see Ecology). Ecological studies on Margarita (see Measures Taken) have already indicated the importance of cactus fields in the lowlands of Macanao and of palosano stands in the main riverbeds (see Ecology), and it is imperative that these receive full protection. While these studies are progressing on Margarita, parallel work is long overdue on Bonaire, for example to elucidate alleged food competition from Brown-throated Parakeets and nest-site competition from Pearly-eyed Thrashers (Voous 1983); such studies are also merited on La Blanquilla, which Desenne and Strahl (1991) have urged to be declared a protected area. From this ecological work and the proposed surveys a broad plan for protected area development, habitat management and local education can be generated for, as Low (1983) asserted, the bird must be protected in all parts of its range. Following STINAPA's action in importing fruit to Bonaire in the 1978 drought, a fund for use in future droughts on the island has been called for (Low 1981, Silva 1989a) as well as the planting of drought-resistant food trees (Silva 1989a). Captive breeding from Bonaire's conservatively estimated 100 birds (in the late 1970s) could (a) produce young to meet local demand and (b) highlight the plight of the species (Low 1981); the value of a captive-breeding programme is endorsed by Noegel (1986), Silva (1989a) and Lantermann and Schuster (1990) but, unless it is specifically targeted at filling the market and replacing the illegal pressure on wild birds (see comments in Desenne and Strahl 1991: 166), there is little need for the effort and expense involved (a view also expressed for Margarita by Silvius 1989). Indeed, there should first be a very careful evaluation of local bird-keeping traditions and the chances of influencing it – and hence of shrinking demand – by education and enforcement. Meanwhile, the collection of further live specimens should not be permitted (Silva 1989a).

A general blueprint for parrot conservation in Venezuela has called for several measures outlined above, but has also highlit the importance of evaluating trade data to determine smuggling patterns and trends, the value of using parrots as ecological indicators by their inclusion in plans for monitoring and managing protected areas, the need for public education campaigns both at the source areas and in the major centres of consumption, and the particular necessity of training enforcement personnel in trade-related issues (Desenne and Strahl 1991).

REMARKS (1) The subspecies *rothschildi* on Margarita, La Blanquilla and Bonaire is invalid (Voous 1957, 1983, Low 1981, 1983, Forshaw 1989, Silva 1989a). (2) Voous (1957) cites "J. Racenis, Doc. Int. Un. Prot. Nat. 3rd Gen. Ass., Caracas, 1952, p.26" for the information that the Península de Paraguaná is particularly important for the species on the Venezuelan mainland; however, inquiries of the IUCN library and of K. H. Voous himself have failed to trace the reference as cited. (3) Several curiosities attend the report from west of Barquisimeto: Low (1981) called the state Tara; Silva (1989a) added that the site in question is "near Aritagua", which most resembles Yaritagua, to the east of Barquisimeto (see TAW 1986); but A. B. Altman (*in litt.* 1991) has affirmed that the town in question is Atarigua, west of Barquisimeto and near Puente Torres. (4) A record from El Valle on the main part of Margarita (Lowe 1907b) is referable to the Orange-winged Amazon *Amazona amazonica*, found on the island by Robinson and Richmond (1895), Clark (1902) and evidently also Fernández Yépez *et al.* (1940; see Remarks 6), although the species had disappeared by the time it was searched for by Vierheilig and Vierheilig (1988). This was a bird which was found in "many large flocks" in 1895 (Robinson and Richmond 1895), and while the causes of its disappearance remain unclear, Clark (1902) referred to it as "a very popular cage bird with the natives" as well as to its behaviour "on the approach of a hunter", which certainly suggests that direct human pressure may have been responsible. This local extinction of a congeneric emphasizes the risks run by the Yellow-shouldered Amazon on Margarita. (5) Where Silva (1989a) had Boca de Pozo, which is just south of Robledar, Low (1981) had Boca de Río, which is on the opposite side of the peninsula; Yépez Tamayo (1964) had Boca de Río. (6) It seems probable that the amazons sometimes enter the mangroves at Restinga, even if Vierheilig and Vierheilig (1988) and Arndt (1989) misunderstood which species they were told nested there. For example, Lowe (1907b) saw "several parties round the lagoon at the west end of the island", and by this he presumably meant the west end of the main island. Incidentally, the confusion he started over the existence of *barbadensis* on the main island (by assuming that birds he saw at El Valle were the same as those at the lagoon) was not entirely dispelled by Fernández Yépez *et al.* (1940) or Yépez Tamayo (1964), so that Rojas (1991) repeated the mistake of believing that *barbadensis* had once occurred at El Valle and thus had suffered a significant range contraction. (7) The "probably 800-1,000" in Desenne and Strahl (1991) was an early guess based on the unanalysed results of the third survey (K. M. Silvius *in litt.* 1992). (8) It is curious that Silva (1989a) referred to a Venezuelan ornithologist failing to find the species on Blanquilla several decades after Lowe's visit. (9) The figures in Reijns and van der Salm (1981), which chronicle numbers at the two main roosts, indicate the the sites were not checked simultaneously (except once) and that the peak of 180 at one site occurred before the second site was even discovered; if the total of 375 included the simple addition of 180 and 120, it is patently unreliable.

RED-TAILED AMAZON *Amazona brasiliensis* E[2]

At the end of the 1980s some 3,000 of these parrots survived in a very small area of coastal São Paulo and adjacent Paraná states, Brazil, moving daily between Atlantic Forest feeding areas and mangrove and littoral forest roosting and breeding areas. Despite some formal protection within reserves, the remaining populations are declining precipitously as a result of trapping, hunting, loss of nest-trees, and land development.

DISTRIBUTION The Red-tailed Amazon (see Remarks 1) is confined to an area of some 600,000 ha on the eastern slopes of the Serra do Mar, including coastal lowlands and islands, in south-eastern São Paulo and eastern Paraná states, Brazil, specifically between (and including) the areas around Itanhaém in the north (see Remarks 2) and Guaratuba in the south (to 25°52'S) (Sick 1985, Scherer Neto 1989, Straube 1990; also P. Martuscelli *in litt.* 1991). That it formerly extended into Santa Catarina and Rio Grande do Sul (Camargo 1962, Sick 1969, Pinto 1978) seems to be completely mistaken, since the positive evidence is tenuous and the negative evidence (the three records in question are all from upland *Araucaria*-rich habitat: Camargo 1962), when set against information in Ecology below, overwhelming. Forshaw (1989) nevertheless continued to indicate a range from São Paulo to Rio Grande do Sul.

São Paulo The species occurs throughout the coastal belt from the municipalities of Itanhaém and Cananéia down to Ariri and the Ilha do Cardoso (Scherer Neto 1989). Prior to this elucidation, records were from near Iguape on the ribeirão do Braço Grande (not "Rio Branco" as in Silva 1989a), municipality of Pariquera-Açu (Camargo 1962), July 1898 (two specimens in MZUSP), this then being a regular breeding locality (von Ihering 1898); and Morrete (on the mainland, not on Ilha do Cardoso, as in Pinto 1938), 15 km south of Cananéia, September 1934 (Camargo 1962; specimen in MZUSP; see Remarks 3). A claim that an article and letters by a Brazil-based aviculturist reveal, in combination, that he obtained birds from along the rio Paranapanema some 500 km west of São Paulo (Bertagnolio 1983) is difficult to accept (see also Remarks 4).

Paraná The species occurs along almost the entire coastal belt, mostly at under 700 m, from Guaraqueçaba through Antonina and Paranaguá to Guaratuba, including the islands of Baía de Paranaguá, namely Ilha do Mel, Ilha das Peças, Ilha Rasa da Cotinga, Ilha do Superagüi, Ilha do Pinheiro and others (Scherer Neto 1989). Prior to this elucidation, the only record was of a bird collected in January 1821 from a flock on the Ilha do Mel, where the species was frequent (von Pelzeln 1868-1871).

Santa Catarina The only record from Santa Catarina is a specimen from Lages (Lajes) (von Ihering 1899a), as clarified by Camargo (1962; see Remarks 5); there have been no more recent records in Santa Catarina (Sick *et al.* 1981 *contra* King 1978-1979; see Remarks 6), and this one seems highly improbable. However, the species's occurrence as far south as Guaratuba in Paraná (see above) suggests the possibility of its at least occasional presence across the border; indeed, a range map in Scherer Neto and Martuscelli (1992) includes the north-easternmost corner of the state.

Rio Grande do Sul Von Ihering (1899a) reported seeing a specimen from São Francisco de Paula (he actually wrote "Cima da Serra" and indicated it was close to the Santa Catarina border), in the north-east highlands (Camargo 1962, Belton 1984-1985). The species has never been found since (Belton 1984-1985, Scherer Neto 1989); this record seems highly improbable, but in any case most or all potentially suitable habitat in the state has been destroyed (Ridgely 1981a).

POPULATION Because it was so little known (it is extremely rare in museum collections), as recently as 10 years ago the Red-tailed Amazon was considered probably the most endangered mainland Neotropical parrot after the possibly extinct Glaucous Macaw *Anodorhynchus glaucus*; for, although in the past it was presumably at least locally numerous, a major decrease in numbers was assumed to have occurred in this century, brought about by the near-total deforestation of most of its (assumed former) range (Ridgely 1981a). In fact, subsequent fieldwork indicated that the total population stood at around 3,000 (Scherer Neto 1988), this somewhat upgrading the estimate of 2,000-2,500 in Diefenbach and Goldhammer (1986) and tending to indicate that the assumption of a major decrease may, in fact, have been mistaken. Nevertheless, new studies in 1991/1992 have shown that there is indeed a major population decline under way, such that in the near future the species will be reduced to a few hundred birds, like certain Caribbean amazons (Scherer Neto and Martuscelli 1992).

The major aggregations found in São Paulo in 1984/1985 were in the municipality of Iguape, where a maximum of 120 birds in several groups was seen; the biggest single flock, at a site 35 km from Iguape (on the road to Pariquera-Açu), consisted of 96 birds (Scherer Neto 1989). Small numbers roosted in the vicinity of the headquarters at Ilha do Cardoso State Park in December 1987, when a maximum of six birds was seen; at this time there was a report from local people that these parrots were much commoner in winter, with "hundreds" present, which requires confirmation (D. F. Stotz *in litt.* 1988); the island's population has subsequently been reported as around 145 birds (P. Martuscelli *in litt.* 1991).

The highest numbers in Paraná in this same period were found on the islands in Baía de Paranaguá: Ilha das Peças (179-343), Ilha do Mel (69-241) (where the species was frequent and in flocks, 1821: von Pelzeln 1868-1871), Ilha Rasa da Cotinga (45-188) and Ilha do Superagüi (0-250) (Scherer Neto 1989). A separate count was carried out monthly from December 1984 to December 1985 on the small Ilha do Pinheiro, an important "roosting island" to which birds come from Ilha das Peças and Ilha do Superagüi: numbers varied from 370 in February to 754 in August, with a second peak of 650 in January (Scherer Neto 1989).

ECOLOGY The Red-tailed Amazon may be characterized as an Atlantic Forest endemic, but it is no less dependent on the adjacent vegetation ("sand-plain forest") along coasts and on inshore estuarine islands including mangroves, where most breeding and roosting (seasonally in large flocks, e.g. up to 400 pairs) occurs (Scherer Neto 1988, P. Martuscelli *in litt.* 1991). It keeps strictly to the lowlands, ranging mainly up to 300-400 m in the low foothills, and hence does not occur in *Araucaria* forest and is nowhere sympatric with Red-spectacled Amazon *Amazona pretrei* (*contra* Sick 1969, 1972, Forshaw 1978), although it is marginally sympatric with Vinaceous Amazon *A. vinacea*, apparently (e.g.) in the Jacupiranga State Park (Diefenbach and Goldhammer 1986, Scherer Neto 1989; see relevant accounts). Characteristic trees of the habitat are *Luehea* and *Andira* spp. as well as species from the Lauraceae and Sapotaceae; common palms are *Arecastrum* and *Euterpe edulis* (Diefenbach and Goldhammer 1986). Habitat on the islands to which the birds move to breed and roost is restinga and halophytic flora (Ilha do Mel) (Camargo 1962); Ilha Comprida is a sandy, deltaic island with mangrove, caixeta *Tabebuia* and gerivá palms *Arecastrum romanzoffianum* growing on swampy terrain (C. Yamashita *in litt.* 1991); Ilha do Cardoso is a massif covered with wet forest with mangrove in the swampy lower areas (C. Yamashita *in litt.* 1991).

Food is chiefly found in thick forest, with fruit of over 42 species of tree being identified to date (in four cases also the leaves; in five others also the flowers); guanandi *Callophyllum brasiliense* is an important resource, being involved in six out of 83 feeding records, and also being a frequent nest-tree (Scherer Neto 1989). Earlier reports mention flowers of *Erythrina speciosa* being consumed during the summer at roosts in mangroves, as well as *Euphorbia* and *Myrcia* fruits (Scherer Neto 1988, 1989; also P. Scherer Neto *in litt.* 1986). Birds were noted to feed in pairs or flocks up to and over 20 (Scherer Neto 1989).

They nest in holes usually high in both live and dead trees (often in groups of dead, hollow *Mauritia* palms in swampy areas: confirmed in Bertagnolio 1981, 1983), on average the cavity being 8 m above ground (highest 16 m), although nests have been found only 1.5 m up in small trees; inaccessible sites in thick forest, swamp or floodplain protect nests against predators (Scherer Neto 1988; also Diefenbach and Goldhammer 1986). Six of a total of 18 nests were in guanandi trees on the Ilhas do Mel and Rasa da Cotinga, with two in gerivá palms on the Ilha Comprida and two in fig trees *Ficus enormis* at mainland sites; other trees included jacarerama *Laplacea fruticosa*, pau-óleo *Copaifera trapezifolia* and guape *Eugenia hiemalis* (Scherer Neto 1989). Nests can be as close as 40 m (average of six nests 79 m) on the Ilha do Mel (Scherer Neto 1989). Breeding runs from September through to February (although the extremes for nest finds are 6 August and 5 March), when the last birds fledge; clutch-size is 2-4 (maximum young seen fledged is three), incubation lasts 28-30 days, and the fledging period is 50-55 days (Scherer Neto 1988, 1989; also P. Scherer Neto *in litt.* 1986, Diefenbach and Goldhammer 1986).

THREATS A decade ago the Red-tailed Amazon was believed highly threatened by habitat destruction (Sick and Teixeira 1979, Ridgely 1981a); this is now recognized to be true only in São Paulo, where there is rapid forest loss (Scherer Neto 1989), while forest cover in Paraná is now known to be relatively stable (P. Scherer Neto *in litt.* 1986). Intensive wood exploitation on Ilha Comprida was a cause for concern in the mid-1980s because of its impact on nest-site availability (P. Scherer Neto *in litt.* 1986). Indeed, the island was then reportedly being divided into housing lots (C. Torres *in litt.* 1985) and being developed as a weekend resort with a bridge planned (Diefenbach and Goldhammer 1986); all of this is now accelerating (Scherer Neto 1989, C. Yamashita *in litt.* 1991), and by 1992 half the island was deforested or otherwise disturbed, while the other half was largely parcelled out in illegal plots of land (Scherer Neto and Martuscelli 1992). The creation of pasture for buffalo leads to competition between this animal and the parrots for the fruit of *Erythrina speciosa* along stream margins, and the former push over gerivá palms to get at their fruit, thus reducing both food-supply and nest-sites (Scherer Neto and Martuscelli 1992). However, the wholesale clearance of forest is less an immediate problem than: cutting of palms and of guanandi (used by the species for nesting) to make fishing boats, since the albeit low human population of the region subsists on fish (Scherer Neto 1988, 1989); cutting of *Euterpe* palms (used by the species for food and roosting) to make salads (see, e.g., Threats under Blue-bellied Parrot *Triclaria malachitacea*); exploitation of caixeta trees for the pencil industry, as these are also used for nesting (P. Martuscelli *in litt.* 1991). Clearance of trees for crops on the 15 ha Ilha do Pinheiro was a cause for alarm in October 1983 (W. Belton *in litt.* 1983).

Illegal trade in the species has long been a problem, and has resulted in the diminution of the wild population (Scherer Neto 1988), although until around 1988 (see below) it almost exclusively served internal markets: a bird acquired in the U.K. (presumably in the 1950s) from a merchant navy steward (Maxwell 1960) presumably derived from a chance transaction in Brazil. In the early 1980s in the markets of southern São Paulo state the species sold for as little as $10 a bird, although elsewhere in Brazil it was much more expensive (C. Torres *in litt.* 1985). Most of the birds seen in the late 1970s being offered for sale came from the Ilha Comprida (P. Scherer Neto *in litt.* 1986), but it is now known that young are taken from nests also in Cananéia and Iguape municipalities and on Ilhas do Mel, das Peças and Rasa da Cotinga, with fishermen and other locals fixing steps up to certain nests so as to take the young annually without cutting the trees (Scherer Neto 1989); in 1984/1985 the actions of trappers resulted in the failure of every nest being studied (Diefenbach and Goldhammer 1986), and this happened again in 1991/1992 when all seven nests under study were "destroyed" to capture the young (P. Scherer Neto *in litt.* 1992 to R. Wirth). Thus illegal trade continues (P. Martuscelli *in litt.* 1991); in the late 1980s the number in captivity was known to exceed 50 (Silva 1989a), but has now risen: Scherer Neto (1989) knew of 50 inside Brazil, 30 outside, but he indicated several hundred inside Brazil and a large number of birds being smuggled to Europe in the period 1988-1990 (Scherer Neto 1991a). The latest evidence is of a major illicit exploitation, 20% simply for "personal" local consumption, 80% for commerce, most of it abroad (to the U.S.A. and Europe, mainly Germany): in the municipality of Cananéia alone (one quarter of the species's range), 356 birds were taken from the wild for either eating or trade in the 1991/1992 breeding season (Scherer Neto and Martuscelli 1992).

A further factor of concern is hunting: in 1982 50 birds were reportedly shot dead at the roost on Ilha do Pinheiro and many others left dying, apparently for no other reason than pleasure (Scherer Neto 1988, 1989). However, it was believed that birds may also be shot for food in southern São Paulo (C. Torres *in litt.* 1985), and this was confirmed by experience in 1989 again on Ilha do Pinheiro and 1990 at Ariri when some 100 birds were killed at each site (Scherer Neto and Martuscelli 1992).

Owls can reportedly reduce breeding success to near-zero in some cases where birds nest semi-colonially in more open situations in marshes (Bertagnolio 1981, 1983); moreover, dead palms snap off in bad weather, and in 1983 nine young died at one site through this cause (Diefenbach and Goldhammer 1986; also Scherer Neto and Martuscelli 1992).

MEASURES TAKEN The species is protected under Brazilian law (Bernardes *et al.* 1990), listed on Appendix I of CITES, and treated as endangered under the U.S. Endangered Species Act (Nowak 1990). The lack of protected areas within its range noted by Ridgely (1981a) appears to have been rectified: there are now at least 12, namely (in São Paulo) the Juréia Ecological Station (presence not proved but probable), Chuá Ecological Station, Cananéia–Iguape–Peruíbe Environmental Protection Area, Jacupiranga State Park (150,000 ha), Serra do Mar State Park and Ilha do Cardoso State Park (22,500 ha), and (in Paraná) the Superagüi National Park (21,400 ha; only decreed on 25 April 1989), Guaraqueçaba Ecological Station, Guaraqueçaba Environmental Protection Area, Ilha do Mel Ecological Station, Serra Negra State Park and the recently declared Ilha do Pinheiro "Area of Relevant Ecological Interest" (Scherer Neto 1989). Scherer Neto (1988, 1989) also referred to a scheme for erecting nest-boxes at certain sites, although the success of this measure has not yet been indicated. In 1991, further work on the species, reported in Scherer Neto and Martuscelli (1992), was initiated as a joint project of The Nature Conservancy and Fundação SOS-Mata Atlântica.

MEASURES PROPOSED The Red-tailed Amazon was considered a species for which a concerted captive programme might be genuinely worthwhile, using already captive birds (Ridgely 1981a), and given the steep decline currently in progress this has also been called for in order to create and maintain a gene bank for the species (Scherer Neto and Martuscelli 1992). However, Scherer Neto's (1988, 1989) work has shown that the priorities for this species lie in adequate protection of habitat, proper management of existing protected areas, and the identification and protection of key sites, plus the continued vigilance of authorities against illegal poaching, hunting and cutting of trees; he has called for continued monitoring and study of the populations in the known breeding and roosting sites, linked with a special education programme for guards and local inhabitants (these are also proposed in Scherer Neto and Martuscelli 1992). Despite its recent protection (see Measures Taken), the tiny but critically important Ilha do Pinheiro surely merits inclusion in the adjacent Superagüi National Park.

REMARKS (1) Camargo (1962) treated the Red-tailed Amazon as a race within a polytypic species that also includes Blue-cheeked Amazon *A. dufresniana* and Red-browed Amazon *A. rhodocorytha*, and in this he was followed by Meyer de Schauensee (1966, 1982); but King (1978-1979), Ridgely (1981a), Sick (1985) and Forshaw (1989) all preferred to maintain its specific identity, and their judgement is followed here. (2) Silva (1989a) gave "Vale do Ribeira" as the northern limit, and both Sick and Teixeira (1979) and Diefenbach and Goldhammer (1986) also mentioned the rio Ribeira valley for the species; Itanhaém is further north, and the Ribeira valley is a generalization for the Pariquera-Açu, near Iguape. (3) MZUSP also has a São Paulo skin from "Ilha Grande", dated July 1970, which cannot be traced; it is possibly a mistake for Ilha Comprida. (4) Finsch (1867-1868) and von Pelzeln (1868-1871) began publishing their work simultaneously, so the former was in correspondence with the latter over J. Natterer's observations of parrots. Under the entry for *Amazona brasiliensis* Finsch cited a letter from von Pelzeln that mentioned not only the details about Ilha do Mel as published in von Pelzeln (1868-1871) but also a locality "an Bord von Menalha" (possibly "on the bank of the rio Menalha"). The itinerary at the start of von Pelzeln (1868-1871) reveals that this "site" was visited on 20 January 1821 between stays at (and therefore obviously close to) Itararé, and indicates, as some kind of geographical qualifier, that it was in or close to "Höhe von Guairussu" (Guairussu heights). This curious record would tend to support the supposed report of breeding inland in Bertagnolio (1983), were it not for the fact that elsewhere in von Pelzeln (1868-1871) he used "an Bord" to indicate "aboard ship". Evidently the Menalha was one; in other words a total misunderstanding originally surrounded J. Natterer's notes about this part of his journey, compounded by the single date involved, by the mention of "Guairussu heights", and by the association with this parrot (none of which makes any sense even now). (5) Lages is not in Rio Grande do Sul (*contra* Pinto 1978). (6) King (1978-1979) stated that "most of the recent records are from Santa Catarina", and although Ridgely (1981a) pointed out that this seems to have no foundation, it may derive from a mistaken translation of Sick (1969), who wrote that more (meaning further) records in the literature refer to Santa Catarina and Rio Grande do Sul.

ST VINCENT AMAZON *Amazona guildingii* **R**[11]

Endemic to moist forest on the upper west and east ridges of St Vincent, this parrot has declined owing to habitat loss, hunting, hurricanes and trade, but following recent action by government and non-government agencies the species is now relatively secure, with some 440-500 individuals extant.

DISTRIBUTION The St Vincent Amazon was evidently always confined to areas of moist forest on St Vincent, this habitat now (and evidently for most of this century) surviving on the upper slopes to the east and to the west of the central ridge of the island (Lawrence 1879, Lister 1880, Anon. 1904, Clark 1905, Lack *et al.* 1973, and references below; see map in Butler 1988: 49; for possible genetic variation between the the two areas, see the third paragraph under Population). Although once reported to be most numerous in the north of the island (Bond 1928b), only one recent report refers to the species's presence on the dominant northern Mount Soufrière (Andrle and Andrle 1975), others indicating its absence even before the 1979 eruption (see Threats) (Gochfeld 1974, Laidler 1977, Nichols 1981, Lambert 1984). A record of birds coming down to feed in a garden among the hills (apparently near Chateaubelair) and of breeding near Kingstown (see Ecology for both), combined with Lister's (1880) report that in the late 1870s forest covered peaks and, on the western side, reached almost to sea level, indicates that the species's range on the island must have contracted and fragmented substantially in the past hundred years. Major localities where the species concentrates are listed under Population.

POPULATION Assessments of population status have varied not only with real variations in numbers resulting from adversities but also, evidently, with observer judgement. The earliest appraisal seems to have been that of a resident in the early 1870s who, in seeking to procure specimens for London Zoo, found it "now scarce" and only obtained a bird "after many inquiries" (*Proc. Zool. Soc. London* 1874: 324). Against this it was regarded as "formerly very numerous, and... still common at the time of the great hurricane (1898)", but this storm, along with the eruption of Soufrière four years later (see Threats), led to its being "not at all abundant" and even "now decidedly rare" in 1903–1904 (Anon. 1904, Clark 1905; but see Remarks 1), which was possibly the reason that Rothschild (1905) regarded it as "almost extinct". However, in 1908 it was found to occur "in sufficient numbers... to make its preservation a matter of certainty if proper care is exercised", with several large flocks known and the impact of the eruption being thought "moderate" (Lowe 1909). Despite Knobel (1926) calling it "exceedingly rare" and Phillips (1929) reporting (at second hand) "only one or two flocks left" in 1924, Bond (1928b) found it "not as rare as expected" and guessed that several hundred still existed, this being the first attempt at indicating a total population size; Porter (1930a) also had evidence that it was still to be "found in small numbers" in the 1920s, but by the 1950s it was reported to be "becoming less and less", such that without protection it would be extinct before the Imperial Amazon *Amazona imperialis* (Frost 1959).

A succession of studies in the 10 years from 1973 to 1982 sought to achieve clarity on the numbers of birds remaining. In April and May 1973 the species was seen in small numbers, though with flocks of up to 50 reported, so that a total of some 200 birds seemed possible (Andrle and Andrle 1975). In September 1973 observations in the upper Buccament valley yielded a conservative estimate of 100 birds (Snyder 1973). Estimations based on surveys in 1975 and 1976 were of "several hundred to a thousand" (Laidler and Laidler 1977) or of "a few thousand" (Laidler 1977; see Remarks 2), although another team in 1974 gave an estimate of 400 (Nichols 1975), in 1975 450 (Nichols 1976), while further fieldwork by the same team to 1978 arrived at a figure of 525±75, distributed in the various valley-head forests as follows: Buccament 80, Wallilabou 50, Cumberland 60, Linley 50, Richmond 50, Wallibou 30, Locust valley to Colonarie valley 150, Mesopotamia 30, scattered elsewhere 25 (Nichols 1981).

In 1982, the total estimated was 421±52, distributed as: Buccament 85±20, Cumberland–Wallilabou 186±12, Linley–Richmond–Wallibou 50, Locust valley to Colonarie valley 100±20, Mesopotamia 0, scattered elsewhere 0 (Lambert 1983, 1984); this 20% decline since 1978 was attributed to the 1979 Soufrière eruption and the 1980 Hurricane Allen (see Threats). The 1982 survey disclosed that the small windward (eastern) population (perhaps only 80 birds) might be genetically somewhat isolated from the leeward birds, since while some birds might cross (or be blown) from east to west there seemed little opportunity for the reverse passage; windward birds had a higher frequency of green morphs and higher-pitched voices (Lambert 1983, 1984; also Butler 1990). The 1982 survey also noted, however, that little exchange might occur between birds in the various leeward valleys, whose lateral ridges formed greater barriers than those of windward valleys (Lambert 1983, 1984).

In 1988 two censuses were undertaken, using a methodology that could be repeated to detect trends even if the absolute totals could be no more than "guesstimated": in March, results were Buccament 100, Cumberland 125, Colonarie 65, Congo–Jennings–Perseverance 80, Richmond 45, scattered elsewhere 25; in August and September a second census, which was intended to train forest officers in the methodology, detected no significant differences in the frequency of records from the various watch-points, establishing the view that during that year the total wild population of St Vincent Amazons lay between 440 and 500 (Butler 1988).

ECOLOGY Although clearly a bird of mature moist forest (e.g. Lister 1880, Lack *et al.* 1973) that extends from between 125 and 500 m up to c.1,000 m, the St Vincent Amazon shows some preference within this for lower elevations where trees grow that are large enough to nest in (Andrle and Andrle 1975). Reports exist of occasional visits to partially cultivated sectors outside the main mountain core (Andrle and Andrle 1975), and birds were said to come regularly to a garden among the hills to feed (Lowe 1909), but clearly the species remains directly allied to the island's forest habitat.

Food includes the flowers, fruit and seeds of *Cordia sulcata*, *Dacryodes excelsa* (tabonuco), *Mangifera indica*, *Krugiodendron ferreum*, *Micropholis chrysophylloides*, *Pouteria multiflora*, *Dussia martinicensis*, *Talauma dodecapetala*, *Inga ingoides*, *Chione verosa*, *Simaruba amara*, *Ixora ferrea*, *Sloanea*, *Richeria grandis*, *Psidium guajava*, *Clusia*, *Annona muricata*, *Calophyllum brasiliense*, *Andira inermis*, *Cordia alliodora* (flowers only), *Aiphanes erosa*, *Acrocomia aculeata*, *Euterpe globosa*, *E. hagleyi*, *Ficus clusiifolia*, *F. insipida*, *F. trigonata* and *F. citrifolia* (Nichols 1981). Of these it appears that *Pouteria multiflora* is especially favoured (Nichols and Nichols 1973, Gochfeld 1974, Laidler 1977) and that tabonuco, important for breeding (see below), is also much utilized, at least in August (Lambert 1983). The report that *Manilkara bidentata* is taken (Laidler 1977, also Forshaw 1989) could not be confirmed (Nichols 1981), but local woodsmen identified *Byrsonima coriacea* var. *spicata* and *Rudgea caribea* in addition to *Clusia alba*, *Sloanea massoni*, two *Ficus* and an *Inga* as food-plants, although *Clusia* was rejected by captive birds (Lambert 1983); Butler (1988) added *Cecropia peltata* and *Meliosma virescens* to the list of food-plants.

Birds "mate" in February/March, and breed in April/May (Lawrence 1878a, Lister 1880), and although in rainy years (such as 1974) the breeding season may be curtailed (many pairs evidently not even attempting to nest), in dry ones (such as 1975) eggs may be laid through into July (Nichols 1974, 1976); eggs may even be laid as early as January and February (Butler 1988). Nests are holes in trees, chiefly tabonuco owing to its propensity to become hollow with maturity and the consequent brittleness of its limbs, which after falling leave natural cavities; of 20 nest-trees inspected, 17 were this species (Laidler 1977; also Nichols and Nichols 1973, Lambert 1984, and tabulation of nest-site data in Silva 1989a); one nest examined was 6.35 m deep and pitch dark at the bottom (Snyder *et al.* 1987: 108). A pair was reported breeding in an old estate chimney near Kingstown (Clark 1905). In the breeding season "loose nesting assemblages of approximately a dozen birds" form, and although each constituent pair defends its own nest-site (sometimes in spectacular battles) from the others, it also tolerates the close proximity of other constituent pairs, often feeding or roosting with them (Nichols 1975); there is a record of two active nests in the same tabonuco, only 5.6 m apart (Snyder *et al.* 1987: 100). Nest-site fidelity is strong (Butler 1988). Clutch-size is two, very rarely three (Frost 1959, Nichols 1981 *contra* Laidler 1977). In captivity, incubation was around 24 days and fledging 67-69 days (Forshaw 1989, Silva 1989a). In the wild only one or two young are raised even in the best years (Nichols 1974; also Low 1984), and a 50% nest failure owing to natural causes was estimated (Nichols 1976), figures which accord well with the evidence of slow breeding rate advanced in Porter (1930a). In captivity, pairs seldom lay fertile eggs before they are five years old (Butler 1988).

Birds show flight activity from 06h15 to 08h00, after which they become quiet and feed in the canopy; after a minor peak in flight activity soon after midday, birds remain quiet again until around 16h00 when activity again increases, lulling after 17h15 before a final peak just before dark (Butler 1988). Rain can disrupt this pattern, with birds remaining quiet throughout downpours but calling and flying short distances as soon as they stop (Butler 1988). Daily dispersal is outwards to the periphery of the forest during the day, inwards to the centre for the night (Butler 1988).

THREATS The chief threats to the species, identified over the years, are habitat destruction, the cagebird market, hunting and a variety of natural causes.

Habitat destruction The retreat of St Vincent's moist forests appears to have been poorly documented; while Lister (1880) could write of forest reaching the peaks and extending to near sea level on the leeward side, Lack *et al.* (1973) referred to "rather small areas" remaining at the heads of the main valleys; and although Andrle and Andrle (1975) considered some 100 km^2 of such forest to remain, they thought only 30 km^2 to be suitable for breeding habitat, in disjunct areas. Studies in 1982 showed that moist forest still occupied much the same area as that documented in 1949 (Lambert 1983), tending to vindicate the report in Forshaw (1978) that the situation was stable; nevertheless, Lack *et al.* (1973) had witnessed some clearance in 1971, Andrle and Andrle (1975) noted that commercial lumbering and local people had reduced the habitat considerably, and Lambert (1983) found that agricultural developments for banana production had resulted in the loss of almost all forest at Mesopotamia by 1982, when in 1978 the region had supported 30 parrots. Because it concentrates on middle-aged tabonuco, charcoal production was seen as a threat that had eliminated many potential nest-trees in the Colonarie valley in 1982 (Lambert 1983, 1984), and trappers had also damaged or destroyed nest-sites (five out of 12 examined in 1973, with only one of the five being reoccupied) by cutting open the trees to obtain the young (Snyder 1973, Snyder *et al.* 1987: 127). A study in 1984 determined that of the island's 340 km^2, only 16 km^2 were under primary forest, with 37 km^2 and 35 km^2 under secondary and young secondary forest respectively, and another 40 km^2 under palm, elfin or dry scrub forest; and the trend of steady forest loss was continuing (Butler 1988).

Trade The species has for many years been in demand as a cagebird, as much locally as internationally; Porter (1930a) remarked that natives sometimes caught the birds asleep in their roost-trees (although this could equally well have been in order to eat them) and sometimes also took young birds to hand-rear them. Over-exploitation by trapping was identified as a problem as long ago as 1964, when birds were known to be held on Martinique, Grenada and Trinidad as well as St Vincent itself (Vincent 1966-1971). Demand from private zoos and aviaries was still obvious in 1972, when 23 birds were found at two local hotels (Gochfeld 1974). The following year, 29 birds were found in captivity on the island and two trappers in one area admitted taking 10 young that year and knew of five others caught elsewhere (Andrle and Andrle 1975); another researcher had similar results and considered trade an increasing problem as more local people realized its value (each young sold for the equivalent of a week's wage) (Snyder 1973); and a third researcher then estimated that 30-40 were lost annually to collectors, through both the taking of nestlings and the wing-shooting of adults (Nichols 1977a). In 1974 two out of four nests being monitored had their young stolen for either food or the pet trade (Nichols 1974) and an illegal shipment of 20 birds apparently went to the pet markets in Trinidad (Nichols 1975). In 1976 "the entire population of a small valley – fifteen birds" were shot dead by a hunter in an attempt to capture one alive for a foreigner – see Threats: Trade under Imperial Amazon – offering (presumably US) $1,000 for a bird (Nichols 1986). In 1980 between 30 and 40 birds were believed to be in captivity on the island (Low 1984), and in 1982 23 were found, at least eight having been taken that year from nests; it was then reported that many young go to the Grenadines, especially Bequia, to be sold to tourists (Lambert 1983, 1984).

Hunting "Illicit gunning" remained a threat in the 1920s to all Lesser Antillean parrots (Bond 1928b); it was still considered the prime cause of the St Vincent Amazon's decline from the late 1950s to the early 1970s (Frost 1959, Bond 1961, Sjögren 1963, Vincent 1966-1971, Nichols 1974). One hunter was reported to have shot 20 in one valley in 1971 (King 1978-1979), and in 1974 a hunter reported shooting about a dozen each year (Nichols 1975), but owing to the growing exploitation of young in the early 1970s the trappers themselves began to restrict hunting activities (Snyder 1973), and by 1982 the problem was not judged serious (Lambert 1983).

Natural causes St Vincent is only 345 km^2 and is dominated by Mount Soufrière, which erupted 4,000 years ago with the force equivalent to that of Mount St Helens in 1980, and in 1718 with sufficient violence to leave a mile-wide, 500 m deep crater (Sigurdsson 1982): how the amazon survived such events is mystifying. In 1902 an eruption that killed 1,500 people (Sigurdsson 1982) "probably killed many" parrots, as that part of the island best suited to them was destroyed (Clark 1905), and in 1979 gas and ash from an eruption caused the death of some birds as far south as Buccament valley (Nichols 1981). The island is also prone to being struck by hurricanes, e.g. in 1898, when many parrots were killed outright (two even being found dead on beaches in St Lucia), others dying later seeking food in towns or else being captured by locals for food (Thompson 1900, Clark 1905). The temporal proximity of eruption and hurricane, as in 1898 and 1902, and 1979 and 1980 (Hurricane Allen), would appear particularly dangerous; yet the species seems to have the capacity to survive and recover quite rapidly. Porter (1930a) was told that the 1898 eruption did not kill birds but that a "recent" hurricane, presumably that of 1928 (see, e.g., Threats under Imperial Amazon or Puerto Rican Amazon *Amazona vittata*), had swept "quite a few... to their doom". Non-human predators of birds or their nests are (or may be) opposums *Didelphis marsupialis*, Broad-winged Hawks *Buteo platypterus*, thrashers *Margarops* and black rats *Rattus rattus* (Laidler 1977). Only the first of these was regarded seriously by Nichols (1981) (see also Nichols 1975), but Lambert (1983) reported swoops at flocks of parrots by the hawk; certainly the thrasher in question (Scaly-breasted *M. fuscus*) is not known to pose a problem (Lambert 1983). There may be some nest-site competition from bees (Laidler 1977), which were reported in one case to have taken over a parrot nest while it still contained nestlings (Snyder *et al.* 1987: 175), and if the commonly imported Orange-winged Amazon *A. amazonica* becomes feral on the island this may become a general competitor (Lambert 1983) or spread disease to the more vulnerable insular congener.

MEASURES TAKEN The species was for long protected by law from capture or export (the latter since 1920: Nichols 1977a), but the law was not enforced (Porter 1930a, Andrle and Andrle 1975). Registration of all captive birds on St Vincent was a recommendation of the 1982 expediton that was immediately implemented, with the result that seven birds (four of them in the process of being smuggled via a yacht) were confiscated in the second half of the year (Lambert 1983). A captive breeding consortium was established in 1980 (Jeggo 1984) and ecological studies, funded by SAFE International (a branch of JWPT), were conducted in the mid-1970s (Nichols 1974, 1977a).

Some detailed proposals for forest conservation were made by Andrle and Andrle (1975), these stressing in particular the need to preserve large trees at lower altitudes. Laidler and Laidler (1977) also offered detailed proposals and identified the Buccament valley as a potential reserve. Lambert (1983) likewise proposed a reserve to embrace the entire upper Buccament, upper Cumberland and Wallilabou catchments, pointing out that this area (a) comprises a major watershed of great importance for human populations in that part of the island, (b) then supported over half the island's parrots, (c) is remote from Soufrière, (d) remains accessible for nature tourism, and (e) holds a wide variety of the island's wildlife. In order to curb trade and promote conservation education, in line with the earlier recommendations of Gochfeld (1974) and Laidler (1977), Lambert (1983) also called for the improvement and enforcement of laws, with larger fines, compulsory registration and the building of a large aviary to breed from existing captive stock, with a concomitant public awareness campaign and further habitat surveys. Butler and Charles (1982), in response to WWF interest in a 1981 proposal from the St Vincent government itself for a parrot reserve and aviary, complemented Lambert's (1983) proposals with the case for an island-wide forest reserve (basically embracing all existing forest).

All these ideas were duly accommodated in a far-reaching conservation programme for both the forests and the parrot developed by the St Vincent government with the various support of CIDA (forestry management plan), WWF (drafting of a wildlife protection ordinance, promotion of ratification of CITES, provision of vehicle, training and other funds), JWPT (support for central captive breeding aviary) (all of which are documented in Butler and Charles 1986) and RARE (environmental education campaign) (Butler 1988, Johnson 1988). The initial achievements of this programme have been detailed in Butler (1988), which outlines the 1987 Wildlife Protection Act (which provides a complete framework for conservation on St Vincent) and describes a year (1988) of intensive activity (coordinated and fronted by P. J. Butler, funded by RARE Center) addressing the implementation of this act, registering all captive parrots on the island, creating a breeding centre for some of them, censusing the wild parrots (see Population), demarcating and drawing up a management plan for a 40 km^2 parrot reserve in the middle of the island, undertaking an island-wide campaign of public education and sensitization to the problems of forest and wildlife conservation, with particular emphasis on the parrot, and not least bringing these developments to international attention so that the position and commitment of the St Vincent government (which in due course became a party to CITES) would be clearly understood not only by conservationists but also by bird-fanciers with an interest in adding the St Vincent Amazon to their collections.

MEASURES PROPOSED Continued monitoring of the wild parrot population, and strong enforcement of CITES so that illegally held birds can be returned to St Vincent whenever requested by the government, are among the measures needed to maintain the relatively secure status of the St Vincent Amazon at present.

Captive breeding One of the declared intentions of the fieldwork initiated in the mid-1970s was to take a sufficient number of birds to "establish a viable captive population", and two birds were taken in 1974 to Houston Zoo (Nichols 1974, 1975). However, at that time the government was making small numbers available to various institutions, a policy considered mistaken (Nichols 1977a) for, as noted by Jeggo (1981), "there is a grave danger that uncoordinated attempts will only be to the detriment of the species"; meanwhile, the owner of a facility on Barbados with the largest collection of captive birds was "completely uncooperative" (Nichols 1977a), although evidently not with Vogelpark Walsrode (see Robiller and Trogisch 1985). However, in 1980 an international captive breeding consortium for the St Vincent Amazon was established to foster cooperation between holders of the species, and seven institutions, holding 15 birds between them, joined (Paradise Park [U.K.], Houston Zoo, JWPT, the National Zoo in Washington, New York Zoo, T. D. Nichols of the James Bond Research Foundation, and the St Vincent government), although several others that then held or subsequently acquired birds (e.g. W. Miller on Barbados, R. Noegel of Life Fellowship, Vogelpark Walsrode and Loro Parque) have remained outside the formal agreement (Jeggo 1990), Walsrode joining in late 1991 (D. F. Jeggo verbally 1992). The rearing of a bird at Paradise Park in 1991 was the first breeding success within the consortium (D. F. Jeggo *in litt.* 1992). An amnesty on St Vincent in 1988 resulted in the registration of some 80 birds in captivity on the island, of which 20 are in a new government facility in the Botanical Gardens, Kingstown (four young were reared in 1991: D. F. Jeggo *in litt.* 1992); in 1990 there were an additional 50 birds in captivity outside St Vincent (Jeggo 1990; for the Kingstown facility, see Amberger 1989b). It is clear that further efforts are needed to involve other holders of the species and to begin breeding birds in numbers before the captive population indeed becomes viable.

REMARKS (1) The value of these post-hurricane assessments from so long ago is always open to doubt; and another testimony, that of Thompson (1900), is that although the species suffered losses in the 1898 storm the species had already shown itself well recovered by 1900, birds being seen "in their usual numbers in their usual haunts". (2) Estimates of a thousand or more were disputed by Nichols (1981) on the grounds that they resulted from extrapolation from estimates of numbers in upper Buccament valley, already shown in September 1973 to be an area of unusually high density.

IMPERIAL AMAZON *Amazona imperialis* E[1]

The Imperial Amazon is highly endangered on its native Dominica, where it occurs now only in the forests of Morne Diablotin, and, having suffered from a combination of habitat loss, hunting, trade and hurricanes, now numbers only around 80 individuals, although in recent years it has benefited from joint government and non-government efforts to protect its habitat and sensitize local citizens to its needs.

DISTRIBUTION The Imperial Amazon is endemic to Dominica, West Indies, where it is now seemingly confined to the east, north and west slopes on the upper reaches of Morne Diablotin (1,421 m) in the north of the island (see Figure 4 in Evans 1991). Its centre of abundance may have always been Morne Diablotin, where it was "found more commonly than in any other part of the island" by Bond (1941b), but vague early records of its presence "in the very centre and most mountainous part of the island" (*Proc. Zool. Soc. London* 1865: 437) doubtless reflect accurately its original distribution throughout the mountain chain of Dominica as far south as Morne Anglais, in the region of which (together with Morne Watt and Morne Jaune) an ever-dwindling population, separated from that on Morne Diablotin well before 1950 (see Figure 2 in Evans 1991, based largely on localities cited in Nichols *et al.* 1976), finally appeared to have died out in the early 1980s, the last verified sighting being around 1983 (Evans 1988a, 1991).

On Morne Diablotin itself, there has been a steady if uneven retreat upwards. Bond (1928b) referred to birds in the forests to the south and south-east of the mountain. Around 1945 the range followed a line running just above Syndicate Estate, along Morne Turner Ridge, between Foundland and Chilenbain Estate, north of Chaudière Estate, to Grand Bambou, Never Fail and Gros Bois, just north of a peak (670 m) between Gros Bois and Coffee, west of Main Ridge, to Entwistle, south to include Dleau Gommier, just north of Bambou Ettor, to Fond Trouve, including McFarlin to the heights of upper Petit Macocoucheri, between Jean and En Haut Jean, to Kachibona, Savanne Gommier, and back to Syndicate, this being something like double the area occupied in 1975 (Nichols *et al.* 1976). Even in 1981 the species was being reported from the south slopes of the mountain (Anon. 1981b), but accumulated evidence through the decade indicates its absence there now, with the area north-west of the mountain in the upper Picard river valley (or Devil's valley), notably the Morne Plaisance and Dyer estates, being critically important (Anon. 1981b, Nichols 1981c, Evans 1988a, 1991). Fieldwork in early 1992 indicated the population was still chiefly confined to elevations between 450 and 1,000 m, but with regular sightings within the newly acquired nature reserve (see Measures Taken: Habitat protection) at 300 m and one observation as low as 200 m above Wesley in the north-east (P. G. H. Evans *in litt.* 1992).

POPULATION Estimates and assessments have varied with observer, in part at least in relation to degree of penetration of habitat; however, a comment by the guide used by Gochfeld (1974), that the species was to be found in relatively few, discrete areas of montane forest, suggests that human judgement of its abundance would depend on the extent of penetration of those particular areas of habitat. Even today there are areas of forest that require investigation (see Measures Proposed) and about which assumptions have been made that influence recent and current estimates (see below).

It was surely the inaccessibility of the Imperial Amazon's habitat that gave rise to the earliest account of its status as "very rare" and "seldom seen", with "only one or two... caught during the year" (*Proc. Zool. Soc. London* 1865: 437), for in fact when properly investigated it was described as abundant in the high mountains in the 1870s (Lawrence 1878) and common in the interior and on the windward side, 1890 (Verrill 1892). Despite Verrill's (1905) observation that the species had become rarer than the Red-necked Amazon *Amazona arausiaca* and the gloomy prognostications in Beebe (1912), much the same situation appears to have obtained into the

1920s, with investigators worrying whether the species survived at all and being told that it was "excessively rare" (e.g. Porter 1929), only to conclude that, despite being so poorly known to Dominicans themselves, the species had maintained itself in its fastnesses "in limited numbers" (Wood 1924) or "in some numbers" (Bond 1928b). A flock of 100-200 seen in a valley after a hurricane in 1928 was judged possibly to have been the entire population of the species (Porter 1929), although there seems to be no good reason why this should have been so; nor does there seem to be anything more than guesswork in the view that there were 200-275 birds on the island in 1918 (Anon. 1981b). A non-specialist's remark that the bird was "scarce" at this time (Howes 1929) would be much as expected. Once again, although described as very rare by an outside observer in the 1950s (Frost 1959), "small flocks... sparsely distributed" still remained in 1966 (Gochfeld 1974), and D. Lack (*in litt.* 1971 to P. Barclay-Smith) found it "in reasonably large numbers on Diablotin and reasonably safe".

Fieldwork targeted at or at least encompassing the species has been more or less continuous since the mid-1970s, resulting initially in informed guesses by three observers of 250, 150 and 150 birds remaining in 1975 (Nichols *et al.* 1976), the latter figure gaining the greater currency through several repetitions (e.g. in Nichols 1976, 1977b; see Remarks 1). The isolated southern population based around Morne Anglais was believed to have suffered a marked decline since around 1970, when as many as 15 had been seen together at one time, and it was agreed that no more than 24 and probably only about eight remained there (Nichols *et al.* 1976); but either the population there recovered somewhat, or the observers had simply overlooked the birds (evidently extremely easy; but it throws into doubt all attempts to put figures on the population), or the following report was mistaken, for in early 1979 16 were reported in one valley near Morne Anglais and possibly more were still extant in another near Morne Watt (Snyder and Snyder 1979; *ICBP Newsletter* 2[1], 1980; see Remarks 1).

The effect of hurricanes in 1979 and, to a lesser degree, 1980 (see Threats), was to reduce the southern population to unviable status ("possibly not more than a dozen birds") (Snyder and Snyder 1979, Anon. 1981a,b) and indeed, although some lingered for a few years, it appears that by 1985 all birds away from Morne Diablotin had disappeared (Evans 1986a). The northern population was thought to have been halved, so that 70-100 was the figure for 1980 and 1981 (Anon. 1981a,b), although another fieldworker put the figure at 75 in 1979 and, following clear-cutting of feeding areas in the upper Picard valley (see Threats), 40-60 in 1981 (Nichols 1986; for upper Picard valley, 1978-1990, with the clear effect of the 1979 hurricane, see Figure 6 in Evans 1991). By 1985 preliminary analysis of survey data indeed suggested that as few as 50 survived (Evans 1986a), but further work showed that in 1987 some 60 birds could be estimated (Evans 1988a), with a slight recovery to 80 in 1990 (Evans 1991) and possibly more (but still less than 100) in 1992 (P. G. H. Evans *in litt.* 1992).

ECOLOGY The Imperial Amazon occupies the canopy of primary rainforest on interior mountain slopes; it has always been regarded as a montane species (e.g. Verrill 1892, Porter 1929, Gochfeld 1974, Nichols *et al.* 1976), and more recent work has confirmed that it occurs primarily between 600 and 1,300 m (Evans 1988a, 1991). However, Lawrence (1878) reported that "it descends to the valleys in the rainy season to some extent"; three skins dated September 1899 in AMNH are marked as taken at 1,000 feet (300 m), and even in the 1980s there have been observations from as low as 150 m (see Figure 9 in Evans 1991), all such records presumably resulting from either food shortages (Evans 1988a) or at least foraging preferences. There is, nevertheless, evidence that the species's range has retreated upwards in recent years (see Distribution). Birds may also penetrate elfin forest at 1,200 m and above (Nichols 1981c). Ecological separation from the also threatened Red-necked Amazon (see relevant account) is partially altitudinal, the latter chiefly occurring between 300 and 800 m (Evans 1988a, 1991), and partially dietary (see below and under Red-necked Amazon), but there is considerable overlap in both variables which renders the issue problematic (indeed, the two species show maximum densities at the same altitudes, 500-600 m: Evans 1991). Moreover, studies have shown that certain parts of the forest (with associations of particular tree species such as mature gommiers *Dacryodes excelsa*) are much more important than others for both species, so that no easy assumptions can be made based purely on the amount of habitat remaining (Evans 1986a). However, the Imperial Amazon seems much less able to tolerate disturbance of habitat than the Red-neck (Nichols *et al.* 1976).

Both species eat the fruits of gommier (an important item for both), bois diable *Licania ternatensis*, bois bande *Richeria grandis*, carapite *Amanoa caribaea*, bois blanc *Simarouba amara*, mangle *Symphonia globulifera*, bois rivière *Chimarrhis cymosa* (also flowers) and balate *Pouteria (Oxythece) pallida* (this apparently being the *Manilkara bidentata* of other authors), with Imperial Amazon alone taking also bois cote *Tapura antillana*, the palm *Euterpe globosa* and kaklin *Clusia venosa* (Evans 1988a). Of these, the three last and *S. globulifera* appeared to be favoured, plus the palm *E. dominicana* (Anon. 1981b), a plant also identified as food by Ober (1880) and Nichols *et al.* (1976). Verrill (1892) indicated that the species particularly favoured areas where mountain palms and gommiers grew, consuming (as "a large part of its diet") their seeds and fruit, plus the young shoots of the former; Lawrence (1878) reported much the same, adding bois diable to the list. In the months following Hurricane Allen, birds were seen feeding on vines and shrubs near ground level (Anon. 1981a). As evidence that the species seemed adapted to cope with food shortages as might occur on any island, but particularly one prone to storm damage, Porter (1929) recorded a wounded bird that went 13 days without food before making a near-full recovery.

The main breeding season for both species of Dominican amazon is February–June (particularly March–May), coinciding with the dry season and perhaps therefore related to greater food abundance during the nestling and fledgling period (Evans 1988a). In the Imperial Amazon, defence of a nesting territory probably occurs throughout the year (P. G. H. Evans *in litt.* 1992) and has certainly been witnessed as early as mid-December; data from 1980 and 1981 suggest that pairs rarely leave this territory for long periods, and indeed occupy it (with self-advertising display-flights) throughout the year, but with more frequent absences from September to mid-December (Anon. 1981b). Although reported generally to place the nest in the top of a dead (broken shaft) palm (Ober 1880, Verrill 1892) this has not been confirmed; instead, records of nest-sites are from high in the trunks of the dominant forest trees chataignier *Sloanea berteriana* and gommier (Nichols *et al.* 1976, Evans 1988a), although breeding was also reported from a spur high enough to be in the elfin forest zone (Bond 1941b). The reproductive rate is low, with two eggs being laid perhaps only every second year and pairs seldom raising more than one young per clutch (Gregoire 1981; also Frost 1959, Evans 1988a); comments by locals that only one egg is laid (Porter 1929) might be based on the usual number of young seen. Age of first breeding and whether nest-sites are limiting remain unknown (Evans 1988a). From July (and certainly September: P. G. H. Evans *in litt.* 1992) to November, birds are very unobtrusive, feeding quietly (Anon. 1981b). Activity is greatest 06h00-10h00 and 16h00-19h00, with 95% of feeding observations being made within these periods, although the birds' relative silence between the two means that feeding activity may then go unobserved (Evans 1988a). Roosting is at traditional sites, commonly large gommier or chataignier trees, but although used from year to year they are not necessarily used throughout the year (Evans 1988a).

THREATS The most important threat by far at this stage is habitat destruction, but hunting played a major part in suppressing numbers when habitat was still extensive, and by 1981 hunting for the pet trade was considered a threat of only slightly less significance than deforestation (Anon. 1981a); meanwhile, another hurricane with the force and path of David in 1979 could be conclusive. Some of these factors work to promote others, of course: hurricanes kill birds, destroy habitat and promote habitat destruction; a road through the forest in the 1880s allowed hunters in "and one collector shot a dozen specimens" (Beebe 1912). The following enumeration includes two headings for "natural causes", but it is particularly worth stressing in this instance that in most cases what is prima facie "natural" has behind it the insidious influence of man, by reducing habitat to the critical point where it or its constituents become vulnerable to natural processes, by suppressing natural population levels in a way that lends competitive advantage to other species, by introducing species whose natural activities affect the habitat or its constituents, or a combination of any of these.

Habitat destruction "The remoteness and inaccessibility of its native haunts" was a reason to regard the species as relatively secure "for many years" (Wood 1924, Bond 1928b, 1961, Porter 1929), and even as late as the mid-1970s this impregnability of habitat lay behind the belief that "this species will undoubtedly survive in the wild" (Nichols 1977b). The excessive expense of transporting timber down from the mountains led to a Canadian company abandoning rights to extract timber from the island in the 1960s (Gochfeld 1974). In the 1970s this scenario seems to have been repeated, with "irreparable damage" being avoided only by failure to reach agreement between the government and a logging company to clear-cut a very large area of the island (Nichols *et al.* 1976). However, at that time it was the piecemeal destruction of forest through selective logging, charcoal production and agricultural clearance that caused greater concern, being more relentless and more difficult to control (Nichols *et al.* 1976). Selective felling of the patchily abundant gommier (important for parrots: see Ecology above, and under Red-necked Amazon) in large quantities was a practice thought likely to disrupt links in the ecosystem (Evans 1986a). Since 1980, interest has focused on the high-quality forests (and their high-quality agricultural soils) north-west of Morne Diablotin (details in Evans 1988a, 1991). Thus in early 1980, prime forest land bordering Imperial habitat at Syndicate was sold and converted to agriculture, affecting birds' foraging ability and increasing hunting pressure (Zamore 1980), this presumably the feeding area lost to banana production after 1978 referred to by Nichols (1981c). A planned feeder road in the Syndicate area would result in the loss of 540 ha of forest to agriculture, depriving the species of a major feeding area and eliminating a necessary buffer between it and agricultural holdings (Anon. 1981b). Then in 1982 attention shifted to the 375 ha Morne Plaisance Estate, part of which has now been logged in what was recommended as the least ecologically damaging manner (see Evans 1991). Pressure then built up to clear the neighbouring Dyer Estate, and in July 1989 a timber company began selectively felling gommiers there, at which point national and international forces coalesced in successful opposition (Evans 1991; see Measures Taken: Habitat protection). It has been estimated that in the decade of the 1980s a greater area of forest was destroyed on Dominica than in the previous thousand years (Evans 1989). As a further twist in the forest-to-farm development, aerial spraying of banana crops next to foraging areas has led to reports of poisoning and blindness in parrots (Anon. 1981a; also Nichols 1981c).

Hunting Hunting was possibly the most serious factor limiting the population through into the 1970s. In the nineteenth century birds were much hunted for food, especially in the rainy season when they were very fat and excellent eating, occasionally reaching Roseau market (Lawrence 1878, 1880a, Verrill 1892). Porter (1929), in remarking that they used to be shot and eaten in fair quantities, added that this happened occasionally in the present, but in fact what he then related suggests considerable continuing exploitation: apart from stories of many birds being shot while he was on the island (some in attempts to capture them alive), he discovered that 38 were killed or captured between October 1928 and February 1929 in the wake of a major hurricane. Hunting was blamed for the species being (as was believed) almost extinct in the 1950s (Frost 1959) and, despite the reassurance that the cost of cartridges had reduced pressure on the bird in 1966 (Gochfeld 1974), in 1973 hunting was again perceived as the major problem, with almost everyone met admitting to being a former or current shooter of parrots, and with one instance of a pair being killed while young were in the nest and in spite of pleas from a local guide (Snyder 1973). Subsequent workers (Nichols *et al.* 1976) agreed that hunting continued to be the most serious threat, with evidence that in 1975 another pair had been shot. Even after the 1979 hurricane and in spite of Forestry Division efforts, there were believed to be "strong hunting pressures" on the species (Snyder and Snyder 1979; *ICBP Newsletter* 2[1], 1980; Zamore 1980, Gregoire 1981), and in November 1981 four Frenchmen from Guadeloupe were apprehended while hunting in the

Forest Reserve (Anon. 1981b); nevertheless, throughout the rest of the 1980s there was little evidence of other than occasional shooting (P. G. H. Evans *in litt.* 1992).

Trade Owing at least in part to the inaccessibility of nests from which to take young, hunting for cagebirds involved the highly destructive practice of "wing-shooting", which resulted in the accidental deaths of many birds (as reported, e.g., by Lawrence 1878, Porter 1929). An offer, apparently in the early 1960s, of US$300 for a live bird led to many islanders going out and attempting to wing-shoot individuals (Gochfeld 1974), and Gregoire (1981) estimated that 40 birds (of each species) were being shot every year (i.e. even in the 1970s) as a consequence of this practice; much of this was apparently from local rather than international interest (Nichols *et al.* 1976), but Nichols (1986) reported that in 1976 C. Cordier was involved in obtaining Imperials (and simultaneously St Vincent Amazons *A. guildingii*: see relevant account) by implication for Vogelpark Walsrode in (West) Germany. This appears to be unrelated to the story in Butler (1989) of the importation into (West) Germany in 1979 of a number of both Red-necked and Imperial Amazons with incorrect papers via Guadeloupe, which, however, had a satisfactory outcome (see Measures Taken). The fact that illegally exported birds had been able to remain in foreign hands (Christian 1991) had been noted by other European aviculturists, and this was thought to be likely to contribute to further attempts to capture and smuggle birds abroad (Nichols 1981c). However, the situation is now considered under control (see Measures Taken).

Natural causes: hurricanes Clearly the wildlife of the Caribbean islands is to some extent adapted to the effects of hurricanes, and the long-term damage to species on pristine islands was perhaps always negligible. However, when species become isolated by habitat destruction or rare through human exploitation, their immunity to hurricane damage is greatly reduced (Nichols *et al.* 1976); moreover, hurricanes affecting developing countries result in such things as (a) local people taking the chance to clear and cultivate badly damaged land, and (b) foreign aid programmes directed at rapid recuperation, irrespective of long-term environmental costs (Evans 1988a). On 29 August 1979 the exceptionally powerful Hurricane David struck directly across Dominica from south-east to north-west, destroying five million trees in the southern forests, halving the parrot populations (see Population), stripping trees of fruit and eliminating many nest-sites (see Gregoire 1981, Evans 1991). Even on the relatively sheltered north-west slopes of Morne Diablotin, four out of five known nest-trees of Imperial Amazon were rendered unfit, with similar evidence elsewhere (Zamore 1980). A second, less damaging hurricane (Allen, on 3 August 1980) shook fruit off trees and caused both parrot species to forage on buds and shoots near the ground again (Anon. 1981a), and this may have contributed to the apparent failure of Imperials to breed for two successive years after David (Anon. 1981b, Nichols 1981c).

Natural causes: predators and competitors Possible predators include opossum *Didelphis marsupialis*, rats *Rattus*, boas *Constrictor constrictor* and Broad-winged Hawks *Buteo platypterus*, although only the first, believed introduced in the later nineteenth century, has been thought in any way serious (Nichols *et al.* 1976). Competition for nest-sites from Pearly-eyed Thrashers *Margarops fuscatus* was thought probably insignificant, as the latter seemed not to be as common in the Imperial's as in the Red-necked Amazon's range (Nichols *et al.* 1976; also Evans 1991). The idea that Red-necked Amazons might be in direct competition with Imperials (see, e.g., King 1978-1979) could not be confirmed, with no interactions when seen feeding together ("feeding and living in harmony": Porter 1929) and evidence that both were in steep decline (Nichols *et al.* 1976), although nest-site competition between the species (won by Imperials) was witnessed twice in 1981 and attributed to Red-necks being forced into higher altitudes by habitat destruction below (Anon. 1981b), observations discounted by Evans (1988a), who (reassuringly, since his work is almost all post-1981) has found "no evidence as yet to suggest that one species interferes with the other". Escape of exotic parrot pets might pose a threat in the future (Nichols *et al.* 1976).

MEASURES TAKEN For any measures to be taken they generally first have to be proposed, and it is worth recording that Nichols *et al.* (1976), Snyder and Snyder (1979) and Gregoire (1981) all made recommendations, some of which were implemented, some modified, some superseded, some ignored, and some still relevant; this and the next section conflates these and other current or possible measures. While those already taken are best broken down into separate issues, it is important to credit individuals and organizations that have contributed to these various initiatives: the Dominican Forestry Division for its long-term efforts on all fronts; SAFE International (part of JWPT/WPTI) and WWF-U.S. for support of work by Nichols (1976, 1977b), *et al.* (1976), etc.; WWF-U.S. for emergency support for post-hurricane conservation work; ICBP Pan American Section for support of several key surveys including one that prompted WWF's post-hurricane intervention; P. G. H. Evans (and his many co-workers) for his long-term study (see, e.g., Evans 1986b, 1989) aimed (since 1982) at finding ways to integrate conservation and development needs (something originally called for by Nichols *et al.* 1976), now within the programme of ICBP but receiving the support of many different interest groups, including the James Bond Research Foundation (see Nichols 1986) and Loro Parque (see Low 1988), but always with the full support of the Dominican government (see Gregoire 1987); and RARE (now RARE Center), for providing various types of support through the 1980s culminating in the education and awareness programme "Project Sisserou" conducted by P. J. Butler in 1989.

Legal protection Lawrence (1878) reported the existence of "a very beneficent law" that prohibited hunting of parrots except between September and February, "thus ensuring protection during the breeding season"; evidently this law was replaced with full protection in 1914 (Swank and Julien 1975), although it was further upgraded and defined in 1976 (Porter 1930b took what steps he could to have it enforced). Following Hurricane David, a total ban was imposed on hunting of all wildlife and the Forestry Division recruited (with a grant from WWF-U.S.) four conservation officers to patrol the forests and enforce the law (Anon. 1981a,b, Gregoire 1981, and as recommended by Snyder and Snyder 1979). A significant decrease in the problem of hunting has resulted (Evans 1991), and the compulsory registration (using an amnesty as inducement to declare) in early 1989 of all captive birds on the island has closed the local market in the species (Butler 1989). In 1979 an illegal consignment of both Red-necked and Imperial Amazons was returned from West Germany to Dominica after the latter government's intervention (Butler 1989). Illegal smuggling of birds to the international market, which was investigated by U.S. State Department special agents in 1981 (Anon. 1981b), is currently discounted as a major threat (Evans 1988a). Details of national laws are provided in Butler (1989). The species is listed on Appendix I of CITES.

Habitat protection The protected area system in Dominica, welcome as it is, fails to cater for the parrots of the country: Morne Trois Pitons National Park (for which see Wright 1985) is not the most important area ecologically (the Red-necked Amazon has not been recorded there since 1973: Evans 1991), and the Northern Forest Reserve (for which see Gregoire 1981) does not include the important, relatively flat area of climax forest that occupies the Syndicate, Dyer, Milton, Jude and Morne Plaisance estates and which is an important area for both species (Evans 1988a). Attempts in Washington in 1983 by the Director of Forestry and Wildlife, C. Maximea, to raise the funds to acquire these estates for conservation met with no success (Nichols 1986, Evans 1991). Actual and prospective loss of forest in the upper Picard valley (see Threats: Habitat destruction) became so serious that in August 1988 the government of Dominica, ICBP and RARE Center signed a memorandum of agreement to seek to protect the area, and in July 1989 a vitally important and imminently threatened tract of 80 ha was acquired by the three signatories, to become government property as a nature reserve after three years (Rands and Foster 1989, Evans 1991). Nevertheless, much more needs to be done to protect a wider area of forest (see Measures Proposed).

Environmental education and awareness This was urged as likely to "produce beneficial effects" (Swank and Julien 1975), and since 1980 there have been various initiatives aimed at creating a new conservation consciousness in Dominica, particularly in relation to parrot protection and habitat conservation. Following Hurricane David, the Forestry Division (funded by WWF-U.S.) stepped up its customary educational work with school visits, public lectures, radio broadcasts, the distribution of a RARE-funded poster (with the same motif on tee-shirts), and a play called "Parrot Poachers" (Anon. 1981a,b, Gregoire 1981, Low 1984, Christian 1991, Evans 1991). A conservation education newspaper, "VWA Diablotin", was circulated to every school for several years in the mid-1980s, and the recent creation of an Environmental Education Unit has led to its revival (Christian 1991, Evans 1991). From January to August 1989 P. J. Butler of RARE Center conducted a further campaign of public awareness, promoting the fact that the Imperial Amazon is the country's national bird and emblem, and organizing an amnesty for illegally held parrots, all as part of "Project Sisserou" (Butler 1989, Evans 1991; see Measures Proposed: Captive Breeding).

Ecotourism Development of nature tourism to Dominica was recommended by Nichols *et al.* (1976) and Evans (1986, 1988a) as one step towards underpinning the foundations of conservation in the country; at least one British company now runs specialist tours to the island.

Survey, study and monitoring of birds In response to a recommendation by Snyder and Snyder (1979), WWF-U.S. funded the training of personnel, the construction of forest observation posts, and the subsequent study and monitoring of the two parrot species by Forestry Division staff (cited, e.g., in Ecology from Anon. 1981a,b).

MEASURES PROPOSED Four of Evans's (1988a) nine recommendations (those concerning the protection of the upper Picard valley, the creation of an education unit, the revival of a newspaper and the promotion of ecotourism) have been at least partly fulfilled (see above). The others relate to survey and study of the parrots and are outlined in the following paragraph, with additional points carried over from Nichols *et al.* (1976). Subsequent paragraphs refer to points not addressed by or arising subsequently to Evans (1988a).

Survey, study and monitoring of birds Evans's (1988a) five further recommendations (with parentheses for those of Nichols *et al.* 1976) are (1) to survey the remote eastern slopes of Morne Diablotin to establish the relative abundance of both parrot species; (2) to survey certain mountain areas in the south of the island to establish whether either parrot is present; (3) to determine more precisely the habitat requirements and food preferences of both species (also to clarify the extent and nature of interspecific interactions); (4) to investigate by use of radio-tagging the effects of forest fragmentation on both species (and to assess the extent and causes of seasonal movements); (5) to gather life-history data on both species with particular emphasis on population parameters (and with some emphasis on the problem of possible nest-site competition from Pearly-eyed Thrashers); while a further point (6) is that regular monitoring of the populations, with the involvement of appropriately trained forestry officers, is of critical importance (Butler 1989).

Morne Diablotin National Park The Dominican government and ICBP have now drawn up a proposal to convert lands in the upper Picard valley and the western sector of the existing Northern Forest Reserve, in total an area of over 3,800 ha including the most important area for both parrots and the best tracts of forest with the richest wildlife in the country, into a national park, at a cost of approximately US$800,000 (N. Varty verbally 1992). The idea of a national park in this area, albeit somewhat grander in scope, was first made in Nichols *et al.* (1976); the management plan for the proposed park was expected to be completed in September 1992 by N. Varty and G. Mendelssohn (ICBP), R. Charles and D. Williams (government of Dominica).

Replanting The rapid replanting of areas lumbered for timber or charcoal with slow-growing native climax dominants such as gommier, pommier, penipice and carapite, would be both useful to parrots and valuable economically (Nichols *et al.* 1976); although most such logged areas appear to be converted to agriculture, there are some places where replanting in this way would be feasible.

Captive breeding Consideration of this option was urged by Snyder and Snyder (1979) and Gregoire (1981) in the wake of Hurricane David, and later by Low (1984). The 1989 amnesty (see Measures Taken: Environmental education and awareness) resulted in the surrender of one Imperial and eight Red-necked Amazons, for which an aviary was officially opened in May 1992 in the Botanical Gardens in Roseau, with JWPT providing the appropriate training (D. F. Jeggo *in litt.* 1992, M. G. Kelsey *in litt.* 1992; see Remarks 2); Low (1984), however, felt that birds should not be held on Dominica but placed with experienced aviculturists. While any attempts to breed birds either on or away from Dominica should not distract attention from the other needs outlined in this section, it is clearly worth trying to use existing captive stock throughout the world (if holders will admit to possessing them) in a concerted effort to maximize genetic variation and generate sufficient numbers for more public education programmes. In this regard the crossbreeding experiments of D. Green (as indicated in Nichols 1981b, Gerstberger 1982 and Amberger 1989a) should be stopped as the participation of his birds would be valuable.

Vigilance over trade Attempts to acquire both species of parrot continue to be made by unscrupulous foreign bird fanciers, so control of capture and export must remain a high priority, for which purpose Dominica is urged to accede to CITES (Evans 1991). Linked with this is the recommendation in Nichols *et al.* (1976) to impose stricter rules on the importation of exotic parrots (see Threats: Natural causes: predators and competitors).

REMARKS (1) Anon. (1981a) cited "Nichols and Nichols" as the source of information that there were 150-200 birds present in 1972, something which hence crops up even in Evans (1988a); and Anon. (1981b) referred to the southern population as being estimated at over 50 in 1972 (which crops up in Evans 1991), obviously implying that the Nichols were involved in arriving at this figure; but there is no evidence in any writing by any Nichols that 1972 was a year used for estimating numbers or that "150-200" or "50" were used as population figures as indicated. These figures may therefore be forestry personnel assessments (P. G. H. Evans *in litt.* 1992). (2) According to Butler (1989), a facility of some sort already existed in the 1980s and housed the birds returned from West Germany in 1979 (see Measures Taken).

YELLOW-HEADED AMAZON *Amazona oratrix* V[9]

The most popular and sought-after amazon in trade, this species is known from four discrete areas, three in Mexico (Atlantic lowlands, Pacific lowlands, and the Islas Marías) and one in Belize, but has suffered enormously from trade pressures and habitat loss throughout its Mexican range, and it may also be under pressure in Belize. A suite of actions, including surveys, studies, site protection and management, and local education campaigns, is required.

DISTRIBUTION The Yellow-headed Amazon (see Remarks 1) is confined to Mexico and Belize in four apparently discrete populations, namely the race *tresmariae* on Mexico's Islas Marías ("Tres Marías" islands) off the coast of Nayarit, a population of nominate *oratrix* on the Pacific slope of Mexico in the states of Jalisco, Colima, Michoacán, Guerrero and Oaxaca, another population of nominate *oratrix* (sometimes considered a distinct race, *magna*: but see Remarks 2) on the Atlantic slope of Mexico in the states of Tamaulipas, San Luis Potosí, Veracruz, Tabasco and Chiapas (with records or claims also for Guanajuato, México, Puebla, Campeche and Yucatán), and *belizensis* in Belize (for records concerning Guatemala, see Remarks 3; for other distributional reports, see Remarks 4).

Mexico The following account is organized primarily by discrete populations (*tresmariae*, *oratrix* and "*magna*") and then by state, from north to south and with localities within them from north to south or west to east; unless otherwise stated, coordinates are derived from OG (1956a).

Islas Marías The race *tresmariae* occurs on all four islands – San Juanito, María Madre, María Magdalena and María Cleofas – in the group (Stager 1957, Grant and Cowan 1964), and because nomadic within and between islands (e.g. Konrad 1984, 1986) it has no clearly identified key sites or sites repeatedly mentioned in the literature; nonetheless, in April 1983 "literally hundreds (if not thousands)" of birds congregated daily in the main seaport of Balleto on María Madre, because of the fruit trees in the vicinity, while elsewhere they were hard to find (Hansen 1984), which indicates that there may be some very definite areas of importance for the species.

Jalisco Records are by P. Hubbell near Chamela in the 1960s, and by K. Radamaker, who saw two adults 13 km north of Barra de Navidad in December 1991 (both *per* S. N. G. Howell *in litt.* 1992).

Colima Lawrence (1874) listed the "Tupila River" and the río de Coahuayana as localities where J. Xantus, who was reported to have worked only in the Colima and Manzanillo areas, had collected the species; the former cannot be traced but both are indicated for the state by Ridgway (1916), the latter, at 18°41'N 103°45'W, evidently lying at the frontier with Michoacán. However, all Schaldach's (1963) records were from the base of Cerro del Sacate (with specimens from the adjacent Llano de Garritas, coordinates for both, as read from his map, being almost exactly 19°N 104°W) and other mountain massifs in the central part of the state, the species not being seen elsewhere.

Michoacán Certain authorities, lacking evidence, have resisted including this state in the range of the species, despite its position between Colima and Guerrero (e.g. Ridgway 1916, Friedmann *et al.* 1950, Forshaw 1989), while at the other extreme Monroe and Howell (1966) shaded the entire coastal region of the state as part of the bird's distribution, and AOU (1983) involved it through the phrase "Colima south to Oaxaca"; yet there appear to be only two records, both previously unpublished. A male was taken at La Placita on 8 July 1950 (specimen in UMMZ); however, the collector of this specimen, R. W. Storer (*in litt.* 1992), in indicating that La Placita is a village on the east bank of the río Maquili c.1 km from the sea and c.20 km south-east of the Coahuayana estuary, also reported that he found the species "fairly common in coconuts and small trees" in the vicinity, and he has field notes that suggest that several hundred amazons nearby at Ostula (c.15 km from the sea on the río Ostula, which meets the Pacific south-east of La Placita) may have been this species. In November 1987 R. Bowers saw 25 at Km 100 on the main coastal highway (S. N. G. Howell *in litt.* 1992).

Guerrero Evidence for the listing of this state (Friedmann *et al.* 1950, Forshaw 1989; and by map and by implication – see above – Monroe and Howell 1966 and AOU 1983 respectively) appears to reside with just two records, a specimen from Papayo (Ridgway 1916) and one from Cuajinicuilapa (Monroe and Howell 1966). OG (1956a) lists only two localities called Papayo, but both within this state, at 17°02'N 100°17'W and 17°55'N 100°32'W, the former being perhaps the more likely as seemingly at a lower altitude and closer to the coast (see Ecology); Cuajinicuilapa is listed at 16°28'N 98°25'W, i.e. close to the coast. There are no credible recent reports from the state (S. N. G. Howell *in litt.* 1992).

Oaxaca Birds have been recorded from two disjunct areas: in the south-west at Llano Grande, Minitán, Río Grande (near Puerto Escondido) and 15 km west-north-west of San José Estancia Grande; and in the east at "Petapa" (this probably Santo Domingo Petapa), 16°49'N 95°09'W, and El Barrio, 16°48'N 95°08'W (Binford 1989, whence also the coordinates). Binford (1989) expected the race *magna* to occur in the northern part of the state, but there appear to be no records (but see, e.g., Playa Vicente under Veracruz).

Tamaulipas Records are from the centre of the state southwards, as follows: Villagrán, nineteenth century (specimen in BMNH marked "Villa Gran, N.L." but doubtless from the Tamaulipas locality, which is close to the Nuevo León border; see Remarks 4); Hidalgo (Ridgway 1916, Monroe and Howell 1966); Jiménez (Ridgway 1916, Monroe and Howell 1966); río Cruz (presumably río de la Cruz as in Ridgway 1916; now río Purificación), 23°58'N 98°42'W (Phillips 1911); río Pilón, 23°58'N 98°42'W (Ridgway 1916, Monroe and Howell 1966); río Corona at 250 m (23°55'N 99°00'W in Gehlbach *et al.* 1976; also Ridgely 1981a), including near Güemez (Sutton and Burleigh 1939, also *Amer. Birds* Christmas Bird Count site); (Villa de) Casas, 23°44'N 98°45'W (Vázquez undated); Soto la Marina and the river of the same name (Ridgway 1916, Monroe and Howell 1966, Pérez and Eguiarte 1989, Vázquez undated); La Pesca (Baker and Fleming 1962), also a pair in April 1990 (S. N. G. Howell *in litt.* 1992); Ciudad Victoria and environs, including 35 km to the east (specimen in UMMZ) and the Sierra Madre Oriental above (i.e. to the west) (Ridgway 1916, Sutton and Burleigh 1939, Monroe and Howell 1966, Vázquez undated); Aldama (Ridgway 1916, Vázquez undated) and the Los Colorados Ranch, east-north-east of Aldama (see map in Pérez and Eguiarte 1989); Gómez Farías, 23°03'N 99°09'W, this area including the Rancho Rinconada and the río Frío district (Sutton and Burleigh 1939, Sutton and Pettingill 1942; also an *Amer. Birds* Christmas Bird Count site, specimen in DMNH); 5 km north-west of Acuña, 23°12'N 98°26'W, in the Sierra de Tamaulipas (specimen in DMNH); Tampico (Ridgway 1916, Monroe and Howell 1966). An untraced locality in the state is "S. F. de Presas" (Monroe and Howell 1966), which Ridgway (1916) recorded as "Santa Fé de Presas".

San Luis Potosí Records are from the easternmost part of the state at: El Naranjo (Las Abritas at the centre of this area), 22°30'N 99°24'W (*Amer.* Birds Christmas Bird Count site), this also being "El Salto", where a pair was seen in April 1990 (S. N. G. Howell *in litt.* 1992); Ebano and 15 km west of Ebano; El Bonito (untraced); Hacienda Limón (untraced); and 3 km north of Tamuín (all from Monroe and Howell 1966). A further untraced locality is "El Banito", where a specimen (in FMNH) was collected on 27 June 1940.

Guanajuato Records from this state have been dismissed as referring to escaped cagebirds (Friedmann *et al.* 1950), but this ignores the testimony (and apparently only basis for listing the state) of Dugès (1899), who indicated that the occurrence of flocks around Silao (20°56'N 101°26'W) was abnormal and caused by loss of food to heavy frosts in Veracruz.

Veracruz Records are from throughout the low coastal plains (as indicated by Sumichrast 1869), at: río Tamesí near Rayón (San Antonio Rayón is at 22°25'N 98°25'W) (Ridgway 1916, Monroe and Howell 1966), and near Paso del Haba (specimen in DMNH; also Chapman 1914b); Pánuco (Monroe and Howell 1966); Misantla (Ridgway 1916; see Remarks 5); Jalapa (Ridgway 1916); río Blanco, 20 km west-north-west of Piedras Negras (Lowery and Dalquest 1951); Alvarado (Salvin and Godman 1888-1904); near San Andrés Tuxtla (Sclater 1857b); 12 km north of Catemaco (*Amer. Birds* Christmas Bird Count site, this possibly the same as the preceding area; Playa Vicente (Sclater 1859b), at 17°50'N 95°50'W (in Binford 1989, who placed the locality in this state rather than in Oaxaca (*contra* Sclater 1859b); Zanja Seca, Playa Vicente municipality on Oaxaca border (specimen in DMNH); 10 km south-west of Jimba, 17°55'N 95°25'W (Lowery and Dalquest 1951); 20 km east of Jesús Carranza, at 90 m (Lowery and Dalquest 1951); Paso Nuevo (if this is the "Pasa Nueva" of Ridgway 1916, Monroe and Howell 1966), 18°01'N 94°27'W. Untraced localities include Santa Ana (Ferrari-Perez 1886, Ridgway 1916) and San Juan (Ridgway 1916).

Chiapas Ridgely (1981a) listed the species for north of the state without indicating the evidence, but on 3 March 1987 a single adult was seen by S. N. G. Howell and S. Webb (*in litt.* 1992) along the road to El Cuyo north of Catazajá in the far north-east, i.e. c.17°40'N 91°55'W (as read from PM 1988), and other records of up to four birds have been reported to these observers from this and adjacent areas during the 1980s.

México Records from this state (Ridgway 1916, presumably based on Lawrence 1871) have been dismissed as referring to escaped cagebirds (Friedmann *et al.* 1950).

Puebla Rinconada was listed by Ridgway (1916) based on Lantz (1900), the only such locality in OG (1956a) that occurs in the state being a railway station at 19°06'N 97°40'W.

Tabasco There appear to be two records, from 15 km north of Reforma (which TAW 1986 and PM 1988 place just inside Chiapas against the Tabasco border) (Brodkorb 1943) and from 15 km north of Balancán in the east of the state (Monroe and Howell 1966).

Belize The apparently endemic race *belizensis* is known from the following localities (north to south, coordinates from OG 1956b): St Ann's village (C. Pickup *in litt.* 1989), presumably Santa Ana, 17°49'N 88°19'W; Crooked Tree pine ridge, 17°45'N 88°32'W (Russell 1964, specimen in BMNH), where one was seen in March 1991 (S. N. G. Howell *in litt.* 1992); Mussel Creek, 17°39'N 88°24'W (Miller and Miller 1988); Hill Bank (Russell 1964); Gallon Jug, 17°33'N 89°01'W (Russell 1964, Monroe and Howell 1966); lower reaches of Sibun river, 17°26'N 88°16'W (Russell 1964); near Belize City (Counsell 1988); Monkey Bay Wildlife Sanctuary, c.50 km west of Belize City, February 1992 (S. N. G. Howell *in litt.* 1992); near Dangriga (C. Pickup *in litt.* 1989); lower reaches of Sittee river, 16°48'N 88°15'W; All Pines, 16°47'N 88°18'W (Russell 1964, Monroe and Howell 1966); around Placentia, 16°31'N 88°22'W (D. Weyer *in litt.* 1989); Ycacos Lagoon, 16°18'N 88°37'W, and environs (Russell 1964, Monroe and Howell 1966).

U.S.A. Feral populations of members of the *Amazona ochrocephala* group have become established in various parts of North America and the Caribbean (see Long 1981, Lever 1987), although it is not always clear which race or species is involved, and in any case with the possibility that several are, and that they hybridize (Forshaw 1989). Lever (1987) reported that *oratrix* is the form established on Puerto Rico and in Miami, although in the latter it hybridizes with Green-cheeked Amazon *A. viridigenalis*.

POPULATION This species has undergone one of the most dramatic population declines of any bird in the Americas. Its heartland, in terms of abundance and continuity of populations, was the Atlantic lowlands in Tamaulipas and Veracruz, and although it is possible that the two outlying populations in the Islas Marías and Belize are less seriously affected, and that the numbers on the Pacific slope were never high, it is in the Atlantic lowlands that the birds' disappearance has been both widespread and relentless, giving rise to concern for the long-term prospects of the entire species. In 1976 and 1979 surveys were made and the total population (presumably in Mexico) was then estimated to be no more than 17,000 birds, with all subpopulations declining (C. Schouten *in litt.* 1986). Edwards (1989) called the bird rare.

Islas Marías Although the birds were "very abundant" in 1865, only two years later "their numbers had diminished considerably" (Grayson and Lawrence 1871, Lawrence 1874; see Threats). This oscillation apart, however, the population of *tresmariae* has seemingly maintained itself well, with comments such as "common" (Nelson 1899), "very common" on María Cleofas

(Bailey 1906), "common on all of the four islands" (Stager 1957), and "hundreds (if not thousands)" on María Madre (Hansen 1984). Transects on María Madre in 1984 yielded a mean of four parrots per 8 km route and, with observations including a count of around 150 during morning feeding flights in the north-eastern third of María Magdalena and of about 100 in the orchards of Nayarit and Rehilete villages, María Madre, the total population of *tresmariae* was estimated to be less than 800 (Konrad 1984). Populations move between islands: on 22 January 1985 between 170 and 220 were seen flying between María Madre and San Juanito (Konrad 1986); thus it is not possible to break down numbers of birds by island.

Pacific slope (race oratrix*)* Evidence all points to the species being very local and, at best, uncommon: "uncommon" in Colima (Schaldach 1963), "uncommon and local" in Oaxaca (Binford 1989), and known from a total of three specimens and a handful of records for Jalisco, Michoacán and Guerrero (see Distribution).

Atlantic lowlands (race "magna"*)* In Tamaulipas it was common along the río Corona in February 1938, though less so near Gómez Farías (Sutton and Burleigh 1939), and in Veracruz it was common in the 1850s and the 1940s, with "literally hundreds" in roosting flights (Sclater 1857b, Lowery and Dalquest 1951). Ridgely (1981a), referring to "a striking reduction in numbers... over, as far as is known, all of its range", emphasized the loss of birds from this particular region ("a pair or two where great flocks used to occur"), citing an observer with 20 years' experience there. Even in the 1980s, however, the marked decline has continued, with campesinos reporting that each year it is more difficult to find nests and capture young (Vázquez undated). On the 600 ha (though now 4,000 ha) Los Colorados Ranch, 25 birds were estimated present in 1985, revealing a 90% decline from 1976 to 1979 and an 18% further decline to 1985 (Pérez and Eguiarte 1989). The four localities where the species has been recorded during the *Amer. Birds* Christmas Bird Counts have generally yielded very low numbers (single figures or sometimes none at El Naranjo, Gómez Farías and Catemaco), although near Güemez there were counts of 77 in 1983 and 114 in 1985.

Belize The race *belizensis* was reported by Russell (1964) to be common only in the vicinity of Hill Bank and Ycacos Lagoon and along the lower reaches of the Sibun and Sittee rivers, being considered local elsewhere. However, Forshaw (1989) had a report from 1981 that this was the only parrot to have declined dramatically in the country in recent years, a view repeated by C. Schouten *in litt.* (1986) and supported by resident naturalists (e.g. D. Weyer), who have noted a decline in the population along the Sibun River (J. Clinton-Eitniear *in litt.* 1992). Nevertheless, the species was reported to be still fairly common in the country in 1986 (D. S. Wood *in litt.* 1986; see also last clause in Remarks 6), a view provisionally endorsed by S. N. G. Howell (*in litt.* 1992) on the basis of 70-80 roosting at the Monkey Bay Wildlife Sanctuary in February 1992, and observations between mileposts 29 and 32 on the Western Highway; but see Threats.

ECOLOGY The Yellow-headed Amazon occupies xerophytic vegetation (e.g. dense thorn forest), savanna, tall deciduous forest and humid riverine woodland in tropical lowlands (Lowery and Dalquest 1951, Schaldach 1963, Monroe and Howell 1966); in the northern part of the Atlantic lowlands birds favour gallery forest in semi-arid regions, while to the south they occur in more humid savanna country, also with gallery forest (Ridgely 1981a). The species occasionally ranges as high as 500 m (Ridgely 1981a), in Oaxaca 330 m (Binford 1989). In Belize it roosts in pine ridges and feeds in adjacent humid forest (Russell 1964; see Remarks 6). Birds make flights between roosting and feeding areas, sometimes flying very high (Grayson and Lawrence 1871, Baker and Fleming 1962); in one case, birds fed in "the jungles of the humid division" of the regional life-zone and roosted in the arid coastal plain (Lowery and Dalquest 1951); in another they fed on "forested slopes of the interior" (of María Cleofas) and roosted in a heavy stand of large agaves by the coast, actually settling for the night on the lower spiny leaves less than 2 m from the ground (Stager 1957).

Food consists of fruit such as wild figs (Bailey 1906) and other trees both wild and cultivated, such as *Psidium guajava, Pithecellobium flexicaule, P. dulce, Acacia milleriana, Acacia* sp., *Macuna* sp., *Zuelania guidonia, Bumelia laetivirens, Solanum* sp., *Zea mays* and palms, and also the young buds of trees and shrubs (Vázquez and Maldonado Rodríguez 1990; also Nelson 1899, Lowery and Dalquest 1951, Clinton-Eitniear 1990). In some cases, damage may thus be done to certain crops, e.g. of green bananas (Lowery and Dalquest 1951), and on Islas Marías in the months of March to June (Konrad 1986); on María Madre birds were seen to eat mango flowers and tiny fruit in April 1983 (Hansen 1984). Over the 1991/1992 winter the main food item of a study population in Tamaulipas was the bean of *Pithecellobium ebano* (E. Enkerlin *in litt.* 1992; this is presumably *P. flexicaule* or *P. dulce*). Birds displaced from Veracruz by food privation in March 1899 fed on sweet lemons, avocados and other cultivated fruit, and devastated a lucerne crop (Dugès 1899).

On Islas Marías Grant (1966) reported breeding later than on the mainland and indicated May as against February. However, this seems mistaken: on the islands in 1984 two broods of two nestlings were observed in early April, which meant that eggs must have been laid in mid-February, with hatching in mid-March and an anticipated fledging in mid-May (Konrad 1986); in other cases, half-grown young were found in mid-April (Hansen 1984) and mid-May (Nelson 1899). On the mainland, breeding condition males have been collected in mid-February in Oaxaca (Binford 1989) and at the start of April in Tamaulipas (Sutton and Pettingill 1942), the breeding cycle in the latter state lasting from March till June (Vázquez and Maldonado Rodríguez 1990). This pattern is largely repeated in Belize, where nests with eggs have been found in March and April, a nest with young in May, and a female in February and a male in May both in breeding condition (Russell 1964). Birds nest in holes in living and dead trees, 6-15 m up with the cavities sometimes over 4 m deep, laying two or three eggs usually at the end of March or start of April, incubation lasting 30-35 days with chicks hatching in early May and leaving the nest 30 days or more later (Vázquez and Maldonado Rodríguez 1990). Six nests found on the Los Colorados Ranch in 1985 were 4-10 m up in the trunks of *Pithecellobium ebano* (four), *Bumelia laetivirens* and *Ficus involuta* (Pérez and Eguiarte 1989). On the Islas Marías holes high in large forest trees (one was identified as locally called "palo prieto") are again used (Grayson and Lawrence 1871, Lawrence 1874, Nelson 1899). Records on these islands all refer to two eggs or two nestlings (Lawrence 1874, Nelson 1899, Konrad 1984). On the río Corona, breeding density was 1-2 males per 8 ha (Gehlbach *et al.* 1975), with 0.26 birds per ha in coastal Tamaulipas (see Pérez and Eguiarte 1989). In Belize birds nest in pines (Russell 1964).

The species is non-migratory, but food privation and fire cause occasional wanderings (Dugès 1899; see Distribution: Guanajuato) and on the Islas Marías local, possibly seasonal, movements take place between islands (Konrad 1984). Even within flocks birds keep in pairs, and commonly sit in the tops of tall trees (Nelson 1899, Lowery and Dalquest 1951, Edwards 1989). In Tamaulipas no strong flocking behaviour has been recorded in a resident study population of c.50 birds, only groups of 2-5 or lone individuals (E. Enkerlin *in litt.* 1992).

THREATS The massive decline in the numbers of this species is the product of habitat destruction combined with intensive and relentless exploitation for the cagebird trade (Ridgely 1981a, C. Schouten *in litt.* 1986); the Atlantic lowland populations (race "*magna*") suffered the most, being in the area most devastated by forest clearance and closest to the U.S. border for illegal trafficking (Ridgely 1981a). In Belize these factors may be somewhat less pressing, but are compounded by "considerable hunting pressure" (D. S. Wood *in litt.* 1986).

Habitat destruction Loss of natural habitats has been extensive in north-eastern Mexico (see the relevant section in Threats under Green-cheeked Amazon). Vázquez (undated), discussing Tamaulipas in 1986, referred to continuing cutting and burning of forests, timber extraction, water pollution and insecticide use. In this state, forest destruction has led to birds occupying suboptimal habitat (Pérez and Eguiarte 1989). Elsewhere within the species's range, evidence is much less clear on the status of habitats, except (a) in the case of Belize where, having long remained largely unaffected (D. S. Wood *in litt.* 1986), forests are now suffering conversion in many areas to citrus plantation (and the birds are being persecuted as pests as a consequence) (S. N. G. Howell *in litt.* 1992), and (b) on the Islas Marías, where much forest remains (Konrad 1984, 1986); in general, habitat alteration in the southern part of the species's range (east of Veracruz) has been relatively minor (Ridgely 1981a).

Trade The Yellow-headed Amazon is or at least was "the most in demand of any amazon parrot", all forms being thought "the most tameable and the best talkers among the neotropical parrots" (Ridgely 1981a). This ability has long been known (Chapman 1914b found dealers who rated it second only to the African Grey Parrot *Psittacus erithacus* in this regard), and before the turn of the century birds on the Islas Marías were being sold directly to visitors but also sent to market in mainland ports, those taken when young being most prized as they proved most docile (Nelson 1899; also Lawrence 1874). Although Low (1972) considered *tresmariae* "rare in aviculture", Ridgely (1981a) reported "relatively large numbers" being sold in the U.S.A., prompting the work by Konrad (1984, 1986) who, however, found that on María Madre a limit of 20-30 young parrots per year was set on the number that could be taken for private use within the island and their export entirely prohibited; but he noted that many of these captured birds died through lack of care. Some fluctuations in persecution may have taken place on these islands, as A. J. Grayson found the birds tame and unsuspicious in 1865 but shy and wary of man in 1867 (Grayson and Lawrence 1871, Lawrence 1874), yet they had returned to their confiding ways 30 years later (Nelson 1899) and were once again "as wild as the parrots on the mainland" in 1955 (Stager 1957).

On the mainland, persistent taking of nestlings for the pet market was the suspected cause of the species's scarcity in Colima, with a "great demand" for birds from as far away as Mexico City (Schaldach 1963). In a nine-month period from October 1979 to June 1980 over 2,700 birds were recorded as imports into the U.S.A. (Roet *et al.* 1981), and many more would have been smuggled across the border: "campesinos everywhere are very much aware of how much nestlings are worth" (Ridgely 1981a). Recent studies in Tamaulipas entirely confirm this last point, and indicate that even now trapping is the major factor operating against the species (Vázquez and Maldonado Rodríguez 1990). Even on a relatively well protected site in this state, such as the Los Colorados Ranch, amazon parrot nests (three species) suffered 30% loss to trappers in 1985 (Pérez and Eguiarte 1989). In Belize there is now evidence of considerable trapping for foreign markets (S. N. G. Howell *in litt.* 1992), captive birds being too valuable to be kept as pets (J. Clinton-Eitniear *in litt.* 1992).

Natural causes In Tamaulipas heavy rain can flood nest cavities and drown chicks; and certain reptiles prey on eggs (Vázquez and Maldonado Rodríguez 1990). On the Islas Marías nest predators may include snakes, iguanas and racoons, while Crested Caracaras *Polyborus plancus* and Peregrines *Falco peregrinus* were witnessed attacking adults (Konrad 1986).

MEASURES TAKEN There have been few concrete achievements. In Belize, a seven-year moratorium on commercial trade in wildlife was imposed in 1981, and all but six species of bird are protected from hunting (Inskipp *et al.* 1988). In Mexico, commercial export of most wildlife has been prohibited since 1982 (Inskipp *et al.* 1988). The survey of the race *tresmariae* called for by Ridgely (1981a) was duly carried out (Konrad 1984, 1986), and the birds were found to be "completely protected" there, albeit young were taken from nests for local interest (Hansen 1984). Recent studies in Tamaulipas (Vázquez undated, Vázquez and Maldonado Rodríguez 1990, and by E. Enkerlin) have begun to provide essential data on the species's status and requirements within the state.

MEASURES PROPOSED Clearly a principal need is for a thorough survey of the Yellow-headed Amazon throughout its mainland Mexican range, using interviews with local people as a major source of evidence of past or present occurrence; on present knowledge, the establishment of reserves in which to manage the species should be a target in Colima, Tamaulipas and

Veracruz, in the latter two cases at sites that also hold the threatened sympatric Green-cheeked Amazon (see relevant account for certain possible localities); nest-box deployment at one such site, Los Colorados Ranch in Tamaulipas (see Distribution), has already begun with the support of the Avicultural Society of America; this programme will also involve local education campaigns (see Measures Proposed under Green-cheeked Amazon). A key element in a conservation strategy for both amazons may be the encouragement and commitment of landowners to preserving tracts of habitat and to guarding the birds, particularly when nesting, with the aid of their staff (E. Enkerlin *in litt.* 1992). Surveys should not ignore Jalisco, Michoacán or Guerrero in the west or eastern Veracruz or Tabasco in the east, and some effort to confirm the bird's presence and status in western Campeche (see Remarks 4) and on the Isthmus de Tehuantepec, and in particular in western Oaxaca, is required. Representations are needed with the Mexican authorities to continue the existing policy of non-export from the Islas Marías (at least part of which is a penal settlement: Konrad 1986) and to manage the islands so that this important small population is fully catered for. In Belize a study of the apparently fairly strong but waning status and distribution of the bird would be very timely.

Captive breeding The Yellow-headed Amazon has been bred fairly widely in captivity and efforts are needed to keep subspecies separate (Bosch 1991). Whether there is scope for using confiscated birds for a captive breeding and release programme (as suggested by Vázquez undated) remains to be evaluated, based on several major considerations (as outlined by Black 1991).

REMARKS (1) The *Amazona ochrocephala* complex (discussed by Monroe and Howell 1966) appears to split into three species, the Yellow-headed Amazon *A. oratrix*, the Yellow-naped Amazon *A. auropalliata* and the Yellow-crowned Amazon *A. ochrocephala* (Ridgely 1981a, AOU 1983, Binford 1989, Forshaw 1989, Sibley and Monroe 1990); although at present this arrangement remains tentative, it is accepted here.

(2) Of the four races, *belizensis* is certainly the most distinct (to the point where its place in *oratrix* might be reconsidered, especially in the light of the second paragraph in Remarks 3), *tresmariae* is widely tolerated although opinions vary since some characters seem only to be age-related (Stager 1957 and Monroe and Howell 1966 thought it well differentiated; Nelson 1899, Salvadori 1906 and Grant 1965 did not), while *magna* has been regarded with considerable scepticism (e.g. by Ridgely 1981a, Forshaw 1989). The describers of *magna* (Monroe and Howell 1966) insisted that "the Pacific and Atlantic slope populations are completely separate from one another for their entire range with the possible exception of the Tehuantepec region, and we know of no unequivocal data that demonstrate a continuity of the two populations across the Isthmus". However, the type-locality for *oratrix* is in the same drainage and same lowlands (judging from TAW 1986 and Binford 1989) as the birds in Veracruz from east of Jesús Carranza, some 70 km to the north, and it is very difficult to believe that there could ever have been a barrier to the miscegenation of populations in these localities. Nevertheless, it is evidently at the Isthmus de Tehuantepec that the species *oratrix* divides from the species *auropalliata*, the distance between the type-locality of *oratrix* and the closest western site for *auropalliata* also being only some 70 km (judged again from the sources above).

(3) Inskipp *et al.* (1988) pointed out that the single record of "*Amazona ochrocephala*" from the Petén, north-eastern Guatemala, given (it is not clear on what evidence) by Land (1970), may refer to *A. oratrix* (presumably *belizensis*); the presence of *oratrix* either side of northernmost Guatemala is a curiosity that may be an artefact of observation, despite the distinctive appearance of *belizensis*.

There appears to be a population of birds close to *belizensis* (but with less extensive yellow on the face, concentrated on the crown and lores; i.e. perhaps intermediate between *belizensis* and the yellow-crowned population in the Sula valley of north-west Honduras, for which see Monroe and Howell 1966) in the beach scrub and mangroves north of Puerto Barrios on the Golfo de Honduras (J. Bucklin *per* S. N. G. Howell *in litt.* 1992). Captive birds in Puerto Barrios were said to have been caught locally, and thus represent a case of exploitation in trade prior to formal documentation in the scientific literature (S. N. G. Howell *in litt.* 1992).

(4) In Mexico, Nuevo León has been listed for the species (Salvadori 1895a; hence presumably Friedmann *et al.* 1950, and hence presumably Blake 1953, Ridgely 1981a, AOU 1983, Inskipp *et al.* 1988, Forshaw 1989, Sibley and Monroe 1990), but this seems to be based on a single skin in BMNH marked "Villa Gran, N.L.", discussed above under Tamaulipas (and listed as Villa Grande in Salvin and Godman 1888-1804). Campeche is mentioned as having a population by Ridgely (1981a) but by no-one else. Yucatán was once listed (e.g. by Ridgway 1916, Peters 1935, Friedmann *et al.* 1950) but there appears to be no supporting evidence (Paynter 1955).

(5) Salvin and Godman (1888-1904) and Ridgway (1916) also list "Río Rancho Nuevo" for Veracruz, but this is in fact on the same specimen label (in BMNH) as that responsible for the listing of Misantla.

(6) Monroe and Howell (1966) interpreted this as indicating the species being "confined to the lowland pine savanna and adjacent areas", which may be accurate; Wood *et al.* (1986) listed it for two broad habitat types, coastal savannas (but this includes lowland areas covered in pines) and northern hardwood forests (which includes gallery forests that cross savannas), adding that it is common in the former, uncommon in the latter.

RED-SPECTACLED AMAZON *Amazona pretrei* V/R[10]

This parrot has a small range in south-east Brazil, apparently breeding in Rio Grande do Sul, the more southerly birds migrating to the north of the state, with tiny numbers once occurring in neighbouring Misiones province, north-east Argentina, and possibly eastern Paraguay. Formerly abundant, it is partially dependent on araucaria forest as a food source and roosting cover for much of the year, and its decline is related to habitat fragmentation and trade.

DISTRIBUTION The Red-spectacled Amazon (see Remarks 1) now appears to be confined to the state of Rio Grande do Sul in south-east Brazil, although it has occurred seasonally in very small numbers in Argentina and possibly Paraguay, with no good evidence from Uruguay (see Remarks 2).

Brazil Outside Rio Grande do Sul the species is believed formerly to have ranged north as far as the state of São Paulo, whence there is a single specimen collected at Piracicaba plus reports from Apiahy (Apiaí) in the last decade of the century (von Ihering 1898; also von Ihering and von Ihering 1907, Pinto 1938), although it no longer occurs there (Pinto 1946, 1978; see Remarks 3). Its occurrence in the state of Santa Catarina (Sick and Teixeira 1979, Sick *et al.* 1981, Belton 1984-1985, Nores and Yzurieta 1986) has been affirmed but remains unsubstantiated (its at least seasonal presence just inside Rio Grande do Sul at Espigão Alto State Park indicates the probability that it does), and during several years of searching for it in São Paulo, Paraná and northern Santa Catarina, Diefenback and Goldhammer (1986) only found the Vinaceous Amazon *Amazona vinacea* in the araucaria groves; this has also been the case in at least part of north-eastern Rio Grande do Sul (R. S. Ridgely *in litt.* 1989) where, however, time of year is important (N. Varty verbally 1992).

Rio Grande do Sul The Red-spectacled Amazon seems now (and indeed may always have been) almost entirely restricted to this state, where records both ancient and modern stem roughly from within an area bounded by 28°00' to 31°00'S and 50°30' to 54°00'W, with sightings concentrated in the north-eastern and northern central highlands, thence south through the centre of the state across the central depression to the northern portion of the southern central hill country, although it could occur somewhat beyond these limits in all directions (Belton 1984-1985, which see for map; also Gliesch 1930). It is now found mostly between 300 and 1,000 m (Ridgely 1981a, Belton 1984-1985), although it formerly also occurred lower (and in the south still does so), having been collected at Taquara, 39 m at 29°39'S 50°47'W, and São Lourenço, 3 m at 31°22'S 51°58'W, in the nineteenth century and in 1928 and 1929 (von Ihering 1899a; specimens in AMNH), São Leopoldo, 20 m at 29°47'S 51°10'W (Finsch 1867-1868), Porto Alegre, 10 m at 30°02'S 51°12'W (Gliesch 1930), Pedras Brancas (now Guaíba), 10 m at 30°07'S 51°20'W, and Barra do rio Camaquã, 31°17'S 51°45'W (von Ihering 1899a; all coordinates and altitudes from Belton 1984-1985), with "summer" records from the Serra dos Taipes and the Serra do Herval (both untraced) and speculated "winter" records from Cima da Serra (von Ihering 1899a; see Remarks 4). In the far north of the state, the Indians at Nonoai Indian Reserve remember the species and used to capture it, and it still occurs at Espigão Alto State Park near Barracão (E. Albuquerque *per* N. Varty verbally 1992).

There have been two recent assessments of the breeding and non-breeding distributions of this puzzling species in the state. The first was that outside the breeding season it apparently moves in large numbers from area to area, depending on food supply, but scatters in pairs throughout the entire region for nesting from the end of September to the beginning of January (Belton 1984-1985). The second (apparently developed by W. A. Voss: N. Varty verbally 1992), consistent with other evidence (such as that the species only appeared at Taquara in March, April and May: von Berlepsch and von Ihering 1885; but see Remarks 5), is that the breeding grounds, occupied from August to January, are chiefly in the south of the state, and that there is a post-breeding dispersal, January to August, to the highland plateau of the north and north-east (Silva 1989a).

Current studies have indicated that the truth lies in between: there are essentially two populations, one breeding in the northern part of the state around Carazinho and probably near Vacaria, the other in the south, concentrating around Caçapava do Sul and Santana da Boa Vista (F. Silva *per* N. Varty verbally 1992); birds in the north may move seasonally, while those in the south certainly do, occurring in large numbers in Carazinho's municipal park and thus presumably then mixing with the northern birds (N. Varty verbally 1992).

Large (post-breeding) roosts have been noted in an araucaria grove (now included in the Aracuri-Esmeralda Ecological Station) at 900 m at 28°14'S 51°10'W, 18 km south of Esmeralda (Belton 1984-1985) and in a *Podocarpus* grove a few kilometres away during a period when the first-mentioned roost was deserted (King 1978-1979), and in an araucaria grove at Rincão dos Pereira, 300 m at 30°48'S 53°03'W (Belton 1984-1985), 11 km north-east of Santana da Boa Vista (Belton 1984-1985), although this latter has probably now disappeared (N. Varty verbally 1992). It is possible that the entire population sometimes gathers at the Esmeralda site (King 1978-1979).

Argentina Two males were collected at Santa Ana, Misiones province, in October 1909 (Orfila 1936-1938) and September 1917 (specimen in MACN) respectively, but the only recent records (coordinates from Paynter 1985) are a single bird seen in February 1980 at arroyo Urugua-í, 25°54'S 54°35'W, in Iguazú department (Chebez 1981); two birds in flight over Ruta Nacional 12, 2 km north of Garuhapé, c.26°55'S 54°55'W, in December 1982 (F. Moschione and L. Pastorino *per* J. C. Chebez *in litt.* 1992); and an unspecified number in flight across the río Paraná 2 km from Candelaria, 27°28'S 55°44'W, in July 1987 (F. Moschione and J. Sancristóbal *per* J. C. Chebez *in litt.* 1992).

Paraguay Occurrence in south-eastern Paraguay has been speculated (Forshaw 1978), as a few (but dwindling) araucaria groves are found in that country (Ridgely 1981a, Nores and Yzurieta 1986), and in fact there is a single, neglected record of three birds collected in June 1928 on the "río Pyraty-y (Alto Paraná)" (río Piratiy, 24°08'S 54°22'W in OG 1957a), of which one was later obtained for the national museum (Podtiaguin 1941-1945). "Summer" birds in the serras of Rio Grande do Sul were said to have come from Paraguay (von Ihering 1899a; see also Remarks 5). López (in press) knew of no certain records.

POPULATION Modern attempts at judging numbers only began in the 1970s, but evidence of the species's former abundance, based on reliable witnesses, reveals a previously undocumented and very startling decline: thus in "winter" 1950 a local resident at Vacaria saw a flock estimated to be a kilometre in width which took 45 minutes to pass overhead (E. A. Isaia and A. Kindel *per* N. Varty verbally 1992), and people at Caçapava do Sul have similar stories of great abundance in the 1950s, but all now report an enormous decline in the number of birds observed (N. Varty verbally 1992).

In May 1971 numbers at the Esmeralda roost were put at between 10,000 and 30,000 (Forshaw 1978), and in May 1972 less than 10,000 were estimated (by W. Belton in Silva 1981a) or, in another version, possibly less than 5,000, this apparent decline following the removal of tall araucarias at the site (W. Belton *in litt.* 1974 to W. B. King); no significant flocks were registered there in 1974 (Belton 1984-1985). Silva (1981a) recorded that in May 1975 less than 5,000 were seen at the site, which may or may not have represented a decline, but a decline in other roosting areas was noted, principally the Santana da Boa Vista site, where only 2,000 were seen in February 1976 (Belton 1984-1985). In 1976 the Esmeralda roost was temporarily deserted for reasons unknown (King 1978-1979), but a flock of about 2,000 began to roost in a nearby *Podocarpus* grove (King 1978-1979). In July 1980 c.1,000 birds (Silva 1981a) but in late February and mid-May 1983 c.10,000 birds were estimated at the original Esmeralda roost (Belton 1984-1985). In 1989 no fewer than 14,000 birds were estimated to be present, but in 1991 the highest number recorded was only around 300; this is noted as a decline (Scherer Neto 1991b), although it seems equally possible that the birds had simply moved elsewhere. It is worth noting that 350-500 birds were roosting at the Carazinho park roost in January 1992 prior to the departure of birds from the southern breeding populations (N. Varty verbally 1992).

That the species was probably never common in Misiones, Argentina, as araucaria always had a very limited distribution there (Hueck 1978, Nores and Yzurieta 1986), seems at odds with evidence offered in Threats under Vinaceous Amazon, which, however, indicates that the tree is certainly now extremely limited in extent there; almost complete deforestation in San Pedro and General Belgrano departments has occurred (Chebez 1985a, Nores and Yzurieta 1986).

ECOLOGY Although it has been authoritatively reported that the Red-spectacled Amazon breeds in forested areas where the commonest tree is *Araucaria angustifolia* (Belton 1984-1985), this is not true of the two southern breeding populations, where the habitat is lowland riverine forests (up to 300 m) among the hills (N. Varty verbally 1992) or what Silva (1989a) called dense broadleaved forest. During the non-breeding season it mainly roosts in araucaria groves, though *Podocarpus lamberti* groves may also be used (King 1978-1979, Belton 1984-1985). During the day it frequents *Podocarpus* groves in January and February, while for the rest of the non-breeding season, at least from the end of February to July, it is found in araucaria groves (Belton 1984-1985, Sick 1985, Silva 1989a), although araucaria does not produce ripe fruit until April/May (N. Varty verbally 1992). During the breeding season the Red-spectacled Amazon is found in pairs that may vocalize in flight but often move about silently and are very secretive near their nest (Belton 1984-1985); hence lack of calls at this season does not necessarily signify lack of birds. They possibly gather at food sources even then, as a flock of 12 was seen on 7 October (Silva 1981a), although these may have been younger, non-breeding birds. In contrast they become very noisy during the non-breeding season when they move about in varying-sized flocks of 5-150 birds, fly long distances every day (up to 70 km: E. Albuquerque *per* N. Varty verbally 1992), and gather in enormous roosts at night, sometimes possibly the entire population at one or a few roosts (King 1978-1979, Belton 1984-1985). Birds coming into roosts in May appeared as two categories, one of fairly silent pairs and one of noisy family groups of 2-4 (Sick 1985).

In January and most of February the principal food source is the seeds of *Podocarpus lamberti* (not earlier in the breeding season, as fruiting only occurs in these months: N. Varty verbally 1992), while other favourites are the fruits of a *Eugenia* sp. and a *Campomanesia* sp., both in the family Myrtaceae (Belton 1984-1985, Sick 1985), also berries and fruit of *Nectandra* and *Ocotea* spp. (Silva 1989a). That the cones of *Araucaria angustifolia* ripen from the end of February (Sick 1985) is mistaken (they appear on the trees then but only ripen in April: N. Varty verbally 1992) but they appear to form the principal food source of the parrot at least until July (Belton 1984-1985, Sick 1985), after which the birds (in one account) spread out in smaller groups (Silva 1981a) or (in another) return south to their broadleaved forest breeding zones (Silva 1989a). In October the parrots have been observed feeding on the fruits of *Melia* sp. (Silva 1981a).

Trees used for nesting were, in the five nests recorded, *Casearia* sp. and *Quillaja brasiliensis*, both of the holes being 10 m up (Silva 1981a, Belton 1984-1985), *Ficus* sp., *Cuparia vernalis* and "angico", the holes in these last three being 7.8, 6.1 and 9.2 m up respectively (N. Varty verbally 1992). According to local people, the number of young varies from two to four, but is usually three, and they are always fledged by Christmas (Belton 1984-1985, Silva 1989a). The incubation period of a captive pair was 29-30 days in one case (Diefenback and Goldhammer 1986), 26-27 days in another (Low 1991a,b,c). The young probably fledge when around nine weeks old as in other species of *Amazona* (Forshaw 1978), which would mean that egg-laying in this species commences at the end of September; however, Low (1991a,b,c) recorded fledging as early as around 50 days. Egg-laying (though infertile) by a bird apparently three years of age has been recorded in captivity (Diefenback and Goldhammer 1986). In January the young begin to flock with their parents in parties of 30-50 prior to their movement into the highlands (Silva 1989a), and still larger roosting flocks form at this season (N. Varty verbally 1992).

THREATS The Red-spectacled Amazon is reported to be a rare and little favoured bird in captivity (Ridgely 1981a, Diefenback and Goldhammer 1986), although over a century ago hunters shot at flocks to bring down birds alive and sell, there being a good market for what was considered a good talker (von Berlepsch and von Ihering 1885). The information that 976 were imported into the U.S.A. in 1977 (Anon. 1980) seems doubtful in view of the large number involved, and the fact that the species was protected at the time, all legal trade in it having ceased since its listing on Appendix I of CITES, which came into force on 1 July 1975 (WTMU 1988). However, there is certainly a continuing organized trade in the species, at least at the internal level, with two key dealers in Florianópolis and Fontoura Xavier, and losses of birds to this pressure appear to be significant (N. Varty verbally 1992). Although it is sometimes shot by local people for food (Diefenback and Goldhammer 1986, N. Varty verbally 1992), the other major threat at present appears to be habitat destruction (Sick and Texeira 1978, Sick 1985, Diefenback and Goldhammer 1986, Nores and Yzurieta 1986). In Paraná state the original area forested by araucaria was 73,780 km^2, in 1930 it was reduced to 39,580 km^2 and in 1965 only 15,932 km^2 remained; in Rio Grande do Sul the situation is similar (Sick and Teixeira 1979; see also Hueck 1978). Most reforestation in Brazil from 1966 to 1976 was of the foreign trees *Pinus* sp. and *Eucalyptus* sp., araucaria only being planted in 2.7% of the areas being reforested (Sick and Texeira 1979). Sick (1985) gave the deforestation of traditional roosting sites as the cause of the decline of the parrot, although Ridgely (1981a) doubted that lack of araucaria seeds or roosting sites was responsible and suggested that lack of breeding sites, e.g. trees large enough to have suitable big holes, was the cause.

In Argentina the site where it was observed in 1980 has been flooded by the Urugua-í Reservoir (J. C. Chebez *in litt.* 1992). Loss of araucaria in Misiones is documented in Threats under Vinaceous Amazon.

MEASURES TAKEN The species is protected under Brazilian law (Bernardes *et al.* 1990) and is listed on Appendix I in CITES (King 1978-1979). The largest roosting site has been protected (Belton 1984-1985), and although it was deserted in 1976 (King 1978-1979) it was later again in use (Belton 1984-1985).

MEASURES PROPOSED Although the protection of *Araucaria angustifolia* forests and groves, being the principal food source of these parrots for the winter, seems to be important for preserving the parrot (Sick 1985, Diefenback and Goldhammer 1986, Nores and Yzurieta 1986), attention should also be given to the preservation of mixed forest with *Podocarpus lamberti* groves, as these provide most of its food in January and February, and perhaps during the breeding season (Sick 1985), and nesting trees (Silva 1981a) and habitat should also be secured; such recommendations need local adjustment, as (e.g.) there are many *Podocarpus* trees around Santana de Boa Vista and very few around Caçapava do Sul (N. Varty verbally 1992). Belton's (1984-1985) urging of a full study of the species to find and try to preserve major roosting sites and food resources, and to determine its life history and the factors causing its decline, has been heeded: a project to study the ecology of this and the Vinaceous Amazon in Rio Grande do Sul is now being developed by CNPq and PUC-RS in collaboration with ICBP.

REMARKS (1) The near-threatened Alder Amazon *Amazona tucumana* was previously regarded as a race of *A. pretrei* (Peters 1937), but was separated as a full species on the basis of a (probably erroneous: Ridgely 1981a) record of sympatry in Misiones province, Argentina (SOMA 1935-1942). However, the two forms seem to differ in the juvenile plumage, and also by *pretrei* being sexually dimorphic, while the sexes are alike in *tucumana* (Diefenback and Goldhammer 1986). These differences (see also Low 1991a,b,c), plus their evidently different feeding requirements, tend to support the view that *pretrei* and *tucumana* should be treated as two species, although biochemical and other evidence is needed to disclose their true relationship.

(2) Occurrence in Uruguay was mentioned by Finsch (1867-1868) (inasmuch as he noted a specimen labelled from Montevideo), von Ihering and von Ihering (1907), Brabourne and Chubb (1912), Cory (1918), Peters (1937), Podtiaguin (1941-1945), who specifically mentioned Artigas and Rivera departments, and Barattini (1945), but apart from a single specimen (now in BMNH) unreliably labelled "Rio de la Plata" and in any case probably a cagebird (P. R. Colston verbally 1988), there appears to be no good basis for this and, as no natural araucaria groves are found in the country (a few plantations may now grow in a semi-wild state: Hueck 1978), it seems quite unlikely that it ever occurred (Cuello and Gerzenstein 1962), and it was omitted altogether by Gore and Gepp (1978). Nevertheless, because (a) occurrence so far south as Uruguay would of necessity be in the breeding season, and (b) the species does not require araucaria when breeding (see Ecology), absence of the tree does not prove absence of the parrot.

(3) This (apparently single) specimen record from São Paulo seems to have caused all authorities (e.g. Pinto 1978, Belton 1984-1985, Sick 1985) to indicate that the original distribution extended from that state south to Rio Grande do Sul, whereas the probability is that the São Paulo record was of a wandering bird in the austral winter. However, according to C. Yamashita (*in litt.* 1990) the São Paulo record is simply in error, and the species probably never occurred in Paraná either.

(4) None of these "serra" localities appears to have been traced by Belton (1984-1985), although he gave an Herval in hills in the farthest south of the state, and von Ihering (1899a) himself, in providing a record of Red-tailed Amazon *Amazona brasiliensis* (see relevant account) from Cima da Serra, indicated it as in the north, close to the border with Santa Catarina.

(5) The problem of the migration of this species was not resolved by the accounts of it in either Belton (1984-1985) or Sick (1985). The account provided in Silva (1989a) seems to fit the facts best, although not entirely: thus the large flocks that visited the Serra dos Taipes and environs from January to April were reported by von Ihering (1887) to return in April to their usual region, the pine forests of the province's highlands, implying that they came down from that region in December (although he admitted that the direction and causes of these wanderings were not clear); later (von Ihering 1898) he remarked that the species visited São Lourenço (the southernmost traced locality known for the species) from Paraguay, as if breeding might take place in the latter rather than the former. None of this is entirely clarified by recent studies, but habitat destruction may well have played a role in altering past patterns of dispersal and movement.

RED-BROWED AMAZON *Amazona rhodocorytha* V/R[10]

Now rare and local in isolated patches of primary Atlantic Forest in eastern Brazil between Alagoas and Rio de Janeiro, this parrot still suffers from habitat destruction compounded by exploitation for trade; its presence in six protected areas is only partial mitigation of these pressures.

DISTRIBUTION The Red-browed Amazon (see Remarks 1) is endemic to eastern Brazil in Alagoas and from Bahia and eastern Minas Gerais south locally to Rio de Janeiro (Sick 1985).

Alagoas The species was only found in north-east Brazil in Usina Sinimbu in São Miguel dos Campos, March 1957 (Pinto and de Camargo 1961, Camargo 1962). Although lowland forest is now destroyed (see Threats) the species could still be seen in the remaining forests of the area until the mid-1980s (A. G. M. Coelho *in litt.* 1986), as witness a specimen in MNRJ from São Miguel dos Campos ("Grota do Niquim") shot from a flock of six in April 1984.

Bahia Records (north to south) are from Camamú, 1930s (Pinto 1935); rio Gongogi near the rio Novo confluence, December 1932 (Pinto 1935); Ilhéus in January, February and May 1945, one specimen being from ribeirão de Fortuna (in MNRJ; also Camargo 1962); rio Jequitinhonha at Belmonte (estuary) and on Ilha Cachoeirinha (Wied 1820-1821; see Bokermann 1957); rio Jucurucu, Cachoeira Grande, April 1933 (Pinto 1935); CVRD Porto Seguro Reserve, October 1986 and January 1988 (Gonzaga *et al.* 1987, B. M. Whitney *in litt.* 1988), where in June 1990 a flock of 37 was seen (Gardner and Gardner 1990b); Monte Pascoal National Park (Ridgely 1981a, Gonzaga *et al.* 1987); rio Mucuri (Wied 1820-1821).

Minas Gerais Records are from the eastern quarter of the state at (north to south) Jequitinhonha valley (locality unspecified), recently; Machacalis, December 1954; lower Suaçuí, north of the rio Doce, September 1940; Mantena, recently; Rio Doce State Park, recently; Viçosa, recently; Ibitipoca State Park, recently (Camargo 1962, Monteiro *et al.* 1983, M. A. de Andrade *in litt.* 1986, 1988).

Espírito Santo Records are (north to south) from Córrego Grande (Fazenda Klabin) Biological Reserve, October 1986 (Gonzaga *et al.* 1987); rio Itaúnas, November 1950 (Aguirre and Aldrighi 1983); Córrego do Veado Biological Reserve, October 1986 (Gonzaga *et al.* 1987); Sooretama Biological Reserve (Ridgely 1981a, Scott and Brooke 1985, B. M. Whitney *in litt.* 1990) and adjacent CVRD Linhares Reserve, recently (Collar and Gonzaga 1985, Pacheco and da Fonseca 1987, B. M. Whitney *in litt.* 1987, D. F. Stotz *in litt.* 1988); Lagoa do Durão, Linhares, December 1945 (specimen in MNRJ); Santa Teresa at 750 m, December 1940 (specimen in MNRJ), this record probably being from the present Augusto Ruschi (Nova Lombardia) Biological Reserve, where the species was found in December 1986 (C. E. Carvalho *in litt.* 1987) and in July 1991 (Anon. 1991b); "rio Espírito Santo", meaning present-day Vitória, 1810s (Wied 1820-1821); Marataízes, May 1966 (specimen in MNRJ).

Rio de Janeiro Older records (east to west) are: rio Paraíba; Cabo Frio; "Serra dos Órgãos" (see Remarks 2); Serra de Inoã; Sepetiba (Wied 1820-1821, 1831-1833, von Pelzeln 1868-1871). There followed such a long gap in records that Ridgely (1981a) speculated that the species no longer existed in the state, while O. M. O. Pinto (in Wied 1940) had already regarded it as long extinct there. However, modern observations are (east to west) from: Barra Seca, São João da Barra, north of Travessão, 1987 (J. F. Pacheco verbally 1990); lowlands near Desengano State Park, where pairs have been seen since December 1986 (J. F. Pacheco *in litt.* 1987); Macaé, where a flock of 49 was seen in April 1982 and pairs seen subsequently (N. C. Maciel *in litt.* 1987, J. F. Pacheco *in litt.* 1987); Fazenda União, near Casimiro de Abreu, January 1992 (R. Parrini *per* J. F. Pacheco verbally 1992); Ilha da Marambaia, October 1986 (L. A. R. Bege *per* N. C. Maciel *in litt.* 1987); Ilha Grande, outside the Biological State Reserve of Praia do Sul, 1989 (J. F. Pacheco verbally 1991, following a report by N. C. Maciel). Birds have been seen throughout the year at the Desengano site, and repeatedly at Barra Seca (J. F. Pacheco verbally 1991).

POPULATION The species was evidently always relatively abundant within its range, as testified by Wied's (1850) recollection of finding it in every forest visited during his trip, and Pinto's (1935) records ("very common") from southern Bahia; even today in one extensive tract (the adjacent Sooretama/CVRD Linhares reserves) it remains "fairly common", with "small numbers seen/heard on all or most days in appropriate habitat" (Ridgely 1981a, Scott and Brooke 1985, D. M. R. Fortaleza *in litt.* 1991). Nevertheless, over 20 years ago the species was noted to be scarce (Sick 1969, 1972), and 10 years ago it was considered rare and very local (Ridgely 1981a). Although in the past few years many more records and localities have been accumulated, sometimes with reports of fairly good numbers, it is clear that the fragmentation of populations is so serious that Ridgely's use of "rare" is fully justified.

ECOLOGY The species is found primarily in humid lowland forests, but also occurs in forest in the interior highlands (Sick 1985). That there may be seasonal displacements into more montane areas to about 1,000 m, as surmised by Ridgely (1981a), is at odds with Wied's (1831-1833) report that in winter (i.e. around June) birds moved in flocks to the coast and to estuarine mangroves. Burmeister (1856) referred to the species as only found in dense primary forest; and although Ridgely (1981a) found it at the edge of continuous forest he thought it maladaptive to partially deforested areas. Roosting has been recorded in a large flock in the tallest trees of the forest (Pinto 1935).

Food is fruit, seeds, berries and buds procured in the treetops (Forshaw 1989); in one case the fruit of "cajueira" were taken (Aleixo *et al.* 1991). There are no breeding data from the wild, although Silva (1989a) reported evidence that suggests hatching in October, which fits well with one report of captive breeding undertaken within the range of the species (D. M. R. Fortaleza *in litt.* 1991), and another of pairs with fledglings in January 1991 (Aleixo *et al.* 1991). Up to four eggs have been laid in captivity, with an incubation period of 24 days or a little longer; fledging occurs at around 34 days, and independence at around 100 days (Mann and Mann 1982, D. M. R. Fortaleza *in litt.* 1991).

THREATS Extensive forest clearance throughout its range and over many centuries has been the main cause of this amazon's decline (Sick 1969, Sick and Teixeira 1979, Ridgely 1981a). Monte Pascoal National Park is under severe pressure (Redford 1989), and many of the areas from which the species has been recorded in recent years in Rio de Janeiro state are being cleared, notably around Desengano State Park (J. F. Pacheco verbally 1991).

The Red-browed Amazon commands high prices in the pet trade, since it is considered one of the best "speakers" in its genus (M. Levy verbally 1985; a perception reported long ago by Wied 1831-1833), and it appears regularly in small numbers on the domestic Brazilian market, e.g. in the notorious Caxias bird market in Rio de Janeiro (C. E. Carvalho *in litt.* 1987). Even in a reserve like Sooretama, where considered secure (Ridgely 1981a), this species is not safe from bird trappers, as indicated by 36 birds held by a dealer in Espírito Santo who admitted they had all been taken in the reserve (R. Wirth *in litt.* 1984). In October 1986 birds were seen being offered for sale at the roadside outside Monte Pascoal National Park (LPG, NJC). At the international level the species has been imported into the United States despite the legal protection outlined below (Ridgely 1981a), and into Switzerland, legally, as a subspecies of Blue-cheeked Amazon *A. dufresniana* (listed on CITES Appendix II; see Remarks 1) (C. Yamashita *in litt.* 1986).

MEASURES TAKEN The species is protected under Brazilian law (Bernardes *et al.* 1990) and listed on Appendix I of CITES. Its occurrence in Monte Pascoal National Park (Bahia), the Rio Doce State Park and Ibitipoca State Park (Minas Gerais), Córrego Grande Biological Reserve, the adjacent Sooretama/CVRD Linhares reserves and Augusto Ruschi Biological Reserve (Espírito Santo) is important, but the quality of protection provided is variable, with birds being poached from Monte Pascoal (see also Redford 1989) and Sooretama (see Threats), while Córrego Grande (formerly Fazenda Klabin) is now very small (1,242 ha: Gonzaga *et al.* 1987).

MEASURES PROPOSED The Red-browed Amazon's most pressing need is for the speedy location and immediate protection of additional remnant forest areas within its range (Ridgely 1981a, Silva 1989a). More specifically, it is important that CVRD continue to recognize the biological importance of its Porto Seguro Reserve in Bahia and give it total protection, and that the authorities in Rio de Janeiro state take the necessary steps to protect the forests where the species has been recorded that lie outside existing park boundaries, i.e. at Desengano State Park and on Ilha Grande. The taking of nestlings and capture and shooting of adult birds may be reduced by an education campaign in the areas adjacent to the breeding sites (R. Wirth *in litt.* 1984). Silva's (1989a) declaration that no additional specimens should be taken from the wild is no more than a reaffirmation of the existing Brazilian law; his call for additional pairs to be formed from individuals already in confinement is clearly sensible. Captive breeding reports include Mann and Mann (1982) and Robiller and Trogisch (1984).

REMARKS (1) The Red-browed Amazon has often been treated as a subspecies of Blue-cheeked Amazon (e.g. Forshaw 1978), and both have also been included under Red-tailed Amazon *A. brasiliensis* (see Remarks 1 under that species); however, the modern trend has been to treat all three as good species (Ridgely 1981a, Sick 1985, Forshaw 1989). (2) Wied did not visit the Serra dos Órgãos (see Bokermann 1957 for itinerary, although he does not discuss this fact) and this record probably refers to second-hand information or a misunderstanding of the name for a site (J. F. Pacheco verbally 1991).

ST LUCIA AMAZON *Amazona versicolor* R[11]

Endemic to moist forest on the central-southern mountains of St Lucia, this parrot has experienced depletion of numbers owing to habitat loss, hurricanes, hunting and trade, but recent action by government and non-government agencies has now reversed the situation, with some 300-350 individuals extant and the nation sensitized to the importance of the species.

DISTRIBUTION The St Lucia Amazon is endemic to St Lucia in the West Indies. Its original range on the island is reasonably assumed to have followed the original distribution of moist forest there, and thus prior to 1850 it was "widespread" (Butler 1980, 1981a). During the twentieth century it has been documented in progressive retreat into the core of the central and southern block of mountains, in the 1920s from La Sorcière south (Bond 1928b), in 1971 from the Barre de l'Isle south (Diamond 1973), in 1950 with an estimated 295 km^2 of habitat (clockwise running from Forestière to La Sorcière, St Joseph Estate, Mt Durocher, Blancnard, Saltibus, Fond St Jacques, Mt Tabac and Mt Parasol), in 1969 with only about 82 km^2 (Jovicich 1976, Butler 1980, 1981a; see Remarks 1). Since the mid-1970s its range has been within a roughly 65-70 km^2 area of forest from Millet and Mont Lacombe in the north to Mont Beucop and Calfourc in the east, Piton Cochon, Piton St Esprit, Desrache and Grand Magasin in the south, and Morne Gimie and Mont Houlemon in the west and north-west respectively (Jeggo 1976a,b, 1981, Butler 1980, 1981a); details of localities to and from which birds make daily dispersals are given in Jeggo (1976a) and Butler (1981a). Centres of abundance within this range may vary with time or season: Bond (1928b) found most birds around Piton Lacombe but was told the greatest concentration was between Dennery and Micoud near the windward coast (Danforth 1935 found them only on Piton Lacombe); since the mid-1970s apparent changes in abundance in three key survey areas, Millet, Quilesse and Edmund Forest, have been documented in Jeggo (1987) and Jeggo *et al.* (1989). Survey work in 1990 confirmed that the south-western parts of the remaining forest hold the greatest concentrations of parrots, while those in the north-east support very few (Jeggo and Anthony 1991).

POPULATION Although judged to have been relatively abundant before 1850 (Butler 1980, 1981a), and still described as "not uncommon in the high woods" at the turn of the century (Thompson 1902; see Remarks 2), the species evidently thereafter declined seriously (see Threats) and recovered again, since Porter (1930a) recorded that "twenty years ago the bird was to all intents and purposes practically extinct" but that it was "now fairly common" with flocks of 20 being reported on their way to their feeding areas. An estimated 1,000 birds existed in around 1950 (Jovicich 1976, Butler 1978, 1980, 1981a), and at the end of the decade the species was judged "not as rare as usually thought" (Frost 1959; see Remarks 3), although Bond (1961) detected a marked deterioration in status since his work there in the late 1920s. At the start of the 1960s the species was regarded as in danger of becoming rare through excessive shooting (Sjögren 1963) and by the end of the decade this prediction was evidently coming true, with some 40 estimated being shot every year and the species considered common in only about half its remaining habitat, then c.20 km^2 in extent (Wingate 1969). Survey work in 1975, which included the sighting of a flock of 20, and follow-up studies in 1976, resulted in an estimated 100-150 birds remaining (Jeggo 1976a,b) or plain 125 (Nichols 1976, 1977a) or 150±25 (Jovicich 1976, Butler 1978, 1980, 1981a) or 125-150 (Nichols 1977b) or 100±25 (Jeggo 1981). A study in July–August 1977 concluded that the total population was probably no more than 100 (Butler 1978), a figure that appeared to be valid for the situation up to 1980 (Butler 1980, 1981a; hence also Low 1980b, Silva 1980). Following (but despite) the devastation wrought by Hurricane Allen in 1980 (see Threats) a survey suggested a population level similar to that of 1975/1976, i.e. 150±25, which "would tend to indicate a small increase on the 1977 figure", although the only specific conclusions were that "the hurricane adversely affected the possible recent upward trend of the population" (Butler and Jeggo in Butler 1980) and that "the hurricane had not caused a significant decline in the parrot population" (Jeggo and Taynton 1981). Four subsequent surveys have revealed a steady increase in numbers: the first, in 1982, recorded the species with much greater frequency than that in 1980, the conclusion being that certainly no decline had taken place, that the increased frequency might reflect changes in distribution in response to forest damage, but that it might indicate an increasing population (Jeggo *et al.* 1983); the second, in 1986, though based on the revised opinion that "the sightings in 1982 did not indicate any increase in the population", estimated numbers at 200-250 (Jeggo 1987); the third, in 1988, estimated numbers at 250-300 (Jeggo *et al.* 1989); and the fourth, in August–September 1990, resulted in a further estimated increase to 300-350 (Jeggo and Anthony 1991).

ECOLOGY Habitat is the canopy of tropical moist forest in the montane interior of the island; diurnal movements take the species outwards from the heart of the forest in the early morning, sometimes to the periphery of its habitat and into adjacent areas of secondary growth, birds returning to roost in the later afternoon and evening (Jeggo 1976a,b; see Remarks 4). Jovicich (1976) noted activity to occur typically (although varying in poor weather) from 45 minutes before sunrise, reaching a peak between 07h30 and 08h00, tailing off to nothing by 10h30-11h00, beginning again around 14h30 and culminating in a late afternoon peak at c.17h00, winding down completely 45 minutes before darkness.

Catholic use of the apparently abundant and extensive food-plants has always been assumed (Jeggo 1976a, Butler 1981a) but little has been published. To date, birds have been recorded eating flowers or fruits of strangling fig (aralie) *Clusia* sp., wild breadfruit (bois pain marron) *Talauma dodecapetala*, gri gri palm *Acrocomia irenensis*, pennypiece *Pouteria* sp., bois cote *Miconia mirabilis*, "pomme-de-lien" (*sic*; no scientific name given), by implication the palm *Euterpe globosa* and, after Hurricane Allen, bananas in cultivated areas (Jeggo 1976a, 1977, Butler 1980, 1981a, Jeggo and Taynton 1981, Forshaw 1989). Jovicich (1976) reproduced a list of food sources provided by his respected guide (S. John), as follows (excluding those listed above): balata chien *Manilkara riedleana*, bois tan rouge *Byrsonima martinicensis*, chatagnier *Sloanea massoni*, dalmarie *Pithecellobium jupunba*, gommier *Dacryodes excelsa*, goyavier *Cassipourea guianensis*, l'ensense *Protium attenuatum*, mapon *Torrubia* [*sic*] *fragrans*, paletuvier *Pterocarpus officinalis*, wild mahoe *Sterculia caribaea*. The species's apparent absence from Edmund Forest between late August and late November is possibly due to a lack of fruiting *Clusia* in the area at that time (Butler 1981a). A bird collected in July 1931 contained "a large number of small unidentified fruits and their seeds" (Danforth 1935).

Nests are placed in holes in trees, but despite the report by Mühlhaus and Mühlhaus (1983) that *Dacryodes excelsa* is the most favoured species, it is not preferred to the same degree as by the St Vincent Amazon *Amazona guildingii* (see relevant account): thus of 10 nests, 1975/1976, three were in gommier, two in pennypiece, two in burnline *Sapium caribaeum*, and one each in wild breadfruit, boardwood *Simarouba amara* and "bad job" (scientific name not given) (Jeggo 1977). Breeding coincides with the dry season from February to August; from the evidence of two nestlings found in late May and early June 1975, plus the sighting of a newly fledged bird on 13 June, egg-laying that year would have occurred from the end of February through March (Jeggo 1976a). Clutch-size is two, though generally only one young is reared (Mühlhaus and Mühlhaus 1983); the only two nests found in 1975 each held only one chick (one nestling was later found dead outside the cavity, possibly victim of an opossum *Didelphis marsupialis*, and the other was taken for captive breeding), while in 1976 of seven certain and five suspected nests only three reached nestling stage, these holding two young each (all taken for captive breeding) (Jeggo 1976a,b, 1977). In 1979 and 1980 breeding success was judged to have been better (Jeggo and Taynton 1981), and indeed the recovery of the population, 1980–1988, indicated an increase in numbers of 150-200 birds at an average recruitment of 25-30 per year (Jeggo *et al.* 1989). Maturity is reached at several years (Jeggo 1981); a captive (paired) female laid infertile eggs at four years old, two fertile clutches at six (Jeggo 1983); the incubation period is 28 days, and the first young hatched in captivity flew at 81 days (Jeggo 1983).

THREATS Causes of decline in the St Lucia Amazon may be attributed to habitat loss, hunting (partly for trade), and predation or competition from indigenous or introduced bird and mammal species.

Habitat loss The chief cause of overall decline has been habitat destruction (Mühlhaus and Mühlhaus 1983), a point often overlooked in some of the detailed reviews of the species's status in the past 20 years; for example, the fact that the species's habitat covered 295 km^2 in 1950 and only 65-70 km^2 in 1975 (see Distribution) indicates an inevitable, irretrievable and disastrous loss in numbers. Although in that latter year the forests were under protection for water supplies, considerable fragmentation of forest and inroads into forest reserves were being made by shifting cultivators (Jeggo 1976a,b, Butler 1978, 1981a). Hurricane Allen, on 4 August 1980, apparently killed at least two birds, disabled the tourist walk, and severely damaged the nature reserve established chiefly for the parrot; throughout the island, 39% of trees were considered dead, 41% were recovering and 20% were unaffected, while within the parrot's range the equivalent figures were 56%, 28% and 16%; yet (owing very largely to the pre-existing conservation programme) there was no invasion of forest land by displaced farmers and the forest quickly began regenerating (Butler and Jeggo in Butler 1980, Jeggo and Taynton 1981). A proposed dam proved to offer little threat to existing forest (Jeggo 1987), but monitoring of changes at Millet resulting from its construction remains important (Jeggo and Anthony 1991). It has been proposed that cutting vines for (e.g.) basket-weaving affects the birds by denuding and disturbing the forest (Butler 1978, 1981a), but no evidence has been adduced. Uncontrolled tree-felling since the 1950s may have led to a scarcity of trees with deep, dark cavities such as St Lucia Amazons can use but which Pearly-eyed Thrashers *Margarops fuscatus* avoid, leading to competition between the two (see below).

Hunting and trade The reduction of the species to near extinction around 1910 (see Population) was attributed wholly to hunting for food and trapping for pets, while its recovery (a conservation measure taken that was not sustained) resulted directly from the exaction of severe penalties for such infringements (Porter 1929, 1930a); certainly at the turn of the century dead birds were on sale "almost every week in the market of the little town of Soufrière" (Thompson 1902). However, while the policy of strict protection was known in 1931 to Danforth (1935), he found evidence that "considerable numbers... had been killed for eating within the past few years" and expressed his concern for the future of the species if this trend continued. Both the problem and the species were still present thirty years later (Bond 1961, Sjögren 1963) such that in 1969 it was estimated some 40 were being killed annually, many as accidental victims of "wing-shooting" in which the intention was to bring down the bird alive for the cage-bird market (Wingate 1969, Butler 1978). In 1971 the species was "intensively hunted" (Diamond 1973) and in 1975 hunting was regarded as the bird's chief threat: the whole forest was found intersected with hunters' trails, with birds "extremely wary and nervous" and considered fair game and good eating (Jeggo 1976a); in 1977 the situation was essentially the same (Butler 1978, 1981a). Hunters were also still wing-shooting birds as tourists paid high prices for them, but there was very little evidence of trapping young for pets (Jeggo 1976a). There is a comment that birds were usually caught with lime made from wild breadfruit sap (Frost 1959), this presumably referring to a period when the species's habitat came lower and birds might have visited suitable trees near cultivations.

Predation and competition Indigenous predators include Broad-winged Hawk *Buteo platypterus*, fer-de-lance *Bothrops caribaeus* and boa *Constrictor constrictor*, though none of these can be a serious problem (Jeggo 1976a, Butler 1978); introduced predators include rats *Rattus*, mongoose *Herpestes auropunctatus* and opossum, none of which should be a serious problem either (the mongoose being terrestrial and the opossum being itself greatly hunted: Jeggo 1976a). However, the Pearly-eyed Thrasher, a nest-competitor that was rare on the island in 1950 but which is now common in the forests, was seen repeatedly interfering with parrots in the 1976 breeding season and was then judged to represent a considerable threat (Jeggo 1977, 1981a).

MEASURES TAKEN The recent history of conservation on St Lucia has become a model for other Caribbean countries and reveals an achievement unparalleled elsewhere in the world. Jeggo (1976a), in support of the captive breeding programme he then considered vital to the St Lucia Amazon's survival, called for studies of the species's ecology and the establishment of reserves based on the results, and added that "above all it is important to generate a spirit of enthusiasm for conservation in St Lucia", something he regarded as a long-term option only.

In fact, the spirit in question arrived in human form as P. J. Butler (see, e.g. Wille 1991, Nielsen 1992), whose recommendations (Butler 1978) – for (a) stronger penalties against hunters, trappers and exporters of the parrots, (b) nature reserves in existing forest reserves, (c) environmental education, (d) registration of all captive parrots, (e) a local breeding project with existing captive birds and (f) promotion of nature tourism – all received the endorsement of the government, Butler (1980, 1981a,b) himself being invited back in 1978 to implement them, so that by 1980 (a) the St Lucia Amazon had been declared the national bird, a new Wildlife Ordinance was passing into law raising the fine for killing a parrot from 24 to 5,000 East Caribbean dollars, and a new Forest, Soil and Water Ordinance was poised to bestow stronger powers to conserve forest, (b) a 16 km^2 nature reserve had been established including Morne Gimie, Mont Cochon and almost all the known parrot nesting areas (major support for this coming from WWF), (c) education packs on the parrot, the forest and conservation in general had been produced and targeted on the island's 20,000 school children, a centre was under construction, and broadcasts had spread the message, (d) of 15 known captive birds (nine at JWPT, six on the island) all had been registered, (e) a small aviary had been constructed on the island but no further birds were to be taken from the wild, and (f) two tourist walks had been established that were raising funds for conservation.

Following Hurricane Allen, Butler and Jeggo (in Butler 1980) recommended (i) the protection of natural forests against invasion by new landless farmers, (ii) replanting with native trees, (iii) erection of artificial nest-boxes to compensate for tree losses and to help avoid competition with Pearly-eyed Thrashers (implemented without success: Butler 1982), (iv) closure (immediately implemented) of the open season, (v) continuation of the environmental education programme, and (vi) monitoring of the parrot population (implemented by Jeggo *et al.* 1983, 1989, Jeggo 1987). Progress was reviewed by Jeggo (1987), who particularly identified for praise precisely what he had called for a decade earlier, the continuing education programme, with its high profile of the parrot through tee-shirts, bumper stickers, monthly magazines ("Bush Talk" for adults, "Jacquot" for children) and media coverage, all of which had resulted in "a very great feeling that *A. versicolor* is something very special to St Lucia and that it should be protected and cherished". Further reviews of the history and progress of (conservation education) work on the St Lucia Amazon are in Butler (1991, 1992).

Major organizational support for the conservation of the St Lucia Amazon since the mid-1970s has come from JWPT throughout, WWF in the early stages, and RARE throughout the 1980s. CIDA has funded forest conservation work in relation to the island's water requirements (Jeggo 1987), and a map of the present government forest reserves (total area 7,507 ha) is provided in Butler (1991).

MEASURES PROPOSED Clearly the major initiatives have already been taken, but a scattering of points deserve attention (see Remarks 5). A "Parks and Protected Areas System Plan" is in preparation by the St Lucia National Trust, and the passage of the appropriate legislation deserves priority treatment (Butler 1991). The study of the St Lucia Amazon's ecology is still basically lacking, and this needs to be rectified, particularly in respect of feeding and breeding requirements, so that forestry planning (and planting) can be refined. With regard to this last, Jeggo (1987) anticipated the phasing out of plantations in important forest areas and their reversion to natural forest, with timber needs on the island being met by the planting of suitable yield trees in degraded areas on the periphery of the forest; given this, there seems all the more reason for the ecological study of the parrot (and in fact a two-year JWPT/St Lucia Forestry Division field study of the bird's behaviour and ecology is to begin in September 1992: D. F. Jeggo *in litt.* 1992). Moreover, there is a need to understand better the relationship between the Pearly-eyed Thrasher and the St Lucia Amazon so that any future conflict between the two species can be managed with maximum efficiency.

Captive breeding The establishment of a captive breeding programme for the St Lucia Amazon was considered vital for the species's survival in 1975 (Jeggo 1976a,b), a sentiment fully endorsed by Low (1980b) and Silva (1980). However, developments on St Lucia since then have tended to marginalize this JWPT-funded and -run programme, which now justifies itself more as a reservoir against total failure in the wild population (Jeggo 1981, 1991). The continuing recovery of the wild population, the championing of which is greatly to JWPT's credit, certainly calls into question the authority with which certain pronouncements ("captive breeding will be the only way to save them from extinction": Silva 1980) have been made. Between 1975 and 1978 JWPT assembled nine birds on Jersey, seven nestlings from the wild (Jeggo 1976a, 1977) and two on loan from Bermuda and Britain respectively (details of their care are in Jeggo 1981, 1991), and bred one in 1982 (Jeggo 1983), one in 1985, two in 1986, four in 1987 (Jeggo 1987) and further subsequent successes such that as many as 10 offspring a year were hoped for by 1994 (Jeggo 1991); unfortunately, however, in the period 1990–1992 no young were reared and currently there are 13 in Jersey (seven wild-caught, six captive-bred) and three in St Lucia (two captive-bred in Jersey, returned in 1989, and one wild-caught) (D. F. Jeggo *in litt.* 1992).

REMARKS (1) Silva (1989a) gave incorrect values in square kilometres for the former range. (2) Phillips (1929) referred to a visit by P. Lowe and S. Braach in 1901 from which he apparently derived the view that the bird was rare, but the source for this is not known. (3) Butler (1980, 1981a) gave Frost (1959) as the source for asserting that the species was then rare and declining rapidly, which is mistaken. (4) The view that birds fly *to* their feeding grounds in the late afternoon (Bond 1928b) seems mistaken. (5) While the achievements on St Lucia have been excellent and what is here proposed remains important, it must be pointed out that other birds on the island deserve attention, notably two in their own genus: Semper's Warbler *Leucopeza semperi*, sadly perhaps already extinct, and the White-breasted Thrasher *Ramphocinclus brachyurus*, which desperately needs human intercession (see relevant accounts).

VINACEOUS AMAZON *Amazona vinacea* V/R[10]

Formerly abundant and widespread from Bahia, Brazil, south through eastern Paraguay to northern Argentina and Rio Grande do Sul, this amazon has declined dramatically in numbers as its populations have retreated into isolated pockets of forest, mostly in the south of its range: although perhaps still secure in places (work is needed to identify further key sites), the reasons for its long-term decline and the basic details of its ecological needs remain obscure (work is equally needed to address these matters).

DISTRIBUTION The Vinaceous Amazon is endemic to the Atlantic Forest region of south-eastern South America, extending originally from Bahia to Rio Grande do Sul in Brazil into eastern Paraguay and Misiones and apparently Corrientes, Argentina, but now apparently confined to relatively few, highly scattered sites within this range. A record from Montevideo, Uruguay (Finsch 1867-1868), is discounted here as a trade skin of uncertain provenance.

Brazil Although largely to be regarded as a bird of southern Brazil (São Paulo southwards), the Vinaceous Amazon appears to persist in tiny isolated pockets in all four range states to the north.

Bahia Southern Bahia is cited repeatedly as the northernmost part of the species's range (e.g. Pinto 1938, Meyer de Schauensee 1966, Ridgely 1981a, Forshaw 1989) but the evidence for its former occurrence there (there are no recent records: Ridgely 1981a) appears to derive almost entirely from the testimony of Wied (1831-1833), who reported never finding it in the coastal high forest but rather in the hills of the hinterland ("Sertong", i.e. "sertão"), particularly often near "Vareda", which Bokermann (1957) traced to within 50 km of "Barra da Vareda", now apparently Inhomirim (see Remarks 1). Most interestingly, however, captive specimens seen in July 1990 in Lençóis (northern end of the Chapada Diamantina National Park) were claimed by the owner to have been caught from a local population (R. Parrini verbally 1990). Bosch and Wedde (1981) gave Salvador as a specific locality, without explanation.

Espírito Santo Like Bahia, the evidence for the inclusion of this state in the species's range has been weak, and Ridgely (1981a) could find no recent records. A female was collected at Braço do Sul (rio Jucu Braço Sul) in June 1897 (Hellmayr 1915), and there are four specimens from "Engenheiro Reeve", 400-600 m, March and April 1903 (in AMNH), this apparently being Rive, at 20°46'S 41°28'W (see Remarks 2). In recent years a relict population was located in the municipalities of Agua Doce do Norte and Barra de São Francisco, in the north-west close to the border with Minas Gerais; although the species may be extinct now (see Population), reports continue of birds present at Guararema, 18°50'S 40°43'W (Nova Venécia municipality) and Pedra Torta (untraced) in Barra de São Francisco (D. M. R. Fortaleza *in litt.* 1990, 1991).

Minas Gerais This state has commonly been omitted from the range (e.g. in Meyer de Schauensee 1966, Ridgely 1981a, Forshaw 1989), but there is a specimen (in MZUFV) from Piranga, November 1938, Pinto (1952) saw the species along the Rio Doce (whence a skin in MNRJ from 1917, unless this was in Espírito Santo), and Sick (1985) must have had other reports (see Population). In recent years five sites have been found: Ibitipoca Park, where one or two are frequently seen (M. A. de Andrade *in litt.* 1988); the left bank of the rio São Francisco near Januária and Itacarambi in the north-west, in November 1986 (a startling range extension) (M. A. de Andrade *in litt.* 1988); the Monte Verde area, Camanducaia municipality, in the extreme south (M. A. de Andrade *in litt.* 1988); the Caratinga Reserve at Fazenda Montes Claros (M. A. Brazil and D. R. Waugh *in litt.* 1987, R. S. Ridgely *in litt.* 1991); and Caparaó National Park, April 1991, at 1,600 m (J. F. Pacheco verbally 1991).

Rio de Janeiro Although commonly given as a range state (e.g. in Pinto 1938, Meyer de Schauensee 1966, Forshaw 1989), the evidence for occurrence is very weak and Burmeister (1856) regarded it as naturally absent. However, the species was found around Nova Friburgo in 1828 (see Population), when a juvenile male was collected at Morro Queimado, near Rosário (22°41'S

43°15'W in OG 1963b) (Reinhardt 1870, Krabbe undated). Recently the species was rediscovered in the state 15 km north of Valença (400 m), where a pair was seen in December 1990 and locals reported a small breeding (but seasonally absent) population (J. F. Pacheco verbally 1991).

São Paulo Between 1818 and 1821 the species was collected at "Pahor" (east of Campos do Jordão), "Murungaba" (east of Campinas), Ipanema (west of São Paulo) and Itararé (von Pelzeln 1868-1871; see Remarks 3). There are three specimens from Xiririca or rio Preto, Xiririca (now Eldorado, 24°32'S 48°06'W in OG 1963b), in the Serra Paranapiacaba, dating from August/September 1929 (Pinto 1938, and in MCZ), and another from Iguape, October 1900 (Pinto 1938). In recent years records are from the Campos do Jordão State Park on the north-east slope of the Serra da Mantiqueira, 1,500-2,000 m (Willis and Oniki 1981a); the Jacupiranga State Reserve near Jacupiranga, 750 m (Willis and Oniki 1981a), with a flock of 60 on the boundary of the latter in March 1991 (H. Palo Junior *per* P. Scherer Neto verbally 1991); several pairs along BR 116 in the extreme south of the state bordering Paraná (extensive forest in the region), October 1991 (B. M. Whitney *in litt.* 1991); and a flock of 30 at km 526 on the same road, January 1991 (S. C. Luçolli and Z. Kock *in litt.* 1992). Three unidentified amazons at Boracéia Experimental Station in January 1987 were thought most probably Vinaceous (D. F. Stotz *in litt.* 1988); see also under Santa Catarina concerning the work of Diefenback and Goldhammer (1986).

Paraná The species was collected in 1820 at Pitangui, near Curitiba (von Pelzeln 1868-1871); OG (1963b) indicates a rio Pitangui at 25°01'S 49°59'W, i.e. just south of Castro. Other specimen records are of three birds, Castro, May and August 1907 (Pinto 1938); two, Foz de Iguaçu (one labelled as at 90 m), May 1950 (Aguirre and Aldrighi 1983, and in AMNH); three, Tibagi (two simply labelled Fazenda Monte Alegre, which is the same place), 900 m, August 1907 and March 1930 (in AMNH and MZUSP); one, Rio Claro, Serra da Esperança (from these two qualifiers the locality appears to be Rio Claro do Sul, 25°56'S 50°41'W, in OG 1963b), February 1922 (Sztolcman 1926); and one each at Rio Baile (untraced, but not as defined in Paynter and Traylor 1991) and Cândido de Abreu on consecutive days in November 1929 (in FMNH). Recent records are from Fazenda Santa Rita in Ponta Grossa municipality (untraced) (L. dos Anjos *per* S. C. Luçolli *in litt.* 1992), Fazenda Monte Alegre in Telêmaco Borba municipality (untraced) (R. A. Berndt *per* S. C. Luçolli *in litt.* 1992), and Fazendas São Pedro and Santa Cândida in General Carneiro municipality (untraced), in the extreme south (S. D. Arruda and S. C. Luçolli *in litt.* 1992). The record above from São Paulo state along BR 116 suggests that birds occur there inside Paraná; see also under Santa Catarina concerning the work of Diefenback and Goldhammer (1986).

Santa Catarina Sick (1972, 1985) regarded the state as one in which the species persisted in relatively good numbers, and Sick *et al.* (1981) indicated that it was known there via references in the literature, specimens in state museums and their own observations (no details given); nevertheless, there is very poor documentation of its presence. Five previously unpublished records, the second, third and fifth made during fieldwork by Sick *et al.* (1981), are (in the west, adjacent to Argentina) Parque de São Miguel (not a protected area), São Miguel do Oeste, 8 October 1980; (in the east, north to south) Bom Sucesso, Itaiópolis municipality, 26 October 1978; Sassafrás Biological Reserve, Benedito Novo municipality, same date; Piuras, Serra da Bocaina do Sul, Lages municipality, 15 December 1982; Morro da Palha, Lauro Müller municipality, 16 February 1978 (L. A. R. Bege *in litt.* 1991). A little west of this last, the species was observed in the São Joaquim region in January 1990 (Pacheco and da Fonseca 1990). Moreover, MNRJ has a bird from the rio Uruguay, Porto Feliz (now Mondaí), in August 1928. Diefenback and Goldhammer (1986), in searching for the Red-spectacled Amazon *Amazona pretrei*, encountered only the Vinaceous Amazon in the araucaria groves of the northern part of this state, and also in those of São Paulo and Paraná, but they did not specify their records.

Rio Grande do Sul The species is now confined to the north and north-east of the state (Belton 1984-1985, which see for coordinates of localities below). Specimen records are from Arroio Grande (near Taquara) and Linha Tirajá (near Nova Petrópolis), 1880-1890 (von Berlepsch and von Ihering 1885; specimens in AMNH); two males, Itaquy, February/March 1905 (Pinto

1938); a male from São Francisco de Paula, 900 m, December 1918; a male from São Pedro ("coastal lagoons"), October 1928; a female from Sananduva, 600 m, January 1929; a male and female from Nonohay (Nonoai), Passo da Entrada, 600 m, February 1929; and a female from Passo Fundo, 600 m, March 1929 (all in AMNH). Other older records are from Poço das Antas, Canela and Torres (Gliesch 1930, Belton 1984-1985); Silva (1989a) ignored Belton's (1984-1985) warning that von Ihering's (1902) eggs (see Ecology) sent from São Lourenço did not necessarily originate there. Modern records are from Turvo State Park and Nonoai Indian Reserve (E. Albuquerque *per* N. Varty verbally 1992), Espigão Alto State Park near Barracão (W. A. Voss *per* S. C. Luçolli *in litt.* 1992), Carazinho (N. Varty verbally 1992), Vacaria (Belton 1984-1985), Bom Jesus, where it occurs at times (Forshaw 1978, 1989), Cambará do Sul (N. Varty verbally 1992), Aparados da Serra National Park (Ridgely 1981a, Belton 1984-1985, TAP), Tainhas (W. A. Voss *per* S. C. Luçolli *in litt.* 1992), Canela (W. A. Voss *per* S. C. Luçolli *in litt.* 1992), São Francisco de Paula National Forest (N. Varty verbally 1992, TAP) and the untraced Fazenda Mauro J. Machado (W. A. Voss *per* S. C. Luçolli *in litt.* 1992).

Paraguay The Vinaceous Amazon was evidently once fairly widespread in south-eastern Paraguay (coordinates below are from OG 1957a or Paynter 1989) in the departments of Amambay, Canindeyú, Caaguazú, Alto Paraná, Itapúa and Guaíra, this last based on specimens collected at "Villa Rica" (male, July 1893, in AMNH; also Salvadori 1895b) and "Villa Ricca" (male and female, June 1907, in BMNH), apparently the westernmost point from which the species has been recorded (see Remarks 4). A contraction of range eastwards, southwards and northwards seems to have occurred: thus there is a record from Yhú (24°59'S 55°59'W) (Salvadori 1895b) and a specimen (male) from east of Caaguazú town, 300 m, November 1930 (in AMNH), but birds no longer occur in the department of the same name (Silva 1989a); there are 15 specimens from Capitán Meza, Itapúa (27°01'S 55°34'W), from where the species now seems to have disappeared (Nores and Yzurieta 1983); and the species was not reported in 1988 by inhabitants in Amambay (Silva 1989a; see Remarks 5). However, apart from recent first (but see Remarks 4) records (no details given) for the department of Concepción at Estancia Centurión and Santa María de la Sierra (López in press), the species survives in Canindeyú (despite not being reported to Silva 1989a) and Alto Paraná.

Canindeyú Up to eight birds were seen daily, 16-18 July 1977 in forest east of Celos Parini along the road to Saltos del Guaíra (R. S. Ridgely *in litt.* 1991); many were seen at Arroyo Pozuelo, 2-5 November 1987, many at Catueté, 24 July 1989, many along the río Carapá south of Mbaracayú, 25 July 1989 (F. E. Hayes *in litt.* 1991); it remains numerous in the Mbaracayú Reserve (Sierra de Maracaju) (P.A. Scharf *per* R. S. Ridgely *in litt.* 1991); and morning flights of 30-35 (at least 50 therefore considered present in the area) were seen at the 8,000 ha Guayaki Reserve (Estancia Itabo) in the south-east, June 1991 (R. S. Ridgely *in litt.* 1991).

Alto Paraná Records (north to south) are from the western shores of Itaipu Dam in two forest reserves, Itabo and Limoy (N. Pérez *in litt.* 1988); to the north of Hernandarias (Nores and Yzurieta 1983); east of Puerto Presidente Stroessner, 22 August 1977 (R. S. Ridgely *in litt.* 1991); Puerto Gibaja (25°33'S 54°40'W; specimens in UMMZ); Puerto Bertoni (25°38'S 54°40'W) (Bertoni 1927; see Remarks 6; specimens in UMMZ are from 7 km north); Paranambú (presumably Puerto Paranambú, 25°59'S 54°46'W), where already extinct (Silva 1989a); the Río Ñacunday basin, 26°03'S 54°45'W (Nores and Yzurieta 1983); Colonia Dorada (untraced), where extinction was looming in 1988 (Silva 1988a, 1989a,b); and at Comandacay (untraced) (Nores and Yzurieta 1983); F. E. Hayes (*in litt.* 1991) saw four birds at Puerto Barra, 28 September 1989 (locality untraced).

Argentina All specific Argentine records of the Vinaceous Amazon are from Misiones province, although Canevari *et al.* (1991) also mentioned north-east Corrientes; unless otherwise stated, coordinates are from OG (1968) or Paynter (1985). Specimens have been collected at Iguazú, 1900 (Orfila 1936-1938); Deseado (25°47'S 54°03'W), General Belgrano department, a male, August 1955 (Navas and Bó 1988a); along the Arroyo Urugua-í (25°54'S 54°36'W) at km 10,

1958-1961 (44, of which 35 are in AMNH, three in ANSP, five in LACM and one in YPM); San Antonio, 26°07'S 53°45'W, October 1946 (specimen in IML); Eldorado, 26°24'S 54°38'W, May/June 1962 and July 1963, four (Navas and Bó 1988a,); August 1967, one (Keve and Kovács 1973); Tobunas, 1953 and 1959 (Navas and Bó 1988a, plus 10 skins in LACM, whose labels give 26°28'S 53°54'W: K. L. Garrett *in litt.* 1986); Montecarlo, September 1956 (specimen in IML); San Pedro, 26°38'S 54°08'W, November 1949 (specimens in IML); Santa Ana (27°22'S 55°34'W), 12, 1910-1920 (Orfila 1936-1938, and specimens in AMNH, IML, MACN); Bonpland (or Bonplano), 27°29'S 55°29'W, January 1912 (specimen in IML); Concepción (27°59'S 55°31'W), two males, June 1881 (in BMNH and MNHN; also White 1882); and Villa Lutecia (= Teyú-cuarí: J. C. Chebez *in litt.* 1992), near San Ignacio (27°16'S 55°32'W), July 1910 (one in MNHN). In 1986 it was still reputedly possible to see flocks at Eldorado (Silva 1989a; M. Nores *in litt.* 1992 dissented from this view), but at other localities such as Concepción and San Javier (27°53'S 55°08'W), mentioned by White (1882), the species has disappeared (Silva 1989a); indeed Nores and Yzurieta (1983) questioned whether it survived anywhere in the country, including Iguazú National Park (around 30 years ago it was still present near Iguazú Falls; Eckleberry 1965), the last observation there being in April 1983 (R. J. Straneck *per* J. C. Chebez *in litt.* 1992).

However, in recent years three relictual populations have been found, at Campo Viera, 27°23'S 55°02'W (Oberá department), San Antonio and San Pedro (M. Nores and D. Yzurieta *in litt.* 1986, J. C. Chebez *in litt.* 1986, 1989, 1992; also Silva 1991d); a review of the past and current status of the species in Misiones is in Chebez (in press). It is worth noting that the record from Parque de São Miguel in westernmost Santa Catarina, Brazil, is from "an entirely agricultural area, but on the Argentine side there is undamaged subtropical forest which is perhaps the cause of the occurrence" (L. A. R. Bege *in litt.* 1991); the area in question would be well east of San Pedro, from the coordinates above.

POPULATION The Vinaceous Amazon has now become a rare bird almost everywhere in its range, having once been abundant in many places. Thus for example Wied (1831-1833) saw large roosting flocks in central Bahia, P. Lund (in a hitherto entirely neglected report) found birds "extremely common" at Nova Friburgo in Rio state in 1828 (Reinhardt 1870) although it was absent there 20 years later (Burmeister 1856, Reinhardt 1870), White (1882) referred to "incredible numbers" in one area of Misiones from which it is now extirpated, Bertoni (1927) witnessed skies darkened by immigrating birds in Paraguay in the 1890s, and Silva (1989a, 1991d) reported a trapper in Paraguay telling him of 8,000 or more birds at Colonia Dorada and up to 4,000 at Paranambú, both in 1978; all these populations have disappeared or, in the case of Colonia Dorada, where only around 300 were judged to survive in 1988 (Silva 1988a), will soon do so (Nores and Yzurieta 1983, Silva 1989a). Thus in 10 years Paraguay has moved from being the Vinaceous Amazon's stronghold, even though numbers might be relatively small (Ridgely 1981a; also Forshaw 1989), to the point where the species is now judged the country's most endangered parrot (Silva 1989a); however, it has been reported as numerous at Mbaracayú (see Distribution), and indeed as fairly common throughout Alto Paraná and Canindeyú departments both at the start and end of the 1980s (Nores and Yzurieta 1983, F. E. Hayes *in litt.* 1991, M. Nores *in litt.* 1992), and as commoner than Turquoise-fronted Amazon *Amazona aestiva* in the Itabo and Limoy reserves (N. Pérez *in litt.* 1988), with c.80 seen on the shores of the Itaipu Dam in May 1991 (M. Nores *in litt.* 1992). In Argentina the species appears to hang by a thread, with a very low total population (see Distribution).

In Brazil the situation is confusing: the species may never have been very abundant in the northern half of its range, and must now be close to extinction in Bahia and Rio de Janeiro states, while the relict population in Espírito Santo produced 80, 38, 12 and five chicks in successive years, although there have been no reliable records since 1984 (D. M. R. Fortaleza *in litt.* 1990); moreover, the evidence amassed under Distribution does not reflect encouragingly on the position in Minas Gerais (despite over 30 being found on the first day of a recent visit to Caratinga Reserve: R. S. Ridgely *in litt.* 1991) or to the south, so that Ridgely (1981a) regarded it as local even in the core of its range. Nevertheless, Sick (1972) referred to the species as still most frequent in Santa Catarina and Rio Grande do Sul, and later as still relatively common in Santa Catarina and Minas Gerais (Sick 1985), tending to suggest that he had access to information that has not been filtering out to compilers of data like Ridgely (1981a), Forshaw (1989) or Silva (1989a). The only items of quantified information on the abundance of the species are from two sites in São Paulo state, Campos do Jordão State Park and Jacupiranga State Reserve, where in the late 1970s 113 and 107 individuals were recorded per 100 hours of survey respectively (Willis and Oniki 1981a); the record of 60 from the borders of the latter (see Distribution) is encouraging. At Aparados da Serra the breeding population is probably less than 12 pairs, 2-3 pairs being usually the maximum daily count (TAP), and at São Francisco de Paula there have been counts of up to 20 birds in recent years (TAP) but only 3-4 pairs appear to breed (N. Varty *in litt.* 1992).

ECOLOGY The extent to which the Vinaceous Amazon is allied to araucaria is not clear, although there is an obvious strong preference in Rio Grande do Sul (TAP), and the coincidence of its disappearance from most of Argentina and the loss there of most araucaria (see Threats) seems like a direct correlation, particularly as two of the three remaining small populations in Misiones are linked with relict patches of araucaria (J. C. Chebez *in litt.* 1992). While the species's range originally extended north well beyond the normally understood range of *Araucaria angustifolia* in the Atlantic Forest region, the map of the latter in Hueck (1978: 229) shows pockets extending up the Serra Paranapiacaba through Itatiaia National Park to the east of Belo Horizonte as far as a site just north of the Rio Doce, which conforms fairly well with the evidence under Distribution; and Hueck's (1971, 1978) mistake in implying that araucaria is wholly absent from eastern Paraguay (TAP; see also Distribution: Paraguay under Red-spectacled Amazon) is borne out by a male taken there in July that had been eating "arauci" (Salvadori 1895b; specimen in AMNH). Certainly in Rio Grande do Sul the Vinaceous Amazon is a bird of araucaria forest (Belton 1984-1985), while in São Paulo the habitat in Campos do Jordão State Park is forest of *A. angustifolia* and *Podocarpus lamberti*, although at Jacupiranga State Reserve it is epiphyte- and bamboo-rich humid forest (Willis and Oniki 1981a). At Aparados da Serra and São Francisco de Paula the species occurs almost exclusively in mixed evergreen forest with numerous emergent araucaria (TAP). Thus it appears that some important ecological link exists between the parrot and at least one cone-bearing tree species, this being neither supported nor opposed by evidence in the rest of this paragraph. The specimen collected on the rio Uruguay in Santa Catarina was in "capoeira" (young second growth), and of the five other unpublished records given for the state two were from Atlantic Forest, two from mixed forest, and one (in the west) from "floresta branca" (L. A. R. Bege *in litt.* 1991). Sick (1985) gives its habitat as dry interior forests, pinewoods and forest patches ("capões") surrounded by fields. Ridgely (1981a) noted that in Paraguay and Argentina the species occupies lowland forest whereas in Brazil, owing perhaps mostly to forest clearance, it is largely restricted to foothills up to at least 1,100 m (indeed Campos do Jordão, as noted under Distribution, lies at 1,500-2,000 m).

Birds eat buds, flowers and tender leaves, including eucalyptus and pine leaves (Sick 1985, N. Varty verbally 1992). A July specimen had eaten wild fruits and berries; in August a pair were observed eating araucaria nuts (Belton 1984-1985). Birds have been reported foraging in araucaria in the company of Red-spectacled Amazons and Scaly-headed Parrots *Pionus maximiliani* (Forshaw 1978, 1989). Eating of mineral-rich soil in swamps has been reported (Silva 1989a). A century ago birds evidently caused some damage to orange crops, appearing "very voracious, as they feed all day long" (White 1882) (which actually suggests food-stress, possibly caused by failure of a staple resource). At that time other food noted included the fruits of *Achatocarpus* and seeds of *Pilocarpus* spp. (Bertoni 1927).

From gonad condition of museum specimens Navas and Bó (1988a) judged breeding to occur in Misiones in September/October; this is supported by enlarged testes in two Paraguay specimens from 30 August (in UMMZ), and by egg-laying in August by captive birds, Espírito Santo (D. M. R. Fortaleza *in litt.* 1991). However, variation in the timing of breeding occurs, perhaps between years or between pairs, as other evidence is of inactive testes, late July (Belton 1984-1985), half-developed testes in late October in a Rio Grande do Sul specimen (in AMNH), and nesting in December (Belton 1978; also White 1882). Silva (1989a) gave the breeding period as October to January. A hollow araucaria (Belton 1984-1985), a huge myrtle in which the nest-cavity was 2 m deep (von Ihering 1902) and a cedar *Cedrela odorata* (Reinhardt 1870) have been recorded as nest-trees; but most are in araucarias (N. Varty verbally 1992). There is also a curious report of colonial nesting "in a cliff about 300 km from São Paulo" (Bertagnolio 1981); this is supported by the record of three nests in a single tree in Rio Grande do Sul, reported by foresters to N. Varty (verbally 1992), and it appears that the variation in breeding season noted above may in fact result from delayed breeding in some pairs unable to find a suitable nest-site other than one already occupied (suitably large araucarias are often extremely uncommon): thus, a forester reported a nest-site that for 30 years was occupied twice in a season, with young (usually 3-4) fledging in late December and more young (usually only 1-2) fledging in late March (N. Varty verbally 1992). Silva (1989a) reported 2-4 eggs in a clutch, D. M. R. Fortaleza (*in litt.* 1991) four; the pair in the cedar had three nearly fledged young on 20 November (Reinhardt 1870), and 3-4 young are usual in Rio Grande do Sul (N. Varty verbally 1992). The fledging period is around 70 days (Silva 1991d).

A report in Forshaw (1978, 1989), that the species is "at times" quite common at a locality in Rio Grande do Sul, plus Bertoni's (1927) description of thousands immigrating into Paraguay during cloudy or rainy weather, poses the question of whether significant movements or migrations take place, a point which bears directly on conservation. However, the dates of specimens collected in Misiones (see Distribution) suggest year-round residence (33 of the AMNH specimens from Arroyo Urugua-í were collected in the first half of 1958; the 10 LACM specimens from Tobunas were collected in June, July, August and September). Recent evidence from São Francisco de Paula National Forest, Rio Grande do Sul, suggests that there is some post-breeding dispersal: birds breed in November–December, some remain in January–February but all disappear for March; from April through to July pairs return to feed on araucaria in the 900 ha of native forest, and in July and August they form flocks of up to 30 birds, these breaking down into pairs for the commencement of the breeding season in September–October (N. Varty verbally 1992). If there is a tie-up between the bird and araucaria or another conifer, then its movements would largely be dictated by within- and between-year variations in cone-crop production (see, e.g., Ecology under Thick-billed Parrot *Rhynchopsitta pachyrhyncha*). In Bahia, birds formed large flocks when going to roost in low wooded hills (Wied 1831-1833).

THREATS Deforestation has clearly been the critical factor in the steep decline of this species: Ridgely (1981a) pointed out that possibly the only part of its range where reasonable tracts of habitat remained was in eastern Paraguay, but noted that no protected area in that region was big enough to support a viable population; he also noted that forest destruction was proceeding apace in Paraguay in July/August 1977. Silva (1989a) showed that this destruction continued over the period 1978-1988, during which time a major area reputed to have held at least 8,000 birds was almost totally converted to grassland. Ríos and Zardini (1989) referred to deforestation at the rate of 1,000 km^2 a year, largely in the east. The flooding caused by the Itaipu Dam clearly reduced forest habitat (N. Pérez *in litt.* 1988). In Misiones, where once the inhabitants shot the species for food (White 1882), modification or destruction of habitat has proceeded throughout the 1980s (Ridgely 1981a, Nores and Yzurieta 1983, Navas and Bó 1988a); most significantly, the 210,000 ha of araucaria that remained in the province in 1960 had been reduced by 1988 to two salvageable patches of 400 and 100 ha (Araucaria and Cruce Caballero Provincial Parks), with barely the same amount of dispersed araucaria in San Antonio Strict Nature Reserve and Urugua-í Provincial Park combined (J. C. Chebez *in litt.* 1992). The view that the species simply needs large areas of forest, and that Iguazú National Park's size, cited as "225,000 ha" (it is 49,200 ha: CNPPA 1982, although when combined with Yacuy and Urugua-í Provincial Parks and Iguaçu National Park in Brazil the area under protection reaches 300,000 ha: J. C. Chebez *in litt.* 1992), is "insufficient to support populations of all but the most adaptable of parrots" (Silva 1989a) needs revision in the light of the evidence concerning araucaria. In Brazil the destruction of habitat has been poorly documented by ornithologists, but in Paraná the original area forested by araucaria was 73,780 km^2, in 1930 it was reduced to 39,580 km^2 and in 1965 only 15,932 km^2 remained; in Rio Grande do Sul the situation is similar (Sick and Teixeira 1979; see also Hueck 1978).

Trade at the international level appears not to have had a major impact. Low (1972) thought the Vinaceous Amazon "one of the most desirable of the amazons available in Europe but... imported irregularly and in very small numbers". A shipment of over 100 entered the U.S.A. in the mid-1970s (King 1978). Ridgely (1981a) knew of small numbers being captured in the wild in Paraguay and felt that the bird could no longer tolerate any such pressure; yet as late as 1988 Silva (1988a, 1989a,b) saw the remnants of a once major Paraguayan population being heavily trapped, and indeed met with trappers who claimed to be holding 500 smuggled birds on the Brazilian side of the border from Colonia Dorada. In Argentina persecution for the internal live animal trade (extending back to the last century) probably affected the populations there adversely (Navas and Bó 1988a; also J. C. Chebez *in litt.* 1986). In Brazil, small numbers have recently begun to appear on the domestic market (C. E. Carvalho *in litt.* 1987), and market birds are easily found in Rio Grande do Sul (N. Varty verbally 1992).

The disappearance by the 1840s of what was in the 1820s an evidently healthy population at Nova Friburgo was tentatively explained as the twin impact of heavy persecution first for food (the species being considered "good game") and second for skins from which to manufacture "feather flowers" as ornaments for sale in Rio de Janeiro (Reinhardt 1870).

MEASURES TAKEN The Vinaceous Amazon is protected under Brazilian law (Bernardes *et al.* 1990) and listed on Appendix I of CITES (King 1978-1979). Small populations occur in several protected areas, namely Ibitipoca Park, Caparaó National Park and the Caratinga Reserve (Minas Gerais), Sassafrás Biological Reserve and possibly São Joaquim National Park (since Morro da Palha lies on its border: L. A. R. Bege *in litt.* 1991) (Santa Catarina), Campos do Jordão State Park and Jacupiranga State Reserve (São Paulo), Turvo, Nonoai and Espigão Alto parks, São Francisco National Forest and Aparados da Serra National Park (Rio Grande do Sul), plus Mbaracayú proposed national park (57,000 ha, recently acquired: *Nature Conservancy* September/October 1991: 6) and Itabo and Limoy Biological Reserves (11,200 and 14,828 ha respectively: Ríos and Zardini 1989) in Paraguay; it is presumed extinct in Iguazú National Park, Argentina (see Distribution, Population), but an attempt to help the remnant populations in that country is being made by "Proyecto Nauta" and involving a local education and captive-breeding programme (eggs have been laid and one chick hatched but not reared) at Campo Viera that uses birds reclaimed from local holders of wild-caught birds (J. C. Chebez *in litt.* 1989, 1992). A project to study the ecology of Vinaceous and Red-spectacled Amazons in Rio Grande do Sul is now being developed by CNPq and PUC-RS in collaboration with ICBP.

MEASURES PROPOSED Silva (1989a) called for protection of substantial tracts of forest where this species occurs, and for investigations into its biology. These are clearly important requirements (and for a reforestation project in Minas Gerais see the corresponding section under Blue-chested Parakeet *Pyrrhura cruentata*); however, perhaps the first thing needed is a major survey to determine key sites for the species in São Paulo, Paraná, Santa Catarina, Rio Grande do Sul and, in Paraguay, the departments of Canindeyú and Alto Paraná, particularly with regard to major areas of araucaria. This important work could be carried out as part of a wider survey to identify key sites for other fauna endemic to and rare in the Atlantic Forest region, for example (in birds) Black-fronted Piping Guan *Pipile jacutinga* and Helmeted Woodpecker *Dryocopus galeatus* (see relevant accounts). Meanwhile, support for such reserves as Caratinga in Minas Gerais and Mbaracayú in Paraguay (for the latter see Gauto 1989) is imperative. The population near Valença in Rio de Janeiro is worthy of further study, especially because Golden-capped Parakeet *Aratinga auricapilla* has been found in the same area (see relevant account). The view that captive breeding deserves a greater role (Low 1984, Silva 1989a) cannot be endorsed here, except inasmuch as international support from aviculturists could be given to Proyecto Nauta in Argentina, and as a means of reducing trade pressure on remaining wild populations there.

REMARKS (1) Bokermann (1957) could not trace Vareda precisely, but mapped it at around 15°00'S 41°25'W; OG (1963b) lists no "Vareda" but several places called "Vereda", including a Vereda do Paraíso at 15°28'S 41°27'W. (2) OG (1963b) gives "Reeve" as a former spelling of "Rive", the only locality of this name in Brazil. (3) From the itineraries in von Pelzeln (1868-1871) and by reference to OG (1963b), it can be determined that "Pahor" lies between Areias (22°35'S 44°42'W) and Canas (22°43'S 45°05'W); and that Morungaba (*sic*) is at 22°52'S 46°48'W. (4) There is an anomalous record, apparently backed by a specimen, from the mouth of the río Apa near San Lázaro, i.e. north-westernmost Concepción, where in December 1939 birds were uncommon but in flocks of 4-6 (Podtiaguin 1941-1945). This author also lists the departments of Misiones and Caazapá for the species. Bertoni (1927) mentioned Yaguarasapá, which Paynter (1989) could not trace even to department. (5) Silva (1989a) mentioned Amambay department as having no birds, as if it once did; the recent records from Concepción certainly indicate that occurrence there was possible and, if so, then the adjacent area of southernmost Mato Grosso in Brazil might also hold or have held birds. (6) Bertoni (1927) established the name *paranensis* for birds he found at Puerto Bertoni, but the examples involved were judged to be a colour phase by Peters (1937).

GREEN-CHEEKED AMAZON *Amazona viridigenalis* V[9]

This popular cagebird, confined to tropical evergreen gallery forest and deciduous woodland in north-east Mexico, has been overexploited for trade and suffered from extensive habitat loss. A suite of actions, including surveys, studies, site protection and management, and local education campaigns, is required.

DISTRIBUTION The Green-cheeked (Red-crowned) Amazon is endemic to north-east Mexico in the lowlands and the lower slopes of the Sierra Madre Oriental between 26° (now apparently 24°) and 20°N, this constituting a modern range of only some 40,000 km^2; however, it has also established feral populations in Puerto Rico and in the cities of Miami, Los Angeles, San Diego and Brownsville, U.S.A., and Monterrey, Mexico.

Mexico Modern records are from Tamaulipas and San Luis Potosí; there appear to be no records in the past 50 years from Nuevo León and in the past 40 years from Veracruz, and indeed in his review of the species Clinton-Eitniear (1986) seems to regard Tamazunchale (which he gives as in Veracruz, although it is in San Luis Potosí) as its southernmost limit, with no records from south-east, east or even north-east of there. It is clear that the species now occurs in discontinuous pockets throughout its range, although it probably retains the capacity to disperse between sites (see Ecology); nevertheless, modern knowledge of its status and distribution within Mexico is wholly unsatisfactory. In the following account records are listed roughly from north to south, with coordinates taken from OG (1956a).

Nuevo León The species is known by late nineteenth century specimens from central Nuevo León at Monterrey and China (not Chitra as in Ridgway 1916, Inskipp *et al.* 1987), at around 25°40'N the two most northerly localities recorded (but see Remarks 1), plus Montemorelos and río Camacho (latter untraced, but not Comachio or Comacho as in Salvin and Godman 1888-1904, Salvadori 1891, Ridgway 1916; specimens in BMNH, MCZ, ROM, USNM). The only twentieth-century records of wild birds appear to be from Linares, where a large flock was seen, March 1939, and río Pablillo, 24°57'N 99°20'W (Sutton and Pettingill 1943), and La Unión, 20 km north-east of General Terán, where a specimen (in MVZ) was taken in July 1945 (see Remarks 1). However, since 1980 birds – presumably escapes or their descendants – have been present in San Pedro, a suburb of Monterrey, and since 1984 they have been noted as present throughout the year, nesting in San Pedro and being seen also on at least one occasion in southern Monterrey (A. M. Sada *in litt.* 1992).

Tamaulipas Records are from the centre and south of the state at: Jiménez (specimens in AMNH); Santa Leonor, untraced but at the base of the Sierra Madre Oriental north-west of Ciudad Victoria, judging from Phillips (1911); río Cruz (presumably río de la Cruz as in Ridgway 1916; now río Purificación), 23°58'N 98°42'W (Phillips 1911); río Martínez, close to the preceding (Phillips 1911); río Corona at 250 m (23°55'N 99°00'W in Gehlbach *et al.* 1976; also Sutton and Burleigh 1939, Ridgely 1981a); río Caballeros in the same region (Sutton and Burleigh 1939); Soto la Marina and the river of the same name (Ridgway 1916, Clinton-Eitniear 1986); Ciudad Victoria and the Sierra Madre Oriental above (i.e. to the west) (Ridgway 1916) and 17 km to the north (specimen in MNHUK); 15 km north-east of Zamorina, 23°20'N 97°58'W (specimen each in AMNH, DMNH); (El) Forlon, 23°14'N 98°48'W (Ridgway 1916); Acuña, 23°12'N 98°26'W, plus Santa María in the Sierra de Tamaulipas (Martin *et al.* 1954; also specimens in MLZ); the Presa de Español (Español dam) north of Aldama (Clinton-Eitniear 1986; but see Population); the Los Colorados Ranch, east-north-east of Aldama (see map in Pérez and Eguiarte 1989); Gómez Farías, 23°03'N 99°09'W (specimens in CM, DMNH, USNM), this area including the río Sabinas, 22°59'N 98°58'W (Clinton-Eitniear 1986), and specifically Rancho Rinconada (Sutton and Pettingill 1942), El Encino (Clinton-Eitniear 1988), Pano Ayuctle "sugar camp" and El Limon (specimens in AMNH, DMNH, FMNH and YPM; Pano Ayuctle is described in Eaton and

Edwards 1948); Antiguo Morelos (specimen in MNHUK); Tampico (Ridgway 1916; see also under Veracruz).

San Luis Potosí Records are from the easternmost part of the state at: río del Naranjo, centred on Las Abritas, at 22°30'N 99°24'W (Clinton-Eitniear 1986); Ciudad del Maiz, March 1942 (specimen in MLZ); Rancho Martínez, 25 km south of Naranjo (see Remarks 2), October 1945 (specimen in MLZ); (Ciudad de) Valles, San Luis Potosí (Ridgway 1916), one specimen (in CM) from 13 km south, and another (in UMMZ) from 20 km east; Axtla (now Alfredo M. Terrazas), 21°28'N 98°51'W (specimen in CM) and along río Axtla (Sutton and Burleigh 1940b), though none was seen in 1983 (Clinton-Eitniear 1986); Xilitla (Davis 1952); along río Moctezuma, 6-8 km upstream from Tamazunchale (Sutton and Burleigh 1940b, Clinton-Eitniear 1986); and El Sol, 1.5 km north of Tamazunchale (specimen in ANSP). There is one wholly untraced locality in the state, this being "El Banito", where a male (in FMNH) was collected on 30 June 1940.

Veracruz Records are from the north and centre of the state at: río Tamesí near Rayón (San Antonio Rayón is at 22°25'N 98°25'W) in northern Veracruz (specimens in AMNH); "Tamesi near Tampico" (specimen in BMNH) and nearby on the río Tamesí at Paso del Haba (Chapman 1914b); Altamira (Richmond 1895); Laguna de Tamiahua, 50 km south of Tampico, where a male was taken in May 1944 (specimen in MLZ), and 30 km north of Naranjos (latter at 21°21'N 97°41'W), where two birds were taken in April 1960 (specimens in MVZ); "Tantina, near Tampico", June 1888 (female in BMNH; see also Salvin and Godman 1888-1904), i.e. presumably Tantima, 21°20'N 97°50'W; Potrero (del) Llano, 21°03'N 97°41'W, and 9 km north-west of Nautla (Lowery and Dalquest 1951); Colipa, 19°55'N 96°42'W (Salvin and Godman 1888-1904, Salvadori 1891; see Remarks 3); and, some 200 km further south and somewhat anomalously (though possibly as wintering birds), around San Andrés Tuxtla (Sclater 1857b).

U.S.A. Feral populations exist in a good number of localities in the U.S.A., notably (*California*) Los Angeles (Temple City district: Forshaw 1989), San Diego (J. Clinton-Eitniear *in litt.* 1987) and the San Gabriel valley (AOU 1983; also Froke 1981); (*Florida*) the Florida Keys, Miami, Fort Lauderdale and West Palm Beach (Owre 1973, Silva 1989a); (*Texas*) Brownsville (Lever 1987, J. Clinton-Eitniear *in litt.* 1987), although here the birds have proven to be winter visitors (October to March) and may represent genuine wanderers from Tamaulipas rather than part of a resident group whose summer quarters are unknown (Neck 1986, also Ridgely 1981a; *contra* Forshaw 1989, who attributed them to smugglers' panic releases: see Threats); and there are small ones on Puerto Rico (Lever 1987, Raffaele 1989) and Oahu in the Hawaiian Islands (AOU 1983, though not mentioned by Pratt *et al.* 1987).

POPULATION At the southernmost locality known for the species, around San Andrés Tuxtla, it was "common in the *tierra caliente*" some 140 years ago (Sclater 1857b); there have been no further reports from this area. However, the species's overall abundance seems unlikely to have altered drastically for another century: from the major period of bird study in the region, the late 1930s to early 1950s (e.g. Sutton and Burleigh 1939, 1940a,b, Sutton and Pettingill 1942, 1943, Sutton *et al.* 1942, Lowery and Dalquest 1951, Davis 1952, Martin *et al.* 1954, Zimmerman 1957), it is clear that the Green-cheeked Amazon was then generally relatively common ("abundant about Gómez Farías, where... considered a pest": Sutton and Burleigh 1939; "literally hundreds of them": Sutton 1951) in appropriate habitat from central Tamaulipas south to eastern San Luis Potosí and northern Veracruz (much less common in central Veracruz), and this view is reflected in the generalizing literature (e.g. Blake 1953, Edwards 1972). Even in the 1970s the species was regarded as "fairly common locally" (Ridgely 1981a), with one study (at río Corona) yielding figures of five males per 8 ha of riverine forest (Gehlbach *et al.* 1976) and another of 0.26 birds per ha in coastal Tamaulipas (see Pérez and Eguiarte 1989). Nevertheless, Ridgely (1981a) reported a consensus "that a large overall decline in the numbers of this species has taken place in the past several decades" so that "where formally hundreds could be seen, now one sees scattered pairs, or at most small flocks". Clinton-Eitniear (1986, 1988) provided figures from the

American Birds Christmas Bird Counts since the early 1970s, but these do not help delineate any trend; on the other hand, he recorded a population at Presa de Español reducing from 30 pairs in 1979 through 14 pairs in 1983 to none at all in 1988, and he also indicated that while numbers are relatively low and declining in the north at río Corona, they remain healthy in the río Sabinas region (Neck 1986 reported an increase in numbers in this area in the 1970s, but a decrease at Gómez Farías). On the 600 ha (though now 4,000 ha) Los Colorados Ranch, 67 birds were estimated present in 1985, a 55% decline since 1976 (Pérez and Eguiarte 1989).

Of the feral populations, that in Los Angeles is known to comprise several hundred birds (Forshaw 1989), that in (or near) Miami is at least 150 strong (Silva 1989a), being "commonly seen throughout metropolitan Miami and in Ft Lauderdale" (Owre 1973), while those in Brownsville, on Puerto Rico and on Oahu remain small (Lever 1987, Raffaele 1989). That in Monterrey, Nuevo León, is thought to number a few hundred birds (A. M. Sada *in litt.* 1992).

ECOLOGY The Green-cheeked Amazon is a bird of the lusher parts of generally arid lowlands and foothills, thus occupying tropical evergreen gallery forest, deciduous woodland on slopes and in canyons, partially cleared and cultivated landscapes with woodlots and woodland patches (i.e. in forest edge) ranging up onto dry open pine-oak ridges as high as 1,200 m at least seasonally (Davis 1952, Martin *et al.* 1954, Edwards 1972, Forshaw 1978, Ridgely 1981a, Clinton-Eitniear 1988). The species will even occur, albeit in reduced numbers, in agricultural areas if a few large trees, needed for nesting and roosting, remain standing (Ridgely 1981a). The habitat at río Corona consists (or consisted) of tropical evergreen forest dominated by ebony *Pithecellobium flexicaule* with *Ehretia*, *Bumelia* and *Condolia* subdominant (Gehlbach *et al.* 1976); at río el Naranjo of montane wet-oak/sweetgum forest, brushland, arid upland grassland and dry oak forest (Clinton-Eitniear 1988). Forest destruction has led to birds occupying suboptimal habitat (Pérez and Eguiarte 1989). A feral population in the suburban San Gabriel valley, Los Angeles County, California, appeared to be self-sustaining in mature suburban vegetation, though concentrated to some degree on a large arboretum (Froke 1981). That in Puerto Rico occupies (at least in part) dry forest in the south of the island (see Remarks 1 under Puerto Rican Amazon *Amazona vittata*).

At río Corona, birds were seen feeding on *Pithecellobium* beans and *Ehretia anaqua* berries (Gehlbach *et al.* 1976, Gehlbach 1987), at río Naranjo on acorns and "exotic China Berries" *Melia azedarach* (Clinton-Eitniear 1988), and food generally appears to be taken opportunistically, with nuts, berries, buds, flowers and various fruit being consumed according to season, and pine-seeds being important at least for some populations (Sutton and Pettingill 1942, Martin *et al.* 1954, Clinton-Eitniear 1986). *Pithecellobium* seeds have also been recorded as food in Texas (Neck 1986). The feral San Gabriel valley population fed with feral Lilac-crowned Amazons *A. finschi* on at least 34 tree and shrub species, most commonly English walnut *Juglans regia* and sweetgum *Liquidambar styraciflua*; foraging mostly took place from 06h00 to 09h00 and from 16h00 to roosting, which occurred soon after sunset, and the period from 10h00 to 16h00 was spent resting in the shade (Froke 1981). In these feral birds there was a general increase in foraging flock size from summer through to winter (July–January), with greatest mean in December (32.5), reducing sharply in spring (March–June), with smallest mean in April (5.5); during the spring, one pair ate more flowers than seeds of *Chorisa*, and while feeding nestlings foraged on the flowers of ironbark *Eucalyptus sideroxylon* (Froke 1981). In Miami birds were seen to feed and breed in casuarina trees (Owre 1973).

Breeding activity (courtship, nest-hole occupation) commences in March (Sutton and Pettingill 1942; see also Sutton and Burleigh 1940b, Gehlbach *et al.* 1976), a female in DMNH taken 24 March (1957, río Sabinas) held an egg ready to lay, and another in MVZ taken 9 April (1960, Laguna de Tamiahua) had fully developed ovaries; moreover, three clutches of four, four and three eggs were taken near Ciudad Victoria (one) and northern Veracruz (two) in April 1953 and April 1960 respectively (specimens in WFVZ). However, courtship-flights are also recorded in mid-April (Martin *et al.* 1954), a female from 25 March had undeveloped ovaries (Sutton and Burleigh 1940a) and two male specimens from mid-April (1952, río Sabinas) in AMNH are labelled "not breeding condition" and "not full breeding". Feral birds in Los Angeles also start to breed in March/April (Forshaw 1978), although they show territorial or at least proprietorial interest in the nest-tree from the preceding September; in one case a pair evicted all other pairs (including those of Lilac-crowned Amazons) from the tree and its vicinity (an area of c.250 m^2), but after the eggs were laid they began to tolerate a second pair that took up residence in a hole 10 m away in the same tree, and eventually shared its territorial defence with them, the second pair fledging their young four weeks after the first (Froke 1981). In the wild one pair was seen to occupy an old hole of Lineated Woodpeckers *Dryocopus lineatus* c. 20 m up in a large cypress (Sutton and Pettingill 1942), and along the río Corona the species requires either abandoned nests of this woodpecker or large natural cavities in Montezuma cypress *Taxodium mucronatum* (Gelhbach 1987). However, six nests found on the Los Colorados Ranch in 1985 were 6-14 m up in the trunks of either *Bumelia laetivirens* or *Brosimum alicastrum* (Pérez and Eguiarte 1989). In captivity, the incubation period was 28 days and the fledging period about nine weeks (Lantermann 1982, Wozniak and Lantermann 1984). Feral birds incubated for about 25-30 days and showed a fledging period of at most 55 days; parents began to resist food-begging demands of their young 2-3 months after fledging (Froke 1981).

The species is evidently nomadic in winter, being notably more abundant then at higher elevations and easily able to range over considerable distances between lusher areas to forage (Clinton-Eitniear 1986). This has been confirmed by recent studies showing that while the sympatric conspecific Yellow-headed Amazon *A. oratrix* (also threatened) and Red-lored Amazon *A. autumnalis* are year-round residents where they occur in Tamaulipas the Green-cheek gathers in large flocks and moves south (though possibly also north: see Distribution: U.S.A.) outside the breeding season, returning in February (E. Enkerlin *in litt.* 1992). Winter flocks in Veracruz reached up to 100 birds, these being active throughout the day (Lowery and Dalquest 1951). The species has been described as irregular in Nuevo León (Sutton and Pettingill 1943).

THREATS The Green-cheeked Amazon has suffered over the long term from habitat loss and in the past 20 years from a high level of exploitation for trade. However, in the Sierra de Tamaulipas, farmers shoot (or shot) many parrots raiding the maizefields for corn (Martin *et al.* 1954). The only natural predator reported is the Ornate Hawk-eagle *Spizaetus ornatus* (Sutton and Pettingill 1942).

Habitat loss Much of the species's range has been or is being modified for agricultural use, especially now for sorghum, and the gallery forests are gradually being degraded or cleared outright (Ridgely 1981a). Over 80% of the Tamaulipas lowlands have been cleared for agriculture and pasture (E. Enkerlin *in litt.* 1992). The apparent loss of the species from Nuevo León (see Distribution) is presumably attributable to habitat destruction, but the literature is weak on specific instances: the flooding of the río Corona valley through the Las Adjuntas dam submerged a considerable extent of important floodplain forest (Gehlbach *et al.* 1976, Ridgely 1981a), this area also being affected by lumbering, extensive clearance, gravel dredging, and increasing public use for bathing, washing and swimming (Gehlbach *et al.* 1976, Clinton-Eitniear 1986). Near another dam, the Presa de Español, habitat destruction was responsible for the local population decline to apparent extinction (Clinton-Eitniear 1986; see Population).

Trade Trade apparently developed as a major factor in the late 1960s, with well over 2,000 birds being imported legally into the U.S.A. between 1968 and 1972 (Lever 1987), and towards the end of the 1970s thousands or even tens of thousands of birds were still being imported almost exclusively into the U.S.A. (Ridgely 1981a). Between October 1979 and June 1980, 3,279 were legally imported into the U.S.A. (Roet *et al.* 1981), and over the period 1977-1980 the figure was 7,452 (Clinton-Eitniear 1988, 1989). Despite a ban on this trade (see Measures Taken), smuggling has kept the threat alive with (e.g.) only pairs nesting in the remotest sites at Gómez Farías managing to fledge young (Clinton-Eitniear 1988). Even on a relatively well protected site such as the Los Colorados Ranch, amazon parrot nests (three species) suffered 30% loss to trappers in 1985 (Pérez and Eguiarte 1989). The smugglers' habit of releasing birds at the first sign of detection (Forshaw 1989) compromises any hope of releasing confiscations back into the wild. The trappers' inevitable damage of nests when taking chicks usually results in the site being permanently abandoned (Gildardo 1976).

MEASURES TAKEN There are no protected areas for the species other than a few small tracts of habitat preserved through private ownership and management (Ridgely 1981a). At río el Naranjo, a patch of forest used as a roost adjacent to the El Salto hydroelectric plant is protected by the army (Clinton-Eitniear 1986). Commercial export was banned (as urged by Ridgely 1981a) on 20 September 1982, and appears to have been effective: thus net imports recorded by CITES officials were 586 in 1981, 1,727 in 1982, 99 in 1983, and two in 1984 (Inskipp *et al.* 1987); nevertheless, smuggling continues (see Threats).

MEASURES PROPOSED Protection of certain key areas has been urged, such as in the río Sabinas valley (Ridgely 1981a) and at Gómez Farías (Clinton-Eitniear 1986); see Remarks 4. A comprehensive survey and a detailed study of the species are warranted, to determine the best and most feasible sites for conservation, bringing to bear the relevant biological information on the species's year-round requirements and capacity for long-term population maintenance; the detailed study, by E. Enkerlin (supported by AFA), has already started. Apart from this, the planting of appropriate fruiting shrubs and trees, the financial reward of local people for allowing birds to fledge, a campaign to generate local pride in the species by indicating its endemism in north-eastern Mexico, and the erection of nest-boxes where they are unlikely to be robbed are all proposed (Clinton-Eitniear 1988, J. Clinton-Eitniear *in litt.* 1988). Some of these measures now form the basis of a joint programme between the Universidad Autónoma de Tamaulipas and the Center for the Study of Tropical Birds: thus the nest-box deployment, at Los Colorados Ranch in Tamaulipas (see Distribution) where Yellow-headed Amazons also stand to benefit), has already begun with the support of the Avicultural Society of America (*AFA Watchbird* 18,1 [1991]: 51), an educational poster is being produced (J. Clinton-Eitniear *in litt.* 1991), and a scheme is being developed to return confiscated birds to the wild (*AFA Watchbird* 18,4 [1991]: 56). A key element in a conservation strategy for both amazons may be the encouragement and commitment of landowners to preserving tracts of habitat and to guarding the birds, particularly when nesting, with the aid of their staff (E. Enkerlin *in litt.* 1992). Study of certain feral populations, such as that in Monterrey, is to be encouraged.

Captive breeding If this is to be of help (by replacing demand for wild-caught birds), as many holders as possible should cooperate and accurate records must be kept (Clinton-Eitniear 1988); in a survey in 1989 the number of captive pairs in the U.S.A. was 184, their total offspring 271, and the total number of birds 1,096, giving strong hope of a minimum sustainable population of 200 pairs (Clinton-Eitniear 1989); a (regional) studbook is being developed (*AFA Watchbird* 18,1 [1991]: 50).

REMARKS (1) The specimen from China was actually taken at a river 15 "leagues" (i.e. 75 km) to the south; the previous day (18 April 1891) the same collector (W. Lloyd) took a specimen (also in USNM) at "El Union" in Tamaulipas, which may be the same as the "La Unión" north-east of General Terán at which a specimen was taken in 1945, although not in Tamaulipas. (2) It is assumed here that the Naranjo in question is that just north of the state border inside Tamaulipas. (3) Ridgway (1916) gives Misantla (south of Colipa) as a locality, but this appears to be a misinterpretation of Salvin and Godman (1888-1904), who found the species to the north of Misantla (i.e. Colipa). (4) Since the Green-cheeked Amazon is partially sympatric with the also threatened Yellow-headed Amazon, the choice of areas to protect may to some extent be determined by sites at which both species occur; the río Corona valley is one such area (Ridgely 1981a). The río Corona floodplain forest is in fact part of a major biome (Tamaulipan Dry Forest) which in the mid-1970s was not represented even in a planned reserve, and is of further interest for being part of the drainage system that demarcates the Neotropical from the Nearctic avifauna (Gehlbach *et al.* 1976).

PUERTO RICAN AMAZON *Amazona vittata* (E)[5]

This species has been the subject of the most intensive conservation programme ever conducted on a parrot. Endemic to and probably originally present throughout Puerto Rico, it suffered from the almost total loss of its forest habitat and the crippling effects of being taken for pets and food, so that by the 1930s its population of c.2,000 was confined to rainforest in the Luquillo Mountains in the north-east of the island. Here it endured a long decline towards extinction that was only halted through major intervention beginning in 1968 and involving experiments with artificial nest-sites, controlling nest predators and competitors, and captive breeding. Recovery since the all-time population low of 13 birds in 1975 has been steady except for the impact of Hurricane Hugo in September 1989, and by the beginning of 1992 the population stood at a minimum 22-23 in the wild and 58 in captivity; after a record fledging success in July 1992, the wild population was 39-40.

DISTRIBUTION (All information in this section is derived from Snyder *et al.* 1987.) It is probable that the Puerto Rican Amazon originally occurred throughout Puerto Rico, since lack of distributional precision in early accounts may well have reflected its breadth of range, while in any case *Amazona* parrots are well known to wander widely from their most usual haunts. Certainly the evidence reveals its former presence in all major vegetation types on the island except the dry forests of the southern coastal strip, although even there it is probable that the bird occurred (see Remarks 1). The current range in the Luquillo Mountains, covering some 1,600 ha, represents a mere 0.2% of its former area of distribution (see Remarks 2).

A subspecifically distinct population, *gracilipes*, formerly occurred on Culebra off the east coast (it was common there in 1899 but had disappeared by 1912), bones of the species have been found on Mona, and reports of parrots, presumably of this species, are known from Vieques and St Thomas (the latter in the U.S. Virgin Islands).

POPULATION (Unless otherwise stated, all information in this section is derived from Snyder *et al.* 1987.) Early evidence is that the species was originally abundant on the island, and indeed extrapolation from 1956 figures yields a conservative figure of 84,000 birds for pre-Columbus times, the true number being perhaps several hundred thousand or even a million. Although in the second half of the last century the species was still considered abundant in many areas, it was evidently in steep decline throughout the period, which witnessed the most drastic reduction in forest cover in the island's history (see Threats).

In the twentieth century the species survived in the Guajataca area until about 1918-1920; at Río Abajo until 1925, and not beyond 1928; in the Sierra de Cayey until at least 1936; and in the areas adjacent to the Luquillo Mountains down to around 1960, after which all records are confined to the forest on the mountains themselves (although parrots have sometimes been observed leaving Luquillo's western flanks on long flights, especially during summer). In 1937, when the species was apparently confined to the north-east of the island centred on Luquillo Forest, an estimate of 2,000 birds was made, although the director of the Forest Service in the 1920s felt this to be far lower than the number of birds present during his tenure of office (the decline, if real, might have been attributable to the impact of the 1928 and 1932 hurricanes: see Threats). By the 1950s the population had dropped to around 200, although the error factor in the censuses then may have been ±25%. Then in May 1963 a minimum 130 and possibly over 200 were observed. In December 1966 70 were counted in a single flock, probably with an accuracy of ±10, although there is no evidence that this represented the entire population at the time. However, less than two years later, in November 1968, at the start of the second major study of the species, only 24 birds could be found. Over the next three years the population continued to decline, and in February 1972 two birds were trapped from the wild population of 16; although there was some recruitment in the following three years, other losses led to the population being a firm minimum of 14 at the start of the 1975 breeding season, briefly dipping to 13 with the death of a nesting adult, this figure representing the lowest the species has ever reached in the wild. With six young fledging that year, and with further slight gains in recruitment against mortality, the wild population rose to 25-26 in 1979. In 1980 only 18 birds survived but fledged eight young (including two fostered from captivity), making 26; in 1981 the equivalent figures were 19, 10 (1), 29; in 1982 numbers at the start of the breeding season were unknown, 8 (3), 26; in 1983, 25-27, 6 (3), 31; in 1984 29, 4, 28; in 1985 25, 12, 37; (information hereafter from F. J. Vilella *in litt.* 1992) in 1986 28, 4, 28; in 1987 33, 8, 36; in 1988 36, 4 (2) 30; in 1989, 30, 7 (2) giving a total of 47 in September when Hurricane Hugo struck; in 1990 21, 2, 23; in 1991 23, 7, 30, with six pairs breeding in the wild (the highest since the 1950s: Wilson *et al.* in press); in 1992 21-23 birds were known to be alive before the breeding season (and by early July all 11 chicks, 10 of them wild-born, had fledged, a record for the project, bringing the total wild population to 39-40 birds), but in this case as in that of the low post-breeding total in 1988 and pre-breeding total in 1989 (both 30) the counts may have been influenced negatively by adverse weather.

The development in numbers of the captive flock from two in 1970 to 29 in 1986 and 58 in 1992 is given in Measures Taken: Captive breeding.

ECOLOGY (Unless otherwise indicated, all information in this section is derived from Snyder *et al.* 1987; but see also Rodríguez-Vidal 1962.)

Original parrot habitats In its original state Puerto Rico supported eight major climax vegetation types, all of them forest and in combination extending from the shoreline to the highest peaks of the (predominantly mountainous) island. Of these types, moist coastal forest covered 27% of the island in the north, east and west, moist limestone forest covered 17% in the north and north-west, dry coastal and dry limestone forest covered 13% and 2% in the south, lower Cordillera and lower Luquillo forest covered 32% and 1.5% in the centre, and upper Cordillera and upper Luquillo forest covered 6% and 1%, also in the centre, with 0.5% given over to mangrove and littoral scrub forest; records exist of the Puerto Rican Amazon's occurrence in all but the two dry forest types, although it is believed that it occurred there nevertheless (see Remarks 1), while its presence in mangrove and littoral scrub forest is judged to have been largely seasonal, although some birds may have been resident.

Current parrot habitats The area in which the species now remains is upper Luquillo tropical rainforest, between 200 (150 since 1990: J. M. Meyers *in litt.* 1992) and 600 m, wetter than elsewhere on Puerto Rico and considered a distinct ecological province of the island. Four broad forest types exist in Luquillo in response to soil, rainfall and wind: (1) tabonuco forest, a classic diverse tall rainforest formation, occurs on lower mountain slopes (covering 5,430 ha within the national forest, although only a few hectares are old-growth) and is dominated by tabonuco *Dacryodes excelsa*, which before the largest specimens were logged was extremely important as a source of both food and nest-sites for the parrot; immediately above this lies (2) the palo colorado zone (covering about 3,400 ha), a depauperate upland swamp of short-statured trees, is characterized by palo colorado *Cyrilla racemiflora*, whose susceptibility to heart-rot makes it an important source of nest-sites and hence now the chief zone in which the parrot occurs; (3) sierra palm *Prestoea montana* forest (covering 2,050 ha) forms dense, virtually monocultural patches on highly eroded soils within the altitudinal range of the two previous types, and provides fruit in enormous abundance such that parrot breeding is timed to coincide with fruiting and parrot movements during much of the year are explicable in terms of palm fruit availability; and (4) dwarf forest (covering 450 ha) is the upper limit formation and of no significance to parrots except for occasional perches, although F. J. Vilella (*in litt.* 1992) reported several important food sources – e.g. *Clusia* and *Miconia* – and sufficient frequency of parrot occurrence in this habitat that it must serve the species on occasion for foraging. Analysis of habitats used by breeding and non-breeding parrots in 1991, two years after Hurricane Hugo, detected no significant differences, although such differences did exist between nesting areas themselves (Meyers and Barrow 1992).

Food and feeding Birds feed primarily on fruits, procured with the bill, normally one at a time in a slow deliberate manner, although in quite large amounts in relatively short periods: with spatially concentrated foods such as sierra palm, birds can fill their crops in well under an hour, and in the case of the sierra palm about 130 fruits constitute one meal. The species has been recorded feeding on at least 60 plant species in Luquillo (see Appendix 8 in Snyder *et al.* 1987), with most records being of fruits, seeds or leaves of trees (44 species), shrubs (seven species) and vines (seven species). Birds rarely descend near the ground but have been seen feeding about 2 m up on *Miconia* fruits and *Psychotria* bark; sierra palm accounts for 22% of the records, and the next most frequently observed food, tabonuco, accounts for less than 7% of the total, indicating the catholicity of usage in the species; only 62% of feeding observations come from the top ten species. Non-fruit items (chiefly leaves) are eaten frequently enough to be significant if minor components of the diet, and are associated with the breeding season, possibly because they contain specific nutrients important for reproduction. Flowers of *Piptocarpa tetrantha* and bracts of *Marcgravia sintenisii* are consumed for their nectar. On a species total basis, there may be some avoidance of small fruits, possibly through time/energy and/or predation-risk factors. Although fruiting in many trees is almost year-round, those most favoured by the parrots show pronounced peaks, thus causing variation in use of forest zones by parrots. Sierra palm bears fruit throughout the year, but maximum seed drop (indicating maximum crop of edible fruits) occurs between February and April, and parrots feed heavily on the species from January to May. Towards the end of the breeding season and into summer the species exploits cupeillo *Clusia grisebachiana*, and when this declines they switch largely to tabonuco through the fall and winter. Since the maximum flight time between extremes of the present range within Luquillo is only 10 minutes, much flight activity may provide birds with information on the state of various foods. The species certainly once descended to crops, as it was recorded in 1836 that great flocks destroyed whole fields of corn, and this habit might have led to its extermination on Culebra (but see Threats for alternative explanations). During incubation, females are virtually confined to their nests and their mates provide them with almost all their food, on average 5.4 times a day.

Nest-sites The species breeds in natural cavities in trees produced almost wholly by decay, although it formerly used potholes in limestone cliffs in Río Abajo. Analysis of records indicates that birds are very conservative in their choice of nesting areas in Luquillo, almost all records in the 50 years to 1980 being from five areas, North Fork and South Fork in the west, and East Fork, West Fork and Center Fork in the east, although since Hurricane Hugo two new nesting areas (involving a pair each, with all four birds born since 1986) have been found or have become established, on East Mountain, c.1 km from the East Fork area, and Quebrada Grande, in the next valley south from South Fork (F. J. Vilella *in litt.* 1992). Of 25 nest trees documented in 1945-1986 all but one were in palo colorado, the exception being a laurel sabino *Magnolia splendens*, although older evidence exists that the species has used tabonuco and caimitillo *Micropholis* spp.; elsewhere in Puerto Rico nests have been reported from corcho *Pisonia subcordata*, aguacate *Persea americana*, jácana *Pouteria multiflora* and royal palm *Roystonea borinquena.* In 1991 at the new site in East Mountain the first confirmed use of tabonuco was recorded, the cavity in question being more similar in structure to cavities found in trees of coastal forest currently used by exotics (F. J. Vilella *in litt.* 1992; see Remarks 1). An important factor in re-use of nests is cavity durability; the longest-lasting tree nest cavity recorded survived for 20 years, the average being between 10 and 15 years; qualitative evidence suggests that females select nest-sites. Nest-sites can be very close, once 33 m, once 15.2 m, once 4 m, though this is not usual; however, nests appear to be clumped within the forest, location of parrot nesting areas appears to have no strong relationship with good feeding areas, and the overall breeding distribution appears to reflect cavity availability. Birds seem to prefer deep or possibly dark sites; they also prefer the largest cavities available. Wetness, coupled with deepness, most severely governs the availability of nest-sites. Optimal sites are at least 4.5 m from the ground, and are dry, flat-bottomed, at least 60 cm deep, dark within, with entrance widths of at least 6 cm and internal diameters of at least 23 cm at the bottom; minimal sites may be any height from the ground, as shallow as 25 cm, with internal diameters at least 15 cm; the former are rare, the latter relatively common.

Breeding success and related behaviour In most recent years a substantial fraction of pairs in the population have defended territories in the breeding season, but a substantial fraction of these pairs (nearly half) have failed to lay eggs, a major factor militating against recovery of numbers; from 1976 through to the mid-1980s the number of actual breeding pairs in the wild population remained virtually constant at four, despite a gradually increasing total population, and only when the population reached about 40 individuals in 1989 did new breeding pairs begin to appear (N. F. R. Snyder *in litt.* 1992).

In the past, failure to breed may have reflected failure to find suitable nest-sites, but may also be explained in terms of immaturity and inadequate compatability or other factors. Territorialism can be vigorous but is related primarily to nest defence, with pairs sometimes driving out intruders as far as 140 m from the nest; the frequent abandonment of the nest hole for territorial defence is a major liability in relation to nest-predation by Pearly-eyed Thrashers; moreover, birds take little notice of their surroundings during defence, and probably then are especially vulnerable to predation by hawks. Territories are defended year-round to some extent, but much more vigorously in the breeding season. Because of the apparent abundance of limestone holes at Río Abajo, there seems to have been no strong territorialism in the population there. In almost every observed instance newly territorial pairs have established themselves immediately adjacent to territories of breeding pairs, a tendency that helps explain the extreme stability of nesting areas. Parrot pairs nevertheless check other sites continually, probably as a type of insurance. Timing of breeding coincides with maximum production of sierra palm, but may also be linked to the "dry" season, important because dry cavities are essential to reproductive success. Calculated dates of first eggs are between 11 February and mid-April (most late February to early March), with all evidence pointing to incubation starting with the first egg; on average the hatching interval between eggs is two days, following a 26-day incubation period; although the egg-laying period coincides with the driest time of the year, in lowland Puerto Rico egg-laying occurred considerably earlier and it would seem that other factors, such as fruiting of major foods, are the chief trigger of breeding. Clutch-size varies from two to four, mostly (and mean) three; reports of up to six may have involved two females. Eggs are incubated exclusively by females. All 67 eggs laid in the wild and not predated, 1973-1979, were fertile, 56 hatched, and only one gave rise to an abnormal chick. Adults feed their young on demand, though as the latter grow, their crops expand greatly and feeding frequency declines accordingly; when close to fledging, young actually become reluctant to take food, perhaps in order to make the first flight (which is seemingly haphazard and sometimes disastrous) more buoyant. Length of nestling stage averages about nine weeks, but varies considerably, the fledging date showing an inverse correlation with egg weight. The female stays with the chicks throughout the first week and a half after hatching, but then undertakes morning and sometimes evening foraging trips with her mate; she roosts with the chicks right through to fledging; however, in one case a widowed female fed and reared chicks essentially unaided by a new partner. Adults are extremely circumspect in approaching fledged young, suggesting high risk of predation, and it may be that large broods present difficulties of management through the dependency stage, resulting perhaps in greater risks of mortality to the adults as well as to their offspring. Families stay together after fledging, certainly (in one case) for five weeks and almost certainly (from fragmentary observations) into the fall, tending to disband in winter. A radio-telemetry study of juvenile parrots showed that they stayed 58±29 days in the natal valley (except in one case where the killing by a raptor of one of a brood of two led to the immediate movement by the surviving family to an adjacent valley), ranging over up to 32±10 ha in one year though only 13±6 ha in another, later integrating with adult flocks 33-95 days after fledging, when they then ranged over much larger areas (1,243 ha in 1986 and 822 ha in 1987) (Lindsey *et al.* 1991; see also Lindsey and Arendt 1991). However, first-year birds appear around the natal nest-sites in the early stages of the next breeding season, only to be chased off silently by their parents, and this behaviour is helpful in calculating first-year mortality rates in the species, put in the 1970s at 32.5%. Post-juvenile subadult mortality then appeared to be around 15.2%; and adult mortality was around 9%; however, in the early 1980s while adult mortality was only 6.8%, post-juvenile subadult mortality rose to 29%, for unknown reasons (this was the stimulus for the radio-telemetry study of the mid-1980s, which showed that predation by Red-tailed Hawks *Buteo jamaicensis* was significant: Lindsey *et al.* 1988). In the 1970s nest success increased from a historically low rate of 11-26% to around 69% for pairs laying eggs, i.e. 1.5 young fledged into the wild per egg-laying pair, but only because of a wide variety of measures; this was maintained in the period 1980-1985. Evidence from the wild and captivity suggests that age of first breeding may generally be four.

Social organization (spatial and temporal) The basic social unit is the pair: of 413 sightings of flying parrots in the non-breeding season, 1968-1969, 307 (74%) were of two birds, 73 (18%) of singles, 23 (6%) of trios and 10 (2%) of anything larger; trios were usually a pair plus an extra bird, commonly a juvenile offspring. Members of mated pairs stay close together (less than 2 m when flying) throughout the year, except in the weeks when the female is egg-laying, incubating and tending small young; but pairs do not automatically represent mated pairs, as juveniles of single broods tend to stick together through their first year, even when not with their parents. Pairs usually remain constant over the years; however, when one member of a pair is lost, re-pairing can be rapid, with one case of a male abandoning his injured mate for a healthy, recently widowed female. Most feeding observations (79%) have fallen between 06h00 and 09h00 and between 16h00 and 19h00; 41% between 07h00 and 08h00 and between 17h00 and 18h00, indicating peak foraging times. Birds feed during the morning (they stop calling at 09h30), then retire to roosting trees where they stay over midday, rarely becoming vocal until c.16h00 (some feeding may of course occur over midday). An increase in the number and intensity of calls and flights after 15h30 heralds the afternoon feeding period. Birds have never been observed returning to their roosts after dark, and it is highly unlikely that they ever fly at night. Feeding is relatively gregarious: of 92 feeding observations, 1968-1976, 11 (12%) were solitary, 43 (47%) were in pairs, and 38 (41%) were in groups of three or more; anti-predator sentinels appoint themselves at feeding flocks. Birds do not roost in holes during the non-breeding season, and when breeding the female does so, in the nest cavity. Birds roost in the nesting areas for much of the year, and by the middle of the breeding season assemble there each night, which is when census work can be considered most reliable. Parrots generally leave their roosts an hour after sunrise and return about an hour before dark.

THREATS (Unless otherwise indicated, all information in this section is derived from Snyder *et al.* 1987.) Among important threats to evaluate have been a diversity of man-caused problems, including cutting of the original forests, hunting, harassment in agricultural lands, pet-taking, and the steady selective loss of potential nest holes resulting from (a) competition from introduced honeybees *Apis mellifera* and (b) felling of trees in which bees nest. Among natural threats have been nest predation and competition from Pearly-eyed Thrashers *Margarops fuscatus*, parasitism by warble flies *Philornis pici*, and predation by Red-tailed Hawks. There is now a firm belief that as soon as one problem is brought under control another arises to take its place: complexity and unpredictability are central to the problems faced by the species.

Habitat loss Although European settlement of Puerto Rico was initially slow, with only 880 Spaniards by 1650, the human population was 45,000 by 1770, 100,000 by 1790, 500,000 by 1850 and 1,000,000 by 1900, and it was during the second half of the nineteenth century that the major destruction of habitat occurred, so that by 1912 less than 1% of the island's original forests were virgin. Even Luquillo Forest was reduced to 2,270 ha of virgin habitat by the turn of the century. A timber stand improvement scheme in Luquillo, begun in 1945, led to the selective removal of palo colorado from at least 1,620 ha of prime palo colorado forest, and this may have been highly damaging given the species's dependence on this tree for nest-sites. Moreover, selective felling of trees with cavities, to obtain either nestlings or much more frequently honey, will have had the long-term effect of critically reducing the number of available nest-sites for parrots. There is a recurring proposal to reopen the 191 road through the Luquillo Forest, which it is believed (despite Fish and Wildlife Service findings) would jeopardize the prospects of the parrot recolonizing (predicted to happen soon) the formerly important Icacos valley (J. W. Wiley *in litt.* 1992). The U.S. Forest Service has attempted to increase timber cutting within Luquillo and, although this has been rejected, the issue may be revived (J. W. Wiley *in litt.* 1992).

Hunting Parrots were hunted in the mangroves at Mameyes Swamp only 16 km from Luquillo in 1912, the last lowland locality at which the species was recorded. The race *gracilipes* was exterminated by settlers on Culebra apparently in retaliation for its feeding on crops, although Phillips (1929) considered its loss to have been contributed to by the establishment of a naval base there, and there is good evidence that a hurricane was to blame (see below). Hunting was not, however, significant in the Luquillo region until the mid-1960s, when it apparently became "especially common"; the severe downturn in parrot numbers in the late 1960s may therefore possibly be attributable to this abuse.

Pet-taking Relentless hunting and pet-taking in combination may have caused the final extinction of local populations in many areas, e.g. around Guajataca and at Río Abajo. Pet-taking is implicated in the final extinction of the species in the Sierra de Cayey. Pet-taking was rampant in certain areas around Luquillo during this century until the 1950s, e.g. in the Fajardo valley, Icacos valley and notably on the western side of the mountains, where in 1948 10 trappers each took 6-12 parrots per year, a harvest that may have represented the entire annual reproductive output of the species in the region. Nest-robbing continued in Luquillo into the 1960s at the North Fork nest.

Translocation attempts A large number of nestlings were removed from the population in the mid-1950s in an attempt to reintroduce the species into several other forests; many dozens of chicks were taken in each of the two years of this experiment (1956 and 1957 or 1957 and 1958). Healthy fledglings were released in groups in several forested sites in central and western Puerto Rico including Toro Negro, Maricao and perhaps Guajataca forests, but none is known to have survived. A strong negative impact on the Luquillo population can be assumed.

Radiation and other factors in the late 1960s From January to April 1965 part of Luquillo was deliberately exposed to high-intensity radiation to determine the response of rainforest vegetation. Although no evidence of direct parrot mortality was found, some may have occurred; and although it is not clear how this could explain the precipitous fall in numbers after December 1966 (observations in 1969 indicated that only two pairs were nesting), it cannot be ruled out as a contributory factor. Warfare manoeuvres were undertaken in Luquillo, 1966-1971, but seem unlikely to have been a serious influence. Herbicide experiments in 1967 took place outside the normal range of the parrot and were probably insignificant; construction of the East Peak Road in the late 1960s may have caused disturbance to a parrot area, but seems unlikely to have caused any mortality; and microwave emissions from the East Peak radar station since 1965 has had an unknown impact on parrots.

Hurricanes and drought The population at Río Abajo was considered not to have recovered from the impact of San Ciriaco in 1899, and any remnant population (which had then suffered from trapping and shooting and further logging) would have been annihilated by the great 1928 hurricane San Felipe that directly hit the area. San Ciriaco might well have been responsible for exterminating the last representatives of the Culebra race *gracilipes*, given that the bird was present on the island in February 1899, the storm struck in August, and the following year no birds were seen (Pérez-Rivera and Bonilla 1982). San Ciriaco and San Felipe also devastated the Sierra de Cayey, allowing for rapid opportunistic human settlement. San Felipe, regarded as the worst storm to have struck the island, was followed only four years later by San Ciprián (1932), and both these had major impacts on the Luquillo Mountains, causing direct death to parrots, indirect losses from subsequent starvation and, possibly, reproductive depression through removal of nest-trees (although one effect of hurricanes is to cause a pulse in fruiting, this possibly being the cause of the enhanced reproduction of parrots observed in the years after Hugo, notably in 1991: N. F. R. Snyder *in litt.* 1992). A major drought in 1967 coincided with the period of maximum rate of decline in the Puerto Rican Amazon, but although birds may have been stressed by this it seems unlikely to have been the primary cause of mortality.

On 18 September 1989 Hurricane Hugo tracked directly across Luquillo, with maximum sustained winds of 225 kph: of the 45-47 parrots counted in August, only 21-23 could be found at the end of September, and their behaviour had radically changed, with birds very quiet and in small groups instead of the flocks usually encountered at that time of year (M. H. Wilson *in litt.* 1992). The loss of 50% of the population was probably mostly attributable to the virtual loss of food and cover in Luquillo for 2-3 months afterwards, during which time parrots were observed almost daily leaving the forest in the early morning presumably in search of food and returning in late evening to roost (F. J. Vilella *in litt.* 1992). All five nest trees survived the onslaught, and although breeding in the following year was late, in March three pairs laid a total of eight eggs, all fertile, five hatching and two young fledging (M. H. Wilson *in litt.* 1992).

Bees Introduced honeybees *Apis mellifera* are now common in Luquillo, usually nesting in palo colorado cavities. It is not known if they can evict parrots from nests, but their occupancy of many good potential sites probably reduces nest-site availability for the parrots; in the period 1973-1979 five parrot nests were taken over in the post-breeding period by bees (see Measures Taken: Bees).

Warble-flies Warble-flies or bot-flies *Philornis pici* parasitize birds of several species in Luquillo at relatively high levels, e.g. 11 (25%) of 44 young Puerto Rican Amazons, 1973-1979; of these, four would have died without intervention. Warble-flies may have increased in Luquillo in response to an increase there of their most favoured host, the Pearly-eyed Thrasher. In 1984 a chick was lost to soldier-fly *Hermetia illucens* larvae, not previously noted to behave in a predatory manner.

Non-avian vertebrates The Puerto Rican Boa *Epicrates inornatus* was reported once to have been seen about to enter a nest and it seems highly likely that it is an occasional predator of eggs and young. There is an ever-present risk of monkeys becoming established in the forest, and there are already reports of rhesus monkeys *Macaca mulatta* colonizing the island (there is in fact a feral colony of these monkeys in the Sierra Bermeja, although this is 140 km from Luquillo: R. A. Pérez-Rivera *in litt.* 1992). Cats *Felis catus* are common in Luquillo, but there is only one recorded case of cat predation on parrots, dating from the 1950s, and the threat is not thought significant. The roof rat *Rattus rattus* is common in Luquillo, and was believed in the 1950s to be the single most important threat to the parrot, with four apparent cases of predation of nests out of 16 studied; while reanalysis of these cases in the light of subsequent experience suggests that the rats may have been scavenging in nests deserted or lost for other reasons (Snyder *et al.* 1987), it is still felt that the risk is significant and the rat control programme is important to continue (R. A. Pérez-Rivera *in litt.* 1992). Since 1956 (see Measures Taken: Rats) there have been no clear cases of loss of nests to rats.

Raptors There is no evidence that either of the two threatened endemic raptor subspecies (see Remarks) poses a serious threat to the Puerto Rican Amazon, but two other raptors, the Red-tailed Hawk and Peregrine *Falco peregrinus* give cause for concern. The Red-tailed Hawk is the most abundant raptor in Luquillo and the most important predator faced by the parrot: attacks have been witnessed, a dead female was almost certainly victim of the species, two of three radio-tagged fledglings released in 1985 were apparently killed by the species, and three cases of (attempted) nest-predation have been recorded, the last of which was terminated by an observer from a hide; possibly as many as nine of the nest failures recorded since the 1950s were caused by this species (more recent work has confirmed this species as a particular threat: Lindsey *et al.* 1988). The Peregrine is not regular in winter in Luquillo, but a male once took up residence for three months; if such a bird ever keyed in on parrot foraging flights the population could be rapidly decimated, and in the absence of a solid explanation it is at least possible that the population crash of the late 1960s was caused by such a development.

Pearly-eyed Thrashers These are the most remarkable natural enemy of the parrot, particularly common in the palo colorado zone of Luquillo; they probably do not enter parrot nests in order to prey on the contents (no ingestion of victims has been seen), but quickly attack if they find eggs or young in occupation. In the 1950s only one of the 10 cases of nest failure documented was attributable to thrasher attack, but this reflects much lower density of thrashers then; a five-fold increase in their numbers occurred in the 20 years to 1976, probably in the decade to 1963, and since 1968 at least five nest failures have been attributable to the species; factors limiting thrashers include nest-site availability and warble-fly parasitism. The species may only have arrived on Puerto Rico in the mid-nineteenth century (no subfossil bone deposits are known, despite its habit of nesting in cave entrances), and it was certainly rare there at the end of the century; hence perhaps the parrot's poorly developed defences to the species.

Accidents, injury and disease One cause of nest failure has been tree fall (two cases since 1954) and another is death of young by drowning in the cavity (one case in the 1950s). Recent studies have shown that birds can injure themselves accidentally if panicked or when flying at low light intensities, and damage each other deliberately during disputes over nest-site ownership. Meanwhile, large numbers of exotic psittacines have been imported into Puerto Rico in recent decades, and although no species has yet established itself in Luquillo some have been seen on the fringes (and there have been two sightings inside the forest since 1990: J. M. Meyers *in litt.* 1992); the diseases they may be carrying could easily be transmitted to the endemic (and presumably less resistant) species, and in the absence of a solid explanation it is at least possible that the population crash of the late 1960s was caused by such a development.

Poor breeding performance For reasons that can only be speculated on, the failure of the population in the late 1970s and early 1980s to form more new breeding pairs was discouraging. Moreover, few pairs were then laying eggs and several pairs only fledged young because of fostering captive-bred offspring into their nests. While the pairs laying eggs continued to exhibit good nesting success (69%) through this period (under intensive management), nearly half of all territorial pairs remained non-breeders. The exact causes of failure to lay eggs have remained difficult to document, but in the most recent years have apparently not been a function of nest-site availability, as many suitable nest-sites have been provided in the nesting areas; the upswing in reproductive effort associated with (a) the population reaching a size of about 40 individuals in the late 1980s and (b) the massive fruiting of forest trees post-Hugo suggests the existence of some density-dependent controlling factors and the possible importance of nutritional and perhaps other factors (N. F. R. Snyder *in litt.* 1992). One such factor might be inbreeding depression: DNA fingerprints of successfully captive breeding pairs of Hispaniolan and Puerto Rican Amazons had average bandsharing coefficients of 0.29 and 0.34 respectively, while those of unsuccessful Puerto Rican Amazons had a significantly higher average of 0.47, which suggests that unrelated Puerto Rican Amazons are inbred and that inbreeding depression is partly responsible for the low number of successfully breeding pairs (Brock 1991).

MEASURES TAKEN (Unless otherwise stated, all information in this section is derived from Snyder *et al.* 1987.) Habitat conservation in Luquillo on behalf of the Puerto Rican Amazon was recommended in separate reports in the late 1940s, and for the most part the lands identified have been maintained free of significant development by the Forest Service, although in the 1950s it rapidly became clear that habitat conservation was insufficient to guarantee the preservation of the species. The first study of the Puerto Rican Amazon itself was carried out in 1953-1956 by the Commonwealth of Puerto Rico government supported by the Pittman-Robertson Program of the U.S. Fish and Wildlife Service (see Rodríguez Vidal 1962). The second study began in 1968, following the placing of the species on the Endangered Species List in 1967, as a cooperative programme of the U.S. Fish and Wildlife Service, U.S. Forest Service and the Commonwealth of Puerto Rico government (through its Department of Natural Resources), with important support from WWF, and continues today. This has involved over 20,000 hours of observation (making it possible to identify and evaluate some of the major stresses on the species) and years of thought and analysis, yet a full understanding of the causes of the species's endangerment remains to be achieved; the validity of scientific generalization is greatly compromised by sample size, and with a tiny population dwindling towards extinction the critical factor has been time, so that measures have had to be implemented rapidly "on the basis of incomplete information, intuition and hope".

Hunting Since 1974 increased patrolling of the forest has led to a decline in the frequency of gunshots heard in Luquillo.

Rats In 1956 and 1957 rat control (poisoning and metal guards on nest trees) was practised, and it was reinstituted at the start of the second study in 1968 and continues down to the present.

Bees The five honeybee colonies established in parrot nests after breeding in the period 1973-1979 were simply exterminated. Now the preferred method for ensuring that nest-sites remain available to parrots is to close them off after fledging in June until the end of the swarming season in September.

Pearly-eyed Thrashers Between 1973 and 1976 attempts (successful) were made to guard all parrot nests from thrashers through direct observation and the use of pellet guns (a minimum of 26 thrashers were shot at one nest-site in 1973), while from 1975 experiments were made with the substitution of plaster eggs over the incubation period so as to allow concentration of efforts on other nests. A nest-site design attractive to parrots but not to thrashers was developed and deployed, and the provision of alternative sites for thrashers nearby has resulted in resident pairs of the latter greatly reducing visits from prospecting conspecifics; these two factors in combination appear to have resolved the problem (but the continuing nest-watch programme is important in monitoring the situation in case of complications: J. W. Wiley *in litt.* 1992).

Warble-flies The only effective counter to infestation of chicks is to check them regularly and remove and treat any that are affected, and at least three birds have been saved from certain death in this way. A remarkable drop-off in infestation since 1979, despite no observed decline in warble-fly populations in the forest, may be the result of the deeper, darker nest-cavities made to foil thrashers.

Nest-site increase and enhancement In the belief that very low nest-site availability might be inhibiting birds from breeding, many nest-boxes were installed in the forest in 1969 and 1970, although these were not used, probably because too small. Further nest-boxes were installed over the coming years; from 1973 natural nest-sites were improved by creating artifical substrates or greater space, and since 1975/1976 all breeding pairs have been using sites either created or rehabilitated by man. All parrot nests have been modified to prevent entry by Red-tailed Hawks. In 1989 Hurricane Hugo destroyed most nest-boxes in Luquillo, and the Forest Service elected not to replace them but to focus efforts instead on enhancing natural cavities in living palo colorado trees, scooping existing holes to a greater depth, drilling drainage channels, using chicken wire as a false bottom, and/or attaching a sheet zinc visor to the entrance, all to ensure dry nesting; by mid-1992 47 cavities had been enhanced by the Forest Service in parrot nesting areas, and three of them were adopted by breeding pairs in 1991 and 1992, one of these being in a valley previously not known to be occupied by nesting pairs (E. R. García *in litt.* 1992; also Meyers *et al.* in prep.).

Direct assistance In a case where a chick was so affected by slime inside the cavity that it could not fledge, moulted feathers from a captive bird were "imped" onto its wings and tail to allow it to do so. Interventions from hides have prevented predation of nests by Red-tailed Hawks and Pearly-eyed Thrashers. As many as six nests that were successful between 1973 and 1976 might have been lost to thrashers without intervention. Increased vigilance since 1987 has resulted in further successful interventions (Lindsey *et al.* 1989).

Monkeys A small colony of monkeys *Saimiri sciureus* released into Luquillo Forest by an unknown agent was removed just in time in 1973.

Captive breeding A captive breeding programme for the species was begun in 1970, as a safeguard against extinction, a source of biological information unobtainable from wild birds, and a reserve from which the wild population could be supplemented either in Luquillo or in due course elsewhere. An aviary was established in Luquillo itself in 1973. The original stock consisted of two old zoo birds donated in 1970, two wild birds trapped in 1972 and five young taken as eggs or chicks in 1973; since then the emphasis has fallen on adding representatives of different genetic stock, and as of 1979 every pair that had bred in the wild since 1972 had descendants in captivity. In 1979, when the stock stood at 15 birds, nine females and six males, the first captive breeding occurred and the offspring was fostered into a wild nest where it fledged successfully. In the period 1979-1986, although only four wild birds were added to the stock, it increased to 29, 10 females, seven males and 12 unsexed juveniles.

In 1986-1988 another nine birds were added to the wild stock, but the captive population continued to increase to 47 birds (of which 16 were known to be female, 20 male); the captive flock was unaffected by Hurricane Hugo, with no birds lost and as many eggs laid and young fledged in 1990 as in 1989 (M. H. Wilson *in litt.* 1992), and before the start of the 1992 breeding season the total stood at 58 birds (F. J. Vilella *in litt.* 1992). As in the wild, the number of breeding pairs in the captive flock remained low, around four (Wilson *et al.* in press). Studies of the birds' nutritional requirements and genetic diversity have therefore been undertaken, along with research on artificial insemination techniques and artificial incubation (Lindsey *et al.* 1989). A second captive facility at Río Abajo, constructed with reintroduction there in mind (see Measures Proposed: Reintroduction), is not yet finished, but 12 birds may be moved there by the end of 1992 or at the start of 1993 (J. M. Meyers *in litt.* 1992).

Other developments since the mid-1980s Wild nestlings have been sexed and fitted with steel leg bands; a volunteer nest-watch programme since 1987 has increased coverage of nests substantially; survival, movement and behaviour of parrot young has been studied using radio-telemetry; in 1988 a study of the distribution and territorial behaviour of non-breeding parrots was initiated; and release strategies have been developed for optimizing the survival of captive-raised birds when returned to the wild (Lindsey *et al.* 1989). Studies have also been conducted on the reproductive behaviour of the species, on its territorial behaviour, on its vocalizations, on constant character differences in vocalizations between pairs, and on capture and marking of surrogate psittacines (M. H. Wilson *in litt.* 1992). The Forest Service has built (or, after Hugo, rebuilt) 34 look-out towers for monitoring operations (E. R. García *in litt.* 1992).

A population viability analysis was conducted on the Puerto Rican Amazon in June 1989 under the auspices of CBSG (Lacy *et al.* 1989); although its recommendations for a metapopulation (i.e. several as far as possible self-sustaining subpopulations) were felt inappropriate or at least premature (see Measures Proposed) it has had the effect of intensifying the build-up of the captive population, and this appears in part to have been at the expense of the programme to release captive-bred birds into the wild population, discontinued since 1986 (J. W. Wiley *in litt.* 1992). DNA "fingerprinting" has allowed the development of a genealogy (by K. M. Brock) and hence the planned maximization of available genetic variation; captive pairs are being allowed to rear their own young, aiming at future releases of captive-bred birds (F. J. Vilella *in litt.* 1992).

Following Hurricane Hugo in September 1989 a number of new management techniques have been introduced. New observation blinds have been built at newly active nests; steel leg bands have been coloured through electroplating, and parrot chicks are now individually marked using band combinations; and census methods have been modified to increase precision and sample size (F. J. Vilella *in litt.* 1992).

MEASURES PROPOSED (Unless otherwise stated, the points below derive from Snyder *et al.* 1987).

Miscellaneous Insecticidal treatment of parrot nests might be effective against warble-fly parasitism, but may run certain risks to the parrots themselves, so that careful evaluation of this resort should be made before implementation (a study of such treatment using Pearly-eyed Thrashers concluded that additional work was needed to perfect the technique: LaRue 1987). Rat poisoning is questionable in the long term but its value in forestalling the destruction of eggs early in the season before females have developed incubation constancy, and in preventing the loss of eggs or young in the event of the death of a female later in the cycle, justifies continuation until the parrot population shows fuller recovery. Because only one unscrupulous hunter could yet have a serious impact on the population, intensive enforcement of hunting regulations in Luquillo must remain for many years. Long-term vigilance is also needed for the threats of competition and hybridization posed by other amazons introduced into Puerto Rico. Moreover, the growing populations of exotic psittacines on the island need monitoring and perhaps even control (notably at Río Abajo: see below), given their potential for transmitting disease to the native species (J. W. Wiley *in litt.* 1992). Moves to reopen road 191 through Luquillo and to increase cutting of timber there are likely to be detrimental to the parrot's prospects and need to be subject to careful evaluation (J. W. Wiley *in litt.* 1992; again note Remarks 2). The official target is to establish a population of 500 birds in the Luquillo mountains (USFWS 1987).

Reintroduction (at Río Abajo) If the worrying problems in reproduction in the wild are habitat specific and beyond correction, the species can ultimately be saved only by reintroductions elsewhere, something that needs at some stage to happen in any case in order to guarantee its long-term survival. Preliminary reconnaissance suggests that the karst region of the Río Abajo Commonwealth Forest is the most favourable area, as it is an area which the species previously occupied, which can be patrolled well, and in which relatively few Red-tailed Hawks or Pearly-eyed Thrashers occur (against this, however, is the small size of the reserve, its high percentage of edge habitat, and its intensive timber management: F. J. Vilella *in litt.* 1992); a second promising area is the Cristal-Camandules region of lower Luquillo, with many tabonuco, half the rainfall, and few thrashers; six other possible sites, including the offshore islands of Culebra and Mona, deserve consideration (although habitat destruction on Culebra for housing and tourism is perhaps now too extensive, and Vieques would appear a better alternative: J. W. Wiley *in litt.* 1992). It has been recommended that the Río Abajo aviary should be stocked with non-breeding adults and captive-bred juveniles from the Luquillo aviaries, and that no attempts to establish a second wild flock should be made until the existing wild stock exceeds 70 birds, as to do so would conflict with bolstering the extant wild stock as quickly as possible (Wilson *et al.* in press). Studies of wild juveniles have suggested that the optimal time for integration of captive-bred birds into a wild flock would be at around five months (Lindsey *et al.* 1991). The official target is to establish 500 birds in the Río Abajo forest in addition to the 500 at Luquillo (USFWS 1987).

Third captive population on U.S. mainland Following the population viability analysis in 1989, it was recommended that the species's security and propagation might be enhanced by the establishment of a reserve population at a zoo on the U.S. mainland (Lacy *et al.* 1989). However, this move was opposed and finally ruled out on the grounds that it would greatly escalate the risks of disease transmission as well as compound problems of finding good matches amongst prospective mates (Wilson *et al.* in press).

REMARKS (1) As circumstantial evidence of former occurrence in dry forest, at least two congeners, Green-cheeked Amazon *Amazona viridigenalis* and Hispaniolan Amazon *A. ventralis*, the latter a close relative, are now well established in such habitat in southern Puerto Rico, utilizing trees such as úcar *Bucida buceras* and ceiba *Ceiba pentandra* for breeding, these being quite possibly historical nesting trees for the Puerto Rican Amazon since they are common throughout the coastal forests of the country (F. J. Vilella *in litt.* 1992). (2) Luquillo Forest is also a major area for two threatened endemic subspecies of bird, the Puerto Rican Sharp-shinned Hawk *Accipiter striatus venator* and Puerto Rican Broad-winged Hawk *Buteo platypterus brunnescens* (King 1978-1979; see also Snyder *et al.* 1987).

BLUE-BELLIED PARROT *Triclaria malachitacea* V/R[10]

This unusual shade-loving parrot is restricted to the Atlantic Forest region of south-east Brazil (two records from Argentina), living in low numbers in the moister valleys although venturing out seasonally to lower areas. Its rarity appears to be related to this habitat preference, combined with overall habitat loss and the particular human exploitation of a favoured palm-fruit.

DISTRIBUTION The Blue-bellied Parrot (see Remarks 1) occurs in south-eastern Brazil from southern Bahia south to northern Rio Grande do Sul (Sick and Teixeira 1979, Ridgely 1981a, Sick 1985, Forshaw 1989, Bernardes *et al.* 1990, Robiller 1990), with two recent records from Misiones, Argentina (see Remarks 2). A record from Mato Grosso do Sul is not accepted here (see Remarks 3).

Brazil Forshaw (1989) pointed out that this species has disappeared from parts of its range in south-east Brazil. In the following account, localities are listed from north to south, with coordinates (unless otherwise stated) derived from Paynter and Traylor (1991).

Bahia Despite the repeated listing of this state (e.g. in all the summarizing texts listed above) the only good evidence of occurrence there appears that of Wied (1831-1833), who found the species near Caravelas and in the woods inland from Mucuri to Morro da Arara (where he noted its curious voice: see Remarks 1), including along the rio Peruípe (see Bokermann 1957), all in the southernmost part of the state; he expressed doubt that it occurred further north. There is a specimen labelled "Bahia" from before 1833 in MHNG.

Minas Gerais The few records are from: Lagoa Santa (Burmeister 1856), a perhaps unreliable site if only because so far into the interior; rio Matipó, July 1919 (Pinto 1938); and on the rio Doce (Pinto 1978), although the basis for this is unknown and it might simply represent an error for the site below under Espírito Santo. Recent field observations are implied, though not specified, by de Mattos *et al.* (1985).

Espírito Santo Records are from: rio Doce, April and August 1906 and at an unspecified later date (von Ihering and von Ihering 1907, Pinto 1938, Aguirre 1947); córrego Cupido, rio Barra Seca, i.e. present-day Sooretama Biological Reserve, April 1939 (Aguirre and Aldrighi 1983); three sites in the adjacent municipalities of Santa Teresa, Santa Leopoldina and Domingos Martins in the middle of the state, recently (D. M. R. Fortaleza *in litt.* 1990), of which the first is evidently in or near the Augusto Ruschi (Nova Lombardia) Biological Reserve, where the species has been seen in small numbers on repeated visits, 1980-1990 (TAP), and the second may be Chaves, as a specimen (in MCZ) was taken there in September 1942; Duas Bocas State Reserve, 400-500 m, near Cariacica (Vitória), where the species was recorded in the 1980s (C. E. Carvalho verbally 1987).

Rio de Janeiro Records are from: Nova Friburgo, nineteenth century (Burmeister 1856, von Ihering 1900a), and in the Macaé de Cima area nearby, where local people reported it in 1984 (J. F. Pacheco *in litt.* 1986); Desengano State Park, since 1986 (J. F. Pacheco *in litt.* 1987); Tapebuçu (south of Macaé: see Bokermann 1957), early in the nineteenth century (Wied 1831-1833); Cantagalo, nineteenth century (von Ihering 1900a); Serra do Tinguá, 700 m, 1980-1981 (Scott and Brooke 1985), and subsequently within this range at Xerém, 120-130 m, 1986 (C. E. Carvalho *in litt.* 1987) and in July and August 1987 (J. F. Pacheco *in litt.* 1987); and Parati, a littoral site from which the species has been recorded in the non-breeding season (Sick 1968, 1985). It is not clear if Angra dos Reis, mentioned under Population, is a known or speculated site.

São Paulo Records are from: Serra da Bocaina National Park, 1,200 m, November 1989 (P. S. M. da Fonseca and J. F. Pacheco *in litt.* 1990); Victoria (now Vitoriana), 570 m, August 1902 (five specimens in AMNH, FMNH); Fazenda Barreiro Rico, c.22°45'S 48°09'W, Anhembi, 500-600 m, in the period 1957-1964, although not detected in a remanescent woodlot of 1,400 ha there on three-day visits nearly every month from March 1975 to August 1977, and presumed extinct (Willis 1979, 1980, whence coordinates); Ipanema, 1820s (von Pelzeln 1868-1871); Ubatuba, February and April 1905 (von Ihering and von Ihering 1907, Pinto 1938); Boracéia, near Salesópolis, since November 1945 (Camargo 1946, C. Yamashita *in litt.* 1987, D. F. Stotz *in litt.* 1988); Alambari, 500-600 m, January 1901 (specimen in AMNH); Itapetininga, May 1869 (specimen in UMZC); São Sebastião, September 1898 (specimen in AMNH); Sítio Irapuã, near Juquitiba, 600-900 m, 1983-1988 (R. Antonelli Filho verbally 1988); the 38,000 ha Fazenda Intervales, Capão Bonito, December 1989 to August 1990 (I. Simão, M. A. Pizo and M. Galetti *in litt.* 1991); Carlos Botelho State Park, 24°04'S 47°58'W, March 1992 (Straube and Scherer Neto in prep.); Pedro de Toledo, December 1957 (specimens in LACM); Boa Vista and Barra do Veado, close together on the rio Ipiranga (former at 24°35'S 47°38'W), August 1960 (specimens in FMNH); "Porto V. Travessão" (untraced, but also on the Ipiranga), March 1957 (specimen in YPM); Fazenda Bela Vista, Taquarussu, Iguape, 24°43'S 47°33'W (as given on labels), May 1956 (specimens in LACM); Ilha do Cardoso, March 1905 and August 1934 (Pinto 1938), where still resident in the state park of the same name (P. Martuscelli *in litt.* 1991). It is possible that the species has been recorded at Campo Grande (see Remarks 3).

Paraná Although all the descriptions of the species's range cited in the opening paragraph of this section indicate its extension from Bahia to Rio Grande do Sul, records from Paraná are all very recent: Mananciais da Serra, Piraquara, 950 m, July 1991, six birds; Limeira, Guaratuba, 420 m, May 1992, two birds; Barra do Saí, Guaratuba, January 1991, by local report (all from Straube and Scherer Neto in prep.).

Santa Catarina Records are all from the north-east of the state, at: Palmital (now Garuva), June 1929 (specimen in AMNH); São Francisco do Sul (on Ilha de São Francisco), July 1899 (von Ihering and von Ihering 1907, Pinto 1938); Hansa (now Corupá), 75 m, July 1929 (specimens in AMNH). There are apparently no field observations (Sick *et al.* 1981).

Rio Grande do Sul The map in Belton (1984-1985) shows a range extending inland as far as 53°W but restricted latitudinally to between 29 and 30°S. Records, all consonant with this distribution, are from Cambará do Sul, just north of Aparados da Serra National Park (C. Yamashita *in litt.* 1987); Lagoa do Forno (29°20'S 49°53'W in Belton 1984-1985), near Torres, at sea level, October and November 1928 (specimens in AMNH); Poço das Antas, 29°27'S 51°40'W, in the municipality of São João de Montenegro (Gliesch 1930); Sinimbu, 250 m, September 1928 (specimen in AMNH; see Remarks 4); Sapiranga, 60 m, August 1928 (specimen in AMNH), with birds present there (specifically at Picada Verão) in the 1970s and in May 1992 (M. Sander and G. A. Bencke *in litt.* 1992); Taquara (do Mundo Novo), 1882-1883 (von Berlepsch and von Ihering 1885); Monte Alverne, 29°33'S 52°20'W, near Santa Cruz do Sul, August 1991 and January 1992 (G. A. Bencke *in litt.* 1992, including coordinates).

Argentina A bird was observed in a flock of Reddish-bellied Parakeets *Pyrrhura frontalis* near the falls in Iguazú National Park, Misiones, in April 1983 (Rumboll 1990), and another was seen in the upper basin of the arroyo Urugua-í, November 1986 (Canevari *et al.* 1991), the precise site being inside Urugua-í Provincial Park 30 km west of Bernardo de Irigoyen in General Belgrano department (R. J. Straneck and M. Castelino *per* J. C. Chebez *in litt.* 1992).

POPULATION Considerable difficulty attends the evaluation of the status of this species, partly because of its unobtrusive behaviour – it remains largely silent after dawn (TAP), is extremely shy and keeps motionless on the perch when frightened (Descourtilz 1854-1856, also Ridgely 1981a) and flies at or below canopy level (C. Yamashita *in litt.* 1987) – but also because it appears to be either a low-density species or perhaps one that always occurred very patchily throughout its fairly broad range within the Brazilian Atlantic Forest belt. It has been described as "locally common" (Forshaw 1989) and "often fairly common" (Ridgely 1981a), and the latter authority has judged that while some declines have surely occurred, at least in Espírito Santo and probably elsewhere, the species has suffered less than many other parrots with similar ranges. However, the paucity of modern records, with most stemming from the reserves at Augusto Ruschi (Nova Lombardia) and Boracéia, suggests that some specific habitat requirements may be in play that further restrict the species (see Ecology).

Wied (1831-1833) found it not infrequent at the localities he named (four in Bahia and one in Rio de Janeiro), but indicated it belonged overall to the less abundant birds of these regions. In the 1940s the bird was still common in the mountainous part of Espírito Santo, although even then it was recognized as a threatened species (Pinto 1946). In Augusto Ruschi (Nova Lombardia) it is uncommon, not being recorded on every day of surveys between 1977 and 1986 (TAP). It was uncommon (i.e. occasionally encountered in appropriate habitat) in Serra do Tinguá (Scott and Brooke 1985). The main population probably now occurs on the eastern slopes of the Serra do Mar between Angra dos Reis in Rio de Janeiro and Ubatuba in São Paulo (C. Yamashita *in litt.* 1987). However, immediately to the west of this area, at Boracéia Biological Station, birds seem limited by the availability of nesting sites, being seldom recorded over several years of observation (Camargo 1976) and remaining uncommon there today (seen on six days with a maximum of eight in one day) (D. F. Stotz *in litt.* 1988). The population at Cambará do Sul is small (C. Yamashita *in litt.* 1987) and in Rio Grande do Sul in general the bird is considered a "scarce resident" (Belton 1984-1985).

ECOLOGY The Blue-bellied Parrot inhabits wet (Sick 1985 says dry) lower montane and escarpment forests, chiefly at 300-700 m at least in Rio de Janeiro state (although perhaps 500-1,000 m elsewhere), ranging lower into adjacent lowland forests and at times even into coastal regions outside the breeding season (Sick 1968, Belton 1984-1985, Sick 1985, Forshaw 1989). The evidence under Distribution largely confirms this, though not entirely: thus in Espírito Santo the records from the rio Doce (both at sea level) in April and August are consistent, and in Santa Catarina the São Francisco do Sul record from July involved a sea-level locality (as described in Paynter and Traylor 1991), the Corupá record from July was at only 75 m (elevation on AMNH label), and the Garuva record from June (of a sexually inactive bird as given on AMNH label) refers to a locality at 50 m on the coastal plain (as described in Paynter and Traylor 1991); in Rio Grande do Sul, two birds taken in August and September were at 250 m or below although not in breeding condition, birds in both August and January at Monte Alverne were in plateau forest at 500 m, not venturing into lower (though forested) areas (G. A. Bencke *in litt.* 1992), but two taken in October and November at Lagoa do Forno were at sea level at the start of the breeding season (both had gonads slightly enlarged). Vertical displacements are seen on Ilha do Cardoso, where the species ranges from sea level to 700 m (P. Martuscelli *in litt.* 1991). Outside the breeding period it may enter farmed areas with orchards and plantations or even suburban woodlands and gardens, e.g. on the outskirts of São Paulo (Descourtilz 1854-1856, von Berlepsch and von Ihering 1885, Pinto 1946, Ridgely 1981a, Forshaw 1989). However, it does not occur in either savanna or xerophytic woodland (*contra* Smith 1975: 40). At Augusto Ruschi Biological Reserve the birds have been found from mid-storey to the lower canopy, and have never been seen to fly across even small clearings, let alone open countryside (TAP). Birds are usually found in the canopy of tall, bromeliad-rich forest along watercourses in valleys, and this may be a habitat preference that would explain their relative overall scarcity; they are very active in twilight, both in the early morning and at sunset (C. Yamashita *in litt.* 1987, verbally 1988). In captivity the species seeks shade and shows distress in temperatures above 18°C, and one holder knew of no other parrot that enjoyed cold so much (Low 1972).

Birds feed on fruits, seeds, nuts (araucaria: Belton 1984-1985), berries (myrtaceous: Descourtilz 1854-1856), nectar, buds, and perhaps insects (possibly caught on the wing) and their larvae, generally procured in the treetops (Bertagnolio 1981, Forshaw 1989). Murray (1969) noted that captive birds caught flies, and considered that their remarkable swift flight and beautifully precise landings indicated a possible adaptation to hawking for insects. Small groups are attracted to the small fruits of a forest palm ("palmito", i.e. *Euterpe edulis*) in the period from January to May (Bertagnolio 1981, G. A. Bencke *in litt.* 1992; see also Threats). All records in the Augusto Ruschi Biological Reserve, 1980-1990, were from the same small areas near stands of *E. edulis*

(TAP). In the Duas Bocas State Reserve birds come periodically to feed on oranges and fruits of jabuticaba trees in an orchard close to the forest (C. E. Carvalho verbally 1987). When the species takes the particularly juicy fruits of *Citrus medica* the pulp is discarded and only the seeds are eaten (Forshaw 1989, H. Sick verbally 1990). In a study near Capão Bonito the species's diet showed no overlap with other parrots there (a *Forpus*, *Brotogeris*, *Pyrrhura* and *Pionopsitta*) (I. Simão, M. A. Pizo and M. Galetti *in litt.* 1991). In captivity it has been seen to eat leaves, bark, algae growing on wood, and nectar (Murray 1969, Low 1972), bark also being recorded in Bertagnolio (1981).

Nesting occurs from September to January in a natural hollow in very old, large trees, often a palm trunk (Bertagnolio 1981); however, a nest with three chicks has been found as early as September (Camargo 1976, Forshaw 1989). A male collected on 17 August 1974 had inactive gonads (Belton 1984-1985), as did four birds of both sexes (in AMNH) taken in June, August and September; but as noted above, two others taken in October and November had slightly enlarged gonads. Of four birds collected in late January and mid-February one was very young, two were young and one, a male, was in moult (von Berlepsch and von Ihering 1885). The birds are strongly territorial and respond to taped playback (C. Yamashita *in litt.* 1992; see Threats). Two nests were found in holes in trees situated approximately 2 km from each other in forest at the Boracéia Biological Station: the entrances were 4.5 m and 2.2 m above the foot of the trees; three young were taken in September from one of these nests (Camargo 1976). The same nest-site is reported to be used in consecutive years, which may be the result of a scarcity of hollow trees (Camargo 1976). In captivity the clutch is 2-4, incubation is 28 days, and while the fledgling period remains unknown the young become independent three weeks after fledging (Robiller 1990).

There is a post-breeding movement from the Serra do Mar down into the coastal flats, where the species appears at certain localities, and is caught in great numbers (Sick 1968). Birds move in singles, pairs or small family groups with little fear of man (Descourtilz 1854-1856, Bertagnolio 1981, C. Yamashita *in litt.* 1987).

THREATS The decline of this species has been attributed to hunting, land clearance for farming, urbanization, and the intensive collecting of one of its main foodplants, the "palmito" (see Ecology), which is targeted for its use in salads, soups and puddings, the whole tree being cut to obtain the fruit (Bertagnolio 1981, J. Goerck *in litt.* 1992); this also seems to have been a factor affecting the largely sympatric Black-fronted Piping-guan *Pipile jacutinga* (see Threats in relevant account). Although substantial amounts of forest, mostly too wet and too steep for agricultural purposes, might suggest that the Serra do Mar may still provide a secure refuge for the species (Ridgely 1981a, Forshaw 1989, D. F. Stotz *in litt.* 1988), the moister valleys preferred by the bird are threatened by banana plantations on the lower slopes (C. Yamashita verbally 1988, LPG) and in Rio Grande do Sul also by cutting of wood for curing tobacco, whose production is the major industry around Santa Cruz do Sul (G. A. Bencke *in litt.* 1992). Forest exploitation on Ilha do Cardoso is causing a decline there (P. Martuscelli *in litt.* 1991). The 1983 record from Argentina was assumed to be of a bird displaced by the deforestation of 85% of its habitat in adjacent Brazil (Rumboll 1989).

Trade Although described as very rare in captivity (Ridgely 1981a), Wied (1831-1833) quite often found the species in the houses of local people, and Sick (1968) reported it to be caught "in numbers" during its annual visits to the coastal lowlands. The species is sufficiently tame that it can be caught with a noose on a long pole (Bertagnolio 1981). It is also easily enticed into traps by calling decoys (A. Ruschi verbally 1980), presumably regarding such birds aggressively (see Ecology). Some internal trade persists, as birds have been seen in the notorious Caxias market in Rio de Janeiro (C. E. Carvalho *in litt.* 1987). Moreover, in the mid-1980s a number of birds came into international trade, and were judged an ideal cagebird (Robiller 1990), a point already made by Wied (1831-1833), although the testimony of G. Rossi dalla Riva is that it is a very difficult bird to keep (see Bertagnolio 1981).

MEASURES TAKEN The Blue-bellied Parrot is protected under Brazilian law (Bernardes *et al.* 1990). It occurs in at least eight protected areas, the small (40 km^2) Augusto Ruschi (Nova Lombardia) Biological Reserve and the Duas Bocas State Reserve in Espírito Santo, the Desengano State Park and Tinguá Biological Reserve in Rio de Janeiro, Bocaina National Park (probably also on the Rio side), the privately run albeit extensive Boracéia "Watershed Reserve" (as given in Ridgely 1981a), Carlos Botelho State Park and Ilha do Cardoso State Park in São Paulo. Records from forest now protected as Sooretama Biological Reserve indicate, however, that several such lowland sites may be needed to cater for the species and that the seven reserves named above may not be sufficient in themselves. The two records from Argentina have both been from protected areas, and Urugua-í Provincial Park is notably rich in palmito palms (J. C. Chebez *in litt.* 1992).

MEASURES PROPOSED This bird requires patient and painstaking study to determine the fundaments of its ecological requirements; work could be undertaken at any of the seven protected areas listed under Measures Taken. Surveys and perhaps more detailed studies might also be undertaken in the Serra do Mar between Angra dos Reis and Ubatuba, to confirm whether this area is particularly important for the species (see Population). Birds should be looked for in Aparados da Serra National Park. The nature of the birds' seasonal movements requires elucidation. Any new perceptions and key areas to emerge from such fieldwork need to be brought into considerations for the long-term management of the species. Trade, including internal commerce, should be clamped down on. In Rio Grande do Sul, where the existing protected areas fail to include the species, efforts should be made to conserve the last major continuous tracts of forest within its range, but also to establish a network of small reserves at the municipal level in such areas as Santa Cruz do Sul, Poço das Antas, Sapiranga and northwards into Santa Catarina (G. A. Bencke *in litt.* 1992). Research on the species in the northern part of its range might be extended to cover similar research on the Cinnamon-vented Piha *Lipaugus lanioides*, which appears to utilize the same key food-plant, as does the Black-fronted Piping-guan (see relevant accounts and Ecology above).

REMARKS (1) This species is the only one in its genus and in form, behaviour and voice is like no other Neotropical parrot (Murray 1969, Low 1972, TAP). (2) There is a danger of confusion with the superficially similar female Pileated (Red-capped) Parrot *Pionopsitta pileata*, so that sight records in some cases may conceivably be mistaken (TAP). (3) A note that the bird has been recorded from Mato Grosso do Sul (Sick and Teixeira 1979) has been widely ignored, but Sick (1985) reinforced it with the locality Campo Grande (the state capital). Without further information this record appears wholly improbable; it is possible that there was a confusion with Campo Grande in São Paulo state (C. Yamashita *in litt.* 1990). (4) Belton (1984-1985) gave the elevation of Sinimbu as 80 m, but the specimen is labelled as taken at 800 feet.

RUFOUS-BREASTED CUCKOO *Hyetornis rufigularis* I[7]

Deforestation and hunting seem likely to have contributed to the poor status of this low-density but seemingly unspecialized cuckoo in Haiti and the Dominican Republic, but while there is little hope for its survival in the former, it occurs in four protected areas in the latter; nevertheless it requires fuller study and the implementation of existing plans for further key site conservation.

DISTRIBUTION The Rufous-breasted Cuckoo is endemic to Hispaniola, occurring in both Haiti (including Gonave Island) and the Dominican Republic. In the following account coordinates are taken from DMATC (1972, 1973).

Haiti There are very few records from the country.

Gonave Island Five birds were collected somewhere on the island in February 1918 and four at Etroites (18°52'N 72°52'W) and Anse-à-Galets in March 1920 (Wetmore and Swales 1931); a bird was taken in the hills above Anse-à-Galets in July 1927 (Danforth 1929); there are two skins simply labelled "Gonave Island", February and May 1928 (in ANSP). No birds were observed on the island in February 1985, on a walked transect from Pointe-à-Racquettes to Anse-à-Galets (M. A. McDonald *in litt.* 1991).

Mainland Three birds were taken near Moustique (19°49'N 72°57'W) in March 1917 (Wetmore and Swales 1931), and one bird was observed c.15 km down the road from Seguin (18°19'N 72°14'W) to Marigot (18°14'N 72°19'W) in summer 1983 (M. A. McDonald *in litt.* 1991).

Dominican Republic Records below are organized by province, roughly from west to east.

Dajabón Records are from near Loma Cabrera (19°25'N 71°37'W), where birds were frequently seen and two nests found in April 1983 (A. Stockton de Dod *in litt.* 1991).

Elias Peña Localities are: Los Cerezos (untraced) on the slopes of the río Artibonito (for which see IGU 1979), undated (Stockton de Dod 1978); between Pedro Santana (19°06'N 71°42'W) and Bánica, undated (A. Stockton de Dod *in litt.* 1991); Río Limpio (19°15'N 71°31'W) and Loma Nalga de Maco (19°13'N 71°29'W), recently (SEA/DVS 1992).

Independencia A population once occurred in a wooded area (now cleared) near La Descubierta (18°34'N 71°44'W) (A. Stockton de Dod *in litt.* 1991). Two birds were observed above Duvergé (18°32'N 71°31'W), two more at Puerto Escondido (18°19'N 71°34'W) and a single bird elsewhere at the base of Sierra de Baoruco, all of them in April 1987 (J. E. Pierson *in litt.* 1991); Stockton de Dod (1978, 1981) also mentioned Puerto Escondido as one of the places where the species is to be found and where a bird was taken in 1972; Bond (1984) reported a nest west of Puerto Escondido in March 1976.

San Juan A male was taken at a locality 7 km west of Vallejuelo (18°39'N 71°20'W) in 1963 (Schwartz and Klinikowski 1965); and a male was taken at arroyo Loro (18°49'N 71°16'W) in March 1930 (Moltoni 1932).

Azua The species has been recorded at Orégano Chiquito (18°31'N 70°53'W), undated (Stockton de Dod 1981); and an extensive series was obtained at Túbano (see map in Wetmore and Swales 1931) in December 1916 and February 1917 (Wetmore and Swales 1931).

La Vega At Hondo (Hondo Valle in OG 1963b, at 18°53'N 70°50'W) specimens were taken in May 1919 (Wetmore and Swales 1931); near Constanza (18°55'N 70°45'W) birds were collected in April and May 1919, and at Corralito (untraced, but near Constanza) in April 1919 (Wetmore and Swales 1931). One bird was taken at Loma Tina (18°47'N 70°44'W) in January 1917 (Wetmore and Swales 1931); the species was recorded once between Miranda (untraced, but not far from La Vega, at 19°13'N 70°31'W) and La Vega, sometime between December 1906 and April 1907 (Verrill and Verrill 1909).

Peravia Two birds were obtained at San José de Ocoa (18°33'N 70°30'W) and three at Honduras (18°22'N 70°26'W) in 1895 (Cory 1895, Wetmore and Swales 1931); the species has been recorded at Baní (18°17'N 70°20'W), undated (Stockton de Dod 1981), and at Valdesia (18°24'N 70°16'W) in 1971, 1981 and 1982 (A. Stockton de Dod *in litt.* 1991).

POPULATION The limited evidence indicates a strong decline in overall numbers and range at least during the twentieth century.

Haiti The Rufous-breasted Cuckoo has been considered "very local" on the mainland (Bond 1956b) and is now believed to be extremely rare there (M. A. McDonald *in litt.* 1986). On Gonave Island it was reported as "not uncommon" in February 1928 (Bond 1928a); Wetmore and Swales (1931) reported five birds collected in February 1918 and four in March 1920.

Dominican Republic Judging from the number of specimens taken early in the 1900s (see Distribution) the Rufous-breasted Cuckoo appears once to have been at least locally common, although by the 1970s it was believed to be very rare and on the way to extinction (Stockton de Dod 1981). In 1983, however, A. Stockton de Dod *in litt.* (1991) discovered an area near Loma Cabrera where a "good" population of the species was present, birds being "common" and "frequently seen", two occupied nests being found, while between Bánica and Pedro Santana the species was seen more than twice on one day; nevertheless, she still regarded the species as threatened.

ECOLOGY The Rufous-breasted Cuckoo is found in many different habitat types, from dense broadleaf mountain rainforest to arid lowlands, including dense scrub, patchy broadleaf woodland composed of exotics such as papaya *Carica papaya* and breadfruit *Artocarpus altilis*, yards and gardens (Bond 1928a, 1979, Wetmore and Swales 1931, M. A. McDonald *in litt.* 1991, A. Stockton de Dod *in litt.* 1991). It can be found over a wide range of altitudes but appears to prefer rather dry, deciduous environments (Bond 1979, Stockton de Dod 1981, J. E. Pierson *in litt.* 1991). Its habits are poorly known; it has been observed progressing rapidly through the forest, and appears to prefer the high parts of the trees (Wetmore and Swales 1931, Stockton de Dod 1978).

It feeds on insects (locusts, mantids, bugs and beetles have all been recorded), lizards and small mice (Danforth 1929, Wetmore and Swales 1931, A. Stockton de Dod *in litt.* 1991). The stomach of a bird taken in July 1927 contained lizard remains (92%) and insects (8%) (Danforth 1929).

Reproduction in the species (not a brood-parasite) remains little known: a bird taken near Hondo on 9 May contained an egg ready to lay (Wetmore and Swales 1931); a nest found in late March at Puerto Escondido had a fledging young in May (Bond 1984), and two nests with incubating adults were found in April near Loma Cabrera (A. Stockton de Dod *in litt.* 1991). The nest can be built in any kind of tree that has epiphytes (i.e. bromeliads) or leaves that will conceal the construction (A. Stockton de Dod *in litt.* 1991). The few reported nests were placed about 3-6 m above the ground in a mango *Mangifera* sp. or "jabilla" tree, and the clutch-size according to local people consists of two eggs (Bond 1984, A. Stockton de Dod *in litt.* 1991).

THREATS The Rufous-breasted Cuckoo's apparent scarceness throughout Hispaniola is difficult to attribute to habitat destruction, given the records (see Ecology) from so many different habitats. It is possible, however, that it has certain requirements that are influenced by alterations to habitat, and records from (e.g.) yards, gardens, introduced vegetation, etc., cannot entirely be trusted to indicate that it is adaptable and secure.

Haiti A broad view of habitat loss in the country is in Threats under White-winged Warbler *Xenoligea montana*. In Anse-à-Galets on Gonave extreme deforestation of the nearby hills and ravines has exposed the town to the hazard of flash floods (Paryski *et al.* 1989).

Dominican Republic Notes on habitat loss are in Threats under White-winged Warbler. Like other members of its family, the Rufous-breasted Cuckoo has been considered a medicinal food and is therefore hunted (Wetmore and Swales 1931, A. Stockton de Dod *in litt.* 1991). The impact of pesticides and fertilizers may also have been pronounced in the case of this species (A. Stockton de Dod *in litt.* 1991).

MEASURES TAKEN Some general and specific points are made in the corresponding section under White-winged Warbler, but the Rufous-breasted Cuckoo is not listed in any Haitian wildlife protection law (J. A. Ottenwalder *in litt.* 1992), nor does it occur in either La Visite or Pic Macaya National Parks (Woods and Ottenwalder 1986).

In the Dominican Republic the hunting of the species is prohibited (J. A. Ottenwalder *in litt.* 1992), while more than 10% of the total surface area of the country is within protected areas, and the cuckoo is present in at least three national parks (J. Armando Bermúdez, José del Carmen Ramírez and Sierra de Baoruco) and one scientific reserve (Valle Nuevo) (J. A. Ottenwalder *in litt.* 1992; also Distribution).

MEASURES PROPOSED More ecological and distributional studies are needed throughout Hispaniola in order to establish an appropriate conservation strategy for this and other threatened species on the island. An overview of the importance of conserving the mountain forests in Hispaniola is in the corresponding section under Chat-tanager *Calyptophilus frugivorus*.

BANDED GROUND-CUCKOO *Neomorphus radiolosus* V[9]

This ground-cuckoo inhabits wet foothill forests on the Pacific slope of the Cordillera Occidental of south-west Colombia and north-west Ecuador, where it is known from few localities and threatened by forest destruction. There have been three records (in 1988 and 1989) of single birds in Colombia since 1956, with just one (in 1992) in Ecuador since 1936, suggesting that the bird is truly rare and localized, but possibly overlooked.

DISTRIBUTION The Banded Ground-cuckoo has been recorded from a small number of localities on the Pacific slope of the western Andes in three areas of south-west Colombia, and also in adjacent north-west Ecuador.

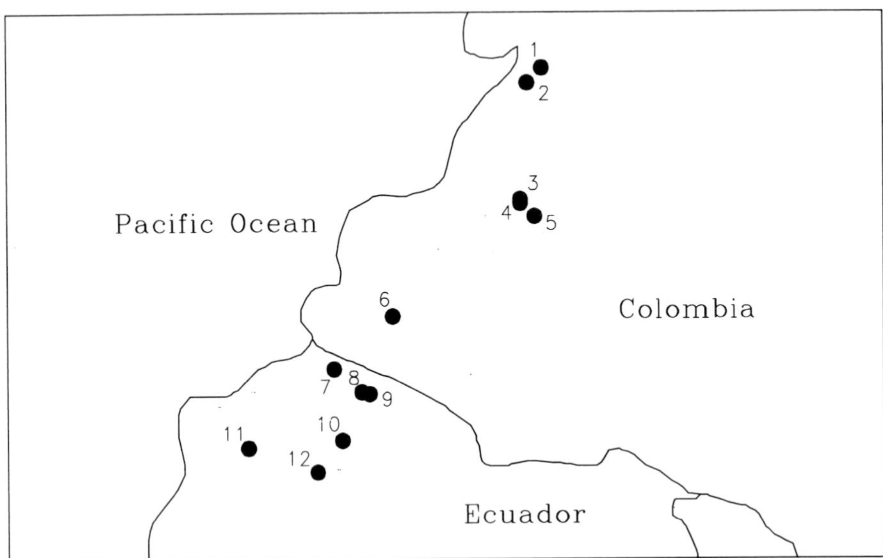

Colombia Records in Colombia come from three areas on the Pacific slope of the Cordillera Occidental in Valle, Cauca and Nariño departments, where localities (north to south, coordinates taken from Paynter and Traylor 1981) are as follows: (*Valle*) near Jiménez[1] (c.3°45'N 76°45'W), where a female (in AMNH) was taken in July 1907 (apparently the first Colombian record) at 885 m; Alto Anchicayá[2] (near El Danubio, at 3°37'N 76°53'W), in Los Farallones de Cali National Park, where a bird was recorded at c.600 m during February 1989 (F. R. Lambert *in litt.* 1989; also *World Birdwatch* 11,2 [1989]: 4); (*Cauca*) Cerro Munchique[3] (2°32'N 76°57'W), where on the western slope a bird was collected at 1,000 m during September 1951 (von Sneidern 1954); La Costa[4] (variously described as 10 km north of or on the western side of Cerro Munchique: Paynter and Traylor 1981), where four specimens have been collected, including a female in January 1936 and two females in January 1937, at 1,000 m (von Sneidern 1954, Negret 1991); río Mechengue[5], near El Tambo (c.2°25'N 76°49'W), where a female (in ANSP) was taken at 730 m in July 1939 (also Bond and Meyer de Schauensee 1940) with another female (in YPM) taken at 800 m in August 1956; La Bermeja (untraced, but within Munchique National Park), where an individual was seen in August 1988 at 800 m (Negret 1991); and (*Nariño*) río Pambí[6] (untraced, but between Junín and Barbacoas), where a bird was seen at 900 m in 1988 (G. Arango verbally 1991).

Ecuador This species has been recorded from just seven localities in north-west Ecuador in Esmeraldas, Imbabura and Pichincha provinces (coordinates from Paynter and Traylor 1977), as follows: (*Esmeraldas*) río Cayapas[7] (c.1°13'N 79°03'W), where a female (in AMNH) was collected in October 1901 (see Remarks); 17.5 km by road past Alto Tambo towards San Lorenzo (c.0°58'N 78°43'W), where a single bird was recorded daily at 450 m, 13-15 February 1992 (NK); Quinindé[11] (= Rosa Zárate; 0°20'N 79°28'W), where a female (in FMNH) was collected in September 1936 (see Remarks); (*Imbabura*) Montes de Achotal[8] (untraced, but apparently near Achotal, at c.0°50'N 78°25'W), where a male and female (in FMNH) were collected in August 1935; Paramba[9] (= Hacienda Paramba; 0°49'N 78°21'W), where a male (in AMNH) was collected in May 1898, with a female (in AMNH) taken in June of the following year, both at 1,065 m (also Hartert 1898a); Intag[10] (c.0°24'N 78°36'W), where the type-specimen was taken in about 1878 (Sclater and Salvin 1878b); and (*Pichincha*) Gualea[12] (0°07'N 78°50'W), where a male (in NRM) was taken at 1,525 m in June 1920 (also Lönnberg and Rendahl 1922).

POPULATION The status of the Banded Ground-cuckoo is essentially unknown, with the only three recent records (i.e. post-1956) coming from Colombia (in 1988 and 1989), and with just one from Ecuador since 1936.

Colombia Although Bond and Meyer de Schauensee (1940) referred to this species as "excessively rare" when they collected a female in the Cerro Munchique area in 1939, this area accounts for seven of the eight Colombian specimens, and von Sneidern (1954) concluded that in this region the species was to be encountered with some frequency. That a population still exists there is confirmed by the observation of an individual within the national park in August 1988 (see Distribution). The recent (February 1989) observations of a bird at Alto Anchicayá, in the vicinity of Jiménez, where a bird was taken in 1907, and of one in Nariño (see Distribution) suggest the survival of two further populations. Hilty and Brown (1986) considered this species to be rare and local, and the evidence appears to confirm this, although it has been suggested (*World Birdwatch* 11,2 [1989]: 4) that it is not so much rare as overlooked.

Ecuador There are apparently just eight specimens of the Banded Ground-cuckoo from Ecuador, with no more than two taken at any of the localities, and with just one record since the last specimen was collected in September 1936 (see above). Hartert (1898a) regarded this species as a "very rare cuckoo". However, local people at the Alto Tambo site recognized the bird from the plate in Hilty and Brown (1986) and claimed that it was fairly common in the area, occurring almost invariably in groups of 3-5 (NK).

ECOLOGY This ground-cuckoo inhabits wet forest, mostly in foothills and on the lower slopes of the Pacific side of the western Andes, from c.600 to 1,000 m in Colombia, and 450 to 1,525 m in Ecuador (Hilty and Brown 1986; see Distribution). At La Costa (Munchique National Park), von Sneidern (1954) described the terrain as broken and covered in forest (for more details of the vegetation in Munchique National Park, see Negret 1991). F. R. Lambert (*in litt.* 1989) described the small patch of forest at Alto Anchicayá as apparently little disturbed (but secondary) moss-forest, isolated from other forest above by a 10 m wide swathe of rough grass (with electric pylons running through) and below by a road (see Threats); this moss-forest was dense, with a thick understorey (mainly of tree-saplings), heavy epiphytic growth, and a canopy height of 8-12 m. The area where the bird was recorded near Alto Tambo supports wet primary forest, c.20-30 m tall (NK). A specimen label (in AMNH) gives this species's local name as "guide of the wild pigs" and Hartert (1898a) likewise translated the local name as "companion of wild boar"; with the collection of a specimen following collared peccaries *Tayassu tajacu* (Hilty and Brown 1986), and the 1988 observation of a bird in Munchique National Park following a band of this same species (Negret 1991), the suggestion could be made that peccaries are an important part of the bird's ecological requirements, and may indicate habits similar to those of the Rufous-vented Ground-cuckoo *Neomorphus geoffroyi*, which often associates with these ungulates and army ants

(Hilty and Brown 1986, LGN). Locals at the Alto Tambo site independently claimed that this species is invariably found in groups of 3-5 birds following army-ant swarms (NK).

THREATS Forest clearance is the main threat to this species and has been intense throughout its Colombian range (LGN), and despite the persistence of large areas of apparently primary or old secondary forest on the Pacific slope in Cauca and Valle departments (F. R. Lambert *in litt.* 1989, G. Kattan *in litt.* 1992, LGN), agricultural and hydroelectric projects are causing local degradation of the vegetation within Munchique National Park (IUCN TFP 1988a), and gold-mining poses a threat to the area around Anchicayá (G. Kattan *in litt.* 1992). In north-west Ecuador, large areas of forest also remain, and human population pressure is not great: however, widespread deforestation has occurred, especially along the rivers and railways, and is becoming more of a problem as the human population increases and agriculture expands (Moore and van der Giessen 1984, Evans 1988b, IUCN TFP 1988b).

MEASURES TAKEN There are several parks encompassing localities where the Banded Ground-cuckoo has been recorded: in Colombia, Munchique National Park (44,000 ha) possibly encompasses all but three of the known localities (CNPPA 1982; see Distribution), and a newly founded private reserve within the buffer zone of this park provides further protection to the area's lowland wet forest (A. J. Negret verbally 1991); the Anchicayá–Verde watershed (covering the area from where both this species and the Yellow-green Bush-tanager *Chlorospingus flavovirens* have been recorded: see relevant account) surrounds two hydroelectric plants, and is protected by the CVC (Hilty 1977); this area is apparently an ecological reserve (but illegal hunting and clearance for agriculture still occur: F. R. Lambert *in litt.* 1989, and Threats), and is within Los Farallones de Cali National Park (150,000 ha: CNPPA 1982, Areas Protegidas 1989, Hernández Camacho *et al.* undated), including large areas of forest on the Pacific slope which may support other populations of the species (G. Kattan *in litt.* 1992), although Hilty (1977) did not encounter it during fieldwork in the area.

In Ecuador, this species has been recorded from a number of localities in what is now the Cotacachi-Cayapas Ecological Reserve (204,400 ha), one of the main forest blocks left in the north-west of the country (CNPPA 1982, Moore and van der Giessen 1984).

MEASURES PROPOSED The guaranteed integrity of forest within the reserves mentioned above is essential if this and other threatened bird species are to survive (see below); where possible, other remaining forest blocks in this area need conserving. A management plan has been drafted for the Cotacachi-Cayapas Ecological Reserve (Moore and van der Giessen 1984), and the conservation of remaining forest in the south-west Colombia/north-west Ecuador region has been identified as of the highest conservation priority (IUCN TFP 1988a,b).

The true distribution, population density and basic ecological requirements of this species are essentially unknown: determining each of these is important, after which it may be possible to assess the bird's conservation needs and act upon them. The range of the Banded Ground-cuckoo overlaps with those of a number of threatened species: at Munchique National Park it probably occurs with Plumbeous Forest-falcon *Micrastur plumbeus* (see relevant account, and for species occurring higher than 1,000 m in this park see the equivalent section under Multicoloured Tanager *Chlorochrysa nitidissima*); at Alto Anchicayá it has been found with Yellow-green Bush-tanager, but in the vicinity of this locality and within the Los Farallones de Cali National Park a number of other threatened species occur, for which see the equivalent section under Multicoloured Tanager. Any conservation initiatives should consider the needs of all these species.

REMARKS The río Cayapas is in the lowlands of Esmeraldas and the exact location where the specimen was taken is unknown, although it seems likely that it was in the foothill forests near the headwaters of this or possibly a tributary river. A similar uncertainty attaches to the specimen locality Quinindé (= Rosa Zárate) which, at c.100 m, is seemingly too low for this species, and may refer to a locality further up the río Quinindé, on somewhat higher ground.

LONG-WHISKERED OWLET *Xenoglaux loweryi* K[12]

This cloud-forest owlet is known from just two localities in the eastern Andes of northernmost Peru, where it was discovered as recently as 1976. Although apparently not yet threatened by habitat destruction, almost nothing is known about its range, ecological needs or population.

DISTRIBUTION The Long-whiskered Owlet (see Remarks) is known from just two localities on the eastern slopes of the eastern cordillera of the Andes in Amazonas and northern San Martín departments, northern Peru (coordinates are from Stephens and Traylor 1983).

The species was first discovered 10 km north-east of Abra Patricia (= Pardo de Miguel, c.5°46'S 77°41'W) on the road to Rioja in the río Mayo drainage (in San Martín department, although this locality is at a pass on the border of San Martín and Amazonas) during late August and early September 1976 (O'Neill and Graves 1977). The species is also recorded from close to the type-locality, east of Bagua (5°40'S 78°31'W) at 2,165 m in the Cordillera de Colán (a large, semi-isolated mountain range), Amazonas (Fjeldså and Krabbe 1990, J. Fjeldså *in litt.* 1992; also Stephens and Traylor 1983).

POPULATION Nothing is known. Three birds (seemingly a mated pair and a female) were collected at the type-locality (August 1976), and others, apparently this species, were heard in the immediate vicinity (O'Neill and Graves 1977), so that it seems likely that the bird is locally not uncommon.

ECOLOGY Records of this little-known owlet come from subtropical forest between 1,890 and 2,350 m where the forest is often shrouded in fog, soaking mist or rain brought in by the prevailing (moisture-laden) easterly winds (O'Neill and Graves 1977, Fjeldså and Krabbe 1990). At Abra Patricia, the resultant elfin or cloud-forest had a canopy at 6-9 m in the sheltered valleys, and only c.4 m on the exposed ridges: all parts of the forest were covered with heavy moss and laden with orchids, bromeliads, strap-leafed ferns and bryophytes, with *Chusquea* bamboo forming dense thickets in canopy openings and along small streams; a great number of tall, slender emergent palms and occasional tree-ferns all gave the forest a characteristic appearance (O'Neill and Graves 1977). The Long-whiskered Owlet was caught and heard (presumably this species) at night (including dusk) on ridge-tops where the forest was slightly more open (O'Neill and Graves 1977). What was presumed to be its song was heard in August 1976, at which time an apparently mated pair was collected: however, all three specimens showed only slightly enlarged gonads, and were deemed to be not breeding (O'Neill and Graves 1977).

THREATS None is known. East of Abra Patricia, in the watershed of the río Mayo, virgin forest stretched eastward to the Amazonian lowlands of north-central Peru (O'Neill and Graves 1977), and it would seem that owing to its inaccessibility the ridge-top elfin forest is currently under little or no threat.

MEASURES TAKEN None is known, although the species may prove to be present in the recently formed Río Abiseo National Park (see Yellow-browed Toucanet *Aulacorhynchus huallagae* account for details).

MEASURES PROPOSED Almost nothing is known about this species's distributional status or ecological requirements, and as such it would be desirable for a survey to concentrate on calling birds in the ridge-top forests of this area, aiming at discovering their distributional range and hence an approximate population size. Although the habitat is at present under little apparent threat, a protected area, perhaps in the Cordillera de Colán, incorporating habitats from the lowlands up to the ridge-top cloud-forest, would help guarantee the survival of this unusual species, and many other montane forest endemics (see Cinnamon-breasted Tody-tyrant *Hemitriccus cinnamomeipectus* account and, for areas to the south of its known range, Remarks under Yellow-browed Toucanet).

REMARKS The Long-whiskered Owlet was described as a new genus *Xenoglaux* (O'Neill and Graves 1977), in which it remains the only representative.

WHITE-WINGED NIGHTJAR *Caprimulgus candicans* E[1]

This distinctive nightjar is known from only two old specimens from open grasslands in Mato Grosso and Sao Paulo in central Brazil, but with even older evidence from Paraguay. The only modern records are from Emas National Park in Goiás, Brazil.

DISTRIBUTION The White-winged Nightjar (see Remarks 1) has only ever been recorded in four localities (north to south; see Remarks 2): near Cuiabá, Mato Grosso, in the mid-1820s (von Pelzeln 1868-1871; also Sclater 1866); Emas National Park, south-western Goiás, currently (Redford 1985, R. S. Ridgely *in litt.* 1992, TAP); "Irisanga" (= Orissanga, 22°12'S 46°57'W in Paynter and Traylor 1991), São Paulo, February 1823 (von Pelzeln 1868-1871; also Sclater 1866; see Remarks 3); and, possibly, somewhere in Paraguay in the eighteenth century (de Azara 1802-1805), but with no confirmed records (F. E. Hayes *in litt.* 1991).

POPULATION The highly distinctive plumage of this species (von Pelzeln 1868-1871 raised but dismissed the possibility of the type being a partial albino) suggests that, although a nightbird and from a poorly known area, it should have been recorded more often if it were at all common or widespread: one general report (in which the identity cannot be confirmed) from the late eighteenth century (de Azara 1802-1805 saw a few – "pocos"), two records of individual birds from the early nineteenth, and one area identified in the late twentieth, is not encouraging evidence. As it is, small numbers of the species were easily found with the aid of a spotlight during night drives through open grassland in Emas National Park almost annually in the 1980s, records being in late August–October, the period when most natural history tour groups visit the park (R. S. Ridgely *in litt.* 1992, TAP). In September 1985 the bird was common (at least a dozen seen) (R. S. Ridgely *in litt.* 1992) and at least six were found on one night in September 1986 along c.3 km of a road north-west of the park headquarters (TAP); yet in September 1989 only two could be found, and in October 1990 only one (R. S. Ridgely *in litt.* 1992). No indication of seasonal or annual changes in abundance can be ascertained from the scanty available information, but it may be that numbers fluctuate with the availability of optimal habitat (R. S. Ridgely *in litt.* 1992). Considering the size of the park (132,000 ha: IBAMA 1989) it is probably safe to assume that the population numbers in the hundreds if not larger.

ECOLOGY The type in São Paulo was found "in grassland on the ground" (von Pelzeln 1868-1871). Birds at Emas have been found in open cerrado that had been burnt in the previous year or two (much like Campo Miners *Geobates poecilopterus*), often favouring areas with a scattering of very low shrubs and prostrate palms, and seemingly avoiding areas with longer grass (R. S. Ridgely *in litt.* 1992); they were observed sitting quietly on small patches of bare ground or atop clumps of grass in open, well-drained campo limpo habitat west and north-west of the park headquarters, where there are extensive areas of open grassland almost devoid of bushes and small trees, but with abundant termite mounds (TAP). Their vocalizations (or other sounds) are unknown, although most grassland bird species at Emas are quite vocal at the beginning of the rainy season in late September-October (TAP). For this reason, it may be that breeding occurs somewhat later in the rainy season (R. S. Ridgely *in litt.* 1992); however, the type, taken in February, was "in very heavy moult" (von Pelzeln 1868-1871). Park staff report that birds are year-round residents, but this needs checking particularly as there may be nomadism in response to fires (R. S. Ridgely *in litt.* 1992, TAP). De Azara (1802-1805) saw what may have been this species only from September to November, and considered it might be migratory.

THREATS The White-winged Nightjar is only known this century from a national park about whose future fears have been expressed, owing to its inappropriate boundaries and the uncontrolled fires set by ranchers outside them (Redford 1985, 1987). The effect of frequent burning of much of the park on the species is unknown: it apparently prefers very open grasslands that are maintained by fire (see Ecology), but the natural burn cycle is presumably not annual, as is now the case in much of west-central Brazil (TAP). The most serious threat to the survival of this species is outright habitat destruction (see also account of Lesser Nothura *Nothura minor*). Extensive, open grasslands on fairly level land like that at Emas are almost non-existent now: this and other protected areas where the species might occur are increasingly becoming tiny islands in a sea of cultivation (TAP). That this and other grassland endemics may be migratory or semi-nomadic in response to fires further complicates their chances of survival.

MEASURES TAKEN The White-winged Nightjar is protected under Brazilian law (Bernardes *et al.* 1990). That the only known locality for this species is a national park offers some comfort, despite comments under Threats; and in recent years the park managers have been able to control the grass fires that affect the area annually (R. S. Ridgely *in litt.* 1992).

MEASURES PROPOSED A census and study of this species at Emas National Park is badly needed, followed by appropriate management (e.g. controlled burning of certain areas if it is shown that the bird does indeed select recently burnt grassland); biological surveys (for which knowledge of the species's voice is obviously desirable) of remaining campo and cerrado localities in Goiás and Mato Grosso are equally urgent, for example in protected areas such as Chapada dos Guimarães National Park north-east of Cuiabá and at the Serra das Araras Ecological Reserve to the west (both Mato Grosso), while extensive campo limpo habitat in Brasília National Park (Distrito Federal) and at Chapada dos Veadeiros National Park also looks suitable for this species (TAP; see Remarks 4). Expansion of the Chapada dos Guimarães National Park to include extensive areas of rolling grassland north of the main highway west of the town might protect populations of this and numerous other grassland endemics, which may also occur on the unprotected serras and adjacent cerrados of northern Mato Grosso (TAP). Further comments are made under Lesser Nothura.

REMARKS (1) The observation that *Caprimulgus candicans* is morphologically like the (also threatened) Sickle-winged Nightjar *Eleothreptus anomalus* (von Pelzeln 1868-1871) deserves further study. Both these apparently allopatric taxa occur in grasslands (the latter more in marshy areas), but lack of behavioural information (and of anatomical material) for either will make such a comparison difficult at present. (2) Two skins tentatively identified as this species from Fazenda Gavião, São Paulo, January 1946 (in FMNH) require re-examination to confirm that they are not. (3) It is worth noting that this is a locality at which J. Natterer obtained specimens of the threatened Lesser Nothura and Dwarf Tinamou *Taoniscus nanus* (see relevant accounts). (4) It is imperative to utilize such fieldwork, both at Emas and beyond, also to search for and study the Bearded Tachuri *Polystictus pectoralis*, of which the nominate race – grasslands of central Brazil southwards into eastern Bolivia (at least formerly), eastern Paraguay, Uruguay and northern Argentina – is now in a highly perilous condition (Fjeldså and Krabbe 1990 pointed out that it might yet be found to constitute a biological species): the only site where it has been found consistently in recent years is Emas National Park, where it seems to be confined to a few small areas of tall grass and dense shrubbery along streams through open grassland, and it is doubtful whether the population (which may not even be resident) exceeds a few hundred individuals (TAP). Other recent localities for this species are mentioned in Remarks 2 under Lesser Nothura and Remarks 3 under Hyacinth Macaw *Anodorhynchus hyacinthinus*.

CAYENNE NIGHTJAR *Caprimulgus maculosus* I[8]

Known with certainty from just one specimen taken in French Guiana during 1917, this nightjar is unknown in life.

DISTRIBUTION The Cayenne Nightjar (see Remarks) is endemic to French Guiana where it is known with certainty from just one record. The type- and apparently the only specimen (a male) was taken at Saut Tamanoir (5°09'N 53°45'W; on the Fleuve Mana, c.10 km above its confluence with Riviere Cokioco: Stephens and Traylor 1985) in April 1917 (Todd 1920). However, J.-L. Dujardin (*in litt.* 1986, 1991) caught a bird at Saül airstrip (3°35'N 53°12'W) in September 1982 which he considered referable to this species, and which J. Ingels (*per* J.-L. Dujardin *in litt.* 1986) thought 75-80% likely to be a female of the species.

POPULATION Nothing is known. However, the closely related and sympatric Blackish Nightjar *Caprimulgus nigrescens* (see Remarks) is common in suitable habitat in the Guianas (Ingels and Ribot 1983, Ingels 1988) and despite recent, quite intensive mist-netting of this species in French Guiana, no Cayenne Nightjars have yet been recorded (J. Ingels *in litt.* 1988).

ECOLOGY Nothing was recorded of the habitat in which the type-specimen was collected, although two basic habitats have been identified at the locality: the lower reaches of the river has many boulder-strewn rapids, and is bordered by (1) closed-canopy forest, or (2) more open areas characterized by large boulders, sandy or stony river banks, and (rare) savanna-like clearings (Ingels 1988). The bird caught by J.-L. Dujardin (*in litt.* 1986, 1991) was in a clearing along the airstrip at Saül. At both the above localities Blackish Nightjar was also present (Dick *et al.* 1984, Ingels 1988).

THREATS None is known.

MEASURES TAKEN None is known.

MEASURES PROPOSED Re-examination of the type may help determine the validity of the species, as would an investigation (e.g. whether or not a specimen was taken) into the bird caught in 1982. Specific efforts should be made to mist-net *Caprimulgus* species at both Saut Tamanoir and Saül, with the aim of confirming the species's continued existence and validity.

REMARKS Although Peters (1940) and Sibley and Monroe (1990) considered the Cayenne Nightjar a full species (following Todd 1920), with so little material on which to base such a conclusion there must remain some doubt: J. M. Thiollay (*in litt.* 1986), J.-L. Dujardin (*in litt.* 1986), and J. Ingels (*in litt.* 1988) all questioned the validity of the taxon, and recognized that the bird would be extremely difficult to identify from Blackish Nightjar in the field, thus perhaps explaining the lack of subsequent records. However, no formal or clearly argued case has been presented questioning the true identity of the specimen, and most recently J.-L. Dujardin (*in litt.* 1991) still considered the nightjar a full species, and that the bird he caught referred to a female.

PUERTO RICAN NIGHTJAR *Caprimulgus noctitherus* R[11]

Believed originally to have occupied the dry forests that once fringed Puerto Rico, this nightbird is restricted to three separate areas of such habitat in the south-west of the island, where the total population is in the order of 670-800 pairs distributed over 10,000 ha of habitat. Despite protected area status for much of the relevant forests, habitat destruction remains a serious threat.

DISTRIBUTION The Puerto Rican Nightjar is endemic to Puerto Rico, where it is now restricted to three separate areas in the south-western portion of the island, namely Guánica Forest (1 km east of Guánica), Susúa Forest (5 km east of Sabana Grande, 18°05'N 66°58'W; coordinates here and below in OG 1958), and the Guayanilla Hills (c.3.5 km east of Guayanilla, 18°01'N 66°47'W, and 2 km from the coast) (Kepler and Kepler 1973, Noble *et al.* 1986, Vilella and Zwank 1987). In addition, since 1986 a number of new nightjar records have been obtained in several areas of south-western Puerto Rico, namely Guánica Forest (section west of Guánica Bay, 17°58'N 66°55'W), the adjacent private lands in Ensenada (Ensenada at 17°58'N 66°56'W), private lands adjacent to Susúa and Maricao Forests (18°09'N 67°00'W) and more recently the Parguera Hills (Parguera at 17°59'N 67°03'W) in 1990 and Sierra Bermeja (c.10 km west of Parguera) in 1992 (Vilella 1989, Vilella and Zwank in press a; see Population, Remarks 1). Former localities (west to east) where the species is known to have occurred include: near Mayagüez, around 1958 (see Reynard 1962); La Cueva Catedral, near Morovís (18°20'N 66°24'W), itself near Bayamón, where bones of this species were examined (Wetmore 1919); near Bayamón, where the type-specimen was taken in October 1888 (Wetmore 1919; also A. Wetmore in Reynard 1962); and Río Piedras (18°24'N 66°03'W), where a possible bird was observed in December 1911 (Wetmore 1919, Bond 1956b). Given the species's present range, former localities and the vegetation-type associated with them, Kepler and Kepler (1973) believed that its original range was coextensive with the moist limestone and coastal forests, the dry limestone forests, the drier sections of the lower cordillera forests and perhaps the dry coastal forest, i.e. it possibly encircled the island, covering most of the coastal plain on both sides of the Cordillera Central and Sierra de Luquillo (see the maps in Kepler and Kepler 1973). Kepler and Kepler (1973) estimated the species's current range to be approximately 3% of its former distribution, although Vilella and Zwank (1988) believed it to be 9-10% (i.e. more than 10,000 ha), and this figure has recently been increased with the post-1986 range extentions (see above); however, it is difficult at present to estimate the total area which should be added to the known range (F. J. Vilella *in litt.* 1992).

POPULATION Prior to 1961, only one specimen of the Puerto Rican Nightjar had been collected, near Bayamón in 1888 (Cory 1889, Wetmore 1919, A. Wetmore in Reynard 1962). Wetmore (1919) saw what he thought was this species in 1911 and it was assumed to be extinct or nearly so (Wetmore 1919, Peters 1940, Bond 1956b) until rediscovered in 1961 in Guánica Forest, where its voice was familiar to local people (Reynard 1962). Soon afterwards the number of birds in Guánica Forest was put at 100 (see Kepler and Kepler 1973). Between 1969 and 1971 Kepler and Kepler (1973) conducted censuses in Guánica and Susúa forests (see Remarks 2), resulting in the estimation of 330 to 470 pairs in the former and 30 in the latter. Further censuses conducted within Guánica Forest and adjacent available habitat and Susúa Forest and suitable adjoining private land in June and July 1984 and January 1985 resulted in the estimation of 324 pairs in the former (one singing bird per 8 ha above 75 m and one per 18.8 ha between 25 and 75 m) and 68 pairs in the latter (one bird per 24.5 ha north of Carretera del Bosque and one per 8.1 ha south of Carretera del Bosque) (Noble *et al.* 1986; which see for survey routes and partial results). The estimation of 324 pairs in Guánica Forest was similar to Kepler and Kepler's (1973) lower estimate of 330 pairs, but substantially less than their higher one of 470 pairs, a discrepancy Noble *et al.* (1986) believed was due to the survey method rather than real population size differences, although Kepler and Kepler's (1973) total estimate of 30 pairs in Susúa Forest was too low as they did not census the northern portion of the forest (see Noble *et al.* 1986). In summary, the total population size estimated by Kepler and Kepler (1973) was of 450 to 500 pairs in approximately 3,200 ha, 80% of the nightjars being in Guánica Forest, while Noble *et al.* (1986) and Vilella and Zwank (1987) estimated a total population of 665 "singing males" (see Remarks 3) in about 7,883 ha, with almost 50% of the total population in the Guánica and adjacent areas. Later estimates given by Vilella and Zwank (1988) are of about 670-800 pairs distributed over approximately 10,000 ha (see Remarks 4). Both in Guánica and Susúa Forests, highest nightjar density was one singing bird per 5 ha (Vilella 1989). Díaz Díaz (1984) suggested that before the Puerto Rican Nightjar could be considered to have "recovered", its population should rise to 600 pairs in Guánica Forest, 400 pairs in the Guayanilla Hills, and 200 pairs in Susúa Forest; however, these figures appear to be above the carrying capacity of the available habitat according to Kepler and Kepler (1973) and Noble *et al.* (1986), who believed that populations in Guánica and Susúa Forests were at equilibrium and possibly at carrying capacity in all suitable public and private habitat. In the Guayanilla Hills rough estimations given by Kepler and Kepler (1973) were of 50-100 pairs on what they believed to be c.500 ha of suitable habitat, although Noble *et al.* (1986) estimated a population of 200 to 260 pairs (but see Remarks 3) on a total of c.1,300 ha. Later censuses conducted in this same area in 1985 and 1986 resulted in densities ranging from 0.04 to 0.12 nightjars per hectare with a total estimated number of 263 singing males (Vilella and Zwank 1987; see Remarks 5). The similar estimate of birds obtained by Kepler and Kepler (1973) and Noble *et al.* (1986) in the Guánica Forest suggests that the species has maintained its numbers for at least 15 years. The later searches which resulted in the discovery of further (previously unreported) areas (see Distribution; Remarks 6) included one individual in the Parguera Hills and five to seven in Sierra Bermeja (all individuals heard); the distribution in this section appeared to be scattered, with a few individuals limited to small fragments of suitable habitat (Vilella 1989).

ECOLOGY The Puerto Rican Nightjar currently inhabits the wooded tropical dry limestone forests of south-western Puerto Rico (Kepler and Kepler 1973; see Remarks 7). However, the species formerly inhabited the moist limestone and moist coastal forests of the northern lowlands of the island (for original forest-types see the maps in Kepler and Kepler 1973). Semi-deciduous vegetation consists of hardwood trees on top of limestone hills; important species include *Bourreria* sp., *Bursera simaruba*, *Bucida buceras*, *Acacia farnesiana*, *Swietenia mahagoni*, *Pisonia albida*, *Coccoloba microstachya*, *Colubrina arborescens*, *Exostema caribaeum*, *Thouinia portoricensis*, with the common shrubs *Croton humilis*, *Eugenia foetida* and *Lantana involucrata* (Kepler and Kepler 1973, Díaz Díaz 1984, Vilella and Zwank 1987). Furthermore, the Puerto Rican Nightjar is also found throughout the highly disturbed forest lands of the Guayanilla-Peñuelas region, wherever the canopy has been retained (F. J. Vilella *in litt.* 1992). No birds were detected below elevations of 25 m in the Guánica Forest during summer, but nightjars occur at low elevations in winter (see Noble *et al.* 1986). Kepler and Kepler (1973) believed that nightjars would not occur at altitudes below 75 m, but Noble *et al.* (1986) considered the limit to be about 25 m, below which they thought that nesting would not take place, probably because (a) steady winds have produced a stunted vegetation providing little cover for the species, (b) insect activity may be reduced under such circumstances, and (c) predation may be important below 25 m (feral cats and mongooses were frequently observed). However, further research in both sections of Guánica Forest (east and west of Guánica Bay) has shown that nightjars also occur at elevations near sea level throughout the year; reproduction can also occur below 100 m but small patches of taller forest with accumulated leaf-litter are required: two nests (out of 23) occurred below 100 m; one of these was located at 55 m elevation (Vilella 1989). No surface water or riparian habitat exists in Guánica Forest, and nightjars did not occur in the riparian habitat in Susúa (Kepler and Kepler 1973, Noble *et al.* 1986).

The Puerto Rican Nightjar captures flying insect prey by flying from perches well above the ground (see Kepler and Kepler 1973). Nesting occurs from late February to early July (Vilella 1989). Calling activity reaches peak levels in February (Kepler and Kepler 1973), eggs having been found from 28 February to 1 July (Kepler and Kepler 1973, Noble and Vilella 1986, Vilella 1989). One or two eggs are laid on the bare ground covered only by fallen leaves, and incubation is mostly performed by the male, in contrast to most members of the genus; in addition, an elaborate nest-relief ceremony was discovered, the only member of the genus for which it is known (Vilella 1989, Vilella and Zwank in prep.; also Kepler and Kepler 1973, Noble and Vilella 1986).

THREATS The mongoose *Herpestes auropunctatus*, introduced in 1877, has long been presumed to have extirpated the Puerto Rican Nightjar from those areas of its former range with sufficient rainfall and standing water to support mongooses (Noble *et al.* 1986), although this has not been proved and it appears to be the nightjar that is limited by the amount of suitable habitat (Vilella 1989, Vilella and Zwank in press b). Deforestation is the single most important factor affecting the species (Vilella and Zwank 1988). The coastal zone is under intense pressure for residential, industrial and recreational development, with the expected onslaught of people, cats, rats, mongooses and the danger of fire (AOU 1976, Vilella and Zwank 1988). Despite its protected area status, Guánica Forest is threatened by road construction, resort development and tremendous industrial expansion to the east and possibly to the west, and nightjars on private land are less secure because much of it is being converted to other uses including goat and cattle raising (Kepler and Kepler 1973, Vilella and Zwank 1987, 1988, Noble *et al* 1988). The species's present restricted range makes it very vulnerable to an expanding human population and natural or man-induced habitat changes (e.g. fires, clearings, parasites and diseases: Díaz Díaz 1984).

MEASURES TAKEN The Puerto Rican Nightjar has been declared endangered and is protected (Díaz Díaz 1984). Guánica, Susúa and Maricao Forests are public lands belonging to the Commonwealth of Puerto Rico, Guánica having also been designated a biosphere reserve; Guánica Forest includes two separate areas (2,759 ha east of Guánica Bay and 700 ha west of Guánica Bay) and the Susúa Forest includes 1,287 ha (Noble *et al.* 1986; see Remarks 8). It is estimated that 53% of the species's current range is protected in the Guánica and Susúa Commonwealth Forests (Vilella and Zwank 1988); but see Threats. Suitable habitat for the species throughout Puerto Rico and offshore adjacent islands was unsuccessfully searched between 1969 and 1971 (for localities and dates of these searches see Kepler and Kepler 1973). The present geographic range of the species has been delineated precisely, and field data have been transferred to maps using an electronic digitizer and planimeter (F. J. Vilella *in litt.* 1992).

MEASURES PROPOSED Further distributional studies are required in order to seek ways of protecting as many possible areas where the species is found. Private land on which the species occurs (i.e. Guayanilla and Parguera Hills, Sierra Bermeja, and the land adjacent to Guánica, Susúa and Maricao Forests and Ensenada) should be protected and managed for optimum benefit to the nightjars. Habitat destruction or modification other than for the management of the species should be prevented. Buffer zones around critical nesting or feeding areas must be delineated and new lands around present habitat protected immediately. Private owners of nightjar habitat should be contacted and encouraged to manage habitat which they control voluntarily. Regular population monitoring is needed for the immediate future to assess general population trends and the effects of management actions. Vilella and Zwank (1988) also recommended that public education and cooperation between government agencies and private landowners will help to ensure the continued existence of the Puerto Rican Nightjar.

REMARKS (1) The three known areas for the species (i.e. Guánica Forest, Susúa Forest and Guayanilla Hills), following the range extension given in Distribution, are better regarded as

Guánica-Bermeja, Susúa-Maricao and Guayanilla-Peñuelas (F. J. Vilella *in litt.* 1992). (2) For a map of the census routes in the Guánica and Susúa Forests and a summary of the results in each route, see Kepler and Kepler (1973). (3) Although Kepler and Kepler (1973) and Noble *et al.* (1986) assumed each singing nightjar represented a breeding pair, Vilella and Zwank (1987) found that unmated males may also sing and thus referred to "singing males" rather than treating each singing nightjar as a breeding pair. (4) This estimation is based on total population counts from which an index of abundance was obtained (F. J. Vilella *in litt.* 1992). (5) A map showing the census routes and partial results can be found in Vilella and Zwank (1987). (6) Searches for the species in the areas from where the species has been recently reported (i.e. Sierra Bermeja and at Parguera Hills) between 1969 and 1970 were unsuccessful (see Kepler and Kepler 1973), but F. J. Vilella (*in litt.* 1992) has indicated that the discovery of the species in these areas was achieved with the additional help of playback recordings, an important aid not available to Kepler and Kepler (1973). (7) The vegetation in Susúa Forest would in the past have belonged to the "lower cordillera forest", but current vegetation there ("secondary scrub vegetation") is similar to the "dry limestone forest" in flora and structure (Kepler and Kepler 1973). (8) According to Noble *et al.* (1986) 240 ha of the Susúa Forest are not occupied by the nightjars, this comprising riparian and man-transformed habitat.

JAMAICAN PAURAQUE *Siphonorhis americanus* **E/Ex**[4]

Endemic to Jamaica, this rare pauraque is known from very few records, the last of which was in 1859, although there have been some recent unconfirmed reports. Almost nothing has been documented about the ecology of the bird, to the extent that it is still uncertain whether it inhabited tall forest or arid scrub.

DISTRIBUTION This species is endemic to Jamaica and is apparently known from just three specimens, all taken before 1860 (Greenway 1958). The localities, which are spread throughout the island, are (from west to east): Savanna-la-Mar (in the Bluefields area) in Westmoreland, where a male (in BMNH) was collected in August 1858 (Osburn 1859, Greenway 1958, Sutton 1981); Freeman's Hall near Albert Town in Trelawney, where a female (in BMNH) was taken in September 1859 (Bond 1956b, Greenway 1958, Sutton 1981); and near Linstead, St Thomas-in-the-Vale (the Worthy Park area of St Catherine), where one of a pair was collected (March 1863, Sutton 1981: see Remarks); the St Catherine Hills themselves were identified as a general area of occurrence by March (1863).

Recent unconfirmed reports (i.e. of birds that could not be ascribed to either of the two other caprimulgids on the island) include: a bird seen several times on one night during February 1975 in the Portland Ridge area (Sutton 1981); and one seen at Milk River in the 1980s (Reynard 1988: see below).

POPULATION The former status of the Jamaican Pauraque is essentially unknown, March (1863) simply reporting it to be "often met with in the St Catherine Hills". Greenway (1958) suggested that it must always have been localized, and Fuller (1987) that it was extremely rare even at an early date, both authors using the fact that the bird was unknown to P. H. Gosse (or his acquaintances) between 1830 and 1840 to justify their conclusions. However, the testimony of March (1863) cited above suggests that historically it was at least locally not uncommon.

As the last record was of a specimen taken in 1859 or 1860, this bird has long been considered possibly or probably extinct (e.g. Sclater 1910, Bangs and Kennard 1920, Greenway 1958, Bond 1979), but the same authors also admit the possibility that a population still exists somewhere on the island. There have indeed been a small number of unconfirmed recent reports: a bird seen in the Portland Ridge area in February 1975 had plumage and physical characteristics incompatible with the other two caprimulgids on the island (Sutton 1981), although it now seems likely that it was a Common Potoo *Nyctibeus griseus* (C. Levy *in litt.* 1992); a bird was seen at Milk River (Reynard 1988); and a hunter in Hellshire Hills described a caprimulgid that appeared likely to be this pauraque (N. Varty *in litt.* 1990).

ECOLOGY Very little is known of the ecology of the species, none of the collectors or observers noting anything referring to habitat or behaviour. Bond (1979) intimated that it occurred (or may still occur) in semi-arid woodland such as in the Hellshire Hills, and AOU (1983) extended this, claiming that it was (or is) a bird of scrubby woodland and partly open situations in arid or semi-arid country: both these statements appear to be based on the habitat requirements of the closely related Least Pauraque *Siphonorhis brewsteri*. The three collecting localities where the species has been taken indicate that it is or was perhaps one of taller forest (see Sutton 1981): however, all the recent unconfirmed records have come from the semi-arid areas along the south coast (see above). Lack (1976) averred that it formerly occurred in lowland woodland, its relatively short wings and tail suggesting that it hunted amongst trees and not in the open. Bangs and Kennard (1920) concluded that it undoubtedly nested on the ground.

THREATS The mongoose *Herpestes auropunctatus* was introduced onto the island during 1872 (Bond 1956b), and Bangs and Kennard (1920) judged that as the bird "undoubtedly nested on the ground... [it] probably fell an easy prey to the mongoose". Greenway (1958) reinforced the idea that introduced mammal species were responsible for the extirpation of this bird, but noted that since the mongoose was not introduced until 1872, it can be assumed that rats *Rattus* spp. were the cause of any decline prior to this date. As it is apparently unknown exactly which habitat type the species preferred, the threat from habitat destruction is difficult to assess. However, the loss of at least 75% of the original forest cover on Jamaica, with remaining forest largely secondary in nature (Haynes *et al.* 1989) presumably had (and perhaps continues to have) an adverse effect: deforestation continues at a rate of 3.3% per year (Eyre 1987, Varty 1991). The threat of habitat destruction was further exacerbated in 1988 when much of remaining forest was damaged by Hurricane Gilbert (Varty 1991), although dry limestone forest was relatively unaffected and occurs at two sites, namely Hellshire Hills and Portland Ridge (Vogel and Kerr in press).

MEASURES TAKEN None is known. The first two Jamaican national parks (one marine and one terrestrial) are being established, although neither includes habitat suitable for this species (N. Varty verbally 1992). The recent rediscovery of a small population of the Jamaican Iguana *Cyclura collei* has led to fieldwork being concentrated in dry limestone forest, during which the pauraque is being searched for (with assistance from the Gosse Bird Club) (C. Levy *in litt.* 1992).

MEASURES PROPOSED The major priority for conservation in Jamaica must be the control of deforestation (Varty 1991), and before specific measures can be outlined for the Jamaican Pauraque, the species has to be rediscovered and an assessment of its ecological requirements made. Only when this has been done can specific areas or habitat types be proposed for protection.

REMARKS The specimen in USNM was collected "near Spanish Town" (on the label) by W. T. March who, however, only mentioned taking one specimen (from near Linstead) in his paper (March 1863): it is therefore probable that "near Linstead" in fact refers to "near Spanish Town", and that the bird is known from just three collecting localities (*contra* Reynard 1988, who suggested that there are four specimens). The specimen in USNM is labelled as a male taken on 19 November 1860, although both the sex and date of collection are questioned in the computerized catalogue.

SICKLE-WINGED NIGHTJAR *Eleothreptus anomalus* K[12]

This curious small nightjar remains very poorly known although it appears to extend over a large range from central and south-eastern Brazil south through eastern Paraguay into the northern parts of Argentina, and is seemingly tied to the fringes of wetland habitats, where it may suffer from farming developments. Its voice needs to be learnt for future survey work.

DISTRIBUTION The Sickle-winged Nightjar has been recorded from central and eastern Brazil, eastern Paraguay and northern Argentina. The repeated inclusion of Uruguay within its range (e.g. Pinto 1938, Olrog 1979, Sick 1985, Collar and Andrew 1988, Bernardes *et al.* 1990) is probably in error, as no specimen is known from the country (F. Achaval *in litt.* 1986) and it remains unlisted in recent national avifaunal reviews (e.g. Cuello and Gerzenstein 1962, Gore and Gepp 1979, Cuello 1985); nevertheless, the record from Colón, immediately across the río Uruguay in Argentina, indicates the likelihood of the species's presence in the country.

Brazil The distribution of this species largely coincides with that of the more southerly Atlantic Forest in the country, but two records, one from Distrito Federal and one from Minas Gerais, indicate a wider range or possibly some migratory movement north or north-westwards into the interior (as shown, for example, by the near-threatened Swallow-winged Cotinga *Phibalura flavirostris*: see Snow 1982), although the dates tend to gainsay this. In the following account, records are given from north to south (or, where at similar latitudes, from east to west) with coordinates taken from Paynter and Traylor (1991).

Distrito Federal A specimen was collected in Brasília National Park[1] in late September 1978 (Straube 1991). The species is listed as inhabiting wetland margins in cerrado by Negret *et al.* (1984), but it is not known whether this was based on anything beyond the foregoing specimen record.

Minas Gerais Two females were collected at Lagoa Santa[2] on 2 August 1847 (Reinhardt 1870, Krabbe undated).

São Paulo Records are from: Orissanga[3] (Irisanga), 22°12'S 46°57'W, January 1823 (von Pelzeln 1868-1871); rio das Pedras[4], 22°17'S 47°02'W, February 1947 (Straube 1991; see Remarks 2); Mato Dentro[5], December 1818 (von Pelzeln 1868-1871); Fazenda Pedras, Avaré[6], November 1963 (Straube 1991; see Remarks 2); Ipanema[7], August, September, November and December in the years 1819-1822 (von Pelzeln 1868-1871); Moji das Cruzes[8], October 1932, July 1933 (Pinto 1938, Straube 1991); Goyao[9] (untraced, but between Moji das Cruzes and São Paulo), January 1819 (von Pelzeln 1868-1871); Ipiranga[10], a suburb of São Paulo, February 1906, December 1931, October 1932 (von Ihering and von Ihering 1907, Pinto 1938); Alambari[11], July 1820 (von Pelzeln 1868-1871; see Remarks 3); Itapetininga[12], October 1964 (specimen in LSUMZ); Paranapiacaba[13] ("Alto da Serra, Cubatão"), 23°47'S 46°19'W, November 1900 (Pinto 1938); Itararé[14], March 1821 (von Pelzeln 1868-1871; see Remarks 4).

Paraná Records are from: Curitiba[15], November 1820 (von Pelzeln 1868-1871); Cambuí Biological Reserve[16], Curitiba, November 1986; Laranjeiras, Piraquara[17], August 1988 (Straube 1991); Umbará, Mandirituba[18], May 1959 (Straube 1991).

Santa Catarina There is a bibliographical source for the occurrence of the species in the state (Sick *et al.* 1981), but it remains untraced.

Rio Grande do Sul The only record is of a road-kill near a marshy reservoir west of Pântano Grande[19] in the middle of the state in October 1971 (Belton 1984-1985). However, von Ihering and von Ihering (1907) mentioned Pelotas as a site.

Paraguay All records are from east of the río Paraguay at: Colonia Risso[20], río Apa, in Concepción department, sometime between the end of August and the start of November 1893 (Salvadori 1895b); Ñu Guazú[21] (8 km north-east of the centre of Asunción, bordering the arroyo Ytay), August 1989 (Contreras and González Romero 1989); Caravini (untraced), Villarrica[22], Guaíra department, April 1924 (specimen in BMNH); Estancia Cerrito Vargas (untraced), Misiones department[23], undated (T. Granizo *per* F. E. Hayes *in litt.* 1991). The species may thus occur throughout eastern Paraguay (F. E. Hayes *in litt.* 1991; see Remarks 5).

Argentina Olrog (1979) listed the provinces of Formosa, Chaco, Santa Fé, northern Buenos Aires and the chaco of Salta, while Short (1975) identified Santa Fé, Chaco and Buenos Aires and probably also eastern Formosa and Corrientes; a record from Catamarca seems likely to be in error (Steullet and Deautier 1939, M. Nores *in litt.* 1992), and the inclusion of Salta on the map in Narosky and Yzurieta (1987) may also be a slip. More specific and mostly recent records are: (*Misiones*) Iguazú National Park[24], one "accidental" female (M. Rumboll *in litt.* 1986) and this or another bird in the "Apto. Viejo" (C. Saibene *per* J. C. Chebez *in litt.* 1992); (*Corrientes*) Estancia Santa Teresa, Mburucuyá[25] (inside the proposed Mburucuyá National Park), September 1989 (J. Hutton *per* J. C. Chebez *in litt.* 1992); Puerto Luján[26], Ituzaingó department, January 1990 (S. Heinonen *per* J. C. Chebez *in litt.* 1992); (*Formosa*) Pilcomayo National Park[27], January 1988, and between Fortín Pilcomayo[28] and Lamadrid, January 1991 (F. N. Moschione and J. San Cristóbal *per* M. Pearman *in litt.* 1992); Estancia El Bagual (untraced), Laishi department[29], two birds in January 1992 (F. N. Moschione and R. Banchs *per* M. Pearman *in litt.* 1992); (*Chaco*)[30] unspecified areas in the east, February and August (Contreras *et al.* 1990; also Lynch Arribálzaga 1920); (*Santiago del Estero*) by a small lagoon 3 km from the Río Hondo Dam[31], where one bird was seen in September 1976 (Nores *et al.* 1991, M. Nores *in litt.* 1992); (*Santa Fe*) (Villa) Ocampo[32], undated but evidently at the start of the century (Hartert and Venturi 1909); Tostado[33], one male from November 1937, 35 km to the north (Pereyra 1939, Giai 1950) and two males from February 1945 (specimens in MACN); (*Entre Ríos*) La Azotea, in Diamante National Park[34], August 1990 (G. Sartori *per* J. C. Chebez *in litt.* 1992); El Palmar National Park[35], by arroyo Palmar, one bird seen on 19 January 1984 and again in 1985 (M. Nores and D. Yzurieta *in litt.* 1986); Colón[36], on the banks of the río Uruguay, January 1979 (M. Nores and D. Yzurieta *in litt.* 1986); Puerto Boca[37], 33°03'S 58°23'W, December 1991 and January 1992, where at least two birds were present, and often (if not always) near the río Gualeguaychu (E. I. Abadie, B. M. López Lanús and M. Pearman *in litt.* 1992, whence coordinates); Ceibas[38], 33°18'S 58°45'W, November 1987 (E. I. Abadie *per* M. Pearman *in litt.* 1992, whence coordinates); (*Buenos Aires*) Quilmes[39], near Buenos Aires, March 1877 (Holmberg 1939).

POPULATION The Sickle-winged Nightjar is an unknown quantity. It appears almost always to have been found singly, and in most cases only a single record has come from each locality. It is widely accepted to be a rare bird (Belton 1984-1985, Contreras *et al.* 1990, Canevari *et al.* 1991; also M. Nores and D. Yzurieta *in litt.* 1986, J. C. Chebez *in litt.* 1986, D. A. Scott *in litt.* 1986, F. E. Hayes *in litt.* 1991), but its seemingly extensive range, from Brasília south to Buenos Aires and from São Paulo west to Santiago del Estero, suggests that it must be seriously overlooked, after the fashion of certain nocturnal, marsh-dwelling rails. Contreras *et al.* (1990) expressed this view, but also speculated that it still appeared to be a very local ("focal" [*sic*]) bird with enormous distances between populations.

ECOLOGY Very little is known. Both Negret *et al.* (1984) and Sick (1985) referred to the species living on the edges of marshes, and this seems to be confirmed by the records from near waterbodies in Distribution for Brazil (Rio Grande do Sul), Paraguay (Ñu Guazú) and Argentina (Santiago del Estero and Entre Ríos); thus the Río Hondo Reservoir record was at a lagoon

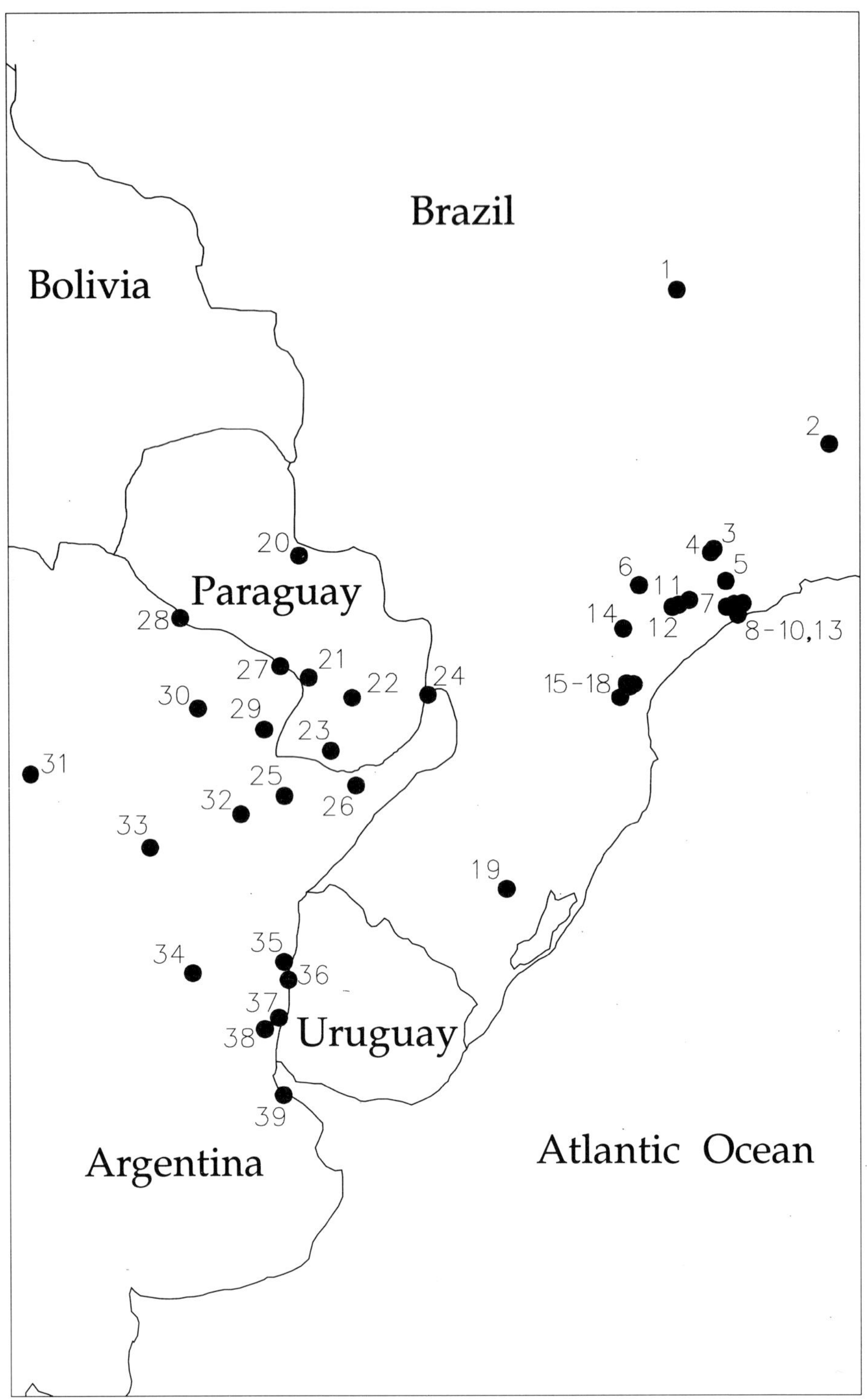
Brazil
Bolivia
Paraguay
Uruguay
Argentina
Atlantic Ocean
1
2
3
4
5
6
7
8-10,13
11
12
14
15-18
19
20
21
22
23
24
25
26
27
28
29
30
31
32
33
34
35
36
37
38
39

ordered by "sunchales" and spiny scrub, the bird in question perching on bushes and wire fencing, those on the río Uruguay, by arroyo Palmar and at Puerto Boca were by gallery forest on a river bank or along a stream (M. Nores and D. Yzurieta *in litt.* 1986, M. Nores *in litt.* 1992, M. Pearman *in litt.* 1992), and that at Ceibas was in chaco-type woodland dominated by *Prosopis affinis* near a small marsh (E. I. Abadie *per* M. Pearman *in litt.* 1992). Moreover, two specimens from Paraná were collected in or near marshes (Straube 1991). Short (1975) listed the species as a chaco-dweller, inhabiting open country and forest edge but favouring the vicinity of water. Contreras *et al.* (1990) named its habitat as humid tropical and subtropical savanna especially with grassland, also along streams, pools, marshes and flooded palm-groves. Reinhardt (1870) stated that the Minas Gerais birds were taken in cerrado, but this may have referred more to the general area rather than to the specific collecting site.

Stomach contents of one specimen were small beetles, moths and ants (Pereyra 1939), and of another (flushed from a clump of thistles) insects (Sclater and Hudson 1888-1889).

Two eggs and a dead bird were acquired in "Alto da Serra" on 17 November (von Ihering 1902). Three just fledged young (not still unfledged, as in Straube 1991) were collected in December (von Pelzeln 1868-1871). The specimen (in LSUMZ) from Itapetininga, October, had developing ovaries, as did those in August from Piraquara (Straube 1991) and Lagoa Santa (Reinhardt 1870). Contreras *et al.* (1990) could not judge from their evidence whether the species was resident or migratory in Chaco, Argentina, and indeed it is not clear if there are any records for the country between March and August; and while Pereyra (1939) described it as sedentary around Tostado in Entre Ríos, Giai (1950) – about whose work Pereyra had been writing – called it very tame (so that it could be caught by hand) when nesting but as wary as other caprimulgids when about to migrate.

THREATS It is possible that stock-raising has taken a toll of this species through grazing and trampling at the borders of lakes and marshes, and that agricultural pressures on wetlands in general (including drainage and reclamation) have caused loss of much habitat (J. C. Chebez *in litt.* 1986, D. F. Stotz *in litt.* 1988). Against this, the sites where the species has been found to date are similar to thousands of others that still exist in Argentina (M. Nores *in litt.* 1992), and the factors behind its (apparent) rarity are thus basically unknown.

MEASURES TAKEN The Sickle-winged Nightjar is protected under Brazilian law (Bernardes *et al.* 1990). There are records of the species from Brasília National Park and Cambuí Biological Reserve in Brazil, and Iguazú, Mburucuyá (still being planned), Pilcomayo, Diamante and El Palmar National Parks in Argentina (see Distribution).

MEASURES PROPOSED The voice of this bird needs to be discovered and recorded, so that ornithologists can be on the alert for the sound during any lacustrine surveys they undertake within its range. Special attention might be given to existing protected areas and the size of the populations they hold. The ecological needs of the species should be determined in the process, and some assessment made of the density at which it is capable of living. Management may then be necessary.

REMARKS (1) The Sickle-winged Nightjar is a distinctive species in its own genus, based largely on the curiously shaped wings of the male (see, e.g., von Ihering 1898, Canevari *et al.* 1991). (2) It is assumed here that rio das Pedras is as located by Paynter and Traylor (1991); Straube (1991) did not map it, but may have intended to under his site 9, which he labels "Ipiranga e Fazenda Pedras", although *Fazenda* Pedras belongs to his site 3, Avaré, suggesting a confusion with *rio das* Pedras. (3) The locality given by von Pelzeln (1868-1871) as

"Cimiterio" is what in his itinerary of J. Natterer's travels he called "Cimeterio do Lambari". Paynter and Traylor (1991) surmised that this may be Alambari, which seems entirely probable (and hence it is mapped thus here), given that Natterer was at the site on a journey between Ipanema and Itararé. However, for some reason Straube (1991) located it north-east of Ipanema. (4) The itinerary in von Pelzeln (1868-1871) contradicts the assertion in the text that Natterer was in Itararé in March in any of his years in Brazil, but 1821 seems the likeliest candidate. (5) There is a possible sighting of a bird at a marsh near Villeta, Central department, January 1990 (J. Escobar *in litt.* 1991).

WHITE-CHESTED SWIFT *Cypseloides lemosi* I[7]

This aerial species is only known with certainty from the southern end of the Cauca valley, southwest Colombia, although a recent unconfirmed record from Napo province in Ecuador suggests that it may range more widely. It has apparently been recorded just once in Colombia since 1966.

DISTRIBUTION The White-chested Swift is, with certainty, known only from the middle and upper Cauca valley, Valle and Cauca departments, south-western Colombia. However, there has recently been an unconfirmed record of birds in Napo province, Ecuador, c.400 km south of the known Colombian range. Unless otherwise stated, coordinates are from Paynter and Traylor (1977, 1981).

Colombia Within the foothills of the Cauca valley, records of this bird come from between Cali and Popayán, where precise localities include: (*Valle*) Cerro de los Cristales ("above Cali", at the west-central part of the city, now within urban limits: LGN), where birds were seen in April 1962 (Eisenmann and Lehmann 1962); (*Cauca*) Hacienda San Julián (untraced, but near Santander, and possibly near San Julián at 3°05'N 76°31'W), where a female (in UV) was collected in June 1966; Santander (3°01'N 76°28'W), where three birds were taken from a flock in April 1961 (Eisenmann and Lehmann 1962); Cerro Coronado (untraced, but apparently very close to Santander), where flocks have been seen, and where specimens were taken in October 1951 and 1957 (Eisenmann and Lehmann 1962); Salvajina hydroelectric plant on the río Cauca near Suárez, where 12 birds were seen in August 1989 (A. J. Negret *in litt.* 1990); Mondomo (2°53'N 76°33'W; 16 km south-south-west of Santander, on the right bank of the río Ovejas), where birds were seen in February 1960 and May 1962 (Eisenmann and Lehmann 1962); and c.8 km south of Pescador (2°47'N 76°33'W), where birds were seen in October 1962 (Eisenmann and Lehmann 1962).

Ecuador At least two birds almost certainly of this species were seen above Archidona (0°55'S 77°48'W) on the road to Loreto, Napo province, in a flock of c.150 *Cypseloides* swifts at 1,060 m on 31 March 1990 (B. M. Whitney *in litt.* 1991).

POPULATION This species is seemingly very rare and localized: Eisenmann and Lehmann (1962) reported flocks of 20-25, sometimes mixed with other swift species, in the Cali–Santander area from 1951 to 1962, suggesting that the White-chested Swift may have been fairly common in the 1950s and early 1960s. All of these flocks were observed between 16h30 and 18h30 (Eisenmann and Lehmann 1962), and therefore perhaps were "roosting" congregations. Since 1966, when a specimen was collected near Santander (see above), searches for the species at several of the historical localities have failed to find it (LGN). However, the observation of 12 birds in August 1989 near Suárez (see Distribution) confirms that the species still exists in small numbers. The probable record of at least two birds in Ecuador may represent either wanderers or non-breeders from Colombia or residents from a previously unknown population (B. M. Whitney *in litt.* 1991).

ECOLOGY The White-chested Swift has been recorded from between 1,000 and 1,300 m in the foothills of the upper Cauca basin; a flock seen in April was flying over pasture in flat country, but all other records have been in hilly or eroded areas where the bare red soil is sparsely covered with coarse grass interspersed with a small melastomataceous bush and a few other scattered bushes and trees including *Lonchocarpus* sp. and *Cecropia* sp. (Eisenmann and Lehmann 1962). Flocks described as "small" and elsewhere given as between 20 and 25 birds were noted as either single-species congregations, or associated with groups of White-collared Swift *Streptoprogne zonaris*, Chestnut-collared Swift *Cypseloides rutilus*, or White-chinned Swift *C. cryptus* (Eisenmann and Lehmann 1962); the birds seen in Ecuador were associated with a loose feeding flock of *Cypseloides*, almost definitely *cryptus* (B. M. Whitney *in litt.* 1991). All flocks seen by Eisenmann and Lehmann (1962) were recorded between 16h30 and 18h30, when they were either feeding (from 15 to 25 m high in the air) or apparently moving through, unless congregating prior to "roosting". The birds seen in Ecuador were observed for c.45 minutes during the early morning, feeding at heights of 50-100 m (B. M. Whitney *in litt.* 1991).

The seasonal movements of this species are unknown: birds have been recorded in the Cauca valley during most months from early February through to the end of October (see Distribution), and are presumably resident (Eisenmann and Lehmann 1962); however, breeding has never been recorded, and the probable record from Ecuador suggests that seasonal movements may occur or even that some individuals are being displaced (B. M. Whitney *in litt.* 1991; see above). Breeding was suspected to occur in the higher hills of the Cauca valley, with immature birds collected in October (Eisenmann and Lehmann 1962). Birds were assumed to build nests in cavities in the soft, bare earth (Eisenmann and Lehmann 1962), although the other members of this genus all nest in rocky ravines and caves, often close to water (F. G. Stiles *in litt.* 1992).

THREATS None is known; however, agrochemical usage in the Cauca valley may have affected the population (A. J. Negret *in litt.* 1990). Also, with the ecological requirements of the species remaining unclear, the effect of the expanding area of eroded ground within its Colombian range is unquantifiable. The type of habitat described in Ecology exists around Santander on both sides of the Cauca valley from the eastern foothills of the West Andes to the western foothills of the Central Andes, being at its widest (c.30 km) near Santander, but it stretches north in two prongs: one along the eastern foothills of the West Andes, narrowing to c.15 km north of Buenos Aires,

Cauca, and to just 3 km at the northern limit in Vijes, Valle; and the other in the western foothills of the Central Andes, north to the río Palo region, a little north-east of Caloto (Eisenmann and Lehmann 1962). This U-shaped area is probably the result of deforestation, and is increasing (Eisenmann and Lehmann 1962). The critical factor, however, is considered to be the availability of safe nest-sites (F. G. Stiles *in litt.* 1992), and until its breeding grounds have been identified, specific threats remain difficult to assess.

MEASURES TAKEN None is known, although Cerro Munchique is situated in the background of one of the habitat photographs in Eisenmann and Lehmann (1962), indicating that the species may occur within the Munchique National Park, which has some of its 44,000 ha within the correct altitudinal range (CNPPA 1982). Los Farallones de Cali National Park is also close to one of the few known localities (i.e. west of Cali), and the bird may well occur there.

MEASURES PROPOSED The first challenge is for ornithologists to begin finding regular sites where this species can be found and, perhaps, studied. The extent to which birds have been overlooked or ignored in the past is hard to judge, but it seems possible that some dedicated swift-watching at known sites or wherever feeding flocks are noted might begin to yield new records. If the breeding areas can then be found, along with the type of habitat that the species prefers to feed over, the extent and causes of the threats that it faces may be determined. Systematic searches for the species's breeding grounds should be undertaken in Munchique and Los Farallones de Cali National Parks (see equivalent section under Multicoloured Tanager *Chlorochrysa nitidissima*).

HOOK-BILLED HERMIT *Glaucis dohrnii* V/R[10]

This rare and little seen hummingbird of the of forest interior has been reduced by habitat loss to a few widely scattered localities in the Atlantic Forest region of Bahia and Espírito Santo, Brazil, and its status remains obscure.

DISTRIBUTION The Hook-billed Hermit (see Remarks 1) is endemic to the Atlantic Forest region of south-eastern Brazil from Bahia (see Remarks 2) south of Salvador south to Espírito Santo and possibly eastern Minas Gerais and Rio de Janeiro state (see Remarks 3), but is now confined to a very few, highly scattered sites within this range. In the following account, coordinates are from Paynter and Traylor (1991).

Bahia Records (north to south) are from: Serra do Palhão, c.14°15'S 39°50'W, rio Gongogi, near Jequié, December 1932 (Pinto 1935); the CVRD Porto Seguro Reserve, October 1987 (Collar 1987, Gonzaga *et al.* 1988), January 1988 (B. M. Whitney *in litt.* 1988), February 1989 (J. F. Pacheco *in litt.* 1991), although not found on a six days' visit in September 1990 (D. Willis *in litt.* 1991; see Threats); Monte Pascoal National Park, 1977 (King 1978-1979, Sick and Teixeira 1979); the valley of the rio Mucuri, October 1947 (Ruschi 1974), although absent there in the early 1960s (Ruschi 1965b).

Espírito Santo Records (unless otherwise indicated, as documented by Ruschi 1974) are (north to south) from: Três de Agosto, 18°08'S 40°07'W, October 1949 (Ruschi 1961); ribeirão (córrego) do Engano, 18°15'S 40°02'W, September 1941 and October 1943; Córrego do Veado Biological Reserve, 1960s (Ruschi 1965b); Fazenda Klabin (now corresponding to the Córrego Grande Biological Reserve), municipality of Conceição da Barra (not São João da Barra as in Sick 1985), October to December 1972, January and July 1973; Boa Lembrança (presumably Fazenda Boa Lembrança, rio Itaúnas, as in Aguirre and Aldrighi 1983), October 1943; Fazenda Roschisky, rio Itaúnas, June 1970 (specimen in MNRJ); rio Itaúnas, September 1950 (specimen in MZUSP) and November 1963 (specimen in AMNH); Pedro Canário, September 1963; São Mateus, September and November 1947; rio São José, September 1942; the CVRD Linhares Reserve (adjacent to Sooretama Biological Reserve), August 1988 (D. F. Stotz *in litt.* 1988), although not found in August 1991 (Stotz 1991); Baixo Guandu (in one case precisely Fazenda União), November 1925, December 1929, and September 1942. An older specimen is from an unspecified locality on the rio Doce, January 1906 (Pinto 1935; in MZUSP). In the 1960s the species was alleged to be restricted either to Fazenda Klabin (Ruschi 1967) or to Córrego do Veado (Ruschi 1969). A decade later Fazenda Klabin was identified as one of only two localities where the species was believed to survive (King 1978-1979, Sick and Teixeira 1979; see Population), but it was not found there in a rapid survey in October 1986 (Collar 1987).

Minas Gerais This state was included in the species's range by Ruschi (1965b), who reported having found it at Nanuque (but see Remarks 3), and by Grantsau (1989). The record from Baixo Guandu just across the border in Espírito Santo (see above) suggests that the species may once have occurred on the eastern fringes of the state.

Rio de Janeiro Although commonly given as a range state (e.g. in Salvin and Hartert 1892, von Ihering and von Ihering 1907, Pinto 1938, 1978, Meyer de Schauensee 1966, Grantsau 1989), the evidence for the species's occurrence there appears to derive entirely from an old, undated specimen in BMNH labelled "Rio de Janeiro" (see Remarks 4).

POPULATION From the scarcity of records it appears that the species was always rare, or at least very local, although King (1978-1979) considered that it "was once vastly more abundant than it is today". Whatever the relative degrees of rarity over the past hundred years, there seems to be little doubt that the species has suffered a great decline in both numbers and distribution as a result of the extensive forest destruction which has taken place in its range, and that it is probably still becoming rarer. Over 20 years ago it was judged the most threatened hummingbird species (Ruschi 1965b, 1967, Sick 1969, 1972) and it has been kept ever since in the "endangered" category of threatened bird lists (King 1978-1979, Sick and Teixeira 1979). A prediction that the species had no more than 10 years left, having reduced in range from 35,000 km^2 to only 100 km^2 in about 30 years (Ruschi 1967) was certainly (and fortunately) only an exaggerated guess to call attention to its plight, but its undoubtedly critical status continued to be acknowledged throughout the 1980s even in identification guides, where it has been called "on verge of extinction" (Meyer de Schauensee 1982) and "one of the rarest Brazilian species" (Grantsau 1989). In the late 1960s the species was said to be restricted to the Córrego do Veado Biological Reserve, where no more than 50 birds were believed to exist (Ruschi 1969); in the following decade, the Fazenda Klabin was elevated to the status of the species's last stronghold, where a population of about 20 was thought to persist (Ruschi 1976), but in 1977 the bird was found in the Monte Pascoal National Park, where it was considered to be uncommon (King 1978-1979). Regardless of this, Ruschi (1982) continued to affirm that the species only survived in Fazenda Klabin, with a population of 40 individuals left. Although it was not found in 1986 either in Monte Pascoal or in what remained of Fazenda Klabin's forest, an apparently strong population of the species was discovered in the CVRD Porto Seguro Reserve, which was then considered to be "evidently a stronghold of the species" (Collar 1987; but see Threats). The status of the species in the CVRD Linhares Reserve remains to be clarified.

ECOLOGY The Hook-billed Hermit inhabits lowland primary forest in Espírito Santo and Bahia (Ruschi 1982, Sick 1985). Birds in Porto Seguro were observed in the interior of closed-canopy forest, and mainly found in damp areas along streambeds, particularly in areas with abundant *Heliconia* plants (Gonzaga *et al.* 1987), but also once visiting a row of ornamental flowering trees near the forest (J. F. Pacheco *in litt.* 1991). This species has been recorded visiting the same flowers (e.g. of lemon trees) as the congeneric Rufous-breasted Hermit *Glaucis hirsuta*, sometimes at the same time (Sick 1985).

There is a great deal of inconsistency in recorded breeding data, incubation period being given as 16 days (Ruschi 1974) or 14-15 days (Ruschi 1982), and fledgling period from 22-30 days (Ruschi 1974) to 20-22 days (Ruschi 1982); another author (Grantsau 1989) states that the nest is similar to that of both Saw-billed Hermit *Ramphodon naevius* and Rufous-breasted Hermit, breeding occurring from September to February, and that the incubation and fledgling periods are, respectively, 15 and 27 days.

THREATS The massive deforestation which has taken place throughout the species's range has been regarded as the cause of its decline (Ruschi 1965b, 1974, 1982, Sick 1985), and even in most of the reserves where it has been found in the last three decades it is seemingly not safe; the privately owned forest at Fazenda Klabin, although now the IBAMA-run Córrego Grande Biological Reserve, has been reduced over the past two decades from 4,000 ha to only 1,200 ha, and now includes no significant watercourse except along its periphery (Gonzaga *et al.* 1987); the Monte Pascoal National Park is also under severe pressure (Redford 1989); the CVRD Porto Seguro Reserve, although generally well maintained, was under considerable pressure from squatters (Gonzaga *et al.* 1987), and has suffered also from fire (J. F. Pacheco *in litt.* 1991) and the construction of forest roads, which has caused many large ponds to form and hence destroy what may have been Hook-billed Hermit habitat (D. Willis *in litt.* 1991); fire spreading from the surrounding farmland is a permanent threat also to the Córrego do Veado Biological Reserve (Mendes 1986), which in any case only possesses a few small streams (Gonzaga *et al.* 1987). The

Itaúnas Forest Reserve that was created in 1948 would have served also for the protection of this species, but it was invaded by squatters and destroyed (Ruschi 1965b, 1967).

MEASURES TAKEN The species is listed on Appendix I of CITES and has been protected by Brazilian law since 1973 (LPG, Bernardes *et al.* 1990). Some of its present remnant populations should persist so long as the forests where they have been found continue to be preserved; but see Threats. On the basis of evidence under Population, the two critical areas for the species are the CVRD Porto Seguro Reserve in Bahia and the CVRD Linhares Reserve (possibly also adjacent Sooretama Biological Reserve) in Espírito Santo, but the former should not be looked upon as a final "safety net" reserve for this species until some better idea of its population size there is obtained (D. Willis *in litt.* 1991; see Threats), and the same could evidently apply to the Linhares site, although this is much larger and better kept than that at Porto Seguro.

MEASURES PROPOSED Establishment of a reserve for this species in the rio Itaúnas area was advocated several times in the past (Ruschi 1965b, Sick 1969, 1972), as well as the preservation and enlargement of the Córrego do Veado Biological Reserve (Ruschi 1969), and it is now evident that those claims have only partially succeeded; ironically, none of the above-mentioned areas seems to be of much present importance for the species, although these and other remaining patches of forest within its range might still harbour small but so far undetected populations, and merit being searched. Support for known key sites remains imperative. More specifically, it is important that CVRD continue recognizing the importance of their reserve at Porto Seguro and give it the excellent standard of protection afforded to their reserve at Linhares.

REMARKS (1) The Hook-billed Hermit has been intermittently treated either in the genus *Ramphodon*, endemic to the Atlantic Forest region of south-eastern Brazil (e.g. Ruschi 1965b, 1967, 1974, Sick 1969, 1972, 1985, Meyer de Schauensee 1982, Sibley and Monroe 1990), or in *Glaucis* (e.g. von Ihering and von Ihering 1907, Cory 1918, Pinto 1935, 1938, 1978, Ruschi 1961, Meyer de Schauensee 1966, Grantsau 1989). (2) Meyer de Schauensee's (1982) citation of this species's range as in Espírito Santo and "probably adjacent Bahia" is obviously mistaken, but it was apparently intended (Meyer de Schauensee 1970) to denote its possible disappearance from this latter state. (3) Although stating that he had never found verification for the species in Minas Gerais (*contra* Ruschi 1965b), Ceará and Rio de Janeiro, Ruschi (1974) implicitly admitted its former occurrence in these states by remarking that "it was extinct there due to habitat destruction". (4) The species's type-locality, mistakenly thought to be Ecuador in its original description, was proposed to be restricted to Rio de Janeiro by Pinto (1938); however, Pinto (1935) himself had included this state in the species's range with reservation and suggested Espírito Santo as the origin of the first specimen. Although certainly more realistic, Ruschi's (1974) defense of his belief that the type actually originated from Bahia (since trade skins mostly came from this state at that time and no material of this species is known from Rio de Janeiro) did not take account of the BMNH specimen (but see Remarks 3).

WHITE-TAILED SABREWING *Campylopterus ensipennis* V/R[10]

This large hummingbird is endemic to the montane forests of the coastal cordillera and Paria Peninsula, north-east Venezuela, and also the island of Tobago. On the mainland, it is threatened by widespread habitat loss, and on Tobago is only just starting to recover from the effects of a hurricane that destroyed much forest in 1963.

DISTRIBUTION The White-tailed Sabrewing is endemic to the Cordillera de Caripe (the eastern coastal mountain range) which runs along the borders of north-easternmost Anzoátegui, northern Monagas and Sucre states, and also the mountains of the Paria Peninsula (Sucre), Venezuela – an area to which five other threatened bird species are restricted (see Threats) – with a separate population on the island of Tobago, Trinidad and Tobago (see Remarks 1).

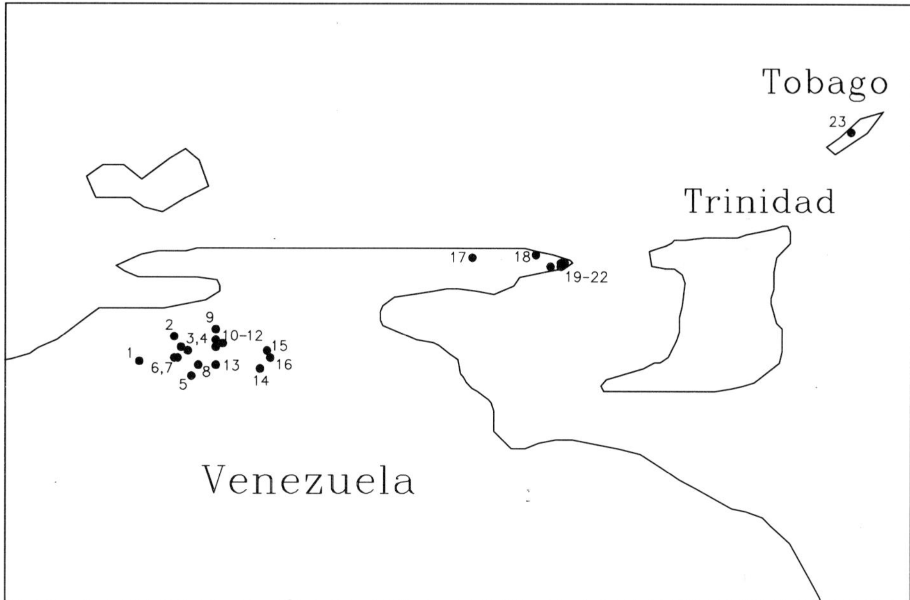

Venezuela Records of this large hummingbird, from roughly west to east and where longitudinal groupings occur, from north to south (treating the Paria Peninsula last), are as follows, with coordinates from Paynter (1982): Cerro Peonía[1] (10°11'N 64°07'W: on the border of all three states, but cited as evidence for the species's occurrence in Anzoátegui), a locality mentioned by Phelps and Phelps (1958); Quebrada Seca[2] (= Villarroel at 10°18'N 63°57'W, Sucre), near where a male (in AMNH) was taken in February 1898; Cumanacoa[3] (10°15'N 63°55'W, Sucre), where a male and two females (in AMNH) were taken in July 1896; San Rafael (c.10°15'N 63°55'W, and near Cumanacoa), and El Yaque[4] (10°14'N 63°53'W, both in Sucre), where six males and two females (in CM) were taken (between 760 and 945 m) in November 1929 and January 1930; Cerro Turumiquire[5] (10°07'N 63°52'W, the summit being in Monagas), where four males and five females (in FMNH) were collected at 1,830 m in February and March 1932, more recent records coming from the Turumiquire "Hydraulic" Reserve (G. Medina-Cuervo *in litt.* 1986: see Measures Taken); La Trinidad[6] (c.10°12'N 63°57'W), which was apparently a coffee plantation (Chapman 1925) on the northern slope of Cerro Turumiquire, where four males and two females (in COP) were taken in February and March 1963 between 1,700 and 1,800 m; Carapas[7] (c.10°12'N

63°56'W; also on the northern slope of Cerro Turumiquire, and adjacent to La Trinidad, Sucre), where a male and female (in AMNH) were taken in March 1925 at 1,700 m; Mirasol[8] (c.10°10'N 63°50'W; likewise on the slopes of Turumiquire), where seven males and two females (in CM, LACM) were taken in December 1929 between 915 and 985 m; Santa Ana[9] (10°20'N 63°45'W, Sucre), where a male (in AMNH) was taken in March 1898; Los Palmales[10] (c.10°17'N 63°45'W, Sucre), where four males (in AMNH, USNM) were taken in a coffee plantation during February and December 1898; Rincón de San Antonio[11] (c.10°16'N 63°43'W, Sucre), where a male (in AMNH) was taken in March 1898; La Tigrera[12] (10°15'N 63°45'W, Sucre), where a female (in AMNH) was collected in February 1898; Campo Alegre[13] (10°10'N 63°45'W, Sucre), where five males and two females (in AMNH) were collected in February and March 1898; El Guácharo[14] (10°09'N 63°32'W, Monagas), where two males (in AMNH, USNM) were taken in November 1898; Cerro Negro[15] (c.10°14'N 63°30'W, on the border of Monagas and Sucre), a locality mentioned by Phelps and Phelps (1958); and Caripe[16] (10°12'N 63°29'W: at 800 m on the eastern slope at the eastern end of the coastal range, Monagas), near where a male (in BMNH) was taken in June 1867 (see Remarks 2).

On the Paria Peninsula (Sucre), records come from: Cerro Humo[17] (c.10°40'N 62°30'W), where observations are from between 800 and 1,220 m (Phelps and Phelps 1958, Gardner and Brisley 1989; also G. Medina-Cuervo *in litt.* 1986, B. Swift *in litt.* 1986, M. Pearman *in litt.* 1991); and on the western end of the peninsula, Pargo[18] (10°43'N 62°03'W), where a male and female (in YPM) were collected in February 1937; Yacua[19] (10°39'N 61°59'W), where a male and female (in YPM) were taken also in Febraury 1937; Cerro “El Olvido” (c.2.5 km west of Cerro Azul, on the ridge between Cerros Patao and Azul), where Bond *et al.* (1989) recorded the species between July and September 1988; Cerro Azul[20] (c.10°40'N 61°56'W), mentioned by Phelps and Phelps (1958); above Cristóbal Colón[21] (= Macuro at 10°39'N 61°56'W, i.e. on the slopes of Cerros El Olvido and Azul), where five males and six females (in AMNH) were taken in May and June 1913 at 460 m; and Cariaquito[22] (c.10°40'N 61°55'W), where a specimen (in ANSP) was taken in 1911 (presumably away from the coast, towards Cerro Azul).

Trinidad and Tobago The presence of the White-tailed Sabrewing has only been confirmed on Tobago[23] (see Remarks 1).

Tobago Records from this island prior to the extensive forest destruction caused by Hurricane Flora in 1963 (see Population and Threats) include: Richmond (March 1897); Englishman Bay; Mondland; Castare; Parret Hall (all records from May 1903) (specimens in AMNH, BMNH, ROM); Hillsborough Stream, and various points along the main ridge between Parlatuvier and Roxburgh where birds were seen in February and June 1934 (Belcher and Smooker 1934-1937); and Pigeon Peak, where birds were found in February 1954 (Junge and Mees 1958). Not until the mid-1970s was the species noted again (see Population), when small groups were increasingly found in isolated pockets of forest on Main Ridge (ffrench 1988), with records coming from the East Tobago National Park (Thelen and Faizool 1980).

POPULATION This species generally seems to be abundant in areas where suitable habitat remains.

Venezuela On the Paria Peninsula, the White-tailed Sabrewing is still found to be common in available habitat, with for example 5-6 birds seen in one day on Cerro Humo in 1978-1979 (G. Medina-Cuervo *in litt.* 1986), six seen on 4 March 1984 (B. Swift *in litt.* 1986), and five seen there on 5 January 1989 (Gardner and Brisley 1989). This fact is also reflected in the study made on Cerro El Olvido in 1988 (Bond *et al.* 1989), when the bird was found to be abundant to 840 m and common to 880 m, with nine territorial males found on the transect which ran up the mountainside (giving a density of 1.5 pairs/ha). The collection of 11 birds above Macuro in 1913 (see Distribution) seems to confirm the species's historic abundance on the peninsula. B. Swift (*in litt.* 1988) suggests that the population of this species in the Paria Peninsula National Park (see Measures Taken) is a viable one.

The situation in the Cordillera de Caripe is less well known: historically the species was common (according to a label on a specimen in AMNH), and certainly the collection of specimens (see Distribution for numbers taken at particular localities) in the area suggests this; however, while there are few recent records, with the bird being judged "not very common" in the Turumiquire reserve in the late 1970s (G. Medina-Cuervo *in litt.* 1986), R. Ramírez (*in litt.* 1988) found it one of the commonest species captured in mist-nets during 1985-1986 fieldwork in forests around the Monagas–Sucre borders.

Trinidad and Tobago The White-tailed Sabrewing was formerly a fairly common to common resident of hill forest (Main Ridge) on Tobago (e.g. "found in some numbers" near the summit of Pigeon Peak in 1954), but in 1963 Hurricane Flora was thought to have destroyed all suitable forest, and indeed the species was not seen for a decade (Junge and Mees 1958, ffrench 1973, R. ffrench *in litt.* 1986, ffrench 1988). However, since 1974-1975, small groups have been increasingly located in small patches of forest that escaped the worst of the storm (R. ffrench *in litt.* 1986, ffrench 1988). Despite the fact that the species apppears to be holding its own in these forest remnants, the area of forest has hardly increased in 10 years and the species remains extremely rare and endangered (Thelen and Faizool 1980, R. ffrench *in litt.* 1986, ffrench 1988).

ECOLOGY In the Cordillera de Caripe, the White-tailed Sabrewing has been recorded from 760 to 1,830 m (Meyer de Schauensee and Phelps 1978 claim 700 to 2,000 m), but on the Paria Peninsula this range is 460 to 1,200 m (see Distribution). The reason for this geographic difference in altitudinal range is that this species (along with the rest of the montane fauna on the peninsula) responds directly to habitat rather than altitude *per se* (Bond *et al.* 1989). On isolated peaks and ridges, and coastal mountains (including peninsulas and islands), the vegetation zones are lower (vertically compressed) than on extensive mountain ranges or those further from the sea: this is known as the "Massenerhebung" effect, and is caused by a combination of high humidity, low nutrient availability and exposure to prevailing winds (these all being factors that effect the Paria Peninsula: Bond *et al.* 1989).

Whether on Tobago, Paria Peninsula or the "mainland", the White-tailed Sabrewing inhabits lower and upper montane forest (i.e. pre-montane and montane tropical forest in the upper tropical and subtropical zones: Phelps and Phelps 1958, G. Medina-Cuervo *in litt.* 1986, Bond *et al.* 1989). Birds have been recorded as common in mature secondary growth and plantations (occurring to c.600 m on the Paria Peninsula: R. Ramírez *in litt.* 1988, Bond *et al.* 1989). On Cerro Humo, B. Swift (*in litt.* 1986) found birds in the wet part of a coffee grove, while Gardner and Brisley (1989) concluded that the species was most obvious at *Heliconia* sp. on the forest edge near a stream. The bird seems to adapt well (at least on Cerro Humo and Cerro El Olvido) to plantations with *Heliconia* and other flowering shrubs (C. Sharpe *in litt.* 1992). The precise requirements of this species remain unknown, but it appears utilize mature secondary forest at lower altitudes, and to flourish in forest of various types and structures higher up (from 35 m tall closed canopy forest to lower, relatively open canopy cloud-forest: Bond *et al.* 1989).

Various food sources have been recorded including flowering bromeliads (ffrench 1973), banana blossoms and other flowering plants (B. Swift *in litt.* 1986), with Bond *et al.* (1989) noting that flowering *Palicourea* sp. trees appeared to be the sole food-plant for the species within the primary forest between July and September 1988; flycatching behaviour has also been observed (Bond *et al.* 1989). Birds perch 1-6 m up (low to middle branches; Meyer de Schauensee and Phelps 1978), and have been seen on exposed twigs in areas opened up by tree-falls and in dense understorey shrubs where the canopy is closed (B. Swift *in litt.* 1986, Bond *et al.* 1989).

Breeding has only been recorded on Tobago: one nest found on 23 February 1934 was placed in the fork of a branch in a coffee-like shrub c.2.5 m above the water of Hillsborough stream (Belcher and Smooker 1934-1937); another nest was discovered with two eggs on 14 February 1954, attached near the end of a pendular twig, c.1.75 m from the forest floor - the female was seen visiting the nest and incubating (Junge and Mees 1958). Also during February 1954 male birds were in "full song" (Junge and Mees 1958) although singing has also been noted as prominent (on Tobago) during April (ffrench 1973). None of the 11 Venezuelan specimens collected near Macuro (see Distribution) during May and June 1913 were in breeding condition, although male birds were noted as "territorial" during surveys from July to September (Bond *et al.* 1989). Interestingly, female birds were rarely seen during the July–September fieldwork on Cerro El Olvido (Bond *et al.* 1989), which may suggest that they were incubating, or feeding young: however, it should be noted that of c.110 sexed specimens, the ratio of males to females was 2:1.

THREATS The threats that the White-tailed Sabrewing faces are representative of those faced by the other five threatened species within its Venezuelan range, namely: Scissor-tailed Hummingbird *Hylonympha macrocerca* (only on the Paria Peninsula), White-throated Barbtail *Margarornis tatei* (on the Cordillera de Caripe and Paria), Venezuelan Flowerpiercer *Diglossa venezuelensis* (on the Cordillera de Caripe and Paria), Paria Redstart *Myioborus pariae* (only on the Paria Peninsula) and Grey-headed Warbler *Basileuterus griseiceps* (only in the Cordillera de Caripe: see relevant accounts), and are thus best treated for each of the discrete areas in question.

In the Cordillera de Caripe, human population pressure is severe: extensive deforestation of montane forest over much of the area has resulted and is the major threat (G. Medina-Cuervo *in litt.* 1986, Ridgely and Tudor 1989). Cutting of forest for agriculture and pasture has taken place (and is increasing), especially in the Turumiquire area (despite its inaccessibility) and, although farmers spare certain lauraceous trees to shade coffee plantations, the remaining forests (particularly palms) have been widely cleared (G. Medina-Cuervo *in litt.* 1986, Bosque and Ramírez 1988). The agricultural practices of campesinos in El Guácharo National Park are one specific cause of habitat destruction (CNPPA 1982), with the park (especially around Cerro Negro, and even more so around Caripe) suffering from repeated burnings and the removal of palm forest (R. Ramírez *in litt.* 1988): unfortunately, these agricultural activities have intensified since the 1970s (Bosque and Ramírez 1988: see following paragraph). In April 1991, a large forest fire devastated 1,760 ha of Cerro Negro (inside the national park), and although this area is being reforested by hand, it is difficult to assess what effects the fire had on the various species known to occur there (e.g. Grey-headed Warbler had been recorded there fairly frequently until that time: see relevant account) (M. L. Goodwin *in litt.* 1992).

On the Paria Peninsula (the information in this paragraph, unless otherwise stated, is from C. Sharpe *in litt.* 1989), almost all suitable habitat occurs in the national park (see Measures Taken): however, a recent increase in cash-crop agriculture practised by the local people has caused the destruction, through uncontrolled burning, of this higher-altitude forest. The main cause of the problem is the cultivation of "ocumo blanco", a root crop which demands completely clear ground for growth – most easily achieved by burning: its cultivation has been expanded on purely economic grounds in response to high market prices, replacing the former widespread cultivation of cacao. The situation progressively worsens with increasing density of farmers as one moves westwards, and unfortunately the richest cloud-forest is also found in the west. The forest destruction has caused landslides on the steep slopes of the peninsula, and streams have dried up. In June 1989 visible changes from 1988 were large areas of forest burned, several obvious recent landslides, and exceptionally dry terrain, many fruit crops having failed and other crops suffering from severe insect damage (thought to be caused by nutrient exhaustion brought on by monocultural farming practices). Cerro Humo, close to the mainland, has been affected by widespread deforestation, accessibility by roads, settlements and agriculture (a reflection of what is happening in the Caripe area), and Cerro Patao from cultivation (up to 800-1,000 m). Fortunately, the easternmost end around Macuro remains inaccessible by road, and fairly untouched although human disturbance is still creating pressure (G. Medina-Cuervo *in litt.* 1986, Bond *et al.* 1989). Perhaps the most serious development in recent years is the "Proyecto Cristobal Colón" proposal to construct a pipeline across the Paria Peninsula to connect gas reserves off the north coast to a port on the south side of the peninsula; some plans have shown that this pipe may run through the national park (C. Sharpe verbally 1991, M. L. Goodwin *in litt.* 1992).

On Tobago, the main threat was and is forest destruction. In 1963, Hurrican Flora destroyed much of the highland forests, and only small isolated patches managed to escape the worst of it: in one of these patches, an apparently stable population of birds was found in 1974-1975 (see Population). Although the forest is now regenerating it has hardly increased in 10 years, and must still be regarded as at risk from future hurricanes or human destruction (R. ffrench *in litt.* 1986, ffrench 1988).

MEASURES TAKEN Within this species's range, two national parks exist: (1) El Guácharo National Park, 82,900 ha (including Alejandro de Humboldt Natural Monument) covering Cerro Negro (CNPPA 1982, *World Birdwatch* 12,1-2 [1990]: 4) was increased to this size in 1989, when Mata de Mango (66,000 ha of primary forest) was added (R. Roca *in litt.* 1992); and (2) Paria Peninsula National Park, 37,500 ha (of which almost 80% maybe primary forest), covering all the montane areas between Cerro Humo and Cerro Azul (Bond *et al.* 1989), however, the south slope of Cerro Humo, which supports excellent cloud-forest habitat and populations of all the threatened species, is not within the boundaries of the park and is under increasing agricultural pressure (C. Sharpe *in litt.* 1992). The extension of El Guácharo National Park in 1989 added a large area of forest, including a hilly region (200-1,600 m) which probably favours (differentially) this species, White-throated Barbtail, Venezuelan Flowerpiercer and Grey-headed Warbler, although records of all four species are lacking (R. Roca *in litt.* 1992). In the Paria Peninsula National Park, the protected status has had little or no practical effect locally: although some people are aware of the park's existence, few understand its significance and hence cannot respect the boundaries or regulations, and there is little control on cultivation or hunting (Bond *et al.* 1989), although there are four park guards (who are hampered by a lack of resources and training: C. Sharpe *in litt.* 1989). At Turumiquire there is a "hydraulic" (presumably watershed) reserve, but this is heavily occupied with scattered human settlements, there is very little control, and this species is no longer common there (G. Medina-Cuervo *in litt.* 1986: see Population).

On Tobago, the White-tailed Sabrewing occurs in the East Tobago National Park (Thelen and Faizool 1980).

MEASURES PROPOSED Within the range of this species, there occur 12 other endemic birds (ICBP 1992, Crosby *et al.* in prep.), of which five are threatened (see accounts of species mentioned in Threats), and any conservation initiative in this area must consider the requirements of all six threatened species present. The ecological needs of these six species are inadequately known, and require work: however, the priorities for this assemblage are to determine the amount of available habitat remaining in the Cordillera de Caripe; ascertain which of the four species reported for the area are still present; and instigate protection for the forest. Such efforts should perhaps focus on obtaining information from the recently enlarged El Guácharo National Park, which may hold viable populations of this species, White-throated Barbtail, Venezuelan Flowerpiercer and Grey-headed Warbler (see relevant accounts). On the Paria Peninsula, almost all suitable areas for the five species that occur (see Threats) are within the national park: again, protection of the forests needs to be ensured; and the distribution of each of the species between Cerro Humo and Cerro Patao needs investigation. The omission of the excellent forest area on the south slopes of Cerro Humo from the park needs to be addressed, and must be incorporated into the park's boundaries as soon as possible. Bond *et al.* (1989) were unable to discover what the objectives of the Paria Peninsula National Park are, and put forward the following: (1) to conserve the montane forest and the fauna of the peninsula as an example of this biotype, and as a representative portion of the Cordillera de Caripe–Paria Peninsula centre of endemism; (2) to achieve the above by increasing the awareness of the local community (an education campaign would be desirable) and national scientists; and (3) to encourage limited, small-scale tourism to provide a small revenue for guides and to spread awarenesss of the park. Various other proposals, survey ideas and methods of implementation have been put forward (Bond *et al.* 1989, C. Sharpe *in litt.* 1989, *Env. Conserv.* 17 [1990]: 367-368)

In Tobago, the primary requirement is the regeneration of the highland forest, which will be most efficiently achieved by protecting the areas involved from encroaching agriculture and grazing animals (it may be appropriate to stress the area's watershed value). Since Trinidad and Tobago calls itself "the land of the hummingbird" (James and Hislop in press), a campaign on Tobago to make this the island's emblem could help focus attention on the need to achieve greater security for its habitat. The conservation and management of forest on the island ought also to benefit the little-known threatened endemic race *oberi* of the Striped Owl *Asio clamator* (see King 1978-1979, ffrench 1992).

REMARKS (1) Cory (1918) and Peters (1945) both suggested that this species is known from Trinidad, although Junge and Mees (1958) and ffrench (1973) stated that it remains unrecorded from Trinidad and the Bocas Islands. Twelve specimens (in BMNH, FMNH, MNHN, USNM, YPM) are all simply labelled "Trinidad" or "Trinity", one having the date of collection, 1860. Whether these birds were taken on Trinidad, or represent trade-skins collected on Tobago or in Venezuela (see Phelps and Phelps 1948) is unknown. The collectors of these birds, where known, were Balston, Elliot (in 1860), and possibly F. T. Jencks. (2) Caripe and Cerro Negro are often referred to as "Cerro Negro, Caripe" (e.g. Phelps and Phelps 1950). In this and other cases (see accounts for the species mentioned under Threats), Caripe (10°12'N 63°29'W, and south-east of Cerro Negro) was probably the base used for collecting on the slopes of the mountain, and not a collecting locality in its own right.

SHORT-CRESTED COQUETTE *Lophornis brachylopha* E[2]

Inhabiting the rapidly decreasing semi-deciduous forest on the slopes of the Sierra Madre del Sur of Guerrero, Mexico, this recently described hummingbird is still only known from a 40 km stretch of road, and is totally unprotected.

DISTRIBUTION Only recently recognized as a full species (Banks 1990; see Remarks), the Short-crested Coquette is known from a c.40 km of road in the Sierra Madre del Sur of Guerrero, Mexico (coordinates below are taken from CETN 1984b). The species was originally described from two adult males taken c.56 km (c.70 km in Banks 1990) north-west of Acapulco, at San Vicente de Benítez (17°18'N 100°17'W) in May 1947 (Moore 1949), and was not found again until a male and two females were collected at Arroyo Grande, 13 km north-east of Paraíso (17°20'N 100°13'W) in 1986 (Ornelas 1987, Howell 1989). Both of these localities are north-west of Acapulco along the Atoyac de Alvarez–Chilpancingo road, Arroyo Grande being c.10 km north-east of the type-locality (Banks 1990). A female was seen (the first observation of the species in the field) at Arroyo Grande on 14 April 1988 (Howell 1989, S. N. G. Howell *in litt.* 1991). Other observations (all during or since 1988) along this road are from: 3.5 km north of San Vicente de Benítez; between San Vicente de Benítez and Paraíso; 12-13 km north-east of Paraíso; 2-3 km south of Nueva Delhi (c.17°25'N 100°12'W, north of Paraíso); and 8-12 km north of Nueva Delhi (Howell 1992).

POPULATION Prior to the race *brachylopha* being given specific status, it was considered to be "apparently very rare in Mexico" (Blake 1953), or (erroneously) "accidental in south-west Guerrero" (Peterson and Chalif 1973; see Remarks). The female seen in April 1988 was observed for c.20 seconds after five days of searching (Howell 1989, 1992), and experiences of other birdwatchers in 1988 and 1989 seemed to confirm that this species (like all other *Lophornis* species: A. G. Navarro and A. T. Peterson *in litt.* 1991) was rare and hard to find.

However, observations of birds during 1990 suggested that the species is in fact relatively common (S. N. G. Howell *in litt.* 1991, Howell 1992): four were found in January, 8-12 km north of Nueva Delhi; three (a male and two females) on 23 March, 2-3 km south of Nueva Delhi; four on 21 May, 3.5 km north of San Vicente de Benítez; and seven on 23 May, between Paraíso and San Vicente de Benítez (making a total of 9-10 birds on this stretch of road) (Howell 1992). The Short-crested Coquette is thus locally common at the right season (Howell 1992), but presumably resident (see below).

ECOLOGY This coquette has been found in semi-deciduous tropical forest at the type-locality and in evergreen subtropical forest at Arroyo Grande (where it occurs sympatrically with the White-tailed Hummingbird *Eupherusa poliocerca*: see relevant account), its habitat generally being considered to be cloud-forest and edge (Ornelas 1987, S. N. G. Howell *in litt.* 1989; see below). San Vicente de Benítez is at about 915 m (not 460 m as given on the 1947 specimen labels: S. N. G. Howell *in litt.* 1989), and Arroyo Grande is at 1,350 m (Ornelas 1987), but with records coming from both north of Arroyo Grande (4-5 km north of Nueva Delhi is at 1,650 m) and south of San Vicente de Benítez, Howell (1992) gave the altitudinal range of the species as 900-1,800 m, although local people near Atoyac de Alvarez suggested that the species is highly seasonal and occurs down to almost 650 m in clear-cut secondary growth (A. G. Navarro and A. T. Peterson *in litt.* 1991). Howell (1992) suspected that this species breeds in cloud-forest from about November to February (this seems to be confirmed by the two specimens taken 29 April and 1 May 1986, which were in moult and had undeveloped gonads: Ornelas 1987), with post-breeding dispersal and the pursuit of flowers taking them to lower altitudes in March–May (there are no records from June to December).

The Short-crested Coquette was recorded flycatching in April 1988, but most subsequent records (from March to May, and in subtropical forest) have been of birds adjacent to the road where they were feeding at the flowers of *Clethra* cf. *mexicana*, *Inga* sp., *Conostegia* cf. *xalapensis* (probably), and *Cecropia* cf. *obtusifolia*; they have not apparently been recorded in or feeding on coffee (see Howell 1992).

THREATS The Short-crested Coquette is at present known from an extremely small area of the Sierra Madre del Sur which is suffering from steady habitat destruction (S. N. G. Howell *in litt.* 1987, Howell 1989; see White-tailed Hummingbird account) with, for example (between Paraíso and Nueva Delhi), the semi-deciduous forest being rapidly cleared for the cultivation of maize, fruit and coffee (Howell 1992, Navarro 1992): this forest-type is apparently the most perturbed in the region (A. G. Navarro *in litt.* 1991).

MEASURES TAKEN None is known.

MEASURES PROPOSED Protection of the forest within the immediate known range of this species is essential for its continued existence, and at the same time specific surveys should be undertaken east and west of the Paraíso area to determine its true distribution. Although a brief survey above Zihuatanejo failed to find the species, this area should perhaps be targeted for further work (A. G. Navarro and A. T. Peterson *in litt.* 1991). Any surveys and subsequent recommendations for protected areas should be coordinated with the measures undertaken for White-tailed Hummingbird and White-throated Jay *Cyanolyca mirabilis* (see relevant accounts): the available evidence suggests that the cloud- and subtropical forest areas in the vicinity of Nueva Delhi are important for all three of the above species, and should be a priority for any conservation efforts in the region. With the jay clearly requiring pine–oak forest, the White-tailed Hummingbird being restricted to cloud-forest, and this species needing semi-deciduous and cloud-forest, a protected area must embrace the full altitudinal complement of these habitats (see relevant accounts).

REMARKS The Short-crested Coquette was originally described as a subspecies of the Rufous-crested Coquette *Lophornis delattrei* (Moore 1949), its occurrence in Mexico being questioned and many ornithologists giving little credence to the 1947 record (Ornelas 1987, Howell 1989), which AOU (1983) totally ignored. The Rufous-crested Coquette was otherwise unknown north of Costa Rica (c.1,900 km away), the centre of abundance being from Panama to north Colombia and eastern Bolivia (Stiles and Skutch 1989). Following the 1988 observation, and having compared the 1986 specimens with other species of coquette, Howell (1989 and *in litt.* 1989) concluded that the Guerrero birds were quite unlike the Rufous-crested or any other coquette, and are obviously specifically distinct: a formal description and proposal for its specific status is given by Banks (1990).

COPPERY THORNTAIL *Popelairia letitiae* I[8]

Known from perhaps three nineteenth-century skins from Bolivia, this hummingbird if a good species – may prove to inhabit the Amazonian lowlands in the north of the country.

DISTRIBUTION The Coppery Thorntail is apparently known from only three nineteenth century specimens simply labelled from Bolivia (see Remarks). The two male specimens reported presumably came from north-eastern Bolivia (Remsen and Traylor 1989).

POPULATION The species has not been seen or collected this century (Remsen and Traylor 1989).

ECOLOGY Nothing is known; however, it could inhabit the Amazonian lowlands of northern Bolivia (Remsen and Traylor 1989), based on the facts that no other *Popelairia* has been recorded there (except for Black-bellied Thorntail *P. langsdorffi* in extreme north-west Pando) and that the other *Popelairia* have lowland distributions (J. V. Remsen *in litt.* 1991).

THREATS None is known.

MEASURES TAKEN None is known.

MEASURES PROPOSED Searches are needed in northern lowland Bolivia for this mysterious species.

REMARKS According to Peters (1945) and Meyer de Schauensee (1966, 1982), two male specimens of this species exist, although it is not clear in which museum(s) they are held; however, AMNH possesses an unsexed and presumably therefore third specimen, which was examined by R. Bleiweiss *in litt.* (1988), who considered it perhaps a late immature and, while expressing due caution on the evidence of a single skin, thought it represented a distinct form.

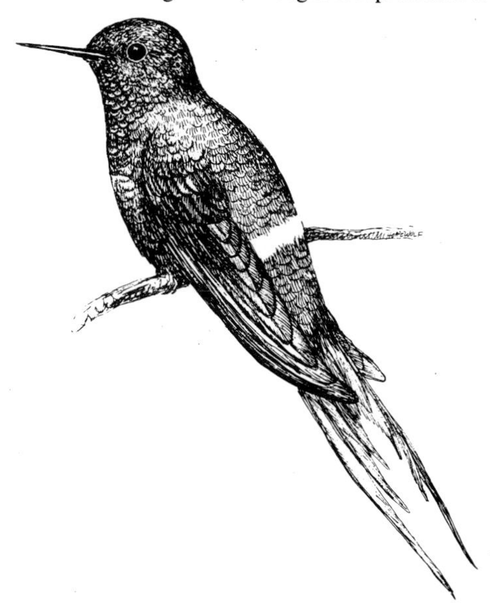

MEXICAN WOODNYMPH *Thalurania ridgwayi* I[7]

Restricted to a small area in western Mexico, this poorly known hummingbird has a patchy distribution in which it may well be threatened owing to habitat destruction.

DISTRIBUTION The Mexican Woodnymph (see Remarks) is only known from the foothills of western Mexico, in Nayarit, Jalisco and Colima states. Field surveys in suitable habitat in central and southern Mexico have not furnished records of the species, and its restricted range seems real and not the result of incomplete knowledge (Escalante-Pliego and Peterson 1992). The relatively few records are as follows:

Nayarit La Bajada, south of San Blas, where the species was recently seen (S. N. G. Howell *in litt.* 1992); Palapita (18 km south of Jalcocotán), where specimens were taken in June and October 1981, and March and June 1982 (Navarro *et al.* 1991, also Escalante-Pliego and Peterson 1992); 10 km from Ejido Las Mesillas (south of the above locality), whence comes a recent specimen (Escalante-Pliego and Peterson 1992);

Jalisco 2.5 km north-east of Puerto Vallarta (1.5 km east of Guapinole) (Escalante-Pliego and Peterson 1992); San Sebastián, where the type-specimen was taken in March 1897 (Nelson 1900); El Refugio, Zuchitlán (1.5 km north of the Chimo road), source of two specimens (Escalante-Pliego and Peterson 1992); La Cumbre (14 km south-south-west of Autlán), source of four (Escalante-Pliego and Peterson 1992); Puerto Los Mazos, Sierra de Manatlán, where five males and two females (in FMNH) were taken in April 1989 (Escalante-Pliego and Peterson 1992), and where there was a recent sighting (S. N. G. Howell *in litt.* 1992);

Colima La Media Luna (north of Puerto Juárez), where two males and a female were taken in February 1959 (Schaldach 1963); Zacatosa, source of one specimen (Escalante-Pliego and Peterson 1992).

POPULATION This species, like most woodnymphs, is seemingly "locally common" within appropriate habitat (Escalante-Pliego and Peterson 1992): however, the bird apparently went unrecorded between 1897 and the 1950s, and was then not seen again until the 1980s (Nelson 1900, Schaldach 1963, Navarro *et al.* 1991, Escalante-Pliego and Peterson 1992), this presumably being attributable at least in part to its local distribution.

ECOLOGY Despite recent attention, almost nothing has been recorded of this species's ecological requirements. Nelson (1900) noted that the type came from an "island" of humid tropical forest on the arid tropical Pacific slope of Jalisco. When the species was next recorded (in Colima), birds were found in a "watered barranca at the upper margin of the tropical deciduous forest on the north slope of La Media Luna" (Schaldach 1963). Schaldach (1963) also reported that A. R. Phillips previously collected this species (at an undisclosed locality) in western Jalisco, apparently "only in the restricted habitat wherein the Green Jay *Cyanocorax yncas* is most abundant": this habitat in Colima consists of dry, wooded barrancas just below oak-dominated woodland, the bird not being found in the higher altitude humid tropical forests. Escalante-Pliego and Peterson (1992) only mentioned that this woodnymph inhabits humid canyons and foothills.

THREATS Escalante-Pliego and Peterson (1992) considered the status of this and other Central American woodnymphs of moderate concern, in the case of Mexican Woodnymph owing to its restricted distribution in an area where suitable habitat has been reduced in recent decades; however, they also mentioned that its habitat is still fairly extensive and that the bird is relatively common. The main problem appears to be ignorance of its patchy distribution, and also its precise ecological requirements: whilst these are undocumented, it remains difficult to assess the impact of habitat loss in the region.

MEASURES TAKEN None is known.

MEASURES PROPOSED A clearer definition of this hummingbird's distributional and ecological limits must be achieved so as to determine the nature of the threats it faces; however, it is clear that protective measures are needed in this area to preserve at least some of the existing habitat within its limited range.

REMARKS Originally described as a full species (Nelson 1900), the Mexican Woodnymph was later merged with the South American Fork-tailed Woodnymph *Thalurania furcata* (from which, however, it is geographically very disjunct) and maintained as a subspecies until very recently (see Escalante-Pliego and Peterson 1992).

SAPPHIRE-BELLIED HUMMINGBIRD *Lepidopyga lilliae* I[6]

Essentially confined to mangroves along the northern coast of Colombia, this hummingbird is extremely rare and threatened by extensive loss of habitat.

DISTRIBUTION The Sapphire-bellied Hummingbird (see Remarks) is endemic to a small area of the coastal strip in Atlántico, Magdalena and La Guajira departments, northernmost Colombia. The few localities where this species has been recorded (coordinates from Paynter and Traylor 1981) are as follows:

Atlántico Bocas de Ceniza (11°07'N 74°51'W), mentioned by Meyer de Schauensee (1948-1952) and also A. J. Negret (*in litt.* 1987);

Magdalena Ciénaga Grande de Santa Marta (10°50'N 74°25'W), on both sides of the río Magdalena estuary (Gochfeld *et al.* 1980, Hilty and Brown 1986); Isla de Salamanca National Park (10°59'N 74°27'W), throughout which there have been scattered observations (Toro *et al.* 1975, Franky and Rodríguez 1977), the most recent of which is from the eastern side (Hilty and Brown 1986); Sevillano (10°56'N 74°15'W; at the north-eastern corner of Ciénaga Grande de Santa Marta) (Darlington 1931); Punta Caimán (untraced, but at the mouth of the Ciénaga Grande de Santa Marta on Isla de Salamanca: see Paynter and Traylor 1981), where a male (in ANSP) was taken in September 1913 (also Stone 1917, Todd and Carriker 1922); and Ciénaga Grande de Santa Marta Sanctuary (10°40'N 74°31'W, in the south-south-west corner of the ciénaga: coordinates from CNPPA 1982), from which there is a report (J. E. Botero *in litt.* 1987);

La Guajira Ríohacha (11°33'N 72°55'W), just east of town at the mouth of the río Ranchería, where two birds were seen in August 1974 (Gochfeld *et al.* 1980); and río Ranchería itself (11°34'N 72°54'W), mentioned by Meyer de Schauensee (1948-1952).

POPULATION Although there are some recent records from the eastern side of Isla de Salamanca National Park (which has been intensively surveyed by several ornithologists during the past few decades: LGN), the population of this species remains essentially unknown, but is presumably very low. Hilty and Brown (1986) considered the bird to be rare, local, and not found with any consistency, S. L. Hilty (*in litt.* 1996) suggesting that this may have always been the case. On the rare occasions that the species is seen, it is usually alone (Gochfeld *et al.* 1980, Hilty and Brown 1986). If the Sapphire-bellied Hummingbird depends on extensive areas of pristine mangrove for sustaining a viable population (see Ecology), it will have undoubtedly declined since the mid-1970s owing to extensive habitat destruction (see Threats).

ECOLOGY The Sapphire-bellied Hummingbird is seemingly restricted to coastal mangroves (Gochfeld *et al.* 1980, Hilty and Brown 1986), although Darlington (1931) recorded the bird from xerophytic thickets; Hilty and Brown (1986) noted that it is usually seen alone at various heights inside the mangroves, although the extent to which the species relies on this habitat is unknown.

THREATS The construction of a highway and pipeline through Isla de Salamanca during the mid-1970s caused an obstruction to both the tidal and freshwater flow between the mangrove swamps and the Ciénaga Grande, thereby increasing the salinity of the outer mangroves and decreasing it in the inland areas: this has resulted in the death of large areas of mangrove (e.g. at least 1,700 ha by 1981) (CNPPA 1982, Scott and Carbonell 1986). Most of the original mangroves on Isla de Salamanca and adjacent Ciénaga Grande de Santa Marta have been destroyed owing to this imbalance in the salinity of some of the lagoons (Scott and Carbonell 1986, LGN).

Urbanization of the Bocas de Ceniza area (i.e. Barranquilla) has also caused the destruction of large areas of natural habitat, including mangroves (A. J. Negret *in litt.* 1987), and pollution from domestic sewage and industrial waste is causing yet further problems to the río Magdalena estuary (Scott and Carbonell 1986).

MEASURES TAKEN Isla de Salamanca National Park (21,000 ha) embraces a majority of the areas where this rare hummingbird has recently been recorded (CNPPA 1982; see Distribution), although wardening, management and enforcement of the park regulations are reported to be inadequate (Scott and Carbonell 1986). Despite the widely recognized threats to the Isla de Salamanca National Park (see above), only minor corrections to the disruption of the tidal flow have so far been undertaken (LGN). The short-term future status of most of the habitats on Isla de Salamanca is uncertain, although biologists at the Instituto de Investigaciones Marinas de Punta de Betín (INVEMAR, Santa Marta) have been documenting the problems during the last few years (Botero and Botero 1987).

The Ciénaga Grande de Santa Marta Sanctuary (23,000 ha) incorporates areas of mangroves in the south-south-west corner of the ciénaga (CNPPA 1982), and the Sapphire-bellied Hummingbird is apparently known to occur there (J. E. Botero *in litt.* 1987).

MEASURES PROPOSED So little is currently known about the ecological requirements or distribution of this bird that a survey, which would also help to clarify the species's population and taxonomic status (see below), is urgently needed. Nevertheless, on present evidence the priority for the species must be the conservation of mangrove areas around the río Magdalena, río Ranchería, and Ciénaga Grande de Santa Marta. The restoration of the mangroves within the Isla de Salamanca National Park is also essential if this species is to maintain a number of viable populations, and a resolution of the third Neotropical Ornithological Congress held in Cali, Colombia, in 1987, urged the Colombian government to take prompt action on such work: however, no adequate conservation strategy for the park has yet been developed.

This whole area (Isla de Salamanca and Ciénaga Grande de Santa Marta) constitutes the most important wetland for waterfowl on the Caribbean coast of Colombia, supporting large concentrations of both resident breeding species and Nearctic migrants (Scott and Carbonell 1986), so any conservation initiatives (restoration, pollution control, protective measures) should allow for the general needs of the waterfowl, as well as the specific needs of the hummingbird. Such measures should also embrace the requirements of the near-threatened Northern Screamer *Chauna chavaria*, which it not uncommon in this region, but is suffering from the widespread loss of its wetland habitat (Hilty and Brown 1986), and also the Bronze-brown Cowbird *Molothrus armenti*, now generally judged only a subspecies of Bronzed Cowbird *M. aeneus* (Ridgely and Tudor 1989), but which has a major part of its range (at least seasonally) within the Isla de Salamanca National Park (Gochfeld *et al.* 1980, Dugand and Eisenmann 1983, Hernández Camacho and Rodríguez-Mahecha 1986).

REMARKS Peters (1945) treated this species as a race of Sapphire-throated Hummingbird *Lepidopyga coeruleogularis*, probably based on the comment by Darlington (1931) who considered *lilliae* a colour phase at that species, which also occurs in the Ciénaga Grande area (Meyer de Schauensee 1948-1952, Hilty and Brown 1986). Meyer de Schauensee (1948-1952) noted that the specific status of *lilliae* must be kept, but in a subsequent account (Meyer de Schauensee 1966) suggested again the possibility of it being an age-related colour-morph of *coeruleogularis*. Sapphire-bellied Hummingbird is here treated as a full species, following Hilty and Brown (1986) and Sibley and Monroe (1990).

MANGROVE HUMMINGBIRD *Amazilia boucardi* V[9]

This uncommon hummingbird is endemic to the Pacific coast of Costa Rica, in areas with a predominance of the Pacific mangrove: it is the indiscriminate destruction of this mangrove habitat that has led to the bird's decline.

DISTRIBUTION The Mangrove Hummingbird is endemic to Costa Rica and distributed along the length of the Pacific coast from the head of Golfo de Nicoya to Golfo Dulce, in effect, virtually anywhere along this coast where Pacific mangrove *Pelliciera rhizophorae* grows abundantly (F. G. Stiles *in litt.* 1991). Localities are treated in order from west to east (all being traced from Slud 1964), and are as follows: Palo Verde (on the río Tempisque, but still tidal and with mangroves), where a male (in BMNH) was collected in June 1906 (Carriker 1910; see Remarks 1); Chomes, where a male and female (in LACM) were taken in January 1928; Tambor (on Península de Nicoya), where a male (in LACM) was taken in November 1928; Puntarenas, whence come a number of specimens (in BMNH; see also Boucard 1878a, Carriker 1910 and Remarks 2) and recent records (Taylor 1990, A. J. Goodwin *in litt.* 1989, M. Pearman *in litt.* 1990, G. J. Speight *in litt.* 1990) from the base of the peninsula and on the north side of the estuary; Zapotal (inland from the base of the Puntarenas peninsula), where a female (in AMNH) was taken in January 1922; Tivives, a locality mentioned by F. G. Stiles (*in litt.* 1989); Pigres, where five males and four females (in USNM: see Carriker 1910), were collected in February and March 1905, with birds recorded nearby between the río La Pita and río Grande de Tárcoles (Taylor 1990), near the Carara Biological Reserve (at Playa Azul near the mouth of the río Grande de Tárcoles: G. J. Speight *in litt.* 1990) and at Estero Guacalillos (ca.5 km from the Carara Biological Reserve, where 12 birds were mist-netted; F. G. Stiles *in litt.* 1989), all these localities being near the mouth of the río Grande de Tárcoles in the same extensive mangrove area (the best developed part of which is in the Pigres–Estero Guacalillos sector: F. G. Stiles *in litt.* 1991); Las Trojas de Puntarenas, where three birds (in BMNH) were taken in July 1933; near Parrita, where Slud (1964) recorded the species, and where a nest was found in January 1985 at the mouth of the river (F. G. Stiles *in litt.* 1989, 1991); Palo Seco, a locality mentioned by F. G. Stiles *in litt.* (1989); Quepos, where D. A. Scott (*in litt.* 1985) found the species in December 1983; Dominical, a locality mentioned by Taylor (1990); Coronado (at the mouth of the río Grande de Térraba), where at least 10 males and 11 females (in AMNH, ANSP, BMNH, CM) were taken in early July 1907 (see also Carriker 1910), with a male (in FMNH) taken in June 1917; Rincón de Osa, where a male and female (in WFVZ) were collected in July 1964, and 1.5 km south-east of Rincón, where a female (in WFVZ) was taken in April 1971; Puerto Jiménez (on Península de Osa), where specimens were taken in September and October 1926 (12 specimens in FMNH, YPM), December 1929 (four males and four females in FMNH, MLZ), and 2 km east of Puerto Jiménez, where nests (in WFVZ) were collected in November 1977 and February 1978 (see Ecology); and Golfito Refuge, a locality mentioned by Taylor (1990), especially in relation to the mangroves along the road to the airport (to the north of town), where at least three birds were seen in March 1983 (B. M. Whitney *in litt.* 1991).

POPULATION This species is generally considered to be a locally common resident of mangroves (Stiles and Skutch 1989), although Carriker (1910) suggested that it was exceedingly rare and local. The bird is apparently common at Puntarenas (Taylor 1990), although most records (see Boucard 1878a, Carriker 1910; also A. J. Goodwin *in litt.* 1989, G. J. Speight *in litt.* 1990) are of just 1-2 birds, and it seems that owing to pollution and deforestation it is less common now; however, the species occurs in several other areas in the Golfo de Nicoya, especially on the east and north-west sides (F. G. Stiles *in litt.* 1991). Carriker (1910) searched for this species at Puntarenas in 1907 but found none. At least nine birds ("about a dozen" in Carriker 1910) were taken at Pigres in February and March 1905, with several localities frequented nearby (see Distribution), and near Parrita (Slud 1964) several individuals were seen every day for an unknown period (on the sandbar: see Ecology), with a pair found nesting there (at the mouth of the river) in 1985 (see Distribution).

The largest series of specimens was taken at Coronado (at the mouth of río Grande de Térraba), where 21 birds were collected over 3-9 July 1907, Carriker (1910) referring to the bird there as being "fairly abundant at one small spot in the mangroves" (see Ecology) and claiming that the region of greatest abundance was likely to be the río Grande de Térraba delta. Birds are still locally common there, although the distribution of *Pelliciera* is patchy, and the hummingbird is similarly localized (F. G. Stiles *in litt.* 1991). At Puerto Jiménez 12 specimens (including an immature male: see Distribution) were taken in September and October 1926, eight birds in December 1929, with two nests found in November 1977 and one in February 1978, suggesting that the species is locally common in the immediate area, this possibly being explained by the lack of tall *Rhizophora* mangroves (due to logging) which often shade out the *Pelliciera* (F. G. Stiles *in litt.* 1991).

ECOLOGY The Mangrove Hummingbird is, as its name suggests, restricted to mangroves on the Pacific coast, where although locally abundant, it is absent from many mangrove areas within its small range (F. G. Stiles *in litt.* 1986). This appears to be explained by its preference for an abundance of Pacific mangrove *Pelliciera rhizophorae* flowers (Stiles and Skutch 1989). It will tolerate much disturbance so long as *Pelliciera* remains common and flowering (e.g. at Puerto Jiménez: see Population), which this species does more or less year round, peaking in September or October–February or March (F. G. Stiles *in litt.* 1989, 1991); however, flowers of other trees (e.g. *Lonchocarpus* sp.), vines, and epiphytes, in and adjoining the mangroves, are also visited (Stiles and Skutch 1989; see also Carriker 1910). The bird taken inland at Palo Verde (see Distribution) was also found in mangroves (the river still being tidal at this point), although the species has been recorded from other habitats (albeit very close or adjacent to mangroves), for example near Parrita where several birds were seen daily on the sandbar that faced the ocean on one side and a mangrove-lined estuary on the other, the vegetation comprising a coconut-palm grove, bushy areas and scattered small trees (Slud 1964). Birds have been seen feeding on mosquitoes (at Pigres) at low tide (Slud 1964), but also at the various flowers mentioned above, where males have been noted to be aggressive but not territorial (Stiles and Skutch 1989). Stiles and Skutch (1989) recorded nesting from October to February, the nests being built on mangrove twigs c.1-4 m up and usually overhanging water. Three nests (in WFVZ) at Puerto Jiménez were collected (all with two eggs in) in mid-November 1977 and at the end of February 1978, the February nest being 1 m above the high-tide line near the tip of a branch (*Laguncularia* sp.) overhanging a channel within the mangroves. Other breeding records include a female at the nest (Puntarenas) in December (A. J. Goodwin *in litt.* 1989), a nest with eggs near the mouth of the río Parrita in January 1985, a bird with young at Chomes in November 1988, and a bird with young at Tivives in January 1988 (all three records from F. G. Stiles *in litt.* 1991); a female (in AMNH) had enlarged ovaries in January 1922 at Zapotal, and nearby (at Puntarenas) an immature male (in BMNH) was taken in June of the same year. Elsewhere, an immature (in BMNH) was collected at Las Trojas in July 1933, with an immature male (in YPM) taken at Puerto Jiménez at the end of September 1926.

THREATS This species is almost totally reliant on mangroves for breeding and feeding (although adjacent habitats may be used when conditions are favourable: see Ecology), and as such is under considerable threat from habitat destruction. Although it will tolerate much disturbance (see Ecology), mangroves are consistently being cleared to make room for salt extraction (salinas) and shrimp ponds (e.g. large areas of mangrove were destroyed for the 405 ha shrimp pond at Chomes), the wood being cut to fuel the stoves that evaporate water from the salinas and to make high-quality mangrove charcoal (Scott and Carbonell 1986, Stiles and Skutch 1989); however, the wood of *Pelliciera* is evidently less desirable than that of *Rhizophora* (F. G. Stiles *in litt.* 1991). Other threats include illegal cutting, dyke and road construction (which have affected the hydrology in a number of places), and pollution (Scott and Carbonell 1986).

MEASURES TAKEN The Mangrove Hummingbird is inadequately protected (F. G. Stiles *in litt.* 1989), although there is a general law (obviously not adhered to) which prohibits the cutting of mangroves (Scott and Carbonell 1986). Tivives (at the mouth of the río Jesús María) is currently (since 1990) protected as a Biological Reserve, although the amount of *Pelliciera* and hence hummingbird habitat there is relatively small (F. G. Stiles *in litt.* 1991).

MEASURES PROPOSED It is essential that a protected area be set up in which a viable population of the Mangrove Hummingbird can survive. The population at Estero Guacalillos (c.5 km from the Carara Biological Reserve, and containing very well developed mangroves) has been suggested as holding a "good protectable population" (F. G. Stiles *in litt.* 1989, 1991). The extension of Carara Biological Reserve to incorporate this area would facilitate the protection of this species, the Yellow-billed Cotinga *Carpodectes antoniae* (see relevant account), and the regionally threatened Scarlet Macaw *Ara macao* (the Carara population of which roosts in the mangroves: F. G. Stiles *in litt.* 1991) without the creation of a new park. Other suitable places for protected areas in which both species occur are Parrita, Palo Seco (although the large tourist population would make protecting particular areas difficult), and possibly Puerto Jiménez (which holds a large population of the species) (F. G. Stiles *in litt.* 1989, 1991), although the status of the hummingbird needs to be determined in the extensive mangroves around Golfo Dulce before suitable areas can be identified. Mangroves around and north of Puntarenas would also appear to support a viable population of this species, which should be considered for protection.

An ecological study is urgently needed to determine the area of mangrove required to sustain a viable population of this species, and indeed to determine where viable populations exist. Once this has been undertaken, areas (where the species is present) with a suitable expanse or a high enough density of *Pelliciera* can be chosen as priority sites. A survey around the mangrove areas of Golfo Dulce (e.g. río Coto and Rincón) is especially needed to determine the species's current status in this area. All measures outlined above should (where appropriate) be integrated with those outlined for Yellow-billed Cotinga.

REMARKS (1) Carriker (1910) mentioned a male specimen taken at Palo Verde in June 1906, although what is presumably the same bird (a male taken at Palo Verde) in BMNH is dated 11 May 1906. (2) Carriker (1910) suggested that this species was discovered at Puntarenas "probably in January 1877" when a few specimens were taken near town. Boucard (1878a) reported that a male and female were collected from Puntarenas in May.

CHESTNUT-BELLIED HUMMINGBIRD *Amazilia castaneiventris* V[9]

This poorly known hummingbird is endemic to lower montane areas in the Serranía de San Lucas and the western slope of the East Andes, Colombia, an area that is now extensively deforested: the bird has apparently gone unrecorded during recent decades.

DISTRIBUTION The Chestnut-bellied Hummingbird has been recorded on the western slope of the East Andes and the Serranía de San Lucas, in Bolívar, Santander and Bojacá departments, Colombia. The few localities (with coordinates, unless otherwise stated, from Paynter and Traylor 1981) are as follows:

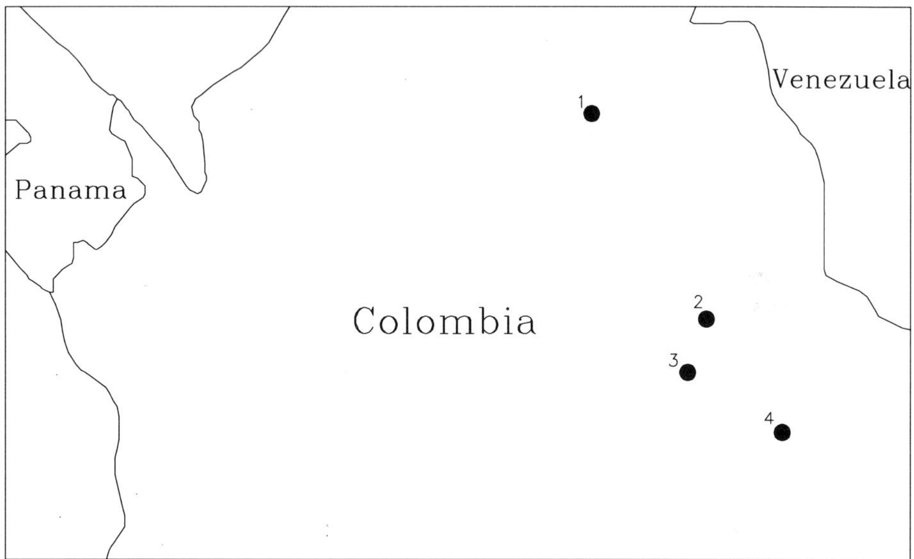

Bolívar Norosí[1] (8°32'N 74°02'W; at c.120 m on the east slope of the Serranía de San Lucas), where a male (in USNM) was collected in March 1947 (also Hilty and Brown 1986);

Santander Lebrija[2] (7°07'N 73°13'W; at c.1,085 m on the west slope of the northern East Andes), where a female (in DMNH) was collected in October 1963; and Portugal[3] (6°45'N 73°21'W, coordinates from LACM specimen labels), where two males (in LACM) were collected in May 1962, with four males and two females (in DMNH, LACM, WFVZ) in May 1963, all between 850 and 950 m;

Bojacá Caseteja[4], near Soatá (6°20'N 72°41'W; on the west slope of the northern East Andes, above the left bank of río Chicamocha), where a bird (in ICN) was taken in August 1949, with 10 (also in ICN) taken during December 1952 and January 1953, all between 1,600 and 2,045 m (also Meyer de Schauensee 1948-1952); and Tipacoque, Vereda Galbán (untraced), where a female (in ICN) was taken in August 1977.

POPULATION The Chestnut-bellied Hummingbird was apparently very common near Soatá during the early 1950s (J. I. Hernández Camacho verbally 1991), and the series of specimens taken there at this time and at Portugal in the early 1960s (see above) seems to confirm that it was at least locally common. This bird appears to have gone unrecorded during the past 30 years although J. I. Hernández Camacho (verbally 1991) suggests that there is no reason to believe it has declined.

ECOLOGY Specimens of Chestnut-bellied Hummingbird come from 850 to 2,045 m (see Distribution), although it may be that the specimen from around Norosí was collected lower than this (Norosí is at 120 m: Paynter and Traylor 1981; see Remarks 1). In this region, the forest between 850 and 2,045 m is best described as lower montane (foothill) humid forest (see Ecology under White-mantled Barbet *Capito hypoleucus*). Birds from Soatá were taken in bushy canyons and at forest borders (LGN), and have commonly been found feeding together with *Colibri* sp. at the flowers of *Salvia* sp. (and other Labiatae) and *Trichanthera gigantea* (ICN label data): birds in this genus are characteristic of scrub and second-growth habitats (F. G. Stiles *in litt.* 1992). The breeding and plumage condition of specimens in ICN suggest a breeding season (in Bojacá) between August and December.

THREATS Deforestation has been progressively affecting the floodplain and foothills of the middle and lower Magdalena valley since the nineteenth century, accelerating over the last 30 years (Graves 1986). However, if the species indeed prefers scrub and forest edge (see Ecology), the reason for it having gone unrecorded for so long may not be attributable to habitat loss, but rather to a lack of observer coverage.

MEASURES TAKEN None is known.

MEASURES PROPOSED It is essential that remnant lower montane forest areas in the Serranía de San Lucas, and on the west slope of the northern East Andes, are afforded some form of protection. An assessment of status and distribution of these remnant forest patches must be a priority which can be combined with searches for and studies of the Chestnut-mantled Hummingbird, whose the current distribution and ecological requirements remain almost unknown, but require urgent attention. Any conservation initiatives in this area should consider the requirements of all sympatric threatened species, which in the Serranía de San Lucas are: White-mantled Barbet, Recurve-billed Bushbird *Clytoctantes alixii* and possibly also Antioquia Bristle-tyrant *Phylloscartes lanyoni*, and on the western slope of the East Andes are listed in the equivalent section under Black Inca *Coeligena prunellei*.

REMARKS (1) Hilty and Brown (1986), based on the altitudes given in Paynter and Traylor (1981), suggested an altitudinal range of 150 to 2,045 m. (2) J. I. Hernández-Camacho (verbally 1991) suggested that this species may be but a subspecies of Rufous-tailed Hummingbird *Amazilia tzacatl*, although both birds overlap in their ranges: further investigation is perhaps warranted to clarify this point.

TACHIRA EMERALD *Amazilia distans* V[9]

Restricted to the foothills of the Andes in westernmost Venezuela, this extremely rare hummingbird inhabits an area undergoing rampant deforestation. First collected in 1954, there have subsequently been just five unconfirmed observations, and the bird remains almost totally unknown.

DISTRIBUTION The Táchira Emerald is endemic to Táchira and westernmost Apure, Venezuela, coordinates here being taken from Paynter (1982). The bird is known from just two specimens (two males in COP and USNM collected on 17 July 1954; see Remarks) taken at El Salao (c.7°26'N 72°00'W) near Burgua in southern Táchira (also Phelps and Phelps 1958). Other records in the vicinity of the type-locality are: an individual "almost certainly this species", seen a few kilometres west of the airport at Santo Domingo (7°34'N 72°05'W: where the road crosses the río Uribante) at c.360 m, on 15 October 1988 (B. M. Whitney *in litt.* 1991); and San Camilo forest, Apure (apparently near Burgua and hence the type-locality), a locality mentioned by Goodwin (1990). Hilty and Brown (1986) mentioned a possible sighting in 1974 on the north slope of the Andes of Táchira, and suggested that the species could occur in adjacent Colombia. Goodwin (1990) recorded the bird from between San Pedro and San Juan de Colón (8°02'N 72°16'W; c.800 m), and north of San Juan de Colón (both localities on the northern slope of the Andes of Táchira).

POPULATION Nothing is known.

ECOLOGY The specimens (in COP and USNM) were collected at 300 m in "selva" (forest), the locality apparently being in the tropical zone rainforest (Meyer de Schauensee 1966, Meyer de Schauensee and Phelps 1978). From the vegetation map of Huber and Alarcón (1988), El Salao is on the boundary of submontane evergreen and foothill semi-deciduous forest. Vegetation on the northern slope of the mountains consists primarily of submontane evergreen and lower altitude semi-evergreen forest (Huber and Alarcon 1988: see below). B. M. Whitney (*in litt.* 1991) recorded an individual (near Santo Domingo) at c.360 m (in October 1988) feeding with several other species of hummingbird on a flowering *Inga* sp., and noted that the native habitat in the area had been cleared or heavily disturbed except on the rather steep slopes above the río Uribante (see Threats). Goodwin (1990) suggested that the species can be found at c.800 m in coffee plantations north of San Juan de Colón.

THREATS None is known, although deforestation is clearly a problem in this area (see above; also Huber and Alarcón 1988), and the extent to which the species can utilize coffee plantations (with or without shade trees), or other secondary habitats is unknown. Forest destruction in the Andes of western Venezuela is so rapid that El Tamá National Park is one of the most threatened protected areas in Venezuela (Desenne and Strahl 1991: see equivalent section under Rusty-faced Parrot *Hapalopsittaca amazonina*).

MEASURES TAKEN The Táchira Emerald apparently occurs in the San Camilo Forest Reserve (see above), and probably in El Tamá National Park (the specimens were taken from a locality adjacent to both areas: DGPOA undated). However, with so little available information on this species, its status within either area remains unknown, as does the status of the relevant habitat in these reserves.

MEASURES PROPOSED The main priority for this species is to determine its precise distribution and ecological requirements so that action can be taken to protect the correct forest areas. Searches should be carried out in southern Táchira around the type-locality and in suitable forests nearby (i.e. between 300 and 800 m, in semi-deciduous forest), and on the north slope of the mountains in semi-evergreen forest (and also coffee plantations). Protection of remaining forest within the region is also an extremely high priority, which could partly be achieved by the extension of the El Tamá National Park to include forested areas to the east of the current reserve boundary. Such actions are essential, and although occurring at much higher altitudes, would also benefit three other threatened species, namely: Rusty-faced Parrot, Táchira Antpitta *Grallaria chthonia* and Hooded Antpitta *Grallaricula cucullata* (see relevant accounts).

REMARKS There are apparently two specimens, a male in USNM (the type) and a male in COP (both taken on the same date). However, Meyer de Schauensee and Phelps (1978) and Hilty and Brown (1986) referred to the species as being known from just one specimen.

HONDURAN EMERALD *Amazilia luciae* E[2]

Although this hummingbird is common in its preferred arid thorn-forest, this habitat has a restricted range within Honduras: unfortunately, these same areas are under severe pressure from agricultural development.

DISTRIBUTION The Honduran Emerald is endemic to Honduras, where its restricted range is explained by an association with the arid interior valleys (Monroe 1968, Howell and Webb 1989a; see Ecology). At present only seven localities have been traced (coordinates from Monroe 1968) and from west to east these are: Santa Bárbara[1] (14°53'N 88°10'W, at c.270-300 m), where a male (in MCZ) was collected in May 1935 (see Threats); Cofradía[2] (15°24'N 88°09'W, c.170 m), where a male (in MCZ) was collected in March 1933 (see Threats); then (further east, along the upper río Aguán valley, in Yoro department) Coyoles[3] (15°29'N 86°41'W, c.75 m), where four males (in AMNH, CM) were taken in June 1948 and 1950; 6 km west-north-west of Coyoles, where the bird was common in June 1988 (Howell and Webb 1989a); 4-4.5 km west of Olanchito[4] (16 km east of Coyoles), where the bird was again common in June 1988 (Howell and Webb 1989a), and in March 1991 (Howell and Webb 1992); then (about 100 km south-east from the Coyoles area) El Boquerón[5] (14°50'N 86°01'W, c.10 km south-west of Catacamas in Olancho department), where two birds (in MCZ) were taken at c.1,220 m in September 1937; and Catacamas[6] (14°53'N 85°55'W, at c.410 m), where a female (in MLZ) was collected in August 1937 (see Moore 1938b). Two other specimens exist: a male (in LSUMZ) was taken at "Las Jabens" (or possibly Las Jabeus; both untraced) in September 1937, Monroe (1968) suggesting that (from the date and collector involved) this is within the Catacamas region; and the type (in AMNH) from "Honduras" (see Lawrence 1867).

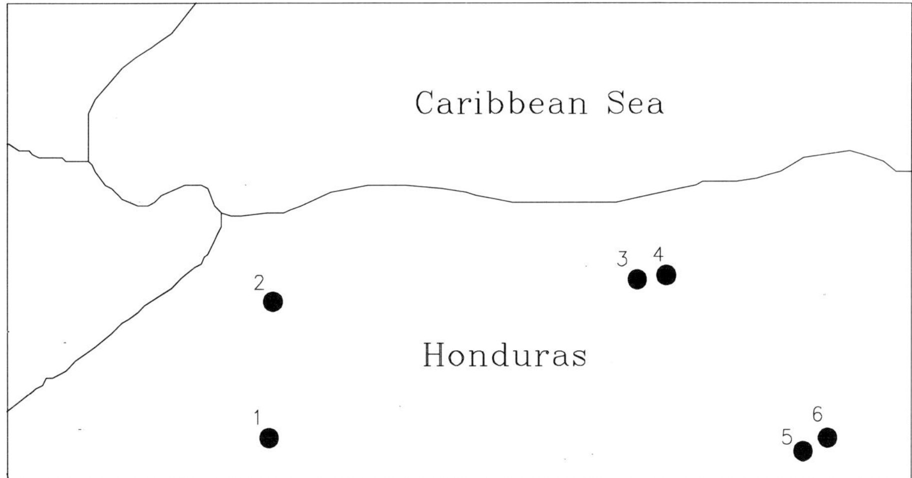

POPULATION Until recently, all that could be said about the population of this poorly known species was that 11 specimens have been collected and it was "possibly common locally" due to the fact that four specimens each have been taken in the Coyoles and Catacamas regions (Monroe 1968). In early June 1988, however, the bird was found to be a common inhabitant of the arid vegetation in the upper río Aguán valley: six birds were found in one hour, just 6 km west-north-west of Coyoles; 12-15 birds were found (easily) in an area of 200 m^2 (one bird holding a territory of 10 m^2), 4 km west of Olanchito (Howell and Webb 1989a); and (4.5 km west of Olanchito)

between 22 and 28 birds were counted in 500 x 50 m of thorn-forest (part of a larger tract) on 16 March 1991 (Howell and Webb 1992). One bird was noted "apparently" singing near Olanchito in 1988 (Howell and Webb 1989a), suggesting that this may be a breeding locality. Nothing is known of any other extant population, apart from the fact that almost all suitable habitat has now been cleared at Santa Bárbara and Cofradía (Howell and Webb 1989a: see Threats).

ECOLOGY The preferred habitat of the Honduran Emerald was unknown until recently, Monroe (1968) presuming it to be a forest inhabitant and AOU (1983) suggesting that the distribution lies generally in the humid lowlands. However, plotting the known localities on the habitat map in Monroe (1968) reveals that they lie close to or within "arid and mixed scrub, and thorn-forest" (Howell and Webb 1989a). In June 1988 it was indeed found that the bird was generally associated with the arid interior valleys where (at two localities: see Distribution) it was found to be a common inhabitant of arid thorn-forest and scrub (Howell and Webb 1989a). Near Coyoles, the thorn-forest was c.6-10 m high and dominated by Mimosaceae, Cactaceae and Euphorbiaceae, the species still being found there despite heavy grazing of the understorey and the apparent lack of flowers (Howell and Webb 1989a). Around Olanchito, birds were seen in similar but more cut-over and heavily grazed thorn-forest and scrub (see Threats), where feeding was noted at several flowering plants, namely *Pithecellobium lentiscifolium*, *Aechmea* cf. *bracteata*, *Pedilanthus* cf. *tithymaloides* and a conspicuous organpipe cactus (probably *Lemaireocereus* or *Cephalocereus*) (Howell and Webb 1989a). The birds fed at heights of 0.5-10 m (insect-catching was also noted) and, earlier, individuals were seen perching at 1.5-8 m in bare trees and bushes (Howell and Webb 1989a). The Honduran Emerald appears to occur at quite high densities in suitable habitat at certain times of the year (i.e. June: see Population), although it is unknown if this situation changes seaonally. "Breeding" records are represented by a bird heard apparently singing on 8 June (Howell and Webb 1989a), and a male with enlarged testes (in AMNH) collected on 13 June (1950).

THREATS The relatively small area of preferred habitat (within the arid interior valleys: see Monroe 1968) explains both the restricted range of this bird and its threatened status, because this habitat is under pressure for conversion to agricultural land (Howell and Webb 1989a). At Santa Bárbara and Cofradía, arid conditions similar to those in the upper río Aguán valley were recorded (in 1988) but most of the thorn-forest had been cleared for grazing, and what little remained was extremely dry with few birds of any species apparent (Howell and Webb 1989a). Despite this, the Honduran Emerald can seemingly tolerate substantial habitat modification, with birds being recorded at Coyoles in understorey heavily grazed by cattle, and at Olanchito where the forest was relatively more cut-over and also heavily grazed (Howell and Webb 1989a). A major threat to the upper río Aguán valley in 1991 appears to be a newly paved road that had opened up the area: much of this valley has been and is continuing to be converted into pineapple plantations (Howell and Webb 1992).

MEASURES TAKEN None is known.

MEASURES PROPOSED Immediate protection needs to be given to a number of tracts of the preferred thorn-forest and scrub habitat where this bird occurs. Its continued survival would probably be ensured in even relatively small areas owing to its seemingly high population density, but an ecological study is necessary in order to confirm this, to identify the bird's year-round needs, to help with the selection of suitable localities, and to suggest an optimum area for the conservation of a viable population. Once areas have been identified, measures need to be taken to prevent (further) degradation. Suitable remaining areas around Coyoles and Olanchito appear to be the current priority for immediate protection, owing to the proven existence of (possibly breeding) populations there and to the urgency caused by agricultural encroachment (see Threats). A search needs to be undertaken to find other populations, for example around Catacamas.

OAXACA HUMMINGBIRD *Eupherusa cyanophrys* V[9]

Endemic to just one mountain range in southernmost Oaxaca, Mexico, this hummingbird is locally common in its preferred cloud-forest habitat which is, however, unprotected and being rapidly destroyed.

DISTRIBUTION The Oaxaca (or Blue-capped) Hummingbird is endemic to the Sierra Miahuatlán, an isolated mountain range in southernmost Oaxaca, Mexico. It has been found in two areas of the Sierra Miahuatlán, separated by c.60-70 km (see map under Distribution in White-tailed Hummingbird *Eupherusa poliocerca*): in the west along the Puerto Escondido road (route 131) where it crosses the sierra; and to the east along the Puerto Angel road (route 175) at its intersection with the río Jalatengo (the species presumably ranges throughout the area between these two roads). Coordinates, distances and altitudes for this account, unless otherwise stated, are taken from Binford (1989).

Along the Puerto Angel road, at río Jalatengo, two female *Eupherusa* were collected in May 1962 (Rowley and Orr 1964) but were attributed to White-tailed Hummingbird (see relevant account); however, as the females of these two species are apparently inseparable (Binford 1989), it seems probable that these specimens pertain to *cyanophrys*. Subsequently, 21 Oaxaca Hummingbirds were seen (four collected) 5 km north of Pluma Hidalgo[1] (15°55'N 96°25'W at 1,525 m) during April and May 1964 (L. C. Binford *in litt.* 1991); a male and a female were taken in February 1965 near río Jalatengo at km 182[2] (15°58'N 96°27'W at 1,525 m, and apparently very close to the previous locality; specimens in AMNH and WFVZ), with 15 birds seen at La Soledad[3] (c.15°53'N 96°25'W at 1,435 m) on one day in April 1988 (S. N. G. Howell *in litt.* 1991) and one seen 11 km south of there[4] (at 1,100 m) in February 1974 (L. C. Binford *in litt.* 1991).

Along the Puerto Escondido road records come from between San Pedro Juchatengo in the north and San Gabriel Mixtepec, 27 km to the south (72 km by road). Localities along this stretch are as follows (distances given are along a straight line south of San Pedro Juchatengo, or north of San Gabriel Mixtepec): San Pedro Juchatengo[5], 840 m (16°20'N 97°06'W); km 179[6], 16 km south (specimen taken at 1,830 m) (16°13'N 97°07'W); km 181 (specimen at 1,770 m); km 182[7], 17.5 km south (34 km south by road) at 1,830 m (16°12'N 97°07'W); km 183 (specimens at 1,585-1,830 m) and La Cima (km 184) (specimens at 1,585-1,830 m) – both localities at 17.5 km south (16°12'N 97°07'W: see Remarks 1); "Barranca Sin Nombre"[8], 19 km south (17.5 km on the specimen) or 8 km north (28-29 km north by road on the specimen) at 1,435 m (c.16°11'N 97°07'W); km 193[9], c.6.5 km north at 1,339 m (c.16°10'N 97°07'W: L. C. Binford *in litt.* 1991); km 195, 6.5 km north at 1,280 m (16°10'N 97°07'W); Jamaica Junction[10] (km 212), 1.5-2.5 km north (6 km north by road) at 730 m (16°07'N 97°07'W); San Gabriel Mixtepec[11], 27 km south at 685 m (16°06'N 97°06'W) (specimens in AMNH, DMNH, FMNH, IBUNAM, MVZ, MZFC, WFVZ; also Rowley and Orr 1964, Rowley 1966, Binford 1989). Records also come from Cerro Verde[12], 17.5 km north-north-east of San Gabriel Mixtepec at 16°14'N 97°02'W, at 2,315-2,620 m (specimens in WFVZ); Cerro Verde has also been described as being 30 km east of Santa Rosa[13] (16°10'N 97°07'W) and 30 km east of Lachao Nuevo – the precise locality of which is unknown but apparently close to Santa Rosa (specimens in AMNH, WFVZ) (Rowley 1966, Binford 1989; see Remarks 2).

POPULATION The Oaxaca Hummingbird is locally a fairly common to common permanent resident (S. N. G. Howell *in litt.* 1987, Binford 1989). Eight specimens (three males, five females) were collected in May 1963 near km 183 (Rowley and Orr 1964); 30 (16 females, 14 males in DMNH) were taken there between 30 November and 13 December 1964, six non-territorial breeding females were found in a 9 ha plot, also at km 183, during a breeding bird survey over 2-12 June 1965 (Webster 1965), and 2-4 birds were seen on four days in May 1964 at km 193 (L. C. Binford *in litt.* 1991). At La Soledad, 15 birds (some of which were singing) were seen in one morning in April 1988 (S. N. G. Howell *in litt.* 1991), and nearby 21 were seen (four collected) in four days (end of April and early May 1964) 5 km north of Pluma Hidalgo (see Distribution). Breeding has been confirmed on four occasions from near La Cima (Rowley 1966), a large percentage of other specimens (not mentioned above) also coming from within a few kilometres of La Cima (km 181-184). This all suggests that the species is indeed locally common at a number of localities along routes 131 and 175, but with the mountains between these two roads (and to the east and west) remaining unexplored (and supporting suitable habitat) and almost certainly harbouring the species, it remains impossible to assess the overall situation.

ECOLOGY The Oaxaca Hummingbird is a permanent resident, restricted primarily to cloud-forest and the upper reaches of tropical semi-deciduous forest, occasionally wandering (possibly seasonally) to lower elevations on adjacent mountain slopes (Binford 1989, S. N. G. Howell *in litt.* 1989). At km 183, near La Cima on the Puerto Escondido road (whence come the majority of records), the habitat is mostly cloud-forest with a thick underbrush in areas where windfalls have opened up the crown; the canopy is irregular owing to the various sizes and heights of the dominant tree species including *Pinus ayacahuite*, *P. oocarpa*, *Quercus brachystachys*, *Garrya laurifolia*, *Oreopanax peltatum*, *Parathesis calophylla*, *Saurauia oreophila*, *Solanum macrantherum*, and *Symplocos* sp., the commonest undershrub being the bamboo *Chusquea longifolia* (Webster 1965). Records from cloud-forest along this stretch of road come from localities at c.1,300-1,950 m (see Distribution). At río Jalatengo, also within this altitude range, the habitat has been described as tropical deciduous forest with gallery forest along the river and tributaries, with a pine-oak association on the steep hillsides (Rowley 1966). Nearby La Soledad is situated within a narrow belt of cloud-forest and coffee fincas between tropical semi-deciduous and pine-forest (S. N. G. Howell *in litt.* 1991). Higher elevations have been recorded on Cerro Verde where the range is c.2,300-2,600 m, lower altitudes being noted on either slope of the Sierra Miahuatlán, at 685-840 m (see Distribution). The vegetation at Jamaica Junction (730 m) on the Pacific slope has been described as tropical evergreen and tropical deciduous forest, with gallery forest along the streams (Rowley 1966). Although the species has also been noted as favouring forest edge (AOU 1983), this is probably a function of the relative ease of observation in such situations (S. N. G. Howell *in litt.* 1991).

Breeding has been confirmed on four occasions, all documented in Rowley (1966): the first nest, containing two young (one week old), was found on 1 October 1964 near La Cima (km 183 at 1,770 m), and was situated at the head of a very steep wet gulch, c.120 cm from the ground in the centre forks of a small bush; a second, containing two eggs, was found on 10 October 1964 at Cerro Verde, and was also in a small bush c.120 cm from the ground; the third, on the exposed root of a pine c.6 m from the ground on a road-cut bank, was located 4 km north of Lachao Nuevo (at 1,280 m between km 181-183 on the Puerto Escondido road: see Remarks 2) on 5 November 1964, and contained one young about a week old; the fourth, containing two eggs, was found on 3 May 1965, also around km 183, about 2.5 m from the ground in a small tree at the head of a small steep, dry canyon. Six females described as non-territorial breeders were recorded at this last site (km 183) over 2-12 June 1965 (Webster 1965), and 15 birds, some of which were "singing strongly", were recorded at La Soledad on 19 April 1988 (S. N. G. Howell *in litt.* 1991). A female collected 5 November 1964 near La Cima was found to contain a "soft egg" (Binford 1989); and a male taken 11 June at Jamaica Junction (the only record from this locality) is apparently an immature (Rowley and Orr 1964, Binford 1989, L. C. Binford *in litt.* 1991). This last record is one of the three lower-altitude records, the others being on 2 March at San Pedro

Juchatengo (in WFVZ), and 15 March 1987 at San Gabriel Mixtepec (in IBUNAM). The record from 11 km south of La Soledad, like these others, may represent post-breeding altitudinal movements, or just the "occasional wanderings to lower elevations" mentioned by Binford (1989).

Rowley (1966) claimed that the species appears to be solitary, it being rare for more than one individual at a time to be seen in a particular place. However, at La Cima in October 1964, several males were seen about 100 m from a brooding female (Rowley 1966), 30 individuals were collected at km 183 (near La Cima) in December 1964 (in DMNH), six non-territorial breeding females were recorded in a 9 ha plot, also at km 183 in June 1965 (Webster 1965), and 15 birds were seen on one day in April 1988 at La Soledad (S. N. G. Howell *in litt.* 1991), all of which seems to indicate that even if "solitary" the birds are locally or seasonally common (see Population).

THREATS In 1963, the Oaxaca Hummingbird occupied an area of cloud-forest essentially unspoiled by human activity (Rowley and Orr 1964). Only a few years later Rowley (1966) was concerned about the future of this species, the cloud-forest habitat in La Cima/Cerro Verde area being destroyed rapidly by the resident Indians, who were cutting and burning huge areas in preparation for planting corn; it was evident that since 1963 much damage had already been done. Even at río Jalatengo, the vegetation was being quickly destroyed by fire and cutting (Rowley 1966). The species being apparently restricted to the Sierra Miahuatlán, steady destruction of the cloud-forest habitat remains its main threat (S. N. G. Howell *in litt.* 1989).

MEASURES TAKEN None is known.

MEASURES PROPOSED Immediate protection must be given to the remaining cloud-forest areas along and between the two roads that at present represent the known "centres" of abundance for this species. A survey of suitable habitat between the Puerto Escondido road, Cerro Verde and the Puerto Angel road should be undertaken to determine the bird's actual distribution and the state of its remaining habitat. An ecological study should be carried out in order to determine the nature of its local/seasonal movements. Once this has been done, a conservation strategy for the species, and indeed the cloud-forest of the Sierra Miahuatlán, can be implemented (see White-throated Jay *Cyanolyca mirabilis* account).

REMARKS (1) La Cima, in Binford (1989), is apparently located at km 184, 17.5 km south of San Pedro Juchatengo (or 38 km south, 34 km north by road) but has variously been described on specimens as 36.5 km north of San Gabriel Mixtepec, and 14.5 km south, 16 km south, 12 km south-east and 14.5 km south-west of San Pedro Juchatengo. Km 183, Barranca Sin Nombre, 4 km north of Lachao Nuevo, and a number of other localities mentioned on specimens are all very close to La Cima, at c.16°11'N 97°07'W.

(2) Lachao Nuevo ("San Juan Lachao Pueblo Nuevo" in Binford 1989) is untraced, but is apparently midway between La Cima and San Gabriel Mixtepec (Rowley 1966). Although Webster (1965) described "Lachao" as 3 km north-east of km 183 on the Puerto Escondido road, Binford (1989) suggested that it is possibly synonymous with (or close to) Santa Rosa near km 199, the coordinates (16°14'N 97°09'W) in OG (1956a) seemingly confirming that this is so.

WHITE-TAILED HUMMINGBIRD *Eupherusa poliocerca* V[9]

This hummingbird is endemic to the Sierra Madre del Sur in Guerrero and western Oaxaca, south-western Mexico, where it is a locally common inhabitant of cloud-forest that is rapidly being destroyed.

DISTRIBUTION The White-tailed Hummingbird is found on the Pacific slope of the Sierra Madre del Sur, in Guerrero and westernmost Oaxaca states, Mexico. A record of the species from Chinantla (Boucard 1895), which AOU (1983) indicated as in Puebla state, is not accepted here (see Remarks 1). Coordinates for Guerrero come from OG (1956a) and for Oaxaca from Binford (1989).

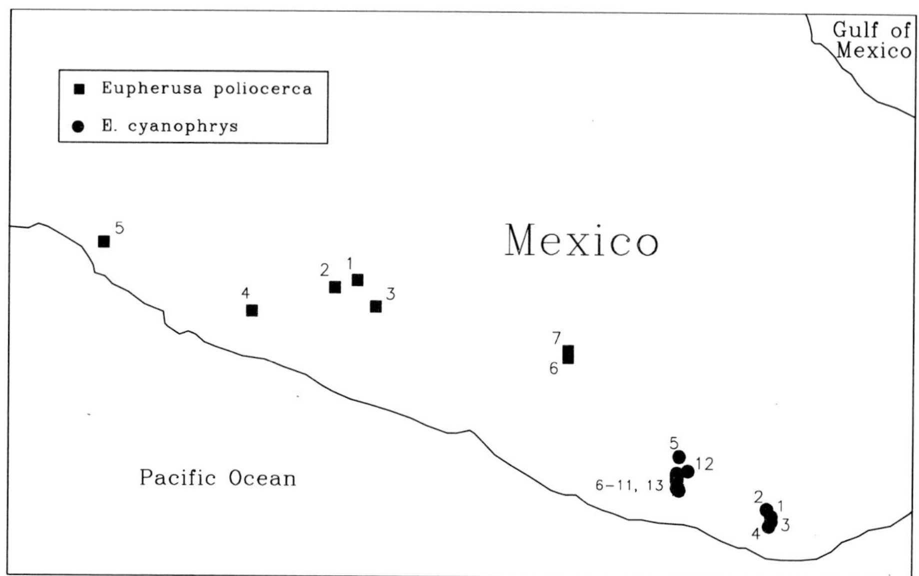

Guerrero Most records for this species in the state are of specimens labelled from the vicinity of Chilpancingo[1] (17°33'N 99°30'W), with eight collected in October (year unknown) (two males in MNHN; six specimens, apparently three males and three females in AMNH: see Remarks 2), plus a male and two females in February 1940 (in MVZ). As Chilpancingo is in an arid valley it seems more likely that these specimens actually came from nearer Omiltemi. At and near Omiltemi[2], in the mountains above and west of Chilpancingo (Salvin and Godman 1888-1904: 17°30'N 99°40'W), specimens were taken in 1936 and 1964 (see Population and Ecology), and more recently (1985) specimens have been taken specifically at Captación Agua Fría, Captación Potrerillos and Hortiguillas (Navarro *et al.* 1991). Acahuizotla[3] is also in this general area with seven specimens (all in DMNH) taken 15 km to the east (17°22'N 99°22'W), between 1964 and 1971. Other localities (along the Atoyac de Alvarez–Teotepec road) are "Atoyac de Alvarez", where five specimens (in MZFC) were apparently collected 22-23 January 1986, between 1,200 and 2,500 m along the road (A. G. Navarro and A. T. Peterson *in litt.* 1991); a number of localities between (and north of) Paraíso and Nueva Delhi[4] (Howell 1992), including (often represented by specimens) El Faisanal (7.5 km north-north-east of Paraíso), Nueva Delhi (8.5 km north-north-east of Paraíso), Retrocesos (5.5 km south of Puerto el Gallo), La Golondrina (13 km north-north-east of Paraíso), El Descanso (2 km south-west of Puerto el Gallo), and El Iris (3 km north-east of Puerto El Gallo) (Navarro *et al.* 1991, Navarro 1992), Arroyo Grande, 13 km north-east of Paraíso (Ornelas 1987), and Chimicotitlan (untraced) where a female and two males were collected December 1978 (in CMN). This species has also been recorded further west along the sierra, inland from Zihuatanejo[5] (A. G. Navarro and A. T. Peterson *in litt.* 1991).

Oaxaca The species was first described from two specimens taken at (or near) Putla de Guerrero[6] in the Sierra Yucuyacua, westernmost Oaxaca (Elliot 1871, Salvin and Godman 1888-1904). Subsequent records are from the road just north of Putla de Guerrero (c.5 km north-east; 9-10 km by road) at km 135, c.17°04'N 97°56'W, in June and July 1965 (specimens in AMNH and WFVZ); Binford (1989) noted the species as present from c.6-18 km (by road) north of Putla de Guerrero[7], and records one from 10 km north (at 915 m) during February 1974 (L. C. Binford *in litt.* 1991); and most recently, S. N. G. Howell (*in litt.* 1991) saw a female (presumably this species) 8 km (by road) north on 5 January 1987 (see Threats). This stretch of road represents the only undisputed locality for the species in Oaxaca (see Remarks 3).

POPULATION Not long after the discovery of the White-tailed Hummingbird, Montes de Oca (1875) regarded it as "rare", a conclusion upheld by subsequent authors (e.g. Friedmann *et al.* 1950, Rowley and Orr 1964). Most recently, Binford (1989) described the species in Oaxaca as a "very uncommon, permanent resident". These assessments appear to be based on distributional rarity, since the specimen data reveal that eight were collected from a breeding population in the mountains around Chilpancingo (five males, three females, a nest and two eggs in AMNH, MNHN: Hartert and Hartert 1894, Rowley and Orr 1964; see Remarks 2), eight were taken at Omiltemi during 1936 (in ANSP, MCZ and MNHN), and three from close by, 22-23 October 1964 (in DMNH), all of which tends to suggest that its local status cannot be judged rare. Indeed recently, in one particular area of the Sierra Madre del Sur of Guerrero, five birds (in MZFC) were taken in two days during January 1986, and observations (and specimens: Navarro *et al.* 1991) there at various times during the 1980s (including April 1988, March and May 1990) revealed this species to be the commonest hummingbird, and it is now generally considered to be fairly common to common, but extremely local (Ceballos-Lascurain 1989, S. N. G. Howell *in litt.* 1989, 1991, A. G. Navarro and A. T. Peterson *in litt.* 1991). Good numbers of this species survive in the Omiltemi State Ecological Park (A. G. Navarro *in litt.* 1991).

ECOLOGY The White-tailed Hummingbird is a permanent resident in cloud-forest, evergreen subtropical and semi-humid forest and forest edge, although it is probably marginal or seasonal at the lower altitudes (c.1,200 m) in tropical semi-deciduous forest and cloud-forest ecotone (Ornelas 1987, Binford 1989, S. N. G. Howell *in litt.* 1989, 1991, A. G. Navarro and A. T. Peterson *in litt.* 1991, Navarro 1992). At Omiltemi, the species is most commonly found in heavily vegetated humid canyons (A. G. Navarro and A. T. Peterson *in litt.* 1991). The AOU (1983) view of it as an inhabitant of open woodland, forest edge and clearings, in semi-arid situations of the subtropical zone, is evidently in error. From March to May (1988 and 1990) birds were common in cloud-forest and adjacent coffee fincas, but notably absent from fincas not close to forest (despite abundant flowers attended by many hummingbirds): while often seen at the edge of forest where flowers may be more concentrated, this species seems to require virgin forest – coffee fincas with shade-trees are not adequate (S. N. G. Howell *in litt.* 1991). It is primarily a cloud-forest or humid montane forest bird that may engage in (little known) seasonal altitudinal movements (S. N. G. Howell *in litt.* 1991): altitudes of 915-1,465 m have been recorded in Oaxaca (Binford 1989) and 1,000-2,440 m in Guerrero (Hartert and Hartert 1894, Ornelas 1987, S. N. G. Howell *in litt.* 1991). Breeding data have only been recorded a small number of times: a nest and two eggs was found in October at Chilpancingo (1,525-2,135 m; Hartert and Hartert 1894); specimens in breeding condition were collected in February 1985 and April 1983 (in

MZFC); two young males were taken at Omiltemi (2,440 m) in October 1936 (in MNHN), with a young female there in October 1985 (in MZFC) and another young male there in June 1985 (in MZFC); and young males were collected at Atoyac de Alvarez in March and April 1983 and 1984 (in MZFC). Many males were "singing strongly" near Arroyo Grande in mid-April 1988 (S. N. G. Howell *in litt.* 1991), and the closely related Oaxaca Hummingbird *Eupherusa cyanophrys* has been recorded breeding in May, October and November (see Remarks 3, and relevant account), suggesting that the breeding season peaks in February–May and again in September–October.

THREATS Despite inhabiting areas within one of the largest tracts of virgin cloud-forest left in Mexico, the White-tailed Hummingbird is threatened by forest destruction, which is causing the steady removal of its habitat, to the point where it has been totally removed in parts of the species's range (S. N. G. Howell *in litt.* 1987, 1989). North of Putla de Guerrero, apart from a remnant arroyo of semi-humid woodland (where a female was seen in January 1987), the whole area (at least near the road) has been deforested and now comprises rocky grassland (S. N. G. Howell *in litt.* 1991). On the slope of the Sierra de Atoyac (from Paraíso to Teotepec), the semi-deciduous forest at the base of the range is being rapidly cleared for cultivation, the cloud-forest zone below 1,800 m is almost completely under cultivation of coffee, and the higher altitude forest (at the upper limit of the range of this species) is being logged at an alarming rate (Navarro 1992: see Threats under White-throated Jay *Cyanolyca mirabilis*).

MEASURES TAKEN None is known, although the Guerrero National Park (Anon. 1989) may harbour the species but is itself poorly protected and suffers from extensive habitat degradation (S. N. G. Howell *in litt.* 1991). The White-tailed Hummingbird is apparently common within the Omiltemi State Ecological Park which covers 9,600 ha of the area to the west of Chilpancingo (Navarro and Muñoz 1990, A. G. Navarro *in litt.* 1991: see equivalent section under White-throated Jay).

MEASURES PROPOSED Any remaining cloud-forest habitat in the Paraíso–Chilpancingo–Putla de Guerrero region (and west of Paraíso) needs to be given some form of protection from indiscriminate cutting and burning, priority being given to the areas where the species is currently known to occur, such as Arroyo Grande where it is common (and where the Short-crested Coquette *Lophornis brachylopha* also occurs at lower elevations; see relevant account): for more comprehensive actions to preserve forest in this region, see the equivalent section under White-throated Jay. Combined with this protection, surveys need to be undertaken in all suitable habitat west of Paraíso, and between there and Putla de Guerrero, in order to determine the actual distribution of the species and the extent of remaining habitat, which is also important for a number of other threatened birds (see under White-throated Jay, which ranges to higher altitudes, and Short-crested Coquette).

REMARKS (1) Boucard (1895) mentioned Chinantla as a locality for *Eupherusa poliocerca*. AOU (1983) regarded this locality as in Puebla state but suspected the record referred to Stripe-tailed Hummingbird *E. eximia*. Binford (1989) located the only traceable Chinantla in southern Puebla in an arid habitat unsuitable for any species of *Eupherusa*. Either, therefore, this record is somehow in error or an untraced Chinantla exists or existed in Oaxaca or Guerrero. (2) There is some confusion as to the number of specimens collected by Baron near Chilpancingo: with two males in MNHN, we must assume that Baron collected five males and three females, presumably three of each sex presently held at the AMNH. (3) Two female *Eupherusa* hummingbirds (in AMNH) were collected at río Jalatengo, Oaxaca, in May 1962 and were identified as *E.*

poliocerca. At this time (1962) *E. cyanophrys* had not been described although it is now known that a population of *cyanophrys* exists at this location. As Binford (1989) considered females of these two species inseparable and suggested that the two forms should be regarded as allopatric until adult males are found together or the characters of females are better defined, the two 1962 specimens almost definitely refer to *cyanophrys*. Four *Eupherusa* specimens collected 3-4 July 1985 (in MZFC) at San Pedro Yosotato, Oaxaca, were also identified as *poliocerca* but probably refer to *cyanophrys* (the sex of these specimens is unknown, and the locality untraced).

SCISSOR-TAILED HUMMINGBIRD *Hylonympha macrocerca* V/R[10]

This hummingbird is endemic to the cloud-forests of the Paria Peninsula, north-eastern Venezuela, a restricted habitat that is under threat from agricultural encroachment.

DISTRIBUTION The Scissor-tailed Hummingbird (see Remarks) is endemic to the mountains of the Paria Peninsula, Sucre state, north-eastern Venezuela, an area which it shares with four other threatened species (see Threats under White-tailed Sabrewing *Campylopterus ensipennis*). Described in 1873 from trade-skins, the origin of this species was not known until 1947, when birds were collected on the Paria Peninsula (Phelps and Phelps 1948).

Records come from two main areas on the peninsula, in the centre and at the easternmost end, the localities involved (coordinates from Paynter 1982) being as follows: Cerro Humo (c.10°40'N 62°30'W), whence come the majority of recent records, specifically from the villages of Manacal and Las Melenas (G. Medina-Cuervo *in litt.* 1986, B. Swift *in litt.* 1986, Goodwin 1990, M. Pearman *in litt.* 1991); Terrón de Azúcar (untraced, but seemingly close to Cerro Humo: Phelps and Phelps 1958, Paynter 1982), a locality mentioned by Phelps and Phelps (1958); Cerro Patao (c.10 km west of Cerro Azul: Bond *et al.* 1989), a locality mentioned by G. Medina-Cuervo (*in litt.* 1986); Cerro "El Olvido" (c.2.5 km west of Cerro Azul, on the ridge between Cerro Patao and Azul: Bond *et al.* 1989), where the species was studied during July to September 1988 (Bond *et al.* 1989); Cerro Azul (c.10°40'N 61°56'W), where five males and nine females were taken during September 1947 (Phelps and Phelps 1948).

POPULATION The shipments of trade-skins to London (the second of which comprised 62 birds of this species) in 1873, and the subsequent series taken on Cerro Azul, led Phelps and Phelps (1948) to consider the Scissor-tailed Hummingbird common. The series of 72 skins in COP includes many taken on the same day, and there are recent observations of 2-7 individuals per day on Cerro Humo, where the bird apparently outnumbers the White-tailed Sabrewing (in March 1984 and July 1990: B. Swift *in litt.* 1986, M. Pearman *in litt.* 1991). On Cerro El Olvido between July and September 1988, Bond *et al.* (1989) recorded this species as "abundant" (absolute numbers estimated at three males and four females) in upper montane forest above 840 m, and rare below this elevation (just three individuals seen between 685 and 785 m): however, the bird was also found to be "abundant" (two males and two females) in mature secondary forest at c.530 m. The density of birds was calculated at between four and eight individuals per hectare, and this was extrapolated to give a population estimate (for the area from Cerro Patao eastwards, above 500 m) of 300 individuals along the ridge, with 700 below this and in secondary growth (Bond *et al.* 1989). The population on Cerro Humo can be assumed to be quite high owing to the numbers recently observed, but there appear to be no recent records of birds from anywhere other than this site and Cerro El Olvido. Further observation is needed in other areas between Cerros Patao and Azul before the estimates outlined above can be used with any confidence.

ECOLOGY The Scissor-tailed Hummingbird has been found between 800 and 1,200 m on Cerro Humo (Meyer de Schauensee and Phelps 1978, G. Medina-Cuervo *in litt.* 1986), whereas further east (where the mountains are no higher than 920 m) birds have mainly been recorded from 685 to 920 m, but the species is known from as low as 530 m on Cerro El Olvido (Phelps and Phelps 1948, Bond *et al.* 1989). It inhabits lower and upper montane rainforest (cloud-forest), and mature and secondary forest (Bond *et al.* 1989). Meyer de Schauensee and Phelps (1978) noted the species as one of forest-edge and small clearings, an assessment reinforced by M. Pearman (*in litt.* 1991), who observed that the bird appears to be one of forest edge rather than the interior. However, the Scissor-tailed Hummingbird was found to be common on the summit of Cerro Azul (in primary cloud-forest) in 1947, and on adjacent Cerro El Olvido the species was much commoner inside the forest of the upper montane zone than in other habitats (Phelps and Phelps

1948, Bond *et al.* 1989), this also being the case on Cerro Humo (C. Sharpe *in litt.* 1992). Within primary cloud-forest (characterized by a lower, more open canopy, luxuriant epiphytic growth, and the presence of small palms in the undergrowth), birds feed mainly at bromeliad flowers and on their insect inhabitants, whereas in secondary forest feeding was associated with the shrubs *Heliconia aurea* and *Costus* sp. (Bond *et al.* 1989). Birds hawk for insects from exposed perches or opportunistically whilst perched (Bond *et al.* 1989). A female that occupied a feeding territory for at least the month of August (this was post-breeding, and no sexual interactions were noted) spent 80-85% of her time perching 3-5 m up (B. Swift *in litt.* 1986 noted perching typically between 10 and 25 m up), and 13% feeding (Bond *et al.* 1989).

THREATS The Scissor-tailed Hummingbird has had its entire range "protected" since 1978 within the Paria Peninsula National Park, but despite this the available habitat is now very restricted, and threatened by agricultural encroachment: Cerro Humo may have no more than 1,500 ha of suitable habitat remaining, this area being very accessible by road, and subjected to much human disturbance (G. Medina-Cuervo *in litt.* 1986). Further details of habitat destruction and threats within the Paria Peninsula National Park are given in the equivalent section under White-tailed Sabrewing.

MEASURES TAKEN This species has only been recorded from areas now within the Paria Peninsula National Park (37,500 ha), which covers all montane areas between Cerro Humo and Cerro Azul (Bond *et al.* 1989: see corresponding section under White-tailed Sabrewing).

MEASURES PROPOSED For the Scissor-tailed Hummingbird the priority has to be the guaranteed protection of the forests on Cerro Humo and those further east, around Cerros Patao and Azul (see Population). The population appears to be healthy (see above), but the status of this species is essentially unknown away from Cerro Humo and Cerro El Olvido. More could be discovered about the bird's ecological requirements, especially with reference to the way it utilizes second-growth forest and forest edge, therefore a study concentrating on these points would be valuable. All studies and initiatives should integrate with work on all five threatened species in this area (see Threats under White-tailed Sabrewing).

REMARKS The Scissor-tailed Hummingbird is the only member of its genus.

PURPLE-BACKED SUNBEAM *Aglaeactis aliciae* I[6]

This rare montane hummingbird is confined to a tiny area of montane shrubbery at just over 3,000 m in the upper Marañón drainage of western Peru, where it is poorly known and in need of investigation.

DISTRIBUTION The Purple-backed Sunbeam (see Remarks 1) is known from a few recent sightings and specimens, and from two older collections, all within 20 km of each other in the upper río Marañón valley, La Libertad department, western Peru, where localities (coordinates from Stephens and Traylor 1983) are as follows: above Succha (Succha was a hacienda at this time, at 7°54'S 77°41'W: see Remarks 2), on the left bank of the río Marañón, Huamachuco province, where the type-series (21 specimens in AMNH, BMNH, FMNH, MCZ, MNHN, USNM and WFVZ) was collected at 3,050-3,200 m in February and March 1895 (Salvin 1896); above Soquián (7°51'S 77°41'W), a hacienda at 2,000 m, just a few kilometres from Succha, where seven specimens (in ANSP and WFVZ) were collected (by M. A. Carriker) in June 1932 (see Remarks 3). Some 20 km north-west of the type-locality at Molino (c.7°45'S 77°46'W: c.10 km north-west of and above Aricapampa, on the road from Trujillo to río Marañón), a few birds were seen and some collected at 3,000 m in October and November 1979 (T. S. Schulenberg *in litt.* 1989).

POPULATION In 1895, 21 specimens were collected in eight days, with seven taken in two days in 1932 (see above), suggesting that the species must then have been at least fairly common (NK). The continued presence of the species near to the type-locality was confirmed in 1979 (see above) although the modern status of the population remains unknown.

ECOLOGY The Purple-backed Sunbeam inhabits shrubbery with alders *Alnus* and other trees at 3,050-3,200 m, and has been observed feeding from an orange-red flowered mistletoe (probably the loranthacean *Tristerix longebrachteatum*: NK) that parasitize these trees in abundance, and from a white-flowered leguminaceous bush with oleander-like leaves, which grows above 2,450 m in Ecuador and Peru (Baron 1897). Other species of the genus *Aglaeactis* have adapted well to human presence, being able to feed from *Eucalyptus*, and regularly feeding from the shrubs that often border fields and villages: this may prove the case with *aliciae* (T. S. Schulenberg *in litt.* 1989). Two males collected in June had slightly enlarged testes, juveniles and immatures being taken in February, March and June (specimens in AMNH, ANSP, FMNH and USNM).

THREATS With its extremely restricted range, the Purple-backed Sunbeam would appear very vulnerable to habitat destruction. However, the status of its habitat remains unknown, and it seems possible that it can tolerate some degree of habitat alteration (T. S. Schulenberg *in litt.* 1989).

MEASURES TAKEN None is known.

MEASURES PROPOSED The status of this species and its habitat should be investigated, and the extent to which it can thrive in secondary habitats needs to be assessed.

REMARKS (1) It has been suggested that the Purple-backed Sunbeam is a well-marked subspecies of the Shining Sunbeam *Aglaeactis cupripennis* (Zimmer 1951, Schuchmann 1985). However, *A. c. cajabambae* occurs at Cajabamba, only some 55 km north-west of Succha (and presumably also at Huamachuco some 45 km west of Succha); *A. c. caumatonotus* occurs at Cochabamba, only 24 km west of Succha and 16 km west-south-west of Molino, and also at Yánac further south, in Ancash department; and *A. c. ruficauda* at Patás on the right bank of the Marañón, only some 16 km from Succha (Zimmer 1951). Thus *aliciae* is surrounded by three forms of *cupripennis* that are more similar to each other than any is to *aliciae*, and as there are no specimens showing any signs of hybridization (Zimmer 1951) and the two may eventually be found to be sympatric, it appears best to retain *aliciae* as a distinct species. (2) Succha was erroneously placed in Ancash department by Peters (1951) and Meyer de Schauensee (1970), and erroneously cited as Huamachuco (see Zimmer 1951). (3) No altitude was given on Carriker's specimens, and although he did collect some species at Soquián between 2,440 m and 2,745 m (Carriker 1933, Bond 1947, 1951a), he may well have collected this sunbeam higher up, perhaps even at the type-locality.

BLACK INCA *Coeligena prunellei* V/R[10]

This hummingbird was originally thought to have a very limited range along the western slope of the East Andes of Colombia. Many recent records indicate that it might have a wider distribution, but its apparent association with now dwindling tracts of oak forest indicates its vulnerability to habitat clearance.

DISTRIBUTION The Black Inca occurs on the western slope of the East Andes in south-east Santander, western Boyacá and western Cundinamarca departments, and also on the western slope of the Central Andes in Quindío department, Colombia. Localities where this hummingbird has been recorded (with coordinates, unless otherwise stated, from Paynter and Traylor 1981) are as follows:

Santander Virolín[1] (6°05'N 73°12'W), where three males (in USNM) were collected at 1,675-1,705 m in August 1943 (28 km south of Charalá on the Duitama road), with two birds (in ICN) taken between 1,840 and 1,970 m during November and December 1978, and within a 5 km radius of which birds were seen during March 1988 (Brooke 1988b); Finca La Argentina (untraced, but in the vicinity of Virolín), where two birds (in ICN) were taken at 2,070-2,150 m in November 1979 and February 1980; and Loma del Rayo (untraced, but also in the vicinity of Virolín), where three birds (in ICN) were collected at 1,980-1,995 m, also in November 1979 and February 1980;

Boyacá Cerro Carare[2] (5°55'N 73°27'W: OG 1964), c.9 km east-south-east of Toqui, where the bird was found to be quite common between 2,300 and 2,500 m during 1978 (King 1978-1979), and where M. Pearman (*in litt.* 1988, 1990) found three birds during February 1987 (on a ridge known locally as "Las Penas");

Cundinamarca Yacopí[3] (c.5°30'N 74°20'W; at 1,415 m, and c.12 km north-north-east of La Palma), and Guaduas[4] (5°04'N 74°36'W; at c.1,000 m), both mentioned by Meyer de Schauensee (1948-1952) and Olivares (1969); La Vega[5] (5°00'N 74°21'W), mentioned by King (1978-1979); on the road to La Vega[6] (4°56'N 74°18'W: coordinates from P. Kaestner), where the species was recorded at 2,100 m in April 1989 (P. Kaestner *in litt.* 1992); Chimbe[7] (4°55'N 74°28'W: OG 1964), a locality mentioned by Geoffroy (1861) and Olivares (1969); Albán[8] (4°53'N 74°27'W; 12 km north-west of Facacativá), mentioned by Nicéforo and Olivares (1967) and Olivares (1969); Facacativá[9] (4°49'N 74°22'W), where the type-specimen was collected at 2,600 m (Bourcier 1843, Meyer de Schauensee 1948-1952); Anolaima[10] (4°46'N 74°28'W; at c.1,500 m, and 14 km south-west of Facacativá), mentioned by Geoffroy (1861) and Olivares (1969); Laguna de Pedropalo[11] (c.4°45'N 74°24'W; at 2,010 m, and 9 km north of Tena), where specimens (in ICN, WFVZ) were collected between 1967 and 1983, and where birds were seen on a number of occasions between 1988 and 1990 (P. Kaestner *in litt.* 1992); near Laguna de Pedropalo at km 28 on the Bogotá–La Mesa road[12] (La Mesa is at 4°38'N 74°28'W), where birds were recently recorded at 1,800 m (P. Kaestner *in litt.* 1992); Bojacá[13] (4°44'N 74°21'W; at 2,845 m), where the species was recorded in 1974 (King 1978-1979); Vereda El Roble (untraced, but in La Vega municipality: see Remarks), where a bird (in ICN) was taken at 2,400 m in September 1965;

Quindío Salento (4°38'N 75°34'W), where a male (in MHNUC) was taken in February 1976 (A. Negret *in litt.* 1992), this being the only record from the Central Andes.

POPULATION The Black Inca is generally rare (S. L. Hilty *in litt.* 1986), and was only infrequently recorded from the turn of the century until the late 1960s (see above). However, recent records from near Virolín, including four observations during a week in March 1988 (Brooke 1988b: see above) suggest that it is not uncommon there (G. Arango verbally 1991). At Cerro Carare, King (1978-1979) reported the species to be quite common (in 1978), with a total population that "must have run into many hundreds", M. Pearman (*in litt.* 1990) finding three birds there on one day in February 1987 and reporting that locals knew the bird well. The Black Inca is also regularly recorded at Laguna de Pedropalo (F. G. Stiles verbally 1991), where P. Kaestner (*in litt.* 1992) saw birds on six out of eight visits to the site between 1988 and 1990; moreover, this hummingbird has been recorded at a number of sites nearby (see Distribution), but cannot be found with any regularity other than at the lake (e.g. P. Kaestner *in litt.* 1992 searched for the species eight times without success in the roadside forest at km 28). The evidence thus suggests that, at best, this species is locally fairly common.

ECOLOGY Recorded elevations at which the Black Inca has been collected or observed are between 1,675 and 2,500 m, although the altitudes of a number of collecting localities are between c.1,000 and 2,845 m (see Distribution). The Black Inca primarily inhabits the interior of humid montane forest, especially oak (*Quercus humboldtii* and *Trigonobalanus excelsa*) forest (Hilty and Brown 1986, M. Pearman *in litt.* 1988, P. Kaestner *in litt.* 1992, LGN). However, at Virolín birds were recorded in open parkland and riverside gallery forest as well as in primary stands of oak (Brooke 1988b), and at Cerro Carare M. Pearman (*in litt.* 1990) reported that locals had observed birds in a flowering garden. The species is a "trap-lining" nectar feeder (but territories are occasionally defended), favouring species with pendant flowers and long corolla tubes, especially vines and climbers (e.g. *Aphelandra*, *Palicourea*, *Psammisia*, *Thibaudia* species), tree-ferns, which it finds from lower mid-levels, in the canopy, and low at forest edges, in parkland, etc. (Snow and Snow 1980, Brooke 1988b, Fjeldså and Krabbe 1990, P. Kaestner *in litt.* 1992), and also *Fuchsia*, *Bomarea* and *Aetanthus*, all of which thrive along forest edge and in old second growth (F. G. Stiles *in litt.* 1992). The gonad condition and moulting sequence of specimens in ICN suggests that breeding takes place between June and October (LGN).

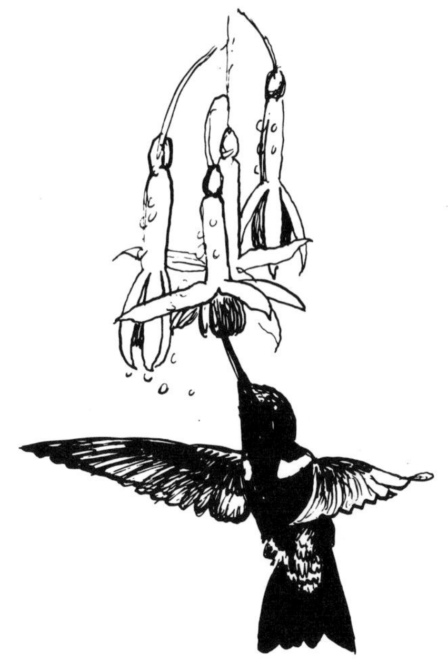

THREATS Although this hummingbird has been seen in tiny relict forest patches (D. W. Snow *in litt.* 1986, P. Kaestner *in litt.* 1992), it appears to be commonest in areas where quite extensive forest remains (see Population), and as such must be considered threatened owing to the serious depletion of humid temperate (especially oak-dominated) forest on the western slope of the East Andes (King 1978-1979, LGN). Many areas (e.g. Virolín, Cerro Carare and Laguna de Pedropalo) are now surrounded by intensive crop cultivation or pastureland (Brooke 1988b, M. Pearman *in litt.* 1990, P. Kaestner *in litt.* 1992). Whether this species can maintain a viable population away from more extensive areas of forest is unknown, although it will probably survive if patches of woodland remain along streams and on steep slopes (as in the Bojacá–Laguna de Pedropalo area: see Ecology) (F. G. Stiles *in litt.* 1992).

MEASURES TAKEN Based on recommendations outlined in Romero-Zambrano (1983) for the conservation of the Gorgeted Wood-quail *Odontophorus strophium* (see relevant account), ICBP and Fundación Natura supported a survey of the oak-dominated forests of the Virolín area in Santander in March 1988, and since this time ICBP, Fundación Natura and INDERENA have been working on a cooperative project to create a protected area there, now to be called the Cachalú Wildlife Sanctuary (Fundación Natura 1990, G. I. Andrade *in litt.* 1990).

MEASURES PROPOSED Apart from the proposal made for the creation of Cachalú Wildlife Sanctuary in the Virolín area (which has yet to be formally designated), since 1990 both the "Grupo Ornis" and the recently founded "Sociedad Bogotana de Ornitología" have been promoting the necessity of giving legal protection to the remnant oak forest that surrounds Laguna de

Pedropalo, where this species, Turquoise Dacnis *Dacnis hartlaubi* and Apolinar's Wren *Cistothorus apolinari* (see relevant accounts) have been recorded in recent years. Formal protection of Laguna de Pedropalo and the Virolín area is an urgent priority, and these current initiatives should be strongly encouraged.

Surveys are needed in the few remnants of upper and lower montane humid forest across the western slope of the East Andes, both of which have suffered extensive deforestation, but are important for a number of sympatric threatened species, e.g. Gorgeted Wood-quail, Chestnut-bellied Hummingbird *Amazilia castaneiventris*, White-mantled Barbet *Capito hypoleucus*, Recurve-billed Bushbird *Clytoctantes alixii*, Turquoise Dacnis, Red-bellied Grackle *Hypopyrrhus pyrohypogaster* (see relevant accounts), and also the near-threatened Sooty Ant-tanager *Habia gutturalis*, so any conservation initiatives should, where possible, consider the needs of all the above species. As well as determining the extent of remaining habitat and current status of the threatened species in this area, the precise ecological requirements of the Black Inca need to be assessed so that its habitat preference, and the extent to which it relies on large areas of forest, can be determined. Although only known from one (recent) record on the western slope of the Central Andes, the immediate area of this is (or at least was) important for six other threatened species, the details and conservation of which are given in the equivalent section under Moustached Antpitta *Grallaria alleni*.

REMARKS Although untraced, "Vereda El Roble" may refer to El Roble (c.4°23'N 74°19'W; at 2,475 m) on the old Bogotá–Fusagasugá trail.

ROYAL SUNANGEL *Heliangelus regalis* K[12]

This hummingbird is known from two localities in northern Peru, where it inhabits subtropical forest-edge shrubbery on very poor soils. At the one locality where it is common, its habitat borders cultivated areas.

DISTRIBUTION The Royal Sunangel is known from 22 specimens taken at two localities in the departments of Cajamarca and San Martín, northern Peru: (*Cajamarca*) above San José de Lourdes (c.5°02'S 78°51'W), at 1,800-2,200 m, east of the río Chinchipe valley in the Cordillera del Condor, where the species was discovered in June 1975 (Fitzpatrick *et al.* 1979, NK); and (*San Martín*) c.15 km on the Balsapuerto trail north-east of Jirillo (c.6°03'S 76°44'W), where two males were collected at 1,450 m in October and November 1983 (Davis 1986). It presumably occurs in part of the intervening region, i.e. in the foothills immediately south of the río Marañón, and possibly also north along the Peru–Ecuador border in Cordillera del Condor (Fitzpatrick *et al.* 1979), although its forest-edge habitat may occur only in the southern end of the mountains.

POPULATION In San Martín only two or three birds were recorded (two collected) during almost a month's survey in October and November 1983 (Davis 1986), while the species was common above San José de Lourdes during June 1975 and July 1976 (Fitzpatrick *et al.* 1979, Parker *et al.* 1982, NK).

ECOLOGY Unless otherwise stated, everything in this section is derived from Fitzpatrick *et al.* (1979). Records of this extremely localized hummingbird come from 1,450 m in San Martín, and between 1,800 and 2,200 m in Cajamarca (see Distribution). The southern extremity of Cordillera del Condor reaches an elevation of about 2,850 m, where it is capped by a dense but stunted cloud-forest growing on a leached, desiccation-prone sandstone substrate, subjected to daily rain almost throughout the year. To the south, this forest gives way abruptly to a mosaic of dense, bushy hillsides, grazed and frequently burnt grassland, and blackwater bogs in the shallow valleys between hills. The Royal Sunangel appears to be most numerous on the brushy slopes bordering the forest edge and along steep ravine banks, where the vegetation is characterized by abundant melastomes (at least three common species) and an undergrowth containing ericaceans and large stands of bracken fern: the brush is extremely dense, up to 1-2 m in height, and reaches heights of 4-5 m along ravines and near the forest border. The hummingbird has occasionally been sighted (and was once netted) inside the forest in areas where sparse canopy permitted a proliferation of understorey plants: the open bogs and burnt pastures to the south, and the forest at 2,450 m to the north, appear not to be frequented by the species. In San Martín, the bird was similarly recorded in mossy, stunted forest (with a canopy height of c.4 m), along the top of a short ridge rising abruptly from the surrounding upper tropical forest (Davis 1986).

In June and July both male and female showed a distinct preference for nectar from the flowers of the melastome *Brachyotum quinquenerve*, and nearly all flower visits were to that species, despite the presence of several other flowering plants, including two other species of melastome. *B. quinquenerve*, a low shrub, has abundant hanging flowers arranged serially along multiple stems, and the Royal Sunangel has to hover directly below and point its bill straight upward to take the nectar, or (as was the case in c.25% of flower visits recorded) by perching on the stem below the flower: nectar was invariably taken through the open end of the corolla. The birds also frequently foraged for small insects by sallying outward or upward several metres from an exposed perch to snatch aerial prey, and usually returned to the same perch. Birds were highly territorial, and male-chases were common: the territory sizes of males were estimated to be about 40-50 m in diameter, and all such territories contained good stands of *Brachyotum* in full bloom. Seven specimens taken in July had active gonads, at which time display was observed, and males were far more visible than females (also the case in early September: NK), all indicating that breeding was taking place (at least in late July), thus coinciding with the onset of the (relatively) dry season. Specimens taken in October and November were not in breeding condition (Davis 1986).

THREATS None is known, but the limited distribution of the species plus the close proximity of cultivated land in Cordillera del Condor renders it vulnerable.

MEASURES TAKEN None is known.

MEASURES PROPOSED A study to disclose the distributional status of this species should be undertaken. A protected area with a wide altitudinal range, so as to hold both the present species, other threatened birds such as Spot-winged Parrotlet *Touit stictoptera*, Ash-throated Antwren *Herpsilochmus parkeri* (hopefully), Cinnamon-breasted Tody-tyrant *Hemitriccus cinnamomeipectus* and perhaps the Orange-throated Tanager *Wetmorethraupis sterrhopteron* (see relevant accounts), and near-threatened species like Bar-winged Wood-wren *Henicorhina leucoptera*, should be established in the Cordillera del Condor.

REMARKS The female plumage and lack of leg-puffs clearly place this species in *Heliangelus*, where, however, it appears to have no very close relatives (Fitzpatrick *et al.* 1979).

TURQUOISE-THROATED PUFFLEG *Eriocnemis godini* E/Ex[4]

Possibly extinct, this poorly known hummingbird is known from just one locality in northern Ecuador, in an area that has now been largely cleared of natural vegetation and where it has not been certainly recorded this century.

DISTRIBUTION The Turquoise-throated Puffleg (see Remarks) is endemic to northern Ecuador where it is confirmed from just one locality, and possibly south-western Colombia (coordinates are taken from Paynter and Traylor 1977, 1981: see Remarks).

Colombia Two "Bogotá" trade-skins (in AMNH) taken during the nineteenth century appear to be the only evidence of this species occurring within Colombia, although Hilty and Brown (1986) and hence Fjeldså and Krabbe (1990) suggested (presumably on the evidence of these skins) that the birds may have been taken south of Pasto (1°13'N 77°17'W) in southern Nariño.

Ecuador Four specimens (in AMNH, BMNH, FMNH) are from "Ecuador", but the type-specimen (a male in BMNH) taken in 1850 appears to be the only one with any locality information, having been taken at Guaillabamba (0°04'N 78°21'W, in Pichincha province) in ravines in the valley of the río Guaillabamba, and south of the town of Perucho (R. Bleiweiss *in litt.* 1982). Since the turn of the century there have been no firm records of this species, although there is an unconfirmed sighting from near Quito in the Chillo valley, made in 1976 (R. Bleiweiss *in litt.* 1982).

POPULATION Nothing has been recorded concerning the past abundance of this hummingbird, and it is now quite possibly extinct, with no confirmed records of it this century.

ECOLOGY The Turquoise-throated Puffleg was recorded at the type-locality between 2,100 and 2,300 m in an area described as a hot (presumably arid) ravine within the valley (Hilty and Brown 1986, Fjeldså and Krabbe 1990). Fjeldså and Krabbe (1990) suggested, on the evidence of the "Bogotá" trade-skins and old unconfirmed statements, that the species may have occurred in temperate zones.

THREATS What is surmised to be this species's native habitat has been almost completely destroyed in the río Guaillabamba valley, although remnants of apparently natural habitat can be found in steep-sided stream-cuts (in the arid upper Guaillabamba drainage), and more extensively in the area of Volcán de Pulalahua and río Blanco (north-west of Quito) (R. Bleiweiss *in litt.* 1982).

MEASURES TAKEN The type-locality is not within any protected area. A search specifically for this species during 1980 at a large number of sites from the head of the Chillo valley north to Perucho, and from west of Perucho to Loma Porotopamba, failed, although remnants of suitable habitat were found and investigated (R. Bleiweiss *in litt.* 1982; see above).

MEASURES PROPOSED It must be hoped that the Turquoise-throated Puffleg still exists within remnant patches of suitable habitat, and should be searched for during fieldwork in any areas near the type-locality.

REMARKS This species closely resembles Glowing Puffleg *Eriocnemis vestitus*, and it has probably been overlooked because of the similarity (Hilty and Brown 1986): however, the taxon appears to be a valid species (Fjeldså and Krabbe 1990; also R. Bleiweiss *in litt.* 1982).

COLOURFUL PUFFLEG *Eriocnemis mirabilis* R[11]

Discovered in 1967, this hummingbird remains known only from the vicinity of the type-locality in south-west Colombia, which, however, lies within a national park, and large tracts of forests in the area remain unexplored.

DISTRIBUTION The Colourful Puffleg is known only from the type-locality, Charguayaco (c.2°40'N 76°57'W, c.12.5 km north of Cerro Munchique: see Remarks), on the Pacific slope of the southern West Andes, Cauca department (Meyer de Schauensee 1967, Dunning 1970, Fjeldså and Krabbe 1990, with coordinates from Paynter and Traylor 1981). In the immediate vicinity of the type-locality, Negret (1991) recorded the bird from Planchón (untraced), at 2,200 m on the road above La Gallera, where a male was seen in September 1990.

POPULATION At the type-locality M. Pearman (*in litt.* 1990) found the species to be very localized, seeing three birds (a male and two females) on one day (1 April 1987). At the time the type-specimen was collected (April 1967), one male was taken and several others were captured and released, with two males (in AMNH, USNM) collected on consecutive days in August 1967 (Meyer de Schauensee 1967). Despite five days' searching for this species in suitable habitat within the Munchique National Park, M. Pearman (*in litt.* 1990) found none away from Charguayaco, and Negret (1991) reported just one bird (see above) after three years of fieldwork in Munchique National Park.

ECOLOGY Records of the Colourful Puffleg come from between 2,195 and 2,440 m (specimens in AMNH, ANSP), although M. Pearman (*in litt.* 1990) suggested that the species may show seasonal altitudinal movements. The few records of this bird have all come from subtropical wet forest and adjacent borders, one bird seen feeding at low flowers in a small clearing near forest (Meyer de Schauensee 1967, Hilty and Brown 1986). M. Pearman (*in litt.* 1990) also recorded the species feeding low down, at tiny yellow flowers, probably similar to those of the *Miconia* sp. which was recorded as a food-plant by Negret (1991). The Munchique National Park, where the type-series was collected, comprises 44,000 ha, including mostly humid (more than 3,000 mm rainfall per year) cloud-forests dominated by *Billia colombiana*, *Clusia* spp., *Persea* sp., *Hyeronima colombiana*, *Quercus humboldtii* and *Weinmannia pubescens* (CNPPA 1982, Hernández Camacho *et al.* undated).

THREATS Despite some clearance of the wet forest close to Cerro Munchique, little disturbance is to be expected at the type-locality. If the bird is distributed over a wider area, the present construction of the new road to López de Micay on the Pacific Coast (LGN) might represent a potential threat from deforestation and other human disturbance.

MEASURES TAKEN The Munchique National Park embraces the only known locality for the Colourful Puffleg (see Ecology), and the recently established Los Tambitos Nature Reserve, an area where this hummingbird might occur, also provides some protection (A. J. Negret verbally 1991).

MEASURES PROPOSED The distribution and ecological needs of this species are essentially unknown, and therefore the priority must be to study it at the type-locality in order to determine at what density the population exists and what its requirements are. Once this has been done, other similar areas nearby can be searched to obtain a more accurate impression of the bird's distributional status. Conservation initiatives in this area must also consider the needs of various other threatened species of bird that occur in or around the park, which at altitudes suitable for this species include Yellow-eared Parrot *Ognorhynchus icterotis*, Golden-plumed Parakeet

Leptosittaca branickii, Giant Antpitta *Grallaria gigantea* (at c.3,000 m) and Tanager-finch *Oreothraupis arremonops* (a number of other threatened species occur within Munchique National Park at altitudes below 2,200 m, and these are listed in the equivalent section under Multicoloured Tanager *Chlorochrysa nitidissima*).

REMARKS The specimen in AMNH is labelled "Charguayaco, eight miles south of Cerro Munchique", although subsequent authors, including Paynter and Traylor (1981), show that this locality is north of the cerro.

BLACK-BREASTED PUFFLEG *Eriocnemis nigrivestis* E[1]

The Black-breasted Puffleg is restricted to two adjacent volcanoes in north-west Ecuador, where it seems to be confined to temperate zone ridge-top elfin forest. Some of these ridges have been subject to cultivation, and unless action is taken the species may soon become extinct.

DISTRIBUTION The Black-breasted Puffleg is confined to Volcán Pichincha and Volcán Atacazo, Pichincha province, north-west Ecuador, where it has been recorded at 2,745-3,050 m (2,440 m) from April to June, and at 3,100-4,570 m (4,725 m) from November to February (Bleiweiss and Olalla 1983; label data on specimens in AMNH, BMNH, NRM and USNM; but see Remarks 1, 2). Some of the localities on Volcán Pichincha given on specimen labels were not traced by Paynter and Traylor (1977), e.g. "Cochabamba" and "Ilambo" (specimens in BMNH), but all sites that have been located are situated on ridge crests on the north side of the volcano: Cerro Pugsi (c.0°06'S 78°36'W), between río Mindo and río Verdecocha; Frutillas (0°05'S 78°34'W); Yanococha (c.0°06'S 78°33'W); and Cerro Alaspungo (c.0°01'N 78°34'W) (Bleiweiss and Ollalla 1983; coordinates read from map in Bleiweiss and Olalla 1983). Evidence of the species's occurrence on Volcán Atacazo seems to rest entirely on three males (specimens in USNM) taken in December 1898 (also Oberholser 1902), although a female hummingbird sighted at the treeline (at 3,500 m) in October 1983 appeared to be of this species (NK).

POPULATION The large number of museum specimens (see Remarks 2) suggests that the species was fairly common to common in the past (NK). However, the rapid disappearance of its specialized habitat (Bleiweiss and Olalla 1983), and the paucity of recent sightings despite intensive searches by many observers (P. Greenfield verbally 1984, NK), seem to indicate that it is now rare and vanishing.

ECOLOGY The habitat description in this paragraph is taken from Bleiweiss and Olalla (1983). The Black-breasted Puffleg inhabits humid temperate forest and edge, and appears to be specialized to the vegetation found on ridge crests (i.e. elfin forest): in September 1980, the vegetation on one of these crests (Cerro Pugsi) at 3,020 m was found to be shorter in height than that on surrounding slopes or in valleys, most trees not exceeding 8-10 m and being heavily laden with epiphytes, with the ground covered in a dense growth of ericaceans. Several areas were grazed by cattle, resulting in local grassy openings and, where grazing was not as intensive, in lush second growth primarily of brambles *Rubus* sp. The most conspicuous plant in bloom in the understorey was the small rubiacean tree *Palicourea huigrensis*, with bright blue flowers borne on large panicles. Among the ericaceans were several species of *Disterigma* that formed large tangles up to canopy height as well as less conspicuous species of scrambling form including *Thibaudia floribunda* and *Macleania macrantha*. The undergrowth was rich in flowering herbaceous plants, creepers and vines. During September, several of the commoner plants were nearing the end of flowering, e.g. *Palicourea huigrensis* and the ericaceans.

The fact that specimens taken or seen from November to February are reported as having been at 3,100-4,725 m and those from April to September at 2,400-3,050 m may suggest seasonal migration; the highest elevation recorded (4,725 m) was of a male, and the lowest (2,440 m) of a female, but both sexes have been recorded at 2,745-4,562 m (Bleiweiss and Olalla 1983; specimens in AMNH, ANSP, BMNH, NRM and USNM; see also Remarks 3), and more evidence is needed to prove a difference in elevational preference between the sexes, although this is known to be the case in a number of species of hummingbird, e.g. Viridian Metaltail *Metallura williami* and Rufous-capped Thornbill *Chalcostigma ruficeps* (NK). During a study on Cerro Pugsi during September, two males and a female were observed and the following flower visits noted for the males, the figure in brackets being the number of visits observed: shrubs and scramblers, *Thibaudia floribunda* (22), *Disterigma* cf. *acuminatum* (12), *D. acuminatum* (4), *Rubus* sp. (12),

Macleania macrantha (4 through holes in the corolla either made by them or, more likely, Glossy Flowerpiercers *Diglossa lafresnayii*), *Miconia hymenanthera* (2), and *Fuchsia* cf. *silvatica* (1); vines or climbers, *Tropaeolum pubescens* (7), *Heppiella ampla* (6), *Burmeistera* sp. (5), and *Manettia recurva* (1); herbs, *Psychotria uliginosa* (7); and small trees, *Miconia corymbiformis* (1) and *Palicourea huigrensis* (92) (Bleiweiss and Olalla 1983). The female was recorded feeding from *Rubus* sp. (1) and *Palicourea huigrensis* (24), but as it was only recorded in a *Palicourea* grove with few alternative nectar sources the difference in male–female diet-breadth may be an artefact (Bleiweiss and Olalla 1983).

The pufflegs often extracted nectar while perched (Bleiweiss and Olalla 1983): a male studied closely spent most time in its feeding area perched atop a small (4 m) tree or on nearby secondary perches, from which it would never vocalize, but did catch insects and chased other hummingbird species and Glossy Flowerpiercers; continuous time on the perch ranged from a few seconds to over nine minutes, but was usually 2-4 minutes; from 07h00 to 15h00 it spent 131 minutes perching and had 60 feeding bouts, while the female for the same period had 17 minutes of perching and 18 feeding bouts and thus spent less time in her feeding area; the female adopted inconspicuous perches and never chased after hummingbirds (Bleiweiss and Olalla 1983). The unpronounced territoriality of the male and complete absence of such in the female may have been a seasonal effect (Bleiweiss and Olalla 1983). Nothing is known on breeding, but most hummingbirds on Volcán Pichincha breed between October and March (J. C. Mathéus verbally 1987). The variety of foodplants used and wide distribution of the favoured *Palicourea* suggest that factors other than nectar sources are responsible for the limited distribution of the Black-breasted Puffleg (Bleiweiss and Olalla 1983).

THREATS The vegetation on the ridge crests is disappearing more rapidly than surrounding vegetation because the crests provide flat ground for cultivation in an otherwise steep terrain; the deforestation of these crests was already noted by Chapman (1926). The crests of both Alaspungo and Frutillas have been almost completely cleared of their natural vegetation and, even if the Black-breasted Puffleg still occurs on these ridges, it is doubtful that they do so in any numbers; searches for it there in recent years have proved negative, and on the only site with recent records, Cerro Pugsi, clearing is now progressing (Bleiweiss 1982, Bleiweiss and Olalla 1983).

MEASURES TAKEN None is known.

MEASURES PROPOSED It is essential that remaining areas of ridge-crest forest and other suitable habitat in these areas is secured for the conservation of this species. A more precise assessment of its ecological requirements, especially with reference to its breeding sites and altitudinal movements, is urgently required.

REMARKS (1) Specimens (in BMNH and FMNH) marked "Napo" and "Sarayacu" have undoubtedly been mislabelled, and some marked "Intag", which is in Imbabura, possibly so (NK). (2) The 100 and more specimens in various museums are believed to have been taken on Volcán Pichincha, although most are insufficiently labelled, e.g. "Ecuador", "N. Ecuador", "Quito", "Tumbaco", "Pichincha", "Gualea" (Bleiweiss and Olalla 1983; specimens in AMNH, ANSP, BMNH, FMNH, NRM, ROM, USMN and ZMUC). (3) Records from above 4,000 m seem somewhat dubious as this is well above the treeline. The only records of the species above 3,000 m are the series collected by W. Goodfellow and C. Hamilton between November 1898 and February 1899, and these specimens are labelled as having been taken at "3,660-4,570 m", "3,960 m", "3,960-4,270 m", "4,170 m" and "near summit" (females), and "4,270 m" and "4,725 m" (males) (specimens in BMNH and USNM).

HOARY PUFFLEG *Haplophaedia lugens* **V/R[10]**

This cloud-forest hummingbird has been poorly recorded throughout its small range in Nariño, Colombia, and north-west Ecuador, but has recently been found not uncommon in suitable habitat. It is threatened by deforestation, and a cross-border biosphere reserve would greatly enhance its chances of long-term survival.

DISTRIBUTION The Hoary Puffleg is known from southern Nariño department, Colombia, and Carchi, Imbabura and Pichincha provinces, Ecuador (see Remarks), where localities (with coordinates, unless otherwise stated, from Paynter and Traylor 1977, 1981) are as follows:

Colombia above Junín (along the Pasto–Tumaco road), where the bird can apparently be found (Hilty and Brown 1986); Ricaurte (east of the previous locality, but along the same road), where 12 birds were collected at 1,190 m during April–May 1941, five at 1,500 m in June 1957, and eight between 2,100 and 2,500 m during April–May 1958 (specimens in ANSP, FMNH, LACM, USNM; also Meyer de Schauensee 1948-1952, Orejuela *et al.* 1982); Piguale (untraced, but apparently near Ricaurte), where three birds (in WFVZ) were collected in July 1959; San Pablo (1°06'N 78°01'W; at 1,400 m) (Meyer de Schauensee 1948-1952); and La Planada Nature Reserve (1°10'N 78°00'W), where birds have been regularly seen (between 1,750 and 1,900 m) in recent years (Orejuela *et al.* 1982, F. R. Lambert *in litt.* 1989, M. Pearman *in litt.* 1991; coordinates from Restrepo 1990);

Ecuador (*Carchi*) "2-3 km west of Maldonado" (c.0°53'N 78°09'W; coordinates read from IGM 1982), apparently in or near the Awá Indigenous Forest (see Measures Taken), where a bird was seen between 1,700 and 1,800 m during July 1983 (O. Læssøe *in litt.* 1984); in the río Cumbe valley, where birds were observed between 1,900 and 2,100 m in 1980 (R. Bleiweiss *in litt.* 1992); (*Imbabura*) Intag (c.0°24'N 78°36'W), where an undated specimen (in MCZ) was collected; (*Pichincha*) Nanegal (0°07'N 78°46'W), whence come two males (in BMNH) taken at 1,525 m; río Saloya, near Mindo (c.0°01'N 78°57'W), where a male (in ANSP) was collected in June 1948; Mindo (0°02'S 78°48'W), where a male (in BMNH) was taken at 1,830 m in January 1914, and from where there are numerous recent sightings (P. Greenfield verbally 1991); "Quito", whence comes the type-specimen (Meyer de Schauensee 1948-1952); Santo Domingo de los Colorados (0°15'S 79°09'W), where a bird (in ANSP) was taken in 1911; near Chiriboga (0°15'S 78°44'W; km 59 from Quito on the Santo Domingo de los Colorados road), where the species was seen at 1,900 m in 1980 and September 1986 (Evans 1988b, R. Bleiweiss *in litt.* 1992).

POPULATION The paucity of records by Orejuela *et al.* (1982) in Nariño, and the suggestion by S. L. Hilty (*in litt.* 1986) that it exists in very low numbers, appear to indicate that the Hoary Puffleg is both local and rare. However, K.-L. Schuchmann (*in litt.* 1986) reported that the bird was not rare in imports into (West) Germany until 1984, and information from the various series of skins collected also suggests that the species was locally common, e.g. at least 34 specimens collected in "Ecuador" last century (in ANSP, BMNH, FMNH, MNHN), while in Colombia 12 were taken in two months at Ricaurte in 1941, five there during one month in 1957, and eight there over two months the following year (see above).

Recent observations at La Planada Nature Reserve, Nariño, tend to confirm the impression of its local commonness: in October 1990, M. Pearman (*in litt.* 1991) found it locally common between 1,750 and 1,900 m, and in fact suggested that at this time the species appeared to be the commonest hummingbird present; 15 birds were banded in July 1991, when it was considered common in secondary growth (F. G. Stiles *in litt.* 1992); and during August and September 1991 several individuals were mist-netted at La Planada, and again the bird was deemed to be fairly common (Barlow *et al.* 1992).

The birds at La Planada are easily observed in secondary habitat, whereas generally they occur singly, feeding low inside forest where they are difficult to find (Hilty and Brown 1986, Barlow *et al.* 1992, F. R. Lambert *in litt.* 1989: see below); however, R. Bleiweiss (*in litt.* 1992) found them in some numbers in Carchi and Pichincha during 1980, and suggested that their apparent scarcity may be due to retiring habits.

ECOLOGY The Hoary Puffleg has been recorded between 1,190 and 2,500 m in Colombia and from 1,525 to 2,100 m in Ecuador (see Distribution). The species inhabits humid and wet premontane forest (cloud-forest), where it usually feeds singly in the lower storey of the forest interior (Hilty and Brown 1986). However, birds have also been recorded at forest borders (Hilty and Brown 1986), and in La Planada Nature Reserve they have been observed in 2-6 year old secondary forest and scrub, especially in the large shrub-dominated grassy clearing bordering the reserve buildings and adjacent forest (F. R. Lambert *in litt.* 1989, Barlow *et al.* 1992). In the primary forest at this reserve birds are seen mostly at small clearings (breaks), along streams and on ridge-tops, only rarely in unbroken forest (F. G. Stiles *in litt.* 1992). In Carchi and Pichincha, R. Bleiweiss (*in litt.* 1992) found that this species favoured the "darkest reaches of thick vegetation growing along rocky, fast-flowing streams within very wet lower montane forest". Birds usually feed in the understorey, taking nectar at small groups of flowers (e.g. *Palicourea*, and species of Marantaceae) or by gleaning from leaves (Hilty and Brown 1986, R. Bleiweiss *in litt.* 1992), although they also feed at flowering shrubs (e.g. *Besleria* sp.) in open areas at La Planada (F. R. Lambert *in litt.* 1989, M. Pearman *in litt.* 1991).

THREATS In Ecuador at least, extensive deforestation within the range of this species (IUCN TFP 1988b) has almost certainly affected its population (J. I. Hernández Camacho verbally 1991). The situation in Nariño, Colombia, is different in that extensive, apparently suitable habitat exists from the Pasto–Tumaco road south to the Ecuador border (M. G. Kelsey verbally 1992), although records in this region are from an extremely small area, and the species must be considered threatened until its distributional status is more thoroughly known. The report that it has been traded internationally (see Population) is also worrying, and any continuing commerce may well present an additional threat on a local scale.

MEASURES TAKEN In Colombia, most recent records come from La Planada Nature Reserve, which is a 3,200 ha private reserve, now officially declared a forest protection zone by INDERENA, and for which there is a long-term management and development plan (Barlow *et al.* 1992; also Orejuela 1987b). Adjacent to this area, in Carchi province, Ecuador, is the Awá Indigenous Forest Reserve, covering an area of 101,000 ha (IUCN 1992), apparently in or very near which one of the most recent Ecuador records was made (see Distribution). Also in Ecuador is the Cotacachi–Cayapas Ecological Reserve, which now covers an area of 204,000 ha (IUCN 1992) and includes apparently suitable areas for this species; and the Centro Científico Las Palmas (incorporating the Chiriboga locality), which preserves at least some suitable habitat (R. Bleiweiss *in litt.* 1992). Around Mindo, this species occurs in several areas receiving at least temporary protection as "Bosque Protector" (NK).

MEASURES PROPOSED It is essential that surveys are carried out to assess better this species's population, distribution, and ecological requirements (especially its ability to survive in secondary habitats).

La Planada Nature Reserve is relatively small and protects an insufficient area to maintain viable populations of most of the species present (Barlow *et al.* 1992): as such, the proposed creation of an international biosphere reserve joining the Awá reserve in Ecuador and La Planada Nature Reserve in Colombia (Poole 1990) is an initiative that must be strongly encouraged, as this would protect the poorly known and still relatively untouched areas in southern Nariño, and therefore populations of this and probably other threatened species such as Plumbeous Forest-falcon *Micrastur plumbeus*, Yellow-eared Parrot *Ognorhynchus icterotis* (at higher elevations), Banded Ground-cuckoo *Neomorphus radiolosus*, Tanager-finch *Oreothraupis arremonops* (at higher elevations) and Scarlet-breasted Dacnis *Dacnis berlepschi* (see relevant accounts), as well as near-threatened species such as Chestnut Wood-quail *Odontophorus hyperythrus*, Tooth-billed Hummingbird *Androdon aequatorialis*, Black-thighed Puffleg *Eriocnemis derbyi*, Blue-whiskered Tanager *Tangara johannae*, Long-wattled Umbrellabird *Cephalopterus penduliger* and Beautiful Jay *Cyanolyca pulchra*. Any conservation actions in this area should seek to take note of the requirements of all of these loosely sympatric species.

REMARKS Old records from eastern Ecuador, i.e. Papallacta (Oberholser 1902), Baeza (specimens in BMNH collected by C. Buckley) and "río Pastassa" (Cory 1918) are undoubtedly based on mislabelled specimens, all recent Ecuadorian records being from the west slope of the Andes, and sympatry with the closely related Greenish Puffleg *Haplophaedia aureliae* being unlikely (NK).

VIOLET-THROATED METALTAIL *Metallura baroni* R[11]

This hummingbird is confined to the edge of the páramo zone above both slopes of the interandean plateau west of Cuenca, Azuay province, southern Ecuador. Until recently it was threatened by habitat destruction, but it may now be safe in some areas.

DISTRIBUTION Only three of the existing 17 museum specimens of the Violet-throated Metaltail (see Remarks 1) are properly labelled with locality, with an additional 12 individuals having been netted and most of them photographed at a different locality. Fourteen specimens collected in Ecuador at the end of last century (Salvin 1893; specimens in AMNH, BMNH and MNHN) were labelled "Cuenca, 12,000'" (3,650 m). There were no subsequent records until 1981, when one was collected and two more seen at 3,400-3,600 m near Miguir, Pacific drainage of Cajas mountains, c.35 km (erroneously given as 25 km) west of Cuenca, at 2°47'S 79°18'W (Ortiz-Crespo 1984; coordinates from OG 1957b). In 1986 an additional specimen (in ANSP) was collected nearby at 3,700 m, and 12 individuals were netted and subsequently released, six of them after having been photographed, at 3,150-3,650 m at Río Mazan, oriental drainage of Cajas mountains, c.14 km west of Cuenca, at 2°52'S 79°08'W (read from LANDSAT 1987 and IGM 1982) (Gretton 1986). A single male (now in MECN) was taken at Paredones, south-west of Molleturo, at 3,250 m, at 2°46'S 79°25'W in March 1991. The type-series may have been collected near Río Mazan, but suitable habitat on isolated páramos apparently also occurs 10 km south-east and 15 km east of Cuenca respectively (from evidence on LANDSAT 1987).

POPULATION Gretton (1986) estimated the population at Río Mazan (the area in question being unspecified, but evidently small) to be between 50 and 100 individuals. In spite of its fairly restricted known range, extrapolation of these numbers to adjacent areas with apparently similar habitat (according to LANDSAT 1987) suggests the total population may number well over 2,000 birds (NK).

ECOLOGY The Violet-throated Metaltail has been recorded at altitudes varying from 3,150 to 3,700 m (Salvin 1983, Ortiz-Crespo 1984, Gretton 1986; specimens in AMNH, ANSP and MECN), where it inhabits elfin forest and treeline shrubbery on humid páramo (Ortiz-Crespo 1984, Gretton 1986, King 1989) and also occurs in open páramo, though generally within 3 km of a *Polylepis* patch (M. Hancock *in litt.* 1989). Ortiz-Crespo (1984) reportedly collected a specimen at the edge of a boggy meadow in a *Polylepis* forest where shrubs and small trees of *Podocarpus*, *Gaiadendron*, *Weinmannia*, *Escallonia* and *Durantha* also grow. He only observed *baroni* feeding on one occasion, from a parasitic loranthacean *Tristerix longebracteatus* (this being chiefly parasitic on *Durantha*), but noted the main nectar sources for hummingbirds in the area to be *Durantha* itself, *Macleania* and other ericaceous shrubs, (Ortiz-Crespo 1984). The specimen collected nearby in 1986 was taken at edge of stunted forest at the treeline (ANSP label data). At Río Mazan the species was reported to be the commonest hummingbird at 3,400 m, where it was seen and netted in shrubs at the edge of a boggy glade near a *Polylepis*-fringed stream; two were also caught in a *Polylepis* patch on the páramo at 3,650 m, and once a bird was netted in shrubby forest at 3,150 m (Gretton 1986). On two occasions it was seen feeding from red flowers of a *Castilleja* shrub (Gretton 1986), although a report based on the same fieldwork referred to it appearing to feed exclusively on the nectar of *Castelleja fissifolia* (King 1989). In 1987, what was possibly this species was seen feeding from a *Puya* sp. (King 1988). At Paredones it was found in disturbed treeline habitat dominated by the proteacean *Oreocallis*, and was seen feeding from flowers of a melastomatacean (NK). The habitat thus apparently closely resembles that reported of Neblina Metaltail *M. odomae* (see relevant account), Coppery Metaltail *M. theresiae*, Fire-throated Metaltail *M. eupogon* and Scaled Metaltail *M. aeneocauda* (Graves 1980, Parker *et al.* 1985), and also that used by Viridian Metaltail *M. williami* in eastern Ecuador (NK). *M.*

williami atrigularis occurs sympatrically with *baroni* at Río Mazan (Gretton 1986), but it is generally found at lower elevations than *baroni* in that valley (A. Gretton verbally 1988; also King 1989; see Remarks 2). Apart from two males with undeveloped gonads in March and August (specimens in ANSP and MECN) there is no indication of breeding season.

THREATS The Violet-throated Metailtail may be threatened by habitat destruction, as the remnant patches of forest in Las Cajas National Recreation Area are (or were) being constantly whittled away (Ridgely 1981a; but see Measures Taken).

MEASURES TAKEN The species is known to occur in Las Cajas National Recreation Area (Ortiz-Crespo 1984; specimen in ANSP) and at Río Mazan, a small reserve at the edge of Cajas National Recreation Area (where it is sympatric with the Golden-plumed Parakeet *Leptosittaca branickii*, Red-faced Parrot *Hapalopsittaca pyrrhops* and probably Bearded Guan *Penelope barbata*: see relevant accounts). The Río Mazan reserve was started as a local initiative by the Cuenca chapter of the national organization Fundación Natura (the local chapter is now called Tierra Viva), which bought the area in 1981 with money donated by Cuenca town council and the civil defence fund, and the forest was thus saved from total felling for furniture manufacture (Robinson 1986). Although some felling continued for a few years, the area is now well protected (A. Gretton and M. Hancock verbally 1988; also M. Hancock *in litt.* 1989).

MEASURES PROPOSED Effective protection of Cajas National Recreation Area should be ensured. Páramos east and south of Cuenca should be surveyed for the possible occurrence of the species.

REMARKS (1) Although described as a species (Salvin 1893), *baroni* was treated as a subspecies of *M. eupogon* by Peters (1945). Zimmer (1952) retained *baroni* as a species, but suggested that *williami*, *baroni*, *theresiae*, *eupogon* and *aeneocauda* should be treated as separate species, an arrangement followed by Graves (1980), who added *odomae* to the assemblage. The discovery in 1986 of sympatry between *williami* (subspecies *atrigularis*) and *baroni* (Gretton 1986), with no apparent hybridization and with some altitudinal segregation (see Ecology), may suggest that *williami* does not belong in this group, or at least that *baroni* and *atrigularis* are not members of the same superspecies in the narrow sense (NK), a view further supported by their possible sympatry east of the central valley (see Distribution). (2) The reported sightings of a single *baroni* in low, shrubby, riparian growth dominated by alders at 1,900 m in the arid Oña valley (Ridgely 1980) may be based on a misidentification or a wandering individual (NK); if reliable and representing a regular phenomenon, this observation would suggest less significance than hitherto thought of dry, interandean valleys as dispersal barriers to members of the *Metallura aeneocauda* superspecies, and might also suggest the presence of *baroni* in Cordillera Cordoncillo immediately east and south-south-east of Oña (NK).

NEBLINA METALTAIL *Metallura odomae* R[11]

This hummingbird inhabits elfin forest and forest edge on the páramo, and is only known from recent sightings in Ecuador and from a single mountain in immediately adjacent Piura, Peru. Despite its small range it appears not to be immediately threatened.

DISTRIBUTION The Neblina Metaltail is known from three sites in Ecuador and one in Peru.

Ecuador On two or three occasions in August and September 1990 the species was observed near Angashcola, 2,750 m, Loja province, at 4°21'S 79°45'W (Williams *et al.* 1991). On 14 March 1991 a male was seen at close range at the treeline, c.3,100 m, above Cajanuma, Podocarpus National Park, Loja province, at c.4°06'S 79°09'W (M. Kessler *in litt.* 1991; coordinates read from IGM 1982), and in late 1991 the species was found around the lagunas above Cajanuma valley in the same park (C. Rahbek *in litt.* 1992). A female was taken on the east slope of Cordillera de Quichiragua along the Jimbura–Zumba road in the southernmost part of the country in December 1991 (R. S. Ridgely *per* C. Rahbek *in litt.* 1992).

Peru Eleven specimens (in FMNH and LSUMZ) have been taken on the páramo of Cerro Chinguela, at c.5°07'S 79°23'W, on the ridge east of Huancabamba and Sapalache, in the upper Huancabamba valley, Piura department near the Cajamarca border (Graves 1980, Parker *et al.* 1985; also Hinkelmann 1987), with subsequent records in June 1987 high on the eastern slopes (four birds in one day: M. Pearman *in litt.* 1989) and in August 1989 (see Ecology).

POPULATION No estimates of the total populations have been made, but it was reported to occur at low densities and was given the status "fairly common", with small numbers of singles seen daily and eight seen during a 4 km walk in its habitat on Cerro Chinguela (Parker *et al.* 1985). This assessment also applies to the population within Podocarpus National Park, where although present in low densities it is nevertheless the most numerous hummingbird in the area above the Cajanuma valley (C. Rahbek *in litt.* 1992).

ECOLOGY The Neblina Metailtail is found at 2,850-3,350 m where it inhabits shrubby growth at the forest–grassland ecotone and patches of shrubs and short trees in the grassland well above the treeline, on windswept, foggy and rainy páramo (Graves 1980, Parker *et al.* 1985). Usually alone, it perches conspicuously atop shrubs, and pursues intruding conspecifics and the occasional Glowing Puffleg *Eriocnemis vestitus* entering its territory (Parker *et al.* 1985). It has been observed feeding by flycatching and from flowers of *Brachyotum* and a *Berberis*-like shrub (Parker *et al.* 1985) and (during a snowstorm) from white flowers of a dwarf ericaceous shrub partly concealed by grass (Graves 1980). Five other species of hummingbird seen during the same snowstorm all foraged in more sheltered ravines (Graves 1980). None of the specimens collected in June/July and on 22 October had enlarged gonads (Graves 1980). However, on 21 August 1989 a nest was found on Cerro Chinguela at about 2,850 m, and consisted of a mossy cup covered with pale lichens (possibly held together with spider webs), about 4 cm deep and 5 cm across, placed c.2 m above ground in a small rock-ledge cavity sheltered from the prevailing wind; the weather was poor and the sitting female was left undisturbed, so presence and number of eggs or chicks were not ascertained (B. M. Whitney *in litt.* 1991).

THREATS None is known, and indeed in Peru the inhospitable climate of the region inhabited by this species offers some protection against intrusion by man. The Cerro Chinguèla páramo is, however, grazed by a small number of cattle, and is burned almost annually by local herders, which must have an adverse effect on various species of grasses and shrubs and may in turn affect population size and distribution of this and other páramo bird species; for example, the Coppery

Metaltail *Metallura theresiae* appears to be considerably more numerous in pristine, tall-grass and shrub-filled páramos than in those that have been burned and grazed for many years (TAP).

MEASURES TAKEN The species is present in Podocarpus National Park in Ecuador, and no burning or grazing currently occurs in the particular area where it was recently recorded (C. Rahbek *in litt.* 1992).

MEASURES PROPOSED Suggestions are included in Remarks under Bearded Guan *Penelope barbata.*

REMARKS Zimmer (1952) considered Viridian Metaltail *Metallura williami*, Violet-throated Metaltail *M. baroni*, Coppery Metaltail, Fire-throated Metaltail *M. eupogon* and Scaled Metaltail *M. aeneocauda* as allospecies of a single superspecies. Graves (1980) considered *odomae* as an additional allospecies in this superspecies, but pointed out that *eupogon* and *aeneocauda* might occur sympatrically in the southern Cordillera Vilcabamba, Cusco, Peru. Sympatry of *williami* and *odomae* in Podocarpus National Park (P. Greenfield and M. Kessler verbally 1991), and of *williami* and *baroni* (at Río Mazan) has now been demonstrated (see account of Violet-throated Metaltail).

GREY-BELLIED COMET *Taphrolesbia griseiventris* V[9]

This rare hummingbird inhabits semi-arid country in north-central Peru, and remains one of the least known members of its family. Although possibly not immediately threatened, it is vulnerable owing to its limited distribution.

DISTRIBUTION The Grey-bellied Comet (see Remarks) is known from some 16 specimens taken at four localities in Peru, one on the Pacific slope in Cajamarca, and three in the río Marañón drainage, Cajamarca and Huánaco departments, as follows (coordinates from Stephens and Traylor 1983):

Cajamarca Paucal (c.7°00'S 79°10'W), on the Pacific slope, the type-locality (Taczanowski 1883, also Plenge 1979); and in the río Marañón drainage, Cajamarca (7°10'S 78°31'W), whence come a specimen (in MNHN) dated December 1893 and two (in AMNH) January 1894 (with one other in ANSP simply "1894"), all from c.2,900 m (also Salvin 1895, Baron 1897, Zimmer 1952, Bond 1954b); near Cajamarca, where four specimens (in AMNH, BMNH) were collected in May 1894 at 3,050 m (also Salvin 1895, Baron 1897, Zimmer 1952); Cajabamba (7°37'S 78°03'W, the town being at 2,655 m), where six specimens (in AMNH, BMNH, MNHN) were collected in January 1894, mostly above the town at 2,750 m, but with one specimen and sightings from below it (also Salvin 1895, Baron 1897, Zimmer 1952);

Huánaco Cullcui (c.9°23'S 76°42'W), on the right bank of the río Marañón at 3,170 m, where a specimen (in FMNH) was collected in December 1922 (also Zimmer 1930, 1952); and c.200 m above the río Marañón, at the point it is crossed by the Huánuco–La Unión road, where three or more were sighted in May 1975 (TAP).

The species presumably occurs along both slopes of the río Marañón in the intervening departments of La Libertad and Ancash, and its range may extend north to southern Amazonas department and west to other regions on the Pacific slope (NK).

POPULATION All but two of the known specimens were collected by O. T. Baron who, after obtaining only eight during a two-week stay at Cajamarca, concluded that it was one of the rarer species of hummingbird (Baron 1897). It was given the status "rare" by Parker *et al.* (1982).

ECOLOGY The Grey-bellied Comet has been found in open semi-arid country on the barren hills surrounding the town of Cajamarca: these hills were partly cultivated by Indians, whose huts were surrounded by fences of cacti and agave, both of which (and other amaryllidaceans) were in bloom in January when *Taphrolesbia* was seen amongst them (Baron 1897). At Cajabamba the hills were covered with small brushwood, only the canyons containing some small trees (Baron 1897). At Cullcui there are steep, dry hills with cacti, agaves and other desert plants that form impenetrable thickets along the streams and, although at 3,170 m, it has been described as being in the arid, subtropical zone (Zimmer 1930). The species lives singly amongst rocky, inaccessible places, and in deep canyons (Baron 1897). It is dominated by the Giant Hummingbird *Patagona gigas* in competition for certain flowers (Baron 1897). Three or more birds observed in the upper río Marañón valley were on a steep slope covered in shrubs, cacti and bromeliads, and were seen at or near the flowers of a *Puya* sp. (TAP). Nothing further is known of its habits.

THREATS None is known, but its apparent rarity and small range may render it vulnerable to any habitat alteration.

MEASURES TAKEN Exports of hummingbirds from Peru are officially controlled (Inskipp 1987), and most species, including *Taphrolesbia*, are on Appendix II of CITES (WTMU 1988).

MEASURES PROPOSED A study of the species is badly needed in order to establish both its distributional status and ecological niche, and therefore whether any management initiatives are required.

REMARKS The Grey-bellied Comet is the sole member of its genus. After receiving a report (from O. T. Baron) that *griseiventris* was not a *Cyanolesbia* (a name used for forms now referred to *Aglaiocercus*, *Lesbia* and *Sappho*), Hartert (1898b) placed this species in *Polyonymus* with *caroli* (a treatment already published by Simon 1897), which he thought it resembled more, by its long, straight, pointed, strong bill, very wide rectrices and style of coloration in both sexes; and indeed although the monotypic *Taphrolesbia* (Peters 1945, Zimmer 1952, Bond 1954b) or *Tephrolesbia* (Simon 1919, 1921, Zimmer 1930, Meyer de Schauensee 1966) has had wide currency, Zimmer (1930) maintained that it is in fact doubtfully separable from *Polyonymus*.

MARVELLOUS SPATULETAIL *Loddigesia mirabilis* V[9]

This uncommon hummingbird is confined to one slope in a single valley of northern Peru. Its small distribution renders it vulnerable, but it is apparently not immediately threatened.

DISTRIBUTION The Marvellous Spatuletail (see Remarks 1) appears to be confined to the right bank of río Utcubamba (an affluent on the right bank of the río Marañón), Bongara and Chachapoyas provinces, Amazonas department, northern Peru. Birds have been recorded from at least seven localities in three general areas, these being (from north to south, with coordinates from Stephens and Traylor 1983):

(*Bongara province*) below an old sawmill c.30 km by road from Pedro Ruiz (= Ingenio, at c.5°56'S 79°59'W) towards Florida (adjacent to Lago Pomacochas, at 5°50'S 77°55'W), where birds were seen at c.2,135 m in December 1974 (Parker 1976) and July 1983 (Gardner 1986), with specimens collected in May 1985, and further sightings in March 1986 (M. Kessler *in litt.* 1988);

(*Chachapoyas area*) Chachapoyas (6°13'S 77°51'W), source of the type-specimen, with another (in BMNH) taken in October 1897, at 2,335 m (Bourcier 1847, Salvin and Hartert 1892, Rothschild 1896, Baron 1897; see Remarks 2); Osmal (untraced, but believed to be near Chachapoyas and Tamiapampa: Vaurie 1972), a source of old sightings (Taczanowski and Stolzmann 1881); Levanto (6°16'S 77°49'W), at 2,590-2,745 m (Baron 1897, Zimmer 1953a, Bond 1954b); Tamiapampa (c.6°20'S 77°52'W), where at 2,680 m, two specimens (in BMNH) were collected in October 1873 and November 1879 (Taczanowski and Stolzmann 1881, Salvin and Hartert 1892; see Remarks 2);

(*Leimebamba area*) north of Leimebamba (c.6°41'S 77°47'W), at 2,200 m, where a male was seen in May 1977 (Boeke 1978, also Baron 1897); and San Pedro (possibly = San Pedro de Leimebamba, both untraced), 4-5 hours south-east of Leimebamba, on the right bank of the río Utcubamba, where birds have been recorded between 2,620 and 2,900 m (Baron 1897, Zimmer 1953a, Ruschi 1964).

The assertion by Greenewalt (1966) that this species occurs in Luya province (mainly situated on the left bank of the Utcubamba) seems based on Ruschi (1965a), who gave a number of thitherto unknown localities, namely: Durasno Pampa, Pomacochas, Chilimbote, Barro Negro, Cordillera Calla-Calla (3,700 m), Montevideo, Maino, Yeso, Luya, Lamud, Santo Tomás, Caclic (1,700 m), Coloco, Colcamar, San Carlos and Puso, all between 5°50' and 7°00'S (see Measures Proposed).

POPULATION Although over 50 specimens have been collected, this hummingbird has been described as "uncommon" (Taczanowski and Stolzmann 1881, Parker *et al.* 1982), albeit with no evidence of any decline during the last 100 years. An average of seven birds were noted daily along 3 km of prime habitat during a five-day survey (Parker 1976). The distance between the northern- and southernmost known localities is c.120 km, and while the width of the zone it inhabits is harder to measure, it probably averages about 10 or 20 km (Ruschi 1965a, NK). An investigation of how much of this c.2,000-3,000 km^2 holds suitable habitat is needed before population estimates can be attempted (see Measures Proposed).

ECOLOGY The Marvellous Spatuletail has been found between 2,100 m and 2,900 m, but at least at one site suitable habitat continues down to 1,830 m (Parker 1976), with Ruschi (1965a) reporting it as low as 1,700 m and as high as 3,700 m (see Distribution). It inhabits forest edge, second-growth and montane scrub, in a general region of open country with fields, pasture and shrubbery and a system of small valleys and gorges supporting more luxuriant vegetation, sometimes even small tree groves, but mainly impenetrable, thorny *Rubus* thickets admixed with a few *Alnus* trees; it is these latter thickets that are most favoured by the bird, especially where they border wooded areas (Taczanowski and Stolzmann 1881, Baron 1897, Ruschi 1964, Parker 1976, Parker *et al.* 1982, M. Kessler *in litt.* 1988).

Birds are usually found alone (Parker 1976), and move constantly throughout the day (Taczanowski and Stolzmann 1881). They move through bushes faster and with greater manoeuvrability than other hummingbirds (Taczanowski and Stolzmann 1881), usually staying hidden within dense, low thickets, and only paying brief foraging visits to flowers (Parker 1976), from which they are easily displaced by other hummingbirds such as Green-tailed Trainbearer *Lesbia nuna*, Green Violetear *Colibri (thalassinus) cyanotus* and Sparkling Violetear *Colibri coruscans* (Taczanowski and Stolzmann 1881, Baron 1897, Ruschi 1965a, Parker 1976). Observations have identified occasional feeding from *Rubus* sp., from a tree called "tolo" (unidentified, but probably a myrtacean), and sometimes the violet flowers of a pepper called "aji" (unidentified, and only seen visited by females), but the most favoured food-plant is apparently the red-flowered lily *Alstroemeria* (*Bomaria formosissima*, Herb.): this flower, which blooms from August to late November, is avoided by *Lesbia* (the only feeding attempt seen by that species was immediately disrupted), and the spatuletail was found wherever *Alstroemeria* occurred, sitting atop the flower while extracting nectar (Taczanowski and Stolzmann 1881). Baron's (1897) only reference to food plants is a note that the dominant *Lesbia* makes it difficult for *Loddigesia* to feed from raspberry flowers *Rubus* sp. Parker (1976) mainly saw females, and noted feeding from a shrub with clusters of small, tubular lavender flowers in late December. Boeke (1978) saw consistent feeding by an adult male from the bright red, tubular flowers of the native labiate *Satureja sericea* in late May, and noted that the spatuletail fed from these flowers only, despite the presence of several other blooms used by hummingbirds. Once an adult male was seen drinking from a waterfall in a small stream just before sunset (Taczanowski and Stolzmann 1881).

Adult males are greatly outnumbered by females and immature males, and are also shier (Taczanowski and Stolzmann 1881). In late December at the northernmost known locality females outnumbered immature males five to one, and only two out of some 35 sightings were of adult males (Parker 1976). At Osmal and Tamiapampa, leks of 2-3 and 5-8 immature males respectively displayed in November: adult males were rarely seen at the leks, but females were usually present; and at Tamiapampa the lek was on an open plateau with scattered bushes and no flowers, the area thus serving only for display (Taczanowski and Stolzmann 1881). Different observations (and interpretations) of the display are described by Taczanowski and Stolzmann (1881), Baron (1897) and Greenewalt (1966). Display has been observed in late October (Baron 1897), November (Taczanowski and Stolzmann 1881) and May (M. Kessler *in litt.* 1988): moss for nest-building was gathered by a female in November (Taczanowski and Stolzmann 1881); a bird with greatly enlarged gonads was taken in February (specimen in AMNH); and nine birds with slightly enlarged gonads in December, January and February (specimens in AMNH, ANSP and USNM), suggesting a breeding period during the rainy season from late October to early May.

THREATS Though continuous forests are being cut throughout the Marañón valley, this hummingbird's apparent preference for forest edge and isolated woodlots high on steep slopes may ensure its survival in spite of heavy cultivation in its restricted range (Parker 1976). The only known capture for aviculture is that of six birds in October 1962 (Ruschi 1964, Greenewalt 1966). If the species were to be taken in large numbers, it might become seriously threatened.

MEASURES TAKEN While exportation from Peru of all hummingbirds inhabiting humid tropical forest is prohibited, export permits can be given for species of other habitats, such as Marvellous Spatuletail: however, all exports are controlled (Inskipp 1987), and at present it seems unlikely that permits to export large numbers of this species would be issued (NK) (see also Measures Proposed). In 1987 all hummingbirds became subject to CITES legislation, with most species, including the present one, going on Appendix II (WTMU 1988). There are apparently no protected areas within the range of the species.

MEASURES PROPOSED A survey to determine the size of the total population and to investigate possible migration and other ecological aspects of the species needs to be made. The extent to which degraded habitat can support viable populations also requires assessment, and a protected area may be appropriate once a suitable site can be identified. Survey and conservation initiatives within the upper Marañón valley should be incorporated into a broader investigation of other sympatric threatened species in the region, for which see the equivalent section under Peruvian Pigeon *Columba oenops*. There appears to be no confirmation of the Marvellous Spatuletail occurring at the localities mentioned by Ruschi (1965a), or indeed anywhere in Luya province (see Distribution), and it would be appropriate to investigate these claims.

REMARKS (1) The Marvellous Spatuletail is the only member of its genus. (2) Concerning O. T. Baron's specimens labelled "Chachapoyas" Baron (1897) included under the name Chachapoyas a former hacienda on a ridge of wooded mountains four hours south-east of Chachapoyas, and stated that this hacienda was once the hunting ground of J. Stolzmann. Stolzmann collected on the farm Tamiapampa, which is situated 12 km south of Chachapoyas, on the edge of the Puma-Urcu forest (given as 4 km south of Chachapoyas by Taczanowski 1884-1886), which connects with the east Andean forested slopes towards the río Huayabamba (Taczanowski 1882), and it seems likely that this is the locality visited by Baron (NK). However, there is a slight possibility that Baron was referring to Osmal, a nearby site (untraced by Stephens and Traylor 1983), where Stolzmann also observed this species (Stolzmann and Taczanowski 1881).

CHILEAN WOODSTAR *Eulidia yarrellii* K[12]

This small hummingbird appears to be confined to two adjacent, heavily cultivated valleys in the desert of Arica department, extreme northern Chile (straggling north into immediately adjacent Peru), and south to northern Antofagasta province. Its small range renders it vulnerable, although birds appear to fare well in gardens.

DISTRIBUTION The Chilean Woodstar is restricted to a very small area on the Pacific coast from Tacna, Peru, to extreme northern Antofagasta, Chile, being found in the few river valleys in a desert practically devoid of life, and possibly breeding only in Lluta and adjacent Azapa valleys, Arica department, Chile.

Peru Four birds were found in December 1977 at Tacna town, 18°01'S 70°15'W (562 m), Tacna department, and the species may also occur in the infrequently visited foothill valleys of Moquegua and Tacna departments (Parker 1982a; elevation and coordinates from Stephens and Traylor 1983): however, it may not be a regular visitor to Tacna, where another observer (R. A. Hughes *in litt.* 1986) only recorded it once despite much searching during many visits.

Chile The species has been consistently reported only from the Lluta and Azapa valleys in Arica department, Tarapacá province, records (coordinates from OG 1967 or read from IFG 1984) being: Lluta valley, c.18°24-25'S 69°50-70°19'W (Johnson 1967, D. A. Scott *in litt.* 1989; specimen in MCZ collected June 1935); Arica town (at the mouth of the Azapa valley) and its northern suburbs Chinchorro and La Chimba (near sea level), 18°29'S 70°20'W, where seven specimens (in BMNH) were taken in the middle of the last century and three (in MCZ and MNHNS) in November 1943, while a nest with young was found there in August 1968 (Salvin and Hartert 1892, Hellmayr 1932, Philippi 1936, Philippi *et al.* 1944, Johnson 1972; see Remarks 1); and Azapa valley, c.18°29-31'S 70°11-14'W, where five specimens (in LACM and USNM) were collected in March 1948, one (in WFVZ) in August 1968 when an incubating bird was photographed, one (in IRSNB) in September 1976, and three (in WFVZ) in June 1986 (also Philippi *et al.* 1944, Johnson 1972), with sightings in November 1986 (D. A. Scott *in litt.* 1989), March 1989 (P. J. Roberts *in litt.* 1989), January-February 1990 (P. Gregory *in litt.* 1990, P. J. Roberts *in litt.* 1990), and January 1991 at 200-720 m (M. Pearman *in litt.* 1991).

Further south in Tarapacá there are sight records from Chupicilca in the Camarones valley, between Conanoxa (19°02'S 69°59'W; at 400 m), and Taltape (18°59'S 69°47'W; at 780 m) (McFarlane 1975), and at Mamiña (20°05'S 69°14'W; at 2,600 m) (Johnson 1970). In Antofagasta province the species has been taken at Cobija, 22°33'S 70°16'W (two specimens in AMNH; also Bonaparte 1854; see Remarks 2), but these records are considered to represent stragglers only (Johnson 1967, McFarlane 1975), as the species does not appear to have colonized the Loa valley in northern Antofagasta.

POPULATION The Chilean Woodstar was reported to be common in 1935 (Philippi 1936), and very abundant in 1948 (Barros 1954). Philippi *et al.* (1944) and Johnson (1967) reported seeing over a hundred at a single flowering tree in the Azapa valley in November 1943; they also found it in Lluta valley at the same time, but only saw a few (Johnson 1967). Although four specimens were collected in Arica town, the statement by Philippi *et al.* (1944) that it was very abundant in Arica, and that there were more Chilean Woodstars than Oasis Hummingbirds *Rhodopis vesper*, may have referred to Arica department as a whole (including the Azapa valley), rather than the town, and Johnson (1967) reported it to be outnumbered 10:1 by the Oasis Hummingbird in the gardens of Arica town in July, making no comments about it having been commoner there in November 1943. Later observers have found the Chilean Woodstar scarce (McFarlane 1975), but whether an actual serious decline for reasons unknown has taken place (McFarlane 1975, King 1978-1979) or whether the observers reporting it abundant (Philippi 1936, Philippi *et al.* 1944,

Barros 1954) simply had the luck to come across a flowering tree favoured by this species, remains unknown.

On 6 October and 1 November 1986 four or more male Chilean Woodstars and eight Oasis Hummingbirds were found near Arica without much searching in just a small part of a large amount of suitable habitat, and on 2 November 1986 three female woodstars and an Oasis Hummingbird were found in Lluta valley, also without much searching (D. A. Scott *in litt.* 1989). In May 1987 some 10-20 Oasis Hummingbirds and two Chilean Woodstars were seen in gardens of Arica town (NK); in March 1989 15 Chilean Woodstars and 30 Oasis Hummingbirds were seen in the Azapa valley (P. J. Roberts *in litt.* 1989), with five (or more) birds in the valley in January 1990, and five in the gardens of the Azapa hotel in February 1990 (P. Gregory *in litt.* 1990, P. J. Roberts *in litt.* 1990). The species was found to be common in January 1991, when it outnumbered both Peruvian Sheartail *Thaumastura cora* and Oasis Hummingbird, with which it was seen feeding: seven birds were seen between 200 and 240 m, with six between 640 and 720 m (M. Pearman *in litt.* 1991).

ECOLOGY The Chilean Woodstar inhabits desert river valleys and gardens, apparently mainly from sea level to c.750 m, but it has once been recorded as high as 2,600 m (see Distribution and Population). Although usually solitary (Parker 1982a, NK), more than a hundred were noted in November at a single flowering tree which, however, was not identified (Philippi *et al.* 1944, Johnson 1967). In the gardens of Tacna it was seen feeding from *Lantana* and *Hibiscus* flowers, and was frequently driven away by the larger Oasis Hummingbirds and Peruvian Sheartails (Parker 1982a). When not foraging it perched inconspicuously within the cover of shrubs and short trees (Parker 1982a). In Arica two males were seen feeding from and fighting over *Lantana* flowers (NK). Birds have also been seen hawking for insects over a watercourse in the Azapa valley (M. Pearman *in litt.* 1991).

Two nests were found in late August 1968, one in an "olivo blanco" tree, containing two eggs (one incubated and normal, the other empty), and one in a "higuerilla" tree, containing two almost fully fledged young fed by the male only, as the female had become entangled in the nest material and died (Johnson 1972). An immature was collected on 13 November (Philippi *et al.* 1944) and one (described as subadult) was seen on 26 December (Parker 1982a).

THREATS The indigenous plants favoured by the species may be severely threatened, as the valleys where this hummingbird occurs are heavily cultivated (King 1978-1979, NK), and it may now, to a large extent, be dependent on garden flowers.

MEASURES TAKEN All exports of hummingbirds from Peru and Chile are controlled (Inskipp 1987).

MEASURES PROPOSED Plants favoured by the species should be identified, and their continued presence in quantities sufficient for maintaining a viable population of the woodstar should be secured. An education campaign stressing the importance of these plants for this and other species of hummingbird in these valleys, and encouraging the planting of appropriate trees and bushes, would be very worthwhile.

REMARKS (1) Of the seven specimens in BMNH one is labelled "Arica" and one "Arica, Peru"; both are from the Gould collection, and were taken before 1869; two other specimens from the Gould collection are labelled "Peru?", and are probably also from Arica. The two types from the Loddiges collection labelled "Montevideo" were presumably taken at Arica (Hellmayr 1932) as is probably the case with an unsexed immature from the same collection, with no locality data. Philippi *et al.* (1944) visited the northern suburbs of Arica, La Chimba and Chinchorro, and reported collecting an immature male and three females at La Chimba on 13 and 14 November 1943. An immature male and a female in MCZ taken on 13 November 1943 are labelled "Chinchorro, Arica"; no collector is given on the label, but these specimens are presumably the same as those reported by Philippi *et al.* (1944). A female in MNHNS taken by Philippi in November 1943 is labelled "Arica" (J. C. Torres-Mura *in litt.* 1988) and is apparently the third of the four specimens reported by Philippi *et al* (1944). The fourth specimen cannot be traced. A female in AMNH without date or collector is labelled "Arica, Peru", and may have been collected last century (NK).

(2) A single specimen labelled "Cobija, Bolivia" (Bonaparte 1854) was taken in the garden of a mining establishment on the Antofagasta coast, Chile (Johnson 1967). The presence of the species this far south was considered exceptional by both Johnson (1967) and McFarlane (1975), who were presumably unaware of the two further specimens in AMNH labelled "Cobija, Peru" with no date or collector given.

ESMERALDAS WOODSTAR *Acestrura berlepschi* E[2]

This rare hummingbird apparently occurs primarily in lowland evergreen moist forest in a small area of western Ecuador, this being one of the most threatened forest types in the Neotropics.

DISTRIBUTION The Esmeraldas Woodstar is known from 12 specimens (in AMNH, ANSP and MNHN), three of which are of uncertain origin (see Remarks), the other nine having been taken at three localities in western Ecuador. The localities, with coordinates from Paynter and Traylor (1977), are as follows: (*Esmeraldas*) Esmeraldas (0°59'N 79°42'W), where three males and three females (in AMNH) were collected from October to December 1912 (also Chapman 1926); (*Manabí*) Chone (0°41'S 80°06'W), where two males (in AMNH) were taken at 20 m in December 1912 (also Chapman 1926); and (*Guayas*) on a ridge near the río Ayampe (1°40'S 80°45'W), on the border of Machalilla National Park (and with Manabí province), where a male was seen by P. Kaestner and R. Jones in March 1990, with one male taken (in ANSP) and three females seen there in January 1991 (R. S. Ridgely *in litt.* 1991).

POPULATION Nothing is known, although this species is obviously very localized and apparently uncommon, searches at the río Ayampe site during June 1992 failing to relocate the species (R. S. Ridgely *in litt.* 1992).

ECOLOGY Beside the río Ayampe the Esmeraldas Woodstar was found in the canopy along borders of semi-humid, second-growth woodland on a ridge at an altitude of 100-150 m, and was seen feeding from flowers of *Muntingia calabura* (Elaeocarpaceae), with the male also flycatching for tiny insects; the Little Woodstar *Acestura bombus* (see relevant account) was also present, but tended to feed lower in the vegetation (R. S. Ridgely *in litt.* 1991). The forest in this area was originally evergreen moist forest (see Dodson *et al.* 1985 for description), patches of which still survive in nearby areas (A. Gentry verbally 1991).

THREATS Widespread deforestation of western Ecuador south of the río Esmeraldas has surely led to a decline in this species (NK, R. S. Ridgely *in litt.* 1991). Dodson and Gentry (1991) discussed the conservation status of different forest types in western Ecuador, of which moist forest is the most threatened. Whereas several species of woodstar *Acestrura* are known to survive in degraded forests and second-growth, much of western Ecuador is devoid of any woody vegetation at all, and thus nearly all forest-dwelling species in the region are ultimately at risk (TAP). Most of the moist forest around the type-locality of this species (Esmeraldas city) has been replaced by pasture with scattered trees (TAP); however, in the vicinity of Chone though the habitat was very patchy, it still (in June 1992) appeared to be adequate for this species (R. S. Ridgely *in litt.* 1992).

MEASURES TAKEN The species occurs in Machalilla National Park (55,000 ha: IUCN 1992), Manabí province (see equivalent section under Grey-backed Hawk *Leucopternis occidentalis*).

MEASURES PROPOSED Effective protection of Machalilla National Park, the only protected area where the Esmeraldas Woodstar is known to occur, should be ensured (see equivalent section under Grey-backed Hawk). Maintaining the integrity of the small areas of moist forest near the coast just south of this park should also be a priority, and the more extensive tracts of forest on the higher ridges inside the park (e.g. Cerro San Sebastián) should receive immediate attention. This hummingbird should be looked for elsewhere in the coastal range, particularly farther north where several "islands" of moist forest survive (e.g. Cerro Pata de Pajaro, and adjacent ridges to the south in Manabí; and on ridges such as Cerro Mutiles, south and east of Esmeraldas city): the large block of wet forest north-east of Muisne in Esmeraldas may also support a population of this species (TAP).

REMARKS Two unpublished specimens in AMNH are labelled "Río Napo" with no other data, and the type-specimen, labelled "Ecuador", was also believed to have come from the río Napo (Chapman 1926). Although it is possible that the species also occurs (perhaps seasonally) in eastern Ecuador (see account of Little Woodstar), it seems safer at present to regard the "Río Napo" specimens as mislabelled (Chapman 1926).

LITTLE WOODSTAR *Acestrura bombus* E[2]

This poorly known hummingbird has been recorded from west-central Ecuador to central Peru at elevations ranging from sea level to 3,050 m. It has been found in humid evergreen forest and, more commonly, in the transitional zone between dry and wet forests, and thus may occur primarily in moist forest, a seriously threatened habitat in western South America, and this may perhaps explain the relative paucity of modern records.

DISTRIBUTION The Little Woodstar has been found in the tropical and subtropical zones of western Ecuador and north-west Peru, and in the upper tropical to the lower temperate zones of eastern Ecuador south to central Peru, where it is mainly found in the middle río Marañón, but also occurs locally in the upper río Huallaga drainage. Part of this range could be represented by vagrants, but there are no data indicating where breeding takes place.

Ecuador Records (with coordinates from Paynter and Traylor 1977) from western Ecuador are as follows: (*Esmeraldas*) Esmeraldas (Chapman 1926); (*Pichincha*) below Hacienda Santa Rosa, at río Cinto, along the new Lloa-Mindo road, where a specimen (in MECN) was collected at 2,030 m in August 1987 (J. C. Mathéus *in litt.* 1989); (*Pichincha*) "Quito" (Hartert 1898a, Zimmer 1953); Santo Domingo de los Colorados (Oberholser 1902); Río Palenque Research Station (P. Greenfield *in litt.* 1991); (*Manabí*) Chone (Chapman 1926); Cordillera de Balzar (see Remarks), where a specimen (in BMNH) was collected in March 1880; Cerro Achi, c.1°23'S 80°38'W, at 550-600 m, recently (TAP); (*Chimborazo*) Citado, untraced, but probably = río Citado c.15 km west of Alausí (Gould 1871); Camipampa, untraced (Cory 1918); Cayandeled (von Berlepsch and Taczanowski 1884-1886); between Chimborazo and Chimbo (Cory 1918); Chimbo (von Berlepsch and Taczanowski 1883, Chapman 1926); Huigra, 2°17'S 78°59'W (Chapman 1926); Pagma forest, untraced, but above Huigra (Chapman 1926); Chunchi (Chapman 1926); (*Los Ríos*) Babahoyo, where two specimens (in MNHN) were collected in September 1891; (*Guayas*) río Ayampe, on the Manabí border, recently (R. S. Ridgely *in litt.* 1991); Yaguachi (Taczanowski 1882); Guayaquil (Oberholser 1902); Durán (= Alfaro) (Chapman 1926); Naranjito, 2°13'S 79°29'W, where a specimen (in BMNH) was collected before 1920; río Pescado or Pogio, untraced (Zimmer 1953); (*Azuay*) Yunguilla valley, at 1,500 m, where four specimens (in BMNH) were collected in July 1939 and February 1940; (*El Oro*) El Bosque, at 1,400 m, where a specimen (in BMNH) was collected in July 1939; 28 km by road west of Catamayo (on the Portovelo road), where two birds were seen at 1,880 m in March 1990 (B. M. Whitney *in litt.* 1991); (*Loja*) Alamor, 4°02'S 80°02'W, and Guainche (between Alamor and Celica) (Chapman 1926).

Eastern Ecuador records come from: (*Napo*) Baisa (= Baeza), where two specimens (in BMNH) were collected in December 1877; below San José (= San José Nuevo) (Chapman 1926); río Napo (Zimmer 1953); (*Tungurahua*) near Baños (specimen in WFVZ); (*Morona-Santiago*) Macas, where two specimens (in BMNH) were collected in September 1937 and October 1940; (*Azuay*) Gima, where three specimens (in BMNH) were collected in March 1877; (*Zamora-Chinchipe*) Sabanillas (Zimmer 1953); Zamora (Chapman 1926); and on the Zumba–Chito trail, where a male was seen in March 1986 (M. Pearman *in litt.* 1990).

Peru Records on the Pacific slope come from: (*Piura*) Porculla (Bond 1954b); (*Lambayeque*) Las Pampas, at 150 m, where a specimen (in LSUMZ) was collected in September 1983; and Seques (Zimmer 1953); in the río Marañón drainage (*Cajamarca*) San Ignacio (Zimmer 1953, Bond 1954b); Huarandosa (Zimmer 1953); Puerto Tamborapa (Bond 1954b); Tambillo (Zimmer 1953); Callacate (Zimmer 1953); (*Amazonas*) Tamiapampa (Taczanowski 1882); Guayabamba (= Santa Rosa de Huayabamba) (Zimmer 1953); Chirimote (Taczanowski 1882); San Pedro (Zimmer 1953); (*La Libertad*) Soquián (Bond 1954b); Succha (Salvin 1895, Baron 1897); in the middle río Huallaga drainage (*San Martín*) Uscho, on the Amazonas border (Zimmer 1953); in the upper río Huallaga drainage (*Huánuco*) Chinchao (Zimmer 1930); and Muña (Zimmer 1953).

POPULATION Despite the large number of old specimens of this hummingbird, there are relatively few recent records, except for recent (mid-1980s) importations into (West) Germany (Collar and Andrew 1988). These imports presumably originated in western Ecuador, whence also came (from Pichincha) a 1987 specimen in MECN, with recent records from the Manabí–Guayas border, two birds in El Oro, and one in Zamora-Chinchipe. There appear to be only two recent reliable records from Peru.

ECOLOGY Although sometimes found in wet evergreen forest and at the edges of cloud-forest, the Little Woodstar apparently prefers moist and semideciduous forests that are only seasonally green (TAP, and habitat descriptions in Taczanowski 1884-1886, Baron 1897, Zimmer 1930, Paynter and Traylor 1977, and Stephens and Traylor 1983). During an El Niño year of heavy rainfall in north-western Peru (1983), the species appeared in scrubby woodland that often remains leafless for up to eight months or more, thus strongly suggesting that the hummingbird may expand its range into dry regions during wet years, and then withdraw into evergreen forests in drier times (TAP). There have been 14 weak to moderate and nine strong to very strong El Niño occurrences from 1900 to 1987 (Quinn *et al.* 1987), and most recently in 1992 (M. B. Robbins *in litt.* 1992). In western Ecuador the bird is found from sea level to c.2,250 m, and from c.900 to 3,050 m in eastern Ecuador and Peru (approximate elevation of localities as given by Paynter and Traylor 1977, Stephens and Traylor 1983, J. C. Mathéus *in litt.* 1989 and on specimen labels in ANSP and BMNH). Most east Ecuadorian specimens were taken from c.900 to 1,800 m, but three from Gima were presumably taken near 3,000 m (Paynter and Traylor 1977). Most Peruvian records are from c.900 m to 2,150 m, but Tamiapampa and San Pedro are at c.2,700-2,750 m (Taczanowski 1884-1886, Baron 1897), and at Succha Baron (1897) found the species from 2,745 to 3,050 m. The 1987 specimen from Pichincha was collected from the canopy of a 20 m tall tree in an area of humid forest with many large *Clusia* and *Cedrela* trees (heavily laden with epiphytes), a large *Alnus* stand near the river, and many bushes such as *Palicourea* (Rubiaceae) and *Cavendishia*, *Psammisia* and other ericaceans; it was taken on 18 August and had a slightly enlarged ovary (J. C. Mathéus *in litt.* 1989). At río Ayampe, Manabí–Guayas, several females were seen feeding at *Muntingia* trees; the threatened Esmeraldas Woodstar *Acestrura berlepschi* was also feeding from the same trees, but tended to be more in the canopy, while *bombus* remained lower, at edge situations, although there was some overlap (R. S. Ridgely *in litt.* 1991): the male seen on the Zumba–Chito trail in March 1986 was trap-lining flowers on a scrubby hillside (M. Pearman *in litt.* 1990). In El Oro during March 1990, a male was seen perching for long periods atop shrubs and low trees in an opening in a heavily wooded quebrada (at a point overlooking the quebrada): this bird performed a display flight on two occasions when approached by a female-plumaged individual (B. M. Whitney *in litt.* 1991).

THREATS Most of the moist forest in western Ecuador has already been destroyed, and only the wettest forest on steep slopes survives in many parts of the Andes in southern Ecuador and northern Peru. The Machalilla National Park is ineffectively protected (TAP: see equivalent section under Grey-backed Hawk *Leucopternis occidentalis*).

MEASURES TAKEN The species occurs at the Río Palenque reserve, Pichincha and Machalilla National Park, Manabí (55,000 ha: IUCN 1992), Ecuador (see equivalent section under Grey-backed Hawk).

MEASURES PROPOSED Proper management of the Machalilla National Park must be initiated to ensure the integrity of the habitat, although much more needs to be learned about the distribution, habitat requirements and behaviour of this enigmatic species before any specific measures can be taken. Details of initiatives proposed to preserve the threatened species endemic to south-west Ecuador and north-west Peru are given in Measures Proposed under Grey-backed Hawk.

REMARKS Concerning the authenticity of the locality Cordillera de Balzar, see Remarks 2 under Saffron Siskin *Carduelis siemiradskii*.

GLOW-THROATED HUMMINGBIRD *Selasphorus ardens* V[9]

This rare hummingbird is restricted to two areas of western and central Panama in the Serranía de Tabasará above 750 m, where it is unprotected and poorly known, in terms of both status and ecology.

DISTRIBUTION The Glow-throated Hummingbird is endemic to Panama, where it is known from very few localities in the Serranía de Tabasará of eastern Chiriquí and Veraguas (see Remarks); coordinates below are from OG (1969).

This species was first recorded in eastern Chiriquí during March 1924 when two males (in AMNH) and a female were collected on Cerro Florés (8°28'N 81°44'W) at 1,100 m (Wetmore 1968). Ridgely and Gwynne (1989) noted that it is found regularly above Cerro Colorado (8°28'N 81°45'W), evidently very close to the collecting locality on Cerro Florés. In Veraguas, specimens were taken (in the late nineteenth century) at Castillo (8°13'N 81°03'W), and Calovévora (presumably "Pico Calovevora" just north of Santa Fé, but still on the Pacific slope, as shown on the map in Salvin 1870) (Salvin and Godman 1888-1904). Other localities, whence come a number of recent records, are: Santa Fé (c.8°31'N 81°05'W; presumably near Calovévora – see above) and the road above (Wetmore 1968, Ridgely and Gwynne 1989), i.e. Cerro Tute (8°29'N 81°06'W) (Stiles 1983, F. G. Stiles *in litt.* 1991, B. M. Whitney *in litt.* 1991).

POPULATION Ridgely and Gwynne (1989) considered this species to be "uncommon", which by their definition implies it has been seen on "less than half of trips in proper habitat", although they noted that it is apparently seen regularly above Cerro Colorado, with a few seen on occasion along the road above Santa Fé (the bird was apparently relocated at Santa Fé during the 1980s, almost 100 years after its first being found there: see Wetmore 1968, Ridgely 1981b, Ridgely and Gwynne 1989). These two localities (i.e. Cerro Colorado/Cerro Florés and Santa Fé/Cerro Tute) represent the only areas where the species has been recorded during the twentieth century (see Distribution). As an indication of abundance near Cerro Tute, B. M. Whitney (*in litt.* 1991) saw just one male in 2.5 days during January 1982, F. G. Stiles (*in litt.* 1991) also seeing just one bird there in January 1984. Ornithologically, the Serranía de Tabasará is among the least known areas in Panama (Stiles 1983) and this is reflected in the paucity of specimens, observations and distributional, population and ecological data available on this bird (see below).

ECOLOGY The Glow-throated Hummingbird apparently inhabits the shrubby second-growth of clearings and forest borders in foothills and lower highlands (750-1,800 m) (Ridgely and Gwynne 1989; also AOU 1983). An adult male seen by B. M. Whitney (*in litt.* 1991) was perched about 4 m above the ground under the forest canopy, but near the edge. At Santa Fé in the east, the species seems to range mainly at higher elevations, and it has been suggested by F. G. Stiles (*in litt.* 1991) that birds may well be more abundant at higher elevations or at least on mountain-crests. Its habits are not well known, but its basic behaviour (and no published information currently exists: Stiles 1983) is probably similar to Scintillant Hummingbird *Selasphorus scintilla* (Ridgely and Gwynne 1989; see Remarks).

THREATS R. S. Ridgely (*in litt.* 1986) indicated that the range of the Glow-throated Hummingbird is largely undisturbed. However, this range is minute and poorly known, the bird's ecological needs are almost totally unknown, and it is seemingly both uncommon and unprotected, and in such circumstances it qualifies as a threatened species (see below).

MEASURES TAKEN None is known. Neither of the two main localities is currently under protection.

MEASURES PROPOSED It is clear that the Serranía de Tabasará is poorly known (see Population), so it is essential that a broad-based survey is undertaken to assess both the actual distribution and habitat needs of the species, as well as to estimate relative abundance levels and status of suitable remaining habitat. In the meantime, protection is vital for both the Cerro Florés and Santa Fé areas, both for this species and the many other species endemic to the Chiriquí/Veraguas highlands (see, e.g., ICBP 1992, Crosby *et al.* in prep.).

REMARKS There has been much confusion over the identification of the *Selasphorus* group of species, many specimens from Costa Rica (e.g. in AMNH, ROM) still labelled as *S. ardens* when they clearly refer to another member of the genus: all such records have been disregarded in this account. Stiles (1983), in reviewing the taxonomic status of Glow-throated Hummingbird and its close relationship to Scintillant Hummingbird, remarked that "while closely related, *scintilla* and *ardens* differ from each other considerably more than do any two members of the *flammula* complex. Especially considering the lack of information on... *ardens*, I think it wisest to continue to recognize them as distinct species. Together *scintilla* and *ardens* might comprise a superspecies".

EARED QUETZAL *Euptilotis neoxenus* I[7]

Although found almost throughout the mountains of western Mexico and even sporadically within Arizona and New Mexico, U.S.A., this trogon is locally distributed in montane pine and pine–oak forests, uncommon and poorly known ecologically, and threatened by the widespread destruction (or modification) of its habitat.

DISTRIBUTION The Eared Quetzal is distributed throughout the Sierra Madre Occidental, Mexico, records of the species coming from Sonora, Chihuahua, Sinaloa, Durango, Nayarit, and Zacatecas states. Away from the main sierra, the bird has been reported from Jalisco and Michoacán, with occasional records from Arizona and New Mexico in the U.S.A. Coordinates for Mexico are taken from OG (1956a).

U.S.A. The records of this species from the U.S.A. are almost certainly examples of sporadic, seasonal migrants (see Ecology), although a pair bred in 1991 (see below).

Arizona Eared Quetzals were first recorded in the U.S.A. when "considerable numbers" were observed at Warsaw Mills (untraced) in early December 1893 (van Rossem 1945). The species was not recorded again until four birds (two males, a female and an immature male) were found in the South Fork of Cave Creek Canyon in the Chiricahua mountains, the birds being observed between mid-October and early December 1977 (Zimmerman 1978). Subsequently, Eared Quetzals have been recorded from this area nearly every autumn/winter (Davis and Russell 1984), for example: one at lower Cave Creek Canyon in November 1978; one in the upper part of South Fork during August and October 1979 (Monson and Phillips 1981); and more recently, birds have been recorded there during June (two birds there 9-10 June, and one staying until 23 June 1991) and August (a female on 8 August 1991) (*Winging It* 3,7 [1991]: 3; 3,8 [1991]: 3; 3,9 [1991]: 3). West of this area, a bird was reported from Madera Canyon (Santa Rita Mountains) on 7 August 1991 (*Winging It* 3,9 [1991]: 3). In 1977, a male was found at Ramsey Canyon in the Huachucas (south-west of the Chiricahuas) in December 1977 (Zimmerman 1978), and up to five were reported there (upper Ramsey Canyon) from 6 August to 31 October 1991, during which period a failed nesting attempt was recorded (*Winging It* 3,12 [1991]: 3; *Amer. Birds* 46 [1992]: 12). A male bird was recorded at upper Carr Canyon (just south of Ramsey Canyon) on 9 August 1989 (*Winging It* 1,9 [1989]: 3).

New Mexico Zimmerman (1978) suggested that the Animas Mountains may well harbour this species, and indeed AOU (1983) reported a sight record for the locality, although no details are given.

Mexico Localities where this species has been recorded are generally from the Pacific side of the mountains (although occasionally on the eastern slope), the overall distribution being similar to that of the Imperial Woodpecker *Campephilus imperialis* (see relevant account).

Sonora There are just two records of the Eared Quetzal from Sonora, referring to a male (in AMNH) taken at El Puerto (see Remarks 1) at 1,920 m in December 1860, El Puerto apparently being close to or synonymous with Rancho La Arizona (at 40 km south-west of Nogales, although this area is a desert locality with no forest: J. T. Marshall *in litt.* 1992); and observations from Pinos Altos (1,420 m) in the Sierra de Nácori (see Remarks 2), during June 1953 (Marshall 1957).

Chihuahua From north to south, localities include: Pacheco (30°06'N 108°21'W), where six birds were collected (four males and two females in AMNH and MCZ) during August 1905, and five (three males and two females in FMNH) between June and August 1909; "Arch valley" and "Strawberry valley" (at roughly 30°10'N 108°10'W in Marshall 1957, and very close to Pacheco), where birds were recorded during August 1951 and June 1952 (Marshall 1957, J. T. Marshall *in litt.* 1992); upper río Gavilán (at roughly 29°58'N 108°25'W in Marshall 1957, and west of Colonia García), where birds were observed at 2,050 m in June 1952 (Marshall 1957); near Colonia García (29°59'N 108°20'W), where five birds were taken (three males and two females in USNM) in June and July 1899; Babicora (29°30'N 108°01'W), where eight birds were taken (three males and five females in FMNH and ROM) during June 1902; and Madera (29°12'N 108°07'W), where a female (in MCZ) was collected in October 1921. East from these northernmost Chihuahua localities the Eared Quetzal has been recorded in the Sierra del Nido (west of Carrizalillo), specimens (all in MVZ) coming from 2,440 m at Arroyo del Nido (29°36'N 106°38'W: female taken in June 1957); Arroyo Mesteño (29°26'N 107°04'W), where at 2,315 m four males and three females were collected in July 1959, and at 2,745 m a male and female were taken here during August 1961; and Cañon del Alamo (29°27'N 106°47'W), where a female was collected at 2,225 m in June 1959. Further south again, the species has been collected (a male in April 1885, in MCZ) at Durasno (probably 28°45'N 107°58'W, and therefore on or close to the río Verde); río Verde (28°43-23'N 107°57-46'W), where a male (in WFVZ) was collected in May 1961; and Pinos Altos (from the map in Lumholtz 1903, this is Pinos Redondeados at 28°15'N 108°17'W: see Remarks 2), where a male and female (in MCZ) were collected in June 1888. Near Barranca del Cobre, at least three pairs and one individual were recorded in a canyon leading to (Cascada) Cusarare (south-west of Creel) during July 1991 (S. N. G. Howell *in litt.* 1991). In the far south of the state, localities include: Jesus María (probably at 26°52'N 107°39'W), where three specimens (in MCZ) were taken from 1883 to 1888; Laguna Juanota (26°30'N 106°29'W), represented by a male (in MLZ) taken during August 1937; and near Guadalupe y Calvo, where four males and three females (in USNM) were taken during August and September 1898. Untraced localities in Chihuahua include Rancho San Miguel (four males and two females in WFVZ, collected during October 1963), and "Mound valley" (a male and female in AMNH and MCZ, collected in September 1905).

Sinaloa In the north of the state, the Eared Quetzal has been collected 12 km north and 50 km east of Sinaloa (25°50'N 108°14'W), a male (in MNHUK) being taken at 1,675 m in April 1962. Further south, specimens (in AMNH, SWC, and YPM) have been collected at Rancho Carrizo, between 12 and 17 km west (by road) of El Palmito (along route 40, near the border with Durango at around km 201: Edwards 1985), with birds taken during February–April 1964 and December 1970, and a female from c.3 km north-west of El Palmito in May 1964. Other localities for sightings along route 40 are: Hortensia's Barranca, near km 212; and Rancho Liebre Barranca north of km 200 and El Palmito (Edwards 1985, J. F. Clements *in litt.* 1989, B. M. Whitney *in litt.* 1991). An untraced locality in Sinaloa is "Babizos", where a male (in MLZ) was collected in December 1935.

Durango Specimens have been collected at Coyotes (either 24°15'N 104°42'W, or 23°49'N 105°20'W), where a male and two females (in FMNH) were taken in August 1904; Mimbres (c.45 km west-south-west of Durango), where a pair was seen in perturbed pine-forest in July 1988 (A. G. Navarro *in litt.* 1991); c.10 km south-west of El Salto (a female in MLZ taken in October 1954); 6 km north-east of Las Adjuntas (23°44'N 105°31'W, also 21 km west of El Salto), where a male (in DMNH) was taken at 2,440 m in May 1972; also, 5 km east of Piedra Gorda (23°46'N 105°54'W, almost on the border with Sinaloa), where a male (in MLZ) was taken in March 1938. These last three localities are along or close to route 40, the main Mazatlán–Durango highway (see above). Further east, two pairs of Eared Quetzal were recorded in La Michilía Biosphere Reserve during July 1980 (A. M. Sada *in litt.* 1992).

Nayarit There are apparently just five specimens (in BMNH, USNM) from this state, four taken at Santa Teresa (apparently 22°28'N 104°44'W) in the north during August 1897, and a male taken in the Sierra Madre de Nayarit at 2,440 m in July 1889.

Zacatecas Specimens come from the south, with a female (in DMNH) taken 8 km west of Monte Escobedo in September 1955, and two males (in USNM) at Plateado (21°57'N 103°06'W) in September 1897. Specimens (in BMNH and MCZ) from the Sierra Valparaiso during July and August 1889 probably originated in this state (the MCZ specimen is labelled "Sierra Valparaiso, Zac"), although on the CETN (1976) map of the area the sierra is situated at c.22°40'N 103°45'W in northernmost Jalisco and south-western Zacatecas (as mentioned under Imperial Woodpecker).

Jalisco The birds collected in 1889 (in BMNH and MCZ) came from the Sierra Valparaiso which straddles the Jalisco–Zacatecas border, but are probably attributable to Zacatecas (see above). Two birds (in BMNH) taken in the mid-nineteenth century were originally believed to be from "Real del Monte" (apparently in Hidalgo), but were later thought to have come from near Bolaños in northern Jalisco (Salvin and Godman 1888-1904). Elsewhere in the state, specimens have been taken at La Barranca de Agua (untraced), 30 km south and 13 km west of Guadalajara, where a male (in MNHUK) was collected at 2,805 m in February 1949 (also Thompson 1962); Mascota (15 km west of Talpa), in the Sierra Juanacatlán, where a female (in AMNH) was taken in May 1892; Cerro Viejo, "Jojotetan" (both untraced), where a male (in AMNH) was taken six days prior to the Mascota bird, suggesting that this locality is also in the Sierra Juanacatlán; near Talpa de Allende (20°23'N 104°51'W), with two birds (in MNHUK) taken 29 km south-east in March 1965, and a male taken "24 km south and 14 km east" (these two localities are presumably the same or very close) at 2,105 m in May 1964. An untraced locality apparently within this state is the Sierra del Alo (possibly "Olo"), where a female (in MNHN) was collected (date unknown).

Michoacán The Eared Quetzal has been recorded from just two localities, both represented by specimens (in USNM) taken in 1903: Patamban (presumably the cerro, at 19°45'N 102°20'W), where three males and two females were collected on 1 February; and Cerro de Tancítaro (19°23'N 102°13'W), where a bird was taken in March.

POPULATION During the nineteenth century, references to the abundance of the Eared Quetzal indicated that it was relatively common: the label on a specimen (in MCZ) taken at Jesus María (see Distribution) in 1883 has "quite common" written on it, and 10 years later, in December 1893, "considerable numbers" were observed in Arizona (van Rossem 1945); Salvin and Godman (1888-1904) considered this species "one of the most characteristic birds" of the sierras, another being the Imperial Woodpecker, which at this time was also relatively abundant (see relevant account). Other examples of apparent past abundance are the collection of seven birds near Guadalupe y Calvo from 27 August to 1 September 1898; five at Patamban on 1 February 1903; six in August 1905 at Pacheco, and eight in June 1902 at Babicora (see Distribution).

Since 1905, the only significant numerical records of this species are of six birds taken at Rancho San Miguel in October 1963; seven taken at arroyo Mesteño, Chihuahua, in July 1959; and three pairs seen in 5 km during surveys in 1953 in the Sierra de Nácori (Marshall 1957: see Distribution), although particular birds (and pairs) were noted to range for at least 3 km along some valleys near Colonia García (J. T. Marshall *in litt.* 1992). Most recently, other than the U.S.A. sightings, records have been concentrated along route 40 near the Sinaloa–Durango border (see Distribution), many birdwatchers visiting Hortensia's and Rancho Liebre Barrancas specifically to see the species (see Edwards 1985). Even at these well known sites, the Eared Quetzal is rare and occurs at low densities: thus J. F. Clements (*in litt.* 1989, 1991) observed it on just two out of seven visits to the Rancho Liebre Barranca (a female in August 1984, with a pair seen and several heard in May 1989), while S. N. G. Howell (*in litt.* 1987, 1991) has not seen it there despite many visits (all months from January to June, and August). However, B. M. Whitney (*in litt.* 1991) recorded one or more individuals at Rancho Liebre Barranca in November 1980, 1981, and 1982, and also in February 1981 and 1983, seven birds (one or two adults, the others possibly immature) having been seen in one tree along the lower part of the trail (above the highway) during February 1981.

Apart from the above observation at Rancho Liebre Barranca, the record of seven adults (at least three breeding pairs) at Cusarare, Chihuahua (a "known site" for this species), in July 1991, and two pairs nesting in La Michilía Biosphere Reserve (see Ecology) are the only other such records suggesting that the bird is common even locally (S. N. G. Howell *in litt.* 1991). Recent observers consider the bird to be rare to uncommon, existing at low densities in localized areas within its large range (Zimmerman 1978, D. A. Scott *in litt.* 1985, S. N. G. Howell *in litt.* 1987). This evidence suggests that the population has decreased during the twentieth century, although no survey has been undertaken (see Measures Proposed) and the seasonal or unpredictable movements of the bird (see Ecology) may well be masking the actual distribution and population.

ECOLOGY Records of the Eared Quetzal come from high temperate zone pine-forests (specimen taken at 2,440 m near El Salto in May, in DMNH: this habitat was considered typical in Miller *et al.* 1957, and AOU 1983), pine–oak woodland (specimens in AMNH and DMNH), and apparently exceptionally in tropical evergreen forest (specimen in AMNH). Birds recorded by Marshall (1957) during June to August (1951-1953) in the mountains along the Sonora–Chihuahua border were found at c.2,050 m in an open-park woodland of apache pine *Pinus engelmanni*, some ponderosa pines *P. ponderosa* and Chihuahua pines *P. leiophylla*, all of which overshadowed the relatively small grey oaks *Quercus grisea*. At another locality in the same area (1,420 m at Pinos Altos), Marshall (1957) recorded the species in an area dominated by blue oak *Q. oblongifolia* and *P. durangensis*; and near Cusarare, the species was found (in July) in a broad rocky canyon with pines, a few oaks, and fewer madrones (S. N. G. Howell *in litt.* 1991). At Rancho Liebre Barranca in May 1989, J. F. Clements (*in litt.* 1989, 1991) found a pair of birds in pine/pine–oak at the rim of the barranca, with several birds heard in the humid canyon just below true pine–oak forest, in woodland comprising broadleaf trees with oaks, sacred fir *Abies* sp., magnolias *Magnolia* sp., numerous *Tillandsia* species, arboreal orchids and other epiphytes. Near Durango, a pair was seen in perturbed but arid pine forest in July 1988 (A. G. Navarro *in litt.* 1991). In Arizona, the habitat at Cave Creek comprised oak thickets, cypress, sycamore and madrones, and was described by Zimmerman (1978) as xeric vegetation, with pine–oak woods above and well developed riparian forest below.

A bird that was "presumably feeding young" (see below) had been feeding primarily on caterpillars and beetles (specimen in DMNH), and the female seen at Rancho Liebre Barranca in August 1984 was consuming both insects and the berry-like fruit of madrones (madroña) *Arbutus arizonica* (J. F. Clements *in litt.* 1991). Marshall (1957) suggested that the species feeds on vegetable matter and arthropods taken from the crowns of pine trees. The bulk of the birds' diet in November in Arizona was found to be madrones – both insects and fruit being secured on the wing (Zimmerman 1978). In 1977, an insufficient food supply was deemed to have prevented the four birds from wintering at Cave Creek, although they may have been able to survive elsewhere in the Chiricahuas (Zimmerman 1978). The Elegant Trogon *Trogon elegans* was noted driving Eared Quetzals away from food trees at Cave Creek, interspecific competition from both this species and Mountain Trogon *T. mexicanus* possibly having some influence on the Eared Quetzal's localized distribution (Elegant Trogon and Eared Quetzal are sympatric in at least one Chihuahua locality; Mountain and Elegant Trogons and Eared Quetzal are sympatric in Durango and Sinaloa, where Mountain Trogon is widespread and common, Eared Quetzal generally rare and local) (Zimmerman 1978, J. F. Clements *in litt.* 1991).

A pair of birds were discovered nesting in a dead maple in Ramsey Canyon (Arizona) during October 1991: unfortunately, although the adults were feeding two young on 15 October, the attempt was unsuccessful (*Winging It* 3,12 [1991]: 3; *Amer. Birds* 46 [1992]: 12). In Michilía Biosphere Reserve, two pairs were nesting (in dead pines) in July 1980 (A. M. Sada *in litt.* 1992). Eared Quetzals singing and inspecting nest holes (one 7 m up) were recorded in June 1952 in Sonora and Chihuahua, with singing noted in the Sierra de Nacorí during August 1951 (J. T. Marshall *in litt.* 1992); birds persistently singing, and apparently courting, were observed near Cusarare during July 1991 (one male singing from a perch c.12 m up, beside a suitable looking nest-hole, in a dead pine: S. N. G. Howell *in litt.* 1992); and TAP found breeding birds in Durango (feeding nestlings) in early September 1973; thus the breeding season is apparently from June to October in much of the species's range. However, specimens that were either about to lay or had just laid have been taken on 14 April (in YPM), 3 June (in MCZ) and 10-15 July (in MVZ). The specimen (in MNHUK) taken at 1,675 m on 16 April was apparently immature ("skull not ossified") and seems particularly early, while the female taken on 20 September and deemed to have laid eggs "within a month" appears to be later than expected.

The Eared Quetzal is restricted to montane areas between 1,675 and 3,050 m, although the majority of records come from 2,100-2,800 m (see Distribution). The records from Sonora appear to be lower, with birds observed in June and August at 1,420 m in the Sierra de Nácori (in pines) (see Distribution). A record from Sinaloa is of a bird (in MNHUK), apparently a juvenile ("skull not ossified"; see below), taken at 1,675 m in April. The records suggest that: (1) birds in the northernmost breeding localities may live at lower altitudes; (2) young birds may wander away from the breeding area (and that this wandering could be altitudinal in nature); and (3) birds may exhibit (sporadic) autumn/winter migrations to lower altitudes, a conclusion reinforced by the unpredictable (although increasingly recorded) occurrence of the species in Arizona and New Mexico, primarily during the months of August–December (see Distribution). At least one immature was present in the Chiricahua mountains in 1977, and although this "influx" involved only five recorded individuals (Zimmerman 1978), considerable numbers were found in December 1893 (van Rossem 1945). Specimens (in AMNH, SWC) taken in December and mid-February at Rancho Carrizo, Sinaloa, were collected in a lush sub-tropical barranca and tropical evergreen woodland respectively: those collected in March and April (AMNH, SWC) at the same locality were found in pine–oak woodland, indicating a localized migration to lower more tropical habitats (in the barrancas or canyons) during the winter months, birds moving uphill again for breeding during late summer (see below). Observations at Rancho Liebre Barranca (J. F. Clements *in litt.* 1991, B. M. Whitney *in litt.* 1991) appear to confirm the above conclusion.

THREATS Specific threats to the Eared Quetzal are difficult to assess owing to a lack of information about its seasonal movements and true distribution. The main threat is logging and the removal of potential nest-site trees (S. N. G. Howell *in litt.* 1987); in many parts of the Sierra Madre Occidental, logging operations have spread to a large number of previously inaccessible areas (see Thick-billed Parrot *Rhynchopsitta pachyrhyncha* and Imperial Woodpecker accounts). Although logging has been selective, the removal of large and dead trees almost invariably reduces the availability of nest-sites (see Thick-billed Parrot account), and often leads to the eventual clear-cutting of forest (J. T. Marshall *in litt.* 1992). It has been found that Elegant Trogons are particularly susceptible to even slight disturbance during the breeding season (Zimmerman 1978), and if Eared Quetzals react in the same way, the disturbance from logging activities and the resultant increase in human population within these remote parts may possibly be a cause of the species's declining population. Along route 40 towards Rancho Liebre Barranca there has recently (since 1984) been development with towns, hotels and restaurants being built (J. F. Clements *in litt.* 1991). Also along this road at around km 200-210, cattle are found roaming through the forest which in turn is being constantly encroached upon by the destructive practice of slash-and-burn agriculture, a consequence of which is that many of the streams are drying up as the pristine forest is gradually destroyed (J. F. Clements *in litt.* 1991). Clearly, the combination of logging, agricultural encroachment and development is collectively threatening most of the forest areas where this species still exists.

MEASURES TAKEN The Eared Quetzal has been recorded in La Michilía Biospere Reserve, Durango (S. N. G. Howell *in litt.* 1991, A. M. Sada *in litt.* 1992), which covers an area (from 1,700 to 3,000 m) of 35,000 ha (Anon. 1989). Apart from this, there are no other protected areas within the immediate range of the species, although the failed nesting attempt in Ramsey Canyon (see Ecology) was within the Nature Conservancy's Mile Hi–Ramsey Canyon preserve (*Nature Conservancy* January/February 1992: 6).

MEASURES PROPOSED The priority action for this species is the preservation of some substantial tracts of pine and pine–oak forest before it all becomes modified. There is also a need to assess the species's precise ecological needs throughout the annual cycle, ideal areas for such studies being La Michilía Biosphere Reserve, where the bird appears to be common, and to a certain extent the Huachucas and Chiricahuas in southern Arizona (where it may now be breeding). These studies should be followed up with surveys in other suitable areas so that a clearer picture of the bird's distribution can be determined and new areas, suitable for protection, identified. Any distributional, and to a certain extent, ecological work, should be combined with the measures proposed for the other threatened species within its range, namely the Imperial Woodpecker and Thick-billed Parrot (see relevant accounts); indeed, the need to preserve several extensive areas of intact forest in the quetzal's range is indicated in the equivalent section under Thick-billed Parrot, and the urgent need to survey certain remote areas is stressed in that under Imperial Woodpecker.

REMARKS (1) An (immature: Allen 1893) male specimen (in AMNH) collected in December 1890 is labelled from "El Pineta, N. Sonora", the locality subsequently changed to "El Puerto"; Allen (1893) and Salvin and Godman (1888-1904) recorded this specimen from "El Pinita, in the state of Chihuahua", van Rossem (1945) finally indicating that in fact it was collected at El Puerto, Sonora. (2) Marshall (1957) mapped his study site of Pinos Altos in the Sierra de Nácori, Sonora, although the Lumholtz (1903) locality is further south and in Chihuahua (apparently the same as Pinos Redondeados at 28°15'N 108°17'W), hence Pinos Altos is treated here as two localities, records prior to Lumholtz (1903) referring to the Chihuahua site, and those from the 1950s to Sonora.

KEEL-BILLED MOTMOT *Electron carinatum* K[12]

Until recently, this seemingly elusive motmot was extremely poorly known, despite a wide distribution from southern Mexico through to Costa Rica. A series of observations since the late 1980s have shown it to be locally not uncommon in lowland and foothill forest: however, there is still no explanation for its patchy distribution even within suitable habitat.

DISTRIBUTION The Keel-billed Motmot has been recorded at a relatively small number of localities scattered over an extensive range in Central America, generally on the Caribbean slope of southern Mexico, Belize, Guatemala, Honduras, Nicaragua and northern Costa Rica. Coordinates are taken from Binford (1989), OG (1956a,b,c, 1965, 1976), Monroe (1968).

Mexico All records of the Keel-billed Motmot are from the Isthmus de Tehuantepec eastward. Evidence from Campeche is discounted here (see Remarks 1).

Veracruz There are only two confident records: in 1948, the species was heard on a number of occasions (but never located) along the ríos Chalchijapa and Solosuchi (c.17°22'N 94°47'W, coordinates from Lowery and Dalquest 1951) near the Oaxaca border (Lowery and Dalquest 1951); it was also recorded south of San José del Carmen (in the south of the state) during the 1950s (D. A. Zimmerman *per* B. W. Miller *in litt.* 1991). Records from Ubero and Tolosa, although attributed to this state, are treated under Oaxaca; and a male (in MNHUK), collected at 90 m 30 km south-south-east of Jesús Carranza (17°26'N 95°02'W) in May 1949, was almost certainly within Oaxaca, close to route 185 near Ubero and Tolosa (Lowery and Dalquest 1951: see below).

Oaxaca The Keel-billed Motmot was twice collected at Tolosa (two specimens in AMNH, one dated December 1901). Although both Veracruz and Oaxaca states possess a town called Tolosa, Binford (1989) suggested that old records from this locality should be referred to Oaxaca and believed that these specimens were probably taken in this state (Tolosa, Oaxaca, is at 17°12'N 95°03'W, and 60 m). A male (in USNM) was taken at Ubero in December 1901 (see Remarks 2), the label suggesting that this is in Veracruz. Again, both states possess an Ubero (Uvero), but that in Oaxaca (at 17°17'N 95°01'W, and at 30 m) is almost on the Veracruz border and in close proximity both to Tolosa and the collecting locality south of Jesús Carranza (see Remarks 2). The only other record from Oaxaca is of a male (in MNHN) taken at "Chuialapa" (= Santa María Chimalapa, 16°55'N 94°42'W, at c.290 m) during February 1952.

Tabasco Only one record exists, a male (in USNM) taken at Teapa in April 1900, although there is an unconfirmed report of a recent specimen from the state (S. N. G. Howell *in litt.* 1987) which, if correct, would be the first record for Mexico since 1952.

Belize Until recently there were very few records from Belize, one specimen (in BMNH) being taken "in the vicinity of Belize" [City] in January 1888. In May of the same year, the same collector (Blancaneaux) took a female (in BMNH) "near San Felipe, Riomakal", a newer label claiming this as in Campeche, Mexico (see Remarks 1). In view of his earlier collection in Belize, it seems likely that this specimen is in fact attributable to this country, and indeed, there is a San Felipe (17°09'N 89°04'W) on the río Macal, just south of San Ignacio. A female (in CM) was taken in the Cockscombe Mountains (at 350 m) in March 1935. Since April 1988, Keel-billed Motmots have been found on the Vaca Plateau in south-western Belize, and a population has been extensively studied around the Caracol Archaeological Site, at 490 m (B. W. Miller *in litt.* 1989, 1990, Miller 1991). In January–February 1991, birds were repeatedly heard and twice seen c.20 km west of the Maya Mountains (13 km south of the Mountain Pine Ridge area, on the río Raspaculo, a continuation of the Chiquibul forest area) (S. Matola *in litt.* 1991, B. W. Miller *in litt.* 1991). A disjunct population was found to the north of Mountain Pine Ridge at Slate

Creek, where two birds were heard in October 1991 (B. W. Miller *in litt.* 1991, also Miller and Miller 1992).

Guatemala The Keel-billed Motmot has been recorded from three areas: in the north (Petén) records come from Laguna Perdida, where a male (in UMMZ) was collected around 1900 (see Remarks 3), and Tikal, where one was seen and filmed in 1958 (E. P. Edwards *in litt.* 1986, 1991, Smithe 1966). Further south, Salvin (Salvin and Godman 1888-1904) believed that he saw this species near the banks of the río Chixoy not far from Santa Ana and the gorge of La Campaña, during March 1874. Santa Ana and the gorge are untraced but presumably near La Campaña (15°19'N 90°31'W), which is very close to the río Chixoy. Land (1970) referred to this sighting as from Santa Ana, Alta Verapaz, the two specimens recorded by Boucard (1878b) from "Vera Paz" presumably being taken near here. More recently, a male (in MNHUK) was taken at El Astillero in February 1955 (apparently at c.7 m); of a number of towns by this name in Guatemala, the most likely is at 15°02'N 90°14'W. In the east, a number of birds (see Population) were recorded between 200 and 700 m on Cerro San Gil (15°40'N 88°47'W) during February 1991 (Howell and Webb 1992).

Honduras Records come from various scattered localities across the country, which from approximately west to east are: Santa Ana (15°29'N 88°03'W, at c.90 m) where two males and a female (in USNM) were taken in January and November 1890; San Pedro Montaña (a mountain range west of San Pedro Sula, which is at 15°28'N 88°01'W), where a male and female (in CM) were taken in January and February 1892 (this mountain range presumably encompasses the previous locality); the east slope of Cerro Santa Bárbara (14°53'N 88°10'W), where two males (in LSUMZ) were taken at 1,220 and 1,555 m in November 1962 and March 1963. In the vicinity of Lago Yojoa, this bird was first recorded between Taulabé (Taulevi, 14°38'N 87°59'W, at 430 m) and Lago Yojoa, where a bird was seen and one collected (in BMNH, but labelled simply "Lake of Yojoa") in 1857 or 1858 (Taylor 1860). Subsequently the species has been taken only once at Lago Yojoa (at 760 m), this being a female (in CM) collected in June 1951.

Along the north-west coast, localities include: near Medina (15°46'N 87°54'W, 5 km south-east of Puerto Cortés), where a bird was seen at 1,500 m in October 1986 (S. Thorn *in litt.* 1991); "near Tela" (J. Clinton-Eitniear *in litt.* 1991), whence come several recent observations; Lancetilla (c.15°42'N 87°28'W), which is the (Tela river) valley running from 3 to 11 km inland of Tela, and where a male and a mated pair (in MCZ) were taken (at 365 m) during March 1928 (Peters 1929), and where birds were recorded during June 1988 and March 1991 (Howell and Webb 1992); La Ceiba (15°47'N 86°50'W), where a male (in MCZ: see Remarks 4) was collected in January 1902. In the east of the country Monroe (1968) listed a female (in UCLA) taken in January 1955 "19 km east of Jalapa, Nicaragua", and interpreted this as 1 km east of Los Paredes (13°56'N 85°58'W), just within Honduras (see below). Records from Arenal are treated under Nicaragua. Two males (in USNM) were collected somewhere along the río Segovia (Coco) in June 1887; as this river forms much of the border between Honduras and Nicaragua, the national origin of these specimens is unknown (see below).

Nicaragua Records come from a number of localities which, from approximately north to south, are as follows: río Segovia (Coco, see above), where two males (in BMNH) were taken (apparently on the Nicaragua side) in March 1898; río Moco (14°39'N 84°17'W), near the village of Moco (untraced), 45 km west-south-west of Waspam, where a male and female (in UCLA) were taken (at 30 m) in February 1962; Eden (14°00'N 84°26'W: Huber 1932), where a female (in ANSP) was collected between 460-760 m in May 1922; and Arenal (13°48'N 85°49'W: Monroe 1968), c.25-27 km "east" (see below) of Jalapa (13°57'N 86°12'W), where two males and a female (in UCLA) were taken between 365 and 515 m in January 1955. From the coordinates it can be seen that Arenal is actually east-south-east of Jalapa, and a female taken just a few days after the Arenal specimens at "19 km east of Jalapa" is also likely to be east-south-east and therefore from Nicaragua, not "1 km east of Los Paredes" in Honduras (*contra* Monroe 1968).

Other localities include: Ocotal (apparently a municipality centred on 13°40'N 86°27'W), where two males (in AMNH) were collected in May 1908; Cum (Kum, 13°42'N 85°17'W), 45 km west-south-west of Siuna, where a female (in UCLA) was taken at 215 m in April 1962; Peña Blanca (Peñas Blancas, presumably the one north-east of Matagalpa), where a male (in AMNH) was taken in May 1909; río Tuma (precise locality along the river unknown), where a male and female (in AMNH) were taken in March-April 1909; río Grande (presumably río Grande de Matagalpa; exact locality unknown) where a male (in BMNH) was taken in February 1898; La Libertad (12°13'N 85°10'W), where a male (in BMNH) was taken in February 1892; and Chontales (a department centred on 12°05'N 85°10'W), where a specimen was taken a short time before 1872 (Salvin 1872).

Costa Rica In Costa Rica, at the southern limit of its range, the Keel-billed Motmot has been recorded from just seven localities, all on the Caribbean slope of the cordilleras (see Remarks 5). Five of these localities come from the north-west, in the cordilleras de Guanacaste and Tilarán, and are as follows: Rincón de la Vieja (two localities on the north-north-east slopes of the volcán), 300-500 m (one specimen in MZUCR collected in November 1988: F. G. Stiles *in litt.* 1991); 4 km north-east of Dos Ríos de Upala (by the río Pizota), where two birds were seen (in 15 days of fieldwork) and a male collected (in MZUCR) during November 1987 (J. Sánchez *in litt.* 1992); La Vijagua (= Bijagua, 10°44'N 85°06'W), c.12 km north-east of Volcán Tenorio, a locality mentioned by Ridgway (1914); El Silencio de Tilarán (10°29'N 84°57'W, just to the south of Lake Arenal), where a male (in DMNH) was collected in February 1954; Peñas Blancas (a valley north of Monteverde on the Caribbean slope of the Cordillera de Tilarán, and south-east of El Silencio), where an individual apparently formed a pair-bond with a Broad-billed Motmot *Electron platyrhynchum* (Stiles and Skutch 1989, S. N. G. Howell *in litt.* 1991; see Population), and where a (questionable) sighting of a bird was recently made (Ridgley and Gwynne 1989, B. W. Miller *in litt.* 1990).

North-east of this general area, the bird has been collected (a female in MNHN) at San Carlos (in the vicinity of Villa Quebrada: the San Carlos region of eastern Alajuela province) in February 1877, representing the first Costa Rica record (Boucard 1878a, Slud 1964, F. G. Stiles *in litt.* 1992). The only other recorded locality is Isla Bonita (c.8 km north-east of Volcán Poás in the Cordillera Central) where a bird (in AMNH) was collected (date unknown).

POPULATION Almost nothing is known about the population of this elusive species, which is generally considered to be the rarest member of its family (D. A. Scott *in litt.* 1986, Miller 1991). Most observations/records have been of pairs or single birds, with normally one record per locality. The exceptions to this are recent observations in Belize, Guatemala and Honduras. The Keel-billed Motmot is apparently widespread but occurs at low density and is generally considered rare to uncommon (see Remarks 6).

Mexico The Keel-billed Motmot in Mexico is represented by 6-7 specimens, the most recent of these being taken in 1952 (see Distribution). This seemingly constitutes the last known record from the country, and indeed the species has been considered extinct there (Miller 1991), although there is a recent unconfirmed report from Tabasco (S. N. G. Howell *in litt.* 1987), and many localities remain to be checked (A. G. Navarro and A. T. Peterson *in litt.* 1991).

Belize Apparently just 2-3 specimens of this bird have been collected in Belize, the last during 1935 (see Distribution). There were a number of observations of breeding birds during the 1970s (D. Weyer *in litt.* 1989), but by 1986 the species had not been recorded for 7-8 years (B. W. Miller *in litt.* 1990). Since 1988, the Keel-billed Motmot has been regularly recorded on the Vaca Plateau (where it is considered locally abundant), and studied in detail around the Caracol Archaeological Site (also on the Vaca Plateau) (B. W. Miller *in litt.* 1989). The current estimate for the area around Caracol (in a forest plot of c.2,400 ha) is of between 17 and 24 birds during the breeding season (B. W. Miller *in litt.* 1991). A focal group of 7-8 breeding birds (in a core area of 1,600 ha) was followed at Caracol (none of which had any reproductive success), this area also supporting 18-20 Blue-crowned Motmots *Momotus momota* (B. W. Miller *in litt.* 1990). In the 1991 breeding season (in the 2,400 ha forest plot) there were 20 pairs of Blue-crowned Motmots to 2-3 pairs of Keel-billed Motmots (B. W. Miller *in litt.* 1991). Elsewhere in Belize, six or seven birds were repeatedly heard (and two seen) during January and February 1991 south of Mountain Pine Ridge: they were not at all common, being localized in one canyon area (S. Matola *in litt.* 1991, B. W. Miller *in litt.* 1991; see Distribution).

Guatemala In referring to the two specimens taken at Vera Paz (possibly the two currently in BMNH, taken during 1872 in "Guatemala" and reported by Salvin 1872), Boucard (1878b) suggested that the Keel-billed Motmot is a rare species seen generally in pairs, although this seems to be based on information taken in Costa Rica (see Boucard 1878a). The possible sighting by Salvin near Santa Ana in 1874 (see Distribution) suggests the presence of at least a small population in the Vera Paz area during the nineteenth century. The type-specimen (see Du Bus 1847: apparently the specimen in MNHN), and the one from Laguna Perdida represented the only other specimen records from Guatemala, while reports from Tikal and more recently unconfirmed reports by P. Hubbell (*in litt.* 1986) were the only records since the turn of the century until a population was found on Cerro San Gil in 1991 (see Distribution; Remarks 3, 4). At least six to eight birds were noted (mostly calling) at Cerro San Gil at the end of February 1991, three birds (apparently two males courting a female) being seen together, and one seen near a probable nest-burrow (Howell and Webb 1992).

Honduras The collection of this species during the 1850s was noted with "much interest" (Sclater 1858), although subsequently it has been considered locally fairly common rather than rare, with as many as five birds seen and heard in June 1988 at Lancetilla and the country seemingly regarded as the species's centre of abundance (S. N. G. Howell *in litt.* 1989, 1991; see also Monroe 1968, Ridgely and Gwynne 1989). There are three main areas of abundance: (1) the San Pedro Montaña area (including Santa Ana), where five birds were taken between 1890 and 1892; (2) Lago Yojoa (including the east slope of Cerro Santa Bárbara), where four birds have been collected, three of them during the 1950s and 1960s; and (3) Tela (including the Tela–Lancetilla river valley) where three birds were taken in 1928 and whence come several recent observations (see Distribution), including that of one bird seen (three to four heard) during early June 1988 and two seen (five to six heard) in mid-March 1991 at Lancetilla (Howell and Webb 1992). In 1928, the species was regarded as "not uncommon" at Lancetilla, despite being easily overlooked (see Remarks 6; Peters 1929).

Nicaragua The Keel-billed Motmot is sparsely distributed across much of northern Nicaragua, but the population is essentially unknown as almost all localities are represented by just one or two specimens. The only exception to this is four birds collected east of Jalapa in January 1955 (see Distribution), which combined with the two taken on the río Moco in February 1962 represent the most recent records from this country.

Costa Rica In 1877 Boucard (1878a), when referring to the collection of birds at San Carlos, claimed that the Keel-billed Motmot was "rare [and] goes by pairs in the forest", subsequent authors (e.g. Slud 1964, Stiles and Skutch 1989) also considering the bird rare. When collected at El Silencio de Tilarán in 1954, however, it was regarded as "not rare" (Slud 1964; see Distribution), and indeed most Costa Rica records come from this general area (i.e. to the north-east at Bijagua, and to the south-east at Peñas Blancas; see Distribution). Slud (1964) suggested that the Broad-billed Motmot (sympatric with Keel-billed Motmot in Costa Rica), although relatively uncommon in the area of overlap, is nevertheless commoner than the Keel-billed Motmot. The record of a bird being fed by a Broad-billed Motmot (the source of the "mixed pairing" mentioned in Stiles and Skutch 1989) in 1986 (the two were possibly seen together in 1985: S. N. G. Howell *in litt.* 1991) seems to suggest that the population is so small in Costa Rica that mates are extremely rare.

ECOLOGY The Keel-billed Motmot is a resident of lowland and foothill areas generally at altitudes of 10-760 m (see below), and exhibits no apparent seasonal variation within this range (see Distribution). Exceptions are two birds at 1,220 and 1,555 m in November 1962 and March 1963 respectively, on Cerro Santa Bárbara, and the observation at 1,500 m near Medina, Honduras (see Distribution). Almost all records come from the Caribbean slope where the bird appears to be an obligate "deep forest" (forest interior) dweller, but may possibly be a tree-fall gap specialist (B. W. Miller *in litt.* 1990, 1991). In Belize, it seems to be limited to one forest type (details unknown) (B. W. Miller *in litt.* 1990), but elsewhere the habitat has variously been described as lowland tropical rainforest, low montane rainforest (the Cerro Santa Bárbara birds were taken in the transition zone between rain- and cloud-forest) (Monroe 1968), and (in Costa Rica) the wetter portions of the subtropical zone (Slud 1964). Many descriptions suggest that the bird prefers the dense (or "heavy") wet/humid forests, especially near streams, rivers and gullies, and where there is a dense shrub layer (Taylor 1860, Huber 1932, Slud 1964, Stiles and Skutch 1989). Singles and pairs of birds have been recorded and are generally seen perching on low branches or undergrowth ("brushwood") close to the ground (Taylor 1860, Huber 1932, Stiles and Skutch 1989), although Peters (1929) recorded one perched high in a tree.

Foraging apparently occurs mostly at low to medium heights (Stiles and Skutch 1989), prey items including cicadas (specimen in MNHUK) and other insect species (B. W. Miller *in litt.* 1991). However, these observations at lower levels may be exceptional as birds observed by S. N. G. Howell (*in litt.* 1991) have usually stayed at mid- to upper levels (often in the canopy) where they have been seen making agile sallies for prey (see Remarks 6). The diet apparently consists of spiders, insects (orthopterans, cicadas etc.) and the occasional anolis lizard (B. W. Miller *in litt.* 1992).

Nesting activities have only been recorded in Belize, although a female (in MNHUK) taken on 17 April in Nicaragua had an incubation patch, and birds at Cerro San Gil, Guatemala, were seen courting and near a probable nest-burrow during February 1991 (Howell and Webb 1992). In Belize, early courtship was recorded during the beginning of March, with pair bonding, copulation, egg-laying and hatching occurring by and during May (B. W. Miller *in litt.* 1990). During this time the birds give a distinct territorial vocalization (see Remarks 6) at first light (generally introducing the dawn chorus along with tinamous, forest-falcons etc.), but continuing at irregular intervals throughout the day between February and June (B. W. Miller *in litt.* 1990, S. N. G. Howell *in litt.* 1991). Around Caracol, the birds prefer the banks and mounds left by the Maya Indians for their nesting sites, and it is in these that they excavate a tunnel c.45 cm long (with a terminal chamber on the left) in which both sexes undertake the incubation of the three eggs (B. W. Miller *in litt.* 1990).

The larger Blue-crowned Motmot is very abundant around Caracol (see Population) and some antagonistic exchanges have been observed, although the two species do not appear to be in direct competition for nesting space, and niche overlap in prey items appears to be minimal (B. W. Miller *in litt.* 1990). In Nicaragua and Costa Rica, the Keel-billed Motmot is sympatric with the relatively more abundant Broad-billed Motmot (Salvin and Godman 1888-1904, Slud 1964), and in Costa Rica, an individual Keel-billed Motmot apparently formed a pair-bond with a Broad-billed Motmot, but no young were produced (Stiles and Skutch 1989).

THREATS This species occurs generally at very low densities and therefore requires large expanses of undisturbed lowland tropical forest in order to sustain a viable population. Wet lowland tropical forest is one of the most threatened habitats in Central America: in Mexico, all suitable habitat is being cleared at an alarming rate, with effectively no forest remaining in sight of the trans-isthmus highway (route 185) on the Veracruz–Oaxaca border (S. N. G. Howell *in litt.* 1987, 1991), although the Chimalapas region of Oaxaca still holds extensive undisturbed lowland forest (A. G. Navarro and A. T. Peterson *in litt.* 1991); while in Costa Rica less than 30% of wet lowland forest remains (a forest type that once covered 30% of the country: Stiles and Skutch 1989), and the area in which the species has most recently been seen is rapidly being cleared

(F. G. Stiles *in litt.* 1991). The same situation obtains to a greater or lesser extent throughout the known range of the Keel-billed Motmot.

The fact that so little is known of this species's requirements means that specific threats are almost impossible to assess, but at Caracol, Belize, one pair of birds was displaced at the start of the breeding season by archaeological work, when their chosen nesting banks were removed with rubble during excavation of the Maya ruins (B. W. Miller *in litt.* 1990), this probably being the explanation for the disappearance of the species from Tikal National Park, Guatemala, where clearance of the Maya ruins was taking place when the bird was seen in 1958 (E. P. Edwards *in litt.* 1991). Only one pair out of 7-8 birds under observation at Caracol laid eggs (human disturbance at the archaeological site possibly causing this poor reproductive effort) but even these eventually failed when the young were killed in the nest burrow, apparently by fire-ants which recently spread into the clearing made by the archaeologists (B. W. Miller *in litt.* 1990). The current threats at Caracol are clearly localized but, as they affect the largest population of this species currently known, they are obviously of some concern. Caracol and the Mountain Pine Ridge locality are both within the same large forest block encompassed by the Chiquibul and Mountain Pine Ridge Forest Reserves, and are therefore set aside for timber (B. W. Miller *in litt.* 1991: see below).

MEASURES TAKEN A number of reserves and parks "protect" areas where the Keel-billed Motmot has previously been recorded, although there are very few where the species has recently been found, or for which information on remaining suitable habitat exists.

Mexico No protected area covers any of the few localities where this species has been found.

Belize The Caracol area is protected as an Archaeological Reserve (and therefore automatically a Wildlife Reserve: D. Weyer *in litt.* 1989), and some areas around it are protected at least to a degree: Mountain Pine Ridge Forest Reserve (c.500 km^2) is too high and within the wrong forest type (details unknown) for this species; Chiquibul Forest Reserve (c.1,850 km^2) is being actively logged but probably harbours the bird; and the Cockscombe Basin Jaguar Reserve (460 km^2) has been extensively logged and is now threatened by "slash-and-burn" agriculture, but may also support this species (*BBC Wildlife* 4 [1984]: 174-178). Almost all the areas whence come records of this species (except for Slate Creek: see below) have recently (December 1991) been designated as the Chiquibul National Park (c.108,055 ha), at the edge of which lies the Caracol site (B. W. Miller *in litt.* 1992): obviously the previous designations will now have changed, but the boundary of the new park is not known, and the degree of overlap is difficult to assess. Slate Creek is currently being established as a private reserve of c.1,400 ha (B. W. Miller *in litt.* 1992). A detailed ecological study of this bird is currently in progress at Caracol and is being followed up with research and analyses in other areas (B. W. Miller *in litt.* 1990).

Guatemala Tikal National Park once harboured the species, although its continued presence there seems to be unlikely owing to clearance around the Maya ruins (see Threats). Cerro San Gil, although an area of special protection, has been proposed (by FUNDAECO) as an ecological reserve, with boundary delimitation (for an area of c.47,400 ha) in progress during 1991 (S. N. G. Howell *in litt.* 1991, D. S. Weber *in litt.* 1992).

Honduras The Jardín Botánico Lancetilla seemingly protects the Tela river basin and contains much untouched forest (in the forest reserve), and although large numbers of people visit the gardens, few venture in the forest where the motmots occur (Cruz 1986, S. N. G. Howell *in litt.* 1991). A well used trail runs through the forest reserve (and possibly the territories of some motmots) to the village of San Francisco, but disturbance away from the path appears to be minimal (S. N. G. Howell *in litt.* 1991). Cusuco National Park protects some of the higher areas of the San Pedro Montaña region, but these may be too high for the Keel-billed Motmot, while the status of the forests (and their protection) lower down is unknown (see Cruz 1986). Similar uncertainty exists in the Santa Bárbara National Park, where although the bird has been collected at 1,220 and 1,555 m (see Distribution) these altitudes are seemingly exceptional, and in any case most of the well preserved areas of the park are above 1,800 m (Cruz 1986). Whether or not the species occurs in this protected area is unknown, and it is also unknown if it occurs in the adjacent "Reserva de Usos Múltiples Lago Yojoa" (although there appears to be limited amount of suitable habitat there: Cruz 1986). WCI's Paso Pantera project aims to link protected areas in Central America (with corridors of habitat), and this may have advantageous effects for populations of the species between Lancetilla and La Muralla Wildlife Refuge (B. W. Miller *in litt.* 1992).

Nicaragua The conservation status of this species in Nicaragua is difficult to determine owing to the imprecise nature of most distribution data. However, it appears that none of the more likely areas are currently protected.

Costa Rica The species has been recorded from Rincón de la Vieja National Park (see Distribution) although there is much habitat clearance around this park (see Threats), while Monteverde National Park apparently includes at least part of the Peñas Blancas valley (see Stiles and Skutch 1989), but whether or not the bird is to be found in the park requires further investigation. Most of Costa Rica's extensive protected areas network covers primarily montane habitats, and therefore many of the known localities for the species fall outside existing areas.

MEASURES PROPOSED The project currently in progress at Caracol is collecting data on tree species diversity, composition and forest type profiles in order to discover the precise niche and area requirements of this bird, with the long-term aim of finding (possibly by using satellite imagery) similar habitats or forest types in the rest of the species's range (B. W. Miller *in litt.* 1990). The census data already collected are to be analysed to give an indication of population viability and eventually to calculate the risk of extinction, taking into account the patchiness of distribution and fragmentation of suitable habitat (B. W. Miller *in litt.* 1990). All of these analyses will be valuable for the effective conservation of the Keel-billed Motmot, especially the identification of suitable remaining forest areas in which surveys should be concentrated in order to assess whether the species is there and, if so, the potential viability of the population: with the species producing a far-carrying call between February and June, surveys (once the call has been learnt) would be relatively easy (S. N. G. Howell *in litt.* 1991). The Caracol area has been proposed as a World Heritage Site on the grounds of its biological and archaeological importance, as has the merging of Chiquibul National Park, Upper Bladen and Cockscombe Basin Reserves into the Maya Mountain Biosphere Reserve (560,000 ha) which would link all the southern half of the country's forests (B. W. Miller *in litt.* 1991, 1992).

Priority areas where (or near where) the species has already been recorded but where further investigation is necessary are all of the reserves mentioned above, more specifically those forests around Caracol as yet unsurveyed (including areas in the Maya Mountains in adjacent Guatemala); the areas whence come recent reports in Guatemala and Honduras; the Honduras–Nicaragua border areas, as well as the still extensive Atlantic forest areas of Nicaragua (which are largely unknown but possibly harbour significant populations; and the region around Lake Arenal, Monteverde and Rincón de la Vieja.

REMARKS (1) A female (in BMNH) was taken "near San Felipe, Riomakal" (untraced, and no country given) in May 1888, a new label on the specimen claiming this to be "San Felipe, Campeche". There are two San Felipes in Campeche, one in the far west on the Tabasco border, and one in the south, bordering on Guatemala. However, "San Felipe, Riomakal" most probably refers to a locality along the río Macal in west-central Belize (see below) and indeed, a specimen was taken by the same collector (Blancaneaux) in January of the same year near Belize City. (2) The specimens taken at Tolosa and Ubero were collected on the same expedition (by A. E. Colburn and P. W. Shufeldt) on 21 and 27 December 1901 respectively, suggesting that the two localities are indeed in close proximity and therefore almost certainly in Oaxaca. (3) The specimen in UMMZ has recently been identified as a male; the original label has been lost but a new one, probably written by J. van Tyne, claims that "this bird was almost certainly collected at Laguna Perdida" in Petén, Guatemala (B. W. Miller *in litt.* 1990). The bird was collected by P. W. Shufeldt, and was therefore presumably taken at around the turn of the century (see Remarks 2). (4) Monroe (1968) could not find the specimen reported from La Ceiba in Bangs (1903) when he searched the MCZ collection and catalogue, but this specimen (a male) was present there in 1987 and, as reported, was collected at La Ceiba, Honduras, on 21 January 1902. (5) Stiles and Skutch (1989) suggested that this species can be found in the Cordilleras de Guanacaste and Talamanca, although this latter is a misprint for Cordillera de Tilarán (F. G. Stiles *in litt.* 1991). It is also suggested that records from further south require confirmation because of possible confusion with young Broad-billed Motmots (Stiles and Skutch 1989). (6) This bird is not easily seen, and may be readily overlooked until the observer is familiar with its voice (Peters 1929). B. W. Miller (*in litt.* 1990) claimed that there are at least five distinct calls, many of which are at very low frequency, the territorial ones being given mostly before sunrise, but also irregularly throughout the day (S. N. G. Howell *in litt.* 1991). The territorial call is very similar to that of the Broad-billed Motmot, and it is possible that this has led to the species being overlooked where these two species are sympatric (S. N. G. Howell *in litt.* 1991). The difficulty of observation (birds most often staying at mid- to upper levels in the forest), and the relatively recent discovery of a full complement of vocalizations, may help to explain the paucity of distributional records.

COPPERY-CHESTED JACAMAR *Galbula pastazae* K[12]

This little known jacamar appears to be patchily distributed along the east slope of the Andes throughout Ecuador (one site in Colombia) in humid subtropical forest, a biome seriously at risk of clearance by farmers.

DISTRIBUTION The Coppery-chested Jacamar is recorded from a single site in southernmost Colombia and through the eastern Andes slopes of Ecuador. A record from lowland Amazonian Brazil (see Remarks) is not accepted here, but the species may well eventually be found in northern Peru (TAP). Unless otherwise stated, coordinates below are from Paynter and Traylor (1977, 1981).

Colombia The only records are four specimens taken at El Carmen, 0°40'N 77°10'W (labels in FMNH say "pipeline"), Nariño department (on the border with Putumayo), at 1,525 m, 2-9 December 1970 (not 1971 as in Hilty and Brown 1986) (Fitzpatrick and Willard 1982).

Ecuador Records, roughly north to south but by province, are from: (*Napo*) km 109 on the Lago Agrio–Baeza road, 1,000 m, July 1976 (two specimens in DMNH); (*Tungurahua*) Ambato, 1°15'S 78°37'W, 1896 (specimen in AMNH); Machay, 1°24'S 78°16'W, on west bank of río Pastaza, and nearby at Hacienda Mapoto, mid-1880s (Taczanowski and von Berlepsch 1885); (*Morona-Santiago*) Macas, 2°19'S 78°07'W, 1,050 m, December 1939 (specimen in AMNH, with two undated others labelled "Macas region" and a fourth, also undated, labelled "Macas-Pitaloma, río Upano" at 1,000-1,200 m; also Chapman 1926); "Yapitya" on the Logroño–Yaupi trail, west slope of the Cordillera de Cutucú, 1,525 m, June 1984 (Robbins *et al.* 1987; specimen in ANSP); (*Zamora-Chinchipe*) Cumbaratza, 3°56'S 78°51'W, 950 m, August 1965 (two specimens in MCZ); Zamora, 610 m, October 1913 (specimens in AMNH, ANSP, MCZ); (*Loja*) the Loja–Sabanilla area by the Loja–Zamora road, 1,500-1,700 m, recently (Bloch *et al.* 1991); the río Bombuscara area, 4°08'S 78°58'W inside Podocarpus National Park and south-west of Zamora, 1,000 m, since the late 1980s (Bloch *et al.* 1991, whence coordinates).

POPULATION There are no details of numbers, but on the evidence under Distribution this species would appear to be rather thinly and patchily distributed, with a low overall population. However, at the one site at which it has been recorded inside Podocarpus National Park it is considered "fairly common", with "quite extensive patches of suitable habitat in the area" (Bloch *et al.* 1991).

ECOLOGY The elevation of records once suggested that this was a bird of the subtropical zone, the only one its family to be found beyond the tropical zone (Chapman 1926), and it certainly appears to have the highest range of any jacamar, with records from 610 to 1,700 m (see Distribution), although Hilty and Brown (1986) mentioned an upper range of 2,100 m and Paynter and Traylor (1977) described Ambato as in a warm valley of interandean tableland in the arid temperate zone at 2,600 m. The usual elevetion seems to be rather narrow, at c.1,000-1,300 m (B. M. Whitney *in litt.* 1992). Elsewhere, habitat has been given as upper cloud-forest (Fitzpatrick and Willard 1982) and humid lower montane forest (Hilty and Brown 1986). If there is indeed some patchiness in the species's distribution, it may be due to some specific habitat requirement, as yet unclear; however, it seems to prefer forest edge and second growth near forest, perching 1.5-4 m up, and darting out after flying prey like other members of the genus (B. M. Whitney *in litt.* 1992). The June specimen from Cordillera de Cutucú (in ANSP) was perched 3 m up at the edge of a clearing in humid forest; its stomach held beetles and wasps, and its testes measured 5×2 mm. The July specimens from Napo province (in DMNH) had gonads 1 mm (female) and 4 mm (male). A nest with young was found at the Río Bombuscara Center, Podocarpus National

Park, in December 1991, being a typical jacamar hole c.1.5 m up in a 2.5 m high earth bank created by the cutting of a trail through forest (C. Rahbek *in litt.* 1992).

THREATS The lower slopes of the eastern Andes, from 1,000 to about 2,500 m, are particularly seriously affected by peasant farmers in ever-increasing numbers, and by coffee and tea growers, and the forest of the region is disappearing at an alarming rate (TAP, B. M. Whitney *in litt.* 1992).

MEASURES TAKEN Podocarpus National Park evidently protects a (possibly quite large) population of this species.

MEASURES PROPOSED The Coppery-chested Jacamar is one of several dozen bird species endemic to the lower montane (subtropical) zone in the Andes, and urgent measures are needed to establish major reserves within this zone in Colombia, Ecuador, Peru and Bolivia (TAP); any such reserve in Ecuador must seek to embrace a good population of this evidently uncommon species, and Podocarpus National Park merits further investigation to determine the number of individuals it harbours. Other species with similar ranges that need to be catered for in a reserve network include the threatened White-necked Parakeet *Pyrrhura albipectus* and Bicoloured Antvireo *Dysithamnus occidentalis* (see relevant accounts), plus Cinnamon Screech-owl *Otus petersoni*, Napo Sabrewing *Campylopterus villaviscensio*, Pink-throated Brilliant *Heliodoxa gularis*, Ecuadorian Piedtail *Phlogophilus hemileucurus*, Rufous-vented Whitetip *Urosticte ruficrissa*, Speckle-chested Piculet *Picumnus steindachneri*, Equatorial Greytail *Xenerpestes singularis*, Ecuadorian Tyrannulet *Phylloscartes gualaquizae* and Red-billed Tyrannulet *Zimmerius cinereicapillus* (ICBP 1992, Crosby *et al.* in prep.).

REMARKS The species has been listed from Arimã, rio Purus, Brazil (Peters 1948, Meyer de Schauensee 1966, 1982, Sibley and Monroe 1990), evidently based on a specimen (in CM) identified as *Galbula pastazae* and dated September 1922.

THREE-TOED JACAMAR *Jacamaralcyon tridactyla* E[2]

Although capable of surviving in badly degraded small woodlots, this distinctive aerial feeder and bank nester has undergone a major decline in overall abundance and a contraction of range in south-east Brazil, where it survives now chiefly in the rio Paraíba valley in Rio de Janeiro state. Much urgent work is needed to clarify its status and needs, and to establish suitable sanctuaries.

DISTRIBUTION The Three-toed Jacamar (see Remarks 1) is endemic to south-eastern Brazil in Espírito Santo (no records since 1940), eastern Minas Gerais, Rio de Janeiro (these two states holding the bulk of modern records), São Paulo (no records since 1945) and northern Paraná (no documented record since 1961). The evidence is that this is a species of the western slopes of the coastal serras and drier interior plateaus. A wholly untraced locality is Estrado de S. Domingos, Conceição, August 1933 (specimen in USNM; see Remarks 2). Specimens from "the vicinity of Bahia" (in BMNH) and "Bahia" (in MNHN) are too vague to trust, but may indicate a (former) extension of range north of Espírito Santo.

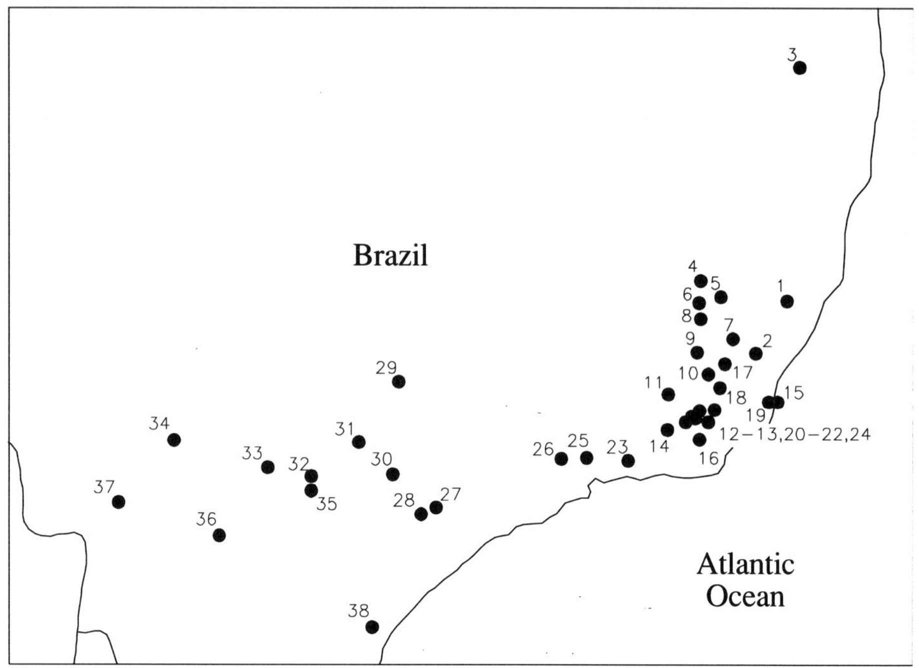

Espírito Santo Three males and two females were collected on the rio de Santa Joana, near Itarana[1], 400 m, 27 August 1940, and one male is from Estação de [Engenheiro] Reeve[2] (= Rive), December 1924 (specimens in MNRJ).

Minas Gerais In the last century birds were found throughout the eastern part of the Serra do Espinhaço (Reinhardt 1870). Specific records (north to south) are: two males collected on the Serra da Mombuca[3], Divisópolis, 930-1,000 m, November 1973 (in CGTM; also G. T. de Mattos *in litt.* 1987); one male and three females from the rio Doce[4] on the lower rio Piracicaba, left bank (i.e. near to the present Rio Doce State Park), August and September 1940 (in MZUSP); Caratinga Reserve[5] (Fazenda Montes Claros), 1977, March, April and July 1983, April and July 1984 (A. Brandt *in litt.* 1987), October 1986 (M. A. Brazil and D. R. Waugh *in litt.* 1986); rio Matipó[6], July and October 1919 (specimens in MZUSP; also Pinto 1938), 1979 (A. Brandt *in litt.* 1987);

one pair from Santa Bárbara do Caparaó[7] (now Caparaó: see Naumburg 1935), 900 m, August 1929 (specimens in AMNH); São Pedro dos Ferros[8], Presidente Bernardes; Serra do Brigadeiro, all in 1979 near Araponga[9] (A. Brandt *in litt.* 1987); two males and one female from Muriaé[10], November and December 1926 (specimens in MNRJ); Rio Novo[11], June 1898 (specimens in MNRJ; also Ribeiro 1927); three males and one female from Volta Grande[12], October 1943 (specimens in MNRJ), with birds observed in January 1980 (J. F. Pacheco *in litt.* 1986); Além Paraíba[13], January 1980 (J. F. Pacheco *in litt.* 1986); Santa Fé[14], 22°06'S 43°09'W (specimen in BMNH; also Sclater 1891). A record from Lagoa Santa in the centre of the state (Burmeister 1856) seems too anomalous to regard as certain (see Reinhardt 1870).

Rio de Janeiro Goeldi (1894) observed the species in the hot lowlands of both margins of the rio Paraíba do Sul valley[15], but not in the forests of the Serra dos Órgãos; there are, however, nineteenth-century records from Nova Friburgo[16] (specimens in BMNH; also Burmeister 1856, Sclater 1891), nearby at Rosário, c.22°16'S 42°32'W (Krabbe undated) and Cantagalo (Cabanis 1874, von Ihering 1900a). Most of the other records, including the modern ones, are from the Paraíba valley at: Bate-pau[17], Porciúncula, December 1988 and February 1990; Miracema[18]; Paraoquena; Campelo[19], all in July 1988; Nossa Senhora do Livramento[20], Carmo, October 1989 (all the foregoing from J. F. Pacheco *in litt.* 1991); Cantagalo[21] (Cabanis 1874); Imitagem[22], Sapucaia, up to six pairs continuously present from March 1988 to 1991 (J. F. Pacheco *in litt.* 1991), although only one was there in May 1992 (M. Pearman *in litt.* 1992); Piraí[23], November 1818 (von Pelzeln 1868-1871). One untraced locality in the state is "Areas", a stream on the way to Minas Gerais (Burmeister 1856), this being between Cantagalo and Itaocara[24] (J. F. Pacheco *in litt.* 1991; see also Paynter and Traylor 1991).

São Paulo Localities (east to west) are: Monjolinha[25] (near Areias), November 1818; Piquete[26], February 1901; Campinas, 1820s or 1830s (Krabbe undated); Ipanema[27], February and July to August 1820; Cemitério[28] (now Alambari), July 1820; Jaboticabal[29], September 1900; Victoria[30] (now Botucatu: see Pinto 1945), 570 m, March to May 1901, March and June 1902; rio Feio[31] (near Bauru: see Pinto 1945), August and September 1905; Fazenda Cayoá[32], Salto Grande, rio Paranapanema (see Pinto 1945), June and July 1903; rio Paranapanema opposite the rio Tibaji confluence[33], May 1945; and Porto Cabral[34], rio Paraná (in the extreme west of the state: Pinto 1945), October 1941 (specimens in AMNH, FMNH, MCZ, MZUSP, ROM, USNM; also von Pelzeln 1868-1871, von Ihering and von Ihering 1907, Pinto 1938). The species has not been found in the state since at least 1975 (E. O. Willis *in litt.* 1986).

Paraná Specimens are from Jacarezinho[35], 1901 (von Ihering and von Ihering 1907, Pinto 1938); Salto do Cobre, rio Ivaí (near Ubaúna)[36], December 1922 (Sztolcman 1926); Porto Camargo[37], January and February 1954 (Pinto and de Camargo 1955); and Ivaté (untraced), January 1961 (in MHNCI). The only recent record, one bird seen at the Guaricana Reserve near Morretes[38] on the eastern slopes of the Serra do Mar, May 1981 (P. Scherer Neto *in litt.* 1986), fails to conform with current evidence on habitat type (see Ecology) and should perhaps be regarded as provisional.

POPULATION The testimony of Danish explorers in the early and mid-nineteenth century is that the Three-toed Jacamar was "very common" in the province of Rio de Janeiro and in the eastern part of the Serra do Espinhaço in Minas Gerais (Reinhardt 1870), a hitherto almost entirely neglected assessment which gives an ominous perspective to the present-day plight of the species. Although it is apparently easily found in at least small numbers where it occurs, to judge from the number of specimens obtained from several localities (see Remarks 3) and from recent observations in what now seems to be the core of its present distribution, it is clearly extremely local and must have suffered a very substantial decline as a result of habitat loss. While it is likely that some populations remain undetected in São Paulo and Paraná (badly degraded woodlots – see Ecology – being understandably unenticing to ornithologists), it is not safe to assume that the species has been greatly overlooked, given its generally conspicuous habits (see Ecology): lack of recent records in most of the places where it has been recorded in the past may reflect its genuine absence.

ECOLOGY The Three-toed Jacamar has been found in remaining patches of secondary growth in northern Minas Gerais and in Rio de Janeiro (J. F. Pacheco *in litt.* 1986, G. T. de Mattos *in litt.* 1987). Sick (1985) referred to the species as inhabiting riversides with shrubs on the mountains in Espírito Santo. In the Caratinga Reserve birds were seen perched in subcanopy of forest in one of the main valleys (M. A. Brazil and D. R. Waugh *in litt.* 1986). Woodlots in the Paraíba do Sul valley are usually dry forest fragments surrounded by pastureland or ricefields, but at least one has a stream running through it; however, for reasons unclear, very few woodlots surveyed have been found to contain the species (J. F. Pacheco verbally 1991). Birds often sit in exposed situations, such as on tall grass stems, wires and leafless twigs, from where they sally for flying prey, and call loudly (Sclater 1882, Sztolcman 1926, Sick 1985, J. F. Pacheco *in litt.* 1986).

Food items include butterflies and other flying insects (J. F. Pacheco verbally 1991). Two specimens from the 1820s had eaten beetles, cicadas and wasps (Krabbe undated); one from December had eaten Hymenopterans (Sztolcman 1926); one in USNM from September contained "vesperas" (probably *vespas*, wasps); one in MNRJ from November simply "insects"; and one in CGTM from November had eaten one wasp and other insects.

The Three-toed Jacamar nests in holes excavated by the birds themselves in riverside or roadside banks (Euler 1900, von Ihering 1900b, Sick 1985); a statement that several entrances to the nest are made to mislead enemies (Goeldi 1894) refers to the members of the family in general, although it has been repeated by Euler (1900) and Sick (1985) as if referring particularly to this species. One pair observed spent more than two months excavating the nest (Euler 1900). Holes are apparently used also for overnight roosting (J. F. Pacheco verbally 1991), and may serve also as roosting sites for swallows (von Ihering 1900b; also Sick 1985). Breeding occurs around October and November, from the available evidence, yet of seven specimens (in AMNH and MNRJ) collected in late August whose gonads were examined, only one male had them slightly enlarged, the other being dormant; however, an early October specimen in MZUSP was labelled as an active male, two specimens in CGTM from early November had enlarged testes, and specimens from June and July had small gonads while ones from August and November had large (Krabbe undated). A nest found in November was in a deep horizontal gallery and contained two white eggs; disturbance of the nest prevented further incubation and the eggs were predated (G. T. de Mattos *in litt.* 1987). Nesting tends to occur gregariously, in small colonies (von Ihering 1900b: 150, B. M. Whitney *in litt.* 1991; see Remarks 1).

THREATS Although the Three-toed Jacamar has been found in very degraded woodlots, it is absent from many such sites and is in general now so rare that some form of habitat loss or disturbance must be assumed: perhaps the most likely explanation is that while like all jacamars it selects forest edge habitat or even habitat that mimics this, such as degraded woodland, it can only survive in the long term at sites which also possess banks in which to breed, and this combination is presumably now extremely uncommon, and becoming ever more so. At this stage collectors could add to the possibility of local extinctions (see Remarks 3).

MEASURES TAKEN The Three-toed Jacamar is protected under Brazilian law (Bernardes *et al.* 1990), but the Caratinga Reserve seems to be the only protected area where the species is known to occur.

MEASURES PROPOSED Surveys in the field are needed as a matter of great urgency to delimit current range and assess conservation status more accurately, and fieldwork on the ecology and breeding success of the populations in the Paraíba valley and the Caratinga Reserve would yield valuable data on the options for managing the species, particularly given the speculation over the causes of its decline (see Threats). Collection of further specimens should not be countenanced.

REMARKS (1) The species is the only one in its genus, and indeed the only jacamar with three toes; however, *Jacamaralcyon* and *Brachygalba* are quite similar in occurring in groups, in their pattern of vocalizations (members of pairs sing together, triggering adjacent pairs to do likewise), in their small size and plumage tones, and in their choice of relatively open arid habitats (B. M. Whitney *in litt.* 1991). (2) This conceivably refers to the road to São Domingos (19°09'S 40°37'W in Paynter and Traylor 1991) leading from Conceição da Barra municipality in northern Espírito Santo. (3) Occurrence of small groups of individuals (or pairs) has been recorded (Sztolcman 1926; J. F. Pacheco *in litt.* 1991) and seems also evident from the museum series. Sztolcman (1926) reported that he obtained three specimens from a "small" group perched on branches of a small tree; according to him, part of the group left the tree after a gunshot, but returned soon after, and in that manner one could kill many birds from a single flock. Nevertheless, a skin (that from Conceição in 1933; see Distribution) indicates that the species's abundance ("freqüencia") at the site was low ("pouca").

WHITE-MANTLED BARBET *Capito hypoleucus* V/R[10]

This polytypic lower montane forest species is endemic to the northern Central Andes and western slope of the East Andes in Colombia; widespread deforestation in the lower Cauca and middle Magdalena drainages mean that since the early 1950s all records come from southernmost Antioquia and northern Caldas.

DISTRIBUTION The White-mantled Barbet is a polytypic species (comprising three subspecies) of the lower Cauca and middle Magdalena drainages, where it occurs on both slopes of the northern Central Andes (including Serranía de San Lucas), and the western slope of the East Andes, Colombia. In the following account, coordinates, unless otherwise stated, are from Paynter and Traylor (1981).

Records of the nominate subspecies are from the following localities: (*Bolívar*) Volador (c.7°58'N 74°15'W; on the eastern slope of Serranía de San Lucas), where two males and three females (in USNM) were collected at 790 m during May 1947 (Graves 1986); (*Antioquia*) Puerto Valdivia (7°18'N 75°23'W; at 180 m on the eastern side of the lower Cauca valley), presumably above which a female (in AMNH) was collected in December 1914 (see Ecology); Valdivia (7°11'N 75°27'W; on the western slope of the north-western Central Andes), where three birds (in BMNH, ROM) were taken at 1,160 m in March 1897, with three males and a female taken at 1,205 m during May 1948 (Salvin 1897, Graves 1986; specimens in USNM); and La Frijolera (c.7°10'N 75°25'W; on the western slope of the Central Andes), where two males and two females (in AMNH, ANSP, MCZ) were taken at 1,525 m in December 1914.

The subspecies *carrikeri* has been recorded as follows: (*Antioquia*) Botero (6°32'N 75°15'W; in the northern Central Andes on the río Porce), where nine birds were taken at 1,095 m during August and September 1950 (Graves 1986); and (either this race or *extinctus*) río Bizcocho (6°18'N 75°02'W; at 1,000 m in San Rafael municipality: Acevedo-Latorre 1971), where specimens were taken at an unstated time (Serna 1980); Jaguas Dam, San Rafael, where three birds were seen at 1,600 m in May 1989 (L. G. Olarte *in litt.* 1992); Punchina Dam, San Carlos (c.6°11'N 74°58'W), where a total of eight birds were recorded at 1,200 m up until April 1991 (P. Velásquez *per* L. G. Olarte *in litt.* 1992); and Cocorna, where a bird was recorded at 1,400 m in February 1992 (P. Velásquez *per* L. G. Olarte *in litt.* 1992).

The subspecies *extinctus* is known from the following localities: (*Antioquia*) Río Claro Natural Reserve, where there have been several recent sightings presumably attributable to this race (F. G. Stiles *in litt.* 1991); (*Caldas*) Hacienda Sofía (= La Sofía, 5°38'N 75°04'W; on the eastern side of the middle Central Andes), where two males and two females were taken at 1,130-1,145 m during May and June 1951 (Graves 1986; specimens in USNM); 3 km west of La Victoria (c.5°19'N 74°55'W; 21 km north-west of Honda), where birds (presumably this subspecies) were seen at 925 m in May 1990 (P. Kaestner *in litt.* 1992); Tasajos (apparently near the previous locality), where presumably this subspecies was seen in May 1990 (F. G. Stiles verbally 1991, P. Kaestner *in litt.* 1992); (*Cundinamarca*) Carmen de Yacopí (= Yacopí, c.5°30'N 74°20'W; at 1,415 m on the western slope of the middle East Andes), where a bird (in AMNH) was taken in August 1914; and (*Tolima*) within 30 km west of Honda (5°12'N 74°45'W; presumably very close to the previous two localities), where two males and a female were collected at 1,525 m during February and March 1907 (Graves 1986; specimens in AMNH).

POPULATION Chapman (1917a) considered this species to be one of the most distinctive forms of the Cauca and Magdalena valleys, and the evidence from the specimens collected during and prior to 1914 suggests that it may have been at least locally common (see above): numbers of specimens collected during the late 1940s and early 1950s also suggest this to have been the case (see above; also Hilty and Brown 1986). Despite this apparent previous abundance, the White-mantled Barbet has been poorly recorded during recent decades: S. L. Hilty (*in litt.* 1986) mentioned that the bird is now rare and local; and Graves (1986) suggested that any remaining populations would be insular and isolated, and named the race *extinctus* in the belief that it had already disappeared. Recent observations by the río Claro, Antioquia, and in two separate patches of remnant forest near La Victoria, Caldas, indicate *extinctus* still exists, and that the subspecies may well be reasonably common (locally), albeit in an increasingly small area of remaining habitat (F. G. Stiles *in litt.* 1991, P. Kaestner *in litt.* 1992). Recent records from further north in Antioquia (between San Rafael and Cocorna (see Distribution) also suggest that the species is still locally not uncommon.

ECOLOGY The White-mantled Barbet has been recorded almost exclusively between 790 and 1,600 m (see Distribution), although the specimen (in AMNH) taken at Puerto Valdivia was labelled as coming from 110 m; Puerto Valdivia is at 180 m (Paynter and Traylor 1981), and this bird was presumably taken on the steep slopes rising behind the town. This barbet inhabits lower montane (foothill) humid forest, and has more recently been recorded in areas with a patchwork of forest, coffee plantations, and pasture, and in "badly cut over forest" (Graves 1986, L. G. Olarte *in litt.* 1992). The recent observations in Caldas have come from a patch of forest c.20 ha in size on a steep slope (P. Kaestner *in litt.* 1992), and in both secondary and heavily disturbed forests (F. G. Stiles *in litt.* 1991). Birds have been recorded in mixed-species flocks, foraging in the forest canopy, but also visiting isolated trees (*Cupania* sp.) in pasture c.50 m from the forest edge (Graves 1986, P. Kaestner *in litt.* 1992, F. G. Stiles *in litt.* 1992). The secondary forest patches where this barbet was recorded between San Rafael and Cocorna were all dominated by *Cecropia* trees in which the species was observed feeding (L. G. Olarte *in litt.* 1992). Graves (1986) noted that one bird was collected amidst large clumps of mistletoe in a tall tree, although information on specimen labels (in AMNH) suggests that the main food sources are insects and seeds. Birds in breeding condition have been collected from the end of May until early September, with an immature taken at the end of August (Graves 1986; specimens as in Distribution).

THREATS The middle and lower Magdalena and Cauca valleys have been heavily deforested since the nineteenth century, and the clearance of the floodplain and foothills of the middle Magdalena valley has almost been completed during the last 30 years (Graves 1986). That the subspecies *extinctus* still exists is perhaps due to the fact that a small area of remnant forest (albeit in patches) has survived on a very steep escarpment near to La Victoria (P. Kaestner *in litt.* 1992), although at río Claro, Antioquia, birds seem to be able to survive in secondary forest (F. G. Stiles *in litt.* 1991). It is possible that the White-mantled Barbet has undergone a historic range loss of greater than 50% due to habitat destruction, and the fragmented state of the remnant lower montane humid forest suggests that remaining populations are insular and genetically isolated (Graves 1986).

MEASURES TAKEN Forested watersheds in some municipalities may provide some protection for local populations, as shown by observations at La Victoria (F. G. Stiles verbally 1991). The forest surrounding the Jaguas and Punchina dams are supposed to be protected by the local electricity company (ISA) (L. G. Olarte *in litt.* 1992), and the bird has also been found in the small (80-100 ha) Río Claro Natural Reserve (see equivalent section under Antioquia Bristle-tyrant *Phylloscartes lanyoni*), although the status of this reserve is unknown, and is in an area undergoing heavy logging activity (L. G. Olarte *in litt.* 1992).

MEASURES PROPOSED It is essential that remnant lower montane forest areas in the northern Central Andes (including the Serranía de San Lucas) are afforded some form of protection (see equivalent section under Chestnut-bellied Hummingbird *Amazilia castaneiventris*). An assessment of status and distribution of these remnant forest patches (and of the species) must be a priority, but the ecological needs of the White-mantled Barbet remain poorly known and require urgent attention, particularly with reference to how well the species survives and reproduces in suboptimal habitats. A sizeable forested area (c.1,000 ha) near Florencia (between río Claro and La Victoria: F. G. Stiles *in litt.* 1992) should be searched for the presence of this and other threatened species (see below), and protected in some way. Any conservation initiatives in the range of this bird should consider the requirements of the other sympatric threatened species (see equivalent section under Chestnut-bellied Hummingbird and Antioquia Bristle-tyrant).

YELLOW-BROWED TOUCANET *Aulacorhynchus huallagae* K[12]

This cloud-forest toucan is confined to a very small area on the eastern slope of the Andes in north-central Peru. It does not appear to be immediately threatened, but its small range renders it vulnerable to habitat destruction.

DISTRIBUTION The Yellow-browed Toucanet (see Remarks 1) is only known from six specimens taken at three localities on the eastern slope of the Andes, in San Martín and south-eastern La Libertad departments, north-central Peru.

The localities (coordinates from Stephens and Traylor 1983) involved are: (*San Martín*) La Playa, near río "El Susto", c.28 km north-east of Pataz in Río Abiseo National Park, where a bird was taken at 2,510 m in August 1989 (E. G. Ortiz *in litt.* 1990); (*La Libertad*) 90 km further south, near the río Mishollo (a tributary on the west bank of the río Huallaga) at "Utcubamba" (8°13'S 77°08'W), where the type-specimen (in ANSP) was taken in May 1932 (although it is labelled from 1,830 m, it was said to be one of a small band at about 2,135 m on the trail to Utcubamba, east of Tayabamba: Carriker 1933); and only a few kilometres away, at Cumpang (c.8°12'S 77°10'W), where four specimens (in LSUMZ) were taken at 2,350-2,450 m in October 1979.

The species probably occurs further north and south, but apparently does not range south to the Carpish mountains in Huánuco (Schulenberg and Parker ms).

POPULATION The species is too little known for its status to be defined clearly. Although Schulenberg and Parker (ms) reported almost daily sightings of pairs or small groups of 3-4 during October and November 1979, the species was given the status "uncommon" by Parker *et al.* (1982). In Río Abiseo National Park no definite observations were made during 31 days of fieldwork between 30 June and 1 August 1988, while in August 1989 only one bird was seen (and collected) there (Leo *et al.* 1988, E. G. Ortiz *in litt.* 1990).

ECOLOGY The Yellow-browed Toucanet inhabits the canopy of humid forest between 2,100-2,450 m (Carriker 1933, Parker *et al.* 1982, Schulenberg and Parker ms; see also Distribution). The forest at Cumpang is lush, epiphyte-laden and dominated by 12-15 m tall trees of the genus *Clusia* (Schulenberg and Parker ms). At La Playa the toucanet was seen in a very humid area on a steep slope with low trees (c.6 m high) and a dense undergrowth (E. G. Ortiz *in litt.* 1990). The species's narrow elevational distribution may be related to the (fairly common) occurrence of the larger Grey-breasted Mountain-toucan *Andigena hypoglauca* above 2,300 m, and perhaps also to the uncommon occurrence of the smaller Emerald Toucanet *Aulacorhynchus prasinus* below 2,100 m, but its restricted geographic range remains unexplained (Schulenberg and Parker ms).

The stomachs of three specimens (in LSUMZ) held fruit (including small green fruit and pulp), and white, 4 mm long seeds. Pairs were twice observed feeding on medium-sized, purple melastome fruits, and one bird was seen probing a cluster of *Clusia* flowers, possibly in search of fruits (Schulenberg and Parker ms). As in other toucans, arthropods and small vertebrates are probably also included in the diet (NK). A male from early October had a brood-patch, while three others at this time had undeveloped gonads (LSUMZ label data).

THREATS Most of the current rapid deforestation of the Huallaga valley is occurring below 2,100 m, the lower limit of this toucan's range (Schulenberg and Parker ms).

MEASURES TAKEN A sizeable population probably occurs in the extensive (274,500 ha) and undisturbed cloud-forest within the recently established Río Abiseo National Park (Schulenberg and Parker ms, IUCN 1992).

MEASURES PROPOSED Surveys are urgently required to determine the precise nature of this species's status and distribution. Such work should concentrate on assessing the population within the Río Abiseo National Park, currently the only protected area in this region. Obviously, fieldwork in the park, and indeed elsewhere, along with initiatives aimed at protecting further montane areas, should consider the requirements of the other sympatric threatened and endemic species (see Remarks 2).

REMARKS (1) The Yellow-browed Toucanet is closely related to the Crimson-rumped Toucanet *Aulacorhynchus haematopygus* of Colombia and Ecuador and to the Blue-banded Toucanet *A. coeruleicinctis* of central Peru and south-east Peru to Bolivia, and is intermediate between them in some respects (Bond 1954a, Schulenberg and Parker ms).

(2) Besides the Yellow-browed Toucanet, the Río Abiseo National Park, and presumably areas to the north and south, may hold other bird species (including some threatened) endemic to montane forest in the eastern Andes of northern Peru, such as: Long-whiskered Owlet *Xenoglaux loweryi*, Russet-mantled Softtail *Thripophaga berlepschi*, Cinnamon-breasted Tody-tyrant *Hemitriccus cinnamomeipectus*, Golden-backed Mountain-tanager *Buthraupis aureodorsalis* (see relevant accounts), plus Rufous-browed Hemispingus *Hemispingus rufosuperciliaris* (see Remarks under Masked Mountain-tanager *Buthraupis wetmorei*), Speckle-chested Piculet *Picumnus steindachneri*, Pale-billed Antpitta *Grallaria carrikeri*, Ochre-fronted Antpitta *Grallaricula ochraceifrons*, Large-footed Tapaculo *Scytalopus macropus*, Bay-vented Cotinga *Doliornis sclateri* and Pardusco *Nephelornis oneilli*; also a large number of more wide-ranging, but rare or local species, e.g. Semicollared Hawk *Accipiter collaris*, Solitary Eagle *Harpyhaliaetus solitarius*, Black-and-chestnut Eagle *Oroaetus isidori*, Banded Snipe *Gallinago imperialis*, Andean Potoo *Nyctibius maculosus* (see Schulenberg *et al.* 1984), White-faced Nunbird *Hapaloptila castanea*, Yellow-vented Woodpecker *Veniliornis dignus*, Chestnut-crested Cotinga *Ampelion rufaxilla*, Scaled Fruiteater *Ampelioides tschudii*, Rufous-winged Tyrannulet *Mecocerculus calopterus*, Green-throated Tanager *Tangara argyrofenges* and White-capped Tanager *Sericossypha albocristata* (Parker and Parker 1982, Schulenberg and Williams 1982, Parker *et al.* 1985, Isler and Isler 1987, Graves and Weske 1987, Schulenberg and Parker ms, NK).

CUBAN FLICKER *Colaptes fernandinae* I[7]

For reasons unclear, through probably related to habitat loss, this once common and widespread ground-feeding woodpecker, endemic to Cuba, has become very rare and localized, with only one relatively strong population (in the Zapata Swamp) and total numbers estimated at only 300 pairs.

DISTRIBUTION The Cuban Flicker is endemic to Cuba, where it was originally found throughout the island, but nowadays is greatly restricted in range, being reduced to a few isolated populations of which the largest is in the Zapata Swamp, Matanzas (see below). Unless otherwise stated, coordinates in the following account are taken from OG (1963a), records (west to east) being:

Pinar del Río c.5 km north-west of Viñales (22°37'N 83°43'W), March 1990 (A. Mitchell *in litt.* 1991); Laguna Media Casa (next to Punta Media Casa, 22°21'N 83°09'W), February 1991 (A. Mitchell *in litt.* 1991); San Diego de los Baños (22°39'N 83°22'W), April 1900 (specimen in USNM); Taco Taco (22°40'N 83°08'W), June 1916 (specimen in UNSM); San Cristóbal (22°43'N 83°03'W), May 1878 (specimen in MNHN); south of San Cristóbal, June 1933 (Rutten 1934); Soroa (22°48'N 83°01'W), November 1987 and February 1989 (A. Mitchell *in litt.* 1991); Loma del Taburete (c.4 km south of Loma del Mulo, 22°53'N 82°59'W), undated (O. H. Garrido *in litt.* 1991); Nortey (22°49'N 82°56'W), where nesting noted (Garrido 1985);

La Habana near "Havana" (Vigors 1827, Ridgway 1914), although Barbour (1943) never found the species in the province and was sceptical of this record;

Matanzas Bacunayagua (23°09'N 81°40'W), 1960 (García undated); Los Cristales (22°33'N 81°30'W), north of the Ciénaga Occidental de Zapata, March 1983 (García and González 1985); "Zapata Swamp", May 1991 (M. Lammertink *in litt.* 1992); "Los Lechuzos" (22°18'N 81°09'W), a nesting pair in May 1984 (coordinates and data in García and González 1985); south-east of Soplillar (22°17'N 81°09'W), currently (A. Mitchell *in litt.* 1991, J. M. Jiménez López *in litt.* 1992); Bermeja (22°38'N 80°16'W), currently; Guamá (on the south-eastern corner of Laguna del Tesoro, this at 22°21'N 81°07'W), undated (both from O. H. Garrido *in litt.* 1991); near Playa Larga (22°16'N 81°10'W), nesting in April 1986 (Jackson 1991), March 1990 (A. Mitchell *in litt.* 1991); Playa Girón (22°04'N 81°02'W), nesting in April 1986 (Jackson 1991); between Playa Girón and Cienfuegos, January 1991 (Sulley and Sulley 1992);

Cienfuegos Aguada de Pasajeros (22°23'N 80°51'W), April 1915 (specimen in MNHN); between Aguada de Pasajeros and Rodas (untraced), where more than 20 birds have been collected (Barbour 1943);

Villa Clara Santo Domingo, where reportedly common (Rutten 1934); near El Dorado (22°54'N 80°03'W), Isabela de Sagua, where nesting noted (Garrido 1985); near Santa Clara, April 1933 (Rutten 1934); near Vega Alta (22°33'S 79°49'W), undated (specimen in USNM); north-west of Vega Alta (less than 1 and 1.5 km respectively), August 1928 (two specimens in UNSM);

Sancti Spíritus Lomas de Trinidad (= Sierra de Trinidad, 21°56'N 80°00'W), undated (García undated); Trinidad, undated (Barbour 1923); pastures south of Sancti Spíritus and north of Zaza del Medio (22°00'N 79°23'W), where the species was reported to be common (Rutten 1934);

Ciego de Avila unspecified (García undated);

Camagüey Santa Rosa (21°26'N 78°00'W), March 1925 (specimen in MNHN); Sibanicu (c.4 km west of Camagüey), March 1948 (specimen in USNM); Camagüey, March 1913 (specimen in USNM); near Camagüey, April 1933 (Rutten 1934); Sierra de la Najasa (21°02'N 77°45'W, in Berovides Alvarez *et al.* 1982), undated (O. H. Garrido *in litt.* 1991); south coast of Camagüey, undated (Barbour 1923);

Holguín Gibara (21°07'N 76°08'W), undated (O. H. Garrido *in litt.* 1991);

Guantánamo Guantánamo, 1884-1919 (six specimens in USNM); Boca de Jaibo (20°02'N 75°14'W), July 1917 and May 1919 (three specimens in USNM); Guantánamo Bay (see ICGC 1978), March 1913 (two specimens in ROM); San Carlos (20°09'N 75°09'W), May 1911 (specimen in USNM); Santa Rita (untraced), Los Caños (20°03'N 75°09'W), January 1911, March 1914 and a large series (see Population) between 1918 and 1919 (specimens in USNM); Manatí (20°05'N 75°06'W), near Los Caños, October 1910 and February 1913 (two specimens in MNHN and USNM); río Seco, San Carlos (20°12'N 75°04'W), April 1912, May 1913 and February 1917 (three specimens in MNHN and USNM); Laguna del Guiral (untraced), October 1911 (specimen in USNM); El Uveral (untraced), December 1918 (specimen in USNM).

POPULATION The sparse nineteenth- and early twentieth-century literature suggests that the species was never very common but locally numerous. Its current status is poorly known but it appears to have suffered a considerable decline, having disappeared from large areas where it was formerly found.

D'Orbigny (1839) and Malherbe (1862) judged it quite rare. Gundlach (1871-1875) found it locally common (also in Cabanis 1856), while Barbour (1923) regarded it as "very rare" yet "locally abundant"; in his later publication (Barbour 1943) the text for the species remains identical except for the deletion of "very rare". Rutten (1934) continued to consider it "locally common", for example in the savannas north of Santa Clara and west of Santo Domingo, and in the pastures south of Sancti Spíritus and north of Zaza del Medio. Bond (1956b) agreed that it was "locally common", adding that it was "numerous" in open country in the provinces of Las Villas and Camagüey. Bond (1971) stated that it is not an "endangered species" as indicated in Vincent (1966-1971). However, Garrido and García Montaña (1977) regarded it as fairly rare, an opinion mantained by García (undated) and again by Garrido (1985), although the latter believed its population to be stable in the limited areas where it occurs, noting that it is commoner in the centre of Cuba than in the western and eastern sections. Nevertheless, M. Lammertink *(in litt.* 1991), conveying the most recent opinion of O. H. Garrido and A. Kirkconnell, reported that the species is known only from three separate areas, two of which hold very small populations while the third and largest persists in the Zapata Swamp (Matanzas province): the total population is perhaps no more than 300 pairs and is believed to be rapidly declining.

It is worth noting that a large series of birds (39 specimens in MNHN, ROM and USNM) was collected in the area of Guantánamo and Guantánamo Bay during the 1910s (20 birds between 1917 and 1919), but that no records have been indicated for the province since 1919. Indeed, apart from Matanzas, the only province where populations are known to survive is Pinar del Río.

ECOLOGY The Cuban Flicker has been reported from different environments in lowlands and at middle elevations, these ranging from savannas, pastures, swamps, palm groves, scrubby semi-arid woodland, forest edge and thick woodland (Gundlach 1871-1875, Rutten 1934, Short 1982, Bond 1985, Garrido 1985, D. Willis *in litt.* 1991). The species has often been observed feeding on the ground, where it uses its bill to find prey (insects, including ants) in the soil or under leaves (Gundlach 1876, Rutten 1934, García undated, Garrido 1985). According to Gundlach (1876), the species starts the excavation of the nest in March, laying four to five eggs, and Short (1982) indicated that the breeding season extends from March to June, although García (undated) reported nest excavation as early as January; a juvenile was taken from the nest in May 1913 (specimen in USNM). The nest-hole is a metre or so above ground, usually in a dead palm (Garrido 1985); in May 1984, García and González (1985) found a pair nesting in a "palma cana" *Sabal parviflora.* Nests can be used from year to year (García undated). Birds have been reported nesting in loose colonies, e.g. up to seven active nests in c.2-3 ha near Playa Girón (Jackson 1991).

THREATS The causes of the species's decline are not well documented; Short (1982) indicated that land-use practices may threaten the species, but Garrido (1985) thought its rarity was not due to human disturbance but possibly to habitat specialization. M. Lammertink (*in litt.* 1991) observed the species in the "Zapata Swamp" at a spot where logging was taking place in order to obtain firewood. Overall, there can be little doubt that habitat conversion over the years will have affected the species adversely, particularly if it has some unidentified specialization.

MEASURES TAKEN None is known except for the populations which may be benefiting from some of Cuba's protected areas (e.g. Ciénaga de Zapata National Park, Taco Taco and Viñales Nature Reserves and Sierra del Rosario Biosphere Reserve).

MEASURES PROPOSED More studies on the ecological requirements and distribution of the species are essential and urgent in order to develop a conservation strategy. The extant populations should be afforded protection, and periodical censuses conducted in order to monitor population trends as well as to estimate overall numbers.

HELMETED WOODPECKER *Dryocopus galeatus* V/R[10]

Records of this rare woodpecker are confined to primary tracts of Atlantic Forest in southern south-east Brazil, eastern Paraguay and northernmost Argentina, where there have been many records in very recent years. It still, however, requires urgent study and survey using voice playback, to clarify its status and ecological niche.

DISTRIBUTION The Helmeted Woodpecker is endemic to the southern Atlantic (Paranense) Forest region of south-east Brazil, eastern Paraguay and north-east Argentina (Misiones). In the following account, records are listed from north to south with coordinates taken, unless otherwise stated, from Paynter (1985, 1989) and Paynter and Traylor (1991).

Brazil The species is known from São Paulo, Paraná, Santa Catarina and at least formerly Rio Grande do Sul, but it is noteworthy that it has been recorded from two and possibly all three frontier areas of southernmost Mato Grosso do Sul (Porto Camargo in easternmost Paraná, Capitán Bado in westernmost Concepción, Paraguay, and possibly the Sierra de Maracaju, northernmost Canindeyú, Paraguay), indicating that it might yet be (or once have been) found in the state.

São Paulo Records are from: Rio Feio, 21°26'S 50°59'W, 1901 (Pinto 1938); Ribeirão Caingang ("Ribeirão dos Bugres"), 21°40'S 51°32'W, April 1901 (Pinto 1938); Vitoriana ("Victoria"), April 1902 (specimen in AMNH); "Aracuahy" mountain near Ipanema, April, May, June and December in the years 1819-1822 (von Pelzeln 1868-1871); Rio Carmo road, Fazenda Intervales, 850 m, 24°17'S 48°25'W, near Capão Bonito, February 1987 (Willis 1987); Iguape, October 1901 (Pinto 1938), this presumably the locality specified as Baurú in von Ihering and von Ihering (1907); Carlos Botelho State Park, 900 m, November 1988 (C. Yamashita *in litt.* 1988); Ilha do Cardoso State Park, recently (P. Martuscelli *in litt.* 1991).

Paraná Records are from: Jacarezinho, March and April 1901 (Pinto 1938; specimens in MZUSP), this being present-day Ourinho (see Distribution: Paraná under Golden-capped Parakeet *Aratinga auricapilla*); Porto Camargo, January 1954 (Pinto and de Camargo 1955; hence King 1978-1979, Sick 1985); Cândido de Abreu, November 1929 (specimen in FMNH); Castro, June 1914 (Pinto 1938); Iguaçu National Park on the Poço Preto trail, October 1988 (TAP, O. Læssøe *in litt.* 1989), November 1988 (P. K. Donahue *in litt.* 1989), May 1989 (M. Pearman *in litt.* 1990) and August and November 1990 (M. Castelino and D. Finch *per* J. C. Chebez *in litt.* 1992).

Santa Catarina Records are from: Canoinhas ("Ouro Verde"), 26°10'S 50°24'W, Serra do Lucindo, 750 m, May 1929 (specimen in AMNH); Poço Preto, 750 m, April 1929 (specimen in AMNH); Joinville, specimen (in BMNH) received in January 1890; Trombudo Alto (untraced, but perhaps near Trombudo Central; the rio Trombudo is an affluent of the Itajaí d'Oeste: J. F. Pacheco *in litt.* 1992), 1946 (Sick 1985).

Rio Grande do Sul Records are from: São Pedro (de Alcântara) at the coastal lagoons, October 1928 (specimen in AMNH); Poço das Antas (Gliesch 1930), presumably around 1920 (Belton 1984-1985); Taquara, August 1883 (von Berlepsch and von Ihering 1885). The species is presumed extinct in the state, but a record inside Argentina (see below), just north across the frontier from the Turvo Forest Reserve (for which see Albuquerque 1977) near the Santa Catarina border, indicates its possible survival in the area (Belton 1984-1985).

Paraguay The species has been recorded from a wide area of the eastern half of the country.

Amambay Single specimens are from Cerro Amambay, near Capitán Bado, August 1938, and from 47 km south-west of Cerro Amambay, October 1938 (Storer 1989b).

Canindeyú Records are from north of Curuguaty: 13 km, specimen, July 1979 (Storer 1989b); 10 km, sighting, 15 September 1989, and 7 km, probable sighting, next day (P. A. Scharf and F. E. Hayes *in litt.* 1991). There was another probable sighting at Estancia La Fortuna near Mbaracayú (Maracaju), June 1991 (R. S. Ridgely *in litt.* 1991; treated as a certain record in *Winging It* 4,4 [1992]: 53).

Caaguazú A specimen was collected at "Piccada de Aios" (= modern-day Coronel Oviedo: Paynter 1989) between the end of June and mid-August 1893 (Salvadori 1895b).

Alto Paraná The species has been recorded recently from the Itaipu area, i.e. near the dam (N. Pérez and A. Colman *in litt.* 1988), and within this general region one was seen 20 km north of Hernandarias in July 1982 (M. Nores and D. Yzurieta *in litt.* 1986) and a pair was seen in or near the Itabo Forest Reserve in June 1991 (R. S. Ridgely *in litt.* 1991). The undated record from Puerto Bertoni, 25°38'S 54°40'W (Bertoni 1939), is presumably that mentioned as from 25°43'S by Bertoni (1901).

Paraguarí Three birds were collected at Sapucaí, 25°40'S 56°55'W, in July and August 1904 (Chubb 1910; specimens in BMNH, MACN).

Itapúa A specimen (in MNHN) was collected in July 1948 at Puerto Edelira, which is on the río Paraná north of Capitán Meza (J. C. Chebez *in litt.* 1992), Capitán Meza being at 27°01'S 55°34'W (Paynter 1989).

Argentina Records are all from Misiones province, as follows:
Puerto Aguirre (now part of Puerto Iguazú), 25°36'S 54°35'W, July 1920 (specimen in MCZ); "Iguazú", October 1900 (specimen in MACN); Iguazú National Park (and possibly environs), e.g. immature seen on the Bernabé Méndez trail, May 1989, and a female seen 500 m from the El Timbo ranger post also near the Bernabé Méndez trail, July 1991 (M. Pearman *in litt.* 1990, 1991), with a further 14 records from 1900 (one), 1985 (two), 1988 (two), 1990 (four) and 1991 (five) compiled and to be published by J. C. Chebez (*in litt.* 1992); Sierra Morena, untraced but in Iguazú department (*per* J. C. Chebez *in litt.* 1992); arroyo Urugua-í, 25°54'S 54°36'W, km 10, March 1958 (two specimens in AMNH), km 30, August 1954 and October 1957 (specimens in AMNH, MACN); near Almirante Brown (Comandante Andresito), untraced but in General Belgrano department, 1989 (*per* J. C. Chebez *in litt.* 1992); Araucaria Provincial Park, San Pedro department, 1989 (*per* J. C. Chebez *in litt.* 1992); arroyo Yabotí-miní, 30 km north of its estuary, at 26°57'S 53°51'W, San Pedro department, close to the Turvo reserve in Brazil, February 1991 (J. Baldo *per* J. C. Chebez and M. Nores *in litt.* 1992, whence also coordinates); San Vicente, untraced but in Guaraní department, 1988 (*per* J. C. Chebez *in litt.* 1992); Lanusse (Colonia Gobernador J. J. Lanusse), 26°00'S 54°17'W, 1979 (C. C. Olrog *per* M. Nores and D. Yzurieta *in litt.* 1986), this probably the same as the record in Lucero and Alabarce (1980); Puerto Rico, untraced but in Libertador General San Martín department, 1988 (*per* J. C. Chebez *in litt.* 1992); Colonia Victoria, untraced but (according to Paynter 1985) probably near Eldorado at 26°24'S 54°38'W, August 1969 (specimen in LSUMZ); Eldorado itself, 1925 (*per* J. C. Chebez *in litt.* 1992); arroyo Piray-miní, near the confluence of arroyo Coral, untraced but in Eldorado department, 1991 (*per* J. C. Chebez *in litt.* 1992); Tobunas, 26°28'S 53°54'W, October 1953 and July 1959 (seven specimens in FMNH, LACM, MACN); Dos de Mayo, 27°02'S 54°39'W, 1979 (C. C. Olrog *per* M. Nores and D. Yzurieta *in litt.* 1986); San Ignacio, January 1942 (Anon. 1942); arroyo Anselmo and Puerto San Juan, both untraced but in Candelaria department and both south of San Ignacio, 1988 and 1991 respectively (*per* J. C. Chebez *in litt.* 1992); Campo San Juan, near San Ignacio, January 1992 (J. Baldo *per* M. Nores *in litt.* 1992); Bonpland (= Bonplano), 27°29'S 55°29'W, 1915 (*per* J. C. Chebez *in litt.* 1992). The record above that corresponds to the one reported by C. C. Olrog (in Belton 1984-1985) as being due north of Rio Grande do Sul's Turvo Forest Reserve appears to be Dos de Mayo, Chebez (1986) indicating that the area in question was at the junction of Guaraní and San Pedro departments; but as indicated above the recent record from arroyo Yabotí-miní was also very close to Turvo.

POPULATION The chronic and common opinion is that the Helmeted Woodpecker is a rare or very rare species (von Berlepsch and von Ihering 1885, Salvadori 1895b, von Ihering 1898, Chubb 1910, Short 1982, Sick 1985, Canevari *et al.* 1991; also D. F. Stotz *in litt.* 1988, F. E. Hayes *in litt.* 1991). However, the speculation that it might even be extinct (Short 1982) has been followed by the expectation (bolstered by the many previously unpublished records above) that it might not prove so very rare as feared (M. Nores and D. Yzurieta *in litt.* 1986, R. S. Ridgely *in litt.* 1991, J. C. Chebez *in litt.* 1992), although caution has been urged in the field identification of the species (B. M. Whitney *in litt.* 1991; see Remarks). The population in the adjacent Iguaçu and Iguazú National Parks in Brazil and Argentina seems likely to be the largest and safest, yet the general failure of birds to respond to tape playback in the former, over many kilometres of track, suggests a genuine rarity even there (TAP); however, it may prove not to be so rare in the Serra de Paranapiacaba (C. Yamashita *in litt.* 1988). Numbers on Ilha do Cardoso appear very small but stable (P. Martuscelli *in litt.* 1991).

ECOLOGY Very little is known. The bird dwells in forest in valleys and on mountains (Sick 1985), and was found in misty cloud-forest at Intervales (Willis 1987) and Carlos Botelho State Park (C. Yamashita *in litt.* 1988). It climbs trunks and central branches of trees, preferably at middle height (Canevari *et al.* 1991): a bird in Iguazú National Park, July 1991, was foraging on large trunks, 4-7 m up, in heavy primary forest (M. Pearman *in litt.* 1991), another in the Sierra Morena was foraging at mid-height on a laurel negro *Nectandra saligna* (J. C. Chebez *in litt.* 1992), and a third in Iguaçu foraged in low-lying forest (understorey dominated by bamboo) c.8-9 m above the ground on trunks of medium-sized trees c.25 m tall, pecking and probing in loose bark covered with mosses and lichens (TAP). This use of the middle storey appears to separate the species from the Lineated Woodpecker *Dryocopus lineatus* and Robust Woodpecker *Campephilus robustus*, which tend to haunt the upper storey (J. C. Chebez *in litt.* 1992), although it has been postulated that the species is a mimic of the latter (Willis 1989). Despite the presence of forest up to 900 m on Ilha do Cardoso (the highests point on the island), the species seems to be restricted to forest at 40-200 m (P. Martuscelli *in litt.* 1991), although it has been recorded in Santa Catarina at 750 m (see Distribution). Many of the recent records from Argentina have been from very modified areas, three of them adjacent to towns, but the species still appears to need patches of pristine forest or at least logged forest which still retains some characteristics of pristine forest (J. C. Chebez *in litt.* 1992).

The diet remains unreported. Because moult is from April to July, the breeding season was anticipated to fall between November and February (Short 1982). In fact, the only confirmed breeding record stems from late September and early October 1985, when a nest was found 2.3 m (presumably; "2.30 cm" in original) up in an unidentified tree at the arroyo Ñandú camp-site in Iguazú National Park (Chebez 1986b). A bird was at an apparent nest-hole in a tree by the side of the road in Iguaçu National Park, November 1988 (P. K. Donahue *in litt.* 1989), and on the same road in August 1990 a pair were behaving very territorially (M. Castelino *per* J. C. Chebez *in litt.* 1992). The record from San Ignacio, January, was of a juvenile male (Anon. 1942).

THREATS The rarity of this species is likely in part to be natural, and may be owing to a particular habitat specialization such as an association with a certain bamboo (B. M. Whitney *in litt.* 1991). It has certainly been observed that it seems to require large tracts of forest, and of course must therefore have suffered from their constant diminution and fragmentation (F. E. Hayes *in litt.* 1991); yet against this are recent observations from Misiones, Argentina, of birds in fairly small and sometimes much disturbed forested areas, suggesting that habitat loss may not be so serious a threat as might be expected. In eastern Paraguay some of the bird's range around the Itaipu Dam was being permanently inundated (N. Pérez and A. Colman *in litt.* 1988), and the areas along the Urugua-í in Argentina have suffered the same fate (J. C. Chebez *in litt.* 1992). The one nest ever recorded apparently failed because, by some extraordinary quirk, the tree was cut down (P. Canevari *in litt.* 1987).

MEASURES TAKEN The Helmeted Woodpecker is protected under Brazilian law (Bernardes *et al.* 1990), and has been recorded from Carlos Botelho State Park, Ilha do Cardoso State Park and Iguaçu National Park in Brazil, the Itabo Reserve in Paraguay, and Iguazú National Park and Araucaria Provincial Park in Argentina, where it probably also occurs in

Urugua-í and Moconá Provincial Parks (J. C. Chebez *in litt.* 1992).

MEASURES PROPOSED Taped voice playback, used sensitively, offers perhaps the most efficient method of determining the presence or absence of the species in particular areas, and any general avifaunal surveys anywhere in the range could include this low-key component. Work is also needed to gather as much as possible on its ecology and needs, so that management can be contemplated; such studies could perhaps best be undertaken in either Iguaçu or Iguazú National Parks, or even both. A survey is needed of Turvo Forest Reserve in Rio Grande do Sul, and at some stage an investigation of the southernmost area of Mato Grosso do Sul south of 22°S might be appropriate. In eastern Paraguay the status of the bird north of Curuguaty and in the Itaipu Dam region requires elucidation. In Argentina the species occurs in four areas that are proposed for protection, namely Yabotí, Puerto San Juan, Piray-miní and Sierra Morena (J. C. Chebez *in litt.* 1992).

REMARKS B. M. Whitney (*in litt.* 1991) pointed out that some recent field observations (not necessarily in this account, as there appear to have been several more from Iguazú National Park) may possibly have involved Lineated Woodpeckers, which in that region have much rusty colour in their underparts not mentioned or depicted in field guides, and he urged all observers to provide full descriptions. However, C. Yamashita (*in litt.* 1988) considered the opposite may also sometimes happen, with Helmeted Woodpeckers being identified as Lineated, and going under-recorded as a result. J. C. Chebez (*in litt.* 1992), aware of these concerns, has reaffirmed his confidence in the veracity of the records he supplied for this account.

The species appears to be morphologically and behaviourally intermediate between *Celeus* and *Dryocopus* woodpeckers: the small pale bill, manner of foraging, and drum pattern are all rather *Celeus*-like, whereas the plumage pattern is certainly like *D. lineatus*, while the strident 4-5 note song is intermediate, having the loudness and pattern of a *Dryocopus* but the emphatic quality of several *Celeus* species (TAP).

IMPERIAL WOODPECKER *Campephilus imperialis* E/Ex[4]

Originally distributed throughout the Sierra Madre Occidental in Mexico, this bird, the largest woodpecker in the world, has suffered from the widespread and almost total destruction of its specialized open pine-forest habitat. Although previously not uncommon, it has not been recorded with certainty since 1958 and may well already be extinct.

DISTRIBUTION Historically the Imperial Woodpecker, the largest member of its family in the world, was found throughout the Sierra Madre Occidental of Mexico in Sonora, Chihuahua, Durango, Nayarit, Zacatecas (possibly) and northern Jalisco, with more isolated populations in western Jalisco and northern Michoacán. Localities are arranged from north to south, with coordinates taken from OG (1956a).

Sonora The Imperial Woodpecker has been recorded from the north-eastern part of the state, where the Sierra Madre Occidental of western Chihuahua extends across the border into Sonora, north of 29°N. The species was first recorded in this area in 1886, when it was found in the pine-forests of the "Sierra Madre de Sonora" within 80 km of the Arizona border (Ridgway 1887c). This is the most northerly record of the species and presumably refers to the most northern part of the sierra around which the río Bavispe flows (i.e. El Tigre), and Marshall (1957) recorded holes "probably made by this woodpecker" in forest on the Sierra Huachinera (30°16'N 108°45'W). Van Rossem (1945) recorded the Sierra de Nácori – apparently referring to the mountains just south of Tres Ríos, which Marshall (1957) placed at roughly 29°50'N 108°45'W – as a locality for the species, but gave no further details, although it probably referred to two birds seen at 1,920 m, c.45-50 km from Nácori, in late 1890 (Lumholtz 1903). Allen (1893) recorded that specimens were taken on the río Bavispe (near the headwaters: van Rossem 1945) during December 1890. Other records include a female (in USNM) taken in the "Sierra Madre de Sonora" (date unknown); and west of Casas Grandes (29°29'N 109°35'W in westernmost Chihuahua) on the summit of the Sierra Madre de Sonora, where a male and female (in LACM) were collected in 1906 (see below). In 1941, the species was "easily found" along the Sonora–Chihuahua "line" (Tanner 1942; see below). An unconfirmed sighting in 1975 by a rancher, who had previously collected a bird and taken a photograph (both lost in a fire at SBMNH), was followed up by the suggestion that the species should be searched for in the mountains between Madera (westernmost Chihuahua), and the headwaters of the río Yaqui in Sonora (Plimpton 1977).

Chihuahua This species has been recorded from a number of scattered localities in the Sierra Madre Occidental of western Chihuahua. From north to south, it has been found along the Sonora–Chihuahua border, where in 1941 it was "easily found" in pine-forests between 2,285-2,745 m on the Chihuahua side (Tanner 1942), localities in this area including Pacheco (30°06'N 108°21'W), where a specimen (in USNM) was taken in March 1902, with a pair and a juvenile (in FMNH) collected in July 1909. An abandoned Imperial Woodpecker nest, taken over by Thick-billed Parrots *Rhynchopsitta pachyrhyncha*, was found in 1905 at "Colonia Pacheco" (= Pacheco, and c.15 km north of Colonia García: Goldman 1951) (Thayer 1906). The records from west of Casas Grandes (on the Chihuahua side of the border) appear to be from Sonora (see above), as they were apparently made on the "summit of the Sierra Madre de Sonora", but travelling west from Casas Grandes high mountains are reached before the border is crossed, so it is impossible to attribute these records to a particular state. Other localities along the border include: three specimens (one female is in AMNH) taken near "Ranchería de los Apachos" at 2,020 m in January 1891 (Allen 1893, Lumholtz 1903), this locality being described as near the río Gavilán with its origin "probably near Chuhuichupa" (29°38'N 108°22'W) (Lumholtz 1903, Marshall 1957), but obviously near the border, as the AMNH specimen has two labels, one with "N. Sonora", the other with "Chihuahua" (see Marshall 1957); near Colonia García (29°59'N 108°20'W), where two males and three females (in USNM) were collected in July 1899, a male and female (in ANSP) in July 1902, a male and two females (in USNM and MCZ) in April 1903, and a male, female and immature (in ROM) during 1903, plus a male and female (in USNM) collected respectively c.8 km and c.25 km west of Colonia García in February 1904; Chuhuichupa (29°38'N 108°22'W), where two males and two females (in AMNH) were taken in January 1892 (see also Allen 1893), with a male and three females (in MCZ) in September 1905; Catalaria (Candelaria) Peak (c.15 km west of Chuhuichupa), where a male (in SDNHM) was collected (date unknown); Babicora (29°30'N 108°01'W), where three males and a female (in FMNH) were taken in June 1902; and in the region of the Sonora–Chihuahua line west of Babicora, where birds were seen around 1940 (K. Simmons *in litt.* to J. T. Tanner 1941 *per* N. Tanner *in litt.* 1991). Further south in the state, the Imperial Woodpecker has been recorded c.80 km west of Terrazas (28°57'N 106°16'W), where 17 were shot in the course of a few months, the area apparently being "much frequented by the species" (Smith 1908); Pinos Altos (from the map in Lumholtz 1903 this is Pinos Redondeados at 28°15'N 108°17'W, and not the same as the locality mentioned by Marshall 1957: see Remarks 2 under Eared Quetzal *Euptilotis neoxenus*), where a male and female (in MCZ) were taken in July 1888; Yahuirachic (28°35'N 108°09'W), where a bird was seen sometime prior to 1961 (A. S. Leopold *in litt.* to J. T. Tanner 1961 *per* N. Tanner *in litt.* 1991), and whence come other unconfirmed reports (Plimpton 1977); and Temochic (27°51'N 107°02'W), where a male (in MCZ) was collected in May 1884 (see Remarks 1). In the vicinity of Temochic, unconfirmed local reports come from Tutuaca, Cebadilla, Pitoreal and Pescados. There is also a rumour of some Mexican biology students reportedly discovering several pairs near Barranca del Cobre in October 1973 (Plimpton 1977), presumably close to where a bird was seen sometime prior to 1961 (B. Villa *in litt.* to J. T. Tanner 1961 *per* N. Tanner *in litt.* 1991). Bennett and Zingg (1935) had old unconfirmed reports from the area around Samachique (27°17'N 107°28'W), although the population was extinct there by the time of their inquiries. In the south of the state, records come from: Laguna Juanota (26°30'N 106°29'W), where a male (in MLZ) was taken at 2,745 m in July 1937; mountains west of Parral (Bergtold 1906), i.e. presumably modern-day Hidalgo del Parral; halfway between Santa Rosa (26°00'N 107°00'W) and Llano Grande (untraced), where one was seen sometime prior to 1962 (C. Pennington *in litt.* to J. T. Tanner 1962 *per* N. Tanner *in litt.* 1991); and "Imperial valley", which is untraced but apparently on the east side of Monte Mohinora (26°06'N 107°04'W) west of Guadalupe y Calvo, where a male (in MLZ) was collected at 3,050 m in May 1937 (see Miller *et al.* 1957), and whence come unconfirmed reports in 1961 (A. Gardner *in litt.* to J. T. Tanner 1961 *per* N. Tanner *in litt.* 1991). Untraced localities in Chihuahua include "Black Cañon", where a male and female (in YPM) were collected in February 1910, and "Mound valley", where two males and five females (in MCZ and CM) were taken in September 1905, a male (in AMNH) in December 1919, and three females (in AMNH) in December 1921.

Durango The Imperial Woodpecker is noted from the western and southern parts of the state, the localities involved being as follows: San Miguel de los Cruces (130 km west-north-west of Durango), with unconfirmed reports (Tanner 1964); río Verde crossing (24°15'N 105°00'W), with unconfirmed reports of a bird in 1961 (A. Gardner *in litt.* to J. T. Tanner 1961 *per* N. Tanner *in litt.* 1991); 200 km west of Durango "at the summit of the sierras", where two females (in AMNH and ROM) were taken at 2,775 m in February 1904; Coyotes (either 24°15'N 104°42'W, or 23°49'N 105°20'W), where a male and two females (in FMNH) were collected in August and September 1904; El Salto, where a male and three females (in USNM) were collected in July 1898; near La Ciudad, where several specimens (male and female taken in January 1882, and a male and female taken in February by the same collector; all in BMNH) were collected (Salvin and Godman 1888-1904); Nievero (Neviero in Miller *et al.* 1957, both untraced but c.6 km west of La Ciudad), where a male and female (in MLZ and LSUMZ) were taken in March 1938; Chavarría (Chavaria in Lumholtz 1903: 23°38'N 105°36'W, and apparently in the immediate vicinity of La Ciudad), where a flock of six was seen in February 1891 (Lumholtz 1903); Pueblo Nuevo (south of El Salto), whence come reports of birds in 1960 (R. Baker *in litt.* to J. T. Tanner 1961 *per* N. Tanner *in litt.* 1991); Rancho Las Margaritas (untraced but apparently 43 km south and 27 km west of Vicente Guerrero at 23°45'N 103°59'W), whence come unconfirmed reports of the species in June 1957 (Fleming and Baker 1963); 46 km south by 31 km west of Vicente Guerrero, where in July 1957 at 2,680 m a nest-hole apparently excavated by the species was found to contain the nest of a Thick-billed Parrot (Baker 1958: see Ecology); Los Cebollos (south of Durango), unconfirmed reports suggesting that the species was present here until 1961 (A. Gardner *in litt.* to J. T. Tanner 1961 *per* N. Tanner *in litt.* 1991); 80 km south of Durango, where a male and female (in MLZ and MNHUK) were taken at 2,440 m in July 1947, with unconfirmed reports coming from the vicinity of "La Guacamayita" (untraced, but also 80 km south of Durango), locals recording the species up to five years prior to 1962 (Tanner 1964); 100 km south of Durango, where a pair was found in 1954, one noted in 1956 and a dead one seen in 1958 (Tanner 1964, Plimpton 1977); near Los Charcos (untraced but 130 km south of Durango), where two old nest-holes were seen at c.2,800 m in June 1962, unconfirmed reports suggesting that the species was present until three years before this date (Tanner 1964). Other reports suggest that the species was present in the northern part of the Sierra de los Huicholes in June 1962 (Tanner 1964), further specimens coming from "Sierra de Durango" (male in SDMNH, date unknown), and the "Durango mountains" (a male in LACM taken in 1912).

Nayarit There appears to be only one record of this bird from Nayarit, represented by a male (in MLZ) taken 16 km north-west of Santa Teresa (22°28'N 104°44'W) at 1,675 m during June 1941. The distribution map given by Tanner (1964) implies that there is an unconfirmed record of the bird from 1961-1962 south-east of the known locality.

Zacatecas The available evidence is inconclusive: Salvin and Godman (1888-1904) suggested that Richardson, "in the Sierra de Valparaíso, in the state of Jalisco, saw a specimen and shot at it", Nelson (1898) mentioned that "Richardson took others in the Sierra de Valparaíso in northern Zacatecas", and both Tanner (1942) and Miller *et al.* (1957) subsequently included Zacatecas within the range of the species. On the CETN (1976) map of the area, however, the Sierra Valparaíso is situated at c.22°40'N 103°45'W in northernmost Jalisco and south-western Zacatecas: the precise locality and state where Richardson recorded the species is therefore unknown.

Jalisco Records of this species from the Sierra de Valparaíso may possibly be from this state (see immediately above). Nelson (1898) recorded the species from near Bolaños (21°41'N 103°47'W) and also suggested that this is the type-locality (see Remarks 2). Lumholtz (1903) mentioned having seen the species as far south as the southernmost point which the Sierra Madre del Norte reaches in the state of Jalisco, north of the río de Santiago. South and west of this river, specimens come from near Mascota (20°32'N 104°49'W) in the Sierra de Juanacatlán, where a female and two juvenile males (in AMNH) were taken in May 1892, with a female in December of the same year. Nelson (1898) described specimens taken by A. C. Buller as coming from (c.240 km) south of Bolaños in the Sierra Juanacatlán, western Jalisco, presumably referring to the specimens that Buller collected at Mascota in 1892, despite the fact that this is c.175 km south-west of Bolaños (calculated from the coordinates). Nelson (1898) also visited this locality (240 km south of Bolaños) in the spring of 1897, recording the scalp of a bird taken a few months previously, and noting unconfirmed reports of the bird in the surrounding mountains.

Michoacán The Imperial Woodpecker has been recorded from just one small area of north-central Michoacán, the most southerly point in the species's distribution. At Pátzcuaro (19°31'N 101°36'W), one bird was killed "a few miles away" in the summer of 1892 (Nelson 1898), this probably referring to a juvenile female (in USNM and labelled "Pátzcuaro") taken in July 1892. In the autumn of the same year, a pair was seen and a male collected at 2,135 m near Nahuatzen (19°42'N 101°50'W), and at a camp to the west of the village five were seen (and all collected), with 5-6 more found in the hills "a mile or so away" (Nelson 1898). Three males, three females and two others (in USNM) were collected at or near Nahuatzen during October 1892, and on the return trip to Pátzcuaro, near the original site, a party of 8-10 were seen (Nelson 1898). In the Nahuatzen district this species's range appears to have been restricted to the rather narrow belt along the top of the main central ridge of the Sierra Madre which lies above 2,135 m (Nelson 1898).

POPULATION The last confirmed record of the Imperial Woodpecker was from Durango in 1958, although there are plausible but unconfirmed records throughout the early 1970s, with nothing having been recorded about the species since 1977. It has been variously described as "greatly reduced in numbers and in danger of extinction" (Miller *et al.* 1957), "virtually extirpated from its native pine-forests in the Sierra Madre Occidental" (Leopold 1959), and "on the brink of extinction if not already extinct" (Short 1982). It was not historically a rare species within its preferred habitat, occurring at a calculated density of 6 birds per 80 km^2, with a group of even 8-10 birds having been recorded (Tanner 1964).

Sonora In 1886, the Imperial Woodpecker was found to be common in the pine-forests of the Sierra Madre de Sonora, within 80 km of the Arizona border (Ridgway 1887c). However, the record of a male and female (in LACM) collected in the "Sierra Madre de Sonora", west of Casas Grandes (westernmost Chihuahua) in 1906 appears to be the last positive record from this state (Miller *et al.* 1957 suggested that there had not been a record since 1902), although the species was easily found along the border on the Chihuahua side in 1941 (Tanner 1942; see below) and an unconfirmed sighting in 1975 may also be from this state (see Distribution).

Chihuahua In the north, almost all records come from between 1892 and 1909 (see Distribution), although in 1941 the species was found easily but was not common across the border from Sonora (Tanner 1942). Further south, c.80 km west of Terrazas, 17 were shot within a few months, this area being "much frequented by the species" (Smith 1908). Even in 1890-1891, Lumholtz (1903) concluded that the bird could be seen in only the remoter parts, but that it was on the point of being exterminated by the Tarahumara and Mexicans. Bergtold (1906) considered it common (in 1903-1904) in the mountains west of Parral. More recent unconfirmed records are from Yahuirachic, 8-14 years prior to 1977; Tutuaca, with reports of "many" in the vicinity during the early 1970s, and one reportedly seen 8 km away in 1977; Cebadilla, 6-8 years prior to 1977, and Pitoreal, where six were reported by woodcutters in 1977 (Plimpton 1977). An interesting rumour of several pairs discovered in the mountains near the Barranca del Cobre in October 1973 is also unconfirmed (Plimpton 1977). A significant population obviously existed at "Mound valley" (see Distribution). There is no information about the population further south in the state.

Durango Fleming and Baker (1963), along with local residents, considered this species rare and elusive in the state. Unconfirmed reports from west of San Miguel de los Cruces indicated that a population died out during the 15 years before 1962 (Tanner 1964). Good numbers appear to have existed in the La Ciudad–Nievero–Chavarría area (see Distribution). In the area south and west of General Vicente Guerrero in 1957, locals (at Rancho Las Margaritas) indicated that (in 1957) birds were only occasionally seen (usually two but sometimes four), being widely spaced with no more than a pair in any one of the large canyons, and indeed in a valley nearby, two birds were reported in June 1957, several trees showing fresh evidence of feeding, and one felled tree having cavities (one of these presumably containing the two young reported taken in that month): residents agreed that the species was less abundant in 1957 than previously, mentioning that a pair in the canyon where La China lumber camp was built in 1956 disappeared soon afterwards (Fleming and Baker 1963). In the south of the state, residents around a new lumber camp in 1953 claimed that 12 individuals were shot in a year (Tanner 1964). In the region 80-130 km south of Durango city, natives who knew the bird agreed (in 1962) that it was once common but no longer present, suggesting that it was last seen around 1957-1959, although other unconfirmed reports indicated that it was still present in the northern part of the Sierra de los Huicholes in June 1962 (Tanner 1964; see Distribution).

Nayarit The only confirmed record refers to a single bird (see Distribution).

Jalisco All records for this state are from the late nineteenth century, the species apparently still being found sparingly in the mountains surrounding Mascota in 1897 (Nelson 1898).

Michoacán In the Pátzcuaro–Nahuatzen district during the summer and autumn of 1892 a group of 8-10 was reported, along with two smaller groups of five or six birds (Nelson 1898). At this same time, the local Indians mentioned other places where they were common, one local leading an observer to a view-point overlooking a great expanse of forested country, and pointing out a number of park-like openings where the birds could assuredly be seen; two nests were found in the area the following year (Nelson 1898). Tanner (1964) calculated the density in this area at c.1 pair per 25 km^2 (or probably more accurately as 6 birds per 80 km^2). There are no records of the bird during the twentieth century, Lea and Edwards (1950) in the Pátzcuaro region during 1947 concluding that the species "is undoubtedly completely absent at present from this section of its former range", the extensive pine-forest between Nahuatzen and Pátzcuaro that existed in the 1890s already having been destroyed.

ECOLOGY Miller *et al.* (1957) asserted that the species was found in mountains from 1,525-3,050 m, but almost all records come from between 1,920 and 3,050 m, and contrary to Tanner (1964) there does not appear to be any significant altitudinal variation between the northern and southern populations (see Distribution). The record from Nayarit (see Distribution), at 1,675 m, is the only one from lower than 1,900 m, and as the specimen was taken in June, it may represent a non-breeding or post-breeding wanderer. The Imperial Woodpecker's preferred habitat can generally be described as open forest consisting of large pines (trees commonly 15-20 m to the lowest limb) with many dead trees intermixed, and broken by grassy park-like areas (Nelson 1898, Tanner 1964). In the north-west of the range, one area for the species (around Casas Grandes between 2,100-2,700 m) is intersected by many ravines and sparsely covered by tall pines (Bergtold 1906), the mountains generally forested with *Pinus montezumae* (Tanner 1942); but in southern Durango, Tanner (1964) found that the dominant tree species (in an area once inhabited by the species) were *P. durangensis*, *P. lutea*, *P. ayacahuite* and *P. montezumae*, the largest pines being found at the higher elevations. Locals in Durango mentioned that the species preferred stands of "yellow" pines with numerous dead but still standing pines intermixed (Fleming and Baker 1963).

In Jalisco, it was found that the undulating mountain summits were forested with several species of pine, oak and madroño (*Arbutus* spp.), park-like basins scattered throughout the area (Nelson 1898). In Michoacán, where the bird's population density was calculated at c.1 pair per 25 km^2, the area was described as upland volcanic country, overgrown with open pine-forest in which grassy parks opened "here and there" (Nelson 1898). A hill which provided a view across this area revealed a succession of pine-covered hills (like a rolling and irregular tableland), broken in places by the dull yellow openings of the grassy parks: here, Imperial Woodpeckers were only found where the forest was almost entirely made up of *Pinus montezumae*, and were not seen to alight on any other tree (Nelson 1898). In the Pátzcuaro district, a pair of birds was seen on a dead pine on the border of an Indian cornfield; although the woodpecker generally roamed through the thin parts of the forest or about the borders of grassy parks, it was also partial to dead trees around partly cleared fields (Nelson 1898).

During February 1891, Lumholtz (1903) noted a group of six birds, concluding that except in this "pairing" season the birds are not seen in such numbers and are normally found in pairs (a conclusion reinforced by an independent observation given by Tanner 1942). However, the six birds may have been a family group from previous seasons (see below), Nelson (1898) recording parties (see Population) during one October, and concluding that the birds remain in family groups during the autumn and winter. Tanner (1964) suggested that as the species produced 1-2 young a year (see below), the flocks of 5-10 birds may have represented young birds from previous breeding seasons, or possibly a chance encounter between two families. In autumn 1892, Nelson (1898) noted a party of five birds that persistently returned to the same roost area each evening, calling from there each dawn and then flying off to a feeding ground amongst the dead pines on an adjacent park-like flat. At that time of year, the birds showed strong local attachments although in the middle of the day the group roamed throughout the open forest (Nelson 1898). Roost-site fidelity was also recorded by Tanner (1942). In western Jalisco, locals claimed that the species was present every summer, but led a more wandering life during the winter (Nelson 1898). In Durango during the winter, birds apparently moved to lower areas in the barrancas when snow fell in the higher country (Fleming and Baker 1963). Also in this area, birds were noted as flying high and often long distances from one side of a steep barranca to another, rarely staying long in one place (Fleming and Baker 1963), although Lumholtz (1903) reported that one of the species's peculiarities was that they "feed on one tree for as long as a fortnight at a time, at last causing the decayed tree to fall".

Imperial Woodpeckers foraged almost exclusively by scaling bark from dead pine trees, and have been observed feeding on partly decayed prostrate trunks and knocking large chunks of outer bark from standing trees (Tanner 1964, Short 1982). The birds fed in this way in order to find large insect larvae (e.g. Cerambycid larvae) (Fleming and Baker 1963, Tanner 1964).

Nest-holes were excavated in dead pine trees, holes having been found c.20 m up in the main trunk, the only tree species recorded being *P. montezumae* (Baker 1958, Fleming and Baker 1963). A local "meat hunter" suggested that the bird may excavate holes in dead oaks or in the dead branches of living oaks (Fleming and Baker 1963), which appears to be the only reference to the species using a broadleaf species and may well involve a misidentification of the bird (see Remarks 3). Breeding has been recorded during February–June: in Michoacán, two eggs were taken in February, a nest with newly hatched young was found on 1 March 1893 (the young flew in April) (Nelson 1898), two young were found in a cavity (in Durango) in June (Fleming and Baker 1963), and juveniles have been collected in May (in AMNH) in Jalisco, and July (in FMNH) in Chihuahua, Short (1982) suggesting that immature birds are known (in Jalisco and Chihuahua) from April to September (birds in the nest in June would still be recognizably immature until September or October: L. L. Short *in litt.* 1991).

THREATS A number of factors have brought about the elimination of this species in the Sierra Madre Occidental, but they can all be summarized as either (initially) hunting pressures or (more recently, and with far greater consequenses) habitat destruction and modification. As early as 1890-1891, Lumholtz (1903) observed that in Chihuahua the Imperial Woodpecker was on the point of being exterminated because (a) the Tarahumara Indians (who at this time ranged throughout the Sierra Madre in Chihuahua) considered the young of the species such a delicacy that they did not hesitate to cut down even large trees in order to get at the nests, and (b) local Mexicans shot them because their plumage was thought to have medicinal properties. Bennett and Zingg (1935) studied the same tribe during the 1930s, the Indians then claiming that they had no knowledge of the species and that it had been wiped out by the Mexicans. Observations in Durango convinced Tanner (1964) that shooting was the main cause of the species's elimination, the locals being dependent on hunting for meat, and indeed the last confirmed record was ironically of a dead bird being carried by a local in southern Durango in 1958 (see Population).

Other examples of the exploitation of this species are the collection of 17 within a few months in Chihuahua on the pretext that the bills had a commercial value (Smith 1908), and the occasional sale of caged birds as pets in the markets of Ciudad Durango (Fleming and Baker 1963), but the collection of over 120 scientific specimens (from museums mentioned in Distribution) is unlikely to have had a significant impact. Two young that were presumably taken from one of the nest-holes noted in a tree felled in June (Fleming and Baker 1963) were obviously sufficiently sought-after (by locals) to warrant the felling of the nest-tree (see below).

The real cause of the hunting problem seems to stem from the expansion of lumber operations into remote parts of the sierra, which brought people into the forest: small ranches were set up, and areas opened up for settlement (Tanner 1964). Residents in a number of areas where lumber operations had started (operations were apparently set up in earnest during the early 1950s) indicated that the Imperial Woodpecker disappeared within a few years (e.g. La China and La Guacamayita; see Population). Although the residents reported this decline, they either gave no reason for it, or blamed it on logging, felling of dead pines or the fact that the birds were shy (contrary to all reliable reports of the bird: Tanner 1964) and "disappear" when man is present (Fleming and Baker 1963). The fact that the species disappeared so rapidly after settlement suggests the influence of hunting rather than habitat modification (e.g. in southern Durango, 12 birds were killed within a year around a new lumber camp: Tanner 1964), although it could also have simply been due to human disturbance.

In Michoacán, there are no records of birds killed by locals, the extinction here being caused by the almost total removal by 1947 of the extensive virgin pine-forests between Nahuatzen and Pátzcuaro (Lea and Edwards 1950). This is the only area where total deforestation (rather than modification) is deemed to be the cause of the species's disappearance, although the widespread felling of trees also used by Military Macaw *Ara militaris* (and Thick-billed Parrot) in Durango (with the intention of obtaining young to sell for pets) may have had a detrimental effect upon the availability of the species's food and nest-trees (Tanner 1964).

In the early 1960s the logging of the Sierra Madre Occidental pine-forests was highly selective and relatively light: many areas still had extensive stands of virgin forest, and logged areas still contained many large pines, enough of which were dead (or would die from natural causes) to supply adequate food (Tanner 1964). It was then believed that if the prevailing policies of selective cutting continued, suitable habitat should remain, and the main problem would be hunting for food. However, it now appears that dead pines are specifically extracted for pulp, and government restrictions only prevent living pines with a breast-height diameter less than 40-50 cm from being felled (see relevant section under Thick-billed Parrot). The relatively recent but widespread modification of primary forest, even in the remotest areas of the species's range, has inevitably (and substantially) reduced the chances of the woodpecker's survival, and if the bird is (or becomes) extinct, this will be the overriding cause of its final destruction.

MEASURES TAKEN Tancítaro and Barranca del Cobre National Parks are both within the range of this woodpecker, although there are no confirmed records from either (see Distribution). There appear to be no protected areas covering localities where this species is known to have occurred, and although the game laws apparently "protect" the bird, they are totally unenforceable (Tanner 1964). There has also been no effort to prevent further pine-forest modification in any areas suitable for the species within the Sierra Madre.

MEASURES PROPOSED Tanner (1964) suggested that the presence of the Imperial Woodpecker in an area of Sierra Madre pine-forest might well be a suitable criterion for the establishment of a national park, although clearly before any such initiative can be implemented, a viable population must first be found. A number of specific searches have been undertaken during and since the 1960s (e.g. Plimpton 1977, A. G. Navarro and A. T. Peterson *in litt.* 1991, L. L. Short *in litt.* 1991), although these have to a large extent concentrated on regions from which the most recent reports came, and are therefore the areas where the species has perhaps been persecuted the most. There are three general areas that appear to be most likely still to harbour individuals of this species: (1) in the north, the area around the Sonora–Chihuahua border where the bird was found easily in 1941, and was probably seen in 1975 (see Distribution); (2) the main part of the Sierra Madre Occidental in northern Durango, north and west of Santiago Papasquiaro, where the species has never been recorded but which is in the middle of its range and appears to be less densely populated than other areas (it appears to be a greatly neglected area in terms of biological investigation); (3) the southern part of the Sierra de los Huicholes, north of the río Grande de Santiago in northern Jalisco (and Nayarit), which also appears to be less densely populated and ornithologically unexplored in recent years. If a remote and as yet relatively unsettled area can be found, this species may well be present in small numbers which would then enable a conservation plan for its survival to be initiated. Obviously, however, with each passing year the prospects of success recede, and it is time that a major international expedition was formed to survey these and other regions exhaustively; with the loss of the closely related Ivory-billed Woodpecker *Campephilus principalis* (see relevant account) to contemplate, the conservation and ornithological communities of North America and indeed the "developed" world would do well at least to avoid posterity's imminent judgement that the planet's largest and most spectacular woodpecker disappeared in a climate of indifference and inertia. The need to preserve several extensive areas of intact forest in this species's range is indicated in the equivalent section under Thick-billed Parrot and Eared Quetzal, species which would also benefit from study in any major new initiative in the Sierra Madre Occidental.

REMARKS (1) Van Rossem (1934) cited a specimen from MCZ collected by McLeod in May 1884 but gave "no locality"; however, inspection of apparently this specimen in 1987 revealed "Temochi" (presumably Temochic) on the label. (2) The type-specimen (one of 5-6) was taken from "that little-explored district of California which borders the territory of Mexico" (*Proc. Zool. Soc. London* 1832: 139-140); Salvin and Godman (1888-1904) suggested that the specimens were taken by Floresi, who apparently collected in the mountains near Bolaños, Jalisco; from this, Nelson (1898) concluded that the type locality was Bolaños. (3) Sclater and Salvin (1866) were the first to recognize the identification "problem" that this large black-and-white woodpecker presented, even a specimen described as this species (Sclater and Salvin 1859) proving on further inspection to be an example of the Pale-billed Woodpecker *Campephilus guatemalensis*. Plimpton (1977) reported that some of the unconfirmed records of the species that he heard of probably referred to Lineated Woodpeckers *Dryocopus lineatus*, and the fact that Tanner (1964) found that the Imperial Woodpecker's common local name ("pitoreal" [*sic*]) was also used for the Pale-billed Woodpecker shows that care needs to be taken with records from locals.

IVORY-BILLED WOODPECKER *Campephilus principalis* E/Ex[4]

The North American population of this large, low-density woodpecker is very probably extinct, and the most recent evidence suggests that there is almost as little hope for the Cuban form, which was last reported in 1987 or 1988 with glimpses in 1991, despite much intensive searching in the Sierra de Moa, the area to which it finally retreated in the course of this century; destruction of its virgin forest habitat, of which each pair evidently needed very large amounts, is chiefly to blame for the loss of the species.

DISTRIBUTION The Ivory-billed Woodpecker formerly occurred throughout the south-east U.S.A. (nominate *principalis*) and Cuba (race *bairdii*; see Remarks 1), but is now virtually or actually extinct in both countries, although evidence for its survival in Cuba is far more recent; for this reason, the following account principally treats the Cuban form, the North American race being judged probably extinct and not to be covered in detail here.

U.S.A. Ivory-bills once ranged through the south-east of the country from south-east North Carolina, southern Kentucky, Illinois, Missouri, Arkansas and Oklahoma to the coast of the Gulf of Mexico and the Florida peninsula, with populations disappearing (as a result of forest destruction, but compounded by commercial collecting, which eliminated certain populations) from the northern and western extremities of its range before 1885, from most of Missouri, Arkansas, Mississippi and Alabama between 1885 and 1900, and from most of Florida, eastern Texas and Louisiana by 1930 (King 1978-1979). The last known population disappeared by 1948 with the clearance of the 311 km^2 Singer (Sewing Machine Company) Tract in Louisiana for soybean cultivation, since when there have only been random observations in scattered localities ranging from Texas to Florida (King 1978-1979); some of these records are assembled in Dennis (1979) and Aldrich (1980). Ten years ago Short (1982) considered the chances of a population surviving in the U.S.A. "virtually nil", and the U.S. Fish and Wildlife Service is now moving to de-list it from the Endangered Species Act as extinct in the country (Shull 1985, L. L. Short *in litt.* 1992). Despite this, "an ongoing survey (to be completed by 1992) holds out hope that Ivory-billed Woodpeckers may yet be found in Louisiana's Atchafalaya Basin or along South Carolina's Santee River, Georgia's Altamaha River, Mississippi's Hyazoo or Pascagoula rivers, or Florida's Suwannee, Withlacoochee, or Ochloconee rivers" (Ehrlich *et al.* 1992). What is apparent from below is that no reintroduction into the U.S.A., speculated as an option if the Cuban population were to be found sufficiently numerous (Ehrlich *et al.* 1992), will take place (see Remarks 2).

Cuba The species was formerly distributed throughout the island (Barbour 1943, Bond 1956b, Alayón and Garrido 1991), although the evidence below indicates that basically it was only ever known to investigators from the western and eastern sectors of the island, and Shull's (1985) assertion that it occurred on the Isle of Pines appears unfounded. During the first half of the twentieth century its range became restricted to the mountains in the (north-)east of the island (e.g. Sierra de Moa, Sierra del Cristal, Sierra de Nipe) and subsequently to the Sierra de Moa. In the following account, records are given roughly from west to east, with coordinates, unless otherwise indicated, taken from OG (1963a), and in most cases records consist of single birds or pairs observed:

Pinar del Río mountains north of San Diego de los Baños (22°39'N 83°22'W), late nineteenth century (see Barbour 1943); Pan de Guajabón (22°48'N 83°22'W), undated (Gundlach 1871-1875); Soroa (= Villa Soroa, a few kilometres north-west of Candelaria, 22°45'N 82°58'W), April 1982 (Garrido 1985), although this is a most doubtful record (TAP, G. Alayón García *in litt.* 1992);

Matanzas río Hanábana (22°33'N 80°58'W), late nineteenth century (see Barbour 1943); Ensenada Cochinos, undated (Gundlach 1871-1875); Calimete (22°32'N 80°54'W) and Banagüises (22°46'N 80°51'W), both late in the nineteenth century (see Barbour 1943);

Holguín Cauto el Embarcadero (presumably on the río Cauto, c.12 km south of Urbano Noris, 20°36'N 76°08'W), undated (Gundlach 1871-1875); highlands of Mayarí (i.e. Sierra de Nipe, 20°28'N 75°49'W), where a nesting pair was collected around 1900 and the species was observed around 1920 (Barbour 1943);

Holguín/Guantánamo (Sierra de Moa area) Sierra de Moa, where a group of six birds was reported in 1941 (see Dennis 1948); "mountains of Oriente province" (presumably Sierra de Moa), March 1988 (Jackson 1991; see Remarks); Cupeyal del Norte Reserve (c.20°29'N 75°02'W: read from ICGC 1978), between 1941 and 1943 (Alayón and Garrido 1991); c.8 km north-west of Cupeyal (20°35'N 75°11'W), February 1968 (Bond 1968, Garrido and García Montaña 1975, Garrido 1985); Monte Cristo (untraced but near Cupeyal), November 1973 (King 1978-1979); Vega Grande (5 km south of Cupeyal), undated (Bond 1968, Garrido and García Montaña 1975, Garrido 1985); La Munición (c.7 km north-east of El Manguito, 20°21'N 75°08'W), December 1984 (Alayón and Garrido 1991); Ojito de Agua area (c.20°28'N 74°59'W: read from ICGC 1978), July 1956 (Lamb 1957); headwaters of Yarey river, Ojito de Agua), March and April 1986 and March 1987 (Short and Horne 1986, Alayón and Garrido 1991; see Population); Cayo Chiquito (within the Bandolero area, which is c.10 km south-west of Moa and south of río Cabañas, 20°39'N 74°55'W), where a pair was reported nesting in 1941 (see Lamb 1957); Bandolero area, where a nesting pair and a subadult were observed in April 1948 (Dennis 1948; also Lamb 1957) and another pair was observed in 1956 (Lamb 1957); "near Moa", 1954, with four pairs in 1956 (see Lamb 1957); headwaters of the río Calentura (c.20°32'N 74°59'W: read from ICGC 1978), July 1956 (Lamb 1957); Nuevo Mundo (c.15 km south of Moa), 1978 (see Garrido 1985); headwaters of the río Jaguaní (c.20°28'N 74°56'W: read from ICGC 1978), 1965 (Lamb 1957); between ríos Moa and Punta Gorda (20°37'N 74°51'W), where two pairs were present between March and June 1956 (Lamb 1957); La Melba (c.20°26'N 74°49'W: read from ICGC 1978), 1970 (Alayón and Garrido 1991); Jaguaní Forest Reserve (c.20°24'N 74°43'W: read from ICGC 1978), 1973 (see Alayón and Garrido 1991); Macanibar (untraced but south of Taco Bay, 20°31'N 74°40'W), between May and June 1985 (Alayón and Garrido 1991);

Guantánamo San Luis de la Cabeza, untraced (Barbour 1923); Yateras (a municipality at 20°12'N 75°09'W), May 1972 (see King 1978-1979); mountains of Yateras, undated (Gundlach 1871-1875); Monte Verde (20°19'N 75°00'W), September 1861 and April 1907 (specimens in USNM).

POPULATION The Cuban Ivory-billed Woodpecker has suffered a steady decline, first indicated by Gundlach (1871-1875), who noted the species's increasing rarity from one year to the next. By the second half of the nineteenth century it was already considered very rare and difficult to observe, having disappeared from several localities where it was once reported, although birds were still present in the mountains of Pinar del Río, in the lowlands of Ensenada Cochinos, Matanzas, and in Yateras, Guantánamo (Gundlach 1871-1875, 1876). Barbour (1943) considered the species to be "virtually extinct" and Garrido and García Montaña (1975) referred to it as "extremely rare" and almost extinct. In the Sierra del Cristal, the last sighting occurred in 1920 (Dennis 1948), searches and enquiries in the area in 1956 obtaining no positive results (Lamb 1957, 1958).

In the Sierra de Moa (the last known refuge for the species), Dennis (1948) heard of a group of six birds in 1941 and himself observed three – including an incubating pair – in April 1948. The species was again recorded in the area in 1954 (one pair) and in 1956 (six pairs), between the watersheds of the río Moa to the west and the río Punta Gorda to the east, along the north coast of north-east Holguín, and in the extreme headwaters of the Calentura and Jaguaní; furthermore, excellent evidence of former nesting (16 nest-holes) was found in 1956 within the Bandolero area south of Moa (Lamb 1957). In the early 1970s the surviving population was estimated at probably fewer than six pairs and certainly no more than eight pairs (King 1978-1979). By around 1980, perhaps based on the foregoing, the population was guessed at "perhaps... a dozen birds" (Short 1982). The last reported observations of the species occurred in the Sierra de Moa in March and April 1986 and April 1987 (Alayón and Garrido 1991) and in March 1988 (see Distribution, Remarks). Thorough searches in 1990 and 1991 in this general area proved unsuccessful (Alayón and Garrido 1991; M. Lammertink *in litt.* 1991); however, fresh barking activity and 2-3 second long glimpses in the Sierra de Moa in April 1991 could well have been by or of the species (J. W. McNeely *in litt.* 1991, McNeely 1992).

The Ivory-billed Woodpecker is now near extinction, and the most recent expedition in March 1992 failed to find it, although fresh signs of foraging (presumably by this species) in the headwaters of the río Jaguaní ("El Toldo") fostered the view that probably one or two birds still existed between río Piloto and Ojito de Agua, and perhaps in other unstudied areas, such as east of La Melba (McNeely 1992, G. Alayón García *in litt.* 1992). Basically, however, the forests in the Sierra de Moa are too degraded, and the last possible refuge in the area is a narrow corridor between the Cupeyal Reserve and Ojito de Agua and the upper reaches of the río Jaguaní (M. Lammertink *in litt.* 1991, 1992). Even if some birds survive, there seems to be no real chance that the species can be saved; the precise date of its extinction, whether passed or impending, is unlikely ever to be determined.

ECOLOGY The Cuban Ivory-billed Woodpecker inhabited forested areas in both lowlands and mountains; however, extensive deforestation in the former restricted the species to the mountains where the best-preserved forests of pines *Pinus cubensis* were present (Bond 1956b, Lamb 1957). In the north-eastern sierras of Holguín and Guantánamo and in the Sierra de los Organos, Pinar del Río, the species inhabited the pine forests, but its former occurrence in the lowlands, e.g. in Matanzas, indicates that it once also locally inhabited dense tropical hardwood forest (Lamb 1957, 1958). Dead trees, especially pines, are of great importance in providing both food and nesting cavities (see below). In the Sierra de Moa, Ivory-bills have been reported in pine, mixed pine with hardwood, and hardwood forests (Lamb 1957, King 1978-1979, Alayón and Garrido 1991). It must be assumed that the Cuban populations existed at similar low densities to those in the U.S.A. (see Remarks 4), itself a biological factor that rendered the species notably extinction-prone.

Cuban Ivory-bills feed mainly on the wood-boring larvae of insects, notably: beetles of the families Cerambicidae, Buprestidae, Scolytidae, Elateridae and Eucmenidae, taken from under the bark of old or rotting trees (Dennis 1948, Lamb 1957, Alayón and Garrido 1991, Jackson 1991); but seasonally the species's diet includes a considerable percentage of seeds and fruits (Alayón and Garrido 1991), this also being true of the former North American population (see, e.g., Cottam and Knappen 1939). By 1956, the Ivory-bills appeared to have adapted to the changing habitat of lumbered areas, where old pines were still standing and food seemed fairly plentiful due to the many fires occurring in the pine forests and the subsequent infestation of the dead trees by beetle larvae (Lamb 1957). Data on food and feeding in the North American population are in Tanner (1942) and Short (1982).

The nesting season extends from March to June, most breeding activity being detected in April; nest-excavation mainly occurs in old and dying pines (Dennis 1948, Lamb 1957, Short and Horne 1986, Alayón and Garrido 1991) but palms appear also to have been utilized (see García undated). Data on breeding in the North American population are in Tanner (1942) and Short (1982).

THREATS Habitat destruction appears to have been the main cause for the Ivory-billed Woodpecker's decline in Cuba (Gundlach 1876, Alayón and Garrido 1991). The species's former haunts have been transformed by clearance for lumber, sugar plantations and charcoal-burning, the most serious depletion of the forests occurring during the first half of the twentieth century (Dennis 1948, Lamb 1957). In the Sierra de Moa, most of the forests inhabited by Ivory-bills were owned by the Bethlehem Cuba Iron Mines Company, but despite its declared sympathy for the plight of the species (Lamb 1957) forests were cleared rapidly right up to the time the company left the area (L. L. Short *in litt.* 1992). Fires also accompanied lumber activities in the

Sierra de Moa in 1948 (Dennis 1948). The last untouched pinewoods in the Sierra de Moa were perhaps those reported as being logged in 1956, the work due to be completed by 1960 (Lamb 1957). Human persecution has also threatened the Ivory-bills: according to Dennis (1948) and Alayón and Garrido (1991), specimens were nailed to the huts of local people to counter witchcraft ("maleficios"), or birds were shot for no other reason than enjoying their beauty in the hand or for adornment (Gundlach 1871-1875, 1876, García undated). In March 1992, McNeely (1992) found unauthorized chromium prospecting only 6 km east of Ojito de Agua (one of the last areas from which the species was reported), and although immediate intervention stopped further activity, the disturbance already caused was presumably irreparable, since the main camp was only a few hundred metres from the previous year's roost or nest cavity.

MEASURES TAKEN Forest reservations have been established within the species's last known range, namely Cupeyal and Jaguaní Natural Reserves. After 1986 the Cuban government closed an area with a radius of 10 km around Ojito de Agua to logging activities (Short and Horne 1986, Alayón and Garrido 1991). Between 1985 and 1992 no less than 17 expeditions to the last known areas were made in order to assess the status of the species (Alayón and Garrido 1991, M. Lammertink *in litt.* 1991, J. W. McNeely verbally 1992).

MEASURES PROPOSED Lamb (1957) suggested the protection of the Bandolero area which in 1956 contained excellent evidence of the species's former nesting (see Population), although it had already been lumbered; the presence of lateritic soil (i.e. not arable) meant that prospective farmers would not suffer; and the suggested area (see the map in Lamb 1957, 1958) supported a good growth of pine which in time would be able to support the Ivory-billed Woodpecker again. Amongst the proposals presented by Short and Horne (1986) after visiting the Ivory-billed Woodpecker area at Ojito de Agua are: a special guard to monitor the birds; exclusion of all but scientists and wildlife management personnel from the area; limited girdling to kill pines along the trails and thereby provide more feeding trees; further searches to locate other possible birds. The 1992 Ivory-billed Woodpecker expedition team (four Cubans, one Chilean and one North American) favoured the last territory being visited as much as possible (contrary to previous recommendations) because ("even with official protection") the area cannot be defended against mining, logging and foraging unless concerned individuals are present (McNeely 1992). The río Yarey valley needs fuller investigation; and satellite images of the region (Jaguaní basin, above La Melba) are needed in order to clarify the status of the remaining forests (McNeely 1992).

REMARKS (1) The differences between the two forms appear minute (see Short 1982). (2) The remark in Ehrlich *et al.* (1992) about reintroduction is best attributed to an understandable despair, as it bears no scrutiny in the face of political and, more emphatically, biological reality. In the latter regard, it is worth noting that Short (1982) considered that competitive interaction with Pileated Woodpeckers *Dryocopus pileatus* played a part in the Ivory-bill's demise once the latter's primary habitat began to disappear in the U.S.A., and he was "pessimistic about chances for establishing a viable Ivorybill population in the presence of Pileated Woodpeckers", hence believing "Cuba, where no *Dryocopus* is found, the main hope for preservation of the Ivorybill". (3) This sighting was not accepted by G. Alayón and O. H. Garrido, who consider the last certain record to have been in late 1987 (L. L. Short *in litt.* 1992). However, birds were glimpsed in April 1991 (McNeely 1992; see Population). (4) The densities at which the Ivory-bill (the second largest of Neotropical woodpeckers after Imperial *Campephilus imperialis*: see relevant account), lived in North America were judged by Tanner (1942), but these seem to have been misinterpreted in various texts: thus Aldrich (1980) referred to suitable habitat being capable of holding one pair per 6-8 km^2, Shull (1985) indicated one pair per 6-17 km^2, and Ehrlich *et al.* (1992) suggested that one pair needed "up to 2,000 acres" (= 8 km^2), although in fact Tanner (1942) considered the species's *maximum* abundance to have been one pair per six and a quarter square miles (= 16 km^2, as given in King 1978-1979), and most of his other data indicated a far lower density even than this.

MOUSTACHED WOODCREEPER *Xiphocolaptes falcirostris* V[9]

This bark-gleaning insectivore occupies a wide range in interior north-eastern Brazil but has become extremely local through the widespread and continuing clearance of its semi-deciduous woodland habitat. A reserve has been proposed in Minas Gerais for one subspecies, but another is needed, perhaps in Maranhão.

DISTRIBUTION The Moustached Woodcreeper (see Remarks 1) is endemic to central and interior north-east Brazil, being known from a scatter of localities in the states of Maranhão, Piauí, Ceará, Paraíba, Pernambuco, Bahia, Minas Gerais (race *franciscanus*) and Goiás.

Maranhão Records are from Cocos (south of Codó), June 1924 (Hellmayr 1929a; hence presumably the reference to "the banks of the middle Itapicuru" in Snethlage 1927-1928: 509); "As Mangueras, Flores" (= Timon), i.e. opposite Teresina (Piauí), May 1926 (four specimens in AMNH), also near Teresina but inside Maranhão, June 1926 (specimen in AMNH); Fazenda Leão, Presidente Dutra (BR 226 at km 48), recently (F. C. Novaes *in litt.* 1987: specimen in MPEG); São Francisco (now São Francisco do Maranhão), July 1925 (Hellmayr 1929a); Sambaíba, recently (J. M. C. da Silva *in litt.* 1988).

Piauí Specimen records are from Amarração (now Luís Correia), May/June 1906 (F. C. Novaes *in litt.* 1987: specimen in MPEG); Ibiapaba, on the upper rio Poti, at the foot of the Serra de Ibiapaba, January 1925 (Hellmayr 1929a); São Gonçalinho (now Amarante), August 1903 (Reiser 1926, Hellmayr 1929a); Belo Horizonte (or Teresina), May and June 1926 (two specimens in AMNH); Parnaguá, 300 m, June 1927 (specimen in AMNH); Corrente, 450 m, May and June 1927 (two specimens in AMNH); and the untraced locality Os Umbús (in the vicinity of Lagoa de Parnaguá), May 1903 (Reiser 1926, Hellmayr 1929a). One bird was observed in Manoel Emídio (Fazenda Bom Recreio) in July 1987 (P. Roth *in litt.* 1987; also Roth 1987c, 1989b). Hellmayr (1929a), for unstated reasons, suggested Oeiras as the type-locality, not indicated in the original description (von Spix 1824).

Ceará Specimens are from Ipu, May 1910 (in MNRJ; also Snethlage 1926); Açudinho, Baturité, August 1958 (Pinto and de Camargo 1961; in MZUSP); Juá (near Iguatu), August and September 1913 (Hellmayr 1929a); and Juazeiro do Norte, 550 m, December 1926 (in AMNH). One sight record is from Guaramiranga, in the Serra de Baturité, March 1987 (R. Otoch *in litt.* 1987).

Paraíba Two females from Curema (Coremas), June 1957 (Pinto and de Camargo 1961) represent the only record.

Pernambuco A female from Fazenda Campos Bons (c.38 km north of Floresta), June 1971 (in MZUSP), is the only record.

Bahia Specimen records are from the rio Preto at Santa Rita de Cássia (in one case specifically Maracujá, c.10°52'S 44°32'W), May and August 1927 and April 1958 (Pinto and de Camargo 1961; specimens in AMNH, LACM, LSUMZ), and the untraced localities Cantinho (possibly Coutinho), Os Mosquins (Moquins) and Fazenda da Porteira on the rio Preto, April 1903 (Reiser 1926); and Fazenda Formoso, Coribe, where nine birds were taken in May and June 1988 (da Silva 1989) (see Remarks 2).

Minas Gerais Records are from Brejo-Januária (not Brejo S. Januário as in Sick 1985; now Brejo do Amparo: de Andrade *et al.* 1986), the holotype of *X. franciscanus* (see Remarks 3), June 1926 (Gonzaga 1989); and Fazenda Olhos d'Água, Itacarambi, July and October 1985, November 1986 (M. A. de Andrade *in litt.* 1986, de Andrade *et al.* 1988, specimens in CGTM), and October 1987, when eight birds were collected (da Silva 1989).

Goiás The only record is one undated specimen in MNRJ obtained by R. Pfrimer in Posse, north-east of the state (not "southern Goiás" as in Teixeira *et al.* 1989, nor "south of Goiás" as in Teixeira 1990; see Remarks 4).

POPULATION Although distributed over a relatively large area, the Moustached Woodcreeper is evidently quite local and its overall numbers have certainly declined as a result of habitat destruction. In Maranhão the species is "distributed only locally and always seems to be uncommon where it occurs" (D. C. Oren *in litt.* 1988). Likewise, a single recent record of the species in the Serra de Baturité, Ceará, seems to indicate that it is not common there either (R. Otoch *in litt.* 1987). In the southern portion of its range the species remained known for over 50 years only from the type-specimen of the race *franciscanus*, although it was observed several times at the type-locality by the original collector (Snethlage 1927), but following its rediscovery, when another specimen was obtained and several other birds were observed (de Andrade *et al.* 1986, 1988), the bird was found to be quite common at both Itacarambi and Coribe, surprisingly so for a woodcreeper that size; a census was performed at Coribe, but the data have not yet been analysed (J. M. C. da Silva *in litt.* 1988).

ECOLOGY The Moustached Woodcreeper has been recorded from semi-deciduous forests (Oren 1988, J. M. C. da Silva *in litt.* 1988, Teixeira 1990), wooded caatinga (Teixeira 1990), and riverine woods (Reiser 1926, Sick 1985). In the region of Manoel Emídio, Piauí, it occurs in the taller forests of depressions ("baixões"), usually wetter than neighbouring areas (P. Roth *in litt.* 1987). Typical trees of semi-deciduous forests in Minas Gerais are amburana *Bursera leptophloeos*, aroeira *Astronium urundeuva*, barrigudas *Chorisia venticosa* and *Cavanillesia arborea*, umbuzeiro *Spondias tuberosa*, jatobá *Hymenaea martiana* and pau-preto *Schinopsis* sp. (de Andrade *et al.* 1986, 1988). Snethlage (1927-1928) considered the species one of monsoon forest, growing in small patches in gorges amidst the hills of Ceará and Piauí, and of dry palm woodland, which he encountered only on the middle Itapicuru in Maranhão (evidently at Cocos: see Distribution). Birds were observed in the forest interior, in groups of 3-6 individuals; sometimes singles were found; other members of the family found in the same areas were Planalto and Scaled Woodcreepers *Dendrocolaptes platyrostris* and *Lepidocolaptes squamatus*; birds forage also on the ground, taking insect larvae, ants, beetles and snails (de Andrade *et al.* 1986, 1988; M. A. de Andrade *in litt.* 1986). Birds collected in Coribe, May/June 1988, were in post-breeding condition (J. M. C. da Silva *in litt.* 1988), and, while the gonads of nine of 11 specimens in AMNH from May and June were not enlarged (two in May were slightly), and those of a specimen in LSUMZ from Santa Rita, August 1927, were not enlarged, two males from Itacarambi, October 1985 and November 1986, had testes enlarged, the former showing a brood patch (specimens in CGTM), and a male in AMNH from December had testes fairly enlarged. A female from near Fazenda da Porteira had a gut parasitic infestation (Reiser 1926).

THREATS Extensive destruction of semi-deciduous forests for charcoal, timber, cultivation and cattle-farming, which has taken place throughout the species's range, is a general concern (de Andrade *et al.* 1986, 1988, R. B. Cavalcanti *in litt.* 1987, G. T. de Mattos *in litt.* 1987, R. Otoch *in litt.* 1987, P. Roth *in litt.* 1987, D. C. Oren *in litt.* 1988, J. M. C. da Silva *in litt.* 1988). In Coribe, Bahia, the species was recorded from an area which "is being converted to irrigation lands with wholesale deforestation, so the record is likely to be of historic value soon" (D. C. Oren *in litt.* 1988). The obvious trend is that the already isolated forests where the species persists, with a distinct population in each, will be greatly reduced in number and size by the end of the century, and no reserve has been created so far to protect this habitat (J. M. C. da Silva *in litt.* 1988, verbally 1991).

MEASURES TAKEN Both *Xiphocolaptes falcirostris* and *X. franciscanus* are protected under Brazilian law (Bernardes *et al.* 1990).

MEASURES PROPOSED The creation of a protected area in the southern portion of the species's range, in the Januária region in Minas Gerais (see Remarks 3), which has been under consideration by governmental organizations (de Andrade *et al.* 1988) and by the non-governmental Fundação Pró-Natureza (J. M. C. da Silva *in litt.* 1988), is an urgent need (G. T. de Mattos *in litt.* 1987, J. M. C. da Silva *in litt.* 1988). However, as regulation of reserves is often poorly implemented, a programme of environmental awareness is also needed and should be directed at landowners, local communities and schools (de Andrade *et al.* 1988). A reserve in the north of the species's range, also embracing a population of Pectoral Antwren *Herpsilochmus pectoralis* (see relevant account), is highly desirable, and in this regard it is worth noting that these two birds were singled out as characteristic of palm woodland found in the middle Itapicuru, Maranhão (Snethlage 1927-1928).

REMARKS (1) Pinto (1952, 1978) suggested that Snethlage's Woodcreeper *X. franciscanus* could be a subspecies of White-throated Woodcreeper *X. albicollis*. Despite this, *X. franciscanus* has been kept separate (e.g. Pinto 1978, Meyer de Schauensee 1966, 1982, Sick 1985, Teixeira and Luigi 1989, Sibley and Monroe 1990), but there now seems to be little doubt that it should rather be treated as a race of *X. falcirostris* (D. C. Oren *in litt.* 1988, da Silva 1988, 1989, Teixeira *et al.* 1989, Teixeira 1990, Willis and Oniki 1991, LPG). (2) *Xiphocolaptes albicollis villadenovae* (*sic*) (Lima 1920), from Villa Nova (now Senhor do Bonfim; see Pinto 1945) in Bahia was considered a synonym of *X. falcirostris* (Cory and Hellmayr 1925, Pinto 1938), but this view has not persisted (Pinto and de Camargo 1961, Pinto 1978). (3) Brejo-Januária is also the type-locality of the threatened Minas Gerais Tyrannulet (see relevant account) and the Januária region is also important for the isolated race of the Caatinga Black-tyrant *Knipolegus (aterrimus) franciscanus*, which deserves consideration as a full species (da Silva 1989). Any reserve must seek to encompass populations of these birds also. (4) Teixeira and Luigi (1989) referred to this specimen as from the "vague locality of Posse, Goiás (probably upper Tocantins [river])", but there seems to be no doubt about this precise location, which was indeed among the places visited by R. Pfrimer in Goiás (see da Silva 1989: 22-23).

ROYAL CINCLODES *Cinclodes aricomae* E[2]

This rare furnariid is confined to a few humid patches of Polylepis *woodland in the Andes of south-east Peru and, at least previously, adjacent Bolivia; its habitat is scarce and has suffered extensive (recent) clearance for firewood and lack of regeneration through burning.*

DISTRIBUTION The Royal Cinclodes (see Remarks 1) is known from four areas in southern Peru and adjacent Bolivia, but may now be gone from the two southern localities (see Threats).

Peru The species is known from Cuzco, Apurímac and Puno departments, and from the evidence below it was apparently once distributed along the entire Cordillera Real, presumably restricted to humid *Polylepis* forest, a habitat now largely destroyed (Fjeldså 1987).

Cuzco A single bird was seen at 3,600 m in the Peñas canyon, near the Ollantaytambo–Quillabamba road, north of Ollantaytambo, Cordillera Vilcanota, in 1982 (Fjeldså *et al.* 1987); later in 1982 the species was photographed in a *Polylepis* woodland at 4,250 m, c.1.5-3.5 km south-west of Abra Málaga (c.13°08'S 72°19'W), a short distance from the Peñas canyon, and in December 1983 a pair in breeding condition was collected in the same wood, with an additional pair observed (Fjeldså *et al.* 1987). There are subsequent reports from the Abra Málaga wood at least up to 1988 (TAP; B. P. Walker *in litt.* 1988).

Apurímac In November 1989 it was discovered at 4,100-4,550 m in remnant patches of mature *Polylepis* woodland in the mountains south-east of Abancay (Fjeldså 1991): ten patches of habitat, each 1-4 ha in size, were found in the Cerro Runtococha and Cerro Morococha region at 13°40-41'S 72°46-47'W, with c.30 patches at 13°41-46'S 72°35-42'W, one of them being a cluster covering c.75 ha on Cerro Balcón at 13°42'S 72°42'W, the rest being only 1-4 ha each (J. Fjeldså *in litt.* 1989; coordinates read from IGM 1978a with the patches indicated by J. Fjeldså).

Puno The type-specimen was collected near the Aricoma Pass (the pass is at 4,815 m), at c.14°17'S 69°47'W, on 17 May 1931 (Carriker 1932; elevation and coordinates from Stephens and Traylor 1983). While surveys in the 1980s failed to find any tracts of habitat (see Threats), the southern parts of the Carabaya mountains were not investigated (Fjeldså 1987), and what is probably suitable *Polylepis* habitat has been seen there from the air (TAP).

Bolivia A specimen in BMNH collected by C. Buckley in 1876, overlooked for many years, is from Tilo Tilo (2,135 m, although the bird was undoubtedly taken higher), at c.16°10'S 68°00'W, Yungas province, La Paz department, Bolivia (Fjeldså *et al.* 1987; elevation and coordinates from Paynter *et al.* 1975).

POPULATION Judging from the paucity of museum specimens and field observations, the species was never common anywhere during this century. It was found to occur at low density in Apurímac in November 1989, with an estimated population of c.40 pairs in the existing (fragmented) 100-200 ha of prime habitat, each pair occupying a territory of 1.5-2 ha (J. Fjeldså *in litt.* 1990). At Abra Málaga one to two pairs have been reported annually since the rediscovery of the species in 1982 (TAP, Fjeldså *et al.* 1987, B. P. Walker *in litt.* 1988). Some of the unexplored small patches of apparently suitable habitat elsewhere in the Vilcanota mountains and the larger woodlands in the Carabaya mountains presumably hold the species, which may also occur in other remote parts of the Cordillera Real (NK). However, the species's habitat is very patchy and scarce (see Threats), so even at best the total population must be very small.

ECOLOGY The species's 1-2 km^2 area of semi-humid woodland at Abra Málaga is mainly *Polylepis* (2-8 m tall, growing in small dense patches rarely covering more than 100 m^2) with a few *Gynoxys* trees, on a steep, north-facing slope with many rocky places, especially under the trees; the ground is covered with coarse grasses *Luzula* and thick layers of moss (Fjeldså *et al.*

1987). For much of the year the mountains are blanketed in clouds; it rains every few days (or for periods of many days), and snow several centimetres deep regularly briefly covers the ground, especially during the dry season (June–September) (Fjeldså *et al.* 1987). In Apurímac the *Polylepis incana* and *P. subsericans* woodlands at 4,100-4,600 m are exceptionally dense and lush (with strong regrowth along most edges and in clearings), most trees being 10-15 m tall with trunks 40-100 cm thick and the larger ones heavily laden with mosses and vines, notably *Salpichroa* (Solanaceae), which forms curtains 5-10 m high hanging from the canopy; the forest floor is shady, with thick litter and moss and an undergrowth of nitrophilous plants in patches (most other *Polylepis* woods, in contrast, represent mosaic habitat with broken canopies, small gnarled trees, and minimal regeneration because of grazing and burning of grass) (Fjeldså 1991).

The bird observed for nearly 30 minutes in the upper part of Peñas canyon hopped on large, lichen-encrusted and moss-covered rocks in a boggy area bordered by shrubs and small trees, probing and flaking off large pieces of moss and earth, presumably to uncover prey items; several Bar-winged Cinclodes *Cinclodes fuscus* in close proximity were foraging in the adjacent bog rather than on the rocks (Fjeldså *et al.* 1987). One individual was observed poking at the mossy bases of *Polylepis* trees at the edge of the Abra Málaga wood in 1985, and a pair was seen probing the bases of many *Polylepis* trees and adjacent, often rocky ground in 1988 (B. P. Walker verbally 1987, *in litt.* 1988). In prime habitat in Apurímac, November 1989, birds vigorously turned over the mossy forest floor with their beaks, typically digging a 500 cm^2 patch down to 5 cm, tossing the moss up to 1 m away and leaving large mounds of it as if pigs had rummaged through the wood; in some places they turned over litter (*Polylepis* bark and leaves) and excavated the decaying wood of fallen trunks; a pair would probably thus work their entire territory of 1-2 ha in a year or two (J. Fjeldså *in litt.* 1990). Presumably only mature (i.e. more or less closed-canopied) woodland provides enough shade for the regeneration of the moss (J. Fjeldså *in litt.* 1990). During a snowstorm a bird was seen digging through the snow with its long beak (Fjeldså 1991). The stomach of a bird collected in Apurímac contained two 1.5 cm long weevils, possibly of the subfamily Otiorrhynchinae (ZMUC label data).

The pair collected in Cuzco in early December 1983 had enlarged gonads, but showed no trace of a brood-patch, so they were presumably at the start of the breeding season (Fjeldså *et al.* 1987), as appeared to be the case with a non-moulting female with somewhat enlarged ovae, taken in Apurímac in late November 1989 (specimen in ZMUC). The closely related Stout-billed Cinclodes *C. excelsior* builds its nest at the end of a tunnel dug in a bank by the bird itself (Graves and Arango 1988).

THREATS The *Polylepis* woodlands near Abra Málaga have been halved in extent during the last 10 years (B. P. Walker *per* J. Fjeldså verbally 1990). During a search for the species in Puno department (including the Aricoma Pass) and La Paz department, Bolivia, in 1987, none of its habitat could be found, and local inhabitants in the Aricoma region confirmed that no *Polylepis* remains there (Fjeldså 1987). The widespread burning of bunch-grass to promote its fresh growth often includes stands growing between *Polylepis* trees, and is believed to be an important factor preventing *Polylepis* from regenerating (Fjeldså 1987). In Apurímac the woodlands are also dwindling owing to widespread cutting for use as firewood, not by the few local inhabitants, who restrict their use to dead branches, but by passing caravans heading for the market in Abancay (J. Fjeldså verbally 1990).

MEASURES TAKEN A poster printed on waterproof paper, showing mature *Polylepis* woodland with some of its characteristic birds, and calling for protection of this habitat, was made by J. Fjeldså in 1990; in January 1991 a batch of these was given to the Asociación Conservación del Selva Sur (a nature conservation group based in Cuzco, Peru) for distribution in target areas; education of local families and placing of posters began in August 1991 around *Polylepis* woodland areas in Apurímac and in the southern Cordillera Vilcabamba (J. Fjeldså verbally 1991).

MEASURES PROPOSED This bird merits further searches: at Abra Málaga the species is rare, even in the woodland where it has been found, so it may occur in similar woodlands in the same region even though investigators have so far failed to detect it (Fjeldså 1987); moreover, the southern Carabaya mountains in Puno department should be investigated (see Distribution). High priority should be given to the mapping and inventory of remaining stands of *Polylepis* (Fjeldså 1987), especially in Cordillera Vilcanota, with special attention going to a large humid tract reported to exist c.50 km north-east of Inquisivi, La Paz, Bolivia (J. Fjeldså verbally 1991). Reforestation with *Polylepis* around existing woods could be initiated, and the local people employed in such efforts: "air-layering" (in which a cut is made in a small branch and kept open with a match-stick or other object, a small polythene bag with moist soil is attached around it, and after two or three weeks roots have formed, and the branch can be cut and planted) has proved the fastest way of propagating *Polylepis* trees (J. Brandbyge verbally 1991). The Tunari National Park in Cochabamba, Bolivia, clearly demonstrates how *Polylepis* regenerates and invades grassland when the latter is kept free of grazing and burning (Fjeldså 1987). Further suggestions are in Measures Proposed under White-cheeked Cotinga *Zaratornis stresemanni*.

REMARKS (1) Although originally described as a species *Upucerthia aricomae* (Carriker 1932), Bond (1945) regarded it as a race of the Stout-billed Cinclodes *Cinclodes excelsior*, a morphologically and to some extent behaviourally similar species of bushy páramo habitats in Colombia and Ecuador (Fjeldså *et al.* 1987). This treatment has been followed by subsequent authors, but the finding of important colour-pattern differences not previously noted, as well as the habitat of the geographically very isolated *aricomae* (Fjeldså *et al.* 1987, Fjeldså and Krabbe 1990), suggest that the latter is perhaps better regarded as a full species. As the main part of *aricomae*'s range appears to have been in Cordillera Real, the vernacular name Royal Cinclodes is invented here. Vaurie (1971, 1980) considered *excelsior* (with *aricomae*) to belong to the genus *Geositta*, a view strongly resisted by observers familiar with the birds in the field (e.g. F. Vuilleumier in Vaurie 1980: 334, Fjeldså *et al.* 1987).

The *Polylepis* woodlands near Abra Málaga and in Apurímac support a rich variety of *Polylepis*-adapted birds (Parker and O'Neill 1980, J. Fjeldså *in litt.* 1990). In addition to several wide-ranging but generally local species, e.g. Tawny Tit-spinetail *Leptasthenura yanacensis*, Line-fronted Canastero *Asthenes urubambensis* (not known from the Apurímac woods), Stripe-headed Antpitta *Grallaria andicola*, Giant Conebill *Oreomanes fraseri* and Thick-billed Siskin *Carduelis crassirostris* (Parker and O'Neill 1980, Fjeldså 1987), they are inhabited by two species known from only a few scattered localities in Peru: Ash-breasted Tit-tyrant *Anairetes alpinus* and White-browed Tit-spinetail *Leptasthenura xenothorax* (see relevant accounts). The threatened White-tailed Shrike-tyrant *Agriornis andicola* may also occur sympatrically with these species at some localities (e.g. in south-central Cuzco), although it has different habitat requirements (see relevant account).

WHITE-BELLIED CINCLODES *Cinclodes palliatus* V[9]

This furnariid is very rare, with a small range above 4,400 m in Huancavelica, Junín and immediately adjacent Lima department, Peru, and appears to have very specific habitat requirements, being found on only a few of the many bogs in this region. It may be in the process of becoming extinct for natural reasons, but this could be greatly accelerated if mining were to commence in these areas.

DISTRIBUTION The White-bellied Cinclodes is confined to the western Andes of central Peru, where it is found at high altitutes from western Junín and eastern Lima departments 250 km south to central Huancavelica department. It is known from c.21 specimens and a number of sightings at the following localities (north to south, with coordinates, unless otherwise stated, from Stephens and Traylor 1983):

Junín Montaña de Vítoc (untraced, but apparently not far from [south of] Hacienda Pacchapata at c.11°17'S 75°16'W), where the type-specimen was collected prior to 1844 (von Tschudi 1844-1846: see Remarks 1); Moyobamba (untraced: see Remarks 2) (Taczanowski 1884-1886); Cerro Ninarupa (c.11°23'S 76°22'W; presumably at the base at c.4,400 m), c.5 km north-west of Marcapomacocha, where three specimens were collected in c.1873 (Taczanowski 1874, 1884-1886: see Population, Remarks 3); 161 km by road from Lima on the Canta–Huarón road (11°01-21'S 76°23-27'W), along which at "4,000 m" five specimens (in MHNJP) were collected in May and June 1948 (T. S. Schulenberg *in litt.* 1989; see Remarks 4); Pampa Pucacocha (11°33'S 76°16'W: coordinates and elevation read from IGM 1973), at 4,400 m on the south-eastern base of Nevada Raujunte, where four birds (in LSUMZ and ZMUC) were taken in July and August 1983, with sightings in November 1983 (NK) (the specimen labels give the altitudes as 4,550 and 4,600 m and misspell the locality as "Pampa Puracocha"); Galera (11°38'S 76°12'W), at 4,800 m at the eastern end of the railroad tunnel through the peak of the western Andes, where a specimen (in BMNH) was collected in February 1899 (Chubb 1906);

Lima just west of Pampa Pucacocha (see above), near the border of Junín department, where two birds were seen in July 1985 (D. F. Stotz *in litt.* 1989); La Viuda (11°18'S 76°31'W), where at 4,480 m a specimen (in MNHN: catalogue entry in MHNJP) was taken in April 1952 (T. S. Schulenberg *in litt.* 1989: see Remarks 5);

Huancavelica near (presumably 10-15 km south-west of) Yauli (c.12°47'S 74°49'W), where at 4,940 m a bird (in BMNH) was taken in July 1947; above (presumably 1.5 km south-west of) Talahuara (at 4,875 m by the glacier on Cerro Ojuijasa), and at Talahuara itself (c.13°04'S 75°04'W), whence come three specimens (in AMNH, BMNH) taken in October and November 1937 (Morrison 1939a); Lira (13°11'S 75°13'W), where a straggling specimen (in BMNH) was taken at 4,460 m during a snowstorm in November 1937 (Morrison 1939a).

The known distribution of this species thus ranges between c.11° and 13°S; although apparently suitable habitat exists in Cordillera Blanca, Ancash department, there are no records of the species there, but it may be found to occur northwards to south-east Ancash and south-west Huánuco departments; however, south of central Huancavelica its habitat is scarce and widely scattered (NK), and a large southward range extension would seem unlikely.

POPULATION The White-bellied Cinclodes is a rare and local bird (Morrison 1939a, Parker *et al.* 1982, Fjeldså and Krabbe 1990), being absent from large areas of apparently suitable habitat (NK). Recent records are of a single individual near Marcapomacocha in August 1983 (B. P. Walker verbally 1983), with five there in July 1985 (B. M. Whitney *in litt.* 1991). Three pairs were recorded on Pampa Pucacocha in July and August 1983 (D. F. Stotz verbally 1983, NK), during which time five birds were collected; however, by November 1983 there were again two pairs on the bog (NK), suggesting recolonization. Immediately west of Pampa Pucacocha, and just inside Lima department, two birds were seen in July 1985 (D. F. Stotz *in litt.* 1989).

Although there may be as much as 10,000 km^2 of habitat, the species appears to breed at only a few sites (NK), and the total population may be very small and declining.

ECOLOGY The White-bellied Cinclodes inhabits boggy terrain from c.4,400 m to the snowline at c.5,000 m. Pampa Pucacocha is a mineral-rich, well-watered cushion-plant bog (most cushions being of *Distichia*), situated below a glacier, with rocky outcrops and stony slopes nearby (NK). The habitat between Marcapomacocha and Ninarupa is similar, but some 5 km east of the nearest glacier (Cordillera de la Viuda). Talahuara is immediately adjacent to a glacier, but near Lira, where the species has been recorded just once and does not normally occur, there being no glacier in the vicinity (Morrison 1939a). While its habitat requirements may be much more specific than in other species of *Cinclodes*, it is also possible that it is in the process of becoming extinct for natural reasons (NK). It is found alone or in pairs, but occasionally three or four birds will gather while calling, in what may be a territorial dispute but which looks more like a social event (NK). The species forages on the bogs, probing into the matted vegetation in search of worms, insects and small frogs (Fjeldså and Krabbe 1990, LSUMZ label data). When alarmed it will fly to a rocky outcrop or hide under rocks (NK). It sleeps and, like most other species of *Cinclodes*, probably also nests in crevices under rocks (NK). Six birds collected in July, August, October and November had undeveloped gonads, while one collected in November had somewhat enlarged testes (specimens in BMNH, LSUMZ and ZMUC). The snow-white underparts of this species render it very conspicuous; while this may enable birds to find each other at very low densities, it probably also makes them more vulnerable to predators such as the Aplomado Falcon *Falco femoralis* (NK).

THREATS Owing to the very high altitude at which the species occurs, its habitat is little disturbed by man. If, however, it breeds at only a few mineral-rich bogs, and these sites were to become centres of mining activity, then it could be severely affected by pollution or any other disturbances.

MEASURES TAKEN None is known.

MEASURES PROPOSED A survey of the species's range should be undertaken in order to decide whether any conservation efforts are required, and a more detailed assessment of its population dynamics and ecological requirements is necessary if this bird is to be saved in the long term.

REMARKS (1) Although no locality was given with the type-description of the species (de Tschudi 1844), it was clearly stated by von Tschudi (1844-1846) that the only specimen he collected was taken at Montaña de Vítoc, where he observed Black-chested Buzzard-eagle *Geranoaetus melanoleucus* at Hacienda Pacchapata: this hacienda is not mentioned under the present species, which may have been taken elsewhere in the region.

(2) A specimen in the Raimondi collection was reported by Taczanowski (1884-1886) to have been taken at Moyobamba (an unlabelled specimen in MHNJP is presumably either this or one of Jelski's: M. A. Plenge *in litt.* 1989): this cannot be the Moyobamba in San Martín, as is often assumed (Peters 1951, Meyer de Schauensee 1966), as none of its habitat exists in that department (NK). Some bird specimens (presumably taken by Raimondi) were labelled "Moyobamba, 11-12°S. Lat." and "Mountain of Moyobamba, 11-12°S. Lat." (Vaurie 1972). J. T. Zimmer (in Vaurie 1972) suggested that the Moyobamba of Raimondi may apply to either of two localities by that name in Ayacucho department, at 13°42'S 73°57'W and 14°20'S 73°58'W respectively, and Vaurie (1972) suggested that the same seemed to be the case with the Moyobamba and Mountain of Moyobamba at "11-12°S. Lat.". It seems a distinct possibility, however, that a fourth Moyobamba exists between 11° and 12°S, as this is the region where most specimens of the White-bellied Cinclodes have been procured. The inclusion of Cajamarca (but not San Martín) in its range (Vaurie 1980) is probably based on this Raimondi specimen.

(3) Jelski collected three specimens in Junín department between 1870 and 1873 (Taczanowski 1874), and Taczanowski (1884-1886) gave Ninarupa as the only locality where Jelski collected the species. One of Jelski's specimens, now in BMNH, is labelled "Central Peru" only (Sclater 1890), the other two specimens possibly being in Warsaw Museum (although they may have been destroyed during the Second World War), as most of Jelski's specimens were deposited there (Taczanowski 1874): however, some of Jelski's specimens remained in Raimondi's collection in Lima (e.g. the now lost type of Grey-bellied Comet *Taphrolesbia griseiventris*: see Taczanowski 1883 and Plenge 1979), and one or both of two unlabelled specimens of *Cinclodes palliatus* in MHNJP may be Jelski's (NK).

(4) The elevation of 4,000 m, given on the label of one of the specimens collected in Junín along the road between Canta and Huarón, is apparently erroneous, as no point in Junín along that road is below 4,400 m (according to IGM 1975).

(5) La Viuda is given as 11°18'S 76°31'W by Stephens and Traylor (1983); however, IGM (1975) places it at 11°21'S 76°26'W, adjacent to the Cordillera de la Viuda, IGM (1978) giving Paso de la Viuda (probably erroneously) as the pass on the border of Lima and Junín departments on the Santa Cruz de Andamarca–Huarón road, although this pass is at c.4,600 m, at c.11°13'S 76°29'W (IGM 1975) and not near the Cordillera de la Viuda.

WHITE-BROWED TIT-SPINETAIL *Leptasthenura xenothorax* E[2]

This furnariid is restricted to a few small patches of humid Polylepis *woodland at 3,700-4,550 m in the departments of Cuzco and Apurímac, south-central Peru: these woodlands are being cleared for firewood, and intervention is urgently required.*

DISTRIBUTION The White-browed Tit-spinetail (see Remarks) is known from a very small area in Cuzco and Apurímac departments, south-central Peru. Coordinates below, unless otherwise stated, are from Stephens and Traylor (1983).

Cuzco The type-specimen (in USNM) was collected in 1915 at 4,267 m (Chapman 1921a,b) above Torontoy (c.13°10'S 72°30'W: presumably the wood situated on Nevada Veronica, c.6 km north-east of Torontoy; B. P. Walker *in litt.* 1989) on the right bank of the río Urubamba, c.12 km upstream from Machu Picchu. This specimen was the only record of the species until August 1974, when it was found nearby in the small *Polylepis–Gynoxys* woodlands far above the treeline (which is at 3,900 m), in the vicinity of Abra Málaga (13°08'S 72°19'W) at: Canchaillo (13°07'S 72°22'W), 10 km north-west of Abra Málaga (elevation 4,315 m on recent tourist maps); and 1.5-3.5 km south-west of Abra Málaga (c.30 km east-north-east of the type-locality) at 3,900 to 4,300 m (Parker and O'Neill 1980). These woodlands were visited by several ornithologists in the 1970s and 1980s, and 12 additional specimens were collected (in AMNH, FMNH, LSUMZ and ZMUC), in three adjacent woods: c.10 km north-north-east of Abra Málaga (B. P. Walker *in litt.* 1988); c.35 km south-east of Abra Málaga, in the valley ending at Urubamba town (c.5 km east-north-east of the town), at an altitude of 3,800-4,500 m (Fjeldså 1987); and Yanacocha lakes (13°17'S 71°59'W), at the head of Huayocari valley, on the slope of Nevada Chicon, at 3,700-3,800 m (B. P. Walker *in litt.* 1989).

Apurímac In November 1989, the White-browed Tit-spinetail was found at 4,100-4,550 m in remnant patches of mature *Polylepis* woodlands in the mountains south-east of Abancay (Fjeldså 1991). Ten patches of habitat, each 1-4 ha, were found in the Cerro Runtacocha–Cerro Morococha region at 13°40-41'S 72°46'W, with c.30 patches at 13°41-46'S 72°35-42'W, one of them being a cluster covering c.75 ha on Cerro Balcón at 13°42'S 72°42'W, the rest covering only 1-4 ha each: this species was found in five of the 10 *Polylepis* woods investigated (J. Fjeldså *in litt.* 1989, 1990: coordinates read from IGM 1978a with the patches indicated by J. Fjeldså).

This species presumably occurs in any patch of *Polylepis* between or near the known localities, but the size and location of these patches has yet to be defined. Searches for the bird in similar woods along the "Inca trail" on the left bank of the río Urubamba have proved fruitless (B. P. Walker verbally 1986), and early collectors failed to find it in the Aricoma Pass, Puno department, a locality now almost devoid of *Polylepis* (Fjeldså 1987). It is absent from other known *Polylepis* woods in Puno (Fjeldså 1987), but may occur in unexplored parts of Cordillera Carabaya, Cuzco (NK), where much habitat has been noted from the air (TAP).

POPULATION In 1987 the population of the wood 1.5-3.5 km south-west of Abra Málaga was estimated at 15 families or c.50 birds, and of the Chaiñapuerto wood at 10 families or c.35 birds (both woods apparently at carrying capacity) (Fjeldså 1987); in 1989 the wood at Yanacocha was estimated to hold about 20 families or c.70 birds (B. P. Walker *in litt.* 1989); however, only one family of three birds was recorded in the Canchaillo wood (Parker and O'Neill 1980), with no numbers estimated for the wood north-north-east of Abra Málaga. Other small woodlands in the Vilcanota mountains may also be found to have dense populations (NK).

In contrast, this bird occurs at very low densities in the woodlands south-east of Abancay, Apurímac department, with a maximum one to two pairs in each, and in November 1989 only 25 pairs were estimated to occur in this entire region (J. Fjeldså *in litt.* 1990).

ECOLOGY All observations of the White-browed Tit-spinetail are from *Polylepis* and *Polylepis–Gynoxys*, save one possibly resident family in *Escallonia* below a *Polylepis* wood (TAP). The woodland at Chaiñapuerto is in a semi-humid glacial cirque valley with *Polylepis weberbaueri* forest at the valley bottom, continuing up ravines and crevices on the surrounding rocky slopes: in the lower part of the forest some of these trees are 0.5 m in diameter, and in certain areas there is *Gynoxys*, *Escallonia* and *Vallea* (Fjeldså 1987). Owing to cutting and grazing, the forest has some open parts with grassland, patches of *Berberis* scrub and dense *Brachyotum*, *Vaccinium* and composite brush, with a variety of herbs; in the upper parts, some coarse grass, moss, and mats of *Muehlenbeckia volcanica* fringe the talus (Fjeldså 1987). The wood 1.5-3.5 km south-west of Abra Málaga is semi-humid, comprising mainly (unidentified) *Polylepis*, with some well-sized trees mixed with some *Gynoxys*, and growing on a steep, north-facing, rocky slope: in several places the rocks are covered with thick layers of moss (Parker and O'Neill 1980, Fjeldså 1987, NK). The Canchaillo and Yanacocha woods are *Polylepis* mixed with *Gynoxys* (Parker and O'Neill 1980, B. P. Walker *in litt.* 1989), with another composed mainly of *Polylepis* (B. P. Walker verbally 1986). In Apurímac, birds were found in four patches of mature woodland, and in one with smaller trees and fewer vines: the mature woodlands (*Polylepis incana* and *P. subsericans*) were exceptionally dense and lush, most trees being 10-15 m tall with trunks 40-100 cm in diameter; dense regrowth existed along most edges and in clearings, and the larger trees were heavily laden with mosses and vines, the most important vine being *Salpichroa* (Solanaceae), which formed curtains 5-10 m high, hanging from the canopy and adorned with yellow tubular flowers (J. Fjeldså *in litt.* 1990). During snow-storms, birds often descend to the lowest parts of the woods, but some have also been seen remaining high (Fjeldså 1991).

The White-browed Tit-spinetail moves in pairs or family groups of three or four, and forages along thicker branches and trunks, picking insects from bark, moss, lichens, twigs, dense masses of hanging dead branches and dead leaves, only rarely probing clusters of green leaves (Parker and O'Neill 1980, Fjeldså and Krabbe 1990, J. Fjeldså *in litt.* 1990, Fjeldså 1991). It is somewhat more deliberate, and spends less time in the thinnest branches and twigs than the near-threatened (longer-billed) Tawny Tit-spinetail *Leptasthenura yanacensis* (Fjeldså and Krabbe 1990), which occurs at the same localities (Parker and O'Neill 1980, Fjeldså 1987): in some *Polylepis* woods in Cuzco and Puno, the White-browed Tit-spinetail is replaced by the Andean Tit-spinetail *L. andicola* (Fjeldså and Krabbe 1990).

The White-browed Tit-spinetails observed at Abra Málaga were very aggressive, constantly chasing conspecifics (Fjeldså and Krabbe 1990), and although this could be the nature of the species, it may be unnaturally frequent as a result of the slowly shrinking habitat (NK). Like most congeners, both sexes are very vocal (Fjeldså and Krabbe 1990), and are easily attracted to playback of their song (NK). No nests have been found, but other tit-spinetails use the abandoned nests of canasteros *Asthenes*, thornbirds *Phacellodomus*, etc., or place their nest in a hole in a bank, tree, rock-crevice or similar cavity (Fjeldså and Krabbe 1990). No definite proof of the breeding season exists, all specimens with data on gonads having been collected in July and December, and all reported inactive: one December specimen, however, was in heavy (probably post-breeding) moult (Fjeldså and Krabbe 1990).

THREATS The major threat is habitat destruction, caused by cutting for firewood and a lack of regeneration due to grazing and burning of grass between the trees. At Abra Málaga, the woods are the only source of fuel for the local community of 3-5 families, and trees or large branches are being cut regularly (J. Fjeldså *in litt.* 1990, NK). The Chaiñapuerto wood is subject to less cutting, as the woodland immediately below it is more easily accessible; however, *Polylepis* is collected daily by a few shepherds and, in contrast to the Abra Málaga woods (where only cattle graze), is being grazed by sheep and goats (Fjeldså 1987). The woodlands in Apurímac, though less important for the present species, are also dwindling (see Threats under Royal Cinclodes *Cinclodes aricomae*).

MEASURES TAKEN So far only the Apurímac woodlands have received attention (see account of Royal Cinclodes).

MEASURES PROPOSED There is an urgent need for the woodlands between the known sites, and in Cordillera Carabaya, to be mapped and surveyed for the presence of this species (Fjeldså *et al.* 1987). Reforestation with *Polylepis* should be initiated around the existing woods (for fastest propagation methods see Measures Proposed under Royal Cinclodes). Above Urubamba town the replacement of native trees with *Eucalyptus* should be prevented, not just for the sake of the survival of the endemic *Polylepis* fauna and flora, but also because of the devastating impact of *Eucalyptus* on soil quality (whereas *Polylepis* forms a very rich soil) (Fjeldså 1987). Nevertheless, planting of *Eucalyptus* on the *Dodonea*-covered slopes lower down the valley should not be opposed, as this may lessen the local exploitation of *Polylepis* (Fjeldså 1987). Various woods in Cuzco and the woodlands in Apurímac department are also inhabited by two other threatened *Polylepis*-adapted bird species: the Ash-breasted Tit-tyrant *Anairetes alpinus* and Royal Cinclodes (see relevant accounts), and any conservation initiatives in these areas should take into consideration the requirements of all three species (the threatened White-tailed Shrike-tyrant *Agriornis andicola* may also occur sympatrically, although apparently with different habitat requirements).

REMARKS On the basis of one specimen, Vaurie (1971, 1980) synonymized *L. xenothorax* with the nominate subspecies of Rusty-crowned Tit-spinetail *L. pileata pileata*, a view that has been accepted elsewhere (e.g. Morony *et al.* 1975). However, the 12 additional specimens obtained since Vaurie's revision, as well as field observations, strongly suggest that this bird is a valid species (Parker and O'Neill 1980, J. P. O'Neill *in litt.* 1986, Fjeldså and Krabbe 1990).

CHESTNUT-THROATED SPINETAIL *Synallaxis cherriei* K[12]

This little-known spinetail occurs in undergrowth in humid forest between 200 and 1,070 m at a handful of localities scattered across Brazil (six), Colombia (one), Ecuador (one) and Peru (four), and may be suffering from habitat loss. Whilst at one site it was only found in bamboo thickets inside at tall forest, which may partly explain its patchy distribution, competition from congeners also evidently plays a part.

DISTRIBUTION The Chestnut-throated Spinetail occurs disjunctly in six areas of Brazil (nominate *cherriei*), with equally disjunct populations of the race *napoensis* (including the synonymized *saturata* of Carriker 1934) scattered through the foothills of the Andes in south-eastern Colombia, Ecuador and Peru. Given the breadth of this range, however, it is inevitable that many more localities will eventually be discovered.

Brazil Localities for the species are as follows:

Rondônia Barão de Melgaço, rio Ji-paraná, where the type-specimen was collected in March 1914 (Cherrie 1916, Gyldenstolpe 1930), this locality (previously part of Mato Grosso) being indicated as at 300 m (Paynter and Traylor 1991);

Mato Grosso Alto Floresta, where a population was found in October 1989 (TAP); rio do Cágado, 250 m, 15°20'S 59°25'W, August 1987 and/or January 1988 (Willis and Oniki 1990, whence also coordinates);

Pará 52 km south-south-west of Altamira on the east bank of the lower rio Xingu, 3°39'S 52°22'W, August/September 1986 (Graves and Zusi 1990, whence coordinates); in and adjacent to the Serra dos Carajás, namely at "Manganês" in the Serra Norte; and also at Gorotire, 7°40'S 51°15'W, near São Felix do Xingu, mid-1980s (Oren and da Silva 1987, whence coordinates).

Colombia Two birds taken on 6 and 10 October 1967 at 300 m at Guascayaco (untraced), Putumayo (specimens in FMNH; identification supported by T. S. Schulenberg and D. E. Willard *in litt.* 1992), i.e. near the border with Ecuador, represent the first record for the country.

Ecuador The species has been collected at 900 m near the río Napo, Napo province (Gyldenstolpe 1930; see Remarks 1). A pair was found (evidently close to this earlier locality) about 2 km south-east of Archidona, Napo, at 0°57'S 77°52'W, at 690 m, in September 1989 (tape-recording by P. Coopmans identified by TAP), with sightings in July 1991 (P. Greenfield and R. S. Ridgely verbally 1991).

Peru Records are from (*San Martín*) Moyobamba, 6°03'S 76°58'W (coordinates from Stephens and Traylor 1983), in July 1912 (Cory and Hellmayr 1925 and specimen in FMNH) and again in October 1933, at 1,070 m (four specimens in ANSP), and río Seco, c.50 km west of Moyobamba at c.900 m (specimens in AMNH); and (*Ayacucho*) the mouth of the río Mantaro on the Cuzco border, at 470 m, where one was taken in August 1975 at 470 m (specimen in AMNH whose label gives 12°17'S 73°44'W), and Hacienda Luisiana, at 600 m, on the left bank of the río Apurímac, where three were taken in August 1965 (Terborgh and Weske 1969; specimens in AMNH, one of whose labels gives 12°39'S 73°44'W).

POPULATION In Peru the species has been considered "local and uncommon" (Parker *et al.* 1982). At Alta Floresta in Brazil at least four pairs held territories along c.400 m of trail through a c.50 ha bamboo thicket inside forest (TAP), which indicates that the species may be locally fairly common in its patchily distributed habitat. At Gorotire Oren and da Silva (1987) found that the Kayapó Indians had a name for the species (*purucheng*) derived from its voice, which suggests that it could not have been rare in the area.

ECOLOGY The Chestnut-throated Spinetail has been recorded at elevations ranging from 200 to 1,070 m, and its selection of habitat appears at least partly to be influenced by sympatric members of its genus, although at one site it exhibits characteristics of a bamboo specialist. In southern Peru it occurs in the understorey of mature humid forest (AMNH label data), and its habitat throughout its Peruvian range is judged to be humid terra firme forest (Parker *et al.* 1982; see Remarks 2); at Hacienda Luisiana it was the only one of four congeners to be limited to high forest (Terborgh and Weske 1969). The elevational range of the species averages higher than its close relative the Ruddy Spinetail *Synallaxis rutilans* (Carriker 1934), which occurs up to 500 m in Colombia (Hilty and Brown 1986) but only below 200 m in Ecuador (R. S. Ridgely *in litt.* 1991), so little competition may be inferred in this part of its range (but see below for Pará). In Ecuador near Archidona the Chestnut-throated Spinetail's habitat consists of the undergrowth of dense humid secondary woodland (R. S. Ridgely *in litt.* 1991, NK), which it shares with the much commoner Dusky Spinetail *S. moesta* and to some degree with the abundant Dark-breasted Spinetail *S. albigularis* (NK). In south-eastern Pará, Brazil, the species was recorded in maturing second growth and forest edge, but not in the interior of high rainforest (from which the Ruddy Spinetail presumably excluded it): thus at Carajás it was in "relatively well-lighted edge zones of the rain forest" covering a manganese deposit, and at Gorotire in the understorey of 25-40 year old second-growth forest with a canopy at about 8 m and at c.200-300 m altitude (Oren and da Silva 1987). At Alta Floresta, Brazil, Chestnut-throated Spinetails were found in an extensive (c.50 ha) area of tall bamboo (*Guadua* sp.) inside evergreen forest about 30 m tall, but were not in extensive bamboo thickets at forest edges bordering roads and large clearings, suggesting that only interior-forest thickets are suitable for them, a habitat they shared with a variety of other patchily distributed bamboo specialists, including Peruvian Recurvebill *Simoxenops ucalayae*, Crested Foliage-gleaner *Automolus dorsalis*, Striated Antbird *Drymophila devillei* (*subochracea*), Manu Antbird *Cercomacra manu*, Dusky-tailed Flatbill *Ramphotrigon fuscicauda*, and Black-and-white Tody-flycatcher *Todirostrum capitale* (TAP). During a return visit to the area in August 1991, three of four pairs were located within 50 m of where they had been found in October 1989, and territories were estimated to be less than 0.5 ha in size; the Ruddy Spinetail was found to be uncommon in adjacent forest with dense undergrowth, and one pair of *rutilans* was heard within earshot of a pair of *cherriei* (TAP).

At Alta Floresta the species was encountered in widely separated pairs that foraged in dense, dark tangles of dead bamboo stalks and fallen tree branches on or within 1 m of the ground, the birds probing and gleaning debris trapped in the tangles, especially dead leaves, and occasionally hopping on the ground and flipping leaves to uncover prey (TAP). In Pará birds were also observed foraging in the understorey, investigating suspended dead leaves near the ground, gleaning the upper and lower surfaces of green leaves usually within 3 m of the ground but up to 8 m on occasion; food included diptera, spiders and lepidoptera larvae (Oren and da Silva 1987).

The only information on breeding season appears to be that adults were accompanied by immatures in May and June in Pará (Oren and da Silva 1987).

THREATS In Peru forests on rich soils along the base of the Andes are being destroyed at an alarming rate, e.g. in the upper drainages of the ríos Apurímac and Huallaga (TAP). Deforestation is also proceeding rapidly in the Amazonian foothill zone in eastern Ecuador (TAP), and presumably in adjacent parts of Colombia. If the Chestnut-throated Spinetail prefers extensive areas of structurally similar habitat such as the bamboo near Alta Floresta, it would be vulnerable to the massive clearance of tall forest that is occurring throughout eastern Pará and northern Mato Grosso, Brazil. Its habitat at "Manganês" in the Serra dos Carajás has now been destroyed by mining operations (Oren and da Silva 1987).

MEASURES TAKEN None is known.

MEASURES PROPOSED At least two areas, each holding populations of substantial size, need to be identified and protected against habitat loss: one such perhaps might be around Alta Floresta, Brazil, and the other in Peru. However, with fuller knowledge of the species's voice there is greater opportunity to investigate its status in all the countries from which it has been recorded, and possibly thus it will prove somewhat more widespread than was previously apparent.

REMARKS (1) A sight record of the species from the lower río Aguarico, Napo province, near the Colombia–Brazil border (Hilty and Brown 1986) is now recognized to have been in error (R. S. Ridgely *in litt.* 1991). (2) Vaurie (1980) lumped the habitat of this species, White-bellied Spinetail *Synallaxis propinqua* and Red-shouldered Spinetail *Gyalophylax hellmayri* as "thick undergrowth in forest and savanna", but given the knowledge now of *propinqua* as a bird of river islands (R. S. Ridgely *in litt.* 1991) this whole assessment can be ascribed to guesswork.

APURIMAC SPINETAIL *Synallaxis courseni* I[6]

The Apurímac Spinetail is confined to the slopes of a single mountain massif in Apurímac department, Peru, where it is a common inhabitant of tangled understorey and shrubbery at 2,450-3,500 m.

DISTRIBUTION The Apurímac Spinetail is known from some 20 specimens (AMNH, FMNH, LSMUZ, MHNJP, ZMUC), all collected immediately north of Abancay, Apurímac department, south-central Peru, at elevations ranging from 2,450 m (Blake 1971) to 3,500 m (Fjeldså 1987). Specimens were collected at Bosque Ampay, a *Podocarpus hermsianus* wood on the south slope of Nevada Ampay, and on the north-slope of a ridge (Cerro Turronmocco) projecting eastwards from the nevada (Blake 1971, Fjeldså and Krabbe 1986, Fjeldså 1987). On the south slope the species has also been found below the *Podocarpus* wood (Fjeldså and Krabbe 1986), as well as in the shrubbery stretching eastwards to where the road from Abancay to Cuzco leaves the valley of Abancay (Fjeldså 1987).

POPULATION Fjeldså and Krabbe (1986) estimated the total population at 250-300 pairs, by extrapolation. With their discovery in 1987 of an additional population on the north slope of Cerro Turronmocco – where, however, the species was far less common than on the south slope (Fjeldså 1987) – the total population may be estimated at 300-400 pairs (NK).

ECOLOGY The Apurímac Spinetail inhabits dense undergrowth, vines, bamboo and tangles in *Podocarpus hermsianus* wood, thickets of composites and other shrubs along small streams below the wood (Fjeldså and Krabbe 1986) and shrubbery on the more shaded areas of the same slope further east, as well as dense shrubbery in the cloud-forest on the north slope of Cerro Turronmocco (Fjeldså 1987), apparently without very specific habitat requirements (Fjeldså and Krabbe 1986), and tolerating somewhat drier conditions than the closely related Azara's and Elegant Spinetails *S. azarae* and *S. elegantior* (Fjeldså and Krabbe 1990). Usually found in pairs or family groups, it forages low, occasionally up to 3 m, within the dense tangles (Fjeldså and Krabbe 1986). Six specimens had insect remains in their stomachs (ZMUC). This fairly vocal species responds to recordings of the indistinguishable song of Azara's Spinetail *S. azarae*, with which it may be conspecific (Fjeldså and Krabbe 1990). The only indications of breeding season are a juvenile taken on 16 November 1989, a male with enlarged gonads and a female with slightly enlarged gonads, collected on 9 December, and an immature collected on 18 March (specimens in ZMUC). Birds collected in May and June had undeveloped gonads (specimens in FMNH, LSUMZ).

THREATS None is known, but the extremely small range of this species renders it vulnerable.

MEASURES TAKEN A local initiative ensured the protection of the *Podocarpus* wood above Abancay, as Santuario Nacional del Ampay, as of August 1987 (P. Hocking *in litt.* 1988). Although most of the spinetails live outside the *Podocarpus* wood, there appear to be enough living within the wood to secure the survival of the species (NK).

MEASURES PROPOSED The native shrubbery and cloud-forest adjacent to the *Podocarpus* wood should not be removed to plant *Eucalyptus* or create pasture, if a large population of the Apurímac Spinetail and other yet unnamed endemic forms, such as a *Taphrospilus* hummingbird, a subspecies of Violet-throated Starfrontlet *Coeligena violifer* and a subspecies of Andean Tapaculo *Scytalopus magellanicus*, that live in this area (Fjeldså and Krabbe 1990) are to be secured. This could be achieved by leaving cloud-forest gallery between the pastures, and by leaving corridors of shrubbery through any *Eucalyptus* woods that are planted.

REMARKS Blake (1971) placed *courseni* between *S. subpudica* and *S. brachyura*, believing them to comprise a superspecies. Vaurie (1980) believed the nearest relatives of *courseni* to be *S. hypospodia*, *infuscata* and *brachyura*. Fjeldså and Krabbe (1986) pointed out that the vocalizations of *courseni*, *elegantior* and *azarae* are indistinguishable and very different from those of *brachyura*, and they believed these former three taxa form a superspecies or are even members of the same species (Fjeldså and Krabbe 1990), a view also held by personnel at LSUMZ (T. S. Schulenberg verbally 1984). The least subtle difference between these forms is the number of tail-feathers, 10 in *courseni* and usually in *elegantior*, eight in the geographically intervening *azarae* (Fjeldså and Krabbe 1986). However M. K. Poulsen and others (*in litt.* 1989) found individuals of *S. elegantior ochracea* in southern Ecuador to have variably 10 or 8 rectrices, and TAP has found the same to be the case in central Peruvian birds. Remsen *et al.* (1988) presented evidence that *Synallaxis superciliosa* of Bolivia and Argentina is also best treated as a subspecies of *S. azarae*. As the distinguishing features of *courseni* thus fall entirely within the variation of the enlarged species *S. azarae*, it may well be preferable to treat it as a subspecies of that form. An additional taxon *S. frontalis* of south-eastern Brazil is closely related to *S. azarae* (Parker *et al.* 1989).

PLAIN SPINETAIL *Synallaxis infuscata* V/R[10]

This small insectivore of forest thickets in north-east Brazil is confined by habitat destruction to just a few very small reserves, although a new race may prove to exist in Maranhão.

DISTRIBUTION The Plain Spinetail (see Remarks 1) is endemic to north-eastern Brazil in the states of Pernambuco and Alagoas. However, five specimens (in LSUMZ) from Maranhão require further evaluation (see Remarks 2).

Pernambuco Although specimens were collected at Palmares in March 1927 (two in AMNH) and at Engenho Pirajá, Ipojuca, in January 1944 (in MNRJ), birds were recognized as distinct (see Remarks 1) only later on the basis of two specimens obtained in September 1950 at Usina Nossa Senhora do Carmo, Vitória de Santo Antão (Pinto 1950b). Other localities where birds have been recorded are: Lagoa do Zumbi, Cabo, April 1961 (specimen in MNRJ); UFPE Ecological Station at Serra (or Brejo) dos Cavalos, Caruaru, 1974-1979; and Saltinho Biological Reserve, Rio Formoso, July 1980 (specimens in MNRJ and UFPE; A. G. M. Coelho *in litt.* 1986).

Alagoas Records are from São Miguel (north bank of the rio São Miguel, opposite Roteiro), where a bird was collected in October 1951; Fazenda Canoas on the rio Pratagí, c.12 km north of Maceió, municipality of Rio Largo, where another specimen was taken in October 1951 (Pinto 1954a); Engenho Riachão, Quebrangulo, where two specimens (in MZUSP and LACM) were taken in April 1957 and birds were seen in the 1980s (Studer 1985, B. C. Forrester *in litt.* 1992); and Pedra ("Serra") Branca, Murici, 500 m, where a bird was collected in January 1986 (specimen in MNRJ) and others were seen in October 1990 (also at Usina Utinga Leão, 5 km from Murici) (J. F. Pacheco *in litt.* 1991) and in April 1992 (also near the junction of BR101 and BR104) (M. Pearman *in litt.* 1992).

POPULATION This species has been considered locally common, or at least not rare (A. G. M. Coelho *in litt.* 1986, D. M. Teixeira *in litt.* 1987, J. Vielliard *in litt.* 1986), but owing to the small size of most of the reserves where it survives overall numbers are likely to be low.

ECOLOGY Very little is known about this species. Birds have been found in patches of Atlantic Forest suffering various degrees of disturbance (Pinto 1950b, 1954a, A. G. M. Coelho *in litt.* 1986, D. M. Teixeira *in litt.* 1987); observations in April 1992 were in second growth in a recently burnt area at forest edge (Murici), and in a coffee plantation mixed with second growth near a remnant forest patch (BR101/104 junction) (M. Pearman *in litt.* 1992). Singles or solitary pairs forage very near the ground in dense tangles and thickets at the edge of forest and in secondary growth, probing in clusters of dead leaves and perch-gleaning from vegetation; the species does not appear to be associated with bamboo (B. M. Whitney *in litt.* 1991).

THREATS Although not rare, the Plain Spinetail is very local and forest-dependent (J. Vielliard *in litt.* 1987, J. F. Pacheco verbally 1991), and even if apparently not immediately threatened, it requires monitoring (D. M. Teixeira *in litt.* 1987). The deforestation throughout its range has been massive (e.g. Teixeira 1986), so that the species is now restricted to a few forest reserves (see Distribution), and even these are not totally secure (A. G. M. Coelho *in litt.* 1986).

MEASURES TAKEN The species is protected under Brazilian law (Bernardes *et al.* 1990). Efforts for the preservation of the forests in the Serra das Guaribas at Quebrangulo (Studer 1985) resulted in the creation in December 1989 of the 4,500 ha Pedra Talhada Biological Reserve (LPG). The occurrence of the species in the 450 ha UFPE Ecological Station and the 500 ha Saltinho Biological Reserve may give it some additional protection.

MEASURES PROPOSED Surveys of the species in the field are needed to assess its conservation status more accurately. The conservation of the Pedra Branca forests at Murici is a self-evident imperative, this being apparently the largest remaining continuous forest area in extreme north-east Brazil (Teixeira 1987) and holding several other threatened birds (see Remarks under Alagoas Foliage-gleaner *Philydor novaesi*).

REMARKS (1) The Plain Spinetail was originally described as a subspecies of the Rufous-capped Spinetail *Synallaxis ruficapilla*, and has been so treated by some subsequent authors (Pinto 1950b, 1954a, 1978, Meyer de Schauensee 1982, Sick 1985), but the view that "they are quite distinct species" on the basis of morphological features (Vaurie 1980) is certainly supported also by their striking differences in voice and their disjunct ranges (LPG; also B. M. Whitney *in litt.* 1991). (2) Five specimens of a *Synallaxis* (in LSUMZ) were collected at Coroatá, Fazenda do Caximbo, Maranhão, in September 1972; with some points of difference (probably subspecific) they match Vaurie's (1980) description of *infuscata* reasonably well (J. V. Remsen *per* B. M. Whitney *in litt.* 1991), and hence may represent a range extension of *infuscata* well to the west. It is worth noting that Fazenda do Caximbo is also a site for Pectoral Antwren *Herpsilochmus pectoralis* (see relevant account).

HOARY-THROATED SPINETAIL *Synallaxis kollari* V[9]

This rare furnariid is known from just six specimens and one observation along four different rivers in northern Roraima, Brazil, where almost nothing is known of its ecology, and where until two birds were seen in August 1992 the last known record was in 1956.

DISTRIBUTION The Hoary-throated Spinetail is known only from northern Roraima in northernmost Brazil. There are just four records of the species as follows (coordinates from Paynter and Traylor 1991): rio Cotingo (a left-bank affluent of the rio Surumu), a locality mentioned by Vaurie (1980), whence there is apparently a specimen; rio Surumu (a right-bank tributary of the lower rio Tacutu), whence comes a specimen taken in July 1956 (Pinto 1966); Conceição do Maú, on the banks of the rio Tacutu (c.2 km from the Guyana border), where a pair of birds was seen in August 1992 (B. C. Forrester *in litt.* 1992); and Fortaleza de São Joaquim (3°01'N 60°28'W: c.28 km north of Boa Vista on the upper rio Branco), where the type-series of four birds was taken in 1831-1832 (von Pelzeln 1868-1871, Sclater 1874, Cory and Hellmayr 1925).

POPULATION The species is apparently known from just six specimens taken during or before 1956, suggesting that it is unlikely to be very common wherever it occurs. It was not seen in 1988 when Rio Branco Antbirds *Cercomacra carbonaria* were found to be relatively common in this area (the upper rio Branco); historically, it was found in lesser numbers than the antbird (see relevant account). Just two birds (apparently a pair) were seen (after several days of searching) on the rio Tacutu during August 1992 (B. C. Forrester *in litt.* 1992), although this still gives little indication of the population density.

ECOLOGY Nothing has been noted of records prior to August 1992, when a pair of birds were located in seasonally flooded riverine forest with an understorey of dense thickets and vines (B. C. Forrester *in litt.* 1992).

THREATS Forest along the rivers in the range of this spinetail is at present relatively untouched and does not appear to be under much pressure (D. F. Stotz *in litt.* 1988); however, with so little known about its limited distribution or ecological requirements the potential exists for threats to take a toll before they are recognized.

MEASURES TAKEN None is known.

MEASURES PROPOSED The priority for this species is to discover the extent of its current distribution, determine its ecological requirements and implement suitable protective measures: such initiatives should be undertaken in conjunction with those outlined for the Rio Branco Antbird.

BLACKISH-HEADED SPINETAIL *Synallaxis tithys* E[2]

This uncommon inhabitant of dense undergrowth of evergreen and deciduous forest in south-west Ecuador and immediately adjacent north-west Peru is seriously threatened both by forest clearance and by the grazing and trampling of roaming cattle in the patches that remain.

DISTRIBUTION The Blackish-headed Spinetail has been recorded in Manabí, Guayas, El Oro, and Loja provinces, south-west Ecuador, and in immediately adjacent Tumbes department, north-westernmost Peru, where the few known localities (coordinates from Paynter and Traylor 1977, Stephens and Traylor 1983, or read from IGM 1989) are as follows:

Ecuador (*Manabí*) in the coastal mountains on Cerro San Sebastián, 300-500 m, at c.1°34'S 80°40'W, in Machalilla National Park (sightings in January 1991 and a specimen now in ANSP taken in August 1991: TAP and R. S. Ridgely *in litt.* 1991); (*Guayas*) Daule, near sea level, at 1°50'S 79°56'W (Chapman 1926); Guayaquil, near sea level, at 2°10'S 79°50'W (Chapman 1926); Cordillera de Chongón (Chapman 1926), including the Cerro Blanco reserve, at c.2°09'S 80°03'W (sightings in July 1991: TAP); (*El Oro*) Santa Rosa (c.100 m), at 3°27'S 79°58'W (Chapman 1926); Arenillas Military Reserve, near sea level, at c.3°30'S near the coast (three individuals seen in July 1991: TAP); (*Loja*) just west of Alamor, 4°00'S 80°05'W (two birds seen and one mist-netted in late September 1991: Williams and Tobias 1991); Guainche (975 m), untraced, but between Alamor and Celica at c.4°02'S 80°00'W (Chapman 1926); 10 km by road below Sabanilla, 4°10'S 80°08'W (recorded in early April 1992: M. B. Robbins *in litt.* 1992); Quebrada Hueco Hondo, 500-1,100 m, Tambo Negro, at 4°24'S 79°51'W (Best and Clarke 1991, Best 1992; also two specimens in MECN collected in March 1991).

Peru (*Tumbes*) Lechugal (= Puerto Lechugal), 3°37'S 80°12'W (type-locality: Taczanowski 1877); and El Caucho (400 m), 3°50'S 80°16'W, and Campo Verde (750 m), c.3°51'S 80°12'W, both in Tumbes National Forest (Wiedenfeld *et al.* 1985).

POPULATION There are relatively few recent records of this species and, allowing for seasonal movements, the population is extremely difficult to assess. On Cerro San Sebastián, Machalilla National Park, the Blackish-headed Spinetail was found to be uncommon in January 1991 (TAP), although some 10-15 individuals were encountered there in August 1991, albeit in a narrow elevational zone (R. S. Ridgely *in litt.* 1991). West of Alamor, two birds were seen and an adult trapped in September 1991, although the significance of these dry season records, from a disturbed habitat (see below), is difficult to ascertain (Williams and Tobias 1991). Near Sabanilla, five birds were recorded in one day during early April 1992 (M. B. Robbins *in litt.* 1992), and at Quebrada Hueco Hondo this spinetail was fairly common from 26 January to 7 February 1991 with up to eight recorded in one morning, although it seemed scarcer or was less vocal in early March 1991 (Best 1992, NK), and probably no more than a few hundred birds persist there (NK). In Peru, the species was common at Campo Verde and El Caucho in June and July 1979, when no fewer than 20 specimens were taken (Wiedenfeld *et al.* 1985).

ECOLOGY The following information is compiled from Wiedenfeld *et al.* (1985), Best and Clarke (1991), Williams and Tobias (1991), Best (1992), R. S. Ridgely (*in litt.* 1991) and personal data (NK, TAP). The Blackish-headed Spinetail inhabits dense undergrowth of undisturbed evergreen and deciduous forest from sea level to 1,100 m. On Cerro San Sebastián it occurs only in the narrow transitional zone between the arid and humid forest at 300 to 500 m, and at Campo Verde it was found in evergreen forest at 750 m. However, west of Alamor, birds were seen in a thick hedgerow between areas of pasture and plantation, although this was at the height of the dry season towards the end of September 1991. That seasonal movements take place is suggested by the temporal changes in abundance at various localities, and the occurrence of the species in seemingly suboptimal habitat during the driest part of the dry season near Alamor: however, these movements, and the extent to which the species utilizes different habitats during the year, remain very poorly known. Pairs or less commonly singles or three together frequent dense viny thickets, almost always less than 2-3 m up (although feeding and calling has been noted at 3-4 m), sometimes searching the leaf-litter on the ground: birds may rarely join mixed-species flocks (especially associating with Black-capped Sparrows *Arremon abeillei*). The species feeds on insects: one stomach contained the head of a grasshopper, one the head of a wasp, and another a whole black beetle and other beetle remains. Although apparently calling throughout the year, the increased song activity at Quebrada Hueco Hondo in January and February suggests that breeding takes place in the wet season, and a female taken there on 10 March 1991 had apparently just finished laying.

THREATS The widespread clearance of forest within its range, as well as the widespread destruction of the undergrowth by roaming cattle in the remaining woodlots, has left this spinetail one of the most threatened birds of the region (Best 1992), although recent records (see above) suggest that it can survive, at least seasonally, in heavily degraded habitats (see Threats under Grey-backed Hawk *Leucopternis occidentalis* and Henna-hooded Foliage-gleaner *Hylocryptus erythrocephalus*).

MEASURES TAKEN The species occurs in four protected areas: Machalilla National Park, where only a relatively small population exists; the Cerro Blanco reserve, where the bird is decidedly rare; Arenillas Military Reserve; and in Tumbes National Forest, where a large and important population still survives (see equivalent section under Grey-backed Hawk).

MEASURES PROPOSED Protection from roaming livestock as well as the preservation of the forest should be ensured at Quebrada Hueco Hondo, and in Tumbes National Park, as they seem to be the most important strongholds for the species (Best 1992), although these measures are also needed at the other protected areas mentioned above. The Blackish-headed Spinetail shares habitat with another threatened species, the Henna-hooded Foliage-gleaner (see relevant account), and a list of the localities that currently harbour all the threatened species endemic to this region of south-west Ecuador and north-west Peru is provided in the equivalent section under Grey-backed Hawk.

RUSSET-BELLIED SPINETAIL *Synallaxis zimmeri* V[9]

This bird of scrub and dense undergrowth is confined to a very small area in the Andes of west-central Peru (the Pacific slope of Cordillera Negra in Ancash department), where it is threatened by habitat destruction by cattle-grazing and farm expansion.

DISTRIBUTION The Russet-bellied Spinetail (see Remarks 1) is restricted to the Pacific slope of Cordillera Negra, Ancash department, west-central Peru (coordinates unless otherwise stated from Stephens and Traylor 1983), where the five known localities are as follows: ridge of Cerro Quitacruz and down the east side of Quebrada de río Seco (9°30'S 77°47'W), above Chacchan on the right bank of the Casma valley, Huaráz province (27 km west of Huaráz), where birds were seen (and tape-recorded) at 2,830-2900 m in August 1983 (NK; coordinates read from IGM 1971); near Colcabamba (c.9°35'S 77°49'W), on the left bank of the Casma valley, Huaráz province (c.20 km west of Huaráz), where the type and paratype (in MHNJP) were collected at 2,800-2,900 m in August 1956 (Koepcke 1957); Bosque San Damián, above San Damián (c.9°51'S 77°47'W), on the right bank of the Huarmey valley, Aija province, where three specimens (in AMNH, MNHJP) were collected in September 1956, with four birds (in LSUMZ) taken in April 1980 and sightings in October 1985, all at 1,830-2,300 m (Koepcke 1957, M. Kessler *in litt.* 1988); Bosque de Noquo near Pararin (c.10°02'S 77°39'W: IGM 1971), Recuay province, where six specimens (in MHNJP) were collected at 2,840 m in May 1988; above Cochabamba (untraced, but still within the Cordillera Negra), where a specimen (in MHNJP) was collected at 2,840 m in June 1985; Huiña Pajatun, below San Juan (untraced, but also in the Cordillera Negra), where two specimens (in MHNJP) were collected at 2,640 m in November 1985.

POPULATION The species was found to be fairly common above Chacchan in August 1983, when seven birds were encountered in 1 ha of habitat (NK). At Bosque San Damián it was found to be uncommon in April 1980 when only four birds were collected during two days of survey (Parker *et al.* 1982; specimens in LSUMZ) and in October 1985, when only two birds were seen at 2,100 m during two days at 2,100-2,600 m (M. Kessler *in litt.* 1988). The six specimens taken in Bosque de Noquo in three days suggest that the species is fairly common there (NK).

ECOLOGY The Russet-bellied Spinetail inhabits 1.5-3 m tall densely tangled, thorny *Croton* scrub, with scattered small trees (some evergreen), on the upper slopes and mountain-tops at 1,800-2,900 m, but is also found in low dry shrubby forest (*Barnadesia*, *Myrsinanthes*), and in the thick undergrowth (mainly *Croton* scrub) within small patches of taller (c.15 m) trees around springs: its habitat is only accessible along the many cattle- and mule-trails traversing it (Koepcke 1957, Fjeldså and Krabbe 1990; also M. Kessler *in litt.* 1988, J. W. Eley *in litt.* 1989, and label data on specimens in AMNH, LSUMZ and MHNJP). Alone or (usually) in pairs, this species forages for insects by hopping along small branches and vines and by probing dry clumps of moss (J. W. Eley *in litt.* 1989, Fjeldså and Krabbe 1990). Stomach contents in five specimens were insects, and in one also seeds (MHNJP label data). A rapid chase followed by a fight was observed in August, and appeared to be a territorial dispute (NK). The only breeding information is of two juveniles taken in May, adults from May, June, August and November all having undeveloped gonads (specimens in MHNJP). In April 1980 local inhabitants above San Damián reported that the slopes are normally green in February but that hardly any rain had fallen for two years (J. W. Eley *in litt.* 1989).

THREATS The dense habitat favoured by this species is being continuously opened and degraded by roaming cattle (M. Kessler *in litt.* 1988, J. W. Eley *in litt.* 1989, NK), a problem facing all the species inhabiting undergrowth on the Pacific slope of south-western Ecuador and north-western and west-central Peru (see Threats under Henna-hooded Foliage-gleaner *Hylocryptus* *erythrocephalus*, Blackish-headed Spinetail *Synallaxis tithys* and Grey-headed Antbird *Myrmeciza griseiceps*). A further threat to the Russet-bellied Spinetail is the encroachment of cultivated fields on this extremely restricted habitat (NK: see Remarks 2).

MEASURES TAKEN None is known.

MEASURES PROPOSED Detailed mapping of the Russet-bellied Spinetail's remaining habitat should be carried out (see Remarks 2), and measures taken to ensure that enough is protected to sustain viable populations of the bird.

REMARKS (1) On the basis of coloration Vaurie (1980) grouped the Russet-bellied Spinetail with Ruddy *S. rutilans*, Chestnut-throated *S. cherriei*, Rufous *S. unirufa*, Black-throated *S. castanea* and Rusty-headed Spinetails *S. fuscorufa*. Vocally and distributionally, however, it more closely resembles the Necklaced Spinetail *S. stictothorax* (NK). (2) On the IGM (1971) map, symbols denoting "matorral" are used at the known sites for the species: these symbols cover some nine patches totalling c.150 km^2 between 9°30' and 10°00'S on the Pacific slope of Cordillera Negra. It is not certain whether the lack of these symbols on adjacent maps to the north and south denotes absence of this habitat there, or whether (as seems to be the case) they were left out for other reasons.

AUSTRAL CANASTERO *Asthenes anthoides* K[12]

This locally distributed furnariid inhabits diverse hillside shrubbery interspersed with mature grassland in Patagonian Argentina and adjacent Chile, a habitat that has been drastically altered for over a century by grazing sheep.

DISTRIBUTION The Austral Canastero (see Remarks 1) breeds from sea level to 1,500 m, from Neuquén, Argentina, and Concepción, Chile, south to Tierra del Fuego and Isla de los Estados, with some birds apparently being partly migratory, occurring rarely as far north as Valparaíso, Chile, in winter (see Remarks 2). Unless otherwise stated, the following localities are those summarized by Cory and Hellmayr (1925), Hellmayr (1932), Olrog (1948), Johnson (1967) and Humphrey *et al.* (1970), and coordinates unless otherwise stated are from OG (1967), Humphrey *et al.* (1970) and Paynter (1985):

Argentina (*Buenos Aires*) Rosas, at 35°58'S 58°56'W (two specimens, one only labelled "Buenos Aires", in MACN: Zotta 1936); (*Neuquén*) Copahue, 3,000 m, at 37°49'S 71°07'W (one seen in January 1990: record and coordinates from M. Babarskas *in litt.* 1992); Sierra Pilpil, 1,500 m, near Lago Nahuel Haupí; 11 km east of Bariloche, 760 m, near Lago Nahuel Haupí, Bariloche being at 41°09'S 71°18'W (also sightings of two c.3 km east of Bariloche in December 1981: D. F. Stotz *in litt.* 1989); (*Chubut*) El Hoyo (= Hoyo de Epuyén), at 42°04'S 71°30'W (two specimens in LSUMZ collected in May 1967 and June 1969); Valle del Lago Blanco, at 45°54'S 71°15'W; (*Santa Cruz*) arroyo Eke (= río Ecker), at 47°04'S 70°45'W, May 1898 (specimen in FMNH), Estancia Killikaike Norte, at 51°34'S 69°28'W, April 1899 (specimen in FMNH); Estancia Monte Dinero, at 52°18'S 68°33'W, December 1960 (two specimens in YPM; coordinates from OG 1968); Cabo Vírgenes, near sea level, at 52°19'S 68°21'W (B. M. Whitney *in litt.* 1988);

Isla Grande–Tierra del Fuego Isla de los Estados, at 54°47'S 64°15'W, where the species is known from the penguin rookery (coordinates from Humphrey *et al.* 1970); around Río Grande, 53°47'S 67°42'W, in various areas including some along the highway to Ushuaia, 54°48'S 68°18'W (B. M. Whitney *in litt.* 1991);

Chile (*Valparaiso*) Concón Bajo, at 32°56'S 71°32'W; Concón Alto, at 32°57'S 71°27'W; Lago de Peñuelas, at 33°10'S 71°31'W (two specimens in YPM collected in July 1938 and May 1943); (*Santiago*) near Santiago town, at 33°27'S 70°40'W (two specimens in USNM collected in July 1865, three in MNHNS, one collected in May 1854, two in May 1862); San Bernardo, at 33°36'S 70°43'W; (*Colchagua*) Cauquenes; (*Concepción*) near Coronel, at 37°01'S 73°08'W; (*Bío-Bío*) road from Lincura (36°52'S 72°23'W) to Estero de Pino Hachado, January 1947 (38°40'S 71°01'W, in Cautín) (specimen in MCZ); (*Cautín*) Lonquimai, at c.38°26'S 71°14'W, January 1947 (specimen in MCZ); río Lolen, 1,100 m, Lonquimai valley, at 38°29'S 71°14'W; Laguna Gualletué, 1,160 m, at 38°42'S 71°16'W; Maquegua, Temuco, at 38°46'S 72°39'W (four specimens in BMNH collected in April 1908 and June 1910); Pelal, Temuco, at 38°50'S 72°40'W, June 1910 (two specimens in BMNH); (*Malleco*) Icalma, c.1,300 m, at 38°48'S 71°16'W, January 1959 (three specimens in WFVZ); (*Valdivia*) Valdivia town, at c.39°46'S 72°51'W (two specimens in MNHNS collected 1899, one in September); (*Llanquihue*) río Ñireguao, 850 m, at 45°10'S 72°09'W; (*Aisén*) Coihaique Alto, at 45°29'S 71°36'W; Chile Chico, 230 m, at 46°33'S 71°44'W, January 1961 (specimen in WFVZ); (*Magallanes*) Torres del Paine National Park, c.51°00'S 72°48'W (fair numbers seen in January 1990: P. Gregory *in litt.* 1990); Ultimo Esperanza, at c.51°34'S 72°45'W, April 1897 (specimen in BMNH); Straits of Magellan (presumed type-locality); Bahía Laredo and Cabeza del Mar, at c.52°57'S 70°51'W; Punta Arenas, at 53°09'S 70°55'W (specimen in CM collected in March 1939; also sighting of one in February 1989: P. J. Roberts *in litt.* 1989).

Isla Grande–Tierra del Fuego Ekewern (= Estancia Nueva de Río Oro), at 52°52'S 69°31'W; Estancia Gente Grande, at 53°04'S 70°16'W; road from Cerro MacPhearson to Estancia China

Creek, at 53°03-09'S 69°11'W; Porvenir, at 53°18'S 70°22'W; Bahía Inútil, at 53°30'S 69°39'W; and Estancia Viamonte, sea level, Río Grande, at c.54°03'S 67°18'W.

POPULATION The species appears to be very local and decreasing in numbers. In Chile, Pässler (1922) found it breeding in Concepción in the period 1914–1918, but many years later there was no sign of it there (Johnson 1967); it was reported to be common at Cauquenes in Colchagua during the last century (Reed 1877), but there are no subsequent records from that province; Olrog (1948) found it only at a single locality in Aisén during 1940. However, fair numbers were found in suitable scrubby habitat within Torres del Paine National Park, Magallanes, in January 1990 (P. Gregory *in litt.* 1990). On Isla Grande it was apparently rare at the turn of the century, when Crawshay (1907) only saw a single bird during six months of ornithological fieldwork. Philippi *et al.* (1954) found it quite common at Estancia Nueva de Río Oro and also heard it at another locality on Isla Grande in 1946, but did not find it elsewhere, either in 1946 or during another expedition in 1952. In north-eastern Isla Grande it is reported to be rare, records being of single birds in winter (April, July and September, 1927 and 1930) (Humphrey *et al.* 1970) and none was found there in April 1940 (Olrog 1948). Olrog (1948) found it common at Cabeza del Mar and near Porvenir in 1940-1941; Philippi *et al.* (1954) found none at Porvenir in 1946 although they searched in the same habitat they had found the species in earlier; B. M. Whitney (*in litt.* 1988) found it to be an uncommon breeder south of Porvenir in December 1987; and P. Gregory (*in litt.* 1990) reported fair numbers there in streamside scrub during January 1990. This canastero was apparently locally common near Cabo Vírgenes in January 1988 (B. M. Whitney *in litt.* 1988), and described as truly common within proper habitat (see below) on Isla Grande, such habitat being commonest on the Argentinian side around Río Grande (various areas including some along the highway to Ushuaia), and perhaps less extensive on the Chilean side (B. M. Whitney *in litt.* 1991). The species is not rare near Bariloche (M. I. Christie *per* M. Nores *in litt.* 1989), where D. F. Stotz (*in litt.* 1989) recorded two in December 1981.

ECOLOGY The Austral Canastero inhabits shrub-steppes (i.e. brush-covered slopes and flats), the dominant shrub being the thorny 0.5-1 m tall "calafate" *Berberis cuneata*, and it appears to prefer areas where a fairly diverse shrub association is interspersed with clumps of native *Festuca*-type grass (Pässler 1922, Olrog 1948, Philippi *et al.* 1954, B. M. Whitney *in litt.* 1988, 1991). At Porvenir it was only found in this habitat in 1987, and did not occur in the disturbed shrubby hills where there was significant grazing and but few species of shrubs (B. M. Whitney *in litt.* 1988). At the penguin rookery at Cabo Vírgenes it has also been found in more homogeneous beach vegetation (B. M. Whitney *in litt.* 1988). The statement by Landbeck (1877) that it inhabits open meadows, damp grassland and well-watered hillsides seems to be somewhat misleading, but may possibly suggest that it was once an inhabitant of long-grass prairie but was forced into secondary habitat by the widespread introduction of sheep, which completely changed the Patagonian landscape over 100 years ago (NK).

The Austral Canastero forages mostly on the ground, hopping or creeping along, sometimes crawling into clumps of grass, quickly reemerging, picking food off the ground and stems, occasionally jumping up to snatch a prey-item off a higher stem, and sometimes huddling at the base of a grass clump, picking intently there for several seconds; it may occasionally forage quite out in the open, on sparse vegetation or even bare earth (B. M. Whitney *in litt.* 1988). Recorded food items include insects of various sizes, such as bugs (Hemiptera: Pentatomidae) and beetles (Coleoptera: Chrysomelidae and Carabidae), and insect larvae (Zotta 1936, Humphrey *et al.* 1970, MCZ label data).

Birds sing from an elevated perch, usually near the top of a shrub (B. M. Whitney *in litt.* 1988), and the nest is placed in a bush (Pässler 1922, Philippi *et al.* 1954). Birds with active gonads have been taken in September (Humphrey *et al.* 1970), in late December and early January (Olrog 1948), and birds apparently feeding young were seen in mid-January (B. M. Whitney *in litt.* 1988), although by January 1946 breeding appeared to have ended at Porvenir (Philippi *et al.*

1954). Five juveniles have been collected in Cautín in February (Hellmayr 1932), and one collected in Santiago in May is labelled as being juvenile (J. C. Torres-Mura *in litt.* 1988). In Concepción its ecology resembled that of Dusky-tailed Canastero *Asthenes humicola*, which had two broods there, one beginning in late September or early October, and one in early December (Pässler 1922).

Although the species appears to be resident on Isla Grande (Humphrey *et al.* 1970), it equally appears to be (at least partly) migratory further north in Chile (Hellmayr 1932). Records from Valparaíso and Santiago all fall from May to September; in Colchagua it was said to be common, but no time of occurrence was given; it was found breeding in Concepción, but was only found from April to September in Malleco, c.100 km south of the Concepción site (Hellmayr 1932: also specimens in MCZ and YPM). Further south, in Bío-Bío and Cautín there are only summer records, but winter records from Temuco, Chubut, Santa Cruz, Magallanes and Tierra del Fuego show the species to be only partly migratory (Hellmayr 1932, Humphrey *et al.* 1970; specimens in AMNH, BMNH, FMNH, LSUMZ and MCZ).

THREATS The rarity of this species can most likely be attributed to habitat destruction by heavy sheep grazing, and a certain amount of burning (NK, B. M. Whitney *in litt.* 1991). While the native herbivore, the guanaco *Lama guanacoe*, bites the grass off, introduced sheep often tear the grass-roots loose from the ground, thus promoting soil erosion, which is rapid in these wind-swept regions, and virtually no areas with long grass now remain in Patagonia, which used to be covered by this habitat (Humphrey *et al.* 1970, NK). Even if long grass is not the preferred nesting habitat, it appears to be important for foraging (see Ecology).

MEASURES TAKEN In Chile, this species has been recorded in Torres del Paine National Park (181,400 ha: IUCN 1992), although it undoubtedly occurs within some the vast protected areas encompassing significant parts of Aisén and Magallanes, e.g. Laguna San Rafael, Bernardo O'Higgins and Alberto de Agostini National Parks (totalling c.6,728,000 ha: IUCN 1992), and Alacalufes and Katalalixar National Reserves (totalling c.2,988,000 ha: IUCN 1992). There have apparently been no records within protected areas in Argentina.

MEASURES PROPOSED Grazing on a rotational basis, or perhaps farming guanaco rather than sheep, would help to maintain suitable habitat for this species, and prevent erosion. One or more localities where the species is known to occur should be fenced off from grazing sheep, not only to preserve the present species, but also other forms of native flora and fauna endemic to this region (see also Measures Proposed under Austral Rail *Rallus antarcticus*, with which it may be sympatric at some localities). Such measures should perhaps be concentrated within the protected areas mentioned above, although some survey work is necessary in many of these to determine the size of populations or even the species's presence there.

REMARKS (1) Olrog (1962) suggested that Streak-backed Canastero *Asthenes wyatti*, Puno Canastero *A. punensis* (and Córdoba Canastero *A. sclateri*) should be treated as subspecies of Austral Canastero, while Navas and Bó (1982) advocated the treatment of *anthoides* and *wyatti* as distinct species and suggested that *punensis* should be treated as subspecies of *sclateri*. Fjeldså and Krabbe (1989) pointed out that the great variability of birds in the zone of contact between *wyatti* and *punensis* suggests that differentiation has only reached megasubspecies level, and presumably both *punensis* and *sclateri* should be treated as subspecies of *wyatti* (NK). However, there seems to be insufficient evidence for treating *wyatti* as a subspecies of *anthoides* (*contra* Olrog 1962); *anthoides* differs from all the other forms by being smaller, having a relatively smaller tail, retaining its pointed tail-feathers in adult plumage, having a less extensive rufous wing-bar, building its nest in a bush rather than in a tussock of grass, and having constant rather than increasingly shorter intervals between notes in its trilled song (NK; tape-recordings by B. M. Whitney and NK, sonagrams printed by National Sound Archive, London). We do not follow the merging of *Asthenes* with *Thripophaga* proposed by Vaurie (1971, 1980; see Remarks under Pale-tailed Canastero *A. huancavelicae* and Russet-mantled Softtail *Thripophaga berlepschi*).

(2) A specimen collected by C. Darwin is labelled "E. Falkland Island" (Sclater 1874). It remains the only record from the Falkland Islands/Islas Malvinas and is considered a mislabelled bird originating in Chile (Woods 1988).

BERLEPSCH'S CANASTERO *Asthenes berlepschi* I[6]

Known from an extremely small area in the semi-arid mountains of north-western Bolivia, this furnariid is reliant on the continued survival of small amounts of natural and man-managed habitat.

DISTRIBUTION Berlepsch's Canastero (see Remarks 1) is only known from the vicinity of Nevado Illampu, in the montane basin of the upper Mapiri valley, La Paz department, north-western Bolivia. The few known localities (coordinates from Paynter *et al.* 1975: see Remarks 2) are as follows: Tacacoma (15°35'S 68°43'W), 20 km north of Sorata, where a bird was taken at 3,495 m in July 1938 (Fjeldså and Krabbe 1989); Chilcani (c.15°44'S 68°40'W), in the río San Cristóbal valley, north-west of Sorata, where a bird was collected at 3,700 m in July 1938 (Fjeldså and Krabbe 1989; also one bird in AMNH); Sorata (15°47'S 68°40'W), where two birds were taken at 2,700 m in July and August 1938 (Fjeldså and Krabbe 1989), with birds recorded on the slopes outside the village in December 1991 (J. Fjeldså *in litt.* 1992); Cotaña (15°49'S 68°37'W), near Sorata, where 10 birds were taken at 3,600 m in July-August 1938 (Fjeldså and Krabbe 1989; also two specimens in AMNH and FMNH); and Monte Illampu (= Nevado Illampu at 15°50'S 68°34'W), on the Tacamara side of which a bird was taken at 3,500 m in July 1938 (Fjeldså and Krabbe 1989).

POPULATION All known specimens of this species originate from a minute area within La Paz department, the majority (15) coming from between Chilcani and Cotaña (see Distribution). During December 1991, the bird was readily found on the slopes just outside the village of Sorata: two nests were found and two birds mist-netted but, although no estimate of numbers was made, the limited extent of suitable habitat in this montane basin suggests that the total population may be just a few hundred pairs (J. Fjeldså *in litt.* 1992).

ECOLOGY Berlepsch's Canastero has only been recorded between 2,600 and 3,700 m on the semi-arid slopes of Nevado Illampu (Fjeldså and Krabbe 1989, 1990). The localities at which specimens were taken in 1938 were variously described as: hilly puna grassland; a rocky area with thorny woodland along a river; a barren stony area with grassy vegetation, some thorny scrub and cultivated fields of maize and potatoes; and an area with some scrub, but widely planted with fig-cactus, mulberry and eucalyptus trees (Fjeldså and Krabbe 1989). Near Sorata, the habitat in December 1991 was noted to be completely converted, with fields, large areas of fallow, shrubs and low scrub, scattered *Eucalyptus* trees and some soil erosion (J. Fjeldså *in litt.* 1992). Birds were seen singly or in pairs, skulking in the hedges separating fields, but at times out in the open, although always near scrub (J. Fjeldså *in litt.* 1992). The two nests found were highly visible, 6-8 m up in *Eucalyptus* trees between fields, c.500 m apart (J. Fjeldså *in litt.* 1992). Two (presumably active) nests were found at the end of December when song activity was generally low, although immature birds have been recorded in July and August (Fjeldså and Krabbe 1990, J. Fjeldså *in litt.* 1992).

THREATS This bird appears to survive well in highly modified habitats (see Ecology), and it is remarkable that nests have been found high up in *Eucalyptus* trees, since the Creamy-breasted Canastero *Asthenes dorbignyi* nests in dense thorn scrub, columnar cacti and *Polylepis* trees (varying between the populations) (J. Fjeldså *in litt.* 1992; also Fjeldså and Krabbe 1990). However, the bird must be regarded as at risk owing to its minute range in one small montane basin, its restricted altitudinal distribution, and the small amount of available vegetation: this semi-arid basin is isolated by mountain slopes with humid yungas scrub and by high cordilleras (J. Fjeldså *in litt.* 1992).

MEASURES TAKEN None is known.

MEASURES PROPOSED Fieldwork is urgently needed to obtain a more detailed assessment of this bird's ecological requirements and population, although its taxonomic status needs to be clarified before any such initiatives are taken (see Remarks 1). Obviously, its long-term survival is dependent on the agricultural practices of the people farming in this area: the importance of hedges, tall trees and scrub along watercourses in preventing soil erosion should be stressed, and local people encouraged to maintain such habitat, or even plant more.

REMARKS (1) Berlepsch's Canastero was considered a full species in Fjeldså and Krabbe (1990) and Sibley and Monroe (1990), and indeed shows a unique combination of "character states"; however, any character may be found in one population or another within the *A. dorbignyi* complex (Fjeldså and Krabbe 1990), which may indicate that *berlepschi* is a relict population from an early phase of dispersal (J. Fjeldså *in litt.* 1992). Species rank is probably justified, although doubts are caused by some tendencies towards *berlepschi* in two specimens of *A. (dorbignyi) arequipae* from near Putina in the northern end of the Lake Titicaca basin, and one from near Río Mauri on the altiplano of western La Paz (J. Fjeldså *in litt.* 1992). A detailed morphological analysis and DNA study is in progress (J. Fjeldså *in litt.* 1992), and should clarify the taxonomy of this complex or superspecies. (2) The type-locality of this bird is given as "Chicani", on the north slope of Cordillera Real (Cory and Hellmayr 1923). Chicani is situated at 16°28'S 68°04'W (in a very humid climate: J. Fjeldså *in litt.* 1992), some distance further south than Nevado Illampu and the upper Mapiri valley (see Distribution). It seems probable, therefore, that Chicani is a typographical error for Chilcani, whence come a number of specimens (see Distribution).

PALE-TAILED CANASTERO *Asthenes huancavelicae* V[9]

The four very local forms composing this species inhabit arid, scrubby intermontane valleys in central Peru, where at least three of them are rare and possibly indirectly threatened by deforestation.

DISTRIBUTION Three or four subspecies, one or two of them previously undescribed, are referred to this species by Fjeldså and Schulenberg (in press: see Remarks 1), all inhabiting arid intermontane valleys in central Peru (coordinates are from Stephens and Traylor 1983).

Northernmost form (description imminent) This is known from the río Santa valley, Ancash department, localities being: below Yánac (8°37'S 77°52'W), where a small population was found at 2,700 m in early May 1979, with a nest c.10 km south-west of Yánac along the Yuracmarca road presumably made by birds from the above population (P. Hocking *in litt.* 1989, NK: two specimens in MHNJP); 19 and 20 km by road from Yuracmarca (8°45'S 77°54'W) towards Yánac, where two specimens (in LSUMZ) were taken at 1,830 and 1,920 m in 1975; just below Huaylas (8°52'S 77°54'W; at 2,720 m), on the left bank of the río Santa, where a small nesting population was found in early May 1979 (P. Hocking *in litt.* 1989). This form may also inhabit the upper río Marañón valley, which is poorly explored ornithologically (NK). In September 1988, two individuals of what appeared to be the present form were observed in the upper Quebrada Ulta at 4,050 m, and 2 km south-west in the Quebrada Matará at 4,200 m, on the eastern slope of the Cordillera Blanca (Frimer and Møller Nielsen 1989).

Huánuco department (undescribed subspecies) The presence of the species in Huánuco department is based on information from P. Hocking (*in litt.* 1989), who was told by an experienced local bird collector of the presence of nests in cacti at 1,980-2,135 m, above Santa María del Valle (9°51'S 76°08'W), c.12 km down river from Huánuco town, on the right bank of the río Huallaga; it is found nowhere else in the Huánuco valley or side valleys.

The subspecies *huancavelicae* is known from the right bank of río Mantaro in Huancavelica and Ayachucho departments, localities being: (*Huancavelica*) slightly above Huancavelica (12°46'S 75°02'W), where four specimens (in BMNH) were taken at 3,600 m in August, September and December 1937 (also Morrison 1938, 1939a); along the railroad from Huancayo to Yauli, especially between Mejorada and Yauli, where nests have been seen (P. Hocking *in litt.* 1989); above Yauli (c.12°47'S 74°49'W), where seven birds (in AMNH, BMNH) were taken in September and December 1937, and three (in FMNH, MHNJP) in 1979, at 3,535 and 3,700 m (also Morrison 1938, 1939a); (*Ayacucho*) above Quinua, between Ayacucho town (13°07'S 74°13'W) and Quinua, where a specimen (in LSUMZ) was taken at 3,475 m; Quebrada del Agua Potable (c.13°13'S 74°14'W), where two specimens (in MHNJP) were collected at 3,000 m in 1976. The bird is also found around the city of Ayacucho, and on the road from Ayacucho towards the coast (P. Hocking *in litt.* 1989).

The subspecies *usheri* inhabits the upper río Apurímac drainage in Ayacucho and Apurímac departments, with records as follows: (*Ayacucho*) at 2,750-3,500 m on Cerros Cuntaya, Larigato and Huayllura, all along río Negro Mayo south of Andamarca (14°23-24'S 73°58'W); between Chipao and Santa Ana de Huaycahnacho, along the río Mayobamba (14°14-22'S 73°52-57'W); and between the Pampachiri and the Soras regions (14°07-11'S 73°32-36'W), the slopes above the lower río Lucanes (near río Mayobamba) south to 14°S, plus the río Soras valley, appearing to hold good habitat (L. Zambrano verbally to J. Fjeldså 1989, J. Fjeldså *in litt.* 1990, NK: coordinates read from IGM 1985); (*Apurímac*) along the ríos Pampas, Chalhuanca and Vilcabamba, specifically: above Ahuayro (13°22'S 73°52'W), in the río Pampas valley at 2,400 m, where three specimens (in BMNH) were collected in September and October 1939; Ninabamba (c.13°28'S 73°49'W), in the río Pampas valley at 2,135 m, where two specimens (in BMNH) were collected in August and September 1939 (also Morrison 1947, 1948), although the bird is now gone from this locality (P. Hocking *in litt.* 1989); 1.5 km west of Mutca, at 2,770 m on the bank of río Chalhuanca, c.15 km north-west of Chalhuanca (at 14°17'S 73°15'W), where a specimen (in ZMUC) was collected in March 1987 (also Fjeldså 1987); Vilcabamba (14°05'S 72°37'W), at 3,300 m in the río Vilcabamba valley, where two specimens (in MHNJP) were collected in 1977; Chuquibambilla (14°07'S 72°43'W), where two specimens in FMNH, MHNJP) were taken at 2,440 m in 1975; Bosque Paragay, and near río Hogonga, both near Piyai (at 14°13'S 72°41'W), where three specimens (in MHNJP) were collected at 3,350 and 3,500 m in 1977.

POPULATION The northernmost subspecies is rare with only a few small populations, the one at Yánac being slightly larger than that at Huaylas (P. Hocking *in litt.* 1988, 1989). The Huánuco population must be very rare, as several collectors working in the region have failed to record the species; and the race *usheri* is also rare, with only small, scattered populations (Morrison 1948, P. Hocking *in litt.* 1988, NK), searches for it at Ninabamba (the type-locality) in 1977 and elsewhere in the río Pampas valley in the 1970s proving fruitless (P. Hocking *in litt.* 1989, Fjeldså and Schulenberg in press). In Ayacucho J. Fjeldså (*in litt.* 1990) estimated 10 pairs along río Negro Mayo, 40-50 pairs along río Mayobamba, and possibly 40 pairs between the Pampachiri and Soras regions.

The subspecies *huancavelicae*, however, has been described as plentiful at Yauli, even abundant in December 1937 (Morrison 1939a), a view not opposed by P. Hocking (*in litt.* 1988), who collected the species close to this same locality, and also found the bird abundant around Ayacucho city, in the countryside around Pampas de Quinua, at Quebrada del Aguas Potable and along the road heading out of Ayacucho towards the coast.

ECOLOGY The Pale-tailed Canastero inhabits arid regions with scattered thorny bushes and cacti, at elevations ranging from 1,830 to 3,700 m, the only exception noted being two singles sighted in *Polylepis* at 4,050 and 4,200 m (Morrison 1939a, 1948, Fjeldså 1987, P. Hocking *in litt.* 1988: see Distribution). Below Huaylas and Yánac, Ancash, it was found in dry shrubby habitat, nesting in *Armatocereus* and *Opuntia* cacti (P. Hocking *in litt.* 1989), and in Huánuco nests were found in *Pseudoespostoa* cacti (P. Hocking *in litt.* 1989). At río Chalhuanca, Apurímac, it was found near the river in a mosaic of stony ground (with some prostrate herbs but generally very little cover) and semi-arid montane scrub-forest, the dominant trees being *Schinus molle*, *Tecoma* and *Carica*, and the scrub comprising *Colletia*, *Dodonea viscosa* and (the introduced) *Spartium junceum*, with many large columnar cacti such as *Cylindropuntia*, *Opuntia*, *Trichocereus* (Fjeldså 1987, J. Fjeldså *in litt.* 1990). Near Andamarca, Ayacucho, it was mostly seen foraging on dry hillsides with little vegetation (dry grass and scattered wilted herbs), scattered thorn bushes (mainly *Colletia*, *Berberis* and thorny solanaceans), and very few branched columnar cacti, these latter being used as nest-sites, with thorny branches (mostly *Colletia*) used as nesting material; its habitat is scarce, and each pair appears to have a large territory (J. Fjeldså *in litt.* 1990).

Usually alone, the species forages for insects on poorly vegetated ground or low in bushes, but sings and observes from small trees or bushes (Morrison 1939a, J. Fjeldså *in litt.* 1990, NK). Although several nests may be found in the same cactus, all have probably been built by the same family, with a new one being added every season (only one ever being in use) (Morrison 1939a, P. Hocking *in litt.* 1989, J. Fjeldså *in litt.* 1990). All nests reported from Ancash, Huánuco, Ayacucho and Apurímac were in columnar cacti (Fjeldså and Schulenberg in press, NK), as were most nests reported from Huancavelica (Morrison 1939a). One cactus with a nest in Ayacucho was identified to *Opuntia* (label data on specimen in LSUMZ: Fjeldså and Schulenberg in press), with *Cylindropuntia*, and to a lesser degree *Pseudoespostoa* given as the preferred genera used for nesting by the species (Fjeldså and Schulenberg in press). A newly built nest found at Yauli, Huancavelica, in December 1939, and the fact that the species was much commoner there than it had been in September that year (Morrison 1939a), may indicate that breeding commences in December; however, at this same locality, birds have been noted to nest in March, and two eggs with developing embryos were found below Yánac, Ancash, in early May 1979 (P. Hocking *in litt.* 1989). A specimen (in BMNH) from Huancavelica, taken in December, appears to be truly juvenile (NK), whilst another (also in BMNH) from Apurímac, taken in September, appears to be moulting from juvenile to immature plumage (NK: see Remarks 2). Three specimens from Ancash and one from Huancavelica, all taken in May, are described as juveniles (Fjeldså and Schulenberg in press), with young found in Apurímac during February (P. Hocking *in litt.* 1989).

THREATS Although little of the species's thorny habitat is being destroyed directly by man, it may be so indirectly: with its very small populations, restricted to small areas, and living in habitats that provide a very limited food-supply owing to the extreme aridity, the Pale-tailed Canastero may be severely affected by even minor decreases in humidity caused by deforestation in adjacent regions (P. Hocking *in litt.* 1988).

MEASURES TAKEN None is known.

MEASURES PROPOSED More study is needed to establish the degree to which regional deforestation affects the amount of local rainfall; however, increased aridity owing to soil erosion and irregular water-supply, both caused by deforestation of water-catchment areas, is a well-known effect, and an education campaign targeted at the local inhabitants of the areas involved might be undertaken aimed at preventing further deforestation. There may also be some benefit in initiating community afforestation schemes to supply the local firewood needs. A protected area in Ayachuco, where the species is most abundant, should also be a priority.

REMARKS (1) Up until 1946, five subspecies of the Creamy-breasted Canastero *Asthenes dorbignyi* had been described. Fjeldså and Schulenberg (in press) have two more subspecies, the northernmost in Ancash, and the darkest in southern Lima, Ayacucho, northern Arequipa, and possibly Apurímac, and they have suggested placing these seven forms in three different species: the pale Rusty-vented Canastero *Asthenes dorbignyi* (with *consobrina*) of lower temperate and upper subtropical arid scrub in Bolivia and Argentina; the dark Dark-winged Canastero *A. arequipae* (with the darkest) of *Polylepis* woodland at high elevations from southern Lima, Peru to western Bolivia and northern Chile (but also locally inhabiting arid scrub on the Pacific slope in Arequipa, Peru); and the pale Pale-tailed Canastero *A. huancavelicae* (including the northernmost form, the as yet uncollected form in Huánuco, and *usheri*) of lower temperate and upper subtropical arid scrub in central Peru.

Either the pale forms represent relict populations of a species that was once widely distributed, or some (or all) may have evolved independently from darker highland forms; however, no significant differences between the darkest form and *usheri* were found in a 300 base-pair sequence in the cytochrome B gene in the mitochondrial DNA (P. Arctander verbally 1990). Vocalizations of the birds from Ancash, Huancavelica and Ayacucho have been described as chattering (P. Hocking *in litt.* 1989), thus resembling those of more south-easterly populations, while those of *usheri* are distinctly different (NK). Vaurie (1971, 1980) did not recognize the present species as even subspecifically distinct from *A. dorbignyi arequipae*; he referred all species of *Asthenes* to *Thripophaga* (and removed two species previously placed in *Thripophaga* to *Phacellodomus*), primarily on the presence of a rufous gular patch in most species of *Asthenes* and in the two remaining species of *Thripophaga*. We here follow the classification used before Vaurie's revision for the following reasons: (a) a rufous gular patch is also present in some species in genera which he placed elsewhere in the system (*Schizoeaca*, *Schoeniophylax*, *Oreophylax* and *Certhiaxis*); (b) at least three, and probably all four species referred to *Thripophaga* before his revision are arboreal (Sick 1985, Fjeldså and Krabbe 1990, NK; see also account of Chestnut-throated Spinetail *Thripophaga cherriei*), whilst species of *Asthenes* are mainly terrestrial (Fjeldså and Krabbe 1990, NK); and (c) Vaurie's often limited material, as well as lack of experience with furnariids in the field, led him to several wrong conclusions (see, e.g., Remarks under Royal Cinclodes *Cinclodes aricomae* and White-browed Tit-spinetail *Leptasthenura xenothorax*).

(2) Some furnariids, notably its close relatives the Dark-winged Canastero and Rusty-vented Canastero, remain in their immature plumage for a considerable period of time (NK) and the distinction between juvenile and immature plumages is not clear in the account of specimens given by Fjeldså and Schulenberg (in press); therefore, no definite indication of the breeding season can be derived from it.

CIPÓ CANASTERO *Asthenes luizae* I[7]

This small rock-haunting insectivore is known to inhabit as yet only a tiny area within the Serra do Cipó, Minas Gerais, Brazil, where it faces possible threats from cattle-grazing, fires and brood-parasitism.

DISTRIBUTION The Cipó Canastero is known only from a restricted area in the Serra do Cipó (part of the Serra do Espinhaço), 1,100-1,500 m, north-east of Jaboticatubas, Minas Gerais, south-east Brazil, where two specimens (including the type) were collected in December 1985 and December 1988 (Vielliard 1990b) and other records obtained in July 1988 (B. C. Forrester *in litt.* 1988), August 1988 and July 1989 (Pearman 1990). The species has not been found outside the Serra do Espinhaço, although it was looked for at Caraça, 19°58'S 43°29'W, 75 km south of Serra do Cipó, in August 1989, in suitable habitat between 1,250 and 1,550 m (Pearman 1990; see Remarks 1); it is likely, however, to be found at other localities in the Serra do Espinhaço to the north of its present range (M. Pearman *in litt.* 1992).

POPULATION The species was considered "not uncommon" in an estimated 10 km^2 area of suitable habitat, where a maximum of seven birds was found on 28 July 1989, using tape playback as a lure (Pearman 1990). In December 1988 twenty birds (nine pairs) were found (Vielliard 1990b; see Ecology), seemingly in the same area.

ECOLOGY Habitat is described as isolated rocky outcrops in grassfields on tablelands (Pearman 1990, Vielliard 1990b). Vegetation on these crags included flowering shrubs (*Vernonia* sp., *Agave* sp., *Yucca* sp.) and various cacti; lichen was present on the rocks (Pearman 1990; see Remarks 2). Birds are mainly terrestrial, often keeping hidden amongst rocks or taking short flights (Pearman 1990, Vielliard 1990b), and preferring the steepest slopes with the most vegetation and crevices; males in full song were strongly territorial, climbing to the tops of bushes (c.1.5 m above the ground) or the most exposed rocks to sing, and responded well to tape playback in late July; non-singing birds were initially lured into the open by playback, but often vanished into crevices (Pearman 1990). Territory size was approximately 10-20 ha (see Remarks 3) and, of the nine territories found in December 1988, four were grouped 200-300 m from each other, three were grouped approximately 1 km from these four, and two were 7 km from these three (Vielliard 1990b). Food is recorded as insects, taken from rocks and crevices (Vielliard 1990b). In early December 1988, two pairs each had a still dependent young, while two other pairs were each feeding a young Shiny Cowbird *Molothrus bonariensis* (Vielliard 1990b). Pairs holding territories were recorded also in July 1988 (B. C. Forrester *in litt.* 1988) and August 1988 (Pearman 1990).

THREATS The species was considered "not to be in immediate danger" as its particular habitat is reasonably extensive and not under any threats (Vielliard 1990b), although it has been noticed that the area is used for cattle-grazing, and grasslands are periodically burnt, large fires having been seen in July 1989, which may represent a threat unless the fires are long-standing features and the bird populations have adapted to cope with them (Pearman 1990); degradation from grazing and fires was also noted as a risk to the habitat in July 1990 (Gardner and Gardner 1990b). Parasitism by the Shiny Cowbird, a recent invader of the rocky fields in the region, is a cause of concern, and there is the potential for over-collecting to affect so highly restricted a population (Vielliard 1990b).

MEASURES TAKEN None is known. The area where the species has been found lies close to the Serra do Cipó National Park (33,800 ha: IBAMA 1989), but it has not yet been recorded from within the park limits (Pearman 1990, Vielliard 1990b).

MEASURES PROPOSED An extension of the Serra do Cipó National Park boundary to enclose an area no more than 20 km^2 is suggested, on the basis of current knowledge of the species's range, to enhance the chances for its survival (M. Pearman *in litt.* 1989). Surveys are needed better to delimit the species's range, possibly using tape playback, and to monitor its status, including further study on the impact of Shiny Cowbird parasitism and fires; given the known, devastating impact of brood-parasitism on isolated populations (see, e.g., accounts of Yellow-shouldered Blackbird *Agelaius xanthomus*, Kirtland's Warbler *Dendroica kirtlandii* and Black-capped Vireo *Vireo atricapillus*), this particular problem requires the most urgent investigation. Collection of further specimens should not be countenanced. Three near-threatened species endemic to the same area deserve to be considered in any conservation initiatives targeted on the Serra do Cipó and/or Serra do Espinhaço (see Remarks 4).

REMARKS (1) The Cipó Canastero is separated from its geographically closest relative, the Short-billed Canastero *Asthenes baeri*, by at least 1,450 km to the south-west (Pearman 1990). If populations are indeed found to the north of its current range, the name "Cipó Canastero" may need to be reconsidered (M. Pearman *in litt.* 1992). (2) It is possible that the plants described for the habitat are primarily species of *Vellozia*, which look like *Agave* and *Yucca* but represent an interesting family (Velloziaceae) endemic to the Brazilian and Guyanan Shields (TAP). (3) An estimate of territory size varying from 15 to 30 m^2 (Pearman 1990) was a typeographical error for 150-300 m^2 (M. Pearman *in litt.* 1992). (4) Two other birds are endemic and one nearly endemic to the Serra do Espinhaço, namely Hyacinth Visorbearer *Augastes scutatus*, Grey-backed Tachuri *Polystictus superciliaris* (also now known from Serra da Canastra National Park: M. Pearman *in litt.* 1992) and Pale-throated Pampa-finch *Embernagra longicauda*: all are considered sufficiently numerous and in such little disturbed habitat as to be considered at far less risk than the Cipó Canastero, but all certainly merit continued monitoring, especially the pampa-finch (which presumably is also liable to suffer brood-parasitism by cowbirds).

RUSSET-MANTLED SOFTTAIL *Thripophaga berlepschi* V/R[10]

This rare and very poorly known bird of elfin forest is confined to Amazonas and La Libertad departments, north-central Peru. It is threatened by deforestation for agriculture, but may exist within a national park.

DISTRIBUTION The Russet-mantled Softtail (see Remarks) is known from some 15-20 specimens taken at five localities south of the río Marañón from central Amazonas department south to eastern La Libertad department, north-central Peru: the bird has not been found in similar habitat further south in Huánuco department (Parker and O'Neill 1976, Schulenberg and Williams 1982). The five known localities (coordinates from Stephens and Traylor 1983) are as follows:

Amazonas south-east of La Peca Nueva (c.5°34'S 78°17'W) in the Cordillera de Colán, where at 2,530 m birds (in LSUMZ) were collected in August or September 1978; Leimebamba (6°41'S 77°47'W), the type-locality, at 3,050 m (Hellmayr 1905); Atuén (c.6°45'S 77°52'W), where six specimens (in ANSP, MCZ) were taken at 3,350 m in July 1932 (also Bond 1945); Lluy (6°45'S 77°49'W), where six specimens (in ANSP, MCZ) were taken at 3,050 m in September 1933 (also Bond 1945);

La Libertad Mashua (c.8°12'S 77°14'W), east of Tayabamba on the trail to Ongón, where a specimen (in LSUMZ) was collected and observations were made at 3,350 m in September 1979 (TAP).

POPULATION The species was considered rare by Parker *et al.* (1982), but the fact that 12 specimens were collected in just seven days in 1932 and 1933 at two localities (specimens in ANSP and MCZ) implies that it was not rare then. In 1979, during more than 20 days of fieldwork in upper montane forest at Mashua, the species was observed only twice, and mist-netted once (TAP), although a sizeable population undoubtedly occurs both to the north and south of Atuén (NK), e.g. in Río Abiseo National Park, situated in south-western San Martín department, and adjacent to the central part of eastern La Libertad department (Leo *et al.* 1988).

ECOLOGY The species inhabits humid elfin forest (Parker *et al.* 1982) at elevations ranging from 2,530 to 3,350 m (see Distribution). The presence of elfin forest as low as 2,500 m (Cordillera de Colán) may be explained by a cool local climate owing to frequent rainfall (NK). At Mashua in La Libertad, this species was observed in the tangled upper parts of *Chusquea* bamboo thickets inside stunted forest near treeline, dominant small trees in this habitat including species of *Clethra*, *Hesperomeles*, *Gynoxys*, and *Weinmannia*, with mosses and bromeliads thickly covering the larger branches of trees; pairs and small groups probed curled, dead leaves trapped amidst branches at 2-3 m, and followed small mixed flocks comprised of Citrine Warbler *Basileuterus luteoviridis*, Black-capped Hemispingus *Hemispingus atropileus* and Plush-capped Finch *Catamblyrhynchus diadema* (TAP). An immature was collected in July, a juvenile and three immatures in September, and an adult with slightly enlarged gonads in September (Bond 1945; specimens in ANSP and LSUMZ), suggesting that breeding takes place at the end of the rainy season and during the "dry" season (June–September).

THREATS In the Chuquibamba district (where Atuén is situated) all land in the quichua and lower jalca (páramo) zones (1,800-3,200 m) is currently cultivated or used by roaming cattle (Schjellerup 1989). It is not known to what degree this is the case in the rest of the species's range, but as elfin forests are generally fairly easily approached from the páramo or puna, they remain very vulnerable (NK). Habitat degradation caused by grazing cattle seriously affects some understorey birds (see accounts of Russet-bellied Spinetail *Synallaxis zimmeri* and Grey-headed Antbird *Myrmeciza griseiceps*), but too little is known about the habitat requirements of this species to estimate the impact of such disturbance. The habitat at Mashua appeared to be relatively undisturbed in 1979, although adjacent páramo grassland was being grazed by a small number of cattle and was burnt almost annually (TAP). Extensive areas of treeline forest and páramo vegetation in the Cordillera de Colán were still pristine in 1978 (T. S. Schulenberg verbally 1990).

MEASURES TAKEN The species probably inhabits Río Abiseo National Park (274,500 ha: IUCN 1992), as it has been found both to the north and the south.

MEASURES PROPOSED Surveys are urgently required to determine the precise nature of this species's status and distribution. Such work should concentrate on searching for and assessing any population within the Río Abiseo National Park, currently the only protected area in this region, although it is recommended that a second reserve ranging from the páramo to the upper tropical zone be established within the range of this species, in order to ensure the integrity of habitat for at least two viable populations of this and other species endemic to the region (see Measures Proposed and Remarks under Yellow-browed Toucanet *Aulacorhynchus huallagae*).

REMARKS Vaurie (1971, 1980) removed *Thripophaga berlepschi* to the thornbirds *Phacellodomus*, despite the somewhat pointed central tail-feathers and the absence of lanceolate chestnut feathers in the forehead of *berlepschi*. His simultaneous merging (Vaurie 1971, 1980) of the canasteros *Asthenes*, including Berlepsch's Canastero *Asthenes berlepschi*, with *Thripophaga* has caused some confusion of names. Vaurie's classification of the furnariids (1971, 1980) has proved wrong or directly misleading in several cases (see, e.g., Remarks under Royal Cinclodes *Cinclodes aricomae*, White-browed Tit-spinetail *Leptasthenura xenothorax* and Pale-tailed Canastero *Asthenes huancavelicae*), and we do not follow it here. The Russet-mantled Softtail appears to be behaviourally and ecologically similar to most members of the genus *Cranioleuca* (TAP).

ORINOCO SOFTTAIL *Thripophaga cherriei* V[9]

Known from just one affluent of the upper río Orinoco, Venezuela, this extremely rare ovenbird has been recorded just twice, although this area does not appear to be under immediate threat from habitat destruction.

DISTRIBUTION The Orinoco Softtail is known only from the vicinity of the type-locality along the upper río Orinoco, Amazonas state, southern Venezuela (coordinates are from Paynter 1982). It was first collected in February 1899, when a male and female (in AMNH) were taken at "Capuano" (= río Capuana, c.4°42'N 67°50'W), a small affluent on the right bank of the upper río Orinoco, c.30 km south of the confluence of the río Vichada (originating in Colombia) (also von Berlepsch and Hartert 1902, Phelps and Phelps 1950). Subsequent specimens (four in AMNH and ANSP), taken in March 1970, also originated from along the río Capuana, at 120 m.

POPULATION Only six specimens of this species have been collected (see above), and there are apparently no other records of the bird: its population remains essentially unknown, as are its distribution limits.

ECOLOGY The río Capuana is at about 100 m (Paynter 1982), and the most recent specimens (in AMNH, ANSP) were apparently taken at 120 m, the bird obviously being one of the lowland tropical zone (also Phelps and Phelps 1950). The habitat of these specimens is described (museum label data) as "caños" (i.e. streams), Meyer de Schauensee and Phelps (1978) giving the habitat as rainforest and clearings along river banks and small caños, where birds actively clamber about in bushes and brush. However, Vaurie (1980) suggested that the Orinoco Softtail is found apparently only on the banks of the ríos Capuana and Orinoco, and not within the forest. The forest in this area (along the rivers), is quite specialized tall (and dense) riverine forest with little undergrowth (Huber and Alarcón 1988); small clearings may be infrequent. This species has only been recorded in February and March, and a male (in ANSP) taken in March 1970 had "gonads small": the male taken in February was in "much worn plumage" (von Berlepsch and Hartert 1902). Whether or not the Orinoco Softtail exhibits any seasonal movements (e.g. to higher ground to the east) is unknown.

THREATS None is known. However, Puerto Ayacucho (c.150 km north of the type-locality) is developing as a trade and tourist centre for the region (see Goodwin 1990), and the situation needs to be monitored with care as this species is only known from a possibly specialized vegetation adjacent to rivers, which may be at more risk than forests of the interior.

MEASURES TAKEN The Sipapo Forest Reserve (12,155 km^2) covers the area of this species's distribution (DGPOA), but it is doubtful if this has resulted in any enforced protection of habitats adjacent to the rivers.

MEASURES PROPOSED It is important to assess the ecological requirements and distributional status of the Orinoco Softtail. Surveys, initially in the vicinity of the type-locality, are required to determine what habitat this bird needs; once this has been done, searches can be made in similar habitat elsewhere along the Orinoco (including areas within Colombia), and a more complete picture of this species's distribution determined. If in fact the species has specific requirements and is as restricted in range as current records suggest, there may be considerable cause for concern, and its habitat will need to be protected from future developments.

STRIATED SOFTTAIL *Thripophaga macroura* V/R[10]

This poorly known ovenbird of lower canopy vine tangles occurs very patchily within a small range in lowland Atlantic Forest in south-east Brazil, where it appears to have suffered from much habitat destruction.

DISTRIBUTION The Striated Softtail is endemic to the Atlantic Forest region of south-east Brazil from Bahia south of Salvador (no records since 1932) through eastern Minas Gerais (no records since 1969) to Espírito Santo and northern Rio de Janeiro state.

Bahia The species was discovered by Wied (1820-1821) near the rio Catolé, an affluent of the rio Pardo (see Remarks), and it was subsequently found at the Engenho da Ponte, Aratuípe, where one female was collected in November 1932 (Pinto 1935), and in forest 11 km east of Boa Nova in August 1989 and July 1990 (B. C. Forrester *in litt.* 1992). Although no other precise localities have been recorded, at least 14 old trade skins in AMNH, ANSP, BMNH, FMNH, MCZ, MZUSP and USNM are labelled "Bahia".

Minas Gerais The only recorded localities are Machacalis, near the border of southern Bahia (not Espírito Santo as in Pinto 1978), where one female was obtained in December 1954 (in MZUSP), and Nanuque, where the species persisted until at least 1969 in the Mata da Cigana (G. T. de Mattos *in litt.* 1987).

Espírito Santo Older records are (north to south) from the rio São José, September 1942; Lagoa Juparanã (in 1925 precisely at Santana), 120 m, August and September 1925, November 1929, and 1941/1942; rio Doce, March 1906 (Pinto 1938) and March 1956; Baixo Guandu (Fazenda da Serra), November 1925; Colatina, November 1940; Pau Gigante (now Ibiraçu), September 1940; Jatiboca (near Itarana), 900-1,000 m, May 1940; and Água Boa, Santa Cruz, October 1940 (specimens in AMNH, LACM, MNRJ, MZUSP, USNM). An untraced old record in the state is "Villa Alegre", January 1912 (Cory and Hellmayr 1925). Recent records (all to the north of the rio São José) are mainly from the Sooretama Biological Reserve, with records almost annually from November 1980 to October 1990 (TAP), plus: November 1986 (J. F. Pacheco *in litt.* 1986), February 1987 (C. E. Carvalho *in litt.* 1987), August 1988 (M. Pearman *in litt.* 1990), September/October 1989 (B. M. Whitney and J. C. Rowlett *in litt.* 1990), July 1990 and January 1991 (Aleixo *et al.* 1991); and from the Córrego das Queixadas, Barra de São Francisco (close to the border of Minas Gerais), where two females were collected in December 1975 and July 1982 (G. T. de Mattos *in litt.* 1987).

Rio de Janeiro Although one male was collected at Aldeia da Pedra (now Itaocara) on 5 July 1828 (Krabbe undated), this record remained overlooked and the state was never included in the species's range (e.g. Cory and Hellmayr 1925, Pinto 1938, 1978, Meyer de Schauensee 1982). Recently birds have been found at up to 800 m in the Desengano State Park, north-east of Santa Maria Madalena (J. F. Pacheco *in litt.* 1986, C. E. Carvalho *in litt.* 1987).

POPULATION It seems evident that the species is now seriously reduced in abundance and distribution as a result of the extensive forest destruction which has taken place in its range (see Threats). It has been considered "locally not rare" (D. M. Teixeira *in litt.* 1987), "reasonably common" near Boa Nova (B. C. Forrester *in litt.* 1992; but see Threats) or even "still abundant" in an unprotected area in Barra de São Francisco (G. T. de Mattos *in litt.* 1987), but at Sooretama, though regularly recorded, birds are apparently restricted to a small portion within the forest (C. E. Carvalho *in litt.* 1987, Aleixo *et al.* 1991) or along forest edges where canopy vines are abundant (TAP). Through use of tape playback, as many as six pairs or families were easily encountered daily (during annual visits from 1980 to 1990) in the latter habitat along the north–south track through the western part of the reserve; however, pairs were very patchily distributed in the forest interior, again occurring where vine tangles were profuse (TAP). The Sooretama population is presumably fairly large, and failure to record the species to date from the adjacent CVRD Linhares

Reserve is a cause of surprise (D. F. Stotz *in litt.* 1991) and a further indication of its apparent patchiness.

ECOLOGY The Striated Softtail has been found in the interior of humid primary or little disturbed forest (Sick 1985, C. E. Carvalho *in litt.* 1987, G. T. de Mattos *in litt.* 1987), but also along forest edges (specimens in MNRJ, G. T. de Mattos *in litt.* 1987, TAP) and in degraded or secondary forest (G. T. de Mattos *in litt.* 1987, Aleixo *et al.* 1991). At Sooretama it was consistently noted in closely associating pairs or (family) groups of 3-5 individuals, two of which always responded vigorously to tape playback of songs (male and female often sing antiphonally, as in the presumably closely related Plain Softtail *Thripophaga fusciceps* of western Amazonia) (TAP). Nearly all of more than 20 observations at that locality involved birds foraging in dense tangles of woody vines in the lower canopy (at 12-16 m) in c.25 m tall forest (TAP; see Population). Wied (1831-1833) also stressed the birds' use of low, thick, interconnecting growth, where it would keep to and call from the darkest, most tangled parts. Records are frequently of single birds or pairs in bird flocks (specimens in MNRJ; also Sick 1985, J. F. Pacheco *in litt.* 1986, C. E. Carvalho *in litt.* 1987, B. M. Whitney and J. C. Rowlett *in litt.* 1990).

The species usually forages in pairs and perhaps family groups with mixed-species understorey flocks (typical members of which at Sooretama are Lesser Woodcreeper *Lepidocolaptes fuscus*, Plain Xenops *Xenops minutus*, Cinereous Antshrike *Thamnomanes caesius*, White-flanked Antwren *Myrmotherula axillaris*, the near-threatened Band-tailed Antwren *M. urosticta* and Olivaceous Flatbill *Rhynchocyclus olivaceus*; although at such times it particularly associates with the similar-looking bromeliad specialist Pale-browed Treehunter *Cichlocolaptes leucophrus*: TAP) in forest and older second growth, from about 2.5 to 7 m above ground, actively climbing in dense vine tangles (to which it generally keeps and in which it is difficult to observe), perch-gleaning arthropods from vines, twigs and branches, sometimes from leaves at the ends of branches (B. M. Whitney *in litt.* 1991); insects were in the stomachs of specimens in CGTM and MNRJ, and brownish, katydid-like orthopterans were seen removed from dead leaves by several individuals at Sooretama (TAP).

Nesting has been recorded in Espírito Santo in September/October (B. M. Whitney and J. C. Rowlett *in litt.* 1990) and December (G. T. de Mattos *in litt.* 1987). The nest is a ball-shaped structure of dry twigs (or in one case possibly rootlets) built on the attenuating limbs of c.10 m tall trees in virgin forest or nearby on isolated trees; clutch-size is three (G. T. de Mattos *in litt.* 1987; also B. M. Whitney *in litt.* 1991). Territories apparently encompass a number of large trees covered with vines, and what were presumably the same pairs were encountered year after year at Sooretama within relatively small areas of less than 1.5 ha; in one area, at least three pairs held territories linearly spaced along a road through tall forest; pairs were usually separated by more than 100 m (TAP).

THREATS The fragmentation of the species's range by extensive forest destruction has certainly had a major impact on its populations; the serious plight of forest around Boa Nova in central-southern Bahia is described in Threats under Slender Antbird *Rhopornis ardesiaca*. Although still present in degraded forests, the species is seemingly unable to survive in capoeira (young secondary growth) and other non-forest habitats (G. T. de Mattos *in litt.* 1987). Furthermore, the species is currently known from only a couple of protected areas, and its recorded numbers in these areas are too low to be confident about the future of the populations they hold.

MEASURES TAKEN The Striated Softtail is protected under Brazilian law (Bernardes *et al.* 1990). Its occurrence in the 24,000 ha Sooretama Biological Reserve and in Desengano State Park is only partially reassuring, since the numbers observed remain so small and the species's ecological requirements are so poorly known.

MEASURES PROPOSED Other remaining patches of forest within the species's range could still harbour small and so far undetected populations, and merit being identified and searched. Surveys of the species in the field are also needed to ascertain and monitor its status in the localities where it has been recorded. Support for the continued protection of these key sites is clearly imperative.

REMARKS The rio Catolé, according to Wied's map, would be a small affluent of the left bank of the rio Cachoeira or Ilhéus; however, recent maps show it as a tributary of the left bank of the rio Pardo (Pinto 1938; also Bokerman 1957).

WHITE-THROATED BARBTAIL *Margarornis tatei* V/R[10]

This uncommon furnariid is restricted to the undergrowth of montane forest in the coastal cordillera and Paria Peninsula, north-east Venezuela, where it is threatened by habitat loss. Although well known on the Paria Peninsula, there have been no recent records from the rest of its range.

DISTRIBUTION The White-throated Barbtail, like five other threatened species (see Threats under White-tailed Sabrewing *Campylopterus ensipennis*), is restricted to the Cordillera de Caripe (in north-eastern Anzoátegui, Sucre and Monagas) and the mountains of the Paria Peninsula, Venezuela.

Records of this species, from roughly west to east, and with coordinates from Paynter (1982), are as follows: Cerro Peonía (10°11'N 64°07'W: on the border of all three states, but cited as evidence for the species's occurrence in Anzoátegui), a locality mentioned by Phelps and Phelps (1950); Cerro Turumiquire (10°07'N 63°52'W, the summit being in Monagas), where two males (including the type-specimen, in AMNH) were collected at 2,410 m in April 1925, and where three males and a female (in FMNH) were taken between 1,525 and 2,135 m during February and March 1932 (also Phelps and Phelps 1950); La Trinidad (c.10°12'N 63°57'W; Sucre), apparently a coffee plantation on the northern slope of Cerro Turumiquire (Chapman 1925), where a male (in COP) was collected at 1,700 m in February 1963; and Cerro Negro (c.10°14'N 63°30'W, on the border on Sucre and Monagas: see Remarks 2 under White-tailed Sabrewing, and Remarks 1), where a male (in BMNH) was taken at 1,500 m in August 1943: also Phelps and Phelps 1950).

On the Paria Peninsula, records come from: Cerro Humo (c.10°40'N 62°30'W: including Irapa, see Remarks 2), where a female (in AMNH) was collected at 1,200 m in November 1947, two males (in AMNH, FMNH) were taken at 1,200 m in May 1948, and whence come recent records between 1,100 and 1,220 m in March 1984, July 1990 and July 1991 (A. B. Altman *in litt.* 1988, M. Pearman *in litt.* 1991, C. Sharpe *in litt.* 1992); Cerro "El Olvido" (on the ridge between Cerro Patao to the west and Cerro Azul c.2.5 km to the east), where Bond *et al.* (1989) recorded the species between 800 and 885 m from June to September 1988; Cerro Azul (c.10°40'N 61°56'W), a locality mentioned by Phelps and Phelps (1950) and Meyer de Schauensee and Phelps (1978).

POPULATION The status of this species is poorly known: during surveys on Cerro El Olvido from June to September 1988, the bird was found infrequently in montane forest above 800 m (commonest between 835 and 885 m) (Bond *et al.* 1989). Approximately four pairs were found along 0.4 km of path, giving a density in this area of 2.4 pairs/ha (Bond *et al.* 1989). On Cerro Humo, A. B. Altman (*in litt.* 1988) found 15 birds (in groups of two, three or four) on 4 March 1984, but M. Pearman (*in litt.* 1991) recorded just two individuals on 3 July 1990 and concluded that the species was uncommon. However, between 1947 and 1952, at least 54 specimens (in COP) were collected from somewhere on the Paria Peninsula (presumably Cerros Humo and Azul), suggesting that in the correct habitat the White-throated Barbtail is (or was) fairly common: the collection of 25 birds (also in COP) during 1943, and apparently from Cerro Negro, seems to back up this assumption. There have been no records of the species from the "mainland" (Cordillera de Caripe) since 1963, B. Swift (*in litt.* 1988) indicating that it is unknown from El Guácharo National Park, and that it has the major part of its range and population within the Paria Peninsula National Park; however, the recent extension of the El Guácharo National Park may have favoured the bird (see Measures Taken under White-tailed Sabrewing).

ECOLOGY In the Cordillera de Caripe, the White-throated Barbtail has been collected between 1,500 and 2,410 m (see Distribution: Meyer de Schauensee and Phelps 1978 gave an altitudinal range of 1,200-1,700 m), whereas on the Paria Peninsula records come from between 1,100 and 1,200 m on Cerro Humo, and 800 to 885 m on Cerro El Olvido (see Distribution; and equivalent section under White-tailed Sabrewing for an explanation of these altitudinal differences). At these elevations (upper tropical and subtropical zones) the habitat is cloud-forest, the canopy is low (15-20 m high) and more open, epiphytic growth is luxuriant (trunks and branches are clothed in mosses and ferns, and bromeliads become conspicuous), and small (3 m tall) palms are increasingly present in the understorey (Bond *et al.* 1989). Birds are invariably found in (fairly dense) undergrowth and low vegetation, from ground level to 2 m up (B. Swift *in litt.* 1986, Bond *et al.* 1989). The White-throated Barbtail is usually found in pairs or groups (Meyer de Schauensee and Phelps 1978, A. B. Altman *in litt.* 1988), but M. Pearman (*in litt.* 1991) recorded only singles on Cerro Humo in July 1990, as did Bond *et al.* (1989) during surveys on Cerro El Olvido from June to September 1988. Breeding is unrecorded.

THREATS Extensive clearance of the White-throated Barbtail's montane forest habitat is the main threat to the species; the fact that it is a bird of the understorey puts it further at risk from habitat alteration caused by coffee cultivation (Ridgely and Tudor 1989). The specific threats to this area are detailed in the corresponding section under White-tailed Sabrewing.

MEASURES TAKEN Two national parks exist within the range of this species and harbour populations of unknown size: (1) El Guácharo National Park (82,900 ha), covering Cerro Negro; and (2) Paria Peninsula National Park (37,500 ha); details of the status of these reserves are given in the corresponding section under White-tailed Sabrewing. At Turumiquire there is a "hydraulic" (presumably watershed) reserve, but this is heavily occupied with scattered human settlements and there is very little control: this species has not been recorded on Cerro Turumiquire in recent years (since 1963), and was not found there during a survey (up to 1,800 m) in 1979 (G. Medina-Cuervo *in litt.* 1986: see Population). The White-throated Barbtail is currently known only from the Paria Peninsula, where the national park covers all localities in which it has been recorded (see above). There are no recent (post-1943) records from El Guácharo National Park (but see Population, and corresponding section under White-tailed Sabrewing).

MEASURES PROPOSED For this species, the priorities must be (1) the guaranteed protection of forest on the Paria Peninsula (i.e. the area where the birds have recently been recorded), combined with: (2) a survey of the Cerro Negro and Cerro Turumiquire areas to determine the current status of the species on the mainland; and (3) an ecological study to discover the precise nature of its habitat requirements. All such studies and initiatives should if possible integrate with work on all five threatened species in this area (see Threats under White-tailed Sabrewing).

REMARKS (1) Phelps and Phelps (1950) use this specimen as evidence of the species's occurrence in Monagas state – the bird presumably coming from the slopes of the cerro, between Caripe and summit. (2) Specimens in AMNH and FMNH are labelled "Cerro Humo, Irapa", and were taken at 1,200 m. Irapa (10°34'N 62°35'W) is at sea level (Paynter 1982) and was presumably used as a base from which collecting trips were made, the specimens obviously being taken on the upper slopes of Cerro Humo.

ALAGOAS FOLIAGE-GLEANER *Philydor novaesi* E^2

The last hope for this small insectivore appears to be an unprotected and rapidly diminishing tract of upland forest, only 1,500 ha in extent, near the type-locality in Alagoas state, Brazil.

DISTRIBUTION The Alagoas Foliage-gleaner (see Remarks 1) is known only from (Fazenda) Pedra Branca ("Serra Branca": see Remarks 2), near Murici (9°19'S 35°57'W), on the south-eastern escarpment of the Borborema plateau in Alagoas, north-eastern Brazil (Teixeira and Gonzaga 1983b, D. M. Teixeira *in litt.* 1987), although it appears now to be present only in the remaining (adjacent) part of this area known as Fazenda Bananeira (see Threats, Measures Proposed). It was described from two adult males mist-netted in February 1979 (Teixeira and Gonzaga 1983b), while four additional specimens, including three females, were obtained at the same locality in November 1983, May 1984 and January 1986, all between 500 and 550 m (Teixeira *et al.* 1987; specimens in MNRJ); there were sight records in 1991 and April 1992 (D. Willis *in litt.* 1991, M. Pearman *in litt.* 1992). The species has not been found in the coastal lowland forests of the region, which have been well explored by ornithologists, although it is not difficult to locate owing to its loud vocalizations (Teixeira and Gonzaga 1983b; also M. Pearman *in litt.* 1992).

POPULATION Numbers are not known. Although described as a relatively conspicuous bird and easy to locate at the time of its discovery (Teixeira and Gonzaga 1983b), very few specimens have been collected since (see Distribution), and efforts made to find the species again in early 1987 and 1988 have failed (D. M. Teixeira verbally 1988), so that it "may be very threatened" (D. M. Teixeira *in litt.* 1987), or at least it seems to be rare.

ECOLOGY The Alagoas Foliage-gleaner has been observed in the forest interior, from the undergrowth to the canopy of the mid-storey trees, also frequenting areas of secondary growth such as selectively logged and old secondary forests (Teixeira and Gonzaga 1983b). Birds are found in pairs or small groups, and also join mixed-species flocks in which Lesser Woodcreepers *Lepidocolaptes fuscus* are particularly frequent (Teixeira and Gonzaga 1983b; for a description of the composition of these flocks, see Teixeira and Gonzaga 1985); all records in April 1992 were of single birds in mixed-species flocks (M. Pearman *in litt.* 1992). Food is obtained on the surface of leaves, branches and trunks, under bark, and amongst the debris jammed in branches, and consists of insects (including larvae taken from dead wood); the stomachs of two specimens contained beetles (perhaps Carabidae), grasshoppers, and ants (Teixeira and Gonzaga 1983b). There is no information on breeding of the species; specimens collected in early February had fairly enlarged testes and were moulting (Teixeira and Gonzaga 1983b), which might indicate a post-breeding condition: an immature female was collected in late January (specimen in MNRJ).

THREATS Destruction of forest in the vicinity of Fazenda Pedra Branca is the single most serious threat to this and all other upland forest species in Alagoas. Sugarcane plantations have replaced all the lower forested areas in Alagoas (see Threats under Alagoas Curassow *Mitu mitu*), and the remaining forests on the higher parts of the ranges, although not under threat from the sugarcane industry, are affected by other pressures such as selective logging, firewood removal and small-scale cultivation (e.g. of bananas), steadily eradicating the remaining forest on steep mountain slopes (Teixeira and Gonzaga 1983b, Teixeira 1986). The critical site for the Alagoas Foliage-gleaner at Pedra Branca, once some 7,000 ha in extent, has largely disappeared in the course of some 15 years of inertia over its protection, such that in 1990 the entire fazenda was found to have been cleared (D. Willis *in litt.* 1991, J. F. Pacheco verbally 1992); the remaining 1,500 ha, called "Bananeira", is protected by law from further felling, but indiscriminate small-scale logging was evidently still occurring in April 1992 (M. Pearman *in litt.* 1992; see Measures Proposed).

MEASURES TAKEN The Alagoas Foliage-gleaner is protected under Brazilian law (Bernardes *et al.* 1990). It was the discovery of and proposal to protect a forested area near Murici (Special Environmental Agency 1977) that led to its investigation in 1979 and hence to the discovery of four new species from this site, the Alagoas Foliage-gleaner itself, Alagoas Antwren *Myrmotherula snowi*, Orange-bellied Antwren *Terenura sicki* and Long-tailed Tyrannulet *Phylloscartes ceciliae* (LPG; see relevant accounts).

MEASURES PROPOSED Although the proposal to protect a forested area of some 5,000 ha near Murici as an ecological station, important to preserve the vegetation in order to sustain several streams rising there (Special Environmental Agency 1977), pre-existed the discovery there of four new birds for science, this discovery apparently made no difference to the urgency (or lack of it) with which the proposal was addressed, and concrete action was only possible (through FBCN) in mid-1992 to establish this as a major protected area in the region. The delay is all the more regrettable, not only because "Pedra Branca" is now known to hold at least 12 threatened bird species (see Remarks 2), but also because in the intervening years the main site in question has been "totally deforested" (J. F. Pacheco verbally 1992), and further because, as of 1987 (when its preservation as apparently the largest remaining continuous forested area in north-east Brazil was described as imperative: Teixeira 1987b), US$200,000 was available to WWF–US through the MacArthur Foundation for the conservation of the area, yet only recently have conditions been suitable to initiate action (M. G. Kelsey verbally 1992). According to one report, all that apparently now remains is an elongated tract of forest, believed to be about 1,500 ha in extent, covering several ridge-tops and belonging to Fazenda Bananeira, which is known to hold this and at least some of the other species listed in Remarks (Alagoas Antwren, Buff-throated Purpletuft *Iodopleura pipra*), and which must now be the subject of urgent action (see Threats) if it, too, is not to disappear (D. Willis *in litt.* 1991); however, FBCN is informed that another 1,400 ha still exists at Usina Bititinga, and the intention is to include both tracts of forest in the park once further surveys have been carried out to demarcate boundaries, etc. (R. B. Pineschi *in litt.* 1992). It is clearly vital that FBCN is successful in this initiative (see Remarks 2), and the strongest international support should attend its efforts and ensure their rapid conclusion.

REMARKS (1) The Alagoas Foliage-gleaner is closely related to the Black-capped Foliage-gleaner *Philydor atricapillus* from south-eastern Brazil, Paraguay and north-eastern Argentina, with which it seems to form a superspecies (Teixeira and Gonzaga 1983b): the English name Greater Black-capped Foliage-gleaner, used for this species in Teixeira *et al.* (1987), indicates this relationship. (2) Although the name of the type-locality of this bird has been given as "Serra Branca" (Teixeira and Gonzaga 1983b, Teixeira *et al.* 1987), this mountain is actually known by local people as Pedra Branca, after the farm that once encompassed a major part of it (P. T. Z. Antas verbally 1988, LPG). One other threatened bird species, the Alagoas Antwren, is known solely from this small area, and another 11, the Golden-tailed Parrotlet *Touit surda*, Plain Spinetail *Synallaxis infuscata*, Orange-bellied Antwren, Scalloped Antbird *Myrmeciza ruficauda*, Black-headed Berryeater *Carpornis melanocephalus*, Buff-throated Purpletuft, White-winged Cotinga *Xipholena atropurpurea*, Long-tailed Tyrannulet (only one other locality known), Forbes's Blackbird *Curaeus forbesi* (recorded in adjacent fields), Seven-coloured Tanager *Tangara fastuosa* and Yellow-faced Siskin *Carduelis yarrellii* (see relevant accounts), have been recorded there, along with the highly threatened subspecies *pernambucensis* of the near-threatened Solitary Tinamou *Tinamus solitarius* (King 1978-1979, LPG), making this one of the most remarkable and important of sites in the Neotropics for threatened species, and one of the most urgent cases to which to attend in Brazilian conservation (see Measures Proposed).

HENNA-HOODED FOLIAGE-GLEANER *Hylocryptus erythrocephalus* I[7]

This moderately common (but possibly seasonal) furnariid inhabits the understorey of deciduous, semi-deciduous and moist evergreen forest (generally from 400 to 1,350 m) in a restricted area of south-west Ecuador and north-west Peru, where it is threatened by habitat destruction and disturbance.

DISTRIBUTION The Henna-hooded Foliage-gleaner (see Remarks) is confined to forests at 400-1,750 m in Manabí, Loja and immediately adjacent El Oro provinces, south-west Ecuador, and Tumbes and Piura departments, north-west Peru. Two subspecies have been described, the nominate form in Ecuador and Tumbes National Forest, Peru, and *palamblae* in the rest of Peru, these together being known from very few areas at the following localities (coordinates from Paynter and Traylor 1977, Stephens and Traylor 1983, or read from IGM 1989):

Ecuador (*Manabí*) Cerro San Sebastián, 400-700 m, c.1°34'S 80°40'W, in Machalilla National Park (sightings in January and August 1991: TAP, R. S. Ridgely *in litt.* 1991); (*El Oro*) just south of Portovelo, 3°44'S 79°37'W (recent sighting: P. Greenfield *in litt.* 1989); (*Loja*) La Puente, 760 m, untraced, but south of Puyango and probably near Quebrada Cebollal at c.3°55'S 80°03'W (male in AMNH taken in October 1921); Quebrada Las Vegas, 1,250 m, 3°59'S 79°57'W, near Alamor (up to three birds seen at the end of August and in September 1991: Williams and Tobias 1991); Hacienda Yamana, 1,100 m, 4°01'S 79°40'W (Paynter 1972b: specimens in MCZ); Alamor, 1,390 m, 4°02'S 80°02'W (Chapman 1919, 1926); 6 km north-west of Catacocha (a few birds found in early March 1991: Best 1992); 2 km north-west of Catacocha, 1,550 m (at least eight birds, plus an active nest, found in April 1992: M. B. Robbins *in litt.* 1992); east and below Celica, 1,350-1,700 m, 4°07'S 79°59'W (one bird recorded in August 1989, and at least four birds calling territorially in April 1992: R. S. Ridgely *in litt.* 1989, M. B. Robbins *in litt.* 1992); El Empalme, 800 m, 4°08'S 79°49'W (one seen in February 1991: Best 1992); near Cruzpampa, 1,200 m, 4°10'S 80°01'W (one bird recorded in August 1989: R. S. Ridgely *in litt.* 1989); 10 km by road below Sabanilla, 500-550 m, 4°10'S 80°08'W (at least eight birds heard in April 1992: M. B. Robbins *in litt.* 1992); Paletillas, 470 m, 4°11'S 80°17'W (two females in AMNH taken in June 1919: Chapman 1926); Quebradas Suquinda and Yaguana, 1,550-1,750 m, at 4°18'S 79°48'W, where there were daily records, 8-12 June 1989 (Rahbek *et al.* 1989), 10 sightings in late August and September 1989 (Best and Clarke 1991), three sightings in August 1990 (R. Williams *in litt.* 1991), and several sightings in February 1991 (Best 1992); Quebrada Hueco Hondo, 600-800 m, Tambo Negro, c.5 km south-west of Sabiango, at 4°23'S 79°51'W (several sightings with birds heard constantly in February and March 1991, and a specimen in MECN collected during March 1991: Best 1992, NK);

Peru (*Tumbes*) El Caucho, 400 m, 3°50'S 80°16'W, and Campo Verde, 750 m, c.3°51'S 80°12'W, both in Tumbes National Forest (Wiedenfeld *et al.* 1985); (*Piura*) Palambla, specimens (in AMNH and FMNH) labelled 1,190-1,980 m, at 5°23'S 79°37'W (also Chapman 1926); (*Lambayeque*) Quebrada Caballito, c.500 m, a side valley to Quebrada Tocto, at 5°48'S 79°40'W (one bird seen in February 1986: M. Kessler *in litt.* 1988); km 21 on the Olmos–Bagua road (one bird seen in June 1987: M. Pearman *in litt.* 1991); km 34 on the Olmos–Abra de Porculla highway, on the border with Piura, south-west of the pass at 5°51'S 79°31'N, altitude given as 1,275 m by Schulenberg and Parker (1981) but as 1,350 m by Krabbe (1984).

This foliage-gleaner was not recorded between Canchaque and Cruz Blanca during extensive surveys in 1974, 1975 and 1980 (Parker *et al.* 1985) and the immediate vicinity of Palambla is devoid of forest (Stephens and Traylor 1983), but some unexplored forest can be seen away from the road (T. S. Schulenberg *in litt.* 1988). The White-winged Guan *Penelope albipennis*, inhabiting fairly similar vegetation, has been found in eight different valley systems between Palambla and Abra de Porculla (see relevant account), and although the Henna-hooded Foliage-gleaner has only been recorded from one of these (Quebrada Tocto), it probably occurs in all those that hold sufficiently green, humid patches of vegetation (NK).

POPULATION In Ecuador, at Cerro San Sebastián in Machalilla National Park, the species was found to be rare during six days of fieldwork in January 1991 (TAP), but an ANSP expedition found eight individuals in two valleys on the same mountain over 3-9 August 1991, and speculated that the population might be fairly large (R. S. Ridgely *in litt.* 1991). Between Sozoranga and Nueva Fátima 8-10 were heard and seen daily along 500 m of trail in mid-June 1989 (Rahbek *et al.* 1989), whilst in August and September the species was never heard calling and was found to be rather uncommon there (seen on one out of three or four days) (Best and Clarke 1991). These differences in recorded numbers may possibly be explained by seasonal movements (B. J. Best *in litt.* 1992). In the Celica area it was scarce in August 1989, and only two birds were recorded: one near Cruzpampa at 1,200 m, and one east of Celica at 1,350 m (R. S. Ridgely *in litt.* 1989). In this same general area (between Catacocha and Sabanilla), the species was found to be common in April 1992, with a minimum of eight birds at two sites (including a breeding pair with two young in the nest) and at least four individuals at a third locality (M. B. Robbins *in litt.* 1992); but this was an El Niño year when bird population numbers may increase in otherwise drier scrubby areas (NK, B. J. Best *in litt.* 1992: see Ecology under Little Woodstar *Acestura bombus*), and this appears to have been the case in 1992, with considerable amounts of rain received beginning in mid-March (M. B. Robbins *in litt.* 1992).

There are too few distributional data to give a realistic estimate for Peru. In spite of procuring 12 specimens between 14 June and 5 July 1979, Wiedenfeld *et al.* (1985) stated it to be "uncommon" in Tumbes National Forest, but M. Kessler (*in litt.* 1988) found it to be fairly common there in late February and early March 1986, with up to 10 recorded per morning, along the Campo Verde–El Caucho trail and around El Caucho; and in late July 1988, 12 were found in two hours along c.1 km of trail between Campo Verde and nearby Cotrina (Parker *et al.* ms). Only scattered patches of forest, few if any larger than 10 km^2 (other than Tumbes National Forest), remain within the Peruvian range of this and other species endemic to the region, and what is almost surely the largest remaining population of this species occurs in the Tumbes National Forest, on forested ridges between río Tumbes and the Ecuador border (Parker *et al.* ms).

ECOLOGY In Peru the Henna-hooded Foliage-gleaner is only known from relatively undisturbed evergreen moist and semi-deciduous forests (Parker *et al.* ms), but at Portovelo and in the Sozoranga region, Ecuador, it has also been found in degraded patches of second-growth woodland and small areas of forest in ravines: north-west and south-east of Sozoranga the species was mostly restricted to dense, tangled forests that were inaccessible to cattle and donkeys, and at Quebrada Hueco Hondo (Tambo Negro) it occurred in *Ceiba*-dominated deciduous forest (P. Greenfield *in litt.* 1989, Rahbek *et al.* 1989, Best and Clarke 1991, Best 1992). Most records range from 400 to 1,350 m, but at Quebradas Suquinda and Yaguana it was only found at 1,550 to 1,750 m (see Distribution). Palambla specimens were collected in September and October 1922 and were each labelled 1,190-1,980 m (specimens in AMNH and FMNH); as all H. Watkins's Palambla specimens examined, regardless of species, were labelled thus (specimens in AMNH), the exact elevation is not certain. At Abra de Porculla the species has been seen in streamside vegetation with tall, large-leaved deciduous trees and scattered evergreen undergrowth; the adjacent slopes have been cleared and are now covered with shrubbery, weeds and scattered small trees (TAP; also Schulenberg and Parker 1981, NK). At Hacienda Yamana in Loja province, Ecuador, the species was found in "dense scrub near a brook" which had thick vegetation, while the valley otherwise was "arid and sparsely vegetated, possibly a result of man's activities" (Paynter 1972b). Near Alamor, also in Loja, birds were seen (in August and September 1991) in small areas with woodland, hedges and mixed banana and coffee plantations (Williams and Tobias 1991), and near Celica and Catacocha, birds were found breeding in recently burnt areas with little vegetation other than small clumps of thorny scrub and dense (c.2-3 m high) second growth restricted to ravines (M. B. Robbins *in litt.* 1992). At El Caucho in Tumbes, Peru, there is deciduous and semi-deciduous forest with a stream that dries out during the dry season (June–December), and the topography is hilly with narrow canyons and steep slopes: the lower part of the forest is composed primarily of large *Ceiba trichistandra*, often reaching 20 m in height, but a variety of smaller trees are also found in the more open, level areas; higher up, where the foliage-gleaner is commonest, *Ceiba* is absent, and the forest is generally more humid; arboreal epiphytes, especially *Tillandsia* spp., are common, the forest understorey is relatively open, but in the narrow canyons vine tangles are common (Wiedenfeld *et al.* 1985, J. W. Eley *in litt.* 1989).

The Henna-hooded Foliage-gleaner is found alone or in pairs, rarely up to four individuals together, and forages on or within 1 m of the ground (Paynter 1972b, Schulenberg and Parker 1981, Wiedenfeld *et al.* 1985, Rahbek *et al.* 1989, Best and Clarke 1991, NK). In the Cordillera Larga, Tumbes, the species occurs alone or with either Stripe-headed Brush-finch *Atlapetes torquatus*, Orange-billed Sparrow *Arremon aurantiirostris* or Black-capped Sparrow *A. abeillei* (Parker *et al.* ms); it sometimes loosely associates with mixed-species flocks, one such including Streak-headed Woodcreeper *Lepidocolaptes souleyetii*, Thick-billed Euphonia *Euphonia laniirostris*, Variable Seedeater *Sporophila americana* and Black-capped Sparrow, and another with Fasciated Wren *Campylorhynchus fasciatus*, Speckle-breasted Wren *Thryothorus (maculipectus) sclateri*, Variable Seedeater and Black-capped Sparrow (J. W. Eley *in litt.* 1989). At Sozoranga in mid-June and from August to September 1989 it readily joined mixed-species flocks for shorter periods, following last in close association with White-winged Brush-finch *Atlapetes leucopterus*, other flock members being Ecuadorian Piculet *Picumnus sclateri*, Streak-headed Woodcreeper, Azara's Spinetail *Synallaxis azarae*, Great Antshrike *Taraba major* and Three-banded Warbler *Basileuterus trifasciatus* (C. Rahbek *in litt.* 1989, Best and Clarke 1991). It often rummages about on the ground, rustling through and tossing dead leaves and twigs into the air, and probes leaf-clusters, low in vine tangles (Wiedenfeld *et al.* 1985, C. Rahbek *in litt.* 1989, Best and Clarke 1991, Best 1992). Stomachs of 14 specimens contained insect parts, one of them also terrestrial isopods, one a large caterpillar and a 1 cm beetle (Wiedenfeld *et al.* 1985: specimens in ANSP and MECN). Although a bird of undergrowth, it may be somewhat dependent on a dense ground cover of fallen leaves from large trees (NK).

On 27 January 1991 three birds were seen violently chasing and attacking each other up to 2 m from the ground, making short flights from branch to branch and calling very loudly in a territorial dispute; during the same week single birds were seen perched 2-3 m up in low trees calling repeatedly (Best 1992). The nest is placed at the end of a c.1 m long burrow in a bank or disturbed slope (M. Kessler *in litt.* 1988, M. B. Robbins *in litt.* 1992). A nest with young was found at El Caucho on 3 March 1986, and at Catacocha on 3 April 1992 (M. Kessler *in litt.* 1988, M. B. Robbins *in litt.* 1992): birds in breeding condition have been taken at Tambo Negro on 10 March, Catacocha on 3 April and Sabanilla on 9 April, and birds with inactive gonads have been collected in June, July and September to November (Paynter 1972b, Wiedenfeld *et al.* 1985; specimens in AMNH, ANSP and FMNH), with immatures taken in June–July (Chapman 1919, Wiedenfeld *et al.* 1985). The behaviour observed near Sozoranga in late January and February 1991 suggests that the birds were nesting (see above). Most species of bird in this region probably breed during the wet season (Marchant 1958), from January to May (Brown 1941).

THREATS Habitat destruction appears to be an immediate threat to species with limited altitudinal and geographical ranges in south-west Ecuador and north-west Peru (Parker *et al.* 1985). Below Cruz Blanca, Peru, forest is being cleared from above and below: with only scattered patches now existing below 2,150 m, and none left at Palambla, this foliage-gleaner has presumably declined dramatically in the region (Parker *et al.* 1985; also Stephens and Traylor 1983). Paynter (1972b) believed man to be a major cause of the aridity in Casanga valley, Loja, Ecuador, a view not shared by R. S. Ridgely (*in litt.* 1989). However, forest clearance and degradation, especially trampling of the undergrowth by cattle and donkeys, is a serious threat to this largely terrestrial species (Best and Clarke 1991, Best 1992), although its occurrence in second-growth scrub and sparsely vegetated areas (during breeding and post-breeding periods: see above) gives some hope for the longer-term survival of the bird (see Measures Proposed). The Machalilla National Park suffers from the activities of numerous families living within its boundaries (TAP, R. S. Ridgely *in litt.* 1991). There is little other than its remoteness to protect the Tumbes National Forest (M. Kessler verbally 1991).

MEASURES TAKEN The major stronghold of this species may be the Tumbes National Forest (75,100 ha: IUCN 1992) in the Cordillera Larga, Peru, which receives some amount of protection by the military authorities, but is far from secure (TAP). The species also occurs in Machalilla National Park (55,000 ha: IUCN 1992) (but see Threats).

MEASURES PROPOSED It is imperative that effective protection of the two large forest reserves where it occurs be ensured. Initiatives specific to Machalilla National Park are outlined in the equivalent section under Grey-backed Hawk *Leucopternis occidentalis*. Efforts should be made to locate additional populations of this foliage-gleaner, and more of its habitat should be protected in some way, especially farther south on the Pacific Andean slope in Piura and Lambayeque (it is of particular interest to determine what populations can be secured through efforts to protect the known habitat of the White-winged Guan). A more precise definition of its ecological requirements is needed, especially the extent to which it can sustain viable populations in second growth or degraded habitats, and the degree to which the population varies in size and habitat preferences during El Niño years. Details on the other threatened species, and additional comments on the conservation status of forests west of the Andes in south-west Ecuador and north-west Peru, are in Measures Proposed under Grey-backed Hawk.

REMARKS Chapman (1919) created the genus *Hylocryptus* for the species; Hellmayr (Cory and Hellmayr 1925) suggested that it was closely related to the (near-threatened) Chestnut-capped Foliage-gleaner *Automolus rectirostris* of south-eastern and central Brazil. Zimmer (1936) agreed with this, and shifted *rectirostris* to *Hylocryptus*. Vaurie (1971) agreed that *rectirostris* is the closest relative of *erythrocephalus*, but merged *Hylocryptus* in *Automolus*, a treatment supported by Paynter (1972b), unopposed by Schulenberg and Parker (1981) and Wiedenfeld *et al.* (1985), but resisted by Parker *et al.* (ms). Vocally, *erythrocephalus* seems fairly different from species of *Automolus* (*sensu stricto*) (R. S. Ridgely *in litt.* 1989).

RUFOUS-NECKED FOLIAGE-GLEANER *Syndactyla ruficollis* E[2]

This generally common furnariid inhabits evergreen, semi-deciduous and deciduous forests from 400 to 2,900 m on the foothills and slopes of the western Andes in south-west Ecuador and north-west Peru, where it is threatened by habitat destruction and disturbance.

DISTRIBUTION The Rufous-necked Foliage-gleaner (see Remarks 1) ranges from El Oro province, south-west Ecuador, to southern Cajamarca department, north-west Peru, at elevations from 400 to 2,900 m, in the foothills and on the Pacific slope of the Andes. Localities (coordinates, unless otherwise stated, from Paynter and Traylor 1977 and Stephens and Traylor 1983) are as follows:

Ecuador (*El Oro*) c.8-10 km west of Piñas, 3°42'S 79°42'W (two birds seen in July 1990: P. K. Donahue *in litt.* 1991) (see Remarks 2); (*Loja*) Cordillera de Celica: Tierra Colorada, 1,400-1,850 m, 4°02'S 79°57'W (sightings in February 1991: Best 1992); Quebrada Cebollal, 945 m, 3°55'S 80°03'W, September 1921; Alamor, 1,390 m, at 4°01'S 80°03'W, August and September 1921; Guachanamá, 2,500 and 2,760 m, at 4°02'S 79°53'W, October 1920; Celica, 1,300-2,000 m, at 4°07'S 79°59'-80°02'W, September 1920 (sources for the preceding four localities being Chapman 1921, 1926; specimens in AMNH, ANSP, BMNH and MCZ; also two in ANSP and one in MECN collected August 1989, and one in WFVZ taken in March 1991); between Celica and Alamor, 1,000-2,550 m (birds seen almost daily in August 1991: Williams and Tobias 1991); 5 km south-east of Gonzanamá, 4°15'S 79°53'W (specimens in MCZ collected in July and August 1965), where an isolated forest exists (LANDSAT 1986); 1 km east-south-east of Cariamanga, 2,300 m, at 4°20'S 79°33'W (specimen in MECN collected in April 1991); Utuana, 2,450 m, at 4°22'S 79°42'W (sightings in August–September 1989 and February 1991: Best and Clarke 1991, Best 1992, NK); between Utuana and Sozoranga, 1,750-1,800 m, at 4°20'S 79°46'W (sightings in February 1991: Best 1992); Quebradas Suquinda and Yaguana, between Sozoranga and Nueva Fátima, at 4°18'S 79°48'W (sightings in June, August and September 1989 and February 1991: Best and Clarke 1991, Bloch *et al.* 1991, Best 1992); Quebrada Hueco Hondo, 600-1,000 m, Tambo Negro, c.5 km south-west of Sabiango, at 4°24'S 79°51'W (sightings in August and September 1989 and February and March 1991; specimen in ZMUC taken in March 1991: Best and Clarke 1991, Best 1992, NK); Angashcola (near Amaluza), 4°34'S 79°22'W (1-2 seen in July 1991: Williams and Tobias 1991); La Laja, 610 m, 3°47'S 80°03'W (specimen in ANSP, taken in June 1933) (see Remarks 2);

Peru (*Tumbes*) El Caucho, 400 m, at 3°50'S 80°16'W (Wiedenfeld *et al.* 1985); Campo Verde, 750 m, at 3°51'S 80°12'W (Wiedenfeld *et al.* 1985), these first two sites being in the Cordillera Larga, a south-western spur of northern Cordillera Chilla; El Angolo, 700 m, 90 km north-west of Sullana (specimen in LSUMZ) at c.4°28'S 80°48'W, in the Cerros de la Brea (= Cerros de Amotape) in Tumbes and Piura departments (situated south-west of Cordillera Larga and probably part of the same geological formation: NK); (*Piura*) near Cerro Chacas, 2,625 m, at c.4°36'S 79°44'W (sightings in September 1989: Best and Clarke 1991); between (and below) Cruz Blanca at 5°20'S 79°32'W and Canchaque at 5°24'S 79°26'W, where there are records from 1,190 to 2,900 m (Chapman 1926, Zimmer 1935, Parker *et al.* 1985, B. M. Whitney *in litt.* 1991; specimens in AMNH, ANSP, FMNH, LSUMZ and MCZ); below (west of) Abra de Porculla, at 1,350 m (given as 1,280 m on label) and 1,600 m, 5°51'S 79°31'W, in south-west Piura near the Lambayeque border (Zimmer 1935; specimens in ANSP, LSUMZ and MCZ, taken in May 1933); (*Lambayeque*) hills east of Olmos, 1,000 m, 5°59'S 79°46'W (sightings in August 1989: B. M. Whitney *in litt.* 1991); Bosque de Chiñama, 2,200-2,500 m, at 6°02'S 79°27'W (6-7 specimens in MHNJP collected in August 1988; coordinates read from IGM 1967); (*Cajamarca*) in the isolated forest on the upper ríos Chanchay and Saña: Chugur, 2,750 m, at 6°40'S 78°45'W; Taulis, 2,700 m, at c.6°54'S 79°03'W; Seques, 1,520 m, at 6°54'S 79°18'W; and Paucal, at 7°00'S 79°10'W

(Taczanowski 1884-1886, Chapman 1926, Zimmer 1935; specimens in AMNH and CM). The species probably also occurs in the isolated forest east of Sapillica at c.4°50'S 79°55'W (LANDSAT 1986; coordinates read from IGM 1982): there appears to be proper habitat along the Andean Pacific slope from c.4°25'S in Loja province, Ecuador, south to c.5°S (LANDSAT 1986), probably continuing south to c.5°25'S (NK).

POPULATION In Ecuador at Celica, the bird was fairly common at 1,300-2,000 m in August 1989, and a fair amount of habitat remained there at the time, the area presumably having a substantial population (R. S. Ridgely *in litt.* 1989). It was judged to be locally common there in March 1991 (L. F. Kiff *in litt.* 1991), and was found to be common and seen almost daily in the Celica–Alamor area between 1,000 and 2,550 m in August 1991 (Williams and Tobias 1991). Between Sozoranga and Nueva Fátima at 1,750 m, it was deemed to be fairly common with 1-3 birds seen several times daily in June 1989 (Bloch *et al.* 1991), and generally in the Sozoranga region it is common above 1,600 m and uncommon below 1,000 m (Best and Clarke 1991, Best 1992). In Peru the species was reported rare at El Caucho in June and July 1979 (Wiedenfeld *et al.* 1985) and uncommon below Cruz Blanca (Parker *et al.* 1985). In late July 1988 it was inconspicuous and apparently uncommon at Campo Verde, where only five individuals were recorded on one day (Parker *et al.* ms). The large number of specimens collected during 1988 in Bosque de Chiñama, Lambayeque, may suggest that the species is common there (T. S. Schulenberg *in litt.* 1989).

ECOLOGY The Rufous-necked Foliage-gleaner inhabits dense to moderately open forest understorey, especially bamboo, and middle storey in humid evergreen forest as well as humid, more or less evergreen patches (e.g. in shaded ravines, at springs or along streams) in semi-deciduous forest, occurring uncommonly in adjacent *Ceiba*-dominated deciduous forest and degraded scrub (e.g. at Tambo Negro): it ranges from 400 to 2,900 m, but is commonest above 1,600 m (Parker *et al.* 1985, Wiedenfeld *et al.* 1985, Best and Clarke 1991, Best 1992). Birds occur singly and in pairs or, during the dry season, in small groups of 3-4 (with 12-15 seen on one occasion), and (especially in the dry season) typically associates with mixed-species flocks, even if only a few other species are present (Parker *et al.* ms, R. S. Ridgely *in litt.* 1989, Best and Clarke 1991, B. M. Whitney *in litt.* 1991, Best 1992). This foliage-gleaner has been found most commonly associating with Scarlet-backed Woodpecker *Veniliornis callonotus*, Spot-crowned Woodcreeper *Lepidocolaptes affinis*, Speckle-breasted Wren *Thryothorus sclateri* and Rufous-browed Peppershrike *Cyclarhis gujanensis*, although the mixed flocks tended to be larger and more diverse than those joined by Henna-hooded Foliage-gleaner *Hylocryptus erythrocephalus*, with (depending on altitude) 14 other species recorded (Best and Clarke 1991: see relevant account).

The species characteristically forages in trees (often in close proximity to stands of bamboo), and probes the bases of arboreal bromeliads (also ferns, mosses and bark) on the larger limbs, as high as 10 m above ground, but it has also been seen hopping through dense tangles of bamboo where it probed the bases of leaf-shoots on stems, and once on the forest floor foraging in the manner of Henna-hooded Foliage-gleaner (Parker *et al.* 1985, Best and Clarke 1991, B. M. Whitney *in litt.* 1991, Best 1992, NK). Most sightings below Cruz Blanca and at Cariamanga were of individuals 2-3 m above ground (Parker *et al.* 1985, NK), while most in the Sozoranga and Celica regions foraged in the understorey and middle strata (Best and Clarke 1991, Best 1992). At Tierra Colorada a bird was seen pecking at the trunk of a burnt tree in a recently planted maize field (Best 1992). One specimen (in LSUMZ) had the remains of large insects in its stomach, and another (in MECN) small insects.

Birds with active gonads have been collected in May (in AMNH and ANSP); with slightly enlarged gonads in April, June, August and October (AMNH, LSUMZ and MECN); with inactive gonads in all months from June to December (AMNH, FMNH, LSUMZ, MCZ and MECN); juvenile or immature birds have been found in April, May and June (AMNH and ANSP), so apparently the species breeds during the wet season, from January to May (Brown 1941), as do probably most species in the region (Marchant 1958). No nest has been found.

THREATS Considerable trampling of the undergrowth by cattle and clearance of bamboo by local people for pack-animal food pose a threat to this and other undergrowth inhabitants such as Grey-headed Antbird *Myrmeciza griseiceps* (see relevant account) that are restricted to a relatively small and densely settled region (Parker *et al.* 1985). Despite the species's ability to tolerate considerable habitat disturbance, its preference for humid high-elevation forest makes it especially vulnerable to the combined effects of trampling, understorey clearance and rampant deforestation occurring throughout its range: all patches of forest holding the species in Ecuador may be gone, critically degraded, or be too small to hold a viable population within 10 years (NK, Best and Clarke 1991).

MEASURES TAKEN The species is known to occur in only one forest reserve, the Tumbes National Forest (75,100 ha: IUCN 1992), where, however, it is rare (Wiedenfeld *et al.* 1985), probably as the park lies at the lower limit of its altitudinal range (see Distribution). Bosque de Chiñama, a forest of some 1,200 ha (read from IGM 1967), is being vigorously protected by the local cooperative (I. Franke *per* T. S. Schulenberg *in litt.* 1989).

MEASURES PROPOSED Although still fairly common in some areas, this species may soon be gone, at least from Ecuador, unless immediate action is taken to protect some of the remaining patches of highland forest in western Loja province, either in the Sozoranga region or on the west slope of the Celica mountains, and preferably both (NK). In Peru continued protection of Bosque de Chiñama should be secured, and the forests near Taulis should be evaluated for conservation. All remaining habitat within the species's range should be mapped and surveyed. Comments on the conservation status of forests and the other threatened and endemic bird species in south-west Ecuador and north-west Peru are given in the equivalent section under Grey-backed Hawk *Leucopternis occidentalis* and Grey-headed Antbird.

REMARKS (1) The Rufous-necked Foliage-gleaner was considered a close relative of the Buff-throated Foliage-gleaner *Automolus ochrolaemus* by Zimmer (1935) and Vaurie (1980), but Parker *et al.* (1985) saw little morphological or behavioural similarity between *ruficollis* and any member of *Automolus*, and suggested that *ruficollis* (and *Simoxenops*), on the basis of streaked pattern, behaviour and strikingly similar vocalizations, might belong in the genus *Syndactyla*, and the case has been formally made out in Parker *et al.* (ms). Ecuadorian specimens have been described as a separate subspecies, *celicae*, with birds from Palambla being intermediate (Chapman 1921, 1926, Zimmer 1935). Birds from Tumbes, and presumably Cerros de la Brea (= Cerros de Amotape) in adjacent Piura, are probably referable to the Ecuadorian form (NK), as also happens with the subspecies of Henna-hooded Foliage-gleaner (Wiedenfeld *et al.* 1985; see relevant account).

(2) Concerning the locality "La Laja": it should be noted that IGM (1982), which is followed here for the position it gives, calls it "Las Lajas", while it is placed at 3°48'S 80°08'W in Tumbes department, Peru, by Stephens and Traylor (1983), and has also been misquoted as La Lejía, Piura, by Peters (1951) and subsequently misinterpreted by Vaurie (1980) as La Lejía in Amazonas department, Peru (NK).

GREAT XENOPS *Megaxenops parnaguae* K[12]

Dry woodland in the heavily populated interior of north-east Brazil is the habitat of this apparently very local and little known mid-storey bark-gleaner, which is presumably suffering from land clearance.

DISTRIBUTION The Great Xenops (see Remarks 1) is known from a few localities thinly scattered over a large area in interior north-eastern and central Brazil. The assumption that it occurs in "probably all the caatinga region of northeastern Brazil" (Vaurie 1980: 325 and map 55) is in need of further supporting evidence, but it is certainly true that very recent records have hugely extended its known range.

Ceará A specimen was collected in March 1925 at Várzea Formosa, near Ipueiras, on the eastern escarpments of the Serra da Ibiapaba (Hellmayr 1929a). Sight records of this bird are known from Chapada do Araripe, recently (Vaurie 1980, Teixeira *et al.* 1989, J. F. Pacheco and B. M. Whitney *in litt.* 1991, M. Pearman *in litt.* 1992), Quixadá in 1982 and Tauá in 1983 (R. Otoch *in litt.* 1986).

Piauí The type-material was two specimens collected in June 1903 on the trail from Parnaguá to Olho d'Agua (untraceable); several other specimens were shot (but not conserved) at the same place on the same day (Reiser 1926). There is a sight record from near Manoel Emídio in July 1987 (P. Roth *in litt.* 1987; also Roth 1987c, 1989b). The species is well represented in Serra da Capivara National Park (Olmos in press). Six specimens (in AMNH, CM) were taken over two days at Parnaguá, 300 m, in June 1927 (see Remarks 2).

Pernambuco A specimen was collected on 2 August 1980 at the border of the Serra Negra Biological Reserve, 1,100 m (8°37'S 30°02'W) (A. G. M. Coelho *in litt.* 1986).

Bahia Eleven specimens (in AMNH, ANSP and LSUMZ) were obtained at "Santa Ritta", 490 m, between May and August 1927, and three (in AMNH) at "Sincorá", 460 m, in mid-October 1927 (also Naumburg 1928; see Remarks 3). There is a sight record from Orobó (12°16'S 40°26'W: see map in Naumburg 1935) in 1927 (Vaurie 1980) and another of a singing bird at Fazenda Brasileira, not far from Serrinha, in June 1991 (D. Willis verbally 1992).

Minas Gerais The species has been recorded in the far north and east of the state, near Mocambinho (c.15°05'S 44°00'W), August/September 1990 (Teixeira *et al.* in press, whence coordinates); on the rio Urucuia at Buritis, February 1989; in the Paracatu region, 1973; and in the Chapadão do Bugre, Uberaba, 1972 (these last three all from de Mattos *et al.* 1990).

Distrito Federal The species was recorded at an unstated locality, recently (Negret *et al.* 1984).

POPULATION Numbers are not known, but the small number of records from an area which has been relatively well explored ornithologically is an indication that the species must be very local, given that its main collector could "hardly understand how such a very conspicuous bird could have been overlooked by former collectors" (Vaurie 1980: see Ecology). It is fairly common in Serra da Capivara National Park (Olmos in press; see Remarks 4). One current opinion is that the species is so much commoner than was once believed that its inclusion on the official list of Brazilian threatened fauna (see Measures Taken) was premature (Teixeira *et al.* in press). That the species may not be rare where it occurs can be judged from the number of specimens obtained at certain places (see Distribution), and indeed in the Chapada do Araripe in September 1991 it was found to be fairly common in 1991 (J. F. Pacheco and B. M. Whitney *in litt.* 1991). Nevertheless, at this same locality it took two observers three days to locate birds even with the advantage of tape playback, April (M. Pearman *in litt.* 1992); moreover, some collectors who have explored the region and visited the known localities have failed to detect it (see Pinto and de Camargo 1961), as have field workers who looked for the bird during expeditions to the region in the 1970s (R. S. Ridgely verbally 1987, H. Sick verbally 1987; see also Sick *et al.* 1987).

ECOLOGY Very little is known about the Great Xenops, which was first discovered in sandy caatinga woodland (Reiser 1926) and seen again in such habitat near Manoel Emídio in 1987 (Roth 1989b), but was observed in fairly dense woodland in the Chapada do Araripe, where trees were perhaps 8-15 m in height, and probably also in dry forest near Orobó (Vaurie 1980). Gallery forest and dry semi-deciduous forest have been indicated as habitat in the Federal District (Negret *et al.* 1984) and in Minas Gerais (de Mattos *et al.* 1990). Snethlage (1927-1928) considered the bird one of "upland forest", which he found only on the Ceará plateau and in central Piauí, and which recalled capoeira (secondary forest), being relatively low and dense, deciduous, and rich in both epiphytes and lianas. In the Serra da Capivara National Park it has been found in all types of caatinga, including low bushes in burnt areas (Olmos in press). It may be found alone, in groups of up to three, or in mixed-species flocks (Teixeira *et al.* in press).

An illustration (in Reiser 1926, who believed the species to be a woodcreeper Dendrocolaptidae) of a bird climbing a tree in the manner of a woodpecker Picidae was considered misleading, judging from the reports of other observers and from the structure of the bird's tail and feet (Vaurie 1980). One bird observed briefly in the Chapada do Araripe was clambering around in medium-sized branches about 3-5 m above ground; it hung under twigs or perched low across them, and inserted its bill under flakes of bark to separate these from the trunk and peck out little insects hiding underneath; other observers reported that this bird picks ants and other insects like an antbird Formicariidae (Vaurie 1980). At the same locality in September 1991 birds were singing shortly before dawn and again toward dusk, travelling in pairs through the day and foraging with mixed-species flocks, staying mostly in the mid-storey 3-8 m up on major limbs and occasionally trunks; foraging was very reminiscent of *Xenops*, involving probing bark and dead branch ends, hanging from and climbing up vines, and sometimes hammering at a crevice with the bill (J. F. Pacheco and B. M. Whitney *in litt.* 1991). The stomach of the bird from Várzea Formosa contained insects (specimen in FMNH).

Fourteen specimens collected between May and August had dormant gonads, while of three taken in mid-October one had slightly enlarged ovaries, another had testes half enlarged and the third (another female) showed no development (specimens in AMNH, CM, LSUMZ). There is no other data on breeding in this bird, other than a note of its singing activity in September (see above); its nest seems to be unknown (Vaurie 1980). Although foraging in all types of caatinga, it may be dependent on taller, arboreal vegetation for nesting (Olmos in press).

THREATS None is known, but within the range of this bird there is much general forest loss and degradation owing to pressure of human numbers on the environment (see equivalent section under, e.g., Hyacinth Macaw *Anodorhynchus hyacinthinus* and Moustached Woodcreeper *Xiphocolaptes falcirostris*). The extent to which the perceived patchiness of the species is the result of some undefined habitat requirement or of the impact of man remains unknown.

MEASURES TAKEN The Great Xenops is protected under Brazilian law (Bernardes *et al.* 1990). The species was collected on the border of the small Serra Negra Biological Reserve, and an apparently good population occurs within the Serra da Capivara National Park in Piauí.

MEASURES PROPOSED Any general ornithological work in the areas from which the species is known, or where it might be expected, should where possible be extended to include searches to locate it, to provide information on its ecology, and to assess its conservation status. Reserves in north-east Brazil have been proposed for the Moustached Woodcreeper in Minas Gerais and Maranhão, in both cases with the proviso that other species also be considered (see relevant account); it is worth noting that the Great Xenops has been found sympatric with this woodcreeper at Manoel Emídio (Piauí) and Santa Rita de Cássia (Bahia). From the evidence gathered to date, the Chapada do Araripe emerges as a key site for the xenops and should be considered for protection. The species should be looked for in the Aiuaba Ecological Station (6°38'S 40°13'W) in Ceará and in the Grande Sertão Veredas National Park in Minas Gerais (LPG).

REMARKS (1) This species is the only one in its genus and has no near relatives (Vaurie 1980), although it had been assumed that *Megaxenops* and *Xenops* are very closely related (e.g. Cory and Hellmayr 1925, Hellmayr 1929a). (2) Despite the statement that specimens "were taken at Corrientes in southern Piauhy not far from Paranagua (*sic*)" (Naumburg 1928), no specimen in E. Kaempfer's collection is known to be labelled from that locality, nor has this indication been followed by subsequent authorities (e.g. Vaurie 1980). (3) Most of Kaempfer's specimens from Bahia are labelled "Santa Ritta", i.e. "Santa Rita do Rio Preto" (see Naumburg 1928, 1935, Pinto 1978, Vaurie 1980) which in more recent maps appears as Santa Rita de Cássia on the left bank of the rio Preto (see Pinto and de Camargo 1961), and which in turn is called Ibipetuba by Paynter and Traylor (1991). On the map showing localities visited by Kaempfer in Bahia (Naumburg 1935), an altitude of 950 m is indicated for Sincorá (13°25'S 41°33'W on this map), while the altitude indicated on the labels of the three specimens (in AMNH) from this locality is "1,500 feet", i.e. 460 m. (4) The voice (presumed song) of the species is loud and distinctive (Olmos in press *contra* Teixeira *et al.* 1989), although not necessarily often used (M. Pearman *in litt.* 1992).

BOLIVIAN RECURVEBILL *Simoxenops striatus* E[2]

This peculiar ovenbird is known from only four specimens and a few sight records from three localities in lower montane forest in the Bolivian departments of La Paz, Cochabamba, and Santa Cruz. It is apparently scarce and confined to a very narrow elevational zone (670-800 m), and may be severely threatened owing to rapid deforestation within its small range.

DISTRIBUTION The Bolivian Recurvebill (see Remarks 1) is known from just three localities in the yungas of Bolivia, in the departments of La Paz, Cochabamba, and Santa Cruz. Until recently it was known only from four specimens collected by M. A. Carriker at two localities in the 1930s (coordinates from Paynter *et al.* 1975): three specimens, including the type (taken in July 1934), are from Santa Ana, 15°50'S 67°36'W, at 670 m on the río Coroico, La Paz department, with one (taken in July 1937) from Palmar, 17°06'S 65°29'W, at 800 m in Cochabamba department (Carriker 1935a, Bond and Meyer de Schauensee 1941, 1942-1943). In August 1989 the species was recorded at 700-800 m along the upper río Saguayo, in Amboró National Park (17°50'S 63°39'W), Santa Cruz department (Parker *et al.* 1992).

POPULATION Little information is available, but the species is presumably rare and declining owing to habitat destruction (see Threats). Of the 385 bird specimens procured at Santa Ana from 11 July to 2 August 1934 only three were of the present species (Bond and Meyer de Schauensee 1942-1943), and Carriker (1935a) therefore considered it rare. Of the 420 bird specimens procured at Palmar, 1-28 July 1937, only one was a Bolivian Recurvebill (Bond and Meyer de Schauensee 1942-1943), so apparently the species was even rarer there (see also Ecology). Along the río Saguayo, at least four individuals, including a territorial pair, were found within an area of c.50 ha (TAP). The Amboró National Park population is presumably large (hundreds to low thousands) and stable, but populations to the north (including those near Santa Ana and El Palmar) are undoubtedly seriously threatened by habitat loss.

ECOLOGY The Bolivian Recurvebill inhabits foothill tropical forest (see Remarks 2) and has been found at 670-800 m (Carriker 1935a: see Distribution). In Amboró National Park, the species was found in the interior and along the edges of 30 m tall forest on steep slopes above the upper río Saguayo: two individuals were noted at 0.5-2 m in dense vegetation (1-3 m tall) covering natural landslides above a small stream at c.800 m, where they were foraging in the tangled branches of fallen trees, and in the shrubby growth and vines that had overgrown them (Parker *et al.* 1992, TAP). Another bird was seen in similar tangles on a steep bank bordering the río Saguayo at 700 m (Parker *et al.* 1992, TAP). In contrast to these was a pair that foraged primarily in vine tangles at 12 to 20 m (in the upper middle storey), in the interior of tall forest: these birds hopped along and up vines and pecked at rotting branches, palm fronds, and large dead leaves trapped in the darkened recesses of extensive tangles; they also probed in large bromeliads and other arboreal epiphytes, such as species of *Philodendron*, growing on trunks and large limbs (Parker *et al.* 1992, TAP). This pair responded strongly to song playback as if territorial, and was noted repeatedly within an area of c.2 ha (TAP). They regularly associated with a large flock of canopy insectivores that included pairs and/or families of the following species: White-throated Woodpecker *Piculus leucolaemus*, Ocellated Woodcreeper *Xiphorhynchus ocellatus*, Rufous-rumped Foliage-gleaner *Philydor erythrocercus*, Ashy Antwren *Myrmotherula grisea* (see relevant account), Slaty-capped Flycatcher *Leptopogon superciliaris*, Tawny-crowned Greenlet *Hylophilus ochraceiceps*, White-shouldered Tanager *Tachyphonus luctuosus*, and other smaller species of *Tangara* tanagers (Parker *et al.* 1992). The area surveyed along the upper río Saguayo is also an important site for the threatened Southern Helmeted Curassow *Pauxi unicornis* (see relevant account).

THREATS Forests in the elevational range of this and other yungas bird endemics (lower montane forest at 500 to 1,500 m), on interior ridges of the Andes in north-western Bolivia, are drier than true montane forest, are easier to burn, and often occur on moderate slopes with rich soils that are well-suited to subsistence agriculture, as well as to the cultivation of cash crops such as coca and coffee: for this reason, they are a favoured target for colonization projects (involving colonists from the altiplano), and large areas in this zone have already been deforested, especially in La Paz and Cochabamba (as around the early localities for this species at Santa Ana and El Palmar) (Remsen and Quintela unpublished, TAP).

MEASURES TAKEN The Bolivian Recurvebill occurs in Amboró National Park in the department of Santa Cruz, a biologically important protected area of 180,000 ha (Parker *et al.* 1992), and also (presumably) in the adjacent Carrasco National Park (1,300,000 ha: IUCN 1992) in Cochabamba. In both parks, suitable habitat for this species is restricted to a narrow band of forest just above the most heavily colonized lands at 300-600 m, and thus remains vulnerable.

MEASURES PROPOSED Satellite images should be analysed to estimate the extent to which the upper tropical zone forest in Bolivia has already been cleared (Remsen and Quintela unpublished), and to locate areas suitable for protection. More reserves in the foothill tropical, upper tropical and lower subtropical zones should be created throughout the Andes in order to save the many species restricted to these elevations: montane forests from Puno, Peru, south to Santa Cruz, Bolivia, have been shown to be especially rich in endemic species of plants and animals, including at least 19 species of bird (ICBP 1992, Crosby *et al.* in prep.). In Bolivia a reserve encompassing the entire range of habitats along the Amazonian slope of the Andes, from the puna zone through the humid montane forests to the Amazonian lowlands, including the mosaic of riverine habitats of a major river system such as the río Beni or río Madre de Dios, would include some 900-1,000 species, or 72-80% of the Bolivian avifauna and most of its threatened or potentially threatened species; the best location would be somewhere in the relatively undisturbed regions of the northern department of La Paz, possibly as a north-eastward extension of the Ulla-Ulla Wildlife Reserve (250,000 ha: IUCN 1992), but if such an "all-elevations" reserve cannot be created, priority should be given to creating one or several areas in the foothills and upper tropical forests of La Paz and Cochabamba, to encompass the full range of montane forest types from c.600 to 3,500 m, a critical (and inadequately protected) habitat for at least 400 species, including 13 species that are threatened or potentially threatened (Remsen and Quintela unpublished, TAP). A forest reserve should be established primarily to protect the watershed of the upper río Beni, where flooding and massive soil erosion will increasingly affect people living along the base of the mountains (TAP).

A large corridor of forest from the headwaters of the upper río Madidi at 400 m to tree-line forests (at 3,500 m) north of Lake Titicaca has recently been proposed as a national park that would protect populations of more than 1,000 species of birds, including most of the yungas endemics (Parker *et al.* 1992).

Financial support (from both national and international development agencies and conservation organizations) for Amboró National Park is an ongoing priority, and similar aid for Carrasco National Park is an urgent necessity. The latter park probably provides the best hope, at present, for endemic species not known as far south as Amboró (see Yellow-rumped Antwren *Terenura sharpei* account). Further clarification of the boundaries of this reserve, as well as of the Serranía Pilon-Lajas Reserve along the La Paz–Beni border, are also imperative. The integrity of habitat within Amboró National Park must be ensured, and hence encroachment upon the park by settlers should be effectively stopped.

Failure to strengthen existing reserves or to establish new ones in the department of La Paz (and elsewhere in Bolivia) will almost certainly result in the extinction of numerous endemic plant and animal taxa, as well as serious socio-economic problems caused directly by destruction of the forested watersheds (TAP). The Southern Helmeted Curassow, Ashy Antwren and Yellow-rumped

Antwren inhabit the same general areas as this species, and should be considered in any conservation initiatives.

REMARKS (1) The vocalizations of the Peruvian Recurvebill *Simoxenops ucayalae* are similar in quality and pattern to those of *Syndactyla* foliage-gleaners (Parker 1982b), indicating the close approach of these genera. Despite morphological and vocal similarities, the Bolivian Recurvebill should continue to be regarded as a species distinct from the (near-threatened) Peruvian Recurvebill, which is a bamboo specialist that occurs patchily in lowland and foothill forest in Amazonia; though long thought to be rare, it has recently been found to occur as far east as the rio Xingu in Brazil (Graves and Zusi 1990; see Ecology under Chestnut-throated Spinetail *Synallaxis cherriei*). (2) Remsen and Quintela (unpublished) defined "foothill tropical forest" in Bolivia as the forest in the foothills of the Andes from about 500 m to 1,100 m, too low in elevation to receive the oreographic rainfall that marks the beginning of true montane forest, the lower (1,100-1,700 m) zone of which they called "upper tropical zone forest".

WHITE-BEARDED ANTSHRIKE *Biatas nigropectus* V/R[10]

Destruction of Atlantic Forest in Brazil and Argentina has reduced the range and numbers of this naturally rare, bamboo-haunting bird, which seems to depend on four or five protected areas (notably Itatiaia and Iguaçu National Parks, Brazil) for its security.

DISTRIBUTION The White-bearded Antshrike (see Remarks 1) is endemic to the Atlantic Forest region of South America, extending from eastern Minas Gerais south through Rio de Janeiro to Santa Catarina (no records this century) in Brazil into Misiones (no records since 1960) in Argentina.

Brazil The occurrence of the species in Espírito Santo, Brazil (Ruschi 1953; see also Meyer de Schauensee 1966), although generally admitted (e.g. Meyer de Schauensee 1970, 1982, Sick and Teixeira 1979, Sick 1985) and quite probable, still awaits confirmation.

Minas Gerais The only records are from Viçosa, 16 May 1934 (specimen in MZUFV; also Monteiro *et al.* 1983, Sick 1985), Itabira, December 1986 (G. T. de Mattos *in litt.* 1987), and São Domingos do Prata, December 1987 (G. T. de Mattos *in litt.* 1988).

Rio de Janeiro Records (east to west) are: Desengano State Park at Rifa, 840 m, October 1986, and ribeirão Vermelho, 830 m, August 1987 (J. F. Pacheco *in litt.* 1987); Cantagalo (Cabanis 1874, von Ihering 1900a); Nova Friburgo (Burmeister 1856, von Ihering 1900a), Pico da Caledônia, 1,300 m, July 1987 (J. F. Pacheco *in litt.* 1987); Sapucaia, Serra do Pião, August 1987 (J. F. Pacheco *in litt.* 1987); Teresópolis, just outside the town on the road to Nova Friburgo, c.700 m, October 1990 and October 1991 (B. M. Whitney *in litt.* 1991), with earlier specimen records from December 1916, June 1926, and at nearby Alpina, June 1914, Fazenda Boa Fé, September 1942 (specimens in MNRJ and MZUSP), and the adjacent Serra dos Órgãos National Park, 1,200 m, December 1986 and August 1991, and Vargem Grande, 1,100 m, September 1987 (J. F. Pacheco *in litt.* 1987, B. C. Forrester *in litt.* 1992); Itatiaia National Park, Maromba, 1,200 m, July and August 1950 (Pinto 1954b), near Véu da Noiva waterfall at c.1,100 m, October 1980 (TAP), near Hotel do Ipê at an unspecified altitude, October 1981 (D. F. Stotz *in litt.* 1991), at two sites, August 1991 (B. C. Forrester *in litt.* 1992), and a few kilometres inside the entrance gate to the park, 700 m, October 1991 (B. M. Whitney *in litt.* 1991).

São Paulo Records (east to west) are from Guarulhos, July 1902 (Pinto 1938), specimen "bought in the market" (in MZUSP); Piracicaba, undated (von Ihering 1898); Ipanema, April, July and August 1819, 1820 or 1821 (von Pelzeln 1868-1871); Itapetininga, April 1966 (specimen in MZUSP; Sick and Teixeira 1979), May 1969 (specimen in CIAL); and Rio Carmo road (24°17'S 48°25'W), 850 m, Fazenda Intervales, Capão Bonito, 1987 (Willis 1989, whence coordinates) and November 1991 (D. F. Stotz *in litt.* 1992).

Paraná Despite the species's inclusion in a state bird-list (Scherer Neto 1985), a male observed at length at the end of the Poço Preto road along the rio Iguaçu in Iguaçu National Park in October 1987 (TAP) was apparently the first documented record for the state; another was heard c.1 km south of the Hotel Cataratas in the same park in October 1990 (TAP), and a pair was seen at Fazenda Santa Rita, Palmeira, 1,000 m, in November 1990 (L. dos Anjos verbally 1991) (see Remarks 2).

Santa Catarina The only record is from Blumenau, 5 May 1910 (Cory and Hellmayr 1924).

Argentina All Argentine records of the White-bearded Antshrike are from Misiones province, where the largest series of specimens has been obtained. Two birds were collected on the arroyo Aguaray-guazú, May 1948, and two others were observed on the arroyo Urugua-í (25°54'S 54°36'W), July 1948 (Giai 1950, 1951), along which specimens were collected at km 10 and 30, many months from May 1952 to August 1960 (Navas and Bó 1988b, and specimens in AMNH, MNRJ). Two other specimens are from Refugio Piñalitos (Piñalitos, at 25°59'S 53°54'W: Paynter

1985), November 1954 (Navas and Bó 1988b; also M. Nores and D. Yzurieta *in litt.* 1986), and four from Tobuna (26°28'S 53°54'W in Paynter 1985), November 1953 (Navas and Bó 1988b).

POPULATION Sparse nineteenth-century evidence indicates this was always considered a rare bird (e.g. Burmeister 1856, von Ihering 1898). This is certainly an easily overlooked species, but the scarcity of records from an area that has been relatively well explored by collectors and birdwatchers suggests that it is indeed rare (a view shared by D. F. Stotz *in litt.* 1988), which led to its being given this status in a Brazilian list of threatened birds (Sick and Teixeira 1979). It is considered scarce also in Argentina (J. C. Chebez *in litt.* 1986, M. Nores and D. Yzurieta *in litt.* 1986, *contra* Sick 1985), where its rarity is probably not directly related to human activities since forests were little disturbed when it was discovered in Misiones (M. Nores and D. Yzurieta *in litt.* 1986). However, the species has seemingly never been the object of direct search in any part of its range, and even the relatively large Argentine series was probably fortuitously obtained.

ECOLOGY This peculiar antbird inhabits the bamboo understorey of lowland and montane forest, occurring primarily in openings and along edges where thickets are most extensive and tall (TAP). At Capão Bonito in São Paulo it was found in the bamboo-rich, dense undergrowth of montane forest in the fog zone, and in the rainshadow zone north of the study area, but not downslope to the south out of the fog belt (Willis 1989). Bamboo (a "large-leaved" species) was also present in all the sites where this species was recorded in Rio de Janeiro (J. F. Pacheco *in litt.* 1987, B. M. Whitney *in litt.* 1991, TAP), in Misiones, Argentina, where it was identified as *Guadua trinii* (Giai 1950, 1951), and in *Araucaria* forest where it was found in Paraná (L. dos Anjos verbally 1991). On the serra of Itabira in Minas Gerais, in the transition zone between Atlantic Forest and cerrado vegetation, the species was in old second growth rich in thorny "taquaruçu" (giant) bamboo formations (G. T. de Mattos *in litt.* 1987). In Itatiaia and Iguaçu National Parks, it was observed only in the most extensive bamboo stands, especially where this plant formed impressive columns of vegetation that climbed into the lower canopy and practically covered numerous medium-sized trees (TAP); tape playback, although possibly not conclusive as evidence, failed to provoke response in certain apparently suitable areas with large-leaved bamboo, suggesting indeed that the species may not be present in all such stands (B. M. Whitney *in litt.* 1991). All of these references to bamboo probably pertain to one or a few large-leaved species, possibly in the genus *Merostachys*, which are a characteristic element in the montane and subtropical forests throughout the range of the White-bearded Antshrike; periodically these large bamboos die off and the bird species confined to them are forced to move elsewhere, and after one such die-off of tall (12 m) *Merostachys* at Itatiaia in 1984 all the bamboo birds disappeared within an elevational range of 900-1,200 m, and many did not reappear until late in 1990, when this same species had grown again in places to a height of 5 m (TAP).

Willis (1989) recorded that the White-bearded Antshrike hops along trunks or on nearby limbs of giant bamboos, principally their horizontal fronds and twigs, pecking insects from dead leaves in the axils or fluttering short distances to foliage nearby. The stomach contents of a specimen in MZUSP from Itatiaia, August, were one spider, legs of another spider, small ants, and many small seeds. On the arroyo Aguaray-guazú the species joined mixed flocks with White-shouldered Fire-eye *Pyriglena leucoptera*, Red-crowned Ant-tanager *Habia rubica*, Black-goggled Tanager *Trichothraupis melanops* and the near-threatened Blackish-blue Seedeater *Amaurospiza moesta* (Giai 1951). At Capão Bonito, pairs of White-bearded Antshrike usually joined flocks of White-collared Foliage-gleaners *Anabazenops fuscus* (see Remarks 2), but at times kept to themselves (Willis 1989). Similarly, in all but one of one observer's records of the species in Rio de Janeiro, it was in the company of this foliage-gleaner (J. F. Pacheco *in litt.* 1987), but the latter has never been recorded at the study area in Paraná (L. dos Anjos verbally 1991) or anywhere in western Paraná or Misiones (TAP).

The only specimen whose gonad condition was recorded had testes undeveloped in mid-May. A pair was recorded building a nest in bamboo in October at Itatiaia (D. F. Stotz *in litt.* 1991), and in Itabira one bird was carrying food for young in mid-December, but the nest could not be found (G. T. de Mattos *in litt.* 1987).

THREATS Although this species appears to be naturally rare wherever it occurs, habitat loss has greatly compounded its poor conservation status. Forest clearance, e.g. in Minas Gerais and much of São Paulo and Paraná, must have caused many local extinctions. The destruction of forest in parts of Misiones (see, e.g., Threats under Brazilian Merganser *Mergus octosetaceus*) must also have resulted in declines in its numbers in Argentina. Because of its apparent restriction to bamboo thickets, whose die-off/regrowth periods create large physical and temporal discontinuities in the distribution of specialist users of such habitat, it would be difficult to maintain in small reserves: it is therefore probably most secure in the largest parks and reserves, especially those that have an abundance of bamboo of different species and at different elevations (e.g. as in Itatiaia National Park).

MEASURES TAKEN The presence of the species in the Desengano State Park, Serra dos Órgãos, Itatiaia and Iguaçu National Parks in Brazil and possibly the recently created Urugua-í Provincial Park on the upper arroyo Urugua-í in Argentina (Chebez and Rolón 1989) may give it some protection (but see Threats).

MEASURES PROPOSED Surveys of the species in the field are needed, particularly now that its calls have been identified and recorded during recent fieldwork (e.g. by P. S. M. da Fonseca and J. F. Pacheco verbally 1988). Its conservation status needs to be better ascertained, and this might best be achieved through a long-term study of bamboo specialist birds in the Atlantic Forest, this to target such other threatened species as Purple-winged Ground-dove *Claravis godefrida*, Fork-tailed Pygmy-tyrant *Hemitriccus furcatus* and the seedeaters *Sporophila falcirostris*, *S. frontalis* and (near-threatened) *Amaurospiza moesta* (see relevant accounts).

REMARKS (1) The White-bearded Antshrike occupies its own genus. (2) The remarkable resemblance in size and female plumage coloration of this antshrike and the largely sympatric White-collared Foliage-gleaner (Sick 1985) has been interpreted as a case of mimicry (Willis 1989), and may be a source of misidentification in the field under the poor light conditions that usually prevail in their bamboo habitat, but also in museum collections (LPG), where specimens are known to have been mistaken for *Anabazenops* (D. F. Stotz *in litt.* 1989). Another source of confusion in the field might stem from the similarity of the songs of the White-bearded Antshrike and the White-shouldered Fire-eye *Pyriglena leucoptera* (TAP).

RECURVE-BILLED BUSHBIRD *Clytoctantes alixii* E[3]

Found in the lowland and foothill forests of westernmost Venezuela and northern Colombia, this furnariid has been recorded from few localities, and has not been recorded in recent years. Deforestation of this area has been extensive, although the bird may be able to survive in dense secondary growth.

DISTRIBUTION The Recurve-billed Bushbird is known from a small number of localities in north-western Venezuela in the Sierra de Perijá, and northern Colombia at the northern ends of the West, Central and East Andes. The type-series, apparently collected in Ecuador, is discussed in Remarks 1. Coordinates (and altitudes in brackets) are from Paynter (1982) and Paynter and Traylor (1981).

Venezuela Records of this bird are restricted to the upper río Negro valley in the Sierra de Perijá, Zulia state, where the few known localities are as follows: Barranquilla (= "Ranchería Julián", at c.10°07'N 72°42'W; 960 m), mentioned by Phelps and Phelps (1963); El Escondido (untraced, but presumably in the region west of Machiques at c.10°04'N 72°34'W; 1,075 m), where a male, two females and a juvenile male were taken (Aveledo and Pons 1952); La Sabana (c.10°00'N 72°50'W; 1,200 m), mentioned by Phelps and Phelps (1963); Cerro Ayapa (c.10°00'N 72°45'W), where a female was collected (Aveledo and Pons 1952); and Panapicho (c.10°00'N 72°45'W; 300 m, and c.7 km downstream from La Sabana), whence comes a single specimen (Aveledo and Pons 1952).

Colombia This species as been found in some of the northern departments, where the scattered records tend to come from the lowlands and foothills at the northern ends of the West, Central and East Andes (see Remarks 2), with localities (essentially from west to east) as follows: (*West Andes*) west of Quebrada Saisa (untraced, but presumably near Saisa), on the eastern slope of Serranía de Abibe, where a female was observed in 1965 (Willis 1988); río Salvajín, 7°45'N 76°16'W (which, via the río Esmeralda, flows into the río Sinú, Córdoba department), where two males and two females (in USNM) were collected at 185 m during May 1949; (*Central Andes*) Puerto Valdivia, 7°18'N 75°23'W (on the eastern side of the lower Cauca valley, Antioquia department), where a male and female were collected at 180 m in December 1914 (Chapman 1917a, Carriker 1955a); Hacienda Belén, c.7°10'N 74°43'W (13 km west of Segovia, Antioquia), where a female (in USNM) was collected at 245 m in April 1948; La Sofía, 5°38'N 75°04'W (on the southern side of río Samaná Sur, i.e. just inside Caldas department), where a male (in USNM) was taken at 1,145 m in May 1951; Santa Rosa, 7°58'N 74°03'W (10 km west of Simití, at the eastern base of the Serranía de San Lucas, Bolívar department), where 10 birds (in USNM) were taken at 610 m in April and May 1947; (*East Andes*) El Cauca, 8°10'N 73°24'W (at 900 m on the west slope, Cesar department), where two males (in CM, USNM) were taken in August 1916 (also Carriker 1955a); and El Tambor, 7°19'N 73°16'W (at c.500 m on the west slope in Santander department), where birds (in CM) were taken in December 1916 and January 1917 (Carriker 1955a).

POPULATION There are very few records of this species, and apparently none since 1965 (see above). However, 10 specimens were collected between 19 April and 2 May 1947 at Santa Rosa, suggesting that the species may at least be locally not uncommon, and Hilty and Brown (1986) mentioned that the species may be more numerous than records otherwise indicate owing to its shy and secretive nature.

ECOLOGY In Venezuela, localities where this species has been collected range from 300 to 1,200 m (as given in Paynter 1982), although it is unknown at precisely what altitude birds were collected, and Meyer de Schauensee and Phelps (1978) give a range of 900-1,000 m: in Colombia, specimens have been collected between 185 and 1,145 m (see Distribution). The Recurve-billed Bushbird occupies the tropical and upper tropical zone where it inhabits rainforest, apparently favouring dense growth close to the ground, thickets, forest borders, and overgrown (young) second growth (Carriker 1955a, Haffer 1975, Meyer de Schauensee and Phelps 1978, Hilty and Brown 1986, Willis 1988). The bird is shy and secretive, and always stays close to the ground, where it has been observed at an ant-swarm with Rufous-vented Ground-cuckoo *Neomorphus geoffroyi*, Ocellated Antbird *Phaenostictus mcleannani* and Spotted Antbird *Hylophylax naevioides* (Carriker 1955a, Meyer de Schauensee and Phelps 1978, Hilty and Brown 1986), and stripping strands from dead stems in the search for insects (Willis 1988). Four breeding condition birds were collected in April and May (Hilty and Brown 1986), and an immature male (in USNM) was taken at the end of April (all in Córdoba and Bolívar departments, Colombia).

THREATS Owing to imprecise knowledge of this species's ecological requirements, the threats it faces are difficult to assess with any confidence, although it is certain that much of the native habitat within its range has been heavily disturbed and cleared during the present century (LGN), and it is thus likely that the population has both declined in number and been fragmented. In both national parks mentioned below, threats to the species arise from agricultural encroachment causing varying degrees of deforestation (CNPPA 1982). However, if this bird really favours dense secondary growth (see Ecology), and can maintain a viable population in such habitat, it may be relatively secure (see Measures Proposed).

MEASURES TAKEN In Venezuela, the Sierra de Perijá National Park, 295,300 ha, embraces the first two localities listed under Distribution (CNPPA 1982). In Colombia, the río Salvajín (where specimens were taken in 1949) is now within the Paramillo National Park, which covers an area of 460,000 ha within Córdoba and Antioquia departments (CNPPA 1982, Hernández Camacho *et al.* undated).

MEASURES PROPOSED The status of this bird within the national parks mentioned above is in urgent need of assessment, as it is on the Colombian side of the Sierra de Perijá; however, it would benefit the species if the Sierra de Perijá National Park were to be extended to embrace all Venezuelan localities, and also to incorporate suitable areas on the Colombian side of the mountains. The Paramillo National Park is known to have harboured populations of this species, Blue-billed Curassow *Crax alberti* and Red-bellied Grackle *Hypopyrrhus pyrohypogaster* (see relevant accounts), although the status of any one of these species there is unknown: clearly, surveys need to be undertaken to resolve this problem. The Serranía de San Lucas has been an important area for this and other threatened bird species (the details of which are given in the equivalent section under Chestnut-bellied Hummingbird *Amazilia castaneiventris*), and therefore may also warrant some form of protection, although surveys are first needed to determine the current status of the threatened species there, and of any remaining habitat. The ecological requirements of the Recurve-billed Bushbird are essentially unknown, but need clarification if conservation actions are to protect known populations or locate new ones with any efficiency. It must be a priority for any surveys to determine the extent to which the species relies on and maintains viable populations within secondary growth.

REMARKS (1) Elliot (1870) described the species and genus from a male and juvenile male apparently collected on the río Napo, Ecuador. Chapman (1926) mentioned that these specimens were actually labelled from "Equateur", and because subsequent records were restricted to Colombia, suggested that there is "no satisfactory evidence of its occurrence in... Ecuador". With the exception of Aveledo and Pons (1952), who reiterated Chapman (1926), the recent literature appears to have ignored these specimens. (2) Some specimens (e.g. in ANSP, BMNH, MCZ) collected during the last century are labelled as from "Bogotá", or in the "vicinity of Bogotá", and Chapman (1926) mentioned (presumably on the evidence of these specimens) that the species is known from the Bogotá region. However, these birds almost certainly represent Bogotá trade skins, and the species's occurrence within this region remains unsubstantiated.

RONDÔNIA BUSHBIRD *Clytoctantes atrogularis* I[8]

This enigmatic antbird is known from a single female specimen and from two sightings of males at the type-locality along the Rio Ji-paraná in Rondônia, Brazil, in 1986. Although its range almost certainly includes adjacent parts of Amazonas and Mato Grosso, rapid deforestation and hydroelectric projects in this part of Brazil must be considered threats to its survival.

DISTRIBUTION All definite records of the Rondônia Bushbird (see Remarks) are from Cachoeira Nazaré, a locality along the west bank of the Rio Ji-paraná, Rondônia, Brazil (9°44'S 61°53'W, elevation 100 m): the type-specimen, a female with a fully ossified skull, was mist-netted on 22 October 1986 (Lanyon *et al.* 1990). One or two male-plumaged individuals were seen at the same locality, the first observation being made on 13 October 1986 (Lanyon *et al.* 1990). However, a male bushbird, presumably of this species (although with an apparently different song: Lanyon *et al.* 1990), was seen along the rio Teles Pires north of Alta Floresta, northern Mato Grosso, in early December 1989 (TAP).

POPULATION This species is presumably rare and local, as suggested by the fact that only one individual was mist-netted during 1,450 net-days and only two others were seen during 1,400 hours of fieldwork by five experienced observers; an additional 375 net-days and 250 field hours at a similar site 70 km away resulted in no further observations (Lanyon *et al.* 1990).

ECOLOGY Little is known of this seemingly elusive antbird. The few records are from mature *terra firme* forest dominated by dense vine tangles. A male was observed "approximately 1 m up in a large tree fall and worked up to 2-5 m in a vine tangle... pounding and digging at the vines with its bill" (Lanyon *et al.* 1990). The male probably of this species near Alta Floresta was observed at 0.5 to 1 m in dense tangles of a tree-fall inside tall *terra firme* forest along a small stream (TAP; "small ravine" in Lanyon *et al.* 1990).

THREATS Deforestation in Rondônia is rapid, proceeding at around 4,000 km^2 per year, and the rate of destruction has increased with the paving of the Cuiabá–Porto Velho highway in 1984 (Fearnside 1987, 1990). A more immediate threat to forest at the type-locality of the Rondônia Bushbird was the construction of a hydroelectric dam nearby (Lanyon *et al.* 1990).

MEASURES TAKEN The Rondônia Bushbird has not yet been found in a protected area of any kind. Pacaás Novos National Park (765,800 ha: IBAMA 1989) may support significant populations of many "Rondônia endemics" (see next section), but data are lacking, and the presence of cerrado habitats within the park suggests that adjacent forests may not be as biologically rich as those to the north of the Cuiabá–Porto Velho highway (TAP). On the other hand, recent avifaunal surveys in the rio Guaporé drainage as far south as 14°35'S in Noel Kempff Mercado National Park, eastern Bolivia, indicate that some Rondônia endemics do occur much farther south than was previously thought (Bates *et al.* 1989, 1992). Nevertheless, on the basis of what is indicated under Threats above, all of the remaining evergreen forest in Rondônia and adjacent portions of Amazonas and Mato Grosso should be considered at great risk of destruction.

MEASURES PROPOSED Current development activities in Rondônia threaten some of the richest bird communities yet reported on earth (nearly 400 species were found at Cachoeira Nazaré: D. F. Stotz *in litt.* 1990), including numerous bird species endemic to forests situated between the upper rios Madeira and Tapajós (see Cracraft 1985). Additional taxa whose small ranges are centred in this part of the Amazon basin (or not far to the north-east) include Dark-winged Trumpeter *Psophia viridis*, Crimson-bellied Parakeet *Pyrrhura rhodogaster*, Black-girdled Barbet *Capito dayi*, White-breasted Antbird *Rhegmatorhina hoffmannsi*, Pale-faced Bare-eye

Skutchia borbae, Snow-capped Manakin *Pipra nattereri* and Tooth-billed Wren *Odontorchilus cinereus*. There is therefore an urgent need for the establishment of various kinds of forest reserve in the biologically rich areas along the northern edge of the Brazilian Shield in northern Rondônia and in adjoining parts of south-eastern Amazonas and northern Mato Grosso, for example along the rios Aripuanã, Juruena, and Teles Pires. Biological (including avifaunal) surveys are desperately needed in this vulnerable and important part of the Neotropics. The gradual elimination by the Brazilian government of incentives for cattle-ranching and inappropriate forms of agriculture should be supported by international development agencies, and this example should be followed by the governments of neighbouring countries. Financial and technological support for extractive reserves of all kinds will increasingly be needed throughout the Amazon basin if large areas of evergreen forest are to survive into the next century.

REMARKS This bird is closely related to the threatened Recurve-billed Bushbird *Clytoctantes alixii* (Lanyon *et al.* 1990); because these are the only members, the genus itself is threatened.

SPECKLED ANTSHRIKE *Xenornis setifrons* K[12]

This lowland forest antshrike is endemic to eastern Panama and north-western Colombia, where it has been recorded infrequently from very few localities (once in Colombia in 1940) and appears to be local and in need of fuller investigation.

DISTRIBUTION The Speckled Antshrike (see Remarks) is endemic to San Blas and eastern Darién provinces, eastern Panama, and Chocó department in north-west Colombia.

Panama Localities where this species has been recorded are restricted to provinces in the east of the country: (*Panama*) Altos de Cerro Azul, on the Cerro Vistamares trail, where a bird was seen in January and February 1992 (Engleman 1992a); Cerro Jefe, where a bird possibly this species was seen during the mid-1980s (Engleman 1992a); Cerro Guagaral (east of Altos de Pacora, but west of Cerro Jefe), where a pair was seen in February–March 1992 (Engleman 1992b); (*western San Blas*) Nusagandi, where a female (netted) and a few others were seen during April and May 1985 (Ridgely and Gwynne 1989), and in February 1989 and January 1992 (Whitney and Rosenberg in prep.); (*eastern San Blas*) Permé (Meyer de Schauensee 1948-1952); Quebrada Venado, in the hills above Armila (a Kuña Indian village), where three males and three females (in AMNH, USNM) were taken in March 1963 (also Wetmore 1972); Obaldía (Meyer de Schauensee 1948-1952); (*eastern Darién*) the middle slopes of Cerro Tacarcuna (Ridgely and Gwynne 1989); at "the old village site" at 580 m on the río Tacarcuna, where the type-specimen was taken in March 1915 (Chapman 1924), with another taken in March 1964 (Wetmore 1972); and La Laguna (on the ridge leading up to the cerro), where a female was taken at 575 m in June 1963 (Wetmore 1972).

Colombia Two females were collected at "Baudó" (= Pizarro; on the coast: Paynter and Traylor 1981) in July 1940, at 550 m (Meyer de Schauensee 1941) apparently beside the río Baudó (ANSP label data) on the lower slopes of the Serranía de Baudó (Meyer de Schauensee 1948-1952).

POPULATION This species is seemingly rare and very local throughout its very limited range (Hilty and Brown 1986, Ridgely and Gwynne 1989): however, in March 1963, once a pair had been located two other pairs were found with relative ease by searching in similar terrain (Wetmore 1972; see Ecology). Recent observations (during and subsequent to 1985) of a number of birds in western and eastern San Blas suggest that, prior to an adequate description of its vocalizations, the bird may previously have been overlooked (Ridgely and Gwynne 1989, B. M. Whitney and G. H. Rosenberg *in litt.* 1991), and although repeated searches at Nusagandi during the past three years failed to relocate the bird (Engleman 1992a), it was seen again during January 1992 and considered to be fairly common at this locality, although generally difficult to detect (Whitney and Rosenberg in prep.). The species's secretive habits (Wetmore 1972), and the lack of fieldwork in the Darién mountains along the border, may also have contributed to the paucity of records, although this cannot account for the lack of records elsewhere in Panama where known localities are relatively well watched.

ECOLOGY Records of this species come from between 150 and 600 m (Meyer de Schauensee 1941, Wetmore 1972, Hilty and Brown 1986, Ridgely and Gwynne 1989, Whitney and Rosenberg in prep.). The Speckled Antshrike inhabits lowland and foothill humid forest, where birds forage in pairs, favouring dense viny undergrowth (Wetmore 1972, Ridgely and Gwynne 1989). Wetmore (1972) recorded birds in a narrow, steep-sloping side-valley (not near the main stream draining the area), and others in similar terrain. The recent sighting from Cerro Azul was of a bird perching 2-3 m above the ground (often on thin saplings), whence it would make a flycatching sally and/or fly to a new perch; it was never seen to skulk in dense undergrowth, but foraged over rather open forest floor (Engleman 1992a).

The Kuña Indian reserve around Nusagandi forms part of the ridge system that makes up the continental divide (on the Caribbean slope), and has an extremely wet climate (in contrast, the Pacific slope just a few kilometres away is remarkably arid for much of the year): this area consists of ridges, steep-sided valleys and ravines with clear, fast-flowing streams (Whitney and Rosenberg in prep.). The forest within this reserve is largely undisturbed with a canopy varying from 15 to 25 m high and generally rather open (i.e. the crowns of the taller trees often do not interlock), and the resultant understorey is dense up to a height of about 2.5 m above which it opens out significantly (Whitney and Rosenberg in prep.). One of the most conspicuous elements of the vegetation in this area is the abundance and variety of palms in the understorey, with some of the species reaching the canopy (Whitney and Rosenberg in prep.). The Speckled Antshrike was found (in February 1987 and January 1992) mostly on the sides of steep slopes below ridges, but was also noted ranging into the damp bottoms of ravines (Whitney and Rosenberg in prep.). Although Ridgely and Gwynne (1989) suggested that this bird does not generally associate with mixed-species flocks, and it is possible that the species undergoes some seasonal shift in foraging strategy (perhaps during breeding activities), Whitney and Rosenberg (in prep.) suggest that this is unlikely, and that it should be regarded as an inveterate member of mixed-species foraging flocks. At Nusagandi, pairs (and in one instance three birds) foraged exclusively as members of such assemblages in the undergrowth of undisturbed forest: the composition of these flocks was fairly constant with respect to at least three "core" species which were present in all flocks (namely Checker-throated Antwren *Myrmotherula fulviventris*, White-flanked Antwren *M. axillaris*, Half-collared Gnatwren *Microbates cinereiventris*), and several other species that were present in most of them, a total of at least 21 species being noted in understorey mixed-species flocks with this bird (Whitney and Rosenberg in prep.). Canopy and subcanopy foraging flocks sometimes appeared to be loosely associated with the understorey flocks, in which the Speckled Antshrike may possibly be a "flock leader"; within these associations, it typically foraged between 0.5 and 2.5 m (most often at c.1 m), but ranged from practically on the ground to as high as 5 m (Whitney and Rosenberg in prep.). Never more than one pair was observed within any particular flock (although on one occasion an adult male and two female-plumaged birds were seen in a single flock), with the two birds usually staying in close proximity to each other: whilst scanning for prey items, birds would sit motionless for an average of 20 seconds (ranging from c.2 to 60 seconds), and would forage by sally-gleans to live foliage, taking prey from the leaf surfaces (Whitney and Rosenberg in prep.).

THREATS The forest in Darién, on the border of Panama and Colombia (including the Cerro Tacarcuna massif), is seemingly mostly unaffected by agricultural or logging activities (CNPPA 1982), but whilst it is expected that large areas of habitat suitable for the Speckled Antshrike remain in easternmost Panama (on the Caribbean slope of San Blas and Darién), it is also likely that these forests will be cleared at the steady rate of deforestation presently going on in San Blas, if they are not in some way protected (Whitney and Rosenberg in prep.). In the Serranía de Baudó there are still large expanses of forest (A. J. Negret *in litt.* 1987); however, both the Colombian side of the border and the Serranía de Baudó (especially around Ensenada Utría) have been identified as of the highest conservation priority (within the Colombian Chocó) owing to the building of roads encouraging settlement, and to timber companies causing further deforestation (IUCN TFP 1988a: see below); aerial observations (as of January 1992) of the Pacific lowlands of Colombia near the Panamanian border and up the río Atrato revealed that practically all of the forest had been cleared (Whitney and Rosenberg in prep.).

MEASURES TAKEN In Panama, the Darién National Park (597,000 ha), which is also a World Heritage Site, covers about 80% of the border area with Colombia, and although it apparently includes much of the Cerro Tacarcuna massif (CNPPA 1982, Ridgely and Gwynne 1989), the Speckled Antshrike has not yet been found in the park (Whitney and Rosenberg in prep.). There are two tribes of Indians (Chocó and Kuña) within the park, but the areas of agriculture and disturbed forest (principally along river courses) are very limited (CNPPA 1982: see Threats). Further west, the area around Nusagandi is protected as a 40,000 ha forest reserve (Ridgely and Gwynne 1989), 12,000 ha of which is a Kuña Indian reserve of largely undisturbed forest in which ecotourism is promoted (Whitney and Rosenberg in prep.).

In Colombia, Los Katíos National Park (72,000 ha) covers areas along the border (CNPPA 1982), and although the bird has not been recorded there or in the surrounding area (on the Colombian side), its location and altitudinal coverage (50-800 m) almost definitely make it an extremely important conservation area for this and other Chocó endemics (Haffer 1975, Whitney and Rosenberg in prep.); and Ensenada Utría National Park (c.50,000 ha) protects some areas of the Serranía de Baudó (IUCN TFP 1988a), although again it is unknown whether the Speckled Antshrike occurs in the immediate area. This latter reserve has been threatened by road-building associated with the construction of a hydroelectric dam (IUCN TFP 1988a), and Fundación Natura is currently undertaking management studies and an inventory in it (M. G. Kelsey *in litt.* 1992).

MEASURES PROPOSED Where possible, conservation efforts for this species should seek to address the needs of the other threatened birds in the region, namely Chocó Tinamou *Crypturellus kerriae* and Baudó Oropendola *Psarocolius cassini* (see relevant accounts), the other 10 lowland endemic birds (ICBP 1992, Crosby *et al.* in prep.), and the Tacarcuna Wood-quail *Odontophorus dialeucos* and Pirre Warbler *Basileuterus ignotus* (endemic to highland forest above 1,050 m on Cerros Tacarcuna, Pirre and Mali), which, although not imminently threatened, need to be considered in any initiatives. The ecological requirements and distributions of all these birds are in urgent need of clarification, which could be attained by fieldwork and surveys in the Cerro Pirre foothills, Cerros de Quía area, Serranía del Darién (including Cerro Tacarcuna), and Serranía de Baudó. The status of each species in the national parks mentioned above also needs to be assessed in order to determine the viability of the populations within them and the effectiveness of the existing protected areas system. The status of this antshrike and the forest it inhabits within San Blas, Panama, also urgently requires assessment and probably protection. A protected area in the Serranía de Baudó, perhaps adjoining the Ensenada Utría National Park, is of the highest conservation priority within the Chocó region owing to its exceptionally high biological diversity (IUCN TFP 1988a; see also equivalent section under Baudó Oropendola).

For several years, INDERENA in Bogotá has been studying the possibility of linking with Panamanian efforts to preserve the Darién area through the creation of a bi-national reserve along the border (LGN), and such a reserve would undoubtedly help to protect this and the other important species mentioned above.

REMARKS The Speckled Antshrike is the only representative of the genus *Xenornis*.

BICOLOURED ANTVIREO *Dysithamnus occidentalis* **V/R**[10]

This retiring bird of regrowth in natural forest clearings in the subtropical Andes of Colombia and Ecuador remains known from only three general areas, and has suffered substantial habitat loss in at least one.

DISTRIBUTION The Bicoloured (Western) Antvireo (see Remarks 1) is known from two areas of Colombia (nominate race) and one in Ecuador (race *punctitectus*), with very recent records from each country following many decades of "absence".

Colombia Nominate *occidentalis* is known from four localities, listed here from north to south, the first in Valle and last three in Cauca in the vicinity of Cerro Munchique (coordinates from Paynter and Traylor 1981): Finca Hato Viejo, 2,200 m, headwaters of río Pance, Farallones de Cali, 3°22'N 76°45'W, November 1990 (adult female collected: H. Alvarez-López and G. Kattan *in litt.* 1991); "río Munchique, El Tambo", 900 m (one female collected: Bond and Meyer de Schauensee 1940, Whitney 1992; see Remarks 2); La Costa (not located, possibly 10 km north of Cerro Munchique), 1,100-1,200 m (two birds collected, one [in ANSP] in October 1939: Gyldenstolpe 1941, Whitney 1992); Cocal, 1,200 m, 2°31'N 77°00'W, June 1911 (type-specimen collected: Cory and Hellmayr 1924, Whitney 1992).

Ecuador The subspecies *punctitectus* is known from the east side of the Andes in Napo province, localities (north to south; see Remarks 3) being: below Oyacachi, 0°10'S 78°07'W (three birds collected: Chapman 1926, Whitney 1992, two of them in AMNH dated January 1923; coordinates from Paynter and Traylor 1977); Baeza, reportedly (specimen in BMNH: Whitney 1992); lower Volcán Sumaco (one male collected in December 1923: Chapman 1926, specimen in AMNH), specifically some 40 km by road west-north-west of Loreto village in January 1990 (Whitney 1992).

POPULATION From the fact that only up to three individuals were ever collected at one site (see above) the Bicoloured Antvireo would appear to be relatively uncommon where it occurs. However, its rediscovery in Ecuador, 1990, involved the use of playback, and resulted in the observation of a moderate number of birds, indicating reasonable densities in the appropriate habitat (as gauged from Whitney 1992).

ECOLOGY In Colombia, altitudes range from 900 to 2,200 m, with birds being known (in Valle) or assumed (in Cauca) to have been taken in forest (see Threats). In Ecuador, altitudes of 500-1,000 m (Hilty and Brown 1986) are presumably based on the apparently erroneous localities given in the same source (see Remarks 3), and Whitney (1992) considered all records in the country stem from above 1,500 m (this is consistent with elevations given in Paynter and Traylor [1977] for the three accepted localities in Distribution), his own being from no lower than 1,675 m. All birds located by Whitney (1992) were along a narrow ridge cloaked in primary subtropical forest, but were only found in places such as tree-falls, landslips or other "light-gaps" where greater-than-average amounts of sunlight penetrated the canopy, creating a locally dense understorey 2-10 m in height; such growth was often dominated by woody plants and herbs with stems under 2 cm in basal width, with a patchy growth of herbs and ferns at floor level on a dense, uniform leaf-litter, and bamboo sometimes conspicuous (although the bird did not appear to be directly associated with it). Birds were encountered in such habitat as solitary individuals or pairs, and at that time of year (January) were quiet and secretive, moving from perch to perch through the understorey and gleaning arthropod prey from leaves and twigs (one foraging movement made every c.30 seconds) always within 2 m of the ground, mostly within 1 m, and occasionally by flipping leaves on the ground, but also often sally-gleaning over short (usually less than 2 m) distances; prey items observed included two small caterpillars, a small adult moth, a 2 cm katydid or mantid and a 4 cm cricket (Whitney 1992). There are no breeding data.

THREATS Whether habitat loss has greatly affected this species in Colombia is unclear, given the consideration in Measures Taken; the recent record from near Cali occurred during work on the effect of fragmentation of woodlots on species number and composition (G. Kattan verbally 1991). In Ecuador, however, most of the type-locality of the race *punctitectus* and much of the suitable habitat elsewhere within its small known range, with the exception of Volcán Sumaco and portions of Huacamayo Ridge, has been cleared (Whitney 1992). Moreover, the local human population on Sumaco has been increasing in recent decades, most families clearing forest to grow naranjilla as a cash-crop, and steadily moving upslope towards the level at which the Bicoloured Antvireo occurs (B. M. Whitney *in litt.* 1991).

MEASURES TAKEN The headwaters of the río Pance appear to be just outside Los Farallones de Cali National Park (see map in Hernández Camacho *et al.* undated), although it seems likely that this largely (ornithologically) unexplored park holds a population of this species. The position of at least two of the localities in Cauca as indicated in Paynter and Traylor (1977) suggests that they lie within the current Munchique National Park (see map in Hernández Camacho *et al.* undated). Volcán Sumaco possesses 100,045 ha of "protected forest" (IUCN 1992) which seems likely to harbour some birds; however, B. M. Whitney (*in litt.* 1991) found no evidence of protection of forest on Sumaco during his work on the species.

MEASURES PROPOSED Now that the voice and habitat of this species has been determined (see Ecology and Whitney 1992), it should be relatively simple to undertake searches in both Colombia and Ecuador to determine its distribution and status, especially within existing protected areas, notably Munchique National Park and Sumaco Protected Forest. It is worth noting that, despite comments made under Threats, Volcán Sumaco is mostly still pristine, with an intact corridor of habitats from the lowlands to above the treeline, and stands in an area of great biological richness, so that its full conservation would represent a major achievement (B. M. Whitney *in litt.* 1991); apart from the Bicoloured Antvireo, the Lesser Collared Forest-falcon *Micrastur buckleyi* has been recorded there (see relevant account) as well as such restricted-range species as Pink-throated Brilliant *Heliodoxa gularis*, Red-billed Tyrannulet *Zimmerius cinereicapillus* and Black-backed Bush-tanager *Urothraupis stolzmanni* (ICBP 1992, Crosby *et al.* in prep.). A number of other threatened species have been recorded in Los Farallones de Cali and Munchique National Parks: these species, and initiatives for their conservation, are presented in the equivalent section under Multicoloured Tanager *Chlorochrysa nitidissima*.

REMARKS (1) The taxonomic history and evidence that indicates this bird belongs to *Dysithamnus* and not *Thamnomanes* or *Thamnophilus* is provided in Whitney (1992). (2) While El Tambo is a well-known site to the east of Cerro Munchique, río Munchique is a Pacific slope stream at c.2°36'N 77°15'W; the qualifier "El Tambo" (ANSP label data) may therefore refer to a general district. (3) The localities "San José, Sarayacú, Zamora" mentioned by Hilty and Brown (1986) for Ecuador appear to be in error, as no source for them can be traced (Whitney 1992).

PLUMBEOUS ANTVIREO *Dysithamnus plumbeus* V/R[10]

This secretive antbird haunts tangles in the lower stratum of tall, primary Atlantic Forest in south-east Brazil, where it has suffered from much habitat loss and seems to depend on a handful of protected areas (notably Sooretama) for its security.

DISTRIBUTION The Plumbeous Antvireo (see Remarks 1) is endemic to the Atlantic Forest region of south-east Brazil from Bahia south of Salvador (one record in 1928) through south-eastern Minas Gerais to Espírito Santo and northern Rio de Janeiro state.

Bahia The only record is from the rio Gongogi at Cajazeiras (14°24'S 39°51'W in Paynter and Traylor 1991), 300 m, 20 June 1928 (Naumburg 1939).

Minas Gerais Older records are from Machacalis, December 1954; rio Doce, right bank, and lower rio Piracicaba at the confluence with rio Doce, August and September 1940; rio Manhuaçu at São Benedito (near Tabaúna), 180 m, January 1930 (Naumburg 1939); rio Matipó, July 1919 (Pinto 1938); around Raul Soares, June 1949, July and August 1957; and Fazendas Barra Alegre and Nova Aurora, São Paulo de Muriahé (now Muriaé), November and December 1926 (where no source before the semi-colon, records are from specimens in FMNH, LACM, MNRJ, MZUSP). Of these, the Piracicaba confluence is close to the present-day Rio Doce State Park (see Pinto 1945), where specimens have been collected (in one case specifically at Lagoa do Aníbal) in September 1975 and August 1978 (in DZMG), and one pair was seen in March 1986 (J. F. Pacheco *in litt.* 1991). The only other locality is the Fazenda Montes Claros (Caratinga Reserve), Caratinga, where one bird was collected in April 1985 (in DZMG) and others were seen in July 1988 (S. G. D. Cook *in litt.* 1988) and in 1990 (A. Whittaker *in litt.* 1991).

Espírito Santo Older records are (north to south) from the rio Itaúnas, September 1950; rio São José, September 1942; Lagoa Juparanã (in 1925 precisely Santana), 120 m, August and October 1925, November 1929 (Snethlage 1927, Naumburg 1939; specimens in AMNH, MNRJ); Baixo Guandu, 120 m, December 1929 (Naumburg 1939); Colatina, November 1940; Pau Gigante (now Ibiraçu), September and November 1940; Jatiboca (near Itarana), 900-1,000 m, December 1940 and January 1941; Porto Cachoeiro (now Santa Leopoldina), November 1905 (von Ihering and von Ihering 1907, Pinto 1938) (where no source before the semi-colon, records are from specimens in MNRJ, MZUSP, USNM). The key site for the species in the state now seems to be Sooretama Biological Reserve, with records in 1980/1981 (Scott and Brooke 1985), November 1986 (J. F. Pacheco *in litt.* 1991) and August 1988 (M. Pearman *in litt.* 1990), and the adjacent CVRD Linhares Forest Reserve, with records from December 1986 (B. M. Whitney *in litt.* 1987) to at least August 1991 (Pacheco and Fonseca 1987, B. M. Whitney *in litt.* 1990, Stotz 1991). The only other recent records are from the Fazenda Vila das Palmas, Barra de São Francisco, in July 1982 (specimen in CGTM), and Augusto Ruschi (Nova Lombardia) Biological Reserve, June 1990 (Gardner and Gardner 1990b).

Rio de Janeiro The inclusion of this state in the species's range, based on "Rio" trade skins (Cory and Hellmayr 1924), is accepted by some authorities (e.g. Pinto 1938, 1978, Sick and Teixeira 1979) but not by others (e.g. Meyer de Schauensee 1982, Sick 1985). However, its occurrence in the extreme north-west has recently been verified at Fazendas São Francisco and São Lourenço on the road between Natividade and Raposo, 140 m, in September/October 1989 and February 1990 (J. F. Pacheco *in litt.* 1991).

POPULATION This species was "not often" encountered by Wied (1831-1833), and remained known from very few specimens until the early 1920s, when it was considered an "exceedingly rare form" (Cory and Hellmayr 1924), a view that continued to be expressed (e.g. by Snethlage 1927, Pinto 1938, Naumburg 1939). Although a fair number of localities have been added to the species's range since, there seems to be little doubt that it is now seriously reduced in abundance and distribution as a result of the extensive forest destruction which has taken place in the region.

Even while not including this bird in their list of rare and threatened species, Sick and Teixeira (1979) considered it prudent to "call attention" to it. Although it has been considered difficult to detect unless its voice is known (Snethlage 1927, B. M. Whitney *in litt.* 1990, J. F. Pacheco *in litt.* 1991), the species was considered "fairly common" (small numbers – under 10 – seen/heard on all or most days in appropriate habitat) at Sooretama in 1980/1981 (Scott and Brooke 1985), but this may apply to only a very limited portion of the reserve (J. F. Pacheco *in litt.* 1991); nevertheless, at least six pairs held territories along c.2 km of one forest trail in the north-west section of the reserve through the 1980s, and on one occasion at least three pairs were heard counter-singing at once within an area of 2 ha, so that it was felt a reasonable population exists in the interior of tall forest in less disturbed parts of the reserve (TAP). It is less easily found in the CVRD Linhares Reserve, where pairs have been detected only after some effort (B. M. Whitney *in litt.* 1987, 1990), e.g. six records in 47 days' fieldwork, July/August 1987 and 1991 (D. F. Stotz *in litt.* 1991), but in the much smaller remaining tract of forest where the species has been detected in Rio de Janeiro it is found with some ease, probably precisely because of the small area where birds concentrate, although numbers cannot be high (J. F. Pacheco *in litt.* 1991).

ECOLOGY The Plumbeous Antvireo inhabits the lower stratum of tall primary or little-disturbed forest (Wied 1831-1833, Snethlage 1927, Scott and Brooke 1985, Sick 1985). Records from CVRD's Linhares Reserve have been of singles and pairs in tall, good forest, sometimes in mixed flocks, sometimes alone (D. F. Stotz *in litt.* 1991, B. M. Whitney *in litt.* 1991). At Sooretama, it is usually encountered in pairs that forage from near the ground up to c.2 m in dense tangles, especially in shaded, old treefalls overgrown with vines and small trees; they also associate with understorey mixed-species flocks, at such times ranging up to 4 m in the lower branches of small trees (TAP). Birds have been considered very secretive, usually keeping amidst tangles of fallen dry twigs on the ground; collection of a small series was only achieved after learning the species's voice (Snethlage 1927); one of these specimens was in a bird flock (in MNRJ). Members of a pair keep in contact with soft call-notes; males sing mostly in the early morning and late afternoon, rarely through the rest of the day (B. M. Whitney *in litt.* 1991).

Individuals forage (and vocalize) in the manner of typical *Dysithamnus* species, hopping along thin branches and vines, scanning and perch-gleaning live foliage, and occasionally probing in clusters of hanging or trapped dead leaves (TAP). Food consists of arthropods up to at least 10 cm in length, including katydids and stick insects taken from leaves and twigs, although birds sometimes perform lunging sally-gleans (B. M. Whitney *in litt.* 1991). Stomach contents of specimens in CGTM and MNRJ are given as "insects", "eggs of insects" and "a chrysalis". Pairs probably regularly follow flocks when they pass through their territories, at such times associating with Lesser Woodcreeper *Lepidocolaptes fuscus*, White-eyed Foliage-gleaner *Automolus leucophthalmus*, Black-capped Foliage-gleaner *Philydor atricapillus*, White-flanked Antwren *Myrmotherula axillaris*, (near-threatened) Band-tailed Antwren *M. urosticta* and Red-crowned Ant-tanager *Habia rubica* (TAP). In some montane forests of Espírito Santo, the Plumbeous Antvireo occurs alongside Plain Antvireo *Dysithamnus mentalis* and Spot-breasted Antvireo *D. stictothorax*, both of which frequent higher strata (Sick 1985).

Of specimens in AMNH, CGTM and DZMG whose gonad condition was recorded, four were dormant in June, July and December, four slightly enlarged in August, December and January, and one half enlarged in November. A nest with two eggs being incubated by a female (no male was seen) was found at the CVRD Linhares Reserve on 23 August 1987; it was 0.3 m from the ground in a 1 m high shrub in closed forest understorey (D. F. Stotz *in litt.* 1991, 1992). Territories appear to be fairly small (less than 1.5 ha) and fixed: several different pairs at Sooretama were easily located every year (for at least five years) by tape playback at the same spots along a trail, the minimum distance between pairs being about 75 m although this was unusually short (TAP).

THREATS The fragmentation of the species's range by extensive forest destruction has been and remains the one significant threat. Even though current records are from a (small) number of protected areas, the species's ecological requirements remain very poorly known and its recorded numbers at these sites are too low to be confident about the future of the populations they hold.

MEASURES TAKEN The Plumbeous Antvireo is protected under Brazilian law (Bernardes *et al.* 1990). Some of its present remnant populations should persist so long as the protected areas where they have been found (Rio Doce, Fazenda Montes Claros, Augusto Ruschi, Sooretama) continue to be preserved; but see Threats.

MEASURES PROPOSED The few remaining patches of forest within the species's range could still harbour small and so far undetected populations, and merit being identified and searched. Surveys of the species in the field are also needed better to ascertain and monitor its status in the localities where it has been recorded, particularly in areas which may prove to be important for its long-term survival, such as the Rio Doce State Park in Minas Gerais and Sooretama/Linhares in Espírito Santo. Support for these existing key sites is clearly imperative to protect this and several other threatened species that occur in the same areas.

REMARKS (1) The case for regarding this south-east Brazilian form as distinct at the specific level from the White-spotted Antvireo *D. leucostictus* (R. S. Ridgely verbally 1987; see also Sibley and Monroe 1990) is accepted here. The species has been treated in the genus *Thamnomanes* (Pinto 1978, Meyer de Schauensee 1982), but is here retained in *Dysithamnus* (Sclater 1890, von Ihering and von Ihering 1907, Cory and Hellmayr 1924, Pinto 1938, Schulenberg 1983, Sick 1985).

RIO DE JANEIRO ANTWREN *Myrmotherula fluminensis* I[8]

This mysterious species is based on a single individual from a degraded woodlot in the middle of Rio de Janeiro state, possibly having straggled from the Serra dos Órgãos and presumably representing populations at risk from forest clearance.

DISTRIBUTION The Rio de Janeiro Antwren is known only from the type-specimen, an adult male from 4 km south-east of Santo Aleixo, Majé, 22°34'45"S, 43°01'39"W, at c.20 m, Rio de Janeiro state, south-east Brazil, on 4 July 1982 (Gonzaga 1988) (see Remarks).

POPULATION The discovery of this bird after seven years of research in the study area was taken as an indication that it was possibly a straggler from the nearby slopes of the Serra dos Órgãos, but that whatever the case the population involved must be local and very small to have avoided detection until so recently (Gonzaga 1988).

ECOLOGY The type was mist-netted in a partially isolated and highly disturbed woodlot in which two other species of the genus, White-flanked Antwren *Myrmotherula axillaris* and the near-threatened Unicoloured Antwren *M. unicolor*, were known to occur, having been regularly recorded in the course of fieldwork there, 1975-1982 (Gonzaga 1988). The specimen's stomach contained anthropod remains, and the gonads were inactive (Gonzaga 1988, LPG).

THREATS None is known in this unique situation, but habitat loss is likely to be the cause of this species's evident rarity. Deforestation has been extensive in the Atlantic Forest region of eastern Brazil, and particularly severe in the lowlands of Rio de Janeiro state, so that only small fragments remain (LPG).

MEASURES TAKEN None is known.

MEASURES PROPOSED Surveys are needed to locate the species and to provide information on its ecology and conservation status. This has been considered "a major challenge to observers and collectors who have the opportunity to work in the foothills and lower-elevation forests of the Serra dos Órgãos or maybe elsewhere in the state of Rio de Janeiro" (Gonzaga 1988).

REMARKS Sibley and Monroe's (1990) only notation on this bird, "known from the unique type, which may be a hybrid *M. axillaris* x *M. unicolor* (Gonzaga 1988)", gives an undue impression of weight to this possibility; whatever the interpretation of the statement in the original description, the likelihood of the type being a hybrid is minimal (LPG). The Rio de Janeiro Antwren seems to be closely related to the bamboo-haunting Ihering's Antwren *M. iheringi* from western Amazonia (see Gonzaga 1988; also D. F. Stotz verbally 1992).

ASHY ANTWREN *Myrmotherula grisea* V/R[10]

This middle-storey and lower canopy antbird is known from six lower cloud-forest localities in La Paz, Cochabamba and Santa Cruz, its small geographic and elevational range (c.500-1,650 m) placing it seriously at risk owing to the current high deforestation in the yungas of north-western Bolivia.

DISTRIBUTION The Ashy Antwren is known from few specimens, and even fewer sightings, from the yungas in the departments of La Paz, Cochabamba and Santa Cruz, Bolivia, where localities from north-west to south-east (coordinates, unless otherwise stated, from Paynter *et al.* 1975) are as follows:

La Paz Santa Ana, 15°50'S 67°36'W, at 670 m (and not found higher or lower) on the río Coroico, where the type-series (seven specimens in ANSP) was collected in July 1934 (Carriker 1935a); along the road to Bolinda, north of Caranavi (at 15°46'S 67°36'W), where three individuals were seen at 1,400 m in September 1979 (Remsen *et al.* 1982); Serranía Bellavista, 35 km by road north of Caranavi, where two males and a female (in LSUMZ) were mist-netted at 1,650 m in lower cloud-forest during June 1979 (Remsen *et al.* 1982); río Beni, c.20 km by river north of Puerto Linares (at c.15°28'S 67°27'W: IGM 1980), where a specimen (in LSUMZ) was collected at 600 m in July 1981;

Cochabamba Alto Palmar (untraced), specimen (in LSUMZ) collected at 1,100 m in 1960; Palmar, 17°06'S 65°29'W, female (in ANSP) collected at 800 m in July 1937 (D. F. Stotz *in litt.* 1989, R. S. Ridgely *in litt.* 1990);

Santa Cruz Santa Rita (untraced), male (in LSUMZ) collected at 500 m in 1961 (Remsen *et al.* 1982); Cerro Hosane, c.17°25'S 64°00'W, on the río Blanco, where two specimens (in CM) were collected at 1,200 m in August and September 1917 (pre-dating the type-series); along the upper río Saguayo (17°50'S 63°39'W), in Amboró National Park, where a few were recorded in March 1992 (Parker *et al.* 1992); and in the Serranía Raigones, 18°10'S 63°32'W, in the extreme south-eastern corner of Amboró National Park, where several individuals were seen at c.800 m (TAP).

POPULATION The paucity of museum specimens and sightings suggests that the species is uncommon, and the bird was certainly scarce at Serranía Bellavista, where only three specimens were mist-netted and none seen during more than 40 days of fieldwork in tall forest at 1,350-1,650 m: similarly, only one individual was collected during a prolonged field effort at 600 m along the río Beni below Puerto Linares (Remsen *et al.* 1982). The only locality where Ashy Antwrens have been found in numbers is the upper río Saguayo valley in Amboró National Park at c.650-1,000 m (Parker *et al.* 1992). In a small area covered daily (c.10 ha) there were two pairs associating with different middle-storey mixed-species flocks at 650-800 m, and a solitary male was seen at 1,000 m (TAP). This was the only *Myrmotherula* species observed at this locality (in contrast to the sites near Puerto Linares and Santa Ana where both White-flanked Antwrens *M. axillaris* and Grey Antwrens *M. menetriesii* were also noted); this suggests that the Ashy Antwren may be most numerous in a narrow elevational zone above the normal upper limits of its congeners (e.g. from 700 to 1,200 m).

ECOLOGY The Ashy Antwren inhabits tall humid forest at elevations ranging from 500 to 1,650 m (Remsen *et al.* 1982). At Serranía Bellavista it occurs at 1,650 m, but apparently not at a nearby lower (1,350 m) but wetter locality, where none was found in 24 days of intensive fieldwork in 1980 (Remsen *et al.* 1982). Remsen and Quintela (unpublished) treated it as a bird of "foothill tropical forest", which they defined as the forest at c.500-1,100 m that is somewhat drier than "true montane forest", the lower zone of which they called "upper tropical zone forest" with approximate elevational limits of 1,100-1,700 m. At all known localities this antwren occurs in the middle storey and lower canopy of tall, humid forest (TAP): four sightings were of birds foraging 3-5 m above ground (Remsen *et al.* 1982), while two specimens are labelled "light forest undergrowth" and "low in forest undergrowth" (specimens in LSUMZ: see below).

Carriker (1935a) noted that it was seen in mixed-species flocks, and indeed along the upper río Saguayo Ashy Antwrens were always noted in flocks that included Tawny-crowned Greenlets *Hylophilus ochraceiceps* and Red-crowned Ant-Tanagers *Habia rubica*, and were often with Golden-crowned Warblers *Basileuterus culicivorus* (TAP). Other regular flock associates, including the Bolivian Recurvebill *Simoxenops striatus*, are listed in Ecology under that species. Both Carriker (1935a) and Remsen *et al.* (1982) noted this antwren in flocks that also contained White-flanked Antwrens and Grey Antwrens; the latter authors also observed Bluish-slate Antshrikes *Thamnomanes schistogynus* with an Ashy Antwren. None of the the latter three associates were noted at the río Saguayo site, although they all occur at lower elevations in Amboró National Park (TAP). The bird seen near Puerto Linares "stood out from other *Myrmotherula* species in its more acrobatic, rapid movements, spending only one-two seconds at isolated small leaf clusters at branch tips before flying to other clusters" (Remsen *et al.* 1982). Two pairs studied at length by Parker *et al.* (1992) "primarily searched clusters of dead leaves that hung from open, slender branches or were trapped in vine tangles, from c. 6-15 m (mainly at 12-14) above the ground; they also occasionally probed balls of moss on branches, and appeared to scan green leaves as well but were not seen to take any prey from them". A pair observed in the Serranía Raigones also searched dead leaves trapped in dense lower canopy tangles at 9-12 m (TAP). All stomachs reported on contained insects (Remsen *et al.* 1982), and prey items at the two Amboró sites included small green orthopterans, small spiders, and a roach (TAP).

A pair behaving nervously, both with small green orthopterans in their bills, were observed on 17 August at río Saguayo, but no nest or fledglings could be found in the area (TAP). All recent Bolivian specimens (LSUMZ) from June–July had ossified skulls and enlarged or slightly enlarged gonads (Remsen *et al.* 1982), although this is not necessarily a sign of breeding (TAP).

THREATS The intensive and expanding cultivation of coca and coffee on the Andean slopes, at elevations inhabited by this species, poses a serious threat, and the species's only chance of survival may be on slopes too steep for cultivation, if such exist (TAP). Because the foothill tropical forest is drier than the upper tropical zone forest, it is easier to clear and burn, and thus is a favoured target for colonization projects; the amount of this forest that has been cleared in the yungas of La Paz and Cochabamba is certainly substantial, and of the 19 species apparently restricted to this type of forest, the Ashy Antwren and the Bolivian Recurvebill are of special concern because of their limited distributions (Remsen and Quintela unpublished, ICBP 1992, Crosby *et al.* in prep.: see relevant account, but also Threats under Yellow-rumped Antwren *Terenura sharpei*).

MEASURES TAKEN The Amboró National Park in Santa Cruz holds the species (see equivalent section under Bolivian Recurvebill).

MEASURES PROPOSED The Ashy Antwren is sympatric with a number of other threatened species, all of which are in urgent need of conservation initiatives to ensure their long-term survival: a strategy for the conservation of the montane forest and its threatened endemic bird in this region is presented in the equivalent section under Bolivian Recurvebill.

ALAGOAS ANTWREN *Myrmotherula snowi* E[2]

The last hope for this small insectivore appears to be an unprotected and rapidly diminishing tract of upland forest, only 1,500 ha in extent, near the type-locality in Alagoas state, Brazil.

DISTRIBUTION The Alagoas Antwren (see Remarks) is known only from (Fazenda) Pedra Branca ("Serra Branca": see Remarks 2 under Alagoas Foliage-gleaner *Philydor novaesi*), near Murici (9°19'S 35°57'W), on the south-eastern escarpment of the Borborema plateau in Alagoas, north-eastern Brazil (see, e.g., Teixeira and Gonzaga 1983; also D. M. Teixeira *in litt.* 1987), although it appears now to be present only in the remaining part of this area known as Fazenda Bananeira (see Threats, Measures Proposed under Alagoas Foliage-gleaner). It was described from one adult male and two adult females collected in February 1979 (Teixeira and Gonzaga 1985), while one additional (juvenile) male was obtained from the same locality in May 1984 (specimen in MNRJ). The species was again recorded at this site in October 1990 (J. F. Pacheco *in litt.* 1991) and in April 1992 (M. Pearman *in litt.* 1992). It seems to be restricted to upland forest (550 m), not having been found in the coastal lowlands (Teixeira and Gonzaga 1985).

POPULATION Numbers are not known.

ECOLOGY The Alagoas Antwren has been recorded in the middle strata of forest, where it often joins mixed-species flocks of insectivorous birds in which White-flanked Antwrens *Myrmotherula axillaris* and a variety of other formicariids may be present (Teixeira and Gonzaga 1985, Teixeira 1987a,b). Another observer has found the species in pairs and small groups, actively foraging 1.5-2 m up in the undergrowth and not associating with other species (M. Pearman *in litt.* 1992). Food consists of arthropods taken from the foliage; the stomachs of specimens collected contained the remains of spiders and insects, including beetles, cockroaches and ants (Teixeira and Gonzaga 1985). Breeding seems to occur around February, as judged from the gonad condition of specimens and the birds' behaviour: one female collected on 9 February had an egg in the oviduct, and juveniles still in the company of their presumed parents were observed in May (Teixeira and Gonzaga 1985).

THREATS Destruction of forest at Pedra Branca is the single most serious threat to this and all other upland forest species in Alagoas (see Threats under Alagoas Foliage-gleaner).

MEASURES TAKEN None is known (but see equivalent section under Alagoas Foliage-gleaner).

MEASURES PROPOSED An initiative to preserve forest and its rich birdlife at Pedra Branca (Fazenda Bananeira) needs urgent impetus (see Measures Proposed and Remarks under Alagoas Foliage-gleaner).

REMARKS This bird was originally described as a subspecies of the Unicoloured Antwren *M. unicolor* from south-east Brazil, but there is growing evidence that it is a good species, with very different vocalizations (D. Willis *in litt.* 1990, B. M. Whitney *in litt.* 1991, M. Pearman *in litt.* 1992).

ASH-THROATED ANTWREN *Herpsilochmus parkeri* E[2]

This recently discovered antwren was fairly common in humid montane forest on a low isolated mountain ridge in San Martín department, northern Peru. Its minute geographic range coupled with rampant deforestation of the adjacent lowlands in the río Huallaga drainage renders it highly vulnerable.

DISTRIBUTION The Ash-throated Antwren (see Remarks 1) is currently known with certainty only from the type-locality, c.15 km by trail north-east of Jirillo to Balsapuerto, 6°03'S 76°44'W, at 1,350 m on the left bank of the río Huallaga, San Martín department, northern Peru, where it was discovered in 1983 (Davis and O'Neill 1986). It was again recorded in June 1987, when a male and female were seen together 3 km north-east of "Jesús del Monte" (untraced), north of Vencedores and Herio (also untraced: see Remarks 2) (M. Pearman *in litt.* 1991). It apparently does not occur immediately to the west, across the Moyobamba valley, and it was found only at 1,350 m even though elevations down to 750 m were studied intensively in the same range of foothills (Davis and O'Neill 1986).

POPULATION This antwren was reported to be fairly common to common at the type-locality, and in October–November 1983 when it was discovered, birds were usually seen in pairs: eight specimens (four of each sex) were taken at this time (Davis and O'Neill 1986, T. S. Schulenberg verbally 1989).

ECOLOGY The habitat at the type-locality is very heterogeneous: the Moyobamba valley directly to the west of the mountain ridge is moderately xeric, owing to a partial rain-shadow effect, and the species was taken at what appeared to be the upper elevational limit of the savanna-like habitat that characterizes much of that valley, which, however, was distributed only in scattered patches at 1,350 m (Davis and O'Neill 1986). There was another distinct habitat, located mostly on ridges in this area, that resulted from the outcropping of poor-quality, sandy soils where vegetation was usually short (c.4 m), extremely dense, and of low floristic diversity: a semi-stunted (canopy height c.12 m), but more diverse forest was also present and seemed to form a transition between the savanna-like vegetation and the tall cloud-forest (averaging 30-35 m in height) present in areas with good soil (Davis and O'Neill 1986): more information on the locality and its avifauna is given by Davis (1986).

The Ash-throated Antwren was noted most commonly in the canopy and mid-levels of the tallest forest, which had a mostly closed canopy, many epiphytes and a moderately open undergrowth, but was only slightly less common in the semi-stunted forest, where it was also found from mid-levels to the canopy, this latter forest having an extremely dense undergrowth and only a slightly closed canopy in which epiphytes were extremely abundant; the species was once netted in some low bushes in the savanna-like habitat at the very abrupt (presumably fire-maintained) border between the savanna and the semi-stunted forest (Davis and O'Neill 1986), an apparently similar situation to where birds were seen in June 1987 (M. Pearman *in litt.* 1991).

Birds usually travel in pairs, often within mixed-species flocks comprising a combination of Slaty Antwren *Myrmotherula schisticolor*, Buff-throated Foliage-gleaner *Automolus ochrolaemus*, Ocellated Woodcreeper *Xiphorhynchus ocellatus*, Streaked Xenops *Xenops rutilans* and Buff-throated Tody-tyrant *Hemitriccus rufigularis*. The stomachs of five individuals contained a variety of insects, primarily Coleoptera (including Curculionidae and Coccinellidae, one of which was tentatively identified as a *Brachiacantha* sp.), Hemiptera (both of which were present in all five stomachs), and Hymenoptera (present in four stomachs); in lower frequencies were Homoptera (including at least one Fulgoroidea), Formicidae, Orthoptera, Dermaptera and one spider of the Araneae (probably Salticidae) (Davis and O'Neill 1986). All known specimens were collected from the end of October to late November (1983): none had active gonads, two had only slightly

(5 and 10%) ossified skulls, most had worn plumage and only two were in light to moderate body moult, all suggesting that most breeding takes place during the drier parts of the year, from about May to September or October (Davis and O'Neill 1986).

THREATS Widespread clearance of the foothill tropical, upper tropical and lower subtropical forest, throughout the Amazonian slopes of the Andes, for the cultivation of both coca and coffee, poses a serious threat to the many species of birds restricted to this zone. Lowland areas in the Huallaga valley to the west of the ridge where this species occurs are almost entirely deforested, and forest clearings are gradually extending further and further up into the surrounding mountains (T. S. Schulenberg verbally 1989). There is no reason to assume that any habitat for the bird will survive for long if steps are not taken to protect some portion of it. The unstable and dangerous political climate that pervades the upper Huallaga valley at the present time probably precludes any conservation action in the next few years, but this area should be placed high on the list of biologically important places to receive attention when the present crisis passes (TAP).

MEASURES TAKEN None is known.

MEASURES PROPOSED A reserve in the low, isolated mountain range east of Moyobamba would also hold several other species that are rare or have very limited distributions, e.g. the threatened Spot-winged Parrotlet *Touit stictoptera* and Royal Sunangel *Heliangelus regalis*, as well as the Napo Sabrewing *Campylopterus villaviscensio* and Bar-winged Wood-wren *Henicorhina leucoptera* (Davis 1986), and should be created as a priority (but see Threats). A study to disclose the distributional status and population of this species should be undertaken.

REMARKS (1) The Ash-throated Antwren is closely related to the Black-capped Antwren *Herpsilochmus pileatus*, which has been treated as three subspecies: *motacilloides*, *atricapillus* and *pileatus*, found from Peru to eastern Brazil; Davis and O'Neill (1986) suggested treating all four taxa as different species, at least until it is known whether any intermediate populations exist between *parkeri* and *motacilloides*, and until the ranges of *pileatus* and *atricapillus* are better known. (2) Jesús del Monte was described as north of Herio village (on the road between Tarapoto and Moyabamba, somewhere between Abra Tangorama and Moyabamba), and thence north of Vencedores: as these localities are untraced, the proximity to the type-locality is unknown.

PECTORAL ANTWREN *Herpsilochmus pectoralis* V[9]

This poorly known and very local antbird is known from three scattered areas of north-eastern Brazil where it survives in unprotected caatinga woodland, secondary woodlots and gallery forest.

DISTRIBUTION The Pectoral Antwren (see Remarks 1) is endemic to north-eastern Brazil in the states of Maranhão, Rio Grande do Norte, Sergipe and Bahia.

Maranhão All the records are from the north-eastern quarter of the state, most of the localities being on the rio Itapicuru basin: Primeira Cruz, May 1906 (Cory 1924); Boa Vista (= Santo Amaro, 2°33'S 43°14'W in Paynter and Traylor 1991), April 1907 (Pinto 1938); Axixá, 1980s (P. Roth verbally 1986); Rosário, 16 April 1926 (Naumburg 1939); Fazenda do Caximbo, Coroatá, September 1972 (specimens in LSUMZ, MPEG; also Oren 1991); Cocos (south of Codó), June 1924 (Hellmayr 1929a; hence presumably the reference to "the banks of the middle Itapicuru" in Snethlage 1927-1928).

Rio Grande do Norte The only record is from near Natal, August 1987 (G. T. de Mattos verbally 1987).

Sergipe A single adult male was seen and tape-recorded at the Itabaiana Ecological Reserve, 175 m, on 25 September 1991 (B. M. Whitney *in litt.* 1991; other observers were J. F. Pacheco, J. L. Rowlett).

Bahia Although most museum skins are from this state, precise localities have rarely been indicated (Pinto 1935; see Remarks 2) and include (all in the north-eastern quarter of the state, here given north to south): Serra Branca (north-east of Canche), a pair seen in January 1979 (LPG; also Sick *et al.* 1987); Jeremoabo, August 1989 (B. C. Forrester *in litt.* 1992) and September 1991 (B. M. Whitney *in litt.* 1991); Santa Bárbara and Itaberaba, January 1988 (B. M. Whitney *in litt.* 1988); Cachoeira, rio Paraguaçu, August 1926 (six specimens in MNRJ); Corupeba (= Curupeba, 12°48'S 38°36'W in Paynter and Traylor 1991), February 1933 (Pinto 1935).

POPULATION The species is clearly extremely local but, although its overall numbers probably cannot be high, it has been considered "locally common" (J. Vielliard *in litt.* 1986), and "not rare" around Axixá (P. Roth verbally 1986).

ECOLOGY The Pectoral Antwren has been recorded from gallery forest (specimens in FMNH) and deciduous forest (Oren 1988) in Maranhão, and in tall caatinga woodland and closed old secondary forest in Bahia (LPG; B. M. Whitney *in litt.* 1988; specimens in MNRJ). Snethlage (1927-1928) only recorded the species in dry palm woodland, and he only found this habitat on the banks of the middle Itapicuru, Maranhão. In two localities in central-eastern Bahia the species was present in remnant woodlots characterized by numerous trees over 10 m and often 15-20 m in height, but was not found in neighbouring habitats with smaller trees; one of the positive sites had been moderately grazed but still showed fairly well developed understorey, with shrubs interlocking in several areas, while the other had had all its understorey cleared, and was "saved" as a shady spot for cattle (B. M. Whitney *in litt.* 1988).

Stomach contents of specimens in FMNH are given as "insects". Birds have been observed foraging by hopping along limbs mostly in the higher parts of trees (canopy and subcanopy about 4 m [2-6 m] up), gleaning arthropods from bark, leaves and twigs (B. M. Whitney *in litt.* 1991).

Two females (in MNRJ) collected on 20 and 31 August in Bahia had well developed ovaries ("ovos muitos desenvolvidos"). There are no other data on breeding except for observations on a family party which included independent immatures in late September (B. M. Whitney *in litt.* 1991).

THREATS Although the species's range and habitat are still insufficiently known, it is apparently dependent upon taller deciduous woodland, which is rare and under pressure in north-eastern Brazil.

MEASURES TAKEN The species is protected under Brazilian law (Bernardes *et al.* 1990). It occurs in the small Itabaiana reserve in Sergipe.

MEASURES PROPOSED Surveys of the species in the field are needed to obtain more accurate knowledge of its distribution and habitat requirements (B. M. Whitney *in litt.* 1988), and should be undertaken in conjunction with efforts to determine an area for the creation of a reserve of deciduous forest in Maranhão, as suggested by Oren and Novaes (1986b), and in central Bahia. The Maranhão reserve should also seek to protect a population of Moustached Woodcreeper *Xiphocolaptes falcirostris* (see relevant account), and in this regard it is worth noting that these two birds were singled out as characteristic of the palm woodland found in the middle Itapicuru, Maranhão (Snethlage 1927-1928); see also Remarks 2 under Plain Spinetail *Synallaxis infuscata.*

REMARKS (1) The species is closely related to Large-billed Antwren *H. longirostris* from northern Bolivia and Central Brazil (Hellmayr 1929a, Davis and O'Neill 1986). (2) The possibility that this species "occurs in all the caatinga region from north and west of Bahia, extending into Maranhão, following the pattern of many other passerines found in the Bahian reconcavo" (Pinto 1935) still needs to be checked.

BLACK-HOODED ANTWREN *Formicivora erythronotos* E[1]

The rediscovery in 1987, after a century or more, of this small undergrowth-dwelling bird has indicated it to be an inhabitant of highly vulnerable secondary forest at sea-level in a single area of southern coastal Rio de Janeiro state, Brazil.

DISTRIBUTION The Black-hooded Antwren (see Remarks 1) is endemic to south-east Brazil in the state of Rio de Janeiro. Its occurrence in Espírito Santo (Ruschi 1953), although admitted by Pinto (1978) and Meyer de Schauensee (1982), has no foundation and is not accepted here. The species was recorded in the middle of the nineteenth century from Nova Friburgo (Burmeister 1856), to whose mountain forests it was thought to be confined (see Remarks 2) until it was rediscovered in September 1987 at sea level near Angra dos Reis, on the southern coast of Rio state (Pacheco 1988a). Further surveys have since succeeded in locating the species at several points around Cunhambebe ("Frade") on the western side of the Baía da Ribeira (F. Carvalho *per* J. F. Pacheco *in litt.* 1991).

POPULATION Known from about 20 nineteenth century skins in European and American museums (Pacheco 1988a) and unrecorded for more than a century, the species has long been on endangered bird lists (Vincent 1966-1971, Sick 1969, 1972, King 1978-1979, Sick and Teixeira 1979, Sick 1985) and indeed feared extinct (King 1978-1979, Scott and Brooke 1985). Following its rediscovery no population surveys have been made, but the species is clearly very local and its extant overall numbers around the Baía da Ribeira are likely to be small, as predicted by King (1978-1979).

ECOLOGY Burmeister (1856) reported this bird living in small groups in forest undergrowth at Nova Friburgo, which sounds unusual in view of what is known of other *Formicivora* species. The site where it was rediscovered was described as a swampy patch of secondary forest near the mangrove line, but its presence was later also verified in dry secondary forest, close to the site of the rediscovery and again at sea level (Pacheco 1988a). In this area birds apparently live in pairs, one of these having been observed foraging in the foliage mainly up to 1 m from the ground, sometimes up to 2 m, with other individuals present nearby; other bird species recorded at the site of the rediscovery were the Uniform Crake *Amaurolimnas concolor*, White-eyed Foliage-gleaner *Automolus leucophthalmus*, White-bearded Manakin *Manacus manacus* and, notably, the near-threatened Salvadori's Antwren *Myrmotherula minor* and Unicoloured Antwren *M. unicolor* (Pacheco 1988a). There is no further information, either on food or breeding of the species.

THREATS The whole region around Angra dos Reis and the Baía da Ilha Grande is one of the most exclusive summer resorts on the coast of Rio de Janeiro and has been subject to extensive real-estate development over the past 20 years. Although the species's range approaches the limits of the Serra da Bocaina National Park, Cairuçu Environmental Protection Area, Tamoios Ecological Station and Tamoios Environmental Protection Area, it has not so far been found in any of these areas.

MEASURES TAKEN The species is protected under Brazilian law (Bernardes *et al.* 1990). Its rediscoverers deliberately refrained from collecting specimens (Pacheco 1988a).

MEASURES PROPOSED Surveys of the species in the field are urgently needed to assess its conservation status more accurately, and this should be done in conjunction with action to protect at least part of its habitat. Further collection of specimens should not be countenanced.

REMARKS (1) The Black-hooded Antwren, originally described in the genus *Formicivora*, was some years later transferred to *Myrmotherula*, where it was retained by all the twentieth-century authorities (e.g. von Ihering and von Ihering 1907, Cory and Hellmayr 1924, Pinto 1938, 1978, Meyer de Schauensee 1982, Sick 1985). Nevertheless, following the species's rediscovery and what has been learnt since of its general behaviour, appearance in life and vocalizations, it appears indeed to belong in *Formicivora* (Pacheco 1988a, B. M. Whitney *in litt.* 1990, LPG). (2) Nova Friburgo has been cited as the only certain locality for this bird throughout the twentieth-century ornithological literature, but Burmeister's (1856) account may be unreliable, and the species may never have been collected there (Pacheco 1988a).

NARROW-BILLED ANTWREN *Formicivora iheringi* V[9]

This poorly known bird inhabits dry forest in a limited area of interior eastern Brazil, living at reasonably high density but under threat from loss of habitat.

DISTRIBUTION The Narrow-billed Antwren is known from only a few localities in interior Bahia and north-east Minas Gerais, eastern Brazil.

Bahia The species was described from "Villa Nova" (Bonfim, Senhor do Bonfim; see Pinto 1938, 1945: 280; also Remarks) (Cory and Hellmayr 1924), where two specimens in MZUSP (including the type) were collected in March 1908. It was next collected at "Iracema" (= Iramaia, 13°17'S 40°58'W in Paynter and Traylor 1991) 700 m, "Giguy" (= Novo Acre, 13°27'S 41°06'W in Paynter and Traylor 1991), 610 m, and Jaguaquara, 760 m, in September and October 1927, and at Boa Nova, 790 m, in June 1928 (Naumburg 1935, 1939). Near this last locality the species was observed again in December 1974 (Willis and Oniki 1981b), October 1977 (Sick and Teixeira 1979, H. Sick verbally 1988), September/October 1982, when four specimens were collected (in MNRJ), July 1988 (M. Pearman *in litt.* 1989), February 1989 (J. F. Pacheco verbally 1992), August 1989 (B. C. Forrester *in litt.* 1992) and June 1990 (Gardner and Gardner 1990b).

Minas Gerais The species is known from Divisópolis, 900-1,000 m, and Almenara in the valley of the rio Jequitinhonha (Sick and Teixeira 1979, Sick 1985), where it was first discovered in December 1973 (specimens in CGTM and MNRJ) and recorded until at least 1986 (G. T. de Mattos *in litt.* 1987).

POPULATION Numbers are not known, but in the localities where it was seen in 1977 in the same woodlands as the threatened Slender Antbird *Rhopornis ardesiaca*, it appeared to be the less numerous of the two (King 1978-1979). However, at Boa Nova in 1974 and 1983 it was considered "common" (Willis and Oniki 1981b, Teixeira 1987c) and in two woodlots at the same site in July 1988 it was "far more numerous" than Slender Antbird, with over 10 (mostly males) being found in one 20 ha woodlot, and five (a male and four females) in one 3 ha woodlot (M. Pearman *in litt.* 1989); this greater abundance was also the clear perception of subsequent observers (Gardner and Gardner 1990b, B. C. Forrester *in litt.* 1992) at this site.

ECOLOGY This species is very little known (Sick and Teixeira 1979). It has been reported from dry forest (King 1978-1979, Willis and Oniki 1981b, Teixeira 1987c, G. T. de Mattos *in litt.* 1987; see Ecology under Slender Antbird), where it is found commonly in the lower mid-levels (Willis and Oniki 1981b). Birds join mixed-species flocks that include Slender Antbird, Rufous Gnateater *Conopophaga lineata*, White-browed Antpitta *Hylopezus ochroleucus*, Bahia Antwren *Herpsilochmus pileatus*, Silvery-cheeked Antshrike *Sakesphorus cristatus*, Flavescent Warbler *Basileuterus flaveolus*, Rufous-browed Peppershrike *Cyclarhis gujanensis*, Pale-legged Hornero *Furnarius leucopus*, Ochre-cheeked Spinetail *Synallaxis scutata* and Streaked Xenops *Xenops rutilans* (M. Pearman *in litt.* 1989). Individuals and pairs noted near Boa Nova and Jequié foraged in dense tangles of thin vines, branches and foliage 2-8 m above the ground (in vine-rich forest c.15 m tall, with closely spaced small and medium trees, and a dense cover of large terrestrial bromeliads): the birds probed in trapped dead leaves and appeared to scan green leaves and stems (TAP). The stomach of one specimen (in CGTM) from Minas Gerais contained "insects". Testes of three specimens (in AMNH, CGTM) obtained in October from central Bahia and in December from northern Minas Gerais were not or only slightly enlarged.

THREATS The Narrow-billed Antwren is believed to face the same threats as the Slender Antbird in south-central Bahia, and to be "surely decreasing as its habitat dwindles" (King 1978-1979), but its range is not so restricted: at least in north-east Minas Gerais and adjacent southern Bahia, where part of its habitat has been cleared for coffee plantations, the species is not considered to be under immediate threat (G. T. de Mattos *in litt.* 1987; but see Threats under Slender Antbird).

MEASURES TAKEN This species was not protected by Brazilian law in the 1970s (*contra* King 1978-1979) but is now (Bernardes *et al.* 1990).

MEASURES PROPOSED The creation of a forest reserve of mata-de-cipó is desirable (Willis and Oniki 1981b, Teixeira 1987c) and could be done in conjunction with an experimental agricultural station, which is needed on the southern Bahian plateau because of its distinctive climate and soils (Willis and Oniki 1981b). Such a reserve would help also to preserve other threatened bird species which occur in the same region (see Remarks 4 under Slender Antbird). Clearly much more work on the biology of this species would be most valuable in determining the principles for its long-term management, and such studies might be combined with any on Slender Antbird.

REMARKS Cory and Hellmayr (1924) indicated this locality as falling within the Serra do Espinhaço, but this is mistaken.

RESTINGA ANTWREN *Formicivora littoralis* E[1]

This newly described antbird occupies a highly restricted range and beach-scrub habitat in Rio de Janeiro state, Brazil, and faces extirpation from the development of the area for holidaymaking.

DISTRIBUTION The Restinga Antwren (see Remarks 1) is confined to restinga and related vegetation in a small number of localities along the coast and offshore islands in Rio de Janeiro state, south-eastern Brazil. The species was discovered in March 1951, when a male was collected in Cabo Frio, but it was described only some 40 years later from a series of specimens obtained in the 1980s from Cabo Frio, Arraial do Cabo, Maçambaba beach, Ilha do Cabo Frio and Ilha Comprida, and observed also at São Pedro da Aldeia and Jaconé beach (Gonzaga and Pacheco 1990). It was not found either farther inland and north of Peró dunes (22°50'S) or west of Jaconé (42°40'W) in apparently suitable habitat in the Maricá region (Gonzaga and Pacheco 1990).

POPULATION In the late 1980s the species was found to occur "at quite high densities over a relatively large area in the Maçambaba region" (Gonzaga and Pacheco 1990), and was seemingly abundant also on Ilha do Cabo Frio (LPG), but no estimate of overall numbers and coverage of optimum habitat has so far been provided.

ECOLOGY The Restinga Antwren is seemingly restricted to the bromeliad-and cactus-rich restinga scrub growing on sandbars and to other scrub vegetation on coastal and island hillsides, where birds keep low in the foliage, foraging on arthropods mainly 1-2 m from the ground, usually in pairs; birds are reluctant to cross openings, seldom leaving thickets (Gonzaga and Pacheco 1990).

Three nests found in June, October and November 1990 on Ilha do Cabo Frio were deep open cups made of vegetable fibres attached to horizontal branch forks 1.7 to 2.1 m from the ground; clutch-size is two, both sexes apparently build the nest and incubate and take care of the young, with parental care continuing after the young leave the nest and are apparently able to obtain food on their own (Soneghet 1991). The breeding season seems to extend nearly all year round, from May to February, judging from the gonadal condition of collected birds (Soneghet 1991).

THREATS The species's small range mostly falls within a "prime holiday development area" (D. Willis *in litt.* 1991) which is under great pressure from real-estate planning (Gonzaga and Pacheco 1990).

MEASURES TAKEN Small portions of its limited range are included in the Jacarepiá and Maçambaba State Reserves and the Maçambaba Environmental Protection Area (IEF/FEEMA/INEPAC 1991); however, these areas apparently lack any effective control. Access to Ilha do Cabo Frio is restricted and controlled by the Brazilian navy, which keeps a lighthouse there.

MEASURES PROPOSED Surveys of the species in the field are needed better to ascertain and monitor its status in the localities where it has been recorded, particularly in the Maçambaba area, which seems important for its long-term survival. Support for this key site is clearly imperative.

REMARKS (1) The Restinga Antwren was originally described as a race of the Serra Antwren *Formicivora serrana*, but the suggestion that it should perhaps be treated as a separate species on the basis of clear morphological and ecological differences (Gonzaga and Pacheco 1990) is accepted here, and this view is shared by others (D. C. Oren, J. M. C. da Silva, D. Willis, D. F. Stotz verbally or *in litt.* 1991).

YELLOW-RUMPED ANTWREN *Terenura sharpei* V[9]

The Yellow-rumped Antwren inhabits entirely unprotected humid forest at a few sites between 1,100 and 1,650 m in the yungas of Bolivia and immediately adjacent Peru. Its habitat is being rapidly cleared for cultivation, mainly of coca and coffee.

DISTRIBUTION The Yellow-rumped Antwren is known from four specimens taken at three different localities, and from sightings at two additional localities, all between 1,100 and 1,650 m in Puno department, south-east Peru, and La Paz and Cochabamba departments, Bolivia. Localities (coordinates from Stephens and Traylor 1983 and Paynter *et al.* 1975) are:

Peru Inca Mine (1,690 m), Santo Domingo, Limbani–Astillero road, Puno, at 13°51'S 69°41'W (Chapman 1901);

Bolivia Serranía Bellavista, 1,650 m, 35 km by road north of Caranavi, Caranavi being at 15°46'S 67°36'W, La Paz (two specimens in LSUMZ from June 1979: Remsen *et al.* 1982); Serranía Bellavista, 1,350 m, 47 km by road north of Caranavi (four sightings of pairs in July 1980: Remsen *et al.* 1982); Quebrada Onda (presumably Q. Honda), east Yungas, Cochabamba, not located (type-specimen collected in July 1892: von Berlepsch 1901); Chaparé, 1,100 m, Cochabamba, at c.16°30'S 65°30'W (male sighted in October 1979: Remsen *et al.* 1982).

POPULATION The paucity of museum specimens may indicate that the species is uncommon, but could also reflect that it is difficult to collect. At 1,650 m in Serranía Bellavista it was noted daily in small numbers from 10 June to 2 July 1979 (Remsen *et al.* 1982); at least four pairs or families were involved in these sightings, which were made along c.2 km of road through tall forest (TAP). Data are unavailable from other localities, but the species presumably survives in small to moderate numbers wherever there is suitable habitat.

ECOLOGY The Yellow-rumped Antwren inhabits humid upper tropical zone forest (see Remarks) at 1,100 to 1,650 m (Remsen *et al.* 1982). While the Ashy Antwren *Myrmotherula grisea* was found at 1,650 m, but not in the wetter forest at 1,350 m in Serranía Bellavista, the Yellow-rumped Antwren was found at both sites (Remsen *et al.* 1982). It is usually found in pairs, in mixed-species flocks of insectivorous birds in the canopy, the most frequent flock associates being Marble-faced Bristle-tyrant *Pogonotriccus ophthalmicus*, Streaked Xenops *Xenops rutilans*, Slate-throated Redstart *Myioborus miniatus* and Buff-banded Tyrannulet *Mecocerculus hellmayri* (Remsen *et al.* 1982).

Most foraging is in areas of very dense foliage 10-20 m above ground and almost always within 1 m of the outer edge of the canopy; of eight observations in which the target substrate could clearly be distinguished, seven were uppersides and one the underside of leaves, from as small as 10x5 cm to as large as 25x15 cm; the species moves very rapidly through the foliage, making frequent lunging and darting movements; twice individuals were seen hanging down from twigs to reach the upper surfaces of leaves below, a behaviour also noted in another member of the genus (Remsen *et al.* 1982). Indeed, the foraging behaviour and vocalizations of the species are very like those of three congeneric antwrens, Rufous-rumped *Terenura callinota*, Chestnut-shouldered *T. humeralis* and Ash-winged *T. spodioptila*, all of which are frequently overlooked owing to their size and habitual use of the uppermost canopy (TAP).

A male collected on 29 June had slightly enlarged testes and a female-plumaged bird collected on 25 June may have been a recently fledged young (Remsen *et al.* 1982). Song was given frequently in June and early July (Remsen *et al.* 1982), but this may not be an indication of breeding.

THREATS The extensive and accelerating clearance of forest in the upper tropical zone along the Amazonian slope of the Andes for cultivation of coffee, coca, tea, citrus fruit, etc., poses a serious threat to the many species of birds (72 in Bolivia) confined to this zone (Remsen and Quintela unpublished). Although the Yellow-rumped Antwren itself occurs at the upper edge of this zone and thus above the preferred elevation for the cultivation of coca and tea, much of its tall forest habitat grows on relatively rich soils suitable for small-scale agriculture, and a recent surge of colonists into the yungas from the altiplano threatens eventually to result in the clearance of most forest on the interior ridges below 2,500 m (TAP: see also Threats under Ashy Antwren *Myrmotherula grisea*).

MEASURES TAKEN Albeit yet to be reported, the species probably occurs in the north-western portion of Amboró National Park in Santa Cruz, and it may do also in Carrasco National Park in Cochabamba, but the forest within the Pilon-Lajas reserve west of San Borja, Beni, is apparently too low for it (TAP: see equivalent section under Bolivian Recurvebill *Simoxenops striatus*).

MEASURES PROPOSED Suggestions that would accommodate the conservation of this species are made in the equivalent section under Bolivian Recurvebill.

REMARKS The song and behaviour of this species is very similar to that of Rufous-rumped Antwren *Terenura callinota*, and the song also to that of Chestnut-shouldered Antwren *T. humeralis*, and they are all probably best considered members of a single superspecies (Remsen *et al.* 1982). Remsen and Quintela (unpublished) gave the limits of the upper tropical zone forest in the yungas of Bolivia as c.1,100 to c.1,700 m, high enough to recieve sufficient rainfall to be classified as true montane forest, and more fertile than what they called foothill tropical forest at c.500 to c.1,100 m.

ORANGE-BELLIED ANTWREN *Terenura sicki* E[2]

The main hope for this small insectivore appears to be an unprotected and rapidly diminishing tract of upland forest, only 1,500 ha in extent, near the type-locality in Alagoas state, Brazil, although three other sites are known, one in Pernambuco.

DISTRIBUTION The Orange-bellied Antwren (see Remarks) is known from three localities on the south-eastern escarpment of the Borborema plateau in Alagoas, north-east Brazil, and at one site to the north along this coastal range in Pernambuco on forested mountain tops (as predicted in Teixeira 1987b).

Pernambuco Eight birds were seen in mountain forest at Água Azul, south of Timbaúba, in January 1989 (Willis and Weinberg 1990).

Alagoas The species was described from a female collected at Pedra Branca ("Serra Branca": see Remarks 2 under Alagoas Foliage-gleaner *Philydor novaesi*), 550 m, near Murici (9°19'S 35°57'W) in February 1979 (Teixeira and Gonzaga 1983a), and five further specimens, including three males, were obtained at this locality in November 1983, May 1984 and January 1986 (Teixeira 1987b), although it appears now to be present only in the remaining part of this area known as Fazenda Bananeira (see Threats, Measures Proposed under Alagoas Foliage-gleaner). The species has been reported also from near Novo Lino (9°01'S 35°40'W), at 300 m, but has not been found in the coastal lowland forests of the region (Teixeira 1987b), which have been well explored ornithologically (Teixeira and Gonzaga 1983a). In August 1989 seven were found and others heard, and in October 1990 two pairs, at Pedra Talhada Biological Reserve at about 700 m (B. M. Whitney *in litt.* 1991, B. C. Forrester *in litt.* 1992).

POPULATION Numbers are not known. Birds are difficult to locate owing to their small size and arboreal habits, having been seen "only four times" when the species was discovered (Teixeira and Gonzaga 1983a), but they call frequently even outside the breeding season, which may be of help in its detection (Teixeira 1987b). In August 1989 it was felt that the species is probably common at Pedra Talhada, but difficult to observe on account of its use of the upper canopy (B. C. Forrester *in litt.* 1992). In April 1992 it was fairly common, based on voice, at Fazenda Bananeira (M. Pearman *in litt.* 1992).

ECOLOGY The Orange-bellied Antwren inhabits the upper strata of forest, moving through the dense foliage looking for food amongst the leaves and amidst the debris adhering to branches (Teixeira and Gonzaga 1983a), and also in arboreal bromeliads (Teixeira 1987b). It is usually seen in the canopy of the middle storey, following mixed-species flocks of upper and middle canopy birds even during the breeding season, isolated pairs being rarely found away from these flocks, which may include more than eighteen species at once (Teixeira and Gonzaga 1983a, Teixeira 1987b; for a description of the composition of these flocks, see Teixeira and Gonzaga 1985). Its diet includes small insects (beetles, cockroaches), as the stomach content of the holotype confirms (Teixeira and Gonzaga 1983a). To judge from the available records of moult and gonadal development of birds collected, breeding probably starts in November and continues into February, when immature birds join adults in mixed-species flocks (Teixeira 1987b). A nest of the species was found on 19 November 1983 in the final stages of construction, attached to a fork in a nearly horizontal branch among the dense foliage of a middle stratum tree, about 10-12 m above the ground; it was a small cup, built with moss and a few filaments of fungi *Marasmius* (Teixeira 1987b).

THREATS Destruction of forest at Pedra Branca is the single most serious threat to this and all other upland forest species in Alagoas (see Threats under Alagoas Foliage-gleaner). Although the Orange-bellied Antwren seemingly survives even in forests which have suffered from severe selective logging, it is not present in degraded secondary growth, which nowadays constitutes an important portion of the few remaining forest areas in north-east Brazil (Teixeira 1987b).

MEASURES TAKEN The Orange-bellied Antwren is protected under Brazilian law (Bernardes *et al.* 1990). A population of the species stands to be secured by the new Pedra Talhada Biological Reserve (see equivalent section under Forbes's Blackbird *Curaeus forbesi*; but also that under Alagoas Foliage-gleaner).

MEASURES PROPOSED An initiative to preserve forest and its rich birdlife at Pedra Branca (specifically now Fazenda Bananeira) needs urgent impetus (see Measures Proposed and Remarks under Alagoas Foliage-gleaner).

REMARKS The full specific status of the Orange-bellied Antwren seems to be confirmed by specimens obtained since its description (Teixeira 1987b). The species is apparently closely related to the Streak-capped Antwren *Terenura maculata* from south-east Brazil to Paraguay and north-east Argentina, with which it forms a superspecies (Teixeira and Gonzaga 1983a).

RIO BRANCO ANTBIRD *Cercomacra carbonaria* V[9]

Endemic to gallery forest on the rio Branco and some of its tributaries in Roraima, Brazil, this antbird is relatively common, but has a minute range and is very poorly known.

DISTRIBUTION The Rio Branco Antbird is known only from northern Roraima in northernmost Brazil, where it has been found on the rio Branco north of Boa Vista and along the rio Mucajaí (see Remarks). The only known localities are as follows: on the east bank of rio Tacutu, c.2 km above its mouth, where the bird was recorded in October 1988 (D. F. Stotz *in litt.* 1988); Fortaleza de São Joaquim (3°01'N 60°28'W; 28 km above Boa Vista: Paynter and Traylor 1991), where the type-series of 22 birds was collected in late 1831 (von Pelzeln 1868-1871, Pinto 1966); on the east bank of rio Branco, 15 km north-east of Boa Vista, and the west bank of rio Branco, 10 km north-east of Boa Vista, birds being recorded at both sites in October 1988 (D. F. Stotz *in litt.* 1988); on Ilha São José and Ilha Boa Água (untraced, but on the rio Branco north of Boa Vista), where birds were noted and one female was collected in October 1988 (D. F. Stotz *in litt.* 1988), birds also being seen on Ilha São José in August 1992 (B. C. Forrester *in litt.* 1992); and on the rio Mucajaí (south of Boa Vista), where one bird was taken in April 1962 (Pinto 1966, 1978), with at least 12 (in FMNH, LACM) taken there in February and March 1963.

POPULATION In 1988, this antbird was found to be relatively common in suitable forest (at least 18 birds seen or heard: D. F. Stotz *in litt.* 1988), an assessment that appears to reflect the abundance encountered when first 22 birds (in 1831) and then 12 (in 1963) were collected in the same general area (see Distribution): five males and a female were found on Ilha São José in August 1992 (B. C. Forrester *in litt.* 1992). D. F. Stotz (*in litt.* 1988) calculated that there was c.150 km (linear) of suitable habitat (of varying widths), supporting a population of between 1,000 and 10,000 birds (c.10 pairs per km^2).

ECOLOGY In 1988 the bird was found exclusively in gallery forest (D. F. Stotz *in litt.* 1988).

THREATS The gallery forest within the range of this antbird appears to be relatively intact and currently under little pressure; however, the fact that such habitat is so limited in extent indicates that the species would be vulnerable to even small changes in forest use (D. F. Stotz *in litt.* 1988).

MEASURES TAKEN None is known.

MEASURES PROPOSED The distributional limits and precise ecological requirements of this species need further elaboration, and areas of gallery forest require protection. Any initiatives for this species should be carried out in conjunction with those for Hoary-throated Spinetail *Synallaxis kollari* (see relevant account).

REMARKS Peters (1951) cited a record of Jet Antbird *Cercomacra nigricans* from Caracaraí (south of Boa Vista): this record should if possible be checked as referring to Jet Antbird rather than Rio Branco Antbird, as it brings the two species to within c.50 km of each other.

FRINGE-BACKED FIRE-EYE *Pyriglena atra* E[3]

The only known area for this undergrowth-haunting ant-follower lies west of the town of Santo Amaro, Bahia, Brazil; loss of habitat there has been substantial and a reserve is now urgently necessary.

DISTRIBUTION The Fringe-backed Fire-eye (see Remarks) is known only from a very restricted area in the vicinity of Salvador, coastal Bahia, eastern Brazil. The type-specimen (in UMZC) was collected in "Pitangua" (Swainson 1825, Cory and Hellmayr 1924): subsequent authors have amended this to "Pitanga" (Pinto 1938, 1978, Meyer de Schauensee 1966, King 1978-1979 – this last has "Piranga" in error), one of them taking this to mean a locality "near Mata de São João" (Pinto 1938) north of Salvador, but most likely the true type-locality is a site bearing this name 8 km west of Santo Amaro, north-west of Salvador (see Pinto 1943: 266), although the species could not be found there despite the use of tape playback, April 1992 (M. Pearman *in litt.* 1992). A bird was later collected at Santo Amaro itself in October 1913 (Cory and Hellmayr 1924; specimen in FMNH), and the species was relocated there again in 1968 (Sick 1972) and in January 1988 (B. M. Whitney *in litt.* 1991). It was studied from 21 November to 1 December 1974 in the Fazendas Timbó and Palma, 15 km south of Santo Amaro, along the road to Cachoeira, north bank of the rio Paraguaçu (Willis and Oniki 1982). One specimen in MNRJ is from Santo Amaro, October 1977 (see Teixeira *et al.* 1989), and another is from Cachoeira, August 1926. The species has never been recorded south of the rio Paraguaçu (King 1978-1979), but may extend or have extended as far north-east as the rio São Francisco (Willis and Oniki 1982).

POPULATION Numbers are unknown. The species may be locally "very common" (Willis and Oniki 1982; see Ecology), but is nonetheless considered endangered (Sick 1969, 1972, King 1978-1979, Sick and Teixeira 1979, Willis and Oniki 1982; see Threats).

ECOLOGY All fire-eyes tend to avoid the very open and vertically oriented undergrowth of tall forests, favouring instead tangled undergrowth, second-growth and other habitats where horizontal perches can be found near the ground; they also avoid sunlight and open vegetation, such as bushy pastures or the extensive semi-open cerrados and caatingas of central Brazil (Willis and Oniki 1982). At Santo Amaro, the Fringe-backed Fire-eye was very common in tall second-growth and uncommon in tall forest, rare in patches of second-growth where most of the vegetation had been cut out, and absent from open zones (Willis and Oniki 1982). Fringe-backed Fire-eyes usually move through tangles of vegetation up to 10 m above the ground searching for insects, and scattered individuals or pairs also favour patches of dense vegetation, around old tree-falls or at the forest edge; they occasionally join interspecific bird flocks, seldom followed for long, a commonly associated species being the Moustached Wren *Thryothorus genibarbis* (Willis and Oniki 1982).

Fire-eyes regularly follow army ant swarms for flushed prey, and 10-16 Fringe-backed Fire-eyes may quickly concentrate at each major swarm of army ants *Eciton burchelli*, which are followed for hours on end across logging roads through dense or open vegetation, but not into sunny clearings (Willis and Oniki 1982). Food is taken almost always (117 of 130 records) from the ground or near it; prey recorded included grasshoppers, winged ants, cockroaches and a 4 cm centipede (Willis and Oniki 1982). The pair found near Santo Amaro in 1988 were following ants, occasionally going to the ground to snatch flushed arthropods, but ranging as high as 4 m into the trees (B. M. Whitney *in litt.* 1988).

The gonads of the October specimen from Santo Amaro were developed (Teixeira *et al.* 1989). Several young Fringe-backed Fire-eyes were out of the nest in late November at Santo Amaro, some nearly independent; both male and female young had dull orange (instead of the adults' bright red) eyes; in several cases only one parent, either the male or the female, fed a young bird or led it away from the observer (Willis and Oniki 1982).

THREATS The major threat is from forest clearance, owing to the species's very restricted range. Forests in which this bird lived have been widely destroyed from the rio Paraguaçu north and, despite its abundance in second growth (see Ecology), it is endangered since not even second growth has been left by the spread of Bahian agriculture in recent years (Willis and Oniki 1982); its close relative in southern Brazil, the White-shouldered Fire-eye *Pyriglena leucoptera* (see Remarks) has been unable to survive in woodlots of 21 and 250 ha, and survives only in woodlots of 300 to 1,400 ha or larger (Willis 1979, Willis and Oniki 1982). The whole area north of Salvador is heavily populated, and government programmes for industrial, agricultural and pastoral expansion will destroy the few remaining forest tracts; forest near Santo Amaro, where the species was found in 1968 and 1974, had been reduced to small patches by 1977 (King 1978-1979), and has suffered still more from recent expansion of oil-palm cultivation, although some tall second-growth could still be found there in 1985 (J. Becker verbally 1988). However, the ridge on which the birds were found in 1988 "held the only forest anywhere near the road for miles in any direction", although other forested ridges were visible in the far distance (B. M. Whitney *in litt.* 1988).

MEASURES TAKEN The Fringe-backed Fire-eye is protected under Brazilian law (Bernardes *et al.* 1990).

MEASURES PROPOSED Creation of a biological reserve has been recommended (Sick 1969, King 1978-1979), but no action has been taken so far. This, however, remains imperative, as it is becoming impossible to identify any suitable tracts of forest in this region of Brazil (B. M. Whitney *in litt.* 1988). Fieldwork to identify potential reserves should be combined with that for the Bahia Tapaculo *Scytalopus psychopompus* and Stresemann's Bristlefront *Merulaxis stresemanni* (see relevant accounts).

REMARKS The Fringe-backed Fire-eye has been treated as a subspecies, either of the White-backed Fire-eye *P. leuconota* (Pinto 1938, 1978) or of the White-shouldered Fire-eye (Zimmer 1931), but this view has not been followed by other authorities (Cory and Hellmayr 1924, Peters 1951, Meyer de Schauensee 1966, Sick 1972, 1979, 1985, Willis and Oniki 1982), and the three may be regarded instead as members of a superspecies (Sick 1972, 1979, 1985). Specimens of Fringe-backed Fire-eyes in Europe from "Bahia" have wingbars that suggest hybridization with White-shouldered Fire-eyes, suggesting that the level of separation between these forms is low (Willis and Oniki 1982); the latter replaces the former south of the rio Paraguaçu (King 1978-1979, Willis and Oniki 1982). Behaviour and vocalizations are very similar in all fire-eyes (Sick 1979, Willis and Oniki 1982, B. M. Whitney *in litt.* 1988); however, antbirds often behave and call similarly even when good sympatric species; future studies in Bahia may locate regions where *atra* occurs with *leuconota* or *leucoptera*, with or without intergradation, but deforestation is so general that few such populations are likely to survive (Willis and Oniki 1982).

SLENDER ANTBIRD *Rhopornis ardesiaca* V[9]

A forest reserve for this species in its native Bahia, Brazil, is urgently needed as the habitat within its small range is very rapidly being cleared, and already only small woodlots remain.

DISTRIBUTION The Slender Antbird (see Remarks 1) is restricted to south-central Bahia, Brazil, where it has been recorded from near Ipaoté (13°10'S 40°00'W), Irajubá (13°14'S 40°04'W), Ituaçu (13°49'S 41°27'W; see Remarks 2), Jequié (13°51'S 40°06'W) and Boa Nova (14°32'S 40°23'W) (King 1978-1979, Sick 1985, Teixeira 1987c). The species was described from a male collected somewhere in eastern Brazil in the early nineteenth century, and rediscovered in 1928, when another male and a female were collected at Ituaçu, 900 m, and Boa Nova, 800 m (Naumburg 1934; see Remarks 2). Most of the recent records of the species are from this latter locality, where it was studied in December 1974 on Fazenda Alvorada (Willis and Oniki 1981b), with six specimens collected there in October 1977, December 1978 and October 1983 (Teixeira 1987c), and February 1989 (J. F. Pacheco verbally 1992); a single bird was at Fazenda Santa Cecilia, north of Boa Nova and probably close to Fazenda Alvorada, in August 1989 (B. C. Forrester *in litt.* 1992). The species was also recorded from the municipality of Irajubá, 900 m, in 1977 (Sick and Teixeira 1979), near Jequié, 900 m, in October 1977 (H. Sick verbally 1988) and in the 1980s (TAP), and from 4 km north of Jequié, January 1988 (B. M. Whitney *in litt.* 1988). It has been speculated that it may also occur to the south of Boa Nova toward Vitória da Conquista and further inland from Ituaçu (King 1978-1979).

POPULATION Numbers are unknown. The species was known until 1974 from only three specimens (Willis and Oniki 1981b), and has consequently been on many lists of threatened birds (Sick 1969, 1972, King 1978-1974, Sick and Teixeira 1979, Willis and Oniki 1981b). In 1974 and 1977 it was found "without difficulty" in its range (King 1978-1979), when "a good, if scattered population" existed in patches of suitable habitat left near Boa Nova (Willis and Oniki 1981b). In a 200 ha woodlot north of Jequié, the species was "fairly common" (eight birds recorded) in January 1988 (B. M. Whitney *in litt.* 1988), but, notwithstanding reports that this bird could be "seen all over inland woodlots, e.g. along the main highway north to Salvador" (R. S. Ridgely verbally 1987), or that it is common where found (Ribeiro 1990a), it should be kept in mind that it is very rare indeed, and its restricted habitat is rapidly being cleared (B. M. Whitney *in litt.* 1988; see Threats).

ECOLOGY The Slender Antbird inhabits dry forest (mesophytic deciduous forest, 800-1,000 mm annual rainfall) with many "cipós" or lianas, such habitat being known as "mata-de-cipó", with a fairly open understorey, blocked here and there by lianas and by patches of huge terrestrial bromeliads *Aechmea* (Willis and Oniki 1981b, Ribeiro 1990a). This vegetation type extends south-west to northern Minas Gerais and typically occurs on deep soils (Rizzini 1979, Eiten 1983); the region of Boa Nova lies on a broad plateau which forms a border between wet coastal forests and the caatinga of the interior, and Slender Antbirds have been observed around terrestrial bromeliads and surrounding undergrowth near the borders between dry forest and caatinga or between dry forest and pastures (Willis and Oniki 1981b; see Remarks 3). In these places – occasionally in tall scrub nearby – the birds hop on the ground, low vines and the tops of bromeliads, tossing the dead leaves trapped in the bromeliads or on the ground (Willis and Oniki 1981b, M. Pearman *in litt.* 1989). However, at one site south-west of Jequié, the species was found on a scrub-covered hillside with (as always) extensive stands of large terrestrial bromeliads, but dominated by short *Acacia*-like trees only about 3 m tall and growing in patches separated by lower growth of bushes and weeds, i.e. certainly not "mata-de-cipó" (TAP). Members of a pair wander separately or together; each pair seems to have a very limited home range, barely 50 m across, usually separated by 100 m or more from the home ranges of other pairs, because patches of bromeliads are seldom close together; maximum densities observed at a study area near Boa Nova were in a rather scrubby second-growth woodlot, where pairs were 100-200 m apart (Willis and Oniki 1981b). In a 200 ha woodlot near Jequié two males were once singing only 30 m apart (B. M. Whitney *in litt.* 1988). A pair observed at Boa Nova seemed to be using an area of roughly 0.84 ha (Teixeira 1987c).

Slender Antbirds were not found to follow either army ants (Willis and Oniki 1981b) or mixed-species flocks (Teixeira 1987c), but such associations certainly occur to some extent, birds being found on one occasion foraging near Ochre-cheeked Spinetail *Synallaxis scutata* and Narrow-billed Antwren *Formicivora iheringi* (see relevant account), and on another with the spinetail, Stripe-backed Antbird *Myrmorchilus strigilatus*, Rufous Gnateater *Conopophaga lineata* and Black-billed Scythebill *Campylorhamphus falcularius* (M. Pearman *in litt.* 1989). The diet includes small grasshoppers and other insects (Willis and Oniki 1981b). Crickets, cockroaches, and small spiders were found in stomach contents, and winged termites *Eutermes* can also be taken at the forest edge (Teixeira 1987c).

Breeding activity seems to start by October, declining from December on; a recently built nest, apparently of this species, was found on 4 October 1983 near the ground among bromeliads; a pair of Slender Antbirds was observed around this nest (Teixeira 1987c). A female in AMNH, collected on 5 June 1928, had undeveloped ovaries.

THREATS In central-southern Bahia primary dry forest is rapidly being cleared for cattle pastures (Willis and Oniki 1981b), being reduced to scattered fragments of 10-15 km^2, which totalled about 965 km^2 in the early 1970s (Teixeira 1987c). Although the initial stages of this clearing, creating many zones of forest edge, probably benefit this bird, patches of forest are decreasing in size and length of edge; cleared slopes can be seen all around Boa Nova, so the survival of the species there is certainly in doubt (Willis and Oniki 1981b). Indeed, three out of four tiny woodlots still standing in July 1989 were highly disturbed by livestock and appeared to face imminent clearance (M. Pearman *in litt.* 1989; also B. C. Forrester *in litt.* 1992) and, overall in this part of Bahia, in 1990 only 5-20% (and nearer 5%) of forest remained (D. Willis *in litt.* 1991; see Remarks 3).

MEASURES TAKEN The Slender Antbird is protected under Brazilian law (Bernardes *et al.* 1990).

MEASURES PROPOSED The creation of a forest reserve of mata-de-cipó is desirable (Willis and Oniki 1981b, Teixeira 1987c) and now urgently needed (Ribeiro 1990a), and could be done in conjunction with an experimental agricultural station, which is needed on the southern Bahian plateau because of its distinctive climate and soils (Willis and Oniki 1981b). Such a reserve would also help to preserve other threatened bird species which occur in the same region (see Remarks 4). Clearly much more work on the biology of this species would be most valuable in determining the principles for its long-term management, and such studies might be combined with any on Narrow-billed Antwren.

REMARKS (1) The Slender Antbird is the only species in its genus. (2) It seems improbable that Naumburg (1934, 1935) would be mistaken over the locality being Ituaçu, yet the specimen in AMNH on which this record is based is labelled "Itirussú", and an Itiruçu is mapped by TAW (1986) just north of Jequié and listed by Paynter and Traylor (1991) on the basis of its mention by Zimmer (1933), who was reviewing *Thamnophilus punctatus pelzelni*; although not stated, it seems very probable that Zimmer's material was provided by the same collector, E. Kaempfer. In terms of its position at 13°31'S 40°09'W, Itiruçu is a slightly more likely locality for the Slender Antbird than Ituaçu. (3) The character of forest in this transition zone can alter within short distances (thus not all the 5-20% of what remains is appropriate for the Slender Antbird): only 11 km east of Boa Nova and at the same altitude a woodlot exists which holds no Slender

Antbirds but an entirely different group of birds, including the near-threatened Rio de Janeiro Antbird *Cercomacra brasiliana* (D. Willis *in litt.* 1991). (4) One other threatened and one near-threatened species, Narrow-billed Antwren and Rio de Janeiro Antbird respectively, are known from dry forests of southern Bahia (see relevant accounts); moreover, these forests are the source of a curious specimen of White-winged Potoo *Nyctibius leucopterus*, a species now known to be widespread in Amazonian forests (R. O. Bierregaard *in litt.* 1989), but the type-locality near Vitória da Conquista (Wied 1820-1821, Greenway 1958) remains the only site for Bahia, and it cannot be assumed that the form in Bahia is identical to that from the Amazon.

GREY-HEADED ANTBIRD *Myrmeciza griseiceps* E[2]

This rare formicariid is confined to patches of bamboo and dense undergrowth in semi-deciduous moist forest and cloud-forest in the Pacific slope foothills of the Andes in south-west Ecuador and north-west Peru, where it is threatened by habitat destruction.

DISTRIBUTION The Grey-headed Antbird (see Remarks 1) is confined to the Pacific slope of the Andes in El Oro and Loja provinces, south-west Ecuador, and Tumbes and Piura departments, north-west Peru, where it is found at elevations ranging from 600 to 2,900 m. The bird is known from few specimens, and is generally distributed in five areas, where localities (coordinates from Paynter and Traylor 1977 and Stephens and Traylor 1983) are as follows:

Ecuador (*El Oro*) La Chonta, 610 m (Chapman 1926, Zimmer 1932), at 3°35'S 79°53'W (see Remarks 2); San Pablo, 1,200 m, at 3°41'S 79°33'W, near Zaruma, where a bird (possibly this species) was heard calling in 1991 (Williams and Tobias 1991); (*Loja*) above Vicentino, 1,250-1,450 m, at c.3°56'S 79°55'W (five males singing in February 1991: Best 1992); Alamor, 1,400 m (Chapman 1926) at 4°02'S 80°02'W; Celica, 2,100 m (Zimmer 1932) at 4°07'S 79°59'W; 8 km west of Celica, 1,900 m (one specimen collected and others seen in August 1989: R. S. Ridgely *in litt.* 1989); near San José de Pozul along the road to Pindal, 1,600 m, at 4°07'S 80°03'W (sightings in April–May 1989: P. Coopmans verbally 1991); Utuana, 2,500 m, at 4°21'S 79°43'W (one male singing in February 1991: Best 1992); Quebrada Hueco Hondo, 1,000 m, Tambo Negro, south-west of Sabiango, at 4°23'S 79°51'W (two birds sighted in February 1991: Best 1992);

Peru (*Tumbes*) Campo Verde, 750 m (Wiedenfeld *et al.* 1985), at c.3°51'S 80°12'W; (*Piura*) Cerro Chacas, 2,625 m, at 4°36'S 79°44'W (several heard and one seen: Best and Clarke 1991); Palambla, 1,200-2,000 m, a few kilometres from Canchaque on the Canchaque–Huancabamba road (Chapman 1923; specimens in AMNH, ANSP, CM and MCZ) at c.5°23'S 79°37'W; c.15 km by road from Canchaque on the Canchaque–Huancabamba road, 1,500-2,900 m (Parker *et al.* 1985; specimens in LSUMZ); 2.8 km by road south-west of Abra de Porculla, 2,000 m (specimen in LSUMZ, also one seen in August 1989: Schulenberg and Parker 1981, B. M. Whitney *in litt.* 1991) at 5°51'S 79°31'W. It may occur east-south-east of Sapillica, at 4°45-50'S 79°50-57'W in Piura department, where isolated patches of habitat apparently exist (read from IGM 1982 and LANDSAT 1986).

POPULATION No estimate has been made, and recent records have added little information on the species's status. In 1974, 1975 and 1980 this antbird was found to be rare, occurring in very small numbers and seen or heard on only one out of six or more days of observation on the Pacific slope in Piura department (Parker *et al.* 1985), presumably owing to the scarcity of its preferred bamboo habitat (NK: see below). In Ecuador it has been found in very low numbers in patchy habitat within a very restricted area (see Distribution), and the overall population must be very small.

ECOLOGY The Grey-headed Antbird inhabits patches of *Chusquea* bamboo and densely tangled undergrowth in humid and semi-humid forest, occasionally being found in deciduous forest (e.g. at Tambo Negro), at elevations ranging from 600 to 2,900 m (Chapman 1926, Parker *et al.* 1985, Wiedenfeld *et al.* 1985, Best and Clarke 1991, Best 1992). In the general region where it occurs in Piura, there is mixed evergreen forest (including *Clusia*, *Oreopanax*, *Podocarpus* and *Polylepis*) between 2,150 and 3,050 m, whilst below 2,150 m, where human pressure is extensive and increasing, only scattered patches of forest exist: arboreal bromeliads are conspicuous, but tree ferns are absent (or very scarce), *Chusquea* bamboo is uncommon, and foggy, cloudy weather conditions occur regularly (Parker *et al.* 1985). At Campo Verde (750 m), Tumbes department, there is mainly a moist evergreen forest, with abundant vine tangles and scattered patches of bamboo (an unidentified genus) (TAP; Wiedenfeld *et al.* 1985). In Ecuador, this antbird has been found in evergreen forest undergrowth, especially bamboo, as well as in dense but low second growth and, rarely, in evergreen patches in otherwise deciduous forest (Best 1992).

The species forages in the undergrowth, usually 1-4 m above ground, often in bamboo, in pairs or family groups, and regularly follows mixed-species flocks (Parker *et al.* 1985, R. S. Ridgely *in litt.* 1989, B. M. Whitney *in litt.* 1991); at Celica it has been seen in flocks with Line-cheeked Spinetail *Cranioleuca antisiensis*, Grey-breasted Wood-wren *Henicorhina leucophrys*, Three-banded Warbler *Basileuterus trifasciatus* and others (R. S. Ridgely *in litt.* 1989). There are no records of its diet, but it presumably feeds on arthropods like other members of the family, and its exceptionally long, slender bill may be specialized for probing internodes and leaf clusters of *Chusquea* bamboo and debris trapped in vine tangles (NK).

Eighteen specimens collected from September to December had inactive gonads (in AMNH, ANSP, LSUMZ and MCZ). Two juveniles were taken in June (ANSP and MCZ). Breeding in this region probably occurs in the wet season (Marchant 1958), which is from January to May (Brown 1941), as is also suggested by several singing males in February 1991 (Best 1992).

THREATS Habitat destruction is a serious threat: in addition to rampant deforestation throughout its range, considerable trampling of the undergrowth by cattle and clearance of bamboo by local people for pack-animal food pose a threat to this and other undergrowth inhabitants such as the threatened Blackish-headed Spinetail *Synallaxis tithys*, Henna-hooded Foliage-gleaner *Hylocryptus erythrocephalus* and Rufous-necked Foliage-gleaner *Syndactyla ruficollis*, all of which have restricted ranges in densely settled regions of south-west Ecuador and north-west Peru (Parker *et al.* 1985, Best and Clarke 1991: see relevant accounts).

MEASURES TAKEN The species is known to occur in only one forest reserve, namely Tumbes National Forest in Peru (75,100 ha: IUCN 1992) (Wiedenfeld *et al.* 1985): however, this park lies at the lower elevational range of the species (see Distribution).

MEASURES PROPOSED Immediate action to protect several large patches of evergreen forest at 1,500-3,000 m on the western slopes of the Andes in south-west Ecuador and north-west Peru should be taken: such forests have been located near Celica, where most recent records of this antbird have been obtained (Best and Clarke 1991). The region south-east of Sapillica, and surviving high-elevation forests between Ayabaca and the Porculla Pass area, should be surveyed to establish the presence of additional populations. Additional comments on the conservation status of the south-west Ecuador and north-west Peru forests, the other threatened species for which they are critically important, and initiatives proposed for their preservation are given in the equivalent section and Remarks under Grey-backed Hawk *Leucopternis occidentalis*.

REMARKS (1) The systematic position of *griseiceps* remains an enigma. Although believed to be closely related to Black-throated Antbird *Myrmeciza atrothorax* by Chapman (1923, 1926) and Cory and Hellmayr (1924), Todd (1927) suggested placing it in *Formicivora*, a view opposed by Zimmer (1932), who pointed out that the widely exposed position of the nostrils, the pattern of wing and tail, and the morphology of the tail closely resembles various species of *Cercomacra*, from which *griseiceps* differs mainly by its more slender bill, a character most closely approached by *Myrmochanes*. Its allocation to *Myrmeciza* was opposed by R. S. Ridgely (*in litt.* 1989), who, on the basis of its behaviour and bamboo association (but still lacking vocal and biochemical data), suspected that it might be better placed in *Drymophila*. Recently its song was recorded at Utuana, and it seems to differ substantially from all other antbird genera (NK). (2) When read on IGM (1982) these coordinates show an elevation of 300 m; according to this map, the nearest site at 600 m on the Santa Rosa–Zaruma road is at 3°41'S 79°45'W.

SCALLOPED ANTBIRD *Myrmeciza ruficauda* V/R[10]

Atlantic Forest destruction has isolated the two races of this ground-haunting insectivore in a few sites in north-east and south-east Brazil; in the latter region it is uncommon where it occurs, while in the former the areas involved are extremely small.

DISTRIBUTION The Scalloped Antbird is endemic to eastern Brazil in three adjacent north-eastern states (race *soror*) and from southern Bahia (no records since 1933) through eastern Minas Gerais (no records since 1930) to Espírito Santo (nominate *ruficauda*).

Paraíba The only record is from Mamanguape, where five birds were obtained in July 1957 (Pinto and de Camargo 1961).

Pernambuco Records (north to south) are: Engenho Água Azul (Usina Cruangi), Timbaúba, June 1971, and recently (specimens in MZUSP, A. G. M. Coelho *in litt.* 1986); Usina São José, Igarassu, March and May 1945 (Berla 1946); Fazenda São Bento, Tapera (corresponding to present-day Tapacurá Ecological Station near São Lourenço da Mata: Coelho 1979), December 1938, March 1945 and recently (Pinto 1940, Berla 1946, A. G. M. Coelho *in litt.* 1986); UFPE Ecological Station at Serra (or Brejo) dos Cavalos, 980 m, Caruaru, and Saltinho Biological Reserve, Rio Formoso, August 1986 (A. G. M. Coelho *in litt.* 1986).

Alagoas Older records are from São Miguel (north bank of the rio São Miguel, opposite Roteiro), September 1951; Fazenda Canoas on the rio Pratagí (c.12 km north of Maceió, municipality of Rio Largo), October 1951; and Usina Sinimbu (near present-day Sinimbu – not Ginimbu as in GQR 1991), October and November 1952, February and March 1957 (Pinto 1954a; specimens in FMNH, LACM and MZUSP). From this latter locality are two birds collected in October 1983 and April 1984 (specimens in MNRJ). Other modern records are from Usina Utinga Leão, Rio Largo, December 1990 (J. F. Pacheco *in litt.* 1991); Pedra ("Serra") Branca, Murici, 550 m, February 1979 and May 1984 (specimens in MNRJ), October 1990 and January 1991 (J. F. Pacheco *in litt.* 1991), and the adjacent Fazenda Bananeira (to which all forest is now reportedly confined), April 1992 (M. Pearman *in litt.* 1992); and Fazendas Pedra Talhada and Riachão (now converted to the Pedra Talhada Biological Reserve: see Measures Taken), Quebrangulo, 1981–1985 (Studer 1985), August 1989 (B. C. Forrester *in litt.* 1992) and October 1990 (J. F. Pacheco *in litt.* 1991).

Bahia Older records (all coordinates from Paynter and Traylor 1991) are from as far north as rio Gongogi at Cajazeiras, 300 m, 14°24'S 39°51'W, June 1928, and rio Pardo at Verruga (rio Verruga confluence, 15°16'S 40°37'W), July 1921 (Naumburg 1939; specimens in AMNH); and from the Braço Sul do rio Jucurucu at Cachoeira Grande (17°15'S 39°25'W), March 1933 (Pinto 1935). At least 14 old specimens in AMNH, ANSP, BMNH, MCZ, UMCZ, and USNM are merely labelled "Bahia" or "Bahia trade skin". No recent records are known.

Minas Gerais The only record is from the rio Doce at Resplendor, 120 m, north shore, January 1930 (Naumburg 1939; specimen in AMNH).

Espírito Santo Older records are (north to south) from the rio Itaúnas, Fazenda Boa Lembrança, October 1950 (Schubart *et al.* 1965, Aguirre and Aldrighi 1983, 1987); Lagoa Juparanã (in one case precisely Santana), August and September 1925 (specimens in MNRJ), October and November 1929 (Naumburg 1939); Linhares, Fazenda Europa, September and October 1939; Colatina, north of rio Doce, November 1940; Baixo Guandu (in one case precisely Fazenda da Serra), October 1925 (specimen in MNRJ), December 1929 and January 1930 (Naumburg 1939); Pau Gigante (now Ibiraçu) (in one case precisely Lauro Müller), February and March 1906 (Pinto 1938), April and August to October 1940; Água Boa, Santa Cruz, October and November 1940; Porto Cachoeiro (now Santa Leopoldina), November and December 1905 (Pinto 1938) (where no source before semi-colon, records are from specimens in LACM, MNRJ, MZUSP, USNM). Two specimens are from an unspecified locality on the rio Doce, July 1906 and December 1913 (Cory and Hellmayr 1924, Pinto 1938). Recent records (all to the north of

Lagoa Juparanã) are from the Córrego do Veado Biological Reserve, October 1986 (Gonzaga *et al.* 1987), and Sooretama Biological Reserve, December 1980/January 1981 (Scott and Brooke 1985), February 1986 and 1987 (C. E. Carvalho *in litt.* 1987), October 1989 (M. Kessler *in litt.* 1989).

POPULATION There seems to be little reason to doubt that a serious decline in numbers and a fragmentation of populations must have taken place owing to habitat destruction, so that the species is now restricted to a few patches of forest. In the largest of these, the Sooretama Reserve, it was considered uncommon (occasionally encountered in appropriate habitat) during a survey in December 1980/January 1981 (Scott and Brooke 1985) and in more recent fieldwork there (B. M. Whitney *in litt.* 1991), although "fairly common" there in October 1989 (M. Kessler *in litt.* 1989). At the adjacent CVRD Linhares Reserve, where it has not yet been recorded, the species must be quite rare if present (D. F. Stotz *in litt.* 1991). Even though numbers in the much smaller reserves listed under Distribution might be expected to be low, the species has been considered locally still fairly common to common (A. G. M. Coelho *in litt.* 1986, J. Vielliard *in litt.* 1986, D. M. Teixeira *in litt.* 1987), but this possibly applies only to the subspecies *soror*, which was fairly common (several pairs located easily) at Murici, while a couple of pairs were found at Pedra Talhada in October 1990 (B. M. Whitney *in litt.* 1991).

ECOLOGY The Scalloped Antbird inhabits primary and secondary forest (Pinto 1954a, Scott and Brooke 1985, Sick 1985, A. G. M. Coelho *in litt.* 1986), but has been found also in much degraded secondary growth (D. M. Teixeira *in litt.* 1987), most of the records being from lowland localities. Birds have been collected and observed mostly in the undergrowth of primary or secondary forest, close to the ground (specimens in MNRJ, A. G. M. Coelho *in litt.* 1986, M. Pearman *in litt.* 1990). At Sooretama the nominate form has been reported from the interior of tall forest (M. Isler and P. Isler verbally 1992), possibly (in the light of what follows) around large treefall gaps, but it has most often been encountered in drier-looking forest along the north–south track through the western side; several territorial pairs were found repeatedly over several years within a few metres of the same spots, and territories thus appear to be well under 1 ha in size, even though pairs are very well spaced (TAP). The undergrowth in these areas was characterized by an abundance of thick, woody vines and small tree trunks (a habitat seemingly also preferred in the reserve by the threatened Striated Softtail *Thripophaga macroura* and the near-threatened Yellow-legged Tinamou *Crypturellus noctivagus*), and birds use vine perches for cover when alarmed and as song-posts (TAP). The race *soror* is similarly almost entirely terrestrial, foraging particularly around light gaps (such as fallen trees and brush piles) and fairly open areas near denser cover in well developed forest; members of a pair have been observed foraging on the ground a few metres apart, often moving into the shelter of a fallen tree or dense understorey (B. M. Whitney *in litt.* 1991).

The birds forage in shady places in the leaf-litter, vigorously flipping leaves to uncover prey items (TAP) but also picking at the lower stems and leaves of understorey plants (B. M. Whitney *in litt.* 1991). The stomach of one specimen contained three spiders, three grasshoppers, one cockroach, one beetle, and other insects (Schubart *et al.* 1965).

A female collected in Espírito Santo on 30 November had a ripe egg in the oviduct, whereas two others from the same locality had slightly enlarged ovaries on 30 October and 17 November; males taken at the same locality on these dates had testes either undeveloped or half-enlarged; of the four birds collected in December and January (also in Espírito Santo), only one male had (slightly) enlarged testes on 28 December; two males collected in Minas Gerais (January) and Bahia (June) had undeveloped testes (specimens in AMNH). From this evidence, breeding seems to occur in Espírito Santo in October/November, whereas in the north-east it apparently takes place between March and May (A. Studer *in litt.* 1987); one nest with two eggs was found on the ground in closed forest at Quebrangulo, 15 April 1985 (A. Studer *in litt.* 1987).

THREATS The massive deforestation which has taken place throughout the species's range has certainly had a major impact on its populations, its present distribution being now heavily fragmented, with most lowland forest localities currently cleared or under pressure, and even reserves not being secure (A. G. M. Coelho *in litt.* 1986, Gonzaga *et al.* 1987).

MEASURES TAKEN The species is protected under Brazilian law (Bernardes *et al.* 1990). Efforts for the preservation of the forests in the Serra das Guaribas at Quebrangulo (Studer 1985) resulted in the creation in December 1989 of the 4,500 ha Pedra Talhada Biological Reserve. The privately owned forest of Engenho Água Azul at Timbaúba is one of the best-kept reserves in Pernambuco (A. G. M. Coelho *in litt.* 1986). The 450 ha UFPE reserve, the 500 ha Saltinho Biological Reserve and the 350 ha Tapacurá Ecological Station might give it some additional protection in the north-east. The species's occurrence in the 24,000 ha Sooretama Biological Reserve and in the 2,200 ha Córrego do Veado Biological Reserve is only partially reassuring, since the numbers observed remain so small.

MEASURES PROPOSED The conservation of the Pedra Branca forests at Murici is clearly important, this being apparently the largest remaining continuous forest area in extreme north-eastern Brazil (Teixeira 1987) and holding several other threatened birds (see Remarks under Alagoas Foliage-gleaner *Philydor novaesi*). Effective protection of already created reserves is obviously an equally urgent need. The few remaining patches of forest within the species's range could still harbour small and so far undetected populations, and merit being identified and searched to assess its conservation status more accurately.

WHITE-MASKED ANTBIRD *Pithys castanea* I[8]

Being known from a single 1937 skin from Amazonian lowlands in Ecuador or Peru, it is impossible to judge the status of this seemingly valid rainforest antbird.

DISTRIBUTION The White-masked Antbird (see Remarks 1) is known from a single specimen (male) collected by the Olalla family at Andoas on the lower río Pastaza, originally (or at least marked by the collectors as) in Oriente province, Ecuador, but now (apparently through changes in the international border) in Loreto in western Peru, on 16 September 1937 (Berlioz 1938, specimen in MNHN; see Remarks 2).

POPULATION Nothing is known.

ECOLOGY The habitat is given as humid forest (Sibley and Monroe 1990). The altitude of Andoas is given as 200 or 250 m (Paynter and Traylor 1977, Stephens and Traylor 1983). Berlioz (1938) noted that "*P. castanea* seems to live side by side in the tropical zone of eastern Ecuador with *P. albifrons peruviana* Tacz., three specimens of which were sent from the same locality".

THREATS The state of forest in this part of western Peru is unknown.

MEASURES TAKEN Understandably, no specific action has been taken other than searches to rediscover the species, e.g. by E. O. Willis (*in litt.* 1991), who visited Andoas (both Andoas Nuevo on the Ecuador frontier and "Andoas Viejo", i.e. the Andoas of the type-locality) in 1979, but who failed to observe the species despite the presence of some large swarms of army ants; and by a team from ANSP, which investigated the region around Taisha, in Morona-Santiago province, Ecuador, about 150 km upriver from the type-locality, in July 1990, without success, although at 600 m this site may have been too high (NK).

MEASURES PROPOSED Further examination of the type-specimen, and the use of biochemical analysis of any DNA extractable from it, would be valuable in determining the taxonomic identity of this bird (see Remarks 1). However, until such work is done searches are still needed in the region of the type-locality and appropriate areas elsewhere in case the species is genuine; concomitant with this, vigilance is needed in case habitat destruction at the type-locality proceeds apace before a firm judgement can be reached on taxonomic status.

REMARKS (1) The only other member of the genus is the White-plumed Antbird *Pithys albifrons*, widespread in the Amazon basin but very little known (there is a useful referenced summary in Hilty and Brown 1986). Berlioz (1938) noted: "The two species are, however, quite different: *P. castanea* is obviously a larger bird than its ally, with uniform chestnut colour (without the grey back and wings of *P. albifrons*), a deep black cap, including the nasal feathers, and apparently (the specimen seems quite adult) nothing recalling the white elongated feathers characteristic of the other species". Nevertheless, the validity of *castanea* as a good species remains in some doubt (see Sibley and Monroe 1990); E. O. Willis (*in litt.* 1991) reported hearing an opinion that it might represent a *Pithys* x *Rhegmatorhina* hybrid. (2) The precise site of the type-locality is unclear; Paynter and Traylor (1977) have a full discussion of the options, concluding that two towns called Andoas exist, a point confirmed by TAW (1986) and by E. O. Willis (*in litt.* 1991), namely one in Ecuador (Andoas Nuevo) on the frontier, and the other (now) in Peru (Andoas or "Andoas Viejo"). It is assumed here, perhaps mistakenly, that the type-locality is the Peruvian Andoas.

RUFOUS-FRONTED ANTTHRUSH *Formicarius rufifrons* V[9]

Riverine floodplain thickets in a restricted area of lowland south-east Peru form the habitat of this ground-dwelling formicariid, which is consequently at some risk from actual and impending development utilizing the soils on which such habitat stands.

DISTRIBUTION The Rufous-fronted Antthrush is known from a very small geographic area in the Amazonian lowlands of south-east Peru near the base of the Andes. The four specimens and a small number of recent sight records are all from floodplain forests along rivers that drain into the río Madre de Dios in the department of the same name. All localities are at elevations of c.300-400 m.

Three of the four specimens were collected at the mouth of the río Colorado (given as 12°30'S 70°25'W by Blake 1957). The type-description is of a female taken in October 1954; an individual obtained at the same place and on the same date is in MHNJP (Parker 1983), while a male (in AMNH) was collected there in October 1958, and another male (in FMNH) was obtained at the mouth of the río Inambari in September 1958. Following these discoveries, the species went unrecorded until September 1982, when one was found along the río Manu near the Cocha Cashu Biological Station (Parker 1983). This record was followed by a small number of sightings annually from 1983 to 1988 along the lower río Manu, especially at Boca Manu (S. L. Hilty, C. A. Munn, S. Robinson verbally 1980s). Most of these observations involved solitary individuals, but "at least three pairs held territories in the vicinity of Cocha Juárez, Manu National Park" in July–August 1990 (P. K. Donahue *in litt.* 1990), where the species was seen again in July 1991 (B. M. Whitney *in litt.* 1991). Another pair was briefly observed (and tape-recorded) in mid-1988 along the lower río Tambopata opposite the mouth of the río La Torre not far upriver from Puerto Maldonado (P. K. Donahue *in litt.* 1988). Recent sight records (mid-1991) are from the Colpa de Guacamayos area along the río Tambopata near the mouth of the río Tavara, where the species is reportedly more numerous than at other known localities (D. Michael *in litt.* 1992), and from Cocha Salvador in Manu National Park (B. M. Whitney *in litt.* 1991).

POPULATION Although population data are unavailable, Rufous-fronted Antthrushes are rare or absent from most of the well-studied localities within the small known range. Most records are of individuals or pairs that were present for only short periods of time. This may reflect the ever-changing structure of their floodplain forest habitat, or may be the result of competitive exclusion by the commoner and apparently dominant Black-faced Antthrush *Formicarius analis* (P. K. Donahue *in litt.* 1988), although Parker (1983) reported a case of no apparent interspecific territoriality. Rufous-fronted Antthrushes may be locally numerous in forests of the right age and structure, as at Cocha Juárez in Manu National Park, where three pairs were found in 1990, or near the Colpa de Guacamayos, where fairly common in 1991 (see Distribution).

ECOLOGY This terrestrial species inhabits shaded thickets of broadleaved plants such as *Heliconia metallica* in young floodplain forests generally within 100 m of rivers or oxbow lakes; these forests are usually dominated by a (relatively) few species of large tree with a canopy height averaging about 25-30 m (Parker 1983, TAP). Common large trees in this habitat in the Madre de Dios drainage include *Ficus insipida*, *Acacia loretensis*, *Cedrela odorata*, *Erythrina* spp., *Sapium* spp. and *Terminalia oblonga* (R. Foster verbally 1991); the middle storey in these forests is fairly open, but there are often tall thickets of spiny bamboo *Guadua* sp. (TAP). Rufous-fronted Antthrushes were regularly found in bamboo thickets in at least two localities (Boca Manu and the Colpa de Guacamayos; S. L. Hilty and D. Michael verbally 1980s), while at Cocha Cashu (Manu National Park) the species was found in tall forest dominated by *Ficus insipida* with a dense ground cover of *Heliconia* (Parker 1983), and at both Cocha Suárez and Cocha Salvador it was in river-edge *Heliconia* thickets (B. M. Whitney *in litt.* 1991). Along the lower río

Tambopata it was found in "second-growth" forest near the riverbank (P. K. Donahue *in litt.* 1988). The morphologically similar Black-faced Antthrush occurs in the floodplain habitat of Rufous-fronted throughout the small range of the latter, and there is evidence (based on song playback experiments) that *analis* may exclude *rufifrons* from some areas apparently suitable to both: *analis* at least occasionally responds strongly and aggressively to songs of *rufifrons* (P. K. Donahue *in litt.* 1988, J. W. Terborgh verbally 1980s). Another plausible explanation for the scarcity of *rufifrons* is that the constantly changing structure and floristic composition (and food resources) of its riverine forest habitat require a more nomadic life-style than is typical of most formicariid species, but why this species is so restricted geographically remains a mystery. The testes of the bird collected in September 1958 were enlarged.

THREATS On paper, this and other floodplain forest bird species (see below) of southern Peru would appear to be relatively safe owing to significant populations of them surely occurring along the rivers within Manu National Park. However, even if this park continues to receive some degree of protection (which is not guaranteed), the extensive riverine forests to the south and east will increasingly become the focus of development schemes and colonization projects: completion and maintenance of the highway through Puerto Maldonado will certainly stimulate development in the department of Madre de Dios, and forests along the rivers will be seriously affected by most types of economic activity (TAP). The species-rich forests along the ríos Madre de Dios, Inambari, and Tambopata have already been selectively logged and – in many areas – degraded by the activities of subsistence farmers, hunters, and gold miners (TAP). Their long-term survival will depend on the degree to which the people of Madre de Dios choose or are allowed to choose sustainable forest activities (selective timber extraction, brazil nut harvesting) over short-term ones (cattle-ranching). Similarly, poorly planned colonization projects will lead (through agriculture and cattle-ranching) to the depletion and erosion of rich alluvial soils within a generation, when with adequate ecological evaluation these could be farmed productively over long periods of time in carefully chosen areas.

MEASURES TAKEN The magnificent Manu National Park (15,330 km^2, parts of which are also constituted as a Biosphere Reserve and World Heritage Site: IUCN 1992) encompasses large areas of lowland and montane rainforest and no doubt protects significant populations of this and other bird species endemic to south-western Amazonia (but see below).

MEASURES PROPOSED Manu National Park needs the full commitment of the world's conservation community: continued financial support (both national and international) for park facilities and park guards is essential if this exceptional area is to survive far into the future, and a campaign to educate the nearby communities concerning the importance of the park (e.g., as a reservoir of economically valuable plants and animals) is badly needed (TAP).

The recently established Tambopata-Candamo Reserve Zone (14,790 km^2: IUCN 1992) covers a large area of land south of the río Madre de Dios between the ríos Heath and Tambopata; although its boundaries and status are still being debated, the reserve includes some of the richest known sites on earth for birds, butterflies and plants – and presumably for all terrestrial life-forms (TAP). Of particular importance is protection for the tall floodplain forests that are being rapidly cleared along the lower Tambopata: these forests – like those in Manu National Park – contain the most diverse bird communities yet reported, with as many as 350 resident bird species in areas of c.1 km^2, and single site lists of over 550 species, e.g. at the Tambopata Reserve (TAP). Recent fieldwork in the adjacent Alto Madidi region of northern Bolivia, where the Rufous-fronted Antthrush must be expected and searched for, revealed similar levels of species diversity for birds and plants, and the area has been proposed as a national park (Parker and Bailey 1991). The observation that floodplain forests are more constrained and not as floristically diverse at the base of the Andes (R. Foster verbally 1991) indicates the importance of preserving large examples of floodplain forest habitat farther out on the Amazon plains, as along the middle and lower río

Tambopata. This in turn underscores the importance of clarifying and seeking increased protection for the that portion of Tambopata-Candamo which lies between the ríos Tavara and La Torre (TAP). The preservation of the tremendous genetic diversity of upper (south-west) Amazonia would also be served by the establishment of additional forest reserves of one kind or another in the headwaters of the río Purus near the Peru–Brazil border, and by increased protection for the Manuripi-Heath Reserve in northern Bolivia.

The Rufous-fronted Antthrush should be looked for along the rivers of south-west Brazil and northern Bolivia.

REMARKS Most of the endemic bird species restricted to south-west Amazonia below 600 m occur primarily in tall floodplain forests along the major rivers (TAP). This makes them all vulnerable to deforestation as well as to more subtle forms of habitat alteration, whereas most upland (terra firme) species tend to be widespread, occurring throughout much of the Amazon basin. In addition to the Rufous-fronted Antthrush, other riverine forest endemics with very similar geographic ranges include the threatened Selva Cacique *Cacicus koepckeae* and the near-threatened Amazonian Parrotlet *Nannopsittaca dachilleae* (see O'Neill *et al.* 1991), Scarlet-hooded Barbet *Eubucco tucinkae* (see Parker *et al.* 1991), Black-faced Cotinga *Conioptilon mcilhennyi* (see Snow 1982) and White-cheeked Tody-flycatcher *Poecilotriccus albifacies* (see Parker 1982b). A number of subspecies are also (curiously) restricted to floodplain forest habitats (e.g., the Emerald Toucanet *Aulacorhynchus prasinus dimidiatus*) (TAP).

MOUSTACHED ANTPITTA *Grallaria alleni* E/Ex[4]

This cloud-forest understorey species is known from just two specimens (representing two subspecies) from the western slopes of the Central and East Andes, Colombia, where it has undoubtedly suffered from widespread deforestation, and is obviously extremely rare.

DISTRIBUTION The Moustached Antpitta (see Remarks) is known only from the type-localities of its two subspecies: the nominate form was described from a single adult female taken in October 1911 at 2,135 m near Salento (in the Boquía valley, c.4°39'N 75°36'W: Paynter and Traylor 1981), on the western slope of the Central Andes (Quindío mountains), Quindío department (Chapman 1912, 1917a, Meyer de Schauensee 1948-1952); and a male (subspecies *andaquiensis*) was collected between c.2,000 and 2,100 m during October 1971 in the vicinity of Cueva de los Guácharos (within the national park at 1°37'N 76°00'W), near the headwaters of the río Suaza, on the western slope of the southern East Andes, Huila department (record and coordinates from Hernández Camacho and Rodríguez 1979).

POPULATION Despite recent ornithological surveys around both known localities, there have been no additional records (Hernández Camacho and Rodríguez 1979), and this antpitta must be regarded as extremely rare.

ECOLOGY Both localities where the species has been collected were originally humid montane forest (low cloud-forest), where it inhabits the undergrowth (Hilty and Brown 1986) and probably stands of bamboo *Chusquea* sp. (LGN).

THREATS Almost all of the cloud-forest (at elevations suitable for this species) along both slopes of the Central Andes, and the western slope of the East Andes, have been logged and replaced by agriculture and settlements (LGN). Extensive clearance of forest in the vicinity of Salento (and Laguneta) was already advanced in 1911 (Chapman 1917a), and is now widespread and thorough (Ridgely 1981a: 339). Such extensive destruction of suitable habitat has undoubtedly caused a decline in the population of this bird.

MEASURES TAKEN There are no protected areas within the elevational range (formerly) occupied by the nominate form of this species within the Central Andes, unless the bird occurs in the lower parts of Ucumarí Regional Park in Risaralda (LGN), or Alto Quindío Acaime Natural Reserve (see equivalent sections under Multicoloured Tanager *Chlorochrysa nitidissima* and Bicoloured Antpitta *Grallaria rufocinerea* respectively). The other subspecies, *andaquiensis*, was described from the Cueva de los Guácharos National Park (9,000 ha: CNPPA 1982, also Distribution).

MEASURES PROPOSED Montane forests (especially those below 2,300 m) in this area of Colombia are in urgent need of protection for both this and a number of other threatened birds. An inventory of remaining forest in each of the areas from which the Moustached Antpitta is known is of the highest priority, and would facilitate effective fieldwork and conservation action. In the vicinity of Salento, Quindío, seven other threatened species have previously been recorded (above c.2,000 m), namely Cauca Guan *Penelope perspicax*, Fuertes's Parrot *Hapalopsittaca fuertesi*, Black Inca *Coeligena prunellei*, Bicoloured Antpitta, Brown-banded Antpitta *Grallaria milleri*, Multicoloured Tanager, and Red-bellied Grackle *Hypopyrrhus pyrohypogaster* (see relevant accounts): searches in any remnant forest in this area should be the highest priority for the present species (which probably occurs too low to survive in the Alto Quindío Acaime Natural Reserve, for details of which see equivalent section under Bicoloured Antpitta). Further south, in the Cueva de los Guácharos National Park, Huila, the Moustached Antpitta apparently co-exists with four other threatened species, namely Black Tinamou *Tinamus osgoodi*, Rusty-faced Parrot *Hapalopsittaca amazonina* (possibly), Yellow-eared Parrot *Ognorhynchus icterotis* and Red-bellied Grackle (see relevant accounts): as one of very few localities from which this antpitta and the Black Tinamou are known, it is essential that the state of suitable habitat in this area is investigated and that the forest is surveyed for the presence of these species and effectively protected wherever possible. Ucumarí Regional Park also merits investigation, and requires more effective protection and expansion at lower altitudes: Cauca Guan, Multicoloured Tanager and Red-bellied Grackle have all been recorded in this park, but for details see equivalent section under Multicoloured Tanager.

REMARKS Hernández Camacho and Rodríguez (1979) suggested that the Moustached Antpitta could be conspecific with Scaled Antpitta *G. guatimalensis* and Variegated Antpitta *G. varia*, owing to the similarity of their plumages and their allopatric distributions.

TACHIRA ANTPITTA *Grallaria chthonia* E^3

Almost totally unknown, this antpitta has been found only at the type- locality in El Tamá National Park in the Andes of western Venezuela, where it has been recorded just twice (during the mid-1950s); deforestation in the area has been proceeding rapidly.

DISTRIBUTION The Táchira Antpitta is endemic to the Andes of westernmost Venezuela where it is apparently known from just four specimens (in COP, USNM: see Remarks), collected in February 1955 and March 1956 at Hacienda La Providencia (c.7°38'N 72°15'W; Paynter 1982) on the río Chiquita, south-western Táchira.

POPULATION Only four specimens (all males) have been collected, these all being taken at the type-locality: there are apparently no sightings since the collection of the second two (A. B. Altman *in litt.* 1988), despite some specific searches in the area (three days were spent at the site looking for this species during September 1990: M. Pearman *in litt.* 1991).

ECOLOGY All the specimens (in COP, USNM) were collected between 1,800 and 2,100 m, Meyer de Schauensee and Phelps (1978) suggesting that the species inhabits the subtropical zone where it forages alone in the mossy undergrowth of high, dense cloud-forest. Nothing else is known.

THREATS The Táchira Antpitta must be considered threatened owing mainly to ignorance of its status: it possesses a putatively tiny range and has not been seen for 35 years. While the forest at the type-locality is essentially virgin above 1,600 m, and receives little or no disturbance (M. Pearman *in litt.* 1991), with so little known about the distribution or ecological requirements of the species, possible threats are difficult to assess, although deforestation in this part of the Venezuelan Andes has been proceeding rapidly and El Tamá National Park is highly threatened (see equivalent section under Rusty-faced Parrot *Hapalopsittaca amazonina*).

MEASURES TAKEN Hacienda La Providencia is within the El Tamá National Park (139,000 ha: IUCN 1992).

MEASURES PROPOSED Further searches are needed in the region of the type-locality in order to assess the current status and ecological requirements of the Táchira Antpitta, after which the species should be looked for in suitable habitat elsewhere to determine its distributional and conservation status. Forests in this region are in urgent need of enforced protection: any fieldwork or other conservation initiatives should be integrated with those undertaken for the Rusty-faced Parrot and Hooded Antpitta *Grallaricula cucullata*, with which this species appears to be sympatric (see relevant accounts, and also equivalent section under Táchira Emerald *Amazilia distans*).

REMARKS Meyer de Schauensee (1966) mentioned that the species is known from just three specimens, although there are apparently three males in COP (one collected on 10 February 1955, and two during March 1956), and a male (the type-specimen) in USNM (also taken on 10 February 1955).

GIANT ANTPITTA *Grallaria gigantea* K[12]

Restricted to swampy areas in the cloud-forest of south-west Colombia and Ecuador, this rare antpitta is known from few localities outside of the Pichincha area, and is notable for the lack of recent records and the extent of deforestation within its range.

DISTRIBUTION The Giant Antpitta is known from three subspecies in the West and Central Andes of Colombia (*lehmanni*), and in Ecuador primarily on the western slope (*hylodroma*: see Remarks 1) and eastern slopes (*gigantea*) of the Andes (Peters 1951: see Remarks 2). Coordinates below are from Paynter and Traylor (1977, 1981), with localities arranged from north to south, as follows:

Colombia (race *lehmanni*) Cerro Munchique (most probably at 2°32'N 76°57'W; in the West Andes of Cauca department: see Remarks 3), where a specimen (in WFVZ) was collected in May 1959; San Marcos (untraced, but on the eastern slope of the Central Andes near Páramo de Puracé at c.2°24'N 76°27'W, i.e. the Moscopán region of Cauca department), where a bird (in USNM) was taken at 3,000 m in November 1941 (Wetmore 1945); Tijeras (2°22'N 76°16'W; at c.3,000 m on the eastern slope of the southern Central Andes, in the Moscopán region of Huila department) (Meyer de Schauensee 1948-1952);

Ecuador (*gigantea*) Pun (= El Pun at 0°40'N 77°37'W; possibly between 2,600 and 2,800 m, Carchi province) (Salvadori and Festa 1899); and much further south, Runtún (1°26'S 78°24'W; on the north-eastern shoulder of Volcán Tungurahua, Tungurahua province), where a female (in ANSP) was taken at 2,200 m in December 1938 (also Meyer de Schauensee 1966); "Hacienda Aragón", on the upper río Cosanga (south of the Cordillera de Huacamayos, Napo province), where a specimen was collected at 2,350 m in June 1992 (R. S. Ridgely *in litt.* 1992); Cordillera de Guacamayos, Napo province (at c.0°40'S), where calls of what was presumably this species were heard at 2,050-2,300 m during 1990 and 1991 (Krabbe 1991, NK: see Ecology);

(*hylodroma*, Pichincha province) Pachijal (= río Tambillo, c.0°18'N 78°59'W), where a specimen (in MNHN) was taken during the 1900s (also Ménégaux 1911); Cerro San José (untraced, but probably in the Montañas de Mindo at 0°10'N 78°55'W), where three birds (in ANSP, BMNH) were collected at 2,000 m in July 1938 and April 1939; Gualea (0°07'N 78°50'W; c.5 km west of Nanegal), where four birds were taken between 1,370 and 1,525 m in 1909, 1910, and 1921 (Chapman 1926; specimens in AMNH, USNM); San Tadeo (0°01'N 78°48'W), where two specimens (in MNHN) were taken in June 1935; río Nambilla (0°00' 78°56'W; a river originating on the western slopes of Pichincha, flowing north) (Meyer de Schauensee 1966); Milpe (0°00' 78°57'W), where a bird (in ANSP) was taken in 1930; Mindo (0°02'S 78°48'W), whence comes a bird (in BMNH) taken at 1,200 m in February 1939; Cerro Castillo (= El Castillo; untraced, but apparently near the previous locality), where the bird was collected in August 1936 (two in AMNH), August 1937 (one in IRSNB), and July 1958 (one in MHNG); Guarumos (0°04'S 78°36'W), whence comes a specimen (in MNHN) taken in June 1936; "Pichincha", where an "immature" (in BMNH) was collected apparently in November 1914; Lloa (0°15'S 78°35'W; on the side of Pichincha mountain), where a male (in BMNH) was apparently taken at 3,350 m in August 1937; Taguaquiri (untraced, but in the Cordillera Occidental), where a specimen (in FMNH) was taken in February 1929; "Bola" or "Tóbalo de Montaña" (untraced), apparently in the Cordillera Occidental, where a bird (in ANSP) was collected in August 1930; El Tambo (c.4°08'S 79°17'W; near the continental divide, Loja province), where a male and female (in ANSP) were taken in March 1938 (also Meyer de Schauensee 1966, Fjeldså and Krabbe 1990; see Remarks 2).

POPULATION Throughout its distribution, this antpitta is poorly known, rare and local, the last record from Colombia being in 1959, with very few recent observations in Ecuador, and just one specimen taken (June 1992) since the previous one was collected in 1958 (Hilty and Brown 1986, Fjeldså and Krabbe 1990; see above). However, the number of specimens (of *hylodroma*) taken in Pichincha during the 1930s (at least 13: see above) suggests that at this time the Giant Antpitta may have been local but not uncommon.

ECOLOGY The Giant Antpitta inhabits humid highland forests in the upper subtropical to temperate zones (Meyer de Schauensee 1966, Hilty and Brown 1986), at altitudes apparently ranging for *hylodroma* from 1,200 to 2,000 m (the record from 3,350 m needing corroboration), for *gigantea* from 2,200 possibly to 2,600 or 2,800 m, whilst *lehmanni* has so far only been recorded at 3,000 m (see Distribution). Almost nothing is known of its ecology, although it has been reported that the bird frequents the floor of humid cloud-forest, especially in swampy places with shallow puddles of stagnant water, where it possibly (based on morphology, comparative observations and characteristics of the old collecting localities) feeds on tadpoles and frogs (Hilty and Brown 1986, Fjeldså and Krabbe 1990, J. Fjeldså *in litt.* 1992). What was presumably this species has been tape-recorded in all months of the year at 2,050-2,300 m in the Cordillera de Guacamayos (along the Baeza–Teng road), Napo province (at c.0°40'S), always near streams on extremely steep slopes with impenetrable wet forest undergrowth (Krabbe 1991, NK).

THREATS Along the Andes of Colombia, cloud-forest above 2,000 m has been the habitat facing the heaviest impact from human disturbance (LGN), and in Pichincha, Ecuador, there seems to have been some alteration of primary forest at this elevation (IUCN TFP 1988b, NK: see Measures Taken). In eastern Ecuador, however, the elevation inhabited by this species is the last to be deforested and remains almost entirely intact (NK).

MEASURES TAKEN The last record of the Giant Antpitta from Colombia was from Cerro Munchique and is presumably referable to the locality in the West Andes (see Remarks 3) now protected by the Munchique National Park (44,000 ha: Hernández Camacho *et al.* undated); also, the record from San Marcos may come from the northern end of Puracé National Park (possibly along the río San Marcos; see map in Hernández Camacho *et al.* undated). In Ecuador, forests around Mindo and Pichincha are designated Protected Forests (covering 27,300 ha: IUCN 1992), although nearby areas where this antpitta has been collected are now almost entirely deforested (NK). The Cotacachi–Cayapas Ecological Reserve (204,400 ha: IUCN 1992) in Esmeraldas may well hold a population of this bird (NK: see equivalent section under Plumbeous Forest-falcon *Micrastur plumbeus*), and in eastern Ecuador, records from Tungurahua and Loja lie just outside two major national parks, namely Sangay (272,000 ha) and Podocarpus (146,300 ha), which along with the Cayambe–Coca Ecological Reserve (403,100 ha) presumably hold populations of this species (NK; sizes from IUCN 1992).

MEASURES PROPOSED The status of the Giant Antpitta needs to be assessed through searches and studies in Munchique and Puracé National Parks, Colombia, and Sangay and Podocarpus National Parks, Ecuador, with fieldwork targeting the specific habitats described in Ecology. An assessment of suitable remaining habitat in Pichincha province needs to be undertaken to determine which areas should be targeted for survey and then be given protected area status. Obviously, all such initiatives in these areas need to consider the requirements of the other threatened species that occur in them, which for Munchique National Park are given in the equivalent section under Colourful Puffleg *Eriocnemis mirabilis*, and for Puracé National Park under Bicoloured Antpitta *Grallaria rufocinerea.*

REMARKS (1) The subspecies *hylodroma* with its distinctive plumage and range at low elevations may be a separate species (R. S. Ridgely verbally 1990). (2) Meyer de Schauensee (1966) mentioned that the subspecies *hylodroma* (presumably referring to the two birds in ANSP collected in March 1938) of the western slope of the Ecuadorian Andes (Peters 1951), had been collected at El Tambo, Loja, on the eastern slope, thus suggesting that a geographic redefinition of the three subspecies might be necessary: however, El Tambo is actually situated west of the continental divide (NK). (3) The record from Cerro Munchique appears to have been overlooked in the recent literature (e.g. Hilty and Brown 1986, Fjeldså and Krabbe 1990), but is significant as it apparently extends the known range of the species into the West Andes. However, there are some problems with the location of "Cerro Munchique": most specimens originated from the mountain in the West Andes, now protected by the Munchique National Park, but some records come from a locality of the same name on the western slope of the Central Andes (at c.3°00'N 76°20'W: see Paynter and Traylor 1981); which of these two localities is the one where M. A. Carriker collected the WFVZ specimen on 27 May 1959 remains uncertain, although it seems more likely that it was the former.

BROWN-BANDED ANTPITTA *Grallaria milleri* E/Ex[4]

This antpitta is endemic to the west slope of the Central Andes, Colombia, where it is known from just 10 specimens taken from two cloud-forest areas. The species was last recorded in 1942, and as most of the original habitat within its range has now been destroyed, it must be considered severely threatened.

DISTRIBUTION The Brown-banded Antpitta is known from the west slope of the Central Andes in Caldas and Quindío departments, Colombia, with localities (coordinates from Paynter and Traylor 1981) as follows: Laguneta (4°35'N 75°30'W, on the trail between Salento and Ibaqué), where the type-series of six specimens (in AMNH, ANSP, BMNH, MCZ) was collected at 3,140 m in August and September 1911 (also Chapman 1912), with two males (in ANSP) also taken there at 2,745 m during April 1942; above Salento (4°38'N 75°34'W), where a male (in AMNH) was taken at 2,745 m in November 1911 (Chapman 1917a referred to specimens collected in 1911 as taken from "at and near Laguneta"); and Sancudo (= El Zancudo; c.5°05'N 75°30'W, at c.2,400 m and 3 km east of Manizales), where an immature female (in CM) was taken in August 1918.

POPULATION This species was last recorded in 1942 when two specimens were collected at the type-locality, in the vicinity of which seven specimens had been collected in 1911: at that time the species was evidently not uncommon. Subsequently, despite intensive surveys both near Manizales (Uribe 1986) and Alto Quindío Acaime Natural Reserve (Renjifo 1988, 1991), the bird has not been observed: however, L. M. Renjifo (*in litt.* 1992) has suggested that there is adequate forest at suitable altitudes for the Brown-banded Antpitta, which almost certainly still survives there.

ECOLOGY Nothing is known of the natural history of this antpitta, but judging from Chapman (1917a), and the current plant cover above Salento and at Alto Quindío, its habitat must be humid montane forest or cloud-forest (with abundant epiphytes) where it presumably inhabits the undergrowth and forest floor (Hilty and Brown 1986, Renjifo 1991, LGN). It has been recorded from the temperate zone, at altitudes between 2,745 and 3,140 m (Paynter and Traylor 1981 gave the altitude of El Zancudo as 2,400 m, so it is possible that the bird occurred as low as this). Four birds taken at Laguneta in August and September (Chapman 1912), and the one from El Zancudo in August, were all immatures: specimens (in the museums noted above) taken between August and November were not in breeding condition.

THREATS The forest around Laguneta, the source of all but one of the specimens, is now mostly destroyed (Fjeldså and Krabbe 1990) apart from that in the Alto Quindío protected areas (see below) and, more generally, widespread deforestation in the Central Andes has caused the removal of much potentially suitable habitat (King 1978-1979, Hilty and Brown 1986: see equivalent section under Moustached Antpitta *Grallaria alleni*).

MEASURES TAKEN Several tracts of apparently suitable habitat for this species still remain in the Central Andes, and are protected within the boundaries of Los Nevados National Park (38,000 ha: CNPPA 1982; but see Threats under Rufous-fronted Parakeet *Bolborhynchus ferrugineifrons*) or smaller reserves such as Ucumarí Regional Park (Risaralda) and Alto Quindío Acaime Natural Reserve (Quindío), which in turn is surrounded by Cañon del Quindío reserve, both of which effectively protect part of the forest in this watershed (Renjifo 1991, L. M. Renjifo *in litt.* 1992, LGN: see equivalent section under Bicoloured Antpitta *G. rufocinerea*).

MEASURES PROPOSED The montane forest in this area is important for a number of threatened bird species, and the conservation of any remaining tracts of forest is of the highest priority. Surveys are urgently needed to determine exactly where such forest exists, especially around Salento, Quindío, which has previously supported seven other threatened species, for details of which see the equivalent section under Moustached Antpitta). A proposal to increase the protection of the Alto Quindío area has been put forward by ICBP and Fundación Herencia Verde, the details of which (including other threatened species found in this area) are given in the equivalent section under Bicoloured Antpitta, and any conservation plan should take into account the needs of all the sympatric threatened species. Meanwhile, a systematic search for this species should be instigated, aiming at its rediscovery and an assessment of its basic ecological requirements.

BICOLOURED ANTPITTA *Grallaria rufocinerea* I[7]

This cloud-forest antpitta is endemic to the Central Andes of Colombia, where it has been recorded from very few localities in an area that has been affected by widespread deforestation.

DISTRIBUTION The Bicoloured Antpitta is known from both slopes of the Central Andes in Colombia, where records of the nominate race come from Antioquia, Caldas, Quindío and Tolima departments, the subspecies *romeroana* being recorded from Cauca and possibly Putumayo (the subspecific identity of the bird seen in Putumayo is uncertain (see Remarks 1). The few localities where this species has been recorded (north to south, with coordinates, unless otherwise stated, from Paynter and Traylor 1981) are as follows:

Antioquia Santa Elena (6°13'N 75°30'W; 8 km east of Medellín on the eastern slope of the Central Andes, at 2,750 m), where the type-specimen was collected (Sclater and Salvin 1879); and Páramo de Sonsón (5°43'N 75°15'W; 65 km south-east of Medellín, and just 20 km north of the Caldas border: Hilty and Brown 1986), where a male (in USNM) was collected between 2,530 and 2,745 m in July 1951;

Caldas río Blanco watershed, north-east of Manizales (on the west slope of the Central Andes), where birds were commonly seen and heard during 1989-1990 (P. Kaestner *in litt.* 1992), with several heard in September 1990 (L. G. Olarte *in litt.* 1992), both records coming from 2,400 m;

Quindío above Calarcá (4°31'N 75°38'W; in the La Línea area of Navarco), where the species has been found fairly regularly between 2,700 and 2,900 m (F. G. Stiles *in litt.* 1992); above Salento (either at 4°39'N 75°36'W, or near El Roble at 4°41'N 75°36'W; on the western slope of the Central Andes), where a male (in AMNH) was taken at 2,745 m in November 1911; Alto Quindío Acaime Natural Reserve (c.4°37'N 75°28'W; on the western slope of the Central Andes, coordinates from Renjifo 1988), where the bird was found commonly between 2,500 and 3,150 m during 1989-1991 (Renjifo 1991, P. Kaestner *in litt.* 1992); Laguneta (c.4°35'N 75°30'W; on the western slope of the Central Andes), where four birds (two males and two females in AMNH) were taken at 3,140 m at the end of August 1911 (also Chapman 1917a);

Tolima La Leona (4°35'N 75°25'W), on the eastern side of the Quindío pass, where the bird was recorded in May 1990 (L. M. Renjifo *in litt.* 1992);

Cauca río Bedón waterfall (2°20'N 76°17'W: coordinates from Hernández Camacho and Rodríguez 1979), west of Versalles in Puracé National Park, where two birds were collected at 3,000 m during November 1970 (Hernández Camacho and Rodríguez 1979) (see Remarks 2);

Putumayo c.20 km east of San Francisco (1°11'N 76°53'W; on the eastern slope of the Andes), whence Hilty and Brown (1986) reported a sighting at 2,450 m in June 1981 (see Remarks 3).

POPULATION This bird is apparently localized and rare, and owing to widespread deforestation within its altitudinal range (see Threats) the population has presumably undergone a significant decline during this century. Although ornithological attention has been focused on Puracé National Park, especially the northern end where this bird has been recorded (e.g. Hilty and Silliman 1983), the Bicoloured Antpitta has not been found there since 1970 (see above). However, recent records on the western slope of the Central Andes near Manizales (several birds heard, and birds seen and heard commonly), above Calarcá (birds found fairly regularly and not uncommon: F. G. Stiles *in litt.* 1992; see Ecology) and at the Alto Quindío Acaime reserve (see Distribution) suggest that viable populations of the nominate race still survive. During intensive fieldwork at the last locality (from June 1989 to July 1990), Renjifo (1991) recorded densities between 1.6 and 5 birds per 10 km transect, with the higher densities in the primary forest at lower altitudes, describing it as uncommon, difficult to see and recorded mainly by vocalization (L. M. Renjifo *in litt.* 1992).

ECOLOGY Records of this antpitta come from between 2,400 and 3,150 m (Hilty and Brown 1986 and Fjeldså and Krabbe 1990 give ranges from 2,100 to 3,300 m), where it inhabits the floor and undergrowth of dense, humid, montane forest and cloud-forest near the tree-line (subpáramo) (Hilty and Brown 1986, Fjeldså and Krabbe 1990). P. Kaestner (*in litt.* 1992) suggested that the species seems to prefer wetter areas in the interior of montane forest. In Quindío, the habitat of the nominate race was described as open temperate-zone forest with small palms, tree-ferns, vines, "climbing bamboo", orchids and other epiphytes, with large trees including oaks *Quercus* sp.; the undergrowth was not dense, except within clearings, and the forest floor was remarkably bare (Chapman 1917a). Renjifo (1991) found the bird in primary and secondary forest, but although birds were heard calling in young second growth, they did not apparently live there. The species at Alto Quindío was found to prefer primary humid forest with young dense vegetation in natural clearings or beside paths, the highest density of birds being noted at lower altitudes (i.e. around 2,500 m) (Renjifo 1991). Above Calarcá, this antpitta was found in an area consisting largely of pine and cypress plantations, with native forest (often highly disturbed) confined to streams and ravines: the birds did not use the plantations to any extent, thus this population is probably very patchy (see Population: F. G. Stiles *in litt.* 1992). At río Blanco (Caldas), the bird was seen in a plantation of native alder *Alnus acuminata*, with a dense, wet understorey; and at La Leona (Tolima) it was recorded in a forest remnant along a ravine (L. M. Renjifo *in litt.* 1992). The type-locality of *romeroana* (in Puracé National Park) was an area of dense forest (with *Clusia* sp., *Clethra* sp., *Weinmannia* sp., and a great abundance of ferns, bromeliads and epiphytic orchids), near its transition to páramo vegetation dominated by *Espeletia hartwegiana* and shrubs (Hernández Camacho and Rodríguez 1979).

The type-specimen had been feeding on insects (Sclater and Salvin 1879). Specimens (in AMNH) collected in Quindío at the end of August and in November 1911 had undeveloped gonads, although the one from Antioquia in June 1951 was in breeding condition (Hilty and Brown 1986).

THREATS The forest around Laguneta is now mostly destroyed (Fjeldså and Krabbe 1990: see equivalent section under Moustached Antpitta *Grallaria alleni*) and, more generally, widespread deforestation (for the sake of agriculture and settlement) on both slopes of the Central Andes has caused the removal of much potentially suitable habitat (King 1978-1979, Hilty and Brown 1986, LGN). Even at the beginning of this century, deforestation and cultivation was noted to have caused a change in conditions near the type-locality at Santa Elena (Chapman 1917a). What little forest remains on the western slope of the Central Andes in Caldas and Quindío is apparently "rich", and at least near Manizales and in the Alto Quindío Acaime Natural Reserve it supports populations of this species (Renjifo 1991, P. Kaestner *in litt.* 1992). This bird seems to tolerate considerable disturbance so long as forest cover is maintained, as in the plantations above Calarcá (F. G. Stiles *in litt.* 1992: see Ecology).

MEASURES TAKEN The nominate race has been recorded from just two areas during the last 40 years, one of which is within the private Alto Quindío Acaime and (departmental) Cañon del Quindío Natural Reserves (see Distribution and Measures Proposed): combined, these areas cover 4,850 ha of which 36% is primary forest, the rest being secondary forest at varying stages of regeneration (L. M. Renjifo *in litt.* 1991). Several tracts of apparently suitable habitat still remain in the northern Central Andes, small areas of which are protected within the boundaries of Los Nevados National Park (38,000 ha: CNPPA 1982; but see equivalent and following section under Rufous-fronted Parakeet *Bolborhynchus ferrugineifrons*), which mostly covers areas at altitudes too high for this species (Hernández Camacho *et al.* undated), or smaller reserves such as Ucumarí Regional Park (Risaralda) (LGN: see equivalent and following section under Multicoloured Tanager *Chlorochrysa nitidissima*). The subspecies *romeroana* was described from Puracé National Park (83,000 ha: CNPPA 1982), and although it has not subsequently been recorded, the park still protects suitable habitat, and surrounding this park there are several forested areas where the species may yet be found, such as the small Finca Merenberg private nature reserve (LGN).

MEASURES PROPOSED Surveys are urgently required in the localities where the species has most recently been recorded (in Caldas and Quindío), but also in Puracé National Park and Putumayo, in order to determine the status of the species and to define more precisely its ecological requirements. The extent of suitable remaining forest cover in these areas is in urgent need of assessment, but once this has been carried out, other populations should be searched for (in, for example, the other protected areas mentioned above), and recommendations to extend protected areas or to designate new ones can be made.

The río Blanco watershed and Alto Quindío area seem to be ideal areas in which to conserve the now dwindling Central Andean montane forest, and efforts should be made to facilitate their protection, and indeed the further protection of this latter area (in five adjacent estates primary forest covers 73% of the 1,800 ha) forms part of a current proposal by ICBP and Fundación Herencia Verde (L. M. Renjifo *in litt.* 1991, M. G. Kelsey *in litt.* 1992). These two areas support a number of other threatened species, namely (at río Blanco) Rusty-faced Parrot *Hapalopsittaca amazonina*, and (at Alto Quindío) Fuertes's Parrot *H. fuertesi*, Rufous-fronted Parakeet, Golden-plumed Parakeet *Leptopsittaca branickii*, Yellow-eared Parrot *Ognorhynchus icterotis* and possibly Brown-banded Antpitta *Grallaria milleri* (see relevant accounts), and any conservation action should consider their needs. The maintenance of primary forest along water courses, even within plantations (e.g. at río Blanco), should be encouraged, as this species is seemingly able to survive in such areas (see Ecology): however, the status of populations in these situations should ideally be monitored to confirm their viability.

Close to the Alto Quindío protected areas (in the vicinity of Salento), the Bicoloured Antpitta is known to have occurred alongside up to seven threatened species, and searches for any other remnant forest patches in this area is a high priority (see Moustached Antpitta for details). At Puracé National Park, this species has been recorded sympatrically with five other threatened species, namely Rusty-faced Parrot, Golden-plumed Parakeet, Yellow-eared Parrot, Giant Antpitta *Grallaria gigantea* and Masked Mountain-tanager *Buthraupis wetmorei* (see relevant accounts); at Páramo de Sonson it occurs sympatrically with Multicoloured Tanager (see relevant account); and near La Leona in Tolima the various sympatric species are listed in the equivalent section under Tolima Dove *Leptotila conoveri*. The initiatives mentioned above that are relevant to these areas should consider the needs of all these species.

REMARKS (1) On the evidence of the remarks below, it appears that this antpitta has been recorded from Antioquia, Caldas, Quindío, Tolima, Cauca and Putumayo departments, although the río Bedón is clearly only a short distance north of the Huila border. (2) Paynter and Traylor (1981) placed the río Bedón and its source (Laguna San Rafael) in Cauca rather than Huila department (*contra* Hernández Camacho and Rodríguez 1979); the citation of the specimens from this locality in Cauca (rather than Huila) was followed by Hilty and Brown (1986), but not by Fjeldså and Krabbe (1990). (3) Hilty and Brown (1986) incorrectly recorded this sighting from Putumayo as from Nariño department, a mistake perpetuated by Fjeldså and Krabbe (1990).

HOODED ANTPITTA *Grallaricula cucullata* V/R[10]

This cloud-forest antpitta is known from very few localities (most recently in two national parks) in the West, Central and East Andes of Colombia, and one area in south-westernmost Venezuela, where suitable habitat has been severely affected by agricultural encroachment and deforestation.

DISTRIBUTION The Hooded Antpitta has been recorded from very few localities on the West, Central and East Andes (Antioquia, Valle, Huila departments) of Colombia (nominate *cucullata*), and in extreme western Venezuela in Táchira and Apure states (race *venezuelana*). Coordinates below are taken from Paynter (1982), and Paynter and Traylor (1981).

Colombia Localities where this species has been collected are as follows: Santa Elena (6°13'N 75°30'W; 8 km east of Medellín, on the east slope of the Central Andes, Antioquia), where a male and female (in BMNH) were collected in September 1878 (also Sclater and Salvin 1879); Ríolima (untraced, but on the eastern slope of the West Andes near San Antonio, 3°30'N 76°38'W, and west of Cali, Valle), where a male (in AMNH) was collected in August 1898; La Candela (c.1°50'N 76°20'W; on the east slope of the Central Andes, 8 km south-south-west of San Agustín, Huila), where a male and female (in AMNH) were collected in May 1912 (also Chapman 1917a), two birds (in ANSP) in September 1942, and a male (in USNM) in May 1952, all between 1,980 and 2,135 m; and the Cueva de los Guácharos National Park (on the west slope of the southern East Andes, Huila), within which specimens (in ICN, IND) have apparently been taken at Acevedo (1°49'N 75°52'W) seemingly between 650 and 800 m (a male in July 1976 and a female in July 1978), above the Guácharos cave (a male at c.1,900 m in September 1975 and a female in June 1976), and 1.5 km south of the previous locality (one female in July 1976 and a male in December 1977) (also Gertler 1977).

Venezuela A second subspecies (*venezuelana*) has been recorded on the río Chiquito (= río Chiquita), apparently at Hacienda La Providencia (c.7°38'N 72°15'W; south-westernmost Táchira), at 1,800 m (Phelps and Phelps 1956, 1963, Meyer de Schauensee and Phelps 1978), which lies within El Tamá National Park (see Measures Taken); and there is a recent sighting from elsewhere in El Tamá National Park, within Apure state, near the border with Táchira (A. B. Altman *in litt.* 1988).

POPULATION Except for the population at the Cueva de los Guácharos National Park in Colombia, where the collection of six birds (and one seen) over a three-year period (Gertler 1977; see above) has led to the judgement that it is common there (Hilty and Brown 1986, Fjeldså and Krabbe 1990, J. I. Hernández Camacho verbally 1991), the Hooded Antpitta appears to be very local (Fjeldså and Krabbe 1990), and seemingly rare. West of Cali, the area around Cerro de San Antonio, where this species was recorded last century (see Distribution), is now highly fragmented, and recent (1990-1991) intensive surveys failed to reveal it even in large (300-400 ha) forest patches along ridge-tops: the bird in this area is now considered locally extinct, although it may well prove to be present within Los Farallones de Cali National Park (G. Kattan, H. Alvarez López and M. Giraldo *in litt.* 1992). The status of this bird in Venezuela is unknown, although it seems likely that El Tamá National Park holds a viable population (see Distribution).

ECOLOGY The Hooded Antpitta has mainly been recorded from 1,800 to 2,135 m, although the lower limit given for Ríolima is 1,500 m, and upper limit for Santa Elena is 2,750 m (Paynter and Traylor 1981), which presumably explains the range of 1,500 to 2,700 m given by Hilty and Brown (1986) and Fjeldså and Krabbe (1990). The records from between 650 and 800 m (see Distribution) appear to be in error, as this is outside the altitudinal range of the Cueva de los Guácharos National Park (Hernández Camacho *et al.* undated), and below the altitude (1,200 m) given for the locality by Paynter and Traylor (1981). Within the subtropical zone, this species inhabits the undergrowth in more open parts of otherwise dense cloud-forest (Meyer de Schauensee and Phelps 1978, Hilty and Brown 1986). Birds are usually seen alone, and hop from perch to perch in low bushes, from ground level to 1.5 m up (Gertler 1977, Meyer de Schauensee and Phelps 1978). At the Cueva de los Guácharos National Park four main habitats are recognized (Hernández Camacho *et al.* undated), of which the Hooded Antpitta inhabits the mixed subandean forest: this forest type has a high diversity of trees, amongst which the commonest are: species of Lauraceae, *Juglans neotropica*, *Cedrela* spp., *Cinchona pubescens*, *Podocarpus* spp., *Ocotea* spp., and *Nectandra* spp. (Hernández-Camacho *et al.* undated). Above c.2,000 m, this forest mingles with moist subandean cloud-forest dominated by oaks such as *Quercus humboldtii* and *Trigonobalanus excelsa* (Hernández Camacho *et al.* undated).

A female bird collected at Santa Elena had been feeding on insects; this same bird (in BMNH), collected in September 1878, was found to contain eggs (Sclater and Salvin 1879). Another female (in AMNH), taken in May, was coming into breeding condition, and a bird (in ICN) taken in July contained an undeveloped egg.

THREATS The bird's habitat (mixed subandean forest) is seriously threatened in Colombia. At the type-locality (Santa Elena, Antioquia), the original forest cover has been cleared since the beginning of this century (Chapman 1917a), and in the Ríolima area (Valle del Cauca) there are only minor tracts of (mostly disturbed) cloud-forest remaining outside of protected areas (Hilty and Brown 1986, M. G. Kelsey verbally 1992). Forest in the western Venezuelan Andes is being destroyed so rapidly that El Táma National Park is one of the most threatened protected areas in Venezuela (Desenne and Strahl 1991: see equivalent section under Rusty-faced Parrot *Hapalopsittaca amazonina*).

MEASURES TAKEN In Colombia, the Cueva de los Guácharos National Park covers 9,000 ha (CNPPA 1982). Also, the Hooded Antpitta may occur at Los Farallones de Cali National Park, a 150,000 ha protected area (CNPPA 1982) largely unexplored by ornithologists (LGN). In Venezuela, El Tamá National Park, 139,000 ha (CNPPA 1982), covers the two localities at which the species has been recorded (see Distribution and Threats).

MEASURES PROPOSED The priority for this species is to ensure the integrity of suitable forest within the Cueva de los Guácharos National Park, and to assess its population size (and hence viability) at this site. Surveys in other likely areas, including Los Farallones de Cali National Park, are needed to determine the overall status of the bird, and with the aim of facilitating the protection of other areas. In Venezuela, the status of the Hooded Antpitta in El Tamá National Park is in urgent need of assessment, as is the state of available habitat there. Conservation initiatives in that area should be integrated with those undertaken for the Rusty-faced Parrot and Táchira Antpitta *Grallaria chthonia* (see relevant accounts, but also equivalent section under Táchira Emerald *Amazilia distans*).

STRESEMANN'S BRISTLEFRONT *Merulaxis stresemanni* I[6]

Almost nothing is known of this bird, which is presumed to live in the undergrowth of the few rapidly diminishing forests in coastal Bahia, where it was recorded once this century and once last.

DISTRIBUTION Stresemann's Bristlefront (see Remarks) is known from two specimens from coastal Bahia, eastern Brazil (King 1978-1979, Sick 1985). The type-specimen (male) was collected between 1831 and 1838 in the vicinity of Salvador, and a second (female) was taken on 8 May 1945 near Ilhéus (Sick 1960).

POPULATION Numbers are unknown, but conceivably very small; the species has aptly been considered rare (Sick and Teixeira 1979, Sick 1985), and recent brief surveys in coastal Bahia (in 1977 and 1987) failed to find it (King 1978-1979, LPG).

ECOLOGY Nothing has been reported concerning the habitat where the specimens were taken, which was presumably the undergrowth of humid forest. A detailed description of the vegetation around Ilhéus in 1944 is given by Veloso (1946).

THREATS Little apparently suitable habitat remains in coastal Bahia owing to extensive deforestation and cacao cultivation (LPG), and remaining forests in the state are now disappearing "at a ferocious rate" (Oliver and Santos 1991). The species was not found during brief surveys in 1986 and 1987 at Una Biological Reserve, the largest protected area close to its range (Gonzaga *et al.* 1987).

MEASURES TAKEN This species was not protected by Brazilian law (*contra* King 1978-1979) until 1989 (Bernardes *et al.* 1990).

MEASURES PROPOSED Fieldwork is needed to rediscover Stresemann's Bristlefront and to provide information on its ecological requirements and status. Searches in coastal Bahia should also target a second endemic rhinocryptid, the Bahia Tapaculo *Scytalopus psychopompus*, and the Fringe-backed Fire-eye *Pyriglena atra* (see relevant accounts). Collection of further specimens should not be countenanced.

REMARKS This species was considered to be a larger sibling of Slaty Bristlefront *Merulaxis ater*, which was collected as close as the rio Jequitinhonha (Belmonte), 120 km south of Ilhéus (Sick 1960). Both probably form a superspecies (Mayr 1971, Sick 1985).

BRASILIA TAPACULO *Scytalopus novacapitalis* R[11]

This small undergrowth-haunting bird survives locally in gallery forest and dense streamside vegetation in a limited area of central Brazil, but may be secure in several protected areas.

DISTRIBUTION The Brasília Tapaculo (see Remarks 1) is known from Goiás, the Federal District and Minas Gerais, Brazil.

Goiás There is a previously unpublished record from Formosa, where two specimens, now lost, were collected in 1963 (J. Hidasi *per* H. Sick verbally 1988).

Federal District The species was described from three specimens collected in May 1957 at 1,100 m in Brasília (Sick 1958), where it was rediscovered only in 1981 (Negret and Cavalcanti 1985, Antas 1989, Vielliard 1990). It occurs in three nature reserves around Brasília (Negret and Cavalcanti 1985, R. B. Cavalcanti *in litt.* 1987; see Measures Taken).

Minas Gerais It has been recorded from the headwaters of the rio São Miguel, 15°50'S 46°30'W, June 1988 (Antas 1989, whence coordinates), the Serra Negra (upper rio Dourados), near Patrocínio, March 1973 (G. T. de Mattos *in litt.* 1987), and from the headwaters of the rio São Francisco, Serra da Canastra National Park, October 1983 (Gonzaga 1984), August 1988 (S. G. D. Cook *in litt.* 1988), August 1989 (M. Pearman *in litt.* 1990) and July 1990 (B. C. Forrester *in litt.* 1992). Reports of its occurrence also in the Serra do Cipó, July 1977 (Negret and Cavalcanti 1985) are now confirmed (Willis and Oniki in press; see Remarks 2).

POPULATION Although the species was once considered rare (Sick and Teixeira 1979, Sick 1985), in the vicinity of Brasília it is found in "reasonable numbers" at least in certain areas (D. M. Teixeira *in litt.* 1987). The existence of 68 birds was confirmed "through an intensive search" using playback techniques in gallery forests around Brasília; results indicate that the species occurs at a "quite low" density (Negret and Cavalcanti 1985), though generally there seems little cause now for concern (Antas 1989).

ECOLOGY The species inhabits swampy gallery forest, occasionally also colonizing disturbed areas near streams with impenetrable secondary growths of fern *Pteridium aquilinum* (Negret and Cavalcanti 1985). The first specimens were collected on the ground and lower branches of the tangles in dense, shady, swampy gallery forest with ferns *Blechnum brasiliense* and palms *Euterpe*; other bird species noticed at the site were Olivaceous Woodcreeper *Sittasomus griseicapillus*, the near-threatened Chestnut-capped Foliage-gleaner *Hylocryptus rectirostris*, Sharp-tailed Streamcreeper *Lochmias nematura*, Sulphur-rumped Flycatcher *Myiobius barbatus* and White-throated Spadebill *Platyrinchus mystaceus* (Sick 1958). The stomach of one specimen contained one small centipede, small spiders, termites, beetles (including larvae), fly larvae and a small gastropod (Schubart *et al.* 1965). The holotype had inactive testes in May, although the population was then very vocal: it seems that singing activity is not strictly linked to the breeding season in the species; the song was heard more frequently during the hotter hours than at dawn (Sick 1958) and served to locate at least four individuals around a site (Sick 1985). A female collected in July 1979 had a "well developed ovary" (Vielliard 1990).

THREATS In view of its apparently very limited range, the species is presumably under threat from habitat loss around Brasília, but its distribution now seems larger that initially thought (D. M. Teixeira *in litt.* 1987) and swampy gallery forests have escaped clearance, which has primarily affected the adjacent cerrado (R. B. Cavalcanti *in litt.* 1987). There are, however, few woodlots in Serra da Canastra National Park, and these are at considerable risk from fires (M. Pearman *in litt.* 1990).

MEASURES TAKEN The Brasília Tapaculo was not protected by Brazilian law in the 1970s (*contra* King 1978-1979) but now is (Bernardes *et al.* 1990). Part of the species's population in the Federal District occurs in the Brasília National Park, which covers 28,000 ha, and in two other nature reserves, Brasília University's Ecological Station, which covers 4,000 ha and the IBGE Ecological Reserve, which covers 1,300 ha (Negret and Teixeira 1983, R. B. Cavalcanti verbally 1988, Antas 1989). Its occurrence in the Serra da Canastra National Park, which covers 72,000 ha, provides additional hope for its survival (see Remarks 3).

MEASURES PROPOSED This species is responsive to taped calls (Negret and Cavalcanti 1985) and an extended population and distribution survey seems feasible using playback techniques (see Population).

REMARKS (1) The Brasília Tapaculo was described as a race of the White-breasted Tapaculo *Scytalopus indigoticus*, but was later recognized as a distinct species (Sick 1960, Meyer de Schauensee 1966, King 1978-1979) forming a superspecies with Mouse-coloured Tapaculo *S. speluncae* (Vielliard 1990). (2) A probably different and as yet undescribed *Scytalopus* has been found in the rocky upland of Caraça Natural Park in Minas Gerais, which some have attributed to *novacapitalis* (B. M. Whitney *in litt.* 1991; see *O Charão* no.15: 14). (3) The threatened Brazilian Merganser *Mergus octosetaceus* also occurs in Minas Gerais in Serra Negra and in Serra da Canastra National Park.

BAHIA TAPACULO *Scytalopus psychopompus* E[2]

This little known ground-haunting bird occurs at two small, unprotected forested sites in coastal Bahia, and must be at great risk from habitat destruction.

DISTRIBUTION The Bahia Tapaculo (see Remarks) is known from only two localities in coastal Bahia, eastern Brazil: Valença, where an adult male and an adult female were collected on 15 and 17 October 1983, and Ilhéus, where a male was obtained on 7 July 1944 (Teixeira and Carnevalli 1989).

POPULATION Numbers are not known.

ECOLOGY Birds have been collected in lowland (45 m) forest fragments, inhabiting "flooded areas of thick vegetation"; the gonads of the pair collected in mid-October, which are recorded as "active", measured 4 (female) and 3 (male) mm; although these birds were "collected beside the nest" (Teixeira and Carnevalli 1989), no other information on breeding has been provided.

THREATS Deforestation has been extensive in the Atlantic Forest region of eastern Brazil (for a full discussion see Sick and Teixeira 1979), and particularly severe in the lowlands of Bahia south of Salvador, such that only small fragments remain (see Threats under Stresemann's Bristlefront *Merulaxis stresemanni*). There is no indication in Teixeira and Carnevalli (1989) that either site for the Bahia Tapaculo enjoys any protection.

MEASURES TAKEN None is known.

MEASURES PROPOSED In view of the very limited knowledge of the Bahia Tapaculo, further fieldwork is needed to rediscover it and to provide information on its ecological requirements and status. Searches for the species in coastal Bahia should also target a second endemic rhinocryptid, Stresemann's Bristlefront, and the Fringe-backed Fire-eye *Pyriglena atra* (see relevant accounts).

REMARKS This species is considered to be closely related to the White-breasted Tapaculo *Scytalopus indigoticus* from south-east Brazil; their distributions seem to parallel those of Stresemann's Bristlefront (see relevant account) and Slaty Bristlefront *M. ater* respectively (Teixeira and Carnevalli 1989).

SHRIKE-LIKE COTINGA *Laniisoma elegans* V/R[10]

This species, as here recognized, is endemic to south-east Brazil where it seemingly undertakes migratory movements and is everywhere rare and mostly confined to a few primary forest sites on the Serra do Mar slopes and in the interior.

DISTRIBUTION The Shrike-like Cotinga, as here defined (see Remarks), is endemic to the Atlantic Forests of south-east Brazil from Bahia (no recent records) south to Paraná (one record in 1984). Although Descourtilz's (1854-1856) attribution of the species to Mato Grosso was dismissed as an error (Hellmayr 1929b), the westernmost locality (Itapura in São Paulo) is directly across the rio Paraná from Mato Grosso do Sul.

Bahia No specific localities are known, but six skins (in AMNH, BMNH, UMZC, USNM) are labelled as from "Bahia". However, Snow (1982) did not admit the state in the species's range.

Espírito Santo Records are from: Augusto Ruschi (Nova Lombardia) Biological Reserve, September 1979 (A. Greensmith *per* D. Willis *in litt.* 1988), October 1980 (TAP), July or August 1987 (Forrester 1987); Segredo do Veado (c.20°35'S 41°45'W in Paynter and Traylor 1991), Serra do Caparaó, 900 m, October 1929 (four specimens in AMNH).

Minas Gerais Records are from: córrego Barra do Ariranha, Mantena, July 1975 (de Mattos *et al.* 1990); "Santa Bárbara de Caparaó, Espírito Santo" (= Caparaó in Minas Gerais, according to Paynter and Traylor 1991), 900 m, October 1929 (two specimens in AMNH); Fazenda Montes Claros (the Caratinga Reserve), near Caratinga, recently, and Caraça Natural Park, recently (both D. B. Trent *per* B. C. Forrester *in litt.* 1992, Caraça being at 19°58'S 43°29'W in Paynter and Traylor 1991); Camanducaia, October 1968 (de Mattos *et al.* 1990).

Rio de Janeiro Apart from four old skins simply labelled "Rio" or "Rio de Janeiro" (in AMNH, BMNH, MCZ, USNM), records (east to west) are from: Desengano State Park, at Morumbeca do Imbé, 550 m, March 1987 (bird singing: C. E. Carvalho *in litt.* 1987, J. F. Pacheco *in litt.* 1987); Fazenda União, near Casimiro de Abreu, under 100 m, July 1990 (J. F. Pacheco *in litt.* 1992); Nova Friburgo, February 1957 (specimen in LACM; old skins in AMNH, BMNH) and specifically at Rio Bonito, October 1985 and November 1990 (J. F. Pacheco *in litt.* 1992); Serra de Macaé, 22°19'S 42°40'W (in Paynter and Traylor 1991), November 1909 (Vieira 1935, Pinto 1944); Teresópolis, 1914 (specimen in MNRJ), specifically at "Grota da Revolta", October 1916 (specimen in MNRJ), "C. Guinle" (Fazenda Comarí), every month between August 1942 and February 1943 (Davis 1945; specimen in MZUSP), Boa Fé and adjacent Canoas, October 1990 and October 1991 (J. F. Pacheco *in litt.* 1992); Petrópolis, at Serra do Couto, 1,000 m, October 1986 (J. F. Pacheco *in litt.* 1986, C. E. Carvalho *in litt.* 1987); near Santo Aleixo, under 50 m, May 1982 (Gonzaga 1986); Xerém, 120 m, July 1986 and June 1988 (J. F. Pacheco *in litt.* 1986, 1992, C. E. Carvalho *in litt.* 1987); Corcovado, Rio de Janeiro city (Descourtilz 1854-1856); Tijuca National Park, near the Corcovado statue in November 1980 (TAP), and elsewhere in September 1988 (J. F. Pacheco *in litt.* 1992); Serra do Tinguá, 1980 or 1981 (Scott and Brooke 1985), this presumably the same as the specimen (in MNRJ) from Nova Iguaçu, February 1981; Itatiaia National Park, May 1967 (specimen in LACM), specifically at Hotel Repouso de Itatiaia (low altitude) at a recent ungiven date (A. Whittaker *in litt.* 1991).

São Paulo Records (east to west) are from: Boracéia "Experimental Station", Salesópolis, November 1945 (three specimens in MZUSP); São Sebastião (i.e. present-day Ilhabela State Park), September 1901 (von Ihering and von Ihering 1907, Vieira 1935, Pinto 1944); the rio Guaratuba at Santos, May 1968 (male in LSUMZ) and May 1973 (female in CIAL); Aparicidinha, near Amparo, June 1945 (Camargo 1946, specimen in MZUSP); Socoraba, recently (da Silva 1991); Ipanema, February 1819 or 1822 (von Pelzeln 1868-1871); Piracicaba, unknown date (von Ihering and von Ihering 1907); Ituverava in the far north, April 1911 (Vieira 1935, Pinto 1944); Ilha do Cardoso State Park in the far south, recently (D. F. Stotz *in litt.* 1988, 1992, P. Martuscelli *in litt.*

1991); Fazenda Barreiro Rico, c.22°45'S 48°09'W, Anhembi, west of Piracicaba, February 1964 (specimen in MZUSP) and sometime between March 1975 and August 1977 (Willis 1979, whence coordinates); Itapura in the far west, July 1904 (von Ihering and von Ihering 1907, Vieira 1935, Pinto 1944).

Paraná The only record is from Curitiba, May 1984 (dos Anjos 1986, L. dos Anjos *in litt.* 1987).

POPULATION This species is easily overlooked, being largely silent and solitary (Wied 1820-1821, D. F. Stotz *in litt.* 1988), so that most recent records in Rio de Janeiro have been of singing birds (J. F. Pacheco *in litt.* 1992), as was the case with at least one of the three birds collected at Boracéia (Camargo 1946). However, the small number of recent records and specimens indicates that the species is genuinely or at least generally rare, as already judged by Pinto (1944). Despite the three specimens collected in three days at Boracéia, the species was not encountered there recently in over 100 days of fieldwork (D. F. Stotz *in litt.* 1992). Monthly totals between October and February at Teresópolis, 1942/1943, ranged from one to 11 birds (Davis 1945), but it was judged rare at the nearby Serra do Tinguá in the early 1980s (Scott and Brooke 1985). The record in Desengano State Park was the only one made in over 20 visits to the site in the late 1980s (J. F. Pacheco *in litt.* 1992). The population on Ilha do Cardoso is evidently small but apparently stable (P. Martuscelli *in litt.* 1991).

ECOLOGY This species, in its wider sense (see Remarks), occurs in low densities in dense hill forest at tropical levels (Snow 1982). Specimens in south-east Brazil have mostly been taken at around 900 m, some lower (Snow 1982). In the Serra do Tinguá this species was found at 680 m in primary forest (Scott and Brooke 1985). On Ilha do Cardoso the species occupies lower forests up to 100 m (P. Martuscelli *in litt.* 1991). Some records under 100 m in the winter must refer to migratory birds (e.g. Gonzaga 1986; see Distribution), as may also records from Fazenda Barreiro Rico in interior São Paulo (Willis 1979). The species was recorded in Teresópolis only during the breeding season there, from August to February (Davis 1945). Birds have been recorded high up in forest canopy trees (Descourtilz 1854-1856, Camargo 1946, J. F. Pacheco *in litt.* 1992), but one specimen (in MNRJ) was collected low in the understorey, and Willis (1979) described the species as an understorey omnivore. A bird at the Augusto Ruschi reserve associated with a large mixed-species flock passing through the crowns of middle-storey and lower canopy trees at c.8-12 m in 25 m tall forest; it perched lethargically on branches, scanning surrounding foliage (TAP). Food has been reported as mainly small insects supplemented by pulpy fruits in season (Descourtilz 1854-1856). The gonads of the six birds (five males, one female) collected in October 1929 in or near the Serra do Caparaó were all half-developed; those of the male from São Paulo in May 1968 were not (specimens in AMNH, LSUMZ). Two eastern Brazilian specimens (males) in advanced stages of moult in November indicate an unusually early start of moult in August and September (Snow 1982).

THREATS Forest destruction within the range of this species has been substantial, and it would appear that few localities remain where populations are secure.

MEASURES TAKEN The species has been recorded from Fazenda Montes Claros (private reserve, Minas Gerais), Augusto Ruschi Biological Reserve (Espírito Santo), Tijuca and Itatiaia National Parks (Rio de Janeiro) and Ilhabela and Ilha do Cardoso State Parks (São Paulo), and it would seem likely to be found in Caparaó National Park on the borders of Espírito Santo and Minas Gerais, Serra dos Órgãos National Park (Teresópolis is at its eastern border), Tinguá Biological Reserve, Serra da Bocaina National Park and Boracéia Ecological Station, although there are no recent records at this last (D. F. Stotz *in litt.* 1988, 1992).

MEASURES PROPOSED Fieldwork is needed to establish the status of this species more clearly, to determine key aspects of its ecology and migratory habits, and to locate populations in hill forests within its range (e.g. in Serra da Bocaina National Park).

REMARKS In this account the nominate race from south-east Brazil is reinstated as a full species, leaving the Andean populations in the races *venezuelensis*, *buckleyi* and *cadwaladeri* to form a second species, Buckley's Cotinga *Laniisoma buckleyi* (as in Hellmayr 1929b, Pinto 1944). The basis for this is mainly the differences in plumage between females of the Andean and Brazilian populations and differences in voice (B. M. Whitney verbally 1991). The Andean species is itself rather rare and merits near-threatened status.

GREY-WINGED COTINGA *Tijuca condita* R[11]

Only two small montane forest areas in the region of Rio de Janeiro city, Brazil, are known to harbour this recently described frugivore, and the populations involved could be very low.

DISTRIBUTION The Grey-winged Cotinga (see Remarks 1) is known from only two mountain localities in the state of Rio de Janeiro, south-east Brazil (Snow 1982, Sick 1985). It was described from a female (apparently adult) collected in October 1942 in Fazenda Guinle (c.22°27'S 42°58'W), Teresópolis (Snow 1980). Speculation concerning the altitude at which the type-specimen was collected, given that Fazenda Guinle (Fazenda Comarí; for details see Davis 1945), now broken up, included part of what is now the town of Teresópolis, at about 800 m, and parts of what is now the Serra dos Órgãos National Park, at altitudes of 900 m upwards (Snow 1980), was effectively ended soon after its formal description when a female was mist-netted at 1,370 m in the Serra do Tinguá (22°36'S 43°27'W), in November 1980, and a small population was found between 1,830 and 1,980 m in the Serra dos Órgãos National Park in December of that year (Snow 1982, Scott and Brooke 1985; see Population, Remarks 2). The species was relocated in July 1990 in the Serra dos Órgãos (Gardner and Gardner 1990b) and again in August 1991 (B. C. Forrester *in litt.* 1992).

POPULATION This species is clearly rare and local, occurring at very low density, and the total area of suitable habitat is small; however, there is little reason to believe that it was ever much more numerous than at present (Scott and Brooke 1985). At least five singing males (see Ecology) and two other birds (including a second trapped female) were located in the Serra dos Órgãos National Park (Snow 1982, Scott and Brooke 1985) and, apart from the female netted in 1980 (see Distribution), a single singing male was also located in the Tinguá area during a brief visit at the end of November 1981 (Scott and Brooke 1985).

ECOLOGY The Grey-winged Cotinga has been recorded from small patches of extremely humid elfin cloud-forest rich in bromeliads and with a rather even canopy 5-10 m above the ground, both on exposed ridge-tops and on sheltered slopes in an otherwise rather open area of bamboo and tussock grass, above the main tree-line (Snow 1982). In August 1991 a calling bird was found in lusher forest habitat at 1,800 m in a tall, fruit-laden tree (B. C. Forrester *in litt.* 1992). Birds have almost always been located by their calls, being remarkably wary and elusive (Snow 1982, Scott and Brooke 1985). Calling was heard sporadically throughout the day but was most frequent in the morning and in the afternoon, under a variety of weather conditions, most frequently during periods of calm with low overcast skies, and almost invariably from a hidden perch within the dense canopy, from which, at the slightest disturbance, the singer would fly off quickly to a similar perch at some distance (Snow 1982). One bird was seen feeding on small red berries exposed on the top of the canopy and calling (Snow 1982). The female caught at 1,370 m on 15 November had a well-developed brood-patch (Snow 1982, Scott and Brooke 1985), which indicates that the species breeds at that season; it is possible that this female was a foraging bird which had moved far down from a larger areas of suitable habitat near the main summit of the Tinguá range, at 1,520 m (Snow 1982).

THREATS Although there are no obvious threats to its habitat (Scott and Brooke 1985), the Grey-winged Cotinga's highly restricted range is likely to be a permanent cause of concern. In the Serra dos Órgãos National Park in July 1990 it was felt that the habitat might be at risk through disturbance by hikers (one bird being seen close to a popular trail) and through fire started by camp fires in the dry season (Gardner and Gardner 1990b, also B. C. Forrester *in litt.* 1992).

MEASURES TAKEN The species occurs in the Serra dos Órgãos National Park, which covers 5,000 ha, and in Tinguá, where the forest has been protected from cutting as a water-catchment area for the city of Rio de Janeiro (Scott and Brooke 1985). The ornithologists who rediscovered the species deliberately refrained from collecting the bird mist-netted at Tinguá (D. A. Scott verbally 1986), which was released (Snow 1982).

MEASURES PROPOSED Further fieldwork is needed to determine the status of this species, and any possible threats it may face. It has been recommended that a biological or equivalent reserve be established in the Serra do Tinguá area (Scott and Brooke 1985). The fact that a bird with so tiny a range so close to a major city remains unprotected under the law of the country to which it is endemic is a curious anomaly that needs attention.

REMARKS (1) The type-specimen of the Grey-winged Cotinga was originally identified as a Black-and-gold Cotinga *Tijuca atra* and remained stored away for over 30 years after being collected (Snow 1980; see also Snow and Goodwin 1974). The plumage colours of the type were sufficiently like those of the females of the Black-and-gold Cotinga to have led to its original misidentification, but results from the analysis of its feather proteins showed the two birds to be quite distinct species and, although not very closely related, to be provisionally treated as congeneric (Snow 1980, Vuilleumier and Mayr 1987; for a description of the male's plumage and voice, see Snow 1982). The main altitudinal ranges of the Grey-winged and (near-threatened) Black-and-gold Cotingas appear to be largely non-overlapping, the latter keeping commonly lower on the same mountain ranges (Snow 1982). (2) Although a number of ornithologists visited the Serra dos Órgãos in the interval between the collection of the type and its description, no-one reported any *Tijuca*-like bird apart from *T. atra* (Snow 1980), although a bird, possibly *condita*, was seen in these mountains in June 1959 (Sick 1985) when it was assumed to be a young Black-and-gold Cotinga that had not yet learned to call correctly (Vuilleumier and Mayr 1987).

BLACK-HEADED BERRYEATER *Carpornis melanocephalus* V/R[10]

As a species of primary lowland Atlantic Forest in eastern Brazil, this largely frugivorous bird has suffered serious habitat loss and depends on a few key protected areas for its survival, notably Sooretama, Ilha do Cardoso and those owned by CVRD.

DISTRIBUTION The Black-headed Berryeater is endemic to the Atlantic Forest region of eastern Brazil in one north-eastern state, Alagoas, and from southern Bahia south to Paraná. In the following account, records are given within states from north to south, with coordinates from Paynter and Traylor (1991) unless otherwise stated.

Alagoas The only recorded locality is Pedra ("Serra") Branca, 550 m, Murici (now with forest only at Fazenda Bananeira), where an adult male was obtained in November 1983 (Teixeira *et al.* 1986), a bird was found there in October 1990 at c.520 m (B. M. Whitney in litt. 1991), and up to six were seen or heard daily, April 1992, at 450 m (M. Pearman *in litt.* 1992).

Bahia Older records are from Pitanga (see Distribution under Fringe-backed Fire-eye *Pyriglena atra*), early in the nineteenth century (Swainson 1820-1823); Cajazeiras (Cajazeira), 14°24'S 39°51'W, on the rio Gongogi, 300 m, June 1928 (specimens in AMNH); Itabuna, July 1919 (Lima 1920, Pinto 1932, 1944); Ilhéus, January 1944 (specimens in MZUSP); Braço Sul do rio Jucurucu at Cachoeira Grande (untraced), March 1933 (Pinto 1932, 1944). Recent records are only from the CVRD Porto Seguro Reserve, January 1988 (B. M. Whitney *in litt.* 1988) and July 1991 (Stotz 1991), and from Monte Pascoal National Park, June 1990 (Gardner and Gardner 1990b).

Espírito Santo Older records are from the Fazenda Boa Lembrança, rio Itaúnas, October 1950 (Aguirre and Aldrighi 1987); rio São José, September and October 1942 (Pinto 1944, specimen in MCZ); Lagoa Juparanã (in one case precisely Santana), September and October 1925 (specimens in MNRJ), November and December 1929 (specimens in AMNH); Linhares, August 1939, October 1941 and January 1942 (specimens in MNRJ); rio Doce, April and September 1906 (von Ihering and von Ihering 1907, Pinto 1944); Colatina, November 1940 (specimen in USNM); Pau Gigante (now Ibiraçu) (in one case precisely Lauro Müller), September and November 1940 (specimens in MNRJ, USNM); Santa Cruz (in one case precisely Água Boa), October 1940 (specimens in MNRJ, USNM); Porto Cachoeiro (now Santa Leopoldina), December 1905 (Pinto 1944); Quartel das Barreiras, c.21°10'S 40°55'W (Wied 1820-1821, Pinto 1944). The key site for the species in the state is Sooretama Biological Reserve (one specimen is from Cúpido, adjacent to present-day Sooretama, August 1939: Aguirre and Aldrighi 1987), with records in September 1945 and October 1967 (Aguirre and Aldrighi 1987), the 1980s (C. E. Carvalho *in litt.* 1987, B. M. Whitney *in litt.* 1987), 1990/1991 (Aleixo *et al.* 1991) and the adjacent CVRD Linhares Reserve, with records since December 1986 (B. M. Whitney *in litt.* 1987, J. F. Pacheco *in litt.* 1987, D. F. Stotz *in litt.* 1988, 1991, G. D. A. Castiglioni verbally 1992). Other recent records are from the Fazenda Klabin (Fazenda São Joaquim) forest (now converted to the Córrego Grande Biological Reserve) in September 1979 (A. Greensmith *per* D. Willis *in litt.* 1988) and October 1986 (Gonzaga *et al.* 1987), and the Duas Bocas State Forest Reserve, west of Cariacica, 700 m, recently (C. E. Carvalho verbally 1987).

Rio de Janeiro There is an old record form Nova Friburgo (Burmeister 1856), and two nineteenth-century skins in BMNH labelled simply "Rio de Janeiro". Recent records are from São Julião (adjacent to Desengano State Park), near Campos, May 1987 (J. F. Pacheco *in litt.* 1987, C. E. Carvalho *in litt.* 1987) and from the Fazenda União, near Rocha Leão, 22°25' 42°01'W, in July, September and November 1990 (J. F. Pacheco *in litt.* 1991, including coordinates).

São Paulo Localities, all in the southern, coastal part of the state, are: Alto da Serra (Paranapiacaba), July 1906 (von Ihering and von Ihering 1907, Pinto 1944, specimen in AMNH): Estação Engenheiro Ferraz (untraced, between São Paulo and Santos), May 1964; ribeirão Fundo, c.24°15'S 47°45'W, July and August 1961, February 1962; Rocha (untraced, north-west of Juquiá),

August and September 1961; Alecrim (now Pedro de Toledo), August 1925 (Pinto 1944); Barro Branco, rio Guaraú (untraced, south of Peruíbe), June 1963; Barra do rio Guaraú, May 1963; Onça Parda (untraced, south of ribeirão Onça Parda), October and November 1962; Barra do ribeirão Onça Parda (tributary of the rio Ribeira de Iguape), November 1964; Fazenda Poço Grande, rio Juquiá, May 1940 (Pinto 1944); Sete Barras State Reserve, February and July 1979 (Willis and Oniki 1981a); Tamanduá (untraced, north-east of Sete Barras), rio Ipiranga, September and October 1962; Quadro Penteado (untraced, west of Sete Barras), October and November 1961; Iporanga (north-west of Juquiá [Paynter and Traylor 1991], therefore not as in GQR 1991), November 1961; Icapara, July 1970; Iguape, May 1893 (von Ihering 1898, Pinto 1944) and recently (D. F. Stotz *in litt.* 1991); Tabatinguara, Cananéia, c.25°01'S 47°57'W, September and October 1934 (Pinto 1944); on the mainland opposite Ilha do Cananéia, July 1991 (B. C. Forrester *in litt.* 1992); Ilha do Cardoso State Park, recently (D. F. Stotz *in litt.* 1988, P. Martuscelli *in litt.* 1991) (where no source before semi-colon, records are from specimens in MZUSP; see Remarks 1).

Paraná The species was not included in the state bird list by Scherer Neto (1985), but P. Martuscelli has recorded it on the mainland of northern Paraná (D. F. Stotz *in litt.* 1991) (see Remarks 2).

POPULATION Although the relative scarcity of recent records might be a result of the species's unobtrusiveness, as Snow (1982) has suggested (Wied 1831-1833 called it "silent, simple-minded and sluggish"), it has certainly suffered an overall decline in numbers and a fragmentation of populations owing to forest destruction within its range. Early last century the species was considered "very rare" by Swainson (1820-1823), whose hunters had never seen it before when they found it (only twice) near Salvador; but early this century it was found to be locally apparently very common ("seen in large numbers") in the vicinity of the rio Jucurucú at a forest fruiting tree, but since the bird was not found elsewhere it was considered not to be common (Pinto 1932). At present the species's stronghold is probably the Sooretama Biological Reserve and the adjacent CVRD Linhares Reserve in northern Espírito Santo. Scott and Brooke (1985) failed to find it at five study sites in Espírito Santo and Rio de Janeiro, in a survey that included a three-week study through early January 1981 at Sooretama. However, it was considered "still relatively common" in Sooretama, where birds were detected at three points in the reserve (C. E. Carvalho *in litt.* 1987). At the Linhares Reserve it was considered "fairly common", being recorded on four out of five days in December 1986, daily totals ranging from a minimum of three to a maximum of six; a conservative total of 15 birds, invariably located by their voice, was estimated to have been found during this survey (B. M. Whitney *in litt.* 1987). Another fieldworker, who found birds calling throughout the reserve, considered the species "common" at Linhares, with records from 37 days, usually of small numbers (4-6 birds) per day (D. F. Stotz *in litt.* 1988, 1991). At Ilha do Cardoso State Park in southern São Paulo, the species is not as common as at Sooretama/Linhares (D. F. Stotz *in litt.* 1991), and has been judged by a resident observer as "uncommon" (occasionally encountered in appropriate habitat) and declining owing to forest destruction (P. Martuscelli *in litt.* 1991); however, even though there is certainly a reasonable population in the forest along the base of the mountain there, and the species is still reasonably widespread in other areas of coastal southern São Paulo, it is not known whether any significant population remains in the rio Ribeira valley which, on the basis of records under Distribution, was clearly a major centre for the species 30 years ago; so little forest remains that the population may be severely reduced (D. F. Stotz *in litt.* 1988, 1991). There is no evaluation of the remaining populations of the species either in Bahia or Rio de Janeiro. It was considered "not rare" in the forests in north-eastern Brazil (Teixeira *et al.* 1986, M. Pearman *in litt.* 1992), where it has only recently been reported.

ECOLOGY The Black-headed Berryeater seems largely confined to lowland forest (see records under Distribution), with the near-threatened Black-hooded Berryeater *Carpornis cucullatus* tending to replace it at higher altitudes and further inland within the Atlantic Forest region (Snow 1982). Birds have been recorded from tall primary forest (Sick 1985, specimens in MZUSP). In the Linhares Reserve, calling birds perched about 8-12 m above the ground in the mid-storey of tall forest, the undergrowth around calling perches being usually rather dense, with many lianas and spiny palms, and the entire area quite dry, on sandy soil, with no water near any of the calling birds located; it appears that the 15 birds, plotted on a map, had grouped into roughly three areas, about five birds in each area, with individuals stationed at least 50 m apart, often 100 m or more, but within earshot and responding vigorously to playback experiments in December, being apparently more vocal in December than in late September–early October; territories appear to be occupied every year, judging from consistent, predictable response to tape playback (B. M. Whitney *in litt.* 1991). Response to the imitation of its voice has been recorded also in southern São Paulo in May and June (specimens in MZUSP).

A bird at Linhares was observed to eat a stick insect about 7 cm long in September/October (B. M. Whitney and J. C. Rowlett *in litt.* 1990), which is evidence against Snow's (1982) speculation that the species of this genus are "apparently exclusively frugivorous", although it is probable that fruits constitute the bulk of their diet. Other food recorded has been given as "always tree fruits, mostly red berries, often also red seeds, apparently *Bixa orellana*" (Wied 1831-1833), "small fruits" (Burmeister 1856, Schubart *et al.* 1965), "large berries" and "berries" (specimens in MNRJ). Birds have been seen at fruiting trees in southern Bahia, March (Pinto 1932), Linhares Reserve (J. F. Pacheco *in litt.* 1991, LPG), and Córrego Grande Biological Reserve (Fazenda Klabin), where one bird arrived in a melastome tree *Henriettea succosa* situated along the margin of Córrego Grande and plucked some fruits from the branches on which it perched; a few minutes after it had departed, the same tree was visited by a Screaming Piha *Lipaugus vociferans*, which fed in the same manner on the berries (Gonzaga *et al.* 1987).

The only data on breeding come from the available records on moult and gonad condition of specimens. Moult records almost exclusively from males show that the (apparently post-breeding) moult begins mainly in September (8) and October (apparently three records), the remainder consisting of one each for May, August, November and December (Snow 1982), while the gonads were not enlarged in two males and a female collected in June or a female in December in Espírito Santo and southern Bahia, and were slightly or half enlarged in two males in December and another in November and a female in June, from the same region (specimens in AMNH). This evidence is apparently consistent with the observed greater vocal activity in December in Espírito Santo (see above), but the moult records are acknowledgedly inconclusive.

THREATS The species's apparent dependence on primary lowland forests, most of which has been extensively cleared throughout its range, remains the one significant threat and cause of concern (E. O. Willis *in litt.* 1986, C. E. Carvalho *in litt.* 1987, B. M. Whitney *in litt.* 1987, D. F. Stotz *in litt.* 1988; for a full discussion of this habitat loss see Sick and Teixeira 1979).

MEASURES TAKEN The species is protected under Brazilian law (Bernardes *et al.* 1990). It has been recorded from Monte Pascoal National Park, Córrego Grande and Sooretama Biological Reserves, the privately owned CVRD reserves at Porto Seguro and Linhares, Duas Bocas and Ilha do Cardoso State Parks, and possibly also occurs in other protected forest areas within its range, where populations should persist so long as they continue to be preserved.

MEASURES PROPOSED Although biological studies of the species are likely to prove difficult, given its evidently retiring nature, they are needed to obtain a clearer picture of its habitat requirements and population dynamics. The Linhares Reserve has been suggested as an ideal place for such studies (B. M. Whitney *in litt.* 1987). Surveys are also needed to locate any new populations of the species, particularly now that its song has been recorded (B. M. Whitney *in litt.* 1987) and could be used to facilitate its detection. The conservation of the Pedra Branca forests at Murici is a self-evident need, this apparently being the largest remaining continuous forest area in extreme north-eastern Brazil (Teixeira 1987) and holding several other threatened birds (see Remarks under Alagoas Foliage-gleaner *Philydor novaesi*).

REMARKS (1) E. O. Willis *in litt.* (1986) mentioned this species from four unspecified localities in the state. (2) A record from a locality on the southern coast of Paraná (Snow 1985: 52) has not been confirmed, and may involve a misidentification (Straube 1990).

WHITE-CHEEKED COTINGA *Zaratornis stresemanni* K[12]

This cotinga is confined to western Peru, at elevations ranging from 3,400 to 4,250 m, where it is a mistletoe specialist inhabiting Polylepis *woodland. These patchily distributed woods are generally small in extent and thus vulnerable, and in places they have diminished owing to cutting by locals; but two areas where the species is common appear to be safe.*

DISTRIBUTION The White-cheeked Cotinga (see Remarks) is known under 15 localities in La Libertad, Ancash, Lima and Ayacucho departments, western Peru, most of which are *Polylepis* or mixed *Polylepis–Gynoxys* woods at 3,250 to 4,250 m, while at least one is a mixed wood at 2,500-2,900 m and apparently not a breeding area (Parker 1981). Coordinates in the following account are from Stephens and Traylor (1983) and IGM (1971, 1972, 1973, 1975, 1978b), with localities as follows:

La Libertad Tayabamba (8°17'S 77°18'W), in the central Andes, whence comes a sight record at 3,250 m (the species presumably also inhabits *Polylepis* woods in the western Andes in this department) (Parker 1981);

Ancash (Cordillera Blanca) above (i.e. south of) Yánac (8°37'S 77°52'W), and Quebrada Tútapac (c.8°40'S 77°49'W), 25 km by trail south of Yánac, whence come specimens (in ANSP, LSUMZ) taken at 3,950-4,550 m (also Parker 1981, NK); Quebrada Paron (c.8°58'S 77°39'W), north-east of Laguna Paron, on the western slope at 4,200-4,400 m, and 1 km south-west of Laguna Paron (9°00'S 77°41'W), also on the western slope at 3,400-4,050 m (Frimer and Møller Nielsen 1989); Quebrada Morococha (c.9°03'S 77°34'W), on the eastern slope (TAP); Quebrada Llanganuco (c.9°05'S 77°39'W), on the western slope between 3,400 and 4,300 m (Parker 1981); Quebrada Ishinca (9°20'S 77°31'W), on the western slope between 3,950 and 4,400 m, and upper Quebrada Rurichinchay (c.9°22-23'S 77°16-19'W), on the eastern slope at 3,800-4,000 m (Frimer and Møller Nielsen 1989); Quebrada Pucavado (9°41'S 77°14'W), on the eastern slope at 4,150 m (Fjeldså 1987; specimen in ZMUC), and at 3,900 m further east in the same valley (Fjeldså 1987);

Lima surroundings of Pueblo Quichas (previously Hacienda Quichas, at c.10°34'S 76°45'W), north of Oyón, whence come records (with specimens in MHNJP, ZMUC) between 3,980-4,200 m (also Fjeldså 1987); Quebrada Quicar (east of Chancay at 11°35'S 77°16'W), at c.3,700 m (Parker 1981); upper Santa Eulalia valley (c.13 km west of Milloc, at c.11°35'S 76°22'W), records (with specimens in AMNH, LSUMZ, MHNJP) from between 3,600 and 4,200 m (Parker 1981, Fjeldså 1987); Zárate (c.11°53'S 76°27'W), near San Bartolomé, with records (specimens in AMNH, LSUMZ, MNHJP) at 2,700-2,900 m (also Koepcke 1954); above (south-west of) Hortigal (c.12°47'S 75°44'W), with records (specimens in MHNJP, ZMUC) between 3,800 and 4,350 m (Fjeldså 1987);

Ayacucho Pampa Galeras (14°40'S 74°23'W), whence come sight records and photos of nests at (3,650) 3,900-3,950 m (Parker 1981, Fjeldså 1987, TAP).

This species undoubtedly occurs in extreme north-western Arequipa department (adjacent to the Ayacucho locality) (Parker 1981), but not further south, as an investigation of the apparently suitable *Polylepis* woods above Chuquibamba in 1987 showed no trace of the bird or its preferred food-plants, although unidentified mistletoes were common in the brushland at lower elevations (Fjeldså 1987), probably dispersed by emberizines like Blue-and-yellow Tanager *Thraupis bonariensis* and Mourning Sierra-finch *Phrygilus fruticeti* (NK).

POPULATION A highly speculative estimate of the entire population would be in the order of 3,000 individuals, but actual numbers may be anywhere between 1,500 and 6,000.

In Lima department, the largest known concentration of the White-cheeked Cotinga is at Pueblo Quichas, where it was found to be common, with a population estimated at 500 birds in 1987 (Fjeldså 1987, NK). It has also been reported as fairly common in the upper Santa Eulalia valley (Parker 1981, Fjeldså 1987) and above Hortigal (Fjeldså 1987). In Ancash department, at least 40 were found at Quebrada Tútapac (TAP), with a sizeable population possibly also on the eastern slope of Cordillera Blanca, where it was found to be fairly common at Quebrada Morococha (TAP), although only a few were recorded at Quebrada Pucavado (Fjeldså 1987). Frimer and Møller Nielsen (1989) only recorded the species at four of 16 *Polylepis* woodlands investigated, most in Quebrada Paron, where five birds were seen. At Pampa Galeras, Ayacucho department, although reported relatively common by Parker (1981), Fjeldså (1987) only found a few birds.

ECOLOGY The White-cheeked Cotinga inhabits *Polylepis* or mixed *Polylepis–Gynoxys* woods at 3,250 to 4,300 m, but during the dry season (August to November) it may also be found down to 2,700 m in mixed woodlands of *Oreopanax*, *Escallonia* and other trees (Parker 1981, Fjeldså 1987, Fjeldså and Krabbe 1990).

It usually occurs alone or in pairs, but may rarely be found in feeding aggregations of four to ten birds (Parker 1981). Although often perching atop a tree on an exposed branch (Parker 1981), it spends most of its time hidden in the foliage (NK), where it feeds on loranthacean mistletoe berries of *Tristerix* and possibly *Ligaria* (Parker 1981). In northern Ancash and central Lima (Santa Eulalia valley) the bird eats *Tristerix chodatianus* (Parker 1981), in central Lima (Zárate) *Tristerix secundus* (Koepcke 1958), in northern and southern Lima *Tristerix longebrachteatum* (Fjeldså 1987); however, these may all be the same species (NK). Parker (1981) gave the food-species in Ayacucho as probably *Ligaria cuneifolia*. The cotinga always regurgitates the (unusually large) seeds of the berries, and may be the only disperser of these plants above 3,000 m (Parker 1981). These mistletoes apparently produce fruit throughout the year, though less abundantly during the dry season (August to October), which may account for the post-breeding dispersal of part of the cotinga population to lower elevations at this time (Parker 1981).

Nest-building has been observed in Lima in March, when birds with enlarged gonads have been collected in Ancash and Lima (Parker 1981; specimens in ZMUC). In May, five nests with eggs and young have been found in Lima and Ancash, all of which were on north-facing slopes and were well-made, rather deep open cups placed within large clumps of mistletoes: the four nests that could be inspected closely all had three eggs or young (Parker 1981).

THREATS Despite its restricted geographical and elevational distribution, the White-cheeked Cotinga does not yet appear to be a seriously threatened species (Parker 1981); however, *Polylepis* woodland is generally a threatened habitat (Fjeldså 1987). Simpson (1977) and Smith (1977) postulated that the patchy distribution of *Polylepis* woodland is largely autecological, but Ellenberg (1958), Ferreyra (1977), Jordan (1983) and Fjeldså (1987) believed man to have had a great impact on its distribution, mainly by clearance for cultivation and grazing, cutting for firewood, roof-beams and fence-rails, burning for maintaining young grass, and extensive grazing by goats and sheep.

In the Tunari National Park, Cochabamba, Bolivia, *Polylepis* has regenerated well in dense, tall grass, and the theory that *Polylepis* is excluded by steppic vegetation must therefore be questioned (Fjeldså 1987). The local people around the large *Polylepis* woods near Hortigal in southern Lima department, where a good population of the cotinga exists, thought of the woods as potential sources for a charcoal-burning industry and were apparently unaware of the danger of soil erosion and rain-catchment loss (Fjeldså 1987). Even within the Huascarán National Park, in the Cordillera Blanca, Ancash department, the *Polylepis* forests are threatened: in general uncontrolled burning for grazing areas and cutting for firewood seems to be the major threat, many woodlands having already been destroyed, and signs of soil erosion can already be seen at several localities; furthermore the woodland which shows the biggest avian uniqueness index, Quebrada Rurichinchay, which prior to 1980 was the most heavily vegetated valley in Cordillera Blanca, has been extensively deforested since this date, owing in part to use of the wood for melting silver at the local mine at Tingo (Frimer and Møller Nielsen 1989). Extensive cutting for a furniture industry in the Huantar area occurs in some of the largest forest tracts within the park, especially in Quebradas Carhuascanchas (around Lake Potrero), Rurec and Rurichinchay (Fjeldså 1987). At Quebrada Llanganuco the *Polylepis* woodlands were noticeably degraded between 1980 and 1987 (P. K. Donahue *in litt.* 1990). The White-cheeked Cotinga must be adversely affected by this development.

MEASURES TAKEN *Polylepis* woodland where this species has been recorded occurs within the Pampa Galeras National Reserve, Ayacucho department (6,500 ha), and in Huascarán National Park, Cordillera Blanca, Ancash department (340,000 ha) (IUCN 1992: see Threats). The planting of *Eucalyptus* around Yánac village in the 1920s and 1930s lessened the local need for *Polylepis* wood, and the *Polylepis* woodland south of Yánac is now left largely untouched (Parker 1981). The *Polylepis* around Pueblo Quichas north of Oyón, northern Lima department, where the largest population of this cotinga exists, is maintained as a mosaic of fields, moderately grazed meadows and forest patches with quite large *Polylepis* trees in certain places (Fjeldså 1987). This area could probably serve as a fine model for the sustainable use of *Polylepis* woodland (Fjeldså 1987).

MEASURES PROPOSED Parker (1981) strongly recommended the establishment of a *Polylepis* reserve in Lima department, as it would greatly facilitate badly needed studies of the flora and fauna of this distinctive environment. The following measures suggested by Frimer and Møller Nielsen (1989) for Cordillera Blanca are largely recommended for the rest of the species's range, given that information campaigns should be carried out at key sites with only a few communities.

Information campaigns about the risk involved in shortsighted exploitation are urgently needed, and local inhabitants should be made aware of the high risk of soil erosion after deforestation, and of the fertile soils formed in *Polylepis* woods.

Cutting for firewood should be dealt with by rotational use, whereby cutting, burning and grazing is temporarily prevented locally to permit regeneration, and to maintain the forests as a renewable resource (the east side of the cordillera has areas with mining of anthracite).

Burning for grazing should be restricted to parts of the flat riverplain grasslands, and not the woods up the valley slopes, with vegetation fringing the main rivers being secured to permit vertical movements for birds (and other wild animals) without having to leave forest habitats.

Planting of eucalyptus (which owing to its high phenol content has a detrimental effect on the soil) is not recommended, the avian species diversity of these plantations is usually low, and planting inside the national park should therefore be prevented. As shade and shelter for the cultivation of crops near houses, *Polylepis* and *Gynoxys* hedges seem valuable and, unlike *Eucalyptus*, apparently give a fine soil. *Polylepis* hedges may also attract some *Polylepis*-adapted birds, although this may depend on the distance of these hedges from other *Polylepis* habitats (Fjeldså 1987: see also Measures Taken).

A special effort should be made to secure the extremely valuable Quebrada Rurichinchay. An information campaign and a dialogue with the families living in the upper reaches as well as in the small villages at the quebrada entrance should include a model for sustainable use of *Polylepis* woodland, and the Tingo mine should be offered an alternative resource for melting silver (e.g. coal).

The *Polylepis* woods in Cordillera Blanca are also inhabited by three other threatened species of bird: Ash-breasted Tit-tyrant *Anairetes alpinus*, Plain-tailed Warbling-finch *Poospiza alticola* and Rufous-breasted Warbling-finch *Poospiza rubecula* (see relevant accounts), and the initiatives outlined above should be extended to and take into consideration the requirements of these species (see also White-tailed Shrike-tyrant *Agriornis andicola* account).

REMARKS The White-cheeked Cotinga was described as a monotypic genus, *Zaratornis* (Koepcke 1954) on the basis of its distinct skull structure. Although later merged with the genus *Ampelion* (Snow 1973), an arrangement followed by Parker (1981), we here use the traditional treatment in accordance with Lanyon and Lanyon (1989), although these authors recommended the transfer of this species and genus to the plantcutters Phytotomidae (see Remarks under Peruvian Plantcutter *Phytotoma raimondii*).

BUFF-THROATED PURPLETUFT *Iodopleura pipra* V/R[10]

It is only in very recent years that this tiny canopy-dwelling frugivore has proved to be surviving in certain areas of north-east and south-east Brazil, but loss of its Atlantic Forest habitat clearly threatens it in both areas, and it requires more detailed study and some rapid intervention to secure key sites, notably around Ubatuba in São Paulo and Pedra Branca in Alagoas.

DISTRIBUTION The Buff-throated Purpletuft is known with certainty only from coastal eastern Brazil in the states of Paraíba, Pernambuco, Alagoas, Espírito Santo (no recent records), Rio de Janeiro and São Paulo; a single inland record from Lagoa Santa[1], Minas Gerais (Burmeister 1856), accepted by several authorities (von Ihering 1898, von Ihering and von Ihering 1907, Hellmayr 1915, Camargo and de Camargo 1964, Meyer de Schauensee 1966, 1982, Snow 1982), doubted by others (Hellmayr 1929b, Pinto 1944, Traylor 1979), and omitted from an ornithological review of the state (Pinto 1952), is treated with suspicion here. Its occurrence in Guyana seems entirely improbable (see Snow 1982, Remarks 1). In the following account, records are given from north to south with coordinates from Paynter and Traylor (1991).

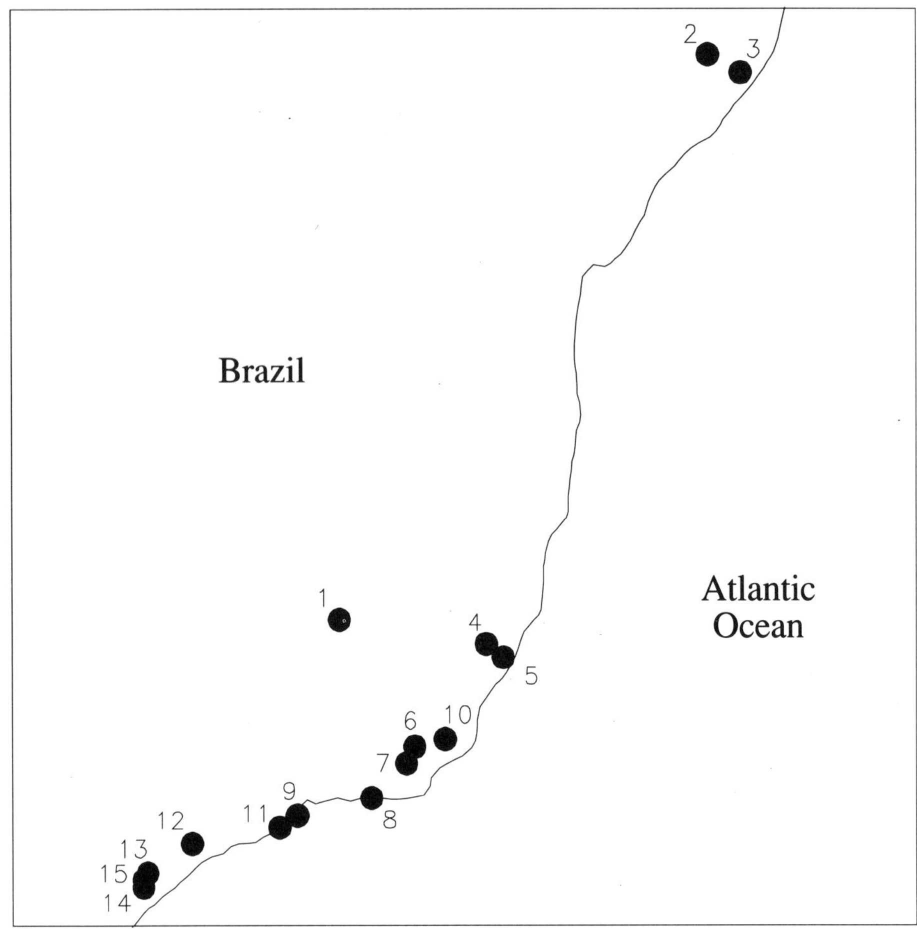

Paraíba Two birds were collected in the vicinity of Mamanguape, May 1989 (Teixeira *et al.* 1990).

Pernambuco A bird was collected at Garanhuns[2], July 1957 (specimen in USNM; see Remarks 1), and the species was recorded again there recently (Teixeira *et al.* 1990). The only other record is from Usina Cruangi, Timbaúba, March 1990 (P. S. M. da Fonseca *per* A. G. M. Coelho *in litt.* 1991).

Alagoas The species was located near Murici in May 1984 (Teixeira *et al.* 1987, 1990; see Remarks 2) and four birds were seen at Pedra Branca[3] ("Serra Branca"), 500 m, near Murici, on 20 and 21 October 1990 (J. F. Pacheco and B. M. Whitney *in litt.* 1991; see Remarks 2 under Alagoas Foliage-gleaner *Philydor novaesi*), with a further record there in January 1991 (J. F. Pacheco verbally 1992).

Espírito Santo Records are from two localities: Jatiboca[4], 20°05'S 40°55'W, 900 m, November 1940 (Camargo and de Camargo 1964; see also Schubart *et al.* 1965: 97) and December 1940 (H. Sick verbally 1988; see Ecology); and "Braço do Sul"[5] (rio Jucu Braço Sul), 500 m, April 1897 (Hellmayr 1915, Camargo and de Camargo 1964; see Remarks 3).

Rio de Janeiro Older specimens are known to have been collected at Cantagalo[6] (Cabanis 1874, von Ihering 1900a), Nova Friburgo[7] (Sclater 1888), the "region of Rio de Janeiro"[8] (presumably the city rather than the state) (Hellmayr 1915), and near Parati[9] in the far south-west on the lower slopes (under 500 m) of the Serra do Mar, June 1941 (Berla 1944). Modern records (east to west) are from Desengano State Park[10], 890 m, October 1986 (J. F. Pacheco verbally 1988), 670 m, October 1989 (B. M. Whitney *in litt.* 1991); Fazenda União, near Casimiro de Abreu, July and November 1990; Macaé de Cima (rio Macaé headwaters, south of Nova Friburgo), 1,000 m, May 1986; Serra dos Órgãos National Park, March and July 1991; Hotel Santa Mônica, rio Bonito, Itatiaia (town), 800 m, August 1988 (all four preceding records from J. F. Pacheco verbally 1992); and near São Roque and Parati around the base of the Serra da Bocaina, several times since October 1989 (B. M. Whitney *in litt.* 1991, J. F. Pacheco verbally 1992).

São Paulo Records are from near Ubatuba[11] (the key site for the species in the state: H. Sick verbally 1988), where it has been found since July 1979 (Willis and Oniki 1981a, 1985, 1988a, B. M. Whitney *in litt.* 1991; see Ecology); near Itapecerica da Serra[12] (the south-western outskirts of São Paulo city), where one specimen was collected at km 60 (now km 314) of highway BR-116 (Willis and Oniki 1985); Ribeirão Fundo[13], c.24°15'S 47°45'W, July and September 1961, and nearby at Boa Vista, 24°35'S 47°38'W, July 1960 (specimen in FMNH), Bela Vista, untraced but like Boa Vista near the rio Ipiranga[14], August 1960, and along the rio Ipiranga, September 1962 (specimens in MZUSP; also Camargo and de Camargo 1964); near Registro[15], at forest edge by highway BR-116, c.110 km from São Paulo city, August 1969 (H. Sick verbally 1988); and Iguape, undated (specimen in MHNG).

POPULATION Numbers are not known, but the relatively sparse records from an area which has been well explored by ornithologists is an indication that it is generally rare and perhaps patchy in abundance. However, its call is similar to those of other purpletufts *Iodopleura* and, once learnt, can be picked out confidently, so that the species has now been seen "numerous times" since 1989 in the Serra da Bocaina lowlands of Rio de Janeiro state (B. M. Whitney *in litt.* 1991). At Ubatuba in August 1986 two pairs nested within 70 m of each other, and a third pair was noted at one stage "wandering together" 500 m away (Willis and Oniki 1988a), suggesting a reasonable local density.

ECOLOGY The Buff-throated Purpletuft is apparently largely a coastal forest species, keeping much to the canopy but also frequenting secondary and disturbed growth, as witness the nesting records from forest underplanted with cocoa (see below). One specimen collected in the mountains in Espírito Santo was 5 m high in a tree in young secondary growth (H. Sick verbally 1988); another, from the south coast of Rio de Janeiro, was sitting on a dead twig of an orange tree in an open area with plantations and young second growth (*capoeira*) near old secondary forest (Berla 1944, Camargo and de Camargo 1964). Two specimens collected in Sao Paulo were perched quietly in branches of leafless trees 8 m in height at the edge of primary forest rich in palms *Euterpe edulis*, nearly at sea level (Camargo and de Camargo 1964). Recent experience in Alagoas, Rio de Janeiro and São Paulo suggests that this purpletuft associates with a single species of tall, fine-leaved leguminous tree, widespread and locally fairly common in eastern Brazilian forests and often holding clumps of mistletoe (B. M. Whitney *in litt.* 1991). Birds are described as resting on the highest branches of trees, favouring dead limbs (mainly those of giant, fine-leaved mimosas), and living in groups of 4-10, feeding on tender berries, especially those of mistletoes (Loranthaceae) growing high in the trees, never chasing insects (but see below) nor descending to the ground (Descourtilz 1854-1856; also Berla 1944).

The stomach of one specimen from Espírito Santo contained a small quantity of vegetable remains (H. Sick verbally 1988), and two others from São Paulo contained several seeds of the mistletoe *Struthantus concinnus* (Camargo and de Camargo 1964). Food of adults is certainly predominantly mistletoe berries (Willis and Oniki 1988a, B. M. Whitney *in litt.* 1991), but birds have also been seen hover-plucking at the leaves of the unidentified leguminous tree with which it seems associated, as if picking off tiny arthropods (B. M. Whitney *in litt.* 1991). Food brought to nestlings consisted of mistletoe berries, but also small insects caught in the air or off a twig or trunk near the nest; early in the morning, one adult regurgitated 14 fruits for a single feed, with feeding peaks occurring from 06h33 to 09h24, 10h12 to 11h13, and 15h08 to 15h48 (Willis and Oniki 1988a). An aggressive interaction with a Sharpbill *Oxyruncus cristatus* over fruit has been witnessed at the Ubatuba site (M. Pearman *in litt.* 1992).

Two (tiny cup) nests of the species, placed on high branches of 20-25 m tall leafless leguminous trees (both "farinha seca", apparently planted to shade cocoa) were found near Ubatuba with one young each on 10 August 1986, and it was judged from the size of the young in relation to the adults and to the nests that the eggs had been laid in early to mid-July (the coldest time of the year in southern Brazil) and that the clutch-size must always be one (Willis and Oniki 1988a). A further nest with a three-quarters grown chick was found near Ubatuba, this time on 11 October 1991, although again on a thin bare limb in the canopy of a nearly bare tree amidst second growth over an extensive patch of "small-leaved" bamboo, some 12 m above ground and fully exposed to the elements (J. L. Rowlett and B. M. Whitney *in litt.* 1991). In the mountains of Espírito Santo the species was only noticed from late October to early December: three birds seen in November were believed newly arrived on migration, one being an adult male in complete moult with slightly enlarged testes; an individual seen in December was in full song (H. Sick verbally 1988). The statement that in Espírito Santo the species "breeds in the mountains, afterwards emigrating and undergoing a complete moult" (Sick 1985) was based on these observations (H. Sick verbally 1988), but is challenged by the discovery of birds nesting on the coast during winter (Willis and Oniki 1988a; see above). However, Willis and Oniki's (1988a) counter-suggestion, that the species nests in winter in coastal forests and occurs in the highlands as a postbreeding summer wanderer, does not seem to fit Sick's observation of a male in full song in December, unless birds are territorial at that time, nor does it entirely square with the recent breeding record from October, nor the records near Casimiro de Abreu in both July and November.

THREATS Accepting that purpletufts appear to require bare trees in which to nest, midwinter breeding may be advantageous because (a) more such trees are available and hence less likely to attract perching avian predators, (b) the midday sun and diurnal temperatures are both lower at that time, and (c) mistletoes may be in greater abundance; against this, such use of relatively unprotected lowland coastal forests renders the species much more at risk than previously thought, since this habitat is rapidly being removed for farms and beach homes (Willis and Oniki 1988a). Destruction of forest at Pedra Branca in Alagoas is also a major problem (see Threats under Alagoas Foliage-gleaner).

MEASURES TAKEN The Buff-throated Purpletuft is protected under Brazilian law (Bernardes *et al.* 1990). It has been recorded from Desengano State Park. There are several forest reserves in mountain localities along the Serra do Mar where the species might occur, perhaps most notably the Bocaina National Park in Rio de Janeiro and São Paulo.

MEASURES PROPOSED This bird requires urgent study to determine its status, distribution (including seasonal displacements) and ecology, something that ought to be achievable given the new insights concerning its voice and ecology. Such work should include forest around Ribeirão Fundo and Registro in the south of São Paulo, forest in the Serra do Mar at Ubatuba and Parati on the São Paulo–Rio de Janeiro border, and the Desengano State Park. Forest in the Ubatuba area needs to be secured from elimination for farms and houses. An initiative to preserve forest at Pedra Branca in Alagoas needs urgent impetus (see Measures Proposed and Remarks under Alagoas Foliage-gleaner). It is not known what forest might remain at Garanhuns in Pernambuco, but it is worth noting that Garanhuns is one of several extensive mountain humid forest refuges surrounded by dry caatinga in the north-east (see de Andrade-Lima 1982).

REMARKS (1) Claims for a distinct subspecies *leucopygia* in British Guyana are based on two specimens obtained in 1877 from a London dealer (Salvin 1885) and described as "trade skins of the characteristic 'Demerara' preparation" (Hellmayr 1929b). However, the provenance of these specimens is problematic, and they may have come, despite their manner of preparation, from the east Brazilian coast somewhere north of the known range of nominate *pipra* (Snow 1982). This view is now greatly supported by the previously undocumented specimen in USNM from Pernambuco (labelled "*leucopygia*" but seemingly identical to nominate *pipra* except for an indistinct off-white line across the rump), and by the recent records of birds in Alagoas (which had conspicuous white rumps: B. M. Whitney *in litt.* 1991) and Pernambuco (see Distribution). However, it seems that the white rump is not a character unique to north-eastern birds, as some south-eastern birds show it (B. M. Whitney *in litt.* 1991), including one museum specimen (see Camargo and de Camargo 1964). (2) The sight record (and nest find) near Murici attributed to the Amazonian White-browed Purpletuft *Iodopleura isabellae* (Teixeira *et al.* 1987) was very surprising, implying that *I. pipra* and *I. isabellae* are sympatric in the north-east Brazilian mountains, but is now assumed to have been a misidentification involving *pipra* (Teixeira *et al.* 1990). (3) Paynter and Traylor (1991) could not trace Braço do Sul precisely, but Camargo and de Camargo (1964) cited a source that indicates its junction with the rio Jucú c.8 km above Viana, i.e. 20°25'S 40°30'W as read from GQR (1991).

KINGLET COTINGA *Calyptura cristata* E/Ex[4]

Deforestation within a range apparently restricted to foothills to the north of Rio de Janeiro city, Brazil, appears to be responsible for the decline to (near) extinction of this remarkable, tiny cotinga, which from the evidence of skins and one nineteenth-century record was not uncommon even in secondary habitat 150 years ago, but which has not been recorded this century.

DISTRIBUTION The Kinglet Cotinga (see Remarks 1) was described from a specimen collected in Brazil and believed to have come from "Rio de Janeiro" (Hellmayr 1929b). This has been interpreted (Pinto 1944, Traylor 1979, Snow 1982) to mean the vicinity of Rio de Janeiro city, and generally accepted thus (Sick and Pabst 1968, Sick and Teixeira 1979, Scott and Brooke 1985, Sick 1985); however, the possibility cannot be discounted that the original collector, Delalande, extended his collecting activities further inland in the state of Rio de Janeiro, visiting for instance the locality of Sumidouro (see, e.g. Pinto 1979: 90-91). The only other accepted localities for the species, which is known from as many as 45 or more nineteenth-century skins (in AMNH, ANSP, BMNH, IRSNB, MCML, MCZ, MNHN, NHMW, UMZC, USNM, ZMB, ZMK; also Fisher 1981, Krabbe undated), are Cantagalo (Cabanis 1874, von Ihering 1990a), Rosário (Fazenda Rosário, c.22°16'S 42°32'W, in Paynter and Traylor 1991), sometime between February 1827 and July 1828 (Krabbe undated; see Remarks 2), and Nova Friburgo (Burmeister 1856, Sclater 1888, von Ihering 1900a), this last having been mistaken as the type-locality by King (1978-1979) and Scott and Brooke (1985). Its listing for the state of Espírito Santo (Ruschi 1953), although admitted by Meyer de Schauensee (1966, 1982), has been called in doubt (King 1978-1979) and is not accepted here. A statement that the species is found in the whole Brazil (Descourtilz 1854-1856) is patently erroneous.

POPULATION Unrecorded for more than a century, the species has long been on lists of threatened birds (Sick 1969, 1972, 1985, King 1978-1979, Sick and Teixeira 1979) and has been feared nearly, if not actually, extinct (King 1978-1979). It was not found during a survey from December 1981 to January 1982 in a tract of forest of about 1,200 ha, 850-1,500 m, at Serra da Sibéria, around the highest peaks in the Nova Friburgo area (Scott and Brooke 1985). These researchers considered that prior to this survey no serious ornithological work had been conducted in the area (see Distribution) for many years, and that it is possible that this was a very local species of intermediate elevations which was exterminated during the main forest clearances earlier this century. Nevertheless, as Collar and Andrew (1988) pointed out, the rediscovery of the Black-hooded Antwren *Formicivora erythronotos*, also originally reported from Nova Friburgo (see relevant account), gives some small hope of the species's survival elsewhere.

ECOLOGY Most information on the Kinglet Cotinga's habits comes from (the not necessarily reliable) Descourtilz (1854-1856), who stated that it inhabited the interior mountains, preferring higher and wilder places, being found in the virgin forests climbing about in all directions on vines or exploring clumps of *Tillandsia* bromeliads in search of small berries or insects and dew (it was fond of "marianeira" fruits, and seemed to be most abundant at their ripening season, although it could be seen throughout the year); most frequently, however, the species was found in second growth in abandoned clearings, where it lived in pairs, always keeping moving among the middle-height foliage, never going up to the treetops, and calling back and forth with a surprisingly loud voice. Notes by P. W. Lund (assembled by Krabbe undated) indicate that he collected immature males on 3 January and 15 June, and that the stomach contents of these and a third bird comprised insects (two cases) and apparently seeds (one) (see Remarks 2).

THREATS Forest clearance has been particularly extensive in the Nova Friburgo region, with very little now left below 1,000 m anywhere in the area, all the valley floors and large patches of hillside having been cleared up to 1,200 m; good primary forest occurs only above 1,150 m, with elfin forest taking over the ridges from 1,420 m to the summits at 1,500 m; there are, however, some good patches of secondary forest down to 920 m (Scott and Brooke 1985). The situation is not different around Cantagalo, where virtually no forest has been left (J. F. Pacheco *in litt.* 1991).

MEASURES TAKEN The species is protected under Brazilian law (Bernardes *et al.* 1990).

MEASURES PROPOSED Renewed surveys are needed to rediscover the Kinglet Cotinga and to provide information on its ecology and status; nothing concerted has been done in this regard, and it is time that a systematic review of forest cover was undertaken in the Nova Friburgo region (including the areas near Cantagalo and extending towards the Serra dos Órgãos and towards Desengano State Park, using up-to-date satellite images and the most recent maps, followed by a major effort to visit and search them all, very much in line with the considerable initiative shown in Oliver and Santos (1991) when reviewing the status of certain mammals further to the north. Such work could, of course, be done with a view to the conservation of other species as well, but certainly making the Kinglet Cotinga the main target. Further collection of specimens should not be countenanced.

REMARKS (1) The allocation of this tiny, highly distinctive kinglet-like species, which occupies its own genus, to the Cotingidae, based on its tarsal scutellation and foot structure, has always been accepted, although from its size and plumage one might suppose it could be placed in the Pipridae or Tyrannidae (Snow 1982). (2) Most birds taken by P. W. Lund at the Swiss colony Rosário were from the adjacent mountain called Morro Queimado (Krabbe undated). For what it is worth, one of Lund's three specimens was noted as "hopping about in shrubbery" and another as "hopping about in a tree and giving an almost sparrow-like chirp" (Krabbe undated).

CINNAMON-VENTED PIHA *Lipaugus lanioides* V/R[10]

Identification problems may have hindered a true appreciation of the range of this cotinga from south-east Brazil, which seems to occupy foothill and lower montane forest and to depend heavily on certain palm fruits. It has become rare, and merits close ecological study.

DISTRIBUTION The Cinnamon-vented Piha (see Remarks 1) is endemic to south-eastern Brazil from Espírito Santo and south-eastern Minas Gerais south to Paraná (no records since 1946) and Santa Catarina (no recent records). A record from Pelotas, Rio Grande do Sul, is usually not accepted (von Ihering 1898, von Ihering and von Ihering 1907, Hellmayr 1929b, Pinto 1944, Snow 1982, Belton 1984-1985), although Sick (1985) included this state in the species's range. Identification problems are such that the more northerly and lowland records, although reproduced here, have to be regarded with severity (even museum specimens have been confused with Screaming Piha *Lipaugus vociferans* – see Remarks 2 – and sight records without tape-recordings, particularly by first-time or one-off visitors to the species's range, need to be scrupulously documented and scrupulously evaluated).

Bahia A bird, probably this species, was seen at the CVRD Porto Seguro Reserve in February 1989 (J. F. Pacheco *in litt.* 1991). This report parallels one of the species from Monte Pascoal National Park, June 1990, following an earlier but uncertain report from A. Greensmith, September 1979, from this same area (Gardner and Gardner 1990b). These require further substantiation before it can be satisfactorily agreed that the bird ranges into the south of the state.

Espírito Santo Records are (north to south) from Sooretama Biological Reserve, January 1981 (Scott and Brooke 1985), in June 1987 (P. K. Donahue *in litt.* 1987), and possibly in February 1986 (C. E. Carvalho *in litt.* 1987; see also Remarks 2); Jatiboca (near Itarana), May and August 1940, January and August 1941 (five specimens in MNRJ); Santa Teresa, between 680 and 850 m, June to August 1940, January 1941, September 1943, October 1964 and May 1966 (eight specimens in DZMG and MNRJ; also Ruschi 1969); Augusto Ruschi (Nova Lombardia) Biological Reserve (at Santa Teresa), September 1979 (A. Greensmith *per* D. Willis *in litt.* 1988), almost annually in small numbers from October 1980 to October 1990 (TAP), with other sightings over the same period in the months of June, July, August, September and October (Gonzaga *et al.* 1987, Gardner and Gardner 1990b, M. Pearman *in litt.* 1990, Whitney *in litt.* 1990, B. C. Forrester *in litt.* 1992); Chaves, Santa Leopoldina, August and September 1942 (Pinto 1944; eight specimens in MCZ and MZUSP); Duas Bocas Forest Reserve (near Cariacica), 700 m, February 1987 (C. E. Carvalho *in litt.* 1987); "Braço do Sul" (rio Jucu, Braço Sul), June 1896 (Hellmayr 1915, 1929b); Segredo do Veado, Serra do Caparaó, 900 m, October 1929 (specimen in AMNH). One undated specimen (in MNRJ) is labelled "Caparaó, Espírito Santo".

Minas Gerais Records (north to south) are: Serra do Cipó National Park, 1980 (A. Brandt *in litt.* 1987); Fazenda Boa Esperança, north of São José da Lagoa (now Nova Era), September and October 1940 (Pinto 1944); Rio Doce State Park, August 1988 (S. G. D. Cook *in litt.* 1988); Fazenda Montes Claros, near Caratinga, recently (D. B. Trent *per* B. C. Forrester *in litt.* 1992); Serra do Caraça (near Santa Bárbara), November 1973, May 1974 (two specimens in DZMG; also Carnevalli 1980), March 1989 (J. F. Pacheco *in litt.* 1991), and undated (A. Whittaker *in litt.* 1991); Mariana, 1906 (von Ihering and von Ihering 1907, Pinto 1944) and March 1926 (specimen in MNRJ from Fazenda Taveira); Serra de Matapau, Ouro Preto, May 1926 (two specimens in MNRJ); Santa Bárbara de Caparaó (now Caparaó), 900 m, October 1929 (two specimens in AMNH and LSUMZ); Porto Seguro, Piranga, September 1936 (specimen in MZUFV); Viçosa, February, April and July 1934, September 1935, August 1936 and May 1937 (eight specimens in MZUFV; also Monteiro *et al.* 1983); Serra do Brigadeiro (near Araponga), August 1991 (G. T. de Mattos verbally 1991).

Rio de Janeiro Records are (east to west) from Agulha and ribeirão Vermelho, Desengano State Park, at 550 m, June 1987 and November 1988 (J. F. Pacheco *in litt.* 1991); Cantagalo

(Cabanis 1874); Teresópolis at Fazendas Boa Fé and Comarí, May, June and September 1942 (Davis 1945, specimens in MNRJ and MZUSP); Fazenda da Serra, Itatiaia, September 1956 (specimen in LACM), this record evidently being close to or in the Itatiaia National Park, where three specimens were collected at Maromba (1,200 m) and "Engenharia" in July and September 1950 (Pinto 1954b), and where a bird was seen at 1,100 m in December 1979 (J. F. Pacheco *in litt.* 1991).

São Paulo One old record is from as far north as Franca, December 1910 (Pinto 1944). Localities in the southern half of the state (north to south) are: Fazenda Barreiro Rico, c.22°45'S 48°09'W, Anhembi, 500-600 m, November 1957, September 1959, November 1964 (four specimens in MZUSP), November 1969 (specimen in MNRJ) and 1975-1977 (Willis 1979, whence coordinates); Victoria (now Vitoriana), March and April 1901 (three specimens in AMNH), May to July 1902 (five specimens in BMNH, MCZ, USNM; also Hellmayr 1929b); Mato Dentro and Ipanema (von Pelzeln 1868-1871, Hellmayr 1929b); Ubatuba Experimental Station, October 1943 (specimen in MZUSP), São Sebastião, May 1990 (specimen in AMNH); Ribeirão Fundo, c.24°15'S 47°45'W, July 1961 (specimen in MZUSP); Fazenda Poço Grande, Juquiá, May 1940 (Pinto 1944); rio Ipiranga (near Juquiá) at several points, August 1960 (five specimens in FMNH), September and October 1962 (three specimens in MZUSP); Iporanga, on rio Ribeira de Iguape, July 1897 and December 1944 (three specimens in MZUSP; also Pinto 1944; see Remarks 3); Fazenda Intervales, Capão Bonito and Iporanga, 400 and 1,100 m, May 1991 (J. F. Pacheco *in litt.* 1991); Ilha do Cardoso State Park, 100-300 m, recently (P. Martuscelli *in litt.* 1991). Untraced localities in the state are: km 118, BR-2 (now BR-116), August 1962; Rocha (at headwaters of ribeirão Fundo), August 1961; Estação Engenheiro Ferraz, May 1964 (specimens in MZUSP); Pai Matias, October 1965 (specimen in CM); Ipiranga, "Port. v. Travessão", March 1957 (specimens in YPM).

Paraná The only record is from Açungui (25°15'S 48°20'W; not the town south-east of Castro as in GQR 1991), Serra Negra (in the present-day Guaraqueçaba Environmental Protection Area), where two birds (in MHNCI) were obtained in August 1946 (F. C. Straube *in litt.* 1991, whence coordinates).

Santa Catarina Records are from the northern coast: Joinville, July 1918 (specimen in FMNH; also Hellmayr 1929b); Hansa-Humboldt (now Corupá), 11 June 1928 and 3 July 1929 (specimens in MNRJ, AMNH); Blumenau (Hellmayr 1929b); Brusque (undated specimen in LACM). No recent records were reported by Sick *et al.* (1981).

POPULATION In general the Cinnamon-vented Piha has become rare and very local. Although it is considered "locally common and difficult to detect when not calling" (D. M. Teixeira *in litt.* 1987), most recent records have involved only a few individuals even at well-known sites, and it is unlikely that many major populations remain to be discovered. In the Augusto Ruschi reserve, the species was found every day in small to moderate numbers of up to 12 individuals, and the population there may number in the low hundreds (TAP).

ECOLOGY This species occurs primarily in foothill and lower montane forest (from c.500 to 1,000 m) in the northern part of its range, but (like many south-east Brazilian endemics) has also been found in lowland forest in São Paulo and to the south. That records from near sea level are perhaps the result of vertical (seasonal) movements (especially the possible coastal records from north of São Paulo) needs to be verified (Snow 1973). There is little doubt that this species primarily occurs above its morphologically similar congener, the Screaming Piha, in the northern part of its range (as suggested by Snow 1982). There may even be no overlap with the Screaming Piha (as suggested by Sick 1985); the evidence that suggests otherwise – i.e. the records from Sooretama and elsewhere in Espírito Santo and in Bahia – deserves consideration but requires corroboration (the once suspected altitudinal separation in congeners such as White-tailed and Mantled Hawks *Leucopternis lacernulata* and *L. polionota* and Golden-tailed and Brown-backed Parrotlets *Touit surda* and *T. melanonota* has not been upheld by new information: see relevant accounts). In the Augusto Ruschi reserve Cinnamon-vented Pihas inhabit mature forest averaging about 25 m in height; middle-storey and undergrowth palms are abundant in many places, especially a *Euterpe* (presumably *edulis*) (TAP). Males typically call/display from the crowns of mid-storey and lower canopy trees within small areas (used annually in at least September/October throughout the 1980s); three display areas were in forest with rather open undergrowth on slopes above more level, poorly drained areas where *Euterpe* was common (TAP). Leks are frequented by one to at least three but usually two males (TAP; also C. E. Carvalho *in litt.* 1987, J. F. Pacheco *in litt.* 1991, A. Whittaker *in litt.* 1991, M. Pearman *in litt.* 1992).

Birds have been observed feeding on the fruits and regurgitating the seeds of *Euterpe edulis* at both the Augusto Ruschi reserve (TAP) and Fazenda Intervales (J. F. Pacheco *in litt.* 1991); foraging sites at the former were also frequented by the threatened Blue-bellied Parrot *Triclaria malachitacea*, and the current distribution of these species might prove to be very similar (TAP). The pihas have also been seen to take smaller fig-like fruits in the tops of tall trees also frequented by Bare-throated Bellbirds *Procnias nudicollis* (TAP). Stomach contents of specimens in MNRJ and MZUFV are given as fruits or large fruits, in one case specifically "assahy" berries (i.e. palmito or juçara palm fruits). One mantid, one beetle and other insect remains, besides vegetable remains, have been recorded as food on two specimen labels (Schubart *et al.* 1965), but this record is probably in error (see Remarks 2); however, the species is listed by Willis (1979) as one which consumes large fruit and insects.

Moult records indicate that a post-breeding moult begins mainly in October and November with no clear difference between sexes, which would signify that both probably attend the nest (Snow 1982), whereas the gonads were not enlarged in a female collected in July in Santa Catarina, but were fairly enlarged in three males obtained in October in the Serra do Caparaó (specimens in AMNH and LSUMZ). This evidence is consistent with the statement that the species was active at Teresópolis in September (Davis 1945), and males were quite vocal in leks from September to November in Espírito Santo (TAP).

THREATS The fragmentation of the species's range by extensive forest destruction has been and remains the one significant threat; even if current records are from a number of protected areas, the species's ecological requirements remain very poorly known and its recorded numbers in those areas are too low to be confident about the future of the populations they hold. Furthermore, some of these reserves, such as Ilha do Cardoso in São Paulo and Desengano in Rio de Janeiro are also suffering from deforestation (P. Martuscelli *in litt.* 1991, J. F. Pacheco *in litt.* 1991). The cutting of *Euterpe* palms within standing forest may have affected populations (see Threats under Blue-bellied Parrot).

MEASURES TAKEN The species is protected under Brazilian law (Bernardes *et al.* 1990). Some of its present remnant populations should persist so long as the protected areas where they have been found continue to be preserved; but see Threats.

MEASURES PROPOSED Surveys of the species in the field are needed to confirm and monitor its continued existence in the localities where it has been recorded, particularly in areas which may prove to be important for its long-term survival (such as the Rio Doce State Park in Minas Gerais, Augusto Ruschi Biological Reserve in Espírito Santo, Itatiaia National Park in Rio de Janeiro and Ilha do Cardoso State Park in São Paulo), as well as to locate any new populations and redefine its range. A research programme into its population dynamics and habitat requirements at various sites should partner a general review of its status in these areas, whose continued protection is obviously an immediate need. Some of this work might be extended to cover similar research on the Blue-bellied Parrot, which appears to utilize the same key food-plant, as does the Black-fronted Piping-guan *Pipile jacutinga* (see relevant accounts and Ecology above).

REMARKS (1) An early suggestion that the Cinnamon-vented Piha was probably conspecific with the Screaming Piha, its range and variation being too little known to admit a final conclusion

(Hellmayr 1929b), has been discounted in the light of further knowledge (Snow 1973). (2) Two birds from Sooretama, November 1944, whose stomach contents are given (see Ecology), were identified as of this species (Schubart *et al.* 1965), but at least one, still in MNRJ, is actually a Screaming Piha (LPG), as already correctly identified in Aguirre and Aldrighi (1987); the second was not conserved (Schubart *et al.* 1965). (3) Von Ihering (1898) and von Ihering and von Ihering (1907) referred to "Iguape" as the provenance of a specimen in Museu Paulista (now MZUSP), evidently that from 1897, whose label reads "Iguape–Iporanga, R. Krone, 21.7.1897".

BANDED COTINGA *Cotinga maculata* R[11]

As a species of primary lowland Atlantic Forest in south-east Brazil, this largely frugivorous bird has suffered serious habitat loss and depends on a few key protected areas for its survival, notably Sooretama and those owned by CVRD.

DISTRIBUTION The Banded Cotinga (see Remarks 1) is endemic to the Atlantic Forest region of south-eastern Brazil from Bahia south of Salvador south through south-eastern Minas Gerais (no records since 1940) to Espírito Santo and formerly Rio de Janeiro state.

Bahia Older records are from as far north as rio Jiquiriçá; rio das Contas (Wied 1831-1833); and rio Gongogi, Cajazeiras, 300 m, June 1928 (specimen in AMNH). It is not known if any populations persist in these areas today, but ones currently exist in the small CEPLAC experimental station on the rio Jequitinhonha at Barrolândia (bird seen in October 1987: LPG) and in the CVRD Porto Seguro Reserve (birds seen in October 1986 and January 1988) (Gonzaga *et al.* 1987, B. M. Whitney *in litt.* 1988). There are two records from Monte Pascoal National Park, in September 1979 (A. Greensmith *per* D. Willis *in litt.* 1988) and in July 1990 (Gardner and Gardner 1990b). Between this park and the border with Espírito Santo records are from the Braço Sul do rio Jucurucu, April 1933 (Pinto 1935), Viçoza (now Nova Viçosa) (Wied 1820-1821), and rio Mucuri (Wied 1831-1833).

Minas Gerais The only records are from São Benedito (corresponding to the present Tabaúna: see Naumburg 1935), rio Manhuaçu, 180 m, January 1930 (specimen in AMNH); and the rio Doce, left bank, on the lower rio Suaçuí, September 1940 (Pinto 1944), i.e. close to the present Rio Doce State Park.

Espírito Santo Older records are from the rio São Mateus in the nineteenth century, and May 1957 (Wied 1831-1833, Aguirre and Aldrighi 1987), and rio Doce, March 1906 (Pinto 1944). The key sites for the species in the state are Sooretama Biological Reserve (whence a specimen in MNRJ, October 1963), with recent records since 1977 (King 1978-1979, Sick and Teixeira 1979, Scott and Brooke 1985, C. E. Carvalho *in litt.* 1987) and the adjacent CVRD Linhares Reserve (see Population), with records since 1984 (Scott 1984, Collar and Gonzaga 1985, Pacheco and Fonseca 1987, B. M. Whitney *in litt.* 1987, 1990). The only other records were from the Fazenda Klabin forest (now much reduced and converted to the Córrego Grande Biological Reserve) in June 1970 and in 1973 (Sick 1972, Sick and Teixeira 1979) and in September 1979 (A. Greensmith *per* D. Willis *in litt.* 1988).

Rio de Janeiro Descourtilz (1854-1856) reported the species near Campos dos Goytacazes (now Campos) and the Morro do Frade (near Frade); it was found at Cantagalo and Nova Friburgo (von Ihering 1900a).

POPULATION Over half a century ago it was already evident that the Banded Cotinga was "far from common" (O. M. O. Pinto in Wied 1940), but this perception had been expressed long before by Wied (1820-1821), who noticed that it was locally less common than the White-winged Cotinga *Xipholena atropurpurea* (see relevant account), and this view persists in modern assessments, compounded by the fact that is it certainly seriously reduced in abundance and distribution as the result of extensive forest destruction within its range (Sick 1969, 1972, King 1978-1979, Sick and Teixeira 1979, Scott and Brooke 1985). It was considered uncommon in Sooretama, where in five sightings a minimum of three birds (all males) were involved in December/January 1980/1981 (Scott and Brooke 1985), while in the Linhares Reserve, November 1984, at least four birds were involved in five records (Scott 1984), with a similar value on 20 December 1986 of at least four individuals (three males and one female) seen from a tower (B. M. Whitney *in litt.* 1987). It has been remarked, however, that this species would appear to be rarer if all observations had to be made from ground-level (C. E. Carvalho *in litt.* 1987, B. M. Whitney *in litt.* 1987). Nevertheless, even though numbers in the much smaller reserves listed under Distribution cannot be high, the species appeared to be fairly common in the CVRD Porto Seguro Reserve in October 1986 when, apart from two females seen on and around a nest, at least four males and two females were watched feeding (Gonzaga *et al.* 1987; see Ecology).

ECOLOGY The Banded Cotinga inhabits the canopy of humid primary lowland forest (Scott and Brooke 1985, Sick 1985, Gonzaga *et al.* 1987), and the statements that it is (was) found even on the highest mountains (Descourtilz 1854-1856) and ranges through the coastal mountains (Meyer de Schauensee 1982) can be largely discounted from the evidence of the records above. There is a tendency for birds to occur very locally within small areas often also frequented by White-winged Cotingas (and often, unless this reflects observational bias, along the edges of clearings), presumably owing to the presence of as yet unidentified fruiting trees attractive to both species (NJC, LPG, TAP).

Food has been generally recorded as many types of seeds, berries and "tree" fruits, some of which colour its flesh (Wied 1831-1833, Gonzaga *et al.* 1987, B. M. Whitney *in litt.* 1987), but also including caterpillars and other insects (Descourtilz 1854-1856). Birds observed in Porto Seguro in October 1986 were feeding (in company with White-winged Cotingas) in fruiting trees around a large cleared area in the centre of the reserve, perching on the highest bare twigs of the canopy or on isolated dead trees and repeatedly flying across the clearing (Gonzaga *et al.* 1987). In Linhares, December 1986, three adult males flocked together while feeding on (possibly green) fruits in a tree (B. M. Whitney *in litt.* 1987).

Calculated dates of the onset of the post-breeding moult are in November and December (Snow 1982), which fits well with records of immature males moulting into adult plumage in January and February (specimen in AMNH; C. E. Carvalho *in litt.* 1987), and with a nest attended by an incubating female at Porto Seguro on 11 October 1986; this nest was a very slight structure of small twigs placed in the fork of an almost horizontal branch in the canopy of a fairly tall tree at the forest border (Gonzaga *et al.* 1987). This appears to be the only record of a nest of this species, apart from a report of one found inside a hollow arboreal termite nest (Sick 1985), and a statement that the nest is placed atop big trees (Descourtilz 1854-1856). That birds keep paired during the breeding season (Descourtilz 1854-1856) seems to be incorrect, on current knowledge of the habits of the genus (Snow 1982, Sick 1985) and given the apparent absence of a male at the nest found in October 1986 (NJC, LPG). Wied (1831-1833) confidently spoke of its appearance in Bahia in the cold season, on the Mucuri for instance in groups of 4-12; although this does not fit current evidence, it is by no means impossible that local movements at least of part of the population occurred when numbers of birds were much higher than today.

THREATS The massive deforestation which has taken place throughout the species's range has been regarded as the main cause of its decline (King 1978-1979, C. E. Carvalho *in litt.* 1987), and indeed the reserves in which it survives are very few and too small to be confident about the future of the populations they hold. The privately owned forest at Fazenda Klabin, although now the IBAMA-run Córrego Grande Biological Reserve, has been reduced over the past two decades from 4,000 ha to only 1,200 ha (Gonzaga *et al.* 1987), and the Monte Pascoal National Park is also under severe pressure (Redford 1989).

The brilliance of the male's plumage made it prized in the past for "feather-flower" craftwork by Indians (Cardim 1925) and Bahian nuns (Wied 1820-1821), with priests collecting 30 or 40 males apiece in the cold season to send to Salvador to support this work (Wied 1831-1833); and it has obviously been a major enticement for modern bird fanciers (Santos 1955). Capture for the cagebird trade, occurring sporadically, has thus been regarded as a threat to the species (Sick and Teixeira 1979, Sick 1985) and, although it has been seldom reported from captivity in recent decades, this is probably a simple consequence of its rarity (a view shared by W. C. A. Bokermann verbally 1991).

MEASURES TAKEN The species is listed in the Appendix I of CITES and has been protected by Brazilian law since 1973 (LPG, Bernardes *et al.* 1990). Some of its present remnant populations should persist so long as the protected areas where they occur continue to be preserved; but see Threats. On the basis of evidence under Population, the two critical areas for the species are the CVRD Porto Seguro Reserve in Bahia and the Sooretama Biological Reserve and adjacent CVRD Linhares Reserve in Espírito Santo, although the Monte Pascoal National Park holds birds and the Rio Doce State Park in Minas Gerais may prove to be important if the species is found there.

MEASURES PROPOSED The few remaining patches of forest within the species's range could still harbour small and so far undetected populations, and merit being identified and searched. Support for existing key sites is clearly imperative. More specifically, it is important that CVRD continue recognizing the importance of their reserve at Porto Seguro in Bahia and give it total protection, as they have done for their excellent reserve at Linhares.

REMARKS The Banded Cotinga is closely related to the Amazonian Purple-breasted Cotinga *Cotinga cotinga*, which it replaces in south-east Brazil, where it is the only species of the genus. An earlier view that the two species were probably conspecific (Hellmayr 1929b) has not prevailed (Traylor 1979, Snow 1982, Sick 1985).

WHITE-WINGED COTINGA *Xipholena atropurpurea* R[11]

As a species of primary lowland and adjacent foothill Atlantic Forest in eastern Brazil, this frugivore has suffered serious habitat loss and depends on a few key sites for its survival, notably Una, Sooretama, Desengano and those owned by CVRD.

DISTRIBUTION The White-winged Cotinga (see Remarks 1) is endemic to the Atlantic forest region of eastern Brazil in three adjacent north-eastern states, from Paraíba (no records since 1957) to Alagoas, and from southern Bahia south to Rio de Janeiro.

Paraíba The only record is from Mamanguape, where five birds were collected on 11, 14 and 22 July 1957 (Pinto and de Camargo 1961).

Pernambuco Two specimens in BMNH (also Sclater 1888) are merely labelled "Pernambuco" and were collected by Craven and Forbes (although the species is not mentioned by Forbes 1881). Another specimen (in AMNH) is from São Lourenço, 28-60 m (probably São Lourenço da Mata, hence close to the present-day Tapacurá Ecological Station), July 1903. The species was not found by Pinto (1940), who believed that it might have disappeared from the state (Pinto 1944), but one specimen was collected at Goiana in December 1943 (in USNM; also Lamm 1948). The only recent record is from Água Preta (A. G. M. Coelho *in litt.* 1986).

Alagoas One specimen was collected in Usina Sinimbu (near present-day Sinimbu – not Ginimbu as in GQR 1991), in March 1957 (in LACM; also Pinto and de Camargo 1961). Modern records are from the Grota do Azevedo, São Miguel dos Campos, November 1983, and Pedra ("Serra") Branca, Murici, 500 m, January 1986 (specimens in MNRJ).

Bahia Records (north to south) are from Santo Amaro, October 1913 (specimens in FMNH; also Hellmayr 1929b); Ilhéus, May 1919, June 1944 (specimens in MZUSP; also Pinto 1944); Una Biological Reserve, October 1986 (Gonzaga *et al.* 1987); Belmonte, August 1919 (Vieira 1935, Pinto 1944; this presumably the record of a pair reported by Lima 1920); CEPLAC "Gregório Bondar" experimental station on the rio Jequitinhonha at Barrolândia (birds seen in October 1987: LPG); CVRD Forest Reserve at Porto Seguro, October 1986, January and July 1988, June 1990 and July 1991 (Gonzaga *et al.* 1987, B. M. Whitney *in litt.* 1988, Gardner and Gardner 1990b, M. Pearman *in litt.* 1990, Stotz 1991); Monte Pascoal National Park, 1977 (King 1978-1979, Sick and Teixeira 1979) and June 1990 (Gardner and Gardner 1990b); Fazenda do Morro da Arara (see Remarks 2) and Mucuri (Wied 1820-1821). At least 22 specimens, in AMNH, BMNH, FMNH, LSUMZ, MCZ, MHNG, MNHN, NHMW and USNM, are merely labelled "Bahia".

Espírito Santo Older records are from the Lagoa da Arara (untraced, but not far from the Mucuri) in the nineteenth century (Wied 1831-1833, Hellmayr 1929b); rio Doce, March 1906 (Pinto 1944); and Pau Gigante (now Ibiraçu), August 1940 (specimen in MZUSP). The key site for the species in the state is Sooretama Biological Reserve (two specimens are from Córrego Joeirana – adjacent to present-day Sooretama – August and September 1939; Aguirre and Aldrighi 1987), with recent records since 1977 (Sick and Teixeira 1979, Scott and Brooke 1985, C. E. Carvalho *in litt.* 1987) and the adjacent CVRD Linhares Reserve (see Population), with records since 1984 (Scott 1984, Collar and Gonzaga 1985, Gonzaga 1986, Pacheco and Fonseca 1987, D. F. Stotz *in litt.* 1988, 1991, B. M. Whitney *in litt.* 1987, 1989, Stotz 1991). The only other fairly recent record was from the Fazenda Klabin forest (now much reduced and converted to the Córrego Grande Biological Reserve) in June 1970 (Sick 1972, who did not then disclose the identity of the site, although this is clear from context).

Rio de Janeiro A recent observation of an immature bird in the Morro da Rifa, 700 m, at Desengano State Park, on 31 August 1986 (J. F. Pacheco *in litt.* 1986, C. E. Carvalho verbally 1986) confirms a nineteenth-century record of the species's occurrence in the state, at Nova Friburgo (Burmeister 1856).

POPULATION Over half a century ago the species was considered to be still common in the forests of Espírito Santo and eastern Bahia, although its persistence in Rio de Janeiro and Pernambuco, the limits of its known range, was doubted (O. M. O. Pinto in Wied 1940). The view that the White-winged Cotinga was frequent in south-eastern Bahian forest, as around Mucuri, where it was commoner than the Banded Cotinga *Cotinga maculata* (see relevant account), had been expressed long before (Wied 1820-1821), and persists in modern records, although the species has certainly suffered an overall decline in numbers and a fragmentation of populations owing to forest destruction, which has fully justified its inclusion in lists of threatened species (King 1978-1979, Sick 1969, Sick and Teixeira 1979, Scott and Brooke 1985, Sick 1985). Although the species has proved to be much less restricted than was previously believed, as in a recent statement that it was "apparently confined to a few areas in Espírito Santo and southern Bahia" (Scott and Brooke 1985), and it is now clear that it has not become extinct at the extremes of its range, the species's stronghold is probably still the Sooretama Reserve and the adjacent CVRD Linhares Reserve in northern Espírito Santo. In Linhares, 22-25 November 1984, at least nine birds were involved in 12 records (Scott 1984), with a slightly larger value of 18 sightings, involving possibly a minimum of 12 birds on 10 different days, in August 1988 (D. F. Stotz *in litt.* 1988). Smaller numbers have been recorded on several occasions (Collar and Gonzaga 1985, Gonzaga 1986, B. M. Whitney *in litt.* 1987, 1989). Even though numbers in the much smaller reserves listed under Distribution might be expected to be low, the species appeared to be quite common in the CVRD Porto Seguro Reserve during a short visit in October 1986 when, apart from an isolated female, at least three adult males, one immature male and four females were watched feeding (see Ecology under Banded Cotinga), and during an equally brief stay in Una Biological Reserve in October 1986 at least two adult males, one immature male and two females were seen (Gonzaga *et al.* 1987); eight birds were seen at the former site on one day in June 1990 (Gardner and Gardner 1990b). However, it has been suggested that this is probably a more conspicuous species than the Banded Cotinga, and the conservation status of both is much the same (B. M. Whitney *in litt.* 1987).

ECOLOGY From the evidence of the records above, the White-winged Cotinga inhabits the canopy of lowland and adjacent foothill Atlantic Forest (e.g. also Sick 1970). Wied (1831-1833) made the interesting observation that it was only to be found in forests near to the coast.

Food has been recorded as fruits, taken in tall forest canopy and around clearings (Gonzaga *et al.* 1987, B. M. Whitney *in litt.* 1987; see Ecology under Banded Cotinga). Snow (1982) reported Sick (1970) as saying that the species was fond of the fruits of caruru *Phytolacca decandra* that grows at forest edges, but this remark appears to apply to the White-tailed Cotinga *Xipholena lamellipennis*. Wied (1831-1833) found red seed stones in stomachs, probably from *Bixa orellana*, and red cherry-like fruit, and noted that these had stained the birds' flesh orange or red. Birds seen in Una in October 1986 were seemingly part of a mixed flock in which Red-legged Honeycreepers *Cyanerpes cyaneus* and Green Honeycreepers *Chlorophanes spiza* were present (Gonzaga *et al.* 1987).

The only two records of (presumably post-breeding) moult available were from March and April (Snow 1982), but a possible (perhaps nuptial) display flight performed by an adult male was observed in Linhares in September 1989 (B. M. Whitney *in litt.* 1989), and a probable nest (not seen), hidden in a huge bromeliad clump about 18 m up in a tree at the forest edge in Sooretama, was visited twice by a female on 26 September 1977 (Sick 1979a, 1985; Snow 1982).

THREATS The massive deforestation which has taken place throughout the species's range has been regarded as the main cause of its decline (Sick and Teixeira 1979, Sick 1985, C. E. Carvalho *in litt.* 1987). The population of the species in the north-east must be at most serious risk from this phenomenon, with almost all lowland forest localities now probably entirely cleared (e.g. Teixeira 1986) and birds restricted to a few remaining but largely still unprotected forest reserves. The situation is now much different in the south, where for example the privately owned forest at Fazenda Klabin, although now the IBAMA-run Córrego Grande Biological Reserve, has been reduced over the past two decades from 4,000 ha to only 1,200 ha (Gonzaga *et al.* 1987), and the formerly 22,500 ha Monte Pascoal National Park is also under severe pressure (Redford 1989). The species has been kept in captivity (Sick 1970, King 1978-1979), and capture for the cagebird trade, where it has appeared sporadically (Sick and Teixeira 1979), is also mentioned as a factor of risk (Sick 1985). However, trade in the species appears to be extremely light, but this fact might merely be a consequence of its increasing rarity.

MEASURES TAKEN The species is protected under Brazilian law (Bernardes *et al.* 1990), and listed in the Appendix I of CITES. Some of its present remaining populations should persist so long as the protected areas where they occur continue to be preserved; but see Threats. On the basis of evidence under Distribution and Population, critical areas for the species seem to be the Pedra Branca areas in Alagoas (see Measures Proposed), Una and Porto Seguro reserves in Bahia, the Sooretama and adjacent Linhares reserves in Espírito Santo, and Desengano State Park in Rio de Janeiro.

MEASURES PROPOSED The conservation of the Pedra Branca forests at Murici is a self-evident imperative, this apparently being the largest remaining continuous forest area in extreme north-eastern Brazil (Teixeira 1987) and holding several other threatened birds (see Remarks under Alagoas Foliage-gleaner *Philydor novaesi*). Effective protection of already created reserves is clearly an equally urgent need. More specifically, it is important that CVRD continue recognizing the importance of their reserve at Porto Seguro and give it total protection, as they have done for their excellent reserve at Linhares. The few remaining patches of forest within the species's range could still harbour small and so far undetected populations, and merit being identified and searched.

REMARKS (1) The White-winged Cotinga is the only member of its genus in eastern Brazil, where it represents the closely related Amazonian allospecies Pompadour Cotinga *Xipholena punicea* and White-tailed Cotinga (Snow 1982, Sick 1985). (2) This is an untraced locality along the rio Mucuri, about 30 km from its estuary in Bahia (not Espírito Santo as in Hellmayr 1929b) according to the text in Bokermann (1957); but on Bokermann's map it is plotted on the rio Peruípe (for Peruíbe), corresponding to rio do Meio in GQR (1991).

YELLOW-BILLED COTINGA *Carpodectes antoniae* V[9]

This rare cotinga is endemic to the Pacific slope of Costa Rica and western Panama, where it relies on extensive areas of mangrove and to a lesser extent (and seasonally) adjacent foothill forests. Little is known about its ecology, but the preferred habitat has been much reduced and is under increasing pressure.

DISTRIBUTION The Yellow-billed Cotinga is found mainly in coastal mangrove and foothill forest areas along the Pacific coasts of Costa Rica and western Panama. Localities in Costa Rica are traced from the map in Slud (1964), and those in Panama from OG (1969).

Costa Rica Records extend rom north-west to south-east, those in the former area coming from: Pigres (Slud 1964), near the mouth of the río Tárcoles (Stiles and Skutch 1989); the mangroves adjacent to río La Pita and río Tárcoles (Taylor 1990); Carara Biological Reserve, through which the río Tárcoles flows (Taylor 1990); Pozo Azul (c.5 km inland of Pirrís; see below), where this species was noted alongside the near-threatened Turquoise Cotinga *Cotinga ridgwayi* in September 1886 (Ridgway 1887a) and subsequently collected there in February and March 1898 (four males and three females in AMNH, MCZ) and May 1902 (five males and two females in AMNH, CM, FMNH, MCZ, ROM) (see Remarks 1); Pirrís (or Parrita, at the mouth of the river), where the type (a male) was taken in May 1883 (Ridgway 1884), and where 22 males, five females and an immature were taken in September 1886 (Ridgway 1887b: see Remarks 2); Santa Rosa de Puriscal (above Parrita), where a post-breeding female (in MZUCR) was collected in May 1979; the estuary of the río Palo Seco (c.5 km east of Pirrís), a locality where Slud (1964) recorded the species in groups (see Population) and which Taylor (1990) mentioned as harbouring the species and having the best mangroves in the area. The most inland record is reported by Skutch (1970), who observed two males and a female over a period of four months in 1940 near Santa Rosa, and nearby across the valley of the río Pacuar (at 760 m, and c.20-25 km from the coast): these were the only places within the El General area (i.e. the mountain-rimmed basin at the head of the río Térraba valley) that he saw the species during 30 years in the area. Further south, all of the other records come from around Golfo Dulce, localities including: río Sierpe, where the species was found to be numerous (mostly males) in June 1987 (Ridgely and Gwynne 1989), and Sierpe estuary, possibly one of the most important areas, where males were seen displaying in May 1977, June 1977 and 1983 (F. G. Stiles *in litt.* 1989, 1991); Golfito, where up to six birds have been seen in mangroves along the road to the airport on the north side of town (Taylor 1990, B. M. Whitney *in litt.* 1991); and Coto, c.10 km up the río Coto estuary/river, a locality mentioned as one of the main nesting areas by F. G. Stiles (*in litt.* 1989). On the Península de Osa side of Golfo Dulce records come from: Rincón [de Osa], where Slud (1964) recorded groups, and where in January 1989 two males were seen in mangroves to the west and a male down a forest track east of town (C. S. Balchin *in litt.* 1989); and Puerto Jiménez, where nine males and three females (in AMNH, FMNH, YPM) were taken on 2-3 October 1926. A single male was seen in January 1986 between La Palmar and Cerro de Oro, on Península de Osa (M. Pearman *in litt.* 1990), and F. G. Stiles (*in litt.* 1991) occasionally recorded the species in Corcovado National Park over a number of years (outside the breeding season, in July, November and February).

Panama Records of this species come almost exclusively from the coastal lowlands of Chiriquí province, where localities include: the head of the río Corotú (behind Puerto Armuelles on Península de Burica), where a male and female were seen in February 1966 (Wetmore 1972), with two further sight records (exact locations unknown), the most recent of which was of a male in June 1982 (Ridgely and Gwynne 1989); Pedregal (8°22'N 82°26'W), where two males (in MCZ, USNM; the only specimens from Panama), were taken in coastal scrub during August 1901 (these were the only ones seen) (Wetmore 1972). Two other published records exist for Panama: to the north, seven *Carpodectes* sp. were seen in the río Cotón valley above Santa Clara (8°50'N

82°45'W: presumably on the border with Costa Rica) in July 1980, Ridgely and Gwynne (1989) presuming them to have been *antoniae* (see Remarks 3); and c.200 km further east one bird was apparently collected (the specimen was subsequently lost) in mangroves near Aguadulce during the 1920s, this record evidently prompting the remark that the species "possibly occurs (or occurred) further east" (Ridgely and Gwynne 1989).

POPULATION The general impression from the evidence below is that the species has suffered a decline that is probably much steeper overall than any one record can indicate.

Costa Rica The Yellow-billed Cotinga appears to be poorly known and very local in its distribution, although in areas where it is found (i.e. extensive mangroves) it can be common (Stiles and Skutch 1989). Despite the collection of 27 birds during September 1886 at Pirrís (see Distribution) it was suggested that the species "cannot be called common", the birds apparently being taken whilst frequenting a particular fruiting tree (Ridgway 1887b). At Pozo Azul seven birds were taken in late February and early March 1898, with a further seven collected in May 1902. Close to both Pirrís and Pozo Azul, Slud (1964) at the estuary of the río Palo Seco saw this species in "groups to the size of small flocks", suggesting that this area, at least in the past, held a significant population of the species: also at this locality, F. G. Stiles (*in litt.* 1991) recorded 2-3 males and at least one female during January of several years between 1985 and 1989. The population (possibly breeding) around Santa Rosa is impossible to assess: just one pair held a territory there (in 1940) but no evidence of breeding was forthcoming (Skutch 1970); whether or not a breeding population exists in these foothills remains unknown, but as this is the only record of apparent attempted breeding in the foothills it seems unlikely (F. G. Stiles *in litt.* 1991). The mangroves around Golfo Dulce have been identified as a key area, with Coto and Sierpe the main nesting areas, Sierpe possibly being the most important (F. G. Stiles *in litt.* 1986). This suggestion is reinforced by Ridgely and Gwynne (1989), who reported that the bird was found to be numerous during June 1987 in mangroves and adjacent fringing lowland forest along the río Sierpe (both sexes were involved but males were more numerous). As at río Palo Seco, "groups to the size of small flocks" have been recorded at Rincón (Slud 1964), but subsequently the only record seems to be of three males seen in January 1986 (C. S. Balchin *in litt.* 1989). The bird was apparently locally common at Puerto Jiménez where 12 were taken in two days during October 1926 (see Distribution).

Panama The two male Yellow-billed Cotingas collected at Pedregal in 1901 (see Distribution) were the only ones seen there at the time, but all of the recent reliable records of this species (involving just a few individuals) come from closer to the Costa Rica border, on Península de Burica (see Distribution). This peninsula is the one place where Ridgely and Gwynne (1989) have suggested that a remnant population could exist, concluding that the bird was probably never very numerous in Panama (a point supported by the paucity of distributional data), and is now very rare and localized owing to habitat destruction within western Chiriquí (see Threats). The record of seven birds in the río Cotón valley needs to be confirmed (see Measures Proposed).

ECOLOGY The majority of records of the Yellow-billed Cotinga come from or near the coast, with just a few sightings originating in the foothills to as high as 760 m (the significance of these latter records remains essentially unknown; see below). The species is normally found within extensive mangroves where it frequents the canopy and often perches in the taller trees (Ridgely and Gwynne 1989, Stiles and Skutch 1989). When not in mangroves, the bird is most often found within habitat adjacent or close to this vegetation type, and has been recorded (almost invariably) in the taller trees of adjacent fringing lowland humid forest, individuals having been seen at woodland borders and in tall treetops within woodland clearings (Slud 1964, Ridgely and Gwynne 1989, Stiles and Skutch 1989), e.g. the male seen near Cerro de Oro in January 1986 was found atop a huge tree by a river, but amongst scrubby secondary growth (M. Pearman *in litt.* 1990), while the two males collected at Pedregal were found within "coastal scrub" (Wetmore 1972; see

Distribution). Especially outside the breeding season, birds are apparently often nomadic, wandering well into the foothills in small groups (F. G. Stiles *in litt.* 1991). The most notable inland record comes from near Santa Rosa, Costa Rica, where birds (possibly attempting to breed; see below) spent much time on prominent trees at the forest edge or within clearings (a similar preference to that shown on the coast), although sometimes flying across large clearings or out of sight over the forest canopy (Skutch 1970; see below). Stiles and Skutch (1989), based presumably on this record, suggested that this species "evidently wanders widely to 760 m in foothills", Snow (1982) judging it to be "evidently rare so high up". The record from near Santa Clara, Panama, needs confirmation but, if correct, reinforces the evidence that the bird prefers rivers when away from mangroves (e.g. at Pozo Azul, near Santa Clara, Coto, near Cerro de Oro, and río Corotú: see Distribution), seemingly using them as corridors to penetrate inland.

In mangroves, at least, this species is relatively sociable, birds often recorded in loose groups (Stiles and Skutch 1989), found to be numerous along the río Sierpe (Ridgely and Gwynne 1989), and occurring in small flocks at río Palo Seco and Rincón (Slud 1964: see Population). They seemingly congregate at particular fruiting trees, Ridgway (1887b) reporting that 27 specimens were collected presumably from the same tree during a period of a few days. The fruits of Lauraceae, mistletoes and Melastomataceae have all been reported as food items taken by this species (Stiles and Skutch 1989).

Breeding data are basically lacking: the male begins to moult from January to April (Snow 1982), with immatures collected on 19 May 1902 at Pozo Azul (specimen in ROM) and in mid-September 1886 at Pirrís (Ridgway 1887b): a post-breeding female (in MZUCR) was collected in May 1979 (see Distribution), and males have been seen displaying during May and June (F. G. Stiles *in litt.* 1991). In 1940, Skutch (1970) observed a male near Santa Rosa (at c.760 m) over a period of four months, and during March and April the bird was observed displaying (this became less frequent as May advanced), and it held a territory against another male that arrived on 3 April; despite the arrival of a female on 27 April, both birds being seen repeatedly, no evidence of breeding was forthcoming. This represents the only evidence that breeding may have occurred inland in the foothills, or indeed of any seasonal migration to such areas (as mentioned by Snow 1982, Ridgley and Gwynne 1989: see above), although the male and female at the head of the río Corotú in February 1966 (Wetmore 1972) and the seven *Carpodectes* above Santa Clara in July 1980 (Ridgely and Gwynne 1989) may also refer to breeding or post-breeding birds. Nevertheless, F. G. Stiles (*in litt.* 1989) suggested that the mangroves around Golfo Dulce, including Sierpe and Coto, are the main nesting areas.

THREATS Accepting that mangroves are essential for the Yellow-billed Cotinga, the bird's habitat is under increasing pressure all along the Pacific coast: in addition to being destroyed to make room for salinas and shrimp ponds, mangroves are cut in order to fuel stoves that evaporate water from the salinas and in order to make mangrove charcoal (Stiles and Skutch 1989). Illegal cutting of mangroves continues in Costa Rica, where road and dyke construction have both affected the hydrology in certain mangrove areas (Scott and Carbonell 1986). In Panama, the mangrove areas in David district are unprotected and threatened by clearance for rice cultivation and ranching, as well as by pollution from pesticide run-off and the oil pipe-line that has been built through the area (Scott and Carbonell 1986). Although the species can tolerate local clearance of woodland (having often been noted in forest clearings: see Ecology), the large-scale destruction of forest in Costa Rica is presumably having a detrimental effect upon the bird (50% of all forest has been destroyed since 1940, and even by 1940 the río Pacuar valley near Santa Rosa had been cleared: Skutch 1970, Stiles and Skutch 1989). In Panama, virtually total deforestation across all of the bird's potential range in Chiriquí suggests that the continued survival of even a remnant population would be unlikely (Ridgely and Gwynne 1989). A small population may still exist on the Panama side of Península de Burica, although the forest there continues to be gradually felled so that most of what remains is on the Costa Rica side of the border (Ridgely and Gwynne 1989).

MEASURES TAKEN This species is not adequately protected within the existing (and reasonably extensive) Costa Rica protected areas system (F. G. Stiles *in litt.* 1986). No extensive mangrove swamps are receiving protection, leaving the Mangrove Hummingbird *Amazilia boucardi* (see relevant account) and sympatric Yellow-billed Cotinga unprotected (Stiles and Skutch 1989). There is a general law in Costa Rica which prohibits the cutting of mangroves (Scott and Carbonell 1986), although this is seemingly widely flaunted and generally ignored (see above: F. G. Stiles *in litt.* 1991). The only reserves where the cotinga occurs are the Carara Biological Reserve (Taylor 1990), although its status and the extent of suitable habitat there are unknown (the reserve seemingly comprises 7,600 ha, primarily tall humid forest: Taylor 1990), and Corcovado National Park, which the species probably uses only seasonally owing to the lack of extensive mangrove habitat (F. G. Stiles *in litt.* 1992). The bird has also been recorded at the Golfito Wildlife Refuge (see Distribution) although the mangroves there are in a poor state (Stiles and Skutch 1989).

In Panama, the Bahía de Muertos Refugio de Vida Silvestre (Morales and Cifuentes 1989) may well have suitable habitat within it but the species has not been recorded from Pedregal or nearby since 1901 (see Population) and its status there as well as the park's are unknown. The Reserva Florestal Chorogo (on Península de Burica: Morales and Cifuentes 1989) may also harbour a population (see Population). No other protected areas appear to cover the few sites where this species has been recorded.

MEASURES PROPOSED Even on the assumption (and more data are clearly needed: see below) that the extensive mangroves around the Golfo Dulce are a key area for this species (F. G. Stiles *in litt.* 1989), it is essential that a protected area is set up in which a viable population can survive. The areas around the río Sierpe, Rincón, and río Coto appear to have retained large enough expanses of mangrove to warrant their protection, which should be carried out as soon as possible. In the north, extension of the Carara Biological Reserve to incorporate some coastal mangrove may facilitate the protection of this species without the creation of another new park, although in order to save the mangroves around río Palo Seco such a park is clearly desirable.

The situation in Panama is somewhat different owing to the lack of recent information about this species, but the Península de Burica (on both sides of the border, but especially in Costa Rica) would appear to be the least deforested area which may yet hold a population, and the protection of what remains should receive the highest priority (Ridgely and Gwynne 1989). Wetmore (1972) recommended that this species should be looked for in mangroves from Pedregal eastward.

An ecological study is urgently needed to show exactly which habitats are used, where the species breeds and whether local migrations are an important part of the life-cycle for a majority of the population. Such a study may show that the bird relies on foothill forest for part of the year, and that protection of such habitat within the bird's range is no less important than measures for the mangrove areas. Obviously, any conservation measures focusing on the mangrove areas of the Pacific coast should be taken in conjunction with those for the Mangrove Hummingbird (see relevant account), and consideration should also then be given to the simultaneous conservation of the near-threatened Turquoise Cotinga and Black-cheeked Ant-tanager *Habia atrimaxillaris*.

REMARKS (1) A male specimen (in ROM) taken at Pozo Azul was apparently collected in "1847" (35 years prior to the collection of the type). This almost certainly represents either a labelling or an interpretation error. (2) Both Pirrís and Pozo Azul were names used by the same collector in the same month and year, suggesting that the differentiation between the two localities (c.5 km apart) was intended. (3) The record of seven *Carpodectes* sp. at Santa Clara (presumed *antoniae*) is a mystery: the justification for their identification as Yellow-billed Cotingas is unknown, although the similar Snowy Cotinga *C. nitidus* occurs primarily on the Caribbean slope in western Bocas del Toro (Ridgely and Gwynne 1989). However, the Snowy Cotinga is poorly known in Panama, occurs throughout adjacent Costa Rica where it wanders widely (Stiles and Skutch 1989), and the río Cotón valley is only just on the Pacific side of the continental divide.

BARE-NECKED UMBRELLABIRD *Cephalopterus glabricollis* V/R[10]

This large cotinga is endemic to Costa Rica and western Panama, where it breeds in adequately protected highland forests, but winters in severely threatened lowland forest. The species is generally uncommon and local throughout its range, although little is known of its status or ecology.

DISTRIBUTION The Bare-necked Umbrellabird is recorded from the tropical belt to well up in the foothills and highlands of chiefly the Caribbean slope of Costa Rica and western Panama.

Costa Rica This species is sparsely distributed in the lowlands and foothills of Cordilleras Guanacaste, Tilarán and Central, and in the Dota mountains (Slud 1964). Localities have been traced from maps in Carriker (1910) and Slud (1964). Records (from approximately north-west to south-east) are from the following localities:

Cordillera Guanacaste La Vijagua (Bijagua) at the headwaters of the río Zapote on the northern slope of Volcán de Miravalles (Carriker 1910), where four birds (in ANSP, MCZ) were taken in February–March and October 1908, and whence come repeated recent records (F. G. Stiles *in litt.* 1991); Rincón de la Vieja, where birds (probably breeding) were seen at 1,500 m in March 1989 (F. G. Stiles *in litt.* 1991);

Cordillera Tilarán El Silencio, where a female (in DMNH) was taken in February 1954; Monteverde Biological Reserve, where the species has been noted in the Peñas Blancas valley (M. P. L. Fogden *per* F. G. Stiles *in litt.* 1991, also Taylor 1990), Slud (1964) recording it from the Pacific-facing slope of the cordillera (although there are no locality data to support this); San Carlos (apparently between Commandancia de San Carlos and the confluence of río Arenal and río San Carlos), where the bird was taken at 915 m in February 1877 (Boucard 1878a, Carriker 1910);

Cordillera Central Cataratas River (apparently part of the upper río San Carlos, and presumably near Cataratas) where a group of males was seen displaying daily during April and May 1942 (Delacour 1943, Wetmore 1972); El Zarcero de Alajuela (Carriker 1910); Barranca (on the west slope of Volcán Poás), where a male (in AMNH) was collected in March 1867; Cariblanco de Sarapiquí, where two males (in ROM) were taken at c.840 m in 1902 and 1903; Finca La Selva, where (between 100 and 220 m) the bird is a non-breeding visitor from August to March (Slud 1960); La Selva Biological Reserve, Rara Avis, and Braulio Carrillo National Park between 300 and 1,100 m (Taylor 1990, B. M. Whitney *in litt.* 1991; see Ecology), a specimen (in MZUCR) being taken at Cantarrana (300 m) low down in the national park in February 1983, with displaying males seen in March each year (1981–1983) at La Montura (F. G. Stiles *in litt.* 1991); San José, over which a bird was seen flying on 4 April 1983 (B. M. Whitney *in litt.* 1991; also Salvin and Godman 1888-1904); Carrillo, where two males (in ROM) were taken during June 1906; La Hondura, where a female (in MCZ) was taken in May 1899, a male (in AMNH) at 915 m in April 1924, and two males (in LACM, YPM) between 1,220 and 1,400 m in March 1929; La Palma de San José, where a female (in USNM) was collected in March 1880; Volcán Irazu, where birds were taken in May 1877 (Boucard 1878a, Carriker 1910); the foothills of the north side of Volcán Turrialba, where birds were noted in August (Slud 1960); Coliblanco, where a bird (in USNM) was taken in May 1905 (Carriker 1910); Naranjo de Cartago (now known as Juan Viñas: Carriker 1910), where a male (in LSUMZ) was taken in March 1888; Tucurriqué (male in BMNH, no date) (Salvin and Godman 1888-1904); Guayabo (apparently a station on the railway between Juan Viñas and Turrialba: Carriker 1910), where a female (in YPM) was taken at 1,220 m in April 1926; Turrialba (the town, not Volcán), where six birds (in BMNH) were collected in 1864, with a seventh (in BMNH) taken in May 1865 (Salvin 1867 referred to these as from "near Turrialba"), and a male (in AMNH) taken in May 1893; Angostura (opposite Turrialba, and just below the Tuís valley), where a female (in USNM) was collected in July 1866;

Bonilla, where a female (in USNM) was taken on 31 March 1905; Hacienda La Iberia, where a male (in LACM) was taken at 300 m in December 1927;

The Old Line Railway La Cristina (presumably close to but north of the railway, along the río Cristina), where a male (in ROM) was taken in February 1907; Jiménez (Carriker 1910); El Hogar, where a male and female (in CM) were collected in March 1907 (also Carriker 1910); Guácimo, where a female (in CM) was taken in October 1903, a female (in BMNH) in November 1905, a male (in BMNH) in February 1907, and a female (in AMNH) at 150 m in March 1925 (also Carriker 1910); Siquirres, where a male and female (in FMNH) were collected in April 1894; Viveros Salsipuedes Farm (18 km east of Siquirres, and through which the río Madre de Díos flows), between 100 and 550 m (Taylor 1990); Limón (seemingly referring to the port, or the hills just behind), where a male (in FMNH) was taken in May 1910;

Dota mountains including a male (in MCZ) from "Dota" taken in February 1867, and a record from Santa Maria de Dota (Carriker 1910); and from sea level somewhere along the río Sicsola (= Sixaola), where a pair was seen (female in CM) in August 1904 (Slud 1964). The birds seen on the río Sixaola suggest that the Bare-necked Umbrellabird is to be found in the Cordillera Talamanca proper (Slud 1964), although whether the birds (on the río Sixaola) originated from the Costa Rica or Panama side of this cordillera is pure speculation. The sighting of a single umbrellabird at Hitoy Cerere Biological Reserve in July 1985, further pointing to the presence of at least a local breeding population on the Caribbean slope of this cordillera (F. G. Stiles *in litt.* 1991).

Panama The Bare-necked Umbrellabird has been found at few localities in the foothills and highlands of the states Bocas del Toro, Chiriquí and Veraguas, descending to the lowlands on the Caribbean slope at least in Bocas del Toro. Coordinates are from OG (1969).

Records (approximately from west to east) come from Boca del Drago (9°25'N 82°20'W) on the coast of Bocas del Toro, where a bird was collected in August 1960 (Wetmore 1972); at the headwaters of the río Changuena (c.9°09'N 84°49'W) between Cerro Fabrega and Cerro Robalo, where a female (in USNM) was taken in July 1960; Chiriquí (at 2,440 m) where the type was taken in 1849 (Gould 1850, Wetmore 1972), Wetmore (1972) adding more detail, saying that this was between Laguna de Chiriquí and David (above Boquete), probably on the north slope at 1,600 m or less (three specimens in AMNH from "Chiriquí"); Boquete (c.8°47'N 82°26'W), where a male and two females (in MCZ) were taken at 1,220 to 1,830 m in March and April 1901 ("above Boquete" in Wetmore 1972), and a female (in AMNH) at 1,070 m in April 1903; Finca Lerida (8°48'N 82°29'W; above Boquete), where two birds were seen at c.1,600 m in July 1964; the Fortuna area (c.8°43'N 82°16'W) of the upper río Chiriquí valley, especially within the drainage of Quebrada de Arena, whence come reports of small numbers in recent years (Ridgely and Gwynne 1989); Cedral (untraced, but in Bocas del Toro), where a male and female (in FMNH) were taken at 1,460 m in July 1933 (see Wetmore 1972); Cordillera de Tolé (c. 8°20'N 81°48'W), where two males (in BMNH, USNM) were taken in 1866 (also Salvin 1867); Calovévora (presumably either at "Pico Calovevora" or in the foothills along the river: see Salvin 1870), where a male (in BMNH) was taken in 1868; Calobre (8°19'N 80°51'W), a locality mentioned by Salvin (1870), but which Wetmore (1972) suggested "may have been in error for Calovévora" as it was not mentioned in any later accounts.

POPULATION A significant number of the localities in both Costa Rica and Panama are represented by small numbers of specimens (quite often just 1-2 old ones), but with the non-breeding population thinly scattered in available habitat, and relatively few localities where (quantitative) repeat observations have been made, more than a rough assessment of the population is almost impossible.

Costa Rica Salvin (1867) claimed that the Bare-necked Umbrellabird appeared to be abundant near Turrialba and in Cordilleras de Tole, although Carriker (1910) wrote that it is "not an abundant bird, and but few individuals are seen". Slud (1964) suggested that the bird is encountered haphazardly and locally, occurring singly in its wintering grounds (see Ecology) but in small groups during its seasonal migrations, and in leks when displaying. At Finca La Selva (a wintering ground) birds were normally seen alone, but at times in twos and threes, the species here assessed as being rare to uncommon when present (Slud 1964), this generally being the case in lowland areas (F. G. Stiles *in litt.* 1991). Wetmore (1972) and M. P. L. Fogden (*per* F. G. Stiles *in litt.* 1991) recorded groups of displaying males on the upper río San Carlos, Monteverde (Peñas Blancas valley) and Braulio Carillo National Park, between 800 and 1,600 m. The size of these groups is generally 3-6 males, but the number of leks and the catchment area of each display site is unknown and consequently the population density or local population sizes are impossible to judge. Stiles and Skutch (1989) summarized the species in Costa Rica as being uncommon and local.

Panama The Bare-necked Umbrellabird is generally considered to be rare (Ridgely and Gwynne 1989), and never seems to have been common (being known from relatively few specimens: see Distribution) (Wetmore 1972), although Salvin (1867) claimed that it appeared to be common in the Cordillera de Chiriquí. The bird is now considered "very rare" in the western Chiriquí highlands, but probably more numerous on the Caribbean side of the mountains, although even here there are relatively few reports (Ridgely 1981b, Ridgely and Gwynne 1989). Small numbers have been found in recent years in the Fortuna area (see Distribution).

ECOLOGY The Bare-necked Umbrellabird undertakes a seasonal vertical migration, breeding in the wetter parts of the cool subtropical belt (occasionally higher) and apparently spending the rest of the year in the foothills down to the edge of the coastal plain (Slud 1964; see below). Despite this migration, birds are always found in (or close to) dense humid primary forest, where they primarily inhabit the upper understorey to mid-canopy (although ground level to treetops have been noted), and sometimes visit fruiting trees in adjacent tall second-growth or semi-open areas (old-style cacao plantations) (Slud 1960, Stiles and Skutch 1989, F. G. Stiles *in litt.* 1991).

Birds feed on the fruits of palms, Lauraceae, Annonaceae, and some large insects (including orthopterans and caterpillars), small lizards and frogs (Stiles and Skutch 1989), and during the non-breeding season have been noted to accompany fruitcrows *Querula* sp. and nunbirds *Monasa* sp. etc. (Ridgely and Gwynne 1989).

The breeding season is between March and June (F. G. Stiles *in litt.* 1991), birds leaving the lowlands (e.g. La Selva) in December–January, and migrating upslope to 800-1,400 m in Costa Rica, and 1,070-1,830 m in Panama (see Distribution: F. G. Stiles *in litt.* 1991). Stiles and Skutch (1989) quoted 800-2,000 m for Costa Rica (rarely to 2,000, but regularly to 1,500-1,600 m: F. G. Stiles *in litt.* 1991); Ridgely (1981b) 1,220-2,440 m and later Ridgely and Gwynne (1989) 900-1,200 m for Panama. Although birds most often occur singly, during seasonal movements they occur in small groups (Slud 1964) which prior to breeding may include displaying males (Stiles and Skutch 1989). Birds generally leave their wintering grounds during March (see Distribution), with almost all birds gone from Finca La Selva by the end of March (one seen in April: Slud 1960). Males have been observed displaying during April and May at 915 m on the upper río San Carlos (Wetmore 1972), and from late March through early April at c.1,300-1,400 m in Monteverde Biological Reserve (Taylor 1990), and during March and the first week of April (1981-1983) at 1,000-1,100 m in Braulio Carrillo National Park, although at La Montura (inside the park), migrating groups of 2-4 males only display for c.1-2 weeks before moving further upslope, breeding mainly at 1,200-1,600 m (e.g. on Volcán Barva) (F. G. Stiles *in litt.* 1991, B. M. Whitney *in litt.* 1991). Stiles and Skutch (1989) stated that the birds display from March to May or June. Displaying is undertaken by loose groups (3-6 birds) of males (leks) perched in the subcanopy (Stiles and Skutch 1989, F. G. Stiles *in litt.* 1991), c.5 m or more above the ground (Wetmore 1972). No nest has ever been described (Ridgely and Gwynne 1989, Stiles and Skutch 1989: see Remarks), although M. P. L. Fogden (*per* F. G. Stiles *in litt.* 1991) has found one in the Peñas Blancas valley.

Birds are noted in the warmer Caribbean lowlands from the end of July (when one seen at Finca La Selva), with most reappearing in August (when a "small wave" is noted at Finca La Selva) (Slud 1960). Other August lowland records include a pair at sea level on río Sixaola (9 August: see Distribution); on the northern side of Volcán Turrialba (Slud 1960); one at sea level from Boca del Drago (25 August: Wetmore 1972); and two together at 300 m in mid-August 1981 in the valley of the río La Patria, Braulio Carrillo National Park (B. M. Whitney *in litt.* 1991). Stiles and Skutch (1989), based on observations over a large number of years, suggested that females winter chiefly below 200 m (nearly all birds at La Selva being females), with the males staying higher up (between 100 and 500 m; also F. G. Stiles *in litt.* 1991).

THREATS The Bare-necked Umbrellabird is seemingly rare over most (or all) of its range, and is threatened by deforestation over significant areas (Ridgely and Gwynne 1989). Although the bird was probably always uncommon to rare, it now faces the problem of lowland forest destruction (F. G. Stiles *in litt.* 1991). Since 1940, half of Costa Rica's forest has been destroyed, and the remainder (primarily lowland forest) is being lost at a rate of 3% of the country's land area per year, the lowlands and foothills of the northern Caribbean slope being one of the regions of most active deforestation (Stiles and Skutch 1989). The problem of deforestation is exacerbated by the fact that this species requires both lowland (for up to eight months of the year) and foothill or highland forests in order to complete each annual cycle: most protected areas in Costa Rica are in the highlands (e.g. the highland area of La Amistad International Park represents half of the land area currently protected within Costa Rica), and at no point is a large lowland park connected by a broad wooded corridor with a highland protected area (Stiles and Skutch 1989). It is anticipated that, owing to continuing deforestation, most of Costa Rica's forest will lie within the current protected areas system within a few years, and consequently the highland avifauna will be relatively more secure than that of the lowlands (Stiles and Skutch 1989). Although La Amistad International Park may harbour a breeding population of this species (though as yet unrecorded), there are no adjacent sizeable tracts of lowland forest to retreat to after the breeding season, and certainly none within a protected area (see Stiles and Skutch 1989), the only suitable area being across the border in Panama (see below).

The situation in Panama in relation to deforestation is similar to that in Costa Rica, although owing to the inaccessible nature of and resultant untouched forest on the Caribbean slope, the Bare-necked Umbrellabird is presumed to be more numerous and less threatened there (Ridgely and Gwynne 1989). Recent highway construction has opened up the La Amistad region area to settlement and land clearance (*Ancon Newsletter* 1 [1988]: 1).

MEASURES TAKEN In Costa Rica, this species is known to occur in Rincón de la Vieja National Park, where it probably breeds (although no lowland areas nearby are protected); Monteverde Biological Reserve, where it breeds; La Selva Biological Reserve, where it winters; Braulio Carrillo National Park, where it breeds; Hitoy Cerere Biological Reserve; and possibly within La Amistad International Park, although there are no records to confirm this (see Distribution). An old record (1867) comes from the area of present-day Volcán Poás National Park, but the species's present status there is unknown. In Panama, the Bare-necked Umbrellabird almost certainly occurs on the Panama side of La Amistad International Park (207,000 ha), and in the contiguous Volcán Baru National Park (14,000 ha) (Morales and Cifuentes 1989).

MEASURES PROPOSED The best chance of saving habitat for altitudinal migrants such as the Bare-necked Umbrellabird lies in preserving and broadening the forest connection between La Selva Biological Reserve and Braulio Carrillo National Park (Stiles and Skutch 1989). Other priority areas for protection should be the lowland forests to the north and east of the Cordillera Central, which must harbour the wintering populations of birds breeding in Cordilleras Central, Guanacaste and Tilarán. A lowland forest area (where the bird occurs during the non-breeding season) close to or continuous with Monteverde Biological Reserve should be identified and become the target of conservation efforts. Population studies are required within all the protected areas mentioned above, but especially in Monteverde, Braulio Carillo and La Selva (and adjacent areas), to determine whether or not the existing areas contain and protect viable numbers of this species.

The year-round distribution for particular populations needs to be discovered before a more detailed strategy can be designed. An obvious priority is to assess the status of the species in La Amistad (Inter-) National Park and, if found there, to determine the major areas on the Caribbean slope (in Costa Rica and Panama) that the population uses during the non-breeding season. The "relatively inaccessible" areas in Caribbean Panama would appear to be ideal for protection and extension of the Panama part of the national park. The recent observations in the Fortuna area (see Distribution) should be followed up with survey work both there and in the Volcán Baru National Park close by.

REMARKS The three nests reportedly found c.1.5-2 m from the ground (Wetmore 1972) appear to be totally (but understandably) dismissed by subsequent authors owing to the fact that no eggs, young or adults were ever recorded at them, and also because the nest of the closely related Amazonian Umbrellabird *Cephalopterus ornatus* has been found 12 m up in a tree.

GOLDEN-CROWNED MANAKIN *Pipra vilasboasi* I[8]

This small forest frugivore remains known only from one primary rainforest locality in south-west Pará, Brazil, although it probably ranges between the rios Tapajós and Xingu and may be safe in one forest reserve.

DISTRIBUTION The Golden-crowned Manakin (see Remarks 1) remains known only from the type-locality, the headwaters of the rio "Cururú" (Cururu, 7°12'S 58°03'W: Paynter and Traylor 1991), a right bank tributary of the upper rio Tapajós, in south-western Pará, Brazil, where five birds (three males, an immature male and a female: see Remarks 1) were taken in July 1957 (Sick 1959a,b; see also Gonzaga 1989). Sick (1959c) called the site "Alto Cururú" and puzzlingly indicated that it was somewhat higher than the Serra do Cachimbo (which he gave as 410 m) some 200 km to the south-east.

Haffer (1970) interpreted the evidence concerning the superspecies to which the Golden-crowned Manakin belongs (see Remarks 2) as indicating that it probably occurs only on the northern edge of the Serra do Cachimbo, but his distribution map for it included a fairly large triangle of land stretching through 8°S between the rios Xingu in the east and the Tapajós and Teles Pires in the west. This larger area is repeated as the probably range in Sibley and Monroe (1990).

POPULATION Nothing is known. Although it is evident that several weeks were spent at the type-locality and that the birds were breeding, Sick (1959c) could find no leks and it appears that the five birds collected were the total found in the area in the entire period of study there.

ECOLOGY The type-series was collected in primary terra firme forest (Sick 1959b). The first specimen was seen and collected 6 m up in a thin sapling in "the deepest high forest", at the edge of a stream also frequented by Fiery-capped Manakin *Machaeropterus pyrocephalus* (Sick 1959c). The stomach contents of the three adult males consisted of fruits (two stomachs) and fruits and insects, the latter predominating (one); those of the female and immature male held small-seeded berries (Sick 1959c). The gonads of the three adult males were strongly or fairly well developed, although those of the immature male and female were not (the skull of the former was ossified); a nest with two eggs was found on 21 July, 1.6 m up in the crown of a small tree in the undergrowth, but the identity of the species involved could not be determined (Sick 1959c).

THREATS None is known. Equally, however, the extent of deforestation in this particular part of Amazonia is unknown.

MEASURES TAKEN The rio Cururu forms the southern boundary of the Mundurucânia Forest Reserve, which appears to extend into the Serra do Cachimbo (see GQR 1991).

MEASURES PROPOSED Clarification is needed concerning the status of forest in the region of the Serra do Cachimbo and in particular at and near the type-locality of the Golden-crowned Manakin. Confirmation that the species occurs within the ample confines of the Mundurucânia Forest Reserve would be valuable.

REMARKS (1) Sick (1959b,c) originally described the males as belonging to *Pipra vilasboasi* and the female and, tentatively, the young male, to a second new species, *Pipra obscura*. However, Mayr (1971) argued that *obscura* was "almost certainly" the female and immature male of *vilasboasi*, a judgement fully accepted in retrospect by Sick (1985). Sibley and Monroe (1990) were mistaken in asserting that *obscura* was based on "females" of *vilasboasi*. (2) The Golden-crowned, Snow-capped *Pipra nattereri* and Opal-crowned Manakins *P. iris* form a southern Lower

Amazon grouping within the White-fronted Manakin *P. serena* superspecies, both Golden-crowned and the far wider spread Snow-capped having evolved in isolated forests on the northern edge of the central Brazilian tableland (the "Madeira–Tapajós Pleistocene Refuge") (Haffer 1970).

BLACK-CAPPED MANAKIN *Piprites pileatus* V/R[10]

This largely montane forest species is, for reasons unclear, very sparsely distributed in south-east Brazil (one record from Argentina) with only a few current localities known (notably Itatiaia and Serra da Bocaina National Parks).

DISTRIBUTION The Black-capped Manakin (see Remarks 1) is endemic to the Atlantic Forest region of south-eastern South America, occurring locally from southern Minas Gerais and adjacent portions of Rio de Janeiro and São Paulo to Paraná, Santa Catarina and Rio Grande do Sul in Brazil into Misiones, Argentina.

Brazil The occurrence of the species in Espírito Santo (Ruschi 1953), although admitted by Meyer de Schauensee (1966, 1982), apparently lacks documentation and is not accepted here.

Minas Gerais The species was included in the state bird list (de Mattos *et al.* 1984) from observations "in forests near Itatiaia National Park" (G. T. de Mattos *in litt.* 1987). Other records from this region are from Bocaina de Minas, near Santo Antonio at Fazenda do Machado (22°13'S 44°30'W), c.1,800 m, December 1984; Alagoa, right bank of stream at Brejo da Lapa (22°42'S 44°42'W), c.2,100 m, July 1984; Passa Vinte at Morro do Chapéu (22°11'S 44°21'W), c.1,700 m, July 1985; and Mirantão at Fazenda Mauá, c.1,500 m, January 1988 (R. B. Pineschi *per* H. Sick verbally 1987, 1988, whence coordinates).

Rio de Janeiro All modern records are from the Itatiaia massif and, except for a record from Visconde de Mauá, 1,200-1,600 m, in 1988 (Pineschi 1990), all are from within the Itatiaia National Park, where two males were collected at Maromba, 1,550 m, in January 1954 (Pinto 1954b), one female was collected at Macieiras, 1,830 m in July 1955 (specimen in CPNI), and elsewhere more recently, thus: almost annually in the 1980s in small numbers (up to six pairs or family groups) in three areas, above Véu da Noiva waterfall, along a track in the upper forest, and along the main road to Agulhas Negras (which may partly pass through Minas Gerais), mostly at 1,550-2,000 m, though as low as 1,400 m (TAP); four in December 1986 between 1,600 and 1,700 m (B. M. Whitney *in litt.* 1987), a minimum of 10 being involved in a display in the forest canopy on 25 October 1987 at 1,700 m (J. F. Pacheco *in litt.* 1987); three in August 1988 (M. Pearman *in litt.* 1990); and "good views of singing males" in September/October 1989 (B. M. Whitney and J. C. Rowlett *in litt.* 1990). An old specimen is from Nova Friburgo; another is labelled simply "Rio" (Hellmayr 1929b).

São Paulo Records are from: Campos do Jordão, where two males were collected in February 1906 (von Ihering and von Ihering 1907, Pinto 1944; specimens in MZUSP), with other birds observed in the Campos do Jordão State Park, 1,500-2,000 m, 1976-1979 (Willis and Oniki 1981a); and the Serra da Bocaina (not in Rio de Janeiro as in Sick 1985), where a male was collected at 1,600 m in May 1951 (specimen in MNRJ), with other birds observed in the Serra da Bocaina National Park, c.1,200 m, November 1989 (Fonseca and Pacheco 1989).

Paraná The species was described from 10 specimens collected in Curitiba, October 1820 (von Pelzeln 1868-1871, Hellmayr 1929b). Other specimen records are of one bird from Tibaji (Fazenda Monte Alegre, 900 m), March 1930 (male in AMNH); Castro, June 1914 (Pinto 1944); and seven from Invernadinha (near Guarapuava), 1,065 m, Cara Pintada (30 km from Invernadinha, north of Guarapuava), 1,007 m, and Vermelho (30 km north of Cara Pintada), 935 m, May and June 1922 (Sztolcman 1926). Scherer Neto (1985) indicated that the bird was known in the state via references in the literature, specimens in museums and his own observations, but no details are given; nevertheless, there is at least one recent record, from the Fazenda Santa Rita, Palmeira, 1,000 m, recently (L. dos Anjos *in litt.* 1987) (see Remarks 2).

Santa Catarina The only records are from Ouro Verde (Meyer de Schauensee 1966), this being based on a female taken there at 750 m on 2 May 1929 (in AMNH), and the São Joaquim area, February 1992 (E. I. Abadie *per* M. Pearman *in litt.* 1992).

Rio Grande do Sul The species has been recorded only three times in the state, from the Fazenda das Amoreiras (29°20'S 50°41'W), between Canela and São Francisco de Paula, 840 m, in September 1972 and January 1976 (Belton 1984-1985, whence coordinates), and in Aparados da Serra National Park in July 1991, when three birds were seen (B. C. Forrester *in litt.* 1992).

Argentina The only Argentine record of the Black-capped Manakin is one specimen collected on 3 September 1959 at Tobunas (Tobuna, 26°28'S 53°54'W: Paynter 1985), Misiones (Partridge 1961, Nores and Yzurieta 1986).

POPULATION This species is apparently rare and local, although there is little reason to believe that it was ever much more numerous than at present (see Threats).

ECOLOGY The Black-capped Manakin is largely confined to montane forest (see records under Distribution) in the *Araucaria angustifolia* and *Podocarpus lamberti* domain. The species has been considered a bird of forest canopy (Meyer de Schauensee 1982, Belton 1984-1985, Sick 1985). At Itatiaia in the 1980s it was found in small numbers in the canopy of dense upper montane forest, primarily at 1,500-2,000 m: nearly all (c.12) observations were of 2-4 individuals foraging inside the crowns of medium-sized trees about 10-14 m tall (TAP). The species was frequently noted in the upper branches of an *Inga*-like tree with rough, blackish bark: individuals often remained in these trees for long periods of time, and even long after the flocks they were following had passed out of earshot (TAP). However, another observer in the same area in 1984/1985 found birds c.1 m from the ground in a dense thicket of *Chusquea* bamboo with 2 m tall treelets (*Roupala* sp.) on hilltops (R. B. Pineschi *per* H. Sick verbally 1988). Three birds seen in August 1988 were in the forest subcanopy, one associating with a mixed flock (M. Pearman *in litt.* 1990). Each of four sightings in December 1986 at Itatiaia National Park involved a bird accompanying a mixed-species flock of frugivores and insectivores; the Black-capped Manakin was always on or near the periphery of the flock, and 8-15 m from the ground; hover-plucking of possibly arthropod prey from the surface of leaves was recorded (B. M. Whitney *in litt.* 1987). Other pairs or small groups of this species in the park were noted with canopy mixed-species flocks that included Buff-fronted Foliage-gleaner *Philydor rufus*, Sharp-billed Treerunner *Heliobletus contaminatus*, Rufous-backed Antvireo *Dysithamnus xanthopterus*, Rufous-crowned Greenlet *Hylophilus poicilotis* and numerous small tanagers, especially the Brassy-breasted Tanager *Tangara desmaresti* (TAP). That the diet of the Black-capped Manakin includes animal food is confirmed by the stomach contents of birds collected in Paraná, which were given as insects, including beetle larvae, and vegetable remains including "chanterelles" (Sztolcman 1926). Fruits taken at the Itatiaia massif included those of four species of *Rapanea* (Pineschi 1990), *Leandra sulfurea* (R. B. Pineschi verbally 1987), and *Geonoma* sp. (R. B. Pineschi *per* H. Sick verbally 1988), all of which were eaten also by a variety of other bird species. Birds foraging for arthropods sallied short distances to glean or hover-glean leaves and twigs (TAP).

The only evidence on breeding comes from a pair engaged in courtship display on 25 September 1972; the male collected that day had much enlarged testes (Belton 1984-1985). The male from Paraná, March, had a three-quarters ossified skull, the female from Santa Catarina, May, an unossified skull (specimens in AMNH). The species was readily located each year using tape playback at known sites, two individuals (presumably a pair) typically responding by flying back and forth calling loudly and almost antiphonally, as if territorial (TAP).

THREATS The species was considered threatened by disappearance of primary araucaria forests (Sick 1969), yet was absent from subsequent lists of threatened birds (Sick 1972, 1985, Sick and Teixeira 1979, 1980). It should be noted, however, that it is not truly an araucaria forest specialist, being found in other mixed subtropical forests within the araucaria range, although it is apparently of restricted occurrence even where these formations remain (TAP).

MEASURES TAKEN The species is protected under Brazilian law (Bernardes *et al.* 1990). It has been recorded from Itatiaia, Serra da Bocaina and Aparados da Serra National Parks and Campos do Jordão State Park in Brazil.

MEASURES PROPOSED Surveys are needed better to assess the species's conservation status and distribution, particularly in the states of Paraná, Santa Catarina and Rio Grande do Sul in Brazil and in Argentina. Special attention should be given to existing protected areas and to monitoring the size of the populations they hold, but other, ornithologically neglected areas within the species's potential range could still harbour so far undetected populations, and merit being searched.

REMARKS (1) The systematic position of this bird, which is atypical of manakins, remains unclear, biochemical studies suggesting the genus is not piprine (see Sibley and Monroe 1990, who proposed the name "Black-capped Piprites". (2) Contrary to what might be expected from the species's occurrence in Paraná and Misiones, it has not been found in the Iguaçu and Iguazú National Parks in Brazil and Argentina respectively, where the Wing-barred Manakin *Piprites chloris* is common (LPG, TAP, B. M. Whitney *in litt.* 1987); however, the mixed broadleaf forest with araucaria and austral conifers that apparently occurs within Iguaçu National Park has not been well surveyed for birds, if at all, but it is in such formations that this bird (along, e.g., with Vinaceous Amazon *Amazona vinacea*) would be most anticipated (TAP).

ASH-BREASTED TIT-TYRANT *Anairetes alpinus* E[2]

This very rare tyrant-flycatcher is confined to humid Polylepis woods in Peru and Bolivia, where two widely disjunct populations exist, one in Cordillera Blanca, Ancash department, and one in southern Peru and adjacent Bolivia. These woodlands suffer from cutting for firewood and lack of regeneration caused by widespread burning.

DISTRIBUTION The Ash-breasted Tit-tyrant is known from two forms in two widely separated upland areas in Ancash department, west-central Peru, and Apurímac and Cuzco departments, southern Peru, and La Páz department, northernmost Bolivia. Coordinates, unless otherwise stated, are from Stephens and Traylor (1983).

Peru Nominate *alpinus* has been collected only above (south of) Yánac (8°37'S 77°52'W) at the northern end of Cordillera Blanca, Ancash department, where two specimens (in ANSP) were taken between 4,000 and 4,500 m in March 1932, with three (in LSUMZ) nearby at Quebrada Tútapac (c.8°40'S 77°49'W) from 3,950 to 4,100 m during May 1976 (also Parker and O'Neill 1980). There are recent sightings at other localities in Ancash department, four on the east slope of Cordillera Blanca, one on the west slope: Quipis Munte (untraced) (TAP); Quebrada Morococha (c.9°03'S 77°34'W: read from IGM 1973) (TAP); Quebrada de Llanganuco (c.9°05'S 77°39'W: IGM 1973), where one was seen at 4,350 m in August 1987 (P. K. Donahue *in litt.* 1990); Quebrada Pucavado (c.9°41'S 77°14'W: IGM 1971), a possible sighting at 4,350 m (Fjeldså 1987); and near Cerro Huansala (c.9°51'S 76°59'W: IGM 1973), at 3,700 m, some 200 km south of Yánac (Fjeldså 1987).

The species presumably occurs throughout the *Polylepis* woods on the east slope in Cordillera Blanca (TAP), but at such low densities that it generally goes undetected (Fjeldså 1987, NK); thus this bird was not recorded during eight days of fieldwork in *Polylepis* woodland in Quebradas Rurichinchay, Rurec and Carhuascancha on the east slope, nor was it recorded on the west slope during 12 days in Quebradas Paron, Ulta, Ishinca and Shallop (Frimer and Møller Nielsen 1989).

The subspecies *bolivianus* is known from three areas, two of which are in Peru: (1) south-east of Abancay, Apurímac department, where it is found in c.40 woodlands, one of 75 ha on Cerro Balcón (13°42'S 72°42'W), the rest of 1-4 ha, 10 of them being in the Cerro Runtacocha–Cerro Morococha region at 13°40-41'S 72°46-47'W, the rest at 13°41-46'S 72°35-42'W (J. Fjeldså *in litt.* 1990; coordinates read from IGM 1978a); (2) Cordillera Vilcanota, Cuzco department, where three specimens were collected in 1974, 1985 and 1987 (in FMNH, LSUMZ and ZMUC), with additional birds sighted regularly from 1974 to 1987 (Fjeldså 1987, P. K. Donahue *in litt.* 1987, TAP) in two small groves near Abra Málaga (13°08'S 72°19'W), one above Canchaillo (13°07'S 72°22'W), at 3,960 m, c.10 km north-west of Abra Málaga, the other 1.5-3.5 km south-west of Abra Málaga at 3,950-4,300 m (Parker and O'Neill 1980, Fjeldså 1987, B. P. Walker *in litt.* 1988, NK, TAP). In 1989 this bird was found at Yanacocha lakes (13°17'S 71°59'W), head of the Huayocari valley, on the slope of Nevada Chicon, Cuzco department, in a mixed *Polylepis–Gynoxys* wood at 3,700-3,800 m (B. P. Walker *in litt.* 1989).

Bolivia The type-specimen (subspecies *bolivianus*) was collected at 4,100 m above km 50 on the Yungas railroad, La Páz department in 1935 (Carriker 1935b), but this region is now virtually devoid of *Polylepis* (Fjeldså 1987) – at least none could be found along the roads leading to the Yungas and Zongo valley in 1984 (NK) and 1987 (Fjeldså 1987).

The Ash-breasted Tit-tyrant was presumably once distributed along the entire Cordillera Real (NK), but in 1987 no habitat was found in the valley from Aricoma Pass to Limbani, Puno department, nor within adjacent valleys 10 km to the south, and local inhabitants reported that no *Polylepis* remains in the entire region, save for tiny patches and planted trees (Fjeldså 1987, NK). Above Cuyocuyo in Sandia valley, Puno department, only tiny patches of *Polylepis* persisted in 1984 (NK). The species presumably occurs in the unexplored parts of the Vilcanota and Carabaya mountains, which can be seen from the air to hold much *Polylepis*, and many suitable patches may remain elsewhere between Cordillera Vilcanota and La Paz (TAP). A park ranger in Tunari National Park, a *Polylepis* reserve in Cochabamba department, Bolivia, claimed that the species occurs there (Fjeldså 1987). Habitat was found c.35 km south-east of Abra Málaga, in the valley of Urubamba town, c.5 km east-north-east of the town, towards Nevada Chaiñapuerto at 3,800-4,500 m, but although the species was not detected during a two-day survey, 1-2 pairs may well exist (Fjeldså 1987).

POPULATION In most of its range the Ash-breasted Tit-tyrant occurs at very low densities with only one pair or family group in each *Polylepis–Gynoxys* grove (Carriker 1933, 1935b, Parker and O'Neill 1980, Fjeldså 1987, Fjeldså and Krabbe 1990). Until recently the largest population was thought to be in Cordillera Blanca, Ancash department, where the species was reported to be "not rare" above Yánac (TAP), the entire population in this cordillera speculatively being as high or higher than 300 individuals; however, the inventory of *Polylepis* woodlands there in 1988 (Frimer and Møller Nielsen 1989; see Distribution) suggested that it is in fact much less. In Cuzco no more than 3-5 pairs have been detected, but perhaps as many as 30 birds may be found by investigating additional *Polylepis* groves between Abra Málaga and Urubamba, with a larger population possibly existing further south, notably in the Cordillera Carabaya (NK). In Apurímac, the species was found to be common in its patchy habitat, with a population of 100 pairs estimated for the c.40 woodlands covering a total of c.2 km^2 (J. Fjeldså *in litt.* 1990).

ECOLOGY The Ash-breasted Tit-tyrant inhabits isolated, semi-humid, mixed *Polylepis–Gynoxys* woods at 3,700 to 4,500 m (Carriker 1933, 1935b, Parker and O'Neill 1980, Fjeldså 1987, Fjeldså and Krabbe 1990, TAP), and there has been one sighting of the species in 1 m tall, scrubby *Polylepis* mixed with *Buddleia* (B. P. Walker *in litt.* 1988). It appears to be common only in Apurímac, where the *Polylepis* woodlands are mature (for description of these forests see Ecology under Royal Cinclodes *Cinclodes aricomae*), and where the several strata may provide a richer supply of insects than can be found in other woods (J. Fjeldså verbally 1989 and *in litt.* 1990).

This species has been seen alone, in pairs and in family groups of two adults and one young (Carriker 1933, 1935b, Parker and O'Neill 1980, Fjeldså and Krabbe 1990; also FMNH label data): it is remarkable that it can survive the low densities in which it occurs at most sites, a *Polylepis* grove of 1 km^2 being inhabited by only 1-2 pairs (Carriker 1933, 1935b, Parker and O'Neill 1980, Fjeldså and Krabbe 1990). Birds, which are often well hidden, flitter restlessly after insects in the outer branches of *Polylepis* and *Gynoxys* brush and trees, where they perch-glean, and make short sallies into the air or to glean foliage and twigs: rarely, they may descend to the ground or climb trunks, and once a bird was seen feeding on thickly moss-clad branches in the subcanopy (Parker and O'Neill 1980, Fjeldså and Krabbe 1990, J. Fjeldså *in litt.* 1990).

Birds collected in Ancash in May and in Cuzco in March had small gonads (specimens in FMNH, LSUMZ and ZMUC): in Cuzco, immatures were caught or collected in March and July (specimen in FMNH; P. Arctander verbally 1987). Two adults taken and others seen in Apurímac during November 1989 were moulting wings and tail, and in early December a pair was seen feeding young, whilst a bird with a minute ovary taken there in December only showed slight body moult (J. Fjeldså *in litt.* 1990; specimens in ZMUC). Breeding thus appears to be late in the dry season, at least in Apurímac. Nesting has not been described, but in other members of the genus the nest is a finely woven, small compact open cup placed in a bush (Fjeldså and Krabbe 1990).

THREATS The major threat to this and other *Polylepis* specialists is habitat destruction, caused by cutting for firewood and a lack of regeneration due to grazing and burning of grass between the trees (for more details of specific threats to particular localities, see Threats under Royal Cinclodes, White-browed Tit-spinetail *Leptasthenura xenothorax* and White-cheeked Cotinga *Zaratornis stresemanni*).

MEASURES TAKEN In Ancash most *Polylepis* occurs within Huascarán National Park, Cordillera Blanca (340,000 ha: IUCN 1992), but is still threatened (see Threats under White-cheeked Cotinga, also Royal Cinclodes). The planting of *Eucalyptus* around the village of Yánac in Cordillera Blanca in the 1920s and 1930s has lessened the local need for *Polylepis* wood (Parker 1981) and is probably responsible for the healthy state of the *Polylepis* woods to the south of the village. In Cuzco no measures are known, but for initiatives carried out in Apurímac see under Royal Cinclodes.

MEASURES PROPOSED The Ash-breasted Tit-tyrant shares habitat with several other threatened *Polylepis*-adapted birds: in Cuzco and Apurímac it is found with White-browed Tit-spinetail and Royal Cinclodes, and in Ancash with White-cheeked Cotinga, Plain-tailed and Rufous-breasted Warbling-finches *Poospiza alticola* and *P. rubecula* (see relevant accounts), and the requirements of all of these species should, where appropriate, be taken into consideration in any conservation proposals. Although occupying a different habitat-type, this species occurs sympatrically with the threatened White-tailed Shrike-tyrant *Agriornis andicola* (at least within Huascarán National Park). Measures Proposed under Royal Cinclodes, White-browed Tit-spinetail and White-cheeked Cotinga outlines possible initiatives to conserve *Polylepis* woodland in this area, and gives a list of some other birds endemic to this specialized habitat.

DINELLI'S DORADITO *Pseudocolopteryx dinellianus* V/R[10]

This very poorly known flycatcher occurs in low numbers in a restricted range in the marshes of northern Argentina (with probably wintering records from adjacent Bolivia and Paraguay) and merits investigation to determine its status and needs.

DISTRIBUTION Dinelli's Doradito occurs in northern Argentina (north-eastern Córdoba, Santiago del Estero and Tucumán). It has been recorded twice in southern Bolivia (Tarija) and three times in south-western Paraguay (Presidente Hayes), these records probably representing wintering birds (see Ecology). Unless otherwise stated, coordinates are taken from Nores *et al.* (1983).

Argentina The species has been recorded from the following provinces: (*Salta*) unspecified (Olrog 1979, Nores *et al.* 1983), this possibly an assumption based on the record from Tarija, Bolivia; (*Tucumán*) río Salí ("Rio Sale"), 27°33'S 64°57'W, October 1903 (two specimens in AMNH), this evidently being the source of all other records from the province (including the type-specimen), since Dinelli (1933) indicated that the species had only been observed along this river "from Tucumán to Santiago del Estero", the other records being: "Tucumán", September 1899 (two specimens in AMNH), January 1901 (specimen in AMNH), October 1904 (type collected: Lillo 1905, Hellmayr 1906b, Esteban 1953b; also Laubmann 1934) and October 1919 (specimen in USNM); (*Santiago del Estero*) western part of the province (Olrog 1979); Bañados de Figueroa, currently (Nores *et al.* 1991); Bañados del río Dulce (30°15'S 62°30'W, extending into Córdoba), October 1971 (T. Narosky *in litt.* 1992) down to the present (Nores *et al.* 1991); (*Santa Fe*) San Carlos (untraced but probably either San Carlos Norte, 31°41'S 61°05'W, San Carlos Centro, 31°44'S 61°06'W or San Carlos Sur, 31°45'S 61°06'W: see Paynter 1985), where two birds were secured in April 1931 (Laubmann 1934); (*Córdoba*) Paso de la Cina (= Limache, 29°49'S 62°48'W), November 1980 (T. Narosky *in litt.* 1992); Bañados del río Dulce (extending from Santiago del Estero), currently (Nores *et al.* 1983, 1991, Molli 1985); río Segundo, south-western Laguna Mar Chiquita (30°42'S 62°36'W: Paynter 1985), where a pair with a nearly fledged young was observed in March 1991 (D. Willis *in litt.* 1991, M. Pearman *in litt.* 1992) and about six singing males were recorded in mid-October 1991 (P. V. Hayman *in litt.* 1992, M. Pearman *in litt.* 1992); Estancia La Africa, south-east Mar Chiquita, October 1991 (M. Pearman *in litt.* 1992); Laguna Ludueña (31°15'S 63°32'W), undated (Nores *et al.* 1983); Embalse del río Tercero (32°13'S 64°30'W), undated (Nores and Yzurieta 1980; also Nores *et al.* 1983); río de los Sauces (32°32'S 64°35'W), undated (Nores and Yzurieta 1980; also Nores *et al.* 1983).

Bolivia The species is known from two specimens collected at Villa Montes, Tarija, in April and May 1926 (Laubmann 1934).

Paraguay There are only three records, all in the department of Presidente Hayes: Escalante (= Laguna Escalante, 23°50'S 60°46'W: Paynter 1989), where a specimen was collected in August 1960 (Steinbacher 1962); Trans Chaco Highway Km 79, where two birds were observed in May 1990, with another seen on the same road (Km 100) in June 1990 (P. A. Scharf *per* F. E. Hayes *in litt.* 1992).

POPULATION Very little is known; in Argentina, Nores *et al.* (1983) reported it to be "more or less common, although not abundant" in the province of Córdoba, while Narosky and Yzurieta (1987) described it as "scarce or difficult to find". In the Bañados de Figueroa and Bañados del río Dulce, Santiago del Estero, the species is considered "frequent" (i.e. often recorded in low or relatively low numbers) (Nores *et al.* 1991). It is known in Santa Fe from two specimens (see Distribution), although it was regarded as common near San Carlos in the early 1930s (Laubmann 1934); however, M. R. de la Peña (*in litt.* 1991) has never recorded it despite having done a great deal of fieldwork in the province. D. Willis (*in litt.* 1991) considered it to be well known to ornithologists at Mar Chiquita, Córdoba, and M. Pearman (*in litt.* 1992) considered it locally common in that same area. In Bolivia the species is known from two specimens collected in autumn, and in Paraguay it is considered a rare winter migrant to the wetlands of the Chaco (F. E. Hayes *in litt.* 1992), the three records there being from the autumn and winter months (see Distribution).

ECOLOGY Dinelli's Doradito inhabits periodically flooded rushy and grassy marsh vegetation and shrubbery near watercourses (Olrog 1979, Canevari *et al.* 1991). Laubmann (1934) indicated that the species was common in lagoon areas of San Carlos, where it almost always associated with the Wren-like Rushbird *Phleocryptes melanops*, nesting in the same habitat (but this appears irrelevant: M. Pearman *in litt.* 1992). Dinelli (1933) found the species always perching in only one type of bush, *Baccharis lanceolata*. Feeding habits are little known other than that it searches nimbly for insects amidst the vegetation (Canevari *et al.* 1991). Breeding occurs during the austral spring and also in autumn; at Laguna Mar Chiquita, a pair of adults with a nearly fledged young was observed in March 1991 (see Distribution), and Laubmann (1934) referred to two nests under construction apparently in April 1931 in Santa Fe. At Laguna Mar Chiquita, several males were singing in a long established breeding locality in October 1991 (P. V. Hayman *in litt.* 1992), a female collected in November 1931 (presumably in Tucumán) contained an egg ready to be laid, the nest being placed in the fork of a bush at 1.2 m above the ground (Dinelli 1933), while another nest was found in the Bañados del río Dulce whose two eggs hatched on 30 November 1983 (Molli 1985). However, the nest can also be placed among rushes and tall grasses (Nores and Yzurieta 1980, Canevari *et al.* 1991; see photographs in Molli 1983). The bird appears to be a year-round resident in Argentina (Nores *et al.* 1983), although records in Bolivia and Paraguay suggest northward displacements during the winter (Short 1975, Canevari *et al.* 1991); Dinelli (1933) noted that the species was present in Tucumán from October to January (i.e. breeding season), but did not know if it was a year-round resident there.

THREATS None is known, but the small range, low numbers and insufficient knowledge of its habits and needs are all causes of concern.

MEASURES TAKEN The Laguna Mar Chiquita has been protected as a WHSRN reserve, which includes a small portion of the Bañados del río Dulce (Scott and Carbonell 1986), and the species is not under immediate pressure there (M. Pearman *in litt.* 1992).

MEASURES PROPOSED A survey should concentrate on accurately delimiting the species's breeding range, the number of subpopulations should be assessed and the numbers they contain estimated. It is also important to gather more general information on habitat requirements, feeding, nesting, seasonal movements, etc., in order to determine possible threats affecting it.

RUFOUS-SIDED PYGMY-TYRANT *Euscarthmus rufomarginatus* I[7]

This flycatcher is known from a small number of widely scattered localities in the cerrado region of central Brazil, from Maranhão south to São Paulo, with an outlying population in southern Surinam; it has recently been found in pristine, shrubby grasslands in western Mato Grosso and eastern Santa Cruz, Bolivia, but remains severely threatened by habitat destruction.

DISTRIBUTION The Rufous-sided Pygmy-tyrant is known from very few sites extending over a vast area in interior Brazil, with one locality in Surinam and one in Bolivia.

Surinam A population in the Sipaliwini savanna (2°06'N 56°02'W in Stephens and Traylor 1985) in the south of the country was discovered in the 1960s and distinguished for its marginally smaller size under the subspecific name *savannophilus* (Mees 1968).

Brazil Localities for the species (north to south, coordinates from Paynter and Traylor 1991) are as follows:

Maranhão Ponto, c.6°10'S 45°10'W, August 1924 (specimen in FMNH; also Cory and Hellmayr 1927, Hellmayr 1929a);

Piauí Correntes, 8°13'S 45°33'W, on the rio Parnaíba, a pair in July 1903 (Reiser 1926; also Hellmayr 1929a);

Pará Serra do Cachimbo, a female in November 1955 (Pinto and de Camargo 1957);

Federal District Brasília National Park, March 1989 (J. F. Pacheco verbally 1992);

Mato Grosso Chavantina, November and December 1946 (Pinto and de Camargo 1948); Pindaíba, September 1946 (specimen in AMNH); Serra das Araras Ecological Station (c.200-700 m) west of Cuiabá, July 1987 (Willis and Oniki 1990) and December 1988 (Teixeira *et al.* in press);

Mato Grosso do Sul Passo do Lontra, August 1991 (J. F. Pacheco verbally 1992); Campo Grande, June and July 1930 (Pinto 1940); Campo Grande, Serra do Norte, without date (Pinto 1940);

São Paulo Calçao do Couro (adjacent to rio Santa Maria) and Rio das Pedras on consecutive days in April 1823 (von Pelzeln 1868-1871), these both being in or near Ituverava (see Threats).

Bolivia A population was found in June and October 1989 at two localities in the Serranía de Huanchaca (c.600-700 m) in extreme north-eastern Santa Cruz, Bolivia (Bates *et al.* 1992).

POPULATION For a species with such an enormous range, this bird is remarkably poorly known and patchily distributed, and hence has been considered "rare" (Pinto and de Camargo 1948). However, birds in the Sipaliwini savanna, Surinam, were frequently ("veelvuldig") found (Mees 1968) and, although data are lacking, the population in the Serranía de Huanchaca of eastern Bolivia may number in the thousands: the top of the serranía inside Noel Kempff Mercado National Park encompasses c.900,000 ha of campo and cerrado habitats, and at one locality in the park at least four territorial pairs were found in a campo sujo area of c.30 ha (TAP). A few additional pairs were located in the Serra das Araras Ecological Reserve in western Mato Grosso (Parker and Willis ms). It seems unlikely that the species survives in São Paulo state (see Threats).

ECOLOGY The observer of the first specimens (J. Natterer) found them on low bushes in grassland (von Pelzeln 1868-1871). Reiser (1926) found his birds hard to collect as they hid in thick grass. Snethlage (1927-1928) simply recorded it (in Maranhão) from "savanna woodland". The habitat on the Serra do Cachimbo was described as if entirely forested ("the entire region is covered in great forests still to be cleared" (Pinto and de Camargo 1957), but there must have been natural grassland openings where the specimen was collected. Sick (1985) reported it in Mato Grosso (he collected the 1946 skin in AMNH) from open cerrado with little vegetation but with many termite mounds (i.e. campo sujo), either low in bushes or hopping on the ground. At Serra das Araras the habitat in one case was semi-open cerrado on grassland (i.e. campo sujo) (Willis and Oniki 1990) and in another open cerrado and campo sujo, where the species was observed foraging on the ground and in the foliage of low and medium shrubs, and singing from the tops of shrubs and small trees (Teixeira *et al.* in press). The pristine campo sujo where this species was studied in the Serranía de Huanchaca, Bolivia, was a level, well-drained area (at 620 m) covered by tall grasses, sedges, and numerous but widely spaced small bushes and trees; the diversity of woody vegetation at this site (which had not been burnt in at least three years) appeared to be great and included shrubby melastomes, dwarf palms, and a variety of small trees including a *Byrsonima* sp., *Curatella americana*, *Eriotheca gracilipes*, and *Tabebuia ochracea* (Parker and Willis ms; see Eiten 1983 for additional description of this habitat). The flycatchers foraged close to the ground in the thick cover of grasses and small bushes, gleaning small insects from the grasses and foliage, occasionally making short sallies to vegetation: three different individuals fed on the small, dark fruits of a shrub and later regurgitated the seeds, and it may therefore be that fruit is important in the species's diet and may partially determine its ecological distribution (Parker and Willis ms). Fruits and small insects were in the stomach of a bird from Serra das Araras, December, whose gonads were not enlarged (Teixeira *et al.* in press). A bird in April, São Paulo, was in heavy moult, while two others were together as a pair (von Pelzeln 1868-1871). Birds in Surinam were always in pairs (Mees 1968).

THREATS Although there appears to be extensive suitable habitat for this species in other protected areas in central Brazil, careful searches by several observers have failed to reveal additional populations (TAP). Destruction of cerrado habitats for agriculture has been massive, and especially at risk are species (such as this) that prefer relatively pristine campo sujo habitat (see Threats under Lesser Nothura *Nothura minor*). Campo sujo habitat that is protected from annual fires is becoming increasingly rare: one area where this species was found in the Serranía de Huanchaca of eastern Bolivia had not burnt for at least three (and possibly many more) years (TAP); but in any case the more subtle habitat changes of the kind caused by intervals between fires are overshadowed in central Brazil by outright conversion of grasslands to farmlands or living space. The campos where Natterer collected the type-series at Calção do Couro and rio das Pedras in São Paulo state have long since been destroyed: the stream that passes through Calcão do Couro is now a concrete storm sewer in modern Ituverava, and the rio das Pedras area nearby to the west has been ploughed under except for a small buriti marsh and cerrado at its junction with rio do Carmo (E. O. Willis *in litt.* 1990). Recent fieldwork by Willis and Oniki (1988b) failed to reveal any significant unmodified campo-cerrado vegetation, let alone populations of Rufous-sided Pygmy-tyrant, in the state of São Paulo.

MEASURES TAKEN Although seemingly suitable habitat for this flycatcher may occur in any or all of the six national parks and several smaller reserves in central Brazil, the Rufous-sided Pygmy-tyrant has only been found in one of them, Brasília National Park, despite coverage by numerous field ornithologists. It has recently been reported from only two other protected areas, the Serra das Araras Ecological Station in western Mato Grosso, Brazil, and Noel Kempff Mercado National Park in eastern Santa Cruz, Bolivia. In Surinam the species presumably finds sanctuary in the Sipaliwini Savanna Nature Reserve, which covers 100,000 ha (see Schulz *et al.* 1977).

MEASURES PROPOSED Unreported populations of this and other campo endemics should be searched for in northern Mato Grosso before all of the remaining campo-cerrado vegetation there is destroyed or thoroughly degraded, and areas should be identified for protection. The mountaintop grasslands on the serras of northern and western Mato Grosso should support populations of some these species (proven in the case of the present species by the record from Serra do Cachimbo), in addition to large numbers of other endemic plants and animals of the

Brazilian Shield. Very good-looking (extensive campo sujo) habitat for the species has been noted in Brasília National Park and north of Chapada dos Guimarães National Park north-east of Cuiabá, Brazil (TAP): this area should be investigated urgently for this and other threatened birds of the region (listed in Threats under Lesser Nothura), and the possibility of including the rolling grasslands north of the main highway west of the town should be pursued at once. Campo sujo habitat in existing parks and reserves should be protected from annual burning and other forms of unnatural disturbance. The status of the isolated northern population in Surinam should also be investigated, particularly as the area is contiguous with savanna in adjacent northern Brazil (see Schulz *et al.* 1977) which presumably also holds the species.

LONG-TAILED TYRANNULET *Phylloscartes ceciliae* E[2]

The last hope for this small insectivore appears to be an unprotected and rapidly diminishing tract of upland forest, only 1,500 ha in extent, near the type-locality in Alagoas state, Brazil.

DISTRIBUTION The Long-tailed Tyrannulet (see Remarks) is known chiefly from (Fazenda) Pedra Branca ("Serra Branca": see Remarks 2 under Alagoas Foliage-gleaner *Philydor novaesi*), near Murici (9°19'S 35°57'W), on the south-eastern escarpment of the Borborema plateau in Alagoas, north-eastern Brazil (see, e.g., Teixeira and Gonzaga 1983; D. M. Teixeira *in litt.* 1987), although it appears now to be present only in the remaining part of this area, Fazenda Bananeira (see Threats, Measures Proposed under Alagoas Foliage-gleaner). It was discovered in November 1983 when one young male was collected; four other specimens (two pairs, including the type) were obtained in May 1984 (Teixeira 1987a). A second population was found in the general Quebrangulo area in February/March 1987 (Teixeira and Luigi 1987: 609), and specifically at Pedra Talhada Biological Reserve in August 1989, when six or more were observed in a mixed-species flock (B. C. Forrester *in litt.* 1992), birds being seen there again in October 1990 (J. F. Pacheco verbally 1992). The species seems to be restricted to highland forest (550 m), not having been found in the coastal lowlands, which had previously been explored ornithologically, but it is difficult to locate on account of its small size and arboreal habits (Teixeira 1987a).

POPULATION Numbers are not known. In the type-locality it was considered "rather common", although difficult to locate (Teixeira 1987a; see Distribution); this seems borne out by other observations referred to in this account (by B. M. Whitney and B. C. Forrester).

ECOLOGY The Long-tailed Tyrannulet inhabits the tops of middle strata trees, often joining mixed-species flocks of other tyrant-flycatchers, woodcreepers, foliage-gleaners, antbirds, gnatwrens and Bananaquits *Coereba flaveola*; its food consists of small insects, which are taken from the surface of leaves and branches (Teixeira 1987a). Birds observed in October 1990 foraged with mixed-species flocks, travelling mostly in pairs in the mid-storey and subcanopy, 6-15 m above ground, taking prey in quick, darting movements from both surfaces of leaves but also sometimes more slowly and methodically searching along limbs (B. M. Whitney *in litt.* 1991). Birds in April 1992 were always in mixed flocks, inside forest or at forest edge (M. Pearman *in litt.* 1992). A breeding period between September and February has been inferred from the observed small size of gonads and intense moult of adult birds collected in May; an immature collected on 20 November was being fed by two adults in the tree-tops; pairs seem to remain together longer than expected, since two of them were collected and several other possible pairs were observed in April and May following mixed flocks (Teixeira 1987a). A nest found in October 1990 was c.45 cm in length, hanging 6 m above ground from the low limb of a 20 m high tree in a rather open area (see Remarks 2); at least one adult was feeding young in the nest, one prey-item being a 3 cm long katydid (B. M. Whitney *in litt.* 1991).

THREATS Destruction of forest at Pedra Branca is the single most serious threat to this and all other upland forest species in Alagoas (see Threats under Alagoas Foliage-gleaner).

MEASURES TAKEN The Long-tailed Tyrannulet is protected under Brazilian law (Bernardes *et al.* 1990; see equivalent section under Alagoas Foliage-gleaner).

MEASURES PROPOSED An initiative to preserve forest and its rich birdlife at Pedra Branca (Bananeira) needs urgent impetus (see Measures Proposed and Remarks under Alagoas Foliage-gleaner).

REMARKS (1) The Long-tailed Tyrannulet is apparently closely related to the Serra do Mar Tyrannulet *Phylloscartes difficilis* from south-eastern and southern Brazil (Teixeira 1987a). However, field observations point to a closer relationship with Oustalet's Tyrannulet *P. oustaleti*, *difficilis* being a highly distinctive bird, dissimilar in voice and behaviour to other *Phylloscartes* (B. M. Whitney *in litt.* 1991). (2) The nest consisted of three parts: a 10 cm long attachment to the limb, the ball-like nest proper (a rounded basket with a 2-3 cm wide entrance hole to one side), and a 20 cm long "tail" of dangling material that may have served to camouflage or stabilize the structure; it was made entirely of one type of moss-like material common on tree-trunks (B. M. Whitney *in litt.* 1991).

ANTIOQUIA BRISTLE-TYRANT *Phylloscartes lanyoni* I[7]

This recently described flycatcher is known from just three localities at the northern end of the Central Andes, Colombia, in an area that has been subjected to widespread deforestation.

DISTRIBUTION The Antioquia Bristle-tyrant (see Remarks) is known from three localities in the Central Andes of Colombia, as follows (coordinates from Paynter and Traylor 1981): (*Antioquia*) El Pescado (c.7°20'N 75°23'W), 12 km below Puerto Valdivia, on the east side of the lower Cauca valley, where the type and holotype (male and female) were collected between 455 and 520 m in May 1948 (Graves 1988); Río Claro Natural Reserve, 10 km east of El Doradal on the east slope of the Central Andes near the Caldas border in the lower Magdalena valley, where the species was apparently seen in July 1987 (T. Cuadros *per* L. G. Olarte *in litt.* 1992), and whence come records in June 1990 (Stiles 1990); and (*Caldas*) 1 km west of La Victoria (5°19'N 74°55'W) somewhat further south in the Magdalena valley, where a bird was seen at 750 m in 1990 (P. Kaestner *in litt.* 1992).

POPULATION Almost nothing is known, although the observation of four birds together in a small clearing at the Río Claro reserve (Stiles 1990) suggests that at least locally this flycatcher may not be uncommon, albeit in an increasingly small area of remaining habitat (see Threats).

ECOLOGY The bristle-tyrant has been recorded from the foothills of the Central Andes between 450 and 750 m (see Distribution), where it inhabits tall second growth and clearings (Stiles 1990, P. Kaestner *in litt.* 1992). At El Pescado, the two birds were found in tall second growth, within an area of pasture, second growth and primary forest on the ridges (Graves 1988). At the Río Claro reserve, four birds were observed in a clearing caused by two trees having fallen some years earlier: this clearing was regenerating, with trees and bushes 2-4 m tall in the middle and surrounded by trees 6-8 m high (Stiles 1990). The birds foraged actively in the foliage, making short sallies to catch small insects from the undersurfaces of leaves and branches (Stiles 1990). The male collected on 15 May 1948 was in breeding condition (Graves 1988).

THREATS Owing to imprecise knowledge of this species's distribution and ecological requirements, the threats it faces are difficult to assess with any confidence; however, the middle and lower Magdalena and Cauca valleys have been heavily deforested since the nineteenth century, and the clearance of the floodplain and foothills of the middle Magdalena valley has been almost total during the last 30 years (Graves 1986).

MEASURES TAKEN The Antioquia Bristle-tyrant has been found in the small (80-100 ha) Río Claro Natural Reserve (Stiles 1990), although the status of this reserve is unknown, and is in an area undergoing heavy logging activity (L. G. Olarte *in litt.* 1992). Forested watersheds in some municipalities may provide some protection (F. G. Stiles verbally 1991), as shown by observations at La Victoria, but the Serranía de San Lucas, with all seven threatened species that have been recorded there (see Measures Proposed), remains totally unprotected.

MEASURES PROPOSED A clearer definition of this species's ecological requirements and distributional status is urgently required. As the species may originally have inhabited a continuous band of foothill forest around the northern Central Andes (including the Serranía de San Lucas: Stiles 1990), the bird should be searched for in remnant patches in this area; all such remnants should be mapped and given some form of protection (see equivalent section under Chestnut-bellied Hummingbird *Amazilia castaneiventris*). The priority areas appear to be the forest above La Victoria, and that at the Río Claro reserve: both of these should enjoy more formal protection, with extensions to all (any) forest patches in their immediate vicinity; the species occurs alongside with the threatened White-mantled Barbet *Capito hypoleucus* in this area, and any conservation initiatives should consider the needs of both. In the vicinity of Valdivia, the Antioquia Bristle-tyrant has been recorded sympatrically with five other threatened species, namely Blue-billed Curassow *Crax alberti*, White-mantled Barbet, Recurve-billed Bushbird *Clytoctantes alixii*, Black-and-gold Tanager *Buthraupis melanochlamys* and Red-bellied Grackle *Hypopyrrhus pyrohypogaster*, and their needs should be considered in any initiatives undertaken in this area.

REMARKS The Antioquia Bristle-tyrant, although collected for the first time in 1948, was only described as a new taxon in 1988, as the two specimens were mistakenly identified as Yellow Tyrannulet *Capsiempis flaveola leucophrys* (Graves 1988).

SÃO PAULO TYRANNULET *Phylloscartes paulistus* V/R[10]

Destruction of its lowland forest habitat has isolated this small flycatcher in a relatively small number of localities spread over a relatively large area of south-east Brazil, eastern Paraguay and northern Argentina.

DISTRIBUTION The São Paulo Tyrannulet is endemic to the Atlantic Forest region of south-eastern Brazil in Espírito Santo (no records since 1942), possibly Minas Gerais (see Remarks), Rio de Janeiro, São Paulo, Mato Grosso do Sul (one record in 1930) and Santa Catarina, ranging into north-east Argentina in Misiones and south-eastern Paraguay. Unless otherwise stated, records in the following account are from north to south, and coordinates are from Paynter (1989) and Paynter and Traylor (1991).

Brazil

Espírito Santo Records are from: Chaves (Santa Leopoldina), August and October 1942 (Pinto 1944; specimens in MCZ, MZUSP); Segredo do Veado (Serra do Caparaó), 1,000 m, c.20°35'S 41°45'W, in or near the border of the present-day Caparaó National Park, October 1929 (specimen in AMNH).

Rio de Janeiro Although the state was included in the species's range by Meyer de Schauensee (1966), the evidence for this remains untraced. However, subsequent records are from: Morumbeca do Imbé, Desengano State Park, 600 m, February 1987 (J. F. Pacheco *in litt.* 1987); Poço das Antas Biological Reserve, under 100 m, October/November 1981 (Scott and Brooke 1985, D. F. Stotz *in litt.* 1991).

São Paulo Records are from: Corredeira das Flores (untraced), on rio Paranapanema, south of Assis, September 1943 (specimen in MZUSP); Victoria (now Vitoriana), 570 m, July 1902 (von Ihering and von Ihering 1907, Pinto 1944; specimen in MZUSP); Fazenda Cayoá (Caiuá, c.22°54'S 49°59'W, not as in GQR 1991), Salto Grande do Paranapanema (now Salto Grande), undated (von Ihering and von Ihering 1907); Ubatuba (Experimental Station), 50-400 m, sometime between June 1977 and July 1979 (Willis and Oniki 1981a), December 1990 and October 1991 (D. F. Stotz *in litt.* 1991); base of Pico do Corcovado, south of Ubatuba, September 1991 (TAP); Boracéia Biological Station, 850 m, January 1987 (D. F. Stotz *in litt.* 1991); Estação Engenheiro Ferraz (untraced, between São Paulo city and Santos), August 1964 (specimen in MZUSP); Carlos Botelho State Park, January 1990 (Pacheco and Fonseca 1990); Sete Barras, 150-400 m, sometime between February and July 1979 (Willis and Oniki 1981a); Laranja Azeda, c.24°20'S 47°52'W, August 1960, and Pousinho, rio Juquiá, c.24°22'S 47°49'W, November 1960 (specimens in FMNH); Fazenda Poço Grande, rio Juquiá, May 1940 (Pinto 1944); Ilha do Cardoso State Park, currently (P. Martuscelli *in litt.* 1991, D. F. Stotz *in litt.* 1988, 1991). E. O. Willis (*in litt.* 1986) had records from six unspecified localities in the state.

Mato Grosso do Sul One specimen from Campanário, 350 m, June 1930 (in AMNH), is the only record.

Paraná Records are from: "Salto do Guayra" (Salto das Sete Quedas, now inundated by a reservoir, 24°02'S 54°16'W), possibly this species, February 1923 (Sztolcman 1926); Guaíra, 200 m, April 1930 (specimens in AMNH); the municipality of Castro (including Caxambú Forest Park), recently (L. dos Anjos *in litt.* 1987); Iguaçu National Park, 1977, 1980-1990 (TAP, R. S. Ridgely verbally 1987), August 1990 (Wilcove 1992) and July 1991 (M. Pearman *in litt.* 1991); Cubatão, 25°50'S 48°48'W, 100-200 m, 1950 (Straube 1990, P. Scherer Neto *in litt.* 1986).

Santa Catarina Records are from a single locality near Joinville: Salto do Pirahy (Piraí), 150 m, June 1929 (specimen in AMNH), and specifically 8 and 9 km north-north-west of Vila Nova, July 1991 (M. Pearman *in litt.* 1991; see Measures Proposed).

Argentina The species is only recorded from northern Misiones, where one bird was banded in September 1978 (Olrog 1979), this having taken place in Iguazú National Park (J. C. Chebez *in* *litt.* 1992), and others were seen in the park in December 1982 and January 1988 (F. N. Moschione *per* J. C. Chebez *in litt.* 1992), December 1986 (B. M. Whitney and R. H. Barth *in litt.* 1986) and January 1990 (B. M. López Lanús *in litt.* 1991); however, in the absence of a photograph or skin these first reports for the country must remain technically open to question (J. C. Chebez *in litt.* 1992).

Paraguay Records are from: (*Canindeyú*) Estancia La Fortuna (untraced), Mbaracayu, recently (R. S. Ridgely *per* M. G. Kelsey verbally 1992); (*Caaguazú*) east of Yhú (lumber camp San Antonio), 300 m, January 1931 (specimen in AMNH); upper río Iguazú, 25°20'S 55°00'W, 300 m, January 1931 (specimen in AMNH); (*Alto Paraná*) Puerto Bertoni, 25°38'S 54°40'W, June 1917 (specimen in FMNH; hence Bertoni 1939).

POPULATION This species, because inconspicuous and difficult to identify, may have been under-recorded; nevertheless it has been considered very local and uncommon in south-east Brazil (M. Pearman *in litt.* 1991). There are no recent records from Espírito Santo and only a few from Rio de Janeiro, where it has been considered locally uncommon (Scott and Broke 1985) or rare (J. F. Pacheco *in litt.* 1987). In São Paulo it is fairly common but local at the base of the Serra do Mar around Ubatuba and on Ilha do Cardoso (P. Martuscelli *in litt.* 1991, D. F. Stotz *in litt.* 1991), and while 13 birds per hundred hours of observation have been recorded at both Ubatuba and Sete Barras (Willis and Oniki 1981a), the species was considered uncommon at Carlos Botelho State Park (Pacheco and Fonseca 1990), though this corresponded to 3-5 birds per ten hours of observation. In Paraná the species is considered rare (P. Scherer Neto *in litt.* 1986, F. C. Straube *in litt.* 1991), although not apparently around Castro (L. dos Anjos *in litt.* 1987). There is a moderately large population, possibly in the low thousands, in Iguaçu National Park, where up to 12 individuals can be noted in a day along the Poço Preto trail, the species doubtless being overlooked owing to its weak voice, small size and preference for shady places well above ground (TAP). In Argentina it is considered a rare and little known species (Canevari *et al.* 1991), very infrequent in Iguazú National Park (M. Pearman *in litt.* 1991), although the fact that it has been recorded from second growth may indicate that the species is commoner there than it is currently recognized (B. M. Whitney and R. H. Barth *in litt.* 1986), and indeed the preceding comments concerning Iguaçu on the Brazilian side probably apply. The population status of the species in Paraguay is not known, but from the scarcity of records it appears that it is rare (F. E. Hayes *in litt.* 1991).

ECOLOGY The São Paulo Tyrannulet has been recorded mainly from under 400 m on the coastal slopes of the Serra do Mar and along rivers of the rio Paraná basin; at least one of the few records above 500 m (see Distribution), at Boracéia, was interpreted as a bird wandering upslope from the base of the mountain (D. F. Stotz *in litt.* 1991). On the higher slopes of Pico do Corcovado, south of Ubatuba, the species seems to be replaced by Oustalet's Tyrannulet *Phylloscartes oustaleti* (TAP). It occurs primarily in the lower canopy and upper middle storeys of fairly mature forest (TAP), usually in the interior (E. O. Willis *in litt.* 1986, D. F. Stotz *in litt.* 1988, 1991, B. M. López Lanús *in litt.* 1991, M. Pearman *in litt.* 1991; specimen in MZUSP), and at Iguaçu and near Ubatuba far from the sunlit edges (TAP), but also at least occasionally along edges (Scott and Brooke 1985, D. F. Stotz *in litt.* 1988, 1991, B. M. Whitney *in litt.* 1991) and even in second growth (Scott and Brooke 1985, B. M. Whitney and R. H. Barth *in litt.* 1986, B. M. Whitney *in litt.* 1991). The interior forest habitat of the species at the base of Pico de Corcovado is tall and epiphyte-laden with numerous large lianas, and is thus (presumably) relatively undisturbed and mature; forest at Iguaçu, although apparently cut over in the distant past, is probably structurally similar to its original state (TAP). All of more than 50 observations (mainly along the Poço Preto road) in Iguaçu National Park (1977, 1980-1990) were of pairs or presumed families of 3-4 individuals that foraged in shady areas at mid-heights (10-14 m) in the crowns of medium-sized trees; they less frequently ranged up into the lower parts of the tallest trees, or down into the upper undergrowth at c.3 m (TAP).

Pairs or families usually foraged within the crown of a single tree or two adjacent trees, staying in close visual and vocal contact, and occasionally perching on thin vines near trunks and sallied to nearby leaves and vinestems; individuals typically perched upright on slender horizontal branches while scanning the surrounding foliage, and made upward vertical or diagonal sallies (up to 0.5 m) to small and medium-sized leaves (TAP). They also hover-glean the tips of leaves and stems, and sometimes clamber under clusters of leaves (B. M. Whitney and R. H. Barth *in litt.* 1986, M. Pearman *in litt.* 1991, B. M. Whitney *in litt.* 1991). Similar behaviour was observed on the lower slopes of Pico do Corcovado south of Ubatuba, where pairs or family parties foraged with mixed-species flocks in the lower canopy of 30 m tall forest (TAP). Prey items were usually too small to identify, but several looked like small green orthopterans (TAP). Birds regularly if not constantly follow mixed-species flocks (M. Pearman *in litt.* 1991, D. F. Stotz *in litt.* 1991; specimen in MZUSP), often comprised at Iguaçu of Ochre-breasted Foliage-gleaner *Philydor liechtensteini*, Streaked Xenops *Xenops rutilans*, Plain Antvireo *Dysithamnus mentalis*, the similar-looking Southern Bristle-tyrant *Pogonotriccus eximius*, Golden-crowned Warbler *Basileuterus culicivorus* and Red-crowned Ant-tanager *Habia rubica* (TAP).

Year after year at Iguaçu pairs or families were encountered in the same relatively small areas (within 1 ha) in shady forest, and such territorial pairs seemed to be widely separated; response to playback of songs (including antiphonal duets of male and female) was strong and prolonged (TAP). Testes of one specimen from Serra do Caparaó, October, were fairly enlarged, while those of specimens from Paraná and Paraguay, April and January, were not enlarged (in AMNH). There is no other information on breeding.

THREATS Forest destruction within the species's range (and specifically within its altitudinal range) has been extensive, so that very little remains on the lowest slopes of the Serra do Mar and adjacent lowlands. Although the species occurs in a few reserves, these are too far apart and numbers observed remain too small to be confident about its long-term conservation.

MEASURES TAKEN The species has been recorded from Desengano, Ilha do Cardoso and Carlos Botelho State Parks, Poço das Antas Biological Reserve in Brazil, and Iguaçu and Iguazú National Parks in Brazil and Argentina (but see Threats).

MEASURES PROPOSED Studies at sites in São Paulo where this species is still relatively common would help provide ecological data valuable both for the management of the species at those sites and for its further study and conservation in areas where it is rarer. Support for the existing protected areas where it occurs must be maintained. Moreover, consideration of a reserve at Salto do Piraí, Santa Catarina, has been suggested, as this is the only locality in the state for the species and one of only two known in the world for Kaempfer's Tody-tyrant *Hemitriccus kaempferi* (see relevant account).

REMARKS A bird closely matching the species was described by a member of a Victor Emanuel Nature Tour during a visit to the Caratinga Reserve (Fazenda Montes Claros) in eastern Minas Gerais in October 1990 (R. S. Ridgely verbally 1992).

MINAS GERAIS TYRANNULET *Phylloscartes roquettei* V[9]

Confined to dry forest patches in one very small area of Minas Gerais in east-central Brazil, this small flycatcher faces extinction from the rapid loss of its semi-deciduous woodland habitat.

DISTRIBUTION The Minas Gerais Tyrannulet is known only from the vicinity of Januária (Brejo-Januária, now Brejo do Amparo: de Andrade *et al.* 1986), left bank of the rio São Francisco, northern Minas Gerais, central Brazil, where the type-specimen was collected on 3 July 1926 (Snethlage 1928a,b). No other specimen is known to have been collected subsequently (see Meyer de Schauensee 1966, Traylor 1979). The species was present in woodlots near the type-locality in 1977 (E. O. Willis *in litt.* 1986), occurring on both sides of the rio São Francisco in September (Willis and Oniki in press).

POPULATION Numbers are unknown, but the species must currently be at best rare in the region of the type-locality, having been missed there by fieldworkers in 1985, 1986 (M. A. de Andrade verbally 1986) and 1987 (J. M. C. da Silva verbally 1988).

ECOLOGY The type-specimen (female), in MNRJ, is labelled as having been collected in caatinga near hills ("serra"), and the stomach contained insects (Gonzaga 1989). In the original descriptions, however, caatinga is not mentioned and forest ("mata", "Bergwald") is indicated instead as the species's habitat (Snethlage 1928a,b). Both caatinga and dry forest (mesophytic deciduous forest) occur in the region of the type-locality around serras and limestone outcrops (de Azevedo 1966, Rizzini 1979, Eiten 1983, M. A. de Andrade *in litt.* 1986). It was in the latter vegetation type that birds were observed in September 1977, when most of the trees were leafless and the species was almost always in pairs, 10-20 m up in the few green trees and bushes; sometimes they descended to the green cotton bushes *Gossypium* of a plantation, always looking for insects on green leaves, hopping constantly and sallying short distances for prey (Willis and Oniki in press).

THREATS The known distribution of the species is very restricted, and its habitat, the (semi-deciduous forest, is possibly the most threatened of all in central Brazil owing to its valuable aroeira *Astronium urundeuva* wood and relatively fertile soils (R. B. Cavalcanti *in litt.* 1987). Charcoal-burners were in full activity in 1985-1986 around the type-locality, where forest cutting for pasture and agricultural development were also rife (M. A. de Andrade *in litt.* 1986, G. T. de Mattos *in litt.* 1987).

MEASURES TAKEN The Minas Gerais Tyrannulet is protected under Brazilian law (Bernardes *et al.* 1990).

MEASURES PROPOSED Further fieldwork is needed to determine the species's status and to provide additional information on its ecology and distribution. The creation of a protected area in the Januária region, which has been under consideration by governmental organizations (de Andrade *et al.* 1988) and by the non-governmental Fundação Pró-Natureza (J. M. C. da Silva *in litt.* 1988) is an urgent need (G. T. de Mattos *in litt.* 1987, J. M. C. da Silva *in litt.* 1988). However, as regulation of reserves is often poorly implemented, a programme of environmental awareness is also needed and should be directed at landowners, local communities and schools (de Andrade *et al.* 1988).

REMARKS Brejo-Januária is also the type-locality of Snethlage's Woodcreeper *Xiphocolaptes franciscanus*, here treated as a race of the threatened Moustached Woodcreeper *X. falcirostris* (see relevant account and, in particular, Remarks 3), and one of the few recorded localities for the

Caatinga (White-winged) Black-tyrant *Knipolegus (aterrimus) franciscanus* (da Silva 1989, Willis and Oniki in press).

CINNAMON-BREASTED TODY-TYRANT *Hemitriccus cinnamomeipectus* V[9]

This rare tyrant-flycatcher is confined to northern Peru and immediately adjacent Ecuador, where it is known from just four localities, and inhabits humid ridge-top elfin forest at 1,700-2,200 m.

DISTRIBUTION The Cinnamon-breasted Tody-tyrant (see Remarks 1) is known from just the following four localities in Zamora-Chinchipe province, southern Ecuador, and Cajamarca, Amazonas and San Martín departments, northern Peru:

Ecuador (*Zamora-Chinchipe*) near Chinapinza, 4°00'S 78°27-28'W, at 1,700 m in the Cordillera del Condor, where three specimens (in ANSP and MECN) were taken in September 1990 (Krabbe 1992);

Peru (*Cajamarca*) above San José de Lourdes, 5°02'S 78°51'W, Cordillera del Condor, where a male and female (type and holotype) were taken in July 1976; (*Amazonas*) 12-20 km by trail east of La Peca Nueva, c.5°34'S 78°17'W, Cordillera de Colán, where a female was collected in June 1978; and (*San Martín*) Abra Patricia (see Remarks 2), 5°46'S 77°42'W, near the border with Amazonas, where four birds were collected in August 1976 (all records and coordinates from Fitzpatrick and O'Neill 1979), with 3-4 birds seen at the last locality in August 1989 (B. M. Whitney *in litt.* 1991). It has not been reported further south-east in San Martín (Davis 1986).

POPULATION It was given the status "rare" by Parker *et al.* (1982), although a substantial population presumably exists along the ridge crests of the Cordillera del Condor. With 3-4 birds seen near Abra Patricia in August 1989 (B. M. Whitney *in litt.* 1991), whence come four specimens taken in 1976 (see above), the species is presumably not uncommon within its specialized habitat.

ECOLOGY The Cinnamon-breasted Tody-tyrant inhabits mossy stunted (elfin) forest on isolated mountain ridges east of the main Andean chain at elevations ranging from 1,700 to 2,200 m (Fitzpatrick and O'Neill 1979, Krabbe 1992: see under Long-whiskered Owlet *Xenoglaux loweryi* for details of the vegetation near Abra Patricia). Most specimens were mist-netted in the dense lower strata of the cloud-forest interior, although one appeared to be associated with a small mixed flock containing antbirds and warblers, in which it foraged with quick sallies, gleaning prey from nearby foliage, about 1.5-2 m off the ground in forest undergrowth (Fitzpatrick and O'Neill 1979). In August 1989 near Abra Patricia, B. M. Whitney (*in litt.* 1991) recorded a number of birds on a low ridge where the vegetation consisted of dense thickets 4-5 m tall with much bamboo and emergent palms: the birds foraged on their own at 0.5-2.5 m above the ground, and generally made darting, upward-directed sally-gleans (usually less than 0.5 m), returning to a different perch each time. A bird taken in Ecuador sang somewhat hidden in the vegetation 1.5 m above the ground, 0.5 m below the canopy, and its songposts suggested a territory no more than 15 m long and only a few metres wide (Krabbe 1992). All Peruvian specimens were collected between 25 June and 27 August of two different years: four of the seven adults had active gonads, one was in the late stage of moulting remiges, two were moulting outer rectrices, only one was in body moult; these data, together with the presence of a bird in juvenile plumage taken on 27 August, suggest that the birds were near the end of their breeding season (Fitzpatrick and O'Neill 1979). A singing male responded vigorously to playback of its song on 12 September (NK).

THREATS The absence of the similar Black-throated Tody-tyrant *Hemitriccus granadensis* in Cordillera del Condor suggests competition with that species (NK), and only near Abra Patricia have both been recorded (Fitzpatrick and O'Neill 1979, Davis 1986). The vegetation on these inaccessible ridge-tops appears to be relatively untouched and safe from the threat of deforestation (see under Long-whiskered Owlet).

MEASURES TAKEN None is known.

MEASURES PROPOSED Further study is needed on many of the elfin forest ridge-tops in this area, to determine the distributional status and population size of this rare species. Any conservation initiatives should be integrated into proposals presented for those species mentioned below. Although the habitat is at present under little apparent threat, a protected area, perhaps in the Cordillera del Condor or Cordillera de Colán, would help to guarantee the survival of this species and many other montane forest endemics. A number of species restricted to north-central and northern Peru have been recorded at the same localities as the present species, e.g. Long-whiskered Owlet, Royal Sunangel *Heliangelus regalis*, Russet-mantled Softtail *Thripophaga berlepschi* (see relevant accounts), and Pale-billed Antpitta *Grallaria carrikeri*, Bar-winged Wood-wren *Henicorhina leucoptera*, Rufous-browed Hemispingus *Hemispingus rufosuperciliaris* (see Remarks under Masked Mountain-tanager *Buthraupis wetmorei*) and Rusty-tinged Antpitta *Grallaria przewalskii* (NK). Many of these species may be found to occur further south in the Río Abiseo National Park, for which see Remarks under Yellow-browed Toucanet *Aulacorhynchus huallagae*.

REMARKS (1) This bird appears to form a superspecies in a relict group with two other threatened flycatchers (see Remarks under Kaempfer's Tody-tyrant *Hemitriccus kaempferi*). There is a sighting of what may be a fourth member of this group from Páramo de Tamá in western Venezuela on 2 January 1984 (C. S. Balchin verbally 1989). (2) The Abra Patricia locality is presumably the same as the type-locality of Long-whiskered Owlet, 10 km north-east of Abra Patricia (= Pardo de Miguel: Stephens and Traylor 1983), as the coordinates given coincide precisely with this (see relevant account).

FORK-TAILED PYGMY-TYRANT *Hemitriccus furcatus* R[11]

This tiny flycatcher is endemic to (and common in) a particular type of bamboo in south-east Brazil where, however, it is currently known from only four localities.

DISTRIBUTION The Fork-tailed Pygmy-tyrant (see Remarks) has been found only in a few localities in the states of Minas Gerais, Rio de Janeiro and São Paulo, south-eastern Brazil. The occurrence of the species in Espírito Santo has been claimed (Ruschi 1953) and repeated (Meyer de Schauensee 1966, 1982, Traylor 1979, Sibley and Monroe 1990), but is not accepted here.

Minas Gerais The only record of the species is from the Serra da Mantiqueira in the south of the state, near Itatiaia National Park (G. T. de Mattos *in litt.* 1987).

Rio de Janeiro The species occurs near Santa Maria Madalena at Desengano State Park between 400 and 850 m, where isolated individuals or pairs have been found regularly since August 1986 (J. F. Pacheco *in litt.* 1987, verbally 1988, B. M. Whitney *in litt.* 1991), having previously been recorded from Cantagalo (Cabanis 1874, von Ihering 1900a) and Nova Friburgo (Cory and Hellmayr 1927) in the same mountainous region. Two specimens in MNRJ were collected in June 1941 near Parati, on the lower coastal slopes (under 500 m) of the Serra do Mar (Berla 1944), and it still occurs there (J. F. Pacheco *in litt.* 1991, B. M. Whitney *in litt.* 1991). Three specimens were collected in July and August 1950 at 1,200 m in the Itatiaia National Park (Pinto 1954b), and the species was observed there in 1990 (D. Finch *per* B. C. Forrester *in litt.* 1992).

São Paulo The species was recorded at Matodentro in 1818 (von Pelzeln 1868-1871) and at Ubatuba (on the northern coast) in February, March and April 1905 (Pinto 1944, 1954b; specimens in AMNH, MCZ, MZUSP, USNM), and is still present at the latter locality (B. C. Forrester *in litt.* 1990, D. Willis *in litt.* 1991, M. Pearman *in litt.* 1992, TAP).

POPULATION Although the species has been considered rare (Berla 1944; Pinto 1954b) and possibly "in real danger" (Scott and Brooke 1985), it is tiny and inconspicuous, so might be often overlooked (C. E. Carvalho *in litt.* 1987), and indeed in one privately owned patch of forest at Ubatuba (Fazenda Angelina) it was considered the commonest bird in its particular habitat, with one pair every 100 m (D. Willis *in litt.* 1991, M. Pearman *in litt.* 1992), and again at Parati in the right habitat it is locally common (B. M. Whitney *in litt.* 1991). Nevertheless, its very limited range and specific habitat needs clearly render the bird very local, since it has eluded many ornithologists who have visited parts of its range.

ECOLOGY This species occurs primarily in bamboo thickets in forest undergrowth and along edges, and its normal habitat may be such thickets growing on natural landslides (TAP): it has been noted to prefer "large-leaved" species of bamboo both at Parati and Desengano, being at lower densities where this bamboo itself is less dense, and nearly or completely absent in stands of smaller-leaved bamboo (B. M. Whitney *in litt.* 1991), and birds have been found in bamboo thickets in forest undergrowth where the White-collared Foliage-gleaner *Anabazenops fuscus* and Drab-breasted Pygmy-tyrant *Hemitriccus diops* also occur (C. E. Carvalho *in litt.* 1987, J. F. Pacheco *in litt.* 1987). Near Ubatuba (Fazenda Capricórnio and at the base of Pico de Corcovado) the species occurs exclusively in extensive thickets of what is presumably the same type of bamboo (possibly *Merostachys*) at the edges of second-growth forest, often in fairly open places with only scattered small trees that barely form a continuous canopy (D. Willis *in litt.* 1991, TAP). Birds there have been found singly, with territorial individuals c.50-100 m apart; three birds observed at length stayed within small areas of c.100 m^2, and most foraging over a period of 30 minutes on different days occurred within c.50 m^2 (TAP). When foraging, birds perch mostly 1-4 m above ground on thin bamboo branches (but "3-14 m up in *Guadua* bamboo and adjacent second growth": M. Pearman *in litt.* 1992; and "usually 8 m up in the tops of bamboo": B. C.

Forrester *in litt.* 1992), usually not in mixed-species flocks, taking small arthropods with frequent darting short-distance (less than 1 m) sallies laterally or diagonally upward to long, hanging bamboo leaves (30+ observations, including a few directed to non-bamboo foliage: TAP; also B. M. Whitney *in litt.* 1991). Prey thus gleaned included two small green caterpillars and (from a stem) a small katydid (TAP). Specimens with insects in the stomach have been collected in second-growth with vine tangles and thorny bushes (Berla 1944). There are no breeding data.

THREATS None is known, though forest clearance would presumably be detrimental to the species. Desengano State Park, largely unprotected, has been under serious threat from extensive deforestation (C. E. Carvalho verbally 1987). The slopes below Pico do Corcovado south of Ubatuba hold numerous patches of bamboo on steep landslides surrounded by tall forest, but these patches persist only for a few decades at most before flowering and dying off, so that the Fork-tailed Pygmy-tyrant and other bamboo specialists of the region must disperse in search of other areas; despite some deforestation possibly having led to an increase in bamboo in recent years, the overall loss of forest means that in the long term bamboo specialists will become severely constrained.

MEASURES TAKEN The Fork-tailed Pygmy-tyrant is protected under Brazilian law (Bernardes *et al.* 1990). Its occurrence in Itatiaia National Park and possibly other protected areas along the Serra do Mar, where much apparently suitable habitat remains, gives some prospect for its long-term survival.

MEASURES PROPOSED Surveys are needed to determine the status of the species and to confirm its current presence in the Itatiaia National Park. The Bocaina National Park on the border between Rio de Janeiro and São Paulo states needs to be fully investigated. Effective forest measures are required at Desengano State Park, and along the lower slopes of the Serra do Mar. This bird would be targeted under a programme of research on (threatened) bamboo specialist birds in Atlantic Forest (see equivalent section under White-bearded Antshrike *Biatas nigropectus*).

REMARKS When in *Ceratotriccus* this species occupied a genus of its own (Cory and Hellmayr 1927), but the general trend has been to consider it a distinctive representative of *Hemitriccus* (Traylor 1979, Sibley and Monroe 1990).

BUFF-BREASTED TODY-TYRANT *Hemitriccus mirandae* V/R[10]

Deforestation is probably the single threat to this forest-haunting flycatcher of north-east Brazil, known from only five areas in three states.

DISTRIBUTION The Buff-breasted Tody-tyrant (see Remarks) is endemic to north-east Brazil in the states of Ceará, Pernambuco and Alagoas, where it is known from five basic areas.

Ceará Three birds (including the type) were collected at São Paulo (not located) on the plateau (c.800 m; but see Ecology) of the Serra da Ibiapaba, in June 1910 (Snethlage 1925), and two other specimens were later obtained in the Serra de Baturité (Pacoti municipality) in July 1958 (Pinto and de Camargo 1961). The species was again encountered in both serras in September 1991, at Fazenda Gameleira, Tianguá, in the former and at Guaramiranga in the latter (J. F. Pacheco *in litt.* 1992).

Pernambuco Cory and Hellmayr (1927) pointed out that there was a possible record from Garanhuns, September 1880 (Forbes 1881), and Zimmer (1953b) confirmed this identification when mentioning two specimens collected at Brejão (some 20 km south of Garanhuns); these were taken at 750 m in February 1927 (specimens in AMNH). Birds "probably of this species" were observed in the Tapacurá Ecological Station, São Lourenço da Mata, November 1976 (Coelho 1979).

Alagoas An adult female was collected at Engenho (Fazenda) Riachão, north of Quebrangulo, in November 1951 (Pinto 1954a), and the species was relocated at the same site, now Pedra Talhada Biological Reserve, in July 1989 (M. Pearman *in litt.* 1991) and October 1990, when the altitude was noted as 710 m (J. F. Pacheco *in litt.* 1992).

POPULATION There is no information on the abundance of this species. It seems, however, to be rather uncommon wherever it has been recorded; Forbes (1881) only found it "once or twice... usually singly".

ECOLOGY That this is a bird of forest in the lowlands (Sibley and Monroe 1990) is wrong: the type-locality, though not located, is known to have been at around 1,000 m (Paynter and Traylor 1991), in Serra de Baturité it was also found in the highlands, not the lower-lying areas (Pinto and de Camargo 1961), while in Alagoas the only altitude recorded is 710 m (see Distribution). Habitat in general is seasonally dry semi-deciduous woodland on isolated serras, 700-860 m (B. M. Whitney *in litt.* 1992): in Pedra Talhada was large-leaved bamboo, in Serra de Baturité it was rather humid forest understorey with little bamboo, in Serra da Ibiapaba it was dry forest understorey with many tall *Orbignya* palms (J. F. Pacheco *in litt.* 1992); but in general the species was to be found in areas of dense, tall vine tangles patchily distributed throughout the woodland, such as around old "light gaps" (B. M. Whitney *in litt.* 1992). In Pernambuco it was found "actively hopping and creeping about the thick scrub which is so prevalent there" (Forbes 1881). The species is said, however, to adapt to secondary formations, surviving in good numbers even in degraded capoeira (Teixeira *et al.* in press), although its very patchy distribution then suggests some other constraint in play. Birds forage from c.1.5 to 10 m above ground, most often at 2-5 m, scanning actively for arthropod prey and making laterally or upwardly directed sally-strike (most less than 1 m) to foliage or vines, taking small prey items (B. M. Whitney *in litt.* 1992). The stomach contents of two specimens in MNRJ are given as "insects". The ovaries of a female in AMNH from Pernambuco, February, were not enlarged.

THREATS The history of north-east Brazil has been one of chronic and continuing deforestation (see, e.g., Teixeira 1986), such that any forest-dependent species endemic to the region – even if capable of surviving in second growth – must be considered at risk. Thus while in 1958 substantial areas of forest still remained in the Serra de Baturité, Ceará (Pinto and de Camargo

1961), 30 years later the massif was being "totally destroyed by advancing agriculture (including banana plantations)", such that a mere 5% of remaining forest (the wettest in the state) was believed to be primary, and the situation in the Serra da Ibiapaba was considered even worse (R. Otoch *in litt.* 1987, 1988).

MEASURES TAKEN Efforts to preserve the forests in the Serra das Guaribas at Quebrangulo (Studer 1985) resulted in the creation, by the Decree No. 98.524 of 13 December 1989, of the 4,500 ha Pedra Talhada Biological Reserve (A. Studer verbally 1990).

MEASURES PROPOSED The relatively gentle climate in the Serra de Baturité was identified as the reason why the area appeared to be rich in endemic forms of wildlife (Pinto and de Camargo 1961), although this presumably refers largely to subspecies and to birds in particular; nonetheless this interesting remark indicates the importance of ensuring the conservation of the area not just for the Buff-breasted Tody-tyrant, and among other birds present are the isolated race *griseipectus* of the White-eared Parakeet *Pyrrhura leucotis* (see Forshaw 1989), the threatened nominate form of the Bearded Bellbird *Procnias averano* (see King 1978-1979), and a population of the threatened Moustached Woodcreeper *Xiphocolaptes falcirostris* (see relevant account). Similar considerations may apply to the Serra da Ibiapaba, which merits closer biological investigation.

REMARKS This bird appears to form a superspecies in a relict group with two other threatened flycatchers (see Remarks under Kaempfer's Tody-tyrant *Hemitriccus kaempferi*). Birds in Ceará differ slightly from those in Alagoas (B. M. Whitney *in litt.* 1992).

KAEMPFER'S TODY-TYRANT *Hemitriccus kaempferi* I[7]

This small flycatcher remains known only from two localities in humid lowland Atlantic Forest in Santa Catarina, Brazil, where further studies are needed to learn more of the bird and to assess options for the creation of a reserve.

DISTRIBUTION The type-specimen of Kaempfer's Tody-tyrant (see Remarks) was collected on 3 June 1929 at nearly 150 m in Salto (do) Piraí (Pirahy), near Joinville, Santa Catarina, southern Brazil (Zimmer 1953, Fitzpatrick and O'Neill 1979). The locality is further described as 9 km north-north-west of Vila Nova by M. Pearman (*in litt.* 1991), who observed an individual of this species there for 10 minutes on 20 July 1991. A second specimen (in MNRJ), apparently only just recognized, was collected c.100 km to the south at Brusque, also in Santa Catarina, in 1950 (Teixeira *et al.* in press).

POPULATION Numbers are not known, but the species must be at best rare in the region of the type-locality, as its collector usually obtained series of specimens in the localities he visited (see Naumburg 1939). In the course of three visits in 1987 to this area one observer failed to rediscover the species (M. A. Da-Ré *in litt.* 1987), and the observation of a bird in 1991, judged less than 1 km from the original collecting site, was the culmination of two days' searching in the area (M. Pearman *in litt.* 1991).

ECOLOGY Humid lowland Atlantic Forest (now partially cleared) occurs at the type-locality at the altitude in which the bird was collected (M. A. Da-Ré *in litt.* 1987, M. Pearman *in litt.* 1991) and is presumed to be the natural habitat of the species (Fitzpatrick and O'Neill 1979). The bird in 1991 actively hover-gleaned in the subcanopy some 6 m up, occasionally dropping to 2 m in trees along a river inside the forest, once at this lower level loosely associating with a lone Golden-crowned Warbler *Basileuterus culicivorus*, and being easily located by its distinctive call; it eventually disappeared into denser forest away from the river (M. Pearman *in litt.* 1991).

THREATS Forest destruction at Salto do Piraí itself is not a problem (see below) and, although the lowest slopes are second growth and the valley bottoms are cleared, there was no evidence in 1991 of recent logging within a 5 km radius of the dam, and forest appeared to be good and extensive in the surrounding hills; nevertheless, logging trucks in nearby Vila Nova indicated the vulnerability of the region to deforestation (M. Pearman *in litt.* 1991).

MEASURES TAKEN The species is protected under Brazilian law (Bernardes *et al.* 1990). Fortuitously CELESC (Centrais Elétricas de Santa Catarina) has established a 400 ha forest reserve off limits to the public, which encompasses the Salto do Piraí hydroelectric power station to assure a water supply from the slopes of the surrounding mountain range (M. A. Da-Ré *in litt.* 1987, M. Pearman *in litt.* 1991).

MEASURES PROPOSED A programme of ornithological studies is needed at Salto do Piraí to learn more of Kaempfer's Tody-tyrant, so that it can be efficiently managed and searched for over a wider area. The possibility of establishing a biological reserve to augment the CELESC reserve merits investigation, particularly as M. Pearman *in litt.* (1991) observed the threatened White-necked Hawk *Leucopternis lacernulata* and São Paulo Tyrannulet *Phylloscartes paulistus*, both (lowland) forest species, at the site (see relevant accounts), as well as the near-threatened upland Saw-billed Hermit *Ramphodon naevius* and Hooded Berryeater *Carpornis cucullatus*.

REMARKS Kaempfer's Tody-tyrant was originally described as a race of the Buff-breasted Tody-tyrant *Hemitriccus mirandae*, but it has subsequently been recognized as specifically distinct

(Fitzpatrick 1976, Traylor 1979, Fitzpatrick and O'Neill 1979), most likely being a member of a superspecies including two other widely disjunct allospecies, the Buff-breasted Tody-tyrant and the Cinnamon-breasted Tody-tyrant *H. cinnamomeipectus* (Vuilleumier and Mayr 1987), both of which are also threatened (see relevant accounts).

BUFF-CHEEKED TODY-FLYCATCHER *Todirostrum senex* I[8]

This small flycatcher is known only from the type collected over 160 years ago at Borba, Amazonas, Brazil.

DISTRIBUTION The Buff-cheeked Tody-flycatcher (see Remarks) remains known from a single male collected at Borba on the right bank of the lower rio Madeira, eastern Amazonas state, Brazil, in June 1830 (von Pelzeln 1868-1871, Hellmayr 1910b).

POPULATION Nothing is known. It is difficult to draw conclusions from evidence over 160 years old, but the fact that J. Natterer collected only a single specimen during a stay of seven or more probably nine months, November 1829 to June or August 1830 (see von Pelzeln 1868-1871), suggests that the bird could not have been common in the region or was perhaps confined to a little explored habitat.

ECOLOGY Nothing is known. Its habitat is "probably humid forest" (Sibley and Monroe 1990), but this could be igapó (permanently flooded), várzea (seasonally flooded) or terra firme (upland) forest.

THREATS None is known. Deforestation generally in Amazonas remains as yet slight (Fearnside 1990), but whether the area around Borba has been particularly affected is unknown.

MEASURES TAKEN None is known.

MEASURES PROPOSED This bird (described in some detail in von Pelzeln 1868-1871, Hellmayr 1910b) should be illustrated as a means of providing a search-image to potential fieldworkers, and then looked for in the environs of Borba in as many types of habitat as are known to have existed there 160 years ago. A modern examination and redescription of the type-specimen would be welcome.

REMARKS Species based on single nineteenth-century specimens tend largely to be considered aberrant or hybrid; however, examination of the type led to the conclusion that this is "a very distinct species" (Cory and Hellmayr 1927).

RUSSET-WINGED SPADEBILL *Platyrinchus leucoryphus* V/R[10]

Although now being found fairly widely in Rio de Janeiro state following the identification of its call, this Atlantic Forest flycatcher of south-east Brazil, eastern Paraguay and northern Argentina occurs at very low densities and remains very poorly known. It has suffered from habitat destruction and is in urgent need of study.

DISTRIBUTION The Russet-winged Spadebill is endemic to the Atlantic Forest region of south-east South America, from Espírito Santo south to northern Rio Grande do Sul (no records from Santa Catarina) in Brazil into eastern Paraguay and north-eastern Argentina.

Brazil In the following account, localities are listed from north to south.

Espírito Santo The species was included in the state bird list by Ruschi (1953), and a specimen, formerly in MNRJ but now missing, was collected in the state (J. F. Pacheco *in litt.* 1991, LPG). Recent records are from the Santa Lucia Reserve (700 ha, kept by MNRJ: see Oliver and Santos 1991: 82), Santa Teresa, October 1986 (J. Vielliard verbally 1986), and the Augusto Ruschi (Nova Lombardia) Biological Reserve, 900 m, 1984-1990 (C. E. Carvalho *in litt.* 1987, TAP), and October 1989 (M. Kessler *in litt.* 1989).

Rio de Janeiro Four old skins in BMNH are labelled "Rio de Janeiro". This state holds the bulk of modern records, all from the late 1980s and early 1990s (and all supplied by J. F. Pacheco *in litt.* 1987, 1991): Desengano State Park, at three sites, 500-1,000 m: Morumbeca do Imbé, February to April, October 1987 to 1989, Marreiros, April 1989, and ribeirão Macapá, April 1989; Mata da Cicuta, Volta Redonda, October 1987; Caiçara, Piraí, July 1989, May 1990; Piraí Ecological Station, December 1987; Serra do Mendanha (north of Campo Grande), August 1988; rio Florestão, Angra dos Reis, December 1990; Horto Florestal (adjacent to Tijuca National Park), September 1988; and Sítio Palmeiras, Parati, September 1989, April and November 1990.

São Paulo Records are from: Rio Feio, Bauru, 1901 (von Ihering 1902, von Ihering and von Ihering 1907, Pinto 1944); Fazenda Barreiro Rico, Anhembi, November 1964 (specimen in MZUSP) and 1975–1977 (Willis 1979); near Ubatuba, September 1991 (D. F. Stotz *in litt.* 1991); Boracéia Biological Station, near Salesópolis, November 1945, September 1963 (specimens in MZUSP) and September and December 1991 (D. F. Stotz *in litt.* 1991, 1992); Casa Grande, February 1968 and in 1972 (specimens in CIAL); Sete Barras State Reserve, 1979 (Willis and Oniki 1981a); and Fazenda Poço Grande, rio Juquiá, May 1940 (Pinto 1944). E. O. Willis *in litt.* (1986) mentioned having found this species at three unspecified localities in the state.

Paraná Scherer Neto (1985) indicated that the species was known in the state from material in museums; this was evidently based on a specimen in MHNCI from Santa Cruz Forest Reserve, 25°35'S 48°35'W, July 1946 (F. C. Straube *in litt.* 1985; coordinates from Straube 1990). Sick's (1985) record of Londrina derived from Steffan (1974), who reported having netted one bird at Água do Quati dam, rio Tibaji, c.20 km east of Londrina, on an unstated date. Other recent records are from the Fazenda de Irmãos Thá, Antonina (25°15'S 49°15'W), December 1986 (SPVS 1988), and Guaraguaçu, near Praia de Leste, c.15 km south of Paranaguá, August 1991 (F. C. Straube *in litt.* 1991). Small numbers were recorded in Iguaçu National Park, 1985-1990 (TAP).

Rio Grande do Sul The only record is from the vicinity of Torres, in subsequently destroyed wet coastal forests, where four birds were collected in October 1928 and September 1973 (Belton 1984-1985; also Sick 1985).

Paraguay Records are from Sapucay, September 1904 (Chubb 1910), and Picada del Monte Caaguazú, November 1930 (specimen in AMNH).

Argentina The only records are those of a bird banded in the Iguazú National Park, April 1978 (Olrog 1979) and of one seen there in January 1989 (P. Cano *per* J. C. Chebez *in litt.* 1992);

however, in the absence of a photograph or skin these first reports for the country must remain technically open to question (J. C. Chebez *in litt.* 1992).

POPULATION This species is apparently rare and local, although it is certainly also very inconspicuous and may therefore be overlooked to a large degree: the number of records in Rio de Janeiro, for instance, has increased significantly since its advertisement call was learnt (J. F. Pacheco verbally 1991). Nevertheless, it has been stated that the species "never seems to be common anywhere, one pair or two at most being present at any given site, which makes it always rare" (D. F. Stotz *in litt.* 1991). It is considered rare at Augusto Ruschi (Nova Lombardia) Biological Reserve (C. E. Carvalho *in litt.* 1987), where during annual visits (1980-1990) individuals or pairs were located (with the aid of tape playback) in only four widely separated areas (TAP). It is also rare in the sites where it has been recorded in Rio de Janeiro (J. F. Pacheco *in litt.* 1991): at Morumbeca, Desengano State Park, an estimated population of at most 10 birds was present in early 1987 (J. F. Pacheco *in litt.* 1987), and numbers at Barreiro Rico and Sete Barras in São Paulo were, respectively, eight and seven birds per 100 hours of fieldwork (Willis 1979, Willis and Oniki 1981a). In extensive good-looking habitat in Iguaçu National Park only four individuals were found, most of them repeatedly in the same areas year after year (TAP). Most of the records at each of the other localities have been of isolated birds or pairs; but while unobtrusiveness of the bird alone may not account for this scarcity of records, it should be noted that several modern records have resulted from the use of mist-nets (specimens in MZUSP, some of the Paraná and the Argentina records at least).

ECOLOGY The Russet-winged Spadebill has been recorded from the understorey of primary and (old) secondary forest both in the coastal mountains and lowlands and in more inland tableland forests. In both Augusto Ruschi and Iguaçu the species occurs in tall (25-30 m) closed-canopy forest with a well developed (and shaded) middle tier of small to medium trees and fairly open undergrowth below: nearly all observations were of individuals perched on slender branches in the crowns of small trees 3-8 m above the ground (thus they do not normally occur near the ground in thick undergrowth or bamboo as does the White-throated Spadebill *Platyrinchus mystaceus*) (TAP). One bird collected near Torres was in a "heavily shaded area of wet coastal forest with only moderate undergrowth at a height of about 1.8 m" (Belton 1984-1985), this description corresponding well to the situation in which the species was found at one site in Desengano State Park in lower montane forest (LPG), but on the Serra do Mendanha birds were in the undergrowth of regenerating forest in an old banana plantation (J. F. Pacheco verbally 1988). Pairs seem to stay far apart when foraging, and indeed are only rarely seen together (e.g. in response to song playbacks at dawn); and although territories seem to be very small (less than 0.5 ha) individuals may spend much time in small portions of a much larger area (TAP). One at Augusto Ruschi was found in the same small area (within 20 m of a few frequently used small trees) every year in September or October from 1984 to 1990, occasionally accompanied by a second individual; this site was characterized by an abundance of small understorey palms and scattered small trees in the full shade of tall forest on a moderately steep slope (TAP). Another bird seen annually from c.1985 to 1990 at Iguaçu was consistently found in the tops of small trees (at 3-6 m) in a shady, level area bordering a small stream: it rarely moved more than 50 m from the centre of its territory and was usually perched in one of a few regularly used trees (TAP). A third bird, also at Iguaçu, frequented similar streamside habitat but ranged up and down a slope and occasionally perched high in a bamboo thicket (TAP).

Birds perch motionless, often for several minutes at a time, scanning surrounding foliage: most foraging movements were diagonal sallies (up to 2 m) to small and medium-sized leaves; an individual watched for 20 minutes in Iguaçu captured two green katydids c.3 cm long (TAP). One bird at Augusto Ruschi was in a mixed-species flock in forest undergrowth (P. K. Donahue *in litt.* 1987).

As with White-crested Spadebill *P. platyrhynchos* of Amazonia, territorial Russet-winged Spadebills rarely if ever occur close to other pairs: the closest adjacent territories in Augusto Ruschi were c.600 m apart (TAP). The only evidence of breeding are that a female collected on 30 September 1973 had an enlarged ovary and follicles (Belton 1984-1985), two males obtained in October and November had testes fairly enlarged, and a female collected with the October male had an ovary slightly enlarged (specimens in AMNH).

THREATS The fragmentation of the species's range by extensive forest destruction has been and remains the one significant threat; even if current records are from a number of protected areas, the species's ecological requirements remain very poorly known and its recorded numbers in those areas are too low to inspire confidence in the future of the populations they hold. Furthermore, some of these areas, such as Desengano in Rio de Janeiro and the southern coast of Paraná, are also suffering from deforestation (Straube 1990, J. F. Pacheco *in litt.* 1991).

MEASURES TAKEN The species is protected under Brazilian law (Bernardes *et al.* 1990). Some of its present remnant populations should persist so long as the protected areas where they have been found continue to be preserved; but see Threats.

MEASURES PROPOSED Surveys of the species in the field are needed to confirm and monitor its continued existence in the localities where it has been recorded, as well as to locate any new populations and to redefine its range, particularly now that its song and calls have been taped (J. Vielliard verbally 1986, LPG) and could be used, perhaps in conjunction with mist-nets, to enhance its detection. It should be noted that this species, like many Neotropical flycatchers, sings primarily at first light, and then normally for only a few minutes; moreover, the most frequently heard call-note (a sharp *queek*) is similar to that of the Rufous-capped Antthrush *Formicarius colma* (TAP). A study programme into its population dynamics and habitat requirements at various sites where it occurs should partner a general review of its conservation status in these areas, whose continued protection is an obvious need.

PACIFIC ROYAL FLYCATCHER *Onychorhynchus occidentalis* E[2]

Confined to humid low-lying forest in western Ecuador and immediately adjacent north-west Peru, this spectacular, low-density flycatcher is now left with virtually no habitat.

DISTRIBUTION The Pacific Royal Flycatcher (see Remarks) was confined to humid lowland forest in western Ecuador and immediately adjacent Peru, but it is now gone from most of its range. The few known localities (coordinates from Paynter and Traylor 1977, Stephens and Traylor 1983) are as follows:

Ecuador (*Esmeraldas*) Esmeraldas (sea level), at 0°59'N 79°42'W (Chapman 1926); (*Manabí*) Chone (Chapman 1926); Cerro San Sebastián, Machalilla National Park, at c.1°34'S 80°40'W (sighting in January 1991: TAP); San José (untraced), 80 m, May 1942 (specimen in BMNH); (*Guayas*) Jauneche reserve, 50-70 m, at c.1°05'S 79°46'W (sightings in July 1991: TAP); nearby at Hacienda Pacaritambo (untraced, but near Quevedo and half-way between Santo Domingo de los Colorados and Babahoyo), May 1962, February 1963 (Brosset 1964; also Vuilleumier 1978); Balzar (100 m), at 1°22'S 79°54'W (Salvadori and Festa 1899); Guayaquil, near sea level (von Berlepsch and Taczanowski 1883); (*Los Ríos*) Vinces (15 m), at 1°32'S 79°45'W (Salvadori and Festa 1899); Babahoyo (5 m), at 1°49'S 79°31'W (Sclater 1860c); (*Cañar*) Manta Real, c.250-500 m, at c.2°30'S 79°17'W (sightings and one specimen now in ANSP collected in 1991: TAP and R. S. Ridgely *in litt.* 1991); (*Azuay*) San Miguel del Azuay, c.900 m,at c.2°48'S 79°30'W (a pair seen at a partially constructed nest in January 1992: M. Whittingham *in litt.* 1992, coordinates from B. J. Best *in litt.* 1992); (*El Oro*) Santa Rosa (c.100 m), at 3°27'S 79°58'W (Chapman 1926); 9 km west of Piñas, 600 m, El Oro, at 3°40'S 79°44'W (Robbins and Ridgely 1990; elevation from M. B. Robbins verbally 1991);

Peru (*Tumbes*) Matapalo, 3°41'S 80°12'W, 60 m, April 1956 (Koepcke 1961); El Caucho, 3°50'S 80°16'W, Tumbes National Forest (recorded during June and July 1979: Wiedenfeld *et al.* 1985).

POPULATION There have been very few recent records of this species: its habitat is now almost gone, and the bird is rare at the few remaining sites, being commonest at Jauneche (TAP), a reserve of only 130 ha (Dodson and Gentry 1991). On Cerro San Sebastián it was reported to be rare in January 1991 (TAP) and none was found there during an intensive survey in August 1991 (R. S. Ridgely *in litt.* 1991). At Manta Real three birds were heard on one day in July 1991 (TAP), but R. S. Ridgely (*in litt.* 1991) reported it to be seemingly rare, and at San Miguel del Azuay only one pair was seen there during fieldwork in January 1992 (M. Whittingham *in litt.* 1992). West of Piñas there were so few records that no abundance was given by Robbins and Ridgely (1990), and in Tumbes National Forest only a few birds were recorded during surveys in June and July 1979 (Wiedenfeld *et al.* 1985). The recent taxonomic split that established this species may have contributed to the paucity of records, although the bird is clearly rare (living naturally at low densities) and has suffered from extensive habitat loss.

ECOLOGY R. S. Ridgely (*in litt.* 1990) described this tyrant flycatcher's habitat as "humid and deciduous forest... favouring deciduous woodland", and on Cerro San Sebastián and at Jauneche there are indeed elements of both humid and deciduous forest (TAP). At Manta Real in 1991 the species was found in cocoa plantations, humid second-growth woods and humid forest lower growth at c.300-550 m (TAP, R. S. Ridgely *in litt.* 1991). The known historic sites all presumably had humid forest, although Esmeraldas, Chone, Guayaquil and Santa Rosa most probably had elements of deciduous forest (NK). Originally occurring down to near sea level, this bird now finds its lowest elevation at Jauneche at 50 to 70 m, whilst its upper limit may be reached at San Miguel del Azuay at 900 m (see Distribution). At the last-mentioned locality (at the edge of primary forest, c.200 m from the village), in January 1992, a pair of birds was seen displaying around a half-constructed nest (built of long twigs, and totalling c.1 m long) which was suspended from a branch overhanging a river (5 m above the water), in trees c.25 m high (M. Whittingham *in litt.* 1992). In a study which judged it a sociable species (i.e. a group was present in the area surveyed), dwelling in the forest understorey at 3-15 m, a male from February had gonads developed (the stomach held a ball of insects), while those of a female from May were dormant (Brosset 1964); the bird (in BMNH) collected in May at San José, Manabí, was juvenile.

THREATS Owing to deforestation and cultivation, low-lying humid forest in western and south-western Ecuador now exists in extremely small and isolated patches (NK), none of which may be large enough to maintain a viable population of this species for much longer (see Threats under Grey-backed Hawk *Leucopternis occidentalis*).

MEASURES TAKEN This flycatcher occurs in Machalilla National Park; Jauneche reserve; and Tumbes National Forest (see equivalent section under Grey-backed Hawk). Plans to establish a reserve at Manta Real are under way (P. Greenfield *in litt.* 1989), but the species only occurs in its lowest part (see Distribution). It is possible that the species also occurs in the Cerros de Amotape National Park that adjoins Tumbes National Forest.

MEASURES PROPOSED The Jauneche and Manta Real reserves should be supported in order to ensure the integrity of the species's habitat there. The few remaining areas on the Pacific slope of Azuay where the forest still reaches down to the coastal plain should be investigated and protected immediately, as this habitat is rapidly disappearing, and may well harbour this species (TAP). A reserve west of Piñas, if large and reaching low enough, might harbour a small population. Both Machalilla National Park and Tumbes National Forest require adequate protection. The Pacific Royal Flycatcher shares habitat with several other threatened species of bird endemic to western Ecuador and north-west Peru: options and actions to preserve all of these species are outlined in Measures Proposed under Grey-backed Hawk.

REMARKS The Pacific Royal Flycatcher has traditionally been regarded a subspecies of Royal Flycatcher *Onychorhynchus coronatus*, found from Mexico to Bolivia, but TAP found *occidentalis* differing enough (e.g. simply in size) to be considered specifically distinct, and R. S. Ridgely (*in litt.* 1990) has suggested that the previously monotypic genus actually may be composed of three or even four allospecies. If this is followed, then the form *O. swainsoni*, Atlantic Royal Flycatcher, of central and south-east Brazil, emerges as an exceptionally rare and little known bird (LPG).

GREY-BREASTED FLYCATCHER *Lathrotriccus griseipectus* V/R[10]

This flycatcher is confined to the viny understorey of tropical deciduous, semi-deciduous and moist forest from sea level to 1,750 m in south-west Ecuador and northern Peru. It has been reported to be common at only two localities, being otherwise uncommon or rare; it is threatened by habitat destruction.

DISTRIBUTION The Grey-breasted Flycatcher (see Remarks 1) is found in the coastal range and western lowlands and on the Pacific slope of the Andes from Esmeraldas and Pichincha provinces, Ecuador, south to at least the region west of Abra de Porculla, Lambayeque department, Peru, also occurring east of the Peruvian Andes in northern Cajamarca department, where it has been found on the left bank of the middle río Marañón.

Ecuador Localities (coordinates and altitudes in parentheses, unless otherwise stated, from Paynter and Traylor 1977) are as follows: (*Esmeraldas*) río Verde, at 1°05'N 79°30'W, specimen collected in July 1951 (Norton *et al.* 1972: see Ecology); (*Pichincha*) "Mindo, 1,830 m", situated on the Pacific slope at 0°02'S 78°48'W (specimen in BMNH collected in January 1914); Río Palenque reserve, 200 m, at c.0°30'S 79°30'W, several recent sightings (P. Greenfield *in litt.* 1989); (*Manabí*) deciduous forest in hills near the coast just south of río Cuaque, c.0°02'S 80°04'W (heard in January 1991: TAP); Cordillera de Balzar (see Remarks 2), at 0°55'S 79°55'W (coordinates from OG 1957b) (specimen in BMNH collected March 1880); Machalilla National Park, several seen in July 1978 (R. S. Ridgely *in litt.* 1989); (*Los Ríos*) Jauneche reserve, 50-70 m, at 1°10'S 79°30'W, many sightings in July, but also records in September and October 1991 (Williams and Tobias 1991, TAP); Babahoyo (5 m), at 1°49'S 79°31'W (Sclater 1888: two specimens in BMNH taken in August 1859); (*Guayas*) Cerro Blanco reserve, at c.2°09'S 80°03'W (sightings in January 1991: TAP, also R. Jones *in litt.* undated); Bucay (300 m), at 2°10'S 79°06'W, on the border of Guayas and Chimborazo provinces (Chapman 1926); Puente de Chimbo (250-925 m), at 2°10'S 79°10'W, on the border of Guayas and Chimborazo provinces (von Berlepsch and Taczanowski 1883, Chapman 1926: two specimens in AMNH taken in November 1882 and August 1922); Naranjito (30 m), at 2°13'S 79°29'W (Chapman 1926: specimen in AMNH taken in May 1913); Isla Puná (Lawrence 1870; type-specimen in USNM); (*Cañar*) Manta Real, 300-600 m, at c.2°30'S 79°17'W, recently (TAP, R. S. Ridgely *in litt.* 1991: see Ecology); (*Azuay*) San Miguel de Azuay, 2°48'S 79°30'W (one seen in January 1992: M. Whittingham and G. J. Morales *in litt.* 1992, coordinates from B. J. Best *in litt.* 1992); (*El Oro*) 9 km west of Piñas (near Buenaventura), 900-950 m, at 3°40'S 79°44'W (specimen in MECN collected in September 1990; one seen in September 1991: Williams and Tobias 1991); Puyango, 275 m, at c.3°52'S 80°05'W, near the border with Loja (Chapman 1926: specimen in AMNH taken in July 1919); (*Loja*) La Puente, 760 m, at c.3°57'S 80°05'W (coordinates read from IGM 1982) (Chapman 1926: specimen in AMNH taken in October 1921); Guainche, 975 m, at c.4°02'S 80°00'W (coordinates read from IGM 1982) (Chapman 1926); Milagros, 670 m, at 4°07'S 80°07'W (Chapman 1926); Paletillas, 470 m, at 4°11'S 80°17'W (Chapman 1926); 4 km south-west of Sabanilla, 500 m, at 4°13'S 80°10'W (specimens in MECN and WFVZ collected in March 1991); Quebrada Suquinda, 1,750 m, near Sozoranga, at 4°18'S 79°51'W (one sighted February 1991: Best 1992); Quebrada Hueco Hondo, 600-1,100 m, Tambo Negro, near Sabiango, at 4°23'S 79°51'W (4-5 birds sighted February and March 1991: Best 1992).

Peru Localities (coordinates from Stephens and Traylor 1983) are restricted to the north-west of the country as follows: (*Tumbes*) El Caucho (450 m), at c.3°50'S 80°16'W (sighting in late July 1988: Parker *et al.* 1989); Campo Verde and nearby Cotrina, 600-750 m, at c.3°51'S 80°12'W (sightings in March 1986 and late July 1988: M. Kessler *in litt.* 1988, Parker *et al.* 1989); (*Piura*) El Angolo, 700 m, on Cerros de Amotape, at c.4°28'S 80°48'W (two specimens in LSUMZ taken in November 1972); Palambla, at 5°23'S 79°37'W, 1922 (Chapman 1926: specimen in AMNH which, like others collected there by H. Watkins, is labelled from between 1,190 and 1,980 m); (*Lambayeque*) Ñaupé, c.150 m, at 5°36'S 79°54'W (sighting in September 1983: NK); Porculla (south-west of the pass: NK), 1,065 m, near the border with Piura, the pass being at 5°51'S 79°31'W (two specimens in MCZ taken in 1933, with sightings nearby in 1979: Meyer de Schauensee 1966, NK); and, east of the Andes (*Cajamarca*), below San José de Lourdes, c.800 m, and 2 km north of San José de Lourdes, 830 m, on the left bank of río Chinchipe, at c.5°03-04'S 78°54'W (two specimens in FMNH and LSUMZ taken in June 1975 and August 1976); and 9 km south of Jaen, 900 m, at 5°42'S 78°47'W (specimen in LSUMZ taken in July 1968).

POPULATION Parker *et al.* (1982) considered this species to be "uncommon" in Peru, and only at two localities has it been reported to be "very common": 2 km north of San José de Lourdes, above the río Chinchipe, (FMNH label data) and at Jauneche reserve, Ecuador (TAP). At this latter site, a c.130 ha reserve with c.25 ha of prime habitat for this species, TAP found a population of c.2 pairs per hectare and estimated that more than 100 individuals were present in July 1991: however, in early September and again in October 1991, several birds and one bird (respectively) were recorded, suggesting seasonality at this site (Williams and Tobias 1991, R. Williams *in litt.* 1992: see below). In moist forest at 500-700 m on Cerro San Sebastián smaller numbers were found in an area of comparable size, but some large tracts of suitable habitat occur on adjacent ridges (TAP). The moist forest habitat in the Tumbes National Forest, Peru, and at other prime sites in Ecuador (e.g. the río Cuaque drainage in Manabí) has not been sufficiently surveyed to determine population densities of this and other semi-deciduous/moist forest endemics.

ECOLOGY The Grey-breasted Flycatcher is apparently most numerous in evergreen moist forest, which is characterized by an abundance and diversity of woody vines that fill much of the understorey and middle storey (TAP; see Dodson *et al.* 1985 for a description of this habitat at Jauneche). It also occurs, at least seasonally, in largely deciduous forests where vines form dense tangles, but it also seems to be resident in small numbers in a narrow band of wet forest along the lower slopes of the Andes in south-west Ecuador, as at Manta Real in Cañar (TAP, R. S. Ridgely *in litt.* 1991). Records range from sea level to 1,750 m, rarely higher (see Distribution), but the bird appears to be most numerous below 700 m (TAP). The apparently rapid decline in numbers at Jauneche reserve between July and October 1991 (see above) further suggests strong seasonal movements.

The flycatcher is found singly or in pairs that stay in shaded tangles of vines and branches in the understorey and at mid-heights, but is regularly noted at 3-8 m, or up into the lower canopy of very tall forest (Best 1992, NK, TAP; also label data on specimens in FMNH, LSUMZ and MECN). One observed for at least 20 minutes employed a variety of foraging manoeuvres as it perched 3-5 m above ground on slender vines and branches of small, partially sunlit trees in forest about 20 m tall; it made short aerial sallies of 15-35 cm into a sunlit gap, and 5-20 cm sallies to leaves, stems and branches within a small area of 5 m^2 (Parker *et al.* 1989). Almost exactly the same behaviour was observed in a pair at Machalilla National Park (R. S. Ridgely *in litt.* 1989). At Jauneche in July (when several males were singing) it was most numerous 2-10 m up in low, 10-15 m tall, viny forest, especially in shady openings under the canopy of vine-covered, medium to small trees, but it also occurred as high as 25 m up in openings in 40 m tall ridge-top forest; it was very active, constantly darting to vines, branches and trunks, occasionally to foliage and air, sallies often as long as 1.5 m forward or down; prey was generally very small, but included two small moths, a small arthropod and a beetle (TAP). Stomachs of two specimens in MECN held insects in one and insects and small bits of bark in the other.

Most recent records (during all seasons) are of vocal individuals or pairs exhibiting territorial behaviour (TAP). One bird was singing near Piñas in September (but had small testes) (NK), as were individuals at Manta Real in July (TAP), at Campo Verde, Peru, in March (M. Kessler *in litt.* 1988), and at Tambo Negro in February (Best 1992). Inactive gonads were found in one bird in late March, five birds in June, one in July, one in August, one in September, one in October and two in November, while two from July were reported to have them slightly enlarged (specimens in AMNH, FMNH, LSUMZ and MECN). An immature was collected in March (specimen in BMNH). Most (perhaps all) bird species in this region probably breed during the wet season (Marchant 1958), which is from January to May (Brown 1941).

THREATS Ecuadorian moist forest is now confined to a few small patches, the Jauneche reserve being perhaps the largest (at 130 ha) surviving below 500 m (TAP). A few larger islands of moist forest persist in the coastal cordillera of Manabí, as at 500-700 m in Machililla National Park (which is, however, ineffectively protected: TAP), and even as far north as Cerro Mutiles near Esmeraldas city, but all remnants of this habitat are being eroded away or otherwise degraded (TAP, A. Gentry verbally 1991). Most of the old specimens of Grey-breasted Flycatcher were collected in forests that no longer exist (TAP). Forests that are floristically like moist forests survive in a narrow transitional zone between deciduous forest and cloud-forest on the lower slopes of the Andes in Piura and Lambayeque, Peru, but these too are gravely threatened by a gradually increasing human population and by unwise land-use practices (TAP). Much of the semi-deciduous forest habitat around Palambla in Piura was destroyed earlier this century, and felling of similar habitat around San José de Lourdes in the middle Marañón drainage of Cajamarca was proceeding rapidly in 1984 (NK).

MEASURES TAKEN In Ecuador, this species occurs in the Río Palenque reserve, Machalilla National Park, Cerro Blanco reserve, and Jauneche reserve; it also inhabits the Tumbes National Forest, Peru (see equivalent section under Grey-backed Hawk *Leucopternis occidentalis*).

MEASURES PROPOSED Proper management and increased protection of existing dry and moist forest reserve areas in western Ecuador is critically important to this and a large number of bird species endemic to that region. The establishment of an additional reserve holding the species, at Manta Real in Cañar, is apparently under way (P. Greenfield *in litt.* 1990). Additional comments on the conservation status of key forests, and details of initiatives proposed to preserve the threatened species endemic to south-west Ecuador and north-west Peru, are given in the equivalent section under Grey-backed Hawk, and under Peruvian Pigeon *Columba oenops* for the upper Marañón valley. Further information on the distributional limits, potential seasonal movements, and behaviour of this and other endemics is urgently needed.

REMARKS (1) The Grey-breasted Flycatcher was previously placed in the genus *Empidonax*. Morphologically and vocally it closely resembles Euler's Flycatcher *Lathrotriccus euleri*, and should be treated as a congener of that species (Parker *et al.* 1989), which was removed from *Empidonax* and placed in a separate genus *Lathrotriccus* by Lanyon and Lanyon (1986). (2) Concerning the location of the Cordillera de Balzar, see Remarks 2 under Saffron Siskin *Carduelis siemiradskii*.

WHITE-TAILED SHRIKE-TYRANT *Agriornis andicola* V/R[10]

This rare tyrant-flycatcher lives high above the treeline in Ecuador, Peru, Bolivia, northern Chile and north-western Argentina. Although reported as "common" in Ecuador last century, there is but one recent report from that country (possibly owing to lack of research at high elevations), but also in Peru and at the type-locality of the southern subspecies, in northern Chile, it appears to have diminished for reasons unknown.

DISTRIBUTION The White-tailed Shrike-tyrant (see Remarks 1) is known from some 42 specimens and a number of sightings at less than 50 localities, scattered throughout the mountains of Ecuador, Peru, Bolivia, north-west Argentina and northern Chile, with nominate *andicola* inhabiting Ecuador (where it has been recorded on most of the páramos), and *albicauda* occurring within the rest of the range. Coordinates below, unless otherwise stated, are from Paynter *et al.* (1975), Paynter and Traylor (1977), Stephens and Traylor (1983), and Paynter (1985, 1988), with records as follows:

Ecuador (*Imbabura*) Ilana, close to but north of Laguna de Yaguarcocha (at 0°22'N 78°06'W), where a specimen (in NRM) was taken at 2,440 m in July between 1900 and 1920 (also Lönnberg and Rendahl 1922); (*Pichincha*) Calacalí (c.0°01'N 78°31'W), in páramo at 3,600 m, on a northern spur of Volcán Pichincha, where a bird was taken in March 1859 (Sclater 1860b: specimen in BMNH now apparently lost); Cumbaya (0°12'S 78°26'W), where a specimen (in AMNH) was collected at 2,400 m in January 1914 (Chapman 1926); Quito (0°13'S 78°30'W), where a specimen (in AMNH) was collected at 2,800 m in August 1922 (Chapman 1926); Guamaní (c.0°20'S 78°13'W), at 3,600-4,200 m, where a specimen (in AMNH, now apparently lost) was presumably collected in 1922 or 1923 (Chapman 1926); (*Napo*) Antisana (c.0°30'S 78°08'W), where a specimen (in AMNH) was collected at 3,660 m in June 1913 (Chapman 1926); (*Chimborazo*) Panza, on the south slope of Volcán Chimborazo (at 1°28'S 78°48'W), where the type-specimen (in BMNH) was collected at 4,275 m in January 1859 (Sclater 1860a); (*Cañar*) Cañar (c.2°33'S 78°56'W), where a specimen (in BMNH) was collected at 3,000 m in April 1899 (Chubb 1919); (*Zamora-Chinchipe*) "Bestion, río Shingata" (presumably = río Shincata on Cerro Bastíon, at 3°25'S 79°01'W: OG 1957b), near the borders of Morona-Santiago and Azuay provinces, where three specimens (in AMNH) were collected at 3,080 m in January 1921 (Chapman 1926; see Remarks 2); (*Loja*) Nudo de Cajanuma (4°05'S 79°12'W), whence comes a specimen (in MCZ) collected at 2,400 m in August 1965;

Peru (*Cajamarca*) 2 km south-east of Cutervo (6°23'S 78°50'W; at 2,650 m), where a specimen (in LSUMZ) was collected in September 1977; Taulis (c.6°54'S 79°03'W), at 3,400 m, where a specimen (in MHNJP) was collected in February 1952 (T. S. Schulenberg *in litt.* 1989); Cajamarca (c.7°10'S 78°31'W), where a specimen (in AMNH) was collected at 3,350 m in January 1894 (Salvin 1895, von Berlepsch 1907, Cory and Hellmayr 1927); (*La Libertad*) Huamachuco (7°48'S 78°04'W), where a specimen (in AMNH) was collected at 3,350 m in March 1895 (Salvin 1895, von Berlepsch 1907, Cory and Hellmayr 1927); mountains near Otuzco (c.7°54'S 78°35'W), at 3,050 m, where a specimen (in FMNH) was collected in March 1912 (Cory and Hellmayr 1927); Hacienda Tulpo (c.8°08'S 78°01'W), at 3,000 m, where two specimens (in AMNH) were collected in May 1900 (von Berlepsch 1907, Cory and Hellmayr 1927); (*Huánuco*) base of Bosque Zapatogocha (c.9°40'S 76°03'W), at c.2,620 m, where a specimen (in LSUMZ) was collected in September 1975; Acomayo (9°46'S 76°05'W), at 2,440 m, where a specimen (in FMNH) was collected in November 1965; (*Ancash*) near Carpa (9°53'S 77°17'W: IGM 1971), at 4,250 m, 5 km west of Ingenio in the Pumapampa valley, where one was seen in February 1987 (Fjeldså 1987); (*Pasco*) La Quinua (10°36'S 76°10'W), at 3,660 m, where a specimen (in FMNH) was collected in May 1922 (Cory and Hellmayr 1927); Rumicruz (c.10°44'S 75°55'W), at 2,950 m, where four specimens (in AMNH) were taken in February and March 1922 (Zimmer 1937); (*Cuzco*)

Cachupata (c.13°17'S 71°22'W), at 3,555 m (Sclater and Salvin 1874); Cordillera Vilcanota, above Calca, whence comes a recently collected specimen (J. Fjeldså verbally 1991); Lucre (= Laguna de Lucre, at 13°31'S 71°59'W), at 3,640 m, 32 km south of Cuzco (von Berlepsch 1907); La Raya (14°29'S 71°05'W), at 4,314 m, on the border of Cuzco and Puno departments, where six specimens (in AMNH and USNM) were collected in April 1917 (Chapman 1921); (*Arequipa*) slopes of Volcán Chachani (c.16°12'S 71°33'W), where a specimen (in MHNJP) was collected in February 1952 (T. S. Schulenberg *in litt.* 1989);

Bolivia (*La Paz*) Iquico, Illimani (c.16°35'S 67°40'W), at 4,000 m (von Berlepsch 1907); Esperanza, Pacajes (17°49'S 68°47'W), at 4,200 m, where a specimen (in LSUMZ) was taken in November 1941; (*Oruro*) c.4 km north-west (or west) of Curahuara (17°52'S 68°26'W: OG 1955a), Carangas, at 3,900 m, where a specimen (in AMNH) was taken in October 1967; (Chuquisaca) near Uzurduy (20°06'S 64°25'W: IGM 1984), at 2,700 m, where a bird was seen in October 1991 (J. Fjeldså verbally 1991); (*Potosí*) Mina Isca-Isca (21°11'S 65°47'W), above La Torre (north of Tupizá), at 4,000 m, where a specimen (in AMNH) was collected in December 1967.

Argentina Records are all from the Sierra del Aconquija in Tucumán and adjacent Catamarca province, localities being: (*Tucumán*) El Infiernillo (c.26°44'S 65°47'W), at 3,000 m, where two birds were seen in May 1948 (Olrog 1949); Cerro Muñoz (26°46'S 65°51'W), at 3,800-4,100 m, where a specimen (in IML) was collected in May 1906 (also Lillo 1909, Olrog 1949, M. Nores and D. Yzurieta *in litt.* 1986); above Tafí del Valle (26°52'S 65°41'W), at 2,900 m, where a specimen (in AMNH) was collected in April 1916, with two (in IML) taken in May and June 1952 (Zimmer 1937, M. Nores and D. Yzurieta *in litt.* 1986); (*Catamarca*) Corral Quemado (27°08'S 66°57'W), at 3,500 m, where a specimen (in MCZ) was taken in December 1918.

Chile The type-specimen of *albicauda* (in MNHNS) was collected in the middle of last century at Putre (18°12'S 69°35'W), in the mountains of Arica department, northernmost Tarapacá province (Philippi and Landbeck 1863, J. C. Torres-Mura *in litt.* 1988), with another specimen (in AMNH) taken there at 3,535 m in July 1924 (Cory and Hellmayr 1927, 1932), and subsequent sightings mentioned by Johnson (1967). In the Lauca National Park, three birds were seen in October 1986 and November 1987 in the vicinity of Laguna Chungará (18°15'S 69°10'W) (B. M. Whitney *in litt.* 1991), with two birds seen between Laguna Chungará and Parinacota (18°12'S 69°16'W) in March 1989 (P. J. Roberts *in litt.* 1989). In Antofagasta province, a specimen (in YPM) was taken at "Linzor, on the outskirts of the Ojalar river" (c.22°13'S 68°01'W), at 4,100 m, in June 1957 (Peña 1961).

POPULATION In Ecuador, the White-tailed Shrike-tyrant was reported to be common on Volcán Chimborazo and the Calacalí páramo on Volcán Pichincha, in the middle of the last century (Sclater 1860a,b), but there appears to be but one recent record from that country (see Distribution), although this could, at least in part, be owing to lack of research at high elevations.

At La Raya in Peru, no less than six birds were collected in 10 days during 1917, so it was then presumably fairly common; however, during five days of intensive searching there in 1983 and 1987 only the Black-billed Shrike-tyrant *Agriornis montana* was found (NK, Fjeldså 1987). The species was considered "uncommon" in Peru by Parker *et al.* (1982), but a four-month survey of its habitat in Peru, Bolivia and Chile in 1987 showed it to be rare, with just one or two records in over 50 localities with apparently suitable habitat, whilst *montana* was recorded at 27 (Fjeldså 1987). In Bolivia, *andicola* is reported to be outnumbered 10:1 by *montana* (Smith and Vuilleumier 1971).

Johnson (1967) reported *andicola* to be "more plentiful" than *montana* in the neighbourhood of Putre in Chile, but he did not report collecting any specimens, and either he misidentified *montana*, or *andicola* has declined seriously there, for eight individuals of *montana* were seen in the same region in May 1987 (NK), when there were no records of *andicola* (Fjeldså

1987): however, P. J. Roberts (*in litt.* 1989) reported two individuals of *andicola* and no *montana* there in March 1989. Near Laguna Chungará in Lauca National Park, B. M. Whitney (*in litt.* 1991) recorded just three birds in October 1986 and November 1987, and considered this species greatly outnumbered by *montana*: P. Gregory (*in litt.* 1990) recorded two birds there in January 1990, and suggested that the species was "very sparse". M. Nores (*in litt.* 1989) believed all reports of *andicola* as common to be caused by confusion with *montana*.

ECOLOGY The White-tailed Shrike-tyrant inhabits the páramo and puna zones, usually above 3,500 m, but in southern Ecuador and north-west Argentina, where the treeline is lower (NK), it occurs down to 3,000 m (see Distribution): records from open areas as low as 2,400 m are undoubtedly of stragglers from higher elevations (NK). It is found on open slopes and valley floors supporting a sparse, xeric vegetation of low shrubs, with scattered rocks and boulders used as observation posts (Smith and Vuilleumier 1971): a bird seen in Ancash, Peru, was perched atop a *Puya raimondii* on a rocky slope with scattered bunchgrass (NK). Like its congeners it is solitary and holds a large territory (Fjeldså and Krabbe 1990).

Its larger congeners take most of their prey from the ground, including large insects, small mammals, lizards, frogs, eggs and nestlings of other birds (Fjeldså and Krabbe 1990). One specimen of *andicola* had a large white grub in its gizzard (Sclater 1860a). Throughout its range the White-tailed Shrike-tyrant occurs sympatrically with the slightly smaller but notably smaller-billed Black-billed Shrike-tyrant (Traylor 1979), and some competition between the two could be expected, although B. M. Whitney (*in litt.* 1991) suggested that *andicola* occurs on average slightly higher than *montana*.

No nest has been described, but congeners build their nest of sticks and grass and line it with wool, placing it in a rock-crevice or low in a bush (Fjeldså and Krabbe 1990). Specimens with inactive gonads have been taken in February and March in Junín; April in Cuzco, Puno and Tucumán; August in Loja; September in Cajamarca; and October in Oruro; one with slightly enlarged gonads was collected in December in Potosí, and one with greatly enlarged gonads in June in Napo (label data on specimens in AMNH, LSUMZ, MCZ and USNM).

THREATS None is known. If the species has truly declined, the cause of this is not apparent, although it is possible that it may have been dependent on the now highly fragmented stands of *Polylepis* and larger species of *Puya*, which are both important refuge habitats for several potential prey species of birds (J. Fjeldså verbally 1991).

MEASURES TAKEN The White-tailed Shrike-tyrant is known to occur in Huascarán National Park in Ancash, Peru (340,000 ha) (Fjeldså 1987, IUCN 1992: see Measures Taken under Ash-breasted Tit-tyrant *Anairetes alpinus*), and in Lauca National Park, northern Chile (137,900 ha) (IUCN 1992).

MEASURES PROPOSED All aspects of this species's ecological requirements need assessment (including the extent to which it may rely on stands of *Polylepis* and *Puya*) before a better explanation for its apparent rarity and specialized habits can be developed. Ecological surveys should perhaps concentrate in the two national parks where the species is known to occur, and aim to assess the size and viability of the populations there: the integrity of the habitats in these two areas also needs to be ensured. In Huascarán National Park, the threatened *Polylepis*-adapted Ash-breasted Tit-Tyrant, White-cheeked Cotinga *Zaratornis stresemanni* and Plain-tailed Warbling-finch *Poospiza alticola* also occur, and elsewhere within its range this species probably occurs sympatrically with Royal Cinclodes *Cinclodes aricomae* and White-browed Tit-spinetail *Leptasthenura xenothorax* (see relevant accounts), both *Polylepis* specialists; any conservation initiatives developed for this species should consider their interests. In Argentina the implementation of the planned national park in the Nevados del Aconquija (Beltrán 1987) would protect populations of this species, Rufous-throated Dipper *Cinclus schulzi* and Tucumán Mountain-finch *Poospiza baeri* (J. C. Chebez *in litt.* 1992; see relevant accounts).

REMARKS (1) Sclater (1860a) described the species under the name *andicola*. Believing *andicola* to be a homonym of *andecola*, a name given to another species of *Agriornis* by d'Orbigny (1835-1844), he later proposed substituting the name *andicola* with *pollens* (Sclater and Salvin 1869), a name used for the species until 1926, when it was shown that the name *albicauda* (Philippi and Landbeck 1861) had been given to the same species (Cory and Hellmayr 1927, 1932). The name *albicauda* has been used for the species by several subsequent authors (e.g. Meyer de Schauensee 1970, Morony *et al.* 1975), although it was pointed out by Zimmer (1937) and again by Traylor (1979) that *andicola* (being derived from the Latin "Andium") and *andecola* (being derived from the French "Andes") are not homonyms.

(2) The locality along río Shingata, Bestion, was not located by Paynter and Traylor (1977), who suggested that it might be the village Bestión at 3°10'S 79°13'W, although Chapman (1926) showed Bestion to be south-east of Oña, which is at 3°32'S 79°10'W (Paynter and Traylor 1977). However, in OG (1957b) it is stated that Bestion is another name for Cerro Bastión at 3°25'S 79°01'W on the border of Azuay, Morona-Santiago and Zamora-Chinchipe provinces, which is in better agreement with Chapman's directions. OG (1957b) lists no río Shingata, but this may be the río Shincata shown on IGM (1981) to rise on Cerro Bastión, run south in Zamora-Chinchipe province along the border of Azuay, and then turn south-east to join río Yacuambi, an affluent of río Zamora.

STRANGE-TAILED TYRANT *Yetapa risora* V[9]

This grassland flycatcher has experienced a catastrophic loss of range in Brazil, Paraguay, Uruguay and Argentina, apparently as a result of the conversion of its habitat to agriculture and cattle-raising land; it remains at all common only in northern Argentina and adjacent Paraguay, and is in urgent need of study and protection along with a suite of similarly placed birds.

DISTRIBUTION The Strange-tailed Tyrant (see Remarks 1) is known from southern Brazil, central and eastern Paraguay, Uruguay and central and north-eastern Argentina. Unless otherwise stated, coordinates in the following account are taken from Rand and Paynter (1981), Paynter (1985, 1989) and Paynter and Traylor (1991); in most cases, records at individual localities are of single birds collected or observed, with records involving a large number of birds generally being discussed under Population.

Brazil Localities (north to south) are: (*Mato Grosso*) Pansecco (= Pau Sêco, 8 km from Caiçara, this at c.16°04'S 57°42'W), June 1826 (von Pelzeln 1868-1871); (*São Paulo*) unspecified (Meyer de Schauensee 1966, Sick 1985); (*Rio Grande do Sul*) unspecified (Wied 1831-1833, Burmeister 1856); São José do Norte, between June and August 1914 (Gliesch 1930).

Paraguay Localities (roughly north to south) include: (*Presidente Hayes*) c.100 km on the Trans-Chaco Highway, May 1991 (R. S. Ridgely *in litt.* 1991, P. A. Scharf *in litt.* 1992); Estancia La Golondrina (= Golondrina, 24°56'S 57°42'W), August and November 1988 (F. E. Hayes *in litt.* 1991); Benjamín Aceval (24°58'S 57°34'W), undated (Bertoni 1930); Pilcomayo, July 1942 (specimen in AMNH); Estancia Santa Catalina, February 1981 (J. Escobar *in litt.* 1991); near Estancia San José near río Confuso, c.15 km south-west of km 75 on the Trans-Chaco Highway, July 1989 (AMN); Villa Hayes, July 1989 (F. E. Hayes *in litt.* 1992); (*Alto Paraná*) unspecified (Bertoni 1939); Puerto Bertoni (25°38'S 54°40'W), March of an unstated year (Bertoni 1926); (*Paraguarí*) Sapucay (= Sapucaí, 25°40'S 56°55'W), April 1903, April and June 1904 (Chubb 1910); (*Guairá*) Villarrica, August 1893 (Salvadori 1895b), October 1905, August 1923 and July 1924 (three specimens in BMNH); (*Ñeembucú*) currently (R. S. Ridgely *in litt.* 1991); (*Misiones*) "Misiones" (Contreras *et al.* 1989); between San Juan Bautista and Santa Elisa (= Estancia Santa Elisa, at c.26°55'S 57°28'W, read from DSGM 1988), March 1990, March and June 1991 (R. S. Ridgely *in litt.* 1991, P. A. Scharf *in litt.* 1992; see Population).

Uruguay Records are few and mainly old: (*Paysandú*) "Paysandú", October 1883 and 1885 (Gibson 1885; two specimens in BMNH; hence presumably Tremoleras 1920, Gore and Gepp 1978); (*Soriano*) April 1955 (Cuello and Gerzenstein 1962); (*Flores*) unspecified (Tremoleras 1920); (*San José*) Playa Pascual (34°45'S 56°35'W), October 1986 (Arballo 1987); (*Maldonado*) "Maldonado", undated (d'Orbigny 1835-1844); near Maldonado, between 1832 and 1836 (Gould 1841).

Argentina Records (north to south) are from:

(*Formosa*) Riacho Pilagá (= Estancia Linda Vista c.25°13'S 59°47'W), August 1920 (Wetmore 1926); c.30 km north to Formosa, December 1986 (B. M. Whitney *in litt.* 1991); Clorinda, October 1991 (T. Narosky *in litt.* 1992; see Population);

(*Chaco*) unspecified, December 1987 (B. M. Whitney *in litt.* 1988); Avia Teraí (26°42'S 60°44'W), May 1916 (specimen in AMNH); Vermejo (= Puerto Bermejo), December 1859 (specimen in USNM); Irarana, untraced but evidently near the ríos Paraguay or Paraná, 1860 (specimen in USNM; see Remarks 2); General Pinedo (27°19'S 61°19'W), May 1916 (two specimens in AMNH);

(*Misiones*) arroyo Urugua-í (25°54'S 54°36'W), July 1960 and August 1961 (Navas and Bó 1988b); río Paranay (= arroyo Paranay-guazú, 26°41'S 54°48'W), September 1926 (specimen in FMNH); Santa Ana (27°22'S 55°34'W), May 1918 (Navas and Bó 1988b); Barra Concepción (28°07'S 55°35'W; coordinates from OG 1968), July 1961 (Navas and Bó 1988b);

(*Corrientes*) Estero Ipucú (27°43'S 57°09'W in OG 1968), Loreto, September 1985 (J. C. Chebez *in litt.* 1992); río Aguapey, October 1984 (T. Narosky *in litt.* 1992); on the road from Corrientes to Posadas, June 1975 (M. Nores and D. Yzurieta *in litt.* 1986; see Population); Itaibaté (= Itá Ibaté, 27°26'S 57°20'W), October 1959 (six specimens in AMNH); 21 km east-south-east of Itá Ibaté, October 1967 (specimen in AMNH); Ituzaingó (27°36'S 56°41'W), October 1959 (two specimens in AMNH); Estancia Garabatá (27°40°S 58°26'W), November and December 1961 (ten specimens in AMNH and LSUMZ); Gobernador Virasoro, November 1975 (T. Narosky *in litt.* 1992); Estancia Las Marías (28°07'S 56°04'W), May 1961 (two specimens in CM); "Esteros de Iberá", August 1972 (four specimens in MHNG); "Pellegrini" (= Colonia Carlos Pellegrini, 28°32'S 57°10'W), November 1979 (T. Narosky *in litt.* 1992); Laguna Iberá, near Colonia Carlos Pellegrini, on the road from the latter to Santo Tomé and on the road from Colonia Carlos Pellegrini to Mercedes, currently (B. M. Whitney *in litt.* 1988, Gardner and Gardner 1990a, M. Pearman *in litt.* 1990, B. M. López Lanús *in litt.* 1991, D. Willis *in litt.* 1991, F. R. Lambert verbally 1992; for this general area see Population); Santa Lucía, currently (J. C. Chebez *in litt.* 1992); La Cruz, November 1976 (T. Narosky *in litt.* 1992); Guayquiraro (30°18'S 59°32'W) (see Cory and Hellmayr 1927); Los Cerros (untraced), July 1985 (T. Narosky *in litt.* 1992);

(*Santiago del Estero*) Girardet (27°37'S 62°10'W), February 1927 (see Nores *et al.* 1991); Selva (29°46'S 62°03'W), January 1900 (Hartert and Venturi 1909);

(*Santa Fe*) Mocoví (28°24'S 59°42'W), September, October and November 1903 and January 1904 (Hartert and Venturi 1909; seven specimens in AMNH and MNHN); Ocampo (= Villa Ocampo, 28°28'S 59°22'W), November 1903 and November 1905 (Hartert and Venturi 1909; three specimens in AMNH); Ceres (29°53'S 61°57'W), January 1900 (Hartert and Venturi 1909); General López (c.40 km from Venado Tuerto, 33°45'S 61°58'W), early this century (Wilson 1926);

(*Entre Ríos*) "Entreríos", before 1912 (two specimens in BMNH); Concepción del Uruguay, September and October 1880 and April 1881 (Barrows 1883; four specimens in MCZ); Estancia La Soledad (32°30'S 58°41'W), February 1899 and January 1902 (Hartert and Venturi 1909);

(*Córdoba*) río Cuarto (33°25'S 63°02'W), undated (Burmeister 1861); "Córdoba", unspecified (Olrog 1959, 1979);

(*San Luis*) in the pampas around San Luis (the town), undated (Burmeister 1860; hence presumably Olrog 1959, 1979);

(*Buenos Aires*) Baradero (33°48'S 59°30'W), November 1897 (specimen in UNP); Campana (34°10'S 58°57'W), Luján bridge, February 1877 (Durnford 1878; three specimens in BMNH); Lomas de Zamora (34°46'S 58°24'W), undated (Withington 1888); La Plata, undated (specimen in BMNH); Estancia Espartilla (c.35°31'S 58°19'W), sometime between 1888 and 1891 (Holland 1891); Carhué (37°11'S 62°44'W), April 1881 (Barrows 1883) and December 1920 (Wetmore 1926); Colina (possibly Estancia Colina, 37°23'S 61°33'W; coordinates from OG 1968), February 1889 (two specimen in BMNH); Estancia Santa Elena (untraced), September 1892 and October 1895 (Holland 1893; two specimens in BMNH); La Rosa (untraced), March 1886 and 1888 (two specimens in BMNH).

POPULATION The Strange-tailed Tyrant is now very rare or has virtually disappeared from large areas of its former range. Although its numbers still appear to be fairly healthy in southern Paraguay (Ñeembucú and Misiones) and in northern Argentina (Corrientes), it is not known whether these populations are stable or also subject to diminution.

Brazil The Strange-tailed Tyrant is very rare; there appears to be just a single nineteenth-century record from Mato Grosso (see Distribution), and in Rio Grande do Sul it has been recorded only once during the twentieth century (1914), having previously been mentioned only twice in the state (Belton 1984-1985; also Distribution). The listing of São Paulo (Meyer de Schauensee 1966, Short 1975, Sick 1985) is not accompanied by further details, and there are no records or museum skins from Paraná (P. Scherer Neto *in litt.* 1986).

Paraguay The Strange-tailed Tyrant appears to be scarce and local in the humid chaco of Presidente Hayes (F. E. Hayes *in litt.* 1991, AMN). East of the río Paraguay (Región Oriental) it is probably very rare except in the grasslands in the southern departments of Ñeembucú and Misiones, which are still fairly pristine (R. S. Ridgely *in litt.* 1991). Within this area, between San Juan Bautista and Santa Elisa, 12 and 15 birds were observed in March 1990 and March 1991 (P. A. Scharf *in litt.* 1992), and 47 were along c.10 km of road on 6 June 1991 (R. S. Ridgely *in litt.* 1991, P. A. Scharf *in litt.* 1992).

Uruguay Cuello and Gerzenstein (1962) considered the species "very rare" and Gore and Gepp (1978) believed it to be a "rare resident". These assessments were supported by Arballo (1987), who referred to it as one of the rarest birds in the country. By contrast, Gould (1841) reported it "not uncommon" near Maldonado and so did Gibson (1885) at Paysandú, comments that obviously indicate a decrease.

Argentina The species seems to have suffered a great decline and it apparently no longer occurs in some of the provinces where it was once reported (e.g. San Luis, Buenos Aires, Córdoba, Entre Ríos, Santiago del Estero). The extraordinary range contraction suggested by the records (see Distribution) is poorly documented for some of the provinces (e.g. San Luis and Córdoba), as the species's occurrence there was based on single records only; however, its disappearance from Buenos Aires province is particularly noteworthy given the number of localities cited under Distribution and, e.g., Holland's (1893) report that it was "plentiful everywhere" at Estancia Santa Elena in the province. In one area of northern Santa Fe (see Distribution) it was found "common" by Hartert and Venturi (1909), although in the south at General López it was "uncommon" (Wilson 1926). The lack of recent observations in Santa Fe suggests that it has suffered a major decline there (see Remarks 3), this also being true in Santiago del Estero, where Pereyra (1938) found it common on the border with Santa Fe (see Nores *et al.* 1991, Distribution). The species's present range has been reduced to eastern Formosa, eastern Chaco, north-eastern Santa Fe, Corrientes and southern Misiones: 10 immatures were observed in Clorinda, Formosa, in October 1991 (T. Narosky *in litt.* 1992); it is still relatively common in Estero Ipucú, Estero de Santa Lucía (J. C. Chebez *in litt.* 1992) and in the Esteros de Iberá, Corrientes, where sightings of more than 15 birds at a single spot can be made (M. Pearman *in litt.* 1990, D. Willis *in litt.* 1991, F. R. Lambert verbally 1992).

ECOLOGY The Strange-tailed Tyrant inhabits wet grasslands (pajonales) and pastures near or within marshes or "esteros" and "bañados", sometimes near forest edge, bushy vegetation and palm savannas (Short 1975, Olrog 1979, Canevari *et al.* 1991). Records from sites in Misiones (see Distribution) usually associated with Atlantic Forest presumably refer to natural clearings. The species is most reliably found in fields with native grasses, but also occurs in fields of introduced grasses (B. M. Whitney *in litt.* 1991). It feeds on invertebrates (small Coleoptera and *Lycosa* spiders have been reported in stomachs) which are captured in flight or on the ground (Gould 1841, Durnford 1878). Birds have been observed foraging in dense clumps of grass by making short sally-gleans (B. M. Whitney *in litt.* 1991). Nesting has been reported in October (a nest contained three eggs), and it is placed on the ground under a tuft of grasses (Gibson 1885, Holland 1893). On 26 December 1987, a female was observed with two recently fledged young (B. M. Whitney *in litt.* 1991). Single birds, pairs, family groups and small flocks have been reported; de Azara (1802-1805) observed a flock of 30 females, and he believed that every male would mate with eight or ten females, a point that, given the highly distinctive breeding dress of male birds, requires consideration. The species is a year-round resident in most of its range; however, at Estancia Santa Elena, Buenos Aires, Holland (1893) referred to it as migratory, birds arriving in September (i.e. early spring) and departing in February (i.e. late summer), and he mentioned that males arrived a little earlier than females and immatures.

THREATS Habitat destruction, mostly through agriculture and cattle-raising, is probably the major threat to the species (Arballo 1987, D. Willis *in litt.* 1991); the latter has often been accompanied by the introduction of foreign grasses (AMN). There is some uncertainty about the impact of cattle on the species's habitat, however: on the one hand Arballo (1987) remarked that the area where the species was observed in San José, Uruguay, was free of cattle and thus quite unique in such an overgrazed country, and P. Canevari *(in litt.* 1987) could never find the species in the Río Pilcomayo National Park, where cattle overgrazing occurs; on the other, it can be present in fields being grazed by cattle if grasses more than about 50 cm tall are present (B. M. Whitney *in litt.* 1991) and at Estancia La Golondrina, Paraguay, cattle were abundant (F. E. Hayes *in litt.* 1992). Nevertheless, the presence of cattle in Paraguay within the species's range is a reason for concern as the best natural grasslands are rapidly being utilized for pasture (AMN). Other factors, such as the use of pesticides, may be in play.

MEASURES TAKEN The species is protected under Brazilian law (Bernardes *et al.* 1990). In Argentina, the Iberá Provincial Reserve and proposed Mburucuyá National Park (15,000 ha in the Estero de Santa Lucía) are of great importance for the conservation of the species (J. C. Chebez *in litt.* 1992).

MEASURES PROPOSED It is vital to ensure the survival of the populations in the grasslands of Corrientes (Argentina; see corresponding section under Saffron-cowled Blackbird *Xanthopsar flavus*), and of those in Presidente Hayes, Ñeembucú and Misiones (Paraguay). To achieve this goal, a study is needed on the status of these regions' natural and semi-natural grasslands and the effect of cattle-grazing. This should be combined with a study on the species's habitat selection and should consider the habitat requirements of near-threatened grassland specialists whose ranges largely overlap with the Strange-tailed Tyrant, namely Cock-tailed Tyrant *Alectrurus tricolor*, Bearded Tachuri *Polystictus pectoralis* (see Remarks 2), Sharp-tailed Tyrant *Culicivora caudacuta*, Rufous-rumped Seedeater *Sporophila hypochroma* (see relevant account) and Black-masked Finch *Coryphaspiza melanotis* (for other important grassland species with a slightly different distribution, see the corresponding section under Saffron-cowled Blackbird). The aim of these studies should be the creation of some strictly protected and other carefully managed areas in which the presence of cattle is prohibited or controlled. The Strange-tailed Tyrant may prove a good indicator of well preserved areas, in which case any healthy populations may provide guides to those areas of greatest general interest for conservation. The presence of the species in the so-called "Ecorregión Ñeembucú" in southern Paraguay adds to the arguments in favour of creating a protected area there (see Acevedo *et al.* 1990).

REMARKS (1) The Strange-tailed Tyrant occupies its own genus, although it is sometimes regarded as belonging in *Alectrurus* (e.g. Sibley and Monroe 1990). (2) The specimen from Irarana was collected by the same man (T. J. Page) who took the bird at Puerto Bermejo (Page was the man who explored the río Paraná at least twice but appears to have left behind an account only of his first endeavours: see Remarks 5 and 6 under Glaucous Macaw *Anodorhynchus glaucus*); since he also collected a specimen of Bearded Tachuri at Irarana, specifying the month of March (1860), it seems likely that this was fairly close to Puerto Bermejo and thus in Chaco or perhaps Corrientes. (3) Despite the lack of recent records from northern Santa Fe, the species's reasonable current status in adjacent Corrientes suggests that a population may be worth searching for in the north-eastern part of the province.

OCHRACEOUS ATTILA *Attila torridus* E[2]

This large flycatcher occurs at low densities, and is restricted to fragments of humid and semi-humid forest in the lowlands and foothills of western Ecuador and immediately adjacent south-western Colombia, and north-west Peru.

DISTRIBUTION The Ochraceous Atilla (see Remarks 1) is primarily known from western Ecuador from Esmeraldas province south to Loja (see Remarks 2), although there is one record from Nariño department in south-western Colombia, and recent records from Tumbes National Forest in north-western Peru. The known localities (coordinates from Paynter and Traylor 1977, 1981, and Stephens and Traylor 1983) are as follows:

Colombia (*Nariño*) Candelilla, on the río Mira, 1°29'N 78°43'W, at 200 m on the Pacific coastal plain (male in FMNH taken in March 1958; also Blake 1959);

Ecuador (*Esmeraldas*) San Javier, untraced, but possibly San Javier de Cachavi, 100 m, at 1°04'N 78°47'W (Hartert 1902; three specimens in AMNH taken at 20 m in January 1900); Esmeraldas (sea level), at 0°59'N 79°42'W (Chapman 1926); Pambilar, untraced, but possibly near río Pambil (below 300 m), the mouth of this river being at 0°46'N 79°05'W (Hartert 1902; two specimens in AMNH taken at 20 m in August and September 1900); Cabeceras de Bilsa (c.100-300 m), east of Bilsa and north-east of Muisne, at c.0°42'N 79°52'W, recently (TAP); (*Pichincha*) Río Palenque reserve (200 m), at c.0°30'S 79°30'W, recently (P. Greenfield *in litt.* 1991); (*Manabí*) río Peripa (below 100 m; possibly in Pichincha), its estuary being at 0°53'S 79°43'W (Salvadori and Festa 1899); unspecified locality, but apparently on the coast between 0°33' and 0°57'S (Chapman 1926; two specimens in AMNH taken in February 1913); Cerro San Sebastián, 650 m, at 1°35'S 80°40'W, in Machalilla National Park, recently (TAP, R. S. Ridgely *in litt.* 1991); (*Los Ríos*) Jauneche reserve, 80 m, at 1°10'S 79°30'W (one bird recorded in October 1991: Williams and Tobias 1991); Vinces (c.15 m), at 1°32'S 79°45'W (Salvadori and Festa 1899); Babahoyo (5 m), the type-locality (Sclater 1860); Isla Silva, on the río Babahoyo, 1°57'S 79°44'W, September/October 1931 (Berlioz 1932; coordinates as for next locality); (*Guayas*) Hacienda Pacaritambo (untraced, but near Quevedo and half-way between Santo Domingo de los Colorados and Babahoyo), June 1962 (Brosset 1964; also Vuilleumier 1978); Samborondón, 1°57'S 79°44'W (Meyer de Schauensee 1953; coordinates as for last locality); Daule (near sea level), at 2°10'S 79°52'W (Chapman 1926: male in AMNH taken in April 1913; specimens in USNM labelled from Guayaquil may also have been taken there); (*Cañar*) Manta Real, 600 m, near río Tigay, 13 road km from Troncal on the road to Shucay, at c.2°30'S 79°17'W (records in July 1991: TAP, also R. S. Ridgely *in litt.* 1991); (*El Oro*) above (a few kilometers south of) Uzhcurumi, 3°21'S 79°34'W (recent record: NK); Santa Rosa, source of four skins, undated (Meyer de Schauensee 1953); La Chonta, 610 m, at 3°35'S 79°53'W (Chapman 1926: two specimens in AMNH collected in July 1921); Piedras, 3°38'S 79°55'W (Meyer de Schauensee 1953); 9 km by road west of Piñas, 300-1,000 m, at 3°40'S 79°44'W (Robbins and Ridgely 1990, Best 1991); (*Loja*) San Lucas, 3°45'S 79°15'W, undated (Hellmayr 1929b); Quebrada Las Vegas (c.10 km north-east of Alamor, near Vicentino), 1,250-1,400 m, at 3°59'S 79°59'W (birds recorded in February and at the end of August 1991: Best 1991, 1992, Williams and Tobias 1991); Alamor (1,325 m), at 4°02'S 80°02'W (Chapman 1926: two birds in AMNH taken in October 1920); Tierra Colorada, 1,700 m, 13 km east of Alamor, at 4°02'S 79°57'W, recently (NK, Best 1992); junction of Celica, Zapotillo and Alamor roads, 1,700 m, at c.4°06'S 79°59'W, recently (Best 1992);

Peru near the Ecuador border in Tumbes National Forest, where one was seen at Cotrina near Campo Verde, 750 m, c.3°51'S 80°12'W, with another, presumably this species, being heard at El Caucho, 400 m, 3°50'S 80°16'W in July 1988 (TAP).

POPULATION The Ochraceous Attila has been considered rare or uncommon at all but two or three of the areas with recent sightings (TAP, R. S. Ridgely *in litt.* 1991, R. Williams *in litt.* 1991, Best 1992, NK). West of Piñas, 1-2 were recorded almost daily (generally heard, and less frequently seen), and its status was therefore given as "fairly common", although it was noted as a low-density bird (Robbins and Ridgely 1990). Many of the most recent records come from the vicinity of Alamor, with up to four birds heard singing daily within a 3 ha area at Tierra Colorada in February 1991 (NK, Best 1992), and 1-2 daily at Quebrada Las Vegas in August of the same year (Williams and Tobias 1991). At Cerro San Sebastián, Machalilla National Park, it was considered fairly common in January 1991, when small numbers (10-20 birds) were seen on the ridge-tops at 600-800 m (TAP), whilst in August of that year it was described as "distinctly uncommon" (R. S. Ridgely *in litt.* 1991). The widespread destruction of its habitat (see Threats) has undoubtedly diminished its numbers considerably.

ECOLOGY The Ochraceous Attila inhabits humid and (at least during the rainy season) possibly deciduous forest (e.g. at Daule), mostly from sea level to 1,000 m, but like many other lowland birds (e.g. Grey-backed Hawk *Leucopternis occidentalis*: see relevant account) it ascends higher than usual in the Celica Mountains, where near Alamor it can be found up to at least 1,700 m (see Distribution). In Machalilla National Park, birds were seen in moist forest on ridge-tops (600-800 m) during January 1991 (TAP), and in February 1991 four birds were singing in humid gallery forest in two humid, lower montane forest valleys at Tierra Colorada (Best 1992). The species has been found from 2 m above the ground at the forest edge (even sallying to the ground), and up to the canopy within forest, but it also occurs in second growth and sometimes cocoa plantations (Robbins and Ridgely 1990, Best 1992, NK, TAP), the reasons for its scarceness remaining obscure. Some seasonal movement of birds apparently takes place (as is suggested by observations at Machalilla National Park: see Population), although the nature of these is unclear.

It is usually found singly or in pairs, does not follow mixed-species flocks, but occasionally some may gather at a fruiting tree (R. S. Ridgely *in litt.* 1991, Best 1992, NK, TAP). Birds have been noted to sally-glean foliage for large insects, especially "*Orthops*" (TAP), although like other attilas they probably sally short distances, then hover-glean foliage and twigs for both insects and fruit (Hilty and Brown 1986). Brosset (1964) collected a bird with a spider in its bill and saw others hunting spiders, and concluded that these animals were its main prey.

Breeding presumably takes place in the rainy season (January–March) when song activity has been noted to be high in both the Celica and coastal mountains (Best 1992, NK, TAP). Despite several seen, virtually no birds were heard at Cerro San Sebastián in August (R. S. Ridgely *in litt.* 1991), but further south Williams and Tobias (1991) reported 1-2 singing daily near Alamor in late August. In Peru the species was heard singing in late July (TAP). Specimens (in AMNH) in breeding condition have been taken on the coast of Manabí in February (male and female), and at Daula in April (male). The gonads of a specimen from June were undeveloped (Brosset 1964).

THREATS Forest destruction in western Ecuador has been extensive over the past 30-40 years (see Threats under Grey-backed Hawk), and continues rapidly within this species's stronghold in the Celica Mountains (NK), where very few patches of forest greater than 50 ha in size are left (Best 1992).

MEASURES TAKEN The Ochraceous Attila occurs in two large protected areas: Machalilla National Park in southern Manabí province, Ecuador, and in Tumbes National Forest, Peru (from where there are only 1-2 records). It also occurs in the smaller Jauneche and Río Palenque reserves (see Distribution), but these may be too small to hold viable populations (see equivalent section under Grey-backed Hawk for details). Protection of an area at Manta Real in Azuay is under way (P. Greenfield *in litt.* 1990, TAP), but the species is uncommon there (see Population).

MEASURES PROPOSED Initiatives should be taken to ensure the integrity of the existing protected areas within this species's range, as these are also important for a large number of other threatened endemics (see equivalent section under Grey-backed Hawk for details and concomitant plans for conservation in this region). The Machalilla National Park is especially important for a large number of threatened species (see equivalent section under Grey-backed Hawk), and action to guarantee its long-term integrity must be of the highest priority. An area within the attila's range on the west slope of the Cordillera de Celica (in the Alamor area) should also be protected, as this seems to be its stronghold (see also account of Grey-headed Antbird *Myrmeciza griseiceps*). Surveys, at least in Tumbes National Park, should be undertaken during the breeding season when the birds are most vocal (B. J. Best *in litt.* 1992).

REMARKS (1) The species's nearest relative seems to be the Cinnamon Attila *Attila cinnamomeus* of the Amazonian lowlands (Chapman 1926), and it has been considered a subspecies of that form (Hilty and Brown 1986). (2) An untraced locality in Ecuador is Santa Rita, presumably the same as the (untraced) type-locality of the Red-faced Parrot *Hapalopsittaca pyrrhops* (see relevant account).

GIANT KINGBIRD *Tyrannus cubensis* I[7]

A naturally low-density flycatcher, this bird has become much rarer still throughout its native Cuba (there are old records from the southern Bahamas and the Turks and Caicos Islands) for reasons unknown, although the most likely culprit is deforestation.

DISTRIBUTION The Giant Kingbird occurs throughout Cuba including the Isle of Pines (Isla de la Juventud) and was formerly found in the southern Bahamas and Turks and Caicos (AOU 1983, Buden 1987a; see Remarks). An accidental individual on Mujeres Island, Península de Yucatán, Mexico, was also reported in 1886 (Salvin 1889).

Cuba Localities (organized by and within provinces from west to east, with coordinates from OG 1963a) where the species has been recorded are:

Pinar del Río "Pinar del Río", February 1900 (four specimens in USNM); El Veral, Península de Guanahacabibes, where two specimens were collected sometime before 1968 (Garrido and Schwartz 1968); Sierra del Rosario, where it was reported common (Bond 1956b); Pica Pica (22°27'N 83°55'W), undated; Sumidero (22°27'N 83°55'W), undated (both from O. H. Garrido *in litt.* 1991); San Diego de los Baños (22°39'N 83°22'W), April 1900 (specimen in USNM); between La Palma (22°45'N 83°33'W) and San Diego (probably San Diego de los Baños) and between La Palma and La Mulata (22°52'N 83°23'W), where it was commonly found in 1933 (Rutten 1934); La Güira (small population south of Sierra de la Güira, this at 22°40'N 83°26'W), undated; Loma del Mulo (22°53'N 82°59'W), undated; Loma del Taburete (c.4 km south of Loma del Mulo), undated (all from O. H. Garrido *in litt.* 1991);

La Habana "near Havana", where a nest was found in May 1939 (Bond 1941a); Laguna de Ariguanabo (22°56'N 82°33'W), undated; Tapaste (23°02'N 82°08'W), undated (both from O. H. Garrido *in litt.* 1991);

Matanzas río San Juan, near Matanzas, where a bird was collected on an ungiven date (Barbour 1943); Santo Tomás (22°24'N 81°25'W), January 1933 (specimen in ASNP); "about the Ciénaga" (presumably referring to the Ciénaga de Zapata), where a few birds were collected at an ungiven date (Barbour 1943); Guamá (at the south-eastern corner of Laguna del Tesoro, this at 22°21'N 81°07'W), December 1901 (specimen in USNM), where only one sighting has been reported during the last 30 years (O. H. Garrido *in litt.* 1991);

Cienfuegos "Mina Carlota", Cumanayagua (22°09'N 80°12'W), April 1941 (three specimens in CM);

Villa Clara Loma de Jumagua (22°48'N 80°07'W) and Santa Clara, undated (O. H. Garrido *in litt.* 1991); Remedios (22°30'N 79°33'W), where the species was collected in 1864 (Barbour 1943);

Sancti Spíritus Trinidad, March 1892 (four specimens in AMNH); Sierra de Trinidad (21°56'N 80°00'W) and Sierra de Sancti Spíritus (21°58'N 79°38'W), undated (O. H. Garrido *in litt.* 1991); San Pablo (21°46'N 79°46'W), where four birds were collected in March 1892 (Chapman 1892);

Ciego de Avila Loma de Cunagua (22°06'N 78°27'W), undated (O. H. Garrido *in litt.* 1991);

Camagüey "Camaguey", March 1948 (specimen in USNM); "north Camagüey", December 1990 (L. Fazio *in litt.* 1992); Sierra de Cubitas (21°41'N 77°55'W), undated (O. H. Garrido *in litt.* 1991); Sierra de Najasa (21°02'N 77°45'W), where the species was recorded in April 1978 (Berovides Alvarez *et al.* 1982);

Holguín Holguín, March and April 1904 (six specimens in AMNH); Preston (20°46'N 75°39'W), where two birds were collected in 1915 (Barbour 1943); Nicaro (20°42'N 75°33'W), undated (O. H. Garrido *in litt.* 1991); near Mosca Verde (a few kilometres north-west of Culebro, this at 20°35'N 75°26'W), where a bird was observed in June 1986 (Abreu *et al.* 1989); Cupeyal

(20°35'N 75°11'W), undated; Sierra de Moa (mountains south of Moa, this at 20°40'N 74°56'W), undated (both from O. H. Garrido *in litt.* 1991); río Fabrico (untraced but opposite Cayo Grande de Moa), where a bird was taken in March 1930 (Wetmore 1932c); Ojito de Agua (c.10 km north-east of La Munición, for which see ICGC 1978), undated; Farallones (c.20 km south-west of Moa), undated (both from O. H. Garrido *in litt.* 1991);

Granma Cabo Cruz, undated; Birama (20°48'N 77°12'W), undated (both from O. H. Garrido *in litt.* 1991); Bayamo, undated (Barbour 1943);

Santiago de Cuba Sierra Maestra (including the surroundings of Pico Turquino), undated (O. H. Garrido *in litt.* 1991);

Guantánamo "Guantánamo", April 1911 (specimen in AMNH), May 1912, February 1914 and April 1916 (three specimens in USNM); Sierra del Guaso (20°14'N 75°10'W), undated; "Cafetal, Virginia" (untraced), "Yateras" (municipality at 20°12'N 75°09'W), December 1917 (specimen in USNM); Yateras, undated (O. H. Garrido *in litt.* 1991); San Carlos (20°09'N 75°09'W), September 1909 and April 1912 (two specimens in LSUMZ); woods at río Seco (untraced), San Carlos, November 1911, March 1912, January 1913, February 1916 (five specimens in USNM); Santa Rita, Los Caños (20°03'N 75°09'W), February 1919 (five specimen in LSUMZ and USNM); Monte Verde (20°19'N 75°00'W), undated (O. H. Garrido *in litt.* 1991); Cuchillas del Toa Biosphere Reserve, 20°27'N 74°58'W), sometime between 1985 and 1989 (Alayón García *et al.* 1987); Sierra del Purial (20°12'N 74°42'W), undated; Duaba Arriba (20°17'N 74°35'W), undated; Cuchillas de Baracoa (mountains c.10 km south of Baracoa: see, e.g., ICGC 1978), undated; Meseta de Maisí (see, e.g., ICGC 1978), undated (all four from O. H. Garrido *in litt.* 1991);

Isle of Pines Santa Bárbara (21°49'N 83°01'W) (see Todd 1916); Los Indios (21°42'N 83°00'W), where a pair was collected in May 1913 (Todd 1916); "Nuevas River" (río de las Nuevas, at 21°56'N 82°56'W), where the species was reported common (Todd 1916); McKinley (21°53'N 82°55'W), sometime before 1911 (Todd 1916); Los Almácigos (21°46'N 82°49'W), "Santa Fé" (21°45'N 82°45'W), Mal País (untraced, but río Mal País is at 21°49'N 82°44'W) and La Vega, untraced, where six birds were observed and five collected in May 1904 (all four from Bangs and Zappey 1905).

POPULATION Although d'Orbigny (1839) referred to this species as "very common" (an unreliable comment as he reported it from all the Greater Antilles), and Gundlach (1871-1875) as "not rare" in appropriate habitat (see Ecology), the Giant Kingbird has generally been regarded as a rare, low-density species (Bangs and Zappey 1905, Todd 1916, Wetmore 1932c, Barbour 1943, Garrido and García Montaña 1975, García 1987, O. H. Garrido *in litt.* 1991, L. Fazio *in litt.* 1992) or "extremely rare" (Garrido and Schwartz 1968). On the Cuban mainland, however, the species was reported to be common in the pine-forest of the Sierra del Rosario, Pinar del Río (Bond 1956b), a judgement probably derived from Rutten (1934), who described it as common in the high pinewoods between San Diego and La Palma, and between the latter locality and La Mulata. O. H. Garrido (*in litt.* 1991) noted that only a single bird was recorded during 30 years at Guamá, Ciénaga de Zapata, and in his opinion the healthiest surviving populations are to be looked for in the eastern sierras (i.e. Toa, Moa, Baracoa and Maestra). On the Isle of Pines observers agreed that the species was comparatively scarce (Bangs and Zappey 1905, Todd 1916, Barbour 1943), although reportedly fairly common along the río de las Nuevas (Todd 1916); but there appear to have been no records for over 70 or even 80 years.

ECOLOGY The Giant Kingbird inhabits woodlands, in particular pine-forest, also semi-open woodlands with high trees, both in the mountains and lowlands, frequently near borders of swamps (Todd 1916, Rutten 1934, Barbour 1943, Bond 1979, O. H. Garrido *in litt.* 1991). According to Gundlach (1871-1875) and hence Barbour (1943) it feeds on flying insects, lizards, and even little birds; and has also been reported catching insects over the water and occasionally minnows near the surface (Bangs and Zappey 1905, Todd 1916). O. H. Garrido (*in litt.* 1991) added caterpillars and considered that a substantial amount of fruit (e.g. *Ficus*) is taken daily; fruit consumption was previously mentioned by Bangs and Zappey (1905), who found remains of insects and berries in a stomach (see also Todd 1916). Gundlach (1871-1875) noted that the species nests on horizontal branches of large trees (e.g. ceiba *Ceiba pentandra*), and a nest situated at the top of a large ceiba found on 28 May 1936 contained three eggs (Bond 1941a; also Balát and González 1982).

THREATS The causes of the species's rarity (and apparenty decline) are not clear, but deforestation appears to be the major problem (Rutten 1934, Barbour 1943, O. H. Garrido *in litt.* 1991, L. Fazio *in litt.* 1992).

MEASURES TAKEN None is known, except for the populations which may be benefiting from some of Cuba's protected areas (e.g. Sierra Maestra, La Güira and Cubitas National Parks, Los Indios and Sierra del Cristal Natural Reserves, Baconao, Cuchillas del Toa, Península de Guanahacabibes and Sierra del Rosario Biosphere Reserves).

MEASURES PROPOSED Intensive studies of the ecological requirements of the species are essential. Although its range appears to extend throughout Cuba and the Isle of Pines, the areas where reasonable populations still occur should be identified, and efforts made to afford protection to the most important. Such activities should if possible be undertaken in conjunction with work on other threatened species, notably Gundlach's Hawk *Accipiter gundlachi* (see relevant account), which is likely often to be sympatric in pinewoods and lowland forest.

REMARKS During the nineteenth century birds were reported from Great Inagua and and Turks and Caicos (North, Middle and East Caicos), where (although not proven) it was a possible breeder (Buden 1987a; five specimens in the FMNH were collected in 1891). The species has not been seen there since and seems likely no longer to occur.

SLATY BECARD *Pachyramphus spodiurus* E[2]

This rare flycatcher is restricted to lowland western Ecuador and immediately adjacent Peru. Most of its forest habitat is now cleared, and there have been relatively few recent records.

DISTRIBUTION The Slaty Becard is restricted to western Ecuador from Esmeraldas south to Loja province, and north-west Peru in Tumbes, Piura and Cajamarca departments, with recent records also coming from the río Marañón drainage in Amazonas. The known localities (coordinates from Paynter and Traylor 1977, Stephens and Traylor 1983 or read from IGM 1989), few of which are represented by recent records, are as follows:

Ecuador (*Esmeraldas*) Esmeraldas, sea level (Chapman 1926); (*Pichincha*) Santo Domingo de los Colorados (500 m) (Goodfellow 1901-1902; female in LACM taken in June 1929); Río Palenque reserve, c.0°30'S 79°30'W (where the species was recently seen: B. Reed *per* M. Pearman verbally 1992); (*Los Ríos*) Hacienda Mopa, c.5 km south of Valencia, at c.0°56'N 79°21'W (male in LSUMZ collected late August 1974); Vinces (c.15 m), at 1°32'S 79°45'W (Salvadori and Festa 1899); Babahoyo (5 m), the type-locality (Sclater 1860); Chimbo, untraced, but near Babahoyo (von Berlepsch and Taczanowski 1883); Isla Silva, on the río Babahoyo, 1°57'S 79°44'W, September/October 1931 (Berlioz 1932); (*Guayas*) Hacienda Pacaritambo (untraced, but near Quevedo and half-way between Santo Domingo de los Colorados and Babahoyo), once in the period 1962–1963 (Brosset 1964; also Vuilleumier 1978); Yaguachi (5 m), at 2°07'S 79°41'W (Taczanowski and von Berlepsch 1885); Bucay (300 m), at 2°10'S 79°06'W (female in ANSP collected in June 1911; hence presumably Meyer de Schauensee 1953); Daule (near sea level) (Chapman 1926: two specimens in AMNH taken in April 1913); (*Azuay*) Manta Real, c.6 km south of Zhucay, at c.2°30'S 79°17'W (male in ANSP taken at 300 m in August 1991; (*El Oro*) 1-2 km south of Machala, near sea level (male seen in 1992: P. Greenfield verbally 1992); Santa Rosa, at sea level (female in AMNH taken in July 1921); Portovelo (640 m), at 3°43'S 79°39'W (Chapman 1926: female in AMNH taken between 610 and 825 m in July 1920); a few kilometres south of Arenillas, 3°33'S 80°04'W, 50 m (four birds recorded in March 1990: B. M. Whitney *in litt.* 1991); La Laja, 3°47'S 80°03'W (male in ANSP taken in June 1933, erroneously labelled from Peru; also Meyer de Schauensee 1953: see Remarks 2 under Rufous-necked Foliage-gleaner *Syndactyla ruficollis*); (*Loja*) Puyango, 300 m, at 3°52'S 80°05'W (male seen in 1992: P. Greenfield verbally 1992); Milagros, 670 m, 4°07'S 80°07'W (two specimens in AMNH taken in July 1919, erroneously labelled from Peru); Paletillas, 465 m, 4°11'S 80°17'W (male and three females in AMNH taken at the end of June 1919, erroneously labelled from Peru);

Peru (*Tumbes*) (Puesto) Lechugal, 3°37'S 80°12'W, nineteenth century (Taczanowski 1884-1886); recently in Tumbes National Forest: Quebrada Faical, east of El Caucho at 3°49'S 80°17'W (24 km south-east of Pampa de Hospital) (four specimens in LSUMZ taken in June and July 1979: Wiedenfeld *et al.* 1985, TAP), and Campo Verde, 750 m, at 3°51'S 80°11'W (Wiedenfeld *et al.* 1985); (*Piura*) Huabal, below Canchaque, 650-700 m, c.5°21'S 79°39'W (birds recorded in May 1956: Koepcke 1961); (*Cajamarca*) south-east of San Ignacio, km 111.5 km from the Abra de Porculla–Bagua road, c.800 m, at c.5°08'S 78°57'W in August 1983 (NK); and 2 km north of Jaen, 350 m (NK); and (*Amazonas*) Corral Quemado, 5°44'S 78°40'W in the late 1970s (NK; see Remarks).

POPULATION The species is generally rare to locally uncommon in Ecuador (R. S. Ridgely *in litt.* 1991, P. Greenfield verbally 1992), and rare at El Caucho in Peru (Wiedenfeld *et al.* 1985). A serious decline must have taken place as there are very few recent records, especially from the northern part of its range. The record of four birds seen south of Arenillas, El Oro, in March 1990 (B. M. Whitney *in litt.* 1991), seems to be the largest number noted together.

ECOLOGY The Slaty Becard is found below 750 m in deciduous, semi-deciduous and humid woodland, shrubby clearings with scattered taller trees, and along dry washes in arid scrub (R. S. Ridgely *in litt.* 1991, B. J. Best *in litt.* 1992, TAP), but it also occurs in patches of evergreen shrubbery, and second growth in humid forest (P. Greenfield verbally 1992, M. B. Robbins verbally 1992, ANSP label data), and several of the old collecting localities were areas of humid forest before they were cleared (NK). South of Arenillas, birds (in March) were present in xeric, semi-deciduous woodland dominated by large *Ceiba* trees covered in *Usnea*, with numerous other trees averaging c.10 m high, and with a generally dense understorey comprising some cacti (B. M. Whitney *in litt.* 1991). Birds in Tumbes National Forest have been observed foraging in the canopy of semi-deciduous forest (TAP). Nothing is known of the species's habits, but presumably they resemble those of others of the genus, which live on insects and fruit, and like most other birds of the region it probably breeds in the rainy season between January and March (NK). As it apparently tolerates some habitat disturbance, the reasons for its rarity are not well understood, although it may have relied (during at least part of the year) on the highly threatened transitional moist forest that once covered the río Guayas basin and which has long since been destroyed (TAP: see below).

THREATS Forest destruction has been extensive in western Ecuador during the past 30-40 years (see Threats under Grey-backed Hawk *Leucopternis occidentalis*), and is rapidly continuing unchecked (NK).

MEASURES TAKEN The species occurs in a single large protected area, namely Tumbes National Forest, Peru, where, however, it is rare (see Population); there has recently been a record from the small Río Palenque reserve, Ecuador, but this is probably too small to sustain a viable population of the species.

MEASURES PROPOSED Increased protection of the Tumbes National Forest (and other reserves in the region) and the creation of further protected areas is the first priority (see equivalent section under Grey-backed Hawk for details). A clearer definition of this species's ecological requirements is urgently needed. Its presence in the río Marañón drainage is particularly interesting, and its status there needs assessment, although such work must also consider the interests of the other threatened and endemic species there (see equivalent section under Peruvian Pigeon *Columba oenops*).

REMARKS The validity of these sight records from río Marañón drainage in northern Peru is not absolute but rendered more plausible by the presence there of another threatened Tumbesian endemic, namely Grey-breasted Flycatcher *Lathrotriccus griseipectus* (see relevant account).

PERUVIAN PLANTCUTTER *Phytotoma raimondii* E[1]

This rare plantcutter inhabits the coast of northern Peru, where it may require a specific habitat that is now threatened by the almost complete cultivation of the coastal river valleys.

DISTRIBUTION The Peruvian Plantcutter is known from very few coastal localities (at altitudes varying from sea-level to 550 m) in Tumbes, Piura, Lambayeque, La Libertad, Ancash and Lima departments, Peru (coordinates, unless otherwise stated, from Stephens and Traylor 1983) as follows:

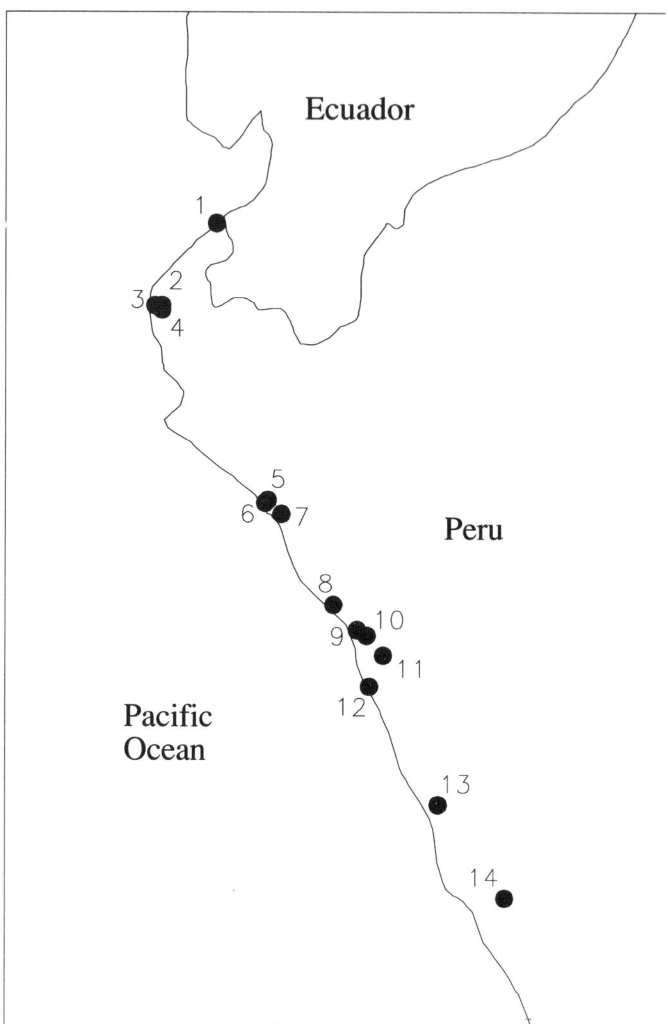

Tumbes Tumbes[1] (3°34'S 80°28'W), whence comes the type-specimen, from near sea-level (Taczanowski 1883);

Piura Quebrada Salada[2] (4°33'S 81°08'W: coordinates given on label), east of Talara, where a specimen (in BMNH) was collected at 90 m in September 1933; near Talara[3] (4°33'S

81°13'W), where a bird (in ROM) was taken at 275 m in March 1934; Quebrada Ancha[4] (4°36'S 81°08'W: coordinates given on label), east-south-east of Talara, where four birds (in BMNH, ROM) were taken at 170 m in January and October 1933, January 1936 and March 1937;

Lambayeque Reque[5] (6°52'S 79°50'W), where 20 birds were seen in August 1989 (B. M. Whitney *in litt.* 1991); Eten[6] (6°54'S 79°52'W), whence come six specimens (in BMNH) collected at 10-15 m in September and October 1899; near río Saña[7], c.5 km north-north-east of Rafan and c.8 km south-west of Mocupé (the latter being at 7°00'S 79°38'W), where a specimen (in LSUMZ) was collected in September 1978 and where six birds were seen in May 1987 (M. Pearman *in litt.* 1990);

La Libertad Trujillo[8] (8°07'S 79°02'W), where at 460 m four were taken in May 1885, four in May 1895, one in October 1912, and two in March 1953 (specimens in AMNH, BMNH, MNHN; also Hellmayr 1929b); Virú[9] (8°25'S 78°45'W), where two specimens (in AMNH) were taken at 45 m in April 1919 (also Hellmayr 1929b); Hacienda Buenavista[10] (c.8°29'S 78°38'W), at 300 m in the Chao valley, where a specimen (in FMNH) was collected in January 1975;

Ancash Suchimán[11] (8°43'S 78°26'W), at 200 m on the río Santa, where two specimens (in ANSP) were taken in March 1932 (also Bond 1956a); Chimbote[12] (9°05'S 78°36'W), where three specimens (in ANSP) were collected at 4 m in March 1932 (also Bond 1956a);

Lima Huaricanga[13] (10°29'S 77°46'W), at 460 m in the Fortaleza valley above Paramonga, where two birds (in AMNH, MHNJP) were collected in August and September 1954 (Koepcke 1961); Chilcon[14], untraced but probably río Chillón (c.11°30-40'S 76°55'-77°00'W), in the Canta valley, where a male and several females were sighted at 550 m in September 1982 (P. Scharf *in litt.* 1989).

POPULATION Unlike the White-tipped Plantcutter *Phytotoma rutila* (see Fjeldså and Krabbe 1990) the present species has never been recorded in large flocks. Although given the status "locally fairly common" by Parker *et al.* (1982), it has been recorded at only five localities since 1933 (see Distribution), and only a few were seen near río Saña/Rafan in January and May 1987 (NK), with three males and three females recorded there (in an area estimated to be c.0.5 ha) by M. Pearman (*in litt.* 1990) in May 1987. In 1989 near Reque, 20 birds were found in a 50 ha patch of suitable habitat (B. M. Whitney *in litt.* 1991).

ECOLOGY The Peruvian Plantcutter inhabits desert scrub and riparian thickets (Parker *et al.* 1982), but must be somewhat specialized, as this habitat type is far more widespread than the bird is (NK). Near Reque, an area of barren coastal dunes, birds were found in an area of habitat consisting of *Prosopis*, *Acacia*, *Capparis* and a variety of unidentified lower shrubs (B. M. Whitney *in litt.* 1991).

Four specimens in ROM had green leaves in their stomachs. Near río Saña the species was frequently observed perching conspicuously in *Prosopis* or *Acacia* trees (especially early in the morning when birds were very vocal), but was only seen feeding (on five occasions) on the succulent leaves of a certain (unidentified) species of bush in 1987, and it was not found during intensive searches in the adjacent agricultural area in 1983 and 1987 (NK, M. Pearman *in litt.* 1990). Other species of plantcutters are known to feed on grass, fruits, buds and tender leaves, occasionally severely damaging crops (Fjeldså and Krabbe 1990).

Two males with active gonads and a laying female have been collected during March (in Ancash), a male with slightly enlarged testes in April (in La Libertad), and three specimens with inactive gonads in April (La Libertad), August (Lima), and September (Lambayeque) (specimens in AMNH and LSUMZ). A male atop a bush with a twig in its bill flew over to a female before being lost from view, in August (B. M. Whitney *in litt.* 1991). The nest has never been described, but in other plantcutters it is an open cup placed in a bush or tree (Fjeldså and Krabbe 1990).

THREATS There may be some form of specialization within its habitat that renders the species particularly vulnerable; however, all the river valleys of western Peru are heavily cultivated (NK) and it may simply be that there is very little of any original habitat left within its range. The 50 ha patch discovered at Reque in 1989 had clearly had many trees removed in the recent past, and most of the larger trees still standing had had their lower limbs removed; this area was heavily grazed every day by cattle and goats, and the general assessment was that the site would soon be destroyed (B. M. Whitney *in litt.* 1991).

MEASURES TAKEN None is known.

MEASURES PROPOSED A study of the species, its habitat and the pressures upon it is urgently needed, and areas where good populations still remain must be conserved as a matter of the highest priority.

REMARKS Fjeldså and Krabbe (1990) noted that, whilst plantcutters Phytotomidae closely resemble cotingas of the genus *Ampelion*, DNA sequencing did not suggest a close relationship; yet Sibley and Monroe (1990) placed the genus *Phytotoma* next to *Ampelion* in the Cotingidae, while Lanyon and Lanyon (1989), also recognizing the similarity of the two genera, proposed moving *Ampelion* and its related genera into the family Phytotomidae (see Remarks under White-cheekd Cotinga *Zaratornis stresemanni*.

OCHRE-BREASTED PIPIT *Anthus nattereri* I[7]

This ground-haunting grassland-dwelling semi-nomadic insectivore has become extremely scarce and local in south-east Brazil, Paraguay and northern Argentina, probably owing to overgrazing and other forms of habitat modification.

DISTRIBUTION The Ochre-breasted Pipit occurs very locally in south-eastern Brazil from southern Minas Gerais south to Rio Grande do Sul, southern Paraguay and north-eastern Argentina.

Brazil In the following account, localities are listed from north to south, with coordinates (unless otherwise stated) derived from Paynter and Traylor (1991).

Minas Gerais De Mattos *et al.* (1984) indicated that the bird was known in the state via reference(s) in the literature and specimens in museums, but no details are given. Specific records are from Monte Belo and Alfenas, in winter, 1983–1985 (J. F. Pacheco *in litt.* 1986), and a female in MNRJ collected on 4 April 1967 at Morro do Ferro, Poços de Caldas (hence Sick 1985).

São Paulo Older records are from: Ipanema (Hellmayr 1935); Villa Prudente (within São Paulo city), January 1900 (specimen in USNM); Ipiranga (within São Paulo city), December 1896 (von Ihering 1898, Pinto 1944); Itapetininga, July 1926 (Pinto 1944); Rio Verde (Sclater 1878, Pinto 1944); Pescaria (untraced, but probably between Ipanema and Itararé: Paynter and Traylor 1991) (Sclater 1878, Pinto 1944); and Itararé, May 1905 (Sclater 1878, Pinto 1944; also Hellmayr 1935). The only post-1926 records appear to be those of E. O. Willis (*in litt.* 1986), who mentioned the species from two unspecified localities in the state, recently.

Paraná Older records are from: Fazenda Monte Alegre, Castro, August 1907 (Pinto 1944; also Hellmayr 1935); and Invernadinha (near Guarapuava), 1,065 m, May 1922 (Sztolcman 1926). Scherer Neto (1985) indicated that the species was known in the state via reference(s) in the literature and his own field records, but no details are given.

Santa Catarina A bird, probably this species, in the vicinity of São Joaquim on 8 January 1990 (Pacheco and Fonseca 1990, J. F. Pacheco verbally 1992) is the only record.

Rio Grande do Sul Older records are from Conceição do Arroio (now Osório), August 1928 (Belton 1984-1985, Sick 1985) and São Lourenço (São Lourenço do Sul), in the last century (von Ihering 1899a). Modern records are from Carazinho, November 1978, and São Francisco de Paula, January 1979 (Belton 1984-1985).

Paraguay Records are from: near Monte Lindo (23°57'S 57°12'W in OG 1957a), Chaco, May 1989 (M. Pearman *in litt.* 1990); Paraguarí, between June and mid-August 1893 (Salvadori 1895b; see Remarks); San Patricio, Misiones, August 1977 (Ridgely and Tudor 1989).

Argentina The only records are from Corrientes in the 1960s: a series of 23 birds was collected between 16 and 22 July 1961 at Estancia San Joaquín (anticipated at c.27°45'S 56°15'W: Paynter 1985) on the río Aguapey near San Carlos (Partridge 1962), with a female from c.14 km north of Ituzaingó, October 1967 (Short 1971, specimen in AMNH), a male from Cuay Grande, 28°40'S 56°17'W, and three males from Torrent, all in May 1962 (specimens in MACN). Records for southern Misiones require confirmation (Olrog 1979, Narosky and Yzurieta 1987).

POPULATION Although pipits can be unobtrusive and difficult to identify in their somewhat unfashionable habitat, it seems evident that this species is genuinely rare and very local (Belton 1984-1985, Ridgely and Tudor 1989). The record from San Carlos, where the species was "abundant" (Partridge 1962), is evidently exceptional, and the reason for the lack of recent records in Argentina is not clear (J. C. Chebez *in litt.* 1986, M. Nores and D. Yzurieta *in litt.* 1986), although Partridge's site itself has apparently not been revisited (see Measures Proposed).

ECOLOGY The Ochre-breasted Pipit is a poorly known species (Sick 1985, Ridgely and Tudor 1989, Canevari *et al.* 1991) which has been recorded in both dry and wet pastures (Belton 1984-1985, Narosky and Yzurieta 1987), rolling grasslands (Ridgely and Tudor 1989), and rocky fields, at times in the vicinity of Hellmayr's Pipit *Anthus hellmayri* (Poços de Caldas, Minas Gerais) or Short-billed Pipit *A. furcatus* (Osório, Rio Grande do Sul) (Sick 1985); J. Natterer reported that it frequented grassy plains and liked "to run on the roads" (Sclater 1878). Birds observed in Minas Gerais in the winters 1983–1985 were in man-made grasses around the Furnas dam in the vicinity of, e.g., Firewood-gatherer *Anumbius annumbi* and Burrowing Owl *Speotyto cunicularia* (Alfenas), in dried-out water-buffalo pastures with streams (Monte Belo) (J. F. Pacheco *in litt.* 1986), and those in Chaco were on a farm track and adjacent grassland (M. Pearman *in litt.* 1990). Studies in São Paulo suggest that the species depends on recently burnt areas within natural grasslands, and that it is semi-nomadic in response to optimal conditions (Willis 1991). Food taken from the stomach of a specimen consisted of insects, mainly (Sztolcman 1926). Breeding data are scarce, and available only from the southern portion of the species's range. Thus, birds collected at Carazinho in November and São Francisco de Paula in January had enlarged gonads; at Carazinho they were displaying and acting strongly territorially in response to play-back of song (Belton 1984-1985). Birds in Corrientes, July, were singing and giving aerial displays (Partridge 1962). A male collected in August at Osório had the testes half-enlarged (specimen in AMNH). A female collected on 22 October at Ituzaingó was flushed from a nest on the ground beside a tussock of grass in a pasture, which contained four eggs in an advanced state of incubation (Short 1971; specimen in AMNH). A nest of unstated origin is described as a shallow cup made of plant stems and grass roots (von Ihering 1900b).

THREATS Overgrazing and/or other forms of modification of its natural grassland habitat has been regarded as a probable threat and cause of the presumed decline of the Ochre-breasted Pipit (Ridgely and Tudor 1989; also J. C. Chebez *in litt.* 1986). However, the critical problem appears to be the species's need for a mosaic of burnt grassland areas, which do not exist within small reserves (Willis 1991). Moreover, natural campos (as well as cerrados) in Brazil are undergoing massive agricultural development with eucalyptus, pines, sugarcane and soybeans (E. O. Willis *in litt.* 1986), and abuse of pesticides over cultivated lands might represent an additional threat to these basically insectivorous birds. Shiny Cowbird *Molothrus bonariensis* parasitism might also eventually be included in this list of possible threats to the species, as it sometimes affects birds of this genus (see Sick 1985).

MEASURES TAKEN The species is protected under Brazilian law (Bernardes *et al.* 1990).

MEASURES PROPOSED General ornithological fieldwork in the areas from which the species is known, or where it might be expected, should be extended to include searches to locate it, to provide information on its ecology, including possible seasonal movements, and to assess its conservation status. Extensive sites which hold the species should be notified to conservation authorities as a matter of urgency. Large reserves that allow for a mosaic of burnt areas, as indicated under Ecology, need to be developed (Willis 1991). A return to Estancia São Joaquín in Corrientes is planned to determine the species's status there 30 years later (M. Nores *in litt.* 1992), and this could result in important perceptions about the needs of the bird in the province. Identification of the species and documentation of records should whenever possible rely on field characters such as voice and tape-recording rather than on the collection of further specimens.

REMARKS It is conceivable that the specimen attributed by Salvadori (1895b) is a Chaco Pipit, which had not then been described (F. E. Hayes *in litt.* 1991); its re-examination is desirable.

RUFOUS-THROATED DIPPER *Cinclus schulzi* K[12]

This dipper is confined to rivers and streams on the slope of the Andes in southernmost Bolivia and north-west Argentina, where it breeds in the alder zone at elevations ranging from 1,500 to 2,500 m. Its small range and general lack of formal conservation render it potentially vulnerable to modern developmental changes.

DISTRIBUTION The Rufous-throated Dipper (see Remarks) is known from one river in Tarija department, southern Bolivia, but in north-west Argentina it has been recorded from a few rivers in the provinces of Salta and Jujuy, and in Tucumán and neighbouring Catamarca provinces birds have been found in all accessible rivers and streams, and probably occur in most streams without such easy access (M. Nores *in litt.* 1989). Localities (with coordinates, unless otherwise stated, from Paynter *et al.* 1975 and Paynter 1985) are as follows:

Bolivia *Tarija* 25 km north-west of Entre Ríos at 21°32'S 64°12'W, 1,650 m (Remsen and Traylor 1983), although the species is apparently genuinely absent further north, where J. Fjeldså (*in litt.* 1991) searched for it in vain during 27 days of fieldwork in September and October 1991 along the río Parapeti, río Pilcomayo and the northern tributaries of río Pilaya in southern Chuquisaca department;

Argentina *Jujuy* the eastern range of Sierra de Zenta, at 3,000 m, 23°03'S 65°05'W, near the border with Salta province, June 1924 (Budin 1931: specimen in USNM); and the vicinity of San Salvador de Jujuy, 24°11'S 65°18'W (río Yala; Termas de Reyes; río la Quesera) (Nores and Yzurieta 1981, Castelino 1985, M. Nores and D. Yzurieta *in litt.* 1986, Chebez and Heinonen Fortabat 1987, B. M. Whitney *in litt.* 1991);

Salta on the río Lipeo, near Lipeo, Santa Victoria department, 1,500 m, 10 August 1992 (A. di Giacomo, G. Gil and others *per* J. C. Chebez *in litt.* 1992); on the río Baritú inside Baritú National Park, same department, 1,700 m, 11-13 August 1992 (A. di Giacomo, G. Gil and others *per* J. C. Chebez *in litt.* 1992); río Santa María, 43 km west of Orán, 23°17'S 64°14'W, Orán department, July 1947 (specimen in MACN); Lesser, c.24°37'S 65°27'W, where three birds were seen on 1 May 1992 (E. Derlindati *per* S. M. Caziani *in litt.* 1992);

Tucumán Trancas department (Cerro Ranchillo; Cerro Negro), Trancas being at 26°13'S 65°17'W (two specimens in AMNH and LSUMZ collected in February 1961 and June 1952 respectively); and the río la Sosa drainage at the following sites (referenced at the end): Aconquija (one specimen in MCZ and five in IML, these latter, collected in August and September, being probably erroneously labelled 3,000 m: M. Nores *in litt.* 1989); Cerro Bayo (possibly Mogote Bayo), the type-locality; Anfama, 1,800 m, at c.26°45'S 65°35'W; La Ciénaga; near Durazno Blanco, Tafí, 1,750 m; near Tafí del Valle; Arroyo La Casita, Quebrada Cañas Horcona, Monteros, 1,800 m; río La Angostura, Monteros, 1,750 m; Punta Carreras, Monteros, 1,700 m; Apeadero General Muñoz, Monteros, 1,600 m (Cabanis 1883, Lillo 1905, Hartert and Venturi 1909, Olrog 1949, Fraga and Narosky 1985, Salvador *et al.* 1986; also M. Nores and D. Yzurieta *in litt.* 1986, R. Vides Almonacid *in litt.* 1986).

Catamarca Cuesta del Clavillo, in Nevados del Aconquija, at 27°20'S 65°57'W, and at Esquina Grande, río Chacras, Andalgalá department, at 27°23'S 65°58'W, both near the border of Tucumán (Fraga and Narosky 1985; M. Nores *in litt.* to W. Belton 1982, 1983, M. Nores and D. Yzurieta *in litt.* 1986: coordinates of río Chacras from M. Nores *in litt.* 1989). The southernmost locality holding suitable habitat, Cerro de los Alisos, is only 30 km from río Chacras (M. Nores *in litt.* 1989).

POPULATION There is no information from Bolivia (see above). Olrog (1949) stated that "this dipper is not rare in [Nevados del] Aconquija, and is also frequent in río la Sosa, e.g. in the subtropical selva". M. Nores and D. Yzurieta (*in litt.* 1986) stated that the species is "more or less common along all streams in alder woods in north-west Argentina", and gave the following counts: along río Yala 6-8 birds on 5 October 1980, 2-3 on 12 October 1980, 2-3 on 12 November 1981; and at Cuesta del Clavillo five were seen on 31 August 1982, and along río la Sosa six were seen on 22 June 1985; moreover, the bird was common along the Baritú near Angosto in Baritú National Park, mid-August 1992 (A. di Giacomo, G. Gil and others *per* J. C. Chebez *in litt.* 1992). However, M. Nores (*in litt.* 1989), who added a count eight birds and three nests along río Yala on 6 and 7 September 1988, reported the distributional gap in southern Salta and parts of Jujuy as apparently genuine, though inexplicable, and noted that on the rivers where it is found its population is probably limited by the number of available nest sites. R. Vides Almonacid (*in litt.* 1986) counted five along 2 km of río La Angostura, at c.1,750 m in November 1982, but only saw a single bird at La Casita, 1,800 m, during 11 trips (45 days of observation) in 1984 and 1985: from his numerous visits to suitable habitat, he concluded that it was a very local bird with very small populations, and expressed fears that numbers would decrease owing to man's activities. At Termas de Reyes eight dippers were encountered on 29 August 1985 (Chebez and Heinonen Fortabat 1987). G. Hoy, an ornithologist resident in Salta province, had seen the species only a very few times during the 30 years before c.1977 (King 1978-1979).

ECOLOGY The Rufous-throated, like other dippers, lives along streams and rivers: it appears to breed only in the alder *Alnus acuminata* zone (Salvador *et al.* 1986, M. Nores and D. Yzurieta *in litt.* 1986), the upper limit of which is given as 2,500 m (Esteban 1969, M. Nores *in litt.* 1989); records of the species from as high as 3,000 m are probably erroneous (M. Nores *in litt.* 1989: see Distribution). The lower limit of the alder zone is given as 1,800 m by Esteban (1969), 1,500 m by M. Nores (W. Belton *in litt.* 1985) and 1,400 m by Salvador *et al.* (1986). Most records where altitude is given, including the three nests described by Salvador *et al.* (1986) and the eight nests found at various localities by C. C. Olrog (Fraga and Narosky 1985), are from between 1,500 and 2,200 m. At the onset of frost birds descend to lower and larger rivers (Dinelli 1918), at least as low as 800 m, although some may remain above 1,500 m (M. Nores *in litt.* 1989).

Like other dippers it perches mostly on boulders and rocky cliffs in or near streams, flies with fast wing-beats and seems to follow the streams as closely as possible (Salvador *et al.* 1986); it has not been reported to perch in trees. The Rufous-throated Dipper usually makes only short flights between foraging sites, frequently calls, and feeds on larvae and insects on the edge of and in the water (Castelino 1985). Reports by Castelino (1985) that it is sometimes completely submerged for short periods are probably erroneous, as other observers, during numerous encounters with the species, have failed to note this behaviour (M. Nores *in litt.* 1989). The dipper has been noted as more active on overcast days or during light rain, when feeding takes place all day: on clear sunny days, birds spend much time standing beneath the shady overhangs of rocks in and along the streams, sometimes not moving for more than one hour (B. M. Whitney *in litt.* 1991). The stomach of one bird contained aquatic insects, mostly beetle imagos (FMNH label data).

The restricted range of the species is somewhat puzzling, as streams in the distributional "gap" (the recent record from Lesser somewhat confounds this concept) in southern Salta and parts of Jujuy were found to be clean and apparently suitable (M. Nores *in litt.* 1989). Suggestions that competition with aquatic furnariids of the genus *Cinclodes* may play some role (Salvador *et al.* 1986) seem doubtful, as at virtually all sites where the dipper has been found it coexists with a *Cinclodes* sp. (and Torrent Duck *Merganetta armata*), and apparently suitable rivers which lack the dipper also lack the *Cinclodes* and Torrent Duck (M. Nores *in litt.* 1989).

Three nests found in late December were placed in niches in rocky walls 95-125 cm above the water: they were bulky globular structures of green moss (two species), grass stems, a few rootlets and pieces of a filamentous green algae; beneath one nest, the remains of an old nest were found, and whilst one of the nests was abandoned with one egg and another was inactive, the third contained two eggs (Salvador *et al.* 1986); it is not clear, however, whether the two eggs comprised a full clutch. Copulation has been observed (on the río Yala) in early January 1988

(B. M. Whitney *in litt.* 1991), and a half-built nest was found in Catamarca on 2 January 1982 (Fraga and Narosky 1985).

THREATS Most if not all of the streams within the Rufous-throated Dipper's range are currently in an acceptable state (M. Nores *in litt.* 1989), but are in serious long-term danger of modification through hydrological control, deforestation, stock-rearing, etc. (R. Vides Almonacid *in litt.* 1986). The fact that only one part of the species's small range enjoys the benefit of protected area status (see below) is of concern if these long-term dangers start to materialize.

MEASURES TAKEN None is known, other than that the bird was very recently (August 1992) found in Baritú National Park in northernmost Salta province, Argentina.

MEASURES PROPOSED While the present state of the species's habitat is relatively good, the absence of any formal conservation of virtually any part of it represents a significant omission in the management of the entire region. The establishment of a system of river management so that populations of the Rufous-throated Dipper have access to rivers with high water quality and adjacent areas of alder *Alnus* in which to breed must become a regional conservation priority. Most desirable is the implementation of the planned national park in the Nevados del Aconquija (Beltrán 1987), which would protect populations of this species and also the Tucumán Mountain-finch *Poospiza baeri* and White-tailed Shrike-tyrant *Agriornis andicola* (J. C. Chebez *in litt.* 1992; see relevant accounts). At río la Quesera, this dipper may be sympatric with the mountain-finch (collected there in October 1950), and any initiatives in this area should take into account the requirements of both species. Consideration should also be given to the near-threatened Alder Amazon *Amazona tucumana*, which at least in Jujuy and Tucumán provinces inhabits a number of the same areas (in the same alder habitat and at the same altitudes) as this dipper (Fjeldså and Krabbe 1990).

REMARKS The Rufous-throated Dipper was regarded as a subspecies of the White-capped Dipper *Cinclus leucocephalus* by Mayr and Greenway (1960), a treatment not followed by other authors. The wing-flicking behaviour of both *schulzi* and *leucocephalus* (as opposed to the bobbing of Palearctic forms, which lack a white wing-patch) does suggest that they are closely related, (S. J. Tyler verbally 1989, NK), but *schulzi* differs from all three forms of *leucocephalus* in its general coloration (greyish rather than blackish), rufous throat, larger white patch on the underside of the wing, and by the absence of a white cap (Fjeldså and Krabbe 1990), and we here follow the majority of authors in treating it as a distinct species.

SUMICHRAST'S WREN *Hylorchilus sumichrasti* V/R[10]

Possibly representing two distinct species, this enigmatic wren is confined to tropical forest on outcropping limestone in two areas of southern Mexico, where it remains poorly known, especially with reference to its distribution and ecology, and is threatened from habitat destruction.

DISTRIBUTION Sumichrast's Wren exists in two disjunct populations in southern Mexico: one in west-central Veracruz and northernmost Oaxaca (nominate *sumichrasti*), and the other to the south-east in easternmost Veracruz and western Chiapas (race *navai*: see Remarks 1). Coordinates for Oaxaca are taken from Binford (1989), the remainder from OG (1956a).

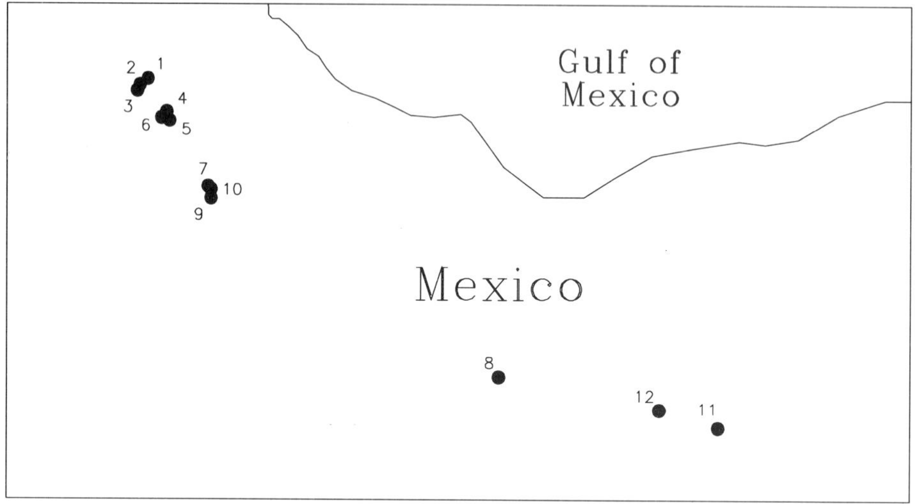

Veracruz In the west-central part of the state, the species is known from a number of sites in a small area around Córdoba: localities include Paraje Nueve[1] (18°52'N 96°52'W), where a male and female (in USNM) were collected in March 1926; 1.5 km south of Amatlán[2] (18°50'N 96°55'W: 5 km south of Córdoba), where birds were seen in January 1984, April 1985, February 1987 and April–May 1990 (Hardy and Delaney 1987, S. N. G. Howell *in litt.* 1991); 10-15 km south of Córdoba[3], where birds were encountered in April 1985 (Hardy and Delaney 1987); Presidio[4] (18°41'N 96°45'W) and nearby, where 38 specimens were taken in March–May 1925 (Bangs and Peters 1927), one in July 1940 (male in DMNH) and another in March 1943 (male in MLZ); Motzorongo[5] (18°38'N 96°44'W) where two specimens (in USNM) were collected between 245 and 365 m during March 1894 (see also Nelson 1897); and La Gloria[6], 16 km south-west of Presidio, which is represented by specimens (two males and a female in MLZ) taken in July 1942 at 915 m (Crossin and Ely 1973). Other localities in this area are "Mata Bejuco" (untraced, but in the same region as Motzorongo: Nelson 1897), where the type-specimen was collected around 1869 (Lawrence 1871: see Remarks 2); and Rancho Caracol[7], 48 km south of Tezonapa (18°36'N 96°41'W), where two specimens (in LSUMZ, MLZ) were collected at the end of August 1945. Rancho Caracol is recorded on the specimens as being in Veracruz, although "48 km south of Tezonapa" places it near the shore of Presa Miguel Alemán, in northernmost Oaxaca (see below). In easternmost Veracruz, Sumichrast's Wren (presumably the race *navai*) has recently been recorded from the limestone areas of the Uxpanapa region[8] (S. N. G. Howell *in litt.* 1992).

Oaxaca Sumichrast's Wren is known only from northernmost Oaxaca, where the population is presumably continuous with that in west-central Veracruz. A female (Miller *et al.* 1957 recorded two specimens) taken in November 1943 by M. del Toro Avilés at Soyaltepec[9] (San Miguel Soyaltepec: 18°12'N 96°29'W) has been doubted (Binford 1989), owing to the known unreliability of this collector's data (L. C. Binford *in litt.* 1991). San Miguel Soyaltepec is now situated on an island in the Presa Miguel Alemán (flooded after del Toro Avilés's specimen was collected), two birds being seen on an adjacent island (8 km west of Temascal[10]: 18°15'N 96°24'W) at 75 m in June 1964 (Binford 1989). The specimens collected at Rancho Caracol, "Veracruz" (in LSUMZ, MLZ), apparently come from Oaxaca, the locality being near the western shore of Presa Miguel Alemán, west of but still very close to the other localities.

Chiapas Records of the species come from the southern side of Lago Malpaso (locally called Presa Nezahualcoyotl) in the central depression of western Chiapas. The species was first discovered there (leading to the description of the race *navai*) in December 1969 when a bird of uncertain identity was seen at 760 m, 26 km north of Ocozocoautla[11] along the Malpaso road (Crossin and Ely 1973). Six specimens were collected there, in a forest block of only a few square miles, during December 1970 and January 1971, and at least 10 were heard and presumably three collected (since nine were taken in total) in the winter of 1971-1972 (Crossin and Ely 1973). More recently, Sumichrast's Wren has been found on the north side of the "canyon of the río La Venta"[12] (c.17°01'N 93°47'W: P. J. Bubb *in litt.* 1991), at 400-500 m in the north-western corner of the El Ocote Ecological Reserve: five birds were seen there on different days in September 1990 along a 2 km path following a tributary of the valley (P. J. Bubb *in litt.* 1991), and c.10 birds (see Population) were recorded along a 2.4 km transect during July and August 1991 (P. Atkinson *in litt.* 1991).

POPULATION The problematic terrain, localized range and quiet post-breeding period make population assessments of Sumichrast's Wren very difficult; location of calling or singing birds gives the easiest opportunity for such assessments, which have yet to be done in any systematic way (see Measures Proposed). Nevertheless, although once described as "one of the rarest and most local of all North American birds" (Bangs and Peters 1927), modern evidence suggests that Sumichrast's Wren is "locally common" (S. N. G. Howell *in litt.* 1987). As noted under Distribution, 38 specimens were taken at and around Presidio, Veracruz, in a three-month period, despite being "hard work to find" (Bangs and Peters 1927), indicating that the species was not uncommon. The study at El Ocote Ecological Reserve in July and August 1991 produced an average of 3.24 birds per kilometre of transect, this being extrapolated to give an approximate population density of 10 to 25 birds per km^2 (the average being c.20/km^2) (Atkinson *et al.* in prep.). In west-central Veracruz near Amatlán, the species was noted as a locally common resident in coffee plantations: records include two seen in April 1985; two seen (one singing) with 4–6 heard singing in a small area on 22 April 1990; a pair seen at a nest (containing young), with 2–3 heard on 11 May 1990 (S. N. G. Howell *in litt.* 1991; also Hardy and Delaney 1987); and between 2.5 and 6.25 birds per kilometre of transect during September 1991 (Atkinson *et al.* in prep). The last record in the adjacent Oaxaca part of the range was in 1964 (see Distribution).

ECOLOGY Sumichrast's Wren is apparently restricted to the lower to middle elevations (75-915 m; see Crossin and Ely 1973, Binford 1989) in steep hill country covered by dense tropical semi-deciduous to evergreen forest (Hardy and Delaney 1987), or coffee with shade-trees (S. N. G. Howell *in litt.* 1991). At río La Venta, Chiapas, the forest canopy (at 15-20 m high) was closed and therefore the understorey was very sparse (P. J. Bubb *in litt.* 1991, Atkinson *et al.* in prep.), this evidently being similar to the habitat described by Nelson (1897) at Motzorongo: however, near Amatlán, the canopy (at 20-30 m, and comprising shade trees) was more open and hence the ground cover (an overgrown coffee plantation) was denser (Atkinson *et al.* in prep.).

All of the known localities are characterized by extensive limestone outcrops, the species spending a majority of its time at or near ground level (never more than 1 m from the top of the nearest rock), always in the shade, and foraging in and around rocks and small caves formed by the outcrops and vegetation (Crossin and Ely 1973, Hardy and Delaney 1987, Atkinson *et al.* in prep.). Birds hop from rock to rock (flying has only been recorded over short distances) and forage on the moss-covered surface of the limestone and in the cracks and crevices of boulders, by peering into crevices and gleaning insects (Atkinson *et al.* in prep.); the long bill obviously facilitates gleaning from such cracks. Recently, the species has been seen in humid coffee plantations (under shade-trees), suggesting that it may in fact be able to adapt to modified habitat as long as limestone outcrops and shade are present (S. N. G. Howell *in litt.* 1987; see Threats). It is generally solitary and shy, although unwary of people (often approaching a tape, when responding to playback, to within "a few feet", even if someone was holding the tape-recorder): at El Ocote, singing birds were usually recorded singly, and only infrequently were two individuals heard at the same time (Atkinson *et al.* in prep.).

Breeding has been recorded on a number of occasions in Veracruz: three nests were found near Presidio in 1925, each containing three eggs, on 6, 17 and 20 May, the last two containing eggs that were at the point of hatching, suggesting that they were laid on about 1 May (Bangs and Peters 1927). All nests were at c.610 m, in mountains where the slopes were rough and broken with immense rocks and deep depressions, two nests being located in crevices in the side of large rocks, and one in a crevice in the roof of a cave (Bangs and Peters 1927). In the Amatlán–Córdoba area, birds were heard singing at the end of April 1985 (Hardy and Delaney 1987); the end of April 1990, with a nest (containing young) found on 11 May 1990 (S. N. G. Howell *in litt.* 1991); and in early September 1991 (Atkinson *et al.* in prep.). Singing at El Ocote has been recorded (throughout the day) in July and August (1991), and although birds were seen at the same locality the previous September they were then just calling (Atkinson *et al.* in prep., P. J. Bubb *in litt.* 1991). A bird trapped at El Ocote on 2 August 1991 was undergoing a complete body moult, indicative of post-breeding (Atkinson *et al.* in prep.). The species is a (presumed) permanent resident (Binford 1989), the northern population being represented by specimens or observations from January to September (the doubtful Soyaltepec specimen was reportedly taken in November), while in the southern population birds have been recorded during July–September and December–January (see Distribution and Population).

THREATS In Veracruz, the steep rocky limestone forested areas the species inhabits are poor for cultivation, which spared them for longer than the adjacent lowlands, but now even these are being attacked, and expansion of limestone quarrying around Amatlán may pose a real threat (S. N. G. Howell *in litt.* 1987). A similar situation exists in Chiapas where the vast majority of the forest along the Malpaso road (between Ocozocoautla and Lago Malpaso) has been cut and converted to grazing and agriculture, the presence of abundant limestone outcroppings apparently being the only reason for the survival of the small forest block where the species was found in the early 1970s (Crossin and Ely 1973). Even here though, there was found to be some cutting for "cafetales" along the edges of the forest (Crossin and Ely 1973), Atkinson *et al.* (in prep.) being unable to find the species in August 1991, and suggesting that the Ocozocoautla–Apic Pac road has opened up surrounding areas for cultivation and caused the rapid reduction of suitable habitat. Much forest within the immediate range of Sumichrast's Wren has presumably been destroyed by the creation of Presa Miguel Alemán and Lago Malpaso.

The species has been found in humid coffee plantations (see Ecology), which suggests that it is the limestone outcrops that are essential and that the coffee plants, presumably as long as shade-trees are present, can act as surrogate forest (S. N. G. Howell *in litt* 1991). Unfortunately, there is an increasing trend to plant coffee that does not require shade (S. N. G. Howell *in litt.* 1991): whether or not the species can adapt to this habitat is unknown. In Chiapas, the most immediate potential impact on this species and its habitat is the proposed Ocozocoautla–Sayula highway, the initial route of which was planned to follow the río La Venta, inside the El Ocote Ecological Reserve, and cross the river at the precise site where Sumichrast's Wren was found in 1990: however, a new route which bye-passes the reserve has recently been approved by presidential decree (P. J. Bubb *in litt.* 1991, verbally 1992). The highway, wherever it cuts through the El Ocote area, will have a detrimental impact in the large, remote and still well forested region of Chimalapas and Uxpanapa, the latter being where the species has recently been found (P. J. Bubb *in litt.* 1991, S. N. G. Howell *in litt.* 1992). Apart from its direct impact, the highway will also inevitably bring secondary deforestation and settlement along the road corridor, potentially destroying most of the species's remaining habitat in this area.

MEASURES TAKEN There is apparently just one existing reserve in which Sumichrast's Wren has been found, this being the El Ocote Ecological Reserve in western Chiapas (called "Reserva Especial de la Biosfera Selva del Ocote" in Anon. 1989). This reserve comprises c.48,000 ha south of Lago Malpaso, with the río La Venta flowing along its southern edge, and includes the area where the species was seen in 1990 (see Distribution). Its current value is diminishing with the development of plans for the Ocozocoautla–Sayula highway (see Threats), although the Mexican environmental body ECOSFERA is actively campaigning against these plans, and is now using Sumichrast's Wren as a figurehead species for the conservation of the reserve (P. J. Bubb *in litt.* 1991). The Cañon del Río Blanco National Park in Veracruz (c.55,700 ha: Anon. 1989) is adjacent to the main area of the species's distribution in west-central Veracruz, although the bird has to date not been recorded from the park.

MEASURES PROPOSED ECOSFERA is working towards producing a management plan for the El Ocote Ecological Reserve, although a survey for new sites for Sumichrast's Wren there has not yet been planned (P. J. Bubb *in litt.* 1991). In view of the potential importance of this reserve for the conservation of the species (see Remarks 1), a systematic survey should be undertaken in order to determine its actual distribution and population within the reserve, and conservation of the bird should be taken into consideration in the subsequent management plan. Determining the bird's status and distribution in the Uxpanapa area is an equally high priority owing to the detrimental effects of the planned highway, and searches should also be aimed at discovering whether the bird occurs in the Chimalapas area of easternmost Oaxaca. More generally, a detailed ecological study of the species may help identify other suitable areas and determine the size of forest necessary to sustain viable populations. This would be particularly pertinent to the forest remnants on limestone outcrops in the Córdoba area, the edges of which are gradually being eroded owing to agricultural encroachment, and also to the forests in and around the Presa Miguel Alemán. The forests around the Presa Miguel Alemán obviously protect the watershed that feeds the reservoir, so any surveys of the surrounding hillsides should take this into consideration (L. C. Binford *in litt.* 1991). An assessment of the species's status, distribution, and remaining habitat in the Córdoba area is also an urgent need before an effective conservation strategy can be designed.

REMARKS (1) Recent observations and studies of birds at El Ocote and in the Uxpanapa region have indicated that *Hylorchilus (sumichrasti) navai* may in fact be a separate species, Nava's Wren (Atkinson *et al.* in prep., *World Birdwatch* 13,4 [1991]: 4, S. N. G. Howell *in litt.* 1992). If the two subspecies are given full specific status, this will present the situation where distributionally Nava's Wren is known from a minute area in part protected by the El Ocote Ecological Reserve, while Sumichrast's Wren, although recorded from a larger area, would be left totally unprotected. From a conservation standpoint such a split would make the situation more urgent: a reserve would be essential to protect a population of Sumichrast's Wren; and the viability of the Nava's Wren population in the El Ocote reserve would need to be determined before habitat destruction in the Uxpanapa area adversely affects the only other known population. (2) Phillips (1991) suggests that "Mata Bejuco" must in fact have been a local name for Sumichrast's Wren, and not a locality; hence the type-locality is unknown although it is obviously in the Motzorongo region (see Distribution).

APOLINAR'S WREN *Cistothorus apolinari* R[11]

This reed-marsh specialist is confined to the dwindling marshes of the East Andes of Colombia, which are threatened by drainage and the influences of agriculture. Key sites include Laguna de Tota in Boyacá and Laguna de Pedropalo in Cundinamarca.

DISTRIBUTION Apolinar's Wren is restricted to the wetlands in the East Andes of northern Boyacá department, and on the Sabana de Bogotá south to Páramo de Sumapaz, Cundinamarca department, Colombia. Coordinates are from Paynter and Traylor (1981), with localities from north to south as follows:

Boyacá Güicán, on the western slope of the Sierra Nevada del Cocuy (Hilty and Brown 1986, Fjeldså and Krabbe 1990); La Cueva (6°25'N 72°21'W; also on the western slope of the Sierra Nevada del Cocuy, at c.3,500 m), where a bird (in ICN) was collected in December 1971; Lagunillas (6°15'N 72°38'W; at 3,300-3,400 m on the south-western slope of the Sierra Nevada del Cocuy), where a female (in CM) was taken in March 1917; Peña Negra (untraced, but on the Páramo de Rechiniga at c.6°16'N 72°23'W), where two females (in CM) were collected in March 1917; Laguna de Tota in 1982 (Varty *et al.* 1986);

Cundinamarca Laguna de Fúquene (J. Fjeldså *in litt.* 1992); Laguna de Cucunubá (5°17'N 73°48'W; at 2,500 m) (J. Fjeldså *in litt.* 1992); Laguna de Palacio (just south of the previous locality), where birds were recorded in February 1992 (L. M. Renjifo *in litt.* 1992); Estación La Caro (4°52'N 74°02'W; at 2,540 m, c.30 km north of Bogotá), where four birds (in ICN) were taken in March 1952; Laguna de Pedropalo (c.4°45'N 74°24'W) (Fjeldså and Krabbe 1990, J. Fjeldså *in litt.* 1992); Suba marsh (4°45'N 74°05'W; at 2,710 m, a northern suburb of Bogotá), where 14 birds (in AMNH, FMNH, MNHN, USNM) were taken between 1913 and 1919 (also Chapman 1917a); Funza (4°43'N 74°13'W; at c.2,600 m, c.20 km north-west of Bogotá), whence come three birds (in AMNH, LACM) taken in 1960; Laguna de la Florida (c.4°43'N 74°09'W; at c.2,600 m on the western outskirts of Bogotá), (Hilty and Brown 1986: see Population); Laguna de la Herrera (c.4°42'N 74°18'W; at c.2,600 m, 20 km west of Bogotá) (Naranjo 1989, J. Fjeldså *in litt.* 1992); Usaquén (4°42'N 74°02'W; at 2,590 m, a north-eastern suburb of Bogotá) (Olivares 1969); Fontibón (4°40'N 74°09'W; at 2,575 m, 10 km north-west of Bogotá) (Olivares 1969); Subia (4°34'N 74°37'W; at 1,800 m), the type-locality (Chapman 1917a); Páramo del Verjón (c.4°32'N 74°04'W; at 3,400-3,600 m, south-east of Bogotá) (Olivares 1969); Chipaque (4°27'N 74°03'W; at 2,470 m, 17 km south-south-east of Bogotá), where a male (in LACM) was collected in January 1960; Lagunas del Chisacal (= Laguna Chisaca at 4°17'N 74°13'W; 45 km south-west of Bogotá on a spur of the Páramo de Sumapaz), whence come numerous specimens (in AMNH, FMNH, ICN, LACM, USNM) taken during the 1950s and early 1960s, and recent records (J. Hernández Camacho verbally 1991); Páramo de Sumapaz (possibly referring to records from the previous locality) (Hilty and Brown 1986, Fjeldså and Krabbe 1990); and Boquerón de Medianaranja (untraced, but apparently on the Páramo de Sumapaz), where a specimen (in ICN) was taken in November 1961.

POPULATION Apolinar's Wren is apparently locally fairly common (Hilty and Brown 1986, Ridgely and Tudor 1989, Fjeldså and Krabbe 1990), but increasingly rare at some localities such as the Laguna Chisaca (J. I. Hernández Camacho and F. G. Stiles verbally 1991), where it was previously common. A substantial population still exists at Laguna de Tota (Ridgely and Tudor 1989), estimated at 30-50 pairs in 1982 (Varty *et al.* 1986). There is very little information on the population of this species, and while King (1978-1979) mentioned that the species was most plentiful at La Florida in Bogotá, recent observations have indicated that the population must be of only a few pairs (LGN), F. R. Lambert (*in litt.* 1989) observing 6-7 birds on 25 February 1989; however, the population of this whole area is probably at least 10-15 pairs (F. G. Stiles *in litt.* 1992). Observations by J. Fjeldså (*in litt.* 1992) in October 1991 recorded three family groups at Laguna Fúquene (noting that the population may be dense in some places, as two males were singing just 10 m apart); a few pairs at Laguna Cucunubá; birds singing at several places around Laguna de la Herrera; and one bird singing at Laguna de Pedropalo. Local populations at La Caro and Usaquén, Cundinamarca (see Distribution), are now apparently extinct (L. M. Renjifo *in litt.* 1992).

ECOLOGY This secretive wren is confined to tall emergent vegetation (reed-beds) fringing marshes and lakes (see Remarks); such vegetation typically comprises bulrushes *Scirpus* sp., cattails *Typha* sp., *Cortadera* sp., and *Polygonum* sp. (Varty *et al.* 1986, J. Fjeldså *in litt.* 1992). Although Hilty and Brown (1986) and Ridgely and Tudor (1989) suggested that Apolinar's Wren occurs primarily in tall cattails, Varty *et al.* (1986) concluded that at Laguna de Tota the bird appeared to favour bulrushes, and at Laguna de Fúquene J. Fjeldså (*in litt.* 1992) found the species inhabiting dense areas of *Scirpus–Polygonum* reed swamp. At Laguna de la Herrera the preference for cattails over bulrushes is evident and appears to segregate the territories of this wren and those of the Yellow-hooded Blackbird *Agelaius icterocephalus bogotensis*, possibly indicating a negative association owing to antagonistic interactions between the species (Naranjo 1989), although L. M. Renjifo (*in litt.* 1992) found one territory in bulrushes overlapping with a colony of the blackbird at this site.

Apolinar's Wrens typically move slowly through dense bulrush–cattail vegetation, by climbing up to 1 m (from the water or ground surface), and dropping to the base of the next stem, where they feed on slow-moving, flightless or emerging insects (Varty *et al.* 1986). Areas of bulrushes *Scirpus* sp. at Laguna de Tota evidently supported the most prey items for the wren, amongst which (in order of preference) were midges Chironomidae, Araneae, Diptera (except Culicidae), Zygoptera and, with much less frequency, Culicidae, Braconidae, and Lepidoptera (Varty *et al.* 1986). Birds spend little time in open areas between patches of suitable reeds, although a juvenile (at Laguna de Tota) was seen to feed in such an area, gleaning from a *Rumex* sp. leaf (Varty *et al.* 1986).

Birds are found in pairs or (family) groups, and may even form loose colonies (Hilty and Brown 1986, Fjeldså and Krabbe 1990). Breeding seems to occur generally between February and October: birds in breeding condition have been noted in most months between February and October (Borrero 1953; specimens in AMNH, ICN, USNM), with eggs in July, juveniles from July to October, a colony and fledglings in October, and singing in the same month (Olivares 1969, Hilty and Brown 1986, Varty *et al.* 1986, Fjeldså and Krabbe 1990, J. Fjeldså *in litt.* 1992).

THREATS Wetland drainage, pollution (sewage and agrochemicals), and reed-harvesting across the Bogotá plateau and adjacent areas is undoubtedly the main reason for the decline of this species (see Colombian Grebe *Podiceps andinus* and Bogotá Rail *Rallus semiplumbeus* accounts for details).

MEASURES TAKEN The wetlands of the Sabana de Bogotá enjoy no legal protection, although the Corporación Autónoma Regional de las Cuencas de los Ríos Bogotá, Ubaté and Suárez (CAR) is charged with the task of providing water for drinking and industrial use, and as such is concerned with conservation initiatives and management plans for the many wetlands within its jurisdiction in Cundinamarca, and Laguna de Tota, Boyacá (Varty *et al.* 1986): however, drainage and other habitat alterations still continue unchecked. Away from the Sabana de Bogotá, Apolinar's Wren occurs in both the El Cocuy National Park, Boyacá (306,000 ha), and Sumapaz National Park, Cundinamarca (154,000 ha) (Hernández Camacho *et al.* undated).

MEASURES PROPOSED The ecological requirements of Apolinar's Wren are already sufficiently well known to allow the design of an effective conservation plan, and the priority must be to secure the long-term future of the larger remaining wetlands. Any initiatives in these areas need to consider the region's other threatened species, namely Colombian Grebe and Bogotá Rail (see relevant accounts), along with threatened and endemic subspecies such as Niceforo's Pintail *Anas (georgica) niceforoi*, Cinnamon Teal *Anas cyanoptera borreroi*, Ruddy Duck *Oxyura jamaicensis andina*, Spot-flanked Gallinule *Porphyriops melanops bogotensis*, Least Bittern *Ixobrychus exilis bogotensis*, Bearded Tachuri *Polystictus pectoralis bogotensis* and Yellow-hooded Blackbird *Agelaius icterocephalus bogotensis* (Varty *et al.* 1986).

Laguna de Tota probably harbours the largest populations of both this species and Bogotá Rail, and is in urgent need of long-term protection from further degradation of suitable habitat.

During the last two years both the "Grupo Ornis" and the recently founded "Sociedad Bogotana de Ornitología" have been campaigning for the legal protection of the remnant oak forest surrounding Laguna de Pedropalo, of critical importance for the Black Inca *Coeligena prunellei* and Turquoise Dacnis *Dacnis hartlaubi*, but also where the Bogotá Rail and Apolinar's Wren have been recorded in recent years (see relevant accounts): these initiatives should be strongly encouraged.

Searches for the wren should perhaps concentrate in the páramo areas which have apparently enjoyed a less disturbed history than the savanna wetlands: the species may well be found to occur widely and in significant populations within these areas. However, an assessment of the population within the savanna wetlands is also important for this species, the status of which is unclear outside of Laguna de Tota.

REMARKS There appears to be some confusion over the habitat preferences of this species, and possibly over its identification: J. I. Hernández Camacho (*in litt.* 1973, and verbally 1991) has stated that some populations on the Bogotá plateau prefer stands of *Alnus acuminata* mixed with *Cortadelia* sp. at the periphery of páramo marshes, and Borrero (1953) noted that the páramo populations are found both in marshes and in patches of *Escallonia myrtillioides* and *Chusquea* sp. with a ground cover of *Sphagnum* sp., and sometimes even in stands of the páramo dominant *Espeletia* spp. However, an analysis of the vocalizations of the birds in such habitat above Bogotá suggest that they belong to a race of the Grass Wren *Cistothorus platensis* (M. Gochfeld *in litt.* undated; also King 1978-1979). There are seemingly no confirmed records of Apolinar's Wren in habitats other than emergent fringing marsh vegetation, despite a number of studies (e.g. Varty *et al.* 1986, J. Fjeldså *in litt.* 1992).

ZAPATA WREN *Ferminia cerverai* V/R[10]

This elusive bird is known only from within a 20 km radius of Santo Tomás in the Zapata Swamp, Cuba, where it appears to have suffered particularly from dry-season burning of its savanna-like habitat and perhaps from introduced predators.

DISTRIBUTION The Zapata Wren is endemic to Cuba, and was not discovered until 1926 (Barbour and Peters 1927). For almost 50 years it was only known to occur in the Zapata Swamp, Matanzas province, in a very restricted area about 13 km^2 and c.5 km north of Santo Tomás (22°24'N 81°25'W in OG 1963a) (King 1978-1979, Bond 1979). In February 1975, two birds were seen and others heard near the mouth of the río Hatiguanico (22°32'N 81°39'W in OG 1963a) (Bond 1984), extending the known range c.15 km to the north-west. In 1988 the species's known range was again extended when on several occasions birds were observed at Hato de Jicarita (22°37'N 81°27'W in OG 1963a) and at La Cola, these two localities being c.20 km north and c.20 km south-east of Santo Tomás respectively (Martínez García and Martínez García 1991). Most skins in AMNH, ANSP, BM, CM, MCZ, MNHN and USNM are simply labelled as "Santo Tomás, Ciénaga de Zapata" or "Santo Tomás, Península de Zapata", but a specimen in ROM is labelled "Represuela (*sic*) de Santo Tomás", which is in the same area north of Santo Tomás (O. H. Garrido *in litt.* 1991).

POPULATION The Zapata Wren was reported to be common within its restricted range soon after its discovery (Bond 1956b, Garrido 1985). Most skins (at least 17) in the museums mentioned above were collected between 1926 and 1934, although one was collected in 1948 (in USNM) and one in 1972 (in ROM). Garrido (1985) reported it to be common in 1962, when several birds could be heard and one was then collected (García undated). However, only after a long trek into the swamp was a bird taken in 1974, and surprisingly no bird was heard singing (Garrido 1980). Subsequent expeditions in 1978, 1979 and 1980 failed to find the species, and it was then believed extinct (Garrido 1985). However in November 1981 a single bird was again reported, in March and April 1982 two birds were seen and in 1985 the species was recorded once more (González 1982, Garrido 1985, C. Wotzkow *in litt.* 1986). Garrido (1985) has suggested that between 1974 and 1981 the Zapata Wren's "disappearance" was related to the fires in the swamp caused by local people (see also Regalado Ruíz 1981, and Threats), although O. H. Garrido (*in litt.* 1991) comment that the Zapata Wren seems to be "just holding up with no signs of increasing" and added that "it has been seen in the same areas for the past six years". Sulley and Sulley (1992) observed two birds in February 1991 near Santo Tomás. The population in the area of Santo Tomás appears to have substantially increased after the protection of the area (H. González Alonso *in litt.* 1991), but its current population is still very low and it is estimated perhaps at less than 30 pairs (L. Fazio *in litt.* 1992).

ECOLOGY The terrain north of Santo Tomás where the Zapata Wren is found, although not firm, is not as soft as the rest of the area (Garrido and García Montaña 1975). The vegetation is savanna-like, mainly formed of sawgrass *Cladium jamaicense*, "macíos" *Typha dominguensis* and rushes with scattered bushes, mostly "arraigán" *Myrica cerifera*, "yana" *Conocarpus erecta*, "yanilla blanca" *Ilex cassine*, "ácana" *Mimusops* sp. and low trees (Barbour 1928, Bruner 1934, Garrido and García Montaña 1975, Garrido 1980, Regalado Ruíz 1981, González 1982). Its habitat within the Santo Tomás area is in part crossed by a ditch or "zanja" known as "La Cocodrila", and the vegetation growing on both sides is rich, owing to the peat that was deposited during its digging (Garrido 1980); this habitat can be either completely covered with water or dried out, depending on the annually variable rainy season, winters tending to be drier (Garrido 1980). The species is hardly ever detected unless its song is heard, and it is rarely seen flying, more usually moving through branches (Garrido 1980, García undated).

It feeds mainly on insects although three stomachs analysed contained lizard bones (Bruner 1934).

The Zapata Wren's nest was first discovered c.2 km north-east of Santo Tomás in 1986, where in due course altogether four nests were found in June 1986, February and March 1988 (Martínez García and Martínez García 1991; see Remarks). Nests were placed in sawgrass tussocks 50 to 70 cm above the ground, and the material used in construction was exclusively sawgrass threads; three of the nests contained two eggs (Martínez García and Martínez García 1991). The dates when nests were discovered plus the following information suggest a wide breeding season which would extend from January to July: a flightless juvenile was collected on 19 May 1933 (specimen in FMNH; see also Garrido 1980), a date that would suggest egg-laying in early May or late April (Balát and González 1982); two birds collected at the beginning of January 1931 had testes swelling (specimens in ANSP); and birds have been reported in full song in January and June, while very few were vocal in April (Balát and González 1982, González 1982).

THREATS Burning of habitat by local people was apparently the cause of the steep decline that evidently took place in the 1970s, and although this practice was believed to have been eradicated (González 1982, Regalado Ruíz 1981) fires still occur year after year (O. H. Garrido *in litt.* 1991). Barbour (1928) and Garrido (1985) both noted the presence of introduced mongoose *Herpestes* and rats *Rattus*, which could constitute a substantial additional threat. Small portions of the swamp have been drained but there is no immediate threat to the integrity of the habitat as a whole (King 1978-1979).

MEASURES TAKEN The 10,000 ha Corral de Santo Tomás Faunal Refuge has been set up in the Zapata Wren's range according to the maps shown in Wright (1988) and also ICGC (1978).

MEASURES PROPOSED A survey of the species is urgently needed, with a special effort to delimit accurately its range, numbers and potential threats (see Remarks under Zapata Rail *Cyanolimnas cerverai*). The protection of other areas where it has recently been found (see Distribution) is obviously necessary. Dry-season burning of the swamp must be investigated and controlled.

REMARKS Local residents described the species's nest as spherical and as containing as many as six eggs (Bond 1979, García undated); this agrees with Martínez García and Martínez García (1991) concerning shape but not clutch-size.

NICEFORO'S WREN *Thryothorus nicefori* I[6]

This species is known only from the type-locality in the East Andes of Santander department, Colombia, where it was originally collected in 1945 and was rediscovered there in 1989 when two birds were found in a remnant patch of acacia.

DISTRIBUTION Nicéforo's Wren (see Remarks) is endemic to the western slope of the East Andes in Santander department, Colombia, where it is known only from the type-locality at San Gil (6°33'N 73°08'W) on the río Fonce, south of Bucaramanga (Meyer de Schauensee 1946, Ridgely and Tudor 1989; coordinates from Paynter and Traylor 1981).

POPULATION Numbers are unknown. Seven specimens (including the type) were taken in October and November 1945 (Meyer de Schauensee 1946, 1948-1952), after which there appear to have been no further records until 1989 when a pair was seen a short distance (c.1 km) east of San Gil (P. Kaestner *in litt.* 1992).

ECOLOGY San Gil is situated in the upper tropical zone at 1,095 m (Meyer de Schauensee 1948-1952, Paynter and Traylor 1981), in a region generally comprising light woodland and coffee plantations (Hilty and Brown 1986); however, the recent observations (see Population) suggest that this species inhabits thick xeric acacia scrub along the río Fonce (P. Kaestner *in litt.* 1992). No birds were found in the coffee plantations that dominate the hills to the north of the type-locality (P. Kaestner *in litt.* 1992).

THREATS The vegetation around the type-locality is highly disturbed, with agriculture dominated by coffee plantations, which in turn are mixed with plantain and sugarcane cultivation and pasture (LGN). Whether this habitat alteration has been at the expense of the apparently favourable acacia scrub, and has therefore had a detrimental effect on the species's population, is unknown.

MEASURES TAKEN None is known.

MEASURES PROPOSED The welcome confirmation of this species's survival must now be followed up with fieldwork to determine its population size and precise ecological requirements (see Remarks). Only with these basic data can a comprehensive conservation strategy be initiated, although it appears that what remains of the acacia scrub at San Gil should be protected if this bird is to survive.

REMARKS Mayr and Greenway (1960) and Ridgely and Tudor (1989) suggested that this bird may be a well-marked subspecies of the widespread Rufous-and-white Wren *Thryothorus rufalbus*, which in Colombia is found from the Caribbean lowlands to the llanos east of the Andes (Hilty and Brown 1986). The recent observations of Nicéforo's Wren showed that it sounds exactly like Rufous-and-white Wren, and indeed responded to a tape of that species (P. Kaestner *in litt.* 1992). The pattern and quality of this bird's song need to be assessed so that these taxonomic doubts can be resolved (Ridgely and Tudor 1989).

WHITE-BREASTED THRASHER *Ramphocinclus brachyurus* E[1]

Habitat destruction and introduced predators are blamed for reducing this distinctive mimid to near-extinction in two dry forest areas on the islands of Martinique and St Lucia respectively, and new initiatives are very urgently needed.

DISTRIBUTION The White-breasted Thrasher (see Remarks 1) is endemic to Martinique (nominate *brachyurus*) and St Lucia (race *sanctaeluciae*), and is today confined to single, very small areas of both.

Martinique The species appears to have been widespread in former times, having once even been found near Forte-de-France (Vincent 1966-1971). It was collected sometime before 1878 (in July and August) at Trois Islets (Lawrence 1878; four specimens in AMNH and USNM), and a bird was observed in the Jardin des Plantes, at St Pierre (date not given) (Lawrence 1878). A bird was taken at Presqu'île de la Caravelle in the north-east in June 1950 (see Bond 1951b), a pair was observed there in February 1966 (Bond 1966), and nowadays the area between Tartane and Le Phare on the peninsula appears to be the only locality for the species on the island (Pinchon 1976, King 1978-1979, Evans 1990).

St Lucia The race *sanctaeluciae* appears to have been once more widespread (see below), but is today restricted to the north-east coast valleys between Petite Anse and Dennery Knob (just south of Louvet) (Babbs *et al.* 1988). Bond (1928b) was told of birds in the southern mountains of the island, and Danforth (1935) also indicated that it had formerly had a "much more general distribution". Bond (1928b) collected the species in the north-east near Le Marquis in April 1927. In April 1932 it was taken at De Barra and Grande Anse, east of Morne La Sorcière (Danforth 1935), being observed again in the latter locality in 1969 (Wingate 1969); in Petite Anse it was collected in January 1950 (Bond 1956b; specimen in ANSP). In March 1951 the species was observed at Morne Fortune, near Castries (see Bond 1967, 1982), this being the only sighting this century away from the north-east coast (see Remarks 2); subsequent searches in that area were unsuccessful (Bond 1982). A survey in 1971 showed it was restricted to five ravines between Grande Anse and Louvet (a distance of less than 8 km, ranging inland no more than 1.5 km) (see King 1978-1979; also Diamond 1973). The investigation conducted by Babbs *et al.* (1988) identified what appears to be the last stronghold of the species, on the north-east coast in river valleys between Petite Anse and Dennery Knob (just south of Louvet) (their map details critical habitat).

POPULATION The White-breasted Thrasher is one of the rarest of West Indian birds; formerly it was much more numerous and widespread, but it has decreased steadily since the mid-nineteenth century (Bond 1957). It needs to be recognized very rapidly in France and on St Lucia that the populations are now critically low, with extinction possibly only a few years away.

Martinique The species appears to have been common and widespread in the nineteenth century (Taylor 1864, Bond 1950), even near Fort-de-France (Vincent 1966-1971, Pinchon 1976). After half a century with no records (specimen in AMNH taken in January 1896) Bond (1950) considered it extinct, but even as he published this opinion the species was rediscovered (in June 1950) on the Presqu'île de la Caravelle (specimen taken), and he modified his judgement of it to "very rare" (Bond 1956b). Of this there is no doubt: one recent estimate of the population on the peninsula gave only 40 pairs (Evans 1990), another a mere 15 pairs (Benito-Espinal and Hautcastel 1988).

St Lucia The species appears to have been reasonably common in the past, given that Semper and Sclater (1872) referred to it as "constantly to be met" in pairs or in small flocks of four or five pairs. Bond (1928b) was also informed that it was "at one time not uncommon" in the southern mountains, but that it was now extinct there. By 1927 it was already considered a "very rare bird" and "decreasing in numbers", Le Marquis being "one of the few localities where it could be found" (Bond 1928b; also Meyer de Schauensee 1941). In 1931 a thorough search of several days to find the species near Le Marquis was unsuccessful, and thus it was feared extinct (Danforth 1935). Further searches in 1932 in a different area (but still on the north-east coast, i.e. De Barra and Grande Anse) resulted in the collection of the species (see Distribution); in this general area Danforth (1935) considered it to be still abundant, though Bond (1950, 1956b) continued to characterize it as "rare and local".

In 1969 the thrashers were found above Grande Anse Bay on the north-east slope of La Sorcière, and appeared to be "reasonably common" (Wingate 1969). A survey in 1971 revealed that the population in the five ravines between Grande Anse and Louvet (i.e. the total population of the island) was about 75 pairs (see King 1978-1979), with a mean 2.4 birds counted per hour on walks (Diamond 1973). In 1987, this population was estimated at 58 pairs maximum in river valleys between Petite Anse and Dennery Knob, no birds being observed elsewhere (Babbs *et al.* 1988; for results of partial censuses within in the species's range see their table 3a). Although this fieldwork slightly increased the known range, the census results compared with 1971 suggested a decline of 24%, and since the species probably occupied the valleys north of Grande Anse and south of Louvet the decline may have been even greater (Babbs *et al* 1988). Ravine la Chaloupe (in the centre of the species's range) contained six confirmed and eight possible breeding pairs, this representing the most suitable habitat (Babbs *et al.* 1988). In March 1992 another census in Ravine la Chaloupe was conducted (not going beyond the fork in the main ravine: see the map in Babbs *et al.* 1988) and resulted in a total of 12 pairs (Burke 1992; see Remarks 3). From late April to mid-June 1992 a survey and census revealed a maximum of 46 pairs in the valleys between Marquis Bay and Dennery Bay, and when comparison was made with the 1987 results an overall rate of decline of 4.1% per year was disclosed (Ijsselstein 1992).

ECOLOGY The White-breasted Thrasher is a ground-haunting bird, living in dense thickets in semi-arid woodland with abundant leaf-litter and in riverine forest (Bond 1928b, 1957, 1979, Danforth 1935, Diamond 1973, Babbs *et al.* 1988). F. A. Ober indicated that the species was found in "deep woods" and along the borders of streams on Martinique (Lawrence 1878), although Pinchon (1976) mentioned that it could be found foraging even in the dry zone at the edge of mangroves. On St Lucia, R. L. Zusi found it in both spindly, short deciduous trees 3-6 m tall and near or on a canyon floor where the trees were 18-21 m tall and greener, this suggesting that the species once occurred in deeper forest than it does today (Storer 1989a). This theory is also bolstered by Taylor's (1864) indication of the species inhabiting "thick forest" and Wingate's (1969) observation of birds in the transitional zone between the dry coastal thickets and the rainforest of the mountains. In St Lucia, Babbs *et al.* (1988) found the species to be highly restricted to a narrow band of riverine forest at the bottom of the valleys.

The species has been reported searching for food in low shrubbery, mostly among leaves on the ground by turning over leaf-litter, vigorously tossing or sweeping leaves aside (Semper and Sclater 1872, Diamond 1973, Babbs *et al.* 1988, Storer 1989a). Semper and Sclater (1872) indicated that it "seems to be strictly insectivorous", but Pinchon (1976) gave its diet as seeds, small insects and myriapods, Diamond (1973) reported one bird picking berries off a twig, and Babbs *et al* (1988) indicated that, while the few identifiable food items brought to the nest were all insects, they also observed it feeding on berries and believed that small vertebrates could possibly be consumed.

The species has been recorded nesting in June (eggs) (Danforth 1935, Bond 1957), July (eggs and nestlings) and early August (nestlings) (Babbs *et al.* 1988), and thus the breeding season appears to occur mainly between April and July (Pinchon 1976, Evans 1990). The nest (a bulky cup) is situated in shrubs or saplings at low or moderate elevations above the ground (2-6 m); two eggs are laid (Bond 1957, 1979, Babbs *et al.* 1988). A description of the vegetation surrounding nests in St Lucia is in Babbs *et al.* (1988). Semper and Sclater (1872) reported seeing the species in pairs or small flocks of four or five pairs. Babbs *et al.* (1988) found it to be largely sedentary, with little evidence of movement between valleys.

THREATS Habitat destruction is presumably one of the major threats affecting the species (Babbs *et al.* 1988). On St Lucia it is certainly the main reason for concern: in the 1970s and 1980s, predictions that cassava growing, charcoal burning and illegal marijuana planting were "likely to continue" and "may increase" (Diamond 1973, Babbs *et al.* 1988) duly came true, and new clearings in Ravine la Chaloupe were detected in April 1992 (W. Burke *in litt.* 1992; also Ijsselstein 1992). The apparent sedentariness of the species may compound its problems as populations become isolated by loss of habitat in intervening valleys (Babbs *et al.* 1988). Clearance of habitat on Martinique is also blamed for the species's decline (Benito-Espinal and Hautcastel 1988), but whether it currently affects any part of the population on the Presqu'île de la Caravelle is unknown.

The species's decline on St Lucia has also been attributed to colonization of the island by the Bare-eyed Thrush *Turdus nudigenis* which proved to be highly aggressive towards other thrush-like birds and was held to be responsible for the near-extinction there of the near-threatened Forest Thrush *Cichlherminia lherminieri* (Bond 1982). The thrasher's terrestrial habits make it a potential prey of the introduced mongoose *Herpestes* (Danforth 1935, King 1978-1979), but this has not been proved (Diamond 1973, Babbs *et al.* 1988); nevertheless, mongoose and rat predation are considered likely causes of decline in Martinique, where the former was introduced in 1893-1894 (Vincent 1966-1971, Pinchon 1976, Benito-Espinal and Hautcastel 1988). The Pearly-eyed Thrasher *Margarops fuscatus* and possibly the Trembler *Cinclocerthia ruficauda* are nest predators that could pose a threat to eggs and nestlings (Babbs *et al.* 1988).

MEASURES TAKEN A reserve on Martinique, perhaps expressly for the species, is a sign that its conservation is at last being taken seriously, yet evidence of thorough distributional and biological work on the bird there is lacking; by contrast, such work has been done on St Lucia (e.g. Babbs *et al.* 1988) but no reserve has yet been established.

Martinique The White-breasted Thrasher occurs within the Caravelle Natural Reserve (see the map in Wright 1988), and it is claimed that the preservation of its habitat is thereby assured, although the area in question is only 517 ha (Benito-Espinal and Hautcastel 1988).

St Lucia The species is legally protected (CCA 1991b). Part of its present distribution gains what in the 1970s was regarded as paper protection by lying within Castries Forest Reserve (King 1978-1979; see the map in Wright 1988). St Lucia's commitment to forest and parrot conservation during the 1980s (see Measures Taken under St Lucia Amazon *Amazona versicolor*) indicates that the legal, social and infrastructural basis exists to carry new initiatives to improve the status of the thrasher.

MEASURES PROPOSED This bird now requires a great deal of work: it needs to be determined very quickly through highly competent study on both islands whether the present critically low numbers are the consequence simply of habitat loss or whether other factors, notably predation by exotic mammals, are involved. Any delay here runs the risk of having to seek the answers as a post mortem exercise. Collaboration between designated researchers on the two islands would be sensible, and indeed the funding agencies involved should require such mutual assistance. These agencies should also be ready to fund practical management initiatives as soon as problems accessible to such management become known. Searches in suitable habitat in both islands from where the species is believed to have disappeared are of great importance in case further populations still exist, but should not deflect the immediate need to manage known populations intensively so as to increase their numerical levels rapidly.

Martinique Surveys of the Presqu'île de la Caravelle should be urgently conducted to ascertain the current status of the species, and biological investigation of its ecology and population dynamics must begin as soon as possible. Actual and potential threats need to be assessed at the same time, along with an evaluation of the efficacy of the existing reserve in meeting the species's requirements.

St Lucia Despite work already done, similar research to that proposed for Martinique is still needed, covering several years. Ravine la Chaloupe has been suggested as a nature reserve as a first step in preventing the extinction of the species (CCA 1991b, Burke 1992), and Ijsselstein (1992) has also suggested the Louvet area for the same treatment; however, the protection of riverine vegetation throughout the north-east coast of the island between Petite Anse and Dennery Knob remains equally important in the long term (Babbs *et al.* 1988, which see for maps of different ravines containing critical habitat; also Ijsselstein 1992). A call for *in situ* captive breeding (Ijsselstein 1992) is premature but, given the rate of decline identified by the same worker, very understandable.

It is important to recognize the great value of the lowland forest of north-east St Lucia, where the species occurs in sympatry with an isolated (subspecifically distinct) population of the Rufous Nightjar *Caprimulgus rufus otiosus* and with the near-threatened endemic St Lucia Oriole *Icterus laudabilis* and Black Finch *Melanospiza richardsoni* (Diamond 1973, Robbins and Parker unpublished, Burke 1992).

REMARKS (1) The White-breasted Thrasher is the sole representative of its genus (Hellmayr 1934, Mayr and Greenway 1960, Storer 1989a). (2) Most of the specimens in museums give no precise collecting locality other than "St Lucia", except of those taken from the north-east after 1932 (e.g. Grande Anse, Petite Anse and De Barra: specimens in ANSP, USNM and YPM). (3) Although the 1992 census method differed from 1987, Burke (1992) believed he had not overestimated or underestimated the number of birds. However, the 1987 census are probably inappropriate as the areas censused were different.

UNICOLOURED THRUSH *Turdus haplochrous* K[12]

Almost nothing is known of this thrush, recorded at three sites in the wooded lowlands of central Bolivia, but more fieldwork may prove it not to be so rare.

DISTRIBUTION The Unicoloured Thrush is a poorly known species which has only been recorded from three localities in the lowlands of central Bolivia. Two specimens (an adult male and female) were collected at the type-locality at Palmarito (16°49'S 62°37'W; coordinates from Paynter and Traylor 1975), río San Julián, Chiquitos province, Santa Cruz department, on 25 May 1918 (Todd 1931, O'Neill 1976); two males were secured 20 years later (12 March and 4 April 1944) on the río Mamoré, Marbán province, Beni department, 250-275 km north-west of the type-locality (O'Neill 1976); and two birds were taken (and the voices of these or other individuals also recorded) in 1984, 6 km south-east of Trinidad, Beni department (J. V. Remsen *in litt.* 1991).

POPULATION Little is known beyond the above records. An attempt to locate the species in 1984 in the nearest suitable-looking area near the type-locality was unsuccessful but little fieldwork has been done in the region, so the scant information does not necessarily imply that the species is rare (J. V. Remsen *in litt.* 1986, 1991).

ECOLOGY Nothing has been published on the habitat of this species; Remsen and Traylor (1989) listed it under the "Non-Amazonian lowlands" life zone, and the 1984 specimens were collected in "semi-open woodland" (J. V. Remsen *in litt.* 1991).

THREATS None is known.

MEASURES TAKEN None is known.

MEASURES PROPOSED A search for the species should be the first requirement in order to find whether it is indeed as rare as it appears to be or has simply been overlooked; such a search would probably be most productive in the areas of the three known localities. If any population can be located, it will need close study to determine the species's ecological needs, which can be used to develop and implement new survey work and any conservation plan.

LA SELLE THRUSH *Turdus swalesi* R[11]

Despite being relatively common where it occurs (and this includes several national parks), this ground-haunting songbird is isolated in poorly protected pockets of habitat in the mountains of Haiti and the Dominican Republic.

DISTRIBUTION The La Selle Thrush is endemic to the high forested mountains of Hispaniola, where it occurs as two distinct subspecies, nominate *swalesi* in the Massif de la Selle (Haiti) and Sierra de Baoruco (Dominican Republic), and *dodae* in the Sierra de Neiba and Cordillera Central (Dominican Republic) (Graves and Olson 1986). Coordinates are taken from DMATC (1972, 1973).

Haiti The species appears to be confined to the Massif de la Selle, with records (west to east) from: La Visite National Park, where it was recorded on several occasions in December 1982 (J. A. Ottenwalder *in litt.* 1992); Morne La Visite (18°21'N 72°19'W), where it was first observed on 11 April 1927 and four birds (including the type) were collected on subsequent days (Wetmore and Swales 1931, Graves and Olson 1986), with several birds observed at the same locality from 1980 to 1985 (P. Y. Roumain *in litt.* 1991; also Woods and Ottenwalder 1986); near Morne Cabaio (18°21'N 72°16'W), where "nests" were found in late May 1941 (Bond 1942); Fonds Verettes (18°24'N 71°51'W), where a bird was observed (at a time when the species was unknown to science) in May 1920 (Wetmore and Swales 1931); Jardins Bois Pin (18°18'N 71°48'W), where the species was present and known to local people in 1927 (Wetmore 1927, Wetmore and Swales 1931); Morne La Selle (18°22'N 71°59'W), where birds were taken in June 1928 and June 1930 (three specimens in ANSP); La Selle plateau (on the ridge of the Massif de la Selle), where it was reported on an ungiven date by Bond (1942).

Dominican Republic Records (west to east) are from:

Sierra de Baoruco Zapotén (Sapotén in DMATC 1972, at 18°19'N 71°41'W), where a bird was observed in April 1978 (A. Stockton de Dod *in litt.* 1991); Loma de Toro, above Zapotén, where a female was collected in September 1972 (Bond 1973; also Stockton de Dod 1978), and another in April 1976 (Graves and Olson 1986); above Puerto Escondido (18°19'N 71°34'W), where four birds were noted in April 1984 and three in April 1987 (J. E. Pierson *in litt.* 1991); Charco de la Paloma (18°13'N 71°33'W), undated (Stockton de Dod 1978); Pueblo Viejo, undated (Stockton de Dod 1981); Pie Pol (18°08'N 71°10'W), where two birds were observed in May 1971 (Bond 1971; also Stockton de Dod 1981); Las Abejas, near Canote, (untraced), where the species was observed in November and December 1980 (A. Stockton de Dod *in litt.* 1991); eastern Sierra de Baoruco, where the species was heard on an ungiven date (Bond 1977);

Sierra de Neiba "Sierra de Neiba", where a female was secured in May 1975 (Graves and Olson 1986), this perhaps the same locality as that given by Bond and Dod (1977) near "Kilómetro 204" (a military outpost, 16 km south-west of Hondo Valle, this latter untraced but c.15 km north of Angel Félix, at 18°38'N 71°46'W), undated;

Cordillera Central on the way to Pico Duarte (19°02'N 70°59'W), undated, reported to Bond (1982); Montazo (probably El Montazo, at 18°52'N 70°59'W), undated (Stockton de Dod 1978); above El Convento (18°52'N 70°41'W), where a bird was trapped in 1977 (A. Stockton de Dod *in litt.* 1991; also Bond 1977); near Alto Bandera (18°49'N 70°37'W), undated (Stockton de Dod 1981).

POPULATION Since the species's discovery in Massif de la Selle in 1927 (Wetmore 1927), most comments in relation to its abundance agree that the bird is and was locally common in the appropriate habitat (see Ecology).

Haiti Although few specimens have been collected in the Massif de la Selle (Wetmore and Swales 1931, Graves and Olson 1986), it appears to have been common at the time the first specimens were secured (Wetmore and Swales 1931). Bond (1942) found the species common on the La Selle plateau, even commoner than the Red-legged Thrush *Turdus plumbeus*, and believed it to be "holding its own very well", an opinion that was subsequently reaffirmed by Woods and Ottenwalder (1983, 1986) and Woods (1987), who found it common in La Visite National Park.

Dominican Republic The first observation of the La Selle Thrush in the country occurred in 1971, in the Sierra de Baoruco (an eastward extension of the La Selle ridge) (Stockton de Dod 1978; also Graves and Olson 1986). Although first considered "very rare" (Stockton de Dod 1981), it was later called "little known", owing to the remoteness of its habitat (Stockton de Dod 1978; see Ecology).

Sierra de Baoruco The species is considered "fairly common" at Zapotén, Loma de Toro and Pueblo Viejo (all within the Sierra de Baoruco National Park) (A. Stockton de Dod *in litt.* 1991).

Sierra de Neiba and *Cordillera Central* constitute the range of the race *dodae*, which appears to be geographically isolated from the nominate population owing to the natural barrier of the Cul-de-Sac–Valle de Neiba depression (Graves and Olson 1986). Bond (1976) was surprised by the "abundance" of the species at "Kilómetro 204", from where four specimens were collected, and it was reported common on the south side of the crest of the Sierra de Neiba (Bond 1978). The species's status within the Cordillera Central remains unclear with only few reported records (see Distribution).

ECOLOGY The La Selle Thrush inhabits the dense understorey of subtropical wet forest and pine forests, at altitudes generally higher than 1,300 m (Stockton de Dod 1978, Bond 1979, Woods and Ottenwalder 1986, J. E. Pierson *in litt.* 1991). In La Visite National Park, Massif de la Selle, Woods and Ottenwalder (1986) found that 75-100% of their records (derived from carefully planned transects through all major habitats) were in areas of "bwa raje" (broadleaved forest in isolated areas unsuitable for agriculture, such as around sinkholes, steep ravines, the steep north face of the massif and areas with numerous blocks of limestone) and "rak bwa" (broadleaved forest where mesic conditions predominate, such as ravines, depressions, limestone outcrops, along streams and rivers and at the mouths of caves and sinkholes), where it was mainly found feeding in trees, especially *Persea anomala*; other observations were from "raje" (severely altered areas) and "jardins" (agricultural areas). In the same La Visite area, Woods and Ottenwalder (1983) found the La Selle Thrush easy to observe when it moved from one mesic pocket to another, commenting that this contrasts with Wetmore and Swales (1931), who found the species secretive, and attributing the difference to loss of habitat forcing the bird to move through open areas from one ravine to another.

The species feeds on the ground on earthworms and arthropods, as well as on wild fruits; feeding has also been reported in the open cultivated gardens near "rak bwa" and "bwa raje" (Stockton de Dod 1978, Woods and Ottenwalder 1986).

Nests found in late May were placed in shrubs at low or moderate elevations above the ground (Bond 1942, 1979). Birds in breeding condition and nests under construction have been found early in June (Bond 1928a, 1943).

THREATS Although the La Selle Thrush is locally common, its very restricted range means that habitat destruction on a large scale represents a major threat (Woods 1987). The species's fate appears to be tied to that of the highland forest, as noted by J. E. Pierson (*in litt.* 1991) and P. Y. Roumain (*in litt.* 1991).

Haiti Woods and Ottenwalder (1986) noted that in La Visite National Park the habitat has been modified in the past by extensive cutting of stands of large pines, and the scrubby broadleaf forest is being rapidly cut as peasant farmers pick new places for gardens; severe habitat loss has been occurring since 1977; "raw bwa" is now restricted to patches of low dense forest as a result of chronic clearing and burning. Very little effort has been made by the Haitian government to follow recommendations for the protection and management of the park; furthermore, the present economic crisis cannot have helped to protect it (J. A. Ottenwalder *in litt.* 1992). A broader view of habitat loss in the country is in Threats under White-winged Warbler *Xenoligea montana*.

Dominican Republic Notes on habitat loss are in Threats under White-winged Warbler. A. Stockton de Dod *in litt.* (1991) noted that the habitat above El Convento in the Cordillera Central and in the area in the Sierra de Neiba where she observed the species is already gone.

MEASURES TAKEN In Haiti, apart from the species's occurrence in La Visite National Park, no other measures are known. In the Dominican Republic, the species has been protected (SEA 1980), and occurs in Sierra de Baoruco and Armando Bermúdez National Parks (Stockton de Dod 1981, Bond 1982, Hoppe 1989).

MEASURES PROPOSED Surveys in both countries should try to delimit accurately the species's range, to determine the extent of remaining habitat both inside and outside protected areas, and to provide more data (e.g. on population densities, ecological needs, threats) in order to establish a clear conservation strategy. Such activities should be combined with similar work on the other threatened and near-threatened birds of Hispaniola. An overview of the importance of the mountain forests in Hispaniola and associated threatened species is in Measures Proposed under Chat-tanager *Calyptophilus frugivorus*.

Haiti The prospects of the La Salle Thrush would be enhanced by the implementation of proposals made by Woods and Ottenwalder (1986) that (1) all cutting of "rak bwa" and "bwa raje" be immediately stopped, and (2) the area west of Morne La Visite all the way to and including the slopes of Morne d'Enfer be included in La Visite National Park.

Dominican Republic Stockton de Dod (1981) remarked that if the natural habitat in Baoruco National Park was adequately protected, the population would have food supplies and enough nesting cover to survive. Enforcement of established regulations in this and the Armando Bermúdez National Park would be a first step to protect the species in the country, while the creation of the first protected area in the Sierra de Neiba (as proposed in DVS 1990) is long overdue.

SIERRA MADRE SPARROW *Xenospiza baileyi* V/R[10]

Originally known from three disjunct bunch-grass areas in Durango, Jalisco and around the Distrito Federal, Mexico, this rare sparrow now appears to be confined to the dwindling expanse of this specialized habitat near México City which, although afforded some official protection, is still subjected to widespread burning and cattle-grazing.

DISTRIBUTION The Sierra Madre Sparrow has been found in three disjunct areas of the Sierra Madre: the high mountains of southern Durango, northern Jalisco and around the Distrito Federal–Morelos border, Mexico. Unless otherwise stated, coordinates are from OG (1956a).

Durango In March 1931, a population was found at c.2,400 m, about 55 km south-south-west (see Remarks 1) of Ciudad Durango, at a locality apparently known locally as "Cienega [sic] Tableterra", c.25 km south of La Casita (23°43'N 104°40'W) (Bailey and Conover 1935, Pitelka 1947). The only other locality recorded in Durango is from San Juan, 8 km west of El Salto, where five specimens were collected between 2,285 and 2,680 m on 16 and 17 June 1951 (Miller *et al.* 1957; three male, two female specimens in MLZ).

Jalisco The first specimens (apparently nine including the type; see Remarks 2) were collected in March 1889, in the "Sierra Bolaños" in the north of the state (Pitelka 1947). The type (a male in MCZ) was collected 8 March 1889 apparently at Bolaños, a village at 21°41'N 103°47'W. Other specimens (a male in USNM, three males and three females in BMNH; see Remarks 2) were collected over 3-10 March 1889 (apparently going unnoticed in the literature: see Remarks 2), these being both the first and last Jalisco records.

Distrito Federal–Morelos Recent records of the Sierra Madre Sparrow have come from a number of places in the bunch-grass area near the highest point on the old road between Cuernavaca, Morelos, and México City, Distrito Federal (Edwards 1968), c.600 km east-south-east of the Jalisco locality (Pitelka 1947). La Cima, at 2,900-3,050 m, is near the crest of the divide (the state border runs just to the south), and appears to be the centre for most recent records, many specimens having been taken there (e.g. in AMNH, CM, CMN, DMNH). Other specimens have been collected north of La Cima near Volcán El Pelado (see Threats), 4 km north of the Morelos border (two males and a juvenile male, August 1956, in DMNH). The road from La Cima runs south for c.10 km to a small town called Tres Marías (also Tres Cumbres, a hill c.2 km to the north-east) (Wilson and Ceballos-Lascurain 1986). Between these two places, the Sierra Madre Sparrow has been collected at 3, 5, and 8 km north of Tres Marías, but mainly around El Capulín at 5 km north (specimens in CM, DMNH, LSUMZ). Edwards (1968) indicated that the sparrow has been found at a number of localities along the new toll road which runs parallel to the old Cuernavaca–México City road. As these two roads are rarely further than 500 m apart (DCW), this is hardly surprising. Other Morelos records include four males from Fierro del Toro, 3,000 m (c.2 km north-west of El Capulín), collected 25-26 June, 12 July and 4 September 1950 (in MVZ, UMMZ; Miller *et al.* 1957). In winter, the species has been noted up to 2 km north of Parres (19°08'N 99°10'W: 4 km north-north-east of La Cima), Tlalpan district, (Distrito Federal); an immature male (in AMNH) was collected 1.5-2 km south of El Guarda (19°09'N 99°11'W: within 1 km of La Cima) on 24 December 1965 (El Guarda is an old name for Parres: R. G. Wilson *in litt.* 1991); and 2-3 birds were seen at 2,750 m on 7 January 1990 c.22 km east of Parres (19°09'N 98°58'W: c.4 km south-east of Santa Ana Tlacotenco) (R. G. Wilson *in litt.* 1991).

POPULATION The Sierra Madre Sparrow is considered rare (Dickerman *et al.* 1967, Wilson and Ceballos-Lascurain 1986) although its specialized habitat requirements and secretive, terrestrial habits (except during the breeding season) (Wilson and Ceballos-Lascurain 1986) suggest that it has probably been under-observed (see Ecology, Measures Proposed).

Durango "A half a dozen or so" Sierra Madre Sparrows were noted by Bailey and Conover (1935) when they collected a male in March 1931 at the small marsh south-south-west of Ciudad

Durango. Bangs (1931) recorded Bailey as telling him of "a dozen or more of the birds" in this same marsh. Which of these two reports is correct is unknown, but Bailey (in Pitelka 1947) mentioned that "the few that I saw... were singing", suggesting a small breeding population of a few pairs in a marsh of a mere 90 m^2 (50 feet by 20 feet: Pitelka 1947; see Remarks 3). The only information about the El Salto population is that five specimens were collected, presumably at the same locality, on 16 and 17 June 1951 (see Distribution), and that none was found there (indeed, no suitable habitat was found: see Threats) in June 1991 (S. N. G. Howell *in litt.* 1991).

Jalisco All that is known about the Sierra Madre Sparrow from this state is that nine specimens (three males and five females, with one unlocated; see Remarks 2) were collected within the Sierra de Bolaños over 3-10 March 1889 (Pitelka 1947).

Distrito Federal–Morelos Wagner (in Pitelka 1947), writing of the first observation of this species south of Jalisco, mentioned that on 23 April 1945 he saw a pair and two individuals at La Cima, where an adult male was collected on the same day. One of the observed birds was singing, indicating that the site probably held a breeding population. The next specimens to be collected from this region were six (including a juvenile) taken 2 km south of La Cima over 17-21 August 1950 (Miller *et al.* 1957). With five specimens (three males, two females in AMNH) taken in June 1962 and four juveniles on 3 September 1962 (in CM, DMNH) at La Cima, a significant population must exist or have existed in the immediate vicinity. Since specimens have been collected at a number of localities along the La Cima–Tres Marías road (see Distribution) (e.g. four adults and a juvenile, 5 km south of La Cima, during June/July 1954: in CM, DMNH, LSUMZ), the population obviously extends for some distance. Up to 15-20 birds have been seen at La Cima in winter (S. N. G. Howell *in litt.* 1991), and the density of breeding birds here has been estimated at c.1 pair/4-5 ha (R. G. Wilson *in litt.* 1991), or as much a 1 pair/1-2 ha in the densest areas (S. N. G. Howell *in litt.* 1991). No formal estimate has been made of the (local) population in this area although Wilson and Ceballos-Lascurain (1986) suggested that a significant proportion of it breeds in the vicinity of La Cima. Although locally common around La Cima, the species appears to occur very sparsely within the zacatón (bunch-grass) (S. N. G. Howell *in litt.* 1991), R. G. Wilson (*in litt.* 1991) suggesting that the population in this area (remaining habitat in Distrito Federal–Morelos being contained within an area of c.200-250 km^2) is probably no more than a few hundred pairs. The area around El Capulín has now largely been cultivated for agriculture (see Threats), recent records of the Sierra Madre Sparrow being confined to within a few kilometres of La Cima–Parres, and near Santa Ana Tlacotenco (R. G. Wilson *in litt.* 1991).

ECOLOGY The individuals that Bailey found in March were in a small marsh fed by a series of springs, at 2,400 m (Bangs 1931, Bailey and Conover 1935). This marsh was "grown to tall grass, dead at this season" (Pitelka 1947). The immediate surrounding area was described as "a rugged mountain region, broken by canyons, and with wide expanses of park... [with] much pine, thorny shrubs and some gnarled oaks intermixed" (Bangs 1931). This one recorded occurrence of the species in a marshy area has been generalized as a habitat requirement (e.g. Edwards 1968, Peterson and Chalif 1973) despite the lack of subsequent records from similar habitats (see Remarks 3): in fact, as suggested by Pitelka (1947), the habitat is not necessarily marsh (see Remarks 3).

More information has been published about the habitat around La Cima, which differs slightly from that described by Bailey (e.g. Pitelka 1947, Blake 1953 and Bangs 1931). Dickerman *et al.* (1967) indicated that at La Cima, the habitat of the Sierra Madre Sparrow is "a primary association of medium and tall bunch-grasses, *Epicampes macrura*, *Festuca amplisima*, *Stipa ichu*, and *Muhlenbergia affinis*, interspersed with park-like stands of *Pinus montezumae* on the ridges and knolls" (bushes being absent in the grassland areas). Refining this description of La Cima, R. G. Wilson (*in litt.* 1991) noted that *Pinus hartwegii* and *P. teocote* are at least as common as *P. montezumae*, and recorded *Muhlenbergia robusta* (possibly a synonym for *M. affinis*) as common. East of Parres (at 2,750 m) the habitat is an open pine–oak woodland (mainly oak including *Quercus rugosa*), with a strong growth of zacatón beneath (R. G. Wilson *in litt.* 1991).

The lack of shrubs and marshy areas differs from the Durango locality, but the common denominator for all reports of the habitat is the bunch-grass or "zacatón" (also zakaton and sacaton; a local name for the grass species involved: D. J. Bell verbally 1991: see Remarks 3) (Pitelka 1947, Wilson and Ceballos-Lascurain 1986). Wagner (in Pitelka 1947) described the zacatón as being 60-80 cm high (this is probably an average as clumps may easily grow to 1.5 m or even 2 m high: R. G. Wilson *in litt.* 1991), covering a dry, secondary plain with some pine trees; labels from specimens taken in the area relate to the dense zacatón meadow with few, scattered and small pines (sometimes in groves) and rocky outcrops (lava).

This subalpine pine/zacatón association is a habitat limited to temperate areas at altitudes of 2,650-4,250 m, across the central volcanic portion of Mexico, and is also the habitat of the Volcano Rabbit *Romerolagus diazi* (Hoth *et al.* 1987, Fa and Bell 1990: see Threats, Measures Proposed). Almost all records of the Sierra Madre Sparrow have been between 2,800 and 3,050 m, although the Durango populations have been recorded from 2,285, 2,400 and 2,680 m (see Threats, Remarks 3). Fields in the La Cima area (see Threats) are used as feeding areas by the species to a varying degree during the year (Dickerman *et al.* 1967), although B. M. Whitney (*in litt.* 1991) saw four birds (c.1.5 km north of La Cima) singing from the tops of zacatón clumps in a heavily grazed and poorly drained field (see Remarks 3). A juvenile male taken at La Cima on 3 September 1962 (in CM) was feeding in a mustard and alfalfa field. The gizzard of an adult male taken in November 1962 (in DMNH) contained a fine gravel, a small coleopteran and the remains of a small spider (Dickerman *et al.* 1967), although it is unclear whether this individual had been feeding in zacatón or fields. Unfledged young were seen being fed with small caterpillars at La Cima in August 1984 (R. G. Wilson *in litt.* 1991)

Bailey, commenting on the Durango birds (in Pitelka 1947), said that the birds were "not skulking" and "were on top of the vegetation, possibly two or three feet high, and were singing". Wagner (in Pitelka 1947) corroborated Bailey's observation of birds singing from tall grass blades but added that they were shy. In spring and summer, males are conspicuous, singing from tall grass or even telephone wires; at this time an occasional alarmed bird may even perch in a pine tree (Dickerman *et al.* 1967). Singing has been recorded from 22 March in Durango and 24 April in Distrito Federal (Pitelka 1947). At La Cima, singing was noted as "slight" during mid-March, but with many individuals heard during late May (S. N. G. Howell *in litt.* 1991). Eggs (a clutch of three has been noted) and juveniles have been observed in June and July: adults seen carrying food to presumed nests on 7 July; a nest with young found 23 August; eggs still noted as being incubated on 31 July; and juveniles recorded in August and September (Miller *et al.* 1957, Dickerman *et al.* 1967, S. N. G. Howell *in litt.* 1991, R. G. Wilson *in litt.* 1991). Four birds were seen singing from zacatón clumps on 11 August 1980 (just north of La Cima), the singing being attributed to the fact that it was raining (B. M. Whitney *in litt.* 1991). Nests are close to (but not on), the ground, between or set into the zacatón clumps (Dickerman *et al.* 1967, R. G. Wilson *in litt.* 1991). Wagner (in Pitelka 1947) indicated that the species occurs scatteredly on the bunch-grass plain; outside the breeding season it is secretive, being almost entirely terrestrial and hardly ever permitting close observation (Wilson and Ceballos-Lascurain 1986; see also Dickerman *et al.* 1967). It has also been suggested that this species undertakes a localized winter dispersal (Wilson and Ceballos-Lascurain 1986), although the evidence for this is based on records just north of Parres/El Guarda (see Distribution), which, at just c.6 km north of La Cima, is a very localized dispersal indeed – records from La Cima in November and December (specimens in UMMZ) suggest that in fact the species is resident there.

THREATS Sizeable areas of the subalpine pine/zacatón habitat are limited to altitudes between 2,650 and 4,250 m on the slopes of three discontinuous volcanic sierras close to Mexico City (see Measures Proposed) (Hoth *et al.* 1987, Fa and Bell 1990). The El Pelado area, at 48 km^2, is one of these and represents the best remaining forest/zacatón habitat in central Mexico (Hoth *et al.* 1987). During a brief visit to this area in April 1985, evidence of extensive, recent fire burns was recorded, with cattle-grazing on recently burnt zacatón; there was also evidence of forest infestation by bark beetle and cutting of zacatón (*Muhlenbergia* spp.) for thatch and brushes (Hoth *et al.* 1987). Overgrazing and forest fires represent the major threat to the habitat (Hoth *et al.* 1987): 98% of these forest fires are started by man, many originating from the uncontrolled burning of zacatón, done to promote new growth of grazing pasture for cattle and sheep, but causing the deterioration and depauperization of the zacatón (Fa and Bell 1990). Land tenancy is undefined in the El Pelado area: villagers from Topilejo, Parres and other smaller villages can acquire rights to grow crops (mainly oats in this area) on Volcán El Pelado without prior assessment of the impact on the land, leading inevitably to agricultural encroachment (Hoth *et al.* 1987, Fa and Bell 1990). In the period since 1954, when Phillips and Warner first collected in the La Cima/Pelado area, a large proportion of the tillable area of this habitat has been ploughed and destroyed as nesting cover, 25-35% of the habitat visited being destroyed in the 12 years after 1954 (Dickerman *et al.* 1967). Extraction of soil is largely uncontrolled; permits are issued by local village authorities often without liaison with the conservation authorities (Fa and Bell 1990). These threats are common to the largest remaining areas of habitat in all three sierras close to Mexico City, namely Nevado de Toluca, Sierras Chichinautzin and Ajusco (Volcán El Pelado/ Tlaloc area) and "Sierra Nevada" (i.e. Volcanes Iztaccihuatl-Popocatépetl) (Hoth *et al.* 1987, Fa and Bell 1990). These sierras are also the last remaining areas where the threatened endemic Volcano Rabbit exists, also in the zacatón vegetation (Hoth *et al.* 1987). However, the area east of La Cima, and extending as far as Santa Ana Tlacotenco (and including Volcanes Chichinautzin and Tlaloc), still supports quite extensive forest areas with much zacatón, and may harbour an undiscovered population of Sierra Madre Sparrow (all of this suitable remaining habitat is contained within an area of just c.200-250 km^2) (R. G. Wilson *in litt.* 1991).

Little has been written about the state of the habitat in the Jalisco/Durango populations of the species, although S. N. G. Howell (*in litt.* 1991) noted that in June 1991 near El Salto, Durango, there was nothing suitable for the species ("odd clumps of bunch-grass"), the area generally having been intensively cultivated and/or logged.

MEASURES TAKEN Hoth *et al.* (1987) suggested that there was "adequate forestry management and close vigilance of forest fires" in the Tlaloc/Pelado area, with the Forestry Division producing posters in an attempt to reduce the incidence of these fires. The existing reserves in this area have been outlined above (see Measures Proposed) and SEDUE (Secretaria de Desarrollo Urbano y Ecología) is currently reviewing the idea of a protection corridor from Tepozteco National Park across the Chichinautzin range to the Desierto de los Leones National Park (now largely destroyed: A. R. Phillips *in litt.* 1991). Despite these measures, greater protection is needed in some select areas to guarantee the survival of the Sierra Madre Sparrow.

MEASURES PROPOSED Rigorous conservation of the bunch-grass habitat near and east of La Cima is necessary in order to protect this and other species from extinction (Wilson and Ceballos-Lascurain 1986, R. G. Wilson *in litt.* 1991). A detailed assessment should be undertaken to determine the population of the Sierra Madre Sparrow in the La Cima area, combined with a detailed search for the species in the extensive areas of similar pine/zacatón habitat that remain around Volcán El Pelado (48 km^2), Volcán Tlaloc (86 km^2; 20 km east of Pelado) and the Sierra Nevada (146 km^2). Fieldwork has already been carried out to determine the distribution of pine/ zacatón habitat in relation to the Volcano Rabbit (see Threats) (Hoth *et al.* 1987, Fa and Bell 1990) – the areas identified now need to be surveyed for the presence of the Sierra Madre Sparrow, and the conservation of both species ensured. There is a serious need for a search for the sparrow in Durango and Jalisco (see Population).

Measures proposed for zacatón conservation and hence the Volcano Rabbit in this area include: (1) assessment of the dynamics of the pine/zacatón vegetation, e.g. the nature of the vegetational succession and the effects of livestock-grazing and fire-burns on the vegetation; (2) implementation of management and wardening of the existing national park (Sierra Nevada) and special protected zones (Volcán El Pelado and Volcán Tlaloc); (3) rational exploitation of natural resources compatible with wildlife protection, e.g. controlled burning at regulated densities to be made compatible with the recovery of other areas and the conservation of wildlife; (4) implementation of educational campaigns at local and national level (information on the impact of land-use methods incompatible with sustained development and conservation should be made available to villages adjacent to the core habitats) (Hoth *et al.* 1987, Fa and Bell 1990). As the Volcano Rabbit has similar habitat requirements, these measures must also apply to the Sierra Madre Sparrow.

REMARKS (1) The journey to Ciénaga Tableterra is described (Bailey and Conover 1935) as 15 miles south-west of Durango to La Casita, and then 15 miles south from there, Bangs (1931) interpreting this as 30 miles south-west. From the coordinates, it is clear that Ciénaga Tableterra is in fact about 35 miles (55 km) south-south-west of Ciudad Durango.

(2) Pitelka (1947) reported nine specimens taken by Richardson; one (the type) is in MCZ, one is in USNM and six are in BMNH, though seven were reported there by Hellmayr (1938) and Pitelka (1947).

(3) The marsh where Bailey observed and collected the species in 1931 cannot have been as small as 50 feet by 20 feet if it held "a dozen or more of the birds" as he claimed, and either some miscalculation or a misprint must have been involved. It was grown to tall grass (Pitelka 1947) although the surrounding area had wide expanses of park (Bangs 1931), which suggests that the tall grass in the marsh was exceptional in relation to the surrounding vegetation and that the concentration of birds there was due to the tall grass rather than the presence of water. At 2,400 m, this marsh is below the documented altitudinal range for the zacatón habitat and most other populations of the sparrow. The other Durango records are also from below the altitudinal range of the zacatón habitat (2,285 and 2,680 m), but from vegetation remnants seen near El Salto in 1991 the habitat used to be typical zacatón (S. N. G. Howell *in litt.* 1991). North of La Cima, four birds were recorded in a poorly drained (but heavily grazed) field with zacatón clumps (B. M. Whitney *in litt.* 1991), this apparently being the only other reference to the species occurring in a "damp" area.

CUBAN SPARROW *Torreornis inexpectata* V/R[10]

Three racially distinct populations of this scrub-dwelling emberizid occur in Cuba, in the Zapata Swamp, on Cayo Coco and on a small stretch of the south-east coast, and the total numbers appear small; each population occupies a somewhat different habitat and faces a different threat.

DISTRIBUTION The Cuban Sparrow (see Remarks 1) is endemic to Cuba and restricted to three isolated and subspecifically distinct populations in Matanzas, Camagüey and Guantánamo provinces, although fossils from caves in Oriente (see Remarks 2) and Habana provinces indicate that these populations are remnants of a once wider distribution (Pregill and Olson 1981, Regalado Ruíz 1981, Morton and González Alonso 1982).

Matanzas Nominate *inexpectata* was known principally for almost 50 years from an area north of Santo Tomás (22°24'N 81°25'W in OG 1963a) in the Zapata Swamp (Ciénaga de Zapata) which was believed to be no larger than 5-10 km^2 (Paynter and Storer 1970, Garrido 1980, Regalado Ruíz 1981). Skins in AMNH, BMNH, CM and MNHN simply give "Santo Tomás", although those in USNM add "2 km north-west". The species is still present in the area albeit in small numbers (see Population). In October 1955 a population was discovered to the south-west at Las Mercedes (22°22'N 81°28'W in OG 1963a) (five skins in YPM; see also Ripley and Watson 1956), and in 1980–1982 a study further expanded the known range of this subspecies c.25 km to the west (González Alonso *et al.* 1986), new localities being: Canal de la Mueca (22°25'N 81°39'W); La Estricnina (22°24'N 81°39'W); Laguna El Palmar (22°23'N 81°43'W); Cayos de Gervedero (22°23'N 81°44'W); Cayo Corral (22°22'N 81°45'W) (all coordinates from González Alonso *et al.* 1986). Additional records are from Hato de Jicarita (22°37'N 81°27'W in OG 1963a), undated (O. H. Garrido *in litt.* 1991).

Camagüey In the Archipiélago de Camagüey the race *varonai* is only known from Cayo Coco (Regalado Ruíz 1981).

Guantánamo The race *sigmani* is restricted to the south coast of the province, the type having been collected 2.3 miles (c.3.7 km) west of Baitiquirí (20°01'N 74°53'W in OG 1963a) (Spence and Smith 1961). The western limit for this subspecies is 5 km east of Tortuguilla (19°58'N 74°59'W in OG 1963a) (González Alonso *et al.* 1986), with the eastern limit at Cajobabo (20°04'N 74°30'W in OG 1963a) (Garrido 1985), but not all habitats in the 27 km between these two points are suitable (González Alonso *et al.* 1986). Three specimens in USNM are labelled "3 km east of Imias", which is within the range mentioned above. There are no reports inland, even though similar habitat extends 50 km inland from the coast (E. S. Morton *in litt.* 1991).

POPULATION The Cuban Sparrow has been considered common but extremely local (Garrido 1985). That it was not discovered until 1927 (Barbour and Peters 1927), and subsequent populations (which proved racially distinct) not until the late 1950s (Spence and Smith 1961) and mid-1970s (Regalado Ruíz 1981), indicates its true patchiness and relatively small numbers.

Matanzas The nominate subspecies was encountered frequently in 1931 (Bond 1973) and from the evidence derived from the specimens collected in April 1927 (at least eight in AMNH, BM, CM and MNHN, with one skin in ANSP taken in February) and October 1955 at Las Mercedes (five in YPM), it seems likely that the bird was common within its very restricted range. García (undated) commented that the species was common in 1962 in the Santo Tomás area, having observed as many as 12 birds on one of his visits. Garrido (1980) also recorded having seen the Cuban Sparrow on "every expedition to the locality" up to 1965, but after that date he could not find it. García (undated) also mentioned a decline in numbers and pointed out that in 1973 none could be found, although in 1977 a flock of 12 birds was observed; and while Regalado Ruíz (1981) located this subspecies with ease, García (undated) still considered it, like *sigmani*, to be "very scarce and in danger of extinction". The first population estimate was of about 250 individuals (Morton and González Alonso 1982); however the new localities found by González

Alonso *et al.* (1986) (see Distribution) obviously imply that the actual figure is higher. According to H. González Alonso (*in litt.* 1991), the nominate race has substantially increased within the area of Santo Tomás as a result of the area being protected (see Threats, Measures Taken) and it is still present in the area of Santo Tomás although difficult to find (O. H. Garrido *in litt.* 1991, Sulley and Sulley 1992).

Camagüey Regalado Ruíz (1981) reported the race *varonai* to be numerous and very common and its population by far the least at risk of the three subspecies, although no estimate of numbers exists.

Guantánamo The race *sigmani* is thought to consist of 55 to 100 pairs (Morton and González Alonso 1982) and no evidence of decline has been detected (King 1978-1979), although it is the most imperilled of the three populations (E. S. Morton *in litt.* 1991, also Garrido 1985; see Threats).

ECOLOGY The Cuban Sparrow occurs in three remarkably different habitats. Nominate *inexpectata* is restricted to shrubbery in the Zapata Swamp near the higher ground of Santo Tomás (Bond 1979), where sawgrass *Cladium jamaicense* swamp filled with "arraigán" *Myrica cerifera* hummocks and "yana" *Conocarpus erecta* are present (Garrido and García Montaña 1975, Regalado Ruíz 1981, Morton and González Alonso 1982). The Santo Tomás area is the least swampy part of the region (Garrido and García Montaña 1975), and practically dries up at certain times of the year, making the habitat of the nominate population more like that of scrub grassland (Pregill and Olson 1981). The *sigmani* subspecies is restricted to an extremely hot, dry area of Cuba, on the southern Guantánamo coast, where old marine terrace is covered with xerophytic plants like acacia and cacti, backed by a cliff at whose base is a dense tangle of vines, shrubs and a few large trees (Spence and Smith 1961, Schwartz and Klinikowski 1963); suitable habitat is indicated by coastal incense *Tournefortia gnaphalodes,* as it offers a major part of the food (see below); many of the same plant species occur in the non-*Torreornis* areas but the phytophysiognomy is different, and apparently unacceptable to the bird (Morton and González Alonso 1982). The *varonai* subspecies inhabits semi-deciduous forest, and also coastal xerophytic thorn-scrub known as "manigua" and mangroves (only where "yana" is present) (Regalado Ruíz 1981). The manigua and mangroves are believed to be occupied by the species only during winter months (Regalado Ruíz 1981). It thus seems that the original habitat of the Cuban Sparrow was arid scrub, and that this habitat must have been continuous across much of Cuba in the late Pleistocene (Pregill and Olson 1981).

Observations and stomach analysis conducted by González Alonso *et al.* (1986) on the nominate subspecies in the early 1980s revealed that during the dry season (November to the beginning of May) birds were feeding on seeds and flowers of small plants of the family Polygonaceae (*Polygonum densiflorum*) and Cyperaceae (*Rhynchospora ciperoides*, *Eleocharis elegans* and *Dichromena colorata*) as well as "arraigán" and "yanilla blanca" *Ilex cassini* fruits; during the rainy season (May–October) the nominate subspecies widens its diet to include snail eggs *Pomacea paludosa* (previously observed by E. S. Morton *in litt.* 1991), and indeed spends almost 54% of its time in foraging for them; six stomachs from this season contained an average of 40 embryonic snails, plus "yanilla blanca" fruits and sawgrass seeds. The eastern race *sigmani* is closely associated with the coastal incense shrub, whose small seed pods were its staple (Morton and González Alonso 1982), while González Alonso *et al.* (1986) found remains of mollusc shells and seeds in stomachs analysed during the rainy season. The *varonai* subspecies has been observed foraging on the ground for insects and seeds (Regalado Ruíz 1981), and stomachs of birds collected during the rainy season contained remains of Coleoptera (Tenebrionidae) and seeds and fruits of *Paspalum* sp. (González Alonso *et al.* 1986).

Breeding was reported in April 1935 by Bond (1973), who found a nest with one egg (presumably an incomplete clutch) in a tussock of sawgrass. At the end of August 1960 Schwartz and Klinikowski (1963) commented that the species had already nested but was continuing to do so. González Alonso *et al.* (1982) gave the breeding season for the nominate subspecies from

March to June, reporting a nest on 5 May 1980 that held two chicks; a second nest was started on 25 April and a third on 11 May, these being finished on 27 and 13 May 1981 respectively, although neither was used; a fourth nest found in May 1981 contained eggshells. The nest is constructed in tussocks formed of sawgrass, "arraigán", "yanilla blanca" and "icaco" *Chrysobalanus icaco* (González Alonso *et al.* 1982, which see for further details).

The Cuban Sparrow lives in pairs that appear to defend territories throughout the year and, although the birds were not breeding during a vocalization study in late October and early November, duetting songs occurred and were believed to signify strong selection for mate cooperation in territorial defence throughout the year (González Alonso *et al.* 1982, Morton and González Alonso 1982). These authors never observed more than two birds together in the *sigmani* subspecies, but they found groups up to three or four as well as pairs of the nominate subspecies at the end of October and beginning of November 1979, and consequently they suggested that perhaps the breeding season is later in the Zapata Swamp. Morton and González Alonso (1982) never observed more than two birds together in the *sigmani* subspecies whereas *varonai*, although observed mainly in pairs, from time to time forms flocks of up to 10-12 birds (Regalado Ruíz 1981). Observations of the nominate subspecies in 1981 showed that from September to February groups were usually composed of three individuals and that in March they separated in to pairs to start reproduction (González Alonso *et al.* 1982); in the Zapata Swamp, four pairs were found on c.12 ha, which would correspond to c.3 ha per pair (González Alonso *et al.* 1982).

THREATS The future of the nominate subspecies is dependent on the preservation of the part of the Zapata Swamp in which the bird is found, proposals to drain large portions having not yet been implemented (King 1978-1979). Burning of habitat there continues to occur year after year by local people in search of turtles and rodents *Capromys* (Regalado Ruíz 1981, O. H. Garrido *in litt.* 1991). The *sigmani* race is apparently the most endangered of the three populations owing to the vulnerability of its dry habitat to burning, which results in grasses taking over; also, part of this habitat was being fenced in 1980 for sheep, with unforeseeable consequences (E. S. Morton *in litt.* 1991). Regalado Ruíz (1981) noted that in Cayo Coco extensive areas formed mainly of the mangrove *Conocarpus erecta* were being cut for charcoal, but with no clear idea of the possible effect of such habitat loss (Regalado Ruíz 1981), but this practice has now been stopped (P. Regalado Ruíz *in litt.* 1992). According to O. H. Garrido (*in litt.* 1991) and P. Regalado Ruíz (*in litt.* 1992) Cayo Coco is being developed as a tourist centre, but see Measures Taken.

MEASURES TAKEN The three subspecies benefit to some degree from protected areas, the nominate population from the Corral de Santo Tomás Faunal Refuge, which consists of 10,000 ha of protected land (but see Threats); race *varonai* from the 34,000 ha Cayo Coco Faunal Refuge and *sigmani* from the 11,000 ha Baitiquirí-Cajobabo National Park (Wright 1988; see also ICGC 1978).

MEASURES PROPOSED A survey of the species is urgently needed, with a special effort to delimit accurately its range and potential threats (see Remarks under Zapata Rail *Cyanolimnas cerverai*). Dry-season burning of the Zapata Swamp must be investigated and controlled. The Baitiquirí-Cajobabo National Park and Cayo Coco and Corral de Santo Tomás Faunal Refuges in which the species is now found should be carefully managed and activities within them controlled in order to ensure the species's survival. Furthermore, the number of visitors to the interior of Cayo Coco needs regulating and they should always be accompanied by the guards (P. Regalado Ruíz *in litt.* 1992). Periodic censuses should be carried out to determine population trends.

REMARKS (1) This bird was previously referred to as the Zapata Sparrow, since for many years it was only known to occur in the Zapata Swamp. However, as suggested by P. Regalado Ruíz (*in litt.* 1992), "Cuban Sparrow" is perhaps more appropriate considering its current known range.

(2) Oriente is the old name for a province that at present has been split in the following provinces: Las Tunas, Granma, Holguín, Santiago de Cuba and Guantánamo.

SLENDER-BILLED FINCH *Xenospingus concolor* V[9]

This generally scarce finch is confined to the few scattered river valleys and coastal lagoons in the desert on the Pacific slope from central Peru to northern Chile, where it inhabits riparian shrubbery, mainly at low elevations, but locally up to nearly 2,300 m. Changes in land use in these almost completely cultivated valleys could severely affect the species.

DISTRIBUTION The Slender-billed Finch (see Remarks 1) is confined to the Pacific slope of the Andes, where c.150 specimens have been taken from Lima department, central Peru, south to northern Antofagasta province, northern Chile. In Peru it has been recorded from eight of the 22 river valleys distributed from central Lima to the Chilean border, but may well occur in most of them, and in Chile it is known from four valleys and an oasis. Localities from north to south (organized by numbered drainage, with coordinates from OG 1967 and Stephens and Traylor 1983) are:

Peru (*Lima*) (1) río Rímac drainage: Callao, sea-level, 12°04'S 77°09'W (specimen in BMNH collected 1900); and Lima (two specimens in AMNH collected in 1913, and two possibly captive birds in MHNJP, one dated July 1927); also simply Lima department (no localities given: Koepcke 1970);

(*Ica*) (2) río Pisco drainage: Huancano (1,020 m), 13°36'S 75°37'W, 1931 (Bond 1951a: specimen in ANSP); 0.5 km east of km 235 on the Panamerican highway, 100 m, 13°41'S 76°12'W, 1983 (specimen in LSUMZ); Pisco (17 m), 13°42'S 76°13'W (Bond 1951a: two specimens in AMNH collected in 1920, five in ANSP and CM collected in 1931; also many recent sightings at the mouth of the river: Parker and O'Neill 1976, Parker *et al.* 1982, NK); and 5 km west-north-west of Pozo Santo, 13°54'S 76°05'W (specimen in LSUMZ collected in 1975, with two in MHNJP collected at km 260 in January 1960); (3) río Ica drainage: Ica (406 m), 14°04'S 75°42'W (von Berlepsch and Stolzmann 1892: also specimen in AMNH collected in 1920); (4) río Grande drainage: río Blanco, 610 m, near Nazca, at 14°50'S 74°57'W (Bond 1951a: four specimens in ANSP collected in 1931, four in FMNH collected in 1970; a male, female and juvenile observed in trees in hotel grounds in April 1982: D. F. Stotz *in litt.* 1989);

(*Arequipa*) (5) río Acarí drainage: Acarí, 120 m, 15°26'S 74°37'W, 1969 and 1970 (two specimens in FMNH); (6) río Sihuas drainage (río Vítor): Vítor (1,631 m), 16°26'S 71°49'W, 1920 (eight specimens in AMNH); and Arequipa, possibly at 1,980 m at 16°27'S 71°36'W, 1931 (see Remarks 2) (Bond 1951a: specimen in ANSP); (7) río Tambo drainage (all records near sea level from the Panamerican highway along the river to the coast and north along the coastal lagoons): El Fiscal, where the Panamerican highway crosses the río Tambo, c.17°03'S 71°43'W (many recent sightings down to 1987: R. A. Hughes verbally 1987, Fjeldså 1987); Hacienda Chucarapi, 17°06'S 71°46'W, 1920 (12 specimens in AMNH and USNM); Cocachacra, 17°06'S 71°46'W (one undated specimen in WFVZ); Punta de Bombón ("La Punta"), 17°11'S 71°48'W, 1931 (Bond 1951a: two specimens in ANSP and CM); Tambo valley, 1867 (Sclater and Salvin 1868: seven specimens in BMNH); Tambo, 10 m, 17°10'S 71°51'W (specimen in LSUMZ collected in 1974; also regular sightings from 1960 to 1987: R. A. Hughes verbally 1987);

(*Moquegua*) (8) río de Osmore drainage: Moquegua, 415 m, 17°12'S 70°56'W, 1920 (six specimens in AMNH and WFVZ), and Ilo, sea level, 17°38'S 71°20'W, 1920 (five specimens in AMNH);

Chile (*Tarapacá*) (1) río Lluta drainage (see Remarks 2): Lluta valley (sightings: Johnson 1967, 1972; also in the lower valley during August 1985 and October-November 1988: B. M. Whitney *in litt.* 1991); near Molinos, 18°23'S 69°57'W, in the Lluta valley (sightings of four birds in January 1990: P. Gregory *in litt.* 1990); Chacalluta (near sea level), 18°24'S 70°19'W (six specimens in FMNH collected in 1924, one collected in 1943; Philippi *et al.* 1944, also Hellmayr 1932); (2) río Azapa drainage: Las Maitas, 18°31'S 70°12'W, 1978 and 1979 (five specimens in

MNHNS); Arica (= Azapa valley: Hellmayr 1938), type-locality (d'Orbigny and Lafresnaye 1837, d'Orbigny 1835-1844, Johnson 1967, 1972: specimen in MNHNS collected in 1949; also 43 specimens in WFVZ collected "near Arica" in June 1986); (3) río Camarones drainage: Camarones valley, c.19°S (sightings: Johnson 1972; also four specimens in WFVZ collected in June and July 1986); Parca, near Mamiña, 2,700 m, 20°01'S 69°12'W, July 1985 (one specimen in WFVZ); Mamiña, 2,735 m, 20°05'S 69°14'W, June 1985 (specimen in WFVZ); Pica, 1,220 m, an oasis at Quebrada de Quisma, 20°30'S 69°21'W (Sclater 1891, Hellmayr 1932: six and two specimens in BMNH and FMNH from 1890 and 1924 respectively);

(*Antofagasta*) (4) río Loa drainage: río Loa, 2,285 m, 1924 (Hellmayr 1932: specimen in FMNH); and Quillagua, 21°39'S 69°33'W (Johnson 1967: specimen in MNHNS collected in 1944).

POPULATION This species appears to be generally rare, although it is common at a few sites. It was described as "locally fairly common" in Peru by Parker *et al.* (1982), although in Lima department it is rare (Koepcke 1970). In Ica department, the bird is regularly encountered along the río Pisco (Parker and O'Neill 1976, Parker *et al.* 1982, NK), usually only one or two at a time (NK), although west-north-west of Pozo Santo, 6-8 birds were seen together in June 1975 (LSUMZ label data). In Arequipa department it is rare at the Mejía lagoons north of the mouth of the río Tambo, but locally common along the río Tambo itself (R. A. Hughes verbally 1987), and 3-4 pairs were seen in a 100 m stretch along the river at El Fiscal in May 1987 (Fjeldså 1987).

In Chile, the Slender-billed Finch was reported to be common in the lower part of Lluta valley, and less common in Azapa and Camarones valleys (Johnson 1972). B. M. Whitney (*in litt.* 1991) reported it to be common in the lower Lluta valley during visits from August 1985 to October and November 1988. No less than 43 specimens were taken near Arica in June 1986 (WFVZ), at which time the species must have been fairly common in the Azapa valley as a whole.

ECOLOGY The Slender-billed Finch is primarily a bird of dense riparian shrubbery, e.g. *Salix humboldti* and *Prosopis limensis* (often overhanging the water), but it may also frequent adjacent mesquite groves and shrubbery, on sand-dunes or bordering fields and pasture, even patches of *Prosopis* bushes in the desert, and has been noted in fields and reedbeds (Philippi *et al.* 1944, Johnson 1967, Koepcke 1970, Parker and O'Neill 1976, Parker *et al.* 1982, NK; also label data on specimens in BMNH, LSUMZ and MHNJP). Though primarily a bird of low elevations, it occurs up to c.2,000 m in Arequipa, to 2,700 m in southern Tarapacá, and nearly 2,300 m in Antofagasta, and has been reported once (probably erroneously: R. A. Hughes *in litt.* 1989) at 3,500 m at Putre, Tarapacá (see Remarks 3). It is found alone, in pairs or family groups, and forages very actively for insects and sometimes seeds, usually well concealed, low down in dense shrubbery, but occasionally, when undisturbed, birds may perch on an outer branch or even a telephone-line (d'Orbigny 1835-1844, Johnson 1967, D. F. Stotz *in litt.* 1989, NK; also label data on specimens in BMNH and LSUMZ): males sing from the tops of shrubs, and have also been noted singing from telephone-lines and fences (B. M. Whitney *in litt.* 1991). The nest has never been found (NK). The distinction between juveniles and immatures on specimen labels is not certain: birds in juvenile or immature plumage have been taken in October (1), November (2), March (3), April (4), May (5), June (4) and July (1), whilst the only collector distinguishing between the two plumages collected two juveniles in March, two in April, and two immatures in March; a bird with active gonads was taken in March, and birds with slightly enlarged gonads in March (1), May (1) and June (3) (label data on specimens in AMNH, ANSP, BMNH, CM, FMNH, LSUMZ and MNHNS). High song activity has been recorded in early May (NK), and November (in northern Chile) (B. M. Whitney *in litt.* 1991).

THREATS Although superficially the Slender-billed Finch has accepted and survived the almost complete loss to farming of the original habitat in the valleys it inhabits, these valleys are so intensively irrigated and cultivated (e.g. for cereals, cotton) that only narrow strips of vegetation (canegrass, willow) persist along the rivers themselves, and very few humid willow thickets survive (J. Fjeldså verbally 1992); the species could therefore be severely affected by any further changes in land use at the few sites where it is common.

MEASURES TAKEN The species is known to occur at the protected Mejía lagoons in Arequipa, Peru, but is rare at this site (see Population).

MEASURES PROPOSED The absence of any formal protection for any of the river drainages inhabited by this finch represents a serious omission in water resource management for the entire region. Measures to manage these watercourses and the vegetation in their immediate catchment areas should be taken to prevent deterioration of this specialized riparian habitat. Such initiatives should at least initially concentrate on the areas where the finch is commonest, i.e. the río Pisco in Ica, río Tambo in Arequipa and, in Chile, the lower Lluta valley and Azapa valley (see Population). Further work aimed at clarifying the precise ecological requirements and population of this species, at least in the valleys where it is commonest, should also be undertaken as a priority.

REMARKS (1) The Slender-billed Finch is the only member of its genus. (2) Specimens of the present species collected by M. A. Carriker in March and April 1931 are labelled "Pisco, Peru", "Nazca, Peru", "Huancano, Peru", "Arequipa, Peru" and "La Punta, Tambo valley, Peru" (specimens in ANSP and CM). It therefore seems likely that "Arequipa, Peru" refers to the town rather than the department of that name. According to Stephens and Traylor (1983), M. A. Carriker collected at Tiabaya, c.6 km south-west of Arequipa, on a tributary of the río Vítor, at 6,500 feet (1,980 m). (3) Sightings reported from Putre, 3,500 m, at 18°12'S 69°35'W by Philippi *et al.* (1944), are probably misidentifications (R. A. Hughes verbally 1987), although Johnson (1967), possibly based on this record, reported the bird to be scarce there.

GREY-WINGED INCA-FINCH *Incaspiza ortizi* V[9]

This rare finch is confined to the northern part of the western Andes of Peru, where it inhabits arid scrub at 1,800-2,300 m. Although rendered vulnerable by its small distribution (known from three sites in two departments), it appears to be under no immediate threat.

DISTRIBUTION The Grey-winged Inca-finch has been found on both slopes of the western Andes, in the departments of Piura and Cajamarca, northern Peru.

Birds are known from three localities (coordinates from Paynter and Traylor 1983) as follows: (*Piura*) 2 km by road north-east of Huancabamba (5°14'S 79°28'W), on the road to Sapalache, where six specimens (in LSUMZ) were collected at 2,125 m in June and July 1980 (also Parker *et al.* 1985), with a minimum of eight birds (three males singing) seen in August 1989 (B. M. Whitney *in litt.* 1991); (*Cajamarca*) La Esperanza (6°36'S 78°54'W), c.5 km north-east of Santa Cruz, at 1,800 m on the upper río Chancay, whence comes the type-specimen (Zimmer 1952); Hacienda Limón (c.6°50'S 78°05'W), on the road from Celendin to Balsas (río Marañón drainage), where a specimen (in ANSP) was collected in September 1933, with 12 others (in AMNH, LSUMZ) taken in August 1975, all between 2,000 and 2,300 m (also Zimmer 1952, Parker *et al.* 1985, NK).

The Grey-winged Inca-finch undoubtedly occurs elsewhere in the region, although the presence of the Buff-bridled Inca-finch *Incaspiza laeta* at 1,500-2,750 m in the upper río Marañón drainage and Great Inca-finch *I. pulchra* at 1,000-2,750 m on the Pacific slope from Lima department north to at least northern Ancash department (Fjeldså and Krabbe 1990) makes it unlikely that *ortizi* occurs much further south.

POPULATION This finch was described as "uncommon" by Parker *et al.* (1982) and as "rare" (generally) and "uncommon" (where found) by Parker *et al.* (1985). However, the collection of six birds (in June and July 1980) and observation of at least eight (in August 1989) near Huancabamba, and the collection of 12 (in August 1975) at Hacienda Limón, seem to suggest that at least locally this species is not uncommon (see above).

ECOLOGY The Grey-winged Inca-finch inhabits dense, arid, montane scrub (Parker *et al.* 1982, 1985, Fjeldså and Krabbe 1990) at elevations ranging from 1,800 to 2,300 m (see Distribution). Near Huancabamba (basically a single rocky hilltop) birds were found in dense herbaceous scrub that averaged 1.5 m high: small *Acacia*, various cacti, including a large columnar *Cereus*-like species and an *Opuntia* sp., with terrestrial bromeliads common (Parker *et al.* 1985, B. M. Whitney *in litt.* 1991). At Hacienda Limón there is open *Acacia* wood, grass and thorny scrub, but no cacti or bromeliads, and the species has been observed in dense, thorny hedgerows (NK). Usually in pairs, it mainly forages on the ground under dense thorny scrub, only occasionally venturing into the open, though never more than a few metres from cover, in which it seeks shelter when alarmed (Parker *et al.* 1985, Fjeldså and Krabbe 1990).

Stomach contents of six specimens (in AMNH and LSUMZ: taken in June and August) were recorded as follows: seeds, gravel, vegetable (plant) matter, and insect remains (parts); one bird found to contain plant and insect matter was earlier seen carrying a caterpillar about 2 cm long (Parker *et al.* 1985).

Near Huancabamba most bird species were breeding in mid-June, males of the present species (which perch conspicuously atop bushes or short trees) were singing, and a female was seen carrying a caterpillar, while at the end of October, when conditions were much drier, most reproductive behaviour had ceased, and only a single male *ortizi* was singing (Parker *et al.* 1985); in mid-August at this locality, three males were found singing, which although the dry season was well advanced may have been a result of recent rains; no juveniles were recorded at this time (B. M. Whitney *in litt.* 1991). Juveniles have been collected in Piura in July, and Cajamarca in

August and September; two birds with slightly enlarged gonads and one with enlarged gonads were taken in Piura in June (specimens in AMNH and LSUMZ), so breeding apparently mainly takes place from May to July. No nest of the genus has been described.

THREATS None is known, although near Huancabamba the valley and slopes across a broad altitudinal range have been cleared for cultivation and pasture, and there appears to be no other suitable habitat in the vicinity: if this single hilltop should be burned, this northernmost population of Grey-winged Inca-finch would surely be lost (B. M. Whitney *in litt.* 1991).

MEASURES TAKEN None is known.

MEASURES PROPOSED The priority for this rare and localized finch is to ensure the integrity of some suitable habitat at the sites from which it is currently known: surveys of such habitat in the intervening areas should also be initiated to determine more precisely its conservation status. This is one of a suite of birds meriting investigation and conservation in the upper Marañón valley (see equivalent section under Yellow-faced Parrotlet *Forpus xanthops*).

PLAIN-TAILED WARBLING-FINCH *Poospiza alticola* V/R[10]

This warbling-finch is a rare bird of shrubby forest and mixed Polylepis–Gynoxys *woodland at 3,200-4,300 m in western Peru, and at least in some areas it appears to be a* Gynoxys *(Compositae) specialist, feeding on the sugary secretions and insects on the undersides of the leaves.*

DISTRIBUTION The Plain-tailed Warbling-finch is known from c.11 specimens taken at six different localities in three departments (Cajamarca, La Libertad and Ancash) along the upper río Marañón in western Peru, and has been sighted at eight more places in the same region, records ranging from 2,900 to 4,300 m (most at 3,500-4,300 m) and localities (north to south, by department, and with coordinates unless otherwise stated from Stephens and Traylor 1983) being:

Cajamarca shrubby patch near Balsas–Celendín road, 10 km east of Celendín, 2,900 m, at c.6°51'S 78°04'W (sightings by TAP; coordinates and altitude read from IGM 1969a); Sendamal, 3,500 m, 30 km south-west of Celendín, at c.6°58'S 78°13'W (specimen in LSUMZ);

La Libertad Cajamarquilla, 3,350 m, at 7°18'S 77°48'W (specimen in ANSP); above Los Alisos, somewhere between 3,200 and 3,700 m, Pataz–Pajaten trail, Pataz being at 7°44'S 77°37'W (sightings by D. F. Stotz, four on 29 July and two on 25 August 1981: T. S. Schulenberg *in litt.* 1988, 1989); Quebrada La Caldera, 3,500 m, 7 km north-east of Tayabamba, at c.8°13'S 77°15'W (specimen in LSUMZ); Huamachuco, 3,170 m, at 7°48'S 78°04'W (Salvin 1895; three specimens including type, in BMNH);

Ancash Quebrada Tútapac, 3,660 m, c.25 km by trail south of Yánac, at c.8°40'S 77°49'W (recent sightings by TAP); Laguna Paron, near río Paron, 4,050 m, west slope of Cordillera Blanca, at 9°00'S 77°41'W (one sighting: Frimer and Møller Nielsen 1989; coordinates read from IGM 1972); Quebrada Morococha, east slope of Cordillera Blanca, at c.9°03'S 77°34'W (recent sightings by TAP; coordinates read from IGM 1973); Quebrada de Llanganuco, 3,600-4,000 m, west slope of Cordillera Blanca, at c.9°05'S 77°39'W (four specimens in MHNJP; also recent sightings by TAP; M. Kessler *in litt.* 1988, P. K. Donahue *in litt.* 1990; coordinates read from IGM 1973); upper Quebrada Rurichinchay, at 3,700 m (Andavite), 3,800 m and 3,800-4,000 m (near the glacier), east slope of Cordillera Blanca, at 9°22-23'S 77°16-19'W (three sightings of singles in 1988 sightings: Frimer and Møller Nielsen 1989; coordinates read from IGM 1978b); Quebrada Carhuascanchan, 3,900 m, east slope of Cordillera Blanca, at 9°28'S 77°16'W (two sighted in 1988: Frimer and Møller Nielsen 1989; coordinates read from IGM 1978); Quebrada Pucavada, 4,300 m, east slope near crest of Cordillera Blanca, at c.9°41'S 77°14'W (Fjeldså 1987; specimen in ZMUC; coordinates read from IGM 1971); Cerro Huansala, 3,700 m, south-eastern Cordillera Blanca, at c.9°51'S 76°59'W (recent sightings by TAP; altitude from Fjeldså 1987; coordinates read from IGM 1973).

POPULATION The Plain-tailed Warbling-finch is considered local and uncommon by Parker *et al.* (1982) and Fjeldså and Krabbe (1990). Frimer and Møller Nielsen (1989) recorded only an average of one individual per day in what appears to be its optimal habitat. Around Laguna Llanganuco a maximum of three was reported in a day during visits in September 1979, July 1980 and August 1987 (P. K. Donahue *in litt.* 1987, 1990), and above Los Alisos up to four were recorded in a day (D. F. Stotz *per* T. S. Schulenberg *in litt.* 1989). Both Quebrada Pucavado and Quebrada Carhuascanchan have dense populations of Tit-like Dacnis *Xenodacnis parina* (Fjeldså 1987, O. Frimer *in litt.* 1988), apparently a competitor (see Ecology), but at other localities with smaller populations of *Xenodacnis* (Laguna Paron, Quebrada Rurichinchay), the warbling-finch appeared to be equally scarce (O. Frimer *in litt.* 1988), so competition does not appear to be a major factor governing the size of the population. Unless the Plain-tailed Warbling-finch is found to be locally numerous or widely using a different habitat north of Cordillera Blanca in La Libertad and Cajamarca, the total poulation is very small.

ECOLOGY The Plain-tailed Warbling-finch mainly inhabits mixed *Polylepis–Gynoxys* woodland (Parker *et al.* 1982, Fjeldså and Krabbe 1990), but has also been encountered in scrubby forest composed largely of *Gynoxys* and, at one locality, in an *Alnus* thicket admixed with a little *Gynoxys* and other shrubs (TAP), at elevations ranging from 3,500 to 4,300 m, occasionally as low as 2,900 m (see Distribution). In Quebrada Rurichinchay it was found at 3,700 m in the transition from humid, 8-15 m tall *Polylepis* woodland to shrubbery composed of *Gynoxys*, *Buddleia*, *Berberis*, *Baccharis*, *Miconia*, *Brachyotum*, *Ribes* and others, but higher up in the valley, near 4,000 m, it was observed in *Polylepis* and *Buddleia* woodland and shrub (Frimer and Møller Nielsen 1989). In Quebrada Carhuascanchan and at Laguna Paron it was found in mixed *Polylepis weberbaueri*, *P. sericea* and *Gynoxys* woodland and shrub (at the latter locality also with many *Berberis* bushes) (Frimer and Møller Nielsen 1989). It is found singly, in pairs or small family groups, and forages in dense, low shrubbery (Fjeldså and Krabbe 1990). The species has been observed taking insects from leaf-clusters of *Polylepis sericea* and *weberbaueri* (O. Frimer *in litt.* 1988), but apparently mainly feeds on the sugary secretions and associated insects on the undersides of *Gynoxys* leaves, thus competing with Tit-like Dacnis and Blue-mantled Thornbill *Chalcostigma stanleyi* (TAP in Fjeldså and Krabbe 1990; O. Frimer *in litt.* 1988), but it also gleans insects from leaves and stems of other shrubs (TAP). Breeding probably takes place from December to February, as juveniles have been recorded in February (in Ancash) and March (in La Libertad) (Fjeldså and Krabbe 1990).

THREATS Although probably less at risk than birds that require taller trees, the species may be threatened by habitat destruction. The mixed *Polylepis–Gynoxys* woods are shrinking as a result of cutting for firewood, as well as lack of regeneration caused by grazing sheep and goats, and by the burning of mature grass between the trees (Fjeldså 1987), even on the steepest slopes (P. K. Donahue *in litt.* 1990). Even in Huascarán National Park the woods are dwindling due to the activities of man (Fjeldså 1987, P. K. Donahue *in litt.* 1987, Frimer and Møller Nielsen 1989).

MEASURES TAKEN Much of the range of the Plain-tailed Warbling-finch falls within Huascarán National Park, Ancash department (but see Threats).

MEASURES PROPOSED Relevant ideas are in Measures Proposed under White-cheeked Cotinga *Zaratornis stresemanni*.

REMARKS The species's overlaps in its *Polylepis* habitat with two other threatened bird species, Ash-breasted Tit-tyrant *Anairetes alpinus* and, to a lesser extent, White-cheeked Cotinga (see relevant accounts).

TUCUMAN MOUNTAIN-FINCH *Poospiza baeri* V/R[10]

This rare mountain-finch is confined to scrubby ravines in a small area of mountain slopes in north-western Argentina, where it is known from relatively few localities, and the total population may be extremely small.

DISTRIBUTION The Tucumán Mountain-finch (see Remarks) has been found at relatively few localities in the Sierra del Manchao and Sierra de Ambato, Catamarca province, on the east slope of Sierra del Aconquija and Sierra de Medina in Tucumán province, and in adjacent Salta, Jujuy and La Rioja provinces, north-western Argentina, as follows (with coordinates, unless otherwise stated, from Paynter 1985):

Jujuy río de la Quesera (c.24°11'S 65°26'W), where a female (in MCNAS) was collected in October 1950 (also Chebez and Heinonen Fortabat 1987); unspecified quebradas of streams in the prepuna in Valle Grande and Humahuaca departments, August 1991 (C. G. Ostrosky *per* J. C. Chebez *in litt.* 1992);

Salta above Chicoana (c.25°06'S 65°33'W), on the east slope of Cumbre de Obispo, along the road to Cachi, Chicoana department, where one was seen at c.2,600 m in November 1984 (M. Rumboll *in litt.* 1986, R. S. Ridgely *in litt.* 1988); El Alisal, untraced but at 2,800 m in the Sierra del Cajón in the southernmost part of the centre of the province, January 1914, where nine were collected (Navas and Bó 1991);

Tucumán Las Cuchillas (c.26°23'S 64°54'W), at 2,000 m on the east slope of Sierra de Medina, Burruyacú department (Olrog 1958c); Lagunita (26°38'S 65°34'W), at 3,000 m (Oustalet 1904, Olrog 1958c; specimens in AMNH); El Infiernillo (c.26°44'S 65°47'W), at 3,000 m above Tafí del Valle, (Narosky and Yzurieta 1987; specimen in LSUMZ), while birds labelled "Tafi del Valle, 2,135 and 2,200-2,500 m" and "above Tafi del Valle, 2,900 m" (Olrog 1958c; specimens in AMNH, NRM) were probably taken nearby, but possibly closer to Tafí del Valle, at 26°52'S 65°41'W, and those labelled "Aconquija" (ANSP and FMNH; also Navas and Bó 1991) may have been taken at c.27°00'S 65°53'W; Las Pavas (27°15'S 65°52'W), at 2,100 m (Olrog 1958c; specimens in FMNH, USNM); Concepción (27°20'S 65°35'W; Paynter 1985 accidentally has 63°35'W), August 1927 (Navas and Bó 1991);

Catamarca Sierra de Ambato (exact location unknown, but these mountains stretch from c.27°50' to c.29°00'S at c.66°W: IGM 1963, 1965b), where specimens (in MCZ) were collected in December 1920; Sierra del Manchao, a continuation of Sierra de Ambato, whence come eight specimens collected in the last few years (M. Nores *in litt.* 1989); Chumbicha (28°52'S 66°14'W), August 1918 (Navas and Bó 1991), this being at 3,000 m on the eastern slope of the Sierra de Ambato (J. C. Chebez *in litt.* 1992);

La Rioja an unspecified locality in the Sierra de Velasco, in around 1990 (A. Serret *per* J. C. Chebez *in litt.* 1992).

POPULATION M. Nores (*in litt.* 1985) estimated a population of not much more than 180-200 birds in the six ravines in Tucumán known to hold the species at the time. With suitable habitat in these (4-6) ravines possibly amounting to only a few hundred hectares (the longest ravine in the area is c.10 km long), the population there may well be only c.20 pairs (M. Pearman *in litt.* 1990, B. M. Whitney *in litt.* 1991). No estimate of the total population has been made since the latest range extensions to the north and the south became known: the extent of remaining habitat in these areas is unknown (see Threats).

ECOLOGY The Tucumán Mountain-finch is found at 2,000-3,000 m, and inhabits semi-humid watered (steep-sided) ravines with dense growths of bushes, within an area of rocky scrubland and pasture, but may also frequent forest edge (Narosky and Yzurieta 1987, M. Nores *in litt.* 1985, 1986), or shrubbery admixed with patches of grass and trees such as *Polylepis* and *Alnus* (Fjeldså and Krabbe 1990). It has been recorded singly and in loose groups (members of a pair keeping in contact with a quiet call), and forages within bushes, close to or on the ground itself, picking (often intently) at the woody bases and bark of the scattered shrubs in the ravines: when alarmed, birds may perch atop bushes (Narosky and Yzurieta 1987, Fjeldså and Krabbe 1990, B. M. Whitney *in litt.* 1990). No information exists on its diet, but it probably eats seeds and a few insects like its close relative the Cochabamba Mountain-finch *Poospiza garleppi* (see relevant account).

Males sing from perches usually just under the tops of shrubs on the sides of ravines (B. M. Whitney *in litt.* 1991). The nest has never been found, but recently fledged young have been collected in March and April (specimens in AMNH, NRM); a bird with slightly enlarged gonads was taken in December, and one with enlarged gonads in March (four others taken in March and April were reproductively inactive) (specimens in AMNH, LSUMZ), hence the main breeding season appears to be from January to March.

THREATS Relatively few of the ravines along the east slope of Sierra del Aconquija (which provides the majority of sightings and specimens: see Distribution) have suitable habitat (M. Nores *in litt.* 1985). The few ravines in Tucumán which hold both suitable habitat and the species (possibly as few as 20 pairs: see Population) are seemingly easily accessible, with the surrounding grasslands susceptible to fire which in turn could present a threat to vegetation within the gullies (M. Pearman *in litt.* 1990). The species's restricted range, limited habitat and small population render it vulnerable to both habitat destruction and trapping for the pet trade (the bird is attractive, lethargic and approachable) (M. Pearman *in litt.* 1990). M. Nores (*in litt.* 1986) suggested that it receives some protection through the inaccessibility of its habitat, but although this may be true at a number of localities it does not generally seem to be the case in Tucumán (see above).

MEASURES TAKEN A reserve holding some ravines inhabited by this species has been created at El Infiernillo in Tucumán (M. Nores *in litt.* 1989), this being an area that was included in the projected Aconquija National Park (J. C. Chebez *in litt.* 1992).

MEASURES PROPOSED There is an urgent need for the distributional status and ecological requirements of this rare species to be better defined. An assessment of the state and distribution of suitable habitat is also needed, after which measures are essential to ensure the protection of small but presumably viable populations. Educational initiatives may be necessary to impress upon the relevant local communities the importance of conserving the vegetation within the ravines for protecting the watercourses and preventing erosion, and thereby aiding the conservation of this species. The effectiveness of the reserve at El Infiernillo, and the status of the mountain-finch within it, also require investigation; meanwhile, the projected Aconquija National Park (covering parts of both Tucumán and Catamarca) would help protect not only this species but also the Rufous-throated Dipper *Cinclus schulzi* and White-tailed Shrike-tyrant *Agriornis andicola* (J. C. Chebez *in litt.* 1992; see relevant accounts). In Jujuy, the mountain-finch was collected at the same locality as the dipper, and initiatives in this area should consider the requirements of both species.

REMARKS The Tucumán Mountain-finch is closely related to the Cochabamba Mountain-finch, and may possibly be conspecific with it (Hellmayr 1938). They were separated from the warbling-finches *Poospiza* as the genus *Compsospiza* (von Berlepsch 1893, Hellmayr 1906b); however, Bond (1951a) suggested their inclusion in *Poospiza*, a treatment followed by some (e.g. Paynter and Storer 1970), but not by others (e.g. Meyer de Schauensee 1966, Narosky and Yzurieta 1987). B. M. Whitney (*in litt.* 1991) favours the retention of *Compsospiza* owing to the larger size and different song pattern (and quality) of *baeri* and *garleppi* when compared to the true warbling-finches, although Fjeldså (in press), in an analysis of the evolution of warbling-finches, places the two species together with Chestnut-breasted Mountain-finch *Poospiza caesar* and (the threatened) Rufous-breasted Warbling-finch *P. rubecula*.

CINEREOUS WARBLING-FINCH *Poospiza cinerea* I[7]

This cerrado emberizid occurs patchily and at inexplicably low density across central Brazil, and although recently found in three national parks it merits study to determine its true status and the causes of its rarity.

DISTRIBUTION The Cinereous Warbling-finch has been recorded from a remarkably large area of south-central Brazil (see map in Ridgely and Tudor 1989), being described as "a characteristic species peculiar to the highlands of inner Brazil" (Naumburg 1930). However, records are extremely scarce within this region, with just three localities in Mato Grosso (no record since 1904), one in Mato Grosso do Sul (in 1937), four in Goiás (two records since 1906), one recently from Distrito Federal, three in São Paulo (last record in 1901) and eight in Minas Gerais (four very recent). Burmeister's (1856) claimed sight-record for Nova Friburgo in Rio de Janeiro is not accepted here. Records may be arranged from west to east, as follows:

Mato Grosso Cuiabá[1], July probably 1824 (von Pelzeln 1868-1871) and April or August 1882 (specimen in BMNH); Santa Anna da Chapada[2] (Hellmayr 1938), this locality being (a) the same as Chapada (Allen 1891-1893), for which there are two skins in AMNH dated August 1882, (b) presumably the same as "Santa Anna, near Cuiabá" (Naumburg 1930, based on an old skin in MNHN) and (c) now called Chapada dos Guimarães (Paynter and Traylor 1991); Porto Faia, November 1904 (von Ihering and von Ihering 1907, Pinto 1944; skin in MZUSP has "Fazenda Faya"), somewhere on the rio Paraná (see Paynter and Traylor 1991);

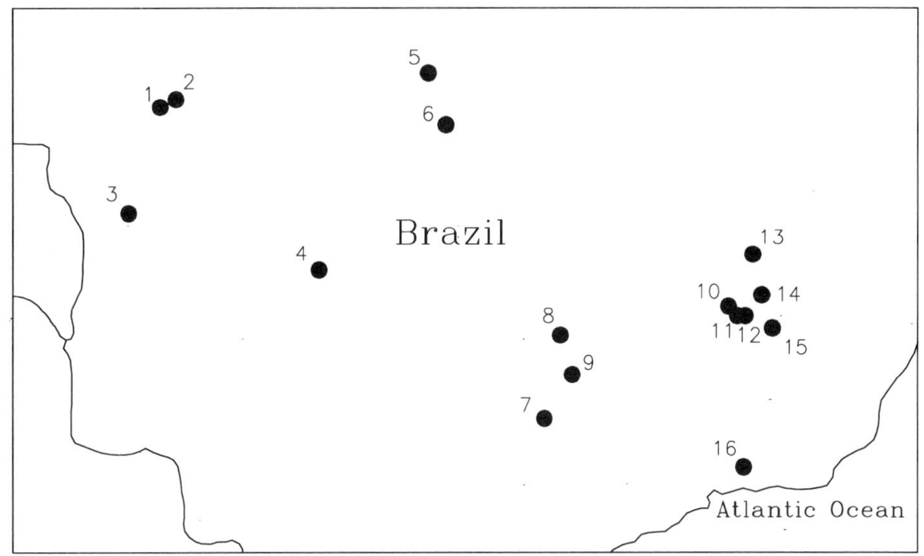

Mato Grosso do Sul Fazenda Recreio[3], Coxim, August 1937 (Pinto 1944);

Goiás Emas National Park[4], July 1988 (R. Byrne *per* B. C. Forrester *in litt.* 1992); rio Tesouras[5], May 1906 (Hellmayr 1908, 1938); Goiás[6], August 1823 (von Pelzeln 1868-1871, Hellmayr 1908, 1938), with this locality (unclear whether town or state is intended) also in March–May 1906 (Hellmayr 1908); Minaçu, October 1986 (R. B. Cavalcanti *in litt.* 1987);

Federal District Brasília National Park, March 1989 (J. F. Pacheco verbally 1992);

São Paulo Rincão[7], February 1901 (von Ihering 1902, von Ihering and von Ihering 1907, Pinto 1944); rio das Pedras[8] (i.e. close to rio Grande at around 20°00'S 47°45'W: Paynter and

Traylor 1991), April 1823 (von Pelzeln 1868-1871); rio Sapucaí[9] (probably on upper third: Paynter and Traylor 1991; i.e. at c.20°45'S 47°30'W), April 1823 (von Pelzeln 1868-1871);

Minas Gerais Sete Lagoas[10] (Reinhardt 1870, Pinto 1952); Pedro Leopoldo[11] (specifically Lapa Vermelha), November 1971 (specimen in DZMG); Parque das Mangabeiras, near Belo Horizonte, recently (A. Whittaker *per* B. C. Forrester *in litt.* 1992); Lagoa Santa[12] (Burmeister 1856, Pinto 1952); Gouvea[13], July 1990 (Forrester 1990); Serra do Cipó National Park[14], July and October 1990 (Forrester 1990, R. S. Ridgely *per* B. C. Forrester *in litt.* 1992); Peti Reserve[15] (c.19°52'S 43°20'W in Paynter and Traylor 1991), August 1990 (Forrester 1990; see Remarks); Vargem Alegre[16], where breeding was apparently recorded, 1900 (von Ihering 1902, von Ihering and von Ihering 1907, Pinto 1944, 1952).

POPULATION Ridgely and Tudor's (1989) expression of concern that the species had "gone virtually unrecorded in recent years" came just as it began to be found in the areas east of Belo Horizonte, but their conclusion that the bird is "inexplicably scarce and local" still seems valid. The number of encounters in recent years give some cause for hope that it is faring better than had been thought, but the numbers encountered remain small, from which it appears that the density is very low.

ECOLOGY Habitat is stated to be fairly open deciduous woodland and cerrado, mostly at 600-1,200 m (Ridgely and Tudor 1989), but it is not clear if this is based on assumption or recent unpublished evidence. Birds were in pairs on low grassland trees near gallery forest along the rio Sapucaí in April 1823, when a young female was collected; seeds were in the stomach of this or another bird taken there (von Pelzeln 1868-1871). In 1900 von Ihering (1902) was sent two eggs from Vargem Grande, Minas Gerais, but there was no indication of time of year nor whether they formed part of a clutch or a complete clutch, or indeed came from separate nests. A specimen from "Minas Gerais" (in DZMG) had testes developed in November. A female from Goiás, May, was in moult, and another from the same month and state was juvenile (skins in AMNH).

THREATS Ridgely and Tudor (1989) referred to this species's "present rarity", finding this difficult to explain through loss of some of its cerrado habitat to agriculture. However, the evidence seems to indicate that this has always been a very scarce bird, doubtless being rendered the more so by conversion of habitat.

MEASURES TAKEN The species is protected under Brazilian law (Bernardes *et al.* 1990). Recent records from Emas National Park in Goiás, Brasília National Park in the Federal District and Serra do Cipó National Park in Minas Gerais, plus that from the Peti Reserve (see Remarks), gives some hope that some populations of this rare bird obtain some security from the Brazilian protected areas system.

MEASURES PROPOSED Searches are needed in the remoter regions of the range states to rediscover this elusive creature and make some effort to plot its distribution. Populations in the three main protected areas mentioned above require careful evaluation. The species should be targeted for study to determine the likely causes of its scarcity.

REMARKS What is here called the "Peti Reserve" is "Reserva Natural Parque do Peti" in Paynter and Traylor (1991) and "Estação Ambiental de Peti" according to B. C. Forrester (*in litt.* 1992); the legal status and effective protection of the site remains unclear.

COCHABAMBA MOUNTAIN-FINCH *Poospiza garleppi* E[2]

Restricted to the mountain slopes surrounding Cochabamba city, Bolivia, this rare and beautiful mountain-finch is rendered vulnerable by its extremely limited distribution.

DISTRIBUTION The Cochabamba Mountain-finch (see Remarks under Tucumán Mountain-finch *Poospiza baeri*) is restricted to the slopes of the mountains surrounding Cochabamba city, in southern Cochabamba department, Bolivia, at 17°10-39'S 65°23'-66°29'W. The bird is known from a large number of specimens (c.85) taken at just the following 10-11 localities (coordinates, unless otherwise stated, from Paynter *et al.* 1975): Cerro Cheñua Sandra (c.17°39'S 66°29'W: IGM 1965a), adjacent to Cerro Pararani, 70 km from Cochabamba on the Oruro road, two birds (in ZMUC) taken at 3,800-3,900 m; Toncoma (c.17°15'S 66°20'W), two birds (in NRM) taken at 3,200-3,250 m; Liriuni (17°19'S 66°20'W), on Monte Tunari, nine birds (in BMNH, NRM) taken at 3,000-3,200 m; Cerro Huacanqui (c.17°21'S 65°52'W), 19 birds (in NRM) taken at 3,800 m; Colomi (17°21'S 65°52'W: the same as for the previous locality), two birds (in CM, MCZ) taken at 3,075 and 3,600 m; Faldas del Monte del Abra (c.17°10'S 65°45'W), one bird (in NRM) taken at 3,200-3,260 m; north of Quillacollo, where two were seen in April 1989 (M. Pearman *in litt.* 1990); Tiraque (17°25'S 65°43'W), where 34 birds (in AMNH, ANSP, FMNH, MCZ, ROM, UMMZ, USNM and ZMUC) were taken between 3,250 and 3,500 m (also Bond and Meyer de Schauensee 1942-1943, Remsen *et al.* 1988); Vacas (17°32'S 65°35'W), at 3,650 m (von Berlepsch 1893); between Pocona and Vacas, at 3,000 m (one in CM); Pocona (17°39'S 65°24'W), two birds (in CM, ZFMK) taken at 2,700 m (Remsen *et al.* 1988); Quebrada Majón (c.17°24'S 65°23'W: MC 1933), near Quehuiñapampa (6.6 km by road beyond López Mendoza, and 98 km by road from Cochabamba on the Santa Cruz road, Carrasco province), eight birds (in EBD, LSUMZ) taken at 2,950-3,150 m (also Remsen *et al.* 1988); and 120 km from Cochabamba towards Santa Cruz de la Sierra, Carrasco province (Remsen *et al.* 1988).

The species was not found in apparently suitable habitat further south, in Chuquisaca department, despite an intensive search in September 1991 (J. Fjeldså verbally 1991).

POPULATION At Cerro Huacanqui 19 specimens were collected in just two days (Fjeldså and Krabbe 1989), and at Tiraque seven were collected in a day (specimens in MCZ), although it was found to be uncommon there in January 1984 (NK). At Quebrada Majón it was noted on 10 of 16 field-days (Remsen *et al.* 1988). During recent visits to most of the known localites, no more than 1-2 pairs were found per locality (S. Arías verbally 1991), and with present distributional knowledge the entire population may be estimated to number between several hundred and a few thousand individuals (NK).

ECOLOGY The Cochabamba Mountain-finch inhabits watered ravines with dense bushes and scattered trees such as *Polylepis* and *Alnus*, and a variety of dense, thorny bushes (von Berlepsch 1893, Remsen *et al.* 1988, Fjeldså and Krabbe 1989, 1990), primarily between 3,000 and 3,800 m (once at 2,700 m and once at 3,900 m: see Distribution). It is possible that the coloration of the bird's plumage is specially adapted to *Polylepis* (NK). Birds are found alone or in pairs, and are secretive and shy (von Berlepsch 1893, Fjeldså and Krabbe 1990); however, it was reported to be rather tame and easily approached in Quebrada Majón by Remsen *et al.* (1988). This mountain-finch forages within dense shrubbery (occasionally on the ground), but may scold from a tree-top when disturbed near the nest (Remsen *et al.* 1988, Fjeldså and Krabbe 1990).

Food (from stomach contents of eight specimens in LSUMZ, ZMUC) appears to be primarily seeds (black, yellow and buff seeds, with wheat or barley and wheat chaff), but insect parts along with grit have also been recorded. Two adults have been observed feeding what appeared to be insect larvae to a recently fledged juvenile (Remsen *et al.* 1988). Birds with active gonads have been taken in January and April, recently fledged young in April and May, with others still in juvenile plumage in July and August; an adult with inactive gonads was taken in August (specimens in LSUMZ, NRM, ZMUC; Remsen *et al.* 1988).

THREATS The main threat to this species is the traditional burning of the mountain slopes to stimulate regrowth of grass: *Polylepis* trees are very sensitive to burning, and in most places this practice has led to the restriction of woodlands to steep ravines, the exception being a few places where land use includes the maintenance of mosaics of small fields and thickets (J. Fjeldså *in litt.* 1992). Cutting of *Polylepis* may be a threat, and M. Pearman (*in litt.* 1990) suggested that suitable habitat is now extremely limited within the Cochabamba basin. The species's minute range renders it vulnerable to any habitat alteration.

MEASURES TAKEN Tunari National Park (6,000 ha: IUCN 1992) holds a fair-sized *Polylepis* wood (Fjeldså 1987), and although the Cochabamba Mountain-finch has not yet been recorded there it is probably present (NK).

MEASURES PROPOSED Remsen *et al.* (1988) strongly recommended that conservation efforts be taken on this mountain-finch's behalf, suggesting that a survey of the extent of *Polylepis* woodlands in the region would be particularly important. A more detailed definition of the species's ecological requirements and population should be carried out in parallel with habitat surveys. However, until a viable population is discovered in the Tunari National Park, strong measures are needed for all remaining habitat, which presumably also protects the various watercourses from erosion. An education campaign in the relevant local communities to emphasize the importance of the vegetation in the mountain-slope gullies inhabited by this species would certainly aid the conservation of the bird.

RUFOUS-BREASTED WARBLING-FINCH *Poospiza rubecula* E[2]

This extremely rare warbling-finch is confined to western Peru, where it has been found at a few scattered localities at elevations ranging from 2,500 to 3,700 m. It remains virtually unknown.

DISTRIBUTION The Rufous-breasted Warbling-finch is known from few specimens and even less sightings at a number of localities from southern Cajamarca to Lima departments, western Peru. The localities (coordinates, unless otherwise stated, from Stephens and Traylor 1983) are:

Cajamarca Cajabamba (7°37'S 78°03'W), where two males (one immature: in BMNH) were collected at 2,750 m in January 1894 (Salvin 1895);

La Libertad Huamachuco (7°48'S 78°04'W), where the type-specimen (in BMNH) was taken at 3,170 m in February 1894 (Salvin 1895);

Ancash Quitacocha (c.8°52'S 77°55'W), above Huaylas in the río Santa valley, where an immature male (in FMNH) was collected at 3,350 m in May 1978 (P. Hocking *in litt.* 1988); Andavite (9°23'S 77°16'W: IGM 1978b), on the Quebrada Rurichinchay, río Marañón drainage, where an adult was seen at 3,700 m in October 1988 (Frimer and Møller Nielsen 1989); Bosque San Damián (c.9°51'S 77°47'W: IGM 1971), in the río Huarmey valley, Cordillera Negra, where two were seen at 2,350 and 2,400 m in October 1985 (M. Kessler *in litt.* 1988);

Lima upper Santa Eulalia valley (c.11°53'S 76°40'W), an affluent of río Rímac, where one was seen at c.2,400 m in August 1980 (J. W. Eley *in litt.* 1988), one at 3,020 m in August 1984 (R. S. Ridgely *in litt.* 1989), one at 3,650 m (P. Hocking *in litt.* 1988), with a pair at 3,000 m in July 1985 (B. M. Whitney *in litt.* 1991); Obrajillo (c.11°23'S 76°41'W), in the Chillón valley, where a male (in ANSP) was collected at c.2,500 m in November 1929 (also Bond 1951a); and in the Rímac valley (at 11°52-53'S 76°27-28'W) at Surco, where a male (in BMNH) was collected in February 1900 with a female (in MHNJP) taken in April 1953, at 2,500 and 2,600 m (also Hellmayr 1938, Koepcke 1958), and at Bosque Zárate, where birds were seen in March 1956 (Koepcke 1958) and an immature female (in MHNJP) was taken in October 1982, at 2,600-2,900 m.

There is a possible sight record from the upper Pisco valley on the border of Ica and Huancavelica departments (Koepcke 1958).

POPULATION This warbling-finch is very rare, occurring at low density, hence despite its wide distribution the total population must be very small. However, owing to its retiring habits, it may be commoner than the scarcity of sightings and museum specimens suggests (P. Hocking *in litt.* 1988).

ECOLOGY The Rufous-breasted Warbling-finch occurs between 2,350 and 3,700 m (see Distribution), inhabiting composite scrub (*Eupatorium*), woodland, "thick páramo sage" (possibly composite *Gynoxys*: NK), and dry scrub-forest at the edge of *Polylepis* woodland with other bushes admixed (Fjeldså and Krabbe 1990). More generally, its habitat has been described as "remnant forests and forested gorges" (P. Hocking *in litt.* 1988).

The habitat at Bosque Zárate was mixed woodland, the dominant trees being *Oreopanax* and *Escallonia*, with the warbling-finch found in bushy undergrowth at the edge of the wood (Koepcke 1958, I. Franke verbally 1987). The slopes where it was observed in the upper Santa Eulalia valley at 2,400 m had low bushes and scattered small trees (a *Polylepis* wood is situated higher up at c.3,500 m on the same slope: NK); one bird seen at 09h30 was preening low in a bush, and flew down into a canyon of dense bushy vegetation (J. W. Eley *in litt.* 1988). In the shrub zone of this same valley (at c.3,000 m), where the habitat in a steep-sided, rocky, arid ravine was described as a medium cover of low woody shrubs, with some *Puya* bromeliads and cacti, a bird perched quietly for some time, not feeding, and ignoring all the commotion of Mourning Sierra-finches *Phrygilus fruticeti*, *Catamenia* seedeaters and other finches around it (R. S. Ridgely *in litt.*

1989, B. M. Whitney *in litt.* 1991): at 3,650 m, one was seen warming itself on a rock bluff at 06h00, but quickly darted away into a nearby bush not far from the *Polylepis* woods (P. Hocking *in litt.* 1988). At Quitacocha, the bird was found at 06h30 in a ravine with dense bushes and 3-5 m tall trees: a pair was hopping about on large rocks near the bushes; they were fast and active, and seemed to hide in heavily leaved bushes near the ground, never venturing higher up into the trees (P. Hocking *in litt.* 1988). At Andavite one was seen at 11h00 low in *Gynoxys* bushes among mixed shrubs along a stream, the general vegetation being transition from shrubs to humid *Polylepis* forest, and composed of 8-15 m tall *Polylepis* trees, *Gynoxys*, *Buddleia*, *Berberis*, *Baccharis*, *Miconia*, *Brachyoton*, *Ribes* and other shrubs (O. Frimer *in litt.* 1988, Frimer and Møller Nielsen 1989). At Bosque San Damián both birds observed were young, sitting in the sun at 08h00, c.2 m up in the 4-5 m tall vegetation, and quickly darted away when approached (M. Kessler *in litt.* 1988).

"It has been found singly, but probably also occurs in pairs or family groups", and it "forages within the vegetation"; birds will apparently on occasion follow mixed-species flocks composed other finches (Koepcke 1958). One specimen had seeds in its stomach (Koepcke 1958), although according to P. Hocking (*in litt.* 1988) the species probably feeds primarily on young leaf buds and berries.

A female in breeding condition was collected in October, and a singing male was observed in late March 1956 at Bosque Zárate (Koepke 1958). Immatures have been collected in January in Cajamarca, April in Lima and May in Ancash (specimens in BMNH, FMNH and MHNJP). The bird collected in October 1953 had white, dark-streaked underparts and was a female in breeding condition; however, the bird collected in April 1982 was changing from streaked to rufous below and was sexed as a female, so apparently the sexes are alike and at least the female is able to breed whilst still in immature plumage (Fjeldså and Krabbe 1990).

THREATS The species may be naturally declining or rare, and according to P. Hocking (*in litt.* 1988) is threatened by habitat destruction. Further details of the plight of *Polylepis* woodland in the region are in Threats under White-cheeked Cotinga *Zaratornis stresemanni.*

MEASURES TAKEN None is known.

MEASURES PROPOSED Further research to disclose more about the habits and ecological requirements of this bird is desirable. Protective measures should be instigated in areas of remaining habitat where it is known to occur. The conservation of *Polylepis* woodland, which is an urgent priority in this region, is outlined in Measures Proposed under White-cheeked Cotinga.

TEMMINCK'S SEEDEATER *Sporophila falcirostris* V/R[10]

This small bird is a bamboo specialist within its limited range in south-east Brazil, Paraguay and Argentina, and is consequently difficult to find and probably genuinely rare, suffering from both habitat loss and the cagebird trade.

DISTRIBUTION Temminck's Seedeater is endemic to the Atlantic Forest region of south-east South America, extending from Bahia to Paraná in Brazil into eastern Paraguay and Misiones, Argentina, these last two countries having only recently been included in its range.

Brazil The map in Ridgely and Tudor (1989) indicates a range extending continuously from central coastal Bahia south through all Espírito Santo and Rio de Janeiro (and easternmost Minas Gerais) through eastern São Paulo and across the entire central region of Paraná; yet all of this is based on very few records, and for some states only one.

Bahia Apart from nineteenth-century reports from coastal forests (Wied 1831-1833, Burmeister 1856, Cabanis 1874, Stresemann 1954), the species has been recorded only once, in Una Biological Reserve, 8 October 1987 (LPG).

Espírito Santo Records (north to south) are from: São Mateus, undated (specimen in MNRJ); Lagoa Juparanã, Linhares, "July" (Sick 1985); and Pau Gigante (now Ibiraçu), October 1940 (specimen in USNM; also Pinto 1944).

Minas Gerais One specimen in MNRJ from the Lagoa Piçarra, rio Casca, Caratinga, 15 July 1936, represents the only known record.

Rio de Janeiro Localities (east to west) include: Ribeirão Vermelho, Santa Maria Madalena, 700 m (i.e. in Desengano State Park), August 1986 (J. F. Pacheco *in litt.* 1987); Nova Friburgo (von Pelzeln 1872, Cabanis 1874); Teresópolis (Sick 1985); Santo Aleixo, July 1975, April and July 1976, July 1981 (LPG; also Gonzaga 1986); Tinguá, March 1955 (specimen in MNRJ) and February 1981 (J. F. Pacheco *in litt.* 1986); Itatiaia National Park, October 1981 (D. F. Stotz *in litt.* 1988; also Ridgely and Tudor 1989) and August 1989 (D. Macdonald *per* B. C. Forrester *in litt.* 1992); and São Roque, Parati, November 1990 (J. F. Pacheco *in litt.* 1991).

São Paulo Records (north to south) are: Lagoinha, October 1991 (D. F. Stotz *in litt.* 1991); Picinguaba, December 1990 (D. Willis *per* J. F. Pacheco *in litt.* 1991); near Ubatuba, November 1943 (Pinto 1944) and October 1991 (B. M. Whitney *in litt.* 1991; see Population) and March 1992 (M. Pearman *in litt.* 1992); Ribeirão Pires, December 1921; Alto da Serra (near Ribeirão Pires; see Pinto 1945), July 1906; Fazenda Poço Grande, Juquiá, May 1940 (these last three sites all in Pinto 1944); Fazenda Palmeira, Iguape, February 1977 (specimen in MZUSP); and Cajati, March 1977 (specimens in CIAL). Sick (1985) mentioned Santos as a locality from which the species has been extirpated.

Paraná The only documented record seems to be one from Fazenda Monte Alegre, Tibaji, 900 m, 11 March 1930 (specimen in AMNH). However, the record from Iguazú Falls in Argentina (see below) suggests the likelihood of its occurrence across the river in the Brazilian Iguaçu National Park.

Argentina Records are from arroyo Urugua-í km 10 and km 30, November 1957 and August 1958 (Navas and Bó 1987), and Iguazú National Park, Misiones, where the species "can at times be found" (Ridgely and Tudor 1989), e.g. August 1977 (R. S. Ridgely *in litt.* 1992), October 1989 and October 1990 (B. M. Whitney *in litt.* 1990, 1991), with breeding recorded in August 1988 (Castelino 1990).

Paraguay Ridgely and Tudor (1989) mentioned Canindeyú department, this being based on observations of the species (common, singing) in bamboo-dominated forest along the road to Salto de Guairá, 14-18 July 1977, although less forest and no birds were present along the same road in May/June 1991 (R. S. Ridgely *in litt.* 1991).

POPULATION From the evidence of the records above, mostly based on the collection or observation of single or a few individuals at any given locality, the view that Temminck's Seedeater is a rare species (Hellmayr 1938, Ridgely and Tudor 1989) seems fully justified; indeed, it has already been on lists of threatened birds (Greenway 1958, Sick 1969). Although it has also been considered common locally (J. Vielliard *in litt.* 1986, D. M. Teixeira *in litt.* 1987), with 5-20 seen daily over four days in Canindeyú (R. S. Ridgely *in litt.* 1991; see Distribution) and "more than 30 individuals... seen and/or heard" near Ubatuba in October 1991 (B. M. Whitney *in litt.* 1991), it has been pointed out that this species never seems to have been as numerous as the similarly distributed Buffy-throated Seedeater *Sporophila frontalis* (see relevant account), being at best uncommon, and usually irregular at any single locality (Ridgely and Tudor 1989). At both Tinguá and Itatiaia in 1981, as well as at Ubatuba in 1991, the species was much less common than the Buffy-throated Seedeater (J. F. Pacheco *in litt.* 1986, D. F. Stotz *in litt.* 1988, B. M. Whitney *in litt.* 1991), which would make it appear more vulnerable than the latter (D. F. Stotz *in litt.* 1988). A statement that the species has disappeared from certain localities, e.g. Santos and Iguape (Sick 1985), seems at least partially based on a misevaluation of its nomadic habits (see Ecology).

ECOLOGY The species has been recorded around stands of bamboo crops (in one case identified as *Chusquea bambusoides*: Gonzaga 1986; in another *Guadua* sp.: M. Pearman *in litt.* 1992) in secondary or disturbed forest and at forest borders (J. F. Pacheco *in litt.* 1986, E. O. Willis *in litt.* 1986, D. F. Stotz *in litt.* 1988, B. M. Whitney *in litt.* 1990, 1991, LPG; also Ridgely and Tudor 1989), where it keeps in the middle and higher strata (Sick 1985, J. F. Pacheco *in litt.* 1991, B. M. Whitney *in litt.* 1991, LPG), thus being rather an arboreal seedeater (Ridgely and Tudor 1989). In the hot lowlands around Lagoa Juparanã in July it was associated with Capped and Rusty-collared Seedeaters *S. bouvreuil* and *S. collaris*, meeting Buffy-throated (see Ecology in relevant account) in the mountains of Rio de Janeiro and São Paulo (Sick 1985).

This bird eats bamboo seeds (Sick 1985, Ridgely and Tudor 1989), being watched at Ubatuba foraging in dense bamboo stands surrounding the trunks of large trees, sometimes clinging head-down apparently to take the seeds, mostly about 5-10 m above ground (B. M. Whitney *in litt.* 1991). In Iguazú National Park its presence coincided with the flowering of *Guadua trinii* (Castelino 1990). It is said to be fond of the seeds of the navalha-de-macaco *Hypolitrum* sp. (Cyperaceae), which grows in forest clearings, and to travel from the forest, flying high over open ground, to swampy areas and rice plantations (Sick 1985).

The nest is placed high up in the vegetation at the forest edge (Sick 1985); but the only one found in Argentina (August) was in a small specimen of *Sorocea ilicifolia* (= *S. bonplandi*) 5 m from the ground (Castelino 1990). There are no further data on breeding, except that the testes of the AMNH specimen from Paraná, March, were fairly enlarged, while the gonads of a pair from São Paulo, also March, were undeveloped. In October at Ubatuba many birds were singing, including several in subadult plumage (B. M. Whitney *in litt.* 1991).

It is clear that the species undertakes movements following bamboo flowerings, as it disappears afterwards (Gonzaga 1986; also Sick 1985).

THREATS This and two other bamboo-specialists (Purple-winged Ground-dove *Claravis godefrida* and Buffy-throated Seedeater; see relevant accounts) seem to be in difficulties even with moderate deforestation, which extends the intervals between major bamboo flowerings and nestings (E. O. Willis *in litt.* 1986), and it seems also that its erratic wanderings must render it more vulnerable and not fully protectable even in reserves. That the species is uncommon or infrequent in the cagebird trade (Sick 1969, C. E. Carvalho *in litt.* 1987) must not be taken as evidence that "it was never in demand as a cagebird" (Ridgely and Tudor 1989: 36), but as a probable consequence of its relative rarity, as is also the case, for instance, with the Black-legged Dacnis *Dacnis nigripes* (see relevant account). Specimens offered for sale in Rio de Janeiro were said to come from Espírito Santo, Rio de Janeiro (Tinguá) and Paraná, and were sometimes alongside its Amazonian representative, the Slate-coloured Seedeater *S. schistacea* (Sick 1969). The species was seen in cages but not in the wild during a survey in 1980/1981 (Scott and Brooke 1985). In Santa Maria Madalena, close to the Desengano State Park, caged birds were reportedly trapped in and around the locality (J. F. Pacheco *in litt.* 1987).

MEASURES TAKEN The species is protected under Brazilian law (Bernardes *et al.* 1990). Occurrence in Desengano State Park, Una and Tinguá Biological Reserves, Itatiaia and Iguaçu National Parks, and possibly several other parks and reserves along the Serra do Mar, may give it partial protection but cannot avert trapping and problems with deforestation elsewhere in its range. Its presence in Iguazú National Park on at least an occasional (but perhaps regular) basis is encouraging.

MEASURES PROPOSED A complete ban on the capture of wild birds for the pet trade, as partial controls would be so open to abuse as to be ineffective, has been called for, very much with this species in mind (Scott and Brooke 1985). Effective control in and around already created forest reserves, mainly during bamboo flowerings, would almost certainly enhance its chances of survival, but, on current knowledge at least, identification and protection of stands of even secondary forest in areas outside reserves (such as the Santo Aleixo area) seem to be of equal importance in view of the species's movements, a better understanding of which, through further study, is probably crucial to its long-term conservation. This bird would be targeted under a programme of research on (threatened) bamboo specialist birds in Atlantic Forest (see the equivalent section under White-bearded Antshrike *Biatas nigropectus*).

BUFFY-THROATED SEEDEATER *Sporophila frontalis* V/R[10]

Deforestation within its range in south-east Brazil (a few records exist for Paraguay and Argentina), perhaps combined with trade, appears to have rendered this bamboo specialist seedeater very patchily distributed and much reduced from its former numbers, with the majority of modern records stemming from Rio de Janeiro state.

DISTRIBUTION The Buffy-throated Seedeater is endemic to the Atlantic Forest region of south-eastern South America, extending from extreme southern Espírito Santo and south-east Minas Gerais south through Rio de Janeiro (this state holding the bulk of modern records) to Rio Grande do Sul (no records this century) in Brazil into eastern Paraguay (no recent records) and Misiones, Argentina.

Brazil Records suggest that the heart of this (evidently somewhat nomadic) species's range lies in and around the state of Rio de Janeiro.

Espírito Santo This state is included in the range by several authorities (Meyer de Schauensee (1966, 1982, Sick 1985, Ridgely and Tudor 1989), but the only recorded localities seem never to have been published: Augusto Ruschi (Nova Lombardia) Biological Reserve, September 1979 (A. Greensmith *per* B. C. Forrester *in litt.* 1992), and Bom Jesus do Norte in the extreme south, where a few individuals were seen in January 1984 (J. F. Pacheco *in litt.* 1991).

Minas Gerais Localities (north to south) include: Fazenda Campo Grande, Passa Tempo, 1984 (de Mattos *et al.* 1990); Araponga; Serra do Brigadeiro (near Araponga); São Miguel do Anta; Rio Preto, these four all in 1979 (and all from A. Brandt *in litt.* 1987); Fazenda Ponderosa, Volta Grande, a concentration in December 1979 (J. F. Pacheco *in litt.* 1991); Bocaina de Minas, near Itatiaia National Park, 1,800 m, one bird mist-netted in October 1985 (de Mattos *et al.* 1990).

Rio de Janeiro Older records are from Cantagalo (Cabanis 1874) and Nova Friburgo (von Pelzeln 1868-1871). Twentieth-century records (east to west) are from Rosal, January 1984, a few birds seen; ribeirão Vermelho, Desengano State Park, 800 m, October 1987; Lumiar, July 1979, a recently trapped bird; Fazenda Bandeirantes, Silva Jardim (adjacent to the Poço das Antas Biological Reserve), 50 m, August 1988; Volta do Pião, March 1988 and August 1989; Teresópolis (see below); Petrópolis, January 1985 and (near Correias) June 1990; Tijuca National Park (see below); Tinguá (near present-day Tinguá Biological Reserve), December 1980 and January 1981; Mazomba, Itaguaí, November 1980, many recently trapped; Serra das Araras, Piraí, March 1990; and Itatiaia National Park (see below) (all from or *per* J. F. Pacheco *in litt.* 1991). There is a concentration of records around Teresópolis: at Fazenda Boa Fé, May 1942 and December 1942 to March 1943 (Davis 1945, 1946, specimens in MNRJ, MZUSP); Serra dos Órgãos National Park, June/July 1986 (C. E. Carvalho *in litt.* 1987); Teresópolis–Nova Friburgo road, September 1987; Sobradinho, December 1990; Alto da Posse and Quebra-frasco, February/March 1991 (all three from J. F. Pacheco *in litt.* 1991). In Tijuca National Park birds have been recorded in November 1959 (Sick and Pabst 1968), on several days in September 1982 (J. F. Pacheco *in litt.* 1991), and in September 1991 (P. S. M. da Fonseca verbally 1991). From Itatiaia there are records in July/August 1950, June 1951 (Pinto 1954b), June/July 1952 (Sick 1968, 1984), October 1977 and October 1980 (TAP), October 1981 (D. F. Stotz *in litt.* 1988), April and July 1985 (J. F. Pacheco *in litt.* 1991, C. E. Carvalho *in litt.* 1986), September/October 1985 and October 1987 (TAP). Birds were formerly recorded also in the Barra da Tijuca and Marambaia, Rio de Janeiro (Sick and Pabst 1968).

São Paulo Old records are: Mato Dentro, December 1818, and Porto do Rio Paraná, c.19°59'S 47°46'W, 1823 (von Pelzeln 1868-1871); Alto da Serra (near Ribeirão Pires; see Pinto 1945), August 1906; Moji das Cruzes, March 1933; Iporanga, rio Betari, January 1944 (all three sites in Pinto 1944); Ipiranga, São Paulo, February 1949; Primeiro Morro, rio Ipiranga (near Juquiá), July 1961; Baicô, Iguape, June 1977 (all three sites based on specimens in CIAL, MZUSP). Recent records are only from the Fazenda Albion, Serra da Bocaina, Bananal, where one bird was seen in December 1990 (J. F. Pacheco *in litt.* 1991); near Ubatuba, August 1991 (B. C. Forrester *in litt.* 1992), September and October 1991 (TAP, D. F. Stotz *in litt.* 1991, B. M. Whitney *in litt.* 1991); and Ilha do Cardoso State Park, where the species is an annual visitor (P. Martuscelli *in litt.* 1991; also M. R. Bornschein verbally 1991).

Paraná The species is listed by Scherer Neto (1985) without further details.

Santa Catarina The species is included in the state list, but no recent record is indicated (Sick *et al.* 1981).

Rio Grande do Sul Two specimens were obtained near Taquara (von Berlepsch and von Ihering 1885); in 1883 this species appeared in huge numbers in German colonies north of 30°S (von Ihering 1887); no further record is known (Belton 1984-1985; see Remarks).

Paraguay One specimen was collected on the upper rio Paraná at 25°40'S on an ungiven date (Bertoni 1901). Another undated locality is Puerto Bertoni (Bertoni 1914). There are no recent records (Ridgely and Tudor 1989, F. E. Hayes *in litt.* 1991).

Argentina The species has been recorded from Misiones (Dabbene 1914, SOMA 1935-1942), but the only concrete record appears to be that of a bird ringed in Iguazú National Park in 1978 (Olrog 1979, J. C. Chebez *in litt.* 1986, 1992). It is probably only occasional in Argentina (M. Nores and D. Yzurieta *in litt.* 1986).

POPULATION In south-east Brazil the species is (or was) known to occur in large numbers locally in rice-fields and at bamboo-flowerings (Sick 1985), but its overall numbers are certainly much reduced owing to deforestation and heavy trapping (Ridgely and Tudor 1989), and this seedeater is now more frequently seen in cages than in the wild (J. F. Pacheco *in litt.* 1986, C. E. Carvalho *in litt.* 1987), although it has also been considered still locally common (D. M. Teixeira *in litt.* 1987) or very common (J. Vielliard *in litt.* 1986); nevertheless, numbers are seemingly greatly reduced from their levels 100 or even 40 years ago.

In Rio Grande do Sul it was reported to have appeared in 1883 in rice-fields in such enormous numbers that the crop would have been lost had birds not suddenly disappeared (von Berlepsch and von Ihering 1885, von Ihering 1887, Belton 1984-1985). During a bamboo flowering in Itatiaia, June/July 1952, "thousands" of birds were present (Sick 1968, 1984, 1985), and an apparently similar concentration (hundreds if not thousands) occurred there again as recently as September/October 1985, at 1,100-1,300 m, with dozens of individuals inside single patches of bamboo, and flocks of up to 30 or more constantly flying back and forth (TAP). Up to 76 birds were counted in January 1943 at Fazenda Boa Fé, Teresópolis (Davis 1945); at Sobradinho birds were in a "small concentration" around an extensive bamboo formation in December 1990 (J. F. Pacheco *in litt.* 1991), but only small numbers (1-6) were seen in the Serra dos Órgãos National Park in June/July 1986 (C. E. Carvalho *in litt.* 1987). "Moderate numbers" were recorded by one observer near Ubatuba in early September 1991 (D. F. Stotz *in litt.* 1991), while others found "more than 100 (possibly many more) of these seedeaters" one month later at the same locality (B. M. Whitney *in litt.* 1991). The species has been found to be periodically fairly common in the Ilha do Cardoso State Park in São Paulo (P. Martuscelli *in litt.* 1991) and at São Miguel do Anta in Minas Gerais (de Mattos *et al.* 1990), and until recently it was common also at Passa Tempo (M. A. de Andrade *in litt.* 1986). Most of the other recent records in Rio de Janeiro were of single or a few (2-3) birds, exceptions being the approximately 100 that had been trapped near Itaguaí in November 1980 and "a large group" present at Tinguá in December 1980/January 1981 (J. F. Pacheco *in litt.* 1991). It is remarkable that the species was only seen in cages, not in the wild, during a survey in Rio de Janeiro that included several one-month stays at Tinguá, Serra dos Órgãos, Poço das Antas reserve and the Nova Friburgo area, October to January, 1980/1981 and 1981/1982 (Scott and Brooke 1985).

ECOLOGY The Buffy-throated Seedeater inhabits forest interior and borders, secondary growth and cultivated and other open areas near forest (Sick 1985, Ridgely and Tudor 1989). Records, at least those of any local concentration of birds, are usually tied to periodic bamboo flowerings, which are regularly attended also by Uniform Finches *Haplospiza unicolor* (Davis 1945, Sick and Pabst 1968, Sick 1984, 1985, C. E. Carvalho *in litt.* 1987, D. F. Stotz *in litt.* 1988, de Mattos *et al.* 1990, J. F. Pacheco *in litt.* 1991). On one occasion, at Itatiaia, the bamboo was identified as *Merostachys* sp., and Sooty Grassquits *Tiaris fuliginosa* were also present (Sick 1984, 1985); on another occasion the bamboo was certainly large-leaved, and believed to be *Merostachys*, the birds plucking the seeds from near the ends of branches, and feeding and flying about in all directions with such intensity that two birds even flew in through the open window of a hotel bedroom (TAP). Near Ubatuba in 1991, Temminck's Seedeaters *Sporophila falcirostris* (see relevant account) were in the same bamboo flowering (a "small-leaved" species), but not concentrated in the same areas as Buffy-throateds (D. F. Stotz *in litt.* 1991, B. M. Whitney *in litt.* 1991). At Teresópolis in 1942/1943, the species was accidental in bird flocks outside the breeding season (Davis 1946). The species is remarkably arboreal, rarely if ever descending to the ground (Ridgely and Tudor 1989), as did the bird collected by Bertoni (1901).

During the September/October 1985 bamboo flowering at Itatiaia, very vocal and seemingly territorial (presumed) males sang persistently throughout the day from a few preferred perches high in the thickets or from the middle branches of nearby trees: several presumed females were observed building ball-like nests of dried grasses or other plant fibres, two being placed c.4 and c.8 m up in the branches of ornamental pine-trees in a clearing near bamboo (TAP). In October at Ubatuba many individuals were singing while foraging on the fruiting bamboo (B. M. Whitney *in litt.* 1991). The species was believed to follow the breeding pattern of its family in Teresópolis, with gonads being progressive in September, active in October and regressive in December (Davis 1945). There are no other data on breeding, except that the gonads of one male and one female (in CIAL) from São Paulo, June, were undeveloped.

THREATS This and two other bamboo specialists (Purple-winged Ground-dove *Claravis godefrida* and Temminck's Seedeater; see relevant accounts) seem to be in difficulties even with moderate deforestation, which extends the intervals between major bamboo flowerings and nestings (E. O. Willis *in litt.* 1986). In addition, birds are systematically persecuted and trapped in numbers for the pet trade: in the popular Caxias bird market in Rio de Janeiro lots of 100-200 birds may often be offered for sale at certain times, when numbers of other bamboo-followers (Temminck's Seedeaters, Uniform Finches and Sooty Grassquits) also increase in the trade (C. E. Carvalho *in litt.* 1987). Although both the core of the species's current distribution and the centre of its exploitation in trade seems to be the state of Rio de Janeiro, it is also persecuted by bird dealers in Minas Gerais (M. A. de Andrade *in litt.* 1986) and doubtless wherever it still occurs.

MEASURES TAKEN The species is protected under Brazilian law (Bernardes *et al.* 1990). Its occurrence in the Tijuca, Serra dos Órgãos and Itatiaia National Parks, Desengano and Ilha do Cardoso State Parks, and possibly several other protected areas along the Serra do Mar, may give it partial protection but cannot avert trapping and problems with deforestation elsewhere in its range. The record from Augusto Ruschi seems not to have been repeated, and may refer to vagrancy in the species.

MEASURES PROPOSED A complete ban on the capture of wild birds for the pet trade, as partial controls would be so open to abuse as to be ineffective, has been called for, very much with this species in mind (Scott and Brooke 1985). Effective control in and around already created forest reserves, mainly during bamboo flowerings, would almost certainly enhance its chances of survival, but, on current knowledge at least, identification and protection of stands of even secondary forest in areas outside reserves (such as those around Teresópolis) seem to be of equal importance in view of the species's movements, a better understanding of which, through further study, is probably crucial to its long-term conservation. This bird would be targeted under a programme of research on (threatened) bamboo specialist birds in Atlantic Forest (see the equivalent section under White-bearded Antshrike *Biatas nigropectus*).

REMARKS Two specimens (in BMNH) from "Pelotas, Rio Grande do Sul" (Sharpe 1888) are from the discredited Joyner collector, and this locality is usually not accepted (e.g. Hellmayr 1938, Belton 1984-1985).

RUFOUS-RUMPED SEEDEATER *Sporophila hypochroma* K[12]

Although distributed over a wide area in Brazil, Paraguay, Bolivia and Argentina, this grassland seedeater appears to be very local and remains too little known for confidence, especially given the pressures of trapping on members of its genus and the mass conversion of its habitat in most parts of Central South America.

DISTRIBUTION The Rufous-rumped Seedeater is known to occur locally in north-east Argentina (Corrientes and Entre Ríos), Paraguay (including the humid chaco), north and east Bolivia and south-west Brazil, and its range appears to be continuous between these areas. Unless otherwise stated coordinates below are taken from OG (1955a), Paynter (1985, 1989), Paynter and Traylor (1991) and Paynter *et al.* (1975).

Argentina The Rufous-rumped Seedeater has only been recorded from Corrientes and Entre Ríos provinces, where records (north to south) are from:

Chaco Isla Cerrito (27°20'S 58°40'W: J. C. Chebez *in litt.* 1992), río Paraná, where a male was observed several times in January 1987 (Herrera 1988);

Corrientes Paso Mbaracayá (c.27°25'S 56°45'W), where a bird was observed in January 1978 (Nores 1986); marshy area 21 km east-south-east of Itá-Ibaté (27°26'S 57°20'W), where a male was taken in October 1967 (Short 1969); the projected Mburucuyá National Park (28°01'S 58°01'W), where the species was observed in April 1990 (J. Hutton *per* S. Krapovickas *in litt.* 1992, whence coordinates) and in March 1992 (D. A. Gómez *per* S. Krapovickas *in litt.* 1992); south of Laguna Iberá, where c.10 males were observed in January 1991 (D. Willis *in litt.* 1991);

Entre Ríos Puerto Boca (33°03'S 58°23'W), where a maximum of one male (possibly two) and two females (the latter presumably of this species) were observed on different occasions between 28 December 1991 and 21 January 1992 (E. I. Abadie, B. M. López Lanús and M. Pearman *in litt.* 1992).

Bolivia Records (west to east) unless otherwise stated refer to males, and are from:

Beni Reyes (14°19'S 67°23'W), where a bird was taken in December 1937; Bresta (c.14°33'S 67°20'W), where four birds (one juvenile) were taken in January 1938; El Consuelo (c.14°20'S 67°15'W), where a bird was procured in December 1937 and two more in January 1938 (all three from Gyldenstolpe 1945); Estancia Inglaterra, río Yata (c.13°30'S 66°30'W), where the species was regularly observed ("medio común", i.e. 3-10 birds per day) from 22 November to 26 December 1976 (Remsen 1986a);

Santa Cruz Buena Vista (17°27'S 63°40'W), where the type was collected in January 1912 (Todd 1915a), two in mid-January 1915 and one in May 1915, one in January 1920, one in January 1926, and a female in February 1927 (specimens in ASNP, CM and FMNH); Viru Viru airport, near Santa Cruz, where two males accompanied by six unidentified females were observed in early May 1991 (T. Bakker *in litt.* 1992); Palmarito (16°49'S 62°37'W), on the río San Julián, where five birds (three females) were collected between 21 and 24 May 1918 (specimens in AMNH and CM); western base of the Serranía de Huanchaca, south of Los Fierros (14°35'N 60°50'W; coordinates from Cabot *et al.* 1988), where 10-20 males were observed in August 1989 (Bates *et al.* 1992).

Brazil The species has only been recorded from the pantanal east of Corumbá, Mato Grosso do Sul, in October 1979 (Ridgely and Tudor 1989) and at Emas National Park (17°49'-18°28'W 52°39'-53°10'W: IBAMA 1989), in extreme south-west Goiás, in October 1984 (IBGE undated, Redford 1987; also Ridgely and Tudor 1989).

Paraguay Records (north to south) are from: (*Presidente Hayes*) near km 100, Trans-Chaco Highway, where two males and an unidentified female were observed in February 1991 (F. E. Hayes *in litt.* 1992); (*Central*) 5 km south-south-east of Villeta, where two males (c.200 m apart) were observed in October 1989 (F. E. Hayes *in litt.* 1992); (*Misiones*) between Santiago and Ayolas (27°24'S 56°54'W), recently (Contreras *et al.* 1989).

POPULATION The status of this little-known species is far from clear. Its breeding grounds and migratory behaviour are poorly known, and hence no judgement of population size or trend is possible. Confusion with the similar and largely sympatric Tawny-bellied Seedeater *Sporophila hypoxantha* (M. Nores *in litt.* 1986, J. C. Chebez *in litt.* 1992), the difficulty of field identification of mixed groups of females and juveniles, and the low level of ornithological investigation in large areas of northern and eastern Bolivia, all lie behind the paucity of records.

Argentina Most records are of just one or two birds (see Distribution), Esteros de Iberá seeming to be the key centre, with c.10 males and numerous females and immatures present in January 1991, although only adult males were identified with certainty (D. Willis *in litt.* 1991).

Bolivia The species appears to have been greatly overlooked, given the scatter of localities at which it has been observed or collected (see Distribution). The records from Estancia Inglaterra, Beni, and near Los Fierros, Santa Cruz, indicate that it is at least locally common.

Brazil Its status in the country is unclear; the number of individuals recorded in the two known areas was not specified, although in Emas National Park it was considered uncommon (IBGE undated), and the birds observed east of Corumbá were apparently in mixed flocks with other seedeaters (Ridgely and Tudor 1989).

Paraguay Nothing is known beyond what is recorded under Distribution.

ECOLOGY The Rufous-rumped Seedeater has been reported near marshes, seasonal flooded grasslands, pastures, and savanna-like areas up to c.1,100 m (Remsen 1986a, Ridgely and Tudor 1989, Bates *et al.* 1992, M. Pearman *in litt.* 1992). In Emas National Park, Brazil, it is said to occur in buriti palm *Mauritia flexuosa* swamp and grassland (IBGE undated). Feeding habits are little known, but it has been reported foraging on grass seeds both in dry and near marshy areas (Ridgely and Tudor 1989, Bates *et al.* 1992). The breeding season has not been reported, but birds appeared to be paired in January (D. Willis verbally 1991) and frequent territorial disputes were observed at Puerto Boca in January 1992 between Rufous-rumped Seedeaters and both Entre Ríos *S. zelichi* and Marsh Seedeaters *S. palustris* (see relevant accounts), whose habitat requirements (at that locality) appeared to be identical. The gonadal condition of a bird taken on 28 October 1967 in Argentina suggested that it had already bred (Short 1969), although birds have been observed in mixed flocks with other seedeaters in October (see Distribution). The Rufous-rumped Seedeater may be "an austral migrant northwards" (Ridgely and Tudor 1989), although the available data are as yet inconclusive. Non-breeding birds appear to gather in mixed flocks of seedeaters (Ridgely and Tudor 1989, Bates *et al.* 1992).

THREATS Male seedeaters of various species are popular cagebirds in Brazil and Argentina, where heavy trapping pressure has led to serious declines in several species, especially the group (of which Rufous-rumped is one) known locally in Argentina as "capuchinos" (Narosky and Salvador 1985, Ridgely and Tudor 1989). The Esteros de Iberá are grazed by cattle, and the Iberá Natural Reserve is still inadequately protected (D. Willis verbally 1991, J. C. Chebez *in litt.* 1992). Threats affecting the grasslands of Mato Grosso, Goiás and adjacent states are outlined in Threats under Lesser Nothura *Nothura minor*.

MEASURES TAKEN None is known other than it occurs in the following protected areas: Iberá Natural Reserve and the projected Mburucuyá National Park, Argentina, and Emas and Pantanal Matogrossense National Parks, Brazil.

MEASURES PROPOSED Although the species cannot perhaps be considered under immediate threat, further investigation is required in order to clarify its range; it is particularly important to ascertain its breeding range in order to discover possible threats affecting it (see also Measures Proposed under Entre Ríos Seedeater and Strange-tailed Tyrant *Yetapa risora*).

TUMACO SEEDEATER *Sporophila insulata* E/Ex[4]

This small finch is known solely from four birds collected in 1912 on the island of Tumaco, south-west Colombia, a site now so heavily developed that it seems doubtful whether it still survives there.

DISTRIBUTION The Tumaco Seedeater (see Remarks) is only known from Isla de Tumaco (1°49'N 78°46'W; at sea level), less than 1 km from the coast of Nariño department, south-western Colombia (Chapman 1921a; coordinates from Paynter and Traylor 1981).

POPULATION The type-series consists of four specimens (a male, female, and two immature males) collected between 26 and 30 July 1912 (Chapman 1917a, 1921a): there have been no subsequent records, and it seems likely that the bird is now extinct (Ridgely and Tudor 1989).

ECOLOGY Nothing has been recorded of the life history of this species, although Chapman (1917a) described the island as dry and sandy with only stunted vegetation and mangroves on one side. Hilty and Brown (1986) suggested that the type-series was taken in open grassy and shrubby areas. Two of the specimens (collected at the end of July) were immatures, although it is apparently difficult to determine breeding season from the age of young *Sporophila* (Meyer de Schauensee 1952).

THREATS Open habitat, apparently suitable for seedeaters, is still available on this island, although the area where the type-series was collected is now heavily settled and covered by the town of Tumaco, the second largest harbour (and the area supporting the largest shrimp farms) on the Pacific coast of Colombia (LGN).

MEASURES TAKEN None is known: the development of the island appears to have proceeded unchecked and without any conservation initiatives. However, there have been several recent, unsuccessful searches for this species (G. Arango and B. Ortiz verbally 1991).

MEASURES PROPOSED The most obvious priority for the Tumaco Seedeater is to undertake systematic searches across all remaining habitat on the island of Tumaco. If it is found, and if it is to continue to survive, suitable habitat will have to be set aside. Searches may also be warranted throughout the adjacent mainland in Nariño department, Colombia, and Esmeraldas province, Ecuador.

REMARKS Ridgely and Tudor (1989) concluded that this species is almost certainly more nearly allied to (and possibly just an isolated population of) Chestnut-throated Seedeater *Sporophila telasco* than it is to Ruddy-breasted Seedeater *S. minuta*, with which it has traditionally been associated: however, they also suggested that the Tumaco Seedeater may represent a hybrid population between these other two species. These points need investigation, and studies of plumage variation within the Chestnut-throated Seedeater, which has been seen on the mainland adjacent to Tumaco (Ridgely and Tudor 1989), may help to clarify the situation.

HOODED SEEDEATER *Sporophila melanops* E/Ex[4]

Assuming that the type taken in western Goiás in 1823 is not an aberrant or a hybrid, this seedeater needs to be looked for near the type-locality and elsewhere in central Brazil.

DISTRIBUTION The Hooded Seedeater (see Remarks 1) is known only from a single bird (adult male) collected at a lake 15 km (see Remarks 2) north of "Porto do Rio Araguay", i.e. modern-day Registro do Araguaia, on the east bank of the rio Araguaia in extreme central-western Goiás, Brazil, 19 October 1823 (von Pelzeln 1868-1871, Hellmayr 1938). De Azara (1802-1805) had described a "pico grueso variable" among other seedeaters in Paraguay, which Bertoni (1914) assumed to be Hooded Seedeater, but Hellmayr (1938) regarded this to be unproven without specimens.

POPULATION Nothing is known.

ECOLOGY The type-specimen was taken from a flock of other finches at a lake; it was in heavy moult (von Pelzeln 1868-1871).

THREATS None is known.

MEASURES TAKEN None is known.

MEASURES PROPOSED Re-examination of the type would help determine its validity, while its colour reproduction in a field guide would stimulate interest in its rediscovery (that there are rare central Brazilian seedeaters is borne out by the case of Black-and-tawny Seedeater *Sporophila nigrorufa*: see relevant account). Seedeater flocks in Goiás and adjacent Mato Grosso require careful scrutiny; and, forlorn an undertaking as it may be, the type-locality needs to be revisited for its modern condition, with fieldwork ranging out to the nearest undisturbed lacustrine sites.

REMARKS (1) Ridgely and Tudor (1989) expressed doubts that this species was but an aberrant Yellow-bellied Seedeater *S. nigricollis* or otherwise a hybrid, a view repeated by Sibley and Monroe (1990), although both works continued to list it as valid. However, Hellmayr (1904, 1938), who had examined the specimen, described *melanops* as "a very distinct species [which] bears some resemblance to *S. n. nigricollis*, but differs at a glance [in various characters]". (2) The collector, J. Natterer, referred to the lake as "drei Meilen" north of the town, a "Meile" being equivalent to a league and hence 4.8 km.

BLACK-AND-TAWNY SEEDEATER *Sporophila nigrorufa* I[7]

Apparently known as yet from only five certain areas in extreme eastern Bolivia and adjacent west-central Brazil, this very local seedeater is at risk owing to the continuing conversion of its remaining areas of campo grassland.

DISTRIBUTION All five areas in which the Black-and-tawny Seedeater (see Remarks 1) has been recorded lie in the block which falls athwart the Bolivia–Brazil border at 13-19°S 56-61°W. The listing of Goiás by von Ihering and von Ihering (1907) was in error.

Bolivia Records are from three sites, all in eastern Santa Cruz department: in a small area of grassland at Flor de Oro, a ranch on the Bolivian side of the río Guaporé at the north end of the Serranía de Huanchaca, opposite the Brazilian town of Pimenteiras in Rondônia, where the species was the most numerous *Sporophila* noted in late May and June 1991 (TAP) and where two flocks of 15 and 10 were seen in late March 1992, birds having been observed there by a fish biologist since at least February (B. M. Whitney *in litt.* 1992); in the Los Fierros grasslands along the western base of the Serranía de Huanchaca, where at least two adult males were identified among large numbers of seedeaters in August 1989 (Bates *et al.* 1992); "Chiquitos", a province at 16°S 60°W, second half of 1831, where the type-material was obtained (Hellmayr 1938, Paynter *et al.* 1975).

Brazil The species has been found with certainty in only two areas, although birds likely to be this species have been reported from three others, which are included below (the last three under Mato Grosso) with their provisional nature indicated:

Mato Grosso just outside Mato Grosso city (now called Vila Bela da Santíssima Trindade) at "an open hut" called Poruti, where eight specimens were collected in October 1826 (von Pelzeln 1868-1871; see Remarks 2), and somewhat further east on the road towards Pontes e Lacerda, where birds were seen in January 1988 (Willis and Oniki 1990; see Population); Recanto Passárgada, 15°44'S 56°05'W, 1987 or 1988, possibly; Porto Limão, 16°10'S 58°05'W, late 1980s, possibly; between Poconé and Porto Jofre, late 1980s, possibly (Willis and Oniki 1990);

Mato Grosso do Sul east of Corumbá, where a male was seen in October 1979 (Ridgely and Tudor 1989). Two juveniles collected at Corumbá in September 1893 were suspected of being this species (Salvadori 1895b).

POPULATION There are no published estimates of population size in this species, and evidence on abundance is largely as given in Distribution above. At Flor de Oro, Bolivia, in a grassland of c.20 km^2 there were probably several hundred individuals in late May 1991, since up to 12 singing males (and numerous probable females) were located easily during walks of c.2 km through the preferred habitat (TAP); against this, the species was outnumbered by four other *Sporophila* species in the Los Fierros savanna to the south-west in late August 1989 (TAP). On the grasslands east of Vila Bela da Santíssima Trindade 55 birds were counted over 18-19 January 1988 (Willis and Oniki 1990).

ECOLOGY At Flor de Oro, Bolivia, this species was found in late May and June 1991 in seasonally flooded grassland with scattered clumps of bushes and trees, a habitat heavily grazed by cattle, and the evenly spaced patches of woody vegetation appeared to be growing on decomposing termite mounds; territorial males sang from exposed perches atop small trees in these patches, territories being small, as up to three or four males were counter-singing within small areas of c.1-2 ha (TAP). Lesser numbers of singing Plumbeous Seedeaters *Sporophila plumbea* were observed in the same areas, and their territories appeared to overlap with those of *S. nigrorufa*; both species clung to stalks and fed on seeds of several species of grasses that were in flower (TAP). In mid-August of the same year no male *nigrorufa* was found at this locality, although male *plumbea* and numerous unidentified female-plumaged *Sporophila* were still present, suggesting that the species may be migratory or nomadic, although in August 1989 two adult male *nigrorufa* were observed in the Los Fierros savanna not far to the south-west of Flor de Oro: these birds were in large mixed flocks of up to several hundred individuals of at least four additional *Sporophila* seedeaters (Dark-throated *S. ruficollis*, Rufous-rumped *S. hypochroma*, Tawny-bellied *S. hypoxantha*, and Plumbeous in order of abundance), all feeding on grass seeds in relatively undisturbed, seasonally inundated grassland at the edge of Noel Kempff Mercado National Park (TAP; also Bates *et al.* 1992). The grasslands at both Flor de Oro and Los Fierros are surrounded by tall tropical evergreen forest; to reach the nearest similar habitat to the south or east, grassland species such as the above *Sporophila* must fly over extensive areas of such forest; similarly, the grasslands near San José de Chiquitos (if this in particular was signified by the "Chiquitos" of the type-locality) are surrounded by deciduous forests and dense cerrados (TAP). In January 1988 (summer) the Black-and-tawny Seedeater was the only bird singing in partially inundated grasslands at Campos do Encanto (Willis and Oniki 1990), but little singing was noted in birds in Noel Kempff Mercado in March 1992 (B. M. Whitney *in litt.* 1992).

THREATS The devastation wrought by farming on the grassland ecosystems of central Brazil and hence on the populations of species endemic to them is outlined in Threats under Lesser Nothura *Nothura minor*. Unfortunately, portions of the protected areas identified below are still being grazed and/or burnt almost annually, and a growing human population is placing more and more pressure on the Brazilian pantanal (TAP). The problem of conserving the Black-and-tawny Seedeater appears to be compounded by its possibly nomadic or migratory behaviour, which means that single-site protection will be inadequate.

MEASURES TAKEN Much of the known habitat of this species lies in or near the Noel Kempff Mercado National Park in Bolivia and the Pantanal Matogrossense National Park in Brazil. The authorities at Noel Kempff Mercado have decided gradually to remove cattle and to restrict burning of the grassland at Flor de Oro; they are also aware of the biological importance of the seasonally flooded grassland near Los Fierros (many vertebrates and presumably plants that do not occur elsewhere in the park occur in these two localities) and have expressed a desire to acquire it from local ranchers (TAP).

MEASURES PROPOSED It seems obvious that this species will be found in many new localities within its restricted range, and should, for example, be expected in Rondônia; but it may also be the case that its centre of abundance lies in the small area defined by 14-16°S 59-61°W, focused on the Serranía de Huanchaca and its adjacent grasslands, notably to the south-east (east of Vila Bela de Santíssima Trindade). Biological surveys of these extensive flooded grasslands and forests in the headwater region of the rio Guaporé south-east of Serra Ricardo Franco in western Mato Grosso are thus urgently needed; it is hoped that, in the absence of government action, private reserves will be established in this region and to the south in the Bolivian pantanal, where vast areas of seasonal grasslands and dry forests survive in good condition (TAP). Furthermore, cattle must eventually be removed from the drier portions of the Pantanal Matogrossense National Park and adjacent areas so that the original flora and fauna will have a chance to recover from the effects of constant grazing and over-burning, for although the belief has been expressed that cattle and wildlife can co-exist harmlessly, the long-term effects of ranching practices on most native grassland plants and animals is probably devastating. Upland grasslands in the San José de Chiquitos area of eastern Bolivia will hopefully be included in a recently proposed national park that would encompass much of the Serranía de Santiago; such a park would protect outlying populations of numerous Brazilian Shield endemics (TAP).

REMARKS (1) The taxonomic status of this and numerous other *Sporophila* species needs to be clarified through behavioural, morphological and biochemical studies. Several of the taxa currently recognized as full species may prove to be colour morphs or well-marked subspecies of other species; likewise, some isolated forms of widespread species may prove to be specifically distinct. Because the breeding ranges and habitats of many *Sporophila* species are restricted and subject to habitat destruction, such studies are urgently needed. A general taxonomic revision of the entire genus would be of great value to bird conservationists. (2) Poruti and (Vila Bela de) Mato Grosso have usually been cited as two different sites (e.g. in von Ihering and von Ihering 1907, Hellmayr 1938), and indeed Hellmayr (1938) reported skins labelled from the two places; yet it appears that the latter was intended as a geographical qualifier of the former, and certainly the two were so close together (see von Pelzeln 1868-1871, Paynter and Traylor 1991) that they count here as one place.

MARSH SEEDEATER *Sporophila palustris* K[12]

This small bird of marshes and grasslands in central-southern South America (Brazil, Paraguay, Uruguay and Argentina) appears to be extremely local owing to habitat loss and trade, but may be under-recorded.

DISTRIBUTION The Marsh Seedeater (see Remarks 1) occurs to about 1,100 m in south-central South America, being recorded very locally from south-central Brazil, north-central Paraguay, north-eastern Argentina and Uruguay; it is probably an austral migrant, and apparently only a summer resident (November to April) in the southern portion of its breeding range (Ridgely and Tudor 1989).

Brazil The northernmost records must refer to wintering migrants (Sick 1985).

Minas Gerais The only record is from an island on the rio São Francisco near Pirapora, where a male was collected on 21 September 1973 (specimen in MNRJ; also Sick 1985).

Goiás Records are only from Emas National Park, October 1979-1981 (Ridgely and Tudor 1989), and again in 1984 (R. A. Rowlett *per* B. C. Forrester *in litt.* 1992).

Mato Grosso The species has been recorded recently from Poconé (C. Yamashita verbally 1987).

Mato Grosso do Sul There are records from Campo Grande (Sick 1985), Corumbá and Porto Murtinho, the last consisting of one male in a group of other seedeaters in November 1987 (C. Yamashita verbally 1987).

Rio Grande do Sul Belton (1984-1985) recorded it from "scattered marshy localities in south and west between November 3 and February 19"; although four of these localities are indicated on a map, only two are specified: Fazenda Casa Branca, 29°36'S 56°15'W, Alegrete, where a pair was collected on 20 (*sic*) February 1975; and near Canal de São Gonçalo across from Santa Isabel (Santa Isabel do Sul), where one bird was seen on 7 January 1976 (Belton 1984-1985, whence coordinates). An older record is from Itaqui, where four males and one female were obtained in November 1914 (specimens in MZUSP; also Pinto 1944).

Paraguay Older records are from Villa Concepción (Kerr 1901; see Remarks 2), Estancia Hermosa and río Siete Pontas (Meyer de Schauensee 1966). The species was seen in pantanal habitat at Surubi-y (untraced), Central department, March 1990 (J. Escobar *in litt.* 1991); it was found in grasslands south-west of San Juan Bautista in Misiones, March 1991 (P. A. Scharf *per* R. S. Ridgely *in litt.* 1991), with a sighting in the former (at Estancia Ñu Pora) of two in March 1989 (F. E. Hayes *in litt.* 1991); and a bird has been seen in Mbaracayú National Park, Canindeyú department (P. A. Scharf *per* F. E. Hayes *in litt.* 1991).

Argentina Records are from: (*Misiones*) on the Argentine side of Iguazú Falls, recently (D. Finch per B. C. Forrester *in litt.* 1992), and otherwise by the reports of local bird-trappers near Posadas, although searches there have been fruitless (A. Garello *per* J. C. Chebez *in litt.* 1992); (*Chaco*) Chaco National Park, 1985 (Saibene 1985; also J. C. Chebez *in litt.* 1986, Ridgely and Tudor 1989); (*Corrientes*) Mburucuyá, 28°03'S 58°14'W, January 1991 (J. Hutton *per* J. C. Chebez *in litt.* 1992; coordinates from Paynter 1985); in the Esteros del Iberá zone north of Mercedes, February 1983 (J. C. Chebez *in litt.* 1986) and January 1991 (D. Willis *in litt.* 1991); Colonia Carlos Pellegrini, 28°32'S 57°10'W, where breeding proved, November 1976 (S. Narosky *per* J. C. Chebez *in litt.* 1992; coordinates from Paynter 1985); (*Entre Ríos*) an undated locality, November 1983 (D. F. Stotz *in litt.* 1988); the type-locality, Concepción del Uruguay, 1880/1881 (Barrows 1883, Hellmayr 1938; specimens in BMNH, MCZ); río Mandisoví, 30°56'S 57°55'W, March 1939 (specimen in MNHNM; coordinates from Paynter 1985); from the vicinity of arroyo Barú, untraced, 1968; and Paranacito, untraced, 1968 (M. Nores and D. Yzurieta *in litt.* 1986); Federal department near arroyo Feliciano, January 1987 (Chebez *et al.* in prep.); arroyo Capilla (c.33°00'S

58°28'W), repeatedly in summer (breeding) since 1988; Balneario Ñandubaysal (c.33°02'S 58°16'W), January 1990; Colonia Ubajay (c.33°02'S 58°16'W), December 1990; Puerto Boca (33°03'S 58°23'W), December/January 1991/1992, where breeding proved (all records at these four sites and coordinates from E. I. Abadie, B. M. López Lanús and M. Pearman *in litt.* 1992); (*Buenos Aires*) Otamendi Strict Nature Reserve (A. G. di Giacomo *per* J. C. Chebez *in litt.* 1992). An untraced locality is Isla Ella (two specimens in BMNH), somewhere in the Paraná delta (J. C. Chebez *in litt.* 1992), also a site for Dot-winged Crake *Porzana spiloptera*, as is the Otamendi reserve (see relevant account).

Uruguay Records are from Colonia Palma, on the río Uruguay, Artigas department, where one male was collected in November 1955; north-west of Laguna Negra, Rocha department, where six or seven birds were seen daily between 24 and 27 February 1961 (both from Vaz-Ferreira and Gerzenstein 1961); and Bañados de India Muerta, also in Rocha, where two birds were seen on each of three occasions in October 1985, November 1986 and December 1987 (Arballo 1990). A. R. M. Gepp (*in litt.* 1986) referred to its local occurrence in November–February close to the río Uruguay in Salto and Artigas departments.

POPULATION The population status of the Marsh Seedeater is not clear. The species is certainly very local and, although Narosky and Yzurieta (1987) included it in the category "rare or very difficult to see" (in Argentina), it was considered locally "fairly common" by Ridgely and Tudor (1989), who noted, however, that it is apparently declining as a result of cagebird trafficking. It is indeed considered "very scarce in Argentina" (M. Nores and D. Yzurieta *in litt.* 1986) and, from the results of a recent survey, it seems clear that the species has declined substantially on its breeding grounds in north-eastern Argentina, thus deserving endangered status (Narosky and Salvador 1985, Ridgely and Tudor 1989), a conclusion endorsed by M. Nores and D. Yzurieta (*in litt.* 1986) and, for Uruguay, by A. R. M. Gepp *in litt.* (1986). In Brazil, it is apparently not rare locally in the pantanal (C. Yamashita verbally 1987), and it may be that this and other *Sporophila* species are not so much rare as poorly known (D. F. Stotz *in litt.* 1988).

ECOLOGY The Marsh Seedeater has been recorded in marshes and grasslands (Vaz-Ferreira and Gerzenstein 1961, Sick 1985, Ridgely and Tudor 1989), the type-locality being described as "an indescribable mixture of land, water, and grass – the latter predominating" (Barrows 1883). In Uruguay, it was found in the same habitat as the near-threatened Dark-throated Seedeater *S. ruficollis* (Vaz-Ferreira and Gerzenstein 1961); at Emas National Park, Goiás, the species has been found to be a regular member of mixed non-breeding *Sporophila* flocks (Ridgely and Tudor 1989); in September it was recorded on an island on the upper rio São Francisco with 10 other species of this genus, forming a concentration of "hundreds" of migrating birds in seeding *Echinochloa crus-pavonis* grasslands (Sick 1985); at the Esteros del Iberá it was recorded together with the near-threatened Chestnut Seedeater *S. cinnamomea* and two other species of the genus (D. Willis *in litt.* 1991). In Entre Ríos it inhabits both marshes along rivers and isolated humid marshes, dominated by *Panicum grumosum* which, together with other marsh vegetation such as *Cortaderia selloana*, *Scirpus californicus* and *Eryngium* spp. and bushes such as *Acacia caven*, *Salix humboldtiana* and *Cephalantus glabratus*, are used for perching and song-posts, with seeds of *Paspalum dilatatum*, *C. selloana* and others being taken as food (M. Pearman *in litt.* 1992). Its seasonal movements have been considered a post-breeding wandering, particularly as wet areas dry up in autumn and winter (Short 1975). Breeding has been recorded in north-eastern Argentina (Narosky and Salvador 1985, Ridgely and Tudor 1989). Birds collected in high, dense grass in a marsh, November, were considered to be breeding there (Barrows 1883). A nest with two eggs, apparently a full clutch, was found in late December 1991 and dependent fledged young have been observed in February (E. I. Abadie and M. Pearman *in litt.* 1992). A male collected on 20 February 1975 in Rio Grande do Sul had enlarged testes, but a female on the same date had inactive ovaries (Belton 1984-1985). At arroyo Capilla, where the species was present at a high density, one territory was estimated to be 50x30 m (M. Pearman *in litt.* 1992).

THREATS Male seedeaters of various species are popular cagebirds in Brazil and Argentina, where heavy trapping pressure has led to serious declines in several species, especially the group known locally in Argentina as "capuchinos" (Narosky and Salvador 1985, Ridgely and Tudor 1989). Failure to find the species at Posadas, Misiones, Argentina, was suspected to reflect exhaustion of the population there by bird-trappers (J. C. Chebez *in litt.* 1992). Vaz-Ferreira and Gerzenstein (1961) recorded that, in the area where a specimen was obtained (Colonia Palma, Artigas) in Uruguay, every year birds are captured to be kept in captivity. The Esteros del Iberá, judged by one well travelled observer to be the finest grassland seen anywhere in South America, are much grazed by cattle and suffer much annual burning (D. Willis verbally 1991).

MEASURES TAKEN The species is protected under Brazilian law (Bernardes *et al.* 1990) and has been recorded from Emas National Park. In Paraguay there is a record from Mbaracayú National Park, and in Argentina reports from the planned Mburucuyá National Park and the existing Chaco National Park, Iberá Provincial Park and Otamendi Strict Nature Reserve. The Iberá grasslands in Argentina (about 20,000 km^2 including at least one city) is grazed by cattle and outside the provincial park boundary at least burning is a standard practice (D. Willis *in litt.* 1991). At one south-east Entre Ríos breeding locality the population and its habitat is protected by the landowner (M. Pearman verbally 1992).

MEASURES PROPOSED Narosky and Salvador (1985) urged the prohibition of the trapping, trading and keeping of the "capuchino" seedeaters, namely Marsh, Tawny-bellied *S. hypoxantha*, Dark-throated, Chestnut, Rufous-rumped *S. hypochroma* and Entre Ríos *S. zelichi* (see relevant account). Surveys should be conducted in order to determine better the species's range and status, and in Argentina it would seem important to target those areas in Entre Ríos, namely Puerto Boca and arroyo Capilla, where the species has been found at reasonably high densities and where the other threatened or near-threatened seedeaters, Entre Ríos, Rufous-rumped and Chestnut, have also been recorded (M. Pearman *in litt.* 1992); in Corrientes three of these (not Entre Ríos Seedeater) occur together around Laguna Iberá (D. Willis *in litt.* 1991) and should clearly be studied and conserved as a group. The conservation of Puerto Boca would be particularly satisfying, as it also holds the threatened Sickle-winged Nightjar *Eleothreptus anomalus* and Saffron-cowled Blackbird *Xanthopsar flavus* as well as the near-threatened Black-and-white Monjita *Heteroxolmis dominicana* (M. Pearman *in litt.* 1992).

REMARKS (1) Short (1975) provisionally included this bird and *S. ruficollis* within *S. hypoxantha*, which would be a polymorphic species, with rufous-, black- and white-throated phases in males, the *palustris* form occurring rarely and totally within the range of the others; while Sick (1985) and other authorities did not follow this treatment, Ridgely and Tudor (1989) partially agreed, considering *S. palustris* and *S. ruficollis* closely related and possibly only colour phases of a single species (though never having found them at the same locality), but pointing out that neither seems to be especially close to *S. hypoxantha*, a considerably more numerous and widespread species. (2) The identification of the specimen (lost) from Villa Concepción has been considered doubtful (Hellmayr 1938).

ENTRE RIOS SEEDEATER *Sporophila zelichi* E[2]

Restricted as a breeding bird to a small part of Entre Ríos province, Argentina, and wintering in areas unknown, this handsome but very poorly known seedeater may be at considerable risk from bird-trappers as well as from the burning of its summer habitat.

DISTRIBUTION The Entre Ríos Seedeater (see Remarks) is known only from a few localities in Entre Ríos province, Argentina, although like other closely related species in its genus it is believed to be a migrant whose wintering areas remain unknown but are presumably to the north (Narosky 1977, Olrog 1979, Narosky and Salvador 1985, Ridgely and Tudor 1989). Coordinates below are taken from Paynter (1985).

The few localities where the species has been found (as listed in Narosky 1977) are: arroyo Perucho Verne (arroyo Perucho Verna at 32°10'S 58°10'W), where an adult male (the type-specimen) was collected on 28 February 1969 and where birds are known to have nested (see Ecology); Puerto Liebig (c.32°08'S 58°16'W), where an adult male was taken on 3 February 1975; and 30 km north of Concordia, where two males (adult and immature) were kept in captivity, having been captured in February 1971 and February 1973 respectively. The species has also been recorded once in El Palmar National Park (c.31°49'S 58°15'W), in May (year not given) (Baliño 1984), and recently at Puerto Boca (33°03'S 58°23'W), where a male (apparently paired with a female) and a subadult male were observed during December 1991 and January 1992 (E. I. Abadie, B. M. López Lanús and M. Pearman *in litt.* 1991). Canevari *et al.* (1991) included Federación (31°00'S 57°54'W) as a locality where the species can be found, but did not provide further details.

POPULATION The Entre Ríos Seedeater was known to M. R. Zelich, for whom it was named, some 60 years ago, and he described it as "rare" between 1925 and 1935 (Narosky 1977). However, during investigations in the 1970s and 1980s it proved to be well known to bird-trappers and collectors by whom it was "regularly observed" and collected in marshy areas in central and eastern parts of Entre Ríos province, although only three captive birds and no wild ones could then be found (Narosky and Salvador 1985).

ECOLOGY The Entre Ríos Seedeater is reported to occur in semi-open areas near small, clear streams, especially where there are small patches of low woodland (Narosky 1977; also Ridgely and Tudor 1989). The male at Puerto Boca had a territory delimited by *Acacia* sp. (used as song posts) at the edge of a large stand of *Panicum grumosum* in a marsh with 20-40 cm surface water (drying out by 19 January 1992). Other important plants used for perching or song posts within the territory were *Eryngium* spp.; the males at Puerto Boca fed on seeds of *Paspalum dilatatum* and other grasses (E. I. Abadie, B. M. López Lanús and M. Pearman *in litt.* 1992). The breeding season falls sometime between November and March (Narosky 1977). Nesting was reported in 1967 at arroyo Perucho Verna, although with no further details (Narosky 1977). On 28 December 1991, the male at Puerto Boca sang infrequently and territory was ill-defined; on 9 January 1992, it sang very frequently, and kept strictly to its territory, which was estimated to be 70 by 50 m, and in late January 1992 a pair was observed feeding a dependent juvenile at the site; territorial interactions were observed with male Marsh Seedeater *Sporophila palustris* and particularly with Rufous-rumped Seedeater *S. hypochroma* (E. I. Abadie, B. M. López Lanús and M. Pearman *in litt.* 1992), both of which have problems of their own (see relevant accounts). In March, birds are known to gather in mixed flocks of adults and juveniles with other closely related *Sporophila* species (Narosky 1977). At Puerto Boca, the three specimens of *zelichi* had departed by early March, but many Marsh Seedeaters remained on the breeding grounds (E. I. Abadie, B. M. López Lanús and M. Pearman *in litt.* 1992).

THREATS Male seedeaters of various species are popular cagebirds in Brazil and Argentina, where heavy trapping pressure has led to serious declines in several species, especially the group known locally as "capuchinos" (Narosky and Salvador 1985, Ridgely and Tudor 1989), to which the Entre Ríos Seedeater belongs; indeed, according to Narosky and Salvador (1985), this species may be especially targeted by bird collectors as its plumage is one of the most conspicuous of the group. Overgrazing and fires in stands of tall natural grasses present serious threats on the breeding grounds (E. I. Abadie, B. M. López Lanús and M. Pearman *in litt.* 1992).

MEASURES TAKEN None is known. The species has been recorded in El Palmar National Park (see Distribution).

MEASURES PROPOSED Narosky and Salvador (1985) urged the prohibition of the trapping, trading and keeping of the "capuchino" seedeaters, namely Tawny-bellied *Sporophila hypoxantha*, Dark-throated *S. ruficollis*, Rufous-rumped, Chestnut *S. cinnamomea* (near-threatened), Marsh and Entre Ríos. Surveys should be conducted in order to locate and estimate surviving populations in those areas where the species has been recorded, and in adjacent regions where habitat is favourable, including the adjacent area of Uruguay where the bird could be present. Preliminary survey work shows Puerto Boca to be an important locality for the species, where it breeds and occurs alongside four other threatened birds, Marsh Seedeater, Rufous-rumped Seedeater, Saffron-cowled Blackbird *Xanthopsar flavus* and Sickle-winged Nightjar *Eleothreptus anomalus* (see relevant accounts) and the near-threatened Black-and-White Monjita *Heteroxolmis dominicanus*. At this locality preferred breeding habitat covers less than 2 ha and requires immediate protection (E. I. Abadie, B. M. López Lanús and M. Pearman *in litt.* 1992). Vigilance is urged in those countries where the species is likely to occur during the austral winter (e.g. Bolivia, Brazil and Paraguay) in order to determine its year-round distribution.

REMARKS The taxonomic status of this species has been controversial, owing to its affinities to others in the group, but at present its specific rank is accepted (e.g. Narosky 1977, Ridgely and Tudor 1989, Sibley and Monroe 1990, Canevari *et al.* 1991).

YELLOW-HEADED BRUSH-FINCH *Atlapetes flaviceps* I[7]

This very rare species is endemic to the Central Andes of Colombia, where it is known from four specimens taken in 1911 and 1942, a bird mist-netted in 1967, and a population discovered in 1989. Clearance of most of the natural vegetation within its limited range seems likely to have caused a population decline.

DISTRIBUTION The Yellow-headed Brush-finch has been recorded from three localities along the upper Magdalena valley in Tolima and Huila departments, on the eastern slope of the Central Andes, where localities (coordinates from Paynter and Traylor 1981) include: (*Tolima*) río Toche (4°26'N 75°22'W; east of Quindío on the Quindío trail), where the type-series (a male and juvenile female in AMNH) was taken at 2,075 m in October 1911 (Chapman 1912); Toche (4°32'N 75°25'W), where a male and female (in ANSP) were collected at 2,255 m in May 1942; between Toche and km 27 (east of Tapias, on the road from Ibagué), where a population was found at c.2,000 m in 1989 (P. Kaestner *in litt.* 1992); and (*Huila*) La Plata Vieja (= La Plata, at 2°23'N 75°53'W; in the middle of the río La Plata Vieja valley), where a single bird was mist-netted and photographed on 18 December 1967 at c.1,300 m (Dunning 1982, Hilty and Brown 1986, H. W. Dunning *in litt.* 1991).

POPULATION Until 1989, the Yellow-headed Brush-finch was only known from two specimens taken in 1911, two more taken near the type-locality in 1942, and a bird trapped in 1967 (see above): however, the species was found to be common (although hard to see) along a 30 km stretch of road between (south-east of) Toche and km 27, with birds seen (usually commonly) in small flocks on all of six visits to the area between March 1989 and June 1990 (P. Kaestner *in litt.* 1992). Despite its apparent abundance at this site, the size of the population remains unknown (P. Kaestner *in litt.* 1992).

ECOLOGY The specimens of this bird were taken at 2,075 and 2,255 m, with the mist-netted birds apparently trapped at c.1,300 m (Hilty and Brown 1986), and recent observations from c.2,000 m (see Distribution). The type-series was collected upriver on the río Toche, which was generally "heavily forested, humid and luxuriant", although the two specimens were taken from the "brush covering the cleared mountainsides of the open valley" (Chapman 1917a). The ANSP specimens were apparently taken in "forest" (Ridgely and Tudor 1989), but Hilty and Brown (1986) suggested that the habitat of this species is apparently similar to that of the Dusky-headed Brush-finch *A. fuscoolivaceus*, i.e. second growth, shrubby forest borders, and bushy overgrown pastures. This suggestion appears to have been confirmed by recent observations near Toche, where birds were seen on highly disturbed hillsides with thick secondary vegetation, especially where there were vines and some remnant forest trees still standing (P. Kaestner *in litt.* 1992). Small flocks of the brush-finch (rarely in mixed bird flocks) foraged in the vines and bushes, calling only infrequently (P. Kaestner *in litt.* 1992). Birds seen in March were all deemed to be adults (with yellow heads), whereas in November many presumably young birds (with olive heads: see Remarks) were present (P. Kaestner *in litt.* 1992), suggesting a breeding season during the middle of the year.

THREATS It is likely that habitat disturbance and, mainly, forest clearance along the foothills of the eastern slope of the Central Andes has been the main, if not the only cause of decline of this upper Magdalena valley endemic (LGN; also Ridgely and Tudor 1989).

MEASURES TAKEN None is known.

MEASURES PROPOSED Surveys should be undertaken to determine the current range and ecological requirements of this species. In particular, studies are needed on populations that appear to exist in secondary habitats (e.g. near Toche) in order to determine whether they are viable, and consequently to assess the true extent and nature of the threats that the species faces. Patches of remaining primary habitat in the foothill areas on the eastern slope of the Central Andes, in both Tolima and Huila, need protected area status to ensure that this and other bird species (see below) are conserved. Obviously, any fieldwork or conservation initiatives should take into account proposals for the Tolima Dove *Leptotila conoveri* (see relevant account), which is sympatric with the Yellow-headed Brush-finch between Toche and Ibagué, and has also been observed in secondary habitats. Other sympatric species and conservation initiatives relevant to this area are mentioned in the equivalent section under Tolima Dove.

REMARKS The type-specimen in AMNH has an olive-yellow head, but the other bird there is mostly olive (it has a scattering of yellow feathers with yellow lores and eye-ring): the bird photographed in December 1967 is like the latter but with less yellow, and the specimens in ANSP show equal variation with the female having a yellower head than the (second) male (Ridgely and Tudor 1989). Recent observations (see Ecology) suggest that the usual head coloration (i.e. mature adult) is yellow, with immature birds showing varying degrees of olive, apparently confirming that the type-series is representative, and that the English name should be Yellow-headed rather than Olive-headed Brush-finch (see Hilty and Brown 1986, Ridgely and Tudor 1989).

PALE-HEADED BRUSH-FINCH *Atlapetes pallidiceps* E/Ex[4]

This finch is known from southern Ecuador, where it inhabits oases in the arid intermontane valleys at elevations ranging from c.1,500 to 2,100 m. The human pressure on areas with water in this region is great, and if it is not extinct the species survives only in small patches of shrubbery bordering streams and irrigated farmland.

DISTRIBUTION The Pale-headed Brush-finch (see Remarks 1) is known from c.24 specimens, taken at five different localities in Azuay and Loja provinces, southern Ecuador. The four Azuay localities are in the upper río Jubones drainage, while the one Loja site appears to be in the drainage of the río Catamayo, an affluent of río Chira. Localities (from north to south, coordinates unless otherwise stated from Paynter and Traylor 1977) are:

Azuay Girón, 2,100 m, río Girón drainage, at c.3°10'S 79°08'W (specimen in ANSP collected in June 1939: Meyer de Schauensee 1948-1952); Yunguilla valley, 1,500 m, río Yunguilla drainage, at c.3°18'S 79°18'W (one specimen in ANSP and two in MECN, collected in July 1939, also two specimens in MCZ collected in August 1955 and in April 1961: Meyer de Schauensee 1948-1952); 10 km north-north-west of Oña, 1,900 m, río León drainage, at c.3°27'S 79°11'W (nine specimens in MCZ collected in November 1965: Paynter 1972a); Guishapa, Oña, 1,830 m, the type-locality, untraced (see Remarks 2), but presumably near Oña, which is in the río León drainage, at 3°32'S 79°10'W (three specimens in BMNH collected in May 1899: Sharpe 1900, Chubb 1919, Hellmayr 1938);

Loja Casanga valley, río Casanga drainage, a tributary of río Catamayo, at c.3°57'S 79°36'W (two specimens in AMNH and four in MECN, collected between 31 December 1968 and 6 January 1969: coordinates estimated from IGM 1989). If the specimens from Casanga valley are correctly labelled (see Remarks 1), then the species may also occur in the intermediate valley, the upper drainage of the río Puyango (an affluent of the río Tumbes) in Loja and adjacent western El Oro provinces.

POPULATION The species was found to be fairly common in a small patch of habitat in 1965 (Paynter 1972a): however, suitable habitat is scarce in the dry interandean valleys of southern Ecuador (NK), so even if this species is confirmed to range south to the Casanga valley, the total population must be very small. Recent searches in the Oña region and near Abdon Calderón and Santa Isabel along the río Jubones, as well as a brief search (at too low an elevation) in the Casanga valley, have been in vain but are inconclusive (R. S. Ridgely *in litt.* 1990, NK): for example, B. M. Whitney (*in litt.* 1991) searched the Oña areas of the río León drainage in March 1990, as did B. J. Best (*in litt.* 1992) in February 1991 and L. F. Kiff (*in litt.* 1991) in March 1991, all three expeditions failing to find any evidence of the species. Most recently (March 1992), M. B. Robbins (*in litt.* 1992) searched in relatively good stands of *Acacia* scrub, the two best areas being in quebradas above the río León (below and to the north of Oña) at 1,950 and 2,100 m: one of these areas was very likely the same quebrada where Paynter (1972a) found the species fairly common in November 1965, and the understorey in both quebradas seemed dense enough to support several pairs of *Atlapetes*: every bird species encountered in this area was singing (i.e. breeding or had just finished), yet no *Atlapetes* were vocalizing in the areas covered (M. B. Robbins *in litt.* 1992). An extensive *Acacia* scrub woodland, continuous from 1,500 to 1,800 m, c.2 km west-north-west of Catacocha in the Casanga valley, was searched in April 1992, and as in the Oña area all birds were vocalizing, yet only White-winged Brush-finch *A. leucopterus* and, lower down, White-headed Brush-finch *A. albiceps* were recorded (M. B. Robbins *in litt.* 1992): it seems likely therefore that this brush-finch is not present in the Casanga valley or indeed near Oña, at least during the normal breeding period.

ECOLOGY In 1965 the species was found in an oasis where a few hectares of artificially irrigated fields were interlaced with shrubs, and where some low trees and humid scrub bordered a brook; there was little thick undergrowth present, and the species occurred mainly in "tree-sized acacias"; it is not known whether it normally frequents trees or was forced to be more arboreal than congeners because of the absence of thickets (Paynter 1972a). Although shy, it was fairly conspicuous as it flew from tree to tree: it usually occurred singly, sometimes in pairs, and only on one occasion were three seen together (Paynter 1972a). A single bird was seen on the ground in an area with coffee bushes and shade trees, and appeared to be turning dead leaves with its bill (Paynter 1972a).

Paynter (1972a) examined the stomachs of eight individuals: all contained a good deal of sand, which at times made up almost half of the material in a full stomach; insect remains were found in six, varying from very little to 25% of the recognizable material; most birds had relatively large pieces of what appeared to be endosperm from a big seed, the outer coating of which was never attached, and it seems likely that the seed was cracked before ingestion and the endosperm extracted in chunks; a few very small seeds (2 mm or less) of several types were also noted; and a minute cocoon (2x5 mm) and tiny (3x8 mm) larval coat of something like a fly larva were found in one specimen.

The only information on breeding is from specimens: of four taken in early January three males had small testes, while one female had a medium to large ovary, one of them (a male) being in fresh plumage, the others worn (skins in MECN); one taken in June or July is immature (Meyer de Schauensee 1948-1952), as is one (in MECN) collected in July 1939 (see Remarks 3). Skull ossification appears to be slow in the species, as all eight November specimens examined for this feature had incompletely (though almost fully) ossified skulls (MCZ label data).

THREATS The species is critically threatened (if still extant) by habitat destruction. The intensive cultivation wherever water is available in these arid valleys has presumably already forced it into marginal habitat. Large numbers of goats have stripped almost the entire valley of vegetation, leaving an eroded, desert-like landscape (NK). Nevertheless, apparently suitable patches of *Acacia* scrub were found north of Oña along two quebradas in March 1992 (M. B. Robbins *in litt.* 1992), and indeed B. M. Whitney (*in litt.* 1991) noted patches of woodland with "tree-sized acacias", other trees and woody shrubs (*Tillandsia*-covered) and a healthy understorey growth, totalling an estimated c.100 ha, in this area: an extensive area of *Acacia* scrub woodland was also found in the Casanga valley in April 1992 (M. B. Robbins *in litt.* 1992: see Population).

MEASURES TAKEN None is known.

MEASURES PROPOSED An intensive search for the species should be started immediately in order to establish its current status, identify its precise ecological requirements and evaluate the status of its preferred habitat, and any threats it may face. Searches should be undertaken in the apparently suitable habitat that remains near Oña (see Population), preferably in November, or at least prior to the wet season and the onset of the breeding season in this area (searches in February–March drew blank, yet the last records there stem from November). It is likely that the species's rediscovery would have to be followed immediately by an intensive programme of habitat conservation in close liaison with local communities.

REMARKS (1) Paynter (1972a) regarded the Pale-headed Brush-finch as a close relative of the smaller White-winged Brush-finch, which occurs as three subspecies: nominate *leucopterus* at 600-2,900 m on the interandean plateau and west slope of the Andes in Ecuador from Imbabura province south to western Azuay, *paynteri* at 1,700-2,200 m in southernmost Cordillera del Condor and the Huancabamba region, Cajamarca and Piura departments, Peru, and *dresseri* at 700-2,500 m on the Pacific slope from south-west Cajamarca, Peru, north to Cerros de Amotape, Cordillera Larga, Cordillera de Alamor, Cordillera de Celica, and Casanga valley, north-west Peru and south-west Ecuador (Chapman 1926, Paynter 1972a, Fitzpatrick 1980). Paynter (1972a) believed *pallidiceps* to be restricted to the upper río Jubones drainage, and argued that its isolation in this valley undoubtedly prevented it from being absorbed into the population now constituting *A. leucopterus dresseri*. Chapman (1926) suggested that *pallidiceps* might be albinistic examples of the White-headed Brush-finch, which is found at 250-1,500 m from west-central Cajamarca in northern Peru north to the Casanga valley in south-west Ecuador (Paynter 1972a). Paynter (1972a) treated *albiceps* in the same species-group as *pallidiceps*. In view of the close relationship between these species, it is of considerable interest that *pallidiceps* has been reported from the Casanga valley, where *albiceps* and *leucopterus dresseri* also occur, and a study to prove the authenticity of *pallidiceps* at this locality, as well as a study of the interactions and possible hybridizations between the three species there, would be desirable; however, given the fact that the Olallas have a reputation for mislabelled specimens, the presence of the Pale-headed Brush-finch in the Casanga valley (all specimens of which were collected by M. Olalla) must be questionable (M. B. Robbins *in litt.* 1992).

(2) According to Brown (1941) Guishapa is the same as Paguishapa, a subtropical station (at 2,400 m) on the trail from Cuenca to Loja, where it follows the río Jubones at c.3°21'S 79°21'W. Paynter (1972a) inquired in the town of Oña, and found no-one with any knowledge of a locality named Guishapa; he suggested that it was either a hacienda, now gone, or an incorrect transliteration from the Quechua, the suffix -shapa or -chapa, meaning "sentry", being common in placenames in the region.

(3) Since Meyer de Schauensee (1948-1952) referred to this immature as being in AMNH, where it can no longer be found, it is conceivably the same as the July 1939 immature from Yunguilla, now in MECN.

TANAGER-FINCH *Oreothraupis arremonops* V/R[10]

This cloud-forest undergrowth species has a poorly known and patchy distribution in the West Andes of Colombia and in north-western Ecuador, with few recent records. However, large tracts of apparently suitable habitat remain in protected areas, the reason for its apparent rarity being essentially unknown.

DISTRIBUTION The Tanager-finch (see Remarks 1) is known from just a few apparently disjunct areas on the West Andes in Antioquia, Valle, Cauca and Nariño departments, Colombia, and also from Imbabura and Pichincha provinces, north-western Ecuador, where localities (coordinates from Paynter and Traylor 1977, 1981) are as follows:

Colombia (*Antioquia*) Hacienda Potreros (c.6°39'N 76°09'W; on the western slope of the West Andes, south-west of Frontino), where a male (in USNM) was taken at 1,980 m in June 1950 (also Carriker 1959); (*Valle*) in the region of Alto Anchicayá (c.3°37'N 76°53'W), where the species has fairly recently been recorded (Orejuela 1983); (*Cauca*) in the vicinity of Cerro Munchique (2°32'N 76°57'W), where the bird is regularly found on the western slope (Hilty and Brown 1986), specific localities including: La Costa (untraced, but c.10 km north of Cerro Munchique), where a female (in ANSP) was taken at 1,830 m in March 1938 (also Meyer de Schauensee 1948-1952), Cocal (2°31'N 77°00'W; north-west of Cerro Munchique), where two specimens were collected at 1,830 m (Chapman 1917a), El Tambo (2°25'N 76°49'W; on the east slope of the West Andes), whence come specimens taken at 1,370 m (Bond and Meyer de Schauensee 1940) and four others (in ANSP) taken from 1,830 to 2,285 m between 1937 and 1940, La Romelia (untraced, but within the Munchique National Park), where this species is seen with relative frequency at 2,200 to 2,600 m (Negret 1991), and El Planchón (untraced, but also within the park), where a male was collected at 2,200 m in November 1990 (Negret 1991); and (*Nariño*) La Planada (1°13'N 77°59'W; 1,250 m), where the bird was recorded by Orejuela (1987);

Ecuador (*Imbabura*) Intag (c.0°24'N 78°36'W), where two specimens (in BMNH) were taken in December 1877; (*Pichincha*) on the road to Nanegal (c.0°07'N 78°46'W), whence comes a male specimen (Chapman 1926); Milpe (0°00' 78°57'W), where a specimen was taken in March 1938 (Krabbe 1991); above Tandayapa (0°01'S 78°46'W), where the species was seen (by T. Læssøe) during July 1987 (Krabbe 1991); Mindo (0°02'S 78°48'W), where the bird was collected at 1,260 m (Goodfellow 1901-1902), with a male (in BMNH) taken at 1,200 m in March 1939; and Castillo (untraced, but near Mindo) (Stresemann 1938).

POPULATION Ridgely and Tudor (1989) suggested that the Tanager-finch is very local and extremely scarce, while Hilty and Brown (1986) considered it infrequently seen (as the species is shy and inconspicuous), but at least fairly common locally (on voice). With most recent records coming from a small area in Cauca department, and with just one recent record from Ecuador, the species indeed appears to have an extremely localized distribution, and is seemingly absent from numerous "suitable" areas (Ridgely and Tudor 1989).

Colombia Recent records, apart from the report at Alto Anchicayá and La Planada, are exclusively from the Cerro Munchique area, and perhaps more specifically from the Munchique National Park where the bird is seen with relative frequency (Negret 1991). The Tanager-finch is most regularly found on the west side of the cerro (Hilty and Brown 1986), where groups of up to six birds are not infrequently seen (e.g. around La Romelia: Negret 1991). However, on the eastern slope of the cerro, the species probably occurs at low densities: although two birds were seen there in March 1987, no more were located during five subsequent days of searching (M. Pearman *in litt.* 1990);

Ecuador This species is presumably rare and local as there are very few specimens from the country, the last being taken in 1939, after which there has apparently been just one sighting, in 1987.

ECOLOGY The Tanager-finch has been recorded between 1,200 and 2,600 m (see Distribution; also Remarks 2), where it inhabits primary humid forest (most often dense, wet, mossy cloud-forest) and occasionally forest borders (Hilty and Brown 1986, Ridgely and Tudor 1989). The area within the boundaries of the Munchique National Park is covered mostly by humid (c.5,000 mm annual rainfall) cloud-forests dominated by *Billia colombiana*, *Clusia* spp., *Persea* sp., *Hyeronima colombiana*, *Quercus humboldtii* and *Weinmannia pubescens* (Hernández Camacho *et al.* undated).

Single birds, but most often close pairs or (family) groups of 3-6, "rummage sluggishly" on or near the ground (in leaf-litter and on mossy logs), in thick undergrowth (including bamboo), where they peer and peck at foliage, stems and fruit (Hilty and Brown 1986, Fjeldså and Krabbe 1990, M. Pearman *in litt.* 1990, P. Kaestner *in litt.* 1992). The species is apparently most often found independent of mixed-species flocks (Ridgely and Tudor 1989), although near La Romelia (Munchique National Park), the species has been observed with mixed flocks led by Rufous Wren *Cinnycerthia unirufa* (Negret 1991).

A male (in USNM) in breeding condition was collected in Antioquia on 8 June 1950, and a juvenile following two adults was also noted during June, in Cauca (Hilty and Brown 1986). Negret (1991) recorded the occurrence of pairs in Munchique National Park during October and November 1990, although other observations (see above, and Population) suggest that this may be a year-round phenomenon.

THREATS Forest clearance is the main threat to this species and has been intense throughout its Colombian range, although large areas of apparently primary or old secondary forest still exist in Valle (F. R. Lambert *in litt.* 1989), while localities in Cauca (e.g. Munchique National Park) have not been severely affected (LGN), despite the fact that agricultural and hydroelectric projects are causing local degradation of the vegetation within the park (IUCN TFP 1988a). In north-west Ecuador, large areas of forest also remain; however, widespread deforestation has occurred, especially along rivers and railways, and is becoming more of a problem as the human population increases (Moore and van der Giessen 1984, Evans 1988b, IUCN TFP 1988b). The Tanager-finch is apparently absent from numerous "suitable" areas, and the reasons for its rarity remain unknown (Ridgely and Tudor 1989). P. Greenfield (verbally 1991) suggested that a general decrease in rainfall may be the cause of its apparent decline in Ecuador.

MEASURES TAKEN Most records of the Tanager-finch come from the Munchique National Park (44,000 ha), which covers the area to the north and west of Cerro Munchique (Hernández Camacho *et al.* undated). Other records come from the Alto Anchicayá area, which is protected by the CVC and is within the Farallones de Cali National Park (150,000 ha) (CNPPA 1982, Hernández Camacho *et al.* undated); and from La Planada Nature Reserve (3,200 ha), an area of mature forest privately owned and now legally protected as a forest protection zone (Barlow *et al.* 1992). In Ecuador, the Cotacachi–Cayapas Ecological Reserve (204,400 ha) protects suitable areas near where the species was collected last century (see Distribution), as does the Awá Indiginous Forest Reserve (over 100,000 ha), on the border with Colombia (IUCN 1992).

MEASURES PROPOSED The guaranteed integrity of forest within the reserves mentioned above is essential if this and other threatened bird species are to survive (see below); where possible, these reserves should be extended, and other remaining forest blocks conserved. There have been recommendations for the establishment of a Biosphere Reserve (for the Awá Indians) in Colombia, to link up with the reserve in Ecuador (Barlow *et al.* 1992: see above): such a large trans-border reserve should be strongly encouraged.

The true distribution, population density and ecological requirements of this species need clarification: determining each of these, especially its status within the various protected areas, is a priority, after which it may be possible to assess its conservation needs and act upon them. The range of the Tanager-finch overlaps with those of a number of other threatened species, which for Alto Anchicayá and Los Farallones de Cali National Park are given in the equivalent section under Multicoloured Tanager *Chlorochrysa nitidissima*, for Munchique National Park under Colourful Puffleg *Eriocnemis mirabilis*, and for La Planada and surrounding areas under Hoary Puffleg *Haplophaedia lugens*; any conservation initiatives should consider the needs of all the sympatric threatened species.

REMARKS (1) The genus *Oreothraupis* is monotypic, and its taxonomic position has been uncertain since it resembles both tanagers and finches (see Meyer de Schauensee 1966). However, following Storer (1958) there has been a general acceptance of its location among the latter, and indeed its behaviour is seemingly much like that of a brush-finch *Atlapetes* (Ridgely and Tudor 1989). (2) The altitudes given by Bond and Meyer de Schauensee (1940) for specimens collected at Munchique are from 580 to 2,285 m, significantly lower than any other record of the species; whether this lower figure is correct is unknown. Blake (1959) considered 3,000 m the bird's upper limit.

YELLOW CARDINAL *Gubernatrix cristata* V[9]

Formerly very widespread in Argentina and common in Uruguay, with outlying populations in Paraguay (possibly now extinct) and southernmost Brazil, this distinctive emberizid has been trapped intensively as a cagebird for over a century and is now rare everywhere except locally in the southern parts of its range.

DISTRIBUTION The Yellow Cardinal (see Remarks 1) has been recorded from Paraguay, extreme southern Brazil (Rio Grande do Sul), Uruguay and eastern Argentina from Salta south to Río Negro. Unless otherwise indicated, coordinates in the following account are taken from OG (1968), Paynter (1985) and Rand and Paynter (1981) and records at individual localities are of single birds, pairs or an unspecified number of birds collected or observed.

Paraguay Sclater and Hudson (1888-1889) gave Paraguay as a range state, but this was presumably a guess. Bertoni (1914) questioned its occurrence (although he later ambiguously claimed it for the "Chaco": Bertoni 1939), Hellmayr (1938) believed no authentic record existed, and neither Ridgely and Tudor (1989) nor Hayes *et al.* (1991) listed it for the country. However, two specimens in BMNH were taken at "Villa Rica" (Villarrica), Guairá department, on 12 May and 10 October 1905 (see Population), and two others (in BMNH and MCZ) are simply labelled "Paraguay" (that in BMNH before 1886).

Brazil There appear to be just a few records, all from Rio Grande do Sul:
between Tapes and Camaquã, November 1980 (see Belton 1984-1985), apparently the northernmost record in the country; São Lorenço (= São Lorenço do Sul), undated (Hellmayr 1938, Belton 1984-1985); Jaguarão, a nineteenth century record (von Ihering 1899); a cattle ranch north of "Tahym" (Taim), July 1931 (specimen in AMNH); on the Uruguayan border south of Santa Victoria (Santa Vitória do Palmar), August 1931 (three specimens in AMNH); the westernmost part of the state, occasionally (Belton 1984-1985).

Uruguay Records (roughly from north to south) are: (*Paysandú*) near río Daymán, where eight birds were observed on 2 May 1978 (Arballo 1990); (*Tacuarembó*) Caraguatá (= Cuchilla Caraguatá, 32°14'S 54°59'W), April 1930 (specimen in MCZ); (*Cerro Largo*) arroyo del Cordobés (32°30'S 55°19'W), 28 km north of Cerro Chato (untraced), March 1970 (specimen in MNHNM); (*Río Negro*) Rincón de Baygorria (c.32°50'S 56°50'W), April 1960 (specimen in MNHNM); (*Treinta y Tres*) unspecified (Cuello and Gerzenstein 1962); (*Soriano/Flores*) rincón of Arroyo Grande and Arroyo Ojosmín (33°08'S 57°09'W), May 1893 (Aplin 1894); (*Lavalleja*) "Minas" (= Lavalleja department), undated (Tremoleras 1920); (*Colonia*) Nueva Palmira, April 1927 (specimen in MACN); arroyo de las Limetas, Estancia San Jorge (c.34°10'S 58°13'W), January 1970 (three specimens in MNHNM); (*Canelones*) unspecified (Tremoleras 1920); (*Maldonado*) north of Gruta la Salamanca (untraced), May 1964 (specimen in MNHNM); (*Rocha*) Lazcano, February 1921 (Wetmore 1926); Paso Alamo, on the arroyo Sarandi (33°47'S 53°35'W), February 1921 (Wetmore 1926); San Vicente (= Castillos, 34°12'S 53°50'W), January 1921 (Wetmore 1926).

Argentina Records by provinces (roughly from north to south) are:

(*Salta*) Rivadavia, where the species was found nesting in 1967 (Hoy 1969);

(*Formosa*) "eastern Formosa" (no further details given) (Olrog 1979, hence presumably Nores *et al.* 1983, Ridgely and Tudor 1989);

(*Chaco*) occurrence assumed (Lynch Arribálzaga 1920; hence or also the distribution maps in Narosky and Yzurieta 1987, Ridgely and Tudor 1989, and Canevari *et al.* 1991);

(*Misiones*) savannas in the south of Misiones, undated (Olrog 1979, hence presumably Ridgely and Tudor 1989);

(*Tucumán*) "Tucuman", October 1899 (Lillo 1902, Hartert and Venturi 1909) and February 1904 (specimen in AMNH);

(*Santiago del Estero*) Gramilla (27°18'S 64°37'N), November 1963 (Nores *et al.* 1991, whence coordinates);

(*Corrientes*) Esteros de Iberá, August 1972 (specimen in LSUMZ); at 29°S, where three pairs were observed (de Azara 1802-1805), these records being attributed to this province by Wetmore (1926); Mercedes, January and February 1953 (two specimens in MACN); Estancia Rincón del Ombú (29°28'S 57°50'W), September 1961 (three specimens in AMNH), October 1961 (six specimens in AMNH and LSUMZ); Curuzú-Cuatiá, between April and May 1917 (Marelli 1918); Estancia Barrancas (untraced but apparently on the right – i.e. Corrientes – side of the río Guayquiraró: Paynter 1985), January-February 1873 (Doering 1874);

(*Santa Fe*) northern Santa Fe, where the species was reported nesting (Pereyra 1938); Nueve de Julio department (28°50'S 61°20'W), undated (Giai 1950); La Gallareta (29°34'S 60°23'W), where two nests were found in November 1974 (de la Peña 1987); Estancia Los Molles (30°02'S 60°46'W), "summer" (presumably 1924) (Renard 1924) and September 1932 (Freiberg 1943); Esperanza (presumably the large town in Santa Fe), June 1902 (specimen in MZUSP); banks of the río Paraná near Santa Fe, undated (Gould 1841);

(*Entre Ríos*) "Entrerios", sometime before 1912 (three specimens in BMNH); San Joaquín (presumably Estancia San Joaquín at 30°44'S 59°59'W: see Remarks 2), January 1924 (Friedmann 1927); Santa Elena (30°57'S 59°48'W), November (presumably 1922), (Serié and Smyth 1923) and February 1924 (Friedmann 1927; specimen in MCZ); near Federal, where two pairs were observed in June 1986 (J. C. Chebez *in litt.* 1992); Estancia Vizcacheras (31°08'S 59°46'W), April 1961 (15 specimens in AMNH, CM and YPM); San Salvador (31°37'S 58°30'W), January 1914 (specimen in MACN); Paraná department (31°40'S 60°00'W), where three birds were collected in January 1927, December 1932 and December 1929 (Freiberg 1943); Paraná, in the 1850s (Burmeister 1861); Ceibas (32°26'S 58°45'W), recently (E. I. Abadie *per* M. Pearman *in litt.* 1992); Concepción del Uruguay, 1879 (Barrows 1883); "La Soledad" (= Estancia La Soledad, 32°30'S 58°41'W; see Paynter 1985), January 1899 (specimen in AMNH);

(*La Rioja*) listed without detail by Nores *et al.* (1983) and shaded on maps in Ridgely and Tudor (1989) and Canevari *et al.* (1991);

(*San Juan*) Valle Fertil (Valle Fertil = San Agustín de Valle Fértil 30°38'S 67°27'W), undated (Haene 1987);

(*Córdoba*) San Francisco del Chañar, present around 1983 (Nores *et al.* 1983); Capilla del Monte, December 1894 (specimen in BMNH), June 1913 (specimen in ROM); Cosquín (31°15'S 64°29'W), between July and October 1882 (White 1883; also BMNH label data); near Córdoba in the 1850s (Burmeister 1861); Valle de los Reartes (31°55'N 64°34'W), where the species nested in the "spring" of 1903 and it was hunted and observed in November 1916 (Castellanos 1931-1934); Los Cóndores (32°20'S 64°16'W), November 1982 (Nores *et al.* 1983); San Roque (untraced but presumably near the Lago de San Roque, 31°23'S 64°29'W), Sierra de Córdoba, at 700 m, December 1915 (specimen in CM);

(*San Luis*) San Martín, 1987 (Bascarán 1987); Sierra de las Quijadas National Park (32°33'S 67°02'W), currently (J. C. Chebez *in litt.* 1992); Villa General Roca, 1987 (Bascarán 1987); Papagayos (32°41'S 65°00'W), November 1958 (specimen in UNP); near El Trapiche (33°07'S 66°05'W), September 1990 (G. Gil and E. Haene *per* J. C. Chebez *in litt.* 1992); Chischaca (33°52'S 66°15'W), December 1925 (two specimens in MACN); Batavia, 1987 (Bascarán 1987); "Nabia" (presumably Navia, at 34°47'S 66°35'W), 1987 (Bascarán 1987); Estancia El Bosque (c.35°07'S 65°15'W), September 1916 (four specimens in MACN); Anchorena (35°41'S 65°27'W), Arizona, Bagual and Esperanza (untraced), all four in 1987 (Bascarán 1987);

(*Buenos Aires*) Escobar (Belén de Escobar, 34°21'S 58°47'W), July 1929 (specimen in MACN); Barracas al Sud (= Avellaneda), November 1900 (Hartert and Venturi 1909); "Conchitas" (= Guillermo E. Hudson, 34°47'S 58°10'W), October 1868 (Sclater and Salvin 1868-1869; specimen in AMNH); La Plata, March 1898 (specimen in FMNH) and October 1903 (specimen in MACN); Atalaya (35°02'S 57°32'W), May 1908 (specimen in AMNH); Monte Veloz (35°27'S 57°17'W), August and October 1919 (two specimens in UNP); Bosque del Meridiano (untraced but near "Darregueira" = Darragueira), where nesting in November 1988, this perhaps being the most northern breeding record in the province (Narosky *et al.* 1990); Villa Iris, November 1958 (specimen in UNP); 20-30 km south of Bahía Blanca, Montes de Oca (38°55'S 63°21'W), Pedro Luro and Villa Longa, currently in all four (Bascarán 1987); "Casas" (= José B. Casás, 40°25'S 62°33'W), October 1960 (specimen in YPM); Carmen de Patagones, currently (Bascarán 1987);

(*La Pampa*) Parera and Caleufú, currently (Bascarán 1987); General Pico, December 1938 and June 1943 (two specimens in MACN); Conhello (36°01'S 64°36'W), where the species was found "very common" in November 1922 (Pereyra 1923); Luan Toro (36°12'S 65°02'W), December 1935 (specimen in MACN); Victorica, December 1920 (Wetmore 1926) and currently (Bascarán 1987); Santa Isabel, Telén, Algarrobo de Aguila, La Copelina, Mahuida and Veinticinco de Mayo, currently in all six (Bascarán 1987); Lihué-Calel National Park (38°02'S 65°33'W), currently (Canevari *et al.* 1991, M. Babarskas *in litt.* 1992, G. Gil *per* J. C. Chebez *in litt.* 1992); Puelches, currently (Bascarán 1987);

(*Río Negro*) from Contralmirante Cordero (38°44'S 68°10'W) in the west to Viedma in the east (range as given by Bascarán 1987), specifically: "valley of the Rio Negro" (see Remarks 3), September 1871 (Hudson 1872; two specimens in BMNH); in the area between General Conesa, San Antonio Oeste, and Viedma, currently (W. N. Paz *per* P. González *in litt.* 1992); Laguna del Monte (45 km east of the San Antonio to Viedma road), January 1989 (M. Pearman *in litt.* 1992), March 1991 (F. R. Lambert verbally 1992); 37 km south of río Negro ("Rute 3", i.e. along the San Antonio to Viedma road), October 1960 (specimen in YPM); El Bolson, August 1957 (specimen in LACM; see Remarks 4).

POPULATION The Yellow Cardinal is known to have declined greatly, and to have disappeared from or become very rare in much of its range (Ridgely and Tudor 1989; see below).

Paraguay Despite the scant information available on the species in the country and indeed the general view that it is absent there (see Distribution), it is remarkable that the label of the specimen taken in Villarrica in October 1905 (a date which could indicate breeding) also states: "fairly common". The complete lack of observations in recent times suggests a clear decline.

Brazil The species is considered to be a scarce resident, being found occasionally throughout the year in southern Rio Grande do Sul near the Uruguayan border (Belton 1984-1985).

Uruguay Gore and Gepp (1978) described the Yellow Cardinal as formerly "very common" in the right habitat but that it had become a scarce resident, a view taken earlier by Alvarez (1933) and Cuello and Gerzenstein (1962). It is nowadays considered to be a very rare bird (R. Vaz-Ferreira verbally 1992).

Argentina Although the Yellow Cardinal has extends widely in the country, it appears to have always been rather uncommon or occasional in most of the northern part of its range, where there are just a few records (e.g. Salta, Tucumán, Santiago del Estero and Misiones, with no precise records from Formosa or Chaco; see Distribution). It is generally accepted that the species has suffered a steep decline elsewhere in its northern range, mainly in Corrientes, Santa Fe, Córdoba, Entre Ríos and northern Buenos Aires (Nores *et al.* 1983, Narosky and Yzurieta 1987, Bucher and Nores 1988, Krapovickas 1990, Narosky *et al.* 1990, Canevari *et al.* 1991; see below). It was presumably once common in Corrientes, Marelli (1918) having found it "common" at Curuzú Cuatía between April and May 1917, and nine specimens (in AMNH and LSUMZ) were taken at Mercedes between 28 September and 6 October 1961. Burmeister (1861) found it common (with "many birds observed") near Córdoba, although White (1883) referred to is as "uncommon" in the Cosquín area in 1882 and Castellanos (1934) considered it "not abundant" and "rarely seen" in the same province; more recently, Nores *et al.* (1983) could only find the species in a few localities (see Distribution). In Santa Fe and La Pampa it was considered "very common"

(Pereyra 1938), e.g. around Conhello in the latter in November 1922 (Pereyra 1923), but no more reports suggest it remains so. In Entre Ríos it was also considered "very common" (Pereyra 1938), although in more site-specific reports it was "not rare" in Paraná (Burmeister 1861), "in small numbers" at Concepción del Uruguay (Barrows 1883), "common" at Santa Elena in November (probably 1922) (Serié and Smyth 1923) but "very local and rather scarce" there in February 1924 (Friedmann 1927), with 15 specimens taken at Estancia Las Vizcacheras during the second half of April 1961 (see Distribution); however, a great decline appears to have occurred, as it is now very difficult to find in the province (M. Pearman *in litt.* 1992), and there appear to be only two recent observations (see Distribution). In most of Buenos Aires the species appears to have been a rather rare bird (Sclater and Hudson 1888-1889), with just a few old records from the north; it is now only present in the south (see below), and it appears that the central-eastern part of the province is out of the species's range.

The Yellow Cardinal is now only to be found locally common in the southern parts of its range in southern Buenos Aires, La Pampa and Río Negro (Bascarán 1987, M. Pearman *in litt.* 1992), notably in the area between General Conesa, San Antonio Oeste and Viedma, where according to W. N. Paz (*per* P. González *in litt.* 1992) it is still usual to see flocks of 15-20 birds, and during the breeding season flocks can even increase to 40-50 birds (see Remarks 5).

ECOLOGY The Yellow Cardinal inhabits open woodland extending into foothills (to about 700 m: see Distribution), semi-open scrub, savannas and shrubby steppes (White 1883, Gore and Gepp 1978, Belton 1984-1985, Narosky and Yzurieta 1987, Ridgely and Tudor 1989). In southern Buenos Aires, La Pampa and eastern Río Negro it is known to be closely associated with the "chañares" *Geoffroea decorticans* (W. N. Paz *per* P. González *in litt.* 1992). The species feeds on grains and seeds (e.g. "verdolaga", "diente de león", "acelga silvestre", "achicoria silvestre"), berries and insects (Bascarán 1987, Canevari *et al.* 1991). Breeding has been reported in "spring" (Castellanos 1934) and nests have been found in November (de la Peña 1987, Narosky *et al.* 1990). The nest is placed in a fork of a branch (e.g. in *Robinia pseudoacacia*: Castellanos 1934), and three to four eggs are laid (Alvarez 1933, Bascarán 1987, Canevari *et al.* 1991). The incubation period (in captivity) is 13-14 days, by the female only (Bascarán 1987, Röder 1990). The Yellow Cardinal is generally found singly, in pairs or in small groups (Canevari *et al.* 1991) but flocks sometimes occur (see Population).

THREATS Constant and chronic exploitation of the Yellow Cardinal as a songbird for the cagebird market has been and remains the most significant threat throughout its range (Barrows 1883, Sclater and Hudson 1888-1889, Gore and Gepp 1978, Carvalho 1985, Ridgely and tudor 1989, Canevari *et al.* 1991). In Uruguay inidividual birds sell for 100,000 pesos (c.US$35) (R. Vaz-Ferreira verbally 1992). Other possible threats affecting the species are unknown, so it is not entirely clear whether trapping is responsible for the species's decline throughout. It seems likely that much habitat would have been converted for or affected by cattle production, but this has not been reported.

MEASURES TAKEN The species is known to be present in the Lihué Calel and Sierra de las Quijadas National Parks, Argentina (see Distribution). It is listed on Appendix II of CITES, and on Appendix III for Uruguay (Amos 1985, Bascarán 1987).

MEASURES PROPOSED The trapping of this species has to be curtailed. To achieve this, an investigation will be needed of the trapping business itself and of the market involved, furnishing clearer evidence of the impact of the trade. Specific legal measures may need to be drafted and enforced in Argentina, but this should be matched by a campaign to sensitize consumers to the bird's plight, and by moves to persuade entrepreneurial aviculturists to meet any demand by breeding from existing captive stock. Surveys and studies of the species's distribution and ecology are important in order determine more clearly its status, optimal habitat, year-round needs, and any other threats that may be adversely affecting it. If small protected areas can be established and well wardened in the few areas in the south of its range where it still survives in some numbers, this would contribute to its greater overall security.

REMARKS (1) The Yellow Cardinal is the only representative of its genus. (2) Although there are two localities in Entre Ríos bearing this name, the other being at 31°57'S 58°42'W, the one listed is likely to be the locality intended, since it is near Santa Elena, which was visited briefly after San Joaquín (see Friedmann 1927). (3) Although a specific locality is not given, Hudson (1872) indicated that all his collecting took place in the valley and the adjacent high grounds "not much over a hundred miles [c.160 km] from the sea". (4) This record from the extreme south-west of the province, near the border with Chile, is well away from the known range and perhaps represents an escape rather than a true record. (5) These numbers are noteworthy, and appear to be the largest flocks ever reported, most sources generally referring to either single birds or pairs.

RUFOUS-BELLIED SALTATOR *Saltator rufiventris* V/R[10]

This rare saltator is confined to the temperate zone of central Bolivia, and Jujuy and Salta provinces in north-western Argentina. It may feed predominantly on mistletoe berries of Polylepis *and* Alnus *woodlands, which are now highly fragmented within most of its range.*

DISTRIBUTION The Rufous-bellied Saltator is known from several recent sightings and a large number of specimens, being predominantly recorded in Cochabamba department, but also La Paz and Chuquisaca departments, Bolivia, and in Jujuy and Salta provinces, Argentina, all at elevations between c.2,500 and 4,000 m. Records of this species (coordinates, unless otherwise stated, from Paynter *et al.* 1975 and Paynter 1985) are as follows:

Bolivia (*La Paz*) near Inquisivi, c.17°22'S 67°45'W, at 3,975 m in Sicasica province, the type-locality (d'Orbigny and Lafresnaye 1837); (*Cochabamba*) near Palca (= Independencia), c.17°07'S 66°53'W, at 2,770 m in Ayupayo province (erroneously placed in Chuquisaca department by Hellmayr 1938) (d'Orbigny 1835-1844); Caluyo, 17°13'S 66°01'W, at 3,500 m (specimen in CM); Toncoma, c.17°15'S 66°20'W, at 3,200-3,250 m (Fjeldså and Krabbe 1989); Liriuni, 17°19'S 66°20'W, at 3,000-3,200 m, where a male (in FMNH) was taken in July 1939 (Fjeldså and Krabbe 1989, S. Arías verbally 1991); Tutimayo, c.17°25'S 66°10'W, at 3,200 m (Bond and Meyer de Schauensee 1942-1943); Cochabamba, at 2,570 m (Remsen *et al.* 1988); Tunari National Park, 20-25 km north-east of Cochabamba, between 2,700 and 3,300 m (Remsen *et al.* 1988, S. Arías verbally 1991); Tiraque, 17°25'S 65°43'W, at 3,200 m (Bond and Meyer de Schauensee 1942-1943); Pocona, 17°39'S 65°24'W, at 2,700 m where 15 specimens (in CM and FMNH) were taken in December 1926 and February 1927; Cerro Cheñua Sandra (c.17°39'S 66°29'W: read from IGM 1965a), at 3,800 m (Fjeldså 1987, S. Arías verbally 1991); 8 km east of Pojo, 17°45'S 64°49'W, at c.2,800 m (Nores and Yzurieta 1984); Quebrada Majon, 6.6 km by road beyond López Mendoza, at km 98 on the Cochabamba–Santa Cruz de la Sierra road, Carrasco province (Remsen *et al.* 1988); Pilpina, 17°58'S 65°33'W, at 3,215 m (Fjeldså and Krabbe 1989); (*Chuquisaca*) Bellavista, c.18°40'S 64°17'W, 25 km north of Quillacollo (Remsen *et al.* 1988); El Cabrada, Posta, at 19°05'S 65°05'W (Remsen *et al.* 1988; specimen in BMNH taken at 3,500 m in September 1900); río San Francisco, 20°43'S 64°39'W, at 2,700 m, and río Puca Laja, 20°43'S 64°36'W, at 2,700 m, both in the Cerros Chapeados, where two singles were seen in September 1991 (J. Fjeldså verbally 1991: coordinates read from IGM 1976); near Azurduy village, 20°06'S 64°25'W, at 2,700 m, where a pair and juvenile were seen in October 1991 (J. Fjeldså verbally 1991: coordinates read from IGM 1984);

Argentina (*Jujuy*) El Duraznillo, c.23°35'S 64°55'W, at 3,000 m, Alto Calilegua (Olrog and Contino 1970; correct elevation from Remsen *et al.* 1988); (*Salta*) above Chicoana, c.25°06'S 65°33'W, at c.2,600 m along the road to Cachi, on the east slope of Cumbre de Obispo, where one was seen in November 1985 (R. S. Ridgely *in litt.* 1989); and below Cachi, where a pair was seen at c.2,630 m in November 1990 (B. M. Whitney *in litt.* 1991).

POPULATION This species was described as being very common near Palca and Inquisivi in September 1830 (d'Orbigny 1835-1844), but only two or three pairs were found in a c.4 ha *Polylepis* woodland at Cerro Cheñua Sandra in April 1987, where their retiring habits made them difficult to detect (NK). In Quebrada Majon the bird was noted on 10 of 16 field days (Remsen *et al.* 1988), and in Tunari National Park as many as 50 birds have been recorded moving between a nightly roost in the *Eucalyptus* plantation and a bushy ravine just above the town of Cochabamba, although other Cochabamba localities are inhabited by very few pairs (S. Arías verbally 1991). The species was still found to be common on Cerro Tunari during February and March 1992 (B. M. Whitney and J. L. Rowlett *in litt.* 1992). At the known sites in Chuquisaca department the species appears to be scarce (J. Fjeldså verbally 1991). There are very few records from Argentina, and the species's status there remains unknown (see above).

ECOLOGY In most of its range the Rufous-bellied Saltator inhabits semi-arid regions where it frequents woodland and bushy, often steep-sloped watered valleys with small woodlands, as well as riparian thickets and hedgerows in agricultural areas, sometimes even entering villages (d'Orbigny 1835-1844, Fjeldså and Krabbe 1990). In Bolivia, the bird has rarely been found far from *Polylepis* trees (Remsen and Quintela unpublished), whilst at Serranía de Calilegua and Cachi, Argentina, it was found in bushes and hedgerows in the alder *Alnus acuminata* zone (Olrog and Contino 1970, B. M. Whitney *in litt.* 1991), the species being found in Argentina, as well as at its easternmost known site (Pojo, Bolivia), in what has been described as humid montane forest and edge (M. Nores *in litt.* 1989).

It occurs in pairs and small groups, sometimes mixing with Golden-billed Saltator *Saltator aurantiirostris* and White-tipped Plantcutter *Phytotoma rutila*, and secretively and slowly forages for berries, especially those of mistletoes and *Schinus molle*, but is also said to eat seeds and insects (d'Orbigny 1835-1844, Fjeldså and Krabbe 1990, S. Arías verbally 1991). In May it has been seen eating the purplish-red fruits of a 1.5-3 m tall *Berberis* sp. shrub as well as those of *Heteromelas* sp.: other birds feeding on these fruits were Great Thrush *Turdus fuscater*, Red-crested Cotinga *Ampelion rubrocristatus* and Golden-billed Saltator (Remsen *et al.* 1988). On one occasion a group of five birds was observed pecking the ground in a ploughed field (Remsen *et al.* 1988), and the pair seen below Cachi was picking intently at small areas on the ground beneath *Alnus* hedgerows (surrounding stone walls) (B. M. Whitney *in litt.* 1991). Stomach contents of 15 birds taken in May and August were vegetable matter, either green plant fibres or fruit seeds ranging in size from 6x3 to 7x4 mm (Remsen *et al.* 1988). The species may depend strongly on mistletoe fruit, and although it uses alternative food sources, viable populations may require habitat patches with large numbers of mistletoes: apparently the mistletoes on *Alnus* trees fruit only during the rainy season when the trees have leaves, whilst the evergreen *Polylepis* may provide a more constant supply of the berries (J. Fjeldså verbally 1991).

A pair taken in Cochabamba in April had slightly enlarged gonads (specimens in ZMUC), as did a female taken in May (Remsen *et al.* 1988); juveniles have been taken in Cochabamba in May, August and September (d'Orbigny 1835-1844, Hellmayr 1925, Remsen *et al.* 1988). In Cochabamba, birds were noted singing and showed territorial response (to playback) in mid-February 1992, but not in mid-March: with the wet season having just ended in mid-February, it seems likely that nesting occurs during December and January (B. M. Whitney *in litt.* 1992).

THREATS If the species is truly dependent on mistletoes, it may be threatened, as the *Polylepis* and *Alnus* woods are dwindling, becoming restricted to watered ravines and steep slopes, owing both to clearance for cultivation and to regular burning for pasture throughout the semi-arid temperate zone of Bolivia and Argentina (J. Fjeldså verbally 1991, B. M. Whitney *in litt.* 1991).

MEASURES TAKEN The species occurs in Tunari National Park (6,000 ha: IUCN 1992), a reserve situated on the slope immediately north of Cochabamba town (but the management of this park does not seem very adequate: J. Fjeldså verbally 1991), and in Calilegua National Park (76,000 ha: IUCN 1992) in Argentina (see Distribution).

MEASURES PROPOSED A study of this species should be undertaken to determine more clearly its ecological requirements (e.g. the extent to which birds rely on mistletoes in *Polylepis* and *Alnus* woods). The best way of protecting its habitat may be to launch an information campaign aimed at educating local people about the soil-degrading impact of burning the mountain slope vegetation (which also leads to loss of water catchment), and developing alternative ways of more intensive land use: suitable target areas could be Cerro Cheñua Sandra, near Azurduy (where a reforestation programme with *Alnus* has already been started) and in Cerros Chapeados

(J. Fjeldså verbally 1991). The bird's continued presence near Inquisivi should be established, and the populations and state of habitat must be determined within the two national parks frequented by the species; the integrity of habitat within these parks must be ensured.

At several localities where this species occurs the Cochabamba Mountain-finch *Poospiza garleppi* (see relevant account) is also found, and in Chuquisaca its habitat overlaps that of the near-threatened Alder Amazon *Amazona tucumana*: the best interests of all these species should be considered in any conservation initiatives undertaken.

CONE-BILLED TANAGER *Conothraupis mesoleuca* E[4]

Known only from a single specimen collected in 1938 in dry forest in Mato Grosso, Brazil, this small bird needs to be searched for in two nature reserves in the region.

DISTRIBUTION The Cone-billed Tanager is known only from the type-specimen from Mato Grosso, central Brazil (Meyer de Schauensee 1966), collected on 25 August 1938 (Berlioz 1939). The stated type-locality, "Juruena, north-east of Cuyaba" (Berlioz 1939, 1946), cannot be traced but probably does not refer to the rio Juruena (J. Berlioz *per* H. Sick verbally 1988), in whose proximity lies the only locality with this name in the state of Mato Grosso (12°51'S 58°56'W in Paynter and Traylor 1991), about 400 km north-west of Cuiabá. The designation of the city of Mato Grosso (15°01'S 59°57'W), about 400 km west of Cuiabá, as the type-locality of this bird (Sick 1985, Isler and Isler 1987), is in error (H. Sick verbally 1988).

POPULATION Numbers are not known, although the species must be rare and local to have avoided detection for so long.

ECOLOGY Nothing is known other than that the type was taken amidst bushy vegetation in dry forest in a seemingly transitional zone between Amazonian rainforest and central Brazilian open woodland (Berlioz 1946). The rarity of the Cone-billed Tanager suggests some unknown factors influencing the species in what appears to be (at least until recently) extensive areas of various possible habitats in central Mato Grosso (a similar consideration affects the Blue-eyed Ground-dove *Columbina cyanopis*: see relevant account). Obviously if this bird is dependent on open cerrado it might be particularly vulnerable to the clearance and degradation of habitat through agricultural expansion in the region (see Threats under Lesser Nothura *Nothura minor*).

THREATS None is known.

MEASURES TAKEN The species is protected under Brazilian law (Bernardes *et al.* 1990).

MEASURES PROPOSED Surveys are needed to rediscover the species and to provide information on its ecology and status. Any ornithological work in the state of Mato Grosso, including the only two nature reserves in the region, the Iquê-Juruena Ecological Station (12°00'S 59°00'W) and Serra das Araras Ecological Station (15°45'S 57°15'W), and other areas where the species might be expected, should where possible be extended to include searches to locate it (also the Blue-eyed Ground-dove and other species listed in the equivalent section under Lesser Nothura).

REMARKS Although originally placed in its own genus (*Rhynchothraupis*), the Cone-billed Tanager is clearly related to the (curiously scarce, hence near-threatened) Black-and-white Tanager *Conothraupis speculigera* (Zimmer 1947, Storer 1960), and indeed it has been claimed that the differences between the two birds "can be no more than subspecific" (Zimmer 1947); nevertheless, subsequent authors have preferred to consider them distinct species (Storer 1960, Meyer de Schauensee 1966, Sick 1985) whose known ranges are separated by about 1,500 km (Isler and Isler 1987; not 1,500 miles as in Storer 1960), although this gap may actually prove smaller given the nomadic tendencies of the Black-and-white Tanager (Isler and Isler 1987). Not having been seen in the wild for over 50 years, by CITES criteria the Cone-billed Tanager could now be considered extinct.

YELLOW-GREEN BUSH-TANAGER *Chlorospingus flavovirens* K[12]

Only known from two areas in north-west Ecuador and one in south-west Colombia, this species of humid moss-forest seems to be restricted to a narrow elevational belt; in Colombia it is common on the single ridge where it has been recorded.

DISTRIBUTION The Yellow-green Bush-tanager is known from just three areas: one ridge on the Pacific slope of the West Andes in Valle department, Colombia; and very locally in Imbabura and Pichincha provinces, northern Ecuador. Coordinates are taken from Paynter and Traylor (1977, 1981).

Colombia The species was discovered in Colombia in 1972 (Hilty 1977), where localities are as follows: "Alto Yunda" (3°32'N 76°48'W; 3.5 km south of La Cascada), where at around 1,000 m the bird was collected and observed between 1972 and 1975 (Hilty 1977); and "Alto Anchicayá" (near El Danubio, at 3°37'N 76°53'W), where F. R. Lambert (*in litt.* 1989) found a bird at 680 m in February 1989. Both of the above localities are from a single ridge near the río Anchicayá–río Verde watershed, on the east side of the upper Anchicayá valley (the Pacific slope of the West Andes), Valle department.

Ecuador The undated type-specimen was described simply from "Ecuador" (Chapman 1926), although another specimen was later found to have been collected at Santo Domingo (= Santo Domingo de los Colorados, at 0°15'S 79°09W; Pichincha province) in July 1914, apparently at 490 m but perhaps on the slopes "above" this locality (Griscom 1935): Isler and Isler (1987) suggested that the species was described from two specimens originating in Pichincha, implying that the type also came from this province. Recent sighting of the bird come from eastern Esmeraldas province on the ridges at El Placer (along the railroad to San Lorenzo) (R. S. Ridgely *in litt.* 1992).

POPULATION Very little is known of the population of this species: Ridgely and Tudor (1989) considered the bird to be very local and uncommon, but at least in the upper Anchicayá valley of Colombia, even if the population is extremely localized, the species was found to be relatively common between 1972 and 1975 (Hilty 1977, Hilty and Brown 1986). At this same locality, three birds (in AMNH, LSUMZ) were collected and several others mist-netted, banded and released during 1972 and 1975, when pairs or groups of 3-5 individuals were observed: over 90 feeding observations were made during fieldwork in these two years (Hilty 1977, Isler and Isler 1987). The 1989 record in the upper Anchicayá valley confirmed that this population is still extant. Almost nothing is known of the status of either Ecuadorian population, other than the generalization made above by Ridgely and Tudor (1989).

ECOLOGY The often quoted altitudinal range of this species is 950-1,050 m (Hilty and Brown 1986, Isler and Isler 1987), or 900-1,100 m (Ridgely and Tudor 1989): however, the specimen taken at Santo Domingo de los Colorados may have been collected at 490 m (see Distribution), and F. R. Lambert (*in litt.* 1989) observed a bird at 680 m in the upper Anchicayá valley. The species occurs in wet, mossy cloud-forest, and is also recorded from forest edge and adjacent tall trees in clearings (Hilty and Brown 1986).

It is conspicuous and highly vocal (making it easy to locate in feeding flocks), and almost always occurs in pairs or groups of 3-5 birds, often associated with mixed-species feeding-flocks (Hilty 1977, Hilty and Brown 1986). Most foraging is done well above 7 m (although F. R. Lambert *in litt.* 1989 observed a bird feeding at 3-4 m above the ground), and often at canopy heights (22-30 m), and birds appear to be reluctant to descend into thickets or lower vegetation, although they readily forage out into large isolated trees in clearings (Hilty 1977); the median foraging height was calculated as 12 m (Isler and Isler 1987). Of 91 observations of feeding birds, 45% were taking fruit, 34% insect searching, and 21% at flowers (Isler and Isler 1987). Fourteen species of fruit have been recorded as eaten by this bird, 75% of which are melastomes (especially *Miconia* spp.), and 13% are from epiphytic and parasitic plants (Isler and Isler 1987). Fruits are taken from a perched position, and insects generally searched for on the sides of large mossy branches and tree-trunks (Isler and Isler 1987).

In the upper Anchicayá valley, nests have been found in March and April, and nest-building has been recorded in August, with a breeding-condition male collected in October (Hilty and Brown 1986). The breeding season of March to May suggested by Isler and Isler (1987) thus appears an over-simplification. The two nests found were placed 5 and 7 m up, one in a mossy tree-fork, and the other at the base of palm fronds (Hilty and Brown 1986).

THREATS None is known. The upper Anchicayá valley is still extensively forested, and seemingly safe (see below), and large areas of apparently primary or old secondary forest still exist in Valle department (F. R. Lambert *in litt.* 1989); nevertheless, with such a localized and poorly known distribution, in Ecuador at least, this bird must be potentially at great risk from forest destruction.

MEASURES TAKEN The Anchicayá–Verde watershed (covering an area where this species is recorded) surrounds two hydroelectric plants, and is protected by the CVC (Hilty 1977); this area functions as an ecological reserve, although illegal hunting and clearance for agriculture still occur (F. R. Lambert *in litt.* 1989), and it lies within Los Farallones de Cali National Park (150,000 ha: CNPPA 1982, Hernández Camacho *et al.* undated, Areas Protegidas 1989), which may support other populations of the species, although Hilty (1977) did not encounter it elsewhere during fieldwork in the area. In Ecuador, there are apparently no protected areas within the bird's range (CNPPA 1982): however, it undoubtedly occurs in the Cotacachi–Cayapas Ecological Reserve (NK), for which see equivalent section under Plumbeous Forest-falcon *Micrastur plumbeus*.

MEASURES PROPOSED There is an urgent need to determine the status of this bush-tanager within both Colombia and Ecuador. Formal designation of the Anchicayá forest region as a protected area, perhaps forming an extension to the Los Farallones de Cali National Park, would hopefully ensure the survival of at least one apparently viable population, and perhaps facilitate further work in this important area, where conservation initiatives should be integrated with those proposed for the Banded Ground-cuckoo *Neomorphus radiolosus* (see relevant account), which was also recorded at Alto Anchicayá in 1989, and for other threatened species known to occur in or near to this national park (see the equivalent section under Multicoloured Tanager *Chlorochrysa nitidissima*). The ecological requirements of the Yellow-green Bush-tanager are relatively well known although the evidence that the bird occurs at lower altitudes than usually thought suggests that further work could be undertaken to determine whether vertical migrations are in play.

REMARKS Ridgely and Tudor (1989) reported this species Ibarra, Imbabura province, although this is evidently in error (R. S. Ridgely *in litt.* 1992).

SLATY-BACKED HEMISPINGUS *Hemispingus goeringi* V/R[10]

This poorly known tanager is a cloud-forest specialist of the Cordillera de Mérida, western Venezuela, where it has been recorded from just four discrete areas. Although habitat destruction has mainly been concentrated in areas too low for the bird, montane forests have been adversely affected.

DISTRIBUTION The Slaty-backed Hemispingus is endemic to the south-western half of Cordillera de Mérida in northern Táchira and Mérida states, Venezuela, where the few known localities (coordinates from Paynter 1982) are as follows: (*Táchira*) Páramo Zumbador (c.8°00'N 72°05'W), where the bird was reported by Phelps and Phelps (1950), and whence come two recent records (Ridgely and Tudor 1989); (*Mérida*) Páramo La Negra (c.8°15'N 71°40'W) (Phelps and Phelps 1963); Páramo Escorial (c.8°38'N 71°05'W: 10 km north-east of Mérida), where two males and a female (in MHNG) were collected at 3,000 m prior to 1907 (also Phelps and Phelps 1950); "Pico Humboldt trail" near Tabay (8°38'N 71°04'W: the previous record was presumably from along this trail), where birds have been seen regularly in recent years (C. S. Balchin *in litt.* 1988, D. Willis verbally 1992); above La Mucuy (8°37'N 71°01'W: c.10 km north-east of Mérida, and also presumably along the Pico Humboldt trail), where birds were seen in October 1981 (F. G. Stiles *in litt.* 1992); and Páramo de Aricagua (probably between El Muerte at 8°20'N 71°11'W and c.8°13'N 71°08'W) (Phelps and Phelps 1950).

POPULATION Almost nothing is known, although Ridgely and Tudor (1989) considered the species to be "apparently rare", and indeed mentioned that the two recent records from Táchira were of single birds. However, this species has recently been regularly seen along the Pico Humboldt trail (north-east of Mérida) in small parties of up to five birds (C. S. Balchin *in litt.* 1988, Fjeldså and Krabbe 1990, F. G. Stiles *in litt.* 1992, D. Willis verbally 1992) with up to seven birds being seen in two days on this trail (S. Whitehouse *in litt.* 1990), and it is apparently locally common. B. Swift (*in litt.* 1988) suggested that there is a viable population of this species within the Sierra Nevada National Park.

ECOLOGY The Slaty-backed Hemispingus is restricted to the subtropical and temperate zones between 2,600 and 3,200 m (Meyer de Schauensee and Phelps 1978: Ridgely and Tudor 1989 give the lower altitudinal limit as 2,400 m). It inhabits humid montane forest (cloud-, dwarf and elfin forest), especially towards the upper edge of this zone in areas of scattered trees and at the edge of the humid páramos (Meyer de Schauensee and Phelps 1978, Fjeldså and Krabbe 1990). It forages for insects and berries in the lower growth of the forest, near or perhaps on the ground (two birds were seen moving within 1 m of the ground), usually under dense cover (e.g. along streams) and apparently closely associated with bamboo (C. S. Balchin *in litt.* 1988, Ridgely and Tudor 1989, Fjeldså and Krabbe 1990, F. G. Stiles *in litt.* 1992). Single birds and small groups of up to five have been noted, sometimes feeding with mixed-species flocks (Isler and Isler 1987, Ridgely and Tudor 1989; also C. S. Balchin *in litt.* 1988).

THREATS The Slaty-backed Hemispingus has recently been seen only at the Táchira locality and on the Pico Humboldt trail (see Distribution), but almost nothing is known of its current status between these areas, or indeed of its precise ecological requirements (see above). Possible threats to this species are difficult to assess, although it is clear from Huber and Alarcón (1988) that habitat destruction in this cordillera south-west of Mérida has been dramatic (mainly below 2,000 m, but including some cloud-forest areas), with cloud-forest areas between Mérida and San Cristóbal restricted to two large blocks, but with a more extensive area surrounding the páramo north-east of Mérida; further depletion of this habitat could seriously threaten this tanager.

Desenne and Strahl (1991) suggested that, owing to rapid deforestation in this area, the Sierra Nevada National Park is one of the most threatened parks in Venezuela.

MEASURES TAKEN The Sierra Nevada National Park (267,200 ha) covers a large area of suitable habitat to the north and east of Mérida, and embraces the records from along the Pico Humboldt trail (CNPPA 1982; see Distribution, and also Threats).

MEASURES PROPOSED The precise ecological requirements of the Slaty-backed Hemispingus are in urgent need of attention: if in fact the bird relies on bamboo-dominated cloud-forest, or areas just on the forest–páramo interface, its effective range could be minute and therefore may be at even greater risk from habitat perturbation. The distributional status of this bird also needs attention, particularly inside Sierra Nevada National Park, along with the state of remaining habitat both inside and outside the park. Conservation initiatives in this area should consider the needs of other endemic birds including the Rusty-faced Parrot *Hapalopsittaca amazonina* (see equivalent section under that species).

CHERRY-THROATED TANAGER *Nemosia rourei* E/Ex[4]

This mysterious bird is known from the nineteenth-century type from south-east Minas Gerais, Brazil, and a 1941 sighting from adjacent Espírito Santo, and is likely to be extinct given the deforestation and the high level of ornithological coverage at the forested sites in the region.

DISTRIBUTION The Cherry-throated Tanager (see Remarks 1) is known only from the type-specimen, collected around the mid-nineteenth century at Muriaé, Minas Gerais (see Remarks 2), and from a flock of eight seen in the region of Jatiboca (Jatibocas, 20°05'S 40°55'W in Paynter and Traylor 1991), Espírito Santo, 900 m (see Remarks 3), on 8 August 1941 (Sick 1979d).

POPULATION The type-specimen was sent to C. Euler by J. de Roure, and Euler reported that in 30 years of collecting birds de Roure had no previous knowledge of the species, (Euler) adding that it was also unknown around Cantagalo in Rio de Janeiro (Cabanis 1870); in other words it was clearly recognized (in part simply because it is so distinctive and memorable a form, as expressed by Cabanis 1870) to be a rarity in Brazil even then. Apparently unrecorded for more than a century since it was described, the species was presumed extinct or at best probably close to extinction (King 1978-1979, Scott and Brooke 1985) at the very time that its rediscovery in 1941 (Sick 1979d) first came to light; however, another fifty-year period has passed since that second record and, by CITES criteria, the species could be considered extinct. If it survives, it can only be in very small numbers.

ECOLOGY The only available information is that the August 1941 sighting referred to a flock of eight birds in the canopy of montane forest, 900-1,000 m, and that they were not associated with other birds (Sick 1979d, 1985).

THREATS The whole of Rio de Janeiro state north-west of the rio Paraíba do Sul and adjacent parts of Minas Gerais have been extensively deforested, so that very few areas now exist that could still harbour a population of this species in its known range (LPG; see Measures Taken). The region in Espírito Santo where birds were seen once is now also deforested (Sick and Teixeira 1979; but see Measures Taken).

MEASURES TAKEN The Caparaó National Park lies between the two localities where the species was recorded and is the main conservation unit in the whole region, but forest there had already been disturbed by human activities before the park was created in 1961, so that almost all of it is secondary vegetation (IBAMA 1989). The small but well protected Augusto Ruschi (Nova Lombardia) Biological Reserve, lying much closer, approximately 30 km east of Jatiboca near Santa Teresa in Espírito Santo, has been frequently visited by observers since the 1970s, but the absence of records there suggests that it harbours no population of the species. The only other significant reserve close by the bird's known range is the Desengano State Park near Santa Maria Madalena, south of the rio Paraíba do Sul: the ornithological survey of this park is in progress (J. F. Pacheco *in litt.* 1987, 1991). The species is protected under Brazilian law (Bernardes *et al.* 1990).

MEASURES PROPOSED Fieldwork is needed to rediscover the bird and to provide information on its ecology and status. Any general ornithological work in the north of Rio de Janeiro, east of Minas Gerais and on the serras of Espírito Santo, including the only nature reserves in the region (see Measures Taken) and other areas where the species might be expected, should be extended to include searches to locate it as a matter of priority. Further collection of specimens should not be countenanced.

REMARKS (1) Cabanis (1870) placed *rourei* in *Nemosia* with confidence tempered by the view that it would have been "easier" to place it in a genus of its own, and it is clearly time that the type was re-examined to confirm or otherwise determine its true affinities. It was, however, seen by Hellmayr (1936), who called it "a very distinct species" and a "remarkable bird", but who retained it in *Nemosia.* It was also seen by Stresemann (1954) and H. Sick (see notes below). It is remarkable that the species was not treated in Pinto (1944) nor in Meyer de Schauensee (1970; included in Appendix in 1982), and consequently it was also absent from Dunning (1982). Its absence from Pinto (1952) is possibly a consequence of the confusion about the type-locality. (2) The attribution of the type-locality to Rio de Janeiro state by Hellmayr (1936), and hence Meyer de Schauensee (1966) and King (1978-1979), derives from the way the locality "Muriahié" was described to Cabanis (1870) as "a still little settled area on the left, therefore north, bank of the rio Paraíba do Sul", no state being indicated: more exactly, however, Muriaé is situated on a left-bank affluent (the rio Muriaé) of the Paraíba do Sul, in south-east Minas Gerais; it is not itself on the Paraíba do Sul (*contra* Sick 1979d, 1985, Isler and Isler 1991). The words on the label of the type-specimen (in Berlin Museum) – "Brasilien Dr C. H. Euler S. Muriahe [Muriahie?], Nordufer der Rio Paraiba do Sul *Journ. Orn.* 18, 1870 459" – are in E. Stresemann's writing, the label certainly not being the original (H. Sick verbally 1986). The "S." after Euler presumably stands for "Senior". (3) According to Schubart *et al.* (1965: 97), Jatiboca lies on the margin of the rio Limoeiro, a tributary of the rio Santa Joana, near Itarana in the municipality of Itaguaçu. Sick (1985) called the place "Limoeiro-Jatiboca", at 900-1,000 m. The two known localities are just over a degree apart in both longitude and latitude, and both positions are misplaced on the map in Isler and Isler (1987), giving the impression of a much wider separation of the sites than is the case.

CHAT-TANAGER *Calyptophilus frugivorus* V/R[10]

This tanager occurs in four races in Haiti (also Gonave Island) and the Dominican Republic, but is everywhere at risk from the clearance of its forest habitat, although the two mainland montane races retain some security in certain protected areas (these need support and others need establishment).

DISTRIBUTION The Chat-tanager (for subspeciation review see Remarks 1) is endemic to Hispaniola, occurring in both Haiti (including Gonave Island) and the Dominican Republic (Isler and Isler 1987). Unless otherwise stated records at individual localities represent single birds collected or observed and coordinates are taken from DMATC (1972, 1973).

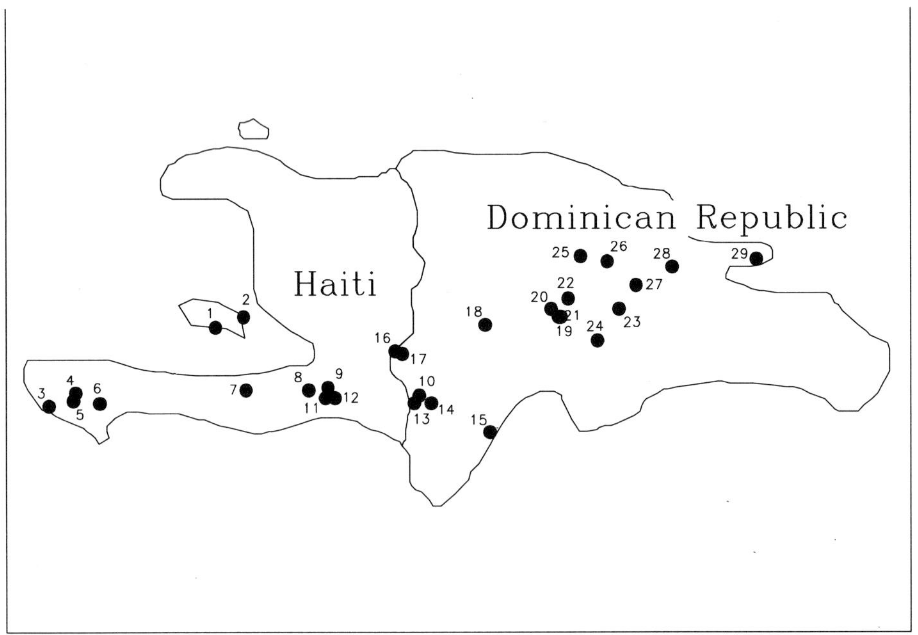

Haiti Records are from:

Gonave Island (race *abbotti*) "Gonave", February 1918 (specimen in USNM), July 1927 (two specimens in USNM), February 1928 (two specimens in AMNH and ANSP) and May 1930 (specimen in ANSP); near La Mahotiérre[1] (18°48'N 73°04'W), where two birds were collected in February 1918 (Wetmore and Swales 1931); between Étroites[2] (18°52'N 72°52'W) and Anse-à-Galets, where two males were collected in July 1927 (Danforth 1929); "Gonave", where two birds were taken in May 1928 (Bond 1928a);

Massif de la Hotte (race *tertius*) higher slopes of Morne La Hotte, behind Les Anglais[3] (18°18'N 74°13'W), June–July 1917 (seven specimens in AMNH, CM and USNM; also Wetmore and Swales 1931); Pic Macaya National Park, where the species was recorded in the area of Pic Macaya[4] (18°23'N 74°02'W) and Plain of Formon[5] (c.18°20'N 74°03'W read from the map in Woods and Ottenwalder 1986, whence the records; also M. A. McDonald *in litt.* 1991); in the latter locality several individuals were heard and observed in April 1992 (J. A. Ottenwalder *in litt.* 1992); Camp Perrin[6] (18°19'N 73°52'W), undated (P. Y. Roumain *in litt.* 1991).

Massif de la Selle (race *tertius*) Morne La Visite[7] (18°24'N 72°51'W), where it has repeatedly been observed (M. A. McDonald *in litt.* 1991); Morne Malanga[8] (18°24'N 72°25'W), January 1928 (specimen in USNM) and undated (Woods and Ottenwalder 1986); La Selle Mountains[9] (these embracing Morne Brouet, probably near Brouet, at 18°25'N 72°17'W; Morne La Selle[10], 18°22'N 71°59'W; Morne Tranchant, untraced but in the vicinity of Kenscoff and Furcy: see, e.g., the map in Wetmore and Swales 1931), where the species was reported to be common, five birds being collected in early June 1928 (Bond 1928a); specifically Morne La Selle, June 1930 (two specimens in AMNH and USNM); specifically Morne Tranchant, January 1928 (specimen in ANSP) and May 1930 (specimen in AMNH); "Nan Nway"[11] (north face of the Massif de la Selle between Morne d'Enfer at 18°21'N 72°21'W and Tête Opaque, which is c.3 km to the south-east of Morne Cabaio, at 18°21'N 72°16'W), where Woods and Ottenwalder (1986) reported it to be common; Morne Tête Bois Pin[12] (Morne Bois Pin, 18°21'N 72°14'W), where a deserted nest was believed to belong to the species, an individual of which was observed nearby, on an ungiven date (Bond 1986).

Dominican Republic Records are from:

Sierra de Baoruco (race *tertius*) Zapotén[13] (18°19'N 71°41'W) (A. Stockton de Dod *in litt.* 1991); Zapotén de Aguacate (probably the same locality as Zapotén), March 1973 (Bond 1973); Loma de Toro, above Zapotén (A. Stockton de Dod *in litt.* 1991); 1 km north of Los Arroyos (between Zapotén and Loma de Toro), undated (Bond 1973); "El Aguacate" (a military post on the road up to Loma de Toro) and above Puerto Escondido[14] (18°19'N 71°34'W), where seven birds were recorded in April 1984 and six in April 1987 (J. E. Pierson *in litt.* 1991); above El Aguacate, where two pairs and two single birds were observed in March 1984 (D. A. Scott *in litt.* 1992); Pie Pol[15] (18°08'N 71°10'W), undated (Bond 1972);

Sierra de Neiba (race *neibae*) near "Kilómetro 204"[16] (a military outpost, 16 km south-west of Hondo Valle, untraced but c.15 km north of Angel Féliz[17] (= Angel Félix, at 18°38'N 71°46'W), where a male (the type of *neiba*) was collected in February 1975 (Bond and Dod 1977); "Sierra de Neiba", May 1975, with two males collected in June 1975 (Bond and Dod 1977);

Cordillera Central (race *neibae*; see Remarks 2) mountains near San Juan[18], where it was reported rare (Wetmore and Swales 1931); 20 km south-east (by road) of Constanza[19] (this being at 18°55'N 70°45'W), where a male and a female were mist-netted in January 1970 (Bond and Dod 1977); Constanza[20], January 1979 (specimen in USNM); Montazo de Constanza[21] (presumably El Montazo, at 18°52'N 70°41'W and near Constanza), undated (Stockton de Dod 1978); El Río[22] (18°59'N 70°38'W), 1919 (Wetmore and Swales 1931); Aguacate[23] (see the map in Wetmore and Swales 1931; also Remarks 3), where three birds were collected in February 1895 (Cherrie 1896); Sierra de Ocoa[24] (see Remarks 4), where the species was reported to be "found in abundance" sometime around 1927 (Wetmore and Swales 1931). Untraced localities include El Mogote de la Horma, Rancho Arriba, Loma de Rodríguez and Los Vedados, all in Stockton de Dod (1978), who gave no further details;

North-eastern lowlands (nominate *frugivorus*; see Remarks 5) La Vega[25], where two birds were collected in July 1883 (specimens in CM and USNM) and others observed in March 1907 (Verrill and Verrill 1909; also Wetmore and Swales 1931); in forest near La Vega, April 1895 (Christy 1897); Miranda[26] (see the map in Wetmore and Swales 1931), March-April 1907 (Verrill and Verrill 1909; also Wetmore and Swales 1931); Cotuí[27], 1921 (Kaempfer 1924); swamps near "Almercen"[28] (= Villa Rivas, 19°11'N 69°55'W) (the type-locality), where eleven birds were collected in late August 1883, one in 1887 and five in January 1924 (Cory 1885; also Wetmore and Swales 1931; specimens in AMNH, ANSP); Arenoso (untraced), March 1884 (Wetmore and Swales 1931); Samaná[29], where a pair was secured in April 1883 (Wetmore and Swales 1931).

POPULATION Two races, *abbotti* and *frugivorus*, appear to be in trouble; the other two fare much better and retain reasonable though isolated and fragmented populations.

Haiti The race *abbotti* was reported to be "fairly common" on Gonave Island in 1918 and "probably not uncommon" in 1927 although difficult to see (Wetmore and Swales 1931), but the two birds collected in May 1928 (Bond 1928a) were apparently the last published record for the island. Although Bond (1956b) considered the species to be "fairly common", Schwartz and Klinikowski (1965) could not find it in a day's visit to the island, nor could M. A. McDonald (*in litt.* 1986) during fieldwork in February 1985 in the area of Anse-à-Galets.

Bond (1956b) reported the race *tertius* to be common in dense thickets on the higher mountains of the Massif de la Hotte and Massif de la Selle in 1930, and Woods and Ottenwalder (1986) also found it common in mesic "rak bwa" in both parks (i.e. Pic Macaya and La Visite) between 1983 and 1985. M. A. McDonald (*in litt.* 1991) heard it on numerous occasions on Morne La Visite and saw it below Pic Macaya, suggesting a relatively healthy population in the area.

Dominican Republic The race *tertius* was reported common to Bond (1973) in the area north-east of Los Arroyos, Sierra de Baoruco, and J. E. Pierson (*in litt.* 1991), after his observations in April 1984 and 1987 above Puerto Escondido, same sierra, assumed it to be fairly common in that area. A. Stockton de Dod (*in litt.* 1991) likewise believed that this race is "quite common" in its restricted range.

The race *neibae* was reported to be rare in the mountains north of San Juan but "in abundance" on the Sierra de Ocoa (Wetmore and Swales 1931). Schwartz and Klinikowski (1965) could not find the species despite intensive work in the Cordillera Central, yet A. Stockton de Dod (*in litt.* 1991) believed that this race was "quite common".

Nominate *frugivorus* is probably the most threatened, as noted by A. Stockton de Dod (*in litt.* 1991), whose many trips to different parts of its range resulted in not a single observation. At the time of its discovery, Cory (1885) reported it "not common".

ECOLOGY On the main island, the Chat-tanager primarily inhabits thick underbrush and dense growth along streams in moist mountain broadleaf forests, at altitudes generally above 1,000 m, although locally at lower elevations on Gonave Island and in north-eastern Hispaniola. On Gonave, it inhabits semi-arid scrub in the lower, hotter parts (Danforth 1929, Wetmore and Swales 1931, Bond 1979, Woods and Ottenwalder 1986, Isler and Isler 1987). In mainland Haiti, Woods and Ottenwalder (1986) found it commonest in the "rak bwa" (broadleaf forest where mesic conditions predominate, such as in ravines, depressions, limestone outcrops, along streams and rivers and at the mouths of caves and sinkholes; see Remarks 6), underneath pines *Pinus occidentalis*; in La Visite National Park, Massif de la Selle, 75% of their records (derived from carefully planned transects through all major habitats) were in "rak bwa" and 25% in "bwa raje" (broadleaf forest in isolated areas unsuitable for agriculture, such as around sinkholes, steep ravines, the steep north face of the massif and areas with numerous blocks of limestone); in the Pic Macaya National Park, Massif de la Hotte, 75% of their records were in "rak bwa", 15% in "bwa raje" and 10% in "bwa pen" (mature pine-forest with scrubby to open understorey vegetation), and on the Plain of Formon (same mountain range) 75% of their records were in "rak bwa" and 25% in "bwa raje". In the Dominican Republic Stockton de Dod (1978) associated the species with the remote high mountains, where it can be found near watercourses with thick vegetation (broadleaf forest); she noted the importance of "cañadas" for the species in the Sierra de Baoruco, describing them as deep dark streams where rainwater has been trapped and moisture preserved (A. Stockton de Dod *in litt.* 1991). The "Kilómetro 204" in the Sierra de Neiba was also reported to Bond (1976) as extremely humid, with a dense growth of broadleaf trees and an undergrowth of tree ferns and abundant moss. The ecological needs of the nominate race have not been described; Cory (1885) simply stated that his specimens were taken "in the swamps" near Almercen.

The Chat-tanager is largely terrestrial in habits (Bond 1928a, Stockton de Dod 1978), scratching among fallen leaves in search of food items (e.g. centipedes, cockroaches, spiders, earthworms) (Stockton de Dod 1981); according to Danforth (1929), stomachs contained 10% vegetable matter (two seeds in one stomach), and 90% animal matter (a moth, an ant *Pheidole megacephala*, two hairy spiders, a thrip, and the ootheca of a cockroach).

One nest, believed to pertain to this species, was built 60 cm above ground in a fern (Isler and Isler 1987). Birds were reported breeding in June (Bond 1928a); birds collected in late May 1930 in the Massif de la Selle and in late June and early July 1917 in Massif de la Hotte were in breeding condition (specimens in AMNH; also Bond 1943); two males collected in mid-July 1927 on Gonave Island had "testes large" (specimens in USNM).

The species is often reported to be shy and secretive (Kaempfer 1924, Wetmore and Swales 1931, Stockton de Dod 1978, Woods and Ottenwalder 1986), although natives at Camp Perrin assured P. Y. Roumain (*in litt.* 1991) that it was very tame and often approached houses.

THREATS Although reported locally common (see Population), the Chat-tanager cannot be considered safe as deforestation has been enormous throughout Hispaniola.

Haiti Severe habitat loss has occurred since 1977 and "rak bwa" is now restricted to low dense patches as a result of chronic clearing and burning (Woods and Ottenwalder 1986). In Anse-à-Galets on Gonave Island, extreme deforestation of the nearby hills and ravines has exposed the town to the hazard of flash floods (Paryski *et al.* 1989). Woods and Ottenwalder (1986) considered the species to be threatened because it is only found in dense wild wet places. A broader view of habitat loss in the country is in Threats under White-winged Warbler *Xenoligea montana.*

Dominican Republic Notes on habitat loss are in Threats under White-winged Warbler. A. Stockton de Dod (*in litt.* 1991) noted that large areas where she observed the Chat-tanager are already gone and the type-locality in the north-east of the island has suffered "unbelievable" destruction.

MEASURES TAKEN In Haiti, besides the species's occurrence in the La Visite and Pic Macaya National Parks, no measures are known. In the Dominican Republic, A. Stockton de Dod (*in litt.* 1991) noted that the species is vulnerable, but that if the habitat in the national parks in the Sierra de Baoruco and Cordillera Central is adequately preserved it should be able to survive. Furthermore, two additional and extremely important areas for the species in the Sierra de Neiba and Sierra de Baoruco have already been proposed for protection (see DVS 1990).

MEASURES PROPOSED Surveys in both countries should attempt to determine the present status of each of the four races, whose ranges should be precisely delimited and their ecological requirements identified. It is essential to recognize the great importance of the national parks in the Massif de la Hotte and Massif de la Selle in Haiti and in the Sierra de Baoruco and Cordillera Central in the Dominican Republic, plus the proposed protected area in the Sierra de Neiba and the proposed protected area in the Sierra de Baoruco, namely Loma La Trocha de Pey (see DVS 1990), where the Chat-tanager, the threatened White-winged Warbler and La Selle Thrush *Turdus swalesi* (absent from the Massif de la Hotte) (see relevant accounts) share almost identical ranges and habitat requirements (i.e. the last remaining mountain cloud-forests in Hispaniola). All of these extant and proposed parks should be carefully managed to ensure the conservation of the last fairly well-preserved habitat within their boundaries, on which the Chat-tanager and the above-mentioned species ultimately depend. Furthermore, this conservation effort would also benefit other threatened species whose ranges partly overlap, namely Hispaniolan Hawk *Buteo ridgwayi*, Plain Pigeon *Columba inornata*, Rufous-breasted Cuckoo *Hyetornis rufigularis* (see relevant accounts), and the near-threatened Hispaniolan Parakeet *Aratinga chloroptera*, Grey-headed Quail-dove *Geotrygon caniceps*, Palm Crow *Corvus palmarum* and White-necked Crow *C. leucognaphalus*. Searches are needed for the race *abbotti* on Gonave Island and *frugivorus* in any of its known localities (see Distribution) or in nearby areas, although searches in the Península de Samaná and Los Haitises National Park have already failed to locate it (A. Stockton de Dod *in litt.* 1991).

REMARKS (1) The taxonomy of this species, which occupied its own genus, is convoluted: originally, two distinct species were admitted, *frugivorus* (from north-east Dominican Republic) and *tertius* (south-west Haiti), which Hellmayr (1936) later considered members of one species together with *abbotti* (Gonave Island) and *selleanus* (Massif de la Selle). The latter has been considered a synonym of *tertius* (Bond 1936, 1956b), an opinion adopted by Paynter (1970) and reaffirmed by Bond and Dod (1977) who, however, described another subspecies *neibae*. Subsequently, Pregill and Olson (1981) again suggested that *tertius* and *frugivorus* should probably be considered separate species. AOU (1983) considered *tertius* and *frugivorus* as two groups, and in this were followed by Isler and Isler (1987) who, however, also contemplated the possibility of their being distinct species ("*tertius*" including *abbotti* and "*frugivorus*" *neibae*). This arrangement appears to ignore Bond (1982), who remarked that *neibae* more closely resembles *tertius* than the nominate race. The current account refers to the four subspecies listed by Isler and Isler (1987), although it is clear that more taxonomic investigation is needed. (2) Some of the localities within the Cordillera Central, namely Aguacate, El Río, mountains north of San Juan and Sierra de Ocoa, were initially attributed to the nominate race (Wetmore and Swales 1931) at a time when *neibae* was not described; however, Bond and Dod (1977) and A. Stockton de Dod (*in litt.* 1991) are of the opinion that *neibae* is the widespread race in the Cordillera Central. (3) From the description of his trip (Cherrie 1896), it is clear that Aguacate is located south-east of Bonao. (4) This sierra (north of San José de Ocoa) can be considered a southwards extension of the Cordillera Central. (5) The limits of *neibae* and the nominate subspecies are not completely clear as, for instance, the specimen collected at La Vega (still in a mountainous area) is believed to belong to *neibae* (A. Stockton de Dod *in litt.* 1991). (6) According to these authors, within the boundaries of La Visite National Park such habitat now occurs as patches of low, dense forest as a result of long continued clearing and burning.

GOLD-RINGED TANAGER *Buthraupis aureocincta* V[9]

This rare cloud-forest species was until recently known from just four specimens collected in or before 1946 on Cerro Tatamá, on the Pacific slope of the West Andes, Colombia, and although threatened by forest destruction, records during 1992 show that a population still exists some 40 km north of this area.

DISTRIBUTION The Gold-ringed Tanager was until recently known from just four specimens taken on three occasions in or before 1946, in the vicinity of Cerro Tatamá, at the boundary of Risaralda, Chocó and Valle departments on the Pacific slope of the West Andes, Colombia. These specimens come from the following localities (coordinates from Paynter and Traylor 1981): Cerro Tatamá (5°00'N 76°05'W), where the type (an adult male) was collected at 2,040 m during October 1909 (Hellmayr 1910a); on the Cartago–Nóvita trail, near Cerro Tatamá, where a male and female (in AMNH) were collected at 2,195 m in December 1911 (Chapman 1917a); and La Selva (4°55'N 76°09'W; Risaralda department *contra* Ridgely and Tudor 1989), on the north-west slope of Cerro Tatamá, where a female (in ANSP) was collected at 2,135 m in January 1946 (Meyer de Schauensee 1948-1952). The bird remained unrecorded until May–June 1992, when a population was found on the mountain ridge of Alto de Pisones, 24 km north-west of Mistrató, Risaralda (i.e. c.40 km north of Cerro Tatamá), between 1,600 and 1,800 m (F. G. Stiles *in litt.* 1992).

POPULATION M. Pearman (*in litt.* 1990) unsuccessfully searched the south-west slope of Cerro Tatamá (in suitable habitat at correct altitudes) during August 1987, concluding that the bird at best must be rare, and scarcer than the Black-and-gold Tanager *Buthraupis melanochlamys* with which it is sympatric but which may occur at slightly lower altitudes (F. G. Stiles *in litt.* 1992; see relevant account, also Ecology). However, at Alto de Pisones (c.40 km north of Cerro Tatamá, and near Mistrató) the species was found to be abundant, with numerous individuals seen daily between the end of May and beginning of June 1992: birds were seen in pairs and post-breeding family groups, and six were mist-netted with a further three (male, female and juvenile) collected (F. G. Stiles *in litt.* 1992).

ECOLOGY On Cerro Tatamá, this tanager has been recorded between 2,040 and 2,195 m (see Distribution), inhabiting humid, mossy cloud-forests (Hilty and Brown 1986; see also Chapman 1917a). At Alto de Pisones (from 28 May to 8 June 1992), the species was found to be numerous, but restricted to the ridges between 1,600 and 1,800 m (never occurring lower), in an area of dense cloud-forest extending from the ridge-tops (c.2,000 m) down to 1,400 m and lower, although the character of the forest changed to a more subtropical type below c.1,500 m (F. G. Stiles *in litt.* 1992). Birds were seen in pairs and post-breeding family groups, often associating with mixed-species flocks, and were seen feeding at *Clusia* and *Miconia* (F. G. Stiles *in litt.* 1992). Although the Black-and-gold Tanager was seen at the same site, these were generally found between 1,400 and 1,600 m (see equivalent section under that species), and were usually not associated with the same mixed flocks as the present species in the zone of overlap (at c.1,600 m) (F. G. Stiles *in litt.* 1992). The Gold-ringed Tanager had apparently just finished breeding by the beginning of June 1992 (no singing was heard; see Population); thus the breeding season seems to coincide with that of the Black-and-gold Tanager (F. G. Stiles *in litt.* 1992). The two birds taken in December 1911 (in AMNH) were not in breeding condition.

THREATS S. L. Hilty (*in litt.* 1986) cited deforestation, colonization and mining activities as potential threats to this species. In 1987, M. Pearman (*in litt.* 1990) found evidence of tree-felling inside the forest on the south-west slope of Cerro Tatamá (within the national park). The slopes of Cerro Tatamá are apparently much more deforested than the area around Alto de Pisones, where a significant tract of forest is almost virgin above 1,500 m, with small clearings along the river bottoms between 1,200 and 1,400 m (F. G. Stiles *in litt.* 1992), but this entire area appears otherwise to have suffered from widespread deforestation.

MEASURES TAKEN In 1987, the area surrounding the type-locality was declared the Tatamá National Park, 51,900 ha (Hernández-Camacho *et al.* undated; but see Threats).

MEASURES PROPOSED Surveys at Alto de Pisones and more generally in the Mistrató area are essential to determine the status of the bird and its habitat there: this area is apparently suitable for a reserve (being important for the Black-and-gold Tanager, and critical for the present species), and the Corporación Autónoma Regional de Risaralda (CARDER) has been informed to this effect (F. G. Stiles *in litt.* 1992). Protection of this seemingly significant tract of virgin forest must be of the highest priority. Systematic searches for both this species and Black-and-gold Tanager are urgently needed within the Tatamá National Park in order to determine the current status and ecological requirements of both birds there. It must also be a priority to prevent any deforestation from encroaching onto the lower (c.2,000 m) slopes of the park, as these areas are presumably the most important for this species. Extension of the park to provide an effective buffer-zone to the lowest areas of cloud-forest (above c.1,000 m) would also be advantageous to both Gold-ringed and Black-and-gold Tanagers. The threatened Multicoloured Tanager *Chlorochrysa nitidissima* and Red-bellied Grackle *Hypopyrrhus pyrohypogaster* have both been recorded in Tatamá National Park, and near to the Mistrató area (at Siató and Pueblorrico), and hence any conservation action in this region should also consider their needs (see relevant accounts).

GOLDEN-BACKED MOUNTAIN-TANAGER *Buthraupis aureodorsalis* K[12]

This rare tanager inhabits elfin forest at over 3,000 m in the departments of San Martín, La Libertad and Huánuco, north-central Peru. Several other species have a similar range, and reserves should be established before human pressure becomes a threat to this habitat.

DISTRIBUTION The Golden-backed Mountain-tanager is known from c.40 specimens and additional sightings, from three areas in three departments of north-central Peru, where localities (coordinates from Stephens and Traylor 1983) are as follows: (*San Martín*) Puerto del Monte (7°32'S 77°10'W), where birds were seen at the treeline in August 1981 (D. F. Stotz *in litt.* 1989); (*La Libertad*) Mashua (c.8°12'S 77°14'W), between 3,140-3,350 m east of Tayabamba on the trail to Ongón; and (*Huánuco*) in the Cordillera Carpish at Bosque Unchog, Quillacocha, and Sariapunta (9°41-43'S 75°54'-76°07'W), between 3,050 and 3,500 m (possibly 2,750-3,700 m) (Blake and Hocking 1974, Parker and O'Neill 1976, Isler and Isler 1987; specimens in AMNH, ANSP, FMNH, LSUMZ, MHNJP, USNM, and ZMUC). The birds presumably also occurs in the unexplored intervening region, but has not been found in similar habitat further north, in Cordillera de Colán, Amazonas department (Isler and Isler 1987).

POPULATION This species was considered uncommon by Parker *et al.* (1982), and during 27 days of fieldwork at Puerto del Monte, San Martín department, it was only recorded three times (three, two and two birds) (D. F. Stotz *in litt.* 1989).

ECOLOGY The Golden-backed Mountain-tanager is found at 3,050-3,500 m, where it inhabits elfin forest (notably *Clusia* and *Escallonia* trees: Fjeldså and Krabbe 1990), especially large islands of forest surrounded by grassland, but occasionally occurring in scattered low trees and scrub in open areas near forest (Isler and Isler 1987). It travels in pairs or small groups of 3-5 (sometimes up to seven), usually by themselves, but sometimes (probably for short periods only) with mixed-species flocks (Isler and Isler 1987). It flies just above the tree-tops between widely separated foraging sites, and after settling into the vegetation becomes difficult to observe (Isler and Isler 1987). Birds sometimes rest quietly for long periods whilst looking around: prior to flight, one bird will begin calling, and after taking off, be quickly followed by others, one at a time (Isler and Isler 1987).

The tanagers forage from the ground to the tree-tops, but most often at mid-heights in small trees and bushes, feeding on berries, fruit (e.g. of *Miconia* and *Cecropia*) and insects: a flock of five (studied for over 45 minutes) was feeding in moss-laden trees less than 3 m high scattered across grassland at the edge of a bog; each bird foraged for some time in one tree (without much movement) before flitting on to the next; they hung or leaned down to pick food out of mosses and lichens on branches, less often gleaning leaves, and then flew from shrubs to nearby stubble to glean twigs, leaning over to pick food (presumably insects) from grass (Isler and Isler 1987). The stomachs of six specimens (in LSUMZ, ZMUC) contained vegetable matter (in one case identified to *Phrygilanthus* fruit), with two also holding animal matter (including an 8 mm beetle) (Isler and Isler 1987). No nest has been found. Two females with brood-patches were collected in September, while four juveniles or immatures were taken in July, October and November (specimens in FMNH, LSUMZ, and ZMUC).

THREATS None is known. The region inhabited by the species is at present largely uninhabited by man.

MEASURES TAKEN Although it is rare there, this species is known to occur in the Río Abiseo National Park in San Martín department (D. F. Stotz *in litt.* 1989), a large reserve (274,000 ha: IUCN 1992) which holds a number of threatened species, some with restricted geographical and altitudinal ranges, and a number of wider-ranging but rare and local species (see Yellow-browed Toucanet *Aulacorhynchus huallagae* account for details).

MEASURES PROPOSED An additional reserve holding a viable population of this rare tanager would be desirable. Obviously any initiatives within its range should take into consideration the requirements of the threatened and endemic species mentioned in the account for Yellow-browed Toucanet (see also Remarks).

REMARKS The range of this tanager overlaps almost precisely with that of the near-threatened Rufous-browed Hemispingus *Hemispingus rufosuperciliaris*, which is uncommon, secretive, and stays low in bamboo *Chusquea* and thickets of dense shrubs and small trees, at the tree-line and in upper montane forest down to c.2,600 m (Blake and Hocking 1974, Ridgely and Tudor 1989, TAP): conservation efforts in this region should therefore also consider the interests of this species.

BLACK-AND-GOLD TANAGER *Buthraupis melanochlamys* V/R[10]

This little-known cloud-forest tanager is endemic to two disjunct areas of western Colombia, in one of which it has not been recorded since 1948, while in the other it survives in and around Tatamá National Park; birds have been recorded foraging in secondary habitats.

DISTRIBUTION The Black-and-gold Tanager is known from two disjunct areas in western Colombia, namely: on the north and western slopes of the Central Andes in Antioquia; and the western slopes of the West Andes in Chocó, Risaralda and Valle departments.

In Antioquia, the few localities where this species has been recorded are as follows (unless otherwise stated, coordinates are from Paynter and Traylor 1981): La Frijolera (c.7°10'N 75°25'W), where a male and two females (in AMNH) were taken at 1,525 m in December 1914 and January 1915 (also Chapman 1917a); in the vicinity of Valdivia (7°11'N 75°27'W; i.e. on the saddle between the Cauca and Nechí drainages), where birds (eight males and seven females, in USNM) were taken at 2,075-2,285 m near Ventanas (c.7°05'N 75°27'W) and at 1,525-1,675 m above Sevilla (untraced) during June 1948; and Yarumal (6°58'N 75°24'W; on the east slope of the Central Andes), a locality mentioned by Nicéforo-María and Olivares (1978).

Further south, this species has only been recorded in Risaralda at San Antonio de Chamí (Quebrada Sutú, north of Mistrató), where a bird was netted and others seen at 1,300 m (F. G. Stiles *in litt.* 1992); Alto de Pisones (24 km north-west of Mistrató), where birds were found between 1,400 and 1,750 m in May–June 1992 (F. G. Stiles *in litt.* 1992); above Mistrató (on the Pacific slope), where two birds were collected and others seen between 1,700 and 1,950 m in April–June 1992 (F. G. Stiles *in litt.* 1992); and from the vicinity of Cerro Tatamá (on the border of Chocó, Risaralda and Valle departments), where localities include: La Selva (4°55'N 76°09'W, on the Quebrada Jamarraya), where the type (a female collected in October 1909: Hellmayr 1910a) and subsequent specimens (in ANSP, ICN, LSUMZ, USNM) were taken between 1,380 and 2,135 m; and at c.1,500 m on the south-west slope in August 1987 (M. Pearman *in litt.* 1990); and nearby, at Alto del Oso (4°52'N 76°20'W: Vereda la Italia, municipality of San José del Palmar), where a specimen (in UV) was collected at 1,000 m in October 1987 (LGN; coordinates from M. S. Alberico verbally 1992).

POPULATION The Black-and-gold Tanager was, at least formerly, not uncommon in parts of its limited range (Hilty and Brown 1986): for example, 15 birds were taken near Valdivia during June 1948 (see above), although this northern population may now be extinct (see Threats). On Cerro Tatamá 11 birds were taken at La Selva in 1945 (Ridgely and Tudor 1989), and the bird was common in secondary forest undergrowth and plantain cultivations at Alto del Oso in Chocó department during October 1987 (groups of two, two, three and five individuals seen in three days: LGN); however, M. Pearman (*in litt.* 1990) saw just one during two days' searching in the same region and year. At La Selva, Ridgely and Tudor (1989) suggested that this species has been recorded with but is much commoner than Gold-ringed Tanager *Buthraupis aureocincta* (see relevant account). Above Mistrató, northern Risaralda, this species was found to be fairly common (in pairs and breeding) during April 1992 (two birds collected and various others seen), and at Alto de Pisones it was found to be common from 1,400 to 1,600 m, but uncommon to rare higher up during May and June 1992 (F. G. Stiles *in litt.* 1992).

ECOLOGY Records of this tanager come from between 1,000 and 2,285 m (Hilty and Brown gave its upper limit as 2,450 m), where it inhabits subtropical humid forest (cloud-forest) with heavy undergrowth (Hilty and Brown 1986), although it has also been recorded from disturbed primary and secondary forest, forest patches (down to c.4 ha in area), forest borders and cultivated land surrounded by primary forest (LGN, F. G. Stiles *in litt.* 1992). Near Mistrató in April–June 1992, F. G. Stiles (*in litt.* 1992) found the species to be most numerous between 1,400 and

1,600 m (the zone in which the forest changes from cloud- to subtropical forest), although he recorded it up to 1,750 m. On the south-western slope of Cerro Tatamá, M. Pearman (*in litt.* 1990) described the bird seen in August 1987 as inhabiting mossy cloud-forest (c.1,500 m), the individual being discovered preening in the subcanopy, and then observed foraging from this height down to 3 m (associated with a mixed feeding flock containing Wedge-billed Woodcreeper *Glyphorynchus spirurus*, Red-headed Barbet *Eubucco bourcierii*, Scaly-throated Foliage-gleaner *Anabacerthia variegaticeps*, and Yellow-throated Bush-tanager *Chlorospingus flavigularis*); the bird was seen to feed on small clumps of berries. Near Mistrató, in the zone of overlap at c.1,600 m, the Black-and-gold Tanager was not usually associated with the same feeding flocks as Gold-ringed Tanager (see Ecology under this species). Also in 1987, pairs or groups of up to five individuals were seen searching actively for small fruit and insects at mid-levels, and on low palms and saplings in the undergrowth (LGN). Birds in breeding condition have been collected in Antioquia in June (seven males and three females in USNM), and December (one male in AMNH), and F. G. Stiles *in litt.* (1992) mentioned that birds were breeding (singing and carrying nest material) in the vicinity of Mistrató in April, with others singing at the end of May and beginning of June 1992 when also a juvenile was mist-netted; this could all indicate a two-peak breeding schedule coinciding with the rainy seasons, which run from May to June and September to October (Hilty and Brown 1986).

THREATS The almost complete deforestation of the area around Valdivia (Hilty and Brown 1986) has been cited as the cause for the possible extirpation of the northern population of the Black-and-gold Tanager (Isler and Isler 1987), and indeed there appear to be no records from this region since the 1940s (see Distribution). Evidence from around Cerro Tatamá and above Mistrató suggests that birds can utilize fragmented, disturbed or secondary habitat, at least for foraging (F. G. Stiles *in litt.* 1992; see Ecology), although nesting has only been recorded from lightly disturbed forest (F. G. Stiles *in litt.* 1992), and it therefore remains doubtful that the species can sustain viable populations without primary forest. The slopes of Cerro Tatamá are much more deforested than is the area around Mistrató (c.35-40 km north), which still comprises virgin forest above c.1,500 m (F. G. Stiles *in litt.* 1992).

MEASURES TAKEN The Tatamá National Park (51,900 ha), on the boundary of Chocó, Risaralda and Valle departments, established in 1987 (Hernández Camacho *et al.* undated), harbours a population of this species (see Threats).

MEASURES PROPOSED The integrity of forest within the Tatamá National Park needs to be ensured, and an extension to embrace more forest above 1,000 m is a priority. The status of the species and its habitat in the northern part of its range requires investigation in order to determine whether or not it still survives there, and whether any forest needs urgent protection. Surveys in the Mistrató area (including Alto de Pisones) are also warranted to determine the status of the bird and its habitat there: this area is apparently suitable for a reserve (and critical for the Gold-ringed Tanager), and the Corporación Autónoma Regional de Risaralda (CARDER) has been informed to this effect (F. G. Stiles *in litt.* 1992). The precise ecological requirements of this species need to be studied, notably the effects that secondary and disturbed habitats have upon its breeding success, but any studies within the Tatamá National Park and the Mistrató area should be undertaken in conjunction with those proposed for the Gold-ringed Tanager and ideally also the Multicoloured Tanager *Chlorochrysa nitidissima* and Red-bellied Grackle *Hypopyrrhus pyrohypogaster*, which have all been recorded in this area (see relevant accounts). Details of threatened species and proposals referring to Serranía de San Lucas, Antioquia, are given in the equivalent section under Chestnut-bellied Hummingbird *Amazilia castaneiventris*.

MASKED MOUNTAIN-TANAGER *Buthraupis wetmorei* V/R[10]

This little-known, secretive tanager inhabits humid páramo forest ecotone in the Andes of eastern Ecuador and immediately adjacent Peru and Colombia. The ubiquitous tradition of burning páramo grassland has almost completely destroyed its habitat.

DISTRIBUTION The Masked Mountain-tanager (see Remarks 1) is known from six areas in southern Colombia, Ecuador and northernmost Peru.

Colombia The five records comprise two specimens, taken at 3,300 and 3,450 m, and three sightings, one of them at 3,000 m; all are from what is now Puracé National Park in the Volcán Puracé region at the southern end of the Central Andes in eastern Cauca department; one of the specimens was taken above Puracé, the other at Páramo de Puracé, near Laguna San Rafael (where Willis 1988 recorded the species in April 1962), while one of the sightings was at km 143 on the Popayán–Neiva road in July 1976, and the other was at km 35 (Paletará) on the Coconuco road in June 1980 (Hilty and Silliman 1983, Hilty and Brown 1986). A population may exist at the northern end of the Central Andes, from where there is a recent sighting by Colombian ornithologists of the Bay-vented Cotinga *Doliornis sclateri* (TAP), a species known to share habitat with the Masked Mountain-tanager in Ecuador (Bloch *et al.* 1991, Robbins *et al.* in prep.).

Ecuador The species is known only from the eastern Andes, records being: west slope of Cerro Mongus, 3,400-3,500 m, south-eastern Carchi province, at c.0°22'N 77°52'W, March 1992 (Robbins *et al.* in prep.); south-eastern end of Culebrillas valley (not located, but 20° north of west of Mt Sangay [c.2°00'S 78°20'W] in what is now Sangay National Park), elevation not specified but above 3,350 m, August 1929 (Moore 1934a,b); Cordillera Zapote-Najda on the border of Azuay and Morona-Santiago provinces near the Gualaceo–General P. Limón G. road, c.3°01'S 78°38'W, 3,250-3,350 m, June 1984 (two specimens in ZMUC) and subsequently (P. Coopmans verbally 1990, R. A. Rowlett and J. C. Arvin *per* B. M. Whitney *in litt.* 1991); Podocarpus National Park, in the border area of Loja and Zamora-Chinchipe provinces, at 4°06'11"S 79°06'09"W, from mid-1980s down to the present (D. Platt *in litt.* 1987, Bloch *et al.* 1991, J. Fjeldså verbally 1991). It undoubtedly occurs more widely in the eastern Andes, though in dwindling numbers, and a sizeable population may occur in the ornithologically poorly explored Cordillera de los Llanganates, northern Tungurahua and south-eastern Napo provinces, where much habitat may remain (NK).

Peru The species was found on Cerro Chinguela, 2,900 m, Piura, near the border of Cajamarca department, at 5°07'S 79°23'W, July 1980 (Parker *et al.* 1985; coordinates from Graves 1980), although searches there in August 1989 were unsuccessful (B. M. Whitney *in litt.* 1991). It seems doubtful that the species occurs further south, where several intensive expeditions by LSUMZ in its habitat have failed to find it (TAP).

POPULATION The species has generally been reported to be rare or uncommon (Parker *et al.* 1985, Hilty and Brown 1986, Bloch *et al.* 1991, Robbins *et al.* in prep.). Its secretive habits may have led to its being somewhat overlooked (see Ecology), and in the right habitat (at Cajanuma) it could be judged fairly common, with 4-5 individuals along a 2 km trail (C. Rahbek *in litt.* 1992), but it seems highly doubtful that the population exceeds 5,000 birds (three pairs per km straight line), and it may well be considerably smaller; furthermore, numbers must be dwindling rapidly as regular burning causes the grassland–forest ecotone to narrow to a few metres and the altitude of the treeline to descend (NK).

ECOLOGY The Masked Mountain-tanager inhabits very humid areas, where it frequents mossy stunted elfin and treeline forest, as well as scattered bushes, mountain bamboo, giant grasses and dense brush above the forest (Moore 1934b, Hilty and Silliman 1983, Parker *et al.* 1985, Hilty and

Brown 1986, Fjeldså and Krabbe 1990, Bloch *et al.* 1991, Robbins *et al.* in prep.). Although records range from as low as 2,900 m to no higher than 3,550 m (see Distribution), the species is nearly always found (an exception being Cajanuma, where birds penetrate elfin forest in mixed-species flocks: C. Rahbek *in litt.* 1992) at or above the treeline (Moore 1934b, Parker *et al.* 1985, Hilty and Brown 1986, Fjeldså and Krabbe 1990, Bloch *et al.* 1991), which naturally occurred up to near 4,000 m in some parts of northern Ecuador, lower in southern Ecuador and northernmost Peru, but which has now been lowered considerably by the activities of man in most places (NK). Singles, pairs, or groups of up to four may follow mixed-species flocks with other frugivores such as Black-chested Mountain-tanager *Buthraupis eximia*, Pale-naped Brush-finch *Atlapetes pallidinucha* and Black-backed Bush-tanager *Urothraupis stolzmanni*; it is a very furtive species, and it may forage silently and rather slowly along thick, moss-covered branches or in the interior or near the top of dense bushes and shrubs, eating berries at the tips of branches in treetops or sallying clumsily for flying insects, and crossing openings quickly, occasionally flying as far as 25 m while following a mixed-species flock (Moore 1934b, Parker *et al.* 1985, Hilty and Brown 1986, Isler and Isler 1987, Fjeldså and Krabbe 1990, Bloch *et al.* 1991, J. Fjeldså verbally 1991, B. M. Whitney *in litt.* 1991, Robbins *et al.* in prep.). Stomach contents have included seeds and green fruit (Isler and Isler 1987, Robbins *et al.* in prep.); birds have been seen to take a small reddish berry (B. M. Whitney *in litt.* 1991). A female in breeding condition was taken in Colombia on 28 February (Hilty and Brown 1985). Food-begging by a recently fledged juvenile was observed in February 1990 (R. A. Rowlett and J. C. Arvin *per* B. M. Whitney *in litt.* 1991). Immatures have been collected in Carchi on 22 March (Robbins *et al.* in prep.) and in Morona-Santiago on 12 June (specimen in ZMUC).

THREATS The consistent burning of páramo grasslands in most parts of the high Andes has prohibited regeneration of bushes and trees, lowered the treeline several hundred metres, and almost completely destroyed the species's habitat; reasons for this burning vary from promotion of fresh growth for (generally very few) cattle to beliefs that the fire will cause rain (NK).

MEASURES TAKEN The species occurs within three national parks (see Distribution). However, records from as low as 3,000 m in Puracé National Park in Colombia suggest that burning of the páramo grasslands may occur there (NK). No burning currently seems to take place in Podocarpus National Park in southern Ecuador (D. Espinosa verbally 1991). There is no available data on burning from Sangay National Park, although suitable habitat for the species is restricted to the eastern part of the park, and burning certainly takes place in some other Ecuadorian protected areas (NK).

MEASURES PROPOSED Burning of páramo grassland within national parks should be strictly prohibited and these areas not used for domestic animals. Initiatives to explain to local communities why this action is being taken, and to seek to find acceptable alternatives for the farmers thus affected, will certainly also be necessary. Surveys are needed of the areas in Colombia and Ecuador where this species is anticipated (see Distribution). In all the above, consideration should also be given to other species with similar habitat needs (see Remarks 2) or distributions. For example, in Puracé National Park this tanager occurs with five other threatened species, the details of which are given in the equivalent section under Bicoloured Antpitta *Grallaria rufocinerea*.

REMARKS (1) A separate genus *Tephrophilus* was erected for *wetmorei*, mainly on the basis of its bill shape and relatively strong feet, and the Buff-breasted Mountain-tanager *Dubusia taeniata*, with its somewhat similar colour pattern and wing-formula, was believed to be its closest relative (Moore 1934a). However, later authors (e.g. Meyer de Schauensee 1970) have placed *wetmorei* in *Buthraupis* and retained *Dubusia* as a valid genus. (2) The almost complete destruction of the entire ecosystem forming this species's habitat has undoubtedly seriously affected other species of bird with similar habitat requirements, such as the Black-backed Bush-tanager *Urothraupis stolzmanni* and the Bay-vented Cotinga. The latter, however, also occurs south and east of the río Marañón, where a sizeable tract of habitat still occurs from San Martín to Huánuco (see account of Golden-backed Mountain-tanager *Buthraupis aureodorsalis*).

ORANGE-THROATED TANAGER *Wetmorethraupis sterrhopteron* V[9]

This tanager is only known from Zamora-Chinchipe province, Ecuador, and northern Amazonas department, Peru, where it inhabits mature humid forest in the upper tropical zone. It remains vulnerable owing to its small distribution at elevations where the forested slopes are not steep or wet, and are therefore ideal for cultivation.

DISTRIBUTION The Orange-throated Tanager (see Remarks) is known from the southern upper reaches of río Zamora in Zamora-Chinchipe province, Ecuador, and along the middle río Marañón valley in northern Amazonas department, Peru.

Ecuador In July and August 1990 this species was discovered in Zamora-Chinchipe province, at 1,000 m along the upper río Nangaritza at Shaime, c.04°20-25'S 78°40'W (M. Marin, R. Corado and J. M. Carrión verbally 1990; four specimens in MECN and WFVZ).

Peru The type-specimen was procured from Aguaruna Indians in July 1963 at Chávez Valdivia, 4°26'S 78°11'W, and had presumably been taken in the foothills of Cordillera del Condor to the west or north-west (Lowery and O'Neill 1964). In 1964 the species was found chiefly at elevations above 600 m (and 50 specimens were then collected) along the río Cenepa (at Tutinum and Suwa), río Comaina (at Kusú and an unspecified locality), and río Kangka (at Bashuim), all at 4°27-33'S 78°12-16'W; on the left bank of the río Marañón (at Chiangkus, Chicais, and Chipi), all at 4°39-48'S 78°12-18'W; and on the right bank of the río Marañón in the hills 3 km west of Urakusa, c.4°42'S 78°03'W, and at Nazaret, 5°09'S 78°19'W (O'Neill 1969), this latter locality being only some 86 km south of Chávez Valdivia.

The species was not found during 16 days of fieldwork in humid forest at 750 m, north-east of Tarapoto, San Martín department (Davis 1986), and may well be genuinely restricted to the hills bordering the middle río Marañón.

POPULATION O'Neill (1969) noted that the species "seems to be common", although it was given the status "uncommon" by Parker *et al.* (1982).

ECOLOGY The Orange-throated Tanager inhabits mature humid terra firme and montane forest, chiefly at elevations from 600 to 800 m (O'Neill 1969, Parker *et al.* 1982, Isler and Isler 1987). It travels in pairs or small groups of up to five individuals, sometimes joining mixed-species flocks, and forages in the canopy, seemingly over a large area (Isler and Isler 1987). Birds scan leaves and search mosses and small bromeliads on branches, and may also hover, presumably to pick hanging fruits from the tips of branches (O'Neill 1969, Isler and Isler 1987). One of a flock of three was collected in the mid-canopy of disturbed forest (specimen in MECN). One stomach contained seeds, fruit pulp and a beetle (Isler and Isler 1987), and another fruit remains and insects (MECN label data). There are no data on breeding, except that a bird (with an incompletely ossified skull) collected in August had small testes (specimen in MECN).

THREATS None is known, save the general widespread and increasing forest clearance (mainly along roads) within the bird's altitudinal range. The range of the species falls almost entirely within Aguaruna Indian territory, but the planned improvement and eastward extension of the road south of the río Marañón (Parker *et al.* 1982) will undoubtedly attract new settlers, and the lower hills along the road between ríos Nieva and Chiriaco (Imaza) may soon look like the lower foothills along the northern road between ríos Chiriaco and Utcubamba, which are being rapidly cleared (Parker *et al.* 1982, NK).

MEASURES TAKEN None is known.

MEASURES PROPOSED A protected area (perhaps within the Cordillera del Condor) with a wide altitudinal range, so as to hold both the present species and other threatened birds, such as Spot-winged Parrotlet *Touit stictoptera*, Royal Sunangel *Heliangelus regalis* and Cinnamon-breasted Tody-tyrant *Hemitriccus cinnamomeipectus*, should be created as a priority. A study to disclose the distributional status of this species should be undertaken in collaboration with work on these other species (see relevant accounts): such work should concentrate on finding areas of sympatry that would be suitable for protection.

REMARKS The Orange-throated Tanager is a distinctive bird, the only member of its genus.

MULTICOLOURED TANAGER *Chlorochrysa nitidissima* V/R[10]

This montane forest tanager, formerly common and still moderately so where it occurs, is found chiefly in the West but also to a lesser extent (one record since 1951) in the Central Andes of Colombia, where it is threatened by habitat fragmentation.

DISTRIBUTION The Multicoloured Tanager is restricted to scattered areas in the West Andes, with some records from the Central Andes, Colombia. It has been recorded from six departments, where localities (coordinates, unless otherwise stated, from Paynter and Traylor 1981) are as follows:

Antioquia Jericó (5°47'N 75°47'W; at 1,965 m on the eastern slope of the West Andes), where a male (in BMNH) was collected in 1876 (also Sclater and Salvin 1879); and La Bodega (c.5°42'N 75°07'W; on the western slope of the Central Andes, c.17 km east of Sonsón), where three birds (in USNM) were taken at 1,770 m during June 1951;

Caldas Hacienda Sofía (= La Sofía at 5°38'N 75°04'W; on the eastern slope of the Central Andes, and on the south side of the río Samaná), where a female (in USNM) was taken at 1,140 m during May 1951;

Risaralda Siató (c.5°13'N 76°07'W; at 1,600 m on the western slope of the West Andes, and very close to the following locality) (Hellmayr 1911); Pueblorrico (5°12'N 76°08'W; at 1,560 m on the western slope of the West Andes, 25 km north-west of Cerro Tatamá) (Hellmayr 1911); La Selva (c.4°55'N 76°09'W; on the north-western slope of Cerro Tatamá), where six males and four females (in AMNH, plus two in ICN) were taken between 1,525 and 2,135 m from December 1945 until February 1946 (also Meyer de Schauensee 1948-1952); and at the Ucumarí Regional Park (4°43'N 75°35'W; in the Central Andes, 14 km north-east of Pereira), where the species has been recorded at 1,850 m (L. M. Renjifo verbally 1991, LGN);

Quindío El Roble (4°41'N 75°36'W; on the western slope of the Central Andes, and 5 km north-west of Salento), where two males (in AMNH, BMNH) were taken at 2,195 m in November 1911 (also one male in ICN); and Salento (4°38'N 75°34'W; at 1,895 m on the western slope of the Central Andes), whence come two specimens (Chapman 1917a);

Valle "Lago Calima" (Calima = Darién, which is at 3°56'N 76°31'W; on the western slope of the West Andes), where a female (in DMNH) was taken at 1,300 m in December 1975; Bosque de Yotoco Reserve (3°52'N 76°33'W; on the eastern slope of the West Andes: Orejuela *et al.* 1979), where the bird has been recorded between 1,400 and 1,600 m (Orejuela *et al.* 1979); Zelandia (untraced, but in Dagua municipality at c.3°40'N 76°40'W, and on the western slope of the West Andes), where a female (in UV) was collected at 1,750 m; La Cumbre (3°39'N 76°33'W; at 1,580 m on the Pacific slope at the crest of the West Andes, 21 km north-north-west of Cali), where five birds (in CM) were taken in July and August 1918; Lomitas (3°38'N 76°38'W; on the Pacific slope of the West Andes, 13 km south-west of La Cumbre), where three males (in AMNH) were collected at 1,525 m in February and March 1911 (also Chapman 1917a); "km 18" or "El Dieciocho" (on the old Cali–Buenaventura road near the crest of the West Andes at c.1,800 m), whence come numerous recent records (Hilty and Brown 1986; also F. R. Lambert *in litt.* 1989, M. Pearman *in litt.* 1990, P. Kaestner *in litt.* 1992, G. Kattan *in litt.* 1992, L. G. Olarte *in litt.* 1992); Bitaco (3°36'N 76°36'W; at 1,350 m on the western slope of the West Andes), where four birds (in CM) were taken in July and August 1918; Mares (c.3°32'N 76°38'W; on the eastern slope near the crest of the West Andes, 12 km north-west of Cali), whence come two males (in UV); Ríolima (untraced, but apparently on the eastern slope of the West Andes near the following locality), where five birds (in AMNH) were taken between 1,220 and 1,525 m in June and August 1898 (also Meyer de Schauensee 1948-1952); San Antonio (3°30'N 76°38'W; on the eastern slope of the West Andes, 10 km north-west of Cali), where two males (in AMNH, USNM) were collected at 2,135 m in November 1907 and January 1911 (also Chapman 1917a), with more recent records from Miller (1963); La Castilla (3°30'N 76°35'W; at 1,600 m on the eastern slope of the West Andes), where a female (in AMNH) was collected in June 1898; and Pichindé (3°26'N 76°37'W; on the eastern slope of the West Andes, 10 km west-south-west of Cali), where a male (in YPM) was taken in February 1957, and near "Peñas Blancas" (untraced, but c.7 km from Pichindé), where birds have been seen as recently as March 1987 (M. Pearman *in litt.* 1990);

Cauca La Gallera (c.2°35'N 76°55'W; on the western slope of the West Andes), where a male (in AMNH) was collected in June 1911 (also Chapman 1917a); río Munchique (c.2°35'N 77°15'W: on the western slope of Cerro Munchique), whence comes a record at 900 m (Meyer de Schauensee 1948-1952); and El Tambo (2°25'N 76°49'W; on the eastern slope of the West Andes, below Cerro Munchique), where a male (in ANSP) was collected at 900 m in July 1938.

POPULATION The number of specimens taken at single localities (see above) suggests that the Multicoloured Tanager was historically at least locally common. Records from the second half of the twentieth century are almost exclusively from the Buga–Cali–Dagua area (i.e. Darién, Bosque de Yotoco, Pichindé and "km 18") in the West Andes (see above), where the bird is found readily in the remnant forest patches, and is reported to be "still fairly numerous" and "fairly common locally" (Hilty and Brown 1986, Ridgely and Tudor 1989). This conclusion is reinforced by the most recent records (all years from 1987 to 1991) from Pichindé and km 18, where small groups of 2-5 birds can often be seen (F. R. Lambert *in litt.* 1989, M. Pearman *in litt.* 1990, P. Kaestner *in litt.* 1992, L. G. Olarte *in litt.* 1992), although the species is clearly present at much lower densities than other similar-sized tanagers (G. Kattan *in litt.* 1992). Despite intensive recent ornithological surveys on both slopes of the Central Andes (LGN), the record from Ucumarí Regional Park appears to be the only one from this mountain range since 1951, although the bird was apparently never widespread or common there (see above).

ECOLOGY The Multicoloured Tanager occurs in the subtropical zone primarily between 1,300 and 2,195 m, although there are records from 1,140 m in the Central Andes, and as low as 900 m in the West Andes (not the Pacific slope, *contra* Hilty and Brown 1986, Ridgely and Tudor 1989: see Distribution). The species inhabits humid, mossy, montane forest (cloud-forest), and is recorded regularly in mixed-species flocks at forest borders, adjacent tall second-growth woodland and clearings with a few large trees left standing (Hilty and Brown 1986, Ridgely and Tudor 1989, G. Kattan *in litt.* 1992); the area around km 18, near Cali (where the species is a permanent resident, and whence come most recent observations) is highly fragmented with forest patches ranging from 10 to 400 ha, in a matrix of second growth, pastures with scattered trees, and suburban houses (G. Kattan *in litt.* 1992).

Birds forage from middle to upper levels (upper understorey to subcanopy) in the forest, mostly in the crowns of trees (the median foraging height has been recorded at c.10 m, rarely descending below 4.5 m), where they typically cling to leaves of the outer foliage to glean the undersides of leaves in a warbler or vireo-like manner (Hilty and Brown 1986, Isler and Isler 1987, Ridgely and Tudor 1989). The Multicoloured Tanager is mostly recorded in pairs, less often singly or in small (family) groups (2-5 individuals: never in monospecific flocks), and is very often found in pairs associating with mixed-species flocks dominated by other tanagers (Isler and Isler 1987, Ridgely and Tudor 1989). Around km 18, G. Kattan (*in litt.* 1992) recorded lone birds (or pairs) comprising 42% of feeding records, of which 87% involved fruits (*Cordia*, *Miconia*, *Palicourea* and *Ficus*), and 13% insects; with the other 58% being of pairs (always) in large mixed flocks, of which 91% involved insects and 9% fruits. Other observations are of the bird eating arillate fruit (*Tovomita* sp.), pecking at green 10-12 mm berries, and feeding on flower clusters and small *Ficus* fruits, with insects comprising small larvae and hairy caterpillars (Miller 1963, Isler and Isler 1987). Birds move actively and rarely remain long in one tree (Isler and Isler 1987, Ridgely and Tudor 1989).

Miller (1963) suggested that the non-breeding period above Cali embraced the months from September to December, although in this same region G. Kattan (*in litt.* 1992) observed adults feeding juveniles in August 1990, and Hilty and Brown (1986) reported a stub-tailed juvenile with two adults on 1 November and a grown juvenile on 8 January; a male in breeding condition (in AMNH) was taken nearby on 28 January. In the Central Andes, three birds in breeding condition (and an immature) were collected in May and June (specimens in USNM), and a male (in AMNH) not in breeding condition was taken in November.

THREATS The Multicoloured Tanager is apparently threatened by habitat destruction (Isler and Isler 1987), and indeed its range is highly fragmented (Hilty 1985). To the west of Cali along the old Cali–Buenaventura road, and at Pichindé, the forest exists only in small remnant patches (10-400 ha) that are being sold for conversion to building land and for cattle-grazing, and therefore this area is insecure (F. R. Lambert *in litt.* 1989, M. Pearman *in litt.* 1990, G. Kattan *in litt.* 1992). However, there are still extensive areas of seemingly suitable forest away from the roads in this area (M. G. Kelsey verbally 1992), and the species may well be relatively safe within such sites (see Ecology).

MEASURES TAKEN The species has been or may be recorded from several areas that are currently protected either within the national parks system or as other (often private) reserves, and are as follows:

Tatamá National Park (51,900 ha, in the Central Andes of Risaralda), which may well protect a number of the Risaralda department localities and apparently embraces suitable habitat (and altitudes) for the species, although there have been no records from the immediate vicinity of Cerro Tatamá since 1946 (Hernandéz Camacho *et al.* undated; see Distribution);

Ucumarí Regional Park (also in the Central Andes of Risaralda: see Distribution), protecting 4,240 ha of the buffer zone of Los Nevados National Park, and administered (protected and managed) by the Corporación Autónoma Regional de Risaralda (CARDER): the area includes primary and secondary forest (where this species has recently been seen) and pastures (which are currently being reforested), and is used for research, education and recreation (LGN);

Bosque Bremen (Quindío); a private "reserve" of unknown size (P. Ruiz verbally 1991);

Farallones de Cali National Park (150,000 ha, south-west of Cali, Valle), which is bounded along at least part of its northern edge by the old Cali–Buenaventura road, and as such incorporates localities where this species has been recorded (Reserva Hato Viejo, Pichindé–Peñas Blancas and Reserva La Teresita: G. Kattan *in litt.* 1992, Hernandéz Camacho *et al.* undated), the park itself being relatively inaccessible, protecting large areas of pristine and poorly known habitat where this species may well occur (M. G. Kelsey verbally 1992);

Bosque de Yotoco Reserve (559 ha) is a site where this species has recently been recorded, and is administered by the Corporación Autónoma Regional de Cauca (CVC) and Universidad Nacional de Colombia, which effectively protect it against poachers and colonists: the area is used for permanent environmental education programmes and some research (Areas Protegidas 1989, LGN);

Munchique National Park (44,000 ha, Cauca) which is in the immediate proximity of both Cauca records (although neither is actually from inside the park) and protects areas with suitable habitat (Hernández Camacho *et al.* undated), suggesting that the tanager may well occur within its boundaries.

MEASURES PROPOSED The priority for this tanager, which is relatively well known ecologically, is to determine its status in the protected areas mentioned above, and to assess the extent of remaining suitable habitat both in these areas and nearby. Any surveys in these areas, whether of this bird or of suitable habitats, should if possible also target other (at least partly sympatric) threatened species occurring there: these species are listed below under the protected areas in which they have been recorded:

Tatamá National Park: see equivalent section under Black-and-gold Tanager *Buthraupis melanochlamys*;

Ucumarí Regional Park: Cauca Guan *Penelope perspicax*, Yellow-eared Parrot *Ognorhynchus icterotis*, Golden-plumed Parakeet *Leptosittaca branickii* and Red-bellied Grackle *Hypopyrrhus pyrohypogaster* (see also Moustached Antpitta *Grallaria alleni*);

Farallones de Cali National Park (including Alto Anchicayá): possibly White-chested Swift *Cypseloides lemosi* (should be searched for), Banded Ground-cuckoo *Neomorphus radiolosus*, Bicoloured Antvireo *Dysithamnus occidentalis*, Turquoise Dacnis *Dacnis hartlaubi* (possibly), Yellow-green Bush-tanager *Chlorospingus flavovirens* and Tanager-finch *Oreothraupis arremonops*;

Bosque de Yotoco: Cauca Guan and Turquoise Dacnis;

Munchique National Park (below 2,200 m) Cauca Guan *Penelope perspicax*, Bicoloured Antvireo and possibly White-chested Swift (the threatened species in this park occurring above 2,200 m are given in the equivalent section under Colourful Puffleg *Eriocnemis mirabilis*, and those below 1,000 m under Plumbeous Forest-falcon *Micrastur plumbeus*).

AZURE-RUMPED TANAGER *Tangara cabanisi* V/R[10]

Endemic to the Sierra Madre de Chiapas, Mexico, and neighbouring Guatemala, this rare tanager is restricted to humid evergreen forest in a narrow elevational band primarily on the Pacific slope. Unfortunately, this very same habitat is at the preferred height for coffee cultivation, and in Mexico the species is now limited to less than 1,300 km² of remaining forest.

DISTRIBUTION (Information in this section, unless otherwise stated, derives from Heath and Long 1991). The Azure-rumped Tanager (or Cabanis's) is endemic to the Sierra Madre de Chiapas, Mexico, and neighbouring Guatemala, and has been recorded from just seven discrete areas.

Mexico From north-west to south-east, the five localities (all in Chiapas state) where this species has been recorded are as follows: (1) above San Antonio Miramar (15°40'N 92°59'W; between 1,100 and 1,400 m on the path to Finca Custepec); (2) close to and along a section of the El Triunfo trail (from 1,000 to 1,700 m) between El Limonar on the Pacific slope to above Finca Prusia on the Gulf slope, but especially around Cañada Honda (15°37'N 92°48'W; at c.1,450 m on the Pacific slope), where birds have been recorded annually (since 1973: the first record there was in 1965), but also between Palo Gordo and Loma Bonita (15°39'N 92°51'W; at 1,200 m), and on the Gulf slope, south of Ejido Santa Rita (15°41'N 92°48'W; at 1,450 m) and at Finca El Porvenir (15°42'N 92°58'W; between 1,400 and 1,600 m above Finca Custepec); (3) Monte Ovando (15°24'N 92°36'W), where a specimen was taken at 1,675 m in August 1937; (4) Volcán Tacaná (15°07'N 92°06'W), where a specimen was collected at c.1,000 m sometime between 1955 and 1965; (5) and "Cacahoatán" (c.14°59'N 92°09'W), where two specimens were taken in April and May 1943, apparently at 600 m (see Remarks 1).

Guatemala Records come from two areas (or perhaps only one: see Remarks 2): Costa Cuca (= Flores Costa Cuca) district (c.14°39'N 91°47'W), where the type-specimen was collected in 1866, apparently at 600 m (see Remarks 2); and on the south-western slope of Volcán Santa María (c.14°42'N 91°32'W), where birds have been seen between 1,280 and 1,450 m since 1976, specific localities including Finca El Faro Reserve (a small flock seen in 1987 at 1,450 m: P. Rockstroh *in litt.* 1988), Finca El Patzulin (adjacent to Finca El Faro) (C. Leahy *in litt.* to A. Long 1990), and another unnamed locality in the immediate vicinity of the other two fincas (B. M. Whitney *in litt.* to A. Long 1990), presumably along the road to Quetzaltenango that borders the two fincas.

POPULATION (Information in this section, unless otherwise stated, derives from Heath and Long 1991). In its preferred habitat (see Ecology), the Azure-rumped Tanager is quite common and generally found quickly: however, the extent of this habitat in Chiapas is very small, being less than 1,300 km². Along the El Triunfo trail (whence come the majority of sightings and population data), birds were observed daily during fieldwork between April 1989 and June 1990, with several nests found within the 1,250 to 1,650 m section of the trail (on the Pacific slope). The species is usually noted in groups of up to six individuals (although sometimes 16 or even 30 birds). Population data from Guatemala are generally lacking, the species being known from few sightings: a small flock was seen in 1987 at Finca El Faro Reserve, with two pairs seen near there in March 1989 (B. M. Whitney *in litt.* to A. Long 1989).

ECOLOGY (Information in this section, unless otherwise stated, derives from Heath and Long 1991). The Azure-rumped Tanager occurs chiefly on the Pacific but also on the Gulf slopes (in humid sheltered valleys) of the Sierra Madre de Chiapas (Mexico and Guatemala). In Chiapas, the species is found between 1,000 and 1,700 m on the Pacific slope, with most sightings from between 1,250 and 1,650 m (see Remarks 3), and records from between 1,400 and 1,600 m on the Gulf slope.

The preferred habitat of this species in Guatemala has been described as wet subtropical evergreen forest, but more precisely (along the El Triunfo trail, Mexico: this paragraph) as medium-height broadleaf forest with a canopy up to 25 m and occasional trees to 35 m. It is essentially an evergreen formation although a number of trees shed their leaves towards the end of the dry season in February (this period of flushing is short, with new leaves fully grown by late March). The canopy cover is complete but, with tree falls common, natural disturbance to the forest can give the appearance of an open, discontinuous canopy. The dominant tree species at El Triunfo are: *Ficus cookii*, *Coccoloba matudae* and *Dipholis minutiflora*. The understorey is well-developed with small trees and shrubs, especially rich in species from the Rubiaceae, Compositae and Solanaceae, and containing a high density of *Chamaedorea* palms. Epiphytes are prominent but are significantly less abundant than in the cloud-forest community above 1,700 m. Mosses are sparse and are replaced by lichen which covers many of the trunks and branches. On the Gulf slope of the El Triunfo trail, the birds were found in habitat similar to that identified on the Pacific slope, although it is generally restricted to humid sheltered valleys and contains more sweetgum. Outside of these Gulf slope valleys, sweetgum–pine–oak forest is the dominant formation and the bird has never been seen in it. It seems likely that 1,700 m is a genuine upper limit for the species as this altitude marks the upper limit of the tropical elements which are characteristic components of its habitat. Although the plant species composition of forest occurring below 1,000 m (on the Pacific slope) is distinct from known Azure-rumped Tanager habitat, it remains possible that such forest supports the species as it shares with the higher formations some physiognomic characteristics and certain species such as *Ficus cookii* (the dominant tree in tanager habitat); if the bird is found below 1,000 m, it will probably be restricted to the humid river valleys where tree species characteristic of its habitat are commoner.

The Azure-rumped Tanager has been seen at forest edges and in areas where limited human activities have degraded the forest, but never in coffee plantations. Observations at El Triunfo (during 1989 and 1990) suggest that it does not frequently use fruiting shrubs in cleared areas; despite on occasions being more visible in open patches or forest edge, it was seen more often foraging in pristine forest. The majority of its time is spent in the upper strata and canopy of the tallest trees. The birds are most often encountered in small groups (see Population), but are also seen in pairs and singly, rarely travelling with mixed-species flocks (Hilty and Simon 1977, A. Long *in litt.* 1991). Food, including fruit (*Ficus* and melostome fruits have been recorded) and mostly insects, is obtained primarily in the canopy, but sometimes lower (Hilty and Simon 1977, A. Long *in litt.* 1991). In Mexico, breeding has been recorded from April to June, with a majority of nests being recorded in *Ficus cookii* trees (one being 12 m up near the end of a 6 m long branch, and overhanging a canyon) (Isler and Isler 1987, A. Long verbally 1992).

THREATS (Information in the section, unless otherwise stated, derives from Heath and Long 1991). The major threat to the Azure-rumped Tanager is habitat destruction which, in Chiapas is a serious problem, owing to the fact that the altitudinal range of the species coincides with the optimal land for coffee cultivation (Chiapas produces more than 30% of Mexico's coffee). During the present century, the primary centre for coffee production in Chiapas has been the Pacific slope of the Sierra Madre from the Guatemala border to about 100 km into the state. Development in this region, and the establishment of important coffee plantations (e.g. Fincas Prusia and Custepec) along the main river valleys on the Gulf slope, has resulted in the destruction of more than 15% of the Azure-rumped Tanager's total range (it is possible that this figure is actually higher owing to the lack of information regarding partially degraded or small patches of agricultural land). Agriculture, especially coffee cultivation, is continually expanding in the Sierra Madre; recently this has been due to new peasant farming communities or "ejidos". Mexican law states that any land that is national territory and not officially protected or in use can be leased out to a group of families to live from. In the Sierra Madre, ejidos have been granted large land parcels (often greater than 5,000 ha) and, although much of this land usually remains forested, clearance for cultivation occurs quickly (as farming is the ejidos' major source of food and income). Most of the mid-elevation cloud-forest on Volcán Tacaná is severely fragmented (on the Mexican side), although some large patches persist on the higher peaks on the Guatemalan side of the volcano (A. G. Navarro and A. T. Peterson *in litt.* 1991).

In Guatemala, the main problems of habitat destruction caused by agricultural encroachment (primarily coffee production) appear to be the same as those found in Chiapas. The Azure-rumped Tanager is distributed within the primary region of coffee production (i.e. along the Pacific slope of the sierra) where, between 1950 and 1977, land under coffee expanded from 1,600 to 2,700 km^2 (Colchester 1991).

MEASURES TAKEN (Information in this section, unless otherwise stated, derives from Heath and Long 1991). In Chiapas, the only protection for the species is the El Triunfo Biosphere Reserve which, however, contains as much as 39% (437 km^2) of the total probable and possible habitat within the state. This reserve spans both Pacific and Gulf slopes in the central portion of the Sierra Madre de Chiapas, but most suitable habitat for the species is found within the reserve's buffer zone, an area in which there are several small but expanding communities. The future status of the tanager rests heavily on the conservation of this habitat within the reserve, which in many areas is currently inadequate.

In Guatemala, the only protected area where the Azure-rumped Tanager has been recorded is Finca El Faro (670 ha), an experimental private reserve whose elevational range is c.800 to 2,500 m and which comprises 300 ha of forest from 1,500 to 2,200 m, remnant gallery forest in river canyons below 1,500 m, and plantation crops including coffee, cardamon *Elettaria cardamomum* and macadamia nuts *Macadamia integrifolia* (Vannini and Morales 1990).

MEASURES PROPOSED Generally, the range of the Azure-rumped Tanager is poorly understood: the western limits are unknown (but the bird should be searched for in the Sierra Atravesada of the Chimalapas region of Oaxaca: A. G. Navarro and A. T. Peterson *in litt.* 1991), and in Guatemala the bird has been recorded from just two (or perhaps one: see Remarks 2) areas. For these reasons, more surveys are needed within suitable habitat (as defined in the second paragraph under Ecology) to try and locate other populations of the bird, which, if (or when) found, will probably require protection. More specifically, the effective conservation of suitable habitat for the species within the El Triunfo Biosphere Reserve is essential for the species's continued survival: collaboration in favour of conservation (i.e. which provides viable, less damaging alternatives to present agricultural practices) between local people of the buffer zone and the Instituto de Historia Natural (IHN) staff is needed to ensure the adequate protection of suitable remaining habitat (Heath and Long 1991). Proposals put forward by the reserve management state that forest vigilance and relations with local people will be developed in other parts of the reserve where current protection is inadequate (management efforts are currently concentrated around one core area) (Heath and Long 1991).

In Guatemala, apart from locating new populations, the remaining forest on the slopes of Volcán Santa María is in urgent need of protection (apart from that within Finca El Faro) and of extensive ecological survey (in order to determine the status of both suitable habitat and the species). This area (i.e. Volcanes Chicabal and Santa María) has been officially proposed as a protected area (P. Hubbell *in litt.* 1989) which, if granted and ensured, would provide adequate protection for the tanager in the country.

REMARKS (Information in this section comes from Heath and Long 1991) (1) Two specimens in MLZ (collected by M. del Toro Avilés) are labelled "Cacahoatán", and from c.600 m: the town of Cacahoatán (at c.600 m) also gives its name to the small municipality in which it lies, and which encompasses much land over 1,000 m (including the southern slope of Volcán Tacaná). The validity of label data on specimens collected by M. del Toro Avilés has been questioned, and given the evidence concerning the species's altitudinal range (see Ecology) the MLZ specimens may well have come from near Volcán Tacaná whence comes another record (see Distribution).

(2) The type-specimen was collected in the district of Costa Cuca which remains untraced, although a village named Flores Costa Cuca appears on recent maps and lies at 550 m in the foothills above the Pacific coastal plain: Volcán Santa María is found just 30 km west-south-west of this locality (see Distribution), and it is clearly conceivable that the Costa Cuca specimen originated on or near Volcán Santa María. (3) The specimens collected from below 1,000 m (i.e. those from Costa Cuca and Cacahoatán) are not considered here owing to the imprecise nature of the localities given (see Remarks 1 and 2).

SEVEN-COLOURED TANAGER *Tangara fastuosa* V/R[10]

Although still numerous at a few localities in its native north-east Brazil, this forest-associated small frugivore has suffered the twin threats of habitat loss and exploitation for trade, and now requires considerable management to be secured.

DISTRIBUTION The Seven-coloured Tanager, first mentioned and illustrated by Marcgrave (1648), is endemic to north-eastern Brazil in the states of Paraíba, Pernambuco and Alagoas in lowland forests to at least 980 m. Its presence in Rio Grande do Norte remains a possibility (Hellmayr 1936).

Paraíba Its occurrence in this state was long ago anticipated (Hellmayr 1936), but the only records are from the vicinities of Serrotinho (untraced) in the municipality of Alagoa Grande (Zenaide 1953), and João Pessoa, where birds were seen in small patches of forest in the campus of the Universidade Federal da Paraíba (M. T. Rodrigues *per* C. Torres *in litt.* 1985).

Pernambuco At least 15 nineteenth-century skins, in AMNH, BMNH and MCZ, are merely labelled "Pernambuco". Forbes (1881) recorded what he believed to be this species once at Quipapá and collected a specimen near Macuca (untraced; between Quipapá and Garanhuns); he considered a bird freshly shot at Cabo as evidence of the species's occurrence nearer the coast. In this century records (north to south) are from: Usina São José, Goiana; Charles Darwin Ecological Refuge, near Goiana; Tapacurá Ecological Station, São Lourenço da Mata; Várzea, 8°04'S 34°57'W; Horto Florestal de Dois Irmãos, Recife; Engenho Pirajá, c.8°19'S 35°06'W, Mercês; UFPE Ecological Station at Serra (or Brejo) dos Cavalos, Caruaru; Saltinho Biological Reserve, Rio Formoso; Garanhuns; Brejão (Berla 1946, A. G. M. Coelho *in litt.* 1986, de Azevedo Junior 1990, specimens in AMNH, NHMW; coordinates from Paynter and Traylor 1991).

Alagoas Its occurrence in this state was again long since anticipated (Hellmayr 1936), but the only recorded localities are: Engenho Riachão (now included in the Pedra Talhada Biological Reserve: see Measures Taken), Quebrangulo, April 1957 (Pinto and de Camargo 1961) and currently (Studer 1985, M. Pearman *in litt.* 1990, B. M. Whitney *in litt.* 1991); Pedra ("Serra") Branca, Murici, November 1983, May 1984 and January 1986 (specimens in MNRJ) and October 1990 (B. M. Whitney *in litt.* 1991); junction of BR101 and BR104, April 1992 (M. Pearman *in litt.* 1992); and São Miguel dos Campos, 1979 (Sick and Teixeira 1979).

POPULATION The Seven-coloured Tanager did not appear to be common in Pernambuco over a century ago (Forbes 1881), and in the first half of this century it was considered to be both "not very common" near Recife (Lamm 1948) and "very common" in the region of Mercês (Berla 1946). Although discrepancies recur in modern assessments, it seems widely accepted that a serious decline in numbers and a fragmentation of populations have taken place owing to habitat destruction and cagebird exploitation, so that the species has become restricted to a few patches of forest where it may be still common but remains vulnerable (King 1978-1979, Coelho 1986, Ridgely and Tudor 1989; also J. Vielliard *in litt.* 1986, D. M. Teixeira *in litt.* 1987; see Threats). In the late 1980s the species persisted in good numbers at Pedra Branca in Alagoas (Ridgely and Tudor 1989) and was common at the Charles Darwin and UFPE reserves in Pernambuco, but not at the others (A. G. M. Coelho *in litt.* 1986).

ECOLOGY The species is found primarily in the canopy and edges of lowland and montane forests, but also occurs in second growth, often associating with other birds in mixed flocks (Forbes 1881, Lamm 1948, Zenaide 1953, Coelho 1986, A. Studer *in litt.* 1987, specimens in MNRJ). It may be commonest in well developed second growth rather than tall forest (B. M. Whitney *in litt.* 1991). Birds at Pedra Talhada were in open agricultural land with scattered trees (B. C. Forrester *in litt.* 1992).

Stomach contents of specimens in LSUMZ and MNHN are given as vegetable matter, seeds and fruit remains. Food seen taken includes fruits of bromeliads, *Cecropia* fruit, mandacaru *Cereus* sp., small berries of low melastome shrubs, cultivated red pepper and guava; in drier times birds drink water accumulated in mulungu *Erythrina* flowers (Coelho 1986, A. Studer *in litt.* 1987, Azevedo Junior 1990, B. M. Whitney *in litt.* 1991).

Of the five specimens (in AMNH) collected in early February whose gonad condition was recorded, two were "fairly enlarged", one "half enlarged" and two "not enlarged". The breeding season is stated to correspond to the southern spring and summer, approximately from October to March (Teixeira and Pinto 1988). The statement that nests are built inside dense clumps of bromeliads or other plants high in the middle storey of forest (Coelho 1986) corresponds to the record of two nests that were semi-hidden in the bases of arboreal bromeliads, 7-9 m from the ground (Teixeira and Pinto 1988), while a nest with two eggs found on 1 March 1987 at Quebrangulo was only 2 m from the ground, fixed where a banana leaf brushed against a banana trunk, near a stream in a clearing inside forest; two young fledged and left this nest on 31 March (A. Studer *in litt.* 1987).

THREATS Heavy trade in this species has been regarded as the main cause of its decline, and forest clearance throughout its limited range has also clearly contributed to its current status (King 1978-1979, Sick and Teixeira 1979, Sick 1985, Coelho 1986, Charity 1988, Ridgely and Tudor 1989); the continued clearance of even secondary habitats for sugarcane production in north-east Brazil must still itself greatly threaten the species (B. M. Whitney *in litt.* 1991).

Trade The Seven-coloured Tanager commands high prices in the pet trade, since its bright colours make it a very attractive cagebird. Importations into Europe and North America began in the nineteenth century, when skins were occasionally received from Pernambuco by dealers in Paris and elsewhere, and live specimens were often seen in the larger zoological gardens and other aviaries (Forbes 1881; also specimens in FMNH, LACM, LSUMZ, MNHN). Birds are sold "in large numbers" all over the north-east of Brazil, and especially in Recife, from where they have been sent to buyers in the south (W. C. A. Bokermann *per* C. Torres *in litt.* 1984). The species was common in the bird market in Rio de Janeiro in the 1950s and 1960s, but declined to the point of being considered a rarity in the late 1970s (Sick 1969, Sick and Teixeira 1979), but in the north-east numbers in trade have evidently not decreased, unless perhaps as a mere consequence of the species's own growing scarcity: in December 1983 50 birds were seen being offered for sale at the roadside between Maceió and Recife, and more than 30 others were in a "birdshop" at Agrestina, in the interior of Pernambuco (A. Studer *in litt.* 1987). The traffic remains intensive in both the interior (e.g. Caruaru) and the capitals of the north-eastern states, as demonstrated by the 22 birds at least that were being offered for sale in the famous "Mercado de Madalena" at Recife, in October 1987, the price of a single bird reaching approximately US$30; these birds had been trapped "in the woods of Alagoas" according to dealers (Charity 1988); but see the next section. It has been reported that a single trapper may obtain 50-100 birds in the appropriate season (summer) in Alagoas (L. C. Marigo verbally 1986). Even in a reserve like the UFPE's at Caruaru this species is not safe, for its forests have been destroyed, there is no adequate vigilance and trapping of the species was continuing in the mid-1980s: it is undoubtedly from this site that birds that have been taken to be sold at Recife, and even at Fortaleza, Ceará (Coelho 1986, A. G. M. Coelho *in litt.* 1986).

MEASURES TAKEN The species is protected under Brazilian law (Bernardes *et al.* 1990). The creation of the Pedra Talhada Biological Reserve is described in the equivalent section under Scalloped Antbird *Myrmeciza ruficauda*. The species's occurrence in the 450 ha UFPE reserve, in the 500 ha Saltinho Biological Reserve, the 350 ha Tapacurá Ecological Station and the privately owned Charles Darwin Ecological Refuge might give it some additional protection, but vigilance is minimal in almost all. Seizing captive birds and releasing them into forest reserves, as has been done under the auspices of the Fundação Pró-Natureza (Funatura) at Caruaru,

Pernambuco (Coelho 1986, also Charity 1988), can only succeed if the protection of such areas is improved (see, however, Measures Proposed); but apparently owing to increased policing of markets the number of birds being offered for sale has diminished, while the population at Caruaru has increased (S. Charity *per* M. G. Kelsey *in litt.* 1992). Research on this and other threatened species has been carried out at the UFPE Ecological Station at Caruaru (Charity 1988), and releases of confiscated birds have started at a second site, the Saltinho reserve (S. Charity *per* M. G. Kelsey *in litt.* 1992).

MEASURES PROPOSED The species urgently needs a special recovery programme (J. Vielliard *in litt.* 1986). The conservation of the Pedra Branca forests at Murici is a self-evident imperative, this apparently being the largest remaining continuous forest area in extreme north-eastern Brazil (Teixeira 1987) and holding several other threatened birds (see Remarks under Alagoas Foliage-gleaner *Philydor novaesi*), but the effective protection of existing reserves is clearly an equally urgent need. A call for a complete ban on the capture of wild birds for the pet trade, as any partial controls would be so open to abuse as to be ineffective (Scott and Brooke 1985), obviously applies in this case. Meanwhile, the species's full protection under Brazilian law needs validation by the enforcers.

GREEN-CAPPED TANAGER *Tangara meyerdeschauenseei* K[12]

This tanager is confined to the arid region at the headwaters of río Inambari in south-eastern Peru, where it inhabits forest edge, riverine scrub and gardens in the subtropical zone. Although its small known distribution renders it vulnerable, it does not appear to be immediately threatened.

DISTRIBUTION The Green-capped Tanager (see Remarks) is known from four specimens taken at two localities and sightings at a third, all at the head of río Inambari (a tributary of río Madre de Dios), in Sandia province, Puno department, south-eastern Peru. Records (with coordinates, unless otherwise stated, from Schulenberg and Binford 1985) are from: Azalay (14°14'S 69°17'W; at 1,750 m: Stephens and Traylor 1983), c.13 km north-north-east of Sandia, where a specimen was taken in November 1960 (Schulenberg and Binford 1985); 2 km north-east of Sandia, where at c.2,175 m two specimens were collected, and additional sightings made in November 1980 (Schulenberg and Binford 1985); Sandia (14°17'S 69°26'W; at 2,180 m), where a specimen was collected in November 1960 (Schulenberg and Binford 1985); west side of Abra de Maruncunca (c.14°14'S 69°17'W; at c.2,000 m), c.20 km east of Sandia, where sightings were made in November 1980 (Schulenberg and Binford 1985). It may be found at similar elevations in other arid valleys in south-eastern Peru, but does not occur at Pampas de Heath, Madre de Dios, the nearest lowland site with a similar habitat (Schulenberg and Binford 1985).

POPULATION The species was reported to be fairly common near Sandia and west of Abra de Maruncunca in early November 1980 (Schulenberg and Binford 1985). However, despite some searching during a two-day visit in late December 1983, none was seen in the riverine scrub at Sandia, although a few birds may have been present (NK).

ECOLOGY The Green-capped Tanager inhabits semi-arid regions, in which it frequents riparian scrub, garden trees and forest-edge (Schulenberg and Binford 1985). It has been recorded between 1,750 and 2,180 m (see Distribution), but its true elevational range may be similar to that of its close relative the Scrub Tanager *Tangara vitriolina*, which occurs from 1,100 to 2,400 m (occasionally as low as 500 m) in western Colombia and northern Ecuador (Schulenberg and Binford 1985).

It typically occurs singly or in pairs, and may frequent fruiting trees in gardens (Schulenberg and Binford 1985), and like the Scrub Tanager probably also regularly picks up fallen fruit from the ground (NK). The stomachs of two specimens contained fruit pulp and seeds as large as 8x4 mm (Schulenberg and Binford 1985). The four specimens collected in November showed no excessive feather wear or moult: gonads were slightly enlarged in the two specimens for which there is data, and although these data are not conclusive, the fact that several forest-inhabiting *Tangara*, e.g. Saffron-crowned *T. xanthocephala*, Blue-and-black *T. vassorii* and Silvery Tanager *T. viridicollis*, were breeding at Abra de Maruncunca in November 1980 supports the likelihood that the Green-capped Tanager was also breeding at this time (Schulenberg and Binford 1985).

THREATS Despite the small extent of its known range, Schulenberg and Binford (1985) doubted that the species is in any immediate danger of extinction, and pointed out that because it appears to inhabit semi-open rather than forested regions (including the edges of cleared areas), it may actually be favoured by continued forest clearance.

MEASURES TAKEN None is known.

MEASURES PROPOSED Further study of the species will establish whether any conservation efforts are needed. Such studies should especially concentrate on the population size, and the extent to which a viable population can be supported in areas degraded by forest clearance: any reliance on primary habitat would render this species threatened (see Schulenberg and Binford 1985).

REMARKS The Green-capped Tanager is very similar to the Burnished-buff Tanager *T. cayana* and the Scrub Tanager; while it comes closest to the former geographically, it resembles the latter more in habitat and elevational distribution, but which of the two is its nearer relative remains open to debate (Schulenberg and Binford 1985).

BLACK-BACKED TANAGER *Tangara peruviana* V/R[10]

Although not uncommon in some localities, this small frugivore faces serious difficulties from the rapid loss (largely to beachfront housing) of its coastal forest and restinga habitat in south-east Brazil, where its seasonal movements require fuller study and understanding.

DISTRIBUTION The Black-backed Tanager (see Remarks 1) is endemic to the coastal Atlantic Forest region of south-east Brazil, with records from Rio de Janeiro, São Paulo, Paraná and Santa Catarina (see Remarks 2). Its occurrence further to the north in Espírito Santo (Ruschi 1953), although admitted by Meyer de Schauensee (1966, 1982), has not been accepted by subsequent authorities (e.g. Sick 1985, Isler and Isler 1987, Ridgely and Tudor 1989) and is also discounted here. In the following account, records are given within states from north to south (east to west in Rio de Janeiro) with coordinates from Paynter and Traylor (1991) unless otherwise stated.

Rio de Janeiro Records are from: rio Mocotó, near Campos, July 1987; Desengano State Park at ribeirão Vermelho, 650 m, August 1987 (J. F. Pacheco *in litt.* 1987); Ilha de Santana (off Macaé), June 1984 and April 1986 (V. S. Alves *in litt.* 1987); Ilha do Cabo Frio, recently (J. B. Nacinovic verbally 1990; specimens in MNRJ); Saquarema, August 1953 (Mitchell 1957); Fazenda Boa Vista, Carmo, August 1988 (J. F. Pacheco verbally 1988); Maricá restinga (near Zacarias), regularly in winter (from June to August) since 1983 to at least 1990 (F. S. Porto verbally 1984, J. F. Pacheco *in litt.* 1986, C. E. Carvalho *in litt.* 1987, G. D. A. Castiglioni verbally 1990); Itaboraí, July 1961 (Aguirre and Aldrighi 1987); Porto das Caixas (Descourtilz 1854-1856); Inhaúma, 25°50'S 43°20'W (Descourtilz 1854-1956); Tijuca National Park above Alto da Boa Vista, July 1979 (A. Greensmith *per* D. Willis *in litt.* 1988); Rio Botanical Garden, July 1988 (B. C. Forrester *in litt.* 1988); Sernambetiba, 23°02'S 43°29'W, August 1946, September 1947 (Novaes 1950); Sepetiba ("Sapitiba"), 22°58'S 43°42'W (von Pelzeln 1868-1871).

São Paulo Records (see Remarks 3, 4) are from: Mato Dentro (von Pelzeln 1868-1871); Itatiba, September 1907 (Hellmayr 1936, Pinto 1944); Cantareira, a northern suburb of São Paulo, March 1976 (specimen in CIAL); Boracéia, 23°39'S 45°54'W, May 1964 and April 1966 (specimens in ANSP and MZUSP); Ipiranga, a suburb of São Paulo, undated (von Ihering and von Ihering 1907); São Sebastião, October 1902 (specimen in AMNH); Santos, August 1902 (von Ihering and von Ihering 1907, Pinto 1944); Itararé, June 1903 (von Ihering and von Ihering 1907, Pinto 1944); Peruíbe, February, April, May and September 1991 (D. F. Stotz *in litt.* 1991); Barra do rio das Corujas, 24°09'S 47°39'W, November and December 1964; Barra do ribeirão Onça Parda, 24°19'S 47°51'W, November 1964; Onça Parda (untraced), October 1962; rio Ipiranga, 24°22'S 47°50'W, September and October 1962; Primeiro Morro (left bank of rio Ipiranga), July and September 1961; Morretinho (untraced), September 1961; Barra do rio Ribeira (rio Ribeira de Iguape, 24°40'S 47°29'W), July 1964; Serra da Juréia (untraced: presumably in or near the present-day Juréia Ecological Station), July 1966; Barra do Icapara (Icapara), August 1966 (specimens from the preceding nine localities in MZUSP); Iguape (in one case precisely Baicô), January and February 1898 (von Ihering 1898, von Ihering and von Ihering 1907, Pinto 1944), July 1969 (specimens in MZUSP), July 1977 (specimens in CIAL), undated (specimen in MNRJ), and recently (D. F. Stotz *in litt.* 1991); Ilha Comprida, January and April 1988 (D. F. Stotz *in litt.* 1991); Ilha da Cananéia (in one case precisely Tabatinguara), September 1934 (Pinto 1944), January and April 1988; on the mainland opposite Ilha da Cananéia, June 1991 (D. F. Stotz *in litt.* 1991); Ilha do Cardoso State Park, recently (D. F. Stotz *in litt.* 1988, 1991, P. Martuscelli *in litt.* 1991).

Paraná Although several of the descriptions of the species's range (e.g. Meyer de Schauensee 1982, Isler and Isler 1987, Ridgely and Tudor 1989) indicate its extension from Rio de Janeiro to Santa Catarina, and Scherer Neto (1985) noted that this bird was known in Paraná from references in the literature, material in museums and his own observations, there appear to be no records in this state (see Remarks 5) before those from: Fazenda Santa Rita, Palmeira, regularly since 1984 (L. dos Anjos *in litt.* 1987 and verbally 1992, F. C. Straube *in litt.* 1987); Ilha do Mel, June 1986 (A. de Meijer *in litt.* 1987); São Mateus do Sul, April 1986 (F. C. Straube *in litt.* 1987).

Santa Catarina The only certain localities still seem to be those recorded by Hellmayr (1936) and repeated by Pinto (1944), based on specimens from Joinville (e.g. May 1930; in MCZ), Blumenau and Araranguá. Sick *et al.* (1981) indicated that there are records for the state in the literature, material in museums and their own field observations, but it is evident that they considered the Black-backed and the Chestnut-backed Tanager *Tangara preciosa* together (see Remarks 1).

POPULATION The species is generally considered not rare, with periodic local fluctuations in numbers due to seasonal movements at least in Rio de Janeiro and São Paulo, which provide the bulk of records. There are no unequivocal records from Santa Catarina since the 1930s; but it is apparently neither rare nor seasonal in Paraná (L. dos Anjos *in litt.* 1987, F. C. Straube *in litt.* 1987). At Ilha do Cardoso it is fairly common, but numbers decline dramatically in the winter; it is uncommon on Ilha da Cananéia and Ilha Comprida, fairly common at Peruíbe; further north in São Paulo it appears to be much rarer; the habitat around Iguape, where a large series was obtained in the 1960s and early 1970s (see Distribution), is mostly intact, but it is doubtful whether the species still occurs inland in this state, except perhaps in the rio Ribeira de Iguape valley, or in winter in small numbers (D. F. Stotz *in litt.* 1988, 1991). In Rio de Janeiro the species appears only in winter months, when it has been recorded regularly mainly along the state's south-eastern coast, from Rio de Janeiro to Cabo Frio (see Distribution).

ECOLOGY The Black-backed Tanager seems to be largely confined to lowland forests and restinga (littoral scrub) along the coast. Most modern records in Rio de Janeiro are from restinga, but the species has also been recorded from the Paraíba do Sul river valley in a fruiting tree at the edge of secondary forest, with other local winter visitors such as Fawn-breasted Tanager *Pipraeidea melanonota* and Yellow-legged Thrush *Platycichla flavipes* (J. F. Pacheco verbally 1988), and at up to 650 m in secondary forest at Desengano State Park (J. F. Pacheco *in litt.* 1987). Recent records in São Paulo have been exclusively from coastal sand-plain forests, i.e. restinga in its wider sense (D. F. Stotz *in litt.* 1988, 1991, P. Martuscelli *in litt.* 1991), and the habitat in which birds have been collected on the southern coast of the state has been recorded as "primitive forest", "interior of primitive forest", "old secondary forest" and "young secondary forest" (specimens in MZUSP). In this region the species does not go into the "true" forests at all, and has not been seen on any of the mountain slopes; but on Ilha da Cananéia and Ilha Comprida it occurs in fairly disturbed habitat as well as undisturbed forest (D. F. Stotz *in litt.* 1988, 1991). Birds have been recorded singly, in pairs (Descourtilz 1854-1956, specimens in MZUSP) or in flocks with other species (P. Martuscelli *in litt.* 1991). Seasonal displacements occur (see Population), with birds appearing in the vicinity of Rio at the beginning of the cold season, when the aroeira *Schinus* fruits were ripe, and disappearing after the winter months of May to July (Descourtilz 1854-1956). There is no information on breeding.

THREATS Deforestation on the lower slopes of the Serra do Mar has been regarded as a probable threat to the species (Ridgely and Tudor 1989) and, given its decided preference for the coastal restinga vegetation, one of the most restricted and threatened habitats in south-eastern Brazil (LPG), this concern seems fully justified. Destruction of the restinga in São Paulo for beachfront housing has been described as "almost unbelievable": from Santos south to Peruíbe, an area which four years before had development just around the towns of Mongaguá and Itanhaém, there is now a nearly continuous strip of development on the beach side of the highway, and it has now started on the inland side (D. F. Stotz *in litt.* 1991). Real-estate development is massive also on Ilha Comprida (C. Yamashita *in litt.* 1991), and deforestation has been considered a threat to the species also on Ilha do Cardoso (P. Martuscelli *in litt.* 1991). The main area of occurrence of the species in Rio de Janeiro is also a "prime holiday development" (D. Willis *in* *litt.* 1991) and is under no less pressure from real-estate onslaught (Gonzaga and Pacheco 1990). Very little habitat remains now where the species has been recorded in the vicinity of Rio city, and even this is disappearing (LPG).

The species occasionally appears in the illegal cagebird trade, both in São Paulo (P. Martuscelli *in litt.* 1991) and in Rio, where "one or two birds" are offered for sale from time to time (C. E. Carvalho *in litt.* 1987). A bird, seen in a cage in August 1953 at Saquarema, was said to have been caught locally (Mitchell 1957). Trade of the species seems to represent a minor, if any, threat at this stage, but it could compound problems in the future with continuing habitat loss.

MEASURES TAKEN Small portions of the species's limited range in Rio de Janeiro are included in the Jacarepiá and Maçambaba State Reserves and the Maçambaba and Maricá Environmental Protection Area near Arraial do Cabo (IEF/FEEMA/INEPAC 1991); however, these areas apparently lack any effective control (LPG). Access to Ilha do Cabo Frio is restricted and controlled by the Brazilian navy, which keeps a lighthouse there. In São Paulo the species's possible occurrence in the Juréia Ecological Station may give it some protection but, to judge from the situation described in Threats, the Cananéia–Iguape–Peruíbe Environmental Protection Area (see CONSEMA 1985) seems to be ineffective to protect the species's habitat. The Ilha do Cardoso State Park may provide some additional security, although appropriate habitat there is somewhat limited and it, too, is inadequately protected (see Threats).

MEASURES PROPOSED Surveys of the species in the field are needed to obtain a fuller understanding of its seasonal movements, which is probably crucial to its long-term conservation. However, enforcement of existing legislation concerning the protection of coastal areas in Rio de Janeiro and São Paulo is clearly imperative. These areas are of singular importance for at least two other endemic threatened birds, the Restinga Antwren *Formicivora littoralis* and the Red-tailed Amazon *Amazona brasiliensis* (see relevant accounts).

REMARKS (1) Following a suggestion by Hellmayr (1936), Sick (1985) judged this bird to form a single polymorphic species with the Chestnut-backed Tanager, but elsewhere they have been and remain treated as distinct, partially sympatric species (Pinto 1944, Meyer de Schauensee 1966, 1982, Isler and Isler 1987, Ridgely and Tudor 1989, Sibley and Monroe 1990, Willis and Oniki 1991). (2) Its occurrence in Misiones and Buenos Aires, Argentina, has been mentioned as accidental (Dabbene 1913, Hellmayr 1936), but these records obviously refer to the Chestnut-backed Tanager (see Isler and Isler 1987, Narosky and Yzurieta 1987, Ridgely and Tudor 1989). Likewise, a record from Pelotas, Rio Grande do Sul, has been discredited (von Ihering 1899b, Hellmayr 1936). (3) Hellmayr (1936) reinterpreted the record "Rio Claro, Goyaz" (Sclater 1886) as indicating the locality in São Paulo, and not the river in Goiás, "where no representative of this group is found". Another old record which would represent a locality very much inland than any of other records is "Rio Paraná" (von Pelzeln 1868-1871), probably now the town of União, 19°59'S 47°46'W (Paynter and Traylor 1991); Pinto (1944) did not consider either of these localities. (4) E. O. Willis *in litt.* (1986) mentioned this species from eight unspecified localities in the state. (5) Von Pelzeln (1868-1871) listed Jaguariaíva as the source of a specimen from Paraná, but Hellmayr (1936), who examined the material in question, apparently considered the bird involved was a Chestnut-backed Tanager.

SIRA TANAGER *Tangara phillipsi* K[12]

This tanager appears to be confined to humid forest in Cerros del Sira, in east-central Peru. Although apparently safe at present, it is vulnerable owing to its small distribution.

DISTRIBUTION The Sira Tanager is known from several sightings and four specimens taken in July 1969, all on the slopes of Cerros del Sira (9°26'S 74°45'W), a series of isolated peaks (connected by a low-elevation ridge to the eastern Andes) in Huánuco department, east-central Peru (Graves and Weske 1987).

POPULATION The species is apparently fairly common within its restricted range (Graves and Weske 1987).

ECOLOGY The Sira Tanager inhabits the canopy of humid cloud-forest at elevations ranging from 1,300 to 1,570 m (the Cerros del Sira reach a maximum of 2,450 m). It is usually found 11-25 m above the ground, although three specimens were taken in a mist-net near the ground; it is a fairly common member of mixed-species canopy flocks, and has been seen with Rufous-rumped Foliage-gleaner *Philydor erythrocercus*, Black-and-white Becard *Pachyramphus albogriseus*, Orange-bellied Euphonia *Euphonia xanthogaster*, Orange-eared Tanager *Chlorochrysa calliparaea*, Golden Tanager *Tangara arthus*, Blue-browed Tanager *T. cyanotis*, Beryl-spangled Tanager *T. nigroviridis*, Saffron-crowned Tanager *T. xanthocephala*, Blue-winged Mountain-tanager *Anisognathus flavinuchus*, Vermilion Tanager *Calochaetes coccineus*, White-winged Tanager *Piranga leucoptera* and Purple Honeycreeper *Cyanerpes caeruleus*; no obvious behavioural features differentiated it from the other four species of *Tangara* with which it was observed (Graves and Weske 1987). None of the four specimens taken in July had active gonads (Graves and Weske 1987).

THREATS None is known.

MEASURES TAKEN None is known.

MEASURES PROPOSED Although apparently not immediately threatened, some consideration should be given to protecting the forested Cerros del Sira, the only known locality for this recently discovered tanager, and also important as the prime (and possibly only) locality for a subspecies of the threatened Southern Helmeted Curassow *Pauxi unicornis koepckeae* (see relevant account).

REMARKS The Sira Tanager is very closely related to the Black-capped Tanager *T. heinei* of Venezuela, Colombia and Ecuador, and in the narrow sense they constitute a superspecies (Graves and Weske 1987).

SCARLET-BREASTED DACNIS *Dacnis berlepschi* I[7]

This species is restricted to lowland and foothill forests in south-west Colombia and north-west Ecuador, where it is poorly known, apparently rare and localized, and seemingly threatened by forest destruction.

DISTRIBUTION The Scarlet-breasted Dacnis is endemic to the Pacific slope and plain of south-west Colombia in Nariño department, and north-western Ecuador in Esmeraldas, Imbabura, and Pichincha provinces. Coordinates (unless otherwise stated) are from Paynter and Traylor (1977, 1981).

Colombia This species is only known from the Pacific slope of south-western Nariño department, where localities are as follows: La Guayacana (1°26'N 78°27'W; near the Ecuador border, on the río Cualquer), where birds (two males and a female in ANSP, ROM) were taken in May 1947, with another male in May 1948 (von Sneidern 1954), and 10 km to the east, where two males were collected in August 1959 (Carriker 1959), all between 220 and 250 m; the río Güiza valley (= río Cualquer, 1°22'N 78°36'W), a locality mentioned by Hilty and Brown (1986), but which presumably refers to birds collected at and near Guayacana, although more recently (September 1991) two birds (probably this species) were seen at 600 m beside this river (Barlow *et al.* 1992); above Junín along the road to Tumaco, where the species has recently been recorded at 1,200 m (Hilty and Brown 1986, Ridgely and Tudor 1989); and apparently within La Planada Nature Reserve (J. E. Orejuela *in litt.* 1991).

Ecuador Records are from Esmeraldas, Imbabura and Pichincha provinces, where localities include: very near (south of) San Lorenzo (1°17'N 78°50'W: coordinates from IGM 1982) (R. S. Ridgely verbally 1991); Carondelet (1°06'N 78°42'W; on the coastal plain beside the río Bogotá and the railroad), where six specimens (four males, a female and an immature male in AMNH, BMNH) were collected at 18 m between 17 October and 3 November 1900; San Javier (1°04'N 78°47'W; also on the coastal plain), where a male and female (in AMNH) were taken at 18 m in July 1900; Ventanas (0°59'N 78°40'W; at 27 m, on the railroad), where at least two birds were seen in August 1986 (Evans 1988b); Lita (0°52'N 78°28'W; 900 m), where a male (the type-specimen) and female were collected in October 1899 (Hartert 1900, Chapman 1926); between La Unión and Muisne (0°42'N 79°52'W: coordinates from IGM 1982), where the bird was seen in September 1990 (R. S. Ridgely verbally 1991); and further south, at río Palenque (c.0°30'S 79°22'W: coordinates from IGM 1982), where the bird was recently seen by P. Greenfield (NK). This last record is from southern Pichincha province (NK: also Ridgely and Tudor 1989), but Isler and Isler (1987) referred to it as in northern Los Ríos.

POPULATION The Scarlet-breasted Dacnis has been variously considered uncommon or rare (Hilty and Brown 1986); scarce and/or local (Isler and Isler 1987); and rare, appearing never to be very numerous (Ridgely and Tudor 1989). However, six birds were collected during two weeks at Carondelet in 1900 (see Distribution), and it may be that the species is very localized in its distribution, but (at least formerly) not uncommon where it occurs.

ECOLOGY Records come from between sea level and 1,200 m (see Remarks), and Hilty and Brown (1986) referred to it as occurring at wet forest edges ("cloud-forest") and in tall (mature) secondary growth (reiterated by Isler and Isler 1987 and Ridgely and Tudor 1989). The birds at Ventanas were seen in relatively open habitat comprising an old grassy clearing with some trees, with mature lowland forest nearby (Evans 1988b). Food is unrecorded. The only evidence of breeding season is the immature male collected at Carondelet, Ecuador, on 26 October.

THREATS None is known, although extensive destruction of lowland (coastal plain) and foothill forests (see Threats under Plumbeous Forest-falcon *Micrastur plumbeus*) has caused a rapid decline in suitable habitat, and inevitably therefore in population: if the species only breeds at low elevations (as may be the case) it is severely threatened (NK).

MEASURES TAKEN The Scarlet-breasted Dacnis apparently occurs in La Planada Nature Reserve, a 1,650 ha protected area in Nariño department, south-west Colombia (J. E. Orejuela *in litt.* 1991; LGN). This species has not been recorded from any protected areas in Ecuador, although the Cotacachi–Cayapas Ecological Reserve (45,000 ha) and Awá Indiginous Forest reserve (over 100,000 ha) are within the bird's range (CNPPA 1982, IUCN 1992).

MEASURES PROPOSED The ecological requirements of this species are in urgent need of clarification, so that the nature of the threats it faces can be more precisely assessed. Combined with this, and for the same reasons, the present distribution of the bird needs to be determined, especially with reference to its possible occurrence within various protected areas. Its range overlaps with those of a number of other threatened species (for details of which see the equivalent section under Plumbeous Forest-falcon and Hoary Puffleg *Haplophaedia lugens*), and any conservation initiatives should where possible take into account the requirements of all these species. Proposed plans for a trans-border biosphere reserve (linking the La Planada area with the Awá reserve in Ecuador: Barlow *et al.* 1992) should be strongly encouraged.

REMARKS Hilty and Brown (1986) gave an altitudinal range of between 200 and 800 m (with a sight record up to 1,200 m), as did Isler and Isler (1987) and Ridgely and Tudor (1989): however, all eight specimens taken in 1900 at Carondelet and San Javier, and the two birds seen at Ventanas in 1986, were below 30 m, on the coastal plain (see Distribution). The complete lack of records during intensive surveys of the foothills of Esmeraldas (down to 350 m: NK) may suggest some degree of seasonal movement to lower altitudes.

TURQUOISE DACNIS *Dacnis hartlaubi* V/R[10]

This endemic to Colombia has a very restricted and fragmented distribution in all three Andean ranges, and may be declining further in response to continuing forest clearance.

DISTRIBUTION The Turquoise Dacnis is known from a small number of localities on the western and eastern slopes of the West Andes, and the western slopes of the Central and East Andes, Colombia. Coordinates here are from Paynter and Traylor (1981), and localities are treated from approximately west to east.

Valle Records are from the Pacific slope of the West Andes as follows: near Cisneros (3°47'N 76°46'W; at c.300 m on the right bank of the río Dagua) (Carriker 1955a); Juntas (3°46'N 76°45'W; on the left bank of the río Dagua), where a male (in AMNH) was collected at 365 m during 1904 (Meyer de Schauensee 1948-1952); Jiménez (c.3°45'N 76°45'W; evidently adjacent to the previous locality), where a male (in BMNH) was collected at 885 m in October 1907; Pavas (3°41'N 76°35'W; at 1,350 m), near the headwaters of the río Dagua, where a male was collected in July 1918 (Carriker 1955a, Hilty and Brown 1986); La Cumbre (3°39'N 76°33'W; at 1,580 m), also near the headwaters of the río Dagua, whence come a male and female (in CM) taken in July 1918 (Carriker 1955a); and, on the eastern slope of the West Andes, Bosque de Yotoco (3°52'N 76°33'W; 1,400-1,600 m on the western side of the upper río Cauca valley: Orejuela *et al.* 1979), where a male was seen during August 1979 (Hilty and Brown 1986).

Quindío The sole record is from the western slope of the middle Central Andes at Hacienda Pital (untraced, but apparently in the municipality of Calarcá at c.4°31'N 75°38'W), where a female (in ICN) was taken in August 1969.

Cundinamarca This dacnis has been recorded on the western side of the middle East Andes, where localities are as follows: near Bojacá, recently (F. G. Stiles *in litt.* 1992); Laguna de Pedropalo (c.4°45'N 74°24'W; at 2,010 m), recently (Hilty and Brown 1986, P. Kaestner *in litt.* 1992), and no more than 3 km from which birds were seen between 1975 and 1977 (LGN); near Tena (4°40'N 74°24'W; at 1,385 m), recently (P. Kaestner *in litt.* 1992); San Antonio de Tequendama (= San Antonio de Tena, 4°37'N 74°21'W), recently (F. G. Stiles *in litt.* 1992); Finca Rancho Grande (4°36'N 74°20'W: Munves 1975), where birds were observed between 1,700 and 2,200 m during 1972-1973 (Munves 1975); and El Baldío (= Cordillera de Baldío, 4°19'N 73°45'W), where a specimen (in AMNH) was taken in December 1912.

POPULATION Recent (post-1980) records are all from Cundinamarca, and even so the species is considered very rare and local (Hilty and Brown 1986, Ridgely and Tudor 1989). At Finca Rancho Grande, Munves (1975) noted that the species was scarce (i.e. "not seen every day and rarely more than three at once") at 1,700 m and was present in unknown abundance at 2,200 m: however, close by at Laguna de Pedropalo, it was found to be common (P. Kaestner *in litt.* 1992, L. M. Renjifo *in litt.* 1992; also LGN), with 1-5 birds recorded there on all visits by F. G. Stiles (*in litt.* 1992).

ECOLOGY Most records of this bird come from between 1,350 and 2,200 m, although there are three records from the río Dagua, Valle, at c.300 to 885 m (see Distribution). This species inhabits humid and lower montane forests, forest borders, and clearings with scattered trees and groves (Munves 1975, Ridgely and Tudor 1989), although it has also been recorded in coffee groves with shade-trees (LGN). The forest at Laguna de Pedropalo has been described as wetter than the surrounding patches of oak forest, but not mossy (P. Kaestner *in litt.* 1992), whereas the male seen at Bosque de Yotoco was seen on mossy branches and at bromeliads (Hilty and Brown 1986). The Turquoise Dacnis is a bird of the canopy and subcanopy, where it has been observed following a mixed tanager–honeycreeper feeding flock (Hilty and Brown 1986, P. Kaestner *in litt.* 1992), and (at Laguna de Pedropalo) has frequently been recorded visiting isolated fruiting trees in pasture near to forest (L. M. Renjifo *in litt.* 1992). The stomach contents of one individual was found to consist of fruit, and a male in breeding condition was taken in early August in Cundinamarca (Hilty and Brown 1986).

THREATS The Turquoise Dacnis has become very rare and local due to the great extent of deforestation on the lower slopes of the Andes within its range (Ridgely and Tudor 1989). In the río Bogotá valley, almost the entire area, on both sides of the river, was formerly covered with humid forest, but this has now been converted into fincas for livestock and coffee, with numerous small towns and weekend cottages being built (Munves 1975). On hillsides too steep for human exploitation there are remnant stands of humid forest, and in the area separating the ríos Bogotá and Subía considerable stands of thick secondary humid forest now exist (this area has been cultivated for at least 100 years) (Munves 1975). Although recorded from secondary habitats (see Ecology), it is unknown whether the species can sustain viable populations in such areas.

MEASURES TAKEN The Turquoise Dacnis has been recorded within the 600 ha Bosque de Yotoco Reserve (Areas Protegidas 1989), but is not known to occur in any other protected area. However, localities along the río Dagua are just north of Los Farallones de Cali National Park (150,000 ha) (CNPPA 1982; Hernández Camacho *et al.* undated), and the species may well occur there.

MEASURES PROPOSED The precise ecological requirements, especially the extent to which primary forest areas are required to maintain viable populations, are essentially unknown for this species, and urgently need assessment. However, the priority must be the protection of Laguna de Pedropalo and adjacent oak forests, where the Turquoise Dacnis is sympatric with a number of other threatened species (see equivalent section under Black Inca *Coeligena prunellei* for details), and which has already been the subject of a recent initiative from some environmental groups in Bogotá (LGN). Surveys are needed within the Los Farallones de Cali National Park to discover whether this species is present; in Bosque de Yotoco Reserve and the Laguna de Pedropalo area to determine its status there; and in surrounding areas where suitable remnant forest patches still remain. The two protected areas (mentioned above) are important for up to seven other threatened species, the details of which (including other proposals), are given in the equivalent section under Multicoloured Tanager *Chlorochrysa nitidissima*).

BLACK-LEGGED DACNIS *Dacnis nigripes* V/R[10]

The status of this small bird, endemic to Atlantic Forest in south-east Brazil, is confused by its similarity to a much commoner congener, but there seems little doubt that it is genuinely rare, of restricted range, and at some risk from trade.

DISTRIBUTION The Black-legged Dacnis occurs thinly throughout coastal south-east Brazil, chiefly in the lowlands and adjacent mountains from Espírito Santo south to Santa Catarina. Records of this species are relatively few and several appear to involve wandering individuals (Gonzaga 1983). A single record from Lagoa Santa, Minas Gerais (Burmeister 1856), although accepted by some authorities (e.g. Pinto 1944, Meyer de Schauensee 1966, Gonzaga 1983), is probably an error in specimen labelling (Isler and Isler 1987, LPG); nevertheless, records below from Itatiaia National Park, which extends into Minas Gerais, and Quilombo, which is on the São Paulo side of the border, indicate the likelihood of the species being found in the extreme south-east of the state.

Espírito Santo The only record (Ruschi 1953) is confirmed by one specimen collected at 850 m at Santa Teresa on 9 November 1942 (Gonzaga 1983).

Rio de Janeiro Records (east to west) are from: Santa Maria Madalena (i.e. adjacent to Desengano State Park), 300 m, March 1988 (at least four: J. F. Pacheco verbally 1988); Fazenda União, near Casimiro de Abreu, July 1990 (J. F. Pacheco verbally 1992; see Population); Nova Friburgo, first half of the nineteenth century (ten specimens collected: von Pelzeln 1856); Macaé de Cima (rio Macaé headwaters), October 1985 (one bird seen: J. F. Pacheco *in litt.* 1986); Teresópolis, 1,000 m, October 1916 (specimen in AMNH); Serra dos Órgãos National Park, 1979 (flock of eight on northern limit: A. Greensmith *per* D. Willis *in litt.* 1988), 900 m, April 1984 (flock of five: LPG); foothills of the Serra dos Órgãos near Santo Aleixo, August 1977 and 1981 (Gonzaga 1983, 1986; see Ecology); Petrópolis, May 1953 (specimen in MPEG) and subsequently (the source of captive birds studied in 1978: Gonzaga 1983), and specifically at Samambaia, 800 m, July 1989 (J. F. Pacheco verbally 1992); Tijuca National Park, 500 m, July 1985 and April 1987 (singles seen: J. F. Pacheco *in litt.* 1986, 1987, Pacheco 1988b); Serra do Tinguá, 250 m, once in 1980-1981 (Scott and Brooke 1985), and at c.100 m near Xerém, October 1988 (P. S. M. da Fonseca verbally 1988); Serra das Araras, 600-700 m, Piraí, July 1989 (J. F. Pacheco verbally 1992); Angra dos Reis (at a site for Black-hooded Antwren *Formicivora erythronotos*: see relevant account), October 1988 (P. S. M. da Fonseca verbally 1988) and July 1990 (Gardner and Gardner 1990b); Itatiaia National Park, December 1953 (specimen collected: Gonzaga 1983) and at 1,700 m, October 1987 (pair observed: J. F. Pacheco *in litt.* 1987).

São Paulo Records (east to west) are from: several forests near Ubatuba in early August 1984 (Willis and Oniki 1985), and specifically at Fazenda Capricórnio (23°25'S 45°05'W in Willis and Oniki 1988b), 100 m, August 1988 (C. Yamashita *in litt.* 1988); Quilombo, date unknown (Willis and Oniki 1985); Paranapiacaba (750 m), Santo André, July 1966 (Gonzaga 1983); Campo Grande, date unknown (Willis and Oniki 1985); Alvarenga, São Bernardo do Campo, July 1962 (Gonzaga 1983), these last three localities all being on the south-east outskirts of São Paulo city; rio Ipiranga, on the southern coast, September and October 1962 (Gonzaga 1983); Ilha do Cardoso State Park, recently (P. Martuscelli *in litt.* 1991); Fazenda Intervales, Capão Bonito, 800-1,000 m, January 1989 and February 1990 (Rodrigues and Silva 1991). One specimen, not preserved but seemingly this species, was taken at Ipanema west of São Paulo (von Pelzeln 1868-1871, von Ihering 1898).

Paraná The only record (Scherer Neto 1980) is based on a cage bird reported to have been captured in May 1979 near Antonina (Gonzaga 1983).

Santa Catarina One specimen from Blumenau (von Berlepsch 1873-1874) and another from Joinville (Hellmayr 1935) seem to be the only records (see Sick *et al.* 1981, Sick and Bege 1984).

POPULATION The species has been considered rare (Pinto 1944, Gonzaga 1983), or scarce and local (Isler and Isler 1987), since it is poorly represented in museum collections and almost absent from field reports (Gonzaga 1983), partly owing to its unobtrusiveness and to the great similarity of males to those of the widespread Blue Dacnis *Dacnis cayana* (see Remarks), so that the former can easily be overlooked (Gonzaga 1983, Scott and Brooke 1985, D. M. Teixeira *in litt.* 1987). However, its rarity has been noted also in Rio de Janeiro cagebird markets, where usually only a few individuals occasionally appear alongside many Blue Dacnises (M. V. Dias verbally 1981, C. E. Carvalho *in litt.* 1987; see Threats). Birds may concentrate locally during certain periods, as at Petrópolis from April to June, when "many" can then be captured on fruiting trees, or in the foothills of the Serra dos Órgãos in winter 1981, when seven specimens were collected "from a much larger group" between 29 July and 2 August, though no trace of the species could be found in the same area one month later, nor in the following year (Gonzaga 1983); near Casimiro de Abreu, July 1990, "hundreds" might have been present (J. F. Pacheco verbally 1992). The five birds seen in the Serra dos Órgãos in April might have been part of such a pre-wintering flock (LPG).

ECOLOGY The Black-legged Dacnis has been found in primary or only slightly disturbed Atlantic Forest (Scott and Brooke 1985), as well as in old secondary forest (Gonzaga 1983, J. F. Pacheco verbally 1988, Rodrigues and Silva 1991, LPG), from near sea level up to 1,700 m. One bird from Paranapiacaba was collected in "eucalyptus flowers at the forest edge" (specimen in MZUSP), and a "wintering" pair at Angra dos Reis was watched for 15 minutes feeding towards the top of flowering eucalyptus trees (Gardner and Gardner 1990b). On three occasions at Fazenda Intervales a pair was observed feeding on fruits of *Clusia*, twice at the edge of second growth and once in scrub vegetation on shallow soil near the summit (Rodrigues and Silva 1991). At Santo Aleixo the species was found in flowering trees *Mabea brasiliensis* near clearings and at forest edge in groups, searching for nectar and insects among the inflorescences in the early mornings, when Blue Dacnises also visited the trees for the same purpose; at mid-morning, the birds joined large mixed-species canopy flocks, in which becards *Pachyramphus viridis*, *P. polychopterus* and *P. validus*, Red-eyed Vireo *Vireo olivaceus*, Chestnut-vented Conebill *Conirostrum speciosum*, tanagers *Hemithraupis flavicollis*, *Tachyphonus cristatus* and *Thraupis palmarum*, and Buff-throated Saltator *Saltator maximus* were often present (Gonzaga 1983). In the Tijuca National Park isolated females were seen in mixed-species flocks that included individuals of Blue Dacnis, Green-headed Tanager *Tangara seledon* and Red-necked Tanager *T. cyanocephala* (J. F. Pacheco *in litt.* 1986, 1987), and each of three other records in Rio de Janeiro also involved birds joining mixed-species flocks (J. F. Pacheco and P. S. M. da Fonseca verbally 1988).

Stomach contents of seven specimens included *Miconia* berries, arillated seeds of *Xylopia*, other unidentified berries, coleopterans (Anthicidae), dipterans (Chloropidae and Sciaridae), hymenopterans (Chalcidoidea), and small caterpillars (Gonzaga 1983). The stomach of one specimen (in MPEG) from Petrópolis contained "insects". On Ilha do Cardoso in winter the birds eat *Schinus* berries (P. Martuscelli verbally 1991).

There is no information on breeding (Isler and Isler 1987), but the gonadal condition of specimens collected in late July and early August in Santo Aleixo (Gonzaga 1983) and in early July in Paranapiacaba (in MZUSP) indicated that they were not then breeding. It seems that the species moves seasonally or sometimes erratically between parts of its range, having been found in the Majé lowland study area during some winters but not in others, probably the result of irregular wandering in search of certain favourite food-plants; many apparently immature birds join these parties (Gonzaga 1983; see Population). The species is a winter visitor to Ilha do Cardoso in flocks of five or so which use the sand-plain forest for feeding only (P. Martuscelli *in litt.* 1991).

THREATS None is known, but the species is little known and could suffer from trapping for the cagebird trade, as it is prized for its rarity value (M. V. Dias verbally 1981). In addition, it seems evident that the periodic concentration of individuals in certain unprotected key areas may greatly enhance the ease with which a large number of birds can be obtained at once (see Population). Captive birds have been reported from Rio de Janeiro (Gonzaga 1983), São Paulo (Willis and Oniki 1985, L. O. Marcondes-Machado verbally 1985), Paraná (Gonzaga 1983) and even Maceió in Alagoas in October 1990 (B. M. Whitney *in litt.* 1991). The extent to which habitat destruction is a problem remains undocumented; however, loss of sand-plain forest on Ilha do Cardoso is considered a threat to the species there (P. Martuscelli *in litt.* 1991).

MEASURES TAKEN The Black-legged Dacnis is protected under Brazilian law (Bernardes *et al.* 1990). It has been recorded from the 5,000 ha Serra dos Órgãos National Park, the 3,000 ha Tijuca National Park, the 30,000 ha Itatiaia National Park, the Tinguá Biological Reserve (the creation of which was called for in Scott and Brooke 1985), the 38,000 ha Intervales state reserve and the 22,500 ha Ilha do Cardoso State Park; it presumably also occurs in the Serra do Mar State Park in São Paulo, which covers 310,000 ha, having been recorded from its borders in the very small Paranapiacaba (state) Biological Reserve, and in the Desengano State Park in Rio de Janeiro (sizes of protected areas from CONSEMA 1985, IBAMA 1989).

MEASURES PROPOSED A complete ban on the capture of wild birds for the pet trade has been called for, as any partial controls would be so open to abuse as to be ineffective (Scott and Brooke 1985). Effective protection of already created forest reserves would almost certainly guarantee the survival of this and other bird species along the Serra do Mar, but on current knowledge the identification and protection of stands of even secondary forest in adjacent lowlands and other areas outside of reserves seems to be of equal importance in view of the species's seasonal movements, an understanding of which, through further study, is probably crucial to its long-term conservation. In rather similar need are the Buff-throated Purpletuft *Iodopleura pipra* and Black-backed Tanager *Tangara peruviana* (see relevant accounts).

REMARKS The great similarity in plumage coloration of the males of this species to those of the more widespread and common Blue Dacnis (see Gonzaga 1983) may be a source of misidentification even in museum collections, where several skins of the former have been found that were confused with those of the latter; in the wild it is often easier to detect the species by the presence of females or female-plumaged immature birds among mixed-species flocks, in which both male and female Blue Dacnis are also usually found (LPG).

VENEZUELAN FLOWERPIERCER *Diglossa venezuelensis* I[7]

This little known flowerpiercer is restricted to the montane forests of the coastal cordillera and Paria Peninsula, north-eastern Venezuela. The bird may have specialized habitat requirements which render it even more vulnerable to the widespread degradation and loss of forest in this area.

DISTRIBUTION The Venezuelan Flowerpiercer, like five other threatened species (see Threats under White-tailed Sabrewing *Campylopterus ensipennis*), is restricted to the Cordillera de Caripe and the mountains of western Paria Peninsula, Venezuela.

Records of this species, from roughly west to east, and with coordinates from Paynter (1982), are as follows: La Elevacia (= La Elvicia, c.10°00'N 64°05'W; on the eastern slope of Cerro Peonía), where three males and a juvenile male (in CM) were taken between 1,675 and 1,775 m during January 1930; La Trinidad (c.10°12'N 63°57'W), a coffee plantation on the northern slope of Cerro Turumiquire (Chapman 1925), where two males (in COP) were taken between 1,750 and 1,800 m in January 1963; Carapas (c.10°12'N 63°56'W; also on the northern slope of Cerro Turumiquire, and adjacent to La Trinidad, Sucre), where eight males and three females (in AMNH, MCZ; also Chapman 1925) were taken at c.1,700 m in March and April 1925; Cerro Turumiquire (10°07'N 63°29'W, the summit being in Monagas), where 17 birds (in ANSP, FMNH) were collected between 1,525 and 2,440 m during February and March 1932, with two males and a female (in COP) taken at 2,400-2,450 m during February 1963 (Chapman 1925 referred to the specimens collected at Carapas as from Turumiquire); Los Dos Ríos (c.10°15'N 63°53'W; just south of Cumanacoa, Sucre), where a female (in AMNH) was taken in April 1898; Cerro Negro (c.10°14'N 63°30'W, on the border of Sucre and Monagas: see Remarks 2 under White-tailed Sabrewing), a locality mentioned by Phelps and Phelps (1950), and whence come a number of recent records from around 1,700 m (R. Ramírez *in litt.* 1988, Ridgely and Tudor 1989); and Cerro Humo (c.10°40'N 62°30'W, the westernmost peak on the Paria Peninsula), whence come a number of recent sight records from near Melenas, including one in 1985 (B. Swift *in litt.* 1986, Ridgely and Tudor 1989), and a male at 855 m in January 1989 (Gardner and Brisley 1989). The species is unknown from further along the Paria Peninsula, and was not found during fieldwork near Macuro in 1988 (Bond *et al.* 1989).

POPULATION The status of this species is essentially unknown: Ridgely and Tudor (1989) suggested that it is apparently uncommon, and B. Swift (*in litt.* 1988) maintained that there is a viable population in the El Guácharo National Park. Collections at Carapas (11 birds: see Chapman 1925) in March and April 1925, La Elvicia (four birds) in January 1930, and Cerro Turumiquire (17 birds) during February and March 1932 (see Distribution) suggest that the species was not uncommon 60 years ago. However, there are relatively few recent reports: a survey up to 1,800 m on Cerro Turumiquire (in 1979) failed to locate the bird (G. Medina-Cuervo *in litt.* 1986), while on Cerro Negro, a population (of unknown size) has been found in a narrow vegetation/altitudinal band (R. Ramírez *in litt.* 1988, Ridgely and Tudor 1989: see Ecology), and on Cerro Humo single birds have recently been seen (see Distribution) although none were found during quite extensive work there during 1990-1991 (C. Sharpe *in litt.* 1992).

ECOLOGY In the Cordillera de Caripe (i.e. the "mainland"), the Venezuelan Flowerpiercer has been recorded from 1,525 to 2,450 m (records away from Cerro Turumiquire are between 1,675 and 1,775 m), and on the Paria Peninsula (Cerro Humo) birds have been seen at 885 m (see Distribution; also Ecology under White-tailed Sabrewing for an explanation of this altitudinal anomaly). Almost nothing is known about the ecology of this species: records come from the subtropical zone, where it apparently inhabits cloud-forest, forest edge, second-growth woodland and shrubbery within the forest (Meyer de Schauensee and Phelps 1978, Isler and Isler 1987,

Ridgely and Tudor 1989); however, on Cerro Negro, the bird is seemingly associated with a small zone (a fringe c.200 m wide around the mountain) of transition between *Clusia*-dominated forest and an area of herbaceous vegetation at 1,700 m (R. Ramírez *in litt.* 1988), an association also recorded on Cerro Humo (Ridgely and Tudor 1989). Birds feed amidst the foliage at "middle" heights (Meyer de Schauensee and Phelps 1978), Gardner and Brisley (1989) observing a male foraging in the middle part of a tall exposed tree (on Cerro Humo). Breeding has not been recorded, although Chapman (1925) collected three males described as immatures in March and April (at Carapas), and a juvenile male was taken in January (at Elvicia: see Distribution).

THREATS The threats faced by this species are essentially the same as those for the White-tailed Sabrewing (i.e. widespread degradation and loss of montane forest: see relevant account), although because it has a more restricted range and essentially unknown ecological needs, this species is potentially at far greater risk. The suggestion of specialized habitat and altitudinal requirements, such as those noted on Cerro Negro (see above), and which may even be seasonal in nature, simply adds to the danger.

MEASURES TAKEN Two national parks exist within the range of this species and harbour populations of unknown size: (1) El Guácharo National Park (82,900 ha), covering Cerro Negro; and (2) Paria Peninsula National Park (37,500 ha); details of the status of these reserves are given in the corresponding section under White-tailed Sabrewing. At Turumiquire there is a "hydraulic" (presumably watershed) reserve, but this is heavily occupied with scattered human settlements and there is very little control: the species has not been recorded on Cerro Turumiquire in recent years, and was not found there during a survey (up to 1,800 m) in 1979 (G. Medina-Cuervo *in litt.* 1986: see Population).

MEASURES PROPOSED For this species, the priority must be the guaranteed protection of forest on Cerro Negro and Cerro Humo (i.e. the only two localities where the bird has recently been recorded), combined with an ecological study to discover the nature of its habitat requirements. All studies and initiatives should if possible integrate with work on all five threatened species in this area (see Threats under White-tailed Sabrewing).

BLACK-POLLED YELLOWTHROAT *Geothlypis speciosa* V[9]

Restricted to the river and lake marshes of central Mexico, this warbler, although common in suitable habitat, has suffered from extensive wetland drainage which has resulted in a number of populations becoming extinct.

DISTRIBUTION The Black-polled Yellowthroat is restricted to a small number of lake and river marshes in southern Guanajuato and northern Michoacán (race *limnatis*) and México state (race *speciosa*) on the central plateau of Mexico. Currently, the main area of distribution is within the lake region of the río Lerma drainage. Coordinates are taken from OG (1956a).

Guanajuato Records come from two lakes within the río Lerma drainage in the south of the state: Lago Yuriria (on the south side), where birds were most recently recorded in July 1991 (S. N. G. Howell *in litt* 1991: also Dickerman 1970), one specimen (in MNHUK) being taken 2 km east of Yuriria in January 1955; and at the northern end of Presa Solis where a male (in LSUMZ) was collected in January 1966.

Michoacán Again, records come from two lakes along the río Lerma drainage in the north of the state. At Lago de Cuitzeo, the species has been collected: 1 km west of Uruétaro, 7.5 road km west of Alvaro Obregón (an immature male in DMNH taken in December 1958: see Remarks 1); from Huingo (19°55'N 100°50'W, at the easternmost end of the lake), where a male (in USNM) was taken in July 1904; more recently, three specimens were taken 4 km north of Zinapécuaro in June 1987 (Navarro *et al.* 1991); and four specimens were collected 4 km west of Araró, also during June 1987 (Navarro *et al.* 1991). Further south the species has been recorded from a number of localities around Lago Pátzcuaro, which include: Erongarícuaro, at the westernmost point of the lake (male in DMNH, February 1949); 8 km west of Pátzcuaro on the southern shore at the "marshy lake edge near a lava flow" (female in DMNH, June 1948); along the south-east arm of the lake, c.5 km north-east of Pátzcuaro, and along a nearby inlet-stream marsh (specimens in DMNH, March and May 1947, February, May and June 1948; see also Lea and Edwards 1950, Edwards and Martin 1955); 4 km north of Pátzcuaro, where three specimens were collected in June 1987 (Navarro *et al.* 1991); and near the limnological station (untraced) (specimens in DMNH, February 1949).

México Records from San Mateo, Lago de Zumpango and Lago de Texcoco are treated here and not from Distrito Federal, *contra* Miller *et al.* (1957) and Dickerman (1970) (see Wilson and Ceballos-Lascurain 1986). In the west of the state the Black-polled Yellowthroat has been recorded at the headwaters of the río Lerma from three main areas: (1) just north of Lerma (= Lerma de Villada, 19°17'N 99°30'W; i.e. south-west of San Nicolás Peralta, 19°22'N 99°29'W), where eight males and a female (in USNM) were taken in July 1907, a male and female (in USNM) in February 1926, four males and a female (in MLZ) in January 1945, seven males (in LACM, MLZ, USNM) in February 1945, with birds observed in 1984, December 1986, January 1987, and 1988 (P. Escalante *in litt.* 1988, S. N. G. Howell *in litt.* 1989, R. G. Wilson *in litt* 1991); (2) San Mateo (= San Mateo Atenco, 19°17'N 99°32'W, near San Pedro Tultepec: see Remarks 2), c.13 km east-south-east of Toluca and just a few kilometres from Lerma, where at least 60 specimens (in AMNH, ANSP, FMNH, MCZ) were collected in November 1910 (with three more in ANSP, MCZ during December 1910); and (3) Almoloya del Río–Texcalyacac–San Pedro Techuchulco (centred on 19°08'N 99°30'W), where specimens (in DMNH, LSUMZ) were taken 1.5 km north of San Pedro Techuchulco (also described as the "marsh at the north side") in September 1961, November 1962, and June 1964, and a male was recorded in July 1988 (R. G. Wilson *in litt.* 1991), with a larger population (see below) inhabiting the marsh along the south edge of this lake between Almoloya del Río and Texcalyacac (R. G. Wilson *in litt.* 1991). North and east of Distrito Federal, this bird has been recorded from Lago de Zumpango in January 1966 and from the north end of Lago de Texcoco in October 1956 (Dickerman 1970). This latter lake in its original undrained state may have supported populations of this species within the Distrito

Federal, but the northern end, which appears to be the only recorded area of distribution, lies outside the state (see Wilson and Ceballos-Lascurain 1986).

POPULATION There is little recent information from the various historical localities where the Black-polled Yellowthroat has been recorded, and currently it is known from just four areas. In the past this bird was evidently abundant in suitable habitat (a fact indicated by the collection of over 60 specimens during November 1910 near Lerma: see Distribution), and it appears to have remained so in its preferred but ever decreasing habitat (see Threats).

Guanajuato An apparently healthy population of this species was found on the south side of Lago Yuriria during July 1991 (R. G. Wilson *in litt* 1991), although in 1987 and 1988, P. Escalante (*in litt.* 1991) found the population to be small (Common Yellowthroat *Geothlypis trichas* being much commoner here, occurring at a ratio of 7:1). There are no details of populations at Presa Solis.

Michoacán The Black-polled Yellowthroat is apparently "quite abundant" at Lago de Cuitzeo, with the bird outnumbering Common Yellowthroat by 3:1 (P. Escalante *in litt.* 1987, 1991): however, this lake has dried out at least once during the mid-1980s and water levels fluctuate widely – the species's survival there must be threatened (P. Escalante *in litt.* 1991, R. G. Wilson *in litt.* 1991). A small population still survives at Lago Pátzcuaro (P. Escalante *in litt.* 1987, 1991), birds being recorded there on a number of occasions during the 1980s (Navarro *et al.* 1991, R. G. Wilson *in litt.* 1991), but the only indication of population size was given by Lea and Edwards (1950) who noted that a few were seen (apparently in pairs) on the south-east arm during March, April and May 1947, Edwards and Martin (1955) concluding that the bird (at that same site) was "breeding in abundance". The Black-polled Yellowthroat now occurs at Lago Pátzcuaro with the far more abundant Common Yellowthoat at a ratio of 7:1 (P. Escalante *in litt.* 1991).

México S. N. G. Howell (*in litt.* 1989) found the bird to be "still common" on the upper río Lerma in 1984, 1986, 1987 and 1988, in an area where the species was historically abundant (see Distribution). More specifically, an extensive reed-bed (c.6 km^2) still exists just north of Lerma de Villada, a population of Black-polled Yellowthroats being found there in December 1986 and January 1987 (R. G. Wilson *in litt.* 1991). The marsh south of the México–Toluca highway (near San Mateo Atenco) still exists, is visible from the road, but is relatively inaccessible; consequently, there appear to be no records of the species from this marsh since the collection of 60 specimens during 1910 (R. G. Wilson *in litt.* 1991: see Distribution). North of San Pedro Techuchulco, despite records from the 1960s and more recently a male during July 1988 (see Distribution), the marsh is very small ("probably only a couple of hectares": R. G. Wilson *in litt.* 1991), as presumably is the species's population. A larger population exists in the more extensive marsh along the south side of the lake between Almoloya and Texcalyacac, and since being rediscovered in 1983 there has been no noticeable change in status there; however, the lake is still shrinking slowly (owing to water extraction) and the area of reeds is "at most a couple of square kilometres in extent", thus the survival of the species there is precarious (R. G. Wilson *in litt.* 1991: see Threats). The last record from Lago de Texcoco appears to that of the specimens taken in 1956 (see Distribution), Dickerman (1970) suggesting that the breeding population had probably become extinct by about 1958 when the north end was finally drained (see Threats). There is no recent information from Lago de Zumpango, specimens taken during 1966 (see Distribution) representing the last confirmed records.

ECOLOGY The Black-polled Yellowthroat is resident in and restricted to lake shore and river marshes comprising cattails and hard-stemmed bulrushes (Dickerman 1970). This habitat is locally known as "tule", and comprises plants (especially those over 1.5 m tall) of the genera *Typha* (*T. angustifolia* and *T. latifolia*), *Scirpus* (*S. lacustris*), and to a lesser extent *Heleocharis* and *Cyperus* (R. G. Wilson *in litt.* 1991). Birds are apparently able to survive even in the driest months when the marshes can temporarily dry out (e.g. in the areas near Lerma during 1988: P. Escalante *in litt.* 1988), although it has been doubted whether they can survive when whole lakes dry out (e.g. Lago de Cuitzeo during the late 1980s) (R. G. Wilson *in litt.* 1991). Paired birds were recorded at Lago Pátzcuaro during March–May 1947 (Lea and Edwards 1950), and the following year were noted as "breeding in abundance" during late May and June (Edwards and Martin 1955). Juveniles have been collected in June, July and September (Dickerman 1970).

THREATS This species, reliant on marshes, is threatened almost exclusively by the drainage of its already limited habitat. The breeding population at Lago de Texcoco probably became extinct in about 1958 when the northern end was finally drained and planted with crops (Dickerman 1970). The drainage and contraction of marshes in the upper río Lerma have left the village of San Mateo "several miles" from habitat suitable for Black-polled Yellowthroat (Dickerman 1965), and this development is probably the reason for the extinction (at the beginning of the twentieth century) of the Slender-billed Grackle *Quiscalis palustris.* Although the Black-polled Yellowthroat is common on the upper río Lerma, there is much drainage being undertaken and the bird remains greatly threatened there (S. N. G. Howell *in litt.* 1989: see Population), much water also being extracted to supply the needs of México City and Toluca (R. G. Wilson *in litt* 1991). Lagos Yuriria, Pátzcuaro and Cuitzeo are shallow lakes at a late stage of development, which has resulted in changes in their water capacities, this in turn affecting the area of marsh and cattail (P. Escalante *in litt.* 1987). The western end of Lago de Cuitzeo dries completely during the dry season, and although birds occupy a relatively large area the species is critically threatened here (P. Escalante *in litt.* 1987, 1988, 1991).

MEASURES TAKEN None is known, although Lagos de Texcoco and Zumpango are currently being "restored" (an ecological commission is working at Lago de Texcoco) (P. Escalante *in litt.* 1991).

MEASURES PROPOSED Government agencies have apparently shown an interest in measures to preserve the environment at Lago de Cuitzeo (P. Escalante *in litt.* 1987), although little seems to have been initiated. Clearly, with an entire catchment area involved (the río Lerma basin), an integrated approach needs to be taken in order to determine the effects of selective drainage and protection of areas on the whole basin. From this point of view, the upper río Lerma marshes must be a priority while the population of Black-polled Yellowthroat is still healthy there and the marshes are (presumably) a source of water for areas lower down the river system: however, land ownership in this area is communal (ejidal), and the water is used to feed México City, making protection of the marshes a difficult undertaking (P. Escalante *in litt.* 1991). Obviously, new water extraction and drainage schemes need to be halted where possible so that suitable areas of habitat can be saved, especially where the larger populations of the bird exist, such as at Lago de Cuitzeo. P. Escalante (*in litt.* 1991) suggested that yellowthroats could be reintroduced to Lagos de Texcoco and Zumpango once they have been restored (see Measures Taken).

REMARKS (1) A specimen in DMNH taken in December 1958 is labelled from west of Uruétaro, and west of Alvaro Obregón. In OG (1956a), however, Uruétaro is at 20°31'N 101°11'W which places it in Guanajuato near Lago Yuriria. (2) There has been much confusion as to the true location of San Mateo where various species (including Slender-billed Grackle and Black-polled Yellowthroat) were collected, but Dickerman (1965) managed to trace it to the San Mateo on the upper río Lerma for which coordinates are given.

SEMPER'S WARBLER *Leucopeza semperi* E/Ex[4]

Almost nothing is known about this extremely rare warbler, which is (or was) confined to montane forest undergrowth on St Lucia and has eluded almost all recent efforts to find a population, there being just a handful of records since the 1920s. It may have been exterminated by introduced mangooses.

DISTRIBUTION Semper's Warbler is endemic to the island of St Lucia in the Lesser Antilles, most records of the species coming mainly from the Barre de l'Isle ridge between Piton Flore and Piton Canaries (King 1978-1979).

Localities where this species has been recorded, from north to south, are: Louvet (on the east coast), where one was seen on 21 May 1961 (Bond 1962); between La Sorcière and Piton Flore, where the bird was reported to occur in heavily forested country (Bond 1928b); Piton Flore (c.565 m: Towle and Towle 1991), where a specimen was taken on 20 March 1925 (on the lower part of the mountain), and where the last known specimen was taken (on the summit) on 15 April 1934 (Danforth 1935, also King 1978-1979); south of Piton Flore, on the Barre de l'Isle ridge (along the road between Castries and Dennery), where a pair was seen (the last confirmed sighting) during 1972 (King 1978-1979); Mont Lacombe (c.455 m: Towle and Towle 1991), where the species was reported to be present (Bond 1928b); between Mont Lacombe and Piton Canaries, where a bird was seen during March 1947 (Greenway 1958, Bond 1961); Fond St Jacques (c.2 km east-south-east of Soufrière), where two females were taken on 3 and 5 April 1889 (Benson 1972, Fisher 1981); and Gros Piton, whence comes a recent unconfirmed report of the bird in May 1989 (D. Anthony *in litt.* 1992). A bird that was "obtained" at Castries on 1 December 1887 (Danforth 1935) was presumably collected inland on higher ground towards Piton Flore.

POPULATION Semper's Warbler is currently at best extremely rare, with just five (or six) records since the 1920s (see above). Even in the 1930s, Danforth (1935) reported that the bird was extremely rare and nearly extinct, but added that older collectors seemingly had had no difficulty in obtaining specimens. This appears to be confirmed by the collection of four birds (a male and three females in FMNH) on three days in May and June 1892, and six birds (a male and five females in AMNH, USNM) on three days in February and March 1901.

Many people have searched for this species at localities where it was previously recorded, but with little success: for example, J. Bond spent many weeks searching in 1927 and 1929 without any result; S. T. Danforth failed to find it in 1931; and S. John spent three years searching, but was finally rewarded with the collection of a single female in April 1934 (Danforth 1935). More recently, D. B. Wingate failed to find it on Piton Flore in April 1969 (Wingate 1969); R. F. Andrle (*in litt.* 1988) spent some time searching in April and May 1981 without success; and 10 days of mist-netting (averaging seven hours, and 60 m of netting every day) on Piton Flore, during June and July 1987, also failed to find the species (Babbs *et al.* 1988). The recent (May 1989) report of this bird on Gros Piton (see Distribution) keeps alive hopes that it is still extant.

ECOLOGY Very little has been recorded. Danforth (1935) noted that the female collected in April 1934 on Piton Flore flew up from near the ground and perched on a branch, and he concluded that the bird is mainly (if not exclusively) one of virgin forest. Subsequent authors have formed a consensus that the species is confined to undergrowth in mountain forests (Bond 1956b, Greenway 1958, King 1978-1979), and from the vegetation map in Towle and Towle (1991) it appears that it was distributed mainly in the lower montane rainforest and the small areas of montane thicket/elfin woodland. The recent report from Gros Piton was of a bird seen twice (or possibly two birds) in the undergrowth of "rain-forest" (D. Anthony *in litt.* 1992). Although Danforth (1935) noted that nothing is known of the species's nesting habits, Bond (1961) suggested that it may nest near if not on the ground.

THREATS As so little is known of the ecology of this warbler, it is difficult to assess with any certainty the precise nature of the threats it has clearly experienced. However, with the suggestion that this is an understorey species that may nest near or on the ground (see above), it seems likely that predation by the mongoose *Herpestes auropunctatus* may be a major factor in the bird's decline (Bond 1961, King 1978-1979). The mongoose was introduced to St Lucia during 1884 in an attempt to control the population of fer-de-lance *Bothrops caribbeaus* (Jeggo 1976a), and there seems to be a consensus that since its introduction to the Lesser Antilles it has caused a decline in populations of both reptiles and ground-nesting birds (Clark 1905, Bond 1928b, Towle and Towle 1991). Despite this, both Bond (1962) and Wingate (1969) noted that in the Louvet area, and between Piton Flore and La Sorcière (whence come the most recent records), there was still a high incidence of fer-de-lance, suggesting that mongooses were perhaps uncommon there and therefore not the main threat to the warbler.

Towle and Towle (1991) noted that habitat destruction is a major problem in St Lucia, with rainforest being converted to other land uses (mainly agriculture) at a rate of 2% every year, and almost half of the "deforestation areas" concentrated north of the Castries–Dennery road towards La Sorcière. The construction of agricultural feeder roads has exacerbated the problem of habitat destruction, opening up previously inaccessible areas and rendering them vulnerable to human disturbance (Towle and Towle 1991). Whether predation by mongooses, habitat destruction or increased disturbance have caused the population decline in this species is essentially unknown and will remain so until a population can be found and studied (see Measures Proposed).

MEASURES TAKEN Currently, c.7,500 ha of the woodland on St Lucia is classified (and demarcated) as government forest reserves, with just 170 ha designated as protected forest (Towle and Towle 1991), some of which refers to forest areas where Semper's Warbler has been recorded (e.g. Piton Flore: D. Anthony *in litt.* 1992). The extensive measures taken for the St Lucia Amazon *Amazona versicolor* (see relevant account) are focused on areas to the south of the warbler's historic range, and are probably of little value for the latter's conservation.

MEASURES PROPOSED The highest priority for this species is to find a population and determine its ecological requirements, which will in turn help to identify the precise nature of the threats that it faces. Although the "rediscovery" of the species is of utmost importance, to ensure that the bird has the highest chance of survival the forest in the La Sorcière–Mont Lacombe area needs absolute protection from any agricultural encroachment, and the mongoose numbers need to be monitored (and controlled where necessary). Bond (1928b) believed that the species would be found on La Sorcière, a location identified by R. F. Andrle (*in litt.* 1988) as a target site for surveys along with the forest reserve south of Mont Lacombe, east and west of the Roseau River valley, and the Castries Waterworks forest reserve. An intensive mist-netting programme between La Sorcière and Mont Lacombe may be the only realistic way to find the bird in the near future, and this should perhaps be extended to the forest on Gros Piton, whence comes the most recent report (see Population).

PARIA REDSTART *Myioborus pariae* E^2

This species is known only from the montane forests of the Paria Peninsula, north-eastern Venezuela, where although not uncommon on one mountain, the total population must be very small, and threatened by habitat disturbance.

DISTRIBUTION The Paria (or Yellow-faced) Redstart is endemic to the mountains of the Paria Peninsula, Sucre state, north-eastern Venezuela, an area which it shares with four other threatened species (see Threats under White-tailed Sabrewing *Campylopterus ensipennis*).

Records of this bird come from two main areas on the peninsula, the localities (coordinates from Paynter 1982) being as follows: Cerro Humo (c.10°40'N 62°30'W), whence come the majority of records, with 12 specimens (in AMNH, BMNH, CM, COP, USNM) taken between 800 and 1,150 m on both the north slope and approaching from the south (Irapa), and with recent records from the villages of Manacal and Las Melenas (Gardner and Brisley 1989, Goodwin 1990); Cerro "El Olvido" (on the ridge between Cerros Patao to the west and Azul c.2.5 km to the east), where just one bird was recorded at 685 m during surveys from June to September 1988 (Bond *et al.* 1989); Cerro Azul (c.10°40'N 61°56'W), where a male (in FMNH) was taken at 920 m (above Macuro, 10°39'N 61°56'W) in May 1948. G. Medina-Cuervo (*in litt.* 1986) also mentioned Cerro Patao (c.10 km west of Cerro Azul) as a locality, but on what evidence is unknown.

POPULATION The Paria Redstart has been found to be "fairly" to "very" common on Cerro Humo (G. Medina-Cuervo *in litt.* 1986, M. Pearman *in litt.* 1991), 4-6 birds regularly being recorded on one day in the field, e.g. 5-6 on one day in 1979 (G. Medina-Cuervo *in litt.* 1986), four on 4 March 1984 (B. Swift *in litt.* 1986), and five on 5 January 1989 (Gardner and Brisley 1989). However, further east there are very few records: one specimen from Cerro Azul (in 1948) appears to represent the only record from this mountain (see above), and the observation of just one bird on Cerro El Olvido during extensive surveys from June to September 1988 led to the conclusion that the bird was "clearly very rare" on this mountain (Bond *et al.* 1989); hence possibly also on the Cerros Patao–Azul ridge. If this is the case, and with the area of suitable habitat on Cerro Humo perhaps no more than 1,500 ha (G. Medina-Cuervo *in litt.* 1986), the total population of this redstart could be extremely small.

ECOLOGY On Cerro Humo, the Paria Redstart has been recorded from between 800 and 1,150 m, although further east (where the mountains are no higher than 920 m), records come from 685 m on Cerro El Olvido and 920 m on Cerro Azul (see Distribution). Almost nothing has been published concerning the ecology of this species: birds have been found in upper tropical and subtropical cloud-forest (lower and upper montane rainforest) within open coffee groves (under the forest canopy) and especially at the forest edge (Phelps and Phelps 1950, Meyer de Schauensee and Phelps 1978, Goodwin 1990; also B. Swift *in litt.* 1986, M. Pearman *in litt.* 1991). The species is not shy, and birds have been observed foraging (alone or in pairs) for insects at 1-5 m up in coffee groves and lower second growth (G. Medina-Cuervo *in litt.* 1986, B. Swift *in litt.* 1986). From the scant information available, the assumption made by Meyer de Schauensee and Phelps (1978) (also Ridgely and Tudor 1989) that its habits are similar to Slate-throated Redstart *Myioborus miniatus* or other congeners (i.e. occurring in pairs or groups, foraging from medium heights to the tree-tops, and joining mixed feeding flocks) remains unsubstantiated.

THREATS The Paria Redstart has had its entire range "protected" since 1978 within the Paria Peninsula National Park, but despite this the available habitat is now very restricted: Cerro Humo, which seemingly harbours the main population of the species, may have no more than 1,500 ha of suitable habitat remaining, this area being very accessible by road, and subjected to much human disturbance (G. Medina-Cuervo *in litt.* 1986). Unfortunately, the population in the easternmost part of the park appears to be very small (see above); further details of habitat destruction and threats within the Paria Peninsula National Park are in the equivalent section under White-tailed Sabrewing. In 1979, G. Medina-Cuervo (*in litt.* 1986) noted that this species was being caught for sale as an exotic cage-bird, and although the scale of this trade is unknown any collecting must be regarded as detrimental and unacceptable.

MEASURES TAKEN The Paria Redstart has only been recorded from areas now within the Paria Peninsula National Park (37,500 ha), which covers almost all montane areas between Cerro Humo and Cerro Azul (Bond *et al.* 1989: see corresponding section under White-tailed Sabrewing).

MEASURES PROPOSED For the Paria Redstart, the priority has to be the guaranteed protection of the forest on Cerro Humo, the south slopes of which are not currently within the boundaries of the park (see equivalent section under White-tailed Sabrewing), and to a lesser extent the forests further east around Cerros Patao and Azul. Little is known of this bird's ecological requirements or indeed its current population, and therefore a study concentrating on these points is desirable. That this species has been and possibly still is being traded (see Threats), regardless of the scale, is of concern: the current situation should be investigatted and any continuing exploitation stopped at once. All studies and initiatives should integrate with work on all five threatened species in this area (see Threats under White-tailed Sabrewing).

GREY-HEADED WARBLER *Basileuterus griseiceps* I[7]

With a minute range in the montane forests of north-east Venezuela, this warbler is currently known from just one area within a national park. The forests in this region are being extensively depleted.

DISTRIBUTION The Grey-headed Warbler, like a number of other threatened birds (see White-tailed Sabrewing *Campylopterus ensipennis* account for details), is restricted to the Cordillera de Caripe which runs along the borders of north-easternmost Anzoátegui, Monagas and Sucre states of north-east Venezuela.

This species has been recorded from an area of c.350 km^2, with localities (roughly from south-west to north-east and coordinates from Paynter 1982) as follows: Cerro Peonía (10°11'N 64°07'W), November 1941 (see Remarks); Cerro Turumiquire (10°07'N 63°52'W, the summit being in Monagas), where a male was taken at 2,410 m in 1925 (Chapman 1925), with five males and 10 females (in FMNH, LSUMZ) taken between 1,525 and 2,440 m during February and March 1932, and five birds (in COP) taken between 1,850 and 1,950 m in February 1963; La Trinidad (c.10°12'N 63°57'W), which was apparently a coffee plantation (Chapman 1925) on the northern slope of Cerro Turumiquire, where three birds were collected in 1925 (Chapman 1925) with another three (in COP) taken between 1,700 and 1,750 m from late January to early February 1963; Carapas (c.10°12'N 63°56'W; also on the northern slope of Cerro Turumiquire, and adjacent to La Trinidad, Sucre), where three birds were taken at c.1,700 m in 1925 (Chapman 1925); "Los Palmales" (c.10°17'N 63°45'W; apparently in the mountains near San Antonio, between Campo Alegre and Caripe), where a specimen was taken in December 1898 (Chapman 1899); Cerro Negro (c.10°14'N 63°30'W), where 15 birds (in COP, USNM) were collected between 1,400 and 1,600 m during August 1943, with birds recorded fairly frequently there until April 1991 (M. L. Goodwin *in litt.* 1992: see Threats under White-tailed Sabrewing); "in the neighbourhood of Caripe" (c.10°12'N 63°29'W; on the eastern slope at the eastern end of the coastal range, Monagas), where the type-specimen was collected in June 1867 (Sclater and Salvin 1868a), presumably on the slopes of Cerro Negro (10 km to the north-west).

POPULATION Almost nothing has been published concerning the abundance of this species, although Sclater and Salvin (1868a) reported the original collector finding the bird "very rare" in 1867. Ridgely and Tudor (1989) maintained that it is "scarce in what little remains of its... habitat": this conclusion is certainly supported by the almost total absence of recent observations, but the fact that 15 birds were taken between 20 February and 9 March 1932 on Cerro Turumiquire with another 15 between 7 and 25 August 1943 on Cerro Negro suggests that in suitable habitat the Grey-headed Warbler was not uncommon. The species was recorded relatively frequently on Cerro Negro until April 1991 (M. L. Goodwin *in litt.* 1992), although the numbers involved are unknown. Ridgely and Tudor (1989) suggested that habitat destruction has had a severe impact on the overall numbers of this species.

ECOLOGY This warbler is essentially unknown in life (Ridgely and Tudor 1989), although Meyer de Schauensee and Phelps (1978) mentioned that it has been recorded from cloud-forest, second growth and clearings where it forages in "the lower tier of the trees"; however, contrary to both these sources (which give elevations of 1,200-1,600 m), the Grey-headed Warbler has been recorded from between 1,200 and 2,440 m, with the majority of specimens taken between 1,400 and 2,100 m (see Distribution). Chapman (1925) described the area around Carapas (1,700 m) and the adjacent coffee plantation at La Trinidad as having "a few natural clearings filled with bramble and bracken-fern... between extensive stands of forest"; at this altitude the first tree-ferns appeared. The slopes of Cerro Turumiquire were described as precipitous and covered with "tangled vegetation", the upper slopes carrying heavy forest (Chapman 1925). The humid forest of El Guácharo National Park contains the following common trees: *Eugenia* sp., *Byrsonima martinicensis*, *Gustavia augusta*, with species of Lecthidaceae dominating; and associated with these trees are tree-ferns, many epiphytes, *Peperomia* spp., Araceae spp., Piperaceae spp., Orchidaceae spp., Ericaceae spp., with *Blechnum l'herminieri* apparently the commonest species (CNPPA 1982). Unfortunately, no details have been published on the recent observations around Cerro Negro (see Population), although these could obviously add significantly to current knowledge.

THREATS Extensive deforestation of this species's montane forest habitat over much of its known range is the main threat to the Grey-headed Warbler, and has presumably had a great impact on its abundance; the fact that forest understorey, possibly its chief habitat, is often cleared (for coffee cultivation) also suggests that it is at grave risk (Ridgely and Tudor 1989: see equivalent section under White-tailed Sabrewing for details of the threats in the Cordillera de Caripe).

MEASURES TAKEN El Guácharo National Park (82,900 ha) covers Cerro Negro and nearby areas, where birds were recorded up until April 1991 (see Population; also Threats and equivalent section under White-tailed Sabrewing).

MEASURES PROPOSED The current status of the Grey-headed Warbler is in urgent need of assessment: surveys must be undertaken on and around Cerro Negro (as a priority) to determine whether a viable population exists in the national park, and also on Cerro Turumiquire, which appears to have been the bird's other main "stronghold" (see Distribution). Its ecological requirements are essentially unknown, as is the status of remaining habitat. All studies and initiatives should if possible integrate with work on all five threatened species in this area (see Threats under White-tailed Sabrewing).

REMARKS Two specimens (in COP) collected at 1,200 m on 30 November 1941 are seemingly labelled "Cerro Peonía, Bergantín": Bergantín (10°01'N 64°22'W, and at c.300 m) is c.35 km south-west (calculated from the coordinates) of Cerro Peonía (10°11'N 64°07') and was presumably used as a base for collecting trips to the cerro (which stands astride the borders of Anzoátegui, Monagas and Sucre).

WHITE-WINGED WARBLER *Xenoligea montana* V/R[10]

The loss of its montane forest habitat threatens this undergrowth-dwelling bird in both Haiti and the Dominican Republic, although it occurs in up to four protected areas in the latter; nevertheless it requires fuller study and the implementation of existing plans for further key site conservation.

DISTRIBUTION The White-winged Warbler (see Remarks 1) is endemic to Hispaniola, being restricted to the main mountainous areas, in both Haiti and the Dominican Republic (Bond 1979). Unless otherwise stated, records at individual localities refer to single birds collected or observed, with coordinates taken from DMATC (1972, 1973).

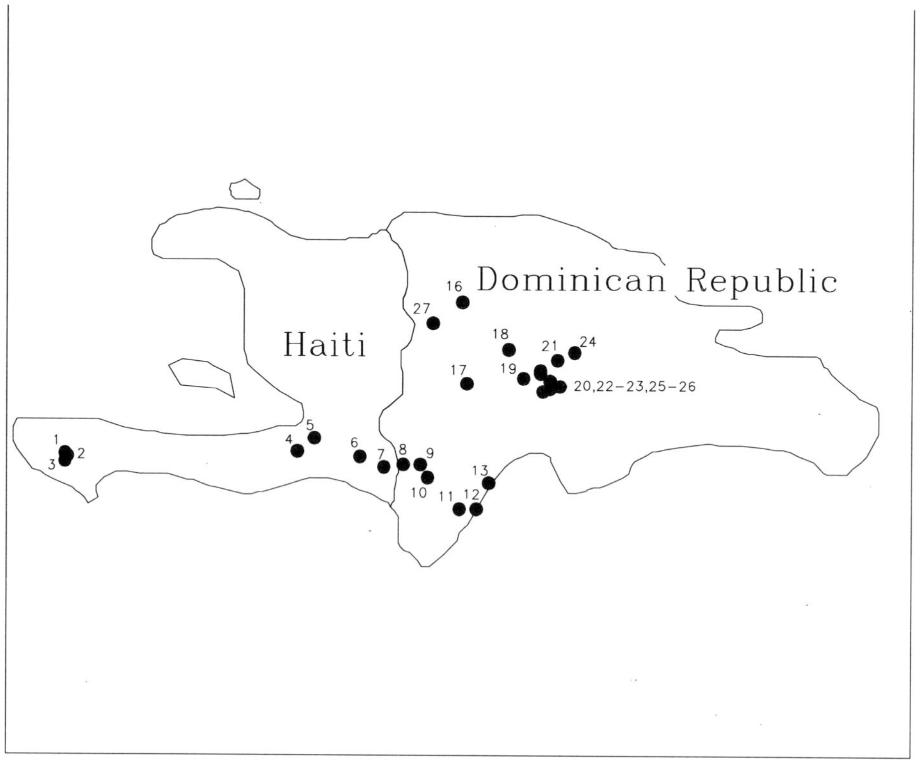

Haiti Records are from:

Massif de la Hotte Unspecified, June 1917 (three specimens in AMNH); around Pic Macaya[1] (18°23'N 74°02'W), April 1931 (six specimens in USNM); "Ridge of Macaya"[2] (see the map in Woods and Ottenwalder 1986), May 1977; "Ridge Formon"[3] (18°20'N 74°02'W), January 1973 (Woods and Ottenwalder 1983); Pic Formon (c.18°22'N 74°02'W as read from the map in Woods and Ottenwalder 1986), December 1982 and January 1984 (M. A. McDonald *in litt.* 1986);

Massif de la Selle Morne Malanga[4] (18°24'N 72°25'W), where two birds were collected in January 1928 (Wetmore and Swales 1931); Morne Tranchant[5] (untraced, but in the vicinity of Kenscoff and Furcy: see, e.g., the map in Wetmore and Swales 1931), where two birds were collected (Bond 1928a); Morne La Selle[6] (18°22'N 71°59'W), April 1927 (two specimens in USNM; also Wetmore and Swales 1931) and June 1928 (two specimens in ANSP, YPM); La

Visite plateau (a broad plateau on the ridge of the Massif de la Selle), May 1975 (Woods and Ottenwalder 1983); Forêt des Pins[7], north-east of Marie Claire (18°18'N 71°49'W), March 1959 (two specimens in YPM).

Dominican Republic Records are from:

Sierra de Baoruco Zapotén[8] (Sapotén, at 18°19'N 71°41'W), July 1986 (A. Stockton de Dod *in litt.* 1991); on the road up from Aguacate (a military post above Zapotén), where five birds were observed in March 1984 (D. A. Scott *in litt.* 1992); between Zapotén and Loma de Toro (a few kilometres to the west of Pueblo Viejo, 18°14'N 71°31'W), where small numbers (one or two at a time) were recorded in 1982 and 1984 (A. Stockton de Dod *in litt.* 1991); above Puerto Escondido[9] (18°19'N 71°34'W), in Loma de Toro, where five to six birds were recorded in April 1984 and up to 30 in April 1987 (J. E. Pierson *in litt.* 1991); Pueblo Viejo[10] (Stockton de Dod 1981); Loma Bretón[11] (18°02'N 71°18'W), where several birds were observed in December 1972 (Stockton de Dod 1978); near "La Lanza"[12] (18°02'N 71°11'W), where four or five birds were observed in 1971 (Stockton de Dod 1978); near Barahona[13] (18°12'N 71°06'W), where a bird was collected in April 1984 at the unusual elevation of c.350 m (F. Sibley *per* A. Stockton de Dod *in litt.* 1991; see Ecology);

Sierra de Neiba the south side of the crest of the Sierra de Neiba, at elevations of c.1,500-1,750 m, where common (Bond 1978);

Cordillera Central Loma Nalga de Maco[14] (19°13'N 71°29'W), recently (SEA/DVS 1992); Loma Tina[15] (18°47'N 70°44'W), where a good series including the type was collected from 12 January to 3 February 1917 (at least 24 specimens in six museums: AMNH, ANSP, BMNH, CM, FMNH and USNM); Monte Viejo (untraced, but in Azua province), August 1929 (Moltoni 1929); La Leonor[16] (19°21'N 71°17'W), where several observations were made in February 1973 (A. Stockton de Dod *in litt.* 1991); mountains north of San Juan[17] (18°50'N 71°15'W), 1929 (Wetmore and Swales 1931); Loma Rucilla[18] (19°3'N 70°58'W), February 1917 (two specimens in AMNH and CM); La Cañita[19] (Las Cañitas, 18°52'N 70°52'W; see Remarks 2), March 1917 (specimen in AMNH); Valle Nuevo[20] (18°48'N 70°41'W), undated (Stockton de Dod 1981); El Río[21] (18°59'N 70°38'W), May 1919 (specimen in USNM) and May 1927 (Wetmore and Swales 1931); close to El Río in the vicinity of Constanza[22] (18°55'N 70°45'W), where two birds were seen and two collected in May 1927 (Wetmore and Swales 1931); La Vega County[23] (c.1.5 km south of Constanza), July 1963 (specimen in FMNH); Casabito[24] (19°02'N 70°31'W), 1973 (Stockton de Dod 1978); Alto Bandera[25] (18°49'N 70°37'W) and Aguas Blancas[26] (18°51'N 70°41'W), undated (Stockton de Dod 1981).

POPULATION Since the White-winged Warbler was first discovered in 1917 (Chapman 1917b) its population has declined rapidly, apparently because of habitat destruction (see Threats), although its habit of joining mixed-species feeding flocks (and thus becoming patchily distributed within its habitat) could explain why it sometimes goes unrecorded (J. E. Pierson *in litt.* 1991).

Haiti It is now very rare, and regarded as the most endangered species of bird in the country (Woods 1987).

Massif de la Hotte At least nine birds were collected between 1917 and 1931, at a time when the species was reported to be fairly common (Wetmore and Lincoln 1933). Subsequently it was observed again at Ridge Formon in January 1973 and Ridge Macaya in May 1977 (Woods and Ottenwalder 1983), a bird was observed near Pic Macaya in December 1982, and one was netted in January 1984 (M. A. MacDonald *in litt.* 1986).

Massif de la Selle Early records referred to three birds (two taken and one seen) in April 1927 (Wetmore and Swales 1931); Bond (1928a) observed it in January 1928 "in small numbers" on Morne Malanga and on Morne Trenchant (*sic*), but reported it to be much more numerous on Morne La Selle, where it roughly equalled Green-tailed Warbler *Microligea palustris* in abundance. More recent records in May 1975 are from La Visite plateau (Woods and Ottenwalder 1983), these same authors commenting that the White-winged Warbler "is by far less common than the Ground [= Green-tailed] Warbler" when discussing the Morne la Visite region. Later, Woods and Ottenwalder (1986) regarded the species as "rare and possibly extirpated" from La Visite National Park.

Dominican Republic The species is considerably less critical than in Haiti.

Sierra de Baoruco Four or five birds were seen together near "La Lanza" in 1971 and several birds at Loma Bretón in December 1972 (A. Stockton de Dod *in litt.* 1991), where local people reported it to be common because of its association with the Cuba tree *Trema micrantha* (Stockton de Dod 1978); 5-6 birds in one flock with other species (see Ecology) were observed above Puerto Escondido in 8 April 1984, and up to 30 birds were recorded primarily in flocks with other species at the same locality in April 1987, when it was judged "the commonest passerine in the forest" that day (J. E. Pierson *in litt.* 1991).

Sierra de Neiba The species was reported "common" on the south side of the crest of Sierra de Neiba (Bond 1978).

Cordillera Central This is the part of its range where most individuals in museums come from (at least 30 specimens in AMNH, BMNH, CM, FMNH and USNM), owing in part to greater ornithological investigation, and to less population pressure (see Threats). It has been considered "fairly common" at high elevations in the Cordillera Central, being "particularly numerous" on the higher slopes of Loma Tina (Bond 1956b). From January to March 1917, R. H. Beck collected no fewer than 27 birds, and clearly from this evidence the species was not rare at the few localities where it was found (see Distribution). Later records from the Cordillera Central offer little information about population densities, except that in February 1973 at La Leonor up to three birds were frequently seen feeding around broadleaf trees (Stockton de Dod 1978, A. Stockton de Dod *in litt.* 1991); however, this author could only find the bird once at Casabito (in 1972), even though she returned to the same area many times subsequently.

ECOLOGY The White-winged Warbler is resident in the mountainous regions of Hispaniola, generally above 1,200 m (Stockton de Dod 1981) and most numerous from 1,300 to 1,800 m (Wetmore and Lincoln 1933, Woods 1987), but three observations fall below this range: in January 1973 at La Leonor (875 m), in December 1972 near "La Lanza" at c.925 m (Stockton de Dod 1978) and in April 1984 near Barahona at c.350 m (A. Stockton de Dod *in litt.* 1991). Although the species can live in pine habitats (Stockton de Dod 1981), it is most often found in dense stands of broadleaved vegetation (Wetmore and Lincoln 1933, Woods and Ottenwalder 1986), including, e.g., low trees, open thickets or the edges of clearings (Wetmore and Swales 1931, Bond 1979, Woods and Ottenwalder 1986) and humid shrubbery, either alone or as an understorey component among pines or other tall trees (J. E. Pierson *in litt.* 1991).

Stockton de Dod (1978) pointed out the importance of seeds of *Trema micrantha* for feeding purposes, and remarked that, because of this, local people at Polo call the White-winged Warbler "cubera", although the species has also been observed searching for insects in broadleaf trees. It is seldom found high above the ground, but does not forage as low as the related Green-tailed Warbler (Wetmore and Swales 1931). It has been observed in mixed feeding flocks with other species such as Green-tailed Warbler and Flat-billed Vireo *Vireo nanus* (J. E. Pierson *in litt.* 1991).

Breeding is thought to occur in April and May (Woods and Ottenwalder 1986), but to date there have been no unequivocal records of nesting and the fact that 5-6 birds were observed in mixed flocks on 8 April 1984 and on 23 April 1987 (J. E. Pierson *in litt.* 1991) may indicate that they, at least, were not then breeding. One of three birds collected on the Massif de la Hotte on 20 and 22 June 1917 was a juvenile moulting into first fall dress (Wetmore and Swales 1931). The birds are found alone, in pairs or in mixed flocks (Wetmore and Swales 1931, Stockton de Dod 1978, J. E. Pierson *in litt.* 1991).

THREATS Habitat destruction on a major scale has been the cardinal threat to the White-winged Warbler throughout Hispaniola.

Haiti The ecological situation is disastrous, in part owing to high human population densities, resulting in deforestation for farming and for the provision of timber for firewood and house construction (Wright 1988; also Woods and Ottenwalder 1986). The country's agriculture cannot feed six million people, and the population may double in another 25 years (Kurlasky 1988); this increase suggests that deforestation would be complete by the year 2000 (Paryski *et al.* 1989); the country is reported to be the worst case of desertification in the Western Hemisphere and there has been a complete lack of governmental interest in the environment (Pellek 1988). The country's tropical rainforest was largely destroyed by the end of the nineteenth century, and by 1954 it was estimated that only 8-9% of the land remained under forest (Lewis and Coffey 1985). After a visit to the country, Bond (1928a) commented: "there has been considerable deforestation, and one encounters virgin forest only about the tops of the higher mountains". The White-winged Warbler also faces serious threats because hillsides have recently come under cultivation (Pellek 1988), with deforestation rates significantly increasing after 1986 (Paryski *et al.* 1989). Habitat loss in the important wildlife area of the Massif de la Hotte is evident from transects which revealed only 2.4% of the region consisted of virgin forest (Cohen 1984). Deforestation has been almost total on the western ridges of Pic Macaya and the southern margin of Pic Formon (Woods and Ottenwalder 1986), while Lewis and Coffey (1985) pointed out an accelerating land and vegetation degradation in the Morne Macaya, one of the "most remote and inaccessible areas in the country".. In La Visite National Park in the Massif de la Selle, the habitat has also been modified in the past by extensive cutting of stands of large pines, and the scrubby broadleaf forest is being rapidly cut as peasant farmers pick new places for gardens; deforestation is also occurring on the north slope of the Massif de la Selle between Morne La Visite and Morne Cabaio; to the west of Morne La Visite is Morne d'Enfer, which forms the most westerly terminus of the high ridges of the Massif de la Selle, this mountain having been almost completely denuded, with severe habitat loss since 1977 (Woods and Ottenwalder 1983). Bond (1942) noted a decrease in the birds of the Massif de la Selle and associated it with the introduction in 1934 of the mongoose *Herpestes*, which would soon have reached the massif; he believed that the ground warblers (both *Microligea* and *Xenoligea*) would particularly have suffered.

Dominican Republic Although the situation is not so extreme as in Haiti, similar deforestation problems exist. A land survey by the Secretaria de Estado de Agricultura in 1979 indicated that 14% of the land was covered by forest and, again, peasant farms constitute an increasing pressure on the forest (Wright 1988), with slash-and-burn methods of farming still being used (A. Stockton de Dod *in litt.* 1986). Forests in the Cordillera Central and Sierra de Baoruco have almost disappeared, except for remnants contained in the national park that surrounds Pico Duarte (J. W. Terborgh *in litt.* 1989).

MEASURES TAKEN Haiti and the Dominican Republic are members of the Organization of American States (OAS), which in 1986 designated two projects to be of the highest priority in achieving regional development in Hispaniola: training, and the development of marine and terrestrial parks.

Haiti Legislation exists that protects natural areas and regulates the cutting, transport and selling of wood (Wright 1988), but obviously enforcement has been negligible (see Threats). In 1983 a decree led to the establishment of La Visite and Pic Macaya National Parks (Wright 1988), whose areas certainly once held White-winged Warblers (see Distribution), but where human population pressure is apparently still a major problem: and the species may have disappeared from the former (Woods and Ottenwalder 1986). The U.S. Agency for International Development (USAID) oversees a reforestation programme that has handed out 22 million tree seedlings to 40,000 peasants (Kurlasky 1988), but about 30 million trees were cut down in 1986 alone, merely for charcoal production (Wright 1988).

Dominican Republic Legislation concerned with forests and wildlife management exists, but the primary focus of the forest law of 1962 is forest production (Wright 1988) and there is a lack of enforcement (J. A. Ottenwalder *in litt.* 1992). At present, three of the country's nine national parks and one of its four scientific reserves are set up in both the Cordillera Central and the Sierra de Baoruco, namely the contiguous (and in conjunction massive) Armando Bermúdez and José del Carmen Ramírez National Parks and the Valle Nuevo Scientific Reserve in the Cordillera Central, and the Sierra de Baoruco National Park; from the map and information in Hoppe (1989) and the information under Distribution it is clear that the White-winged Warbler occurs in all four.

MEASURES PROPOSED More studies are needed to clarify the real situation of the White-winged Warbler in Hispaniola. An overview of the importance of conserving the island's mountain forests is in Measures Proposed under Chat-tanager *Calyptophilus frugivorus*.

Haiti The prospects of the White-winged Warbler would be enhanced by the implementation of proposals, made for other reasons, by Woods and Ottenwalder (1983, 1986), namely (1) the cessation of all cutting of the broadleaved forest above the Plain of Formon and Pic Macaya National Park in the Massif de la Hotte; (2) the incorporation into the Pic Macaya National Park of 1,000 ha of habitat between Caye Formon and Sou Bois on the plateau south of the Ridge of Formon; (3) the preservation of the habitats on the cliffs of La Visite between Morne La Visite and Tête Opaque; (4) the inclusion in La Visite National Park of the area west of Morne La Visite as far as and including Morne d'Enfer.

Dominican Republic Hartshorn *et al.* (1981) mentioned moves to develop new wildlife legislation to be administered by the Departamento de Vida Silvestre and aimed at establishing wildlife management as a goal in itself. The creation of a first protected area in the Sierra de Neiba and a second in the Sierra de Baoruco (see Measures Taken) is long overdue and most important for the conservation of the species.

REMARKS (1) The White-winged Warbler is the sole representative of its genus. (2) Wetmore and Swales (1931) referred to both La Cañita and Las Cañitas, but these appear to be identical as both are described as on the río del Medio (see, e.g., IGU 1979).

TAMARUGO CONEBILL *Conirostrum tamarugense* I[7]

This conebill is confined to a small area in southern Peru and northern Chile, where it appears to be an altitudinal migrant, with breeding grounds and ecological needs as yet to be positively identified, although destruction of Polylepis *is a threat.*

DISTRIBUTION The Tamarugo Conebill is known from several sightings and at least 25 specimens, seen or taken at a number of localities in Arequipa and Tacna departments, Peru, and Tarapacá province, Chile. The known localities (with coordinates from Stephens and Traylor 1983, Paynter 1988, or read from the map in McFarlane 1975), are as follows:

Peru (*Arequipa*) south-eastern slope of Nevado Chachani (c.16°12'S 71°33'W), where birds were seen at 3,950 m in July 1986 and 1987 (T. S. Schulenberg *in litt.* 1988); the slope of Picchupicchu, on the road to Puno (c.43 km by road from Arequipa, and c.20 km by road from Chiguata), where records range from 3,400 to 3,900 m (Schulenberg 1987); (*Tacna*) c.25 km by road from Tarata on the Tacna-Llave road, where the bird has been recorded at 4,050 m (Schulenberg 1987);

Chile (*Tarapacá*) head of Lluta valley, where a birds was seen in March 1989, with six seen at two sites in February 1990 (P. J. Roberts *in litt.* 1989, 1990); (in Quebrada Azapa) San Miguel (c.18°29'S 70°14'W), where a bird was seen in February 1991 (G. Kirwan *in litt.* 1991), Azapa (c.18°31'S 70°11'W), and Ausipar (18°35'S 69°53'W), whence come specimens (in LSUMZ) taken between 195 and 1,200 m; Quebrada Vitor, near Vitor (c.18°45'S 70°20'W) at sea level (McFarlane 1975); (in Camarones valley, Arica department) Taltape (c.19°00'S 69°46'W), where birds have been seen at 780 m, and Conanoxa (19°03'S 69°58'W), where birds have been seen at 400 m (McFarlane 1975); and further south, Mamiña (20°05'S 69°14'W), between 2,600 and 2,950 m (Johnson and Millie 1972, McFarlane 1975); Pica, at 1,355 m (McFarlane 1975); and near the Panamerican Highway (c.20°30'S), c.50 km from Pica, whence comes the type-specimen (Johnson and Millie 1972).

POPULATION Too little is known to give an estimate. Largest numbers recorded were in Arequipa, where a flock of 20 birds was recorded in July 1983 (NK), and the species appears to be at least locally not uncommon (see Distribution and Ecology).

ECOLOGY In Peru, where the Tamarugo Conebill has been found in arid *Gynoxys* and *Polylepis* scrub, records range from 3,400 to 4,050 m; however, in Chile records come from near sea level up to 2,950 m (Schulenberg 1987: see Distribution). In Arequipa, during June 1983, the bird was common in *Gynoxys* at 3,600 m, but less common in the *Polylepis* at 3,900 m (Schulenberg 1987); however, in July 1983 only two birds were sighted in *Gynoxys* at 3,400 m, while a flock of 20 was seen in *Polylepis* at 3,650 m at the same locality (NK). In July 1986, 1987 and 1988, birds were seen in shrubs on Chachani, the 1987 sighting being a flock of 12 or more in the uppermost *Polylepis* at 3,950 m where no Cinereous Conebills *Conirostrum cinereum* were present (T. S. Schulenberg *in litt.* 1988). In Tacna small numbers were seen in low, open *Polylepis* woodland (Schulenberg 1987).

In Chile, the conebill has been found in tree plantations of tamarugal *Prosopis tamarugo*, as well as in riverine scrub, agricultural areas, and citrus groves (Schulenberg 1987). Johnson and Millie (1972) and Tallman *et al.* (1978) suggested that it breeds at high elevations and may wander to adjacent lowlands in the non-breeding season, but in Peru it appears to be almost totally absent from the known highland site in Arequipa during the presumed breeding season (late December to early March) (Schulenberg 1987); the only record from February was of a single bird (Schulenberg 1987) in 1983, an anomalous year with copious rain on the coast and severe drought in the Andes (R. A. Hughes *in litt.* 1988). Tamarugo Conebills have been recorded foraging in groups of 4-20 individuals, resembling Cinereous Conebills in the manner they gleaned insects from leaf surfaces and twigs of trees and shrubs (Tallman *et al.* 1978, NK). Six specimens had insects in their stomachs (Schulenberg 1987), and one had what appeared to be pollen (ZMUC).

In the *Gynoxys* shrubs in Arequipa, Tamarugo Conebills were common in flocks with smaller numbers of Cinereous Conebills: in *Polylepis* woodland at higher elevations they were recorded in conspecific groups that foraged by themselves or in loose association with mixed-species flocks that contained Plain-breasted and Straight-billed Earthcreepers *Upucerthia jelskii* and *U. ruficauda*, Andean and Streaked Tit-spinetails *Leptasthenura andicola* and *L. striata*, and Black-hooded Sierra-finch *Phrygilus atriceps* (Schulenberg 1987). In Chile the species has been found with but outnumbered by Cinereous Conebills (Johnson and Millie 1972, McFarlane 1975).

The breeding season was assumed to be between late December and early March (Schulenberg 1987), but the three known immature or juvenile females were collected in August and September (1984) in Peru (specimens in LSUMZ), and during December (1971) in Chile (Johnson and Millie 1972), with two immature or juvenile males (unossified skulls) collected in August (1984) (LSUMZ). Two not fully adult males (in LSUMZ: 50% ossified skulls) were collected in June (1983) and August (1984), and some of the birds seen on Chachani in July (1986) were in immature plumage (T. S. Schulenberg *in litt.* 1988). Rain usually falls from January to March in Arequipa (R. A. Hughes *in litt.* 1988), with just one record there from late December to early March (a bird recorded in mid-February at 3,400 m) (Schulenberg 1987). Recent records from Chile involve six birds thought to be breeding in the Lluta valley in February 1990 (where a bird has also been seen in early March), with one seen in Quebrada Azapa in February 1991 (P. J. Roberts *in litt.* 1989, 1990, G. Kirwan *in litt.* 1991). Proof of breeding has yet to be obtained, and the precise location of the breeding grounds remains a puzzle.

THREATS *Polylepis* is widely, although illegally, cut and used for charcoal, and for this reason it is almost impossible to find mature trees in accessible areas on Picchupicchu (R. A. Hughes *in litt.* 1988). It is not known if the lack of large trees has a direct effect on the conebill, but widespread destruction of suitable habitat appears to be a major problem.

MEASURES TAKEN None is known.

MEASURES PROPOSED The altitudinal movements and more generally the ecological requirements of this bird are in urgent need of assessment before any realistic conservation initiative can be designed. However, the destruction of *Polylepis* woodland is clearly a threat, and the integrity of remaining blocks of both this and *Gynoxys* (within this species's range) need to be ensured as a priority, preferably in areas where forest over a broad altitudinal range can be preserved.

SAN ANDRES VIREO *Vireo caribaeus* I[7]

Endemic to the densely populated Colombian tourist island of San Andrés in the western Caribbean, this vireo is apparently now restricted to an area of 17 km², where it is threatened by encroaching urbanization, agriculture and coconut palm cultivation.

DISTRIBUTION The San Andrés Vireo is endemic to the island of San Andrés in the western Caribbean (belonging to Colombia), c.200 km east of Nicaragua, Hilty and Brown (1986) implying, without any evidence, that the species occurs on Isla Providencia. San Andrés is only c.13 x 4 km, and records of this species come predominantly from the southern third (Barlow and Nash 1985), although Tye and Tye (1991) recorded it in the northern central area, and Bond (1979) suggested that it is widespread.

POPULATION This vireo is a common resident, having a breeding territory size of as little as 0.5 ha (10 singing males in an area of 5 ha); its abundance appears to have remained unchanged since 1948 (Russell *et al.* 1979, Barlow and Nash 1985). However, the northernmost 20% of the island is urbanized and the southern half is converted to coconut palm *Cocos nucifera* plantations (Tye and Tye 1991), and Barlow and Nash (1985) suggested that records are restricted to an area of 17 km².

ECOLOGY The species is generally recorded from brushy pastures and adjacent inland mangrove swamps, where birds actively forage by gleaning for arthropods and caterpillars from almost ground level to 5 m in shrubby vegetation, and very occasionally to 10 m in tall trees (Barlow and Nash 1985). Males are in full song during April (Russell *et al.* 1979), although nests (two have been found) with eggs and young in have been recorded only in June (Barlow and Nash 1985). One nest was built c.2 m above the ground in a fork of a small branch in a c.4 m high black mangrove *Avicennia marina* situated in a swampy area with large clumps of scrubby mangrove growth, whereas the other (very close to the first) was in an area of pasture with scattered trees, suspended 1 m up from a terminal fork in a 1.3 m broad-leafed shrub which in turn was shaded by a large breadfruit *Artocarpus altilis*; both contained two eggs or young (Barlow and Nash 1985).

THREATS The northernmost 20% of the island (around the capital San Andrés) is urbanized (Tye and Tye 1991), and is the island's centre for tourism (Johnson 1987): little habitat for scrub-dwelling birds remains in or around the capital (Barlow and Nash 1985). The indigenous population of San Andrés, concentrated in the northern two-thirds of the island (Barlow and Nash 1985), increased from 17,000 in 1967 (Emmel 1975) to over 50,000 by 1984 (Johnson 1987). During the seventeenth and eighteenth centuries, San Andrés supported apparently extensive natural stands of "cedar" (possibly *Cedrela odorata*), which were decimated by early colonists (Emmel 1975): the current vegetation cover is mainly coconut palm (covering the southern half of the island) with farmland in between, the native vegetation being restricted to small patches of trees (associated with inland mangrove swamps: Barlow and Nash 1985) and scrub amongst the farmland and settlements (Tye and Tye 1991).

Apart from the inevitable encroachment caused by urbanization (from an expanding resident and tourist population) and agriculture, coastal mangrove areas are being destroyed (on the east coast) by waste oil and the outflow of hot cooling water (Wells 1988), although the extent to which this is affecting the vireo is unknown.

MEASURES TAKEN None is known (see Johnson 1988).

MEASURES PROPOSED A detailed survey of the whole island must determine the precise distribution and abundance of this vireo. Its optimal ecological requirements remain unclear and need definition so that the impact of increasing tourist and commercial pressures can be accurately assessed. For this same reason, the extent and status of remaining native habitats urgently require attention. Any substantial areas of native habitat, especially inland mangroves with their associated stands of native trees, need protection. Various proposals for the control of discharges (oil, hot cooling water, sewage etc.) which affect the marine life (especially the coral formations), lagoon areas, and the mangroves, were put forward by Wells (1988).

BAUDO OROPENDOLA *Psarocolius cassini* I[7]

This large icterid is known from just three localities in the lowlands of Chocó department, north-western Colombia, where four specimens were taken in 1858, 1940 and 1945; there have been no further observations of this seemingly very rare bird.

DISTRIBUTION Records of Baudó (Chestnut-mantled) Oropendola (see Remarks 1) come from three localities in the vicinity of the isolated Serranías de los Saltos and de Baudó, Chocó department, north-western Colombia. The localities involved (coordinates from Paynter and Traylor 1982) are: Camp Albert (= Camp Abert; untraced) on the middle río Truandó (7°26'N 77°07'W), apparently "within the lowland where the Truandó begins to form sandy depositories" (Paynter and Traylor 1982), where the type-specimen (an adult male in USNM) was taken at c.100 m in 1858 (Richmond 1898, Paynter and Traylor 1982); the upper río Baudó, which flows south from the Alto del Buey (6°06'N 77°13'W), where two specimens (in ANSP) were taken at 275 and 365 m during July 1940 (Meyer de Schauensee 1948-1952; see Remarks 2); and beside the río Dubasa (5°19'N 76°57'W), an affluent of the upper río Baudó 60 km upstream from Pizarro, where at 100 m a female (in MHNUC; labelled as from Tubazá) was collected and nine others seen on 2 September 1945 (von Sneidern 1954: see Remarks 3). Rodríguez (1982) mentioned that the species occurs in the río Jurado valley (7°06'N 77°46'W), although he presented no evidence for this.

POPULATION Numbers are essentially unknown, and the species has apparently been recorded on just three occasions (see above). Richmond (1898) reported that only one bird (later to become the type-specimen) was seen on the río Truandó expedition. However, von Sneidern (1954) observed 10 birds together (prior to collecting a female), and suggested that the species was possibly abundant on the ríos Baudó and Dubasa, but that it had not been collected or observed more frequently owing to the difficulty in distinguishing it from other oropendolas when high up in trees or flying. Since 1945 there have been no confirmed records and either the identification of the species remains a problem or the bird is extremely rare or localized.

ECOLOGY The Baudó Oropendola is known from humid lowland forest and forest edge, between 100 and 365 m (Meyer de Schauensee 1970, Hilty and Brown 1986: see Distribution). Von Sneidern (1954) observed birds together in high trees on the banks of the río Dubasa, and the occurrence of the species at Camp Abert (also beside a river) suggests that it may have a preference for forest growing on sandy deposits (see Distribution). Richmond (1898), referring to the sole individual seen, said that it was "very shy".

THREATS It is highly probable that the extensive deforestation occurring throughout north-western Colombia (Ridgely and Tudor 1989) has caused a decline in the population of this species but, with so little known about it, specific threats are difficult to identify or assess. The Serranía de Baudó still retains large expanses of forest (A. J. Negret *in litt.* 1987), but has nevertheless been identified as the highest conservation priority within the Colombian Chocó (especially around Ensenada Utría) owing to the incursion of roads encouraging settlement, and to timber companies causing further deforestation (IUCN TFP 1988a).

MEASURES TAKEN None is known. The Ensenada Utría National Park (c.50,000 ha) protects some areas of the Serranía de Baudó (IUCN TFP 1988a), but it is unknown whether the Baudó Oropendola occurs in the immediate area. In any case, this reserve is threatened by road building associated with the construction of a hydroelectric dam (IUCN TFP 1988a). Fundación Natura is currently undertaking management studies and an inventory in this park (M. G. Kelsey *in litt.* 1992).

MEASURES PROPOSED The rediscovery of the Baudó Oropendola is of the highest priority, and searches should obviously be concentrated in the vicinity of the three known localities and where forest still occurs along rivers. Details of this species's ecological requirements are also urgently needed if an effective conservation plan is to be developed. Any measures for this species should be undertaken in conjunction with those proposed for the Chocó Tinamou *Crypturellus kerriae* (see equivalent section under this species for details). A protected area in the Serranía de Baudó, especially covering forest along the ríos Baudó and Dubasa, rivers originating in the Sierra de los Saltos, and perhaps adjoining the Ensenada Utría National Park, is urgently required, owing to the threats it faces and its exceptionally high biological diversity (IUCN TFP 1988a) (see equivalent section under Speckled Antshrike *Xenornis setifrons* for further initiatives proposed for this area).

REMARKS (1) Meyer de Schauensee (1966) suggested that this bird should be considered conspecific with the Black Oropendola *Psarocolius guatimozinus*, Montezuma's Oropendola *P. montezuma* and Olive Oropendola *P. bifasciatus*. However, Ridgely and Tudor (1989), after examining the specimen (collected on the río Salaquí) supposedly intermediate between *cassini* and *guatimozinus* (Haffer 1975), concluded that it was a typical representative of the latter, and thus retained specific status for both. Ridgely and Tudor (1989) suggested the common name "Baudó Oropendola" in preference to Chestnut-mantled Oropendola, first to avoid confusion with Black Oropendola (both species have chestnut mantles), and second to indicate the species's restricted range. (2) Von Sneidern (1954) it is suggested that only one bird was collected in that year. (3) This record of a specimen and nine birds observed on the río Dubusa in 1945 appears to have been missed in recent literature that mentions the oropendola (e.g. Haffer 1975, Hilty and Brown 1986, Ridgely and Tudor 1989), all of which suggests that the bird is unrecorded in life and known from just three specimens taken at two localities.

SELVA CACIQUE *Cacicus koepckeae* K[12]

Only known from the type-locality (though probably also Manu National Park) in the lowlands of Peru, this icterid may be genuinely rare and, if a riverine species, possibly at some risk of habitat loss.

DISTRIBUTION The Selva Cacique is only known from the type-locality in the lowlands of south-east Peru, where two specimens were secured at Balta, c.10°08'S 71°13'W (coordinates in Lowery and O'Neill 1965), in the valley of río Curanja, Loreto, on 23 July 1963 (specimen in LSUMZ) and on 22 March 1965 (Lowery and O'Neill 1965), with a "possible sighting" from Manu National Park (c.12°00'S 71°30'W; coordinates here and below from Stephens and Traylor 1983), Madre de Dios (Ridgely and Tudor 1989); the source of this latter record is unclear but Terborgh *et al.* (1984) referred to an "almost certain" record from Cocha Cashu Biological Station, at c.11°51'S 71°19'W, Manu National Park, where a bird was repeatedly flushed on 26 September 1981, and M. Kessler *in litt.* (1988) also observed a possible bird at an old arm of the río Manu, just beyond Manu village (12°15'S 70°50'W) on 29 July 1983.

POPULATION The few records suggest that the species is very rare, although this need not necessarily be so. The type-specimen was collected from a group of six individuals (which is the largest number ever observed) (Ridgely and Tudor 1989).

ECOLOGY The Selva Cacique apparently inhabits humid low-lying forests, such as are found at the type-locality (Parker *et al.* 1982); probably it is an arboreal bird occurring mostly at forest borders (Ridgely and Tudor 1989), but it appears to be restricted to riverine habitats in the region (TAP). One of the birds observed at Manu was flushed from open secondary woods near water (M. Kessler *in litt.* 1988), and the other was on the ground under a dense stand of *Heliconia* and bamboo near a stream (Terborgh *et al.* 1984). The type-specimen was likewise on the ground (apparently bathing in a pool along a stream), its five companions retreating into a *Heliconia* thicket when it was shot (Ridgely and Tudor 1989).

THREATS None is known, but if it is a riverine species then it may face loss of habitat in the same manner as that feared for the Rufous-fronted Antthrush *Formicarius rufifrons* (see Threats in relevant account).

MEASURES TAKEN The species has been reported from Manu National Park.

MEASURES PROPOSED The first requirement must be to identify one or more general areas in which some reasonable population exists; these will then need study to determine the species's ecological needs, which can be used to develop and implement further measures, if deemed necessary. The importance of planned and existing protected areas in south-east Peru is outlined in Measures Proposed and Remarks under Rufous-fronted Antthrush.

MARTINIQUE ORIOLE *Icterus bonana* E[2]

This icterid is endemic to Martinique, West Indies, where, although present in most habitat types throughout the island, it suffers severe levels of brood-parasitism from the recently established Shiny Cowbird, and the population has declined dramatically.

DISTRIBUTION The Martinique Oriole is endemic to the island of Martinique (to France), West Indies. It was originally distributed throughout the forested areas of the island, below 700 m (Babbs *et al.* 1987), as indicated from the localities mentioned by Lawrence (1878c), on specimen labels (in CM, LSUMZ, ROM, USNM) and in Babbs *et al.* (1987). Bond (1956b) suggested that the bird is most numerous in the southern portion of Martinique (see Remarks).

POPULATION The Martinique Oriole has suffered a severe decline in recent years, and this seems to have been greater in coastal mangrove and dry forest areas where in some cases the species has completely disappeared (Babbs *et al.* 1987). At the five census sites for which there was an estimate of the population size in the mid-1980s, Babbs *et al.* (1987) recorded a 75-100% decline (these sites were mainly on the boundary between mangrove and dry forest). Even local people (including hunters), many of whom knew the bird, commented on the recent decline of the bird (Babbs *et al.* 1987). The breeding density and total population have never been estimated, so the extent of the decline remains essentially unknown. The overall population is certainly now considered small (Benito-Espinal and Hautcastel 1988).

ECOLOGY The Martinique Oriole apparently inhabits all of the island's forest types except cloud-forest, thus: mangrove, dry forest, moist forest, plantations, gardens with trees, and rainforest, with all records coming from below 700 m; the species is primarily a canopy forager, where it takes some fruit and berries, as well as a large diversity of insects (Babbs *et al.* 1987). Breeding (which is not communal) has been recorded from December onwards, but generally starts in February, with most pairs having fledged young by mid-July; there is apparently no post-breeding movement of (adult) birds, and the species does not seemingly form flocks (Babbs *et al.* 1987). In 1986, breeding was recorded in all habitats except rainforest and cloud-forest (no records from above 360 m), the nest being built 2-4 m above the ground and suspended from a large leaf or a bunch of leaves at the end of a branch. The commonest nesting trees are apparently: baliser *Heliconia caribaea*, bread-fruit *Artocarpus altilis* and banana *Musa acuminata* (in agricultural and moist forest areas); trumpet wood *Cecropia peltata* (in moist and rainforest areas); and raisinier grand-feuilles *Coccoloba grandifolia* (in dry forest) (Babbs *et al.* 1987, Benito-Espinal and Hautcastel 1988). Clutch-size is generally three (Benito-Espinal and Hautcastel 1988). Birds were not recorded feeding more than 100 m from the nest, and indeed, the species seemingly defends only a small territory in the immediate vicinity of the nest-site (Babbs *et al.* 1987).

THREATS The main threat is brood-parasitism by the Shiny Cowbird *Molothrus bonariensis*, which colonized Martinique during the late 1940s and is increasing in number every year: it is apparently now responsible for the parasitism of c.75% of Martinique Oriole nests (B. Dewynter *in litt.* 1982, Babbs *et al.* 1987). An indication of the problem lies in the fact that c.60% of birds chased away from nests are Shiny Cowbirds, and that the latter were present at all sites where Martinique Orioles were recorded (in 1986) except the rainforest (Babbs *et al.* 1987). It is also possible that increases in the population of the Carib Grackle *Quiscalus lugubris* may have a secondary effect on oriole nesting success (through the taking of eggs and nestlings), this species probably being the only important natural predator of orioles on the island (Babbs *et al.* 1987). The oriole is apparently unaffected by habitat loss or illegal hunting (Babbs *et al.* 1987), but the expansion of the cowbird may well have been assisted by deforestation (Benito-Espinal and Hautcastel 1988).

MEASURES TAKEN None is known, other than the fact that the Martinique Oriole enjoys legal protection (Benito-Espinal and Hautcastel 1988).

MEASURES PROPOSED Babbs *et al.* (1987) made a number of recommendations, the main one being (1) the control of the Shiny Cowbird population by using decoy traps (and killing the trapped cowbirds), with the simultaneous monitoring of oriole reproductive success within the trapping area, to give an indication of the effectiveness of this approach; they also called for (2) a study of oriole breeding success and levels of cowbird parasitism in different habitats, with the aim of monitoring population trends, and identifying important areas for the species; (3) assessment of the effect of Carib Grackles on the oriole population; and (4) a public awareness campaign, focusing on the species's plight and its importance as Martinique's only endemic bird.

REMARKS Benito-Espinal and Hautcastel (1988) considered the oriole as now limited to a number of localities, naming Grand Rivière, the slopes of Piton La Croix, Anse à l'Ane, Morne Doré, Rivière Pilote and the Caravelle Peninsula. However, it appears that these localities just refer to the published (Babbs *et al.* 1987) sightings of the bird from two years earlier, and do not represent proof of a range contraction.

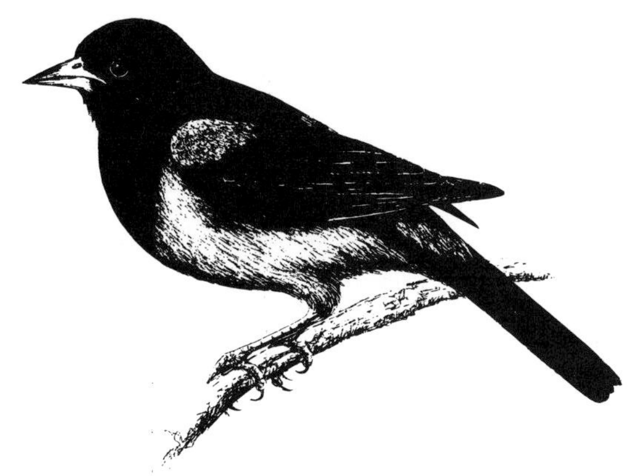

SAFFRON-COWLED BLACKBIRD *Xanthopsar flavus* V[9]

Many different uses of the open country in which this colonial icterid lives are responsible for its steep decline and loss of range in Brazil, Paraguay, Uruguay and Argentina, where it occurs in very few protected areas and is in urgent need of study and survey.

DISTRIBUTION The Saffron-cowled Blackbird occurs in south-eastern Brazil, eastern Paraguay, Uruguay and north-eastern Argentina (Meyer de Schauensee 1966, Ridgely and Tudor 1989). Unless otherwise indicated, in the following account records with dates at individual localities are of single birds collected or observed, with coordinates taken from Paynter (1985, 1989), Paynter and Traylor (1991) and Rand and Paynter (1981).

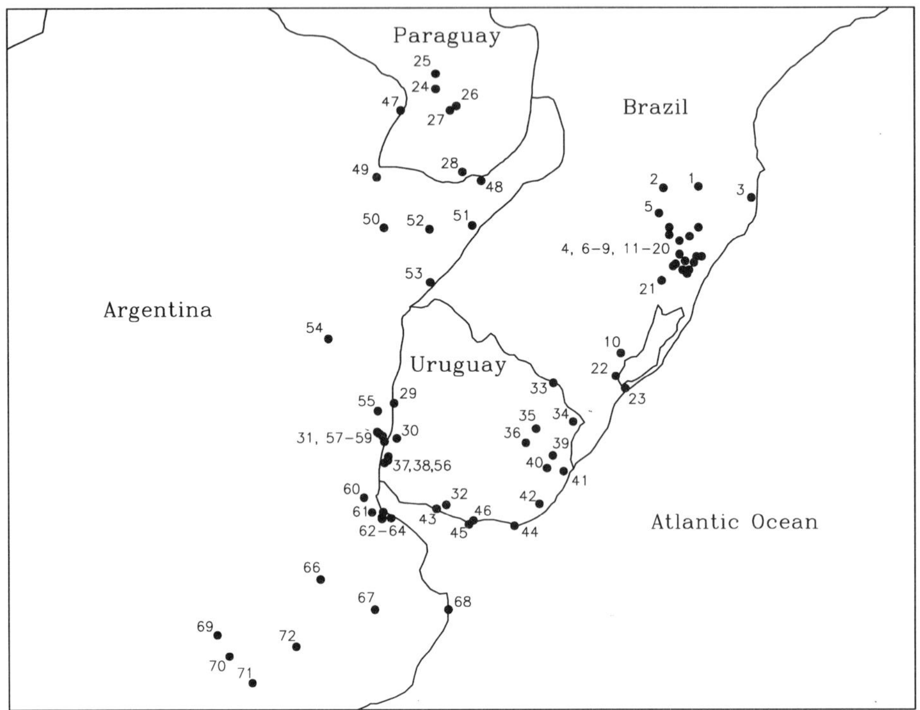

Brazil Records (north to south) include:

(*Santa Catarina*) c.10 km south of Otacílio Costa[1], December 1986 (D. F. Stotz *in litt.* 1991); Anita Garibaldi[2], November 1969 (specimen in MNRJ); Parque Estadual da Serra do Tabuleiro[3] (27°50'S 48°47'W), July 1982 (a few birds observed: M. A. de Andrade *in litt.* 1988); on the border with Rio Grande do Sul, between Bom Jesus and São Joaquim[4], where a flock of six birds was observed (Silva and Fallavena 1988);

(*Rio Grande do Sul*) unspecified, May 1882 (two specimens in MNRJ); between Esmeralda and Muitos Capões[5], where a flock of 24 birds was observed in May-June 1988 (Silva and Fallavena 1988); Vaccaria[6] (= Vacaria), December 1928 (six specimens in AMNH) and December 1974 (specimen in MNRJ); south of Vacaria, December 1986 (D. F. Stotz *in litt.* 1991); between Vacaria and Bom Jesus[7], where flocks of 6-8 birds were observed in August 1988 (Silva and Fallavena 1988); 35 km south of Vacaria[8], where a nest was found in November 1971 (Belton 1984-1985); Bom Jesus[9], January 1990 (Pacheco and da Fonseca 1990); Boa Vista[10], Cambará do

Sul, where a flock of 11 birds was observed in November 1991 (F. Silva *in litt.* 1992); and a flock of six birds in March 1992 (M. Pearman *in litt.* 1992); Lajeado Grande[11], January and November 1960 (five specimens in MCN and MZUSP); between Cambará do Sul and Tainhas[12], where flocks of 8-11 birds were observed in May-June 1988 (Silva and Fallavena 1988); Itaimbezinho area[13] (within Aparados da Serra National Park: see Paynter 1985), currently (Ridgely and Tudor 1989, B. M. Whitney *in litt.* 1991); 11 km north-east of Tainhas[14], September 1970 (specimen in MCN); Várzea do Cedro[15], where two flocks of 5-8 birds were observed in August 1988 (Silva and Fallavena 1988); Saiquí[16] (29°19'S 50°46'W), where nesting activity was detected in November 1972 (Belton 1984-1985); Canela[17], undated (specimen in MNRJ); between Tainhas and São Francisco de Paula[18], where several five flocks of 5-10 birds were observed in May-June 1988 (Silva and Fallavena 1988); near São Francisco de Paula[19], where two flocks of 15-20 birds were observed in February 1980 (M. Nores *in litt.* 1992); 9 km north-east of São Francisco de Paula, December 1986 (four specimens in FMNH); Barragem Blang (untraced but near São Francisco de Paula, September 1958 (specimen in MCN); near Rincão dos Kroeff[20] (29°27'S 50°25'W), December 1970 (specimen in MCN); Novo Hamburgo[21], July 1896 (von Ihering and von Ihering 1907, Pinto 1944; see Remarks); Pelotas[22], undated (two birds taken: Hellmayr 1937, Pinto 1944); Rio Grande[23], 1853 (two specimens in AMNH and BMNH); Campo da Boa Vista (untraced, undated: von Ihering 1899a); between Pelotas and Rio Grande, recently (TAP).

Paraguay Records (north to south) are: (*Presidente Hayes*) "bajo chaco"[24], undated (J. Escobar *in litt.* 1991); (*La Cordillera*) "Cordillera"[25] (Bertoni 1939); (*Guairá*) Villa Rica (= Villarrica), November 1905 (three specimens in BMNH); Caravení (untraced), Villarrica[26], August 1924 (specimen in BMNH); Itapé[27] (25°51'S 56°38'W), October 1927 (two specimens in FMNH); (*Alto Paraná*) Itakyry, Itaipú reservoir, March 1987 (N. Pérez *in litt.* 1992); (*Itapúa*) 10 km west of San Cosme y Damián[28] (c.27°15'S 56°19'W read from DSGM 1988), March 1989 (five birds observed: F. E. Hayes *in litt.* 1991).

Uruguay Records (roughly north to south) are: (*Paysandú*) "Paysandú"[29], October 1883 (specimen in AMNH); (*Río Negro*) Estancia Bopicuá[30] (Bopicuá at c.33°06'S 58°01'W), April 1974 (a flock observed: Gore and Gepp 1978); Fray Bentos[31], November 1967 (a flock of 8-10 birds: Gore and Gepp 1978); southern Río Negro department[32], where according to Alvarez (1933) the species was more commonly found; (*Cerro Largo*) San Diego[33] (c.31°55'S 53°58'W), río Yaguarón, April 1960 (specimen in MNHNM); Ruta (untraced), July 1958 (specimen in MNHNM); (*Treinta y Tres*) Bañados del Este[34], currently (*World Birdwatch* 12,1-2 [1990]: 4), e.g. flock of 20, May 1992 at Los Indios (R. Vaz-Ferreira verbally 1992); marsh near Quebrada de los Cuervos[35] (c.32°54'S 54°25'W), December 1986 (two birds observed: Arballo 1990); arroyo Avestruz[36] (= arroyo Avestruz Grande, at 33°12'S 54°41'W), May 1953 (specimen in MNHNM); Campos de Oscar Pérez (untraced), Río Olimar, August 1958 (specimen in MNHNM); (*Soriano*) c.3 km south-west of Dolores[37], June 1927 (specimen in FMNH); La Concordia[38] (= Colonia La Concordia), at 33°37'S 58°20'W), July and August 1958 (three specimens in MNHNM); (*Rocha*) between Cebollatí and Lascano[39], August 1972, April (six birds observed) and May 1973 (12 birds observed: Gore and Gepp 1978); Arrocera Bonino (untraced), Lascano, undated (specimen in MNHNM); 22 km south-east of Lascano[40], May 1963 (two specimens in AMNH); Bañados de India Muerta[41] (= Bañado de San Miguel, at 33°48'S 53°42'W), where two flocks of 32 and 28 individuals were observed in October and December 1987 respectively (Arballo 1990); marsh near Rocha[42], where a flock of 40 individuals was observed in December 1988 (Arballo 1990); (*Colonia*) "Colonia, Río de la Plata", August 1871 (specimen in BMNH); (*San José*) Arazatí[43] (probably Bañados de Arazatí, at c.34°35'S 57°00'W), August 1956 (specimen in MNHNM); (*Maldonado*) "Maldonado"[44], 1826, January 1837 and December 1866 (three specimens in BMNH, MNHN, UMZC); (*Montevideo*) "Montevideo"[45], undated and 1827 (two specimens in BMNH and MNHN); Bañados de Carrasco[46] (34°50'S 56°03'W), November 1909 (two specimens in MNHNM).

Argentina Records (north to south) are:

(*Formosa*) eastern Formosa (Olrog 1979); Monte Lindo[47] (= Colonia Dalmacia, 25°51'S 57°54'W), November 1944 (Esteban 1953a);

(*Chaco*) unspecified (Freiberg 1943, Ridgely and Tudor 1989); eastern Chaco (Meyer de Schauensee 1966);

(*Misiones*) unspecified (SOMA 1935-1942, Freiberg 1943, Pereyra 1950, Olrog 1979, but based presumably on a female collected in the province and deposited in MACN in March 1932: see Chebez in press); río Paraná[48], Posadas, February 1983 (Chebez in press);

(*Corrientes*) San Cosme[49] (27°22'S 58°31'W), where two birds were collected in November 1947 (Esteban 1953a); Estero Batel[50] (= Esteros del Batel, 28°30'S 58°20'W, in OG 1968), October 1974 (two birds observed: P. Canevari *in litt.* 1987); 18 km north and 4 km west of Santo Tomé[51], Esteros de Iberá, May 1989 (M. Pearman *in litt.* 1990); c.10 km west of Ruta 14[52] (Santo Tomé–Posadas) on the road to Colonia Carlos Pellegrini (28°32'S 57°10'W), where c.105-135 birds arrived to roost in mid-May 1991 (F. R. Lambert verbally 1992); on the way to Paso de los Libres[53], September 1978 (a flock of c.20 birds) (see Klimaitis 1986);

(*Santa Fe*) arroyo Miní (untraced), April 1937 (Freiberg 1943);

(*Entre Ríos*) unspecified (specimen in MNRJ); "Entreríos" (date not given) (specimen in BMNH); Santa Elena[54] (30°57'S 59°48'W), where two nests were found in November 1923 (Smyth 1927-1928); 18 km south of Caseros[55], December 1983 (a flock of c.40 birds) (Klimaitis 1986); Concepción del Uruguay[56], October and November (Barrows 1883; two specimens in MCZ); km 75 (National Road 14), Gualeguaychú Department, November 1990 (Chebez in press); arroyo Gualeyán[57] (32°58'S 58°31'W in OG 1968), at its intersection with National Road 14, 1989 (Chebez in press); Estancia San Luis[58] (33°00'S 58°28'W), where more than 50 birds were observed in January and 16 in March 1992 (E. I. Abadie, B. M. López Lanús and M. Pearman *in litt.* 1992); Puerto Boca[59] (33°03'S 58°23'W), where five birds were observed in October 1987, while in January 1990 two flocks of c.25 and c.15 birds were observed as well as a pair carrying food, in December 1991 two flocks of 30 and c.10 birds, and on different occasions during January 1992 one to five birds (coordinates and data from E. I. Abadie, B. M. López Lanús and M. Pearman *in litt.* 1992);

(*Buenos Aires*) Zelaya[60] (34°21'S 58°52'W), nesting in 1932 (Pereyra 1933); Ribera Norte[61], San Isidro, nesting in 1983, 1984, and 1985 (see Chebez in press); Barracas al Sur[62] (= Barracas, 34°39'S 58°22'W) (Dabbene 1910); Lomas de Zamora[63] (34°46'S 58°24'W), where two birds were collected on an ungiven date (Withington and Sclater 1888); Conchitas[64] (= Guillermo E. Hudson, at 34°47'S 58°10'W), April, August and September 1868 (10 specimens in AMNH, BMNH and USNM; also Sclater and Salvin 1868-1869); Adrogué[65] (34°48'S 58°24'W), January 1881 (White 1882); Alvear[66] (= General Alvear), September 1876 (Durnford 1878); río Vecino[67] (presumably Canal Número Uno, at 36°40'S 58°35'W; see Paynter 1985), no date given (see Hellmayr 1937); Cabo San Antonio[68], where the species was observed on different occasions (Gibson 1885, 1918); between Lavalle[69] (= General Lavalle) and Carhué (37°11'S 62°44'W) (see Hellmayr 1937); Pigué[70] (37°37'S 62°25'W), March 1881 (large flocks observed: Barrows 1883); Sierra de la Ventana[71], which appears to be the southernmost record, although the species no longer occurs there (Fraga 1990); Santa Elena[72] (untraced, but in the north-west of the province), April 1894 (two specimens in BMNH); La Rosa (untraced), April 1886 (specimen in BMNH).

POPULATION The Saffron-cowled Blackbird has become very rare in Argentina, Paraguay and Uruguay, and appears to have diminished seriously since the 1970s in Brazil (Silva and Fallavena 1988, W. Belton *in litt.* 1990).

Brazil The late nineteenth-century literature does not help judge whether the species has diminished or remained stable over the years. In this century it has been considered uncommon in its range (Belton 1984-1985, Sick 1985), although more recently reported to be locally common in Rio Grande do Sul and southern Santa Catarina (W. Belton *in litt.* 1986, D. F. Stotz *in litt.* 1988). After a couple of visits to Rio Grande do Sul around 1986, W. Belton (*in litt.* 1990) noted that the species was scarcer when compared to the 1970s. This decline was corroborated by Silva and Fallavena (1988), who between July 1987 and September 1988 conducted field searches in north-east Rio Grande do Sul and adjacent Santa Catarina: they visited a total of 96 suitable sites, but the species was only present in 17 of them; furthermore, most flocks observed comprised a few individuals and only on one occasion was a flock of as many as 24 birds recorded (see Distribution). Set against the evidence from the 1970s and early 1980s, such as records of "10 to 50 individuals, with occasional bands of 100 or more" (Belton 1984-1985), Silva and Fallavena (1988) interpreted their findings as indicating a recent decline in numbers. Yearly visits to 6-7 colonies between São Francisco de Paula and Itaimbezinho canyon (Aparados da Serra National Park) between 1980 and 1991 resulted in an approximate total of 230 birds, with no noticeable decline in numbers but evidence of cowbird parasitism since 1988; moreover, searches for the species in central and western Rio Grande do Sul during a c.1,500 km drive through grasslands and farmlands in May 1992 were entirely unsuccessful (TAP).

Paraguay The species's status in Paraguay is far from clear, but the few comments found in the literature suggest that it was common at the end of the nineteenth and in the early twentieth centuries: Burmeister (1856) reported it "very common" and de Azara (1802-1805) stated that it was abundant, adding that sometimes it was seen in large flocks. The scarcity of records in recent times (see Distribution) suggests that the species is now very rare.

Uruguay Published evidence suggests that the species was common during the nineteenth century. C. Darwin found large flocks and considered it to be common (Gould 1841), and Gibson (1885) reported it to be "abundant" in the Department of Paysandú. However, Alvarez (1933) noted that the species "is not very abundant" and that it was mainly to be found in the southern parts of Río Negro, while Gore and Gepp (1978) considered it scarce in various parts of the country.

Argentina The species was perhaps never very common (Fraga 1990; also M. I. Christie *in litt.* 1986). Durnford (1878), who collected a bird at Alvear, Buenos Aires, considered it then to be "rare", although Barrows (1883) reported the occurrence of a large flock ("a hundred or more" birds) at Pigué, Buenos Aires, in March 1881. The species was "common" at Santa Elena, Buenos Aires, in April 1894 (BMNH label data). Comments in Sclater and Hudson (1888-1889) and Hudson (1920) suggest that the species was common in the province of Buenos Aires, where flocks of 20-30 birds were reported. After 1882, however, flocks were no longer seen in eastern Buenos Aires, and the southernmost population, in the Sierra de la Ventana, vanished soon after European settlement towards 1900 (Fraga 1990). Pereyra (1933) considered it fairly scarce. Today the species is very rare in the country and declining in most parts (Klimaitis 1984, 1986, Narosky and Yzurieta 1987, Ridgely and Tudor 1989, Fraga 1990; also M. I. Christie *in litt.* 1986, P. Canevari *in litt.* 1987); however, birds are occasionally recorded in southern Misiones, Corrientes, Formosa, Entre Ríos and north-eastern Buenos Aires (J. C. Chebez *in litt.* 1991). The species is still locally common in eastern Corrientes and eastern Entre Ríos, where recent sightings included flocks of more than 50 birds, with 105-135 birds at a roosting site (see Distribution).

ECOLOGY The Saffron-cowled Blackbird has been reported from very different environments ranging from open grasslands, dry bushy areas, agricultural fields, rolling pasture and boggy swales characterized by the presence of *Eryngium* (a plant known as "cardales" in Argentina and "gravatá" in Brazil) (Alvarez 1933, Gore and Gepp 1978, Klimaitis 1984, 1986, Belton 1984-1985, Sick 1985, Ridgely and Tudor 1989, R. I. Orenstein *in litt.* 1991).

Little is known about its feeding requirements; foraging is done by colonies in flocks (TAP), and it has been observed following the plough and feeding on insects and worms (Hudson 1920); maggots have also been reported in its diet (Burmeister 1856). *Eryngium* appears to be of great importance for the species, not only for breeding (see below) but for providing food, since birds have been reported searching for prey items (e.g. locusts) within these clusters (Klimaitis 1986), although they also forage in adjacent grasslands (Ridgely and Tudor 1989).

The Saffron-cowled Blackbird breeds in colonies which are usually situated in patches of *Eryngium* or bushes (e.g. "sarandíes") situated only about 0.3 to 1 m above ground, and have been reported both in dry areas (Gibson 1885, Pereyra 1938, Klimaitis 1986) and in typical upland swales (Brazil) or wet marshes with some standing open water in which *Eryngium* and woody vegetation is present (Barrows 1883, Belton 1984-1985, Ridgely and Tudor 1989). E. I. Abadie, B. M. López Lanús and M. Pearman (*in litt.* 1992) observed a presumed nesting pair in an area of dense marsh vegetation including *Eryngium* and *Acacia caven*. The breeding season starts in October, and most of the nests contain eggs or young by November (Gibson 1885, Smyth 1927-1928, Pereyra 1933, Belton 1984-1985) although, in a colony reported by Barrows (1883), eggs were laid about the third week of December.

The Saffron-cowled Blackbird is a highly sociable species; most records refer to flocks, these sometimes involving more than a hundred birds (Hudson 1920; see also Distribution). Birds are known to associate with other icterids, e.g. Brown-and-yellow Marshbird *Pseudoleistes virescens*, Yellow-rumped Marshbird *P. guirahuro*, Pampas Meadowlark *Sturnella militaris* (see relevant account) and Bay-winged Cowbird *Molothrus badius* (de Azara 1802-1805, Fraga 1990, J. Escobar *in litt.* 1991, F. E. Hayes *in litt.* 1991, E. I. Abadie, B. M. López Lanús and M. Pearman *in litt.* 1992, F. R. Lambert verbally 1992). The species has been reported roosting in large numbers (105-135) mixed with more than 250 Yellow-rumped Marshbirds in reed/long grass beds (F. R. Lambert verbally 1992). An interesting association with the near-threatened Black-and-white Monjita *Heteroxolmis dominicana* has been noted, in which flocks of the blackbird follow and perch around one or two monjitas (Belton 1984-1985, Ridgely and Tudor 1989). This interesting association may well be beneficial for both species, the foraging blackbirds disturbing insects that the monjitas then catch, the prominently perched monjitas serving as anti-predator vigilantes for the blackbirds (TAP). The blackbird's movements are poorly studied and, although it is not considered a migratory species, the data suggest a pattern of irregular eruptions (Fraga 1991), this also being suggested by unsuccessful searches of the species's usual haunts (suitable habitat and known sites throughout Rio Grande do Sul) conducted in late January 1992: such movements should be borne in mind when judging the species's status in a region (TAP).

THREATS The causes of the Saffron-cowled Blackbird's decline in some parts of its range are not clear. According to J. C. Chebez (*in litt.* 1986), the decline in Argentina is related to man-transformed habitats (i.e. expansion of agriculture and cattle-raising) and the associated use of pesticides. Burning of tall grasses in spring for tender pastures has also been indicated as a possible cause of decline in Argentina (M. Rumboll *in litt.* 1986). Extensive pine plantations within the species's range in Rio Grande do Sul are rapidly replacing natural grasslands (TAP). Silva and Fallavena (1988) identified the following threats (all derived from human activities) in apparently suitable habitat in which the species was not recorded during their study in north-eastern Rio Grande do Sul and adjacent Santa Catarina: fires, drainage, human settlements, agriculture and pesticides, cattle and hunting. In eastern Paraguay habitat destruction is probably the species's main threat (F. E. Hayes *in litt.* 1991). In the Bañados del Este, Uruguay, enforcement of existing laws are ignored and some areas have already gone because of draining and development (Scott and Carbonell 1986, *World Birdwatch* 12,1-2 [1990]: 4); the situation there continues to deteriorate and over 40% of the area has already been lost mainly because of rice plantations (P. Canevari *in litt.* 1992). Although not studied, brood-parasitism by Shiny Cowbirds *Molothrus bonariensis* could be an additional problem: Barrows (1883) reported that he found "many" Shiny Cowbird's eggs in Saffron-cowled Blackbird nests, something also recorded in Brazil several times since 1988 (TAP).

MEASURES TAKEN The species is protected under Brazilian law (Bernardes *et al.* 1990). It occurs in the Aparados da Serra National Park in Rio Grande do Sul and in the Bañados del Este

Biosphere Reserve/Ramsar site (but see Threats). In Corrientes, Argentina, the species occurs in the Iberá Provincial Reserve (J. C. Chebez *in litt.* 1992).

MEASURES PROPOSED More distributional and ecological studies are required, to be undertaken year-round so as to determine all the species's needs and to avoid errors in population estimates resulting from any temporary displacements (see Ecology). This work should try to identify remaining breeding areas within the species's range and to ascertain the as yet little known causes of decline. The information derived from these surveys should be used to produce an international conservation strategy to be implemented in an action plan together with the near-threatened Black-and-white Monjita.

It is essential to recognize the great importance in the general area (south-eastern Brazil, southern Paraguay, Uruguay and north-eastern Argentina south to the province of Buenos Aires and Río Negro) of primary dry and wet grasslands and associated marshes, which constitute the main habitat of other partially sympatric threatened species, namely Strange-tailed Tyrant *Yetapa risora*, Pampas Meadowlark and Yellow Cardinal *Gubernatrix cristata*, and the near-threatened Black-and-White Monjita (for other important grassland species with a slightly different distribution, see the corresponding section under Strange-tailed Tyrant). Within this general zone, the Saffron-cowled Blackbird is known to occur sympatrically with the Black-and-White Monjita, Strange-tailed Tyrant, the threatened Rufous-rumped Seedeater *Sporophila hypochroma* (see relevant account) and Yellow Cardinal in the Esteros del Iberá in Corrientes, Argentina, while in the Bañados del Este, Uruguay, it overlaps with the Speckled Crake *Coturnicops notata* (see relevant account) and the near-threatened Straight-billed Reedhaunter *Limnornis rectirostris*, Black-and-White Monjita and Black-bellied Seedeater *Sporophila melanogaster*. Both areas deserve strong conservation management; in the latter, existing regulations should be adequately enforced (see Threats). Other areas where the Saffron-cowled Blackbird and the Black-and-white Monjita are both present but habitat remains unprotected are Puerto Boca in Entre Ríos, Argentina (for the importance of this site, see Measures Proposed under Entre Ríos Seedeater *S. zelichi*), and Itaimbezinho west of the Aparados da Serra National Park, Rio Grande do Sul, Brazil (see Distribution; material on the monjita held on the ICBP database).

REMARKS The labels of two specimens (in MZUSP) from "Novo Hamburgo" (as given in Pinto 1944) actually read: "Boavista Campo, 18 July 1896", apparently Campo da Boa Vista, as in von Ihering (1899a).

YELLOW-SHOULDERED BLACKBIRD *Agelaius xanthomus* (E)[5]

Formerly widespread in various habitats on Puerto Rico and still so on adjacent Mona and Monito islands, this icterid has declined steeply and retreated into two areas on Puerto Rico, in the south-west and the east, having almost vanished in the latter; the total population is under 1,250, having been twice that in 1975. A range of threats, most notably cowbird brood parasitism, and measures to counter them, are identified.

DISTRIBUTION The Yellow-shouldered Blackbird is endemic to Puerto Rico (nominate race) and Mona and Monito islands (race *monensis*) (Barnés 1945, Furniss 1983). The species's population is now concentrated in three centres, namely Mona and Monito islands, coastal south-western Puerto Rico and coastal eastern Puerto Rico (see the map in Post and Wiley 1976). On the mainland it once occurred throughout Puerto Rico, mainly in the lowlands (Post and Wiley 1976). On Mona and Monito island the species can still be found throughout (Furniss 1983, Pérez-Rivera 1983, Hernández-Prieto and Cruz 1987, 1989, Hernández-Prieto *et al.* in prep.). The localities on mainland Puerto Rico (coordinates from OG 1958) to which the species is currently confined are: (south-west population; see Remarks 1), in a narrow coastal zone about 35 km from Ensenada (17°58'N 66°56'W) to Boca Prieta (18°03'N 67°12'W); and (eastern population) Roosevelt Roads Naval Station (3,260 ha) south-east to Ceiba (18°16'N 65°39'W) (Post and Wiley 1976, 1977, Heisterberg and Núñez-García 1988, Wiley *et al.* 1991). However, during the mid- and late 1970s it was still reported from a few isolated localities (west to east; data from Pérez-Rivera 1980): San Germán (18°05'N 67°03'W), where 10-12 pairs nested in 1975 (not present in 1982: Post and Wiley 1977, Wiley *et al.* 1991); Estación Experimental Agrícola de Isabela (18°30'N 67°01'W); Barranquitas (18°11'N 66°18'W), where five birds were observed in July 1979; university campus at Humacao (18°09'N 65°50'W); Toita de Cayey (Cayey at 18°07'N 66°10'W), where a bird was feeding a juvenile in November 1979; mangroves near Bacardí, Cataño (18°27'N 66°07'W), where a blackbird was feeding a juvenile Shiny Cowbird *Molothrus bonariensis* in July 1979; Caño de Martín Peña (18°26'N 66°05'W), where a pair was nesting in July 1979 and several nests were found in October 1979; near río Gurabo (18°17'N 66°01'W). Further marginal nesting localities as indicated by Post and Wiley (1976) included: Boquerón (18°02'N 67°10'W), Boca Prieta, and Carolina (18°23'N 65°57'W).

POPULATION The Yellow-shouldered Blackbird was an abundant and widespread species until the 1940s (Taylor 1864, Post and Wiley 1976), since when its numbers have declined precipitously, probably coincidentally with the arrival of the Shiny Cowbird in Puerto Rico (Post and Wiley 1976, 1977, Wiley *et al.* 1991). The south-western population of Yellow-shouldered Blackbirds was estimated at only about 300 individuals in 1982; censuses of the species's roosts conducted in winter (December to February) in 1974-1975 and 1981-1982 in the south-west population (mainly in Boquerón Forest: Wiley *et al.* 1991) showed that it declined by about 80% in the intervening period (1,663 birds for the former census and 266 for the latter); census results were as follows (numbers in brackets refer to the 1974-1975 and 1981-1982 counts respectively): Pita Haya (1,050, 165); La Parguera (156, 30); Bahía Montalva (284, 14); Bahía Sucia (147, 52); Boca Prieta (9, 0); Boquerón (17, 5) (Wiley *et al.* 1991; see Remarks 1). Subsequent censuses in communal roosts resulted in 343 birds in 1985, 146 in 1986 and 240 in 1987 (McKenzie and Noble 1989). However, in October 1987 approximately 300 blackbirds were counted in two separate mixed-species flocks of icterids c.500 m north-east of Punta Pita Haya in south-west Puerto Rico (McKenzie and Noble 1989; see Remarks 2). About 200 Yellow-shouldered Blackbirds were estimated at Roosevelt Roads in 1975-1976 (Post and Wiley 1976); by 1982, the population at this site had declined to six pairs ("97% decline"; in fact 94%) and in 1985 and 1986 only two nesting pairs were known there (Wiley *et al.* 1991); in this same area Heisterberg and Núñez-García (1988) estimated a total population of at least 31 birds in 1986 (16 adults, eight fledgings and seven of unknown age) and thus believed that this population is perilously close to extirpation. The blackbird population on Mona Island appears to be stable and has not suffered cowbird parasitism (Pérez-Rivera 1983, Hernández-Prieto and Cruz 1987, 1989). Kuns *et al.* (1965) estimated around 15 individuals per c.50 ha on the plateau in the early 1950s. Pérez-Rivera (1983) estimated at least 500 to 600 individuals on Mona in the late 1970s and between 220 and 300 in the early 1980s. A year-round (1987-1988) and several breeding season studies have estimated the minimal population to fluctuate between 400 and 908 individuals (Hernández-Prieto and Cruz 1987, 1989). Thus, the total population of the Yellow-shouldered Blackbird in the period 1982-1986 stood between 771 and 1,212 birds, these figures contrasting with an estimated population of 2,400 birds for 1975 (Post and Wiley 1976, Wiley *et al.* 1991).

ECOLOGY Given its former distribution throughout Puerto Rico, the Yellow-shouldered Blackbird must have inhabited many different habitats types (for original habitats in the island see, e.g., Kepler and Kepler 1973). According to Post and Wiley (1976) and Furniss (1983), the species is known to nest in eight habitat types: (1) mangrove pannes and salinas in the coastal mangrove zone, the trees in question being primarily black mangrove *Avicennia germinans*, red mangrove *Rhizophora mangle*, white mangrove *Laguncularia racemosa* and button mangrove *Conocarpus erectus*; (2) red mangrove cays (100-1,000 km^2) 200-500 m offshore, where aggregates of 2-6 pairs may nest; (3) black mangrove forest in the east, where birds nest near the fringe of the forest by small pools or clearings; (4) lowland pastures in the south-west, where birds nest usually 6-9 m up and often close together in large deciduous trees (mostly 11-14 m high oxhorn bucida *Bucida buceras*) in pastures at the edge of the mangroves; (5) suburban San Germán, where blackbirds nested on the campus of the university 12-15 m up among the fronds of 16-18 m royal palms *Roystonea borinquena* planted around the buildings (Furniss 1983 reported other such sites); (6) coconut *Cocos nucifera* and royal palm plantations, where blackbirds build nests in the axis of the trees, particularly at Boquerón, La Paraguera and Boca Prieta; (7) the dry thorny cactus scrub (dominated by *Philosocereus royenii*) on the central plateau of Mona Island; and (8) coastal cliffs surrounding Mona Island, where nests are placed on ledges or in crevices and in water-surrounded rocks (for this see also Pérez-Rivera 1983).

In Puerto Rico the Yellow-shouldered Blackbird mainly forages in the upper strata of trees, obtaining arthropods by probing and gleaning epiphytes, leaf-clusters and the surfaces of branches and trunks, but also feeds on the ground, where it mostly gathers vegetable material rather than arthropods; the bulk of the diet consists of arthropods (Lepidoptera, Araneae, Orthoptera, Homoptera, Coleoptera, Hymenoptera, Arachnida) (Post 1981, which see for a more detailed inventory of prey items and foraging behaviour). In Mona Island the species forages in monospecific flocks, mainly in the lower strata of the vegetation (Barnés 1946, Hernández-Prieto and Cruz 1987, 1989); birds there have been observed foraging on nectar of a variety of plants such as *Inga laurina*, *Aloe vera*, *Harrisia portoricensis*, *Tabebuia heterophylla*, *Stenocereus histrix*, on fruits and seeds, e.g. *Cissus trifoliata*, *H. portoricensis*, *Reynosia uncinata*, *Paspalum rupestre*, *Bursera simaruba*, *Panicum maximus*, *Lantana involucrata*, *Melocactus intortus*, *Ficus citrifolia*, *Pilosocereus royenii*, *Metopium toxiferum* (Danforth 1926, Furniss 1983, Hernández-Prieto and Cruz 1987, 1989); molluscs *Cepholis gallopavonis*, *Cerion monensis* and *Drymaeus elongatus*, the spider *Argiope argentata*, the homopteran *Icera purchasi*, coleopterans, lepidopterans, orthopterans and even "iguanids" (presumably carcases or hatchlings) have also been recorded (Kuns *et al.* 1965, Hernández-Prieto and Cruz 1987, 1989). Large foraging flocks mixed with other icterids (e.g. Greater Antillean Grackle *Quiscalus niger*, Shiny Cowbird) have been reported feeding in mesquite *Prosopis pallida* woodland and on caterpillars *Mocis latipes* taken from the blades and culms of *Cenchrus ciliaris* and *Bothriochloa pertusa* (McKenzie and Noble 1989).

The breeding season runs from April (in eastern Puerto Rico) and May (in the south-west) to September, but appears to be somehow regulated by the first spring rains (Post and Wiley 1977, Post 1981); however, Pérez-Rivera (1980) reported that breeding activity may begin as early as

February on Mona Island and could last through to November depending on the rainfall pattern during the year. The average clutch-size varies between one and four (Barnés 1945, Post 1981, Pérez-Rivera 1983, Hernández-Prieto and Cruz 1989, Hernández-Prieto *et al.* in prep.). Of 202 nests inspected at Boquerón Forest from 1973 to 1982, 39% were open nests and 61% were in natural or provided cavities and boxes; an overall breeding success ("successful" nests from the standpoint of nest predation or desertion were those fledging at least one host or cowbird chick) of 51% (102/202) was recorded (Post and Wiley 1977, Wiley *et al.* 1991).

THREATS Many factors have contributed to the Yellow-shouldered Blackbird's decline, including disease (see Remarks 3), loss of feeding and nesting habitats, nest predation by the Pearly-eyed Thrasher *Margarops fuscatus* and introduced mammals (e.g. rats, cats, mongooses), but the major cause of decline is the extensive parasitism of nests by the Shiny Cowbird, a recent invader of West Indian islands, recorded for the first time in Puerto Rico in 1955 (Post and Wiley 1976, 1977, Post 1981, Pérez-Rivera 1983, Cruz *et al.* 1985, Wiley *et al.* 1991). Shiny Cowbirds, although detected on Mona since the early 1970s, have not yet been found parasitizing this population (Furniss 1983, Hernández-Prieto and Cruz 1989, Hernández-Prieto *et al.* in prep.). The decrease of the Yellow-shouldered Blackbird in Boquerón Forest and surrounding areas (see Population) was accompanied by an increase of Shiny Cowbirds during the same interval by about 20% (Wiley *et al.* 1991); furthermore, 95% of blackbirds were parasitized from 1973 to 1982 at this site, and the same percentage was determined at Roosevelt Roads between 1975 and 1982 (Wiley *et al.* 1991). The occurrence of nest-mites *Ornithonyssus bursa* and *Androlaelaps casalis* in both natural and artificial cavities and nest-boxes (no differences were found) might lead to premature fledging and to adult desertion (see Wiley *et al.* 1991). Mangroves are particularly vulnerable to exploitation, and large areas have already been destroyed in Puerto Rico (Post and Wiley 1976). The population on Mona Island appears to have avoided predation by introduced mammals (rats and cats) through the use of inaccessible nest-sites (see Ecology); however, natural events such as "storm waves", hurricanes and severe periodic droughts may be responsible for fluctuations in numbers there but these cannot be considered threats in themselves (Pérez-Rivera 1983).

MEASURES TAKEN The species has been recognized as having endangered status by both Federal and Commonwealth of Puerto Rico conservation agencies and thus it receives official protection (King 1978-1979, Wiley *et al.* 1991). The Boquerón Commonwealth Forest, where the blackbirds are now concentrated, is protected by the Department of Natural Resources, and since 1977 the area has been patrolled and the destruction of mangroves and the invasion of cays by squatters has been stopped (Wiley *et al.* 1991). This accomplishment is particularly important in the case of the offshore cays, because they provide the only blackbird habitat that is still relatively cowbird-free (Wiley *et al.* 1991). In 1980 the U.S. Navy, in cooperation with the Fish and Wildlife Service, established a zoning plan for the Roosevelt Roads Naval Station to minimize the impact of their activities on the Yellow-shouldered Blackbird (Furniss 1983; see also Remarks 6 under West Indian Whistling-duck *Dendrocygna arborea*). The species and its habitat receive protection under various Federal and Commonwealth laws which prohibit the disturbance, molesting and capturing of the species, and the disturbance or destruction of mangroves; the Mona Island population receives complete protection from habitat destruction from the Department of Natural Resources personnel on Mona (Furniss 1983); the personnel regularly provide fresh water to blackbirds in that area (E. Hernández-Prieto *in litt.* 1992).

In 1975 conservation techniques to reduce cowbird parasitism and to improve Yellow-shouldered Blackbird breeding success and productivity were developed; this included the instalment of nest-boxes and "modified natural cavities" adjacent to suitable nesting habitat in both Boquerón Commonwealth Forest and Roosevelt Roads Naval Station (Wiley *et al.* 1991; see Remarks 4). Nest success, productivity and parasitism rates were also studied before cowbird removal (Wiley *et al.* 1991). Only 1% of all nests found were in artificial cavities, but nest-boxes proved more successful, with 51% of nests at Boquerón Forest placed in them (Wiley *et al.* 1991). However, cowbirds also parasitized all types of box that were used by the blackbirds, and it is unlikely that a nest-box can be devised that blackbirds will accept but which cowbirds will not enter, partly because the two species are approximately the same size (see Wiley *et al.* 1991). Parasitized artificial cavity nests have, however, the potential advantage of producing more host young than do parasitized open nests, because the incidence of predation is lower than at open sites (Post and Wiley 1977, Wiley *et al.* 1991); furthermore, pairs using open nests fledged fewer blackbird chicks than did pairs using boxes and natural cavities, and fewer cowbirds fledged from parasitized boxes than from open nests in Boquerón Forest (see Wiley *et al.* 1991). An additional advantage of artificial nest-sites is that they can be placed in sites away from trees and fitted with predator-guards; roof rats *Rattus norvegicus* are the main predators of hole-nesting passerine birds in Puerto Rico (Wiley *et al.* 1991). Rats also benefited from the nest-boxes (30% of which were occupied by them in 1977), but this figure dropped to an average of 6% between 1978-1981 after boxes were protected with rat-guards (Wiley *et al.* 1991). Artificial nest cavities can also create new breeding localities in areas adjacent to traditional nesting habitat, such as salt-flats that have no trees (Wiley *et al.* 1991). Larger nest-boxes were also erected for use by other bird species, with the result that competition for nest-sites was reduced (see Wiley *et al.* 1991). The removal experiments of Shiny Cowbirds showed that this measure can improve the breeding success of the blackbirds: nest success in 1975-1982 at Roosevelt Roads was 35%, but increased to 71% during 1983-1986 after removal measures were taken (see Wiley *et al.* 1991). Further removal of cowbirds was conducted in Roosevelt Roads during two consecutive breeding seasons in 1985 and 1986 (Heisterberg and Núñez-García 1988).

MEASURES PROPOSED Mangrove has proved to be of great importance for the species as it constitutes the main breeding habitat of the remaining population, and coastal south-western Puerto Rico contains one of the last extensive, undisturbed tracts of this habitat (Post and Wiley 1976). The habitat being used by the blackbirds in south-western Puerto Rico is believed to belong principally to the Department of Natural Resources, but boundary lines are poorly defined; ownership needs to be determined in order to ensure that all important areas are protected (Furniss 1983).

No nest-boxes should be erected for the species without rat-guards, and some natural cavities (e.g. in trees far enough from other trees that no corridors exist for rats) can and should also be fitted with rat-guards (see Wiley *et al.* 1991). Larger nest-boxes should also be provided in order to reduce interspecific competition for nest-sites. It is necessary to maintain rat-guards and nest-boxes (by removing old nest material) in good condition (see Remarks 5); nest cavities should be treated against mite infestation (see Cruz and Nakamura 1984, Wiley *et al.* 1991). Other arthropods, such as scorpions, wasps and bees, should be destroyed, as they reduce the attractiveness of the nest-boxes to blackbirds (see Wiley *et al.* 1991). Wiley *et al.*'s (1991) recommendation of providing food in the vicinities of the nesting colonies in order to keep blackbirds in the mangrove zone should be carefully considered, as it might also attract more cowbirds to the area. Wiley *et al.* (1991) suggested that any feeding stations would have to be protected from rats. A campaign to eliminate or at least reduce rats near nesting colonies is urgently needed; bird-proof (covered) bait-boxes and rodent traps should be placed in the nesting areas in order to achieve this goal (Cruz and Nakamura 1984), but further experiments in rat control are required.

Control of the Shiny Cowbird population by removal of birds should be conducted around blackbird nesting colonies and adjacent areas (Heisterberg and Núñez-García 1988, Wiley *et al.* 1991). Heisterberg and Núñez-García (1988) found that cowbird removal in Roosevelt Roads in 1985 was not followed by ready replacement by outside cowbirds, as 1986 captures rates were greatly reduced. Similar results were previously obtained in the south-west population, so Wiley *et al.* (1991) believed that cowbird removal has excellent potential for improving Yellow-shouldered Blackbird reproductive success, and should be continued for several years to determine its efficacy. Removal of cowbirds should be started in April and continued throughout the breeding season (Cruz and Nakamura 1984). Although trapping might not be the most effective means of controlling cowbird parasitism on the native avifauna, it is adequate at least as a stop-gap measure until less labour-intensive means can be devised (Wiley *et al.* 1991). More investigation is needed to determine the impact of disease on blackbirds (Furniss 1983).

Periodic censuses should be conducted in order to monitor the trends of the species in the remaining three populations. Communal roosts have proved to be good for censusing the total population in south-western Puerto Rico, but locating and estimating numbers of Yellow-shouldered Blackbirds in foraging concentrations can provide supplementary data to censuses, as shown by McKenzie and Noble (1989). An ongoing long-term study on Mona Island should be maintained to determine possible threats and more data on the breeding biology of the species. Hernández-Prieto and Cruz (1987, 1989) proposed that at least two (hopefully four) censuses that cover all of Mona, and well spaced throughout the year, should be carried out by the Department of Natural Resources, USFWS and other interested researchers; they also proposed that during the breeding season the Department of Natural Resources should open a second station in or at the lighthouse to ensure that (1) hunters (for wild pigs and goats) do not disturb the breeding of the blackbirds, and that (2) a close monitoring of areas identified as active nesting sites in the eastern part of the island is carried out, perhaps with limited access to visitors; furthermore they agree that efforts to eliminate rats and cats from Mona should be made. A study of the phylogenetic relationship of the two subspecies should be undertaken (E. Hernández-Prieto *in litt.* 1992; see Remarks 6).

REMARKS (1) Maps showing the species's current distribution, including nesting areas and roost sites, are in Post and Wiley (1976) and Post (1981), Pérez-Rivera (1983) and Hernández-Prieto and Cruz (1989). (2) McKenzie and Noble (1989) suggested that locating and estimating numbers of Yellow-shouldered Blackbirds in such foraging concentrations could provide supplementary data to censuses taken at communal icterid roosts. (3) Whittaker *et al.* (1970) reported the nematode *Acuaria* in the blackbird at Rio Piedras, and Post and Wiley (1976) noted the incidence of fowl pox in the species: in a total of 305 birds, they found 57 (18.7%) to have tumours, although the magnitude and consequences for the species are not known. Kuns *et al.* (1965) reported no parasites or virus for the blackbirds at Mona. (4) Between 1975 and 1977, 51 nest-boxes and 12 "modified natural cavities" were set up at Roosevelt Roads, and from 1977 to 1982 189 and five at Boquerón Forest (for more details see Wiley *et al.* 1991). (5) Cruz and Nakamura (1984) found that boxes that were not maintained or cleaned were not used by blackbirds, and indicated that rat-guards must be cleaned or replaced on a regular basis in order to maximize their effectiveness against predators. (6) Presumably this would be in order to judge whether introduction of the Mona form to the mainland might be acceptable.

PAMPAS MEADOWLARK *Sturnella militaris* I[7]

Though always rare in Brazil and Uruguay, this pampas-dwelling icterid was once common and widespread in central-eastern Argentina where, however, cultivation (notably of sunflowers) and overgrazing have contributed to a steep decline, with almost no recent records outside the province of Buenos Aires; survey, study and key site protection are now urgent.

DISTRIBUTION The Pampas Meadowlark (Lesser Red-breasted Meadowlark) occurs in central-eastern Argentina (from Corrientes south to La Pampa and Buenos Aires), Uruguay and south-eastern Brazil (see Remarks 1). Unless otherwise stated, coordinates in the following account are taken from Rand and Paynter (1981), Paynter (1985) and Paynter and Traylor (1991), with records within provinces or states organized from north to south.

Brazil The species is known from single records in the state of Paraná and Santa Catarina and from two undated records in Rio Grande do Sul, thus: (*Paraná*) an adult male collected at Pinheirinhos (25°25'S 53°55'W) in April 1923 (Sztolcman 1926); (*Santa Catarina*) a group of more than 35 birds c.1 km north-west of Vila Nova, Joinville, in July 1991 (M. Pearman *in litt.* 1991); (*Rio Grande do Sul*) São Lourenço (= São Lourenço do Sul) and Jaguarão (von Ihering 1899a; also Belton 1984-1985). There is a specimen in USNM simply labelled "Brazil".

Uruguay Records are from: (*Paysandú*) unspecified (Cuello and Gerzenstein 1962); (*Cerro Largo*) unspecified (Tremoleras 1920); (*Durazno*) unspecified (Cuello and Gerzenstein 1962); (*Soriano*) Estancia Santa Elena (c.33°46'S 57°14'W), 1892 (Aplin 1894), February and March 1893 (four specimens in BMNH); (*Flores*) near Porongos (= Trinidad), where many birds were observed in December 1892 (Aplin 1894); Estancia los Mirasoles, Cerro Colorado (c.33°40'S 56°55'W), June 1958 (specimen in MNHNM); (*San José*) "Provincia de San José", June 1909 (specimen in AMNH); Barra de Santa Lucía (34°48'S 56°22'W), July 1914 (specimen in MNHNM); (*Canelones*) "Departamento de Canelones", April 1901 (specimen in MNHNM); Piedra del Toro (34°44'S 55°50'W), May and June 1926, April and May 1928 (11 specimens in FMNH, MNHNM and USNM); (*Montevideo*) "Montevideo", before 1850 (Hellmayr 1937).

Argentina The listing of the provinces of Misiones, Chaco, Tucumán, La Rioja and Mendoza appears to be erroneous (see Remarks 2). Records include:

(*Corrientes*) unspecified (SOMA 1935-1942, Short 1968, Olrog 1979);

(*Santa Fe*) Las Rosas, September and October 1926 (six specimens in FMNH); Estancia La Germania (c.32°33'S 61°24'W), July 1925 (Laubmann 1930); Rosario, undated (Burmeister 1861); General López (c.48 km from Venado Tuerto, 33°45'S 61°58'W), where the species was known to nest early in the twentieth century (Wilson 1926); Los Molles (not located; for options see Paynter 1985), where a birds was collected in December 1929 and another in September 1932 (Freiberg 1943);

(*Entre Ríos*) "Paraná", undated (Burmeister 1861); Santa Elena (30°57'S 59°48'W), where it was reported nesting (Serié and Smyth 1923); Paraná department (31°40'N 60°00'W), where two birds were collected in January 1927 and December 1932 (Freiberg 1943); Villaguay, winter 1986 (C. Bertonatti and S. Heinonen *per* J. C. Chebez *in litt.* 1992); El Brete, Paraná (untraced, but in the central-western part of the province), September 1926 (Freiberg 1943); Pehuajó Norte (untraced, but in Gualeguaychú department), April 1926 (specimen in MACN);

(*Córdoba*) near Saladillo, 1871 (Lee 1873); Estancia La Primavera (34°58'N 65°01'W), where a possible bird was observed sometime in the 1980s (B. Molinuevo *per* J. C. Chebez *in litt.* 1992);

(*Buenos Aires*) "Buenos Aires", 1900 (specimen in MACN, December 1909, December 1910, October 1912 (three specimens in AMNH and MNRJ), 1914, 1921 and 1922 (seven specimens in MACN; Ribera Norte, San Isidro, November 1982 (A. Ronchetti *per* J. C. Chebez *in litt.* 1992); Bernal (34°43'S 58°18'W), August 1898 (two specimens in MZUSP); Zelaya (34°21'S 58°52'W),

April 1922, November 1933 and May and June 1934 (five specimens in AMNH and MACN; Pereyra 1923, 1938); Barracas al Sud (= Barracas, 34°39'S 58°22'W), where two specimens were collected in September 1899 (Hartert and Venturi 1909); Morón (34°39'S 58°37'W), January 1918 (two specimens in MACN); Quilmes, April 1916, November 1917 and January 1918 (six specimens in MACN and one in USNM); Lomas de Zamora (34°46'S 58°24'W), where two nests were reported (Durnford 1877) and three birds collected in September and October 1888 (Withington 1888; specimens in BMNH); Conchitas (= Guillermo E. Hudson, 34°47'S 58°10'W), undated (Sclater and Salvin 1868-1869); six specimens in USNM); Ensenada, March 1915 (Marelli 1919); Villa Elisa (34°51'S 57°55'W) (Marelli 1919); Tolosa (34°53'S 57°58'W), March 1917 (Marelli 1919); La Plata, April 1896, April 1916, August and September 1917, December 1924 and April 1927 (ten specimens in MACN and UNP); Maldonado (untraced but perhaps Bañado Maldonado at 34°55'S 57°51'S in OG 1968), August 1909 (specimen AMNH); San Vicente, March 1894 (specimen in AMNH) and November 1969 (T. Narosky *in litt.* 1992); Poblet (35°04'S 57°57'W), July 1916 (specimen in MACN); surroundings of Punta Indio (untraced, but in the Partido de Magdalena, 35°15'N 57°30'W), undated (Pereyra 1937); Alvarez Jonte (35°19'S 57°28'W), September 1925 (two specimens in MACN); Estancia Juan Gerónimo (= Estancia Juan Jerónimo, c.35°27'S 57°17'W), presumably in October 1942 (Pereyra 1942); Estancia Espartilla (c.35°31'S 58°59'W), September 1889, June 1890 (two specimens in BMNH); Chascomús (35°34'S 58°01'W), August 1917 (specimen in MACN); Rosas (35°58'S 58°56'W), April 1920 (specimen in MACN; Estancia El Toro (36°06'S 58°52'W), May 1920 (Daguerre 1922); Dolores, October 1924 (Aravena 1928); Cacharí (36°24'S 59°33'W), where a nest was found in December 1920 (Smyth 1927-1928) and September 1952 (specimen in MACN); Los Yngleses (= Estancia Los Ingleses, 36°31'S 56°53'W), April, May and October 1909, May 1921 (Grant 1911; specimens in BMNH, CM, FMNH and MCZ); Cabo San Antonio, where considered an autumn visitor (Gibson 1918; an undated specimen in BMNH was collected at Ajó = General Lavalle); Rauch, August 1951 and June 1971 (specimens in MACN and UNP); Sierra Baya (= Sierra Bayas, 36°55'S 60°09'W), November 1922 (specimen in MACN); Guaminí (37°02'S 62°25'W), on 3 March 1921, a date when flocks of a hundred birds or more were observed from this area north to Bolívar (Wetmore 1926) and September 1939 (specimen in MACN); Arano, March 1926 (Aravena 1928); Obligado (possibly Paso Obligado, at 37°08'S 61°43'W in OG 1968), June 1918 (specimen in MACN); Lago Epiquén (= Lago Epecuén), near Carhué, December 1920 (Wetmore 1926); Puan (37°33'S 62°43'W), where large flocks were present in March 1881 (Barrows 1883); La Tinta (Sierra de la Tinta, at 37°37'S 59°33'W) and Collon-Gueyu (untraced but in the vicinity of Sierra de la Tinta), February 1883 (Holmberg 1883-1884; also Paynter 1985); Estancia San Pablo, D'Orbigny (37°41'S 61°43'W), September 1961 (five specimens in AMNH and LSUMZ); c.100 km north of Bahía Blanca, November 1967 (Short 1968); 55 km north of Bahía Blanca (along route 35), where a hundred birds were counted in December 1990 (D. W. Finch *per* P. L. Tubaro *in litt.* 1992); Bahía Blanca, October 1899 (Hartert and Venturi 1909); Estancia La Saudade (37°46'S 62°25'W), present during the breeding season (November) in 1970 and 1971 (Gochfeld 1979; specimen in AMNH); Mar del Plata, September 1914 (specimen in AMNH); "Pampean Sierras" (e.g. Sierra de la Ventana), 1881 (Barrows 1883); between Saavedra and the Sierra de la Ventana, abundant in 1920 (Wetmore 1926); slopes of Sierra de la Ventana, February 1939 (Gavio 1939), November 1967 (Short 1968) and January 1971 (T. Narosky *in litt.* 1992); near Villa Iris, where a dispersed flock of c.20 birds was observed in November 1988 (Narosky *et al.* 1990) with another of c.60 in January 1991 (D. Willis *in litt.* 1991); Nueva Roma (38°18'S 62°39'W), where c.30 birds were observed in December 1990 with a single bird on the same date at San Germán (38°18'S 62°39'W) (coordinates and data from M. Babarskas and T. Narosky *in litt.* 1992); Tres Arroyos (38°23'S 69°17'W), June 1945 (specimen in UNP); Necochea, where c.50 birds were recorded in January 1979 (Narosky *et al.* 1990); Cristiano Muerto (38°38'S 59°37'W), August 1923 (specimen in UNP); Laguna Chasicó (38°38'S 63°06'W), November 1926 (specimen in UNP); Bahía Blanca, October 1899 (specimen in AMNH); 7 km east of Bahía Blanca, November 1970 and 1971 (Gochfeld 1979); east of Médanos, where at least 10 pairs were observed (male taken) on 4 December 1967 (Short 1968); Estancia Santa Elena (untraced), breeding in November (exact year not given) (Holland 1895), March 1893 (specimen in BMNH);

(*San Luis*) "San Luis", November 1897 and September 1898 (two specimens in FMNH; see Remarks 3);

(*La Pampa*) unspecified (SOMA 1935-1942); Macachín (37°09'S 63°39'W in OG 1968), June 1972 (specimen in UNP).

POPULATION The Pampas Meadowlark was always patchily distributed, as suggested by Burmeister (1856), but it has greatly diminished in Argentina, where late nineteenth and early twentieth century authors wrote of flocks of several "hundreds" (see below), a phenomenon never reported from Uruguay or Brazil, where the species was considered rare and to which it is mainly a winter visitor (see Ecology).

Brazil The species is probably a rare winter visitor which has only been recorded a few times, the only recent record being a presumably wintering flock (July) of c.35 birds (see Distribution).

Uruguay Gore and Gepp (1978) considered the species a rare resident, although nesting requires confirmation. Aplin (1894) stated that it "usually breeds around" Santa Elena, but from October 1892 (i.e. the breeding season) he saw a single bird there until early in February when he found a "pair in moult"; later, in December, he found a "good many" near Porongos (presumably a post-breeding flock; see Remarks 4).

Argentina Argentina harbours most of the species's total breeding population, this being mainly confined to the province of Buenos Aires. The Pampas Meadowlark has suffered a steep decline in less than a century, previously being one of the commonest birds in the pampas plains (Narosky *et al.* 1990). This decline is fairly well documented in the province of Buenos Aires: at Zelaya it was considered "fairly common" in April 1922 (Pereyra 1923), at Lomas de Zamora Durnford (1877) recorded it as "very common" and "generally distributed", congregating in winter in "enormous flocks", a finding shared by Withington (1888) who also referred to it as "very common" in the same area; Barrows (1883) found that at Puan, flocks frequently numbered "several hundred" individuals in 1881, and Grant (1911) reported that the species appeared in large flocks after the breeding season at Ajó; Daguerre (1922) reported it "very numerous" in Estancia El Toro, Las Flores municipality, where he also referred to large wintering flocks. Hudson (1920) found it "abundant" in the southern part of the province of Buenos Aires, where flocks in winter were composed of "four or five hundred" to "a thousand or more" individuals. Labels in BMNH of nineteenth century specimens collected at Estancia Santa Elena and Estancia Espartilla read "common". Wetmore (1926) observed flocks of a hundred birds between Empalme Lobos and Bolívar in March 1921, and he believed it to be abundant in the area between Saavedra and the foothills of the Sierra de la Ventana. Short (1968) still found the species "very common" in November 1967 on the grassy slopes of the Sierra de la Ventana, and Gochfeld (1979) reported it "numerous" at La Saudade and at 7 km east of Bahía Blanca in November 1970 and 1971 (11 nests found). However, Narosky *et al.* (1990) noted that there were no recent records in the province except for the above-mentioned, a group of about 50 birds near Necochea in January 1979 and a dispersed group of 20 near Villa Iris in November 1988. However, there are records of c.30 birds at Nueva Roma in December 1990, of c.100 birds 55 km north of Bahía Blanca in December 1990 and of c.60 at Villa Iris in January 1991 (see Distribution). Records outside the province of Buenos Aires give no impression of population status in the past, but it is likely that the species has declined substantially, as it was known to nest in the southern parts of Santa Fe and in northern Entre Ríos during the first two decades of this century (see Distribution). The almost total lack of recent observations outside the province of Buenos Aires also suggests a substantial decline.

ECOLOGY The Pampas Meadowlark, as its name suggests, inhabits the open grasslands of the pampas, both moist and well-drained (Hudson 1920, Short 1968, Gochfeld 1979); short meadows with small shrubs, open bunch-grass, wheat, stubble-fields and mixed grass with arable weeds have also been reported (Wetmore 1926, Narosky *et al.* 1990, D. Willis *in litt.* 1991; also AMNH label data).

Very little is known about its feeding requirements. Birds feed gregariously on the ground taking insects, seeds and tender sprouts (Burmeister 1856, Wetmore 1926, Alvarez 1933). Stomach contents of birds taken around La Plata, Argentina, were given as insects and vegetable remains such as grasses, small beetles and larvae (Marelli 1919); the stomach contents of a bird collected at Dolores was various Coleoptera but no vegetable matter, while two other specimens from Arano had remains of Coleoptera (80%) and seeds (20%) (Aravena 1928).

Breeding occurs in November and nests are built on the ground well concealed under grass; three to four eggs are laid (Holland 1895, Smyth 1927-1928, Gochfeld 1979). Movements are little understood but the species appears to be a year-round resident throughout its range; however, northward dispersion appears to occur in winter, as large flocks (several hundreds) were then commonly observed in the past (Hudson 1920; see also Population). The species is highly sociable, and birds separated from the flock have been observed joining other species, e.g. plovers (Hudson 1920).

THREATS The numbers and overall range of this species have been much reduced by cultivation and overgrazing (Wetmore 1926, Short 1968, Ridgely and Tudor 1989). In Buenos Aires, east of Bahía Blanca, large areas of grassland have been converted to sunflower plantations. Short (1968) remarked that c.100 km north of Bahía Blanca the species was much less common, this probably being related to the heavier grazing and greater cultivation of the region. Competition with congeners such as the White-browed Blackbird *Leistes superciliaris* and the Long-tailed Meadowlark *Sturnella loyca* has been suggested as a possible threat and is to be investigated (P. L. Tubaro *in litt.* 1992).

MEASURES TAKEN The species is protected under Brazilian law (Bernardes *et al.* 1990). There appear to be no records from protected areas.

MEASURES PROPOSED In Argentina surveys should try to delimit the most important breeding grounds and to estimate the populations within them, concentrating initially on the southern part of its range (i.e. southern Buenos Aires and possibly in adjacent La Pampa) where the species may still be found in reasonable numbers. Once all the important areas are identified, threats and habitat requirements must be identified, so that specific areas can be managed appropriately. Investigation of the species's distribution, status, ecology and threats is currently being planned (P. L. Tubaro *in litt.* 1992). In Uruguay, the current status of the species is poorly known, and it would be valuable to gather more information on distribution, numbers, possible key sites and general biology. An overview of the importance of its range in relation to other threatened or near-threatened species is given in Measures Proposed under Saffron-cowled Blackbird *Xanthopsar flavus*.

REMARKS (1) The species has been listed for Paraguay (Burmeister 1856, Bonaparte 1865), probably because de Azara (1802-1805) included it in his work; however, he observed the species between 35° and 36°S, which is south of present-day Paraguay. (2) Canevari *et al.* (1991) mentioned Misiones within the species's range, but their map excluded it; neither Pereyra (1950) nor Ridgely and Tudor (1989) mentioned it. Canevari *et al.*'s (1991) listing of Chaco is also perhaps mistaken inasmuch as the province is not represented on their map and there appears to be no record. The listing of the species in Tucumán, La Rioja and Mendoza (Dabbene 1910, Hellmayr 1937, Freiberg 1943, Olrog 1959) was erroneous and obviously referred to the similar Long-tailed Meadowlark (for taxonomic problems see, e.g., Hellmayr 1937, Short 1968). (3) The name of "San Luis" probably refers to the province; furthermore, the collecting dates of September and November suggest breeding in these unknown localities. (4) It is not possible to ascertain whether these flocks constituted early arrived wintering flocks from further south or local residents flocking after breeding.

RED-BELLIED GRACKLE *Hypopyrrhus pyrohypogaster* I[7]

This grackle is very rare and localized in the West and Central Andes and southern East Andes of Colombia, where it inhabits the severely depleted subtropical forests. Although a few populations have been recorded in recent years, numbers have undoubtedly declined, and the bird is now difficult to find.

DISTRIBUTION The Red-bellied Grackle (see Remarks) has been recorded from Antioquia south to Caquetá department on both slopes of the West and Central Andes, with a disjunct population in the southern East Andes, Colombia. The following records are arranged by locality, mountain range and department from north to south, with coordinates, unless otherwise stated, from Paynter and Traylor (1981):

West Andes (*Antioquia*) Peque (6°59'N 75°51'W; on the eastern slope), one male (in AMNH) taken at 1,525 m in February 1915 (also Chapman 1917a); Hacienda Potreros (6°39'N 76°09'W; on the western slope), five birds (in USNM) taken at 1,980 m in May and June 1950; (*Risaralda*) Siató (c.5°13'N 76°07'W; on the western slope at 1,600 m) (Hellmayr 1911); Pueblorrico (5°12'N 76°08'W; on the western slope at 1,560 m), one bird (in ANSP) taken at 1,525 m in February 1946 (also Hellmayr 1911); La Selva (c.4°55'N 76°09'W; on the north-western slope of Cerro Tatamá), 10 birds (in ANSP, CM) collected between 1,525 and 1,830 m in January 1946 (also Meyer de Schauensee 1948-1952);

Central Andes (*Antioquia*) above Puerto Valdivia (7°18'N 75°23'W), birds seen at 800 m in 1962 (Willis 1972, 1988); Valdivia (7°11'N 75°27'W; on the western slope), 12 birds (in USNM) taken at 1,200 m during May 1948; La Frijolera (c.7°10'N 75°25'W; on the western slope above Puerto Valdivia), five birds (in AMNH, BMNH, USNM) taken at 1,525 m in December 1914; Amalfi (6°55'N 75°04'W; at c.1,500 m on the eastern slope), one bird (in FMNH) from November 1912; Botero (6°32'N 75°15'W), two birds (in USNM) taken at 1,095 m in August 1950; on the Barbosa–Santo Domingo road (c.6°27'N 75°15'W), eight birds recently seen at 1,800 m (L. G. Olarte *in litt.* 1992); Medellín (Serna 1980); Santa Elena (6°13'N 75°30'W; at c.2,750 m on the eastern slope) (Sclater and Salvin 1879); Envigado (6°10'N 75°35'W; on the eastern slope), three birds (in BMNH) taken at 1,525 m in 1872; Angelópolis (6°07'N 75°43'W; at 1,955 m on the western slope) (Serna 1980); Caldas (6°06'N 75°38'W; at c.1,750 m: Acevedo-Latorre 1971), three birds (in USNM; also Serna 1980) taken in February 1974; La Camelia (c.6°05'N 75°45'W; at 1,800 m on the western slope) (Meyer de Schauensee 1948-1952); on the upper río Negro (south of Medellín, and east of Caldas) at Fizebad, El Retiro county, where a flock and nest have recently been recorded between 2,100 and 2,400 m (L. G. Olarte and L. J. Olarte *in litt.* 1992); (*Caldas*) Hacienda Sofía (= La Sofía at 5°38'N 75°04'W; on the eastern slope), two birds (in USNM) taken at 1,135 m in May 1951; (*Risaralda*) La Suiza (Ucumarí Regional Park, 1,900 m), recently (Naranjo undated); (*Quindío*) Filandia (4°41'N 75°40'W; at 1,925 m: Acevedo-Latorre 1971) (Chapman 1917a); El Roble (4°41'N 75°36'W; on the western slope), three birds (in AMNH, USNM) taken at 2,195 m in May and November 1911; "Quindío trail" (between Salento and Ibagué) (Chapman 1917a); Salento (4°38'N 75°34'W; on the western slope), five birds (in AMNH, FMNH) taken at 2,135 m in September and October 1911; (*Tolima*) on the slopes of Nevado del Tolima (4°40'N 75°19'W) (Stone 1899); at El Pie de San Juan (untraced, but along the río Toche), and generally along the río Toche (4°26'N 75°22'W; on the south-south-west slope of Nevado del Tolima) (Chapman 1917a); Gaitania (3°09'N 75°49'W; at 2,100 m on the eastern slope) (specimen in ICN; also Olivares 1960);

East Andes (*Huila*) below Andalucía on the "Caquetá Trail" (1°54'N 75°40'W; on the eastern slope), one female (in AMNH) taken at 2,135 m in June 1912 (also Chapman 1917a); Cueva de los Guácharos National Park (1°35'N 76°00'W; c.2,000 m on the western slope), recently (Hilty and Brown 1986); (*Caquetá*) above Florencia (1°36'N 75°36'W) (Hilty and Brown 1986), and at km 55 north of Florencia where a group of eight birds was seen in 1990 (P. Kaestner *in litt.*

1992). An untraced locality is Soledad (in the upper Magdalena valley), where three birds (in BMNH) were taken at 915 m during the last century.

POPULATION The Red-bellied Grackle was previously not an uncommon bird, and occurred at a relatively large number of localities: Chapman (1917a) found it to be common in small groups along the Quindío trail and beside the río Toche; however, most of the localities where the bird was found in some numbers during the last century and early this century have long since been deforested (see Threats), and it is now a rare, very local, and generally difficult bird to find (Hilty and Brown 1986, Ridgely and Tudor 1989). Recent fieldwork in the Quindío–río Toche area by L. M. Renjifo and P. Kaestner have failed to find the bird (M. G. Kelsey *in litt.* 1992).

Recent records (post-1960), normally referring to groups of up to 10 birds, come from: (1, the Central Andes of Antioquia) above Puerto Valdivia and along the Barbosa–Santo Domingo road (maximum of eight birds) (Willis 1972, 1988, L. G. Olarte *in litt.* 1992); Caldas and nearby on the upper río Negro, where groups (including breeding birds) of up to 15 were recorded in the late 1980s and early 1990s (see Distribution), and in the region of which Serna (1980) suggested that the bird was not uncommon in pine and cypress plantations (see below); (2, Risaralda) in the Ucumarí Regional Park (see Distribution: Naranjo undated); (3, the East Andes of Huila) in Cueva de los Guácharos National Park (Hilty and Brown 1986); and (4, Caquetá) along the road to the north of Florencia, where, amongst other observations, eight birds were seen as recently as 1990 (P. Kaestner *in litt.* 1992; also Hilty and Brown 1986). There are apparently no recent records from the West Andes.

ECOLOGY The Red-bellied Grackle has been found between 800 and 2,400 m, possibly occurring up to 2,750 m (see Distribution), where birds inhabit the canopy and borders of humid montane forest (Hilty and Brown 1986), including scrubby areas (Chapman 1917a) and old second growth (L. G. Olarte *in litt.* 1992). The area on the upper río Negro where the group of c.15 individuals have been watched by members of the Sociedad Antioqueña de Ornitología (SAO) during the past two years is a small patch of old second growth surrounded by a plantation of *Pinus patulla* (L. G. Olarte *in litt.* 1992), and this is perhaps the reason why Serna (1980) suggested that the species was not uncommon in pine and cypress plantations. This grackle usually occurs in small groups of up to 15 (see below), foraging actively (and noisily) in the outer foliage of trees (feeding on insects and fruit: BMNH label data), sometimes with mixed-species flocks (see Willis 1972), or with other large birds such as oropendolas, Green Jays *Cyanocorax yncas*, Blue-winged Mountain-tanagers *Anisognathus flavinucha*, etc. (Hilty and Brown 1986, Ridgely and Tudor 1989).

In the Central Andes, the Red-bellied Grackle has been recorded breeding in January and February (1992), when a nest (which produced three fledglings) was found in the río Negro region (L. G. Olarte *in litt.* 1992), and a breeding condition bird has been taken at the end of December (specimen in AMNH); however, in the same region and elsewhere within the species's range, breeding condition birds (including females ready to lay), immatures and nestlings have been recorded between March and August (Lehmann 1961, Hilty and Brown 1986; specimens in USNM). Hilty and Brown (1986) suggested that the species is solitary when breeding (presumably meaning that it is not colonial), as seemed to be the case with the single nest observed in January and February (see above) by members of SAO, which, however, was attended by at least eight adults out of a group of 15 birds, suggesting cooperative breeding (L. G. Olarte *in litt.* 1992). The nest and eggs of the species were described by Sclater and Salvin (1879).

THREATS Areas of suitable habitat at altitudes and localities where this species was found in some numbers during the nineteenth and early twentieth centuries (e.g. around Medellín and on the slopes of the northern Central Andes) have long since been almost totally cleared (Hilty and Brown 1986, Ridgely and Tudor 1989), and this probably explains the rarity and current localized distribution of the species. However, there are still tracts of forest remaining in the species's range (LGN), although its occurrence in them has in most cases yet to be proven. The usage of old second growth (see above) is encouraging, but whether the species can sustain a viable population in plantations of non-native trees (see Ecology) is unknown. Like many places in the areas around Medellín, the patch of habitat at El Retiro (río Negro region) is protected by the owners, but is in great demand from developers wishing to build on it (L. G. Olarte *in litt.* 1992).

MEASURES TAKEN In the West Andes, this grackle has been recorded from what are now the Paramillo (460,000 ha) and Tatamá (54,300 ha) National Parks (both referring to old records); in the Central Andes from Ucumarí Regional Park (recent records); and in the East Andes from Cueva de los Guácharos National Park (9,000 ha) (Hernández Camacho *et al.* undated, IUCN 1992).

MEASURES PROPOSED Remaining habitat within the range of this species is in urgent need of protection, as a number of national parks (e.g. Los Nevados: see equivalent section under Rufous-fronted Parakeet *Bolborhynchus ferrugineifrons*) only protect areas at too high altitudes (see Hernández Camacho *et al.* undated). Priority should be given to the areas where the bird has been recorded during recent years. Other areas should be investigated for its presence, although such surveys would benefit from a more detailed appreciation of its ecological requirements, which will hopefully be forthcoming from (e.g.) the SAO observations of the breeding group south of Medellín (see Ecology). Where possible, all conservation initiatives should consider the needs of the other threatened species found in this area, as well as near-threatened species such as Sooty Ant-tanager *Habia gutturalis* (see Willis 1972). In Paramillo National Park, the Red-bellied Grackle is sympatric with Blue-billed Curassow *Crax alberti* and Recurve-billed Bushbird *Clytoctantes alixii*, but for the threatened species and proposals made for other important areas see the equivalent sections under Black-and-gold Tanager *Buthraupis melanochlamys* (for Tatamá National Park and the area around Mistrató where this species probably occurs); Multicoloured Tanager *Chlorochrysa nitidissima* (for Ucumarí Regional Park); Moustached Antpitta *Grallaria alleni* (for the area around Salento); Tolima Dove *Leptotila conoveri* (for the río Toche valley, Tolima); and Moustached Antpitta (for Cueva de los Guácharos National Park).

REMARKS The Red-bellied Grackle represents the only member of the genus *Hypopyrrhus*.

FORBES'S BLACKBIRD *Curaeus forbesi* E[2]

Serious difficulties face this icterid, which is known with certainty now from only two localities in Brazil, the Rio Doce State Park, Minas Gerais, where the highest number reported to date is c.30, and a site in Alagoas, where the population of c.150 suffered 100% brood-parasitism in 1987.

DISTRIBUTION Forbes's Blackbird (see Remarks 1) is known from two disjunct regions 1,400 km apart in eastern Brazil in the states of Pernambuco, Alagoas, and Minas Gerais.

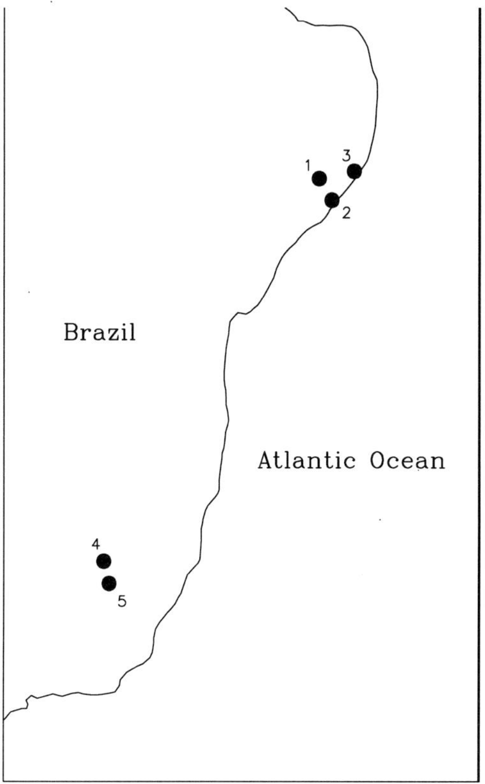

Pernambuco The species was recorded by Forbes (1881) at Vista Alegre and Macuca (both untraced; between Quipapá and Garanhuns), one specimen (the type) being collected at the latter in September 1880 (see Remarks 2). Another specimen was taken at Usina São José, Igarassu, 12 April 1945 (Berla 1946: see Remarks 3). The rio Capibari-mirim (untraced) is included in the range of this species by Sick (1985), but no other detail is given and this record could not be traced to source.

Alagoas Records are known from Quebrangulo[1], November 1951, April 1957 and from 1981 to 1990 (in what is now the Pedra Talhada Biological Reserve: see Measures Taken) (Short and Parkes 1979, Studer and Vielliard 1988, M. Pearman *in litt.* 1990, B. M. Whitney *in litt.* 1991); Usina Sinimbu[2] (near present-day Sinimbu – not Ginimbu as in GQR 1991), February and March 1957 (Short and Parkes 1979, and specimens in MZUSP under Chopi Blackbird *Gnorimopsar chopi* in Pinto [1954a], Pinto and de Camargo [1961] for this and the previous locality); Matriz de Camaragibe[3], February 1986 (specimen in MNRJ); and Pedra Branca (Murici) in a sugarcane plantation, August 1989 (D. Finch *per* B. C. Forrester *in litt.* 1992).

Minas Gerais Older records of the species in this state are: the lower rio Piracicaba at its confluence with the rio Doce[4], August 1940 (specimens in MZUSP under *G. chopi* in Pinto and de Camargo 1961); and Raul Soares[5], July and September 1957 (Short and Parkes 1979), specifically (a) 15 km to the north at córrego da Areia, (b) on the right bank of the rio Matipó, and (c) on the ribeirão Preto (specimens in MACN, also FMNH). The Piracicaba/Doce confluence is close to or in the Rio Doce State Park where the species persists, having been recorded in 1978, 1979 (specimens in DZMG; also G. T. de Mattos *in litt.* 1987), 1983 (Studer and Vielliard 1988), 1987 (M. A. de Andrade *in litt.* 1988, A. Studer verbally 1990) and August 1988 (B. C. Forrester *in litt.* 1992).

POPULATION Uncertainties over the reliability of past and present estimates of this species's abundance inevitably arise from its great similarity to the Chopi Blackbird (see Remarks 1). Forbes (1881) claimed the species "rather abundant at one or two localities", and stated that "though local, the bird was common where it occurred, flying about in large flocks, like starlings, in the neighbourhood of sugar-plantations" (see Remarks 2), this report being paralleled by the earliest accounts in the twentieth century that stated it was "common in Pernambuco in areas of extensive cultivation of sugar-cane" (Berla 1946, Sick 1969, 1972). However, while it remains possible that it has sometimes been overlooked in more recent years, as suggested by Ridgely and Tudor (1989), the species was not found at all during surveys conducted in 1973 and 1982 at the known localities where it had been recorded to that date, and was thus thought to be restricted to Quebrangulo in Alagoas and the Rio Doce State Park in Minas Gerais (Studer and Vielliard 1988). There is no further information on the population at Matriz de Camaragibe in Alagoas. At Quebrangulo, a relict population of about 150 birds was calculated to persist in the early 1980s, but it has decreased since (see Threats). No census of the species seems to have been performed at Rio Doce State Park, where "flocks of 8-10 birds" (G. T. de Mattos *in litt.* 1987), "some individuals" (M. A. de Andrade *in litt.* 1988), "c.30" (S. G. D. Cook *in litt.* 1988), "a flock of 40" (B. C. Forrester *in litt.* 1992) and "4-5 birds" (A. Whittaker *in litt.* 1991) have been reported.

ECOLOGY Despite earlier accounts of the species's abundance in sugar-cane plantations (see Population), most recent observations and specimens are from forested sites. Sick's (1985) statement that it lives in mangroves is apparently linked to his odd record from the rio Capibari-Mirim (see Distribution). At Quebrangulo, the only place where its ecology has been studied, Forbes's Blackbird lives at the forest edge and in marshy areas nearby (Studer and Vielliard 1988). Food includes fruits and insects, but young are fed exclusively insects, more often grasshoppers, larvae, and butterflies (Studer and Vielliard 1988). Timing of breeding depends on the rainy season, which varies from year to year but usually falls between March and June, nests being placed mostly (38 out of 46 observations) in the crown of cultivated mango *Mangifera indica* trees at or near forest edge, 3-12 m (mean 7 m) above ground, with nest material being gathered from an area of c.200 m radius; there is a delay of several (4-10) days between nest construction and laying, which benefits Shiny Cowbird *Molothrus bonariensis* parasitism (see Threats), average clutch-size being 2.84 (1-4) eggs and incubation period c.13 days with usually two clutches per season and almost all breeding pairs being assisted by 2-4 helpers of their species throughout the breeding cycle (Studer and Vielliard 1988). During the dry season (usually from October to January), flocks of 20-30 birds are formed (Studer and Vielliard 1988).

THREATS The species is certainly suffering from habitat loss throughout its range and particularly in the north-east, where deforestation has been massive (e.g. Teixeira 1986). At Quebrangulo, however, it has been found that the population decline in recent years is attributable not only to habitat destruction but also to increasing pressure from the parasitic Shiny Cowbird, which has gradually colonized the region, starting probably in the 1950s and becoming abundant in the 1980s (Studer and Vielliard 1988). Forbes's Blackbird is the preferred host of the Shiny Cowbird at Quebrangulo, where 25 (64%) of all (39) nests studied between 1981 and 1986 were parasitized, this proportion reaching 100% in 1987 when Forbes's Blackbird produced no fledgling of its own from 21 nests observed (Studer and Vielliard 1988).

Although Forbes's Blackbird is not believed to be prized as a songbird pet (Sick 1985), two birds were being offered for sale at Caruaru in 1985 (A. G. M. Coelho *in litt.* 1986). Even if these birds could have been, intentionally or not, mistaken for valued Chopi Blackbirds (see Remarks 1), trade in Forbes's Blackbird should not be underrated as a possible additional factor placing this species at risk.

MEASURES TAKEN The species is protected under Brazilian law (Bernardes *et al.* 1990). Efforts to preserve the forests in the Serra das Guaribas at Quebrangulo (Studer 1985) resulted in the creation, in December 1989, of the 4,500 ha Pedra Talhada Biological Reserve (A. Studer verbally 1990), although it is not yet fully paid for and the danger of some forest clearance still hangs over the site: efforts continue to establish and preserve the integrity of the reserve, involving the Asociação Nordeste (A. Studer verbally 1992). The species's occurrence in the 37,000 ha Rio Doce State Park may be important, but it is not known how widespread and abundant birds are in this reserve. Experiments to verify the effects of systematic destruction of the cowbird's eggs were started in 1987 (Studer and Vielliard 1988).

MEASURES PROPOSED A call for a search of museum collections of the Chopi Blackbird to disclose additional specimens of Forbes's Blackbird (Short and Parkes 1979) is seemingly still valid and might broaden knowledge of the species's (original) range and ecology (see Remarks 1). Surveys of the species's conservation status and ecology at Rio Doce State Park, and continued monitoring of its population at Quebrangulo, as well as a search for other possible relict populations, are the most pressing needs for fieldwork (for example, the records from rio Capibari-mirim, Matriz de Camaragibe and Pedra Branca should be followed up). Further study on the impact of Shiny Cowbird brood-parasitism on the species must be undertaken, and appropriate measures implemented.

REMARKS (1) The great morphological similarity of this species and the widespread Chopi Blackbird has been a permanent source of confusion since its discovery in 1880, affecting identification of museum specimens (Short and Parkes 1979) and in the field (e.g. Sick 1985, G. T. de Mattos *in litt.* 1987), but in the latter case the different voices can be used to distinguish the two (G. T. de Mattos *in litt.* 1987, Studer and Vielliard 1988). Believed known until the late 1960s from only two specimens, the possibility was raised that these birds might represent intergeneric hybrids between species of *Agelaius* and *Gnorimopsar* (Meyer de Schauensee 1966, Short and Parkes 1979). (2) Although Vista Alegre is listed by Meyer de Schauensee (1966) as a sight record of this species, and this locality was in general accepted by other authors (e.g. Hellmayr 1937, Pinto 1944), there remains a strong possibility that most of the birds seen by Forbes at both Macuca and Vista Alegre may have been, as he stated himself, the Chopi Blackbird, an abundant and also gregarious species (Short and Parkes 1979). Pinto's (1944) reference to "type specimens collected at Macuca and Vista Alegre" is in error, since only a single female was collected by Forbes and ever mentioned (Forbes 1881, Sclater 1886, Hellmayr 1937, Short and Parkes 1979). (3) Although this record, based on the second correctly identified specimen known, preceded by 20 years the discussion initiated by Meyer de Schauensee (1966; see Remarks 1), this and subsequent authors (in Paynter 1968, Short and Parkes 1979, Ridgely and Tudor 1989) overlooked it.

RED SISKIN *Carduelis cucullatus* E[2]

Subject to enormous, long-term (but, since the 1940s, illegal) pressure from trappers because of its capacity to hybridize with canaries, this small, semi-nomadic seed- and fruit-eating finch of foothills in northern Venezuela has become extremely rare throughout a now fragmented range, and may not survive if the trapping is not controlled. The species has disappeared from Trinidad; a tiny population exists in Colombia, and another, derived from escaped cagebirds, in Puerto Rico. Fuller field studies, combined with the creation or extension of some protected areas, reintroductions, and a major publicity campaign, are urgently needed.

DISTRIBUTION The Red Siskin is now very patchily distributed in several areas of northern Venezuela, with a tiny outlying population in north-east Colombia and an introduced colony in south-east Puerto Rico; there are a very few records from Trinidad and its islands where it is almost certainly now extinct, while reports from Cuba appear to be based on escaped cagebirds that never established themselves.

Colombia Records are from near Cúcuta, Norte de Santander department. Two specimens were collected at Villa Felisa, 750 m, 20 km south of Cúcuta on the Pamplona highway, in October 1947, with another male and two females seen at the same time, and with a later (November) sighting at 1,500 or 1,700 m in evidently a second area to the south of Cúcuta (Dugand 1948, Meyer de Schauensee 1966, Hilty and Brown 1986; specimens in USNM, which give an altitude of 420 m and 18 km south of Cúcuta, on Pamplona highway). Hilty and Brown (1986) mention a sighting in 1978 in the east of the department, and their map shows two adjacent localities aligned north–south on the Venezuelan frontier.

Venezuela Evidence gathered by Rivero (1983), repeated in less detail in Coats and Rivero (1984) and Coats and Phelps (1985), suggests that the species once extended throughout the northern cordilleras of the country from the Andes of Mérida north-east as far as Miranda, breaking in western Anzoátegui to reappear in Sucre and northern Monagas (see Remarks 1), but that today it is only known with certainty from Falcón and Lara in the west (but see below under Barinas), and Miranda, Distrito Federal, northern Guárico and Anzoátegui in the centre of this former range. In the following breakdown it should be noted that the evidence of Rivero (1983) was based very largely on information from trappers, and that all states except Zulia were mentioned by Coats and Phelps (1985); localities are given roughly from west to east, and coordinates are taken from Paynter (1982).

Zulia Rivero (1983) knew of two sites near San Juan (see Remarks 2). *Mérida* The only site known to Rivero (1983) was evidently that derived from a specimen (in AMNH) taken at "Sabaneta" (La Sabana), 8°35'N 71°28'W, 600 m, in September 1898 (also Hellmayr 1938, Phelps and Phelps, 1950, 1963; specimen om AMNH).

Barinas A male bird was seen in a coffee plantation in the vicinity of Barinitas, March 1984 (S. Whitehouse verbally 1992). Because this record is from a previously unpublished site and extends the range into a new state, it is possibly unknown to trappers; the details are therefore withheld.

Trujillo Rivero (1983) knew of five sites near Carache in the far north-east of the state in the Andean foothills.

Portuguesa Rivero (1983) knew of five sites near Biscucuy in the far north-west of the state in the Andean foothills.

Lara Rivero (1983) knew of 58 sites in the region of Aguado Grande, Duaca, Sanare and Los Humocaros. In a brief survey of 11 of these in January 1981, no birds were found in the wild but six captive birds (three recently taken) were found in mountains near Siquisique, and others were found near El Copey, where many birds, mostly immatures, had been caught in unusual numbers in July–September 1980 (Coats and Rivero 1984). The southernmost part of the Serranía de

Chumuguara just extends into northernmost Lara (Rivero 1983; see under Falcón below), and it would appear that these are those near (just north of) Siquisique. El Copey remains untraced. Rivero (1983) also indicated that (1) the Andean foothills in the west of the state (shared with Zulia, Trujillo and Portuguesa) remained important for the species (see Population), with birds formerly using at least seven sites around Barquisimeto, (2) the Serranía de Ziruma-Baragua in the north-west of the state reportedly held birds until 1975, and that they could recolonize from the mountains to the east (i.e. Chumuguara), and (3) the Serranía de Bobare-Matatere in the east of the state reportedly held birds until 1977, and that birds still visited the area annually in search of food.

Falcón Rivero (1983) knew of 82 sites in the districts of Mene Mauroa, Federación Petit, Zamora, Acosta and Silva, the areas in question being the Sierra or Serranía de San Luis and the Serranía de Churuguara, where important numbers survived in 1981 (see Population).

Yaracuy Rivero (1983) knew of nine sites near Nirgua, 10°09'N 68°34'W. These seem to be different from the extension of the Serranía de Bobare-Matatere into the north-west of the state (see under Lara above) but four of them occurred in the Sierra or Serranía de Aroa, also in the north-west, where the last birds were seen in 1974, and presumably the others were in El Macizo de Nirgua in the central-south of the state, where the last populations were seen in 1976 (Rivero 1983).

Carabobo Rivero (1983) knew of two sites near Valencia.

Aragua Rivero (1983) knew of 13 sites in the districts of Girardot, Ricaurte, San Sebastián and Mariño. Curiously, Coats and Phelps (1985) only listed this as a probable range state.

Distrito Federal Rivero (1983) knew of six sites near Caracas. The species had been recorded from near Caracas in 1867 (Sclater and Salvin 1868a; hence presumably Phelps and Phelps 1950), and reliable reports in 1981 indicated its survival in low numbers in one or two populations, possibly ranging into El Avila National Park (Coats and Rivero 1984).

Miranda Rivero (1983) knew of 43 sites near Ocumare del Tuy. In February 1981 more than 30 sites were visited in the Serranía del Interior, and birds were found at five (see Remarks 3) in this and Guárico state, all roughly aligned east–west, at distances of 14, 10, 42 and 15 km from each other (Coats and Rivero 1984); the study area that was used following this survey was at 9°57'N 65°55'W, on the southern edge of the Serranía del Interior in the Cordillera de la Costa (Coats and Phelps 1985), this seemingly just inside Miranda. M. L. Goodwin (*in litt.* 1992) referred to small groups being seen between February and June in the mountains near Cúa, and this appears to be identical or close to the study area above.

Guárico Rivero (1983) knew of 41 sites near Altagracia de Orituco. Some of these were surveyed in 1981 (see under Miranda above).

Anzoátegui Rivero (1983) knew of 11 sites near Clarines in the north-west of the state, indicating that this was the easternmost point of a once continuous range from the Andes before a natural break until the species reappeared in Sucre. However, there is a skin in USNM taken in 1952 and labelled "probably from Barcelona" in the north-east of the state. In giving a population estimate for the central area, Rivero (1983: 69) implies that birds survive in the west of the state.

Sucre Rivero (1983) knew of nine sites near Cumaná. These doubtless included records based on two specimens (in BMNH) from Carúpano on the north coast of the Paria Peninsula, one dated February 1867 (Sclater and Salvin 1868a), plus those from the plain near Cumaná, plus "Quebrada Secca" (= Villarroel), 10°18'N 63°57'W, Campos Alegre valley, 10°10'N 63°45'W, La Tigrera, 10°15'N 63°45'W, forest of Los Palmales, 10°17'N 63°45'W and Rincón de San Antonio, 10°16'N 63°43'W, all taken in February–April 1898 and all in AMNH (sites listed in Hellmayr 1938, Phelps and Phelps 1963).

Monagas Rivero (1983) knew of six sites near Maturín, these doubtless including San Antonio, Bermúdez, 10°07'N 63°43'W, July 1896, and La Montaña del Guácharo, 10°09'N 63°32'W, February 1898 (specimens in AMNH; sites listed in Hellmayr 1938, Phelps and Phelps

1963; also Phelps 1897). Rivero (1983) also had reports from an ornithologist in the state that the bird no longer occurs there.

Trinidad and Tobago Whether the species was formerly resident in the country remains uncertain (ffrench 1973), with records concentrated in the north-west peninsula and adjacent islands (see map in ffrench 1973): Monos Island, May 1893 (Chapman 1894); Gasparee Island, November 1921 (Belcher and Smooker 1934-1937); Carenage, June 1926 (Belcher and Smooker 1934-1937); Arima valley, May 1960 (ffrench 1973). A nest ("in the stout vertical fork of a small tree at about 12 feet from the ground") believed to be of this species, taken near the River Estate, Diego Martin, in August 1926 (Belcher and Smooker 1934-1937), does not conform well with the scant information that exists on the subject (see Ecology), and this record is better treated as provisional. There are at least 11 skins simply labelled "Trinidad" (in AMNH, ANSP, BMNH, FMNH, MNHN, USNM), but the significance of these in indicating a former population on the island remains unclear; Hellmayr (1906a) dismissed those in BMNH as of the "Orinoco" make and "certainly not from the island". On current evidence, at least, the bird is no longer present (see Population).

Cuba The only concrete record appears to have referred to a cagebird (see Hellmayr 1938; also Population).

Puerto Rico Reports and observations suggest that a population, derived from escaped cagebirds, has established itself in a small area bounded by the towns of Guayama, Coamo and Aibonito in the south-east of the island (Raffaele 1983, 1989). However, two specimens (in USNM; see Remarks 4) taken in June 1977 are from north-east of Salinas, which is south-west of the area covered by the three towns mentioned above.

POPULATION The total number of wild Red Siskins remaining is unknown, but it is certain that an enormous decline has taken place (King 1978-1979). Studies in Venezuela in the early 1980s, although undertaken by co-workers, appear to have resulted in very different assessments of status.

Colombia From a remark in Stepan (1966), it appears that bird fanciers were aware of small numbers coming out of the country, apparently fairly continuously, in the 1960s. The modern status of the species is uncertain, birds being very local although still seen in small numbers, e.g. one small flock in 1978 (Hilty and Brown 1986). Fieldwork around Cúcuta in 1986 indicated that the species was indeed very rare there (some birds being reported) and apparently declining owing to trapping (G. Arango *in litt.* 1986).

Venezuela The Red Siskin is considered the most threatened bird in the country (G. Medina-Cuervo *in litt.* 1986). Its plight came to national attention in the 1940s following a period of three decades in which thousands were trapped and exported (see Measures Taken), but even during the 1940s and 1950s "hundreds, even thousands, ...were sent to Curaçao annually" (Coats and Phelps 1985); indeed Phelps (1952) commented that ten years before it had been relatively common but that at the time of writing it was almost extinct. Similarly, Muñoz-Tébar (1952) indicated that the species was formerly common in bird shops in the country and was often flown to foreign markets in lots of 500, but that now people had to queue to buy a single bird.

Coats and Phelps (1985) divided the Venezuelan range into three areas (although their map shows six) and by extrapolation from fieldwork they presented estimates for the two areas they studied, namely the west, in which they suggested 350-500 birds survived, and the centre, for which they suggested a total of 250-300, while for the east (Sucre, Monagas) they reported the claims of bird-dealers that the species was already extinct, thus yielding a possible national total of only 600-800 birds. These findings generally conform with data in Coats and Rivero (1984), who also indicated roughly 300 birds in the central region, although they speculated that the reason the eastern population was judged extirpated by dealers in Caracas was that trappers might have found other trading routes for their birds (but they agreed that any surviving populations there would be in poor condition; and see Distribution: Monagas).

The most curious challenge to the figures in Coats and Phelps (1985) comes from Rivero (1983), who only addressed in detail the situation in the western area: as indicated under Distribution, he reported apparent extinction of birds in the serranías of Ziruma-Baragua (Lara) and of Bobare-Matatere (Lara, Yaracuy), Sierra de Aroa (Yaracuy) and Macizo de Nirgua (Yaracuy), but reported its survival in the Sierra de San Luis, where he judged 1,000 birds to be present (despite 200 being trapped in 1981; see Remarks 5), the Serranía de Churuguara, which he judged to hold almost half of the entire western area's population, i.e. some 3,000 birds, and the north-eastern Andean foothills, where he thought some 500 birds might survive. Later in the same work he referred to Lara and Falcón holding 4,500 birds, apparently indicating that this is 75% of the western area's total (i.e. again implying some 6,000 birds there; but see Remarks 6), and added that some 1,500 might occupy the central area; he also indicated (somewhat paradoxically) that the Venezuelan population lies between 2,000 and 20,000 birds; finally he suggested that the total was around 6,000 (Rivero 1983). If his figures of captured birds in the period 1975-1982 (see third paragraph under Threats) approximate to the truth, it certainly appears impossible to accept the total figures proposed for the wild population in Coats and Phelps (1985), if only because in 1982 alone more birds were trapped than Coats and Phelps credit for the entire country.

Whether in the high hundreds or the low thousands, however, the total population is clearly very small indeed; Coats and Phelps (1985) felt that it was probably doomed to extinction, and the evidence from campesinos in 1986 was that the trapping pressure was still present and the trend still down (S. Coats *in litt.* 1986). This is a point that is also stressed in Rivero (1983), who argued that the species could be extinct in the country as soon as 1984.

Trinidad and Tobago The species is probably now extirpated from the country, where it was never anything but rare; even the bird-trappers of the island do not know it (R. ffrench *in litt.* 1986, V. C. Quesnel *in litt.* 1986).

Cuba It is very doubtful that any feral populations exist now or ever became established in Cuba (O. H. Garrido *in litt.* 1991).

Puerto Rico Some 12 birds were seen at one site in June 1976 (Raffaele 1983), but despite speculation that the population on the island "may well represent the largest remaining pool" (Raffaele 1983; hence also Diebold 1986) the species has been described as "very rare and local" (Raffaele 1989). Although records go back into the last century, the species was probably an introduction and it seems likely that it became established on the island in the 1930s when South American populations were still high and there was probably heavy demand for the bird in Puerto Rico (Raffaele 1983). Small numbers were seen in 1982 (Coats and Phelps 1985).

ECOLOGY The Red Siskin is a semi-nomadic inhabitant of the foothills and lower montane slopes, ranging altitudinally between 280 and 1,300 m, occupying a variety of habitats from moist evergreen forest to shrubby grassland and pastures (Coats and Phelps 1985; also King 1978-1979); its characterization as a bird of open forest and forest edge (Stepan 1966) appears accurate. In the main study area in Cordillera de la Costa, 1981-1982, birds used two distinct habitat zones: dry deciduous woodland and shrubby grassland at 220-650 m, and mixed deciduous and evergreen forest with cafetals (small coffee plantations), small gardens and clearings, from 650 m upwards, and it was in this zone, from 750 to 1,300 m, that the breeding area lay (Coats and Rivera 1984, Coats and Phelps 1985). Habitat choice appeared to depend on several factors including the availability of food, water for drinking and bathing, song perches (these were preferably at least 4 m above ground), roost trees and nesting sites; all sites where the species was found had in common the presence of food-plants, water, and nearby trees at least 8-9 m high (Coats and Rivero 1984). In Colombia birds occupy open grassy areas with bushes and low trees, favouring drier areas (Hilty and Brown 1986); in Puerto Rico they are found in "scrubby foothills well removed from urban areas" (Raffaele 1983).

On Monos Island Chapman (1894) saw two birds feeding on the fruit of a large cactus. In the 1981-1982 study birds were observed feeding on the dry seeds and fleshy fruits of five species of plant: *Urera baccifera*, which grows in moist, partly shaded areas usually above 600 m and is particularly abundant in cafetals and forest openings, fruiting in February–April when it appears to be the most favoured food, birds in one instance flying a circuit of c.10 km each day to visit several stands in turn; *Trixis divaricata*, a scandescent shrub of dry deciduous forest and savanna above 400 m, most abundant at woodland edge including roadcuts and streamsides, fruiting in December–January; *Eupatorium odoratum*, which grows up to 950 m as a low compact shrub 1-2 m tall at woodland edge, along woodland streams and in savannas (i.e. frequently near *T. divaricata*), often abundant in areas cleared for grazing, fruiting in January–February; *Wedelia caracasana*, an erect, tough-stemmed herb 1-2 m tall in sunny, rocky areas usually above 600 m, abundant in areas cleared for roads and pastures, especially on ridge-tops and slopes of interior valleys, producing seeds from late July to November or December (this plant, under the name *W. calycina*, being considered an "indicator" species for the presence of Red Siskins by Rivero 1983); *Cordia currasavica*, a compact shrub up to 1.5 m tall that grows on rocky soils in open areas and savannas above 650 m, commonest in interior valleys cleared for pasture and in transition zones between savannas and gallery forest, often near *W. caracasana* and fruiting from August to early October (Coats and Rivero 1984; also Coats and Phelps 1985; see Remarks 7). Plants reported by trappers to be used by Red Siskins (times of fruiting in parentheses) are: *Panicum maximum* (probably all year), *Urera caracasana* (September–October), *Coccoloba caracasana* (probably June–August), *Amaranthus dubius* (September–November), *A. spinosus* (February–April), *Xylopia aromatica* (November–March), *Brassica vulgaris* (unknown), *Capparis hastata* (probably July–October), *Senna bacillaris* (perhaps February–May), *Bursera simaruba* (perhaps September–December), *Cochiospermum orinocense* (May–August), *Lemaireocereus deficiens* (unknown; but, as *Ritterocereus*, it is said to ripen after the main rains by Rivero 1983), *Hyptis suaveolens* (December–February), *Borreria verticillata* (November–June), *Brickellia diffusa* (December–April), *Lagascea mollis* (August) (described as the main and most sought-after food for the bird and its young), *Mikania micrantha* (October–January), *Synedrella nodiflora* (unknown; but Rivero 1983 gives September–November), *Trixis frutescens* (February–April), *Wedelia parviflora* (unknown) (Coats and Rivero 1984). In addition to these, Rivero (1983) mentions *Wedelia ambigens* as an important food-source in the driest periods, *Sclerocarpus coffaecolus* (June–August), *Oyedaea verbesinoides* (period not given), *Bidens pilosa*, *Elephantopus mollis*, *Taraxacum officinale* (all three September–November), flowers of *Chamissoa altissima* (March–May), flowers of *Parthenium hysterophorus* (October–December), *Rubus robustus* (August–November), nectar of *Erythrina poeppigiana* (an important shade-tree for coffee; February–May), *Acanthocereus tetragonus* (after the main rains), *Capparis odoratissima* (July, August), *Pithecellobium unguis-cati* (period not given), flowers of *Cedrela odorata* (March–May), nectar of *Bursera simaruba* (April–June), fruits and flowers of *Acalpypha carpinifolia* (March–May).

The main breeding period is from May to early July, with a second period in November–December, many fewer juveniles being seen in January–February than in August–September (Coats and Phelps 1985); the rainy season extends from May to the end of November (Coats and Rivero 1984). The two birds collected in October in Colombia were in breeding condition (Hilty and Brown 1986), as was at least one of the birds collected in June in Puerto Rico (data on label in USNM; see also below). Data from captive breeding indicate that a single nesting cycle (from nest-building to self-feeding young) takes at least 45 days, and therefore there is probably only one brood per breeding period (Coats and Rivero 1984, Coats and Phelps 1985). There are reports of males being serially polygamous (Rivero 1983, Coles 1986); in captivity, a male took no part in nest-building, incubation or care of the young, but he was on hand throughout to provide the female with food (Amsler 1912). In moister areas the nest is constructed in tall trees such as

Erythrina poeppigiana and *Inga* sp.; in semiarid areas in trees such as *Guazuma ulmifolia* and *Prosopis juliflora* (Rivero 1983). Within the tree itself the nest is reportedly placed in clumps of bromeliads *Tillandsia usneoides* (also *T. barbata*: Rivero 1983) hanging from tall (25 m high or more) trees; and certainly tall trees festooned with this epiphyte are commonly used as song perches, February–June (Coats and Rivero 1984). On Puerto Rico in June 1976, a female was seen carrying *Tillandsia* to a nest apparently under construction roughly 1.5 m below the crown of a gumbo limbo *Bursera simaruba* (Raffaele 1983). In captivity, where it has been noted that the female prefers to nest very high up within an aviary (Frey 1985), clutches range from three to five eggs, incubation starts with the last or penultimate egg and lasts 11-13 days, and fledging occurs at 14-16 days (Coats and Rivero 1984, Coats and Phelps 1985). Family groups stay together for several weeks after fledging; during the 1981-1982 study a mean of 1.4 offspring per successful pair was determined during the first month after fledging, but allowing for total failure the true productivity is probably more like 0.5-1 (Coats and Rivero 1984, Coats and Phelps 1985).

During the post-breeding period at the 1981-1982 study site, birds travelled many kilometres daily, often feeding in the lower, dryer zone but usually moving up the mountainsides to communal roosts in the evening; in one case the roost-trees were an *Inga* and an adjacent *Acacia* in the lower part of the wet forest zone (Coats and Rivero 1984, Coats and Phelps 1985). The extent to which birds wander widely after breeding, as implied in King (1978-1979), is not clear, although Rivero (1983) reported localities at which birds were only known to use for feeding, for example the Serranía de Bobare-Matatere, and those apparently far from wet forest near Barquisimeto, in Lara, and concluded that migrations over 50 km took place. On Monos Island, Trinidad, Chapman (1894) was told birds were common there at times, suggesting seasonal influxes. Birds are generally gregarious, foraging throughout the year in groups of 10 or more, although the usual observed flock-size, 1981-1982, was around 2-4; birds may remain in mated pairs throughout the year (Coats and Rivero 1984).

THREATS Excessive and relentless trapping for the cagebird trade since at least 1835 is the single known cause of the decline of the Red Siskin towards extinction: although part of the problem was the use of skins or feathers in the manufacture of ladies' hats (mid-nineteenth century), it is particularly because the species hybridizes with the domestic canary to produce fertile offspring of various reddish colours and with enhanced singing capacity, much prized by bird fanciers and widely known to them since the start of the twentieth century (Amsler 1935, Muñoz-Tébar 1952, King 1978-1979, Coats and Phelps 1985). At that time, there was no trapping from the onset of the rainy season until after the end of the main breeding period, since the nesting areas were relatively inaccessible, so that most trapping took place in July–September when flocks were feeding at the base of the mountains; young birds were preferred as they adapted better and sold better (they could be seen to have a long life-span ahead of them), while most females were released, although the high mortality among the birds meant that more had to be captured than were intended to be sold (Coats and Phelps 1985). The popularity of the species very rapidly grew (big numbers were first imported into Germany in 1909-1911: Stepan 1966), and was intensified with the outlawing of the capture of native birds in the U.S.A. and Europe; ironically, however, following the protection of the species in Venezuela in the mid-1940s interest in it merely redoubled, and trade went underground, with hundreds and even thousands being reputedly smuggled out of the country via the Dutch offshore island of Curaçao (Coats and Phelps 1985). The failure of the Netherlands to accede to CITES meant that this trade route remained open for many years after the species was placed on Appendix I (see Measures Taken).

In recent years new roads have opened up many breeding areas so that now birds are taken at all times of the year, and females are also retained to be hybridized; although other birds are easier and more plentiful to trap, the high prices fetched by Red Siskins (approaching US$1,000 in the mid-1980s for a single bird) maintain the pressure on them and in fact some trappers – many of them originally from the Canary Islands, where the longest tradition of crossing them with canaries exists (see, e.g., Astley 1902, Hopkinson 1920) – pursue them as a kind of sport, following them around in jeeps and trucks, buying them up from campesinos (Coats and Phelps 1985). Although habitat is more extensive in the western part of its now disjunct range, hunting pressure is also greater; meanwhile the eastern part, which was once a major source of birds, may have been completely depleted (Coats and Phelps 1985; but see Population). The preferred food-plants (i.e. the five known species) are very common species of secondary and disturbed vegetation in the more seasonal regions of Venezuela, which obviously helps make the bird a prime target for trappers (A. M. Sugden *in litt.* 1986).

Rivero (1983) devotes two pages of tables to reported captures of birds in each of its known states in each year from 1975 to 1982, condensed with western area first, central area second, as follows: 2,400 and 450 (1975), 2,350 and 250 (1976), 1,500 and 300 (1977), 1,800 and 450 (1978), 1,250 and 550 (1979), 1,750 and 700 (1980), 1,600 and 800 (1981), 300 and 750 (1982) (see Remarks 8). As an example of the interest in the species at national level, a birdwatcher stopping at random at a garage for repairs in Caracas in 1984 counted 10 Red Siskins in cages around the walls of the establishment (S. Whitehouse verbally 1992). The pressure of trade was still very strong inside and outside the country in 1986, with campesinos reporting trapping despite the arrest of bird-catchers (S. Coats *in litt.* 1986).

The species appears always to have been under pressure in Colombia, Stepan (1966) referring to the country as a source of birds for Europe because of the tightening of the laws in Venezuela (although this is barely consistent with the above), and Venezuelan trappers themselves crossing into the Cúcuta area to take birds in the 1980s (G. Arango *in litt.* 1986). Even on Puerto Rico, where the population is almost certainly derived from escaped cagebirds, birds are apparently under trapping pressure, as a boy was reported to be selling them by the roadside near a known site in early 1976 (Raffaele 1983). Nevertheless, the idea that "populations formerly thought safe on several Caribbean islands have been discovered by illegal traffickers and have been systematically decimated" (Amos 1986) seems to be mistaken.

Other threats Rivero (1983) pointed out that while traditional campesino clearance of land had apparently favoured the species (witness the known food-plants: see Ecology), intensive agriculture and the clear-felling of large areas have affected it adversely. Rivero (1983), Coats and Rivero (1984) and Coats and Phelps (1985) listed the species's most likely natural enemies.

MEASURES TAKEN The first prohibitions on sale and export from the mid-1940s, achieved through the agitation of the Phelps family, only had the effect of increasing demand and sending the trade under ground (Coats and Phelps 1985), though by 1952, when the species was designated threatened at the IUCN General Assembly in Caracas (see Muñoz-Tébar 1952, Coats and Phelps 1985), it was almost impossible to obtain an export permit and there were real hopes for a recovery (Phelps 1952). The species was placed on Appendix I of CITES in July 1975 and on the U.S. Endangered Species Act (as "endangered") in June 1976 (Coats and Phelps 1985). The 1981-1982 field study of the species was organized by the Sociedad Venezolana de Ciencias Naturales with a grant from the country's ministry for renewable resources, MARNR (Coats and Phelps 1985). The smuggling of birds through Curaçao, common since the 1940s and undiminished by the Appendix I listing of the species (Coats and Phelps 1985), was presumably rendered less easy with the accession of the Netherlands to CITES in July 1987. Throughout the 1980s the non-governmental conservation group FUDENA has worked to initiate a programme of conservation and reintroduction, and the Venezuelan Audubon Society and the Federación Ornitológica Venezolana have also conducted publicity work to highlight the need for action to save the species (M. L. Goodwin verbally 1987). Birds are not known to occur in any protected area (but see Measures Proposed).

In certain published accounts the names of specific sites in Venezuela have been suppressed in order to give them greater security (e.g. in Meyer de Schauensee and Phelps 1978, Rivero 1983, Coats and Phelps 1985), yet it is perfectly clear from the latter two references and others that the trappers know all the sites already while the conservationists and ornithologists know hardly any. Raffaele (1983) also suppressed names of localities on Puerto Rico for fear of "collectors", but if the area is to be secured in the manner he suggested (see Measures Proposed) these details will quickly become available.

Captive breeding An increase in breeding effort as a means of taking the pressure off wild populations was proposed as long ago as the mid-1960s (Stepan 1966), and this call was repeated in the early 1980s by Venezuelan conservationists (e.g. Goodwin 1982). The American Federation of Aviculture duly responded with an attempted worldwide survey of captive stock (Amos 1986, Coles 1986) and the establishment of a consortium to build a self-sustaining population (Diebold 1986), this project now issuing its own newsletter, *Siskin News*, and expanding to protect habitat in the wild and reintroduce birds where feasible (Gorman 1990, 1992). In Europe both Kühn (1987) and Radtke (1991) reported that an exceptionally high, healthy breeding stock had been built up over 30 years, especially in Germany, and had made importations redundant (but see Measures Proposed). Rivero (1983) indicated that countries with major captive stocks of the species are Germany, Argentina, Belgium, Spain and the Netherlands. Captive breeding information is given in Stepan (1966), Rivero (1983), Galliano (1984), Frey (1985), Coles (1986), Märzhäuser (1986), Kühn (1987) and Radtke (1991); as an example of reproductive capacity in captivity, Coles (1986) reported on three Italian breeders who in 1984 obtained respectively 129 young from 18 pairs, 59 young from eight pairs, and 124 young from 12 males and 15 females.

MEASURES PROPOSED Small populations are reputed to occur in Guatopo and Terepaima National Parks (B. Swift *in litt.* 1988), and there is a possibility that another occurs in El Avila National Park (Coats and Rivero 1984); these three areas need to be carefully surveyed as soon as possible. The recommendations of Coats and Phelps (1985) were to undertake (1) the creation of one or more reserves of sufficient size to give the species year-round protection (something that might best be achieved by an extension of the boundaries of Guatopo National Park, if the birds prove not to be present but only in an adjacent area: Coats and Rivero 1984); (2) further field studies, involving radiotelemetry, to determine daily and seasonal movements of local populations and to define the area to be encompassed by a reserve; (3) the promotion of public concern and involvement through campaigns; and (4) training of staff in Guatopo National Park concerning the Red Siskin and its plight. Obviously the situation in the eastern area of occurrence, which was not addressed in the 1981-1982 fieldwork, needs to be investigated (Coats and Rivero 1984). In response to these points, FUDENA has a proposal to study and protect the species in the wild, control commerce, promote public awareness, breed the species in captivity and reintroduce it where possible, all of which requires financial backing (G. Medina-Cuervo *in litt.* 1987). It is worth noting that, in spite of Europe being reportedly self-sufficient in Red Siskins, there seems to be little contact between countries or continents in order to agree and coordinate future work, and there ought to be sufficient resources, in terms of both stock and finances, for the avicultural communities of the developed world to support work such as outlined above. It is also worth noting that the localities identified but not named by Rivero (1983) need to be catalogued and deposited with Venezuelan government and non-government authorities and with ICBP, so that they can be used responsibly by conservationists.

Outside Venezuela, further fieldwork in Colombia might help elucidate the bird's status there: the area from which it is recorded is apparently relatively unspoilt (G. Arango *in litt.* 1986), suggesting that control of trapping, especially if done by Venezuelans, might lead to the recovery of the population(s) there. In Puerto Rico its status requires fuller investigation, and consideration should be given to declaring its range critical habitat under the U.S. Endangered Species Act (Raffaele 1983), although the idea of reintroducing birds to Venezuela (Raffaele 1983) sounds perhaps too generous (at least at present) with what is a very valuable reserve stock, which merits being managed as such in perpetuity.

REMARKS (1) There is an undated skin in USNM labelled "Orinoco", which is probably simply a mistake but might represent some extension further east than otherwise known. (2) This is presumably the source for the only area mapped in the state by Coats and Phelps (1985), although they mark an area in the foothills of the Sierra de Perijá whereas the coordinates (10°08'N 72°21'W) for the only locality of this name in the state given by Paynter (1982) suggest a lowland area further east. Meanwhile, Rivero (1983) referred to the former range of the species in the north-eastern foothills of the Andes, involving the states of Lara, Portuguesa, Trujillo and Zulia, so it is possible that the area intended by his "San Juan" lies to the east of the Lago de Maracaibo, which is consistent with another map (Figure 3) in Rivero (1983), which shades in an area of foothills in Zulia at roughly 9°N 71°10'W. Curiously, the main text in Coats and Phelps (1985) omits any mention of Zulia. OG (1961) lists a San Juan at 8°54'N 71°41'W. (3) Coats and Phelps (1985) referred to this fieldwork finding the species at six sites rather thsan five, all in the central part of its range. (4) These skins presumably replaced the ones lost in 1976 (see Raffaele 1983). (5) It is evident that the figure for the Sierra de San Luis was guesswork, since Coats and Rivero (1984) mentioned that their planned visit there in May 1981 was prevented by landslips. (6) Rivero (1983) is vague and ambiguous at key places when giving population estimates: the figure of 3,000 for Serranía de Churuguara could, for example, refer to the total population of the western area or, as assumed based on other pronouncements, half of that total; at any rate, in his concluding summary he indicated that the western area held 75% and the central area 25% of the country's populations, which implies that his preferred total for the west was 4,500, not 6,000. (7) These names are as given in Coats and Phelps (1985); Coats and Rivero (1984) give *Wedelia calycina* and use the spelling *curasavica*. (8) Paradoxically, in his final recommendations Rivero (1983) ignored this table and referred to a total of 400 being captured in 1980 and 200 in 1981.

SAFFRON SISKIN *Carduelis siemiradskii* V[9]

This rare finch is confined to south-west Ecuador and adjacent north-west Peru, where it inhabits semi-arid scrub and dry forest up to 750 m. Only two areas are known where it appears even fairly common, but too little is known to assess how seriously it is threatened.

DISTRIBUTION The Saffron Siskin (see Remarks 1) is found in the coastal ranges of west and south-west Ecuador (Manabí, Guayas and Loja provinces) and north-west Peru (Tumbes department), and locally in the intermediate lowlands. Localities where the species has been recorded (coordinates from Paynter and Traylor 1977, Stephens and Traylor 1983, OG 1957b, or read from IGM 1989) are as follows:

Ecuador (*Manabí*) Cordillera de Balzar (0°55'S 79°55'W), where a female-plumaged specimen (in BMNH) was taken (also Sharpe 1888; see Remarks 2); between Jipijapa and Puerto de Cayo (c.1°23'S 80°42'W), on the Pacific slope of the coastal range, where the bird was seen at 320 m in February 1991 (P. Coopmans verbally 1991); río Ayampe (1°40'S 80°45'W), where two flocks were seen in December 1990 (NK); (*Guayas*) near Machalilla National Park, where a male (in ANSP) was collected in January 1991; 40 km west of Guayaquil, where three birds were seen in July 1990 (P. K. Donahue *in litt.* 1990); Cerro Blanco reserve (2°09'S 80°02-03'W), 14 km west of Guayaquil in the Cordillera de Chongón, whence come several recent sightings (P. Greenfield *in litt.* 1989, P. K. Donahue *in litt.* 1990, TAP); Guayaquil, at 0-10 m (von Berlepsch and Taczanowski 1883, Chapman 1926; specimens in AMNH, BMNH, MCZ, USNM); Isla Puná, near sea level (Chapman 1926; specimen in AMNH taken in July 1922); Huerta (Puerto) Negra (c.3°00'S 79°44'W), 20 km east-south-east of Balao, and east of Tenguel, on the border of Guayas and Azuay provinces, whence come three specimens (in USNM) taken in August and September 1974 and October 1976; (*Loja*) 10 km by road south of Sabanilla (c.20 km by road north of Zapotillo), where the bird was fairly common at 525 m in April 1992 (M. B. Robbins *in litt.* 1992);

Peru (*Tumbes*) Quebrada Faical (3°49'S 80°17'W), east of El Caucho at 400 m (Wiedenfeld *et al.* 1985; specimens in LSUMZ taken in June 1979); Campo Verde, and nearby Cotrina and Cerro San Carlos (c.3°51'S 80°11'W), whence come sightings at 600-750 m (Wiedenfeld *et al.* 1985, Parker *et al.* ms); and Tumbes, where the bird was seen at 7 m (Taczanowski 1884-1886).

POPULATION In Ecuador, the region where the Saffron Siskin occurs has not been extensively collected ornithologically (Paynter and Traylor 1977), so the scarcity of museum specimens does not reflect its true status; thus at the Cerro Blanco reserve in the Cordillera de Chongón a flock of 25 was seen in December, and on another occasion at the same locality a flock of 18 was seen (P. Greenfield *in litt.* 1989). However, R. S. Ridgely (*in litt.* 1989) believed collecting around Guayaquil to have been sufficient enough to judge the species "not common", and noted that the Cordillera de Chongón may be a stronghold of the siskin, and even there he had not encountered it daily, with no more than 8-10 seen in a day. At río Ayampe two flocks of 5-6 individuals were seen along 1 km of river in December 1990 (NK). In Loja province (see Distribution), the bird was found to be fairly common in April 1992, when over 20 were recorded in a day, with adults feeding young, and five adult males and two immatures collected (in ANSP, MECN): this led to the conclusion that the area was possibly a stronghold for the species (M. B. Robbins *in litt.* 1992). However, it must be stressed that these observations were made in an El Niño year, and no birds were apparently found in the area in 1991 (Best 1992).

In Peru, this species was rare at El Caucho in June and July 1979 (Wiedenfeld *et al.* 1985), and in late July 1988 only three flocks of 4-8 birds were seen in the vicinity (Parker *et al.* ms).

ECOLOGY The localities where this species has been found are semi-arid scrub and dry, deciduous forest (Paynter and Traylor 1977, Wiedenfeld *et al.* 1985, R. S. Ridgely *in litt.* 1989), with birds also being encountered in tall grass and weeds at forest edge (Parker *et al.* ms), from near sea level to 750 m (see Distribution). The flock of over 20 birds, Loja, April (including adult males and immatures), was seen feeding on the seeds of weeds along or near the roadside: adults were feeding fledged young as they sat in second-growth trees or on wire fences within a few metres of the road (M. B. Robbins *in litt.* 1992). Three specimens (in LSUMZ and USNM) from June, August and September had inactive gonads, and juveniles (in ANSP, LSUMZ) with unossified skulls were taken in April and June. The species thus apparently breeds during the wet season, which is January to May (Brown 1941) as do probably most or all species in this region (Marchant 1958).

THREATS Too little information exists about the species, but as it appears to inhabit arid scrub, forest edge and second growth, it may not be threatened. If, however, as may well turn out to be the case, it depends on deciduous forest (at least for breeding), it may be seriously at risk.

MEASURES TAKEN The species occurs in three protected areas: Machalilla National Park, Manabí, Cerro Blanco reserve, Guayas, and Tumbes National Forest, Peru (see equivalent section under Grey-backed Hawk *Leucopternis occidentalis*).

MEASURES PROPOSED More study on this poorly known species is needed in order to decide whether any species-specific intervention should be undertaken. Proper management of the Machalilla National Park should be encouraged, this site being of paramount importance for conservation in the region. Details of initiatives proposed to preserve the threatened species endemic to western Ecuador and north-west Peru are given in the equivalent section under Grey-backed Hawk. The area in Loja south of Sabanilla, consisted of fairly good deciduous forest and, as one of the strongholds for the Saffron Siskin, it should receive a high conservation priority: the area is also inhabited by other threatened species and by rare (near-threatened) endemics like Pale-browed Tinamou *Crypturellus transfasciatus* (M. B. Robbins *in litt.* 1992: see equivalent section under Grey-backed Hawk).

REMARKS (1) The Saffron Siskin was described as a species (von Berlepsch and Taczanowski 1883), but Chapman (1926) suggested that it might be a subspecies of Hooded Siskin *Carduelis magellanica*, as did Hellmayr (1938) and Meyer de Schauensee (1966). All three, however, maintained it as a species, a treatment followed by all subsequent authors except Dunning (1982), who tentatively treated it as a subspecies of Hooded Siskin. *C. magellanica paula* of the Peruvian coast has been taken as far north as Milagros, Loja province, Ecuador, only some 30 km south-south-east of Campo Verde (Chapman 1926), but M. B. Robbins (*in litt.* 1992) has reported that Saffron Siskin is significantly smaller than even this race, and is undoubtedly a good species.

(2) Concerning the Cordillera de Balzar, Paynter and Traylor (1977) stated that "Balzar" has been erroneously called "Balzar Mts" in the literature, but it is to be noted that "Balzar Mts" is written on the label of the BMNH specimen referred to above; accordingly the cordillera of that name (in Manabí province) and its coordinates (as given in OG 1957b) is preferred here to the town at 1°22'S 79°54'W in Guayas province suggested by Paynter and Traylor (1977). Hellmayr (1938) suggested that the specimen labelled "Balzar Mts" by Illingworth, a native collector in the service of C. Buckley, had no doubt been subject to a confusion of labelling, as this man had also visited Isla Puná. Similarly labelled specimens (in BMNH), however, exist for Grey-backed Hawk, Little Woodstar *Acestrura bombus* and Grey-breasted Flycatcher *Lathrotriccus griseipectus*, and the origin of all these specimens may well be correctly indicated.

YELLOW-FACED SISKIN *Carduelis yarrellii* V/R[10]

Little known in Venezuela and traded in high volume in north-east Brazil, this small open-country finch needs to be studied to determine more of its ecology and needs, particularly at sites where it remains locally common.

DISTRIBUTION The Yellow-faced Siskin (see Remarks 1) is known from two widely disjunct regions 3,500 km apart in northern Venezuela and north-eastern Brazil (see Remarks 2).

Venezuela The species's occurrence in the country is poorly documented, specimens being known from only two localities, the Hacienda El Trompillo, in the vicinity of Lake Valencia, April and May 1914 (Todd 1926, Hellmayr 1938, Meyer de Schauensee and Phelps 1978; specimens in CM, MCZ), and Hacienda La Araguata, Pirapira (Ridgely and Tudor 1989), both in south-eastern Carabobo state (see Remarks 3).

Brazil Records within states (north to south) are:

Ceará The species occurs all over the state, including the serras (R. Otoch *in litt.* 1986). Specimens are from Açudinho, Baturité, August 1958 (in MZUSP; also Pinto and de Camargo 1961); São Paulo, Serra de Ibiapaba, February 1910 (in MNRJ and MPEG; also Snethlage 1926); Juá, near Iguatu, August 1913 (Hellmayr 1929a, 1938); Serra Verde, Joazeiro (corresponding to present-day Juazeiro do Norte; see Naumburg 1935), 560 m, December 1926 (in AMNH).

Paraíba A specimen obtained alive "at Paraíba" and sent to the Zoological Gardens of London in 1880 (Forbes 1881) and another from Uruba, Mamanguape, July 1957 (in MZUSP; also Pinto and de Camargo 1961), are the only records.

Pernambuco Older records (east to west) are: Recife, a pair seen close to the city in a cultivated area and a single bird seen about 80 km to the south (Lamm 1948); Fazenda São Bento, Tapera (corresponding to the present-day Tapacurá Ecological Station: Coelho 1979), one bird collected in December 1938 (Pinto 1940, 1944); a pair seen close to Quipapá in September 1880 (Forbes 1881); São Caitano, undated (Lamm 1948); Garanhuns, one bird seen in September 1880 (Forbes 1881), three specimens collected in February 1927 at 900 m (in AMNH) and two obtained in November 1957 (in USNM); and Brejão, 750 m, February 1927 (two specimens in AMNH). Modern observations are (east to west) from the Tapacurá Ecological Station, São Lourenço da Manta, September 1977 (Coelho 1979), Saltinho Biological Reserve, Rio Formoso; Caruaru; Catimbau, March 1970; Ibimirim; and Serra Negra Biological Reserve, Inajá (A. G. M. Coelho *in litt.* 1986).

Alagoas The species has been recorded from Quebrangulo, where one specimen was collected in November 1951 (Pinto 1954a) and three others in March and April 1957 (Pinto and de Camargo 1961), the species still being present in the first half of the 1980s (Studer 1985) and found there (in crop fields) in August 1989 (B. C. Forrester *in litt.* 1992); Pedra ("Serra") Branca, Murici, where one bird was seen in October 1990 (J. F. Pacheco *in litt.* 1991) and small groups of up to five were present at forest edge and in a recently burnt clearing of the remaining forest at Fazenda Bananeira on two dates in April 1992 (M. Pearman *in litt.* 1992); and Usina Laginha, União dos Palmares, where two pairs were seen in January 1991 (J. F. Pacheco *in litt.* 1991).

Bahia At least 15 specimens, in AMNH, BMNH, MCZ, MHNG, MPEG and USNM, are merely labelled "Bahia" (see Remarks 2). Specimens with indication of locality are from Leopoldina (untraced) (Cabanis 1865-1866, Todd 1926; see Remarks 4) and Fazenda da Serra (probably near Barra), on the rio Grande, 1903 (Reiser 1926, Hellmayr 1938). One bird was seen near Jeremoabo in May 1986 (C. Yamashita *in litt.* 1986) (see Population).

POPULATION The species has been considered extremely hard to find in Venezuela (M. L. Goodwin *in litt.* 1986). In Brazil it was judged to be common but in steep decline in most of its range in Ceará, having disappeared from some localities where it used to be fairly common as a result of intensive trapping (R. Otoch *in litt.* 1986 and verbally 1988; see Threats), but apparently it remains locally common in Pernambuco and Alagoas (A. G. M. Coelho *in litt.* 1986, D. M. Teixeira *in litt.* 1987), and had not yet become rare in northern Bahia by the 1970s (Sick 1985).

ECOLOGY Despite the species's seemingly reasonable abundance in much of its range, very little has been reported on its biology. In Venezuela its habitat is given as "open terrain and cultivated areas, up to 400 m" (Meyer de Schauensee and Phelps 1978). In north-eastern Brazil, it has been found in caatinga (Pinto 1954a), forest edge (M. Pearman *in litt.* 1992), crop fields (B. C. Forrester *in litt.* 1992), second growth, plantations and even large urban centres (D. M. Teixeira *in litt.* 1987). This may be a bird which, like its congener the Red Siskin *Carduelis cucullatus* (see relevant account), utilizes forest at certain seasons or at certain periods of the day. The stomach of one specimen in MNRJ contained fruits. There are no data on breeding, except that of the four specimens in AMNH collected in Pernambuco and Ceará whose gonad condition was recorded, two had them "slightly" or "half" enlarged and one "not enlarged" in February, and the other "slightly enlarged" in December.

THREATS The Yellow-faced Siskin has been under pressure from trapping in numbers for the cagebird trade in Brazil (see below), and even in Venezuela, where it is very hard to find, canary breeders seek it (M. L. Goodwin *in litt.* 1986). It has been suggested that it may be threatened owing to this traffic (Ridgely and Tudor 1989) and its very limited range (Sick 1985). Although Sick (1985) asserted that the time is past when skins of handsome species such as this were exported to Europe as decoration material, trade in live birds obviously still flourishes: at the Sunday bird market at Fortaleza (judged to be the second in importance in Brazil after Rio's Caxias) lots of hundreds (e.g. 700) Yellow-faced Siskins may be offered for sale every week (R. Otoch verbally 1988). Many of these birds are already sick when they arrive in Fortaleza and soon die (most often from coccidiosis); in recent years traders have begun marking females and young males on the crown with black ink so that they can be sold as subadult males about to become valued singing adult males, a trick that has allowed trappers to profit from the post-breeding wandering of immatures in April/May (R. Otoch verbally 1988). This trade in Ceará is thought to feed both internal and the international demand, possibly through Belém and Guyana (R. Otoch verbally 1988). The species is heavily traded also in Pernambuco (A. G. M. Coelho *in litt.* 1986) and in Rio de Janeiro, where in the 1980s it was relatively common in Caxias market, appearing seasonally in lots of 60-100 birds (C. E. Carvalho *in litt.* 1987).

MEASURES TAKEN The species is listed on Appendix II of CITES and is protected under Brazilian law (Bernardes *et al.* 1990). The creation of the Pedra Talhada Biological Reserve is described in the equivalent section under Scalloped Antbird *Myrmeciza ruficauda*. The species's occurrence in the 350 ha Tapacurá Ecological Station, the 500 ha Saltinho Biological Reserve and the 500 ha Serra Negra Biological Reserve might give it some additional protection, but at Saltinho in the mid-1980s vigilance was slight, and at Serra Negra there was none at all (A. G. M. Coelho *in litt.* 1986).

MEASURES PROPOSED Surveys are needed to delimit the current range of the Yellow-faced Siskin and assess its status more accurately: given its relative abundance still in parts of north-east Brazil, a study of its general biology and ecology would be both valuable and apparently straightforward. A call for a complete ban on the capture of wild birds for the pet trade, as any partial controls would be so open to abuse as to be ineffective (Scott and Brooke 1985), clearly applies in this case. Meanwhile, the species's full protection under Brazilian law needs validation by the enforcers; and an initiative to preserve forest and its rich birdlife at Pedra Branca (Bananeira) needs urgent impetus (see Measures Proposed and Remarks under Alagoas Foliage-gleaner *Philydor novaesi*).

REMARKS (1) A suggestion that the Yellow-faced Siskin is probably conspecific with the Andean Siskin *C. spinescens* (Hellmayr 1938) has not found support (Pinto 1944, Meyer de Schauensee 1982, Ridgely and Tudor 1989). (2) The type-locality of this species was originally given as "upper California", but after further clarification Bahia was substituted (Todd 1926). However, the type was received from W. Swainson, who might have secured it on his trip to eastern Brazil (Hellmayr 1938) and it has been suggested that it may have come from Pernambuco, since Swainson did not venture far from the coast in Bahia (Pinto 1944). (3) A suggestion that Venezuelan records may refer to escaped cagebirds (A. B. Altman *in litt.* 1988; also Ridgely and Tudor 1989) requires further consideration, taking into account the fairly large series of 28 specimens (Todd 1926; 24 still in CM and MCZ) obtained by S. M. Klages between 25 April and 23 May 1914 (specimens in CM and MCZ). (4) It is not certain that the untraced Leopoldina was in Bahia. Cabanis (1865-1866) gave the range of the species as Bahia and mentioned two birds from the state, but then added that a skin in Hamburg was labelled "Leopoldina" without clarifying whether a state was given.

WHITE-THROATED JAY *Cyanolyca mirabilis* V[9]

Endemic to the upper cloud- and pine–oak forests of Guerrero and Oaxaca, south-western Mexico, this jay is locally common in undisturbed forest but threatened by widespread habitat destruction.

DISTRIBUTION The White-throated or Omiltemi Jay is endemic to Mexico, being restricted to the Sierra Madre del Sur of Guerrero and to two isolated sierras in Oaxaca. Coordinates in the account below are taken from OG (1956a) for Guerrero and from Binford (1989) for Oaxaca.

Guerrero The species is a permanent resident of the Sierra Madre del Sur in the southern part of the state. The type and most subsequent specimens are from the vicinity of Omiltemi (17°30'N 99°40'W), e.g. 5 km west (specimens in MVZ) and 1 km south-west (Nelson 1903, Hardy 1964). Omiltemi, at between 2,195 and 2,260 m, is a village at the head of a wide canyon on the leeward side of the sierra from the Pacific (Hardy 1964). In the vicinity of Omiltemi, the species has been extensively collected at Cuapango (also referred to as Cuapongo, Coapango, Coapanco and Guapango; specimens in LACM, MCZ, MLZ, MVZ), with one specimen (in AMNH) taken at Puentecilla: the former (and most likely the latter) locality is between Omiltemi and Chilpancingo (A. T. Peterson *in litt.* 1991; see also CETN 1984a). Recent specimens (May and September 1985) taken in the vicinity of Omiltemi come from Cañada de Agua Fría, "camino a Conejos" and Las Joyas (Navarro *et al.* 1991). East of Omiltemi, specimens (in FMNH, LSUMZ, MVZ) come from "Chilpancingo" (17°33'N 99°30'W) and at 1,525 m in the "mountains near" Chilpancingo (specimens in MVZ). The records from "Chilpancingo" need to be qualified, as these collections were made by W. W. Brown who lived in the town and frequently collected in the mountains to the west; consequently, the specimens probably came from nearer Omiltemi (A. T. Peterson *in litt.* 1991). West of this area records are from numerous localities along the road between El Jilguero and Paraiso (the Atoyac de Alvarez–Chilpancingo road) (Ceballos-Lascurain 1989), including 12 km south of Filo de Caballo (Ceballos-Lascurain 1989, S. N. G. Howell *in litt.* 1991), and Cerro Teotepec (17°27'N 100°10'W), probably from the lower parts of the slopes of the Sierra de Atoyac (A. T. Peterson *in litt.* 1991) to as high as 3,500 m (Miller *et al.* 1957), with specimens collected in May and June 1947 (in LACM, MLZ). Near Cerro Teotepec, records come from c.15 km (by road) north of Nueva Delhi at c.2,075 m (S. N. G. Howell *in litt.* 1991), and more generally from cloud-forest at 1,800 m to the top of Cerro Teotepec (A. G. Navarro and A. T. Peterson *in litt.* 1991), specific localities (a number of which are represented by specimens taken in 1983) including La Golondrina (13 km north-north-east of Paraiso, at 1,800 m), El Descanso (2 km south-west of Puerto El Gallo, at 2,000 m), El Iris (3 km north-east of Puerto El Gallo, at 2,200 m) and Puerto El Gallo (15.5 km north-north-east of Paraiso, at 2,500 m) (Navarro *et al.* 1991, Navarro 1992).

Oaxaca The White-throated Jay is a permanent resident in Sierras de Miahuatlán and de Yucuyacua (Binford 1989), but is apparently recorded from just three localities, these being: 1.5 km north of San Andrés Chicahuaxtla (17°11'N 97°53'W), near the highest point on the Putla de Guerrero road (three specimens taken May 1964 in LSUMZ); río Molino, 3 km south-west of San Miguel Suchixtepec at its intersection with the Puerto Angel road (16°04'N 96°28'W; specimens taken April 1962 and November 1964 in AMNH, DMNH); río Guajolote, 8 km south of San Miguel Suchixtepec at its intersection with the Puerto Angel road, between ríos Molino and Jalatengo (16°00'N 96°28'W; specimen taken November 1964 in DMNH; see also Phillips 1966, Rowley 1966, Binford 1989).

POPULATION Despite the large numbers of specimens of White-throated Jay that have been collected, very little has been published regarding the population of the species, although it is apparently not uncommon in what habitat remains in Guerrero (S. N. G. Howell *in litt.* 1987; see Threats).

Guerrero The species is locally common in the Sierra Madre del Sur (in Guerrero) (Miller *et al.* 1957), and in the vicinity of Omiltemi this certainly appeared to be the case, with c.70 specimens (in MCZ, MLZ, MVZ) taken at Cuapango during 1936-1941, and over 190 (in ANSP, BMNH, CAS, DMNH, LSUMZ, MCZ, MLZ, WFVZ) taken at Omiltemi itself in the period 1943–1953 (a maximum of 10 taken in five days May 1945, and c.50 during 1949). In July 1963, Hardy (1964) made two observations of pairs and one of a group of three or four birds c.1 km south-west of the village. While Phillips (1986) says that here it "now seems scarce" at Omiltemi (his field experience does not appear to be recent), recently it has been found common on the humid slopes above the village (several groups seen daily: A. T. Peterson *in litt.* 1991), and it persists in good numbers within the Omiltemi State Ecological Reserve (A. G. Navarro *in litt.* 1991). Elsewhere, 12 specimens were taken in eight days during May and June 1947 at Cerro Teotepec (nine males, three females in LACM, MLZ), and flocks of c.6 birds were readily found along the road between Puerto el Gallo and Paraiso (Ceballos-Lascurain 1989). Clearly from this evidence, the White-throated Jay was not rare at the few localities where it was collected, and is still seemingly common at Omiltemi, fairly common just north of Nueva Delhi, and common between Nueva Delhi and Cerro Teotepec (S. N. G. Howell *in litt.* 1991, A. T. Peterson *in litt.* 1991).

Oaxaca The White-throated Jay was (in 1964) common at the San Andrés Chicahuaxtla site, where 13 were seen on 24 May, but very uncommon or rare at ríos Molino and Guajolote (Binford 1989, L. C. Binford *in litt.* 1991). There are seemingly only seven specimens from Oaxaca, all taken in 1962 and 1964 (in AMNH, DMNH, LSUMZ).

ECOLOGY Despite its small range and localized distribution, the White-throated Jay apparently has a wide ecological tolerance: near Omiltemi, two pairs and a small flock were seen in much disturbed pine–oak woodland, but the species was also found to range into dense humid forest lacking pine and resembling cloud-forest (except for the lack of tree-ferns and sweetgum); also in these mountains the species inhabits fir forests which appear at c.2,700 m (Hardy 1964). Other reports identify the habitat as humid pine–oak forest and possibly cloud-forest (Binford 1989); oak forest (Blake 1953); and cloud-forest (Phillips 1986). The habitat at San Andrés Chicahuaxtla was described as a high pine–oak association within the cloud-forest, and at río Molino as a pine–oak association in what was formerly a semi-cloud-forest area (Rowley 1966). In Guerrero it seems that the bird is clearly restricted to undisturbed cloud- and pine–oak forest, generally above 1,800 m (although below this altitude the cloud-forest has been almost completely cultivated: see Threats) (Navarro 1992). In Guerrero during June 1986, pairs were seen in mixed-species flocks including Unicoloured Jays *Aphelocoma unicolor* and Emerald Toucanets *Aulacorhynchus prasinus*, although no White-throated Jays were seen there in December (and no Unicoloured Jays in January) suggesting that at least local seasonal movements might occur (S. N. G. Howell *in litt.* 1991); however, fieldwork in all months (other than December) in suitable habitat suggests that the birds may be resident (A. G. Navarro *in litt.* 1991). Pairs and a group of three to four birds were observed near Omiltemi in July (Hardy 1964), and S. N. G. Howell (*in litt.* 1991) reported that they can occur in flocks of six to eight birds, often as part of mixed-species flocks. Specimens have been taken between 1,525 and 3,500 m in Guerrero, and between c.2,000 and 2,600 m in Oaxaca. Nothing has been reported concerning diet, but breeding has been recorded during May and June at Cerro Teotepec (Miller *et al.* 1957); eggs were noted in April, May and June at Omiltemi, and in August at Chilpancingo, breeding being recorded in June and July at Cuapongo (specimens in MVZ).

THREATS The habitat of this species within its restricted, local range is being cleared and rapidly grazed out (S. N. G. Howell in litt. 1987; see Population). Just north of San Andrés Chicahuaxtla, Rowley (1966) noted that the vegetation, a high pine–oak association in cloud-forest, was being destroyed rapidly by the agricultural practices of the Trique Indians who inhabit this area; a similar situation obtained at río Molino where the forest was being cut rapidly and burnt out for agriculture. Between Atoyac and Teotepec, the semi-deciduous forest at the base of the range (important for the Short-crested Coquette *Lophornis brachylopha*) is being rapidly cleared for cultivation of maize, fruit and coffee; the cloud-forest zone (important for White-throated Jay and the White-tailed Hummingbird *Eupherusa poliocerca*) has been almost completely cultivated for coffee below 1,800 m (with undisturbed forest only on the steepest slopes); and the higher altitude forests of pine–oak and fir (important for this jay) are being cut for timber at an alarming rate (Navarro 1992). The extensive collections of W. W. Brown may also have contributed to the scarcity of this species in certain areas (A. G. Navarro *in litt.* 1991).

MEASURES TAKEN In 1963, the pine–oak woodland near Omiltemi was noted as greatly disturbed and altered by lumbering (Hardy 1964), although at about this time lumbering was stopped to protect the watershed that supplied Chilpancingo, the result being that the forest there has regenerated (A. T. Peterson *in litt.* 1991). Around Omiltemi, the main conservation area is the Omiltemi State Ecological Park (embracing 9,600 ha, and supported by the government of the state of Guerrero), the main objective of which is to preserve the Omiltemi watershed but which also harbours good numbers of this jay and the White-tailed Hummingbird (see relevant account) (Navarro and Muñoz 1990, A. G. Navarro and A. T. Peterson *in litt.* 1991).

MEASURES PROPOSED An extension of the park (mentioned above) over the mountains to the lowlands of the Sierra de Atoyac has already been suggested in various reports (A. T. Peterson *in litt.* 1991), and this is clearly the best way in which the three threatened endemics can be preserved. Surveys are needed in suitable remaining habitat in the Sierra Madre del Sur (especially west of Nueva Delhi, in the Atoyac drainage and north of Tecpan: A. T. Peterson *in litt.* 1991) and the Sierras de Miahuatlán and Yucuyacua. It is imperative that protection from agricultural encroachment be given to the remaining areas where the species is currently known to occur, especially around Omiltemi, between Nueva Delhi and Cerro Teotepec, and near San Andrés Chicahuaxtla. Special consideration should be given to the protection of localities where this species occurs on the same slopes as the Short-crested Coquette, White-tailed Hummingbird or Oaxaca Hummingbird *E. cyanophrys* (see relevant accounts, also Remarks), e.g. along the Atoyac de Alvarez–Chilpancingo road, the Puerto Angel road, the Putla de Guerrero road and around Omiltemi. The recommended surveys and proposed protected areas must incorporate the requirements of these hummingbirds, but should also consider the recently described White-fronted Swift *Cypseloides storeri*, which is only currently recorded from Tacámbaro in Michoacán and the Sierra de Atoyac in Guerrero, and although probably not threatened (presumably nesting in rocky canyons, etc.), remains virtually unknown (Navarro *et al.* 1992).

REMARKS The altitudinal ranges of the White-tailed Hummingbird and White-throated Jay overlap, and the two species have been noted occurring sympatrically near Puerto el Gallo (Ceballos-Lascurain 1989, Navarro 1992).

DWARF JAY *Cyanolyca nana* E[2]

Known only from temperate zone forests in Veracruz and Oaxaca, Mexico, this rare jay is currently to be found in just one area of Oaxaca, and has apparently been extirpated from much of its historical range by widespread habitat destruction and fragmentation.

DISTRIBUTION The Dwarf Jay is endemic to south-eastern Mexico in the mountains on the Veracruz side of the border with Puebla, and in the sierras de Juárez, Aloapaneca and Zempoaltepec, Oaxaca. AOU (1983) listed the species also for Puebla, but there seems to be no evidence for this. A specimen reportedly from the state of México is not considered here (see Remarks). Unless otherwise stated, coordinates for Veracruz are from OG (1956a) and for Oaxaca from Binford (1989).

Veracruz Localities are from two general areas where the high mountains of central Puebla extend into Veracruz. The northernmost area of the species's range includes Cofre de Perote (19°29'N 97°08'W), where two males were collected in July 1888 (in BMNH), and Las Vigas–Jalapa. Jalapa is a locality given on specimens in ANSP and BMNH, Sclater (1857a, 1859a) qualifying this as in the "vicinity of" or within the "environs of" Jalapa. Las Vigas (19°38'N 97°05'W), where a male (in BMNH) was taken during August 1888, is situated in "pine forest, devoid of undergrowth" at 2,440 m (Chapman 1898), the specimen presumably being taken slightly lower within the pine–oak association (see Ecology). Further south in Veracruz, the situation is similarly confused by poor labelling of skins. A specimen (in BMNH) taken reportedly at Córdoba by R. Montes de Oca (who was responsible for most of the specimens labelled "Jalapa": see Chapman 1898) seems unlikely, as Córdoba lies below 1,000 m and the bird was probably therefore collected nearer to Orizaba. Two specimens (in USNM) are labelled Orizaba, but both have other locality names, both untraced: one in December (year unknown) from "C. de Sepuxtlan", the other in October 1864 from "Mt. Azul". More recently (1942), specimens (in MLZ; see also Hardy 1971) have been taken at La Puerta; La Puerta remains untraced, but is situated somewhere at the top of the Acultzingo grade, c.50-55 km south-west of Orizaba, the distances quoted here being presumably by road, as the evidence from the coordinates is that Orizaba (18°51'N 97°06'W) and Acultzingo (18°43'N 97°19'W) are c.30 km apart. La Puerta is thus situated somewhere near the Puebla–Veracruz border but, according to the specimen and Hardy (1971), is still just within Veracruz state (apparently along route 150).

Oaxaca In the Sierra de Juárez, a male (in USNM) was collected in October 1894 at Reyes (Santos Reyes Pábalo at 17°51'N 96°52'W: Binford 1989), and a male and female (in BMNH) were taken in April 1961, at the highest pass, 60 road km south-west of Valle Nacional (L. C. Binford *in litt.* 1991); a female (in SWC) was taken "on the road to Valle Nacional from Ciudad Oaxaca" in January 1968; and another female (in MLZ) was collected 3 km west of km 211 on route 175 (untraced) in July 1963. South from here is the Sierra de Aloapaneca, where the species has been recorded exclusively in the vicinity of Cerro San Felipe. The localities involved are Cerro San Felipe (17°10'N 96°40'W), La Cumbre (part of Cerro San Felipe, near km 20), and various points in-between (see Short 1961, Hardy 1971; specimens in AMNH, CAS, LSUMZ, MLZ, MVZ, WFVZ). More generally, the species has been recorded in temperate forest near route 175 from Ciudad Oaxaca into Veracruz (Hardy 1964). The south-easternmost area in the Dwarf Jay's range is the Sierra de Zempoaltepec. Most specimens were collected in April and May 1942 near Totontepec (17°13' 96°03'), a village on the north-west slope of Cerro Zempoaltepec (in AMNH, CM, DMNH, FMNH, LACM, MLZ, MNHUK, ROM). Older records (specimens taken July 1894, in USNM) are more generally from Cerro Zempoaltepec, seemingly on the west slope of the mountain between 2,350 m and 3,200 m (Binford 1989, L. C. Binford *in litt.* 1991). Llano Verde, a collecting locality mentioned by Sclater (1859b), is untraced but apparently either in the Sierra de Juárez, or Sierra de Zempoaltepec (see Binford 1989; L. C. Binford *in litt.* 1991), but probably in the former (A. G. Navarro and A. T. Peterson *in litt.* 1991).

POPULATION Very little is known about the population of this species, especially in the Veracruz part of its range, Peterson and Chalif (1973) simply considering it rare.

Veracruz Writing before the La Puerta records were made (see Distribution), Loetscher (1941) regarded the species as a little known and apparently rare resident, having not been found in Veracruz for at least 50 years. A juvenile, two females and a male were taken in July 1942 at La Puerta, but another 50 years have now passed with no records from this state, AOU (1983) concluding that the species was resident at least formerly in the mountains of Veracruz, but is now possibly extinct there. Extensive habitat destruction at Jico, Jico Viejo, Ticuahutipan, Teocelo, etc., make it almost certain that this jay is no longer present within the state, unless they range higher into pine–fir forest than is generally thought (A. G. Navarro and A. T. Peterson *in litt.* 1991).

Oaxaca The Dwarf Jay was noted as a fairly common permanent resident (Binford 1989), although apparently very localized in its distribution (but see below). Population data come almost exclusively from the Cerro San Felipe area, c.12 km north-north-east of Ciudad Oaxaca. Between La Cumbre and Cerro San Felipe, Short (1961) made a number of observations of post-breeding flocks: on 28 August 1954, 12 Dwarf Jays were seen within a mixed-species flock in a small valley, two being seen 1.5 km north later in the day; next day, in the same area (within 2-3 km), three mixed-species flocks were located in which were four, 5-6, and 10-12 Dwarf Jays respectively. On three days over 4-8 July 1963 at Cerro San Felipe, Hardy (1971) observed flocks of 5-10 birds (associated with other species: see Ecology). Also on Cerro San Felipe, Hardy (1971) located active nests in three consecutive years: five in 1965, three in 1966 and two in 1967. At the same site, four nests were found in or near four 100 m^2 quadrats within second-growth *Quercus rugosa–Q. laurina* association (Hardy 1971). Hardy (1971) considered the density of nesting Dwarf Jays at Cerro San Felipe to be the lowest in this (oak) association (in comparison to other associations where the species was found nesting), the four pairs being completely free of interference from other pairs within their territories. The species was found to be more abundant in the pine–oak–fir association at 2,800 m, where other individuals could frequently be heard calling whilst activities at nests in these areas were being observed (Hardy 1971). By walking no more than 90 m from a nest-site, other jays were found foraging, some of which seemed to be non-breeders travelling in flocks of four or five birds, but others occurred regularly in certain nearby places, singly or in pairs, and were probably established breeders (Hardy 1971). Dwarf Jays were easily found and common in this area during the 1980s and December 1990 (S. N. G. Howell *in litt.* 1991). All of this information suggests that there is a substantial breeding population of Dwarf Jays in the Cerro San Felipe area, the species being quite common in suitable habitat, which is however suffering from increasing destruction (A. G. Navarro and A. T. Peterson *in litt.* 1991). The only available data from Totontepec, c.75 km east of Cerro San Felipe, is that 16 females and 20 males were collected there purportedly during April and May 1942 (in AMNH, CM, DMNH, FMNH, LACM, MLZ, MNHUK), suggesting that here, too, the species was quite common. Recent fieldwork by ornithologists (from MZFC) in Sierra de Juaréz produced no evidence of the species, and more limited work in the Sierra de Zempoaltepec also failed to locate the bird, almost all recent records coming from the vicinity of Cerro San Felipe (A. G. Navarro and A. T. Peterson *in litt.* 1991).

ECOLOGY The Dwarf Jay is a permanent resident in the humid montane forest of the temperate zone (see below: Goodwin 1976, AOU 1983). In the Cerro San Felipe area, it has been recorded at altitudes of between 2,440 and 3,050 m (Hardy 1964; specimens in AMNH, LSUMZ). Totontepec is situated at c.1,850 m, specimens here probably coming from above the village (in the upper cloud-forest and pine–oak zone), as this altitude is the lower limit of the temperate zone (in lower cloud-forest) (Hardy 1971, A. G. Navarro and A. T. Peterson *in litt.* 1991), the lower limit in Veracruz (of the "humid alpine zone") being c.1,670 m (Chapman 1898). The range of "1,525 m up" given by Miller *et al.* (1957) seems particularly low.

The Dwarf Jay has been observed in a number of humid montane forest associations where oak (*Quercus* spp.), pine (*Pinus* spp.) and fir (*Abies* spp.) variously make up the dominant tree species (Hardy 1971). One of these associations, where four nests were found in 1965, consisted of *Quercus rugosa* and *Q. laurina*, with fir and pine species as scattered components of the layers below the canopy; this particular association was found on the drier slopes and near the crests of ridges above 1,830 m (Hardy 1971). However, of the associations where Dwarf Jay occurred, it was sparsest in the *Quercus*, being more abundant in the pine–oak–fir habitat at c.2,800 m (see Population; Hardy 1971); areas of "equal pine and oak" are also favoured (Hardy 1964). Laurel *Litsea* spp. are also a characteristic of these associations, as is an abundant epiphytic growth of lichens, mosses and ferns (Hardy 1971). Birds were found rarely to enter the open pine forest, although one was seen to forage briefly this habitat (Hardy 1971). In early April, Dwarf Jays were occasionally seen foraging in the uppermost parts of the subtropical zone in barrancas near Cerro San Felipe: this habitat is very different in character to the pine–oak–fir association, and after nest-building was completed no jays were seen so low, breeding certainly not occurring in this zone (Hardy 1971).

The species is not restricted to undisturbed forest, frequently being found in secondary growth, as long as the preferred tree associations predominate and tracts of primary forest are nearby (Hardy 1971; see Threats). The necessary constituent of Dwarf Jay breeding habitat is a prominent subcanopy (formed by the crowns of the tallest second-layer trees and the lower branches of primary canopy trees), the primary canopy being sufficiently open to allow the development of a dense second-layer (Hardy 1971). Over 80% of foraging time is spent from the bottom of the subcanopy to the top of the shrub layer, during which invertebrates are gleaned (Coleoptera, Diptera, Hymenoptera, insect larvae and eggs have all been recorded) from and around epiphytes (Hardy 1971). Dwarf Jays occasionally enter the subcanopy but do not often forage at these upper levels (Hardy 1971).

At Cerro San Felipe, the breeding season starts in early April, when feeding flocks break up and territorial aggression, courtship feeding and nest-building begin (Hardy 1971). Between 1965 and 1967, a nearly complete nest was seen on 4 April, eggs (clutch-size three) recorded between 12 April and 5 May, with young found in the nest 16 May: of the 10 nests found during this period, all were in *Quercus* species situated either in the crown/subcrown, or on the end of a branch at 3-15 m high (averaging 7 m), i.e. all nests were in the second-layer vegetation (Hardy 1971). Two "prejuveniles" were collected at Totontepec, supposedly on 12 and 18 April 1942 (in MLZ), Hardy (1971) suggesting that they may represent an early season, but Binford (1989) concluding that the dates are probably erroneous (due to the known unreliability of M. del Toro Aviles's data); however, a male specimen apparently carrying insects and feeding young, taken on 3 April 1948 at La Cumbre (in MVZ), indicates that breeding may indeed start earlier in the year, apparently coinciding with the end of the dry season (A. G. Navarro and A. T. Peterson *in litt.* 1991). Feeding of young has also been noted as late as 21 June (1966) at Cerro San Felipe (Binford 1989), although all breeding activity appears to cease before early July (Hardy 1971).

In the non-breeding season, Dwarf Jays move about and forage in loose aggregations of 4-10 individuals, which in turn are part of mixed-species flocks (Hardy 1971). At the end of August such flocks, travelling up to 1.5 km in several hours, contained 2-12 Dwarf Jays, the main constituent species being Grey-barred Wrens *Campylorhynchus megalopterus* and Spot-crowned Woodcreepers *Lepidocolaptes affinis* (Short 1961). Between December and March, these mixed-species flocks have been recorded comprising mainly Steller's Jays *Cyanocitta stelleri*, Grey-barred Wrens, woodcreepers and orioles *Icterus* spp. (S. N. G. Howell *in litt.* 1991). The onset of the breeding season is evident in the pairing of individuals, small groups or pairs being present in breeding habitat in the mornings when courtship and nest-building occurs, the birds moving to forage in the barrancas until evening (Hardy 1971). This pattern continues until eggs are laid, flocks reforming when the young are fully independent of their parents, in early July (Hardy 1971).

THREATS The humid pine–oak forests of Oaxaca in which the Dwarf Jay lives have suffered greatly from clearance, small farm agriculture and other pressures of human activity; the species seems to exist only where most of the forest is of climax tree species (Hardy 1971; see Ecology). At Cerro San Felipe, Hardy (1971) noted evidence of the larger trees having been removed from a number of his study sites, stating that where disturbance has been especially severe, the basic character of the vegetation is so completely altered that only remnant components of the original avifauna (not including Dwarf Jay) persist. Human disturbance at the nest-site led to the immediate desertion of the nest, this reaction suggesting that either the species has few predators or when disturbance does occur it is almost always by a predator that robs the nest, removing any reason for the birds to return to it (Hardy 1971). Damage to the habitat at Cerro San Felipe is apparently increasing, and the lack of recent observations of the bird from areas in the Sierras de Juárez and Zempoaltepec (in fact almost anywhere in Oaxaca other than Cerro San Felipe) must surely be cause for concern (see Population). Extensive habitat destruction and fragmentation in Veracruz has probably led to the species's extinction there (A. G. Navarro and A. T. Peterson *in litt.* 1991).

MEASURES TAKEN There are four national parks within the immediate range of the species, three in Veracruz, one in Oaxaca. In Veracruz, Cofre de Perote is a national park although agricultural practices are carried out in at least part of the area (Vargas Márquez 1984) and the jay has apparently not been seen there since 1888 (see Distribution). Further south in the state is the Cañon del Río Blanco National Park (55,690 ha), situated along route 150 from Orizaba to the Puebla border (Anon. 1989) and apparently covering the La Puerta population last recorded in 1942 (see Population). The Pico de Orizaba National Park (19,750 ha, straddling the Puebla–Veracruz border: Anon. 1989) may well incorporate the Orizaba/Córdoba localities where the species was collected in the late 1800s (see Distribution). Despite these, the Dwarf Jay has not been seen in Veracruz for over 50 years, and it seems that it may already be extinct there (A. G. Navarro and A. T. Peterson *in litt.* 1991). In Oaxaca, the species may occur within the Benito Juárez National Park, which is apparently situated just north of Cerro San Felipe, covering 2,737 ha (Anon. 1989); however, this protected area was apparently never officially approved, has no borders, no staff, and appears to be a classic "paper park"; meanwhile, no highland habitat (suitable for this species) is protected within Oaxaca, and Cerro San Felipe is in constant danger from logging operations (A. G. Navarro and A. T. Peterson *in litt.* 1991: see Threats).

MEASURES PROPOSED Almost all recent records of the Dwarf Jay have come from the Cerro San Felipe area, although its presence in the adjacent Benito Juárez National Park still needs to be confirmed (but see Measures Taken), suggesting that a suitable measure would be to extend the park by incorporating this area (and by giving the park itself full status and support): the protection of forest on and around Cerro San Felipe is by far the highest priority to ensure the continued survival of this jay. Basic surveys in the Sierra de Juárez and on Cerro Zempoaltepec have already drawn blank (A. G. Navarro and A. T. Peterson *in litt.* 1991); however, it is still possible that habitat suitable for this species may be found in these areas (e.g. by aerial surveys), and these forests will need to be investigated for viable populations. The status of the species in Veracruz (and its parks) needs to be confirmed, although it seems likely that it now only survives within Oaxaca (see Population).

REMARKS A specimen collected in 1867 (in BMNH) is apparently from "near Mexico City", and has led to the inclusion of México state in the range of the species (Salvin and Godman 1888-1904, hence Ridgway 1904, Hellmayr 1934, Miller *et al.* 1957, Goodwin 1976). AOU (1983) suggested that the report from this state is open to question, a conclusion that seems justified owing to the large distance between here and the Veracruz part of the species's range.

APPENDIX A

Threatened birds of North America and the "Neotropical Pacific": summary accounts

TOWNSEND'S SHEARWATER *Puffinus auricularis* I[7]

An endemic breeder to the Revillagigedo Islands (c.650 km west of the Mexican state of Colima), Mexico, Townsend's Shearwater faces problems on all three of the islands where it is known to have bred (for a detailed description of its biology see Jehl 1982). On Isla Clarión, numerous unoccupied burrows were found in several areas of the highlands in January 1986 (Everett 1988); in February 1988 c.80 birds were seen on the approach to the island, but on land all the nest-sites found were marked by severe pig rooting, and numerous shearwater remains littered the destroyed burrows (Howell and Webb 1989b, 1990); and by May 1990, all burrows found were old and occupied by rabbits or destroyed by pigs, with neither bones nor feathers seen and only a few birds noted at night (Santaella and Sada 1991). Domestic pigs were introduced shortly after 1979 (Everett and Anderson 1991), and it now appears that the birds have all but abandoned the island in response (Santaella and Sada 1991). On Socorro, the species was common in April 1981 when hundreds were seen at 500 to 650 m (evidently the altitude of the major breeding sites) (Jehl and Parkes 1982): the population at this time was estimated at 1,000 pairs (Jehl 1982), although no nests were found in the many burrows checked (Jehl and Parkes 1982). In February 1988, c.550 birds were seen 1-4 km off the north-west side of the island (Howell and Webb 1990, S. N. G. Howell *in litt.* 1991). What appeared to be a "healthy" breeding population of this species was found in the northern forests during 1990 (L. F. Baptista *in litt.* 1992), but although Santaella and Sada (1991) knew of the "three colonies" recently found in the north, they found no evidence of breeding in May 1990. The remains of four shearwaters (almost certainly killed by feral cats) were found close to the path up Cerro Everman in April 1981, and although the number of kills was small, it was suspected that the carnage away from the trail was extensive (Jehl and Parkes 1982): feral cats occur up to the peak of Cerro Everman (S. N. G. Howell *in litt.* 1991). Townsend's Shearwater bred on Isla San Benedicto until the devastating volcanic eruption of 1952 (Jehl 1982): in February 1988, 11 birds were seen just a few kilometres north of the island, although no nesting burrows were seen (Howell and Webb 1990), and in May 1990 up to 20 birds were again seen at the north end, suggesting that the species may be recolonizing (Santaella and Sada 1991); however, none was found in April 1992 (although this survey was not comprehensive: S. N. G. Howell *in litt.* 1992). Obviously the major threats to this species are feral cats on Socorro and pigs on Clarión: measures need to be taken immediately to eradicate the populations of both species, and should be combined with surveys of the shearwater at each of its breeding colonies.

PINK-FOOTED SHEARWATER *Puffinus creatopus* V/R[10]

Breeding only on Isla Robinson Crusoe and Isla Santa Clara, Juan Fernández Islands, and Isla Mocha (38°22'S 73°56'W; 33 km from the coast of Arauco province: Paynter 1988), Chile, the Pink-footed Shearwater migrates north to western North America where it is present from April to November (Harrison 1983, Schlatter 1984). On Isla Robinson Crusoe, the main colony is on the north-west coast, the total population there (in 1986) being a few thousand pairs (Brooke 1987). On Isla Santa Clara (223 ha), there were 10 main clusters of burrows (covering 30-40% of the island), each with 100-400 burrows, and the population in 1986 (and in 1991) was estimated at 2,000-3,000 pairs (Brooke 1987, M. Pearman *in litt.* 1991). The status on Isla Mocha is unknown. Schlatter (1984) suggested that the species is decreasing in number. The birds arrive at the colonies during November–December, eggs being laid in December–January with fledging and dispersal (to the coast of North America) during March–April (Harrison 1983, Brooke 1987). Nesting on Isla Robinson Crusoe was noted in burrows scattered throughout a badly eroded, sparsely vegetated region between 150 and 300 m (Brooke 1987). Although Schlatter (1984) indicated that the numbers of this shearwater are decreasing, he did not identify any threats: however, coatis *Nasua narica* and feral cats occur throughout Isla Robinson Crusoe (Schlatter 1984) and presumably prey on this species. Isla Santa Clara is uninhabited by humans, and is apparently free of predatory animals (M. Pearman *in litt.* 1991). The Juan Fernández group is a national park, and included in the World Heritage list, although it is clear that much conservation action is required on the islands (Schlatter 1984). Predator control should be undertaken by local authorities but with specialist advice and assistance to eradicate coatis and feral cats (also goats and rabbits), and surveys are needed to determine the distribution and density of this species (Schlatter 1984) and the extent to which it is succumbing to predators: actions on these islands should also consider the threatened Defilippe's Petrel *Pterodroma defilippiana*. Isla Mocha (or at least part of it) should be declared a national park or strictly protected (Schlatter 1984).

DEFILIPPE'S PETREL *Pterodroma defilippiana* V[9]

Defilippe's Petrel is an endemic breeder on the Desventuradas and Juan Fernández Islands, Chile. In the Desventuradas Islands, nesting has been recorded on San Ambrosio (and González islet) where in 1962 Millie (1963) found a cavern containing 300-400 birds, but where in 1970 Jehl (1973) noted the cliffs to be teeming with 10,000 or more birds. Birds also nest on San Félix, but Jehl (1973) estimated just 150-200 pairs there in 1970. Schlatter (1984) suggested that the population on the Desventuradas was more or less 400 individuals, but this obviously did not take into account the evidence from 1970. Within the Juan Fernández archipelago, birds have been found nesting on Isla Robinson Crusoe, although the population is now very small (if indeed it still exists) (M. Pearman *in litt.* 1991). On the adjacent but much smaller (223 ha) Isla Santa Clara, Brooke (1987) suggested a population in 1986 of "hundreds, possibly thousands"; however, in 1991 M. Pearman (*in litt.* 1991) found that suitable nesting habitat was limited to 10% of the island and estimated a population of 100-200 individuals. Schlatter (1984) asserted that the population is decreasing. In the Desventuradas Islands, the breeding season runs from July to December (Millie 1963), Jehl (1973) noting birds courting and setting up territories in June: eggs have been found in August, and most pairs have young during October (on San Ambrosio), although they have been reported as late as February on San Félix (Millie 1963, Jehl 1973). On the Juan Fernández Islands, displaying starts in June, but breeding commences in August and September (Jehl 1973, Brooke 1987): nestlings have been found in November, and by early January nest-sites have been vacated (Brooke 1987, M. Pearman *in litt.* 1991). Nests are built on ledges, under rocks, in crevices, on cliffs, in caves, or in simple scrapes in vegetation (Millie 1963, Jehl 1973). Feral cats were apparently introduced on Isla San Félix prior to 1960, and have caused extensive mortality: although no cats were seen in 1970, the remains of many dead petrels were discovered (Jehl 1973). It seems unlikely that there are predators on San Ambrosio, but there is now apparently a human settlement on one of the islands (Schlatter 1984), and this may have severe implications. Schlatter (1984) also cited rats as predator, but on which island is unknown. This petrel has almost been eradicated from Isla Robinson Crusoe due to predation by introduced coatis *Nasua narica* and feral cats, but Isla Santa Clara is apparently predator-free (Schlatter 1984, M. Pearman *in litt.* 1991). Conservation measures relevant to the Juan Fernández Islands are briefly discussed under Pink-footed Shearwater *Puffinus creatopus*. As the stronghold for the species, the Desventuradas Islands must be protected from further introduction of predators, and those that are already present must be eliminated before the population suffers any further. Surveys to determine the population and local distribution of the bird are needed.

DARK-RUMPED PETREL *Pterodroma phaeopygia* (E)[5]

Existing as two distinct subspecies, the Dark-rumped Petrel breeds in Hawaii and the Galápagos archipelagos. Major sources of information referring to this species, and those used in the following account, are Harris (1970, 1973), Bell and Keith (1983), Coulter *et al.* (1985a,b), Simons (1985), Tomkins (1985), Hayes and Baker (1989) and Podolsky and Kress (1992). In the Galápagos archipelago nominate *phaeopygia* breeds in the highlands of Santa Cruz, Santiago, Floreana and San Cristóbal (and probably Isabela), being most frequently encountered at sea between Isabela and Santa Cruz. The breeding population on Galápagos has been estimated at c.9,000 pairs on Santa Cruz and 1,000 pairs on Floreana (in 1980; but see Tomkins 1985), the population on Floreana being c.1,900 birds in 1981 (1,500 of which were in one area on Cerro Pajas): the populations on these two islands (in 1981) were calculated to have been declining at 33% per year over the previous four years and in 1982 the Floreana population had declined by another 27%, primarily due to low reproductive success (5% on Santa Cruz and 15-30% on Floreana) and to a lesser extent adult mortality on the breeding grounds, both attributable to introduced mammalian predators. Breeding seasons vary between island populations, nests being burrowed in the highlands at low density amongst vegetation: just one egg is laid which, if lost, will not be replaced. Feeding ecology and food are described by Imber *et al.* (1992). The subspecies in Hawaii (*sandwichensis*) was once common with large colonies on all the main islands: numbers are now reduced to several small relict populations totalling c.900 pairs (of which c.50% are breeding adults), 85% of which are in or around Haleakala National Park on Maui (see Simons 1985). This petrel is threatened by clearance of nesting areas for agriculture, possibly the invasive introduced plant supirosa *Lantana camara* (see Cruz *et al.* 1986), but primarily (on both Galápagos and Hawaii) by introduced mammalian predators (dogs, cats, pigs, rats), and habitat destruction (including the inadvertent trampling of nest areas) by goats, donkeys, cattle and horses: obviously the degree to which each of these affects the birds varies between islands, predation being especially severe on Santa Cruz. After controlling feral animals and eliminating rat predation at a colony on Floreana, breeding success increased from 34% in 1982 to 70% in 1984, suggesting that a systematic programme of feral mammal control is the only effective way to ensure long-term survival and allow recovery to natural conditions. Rats (*Rattus rattus* and *R. norvegicus*) are a continuing and increasing threat that will be impossible to remove on anything other than a local scale. Other proposals for protecting populations, finding new ones, removing feral mammals, etc., are given by Bell and Keith (1983) and Tomkins (1985). Podolsky and Kress (1992) outlined a system using playback to attract first-time breeders to artificial burrow clusters that would be more easily protected.

GUADALUPE STORM-PETREL *Oceanodroma macrodactyla* E/Ex[4]

Only known from Isla de Guadalupe, c.280 km west of northern Baja California, Mexico, the Guadalupe Storm-petrel originally nested in burrows in forested areas at the northern end of the island (this and the following information, unless otherwise stated, comes from Jehl and Everett 1985). The species was abundant in the nesting colony as late as 1906, but the last record was of a breeding bird in August 1912. Searches were undertaken in midsummer 1922, after which it was declared extinct; in April 1925 (but not on the breeding grounds); and during the early 1970s (although not all the forested areas were searched). There has been no thorough survey made in the appropriate season since 1906: recent reports of storm-petrels calling at night, and the apparent persistence of Leach's Storm-petrel *O. leucorhoa* breeding on the island, raises some hope that the Guadalupe Storm-petrel may still exist (also Everett and Anderson 1991). This species nested in burrows amongst the pines *Pinus radiata* var. *binata* at the north end of the island and in the cypress *Cupressus guadalupensis* grove in the north-central part of the island, laying eggs from early March but sometimes as late as June (chicks were found in August 1912). The cypress grove is just a remnant of a formerly large forest, and currently shows no sign of regeneration, but *contra* Jehl and Everett (1985) in 1988 the island was not devoid of vegetation (S. N. G. Howell *in litt.* 1992). The destruction of the island's forests has been caused by thousands of introduced goats, although the main cause of the storm-petrel's demise was presumably heavy predation by domestic cats (also Jehl 1972). Recent measures to reduce or prevent further damage to vegetation have included the removal of 20,000 goats (L. F. Baptista *in litt.* 1991); however, there appears to have been no action taken to control cats, which are still common (S. N. G. Howell *in litt.* 1988). Clearly, surveys need to be targeted on the remaining forest areas at the appropriate time of year (March and April) to determine whether or not this species still exists. A programme aimed at eradicating the feral cat population should in any case be undertaken as this would benefit other species such as the Guadalupe Junco *Junco insularis* (see relevant account).

GALAPAGOS CORMORANT *Nannopterum harrisi* — R[11]

Endemic to the Galápagos archipelago, Ecuador, the Galápagos (Flightless) Cormorant is restricted to c.370 km of coastline on Fernandina and Isabela islands (Harris 1974). The small population is on the whole thriving, and although calculated to be c.700-800 pairs in 1970-1971 (Harris 1974), since 1977 it appears to have remained mostly stable at c.650-800 adult birds (Valle and Coulter 1987), with the adult population estimated at 1,000 individuals in 1986 (Rosenberg *et al.* 1990). There was a sharp c.50% decline in 1983, caused by a reduction in marine productivity resulting from El Niño (and thus causing heavy mortality and a lack of breeding), although since 1984 numbers counted have been similar to the pre-1983 figures (Valle and Coulter 1987, Rosenberg *et al.* 1990). The species's restricted distribution remains essentially unexplained although it appears to be confined to the coldest, richest waters and rarely ventures farther than 100 m from the shore (Harris 1974). Birds nest in small "colonies" of just a few pairs, mainly during the cold season (July to October), thus avoiding heat stress for the chicks or for incubating/guarding parents on land, and taking advantage of the peak marine productivity (Harris 1974, Trillmich *et al.* 1983): however, Harris (1974) suggested that breeding may occur throughout the year, with some pairs nesting twice. The fact that this cormorant is restricted to a small area, is flightless and exhibits no tendencies to disperse (even post-breeding: Harris 1974) renders it extremely vulnerable to changes in its environment, such as human disturbance or oil pollution. The thriving commercial crawfish *Palinurus* sp. fishery (until now caught by divers) has suffered a fall-off in catch owing to over-exploitation, and may lead to a change in fishing methods such as the introduction of nets, which have already been used experimentally in Galápagos (Harris 1974): any use of nets (which have been shown to drown cormorants) near the colonies would greatly deplete the population. Feral dogs on Isabela have justly been cause for concern, although there is no evidence of them influencing cormorant numbers (Coulter 1984), and they have now almost been eradicated. The population of this species must be monitored every year (see Rosenberg *et al.* 1990), human disturbance must be minimized, net fishing must not be allowed within range, and the feral dog population should be completely removed. All these measures should consider the needs of the similarly distributed Galápagos Penguin *Spheniscus mediculus* which, although not exposed to the same degree, is susceptible to the same threats.

CALIFORNIA CONDOR *Gymnogyps californianus* — (E)[5]

Until the late Pleistocene c.11,000 years ago, the California Condor was widely distributed throughout much of North America, from northern Mexico to southern Canada, east across southern U.S.A. to Florida and even up to New York state, being able to thrive in both warm temperate and cold boreal climates; however, about 10,000 years ago the species underwent a period of major decline, coinciding with (and, since its food supply was accordingly reduced, possibly caused by) the extinction of many of the continent's large mammals (Steadman and Miller 1987, Kiff 1990). Condors became confined to the Pacific coast from southern British Columbia, Canada, to northern Baja California, Mexico, and persisted there until a subsequent more rapid decline took place associated with the expansion of the human population (Kiff 1990). Condors were all but absent north of California by 1850, and during the twentieth century the main area of distribution was a U-shaped range in central California in the mountains surrounding the south end of the San Joaquin valley (King 1978-1979). The bird's population in northern Baja California became isolated at about the start of the twentieth century, with no confirmed records since 1937 (the recent history of this population is documented by Wilbur and Kiff 1980). The species declined rapidly during the twentieth century (see Snyder and Johnson 1985 for details of the population during this time), and by April 1985 just nine birds remained in the wild: one of these died, and the remaining eight were captured (the last in April 1987) for a captive breeding programme (Jurek 1990). The lowest point for the species was in 1982, when the total wild and captive population may have numbered just 22 individuals (L. F. Kiff *in litt.* 1992). In 1987, the captive population was 27 birds (including nine wild-caught, one caught in 1967 as a fledgling and 17 removed from wild nests as eggs or nestlings) but by 1991 this had increased to 52, and to 64 by July 1992, the individuals split between San Diego Wild Animal Park and Los Angeles Zoo (Jurek 1990, Ehrlich *et al.* 1992, L. F. Kiff *in litt.* 1992). Details of the ecology of this species are presented at length in Snyder and Snyder (1989), but also in Koford (1953) and Miller *et al.* (1965), with the behaviour of the last 23 wild birds, between 1982 and 1987, discussed by Meretsky and Snyder (1992). It is generally accepted that shooting and lead poisoning (from ingested shot in carrion) have been the single most serious causes of decline, although DDT, other pesticides and poisons may have had a detrimental effect (Kiff 1990; also King 1978-1979). A brief history of conservation and recovery efforts since the 1930s is given by Jurek (1990). In January 1992, two birds were released into Los Padres National Forest (north of Los Angeles), various sites having previously been tested by releasing Andean Condors *Vultur gryphus*, and it is hoped that others can be reintroduced in the winter of 1992-1993 and more each subsequent year: the ultimate aim (by 2020) is to downlist the species to "threatened" by establishing two wild communities of c.150 birds each (each with at least 15 breeding pairs) in the most recent historical range in California, and somewhere else (probably northern Arizona), with insurance stock in Los Angeles and San Diego Zoos (Kiff 1990, *Amer. Birds* 46 [1992]: 13, L. F. Kiff *in litt.* 1992).

GALAPAGOS HAWK *Buteo galapagoensis* **R**[11]

Known only from the Galápagos Islands, Ecuador, the Galápagos Hawk was apparently once common on all the main islands except Tower, Culpepper and Wenman (this and the following information is summarized from Harris, 1973, 1982, Faaborg *et al.* 1980, Faaborg 1984, 1986 and de Vries 1984). The species is now extinct in Floreana and San Cristóbal (although its occurrence on them was questioned by de Vries 1984), and also Seymour, Baltra and Daphne (being very reduced in numbers in Santa Cruz: see below). However, it is apparently still quite common on Santiago, Española, Isabela, Fernandina, Pinta, Marchena and Santa Fé. Some 130 breeding territories are still occupied in Galápagos, with c.50 on Santiago, c.17 on Santa Fé, but only 2-3 left from the previously large population on Santa Cruz. The number of breeding territories does not, however, give an obvious indication of the number of individuals in the population, as the Galápagos Hawk shows cooperative polyandry, in which as many as four males may mate with one female and share a single territory and nest, so that on Santiago, for example, the c.50 territories represent c.180 breeding adults. There is often a large non-breeding, non-territorial population (comprising immatures and adult females) which on Santiago may exceed 100 birds, the total population on the island being possibly as high as 250 individuals. Birds breed in all months of the year but the peak in activity is between May and July, nests of twigs being built on rocky outcrops or in trees. Territories are generally occupied by polyandrous groups (two or more males), monogamous pairs probably representing the remnants of polyandrous groups, as all territorial birds seem to remain on the territories for life. Polyandrous groups produce, on average, more young than monogamous pairs, and territorial breeding birds show a higher yearly survivorship (90%) than non-territorial non-breeding birds (50% or less). Birds feed on a wide variety of sea- and landbirds (especially doves and finches), native and introduced rats, lizards, iguanas, invertebrates and carrion. The availability of suitable food, owing to a reduction caused by introduced predators, may be one cause for the decline and elimination of the hawk from many islands, although human persecution is probably the single most important factor. With such a large non-breeding population, the removal of birds (up to 30 per year would have little effect on even a single year's population level) to reintroduce on islands previously occupied has been proposed, but advised against for ecological reasons (de Vries 1984). Clearly, however, killing of birds must be stopped if populations are to be maintained within the current area of distribution.

WHOOPING CRANE *Grus americana* **(E)**[5]

Whooping Cranes exist in two wild populations and in captivity at three locations: the only self-sustaining wild flock nests in Wood Buffalo National Park, south-western Mackenzie and northern Alberta provinces, Canada, and winters on the central Gulf coast of Texas, U.S.A., at Aransas National Wildlife Refuge, Matagorda Island and adjacent areas (the following information is taken from Lewis 1986 and Ehrlich *et al.* 1992; but see also Doughty 1989). The breeding range was formerly larger, extending south to north Dakota and Iowa, and along the coast of Texas and Louisiana, this latter area also being a former wintering ground as was northern Mexico. Another population was established in 1975 by introducing eggs into the nests of "foster parent" Sandhill Cranes *Grus canadensis* at Gray's Lake National Wildlife Refuge, Idaho, these birds wintering mostly in the Bosque del Apache National Wildlife Refuge along the río Grande in New Mexico. Numbers of the species increased from an all-time low of 15-16 birds in 1941 to 160 (including captives) by 1986: the total current population is assumed to be about 200 individuals, about 50% in the Canadian breeding population (which shows an unexplained 10 year population cycle) and the remainder divided more or less evenly between the Idaho population (which as yet has not bred) and three captive flocks at the Patuxent Wildlife Research Center, Laurel, Maryland, the International Crane Foundation, Baraboo, Wisconsin, and the San Antonio Zoo, Texas (see below). The nesting habitat required by the Whooping Crane consists of freshwater marshes and sloughs around potholes and lake margins and in wet prairies of wilderness wetlands. The Canadian population is at risk of oil and chemical contamination in its small Texas winter range, and the Aransas area in undergoing slow chronic erosion. Historically, the species declined owing to over-hunting (1870s to the 1920s) and habitat loss (especially the conversion of prairie wetlands to agriculture) throughout its range, including stopover sites in Saskatchewan, Colorado and Utah, while more recently the chief cause of death in fledged birds has been collision with overhead powerlines. The Whooping Crane is extremely sensitive to intrusion and human disturbance, especially during in the breeding season. In cooperation with Patuxent, the Canadian Wildlife Service started a captive breeding programme in 1990: reintroduction using subadult birds is scheduled for 1992 at Kissimmee Prairie, Florida. Clearly, the population is being carefully monitored and captive populations sensibly managed; however, the wintering grounds at Aransas require constant monitoring and management to prevent further degradation.

ESKIMO CURLEW *Numenius borealis* **E/Ex[4]**

Formerly breeding in a narrow band across the Northwest Territories, Canada, and possibly in Alaska, U.S.A., the Eskimo Curlew – now virtually extinct – migrated south in autumn along the Atlantic coast (large numbers were occasionally blown onshore in Labrador), across the Caribbean to winter in South America in Uruguay and the southern half of Argentina and Chile (possibly also Paraguay and southern Brazil) (this and subsequent information is summarized from Gollop *et al.* 1986, Gollop 1988 and Faanes and Senner 1991). The spring migration route apparently went through Central America, then following a relatively narrow corridor from the Texas coast north through the plains states in the Missouri–Mississippi river drainages to the prairie provinces in Canada and north-west to the Arctic. Owing primarily to organized hunting during the spring migration (but also in winter and opportunistically in autumn), and also to habitat loss on the wintering grounds of the Argentine pampas and at migration stops in the North American prairies, the originally massive population of Eskimo Curlew was noted to be in decline by the 1870s, had almost disappeared by the 1890s, and has evidently never recovered. Although not recorded every year, the Eskimo Curlew is still regularly reported (although rarely verified by specimen – not that this is desirable – or photographic evidence), mostly in Texas in spring (occurrences in 12 years between 1945 and 1988, with 23 reported in 1981). In four years between 1982 and 1987, 18 birds were recorded, with four apparently reliable reports made in 1987, including two birds together in the Northwest Territories (raising hopes of a breeding pair being located); and four birds were also reported by P. L. Michelutti at the Mar Chiquita, Córdoba, Argentina, in October 1990 (Jaramillo 1992). Nevertheless, the prospects of the species surviving the next 100 years with a population perhaps as low as 50 birds, and without intervention, seem slim. The Eskimo Curlew is protected by law in Canada, U.S.A. and Mexico, and parts of its historical breeding range are within protected areas. In 1987, a recovery plan was devised (advocating captive breeding or propagation using Little Curlews *Numenius minutus*, once a nest could be found), and in 1990 an advisory group was formed. Proposals for the species's conservation are outlined in the above references; however, the fact that its population never recovered, once it became so small that hunting could not be expected to affect it, strongly suggests that a major ecological factor has been in play, rendering all plans and hopes for the species ultimately in vain.

BRISTLE-THIGHED CURLEW *Numenius tahitiensis* **V/R[10]**

This rare wader is only known to breed in the remote mountains of westernmost Alaska, U.S.A., where there appear to be two disjunct core areas: the Nulato hills of south-eastern Norton Sound and the mountains of the west-central Seward Peninsula (this and the following information is summarized from detailed accounts of the species's ecology in McCaffery and Peltola 1986, Gill and Handel 1990, Gill *et al.* 1991, Ehrlich *et al.* 1992, Gill and Redmond 1992). Via staging grounds (where from late June to late August birds spend 2-3 weeks) on the Yukon-Kuskokwim delta (and to a lesser extent on the Nushagak Peninsula in Bristol Bay), the species migrates to winter in the Central and South Pacific (including Laysan Islands, Marquesas and Tuamotu Islands, Fiji, Tonga and Samoa). The breeding population has been recently estimated at c.7,000 birds, although with subadults oversummering in the Pacific (where they remain until nearly three years old), the total population may be as high as 10,000; with population estimates only being made very recently, it is not known if or by how much the population may have declined. Birds are long-lived (more than 22 years has been recorded) and highly faithful to nesting areas, in which, however, they show seasonal variation in habitat preferences, presumably resulting from their dietary needs. Birds nest at the end of May, the species's eggs and young seemingly being very susceptible to avian predators. Habitat preferences on the wintering grounds are described by Gill and Redmond (1992). Adult curlews undergo a flightless moult during the autumn and are then highly vulnerable to predation by introduced cats and dogs (possibly pigs), while residents throughout the Tuamotus have traditionally trapped them for food: thus the distribution and abundance of the species in the Pacific is directly related to human distribution, the distribution of introduced mammals (e.g. the recent eradication of cats from the Line Islands resulted in an increase of curlews; and the annual survival on predator-free Laysan Island is 80-88%), and the availability of habitat. On the Seward Peninsula breeding grounds, birds are potentially threatened by off-road hunting and activities associated with gold-mining; however, the main staging post and Nulato hills breeding area are protected within the Yukon Delta National Wildlife Refuge. Conservation actions already carried out and proposed are outlined by Gill and Handel (1990) and Gill and Redmond (1992), although it is clear that any disturbance to the breeding grounds must be minimized, that subsistence hunting of wintering birds must be discouraged, and that predators in the Pacific should if possible be eradicated.

PIPING PLOVER *Charadrius melodus* **V/R**[10]

The Piping Plover inhabits open beaches, alkali flats and sandflats in North America, breeding primarily along the Atlantic coast from North Carolina, U.S.A., to southern Canada, along rivers and wetlands of the northern Great Plains from Nebraska to the southern prairie provinces and along patches of the western Great Lakes (this and the following information comes from Haig 1992 and Haig and Plissner in press). In winter most individuals are found on coastal beaches and sandflats from the Carolinas to Yucatán, Mexico, with some birds scattering throughout the Bahamas and the West Indies (see Haig 1992 for a detailed analysis). Numerous breeding studies have been conducted across its range, yet habitat requirements and limiting factors remain poorly known (Haig 1992 summarizes current knowledge). Fewer than 2,500 breeding pairs were recorded in 1991, these being geographically split as follows: Canadian prairie 500 pairs; U.S. Great Plains 872; Great Lakes 16; Atlantic coast of Canada 245; Atlantic coast of U.S.A. 701. The northern Great Plains birds may be declining owing to severe drought and inappropriate water management practices; the Atlantic coast populations are maintained via intense predator control and human management; and the Great Lakes numbers continue to decline despite all efforts. Conservation work is well organized in breeding areas across North America, whereas little has been attempted in wintering areas, where potential threats have not yet been assessed. Broad-scale conservation actions include formation of inland and Atlantic Piping Plover recovery teams in the U.S.A. and Canada that set conservation priorities for restoring populations. The bird's survival is increasingly dependent on local conservation efforts and management, including closing portions nesting beaches (and restricting off-road vehicle access), construction of predator exclosures around nests, avian and mammalian predator control, mitigation of water-level control policies, vegetation control and, in some cases, the creation of artificial habitat.

SOCORRO DOVE *Zenaida graysoni* **(E)**[5]

Endemic to Isla Socorro in the Revillagigedo Islands, Mexico, the Socorro Dove (confirmed as a full species by Baptista *et al.* 1983) was last seen in the wild in January 1958 (this and the following information is summarized from Jehl and Parkes 1982, 1983, Baptista 1987, 1991, Baptista *et al.* undated and Santaella and Sada 1991). It was common in forests, especially above 500 m, and observations in March 1957 and January 1958 gave no indication that it was declining, yet there have been no subsequent records despite specific searches in April 1978, 1981 and over a number of years recently; however, there has been no systematic search of the entire island, especially at the remote, heavily wooded northern end, and a few individuals may survive. Fortunately a captive population exists in a relatively healthy state, with c.200 birds held in collections in the U.S.A. and Europe (this is a notable instance where aviculture has, albeit unwittingly, stood directly between a species and extinction; the greater involvement of zoos, and the management of stock according to a CBSG population viability analysis, would now seem highly timely). In the wild, the Socorro Dove apparently bred in May, preferring the more heavily wooded areas at 500-600 m, although there may have been some (seasonal) preference for lower altitudes. It was highly terrestrial and was recorded feeding on fruits of *Bumelia socorrensis* and *Prunus capuli*. Its demise may be attributed chiefly to predation by cats, which became feral on the island in the 1950s, although grazing by sheep has reduced the forest understorey (once a carpet of ferns and euphorbias, and presumably good cover for the dove) in the south of the island. A recovery plan (with input from CAS, UCLA, Centro de Investigaciones Biológicas and Secretaria de Desarollo Urbano y Ecología) has been devised, starting with a captive breeding programme aimed at the eventual release of birds onto Socorro in the late 1990s (L. F. Baptista *in litt.* 1992). Obviously, conditions on the island need to be such that the birds are able to thrive, and a priority (for this and Townsend's Shearwater *Puffinus auricularis*, Socorro Parakeet *Aratinga brevipes* and Socorro Mockingbird *Mimodes graysoni*: see relevant accounts) has been put on eradicating the cats and sheep, and, by the judicious planting of native trees, on restoring the natural vegetation cover.

SOCORRO PARAKEET *Aratinga brevipes* **K**[12]

This parakeet, treated as a full species in Collar and Andrew (1988), is endemic to Isla Socorro in the Revillagigedo Islands, Mexico, where its population (in 1990-1991) was estimated to be 400-500 birds, at a density of 8.9 birds per km^2 in the c.35 km^2 of suitable forest habitat (this and all the following information comes from Rodríguez-Estrella *et al.* 1992). Birds are most commonly found in forest of *Bumelia socorrensis*, *Ilex socorrensis* and *Guettarda insularis*, which between 350 and 850 m covers c.22% of the island's total area, predominantly around Cerro Everman (the parakeet being mostly in forest above 500 m and where the trees are c.8 m tall). When forest was well represented on the south side of the island and vegetation was less disturbed, this species was probably found below 450 m. Birds have been recorded feeding on the seeds and fruit pulp of *Bumelia* (51% of feeding records), *Guettarda* (19.5%), *Ilex* (16.7%) and *Psidium socorrensis* (12.7%). The breeding season apparently starts in November, when nests (cavities) have been found in live *Bumelia* trees. Potential predators of the species include the Red-tailed Hawk *Buteo jamaicensis socorroensis* (which the parakeets have been seen mobbing) and domestic (feral) cats, although the remains of this bird were not found in scats of these animals and the parakeets were recently still found to be tame and seen feeding on the ground. There is no evidence of a population decline (when the 1990-1991 findings were compared with those in the literature), but the species's distribution on the island may have been reduced in the last 30 years and, although it is not immediately threatened, the spread of erosion, and in places the lack of forest regeneration caused by sheep overgrazing, could be deleterious. It should benefit from the eradication of cats and sheep proposed for the conservation of Townsend's Shearwater *Puffinus auricularis*, Socorro Dove *Zenaida graysoni* and Socorro Mockingbird *Mimodes graysoni* (see relevant accounts).

JUAN FERNANDEZ FIRECROWN *Sephanoides fernandensis* **V/R**[10]

Endemic to the Juan Fernández archipelago in the eastern Pacific (c.670 km off the coast of Chile), the Juan Fernández Firecrown is now confined to c.1,100 ha on Isla Robinson Crusoe (Masatierra) (Meza 1989). The species (race *leyboldi*) is believed extinct on Isla Alejandro Selkirk (Masafuera), where it has not been recorded since 1908 (Brooke 1987, Colwell 1989, Meza 1989). Historical records indicate that densities on Masatierra were once much greater (Colwell 1989), but by late 1985 and early 1986 the population was estimated to consist of just 250 birds (Brooke 1987), with 200 to 500 birds estimated in 1987 (Stiles 1987); however, more precise year-round censuses conducted between 1988 and 1989 revealed a estimated total of 684 individuals (numbers varying between 804 birds in summer and 445 in autumn) (Meza 1989).

The species inhabits what remains of the native forests (with a high degree of endemic plants), and periodically it benefits from some exotics of urban areas, mainly in autumn and winter when flowers in the forest are scarcer (Meza 1989). The bird is nectarivorous, but also takes small insects from leaves or in flight (further information on plant species utilized and other aspects of the species's biology is given in Brooke 1987, Stiles 1987, Colwell 1989, Meza 1989). Degradation of the natural vegetation cover resulting from human activity and introduced plants (e.g. *Aristotelia chilensis* and *Rubus ulmifolius*, the latter being apparently heavily used by the Green-backed Firecrown *Sephanoides sephaniodes*, increasing interspecific competition) and animals such as cattle, rats, cats and the coati *Nasua narica* (introduced in 1940) are the main reasons for concern (Colwell 1989, Meza 1989). Some 90% of the archipelago's surface is protected within the Archipiélago de Juan Fernández National Park (established in 1935, and a Biosphere Reserve since 1977); afforestation programmes to protect and propagate the endemic endangered vegetation, education campaigns and continuous surveys on the Juan Fernández Firecrown are all being conducted by CONAF with financial support from WWF and the ICBP Pan American Section (Meza 1989). Further studies on the effects of introduced plants and predators on this hummingbird are required and the elimination of coatis, control of other introduced animals and perhaps the elimination of the bramble may well help the species to recover (Colwell 1989, Meza 1989).

RED-COCKADED WOODPECKER *Picoides borealis* E^2

The species was originally distributed throughout the south-eastern U.S.A. in the region dominated by shortleaf *Pinus echinata*, slash *P. elliotti*, longleaf *P. palustris* and loblolly *P. taeda* pines (see Jackson 1988 for distribution of this habitat), but is now limited to about 30 isolated populations, the largest being in South Carolina and north Florida (unless otherwise stated, the following is summarized from Jackson 1986, 1988, and Ehrlich *et al.* 1992; a popular account of the bird is given by McFarlane 1992). The species has an unusual social structure in which it lives in groups or "clans" (see below), and prior to Hurricane Hugo (September 1989) the entire population comprised 2,000 active clans. About 560 clans (constituting three main population centres and containing 25% of the entire wild population) were within Francis Marion National Forest, South Carolina: Hurricane Hugo destroyed 40,000 ha of this forest (including cavity trees of c.50% of the resident clans, and leaving just 1% of the clans completely unscathed), and although the subsequent erection of 100 artificial cavities greatly reduced the impact (*Auk* 108 [1991]: 200-201), the largest population centre (representing more than 33% of remaining birds) is now found in Apalachicola National Forest, northern Florida, although even this is showing imminent signs of collapse (but see *Auk* 108 [1991]: 200-201 for disagreement on population estimates in this area). The total wild population is now estimated at about 7,400 individuals (Ehrlich *et al.* 1992). The bird requires fire-sustained open pine-forest with old-growth pine trees (75-100 years old depending on species), and each clan needs a territory averaging 80 ha (often more): to provide population stability and genetic variability, several clans need to be present in any one continuous forest block. Nesting requires dead, resin-free heartwood in mature trees (especially pines infected with heart disease which eases excavation of the nest-hole). Each clan comprises a strongly territorial family group, numbering up to 10 birds (male, female, young, and occasional male helpers), although only one female breeds: the species has a low fecundity, a long period of parental care, high site-tenacity and low ability to colonize new habitats. An estimated 85% of all colonies are now restricted to federal land (including national forests); however, current forestry policies that prevent fire (thus allowing underbrush and hardwoods to establish) and encourage the harvest of immature trees, are all incompatible with sustaining populations of this woodpecker, and numbers continue to decline and colonies are still being lost. The longleaf pine-forest ecosystem is now reduced to 10% of its original extent (and only 2.5% of this percentage provides suitable woodpecker habitat). Much criticism has been levelled at federal recovery plans which seem to be ineffectual. This species can only be saved by increasing the extent of available nesting habitat, encouraging the perpetuation of old-growth pine, and maintaining corridors between sites. A moratorium on clear-cutting within 1 km of active colonies, cutting rotations of 75 to 90 years in some areas, and control of hardwoods that compete with the pines, are all measures central to the survival of this species.

MASAFUERA RAYADITO *Aphrastura masafuerae* **K**[12]

Endemic to Isla Alejandro Selkirk (Masafuera) in the eastern Pacific Juan Fernández archipelago, c.800 km off the coast of Chile, the Masafuera Rayadito is a poorly known furnariid (the following information comes from Brooke 1988a). Apparently found in small flocks in woods in the middle of the nineteenth century, it was subsequently reported scarce in 1916-1917. Only three birds were seen in 1928, and none was found in 1955: it remained unrecorded (and presumed extinct) until four were seen and others heard in 1983. A survey of the island in January and February 1986 showed the species to be present in 33 25-ha grid squares, with 77 individuals recorded and the total population estimated at c.500 birds (but not exceeding 1,000). Although the bird is not numerous, there is little reason to suppose its population has altered substantially in the past century. In 1986 it was recorded between 600 and 1,300 m (although in the eighteenth century when the island's lower slopes were well wooded, it may have lived at lower altitudes), primarily in the *Dicksonia externa* fern forest and always where there was a complete cover of *Lophosauria quadripinnata*: where the fern cover was broken into clumps by patches of *Rumex acetosella* and *Authoxanthum odoratum*, there were no rayaditos. This species, met singly or in pairs (never in flocks), is a gleaning insectivore, and was most readily found along stream courses where luxuriant *Dicksonia* grew to a height of 5 m and intermingled with *Drimys confertifolia*. No nest was found and no family parties seen during the January-February survey. The future of the species is probably secure for as long as tracts of the ferns *Dicksonia* and *Lophosauria* remain intact; however, although these are not grazed directly by goats, goat trampling may be acting to open up areas currently covered. Such fragmentation of fern forest could be adversely affecting the species, which is already absent from the low-altitude woodlands (depleted of understorey by goats). A study is needed to determine the effect of goat trampling on the ferns: beside its relevance to the future of the rayadito, such a study is long overdue botanically (details of which plant species are particularly vulnerable, or their rates of disappearance under goat grazing, are unknown). It may also be prudent to fence off some areas of pristine fern forest.

SOCORRO MOCKINGBIRD *Mimodes graysoni* **E**[1]

The only member of the genus, this species is endemic to Isla Socorro in the Revillagigego Islands, Mexico. In 1925, it was the most abundant and widely distributed bird on the island, being particularly numerous about the spring at Caleta Grayson and in the heavily wooded canyons (Jehl and Parkes 1982, 1983). Although common at lower elevations in March 1953, it appeared rare at such elevations (on the south side) but common in forested areas at higher elevations and in canyons (on the north side) in November 1953; it was abundant in the higher wooded areas during January 1958; but 20 years later, in April 1978, in the vicinity of coastal fig groves, a mere 4-5 could be found at Playa Blanca, one at Caleta Grayson, one at Academy Bay, and two near the airstrip (Jehl and Parkes 1982, 1983). In 1981, the species was thought be to approaching extinction (Jehl and Parkes 1983); however, in August 1987, 20 individuals were found in a relatively inaccessible part of the island (Santaella and Sada 1991); three possible territories (with c.4-5 pairs) were found in one spot during February 1988 (S. N. G. Howell *in litt.* 1988); 16 birds were found early in 1990, with a family of four and two others recorded in May 1990 (Santaella and Sada 1991); and 19 (attracted by playback) noted in November 1990, leading to a provisional population estimate of 100-150 birds (L. F. Baptista *in litt.* 1988). The mockingbird occurs from sea level to 900 m (S. N. G. Howell *in litt.* 1988), and although Jehl and Parkes (1982) suggested that birds were almost entirely restricted to the vicinity of large coastal fig groves *Ficus continifolia*, recent records (see above) indicate at least some degree of altitudinal movement in response to the breeding season. L. F. Baptista (*in litt.* 1992) suggested that birds prefer the ecotone between brush and forest, or the brush in the arroyos. Singing has been noted in November, with birds on territory, in pairs and with young from February to May (Jehl and Parkes 1982, S. N. G. Howell *in litt.* 1988, Santaella and Sada 1991), primarily away from the coast in mixed woodland of *Ficus*, *Bumelia socorrensis*, *Ilex socorrensis*, *Guettarda insularis* and *Psidium socorrensis* (Santaella and Sada 1991). Food includes young leaves, fruit (e.g. *Bumelia*), large insects, dead land-crabs and possibly small passerines (Parkes 1990, Santaella and Sada 1991). Jehl and Parkes (1982) noted birds foraging on the ground along the beach at the edge of vegetation, and in low shrubs and trees farther inland; however, Santaella and Sada (1991) found birds mostly arboreal, possibly in response to feral cat predation which is thought to be the major cause of this species's decline. Some of the woodland, owing to widespread overgrazing by sheep, has an impoverished understorey and shows no sign of regeneration, although ungrazed forest still persists high on Cerro Everman (Santaella and Sada 1991). It has been proposed to remove two pairs for captive breeding as an insurance (L. F. Baptista *in litt.* 1991), but the priority for this species must be the immediate eradication of cats and sheep, thus also benefiting the threatened Townsend's Shearwater *Puffinus auricularis* and Socorro Parakeet *Aratinga brevipes*.

FLOREANA MOCKINGBIRD *Nesomimus trifasciatus* (E)[5]

Now confined to the islands of Champion and Gardner in the Galápagos archipelago, the Floreana Mockingbird became extinct on Floreana around 1880 (Curry 1986). The species was still common when last seen on Floreana in 1868, but none was found in 1888 or 1891, and it seems likely that it succumbed to non-native rats which ere introduced in the 1830s (Curry 1986). The population on Gardner stands at 200-300 birds (P. R. Grant *in litt.* 1988); and on Champion, between 1980 and 1991, the numbers remained close to 50 birds (ranging from 28 to 53), with the annual adult survival rates averaging 76% for males and 58% for females (Curry and Grant 1991). On Champion, breeding was successful in all years (except during a severe drought), and each female averaged one yearling per year with the juvenile sex ratio averaging 41% males (Curry and Grant 1991). An evaluation of the population viability on Champion suggested that it has less than a 50% chance of persisting 100 years, although prospects improve if one assumes the data underestimate fecundity or female survivorship (Curry and Grant 1991). The population dynamics on Gardner are unknown. On Champion, birds feed and nest primarily in *Opuntia* trees, which are still common, but they are not dependent on *Opuntia* and nest successfully in *Parkinsonia*, *Cordia* and *Croton* (Curry 1986). On Gardner, *Opuntia* is less common and the trees smaller, most nests being in *Croton* and *Cordia*, and on both islands birds spend much time foraging on the ground and in vegetation other than *Opuntia* (Curry 1986). Although protected within the Galápagos National Park, it is essential that these two remnant populations of the mockingbird are monitored and that constant vigilance is exercised with reference to the transportation of rats to the two islands.

GUADALUPE JUNCO *Junco insularis* E[2]

Endemic to Isla de Guadalupe, c.280 km west of northern Baja California, Mexico, the Guadalupe Junco (here considered to be a full species: see Mirsky 1978) was at one time one of the most abundant birds on the island (Jehl and Everett 1985). Although Jehl (1972) mentioned that most of the landbirds existed in fair numbers in 1970 , Jehl and Everett (1985) concluded that the junco was uncommon and much less abundant than the House Finch *Carpodacus mexicanus* and Rock

Wren *Salpinctes obsoletus*. This bird is apparently found scattered along the northern half of the island wherever there is vegetation (Jehl and Everett 1985), and in 1988 S. N. G. Howell (*in litt.* 1988) found 30-40 birds present in the largest tract of forest (although just two birds were found there in November 1989: Mellink and Palacios 1990), with a further 2-3 pairs in an arroyo behind the north-east anchorage, suggesting that the population may be c.100 birds or more. In 1988 the species was noted primarily within the main stand of cypress *Cupressus guadalupensis*, but it has been observed feeding on the ground in litter at the base of pines *Pinus radiata* var. *binata* and oaks *Quercus tomentella*, and now occupies stands of *Nicotiana glauca* on the beach, suggesting a relatively high level of adaptability (Jehl and Everett 1985, S. N. G. Howell *in litt.* 1988). Its precise habitat requirements, especially during the breeding season (late January to at least late April: Jehl and Everett 1985) remain essentially undocumented. Jehl and Everett (1985) estimated the largest tract of (remnant cypress) forest to be c.3 km long (in 1971), but by 1988 this was only c.1 km in length (S. N. G. Howell *in litt.* 1988), and the other smaller forest patches had presumably suffered from similar overgrazing (leading to a total lack of regeneration) by goats. Although Jehl (1972) suggested that most of the feral cats had died of starvation, S. N. G. Howell (*in litt.* 1988) noted that they appeared common but mainly nocturnal. In 1988, a fence around the cypress grove (presumably aimed at keeping goats out) was found to be too low to be effective; however, a more direct approach to the problem of overgrazing led to the apparent removal (in 1990) of 20,000 goats (L. F. Baptista *in litt.* 1991). Whether this represented the entire population is unknown, but it will certainly have widespread beneficial effects on the vegetation. This significant conservation initiative must be followed up with comprehensive surveys to monitor regeneration of forest areas; numbers of remaining goats; the impact and population size of feral cats; and the status of the junco (see also Guadalupe Storm-petrel *Oceanodroma macrodactyla*).

MANGROVE FINCH *Camarhynchus heliobates* **I**[7]

One of "Darwin's finches", this bird is only known from Fernandina and Isabela islands in the Galápagos archipelago, Ecuador. It is restricted to dense mangrove swamps on eastern Fernandina, being seen in 1971 at Punta Mangle but not for many years at Punta Espinosa (Harris 1973, 1982, R. Naveen *in litt.* 1988). On Isabela, it has been recorded on the west coast from just north of Punta Tortuga (at Caleta Black) in short stretches of available habitat to just east of Punta Moreno, and in the south-east from Cartago Bay (Harris 1973, 1982). At Cartago Bay, specimens (in ANSP, YPM) were taken in February 1937 and August 1957, another bird being recorded in 1971; there have apparently been no other records there (Harris 1973). Most records come from Punta Tortuga, where a density of 1-2 pairs per hectare was noted in 1962, and where singles were seen in May-June 1985 and 1986 (King 1978-1979, R. Naveen *in litt.* 1988). Potentially suitable habitat on the two islands totals c.500 ha, although the species does not inhabit the whole of it, and there appears to be no way to confirm the estimated population (in 1974) of 100 to 200 individuals (King 1978-1979, R. Naveen *in litt.* 1988), although it must clearly be very small (Harris 1973, 1982). The Mangrove Finch inhabits dense mangroves (although the reason for it not occupying all apparently suitable habitat is unknown) where it feeds on insects, spiders, some vegetable matter (mangrove leaves), sometimes using a twig to poke out insects (Harris 1982, also King 1978-1979). Although protected within the Galápagos National Park (and there are no apparent threats), almost nothing is known about the current status and distribution of the bird (the many mangrove-fronted beaches on Isabela are hardly ever visited by biologists: R. Naveen *in litt.* 1988), or even its ecological requirements. Obviously fieldwork needs to be carried out to rectify these deficiencies in information, and could possibly be coordinated with the annual surveys of the Galápagos Cormorant *Nannopterum harrisi* which inhabits the same coastlines (see relevant account).

GOLDEN-CHEEKED WARBLER *Dendroica chrysoparia* **V/R**[10]

The Golden-cheeked Warbler is an endemic breeder in Texas, U.S.A., wintering in southernmost Mexico, Guatemala, Honduras and Nicaragua (the following information is summarized from Jahrsdoerfer 1990 and Ehrlich *et al.* 1992, although other major references include Pulich 1976 and Braun *et al.* 1986). The species breeds in central Texas from Palo Pinto and Bosque counties, south through the eastern and south-central portions of the Edwards Plateau, coinciding closely with the distribution of mature ashe juniper *Juniperus ashei* stands on which it is totally dependent for nesting habitat, relying on several old-growth attributes of ashe juniper–oak woodland including nearly closed canopy, canopy height, and the shredding bark of older junipers. Various (especially deciduous) species of oak *Quercus* apparently provide foraging habitat. In contrast to its requirements on the breeding grounds, wintering birds appear to have a wide ecological tolerance, primarily occurring in pine or pine–oak, but recently also recorded in broadleaf associations in lower montane wet and tropical forest (J. P. Vannini *in litt.* 1992). Birds arrive in Texas on the breeding grounds in mid-March, returning to the same territories each year and nesting between April and May, leaving Texas in early August (one of the first migrants to appear in Chiapas, Mexico, with birds being noted from the first week of August: P. J. Bubb *in litt.* 1991), migrating through a narrow band of cloud-forest along the eastern slope of the Sierra Madre Oriental, Mexico. While the population in 1974 was estimated at 15,000-17,000 birds and a 1990 reassessment of available breeding habitat suggested that only 4,800-16,000 pairs could be supported (recognizing that not all birds are paired, and not all habitat is occupied), Ehrlich *et al.* (1992) indicated a 1990 population of as few as 2,200-4,600 birds. Brown-headed Cowbird *Molothrus ater* parasitism appears to be an increasing threat as habitat becomes more fragmented, and in one year a 63% nest desertion rate was recorded owing to this problem: with nest desertion also caused by other factors, breeding success for the species appears to be low. This problem stems from the widespread destruction of juniper from c.1950 to the 1970s (c.50% of the juniper area was cleared) for pasture and urbanization, and these factors (along with various development schemes) continue to threaten the species's breeding habitat. The threats to the species in Central America are poorly known, but its wider ecological tolerance there suggests that habitat loss is not a serious problem; however, the proposed widespread Mediterranean fruit-fly eradication programme (using malathion spray) in Guatemala may seriously affect the supply of invertebrates for wintering birds (K. Young *in litt.* 1991). Although protected under the Endangered Species Act, it is clear that the bird requires urgent "on the ground" protection of private, state- and federal-owned land. Surveys and research are still required on the bird's ecology, distribution and abundance, both in Texas and on the wintering grounds.

KIRTLAND'S WARBLER *Dendroica kirtlandii* **(E)**[5]

Kirtland's Warbler is an endemic breeder to a small area within central Michigan and also in Wisconsin, U.S.A., with just a few pairs breeding on occasion in Ontario and Quebec, Canada; it winters in the Bahama Islands and Turks and Caicos (Collar and Andrew 1988) (unless otherwise stated, the following information is taken from Weinrich 1989 and Ehrlich *et al.* 1992; see also Huber 1982). Most breeding pairs are distributed within Oscoda and Crawford counties, Michigan (75% in 1988), with up to eight pairs in Wisconsin in 1988, but just single pairs in Ontario and Quebec during (some) recent years. From a North American population of 502 territorial males in 1961, numbers dropped to just 167 in 1974 (also in 1987), increasing steadily to a total of 347 in 1991. The nesting requirements of Kirtland's Warbler are highly specialized: it nests only on level or gently rolling sandy soil among young jack pine *Pinus banksiana* when they are about 2-4 m tall (8-20 years old) in nearly homogenous stands, such conditions occurring naturally only after extensive fires (Mayfield 1988). Very large tracts of potential habitat are necessary to provide a sufficient amount of forest in exactly the right successional stage, at all times, to sustain the population: at any one time, this warbler has utilized only c.4,000 ha within the c.100,000 ha of jack-pine forest in its historical breeding range (Mayfield 1988). Breeding takes place from mid-May to mid-July, young of the year departing in mid-August to early September and adults leaving in late September (Sykes *et al.* 1989). Kirtland's Warbler is threatened owing mainly to its specific nesting habitat requirements: forest management policies have reduced the size and frequency of fires, and replaced jack pine with other pine species or hardwoods, so that currently only c.1,800 ha of suitable nesting habitat remains (c.33% of that available in the 1950s and 1960s). The other major threat (caused primarily by the reduction and fragmentation of forest areas) has been the expansion of the Brown-headed Cowbird *Molothrus ater* into areas where it now frequently parasitizes warbler nests: from the 1930 to the 1970s, c.60% of warbler nests (examined) were parasitized; however, since a cowbird control programme was started in 1972, parasitism has ranged from 0 to 9%, with c.3,000 cowbirds removed each year during the 1970s (Kelly and DeCapita 1982), although this recently rose to 8,000 birds in 1989. Little has been recorded of the habitat requirements or potential threats to the species in its wintering range. Cowbird removal is a major part of the Kirtland's Warbler recovery plan, but other initiatives include the planting of trees to provide suitable habitat (1.3 million were planted in 1991), the use of fire to maintain and encourage favourable habitat, and the prevention of hunting, logging and other activities in breeding habitat from early May until mid-September. Constant vigilance is needed to minimize the effects of cowbird parasitism, and the planting of trees may (amongst other obvious benefits) in many areas create more continuous tracts of forest and thus discourage cowbirds. Surveys on the wintering grounds should aim at determining whether there are any threats in this important part of the species's life-cycle.

BACHMAN'S WARBLER *Vermivora bachmani* **E/Ex[4]**

Breeding Bachman's Warblers were recorded in Missouri, Arkansas, Kentucky, Alabama and South Carolina states, with other records from elsewhere in the lowlands of south-eastern U.S.A. (King 1978-1979, Hamel 1988a). The species migrated through Florida, wintering throughout Cuba and occasionally in mainland Florida (King 1978-1979, Hamel 1988a); a record from the Isle of Pines (Isla de la Juventud) is discussed by Hamel (1986). Its former population is difficult to assess: owing to the inaccessible and inhospitable nature of its preferred breeding areas (see below), nesting records and localities were probably under-recorded; however, the bird appears to have been locally common until the start of the twentieth century, and relatively large numbers were recorded on migration in Florida during the late 1880s (King 1978-1979). It is now so reduced in numbers that it might already be extinct: the last nest was found in 1937 and there are currently no known breeding populations, with sightings reduced to just one in the U.S.A. during the 1980s (in Louisiana in August 1988), and a number in the 1970s (in Louisiana and South Carolina) (King 1978-1979, Hamel 1988b), with eight unconfirmed records between 1978 and 1988 on the wintering grounds in Cuba (Hamel 1988a,b). Its precise winter habitat preferences are unknown, but it appears to have been quite catholic (see Hamel 1986). In the south-eastern U.S.A., the bird was restricted to breeding in seasonally flooded swamp-forest, and it seems likely that it had a strong association with canebrakes of the bamboo *Arundinaria gigantea* that occurred in vast stands throughout its breeding range (Remsen 1986b). Although the riverine swamps of the south-eastern U.S.A. have been extensively logged and drained, there is no indication that Bachman's Warbler was restricted to virgin forest; however, large areas of cane were cleared for flood control reasons and by cultivation and overgrazing, so that the vast canebrakes stands have all but disappeared (Remsen 1986b). Expansion of the sugarcane industry in Cuba, which has contributed to a reduction of the forest area to just 14%, is also cited as a reason for this species's disappearance (Hamel 1988a,b). Unsuccessful searches were undertaken in Cuba during the 1980s (Hamel 1988b), but a systematic search for large stands of cane within the historical breeding range may help focus efforts to rediscover the species.

BLACK-CAPPED VIREO *Vireo atricapillus* **E[2]**

Historically, the Black-capped Vireo bred from south-central Kansas, through central Oklahoma, south through central Texas to the Edwards Plateau and Big Bend National Park, U.S.A., then south and west to central Coahuila, Mexico (unless otherwise stated, the following is summarized from Grzybowski *et al.* 1986 and Grzybowski 1991). The winter range is less well known, but records are primarily from Durango, Sinaloa, Nayarit and Jalisco on the Pacific coast of Mexico. Currently, in the U.S.A. breeding is only known from Oklahoma and Texas: in the former, the range has been reduced to three focal areas in the west-central part of the state, two of which support less than 10 pairs, the third c.300 individuals; in the latter, c.620 pairs still breed at a number of localities. Controversy surrounds estimates of the breeding population in Coahuila, Mexico (see Benson and Benson 1990, 1991, Scott and Garton 1991): although less than 30 birds have been seen during the two main surveys of its breeding range, estimates vary from several hundred pairs to between 3,139 and 9,463 pairs. Areas with extirpated or declining populations comprise over 50% of the historical range. Birds arrive in Texas from late March to mid-April, and in Oklahoma from mid-April to early May, migrating south by late August to September from Oklahoma and by mid-September from Texas: they nest in areas of shrubby growth in the forest–grassland ecotone, where the shrubs are of irregular height and distribution, with spaces between the small thickets and clumps, and with vegetation cover extending to ground level (most usually in rocky gullies, on the edges of ravines and on eroded slopes). No single plant species dominates localities with vireos, but oaks *Quercus* spp. are most frequent, and birds seem to prefer areas with very little juniper *Juniperus* sp. Winter preferences seem to be less specific, and birds have been seen in a variety of habitats. The Black-capped Vireo is threatened by increasing levels of nest parasitism by Brown-headed Cowbirds *Molothrus ater* (exceeding 90% in some areas in some years). Habitat destruction due to urbanization, development projects, range management, agriculture and overgrazing have all reduced available nesting areas for the species, the fragmentation and conversion of the vegetation helping to encourage cowbirds into remnant patches of its habitat. Habitat loss through natural succession and juniper invasion is also a problem (other threats to this species and its breeding areas are outlined in the references above). Cowbird control has been initiated at a number of nesting localities; a National Wildlife Refuge managed specifically for the vireo is being established near Austin, Texas, and the Balcones Canyonlands Conservation Plan has been proposed, aimed at maintaining a viable population of birds in this area: other proposed recovery actions are outlined in Grzybowski (1991). Clearly, apart from the comprehensive action being taken and planned in the U.S.A., a high priority must be given to determining the true size and precise distribution of the population breeding in Coahuila, Mexico, and the threats it faces.

APPENDIX B

Threatened birds of the Americas, by category of threat

IUCN has come to use the word "threatened" as a generic term to denote any form that qualifies for inclusion in a Red Data Book. This usage is followed throughout ICBP's work, sometimes with the substitution of the phrases "at risk" or "in peril". IUCN's specific status categories for Red Data Books are as follows.

Extinct (Ex) is used for "species not definitely located in the wild during the past 50 years". However, in this volume we have not used the category nor sought to reapply its criterion. The one species regarded as recently extinct, the Atitlán Grebe *Podilymbus gigas* (see Hunter 1988, LaBastille 1990), is not included in the book. We have, however, combined Extinct with Endangered for species which are either one or the other (see below).

Endangered (E) applies to "taxa in danger of extinction and whose survival is unlikely if the causal factors continue operating".

Vulnerable (V) is used for "taxa believed likely to move into the Endangered category in the near future if the causal factors continue operating".

Indeterminate (I) covers "taxa known to be Endangered, Vulnerable or Rare but where there is not enough information to say which of the three categories is appropriate". Collar and Stuart (1985) also used this category to cover the possibility of extinction, but this is not followed here. However, as they pointed out, it needs to be noted that Indeterminate should be regarded as a higher category than Rare (since any bird so classified is *at best* Rare).

Rare (R) is for "taxa with small world populations that are not at present Endangered or Vulnerable, but are at risk" (often simply as a function of their restricted range).

Insufficiently Known (K) is used for "taxa that are suspected but not definitely known to belong to any of the above categories, because of lack of information" (whether or not technically correct, in practice species in this category have to be counted as "threatened").

In reviewing the 327 species in this book to see how they break down into groups based on priorities for action (in an exercise independent of attempting to classify them by IUCN criteria), 12 groupings emerged. They are as follows: (1) species at critically low levels which need immediate intervention; (2) species which need urgent assistance; (3) species confidently believed to be extant but which have first to be found and then urgently assisted; (4) species (a few of which also need taxonomic clarification) for which action will be urgent if a viable population or even evidence of survival is found (these birds are really beyond the highest category of threat by virtue of their possible extinction, so that even the highly desirable action of searching for them has implications that must be carefully considered, at least in the case of formerly wide-ranging species); (5) species at critically low levels that are already being very fully assisted; (6) species for which action is urgent so long as their taxonomic status is confirmed; (7) species for which there is conflicting or insufficient evidence but which could well prove to be in urgent need; (8) species possibly or probably needing attention if and when they are rediscovered (most of these are Amazonian birds known from one specimen or one locality, and most have some taxonomic uncertainty); (9) species that remain largely unprotected throughout their ranges, and which need substantial management either directly or via the conservation of key sites and habitats; (10) species that are partially protected throughout their ranges, but which merit further intervention; (11) species which are largely protected, but for which vigilance (mostly in the form of protected area management) is constantly needed; (12) species that seem unlikely to be in serious danger, but for which certain levels of protection are clearly prudent.

These classifications were not intended to serve as subdivisions of existing IUCN categories, but it turns out that the two sets can crudely be made to interlock. Thus groupings 1-3 correspond to E, 4 to E/Ex, 5 to E (but because of the existing measures this goes in parentheses), 6-8 to I, 9 to V, 10 to V/R, 11 to R, and 12 to K. Both letter and number are given at the head of each species account.

Several points arise. First, the listing 1-12 clearly reflects in some degree a order of priority, but it must be obvious that some groupings are parallel: in particular, group 3 must contain species whose situation is as critical as some in group 1, while if only some of the birds in group 4 could be relocated they would inevitably and immediately move into group 1. Second, these groupings were undertaken very much as a last-minute aid to interpretation, not with the intention of creating some authoritative new system of classification. Third, precisely because last-minute in nature, it has not had the benefit of comment or adjustment by "outposted" co-authors (LPG, NK, LGN, TAP).

1. Situation critical: action urgent Endangered

Junín Grebe	*Podiceps taczanowskii*
Brazilian Merganser	*Mergus octosetaceus*
White-winged Guan	*Penelope albipennis*
Alagoas Curassow	*Mitu mitu*
Grenada Dove	*Leptotila wellsi*
Lear's Macaw	*Anodorhynchus leari*
Spix's Macaw	*Cyanopsitta spixii*
Fuertes's Parrot	*Hapalopsittaca fuertesi*
Imperial Amazon	*Amazona imperialis*
White-winged Nightjar	*Caprimulgus candicans*
Black-breasted Puffleg	*Eriocnemis nigrivestis*
Black-hooded Antwren	*Formicivora erythronotos*
Restinga Antwren	*Formicivora littoralis*
Peruvian Plantcutter	*Phytotoma raimondii*
White-breasted Thrasher	*Ramphocinclus brachyurus*
Socorro Mockingbird	*Mimodes graysoni*

2. Situation serious: action urgent Endangered

Grey-backed Hawk	*Leucopternis occidentalis*
Trinidad Piping-guan	*Pipile pipile*
Northern Helmeted Curassow	*Pauxi pauxi*
Bearded Wood-partridge	*Dendrortyx barbatus*
Plain-flanked Rail	*Rallus wetmorei*
Junín Rail	*Laterallus tuerosi*
Ochre-bellied Dove	*Leptotila ochraceiventris*
Red-faced Parrot	*Hapalopsittaca pyrrhops*
Red-tailed Amazon	*Amazona brasiliensis*
Short-crested Coquette	*Lophornis brachylopha*
Honduran Emerald	*Amazilia luciae*
Esmeraldas Woodstar	*Acestrura berlepschi*
Little Woodstar	*Acestrura bombus*
Three-toed Jacamar	*Jacamaralcyon tridactyla*
Red-cockaded Woodpecker	*Picoides borealis*
Royal Cinclodes	*Cinclodes aricomae*
White-browed Tit-spinetail	*Leptasthenura xenothorax*
Blackish-headed Spinetail	*Synallaxis tithys*

Alagoas Foliage-gleaner	*Philydor novaesi*
Rufous-necked Foliage-gleaner	*Syndactyla ruficollis*
Bolivian Recurvebill	*Simoxenops striatus*
Alagoas Antwren	*Myrmotherula snowi*
Ash-throated Antwren	*Herpsilochmus parkeri*
Orange-bellied Antwren	*Terenura sicki*
Grey-headed Antbird	*Myrmeciza griseiceps*
Bahia Tapaculo	*Scytalopus psychopompus*
Ash-breasted Tit-tyrant	*Anairetes alpinus*
Long-tailed Tyrannulet	*Phylloscartes ceciliae*
Pacific Royal Flycatcher	*Onychorhynchus occidentalis*
Ochraceous Attila	*Attila torridus*
Slaty Becard	*Pachyramphus spodiurus*
Guadalupe Junco	*Junco insularis*
Cochabamba Mountain-finch	*Poospiza garleppi*
Rufous-breasted Warbling-finch	*Poospiza rubecula*
Entre Ríos Seedeater	*Sporophila zelichi*
Paria Redstart	*Myioborus pariae*
Black-capped Vireo	*Vireo atricapillus*
Martinique Oriole	*Icterus bonana*
Forbes's Blackbird	*Curaeus forbesi*
Red Siskin	*Carduelis cucullatus*
Dwarf Jay	*Cyanolyca nana*

3. Situation critical: action urgent when population found Endangered

Blue-billed Curassow	*Crax alberti*
Blue-eyed Ground-dove	*Columbina cyanopis*
Blue-throated Macaw	*Ara glaucogularis*
Yellow-eared Parrot	*Ognorhynchus icterotis*
Recurve-billed Bushbird	*Clytoctantes alixii*
Fringe-backed Fire-eye	*Pyriglena atra*
Táchira Antpitta	*Grallaria chthonia*

4. Situation terminal: action urgent if population extant Endangered/Extinct

Magdalena Tinamou	*Crypturellus saltuarius*
Kalinowski's Tinamou	*Nothoprocta kalinowskii*
Colombian Grebe	*Podiceps andinus*
Jamaica Petrel	*Pterodroma caribbaea*
Guadalupe Storm-petrel	*Oceanodroma macrodactyla*
Austral Rail	*Rallus antarcticus*
Eskimo Curlew	*Numenius borealis*
Purple-winged Ground-dove	*Claravis godefrida*
Glaucous Macaw	*Anodorhynchus glaucus*
Jamaican Pauraque	*Siphonorhis americanus*
Turquoise-throated Puffleg	*Eriocnemis godini*
Imperial Woodpecker	*Campephilus imperialis*
Ivory-billed Woodpecker	*Campephilus principalis*
Moustached Antpitta	*Grallaria alleni*

Brown-banded Antpitta	*Grallaria milleri*
Kinglet Cotinga	*Calyptura cristata*
Tumaco Seedeater	*Sporophila insulata*
Hooded Seedeater	*Sporophila melanops*
Pale-headed Brush-finch	*Atlapetes pallidiceps*
Cone-billed Tanager	*Conothraupis mesoleuca*
Cherry-throated Tanager	*Nemosia rourei*
Bachman's Warbler	*Vermivora bachmani*
Semper's Warbler	*Leucopeza semperi*

5. Situation serious but in progress (Endangered)

Cahow or Bermuda Petrel	*Pterodroma cahow*
Puerto Rican Amazon	*Amazona vittata*
Yellow-shouldered Blackbird	*Agelaius xanthomus*
Dark-rumped Petrel	*Pterodroma phaeopygia*
California Condor	*Gymnogyps californianus*
Whooping Crane	*Grus americana*
Socorro Dove	*Zenaida graysoni*
Floreana Mockingbird	*Nesomimus trifasciatus*
Kirtland's Warbler	*Dendroica kirtlandii*

6. Situation unclear: action urgent if taxonomic status confirmed Indeterminate

Sapphire-bellied Hummingbird	*Lepidopyga lilliae*
Purple-backed Sunbeam	*Aglaeactis aliciae*
Apurímac Spinetail	*Synallaxis courseni*
Berlepsch's Canastero	*Asthenes berlepschi*
Stresemann's Bristlefront	*Merulaxis stresemanni*
Niceforo's Wren	*Thryothorus nicefori*

7. Conflicting evidence: possibly urgent Indeterminate

Chocó Tinamou	*Crypturellus kerriae*
Lesser Nothura	*Nothura minor*
Dwarf Tinamou	*Taoniscus nanus*
Black-capped Petrel	*Pterodroma hasitata*
Townsend's Shearwater	*Puffinus auricularis*
Hispaniolan Hawk	*Buteo ridgwayi*
Wattled Curassow	*Crax globulosa*
Zapata Rail	*Cyanolimnas cerverai*
Dot-winged Crake	*Porzana spiloptera*
Speckled Crake	*Coturnicops notata*
Plain Pigeon	*Columba inornata*
Blue-headed Quail-dove	*Starnoenas cyanocephala*
Rufous-breasted Cuckoo	*Hyetornis rufigularis*
White-chested Swift	*Cypseloides lemosi*
Mexican Woodnymph	*Thalurania ridgwayi*
Eared Quetzal	*Euptilotis neoxenus*
Cuban Flicker	*Colaptes fernandinae*

Cipó Canastero	*Asthenes luizae*
Henna-hooded Foliage-gleaner	*Hylocryptus erythrocephalus*
Bicoloured Antpitta	*Grallaria rufocinerea*
Rufous-sided Pygmy-tyrant	*Euscarthmus rufomarginatus*
Antioquia Bristle-tyrant	*Phylloscartes lanyoni*
Kaempfer's Tody-tyrant	*Hemitriccus kaempferi*
Giant Kingbird	*Tyrannus cubensis*
Ochre-breasted Pipit	*Anthus nattereri*
Cinereous Warbling-finch	*Poospiza cinerea*
Black-and-tawny Seedeater	*Sporophila nigrorufa*
Mangrove Finch	*Camarhynchus heliobates*
Yellow-headed Brush-finch	*Atlapetes flaviceps*
Scarlet-breasted Dacnis	*Dacnis berlepschi*
Venezuelan Flowerpiercer	*Diglossa venezuelensis*
Grey-headed Warbler	*Basileuterus griseiceps*
Tamarugo Conebill	*Conirostrum tamarugense*
San Andrés Vireo	*Vireo caribaeus*
Baudó Oropendola	*Psarocolius cassini*
Pampas Meadowlark	*Sturnella militaris*
Red-bellied Grackle	*Hypopyrrhus pyrohypogaster*

8. Birds perhaps in need if and when found Indeterminate

Cayenne Nightjar	*Caprimulgus maculosus*
Coppery Thorntail	*Popelairia letitiae*
Rondônia Bushbird	*Clytoctantes atrogularis*
White-masked Antbird	*Pithys castanea*
Rio de Janeiro Antwren	*Myrmotherula fluminensis*
Golden-crowned Manakin	*Pipra vilasboasi*
Buff-cheeked Tody-flycatcher	*Todirostrum senex*

9. Birds largely unprotected and needing attention Vulnerable

Taczanowski's Tinamou	*Nothoprocta taczanowskii*
Defilippe's Petrel	*Pterodroma defilippiana*
Peruvian Diving-petrel	*Pelecanoides garnotii*
West Indian Whistling-duck	*Dendrocygna arborea*
Crowned Eagle	*Harpyhaliaetus coronatus*
Plumbeous Forest-falcon	*Micrastur plumbeus*
Rusty-flanked Crake	*Laterallus levraudi*
Ring-tailed Pigeon	*Columba caribaea*
Peruvian Pigeon	*Columba oenops*
Red-fronted Macaw	*Ara rubrogenys*
Golden-capped Parakeet	*Aratinga auricapilla*
Cuban Parakeet	*Aratinga euops*
Golden Parakeet	*Guaruba guarouba*
Thick-billed Parrot	*Rhynchopsitta pachyrhyncha*
Maroon-fronted Parrot	*Rhynchopsitta terrisi*
Yellow-faced Parrotlet	*Forpus xanthops*
Yellow-headed Amazon	*Amazona oratrix*

Green-cheeked Amazon	*Amazona viridigenalis*
Banded Ground-cuckoo	*Neomorphus radiolosus*
Mangrove Hummingbird	*Amazilia boucardi*
Chestnut-bellied Hummingbird	*Amazilia castaneiventris*
Táchira Emerald	*Amazilia distans*
Oaxaca Hummingbird	*Eupherusa cyanophrys*
White-tailed Hummingbird	*Eupherusa poliocerca*
Grey-bellied Comet	*Taphrolesbia griseiventris*
Marvellous Spatuletail	*Loddigesia mirabilis*
Glow-throated Hummingbird	*Selasphorus ardens*
Moustached Woodcreeper	*Xiphocolaptes falcirostris*
White-bellied Cinclodes	*Cinclodes palliatus*
Hoary-throated Spinetail	*Synallaxis kollari*
Russet-bellied Spinetail	*Synallaxis zimmeri*
Pale-tailed Canastero	*Asthenes huancavelicae*
Orinoco Softtail	*Thripophaga cherriei*
Pectoral Antwren	*Herpsilochmus pectoralis*
Narrow-billed Antwren	*Formicivora iheringi*
Yellow-rumped Antwren	*Terenura sharpei*
Rio Branco Antbird	*Cercomacra carbonaria*
Slender Antbird	*Rhopornis ardesiaca*
Rufous-fronted Antthrush	*Formicarius rufifrons*
Yellow-billed Cotinga	*Carpodectes antoniae*
Minas Gerais Tyrannulet	*Phylloscartes roquettei*
Cinnamon-breasted Tody-tyrant	*Hemitriccus cinnamomeipectus*
Strange-tailed Tyrant	*Yetapa risora*
Slender-billed Finch	*Xenospingus concolor*
Grey-winged Inca-finch	*Incaspiza ortizi*
Yellow Cardinal	*Gubernatrix cristata*
Gold-ringed Tanager	*Buthraupis aureocincta*
Orange-throated Tanager	*Wetmorethraupis sterrhopteron*
Black-polled Yellowthroat	*Geothlypis speciosa*
Saffron-cowled Blackbird	*Xanthopsar flavus*
Saffron Siskin	*Carduelis siemiradskii*
White-throated Jay	*Cyanolyca mirabilis*

10. Birds with populations only partly protected Vulnerable/Rare

Pink-footed Shearwater	*Puffinus creatopus*
Gundlach's Hawk	*Accipiter gundlachi*
White-necked Hawk	*Leucopternis lacernulata*
Bearded Guan	*Penelope barbata*
Chestnut-bellied Guan	*Penelope ochrogaster*
Black-fronted Piping-guan	*Pipile jacutinga*
Horned Guan	*Oreophasis derbianus*
Southern Helmeted Curassow	*Pauxi unicornis*
Gorgeted Wood-quail	*Odontophorus strophium*
Bogotá Rail	*Rallus semiplumbeus*
Rufous-faced Crake	*Laterallus xenopterus*
Bristle-thighed Curlew	*Numenius tahitiensis*
Piping Plover	*Charadrius melodus*

Tolima Dove	*Leptotila conoveri*
Hyacinth Macaw	*Anodorhynchus hyacinthinus*
Golden-plumed Parakeet	*Leptosittaca branickii*
Flame-winged Parakeet	*Pyrrhura calliptera*
El Oro Parakeet	*Pyrrhura orcesi*
Rufous-fronted Parakeet	*Bolborhynchus ferrugineifrons*
Brown-backed Parrotlet	*Touit melanonota*
Golden-tailed Parrotlet	*Touit surda*
Rusty-faced Parrot	*Hapalopsittaca amazonina*
Red-spectacled Amazon	*Amazona pretrei*
Red-browed Amazon	*Amazona rhodocorytha*
Vinaceous Amazon	*Amazona vinacea*
Blue-bellied Parrot	*Triclaria malachitacea*
Hook-billed Hermit	*Glaucis dohrnii*
White-tailed Sabrewing	*Campylopterus ensipennis*
Scissor-tailed Hummingbird	*Hylonympha macrocerca*
Black Inca	*Coeligena prunellei*
Juan Fernández Firecrown	*Sephanoides fernandensis*
Hoary Puffleg	*Haplophaedia lugens*
White-mantled Barbet	*Capito hypoleucus*
Helmeted Woodpecker	*Dryocopus galeatus*
Plain Spinetail	*Synallaxis infuscata*
Russet-mantled Softtail	*Thripophaga berlepschi*
Striated Softtail	*Thripophaga macroura*
White-throated Barbtail	*Margarornis tatei*
White-bearded Antshrike	*Biatas nigropectus*
Bicoloured Antvireo	*Dysithamnus occidentalis*
Plumbeous Antvireo	*Dysithamnus plumbeus*
Ashy Antwren	*Myrmotherula grisea*
Scalloped Antbird	*Myrmeciza ruficauda*
Hooded Antpitta	*Grallaricula cucullata*
Shrike-like Cotinga	*Laniisoma elegans*
Black-headed Berryeater	*Carpornis melanocephalus*
Buff-throated Purpletuft	*Iodopleura pipra*
Cinnamon-vented Piha	*Lipaugus lanioides*
Bare-necked Umbrellabird	*Cephalopterus glabricollis*
Black-capped Manakin	*Piprites pileatus*
Dinelli's Doradito	*Pseudocolopteryx dinellianus*
São Paulo Tyrannulet	*Phylloscartes paulistus*
Buff-breasted Tody-tyrant	*Hemitriccus mirandae*
Russet-winged Spadebill	*Platyrinchus leucoryphus*
Grey-breasted Flycatcher	*Lathrotriccus griseipectus*
White-tailed Shrike-tyrant	*Agriornis andicola*
Sumichrast's Wren	*Hylorchilus sumichrasti*
Zapata Wren	*Ferminia cerverai*
Sierra Madre Sparrow	*Xenospiza baileyi*
Cuban Sparrow	*Torreornis inexpectata*
Plain-tailed Warbling-finch	*Poospiza alticola*
Tucumán Mountain-finch	*Poospiza baeri*
Temminck's Seedeater	*Sporophila falcirostris*
Buffy-throated Seedeater	*Sporophila frontalis*

Tanager-finch	*Oreothraupis arremonops*
Rufous-bellied Saltator	*Saltator rufiventris*
Slaty-backed Hemispingus	*Hemispingus goeringi*
Chat-tanager	*Calyptophilus frugivorus*
Black-and-gold Tanager	*Buthraupis melanochlamys*
Masked Mountain-tanager	*Buthraupis wetmorei*
Multicoloured Tanager	*Chlorochrysa nitidissima*
Azure-rumped Tanager	*Tangara cabanisi*
Seven-coloured Tanager	*Tangara fastuosa*
Black-backed Tanager	*Tangara peruviana*
Turquoise Dacnis	*Dacnis hartlaubi*
Black-legged Dacnis	*Dacnis nigripes*
Golden-cheeked Warbler	*Dendroica chrysoparia*
White-winged Warbler	*Xenoligea montana*
Yellow-faced Siskin	*Carduelis yarrellii*

11. Birds largely protected, but for which vigilance is needed Rare

Galápagos Cormorant	*Nannopterum harrisi*
Galápagos Hawk	*Buteo galapagoensis*
Cauca Guan	*Penelope perspicax*
Red-billed Curassow	*Crax blumenbachii*
Blue-chested Parakeet	*Pyrrhura cruentata*
Red-necked Amazon	*Amazona arausiaca*
St Vincent Amazon	*Amazona guildingii*
St Lucia Amazon	*Amazona versicolor*
Puerto Rican Nightjar	*Caprimulgus noctitherus*
Colourful Puffleg	*Eriocnemis mirabilis*
Violet-throated Metaltail	*Metallura baroni*
Neblina Metaltail	*Metallura odomae*
Brasília Tapaculo	*Scytalopus novacapitalis*
Grey-winged Cotinga	*Tijuca condita*
Banded Cotinga	*Cotinga maculata*
White-winged Cotinga	*Xipholena atropurpurea*
Fork-tailed Pygmy-tyrant	*Hemitriccus furcatus*
Apolinar's Wren	*Cistothorus apolinari*
La Selle Thrush	*Turdus swalesi*

12. Birds for which further protection is desirable Insufficiently Known

Black Tinamou	*Tinamus osgoodi*
Lesser-collared Forest-falcon	*Micrastur buckleyi*
Horned Coot	*Fulica cornuta*
Olrog's Gull	*Larus atlanticus*
Socorro Parakeet	*Aratinga brevipes*
White-necked Parakeet	*Pyrrhura albipectus*
Spot-winged Parrotlet	*Touit stictoptera*
Yellow-shouldered Amazon	*Amazona barbadensis*
Long-whiskered Owlet	*Xenoglaux loweryi*
Sickle-winged Nightjar	*Eleothreptus anomalus*

Royal Sunangel	*Heliangelus regalis*
Chilean Woodstar	*Eulidia yarrellii*
Keel-billed Motmot	*Electron carinatum*
Coppery-chested Jacamar	*Galbula pastazae*
Yellow-browed Toucanet	*Aulacorhynchus huallagae*
Masafuera Rayadito	*Aphrastura masafuerae*
Chestnut-throated Spinetail	*Synallaxis cherriei*
Austral Canastero	*Asthenes anthoides*
Great Xenops	*Megaxenops parnaguae*
Speckled Antshrike	*Xenornis setifrons*
Giant Antpitta	*Grallaria gigantea*
White-cheeked Cotinga	*Zaratornis stresemanni*
Rufous-throated Dipper	*Cinclus schulzi*
Unicoloured Thrush	*Turdus haplochrous*
Rufous-rumped Seedeater	*Sporophila hypochroma*
Marsh Seedeater	*Sporophila palustris*
Yellow-green Bush-tanager	*Chlorospingus flavovirens*
Golden-backed Mountain-tanager	*Buthraupis aureodorsalis*
Green-capped Tanager	*Tangara meyerdeschauenseei*
Sira Tanager	*Tangara phillipsi*
Selva Cacique	*Cacicus koepckeae*

APPENDIX C

Threatened birds of the Americas, by country

In compiling this list by reference to the main text, discretion has been used in determining the weight to be given to particular records: records of passage migrants (e.g. Eskimo Curlew *Numenius borealis* in the Guianas) have been excluded where they are known to be such, as have unconfirmed records (e.g. White-chested Swift *Cypseloides lemosi* in Ecuador, Turquoise-throated Puffleg *Eriocnemis godini* in Colombia), and records for countries where the species concerned is likely or known no longer to occur (e.g. California Condor *Gymnogyps californianus* in Canada and Mexico). This reduction (albeit small) is aimed at clarifying for the conservationist which the countries are that individual species truly depend on: however, single confirmed records of species in a particular country have been included for regions where the distributional status of species is poorly known, as with further fieldwork these countries may prove to be critically important for a species's continued existence. The asterisk after a species's name indicates that it is endemic to the country involved.

Alaska (U.S.A.)

Eskimo Curlew	*Numenius borealis*
Bristle-thighed Curlew	*Numenius tahitiensis*

Antigua and Barbuda

West Indian Whistling-duck	*Dendrocygna arborea*

Argentina

Dwarf Tinamou	*Taoniscus nanus*
Brazilian Merganser	*Mergus octosetaceus*
Crowned Eagle	*Harpyhaliaetus coronatus*
Black-fronted Piping-guan	*Pipile jacutinga*
Austral Rail	*Rallus antarcticus*
Dot-winged Crake	*Porzana spiloptera*
Speckled Crake	*Coturnicops notatus*
Horned Coot	*Fulica cornuta*
Eskimo Curlew	*Numenius borealis*
Olrog's Gull	*Larus atlanticus*
Purple-winged Ground-dove	*Claravis godefrida*
Glaucous Macaw	*Anodorhynchus glaucus*
Red-spectacled Amazon	*Amazona pretrei*
Vinaceous Amazon	*Amazona vinacea*
Blue-bellied Parrot	*Triclaria malachitacea*
Sickle-winged Nightjar	*Eleothreptus anomalus*
Helmeted Woodpecker	*Dryocopus galeatus*
Austral Canastero	*Asthenes anthoides*
White-bearded Antshrike	*Biatas nigropectus*
Black-capped Manakin	*Piprites pileatus*
Dinelli's Doradito	*Pseudocolopteryx dinellianus*
São Paulo Tyrannulet	*Phylloscartes paulistus*
Russet-winged Spadebill	*Platyrinchus leucoryphus*
White-tailed Shrike-tyrant	*Agriornis andicola*

Strange-tailed Tyrant	*Yetapa risora*
Ochre-breasted Pipit	*Anthus nattereri*
Rufous-throated Dipper	*Cinclus schulzi*
Tucumán Mountain-finch	*Poospiza baeri* *
Temminck's Seedeater	*Sporophila falcirostris*
Buffy-throated Seedeater	*Sporophila frontalis*
Rufous-rumped Seedeater	*Sporophila hypochroma*
Marsh Seedeater	*Sporophila palustris*
Entre Ríos Seedeater	*Sporophila zelichi* *
Yellow Cardinal	*Gubernatrix cristata*
Rufous-bellied Saltator	*Saltator rufiventris*
Saffron-cowled Blackbird	*Xanthopsar flavus*
Pampas Meadowlark	*Sturnella militaris*

Bahama Islands

West Indian Whistling-duck	*Dendrocygna arborea*
Piping Plover	*Charadrius melodus*
Kirtland's Warbler	*Dendroica kirtlandii*

Belize

Yellow-headed Amazon	*Amazona oratrix*
Keel-billed Motmot	*Electron carinatum*

Bermuda (to U.K.)

Cahow or Bermuda Petrel	*Pterodroma cahow* *

Bolivia

Crowned Eagle	*Harpyhaliaetus coronatus*
Southern Helmeted Curassow	*Pauxi unicornis*
Wattled Curassow	*Crax globulosa*
Horned Coot	*Fulica cornuta*
Hyacinth Macaw	*Anodorhynchus hyacinthinus*
Blue-throated Macaw	*Ara glaucogularis* *
Red-fronted Macaw	*Ara rubrogenys* *
Coppery Thorntail	*Popelairia letitiae* *
Royal Cinclodes	*Cinclodes aricomae*
Berlepsch's Canastero	*Asthenes berlepschi* *
Bolivian Recurvebill	*Simoxenops striatus* *
Ashy Antwren	*Myrmotherula grisea* *
Yellow-rumped Antwren	*Terenura sharpei*
Ash-breasted Tit-tyrant	*Anairetes alpinus*
Dinelli's Doradito	*Pseudocolopteryx dinellianus*
Rufous-sided Pygmy-tyrant	*Euscarthmus rufomarginatus*
White-tailed Shrike-tyrant	*Agriornis andicola*
Rufous-throated Dipper	*Cinclus schulzi*
Unicoloured Thrush	*Turdus haplochrous* *
Cochabamba Mountain-finch	*Poospiza garleppi* *
Rufous-rumped Seedeater	*Sporophila hypochroma*
Black-and-tawny Seedeater	*Sporophila nigrorufa*
Rufous-bellied Saltator	*Saltator rufiventris*

Brazil

Lesser Nothura	*Nothura minor* *
Dwarf Tinamou	*Taoniscus nanus*
Brazilian Merganser	*Mergus octosetaceus*
White-necked Hawk	*Leucopternis lacernulata* *
Crowned Eagle	*Harpyhaliaetus coronatus*
Lesser Collared Forest-falcon	*Micrastur buckleyi*
Chestnut-bellied Guan	*Penelope ochrogaster* *
Black-fronted Piping-guan	*Pipile jacutinga*
Alagoas Curassow	*Mitu mitu* *
Red-billed Curassow	*Crax blumenbachii* *
Wattled Curassow	*Crax globulosa*
Rufous-faced Crake	*Laterallus xenopterus*
Speckled Crake	*Coturnicops notata*
Blue-eyed Ground-dove	*Columbina cyanopis* *
Purple-winged Ground-dove	*Claravis godefrida*
Glaucous Macaw	*Anodorhynchus glaucus*
Hyacinth Macaw	*Anodorhynchus hyacinthinus*
Lear's Macaw	*Anodorhynchus leari* *
Spix's Macaw	*Cyanopsitta spixii* *
Golden-capped Parakeet	*Aratinga auricapilla* *
Golden Parakeet	*Guaruba guarouba* *
Blue-chested Parakeet	*Pyrrhura cruentata* *
Brown-backed Parrotlet	*Touit melanonota* *
Golden-tailed Parrotlet	*Touit surda* *
Red-tailed Amazon	*Amazona brasiliensis* *
Red-spectacled Amazon	*Amazona pretrei*
Red-browed Amazon	*Amazona rhodocorytha* *
Vinaceous Amazon	*Amazona vinacea*
Blue-bellied Parrot	*Triclaria malachitacea*
White-winged Nightjar	*Caprimulgus candicans* *
Sickle-winged Nightjar	*Eleothreptus anomalus*
Hook-billed Hermit	*Glaucis dohrnii* *
Three-toed Jacamar	*Jacamaralcyon tridactyla* *
Helmeted Woodpecker	*Dryocopus galeatus*
Moustached Woodcreeper	*Xiphocolaptes falcirostris* *
Chestnut-throated Spinetail	*Synallaxis cherriei*
Plain Spinetail	*Synallaxis infuscata* *
Hoary-throated Spinetail	*Synallaxis kollari* *
Cipó Canastero	*Asthenes luizae* *
Striated Softtail	*Thripophaga macroura* *
Alagoas Foliage-gleaner	*Philydor novaesi* *
Great Xenops	*Megaxenops parnaguae* *
Rondônia Bushbird	*Clytoctantes atrogularis* *
White-bearded Antshrike	*Biatas nigropectus*
Plumbeous Antvireo	*Dysithamnus plumbeus* *
Alagoas Antwren	*Myrmotherula snowi* *
Pectoral Antwren	*Herpsilochmus pectoralis* *
Black-hooded Antwren	*Formicivora erythronotos* *
Narrow-billed Antwren	*Formicivora iheringi* *
Restinga Antwren	*Formicivora littoralis* *

Orange-bellied Antwren	*Terenura sicki* *
Rio Branco Antbird	*Cercomacra carbonaria* *
Fringe-backed Fire-eye	*Pyriglena atra* *
Slender Antbird	*Rhopornis ardesiaca* *
Scalloped Antbird	*Myrmeciza ruficauda* *
Rio de Janeiro Antwren	*Myrmotherula fluminensis* *
Stresemann's Bristlefront	*Merulaxis stresemanni* *
Brasília Tapaculo	*Scytalopus novacapitalis* *
Bahia Tapaculo	*Scytalopus psychopompus* *
Shrike-like Cotinga	*Laniisoma elegans* *
Grey-winged Cotinga	*Tijuca condita* *
Black-headed Berryeater	*Carpornis melanocephalus* *
Buff-throated Purpletuft	*Iodopleura pipra* *
Kinglet Cotinga	*Calyptura cristata* *
Cinnamon-vented Piha	*Lipaugus lanioides* *
Banded Cotinga	*Cotinga maculata* *
White-winged Cotinga	*Xipholena atropurpurea* *
Golden-crowned Manakin	*Pipra vilasboasi* *
Black-capped Manakin	*Piprites pileatus*
Rufous-sided Pygmy-tyrant	*Euscarthmus rufomarginatus*
Long-tailed Tyrannulet	*Phylloscartes ceciliae* *
São Paulo Tyrannulet	*Phylloscartes paulistus*
Minas Gerais Tyrannulet	*Phylloscartes roquettei* *
Fork-tailed Pygmy-tyrant	*Hemitriccus furcatus* *
Buff-breasted Tody-tyrant	*Hemitriccus mirandae* *
Kaempfer's Tody-tyrant	*Hemitriccus kaempferi* *
Buff-cheeked Tody-flycatcher	*Todirostrum senex* *
Russet-winged Spadebill	*Platyrinchus leucoryphus*
Strange-tailed Tyrant	*Yetapa risora*
Ochre-breasted Pipit	*Anthus nattereri*
Cinereous Warbling-finch	*Poospiza cinerea* *
Temminck's Seedeater	*Sporophila falcirostris*
Buffy-throated Seedeater	*Sporophila frontalis*
Rufous-rumped Seedeater	*Sporophila hypochroma*
Hooded Seedeater	*Sporophila melanops* *
Black-and-tawny Seedeater	*Sporophila nigrorufa*
Marsh Seedeater	*Sporophila palustris*
Yellow Cardinal	*Gubernatrix cristata*
Cone-billed Tanager	*Conothraupis mesoleuca* *
Cherry-throated Tanager	*Nemosia rourei* *
Seven-coloured Tanager	*Tangara fastuosa* *
Black-backed Tanager	*Tangara peruviana* *
Black-legged Dacnis	*Dacnis nigripes* *
Saffron-cowled Blackbird	*Xanthopsar flavus*
Pampas Meadowlark	*Sturnella militaris*
Forbes's Blackbird	*Curaeus forbesi* *
Yellow-faced Siskin	*Carduelis yarrellii*

Canada

Whooping Crane	*Grus americana*
Piping Plover	*Charadrius melodus*

Eskimo Curlew	*Numenius borealis*
Kirtland's Warbler	*Dendroica kirtlandii*

Cayman Islands (to U.K.)

West Indian Whistling-duck	*Dendrocygna arborea*

Chile (see also Desventuradas Islands, Juan Fernández Islands)

Pink-footed Shearwater	*Puffinus creatopus* *
Peruvian Diving-petrel	*Pelecanoides garnotii*
Austral Rail	*Rallus antarcticus*
Horned Coot	*Fulica cornuta*
Eskimo Curlew	*Numenius borealis*
Chilean Woodstar	*Eulidia yarrellii*
Austral Canastero	*Asthenes anthoides*
White-tailed Shrike-tyrant	*Agriornis andicola*
Slender-billed Finch	*Xenospingus concolor*
Tamarugo Conebill	*Conirostrum tamarugense*

Colombia (see also San Andrés Island)

Black Tinamou	*Tinamus osgoodi*
Chocó Tinamou	*Crypturellus kerriae*
Magdalena Tinamou	*Crypturellus saltuarius* *
Colombian Grebe	*Podiceps andinus* *
Plumbeous Forest-falcon	*Micrastur plumbeus*
Cauca Guan	*Penelope perspicax* *
Northern Helmeted Curassow	*Pauxi pauxi*
Blue-billed Curassow	*Crax alberti* *
Wattled Curassow	*Crax globulosa*
Gorgeted Wood-quail	*Odontophorus strophium* *
Bogotá Rail	*Rallus semiplumbeus* *
Speckled Crake	*Coturnicops notata*
Tolima Dove	*Leptotila conoveri* *
Golden-plumed Parakeet	*Leptosittaca branickii*
Yellow-eared Parrot	*Ognorhynchus icterotis*
Flame-winged Parakeet	*Pyrrhura calliptera* *
Rufous-fronted Parakeet	*Bolborhynchus ferrugineifrons* *
Spot-winged Parrotlet	*Touit stictoptera*
Rusty-faced Parrot	*Hapalopsittaca amazonina*
Fuertes's Parrot	*Hapalopsittaca fuertesi* *
Banded Ground-cuckoo	*Neomorphus radiolosus*
White-chested Swift	*Cypseloides lemosi* *
Sapphire-bellied Hummingbird	*Lepidopyga lilliae* *
Chestnut-bellied Hummingbird	*Amazilia castaneiventris* *
Black Inca	*Coeligena prunellei* *
Colourful Puffleg	*Eriocnemis mirabilis* *
Hoary Puffleg	*Haplophaedia lugens*
Coppery-chested Jacamar	*Galbula pastazae*
White-mantled Barbet	*Capito hypoleucus* *
Chestnut-throated Spinetail	*Synallaxis cherriei*
Recurve-billed Bushbird	*Clytoctantes alixii*
Speckled Antshrike	*Xenornis setifrons*

Bicoloured Antvireo	*Dysithamnus occidentalis*
Moustached Antpitta	*Grallaria alleni* *
Giant Antpitta	*Grallaria gigantea*
Brown-banded Antpitta	*Grallaria milleri* *
Bicoloured Antpitta	*Grallaria rufocinerea* *
Hooded Antpitta	*Grallaricula cucullata*
Antioquia Bristle-tyrant	*Phylloscartes lanyoni* *
Ochraceous Attila	*Attila torridus*
Apolinar's Wren	*Cistothorus apolinari* *
Niceforo's Wren	*Thryothorus nicefori* *
Tumaco Seedeater	*Sporophila insulata* *
Yellow-headed Brush-finch	*Atlapetes flaviceps* *
Tanager-finch	*Oreothraupis arremonops*
Yellow-green Bush-tanager	*Chlorospingus flavovirens*
Gold-ringed Tanager	*Buthraupis aureocincta* *
Black-and-gold Tanager	*Buthraupis melanochlamys* *
Masked Mountain-tanager	*Buthraupis wetmorei*
Multicoloured Tanager	*Chlorochrysa nitidissima* *
Scarlet-breasted Dacnis	*Dacnis berlepschi*
Turquoise Dacnis	*Dacnis hartlaubi* *
Baudó Oropendola	*Psarocolius cassini* *
Red-bellied Grackle	*Hypopyrrhus pyrohypogaster* *
Red Siskin	*Carduelis cucullatus*

Costa Rica

Mangrove Hummingbird	*Amazilia boucardi* *
Keel-billed Motmot	*Electron carinatum*
Yellow-billed Cotinga	*Carpodectes antoniae*
Bare-necked Umbrellabird	*Cephalopterus glabricollis*

Cuba

Black-capped Petrel	*Pterodroma hasitata*
West Indian Whistling-duck	*Dendrocygna arborea*
Gundlach's Hawk	*Accipiter gundlachi* *
Zapata Rail	*Cyanolimnas cerverai* *
Plain Pigeon	*Columba inornata*
Blue-headed Quail-dove	*Starnoenas cyanocephala* *
Cuban Parakeet	*Aratinga euops* *
Cuban Flicker	*Colaptes fernandinae* *
Ivory-billed Woodpecker	*Campephilus principalis* *
Giant Kingbird	*Tyrannus cubensis* *
Zapata Wren	*Ferminia cerverai* *
Bachman's Warbler	*Vermivora bachmani*
Cuban Sparrow	*Torreornis inexpectata* *

Desventuradas Islands (to Chile)

Defilippe's Petrel	*Pterodroma defilippiana* *

Dominica

Black-capped Petrel	*Pterodroma hasitata*
Red-necked Amazon	*Amazona arausiaca* *

Imperial Amazon	*Amazona imperialis* *

Dominican Republic

Black-capped Petrel	*Pterodroma hasitata*
West Indian Whistling-duck	*Dendrocygna arborea*
Hispaniolan Hawk	*Buteo ridgwayi*
Plain Pigeon	*Columba inornata*
Rufous-breasted Cuckoo	*Hyetornis rufigularis*
La Selle Thrush	*Turdus swalesi*
Chat-tanager	*Calyptophilus frugivorus*
White-winged Warbler	*Xenoligea montana*

Ecuador (see also Galápagos Islands)

Grey-backed Hawk	*Leucopternis occidentalis*
Lesser Collared Forest-falcon	*Micrastur buckleyi*
Plumbeous Forest-falcon	*Micrastur plumbeus*
Bearded Guan	*Penelope barbata*
Wattled Curassow	*Crax globulosa*
Ochre-bellied Dove	*Leptotila ochraceiventris*
Golden-plumed Parakeet	*Leptosittaca branickii*
Yellow-eared Parrot	*Ognorhynchus icterotis*
White-necked Parakeet	*Pyrrhura albipectus* *
El Oro Parakeet	*Pyrrhura orcesi* *
Spot-winged Parrotlet	*Touit stictoptera*
Red-faced Parrot	*Hapalopsittaca pyrrhops*
Banded Ground-cuckoo	*Neomorphus radiolosus*
Turquoise-throated Puffleg	*Eriocnemis godini* *
Black-breasted Puffleg	*Eriocnemis nigrivestis* *
Hoary Puffleg	*Haplophaedia lugens*
Violet-throated Metaltail	*Metallura baroni* *
Neblina Metaltail	*Metallura odomae*
Esmeraldas Woodstar	*Acestrura berlepschi* *
Little Woodstar	*Acestrura bombus*
Coppery-chested Jacamar	*Galbula pastazae*
Chestnut-throated Spinetail	*Synallaxis cherriei*
Blackish-headed Spinetail	*Synallaxis tithys*
Henna-hooded Foliage-gleaner	*Hylocryptus erythrocephalus*
Rufous-necked Foliage-gleaner	*Syndactyla ruficollis*
Bicoloured Antvireo	*Dysithamnus occidentalis*
Grey-headed Antbird	*Myrmeciza griseiceps*
Giant Antpitta	*Grallaria gigantea*
Slaty Becard	*Pachyramphus spodiurus*
Cinnamon-breasted Tody-tyrant	*Hemitriccus cinnamomeipectus*
Pacific Royal Flycatcher	*Onychorhynchus occidentalis*
White-tailed Shrike-tyrant	*Agriornis andicola*
Ochraceous Attila	*Attila torridus*
Pale-headed Brush-finch	*Atlapetes pallidiceps* *
Tanager-finch	*Oreothraupis arremonops*
Yellow-green Bush-tanager	*Chlorospingus flavovirens*
Masked Mountain-tanager	*Buthraupis wetmorei*
Orange-throated Tanager	*Wetmorethraupis sterrhopteron*

	Scarlet-breasted Dacnis	*Dacnis berlepschi*
	Saffron Siskin	*Carduelis siemiradskii*
French Guiana		
	Cayenne Nightjar	*Caprimulgus maculosus* *
Galápagos Islands (to Ecuador)		
	Dark-rumped Petrel	*Pterodroma phaeopygia*
	Galápagos Cormorant	*Nannopterum harrisi* *
	Galápagos Hawk	*Buteo galapagoensis* *
	Floreana Mockingbird	*Nesomimus trifasciatus* *
	Mangrove Finch	*Camarhynchus heliobates* *
Grenada		
	Grenada Dove	*Leptotila wellsi* *
Guadalupe Island (to Mexico)		
	Guadalupe Storm-petrel	*Oceanodroma macrodactyla* *
	Guadalupe Junco	*Junco insularis* *
Guadeloupe (to France)		
	Black-capped Petrel	*Pterodroma hasitata*
Guatemala		
	Horned Guan	*Oreophasis derbianus*
	Keel-billed Motmot	*Electron carinatum*
	Azure-rumped Tanager	*Tangara cabanisi*
	Golden-cheeked Warbler	*Dendroica chrysoparia*
Guyana		
	Speckled Crake	*Coturnicops notata*
Haiti		
	Black-capped Petrel	*Pterodroma hasitata*
	West Indian Whistling-duck	*Dendrocygna arborea*
	Hispaniolan Hawk	*Buteo ridgwayi*
	Plain Pigeon	*Columba inornata*
	Rufous-breasted Cuckoo	*Hyetornis rufigularis*
	La Selle Thrush	*Turdus swalesi*
	Chat-tanager	*Calyptophilus frugivorus*
	White-winged Warbler	*Xenoligea montana*
Honduras		
	Honduran Emerald	*Amazilia luciae* *
	Keel-billed Motmot	*Electron carinatum*
	Golden-cheeked Warbler	*Dendroica chrysoparia*
Jamaica		
	Jamaica Petrel	*Pterodroma caribbaea* *
	West Indian Whistling-duck	*Dendrocygna arborea*
	Ring-tailed Pigeon	*Columba caribaea* *

Plain Pigeon	*Columba inornata*
Jamaican Pauraque	*Siphonorhis americanus* *

Juan Fernández Islands (to Chile)

Pink-footed Shearwater	*Puffinus creatopus* *
Defilippe's Petrel	*Pterodroma defilippiana* *
Juan Fernández Firecrown	*Sephanoides fernandesis* *
Masafuera Rayadito	*Aphrastura masafuerae* *

Martinique (to France)

Black-capped Petrel	*Pterodroma hasitata*
White-breasted Thrasher	*Ramphocinclus brachyurus*
Martinique Oriole	*Icterus bonana* *

Mexico (see also Guadalupe Island, Revillagigedo Islands)

Horned Guan	*Oreophasis derbianus*
Bearded Wood-partridge	*Dendrortyx barbatus* *
Piping Plover	*Charadrius melodus*
Thick-billed Parrot	*Rhynchopsitta pachyrhyncha* *
Maroon-fronted Parrot	*Rhynchopsitta terrisi* *
Yellow-headed Amazon	*Amazona oratrix*
Green-cheeked Amazon	*Amazona viridigenalis* *
Short-crested Coquette	*Lophornis brachylopha* *
Mexican Woodnymph	*Thalurania ridgwayi* *
Oaxaca Hummingbird	*Eupherusa cyanophrys* *
White-tailed Hummingbird	*Eupherusa poliocerca* *
Eared Quetzal	*Euptilotis neoxenus*
Keel-billed Motmot	*Electron carinatum*
Imperial Woodpecker	*Campephilus imperialis* *
Sumichrast's Wren	*Hylorchilus sumichrasti* *
Sierra Madre Sparrow	*Xenospiza baileyi* *
Azure-rumped Tanager	*Tangara cabanisi*
Golden-cheeked Warbler	*Dendroica chrysoparia*
Black-polled Yellowthroat	*Geothlypis speciosa* *
Black-capped Vireo	*Vireo atricapillus*
White-throated Jay	*Cyanolyca mirabilis* *
Dwarf Jay	*Cyanolyca nana* *

Netherlands Antilles (to Netherlands)

Yellow-shouldered Amazon	*Amazona barbadensis*

Nicaragua

Keel-billed Motmot	*Electron carinatum*
Golden-cheeked Warbler	*Dendroica chrysoparia*

Panama

Chocó Tinamou	*Crypturellus kerriae*
Glow-throated Hummingbird	*Selasphorus ardens* *
Speckled Antshrike	*Xenornis setifrons*
Yellow-billed Cotinga	*Carpodectes antoniae*
Bare-necked Umbrellabird	*Cephalopterus glabricollis*

Paraguay

Brazilian Merganser	*Mergus octosetaceus*
Crowned Eagle	*Harpyhaliaetus coronatus*
Black-fronted Piping-guan	*Pipile jacutinga*
Rufous-faced Crake	*Laterallus xenopterus*
Speckled Crake	*Coturnicops notata*
Purple-winged Ground-dove	*Claravis godefrida*
Glaucous Macaw	*Anodorhynchus glaucus*
Hyacinth Macaw	*Anodorhynchus hyacinthinus*
Vinaceous Amazon	*Amazona vinacea*
Sickle-winged Nightjar	*Eleothreptus anomalus*
Helmeted Woodpecker	*Dryocopus galeatus*
Dinelli's Doradito	*Pseudocolopteryx dinellianus*
São Paulo Tyrannulet	*Phylloscartes paulistus*
Russet-winged Spadebill	*Platyrinchus leucoryphus*
Strange-tailed Tyrant	*Yetapa risora*
Ochre-breasted Pipit	*Anthus nattereri*
Temminck's Seedeater	*Sporophila falcirostris*
Buffy-throated Seedeater	*Sporophila frontalis*
Rufous-rumped Seedeater	*Sporophila hypochroma*
Marsh Seedeater	*Sporophila palustris*
Yellow Cardinal	*Gubernatrix cristata*
Saffron-cowled Blackbird	*Xanthopsar flavus*

Peru

Black Tinamou	*Tinamus osgoodi*
Kalinowski's Tinamou	*Nothoprocta kalinowskii* *
Taczanowski's Tinamou	*Nothoprocta taczanowskii* *
Junín Grebe	*Podiceps taczanowskii* *
Peruvian Diving-petrel	*Pelecanoides garnotii*
Grey-backed Hawk	*Leucopternis occidentalis*
Lesser Collared Forest-falcon	*Micrastur buckleyi*
White-winged Guan	*Penelope albipennis* *
Bearded Guan	*Penelope barbata*
Southern Helmeted Curassow	*Pauxi unicornis*
Wattled Curassow	*Crax globulosa*
Junín Rail	*Laterallus tuerosi* *
Peruvian Pigeon	*Columba oenops* *
Ochre-bellied Dove	*Leptotila ochraceiventris*
Golden-plumed Parakeet	*Leptosittaca branickii*
Yellow-faced Parrotlet	*Forpus xanthops* *
Spot-winged Parrotlet	*Touit stictoptera*
Red-faced Parrot	*Hapalopsittaca pyrrhops*
Long-whiskered Owlet	*Xenoglaux loweryi* *
Purple-backed Sunbeam	*Aglaeactis aliciae* *
Royal Sunangel	*Heliangelus regalis* *
Neblina Metaltail	*Metallura odomae*
Grey-bellied Comet	*Taphrolesbia griseiventris* *
Marvellous Spatuletail	*Loddigesia mirabilis* *
Chilean Woodstar	*Eulidia yarrellii*
Little Woodstar	*Acestrura bombus*

Yellow-browed Toucanet	*Aulacorhynchus huallagae* *
Royal Cinclodes	*Cinclodes aricomae*
White-bellied Cinclodes	*Cinclodes palliatus* *
White-browed Tit-spinetail	*Leptasthenura xenothorax* *
Chestnut-throated Spinetail	*Synallaxis cherriei*
Apurímac Spinetail	*Synallaxis courseni* *
Blackish-headed Spinetail	*Synallaxis tithys*
Russet-bellied Spinetail	*Synallaxis zimmeri* *
Pale-tailed Canastero	*Asthenes huancavelicae* *
Russet-mantled Softtail	*Thripophaga berlepschi* *
Henna-hooded Foliage-gleaner	*Hylocryptus erythrocephalus*
Rufous-necked Foliage-gleaner	*Syndactyla ruficollis*
Ash-throated Antwren	*Herpsilochmus parkeri* *
Yellow-rumped Antwren	*Terenura sharpei*
Grey-headed Antbird	*Myrmeciza griseiceps*
White-masked Antbird	*Pithys castanea* *
Rufous-fronted Antthrush	*Formicarius rufifrons* *
White-cheeked Cotinga	*Zaratornis stresemanni* *
Slaty Becard	*Pachyramphus spodiurus*
Ash-breasted Tit-tyrant	*Anairetes alpinus*
Cinnamon-breasted Tody-tyrant	*Hemitriccus cinnamomeipectus*
Pacific Royal Flycatcher	*Onychorhynchus occidentalis*
Grey-breasted Flycatcher	*Lathrotriccus griseipectus*
White-tailed Shrike-tyrant	*Agriornis andicola*
Ochraceous Attila	*Attila torridus*
Peruvian Plantcutter	*Phytotoma raimondii*
Slender-billed Finch	*Xenospingus concolor*
Grey-winged Inca-finch	*Incaspiza ortizi* *
Plain-tailed Warbling-finch	*Poospiza alticola* *
Rufous-breasted Warbling-finch	*Poospiza rubecula* *
Golden-backed Mountain-tanager	*Buthraupis aureodorsalis* *
Masked Mountain-tanager	*Buthraupis wetmorei*
Orange-throated Tanager	*Wetmorethraupis sterrhopteron*
Green-capped Tanager	*Tangara meyerdeschauenseei* *
Sira Tanager	*Tangara phillipsi* *
Tamarugo Conebill	*Conirostrum tamarugense*
Selva Cacique	*Cacicus koepckeae* *
Saffron Siskin	*Carduelis siemiradskii*

Puerto Rico (to U.S.A.)

West Indian Whistling-duck	*Dendrocygna arborea*
Plain Pigeon	*Columba inornata*
Puerto Rican Amazon	*Amazona vittata* *
Puerto Rican Nightjar	*Caprimulgus noctitherus* *
Yellow-shouldered Blackbird	*Agelaius xanthomus* *
Red Siskin	*Carduelis cucullatus*

Revillagigedo Islands (to Mexico)

Townsend's Shearwater	*Puffinus auricularis* *
Socorro Dove	*Zenaida graysoni* *
Socorro Parakeet	*Aratinga brevipes* *

	Socorro Mockingbird	*Mimodes graysoni* *
San Andrés Island (to Colombia)		
	San Andrés Vireo	*Vireo caribaeus* *
St Croix (to U.S.A.)		
	West Indian Whistling-duck	*Dendrocygna arborea*
St Kitts–Nevis		
	West Indian Whistling-duck	*Dendrocygna arborea*
St Lucia		
	St Lucia Amazon	*Amazona versicolor* *
	White-breasted Thrasher	*Ramphocinclus brachyurus*
	Semper's Warbler	*Leucopeza semperi* *
St Vincent		
	St Vincent Amazon	*Amazona guildingii* *
Surinam		
	Rufous-sided Pygmy-tyrant	*Euscarthmus rufomarginatus*
Trinidad and Tobago		
	Trinidad Piping-guan	*Pipile pipile* *
	White-tailed Sabrewing	*Campylopterus ensipennis*
Turks and Caicos Islands (to U.K.)		
	West Indian Whistling-duck	*Dendrocygna arborea*
	Kirtland's Warbler	*Dendroica kirtlandii*
U.S.A. (see also Alaska, Puerto Rico, St Croix)		
	California Condor	*Gymnogyps californianus* *
	Whooping Crane	*Grus americana*
	Eskimo Curlew	*Numenius borealis*
	Piping Plover	*Charadrius melodus*
	(Thick-billed Parrot	*Rhynchopsitta pachyrhyncha*)
	Eared Quetzal	*Euptilotis neoxenus*
	Red-cockaded Woodpecker	*Picoides borealis* *
	Golden-cheeked Warbler	*Dendroica chrysoparia*
	Kirtland's Warbler	*Dendroica kirtlandii*
	Bachman's Warbler	*Vermivora bachmani*
	Black-capped Vireo	*Vireo atricapillus*
Uruguay		
	Crowned Eagle	*Harpyhaliaetus coronatus*
	Dot-winged Crake	*Porzana spiloptera*
	Speckled Crake	*Coturnicops notata*
	Eskimo Curlew	*Numenius borealis*
	Olrog's Gull	*Larus atlanticus*
	Glaucous Macaw	*Anodorhynchus glaucus*
	Strange-tailed Tyrant	*Yetapa risora*

Marsh Seedeater	*Sporophila palustris*
Yellow Cardinal	*Gubernatrix cristata*
Saffron-cowled Blackbird	*Xanthopsar flavus*
Pampas Meadowlark	*Sturnella militaris*

Venezuela

Northern Helmeted Curassow	*Pauxi pauxi*
Plain-flanked Rail	*Rallus wetmorei* *
Rusty-flanked Crake	*Laterallus levraudi* *
Speckled Crake	*Coturnicops notata*
Rusty-faced Parrot	*Hapalopsittaca amazonina*
Yellow-shouldered Amazon	*Amazona barbadensis*
White-tailed Sabrewing	*Campylopterus ensipennis*
Táchira Emerald	*Amazilia distans* *
Scissor-tailed Hummingbird	*Hylonympha macrocerca* *
Orinoco Softtail	*Thripophaga cherriei* *
White-throated Barbtail	*Margarornis tatei* *
Recurve-billed Bushbird	*Clytoctantes alixii*
Táchira Antpitta	*Grallaria chthonia* *
Hooded Antpitta	*Grallaricula cucullata*
Slaty-backed Hemispingus	*Hemispingus goeringi* *
Venezuelan Flowerpiercer	*Diglossa venezuelensis* *
Paria Redstart	*Myioborus pariae* *
Grey-headed Warbler	*Basileuterus griseiceps* *
Red Siskin	*Carduelis cucullatus*
Yellow-faced Siskin	*Carduelis yarrellii*

Virgin Islands (to U.K.)

West Indian Whistling-duck	*Dendrocygna arborea*

APPENDIX D

Near-threatened birds of the Americas

The dividing line between "threatened" and "secure" is rendered artificially certain by the compilation of lists that simply identify the former. IUCN's "Insufficiently Known" category was a relatively late invention in response to the difficulty Red Data Book compilers often experienced in making the decision to include or exclude a taxon. Nevertheless, this still fails to cater for the genuine borderline cases that lost that decision, even though it lets through a greater percentage than before into "threatened" status. ICBP has therefore adopted the concept of "near-threatened" species as a means of identifying and tracking those birds which, while apparently not (yet) seriously in danger of global extinction, give cause for concern. As noted in the Introduction, ideally the following list should be annotated in order to offer some explanation of inclusion at this level, but considerations of both time and space have precluded this. There has not been time, either, to undertake a major review and revision of this list, which is based on (though considerably amended from) that published in Collar and Andrew (1988), this itself being derived from the judgements and data of the several hundred correspondents who replied to the circulation of the candidate list of threatened species in early 1986. It cannot pretend to comprehensiveness, and the question is immediately begged of how to distinguish "near-threatened" from "secure". Nevertheless, even in this form, it serves to acknowledge the concerns that may be widely felt over these species, and it indicates the (325) birds beyond the main list to which ornithologists and conservationists might most valuably devote their further attentions.

Greater Rhea	*Rhea americana*
Puna Rhea	*Pterocnemia pennata*
Solitary Tinamou	*Tinamus solitarius*
Hooded Tinamou	*Nothocercus nigrocapillus*
Colombian Tinamou	*Crypturellus columbianus*
Yellow-legged Tinamou	*Crypturellus noctivagus*
Pale-browed Tinamou	*Crypturellus transfasciatus*
Peruvian Penguin	*Spheniscus humboldti*
Galápagos Penguin	*Spheniscus mendiculus*
Hooded Grebe	*Podiceps gallardoi*
Galápagos Albatross	*Diomedea irrorata*
Black-vented Shearwater	*Puffinus opisthomelas*
Ringed Storm-petrel	*Oceanodroma hornbyi*
Markham's Storm-petrel	*Oceanodroma markhami*
Red-legged Cormorant	*Phalacrocorax gaimardi*
Agami Heron	*Agamia agami*
Fasciated Tiger-heron	*Tigrisoma fasciatum*
Zigzag Heron	*Zebrilus undulatus*
Andean Flamingo	*Phoenicoparrus andinus*
Puna Flamingo	*Phoenicoparrus jamesi*
Northern Screamer	*Chauna chavaria*
Trumpeter Swan	*Cygnus buccinator*
Ruddy-headed Goose	*Chloephaga rubidiceps*
Orinoco Goose	*Neochen jubata*

White-headed Steamer Duck	*Tachyeres leucocephalus*
Spectacled Duck	*Anas specularis*
Black-headed Duck	*Heteronetta atricapilla*
Semicollared Hawk	*Accipiter collaris*
Grey-bellied Hawk	*Accipiter poliogaster*
Plumbeous Hawk	*Leucopternis plumbea*
Mantled Hawk	*Leucopternis polionota*
Semiplumbeous Hawk	*Leucopternis semiplumbea*
Solitary Eagle	*Harpyhaliaetus solitarius*
Rufous-tailed Hawk	*Buteo ventralis*
Crested Eagle	*Morphnus guianensis*
Harpy Eagle	*Harpia harpyja*
Black-and-white Hawk-eagle	*Spizastur melanoleucus*
Black-and-chestnut Eagle	*Oroaetus isidori*
Orange-breasted Falcon	*Falco deiroleucus*
Striated Caracara	*Phalcoboenus australis*
Rufous-headed Chachalaca	*Ortalis erythroptera*
Highland Guan	*Penelopina nigra*
Red-faced Guan	*Penelope dabbenei*
White-browed Guan	*Penelope jacucaca*
Baudó Guan	*Penelope ortoni*
White-crested Guan	*Penelope pileata*
Wattled Guan	*Aburria aburri*
Black Guan	*Chamaepetes unicolor*
Black-fronted Wood-quail	*Odontophorus atrifrons*
Venezuelan Wood-quail	*Odontophorus columbianus*
Tacarcuna Wood-quail	*Odontophorus dialeucos*
Chestnut Wood-quail	*Odontophorus hyperythrus*
Black-breasted Wood-quail	*Odontophorus leucolaemus*
Dark-backed Wood-quail	*Odontophorus melanonotus*
Ocellated Quail	*Cyrtonyx ocellatus*
Ocellated Turkey	*Agriocharis ocellata*
Brown-backed Wood-rail	*Aramides wolfi*
Galápagos Crake	*Laterallus spilonotus*
Ocellated Crake	*Micropygia schomburgkii*
Colombian Crake	*Neocrex colombianus*
Sandpiper-plover	*Phegornis mitchellii*
Magellanic Plover	*Pluvianellus socialis*
Hudsonian Godwit	*Limosa haemastica*
Imperial Snipe	*Gallinago imperialis*
Strickland's Snipe	*Gallinago stricklandii*
Lava Gull	*Larus fuliginosus*
Craveri's Murrelet	*Brachyramphus craveri*
Xantus's Murrelet	*Brachyramphus hypoleuca*
Marbled Murrelet	*Brachyramphus marmoratus*
Chilean Pigeon	*Columba araucana*
Grey-headed Quail-dove	*Geotrygon caniceps*
Russet-crowned Quail-dove	*Geotrygon goldmani*
Bridled Quail-dove	*Geotrygon mystacea*
Crested Quail-dove	*Geotrygon versicolor*
Blue-winged Macaw	*Ara maracana*

Hispaniolan Parakeet	*Aratinga chloroptera*
Red-masked Parakeet	*Aratinga erythrogenys*
Rose-crowned Parakeet	*Pyrrhura rhodocephala*
Santa Marta Parakeet	*Pyrrhura viridicata*
Slender-billed Conure	*Enicognathus leptorhynchus*
Grey-cheeked Parakeet	*Brotogeris pyrrhopterus*
Amazonian Parrotlet	*Nannopsittaca dachilleae*
Red-fronted Parrotlet	*Touit costaricensis*
Pileated Parrot	*Pionopsitta pileata*
Black-billed Amazon	*Amazona agilis*
Yellow-billed Amazon	*Amazona collaria*
Blue-cheeked Amazon	*Amazona dufresniana*
Cuban Amazon	*Amazona leucocephala*
Alder Amazon	*Amazona tucumana*
Hispaniolan Parrot	*Amazona ventralis*
Yellow-faced Parrot	*Amazona xanthops*
Cocos Cuckoo	*Coccyzus ferrugineus*
Scaly Ground-cuckoo	*Neomorphus squamiger*
Bridled Screech-owl	*Otus barbarus*
Spotted Owl	*Strix occidentalis*
Unspotted Saw-whet Owl	*Aegolius ridgwayi*
Buff-fronted Owl	*Aegolius harrisii*
Hispaniolan Least Pauraque	*Siphonorhis brewsteri*
Eared Poorwill	*Otophanes mcleodii*
Yucatán Poorwill	*Otophanes yucatanicus*
Pygmy Nightjar	*Caprimulgus hirundinaceus*
Roraiman Nightjar	*Caprimulgus whitelyi*
Long-trained Nightjar	*Macropsalis creagra*
Rothschild's Swift	*Cypseloides rothschildi*
White-fronted Swift	*Cypseloides storeri*
Tooth-billed Hummingbird	*Androdon aequatorialis*
Saw-billed Hermit	*Ramphodon naevius*
Koepcke's Hermit	*Phaethornis koepckeae*
Long-tailed Sabrewing	*Campylopterus excellens*
Santa Marta Sabrewing	*Campylopterus phainopeplus*
Napo Sabrewing	*Campylopterus villaviscensio*
Fiery-tailed Awlbill	*Avocettula recurvirostris*
Spangled Coquette	*Lophornis stictolopha*
Pirre Hummingbird	*Goethalsia bella*
Blossomcrown	*Anthocephala floriceps*
Ecuadorian Piedtail	*Phlogophilus hemileucurus*
Peruvian Piedtail	*Phlogophilus harterti*
Pink-throated Brilliant	*Heliodoxa gularis*
Wedge-tailed Hillstar	*Oreotrochilus adela*
Black-thighed Puffleg	*Eriocnemis derbyi*
Bronze-tailed Comet	*Polyonymus caroli*
Perijá Metaltail	*Metallura iracunda*
Hooded Visorbearer	*Augastes lumachellus*
Hyacinth Visorbearer	*Augastes scutatus*
Beautiful Hummingbird	*Calothorax pulcher*
Magenta-throated Woodstar	*Calliphlox bryantae*

Bee Hummingbird	*Calypte helenae*
Baird's Trogon	*Trogon bairdii*
Hispaniolan Trogon	*Temnotrogon roseigaster*
Resplendent Quetzal	*Pharomachrus mocinno*
Narrow-billed Tody	*Todus angustirostris*
Sooty-capped Puffbird	*Bucco noanamae*
Lanceolated Monklet	*Micromonacha lanceolata*
Chestnut-headed Nunlet	*Nonnula amaurocephala*
Five-coloured Barbet	*Capito quinticolor*
Scarlet-hooded Barbet	*Eubucco tucinkae*
Toucan Barbet	*Semnornis ramphastinus*
Pale-mandibled Araçari	*Pteroglossus erythropygius*
Saffron Toucanet	*Baillonius bailloni*
Hooded Mountain-toucan	*Andigena cucullata*
Grey-breasted Mountain-toucan	*Andigena hypoglauca*
Plate-billed Mountain-toucan	*Andigena laminirostris*
Black-billed Mountain-toucan	*Andigena nigrirostris*
Tawny Piculet	*Picumnus fulvescens*
Mottled Piculet	*Picumnus nebulosus*
Spot-crowned Piculet	*Picumnus subtilis*
Speckle-chested Piculet	*Picumnus steindachneri*
Hispaniolan Piculet	*Nesoctites micromegas*
White-browed Woodpecker	*Piculus aurulentus*
Black-bodied Woodpecker	*Dryocopus schulzi*
Greater Scythebill	*Campylorhamphus pucheranii*
Bolivian Earthcreeper	*Upucerthia harterti*
Araucaria Tit-spinetail	*Leptasthenura setaria*
Tawny Tit-spinetail	*Leptasthenura yanacensis*
Perijá Thistletail	*Schizoeaca perijana*
Cactus Canastero	*Asthenes cactorum*
Chestnut Canastero	*Asthenes steinbachi*
Line-fronted Canastero	*Asthenes urubambensis*
Great Spinetail	*Siptornopsis hypochondriacus*
Chestnut-backed Thornbird	*Phacellodomus dorsalis*
Bay-capped Wren-spinetail	*Spartonoica maluroides*
Canebrake Groundcreeper	*Clibanornis dendrocolaptoides*
Straight-billed Reedhaunter	*Limnornis rectirostris*
Equatorial Greytail	*Xenerpestes singularis*
Beautiful Treerunner	*Margarornis bellulus*
White-browed Foliage-gleaner	*Philydor amaurotis*
Russet-mantled Foliage-gleaner	*Philydor dimidiatus*
Peruvian Recurvebill	*Philydor ucalayae*
Chestnut-capped Foliage-gleaner	*Hylocryptus rectirostris*
Cocha Antshrike	*Thamnophilus praecox*
Spot-breasted Antvireo	*Dysithamnus stictothorax*
Klages's Antwren	*Myrmotherula klagesi*
Salvadori's Antwren	*Myrmotherula minor*
Unicoloured Antwren	*Myrmotherula unicolor*
Band-tailed Antwren	*Myrmotherula urosticta*
Black-capped Antwren	*Herpsilochmus pileatus*
Serra Antwren	*Formicivora serrana*

Rufous-tailed Antbird	*Drymophila genei*
Ochre-rumped Antbird	*Drymophila ochropyga*
Rio de Janeiro Antbird	*Cercomacra brasiliana*
Yapacana Antbird	*Myrmeciza disjuncta*
Bare-eyed Antbird	*Rhegmatorhina gymnops*
White-breasted Antbird	*Rhegmatorhina hoffmannsi*
Chestnut Antpitta	*Grallaria blakei*
Elusive Antpitta	*Grallaria eludens*
Great Antpitta	*Grallaria excelsa*
White-browed Antpitta	*Hylopezus ochroleucus*
Crescent-faced Antpitta	*Grallaricula lineifrons*
Scallop-breasted Antpitta	*Grallaricula loricata*
Ochre-fronted Antpitta	*Grallaricula ochraceifrons*
Peruvian Antpitta	*Grallaricula peruviana*
Hooded Gnateater	*Conopophaga roberti*
Marañon Crescentchest	*Melanopareia maranonica*
Spotted Bamboowren	*Psilorhamphus guttatus*
Slaty Bristlefront	*Merulaxis ater*
Swallow-tailed Cotinga	*Phibalura flavirostris*
Turquoise Cotinga	*Cotinga ridgwayi*
Black-and-gold Cotinga	*Tijuca atra*
Hooded Berryeater	*Carpornis cucullatus*
Fiery-throated Fruiteater	*Pipreola chlorolepidota*
Scarlet-breasted Fruiteater	*Pipreola frontalis*
Black-chested Fruiteater	*Pipreola lubomirskii*
Scaled Fruiteater	*Ampelioides tschudii*
Purple-throated Cotinga	*Porphyrolaema porphyrolaema*
White Cotinga	*Carpodectes hopkei*
Black-faced Cotinga	*Conioptilon mcilhennyi*
Long-wattled Umbrellabird	*Cephalopterus penduliger*
Three-wattled Bellbird	*Procnias tricarunculata*
Bare-throated Bellbird	*Procnias nudicollis*
Grey-headed Manakin	*Piprites griseiceps*
Salinas Monjita	*Xolmis salinarum*
Black-and-white Monjita	*Heteroxolmis dominicana*
Rufous-bellied Bush-tyrant	*Myiotheretes fuscorufus*
Santa Marta Bush-tyrant	*Myiotheretes pernix*
Piura Chat-tyrant	*Ochthoeca piurae*
Cock-tailed Tyrant	*Alectrurus tricolor*
Hudson's Black-tyrant	*Knipolegus hudsoni*
Shear-tailed Grey-tyrant	*Muscipipra vetula*
Tumbes Tyrant	*Tumbezia salvini*
Ochraceous Pewee	*Contopus ochraceus*
Belted Flycatcher	*Xenotriccus callizonus*
Pileated Flycatcher	*Aechmolophus mexicanus*
Black-billed Flycatcher	*Aphanotriccus audax*
Tawny-chested Flycatcher	*Aphanotriccus capitalis*
Orange-banded Flycatcher	*Myiophobus lintoni*
White-cheeked Tody-flycatcher	*Poecilotriccus albifacies*
Short-tailed Tody-flycatcher	*Todirostrum viridanum*
Hangnest Tody-tyrant	*Idioptilon nidipendulum*

Eye-ringed Tody-tyrant	*Idioptilon orbitatum*
Boat-billed Tody-tyrant	*Microcochlearius josephinae*
White-breasted Pygmy-tyrant	*Myiornis albiventris*
Zimmer's Tody-tyrant	*Hemitriccus aenigma*
Buff-throated Tody-tyrant	*Hemitriccus rufigularis*
Southern Bristle-tyrant	*Pogonotriccus eximius*
Venezuelan Bristle-tyrant	*Pogonotriccus venezuelanus*
Bay-ringed Tyrannulet	*Leptotriccus sylviolus*
Oustalet's Tyrannulet	*Phylloscartes oustaleti*
Serra do Mar Tyrannulet	*Phylloscartes difficilis*
Reiser's Tyrannulet	*Phyllomyias reiseri*
Grey-capped Tyrannulet	*Oreotriccus griseocapillus*
Bearded Tachuri	*Polystictus pectoralis*
Grey-backed Tachuri	*Polystictus superciliaris*
Sharp-tailed Tyrant	*Culicivora caudacuta*
Sinaloa Martin	*Progne sinaloae*
Bahama Swallow	*Tachycineta cyaneoviridis*
Golden Swallow	*Tachycineta euchrysea*
Chaco Pipit	*Anthus chacoensis*
Socorro Wren	*Thryomanes sissonii*
Clarión Wren	*Troglodytes tanneri*
Bar-winged Wood-wren	*Henicorhina leucoptera*
Cuban Solitaire	*Myadestes elisabeth*
Rufous-brown Solitaire	*Myadestes leucogenys*
Grayson's Thrush	*Turdus graysoni*
Forest Thrush	*Cichlherminia lherminieri*
Black Catbird	*Melanoptila glabrirostris*
Creamy-bellied Gnatcatcher	*Polioptila lactea*
Cuban Gnatcatcher	*Polioptila lembeyei*
Rosita's Bunting	*Passerina rositae*
Henslow's Sparrow	*Ammodramus henslowii*
Oaxaca Sparrow	*Aimophila notosticta*
Sumichrast's Sparrow	*Aimophila sumichrasti*
Worthen's Sparrow	*Spizella wortheni*
Peg-billed Finch	*Acanthidops bairdii*
Blue Finch	*Porphyrospiza caerulescens*
Coal-crested Finch	*Charitospiza eucosoma*
Black-throated Finch	*Melanodera melanodera*
Little Inca-finch	*Incaspiza watkinsi*
Lesser Grass-finch	*Emberizoides ypiranganus*
Black-masked Finch	*Coryphaspiza melanotis*
Citron-headed Yellow Finch	*Sicalis luteocephala*
Buff-throated Pampa-finch	*Embernagra longicauda*
Chestnut Seedeater	*Sporophila cinnamomea*
Black-bellied Seedeater	*Sporophila melanogaster*
Dark-throated Seedeater	*Sporophila ruficollis*
Greater Large-billed Seed-finch	*Oryzoborus maximiliani*
Lesser Large-billed Seed-finch	*Oryzoborus crassirostris*
Blackish-blue Seedeater	*Amaurospiza moesta*
Slate-blue Seedeater	*Amaurospiza relicta*
St Lucia Black Finch	*Melanospiza richardsoni*

Floreana Tree-finch	*Camarhynchus pauper*
Santa Marta Seedeater	*Catamenia oreophila*
Dusky-headed Brush-finch	*Atlapetes fuscoolivaceus*
White-rimmed Brush-finch	*Atlapetes leucopis*
Rufous-eared Brush-finch	*Atlapetes rufigenis*
Masked Saltator	*Saltator cinctus*
Thick-billed Saltator	*Saltator maxillosus*
Green-throated Euphonia	*Euphonia chalybea*
Brown Tanager	*Orchesticus abeillei*
Rufous-browed Hemispingus	*Hemispingus rufosuperciliaris*
Azure-shouldered Tanager	*Thraupis cyanoptera*
Blue-and-gold Tanager	*Buthraupis arcaei*
Blue-whiskered Tanager	*Tangara johannae*
Dotted Tanager	*Tangara varia*
Black-cheeked Ant-tanager	*Habia atrimaxillaris*
Sooty Ant-tanager	*Habia gutturalis*
Black-and-white Tanager	*Conothraupis speculigera*
Chestnut-bellied Flowerpiercer	*Diglossa gloriosissima*
White-bellied Dacnis	*Dacnis albiventris*
Viridian Dacnis	*Dacnis viguieri*
Tit-like Dacnis	*Xenodacnis parina*
Pearly-breasted Conebill	*Conirostrum margaritae*
Giant Conebill	*Oreomanes fraseri*
Colima Warbler	*Vermivora crissalis*
Elfin Woods Warbler	*Dendroica angelae*
Vitelline Warbler	*Dendroica vitellina*
Whistling Warbler	*Catharopeza bishopi*
Belding's Yellowthroat	*Geothlypis beldingi*
Altamira Yellowthroat	*Geothlypis flavovelata*
Pink-headed Warbler	*Ergaticus versicolor*
Grey-throated Warbler	*Basileuterus cinereicollis*
Pirre Warbler	*Basileuterus ignotus*
Chestnut-sided Shrike-vireo	*Vireolanius melitophrys*
Slaty Vireo	*Vireo brevipennis*
Dwarf Vireo	*Vireo nelsoni*
Blue Mountain Vireo	*Vireo osburni*
St Lucia Oriole	*Icterus laudabilis*
Montserrat Oriole	*Icterus oberi*
Jamaican Blackbird	*Nesopsar nigerrimus*
Mountain Grackle	*Macroagelaius subalaris*
Nicaraguan Grackle	*Quiscalus nicaraguensis*
Azure Jay	*Cyanocorax caeruleus*
Tufted Jay	*Cyanocorax dickeyi*
Beautiful Jay	*Cyanolyca pulchra*
White-necked Crow	*Corvus leucognaphalus*
Palm Crow	*Corvus palmarum*

References

Abramson, J. (1991) Macaw breeding and conservation. *AFA Watchbird* 18(3): 40-42.

Abreu, R. M., de la Cruz, J., Rams, A. and García, M. E. (1989) Vertebrado [*sic*] del complejo montañoso "La Zoilita", Holguín, Cuba. *Poeyana* 370.

ACB (1976) = *Atlas of the Commonwealth of the Bahamas*. Kingston, Jamaica: Ministry of Education, Nassau, Bahamas.

Acevedo, C., Fox, J., Gauto, R., Granizo, T., Keel, S., Pinazzo, J., Spinzi, L., Sosa, W. and Vera, V. (1990) *Areas prioritarias para la conservación en la región oriental del Paraguay*. Asunción: Centro de Datos para la Conservación.

Acevedo-Latorre, E. (1971) *Diccionario geográfico de Colombia*. Bogotá: Instituto Geográfico Agustín Codazzi.

Acosta, M. and Berovides, V. (1984) Ornitocenosis de los cayos Coco y Romano, Archipiélago de Sabana-Camagüey, Cuba. *Poeyana* 274.

Acosta, M., Ibarra, M. E. and Fernández, E. (1988) Aspectos ecológicos de la avifauna de Cayo Matías (grupo insular de los Canarreos, Cuba). *Poeyana* 360.

Acosta Cruz, M. and Mugica Valdés, L. (1988) Estructura de las comunidades de aves que habitan los bosques cubanos. *Cienc. Biol.* 19-20: 9-19.

AGSNY (1940) = American Geographical Society of New York (1940) South America, 1:1,000,000. Sucre, provisional edition SE-20. New York: American Geographical Society of New York.

AGSNY (1954) = American Geographical Society of New York (1954) North America, 1:1,000,000. Monterrey, provisional edition NG-14. New York: American Geographical Society of New York.

Aguirre, A. (1947) Sooretama. *Bol. Min. Agric.* (Rio de Janeiro) 36(4-6): 1-52.

Aguirre, A. (1958) *A caça e a pesca no pantanal de Mato Grosso*. Rio de Janeiro: Ministério de Agricultura.

Aguirre, A. C. and Aldrighi, A. D. (1983) *Catálogo das aves do Museu da Fauna*. Primeira parte. [Rio de Janeiro:] Instituto Brasileiro de Desenvolvimento Florestal, Delegacia Estadual do Estado do Rio de Janeiro.

Aguirre, A. C. and Aldrighi, A. D. (1987) *Catálago das aves do Museu da Fauna*. Segunda parte. Rio de Janeiro: Instituto Brasileiro do Desenvolvimento Florestal.

Alayón, G. and Garrido, O. H. (1991) Current situation of the Ivory-billed Woodpecker (*Campephilus principalis*) in Cuba. Unpublished.

Alayón García, G. (1987) Lista de las aves observadas en la Reserve Natural de Cupeyal, Provincia de Guantánamo, Cuba. *Misc. Zool. Acad. Cienc. Cuba* 31: 1-2.

Alayón García, G., Estrada, A. R. and Torres Leyva, A. (1987) Lista de las aves observadas en la Reserva de la Biosfera "Cuchillas del Toa", provincia de Holguín y Guantánamo, Cuba. *Garciana* 6: 1-3.

Albin, E. (1738) *A natural history of birds*, 2. London: W. Innys and R. Manby.

Albuquerque, E. P. (1981) Lista preliminar das aves observadas no Parque Florestal Estadual do Turvo. *Rosseleria* 4: 107-122.

Albuquerque, J. L. B. (1986) Conservation and status of raptors in southern Brazil. *Birds of Prey Bull.* 3: 88-94.

Alderton, D. (1985) More about macaws. *Cage and Aviary Birds*, 16 February: 4-5.

Aleixo, A. L. P., de Lima, F. C. T. and Fortaleza, D. M. R. (1991) Resultados de uma excursão ornitológica à Reserva Biológica de Sooretama. Centro de Preservação dos Psitacídeos do Espírito Santo e Sul Bahia, unpublished.

Alfonso Sánchez, M. A., Berovides Alvarez, V. and Acosta Cruz, M. (1988) Diversidad ecológica y gremios en tres comunidades de aves cubanas. *Cienc. Biol.* 19-20: 20-29.

Alho, C. J. R. and Rondon, N. L. (1987) Habitats, population densities, and social structure of capybaras (*Hydrochaeris hydrochaeris*, Rodentia) in the Pantanal, Brazil. *Revta. Bras. Zool.* 4: 139-149.

Allen, J. A. (1889) List of the birds collected in Bolivia by Dr H. H. Rusby, with field notes by the collector. *Bull. Amer. Mus. Nat. Hist.* 2: 77-112.

Allen, J. A. (1891-1893) On a collection of birds from Chapada, Mato Grosso, Brazil, made by Mr H. H. Smith. *Bull. Amer. Mus. Nat. Hist.* 3:337-380; 4: 330-350; 5: 107-158.

Allen, J. A. (1893) List of mammals and birds collected in northeastern Sonora and northwestern Chihuahua, Mexico, on the Lumholtz Archaeological Expedition. *Bull. Amer. Mus. Nat. Hist.* 5: 27-42.

Allen, J. A. (1900) List of birds collected in the district of Santa Marta, Colombia, by Mr Herbert H. Smith. *Bull. Amer. Mus. Nat. Hist.* 13: 117-183.

Allen, J. A. (1904) Black-capped Petrel in New Hampshire. *Auk* 21: 383.

Allen, R. P. (1962) *Birds of the Caribbean.* London: Thames and Hudson.

Alvarez, T. (1933) Observaciones biológicas sobre las aves del Uruguay. *An. Mus. Hist. Nat. Montevideo* (2)4: 1-50.

Alvarez del Toro, M. (1976) Datos biológicos del Pavón (*Oreophasis derbianus* G. R. Gray). *Revta. Univ. Auton. Chiapas* 1: 43-54.

Alvarez del Toro, M. (1981) Aves notables en Chiapas y problemas para la conservación de la avifauna local. *Centzontle* 1(2): 79-88.

Amadon, D. (1964) Taxonomic notes on birds of prey. *Amer. Mus. Novit.* 2166.

Amberger, F. (1989a) Im Lebensraum der Dominica-Amazonen. *Gefied. Welt* 113: 244-246.

Amberger, F. (1989b) Schau- und Zuchtvolieren auf St Vincent. *Papageien* 3/89: 82-83.

Amos, E. J. R. (1991) *A guide to the birds of Bermuda.* Warwick, Bermuda: Eric J. R. Amos.

Amos, S. H. (1985) Breeding the Yellow Cardinal *Gubernatrix cristata* at the National Aquarium in Baltimore, Maryland, USA. *Avicult. Mag.* 91: 119-203.

Amos, S. H. (1986) Efforts to aid the endangered Black-hooded Red Siskin. *AFA Watchbird* 12(6): 19.

Amsler, M. (1912) Breeding of the Hooded Siskin. *Avicult. Mag.* (3)4: 51-54.

Amsler, M. (1935) Fertility of the Hooded Siskin and Canary hybrid. *Avicult. Mag.* (4)13: 229-232.

de Andrade, M. A., de Freitas, M. V. and de Mattos, G. T. (1986) A redescoberta de "*Xiphocolaptes franciscanus*" Snethlage 1927 no estado de Minas Gerais, Brasil. *An. Soc. Sul-Riogr. Orn.* 7: 18-20.

de Andrade, M. A., de Freitas, M. V. and de Mattos, G. T. (1988) O arapaçu-do-São-Francisco 60 anos depois. *Ciência Hoje* 8(44): 78-79.

Andrade, N. C. (1987) Land use management plan for Venezuela's Margarita Island. *Caribbean Conserv. News* 4(12): 2.

de Andrade-Lima, D. (1982) Present-day forest refuges in northeastern Brazil. Pp.245-251 in G. T. Prance, ed. *Biological diversification in the tropics.* New York: Columbia University Press.

Andrle, R. F. (1967) The Horned Guan in Mexico and Guatemala. *Condor* 69: 93-109.

Andrle, R. F. (1969) Biology and conservation of the Horned Guan. *Amer. Phil. Soc. Year Book* 1968: 276-277.

Andrle, R. F. and Andrle, P. R. (1975) Report on the status and conservation of the Whistling Warbler on St Vincent, West Indies, with additional observations on the St Vincent Parrot and Rufous-throated Solitaire. *XII Bull. Internatn. Coun. Bird Preserv.*: 245-251.

Anon. (1904) The birds of St Vincent. *West Indian Bull.* 5(1): 75-95.

Anon. (1931) Las colecciones ornitológicas del Museo Nacional. *Hornero* 4: 458.

Anon. (1942) Algunas observaciones obtenidas en el viaje a Misiones. *Hornero* 8: 271-276.

Anon. (1980) Neotropical psittacines in trade. TRAFFIC (U.S.A.) for World Wildlife Fund-U.S. Unpublished.

Anon. (1981a) Emergency protection for the *Amazona* parrots of Dominica following the passage of Hurricane David. Final [first-year] report [by Forestry Division, Dominica] to World Wildlife Fund-U.S, January 1981. Unpublished.

Anon. (1981b) Emergency protection for the *Amazona* parrots of Dominica following the passage of Hurricane David. Second annual report to World Wildlife Fund-U.S., December 1981, [by] Forestry Division, Dominica. Unpublished.

Anon. (1989) *Información básica sobre las áreas naturales protegidas de México.* Dirección General de Conservación Ecológica de los Recursos Naturales.

Anon. (1991a) Mexico's most endangered parrot. *Psittascene* 3(1): 8.

Anon. (1991b) Relatório de uma excursão à Reserva Biológica de Nova Lombardia. Centro de Preservação dos Psitacídeos do Espírito Santo e Sul Bahia, unpublished.

Antas, P. T. Z. (1989) Situação de vulnerabilidade de duas aves endêmicas do Brasil central. Pp.146-147 in *Resumos, XVI Congresso Brasileiro de Zoologia.* João Pessoa: Universidade Federal de Paraíba.

AOU (1976) = American Ornithologists' Union (1976) Report of the Committee on Conservation. *Auk* 93 (4th Suppl.): 1DD-19DD.

AOU (1983) = American Ornithologists' Union (1983) *Check-list of North American birds*. Sixth edition. American Ornithologists' Union.

Aplin, O. V. (1894) On the birds of Uruguay. *Ibis* 6(6): 149-215.

Apolinar-María, Hno. (1946) Vocabulario de términos vulgares en historia natural colombiana. *Revta. Acad. Colomb. Cienc. Exact. Fís. Nat.* 7(25-26): 14-33.

Aravena, R. (1928) Notas sobre la alimentación de las aves. *Hornero* 4: 38-49, 153-166.

Araya Mödinger, B. and Duffy, D. C. (1987) Animal introductions to Chañaral Island, Chile; their history and effect on seabirds. *Cormorant* 15: 3-6.

Araya Mödinger, B. and Millie Holman, G. (1986) *Guía de campo de las aves de Chile*. Santiago: Editorial Universitaria.

Arballo, E. (1987) Registro de la Tijereta de las Pajas para el Uruguay. *Nuestras Aves* 13: 16-17.

Arballo, E. (1990) Nuevos registros para avifauna uruguaya. *Hornero* 13: 179-187.

Areas Protegidas (1989) Areas protegidas en el territorio de jurisdicción de la C.V.C. Colombia. *Flora, Fauna y Areas Silvestres* 3(11): 20-22.

Arndt, T. (1986) *Südamerikanische Sittiche: Enzyklopädie der Papageien und Sittiche*, 5. Bomlitz: Horst Müller.

Arndt, T. (1987) Spix-Ara-Tagung auf Teneriffa. *Zool. Ges. Arten- und Populationsschutz Mitglieder Information*, Oktober 1987 [:8-9].

Arndt, T. (1989) Zum Status der Gelbschulter-amazone. *Papageien* 2/89: 57-60.

Arndt, T., Sojer, A., Strunden, H. and Wirth, R. (1986) 5 Minuten vor 12 für den Spix-Ara (*Cyanopsitta spixii*). *Gefied. Welt* 110: 321-323.

Astley, H. D. (1902) The Hooded Siskin. *Avicult. Mag.* (2)1: 47-51.

Astley, H. D. (1907) Lear's Macaw. *Avicult. Mag.* (2)5: 111-113.

Aveledo, H. R. and Pons, A. R. (1952) Aves nuevas y extensiones de distribución a Venezuela. *Noved. Cient. Mus. Hist. Nat. La Salle*, ser. zool. 7: 3-21.

de Azara, F. (1802-1805) *Apuntamientos para la historia natural de los páxaros del Paraguay y río de la Plata*. Madrid: Imprenta de la Viuda de Ibarra.

de Azevedo, L. G. (1966) Tipos eco-fisionômicos da vegetação da região de Januária (MG). *An. Acad. Bras. Ciênc.* 38 (supl.): 39-57.

de Azevedo, N. V. (1984) As mil e uma utilidades da algaroba. *Ciência Hoje* 3(13): 24.

de Azevedo Junior, S. M. (1990) A estação ecológica do Tapacurá e suas aves. Pp.92-99 in *Anais do Encontro Nacional de Anilhadores de Aves*, 4, Recife, 1988. Recife: Universidade Federal Rural de Pernambuco.

Babbs, S., Buckton, S., Robertson, P. and Wood, P. (1988) *Report of the 1987 University of East Anglia–ICBP St Lucia expedition*. Cambridge, U.K.: International Council for Bird Preservation (Study report 33).

Babbs, S., Ling, S., Robertson, P. and Wood, P. (1987) *Report of the 1986 University of East Anglia Martinique Oriole expedition*. Cambridge, U.K.: International Council for Bird Preservation (Study report 23).

Baepler, D. H. (1962) The avifauna of the Soloma region in Heuhuetenango, Guatemala. *Condor* 64: 140-153.

Baer, G. A. (1904) Note sur une collection d'oiseaux du Tucuman, République Argentine. *Ornis* 12: 209-234.

Bailey, A. M. and Conover, H. B. (1935) Notes from the state of Durango, Mexico. *Auk* 52: 421-424.

Bailey, H. H. (1906) Ornithological notes from western Mexico and the Tres Marías and Isabella Islands. *Auk* 23: 369-391.

Baker, R. H. (1958) Nest of the Military Macaw in Durango. *Auk* 75: 98.

Baker, R. H. and Fleming, R. L. (1962) Birds near La Pesca, Tamaulipas, Mexico. *Southwestern Nat.* 7: 253-261.

Balát, F. and González, H. (1982) Concrete data on the breeding of Cuban birds. *Acta Sci. Nat. Brno* 16(8): 1-46.

Balharry, D. (1989) Aberdeen University ecological expedition to Peru 1986. Unpublished report submitted to ICBP, January 1989.

Baliño, J. (1984) Aves del Parque Nacional El Palmar. Lista sistemática y otras contribuciones a su conocimiento. *Revta. Mus. Arg. Cienc. Nat., Zool.* 13: 499-511.

Bancroft, E. N. (1835) Remarks on some animals sent from Jamaica. *Zool. J.* 5: 80-86.

Bangs, O. (1903) Birds and mammals from Honduras. *Bull. Mus. Comp. Zool.* 39: 141-159.

Bangs, O. (1931) A new genus and species of American buntings [*sic*]. *Proc. New England Zool. Club* 12: 85-88.

Bangs, O. and Kennard, F. H. (1920) *A list of the birds of Jamaica.* Kingston, Jamaica: Government Printing Office (excerpted from "The handbook of Jamaica, 1920").

Bangs, O. and Noble, G. K. (1918) List of birds collected on the Harvard Peruvian Expedition of 1916. *Auk* 35: 442-463.

Bangs, O. and Peters, J. L. (1927) Birds from the rain forest region of Vera Cruz. *Bull. Mus. Comp. Zool.* 67: 471-487.

Bangs, O. and Zappey, W. R. (1905) Birds of the Isle of Pines. *Amer. Nat.* 39: 179-215.

Banks, R. C. (1986) A taxonomic reevaluation of the Plain Pigeon (*Columba inornata*). *Auk* 103: 629-631.

Banks, R. C. (1990) Taxonomic status of the coquette hummingbird of Guerrero, Mexico. *Auk* 107: 191-192.

Baptista, L. F. (1987) Andrew Jackson Grayson and the "Solitary Dove". *Pacific Discovery* 40(2): 30-37.

Baptista, L. F. (1991) Socorro Dove project update from International Dove Society Newsletter, Sept. 1991. *ASA Avicult. Bull.* November: 14-16.

Baptista, L. F., Boardman, W. I. and Kandianidis, P. (1983) Behavior and taxonomic status of Grayson's Dove. *Auk* 100: 907-919.

Baptista, L. F., Horblit, H. M. and Walter, H. S. (undated) The Socorro Island recovery project. Unpublished.

Barattini, L. P. (1945) Las aves de Paysandú. *An. Lic. Dep. Paysandú* 1: 1-60.

Barattini, L. P. and Escalante, R. (1958) *Catálogo de las aves uruguayas, 1: falconiformes.* Montevideo: Concejo Departamental de Montevideo (Museo Dámaso A. Larrañaga).

Barber, R. and Chavez, F. (1983) Biological consequences of El Niño. *Science* 222: 1203-1210.

Barbour, T. (1923) *The birds of Cuba.* Cambridge, Mass.: Nuttall Ornithological Club (Memoirs 6).

Barbour, T. (1928) Notes on three Cuban birds. *Auk* 45: 28-32.

Barbour, T. (1943) *Cuban ornithology.* Cambridge, Mass.: Nuttall Ornithological Club (Memoirs 9).

Barbour, T. and Peters, J. L. (1927) Two more remarkable new birds from Cuba. *Proc. New England Zool. Club* 9: 95-97.

Barlow, J. C. and Nash, S. V. (1985) Behavior and nesting biology of the St. Andrew Vireo. *Wilson Bull.* 97: 265-272.

Barlow, K., Beltrán, W., Downing, C., Kingston, T., Payne, T., Salaman, P. and Serrano, V. H. (1992) The survey and conservation of fauna in south-west Nariño, Colombia. Unpublished draft report.

Barnés, V. (1945) A new form of *Agelaius* from Mona Island, Puerto Rico. *Auk* 62: 299-300.

Barnés, V. (1946) The birds of Mona Island, Puerto Rico. *Auk* 63: 318-327.

Barnicoat, F. (1982) The Boswell parrot collection. *Avicult. Mag.* 88: 101-104.

Baron, O. T. (1897) Notes on the localities visited by O. T. Baron in northern Peru and on the Trochilidae found there. *Novit. Zool.* 4: 1-10.

Barros, O. (1954) Aves de Tarapacá. *Invest. Zool. Chilenas* 2: 35-64.

Barrows, W. B. (1883) Birds of the lower Uruguay. *Bull. Nuttall Orn. Club* 8: 82-94, 129-143, 198-212.

Barrows, W. B. (1884) Birds of the lower Uruguay. *Auk* 1: 20-30, 109-113, 270-278, 313-319.

Bartmann, W. (1988) New observations on the Brazilian Merganser. *Wildfowl* 39: 7-14.

Bascarán, J. L. (1987) El cardenal amarillo *Gubernatrix cristata. Accespa* 6.

Bates, H. W. (1863) *A naturalist on the River Amazons.* London: John Murray.

Bates, J. M., Garvin, M. C., Schmitt, D. C. and Schmitt, G. C. (1989) Notes on bird distribution in northeastern Dpto. Santa Cruz, Bolivia, with 15 species new to Bolivia. *Bull. Brit. Orn. Club* 109: 236-244.

Bates, J. M., Parker, T. A., Capparella, A. P. and Davis, T. J. (1992) Observations on the *campo, cerrado* and forest avifaunas of eastern Dpto. Santa Cruz, Bolivia, including 21 species new to the country. *Bull. Brit. Orn. Club* 112: 86-98.

Bauer, J. (1989) Haltung und Zucht des Kubasittichs *Aratinga euops. Papageien* 4/89: 108-110.

Beard, J. S. (1946) *The natural vegetation of Trinidad.* Oxford: Clarendon Press.

Beatty, H. A. (1930) Birds of St Croix. *J. Dept. Agric. Puerto Rico* 14(3): 134-150.

Beck, R. H. (1921) Bird collecting in the highlands of Santo Domingo. *Nat. Hist.* 21: 36-49.

Beebe, C. W. (1905) *Two bird-lovers in Mexico.* London: Archibald Constable and Company.

Beebe, C. W. (1912) The Imperial Parrot. *Zool. Soc. Bull.* 16 (51): 868-870.

Behn, F. and Millie, G. (1959) Beitrag zur Kenntnis des Rüsselbläßhuhns *Fulica cornuta. J. Orn.* 100: 119-131.

Belcher, C. and Smooker, G. D. (1934-1937) Birds of the colony of Trinidad and Tobago. *Ibis* (13)4: 572-595; (13)5: 279-297; (13)6: 1-35; 792-813; (14)1: 225-249; 504-550.

Bell, B. D. and Keith, J. O. (1983) Effects of feral animals on breeding Dark-rumped Petrels, Galápagos Islands. Unpublished.

Belton, W. (1978) Supplementary list of new birds for Rio Grande do Sul, Brazil. *Auk* 95: 413-415.

Belton, W. (1984-1985) Birds of Rio Grande do Sul, Brazil. *Bull. Amer. Mus. Nat. Hist.* 178(4) and 180(1).

Beltrán, J. (1987) El mirlo de agua (*Cinclus schulzi*). *Nuestras Aves* 5(13): 23-25.

Benito-Espinal, E. and Hautcastel, P. (1988) Les oiseaux menacés de Guadeloupe et de Martinique. Pp.37-60 in J.-C. Thibault and I. Guyot, eds. *Livre rouge des oiseaux menacés des régions françaises d'outre-mer.* Saint-Cloud: Conseil International pour la Protection des Oiseaux ([ICBP] Monogr. 5).

Bennett, A. G. (1926) A list of the birds of the Falkland Islands and dependencies. *Ibis* (12)2: 306-333.

Bennett, W. C. and Zingg, R. M. (1935) *The Tarahumara: an Indian tribe of northern Mexico.* Chicago: University of Chicago Press.

Benson, C. W. (1972) Skins of extinct or near extinct birds in Cambridge. *Bull. Brit. Orn. Club* 92: 59-68.

Benson, R. H. and Benson, K. L. P. (1990) Estimated size of Black-capped Vireo population in northern Coahuila, Mexico. *Condor* 92: 777-779.

Benson, R. H. and Benson, K. L. P. (1991) Reply to Scott and Garton. *Condor* 93: 470-472.

Bent, A. C. (1922) Life histories of North American petrels and pelicans and their allies. *U.S. Natn. Mus. Bull.* 121.

Bent, A. C. (1940) Life-histories of North American cuckoos, goatsuckers, hummingbirds and their allies. *Bull. U.S. Natn. Mus.* 176.

Bergtold, W. H. (1906) Concerning the Thick-billed Parrot. *Auk* 23: 425-428.

Berla, H. F. (1944) Lista das aves colecionadas em Pedra Branca, município de Parati, estado do Rio de Janeiro, com algumas notas sobre sua biologia. *Bol. Mus. Nac. Rio de Janeiro* n.s. Zool. no.18.

Berla, H. F. (1946) Lista das aves colecionadas em Pernambuco, com descrição de uma subespécie n., de um alótipo ♀ e notas de campo. *Bol. Mus. Nac. Rio de Janeiro* n.s. Zool. no.65.

Berla, H. F. (1954) Um novo "Psittacidae" do nordeste brasileiro (Aves, Psittaciformes). *Revta. Bras. Biol.* 14: 59-60.

von Berlepsch, H. (1873-1874) Zur Ornithologie der Provinz Santa Catharina, Süd-Brasilien. *J. Orn.* 21: 225-293; 22: 241-284.

von Berlepsch, H. (1887) Systematisches Verzeichniss der in der Republik Paraguay bisher beobachteten Vogelarten. *J. Orn.* 35: 113-134.

von Berlepsch, H. (1889) Systematisches Verzeichniss der von Herrn Gustav Garlepp in Brasilien und Nord-Peru im Gebiete des oberen Amazonas gesammelten Vogelbälge. *J. Orn.* 37: 289-321.

von Berlepsch, H. (1893) On a remarkable new finch from the highlands of Bolivia. *Ibis* 5(6): 207-210.

von Berlepsch, H. (1901) Mitteilungen über die von den gebrüdern G. und O. Garlepp in Bolivia gesammelten Vögel und Beschreibungen neuer Arten. *J. Orn.* 49: 81-99.

von Berlepsch, H. (1907) Studien über Tyranniden. *Ornis* 14: 463-493.

von Berlepsch, H. and Hartert, E. (1902) On the birds of the Orinoco region. *Novit. Zool.* 9: 1-134.

von Berlepsch, H. and von Ihering, H. (1885) Die Vögel der Umgegend von Taquara do Mundo Novo, Prov. Rio Grande do Sul. *Zeitschr. gesammte Orn.* 2: 97-184.

von Berlepsch, H. and Stolzmann, J. (1892) Résultats des recherches ornithologiques faites au Pérou par M. Jean Kalinowski. *Proc. Zool. Soc. London*: 371-411.

von Berlepsch, H. and Stolzmann, J. (1894) Descriptions de quelques espèces nouvelles d'oiseaux du Pérou central. *Ibis* (6)6: 385-405.

von Berlepsch, H. and Stolzmann, J. (1901) Descriptions d'oiseaux nouveaux du Pérou central recueillis par le voyageur Polonais Jean Kalinowski. *Ornis* 11: 191-195.

von Berlepsch, H. and Stolzmann, J. (1902) On the ornithological researches of M. Jean Kalinowski in Central Peru. *Proc. Zool. Soc. London*: 18-60.

von Berlepsch, H. and Stolzmann, J. (1906) Rapport sur les nouvelles collections ornithologiques faites au Pérou par M. Jean Kalinowski. *Ornis* 13: 63-133.

von Berlepsch, H. and Taczanowski, L. (1883) Liste des oiseaux recueillis par MM. Stolzmann et Siemiradski dans l'Ecuadeur occidental. *Proc. Zool. Soc. London*: 536-577.

von Berlepsch, H. and Taczanowski, L. (1884) Deuxième liste des oiseaux recueillis dans l'Equateur donnée au Muséum par M. Clavery. *Bull. Mus. Natn. Hist. Nat. Paris* 34: 71-78.

Berlioz, J. (1932) Contribution a l'étude des oiseaux de l'Ecuador. *Bull. Mus. Natn. Hist. Nat. Paris* (2)4: 228-242.

Berlioz, J. (1938) [A new species belonging to the family Formicariidae.] *Bull. Brit. Orn. Club* 58: 90-91.

Berlioz, J. (1939) A new genus and species of tanager from central Brazil. *Bull. Brit. Orn. Club* 59: 102-103.

Berlioz, J. (1946) Note sur une collection d'oiseaux du Brésil Central. *Oiseau et R.F.O.* 16: 1-6.

Bernardes, A. T., Machado, A. B. M. and Rylands, A. B. (1990) *Fauna brasileira ameaçada de extinção.* Belo Horizonte: Fundação Biodiversitas para a Conservação da Diversidade Biológica.

Berovides Alvarez, V., González, H. and Ibarra, M. E. (1982) Evaluación ecológica de las comunidades de aves del área protegida de Najasa (Camagüey). *Poeyana* 239.

Bertagnolio, P. (1981) The Red-tailed Amazon and other uncommon South American parrots. *Avicult. Mag.* 87: 6-18.

Bertagnolio, P. (1983) L'Amazzone a coda rossa (*Amazona brasiliensis*). *Boll. Centro Studio e Conserv. Psittaciformi* 1: 1-15.

Bertoni, A. de W. (1901) Aves nuevas del Paraguay: catálogo de las aves del Paraguay. *An. Cient. Paraguay* 1, ser.1: 1-216.

Bertoni, A. de W. (1914) *Fauna paraguaya. Catálogos sistemáticos de los vertebrados del Paraguay.* Asunción: Gráfico M. Brossa.

Bertoni, A. de W. (1926) Apuntes ornitológicos. *Hornero* 3: 396-401.

Bertoni, A. de W. (1927) Nueva forma de psitácidos del Paraguay. *Revta. Soc. Cient. Paraguay* 2(3): 149-150.

Bertoni, A. de W. (1930) Aves del chaco paraguayo colectadas por Felix Posner en la Colonia "Monte Sociedad" hoy Benjamin Aceval. *Revta. Soc. Cient. Paraguay* 2(6): 343-258.

Bertoni, A. de W. (1939) Catálogos sistemáticos de los vertebrados del Paraguay. *Revta. Soc. Cient. Paraguay* 4(4): 1-59.

Best, B. J. (1991) The Ecuadorian dry forest project 1991: preliminary report. Unpublished.

Best, B. J. and Clarke, C. T., eds. (1991) *The threatened birds of the Sozoranga region, southwest Ecuador.* Cambridge, U.K.: International Council for Bird Preservation (Study Report 44).

Best, B. J. (1992) The threatened forests of south-western Ecuador: a biological survey January–March 1991. Unpublished.

Beyer, C. (1886) Mapa de la República del Paraguay, 1:1,000,000. Buenos Aires: Ernst Nolte, Libreria Alemana.

Biaggi, V. (1970) *Las aves de Puerto Rico.* San Juan: Editorial Universitaria, Universidad de Puerto Rico.

Binford, L. C. (1989) *A distributional survey of the birds of the Mexican state of Oaxaca.* Washington, D.C.: American Ornithologists' Union (Orn. Monogr. 43).

Bish, E. (1985) Breeding Lear's Macaw *Anodorhynchus leari* at the Busch Gardens (Tampa, Florida). *Avicult. Mag.* 91: 30-31.
Blaauw, F. E. (1900) Notes on the Zoological Garden of Berlin. *Proc. Zool. Soc. London*: 299-306.
Blake, E. R. (1953) A Colombian race of *Tinamus osgoodi*. *Fieldiana Zool.* 34: 199-200.
Blake, E. R. (1953) *Birds of Mexico: a guide for field identification.* Chicago: University of Chicago Press.
Blake, E. R. (1955) A collection of Colombian game birds. *Fieldiana Zool.* 37: 9-23.
Blake, E. R. (1957) A new species of ant-thrush from Peru. *Fieldiana Zool.* 39: 51-53.
Blake, E. R. (1959) New and rare Colombian birds. *Lozania* 11: 1-10.
Blake, E. R. (1962) Birds of the Sierra Macarena, eastern Colombia. *Fieldiana Zool.* 44: 69-112.
Blake, E. R. (1971) A new species of spinetail (*Synallaxis*) from Peru. *Auk* 88: 179.
Blake, E. R. (1977) *Manual of neotropical birds*, 1. Chicago: University of Chicago Press.
Blake, E. R. and Hocking, P. (1974) Two new species of tanager from Peru. *Wilson Bull.* 86: 321-324.
Bleiweiss, R. (1982) Case studies of two rare and endangered Ecuadorian hummingbirds. Appendix 1 in project proposal on Andean conservation. Unpublished.
Bleiweiss, R. and Olalla P., M. (1983) Notes on the ecology of the Black-breasted Puffleg on Volcán Pichincha, Ecuador. *Wilson Bull.* 95: 656-661.
Bloch, H., Poulsen, M. K., Rahbek, C. and Rasmussen, J. F. (1991) *A survey of the montane forest avifauna of the Loja Province, southern Ecuador.* Cambridge, U.K.: International Council for Bird Preservation (Study Report 49).
Blockstein, D. E. (1988) Two endangered birds of Grenada, West Indies: Grenada Dove and Grenada Hook-billed Kite. *Caribbean J. Sci.* 24: 127-136.
Blockstein, D. E. (1991) Population declines of the endangered endemic birds on Grenada, West Indies. *Bird Conserv. Internatn.* 1: 83-91.
Blockstein, D. E. and Hardy, J. W. (1989) The Grenada Dove (*Leptotila wellsi*) is a distinct species. *Auk* 106: 334-340.
Boeke, J. D. (1978) A food source of the Marvellous Spatuletail *Loddigesia mirabilis*. *Ibis* 120: 551.
Bokermann, W. C. A. (1957) Atualização do itinerario da viagem do Príncipe de Wied ao Brasil (1815-1817). *Arq. Zool. São Paulo* 10: 209-251.
Bonaparte, C. L. (1865) *Conspectum generum avium.* [Leiden:] E. J. Brill.
Bonaparte, C. L. (1854) Notes sur les collections rapportées en 1853, par M. A. Delattre, de son voyage en Californie et dans Nicaragua. *C.R. Acad. Sci. Paris* 38: 660.
Bond, J. (1928a) The distribution and habits of the birds of the Republic of Haiti. *Proc. Acad. Nat. Sci. Philadelphia* 80: 483-521.
Bond, J. (1928b) On the birds of Dominica, St Lucia, St Vincent, and Barbados, B.W.I. *Proc. Acad. Nat. Sci. Philadelphia* 80: 523-545.
Bond, J. (1936) *Birds of the West Indies.* Philadelphia: Academy of the Natural Sciences of Philadelphia.
Bond, J. (1941a) Some West Indian birds' eggs. *Auk* 58: 109-110.
Bond, J. (1941b) Nidification of the birds of Dominica, B.W.I. *Auk* 58: 364-375.
Bond, J. (1942) Additional notes on West Indian birds. *Proc. Acad. Nat. Sci. Philadelphia* 94: 89-106.
Bond, J. (1943) Nidification of the passerine birds of Hispaniola. *Wilson Bull.* 55: 115-125.
Bond, J. (1945) Notes on Peruvian Furnariidae. *Proc. Acad. Nat. Sci. Philadelphia* 97: 17-39.
Bond, J. (1947) Notes on Peruvian Tyrannidae. *Proc. Acad. Nat. Sci. Philadelphia* 99: 127-154.
Bond, J. (1950) *Check-list of birds of the West Indies.* Philadelphia: The Academy of Natural Sciences of Philadelphia.
Bond, J. (1951a) Notes on Peruvian Fringillidae. *Proc. Acad. Nat. Sci. Philadelphia* 103: 65-84.
Bond, J. (1951b) *First supplement to the check-list of birds of the West Indies (1950).* Philadelphia: Academy of Natural Sciences of Philadelphia.
Bond, J. (1954a) Notes on Peruvian Piciformes. *Proc. Acad. Nat. Sci. Philadelphia* 106: 45-61.
Bond, J. (1954b) Notes on Peruvian Trochilidae. *Proc. Acad. Nat. Sci. Philadelphia* 106: 165-183.
Bond, J. (1955) Additional notes on Peruvian birds, 1. *Proc. Acad. Nat. Sci. Philadelphia* 107: 207-244.
Bond, J. (1956a) Additional notes on Peruvian birds, 2. *Proc. Acad. Nat. Sci. Philadelphia* 108: 227-247.

Bond, J. (1956b) *Check-list of the birds of the West Indies*. Fourth edition. Pennsylvania: Academy of Natural Sciences of Philadelphia.
Bond, J. (1957) Notes on the White-breasted Thrasher. *Auk* 74: 259-260.
Bond, J. (1958) *Third supplement to the check-list of birds of the West Indies (1956)*. Philadelphia: Academy of Natural Sciences of Philadelphia.
Bond, J. (1961) Extinct and near-extinct birds of the West Indies. New York: International Council for Bird Preservation Pan-American Section, Research Report 4.
Bond, J. (1962) *Seventh supplement to the check-list of birds of the West Indies (1956)*. Philadelphia: Academy of Natural Sciences of Philadelphia.
Bond, J. (1963) *Eighth supplement to the check-list of birds of the West Indies (1956)*. Philadelphia: Academy of Natural Sciences of Philadelphia.
Bond, J. (1964) *Ninth supplement to the check-list of birds of the West Indies (1956)*. Philadelphia: Academy of Natural Sciences of Philadelphia.
Bond, J. (1966) *Eleventh supplement to the check-list of birds of the West Indies (1956)*. Philadelphia: Academy of Natural Sciences of Philadelphia.
Bond, J. (1967) *Twelfth supplement to the check-list of birds of the West Indies (1956)*. Philadelphia: Academy of Natural Sciences of Philadelphia.
Bond, J. (1968) *Thirteenth supplement to the check-list of birds of the West Indies (1956)*. Philadelphia: Academy of Natural Sciences of Philadelphia.
Bond, J. (1971) *Sixteenth supplement to the check-list of birds of the West Indies (1956)*. Philadelphia: Academy of Natural Sciences of Philadelphia.
Bond, J. (1972) *Seventeenth supplement to the check-list of birds of the West Indies (1956)*. Philadelphia: Academy of Natural Sciences of Philadelphia.
Bond, J. (1973) *Eighteenth supplement to the check-list of birds of the West Indies (1956)*. Philadelphia: Academy of Natural Sciences of Philadelphia.
Bond, J. (1974) *Nineteenth supplement to the check-list of birds of the West Indies (1956)*. Philadelphia: Academy on Natural Sciences of Philadelphia.
Bond, J. (1976) *Twentieth supplement to the check-list of birds of the West Indies (1956)*. Philadelphia: Academy of Natural Sciences of Philadelphia.
Bond, J. (1977) *Twenty-first supplement to the check-list of birds of the West Indies (1956)*. Philadelphia: Academy of Natural Sciences of Philadelphia.
Bond, J. (1978) *Twenty-second supplement to the check-list of birds of the West Indies (1956)*. Philadelphia: Academy of Natural Sciences of Philadelphia.
Bond, J. (1979) *Birds of the West Indies*. Fourth edition. London: Collins.
Bond, J. (1980) *Twenty-third supplement to the check-list of birds of the West Indies (1956)*. Philadelphia: Academy of Natural Sciences of Philadelphia.
Bond, J. (1982) *Twenty-fourth supplement to the check-list of birds of the West Indies (1956)*. Philadelphia: Academy of Natural Sciences of Philadelphia.
Bond, J. (1984) *Twenty-fifth supplement to the check-list of birds of the West Indies (1956)*. Philadelphia: Academy of Natural Sciences of Philadelphia.
Bond, J. (1985) *Birds of the West Indies*. Fifth edition. London: Collins.
Bond, J. (1986) *Twenty-sixth supplement to the check-list of the birds of the West Indies (1956)*. Philadelphia: Academy of Natural Sciences of Philadelphia.
Bond, J. and Dod, A. (1977) A new race of Chat Tanager (*Calyptophilus frugivorus*) from the Dominican Republic. *Notulae Naturae* 451.
Bond, J. and Meyer de Schauensee, R. (1939) Descriptions of new birds from Bolivia. Part II – a new species of the genus *Pauxi*. *Notulae Naturae* 29.
Bond, J. and Meyer de Schauensee, R. (1940) On some birds from southern Colombia. *Proc. Acad. Nat. Sci. Philadelphia* 92: 153-169.
Bond, J. and Meyer de Schauensee, R. (1941) Descriptions of new birds from Bolivia. Part IV. *Notulae Naturae* 93.
Bond, J. and Meyer de Schauensee, R. (1942-1943) The birds of Bolivia. *Proc. Acad. Nat. Sci. Philadelphia* 94: 307-391; 95: 167-221.

Bond, J. and Meyer de Schauensee, R. (1943) A new species of dove of the genus *Leptotila* from Colombia. *Notulae Naturae* 122.

Bond, R., Convey, P., Sharpe, C. and Varey, A. (1989) Cambridge Columbus zoological expedition to Venezuela 1988. Unpublished report.

Bonhote, J. L. (1903) On a collection of birds from the northern islands of the Bahama group. *Ibis* (8)3: 273-315.

Bornschein, M. R. and Straube, F. C. (1991) Novos registros de alguns Accipitridae nos estados do Paraná e Santa Catarina (sul do Brasil). Resúmenes, I Encuentro de Ornitología de Paraguay, Brasil y Argentina, Mayo 1991, Ciudad del Este, Paraguay, Mayo 1991.

Borrero H., J. F. and Hernández C., J. (1958) Apuntes sobre aves colombianas. *Caldasia* 8: 252-295.

Borrero, J. I. (1947) Aves ocasionales en la sabana de Bogotá y las lagunas de Fúquene y Tota. *Caldasia* 4: 491-498.

Borrero, J. I. (1953) Status actual de *Zenaida auriculata* y *Leptotila plumbeiceps* en el Departamento de Caldas y de *Cistothorus apolinari* en la región de Bogotá. *Lozania* 1: 7-12.

Borrero, J. I. (1963) El Lago de Tota. *Revta. Fac. Nac. Agron.* 23: 1-15.

Bosch, K. (1991) Welche Gelbkopfamazone haben Sie? *Gefied. Welt* 115: 342-344.

Bosch, K. and Wedde, U. (1981) *Amazonen: Enzyklopädie der Papageien und Sittiche*, 2. Bomlitz: Horst Müller.

Bosque, C. and Ramirez, R. (1988) Post-breeding migration of Oilbirds. *Wilson Bull.* 100: 675-677.

Botero, J. E. and Botero, L. (1987) La Ciénaga Grande de Santa Marta: una laguna costera en peligro de muerte. Paper presented at III Congreso de Ornitología Neotropical, Cali, Colombia, November, 1987. Unpublished.

Boucard, A. (1878a) On birds collected in Costa Rica. *Proc. Zool. Soc. London*: 37-71.

Boucard, A. (1878b) Liste des oiseaux récoltés au Guatémala. *Ann. Soc. Linnéenne Lyon*: 1-47.

Boucard, A. (1895) *Genera of hummingbirds*. London: Pardy and Sons.

Bourcier, J. (1847) Description de quinze espèces de Trochilidae du cabinet du M. Loddiges. *Proc. Zool. Soc. London*: 42-47.

Bourjot Saint-Hilaire, A. (1837-1838) *Histoire naturelle des perroquets*, 3. Paris: F. G. Levrault.

Bourne, W. R. P. (1965) The missing petrels. *Bull. Brit. Orn. Club.* 85: 97-85.

Bourne, W. R. P. (1983) Shy Albatrosses, elusive Capped Petrels, and great accumulations of shearwaters. *Brit. Birds* 76: 583-584.

Bourne, W. R. P. (1989) Seabird reports received in 1987 and 1988. *Sea Swallow* 38: 7-30.

Bourne, W. R. P. and Dixon, T. J. (1973) Observations of seabirds 1967-1969. *Sea Swallow* 22: 29-60.

Boussekey, M., Saint-Pie, J. and Morvan, O. (1991a) Observation d'une population d'Aras (*sic*) rubrogenys dans la vallée du Rio Caine, Bolivie Centrale. Unpublished.

Boussekey, M., Saint-Pie, J. and Morvan, O. (1991b) Observations on a population of Red-fronted Macaws *Ara rubrogenys* in the Río Caine valley, central Bolivia. *Bird Conserv. Internatn.* 1: 335-350.

Boussekey, M., Saint-Pie, J. and Morvan, O. (1992) Beobachtungen an einer Population des Rotohraras (*Ara rubrogenys*) im Rio-Caine-Tal, Zentral Bolivien. *Papageien* 5: 54-57, 95-99.

Bowdish, B. S. (1902-1903) Birds of Porto Rico. *Auk* 19: 356-366; 20: 193-195.

Brabourne, W. W. K.-H. and Chubb, C. (1912) *The birds of South America*, 1. London: Taylor and Francis.

Brabourne, Lord (1914) Aviculture in Paraguay. *Avicult. Mag.* (3)5: 185-191.

Brack, C. (1987a) Some personal notes on Spix or Little Blue Macaw (*Cyanopsitta spixii*, Wagler 1832) in captivity. *Ratel* 14(2): 50-51.

Brack, C. (1987b) Spix Macaws (*Cyanopsitta spixii*) – footnote to article by Christopher Brack (Vol. 14, no.2). *Ratel* 14(5): 143-144.

Bradlee, T. S. (1906) Audubon's Shearwater and Peale's Petrel breeding in Bermuda. *Auk* 23: 217.

Bradlee, T. S. Mowbray, L. L. and Eaton, W. F. (1931) A list of birds recorded from the Bermudas. *Proc. Boston Soc. Nat. Hist.* 39: 279-382.

Brandt, A. and Machado, R. B. (1990) Área de alimentação e comportamento alimentar de *Anodorhynchus leari*. *Ararajuba* 1: 57-63.

Braun, M. J., Braun, D. D. and Terrill, S. B. (1986) Winter records of the Golden-cheeked Warbler (*Dendroica chrysoparia*) from Mexico. *Amer. Birds* 40: 564-566.
Brock, M. K. (1991) Genetic assessment of the captive breeding programs for the Puerto Rican Parrot *Amazona vittata*, and other Caribbean parrots. Ph.D. thesis, Department of Biology, Queen's University, Kingston, Ontario.
Brodkorb, P. (1938) Further additions to the avifauna of Paraguay. *Occas. Pap. Mus. Zool. Univ. Michigan* 394.
Brodkorb, P. (1943) Birds from the Gulf lowlands of southern Mexico. *Misc. Publ. Mus. Zool. Univ. Michigan* 55: 1-88.
Brooke, M. de L. (1987) *The birds of the Juan Fernandez Islands, Chile*. Cambridge, U.K.: International Council for Bird Preservation (Study Report 16).
Brooke, M. de L. (1988a) Distribution and numbers of the Masafuera Rayadito *Aphrastura masafuerae* on Isla Alejandro Selkirk, Juan Fernandez archipelago, Chile. *Bull. Brit. Orn. Club* 108: 4-9.
Brooke, M. de L. (1988b) The ornithological significance of the Virolín area, Santander, Colombia, with special reference to Gorgeted Wood-quail *Odontophorus strophium*. Unpublished report.
Brosset, A. (1964) Les oiseaux de Pacaritambo (Ouest de l'Ecuador). *Oiseau et R.F.O.* 34: 1-24, 112-135.
Brown, F. M. (1941) A gazetteer of entomological stations in Ecuador. *Ann. Entom. Soc. Amer.* 34: 809-851.
Brown, L. H. and Amadon, D. (1968) *Hawks, eagles and falcons of the world*. London, New York: Hamlyn, McGraw-Hill.
Brudenell-Bruce, P. G. C. (1975) *The birds of New Providence and the Bahama Islands*. London: Collins.
Bruner, S. C. (1934) Observaciones sobre *Ferminia cerverai* (Aves: Troglodytidae). *Mem. Soc. Cubana Hist. Nat.* 8: 97-102.
Bucher, E. H, and Nores, M. (1988) Present status of birds in steppes and savannas of northern and central Argentina. Pp.71-79 in P. D. Goriup, ed. *Ecology and conservation of grassland birds*. Cambridge, U.K.: International Council for Bird Preservation (Techn. Publ. 7).
Buden, D. W. (1987a) *The birds of the southern Bahamas*. London: British Ornithologists' Union (Check-list 8).
Buden, D. W. (1987b) Birds of the Cay Sal Bank and Ragged Islands, Bahamas. *Biol. Sci.* 1: 21-34.
Buden, D. W. (1987c) The birds of Cat Island, Bahamas. *Wilson Bull.* 99: 579-600.
Buden, D. W. (1990) The birds of Rum Cay, Bahama Islands. *Wilson Bull.* 102: 451-468.
Buden, D. W. and Olson, S. L. (1989) The avifaunas of the cayerías of southern Cuba, with the ornithological results of the Paul Bartsch Expedition of 1930. *Smithson. Contrib. Zool.* 477.
Budin, E. (1931) Lista y notas sobre aves del N. O. Argentino (Prov. de Jujuy). *Hornero* 4: 401-411.
Burke, W. (1992) Report on partial census of Ravine la Chaloupe for White-breasted Thrasher (*Ramphocinclus brachyurus*) on March 8, 1992. Unpublished.
Burleigh, T. D. and Lowery, G. H. (1942) Notes on the birds of southeastern Coahuila. *Occas. Pap. Mus. Zool. Louisiana State Univ.* 12: 185-212.
Burmeister, H. (1853) *Reise nach Brasilien, durch die Provinzen von Rio de Janeiro und Minas Geraës*. Berlin: Georg Reimer.
Burmeister, H. (1856) *Systematische Uebersicht der Thiere Brasiliens*, 2: Vögel (Aves). Berlin: Georg Reimer.
Burmeister, H. (1860) Systematisches Verzeichniss der in den La Plata-Staaten beobachteten Vögelarten. *J. Orn.* 8: 241-268.
Burmeister, H. (1861) *Reise durch die La Plata-Staaten*. Halle: H. W. Schmidt.
Butler, P. J. (1978) Saint Lucia Research Report. North East London Polytechnic, unpublished.
Butler, P. J. (1980) The Saint Lucia Parrot *Amazona versicolor*. Its changing status and its conservation. (Including Hurricane Allen damage assessment by P. J. Butler and D. F. Jeggo). Unpublished.
Butler, P. J. (1981a) The St Lucia Amazon (*Amazona versicolor*): its changing status and conservation. Pp.171-180 in R. F. Pasquier, ed. *Conservation of New World parrots*. Washington, D.C.: Smithsonian Institution Press for the International Council for Bird Preservation (Techn. Publ. 1).
Butler, P. J. (1981b) A brighter future for Jacquot. *World Wildlife News*, autumn: 9-11.

Butler, P. (1982) Artificial parrot nestbox project. A summary of 1981/82 breeding seasons. Saint Lucia Forestry Division, unpublished.

Butler, P. J. (1988) *Saint Vincent Parrot* Amazona guildingii*: the road to recovery*. Philadelphia: RARE Center for Tropical Bird Conservation (in conjunction with the Forestry Division of St Vincent and the Grenadines).

Butler, P. J. (1989) *Imperial or Sisserou Parrot* Amazona imperialis *and Red-necked Parrot* Amazona arausiaca*: a new beginning*. Philadelphia: RARE Center for Tropical Bird Conservation.

Butler, P. J. (1990) Some observations on polymorphism in the St Vincent Parrot *Amazona guildingii*. *Dodo* 26 [1989]: 98-107.

Butler, P. J. (1991) *Saint Lucia Parrot* Amazona versicolor*: consolidating a conservation campaign*. Philadelphia: RARE Center for Tropical Conservation.

Butler, P. J. (1992) Parrots, pressures, people, and pride. Pp.25-46 in S. R. Beissinger and N. F. R. Snyder, eds. *New World parrots in crisis: solutions from conservation biology*. Washington, D.C.: Smithsonian Institution Press.

Butler, P. J. and Charles, C. L. (1982) Development of Saint Vincent Parrot Conservation Programme. Consultancy report (WWF no. US 225), unpublished.

Butler, P. and Charles, G. (1986) St Vincent Parrot Conservation Project: a status report. Unpublished.

Cabanis, J. (1856) Dr J. Gundlach's Beiträge zur Ornithologie Cuba's. *J. Orn.* 4: 97-112.

Cabanis, J. (1865-1866) Ueber neue oder weniger bekannte exotische Vögel. *J. Orn.* 13: 406-414; 14: 159-165, 231-235, 305-310.

Cabanis, J. (1867) Ueber die systematische Stellung von *Sylvia concolor* Orb. als Typus einer neuen Gattung *Xenospingus*. *J. Orn.* 15: 347-349.

Cabanis, J. (1874) Uebersicht der von Herrn Carl Euler im District Cantagallo, Provinz Rio de Janeiro, gesammelten Vögel. *J. Orn.* 22: 81-90, 225-231.

Cabanis, J. (1883) [Ueber neue Arten von Herrn F. Schulz in nördl. Argentinien.] *J. Orn.* 31: 102-103.

Cabot, J., Castroviejo, J. and Urios, V. (1988) Cuatro nuevas especies de aves para Bolivia. *Doñana, Acta Vert.* 15: 235-238.

Cabot, J. and Serrano, P. (1982) La comunidad de aves. Pp.40-59 in *Informe sobre la vegetación y fauna de la Reserva Nacional Altoandina "Eduardo Avaroa", Provincia Sud-Lipez, Potosí*. La Paz, Bolivia: MACA, MICT and INFOL (Estudios Especializados no.42).

Camacho Lara, R. R. (1947) *Mapa de la República de Bolivia*. La Paz: Editorial Renacimiento, R. Zumelzu y Cia.

Camacho Lara, R. R. (1958) *Atlas de Bolivia*. Novara (Italy): Istituto Geografico de Agostini.

Camargo, H. F. de A. (1946) Sobre uma pequena coleção de aves de Boracéia e do Varjão do Guaratuba (Estado de S. Paulo). *Pap. Avuls. Dep. Zool. São Paulo* 7: 143-164.

Camargo, H. F. de A. (1962) Sobre as raças geográficas brasileiras de *Amazona brasiliensis* (L., 1758) (Aves, Psittacidae). *Pap. Avuls. Dep. Zool. São Paulo* 15: 67-77.

Camargo, H. F. de A. (1976) Sobre o ninho de *Triclaria malachitacea* (Spix, 1824) (Aves, Psittacidae). *Pap. Avuls. Zool.* 29: 93-94.

Camargo, H. F. de A. and de Camargo, E. A. (1964) Ocorrência de *Iodopleura p. pipra* no estado de São Paulo, Brasil, e algumas notas sôbre *Iodopleura isabellae* (Aves, Cotingidae). *Pap. Avuls. Dep. Zool. São Paulo* 16: 45-55.

Campbell, D. G. (1978) *The ephemeral islands: a natural history of the Bahamas*. London: MacMillan.

Canevari, M., Canevari, P., Carrizo, G. R., Harris, G., Mata, J. R. and Straneck, R. J. (1991) *Nueva guia de las aves argentinas*. Buenos Aires: Fundación Acindar.

Canevari, P. and Caziani, S. M. (1988) Situación de la familia Cracidae en la República Argentina. Unpublished paper presented at the II International Cracid Symposium, Caracas, Venezuela, February/March 1988.

Cardim, F. (1925) *Tratados da terra e gente do Brasil*. Rio de Janeiro: José Leite e Cia.

Carriker, M. A. (1910) An annotated list of the birds of Costa Rica including Cocos Island. *Ann. Carnegie Mus.* 6: 314-915.

Carriker, M. A. (1932) Additional new birds from Peru with a synopsis of the races of *Hylophylax naevia*. *Proc. Acad. Nat. Sci. Philadelphia* 84: 1-7.

Carriker, M. A. (1933) Descriptions of new birds from Peru, with notes on other little-known species. *Proc. Acad. Nat. Sci. Philadelphia* 85: 1-38.
Carriker, M. A. (1934) Descriptions of new birds from Peru, with notes on the nomenclature and status of other little-known species. *Proc. Acad. Nat. Sci. Philadelphia* 86: 317-334.
Carriker, M. A. (1935a) Descriptions of new birds from Bolivia, with notes on other little known species. *Proc. Acad. Nat. Sci. Philadelphia* 87: 313-341.
Carriker, M. A. (1935b) Descriptions of new birds from Peru and Ecuador, with critical notes on other little-known species. *Proc. Acad. Nat. Sci. Philadelphia* 87: 343-359.
Carriker, M. A. (1955a) Notes on the occurrence and distribution of certain species of Colombian birds. *Noved. Colombianas* 2: 48-64.
Carriker, M. A. (1955b) Studies on neotropical Mallophaga XII, Part IV. Lice of the Tinamous. *Bol. Entomol. Venezolana* 11(3-4): 1-35.
Carriker, M. A. (1959) New records of rare birds from Nariño and Cauca and notes on others. *Noved. Colombianas* 1: 196-199.
Carriker, M. A. and Meyer de Schauensee, R. (1935) An annotated list of two collections of Guatemalan birds in the Academy of Natural Sciences of Philadelphia. *Proc. Acad. Nat. Sci. Philadelphia* 87: 411-455.
Carte, A. (1866) On an undescribed species of petrel from the Blue Mountains of Jamaica. *Proc. Zool. Soc. London*: 93-95.
Carvalho, C. E. de S. (1985) Lista preliminar da fauna comercializada na feira de Caxias, RJ. *Bol. FBCN* 20: 90-102.
Casares, J. (1939) Nota sobre la distribución del gaviotón de cola blanca y negra (*Larus belcheri*). *Hornero* 7: 286-287.
Cassin, J. (1859) Notes on the birds collected by the La Plata Expedition. Pp.599-602 [= Appendix J] in T. J. Page, *La Plata, the Argentine Confederation, and Paraguay*. London: Trubner and Co.
Castelino, M. A. (1985) Mirlo de Agua en Jujuy. *Nuestras Aves* 3(8): 26.
Castelino, M. (1990) Un ave nueva para la República Argentina y segunda mención para otra. *Nótulas Faunísticas* 21.
Castellanos, A. (1931-1934) Aves del Valle de los Reartes (Córdoba). *Hornero* 4: 361-391; 5: 1-40, 159-174, 307-338.
Caufield, C. (1985) *In the rainforest*. London: Heinemann.
Cavalcanti, R. B. (1988) Conservation of birds in the *cerrado* of central Brazil. Pp.59-66 in P. D. Goriup, ed. *Ecology and conservation of grassland birds*. Cambridge, U.K.: International Council for Bird Preservation (Techn. Publ. 7).
CCA (1991a) = Caribbean Conservation Association (1991) *Antigua and Barbuda: country environmental profile*. St Michael, Barbados: The Caribbean Conservation Association.
CCA (1991b) = Caribbean Conservation Association (1991) *St Lucia: country environmental profile*. St Michael, Barbados: The Caribbean Conservation Association.
Ceballos-Lascurain, H. (1989) Rare and unusual birds of the Sierra Madre del Sur of Mexico. *Aves Mexicanas* 2(89-2): 1-3.
Cesar, E. (1990) Maior traficante de fauna na "mira" do Ibama. *O Globo* Saturday 17 November: 18.
CETN (1976) = Comisión de Estudios del Territorio Nacional (1976) Huejuquila, 1:50,000, F-13-B-64. First reprinting. [Mexico:] Secretaria de la Presidencia.
CETN (1984a) = Comisión de Estudios del Territorio Nacional (1984) Chilpancingo, 1:50,000, E-14-C-28. First reprinting. [Mexico:] Secretaria de la Presidencia.
CETN (1984b) = Comisión de Estudios del Territorio Nacional (1984) El Paraíso, 1:50,000, E-14-C-36. First reprinting. [Mexico:] Secretaria de la Presidencia.
Chapman, F. M. (1892) Notes on birds and mammals observed near Trinidad, Cuba, with remarks on the origin of West Indian bird-life. *Bull. Amer. Mus. Nat. Hist.* 4: 279-330.
Chapman, F. M. (1894) On the birds of the island of Trinidad. *Bull. Amer. Mus. Nat. Hist.* 6: 1-86.
Chapman, F. M. (1898) Notes on birds observed at Jalapa and Las Vigas, Vera Cruz, Mexico. *Bull. Amer. Mus. Nat. Hist.* 10: 15-43.
Chapman, F. M. (1899) Descriptions of five apparently new birds from Venezuela. *Bull. Amer. Mus. Nat. Hist.* 12: 153-156.

Chapman, F. M. (1901) Descriptions of six apparently new birds from Peru. *Bull. Amer. Mus. Nat. Hist.* 14: 225-228.
Chapman, F. M. (1912) Diagnoses of apparently new Colombian birds. *Bull. Amer. Mus. Nat. Hist.* 31: 139-166.
Chapman, F. M. (1914a) Descriptions of proposed new birds from Ecuador. *Bull. Amer. Mus. Nat. Hist.* 33: 317-322.
Chapman, F. M. (1914b) A naturalist's journey around Vera Cruz and Tampico. *Natn. Geogr. Mag.* 25: 533-562.
Chapman, F. M. (1917a) The distribution of bird-life in Colombia. *Bull. Amer. Mus. Nat. Hist.* 36.
Chapman, F. M. (1917b) Descriptions of new birds from Santo Domingo and remarks on others in the Brewster-Sanford Collection. *Bull. Amer. Mus. Nat. Hist.* 37: 327-334.
Chapman, F. M. (1919) Descriptions of proposed new birds from Peru, Bolivia, Brazil, and Colombia. *Proc. Biol. Soc. Washington* 32: 253-268.
Chapman, F. M. (1921a) Descriptions of new birds from Colombia, Ecuador, Peru and Brazil. *Amer. Mus. Novit.* 18.
Chapman, F. M. (1921b) The distribution of bird life in the Urubamba Valley of Peru. *Bull. U.S. Natn. Mus.* 117: 1-138.
Chapman, F. M. (1923) Descriptions of proposed new Formicariidae and Dendrocolaptidae. *Amer. Mus. Novit.* 86.
Chapman, F. M. (1924) Descriptions of new genera and species of Tracheophonae from Panama, Ecuador, Perú and Bolivia. *Amer. Mus. Novit.* 123.
Chapman, F. M. (1925) Remarks on the life zones of northeastern Venezuela with descriptions of new species of birds. *Amer. Mus. Novit.* 191.
Chapman, F. M. (1926) The distribution of bird-life in Ecuador. *Bull. Amer. Mus. Nat. Hist.* 55.
Chapman, F. M. (1933) *Autobiography of a bird-lover.* New York: Appleton-Century Co.
Charity, S. (1988) Intenso comércio ameaça pintor-verdadeiro. *Bol. Funatura*, Brasília 2(2): 2.
Chebez, J. C. (1981) Las aves del Urugua-í. *Rev. Iguazú* 1: 57-73.
Chebez, J. C. (1984) Nuestras aves amenazadas, 2: el Pato Serrucho (*Mergus octosetaceus*). *Nuestras Aves* 4: 17-18.
Chebez, J. C. (1985a) Nuestras aves amenazadas, 6: el Chorao (*Amazona pretrei*). *Nuestras Aves* 3(6): 17-19.
Chebez, J. C. (1985b) Nuestras aves amenazadas, 7: la Yacutinga (*Aburria jacutinga*). *Nuestras Aves* 3(7): 16-17.
Chebez, J. C. (1986a) Nuestras aves amenazadas, 12: el Guacamayo Violaceo (*Anodorhynchus glaucus*). *Nuestras Aves* 4(9): 17-20.
Chebez [typeset as Chevez], J. C. (1986b) Nuestras aves amenazadas, 13: Carpintero Cara Canela (*Dryocopus galeatus*). *Nuestras Aves* 4(10): 16-18.
Chebez, J. C. (1986c) Nuestras aves amenazadas, 16: Palomita Morada (*Claravis godefrida*). *Nuestras Aves* 4(11): 21-22.
Chebez, J. C. (1989) Nuevos registros de águilas crestadas en el noroeste argentino. *Nuestras Aves* 20: 6-7.
Chebez, J. C. (1990) Los manuscritos de William Henry Partridge, 1. *Nuestras Aves* 22(8): 21-24.
Chebez, J. C. (in press) Notas sobre algunas aves raras o amenazadas de Misiones (Argentina). *Aprona, Bol. Cient.*
Chebez, J. C. and Heinonen Fortabat, S. (1987) Novedades ornitogeográficas argentinas, 2. *Nótulas Faunísticas* (Asunción) no.3.
Chebez, J. C. and Rolón, L. H. (1989) *Parque Provincial Urugua-í.* Posadas, Argentina: Ediciones Montoya.
Cherrie, G. K. (1896) Contribution to the ornithology of San Domingo. *Field Col. Mus. Publ.* Orn. Ser. 1(1): 1-26.
Cherrie, G. K. (1916) Some apparently undescribed birds from the collection of the Roosevelt South America Expedition. *Bull. Amer. Mus. Nat. Hist.* 35: 183-190.
Cheshire, N. G. (1990) Notes on seabirds – reports received in 1989. *Sea Swallow* 39: 18-37.

Christian, C. S. (1991) Parrot conservation efforts in the islands of the Antilles (from Puerto Rico to Grenada). Master's thesis, Clemson University (Department of Parks, Recreation and Tourism Management).

Christy, C. (1897) Field-notes on the birds of the island of San Domingo. *Ibis* (7)3: 317-342.

Chubb, C. (1910) On the birds of Paraguay. *Ibis* 9(4): 53-78, 263-285, 517-534, 571-647.

Chubb, C. (1919) Notes on collections of birds in the British Museum, from Ecuador, Peru, Bolivia, and Argentina. *Ibis* (11)1: 1-55, 256-290.

Clapp, R. B., Banks, R., Morgan-Jacobs, D. and Hoffman, W. A. (1982) Marine birds of the southeastern United States and Gulf of Mexico. Part 1. Gaviiformes through Pelecaniformes. Washington, D.C.: U.S, Department of the Interior (FWS/OBS-82/01).

Clark, A. H. (1902) The birds of Margarita Island, Venezuela. *Auk* 19: 258-267.

Clark, A. H. (1905) Birds of the southern Lesser Antilles. *Proc. Boston Soc. Nat. Hist.* 32: 203-312.

Clark, W. D. (1991) Hyacinth Macaws: nesting habits in the wild. *AFA Watchbird* 18(3): 8-10.

Clarke, R. O. S. and Duran Patiño, E. (1991) The Red-fronted Macaw (*Ara rubrogenys*) in Bolivia: distribution, abundance, biology and conservation. Buena Vista: unpublished report to Wildlife Conservation International and the International Council for Bird Preservation.

Clements, J. F. (1979) Viva Zapata! *Birding* 11(1): 2-6.

Clinton-Eitniear, J. (1986) Status of the Green-cheeked Amazon in north-eastern Mexico. *AFA Watchbird* 12(6): 22-24.

Clinton-Eitniear, J. (1987) Endangered amazon parrots in the Commonwealth of Dominica. *AFA Watchbird* 14(5): 28.

Clinton-Eitniear, J. (1988) Green-cheeked Amazon update. *AFA Watchbird* 15(4): 28-29.

Clinton-Eitniear, J. (1989) Captive status of the Green-cheeked Amazon parrot. *AFA Watchbird* 16(3): 33.

Clinton-Eitniear, J. (1990) *Amazona oratrix belizensis. AFA Watchbird* 17(2): 25-26.

Clubb, K. J. and Clubb, S. L. (1991) Status of macaws in aviculture. *AFA Watchbird* 18(3): 21-23.

CNPPA (1982) = IUCN Commission on National Parks and Protected Areas (1982) *IUCN Directory of Neotropical protected areas*. Dublin: Tycooly International Publishing Limited (published for International Union for Conservation of Nature and Natural Resources).

Coats, S. and Phelps, W. H. (1985) The Venezuelan Red Siskin: case history of an endangered species. Pp.977-985 in P. A. Buckley, M. S. Foster, E. S. Morton, R. S. Ridgely and F. G. Buckley, eds. *Neotropical ornithology*. Washington, D.C.: American Ornithologists' Union (Orn. Monogr. 36).

Coats, S. and Rivero M., A. (1984) Report on the status and natural history of *Spinus cucullatus* (Aves; Fringillidae) in Venezuela. *Bol. Soc. Venezolana Cienc. Nat.* 142: 25-64.

Coelho, A. G. M. (1979) As aves da Estação Ecológica de Tapacurá, Pernambuco. *Notulae Biologicae* (Recife) n.s. no.2.

Coelho, A. G. M. (1986) Pintores e macucos. *Ciência Hoje* 4(24): 38-39.

Coelho, A. G. M. (1987) Aves da Reserva Biológica de Serra Negra (Floresta-PE). Lista preliminar. *Publ. Avuls. Univ. Fed. Pernambuco* no.2.

Cohen, W. B. (1984) *Environmental degradation in Haiti: an analysis of aerial photography*. Port-au-Prince, Haiti: USAID/Haiti.

Coimbra-Filho, A. F. (1970) Sobre *Mitu mitu* (Linnaeus, 1766) e a validez das suas duas raças geográficas (Cracidae, Aves). *Revta. Bras. Biol.* 30: 101-109.

Coimbra-Filho, A. F. (1971) Tres formas da avifauna do nordeste do Brasil ameaçadas de extinção: *Tinamus solitarius pernambucensis* Berla, 1946, *Mitu mitu mitu* (Linnaeus, 1766) e *Procnias a. averano* (Hermann, 1783) (Aves – Tinamidae, Cracidae, Cotingidae). *Revta. Bras. Biol.* 31: 239-247.

Coimbra-Filho, A. F. (1974) Situação mundial de recursos faunísticos na faixa intertropical. *Brasil Florestal* 5: 12-37.

Coimbra-Filho, A. F. and Aldrighi, A. D. (1971) A restauração da fauna do Parque Nacional da Tijuca. *Publ. Avuls. Mus. Nac.* 57.

Coimbra-Filho, A. F. and Aldrighi, A. D. (1972) Restabelecimento da fauna no Parque Nacional da Tijuca (segunda contribuição). *Brasil Florestal* 3(11): 19-33.

Coimbra-Filho, A. F., Aldrighi, A. D. and Martins, H. F. (1973) Nova contribuição ao restabelecimento da fauna do Parque Nacional da Tijuca, GB, Brasil. *Brasil Florestal* 4(16): 7-25.

Coimbra-Filho, A. F. and Magnanini, A. (1968) Animais raros ou em vias de desaparecimento no Brasil. *Anuário Bras. Econ. Florestal* 19: 149-177.

Coker, R. E. (1908) Regarding the future of the guano industry and the guano-producing birds of Peru. *Science* 28: 58-64.

Coker, R. E. (1920) Habits and economic relations of the guano birds of Peru. *Proc. U.S. Natn. Mus.* 56: 449-511.

Colchester, M. (1991) Guatemala: the clamour for land and the fate of the forests. *Ecologist* 21: 177-185.

Coles, D. (1986) Results of the Hooded Siskin census. *Avicult. Mag.* 92: 100-108.

Collar, N. J. (1986) The best-kept secret in Brazil. *World Birdwatch* 8(2): 14-15.

Collar, N. J. (1987) Red data bird: Hook-billed Hermit. *World Birdwatch* 9(1): 5.

Collar, N. J. and Andrew, P. (1988) *Birds to watch: the ICBP world checklist of threatened birds.* Cambridge, U.K.: International Council for Bird Preservation (Techn. Publ. 8).

Collar, N. J. and Gonzaga, L. A. P. (1985) The Red-billed Curassow *Crax blumenbachii* in the CVRD Forest Reserve near Linhares (Espírito Santo), Brazil. Report and recommendations of a consultancy for Companhia Vale do Rio Doce, 27 September to 26 October 1985. Unpublished.

Collar, N. J., Gonzaga, L. A. P., Jones, P. J. and Scott, D. A. (1987) Avifauna da Mata Atlântica. Pp.73-84 in *Desenvolvimento económico e impacto ambiental em áreas de trópico úmido brasileiro: a experiência da CVRD.* Rio de Janeiro: Companhia Vale do Rio Doce.

Collar, N. J. and Gonzaga, L. A. P. (1988) O mutum *Crax blumenbachii* na Reserva Florestal Particular de Linhares – ES. *Espaço, Ambiente e Planejamento* [Bol. Tecn. CVRD] 2(8).

Collar, N. J. and Stuart, S. N. (1985) *Threatened birds of Africa and related islands: the ICBP/IUCN Red Data Book,* 1. Cambridge, U.K.: International Council for Bird Preservation, and International Union for Conservation of Nature and Natural Resources.

Colwell, R. K. (1989) Hummingbirds of the Juan Fernández Islands: natural history, evolution and population status. *Ibis* 131: 548-566.

Cominese Filho, F. R., Cominese, I. T. and Scherer Neto, P. (1986) Reprodução em cativeiro da "jacutinga" no estado do Paraná. *An. Soc. Sul-Riogrand. Orn.* 7: 10-14.

CONAF (1988) Presencia de Tagua Cornuda (*Fulica cornuta*) en la Laguna Santa Rosa, III Región de Atacama. Proyecto Tagua Cornuda: Gestión Anual. Corporación Nacional Forestal, Ministerio de Agricultura. Unpublished.

Conover, B. (1949) A new species of *Tinamus* from Peru. *Fieldiana Zool.* 31: 263-266.

Conover, H. B. (1934) A new species of rail from Paraguay. *Auk* 51: 365-366.

CONSEMA (1985) *Áreas naturais do estado de São Paulo.* São Paulo: Conselho Estadual do Meio Ambiente.

Contreras, J. R. (1978) Ecología de la avifauna de la región de Puerto Lobos, provincias de Río Negro y del Chubut. *Ecosur* 10: 169-181.

Contreras, J. R. (1989) Abundancia y densidad relativa de rapaces (Accipitridae y Falconidae) en Corrientes. *Nuestras Aves* 20: 10-11.

Contreras, J. R., Berry, L. M., Contreras, A. O., Bertonatti, C. C. and Utges, E. E. (1990) *Atlas ornitogeográfico de la provincia del Chaco – República Argentina.* Corrientes: FVSA Capítulo Corrientes (Quadernos Técnicos Félix de Azara 1).

Contreras, J. R. and González Romero, N. (1989) Nuevos datos acerca de la avifauna intraurbana de Ñu Guazú, Asunción, República del Paraguay. *Nótulas Faunísticas* (Asunción) no.18.

Contreras, A. O., Vitale, C., Davies, Y. E. and Ramírez [not Rodríguez], J. L. (1989) La avifauna del Departamento de Misiones, República del Paraguay. Nota preliminar acerca de la zona comprendida entre Santiago y Ayolas. Pp.11-12 in C. Acevedo Gómez, ed. *Resúmenes y programa, II Encuentro Paraguayo-Argentino de Ornitología.* Asunción: Imprenta Graphis S.R.L.

Cordier, C. (1971) The quest for the Horned Curassow. *Animal Kingdom* 74(2): 9-11.

Correa, H. and Oyarzo, H. (1987) Presencia de Tagua Cornuda (*Fulica cornuta*) en la Laguna Santa Rosa, III Región de Atacama. Proyecto Tagua Cornuda. Informe preliminar no.1. Corporación Nacional Forestal, Ministerio de Agricultura. Unpublished.

Cory, C. B. (1880) *Birds of the Bahama Islands; containing many birds new to the islands, and a number of undescribed winter plumages of North American species.* Boston: published by the author.

Cory, C. B. (1885) *The birds of Haiti and San Domingo.* Boston: Estes and Lauriat.

Cory, C. B. (1887) The birds of the West Indies. *Auk* 4: 108-120.

Cory, C. B. (1892) In Cuba with Dr. Gundlach. *Auk* 9: 271-273.

Cory, C. B. (1895) Description of two new species of birds from San Domingo. *Auk* 12: 278-279.

Cory, C. B. (1909) The birds of the Leeward Islands, Caribbean Sea. *Field Mus. Nat. Hist. Orn. Ser.* 1(5): 193-255 (Publ. 137).

Cory, C. B. (1918) Catalogue of birds of the Americas, Part II no.1. *Field Mus. Nat. Hist. Zool. Ser.* 13 (Publ. 197).

Cory, C. B. and Hellmayr, C. E. (1924) Catalogue of birds of the Americas, Part III. *Field Mus. Nat. Hist. Zool. Ser.* 13 (Publ. 223).

Cory, C. B. and Hellmayr, C. E. (1925) Catalogue of birds of the Americas, Part IV. *Field Mus. Nat. Hist. Zool. Ser.* 13 (Publ. 234).

Cory, C. B. and Hellmayr, C. E. (1927) Catalogue of birds of the Americas, Part V. *Field Mus. Nat. Hist. Zool. Ser.* 13 (Publ. 242).

Cottam, C. and Knappen, P. (1939) Food of some uncommon North American birds. *Auk* 56: 138-169.

Coulter, M. C. (1984) Seabird conservation in the Galápagos Islands, Ecuador. Pp.237-244 in J. P. Croxall, P. G. H. Evans and R. W. Schreiber, eds. *Status and conservation of the world's seabirds.* Cambridge, U.K.: International Council for Bird Preservation (Techn. Publ. 2).

Coulter, M. C., Cruz, F. and Cruz, T. (1985a) A programme to save the Dark-rumped Petrel, *Pterodroma phaeopygia*, on Floreana Island, Galápagos, Ecuador. Pp.177-180 in P. J. Moors, ed. *Conservation of island birds: case studies for the management of threatened island species.* Cambridge, U.K.: International Council for Bird Preservation (Techn. Publ. 3).

Coulter, M. C., Cruz, F. and Beach, T. (1985b) The biology and conservation of the Dark-rumped Petrel, *Pterodroma phaeopygia*, on Floreana Island, Galápagos, Ecuador. Unpublished.

Counsell, D. (1988) The RAFOS Expedition to Belize, Feb.–Mar. 1986. *Royal Air Force Orn. Soc. J.* 18: 17-63.

Cox, G. (1990) The unicorn's nest. *WPA News* 29: 8-10.

Cox, G. and Clarke, R. O. (1988) Erste Ergebnisse einer Studie über den Bolivianischen Helmhokko *Pauxi unicornis* in Amboró-Nationalpark, Bolivien. *Trochilus* 9: 96-101.

Cox, U. O. (1895) A collection of birds from Mount Orizaba, Mexico. *Auk* 12: 356-359.

Cracraft, J. (1985) Historical biogeography and patterns of differentiation within the South American avifauna: areas of endemism. Pp.49-84 in P. A. Buckley, M. S. Foster, E. S. Morton, R. S. Ridgely and F. G. Buckley, eds. *Neotropical ornithology.* Washington, D.C.: American Ornithologists' Union (Orn. Monogr. 36).

Cramp, S. and Simmons, K. E. L. (1977) *The birds of the Western Palearctic*, 1. London: Oxford University Press.

Crawshay, R. (1907) *The birds of Tierra del Fuego.* London: Bernard Quaritch.

Crespo, J. A. (1941) La fauna del altiplano jujeño. *Revta. Arg. Zoogeogr.* 1: 17-25.

Crosby, M. J., Heath, M. F., Long, A. J. and Stattersfield, A. J. (in prep.; sequence of authors undecided) *A global directory of endemic bird areas.* Cambridge, U.K.: International Council for Bird Preservation (Techn. Publ.).

Crossin, R. S. (1967) The breeding biology of the Tufted Jay. *Proc. West. Found. Vert. Zool.* 1: 265-300.

Crossin, R. S. and Ely, C. A. (1973) A new race of Sumichrast's Wren from Chiapas, Mexico. *Condor* 75: 137-139.

Cruz, A., Manolis, T. and Wiley, J. W. (1985) The Shiny Cowbird: a brood parasite expanding its range in the Caribbean region. Pp.607-620 in P. A. Buckley, M. S. Foster, E. S. Morton, R. S. Ridgely and F. G. Buckley, eds. *Neotropical ornithology.* Washington, D.C.: American Ornithologists' Union (Orn. Monogr. 36).

Cruz, A. and Nakamura, T. K. (1984) The 1983 nesting season of the Yellow-shouldered Blackbird (*Agelaius xanthomus*) in southwestern Puerto Rico. Unpublished.

Cruz, F., Cruz, J. and Lawesson, J. E. (1986) *Lantana camara* L., a threat to native plants and animals. *Notícias de Galápagos* 43: 10-11.

Cruz, G. A. (1986) *Guia de los parques nacionales, refugios de vida silvestre, reservas biológicas y monumentos naturales de Honduras*. Tegucigalpa: Asosiación Hondureña de Ecología.
CSD (1963) = Cadastrial Survey Department (1963) Bonaire, 1:25,000. Netherlands Antilles: Cadastrial Survey Department.
Cubillas, S., Kirkconnell, A., Posada, R. M. and Llanes, A. (1988) Aves observadas en los Cayos Rosario y Cantiles, Archipiélago de los Canarreos, Cuba. *Misc. Zool. Acad. Cienc. Cuba* 38: 1-2.
Cuello, J. P. (1985) Lista de referencia y bibliografía de las aves uruguayas. *Mus. Dámaso Antonio Larrañaga* Ser. Divulg. no.1.
Cuello, J. and Gerzenstein, E. (1962) Las aves del Uruguay: lista sistemática, distribución y notas. *Com. Zool. Mus. Hist. Nat. Montevideo* 6(93).
Curry, R. L. (1986) Whatever happened to the Floreana Mockingbird? *Noticias de Galápagos* 43: 13-15.
Curry, R. L. and Grant, P. R. (1991) The Floreana Mockingbird: demography and viability of a relict population. Abstract 245 in the Program of the 109th stated meeting of the American Ornithologists' Union, 14-17 August 1991. Montreal: Committee on Local Arrangements (etc.), unpublished.
Dabbene, R. (1910) *Ornitología argentina*. Buenos Aires: Imprenta y Casa Editora "Juan A. Alsina". (*An. Mus. Nac. Buenos Aires* [3]11).
Dabbene, R. (1913) Distribution des oiseaux en Argentine. *Bol. Soc. Physis* 1: 241-261, 293-366.
Dabbene, R. (1920) El "Canindé" de Azara es el *Ara ararauna* (Lin.). *Hornero* 2: 56.
Dabbene, R. (1921) Algunas palabras más sobre el cambio de nombre del Ara caninde auct. *Hornero* 2: 225.
Dabbene, R. (1926) Tres aves nuevas para la avifauna uruguaya. *Hornero* 3: 422.
Daguerre, J. B. (1922) Lista de aves coleccionadas y observadas en Rosas, F.C.S. *Hornero* 2:259-271.
Daguerre, J. B. (1933) Dos aves nuevas para la fauna argentina. *Hornero* 5: 213-215.
Danforth, S. T. (1929) Notes on the birds of Hispaniola. *Auk* 46: 358-375.
Danforth, S. T. (1935) *The birds of Saint Lucia*. Puerto Rico: University of Puerto Rico (Monogr. Univ. Puerto Rico, Ser. B: 3).
Danforth, S. (1936) *Los pájaros de Puerto Rico*. Chicago: Rand McNally and Co.
Dannenberg, R. (1982) Ornithologische Beobachtungen im Nordostatlantik. *Orn. Mitt.* 34: 107-117.
Darlington, P. J. (1931) Notes on the birds of the Río Frío (near Santa Marta), Magdalena, Colombia. *Bull. Mus. Comp. Zool.* 71: 349-421.
Dathe, H. and Fischer, W. (1979-1981) Beiträge zur Ornithologie Kubas. *Beitr. Vogelkd.* 25: 171-203, 27: 100-122.
Davis, D. E. (1941) Notes on Cuban birds. *Wilson Bull.* 53: 37-40.
Davis, D. E. (1945) The annual cycle of plants, mosquitoes, birds, and mammals in two Brazilian forests. *Ecol. Monogr.* 15: 243-295.
Davis, D. E. (1946) A seasonal analysis of mixed flocks of birds in Brazil. *Ecology* 27: 168-181.
Davis, F. W., Hilgartner, W. B. and Steadman, D. W. (1985) Notes on the diets of *Geotrygon montana* and *Columba caribaea* in Jamaica. *Bull. Brit. Orn. Club* 105: 130-133.
Davis, L. I. (1952) Winter bird census at Xilitla, San Luis Potosí, Mexico. *Condor* 54: 345-355.
Davis, T. J. (1986) Distribution and natural history of some birds from the Departments of San Martín and Amazonas, northern Peru. *Condor* 88: 50-56.
Davis, T. J. and O'Neill, J. P. (1986) A new species of antwren (Formicariidae: *Herpsilochmus*) from Peru, with comments on the systematics of other members of the genus. *Wilson Bull.* 98: 337-352.
Davis, W. A. and Russell, S. M. (1984) *Birds in southeastern Arizona*. Tucson: Tucson Audubon Society.
DCM (1958) = Departamento Cartográfico Militar (1958) Estados Unidos Mexicanos, 1: 500,000. México: Comisión Intersecretarial Coordinadora de Levantamiento de la Carta Geográfica de la República.
DCN (1964) = Dirección de Cartografia Nacional (1964) Carta geográfica del Estado Nueva Esparta. República de Venezuela: Ministerio de Obras Públicas.
Decoteau, A. E. (1982) *Handbook of macaws*. Neptune, N.J.: T. F. H. Publications, Inc.
DeDios [*sic*], A. and Hill, P. (1990) Breeding the Spix Macaw. *Bird World* 13(4) (November/ December): 16, 18.

Dejonghe, J. F. and Mallet, B. (1978) Sur la redécouverte de la Pénélope à ailes blanches, *Penelope albipennis*. *Gerfaut* 68: 204-209.
Delacour, J. (1939) Parrots and parrakeets at Clères. *Avicult. Mag.* (5)4: 390-392.
Delacour, J. (1943) A collection of birds from Costa Rica. *Avicult. Mag.* (5)8: 29-32.
Delacour, J. (1959) *The waterfowl of the world*, 3. London: Country Life.
Delacour, J. and Amadon, D. (1973) *Curassows and related birds*. New York: American Museum of Natural History.
DeLoach, J. (1983) Breeding the Red-fronted Macaw. *AFA Watchbird* 9(6): 21.
Dennis, J. V. (1948) A last remnant of Ivory-billed Woodpeckers in Cuba. *Auk* 65: 497-507.
Dennis, J. V. (1979) The Ivory-billed Woodpecker *Campephilus principalis*. *Avicult. Mag.* 85: 75-84.
Descourtilz, J. T. (undated, apparently 1854-1856) *Ornithologie brésilienne ou histoire des oiseaux du Brésil*. Rio de Janeiro: Thomas Reeves.
Desenne, P. and Strahl, S. D. (1991) Trade and the conservation status of the family Psittacidae in Venezuela. *Bird Conserv. Internatn.* 1: 153-169.
Devillers, P. (1977) Observations at a breeding colony of *Larus (belcheri) atlanticus*. *Gerfaut* 67: 22-43.
DGPOA (undated) = Dirección General de Planificación y Ordenación del Ambiente (undated) Mapa de ubicación de las áreas bajo regimen especial actuales. Caracas: Ministério del Ambiente y de los Recursos Naturales Renovables.
Diamond, A. W. (1973) Habitats and feeding stations of St Lucia forest birds. *Ibis* 115: 313-329.
Díaz Díaz, C. A. (1984) Recovery plan for the Puerto Rican Whip-poor-will (*Caprimulgus noctitherus*). Atlanta, Georgia: U.S. Fish and Wildlife Service.
Díaz Montes, V. R. (1991) Status of the highly endangered White-winged Guan. *Cracid Newsletter* 1(1): 1, 6.
Díaz-Soltero, H. (1988) Break-through in recovery of Puerto Rican Plain Pigeon. *Endang. Species Techn. Bull.* 13(9-10): 11.
Dick, J. A., McGillivray, W. B. and Brooks, D. J. (1984) A list of birds and their weights from Saül, French Guiana. *Wilson Bull.* 96: 347-365.
Dickerman, R. W. (1965) The juvenile plumage and distribution of *Cassidix palustris* (Swainson). *Auk* 82: 268-270.
Dickerman, R. W. (1970) A systematic revision of *Geothlypis speciosa* the Black-polled Yellowthroat. *Condor* 72: 95-98.
Dickerman, R. W. and Warner, D. W. (1961) Distribution records from Tecolutla, Veracruz, with the first record of *Porzana flaviventer* for Mexico. *Wilson Bull.* 73: 336-340.
Dickerman, R. W., Phillips, A. R. and Warner, D. W. (1967) On the Sierra Madre Sparrow, *Xenospiza baileyi*, of Mexico. *Auk* 84: 49-60.
Diebold, E. N. (1986) Venezuelan Black-hooded Red Siskin on the brink. *AFA Watchbird* 13(2): 8-11.
Diefenbach, K. H. and Goldhammer, S. P. (1986) Biologie und Ökologie der Rotschwanzamazone (*Amazona brasiliensis*). *Trochilus* 7: 72-78.
Diefenback [*sic*], K. H. and Goldhammer, S. P. (1986) Tracking *Amazona pretrei pretrei*. *Amazona Newsletter* 3(4) [10]: 2-9.
Dinelli, L. (1918) Notas biológicas sobre las aves del noroeste de la República Argentina. *Hornero* 1: 57-68.
Dinelli, L. M. (1933) El tiránido *Pseudocolopteryx dinellianus* y su nido. *Hornero* 5: 221-222.
DMATC (1972) = Defense Mapping Agency Topographic Center (1972) *Dominican Republic: official standard names*. Second edition. Washington, D.C.: Defense Mapping Agency Topographic Center.
DMATC (1973) = Defense Mapping Agency Topographic Center (1973) *Haiti: official standard names*. Second edition. Washington, D.C.: Defense Mapping Agency Topographic Center.
Dodson, C. H. and Gentry, A. H. (1991) Biological extinction in western Ecuador. *Ann. Missouri Bot. Gard.* 78: 273-295.
Dodson, C. H., Gentry, A. H., and Valverde, F. M. (1985) Flora of Jauneche. *Selbyana* 8: 1-512.
Doering, A. (1874) Noticias ornitológicas de las regiones ribereñas del río Guayquiraró. *Period. Zool. Argent.* 1: 237-258.
Dorst, J. (1957a) Contribution à l'étude écologique des oiseaux du haut Marañón (Pérou septentrional). *Oiseau et R.F.O.* 27: 235-269.

Dorst, J. (1957b) Etude d'une collection d'oiseaux rapportée du bassin du Haut Marañon, Pérou septentrional. *Bull. Mus. Natn. Hist. Nat. Paris* (2)29: 377-384.

Doughty, R. W. (1989) *Return of the Whooping Crane*. Austin: University of Texas Press.

Dourojeanni, M., Hofmann, R., García, R., Malleaux, J. and Tovar, Y. A. (1968) Observaciones preliminares para el manejo de las aves acuáticas del Lago Junín, Perú. *Revta. Forestal Perú* 2: 3-52.

Downer, A. and Sutton, R. (1990) *Birds of Jamaica*. Cambridge: Cambridge University Press.

DSGM (1988) = Dirección Servicio Geográfico Militar (1988) Mapa del Paraguay (1: 2,000,000). Séptima edición. Dirección del Servicio Geográfico Militar.

Du Bus, B. (1847) Note sur quelques espèces nouvelles d'oiseaux d'Amérique. *Bull. Acad. Roy. Sci. Lettres Beaux-Arts Belgique* 14(2): 101-108.

Dubs, B. (1983) *Die Vögel des südlichen Mato Grosso*. Bern: Verlag Verbandsdruckerei-Betadruck.

Duffy, D. C., Hays, C. and Plenge, M. A. (1984) The conservation status of Peruvian seabirds. Pp.245-259 in J. P. Croxall, P. G. H. Evans and R. W. Schreiber, eds. *Status and conservation of the world's seabirds*. Cambridge, U.K.: International Council for Bird Preservation (Techn. Publ. 2).

Dugand, A. (1945a) Notas ornitológicas colombianas, I. *Caldasia* 3: 337-341.

Dugand, A. (1945b) Notas ornitológicas colombianas, II. *Caldasia* 3: 397-418.

Dugand, A. (1948) Notas ornitológicas colombianas, IV. *Caldasia* 5: 157-199.

Dugand, A. and Eisenmann, E. (1983) Rediscovery of, and new data on, *Molothrus armenti* Cabanis. *Auk* 100: 991-992.

Dugès, O. (1899) Emigration accidentelle d'oiseaux. *Auk* 16: 287-288.

Dunning, J. S. (1970) *Portraits of tropical birds*. Wynnewood, Pa.: Livingston Publ. Co.

Dunning, J. S. (1982) *South American land birds*. Newtown Square, Penn.: Harrowood Books.

Durnford, H. (1877) Notes on the birds of the province of Buenos Ayres. *Ibis* (4)1: 166-203.

Durnford, H. (1878) Notes on the birds of the Province of Buenos Ayres. *Ibis* (4)2: 58-68.

Dutton, F. G. (1897) Parrot notes. *Avicult. Mag.* 4: 21-24, 63-65.

Dutton, F. G. (1900) The feeding of parrots. *Avicult. Mag.* 6: 240-245.

DVS (1990) = Departamento de Vida Silvestre (1990) *La diversidad biológica en la República Dominicana*. Santo Domingo: Secretaría de Estado de Agricultura/Subsecretaría de Estado de Recursos Naturales/Departamento de Vida Silvestre.

Eaton, S. W. and Edwards, E. P. (1948) Notes on birds of the Gómez Farías region of Tamaulipas. *Auk* 60: 109-114.

Eckleberry, D. R. (1965) A note on the parrots of northeastern Argentina. *Wilson Bull.* 77: 111.

Edwards, E. P. (1968) *Finding birds in Mexico*. Second edition. Sweet Briar, Virginia: Ernest P. Edwards.

Edwards, E. P. (1972) *A field guide to the birds of Mexico*. Sweet Briar, Virginia: Ernest P. Edwards.

Edwards, E. P. (1985) *1985 supplement to finding birds in Mexico (1968)*. Sweet Briar, Virginia: Ernest P. Edwards.

Edwards, E. P. (1989) *A field guide to the birds of Mexico*. Second edition. Sweet Briar, Virginia: Ernest P. Edwards.

Edwards, E. P. and Martin, P. S. (1955) Further notes on birds of the Lake Pátzcuaro region, Mexico. *Auk* 72: 174-178.

Eisenmann, E. and Lehmann, F. C. (1962) A new species of swift of the genus *Cypseloides* from Colombia. *Amer. Mus. Novit.* 2117.

Eiten, G. (1983) *Classificação da vegetação do Brasil*. Brasília: Conselho Nacional de Desenvolvimento Científico e Tecnológico.

Ehrlich, P. R., Dobkin, D. S. and Wheye, D. (1992) *Birds in jeopardy: the imperiled and extinct birds of the United States and Canada, including Hawaii and Puerto Rico*. Stanford: Stanford University Press.

Eley, J. W. (1982) Systematic relationships and zoogeography of the White-winged Guan (*Penelope albipennis*) and related forms. *Wilson Bull.* 94: 241-259.

Ellenberg, (1958) Wald oder Steppe? Die natürliche Pflanzendecke der Anden Perus. *Die Umschau* 21: 645-648, 679-681.

Elliot, D. G. (1870) Descriptions of some new genera and species of birds belonging to the families Formicariidae, Pachycephalidae, and Sylviidae. *Proc. Zool. Soc. London*: 242-244.

Elliot, D. G. (1871) Descriptions of two new species of hummingbirds belonging to the genera *Eupherusa* and *Cyanomyia*. *Ann. Mag. Nat. Hist.* 8: 1-2.
Ellis-Joseph, S., Hewston, N. and Green, A. (1992) *Global waterfowl conservation assessment and management plan.* Captive Breeding Specialist Group and The Wildfowl and Wetland Trust. First review draft, 15 March 1992.
Ely, C. E. (1962) The birds of southeastern Coahuila, Mexico. *Condor* 64: 34-39.
Emmel, T. C. (1975) The butterfly faunas of San Andres and Providencia islands in the western Caribbean. *J. Res. Lepidoptera* 14: 49-56.
Engleman, D. (1992a) Field editor's report. *Toucan* 18(2): 4.
Engleman, D. (1992b) Field editor's report. *Toucan* 18(3): 4.
Escalante, C. C. (1984) Problemas en la conservación de dos poblaciones de láridos sobre la costa atlántica de Sud América: *Larus (belcheri) atlanticus* y *Sterna maxima. Rev. Mus. Arg. Cienc. Nat. (Zoología)* 13(14): 117-152.
Escalante-Pliego, P. and Peterson, A. T. (1992) Geographic variation and species limits in middle American woodnymphs (*Thalurania*). *Wilson Bull.* 104: 205-219.
Escalante, R. (1962) Frequency of occurrence of some seabirds in Uruguay. *Condor* 64: 510-512.
Escalante, R. (1966) Notes on the Uruguayan population of *Larus belcheri. Condor* 68: 507-510.
Escalante, R. (1970) *Aves marinas del río de la Plata y aguas vecinas del Océano Atlántico.* Montevideo: Barreiro y Ramos.
Escalante, R. (1980) Notas sobre algunas aves de la vertiente atlántica de Sud América (Rallidae, Laridae). *Resúmenes, I Jornadas de Ciencias Naturales, Montevideo*: 33-34.
Esteban, J. G. (1953a) Nuevas localidades para las aves argentinas. *Acta Zool. Lilloana* 13: 349-362.
Esteban, J. G. (1953b) Tipos de aves en la colección del Instituto Miguel Lillo. *Acta Zool. Lilloana* 13: 363-365.
Esteban, J. G. (1969) Protección de los recursos naturales en la Provincia de Tucumán (especialmente la fauna). *Acta Zool. Lilloana* 24: 89-98.
Estudillo López, J. (1986) Notes on rare cracids in the wild and in captivity. *World Pheasant Assoc. J.* 11: 53-66.
Euler, C. (1868) Beiträge zur Naturgeschichte der Vögel Brasiliens, 4. *J. Orn.* 16: 182-194.
Euler, C. (1900) Descripção de ninhos e ovos das aves do Brasil. *Revta. Mus. Paulista* 4: 9-148.
Evans, P. G. H. (1986a) Dominica, West Indies. *World Birdwatch* 8(1): 8-9.
Evans, P. G. H. (1986b) Dominica multiple land use project. *Ambio* 15: 82-89.
Evans, P. G. H. (1988a) *The conservation status of the Imperial and Red-necked Parrots on the island of Dominica, West Indies.* Cambridge, U.K.: International Council for Bird Preservation (Study Report 27).
Evans, P. (1989) Dominica multiple land use project. Pp.81-88 in A. E. Lugo, ed. *Wildlife management in the Caribbean.* Rio Pedras, Puerto Rico: Institute of Tropical Forestry and the Caribbean National Forest.
Evans, P. G. H. (1990) *Birds of the eastern Caribbean.* London: MacMillan.
Evans, P. G. H. (1991) Status and conservation of Imperial and Red-necked Parrots *Amazona imperialis* and *A. arausiaca* on Dominica. *Bird Conserv. Internatn.* 1: 11-32.
Evans, R. J., ed. (1988b) An ornithological survey in the province of Esmeraldas in north-west Ecuador – August 1986. Unpublished report of the Durham University expedition.
Everett, W. T. (1988) Notes from Clarión Island. *Condor* 90: 512-513.
Everett, W. T. and Anderson, D. W. (1991) Status and conservation of the breeding seabirds on offshore Pacific islands of Baja California and the Gulf of California. PP.115-139 in J. P. Croxall, ed. *Seabird status and conservation: a supplement.* Cambridge, U.K.: International Council for Bird Preservation (Techn. Publ. 11).
Eyre, L. A. (1987) Jamaica: test case for tropical deforestation. *Ambio* 16: 6.
Fa, J. E. and Bell, D. J. (1990) The Volcano Rabbit *Romerolagus diazi*. Pp.143-146 in J. A. Chapman and J. E. Flux, eds. *Rabbits, hares and pikas: status survey and conservation action plan.* Gland, Switzerland: International Union for Conservation of Nature and Natural Resources.
Faaborg, J. (1984) Potential for restocking Galápagos Hawks on islands where they have been extirpated. *Notícias de Galápagos* 39: 28-30.

Faaborg, J. (1986) Reproductive success and survivorship of the Galápagos Hawk *Buteo galapagoensis*: potential costs and benefits of cooperative polyandry. *Ibis* 128: 337-347.

Faaborg, J. R. and Arendt, W. J. (1985) *Wildlife assessments in the Caribbean*. San Juan, Puerto Rico: Institute of Tropical Forestry.

Faaborg, J., de Vries, T., Patterson, C. B. and Griffin, C. R. (1980) Preliminary observations on the occurrence and evolution of polyandry in the Galápagos Hawk (*Buteo galapagoensis*). *Auk* 97: 581-590.

Faanes, C. A. and Senner, S. E. (1991) Status and conservation of the Eskimo Curlew. *Amer. Birds* 45: 237-239.

Fearnside, P. M. (1987) Deforestation and international economic development projects in Brazilian Amazonia. *Conserv. Biol.* 1: 214-221.

Fearnside, P. M. (1990) The rate and extent of deforestation in Brazilian Amazonia. *Environ. Conserv.* 17: 213-226.

Feilden, H. W. (1894) The deserted domicile of the Diablotin in Dominica. *Trans. Norfolk and Norwich Nat. Soc.* 5: 24-39.

Fernández Yépez, A., Benedetti, F. L. and Phelps, W. H. (1940) Las aves de Margarita. *Bol. Soc. Venezolana Cienc. Nat.* 43: 91-132.

Ferrari-Perez, F. (1886) Catalogue of animals collected by the Geographical and Exploring Commission of the Republic of Mexico. *Proc. U.S. Natn. Mus.* 9: 125-199.

Ferreyra, R. (1976) *Endangered species and plant communities in Andean and coastal Peru*. New York: New York Botanic Garden.

ffrench, R. (1973) *A guide to the birds of Trinidad and Tobago*. Wynnewood, Pennsylvania: Livingston Publishing Company.

ffrench, R. (1988) Supplement to a guide to the birds of Trinidad and Tobago. Unpublished.

ffrench, R. (1992) *A guide to the birds of Trinidad and Tobago*. Second edition. London: Christopher Helm (published in 1991 in U.S.A. by Cornell University).

Finsch, O. (1867-1868) *Die Papageien, monographisch bearbeitet*. Leiden: E. J. Brill.

Fisher, C. T. (1981) Specimens of extinct, endangered or rare birds in the Merseyside County Museums, Liverpool. *Bull. Brit. Orn. Club* 101: 276-285.

Fitter, R. and Fitter, M. (1987) *The road to extinction: problems of categorizing the status of taxa threatened with extinction*. Gland, Switzerland, and Cambridge, U.K.: International Union for Conservation of Nature and Natural Resources.

Fitzpatrick, J. W. (1980) A new race of *Atlapetes leucopterus*, with comments on widespread albinism in *A. l. dresseri* (Taczanowski). *Auk* 97: 883-887.

Fitzpatrick, J. W. and O'Neill, J. P. (1979) A new tody-tyrant from northern Peru. *Auk* 96: 443-447.

Fitzpatrick, J. W. and Willard, D. E. (1982) Twenty-one bird species new or little known from the Republic of Colombia. *Bull. Brit. Orn. Club* 102: 153-158.

Fitzpatrick, J. W., Willard, D. E. and Terborgh, J. W. (1979) A new species of hummingbird from Peru. *Wilson Bull.* 91: 177-186.

Fitzpatrick, J. W. (1976) Systematics and biogeography of the tyrannid genus *Todirostrum* and related genera (Aves). *Bull. Mus. Comp. Zool.* 147: 435-463.

Fjeldså, J. (1981a) Comparative ecology of Peruvian grebes – a study of the mechanisms of evolution of ecological isolation. *Vidensk. Meddr. Dansk Naturh. Foren.* 143: 125-249.

Fjeldså, J. (1981b) *Podiceps taczanowskii* (Aves, Podicipedidae), the endemic grebe of Lake Junín, Peru: a review. *Steenstrupia* 7: 237-259.

Fjeldså, J. (1983a) A black rail from Junín, central Peru. *Steenstrupia* 8: 277-282.

Fjeldså, J. (1983b) Vertebrates of the Junín Area, Central Peru. *Steenstrupia* 8: 285-298.

Fjeldså, J. (1984) Three endangered South American grebes (*Podiceps*): case histories and the ethics of saving species by human intervention. *Ann. Zool. Fennici* 21: 411-416.

Fjeldså, J. (1986a) Report of the ICBP/IWRB grebe specialist group, July 1986. Unpublished.

Fjeldså, J. (1986b) Research and conservation management relating to Lake Junín, C. Peru, and the Junín Flightless Grebe. Proposal submitted to ICBP 20 October 1986, unpublished.

Fjeldså, J. (1987) *Birds of relict forests in the high Andes of Peru and Bolivia*. Copenhagen: Zoological Museum University of Copenhagen, technical report.

Fjeldså, J. (1988) Status of birds of steppe habitats of the Andean zone and Patagonia. Pp.81-95 in P. D. Goriup, ed. *Ecology and conservation of grassland birds.* Cambridge, U.K.: International Council for Bird Preservation (Techn. Publ. 7).

Fjeldså, J. (1991) The activity of birds during snow-storms in high-level woodlands in Peru. *Bull. Brit. Orn. Club* 111: 4-11.

Fjeldså, J. (in press) Biogeographic patterns and evolution of the avifauna of relict high altitude woodlands of the Andes. *Steenstrupia.*

Fjeldså, J. (in prep.) The decline and probable extinction of the Colombian Grebe *Podiceps andinus. Bird Conserv. Internatn.*

Fjeldså, J. and Krabbe, N. (1986) Some range extensions and other unusual records of Andean birds. *Bull. Brit. Orn. Club* 106: 115-124.

Fjeldså, J. and Krabbe, N. (1989) An unpublished major collection of birds from the Bolivian highlands. *Zool. Scripta* 18: 321-329.

Fjeldså, J. and Krabbe, N. (1990) *Birds of the high Andes.* [Copenhagen:] Zoological Museum, University of Copenhagen, and Svendborg: Apollo Books.

Fjeldså, J., Krabbe, N. and Parker T. A. (1987) Rediscovery of *Cinclodes excelsior aricomae* and notes on the nominate race. *Bull. Brit. Orn. Club* 107: 112-114.

Fjeldså, J. and Schulenberg, T. S. (in press) A systematic revision of the *Asthenes dorbignyi* superspecies.

Fleming, P. (1933) *Brazilian adventure.* London: Jonathan Cape.

Fleming, R. L. and Baker, R. H. (1963) Notes on the birds of Durango, Mexico. *Publ. Mus. Michigan State Univ.* 2: 273-304.

Fletcher, J. (1986) Pigeon with banded tail. *Gosse Bird Club Broadsheet* no.46: 6.

Fontana, L. J. (1881) *El Gran Chaco.* Buenos Aires.

Forbes, H. O. and Robinson, H. C. (1897) Catalogue of the parrots (Psittaci) in the Derby Museum. *Bull. Liverpool Mus.* 1: 5-22.

Forbes, W. A. (1881) Eleven weeks in north-eastern Brazil. *Ibis* (4)5: 312-362.

Forcelli, D. O. (1987) El Pato Esquivo ¿Sobrevivirá? *En Peligro de Extinción* 1(1): 2-3.

Forrester, B. C. (1987) Brazil July/August 1987. Unpublished (birdwatching) report.

Forrester, B. C. (1990) Brazil IV, July/August 1990. Unpublished (birdwatching) report.

Forshaw, J. M. (1973) *Parrots of the world.* Melbourne: Lansdowne Editions.

Forshaw, J. M. (1978) *Parrots of the world.* Second (revised) edition. Melbourne: Lansdowne Editions.

Forshaw, J. M. (1989) *Parrots of the world.* Third (revised) edition. London: Blandford Press.

Fraga, R. M. (1990) El Tordo Amarillo al borde de la extinción. *Nuestras Aves* 23: 13-15.

Fraga, R. and Narosky, S. (1985) *Nidificación de las aves argentinas (Formicariidae a Cinclidae).* Buenos Aires: Asociación Ornitológica del Plata.

Franky, S. M. and Rodríguez, P. (1977) *Parque Nacional Natural Isla de Salamanca.* Bogotá: INDERENA.

Freiberg, M. A. (1943) Enumeración sistemática de las aves de Entre Ríos y lista de los ejemplares que las representan en el museo de Entre Ríos. *Mem. Mus. Entre Ríos* (Zoología) 21.

Freud, A. (1980) The discovery of the home of Lear's Macaw. *Avicult. Mag.* 86: 261-263.

Frey, H. (1985) The Black-hooded Red Siskin: an endangered species (an interview with Patricia Demko). *AFA Watchbird* 12(4): 40-42.

Friedmann, H. (1927) Notes on some Argentine birds. *Bull. Mus. Comp. Zool.* 68: 139-236.

Friedmann, H. (1950) The birds of North and Middle America, 11. *Bull. U.S. Natn. Mus.* 50.

Friedmann, H., Griscom, L. and Moore, R. T. (1950) *Distributional checklist of the birds of Mexico,* 1. Cooper Ornithological Society (Pacific Coast Avifauna 29).

Frimer, O. and Møller Nielsen, S. (1989) The status of *Polylepis* forests and their avifauna in Cordillera Blanca, Peru. Technical report from an inventory in 1988, with suggestions for conservation management. Copenhagen: Zoological Museum University of Copenhagen.

Froke, J. B. (1981) Populations, movements, foraging and nesting of feral *Amazona* parrots in southern California. M.Sc. thesis, Humboldt State University.

Frost, K. D. (1959) Three amazon parrots. *Avicult. Mag.* 65: 84-85.

Fry, C. H. (1970) Ecological distribution of birds in north-eastern Mato Grosso state, Brazil. *An. Acad. Bras. Cienc.* 42: 275-318.

Fuller, E. (1987) *Extinct birds.* London: Viking/Rainbird.

Fuller, K. S., Swift, B., Jorgenson, A., Bräutigam, A. and Gaski, A. L. (1987) *Latin American wildlife trade laws.* Second (revised) edition. Washington, D.C.: TRAFFIC (U.S.A.), World Wildlife Fund.

Funck, N. (1875) [Extract of a letter to Mr Sclater.] *Proc. Zool. Soc. London*: 566.

Fundación Natura (1990) Propuesta para la declaración de una unidad de conservación en el area de Virolín, cuenca alta del río Fonce, departamento de Santander. Unpublished.

Furniss, S. B. (1983) *Yellow-shouldered Blackbird recovery plan.* Atlanta, Georgia: U.S. Fish and Wildlife Service.

Galliano, D. (1984) Breeding the Black-hooded Red Siskin *Carduelis cucullatus. Avicult. Mag.* 90: 76-79.

García, F. (undated [c.1984]) *Las aves de Cuba: especies endémicas,* 1. La Habana: Editorial Gente Nueva.

García, F. (1987) *Las aves de Cuba: subespecies endémicas,* 2. La Habana: Editorial Gente Nueva.

García, M. E. and González, H. (1985) Nueva localidad para el Carpintero Churroso (*Colaptes fernandinae*) (Aves: Picidae). *Misc. Zool. Acad. Cienc. Cuba* 25: 4.

García, M. E., González Alonso, H. J. and Rodríguez, D. (1987) Evaluación ecológica de la ornitocenosis de un bosque semicaducifolio en la Península de Zapata, Cuba. *Ciencias Biológicas* 18: 93-101.

Gardner, N. (1986) A birder's guide to travel in Peru. Unpublished.

Gardner, N. J. and Brisley, D. S. (1989) Birding trip to Venezuela: 16 December 1988–8 January 1989. Unpublished report.

Gardner, N. and Gardner, D. (1990a) A birder's guide to travel in Argentina. Unpublished.

Gardner, N. J. and Gardner, D. S. (1990b) Birding trip to Brazil. 1st May 1990–21 July 1990. Unpublished report.

Garrido, O. H. (1967) Nidada del gavilancito cubano, *Accipiter striatus fringilloides* (Aves: Accipitridae). *Poeyana* 50: 1-2.

Garrido, O. H. (1973) Anfibios, reptiles y aves de Cayo Real (Cayos de San Felipe), Cuba. *Poeyana* 119.

Garrido, O. H. (1976) Aves y reptiles de Cayo Coco, Cuba. *Misc. Zool. Acad. Cienc. Cuba* 3: 3-4.

Garrido, O. H. (1980) Los vertebrados terrestres de la Península de Zapata. *Poeyana* 203.

Garrido, O. H. (1984) *Los patos de Cuba.* La Habana: Editorial Científico-Técnica.

Garrido, O. H. (1985) Cuban endangered birds. Pp.992-999 in P. A. Buckley, M. S. Foster, E. S. Morton, R. S. Ridgely and F. G. Buckley, eds. *Neotropical ornithology.* Washington, D.C.: American Ornithologists' Union (Orn. Monogr. 36).

Garrido, O. H. (1986) *Las palomas.* La Habana: Editorial Científico Técnica.

Garrido, O. H., Estrada, A. R. and Llanes, A. (1986) Anfibios, reptiles y aves de Cayo Guajaba, Archipiélago de Sabana-Camagüey, Cuba. *Poeyana* 328.

Garrido, O. H. and García Montaña, F. (1975) *Catálogo de las aves de Cuba.* La Habana: Academia de Ciencias de Cuba.

Garrido, O. H. and Schwartz, A. (1968) Anfibios, reptiles y aves de la Península de Guanahacabibes, Cuba. *Poeyana* 53.

Garrido, O. H. and Schwartz, A. (1969) Anfibios, reptiles y aves de Cayo Cantiles. *Poeyana* 67.

Gauto, R. (1989) Private conservation programs in Paraguay. *Conserv. Biol.* 3: 120.

Gavio, H. S. (1939) Excursión al parque provincial de Sierra de la Ventana. *Hornero* 7: 255-259.

Geerlings, L. (1992) European cracid inventory, autumn 1990. Unpublished.

Gehlbach, F. R. (1987) Natural history sketches, densities, and biomass of breeding birds in evergreen forests of the Rio Grande, Texas, and Rio Corona, Tamaulipas, Mexico. *Texas J. Sci.* 39: 241-251.

Gehlbach, F. R., Dillon, D. O., Harrell, H. L., Kennedy, S. E. and Wilson, K. R. (1976) Avifauna of the Río Corona, Tamaulipas, Mexico: northeastern limit of the tropics. *Auk* 93: 53-65.

Gentry, A. (1989) Northwest South America (Colombia, Ecuador and Peru). Pp.393-399 in D. G. Campbell and H. D. Hammond, eds. *Floristic inventory of tropical countries.* New York: New York Botanical Garden.

Geoffroy, L. (1861) Note sur les Trochilidées (oiseaux-mouches–Tominejas) de la Nouvelle Grenade. Pp.1-16 in E. Uricoechea, ed. *Contribuciones de Colombia a las Ciencias y a las Artes, publicadas con la cooperación de naturalistas neogranadinos.* Bogotá: Imprenta de El Mosaico.

Gerstberger, P. (1982) Expeditionen durch den karibischen Regenwald Dominicas. *Trochilus* 3: 62-68.

Gertler, P. E. (1977) Hooded Antpitta (*Grallaricula cucullata*) in the Eastern Andes of Colombia. *Condor* 79: 389.

Giacomelli, E. (1923) Catálogo sistemático de las aves útiles y nocivas de la Provincia de La Rioja. *Hornero* 3: 66-84.

Giai, A. G. (1950) Notas de viajes. *Hornero* 9: 121-164.

Giai, A. G. (1951) Notas sobre la avifauna de Salta y Misiones. *Hornero* 9: 247-276.

Giai, A. G. (1952) Diccionario ilustrado de las aves argentinas. Part I. *Revta. Mundo Agrario*, 52.

Giai, A. G. (1976) *Vida de un naturalista en Misiones.* Buenos Aires: Editorial Albatros.

Gibson, E. (1885) Notes on the birds of Paisandú, Republic of Uruguay. *Ibis* (5)3: 275-283.

Gibson, E. (1918) Further ornithological notes from the neighbourhood of Cape San Antonio, province of Buenos Ayres, 1. *Ibis* (10)6: 363-415.

Gibson, E. (1920) Further ornithological notes from the neighbourhood of Cape San Antonio, province of Buenos Ayres. *Ibis* (11)2: 1-97.

Gildardo, C. A. (1976) *Estudio de los poblaciones de Cotorra Frente Roja (*Amazona viridigenalis*) y del Loro Cabeza Amarilla (*A. ochrocephala*) en la costa de Tamaulipas, México.* Mexico: Dirección General de la Fauna Silvestre (*Bol. Fauna* 8).

Gill, R. E. and Handel, C. M., compilers (1990) Summary of the proceedings from the workshop on Bristle-thighed Curlews, February 14-16, 1990 Anchorage, Alaska. Anchorage, Alaska: U.S. Fish and Wildlife Service, unpublished.

Gill, R. E., Lanctot, R. B., Mason, J. D. and Handel, C. M. (1991) Observations on habitat use, breeding chronology and parental care in Bristle-thighed Curlews on the Seward Peninsula, Alaska. *Wader Study Group Bull.* 61: 28-36.

Gill, R. E. and Redmond, R. L. (1992) Distribution, numbers and habitat of Bristle-thighed Curlews (*Numenius tahitiensis*) on Rangiroa Atoll. *Notornis* 39: 17-26.

Ginés, H. and Aveledo, R. (1958) *Aves de caza de Venezuela.* Caracas: Editorial Sucre (Sociedad de Ciencias Naturales La Salle Monogr. 4).

Glade, A. A., ed. (1988) *Red list of Chilean terrestrial vertebrates: Proceedings of the Symposium "Conservation Status of Chilean Terrestrial Vertebrate Fauna".* Santiago: Impresiones Comerciales, for CONAF.

Gliesch, R. (1930) Lista das aves colligidas e observadas no estado do Rio Grande do Sul. *Egatea* 15: 276-292.

Gochfeld, M. (1974) Current status of and threats to some parrots of the Lesser Antilles. *Biol. Conserv.* 6: 184-187.

Gochfeld, M. (1979) Brood parasite and host coevolution: interactions between shiny cowbirds and two species of meadowlarks. *Amer. Nat.* 113: 855-870.

Gochfeld, M. and Keith, S. (1977) The Red-billed Curassow. *Oryx* 14: 22-23.

Gochfeld, M., Keith, S., and Donahue, P. (1980) Records of rare or previously unrecorded birds from Colombia. *Bull. Brit. Orn. Club* 100: 196-201.

Godman, F. D. (1899) [Two apparently new species of Peruvian birds.] *Bull. Brit. Orn. Club* 10: 27.

Godman, F. D. (1907-1910) *A monograph of the petrels.* London: Witherby and Co.

Goeldi, E. A. (1894) *As aves do Brasil.* Parte 1. Rio de Janeiro and São Paulo: Livraria Clássica de Alves.

Goeldi, E. A. (1897) Ornithological results of a naturalist's visit to the coast-region of south Guyana. *Ibis* (7)3: 149-165.

Goeldi, E. A. (1903) Ornithological results of an expedition up the Capim River, state of Pará, with critical remarks on the Cracidae of Lower Amazonia. *Ibis* (8)3: 472-500.

Goldman, E. A. (1951) Biological investigations in Mexico. *Smithson. Misc. Coll.* 115.

Gollop, J. B. (1988) The Eskimo Curlew. Pp.582-595 in W. J. Chandler, ed. *Audubon Wildlife Report 1988/1989.* San Diego: Academic Press, Inc.

Gollop, J. B., Barry, T. W. and Iversen, E. H. (1986) *Eskimo Curlew: a vanishing species?* Regina, Saskatchewan: Saskatchewan Natural History Society (Spec. Publ. 17).

Gonzaga, L. P. (1983) Notas sobre *Dacnis nigripes* Pelzeln, 1856 (Aves, Coerebidae). *Iheringia*, sér. zool. 63: 45-58.

Gonzaga, L. A. P. (1984) Voa araponga, voa macuco, que o homem vem aí ... *Ciência Hoje* 2(11): 18-24.

Gonzaga, L. P. (1986) Composição da avifauna em uma parcela de mata perturbada na baixada, em Majé, estado do Rio de Janeiro, Brasil. M.Sc. dissertation, Universidade Federal do Rio de Janeiro.

Gonzaga, L. P. (1988) A new antwren (*Myrmotherula*) from southeastern Brazil. *Bull. Brit. Orn. Club* 108: 132-135.

Gonzaga, L. P. (1989) Catálogo dos tipos na coleção ornitológica do Museu Nacional. II. Passeriformes. *Bol. Mus. Para. Emílio Goeldi* sér. zool. 5(1): 41-69.

Gonzaga, L. A. P. (unpublished) The Red-billed Curassow *Crax blumenbachii* in the CVRD Forest Reserve at Linhares (Espírito Santo), Brazil. Second appraisal. Report and recommendations of a consultancy to the Companhia do Vale do Rio Doce, 17-27 February 1986.

Gonzaga, L. P. and Pacheco, J. F. (1990) Two new subspecies of *Formicivora serrana* (Hellmayr) from south-eastern Brazil, and notes on the type-locality of *Formicivora deluzae* Ménétriès. *Bull. Brit. Orn. Club* 110: 187-193.

Gonzaga, L. P., Scott, D. A. and Collar, N. J. (1987) The status and birds of some forest fragments in eastern Brazil: report on a survey supported by CVRD, October 1986. Unpublished.

Gonzaga, L. P., Scott, D. A. and Collar, N. J. (1988) O beija-flor *Ramphodon dohrnii* na reserva florestal da CVRD em Porto Seguro, Estado da Bahia. P.473 in *Resumos, XV Congresso Brasileiro de Zoologia*. Curitiba: Universidade Federal do Paraná.

González Alonso, H., de las Pozas, G. and González Bermúdez, F. (1982) Aspectos reproductivos y densidad poblacional de *Torreornis inexpectata inexpectata* (Aves: Fringilidae) en la Ciénaga de Zapata, Cuba. *Ciencias Biológicas* 8: 123-129.

González Alonso, H., González Bermúdez, F. and Quesada, M. (1986) Distribución y alimentación del Cabrerito de la Ciénaga *Torreornis inexpectata* (Aves: Fringillidae). *Poeyana* 310.

González Alonso, H., Sirois, J., McNicholl, M. K., Hamel, P. B., Godínez, E., McRae, R. D., Acosta, M., Rodríguez, D., Marcos, C. and Hernández, J. (1990) Preliminary results of a cooperative bird-banding project in the Zapata Swamp, Cuba, January 1988. *Canad. Wildl. Serv. Progr. Notes* no.187.

González, H. (1982) Localización de *Ferminia cerverai* (Aves: Troglodytidae) en la Ciénaga de Zapata. *Misc. Zool. Acad. Cienc. Cuba* 16: 4.

González-García, F. (1984) Aspectos biológicos del Pavón *Oreophasis derbianus* G. R. Gray (Aves: Cracidae) en la reserva natural "El Triunfo", Municipio del Angel Albino Corzo, Chiapas. Tesis de licenciatura, Facultad de Ciencias Biológicas, Universidad Veracruzana, Xalapa, Veracruz.

González-García, F. (1988a) Ecología y distribución del Pavón *Oreophasis derbianus* en México: pasado, presente y futuro. Unpublished paper presented at the II International Cracid Symposium, Caracas, Venezuela, February/March 1988.

González-García, F. (1988b) The Horned Guan. *Animal Kingdom* 91(4): 21-22.

González-García, F. (1991) Observaciones sobre la ecología y biología reproductiva del Pavón *Oreophasis derbianus* en la Reserva de la Biosfera "El Triunfo", Chiapas, México. Paper presented at IV Congreso de Ornitología Neotropical, Quito, Ecuador, November 1991. Unpublished.

González-García, F. and Bubb, P. J. (1989) Estudio y conservación del Pavón (*Oreophasis derbianus*) en la Sierra Madre de Chiapas. Xalapa, México: Informe de actividades (for Instituto de Ecología, A.C., and Wildlife Conservation International), unpublished.

Goodall, J. D., Johnson, A. W. and Philippi, R. A. (1951) *Las aves de Chile, su conocimiento y sus costumbres*, 2. Buenos Aires: Platt Establecimientos Gráficos.

Goodfellow, W. (1901-1902) Results of an ornithological journey through Colombia and Ecuador. *Ibis* (8)1: 300-319, 458-480, 699-715; (8)2: 56-67, 207-233.

Goodwin, D. (1976) *Crows of the world*. London: British Museum (Natural History).

Goodwin, D. (1983) *Pigeons and doves of the world*. Third edition. Ithaca, New York: Cornell University Press.

Goodwin, M. (1982) Letter: the Red Siskin. *Avicult. Mag.* 89: 120-121.

Goodwin, M. L. (1990) *Birding in Venezuela*. Second edition. Caracas: Sociedad Conservacionista Audubon de Venezuela.

Gore, M. E. J. and Gepp, A. R. M. (1978) *Las aves del Uruguay*. Montevideo: Mosca Hermanos.

Gorman, K. M. (1990) Breeding the endangered Venezuelan Black-hooded Red Siskin. *AFA Watchbird* 17(1): 7-12.

Gorman, K. M. (1992) AFA Red Siskin Project. *AFA Watchbird* 18(6): 24-25.

Gosse, P. H. (1847) *The birds of Jamaica*. London: John van Voorst.

Gould, J. (1841) Birds. Part III of C. Darwin, ed. *The zoology of the voyage of H.M.S. Beagle, under the command of Captain Fitzroy, R.N., during the years 1832 to 1836*. London: Smith, Elder and Co.

Gould, J. (1850) Descriptions of new birds. *Proc. Zool. Soc. London*: 91-95.

Gould, J. (1871) [On two species of hummingbirds.] *Proc. Zool. Soc. London*: 803-804.

GQR (1991) = Guia Quatro Rodas (1991) *Guia rodoviário*. São Paulo: Editora Abril.

Graham, F. (1988) A bird in the hand is worth... plenty! *Audubon* 3: 96-99.

de Grahl, W. (1986) Vom Spix' Blauara (*Cyanopsitta spixii* [Wagler 1832]). *Gefied. Welt* 110: 103.

Granizo Tamayo, T. and Hayes, F. E. (in prep.) El Pato Serrucho *Mergus octosetaceus* probablemente extinto en el Paraguay. [*Hornero*]

Grant, C. H. B. (1911) List of birds collected in Argentina, Paraguay, Bolivia, and southern Brazil, with field-notes. *Ibis* (9)5: 80-137.

Grant, P. R. (1965) A systematic study of the terrestrial birds of the Tres Marías Islands, Mexico. *Postilla* 90.

Grant, P. R. (1966) Late breeding on the Tres Marías Islands. *Condor* 68: 249-252.

Grant, P. R. and Cowan, I. M. (1964) A review of the avifauna of the Tres Marías Islands, Nayarit, Mexico. *Condor* 66: 221-228.

Grantsau, R. (1989) *Os beija-flores do Brasil*. Rio de Janeiro: Expressão e Cultura.

Graves, G. R. (1980) A new species of metaltail hummingbird from northern Peru. *Wilson Bull*. 92: 1-7.

Graves, G. R. (1985) Elevational correlates of speciation and intraspecific geographic variation in plumage in Andean forest birds. *Auk* 102: 556-579.

Graves, G. R. (1986) Geographic variation in the White-mantled Barbet (*Capito hypoleucus*) of Colombia (Aves: Capitonidae). *Proc. Biol. Soc. Washington* 99: 61-64.

Graves, G. R. (1988) *Phylloscartes lanyoni*, a new species of bristle-tyrant (Tyrannidae) from the lower Cauca valley of Colombia. *Wilson Bull*. 100: 529-534.

Graves, G. R. and Arango, G. (1988) Nest-site selection, nest, and eggs of the Stout-billed Cinclodes (*Cinclodes excelsior*), a high Andean furnariid. *Condor* 90: 251-253.

Graves, G. R. and Giraldo O., J. P. (1987) Population status of the Rufous-fronted Parakeet (*Bolborhynchus ferrugineifrons*), a Colombian endemic. *Gerfaut* 77: 89-92.

Graves, G. R. and Olson, S. L. (1986) A new subspecies of *Turdus swalesi* (Aves: Passeriformes: Muscicapidae) from the Dominican Republic. *Proc. Biol. Soc. Washington* 99: 580-583.

Graves, G. R. and Uribe Restrepo, D. (1989) A new allopatric taxon in the *Hapalopsittaca amazonina* (Psittacidae) superspecies from Colombia. *Wilson Bull*. 101: 369-376.

Graves, G. R. and Weske, J. S. (1987) *Tangara phillipsi*, a new species of tanager from the Cerros del Sira, eastern Peru. *Wilson Bull*. 99: 1-6.

Graves, G. R. and Zusi, R. L. (1990) Avian body weights from the lower Rio Xingu. *Bull. Brit. Orn. Club* 110: 20-25.

Grayson, A. J. and Lawrence, G. N. (1871) On the physical geography and natural history of the islands of the Tres Marías and of Socorro, off the western coast of Mexico. *Proc. Boston Soc. Nat. Hist.* 14: 261-302.

Greenewalt, C. H. (1966) The Marvelous Hummingbird rediscovered. *Natn. Geogr. Mag*. 130 (July): 98-101.

Greenway, J. C. (1958) *Extinct and vanishing birds of the world*. New York: American Committee for International Wildlife Protection (Spec. Publ. 13).

Greenway, J. C. (1967) *Extinct and vanishing birds of the world*. Second (revised) edition. New York: Dover Publications.

Gregoire, F. W. (1981) The dilemma of the *Amazona imperialis* and *Amazona arausiaca* parrots in Dominica following Hurrican David in 1979. Pp.161-167 in R. F. Pasquier, ed. *Conservation of New World parrots*. Washington, D.C.: Smithsonian Institution Press for the International Council for Bird Preservation (Techn. Publ. 1).

Gregoire, F. (1987) Response to the article on the *Amazona imperialis*, in the Amazona Newsletter, Supplement no.1, September 1986, by T. D. Nichols. *Amazona Newsletter* 4(1): 2-6.

Gretton, A. (1986) Birds. Pp.33-57 in F. Robinson, ed. Río Mazan project 1986 report. Oxford: Department of Plant Sciences, University of Oxford, unpublished.

Griscom, L. (1932) The distribution of bird-life in Guatemala. *Bull. Amer. Mus. Nat. Hist.* 64.

Griscom, L. (1935) The rediscovery of *Chlorospingus flavovirens* (Lawrence). *Auk* 52: 94-95.

Griscom, L. and Greenway, J. C. (1941) Birds of Lower Amazonia. *Bull. Mus. Comp. Zool.* 88: 81-344.

Grzybowski, J. A. (1991) *Black-capped Vireo (*Vireo atricapillus*) recovery plan.* Austin, Texas: U.S. Fish and Wildlife Service.

Grzybowski, J. A., Clapp, R. B. and Marshall, J. T. (1986) History and current population status of the Black-capped Vireo in Oklahoma. *Amer. Birds* 40: 1151-1161.

Guedes, N. M. R. (1991) Observações de ninhos de arara azul (*Anodorhynchus hyacinthinus*) no Pantanal. P.6 in Resumos, I Congresso Brasileiro de Ornitologia. Belém: Museu Paraense Emílio Goeldi.

Guedes, N. M. R. and Harper, L. H. (1991) Nest site characteristics of the Hyacinth Macaw (*Anodorhynchus hyacinthinus*) in the Nhecolândia region of the Brazilian Pantanal. Abstract 261 in the Program of the 109th Stated Meeting of the American Ornithologists' Union, 14-17 August 1991. Montreal: Committee on Local Arrangements (etc.), unpublished.

Gundlach, J. (1852) Description of five new species of birds, and other ornithological notes on Cuban species. *Boston J. Nat. Hist.* 6: 313-319.

Gundlach, J. (1861) Tabellarische Uebersicht aller bisher auf Cuba beobachteten Vögel. *J. Orn.* 9: 321-349.

Gundlach, J. (1871-1875) Neue Beiträge zur Ornithologie Cubas. *J. Orn.* 19: 265-295, 353-378; 20: 401-432; 22: 113-166, 286-303; 23: 293-340, 353-407.

Gundlach, J. (1872) Catálogo de las aves cubanas. *An. Soc. Española Hist. Nat.* 2: 81-191.

Gundlach, J. (1876) *Contribución a la ornitología cubana.* Habana: Imprenta "La Antilla".

Gundlach, J. (1878a) Neue Beiträge zur Ornithologie der Insel Portorico. *J. Orn.* 26: 157-194.

Gundlach, J. (1878b) Apuntes para la fauna Puerto-Riqueña. *An. Soc. Española Hist. Nat.* 7: 135-234, 343-422.

Gundlach, J. (1893) *Ornitología cubana, o catálogo descriptivo de todas las especies de aves tanto indígenas como de paso anual o accidental observadas en 53 años.* Habana: Archivos de la Policlínica.

Gyldenstolpe, N. (1927) Types of birds in the Royal Natural History Museum in Stockholm. *Ark. Zool.* 19(2).

Gyldenstolpe, N. (1930) On a new spine-tail from east Ecuador together with some notes on the forms of the *Synallaxis rutilans* group. *Ark. Zool.* 21A(25): 1-20.

Gyldenstolpe, N. (1941) On some new or rare birds chiefly from south-western Colombia. *Ark. Zool.* 33A(6): 1-17.

Gyldenstolpe, N. (1945) A contribution to the ornithology of northern Bolivia. *Kungl. Svenska Vetenskapakad. Handl.* (3)23(1).

Gyldenstolpe, N. (1951) The ornithology of the Rio Purus region in western Brazil. *Ark. Zool.* (2)2: 1-320.

Haene, E. (1987) Nuevos registros para la avifauna sanjuanina. *Nuestras Aves* 12: 18-19.

Haene, E. and Gil, G. (undated) El proyectado Parque Nacional Sierra de las Quijadas (Provincia de San Luis, República Argentina). Buenos Aires: A.P.N. (unpublished).

Haffer, J. (1967) Some allopatric species pairs of birds in north-west Colombia. *Auk* 84: 343-365.

Haffer, J. (1970) Art-Entstehung bei einigen Waldvögeln Amazoniens. *J. Orn.* 111: 285-331.

Haffer, J. (1975) *Avifauna of north-western Colombia, South America.* Bonn: Zoologisches Forschunginstitut und Museum Alexander Koenig (Bonner Zool. Monogr. 7).

Haig, S. M. (1992) Piping Plover. In A. Poole, P. Stettenheim and F. Gill, eds. *The birds of North America*, no.2. Philadelphia: Academy of Natural Sciences of Philadephia, and Washington, D.C.: American Ornithologists' Union.
Haig, S. M. and Plissner, J. H. (in press) Distribution and abundance of Piping Plovers in 1991. [*Condor.*]
van Halewyn, R. and Norton, R. L. (1984) The status and conservation of seabirds in the Caribbean. Pp.169-222 in J. P. Croxall, P. G. H. Evans and R. W. Schreiber, eds. *Status and conservation of the world's seabirds.* Cambridge, U.K.: International Council for Bird Preservation (Techn. Publ. 2).
Hamel, P. (1986) *Bachman's Warbler: a species in peril.* Washington, D.C.: Smithsonian Institution Press.
Hamel, P. (1988a) Bachman's Warbler. Pp.625-635 in W. J. Chandler, ed. *Audubon Wildlife Report 1988/1989.* San Diego: Academic Press, Inc.
Hamel, P. (1988b) Bachman's Warbler still a mystery. *World Birdwatch* 10(3-4): 9.
Hämmerli, J. (1991) Haltung und Zucht des Spix-Aras (*Cyanopsitta spixii*). *Gefied. Freund* 38: 130-145.
Haney, J. C. (1983) Previously unrecorded and hypothetical species of seabirds on the continental shelf of Georgia. *Oriole* 48: 21-32.
Haney, J. C. (1986) Records of seabirds from South Carolina offshore waters. *Chat* 50: 44-46.
Haney, J. C. (1987) Aspects of the pelagic ecology and behaviour of the Black-capped Petrel *Pterodroma hasitata. Wilson Bull.* 99: 153-168.
Hansen, W. (1984) In search of the Tres Marías Double Yellow-headed Parrot. *AFA Watchbird* 11(1): 17-23.
Hardie, L. C. (1987) Brazilian macaws get second chance. *TRAFFIC (U.S.A.)* 7(4): 7.
Hardy, J. W. (1964) Behavior, habitat, and relationships of jays of the genus *Cyanolyca. Occas. Pap. C. C. Adams Center Ecol. Stud.* 11: 1-14.
Hardy, J. W. (1967) *Rhynchopsitta terrisi* is probably a valid species: a reassessment. *Condor* 69: 527-528.
Hardy, J. W. (1971) Habitat and habits of the Dwarf Jay *Aphelocoma nana. Wilson Bull.* 83: 5-30.
Hardy, J. W. and Delaney, D. J. (1987) The vocalizations of the Slender-billed Wren (*Hylorchilus sumichrasti*): who are its close relatives? *Auk* 104: 528-530.
Hardy, J. W. and Dickerman, R. W. (1955) The taxonomic status of the Maroon-fronted Parrot. *Condor* 57: 305-306.
Hardy, R. (1984) Comunicaciones de la Prodena, no.6, 23 October. Unpublished newsletter.
Hargitt, E. (1890) *Catalogue of birds in the British Museum*, 18. London: Taylor and Francis (printed by order of the Trustees).
Hargrave, L. L. (1939) Bird bones from abandoned Indian villages in Arizona and Utah. *Condor* 41: 206-210.
Harris, G. and Yorio, P. (in press) Actualización de la distribución reproductiva, estado poblacional y de conservación de la Gaviota de Olrog (*Larus atlanticus*). [*Hornero.*]
Harris, M. P. (1970) The biology of an endangered species, the Dark-rumped Petrel (*Pterodroma phaeopygia*) in the Galápagos Islands. *Condor* 72: 76-84.
Harris, M. P. (1973) The Galápagos avifauna. *Condor* 75: 265-278.
Harris, M. P. (1974) A complete census of the Flightless Cormorant (*Nannopterum harrisi*). *Biol. Conserv.* 6: 188-191.
Harris, M. P. (1981) The waterbirds of Lake Junín, Central Peru. *Wildfowl* 32: 137-145.
Harris, M. P. (1982) *A field guide to the birds of Galápagos.* London, U.K.: Collins.
Harrison, P. (1983) *Seabirds: an identification guide.* Beckenham, Kent: Croom Helm.
Harrison, P. (1987) *Seabirds of the world: a photographic guide.* London: Christopher Helm.
Hart, J. K. (1991) Conservation of the Lear's Macaw: management of an endangered species. Pp.48-51 in J. Clinton-Eitniear, ed. *Proceedings of the First Mesoamerican Workshop on the Conservation and Management of Macaws.* San Antonio, Texas: Center for the Study of Tropical Birds, Inc. (Misc. Publ. 1).
Hartert, E. (1893) On the birds of the islands of Aruba, Curaçao, and Bonaire. *Ibis* (6)5: 289-338.

Hartert, E. (1898a) On a collection of birds from northwestern Ecuador, collected by W. F. H. Rosenberg. *Novit. Zool.* 5: 477-505.

Hartert, E. (1898b) Further notes on humming-birds. *Novit. Zool.* 5: 514-520.

Hartert, E. (1900) [Some new South American birds.] *Bull. Brit. Orn. Club* 11: 37-40.

Hartert, E. (1902) Some further notes on the birds of northwest Ecuador. *Novit. Zool.* 9: 599-617.

Hartert, E. and Hartert, C. (1894) On a collection of humming-birds from Ecuador and Mexico. *Novit. Zool.* 1: 43-64.

Hartert, E. and Venturi, S. (1909) Notes sur les oiseaux de la République Argentine. *Novit. Zool.* 16: 159-267.

Hartshorn, G., Antonini, G., Dubois, R., Harcharik, D., Heckadon, S., Newton, H., Quesada, C., Shores, J. and Staples, G. (1981) *The Dominican Republic country environmental profile: a field study.* Virginia: JRB Associates.

Hayes, F. E., Goodman, S. M. and López, N. E. (1990) New or noteworthy bird records from the Matogrosense region of Paraguay. *Bull. Brit. Orn. Club* 110: 94-103.

Hayes, F. E. and Granizo Tamayo, T. (in press) Bird densities along three tributaries of the Paraná river in eastern Paraguay. *Hornero.*

Hayes, F. E., Scharf, P. A. and Loftin, H. (1991) *A birder's field checklist of the birds of Paraguay.* Lake Helen, Florida: Russ's Natural History Books.

Hayes, W. (1794) *Portraits of rare and curious birds with their descriptions.* London: W. Bulmer and Co.

Haynes, A. M. (1987) Human exploitation of seabirds in Jamaica. *Biol. Conserv.* 41: 99-124.

Haynes, A. M., Sutton, R. L. and Harvey, K. D. (1989) Conservation trends, and the threats to endemic birds in Jamaica. Pp.827-838 in C. A. Woods, ed. *Biogeography of the West Indies: past, present, and future.* Gainesville, Florida: Sandhill Crane Press.

Hays, C. (1984) Effects of the 1982-1983 El Niño on Humboldt Penguin colonies in Peru. *Biol. Conserv.* 36: 169-180.

Hays, C. (1989) The Peruvian diving petrel in Peru. *Oryx* 23: 102-105.

Hayward, J. (1983) Caninde Macaw – bred in South Africa. *Cage and Aviary Birds* 9 April: 6.

Hayward, K. J. (1967) Fauna del noroeste argentino, 1. Las aves de Guayapa (La Rioja). *Acta Zool. Lilloana* 22: 211-220.

Heath, M. and Long, A. (1991) Habitat, distribution and status of the Azure-rumped Tanager *Tangara cabanisi* in Mexico. *Bird Conserv. Internatn.* 1: 223-254.

Heisterberg, J. F. and Núñez-García, F. (1988) Controlling Shiny Cowbirds in Puerto Rico. Pp.295-300 in A. C. Crabb and R. E. Marsh, eds. *Proc. Vertebrate Pest Conf.* 13. Davis, California: University of California.

Hellmayr, K.[= C.] E. (1904) Über neue und wenig bekannte Fringilliden Brasiliens. *Verhandl. zool.-bot. Ges. Wien* 54: 516-537.

Hellmayr, C. E. (1905) Description of two new birds discovered by Mr O. T. Baron in northern Peru. *Novit. Zool.* 12: 503-504.

Hellmayr, C. E. (1906a) On the birds of the island of Trinidad. *Novit. Zool.* 13: 1-60.

Hellmayr, C. E. (1906b) Critical notes on the types of little-known species of Neotropical birds, 1. *Novit. Zool.* 13: 305-352.

Hellmayr, C. E. (1906c) Revision der Spix'schen Typen brasilianischer Vögel. *Abhandl. Königl. Bayer. Akad. Wissensch., II Kl.* 22(3): 561-726.

Hellmayr, C. E. (1908) An account of the birds collected by Mons. G. A. Baer in the state of Goyaz, Brazil. *Novit. Zool.* 15: 13-102.

Hellmayr, C. E. (1910a) [Descriptions of two new species of tanagers from western Colombia.] *Bull. Brit. Orn. Club* 25: 111-112.

Hellmayr, C. E. (1910b) The birds of the Rio Madeira. *Novit. Zool.* 17: 257-428.

Hellmayr, C. E. (1911) A contribution to the ornithology of western Colombia. *Proc. Zool. Soc. London*: 1084-1213.

Hellmayr, C. E. (1912) Zoologische Ergebnisse einer Reise in das Mundungsgebiet des Amazonas, II. Vögel. *Abhandl. Königl. Bayer. Akad. Wissensch., Math.-Phys. Kl.* 26(2).

Hellmayr, C. E. (1915) Ein kleiner Beitrag zur Ornithologie des Staates Espirito Santo, Sudöstbrasilien. *Verh. orn. Ges. Bayern* 12: 126-159.
Hellmayr, C. E. (1925) Review of the birds collected by Alcide d'Orbigny in South America (continuation). *Novit. Zool.* 32: 1-30.
Hellmayr, C. E. (1929a) A contribution to the ornithology of northeastern Brazil. *Field Mus. Nat. Hist. Publ. Zool. Ser.* 12, no.18 (Publ. 255).
Hellmayr, C. E. (1929b) Catalogue of birds of the Americas, Part VII. *Field Mus. Nat. Hist. Zool. Ser.* 13 (Publ. 266).
Hellmayr, C. E. (1932) The birds of Chile. *Field Mus. Nat. Hist. Publ. Zool. Ser.* 19 (Publ. 308).
Hellmayr, C. E. (1934) Catalogue of birds of the Americas, Part VII. *Field Mus. Nat. Hist. Zool. Ser.* 13 (Publ. 330).
Hellmayr, C. E. (1935) Catalogue of birds of the Americas. Part VIII. *Field Mus. Nat. Hist. Zool. Ser.* 13 (Publ. 347).
Hellmayr, C. E. (1936) Catalogue of birds of the Americas, Part IX. *Field Mus. Nat. Hist. Zool. Ser.* 13 (Publ. 365).
Hellmayr, C. E. (1937) Catalogue of birds of the Americas, Part X. *Field Mus. Nat. Hist. Zool. Ser.* 13 (Publ. 381).
Hellmayr, C. E. (1938) Catalogue of birds of the Americas, Part XI. *Field Mus. Nat. Hist. Zool. Ser.* 13 (Publ. 430).
Hellmayr, C. E. and Conover, H. B. (1932) Notes on some neotropical game-birds. *Auk* 49: 324-336.
Hellmayr, C. E. and Conover, B. (1942) Catalogue of birds of the Americas, Part I, number 1. *Field Mus. Nat. Hist. Zool. Ser.* 13 (Publ. 514).
Hellmayr, C. E. and Conover, B. (1948) Catalogue of birds of the Americas, Part I, number 2. *Field Mus. Nat. Hist. Zool. Ser.* 13 (Publ. 615).
Hellmayr, C. E. and Conover, B. (1949) Catalogue of birds of the Americas, Part I, number 4. *Field Mus. Nat. Hist. Zool. Ser.* 13 (Publ. 634).
van Helmond, C. A. M. and Wijsman, J. (1988) Populatiedichtheid van *Amazona barbadensis rothschildi* in 1987. CARMABI report, unpublished.
Helwig, V. (1987) *Remembering the tody: a lifetime of bird-watching in Jamaica.* Wakefield, Quebec: Castenchel.
Hernández Camacho, J. I. and Rodríguez-M., J. V. (1979) Dos nuevos taxa del género *Grallaria* (Aves: Formicariidae) del alto valle del Magdalena (Colombia). *Caldasia* 12: 573-580.
Hernández Camacho, J. I. and Rodríguez-Mahecha, J. V. (1986) Status geográfico y taxonómico de *Molothrus armenti* Cabanis 1851 (Aves: Icteridae). *Caldasia* 15: 655-664.
Hernández Camacho, J. I., Sánchez, H., Pardo, J. L. and Castaño Uribe, C., eds. (undated [c.1990]) *Guia del sistema de parques nacionales de Colombia.* Bogotá: INDERENA.
Hernández-Prieto, E. and Cruz, A. (1987) The Yellow-shouldered Blackbird on Mona Island – summer of 1986 field season. Report submitted to the U.S. Fish and Wildlife Service and the Department of Natural Resources, Puerto Rico.
Hernández-Prieto, E. and Cruz, A. (1989) The Yellow-shouldered Blackbird on Mona Island – summer of 1987-1988 season report. Report submitted to the U.S. Fish and Wildlife Service and the Department of Natural Resources, Puerto Rico.
Hernández-Prieto, E., Cruz, A., Pérez-Rivera, R. A. and González Román, M. (in prep.) The Shiny Cowbird (*Molothrus bonariensis*) in Mona Island, Puerto Rico.
Herrera, G. A. (1988) Primeros registros para la provincia del Chaco del picaflor vientre negro *Anthracothorax nigricollis* y de corbatita colorada *Sporophila hypochroma. Garganchillo* 3(8): 7-9.
Herrmann, A. (1989) Die Vogelbeschreibungen Georg Markgrafs in der *Historia naturalis brasiliae. Bonn. zool. Beitr.* 40: 183-196.
Hilty, S. L. (1977) *Chlorospingus flavovirens* rediscovered, with notes on other Pacific Colombian and Cauca Valley birds. *Auk* 94: 44-49.
Hilty, S. L. (1985) Distributional changes in the Colombian avifauna: a preliminary blue list. Pp.1000-1012 in P. A. Buckley, M. S. Foster, E. S. Morton, R. S. Ridgely and F. G. Buckley, eds. *Neotropical ornithology.* Washington, D.C.: American Ornithologists' Union (Orn. Monogr. 36).

Hilty, S. L. and Brown, W. L. (1986) *A guide to the birds of Colombia*. Princeton, New Jersey: Princeton University Press.
Hilty, S. L. and Silliman, J. R. (1983) Puracé National Park, Colombia. *Amer. Birds* 37: 247-256.
Hilty, S. L. and Simon, D. (1977) The Azure-rumped Tanager in Mexico with comparative remarks on the Gray-and-gold Tanager. *Auk* 94: 605-606.
Hinkelmann, C. (1987) Neu beschreibene Kolibriarten. *Trochilus* 8: 93-99.
Hobley, C. W. (1932) Dominica "Diablotin" (*Pterodroma hæsitata*). *J. Soc. Preserv. Fauna Empire*, n.s., part 17: 17-20.
Hoffman, B. (1989) Finding the Altamira Yellowthroat (*Geothlypis flavovelata*) in Nacimiento, Tamaulipas. *Aves Mexicanas* 2(1): 2.
Hohenstein, K. F. (1987) Werkzeuggebrauch bei Papageien *Anodorhynchus hyacinthinus*. *Gefied. Welt* 111: 329-330.
Holland, A. H. (1891) Further notes on the birds of the Argentine Republic. *Ibis* (6)3: 16-20.
Holland, A. H. (1892) Short notes on the birds of the Estancia Espartilla, Argentine Republic. *Ibis* (6)4: 193-214.
Holland, A. H. (1893) Field-notes on birds of Estancia Sta. Elena, Argentine Republic. *Ibis* (6)5: 483-488.
Holland, A. H. (1896) Field-notes on the birds of the Estancia Sta. Elena, Argentine Republic, 3. *Ibis* (7)2: 315-318.
Holman, J. P. (1952) West Indian Black-capped Petrel, *Pterodroma hasitata*, picked up on Fairfield Beach, Connecticut. *Auk* 69: 459-460.
Holmberg, E. L. (1939) Las aves argentinas [reprinted from 1895]. *Hornero* 7: 142-233.
Holmberg, E. L. (1883-1884) Resultados científicos especialmente zoológicos y botánicos de los tres viajes llevados a cabo por el Dr. Holmberg en 1881, 1882, 1883 a la Sierra del Tandil. Aves. *Act. Acad. Cienc. Córdoba* 5: 73-92.
Hopkinson, E. (1920) Hooded Siskin mules. *Avicult. Mag.* (3)11: 150.
Hopkinson, E. (1927) Birds at the Primley Zoo, 1927. *Avicult. Mag.* 5: 317-323.
Hopkinson, E. (1931) The birds at Paignton Zoo. *Avicult. Mag.* 9: 242-251, 307-316.
Hoppe, D. (1988) Noch einiges über den Spix-Ara. *Gefied. Welt* 112: 61-62.
Hoppe, J. (1989) *The national parks of the Dominican Republic*. Santo Domingo: Colección Barceló 1.
Hoth, J., Velázquez, A., Romero, F. J., León, L., Aranda, M. and Bell, D. J. (1987) The Volcano Rabbit – a shrinking distribution and a threatened habitat. *Oryx* 21: 85-91.
Howell, S. N. G. (1989) Hummingbird discoveries. *Point Reyes Bird Observatory Newsletter* 85: 8-9.
Howell, S. N. G. (1992) The Short-crested Coquette: Mexico's least-known endemic. *Birding* 24: 87-91.
Howell, S. N. G. and Webb, S. (1989a) Notes on the Honduran Emerald. *Wilson Bull.* 101: 642-643.
Howell, S. N. G. and Webb, S. (1989b) Additional notes from Isla Clarión, Mexico. *Condor* 91: 1001-1008.
Howell, S. N. G. and Webb, S. (1990) The seabirds of Las Islas Revillagigego, Mexico. *Wilson Bull.* 102: 140-146.
Howell, S. N. G. and Webb, S. (1992) New and noteworthy bird records from Guatemala and Honduras. *Bull. Brit. Orn. Club* 112: 42-49.
Howes, P. G. (1929) The mountains of Dominica. *Natural History* 29: 595-610.
Hoy, G. (1968) Über Brutbiologie und Eier einiger Vögel aus Nordwest-Argentina. *J. Orn.* 109: 425-453.
Hoy, G. (1969) Addendas a la avifauna salteña. *Hornero* 11: 53-56.
Hubbard, J. P. and Crossin, R. S. (1974) Notes on northern Mexican birds. *Nemouria* 14.
Huber, K. R. (1982) *The Kirtland's Warbler* (Dendroica kirtlandii)*: an annotated bibliography 1952-1980*. Ann Arbor: Museum of Zoology, University of Michigan.
Huber, O. and Alarcón, C. (1988) Mapa de vegetación de Venezuela. Caracas: Ministério del Ambiente y de los Recursos Naturales Renovables (División de Vegetación).
Huber, W. (1932) Birds collected in northeastern Nicaragua in 1922. *Proc. Acad. Nat. Sci. Philadelphia* 84: 205-249.
Hudson, W. H. (1870) Letter. *Proc. Zool. Soc. London*: 545-547.
Hudson, W. H. (1872) On the birds of the Río Negro of Patagonia. *Proc. Zool. Soc. London*: 534-550.

Hudson, W. H. (1920) *Birds of La Plata*, 1. London: J. M. Dent and Sons.
Hueck, K. (1971) Mapa de la vegetación de America del Sur. Stuttgart: Gustav Fischer Verlag.
Hueck, K. (1978) *Los bosques de Sudamérica; ecología, composición e importancia económica*. Eschborn, Germany: Sociedad Alemania [*sic*] de Cooperacion [*sic*] Técnica.
Humphrey, P. S., Bridge, D., Reynolds, P. W. and Peterson, R. T. (1970) *Birds of Isla Grande (Tierra del Fuego)*. Lawrence, Kansas: University of Kansas Museum of Natural History, for the Smithsonian Institution, Washington, D.C.
Hunter, L. A. (1988) Status of the endemic Atitlán Grebe of Guatemala: is it extinct? *Condor* 90: 906-912.
Hussey, R. F. (1916) Notes on some spring birds of La Plata. *Auk* 33: 384-399.
IBAMA (1989) *Unidades de conservação do Brasil, 1: parques nacionais e reservas biológicas*. Brasília: Instituto Brasileiro do Meio Ambiente e dos Recursos Naturais Renováveis.
IBGE (1959) *Enciclopédia dos municípios brasileiros*, 26. Rio de Janeiro: Instituto Brasileiro de Geografia e Estatística.
IBGE (undated) Aves do Parque Nacional das Emas – GO. Observações realizadas por Alvaro Negret durante o período de 2 a 17 de outubro de 1984. Unpublished report.
ICBP (1992) *Putting biodiversity on the map: priority areas for global conservation*. Cambridge, U.K.: International Council for Bird Preservation.
ICGC (1978) = Instituto Cubano de Geodesia y Cartografía (1978) *Atlas de Cuba: XX aniversario del triunfo de la revolución cubana*. La Habana: Instituto Cubano de Geodesia y Cartografía.
Idyll, C. P. (1973) The anchovy crisis. *Sci. Amer.* 228: 22-29.
IEF/FEEMA/INEPAC (1991) Tombamento da Serra do Mar/Mata Atlântica (Unidades de conservação e áreas protegidas). 1:400,000.
IFG (1984) Mapa planimétrico de imágenes de satelite 1:250,000, hoja SE 19-10 (Tacna). [Based on LANDSAT images taken on 1 December 1975 and 3 May 1981]. Neu Isenburg, West Germany: Institute for Applied Geosciences.
IGM (1957) Mapa geográfico de la República del Ecuador (1:500,000). Quito: Instituto Geográfico Militar.
IGM (1963) Carta provisional de la República Argentina, 1:500,000, no.2766 (San Miguel de Tucumán). Buenos Aires: Instituto Geográfico Militar.
IGM (1965a) Carta Nacional, Bolivia, 1:50,000, 6341-3 (Parotani). La Paz: Instituto Geográfico Militar.
IGM (1965b) Carta provisional de la República Argentina, 1:500,000, no.2966 (Catamarca). Buenos Aires: Instituto Geográfico Militar.
IGM (1966) Carta Nacional de Perú, 1:100,000, 12d (Olmos). Lima: Instituto Geográfico Militar.
IGM (1967) Carta Nacional de Perú, 1:100,000, 13e (Incahuasi). Lima: Instituto Geográfico Militar.
IGM (1969a) Carta Nacional de Perú, 1:100,000, 14g (Celendín). Lima: Instituto Geográfico Militar.
IGM (1969b) Ecuador: 1:100,000, Series J621. [Map CI-NVI-D,3783: Provincia de Loja: Saraguro, Ecuador.] Quito: Instituto Geográfico Militar.
IGM (1971) Carta Nacional de Perú, 1:100,000, 20h (Huaráz), 20i (Recuay), 21h (Huayllapampa). Lima: Instituto Geográfico Militar.
IGM (1972) Carta Nacional de Perú, 1:100,000, 18h (Corongo). Lima: Instituto Geográfico Militar.
IGM (1973) Carta Nacional de Perú, 1:100,000, 19h (Carhuaz), 20j (La Unión), 24k (Matucana), 26l (Tupe). Lima: Instituto Geográfico Militar.
IGM (1975) Carta Nacional de Perú, 1:100,000, 22j (Oyón), 23k (Ondores). Lima: Instituto Geográfico Militar.
IGM (1976) Map of Bolivia, 1:250,000, SF 20-1 (Camargo). La Paz: Instituto Geográfico Militar.
IGM (1978a) Carta Nacional de Perú, 1:100,000, 19i (Huari), 28q (Abancay [1984 reprint]). Lima: Instituto Geográfico Militar.
IGM (1978b) Mapa fisica politica, 1:1,000,000. Lima: Instituto Geográfico Militar.
IGM (1980) Mapa de la República de Bolivia, 1:500,000, hoja 1. Second edition. La Paz: Instituto Geográfico Militar.
IGM (1982) República del Ecuador. 1:1,000,000 map of Ecuador, updated to 31 March 1981. Quito: Instituto Geográfico Militar.
IGM (1984) Map of Bolivia, 1:250,000, SF 20-2 (Camiri). La Paz: Instituto Geográfico Militar.

IGM (1985) Carta Nacional de Perú, 1:100,000, 29o (Querobamba). Lima: Instituto Geográfico Militar.

IGM (1989) República del Ecuador, 1:1,000,000. Updated to 31 May 1989. Quito: Instituto Geográfico Militar.

IGU (1979) Mapa de la República Dominicana, 1:600,000. Seventh edition. Instituto Geográfico Universitario.

von Ihering, H. (1887) Ornithologische Forschung in Brasilien. *Ornis* 3: 569-581.

von Ihering, H. (1898) As aves do estado de S. Paulo. *Revta. Mus. Paulista* 3: 113-476.

von Ihering, H. (1899a) *As aves do estado do Rio Grande do Sul.* Porto Alegre: Gundlach and Krahe [reprinted from pp.113-154 of *Annuario do Estado do Rio Grande do Sul para o anno de 1900*].

von Ihering, H. (1899b) Critical notes on the zoo-geographical relations of the avifauna of Rio Grande do Sul. *Ibis* (7)5: 432-436.

von Ihering, H. (1900a) Aves observadas em Cantagallo e Nova Friburgo. *Revta. Mus. Paulista* 4: 149-164.

von Ihering, H. (1900b) Catálogo crítico-comparativo dos ninhos e ovos das aves do Brasil. *Revta. Mus. Paulista* 4: 191-300.

von Ihering, H. (1902) Contribuções para o conhecimento da ornithologia de São Paulo. *Revta. Mus. Paulista* 5: 261-329.

von Ihering, H. (1905a) As aves do Paraguay em comparação com as de São Paulo. *Revta. Mus. Paulista* 6: 310-384.

von Ihering, H. (1905b) O Rio Juruá. *Revta. Mus. Paulista* 6: 385-460.

von Ihering, H. and von Ihering, R. (1907) *As aves do Brazil.* São Paulo: Typographia do Diario Official (Catálogos da fauna brazileira, 1).

Ijsselstein, C. (1992) Report on the censusing of the St Lucia White-breasted Thrasher, *Ramphocinclus brachyurus sanctaeluciae.* 6 August 1992. Unpublished.

Imber, M. J. (1991) The Jamaican Petrel – dead or alive? *Gosse Bird Club Broadsheet* no.57: 4-9.

Imber, M. J., Cruz, J. B., Grove, J. S., Lavenberg, R. J., Swift, C. C. and Cruz, E. (1992) Feeding ecology of the Dark-rumped Petrel in the Galápagos Islands. *Condor* 94: 437-447.

Ingels, J. (1988) A review of the Neotropical *Caprimulgus* species *maculosus*, *nigrescens* and *whitelyi.* Unpublished.

Ingels, J. and Ribot, J.-H. (1983) The Blackish Nightjar *Caprimulgus nigrescens* in Surinam. *Gerfaut* 73: 127-146.

Ingels, J., Parkes, K. C. and Farrand, J. (1981) The status of the macaw generally but incorrectly called *Ara caninde* (Wagler). *Gerfaut* 71: 283-294.

Inskipp, T. (1987) Hummingbird trade and protection. *TRAFFIC Bull.* 9: 12-28.

Inskipp, T., Broad, S. and Luxmoore, R. (1988) *Significant trade in wildlife: a review of selected species in CITES Appendix II, 3: Birds.* Cambridge, U.K.: International Union for Conservation of Nature and Natural Resources, and Secretariat of the Convention on International Trade in Endangered Species of Wild Fauna and Flora.

Isler, M. L. and Isler, P. R. (1987) *The tanagers: natural history, distribution, and identification.* Washington, D.C.: Smithsonian Institution Press.

Isler, M. L. and Isler, P. R. (1987) *The tanagers.* Washington, D.C.: Smithsonian Institution Press.

IUCN TFP (1988a) = IUCN Tropical Forest Programme (1988) Colombian Chocó – conservation of biological diversity and forest ecosystems. Cambridge, U.K.: World Conservation Monitoring Centre (unpublished).

IUCN TFP (1988b) = IUCN Tropical Forest Programme (1988) Ecuador – conservation of biological diversity and forest ecosystems. Cambridge, U.K.: World Conservation Monitoring Centre (unpublished).

IUCN (1992) *Protected areas of the world: a review of national systems, 4: Nearctic and Neotropical.* Gland, Switzerland and Cambridge, U.K.: International Union for Conservation of Nature and Natural Resources (draft).

Jackson, J. A. (1986) Biopolitics, management of federal lands and the conservation of the Red-cockaded Woodpecker. *Amer. Birds* 40: 1162-1168.

Jackson, J. A. (1988) The south-eastern pine forest ecosystem and its birds: past, present and future. *Bird Conserv.* 3: 119-158.

Jackson, J. A. (1991) Will-o'-the-Wisp. *Living Bird Q.* 10: 29-32.

Jahncke Aparicio, J. and Riveros-Salcedo, J.C. (1991) Hábitos de anidación del Potoyunco Peruano *Pelecanoides garnotii*. Resúmenes del IV Congreso de Ornitología Neotropical, 3-9 de Noviembre 1991, Quito, Ecuador (resumen 20).

Jahncke, J. and Riveros, J. C. (1989) Biología reproductiva del Potoyunco Peruano (*Pelecanoides garnotii*) en las islas San Gallán. Libro de Resúmenes, I Symposium sobre Ecología y Conservación en el Perú. Lima, 25-29 Julio 1989. Unpublished.

Jahrsdoerfer, S. (1990) Endangered and threatened wildlife and plants; final rule to list the Golden-cheeked Warbler as endangered. *Federal Register* 55 (no.249, December 27): 53153-53160.

James, C. and Hislop, G. (1988) Status and conservation of two cracid species, the Pawi or Trinidad Piping Guan (*Pipile pipile*) and the Cocrico (*Ortalis ruficauda*) in Trinidad and Tobago. Unpublished paper presented at the II International Cracid Symposium, Caracas, Venezuela, February/March 1988.

Jaramillo, A. (1992) Eskimo Curlew: a glimmer of hope. *Birders J.* 1: 202.

JCEP (1987) = *Jamaica Country Environmental Profile*. Kingston, Jamaica: Government of Jamaica, Ministry of Agriculture, Natural Resources Conservation Division.

Jeffrey-Smith, M. (1956) *Bird-watching in Jamaica*. Kingston, Jamaica: Pioneer Press.

Jeggo, D. (1976a) A report on the field study of the St Lucia Parrot *Amazona versicolor* during 1975. *Jersey Wildl. Preserv. Trust 12th Ann. Rep. 1975*: 34-41.

Jeggo, D. (1976b) The Lesser Antillean Parrot Programme at the Jersey Zoological Park. *Avicult. Mag.* 82: 101-105.

Jeggo, D. (1977) Lesser Antillean Parrot Programme, a progress report. *Jersey Wildl. Preserv. Trust 13th Ann. Rep. 1976*: 21-26.

Jeggo, D. (1984) St Vincent Parrots. *On the Edge* 47.

Jeggo, D. F. (1981) The captive breeding programme for Caribbean amazons at the Jersey Wildlife Preservation Trust. Pp.181-196 in R. F. Pasquier, ed. *Conservation of New World parrots*. Washington, D.C.: Smithsonian Institution Press for the International Council for Bird Preservation (Techn. Publ. 1).

Jeggo, D. F. (1983) Captive breeding programme for the St Lucia Parrot *Amazona versicolor*, at Jersey Wildlife Preservation Trust – a report on the first breeding. *Dodo* 19 [1982]: 69-77.

Jeggo, D. F. (1987) The St Lucia Parrot *Amazona versicolor* 1975-1986: turning the tide for a vanishing species. *Dodo* 23 [1986]: 59-68.

Jeggo, D. F. (1990) Preliminary international studbook: St Vincent Parrot *Amazona guildingii*. Unpublished.

Jeggo, D. F. (1991) Captive breeding and the conservation of the St Lucia Parrot *Amazona versicolor* and St Vincent Parrot *A. guildingii*. Pp.18-28 in R. Colley, ed. *Parrots in captivity*. Bristol: Association of British Wild Animal Keepers.

Jeggo, D. F. and Anthony, D. (1991) A report on the 1990 field survey of the St Lucia Parrot *Amazona versicolor*. *Dodo* 27: 102-107.

Jeggo, D. F. and Taynton, K. M. (1981) The effects of Hurricane Allen on the status of the St Lucia Parrot *Amazona versicolor*. *Dodo* 17 [1980]: 11-18.

Jeggo, D. F., Taynton, K. M. and Bobb, M. (1983) A survey of the St Lucia Parrot *Amazona versicolor* in 1982. *Dodo* 19 [1982]: 33-37.

Jeggo, D. F., Anthony, D. and John, L. (1989) A report on the 1988 survey of the St Lucia Parrot *Amazona versicolor*. *Dodo* 25 [1988]: 24-30.

Jeggo, D. (1975) The Thick-billed Parrot *Rhynchopsitta pachyrhyncha* (Swainson) breeding programme at Jersey Zoological Park. *Jersey Wildl. Preserv. Trust 11th Ann. Rep. 1974*: 63-69.

Jehl, J. R. (1972) On the cold trail of an extinct petrel. *Pacific Discovery* 25(6): 24-29.

Jehl, J. R. (1973) The distribution of marine birds in Chilean waters in winter. *Auk* 90: 114-135.

Jehl, J. R. (1982) The biology and taxonomy of Townsend's Shearwater. *Gerfaut* 72: 121-135.

Jehl, J. R. and Everett, W. T. (1985) History and status of the avifauna of Isla Guadalupe, Mexico. *Trans. San Diego Soc. Nat. Hist.* 20: 313-336.

Jehl, J. R. and Parkes, K. C. (1982) The status of the avifauna of the Revillagigedo Islands, Mexico. *Wilson Bull.* 94: 1-19.

Jehl, J. R. and Parkes, K. C. (1983) "Replacements" of landbird species on Socorro Island, Mexico. *Auk* 100: 551-559.

Jehl, J. R. and Rumboll, M. A. E. (1976) Notes on the avifauna of Isla Grande and Patagonia, Argentina. *Trans. San Diego Soc. Nat. Hist.* 18: 145-154.

Jobling, J. A. (1991) *A dictionary of scientific bird names.* Oxford: Oxford University Press.

Johns, A. D. (1986) Effects of habitat disturbance on rainforest wildlife in Brazilian Amazonia. World Wildlife Fund U.S. Project US-302, Final Report.

Johnsgard, P. A. (1973) *Grouse and quails of North America.* Lincoln, Nebraska: University of Nebraska Press.

Johnsgard, P. A. (1988) *The quails, partridges, and francolins of the world.* Oxford: Oxford University Press.

Johnson, A. and Chebez, J. C. (1985) Sobre la situación de *Mergus octosetaceus* (Anseriformes: Anatidae) en la Argentina. *Historia Natural* 1: 1-16.

Johnson, A. W. (1965) *The birds of Chile and adjacent regions of Argentina, Bolivia and Peru,* 1. Buenos Aires: Platt Establecimientos Gráficos.

Johnson, A. W. (1967) *The birds of Chile and adjacent regions of Argentina, Bolivia and Peru,* 2. Buenos Aires: Platt Establicimientos Gráficos.

Johnson, A. W. (1970) Aves observadas en Mamiña (Tarapacá) desde el 15 al 30 de Agosto de 1968 y 1969. *Bol. Orn.* 2(1):1-2.

Johnson, A. W. (1972) *Supplement to the birds of Chile and adjacent regions of Argentina, Bolivia and Peru.* Buenos Aires: Platt Establicimientos Gráficos.

Johnson, A. W. and Millie, W. R. (1972) A new species of conebill (*Conirostrum*) from northern Chile. Pp.3-8 in A. W. Johnson, *Supplement to the birds of Chile and adjacent regions of Argentina, Bolivia, and Peru.* Buenos Aires: Platt Establecimientos Gráficos.

Johnson, T. B. and Snyder, N. F. (1987) A return to the Thick-billed Parrot. *Wildlife Views,* December: 9-10.

Johnson, T. B., Snyder, N. F. R. and Snyder, H. A. (1989) The return of Thick-billed Parrots to Arizona. *Endang. Species Techn. Bull.* 14(4): 1, 4-5.

Johnson, T. B., Snyder, N. F. R. and Franks, M. A. (1991) Thick-billed Parrot Reintroduction Project Progress Report of December 23, 1991. Arizona Game and Fish Department. Unpublished.

Johnson, T. H. (1988) *Biodiversity and conservation in the Caribbean: profiles of selected islands.* Cambridge, U.K.: International Council for Bird Preservation (Monogr.1).

Johnston, D. W., Blake, C. H. and Buden, D. W. (1971) Avifauna of the Cayman Islands. *Q. J. Florida Acad. Sci.* 34: 141-156.

Joordens, J. (1985) Lora-telling 1985: een schatting van het aantal *Amazona barbadensis rothschildi* op Bonaire in de regentijd 1985. Unpublished.

Jordan, E. (1983) Die Verbreitung von *Polylepis*-Beständen in der Westkordillera Boliviens. *Tuexenia* 3: 101-112.

Jovicich, S. A. (1976) *Amazona versicolor,* a study of the St Lucian Parrot. WWF Project 1269 Report, unpublished.

Junge, G. C. A. and Mees, G. F. (1958) *The avifauna of Trinidad and Tobago.* Leiden: E. J. Brill (*Zool. Verhand.* 37).

Juniper, A. T. and Yamashita, C. (1991) The habitat and status of Spix's Macaw *Cyanopsitta spixii. Bird Conserv. Internatn.* 1: 1-9.

Juniper, T. (1991) Last of a kind. *Birds Internatn.* 3: 10-16.

Juniper, T. and Yamashita, C. (1990) The conservation of Spix's Macaw. *Oryx* 24: 224-228.

Juniper, T. (1990) A very singular bird. *BBC Wildlife* 8: 674-675.

Junqueira, C. (1938) Observações práticas sobre a criação de algumas aves indígenas em captiveiro. *Revta. Indust. Animal* 1(1): 95-102.

Jurek, R. M. (1990) An historical review of California Condor recovery programmes. *Vulture News* 23: 3-7.

Kaempfer, E. (1924) Ueber das Vogelleben in Santo Domingo. *J. Orn.* 72: 178-184.

Kear, J. (1979) Wildfowl at risk, 1979. *Wildfowl* 30: 159-161.

Kear, J. and Williams, G. (1978) Waterfowl at risk. *Wildfowl* 29: 5-21.

Keller, C. (1987) Up-to-date information on the Spix Macaw (*Cyanopsitta spixii* [Wagler]) and the environmental situation in Brazil. Unpublished.

Keller, C. (1992) Em busca da ararinha de Spix. *Atualidades Ornitológicas* 45: 5.

Kepler, C. B. and Kepler, A. K. (1973) The distribution and ecology of the Puerto Rican Whip-poor-will, an endangered species. *Living Bird* 11: 207-239.

Kerr, J. G. (1892) On the avifauna of the lower Pilcomayo. *Ibis* (6)4: 120-152.

Kerr, J. G. (1901) On the birds observed during a second zoological expedition to the Gran Chaco. *Ibis* (8)1: 215-236.

Keve, A. and Kovács, A. (1973) Einige Daten sur Ornis von Missiones (Nordöst-Argentinien), II. *Opusc. Zool. Budapest* 11(1-2): 75-77.

Kiessling, W. (1985) Blue-throated Macaws. *AFA Watchbird* 12(1): 13.

Kiessling, W. and Low, R. (1987) Spix-Ara-Kongreß auf Teneriffa. *Gefied. Welt* 111: 330-331.

Kiff, L. (1990) To the brink and back: the battle to save the California Condor. *Terra* 28(4): 6-18.

Kincaid, E. B. (1976) Mesa de las Tablas, Coahuila, Mexico: Christmas bird count. *Amer. Birds* 30: 623.

King, J. (1988) Birds. In Río Mazan project report, 1987. Oxford: Department of Plant Sciences, University of Oxford, unpublished.

King, J. R. (1989) Notes on the birds of the Rio Mazan Valley, Azuay Province, Ecuador, with special reference to *Leptosittaca branickii*, *Hapalopsittaca amazonina pyrrhops* and *Metallura baroni*. *Bull. Brit. Orn. Club* 109: 140-147.

King, W. B. (1978-1979) *Red data book, 2. Aves.* Second edition. Morges, Switzerland: International Union for Conservation of Nature and Natural Resources.

King, W. B. (1981) *Endangered birds of the world: the ICBP bird red data book.* Washington, D.C.: Smithsonian Institution Press and International Council for Bird Preservation [bound reissue of King 1978-1979].

Klimaitis, J. and Moschione, F. (1987) *Aves de la Reserva Integral de Selva Marginal de Punta Lara y sus alrededores.* Buenos Aires: Ministerio de Economía de la Provincia de Buenos Aires.

Klimaitis, J. F. (1984) Hallazgo del Tordo de Cabeza Amarilla en la provincia de Entre Ríos. *Nuestras Aves* 4: 7-8.

Klimaitis, J. F. (1986) Observaciones sobre el Varillero Amarillo *Xanthopsar flavus* en la provincia de Entre Ríos, Argentina. *Garganchillo* 1: 1-4.

Knaggs, L. (1980) My experience with siskins. *AFA Watchbird* 7(2): 8-9.

Knobel, E. M. (1926) Amazon parrots. *Avicult. Mag.* (4)4: 203-213, 229-234.

Koepcke, H.-W. and Koepcke, M. (1963) *Las aves silvestres de importancia económica del Perú.* Lima: Ministerio de Agricultura.

Koepcke, M. (1954) *Zaratornis stresemanni* nov. gen. nov. spec., un cotingido nuevo del Peru. *Publ. Mus. Hist. Nat. "Javier Prado"*, Ser. A. (Zool.) 16.

Koepcke, M. (1957) Una nueva especie de *Synallaxis* (Furnariidae, Aves) de las vertientes occidentales andinas del Perú central. *Publ. Mus. Hist. Nat. "Javier Prado"*, Ser. A (Zool.) 18.

Koepcke, M. (1958) Die Vögel des Waldes von Zárate (Westhang der Anden in Mittelperu). *Bonn. zool. Beitr.* 9: 130-193.

Koepcke, M. (1961) Birds of the western slope of the Andes of Peru. *Amer. Mus. Novit.* 2028.

Koepcke, M. (1970) *The birds of the department of Lima, Peru.* Wynnewood, Penn.: Livingston Publishing Company.

Koford, C. B. (1953) *The California Condor.* New York: Dover Publications.

Konrad, P. M. (1984) Birds of the Tres Marías Islands. Unpublished.

Konrad, P. M. (1986) Birds of the Tres Marías Islands, Mexico. Unpublished.

Koschmann, J. R. and Price, P. L. (1987) The Thick-billed Parrot. *AFA Watchbird* 14(1): 48-53.

Kothe, K. (1912) Trennung der Gattungen *Harpyhaliaetus* und *Urubitornis*. *Orn. Monatsber.* 20(1): 1-5.

Krabbe, N. (1991) Avifauna of the temperate zone of the Ecuadorean Andes. Copenhagen: Zoological Museum University of Copenhagen (techn. report).

Krabbe, N. (in prep.) Avifaunal notes from Cordillera del Condor, south-eastern Ecuador.

Krabbe, N. (undated) A collection of birds from south-eastern Brazil 1825-1855. Unpublished.

Krapovickas, S. (1990) Encuentro Argentino-Paraguayo de ornitología. *Nuestras Aves* 22: 24.

Kühn, G. (1987) Steckbrief: Kapuzenzeisig (*Spinus cucullatus*). *Gefied. Welt* 111: 8-10.

Kuns, M. L., Griffin, T. P., Brenner, T. and Pippin, W. E. (1965) Ecological and epidemiological studies of Mona Island, Puerto Rico. U.S. Air Force, Air Proving Ground Command, Eglin Air Force Base, Florida.

Kurlasky, M. (1988) Haiti's environment teeters on the edge. *Internatn. Wildl.* 18(2): 35-38.

LaBastille, A. (1973) Establishment of a Quetzal cloud-forest reserve in Guatemala. *Biol. Conserv.* 5: 60-62.

LaBastille, A. (1990) And now they are gone. *Internatn. Wildlife* 20(4): 18-23.

Lack, D. (1976) *Island biology.* Oxford: Blackwell.

Lack, D., Lack, E., Lack, P. and Lack, A. (1973) Birds on St Vincent. *Ibis* 115: 46-52.

Lacy, R. C., Flesness, N. R. and Seal, U. S. (1989) *Puerto Rican Parrot* Amazona vittata *population viability analysis and recommendations.* Apple Valley, Minnesota: Captive Breeding Specialist Group.

de Lafresnaye, M. F. (1844) Description de quelques oiseaux de la Guadeloupe. *Revue Zool.* 7: 167-169.

Laidler, E. (1977) The St Vincent Parrot, its status and prospects. *Avicult. Mag.* 83: 34-42.

Laidler, K. and Laidler, E. (1977) Report of the 1975 and 1976 Durham University Expeditions to St Vincent (West Indies). Unpublished.

Lamb, G. R. (1957) *The Ivory-billed Woodpecker in Cuba.* New York: Pan-American Section, International Committee for Bird Preservation (Research Report 1).

Lamb, G. R. (1958) Excerpts from a report on the Ivory-billed Woodpecker (*Campephilus principalis bairdii*) in Cuba. *VII Bull. Internatn. Coun. Bird Preserv.*: 139-144.

Lambert, F. (1983) *Survey of the status of the St Vincent Parrot* Amazona guildingii *in 1982.* Cambridge, U.K.: International Council for Bird Preservation (Study Report 3).

Lambert, F. (1984) The St Vincent Parrot, an endangered Caribbean bird. *Oryx* 19: 34-37.

Lamm, D. W. (1948) Notes on the birds of the states of Pernambuco and Paraíba, Brazil. *Auk* 65: 261-283.

Land, H. C. (1970) *Birds of Guatemala.* Wynnewood, Penn.: Livingston Publishing Company, for the International Committee for Bird Preservation Pan-American Section.

Landbeck, L. (1877) Bemerkungen über die Singvögel Chiles. *Zool. Garten* 18: 233-261.

LANDSAT (1986) 1:1,000,000 satellite photograph of Ecuador, 2 November 1986. Bin 614H, frame 53. Sioux Falls, South Dakota: Earth Observation Satellite Company, c/o Eros Data Center.

LANDSAT (1987) 1:1,000,000 satellite photograph of Ecuador, 26 March 1987. Bin 614H, frame 24. Sioux Falls, South Dakota: Earth Observation Satellite Company, c/o Eros Data Center.

Lanning, D. V. (1978) Letter of 26 February to L. L. Short reporting a study of "Winter habits and range of the Maroon-fronted Parrot, *Rhynchopsitta terrisi*, in northeastern Mexico", as supported by the International Council for Bird Preservation Pan American Section. Unpublished.

Lanning, D. V. (1982) Survey of the Red-fronted Macaw (*Ara rubrogenys*) and Caninde Macaw (*Ara caninde*) in Bolivia, December 1981–March 1982. Unpublished report to the International Council for Bird Preservation and New York Zoological Society.

Lanning, D. V. (1991) Distribution and breeding biology of the Red-fronted Macaw. *Wilson Bull.* 103: 357-365.

Lanning, D. V. and Lawson, P. W. (1977) Observations of the Maroon-fronted Parrot, *Rhynchopsitta terrisi*, in north-eastern Mexico: 1976-1977. Chihuahuan Desert Research Institute preliminary report.

Lanning, D. V. and Shiflett, J. T. (1981) Status and nesting ecology of the Thick-billed Parrot (*Rhynchopsitta pachyrhyncha*). Pp.393-401 in R. F. Pasquier, ed. *Conservation of New World parrots.* Washington, D.C.: Smithsonian Institution Press for the International Council of Bird Preservation (Techn. Publ. 1).

Lanning, D. V. and Shiflett, J. T. (1983) Nesting ecology of Thick-billed Parrots. *Condor* 85: 66-73.

Lantermann, W. and Schuster, A. (1990) *Papageien vom Aussterben bedroht.* Hamburg: Rasch und Röhring.

Lantz, D. E. (1900) A list of birds collected by Col. N. S. Goss in Mexico and Central America. *Trans. Kansas Acad. Sci.* 16: 218-224.

Lanyon, W. E. and Lanyon, S. M. (1986) Genetic status of Euler's Flycatcher: a morphological and biochemical study. *Auk* 103: 341-350.

Lanyon, S. M. and Lanyon, W. E. (1989) The systematic position of the plantcutters, *Phytotoma*. *Auk* 106: 422-432.

Lanyon, S. M., Stotz, D. F. and Willard, D. E. (1990) *Clytoctantes atrogularis*, a new species of antbird from western Brazil. *Wilson Bull.* 102: 571-580.

LaRue, E. L. (1987) Permethrin control of *Philornis pici* (Diptera: Muscidae) on pearly-eyed thrasher nestlings in Luquillo Forest, Puerto Rico. M.Sc. thesis, Ohio State University.

Laubmann, A. (1930) *Wissenschaftliche Ergebnisse der Deutschen Gran Chaco-Expedition.* Stuttgart: Strecker und Schröder.

Laubmann, A. (1934) Weitere Beiträge zur Avifauna Argentiniens. *Verh. Orn. Ges. Bayern* 20: 249-336.

Lawrence, G. N. (1867) Descriptions of five new species of Central American birds. *Proc. Acad. Nat. Sci. Philadelphia* 19: 232-233.

Lawrence, G. (1870) Catalogue of birds from Puna Island, Gulf of Guayaquil, in the museum of the Smithsonian Institution, collected by J. F. Reeve Esq. *Ann. Lyc. Nat. Hist. New York* 9: 234-238.

Lawrence, G. N. (1871) Descriptions of new species of birds of the families Troglodytidae and Tyrannidae. *Proc. Acad. Nat. Sci. Philadelphia* 22: 233-236.

Lawrence, G. N. (1871) Letter. *Ibis* (3)1: 249-251.

Lawrence, G. N. (1874) The birds of western and northwestern Mexico, based upon collections made by Col. A. J. Grayson, Capt. J. Xantus and Ferd. Bischoff, now in the museum of the Smithsonian Institution, at Washington, D.C. *Mem. Boston Soc. Nat. Hist.* 2: 265-319.

Lawrence, G. N. (1878a) Catalogue of the birds of Dominica from collections made for the Smithsonian Institution by Frederick A. Ober, together with his notes and observations. *Proc. U.S. Natn. Mus.* 1: 48-69.

Lawrence, G. N. (1878b) Catalogue of the birds of St Vincent, from collections made by Mr Fred. A. Ober, under the directions of the Smithsonian Institution, with his notes thereon. *Proc. U.S. Natn. Mus.* 1: 185-198.

Lawrence, G. N. (1878c) Catalogue of the birds collected in Martinique by Mr Fred. A. Ober for the Smithsonian Institution. *Proc. U.S. Natn. Mus.* 1: 349-360.

Lawrence, G. N. (1878d) Catalogue of a collection of birds obtained in Guadeloupe for the Smithsonian Institution, by Mr. Fred. A. Ober. *Proc. U.S. Natn. Mus.* 1: 449-462.

Lawrence, G. N. (1880a) Description of a new species of parrot of the genus *Chrysotis*, from the island of Dominica. *Proc. U.S. Natn. Mus.* 3: 254-257.

Lawrence, G. N. (1880b) Descriptions of two new species of parrots and a new pigeon from South America. *Ibis* (4)4: 237-239.

Lawrence, G. N. (1891) Description of a new subspecies of Cypselidae of genus *Chaetura*, with a note on the Diablotin. *Auk* 8: 59-62.

Lawson, P. W. and Lanning, D. V. (1981) Nesting and status of the Maroon-fronted Parrot (*Rhynchopsitta terrisi*). Pp.385-392 in R. F. Pasquier, ed. *Conservation of New World parrots.* Washington, D.C.: Smithsonian Institution Press for the International Council for Bird Preservation (Techn. Publ. 1).

Lea, R. B. and Edwards, E. P. (1950) Notes on birds of the Lake Pátzcuaro region, Michoacán, Mexico. *Condor* 52: 260-271.

Leck, C. F. (1979) Avian extinctions in an isolated tropical wet-forest preserve, Ecuador. *Auk* 96: 343-352.

Lee, D. S. (1977) Occurrence of the Black-capped Petrel in North Carolina waters. *Chat* 41: 1-2.

Lee, D. S. (1984) Petrels and storm-petrels in North Carolina's offshore waters: including species previously unrecorded for North America. *Amer. Birds* 38: 151-163.

Lee, D. S. and Booth, J. (1979) Seasonal distribution of offshore and pelagic birds in North Carolina waters. *Amer. Birds* 33: 715-721.

Lee, D. S. and Rowlett, R. A. (1979) Additions to the seabird fauna of North Carolina. *Chat* 43: 1-9.

Lee, W. B. (1873) Ornithological notes from the Argentine Republic. *Ibis* (3)3: 129-138.

LeGrand, H. E. (1984) Southern Atlantic coast region. *Amer. Birds* 38: 897-899.

Lehmann, F. C. (1957) Contribuciones al estudio de la fauna de Colombia, XII. *Noved. Colombianas* 3: 101-156.

Lehmann, F. C. (1961) Notas generales. *Noved. Colombianas* 1: 523-526.

Leibfarth, H. (1988) Die Zucht des Kaninde-Aras *Ara glaucogularis. Papageien* 2/88: 38-41.
Lembeye, J. (1850) *Aves de la isla de Cuba.* Habana: Imprenta del Tiempo.
Lemire, R. (1991) Aves del área de Vilcabamba, sur del Ecuador. *Parque Nac. Podocarpus, Bol. Inform. Biol. Conserv. Vida Silv.* 2: 5-22.
Leo, M., Ortiz, E. G. and Rodríguez, L. (1988) Results of 1988 fieldwork: faunal inventory, Río Abiseo National Park, Peru. Lima: APECO.
Leopold, A. (1937) The Thick-billed Parrot in Chihuahua. *Condor* 39: 9-10.
Leopold, A. S. (1959) *Wildlife of Mexico: the game birds and mammals.* Berkeley and Los Angeles: University of California Press.
Léotaud, A. (1866) *Oiseaux de l'île de la Trinidad.* Port d'Espagne: Chronicle Publishing Office.
Lesson, R. P. (1828) *Manual d'ornithologie ou description des genres et des principales espèces d'oiseaux.* 2. Paris: Roret.
Lever, C. (1987) *Naturalized birds of the world.* Harlow (Essex, U.K.): Longman Scientific and Technical, and New York: John Wiley and Sons.
Levy, C. (1989) Bird notes: West Indian Whistling Duck. *Gosse Bird Club Broadsheet* no.53: 23.
Lewis, J. C. (1986) The Whooping Crane. Pp.659-676 in R. L. Di Silvestro, ed. *Audubon Wildlife Report 1986.* New York: National Audubon Society.
Lewis, L. A. and Coffey, W. J. (1985) The continuing deforestation in Haiti. *Ambio* 14: 158-160.
van Liefde, M. (1992) Status of the West Indian Whistling Duck in the Cayman Islands. *IWRB Threatened Waterfowl Research Group Newsletter* 2: 11-12.
Lillo, M. (1902) Enumeración sistemática de las aves de la provincia de Tucumán. *An. Mus. Nac. Buenos Aires* 8(3), 1, 1: 169-221.
Lillo, M. (1905) Fauna tucumana: Aves, catálogo sistemático. *Revta. Letras y Cienc. Soc.* 3: 3-41.
Lillo, M. (1909) Notas ornitológicas. *Apuntes Hist. Nat. Buenos Aires* 1: 21-26.
Lima, J. L. (1920) Aves colligidas no estado de S. Paulo, Matto-Grosso e Bahia, com algumas formas novas. *Revta. Mus. Paulista* 12: 93-106.
Lindsey, G. D. and Arendt, W. J. (1991) Radio-tracking Puerto Rican Parrots: assessing triangulation accuracy in an insular rain forest. *Carib. J. Sci.* 27: 46-53.
Lindsey, G. D., Arendt, W. J. and Kalina, J. (1988) Radio-tracking Puerto Rican Parrots: survival and causes of mortality in post-fledging birds. Unpublished.
Lindsey, G. D., Arendt, W. J., Kalina, J. and Pendleton, G. W. (1991) Home range and movements of juvenile Puerto Rican Parrots. *J. Wildl. Mgmt.* 55: 318-322.
Lindsey, G. D., Brock, M. K. and Wilson, M. H. (1989) Current status of the Puerto Rican Parrot conservation program. Pp.89-99 in A. E. Lugo, ed. *Wildlife management in the Caribbean islands.* Rio Pedras, Puerto Rico: Institute of Tropical Forestry and the Caribbean National Forest.
Lister, C. E. (1880) Field-notes on the birds of St Vincent, West Indies. *Ibis* (4)4: 38-44.
Llanes Sosa, A., Kirkconnell, A., Posada, R. M. and Cubillas, S. (1987) Aves de Cayo Saetía, archipiélago de Camagüey, Cuba. *Misc. Zool. Acad. Cienc. Cuba* 35: 3-4.
Loetscher, F. W. (1941) Ornithology of the Mexican state of Veracruz with an annotated list of the birds. Ph.D. thesis, Cornell University.
Long, A. and Heath, M. (1991) Flora of the El Triunfo Biosphere Reserve, Chiapas, Mexico: a preliminary floristic inventory and the plant communities of Polygon I. *An. Inst. Biol. Univ. Nac. Autón. México*, Ser. Bot. 62: 133-172.
Long, J. L. (1981) *Introduced birds of the world.* Newton Abbot, Devon: David and Charles.
Lönnberg, E. and Rendahl, H. (1922) A contribution to the ornithology of Ecuador. *Ark. Zool.* 14(25): 1-87.
López, N. E. (in press) Observaciones sobre la distribución de psitácidos en el departamento de Concepción, Paraguay.
Low, R. (1972) *The parrots of South America.* London: John Gifford.
Low, R. (1980a) *Parrots: their care and breeding.* Poole, Dorset: Blandford Press.
Low, R. (1980b) The St Lucia Parrot. *AFA Watchbird* 7(5): 10-15.
Low, R. (1981) The Yellow-shouldered Amazon (*Amazona barbadensis*). Pp.215-225 in R. F. Pasquier, ed. *Conservation of New World parrots.* Washington, D.C.: Smithsonian Institution Press for the International Council for Bird Preservation (Techn. Publ. 1).

Low, R. (1983) The Yellow-shouldered Amazon *Amazona barbadensis*. *Avicult. Mag.* 89: 9-21.
Low, R. (1984) *Endangered parrots*. Poole, Dorset: Blandford Press.
Low, R. (1986) *Parrots: their care and breeding*. Revised edition. Poole, Dorset: Blandford Press.
Low, R. (1987) Attempt to save Spix's Macaw. *Cage and Aviary Birds* 3 October 1987: 2.
Low, R. (1988) Rasche Hilfe für die Papageien von Dominica. *Gefied. Welt* 112: 223-224.
Low, R. (1990) *Macaws: a complete guide*. London: Merehurst Press.
Low, R. (1991a) Appendix I profile: Pretre's Amazon. *Psittascene* 3(1): 4-5.
Low, R. (1991b) Die Zucht der Prachtamazone *Amazona pretrei* im Palmitos Park. *Papageien* 1/91: 6-8.
Low, R. (1991c) Breeding Pretre's Amazon at Palmitos Park, Gran Canaria. *AFA Watchbird* 18(3): 56-58.
Low, R. (1991d) Im Palmitos-Park ziehen Hyazintharas Junge auf. *Gefied. Welt* 115: 80-83.
Low, R. (1991e) Repay the debt while time is left. *Bird Talk* 9(3): 26-32.
Lowe, P. R. (1907a) On the birds of Blanquilla Island, Venezuela. *Ibis* (9)1: 111-122.
Lowe, P. R. (1907b) On the birds of Margarita Island, Venezuela. *Ibis* (9)1: 547-570.
Lowe, P. R. (1909) Notes on some birds collected during a cruise in the Caribbean Sea. *Ibis* (9)3: 304-347.
Lowe, P. R. (1911) *A naturalist on desert islands*. London: Witherby.
Lowery, G. H. and Dalquest, W. W. (1951) Birds of the state of Veracruz, Mexico. *Univ. Kansas Publ. Mus. Nat. Hist.* 3: 531-649.
Lowery, G. H. and Newman, R. J. (1951) Notes on the ornithology of south-eastern San Luis Potosí. *Wilson Bull.* 63: 315-322.
Lowery, G. H. and O'Neill, J. P. (1964) A new genus and species of tanager from Peru. *Auk* 81: 125-131.
Lowery, G. H. and O'Neill, J. P. (1965) A new species of *Cacicus* (Aves, Icteridae) from Peru. *Occas. Pap. Mus. Zool. Lousiana State Univ.* 33.
de Lucca, E. R. (1992) El Aguila Coronada *Harpyhaliaetus coronatus* en San Juan. *Nuestras Aves* 26: 25.
Lucero, M. M. and Alabarce, E. A. (1980) Frecüencia de especies e individuos en una parcela de la selva misionera (Aves). *Revta. Mus. Arg. Cienc. Nat. "Bernardino Rivadavia"* Ecol. 2(7): 117-127.
Luigi, G. (1988) Sobre a avifauna do município de Nova Friburgo, RJ. P.488 in *Resumos, XV Congresso Brasileiro de Zoologia*. Curitiba: Universidade Federal do Paraná.
Lumholtz, C. (1903) *Unknown Mexico*. London: MacMillan.
Lusk, R. D. (1900) Parrots in the United States. *Condor* 2: 129.
Luthin, C. (1988) Argentina: La Reserva "Selva Misionera". *Boletín Panamericano* 3(2): 1.
Lynch Arribálzaga, E. (1920) Las aves del Chaco. *Hornero* 2: 85-98.
Mabberley, D. J. (1987) *The plant-book*. Cambridge, U.K.: Cambridge University Press.
Mace, G. M. and Lande, R. (1991) Assessing extinction threats: toward a reevaluation of IUCN threatened species categories. *Conserv. Biol.* 5: 148-157.
de Macedo, H. (1978) Redécouverte du cracidé *Penelope albipennis* dans les forêts seches du nord-ouest du Pérou. *C. R. Acad. Sci. Paris* 287 Ser. D: 265-267.
de Macedo-Ruiz, H. (1979) "Extinct" bird found in Peru. *Oryx* 15: 33-37.
Machado, R. B. and Brandt, A. (1990) Projeto ararinha azul: relatório final. Belo Horizonte: Fundação Biodiversitas, unpublished.
MAG (1954) = Ministerio de Agricultura y Ganadería (1954) Ley No. 13,908 de caza y protección a la fauna y Decreto Reglamentario No. 15,501/53. *Public. Miscelánea* 383. (Buenos Aires).
de Magalhães, J. C. R. (1978) Espécies cinegéticas e proteção à fauna na região sudeste, com especial referência ao estado de São Paulo. Pp.62-67 in *Seminário sobre caça amadorista*. Rio de Janeiro: Fundação Brasileira para a Conservação da Natureza.
Magno, S. (1971) Avifauna argentina. Familia Laridae: gaviotas y gaviotines. *Hornero* 11: 65-84.
Malherbe, A. (1862) *Monographie des picidées*, 2. Typographie de Jules Verronnais. Société d'Histoire Naturelle de la Moselle.
Mann, R. and Mann, R. (1982) Breeding the Red-topped Amazon Parrot *Amazona dufresnia* [*sic*] *rhodocorytha*. *Avicult. Mag.* 88: 12-14.
Marcgrave, G. (1648) *Historia naturalis brasiliae* [etc.]. [Amsterdam.]

March, W. T. (1863) Notes on the birds of Jamaica. *Proc. Acad. Nat. Sci. Philadelphia* 15: 150-154, 283-304.

Marchant, S. (1958) The birds of the Santa Elena Peninsula, S.W. Ecuador. *Ibis* 100: 349-387.

Marelli, C. A. (1918) Aves de Curuzú Cuatiá. *Hornero* 1: 74-80.

Marelli, C. A. (1919) Sobre el contenido del estómago de algunas aves. *Hornero* 1: 221-228.

Marsden, J. W. (1927) The smaller macaws. *Avicult. Mag.* (4)5: 246-247.

Marshall, J. T. (1957) *Birds of pine–oak woodland in southern Arizona and adjacent Mexico*. Berkeley: Cooper Ornithological Society (Pacific Coast Avifauna 32).

Martin, P. S., Robins C. R. and Heed, W. B. (1954) Birds and biogeography of the Sierra de Tamaulipas, an isolated pine–oak habitat. *Wilson Bull.* 64: 38-57.

Martin de Moussy, V. (1860) *Description géographique et statistique de la Confédération Argentine*, 2. Paris: Firmin Didot Frères, Fils et Cie.

Martínez García, O. and Martínez García, A. (1991) Primer reporte de nidificación y observaciones de *Ferminia cerverai* (Aves: Troglodytidae) para Cuba. *Pitirre* 4(2): 10.

Martuscelli, P. (1991) Predação de *Megalobulimus paranaguensis* Pelsbry & Ihering, 1900 (Megalobulimidae, Mollusca) por *Leucopternis lacernulata*. P.29 in Resumos, 1 Congreso Brasileiro de Ornitologia. Belém: Museu Paraense Emílio Goeldi.

Märzhäuser, H. (1986) Meine Haltung und Zucht des Kapuzenzeisigs und seiner Mischlinge. *Gefied. Welt* 110: 242-243.

Mathews, G. M. (1934) A check-list of the order procellariiformes. *Novit. Zool.* 39: 151-206.

de Mattos, G. T. and de Andrade, M. A. (1988) Contribuição à bionomia de *Pyrrhura cruentata* (Wied, 1820). Paper presented at Second International Meeting of the ICBP/IUCN Parrot Specialist Group, Curitiba, Paraná, 13-18 October 1988. Unpublished.

de Mattos, G. T., de Andrade, M. A. and de Freitas, M. V. (1990) Acréscimos à lista das aves do estado de Minas Gerais, Brasil. Unpublished.

de Mattos, G. T., de Andrade, M. A., Castro, P. de T. A. and de Freitas, M. V. (1984) *Lista preliminar das aves do estado de Minas Gerais*. Belo Horizonte: Instituto Estadual de Florestas.

de Mattos, G. T., de Andrade, M. A., Castro, P. de T. A. and de Freitas, M. V. (1985) Aves do estado de Minas Gerais. *SOM–Orgão da Sociedade Ornitológica Mineira* 31: 19-22.

Maxwell, P. H. (1960) My Blue-faced or Red-tailed Amazon Parrot (*Amazona brasiliensis* (Linn.)). *Avicult. Mag.* 66: 1-2.

Mayfield, H. F. (1988) Where were Kirtland's Warblers during the last ice age? *Wilson Bull.* 100: 660-663.

Mayr, E. (1971) New species of birds described from 1956 to 1965. *J. Orn.* 112: 302-316.

Mayr, E. and Cottrell, G. W., eds. (1979) *Check-list of birds of the world*, 1. Second edition. Cambridge, Mass.: Museum of Comparative Zoology.

Mayr, E. and Greenway, J. C., eds. (1960) *Check-list of birds of the world*, 9. Cambridge, Mass.: Museum of Comparative Zoology.

MC (1933) Carta No. 1333 de la Mapoteca Vica, 1:250,000, no.33 (Valle de Cochabamba). La Paz: Ministério de Colonización.

McCaffery, B. J. and Peltola, G. (1986) The status of Bristle-thighed Curlew on the Yukon Delta National Wildlife Refuge, Alaska. *Wader Study Group Bull.* 47: 22-25.

McFarlane, R. W. (1975) The status of certain birds in northern Chile. *XII Bull. Internatn. Coun. Bird Preserv.*: 300-309.

McFarlane, R. W. (1992) *A stillness in the pines: the ecology of the Red-cockaded Woodpecker*. New York: W. N. Norton.

McKenzie, P. M. and Noble, R. E. (1989) Notes on a large foraging concentration of the endangered Yellow-shouldered Blackbird (*Agelaius xanthomus*) in southwestern Puerto Rico. *Carib. J. Sci.* 25: 90-91.

McNeely, J. (1992) 1992 Ivory-billed Woodpecker expedition report. Unpublished.

Mees, G. F. (1968) Enige voor de avifauna von Suriname nieuwe vogelsoorten. *Gerfaut* 58: 101-107.

Mellink, C. and Molina, R. (1984) Reproduktiesukses van *Amazona barbadensis rothschildi* op Bonaire. Unpublished.

Mellink, E. and Palacios, E. (1990) Observations on Isla Guadalupe in November 1989. *Western Birds* 21: 177-180.

Ménégaux, A. (1908) Étude d'une collection d'oiseaux de l'Équateur. *Bull. Soc. Philomath. Paris* (9)10: 84-100.

Ménégaux, A. (1909) Étude d'une collection d'oiseaux provenant des hauts plateaux de la Bolivie et du Pérou Méridional. *Bull. Soc. Philomath. Paris* (10)1: 205-229.

Ménégaux, A. (1910) Étude d'une collection d'oiseaux du Pérou. *Rev. franc. Orn.* 1: 318-322.

Ménégaux, A. (1911) Étude des oiseaux de l'Équateur rapportés par le Dr. Rivet, dans mission du Service Géographique de l'Armée pour la mésure d'un arc de méridien équatorial en Amérique du Sud sous le controle scientifique de l'Académie des Sciences de France, 1899-1906. *Zoölogie* 9: 1-28.

Ménégaux, A. (1925) Étude d'une collection d'oiseaux faite par M. E. Wagner dans le chaco argentine. *Rev. franc. Orn.* 9: 221-238, 279-297, 322-329.

Meretsky, V. J. and Snyder, N. F. R. (1992) Range use and movements of California Condors. *Condor* 94: 313-335.

Mertens, R. and Steinbacher, J. (1955) Die im Senckenberg-Museum vorhandenen Arten ausgestorbener, aussterbender oder seltener Vögel. *Senckenb. Biol.* 36: 241-265.

Meyer de Schauensee, R. (1941) Rare and extinct birds in the collections of the Academy of Natural Sciences of Philadelphia. *Proc. Acad. Nat. Sci. Philadelphia* 93: 281-324.

Meyer de Schauensee, R. (1946) A new species of wren from Colombia. *Notulae Naturae* 182.

Meyer de Schauensee, R. (1948-1952) The birds of the Republic of Colombia. *Caldasia* 5(22): 251-380; (23): 381-644; (24): 645-871; (25): 873-1112; (26): 1115-1214.

Meyer de Schauensee, R. (1950) Colombian Zoological Survey. Part VII. A collection of birds from Bolivar, Colombia. *Proc. Acad. Nat. Sci. Philadelphia* 102: 111-139.

Meyer de Schauensee, R. (1951) Notes on Ecuadorian birds. *Notulae Naturae* 234.

Meyer de Schauensee, R. (1952) A review of the genus *Sporophila*. *Proc. Acad. Nat. Sci. Philadelphia* 104: 153-196.

Meyer de Schauensee, R. (1953) Manakins and cotingas from Ecuador and Peru. *Proc. Acad. Nat. Sci. Philadelphia* 105: 29-43.

Meyer de Schauensee, R. (1959) Additions to the birds of the Republic of Colombia. *Proc. Acad. Nat. Sci. Philadelphia* 111: 53-75.

Meyer de Schauensee, R. (1962) Notes on Venezuelan birds, with a history of the rail, *Coturnicops notata*. *Notulae Naturae* 357.

Meyer de Schauensee, R. (1964) *The birds of Colombia and adjacent areas of South and Central America*. Narberth, Penn.: Livingston Publishing Company.

Meyer de Schauensee, R. (1966) *The species of birds of South America and their distribution*. Narberth, Penn.: Livingston Publishing Company for the Academy of Natural Sciences Philadelphia.

Meyer de Schauensee, R. (1967) *Eriocnemis mirabilis*, a new species of hummingbird from Colombia. *Notulae Naturae* 402.

Meyer de Schauensee, R. (1970) *A guide to the birds of South America*. Wynnewood, Penn.: Livingston Publishing Company for the Academy of Natural Sciences of Philadelphia.

Meyer de Schauensee, R. (1982) *A guide to the birds of South America*. Wynnewood, Penn.: Livingston Publishing Company for the Academy of Natural Sciences of Philadelphia (reprinted with addenda by ICBP Pan-American Section).

Meyer de Schauensee, R. and Phelps, W. H. (1978) *A guide to the birds of Venezuela*. Princeton, New Jersey: Princeton University Press.

Meyers, J. M. and Barrow, W. C. (1992) Habitat of breeding and nonbreeding pairs of Puerto Rican Parrots (*Amazona vittata*) after Hurricane Hugo. Program abstract, Society of Conservation Biology, June 27–July 1 1992. Blacksburg, VA: Virginia Polytech Institute and State University.

Meyers, J. M., Vilella, F. J. and Barrow, W. C. (in prep.) Positive impacts from Hurricane Hugo: record year for nesting Puerto Rican Parrots. [*Endang. Spec. Techn. Bull.*]

Meza, J. (1989) Informe anual del proyecto "conservación del Picaflor de Juan Fernández *Sephanoides fernandensis*". Invierno 1988 – otoño 1989. [Santiago]: Corporación Nacional Forestal.

Miller, A. H. (1963) Seasonal activity and ecology of the avifauna of an American equatorial cloud forest. *Univ. California Publ. Zool.* 66: 1-74.
Miller, A. H., Friedmann, H., Griscom, L. and Moore, R. T. (1957) *Distributional checklist of the birds of Mexico*, 2. Cooper Ornithological Society (Pacific Coast Avifauna 33).
Miller, A. H., McMillan, I. I. and McMillan, E. (1965) *The current status and welfare of the California Condor*. New York: National Audubon Society (Research Report 6).
Miller, B. W. and Miller, C. M. (1988) Mussel Creek Drainage: a report with recommendations resulting from 1987 surveys as requested by the Belize Heritage Society. Unpublished.
Miller, B. M. and Miller, C. M. (1992) Distributional notes and new species records for birds in Belize. *Occas. Pap. Belize Nat. Hist. Soc.* 1(1): 6-25.
Miller, C. M. (1991) Keel-billed Motmot: Belize's rarest bird. *Belize Audubon Soc. Newsletter* 23(1): 12.
Miller, W. de W. (1906) List of birds collected in northwestern Durango, Mexico, by J. H. Batty, during 1903. *Bull. Amer. Mus. Nat. Hist.* 22: 161-183.
Millie, W. R. (1963) Brief notes on the birds of San Ambrosio and San Felix Islands, Chile. *Ibis* 105: 563-566.
Mirsky, E. N. (1976) Song divergence in hummingbird and junco populations on Guadalupe Island. *Condor* 78: 230-235.
Mitchell, M. H. (1957) *Observations on birds of southeastern Brazil*. Toronto: University of Toronto Press.
Mitchell, I. (1991) Yellow-faced Parrotlets (*Forpus xanthops*). *Mag. Parrot Soc.* 15: 56-57.
Mittermeier, R. A., Coimbra-Filho, A. F. and Valle, C. (1982) Highest priority areas in the Atlantic Forest region of eastern Brazil. WWF Tropical Forest and Primates Program, unpublished.
Molli, A. F. (1985) Notas nidobiológicas sobre aves argentinas: nido de Doradito Tucumano. *Nuestras Aves* 8: 12.
Moltoni, E. (1929) Primo elenco degli uccelli dell' isola di Haiti. *Atti Soc. Ital. Sci. Nat.* 68: 306-326.
Moltoni, E. (1932) Secondo elenco degli uccelli dell' isola di Haiti. *Atti Soc. Ital. Sci. Nat.* 71: 1-11.
Monroe, B. L. (1968) *A distributional survey of the birds of Honduras*. American Ornithologists' Union (Orn. Monogr. 7).
Monroe, B. L. and Howell, T. R. (1966) Geographic variation in Middle American parrots of the *Amazona ochrocephala* complex. *Occas. Pap. Mus. Zool. Louisiana State Univ.* 34.
Monson, G. (1965) A pessimistic view – the Thick-billed Parrot. *Audubon Field Notes* 19: 389.
Monson, G. and Phillips, A. R. (1981) *Annotated checklist of the birds of Arizona*. Second edition. Tucson: University of Arizona Press.
Montes de Oca, R. (1875) *Ensayo ornitológico de los troquilideos ó colobríes de México*. México [City]: Ignacio Escalante.
Moojen, J. (1943) Fauna de Minas Gerais. *Ceres* 5(26): 115-120.
Moojen, J., Carvalho, J. M. C. and Lopes, H. S. (1941) Observações sobre o conteúdo gástrico das aves brasileiras. *Mem. Inst. Oswaldo Cruz* 36(3): 405-444.
Moore, A. and van der Giessen, R. (1984) Cotacachi–Cayapas Ecological Reserve (project 1543). *World Wildlife Fund Monthly Report* September: 243-245.
Moore, H. E. (1977) Endangerment at the specific and generic levels in palms. Pp.267-282 in G. T. Prance and T. S. Elias, eds. *Extinction is forever*. New York: New York Botanical Garden.
Moore, R. T. (1934a) A new genus and species of tanager from Ecuador. *Auk* 51: 1-7.
Moore, R. T. (1934b) The Mt Sangay labyrinth and its fauna. *Auk* 51: 141-156.
Moore, R. T. (1935) A new jay of the genus *Cyanocorax* from Sinaloa, Mexico. *Auk* 52: 274-277.
Moore, R. T. (1938a) Discovery of the nest and eggs of the Tufted Jay. *Condor* 40: 233-241.
Moore, R. T. (1938b) Rediscovery of *Agyrtria luciae* (Lawrence). *Auk* 55: 534.
Moore, R. T. (1947) New species of parrot and race of quail from Mexico. *Proc. Biol. Soc. Washington* 60: 27-28.
Moore, R. T. (1949) A new hummingbird of the genus *Lophornis* from southern Mexico. *Proc. Biol. Soc. Washington* 62: 103-104.

Morales, R. and Cifuentes, M., eds. (1989) *Sistema regional de áreas silvestres protegidas en América Central: plan de acción 1989-2000.* Turrialba: Centro Agronómica Tropical de Investigación y Enseñanza.

Morony, J. J., Bock, W. J. and Farrand, J. (1975) *Reference list of birds of the world.* New York: American Museum of Natural History (Department of Ornithology).

Morrison, A. (1938) Three new birds from the department of Huancavelica, central Peru. *Ibis* (14)2: 774-775.

Morrison, A. (1939a) The birds of the department of Huancavelica, Peru. *Ibis* (14)3: 453-486.

Morrison, A. (1939b) Notes on the birds of Lake Junín, Central Peru. *Ibis* (14)3: 643-653.

Morrison, A. (1947) A new race of spine-tail from Peru. *Bull. Brit. Orn. Club* 67: 80-81.

Morrison, A. (1948) Notes on the birds of the Pampas River Valley, south Peru. *Ibis* 90: 119-126.

Morton, E. S. (1979) Status of endemic birds of the Zapata Swamp, Cuba. Memorandum to S. D. Ripley, 6 November (unpublished).

Morton, E. S. and González Alonso, H. T. (1982) The biology of *Torreornis inexpectata*, I. A comparison of vocalizations in *T. i. inexpectata* and *T. i. sigmani*. *Wilson Bull.* 94: 433-446.

Mörzer Bruyns, W. F. J. (1967a) Black-capped Petrels (*Pterodroma hasitata*) in the Caribbean. *Ardea* 55: 144-145.

Mörzer Bruyns, W. F. J. (1967b) Black-capped Petrels (*Pterodroma hasitata*) in the Atlantic Ocean. *Ardea* 55: 270.

Mühlhaus, J. and Mühlhaus, G. (1983) St Lucia–Ornithologische Beobachtungen auf einer Karibikinsel. *Trochilus* 4: 64-97.

Müller, L. (1912) Zoologische Ergebnisse einer Reise in das Mündungsgebiet des Amazonas, I. Allgemeine Bermerkungen über Fauna und Flora des bereisten Gebietes. *Abhandl. Königl. Bayer. Akad. Wissensch., Math.-Phys. Kl.* 26(1).

Müller-Bierl, M. and Cordier, C. (1991) Auf den Spuren des Rotohraras *Ara rubrogenys*. *Gefied. Welt* 115: 413-416.

Munn, C. A., da Silva, C. P., Renton, K. and Valqui, M. (1991) Eine kurze Studie über nistende Hyazintharas im Pantanal. *Papageien* 5/91: 145-148; 6/91: 178-181.

Munn, C. A., Thomsen, J. B. and Yamashita, C. (1987) Survey and status of the Hyacinth Macaw (*Anodorhynchus hyacinthinus*) in Brazil, Bolivia, and Paraguay. Unpublished.

Munn, C. A., Thomsen, J. B. and Yamashita, C. (1989) The Hyacinth Macaw. Pp.405-419 in W. J. Chandler, ed. *Audubon Wildlife Report 1989/1990.* San Diego: Academic Press, Inc.

Muñoz-Tébar B., R. (1952) El Cardenalito: un ave en peligro. *El Farol* 43: 20-22.

Munves, J. (1975) Birds of a highland clearing in Cundinamarca, Colombia. *Auk* 92: 307-321.

Murphy, R. C. (1936) *Oceanic birds of South America.* New York: American Museum of Natural History.

Murphy, R. C. (1952) Bird islands of Venezuela. *Geogr. Rev.* 42: 551-561.

Murphy, R. C. and Harper, F. (1921) A review of the diving petrels. *Bull. Amer. Mus. Nat. Hist.* 44: 495-554.

Murphy, R. C. and Mowbray, L. S. (1951) New light on the Cahow, *Pterodroma cahow*. *Auk* 68: 266-280.

Murray, H. (1969) Breeding notes – season 1968. *Avicult. Mag.* 75: 17-20.

des Murs, O. (1855) Oiseaux. In F. de Castelnau, *Animaux nouveaux ou rares... de l'Amérique du Sud...* [etc.] [part 7 – Zoology – of *Expédition dans les parties centrales de l'Amérique du Sud.*] Paris: P. Bertrand.

Myers, P. and Hansen, R. L. (1980) Rediscovery of the Rufous-faced Crake (*Laterallus xenopterus*). *Auk* 97: 901-902.

Naranjo, L. G. (undated) Inventario preliminar y estructura de comunidades aviarias en el Parque Regional Ucumarí. Pereira: Corporación Autónoma Regional de Risaralda, unpublished.

Naranjo, L. G. (1989) Territory quality, male behavior, and the polygyny threshold in the Yellow-hooded Blackbird. Ph.D. dissertation, New Mexico State University, Las Cruces, New Mexico.

Narosky, S. (1973) Una nueva especie de *Sporophila* para la avifauna argentina. *Hornero* 11: 169-171.

Narosky, S., di Giacomo, A. G. and López Lanús, B. (1990) Notas sobre aves del sur de Buenos Aires. *Hornero* 13: 173-178.

Narosky, T. (1977) Una nueva especie del género *Sporophila* (Emberizidae). *Hornero* 11: 345-348.
Narosky, T. (1985) *Aves argentinas: guía para el reconocimiento de la avifauna bonaerense.* Buenos Aires: Editorial Albatros.
Narosky, T. (1990) El nordeste de Chile a vuelo de pájaro. *Nuestras Aves* 21: 30-32.
Narosky, T. and di Giacomo, A. G. (in prep.) *Avifauna bonaerense.*
Narosky, T. and Fiameni, M. (1987) Aves de Costa Bonita. *Nuestras Aves* 12: 16-17.
Narosky, T. and Salvador, S. (1985) Informe *Sporophila.* Unpublished.
Narosky, T. and Yzurieta, D. (1987) *Guía para la identificación de las aves de Argentina y Uruguay.* Buenos Aires: Asociación Ornitológica del Plata.
Naumburg, E. M. B. (1928) Remarks on Kaempfer's collections in eastern Brazil. *Auk* 45: 60-65.
Naumburg, E. M. B. (1930) The birds of Mato Grosso: a report on the birds secured by the Roosevelt-Rondon Expedition. *Bull. Amer. Mus. Nat. Hist.* 60: 1-432.
Naumburg, E. M. B. (1934) Rediscovery of *Rhopornis ardesiaca* (Wied). *Auk* 51: 493-496.
Naumburg, E. M. B. (1935) Gazetteer and maps showing stations visited by Emil Kaempfer in eastern Brazil and Paraguay. *Bull. Amer. Mus. Nat. Hist.* 68: 449-469.
Naumburg, E. M. B. (1939) Studies of birds from eastern Brazil and Paraguay, based on a collection made by Emil Kaempfer. *Bull. Amer. Mus. Nat. Hist.* 76: 231-276.
Navarro, A. G. (1992) Altitudinal distribution of birds in the Sierra Madre del Sur, Guerrero, Mexico. *Condor* 94: 29-39.
Navarro, A. G. and Muñoz, A. (1990) Aves, reptiles y anfibios del Parque Estatal Omiltemi, Chilpancingo, Guerrero. Pp.247-258 in J. L. Camarillo and F. Rivera, eds. *Areas naturales protegidas en México y especies en extinción.* [México City:] Unidad de Investigación ICSE, ENEP Iztacala, UNAM.
Navarro, A. G., Torres, M. G. and Escalante, B. P. (1991) *Catálogo de aves, Museo de Zoología, Facultad de Ciencias, Universidad Nacional Autónoma de México.* México [City]: Museo de Zoología "Alfonso L. Herrera", Facultad de Ciencias, UNAM.
Navarro, A. G., Peterson, A. T., Escalante, B. P. and Benítez, H. (1992) *Cypseloides storeri*, a new species of swift from Mexico. *Wilson Bull.* 104: 55-64.
Navas, J. R. (1962) Reciente hallazgo de *Rallus limicola antarcticus* King (Aves, *Rallidae*). *Neotrópica* 8(26): 73-76.
Navas, J. R. (1991) Gruiformes. *Fauna de agua dulce de la República Argentina*, 43(3): 1-80.
Navas, J. R. and Bó, N. A. (1982) La posición taxonómica de *Thripophaga sclateri* y *T. punensis* (Aves, Furnariidae). *Com. Mus. Arg. Cienc. Nat. "Bernardino Rivadavia"* 4: 85-93.
Navas, J. R. and Bó, N. A. (1986) Aves nuevas o poco conocidas de Misiones. Argentina, 1. *Neotrópica* 32(87): 43-44.
Navas, J. R. and Bó, N. A. (1987) *Sporophila falcirostris*, nueva especie para la Argentina. *Neotrópica* 33(90): 96.
Navas, J. R. and Bó, N. A. (1988a) Aves nuevas o poco conocidas de Misiones, Argentina, 2. *Com. Zool. Mus. Hist. Nat. Montevideo* 166(12): 1-9.
Navas, J. R. and Bó, N. A. (1988b) Aves nuevas o poco conocidas de Misiones, Argentina, 3. *Revta. Mus. Arg. Cienc. Nat. "Bernardino Rivadavia"* (Zool.) 15: 11-37.
Navas, J. R. and Bó, N. A. (1991) Anotaciones taxonómicas sobre Emberizidae y Fringillidae de la Argentina. *Revta. Mus. La Plata* (n.s., Zool.) 14(158): 119-134.
Neck, R. W. (1986) Expansion of Red-crowned Parrot, *Amazona viridigenalis*, into southern Texas and changes in agricultural practices in northern Mexico. *Bull. Texas Orn. Soc.* 19: 6-12.
Negret, A. J. (1987) Aves colombianas amenazadas de extinción. Primera aproximación. Anotaciones bibliográficas y observaciones personales. Unpublished.
Negret, A. J. (1991) Reportes recientes en el Parque Nacional Munchique de aves consideradas raras o amenazadas de extinción. *Noved. Colombianas* (nueva epoca) 3: 39-45.
Negret, A. J. and Acevedo, C. I. (1990) Reportes recientes de *Leptosittaca branickii*, ave colombiana amenazada de extinción. *Noved. Colombianas* (nueva epoca) 2: 70-71.
Negret, A. J. and Cavalcanti, R. (1985) Censo poblacional de duas aves da região de Brasília: *Scytalopus novacapitalis* e *Melanopareia torquata* (Rhinocryptidae). Pp.271 in A. C. Z. Amaral and

E. H. M. do Amaral, eds. *Resumos, XII Congresso Brasileiro de Zoologia*. Campinas: Editora da UNICAMP.

Negret, A., Taylor, J., Soares, R. C., Cavalcanti, R. B. and Johnson, C. (1984) *Aves da região geopolítica do Distrito Federal: lista (check list) 429 espécies*. Brasília: Ministério do Interior, Secretaria Especial do Meio Ambiente.

Negret, A. J. and Teixeira, D. M. (1983) Notas sobre duas aves brasileiras ameaçadas de extinção: *Scytalopus novacapitalis* (Rhinocryptidae) e *Taoniscus nanus* (Tinamidae). Pp.357-358 in *Resumos, X Congresso Brasileiro de Zoologia*. Belo Horizonte: Imprensa Universitária.

Negret, A. J. and Teixeira, D. M. (1984) Notas sobre duas espécies de aves raras: *Micropygia schomburgkii* e *Laterallus xenopterus* (Rallidae) na região de Brasília–DF. P.337 in *Resumos, XI Congresso Brasileiro de Zoologia*. Belo Horizonte: Imprensa Universitária.

Nelson, E. W. (1897) Preliminary descriptions of new birds from Mexico and Guatemala in the collection of the United States Department of Agriculture. *Auk* 14: 42-76.

Nelson, E. W. (1898) The Imperial Woodpecker, *Campephilus imperialis* (Gould). *Auk* 15: 216-223.

Nelson, E. W. (1899) Birds of the Tres Marias Islands. Pp.21-62 in C. H. Merriam, ed. *Natural history of the Tres Marias Islands, Mexico*. Washington, D.C.: Government Printing Office (*North American Fauna* 14).

Nelson, E. W. (1900) Descriptions of thirty new North American birds, in the biological survey collection. *Auk* 17: 253-270.

Nelson, E. W. (1903) Descriptions of new birds from southern Mexico. *Proc. Biol. Soc. Washington* 16: 151-160.

Neris, N. and Colman, F. (1991) Observaciones de aves en los alrededores de Colonia Neuland, Departamento Boquerón, Paraguay. *Bol. Mus. Nac. Hist. Nat. Paraguay*. 10: 1-10.

Neunzig, K. (1921) *Die fremdländischen Stubenvögel*. Magdeburg: Creutz'sche Verlagsbuchhandlung.

Newton, E. (1859) Observations on the birds of St Croix, West Indies, made between February 20th and August 6th 1857 by Alfred Newton, and between March 4th and September 28th 1858 by Edward Newton. *Ibis* 1: 59-69, 138-150, 252-264, 365-379.

Nicéforo María, H. (1947) Notas sobre aves de Colombia, II. *Caldasia* 4: 317-377.

Nicéforo María, H. (1955) Una crácida nueva para la avifauna colombiana. *Caldasia* 7: 177-184.

Nicéforo-María, H. and Olivares, A. (1964) Adiciones a la avifauna colombiana, I (Tinamidae-Falconidae). *Bol. Inst. La Salle* 204: 5-27.

Nicéforo María, H. and Olivares, A. (1965) Adiciones a la avifauna colombiana, II (Cracidae–Rynchopidae). *Bol. Soc. Venezolana Cienc. Nat.* 26: 36-58.

Nicéforo-María, H. and Olivares, A. (1978) Adiciones a la avifauna colombiana, VII (Vireonidae-Fringillidae). *Revta. Univ. Soc. Católica La Salle* 1: 69-113.

Nichols, H. A. J. (1974) [The ecology of the endangered St Vincent parrot.] *SAFE International Newsletter* 2: 1-6.

Nichols, H. (1975) Lesser Antillean amazon parrot programme. *Jersey Wildl. Preserv. Trust 11th Ann. Rep. 1974*: 23-26.

Nichols, H. A. J. (1976) Parrot watching in the Caribbean. *SAFE International Newsletter* 6: 1-8.

Nichols, H. A. J. (1977a) Captive breeding programs for *Amazona* parrots. Pp.263-271 in S. A. Temple, ed. *Endangered birds: management techniques for preserving threatened species*. Madison: University of Wisconsin Press.

Nichols, H. A. J. (1977b) The amazon parrots of the Lesser Antilles. Wildlife Preservation Trust International, Report 1 (unpublished).

Nichols, H. A. J. and Nichols, T. D. (1973) St Vincent Parrot: plumage polymorphism, juvenile plumage and nidification. *Bull. Brit. Orn. Club* 93: 120-123.

Nichols, H. A. J., Nichols, C. A., VanVliet [*sic*], G. B. and Gray, G. S. (1976) Endangered amazons of Dominica: the Imperial and Arausiaca Parrots. Unpublished typescript.

Nichols, J. T. (1913) Notes on offshore birds. *Auk* 30: 505-511.

Nichols, J. T. and Mowbray, L. L. (1916) Two new forms of petrels from the Bermudas. *Auk* 33: 194-195.

Nichols, T. D. (1981a) St Vincent Amazon (*Amazona guildingii*): predators, clutch size, plumage polymorphism, effect of the volcanic eruption, and population estimate. Pp.197-208 in R. F.

Pasquier, ed. *Conservation of New World parrots.* Washington, D.C.: Smithsonian Institution Press for the International Council for Bird Preservation (Techn. Publ. 1).

Nichols, T. D. (1981b) An unusual amazon hybrid. Pp.169-170 in R. F. Pasquier, ed. *Conservation of New World parrots.* Washington, D.C.: Smithsonian Institution Press for the International Council for Bird Preservation (Techn. Publ. 1).

Nichols, T. D. (1981c) Observation on *Amazona imperialis* during the second nesting season after Hurricane David. Report to ICBP, July 1981. Unpublished.

Nichols, T. D. (1986) *Amazona imperialis* and a story of an albatross. *Amazona Newsletter* Supplement 1.

Nicoll, M. J. (1904) Ornithological journal of a voyage round the world in the "Valhalla" (November 1902 to August 1903). *Ibis* (8)4: 22-67.

Nieboer, E. (1966) Notes on sea-birds, 15. Probable sight record of *Pterodroma hasitata* in the western Sargasso Sea. *Ardea* 54: 88.

Nielsen, B. (1992) Paul Butler sells parrots. *Wildlife Conserv.* 95(1): 67-71.

Niles, J. J. (1981) The status of psittacine birds in Guyana. Pp.431-438 in R. F. Pasquier, ed. *Conservation of New World parrots.* Washington, D.C.: Smithsonian Institution Press for the International Council for Bird Preservation (Techn. Publ. 1).

Nilsson, G. (1985) U.S. import and mortality data for Neotropical parrots. *TRAFFIC (U.S.A.) Newsletter* 6(2): 19-24.

Nilsson, G. and Mack, D. (1980) *Macaws: traded to extinction?* Washington, D.C.: TRAFFIC (U.S.A.), Special Report 2.

Noble, G. K. (1916) The resident birds of Guadeloupe. *Bull. Mus. Comp. Zool.* 60: 359-396.

Noble, R. E. and Vilella, F. J. (1986) Apuntes sobre el anidamiento del Guabairo. *Carib. J. Sci.* 22: 223.

Noble, R. E., Vilella, F. J. and Zwank, P. J. (1986) Status of the endangered Puerto Rican Nightjar in 1985. *Carib. J. Sci.* 22: 137-143.

Noegel, R. (1986) First captive breeding of the Yellow-shouldered Amazon. *AFA Watchbird* 13(5): 4-7.

Nogueira-Neto, P. (1973) *A criação de animais indígenas vertebrados.* São Paulo: Edições Tecnapis.

Nores, M. (1986) Nuevos registros para aves de Argentina. *Hornero* 12: 304-307.

Nores, M. and Yzurieta, D. (1975) Sobre aves de la provincia de Córdoba. *Hornero* 11: 312-314.

Nores, M. and Yzurieta, D. (1980) *Aves de ambientes acuáticos de Córdoba y centro de Argentina.* Córdoba, Argentina: Secretaría de Estado de Agricultura y Ganadería (Dirección de Caza, Pesca y Actividades Acuáticas).

Nores, M. and Yzurieta, D. (1981) Nuevas localidades para aves argentinas. *Hist. Nat.* (Mendoza) 2: 40.

Nores, M. and Yzurieta, D. (1984a) Registro de aves en el sur de Bolivia. *Doñana, Acta Vert.* 11: 327-337.

Nores, M. and Yzurieta, D. (1984b) Distribución y situación actual de las parabas y parabachis en Bolivia. Consejo Internacional para la Preservación de las Aves, unpublished.

Nores, M. and Yzurieta, D. (1986) Distribución y situación actual de grandes psittácidos en Sudamérica central. Unpublished.

Nores, M. and Yzurieta, D. (1988a) Situación y conservación de los crácidos de Argentina. Unpublished paper presented at the II International Cracid Symposium, Caracas, Venezuela, February/March 1988.

Nores, M. and Yzurieta, D. (1988b) The status of Argentine parrots. Unpublished typescript.

Nores, M., Yzurieta, D. and Miatello, R. (1983) *Lista y distribución de las aves de Córdoba, Argentina.* Córdoba, Argentina: Academia Nacional de Ciencias (*Bol. Acad. Nac. Cienc.* 56, 1, 2).

Nores, M., Yzurieta, D. and Salvador, S. A. (1991) Lista y distribución de las aves de Santiago del Estero, Argentina. *Bol. Acad. Nac. Cienc. Córdoba* 59 (3a-4a): 157-196.

Northrop, J. (1891) The birds of Andros Island, Bahamas. *Auk* 8: 64-80.

Norton, D. W., Orcés V., G. and Sutter, E. (1972) Notes on rare and previously unreported birds from Ecuador. *Auk* 89: 889-894.

Norton, R. L. (1983) The spring migration, West Indies Region. *Amer. Birds* 37: 916-917.

Norton, R. L. (1984) The winter season, West Indies Region. *Amer. Birds* 38: 361-362.

Norton, R. L. and Clarke, N. V. (1987) Species accounts of wetland birds observed in the Turks and Caicos Islands (July 17-26, September 26–October 4, 1987). Unpublished.

Norton, R. L., Yntema, J. A. and Sladen, F. W. (1986) Abundance, distribution and habitat use by anatids in the Virgin Islands. *Carib. J. Sci.* 22: 99-106.

Novaes, F. C. (1950) Sobre as aves de Sernambetiba, Distrito Federal, Brasil. *Revta. Bras. Biol.* 10(2): 199-208.

Novaes, F. C. (1958) Sobre uma coleção de aves do sudeste do estado do Pará. *Arq. Zool. São Paulo* 11: 133-146.

Novaes, F. C. (1978a) Ornitologia do território do Amapá, 2. *Publ. Avuls. Mus. Para. Emílio Goeldi* 29.

Novaes, F. C. (1978b) Sobre algumas aves pouco conhecidas da Amazônia brasileira II. *Bol. Mus. Para. Emílio Goeldi* n.s. Zool. no.90.

Nowak, R. M. (1990) Endangered and threatened wildlife and plants; endangered status for six foreign birds. *Federal Register* 55 (no.189, September 28): 39858-39860.

Oates, E. W. (1901) *Catalogue of the collection of birds' eggs in the British Museum*, 1. London: Taylor and Francis.

Ober, F. A. (1880) *Camps in the Caribbees: the adventures of a naturalist in the Lesser Antilles.* Edinburgh: David Douglas.

Oberholser, H. C. (1902) Catalogue of a collection of hummingbirds from Ecuador and Colombia. *Proc. U.S. Natn. Mus.* 24: 309-342.

OG (1955a) = Office of Geography (1955) *Gazetteer no.4: Bolivia.* Washington, D.C.: Department of the Interior.

OG (1955b) = Office of Geography (1955) *British West Indies and Bermuda: official standard names approved by the U.S. Board on Geographic Names.* Washington, D.C.: Department of the Interior.

OG (1956a) = Office of Geography (1956) *Mexico: official standard names approved by the U.S. Board on Geographic Names.* Washington, D.C.: Department of the Interior.

OG (1956b) = Office of Geography (1956) *Gazetteer no.16: British Honduras.* Washington, D.C.: Department of the Interior.

OG (1956c) = Office of Geography (1956) *Gazetteer no.18: Costa Rica.* Washington, D.C.: Department of the Interior.

OG (1957a) = Office of Geography (1957) *Gazetteer no.35: Paraguay.* Washington, D.C.: Department of the Interior.

OG (1957b) = Office of Geography (1957) *Gazetteer no.36: Ecuador.* Washington, D.C.: Department of the Interior.

OG (1958) = Office of Geography (1958) *Gazetteer no.38: Puerto Rico, the Virgin Islands and other islands banks in the Caribbean.* Washington, D.C.: Department of the Interior.

OG (1961) = Office of Geography (1961) *Gazetteer no.56: Venezuela.* Washington, D.C.: Department of the Interior.

OG (1963a) = Office of Geography (1963) *Gazetteer no.30: Cuba.* Second edition. Washington, D.C.: Department of the Interior.

OG (1963b) = Office of Geography (1963) *Gazetteer no.71: Brazil.* Washington, D.C.: Department of the Interior.

OG (1964) = Office of Geography (1964) *Gazetteer no.86: Colombia.* Washington, D.C.: Department of the Interior.

OG (1965) = Office of Geography (1965) *Gazetteer no.94: Guatemala.* Washington, D.C.: Department of the Interior.

OG (1967) = Office of Geography (1967) *Chile: official standard names approved by the U.S. Board on Geographic Names.* Washington, D.C.: Department of the Interior.

OG (1968) = Office of Geography (1968) *Gazetteer no.103: Argentina.* Washington, D.C.: Department of the Interior.

OG (1969) = Office of Geography (1969) *Panama: official standard names approved by the U.S. Board on Geographic Names.* Washington D.C.: Department of the Interior.

OG (1976) = Office of Geography (1976) *Nicaragua: official standard names approved by the U.S. Board on Geographic Names.* Washington D.C.: Department of the Interior.

Ogilvie-Grant, W. R. (1893) *Catalogue of birds in the British Museum*, 22. London: Taylor and Francis (printed by order of the Trustees).

Ogilvie-Grant, W. R. (1897) *A hand-book to the game-birds*, 2. London: Edward Lloyd.

Olivares, A. (1959) Cinco aves que aparentamente no habian sido registradas en Colombia. *Lozania* 12: 51-56.

Olivares, A. (1960) Algunas aves de Gaitania (Municipio de Ataco, Tolima, Colombia). *Caldasia* 8: 379-382.

Olivares, A. (1969) *Aves de Cundinamarca*. Bogotá: Universidad Nacional de Colombia.

Olivares, A. (1971) Aves de la ladera oriental de los Andes Orientales, alto río Cusiana, Boyacá, Colombia. *Caldasia* 11: 203-226.

de Oliveira, R. G. (1982) O jacutinga (*Pipile jacutinga*) no Rio Grande do Sul. *An. Soc. Sul-Riogrand. Orn.* 3: 16-19.

Oliver, W. L. R. and Santos, I. B. (1991) *Threatened endemic mammals of the Atlantic Forest region of south-east Brazil*. Jersey, Channel Islands: Jersey Wildlife Preservation Trust (Spec. Sci. Report 4).

Olmos, F. (in press) Birds of Serra da Capivara National Park, north-east Brazil. *Bird Conserv. Internatn.*

Olney, P. J. S., ed (1977) Census of rare animals in captivity, 1976. *Internatn. Zoo Yearbook* 17: 333-371.

Olrog, C. C. (1948) Observaciones sobre la avifauna de la Tierra del Fuego y Chile. *Acta Zool. Lilloana* 5: 437-531.

Olrog, C. C. (1949) Breves notas sobre la avifauna del Aconquija. *Acta Zool. Lilloana* 7: 139-159.

Olrog, C. C. (1958a) Notas ornitológicas sobre la colección del Instituto Miguel Lillo de Tucumán. III. *Acta Zool. Lilloana* 15: 5-18.

Olrog, C. C. (1958b) Observaciones sobre la avifauna antártica y de alta mar desde el Río de la Plata hasta los 60° de latitud sur. *Acta Zool. Lilloana* 15: 19-33.

Olrog, C. C. (1958c) Notas ornitológicas sobre la colección del Instituto Miguel Lillo (Tucumán), 4. *Acta Zool. Lilloana* 16: 83-90.

Olrog, C. C. (1959) *Las aves argentinas, una guía de campo*. Tucumán: Universidad Nacional de Tucumán (*Opera Lilloana* IX).

Olrog, C. C. (1962) Notas ornitológicas sobre la colección del Instituto Miguel Lillo (Tucumán), 6. *Acta Zool. Lilloana* 18: 111-120.

Olrog, C. C. (1963) *Lista y distribución de las aves argentinas*. Tucumán: Universidad Nacional de Tucumán. (*Opera Lilloana* 9).

Olrog, C. C. (1967) Breeding of the Band-tailed Gull *Larus belcheri* on the Atlantic coast of Argentina. *Condor* 69: 42-48.

Olrog, C. C. (1968) *Las aves sudamericanas: una guia de campo*. Tucumán: Instituto Miguel Lillo.

Olrog, C. C. (1979) *Nueva lista de la avifauna argentina*. Tucumán: Ministerio de Cultura y Educación, Fundación Miguel Lillo (*Opera Lilloana* 27).

Olrog, C. C. (1984) *Las aves argentinas*. Buenos Aires: Administración de Parques Nacionales.

Olrog, C. C. and Contino, F. (1970) Dos especies nuevas para la avifauna argentina. *Neotrópica* 16: 94-95.

Olson, S. L. (1974) A new species of *Nesotrochis* from Hispaniola, with notes on other fossil rails from the West Indies (Aves: Rallidae). *Proc. Biol. Soc. Washington* 87: 437-450.

Olson, S. L. and Hilgartner, W. B. (1982) Fossil and subfossil birds from the Bahamas. *Smithson. Contrib. Paleobiol.* 48: 22-56.

O'Neill, J. P. (1969) Distributional notes on the birds of Peru, including twelve species previously unreported from the Republic. *Occas. Pap. Mus. Zool. Louisiana State Univ.* 37: 1-11.

O'Neill, J. P. (1976) Notes on two species of Bolivian birds. *Wilson Bull.* 88: 492-493.

O'Neill, J. P. (1981) Comments on the status of the parrots occurring in Peru. Pp.419-424 in R. F. Pasquier, ed. *Conservation of New World parrots*. Washington, D.C.: Smithsonian Institution Press for the International Council for Bird Preservation (Techn. Publ. 1).

O'Neill, J. P. (1987) A discussion of the birds of Peru, with comments on groups of special interest to aviculturists. Pp.240-249 in *Proceedings 1987 Jean Delacour/IFCB Symposium on Breeding Birds in Captivity*. North Hollywood, California: International Foundation for the Conservation of Birds.

O'Neill, J. P. and Graves, G. R. (1977) A new genus and species of owl (Aves: *Strigidae*) from Peru. *Auk* 94: 409-416.

O'Neill, J. P. and Pearson, D. L. (1974) Estudio preliminar de las aves de Yarinacocha, Departamento de Loreto, Perú. *Publ. Mus. Hist. Nat. Javier Prado* Ser. A, Zool., no.25: 1-13.
d'Orbigny, A. (1835) *Voyage dans l'Amérique méridionale*, 1. Paris: Pitois-Levrault; and Strasbourg: V. Levrault.
d'Orbigny, A. (1835-1844) *Voyage dans l'Amérique méridionale*, 4 (Part 3), Oiseaux. Paris: P. Bertrand.
d'Orbigny, A. (1839) *Historia física, política y natural de la isla de Cuba, por D. Ramón de la Sagra: Aves*. Paris: Arthus Bertrand.
d'Orbigny, A. and de Lafresnaye, F. (1837) Synopsis avium. *Mag. Zool.* 7, cl.2.
Orejuela, J. E. (1983) Prospectus for conservation of several critical natural areas rich in endemic organisms in Colombia, South America. Unpublished.
Orejuela, J. E. (1985) Loras colombianas en peligro de extinción. *Rupicola* 5(7-8): 1-4.
Orejuela, J. E. (1987a) La Reserva Natural "La Planada" y la biogeografia andina. *Humboldtia* 1: 117-148.
Orejuela, J. E. (1987b) Conservation of endemic birds of the department of Nariño, Colombia. Pp.469-498 in *Proceedings 1987 Jean Delacour/IFCB Symposium on Breeding Birds in Captivity*. North Hollywood, California: International Foundation for the Conservation of Birds.
Orejuela, J. E. and Alberico, M. S. (1980) Ecological relationships of endemic bird species in the major centres of endemism of Colombia. Research proposal submitted to ICBP, WWF, and to COLCIENCIAS, unpublished.
Orejuela, J. E., Cantillo, G. and Alberico, M. S. (1982) Estudio de dos comunidades de aves y mamíferos en Nariño, Colombia. *Cespedesia* 41-42(3): 41-67.
Orejuela, J. E., Raitt, R. J. and Alvarez, H. (1979) Relaciones ecológicas de las aves en la reserva forestal de Yotoco, Valle del Cauca. *Cespedesia* 29-30(8): 7-27.
Oren, D. C. (1988) Uma reserva biológica para o Maranhão. *Ciência Hoje* 8(44): 36-45.
Oren, D. C. (1991) As aves do estado do Maranhão, Brasil. *Goeldiana, Zool.* no.9.
Oren, D. C. and Novaes, F. C. (1986a) Observations on the Golden Parakeet *Aratinga guarouba* in northern Brazil. *Biol. Conserv.* 36: 329-337.
Oren, D. C. and Novaes, F. C. (1986b) Prioridades para a conservação da natureza nas florestas do Estado do Maranhão. Belém: MPEG. Unpublished report.
Oren, D. C. and da Silva, J. M. C. (1987) Cherrie's Spinetail (*Synallaxis cherriei* Gyldenstolpe) (Aves: Furnariidae) in Carajás and Gorotire, Pará, Brazil. *Bol. Mus. Para. Emílio Goeldi* Ser. Zool. 3(1): 1-9.
Oren, D. C. and Willis, E. O. (1981) New Brazilian records for the Golden Parakeet (*Aratiga guarouba*). *Auk* 98: 394-396.
Orfila, R. N. (1936-1938) Los psittaciformes argentinos. *Hornero* 6: 197-225, 365-382; 7: 1-21.
Ornelas, J. F. (1987) Rediscovery of the Rufous-crested Coquette (*Lophornis delattrei brachylopha*) in Guerrero, Mexico. *Wilson Bull.* 99: 719-721.
Ortiz T., E. (1980) Estudio preliminar sobre la "Pava de Ala Blanca" (*Penelope albipennis*). Unpublished.
Ortiz T., E. (1988) [Status of cracids in Peru.] Unpublished paper presented at the II International Cracid Symposium, Caracas, Venezuela, February/March 1988.
Ortiz-Crespo, F. I. (1984) First twentieth-century specimen of the Violet-throated Metailtail *Metallura baroni*. *Bull. Brit. Orn. Club* 104: 95-97.
Osburn, W. (1859) Notes on the birds of Jamaica. *Zoologist*: 6368-6373.
Ottenwalder, J. A. (1989) A summary of conservation trends in the Dominican Republic. Pp.845-850 in C. A. Woods, ed. *Biogeography of the West Indies*. Gainesville, Florida: Sandhill Crane Press.
Ottenwalder, J. A. and Vargas M., T. (1979) Nueva localidad para el Diablotín en la República Dominicana. *Naturalista Postal [Carta Ocasional del Herbario UASD]* No.36.
Oustalet, E. (1891) *Mission scientifique du Cap Horn 1882-83*, 6. Zoologie, Oiseaux. Paris: Gauthier-Villars.
Oustalet, [E.] (1904) Description d'espèces nouvelles d'oiseaux rapportés par M. G.-A. Baer du Tucuman (République Argentine). *Bull. Mus. Hist. Nat. Paris* 10: 43-45.
Owre, O. T. (1973) A consideration of the exotic avifauna of southeastern Florida. *Wilson Bull.* 85: 491-500.

Oyarzo, H. and Cisternas, G. (1990) Proyecto conservación de la Tagua Cornuda (*Fulica cornuda*) en la Laguna Santa Rosa. Informe no.2. Corporación Nacional Forestal, Ministerio de Agricultura. Unpublished.

Oyarzo, H. and Cisternas, G. (1991) Proyecto "Conservación de la Tagua Cornuda (*Fulica cornuta*) en la Laguna Santa Rosa, III Región de Atacama, Chile". Primer informe semestral 1991. Corporación Nacional Forestal, Ministerio de Agricultura. Unpublished.

Pacheco, F. (1988a) Black-hooded Antwren *Formicivora [Myrmotherula] erythronotos* re-discovered in Brazil. *Bull. Brit. Orn. Club* 108: 179-182.

Pacheco, J. F. (1988b) Acrésimos à lista de aves do município do Rio de Janeiro. *Bol. FBCN* 23: 104-120.

Pacheco, J. F. and da Fonseca, P. S. M. (1987) Aves observadas na Reserva Florestal da CVRD – Linhares, ES, 6-10 de janeiro de 1987. Unpublished.

Pacheco, J. F. and da Fonseca, P. S. M. (1990) Resultados de excursão ornitológica à determinadas áreas dos estados de São Paulo, S. Catarina e R. G. do Sul, Janeiro 1990. Unpublished.

Pádua, M. T. J. (1983) *Os parques nacionais e reservas biológicas do Brasil.* Brasília: Instituto Brasileiro de Desenvolvimento Florestal.

Page, T. J. (1859) *La Plata, the Argentine Confederation, and Paraguay.* London: Trubner and Co.

Parchappe, M. and d'Orbigny, A. (1835) *Carte d'une partie de la Rép.que Argentine comprenant les provinces de Corrientes et des Missions dressé sur les lieux en 1828.* Paris: F. G. Levrault.

Parker, T. A. (1976) Finding the Marvelous Spatuletail. *Birding* 8: 175.

Parker, T. A. (1981) Distribution and biology of the White-cheeked Cotinga *Zaratornis stresemanni*, a high Andean frugivore. *Bull. Brit. Orn. Club* 101: 256-265.

Parker, T. A. (1982a) First record of the Chilean Woodstar *Eulidia yarrellii* in Peru. *Bull. Brit. Orn. Club* 102: 86.

Parker, T. A. (1982b) Some observations of unusual rainforest and marsh birds in southeastern Peru. *Wilson Bull.* 94: 477-493.

Parker, T. A. (1983) Rediscovery of the Rufous-fronted Antthrush (*Formicarius rufifrons*) in southeastern Peru. *Gerfaut* 73: 287-289.

Parker, T. A., and Bailey, B. (1991) *A rapid biological assesssment of the Alto Madidi region, and adjacent areas in northern La Paz, Bolivia.* Washington, D.C.: Conservation International.

Parker, T. A., Bates, J. and Cox, G. (1992) Rediscovery of the Bolivian Recurvebill with notes on other little-known species of the Bolivian Andes. *Wilson Bull.* 104: 173-177.

Parker, T. A., Castillo U., A., Gell-Mann, M. and Rocha O., O. (1991) Records of new and unusual birds from northern Bolivia. *Bull. Brit. Orn. Club* 111: 120-138.

Parker, T. A., Hilty, S. and Robbins, M. (1976) Birds of El Triunfo cloud forest, Mexico, with notes on the Horned Guan and other species. *Amer. Birds* 30: 779-782.

Parker, T. A. and O'Neill, J. P. (1976) An introduction to bird finding in Peru. *Birding* 8: 140-144, 205-216..

Parker, T. A. and O'Neill, J. P. (1980) Notes on little known birds of the upper Urubamba valley, southern Peru. *Auk* 97: 167-176.

Parker, T. A. and Parker, S. A. (1982) Behavioural and distributional notes on some unusual birds of a lower montane cloud forest in Peru. *Bull. Brit. Orn. Club* 102: 63-70.

Parker, T. A., Parker, S. A. and Plenge, M. A. (1982) *An annotated checklist of Peruvian birds.* Vermillion, South Dakota: Buteo Books.

Parker, T. A. and Remsen, J. V. (1987) Fifty-two Amazonian bird species new to Bolivia. *Bull. Brit. Orn. Club* 107: 94-107.

Parker, T. A., Schulenberg, T. S., Graves, G. R. and Braun, M. J. (1985) The avifauna of the Huancabamba region, northern Peru. Pp.169-197 in P. A. Buckley, M. S. Foster, E. S. Morton, R. S. Ridgely and F. G. Buckley, eds. *Neotropical ornithology.* Washington, D.C.: American Ornithologists' Union (Orn. Monogr. 36).

Parker, T. A., Schulenberg, T. S., Kessler, M. and Wust, W. (1989) Species limits, natural history, and conservation of some endemic birds in north-west Peru. Unpublished.

Parker, T. A. and Willis, E. O. (ms) Notes on the grassland flycatchers *Euscarthmus rufomarginatus* and *Polystictus pectoralis*, with comments on the disastrous decline of South American savannas. Unpublished.

Parkes, K. C. (1990) Was the Socorro Mockingbird (*Mimodes graysoni*) a predator on small birds? *Wilson Bull.* 102: 317-320.

Partridge, W. H. (1956) Notes on the Brazilian Merganser in Argentina. *Auk* 73: 473-488.

Partridge, W. H. (1961) Aves de Misiones nuevas para Argentina. *Neotrópica* 7: 25-28, 58.

Paryski, P., Woods, C. A. and Sergile, F. (1989) Conservation strategies and the preservation of biological diversity in Haiti. Pp.855-878 in C. A. Woods, ed. *Biogeography of the West Indies.* Gainesville, Florida: Sandhill Crane Press.

Pässler, R. (1922) In der Umgebung Coronel's (Chile) beobachtete Vögel. Beschreibung der Nester und Eier Brutvögel. *J. Orn.* 70: 430-482.

Patzwahl, S. (1991) Vogelpark Walsrode places Spix's Macaw in breeding program. *AFA Watchbird* 18(3): 4, 7.

Paynter, R. A. (1955) The ornithogeography of the Yucatán Peninsula. *Peabody Mus. Nat. Hist. Bull.* 9.

Paynter, R. A., ed. (1968) *Check-list of birds of the world*, 14. Cambridge, Mass.: Museum of Comparative Zoology.

Paynter, R. A. (1972a) Biology and evolution of the *Atlapetes schistaceus* species-group (Aves: Emberizinae). *Bull. Mus. Comp. Zool.* 143: 297-320.

Paynter, R. A. (1972b) Notes on the furnariid *Automolus* (*Hylocryptus*) *erythrocephalus. Bull. Brit. Orn. Club* 92: 154-155.

Paynter, R. A. (1982) *Ornithological gazetteer of Venezuela.* Cambridge, Mass.: Museum of Comparative Zoology.

Paynter, R. A. (1985) *Ornithological gazetteer of Argentina.* Cambridge, Mass.: Museum of Comparative Zoology.

Paynter, R. A. (1988) *Ornithological gazetteer of Chile.* Cambridge, Mass.: Museum of Comparative Zoology.

Paynter, R. A. (1989) *Ornithological gazetteer of Paraguay.* Second edition. Cambridge, Mass.: Museum of Comparative Zoology.

Paynter, R. A. and Storer, R. W. (1970) *Check-list of birds of the world*, 13. Cambridge, Mass.: Museum of Comparative Zoology.

Paynter, R. A. and Traylor, M. A. (1977) *Ornithological gazetteer of Ecuador.* Cambridge, Mass.: Museum of Comparative Zoology.

Paynter, R. A. and Traylor, M. A. (1981) *Ornithological gazetteer of Colombia.* Cambridge, Mass.: Museum of Comparative Zoology.

Paynter, R. A. and Traylor, M. A. (1983) *Ornithological gazetteer of Peru.* Cambridge, Mass.: Museum of Comparative Zoology.

Paynter, R. A. and Traylor, M. A. (1991) *Ornithological gazetteer of Brazil.* Cambridge, Mass.: Museum of Comparative Zoology.

Paynter, R. A., Traylor, M. A. and Winter, B. (1975) *Ornithological gazetteer of Bolivia.* Cambridge, Mass.: Museum of Comparative Zoology.

Pearman, M. (1990) Behaviour and vocalizations of an undescribed canastero *Asthenes* sp. from Brazil. *Bull. Brit. Orn. Club* 110: 145-153.

Pellek, R. R. (1988) Misperceptions of deforestation in Haiti: problems of available data and methodology. *Ambio* 17: 245-246.

von Pelzeln, A. (1856) Neue und wenig gekannte Arten der Kaiserlichen ornithologischen Sammlung. *Sitzungsber. Akad. Wissensch. Wien Math.-natur. Kl.* 20(1): 153-166.

von Pelzeln, A. (1868-1871) *Zur Ornithologie Brasiliens: Resultate von Johann Natterers Reisen in den Jahren 1817 bis 1835.* Wien: A. Pichler's Witwe und Sohn.

von Pelzeln, A. (1872) Verzeichniss einer an Dr L. W. Schaufuss gelangten Sendung Vögel aus Neu-Freiburg in Brasilien. *Nunquam Otiosus* 2: 291-292.

Peña, L. E. (1961) Exploration in the Antofagasta range, with observations on the fauna and flora. [And] Results of research in the Antofagasta ranges of Chile and Bolivia. *Postilla* 49: 3-42 [and] 139-159.

de la Peña, M. R. (1977a) *Aves de la provincia de Santa Fe.* (Fasc. 2). Second edition. Santa Fe, Argentina: Librería y Editorial Castellvi.

de la Peña, M. R. (1977b) *Aves de la provincia de Santa Fe.* (Fasc. 3). Second edition. Santa Fe, Argentina: Librería y Editorial Castellvi.

de la Peña, M. R. (1985) *Guía de aves argentinas, 2. Falconiformes.* Santa Fe, Argentina: Fundación Banco Bica.

de la Peña, M. R. (1987) *Nidos y huevos de aves argentinas.* Santa Fe, Argentina: Talleres Gráficos de Imprenta Lux.

de la Peña, M. R. (1989) *Guia de aves argentinas, 4. Passeriformes.* Buenos Aires: Literature of Latin America.

Pereyra, J. A. (1923) Las aves de la región ribereña de la provincia de Buenos Aires. *Hornero* 3: 159-174.

Pereyra, C. B. (1927) Segunda lista de aves colectadas en la región ribereña de la provincia de Buenos Aires. *Hornero* 4: 23-34.

Pereyra, J. A. (1933) Nuestros tordos de bañado del género *Agelaius. Hornero* 5: 189-192.

Pereyra, J. A. (1937) Miscelánea ornitológica. *Hornero* 6: 437-449.

Pereyra, C. B. (1938) Aves de la zona ribereña nordeste de la provincia de Buenos Aires. *Mem. Jardín Zool. La Plata* 9: 1-304.

Pereyra, J. A. (1939) Miscelánea ornitológica. *Hornero* 7: 234-243.

Pereyra, J. A. (1942) Miscelánea ornitológica. Excursión a «Juan Gerónimo». *Hornero* 8: 218-231.

Pereyra, J. A. (1943) *Nuestras aves.* La Plata: Tailler de Impresiones Oficiales.

Pereyra, J. A. (1950) Las aves del territorio de Misiones. *An. Mus. Nahuel Huapí* 2: 3-38.

Pérez, J. and Eguiarte, L. E. (1989) Situación actual de tres especies del género *Amazona* (*A. ochrocephala, A. viridigenalis,* y *A. autumnalis*) en el noroeste de México. *Vida Silvestre Neotropical* 2: 63-67.

Pérez-Rivera, R. A. (1977a) Nuevos datos sobre la Paloma Sabanera. *Science-Ciencia* 4(3): 77-78.

Pérez-Rivera, R. A. (1977b) El "status" de la Paloma Sabanera (*Columba inornata wetmorei*) en Puerto Rico. *Science-Ciencia* 5(1): 39-40.

Pérez-Rivera, R. A. (1978) Preliminary work on the feeding habits, nesting habitat and reproductive activities of the Plain Pigeon (*Columba inornata wetmorei*) and the Red-necked Pigeon (*Columba squamosa*), sympatric species: and analysis of their interaction. *Science-Ciencia* 5(3): 89-98.

Pérez-Rivera, R. A. (1980) Algunas notas sobre la biología y estatus de la Mariquita (*Agelaius xanthomus*), con especial énfasis en la subespecie de Mona. [Humacao:] Universidad de Puerto Rico (Memorias del Segundo Coloquio sobre la Fauna de Puerto Rico).

Pérez-Rivera, R. A. (1981) Notas adicionales sobre la distribución geográfica de la Paloma Sabanera (*Columba inornata wetmorei*) en Puerto Rico. *Science-Ciencia* 8(2): 19-24.

Pérez-Rivera, R. A. (1983) Sobre el estatus de la Mariquita de Mona (*Agelaius xanthomus monensis*). [Humacao:] Universidad de Puerto Rico (Memorias del Cuarto Simposio sobre la Fauna de Puerto Rico y el Caribe, Septiembre 1983).

Pérez-Rivera, R. A. (1984) El estatus de la paloma sabanera (*Columba inornata wetmorei*) y de la calandria (*Icterus dominicensis portoricensis*) en las partes centrales de Puerto Rico. Humacao, Puerto Rico: Universidad de Puerto Rico, Colegio Universitario de Humacao (Memorias del Quinto Simposio de la Fauna de Puerto Rico y el Caribe).

Pérez-Rivera, R. A. (1985) Crianza y mantenimiento en cautiverio de una población de palomas sabaneras (*Columba inornata wetmorei*). Humacao, Puerto Rico: Universidad de Puerto Rico, Colegio Universitario de Humacao (Memorias del Sexto Simposio de la Fauna de Puerto Rico y el Caribe).

Pérez-Rivera, R. A. (1990) Sobre la situación de la Paloma Ceniza o Sabanera (*Columba inornata*) en las Antillas Mayores. *Science-Ciencia* 17(1): 21-25.

Pérez-Rivera, R. A. and Bonilla, G. (1982) Los huricanes: algunos de sus efectos sobre aves en Puerto Rico incluyendo sus patrones de comportamiento. Humacao, Puerto Rico: Universidad de Puerto Rico (Memorias del Tercero Simposio sobre la Fauna de Puerto Rico).

Pérez-Rivera, R. A. and Collazo Algarín, J. (1976) Ciclo de vida y algunos problemas a que se enfrenta la Paloma Sabanera de Puerto Rico. *Science-Ciencia* 4(1): 10-19.

Pérez-Rivera, R. A., Rodríguez, A., Ruiz, J. L. and Ruiz-Lebrón, C. (1988) Maintenance and captive breeding of the Puerto Rican Plain Pigeon (*Columba inornata wetmorei*). Humacao, Puerto Rico: Universidad de Puerto Rico, Colegio Universitario de Humacao, Departamento de Biología (Memorias del Octavo y Noveno Simposio sobre la Fauna de Puerto Rico y el Caribe).

Pérez-Rivera, R. A. and Ruiz-Lebrón, C. R. (1992) Situación actual de la población de palomas sabaneras (*Columba inornata wetmorei*) en Cidra, Puerto Rico. Humacao, Puerto Rico: Universidad de Puerto Rico, Colegio Universitario de Humacao, Departamento de Biología (Memorias del Décimo Simposio sobre la Flora y Fauna de Puerto Rico y el Caribe).

Peters, J. L. (1917) Birds of the northern coast of the Dominican Republic. *Bull. Mus. Comp. Zool.* 61: 391-426.

Peters, J. L. (1929) An ornithological survey in the Caribbean lowlands of Honduras. *Bull. Mus. Comp. Zool.* 69: 397-478.

Peters, J. L. (1931) *Check-list of birds of the world*, 1. Cambridge, Mass.: Museum of Comparative Zoology.

Peters, J. L. (1935) The range of *Amazona oratrix. Auk* 52: 449-450.

Peters, J. L. (1937) *Check-list of birds of the world*, 3. Cambridge, Mass.: Harvard University Press.

Peters, J. L. (1940) *Check-list of birds of the world*, 4. Cambridge, Mass.: Harvard University Press.

Peters, J. L. (1945) *Check-list of birds of the world*, 5. Cambridge, Mass.: Harvard University Press.

Peters, J. L. (1951) *Check-list of birds of the world*, 7. Cambridge, Mass.: Museum of Comparative Zoology.

Peters, J. L. and Griswold, J. A. (1943) Birds of the Harvard Peruvian expedition. *Bull. Mus. Comp. Zool.* 92: 279-327.

Peterson, R. T. and Chalif, E. L. (1973) *A field guide to Mexican birds*. Boston: Houghton Mifflin.

Phelps, W. H. (1897) Birds observed on a collecting trip to Bermudez, Venezuela. *Auk* 14: 357-371.

Phelps, W. H. (1948) Las aves de la isla La Blanquilla y de los Morros el Fondeadero y la Horquilla del Archipiélago de los Hermanos. *Bol. Soc. Ven. Cienc. Nat.* 11: 85-118.

Phelps, W. H. (1952) Informe del Comité Nacional Venezolano. *VI Bull. Internatn. Coun. Bird Preserv.*: 233-237.

Phelps, W. H. and Phelps, W. H. (1948) The discovery of the habitat of Gould's Hummingbird *Hylonympha macrocerca. Auk* 65: 62-66.

Phelps, W. H. and Phelps, W. H. (1950) Lista de las aves de Venezuela con su distribución. 2: passeriformes. *Bol. Soc. Venezolana Cienc. Nat.* 12.

Phelps, W. H. and Phelps, W. H. (1951) Las aves de Bonaire. *Bol. Soc. Venezolana Cienc. Nat.* 13: 161-187.

Phelps, W. H. and Phelps, W. H. (1958) Lista de las aves de Venezuela con su distribución, I: no passeriformes. *Bol. Soc. Venezolana Cienc. Nat.* 19.

Phelps, W. H. and Phelps, W. H. (1961) A new subspecies of warbler from Cerro de la Neblina, Venezuela, and notes. *Proc. Biol. Soc. Washington* 74: 245-247.

Phelps, W. H. and Phelps, W. H. (1962) Two new subspecies of birds from Venezuela, the rufous phase of *Pauxi pauxi*, and other notes. *Proc. Biol. Soc. Washington* 75: 199-204.

Phelps, W. H. and Phelps, W. H. (1963) Lista de las aves de Venezuela con su distribución, Parte II: Passeriformes, segunda edición. *Bol. Soc. Venezolana Cienc. Nat.* 24.

Philippi, R. A. (1858) Kurze Beschreibung einer neuen Chilenischen Ralle. *Arch. Naturges.* 24: 83-84.

Philippi, R. A. (1888) Der Wüste Atacama und der Provinz Tarapacá. *Ornis* 4: 155-160.

Philippi, R. A. and Landbeck, L. (1863) Beiträge zur Fauna von Peru. *Arch. Naturges.* 29: 119-138.

Philippi B., R. A. (1936) Aves de Arica y alredores (extremo norte de Chile). *Hornero* 6: 225-239.

Philippi B., R. A., Johnson, A. W. and Goodall, J. D. (1944) Expedición ornitológica al norte de Chile. *Bol. Mus. Nac. Hist. Nat. Chile* 22: 65-120.

Philippi B., R. A., Johnson, A. W., Goodall, J. D. and Bahn, F. (1954) Notas sobre aves de Magallanes y Tierra del Fuego. *Bol. Mus. Nac. Hist. Nat. Chile* 26(3): 1-65.

Philippi B., R. A. (1941) Notas sobre aves observadas en la provincia de Tarapacá. *Bol. Mus. Nac. Hist. Nat. Chile* 19: 43-77.

Philipson, W. R., Doncaster, C. C. and Idrobo, J. M. (1951) An expedition to the Sierra de la Macarena, Colombia. *Geogr. J.* 117: 188-199.

Phillips, A. R. (1966) Further systematic notes on Mexican birds. *Bull. Brit. Orn. Club* 86: 86-94, 103-112, 125-131.

Phillips, A. R. (1986) *The known birds of North and Middle America*, 1. Denver, Colorado: Allan R. Phillips.

Phillips, A., Marshall, J. and Monson, G. (1964) *The birds of Arizona*. Tucson: University of Arizona Press.

Phillips, J. C. (1911) A year's collecting in the state of Tamaulipas, Mexico. *Auk* 28: 67-89.

Phillips, J. C. (1929) An attempt to list the extinct and vanishing birds of the Western Hemisphere with some notes on recent status, location of specimens, etc. Pp.503-534 in F. Steinbacher, ed. *Verhandlungen des VI. Internationalen Ornithologen-Kongresses in Kopenhagen 1926*. Berlin: [no publisher given].

Pinchon, R. (1976) *Faune des Antilles Françaises: les oiseaux*. Second edition. Fort-de-France: [no publisher given].

Pineschi, R. B. (1990) Aves como dispersores de sete espécies de *Rapanea* (Myrsinaceae) no maciço do Itatiaia, estados do Rio de Janeiro e Minas Gerais. *Ararajuba* 1: 73-78.

Pinto, O. M. O. (1932) Resultados ornithológicos de uma excursão pelo oeste de Sao Paulo e sul de Matto-Grosso. *Revta. Mus. Paulista* 17(2): 689-826.

Pinto, O. M. O. (1935) Aves da Bahia. *Revta. Mus. Paulista* 19: 1-325.

Pinto, O. (1936) Contribuição à ornitologia de Goyaz. *Revta. Mus. Paulista* 20: 1-171.

Pinto, O. (1937) A rôlinha *Oxypelia cyanopis* Pelzeln, só conhecida do Brasil, é uma das aves mais raras que existem. *Bol. Biológico*, n.s. 3(5): 17-18.

Pinto, O. M. de O. (1938) Catálogo das aves do Brasil e lista dos exemplares que as representam no Museu Paulista. *Revta. Mus. Paulista* 22.

Pinto, O. (1940) Aves de Pernambuco. *Arq. Zool. São Paulo* 1: 219-282.

Pinto, O. (1941) Nova contribuição à ornitologia de Mato-Grosso. *Arq. Zool. São Paulo* 2: 1-37.

Pinto, O. (1943) Nova contribuição à ornitologia do Recôncavo (Baía). *Pap. Avuls. Dep. Zool. São Paulo* 3: 265-284.

Pinto, O. M. de O. (1944) *Catálogo das aves do Brasil*. 2a. Parte. São Paulo: Departamento do Zoologia.

Pinto, O. (1945) Cinqüenta anos de investigação ornitológica. *Arq. Zool. São Paulo* 4: 261-340.

Pinto, O. M. O. (1946) Aves brasileiras da família dos papagaios. *Relat. An. Inst. Bot. São Paulo*: 126-129.

Pinto, O. (1949) Esboço monográfico dos Columbidae brasileiros. *Arq. Zool. São Paulo* 7: 241-324.

Pinto, O. (1950a) Peter W. Lund e sua contribuição à ornitologia brasileira. *Pap. Avuls. Dep. Zool. São Paulo* 9: 269-283.

Pinto, O. (1950b) Miscelânea ornitológica, V. Descrição de uma nova subespécie nordestina em *Synallaxis ruficapilla* Vieillot (Fam. Furnariidae). *Pap. Avuls. Dep. Zool. São Paulo* 9: 361-364.

Pinto, O. (1950c) Miscelânea ornitológica, VI. Sobre a verdadeira pátria de *Anodorhynchus leari* Bonap. *Pap. Avuls. Dep. Zool. São Paulo* 9: 364-365.

Pinto, O. (1951) Aves do Itatiaia. *Pap. Avuls. Dep. Zool. São Paulo* 10: 155-208.

Pinto, O. (1952) Súmula histórica e sistemática da ornitologia de Minas-Gerais. *Arq. Zool. São Paulo* 8: 1-51.

Pinto, O. M. de O. (1952) Redescobrimento de *Mitu mitu* (Linné) no nordeste do Brasil (est. de Alagoas). Provada a independência de *Mitu tuberosus* (Spix) como espécie à parte. *Pap. Avuls. Dep. Zool. São Paulo* 10: 325-334.

Pinto, O. (1954a) Resultados ornitológicos de duas viagens científicas ao estado de Alagoas. *Pap. Avuls. Dep. Zool. São Paulo* 12: 1-98.

Pinto, O. (1954b) Aves do Itatiaia. Lista remissiva e novas achegas à avifauna da região. *Bol. Parq. Nac. Itatiaia* no.3.

Pinto, O. M. de O. (1964) *Ornitología brasiliense*, 1. São Paulo: Departamento de Zoologia da Secretária de Agricultura do Estado de São Paulo.

Pinto, O. M. de O. (1978) *Novo catálogo das aves do Brasil*. Primeira parte. São Paulo: Empresa Gráfica da Revista dos Tribunais.

Pinto, O. M. O. (1979) A ornitologia do Brasil através das idades (Século XVI a Século XIX). *Brasiliensia Documenta* 13: 1-117.
Pinto, O. M. O. and de Camargo, E. A. (1948) Sobre uma coleção de aves do Rio das Mortes (estado de Mato Grosso). *Pap. Avuls. Dep. Zool. São Paulo* 8: 287-336.
Pinto, O. M. O. and de Camargo, E. A. (1952) Nova contribuição à ornitologia do Rio das Mortes. *Pap. Avuls. Dep. Zool. São Paulo* 10: 213-234.
Pinto, O. M. O. and de Camargo, E. A. (1955) Lista anotada de aves colecionadas nos limites occidentais do Estado do Paraná. *Pap. Avuls. Dep. Zool. São Paulo* 12: 215-234.
Pinto, O. M. O. and de Camargo, E. A. (1957) Sobre uma coleção de aves da região de Cachimbo (sul do estado do Pará). *Pap. Avuls. Dep. Zool. São Paulo* 13: 51-69.
Pinto, O. M. O. and de Camargo, E. A. (1961) Resultados ornitólogicos de quatro recentes expedições do Departamento de Zoologia ao Nordeste do Brasil, com descrição de seis novas subespecies. *Arq. Zool. São Paulo* 11: 193-284.
Pitelka, F. A. (1947) Taxonomy and distribution of the Mexican Sparrow *Xenospiza baileyi*. *Condor* 49: 199-203.
Plath, K. (1930) Mr Karl Plath's collection. *Avicult. Mag.* (4)8: 134-135.
Plath, K. (1934) Notes from a Chicago aviary. *Avicult. Mag.* (4)12: 33-41.
Plath, K. (1937) The birds at the New Chicago Zoological Park. *Avicult. Mag.* (5)2: 285-293.
Plath, K. (1969) The Spix Macaw, or Little Blue Macaw (*Ara spixii*). *Avicult. Mag.* 75: 139-140.
Plenge, M. A. (1979) Type specimens of birds in the Museo de Historia Natural "Javier Prado", Lima, Peru. *Occas. Pap. Mus. Zool. Louisiana State Univ.* 53.
Plimpton, G. (1977) Un gran pedazo de carne. *Audubon* 79(6): 10-25.
PM (1988) = Petróleos Mexicanos (1988) *México: atlas de carreteras y ciudades turísticas*. Second edition. México, D.F.: HFET Cartografia y Servicios Editoriales.
Podolsky, R. and Kress, S. W. (1992) Attraction of the endangered Dark-rumped Petrel to recorded vocalizations in the Galápagos Islands. *Condor* 94: 448-453.
Podtiaguin, B. (1941-1945) Catálogo sistemático de las aves del Paraguay. *Revta. Soc. Cient. Paraguay* 5(5): 3-109; 6(3): 7-119; 6(6): 63-79.
Poole, P. (1990) *Desarrollo de trabajo conjunto entre pueblos indígenas, conservacionistas y planificadores del uso de la tierra en América Latina*. Turrialba, Costa Rica: CATIE.
Porter, S. (1929) In search of the Imperial Parrot. *Avicult. Mag.* (4)7: 240-246, 267-275.
Porter, S. (1930a) Notes on the rare parrots of the genus *Amazona*. *Avicult. Mag.* (4)8: 2-12.
Porter, S. (1930b) Bouquet's Parrot (*Amazona bouqueti*). *Avicult. Mag.* (4)8: 36-44.
Porter, S. (1930c) Notes on the birds of Dominica. *Avicult. Mag.* (4)8: 114-126, 146-158.
Porter, S. (1938) Notes from South America. *Avicult. Mag.* (5)3: 207-213, 245-254, 289-298.
Post, W. (1981) Biology of the Yellow-shouldered Blackbird – *Agelaius* on a tropical island. *Bull. Florida State Mus., Biol. Sci.* 26: 125-202.
Post, W. and Wiley, J. W. (1976) The Yellow-shouldered Blackbird – present and future. *Amer. Birds* 30: 13-20.
Post, W. and Wiley, J. W. (1977) Reproductive interactions of the shiny cowbird and the yellow-shouldered blackbird. *Condor* 79: 176-184.
de las Pozas, G. and González, H. (1984) Disminución de los sitios de nidificación de cotorra y catey (Aves: Psittacidae) por la tala de palmas en Ciénaga de Zapata, Cuba. *Misc. Zool. Acad. Cienc. Cuba* 18: 4.
Pratt, J. D., Bruner, P. L. and Berrett, D. G. (1987) *A field guide to the birds of Hawaii and the tropical Pacific*. Princeton: Princeton University Press.
Pregill, G. K. and Olson, S. L. (1981) Zoogeography of West Indian vertebrates in relation to Pleistocene climate cycles. *Ann. Rev. Ecol. Syst.* 12: 75-98.
Prestwich, A. A. (1930a) The foreign birds at the Crystal Palace. *Avicult. Mag.* (4)8: 70-74.
Prestwich, A. A. (1930b) The new parrot house at London Zoological Gardens. *Avicult. Mag.* (4)8: 215-218.
Prestwich, A. A. (1931) The foreign birds at the Crystal Palace. *Avicult. Mag.* (4)9: 74-79.
Pulich, W. M. (1976) *The Golden-cheeked Warbler*. Austin, Texas: Texas Parks and Wildlife Department.

Pulido, V. (1991) *El libro rojo de la fauna silvestre del Perú*. Lima: Maijosa Editorial.
Quinn, W. H., Neal, V. T. and Antunez de Mayolo, S. E. (1987) El Niño occurrences over the past four and a half centuries. *J. Geophys. Res.* 92(C13): 14449-14461.
Radtke, G. A. (1991) Haltung und Zucht des Kapuzenzeisigs (*Spinus cucullatus*). *Voliere* 14: 59-61.
Raffaele, H. A. (1983) The raising of a ghost – *Spinus cucullatus* in Puerto Rico. *Auk* 100: 737-739.
Raffaele, H. A. (1989) *A guide to the birds of Puerto Rico and the Virgin Islands*. Revised edition. San Juan: Fondo Educativo Interamericano.
Rahbek, C., Bloch, H., Poulsen, M. K. and Rasmussen, J. F. (1989) *Zoologisk Museums ornithologiske ekspedition til Sydamerikas Andesbjerge 1989*. Copenhagen: Zoological Museum, University of Copenhagen.
Rand, D. M. and Paynter, R. A. (1981) *Ornithological gazetteer of Uruguay*. Cambridge, Mass.: Museum of Comparative Zoology.
Rands, M. and Foster, M. (1989) ICBP in the Americas. *World Birdwatch* 11(3): 6-8.
Redford, K. H. (1985) Emas National Park and the plight of the Brazilian cerrados. *Oryx* 19: 210-214.
Redford, K. H. (1987) Parque das Emas. *Ciencia Hoje* 7(38):42-48.
Redford, K. H. (1989) Monte Pascoal – indigenous rights and conservation in conflict. *Oryx* 23: 33-36.
Reed, C. S. (1916) *Las aves de la provincia de Mendoza, 1. (Lista sistemática)*. Mendoza, Argentina: Museo Educacional de Mendoza.
Reed, E. C. (1877) Apuntes de la zoología de la Hacienda de Cauquenes, provincia de Colchagua. *An. Univ. Chile* 49: 535-569.
Regalado Ruíz, P. (1981) El género *Torreornis* (Aves: Fringillidae), descripción de una nueva subespecie en Cayo Coco, Cuba. *Centro Agrícola* 2: 87-112.
Reichenow, A. (1882) *Conspectus Psittacorum: Systematische Uebersicht aller bekannten Papageienarten*. Berlin: published by the author.
Reichholf, J. (1974) Artenreichtum, Häufigkeit und Diversität der Greifvögel in einigen Gebieten von Südamerika. *J. Orn.* 115: 381-397.
Reijns, P. and van der Salm, J. (1980) Het voorkomen en voedsel van *Amazona barbadensis rothschildi* op Bonaire. Unpublished.
Reijns, P. J. and van der Salm, J. N. C. (1981) Some ecological aspects of the Yellow-shouldered Amazon (*Amazona barbadensis rothschildi*). Pp.227-231 in R. F. Pasquier, ed. *Conservation of New World parrots*. Washington, D.C.: Smithsonian Institution Press for the International Council for Bird Preservation (Techn. Publ. 1).
Reinhardt, J. (1870) Bidrag til kundskab om fuglefaunaen i Brasiliens campos. *Vidensk. Meddel. Naturhist. Foren. Kjöbenhavn*: 1-124, 315-457.
Reiser, O. (1926) Liste der Vogelarten welche auf der von der Kaiserl. Akademie der Wissenschaften 1903 nach Nordostbrasilien entsendeten Expedition unter Leitung des Herrn Hofrates Dr F. Steindachner gesammelt wurden. [And] Vögel. *Denkschr. Akad. Wiss. Wien, math.-naturwiss. Kl.* 76: 55-100 [and] 107-252.
Remsen, J. V. (1986a) Aves de una localidad en la sabana húmeda del norte de Bolivia. *Ecol. Bolivia* 8: 21-35.
Remsen, J. V. (1986b) Was Bachman's Warbler a bamboo specialist? *Auk* 103: 216-219.
Remsen, J. V., Parker, T. A. and Ridgely, R. S. (1982) Natural history notes on some poorly known Bolivian birds. *Gerfaut* 72: 77-87.
Remsen, J. V. and Quintela, C. E. (unpublished) A preliminary conservation strategy for the birds of Bolivia.
Remsen, J. V. and Ridgely, R. S. (1980) Additions to the avifauna of Bolivia. *Condor* 82: 69-75.
Remsen, J. V., Schmitt, C. G. and Schmitt, D. C. (1988) Natural history notes on some poorly known Bolivian birds. Part 3. *Gerfaut* 78: 363-381.
Remsen, J. V. and Traylor, M. A. (1983) Additions to the avifauna of Bolivia, part 2. *Condor* 85: 95-98.
Remsen, J. V. and Traylor, M. A. (1989) *An annotated list of the birds of Bolivia*. Vermillion, South Dakota: Buteo Books.
Remsen, J. V., Traylor, M. A. and Parkes, K. C. (1985) Range extensions for some Bolivian birds, 1 (Tinamiformes to Charadriiformes). *Bull. Brit. Orn. Club* 105: 124-130.

Remsen, J. V., Traylor, M. A. and Parkes, K. C. (1986) Range extensions for some Bolivian birds, 2 (Columbidae to Rhinocryptidae). *Bull. Brit. Orn. Club* 106: 22-32.

Renard, A. (1924) Notas sobre aves de la provincia de Santa Fe. *Hornero* 3: 286-287.

Renjifo, L. M. (1988) *Composición y estructura de la comunidad aviaria de bosque andino primario y secundario en la reserva del Alto Quindío "Acaime", Colombia.* Dissertation, Universidad Javeriana, Bogotá.

Renjifo, L. M. (1991) Evaluación del estatus de la avifauna amenazada del Alto Quindío. Informe final. Unpublished.

Ress, P. E. (1987) A tale of two parrots...or the real macaw. *IUCN Bull.* 18(4-6): 3-4.

Restrepo, C. (1990) Ecology and cooperative breeding in a frugivorous bird, *Semnornis ramphastinus.* M.Sc. thesis, University of Florida, Gainesville.

Reynard, G. B. (1962) The rediscovery of the Puerto Rican Whip-poor-will. *Living Bird* 1: 51-60.

Reynard, G. B. (1988) Some rare birds in the Greater Antilles, lost and found. *Gosse Bird Club Broadsheet* no.51: 8-9.

Reynard, G. B., Short, L. L., Garrido, O. H., and Alayón García, G. (1987) Nesting, voice, status, and relationships of the endemic Cuban Gundlach's Hawk (*Accipiter gundlachi*). *Wilson Bull.* 99: 73-77.

Ribeiro, A. de M. (1920) Revisão dos psittacídeos brasileiros. *Revta. Mus. Paulista* 12(2): 1-82.

Ribeiro, A. de M. (1927) Notas ornithologicas vi–a. *Bol. Mus. Nac. Rio de Janeiro* 3: 19-37.

Ribeiro, C. (1990a) *Rhopornis ardesiaca*, a ave que se esconde. *Ciência Hoje* 11(66): 62.

Ribeiro, C. (1990b) The Bahia blues. *BBC Wildlife* 8: 433-435.

Richmond, C. W. (1895) Partial list of birds collected at Alta Mira, Mexico, by Mr Frank B. Armstrong. *Proc. U.S. Natn. Mus.* 18: 627-632.

Richmond, C. W. (1898) Description of a new species of *Gymnostinops*. *Auk* 15: 326-327.

Ridgely, R. S. (1979) The status of Brazilian parrots – a preliminary report. Unpublished.

Ridgely, R. S. (1980) Notes on some rare or previously unrecorded birds in Ecuador. *Amer. Birds* 34: 242-248.

Ridgely, R. S. (1981a) The current distribution and status of mainland Neotropical parrots. Pp.233-384 in R. F. Pasquier, ed. *Conservation of New World parrots.* Washington, D.C.: Smithsonian Institution Press for the International Council for Bird Preservation (Techn. Publ. 1).

Ridgely, R. S. (1981b) *A guide to the birds of Panama.* Princeton: Princeton University Press.

Ridgely, R. S. (1983) Hyacinth Macaw and Brazil's Pantanal. *Birding* 15: 179-185.

Ridgely, R. S. (1989) First among parrots: Hyacinth Macaws in the wild. *Birds Internatn.* 1: 9-17.

Ridgely, R. S. and Gaulin, J. C. (1980) The birds of Finca Merenberg, Huila department, Colombia. *Condor* 82: 379-391.

Ridgely, R. S. and Gwynne, J. A. (1989) *A guide to the birds of Panama with Costa Rica, Nicaragua, and Honduras.* Second edition. Princeton: Princeton University Press.

Ridgely, R. S. and Robbins, M. B. (1988) *Pyrrhura orcesi*, a new parakeet from southwestern Ecuador, with systematic notes on the *P. melanura* complex. *Wilson Bull.* 100: 173-182.

Ridgely, R. S. and Tudor, G. (1989) *The birds of South America*, 1. Austin: University of Texas Press.

Ridgway, R. (1884) On a new *Carpodectes* from south-western Costa Rica. *Ibis* (5)2: 27-28.

Ridgway, R. (1887a) Description of a new species of cotinga from the Pacific coast of Costa Rica. *Proc. U.S. Natn. Mus.* 10: 1-2.

Ridgway, R. (1887b) Description of the adult female of *Carpodectes antoniae* Zeledon; with critical remarks, notes on habits, etc., by José C. Zeledon. *Proc. U.S. Natn. Mus.* 10: 20.

Ridgway, R. (1887c) The Imperial Woodpecker (*Campephilus imperialis*) in northern Sonora. *Auk* 4: 161.

Ridgway, R. (1895) Description of a new species of ground warbler from eastern Mexico. *Proc. U.S. Natn. Mus.* 18: 119-120.

Ridgway, R. (1901) The birds of North and Middle America. *Bull. U.S. Natn. Mus.* 50(1).

Ridgway, R. (1904) The birds of North and Middle America. *Bull. U.S. Natn. Mus.* 50(3).

Ridgway, R. (1914) The birds of North and Middle America. *Bull. U.S. Natn. Mus.* 50(6).

Ridgway, R. (1916) The birds of North and Middle America. *Bull. U.S. Natn. Mus.* 50(7).

Ridgway, R. and Friedmann, H. (1941) The birds of North and Middle America. *U.S. Natn. Mus. Bull.* 50(9).

Riker, C. B. and Chapman, F. M. (1890-1891) A list of birds observed at Santarem, Brazil. *Auk* 7: 131-137, 265-271; 8: 24-31, 158-164.

Ríos, E. and Zardini, E. (1989) Conservation of biological diversity in Paraguay. *Conserv. Biol.* 3: 118-120.

Ripley, S. D. (1957) Notes on the Horned Coot *Fulica cornuta. Postilla* 30.

Ripley, S. D. (1977) *Rails of the world.* Toronto: M. F. Feheley.

Ripley, S. D. and Beehler, B. M. (1985) Rails of the world, a compilation of new information, 1975-1983 (Aves: Rallidae). *Smithson. Contrib. Zool.* 417.

Ripley, S. D. and Watson, G. E. (1956) Cuban bird notes. *Postilla* 26.

Rivera-Milán, F. F. (1992) Distribution and relative abundance patterns of columbids in Puerto Rico. *Condor* 94: 224-238.

Rivero M., A. (1983) *El Cardinalito de Venezuela: ecología y comportamiento en la región centro occidental.* Barquisimeto: [apparently privately printed].

Riveros Salcedo, J. C., Sánchez S., R. and Ascensios V., D. (1991) Distribución y status del Pachaloro *Forpus xanthops*. Resúmenes del IV Congreso de Ornitología Neotropical, 3-9 de Noviembre 1991, Quito, Ecuador (resumen 160).

Riviere, S. D., Clubb, S. L. and Clubb, K. J. (1986) The elusive Caninde. *AFA Watchbird* 13(1): 6-9.

Rizzini, C. T. (1979) *Tratado de fitogeografia do Brasil*, 2. São Paulo: HUCITEC, Editora da Universidade de São Paulo.

Robbins, M. B. and Parker, T. A. (unpublished) Comments on St Lucia Nightjar *Caprimulgus otiosus.*

Robbins, M. B. and Ridgely, R. S. (1990) The avifauna of an upper tropical cloud forest in southwestern Ecuador. *Proc. Acad. Nat. Sci. Philadelphia* 142: 59-71.

Robbins, M. B., Ridgely, R. S., Schulenberg, T. S. and Gill, F. B. (1987) The avifauna of the Cordillera de Cutucú, Ecuador, with comparisons to other Andean localities. *Proc. Acad. Nat. Sci. Philadelphia* 139: 243-259.

Robiller, F. (1990) *Papageien, 3: Mittel- und Süd-amerika.* Berlin: Deutscher Landwirtschaftsverlag, and Stuttgart: Verlag Eugen Ulmer.

Robiller, F. Maxion, I. and Neumann, N. (1988) Der Rotohrara *Ara rubrogenys* (Lafresnaye, 1847). *Papageien* 1/88: 9-11.

Robiller, F. and Trogisch, K. (1984) Seltenheitszucht der Rotscheitel-Amazone (*Amazona dufresniana rhodocorytha*). *Gefied. Welt* 108: 248-250.

Robins, C. R. and Heed, W. B. (1951) Bird notes from La Joya de Salas, Tamaulipas. *Wilson Bull.* 63: 263-270.

Robinson, F. (1986) Introduction. Pp.4-7 in F. Robinson, ed. Río Mazan project. 1986 report. Oxford: Department of Plant Sciences, University of Oxford, unpublished.

Robinson, F., ed. (1988) Río Mazan project report, 1987. Oxford: Department of Plant Sciences, University of Oxford.

Robinson, W. and Richmond, C. W. (1895) An annotated list of the birds observed on the island of Margarita, and at Guanta and Laguayra, Venezuela. *Proc. U.S. Natn. Mus.* 18: 649-685.

Rocha O., O. (1990a) *Diagnóstico de los recursos naturales de la Reserva Nacional de Fauna Andina Eduardo Avaroa.* La Paz, Bolivia: Instituto de Ecología, Museo de Historia Natural, y Centro de Estudios Ecológicos y de Desarrollo Integral.

Rocha O., O. (1990b) Avifauna de la Reserva Nacional de Fauna Andina "Eduardoavaroa" [*sic*]. *Mus. Nac. Hist. Nat. (Bolivia) Com.* no.9: 54-64.

Rocha O., O. (1990c) Lista preliminar de aves de la Reserva de la Biosfera "Estación Biológica Beni". *Ecología en Bolivia* no.15: 57-68.

Röder, J. (1990) Beobachtungen bei der Haltung und Zucht des Grünkardinals. *Voliere* 13: 184-186.

Rodrigues, M. and Silva, W. R. (1991) Notes on threatened and rare tanagers of southeastern Brazil. Unpublished.

Rodríguez, D. and Sánchez, B. (1991) Ecología de las palomas terrestres cubanas (géneros: *Geotrygon* y *Starnoenas*). Unpublished.

Rodriguez-Estrella, R., Mata, E. and Rivera, L. (1992) Ecological notes on the Green Parakeet of Isla Socorro, Mexico. *Condor* 94: 523-525.

Rodríguez-M., J. V. (1982) *Aves del Parque Nacional Los Katíos.* Bogotá: INDERENA.

Rodríguez, J. V. and Hernández Camacho, J. (1988) La familia Psittacidae en Colombia: una aproximación del conocimiento de su estado actual. Unpublished.

Rodríguez Vidal, J. A. (1962) La Cotorra Puertorriqueña (*Amazona vittata vittata* Boddaert). *Revta. Agric. Puerto Rico* 49: 67-79.

Roet, E. C., Mack, D. S. and Duplaix, N. (1981) Psittacines imported by the United States (October 1979–June 1980). Pp.21-55 in R. F. Pasquier, ed. *Conservation of New World parrots*. Washington, D.C.: Smithsonian Institution Press for the International Council for Bird Preservation (Techn. Publ. 1).

Rojas, F. (1991) Biología reproductiva de la cotorra: *Amazona barbadensis* (Aves: Psittaciformes) en la Península de Macanao, Edo. Nueva Esparta. Lic. Biol. thesis, Universidad Central de Venezuela.

Romero, R. (1974a) The Red-fronted Macaw: one of the rarest psittacines in the world. *Game Bird Breeder's Gazette* 34: 38.

Romero, R. (1974b) Notes on the Red-fronted or Red-cheeked Macaw *Ara rubrogenys*. *Avicult. Mag.* 80: 131.

Romero-Zambrano, H. (1983) Revisión del status zoogeográfico y redescripción de *Odontophorus strophium* (Gould) (Aves: Phasianidae). *Caldasia* 13: 777-786.

Rooth, J. (1968) Over het voorkomen van de Geelvleugelamazone, *Amazona barbadensis rothschildi*, op Bonaire. *Ardea* 56: 280-283.

Rosenberg, D. K., Valle, C. A., Coulter, M. C. and Harcourt, S. A. (1990) Monitoring Galápagos Penguins and Flightless Cormorants in the Galápagos Islands. *Wilson Bull.* 102: 525-532.

van Rossem, A. J. (1934) Critical notes on Middle American birds. *Bull. Mus. Comp. Zool.* 77: 387-490.

van Rossem, A. J. (1945) A distributional survey of the birds of Sonora, Mexico. *Occas. Pap. Mus. Zool. Louisiana State Univ.* 21.

Roth, P. (1985) Notes on Spix's Macaw and observations on some other bird species of northeastern Brazil. Report on the excursion in search of Spix's Macaw, June 22 to July 24, 1985. Unpublished.

Roth, P. (1986) Report on the second half of the project in search of Spix's Macaw. Unpublished.

Roth, P. (1987a) A last chance to save Spix's Macaw. *Oryx* 21: 73.

Roth, P. (1987b) Bericht über die Reise vom 28 April bis zum 10 Mai 1987 in die Region von Curaçá. *Zoologische Gesellschaft für Arten- und Populationsschutz Mitglieder Information* Oktober 1987 [:5-7].

Roth, P. (1987c) Ararinha azul: a um passo da extinção. *Ciência Hoje* 5(30): 74.

Roth, P. (1987d) Distribution, actual status and biology of Spix's Macaw *Cyanopsitta spixii*: report on the 1987 activities. Unpublished.

Roth, P. (1988a) Distribution, biology and actual status of Spix's Macaw. Unpublished.

Roth, P. (1988b) Populations, actual status and biology of Spix's Macaw (*Cyanopsitta spixii*). Unpublished.

Roth, P. (1988c) Der Hyazinth-Ara *Anodorhynchus hyacinthinus*. *Zool. Soc. Conserv. Species and Popul.* [Newssheet]

Roth, P. (1989a) Der Hyazinthara *Anodorhynchus hyacinthinus*. *Papageien* 1/89: 20-24.

Roth, P. (1989b) Spix's Macaw: population, actual status and biology of Spix's Macaw *Cyanopsitta spixii*. Unpublished.

Roth, P. (1990) Spix-Ara *Cyanopsitta spixii*: was wissen wir heute über diese seltenen Vögel? Bericht über ein 1985-1988 durchgeführtes Projekt. *Papageien* 3/90: 86-88; 4/90: 121-125.

Rothschild, W. (1896) [Several examples of *Loddigesia mirabilis* collected by Baron at Chachapoyas]. *Ibis* (7)2: 567.

Rothschild, W. (1905) [Extinct parrots from the West Indies.] *Bull. Brit. Orn. Club* 16: 13-15.

Rowley, J. S. (1966) Breeding records of birds of the Sierra Madre del Sur, Oaxaca, Mexico. *Proc. West. Found. Vert. Zool.* 1: 107-204.

Rowley, J. S. (1984) Breeding records of land birds in Oaxaca, Mexico. *Proc. West. Found. Vert. Zool.* 2: 73-221.

Rowley, J. S. and Orr, R. T. (1964) A new hummingbird from southern Mexico. *Condor* 66: 81-84.

Rumboll, M. A. E. (1990) Tres aves nuevas para la Argentina. *Nuestras Aves* 22(8): 28.

Ruschi, A. (1953) Lista das aves do estado do Espírito Santo. *Bol. Mus. Biol. Prof. Mello Leitão*, Sér. Zool. no.11.

Ruschi, A. (1961) A coleção viva de Trochilidae do Museu de Biologia Prof. Mello Leitão, nos anos de 1934 até 1961. *Bol. Mus. Biol. Prof. Mello Leitão*, Sér. Biol. no.30.

Ruschi, A. (1964) Nidificação de *Loddigesia mirabilis* (Bourcier) em cativeiro e algumas observações sobre sua hibridação com *Myrtis fanny fanny* (Lesson). *Bol. Mus. Biol. Prof. Mello Leitão*, Sér. Biol. no.43.

Ruschi, A. (1965a) A atual distribuição geográfica de *Loddigesia mirabilis* (Bourcier) e algumas observações a seu respeito. *Bol. Mus. Biol. Prof. Mello Leitão*, Sér. Biol. no.46.

Ruschi, A. (1965b) O beija-flor *Ramphodon dohrnii* e o perigo iminente de sua extinção. *Bol. Mus. Biol. Prof. Mello Leitão*, Sér. Prot. Nat. no.26.

Ruschi, A. (1967) Beija-flores raros ou ameaçados de extinção. *Bol. Mus. Biol. Prof. Mello Leitão*, Sér. Prot. Nat. no.29.

Ruschi, A. (1969) As aves do recinto da sede do Museu de Biologia Prof. Mello Leitão, na cidade de Santa Teresa, observadas durante o ano de 1968-1969, e a influência das áreas circunvizinhas. *Bol. Mus. Biol. Prof. Mello Leitão*, Série Prot. Nat. no.31.

Ruschi, A. (1974) Beija-flores do Brasil–II. Gêneros: *Doryfera* e *Ramphodon*. *Bol. Mus. Biol. Prof. Mello Leitão*, Sér. Zool. no.76.

Ruschi, A. (1979) *Aves do Brasil*. São Paulo: Editora Rios.

Ruschi, A. (1982) *Beija-flores do estado do Espírito Santo*. São Paulo: Editora Rios.

Russell, S. M. (1964) *A distributional study of the birds of British Honduras*. American Ornithologists' Union (*Orn. Monogr.* 1).

Russell, S. M., Barlow, J. C. and Lamm, D. W. (1979) Status of some birds on Isla San Andres and Isla Providencia, Colombia. *Condor* 81: 98-100.

Rutten, M. G. (1931) Over de vogels van de Hollandsche Benedenwindsche Eilanden (Antillen). *Ardea* 20: 91-143.

Rutten, M. (1934) Observations on Cuban birds. *Ardea* 23: 109-126.

Sada, A. M. (1987) Locating the Maroon-fronted Parrot (*Rhynchopsitta terrisi*) in Nuevo León. *MBA "Bulletin Board"* 1(87-3): 1-2.

Saibene, C. (1985) Registros nuevos para el Chaco. *Nuestras Aves* 3(7): 6.

de Saint-Hilaire, A. (1830) *Voyage dans les provinces de Rio de Janeiro et de Minas Gerais*. Paris: Grimbert et Dorez.

de Saint-Hilaire, A. (1833) *Voyage dans le district des diamans et sur le littoral du Brésil*. Paris: Librairie-Gide.

de Saint-Hilaire, A. (1851) *Voyage dans les provinces de Saint-Paul et de Sainte-Catherine*, 2. Paris: Arthus Bertrand.

Salmon, L. (1986) Ring-tailed Pigeons. *Gosse Bird Club Broadsheet* no.46: 9.

Salvador, S., Narosky, S. and Fraga, R. (1986) First description of the nest and eggs of the Rufous-throated Dipper (*Cinclus schulzi*) in northwestern Argentina. *Gerfaut* 76: 63-66.

Salvadori, T. (1891) *Catalogue of birds in the British Museum*, 20. London: Taylor and Francis (printed by order of the Trustees).

Salvadori, T. (1893) *Catalogue of birds in the British Museum*, 21. London: Taylor and Francis (printed by order of the Trustees).

Salvadori, T. (1895a) *Catalogue of birds in the British Museum*, 27. London: Taylor and Francis (printed by order of the Trustees).

Salvadori, T. (1895b) Viaggio del dott. Alfredo Borelli nella Republica Argentina e nel Paraguay. Uccelli raccolti nel Paraguay, nel Matto Grosso, nel Tucuman e nella Provincia di Salta. *Boll. Mus. Zool. Anat. Comp. Torino* 10(208): 1-24.

Salvadori, T. (1906) Notes on the parrots. *Ibis* (8)6: 124-130, 326-332, 451-464, 642-659.

Salvadori, T. and Festa, E. (1899) Viaggio del Dr Enrico Festa nell' Ecuador, 2. Passeres clamatores. *Boll. Mus. Zool. Anat. Comp. Torino* 15(362): 1-34.

Salvadori, T. and Festa, E. (1900) Viaggio del Dr Enrico Festa nell' Ecuador, 3. Trochili–Tinami. *Boll. Mus. Zool. Anat. Comp. Torino* 15(368): 1-54.

Salvin, O. (1860) History of the Derbyian Mountain-pheasant (*Oreophasis derbianus*). *Ibis* 2: 248-253.

Salvin, O. (1867) On some collections of birds from Veragua. Part 1. *Proc. Zool. Soc. London*: 129-161.

Salvin, O. (1870) On some collections of birds from Veragua. Part 2. *Proc. Zool. Soc. London*: 175-219.

Salvin, O. (1872) Notes on the birds of Nicaragua, based upon a collection made at Chontales by Mr Thomas Belt. *Ibis* (3)2: 311-323.
Salvin, O. (1876) On some new species of birds from western Ecuador. *Ibis* (3)6: 493-496.
Salvin, O. (1883) A list of the birds collected by Captain A. H. Markham on the west coast of America. *Proc. Zool. Soc. London*: 419-432.
Salvin, O. (1885) A list of the birds obtained by Mr Henry Whitely in British Guiana. *Ibis* (5)3: 195-219, 291-305.
Salvin, O. (1889) A list of the birds of the islands of the coast of Yucatan and of the Bay of Honduras. *Ibis* (6)1: 359-379.
Salvin, O. (1893) [Descriptions of two new species of *Metallura* from Ecuador.] *Bull. Brit. Orn. Club* 1: 49-50.
Salvin, O. (1895) On birds collected in Peru by Mr O. T. Baron. *Novit. Zool.* 2: 1-22.
Salvin, O. (1896) [Description of a new species of hummingbird from northern Peru.] *Bull. Brit. Orn. Club* 4: 24-25.
Salvin, O. (1897) [Descriptions of five species of South American birds.] *Bull. Brit. Orn. Club* 5: 15-17.
Salvin, O. and Godman, F. D. (1888-1904) *Biologia Centrali-Americana. Aves* 2. London: privately published.
Salvin, O. and Hartert, E. (1892) *Catalogue of the birds in the British Museum*, 16. London: Taylor and Francis (printed by order of the Trustees).
Sánchez Labrador, J. (1767) *Peces y aves del Paraguay natural ilustrado*, ed. M. N. Castex (1968). Buenos Aires: Compañia General Fabril Editora.
Santaella, L. and Sada, A. M. (1991) The avifauna of the Revillagigedo Islands, Mexico: additional data and observations. *Wilson Bull.* 103: 668-675.
Santana, E. C. (1991) Nature conservation and sustainable development in Cuba. *Conserv. Biol.* 5: 13-16.
Santos, E. (1955) *O amador de pássaros, captura, manutenção e criação.* Rio de Janeiro: F. Briguiet.
Schäfer, E. (1953) Estudio bio-ecológico comparativo sobre algunos Cracidae del norte y centro de Venezuela. *Bol. Soc. Venezolana Cienc. Nat.* 15: 30-63.
Schäfer, E and Phelps, W. H. (1954) Las aves del Parque Nacional "Henri Pittier" (Rancho Grande) y sus funciones ecológicas. *Bol. Soc. Venezolana Cienc. Nat.* 16: 3-167.
Schaldach, W. J. (1963) The avifauna of Colima and adjacent Jalisco, Mexico. *Proc. West. Found. Vert. Zool.* 1: 1-100.
Schalow, H. (1898) Die Vögel der Sammlung Plate. *Zool. Jahrb.* 4th suppl.: 641-748.
Scheffler, W. J. (1931) Aviculturists seek the Masked Bob White (*Colinus ridgwayi*) in Mexico. *Aviculture*: (June) 135-138; (July) 164-167.
Scherer Neto, P. (1980) *Aves do Paraná.* Rio de Janeiro: Zoobotânica Mario Nardelli.
Scherer Neto, P. (1985) *Lista das aves do Estado do Paraná.* Curitiba: Prefeitura Municipal de Curitiba.
Scherer Neto, P. (1988) Die Rotschwanz-amazone *Amazona brasiliensis* hat eine ungewisse Zukunft. *Papageien* 1/88: 23-26.
Scherer Neto, P. (1989) Contribuição à biologia do papagaio-de-cara-roxa *Amazona brasiliensis.* M.Sc. dissertation, Universidade Federal do Paraná, Curitiba.
Scherer Neto, P. (1991a) Beitrag zur Biologie der Rotschwanzamazone. *Zool. Ges. Arten-Populationschutz Mitt.* 7(2): 6.
Scherer Neto, P. (1991b) Projektbeschreibung Prachtamazone. *Zool. Ges. Arten- Populationschutz Mitt.* 7(2): 13-14.
Scherer Neto, P. and Martuscelli, P. (1992) Conservação e biologia do Papagaio-da-cara-roxa, *Amazona brasiliensis*, nos estados de São Paulo e Paraná. Segundo relatório parcial. Unpublished report to The Nature Conservancy and Fundação SOS-Mata Atlântica.
Schjellerup, I. (1989) *Children of the stones: a report on the agriculture in Chuquibamba, a district in North-Eastern Peru.* Copenhagen: Royal Danish Academy of Sciences and Letters' Commision for Research on the History of Agricultural Implements and Field Structures. (Publ. 7).
Schlatter, R. P. (1984) Status and conservation of seabirds in Chile. Pp.261-269 in J. P. Croxall, P. G. H. Evans and R. W. Schreiber, eds. *Status and conservation of the world's seabirds.* Cambridge, U.K.: International Council for Bird Preservation (Techn. Publ. 2).

Schlatter, R. P. and Marin, M. (1983) Breeding of Elliot's Storm Petrel *Oceanites gracilis* in Chile. *Gerfaut* 73: 197-199.

Schlegel, H. (1880) *Muséum d'Histoire Naturelle des Pays-Bas: revue méthodique et critique des collections déposées dans cet établissement, 8 (Monographie 41: Tinami).* Leide[n]: E. J. Brill.

Schnell, G. D., Weske, J. S. and Hellack, J. J. (1974) Recent observations of the Thick-billed Parrot in Jalisco. *Wilson Bull.* 86: 463-465.

Schubart, O., Aguirre, A. C. and Sick, H. (1965) Contribuição para o conhecimento da alimentação das aves brasileiras. *Arq. Zool. São Paulo* 12: 95-249.

Schuchmann, K.-L. (1985) Schillerkolibris (*Aglaeactis* sp.). *Trochilus* 6: 2-8.

Schulenberg, T. S. (1983) Foraging behavior, eco-morphology, and systematics of some antshrikes (Formicariidae: *Thamnomanes*). *Wilson Bull.* 95: 505-521.

Schulenberg, T. S. (1987) Observations on two rare birds, *Upucerthia albigula* and *Conirostrum tamarugense*, from the Andes of southwestern Peru. *Condor* 89: 654-658.

Schulenberg, T. S., Allen, S. E., Stotz, D. F., and Wiedenfeld, D. A. (1984) Distributional records from the Cordillera Yanachaga, central Peru. *Gerfaut* 74: 57-70.

Schulenberg, T. S. and Binford, L. C. (1985) A new species of tanager (Emberizidae: Thraupinae, *Tangara*) from southern Peru. *Wilson Bull.* 97: 413-420.

Schulenberg, T. S. and Parker, T. A. (1981) Status and distribution of some northwest Peruvian birds. *Condor* 83: 209-216.

Schulenberg, T. S. and Parker, T. A. (ms) Rediscovery of the Yellow-browed Toucanet *Aulacorhynchus huallagae.*

Schulenberg, T. S. and Williams, M. D. (1982) A new species of antpitta (*Grallaria*) from northern Peru. *Wilson Bull.* 94: 105-113.

Schulz, J. P., Mittermeier, R. A. and Reichart, H. A. (1977) Wildlife in Surinam. *Oryx* 14: 133-144.

Schwartz, A. and Klinikowski, R. F. (1963) Observations of West Indian birds. *Proc. Acad. Nat. Sci. Philadelphia* 115: 53-77.

Schwartz, A. and Klinikowski, R. F. (1965) Additional observations on West Indian birds. *Notulae Naturae* 376.

Schwartz, P. (1972) *Micrastur gilvicollis*, a valid species sympatric with *M. ruficollis* in Amazonia. *Condor* 74: 399-415.

Sclater, P. L. (1857a) List of additional species of Mexican birds, obtained by M. Auguste Sallé from the environs of Jalapa and S. Andres Tuxtla. *Proc. Zool. Soc. London*: 201-207.

Sclater, P. L. (1857b) On a collection of birds received by M. Sallé from southern Mexico. *Proc. Zool. Soc. London*: 226-230.

Sclater, P. L. (1858) List of birds collected by Geo. Cavendish Taylor, Esq., in the Republic of Honduras. *Proc. Zool. Soc. London*: 356-360.

Sclater, P. L. (1859a) On a series of birds collected in the vicinity of Jalapa in southern Mexico. *Proc. Zool. Soc. London:* 362-369.

Sclater, P. L. (1859b) List of birds collected by M. A. Boucard in the state of Oaxaca in south-western Mexico, with descriptions of new species. *Proc. Zool. Soc. London*: 369-393.

Sclater, P. L. (1860a) List of birds collected by Mr Fraser in the vicinity of Quito, and during excursions to Pichincha and Chimborazo, with notes and descriptions of new species. *Proc. Zool. Soc. London*: 73-83.

Sclater, P. L. (1860b) List of birds collected by Mr Fraser in Ecuador, at Nanegal, Calacali, Perucho, and Puellaro, with notes and descriptions of new species. *Proc. Zool. Soc. London*: 83-97.

Sclater, P. L. (1860c) List of birds collected by Mr Fraser at Babahoyo in Ecuador, with descriptions of new species. *Proc. Zool. Soc. London*: 272-290.

Sclater, P. L. (1862) Characters of nine new species of birds received in collections from Bogotá. *Proc. Zool. Soc. London*: 109-112.

Sclater, P. L. (1866) Additional notes on the Caprimulgidae. *Proc. Zool. Soc. London*: 581-590.

Sclater, P. L. (1874) On the species of the genus *Synallaxis* of the family Dendrocolaptidae. *Proc. Zool. Soc. London*: 2-28.

Sclater, P. L. (1878) Preliminary remarks on the Neotropical pipits. *Ibis* (4)2: 356-367.

Sclater, P. L. (1882) *A monograph of the jacamars and puffbirds*. London: R. H. Porter, and Dulan and Co.
Sclater, P. L. (1886) *Catalogue of the birds in the British Museum*, 11. London: Taylor and Francis (printed by order of the Trustees).
Sclater, P. L. (1888) *Catalogue of the birds in the British Museum*, 14. London: Taylor and Francis (printed by order of the Trustees).
Sclater, P. L. (1890) *Catalogue of the birds in the British Museum*, 15. London: Taylor and Francis (printed by order of the Trustees).
Sclater, P. L. (1891) On a second collection of birds from the province of Tarapacá, northern Chili. *Proc. Zool. Soc. London*: 131-137.
Sclater, P. L. (1910) *Revised list of the birds of Jamaica*. Kingston, Jamaica: Institute of Jamaica.
Sclater, P. L. and Hudson, W. H. (1888-1889) *Argentine ornithology*. London: R. H. Porter.
Sclater, P. L. and Salvin, O. (1859) On the ornithology of Central America, Part 2. *Ibis* 1: 117-138.
Sclater, P. L. and Salvin, O. (1866) Corrections to the former papers on the ornithology of Central America. *Ibis* (2)1: 201-207.
Sclater, P. L. and Salvin, O. (1867) List of birds collected by Mr Wallace on the Lower Amazons and Rio Negro. *Proc. Zool. Soc. London*: 566-596.
Sclater, P. L. and Salvin, O. (1868a) On Venezuelan birds collected by Mr A. Goering. *Proc. Zool. Soc. London*: 165-173.
Sclater, P. L. and Salvin, O. (1868b) On Peruvian birds collected by Mr H. Whitely. Part 2. *Proc. Zool. Soc. London*: 173-178.
Sclater, P. L. and Salvin, O. (1868c) Synopsis of the American rails (Rallidae). *Proc. Zool. Soc. London*: 442-470.
Sclater, P. L. and Salvin, O. (1869) On Peruvian birds collected by Mr Whitely. Part 4. *Proc. Zool. Soc. London*: 151-158.
Sclater, P. L. and Salvin, O. (1868-1869) [List of birds collected at Conchitas, Argentine Republic, by Mr William H. Hudson.] *Proc. Zool. Soc. London*: [1868] 137-146; [1869] 158-163, 631-636.
Sclater, P. L. and Salvin, O. (1870) Synopsis of the Cracidae. *Proc. Zool. Soc. London*: 504-544.
Sclater, P. L. and Salvin, O. (1873) On the birds of eastern Peru. *Proc. Zool. Soc. London*: 252-311.
Sclater, P. L. and Salvin, O. (1874) On Peruvian birds collected by Mr Whitely. Part 8. *Proc. Zool. Soc. London*: 677-680.
Sclater, P. L. and Salvin, O. (1876) A revision of the Neotropical Anatidae. *Proc. Zool. Soc. London*: 358-412.
Sclater, P. L. and Salvin, O. (1878a) Reports on the collections of birds made during the voyage of H.M.S. "Challenger" – no.9. On the birds of Antarctic America. *Proc. Zool. Soc. London*: 431-438.
Sclater, P. L. and Salvin, O. (1878b) Descriptions of three new birds from Ecuador. *Proc. Zool. Soc. London*: 438-440.
Sclater, P. L. and Salvin, O. (1879) On the birds collected by the late Mr T. K. Salmon in the state of Antioquia, United States of Colombia. *Proc. Zool. Soc. London*: 486-550.
Sclater, W. L. (1918) [New hawks from South America]. *Bull. Brit. Orn. Club* 38: 43-45.
Scott, D. A. (1985) Nature conservation and faunal research by Companhia Vale do Rio Doce: some observations and suggestions. Unpublished.
Scott, D. A. and Brooke, M. de L. (1985) The endangered avifauna of southeastern Brazil: a report on the BOU/WWF expedition of 1980/81 and 1981/82. Pp.115-139 in A. W. Diamond and T. E. Lovejoy, eds. *Conservation of tropical forest birds*. Cambridge, U.K.: International Council for Bird Preservation (Techn. Publ. 4).
Scott, D. A. and Carbonell, M. (1986) *A directory of Neotropical wetlands*. Cambridge, U.K.: International Union for Conservation of Nature and Natural Resources, and Slimbridge, U.K.: International Waterfowl Research Bureau.
Scott, J. M. and Garton, E. O. (1991) Population estimates of the Black-capped Vireo. *Condor* 93: 469-470.
Scott, W. E. D. (1891-1893) Observations on the birds of Jamaica, West Indies. *Auk* 8: 249-256, 353-365; 9: 9-15, 120-129, 273-277, 369-375; 10: 177-181, 339-342.

Scott, W. E. D. and Sharpe, R. B. (1904) *Reports of the Princeton University Expeditions to Patagonia, 1896-1899*, 2: Ornithology, Part 1. Princeton, N.J.: Princeton University Press.

SEA (1980) = Secretaría de Estado de Agricultura (1980) *Animales protegidos.* Santo Domingo: Secretaría de Estado de Agricultura.

SEA/DVS (1992) *Reconocimiento y evaluación de los recursos naturales en Loma Nalga de Maco.* Santo Domingo, República Dominicana: Secretaría de Estado de Agricultura, Departamento de Vida Silvestre.

Seitre, R. (1990) La quête de l'oiseau bleu. *Terre Sauvage* 39: 60-67.

Semper, J. E. and Sclater, P. L. (1872) Observations on the birds of St. Lucia. *Proc. Zool. Soc. London*: 647-653.

Serié, P. (1923) Miscelánea ornitológica. *Hornero* 3: 189-191.

Serié, P. and Smyth, C. H. (1923) Notas sobre aves de Santa Elena (E. Ríos). *Hornero* 3: 37-55.

Serna D., M. A. (1980) *Catálogo de aves, Museo de Historia Natural.* [Medellin, Colombia: Museo de Historia Natural del Colegio de San José de Medellin.]

Seth-Smith, D. (1926) Foreign birds at Paignton. *Avicult. Mag.* (4)4: 16-17.

Seth-Smith, D. (1927) Foreign birds at the Crystal Palace bird show. *Avicult. Mag.* (4)5: 84-86.

Seth-Smith, D. (1932) Foreign birds at the Crystal Palace. *Avicult. Mag.* (4)10: 66-69.

Sharpe, R. B. (1881) Account of the zoological collections made during the survey of H.M.S. "Alert" in the Straits of Magellan and on the coast of Patagonia, 2: birds. *Proc. Zool. Soc. London*: 6-18.

Sharpe, R. B. (1894) *Catalogue of the birds in the British Museum*, 23. London: Taylor and Francis (printed by order of the Trustees).

Sharpe, R. B. (1900) [Descriptions of new species of birds in the collection of the British Museum.] *Bull. Brit. Orn. Club* 11: 2.

Sheean, O. (1992) Fool's gold in Ecuador. *WWF News* 75: 2.

Short, L. L. (1961) Interspecies flocking of birds of montane forest in Oaxaca, Mexico. *Wilson Bull.* 73: 341-347.

Short, L. L. (1968) Sympatry of Red-breasted meadowlarks in Argentina, and the taxonomy of meadowlarks (Aves: *Leistes*, *Pezites*, and *Sturnella*). *Amer. Mus. Novit.* 2349.

Short, L. L. (1969) Relationships among some South American seedeaters (*Sporophila*), with a record of *S. hypochroma* for Argentina. *Wilson Bull.* 81: 216-219.

Short, L. L. (1971) Aves nuevas o poco comunes de Corrientes, República Argentina. *Revta. Mus. Arg. Cienc. Nat. "Bernardino Rivadavia" Inst. Natn. Invest. Cienc. Nat. (Zool.)* 9(11): 283-309.

Short, L. L. (1974) Nesting of southern Sonoran birds during the summer rainy season. *Condor* 76: 21-32.

Short, L. L. (1975) A zoogeographic analysis of the South American chaco avifauna. *Bull. Amer. Mus. Nat. Hist.* 154: 165-352.

Short, L. L. (1982) *Woodpeckers of the world.* Delaware: Delaware Museum of Natural History (Monogr. Ser. 4).

Short, L. L. and Horne, J. F. M. (1986) The Ivorybill still lives. *Nat. Hist.* 7: 26-28.

Short, L. L. and Parkes, K. C. (1979) The status of *Agelaius forbesi* Sclater. *Auk* 96: 179-183.

Shufeldt, R. W. (1916) The bird-caves of the Bermudas and their former inhabitants. *Ibis* (10)4: 623-635.

Shull, A. M. (1985) Endangered and threatened wildlife and plants; review of the status of the Ivory-billed Woodpecker. *Federal Register* 50 (no.69, April 10): 14123-14124.

Sibley, C. G. and Monroe, B. L. (1990) *Distribution and taxonomy of birds of the world.* New Haven: Yale University Press.

Sick, H. (1955) O aspecto fitofisionómico da paisagem do médio Rio das Mortes, Mato Grosso, e a avifauna da região. *Arq. Mus. Nac. Rio de Janeiro* 42: 541-566.

Sick, H. (1958) Resultados de uma excursão ornitológica do Museu Nacional à Brasília, novo Distrito Federal, Goiás, com a descrição do um novo representante de *Scytalopus* (Rhinocryptidae, Aves). *Bol. Mus. Nac. Rio de Janeiro*, n.s. zool. no.185.

Sick, H. (1959a) Um novo piprídeo do Brasil central: "*Pipra vilasboasi*" sp.n. (Pipridae, Aves). *Revta. Bras. Biol.* 19: 13-16.

Sick, H. (1959b) Zwei neue Pipriden aus Brasilien. *J. Orn.* 100: 111-112.

Sick, H. (1959c) Zur Entdeckung von *Pipra vilasboasi*. *J. Orn.* 100: 404-412.

Sick, H. (1960) Zur Systematik und Biologie der Bürzelstelzer (Rhinocryptidae), speziell Brasiliens. *J. Orn.* 101: 141-174.

Sick, H. (1965) A fauna do cerrado. *Arq. Zool. São Paulo* 12: 71-93.

Sick, H. (1968) Vogelwanderungen im kontinentalen Südamerika. *Vogelwarte* 24: 217-242.

Sick, H. (1969) Aves brasileiras ameaçadas de extinção e noções gerais de conservação de aves no Brasil. *An. Acad. Brasil. Ciênc.* 41 (suppl.): 205-229.

Sick, H. (1970) Ueber Eier und Lebensweise der Weissflügel-Kotinga, *Xipholena atropurpurea*. *J. Orn.* 111: 107-108.

Sick, H. (1970) Notes on Brazilian Cracidae. *Condor* 72: 106-108.

Sick, H. (1972) A ameaça da avifauna brasileira. Pp.99-153 in *Espécies da fauna brasileira ameaçadas de extinção*. Rio de Janeiro: Academia Brasileira de Ciências.

Sick, H. (1979a) Zur Nistweise der Cotingiden *Iodopleura* und *Xipholena*. *J. Orn.* 120: 73-77.

Sick, H. (1979b) Découverte de la patrie de l'Ara de Lear *Anodorhynchus leari*. *Alauda* 47: 59-60.

Sick, H. (1979c) Die Herkunft von Lear's Ara (*Anodorhynchus leari*) entdeckt! *Gefied. Welt* 103: 161-162.

Sick, H. (1979d) Notes on some Brazilian birds. *Bull. Brit. Orn. Club* 99: 115-120.

Sick, H. (1979e) A voz como caráter taxonômico em aves. *Bol. Mus. Nac. Rio de Janeiro*, n.s. zool. no.294.

Sick, H. (1980) Characteristics of the Razor-billed Curassow *Mitu mitu mitu*. *Condor* 82: 227-228.

Sick, H. (1981) About the blue macaws, especially the Lear's Macaw. Pp.439-444 in R. F. Pasquier, ed. *Conservation of New World parrots*. Washington, D.C.: Smithsonian Institution Press for the International Council for Bird Preservation (Techn. Publ. 1).

Sick, H. (1983) Aves da Mata Atlântica em extinção. *Revta. Serv. Público* 111: 155-157.

Sick, H. (1984) *Migrações de aves na América do Sul Continental*. Brasília: Instituto Brasileiro de Desenvolvimento Florestal (CEMAVE Publ. Técn. 2).

Sick, H. (1985) *Ornitologia brasileira, uma introdução*. Brasília: Editora Universidade de Brasília.

Sick, H. (1986) Memorandum to Jersey Wildlife Preservation Trust. Unpublished.

Sick, H. (1987) A guarouba: novo símbolo nacional? *Ciência Hoje* 5(29): 76-77.

Sick, H. (1990) Notes on the taxonomy of Brazilian parrots. *Ararajuba* 1: 111-112.

Sick, H., and Bege, L. A. do R. (1984) Novas informações sobre as aves do estado de Santa Catarina. *An. Soc. Sul-Riogrand. Orn.* 5: 3-6.

Sick, H., Gonzaga, L. P. and Teixeira, D. M. (1987) A Arara-Azul-de-Lear, *Anodorhynchus leari* Bonaparte, 1856. *Revta. Bras. Zool.* 3(7): 441-463.

Sick, H. and Pabst, L. F. (1968) As aves do Rio de Janeiro (Guanabara). Lista sistemática anotada. *Arq. Mus. Nac. Rio de Janeiro* 53: 99-160.

Sick, H., do Rosário, L. A. and de Azevedo, T. R. (1981) Aves do estado de Santa Catarina. *Sellówia* Ser. Zool. no.1.

Sick, H. and Teixeira, D. M. (1979) Notas sobre aves brasileiras raras ou ameaçadas de extinção. *Publ. Avuls. Mus. Nac.* 62.

Sick, H. and Teixeira, D. M. (1980) Discovery of the home of the Indigo Macaw in Brazil. *Amer. Birds* 34: 118-119, 212.

Sick, H. and Teixeira, D. M. (1983) The discovery of the home of the Indigo Macaw *Anodorhynchus leari* Bonaparte, 1856. *Hornero* no. extraord.: 109-112.

Sick, H., Teixeira, D. M. and Gonzaga, L. P. (1979) A nossa descoberta da pátria da arara *Anodorhynchus learei* [*sic*]. *An. Acad. Bras. Ciênc.* 51: 575-576.

Sigurdsson, H. (1982) In the volcano. *Natural History* 91(3): 61-68.

da Silva, C. P., Munn, C. A., Cintra, R., Renton, K., Valqui, M. and Yamashita, C. (1991) Breeding ecology of Hyacinth Macaws. *Psittascene* 3(3): 1-3.

Silva, F. (1981) Contribuição ao conhecimento da biologia do papagaio charão, *Amazona pretrei* (Temminck, 1830) (Psittacidae, Aves). *Iheringia* Ser. Zool. (58): 79-85.

Silva, F. and Fallavena, M. A. B. (1988) Censo de *Xanthopsar flavus* no Rio Grande do Sul. Unpublished.

da Silva, G. L. and Nacinovic, J. B. (1991) Birds as indicator [*sic*] for the conservation of Atlantic Forests in Bahia, Brazil. Interim project report to WWF for the period July 1990–July 1991.

da Silva, J. M. C. (1989) Análise biogeográfica da avifauna de florestas do interflúvio Araguaia–São Francisco. M.Sc. dissertation, Universidade de Brasília, Brasília.

da Silva, J. M. C. and Willis, E. O. (1986) Notas sobre a distribuição de quatro espécies de aves da Amazônia brasileira. *Bol. Mus. Para. Emílio Goeldi* 2(2): 151-158.

Silva, T. (1980) The St Lucian Amazon Parrot. *Avicult. Mag.* 86: 248-249.

Silva, T. (1981) The status of *Aratinga euops. AFA Watchbird* 8(2): 10.

Silva, T. (1988a) Bird watching in Paraguay. *Bull. Amazona Soc.* 5(4) [18]: 2-6.

Silva, T. (1988b) The survival of parrots in the wild. *Bird Talk* November: 108-111.

Silva, T. (1989a) *A monograph of endangered parrots*. Ontario: Silvio Mattacchione and Co.

Silva, T. (1989b) Bei Vogelfängern in Paraguay. *Gefied. Welt* 113: 247-248.

Silva, T. (1990a) Der Spix-Ara (*Cyanopsitta spixii*) – gelingt seine Rettung durch Gefangenschaftszucht? *Papageien* 2/90: 57-60.

Silva, T. (1990b) Some news from Brazil. *Bull. Amazona Soc.* 7(4) [26]: 7-8 [incorrectly dated 1991].

Silva, T. (1990c) [Untitled.] *Loro Parque Newsletter* no.21.

Silva, T. (1991a) Der Spix-Ara (*Cyanopsitta spixii*) – gelingt seine Rettung durch Gefangenschaftszucht? *Voliere* 14: 87-90.

Silva, T. (1991b) Treffen des Spix-Ara-Komitees. *Papageien* 1/91: 5.

Silva, T. (1991c) [Untitled.] *Loro Parque Newsletter* no.22.

Silva, T. (1991d) Zucht der Taubenhalsamazone *Amazona vinacea* im Loro Parque. *Gefied. Welt* 115: 164-166.

da Silveira, C. L. and Pais, J. A. (1986) Breeding and hand-rearing the Red-billed Curassow *Crax blumenbachii* at Rio de Janeiro Zoo. *Internatn. Zoo Yearbook* 24/25: 244-247.

da Silveira, E. K. P. (1967) Distribuição geográfica do inhambú-carapé no sudeste de Goiás e Brasília, Brasil central. *Bol. Geogr. Rio de Janeiro* 200: 38-41.

da Silveira, E. K. P. (1968) A brief note on the Little Tinamou *Taoniscus nanus* in Brasília Zoo. *Internatn. Zoo Yearbook* 8: 212.

Silvius, K. M. (1989) Resultados preliminares del proyecto "Ecología, biología, y situación actual de la Cotorra (*Amazona barbadensis*: Psittacidae) en la Isla de Margarita, Nueva Esparta". FUDENA and WCI unpublished report.

Silvius, K. M. (1991) Ecology and conservation of *Amazona barbadensis* on Margarita Island, Venezuela. Summary report of activities and results, 1989-1991. Unpublished.

Simmons, K. E. L. (1962) Some recommendations for a revised checklist of the genera and species of grebes (Podicipedidae). *Bull. Brit. Orn. Club* 82: 109-116.

Simon, E. (1897) *Catalogue des espèces actuellement connues de la famille des Trochilidés*. Paris.

Simon, E. (1907) Liste des Trochilidés observés par M. le Dr Rivet dans la République de l'Ecuador. *Bull. Mus. Natn. Hist. Nat. Paris* 13: 16-23.

Simon, E. (1919) Notes critiques sur les Trochilidés. *Rev. Franç. Orn.* 6: 52-54.

Simon, E. (1921) *Histoire naturelle des Trochilidae* (Synopsis et Catalogue). Paris: Mulo.

Simons, T. R. (1985) Biology and behavior of the endangered Hawaiian Dark-rumped Petrel. *Condor* 87: 229-245.

Simpson, B. B. (1977) A revision of the genus *Polylepis* (Rosaceae: Sanguisorbeae). *Smithson. Contrib. Bot.* 43.

Sissons [= Sissen], H. (1991) Breeding macaws and other endangered parrots. Pp.29-34 in R. Colley, ed. *Parrots in captivity*. Bristol: Association of British Wild Animal Keepers.

Sjögren, B. (1963) Västindiens sista papegojor. *Naturen* 7: 439-447.

Skutch, A. F. (1970) The display of the Yellow-billed Cotinga *Carpodectes antoniae*. *Ibis* 112: 115-116.

Slud, P. (1960) The birds of Finca "La Selva", Costa Rica, a tropical wet forest locality. *Bull. Amer. Mus. Nat. Hist.* 121.

Slud, P. (1964) The birds of Costa Rica: distribution and ecology. *Bull. Amer. Mus. Nat. Hist.* 128.

Smith, A. P. (1907) The Thick-billed Parrot in Arizona. *Condor* 9: 104.

Smith, A. P. (1908) Destruction of Imperial Woodpeckers. *Condor* 10: 91.

Smith, A. P. (1977) Establishment of seedlings of *Polylepis sericea* in the paramo (alpine) zone of the Venezuelan Andes. *Bartonia* 45: 11-14.

Smith, G. A. (1975) Systematics of parrots. *Ibis* 117: 18-68.

Smith, G. A. (1975-1978) Notes on some species of parrot in captivity. *Avicult. Mag.* 81: 200-211; 82: 22-32, 73-83, 143-150; 83: 21-27, 160-166; 84: 200-205.

Smith, G. A. (1991a) Spix's Macaw *Ara (Cyanopsitta) spixii. Mag. Parrot Soc.* 15: 164-165.

Smith, G. A. (1991b) The Glaucous Macaw *Anodorhynchus g. glaucus. Mag. Parrot Soc.* 15: 236-237.

Smith, G. A. (1991c) The Hyacinthine Macaw *Anodorhynchus hyacinthinus. Mag. Parrot Soc.* 15: 340-341.

Smith, R. W. (1968) Jamaicas's own birds. *Jamaica J.* 2(4): 18-21.

Smith, W. J. and Vuilleumier, F. (1971) Evolutionary relationships of some South American ground tyrants. *Bull. Mus. Comp. Zool.* 141: 179-268.

Smithe, F. B. (1966) *The birds of Tikal.* New York: Natural History Press.

Smyth, C. H. (1927-1928) Decripción de una colección de huevos de aves argentinas. *Hornero* 4: 1-16, 125-152.

von Sneidern, K. (1954) Notas sobre algunas aves del Museo de Historia Natural de la Universidad del Cauca, Popayán, Colombia. *Noved. Colombianas* 1: 3-13.

Snethlage, E. (1908) Sobre uma collecção de aves do Rio Purús. *Bol. Mus. Goeldi* 5: 43-78.

Snethlage, E. (1913) Über die Verbreitung der Vogelarten in Unteramazonien. *J. Orn.* 61: 469-539.

Snethlage, E. (1914) Catálogo das aves amazônicas. *Bol. Mus. Goeldi* 8.

Snethlage, E. (1925) Neue Vogelarten aus Nord-Brasilen [*sic*]. *J. Orn.* 73: 264-274.

Snethlage, E. (1926) Resumo de trabalhos executados na Europa de 1924 a 1925, em museus de história natural. *Bol. Mus. Nac. Rio de Janeiro* 2(6): 35-70.

Snethlage, E. (1927) Algumas observações sobre pássaros raros or pouco conhecidos do Brasil. *Bol. Mus. Nac. Rio de Janeiro* 3(3): 60-64.

Snethlage, E. (1928a) Novas espécies e subespécies de aves do Brasil central. *Bol. Mus. Nac. Rio de Janeiro* 4(2): 1-7.

Snethlage, E. (1928b) Neue Vogelarten und Unterarten aus Innerbrasilien. *J. Orn.* 76: 581-587.

Snethlage, E. (1935) Beiträge zur Brutbiologie brasilianischer Vögel. *J. Orn.* 83: 1-24, 532-562.

Snethlage, H. (1927-1928) Meine Reise durch Nordostbrasilien. *J. Orn.* 75: 453-484; 76: 503-581, 668-738.

Snow, D. (1973) The classification of the Cotingidae (Aves). *Breviora* 409: 1-27.

Snow, D. W. (1980) A new species of cotinga from southeastern Brazil. *Bull. Brit. Orn. Club* 100: 213-215.

Snow, D. W. (1982) *The cotingas.* London: British Museum (Natural History), and Oxford: Oxford University Press.

Snow, D. W. and Goodwin, D. (1974) The Black-and-gold Cotinga. *Auk* 91: 360-369.

Snow, D. W. and Snow, B. K. (1980) Relationships between hummingbirds and flowers in the Andes of Colombia. *Bull. Brit. Mus. Nat. Hist.* 38: 105-139.

Snyder, N. F. R. (1973) Activities from 15 September to 9 October: trip to St Vincent, St Lucia, and Dominica. Unpublished report 12 October 1973 to Director, Patuxent Wildlife Research Center.

Snyder, N. F. R. and Johnson, E. V. (1985) Photographic censusing of the 1982-1983 California Condor population. *Condor* 87: 1-13.

Snyder, N. F. R. and Johnson, T. B. (1988) Parrot release – news from the field. *On the Edge* 56: [2-3].

Snyder, N. F. R. and Johnson, T. V. [*sic*] (1989) Reintroduction of Thick-billed Parrot *Rhynchopsitta pachyrhyncha* in Arizona. *Dodo* 25 [1988]: 15-24.

Snyder, N. F. R. and Snyder, H. A. (1979) An assessment of the status of parrots of Dominica following Hurricane David. Unpublished report to ICBP.

Snyder, N. F. R. and Snyder, H. A. (1989) Biology and conservation of the California Condor. Pp.175-267 in D. M. Power, ed. *Current ornithology*, 6. New York and London: Plenum Press.

Snyder, N. F. R. and Wallace, M. P. (1987) Reintroduction of the Thick-billed Parrot in Arizona. Pp.360-384 in *Proceedings 1987 Jean Delacour/IFCB Symposium on Breeding Birds in Captivity.* North Hollywood, California: International Foundation for the Conservation of Birds.

Snyder, N. F. R., Snyder, H. A. and Johnson, T. B. (1989a) Parrots return to the Arizona skies. *Birds Internatn.* 1(2): 41-52.

Snyder, N. F. R., Snyder, H. A. and Johnson, T. B. (1989b) Thick-billed Parrots released and raised in the wilds of Arizona. *AFA Watchbird* 16(2): 40-45.

Sojer, A. (1989) Spix-Ara (*Cyanopsitta spixii*). *Zool. Ges. Arten- und Populationsschutz Mitglieder Information* März 1989: 5-6.

Sojer, A. and Wirth, R. (1989) Zur situation des Spix-Ara. *Voliere* 12: 139-140.

SOMA (1935-1942) = Sección Ornitológica del Museo Argentino de Ciencias Naturales (1935-1942) Lista sistemática de las aves argentinas. *Hornero* 6: 151-196, 343-364, 531-554; 7: 89-124, 299-326, 447-472; 8: 137-153, 309-344.

Soneghet, M. (1991) Sobre a biologia reprodutiva do "com-com" *Formicivora serrana littoralis* (Formicariidae) na ilha do Cabo Frio–Arraial do Cabo, RJ. P.13 in Resumos, I Congresso Brasileiro de Ornitologia. Belém: Museu Paraense Emílio Goeldi.

Spaans, A. L. (1973) Het voorkomen van de Geelvleugelamazone, *Amazona barbadensis*, op Bonaire: een pleidooi voor nader onderzoek. Unpublished.

Special Environmental Agency (1977) *Program of ecological stations.* Brasília: Ministry of the Interior.

Spence, M. J. and Smith, B. L. (1961) A subspecies of *Torreornis inexpectata* from Cuba. *Auk* 78: 95-97.

Spence, S. (1973) Plain or Blue Pigeon. *Gosse Bird Club Broadsheet* no.21: 21.

Spence, S. (1977) A study of Jamaican pigeons and doves. *Gosse Bird Club Broadsheet* no.29: 2-4.

Spenkelink-van Schaik, J. L. (1984) Blue-throated Conures (*Pyrrhura cruentata*). *AFA Watchbird* 11(3): 28.

von [= de] Spix, J. B. (1824) *Avium species novae, quas in itinere per Brasiliam annis MDCCCXVII–MDCCCXX jussu et auspiciis Maximiliani Josephi I Bavariae regis suscepto* [etc.]. Munich: F. S. Hübschmann.

SPVS (1988) Considerações sobre a fauna de vertebrados e fitofisionomia da Área Especial de Interesse Turístico do Marumbi, Curitiba. Unpublished.

Stager, K. E. (1954) Birds of the Barranca de Cobre region of southwestern Chihuahua, Mexico. *Condor* 56: 21-32.

Stager, K. E. (1957) The avifauna of the Tres Marías Islands, Mexico. *Auk* 74: 413-432.

Stager, K. E. (1961) The Machris Brazilian Expedition, ornithology: non-passerines. *Contrib. Sci. (Los Angeles Co. Mus.)* 41.

Steadman, D. W. and Miller, N. G. (1987) California Condor associated with spruce–jack pine woodland in the late pleistocene of New York. *Quaternary Res.* 28: 415-426.

Steffan, K. (1974) Vogelleben am Agua do Quati (Brasilien). *Gefied. Welt* 98: 102-104.

Steinbacher, J. (1962) Beiträge zur Kenntnis der Vögel von Paraguay. *Abhandl. Senckenb. Naturforsch. Ges.* 502: 1-106.

Steinbacher, J. (1968) Weitere Beiträge über Vögel von Paraguay. *Senckenbergiana Biol.* 49: 317-365.

Stempelmann, H. and Schulz, F. (1890) Enumeración de las aves de la provincia de Córdoba, República Argentina. *Bol. Acad. Nac. Cienc. Córdoba* 10: 393-408.

Stepan, R. (1966) Der Kapuzenzeisig (*Spinus cucullatus*). *Gefied. Welt* 90: 223-226.

Stephens, L. and Traylor, M. A. (1983) *Ornithological gazetteer of Peru.* Cambridge, Mass.: Museum of Comparative Zoology.

Stephens, L. and Traylor, M. A. (1985) *Ornithological gazetteer of the Guianas.* Cambridge, Mass.: Museum of Comparative Zoology.

Stern, J. and Stern, M. (1990) A reporter at large: parrots. *New Yorker* July 30: 55-73.

Steullet, A. B. and Deautier, E. A. (1935-1946) *Catálogo sistemático de las aves de la República Argentina.* Buenos Aires: Imprenta y Casa Editora "Coni" (Obra del Cincuentenario del Museo de la Plata).

Stiles, F. G. (1983) Systematics of the southern forms of *Selasphorus* (Trochilidae). *Auk* 100: 311-325.

Stiles, F. G. (1987) Observaciones sobre la situación actual del Picaflor Rojo de Juan Fernández (*Sephanoides fernandensis*), con recomendaciones para un estudio integral de su ecología y biología poblacional. Santiago, Chile: Organización de las Naciones Unidas para la Agricultura y la

Alimentación, Organización de las Naciones Unidas para el Medio Ambiente. (Report to Corporación Nacional Forestal).

Stiles, F. G. (1990) Un encuentro con el Mosquerito Antioqueño, *Phylloscartes lanyoni* Graves. *Bol. SAO* 1(2): 12-13.

Stiles, F. G. and Skutch, A. F. (1989) *A guide to the birds of Costa Rica*. London: Christopher Helm.

Stockton de Dod, A. (1978) *Aves de la República Dominicana*. Santo Domingo: Museo Nacional de Historia Natural.

Stockton de Dod, A. (1981) *Guía de campo para las aves de la República Dominicana*. Santo Domingo: Editora Horizontes de América.

Stokes, H. S. (1930) A tour of France. *Avicult. Mag.* (4)8: 254-258, 282-288.

Stokes, S. (1932) The zoo at Mossley Hill, Liverpool. *Avicult. Mag.* (4)10: 172-173.

Stone, W. (1899) On a collection of birds from the vicinity of Bogotá, with a review of the South American species of *Speotyto* and *Troglodytes*. *Proc. Acad. Nat. Sci. Philadelphia* 51: 302-313.

Stone, W. (1917) A new hummingbird from Colombia. *Proc. Acad. Nat. Sci. Philadelphia* 69: 204.

Stone, W. and Roberts, H. R. (1935) Zoological results of the Mato Grosso Expedition to Brazil in 1931 – III. Birds. *Proc. Acad. Nat. Sci. Philadelphia* 86: 363-397.

Storer, R. W. (1958) The affinities of *Oreothraupis arremonops*. *Auk* 75: 352-354.

Storer, R. W. (1960) Notes on the systematics of the tanager genus *Conothraupis*. *Auk* 77: 350-351.

Storer, R. W. (1967) Observations on Rolland's grebe. *Hornero* 10: 339-350.

Storer, R. W. (1981) The Rufous-faced Crake (*Laterallus xenopterus*) and its Paraguayan congeners. *Wilson Bull.* 93: 137-144.

Storer, R. W. (1989a) Geographic variation and sexual dimorphism in the tremblers (*Cinclocerthia*) and White-breasted Thrasher (*Ramphocinclus*). *Auk* 106: 249-258.

Storer, R. W. (1989b) Notes on Paraguayan birds. *Occas. Pap. Mus. Zool. Univ. Michigan* 719.

Stotz, D. (1991) Aves observadas durante curso de campo (UNICAMP) 1991 em Espírito Santo e Bahia. Unpublished report.

Strahl, S. D. (1991) Cracid news. *WPA News* 33: 33-34.

Strahl, S. D. and Silva, J. L. (1987) Pauji copete de piedra. *Pro Vita* (Caracas) 1(2): 3-4.

Straube, F. C. (1988) Contribuições ao conhecimento da avifauna da região sudoeste do estado do Paraná (Brasil). *Biotemas* 1(1): 63-75.

Straube, F. C. (1990) Conservação de aves no litoral-sul do estado do Paraná (Brasil). *Arq. Biol. Tecnol.* 33: 159-173.

Straube, F. C. (1991) Notas sobre a distribuição de *Eleothreptus anomalus* (Gould, 1837) e *Caprimulgus longirostris longirostris* Bonaparte, 1825 no Brasil (Aves; Caprimulgidae). *Acta Biol. Leopoldensia* 12: 301-312.

Straube, F. C. and Bornschein, M. R. (1989) A contribuição de André Mayer à história natural no Paraná (Brasil), I. Sobre uma coleção de aves do extreme noroeste do Paraná e sul do Mato Grosso do Sul. *Arq. Biol. Tecnol.* 32: 441-471.

Straube, F. C. and Bornschein, M. R. (1991) Sobre *Leucopternis polionota* (Kaup, 1847) nos estados do Paraná e Santa Catarina (sul do Brasil). Resúmenes, I Encuentro de Ornitología de Paraguay, Brasil y Argentina, Mayo 1991, Ciudad del Este, Paraguay.

Straube, F. C. and Scherer Neto, P. (in prep.) Novas observações sobre *Triclaria malachitacea* (Spix, 1824) nos estados do Paraná e São Paulo.

Stresemann, E. (1935) Ueber *Mergus squamatus* und *Mergus octosetaceus*. *Orn. Monatsber.* 43: 121.

Stresemann, E. (1938) Ueber einige seltene Vögel aus Ecuador, 2. *Orn. Monatsber.* 46: 115-118.

Stresemann, E. (1948) Der Naturforscher Friedrich Sellow und sein Beitrag zur Kenntnis Brasiliens. *Zool. Jahrb. Syst. Okol. Geogr.* 77: 401-425.

Stresemann, E. (1950) Die brasilianischen Vogelsammlungen des Grafen von Hoffmannsegg aus den Jahren 1800-1812. *Bonn. Zool. Beitr.* 1: 126-143.

Stresemann, E. (1954) Ausgestorbene und Aussterbende Vogelarten, Vertreten im Zoologischen Museum zu Berlin. *Mitt. Zool. Mus. Berlin* 30: 38-53.

Struhsaker, T. T. (1976) The dim future of La Macarena. *Oryx* 13: 298-302.

Strunden, H. (1974) Papageien im Zoo von Rio de Janeiro. *Gefied. Welt* 98: 104-105.

Strunden, H., Arndt, T., Wirth, R. and Sojer, A. (1986) Keine Chance für den Spix-Ara? *Zool. Ges. Arten- und Populationsschutz Mitglieder Information* Dezember 1986 [:1-3].

Studer, A. (1985) Estudo ecológico do conjunto florestal da serra das Guaribas e da serra do Cavaleiro. Pedido para a salvaguarda desta floresta. Unpublished.

Studer, A. and Vielliard, J. (1988) Premières données étho-écologiques sur l'Ictéridé brésilien *Curaeus forbesi* (Sclater, 1886) (Aves, Passeriformes). *Rev. Suisse Zool.* 95: 1063-1077.

Sugden, A. M. (1982) The vegetation of the Serranía de Macuira, Guajira, Colombia: a contrast of arid lowlands and an isolated cloud forest. *J. Arnold Arboretum* 63: 1-30.

Sulley, S. C. and Sulley, M. E. (1992) *Birding in Cuba.* Derbyshire, U.K.: Worldwide Publications.

Sumichrast, F. (1869) The geographical distribution of the native birds of the department of Vera Cruz, with a list of the migratory species. *Mem. Boston Soc. Nat. Hist.* 1: 542-563.

Sumichrast, F. (1881) Enumeración de las aves observadas en el territorio de la República Mexicana. *La Naturaleza* 5: 227-250.

Summerhayes, W. (1874) Letter. *Proc. Zool. Soc. London*: 420.

Sutton, G. M. (1951) *Mexican birds: first impressions.* Norman, Oklahoma: University of Oklahoma Press.

Sutton, G. M. and Burleigh, T. D. (1939) A list of birds observed on the 1938 Semple Expedition to northeastern Mexico. *Occas. Pap. Mus. Zool. Louisiana State Univ.* 3: 15-46.

Sutton, G. M. and Burleigh, T. D. (1940a) Birds of Valles, San Luis Potosí, Mexico. *Condor* 42: 259-262.

Sutton, G. M. and Burleigh, T. D. (1940b) Birds of Tamazunchale, San Luis Potosí. *Wilson Bull.* 52: 221-233.

Sutton, G. M. and Pettingill, O. S. (1942) Birds of the Gómez Farías region, southwestern Tamaulipas. *Auk* 59: 1-34.

Sutton, G. M. and Pettingill, O. S. (1943) Birds of Linares and Galeana, Nuevo León, Mexico. *Occas. Pap. Mus. Zool. Louisiana State Univ.* 16: 273-291.

Sutton, J. M. (1940) Black-capped Petrel in New York. *Auk* 57: 244.

Sutton, R. L. (1981) Hunting the Jamaican Pauraque. *Gosse Bird Club Broadsheet* no.37: 4-5.

Swainson, W. (1820-1823) *Zoological illustrations* [etc.]. London: Baldwin, Cradock and Joy; and W. Wood.

Swainson, W. (1825) On two new genera of birds, *Formicivora* and *Drymophila*, with descriptions of several species. *Zool. J.* 2: 145-154.

Swank, W. G. and Julien, C. R. (1975) Distribution and status of wildlife on Dominica. Rome: Food and Agriculture Organization of the United Nations (FO:DP/DMI/74/001 Project working document no.1).

Swann, H. K. (1920) *A synoptic list of the Accipitres.* London: John Wheldon and Co.

Sykes, P. W. (1983) Field notes of birding holiday on Jamaica. *Gosse Bird Club Broadsheet* no.41: 1-5.

Sykes, P. W., Kepler, C. B., Jett, D. A. and De Capita, M. E. (1989) Kirtland's Warblers on the nesting grounds during the post-breeding period. *Wilson Bull.* 101: 545-558.

Sztolcman, J. (1926) Étude des collections ornithologiques de Paraná. *Prace Zool. Pol. Państ. Muz. Przyr.* [*Ann. Zool. Mus. Pol. Hist. Nat.*] 5(3): 107-196.

Taczanowski, L. (1874) Liste des oiseaux recueillis par M. Constantin Jelski dans la partie centrale du Pérou occidental. *Proc. Zool. Soc. London*: 501-565.

Taczanowski, L. (1877) Liste des oiseaux recueillis en 1876 au nord de Pérou occidental par MM. Jelski et Stolzmann. *Proc. Zool. Soc. London*: 319-333, 744-754.

Taczanowski, L. (1879) Liste des oiseaux recueillis au nord du Pérou par MM. Stolzmann et Jelski en 1878. *Proc. Zool. Soc. London*: 220-245.

Taczanowski, L. (1882) Liste des oiseaux recueillis par M. Stolzmann au Pérou nord-oriental. *Proc. Zool. Soc. London*: 2-49.

Taczanowski, L. (1883) Description des espèces nouvelles de la collection péruvienne de M. le Dr Raimondi de Lima. *Proc. Zool. Soc. London*: 70-72.

Taczanowski, L. (1884-1886) *Ornithologie du Pérou.* Paris: Oberthur.

Taczanowski, L. and Stolzmann, J. (1881) Notice sur la *Loddigesia mirabilis* (Bourc.). *Proc. Zool. Soc. London*: 827-834.

Taczanowski, L. and von Berlepsch, H. (1885) Troisième liste des oiseaux recueillis par M. Stolzmann dans l'Ecuadeur. *Proc. Zool. Soc. London*: 67-124.

Taibel, A. M. (1968) Osservazioni sulla riproduzione e allevamento di *Pipile jacutinga* (Spix) (Cracidae–Galliformes) realizzata per la prima volta con esemplari in cattività. *Ann. Civ. Mus. Stor. Nat.* 77: 33-52.

Tallman, D. A., Parker, T. A., Lester, G. D. and Hughes, R. A. (1978) Notes on two species of birds previously unreported from Peru. *Wilson Bull.* 90: 445-446.

Tanner, J. T. (1942) *The Ivory-billed Woodpecker*. New York: Dover Publications (1966 republication of Research Report 1 of National Audubon Society).

Tanner, J. T. (1964) The decline and present status of the Imperial Woodpecker of Mexico. *Auk* 81: 74-81.

Tavistock, Marquess of (1926) Macaws. *Avicult. Mag.* (4)4: 156-158.

Tavistock, Marquess of (1929) *Parrots and parrot-like birds in aviculture*. London: F. V. White and Co.

TAW (1986) = *The Times atlas of the world*. Comprehensive (seventh) edition with revisions. London: Times Books.

Taylor, E. C. (1864) Five months in the West Indies. *Ibis* 6: 73-97, 157-173.

Taylor, G. C. (1860) On birds collected or observed in the Republic of Honduras, with a short account of a journey across that country from the Pacific to the Atlantic Ocean. *Ibis* 2: 10-24, 110-122, 222-228, 311-317.

Taylor, J. A. (1975a) The Northern Helmeted Curassow *Pauxi pauxi*. *Avicult. Mag.* 81: 195-196.

Taylor, J. A. (1975b) [Letter to J. Delacour.] *Avicult. Mag.* 81: 231.

Taylor, K. (1990) *A birder's guide to Costa Rica*. Revised second edition. Privately published.

Teixeira, D. M. (1986) The avifauna of the north-eastern Brazilian Atlantic forests: a case of mass extinction? *Ibis* 128: 167-168.

Teixeira, D. M. (1987a) A new tyrannulet (*Phylloscartes*) from northeastern Brazil. *Bull. Brit. Orn. Club* 107: 37-41.

Teixeira, D. M. (1987b) Notas sobre *Terenura sicki* Teixeira and Gonzaga, 1983 (Aves, Formicariidae). *Bol. Mus. Para. Emílio. Goeldi*, sér. zool., 3(2): 241-251.

Teixeira, D. M. (1987c) Notas sobre o "gravatazeiro", *Rhopornis ardesiaca* (Wied, 1831) (Aves, Formicariidae). *Revta. Bras. Biol.* 47: 409-414.

Teixeira, D. M. (1990) Notas sobre algumas aves descritas por Emile Snethlage. *Bol. Mus. Nac. Rio de Janeiro* n.s., Zool. no.337.

Teixeira, D. M. and Antas, P. T. Z. (1982) Notes on endangered Brazilian Cracidae. Pp.176-186 in *Primer Simposio Internacional de Familia Cracidae*, 1981. [Mexico City:] Universidad Nacional Autónoma de México.

Teixeira, D. M. and Carnevalli, N. (1989) Nova espécie de *Scytalopus* Gould, 1837, do nordeste do Brasil (Passeriformes, Rhinocryptidae). *Bol. Mus. Nac. Rio de Janeiro*, n.s. Zool. no.331.

Teixeira, D. M. and Gonzaga, L. P. (1983a) A new antwren from northeastern Brazil. *Bull. Brit. Orn. Club* 103: 133-135.

Teixeira, D. M. and Gonzaga, L. P. (1983b) Um novo Furnariidae do nordeste do Brasil: *Philydor novaesi* sp. nov. (Aves, Passeriformes). *Bol. Mus. Para. Emílio Goeldi*, n.s., Zool. no.124.

Teixeira, D. M. and Gonzaga, L. P. (1985) Uma nova subespécie de *Myrmotherula unicolor* (Ménétries, 1835) do nordeste do Brazil. *Bol. Mus. Nac. Rio de Janeiro*, n.s., Zool. no.310.

Teixeira, D. M. and Luigi, G. (1989) Notas sobre *Cranioleuca semicinerea* (Reichenbach 1853) (Aves, Furnariidae). *Revta. Bras. Biol.* 49: 605-613.

Teixeira, D. M., Luigi, G. and Almeida, A. C. C. (1990) A redescoberta de *Iodopleura pipra leucopygia* (Salvin, 1885) no nordeste do Brasil (Passeriformes, Cotingidae). Pp.179 in *Resumos, XVII Congresso Brasileiro de Zoologia*. Londrina: Universidade Estadual de Londrina.

Teixeira, D. M. and Nacinovic, J. B. (1990) A plumagem natal de *Taoniscus nanus*. *Ararajuba* 1: 113-114.

Teixeira, D. M., Nacinovic, J. B. and Luigi, G. (1989) Notes on some birds of northeastern Brazil (4). *Bull. Brit. Orn. Club* 109: 152-157.

Teixeira, D. M., Nacinovic, J. B. and Pontual, F. B. (1987) Notes on some birds of north-eastern Brazil (2). *Bull. Brit. Orn. Club* 107: 151-157.

Teixeira, D. M., Nacinovic, J. B. and Schloemp, I. M. (in press) Notas sobre alguns passeriformes brasileiros pouco conhecidos. *Ararajuba* 2: 97-100.

Teixeira, D. M. and Negret, A. (1984) The Dwarf Tinamou (*Taoniscus nanus*) of central Brazil. *Auk* 101: 188-189.

Teixeira, D. M. and Pinto, F. J. M. (1988) Sobre a reprodução do pintor-verdadeiro *Tangara fastuosa* (Lesson, 1831). P.484 in *Resumos, XV Congresso Brasileiro de Zoologia.* Curitiba: Universidade Federal do Paraná.

Teixeira, D. M. and Puga, M. E. M. (1984) Notes on the Speckled Crake (*Coturnicops notata*) in Brazil. *Condor* 86: 342-343.

Teixeira, D. M. and Sick, H. (1981) Notes on Brazilian Cracidae: the Red-billed Curassow, *Crax blumenbachii* Spix, 1825, and the Wattled Curassow, *Crax globulosa* Spix, 1825. *Bol. Mus. Nac. Rio de Janeiro*, n.s. Zool. no.299.

Teixeira, D. M. and Snow, D. W. (1982) Notes on the nesting of the Red-billed Curassow *Crax blumenbachii. Bull. Brit. Orn. Club* 102: 83-84.

Temminck, C. J. (1838) *Nouveau recueil de planches coloriées d'oiseaux*, 1. Paris: F. G. Levrault.

Terborgh, J., Fitzpatrick, J. W. and Emmons, L. (1984) Annotated checklist of bird and mammal species of Cocha Cashu Biological Station, Manu National Park, Peru. *Fieldiana Zool.* 21.

Terborgh, J. and Weske, J. S. (1969) Colonization of secondary habitats by Peruvian birds. *Ecology* 50: 765-782.

Thayer, J. E. (1906) Eggs and nests of the Thick-billed Parrot (*Rhynchopsitta pachyrhyncha*). *Auk* 23: 223-224.

Thelen, K. D. and Faizool, S. (1980) *Plan for a system of national parks and other protected areas in Trinidad and Tobago.* Port of Spain: Forestry Division, Ministry of Agriculture, Lands and Fisheries.

Thiollay, J.-M. (1984) Raptor community structure of a primary rain forest in French Guiana and effect of human hunting pressure. *Raptor Research* 18: 117-122.

Thompson, H. L. (1900) Notes on the St Vincent Parrot. *Avicult. Mag.* (2)6: 147-149.

Thompson, Lady (1902) The St Lucia Parrot. *Avicult. Mag.* (2)8: 275-276.

Thompson, M. C. (1962) Noteworthy records of birds from the Republic of Mexico. *Wilson Bull.* 74: 173-176.

Thomsen, J. B. and Munn, C. A. (1988) *Cyanopsitta spixii*: a non-recovery report. *Parrotletter* 1: 6-7.

Todd, W. E. C. (1915a) Preliminary diagnoses of apparently new South American birds. *Proc. Biol. Soc. Washington* 28: 79-82.

Todd, W. E. C. (1915b) Preliminary diagnoses of seven apparently new Neotropical birds. *Proc. Biol. Soc. Washington.* 28: 169-170.

Todd, W. E. C. (1916) The birds of the Isle of Pines. *Ann. Carnegie Mus.* 10: 146-296.

Todd, W. E. C. (1920) Descriptions of apparently new South American birds. *Proc. Biol. Soc. Washington* 33: 71-76.

Todd, W. E. C. (1926) A study of the neotropical finches of the genus *Spinus. Ann. Carnegie Mus.* 17: 11-82.

Todd, W. E. C. (1927) New gnateaters and antbirds from tropical America, with a revision of the genus *Myrmeciza* and its allies. *Proc. Biol. Soc. Washington* 40: 149-178.

Todd, W. E. C. (1931) Critical notes on the neotropical thrushes. *Proc. Biol. Soc. Washington* 44: 47-54.

Todd, W. E. C. and Carriker, M. A. (1922) The birds of the Santa Marta Region of Colombia: a study in altitudinal distribution. *Ann. Carnegie Mus.* 14.

Todd, W. E. C. and Worthington, W. W. (1911) A contribution to the ornithology of the Bahama Islands. *Ann. Carnegie Mus.* 7: 388-464.

Tokunaga, H. (1987) Trade in curassows from Colombia. TRAFFIC (Japan): unpublished memorandum.

Tomkins, R. J. (1985) Breeding success and mortality of Dark-rumped Petrels in the Galápagos and control of their predators. Pp.159-175 in P. J. Moors, ed. *Conservation of island birds.* Cambridge, U.K.: International Council for Bird Preservation (Techn. Publ. 3).

Toro, G., Borrero, J. I., Russell, S., Chiriví, H., León, C. A. and Hernández Camacho, J. I. (1975) Lista general de las aves de la Isla de Salamanca. Bogotá: INDERENA (unpublished).

Torres Leyva, A., Wotzkow Alvarez, C. and Rams Beceña, A. (1988) Algunas consideraciones sobre la biología del Gavilán Colilargo Oriental, *Accipiter gundlachi wileyi* (Wotzkow) en las provincias orientales. *Garciana* 10: 1-2.

Towle, J. A. and Towle, E. L., eds. (1991) *St Lucia country environmental profile.* St Michael, Barbados: Caribbean Conservation Association.

Toyne, E. P., Flanagan, N. J. and Jeffcote, M. T. (in prep.) Status, ecology and conservation of the Red-faced Parrot *Hapalopsittaca pyrrhops* in southern Ecuador.

Toyne, E. P. and Jeffcote, T. M. (1992) Parrots in peril: Ecuador 1990. Imperial College London draft expedition report.

Traylor, M. A. (1948) New birds from Peru and Ecuador. *Fieldiana Zool.* 31: 195-200.

Traylor, M. A. (1952) Notes on birds from the Marcapata Valley, Cuzco, Peru. *Fieldiana Zool.* 34: 17-23.

Traylor, M. A. (1958) Birds of northeastern Peru. *Fieldiana Zool.* 35: 87-141.

Traylor, M. A., ed. (1979) *Check-list of birds of the world,* 8. Cambridge, Mass.: Museum of Comparative Zoology.

Tremoleras, J. (1920) Lista de aves uruguayas. *Hornero* 2: 10-25.

Trillmich, F., Trillmich, K., Limberger, D. and Arnold, W. (1983) The breeding season of the Flightless Cormorant *Nannopterum harrisi* at Cabo Hammond, Fernandina. *Ibis* 125: 221-221.

de [= von] Tschudi, J. J. (1844) Avium conspectus quae in Republica Peruana reperiuntur et pleraeque observatae vel collectae sunt in itinere. *Arch. Naturges.* 10: 262-317.

von Tschudi, J. J. (1844-1846) *Untersuchungen über die Fauna Peruana, Ornithologie.* St Gallen, Switzerland: Scheitlin und Zollekofer.

Tye, A. and Tye, H. (1991) Bird species on St Andrew and Old Providence islands, west Caribbean. *Wilson Bull.* 103: 493-497.

Urban, E. K. (1959) Birds from Coahuila, Mexico. *Univ. Kansas Publ. Mus. Nat. Hist.* 11: 443-516.

Uribe, D. A. (1986) Contribución al conocimiento de la avifauna del bosque muy húmedo montano bajo en cercanías de Manizales. Thesis, Universidad de Caldas, Manizales.

USFWS (1982) = U.S. Fish and Wildlife Service (1982) *Puerto Rican Plain Pigeon recovery plan.* Atlanta: U.S. Fish and Wildlife Service.

USFWS (1987) = U.S. Fish and Wildlife Service (1987) *Recovery plan for the Puerto Rican parrot (*Amazona vittata*).* Atlanta: U.S. Fish and Wildlife Service.

USGS (1951) = United States Geological Survey (1951) Puerto Rico e Islas limítrofes. Gobierno de Puerto Rico, Departamento del Interior ([issued or reprinted by] Interior Geological Survey, Reston, Virginia 1982).

Valdés Miró, V. (1984) Datos de nidificación sobre las aves que crían en Cuba. *Poeyana* 282.

Valenzuela, N., Coffey, M. and Nichols, T. D. (1981) Observations on *Rhynchopsitta terrisi.* Report to ICBP (unpublished).

Valle, C. A. and Coulter, M. C. (1987) Present status of the Flightless Cormorant, Galápagos Penguin and Greater Flamingo populations in the Galápagos Islands, Ecuador, after the 1982-1983 El Niño. *Condor* 89: 276-281.

Vannini, J. P. and Rockstroh, P. M. (1988) The status of cracids in Guatemala. Unpublished paper presented at the II International Cracid Symposium, Caracas, Venezuela, February/March 1988.

Vargas Márquez, F. (1984) *Parques nacionales de México y reservas equivalentes.* Universidad Nacional Autónoma de México: Instituto de Investigaciones Económicas.

Vargas Mora, T. A. and González Castillo, M. (1983) Estudios en las áreas silvestres de la Península de Barahona e Isla Beata: propuesta para la creación de una zona protegida (Parque Nacional). Santo Domingo: Secretaría de Estado de Agricultura (unpublished).

Varty, N. (1991) The status and conservation of Jamaica's threatened and endemic forest avifauna and their habitats following Hurricane Gilbert. *Bird Conserv. Internatn.* 1: 135-151.

Varty, N., Adams, J., Espin, P. and Hambler, C., eds. (1986) *An ornithological survey of Lake Tota, Colombia, 1982.* Cambridge, U.K.: International Council for Bird Preservation (Study Report 12).

Vaurie, C. (1957) Field notes on some Cuban birds. *Wilson Bull.* 69: 301-313.

Vaurie, C. (1966a) Systematic notes on the bird family Cracidae, no.5: *Penelope purpurascens, Penelope jaquacu* and *Penelope obscura. Amer. Mus. Novit.* 2250.

Vaurie, C. (1966b) Systematic notes on the bird family Cracidae, no.6: reviews of nine species of *Penelope*. *Amer. Mus. Novit.* 2251.

Vaurie, C. (1967a) Systematic notes on the bird family Cracidae, no.7: the genus *Pipile*. *Amer. Mus. Novit.* 2296.

Vaurie, C. (1967b) Systematic notes on the bird family Cracidae, no.9: the genus *Crax*. *Amer. Mus. Novit.* 2305.

Vaurie, C. (1967c) Systematic notes on the bird family Cracidae, no.10: the genera *Mitu* and *Pauxi* and the generic relationships of the Cracini. *Amer. Mus. Novit.* 2307.

Vaurie, C. (1968) Taxonomy of the Cracidae (Aves). *Bull. Amer. Mus. Nat. Hist.* 138: 131-260.

Vaurie, C. (1971) *Classification of the ovenbirds (Furnariidae)*. London: H. F. and G. Witherby.

Vaurie, C. (1972) An ornithological gazetteer of Peru (based on information compiled by J. T. Zimmer). *Amer. Mus. Novit.* 2491.

Vaurie, C. (1980) Taxonomy and geographical distribution of the Furnariidae (Aves, Passeriformes). *Bull. Amer. Mus. Nat. Hist.* 166(1).

Vaz-Ferreira, R. and Gerzenstein, E. (1961) Aves nuevas o poco conocidas en la república oriental del Uruguay. *Com. Zool. Mus. Hist. Nat. Montevideo* 5(92).

Vázquez, M. A. (undated) Estudio y acciones sobre el Loro Cabeza Amarilla (*Amazona ochrocephala*) en el centro de Tamaulipas, México. Unpublished.

Vázquez, M. A. and Maldonado Rodríguez, D. M. A. (1990) Loro Cabeza Amarilla (*Amazona ochrocephala*) en el estado de Tamaulipas. Unpublished.

Veloso, H. P. (1946) A vegetação no município de Ilhéus, estado da Bahia, I. Estudo sinecológico das áreas de pesquisas sobre a febre amarela silvestre realizado pelo SEPFA. *Mem. Inst. Oswaldo Cruz* 44: 13-105.

Verrill, A. E. (1902) The "Cahow" of the Bermudas, an extinct bird. *Ann. Mag. Nat. Hist.* 7: 26-31.

Verrill, A. E. and Verrill, A. H. (1909) Notes on the birds of San Domingo, with a list of the species, including a new hawk. *Proc. Acad. Nat. Sci. Philadelphia* 61: 352-366.

Verrill, A. H. (1905) Addition to the avifauna of Dominica. Notes on species hitherto unrecorded with descriptions of three new species and a list of all birds now known to occur on the island. Barbados: privately published.

Verrill, G. E. (1892) Notes on the fauna of the island of Dominica, British West Indies, with lists of the species obtained and observed by G. E. and A. H. Verrill. *Trans. Connecticut Acad. Arts Sci.* 8: 315-355.

Vestner, J. (1987) Spix-Aras in Jugoslawien. *Zool. Ges. Arten- und Populationsschutz Mitglieder Information* Oktober 1987 [:9].

Vides-Almonacid, R. (1988) Notas sobre el estado de las poblaciones de la Gallareta Cornuda *Fulica cornuta* en la provincia de Tucumán, Argentina. *Hornero* 13: 34-38.

Vides-Almonacid, R. (1990) Observaciones sobre la utilización del hábitat y la diversidad de especies de aves en una laguna de la puna argentina. *Hornero* 13: 117-28.

Vielliard, J. (1979) Commentaires sur les aras du genre *Anodorhynchus*. *Alauda* 47: 61-63.

Vielliard, J. (1990a) Estudo bioacústica das aves do Brasil: o gênero *Scytalopus*. *Ararajuba* 1: 5-18.

Vielliard, J. (1990b) Uma nova espécie de *Asthenes* da serra do Cipó, Minas Gerais, Brasil. *Ararajuba* 1: 121-122.

Vieira, C. da C. (1935) Os cotingídeos do Brasil. *Revta. Mus. Paulista* 19: 329-397.

Vierheilig, M. B. and Vierheilig, H. (1988) Beiträge zu Status und Biologie von Papageien der Insel Margarita, Venezuela. *Gefied. Welt* 112: 50-52, 91.

Vigors, N. A. (1827) On some species of birds from Cuba. *Zool. J.* 3: 432-448.

Vilella, F. J. (1989) The reproductive ecology and population biology of the Puerto Rican Nightjar *Caprimulgus noctitherus*. Ph.D. dissertation, Lousiana State University, Baton Rouge, Louisiana.

Vilella, F. J. and Zwank, P. J. (1987) Density and distribution of the Puerto Rican Nightjar in the Guayanilla Hills. *Carib. J. Sci.* 23: 238-242.

Vilella, F. J. and Zwank, P. J. (1988) Red data bird: Puerto Rican Nightjar. *World Birdwatch* 10(3-4): 9.

Vilella, F. J. and Zwank, P. J. (in press a) Geographic distribution and abundance of the Puerto Rican Nightjar. [*J. Field Orn.*]
Vilella, F. J. and Zwank, P. J. (in press b) Small indan mongoose in sympatry with the Puerto Rican Nightjar. [*Carib. J. Sci.*]
Vilina, Y. A. (in press) Status of the Peruvian Diving-petrel, *Pelecanoides garnoti*, on Chañaral Island, Chile. *Colonial Waterbirds* 15.
Vilina, Y. A. and Capella, J. J. (1991) Estado de conservación del Pato Yunco, *Pelecanoides garnoti*, en Chile. Resúmenes del IV Congreso de Ornitología Neotropical, 3-9 de Noviembre 1991, Quito, Ecuador (resumen 136).
Vincent, J. (1966-1971) *Red data book, 2. Aves.* Morges, Switzerland: International Union for Conservation of Nature and Natural Resources.
Vogel, P., Downer, A., Levy, C. and Strong, Y. (1989) The legislation and conservation of pigeons and doves in Jamaica. *Gosse Bird Club Broadsheet* no. 53: 11-18.
Vogel, P. and Kerr, R. (in press) The Jamaican Iguana: survival in a threatened habitat. *Proc. Fourth Ann. Conference Sci. Techn.* 1990.
Vooren, C. M. and Chiaradia, A. (1990) Seasonal abundance and behaviour of coastal birds on Cassino Beach, Brazil. *Ornitología Neotropical* 1: 9-24.
Voous, K. H. (1957) *The birds of Aruba, Curaçao, and Bonaire.* The Hague: Martinus Nijhoff (Studies on the fauna of Curaçao and other Caribbean islands 7, no.29).
Voous, K. H. (1965) Specimens of Lear's Macaw in the Zoological Museum of Amsterdam. *Oiseau et R.F.O.* 35 (spec. no.): 153-155.
Voous, K. H. (1983) *Birds of the Netherlands Antilles.* [No place of publication:] De Walberg Pers.
Vorhies, C. T. (1934) Arizona records of the Thick-billed Parrot. *Condor* 36: 180-181.
de Vries, T. (1984) Problems of reintroducing native animals on islands where they have been exterminated. *Notícias de Galápagos* 40: 12.
Vuilleumier, F. (1978) Remarques sur l'echantillonage d'une riche avifaune de l'ouest de l'Ecuador. *Oiseau et R.F.O.* 48: 21-36.
Vuilleumier, F. and Mayr, E. (1987) New species of birds described from 1976 to 1980. *J. Orn.* 128: 137-150.
Wagner, H. O. (1953) Die Hockohuhner der Sierra Madre de Chiapas, Mexico. *Veroffentl. Mus. Bremen* A 2(2): 105-128.
Wall, J. W. (1992) Worldtwitch. *Winging it* 4(4): 53.
Wallace, A. R. (1853a) *A narrative of travels on the Amazon and Rio Negro* [etc.]. London: Reeve and Co.
Wallace, A. R. (1853b) *Palm trees of the Amazon and their uses.* London: John van Voorst.
Warham, J. (1990) *The petrels: their ecology and breeding systems.* London: Academic Press.
Warming, E. (1908) *Lagoa Santa: contribuição para a geographia phytobiológica, com uma lista dos animaes vertebrados da Lagoa Santa, communicada pela primeira secção do Museu Zoologico da Universidade.* Belo Horizonte: Imprensa Official do Estado de Minas Gerais (Facsimile edition, 1973: Belo Horizonte: Livraria Itatiaia).
Webster, J. D. (1965) [Twentyninth Breeding-Bird Census] Cloud-forest. *Audubon Field Notes* 19: 598-599.
Weinrich, J. A. (1989) Status of the Kirtland's Warbler, 1988. *Jack-Pine Warbler* 67: 69-72.
Wells, J. G. (1886) A catalogue of the birds of Grenada, West Indies, with observations thereon. *Proc. U.S. Nat. Mus.* 39: 609-633.
Wells, S. M., ed. (1988) *Coral reefs of the world, 1: Atlantic and eastern Pacific.* Cambridge, U.K.: United Nations Environment Programme and International Union for Conservation of Nature and Natural Resources.
Weske, J. S. and Terborgh, J. W. (1971) A new subspecies of curassow of the genus *Pauxi* from Peru. *Auk* 88: 233-238.

West, S. (1979) *Preliminary checklist to the birds of the republic of Bolivia*. Alpine, Texas: Ross State University.

Wetmore, A. (1916) The birds of Vieques Island, Porto Rico. *Auk* 33: 403-419.

Wetmore, A. (1919) Description of a Whippoorwill from Porto Rico. *Proc. Biol. Soc. Washington* 32: 235-238.

Wetmore, A. (1922) Bird remains from the caves of Porto Rico. *Bull. Amer. Mus. Nat. Hist.* 46: 297-333.

Wetmore, A. (1926) Observations on the birds of Argentina, Paraguay, Uruguay and Chile. *Bull. U.S. Natn. Mus.* 133: 1-448.

Wetmore, A. (1927) A thrush new to science from Haiti. *Proc. Biol. Soc. Washington* 40: 55-56.

Wetmore, A. (1931) Early records of birds in Arizona and New Mexico. *Condor* 33: 35.

Wetmore, A. (1932a) Notes from Dr R. Ciferri on the birds of Hispaniola. *Auk* 49: 107-108.

Wetmore, A. (1932b) The Diablotin in Dominica. *Auk* 49: 456-457.

Wetmore, A. (1932c) Birds collected in Cuba and Haiti by the Parish-Smithsonian Expedition of 1930. *Proc. U.S. Natn. Mus.* 81(2): 1-40.

Wetmore, A. (1935) The Thick-billed Parrot in southern Arizona. *Condor* 37: 18-21.

Wetmore, A. (1938) Bird remains from the West Indies. *Auk* 55: 51-55.

Wetmore, A. (1939) A record of the Black-capped Petrel from Haiti. *Auk* 56: 73.

Wetmore, A. (1945) A review of the Giant Antpitta *Grallaria gigantea*. *Proc. Biol. Soc. Washington* 58: 17-20.

Wetmore, A. (1950) Additional forms of birds from the republics of Panama and Colombia. *Proc. Biol. Soc. Washington* 63: 171-174.

Wetmore, A. (1952) A record for the Black-capped Petrel, *Pterodroma hasitata*, in Martinique. *Auk* 69: 460.

Wetmore, A. (1968) *Birds of the Republic of Panamá*. Washington, D.C.: Smithsonian Institution Press (Smithson. Misc. Coll. 150, Part 2).

Wetmore, A. (1972) *Birds of the Republic of Panamá*. Washington, D.C.: Smithsonian Institution Press (Smithson. Misc. Coll. 150, Part 3).

Wetmore, A. and Lincoln, F. C. (1933) Additional notes on the birds of Haiti and the Dominican Republic. *Proc. U.S. Natn. Mus.* 82(25): 1-68.

Wetmore, A., Pasquier, R. F., and Olson, S. L. (1984) *Birds of the Republic of Panamá*. Washington, D.C.: Smithsonian Institution Press (Smithsonian Misc. Coll. 150, Part 4).

Wetmore, A. and Phelps W. H. (1943) Description of a third form of curassow of the genus *Pauxi*. *J. Washington Acad. Sci.* 33: 142-146.

Wetmore, A. and Swales, B. H. (1931) The birds of Haiti and the Dominican Republic. *Bull. U.S. Natn. Mus.* 155.

Wetterburg, G. B., Prance, G. T. and Lovejoy, T. E. (1981) Conservation progress in Amazonia: a structural review. *Parks* 6(2): 5-10.

White, E. W. (1882) Notes on the birds collected in the Argentine Republic. *Proc. Zool. Soc. London*: 591-629.

White, E. W. (1883) Supplementary notes on the birds of the Argentine Republic (with remarks by P. L. Sclater). *Proc. Zool. Soc. London*: 37-43.

Whitney, B. M. (1992) Observations on the systematics, behavior, and vocalizations of *"Thamnomanes" occidentalis* (Formicariidae). *Auk* 109: 302-308.

Whitney, B. M. and Rosenberg, G. H. (in prep.) Observations on the behaviour, vocalizations, and possible relationships of *Xenornis setifrons*, a little known Chocó endemic.

Whittaker, F. H., Schmidt, G. D. and García Díaz, J. (1970) Helminth parasites of some birds in Puerto Rico. *Proc. Helminthol. Soc. Washington.* 37: 123-124.

Wied [-Neuwied], M. Prinz zu (1820-1821) *Reise nach Brasilien in den Jahren 1815 bis 1817*. Frankfurt [am Main]: Heinrich Ludwig Brönner.

Wied, M. Prinz zu (1831-1833) *Beiträge zur Naturgeschichte von Brasilien*, 3-4. Weimar: Landes-Industrie-Comptoirs.

Wied, M. Prinz zu (1850) *Nachträge, Berichtigungen und Zusätze zu der Beschreibung meiner Reise in östlichen Brasilien.* Frankfurt am Main: Heinrich Ludwig Brönner.

Wied, M. Prinz zu (1940) *Viagem ao Brasil.* [Translation by E. S. de Mendonça and F. P. de Figueiredo, with notes by O. Pinto.] São Paulo: Companhia Editora Nacional (Brasiliana Grande Formato 1).

Wiedenfeld, D. A., Schulenberg, T. S. and Robbins, M. B. (1985) Birds of tropical deciduous forest in extreme northwestern Peru. Pp.305-315 in P. A. Buckley, M. S. Foster, E. S. Morton, R. S. Ridgely and F. G. Buckley, eds. *Neotropical ornithology.* Washington, D.C.: American Ornithologists' Union (Orn. Monogr. 36).

Wilbur, S. R. and Kiff, L. F. (1980) The California Condor in Baja California, Mexico. *Amer. Birds* 34: 856-859.

Wilcove, D. S. (1992) In praise of obscurity. *Living Bird* 11: 36-37.

Wiley, J. W. (1985a) Status and conservation of forest raptors in the West Indies. Pp.199-204 in I. Newton and R. D. Chancellor, eds. *Conservation studies on raptors.* Cambridge, U.K.: International Council for Bird Preservation (Techn. Publ. 5).

Wiley, J. W. (1985b) Bird conservation in the United States Caribbean. *Bird Conserv.* 2: 107-159.

Wiley, J. W. (1986) Status and conservation of raptors in the West Indies. *Birds of Prey Bull.* 3: 57-70.

Wiley, J. W. (1991) The status and conservation of parrots and parakeets in the Greater Antilles, Bahama Islands, and Cayman Islands. *Bird Conserv. Internatn.* 1: 187-214.

Wiley, J. W., Post, W. and Cruz, A. (1991) Conservation of the Yellow-shouldered Blackbird *Agelaius xanthomus*, an endangered West Indian species. *Biol. Conserv.* 55: 119-138.

Wiley, J. W. and Ottenwalder, J. A. (1990) Birds of islas Beata and Alto Velo, Dominican Republic. *Studies on Neotropical Fauna and Environment* 25(2): 65-88.

Wiley, J. W. and Wiley, B. N. (1981) Breeding season ecology and behaviour of Ridgway's Hawk *Buteo ridgwayi. Condor* 83: 132-151.

Wille, C. (1991) Paul Butler: parrot man of the Caribbean. *Amer. Birds* 45: 26-35.

Williams, M. D. (1980) First description of the eggs of the White-winged Guan *Penelope albipennis*, with notes on its nest. *Auk* 97: 889-892.

Williams, R. and Tobias, J. (1991) Preliminary report of the Amaluza '91 project, July–November 1991. Unpublished.

Williams, R., Tobias, J. and Wann, J. (1991) Cloud forest birds in southern Ecuador. Ornithological and botanical observations of the Amaluza '90 Project. Cardiff, U.K.: University of Wales College of Cardiff, unpublished.

Williams Linera, G. (1991) Nota sobre la estructura del estrato arboreo del bosque mesófilo de montaña en los alrededores del campamento "El Triunfo", Chiapas. *Acta Bot. Mexicana* 13: 1-7.

Willis, E. O. (1972) Taxonomy, ecology and behavior of the Sooty Ant-tanager (*Habia gutturalis*) and other ant tanagers. *Amer. Mus. Novit.* 2480.

Willis, E. O. (1979) The composition of avian communities in remanescent woodlots in southern Brazil. *Pap. Avuls. Dep. Zool. São Paulo* 33: 1-25.

Willis, E. O. (1980) Species reduction in remanescent woodlots in southern Brazil. Pp.783-786 in R. Nöhring, ed. *Acta XVII Congr. Internatn. Orn.* Berlin: Verlag der Deutschen Ornithologen-Gesellschaft.

Willis, E. O. (1987) Redescoberta de *Dryocopus galeatus* no estado de São Paulo. P.835 in Resumos de Reunião Anual SBPC, 39, Brasília.

Willis, E. O. (1988) Behavioral notes, breeding records, and range extensions for Colombian birds. *Revta. Acad. Colomb. Cienc. Exact. Fís. Nat.* 16: 137-150.

Willis, E. O. (1989) Mimicry in bird flocks of cloud forests in southeastern Brazil. *Revta. Bras. Biol.* 49: 615-619.

Willis, E. O. (1991) Desaparecimento de aves semi-nomádicas com desmatamentos no cerrado brasileiro. Resúmenes, I Encuentro de Ornitología de Paraguay, Brasil y Argentina, and IV Encuentro Paraguayo-Argentino de Ornitología, Mayo 1991, Ciudad del Este, Paraguay.

Willis, E. O. and Oniki, Y. (1981a) Levantamento preliminar de aves em treze áreas do estado de São Paulo. *Revta. Bras. Biol.* 41: 121-135.

Willis, E. O. and Oniki, Y. (1981b) Notes on the Slender Antbird. *Wilson Bull.* 93: 103-107.

Willis, E. O. and Oniki, Y. (1982) Behaviour of Fringe-backed Fire-eyes (*Pyriglena atra*, Formicariidae): a test case for taxonomy versus conservation. *Revta. Bras. Biol.* 42: 213-223.

Willis, E. O. and Oniki, Y. (1985) Bird specimens new for the state of São Paulo, Brazil. *Revta. Bras. Biol.* 45: 105-108.

Willis, E. O. and Oniki, Y. (1988a) Winter nesting of *Iodopleura pipra* (Lesson, 1831) (Aves, Cotingidae) in southeastern Brazil. *Revta. Bras. Biol.* 48: 161-167.

Willis, E. O. and Oniki, Y. (1988b) Bird conservation in open vegetation of São Paulo state, Brazil. Pp.67-70 in P. D. Goriup, ed. *Ecology and conservation of grassland birds.* Cambridge, U.K.: International Council for Bird Preservation (Techn. Publ. 7).

Willis, E. O. and Oniki, Y. (1990) Levantamento preliminar das aves de inverno em dez áreas do sudoeste de Mato Grosso, Brasil. *Ararajuba* 1: 19-38.

Willis, E. O. and Oniki, Y. (1991) *Nomes gerais para as aves brasileiras.* São Paulo: Américo Brasil.

Willis, E. O. and Oniki, Y. (in press) Avifaunal transects across the open zones of northern Minas Gerais, Brazil. *Ararajuba* 2: 41-58.

Willis, E. O., Wechsler, D. and Stiles, F. G. (1983) Forest-falcons, hawks, and a pygmy-owl as ant followers. *Revta. Bras. Biol.* 43: 23-28.

Willis, E. O. and Weinberg, L. F. (1990) *Terenura sicki* em Pernambuco. *O Charão* 16: 14.

Wilson, A. S. (1926) Lista de las aves del sur de Santa Fe. *Hornero* 3: 349-363.

Wilson, M. H., Snyder, N. F. R., Derrickson, S. R., Dein, F. J., Wiley, J. W., Wunderle, J. M., Kepler, C. B., Lugo, A. E., Graham, D. L. and Toone, W. D. (in press) Puerto Rican Parrots and potential limitations of the metapopulation approach to species conservation.

Wilson, R. G. and Ceballos-Lascurain, H. (1986) *The birds of Mexico City: an annotated checklist and bird-finding guide to the Federal District.* Burlington, Ontario: BBC Printing and Graphics Ltd.

Wingate, D. B. (1960) Cahow, living legend of Bermuda. *Canad. Audubon* 22: 145-149.

Wingate, D. B. (1964a) Discovery of breeding Black-capped Petrels on Hispaniola. *Auk*: 81: 147-159.

Wingate, D. B. (1964b) Does the "Blue Mountain Duck" of Jamaica survive? *Gosse Bird Club Broadsheet* no.2: 1-2.

Wingate, D. B. (1964c) John Tavernier Bartram, naturalist of 19th. century Bermuda. *Bermuda Hist. Q.* 21: 85-96.

Wingate, D. B. (1969) A summary of the status of the St Lucia Parrot *Amazona versicolor* and other rare native birds of St Lucia based on a survey of the island from April 22 to May 15, 1969, conducted under a grant from the International Committee for Bird Protection [*sic*]. Unpublished report.

Wingate, D. B. (1972) First successful hand-rearing of an abandoned Bermuda Petrel chick. *Ibis* 114: 97-101.

Wingate, D. B. (1973) *A checklist and guide to the birds of Bermuda.* Hamilton: Bermuda Press.

Wingate, D. B. (1978) Excluding competitors from Bermuda Petrel nesting burrows. Pp.93-102 in S. A. Temple, ed. *Endangered birds: management techniques for preserving threatened species.* Madison: University of Wisconsin Press.

Wingate, D. B. (1982) Report of the ICBP Representative of Bermuda for the ICBP World Conference. Unpublished.

Wingate, D. B. (1985) The restoration of Nonsuch Island as a living museum of Bermuda's pre-colonial terrestrial biome. Pp.225-238 in P. J. Moors, ed. *Conservation of island birds.* Cambridge, U.K.: International Council for Bird Preservation (Techn. Publ. 3).

Withington, F. and Sclater, P. L. (1888) On the birds of Lomas de Zamora, Buenos Aires, Argentine Republic. *Ibis* (5)6: 461-473.

Witt, C. R. (1978) Mexican Thick-billed Parrots (*Rhynchopsitta pachyrhyncha pachyrhyncha*). *AFA Watchbird* 5(4): 6-10.

Wood, C. A. (1924) My quest of the Imperial Parrot. *Avicult. Mag.* (4)2: 57-59, 77-81.

Wood, D. S., Leberman, R. C. and Weyer, D. (1986) *Checklist of the birds of Belize.* Pittsburgh: Carnegie Museum of Natural History (Spec. Publ. 12).

Woodard, D. W. (1980a) *Selected vertebrate endangered species of the seacoast of the United States – Ivory-billed Woodpecker.* Washington, D.C.: Fish and Wildlife Service, U.S. Department of the Interior: Biological Services Program (FWS/OBS-80/01.8 March 1980).

Woodard, D. W. (1980b) *Selected vertebrate endangered species of the seacoast of the United States – Thick-billed Parrot.* Washington, D.C.: Fish and Wildlife Service, U.S. Department of the Interior: Biological Services Program (FWS/OBS-80/01.54 March 1980).

Woods, C. A. (1987) The threatened and endangered birds of Haiti: lost horizons and new hopes. Pp.385-429 in *Proceedings 1987 Jean Delacour/IFCB Symposium on Breeding Birds in Captivity.* North Hollywood, California: International Foundation for the Conservation of Birds.

Woods, C. A. and Ottenwalder, J. A. (1983) The montane avifauna of Haiti. Pp.607-622 in *Proceedings Jean Delacour/IFCB Symposium on Breeding Birds in Captivity.* North Hollywood, California: International Foundation for the Conservation of Birds.

Woods, C. A. and Ottenwalder, J. A. (1986) *Birds of the national parks of Haiti.* Gainsville: University of Florida.

Woods, R. W. (1988) *Guide to birds of the Falkland Islands.* Oswestry, U.K.: Anthony Nelson Ltd.

Woolfenden, G. E. (1974) A Black-capped Petrel specimen from Florida. *Florida Field Nat.* 2: 17-19.

Wotzkow, C. (1985) Status and distribution of falconiformes in Cuba. *Bull. World Working Group on Birds of Prey* 2: 1-10.

Wotzkow, C. (1986) Ecological observations of Gundlach's Hawk *Accipiter gundlachi* in Cuba. *Birds of Prey Bull.* 3: 111-114.

Wotzkow Alvarez, C. (1988) Nueva subespecie de Gavilán Colilargo en la región oriental de Cuba. *Garciana* 9: 2-3.

Wotzkow, C. (1991) New subspecies of Gundlach's Hawk, *Accipiter gundlachi* (Lawrence). *Birds of Prey Bull.* 4: 271-292.

Wozniak, S. and Lantermann, W. (1984) Breeding the Green-cheeked Amazon Parrot *Amazona viridigenalis* at the Ornithological Institute, Oberhausen, Germany. *Avicult. Mag.* 90: 195-197.

Wright, C. (1988) *Review of protected areas legislation and systems in the Caribbean islands.* Cambridge, U.K.: World Conservation Monitoring Centre (Protected Areas Data Unit).

Wright, R. M. (1985) Morne Trois Pitons National Park in Dominica: a case study in park establishment in the developing world. *Ecol. Law Q.* 12: 747-778.

WTMU (1988) = Wildlife Trade Monitoring Unit (1988) *Annotated CITES appendices and reservations.* Cambridge, U.K.: IUCN Conservation Monitoring Centre.

Wurster, C. F. and Wingate, D. B. (1968) DDT residues and declining reproduction in the Bermuda Petrel. *Science* 159(3181): 979-981.

Yamashita, C. (1987) Field observations and comments on the Lear's Macaw (*Anodorhynchus leari*), a highly endangered species from northeastern Brazil. *Wilson Bull.* 99: 280-282.

Yamashita, C. and França, J. T. (in press) A range extension of the Golden Conure *Guaruba guarouba* to Rondônia state, western Amazonia. *Ararajuba* 2.

Yamashita, C. and Valle, M. de P. (1990) Ocorrência de duas aves raras no Brasil central: *Mergus octosetaceus* and *Tigrisoma fasciatum fasciatum*. *Ararajuba* 1: 107-109.

Yépez Tamayo, G. (1964) Ornitología de las Islas Margarita, Coche y Cubagua (Venezuela): segunda parte (continuación). *Mem. Soc. Cienc. Nat. Salle* 24: 5-39.

Zamore, M. P. (1980) Progress report (WWF Parrot Project), January–June 1980. Unpublished.

Zamore, M. P. (1982) Effect of Rotary (logging) operations at Morne Plaisance on parrot populations. Forestry Division, Dominica, internal report.

Zenaide, H. (1953) *Aves da Paraíba*. João Pessoa: Editora Teone.

Zimmer, J. T. (1930) Birds of the Marshall Field Peruvian Expedition, 1922-1923. *Field Mus. Nat. Hist. Zool. Ser.* 17: 233-480 (Publ. 282).

Zimmer, J. T. (1931) Studies of Peruvian birds, II. Peruvian forms of the genera *Microbates*, *Ramphocaenus*, *Sclateria*, *Pyriglena*, *Pithys*, *Drymophila*, and *Liosceles*. *Amer. Mus. Novit.* 509.

Zimmer, J. T. (1933) Studies of Peruvian birds, X. The formicarian genus *Thamnophilus*, part II. *Amer. Mus. Novit.* 647.

Zimmer, J. T. (1935) Studies of Peruvian birds, XVII. Notes on the genera *Syndactyla*, *Anabacerthia*, *Philydor*, and *Automolus*. *Amer. Mus. Novit.* 785.

Zimmer, J. T. (1936) Studies of Peruvian birds. XXI. Notes on the genera *Pseudocolaptes*, *Hyloctistes*, *Hylocryptus*, *Thripadectes*, and *Xenops*. *Amer. Mus. Novit.* 862.

Zimmer, J. T. (1937) Studies of Peruvian birds, XXVI. Notes on the genera *Agriornis*, *Muscisaxicola*, *Myiotheretes*, *Ochthoeca*, *Colonia*, *Knipolegus*, *Phaeotriccus*, *Fluvicola* and *Ramphotrigon*. *Amer. Mus. Novit.* 930.

Zimmer, J. T. (1947) Studies of Peruvian birds, 52. The genera *Sericossypha*, *Chlorospingus*, *Chemoscopus*, *Hemispingus*, *Conothraupis*, *Chlorornis*, *Lamprospiza*, *Cissopis*, and *Schistochlamys*. *Amer. Mus. Novit.* 1367.

Zimmer, J. T. (1951) Studies of Peruvian birds, 61. The genera *Aglaeactis*, *Lafresnaya*, *Pterophanes*, *Boissonneaua*, *Heliangelus*, *Eriocnemis*, *Haplophaedia*, *Ocreatus*, and *Lesbia*. *Amer. Mus. Novit.* 1540.

Zimmer, J. T. (1952) A new finch from northern Peru. *J. Washington Acad. Sci.* 42: 103-104.

Zimmer, J. T. (1952) Studies of Peruvian birds, 62. The hummingbird genera *Patagona*, *Sappho*, *Polyonymus*, *Ramphomicron*, *Metallura*, *Chalcostigma*, *Taphrolesbia*, and *Aglaiocercus*. *Amer. Mus. Novit.* 1595.

Zimmer, J. T. (1953a) Studies of Peruvian birds, 63. The hummingbird genera *Oreonympha*, *Schistes*, *Heliothryx*, *Loddigesia*, *Heliomaster*, *Rhodopis*, *Thaumastura*, *Calliphlox*, *Myrtis*, *Myrmia*, and *Acestrura*. *Amer. Mus. Novit.* 1604.

Zimmer, J. T. (1953b) Notes on tyrant flycatchers (Tyrannidae). *Amer. Mus. Novit.* 1605.

Zimmer, J. T. and Phelps, W. H. (1944) New species and subspecies of birds from Venezuela. Part 1. *Amer. Mus. Novit.* 1270.

Zimmerman, D. A. (1957) Notes on Tamaulipan birds. *Wilson Bull.* 69: 273-277.

Zimmerman, D. A. (1978) Eared Trogon – immigrant or visitor? *Amer. Birds* 32: 135-139.

Zimmerman, D. R. (1975) *To save a bird in peril*. New York: Coward, McCann and Geoghegan Inc.

Zorrilla de San Martín, J. C. (1959) Ampliación de la distribución de *Larus belcheri* hasta el territorio uruguayo. *Bol. Soc. Taguató* 1(2): 57-60.

Zotta, D. A. (1936) Sobre el contenido estomacal de aves argentinas. *Hornero* 6: 261-270.

Index